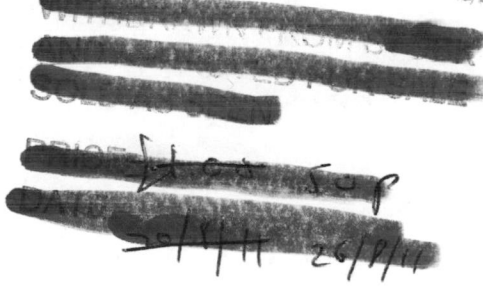

THE BREEDON BOOK OF
FOOTBALL LEAGUE RECORDS

THE BREEDON BOOK OF FOOTBALL LEAGUE RECORDS

GORDON SMAILES

BREEDON
BOOKS
SPORT

First published in Great Britain by
The Breedon Books Publishing Company Limited
44 Friar Gate, Derby DE1 1DA
1991.
Second edition published 1992

ISBN 1 873626 33 9

Printed and bound by The Bath Press Limited, Bath and London.
Jacket printed by BDC Printing Services Ltd of Derby.

Contents

This page: Lol Chappell scores for Barnsley against Darlington at Oakwell in 1954.

Title page: A Sheffield United shot crashes against the Wednesday crossbar during the South Yorkshire local derby game at Bramall Lane in 1954.

Foreword

IT WAS Lloyd George who said early this century: "You cannot feed the hungry on statistics", but Breedon Books in general, and Gordon Smailes in particular, continue to do their best to provide the committed football follower with works of reference which are more than mere argument settlers.

With the game changing rapidly and the almost inevitable advent of a new Premier League, it is an unenviable task to keep pace with the myriad of factual information which association football throws up, and which the ardent supporter devours, as one season seems to run into the next.

Records have been set, and some of them protected, ever since the Football League stirred into life in September 1888. There were just five matches on the opening day (there was certainly no *Sports Report* to give the results at five o'clock) and it would be nearly forty years later before such relevant facts as attendance figures would be properly recorded.

However, the achievement of Preston North End in winning the League Championship that first season without losing a single game has never been matched, although Arsenal came as near to it in the 1990-91 season as had any other Championship side over the century.

Although it is generally agreed that the modern game is harder, faster and more demanding than in years gone by, records continue to fall and new ones are set. It is frequently the more recent achievements that play tricks with the memory.

But for glancing through this volume I would have struggled to nominate John Aldridge as the player to have scored in the most consecutive games, and to pinpoint the year in which Brian Clough's Nottingham Forest set the League record of 42 unbeaten matches. The latter achievement is one to which Clough proudly referred in a BBC interview prior to the 1991 FA Cup Final.

Thinking of the FA Cup, the inclusion here of all the results from the two major knockout competitions gives the book added weight and authenticity. Across the spectrum of the three leading domestic outlets — League, League Cup and FA Cup — Gordon Smailes has not only pulled together the full story of some 120 years of first-class football in England, but has also managed to correct the irritating, yet inevitable, inaccuracies which at times have appeared elsewhere.

In short, it is another in the series of labours of love for which Breedon, with their *Complete Record* series featuring individual clubs, seem able to come up with authors who are either fanatics, insomniacs, or just plain football daft.

Without them, for sure, those of us who depend on reliable works of reference would be totally lost. I only hope that their job satisfaction is not tempered by the thought that in just one year's time, the volume can be out of date!

Fortunately, the constant updating of the series has meant more editions, and more space to be found on the now overcrowded bookshelf of the soccer collector. Allocating space for this one, however, will be both a necessity and a pleasure.

John Motson
St Albans
May 1991

Introduction

THERE have been many statistical books covering the story of the Football League since its foundation in 1888. The League's official history *The Story of the Football League,* published in 1938, gave the dates and results of all games played up to the end of the 1937-8 season; and Ian Laschke's *Rothmans Book of Football League Records 1888-89 to 1978-79* extended that work when it was published and added to it the Football League tables.

This second edition of *The Breedon Book of Football League Records,* a work first published in 1991 and now corrected and updated, not only extends the subject still further, now taking in the 13 seasons since the Laschke book, it also attempts to correct a few earlier errors which inevitably have crept into books of this sort.

For instance, the result of the Notts County-Derby County game in the League's first season had always been given as 5-2 in Derby's favour and with a date of 17 November 1888; it is now known that the score was 5-3 to the Rams and that the game was played on 16 March 1889; similarly, the Woolwich Arsenal-Loughborough Town game on 4 January 1896 ended 5-0 to the Gunners, not 6-0 as always previously published. For that piece of information we are indebted to Arsenal historian, Fred Ollier.

All this is not to smugly suggest that this book has righted all previous wrongs and is 100 per cent accurate, simply to illustrate that there are so many areas where the researcher has to tread carefully and not blindly accept what has been accepted before. To attempt this, Gordon Smailes has gone back to primary sources of research and both he and the publishers believe this book to be more accurate than anything that has gone before. Anyone with additional information is cordially invited to contact the author through Breedon Books.

This book also includes the results of all FA Cup ties (from the competition proper) and all Football League Cup games in a bid to present as broad a picture of English first-class football as possible. And it is hoped that the inclusion of a records section and the many illustrations will also enhance this work.

The author and publishers are most grateful to John Motson for his kind foreword and to football statisticians and historians everywhere who have shown enthusiasm for this project.

Note: In the results tables for each Football League division, 'A' refers to August, 'a' to April; 'm' refers to May, 'M' to March; and 'j' refers to June and 'J' to January. All the other capital letters are the initial letters of the month concerned (ie 'F' refers to February). The notes at the head of each season tell how the make-up of the League was achieved for that campaign. Thus 'Doncaster Rovers failed to gain re-election' at the head of 1905-06 means that they were voted out at the 1905 annual meeting.

William McGregor, the Birmingham draper who suggested the idea of a Football League.

The Football League

IN 1888, organized football was still an infant, albeit a lusty one, with professionalism having been legalized only three years earlier and the FA Cup only 16 years old. And apart from that competition, then known as the 'English Cup', and the mushrooming local cup competitions, football clubs still had to rely on prestigious friendly games to bring in the crowds. It was a state of affairs which was beginning to pose problems for the leading sides.

Once the thrill of truly competitive cup football had been experienced, friendly matches between even the top teams of the day, had no cutting edge, no real excitement. Further down the scale, the game was often being conducted in a haphazard manner. It was not uncommon for people to arrive and find that the opposition had not turned up, or matches kicked-off so late that spectators had drifted home long before the end.

At the top end of the scale, those clubs which had embraced professionalism now needed money to pay their players. These were the days long before outside commercial activity in football and the clubs could see only one way to finance the signing of better players. The money had to come through the gate, handed over by the paying spectator. It was vital for clubs to find a regular source of income.

One such club was Aston Villa and one of their committee members, William McGregor, a draper with premises near Aston Park, fearing that his club might lose its place as one of the leading sides in the country, suggested a league competition similar to that used in American baseball, although much nearer to home the County Cricket Championship could have provided an example.

His argument was strong: a league would guarantee a definite list of games — what McGregor called a 'fixity of fixtures'. And it would provide additional competitive football.

On 2 March 1888, he sent out his now famous letter to Blackburn Rovers, Bolton Wanderers, Preston North End, West Bromwich Albion and to the secretary of his own club, Aston Villa, asking them if they would be interested in forming a football league.

An initial meeting was held on the eve of that year's FA Cup Final, on Friday, 23 March at Anderton's Hotel in Fleet Street, London. Officially in attendance were representatives of Aston Villa, Blackburn Rovers, Burnley, Stoke (who weren't 'City' until 1925), Notts County, West Bromwich Albion and Wolverhampton Wanderers. Preston, who were playing in the Cup Final, did not attend. Nor did Bolton, although as their secretary, John Bentley, had been the only one to respond to McGregor's request for lists of prospective founder-members, presumably McGregor was not too concerned at the Trotters' absence. Derby County's secretary, John Richardson, attended but 'only to observe'.

A further meeting was held on 17 April at Manchester's Royal Hotel. According to the minutes, 11 clubs were represented — all the founder-members except Accrington, although they may have been there — and a name for the competition was settled. McGregor suggested the 'Football Association Union', but this was rejected because of possible confusion with the Rugby Football Union. McGregor's own objection to the name 'Football League' (he thought it might be confused with politically unpopular organizations, the Irish Home Rule League and the Land League) was overruled.

So the Football League began with 12 clubs. They comprised six from Lancashire: Accrington, Blackburn Rovers, Bolton Wanderers, Burnley, Everton and Preston North End; and six from the Midlands: Aston Villa, Derby County, Notts County, Stoke, West Bromwich Albion and Wolverhampton Wanderers. Remarkably, of those dozen founder-members over a century ago, only Accrington (no relation to the later Accrington Stanley) have gone to the wall. Nottingham Forest, The Wednesday (they did not adopt 'Sheffield' until 1929) and a Lancashire side called Halliwell were not accepted by the new organization.

William McGregor was elected chairman, Harry Lockett of Stoke was the first secretary, and Major William Sudell of Preston North End was the first treasurer. The annual subscription for each club was two guineas (£2.10) and two points were to be awarded for a win and one for a draw. Teams finishing on the same number of points would have to submit to the goal-average, whereby the number scored was divided by the number conceded. It is ironic that this prevailed until 1976 — the dawn of the pocket calculator age — when it was replaced by the much simpler goal-difference used today. Two points for a win continued until 1981, when it was replaced by three points for victory, a move which arguably made the game more entertaining and deterred visiting teams from settling for a draw and only one point.

The first matches in the Football League — five at the onset — were staged on Saturday, 8 September 1888.

Until the League began to keep such records in 1925, football attendance figures were notoriously inaccurate and it apparently relied upon a local journalist casting an eye around a not-always familiar stadium. Indeed, if the exact figure was known, the League ordered that it should not be published. Nevertheless, one has to record that apparently some 26,000 people watched the five opening games, an average of just over 5,000 per match.

The highest 'gate' of the day was the 10,000 who saw Everton beat Accrington 2-1; the lowest, suprisingly, was the local derby game between Wolves and Aston Villa, where 2,500 turned up at Dudley Road.

There were few shocks, although Derby County managed to beat Bolton Wanderers 6-3 at Pikes Lane after trailing 3-0 after only 15 minutes. And the first League game on Merseyside started an hour after the scheduled kick-off when Accrington were late arriving at Anfield — where Everton then played.

The identity of the first Football League goalscorer is not known, although it was probably either Preston's Jack Gordon or his amateur teammate Fred Dewhurst, depending on which account one reads.

A week later Notts County and Blackburn Rovers made their League debuts. County attracted only 3,000 to Anfield. Blackburn drew 5-5 with Accrington before a 5,000 crowd at Ewood Park.

Until 1891, the referee stood on the touch-line and arbitrated only when the umpires, one from each club, could not agree. Players were not numbered until 1939 and there were no programmes.

The first player to be cautioned in a Football League game was Alec Dick, an Everton full-back who, on 13 October 1888, apparently hit a Notts County player and used foul language. The first offence was not proven and Dick was simply ordered to apologize for using ungentlemanly language.

At the end of the first season, Preston North End were declared League Champions. They were unbeaten in their 22 games and also won the FA Cup without conceding a goal. The four bottom clubs — Stoke, Burnley, Derby and Notts County — were all re-elected. A total of 586 goals were scored at an average of 4.43 per game and only two matches ended scoreless in that first season.

Preston retained the title the following season, at the end of which the Football League lost its first club when Stoke finished bottom and were replaced by Sunderland. It was a particular blow for the League secretary Harry Lockett of Stoke FC. Thus, the position of secretary was now held by a truly impartial individual, a situation that has remained so ever since.

In that second season, the Football League had begun to raise more and more funds by fining clubs for breaches of the regulations, mostly for ineligible players.

That season also saw the League Committee rule that since Aston Villa and Bolton Wanderers, who had both finished on 19 points, were separated by only the tiniest fraction of a goal (0.84314 and 0.84375 respectively) they should be declared as having finished equal eighth, which thus avoided the embarrassment of McGregor's Villa having to apply for re-election.

In 1890-91, a new name appeared on the Football League trophy when Everton took top place. During this season, newcomers Sunderland became the first club to have two points deducted when they fielded goalkeeper Teddy Doig before his qualifying period was ended.

The League also imposed a minimum admission charge of 6d (less than 3p) to games, although they let in ladies free.

In December 1891, concerned at the 'poaching' of players, the Football League and the newly-formed Football Alliance agreed a maximum signing-on fee of £10. It remained so for the next seven decades. A bid to impose a maximum wage in 1891 failed for the time being.

In April 1891 the first inter-League game took place between the Football League and the Football Alliance at Olive Grove, Sheffield. Other fixtures were added and the games were used primarily as fund-raisers for the participating competitions.

At the end of the League's third season Stoke, who had played a season in the Football Alliance, were voted back in with Lancashire club, Darwen. This time there was no team dropping out, the League being extended to 14 clubs.

In their second season of membership, Sunderland took the title and at the 1892 annual meeting it was decided to form a Second Division (although it initially referred to as the 'Second League') by incorporating many of the clubs from the Football Alliance. West Brom, incidentaly, having just won the FA Cup, were exempted from having to apply for re-election even though they had finished in the bottom four.

Nottingham Forest, Newton Heath (later Manchester United) and The Wednesday went straight into what was now effectively the First Division; Darwen, who had just finished bottom, joined the Second Division.

Newcastle East End, Middlesbrough and Middlesbrough Ironopolis (who would amalgamate if accepted) applied for the First Division and, having been rejected, each turned down a Second Division place. Liverpool, a newly-formed club, were also turned down and spent their first season in the Lancashire League, which they won.

The Football League was now expanding into new areas and William McGregor resigned, to be replaced by the Bolton-based referee and journalist John Bentley who was to have such an enormous impact on the League's affairs.

Now a two-division affair, the Football League had to address the problem of promotion and relegation. In April 1892, with Sunderland again the League Champions, six clubs fought out a 19th-century version of today's play-offs, which were resurrected in 1987. Three from the top of Division Two and three from the bottom of Division One played what were called 'test matches,' whilst the bottom four clubs in Division Two had to submit to re-election.

The outcome was that Accrington and Notts County were relegated and Darwen and Sheffield United promoted. Bootle, who had finished outside the re-election zone, resigned anyway and the Second Division was enlarged to 15 clubs with the election of Newcastle United, Rotherham County and Middlesbrough.

The test match idea was eventually dropped in favour of automatic promotion/relegation after the infamous 'game without a shot at goal', when Stoke and Burnley, each needing a point, blatently contrived a goalless draw at the end of the 1897-8 season.

In 1898-9, the first season of automatic ups and downs, there was a quite remarkable situation when the game between Aston Villa (the eventual Champions) and The Wednesday (who were to finish bottom) on 26 November was abandoned because of bad light with Villa leading 3-1 and just over ten minutes to play. The remaining minutes were played out on 13 March the following year, when Villa added another goal.

New names were now being engraved on the Football League Championship trophy. Aston Villa were the giants up to the turn of the century with five successes, whilst Liverpool and Sheffield United also won the title in that time. Villa were the true football giants of that decade and in 1896-7 they became the second team (and the last for over 60 years) to win the League and FA Cup double. They did it with the names of Athersmith, Devey, Spencer, Reynolds and the Cowans making the headlines, for soccer was now receiving much greater newspaper coverage.

Still there were many changing names in the League's membership and in 1893, Woolwich Arsenal became the first Football League club in London. Meanwhile, the League was being steadily increased in numbers and by 1900 the First and Second Divisions each stood at 18 clubs.

In the early years of this century, Liverpool twice won the title and were relegated in between, and The Wednesday were League Champions in consecutive years.

Liverpool's first title came in 1900-01, despite few changes in playing personnel from the side which had finished in tenth place the previous season. Despite winning their first three games, Liverpool had fallen to eighth by the middle of January and an early exit from the FA Cup meant that the Anfielders had lost three consecutive games. But from 9 February until the end of the season on 29 April, they were unbeaten, conceding only four goals in their last 12 matches. The Merseysiders were thus Champions only eight seasons after joining the Football League.

The Reds were relegated at the end of the 1903-04 season, but in 1905-06 they became the first club to win the First and Second Divisions in consecutive seasons. And they took their second League Championship with the addition of only two players — goalkeeper Sam Hardy and half-back James Bradley — to the side which had stormed to the Second Division title.

Yet a strange twist perhaps helped Liverpool to this second title. On the opening day of the season, centre-forward Jack Parkinson broke his wrist at Woolwich Arsenal's Plumstead ground. Joe Hewitt took over and ended the season as the Reds' leading scorer with 23 goals from only 37 games. Early in the season, Liverpool had languished in the bottom

Aston Villa attacking the Everton goal in September 1901, when a crowd of 20,000 saw a 1-1 draw. Everton finished the season runners- up.

Liverpool's Jack Parkinson breaks his wrist in a collision with the Woolwich Arsenal goalkeeper in September 1905 but Liverpool went on to win the title.

two before an unbeaten run of 16 games swept them to the top.

On 2 September 1899, The Wednesday opened their new ground at Owlerton with a Second Division game against Chesterfield. The ground became known as Hillsborough and Wednesday celebrated the move by winning the Second Division title that season.

After a period of consolidation it was Wednesday's turn to write their name on the Football League trophy. They topped the First Division in 1902-03 and retained the title the following season. Their first success was a close-run affair. When the Owls had completed their programme, Sunderland, the other contenders, still had a game to play. In the event the Wearsiders suffered an unexpected setback at Newcastle.

On the day their fate was decided, Wednesday were helping to promote professional football in Devon, playing Notts County at Home Park where a 3-0 win earned them the Plymouth Bowl. They retained the League Championship in more comfortable fashion, finishing three points ahead of Manchester City in a season when there was talk of a League and Cup double at Owlerton. They lost to Manchester City in the FA Cup semi-final at Goodison Park. And then City beat Bolton in the Final, having, of course, themselves missed out on the double by losing the title to Wednesday.

Manchester United, inspired by the great Billy Meredith, won the First Division title for the first time in 1907-08, the season that United were floated as a public company. Meredith had joined them in May 1906, in the wake of a bribes and illegal payments scandal surrounding his previous club, Manchester City, which had seen him and others receive lengthy suspensions.

Meredith made his United debut after the ban had been lifted on 1 January 1907 and the following season, along with former City colleagues Burgess, Bannister and Sandy Turnbull, all of whom had also been suspended, he helped United to the title.

They were by far the First Division's outstanding team, finishing nine points clear of runners-up Aston Villa, who were themselves only 13 points clear of the bottom club, Birmingham. Between them Meredith, Sandy Turnbull and the England winger George Wall scored over 50 of United's goals. Vittorio Pozzo, the man who was to guide Italy to two World Cup triumphs in the 1930s, was then a poor student living in England. He watched United during their Championship season and used some of their techniques in his successful Italian teams.

But the great name in Edwardian soccer was that of Newcastle United, who enjoyed three Championship successes in five seasons as well as appearing in five FA Cup Finals before World War One.

In 1905 they won the title for the first time and almost did the double, losing to Aston Villa in the FA Cup Final. The following season they were again beaten in the Cup Final but lifted another First Division title in 1907. Twelve months later the Magpies lost yet another Cup Final but in 1909 they achieved another Championship triumph, despite an amazing 9-1 defeat by arch-rivals Sunderland at St James' Park. The Cup eventually went to Gallowgate in 1910 when Newcastle beat Barnsley in a replayed Final at Goodison Park. A year later, by now the most consistent team of the decade, they reached the Cup Final once more, this time losing to Barnsley.

There were some great names in the famous black and white stripes — long-serving goalkeeper Jimmy Lawrence, full-backs Carr, McCombie and McCracken, half-backs Veitch, McWilliam and Gardner, and a forward line of Rutherford, Shepherd, Appleyard and Howie. In the history of the game only a handful of clubs can match the dominance which Newcastle United enjoyed in their Edwardian heyday.

Before the Football League closed down during World War One, Manchester United, Aston Villa, Sunderland and Everton had added to their earlier wins and Blackburn Rovers were First Division champions for the first time in 1911-12.

For so long, Blackburn supporters had criticized their club for being too frugal with money. Now the Rovers' board spent on strengthening the team and were rewarded with the League Championship. The major signing was that of Jock Simpson, a right winger who joined Blackburn from Falkirk. This former driver of a horse-drawn omnibus cost Rovers a record £1,800 and he repaid them with some fine performances in the Championship season.

Two seasons later, Blackburn were Champions again. They began the season with five straight wins and that set the pattern for the rest of the campaign. Simpson, Danny Shea (a £2,000 signing from West Ham), Eddie Latheron (a £25 'snip' from non-League football) and Joe Hodkinson (from Second Division Glossop) blended well together. Behind them, one of the League's finest full-back partnerships of long-serving England

Sheffield Wednesday, League Champions in 1902-03. Back row (left to right): Ferrier, Hemingfield, Thackery. Middle row (players only): Layton, Langley, Lyall, Crawshaw, Ruddlesdin. Front row: V.Simpson, Davies, Chapman, Wilson, Mallock, Spiksley, G.Simpson.

Action from the game between Sheffield Wednesday, the League Champions, and Aston Villa at Villa Park on Boxing Day 1904. A crowd of nearly 50,000 saw Villa win 2-1.

player Bob Crompton and Arthur Cowell was as reliable as ever.

One outrageous piece of business had been conducted in 1919 when Arsenal, sixth in Division Two in the last prewar season and heavily in debt after moving to their new stadium at Highbury, were engineered into the First Division by their owner, Sir Henry Norris MP. Each division was to be extended by two clubs but there was never any justification for Arsenal to be moved up to Division One, where they have remained ever since.

West Brom and Burnley added their names in the first two seasons of postwar football before Liverpool won the title twice in succession. And in 1920-21, the Third Division was formed, by incorporating clubs from the Southern League, although Cardiff City went straight into Division Two and Grimsby Town made up the numbers in the new Third Division with the prospect of some long journeys.

Twelve months later the new section became the Third Division South with the creation of the Third Division North, to which Grimsby where thankfully switched. Now the Football League had four divisions and numbered 88 clubs in all, although the Third Division sides were 'associate members' only.

In 1923-4, Huddersfield Town won the first of three successive Football League Championship titles. The man who started them on that historic road was a former Northampton Town player called Herbert Chapman. Before Town's third title win, Chapman had moved to Highbury, where he set the Gunners on the road to a similar feat, although he was to die before it was completed.

Huddersfield's first success was not resolved until the very last day of the season, when their 3-0 win over Nottingham Forest, coupled with Cardiff City's 0-0 draw at St Andrew's, was sufficient to give the Yorkshire club the title by 0.024 of a goal. An eight-match run, during which they dropped only four points, clinched the title 12 months later. And the third Championship was achieved after Town again opened the season with ten unbeaten games and finally took the title with a 3-0 win over their 'bogey' team. Bolton Wanderers. There was something of an anticlimax after that when Town lost their last two games.

The Huddersfield team which achieved this treble was skippered by the former Aston Villa forward, Clem Stephenson, who scored 20 goals in 105 appearances in that time. Other stalwarts were Tommy Wilson, Billy Watson, Billy Smith, Sam Wadsworth, George Brown (leading overall scorer with 63 goals), David Steele, Ray Goodall, George Cook, Ted Taylor, Charlie Wilson and Alex Jackson, one of the most gifted forwards of the inter-war period, who joined

Manchester United, League Champions 1907-08. Back row (left to right): Mr J.E.Mangnall (secretary), Bacon, Picken, Edmonds, Mr Murray (director), Moger, Mr H.Davies (chairman), Homer, Mr Lawton (director), Bell, Mr Deakin (director). Middle row: Meredith, Duckworth, Roberts, J.Turnbull, West, Stacey. Front row: Whalley, Hofton, Halse, Wall.

Liverpool in 1923, after their consecutive League Championship titles. Back row (left to right): Wadsworth, Connell (trainer), McNab, Scott, Walsh, unknown director, Bromilow. Front row: Longworth, Gilhespy, Forshaw, McKinlay, Chambers, Hopkin. Jimmy Walsh had replaced Dick Johnson at centre-forward.

Huddersfield for a club record fee of £5,000 from Aberdeen.

After Huddersfield's feat, the League trophy ended the 1920s in familiar hands with Newcastle, Everton and Sheffield Wednesday all regaining it. Arsenal began the 1930s with their first Championship and after Everton had interrupted their run in 1931-2, the Gunners were Champions for three seasons on the trot.

Everton's title had been won with the epic contribution of centre-forward Dixie Dean, who scored 45 League goals that season. Of course, that was relatively small beer to Dean, who had netted a record 60 goals in the 1927-8 season and would end his career with 349 League goals in only 399 matches. He also scored a record 37 hat-tricks during his career.

But it was Arsenal who were perhaps the first truly 'national' club, stamping their name indelibly on English football during the 1930s.

Besides the innovative Herbert Chapman — amongst many other things he is credited with evolving the 'stopper' centre-half system to counter the 1925 change in the offside law — there were great players like Alex James and Cliff Bastin, Eddie Hapgood and George Male, Jack Crayston and Wilf Copping, Jack Lambert and then Ted Drake, all of whom became household names. Seven Arsenal players turned out in one England team.

When the Gunners won the title for the first time in 1930-31 they were the first southern club to lift the Championship. The following season they finished two points behind top club Everton and lost a controversial FA Cup Final to Everton. Then came another Championship, in a season also marked by a sensational FA Cup defeat at the hands of Third Division Walsall, and two more titles quickly followed.

In January 1934, Hebert Chapman died after a short illness. It is impossible to overestimate his contribution to the game

Arsenal skipper Eddie Hapgood (left), gets the ball away from a Sheffield Wednesday forward in the 1930s.

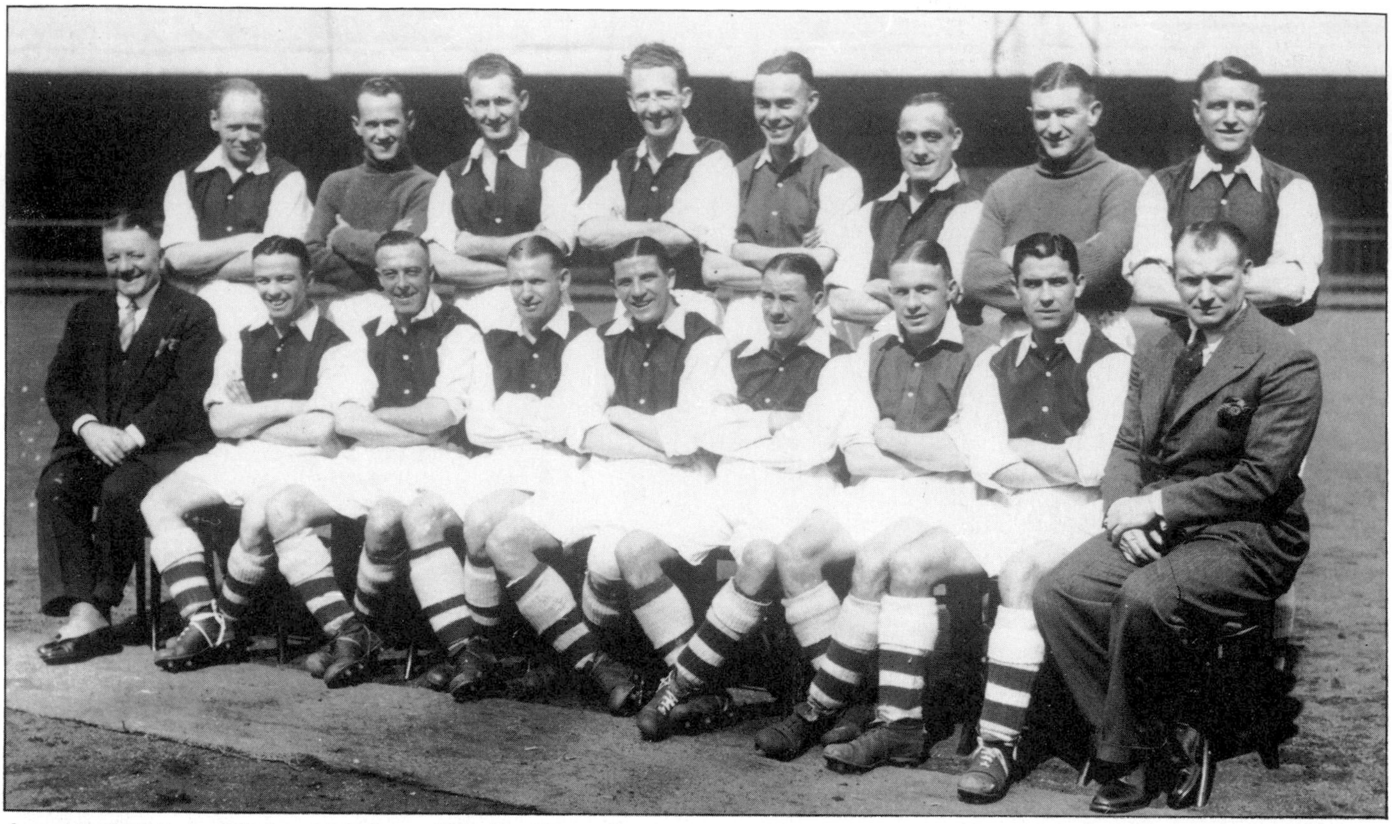

Arsenal in 1936. Back row (left to right): George Male, Alex Wilson, Jack Crayston, Herbie Roberts, Norman Sidey, Wilf Copping, Frank Moss, Eddie Hapgood. Front row: George Allison (manager), Bobby Davidson, Joe Hulme, Cliff Bastin, Ted Drake, Alex James, Pat Beasley, Jackie Milne, Tom Whittaker (trainer).

Everton in 1938-9, the last League Champions before World War Two. Back row (left to right): Lawton, Jones, Sagar, Cook (trainer), Mercer, Greenhalgh. Front row: Cook, Gillick, Bentham, Thomson, Stevenson, Boyes. J.Shannon is the club mascot.

and the period 1929-34 will always be known as the 'Chapman Era'. George Allison, one of the club's directors and a well-known journalist, took over as manager of Arsenal and saw the Gunners through to their historic treble.

During the 1920s and '30s, transfer fees had spiralled. In 1928, Arsenal paid a record £10,000 for centre-forward David Jack from Bolton. His fee was 50 per cent higher than the previous record, paid by Aston Villa for Partick Thistle's Jimmy Gibson. And it had all started with the £1,000 which Middlesbrough had paid Sunderland for centre-forward Alf Common in 1905, when 'Boro were criticized for 'buying' their way out of trouble, as though it was not a gentlemanly thing to do. It was an upward trend that would continue until fees approached the £2 million mark in the 1980s.

Although Arsenal remained the country's leading club up to World War Two, they won the title only once more, in 1937-8, with Sunderland, Manchester City (for the first time) and Everton all taking their turn before the competition

Dixie Dean, Everton's prolific goalscorer.

Herbert Chapman, the manager who gave his name to an era.

was again suspended. In the Everton side which won the last post-war League Championship, a 19-year-old centre-forward called Tommy Lawton scored 34 goals. Sadly, like so many of his generation, Lawton was about to lose six years of his career to the war.

Although Liverpool were the first post-war Champions — this was the team of Billy Liddell, Jack Balmer, Albert Stubbins, Phil Taylor, Bob Paisley and company — Arsenal again lifted the title in 1947-8. Their heroes were now Joe Mercer (a member of Everton's pre-war Championship side), George Swindin, Wally Barnes, Laurie Scott, the Compton brothers, Jimmy Logie, Reg Lewis and the veteran centre-forward Ronnie Rooke.

Then a vibrant Portsmouth team, led by Jimmy Dickinson and containing exciting players like Jack Froggatt and Phil Harris, topped the First Division in successive seasons before the 1950s began with Arthur Rowe's newly-promoted Tottenham side, with its delightful 'push and run' style, going straight to the top of the tree.

Rowe's Tottenham side was one of the most purely 'footballing' teams the game has ever seen. They began the 1949-50 season with a long unbeaten run, including two spells of seven consecutive victories. That was enough to give them the Second Division title and they went straight on to head Division One in 1950-51. Despite losing the first game of that season, 4-1 at home to Blackpool, they enjoyed an eight-match winning sequence in October and November and during that time beat Portsmouth (Champions for the previous two seasons) 5-1, Newcastle United 7-0 and Stoke City 6-1. There is always a hiccup, however, and bottom club Huddersfield were the only team to take all the points off Spurs that season — and also knocked them out of the FA Cup for good measure.

That great Spurs team included the skilful wing-halves Bill Nicholson and Ronnie Burgess, and delightful forward play from Eddie Baily, Len Duquemin, Les Bennett and Les Medley. Ted Ditchburn kept goal behind full-backs Alf Ramsey and Arthur Wilis.

Spurs' reign was brief, however, as Matt Busby's Manchester United (a club Busby had inherited when they had no ground in the aftermath of the war) and then Arsenal again took the title.

Those early post-war days had been a boom time for soccer attendances. After the deprivations of war, people wanted entertainment and there were queues everywhere — at cinemas and into speedway, cricket and boxing tourna-

Portsmouth, League Champions for the second year in succession in 1949-50. Back row (left to right): Scoular, Hindmarsh, Reid, Butler, Dickinson, Thompson. Front row: Harris, Clarke, Ferrier, Barlow, Froggatt.

Tottenham's 'push and run' side of the early 1950s. Back row (left to right): C.Poynton (trainer), Ramsey, Duquemin, Murphy, Ditchbum, Clarke, Bennett, Withers. Front row: Nicholson, Walters, Willis, Burgess, Baily, Medley.

ments. Football, as the true national sport, benefited most and this was a golden age of great stars and huge crowds.

Manager Stan Cullis and England skipper Billy Wright steered Wolves to the Championship in 1953-4 and nobody much begrudged Chelsea, for so long a music-hall joke, their lone success the following season before Manchester United took up the reins again.

This was the United team of Tommy Taylor and Duncan Edwards, Roger Byrne and Eddie Colman. The United team that was to be decimated and then immortalized by the Munich air disaster. In the season that United's dreams came crashing down at the end of an icy German runway, Wolves took the title and retained it the following year.

In 1958 the League format was altered significantly. The top halves of the Third Divisions North and South formed a new Third Division. The rest went into a national Fourth Division. Re-election still had to be avoided until 1987 when the bottom club had no choice but was simply relegated to what is now the GM Vauxhall Conference. It was a shock for Burnley, founder-members of the Football League, when, in the first year of play-offs and relegation from Division Four, they came within one game of going out of the League altogether.

In 1959-60, however, Burnley lifted the Championship before another great Tottenham side blossomed into full fruit. Danny Blanchflower led Bill Nicholson's side to the first modern League and FA Cup double in 1960-61 before Ipswich Town took the title in 1961-2. The names of that Spurs team rolled off the tongue like honey, names like Brown, Baker and Henry, Blanchflower, Norman and Mackay, Jones, Medwin, White, Smith, Greaves, Allen and Dyson.

This was an important era for the Football League. In 1961, led by its chairman, Jimmy Hill, the Professional Footballers' Association successfully campaigned for the abolition of the maximum wage. Now the best players could earn more by moving on and the game was to see the end of such long-serving one-club stars as Tom Finney and Nat Lofthouse. The effect was enormous. The removal of the maximum wage, whilst a move of obvious natural justice, saw the powerful big-city clubs grow more powerful still. Only they could afford the major stars and coupled, eventually, with television saturation of the game, mass car ownership and good motorway links, it began to polarize support for the big clubs. Freedom of contract and the end of the outdated (in labour terms) retain-and-transfer system would also contribute to this development.

The famous Spurs double-winning side of 1960-61. Back row (left to right): Henry, Norman, Brown, Smith, Baker. Front row: Jones, White, Blanchflower, Allen, Dyson, Mackay.

Manchester City in their Championship season of 1967-8. Back row (left to right): Book, Horne, Heslop, Ogley, Dowd, Oakes, Pardoe, Doyle. Front row: Summerbee, Connor, Bell, Crossan, Jones, Young, Coleman.

That, though, was still some way down the line. Meanwhile, down in the soccer backwater of rural Suffolk, Alf Ramsey, the former Tottenham full-back, was creating a tactical football revolution. Using a withdrawn 'winger' in Jimmy Leadbetter and two fine goalscorers in Ray Crawford and Ted Phillips, he took Ipswich Town from the Second Division to the League Championship. Four years later, Ramsey was weaving a similar tactical plan to take England to World Cup glory.

Everton, Liverpool (the first of Bill Shankly's major successes) and Manchester United all took the title in the early 1960s, and before the decade was out the Championship had gone back to Anfield and then Old Trafford. After Manchester United won it in 1967 they went on to become the first English club to win the European Cup on a night of high emotion at Wembley.

The first of Busby's successful teams had included several players who were on the books when war broke out — men like Johnny Morris, Stan Pearson, Charlie Mitten, Jack Rowley, Allenby Chilton and Johnny Carey. Now the post-Munich team paraded the skills of Munich survivor Bobby Charlton together with the ultimately wayward genius of George Best and the fiery Denis Law.

Then it was Manchester City's turn for League glory under Joe Mercer and Malcolm Allison, with United finishing runners-up to make it Manchester's season, before Don Revie carried on his Leeds United miracle. Revie had taken a club wallowing in Divison Two and eventually turned it into Championship-winning material, the first success coming in 1968-9. Leeds United, born out of the disgraced Leeds City, who were kicked out of the League in 1919 for, the cynics may say, being found out when they paid illegal bonuses, were a club who had acheived very little up to then.

Revie changed all that and his side, led by another fiery Scot in Billy Bremner, could practically be pencilled-in every week during that first Championship success as Gary Sprake, Paul Reaney, Terry Cooper, Billy Bremner, Jack Charlton, Norman Hunter, Peter Lorimer, Paul Madeley, Johnny Giles, Eddie Gray, Mick Jones and Mike O'Grady held sway.

After Everton, with their magnificent midfield of Colin Harvey, Howard Kendall and Alan Ball, had another brief

Tommy Smith (Liverpool) and Frank Gray (Leeds United) do battle at Anfield in April 1969. Chris Lawler and Ian Callaghan are in the background.

Arsenal's double-winning squad. Back row (left to right): McNab, Kennedy, Wilson, Roberts, Barnett, Simpson, Marinello. Front row: Nelson, Storey, Radford, Kelly, McLintock, Rice, Graham, Armstrong. George and Sammels are not pictured.

taste of success, Arsenal, under manager Bertie Mee, did the double in 1970-71. Many people outside Highbury said they were 'boring' — just as many people outside Elland Road had labelled Leed 'unscrupulous' — but the feat had been achieved and new Arsenal heroes like Charlie George, John Radford, George Graham, Peter Storey, Ray Kennedy and Frank McLintock were the darlings of Highbury.

Brian Clough took Derby to their first title in 1971-2 — they were to win it again in 1974-5 under former Tottenham star, Dave Mackay — but now the Football League was entering the age of Liverpool. Since 1975-6, Liverpool have won the Football League Championship on no less than ten occasions. Occasionally there have been interlopers — Aston Villa, Nottingham Forest, Everton and Arsenal, who won the title in 1988-9 and lifted it again in 1990-91 — but Liverpool have been the most remarkably consistent club in the history of the competition. Successive managers — Bob Paisley, Joe Fagan and Kenny Dalglish — have inherited Bill Shankly's legacy and built upon it.

In 1975-6, Paisley steered Liverpool to the League Championship and the UEFA Cup, first won three years earlier. The title was retained the following year and if Liverpool's away form concerned their supporters, their results at the citadel which Anfield had become more than allayed any fears. It has been a familar story ever since — Liverpool were Champions in 1978-9, 1979-80, 1981-2, 1982-3, 1983-4, 1985-6, 1987-8 and 1989-90.

During that time there have been many Anfield heroes: Keegan, Toshack, Heighway, Callaghan, Hughes, Thompson, Clemence, Neal, Jones, Dalglish, Souness, Smith, the Kennedys, McDermott,

Hansen, Johnson, Johnston, Case, Fairclough, Grobbelaar, Lee, Whelan, Lawrenson, Rush, Nicol, Molby, Barnes, Beardsley, Aldridge, McMahon, Gillespie, Houghton. One could go on and on, for there have been so very many headline-making names to come out of Anfield.

And all this, of course, has been achieved by the tremendous consistency of the Liverpool approach, the famous 'boot-room' brigade who have plotted the Reds' seemingly inexorable march over these past two decades.

Indeed, it is now hard to imagine a time when Liverpool were not dominating English football, although the 1991-2 season saw the Reds suffer injury and uncharacteristically fall away in the First Division.

It may be, of course, that they will recover to dominate it for years to come. It may be that Arsenal will emerge as the dominant force once more.

But already, new challengers in the shape of Leeds United, who lifted the Football League Championship in 1991-2 under Howard Wilkinson, have appeared to confirm that there is still a chance for a team from outside the ring of Merseyside and London clubs, who have, by and large, made the Football League title their preserve for so many years now.

It may be, of course, that the FA's new 'Super League' will render such speculation superfluous. Perhaps the fairy-story rise of clubs like Oxford United and Wimbledon, both of whom made it from the Southern League to the First Division in truly testing times, will never be repeated.

The effects of the advent of the Premier League have not been so far-reaching as was first thought. The existing Second Division clubs and the players' union, the Professional Footballers' Association, have seen to that.

Far from being a small élite group, the Premier League will not look much different from the old First Division after all. The Football League has proved too lusty a centenarian to be casually swept aside.

Indeed, the story of the Football League is a remarkable one and a tale that even that great 19th-century visionary, William McGregor, could hardly have foreseen. Would McGregor approve of the Premier League? Perhaps he would, for he was ever the visionary. After all, was not the original Football League of 1888 just that — a premier competition for the best in the land?

Liverpool with the Milk Cup in 1982, in the middle of a hat-trick of League Championships. Back row (left to right): Lawrenson, Fairclough, Hansen, Whelan, Rush, Grobbelaar. Front row: Johnston, Dalglish, Neal, Souness, Lee, Kennedy.

Football League Records

HIGHEST WINS

(HOME)

Division 1	West Bromwich A	12	Darwen	0	4 Apr 1892
	Nottingham F	12	Leicester Fosse	0	21 Apr 1909
Division 2	Newcastle U	13	Newport Co	0	5 Oct 1946
Division 3(S)	Luton T	12	Bristol R	0	13 Apr 1936
Division 3(N)	Stockport Co	13	Halifax T	0	6 Jan 1934
Division 3	Gillingham	10	Chesterfield	0	5 Sep 1987
Division 4	Oldham Ath	11	Southport	0	26 Dec 1962

(AWAY)

Division 1	Newcastle U	1	Sunderland	9	5 Dec 1908
	Cardiff C	1	Wolverhampton W	9	3 Sep 1955
Division 2	Burslem PV	0	Sheffield U	10	10 Dec 1892
Division 3(S)	Northampton T	0	Walsall	8	2 Feb 1947
Division 3(N)	Accrington S	0	Barnsley	9	3 Feb 1934
Division 3	Halifax T	0	Fulham	8	16 Sep 1969
Division 4	Crewe Alex	1	Rotherham U	8	8 Sep 1973
Aggregate Division 3(N)	Tranmere R	13	Oldham Ath	4	26 Dec 1935

League Championship Hat-tricks

Huddersfield T 1923-24 to 1925-26
Arsenal 1932-33 to 1934-35
Liverpool 1981-82 to 1983-84

Most Goals For in a Season

		Goals	Games	
Division 1	Aston Villa	128	42	1930-31
Division 2	Middlesbrough	122	42	1926-27
Division 3(S)	Millwall	127	42	1927-28
Division 3(N)	Bradford C	128	42	1928-29
Division 3	Queen's Park R	111	46	1961-62
Division 4	Peterborough U	134	46	1960-61

Middlesbrough in 1926-7, Second Division champions and scorers of most goals in a Division Two season. Back row (left to right): Miller, Smith, Mathieson, Freeman, Ashman. Front row: Pease, Birrell, Camsell, Carr, Williams, Holmes.

Least Goals For in a Season

(Minimum 42 games)

		Goals	Games	
Division 1	Stoke C	24	42	1984-85
Division 2	Watford	24	42	1971-72
Division 3(S)	Crystal Palace	33	42	1950-51
Division 3(N)	Crewe Alex	32	42	1923-24
Division 3	Stockport Co	27	46	1969-70
Division 4	Crewe Alex	29	46	1981-82

Most Goals Against in a Season

		Goals	Games	
Division 1	Blackpool	125	42	1930-31
Division 2	Darwen	141	34	1898-99
Division 3(S)	Merthyr T	135	42	1929-30
Division 3(N)	Nelson	136	42	1927-28
Division 3	Accrington S	123	46	1959-60
Division 4	Hartlepools U	109	46	1959-60

Least Goals Against in a Season

(minimum 42 games)

		Goals	Games	
Division 1	Liverpool	16	42	1978-79
Division 2	Manchester U	23	42	1924-25
Division 3(S)	Southampton	21	42	1921-22
Division 3(N)	Port Vale	21	46	1953-54
Division 3	Middlesbrough	30	46	1986-87
Division 4	Lincoln C	25	46	1980-81

Most Points in a Season

(two points for a win)

		Points	Games	
Division 1	Liverpool	68	42	1978-79
Division 2	Tottenham H	70	42	1919-20
Division 3(S)	Nottingham F	70	46	1950-51
	Bristol C	70	46	1954-55
Division 3(N)	Doncaster R	72	42	1946-47
Division 3	Aston V	70	46	1971-72
Division 4	Lincoln C	74	46	1975-76

(three points for a win)

Division 1	Everton	90	42	1984-85
	Liverpool	90	40	1987-88
Division 2	Chelsea	99	46	1988-89
Division 3	Bournemouth	97	46	1986-87
Division 4	Swindon T	102	46	1985-86

Fewest Points in a Season

(minimum 34 games)

		Points	Games	
Division 1	Stoke C	17	42	1984-85
Division 2	Doncaster R	8	34	1904-05
	Loughborough T	8	34	1899-1900
Division 3(S)	Merthyr T	21	42	1924-25 & 1929-30
	Queen's Park R	21	42	1925-26
Division 3(N)	Rochdale	11	40	1931-32
Division 3	Rochdale	21	46	1973-74
	Cambridge U	21	46	1984-85
Division 4	Workington	19	46	1976-77

Most Wins in a Season

		Wins	Games	
Division 1	Tottenham H	31	42	1960-61
Division 2	Tottenham H	32	42	1919-20

Tottenham's 1919-20 line-up, the season in which Spurs won a record 32 matches. Back row (left top right): Archibald, Smith, Jacques, Grimsdell, Lowe, Brown. Front row: McDonald, Banks, Seed, Cantrell, Bliss, Chipperfield.

Division 3(S)	Millwall	30	42	1927-28
	Plymouth Arg	30	42	1929-30
	Cardiff C	30	42	1946-47
	Nottingham F	30	46	1950-51
	Bristol C	30	46	1954-55
Division 3(N)	Doncaster R	33	42	1946-47
Division 3	Aston Villa	32	46	1971-72
Division 4	Lincoln C	32	46	1975-76
	Swindon T	32	46	1985-86

Record Home Wins in a Season

Brentford won all 21 games in Division 3 South in 1929-30

Undefeated at Home

Liverpool 85 games (63 League, 9 League Cup, 7 European, 6 FA Cup), Jan 1978-Jan 1981.

Record Away Wins in a Season

Doncaster R won 18 out of 21 games in Division 3 North in 1946-47

Fewest Wins in a Season

		Wins	Games	
Division 1	Stoke	3	22	1889-90
	Woolwich Arsenal	3	38	1912-13
	Stoke C	3	42	1984-85
Division 2	Loughborough T	1	34	1899-1900
Division 3(S)	Merthyr T	6	42	1929-30
	Queen's Park R	6	42	1925-26
Division 3(N)	Rochdale	4	40	1931-32
Division 3	Rochdale	2	46	1973-74
Division 4	Southport	3	46	1976-77

Most Defeats in a Season

		Defeats	Games	
Division 1	Stoke C	31	42	1984-85
Division 2	Tranmere R	31	42	1938-39
Division 3(S)	Merthyr T	29	42	1924-25
	Walsall	29	46	1952-53
	Walsall	29	46	1953-54
Division 3(N)	Rochdale	33	40	1931-32
Division 3	Cambridge U	33	46	1984-85
Division 4	Newport Co	33	46	1987-88

Fewest Defeats in a Season

(minimum 20 games)

		Defeats	Games	
Division 1	Preston NE	0	22	1888-89
	Leeds U	2	42	1968-69
Division 2	Liverpool	0	28	1893-94
	Burnley	2	30	1897-98
	Bristol C	2	38	1905-06
	Leeds U	3	42	1963-64
Division 3(S)	Southampton	4	42	1921-22
	Plymouth Arg	4	42	1929-30
Division 3(N)	Port Vale	3	46	1953-54
	Doncaster R	3	42	1946-47
	Wolverhampton W	3	42	1923-24
Division 3	Queen's Park R	5	46	1966-67
Division 4	Lincoln C	4	46	1975-76
	Sheffield U	4	46	1981-82
	Bournemouth	4	46	1981-82

Most Drawn Games in a Season

		Draws	Games	
Division 1	Norwich C	23	42	1978-79
Division 4	Exeter C	23	46	1986-87

Most Goals in a Game

Division 1	Ted Drake (Arsenal) 7 goals v Aston Villa	14 Dec 1935
	James Ross (Preston NE) 7 goals v Stoke	6 Oct 1888
Division 2	Tommy Briggs (Blackburn R) 7 goals v Bristol R	5 Feb 1955
	Neville Coleman (Stoke C) 7 goals v Lincoln C (a)	23 Feb 1957
Division 3(S)	Joe Payne (Luton T) 10 goals v Bristol R	13 Apr 1936
Division 3(N)	Bunny Bell (Tranmere R) 9 goals v Oldham Ath	26 Dec 1935
Division 3	Steve Earle (Fulham) 5 goals v Halifax T	16 Sep 1969
	Barrie Thomas (Scunthorpe U) 5 goals v Luton T	24 Apr 1965
	Keith East (Swindon T) 5 goals v Mansfield T	20 Nov 1965
	Alf Wood (Shrewsbury T) 5 goals v Blackburn R	2 Oct 1971
	Tony Caldwell (Bolton W) 5 goals v Walsall	10 Sep 1983
	Andy Jones (Port Vale) 5 goals v Newport Co	4 May 1987
	Steve Wilkinson(Mansfield T) 5 goals v Birmingham C	3 Apr 1990
Division 4	Bert Lister (Oldham Ath) 6 goals v Southport	26 Dec 1962

Neville Coleman (left) scored seven goals for Stoke City at Lincoln. Joe Payne (right) hit ten for Luton Town against Bristol Rovers.

Most League Goals in a Season

		Goals	Games	
Division 1	Dixie Dean (Everton)	60	39	1927-28
Division 2	George Camsell (Middlesbrough)	59	37	1926-27
Division 3(S)	Joe Payne (Luton T)	55	39	1936-37
Division 3(N)	Ted Harston (Mansfield T)	55	41	1936-37
Division 3	Derek Reeves (Southampton)	39	46	1959-60
Division 4	Terry Bly (Peterborough U)	52	46	1960-61

Most League Goals in a Career

		Goals	Games	
Arthur Rowley	West Bromwich A	4	24	1946-48
	Fulham	27	56	1948-50
	Leicester C	251	303	1950-58
	Shrewsbury T	152	236	1958-65
		434	619	

Longest Winning Sequence

		Games	
Division 1	Tottenham H	13	1959-60(2) & 1960-61(11)
Division 2	Manchester U	14	1904-05
	Bristol C	14	1905-06
	Preston NE	14	1950-51
Division 3	Reading	13	1985-86
From season's start			
Division 1	Tottenham H	11	1960-61

Longest Sequence Without a Win From Season's Start

		Games	
Division 1	Sheffield U	16	1990-91

Longest Sequence of Consecutive Scoring

(individual)

		Games	
Arthur Chandler	(Leicester C)	16	1924-25

Longest Winning Sequence in a Season

		Games	
Division 1	Tottenham H	11	1960-61
	Liverpool	11	1981-82
Division 2	Manchester U	14	1904-05
Division 2	Bristol C	14	1905-06
Division 2	Preston NE	14	1950-51

Longest Unbeaten Sequence

		Games	
Division 1	Nottingham F	42	Nov 1977-Dec 1978

Longest Unbeaten Sequence in a Season

		Games	
Division 1	Burnley	30	1920-21

Longest Unbeaten Start to a Season

		Games	
Division 1	Leeds U	29	1973-74
Division 1	Liverpool	29	1987-88

Longest Sequence Without a Win in a Season

		Games	
Division 2	Cambridge U	31	1983-84

Longest Sequence of Consecutive Defeats

		Games	
Division 3(N)	Rochdale	17	1931-32

Goalkeeping Records

(without conceding a goal)

Steve Death (Reading) 1,103 minutes from 24 March to 18 August 1979.

Penalties

Most in a season (individual)

		Goals	
Division 1	Francis Lee (Manchester C)	13	1971-72

Most awarded in one game

Five Crystal Palace (4-1 scored, three missed) v Brighton & HA (1 scored), Div 2 ... 1988-89

Most Saved in a season

Division 1 Paul Cooper (Ipswich T) 8 (out of 10) 1979-80

Steve Death (left) went 1,103 minutes without conceding a goal. Paul Cooper (right) saved eight penalties in one season.

Most League Appearances

968 Peter Shilton(286 Leicester City, 110 Stoke City, 202 Nottingham Forest, 188 Southampton, 175 Derby County, 7 Plymouth Argyle) ... 1966-92
824 Terry Paine (713 Southampton, 111 Hereford United) ... 1957-77
790 Tommy Hutchison (165 Blackpool, 314 Coventry City, 46 Manchester City, 92 Burnley, 173 Swansea City, also 68 Alloa 1965-68) ... 1968-90
777 Alan Oakes (565 Manchester City, 211 Chester City, 1 Port Vale) 1959-84
770 John Trollope (all for Swindon Town) ... 1960-80*
764 Jimmy Dickinson (all for Portsmouth) ... 1946-65
761 Roy Sproson (all for Port Vale) ... 1950-72
758 Ray Clemence (48 Scunthorpe United, 470 Liverpool, 240 Tottenham Hotspur) ... 1966-87
757 Pat Jennings (48 Watford, 472 Tottenham Hotspur, 237 Arsenal) 1963-86

*record for one club

Consecutive

401 Harold Bell (401 Tranmere R; 459 in all games) ... 1946-55

Youngest Players

Football League

Albert Geldard, 15 years 158 days, Bradford v Millwall, Division 2, 16 Sep 1929; and Ken Roberts, 15 years 158 days, Wrexham v Bradford, Division 3 North, 1 Sep 1951.

Football League goalscorer

Ronnie Dix, 15 years 180 days, Bristol Rovers v Norwich City, Division 3 South, 3 Mar 1928.

Ronnie Dix (left) is the youngest-ever Football League goalscorer. Albert Geldard (right) is the youngest-ever League debutant.

Division 1

Derek Forster, 15 years 185 days, Sunderland v Leicester City, 22 Aug 1984.

Division 1 goalscorer

Jason Dozzell, 16 years 57 days Ipswich Town v Coventry City (substitute) 4 Feb 1984.

Division 1 hat-tricks

Alan Shearer, 17 years 240 days, Southampton v Arsenal 9 Apr 1988.
Jimmy Greaves, 17 years 308 days, Chelsea v Portsmouth, 25 Dec 1957.

Chelsea's Jimmy Greaves (left), the youngest player to hit a First Division hat-trick until Alan Shearer beat that record. Jason Dozzell (right) is the youngest-ever First Division scorer.

Oldest Players

Football League

Neil McBain, 52 years 4 months, New Brighton v Hartlepools United, Division 3 North, 15 Feb 1947 (McBain was New Brighton's manager and had to play in goals in an emergency).

Division 1

Stanley Matthews, 50 years 5 days, Stoke City v Fulham, 6 Feb 1965.

Football League Records Seasons 1888-89 & 1889-90

Top scorer: J.Goodall (Preston North End) 21 goals.

DIVISION 1

	ACCRINGTON	ASTON VILLA	BLACKBURN R	BOLTON W	BURNLEY	DERBY CO	EVERTON	NOTTS CO	PRESTON N.E.	STOKE	W.B.A.	WOLVERHAMPTON W
1 ACCRINGTON		D15 1-1	J19 0-2	M23 2-3	D01 5-1	O13 6-2	D29 3-1	J26 1-2	O20 0-0	a20 2-0	N24 2-1	O06 4-4
2 ASTON VILLA	O27 4-3		O13 6-1	J12 6-2	D22 4-2	D29 4-2	S22 2-1	S29 9-1	F09 0-2	S15 5-1	J19 2-0	N24 2-1
3 BLACKBURN R	S15 5-5	N17 5-1		D08 4-4	F04 4-2	a15 3-0	N10 3-0	D15 5-2	J12 2-2	O27 5-2	S22 6-2	O20 2-2
4 BOLTON W	D22 4-1	O20 2-3	J26 3-2		S15 3-4	S08 3-6	S29 6-2	M09 7-3	N24 2-5	O13 2-1	N17 1-2	D29 2-1
5 BURNLEY	J12 2-2	J05 4-0	N03 1-7	O06 4-1		J19 1-0	N17 2-2	D29 1-0	D15 2-2	D08 2-1	N10 2-0	O13 0-4
6 DERBY CO	S22 1-1	M09 5-2	N24 0-2	D26 2-3	M02 1-0		O20 2-4	D22 3-2	S29 2-3	J26 2-1	S15 1-2	J12 3-0
7 EVERTON	S08 2-1	O06 2-0	M30 3-1	N03 2-1	N24 3-2	O27 6-2		S15 2-1	J19 0-2	J12 2-1	D01 1-4	F09 1-2
8 NOTTS CO	N10 3-3	D08 2-4	O06 3-3	M05 0-4	O27 6-1	M16 3-5	O13 3-1		N03 0-7	N24 0-3	J12 2-1	J19 3-0
9 PRESTON N.E.	N17 2-0	N10 1-1	D29 1-0	S22 3-1	S08 5-2	D08 5-0	D22 3-0	J05 4-1		O06 7-0	O13 3-0	O27 5-2
10 STOKE	S29 2-4	N03 1-1	D01 2-1	J19 2-2	O20 4-3	a06 1-1	D15 0-0	S22 3-0	N12 0-3		S08 0-2	N17 0-1
11 W.B.A.	N03 2-2	J26 3-3	D22 2-1	N05 1-5	S29 4-3	O06 5-0	F23 1-0	O20 4-2	D26 0-5	D29 2-0		J05 1-3
12 WOLVERHAMPTON W	D08 4-0	S08 1-1	S29 2-2	N10 3-2	S22 4-1	N03 4-1	J26 4-0	F23 2-1	S15 0-4	D22 4-1	D15 2-1	

1888-89

LEAGUE TABLE
FOOTBALL LEAGUE

	P	W	D	L	F	A	W	D	L	F	A	Pts
Preston NE	22	10	1	0	39	7	8	3	0	35	8	40
Aston Villa	22	10	0	1	44	16	2	5	4	17	27	29
Wolves	22	8	2	1	30	14	4	2	5	20	23	28
Blackburn R	22	7	4	0	44	22	3	2	6	22	23	26
Bolton W	22	6	0	5	35	30	4	2	5	28	29	22
WBA	22	6	2	3	25	24	4	0	7	15	22	22
Accrington	22	5	3	3	26	17	1	5	5	22	31	20
Everton	22	8	0	3	24	17	1	2	8	11	29	20
Burnley	22	6	3	2	21	19	1	0	10	21	43	17
Derby Co	22	5	1	5	22	20	2	1	8	19	41	16
Notts Co	22	4	2	5	25	32	1	0	10	15	41	12
Stoke	22	3	4	4	15	18	1	0	10	11	33	12

Top scorer: J.Ross (Preston North End) 24 goals.

DIVISION 1

	ACCRINGTON	ASTON VILLA	BLACKBURN R	BOLTON W	BURNLEY	DERBY CO	EVERTON	NOTTS CO	PRESTON N.E.	STOKE	W.B.A.	WOLVERHAMPTON W
1 ACCRINGTON		N30 4-2	S28 2-2	J04 3-1	O19 2-2	N16 6-1	F22 5-3	O12 1-8	M15 2-2	D28 2-1	F08 0-0	J01 6-3
2 ASTON VILLA	D26 1-2		M31 3-0	J25 1-2	S07 2-2	O12 7-1	N23 1-2	S14 1-1	S21 5-3	D07 6-1	O26 1-0	N02 2-1
3 BLACKBURN R	N23 3-2	O19 7-0		D21 7-1	O26 7-1	S21 4-2	D28 2-4	N16 9-1	N02 3-4	J04 8-0	N30 5-0	S14 4-3
4 BOLTON W	S14 2-4	N16 2-0	N09 3-2		M17 2-2	N30 7-1	S21 3-4	O26 0-4	O12 2-6	F08 5-0	D07 7-0	F24 4-1
5 BURNLEY	S21 2-2	O05 2-6	F22 1-2	M01 7-0		M08 2-0	F08 0-1	M15 3-0	S28 0-3	J11 1-3	O12 1-2	N09 1-2
6 DERBY CO	F15 2-3	D28 5-0	F08 4-0	D26 3-2	J04 4-1		O05 2-2	S28 2-0	O19 2-1	O26 2-0	S14 3-1	N23 3-3
7 EVERTON	O26 2-2	J04 7-0	S07 3-2	S28 3-0	S14 2-1	M15 3-0		D07 5-3	N16 1-5	N02 8-0	M08 5-1	S30 1-1
8 NOTTS CO	M13 3-1	N09 1-1	F18 1-1	J11 3-5	N02 1-1	D21 3-1	O19 4-3		M27 0-1	O05 3-1	S21 1-2	D14 0-2
9 PRESTON N.E.	N09 3-1	D25 3-2	D07 1-1	N23 3-1	N30 6-0	J11 5-0	D21 1-2	M01 4-3		S14 10-0	O05 5-0	O26 0-2
10 STOKE	M01 7-1	M17 1-1	D23 0-3	O19 0-1	M10 3-4	S07 1-1	N09 1-2	M24 1-1	N11 1-2		N16 1-3	S28 2-1
11 W.B.A.	D21 4-1	S28 3-0	J11 3-2	N04 6-3	N23 6-1	N09 2-3	M22 4-1	J04 4-2	D26 2-2	M15 2-1		O19 1-4
12 WOLVERHAMPTON W	O05 2-1	D21 1-1	D26 2-4	M15 5-1	D07 9-1	J25 2-1	S16 2-1	S07 2-0	J04 0-1	O12 2-2	D28 1-1	

1889-90

LEAGUE TABLE
FOOTBALL LEAGUE

	P	W	D	L	F	A	W	D	L	F	A	Pts
Preston NE	22	8	1	2	41	12	7	2	2	30	18	33
Everton	22	8	2	1	40	15	6	1	4	25	25	31
Blackburn R	22	9	0	2	59	18	3	3	5	19	23	27
Wolves	22	6	3	2	28	14	4	2	5	23	24	25
WBA	22	8	1	2	37	20	3	2	6	10	30	25
Accrington	22	6	4	1	33	25	3	2	6	20	31	24
Derby Co	22	8	2	1	32	13	1	1	9	11	42	21
Aston Villa	22	6	2	3	30	15	1	3	7	13	36	19
Bolton W	22	6	1	4	37	24	3	0	8	17	41	19
Notts Co	22	4	3	4	20	19	2	2	7	23	32	17
Burnley	22	3	1	7	20	21	1	4	6	16	44	13
Stoke	22	2	3	6	18	20	1	1	9	9	49	10

Preston North End, first winners of the Football League and victorious in the FA Cup Final the same season. Back row (left to right, players only): Drummond, Howarth, Russell, Holmes, Graham, Dr Mills-Roberts. Front row: Gordon, J.Ross, Goodall, Dewhurst, Thomson.

Football League Records Seasons 1890-91 & 1891-92

Top scorer: J.Southworth (Blackburn Rovers) 26 goals.
Sunderland were elected in place of Stoke.

DIVISION 1

	ACCRINGTON	ASTON VILLA	BLACKBURN R	BOLTON W	BURNLEY	DERBY CO	EVERTON	NOTTS CO	PRESTON N.E.	SUNDERLAND	W.B.A.	WOLVERHAMPTON W
1 ACCRINGTON		M21 1-3	M04 0-4	J10 2-1	S06 1-1	N08 4-0	S27 1-2	O25 3-2	O11 1-3	N22 4-1	a18 1-0	J01 1-2
2 ASTON VILLA	N15 3-1		D13 2-2	N22 5-0	N08 4-4	O25 4-0	O11 2-2	S13 3-2	M09 0-1	D26 0-0	S27 0-4	M14 6-2
3 BLACKBURN R	S13 0-0	D06 5-1		M07 0-2	N22 5-2	J03 8-0	N08 2-1	M14 1-7	O25 1-0	O11 3-2	D20 2-1	S27 2-3
4 BOLTON W	D13 6-0	O04 4-0	M28 2-0		M21 1-0	S13 3-1	S20 0-5	S06 4-2	N15 1-0	O25 2-5	M14 7-1	D29 6-0
5 BURNLEY	N29 2-0	S20 2-1	O18 1-6	O11 1-2		N15 6-1	M14 3-2	D20 0-1	M07 6-2	S27 3-3	D06 5-4	N01 4-2
6 DERBY CO	D06 1-2	O18 5-4	S06 0-5	D26 1-1	J24 2-4		D13 2 6	D27 3 1	S20 1 3	F07 3-1	N22 3-1	J10 9-0
7 EVERTON	D26 3-2	J01 5-0	N29 3-1	O18 2-0	D27 7-3	O04 7-0		J03 4-2	J10 0-1	N15 1-0	O25 2-3	S13 5-0
8 NOTTS CO	S20 5-0	N29 7-1	N15 1-2	O02 3-1	F10 4-0	S27 2-1	N01 3-1		D06 2-1	D15 2-1	O11 3-2	N22 1-1
9 PRESTON N.E.	N01 1-1	J24 4-1	O04 1-2	S27 1-0	F05 7-0	D20 6-0	N22 2-0	N08 0-0		F21 0-0	S13 3 0	O18 5 1
10 SUNDERLAND	O18 2-2	J10 5-1	N01 3-1	F10 2-0	**S13 2-3**	M21 5-1	D20 1-0	J24 4-0	M14 3-0		N08 1-1	S15 3-4
11 W.B.A.	M07 5-1	N01 0-3	M09 1-0	N03 2-4	O04 3-1	N29 3-4	S06 1-4	O18 1-1	F07 1-3	S20 0-4		D13 0-1
12 WOLVERHAMPTON W	O04 3-0	S06 2-1	D26 2-0	N08 1-0	O25 3-1	O11 5-1	D06 0-1	S22 1-1	N29 2-0	D27 0-3	J03 4-0	

1890-91

LEAGUE TABLE
FOOTBALL LEAGUE

	P	W	D	L	F	A	W	D	L	F	A	Pts
Everton	22	9	0	2	39	12	5	1	5	24	17	29
Preston NE	22	7	3	1	30	5	5	0	6	14	18	27
Notts Co	22	9	1	1	33	11	2	3	6	19	24	26
Wolves	22	8	1	2	23	8	4	1	6	16	42	26
Bolton W	22	9	0	2	36	14	3	1	7	11	20	25
Blackburn R	22	7	1	3	29	19	4	1	6	23	24	24
Sunderland	22	7	2	2	31	13	3	3	5	20	18	*23
Burnley	22	7	1	3	33	24	2	2	7	19	39	21
Aston Villa	22	5	4	2	29	18	2	0	9	16	40	18
Accrington	22	5	1	5	19	19	1	3	7	9	31	16
Derby Co	22	6	1	4	38	28	1	0	10	9	53	15
WBA	22	3	1	7	17	26	2	1	8	17	31	12

**Sunderland deducted two points for unapproved registration*

Top scorer: J.Campbell (Sunderland) 32 goals.
Darwen joined, Stoke rejoined League.

DIVISION 1

	ACCRINGTON	ASTON VILLA	BLACKBURN R	BOLTON W	BURNLEY	DARWEN	DERBY CO	EVERTON	NOTTS CO	PRESTON N.E.	STOKE	SUNDERLAND	W.B.A.	WOLVERHAMPTON W
1 ACCRINGTON		J04 3-2	F27 1-0	N07 0-3	S05 1-0	O10 1-1	a02 1-1	S26 1-1	N21 2-0	J02 1-3	J09 3-0	M05 3-5	J23 4-2	O24 3-2
2 ASTON VILLA	M12 12-2		S05 5-1	O10 1-2	D05 6-1	D26 7-0	J09 6-0	D28 3-4	N07 5-1	a16 3-1	N21 2-1	S28 5-3	S12 5-1	a18 3-6
3 BLACKBURN R	D26 2-2	M05 4-3		N21 4-0	S26 3-3	D25 4-0	J02 0-2	D05 2-2	S12 5-4	O24 2-4	M19 5-3	N07 3-1	M12 3-2	O10 2-0
4 BOLTON W	O03 3-4	a02 1-2	O31 4-2		O24 2-0	S12 1-0	J01 3-1	O17 1-0	M26 2-0	S26 3-0	N14 1-1	S19 4-3	D19 1-1	D05 3-0
5 BURNLEY	N14 2-1	O17 4-1	D12 3-0	M05 1-2		J09 9-0	a16 2 4	F13 1 0	a15 1-0	S07 2-0	S19 4-1	a30 1-2	N28 3-2	M26 1-1
6 DARWEN	S19 5-2	O31 1-5	O17 3-5	S05 1-2	a02 2-6		N28 2-0	N14 3-1	F27 2-3	J01 0-4	O03 9-3	a23 1-7	a16 1-1	M01 1-4
7 DERBY CO	S12 3-1	O03 4-2	M26 1-1	D26 3-2	D19 0-1	N21 7-0		O24 0-3	S19 3-0	D05 1-2	O17 3-3	M19 0-1	F06 1-1	O31 2-1
8 EVERTON	M19 3-0	N28 5-1	S19 3-1	a18 2-5	J02 1-1	S07 5-3	a15 1-2		a16 4-0	O10 1-1	M05 1-0	D25 0-4	N07 4-3	D12 2-1
9 NOTTS CO	N28 9-0	J02 5-2	D19 2-2	O01 2-0	M01 5-1	O24 5-0	F20 2-1	J09 1-3		S05 2-0	S26 1-1	a09 1-0	O10 4-0	N14 2-2
10 PRESTON N.E.	a15 4-1	S19 0-1	N14 3-2	N28 4-0	S21 5-1	a18 4-0	M05 3-0	O31 4-0	D12 6-0		**D25 3-2**	S12 3 1	J09 1 0	**O03 2 0**
11 STOKE	D19 3-1	O24 2-3	N09 0-1	D12 0-1	O10 3-0	D05 5-1	S05 2-1	M12 0-1	F06 1-3	N07 0-1		N28 1-3	a23 1-0	S12 1-3
12 SUNDERLAND	O31 4-1	M26 2-1	a16 6-1	M01 4-1	N21 2-1	D12 7-0	N14 7-1	O03 2-1	D05 4-0	M12 4-1	a02 4-1		O24 4-0	S05 5-2
13 W.B.A.	D05 3-1	N14 0-3	O03 2-2	N02 0-2	D26 1-0	a04 12-0	D12 4-2	S05 4-0	O31 2-2	N21 1-2	a11 2-2	O17 2-5		S19 4-3
14 WOLVERHAMPTON W	S14 5-0	D19 2-0	N28 6-1	a16 1-2	N07 0-0	S28 2-2	S26 1-3	N21 5-1	O17 2-1	a02 3-0	J02 4-1	D26 1-3	D28 2-1	

1891-92

LEAGUE TABLE
FOOTBALL LEAGUE

	P	W	D	L	F	A	W	D	L	F	A	Pts
Sunderland	26	13	0	0	55	11	8	0	5	38	25	42
Preston NE	26	12	0	1	42	8	6	1	6	19	23	37
Bolton W	26	9	2	2	29	14	8	0	5	22	23	36
Aston Villa	26	10	0	3	63	23	5	0	8	26	33	30
Everton	26	8	2	3	32	22	4	2	7	17	27	28
Wolves	26	8	2	3	34	15	3	2	8	25	31	26
Burnley	26	9	1	3	34	14	2	3	8	15	31	26
Notts Co	26	9	3	1	41	12	2	1	10	14	39	26
Blackburn R	26	8	3	2	39	26	2	3	8	19	39	26
Derby Co	26	6	3	4	28	18	4	1	8	18	34	24
Accrington	26	7	3	3	24	20	1	1	11	16	68	20
WBA	26	6	3	4	37	24	0	3	10	14	34	18
Stoke	26	5	0	8	19	19	0	4	9	19	42	14
Darwen	26	4	1	8	31	43	0	2	11	7	69	11

Everton's 1890-91 line-up. Back row (left to right, players only): Hannah, Smalley, Doyle. Middle row: Brady, Kirkwood, Holt, Parry, Chadwick. Front row: Latta, Geary, Millward. Goalkeeper Smalley made only one appearance as the Goodison club became the second club to write their name on the Football League Championship trophy. The regular 'keepers were Jardine and Angus.

Football League Records Season 1892-93

Top scorers: Div 1, J.Campbell (Sunderland) 31 goals; Div 2, G.Wheldon (Small Heath) 24 goals.
Test Matches: 22 Apr Sheffield United 1 Accrington 0 (Nottingham); Darwen 3 Notts County 2 (Ardwick); Small Heath 1 Newton Heath 1 (Stoke); 27 Apr Newton Heath 5 Small Heath 2 (Sheffield). Darwen and Sheffield United promoted, Notts County relegated.
Bootle, Burton Swifts, Crewe Alexandra, Grimsby Town, Lincoln City, Ardwick, Northwich Victoria, Burslem Port Vale, Sheffield United, Small Heath and Walsall Town Swifts were elected to the new Division Two; Newton Heath, Nottingham Forest and Sheffield Wednesday elected straight into Division One.

DIVISION 1

	ACCRINGTON	ASTON VILLA	BLACKBURN R	BOLTON W	BURNLEY	DERBY CO	EVERTON	NEWTON HEATH	NOTTINGHAM F	NOTTS CO	PRESTON N.E.	SHEFFIELD W	STOKE	SUNDERLAND	W.B.A.	WOLVERHAMPTON W
1 ACCRINGTON		a15 1-1	J02 1-1	O08 1-1	J14 0-4	M31 0-3	F25 0-3	N26 2-2	M18 1-1	D10 4-2	N05 1-2	S24 4-2	D26 5-2	S03 0-6	D17 5-4	D31 4-0
2 ASTON VILLA	M25 6-4		D10 4-1	D24 1-1	a04 1-3	O29 6-1	S10 4-1	M06 2-0	O15 1-0	M18 3-1	N26 3-1	J07 5-1	O10 3-2	S17 1-6	N05 5-2	a03 5-0
3 BLACKBURN R	O01 3-3	F11 2-2		N26 3-0	D17 2-0	J07 2-2	S17 2-2	S03 4-3	D31 0-1	D24 1-0	O29 0-0	O15 0-2	F25 3-3	M31 2-2	J28 2-1	N12 3-3
4 BOLTON W	M04 5-2	S24 5-0	M18 2-1		F25 1-0	J02 0-3	O29 4-1	D03 4-1	M31 3-1	M25 4-1	N01 2-4	S17 1-0	O15 4-4	a01 2-1	S10 3-1	O01 3-1
5 BURNLEY	O29 1-3	S05 0-2	D03 0-0	F11 3-0		O08 2-1	a08 3-0	S17 4-1	N26 1-1	O22 3-0	M18 4-2	M31 4-0	S24 3-2	a15 2-3	D31 5-0	a01 2-0
6 DERBY CO	D03 3-3	D17 2-1	O22 3-0	**D26 1-1**	N12 1-0		N05 1-6	F11 5-1	O01 2-3	O19 4-5	S10 1-2	M25 2-2	D24 1-0	a08 1-1	S24 1-1	N26 2-2
7 EVERTON	O22 1-1	O01 1-0	a01 4-0	a03 3-0	D24 0-1	a15 5-0		S24 6-0	S03 2-2	J07 6-0	F11 6-0	N26 3-5	N12 2-2	O08 1-4	J14 1-0	**D10 3-2**
8 NEWTON HEATH	a08 3-3	N19 2-0	N05 4-4	D10 1-0	S10 1-1	D31 7-1	O19 3-4		J14 1-3	N12 1-3	a01 2-1	D24 1-5	M31 1-0	M04 0-5	O08 2-4	O15 10-1
9 NOTTINGHAM F	J07 3-0	N12 4-5	M11 0-1	O20 2-0	D10 2-2	J28 1-0	J12 2-1	O29 1-1		F25 3-1	S24 1-2	D01 2-0	S10 3-4	D03 0-5	M02 3-4	D24 3-1
10 NOTTS CO	F11 2-0	D31 1-4	J14 0-0	O06 2-2	D08 3-1	S17 1-1	D17 1-2	J26 4-0	O08 3-0		O01 3-1	S03 0-1	N05 0-1	N26 3-1	N19 8-1	a08 3-0
11 PRESTON N.E.	a03 0-0	O22 4-1	O08 2-1	S03 2-1	O15 2-0	a17 0-1	D03 5-0	D26 2-1	S17 1-0	M31 4-0		S12 4-1	D31 2-1	J07 1-2	a13 1-1	a10 4-0
12 SHEFFIELD W	S10 5-2	D03 5-3	N19 0-3	N05 4-2	O01 2-0	D10 3-3	F13 0-2	O22 1-0	O03 2-2	a03 3-2	J14 0-5		a01 0-1	O29 3-2	J02 6-0	M11 0-1
13 STOKE	S17 2-2	S12 0-1	a03 2-2	J14 6-0	N19 4-1	S03 1-3	J28 0-1	J07 7-1	O22 3-0	M11 1-0	N14 2-1	D17 2-0		M18 0-1	F11 1-2	O29 2-1
14 SUNDERLAND	O15 4-2	J14 6-0	S24 5-0	F14 3-3	N05 2-0	M11 3-1	J03 4-3	a04 6-0	N19 1-0	S10 2-2	D17 2-0	J28 4-2	O01 3-1		O22 8-1	J02 5-2
15 W.B.A.	N12 4-0	S19 3-2	D26 1-2	N07 1-0	J07 7-1	a01 3-1	O15 3-0	O01 0-0	a03 2-2	O29 4-2	D10 0-1	M18 3-0	N26 1-2	D24 1-3		S17 2-1
16 WOLVERHAMPTON W	N19 5-3	O08 2-1	S10 4-2	O22 1-2	S03 1-0	F25 2-1	M18 2-4	D17 2-0	N05 2-2	S24 3-0	a15 2-1	F11 2-0	D03 1-0	D26 2-0	D27 1-1	

DIVISION 2

	ARDWICK	BOOTLE	BURSLEM P.V.	BURTON S	CREWE A	DARWEN	GRIMSBY T	LINCOLN C	NORTHWICH V	SHEFFIELD U	SMALL HEATH	WALSALL T.S.
1 ARDWICK		S03 7-0	S12 2-0	N26 1-1	F18 3-1	D17 4-2	J30 0-3	a08 3-1	S24 1-1	M04 2-3	O22 2-2	O01 2-0
2 BOOTLE	J21 5-3		S17 1-1	F25 3-2	M25 2-1	D31 5-1	D17 3-1	a15 4-1	D03 2-5	S10 2-0	N05 1-4	M18 7-1
3 BURSLEM P.V.	O10 1-2	N12 0-0		O08 1-0	S24 4-1	O01 2-4	F11 0-1	D03 1-2	M04 4-0	D10 0-10	M25 0-3	D31 3-0
4 BURTON S	J14 2-0	S24 2-1	M18 3-3		S03 7-1	D24 0-2	a08 5-1	D17 4-2	N05 2-0	a01 0-3	O03 2-3	F04 3-2
5 CREWE A	F04 4-1	J07 2-1	N26 5-0	O01 2-4		**F25 2-2**	S10 1-0	J28 4-1	S17 4-2	a12 0-4	D31 1-3	N05 5-6
6 DARWEN	O08 3-1	O22 3-0	N05 4-1	S10 2-3	D03 7-3		M18 6-1	J14 3-1	F14 3-1	N19 3-1	D10 4-3	S24 5-0
7 GRIMSBY T	N05 2-0	O08 3-0	J14 2-0	D03 4-0	D24 4-0	S17 0-1		**F18 2-2**	**S03 2-1**	**M31 0-1**	**O01 3-2**	a01 3-0
8 LINCOLN C	D24 2-1	a01 5-1	O22 3-4	F11 5-1	D26 1-1	N12 1-1	M04 1-3		F25 5-1	O01 1-0	J07 3-4	M31 3-1
9 NORTHWICH V	S10 0-3	O01 3-2	a08 2-4	M25 2-1	O22 4-1	a15 1-0	J07 5-3	D31 2-1		F18 1-3	D24 0-6	N26 5-2
10 SHEFFIELD U	M25 2-1	N26 8-3	D17 4-0	F06 3-1	M18 4-0	O15 2-0	S27 2-0	S03 4-2	J23 1-1		S17 2-0	J07 3-0
11 SMALL HEATH	a01 3-2	F18 6-2	S03 5-1	N12 3-2	O08 6-0	O29 3-2	F25 8-3	S24 4-1	J14 6-2	D03 1-1		D17 12-0
12 WALSALL T.S.	S17 2-4	D24 4-4	F18 3-0	M04 3-2	J14 3-3	S03 1-2	O22 3-1	O08 2-1	F11 2-3	a15 1-1	S10 1-3	

LEAGUE TABLES

DIVISION 1

	P	W	D	L	F	A	W	D	L	F	A	Pts
Sunderland	30	13	2	0	58	17	9	2	4	42	19	48
Preston NE	30	11	2	2	34	10	6	1	8	23	29	37
Everton	30	9	3	3	44	17	7	1	7	30	34	36
Aston Villa	30	12	1	2	50	24	4	2	9	23	38	35
Bolton W	30	12	1	2	43	21	1	5	9	13	34	32
Burnley	30	10	2	3	37	15	3	2	10	14	29	30
Stoke	30	8	2	5	33	16	4	3	8	25	32	29
WBA	30	9	2	4	35	17	3	3	9	23	52	29
Blackburn R	30	5	8	2	29	24	3	5	7	18	32	29
Nottingham F	30	7	2	6	30	27	3	6	6	18	25	28
Wolves	30	11	2	2	32	17	1	2	12	15	51	28
Sheffield W	30	8	2	5	34	28	4	1	10	21	37	27
Derby Co	30	5	6	4	30	28	4	3	8	22	36	27
Notts Co	30	8	3	4	34	15	2	1	12	19	46	24
Accrington	30	5	5	5	29	34	1	6	8	28	47	23
Newton Heath	30	6	3	6	39	35	0	3	12	11	50	18

DIVISION 2

	P	W	D	L	F	A	W	D	L	F	A	Pts
Small Heath	22	10	1	0	57	16	7	1	3	33	19	36
Sheffield U	22	10	1	0	35	8	6	2	3	27	11	35
Darwen	22	10	0	1	43	15	4	2	5	17	21	30
Grimsby T	22	8	1	2	25	7	3	0	8	17	34	23
Ardwick	22	6	3	2	27	14	3	0	8	18	26	21
Burton S	22	7	1	3	30	18	2	1	8	17	29	20
Northwich V	22	7	0	4	25	26	2	2	7	17	32	20
Bootle	22	8	1	2	35	20	0	2	9	14	43	19
Lincoln C	22	6	2	3	30	18	1	1	9	15	33	17
Crewe A	22	6	1	4	30	24	0	2	9	12	45	15
Burslem PV	22	4	1	6	16	23	2	2	7	14	34	15
Walsall TS	22	4	3	4	25	24	1	0	10	12	51	13

Small Heath, the first champions of the Second Division. Back row (left to right, players only): Bayley, Charsley, Pumfrey, Short, Weston. Middle row: Hallam, Walton, Mobley, Jenkyns, Wheldon, Hands. Front row: Ollis, Devey. Goalkeeper Chris Charsley, an amateur throughout his career, won an England cap and later became chief constable of Coventry and deputy mayor of Weston-super-Mare.

Edgar Chadwick was one of the great names in football in the 1890s. Born in Blackburn, he had one season with Blackburn Rovers before joining Everton for the inaugural Football League season. He won seven England caps at inside-forward and Championship medals with Everton and Southern League Southampton, whom he joined in 1900 after one season with Burnley.

Football League Records Season 1893-94

Top scorers: Div 1, J.Southworth (Everton) 27 goals; Div 2, F.Mobley (Small Heath) 23 goals.
Test Matches: 28 Apr Small Heath 3 Darwen 1 (Stoke); Liverpool 2 Newton Heath 0 (Blackburn); Preston North End 4 Notts County 0 (Sheffield). Liverpool and Small Heath promoted, Darwen and Newton Heath relegated.
Accrington and Bootle resigned. Liverpool, Middlesbrough Ironopolis, Newcastle United, Rotherham Town and Woolwich Arsenal elected to League.

DIVISION 1

	ASTON VILLA	BLACKBURN R	BOLTON W	BURNLEY	DARWEN	DERBY CO	EVERTON	NEWTON HEATH	NOTTINGHAM F	PRESTON N.E.	SHEFFIELD U	SHEFFIELD W	STOKE	SUNDERLAND	W.B.A	WOLVERHAMPTON W
1 ASTON VILLA		M24 2-1	M03 2-3	O28 4-0	D26 9-0	S30 1-1	S23 3-1	F03 5-1	a14 3-1	N25 2-0	O30 4-0	D09 3-0	S11 5-1	N11 2-1	S02 3-2	M26 1-1
2 BLACKBURN R	N04 2-0		D02 0-1	N18 3-2	D25 4-1	M23 0-2	D16 4-3	M26 4-0	F03 6-1	O07 1-0	J15 4-1	S09 5-1	a14 5-0	O21 4-3	J13 3-0	S23 3-0
3 BOLTON W	N18 0-1	S16 2-1		J06 2-0	O07 1-0	J01 1-1	a16 0-1	D09 2-0	M23 1-1	S30 0-3	O14 0-1	D25 1-1	S02 4-1	a23 2-0	a07 0-3	O21 2-0
4 BURNLEY	a07 3-6	D23 1-0	F03 2-1		S04 5-1	M10 3-1	O07 2-1	O21 4-1	N04 3-1	S09 4-1	D25 4-1	M23 0-1	S30 4-0	D02 1-0	D09 3-0	a14 4-2
5 DARWEN	O14 1-1	S02 2-3	O28 1-3	F06 0-0		a14 2-3	J01 3-3	S30 1-0	D23 0-4	F03 2-1	J06 3-3	D11 2-1	S16 3-1	a07 0-3	N11 2-1	M10 3-1
6 DERBY CO	D02 0-3	M31 5-2	D26 6 1	a02 3 3	N18 2-1		S09 7-3	O07 2-0	D09 3-4	J06 2-1	N04 2-1	O21 3-3	D23 5-2	M07 1-4	S16 2-3	F03 4-1
7 EVERTON	S16 4-2	O14 2-2	M26 3-2	N25 4-3	O21 8-1	N11 1-2		J06 2-0	S04 4-0	O28 2-3	S02 2-3	D23 8-1	a07 6-2	S30 7-1	D30 7-1	M24 3-0
8 NEWTON HEATH	D16 1-3	M12 5-1	M24 2-2	S02 3-2	N04 0-1	M17 2-6	D02 0-3		S23 1-1	a14 1-3	M10 0-2	J13 1-2	M23 6-2	M03 2-4	O14 4-1	N11 1-0
9 NOTTINGHAM F	O07 1-2	N25 0-0	O05 1-0	S16 5-0	M15 4-1	D30 4-2	J18 3-2	a07 2-0		M24 4-2	N18 1-1	O28 1-0	O21 2-0	J13 1-2	S30 2-3	S02 7-1
10 PRESTON N.E.	J18 2-5	N11 0-1	N04 1-0	O14 1-2	S23 4-1	S02 1-0	J13 2-4	D23 2-0	D02 0-2		a07 3-0	M26 1-0	D25 3-3	S16 1-2	M03 3-1	D16 1-3
11 SHEFFIELD U	O02 3-0	M03 3-2	S23 4-2	M26 1-0	S09 2-1	S04 1-2	D09 0-3	N25 3-1	J01 0-2	N20 1-1		O16 1-1	F03 3-3	O07 1-0	O28 0-2	J13 3-2
12 SHEFFIELD W	J06 2-2	S30 4-2	D16 2-1	D26 0-1	J15 5-0	O14 4-0	N04 1-1	S16 0-1	M05 1-0	F06 3-0	N13 1-2		D07 4-1	S02 2-2	S25 2-4	D02 1-4
13 STOKE	O16 3-3	O28 3-1	J13 5-0	N11 4-2	D02 3-1	S23 3-1	M03 3-1	M31 3 1	S09 2-1	N13 2-1	D16 5-0	O07 4-1		M24 2-0	J20 3-1	D30 0-3
14 SUNDERLAND	S09 1-1	D09 2-3	D30 2-1	D16 2-2	M27 4-0	O28 5-0	F06 1-0	D06 4-1	M17 2-0	J01 6-3	J20 4-1	S23 1-1	O14 4-0		N25 2-1	N04 6-0
15 W.B.A.	O21 3-6	J06 2-1	N06 5-2	S23 1-1	D16 2-2	M24 0-1	F03 3-1	S09 3-1	M26 3-0	D04 2-0	D26 3-1	N27 2-2	N04 4-2	D23 2-3		O07 0-0
16 WOLVERHAMPTON W	D23 3-0	D26 5-1	S09 2-1	M03 1-0	S18 2-1	J20 2-4	D04 2-0	O28 2-0	O14 3-1	D09 0-0	S30 3-4	S04 3-1	N25 4-2	J06 2-1	D27 0-8	

DIVISION 2

	ARDWICK	BURSLEM P.V.	BURTON S	CREWE A	GRIMSBY T	LINCOLN C	LIVERPOOL	MIDDLESBROUGH I	NEWCASTLE U	NORTHWICH V	NOTTS CO	ROTHERHAM T	SMALL HEATH	WALSALL T.S.	W ARSENAL
1 ARDWICK		O07 8-1	S11 1-4	a07 1-2	D09 4-1	M31 0-1	S16 0-1	S09 6-1	O21 2-3	J27 4-2	O28 0-0	D26 3-2	S30 0-1	N18 3-0	D30 0-1
2 BURSLEM P.V.	S02 4-2		D16 3-1	S16 4-2	D04 6-1	M10 5-3	a07 2-2	S18 4-0	F03 1-1	S30 3-2	N25 1-0	O21 2-3	S25 5-0	F10 1-2	J06 2-1
3 BURTON S	S20 5-0	J13 5-3		M31 6-1	a07 0-3	F10 1-3	O21 1-1	M17 7-0	S23 3-1	O02 6-2	D30 0-2	S30 4-1	D09 0-2	F24 8-5	N18 6-2
4 CREWE A	F24 1-1	D09 1-1	O07 1-2		J20 3-3	O21 1-1	D28 0-5	S30 5-0	D27 1-1	O28 3-0	S02 0-2	J27 2-0	J13 3-5	D02 1-1	M03 0-0
5 GRIMSBY T	J13 5-0	D02 4-0	S16 2-1	M10 3-2		O28 2-4	M31 0-1	F03 2-1	a14 0-0	S02 7-0	O21 5-2	F10 7-1	M03 2 1	S30 5 2	D26 3-1
6 LINCOLN C	M24 6-0	F24 2-2	D23 1-1	D25 6-1	S23 1-2		M17 1-1	D26 2-3	O07 2-1	S16 4-1	M23 0-2	S02 1-1	N11 2-5	a07 0-2	F03 3-0
7 LIVERPOOL	D02 3-0	a14 2-1	M03 3-1	M24 2-0	D30 2-0	S09 4-0		O07 6-0	N04 5-1	F03 4-0	N18 2-1	J13 5-1	S23 3-1	D09 3-0	J01 2-0
8 MIDDLESBROUGH I	S23 2-0	J01 3-1	O28 2-1	J06 2-0	N11 2-6	J13 0-0	S02 0-2		D25 1-1	M03 2-1	D16 0-0	D09 6-1	N25 3-0	D30 1-1	F24 3-6
9 NEWCASTLE U	J06 2-1	D30 2-1	M24 4-1	M23 2-1	F24 4-1	J01 5-1	N25 0-0	J02 7-2		J13 3-0	D09 3-0	F17 4-0	O28 0-2	M10 2-0	S30 6-0
10 NORTHWICH V	F10 1-4	S23 1-5	M10 1-1	S09 1-2	F17 0-1	J20 0-3	M28 2-3	a07 2-1	N18 5-3		S11 0-1	M31 1-1	J06 0-7	O07 1-0	D09 2-2
11 NOTTS CO	M15 5-0	O26 6-1	N30 6-2	F17 9-1	O05 3-0	N16 1-2	S30 1-1	N04 3-0	O14 3-1	N23 6-1		J11 4-2	F03 3-1	J20 2-0	S09 3-2
12 ROTHERHAM T	M26 1-3	O28 0-1	N11 2-5	a09 1-4	S09 4-3	D02 2-8	J06 1-4	a14 4-1	J20 2-1	D30 5-4	S16 0-2		M23 2-3	F03 3-2	F06 1-1
13 SMALL HEATH	M17 10-2	M24 6-0	S09 6-1	D06 6-1	O07 5-2	D30 6-0	O14 3-4	D23 2-1	D16 1-4	D02 8-0	a07 3-0	S04 4-3		S16 4-0	O21 4-1
14 WALSALL T.S.	a14 5-2	S09 0-5	J06 3-4	S23 5-1	M24 5-0	M26 5-2	N11 1-1	O21 1-0	D26 1-2	D23 3-0	M12 2-1	S26 3-0	S02 1-3		F12 1-2
15 W ARSENAL	N11 1-0	D25 4-1	a14 0-2	F10 3-2	S25 3-1	F17 4-0	O28 0-5	M10 1-0	S02 2-2	M23 6-0	M24 1-2	N13 3-0	M31 1-4	S11 4-0	

LEAGUE TABLES

DIVISION 1

	P	W	D	L	F	A	W	D	L	F	A	Pts
Aston Villa	30	12	2	1	49	13	7	4	4	35	29	44
Sunderland	30	11	3	1	46	14	6	1	8	26	30	38
Derby Co	30	9	2	4	47	32	7	2	6	26	30	36
Blackburn R	30	13	0	2	48	15	3	2	10	21	38	34
Burnley	30	13	0	2	43	17	2	4	9	18	34	34
Everton	30	11	1	3	63	23	4	2	9	27	34	33
Nottingham F	30	10	2	3	38	16	4	2	9	19	32	32
WBA	30	8	4	3	35	23	6	0	9	31	36	32
Wolves	30	11	1	3	34	24	3	2	10	18	39	31
Sheffield U	30	8	3	4	26	22	5	2	8	21	39	31
Stoke	30	13	1	1	45	17	0	2	13	20	62	29
Sheffield W	30	7	3	5	32	21	2	5	8	16	36	26
Bolton W	30	7	3	5	18	14	3	1	11	20	38	24
Preston NE	30	7	1	7	25	24	3	2	10	19	32	23
Darwen	30	6	4	5	25	28	1	1	13	12	55	19
Newton Heath	30	5	2	8	29	33	1	0	14	7	30	14

DIVISION 2

	P	W	D	L	F	A	W	D	L	F	A	Pts
Liverpool	28	14	0	0	46	6	8	6	0	31	12	50
Small Heath	28	12	0	2	68	19	9	0	5	35	26	42
Notts Co	28	12	1	1	55	14	6	2	6	15	17	39
Newcastle U	28	12	1	1	44	10	3	5	6	22	29	36
Grimsby T	28	11	1	2	47	16	4	1	9	24	42	32
Burton S	28	9	1	4	52	26	5	2	7	27	35	31
Burslem PV	28	10	2	2	43	20	3	2	9	23	44	30
Lincoln C	28	5	4	5	31	22	6	2	6	28	36	28
W Arsenal	28	9	1	4	33	19	3	3	8	19	36	28
Walsall TS	28	8	1	5	36	23	2	2	10	15	38	23
M'brough Iron	28	7	4	3	27	20	1	0	13	10	52	20
Crewe A	28	3	7	4	22	22	3	0	11	20	51	19
Ardwick	28	6	1	7	32	20	2	1	11	15	51	18
Rotherham T	28	5	1	8	28	42	1	2	11	16	49	15
Northwich V	28	3	3	8	17	34	0	0	14	13	64	9

Liverpool, Second Division champions in 1893-4. Back row (left to right, players only): McCartney, M.McQueen, Hannah, McOwen, McLean, Dick, Henderson. Front row: Gordon, McVean, McQue, McBride, Bradshaw, Stott, H.McQueen.

John Devey of Aston Villa, the Football League Champions' leading scorer with 20 goals in 1893-4. In all, Devey won five Championship medals with Villa and appeared in three FA Cup Finals, twice on the winning side. He was restricted to two England caps by the presence by Steve Bloomer and John Goodall. Devey was also a fine cricketer who played for Warwickshire.

Football League Records
Season 1894-95

Top scorers: Div 1, J.Campbell (Sunderland) 22 goals; Div 2, D.Skea (Leicester Fosse) 22 goals.
Test Matches: 27 Apr Bury 1 Liverpool 0 (Blackburn); Derby County 2 Notts County 1 (Leicester); Stoke 3 Newton Heath 0 (Burslem). Bury promoted, Liverpool relegated.

Middlesbrough Ironopolis and Northwich Victoria resigned. Burton Wanderers, Bury and Leicester Fosse elected in their place.

DIVISION 1

	ASTON VILLA	BLACKBURN R	BOLTON W	BURNLEY	DERBY CO	EVERTON	LIVERPOOL	NOTTINGHAM F	PRESTON N.E.	SHEFFIELD U	SHEFFIELD W	SMALL HEATH	STOKE	SUNDERLAND	W.B.A.	WOLVERHAMPTON W
1 ASTON VILLA		D08 3-0	J26 2-1	a06 5-0	J05 4-0	a24 2-2	O27 5-0	N24 4-1	N10 4-1	N12 5-0	D03 3-1	S01 2-1	D26 6-0	S15 1-2	O13 3-1	a15 2-2
2 BLACKBURN R	D01 1-3		O13 2-1	N17 1-0	a12 0-0	O20 4-3	S01 1-1	J01 0-0	O27 1-1	D26 3-2	S29 3-1	J05 9-1	S15 6-0	N10 1-1	D22 3-0	M23 5-1
3 BOLTON W	M23 4-3	N03 1-3		O20 1-1	J01 6-0	O06 1-3	D25 1-0	a12 4-1	S15 1-2	J14 6-2	J07 2-2	N24 1-2	S01 2-2	S29 4-1	a13 5-0	D15 6-1
4 BURNLEY	F23 3-3	J12 2-1	J05 1-0		S29 2-0	M16 2-4	S03 3-3	O27 0-1	D08 2-1	D22 2-4	N10 3-0	O13 3-1	a20 1-2	a13 0-3	N24 2-0	S22 2-1
5 DERBY CO	S22 0-2	a06 0-0	D26 2-2	D12 0-2		J12 2-2	J09 0-1	S08 4-2	N24 2-1	D15 4-1	S15 1-2	M30 4-1	J19 1-1	O13 1-2	O27 1-1	J26 1-3
6 EVERTON	J17 4-2	N24 2-1	D08 3-1	M21 3-2	a13 2-3		O13 3-0	S15 6-1	F23 4-2	J26 1-1	S01 3-1	S03 5-0	J07 3-0	O27 2-2	S29 4-1	a08 2-1
7 LIVERPOOL	S08 1-2	S22 2-2	S13 1-2	N03 0-3	M02 5-1	N17 2-2		**J12 5-0**	**a20 2-5**	**O06 2-2**	**M30 4-2**	**D15 3-1**	**O20 2-0**	**M25 2-3**	**J01 4-0**	D01 3-3
8 NOTTINGHAM F	O06 2-1	D29 2-3	M16 3-3	S01 2-1	N03 2-1	S22 2-3	a06 3-0		O04 0-2	N17 3-0	J19 2-1	J26 2-0	F23 3-1	D27 2-1	D08 5-3	a13 0-2
9 PRESTON N.E.	J12 0-1	O06 1-1	D01 2-2	J26 4-0	N17 3-2	D15 1-2	a12 2-2	M23 3-1		S08 2-1	a13 3-1	S22 0-1	D25 3-0	D29 1-0	F26 5-0	O20 2-0
10 SHEFFIELD U	O22 2-1	O08 3-0	a15 5-0	S15 2-2	D25 1-4	F26 4-2	D08 2-2	S29 3-2	O13 0-1		J12 1-0	a13 0-2	F09 3-0	M09 4-0	S01 2-1	J19 1-0
11 SHEFFIELD W	N03 1-0	S08 4-1	S22 2-1	O06 4-3	D27 1-1	J01 3-0	J05 5-0	D15 0-0	S03 3-1	O27 2-3		D26 2-0	a17 2-4	M23 1-2	a01 3-2	N17 3-1
12 SMALL HEATH	O20 2-2	M02 1-1	S08 2-0	M23 1-0	M16 3-5	N03 4-4	D29 3-0	D22 1-2	S29 4-4	D01 4-2	M25 0-0		N17 4-2	F09 1-1	F23 1-2	O06 4-3
13 STOKE	S29 4-1	a13 5-1	J12 5-0	M30 5-1	M23 4-1	S08 1-3	N10 3-1	O13 0-3	N12 2-1	S22 1-3	D08 0-2	O27 2-2		J26 2-5	M25 1-1	F04 0-0
14 SUNDERLAND	J02 4-4	D15 3-2	N17 4-0	S08 3-0	S01 8-0	a20 2-1	N24 3-2	J05 2-2	J01 2-0	F23 2-0	F26 3-1	D08 7-1	O06 3-1		S22 3-0	N03 2-0
15 W.B.A.	N17 3-2	J26 2-0	N05 1-1	D29 0-1	O20 2-2	D01 1-4	S15 5-0	a15 1-0	J05 4-5	N03 1-0	a22 6-0	N10 4-1	D15 3-2	D26 0-2		S08 5-1
16 WOLVERHAMPTON W	D22 0-4	F23 3-3	O27 4-2	D26 1-0	D08 2-2	J05 1-0	S29 3-1	N10 1-1	**S01 1-3**	S03 0-3	O13 2-0	S15 2-1	N24 0-0	J12 1-4	D27 3-1	

DIVISION 2

	BURSLEM P.V.	BURTON S	BURTON W	BURY	CREWE A	DARWEN	GRIMSBY T	LEICESTER F	LINCOLN C	ARDWICK	NEWCASTLE U	NEWTON HEATH	NOTTS CO	ROTHERHAM T	WALSALL T.S.	W ARSENAL
1 BURSLEM P.V.		M04 2-0	O20 1-0	S15 1-2	a20 4-0	N17 0-3	a06 5-0	F23 1-1	M16 7-1	F02 1-2	O06 4-4	D24 2-5	S17 0-3	F16 1-1	S01 1-0	J19 0-1
2 BURTON S	S29 1-0		F16 2-2	a06 0-1	S01 4-0	M16 3-0	S19 2-1	M02 0-5	J26 6-1	N10 2-1	J05 5-3	O20 1-2	D22 2-2	M30 2-0	O01 1-2	S15 3-0
3 BURTON W	M09 4-0	O27 1-2		N17 1-2	J19 4-0	M23 2-2	a13 0-0	F09 1-1	F23 4-1	D26 8-0	a15 9-0	S08 1-0	D08 1-0	O06 4-0	J12 7-0	a20 2-1
4 BURY	N10 4-0	D01 2-0	D22 4-0		S08 4-1	S29 1-0	O06 5-1	D25 4-1	J12 4-1	S01 4-2	N03 4-1	a15 2-1	J01 2-1	S18 2-1	a02 4-1	M02 2-0
5 CREWE A	J05 2-2	O06 1-3	M16 1-2	O20 1-5		F23 2-2	F09 2-1	J12 2-2	O27 1-4	D31 2-3	M09 2-1	D01 0-2	J16 0-3	S22 2-1	S29 2-3	M23 0-0
6 DARWEN	O27 2-0	a20 5-0	S22 2-0	D15 0-1	F16 5-0		J12 4-1	J15 8-2	S08 6-0	a06 4-0	S01 5-0	O06 1-1	J26 2-1	M09 4-3	D01 2-0	J01 3-1
7 GRIMSBY T	J26 4-1	M09 7-1	S29 7-2	J05 3-2	D08 5-0	M30 2-1		S01 4-3	N10 3-0	a20 2-1	S15 3-0	N17 2-1	F05 0-1	O27 4-1	M16 1-0	D26 4-2
8 LEICESTER F	M23 2-1	N17 2-2	S15 1-2	a20 1-0	F18 4-0	N10 2-1	a15 1-0		M04 2-1	M16 3-1	O20 4-4	S22 2-3	D01 5-1	S08 4-2	J05 9-1	J07 3-1
9 LINCOLN C	D08 6-1	S22 3-2	M30 0-2	D26 1-3	a13 5-2	J05 0-2	O20 1-5	a06 1-2		M02 0-2	N17 3-1	D29 3-0	a12 1-3	D25 2-0	F16 1-0	S01 5-2
10 ARDWICK	S08 4-1	a13 4-1	S03 1-1	D08 3-3	a12 4-1	O20 2-4	S22 2-5	M30 1-1	M23 11-3		F09 4-0	N03 2-5	M09 7-1	J01 1-0	O06 6-1	D15 4-1
11 NEWCASTLE U	a12 1-2	S08 6-3	N10 3-1	M16 1-0	D25 6-0	O13 3-2	D01 1-4	S29 2-0	J01 4-2	O27 5-4		a13 3-0	S22 2-2	D15 5-2	D22 7-2	N24 2-4
12 NEWTON HEATH	J01 3-0	D08 5-1	M02 1-1	a12 2-2	S15 6-1	N24 1-1	M23 2-0	O27 2-2	D22 3-0	J05 4-1	a06 5-1		a20 3-3	N10 3-2	a03 9-0	O13 3-3
13 NOTTS CO	F26 10-0	J12 5-1	J05 2-0	N24 2-1	N10 5-1	S15 2-1	O04 3-2	O06 3-0	S29 3-0	O13 1-3	M23 2-1	D15 1-1		M16 4-2	D25 5-0	O27 2-2
14 ROTHERHAM T	M02 2-1	D29 4-1	S01 1-3	N06 2-3	a15 2-0	a13 4-1	J07 3-2	J26 0-1	S15 5-2	O01 3-2	D26 1-0	J12 2-1	N05 1-2		N17 6-1	O20 1-2
15 WALSALL T.S.	S22 2-0	M23 4-1	a16 3-1	O27 0-3	J26 4-0	a15 5-1	S08 4-3	D08 1-3	a20 1-2	S15 1-2	D29 2-3	D26 1-2	M25 2-1	S24 1-2		N10 4-1
16 W ARSENAL	D25 7-0	F23 3-0	J26 1-1	S22 4-2	a06 7-0	D08 4-0	S10 1-3	M09 3-3	O06 5-2	S29 4-2	J12 3-2	M30 3-2	N03 2-1	F09 1-1	a12 6-1	

LEAGUE TABLES

DIVISION 1

	P	W	D	L	F	A	W	D	L	F	A	Pts
Sunderland	30	13	2	0	51	14	8	3	4	29	23	47
Everton	30	12	2	1	47	18	6	4	5	35	32	42
Aston Villa	30	12	2	1	51	12	5	3	7	31	31	39
Preston NE	30	9	3	3	32	14	6	2	7	30	32	35
Blackburn R	30	9	5	1	40	15	2	5	8	19	34	32
Sheffield U	30	10	2	3	33	17	4	2	9	24	38	32
Nottingham F	30	10	1	4	33	22	3	4	8	17	34	31
Sheffield W	30	10	2	3	36	19	2	2	11	14	36	28
Burnley	30	8	2	5	28	24	3	2	10	16	32	26
Bolton W	30	8	3	4	45	23	1	4	10	16	39	25
Wolves	30	7	4	4	24	25	2	3	10	19	38	25
Small Heath	30	6	6	3	35	28	3	1	11	15	46	25
WBA	30	9	2	4	38	21	1	2	12	13	45	24
Stoke	30	7	3	5	35	25	2	3	10	15	42	24
Derby Co	30	4	5	6	23	23	3	4	8	22	45	23
Liverpool	30	6	4	5	38	28	1	4	10	13	42	22

DIVISION 2

	P	W	D	L	F	A	W	D	L	F	A	Pts
Bury	30	15	0	0	48	11	8	2	5	30	22	48
Notts Co	30	12	2	1	50	15	5	3	7	25	30	39
Newton Heath	30	9	6	0	52	18	6	2	7	26	26	38
Leicester F	30	11	2	2	45	20	4	6	5	27	33	38
Grimsby T	30	14	0	1	51	16	4	1	10	28	36	37
Darwen	30	13	1	1	53	10	3	3	9	21	33	36
Burton W	30	10	3	2	49	9	4	4	7	18	30	35
W Arsenal	30	11	3	1	54	20	3	3	9	21	38	34
Ardwick	30	9	3	3	56	28	5	0	10	26	44	31
Newcastle U	30	11	1	3	51	28	1	2	12	21	56	27
Burton S	30	9	2	4	34	20	2	1	12	18	54	25
Rotherham T	30	10	0	5	37	22	1	2	12	18	40	24
Lincoln C	30	8	0	7	32	27	2	0	13	20	65	20
Walsall TS	30	8	0	7	35	25	2	0	13	12	67	20
Burslem PV	30	6	3	6	30	23	1	1	13	9	54	18
Crewe A	30	3	4	8	20	34	0	0	15	6	69	10

Sunderland, the 1894-5 Football League Champions. Back row (left to right, players only): McNeil, Doig, Wilson, Gow, McCreadie. Middle row: Dunlop, Miller, Hannah, Harvie. Front row: Auld, Gillespy, Campbell, Scott, Johnston.

Scottish international forward John Bell, who scored 15 goals for runners-up, Everton. He was a 'masterful dribbler' who joined Everton from Dumbarton and later had spells with Spurs, Celtic, New Brighton Tower, Everton (again) and Preston, where he became player-coach.

Football League Records Season 1895-96

Top scorers: Div 1, J.Campbell (Aston Villa), S.Bloomer (Derby County) 20 goals; Div 2, G.Allan (Liverpool) 26 goals.
Test Matches: 18 Apr Ardwick 1 West Bromwich Albion 1; Liverpool 4 Small Heath 0; 20 Apr West Bromwich Albion 6 Ardwick 1; Small Heath 0 Liverpool 0; 25 Apr Ardwick 3 Small Heath 0; Liverpool 2 West Bromwich Albion 0; 27 Apr Small Heath 8 Ardwick 0; West Bromwich Albion 2 Liverpool 0. Liverpool promoted. Small Heath relegated. Loughborough Town elected in place of Walsall Town Swifts.

DIVISION 1

	ASTON VILLA	BLACKBURN R	BOLTON W	BURNLEY	BURY	DERBY CO	EVERTON	NOTTINGHAM F	PRESTON N.E.	SHEFFIELD U	SHEFFIELD W	SMALL HEATH	STOKE	SUNDERLAND	W.B.A.	WOLVERHAMPTON W
1 ASTON VILLA		O19 3-1	D14 2-0	N02 5-1	D28 2-0	S21 4-1	S30 4-3	J25 3-1	J11 1-0	N16 2-2	M14 2-1	S07 7-3	F22 5-2	O05 2-1	S02 1-0	a06 4-1
2 BLACKBURN R	S28 1-1		D07 3-2	O05 1-0	J04 0-2	F22 0-2	J01 2-3	S14 2-0	O12 3-0	J25 1-0	N23 2-1	M21 2-1	a03 3-1	O26 2-4	F17 1-0	N09 3-1
3 BOLTON W	M07 2-2	N30 1-1		S21 1-0	O05 2-4	J01 2-1	S14 3-1	O19 2-1	M14 1-0	a03 4-1	a25 2-0	F22 4-1	O26 3-1	D21 1-0	a04 2-1	J04 4-0
4 BURNLEY	N23 3-4	a18 6-0	O12 1-2		S14 3-0	a04 2-2	O26 1-1	D21 0-0	S28 1-0	F03 5-0	J04 2-0	a03 1-1	M16 2-0	S09 0-0	J11 3-0	F22 3-1
5 BURY	M21 5-3	a25 2-0	S07 0-3	J01 3-4		N23 1-2	J11 1-1	M24 1-0	D14 1-2	S21 1-0	N09 6-1	O12 4-5	N30 0-1	a03 1-2	N02 3-0	F18 3-0
6 DERBY CO	F08 2-2	a11 0-0	D26 2-1	N09 5-1	O19 2-1		a07 2-1	D07 4-0	M04 1-0	M14 0-2	S28 3-1	N30 8-0	O12 2-1	S14 2-0	D14 4-1	O26 5-2
7 EVERTON	D21 2-0	S21 0-2	a06 1-1	N30 2-1	S09 3-2	a03 2-2		S07 6-2	M07 3-2	O05 5-0	S02 2-2	F03 3-0	D14 7-2	N16 1-0	O19 1-1	N02 2-0
8 NOTTINGHAM F	a03 0-2	D28 4-2	J11 0-0	M07 2-1	S05 5-0	O05 2-5	O12 2-1		O26 0-1	D14 3-1	a07 1-0	S21 3-0	N28 4-0	J18 3-1	N16 2-0	a04 3-2
9 PRESTON N.E.	D07 4-3	N02 1-1	N09 1-0	O19 1-1	a04 1-1	M28 1-0	J25 1-1	F22 6-0		N30 4-3	a06 0-1	O05 3-2	D25 0-1	J04 4-1	a03 0-0	S07 4-3
10 SHEFFIELD U	S14 2-1	M07 1-1	D30 1-0	M30 1-1	a06 8-0	D21 1-1	N09 1-2	N23 2-1	S30 2-1		D26 1-1	S02 2-0	S28 1-0	O07 1-2	J04 2-0	F08 2-1
11 SHEFFIELD W	J18 1-3	J11 3-0	N02 1-1	D14 1-0	F22 1-3	D28 0-4	F18 3-1	N30 3-0	J01 1-1	S07 1-0		a04 3-0	N16 2-1	O19 3-0	O05 5-3	O12 3-1
12 SMALL HEATH	O26 1-4	F29 2-1	S28 1-2	D26 1-0	M07 1-0	J04 1-3	D07 0-3	N09 1-0	N23 5-2	a07 2-1	F08 1-1		S14 1-2	a11 0-1	D21 2-2	J18 3-2
13 STOKE	J04 1-2	a04 3-0	S02 2-0	D07 2-1	D26 0-2	S07 2-1	a11 1-2	M21 1-0	N11 4-0	N02 4-0	F21 5-0	O19 6-1		M14 5-0	S21 3-1	N23 4-1
14 SUNDERLAND	N09 2-1	S07 2-1	N23 1-0	F18 3-1	S28 0-0	N02 2-2	F22 3-0	F08 1-1	S02 4-1	J11 1-1	M07 2-1	D14 2-1	M28 4-1		J25 7-1	S21 2-2
15 W.B.A.	O12 1-1	a29 3-2	N04 2-3	S07 0-2	M09 1-3	J18 0-0	N23 0-3	S28 3-1	S14 1-2	F22 1-0	O26 2-3	a06 0-0	N09 1-0	D26 1-1		N30 2-1
16 WOLVERHAMPTON W	D26 1-2	D14 1-2	a11 5-0	S02 5-1	a07 1-0	N16 2-0	S28 2-3	M28 6-1	D21 2-1	O19 4-1	S14 4-0	J25 7-2	O05 1-0	D27 1-3	M07 1-2	

DIVISION 2

	BURSLEM P.V.	BURTON S	BURTON W	CREWE A	DARWEN	GRIMSBY T	LEICESTER F	LINCOLN C	LIVERPOOL	LOUGHBOROUGH T	ARDWICK	NEWCASTLE U	NEWTON HEATH	NOTTS CO	ROTHERHAM T	W ARSENAL
1 BURSLEM P.V.		J11 1-0	J18 2-2	O26 2-1	O05 3-3	N16 1-4	M07 1-1	F22 0-1	O21 5-4	a07 1-1	F10 0-1	a20 2-0	M23 3-0	S14 0-4	J25 4-0	F15 0-2
2 BURTON S	M14 2-1		O26 0-2	J04 1-1	a11 1-2	N09 2-1	M28 0-2	S30 4-0	F29 0-7	S28 1-2	N30 1-4	D07 3-1	F08 4-1	J18 0-0	S14 2-0	D21 3-2
3 BURTON W	S21 2-1	J25 2-1		D28 4-0	S07 3-0	O05 2-1	O19 0-0	a04 4-1	M07 2-1	J20 4-0	N16 4-1	F22 0-3	M18 5-1	a06 1-3	M21 6-1	D14 4-1
4 CREWE A	M25 3-2	N16 1-3	S14 0-1		D07 3-1	M07 0-1	F22 1-1	F08 2-2	M28 0-7	a03 1-2	O19 0-2	J25 3-0	S28 0-2	O05 5-1	N09 3-2	D23 0-1
5 DARWEN	O19 8-2	F15 3-0	J04 3-0	N30 6-1		S14 3-3	S21 4-1	M28 5-0	D14 0-4	F22 1-1	N02 2-3	N09 4-4	D21 3-0	J01 2-0	J13 10-2	M14 1-1
6 GRIMSBY T	J04 6-1	D28 3-0	M28 2-1	F29 2-0	J25 5-0		a11 7-1	S07 4-2	O19 1-0	N30 2-0	S21 5-0	D26 2-1	M14 4-2	M21 3-0	M03 4-0	a04 1-1
7 LEICESTER F	M21 5-0	S07 2-1	S28 1-3	D21 4-1	O26 2-3	a06 1-2		F29 1-3	N30 2-0	O05 5-0	a04 1-2	a07 2-0	J04 3-0	J11 2-1	a03 8-0	J25 1-0
8 LINCOLN C	a18 4-2	O05 1-2	N30 1-2	D26 6-2	M07 1-0	S28 2-5	F15 2-3		D21 0-1	N09 4-1	J11 1-2	D28 4-0	a11 2-0	a03 2-3	F01 5-0	S14 1-1
9 LIVERPOOL	S28 5-1	M21 6-1	S30 4-1	O07 6-1	N23 0-0	F22 3-1	N09 3-1	J25 6-1		D07 1-0	J01 3-1	S14 5-1	O12 7-1	O26 3-0	F18 10-1	J11 3-0
10 LOUGHBOROUGH T	a11 3-0	D26 2-2	N15 1-1	a18 4-1	M21 4-1	D21 0-1	N16 1-4	O26 3-0	S21 2-4		F01 2-4	M07 1-0	S14 3-3	D28 1-3	a06 3-0	F29 2-1
11 ARDWICK	F17 1-0	M07 1-1	N23 1-1	F15 4-0	O12 4-1	O26 2-1	S14 2-0	M14 4-0	a03 1-1	F24 5-1		J04 5-2	D07 2-1	a08 2-0	S09 2-0	S28 1-0
12 NEWCASTLE U	a03 4-2	a04 5-0	F08 4-0	D25 6-0	N16 7-2	J11 1-5	J01 1-0	J02 5-0	O05 1-0	S07 3-0	M21 4-1		O26 2-1	S21 5-1	D21 6-1	J18 3-1
13 NEWTON HEATH	a06 2-1	S21 5-0	F29 1-2	S07 5-0	a03 4-0	J01 3-2	F03 2-0	N16 5-5	N02 5-2	a04 2-0	O05 1-1	O19 2-1		D14 3-0	J11 3-0	N30 5-1
14 NOTTS CO	D07 7-2	F22 5-0	N09 1-4	a04 6-0	S28 4-1	O03 5-3	F08 1-2	O19 2-0	S07 2-3	D25 2-0	F29 3-0	M14 0-1	N23 0-2		N30 0-0	N02 3-4
15 ROTHERHAM T	S07 0-2	S23 1-4	D07 1-6	S21 4-0	D26 3-0	F08 1-0	J18 2-0	M16 2-2	J04 0-5	M14 4-0	N04 2-3	S28 1-1	M07 2-3	N16 1-0		O26 3-0
16 W ARSENAL	D25 2-1	O19 5-0	O12 3-0	M21 7-0	a18 1-3	S02 3-1	D07 1-1	S21 4-0	N16 0-2	J04 5-0	S07 0-1	a06 2-1	N09 2-1	M07 2-0	O05 5-0	

LEAGUE TABLES

DIVISION 1

	P	W	D	L	F	A	W	D	L	F	A	Pts
Aston Villa	30	14	1	0	47	17	6	4	5	31	28	45
Derby Co	30	12	2	1	42	13	5	5	5	26	22	41
Everton	30	10	4	1	40	17	6	3	6	26	26	39
Bolton W	30	12	2	1	34	14	4	3	8	15	23	37
Sunderland	30	10	5	0	36	14	5	2	8	16	27	37
Stoke	30	12	0	3	43	11	3	0	12	13	36	30
Sheffield W	30	10	2	3	31	18	2	3	10	13	35	29
Blackburn R	30	10	1	4	26	18	2	4	9	14	32	29
Preston NE	30	8	5	2	31	18	3	1	11	13	30	28
Burnley	30	8	5	2	33	11	2	2	11	15	33	27
Bury	30	7	1	7	32	24	5	2	8	18	30	27
Sheffield U	30	9	4	2	28	12	1	2	12	12	38	26
Nottingham F	30	11	1	3	34	16	0	2	13	8	41	25
Wolves	30	10	0	5	43	18	0	1	14	18	47	21
Small Heath	30	7	2	6	22	24	1	2	12	17	55	20
WBA	30	5	4	6	18	22	1	3	11	12	37	19

DIVISION 2

	P	W	D	L	F	A	W	D	L	F	A	Pts
Liverpool	30	14	1	0	65	11	8	1	6	41	21	46
Ardwick	30	12	3	0	37	9	9	1	5	26	29	46
Grimsby T	30	14	1	0	51	9	6	1	8	31	29	42
Burton W	30	12	1	2	43	15	7	3	5	26	25	42
Newcastle U	30	14	0	1	57	14	2	2	11	16	36	34
Newton Heath	30	12	2	1	48	15	3	1	11	18	42	33
W Arsenal	30	11	1	3	42	11	3	3	9	16	31	32
Leicester F	30	10	0	5	40	16	4	4	7	17	28	32
Darwen	30	9	4	2	55	22	3	2	10	17	45	30
Notts Co	30	8	1	6	41	22	4	1	10	16	32	26
Burton S	30	7	2	6	24	26	3	2	10	15	43	24
Loughboro' T	30	7	3	5	32	25	2	2	11	8	41	23
Lincoln C	30	7	1	7	36	24	2	3	10	17	51	22
Burslem PV	30	6	4	5	25	24	1	0	14	18	54	18
Rotherham T	30	7	2	6	27	26	0	1	14	7	71	17
Crewe A	30	5	2	8	22	28	0	1	14	8	67	13

Derby County's side that finished First Division runners-up in 1895-6. Back row (left to right): Methven, A.Staley (trainer), Leiper. Middle row: W.D.Clark (secretary), Cox, A.Goodall, Robinson, Kinsey, J.Staley. Front row: J.Goodall, Paul, Miller, Stevenson, McQueen. On ground: Bloomer, McMillan. Johnny McMillan's son, Stuart, managed the Rams when they won the FA Cup in 1946.

Scottish international Johnny Campbell spent only two seasons with Aston Villa but he scored 39 goals in that time and netted the first-ever goal at Villa Park, in April 1897. He won two Championship medals and an FA Cup winners' medal with them before returning to Celtic.

Football League Records Season 1896-97

Top scorers: Div 1, S.Bloomer (Derby County) 22 goals; Div 2, T.Boucher and J.Murphy (both Notts County) 22 goals.
Test Matches: 17 Apr Notts County 1 Sunderland 0; 19 Apr Sunderland 0 Notts County 0; Burnley 2 Newton Heath 0; 21 Apr Newton Heath 2 Burnley 0; 24 Apr Newton Heath 1 Sunderland 1; 26 Apr Burnley 0 Notts County 1; Sunderland 2 Newton Heath 0. Notts County promoted. Burnley relegated. Blackpool, Gainsborough Trinity and Walsall replaced Crewe Alexandra, Burslem Port Vale and Rotherham Town. Ardwick became Manchester City.

DIVISION 1

	ASTON VILLA	BLACKBURN R	BOLTON W	BURNLEY	BURY	DERBY CO	EVERTON	LIVERPOOL	NOTTINGHAM F	PRESTON N.E.	SHEFFIELD U	SHEFFIELD W	STOKE	SUNDERLAND	W.B.A.	WOLVERHAMPTON W
1 ASTON VILLA		a17 3-0	M22 6-2	J02 0-3	N07 1-1	O24 2-1	S26 1-2	M13 0-0	D19 3-2	F22 3-1	S12 2-2	N21 4-0	S02 2-1	J16 2-1	O10 2-0	a19 5-0
2 BLACKBURN R	N28 1-5		O17 1-0	O03 3-2	F20 1-2	J16 5-2	M06 4-2	S05 1-0	N14 0-0	O31 0-4	F06 1-3	S19 4-0	M20 2-1	D25 1-2	S01 1-2	J02 2-0
3 BOLTON W	M27 1-2	S12 0-0		M13 2-1	O10 2-0	M06 1-3	D07 2-0	J01 1-4	M20 0-0	O03 3-1	a16 0-2	a10 2-1	O24 4-0	S26 1-0	D19 2-2	a05 1-2
4 BURNLEY	F08 3-4	N07 0-1	F06 0-2		S12 1-0	a05 2-3	O10 2-1	D26 4-1	S19 2-2	O17 2-2	J16 1-1	D19 1-1	J09 1-3	S07 1-1	a10 5-0	M20 0-3
5 BURY	F06 0-2	M27 3-0	O31 2-2	J01 1-1		a10 1-0	M02 3-1	S19 1-2	D25 2-0	S05 0-0	M20 0-1	O17 1-1	N14 4-2	a16 1-1	M13 3-0	N28 3-2
6 DERBY CO	O17 1-3	N21 6-0	D26 1-0	N14 3-2	S26 7-2		a20 0-1	D19 3-2	S05 1-1	M27 2-2	O10 1-3	J09 2-1	N07 5-1	J23 1-0	D25 8-1	S19 4-3
7 EVERTON	S19 2-3	M13 0-3	N14 2-3	N28 6-0	a24 1-2	a16 5-2		O03 2-1	J09 3-1	F06 3-4	O17 1-2	S05 2-1	D19 4-2	D26 5-2	a17 6-3	O31 0-0
8 LIVERPOOL	D25 3-3	O24 4-0	S07 0-2	M27 1-2	D12 3-1	S12 2-0	N21 0-0		O10 3-0	a10 0-0	J02 0-0	a03 2-2	J16 1-0	N07 3-0	S26 0-0	M04 3-0
9 NOTTINGHAM F	M06 2-4	D12 2-1	J16 2-0	O24 4-1	D28 3-0	N18 1-2	M10 3-0	N28 2-0		a08 0-0	S26 2-2	O31 2-2	S12 4-0	N21 2-1	J02 0-1	a10 1-2
10 PRESTON N.E.	a26 0-1	O10 3-1	N21 2-3	S26 5-3	D26 2-2	a19 0-2	a03 4-1	N14 1-1	N07 3-2		O24 1-0	F20 2-2	N28 3-0	S12 5-3	a16 0-0	J16 4-0
11 SHEFFIELD U	O03 0-0	J09 7-0	D29 1-0	S05 1-0	N21 2-2	O31 2-2	J01 1-2	O19 1-1	F20 0-3	M13 0-2		D26 2-0	M27 1-0	S19 3-0	D05 0-1	J23 1-3
12 SHEFFIELD W	N14 1-3	D28 6-0	F27 0-0	M06 1-0	a17 2-0	N28 2-0	O24 4-1	S01 1-2	a05 3-0	J02 1-0	M02 1-1		S26 4-3	O10 0-0	S12 3-1	D12 0-0
13 STOKE	O31 0-2	a10 1-0	S19 2-3	F27 3-2	a12 3-0	D05 2-2	J02 2-3	F06 6-1	O17 3-0	N09 2-1	a15 2-0	J23 0-0		a03 0-1	N21 2-2	S05 2-1
14 SUNDERLAND	J09 4-2	D19 0-1	S05 1-1	M02 1-1	S01 0-1	J02 1-2	D12 1-1	O17 4-3	M13 2-2	J01 1-1	F27 0-1	D05 0-0	F20 4-1		M06 2-1	O03 0-3
15 W.B.A.	S05 3-1	D26 1-0	N02 1-0	a03 3-0	O24 0-0	F06 1-4	J16 1-4	O31 0-1	J23 4-0	S19 1-1	N14 0-1	O03 0-2	D12 1-2	N28 1-0		O17 1-0
16 WOLVERHAMPTON W	D26 1-2	S26 1-1	a20 4-0	N21 2-0	F27 1-1	S01 1-0	S12 0-1	J09 1-2	D05 4-1	D19 1-1	M06 1-1	M13 2-0	O10 1-2	O24 0-1	D28 6-1	

DIVISION 2

	BLACKPOOL	BURTON S	BURTON W	DARWEN	GAINSBOROUGH T	GRIMSBY T	LEICESTER F	LINCOLN C	LOUGHBOROUGH T	MANCHESTER C	NEWCASTLE U	NEWTON HEATH	NOTTS CO	SMALL HEATH	WALSALL	W ARSENAL
1 BLACKPOOL		a19 3-0	S19 5-0	a16 1-0	a24 1-1	J01 1-0	F27 3-0	N14 3-1	M27 4-1	S26 2-2	M13 4-1	O17 4-2	N28 3-2	J23 1-3	F13 3-2	J04 1-1
2 BURTON S	O24 2-2		a16 1-1	N28 2-0	a17 4-0	J16 0-0	S19 2-1	F06 4-0	N07 3-1	D26 5-0	a12 3-0	S05 3-5	J02 1-4	S26 1-1	O05 1-3	M13 1-2
3 BURTON W	M29 3-1	D25 1-0		N14 1-0	J23 3-2	S12 5-1	D19 2-1	a03 2-0	a19 0-1	M06 1-1	D05 0-1	M20 1-2	O03 0-3	F13 2-6	J09 1-0	S14 0-3
4 DARWEN	S12 2-3	O17 5-1	S26 3-0		a10 3-2	M20 3-1	O24 4-1	D19 4-1	F13 5-1	J09 3-1	N07 2-1	M13 0-2	F27 2-1	N21 2-0	D26 12-0	J01 4-1
5 GAINSBOROUGH T	a03 2-0	F13 4-1	N07 2-1	D25 2-4		O03 1-1	F06 0-2	M27 7-0	D05 2-0	S12 1-1	D28 2-0	O21 2-0	M06 3-2	J02 1-3	S26 2-0	D26 4-1
6 GRIMSBY T	F20 2-2	a03 3-0	J02 3-0	M06 4-2	S05 1-1		J23 4-1	S26 3-1	O17 8-1	O24 3-1	D26 3-2	S19 2-0	N21 3-1	D12 2-1	M13 0-1	a08 3-1
7 LEICESTER F	O03 2-1	M06 3-0	J16 2-1	S05 4-1	a19 0-0	D05 4-2		N07 4-1	D25 4-2	a12 3-3	J09 5-0	D28 1-0	S12 2-3	M27 0-1	N28 4-1	F13 6-3
8 LINCOLN C	S05 3-1	M20 1-1	D26 2-3	J16 1-0	F20 0-2	J09 0-3	a10 2-1		O03 0-2	F13 0-1	O24 1-2	a01 1-3	M31 1-1	M13 1-3	a16 2-1	D03 2-3
9 LOUGHBOROUGH T	J30 4-1	S12 0-2	a17 6-0	J02 4-2	N14 1-0	S02 1-4	S26 0-2	M06 3-0		M17 2-0	F20 3-0	a10 2-0	O24 0-1	D19 2-0	O10 1-2	D12 8-0
10 MANCHESTER C	N07 4-2	N14 3-1	N28 2-1	S19 4-1	F27 4-1	D19 3-1	M13 4-0	S21 3-0	a16 1-1		O17 1-2	O03 0-0	O31 1-4	J01 3-0	J06 5-0	S05 1-1
11 NEWCASTLE U	J16 4-1	M27 2-1	a10 3-0	O03 5-1	M20 1-2	O10 3-0	N14 3-1	J02 2-1	N28 4-1	F06 3-0		J01 2-0	D12 2-2	S12 4-3	M06 2-0	J23 2-0
12 NEWTON HEATH	D26 2-0	J09 1-1	O24 3-0	M02 3-1	S01 2-0	N07 4-2	F20 2-1	S12 3-1	F06 6-0	D25 2-1	S26 4-0		M27 1-1	O10 1-1	S07 2-0	M22 1-1
13 NOTTS CO	M20 3-1	D05 6-1	M13 5-0	F06 4-0	J09 2-0	O01 1-3	O17 6-0	J23 8-0	S05 3-1	O10 3-3	S19 3-1	J19 3-0		a03 1-2	N14 5-2	N07 7-4
14 SMALL HEATH	M06 1-3	O03 1-2	F27 3-2	S14 5-1	O17 2-2	O31 0-1	a16 2-2	S19 1-2	M20 3-0	a19 3-1	S05 3-1	N28 1-0	a10 3-1		D25 3-3	N14 5-2
15 WALSALL	a10 2-0	J23 5-2	S05 2-0	a21 4-0	S19 1-1	F27 0-1	M20 1-1	a17 5-0	O31 5-1	N23 3-2	a03 0-2	S21 2-3	J16 1-3	O24 1-6		O17 5-3
16 W ARSENAL	D19 4-2	F20 3-0	O12 3-0	a19 1-0	O24 6-1	N28 4-2	a17 2-1	D25 6-2	S19 2-0	a28 1-2	a16 5-1	a03 0-2	S26 2-3	M29 2-3	S12 1-1	

LEAGUE TABLES

DIVISION 1

	P	W	D	L	F	A	W	D	L	F	A	Pts
Aston Villa	30	10	3	2	36	16	11	2	2	37	22	47
Sheffield U	30	6	4	5	22	16	7	6	2	20	13	36
Derby Co	30	10	2	3	45	22	6	2	7	25	28	36
Preston NE	30	8	4	3	35	21	3	8	4	20	19	34
Liverpool	30	7	6	2	25	10	5	3	7	21	28	33
Sheffield W	30	9	4	2	29	11	1	7	7	13	26	31
Everton	30	8	1	6	42	29	6	2	7	20	28	31
Bolton W	30	7	3	5	22	18	5	3	7	18	25	30
Bury	30	7	5	3	25	15	3	5	7	14	29	30
Wolves	30	6	4	5	26	14	5	2	8	19	27	28
Nottingham F	30	8	3	4	30	16	1	5	9	14	33	26
WBA	30	7	2	6	18	16	3	4	8	15	40	26
Stoke	30	8	3	4	30	18	3	0	12	18	41	25
Blackburn R	30	8	1	6	27	25	3	2	10	8	37	25
Sunderland	30	4	6	5	21	21	3	3	9	13	26	23
Burnley	30	4	5	6	25	25	2	2	11	18	36	19

DIVISION 2

	P	W	D	L	F	A	W	D	L	F	A	Pts
Notts Co	30	12	1	2	60	18	7	3	5	32	25	42
Newton Heath	30	11	4	0	37	10	6	1	8	19	24	39
Grimsby T	30	12	2	1	44	15	5	2	8	22	30	38
Small Heath	30	8	3	4	36	23	8	2	5	33	24	37
Newcastle U	30	13	1	1	42	13	4	0	11	14	39	35
Manchester C	30	10	3	2	39	15	2	5	8	19	35	32
Gainsboro' T	30	10	2	3	35	16	2	5	8	15	31	31
Blackpool	30	11	3	1	39	16	2	2	11	20	40	31
Leicester F	30	11	2	2	44	19	2	2	11	15	37	30
W Arsenal	30	10	1	4	42	20	3	3	9	26	50	30
Darwen	30	13	0	2	54	16	1	0	14	13	45	28
Walsall	30	8	2	5	37	25	3	2	10	16	44	26
Loughboro' T	30	10	0	5	37	14	2	1	12	13	50	25
Burton S	30	7	4	4	33	20	2	2	11	13	41	24
Burton W	30	8	1	6	22	22	1	1	13	9	45	20
Lincoln C	30	4	2	9	17	27	1	0	14	10	58	12

Notts County, Second Division champions in 1896-7. Back row (left to right, players only): Bramley, Smith, Prescott, Toone, Allsop, Gibson. Front row: Langham, Allen, Murphy, Bull. On ground: Boucher.

England's Charlie Athersmith was one of the game's fastest wingers and altogether scored 85 goals in 307 League and Cup appearances for Aston Villa between 1890-91 and 1900-01. In 1896-7 he won every honour going that season, League Championship and FA Cup winners' medals and international caps.

Football League Records Season 1897-98

Top scorers: Div 1, G.Wheldon (Aston Villa) 21 goals; Div 2, H.Boyd (Newton Heath) 23 goals.
Test Matches: 20 Apr Newcastle United 2 Stoke 1; 21 Apr Blackburn Rovers 1 Burnley 3; 23 Apr Stoke 1 Newcastle United 0; Burnley 2 Blackburn Rovers 0; 26 Apr Burnley 0 Stoke 2; 28 Apr Blackburn Rovers 4 Newcastle United 3; 30 Apr Newcastle United 4 Blackburn Rovers 0; Stoke 0 Burnley 0. Burnley and Newcastle United were promoted.
Luton Town were elected in place of Burton Wanderers.

DIVISION 1

	ASTON VILLA	BLACKBURN R	BOLTON W	BURY	DERBY CO	EVERTON	LIVERPOOL	NOTTINGHAM F	NOTTS CO	PRESTON N.E.	SHEFFIELD U	SHEFFIELD W	STOKE	SUNDERLAND	W.B.A.	WOLVERHAMPTON W
1 ASTON VILLA		D11 5-1	O02 3-2	S18 3-1	M05 4-1	N13 3-0	O30 3-1	a30 2-0	O16 4-2	F05 4-0	J15 1-2	S01 5-2	a02 1-1	N27 4-3	S04 4-3	a11 1-2
2 BLACKBURN R	S25 4-3		S11 1-3	M19 1-1	N27 1-1	J01 1-1	J08 2-1	J15 1-1	a09 0-1	O09 1-0	N20 1-1	O23 1-1	a08 1-1	D25 2-1	F05 1-3	F26 2-3
3 BOLTON W	N20 2-0	a14 1-2		J03 0-0	J01 3-3	M26 1-0	D25 0-2	O23 2-0	S18 1-0	S25 1-0	a08 0-1	O09 0-3	N13 2-1	O30 1-0	a02 2-0	M12 2-1
4 BURY	M12 1-2	a16 1-0	D11 2-1		M29 4-0	O23 0-1	M26 0-2	a04 2-2	N27 0-0	F12 1-0	O09 2-5	S11 3-0	J01 3-3	a08 1-0	O02 3-2	N06 2-1
5 DERBY CO	J22 3-1	S04 3-1	D27 1-0	O16 2-2		S11 5-1	a12 3-1	a11 5-0	D25 1-2	M12 3-1	N13 1-1	F19 1-2	N06 4-1	D11 2-2	S18 3-2	J08 3-2
6 EVERTON	D25 2-1	O02 1-1	S04 2-1	M05 4-2	a08 3-0		O16 3-0	a02 2-0	D11 1-0	M21 1-1	O30 1-4	J08 1-0	J17 1-1	a11 2-0	N27 6-1	S18 3-0
7 LIVERPOOL	a16 4-0	D18 0-1	M19 1-1	M31 2-2	O23 4-2	S25 3-1		N06 1-2	M12 2-0	S11 0-0	F05 0-4	a11 4-0	O09 4-0	D27 0-2	J01 1-1	N20 1-0
8 NOTTINGHAM F	M26 3-1	O16 3-1	J08 2-0	a09 3-1	O30 3-4	M12 2-2	N27 2-3		S04 1-1	N13 4-1	S18 1-1	J22 1-0	F19 3-1	O02 1-1	D11 0-1	a08 1-1
9 NOTTS CO	S11 2-3	M05 0-0	N06 1-2	F26 2-1	S25 1-1	J15 3-2	a02 3-2	O09 1-3		O07 1-1	J01 1-3	D04 0-0	O23 4-0	F05 0-1	M19 2-2	D18 2-2
10 PRESTON N.E.	N06 3-1	O30 1-4	O16 0-0	J08 2-1	a09 5-0	N20 1-1	O02 1-1	D25 3-0	a08 3-1		S04 1-3	D18 2-0	M05 0-0	S18 2-0	M31 1-1	N27 1-2
11 SHEFFIELD U	J08 1-0	O04 5-2	F07 4-0	S25 1-1	S01 2-1	F22 0-0	D29 1-2	D04 1-1	F19 0-1	O23 2-1		D27 1-1	S11 4-3	a02 1-0	a11 2-0	J22 2-1
12 SHEFFIELD W	S27 3-0	N13 4-1	N27 3-0	N20 3-0	J15 3-1	F05 2-1	S18 4-2	J01 3-6	O02 3-1	D11 2-1	O16 0-1		D25 4-0	S04 0-1	a09 3-0	M05 2-0
13 STOKE	D18 0-0	S18 2-1	J15 2-0	D27 3-1	O02 2-1	a09 2-0	S04 2-2	N20 1-2	S02 2-0	N08 1-2	D11 2-1	M26 2-1		J08 0-1	O30 0-0	O16 0-2
14 SUNDERLAND	O23 0-0	M12 2-1	F22 2-0	J15 2-1	O09 2-1	D18 0-0	J22 1-0	a23 4-0	J03 2-0	J01 1-0	M05 3-1	S25 1-0	D04 4-0		O16 0-2	S11 3-2
15 W.B.A.	O09 1-1	D27 1-1	N01 2-0	D18 1-0	N20 3-1	N06 2-2	N13 2-1	S11 2-0	a04 0-3	J15 3-1	M26 2-0	M12 0-2	S25 2-0	F19 2-2		O23 2-2
16 WOLVERHAMPTON W	D27 1-1	a02 3-2	a09 2-0	S04 3-0	D04 2-0	O09 2-3	D11 2-1	S25 0-0	O30 3-1	S01 3-0	O02 1-1	a16 5-0	F05 4-2	N13 4-2	D28 1-1	

DIVISION 2

	BLACKPOOL	BURNLEY	BURTON S	DARWEN	GAINSBOROUGH T	GRIMSBY T	LEICESTER F	LINCOLN C	LOUGHBOROUGH T	LUTON T	MANCHESTER C	NEWCASTLE U	NEWTON HEATH	SMALL HEATH	WALSALL	W ARSENAL
1 BLACKPOOL		S11 1-1	O09 2-1	a08 1-0	D18 5-0	a16 1-1	J08 2-1	F19 5-0	a23 4-0	a30 1-0	S18 0-2	D25 2-3	S25 0-1	O16 4-1	a02 1-1	J01 3-3
2 BURNLEY	S04 5-1		O16 2-0	N27 6-1	M12 1-1	D11 6-0	J15 4-0	J01 2-1	M28 9-3	N13 4-0	O30 3-1	O02 3-0	M07 6-3	F05 4-1	S18 4-1	S06 5-0
3 BURTON S	F26 2-1	M05 0-2		F19 2-0	a23 1-1	D01 4-0	N27 2-3	J08 1-1	a08 3-0	D25 2-1	a09 0-0	D18 3-1	S11 0-4	S04 1-3	O02 3-2	J15 1-2
4 DARWEN	N13 3-1	N06 0-1	M26 1-2		J01 2-4	O16 1-0	D18 1-2	S18 3-2	S25 2-1	F26 0-2	S04 2-4	M05 1-3	M19 2-3	O02 1-1	F12 1-2	M12 1-4
5 GAINSBOROUGH T	O02 4-1	a09 0-0	M23 3-2	D24 3-1		S25 2-0	M19 1-0	O16 4-0	M05 4-0	N27 3-3	F26 1-0	D04 1-3	D27 2-1	F19 0-0	J22 1-1	M26 1-0
6 GRIMSBY T	M19 3-0	O23 2-1	F05 7-2	S11 5-0	S04 4-2		S18 0-0	O02 4-2	D04 7-0	J22 1-3	D18 3-4	N06 2-0	a02 1-3	N13 3-1	M05 1-2	F12 1-4
7 LEICESTER F	N06 4-1	O09 0-1	M12 1-1	F05 0-1	a16 3-1	a11 1-0		F12 3-1	D25 4-0	S04 1-1	a02 0-0	a09 1-1	N20 1-1	M26 2-0	O16 3-1	D04 2-1
8 LINCOLN C	F05 3-2	a08 1-1	J29 3-0	O09 2-2	N13 2-1	D25 1-1	M05 1-4		O23 2-3	D04 4-2	M19 2-1	S25 2-3	N06 1-0	J15 1-2	a09 0-2	D27 2-3
9 LOUGHBOROUGH T	M26 0-2	J22 0-2	D27 3-2	J08 0-1	F05 0-5	a09 2-1	N13 1-1	N27 4-2		O16 2-0	O02 0-3	a11 0-1	a16 0-0	S18 0-2	S04 2-1	D18 1-3
10 LUTON T	N29 3-1	M19 2-0	N06 1-1	a11 3-0	S11 4-0	D27 6-0	a08 0-1	D18 9-3	J15 7-0		J01 3-0	F19 3-1	M21 2-2	a02 1-2	F05 6-0	O02 0-2
11 MANCHESTER C	M30 3-3	N20 1-1	a16 9-0	O23 5-0	S01 3-0	O09 3-0	D11 2-1	J24 3-1	S11 3-0	M26 2-1		J08 1-1	D25 0-1	a11 3-3	J03 3-2	S25 4-1
12 NEWCASTLE U	O23 2-0	D27 0-1	S18 3-1	J15 1-0	a02 5-2	M26 4-0	J22 4-2	F26 3-0	J03 3-1	M12 4-1	M16 2-0		O09 2-0	N27 4-0	J01 2-1	S04 4-1
13 NEWTON HEATH	J15 4-0	J12 0-0	J01 4-0	a23 3-2	a08 1-0	N27 2-1	O02 2-0	S04 5-0	M29 5-1	S18 1-2	O16 1-1	N13 0-1		a09 3-1	O30 6-0	F26 5-1
14 SMALL HEATH	J29 2-3	J08 2-2	S25 2-1	D25 5-1	O09 4-3	M12 0-2	S11 2-1	a16 4-0	N06 1-0	F12 4-2	D27 0-1	a12 1-0	O23 2-1		D04 6-0	a23 2-1
15 WALSALL	D27 6-0	S25 1-2	O23 4-0	S27 5-0	a11 3-0	N20 1-1	F26 2-1	M12 3-1	O09 3-0	J08 5-0	J15 2-2	S11 2-3	D11 1-1	D18 1-2		N06 3-2
16 W ARSENAL	N27 2-1	a02 1-1	a11 3-0	a09 3-1	S18 4-0	S01 4-1	O23 0-3	S11 2-2	M19 4-0	O09 3-0	F05 2-2	O16 0-0	J08 5-1	M05 4-2	N13 4-0	

LEAGUE TABLES

DIVISION 1

	P	W	D	L	F	A	W	D	L	F	A	Pts
Sheffield U	30	9	4	2	27	14	8	4	3	29	17	42
Sunderland	30	12	2	1	27	8	4	3	8	16	22	37
Wolves	30	10	4	1	36	14	4	3	8	21	27	35
Everton	30	11	3	1	33	12	2	6	7	15	27	35
Sheffield W	30	12	0	3	39	15	3	3	9	12	27	33
Aston Villa	30	12	1	2	47	21	2	4	9	14	30	33
WBA	30	8	5	2	25	16	3	5	7	19	29	32
Nottingham F	30	7	5	3	30	19	4	4	7	17	30	31
Liverpool	30	7	4	4	27	16	4	2	9	21	29	28
Derby Co	30	10	3	2	40	19	1	3	11	17	42	28
Bolton W	30	9	2	4	18	13	2	2	11	10	28	26
Preston NE	30	7	5	3	26	15	1	3	11	9	28	24
Notts Co	30	4	6	5	23	23	4	2	9	13	23	24
Bury	30	8	3	4	25	19	0	5	10	14	32	24
Blackburn R	30	4	7	4	20	22	3	3	9	19	32	24
Stoke	30	8	3	4	21	14	0	5	10	14	41	24

DIVISION 2

	P	W	D	L	F	A	W	D	L	F	A	Pts
Burnley	30	14	1	0	64	13	6	7	2	16	11	48
Newcastle U	30	14	0	1	43	10	7	3	5	21	22	45
Manchester C	30	10	4	1	45	15	5	5	5	21	21	39
Newton Heath	30	11	2	2	42	10	5	4	6	22	25	38
W Arsenal	30	10	4	1	41	14	6	1	8	28	35	37
Small Heath	30	11	1	3	37	18	5	3	7	21	32	36
Leicester F	30	8	5	2	26	11	5	2	8	20	24	33
Luton T	30	10	2	3	50	13	3	2	10	18	37	30
Gainsboro' T	30	10	4	1	30	12	2	2	11	20	42	30
Walsall	30	9	3	3	42	15	3	2	10	16	43	29
Blackpool	30	8	4	3	32	15	2	1	12	17	46	25
Grimsby T	30	9	1	5	44	24	1	3	11	8	38	24
Burton S	30	7	3	5	25	21	1	2	12	13	48	21
Lincoln C	30	6	3	6	27	27	0	2	13	16	55	17
Darwen	30	4	1	10	21	32	2	1	12	10	44	14
Loughboro' T	30	5	2	8	15	26	1	0	14	9	61	14

Sheffield United, League Champions in 1897-8. Back row (left to right, players only): Hedley, Johnson, Boyle, Foulke, Almond, Morren. Front row: Bennett, Beers, Needham, Thickett, Priest.

Gavin Crawford was one of Woolwich Arsenal's first professional footballers and their skipper for several years. He had already made around 100 senior appearances when the Gunners entered the Football League in 1893. Crawford, a wing-half, later played for Millwall and QPR and was Charlton Athletic's groundsman.

Football League Records Season 1898-99

Top scorers: Div 1, S.Bloomer (Derby County) 23 goals; Div 2, W.Abbott (Small Heath) 33 goals.
From this season automatic two-up/two-down system of promotion/relegation came into operation. Barnsley, Glossop North End, New Brighton Tower and Burslem Port Vale elected to the League.

LEAGUE TABLES

DIVISION 1

	P	W	D	L	F	A	W	D	L	F	A	Pts
Aston Villa	34	15	2	0	58	13	4	5	8	18	27	45
Liverpool	34	12	3	2	29	10	7	2	8	20	23	43
Burnley	34	11	5	1	32	15	4	4	9	13	32	39
Everton	34	10	2	5	25	13	5	6	6	23	28	38
Notts Co	34	9	6	2	33	20	3	7	7	14	31	37
Blackburn R	34	9	5	3	41	23	5	3	9	19	29	36
Sunderland	34	11	3	3	26	10	4	3	10	15	31	36
Wolves	34	9	5	3	30	13	5	2	10	24	35	35
Derby Co	34	11	5	1	46	19	1	6	10	16	38	35
Bury	34	9	5	3	31	18	5	2	10	17	31	35
Nottingham F	34	6	6	5	22	18	5	5	7	20	24	33
Stoke	34	10	4	3	29	17	3	3	11	18	35	33
Newcastle U	34	9	3	5	33	18	2	5	10	16	30	30
WBA	34	11	1	5	28	9	1	5	11	14	48	30
Preston NE	34	10	4	3	29	14	0	5	12	15	33	29
Sheffield U	34	7	8	2	31	20	2	3	12	14	31	29
Bolton W	34	6	5	6	24	21	3	2	12	13	30	25
Sheffield W	34	8	2	7	26	24	0	6	11	6	37	24

DIVISION 2

	P	W	D	L	F	A	W	D	L	F	A	Pts
Manchester C	34	15	1	1	64	10	8	5	4	28	25	52
Glossop NE	34	12	1	4	48	13	8	5	4	28	25	46
Leicester F	34	12	5	0	35	12	6	4	7	29	30	45
Newton Heath	34	12	4	1	51	14	7	1	9	16	29	43
New Brighton	34	13	2	2	48	13	5	5	7	23	39	43
Walsall	34	12	5	0	64	11	3	7	7	15	25	42
W Arsenal	34	14	2	1	55	10	4	3	10	17	31	41
Small Heath	34	14	1	2	66	17	3	6	8	19	33	41
Burslem PV	34	12	2	3	35	12	5	3	9	21	22	39
Grimsby T	34	10	3	4	39	17	5	2	10	32	43	35
Barnsley	34	11	4	2	44	18	1	3	13	8	38	31
Lincoln C	34	10	5	2	31	16	2	2	13	20	40	31
Burton S	34	7	5	5	35	25	3	3	11	16	45	28
Gainsboro' T	34	8	4	5	40	22	2	1	14	16	50	25
Luton T	34	8	1	8	37	31	2	2	13	14	64	23
Blackpool	34	6	3	8	35	30	2	1	14	14	60	20
Loughboro' T	34	5	4	8	31	26	1	2	14	7	66	18
Darwen	34	2	4	11	16	32	0	1	16	6	109	9

Welsh international winger Billy Meredith helped Manchester City into the First Division in 1898-9 and later won League Championship and FA Cup winners' medals with Manchester United.

DIVISION 1

	ASTON VILLA	BLACKBURN R	BOLTON W	BURNLEY	BURY	DERBY CO	EVERTON	LIVERPOOL	NEWCASTLE U	NOTTINGHAM F	NOTTS CO	PRESTON N.E.	SHEFFIELD U	SHEFFIELD W	STOKE	SUNDERLAND	W.B.A.	WOLVERHAMPTON W
1 ASTON VILLA		N19 3-1	O29 2-1	J14 4-0	J07 3-2	N05 7-1	D17 3-0	a29 5-0	D26 1-0	O22 3-0	a22 6-1	O08 4-2	S24 1-1	M25 3-1	S03 3-1	D03 2-0	a24 7-1	D10 1-1
2 BLACKBURN R	M18 0-0		S10 4-1	D26 0-2	O01 0-0	J14 3-0	O29 1-3	D24 1-3	D10 4-2	D31 3-3	J02 6-0	a15 2-2	a01 2-1	F04 2-0	N12 4-1	O15 3-2	S24 4-1	F18 2-2
3 BOLTON W	a17 0-0	J07 0-2		J03 2-0	D17 0-1	M31 2-1	F25 2-4	a01 2-1	M18 0-0	D10 0-2	O15 0-1	N26 2-2	N12 3-0	S17 0-0	F18 0-2	J21 6-1	S03 3-3	O01 2-1
4 BURNLEY	S17 2-4	N26 2-0	N05 2-0		J21 2-1	M11 2-1	a22 0-0	O22 2-1	O08 2-1	M06 1-1	S03 1-1	S05 3-1	M31 1-0	D03 5-0	a17 1-1	a08 1-0	N19 1-1	D17 4-2
5 BURY	S10 2-1	F14 3-2	a15 3-1	S24 1-1		D31 0-0	M18 3-1	N19 3-0	O22 1-1	D03 2-0	a08 2-0	N05 3-1	O08 1-3	J02 0-0	D24 5-2	M31 1-2	J14 1-1	M14 0-2
6 DERBY CO	M04 1-1	S17 0-0	D26 1-1	N12 2-1	S03 1-2		O15 5-5	D10 1-0	N26 3-1	a20 2-0	F18 4-2	a01 1-0	a22 1-0	J21 9-0	O29 1-1	O01 4-2	J07 4-1	F04 6-2
7 EVERTON	a15 1-1	S01 2-1	O08 1-0	D24 4-0	N26 0-1	a03 1-2		S24 1-2	S10 3-0	J02 1-3	a01 1-2	J14 2-0	D31 1-0	N05 2-0	D10 2-0	M11 0-0	O22 1-0	N19 2-1
8 LIVERPOOL	O15 0-3	a22 2-0	D03 2-0	F18 2-0	a20 1-0	a08 4-0	J21 2-0		a03 3-2	M25 0-1	O01 0-0	N12 3-1	O29 2-1	S03 4-0	F04 1-0	J07 0-0	D17 2-2	S17 1-0
9 NEWCASTLE U	O01 1-1	a08 1-0	N19 4-1	F04 4-1	F18 2-0	M25 2-0	J07 2-2	N05 3-0		M11 0-1	S17 1-2	F25 2-1	O15 1-2	D17 2-2	J21 3-0	a22 0-1	D03 3-0	S03 2-4
10 NOTTINGHAM F	F18 1-0	S03 0-1	a08 1-2	O29 0-1	a01 1-2	D17 3-3	O01 0-0	N26 0-3	N12 2-0		F04 0-0	O06 2-2	M04 2-1	J07 1-1	O15 2-1	S17 1-1	a22 3-0	J21 3-0
11 NOTTS CO	D24 1-0	N05 5-3	a03 2-1	D31 2-2	D10 4-1	O22 2-2	D03 0-1	D27 1-1	J14 3-1	O08 2-2		S24 1-0	S10 2-2	M11 1-0	a15 2-0	N19 5-2	M09 0-0	M25 0-2
12 PRESTON N.E.	F04 2-0	D17 1-1	a29 0-1	O15 1-1	D26 3-1	D03 3-1	S17 0-0	M11 1-2	O29 1-0	N19 1-0	M20 2-0		F18 1-0	a22 1-1	O01 4-2	S03 2-3	a08 4-0	J07 2-1
13 SHEFFIELD U	J21 1-3	D03 1-1	M11 3-1	O01 1-1	F04 4-1	N19 2-1	S03 1-1	J02 0-2	S26 2-2	N05 2-2	J07 2-2	O22 1-1		D26 2-1	S17 1-1	D17 2-0	M25 5-0	S12 1-0
14 SHEFFIELD W	M13 4-1	O08 1-2	J14 1-0	a01 1-0	O15 3-2	S24 3-1	M04 1-2	D31 0-3	a15 1-3	S10 2-1	N12 1-1	S19 2-1	O03 1-1		M27 1-3	F18 0-1	F14 1-2	O29 3-0
15 STOKE	D31 3-0	M11 0-1	O22 2-3	S10 4-1	a22 1-1	S01 0-0	a08 2-1	O08 2-1	S24 0-0	D26 2-1	D17 1-1	N14 2-1	J14 4-1	N19 1-0		M25 1-0	N05 2-1	D03 2-4
16 SUNDERLAND	a01 4-2	a03 0-1	S24 0-0	D10 0-1	O29 3-0	J02 1-0	N12 2-1	S10 1-0	D24 2-3	J14 1-1	M18 1-1	D31 1-0	a29 1-0	O22 2-0	N26 2-0		O08 2-0	M04 3-0
17 W.B.A.	N12 0-1	J21 6-2	D31 1-0	M18 0-1	S17 2-0	S10 1-1	N07 3-0	D26 0-1	a01 2-0	D24 2-0	O29 2-0	D10 2-0	N26 3-0	O01 2-0	M04 0-1	F04 1-0		O15 1-2
18 WOLVERHAMPTON W	a03 4-0	O22 2-1	a04 1-0	a15 4-0	N12 1-2	O08 2-2	a29 1-2	J14 0-0	D31 0-0	S24 0-2	N26 1-0	S10 0-0	D24 4-1	F25 0-0	a01 3-2	N05 2-0	D27 5-1	

DIVISION 2

	BARNSLEY	BLACKPOOL	BURSLEM P.V.	BURTON S	DARWEN	GAINSBOROUGH T	GLOSSOP N.E.	GRIMSBY T	LEICESTER F	LINCOLN C	LOUGHBOROUGH T	LUTON T	MANCHESTER C	NEW BRIGHTON	NEWTON HEATH	SMALL HEATH	WALSALL	W ARSENAL
1 BARNSLEY		F11 2-1	D31 2-1	a15 2-0	O08 6-0	O22 1-0	D27 1-1	F25 2-2	S24 3-4	a03 1-0	J28 9-0	S10 2-1	N05 1-1	M25 2-1	a04 0-2	J14 7-2	D03 1-1	D24 2-1
2 BLACKPOOL	M15 3-1		S24 0-4	J14 3-0	M31 6-0	a15 4-0	D31 1-2	F18 3-6	a01 2-2	N12 3-0	O08 2-1	N26 2-3	D24 2-4	M04 1-2	a03 0-1	M08 1-1	S10 1-2	M22 1-1
3 BURSLEM P.V.	S03 2-0	J21 6-1		D24 4-1	M18 3-1	N26 2-1	a03 1-2	O01 2-0	N12 0-2	F18 2-1	S17 3-0	M04 4-1	a01 1-1	O15 0-0	F04 1-0	J07 1-0	a15 0-1	S05 3-0
4 BURTON S	D17 5-0	S17 3-1	J28 2-0		N12 4-0	M18 2-1	a01 1-2	J21 1-2	M04 1-1	a12 2-1	J07 1-1	D26 1-1	N26 3-3	F04 1-1	O01 5-1	S03 2-6	M31 0-2	F18 1-2
5 DARWEN	M21 1-1	a08 0-2	J02 1-3	M11 0-2		F11 0-3	F25 0-2	D17 0-2	O01 3-0	J07 1-2	D03 0-1	a11 4-1	O22 0-2	D31 2-4	a22 1-1	M25 1-1	N05 1-1	S17 1-4
6 GAINSBOROUGH T	F18 2-0	D17 7-0	M25 3-2	O26 1-2	O15 2-2		N05 2-4	a22 5-1	F04 4-0	S17 2-2	D26 3-0	O01 2-3	F25 3-1	J07 3-1	S03 0-2	D03 1-1	M11 0-0	J21 0-1
7 GLOSSOP N.E.	M31 1-0	S03 4-1	a08 0-0	D03 5-0	M07 5-0	M04 5-1		J07 4-2	F18 1-3	O01 2-0	a22 4-0	O15 5-0	N12 1-2	J21 5-0	S17 1-2	D17 1-2	M25 2-0	F04 2-0
8 GRIMSBY T	D26 0-1	O22 2-1	F21 3-1	S24 1-3	a15 9-2	D24 0-2	S10 1-1		M31 1-0	M18 1-1	F11 5-0	a01 5-0	a11 1-2	N12 2-2	M04 3-0	O08 2-0	J14 2-1	N26 1-0
9 LEICESTER F	J21 3-1	D03 4-0	M11 1-1	N05 1-0	D26 4-0	O08 1-0	O22 4-2	a03 2-0		S03 3-2	D27 1-0	S17 1-1	F11 1-1	a22 4-1	D17 1-0	a29 0-0	F25 2-2	J07 2-1
10 LINCOLN C	S01 1-0	M11 0-0	O22 1-0	F11 1-1	S10 2-0	J14 1-0	D26 2-2	a08 1-6	D31 3-1		N05 6-0	D24 2-0	S24 3-1	D27 1-2	M25 2-0	M31 2-2	O08 1-1	a15 2-0
11 LOUGHBOROUGH T	M11 2-0	F04 1-3	J14 0-3	S10 1-0	a01 10-0	a03 0-0	D24 1-3	a17 1-3	N26 0-3	M04 2-4		M18 4-1	D10 1-3	a29 6-0	F18 0-1	S24 1-1	D31 1-1	N12 0-0
12 LUTON T	J07 4-1	M25 3-2	N05 0-1	a03 3-0	S24 8-1	J28 4-2	F11 0-2	D03 3-1	J14 1-6	a22 2-0	M31 2-2		O08 0-3	D17 2-3	a08 0-1	M11 2-3	O22 3-2	S03 0-1
13 MANCHESTER C	M04 5-0	a22 4-1	D03 3-1	M25 6-0	F18 10-0	M31 4-0	J02 0-2	S03 7-2	O15 3-1	F22 3-1	D17 5-0	F04 2-0		S17 1-1	D26 4-0	a08 2-0	N19 2-0	O01 3-1
14 NEW BRIGHTON	N26 2-1	N05 4-0	F11 1-0	O08 2-2	D22 7-0	S10 3-2	S24 2-2	M11 2-0	D24 1-0	a01 4-1	F25 3-0	a15 4-0	J14 0-1		N19 0-3	O22 4-0	J28 6-0	D10 3-1
15 NEWTON HEATH	N12 0-0	D10 3-1	O08 2-1	J02 2-2	D24 9-0	D31 6-1	J14 3-0	N05 3-2	a15 2-2	N26 1-0	O22 6-1	a12 5-0	S10 3-0	M18 1-2		F25 2-0	S24 1-0	a01 2-2
16 SMALL HEATH	S17 3-1	D26 5-0	S10 1-2	D31 4-1	N26 8-0	a01 6-1	a15 1-1	F04 2-1	M18 0-3	S05 4-1	J21 6-0	N12 9-0	D27 4-1	F18 3-2	O15 4-1		D24 2-1	M04 4-1
17 WALSALL	a01 1-1	J07 6-0	D17 1-1	a04 7-1	M04 10-0	N12 6-1	N26 2-0	S17 4-1	S26 1-1	F04 3-2	S03 7-0	F18 6-0	M18 1-1	O01 1-1	J21 2-0	a22 2-0		O15 4-1
18 W ARSENAL	a22 3-0	M18 6-0	F25 1-0	O22 2-1	J14 6-0	S24 5-1	F13 3-0	M25 1-1	S10 4-0	D17 4-2	M13 3-1	D31 6-2	a03 0-1	a08 4-0	D03 5-1	N05 2-0	F11 0-0	

Football League Records Season 1899-1900

Top scorers: Div 1, W.Garraty (Aston Villa) 27 goals; Div 2, J.Wright (Sheffield Wednesday) 24 goals.
Chesterfield and Middlesbrough were elected in place of Blackpool and Darwen.
Glossop dropped the 'North End' part of their name.

DIVISION 1

	ASTON VILLA	BLACKBURN R	BURNLEY	BURY	DERBY CO	EVERTON	GLOSSOP	LIVERPOOL	MANCHESTER C	NEWCASTLE U	NOTTINGHAM F	NOTTS CO	PRESTON N.E.	SHEFFIELD U	STOKE	SUNDERLAND	W.B.A.	WOLVERHAMPTON W
1 ASTON VILLA		S23 3-1	N25 2-0	O07 2-1	F03 3-2	J13 1-1	S04 9-0	M24 1-0	O21 2-1	N04 2-1	D09 2-2	F17 6-2	a07 3-1	M03 1-1	D23 4-1	D30 4-2	S09 0-2	N11 0-0
2 BLACKBURN R	J20 0-4		J01 2-0	D16 3 2	a14 2 0	N25 3-1	M03 2-2	S30 2-0	S02 4-3	S16 2-3	M05 2-1	a28 2-0	O14 3-0	a13 3-3	M10 3-0	N11 1-2	M24 2-0	a07 2-1
3 BURNLEY	M31 1-2	O07 1-0		O21 1-0	F17 1-2	F03 3-1	D30 3-1	D02 2-1	N04 2 0	N18 1 3	D23 2 2	M03 3-0	a21 0-1	a23 1-0	S09 2-2	J13 3-1	S23 2-0	D09 0-1
4 BURY	J01 2-0	a25 2-0	M14 1-1		D23 1-1	D09 4-1	N11 2-1	O14 2-1	S16 1-4	S30 2-1	D25 2-1	J06 0-1	O28 2-0	J20 2-1	a13 0-1	N25 2-0	a07 1-0	S02 3-0
5 DERBY CO	S30 2-0	D09 0-2	O14 4-1	a28 3-0		a07 2-1	D26 4-1	D25 3-2	J06 0-0	J20 2-1	O28 2-2	S02 0-1	a04 2-0	S16 0-1	N11 2-0	M24 2-0	N25 4-1	D16 0-2
6 EVERTON	S16 1-2	M31 0-0	S30 2-0	a14 2-0	D02 3-0		a16 4-1	J20 3-1	a28 4-0	J06 3-2	O14 2-1	D16 0-2	J01 1 0	S02 1-2	D25 2-0	M10 1-0	N11 1-3	M24 0-1
7 GLOSSOP	D16 1-0	F27 4-2	S02 2-0	M17 0-0	a13 1-3	O21 1-1		a28 1-2	M31 0-2	a14 0-0	S16 3-0	N18 0-0	J06 0-2	D02 2-2	F03 1-2	O07 0-2	a24 1-1	J20 2-3
8 LIVERPOOL	N18 3-3	F03 3-1	a07 0-1	a09 2-0	O07 0-2	S23 1-2	D23 5-2		M03 5-2	M17 2-0	a21 1-0	O21 3-1	D09 1-0	N04 2-2	D30 0-0	S09 0-2	J13 2-0	N25 1-1
9 MANCHESTER C	M19 0-2	D30 1-1	M10 1-0	J13 2-2	S09 4-0	D23 1-2	N25 4-1	O28 0-1		O14 1-0	a09 2-0	S23 5-1	N11 3-1	D25 1-2	a07 1-0	D09 2-1	a21 4-0	S30 1-1
10 NEWCASTLE U	M10 3-2	J13 4-1	M24 2-0	F03 2-1	S23 2-0	S09 2-0	M14 1-0	N11 1-1	a13 0-0		a07 3-1	O07 6-0	N25 0-0	O21 0-0	a21 2-2	D23 2-4	D30 4-2	O28 0-1
11 NOTTINGHAM F	a14 1-1	O21 3-2	a28 4-0	N04 2-2	M03 4-1	F17 4-2	J13 5-0	D16 1-0	D27 2-0	D02 1-0		M17 0-3	S02 3-1	M31 4-0	S23 1-0	a17 1-3	O07 6-1	J06 0-0
12 NOTTS CO	O14 1-4	D23 5-1	O28 6-1	S09 2-2	D30 0-0	a21 2-2	M24 0-0	O05 2-1	J20 1-1	a16 0-0	N11 1-2		M10 3-0	S30 1-2	N25 1-3	a07 3-1	D09 1-2	S16 0-0
13 PRESTON N.E.	D02 0-5	a30 2-0	D16 1-1	M03 1-0	O21 0-0	O07 1-1	S09 1-0	a14 1-3	a16 0-2	M31 4-1	D30 3-0	N04 4-3		N18 0-1	J13 3-0	S23 0-1	F03 5-2	a28 2-0
14 SHEFFIELD U	O28 2-1	S09 3-0	N11 0-0	S23 4-0	J13 1-1	D30 5-0	a07 4-0	M10 1-2	O07 3-0	M26 3-1	N25 3-0	F03 1-1	M24 1-0		D09 1-0	O02 2-2	D23 1-1	O14 5-2
15 STOKE	N13 0-2	N04 2-0	D26 3-0	a16 2-0	M17 1-1	O28 1-1	S30 1-0	S02 3-2	D02 1-0	D16 2-2	J20 0-0	M31 1-0	S16 3-1	a14 1-1		M26 1-2	O21 1-0	S18 1-3
16 SUNDERLAND	S02 0-1	a16 1-0	S16 2-1	M31 1-0	M21 2-0	N04 1-0	F24 0-0	J06 1-0	a14 3-1	a28 1-2	S30 1-0	D02 5-0	J20 1-0	D16 1-1	O14 3-0		M03 3-1	J01 1-2
17 W.B.A.	J06 0-2	a02 1-0	J20 2-0	D02 0-1	M31 0-0	D26 0 0	O14 3 3	S16 2-0	D16 0-0	S02 1-1	a16 8-0	a14 0-0	S30 1-0	N06 1-2	M19 4-0	O28 1-0		M10 3-2
18 WOLVERHAMPTON W	a16 0-1	D02 4-0	a14 3-0	D30 1-0	a21 3-0	M17 2-1	S23 4-0	M31 0-1	F03 1-1	M03 1-1	S09 2-2	J13 2-2	D23 1-3	a17 1-2	O07 0-2	D26 1-0	N04 2-0	

LEAGUE TABLES

DIVISION 1

	P	W	D	L	F	A	W	D	L	F	A	Pts
Aston Villa	34	12	4	1	45	18	10	2	5	32	17	50
Sheffield U	34	11	5	1	40	11	7	7	3	23	22	48
Sunderland	34	12	2	3	27	9	7	1	9	23	26	41
Wolves	34	8	4	5	28	16	7	5	5	20	21	39
Newcastle U	34	10	5	2	34	15	3	5	9	19	28	36
Derby Co	34	11	2	4	32	15	3	6	8	13	28	36
Manchester C	34	10	3	4	33	15	3	5	9	17	29	34
Nottingham F	34	12	3	2	42	16	1	5	11	14	39	34
Stoke	34	9	5	3	24	15	4	3	10	13	30	34
Liverpool	34	9	4	4	31	19	5	1	11	18	26	33
Everton	34	11	1	5	30	15	2	6	9	17	34	33
Bury	34	12	2	3	29	14	1	4	12	11	30	32
WBA	34	8	6	3	27	11	3	2	12	16	40	30
Blackburn R	34	12	2	3	38	22	1	2	14	11	39	30
Notts Co	34	5	7	5	29	22	4	4	9	17	38	29
Preston NE	34	9	3	5	28	20	3	1	13	10	28	28
Burnley	34	10	2	5	28	17	1	3	13	6	37	27
Glossop	34	4	6	7	19	22	0	4	13	12	52	18

DIVISION 2

	P	W	D	L	F	A	W	D	L	F	A	Pts
Sheffield W	34	17	0	0	61	7	8	4	5	23	15	54
Bolton W	34	14	2	1	47	7	8	6	3	32	18	52
Small Heath	34	15	1	1	58	12	5	5	7	20	26	46
Newton Heath	34	15	1	1	44	11	5	3	9	19	16	44
Leicester F	34	11	5	1	34	8	6	4	7	19	28	43
Grimsby T	34	10	3	4	46	24	7	3	7	21	22	40
Chesterfield	34	10	4	3	35	24	6	2	9	30	36	38
W Arsenal	34	13	1	3	47	12	3	3	11	14	31	36
Lincoln C	34	11	5	1	31	9	3	3	11	15	34	36
New Brighton	34	9	4	4	44	22	4	5	8	22	36	35
Burslem PV	34	11	2	4	26	16	3	4	10	13	33	34
Walsall	34	10	5	2	35	18	2	3	12	15	37	32
Gainsboro' T	34	8	4	5	37	24	1	3	13	10	51	25
Middlesbrough	34	8	4	5	28	15	0	4	13	11	54	24
Burton S	34	8	5	4	31	24	1	1	15	12	60	24
Barnsley	34	8	5	4	36	23	0	2	15	10	56	23
Luton T	34	5	3	9	25	25	0	5	12	15	50	18
Loughboro' T	34	1	6	10	12	26	0	0	17	6	74	8

DIVISION 2

	BARNSLEY	BOLTON W	BURSLEM P.V.	BURTON S	CHESTERFIELD	GAINSBOROUGH T	GRIMSBY T	LEICESTER F	LINCOLN C	LOUGHBOROUGH T	LUTON T	MIDDLESBROUGH	NEW BRIGHTON	NEWTON HEATH	SHEFFIELD W	SMALL HEATH	WALSALL	W ARSENAL
1 BARNSLEY		D26 1-6	J20 3-0	S02 4-1	a17 0-0	F24 5-0	a21 0-1	J06 1-2	N25 0-4	M10 7-0	S16 2-1	F10 5-2	D09 1-1	N11 0-0	M24 1-0	a07 1-1	S30 2-2	a23 3-2
2 BOLTON W	a13 2-0		J02 5-0	a28 5-0	a14 3-0	a21 3-0	F17 1-2	N04 2-2	S23 4-0	D30 7-0	M17 3-0	D02 3-0	J01 2-1	S09 2-1	J13 1-0	F03 1-1	M31 2-0	O21 1-0
3 BURSLEM P.V.	S23 3-1	a23 0-2		O14 2-1	M10 2-0	N11 1-0	S09 2-3	F03 0-2	a21 2-0	N25 3-1	O07 1-0	S04 3-1	D30 1-1	a07 1-0	F12 0-3	D23 3-0	F24 1-0	J13 1-1
4 BURTON S	D30 4-0	D23 2-5	F17 2-2		M31 2-1	a14 1-1	D02 1-2	J13 2-0	O21 0-0	S09 3-1	F03 3-1	M17 5-0	F10 2-2	S23 0-0	O07 0-5	N04 0-3	a13 2-1	a21 2-0
5 CHESTERFIELD	F17 2-1	D06 3-3	N04 0-4	N25 0-4		a07 3-1	F03 3-1	O21 0-0	S09 2-2	a13 1-0	M26 2-0	J27 7-1	J20 5-2	D23 2-1	D30 1-0	J13 0 0	M17 1 0	O07 0 1
6 GAINSBOROUGH T	O21 1-0	D16 1-1	M17 4-0	D26 4-1	D02 3-5		O07 2-3	M03 3-0	J13 3-1	D23 4-2	N04 2-2	M31 5-0	a18 1-1	D30 0-1	S09 0-2	S23 1-4	a30 2-0	F17 1-1
7 GRIMSBY T	D16 8-1	O14 0-0	J06 1-1	a07 6-0	D25 0-3	F10 3-0		a28 6-1	N11 5-2	F24 3-0	S02 3-3	J20 2-0	N25 1-2	D26 0-7	a13 1-2	M24 2-0	S16 4-2	a14 1-0
8 LEICESTER F	S09 1-0	M10 0-0	S30 2-0	S16 1-0	F24 2-2	a16 5-0	D23 3-0		a07 2 0	D25 6-0	J20 2-2	O14 4-1	a21 1-2	M24 2-0	N25 0-0	a17 2-0	D27 2-1	D30 0-0
9 LINCOLN C	M31 1-1	J20 1-0	D16 1-1	F24 3-0	J06 2-0	S16 2-1	a27 1-1	D02 2-0		S30 3-2	M03 2-0	S02 3-0	N04 0-0	F10 1-0	O14 1-2	a13 0-0	D26 3-1	D25 5-0
10 LOUGHBOROUGH T	N04 0-0	S02 2-3	M31 1-2	J06 2-1	a16 0-4	a28 1-2	O21 0-0	N11 0-2	a23 0-1		a17 1-1	a14 1-1	F17 1-2	J13 0-2	S23 0-0	O07 1-2	D02 0-0	M03 2-3
11 LUTON T	J13 3-0	N11 0-2	F10 1-1	S30 5-2	D26 0-3	M10 4-0	D30 0-4	S23 0 0	a16 0 2	M24 4 0		F24 1 1	D23 1-4	N25 0-1	a07 0-1	a21 1-2	O14 4-0	S09 1-2
12 MIDDLESBROUGH	O07 3-0	a07 0-3	M03 1-0	N11 8-1	M24 0-1	N25 0-0	S23 1-0	F17 0-1	D30 1-1	D09 3-0	O21 0-0		J13 5-2	a21 2-0	D23 1-2	S09 1-3	N04 1-1	F03 1-0
13 NEW BRIGHTON	a25 6-2	a16 3-1	S02 2-0	M24 5-0	N06 2-3	O28 5-0	M31 2-1	D16 2-2	M10 3-0	J27 3-0	a28 5-1	S16 1-1		F24 1-4	D25 2-2	N11 2-2	J06 0-1	D02 0-2
14 NEWTON HEATH	M17 3-0	J06 1-2	D02 3-0	J20 4-0	a28 2-1	S02 2-2	M03 1-0	a13 3-2	O07 1-0	S16 4-0	M31 5-0	D16 2-1	O21 2-1		F03 1-0	F17 3-2	a14 5-0	N04 2-0
15 SHEFFIELD W	F27 5-1	S16 2-1	a14 4-0	M12 6-0	S02 5-1	J06 5-1	J01 2-1	M31 2-0	a17 1-0	J20 5-0	D02 6-0	a28 3-0	M03 4-0	S30 2-1		O21 4-0	D16 2-0	M17 3-1
16 SMALL HEATH	D02 5-0	S30 0-0	J27 2-1	M10 2-0	S16 5-3	J20 8-1	F12 0-1	a14 4-1	O02 5-0	F10 6-0	D16 3-0	J06 5-1	M17 2-0	O14 1-0	F24 4-1		S02 3-2	M31 3-1
17 WALSALL	D25 4-2	N25 2-2	O21 0-1	a16 2-0	N11 6-3	M24 1-0	J13 1-1	S25 1-2	D23 3-1	a07 1-0	F17 7-3	M10 1-1	S09 2-1	a17 0-0	a21 1-1	D30 1-0		S23 2-0
18 W ARSENAL	a28 5-1	F24 0-1	S16 1-0	D16 1-1	F10 2-0	O14 2-1	a16 2-0	S02 0-2	M24 2-1	M12 12-0	J06 3-1	S30 3-0	a07 5-0	M10 2-1	N11 1-2	N25 3-0	J20 3-1	

Wing-half Herrod Ruddlesdin was ever-present when Sheffield Wednesday won the Second Division in 1899-1900. He later won three England caps and two League Championship medals but died in March 1910, when he was only 33.

Football League Records Season 1900-01

Top scorers: Div 1, S.Bloomer (Derby County) 23 goals; Div 2, A.Swann (Barnsley) 18 goals.
Blackpool and Stockport County were elected in place of Loughborough Town and Luton Town.

LEAGUE TABLES

DIVISION 1

	P	W	D	L	F	A	W	D	L	F	A	Pts
Liverpool	34	12	2	3	36	13	7	5	5	23	22	45
Sunderland	34	12	3	2	43	11	3	10	4	14	15	43
Notts Co	34	13	2	2	39	18	5	2	10	15	28	40
Nottingham F	34	10	4	3	32	14	6	3	8	21	22	39
Bury	34	11	3	3	31	10	5	4	8	22	27	39
Newcastle U	34	10	5	2	27	13	4	5	8	15	24	38
Everton	34	10	4	3	37	17	6	1	10	18	25	37
Sheffield W	34	13	2	2	38	16	0	8	9	14	26	36
Blackburn R	34	9	4	4	24	18	3	5	9	15	29	33
Bolton W	34	10	5	2	21	12	3	2	12	18	43	33
Manchester C	34	12	3	2	32	16	1	3	13	16	42	32
Derby Co	34	10	4	3	43	18	2	3	12	12	24	31
Wolves	34	6	10	1	21	15	3	3	11	18	40	31
Sheffield U	34	8	4	5	22	23	4	3	10	13	29	31
Aston Villa	34	8	5	4	32	18	2	5	10	13	33	30
Stoke	34	8	3	6	23	15	3	2	12	23	42	27
Preston NE	34	6	4	7	29	30	3	3	11	20	45	25
WBA	34	4	4	9	21	27	3	4	10	14	35	22

DIVISION 2

	P	W	D	L	F	A	W	D	L	F	A	Pts
Grimsby T	34	14	3	0	46	11	6	6	5	14	22	49
Small Heath	34	14	2	1	41	8	5	8	4	16	16	48
Burnley	34	15	2	0	39	6	5	2	10	14	23	44
New Brighton	34	12	5	0	34	8	5	3	9	23	30	42
Glossop	34	11	2	4	34	9	4	6	7	17	24	38
Middlesbrough	34	11	4	2	38	13	4	3	10	12	27	37
W Arsenal	34	13	3	1	30	11	2	3	12	9	24	36
Lincoln C	34	12	3	2	39	11	1	4	12	4	28	33
Burslem PV	34	8	6	3	28	14	3	5	9	17	33	33
Newton Heath	34	11	3	3	31	9	3	1	13	11	29	32
Leicester F	34	9	5	3	30	15	2	5	10	9	22	32
Blackpool	34	7	6	4	20	11	5	1	11	13	47	31
Gainsboro' T	34	8	4	5	26	18	2	6	9	19	42	30
Chesterfield	34	6	5	6	25	22	3	5	9	21	36	28
Barnsley	34	9	3	5	34	23	2	2	13	13	37	27
Walsall	34	7	7	3	29	23	0	6	11	11	33	27
Stockport Co	34	9	2	6	25	21	2	1	14	13	47	25
Burton S	34	7	3	7	16	21	1	1	15	18	45	20

Sam Raybould, Liverpool's leading scorer with 16 goals when they won the First Division in 1900-01. In 1902-03 he netted 31, a club record for 30 years.

DIVISION 1

	ASTON VILLA	BLACKBURN R	BOLTON W	BURY	DERBY CO	EVERTON	LIVERPOOL	MANCHESTER C	NEWCASTLE U	NOTTINGHAM F	NOTTS CO	PRESTON N.E.	SHEFFIELD U	SHEFFIELD W	STOKE	SUNDERLAND	W.B.A.	WOLVERHAMPTON W
1 ASTON VILLA		O29 3-3	D26 3-0	S10 1-0	S29 2-1	S15 1-2	M16 0-2	D01 7-1	N17 2-2	D15 2-1	O13 1-2	S03 4-0	M30 0-0	M09 2-1	S01 2-0	J19 2-2	J05 0-1	O27 0-0
2 BLACKBURN R	D22 2-2		N24 2-0	a13 0-2	M23 1-0	M09 2-1	D29 3-1	S22 1-0	S08 0-0	O06 1-3	a06 0-2	J01 3-1	J12 1-0	O13 2-2	F23 3-2	N10 0-1	O27 1-1	a20 2-0
3 BOLTON W	O06 1-0	M30 1-0		M16 3-2	S01 0-1	D15 1-0	F16 1-0	N03 0-0	O20 3-2	J01 4-2	a05 0-1	S22 1-1	M02 0-0	J05 1-1	D01 1-0	J02 0-0	a13 3-2	a29 1-0
4 BURY	D08 3-1	S29 0-1	N10 3-0		M09 2-1	J01 3-0	a20 0-0	S08 4-0	D22 1-0	M27 0-1	M23 1-0	N24 2-1	D29 1-1	S15 2-0	a05 3-2	O27 0-0	O13 6-1	a06 0-1
5 DERBY CO	a22 3-0	N17 4-0	D29 4-2	N03 5-2		a13 0-1	O06 2-3	M02 2-0	F16 1-1	M16 0-0	S08 2-1	J12 0-0	O20 4-0	a27 3-1	M30 4-1	D26 1-1	D01 4-0	S22 4-5
6 EVERTON	J12 2-1	N03 0-0	a20 2-3	D26 3-3	D08 2-0		S22 1-1	F16 5-2	a08 0-1	M02 4-1	D22 0-1	D29 4-1	O06 3-1	N24 1-1	M16 3-0	a06 1-0	N17 1-0	S08 5-1
7 LIVERPOOL	N10 5-1	S01 3-0	O13 2-1	D15 1-0	D25 0-0	J19 1-2		a13 3-1	M30 3-0	a27 2-0	a08 1-0	O27 3-2	D01 1-2	M23 1-1	J01 3-1	S29 1-2	S15 5-0	M09 1-0
8 MANCHESTER C	a27 4-0	J19 1-3	M09 1-1	J05 1-0	O27 2-0	O13 1-0	D08 3-4		a20 2-1	S15 1-0	N10 2-0	F23 3-1	D22 2-1	S01 2-2	S29 2-0	D25 1-1	a05 1-0	N24 3-2
9 NEWCASTLE U	a17 3-0	J05 1-0	M27 3-0	a27 0-0	O13 2-1	S29 1-0	N24 1-1	D15 2-1		S01 0-0	O27 2-0	M09 3-5	a13 3-0	a06 0-0	S15 2-1	a24 0-2	J19 1-1	N10 3-1
10 NOTTINGHAM F	a20 3-1	a08 0-1	D25 3-0	S22 1-1	N10 1-0	O27 2-1	D22 0-0	J12 4-2	D29 1-2		N24 5-0	O04 4-1	S08 2-0	S29 1-0	O13 1-1	M09 0-0	M13 2-3	D08 2-1
11 NOTTS CO	F16 2-0	D01 2-1	S15 3-1	N17 1-0	J05 2-1	a09 3-2	O20 3-0	M16 0-0	M02 3-1	D26 1-0		M27 6-1	N03 2-4	J19 2-0	a13 2-4	S01 2-2	D15 1-0	O06 4-1
12 PRESTON N.E.	O20 0-2	D08 4-1	M23 1-3	M30 3-1	S15 3-2	S01 1-2	M02 2-2	N17 0-4	N03 0-1	D01 1-1	S29 0-1		M16 3-1	a05 3-2	D25 4-2	J05 1-1	a15 2-3	F16 1-1
13 SHEFFIELD U	N24 2-2	S15 2-1	O27 0-2	S01 0-3	M11 2-1	D25 2-1	a22 0-2	D26 1-1	D08 2-0	J05 0-1	M09 4-2	N10 2-1		D15 1-0	J19 0-4	O13 2-0	S29 1-1	M25 1-1
14 SHEFFIELD W	N03 3-2	F16 1-1	S08 1-0	J12 1-2	D22 2-1	M30 3-1	N17 3-2	D29 4-1	D01 2-2	a09 4-1	S22 4-1	O06 0-1	a29 1-0		M02 4-0	a13 1-0	M16 2-1	J01 2-0
15 STOKE	D29 0-0	O20 2-0	N12 2-1	O06 1-2	N24 0-1	N10 0-2	S08 1-2	J26 2-1	J12 2-0	F16 0-3	S10 1-1	D26 5-0	S22 0-1	O27 2-1		M23 0-0	M09 2-0	D22 3-0
16 SUNDERLAND	S22 0-0	M16 2-0	a08 5-1	M02 4-1	J01 2-1	D01 2-0	F23 0-1	O20 3-0	O06 1-1	N03 0-1	D29 1-1	S08 3-1	F16 3-0	D08 1-0	N17 6-1		M30 3-0	J12 7-2
17 W.B.A.	S08 0-1	M02 1-1	D08 7-2	F16 1-2	S03 1-1	a22 1-2	a29 0-1	O06 3-2	S22 0-1	O20 1-6	N05 1-0	D22 0-1	a30 0-2	N10 1-1	N03 2-2	N24 1-0		D29 1-2
18 WOLVERHAMPTON W	a08 0-0	D15 2-2	S29 1-1	D01 1-1	J19 0-0	J05 1-1	N03 2-1	M30 1-0	M16 1-0	a13 1-0	S03 3-2	O13 2-2	N17 3-0	D26 1-1	a09 0-2	S15 2-2	S01 0-0	

DIVISION 2

	BARNSLEY	BLACKPOOL	BURNLEY	BURSLEM P.V.	BURTON S	CHESTERFIELD	GAINSBOROUGH T	GLOSSOP	GRIMSBY T	LEICESTER F	LINCOLN C	MIDDLESBROUGH	NEW BRIGHTON	NEWTON HEATH	SMALL HEATH	STOCKPORT CO	WALSALL	W ARSENAL
1 BARNSLEY		S29 0-1	a05 2-1	a06 1-3	S08 3-2	S15 4-1	D22 1-3	a08 2-2	F23 2-3	J01 1-0	O27 0-0	M14 3-1	a20 1-1	a09 6-2	O13 1-2	F09 2-0	D29 2-1	J19 3-0
2 BLACKPOOL	M20 1-1		D08 0-1	a05 2-1	S22 2-0	O13 1-1	S08 1-1	N24 0-0	M09 0-1	D22 1-0	N10 2-0	a06 3-0	D29 1-2	M23 1-2	O27 0-0	F23 3-0	J12 1-0	O06 1-1
3 BURNLEY	M30 4-0	a13 4-0		F16 1-0	S03 2-1	J26 5-1	D25 2-1	J19 5-1	S01 3-0	O20 0-0	J05 1-0	S29 2-0	N03 2-1	S15 1-0	a27 1-0	D15 3-1	M16 0-0	D01 3-0
4 BURSLEM P.V.	D01 3-2	D15 4-0	O13 1-0		M30 4-0	F23 5-1	M16 1-1	S29 0-0	N03 0-0	M02 0-0	S15 2-0	M11 0-2	N17 1-3	J19 2-0	S01 2-2	S03 0-1	D25 2-2	a13 1-0
5 BURTON S	J05 1-1	J19 1-2	M23 1-0	N24 0-2		S01 0-4	a20 1-0	M09 1-3	O13 1-2	O01 0-1	F23 0-0	N10 0-0	D25 1-0	O27 3-1	a15 0-2	S29 3-2	D22 2-1	S15 1-0
6 CHESTERFIELD	J12 1-2	F16 2-0	O06 1-3	O20 1-1	D29 2-0		D01 2-2	S08 0-1	M30 3-3	a05 1-0	a08 2-0	S22 2-3	D26 0-1	D22 2-1	M16 1-1	M02 4-2	a20 1-1	F19 0-1
7 GAINSBOROUGH T	O24 4-2	J05 1-3	M09 3-0	N10 2-1	D15 2-1	a06 2-3		F27 1-1	S29 0-1	M23 0-0	F09 1-1	O27 1-1	N24 4-1	O13 0-1	J19 1-2	S15 2-0	a13 1-0	D29 1-0
8 GLOSSOP	M16 2-1	M30 6-0	S22 0-1	F09 1-2	a05 3-0	D25 1-1	O20 3-1		D15 0-0	O06 3-1	a27 2-0	J12 2-0	F16 0-1	S01 1-0	a13 2-0	D01 6-0	M02 2-0	N17 0-1
9 GRIMSBY T	O20 1-0	J26 2-0	D29 2-1	S08 6-1	F16 5-2	N24 5-2	a05 0-0	a20 1-0		J12 4-1	D01 4-0	D22 2-0	S22 5-2	D08 2-0	N17 1-1	N10 5-1	O06 0-0	M02 1-0
10 LEICESTER F	D25 2-0	a09 3-1	N17 1-1	O27 0-0	D01 5-2	M09 1-3	a08 1-0	F21 1-2	S15 4-0		J19 0-2	O13 1-0	M16 1-1	S29 1-0	J05 1-1	S01 2-2	M30 5-0	D15 1-0
11 LINCOLN C	M02 3-0	M16 3-0	S08 2-0	J12 2-2	O20 2-1	a13 2-0	O06 6-0	D26 1-1	D25 0-1	S22 1-0		D29 1-2	a01 2-0	a05 2-0	M30 3-1	D08 4-0	F16 2-0	J26 3-3
12 MIDDLESBROUGH	D26 3-0	D01 3-1	a09 0-0	O06 4-0	M16 3-1	J19 2-0	M02 9-2	S15 2-2	a27 0-0	F16 2-1	S01 2-0		O20 2-1	J01 1-2	D15 0-1	a13 2-0	M09 2-1	M30 1-1
13 NEW BRIGHTON	D15 2-0	S01 0-0	O27 2-1	M09 1-1	a08 3-1	M23 1-1	M30 3-2	O13 1-0	J19 5-0	N10 0-0	S29 2-0	M25 3-1		F19 2-0	S15 0-0	J01 3-0	D01 5-1	a27 1-0
14 NEWTON HEATH	M13 1-0	D26 4-0	J12 0-1	S22 4-0	M02 1-1	a27 1-0	F16 0-0	D29 3-0	a13 1-0	M20 2-3	D15 4-1	S08 4-0	O06 1-0		D01 0-1	M30 3-1	O20 1-1	M16 1-0
15 SMALL HEATH	F16 3-1	M02 10-1	D22 0-1	D29 2-1	O06 2-0	N10 0-0	S22 6-0	D08 1-0	a01 2-1	S08 0-0	N24 2-0	a20 2-1	J12 4-0	a06 1-0		D26 2-0	a08 2-1	O20 2-1
16 STOCKPORT CO	O06 2-1	O20 0-1	a20 3-2	D22 1-1	a27 2-0	O27 3-1	J12 1-2	a06 1-3	M16 0-1	D29 3-1	M23 1-0	a05 0-1	S08 0-5	N24 1-0	M09 0-0		S22 4-1	F16 3-1
17 WALSALL	S01 3-0	S15 1-2	N10 2-0	M23 2-1	S24 1-5	D15 2-2	D26 3-3	O27 2-1	F09 0-0	N24 2-0	O13 3-0	a22 0-0	a06 3-3	F25 1-1	S29 2-2	J19 1-3		D24 1-0
18 W ARSENAL	S22 1-2	a08 3-1	a06 3-1	D08 3-0	J12 3-1	S29 1-0	S01 2-1	M23 2-0	O27 1-1	N03 2-1	M09 0-0	N24 1-0	D22 2-1	N10 2-1	a22 1-0	O13 2-0	S08 1-1	

Football League Records Season 1901-02

Top scorers: Div 1, J.Settle (Everton) 18 goals; Div 2, C.Simmons (West Bromwich Albion) 23 goals.
New Brighton Tower resigned and Walsall failed to gain re-election. Bristol City and Doncaster Rovers were elected in their place. Burton Swifts and Wanderers amalgamated to become Burton United.

DIVISION 1

	ASTON VILLA	BLACKBURN R	BOLTON W	BURY	DERBY CO	EVERTON	GRIMSBY T	LIVERPOOL	MANCHESTER C	NEWCASTLE U	NOTTINGHAM F	NOTTS CO	SHEFFIELD U	SHEFFIELD W	SMALL HEATH	STOKE	SUNDERLAND	WOLVERHAMPTON W
1 ASTON VILLA		S14 1-1	N09 1-0	J04 2-0	F15 3-2	S28 1-1	D14 4-1	M29 0-1	M31 2-2	D07 0-0	D28 3-0	S09 2-0	S16 1-2	O26 4-1	D26 1-0	J18 0-0	F01 0-1	N23 2-1
2 BLACKBURN R	J11 4-0		D07 2-0	O05 0-3	a19 3-1	O26 3-1	D25 2-0	a26 1-1	a12 1-4	S07 0-0	J01 1-0	M29 4-2	S21 2-1	N23 2-0	N09 3-1	F15 6-1	M01 0-1	D21 2-0
3 BOLTON W	M08 2-2	a05 4-0		N30 2-2	S14 2-1	a19 1-3	O05 4-0	F22 1-0	J01 3-3	N02 3-1	J02 3-0	S28 1-1	M28 1-0	J18 3-1	J04 4-0	D14 2-1	D28 0-0	O19 2-2
4 BURY	S07 0-0	M28 2-0	M29 2-2		N09 2-0	F15 1-0	J01 1-1	F01 0-0	N07 3-0	a26 4-0	S21 1-1	N23 3-0	J11 1-2	M15 2-0	M01 2-0	O12 4-2	O26 1-0	a12 2-1
5 DERBY CO	O19 1-0	N16 1-1	J11 1-2	M08 1-0		N30 3-1	a01 2-0	O05 1-1	S21 2-0	D26 1-0	N02 1-1	S07 2-0	a28 3-1	a26 2-2	M31 0-0	M22 1-0	a05 1-0	D25 3-1
6 EVERTON	D25 2-3	F22 0-2	D21 1-0	O19 1-1	M29 2-0		M08 0-1	J11 4-0	S02 3-1	S21 0-0	M31 1-0	a12 0-1	O05 2-1	D07 5-0	N23 1-0	N02 1-0	M15 2-0	S07 6-1
7 GRIMSBY T	a12 4-1	O12 2-1	F01 4-1	S28 2-0	S03 1-1	N09 0-2		M15 1-1	F15 3-2	M28 3-0	S14 1-0	J18 1-0	D28 0-1	J04 3-1	D07 1-0	O26 1-2	N23 3-3	M01 3-0
8 LIVERPOOL	N30 1-0	D28 1-0	O26 1-1	a19 1-0	a14 0-2	S14 2-2	a21 2-2		M01 4-0	M22 0-1	D14 0-2	F15 0-1	a05 1-0	O12 1-2	S28 3-1	J04 7-0	D26 0-1	N09 4-1
9 MANCHESTER C	F17 1-0	D14 1-1	O12 1-0	a05 2-0	J18 0-0	M17 2-0	O19 3-0	N02 2-3		M08 2-0	N30 3-1	F01 1-0	M22 4-0	M28 0-3	S14 1-4	a19 2-2	J04 0-3	F22 3-0
10 NEWCASTLE U	a05 2-1	J04 0-3	M01 4-1	D28 1-1	O12 0-1	J18 1-1	N30 5-1	N23 1-0	N09 3-0		a19 3-0	O26 8-0	D14 1-1	F15 2-1	F01 2-0	S14 5-1	S28 0-1	M15 3-1
11 NOTTINGHAM F	a01 1-1	S28 3-0	N23 4-1	J18 2-1	M01 3-1	O12 4-0	J11 0-1	a12 1-1	M29 3-1	M19 0-2		D26 1-0	S07 2-1	N09 1-1	O26 1-1	F01 2-0	F15 2-1	D07 2-0
12 NOTTS CO	N02 0-3	N30 3-0	M31 2-1	M22 2-1	J04 3-2	D14 0-2	S21 3-0	O19 2-2	O05 2-0	O03 0-2	N16 3-0		M08 4-0	S14 6-1	D28 6-1	a05 1-1	a19 2-0	M28 5-3
13 SHEFFIELD U	J01 6-0	J18 4-1	a07 2-0	S14 3-1	O26 3-0	F01 0-0	F11 2-2	D07 2-1	N23 5-0	a12 1-0	J04 2-2	N09 3-0		M01 3-0	F15 1-4	S28 1-1	O12 0-1	M29 0-0
14 SHEFFIELD W	F22 1-0	M22 0-1	S21 5-1	N16 4-1	M17 2-0	a05 1-1	S07 3-1	a01 1-1	D26 2-1	O19 0-0	M08 0-2	J11 4-0	N02 1-0		a19 1-2	N30 3-1	D14 1-1	O05 1-1
15 SMALL HEATH	O12 0-2	M08 2-0	S07 2-0	N02 1-0	a12 5-1	M22 0-1	F22 6-0	S02 0-0	J11 1-0	O05 3-1	a05 1-1	a26 0-0	O19 5-1	D21 1-1		F17 1-1	N30 2-3	S21 1-2
16 STOKE	S21 1-0	O19 2-2	a12 4-0	S02 1-2	N23 1-1	M01 1-2	a14 2-0	S07 1-0	J13 3-0	J11 0-0	O05 1-1	D07 3-0	D26 3-2	M29 1-2	M15 1-0		N09 3-0	N11 3-0
17 SUNDERLAND	O05 1-0	N02 3-2	a26 2-1	a16 3-0	J01 1-0	N16 2-4	M22 3-1	S21 1-1	S07 1-0	M31 0-0	O19 4-0	D21 2-1	S02 3-1	a12 1-2	M29 1-1	M08 2-0		J11 2-0
18 WOLVERHAMPTON W	M22 0-2	M31 3-1	F15 1-2	D14 1-0	S28 0-0	D26 2-1	N02 2-0	M08 3-1	O26 0-0	M10 3-0	S02 2-0	O12 3-1	N30 1-1	F01 1-0	J18 2-1	D28 4-1	S14 4-2	

LEAGUE TABLES

DIVISION 1

	P	W	D	L	F	A	W	D	L	F	A	Pts
Sunderland	34	12	3	2	32	14	7	3	7	18	21	44
Everton	34	11	2	4	31	11	6	5	6	22	24	41
Newcastle U	34	11	3	3	41	14	3	6	8	7	20	37
Blackburn R	34	12	2	3	36	16	3	4	10	16	32	36
Nottingham F	34	11	4	2	32	13	2	5	10	11	30	35
Derby Co	34	11	5	1	26	10	2	4	11	13	31	35
Bury	34	11	5	1	31	9	2	3	12	13	29	34
Aston Villa	34	9	5	3	27	13	4	3	10	15	27	34
Sheffield W	34	9	5	3	30	14	4	3	10	18	38	34
Sheffield U	34	10	5	2	38	13	3	2	12	15	35	33
Liverpool	34	8	3	6	28	16	2	9	6	14	22	32
Bolton W	34	10	6	1	38	17	2	2	13	13	39	32
Notts Co	34	12	2	3	44	19	2	2	13	7	38	32
Wolves	34	12	3	2	32	13	1	3	13	14	44	32
Grimsby T	34	11	3	3	33	16	2	3	12	11	44	32
Stoke	34	10	4	3	31	12	1	5	11	14	43	31
Small Heath	34	8	5	4	31	14	3	3	11	16	31	30
Manchester C	34	10	3	4	28	17	1	3	13	14	41	28

DIVISION 2

	P	W	D	L	F	A	W	D	L	F	A	Pts
WBA	34	14	2	1	52	13	11	3	3	30	16	55
Middlesbrough	34	15	1	1	58	7	8	4	5	32	17	51
Preston NE	34	12	3	2	50	11	6	3	8	21	21	42
W Arsenal	34	13	2	2	35	9	5	4	8	15	17	42
Lincoln C	34	11	6	0	26	4	3	7	7	19	31	41
Bristol C	34	13	1	3	39	12	4	5	8	13	23	40
Doncaster R	34	12	3	2	39	12	1	5	11	10	46	34
Glossop	34	7	6	4	22	15	3	6	8	14	25	32
Burnley	34	9	6	2	30	8	1	4	12	11	37	30
Burton U	34	8	6	3	32	23	3	2	12	14	31	30
Barnsley	34	9	3	5	36	33	3	3	11	15	30	30
Burslem PV	34	7	7	3	26	17	3	2	12	17	42	29
Blackpool	34	9	3	5	27	21	2	4	11	13	35	29
Leicester F	34	11	2	4	26	14	1	3	13	12	42	29
Newton Heath	34	10	2	5	27	12	1	4	12	11	41	28
Chesterfield	34	10	3	4	35	18	1	3	13	12	50	28
Stockport Co	34	8	3	6	25	20	0	4	13	11	52	23
Gainsboro' T	34	4	9	4	26	26	0	2	15	4	56	19

Sunderland's Scottish international goalkeeper Teddy Doig, who spent 14 years with the Roker club from 1890 and later starred for Liverpool.

DIVISION 2

	BARNSLEY	BLACKPOOL	BRISTOL C	BURNLEY	BURSLEM P.V.	BURTON U	CHESTERFIELD	DONCASTER R	GAINSBOROUGH T	GLOSSOP	LEICESTER F	LINCOLN C	MIDDLESBROUGH	NEWTON HEATH	PRESTON N.E.	STOCKPORT CO	W.B.A.	W ARSENAL
1 BARNSLEY		M08 2-0	D25 2-2	J01 2-2	O05 4-0	S07 3-2	F08 3-2	a05 3-0	O19 2-0	D26 1-4	J11 2-3	a12 2-2	F22 2-7	M22 3-2	S21 0-4	M31 3-1	a19 0-2	D28 2-0
2 BLACKPOOL	N09 2-1		S07 0-2	M29 2-1	J01 1-0	J11 1-0	a12 0-0	O12 3-1	D21 3-0	F01 1-1	M28 4-0	F15 3-0	a26 0-2	S28 2-4	N23 1-4	J18 1-0	O26 2-2	M01 1-3
3 BRISTOL C	M01 3-1	J04 3-0		a12 1-0	M29 4-0	a26 0-2	D07 5-2	F01 3-0	J25 4-0	S28 2-0	N09 2-1	O12 1-1	D21 1-0	J18 4-0	M15 2-0	S14 3-0	F15 1-2	O26 0-3
4 BURNLEY	S28 2-0	N30 2-0	M22 0-1		F22 4-1	O19 0-0	N02 0-0	D28 7-0	M08 6-0	a19 1-1	F01 1-0	J04 1-0	N16 2-2	M28 1-0	O12 0-3	S09 3-0	S14 0-0	J18 0-0
5 BURSLEM P.V.	F01 2-1	a05 0-1	S09 3-0	O26 1-1		M10 2-1	M08 4-2	J04 2-2	M28 1-1	D28 1-0	O12 3-0	S14 1-2	M22 1-1	a19 1-1	F15 0-0	D14 1-1	J18 2-3	S28 1-0
6 BURTON U	J04 2-1	S14 1-1	D28 2-2	F15 5-2	M01 3-0		M15 0-1	N09 1-1	M29 5-0	O26 1-1	J18 2-0	N23 0-6	a12 3-2	O12 0-0	F01 1-1	S28 3-2	D07 1-3	a19 2-0
7 CHESTERFIELD	O12 1-2	M31 3-1	a05 1-0	M01 3-0	N09 4-3	M28 3-1		S14 0-0	M22 2-0	J04 1-0	F15 3-3	J18 0-1	N30 0-0	M17 3-0	O26 2-0	a19 8-1	S28 0-3	F01 1-3
8 DONCASTER R	D07 0-1	F08 4-3	O05 3-0	a26 3-0	S07 3-3	M08 2-0	J11 4-1		S21 3-0	M31 1-2	a12 2-1	M15 1-1	M28 0-0	F22 4-0	a19 4-0	O19 2-0	N23 2-0	M29 1-0
9 GAINSBOROUGH T	F15 0-0	a19 3-0	a02 2-0	N09 1-1	M15 2-3	N30 1-4	N23 0-0	J18 4-1		S14 2-1	O26 3-3	S28 2-2	a05 1-4	J04 1-1	M01 0-1	D28 1-1	F01 1-1	O12 2-2
10 GLOSSOP	M29 1-1	O05 3-1	M04 1-2	D21 0-0	a26 0-1	F22 2-1	S07 3-1	M01 3-1	J11 0-0		D07 1-1	N09 1-1	S21 1-0	O19 0-0	a12 3-1	F08 2-1	M15 1-2	N23 0-1
11 LEICESTER F	S14 2-0	M15 1-0	M08 0-1	O05 2-1	J25 0-1	S21 4-0	O19 3-0	D26 1-0	F22 2-0	a01 1-1		a19 3-1	N02 0-2	N30 3-2	M31 1-0	N23 1-1	D28 0-3	J04 2-1
12 LINCOLN C	M28 1-1	O19 0-0	a21 1-0	S07 1-0	J11 1-1	M22 0-0	S21 4-0	D25 0-0	a16 3-0	M08 1-0	D21 2-0		O05 2-1	D26 2-0	a26 2-1	F22 5-0	M29 1-0	D07 0-0
13 MIDDLESBROUGH	O26 2-1	D28 2-1	a19 2-0	M15 3-0	N23 3-0	J01 5-0	M29 7-1	S28 6-0	D07 3-1	J18 5-0	M01 5-0	F01 0-0		S14 5-0	N09 2-1	J04 6-0	O12 1-2	F15 1-0
14 NEWTON HEATH	N23 1-0	J25 0-1	S21 1-0	F11 2-0	D21 1-0	a21 3-1	a23 2-0	O26 6-0	S07 3-0	F15 1-0	M29 2-0	M01 0-0	a07 1-2		J01 0-2	O05 3-3	N09 1-2	M15 0-1
15 PRESTON N.E.	D14 4-0	M22 1-1	N30 0-0	a07 3-1	O19 2-0	O05 1-0	F22 5-0	D21 3-0	D25 4-1	M28 2-2	S28 5-0	D28 8-0	M08 0-3	D07 5-1		M29 4-0	J04 1-2	S14 2-0
16 STOCKPORT CO	M15 2-3	S21 3-1	J11 1-1	D07 1-2	a12 4-2	a14 2-0	D21 3-0	F15 1-2	a26 2-1	O12 0-0	M24 2-0	O26 2-1	S07 1-3	F01 1-0	a05 0-2		M01 0-2	N09 0-0
17 W.B.A.	D21 3-1	F22 7-2	O19 2-2	J11 3-0	S21 3-1	a05 2-1	S09 4-0	M22 2-2	O05 7-0	S02 0-1	J06 1-0	D09 4-1	D14 2-0	M08 4-0	S07 3-1	D26 3-0		a12 2-1
18 W ARSENAL	S02 2-1	D25 0-0	F22 2-0	S21 4-0	D26 3-1	D21 0-1	O05 3-2	N30 1-0	F08 5-0	M22 4-0	S07 2-0	a05 2-0	O19 0-3	N16 2-0	J11 0-0	M08 3-0	M31 2-1	

Football League Records Season 1902-03

Top scorers: Div 1, S.Raybould (Liverpool) 31 goals; Div 2, W.Gillespie (Manchester City) 30 goals.
Newton Heath became Manchester United.

LEAGUE TABLES

DIVISION 1

	P	W	D	L	F	A	W	D	L	F	A	Pts
Sheffield W	34	12	3	2	31	7	7	1	9	23	29	42
Aston Villa	34	11	3	3	43	18	8	0	9	18	22	41
Sunderland	34	10	5	2	27	11	6	4	7	24	25	41
Sheffield U	34	11	0	6	36	22	6	5	6	22	22	39
Liverpool	34	11	3	3	48	21	6	1	10	20	28	38
Stoke	34	11	2	4	29	11	4	5	8	17	27	37
WBA	34	10	2	5	37	27	6	2	9	17	26	36
Bury	34	14	1	2	41	14	2	2	13	13	29	35
Derby Co	34	13	2	2	34	11	3	1	13	16	36	35
Nottingham F	34	10	3	4	33	22	4	4	9	16	25	35
Wolves	34	12	2	3	34	17	2	3	12	14	40	33
Everton	34	10	2	5	28	18	3	4	10	17	29	32
Middlesbrough	34	10	3	4	27	16	4	1	12	14	34	32
Newcastle U	34	12	1	4	31	11	2	3	12	10	40	32
Notts Co	34	8	5	4	25	16	4	2	11	16	33	31
Blackburn R	34	9	2	6	27	24	3	3	11	17	39	29
Grimsby T	34	6	5	6	28	22	2	4	11	15	40	25
Bolton W	34	6	2	9	18	20	2	1	14	19	53	19

DIVISION 2

	P	W	D	L	F	A	W	D	L	F	A	Pts
Manchester C	34	15	1	1	64	15	10	3	4	31	14	54
Small Heath	34	17	0	0	57	11	7	3	7	17	25	51
W Arsenal	34	14	2	1	46	9	6	6	5	20	21	48
Bristol C	34	12	3	2	43	18	5	5	7	16	20	42
Manchester U	34	9	4	4	32	15	6	4	7	21	23	38
Chesterfield	34	11	4	2	43	10	3	5	9	24	30	37
Preston NE	34	10	5	2	39	12	3	5	9	17	28	36
Barnsley	34	9	4	4	32	13	4	4	9	23	38	34
Burslem PV	34	11	5	1	36	16	2	3	12	21	46	34
Lincoln C	34	8	3	6	30	22	4	3	10	16	31	30
Glossop	34	9	1	7	26	20	2	6	9	17	38	29
Gainsboro' T	34	9	4	4	28	14	2	3	12	13	45	29
Burton U	34	9	4	4	26	20	2	3	12	13	39	29
Blackpool	34	7	5	5	32	24	2	5	10	12	35	28
Leicester F	34	5	5	7	20	23	5	3	9	21	42	28
Doncaster R	34	8	5	4	27	17	1	2	14	8	55	25
Stockport Co	34	6	4	7	26	24	1	2	14	13	50	20
Burnley	34	6	7	4	25	25	0	1	16	5	52	20

England centre-half Tommy Crawshaw played in two FA Cup winning teams and two League Championship winning sides for Sheffield Wednesday.

DIVISION 1

	ASTON VILLA	BLACKBURN R	BOLTON W	BURY	DERBY CO	EVERTON	GRIMSBY T	LIVERPOOL	MIDDLESBROUGH	NEWCASTLE U	NOTTINGHAM F	NOTTS CO	SHEFFIELD U	SHEFFIELD W	STOKE	SUNDERLAND	W.B.A.	WOLVERHAMPTON W
1 ASTON VILLA		J24 5-0	N15 4-2	S20 2-2	S06 0-0	O18 2-1	D27 2-2	D13 1-2	a27 5-0	N29 7-0	J10 3-1	a15 2-1	a18 4-2	D26 1-0	a13 2-0	O04 0-1	N01 0-3	a04 3-1
2 BLACKBURN R	S27 0-2		a04 4-2	O11 0-3	O18 2-4	N08 3-2	J17 2-0	J03 3-1	S01 0-1	a18 3-1	J31 2-2	N29 1-2	S13 2-0	N15 2-1	N01 1-1	D25 0-2	M21 1-0	J01 1-0
3 BOLTON W	M14 0-1	D06 1-2		M28 1-0	J24 2-0	N01 1-3	J02 0-1	O25 1-1	J31 2-1	O11 0-2	N22 1-1	S20 0-1	F28 1-0	S06 0-2	D20 2-3	a11 2-0	J10 0-1	F14 4-1
4 BURY	J17 0-1	a10 1-1	N29 3-0		O04 1-0	J01 4-2	S13 2-1	D27 3-1	a04 3-1	D13 1-0	S27 3-1	M26 3-1	J03 3-1	a06 4-0	D25 2-1	O18 3-1	N15 1-2	a22 4-0
5 DERBY CO	J03 2-0	F14 1-0	S27 5-0	J31 2-0		M28 0-1	a22 2-2	N22 2-1	O11 3-2	O25 0-0	J17 0-1	S13 4-1	D06 1-0	a11 1-0	M14 2-0	N01 5-2	D27 1-0	N08 3-1
6 EVERTON	F14 0-1	a13 0-3	D27 3-1	F28 3-0	N29 2-1		O11 4-2	S27 3-1	J03 3-0	S13 0-1	O25 1-1	a18 2-0	J31 1-0	a04 1-1	N22 0-1	M14 0-3	D13 3-1	J17 2-1
7 GRIMSBY T	a25 0-2	S20 4-1	N08 1-1	J10 2-1	D20 4-1	D25 0-0		a04 3-1	N15 2-2	M21 1-0	S09 0-1	N01 1-1	D13 1-2	O18 0-1	O04 2-2	J24 2-4	a10 4-0	N29 1-2
8 LIVERPOOL	a11 2-1	S06 5-2	D25 5-1	a25 2-0	M23 3-1	a10 0-0	D06 9-2		N01 5-0	M07 3-0	D20 2-1	O18 0-2	M28 2-4	O04 4-2	S20 1-1	M30 1-1	J01 0-2	N15 4-1
9 MIDDLESBROUGH	N22 1-2	a11 4-0	O04 4-3	D06 1-1	a13 3-1	S06 1-0	M14 2-0	F28 0-2		F14 1-0	M28 2-0	J24 2-1	N08 0-2	J10 2-1	a25 1-1	D20 0-1	S20 1-1	O25 2-0
10 NEWCASTLE U	M28 2-0	D20 1-0	a13 2-0	a11 1-0	a10 2-1	a01 3-0	N22 1-0	N08 1-2	O18 0-1		D06 0-2	O04 6-1	M14 0-0	S20 3-0	S06 5-0	a25 1-0	J24 1-0	F28 2-4
11 NOTTINGHAM F	S13 2-0	O04 2-0	M21 1-2	J24 3-0	S20 2-3	O02 2-2	J03 2-1	a18 1-0	N29 1-0	a04 3-2		N15 0-0	D27 2-2	N01 1-4	O18 1-3	a13 5-2	M07 3-1	D13 2-0
12 NOTTS CO	N08 2-1	M28 4-0	J17 1-3	N22 1-0	J10 2-1	D20 2-0	F28 0-1	F14 1-2	S27 2-0	J31 2-2	D26 1-1		O25 1-1	O03 0-3	a11 3-0	D06 0-0	S06 3-1	O11 0-0
13 SHEFFIELD U	D20 2-4	J10 2-1	D26 7-1	S06 1-0	M30 3-2	O04 0-2	a11 3-0	N29 2-0	M07 1-3	N15 2-1	O13 2-0	a10 3-0		S01 2-3	J24 1-3	S20 1-0	O18 1-2	M21 3-0
14 SHEFFIELD W	J01 4-0	M14 0-0	J03 3-0	N08 2-0	D13 0-1	D06 4-1	F14 1-1	J31 3-1	S13 2-0	J17 3-0	F28 1-0	D27 2-0	O11 0-1		M28 1-0	N22 1-0	a18 3-1	S27 1-1
15 STOKE	O11 1-0	D26 0-2	a18 2-0	O25 1-0	N15 2-0	M21 2-0	J31 1-1	J17 1-0	D27 0-2	J03 5-0	F14 3-2	S15 0-2	S27 0-1	N29 4-0		N08 1-1	a04 3-0	S13 3-0
16 SUNDERLAND	J31 1-0	O25 2-2	D13 3-1	F14 3-1	J01 2-0	N15 2-1	S27 5-1	S13 2-1	a18 2-1	D27 0-0	S01 0-1	a04 2-1	J17 0-0	M21 0-1	a10 0-0		N29 0-0	J03 3-0
17 W.B.A.	F28 1-2	N22 5-3	S13 2-1	a20 1-3	a25 3-0	S01 2-1	O25 1-0	O11 1-2	J17 1-0	S27 6-1	N08 2-0	J03 3-2	F14 3-3	D20 2-3	D06 2-1	M28 0-3		J31 2-2
18 WOLVERHAMPTON W	D06 2-1	D27 2-0	O18 3-1	D20 3-2	S01 3-0	S20 1-1	M28 3-0	a27 0-2	D26 2-0	N01 3-0	a11 2-1	a13 2-0	N22 1-3	J24 2-1	J10 1-0	S06 3-3	O04 1-2	

DIVISION 2

	BARNSLEY	BLACKPOOL	BRISTOL C	BURNLEY	BURSLEM P.V.	BURTON U	CHESTERFIELD	DONCASTER R	GAINSBOROUGH T	GLOSSOP	LEICESTER F	LINCOLN C	MANCHESTER C	MANCHESTER U	PRESTON N.E.	SMALL HEATH	STOCKPORT CO	W ARSENAL
1 BARNSLEY		J10 6-0	a11 2-0	J01 3-0	a10 1-0	D06 4-0	M21 2-2	J24 2-0	M28 2-3	D20 0-1	O18 1-2	O04 0-0	a14 0-3	a25 0-0	M07 3-0	a13 3-0	S06 2-1	S20 1-1
2 BLACKPOOL	S13 3-3		J01 0-1	F07 2-0	J03 2-5	S27 3-3	a13 2-1	D25 4-0	J17 4-0	O11 2-2	a04 2-0	M21 2-3	D13 0-3	F14 2-0	D27 2-2	N29 0-1	O25 2-0	M07 0-0
3 BRISTOL C	D25 3-3	J31 0-1		M21 3-0	a04 3-0	D27 3-1	S06 2-1	O18 4-2	a18 1-0	J10 1-1	M07 6-1	M30 0-2	N15 3-2	S20 3-1	N29 2-1	N01 1-1	J24 7-1	O04 1-0
4 BURNLEY	F28 1-2	D20 1-1	N22 0-0		O25 3-3	M14 4-1	S08 1-1	S06 1-1	N08 3-2	M28 2-1	J24 1-3	J10 1-0	O04 1-1	D06 0-2	F14 1-1	S20 2-1	a11 3-2	N15 0-3
5 BURSLEM P.V.	a20 2-0	S06 1-1	D06 2-0	M30 3-1		M28 4-2	M07 2-1	S20 3-0	N22 3-1	a11 1-0	F07 2-0	J24 5-1	O18 1-4	D20 1-1	S08 0-0	O04 2-2	N10 3-1	J10 1-1
6 BURTON U	a04 1-1	J24 2-0	a25 0-3	S01 0-0	a13 0-0		D20 1-0	F07 1-0	a11 3-0	S06 2-1	D26 2-3	O18 2-2	M07 0-5	J10 3-1	M21 2-1	F21 0-1	S20 5-1	D25 2-1
7 CHESTERFIELD	N22 3-0	F28 1-1	J03 3-0	O11 2-0	N08 3-0	a18 1-0		M28 1-1	D06 0-1	J17 10-0	S13 5-0	a11 1-0	S27 0-1	J31 2-0	O25 4-2	D27 1-1	F14 4-1	M14 2-2
8 DONCASTER R	S27 2-0	M14 3-0	F14 0-0	a10 2-1	J17 3-2	O11 1-1	N29 3-4		J31 0-0	O25 4-1	a18 0-0	a04 2-1	D27 1-2	F28 2-2	S13 1-2	D13 1-0	N08 2-0	N22 0-1
9 GAINSBOROUGH T	M25 1-2	S20 0-0	D20 2-1	M07 3-0	M21 1-1	a10 3-1	a04 3-2	O04 3-0		a25 1-1	F21 5-1	a15 4-0	O22 0-3	S06 0-1	M14 1-0	O18 1-0	F07 0-0	J24 0-1
10 GLOSSOP	a18 2-2	F17 1-0	S13 0-2	D02 2-0	D09 2-1	J03 3-0	S20 0-3	F24 3-0	D27 4-2		a10 1-2	F28 2-0	M21 0-1	J24 1-3	a04 1-0	M07 0-1	D25 3-1	O18 1-2
11 LEICESTER F	F14 1-2	D06 2-1	N08 2-2	S27 2-1	O11 2-0	F28 0-1	J10 0-2	D20 0-1	D25 4-1	M14 3-2		a14 0-0	J17 1-1	N22 1-1	J31 1-1	S06 1-3	M26 0-2	a11 0-2
12 LINCOLN C	J21 1-3	N22 0-2	O25 1-1	S13 4-1	S27 4-1	F14 4-0	D25 0-0	D06 4-2	O11 1-0	D26 1-0	D27 1-2		J03 1-0	N08 1-3	J17 2-3	a10 0-1	S15 3-1	M28 2-2
13 MANCHESTER C	N24 3-2	a11 2-0	M14 2-2	J31 6-0	F14 7-1	N08 2-0	J24 4-2	J01 4-1	F28 9-0	N22 5-2	S20 3-1	S06 3-1		a10 0-2	O11 1-0	F23 4-0	D06 5-0	D20 4-1
14 MANCHESTER U	D27 2-1	D26 2-2	J17 1-2	a04 4-0	a18 2-1	S13 1-0	O04 2-1	a13 4-0	J03 3-1	S27 1-1	M21 5-1	M07 1-2	D25 1-1		M30 0-1	N15 0-1	M23 0-0	M09 3-0
15 PRESTON N.E.	N08 3-0	a10 3-1	M28 1-0	O18 5-0	F28 5-1	N22 1-1	a20 1-1	J10 5-0	a13 0-0	D06 0-0	O04 2-0	S20 0-1	D26 0-2	a11 3-1		J24 2-1	D20 6-1	S06 2-2
16 SMALL HEATH	O11 2-1	M28 5-1	F28 2-0	J17 3-0	J31 5-1	O25 2-0	D26 2-1	a11 12-0	F14 1-0	N08 3-1	J03 4-3	D20 3-1	S13 4-0	a20 2-1	S27 3-1		N22 2-0	D06 2-0
17 STOCKPORT CO	J03 4-1	F21 4-0	S27 0-1	a13 3-0	D13 0-4	J17 0-2	O18 2-2	M07 1-0	J10 1-1	J31 2-3	N29 2-2	M14 3-1	a04 0-2	O11 2-1	a18 1-1	M21 1-2		J01 0-1
18 W ARSENAL	J17 4-0	N08 2-1	O11 2-1	D27 5-1	S13 3-0	J31 3-0	a10 3-0	M21 3-0	S27 6-1	F14 0-0	a13 0-0	N29 2-1	N01 1-0	O25 0-1	J03 3-1	a04 6-1	F28 3-1	

Football League Records Season 1903-04

Top scorers: Div 1, S.Bloomer (Derby County) 20 goals; Div 2, P.Smith (Preston North End) 26 goals.
Bradford City were elected in place of Doncaster Rovers.

DIVISION 1

	ASTON VILLA	BLACKBURN R	BURY	DERBY CO	EVERTON	LIVERPOOL	MANCHESTER C	MIDDLESBROUGH	NEWCASTLE U	NOTTINGHAM F	NOTTS CO	SHEFFIELD U	SHEFFIELD W	SMALL HEATH	STOKE	SUNDERLAND	W.B.A.	WOLVERHAMPTON W
1 ASTON VILLA		D12 2-3	a02 0-2	O10 3-0	S26 3-1	N28 2-1	J13 0-1	M19 2-1	N07 3-1	a16 3-1	O24 4-0	F27 6-1	D26 2-1	J16 1-1	J30 3-1	J02 2-0	S12 3-1	N14 2-0
2 BLACKBURN R	a09 0-3		S05 2-2	N07 2-1	O24 0-2	a23 2-3	M12 2-5	D19 1-1	D05 4-0	J01 3-1	N21 3-0	M26 3-0	S26 0-0	F13 1-1	D25 2-0	J30 1-3	O10 2-0	J09 1-1
3 BURY	D05 2-2	J02 3-0		F27 2-2	F13 0-0	D19 2-2	N07 1-3	a09 1-1	M26 0-3	S12 2-2	J01 3-0	N21 0-1	J16 1-0	O10 1-0	O24 2-2	S26 3-1	J30 2-1	a23 0-0
4 DERBY CO	D28 2-2	a11 3-0	O31 2-2		a16 0-1	D25 2-0	J09 2-3	O17 2-2	O03 1-3	N14 2-6	S19 0-1	J23 3-5	a30 0-2	S01 4-1	D26 5-0	N28 7-2	a02 4-2	S05 2-1
5 EVERTON	J23 1-0	S01 3-1	O17 2-1	D19 0-1		a01 5-2	a25 1-0	O03 2-0	S19 4-1	O31 0-2	S05 3-1	J09 2-0	a04 2-0	N28 5-1	a09 0-1	N14 0-1	a18 4-0	a02 2-0
6 LIVERPOOL	M26 1-1	D26 1-2	a16 3-0	O24 3-1	O10 2-2		F27 2-2	F22 1-0	N21 1-0	J02 0-0	N07 2-1	M12 3-0	S12 1-3	J30 0-2	F13 0-0	J16 2-1	S26 1-3	D12 1-2
7 MANCHESTER C	O17 1-0	N14 1-0	a11 3-0	S12 2-1	D26 1-3	O31 3-2		J01 1-1	a01 1-3	a13 0-0	J23 3-0	O03 0-1	N28 1-1	a16 4-0	J02 2-2	a02 2-1	D12 0-3	S19 4-1
8 MIDDLESBROUGH	N21 2-1	a16 0-2	D12 1-0	F13 0-0	J30 3-0	a02 1-0	O24 6-0		M12 1-3	D26 1-1	F27 1-0	N07 4-1	J02 0-1	S26 3-1	O10 2-0	S12 2-3	J16 2-2	N28 1-2
9 NEWCASTLE U	S02 1-1	a02 2-1	N28 3-2	J30 0-0	J16 1-0	M19 1-1	O10 1-0	N14 2-1		D12 3-1	F13 4-1	O24 0-1	a16 4-0	S12 3-1	S26 1-0	D26 1-3	J02 1-0	O31 3-0
10 NOTTINGHAM F	D19 3-7	S19 0-1	J09 2-2	M12 5-1	F27 0-4	S05 2-1	N21 0-3	a23 1-1	a09 1-0		D25 0-1	D05 1-1	J30 0-1	O24 0-1	N25 4-2	O10 3-0	M30 2-0	J23 5-0
11 NOTTS CO	a01 0-0	M19 4-2	N14 0-0	J16 2-2	J02 0-3	O01 4-2	S26 0-3	O31 3-2	O17 3-2	N28 1-3		a04 2-1	a02 1-0	D26 2-0	S12 1-0	D12 2-1	F20 2-3	O03 0-2
12 SHEFFIELD U	O31 1-2	N28 2-2	M19 0-0	S26 3-2	S12 2-1	N14 2-1	D28 5-3	M28 3-0	D25 2-2	a02 2-0	O10 3-1		D12 1-1	J02 1-1	J16 1-1	a16 1-2	D26 4-0	O17 7-2
13 SHEFFIELD W	a23 4-2	J23 3-1	S19 1-1	N21 1-0	N07 1-0	J09 2-1	M26 1-0	S05 4-1	D19 1-1	O03 2-1	F22 2-0	a09 3-0		F27 3-2	M12 1-0	F13 0-0	O24 1-0	J01 4-0
14 SMALL HEATH	S19 2-2	O17 2-1	a04 1-0	a09 1-0	M26 1-1	O03 1-2	D19 0-3	J23 2-2	J09 3-0	S07 3-3	a23 2-0	S05 1-3	O31 0-0		D05 1-0	M05 2-1	N14 0-1	M19 3-0
15 STOKE	O03 2-0	O31 6-2	S01 4-1	a23 1-1	D12 2-3	O17 5-2	S05 1-2	D28 0-0	J23 2-3	M05 2-3	J09 0-2	S19 3-4	N14 3-1	a02 1-0		M19 3-1	N28 5-0	D19 5-1
16 SUNDERLAND	S05 6-1	O03 2-0	J23 6-0	M26 0-3	M12 2-0	S19 2-1	D05 1-1	J09 3-1	J01 1-1	a04 3-1	S01 4-1	D19 2-1	O17 0-1	N07 3-1	N21 3-0		F27 1-1	a01 2-1
17 W.B.A.	J09 1-3	D28 2-1	O03 3-2	D14 0-0	N21 0-0	J23 2-2	a09 2-1	S19 0-0	S05 1-2	O17 1-1	D19 0-0	a23 2-2	S02 0-1	M12 0-1	M26 3-0	O31 1-1		M05 1-2
18 WOLVERHAMPTON W	M12 3-2	S12 1-0	D26 0-0	J02 2-2	D05 2-2	D28 4-2	M21 1-6	M26 2-2	F27 3-2	S26 3-2	J30 1-1	F13 1-0	O10 2-1	N21 1-0	a04 0-0	O24 2-1	N07 1-0	

LEAGUE TABLES

DIVISION 1

	P	W	D	L	F	A	W	D	L	F	A	Pts
Sheffield W	34	14	3	0	34	10	6	4	7	14	18	47
Manchester C	34	10	4	3	35	19	9	2	6	36	26	44
Everton	34	13	0	4	36	12	6	5	6	23	20	43
Newcastle U	34	12	3	2	31	13	6	3	8	27	32	42
Aston Villa	34	13	1	3	41	16	4	6	7	29	32	41
Sunderland	34	12	3	2	41	15	5	2	10	22	34	39
Sheffield U	34	9	6	2	40	21	6	2	9	22	36	38
Wolves	34	10	6	1	29	23	4	2	11	15	43	36
Nottingham F	34	7	3	7	29	26	4	6	7	28	31	31
Middlesbrough	34	9	3	5	30	17	0	9	8	16	30	30
Small Heath	34	8	5	4	25	19	3	3	11	14	33	30
Bury	34	6	8	3	25	20	1	7	9	15	33	29
Notts Co	34	9	3	5	27	26	3	2	12	10	35	29
Derby Co	34	7	3	7	41	33	2	7	8	17	27	28
Blackburn R	34	7	5	5	29	23	4	1	12	19	37	28
Stoke	34	9	2	6	45	26	1	5	11	9	31	27
Liverpool	34	7	5	5	24	20	2	3	12	25	42	26
WBA	34	4	8	5	19	19	3	2	12	17	41	24

DIVISION 2

	P	W	D	L	F	A	W	D	L	F	A	Pts
Preston NE	34	13	4	0	38	10	7	6	4	24	14	50
W Arsenal	34	15	2	0	67	5	6	5	6	24	17	49
Manchester U	34	14	2	1	42	14	6	6	5	23	19	48
Bristol C	34	14	2	1	53	12	4	4	9	20	29	42
Burnley	34	12	2	3	31	20	3	7	7	19	35	39
Grimsby T	34	12	5	0	39	12	2	3	12	11	37	36
Bolton W	34	10	3	4	38	11	2	7	8	21	30	34
Barnsley	34	10	5	2	25	12	1	5	11	13	45	32
Gainsboro' T	34	10	2	5	34	17	4	1	12	19	43	31
Bradford C	34	8	5	4	30	25	4	2	11	15	34	31
Chesterfield	34	8	5	4	22	12	3	3	11	15	33	30
Lincoln C	34	9	4	4	25	18	2	4	11	16	40	30
Burslem PV	34	10	3	4	44	20	0	6	11	10	32	29
Burton U	34	8	6	3	33	16	3	1	13	12	45	29
Blackpool	34	8	2	7	25	27	3	3	11	16	40	27
Stockport Co	34	7	7	3	28	23	1	4	12	12	49	27
Glossop	34	7	4	6	42	25	3	2	12	15	39	26
Leicester F	34	5	8	4	26	21	1	2	14	16	61	22

DIVISION 2

	BARNSLEY	BLACKPOOL	BOLTON W	BRADFORD C	BRISTOL C	BURNLEY	BURSLEM P.V.	BURTON U	CHESTERFIELD	GAINSBOROUGH T	GLOSSOP	GRIMSBY T	LEICESTER F	LINCOLN C	MANCHESTER U	PRESTON N.E.	STOCKPORT CO	W ARSENAL
1 BARNSLEY		J09 2-2	a04 1-0	F20 1-2	O03 2-0	a09 1-1	M05 1-0	J23 2-1	M26 0-0	S19 2-0	O17 4-0	a23 3-1	S05 1-1	M12 2-1	a05 0-2	D19 1-0	N21 0-0	O31 2-1
2 BLACKPOOL	S12 0-2		O10 1-4	D26 0-1	a02 0-1	F13 0-5	a01 1-0	F20 4-1	J30 0-0	M19 2-1	D25 3-2	F27 3-0	N07 1-2	J16 2-1	M09 2-1	O24 0-3	S26 4-1	J02 2-2
3 BOLTON W	D25 5-1	J01 3-0		a11 1-0	O31 1-1	J09 1-1	J02 5-0	S01 3-0	D26 4-0	O17 5-0	N14 0-1	J23 4-0	O03 3-1	D12 1-2	a25 0-0	S19 0-2	a16 0-1	N28 2-1
4 BRADFORD C	O24 3-1	a23 0-2	N21 3-3		S19 1-0	M26 3-0	D28 1-1	J09 3-0	M12 2-6	S05 1-3	F06 2-1	a09 1-0	D19 4-0	F27 2-1	J23 3-3	D05 1-1	D12 0-0	a19 0-3
5 BRISTOL C	J30 2-0	D05 5-0	F27 2-0	J16 1-1		N07 6-0	a23 2-1	D19 4-0	O24 3-2	a09 2-1	S12 5-0	N21 4-0	M26 4-0	O10 3-1	J02 1-1	M12 3-1	F13 6-0	S26 0-4
6 BURNLEY	a01 2-2	O17 1-4	S12 0-0	N28 3-2	M05 2-3		S19 1-0	D25 2-1	J02 2-1	F20 2-0	M19 2-4	O03 2-0	F06 2-1	a16 3-1	S07 2-0	J23 2-1	D26 2-0	a02 1-0
7 BURSLEM P.V.	N07 3-0	M12 5-0	S07 2-3	O10 5-2	D26 3-1	J16 2-2		a09 3-1	a16 3-0	M26 3-0	S26 1-1	F13 1-2	F27 6-2	N21 2-2	S12 1-0	J30 0-1	D05 2-0	O24 2-3
8 BURTON U	S26 1-1	M26 1-1	O24 2-1	S12 0-2	a16 2-3	F27 1-2	a04 0-0		F13 4-0	D05 2-1	J02 2-0	M12 1-0	N21 0-0	J30 5-2	D26 2-2	D28 0-0	O10 7-0	J16 3-1
9 CHESTERFIELD	a30 1-0	O03 2-1	a13 1-1	a04 1-1	F20 1-0	S05 0-0	D19 1-1	O17 2-1		F06 6-1	M05 0-0	S19 0-1	J23 2-0	a02 0-1	a01 0-2	J09 0-1	D28 4-1	M19 1-0
10 GAINSBOROUGH T	J16 4-2	N21 3-1	F13 3-1	J02 3-0	a01 3-1	O24 1-2	D29 3-0	a02 1-2	O10 1-0		D26 0-1	a06 4-2	M12 4-0	S26 0-0	a16 0-1	F27 2-0	J30 2-2	S12 0-2
11 GLOSSOP	F13 7-0	D19 0-1	M12 3-3	M01 2-0	J09 1-1	N21 6-2	J23 4-1	S05 0-1	N07 0-2	a23 0-2		D05 1-1	a09 5-0	O24 5-0	S19 0-5	M26 2-2	F27 5-1	O10 1-3
12 GRIMSBY T	D26 5-1	a04 4-0	S26 0-0	S01 2-0	M19 2-0	J30 0-0	O17 3-1	a01 4-0	J16 1-0	M05 3-1	a02 2-0		F20 4-3	J02 1-1	a12 3-1	O10 1-1	S12 2-1	a16 2-2
13 LEICESTER F	J02 2-0	M05 5-1	J30 2-2	a16 1-2	F25 1-0	O10 0-0	D25 1-1	M19 1-3	S26 0-0	a04 2-2	D12 4-2	O24 1-1		S12 2-2	a02 0-1	F13 1-4	J16 3-0	D26 0-0
14 LINCOLN C	D28 0-0	S19 0-0	a09 1-0	a01 1-0	M07 2-6	D19 3-1	M19 3-2	O03 1-0	D05 0-2	J23 0-1	F20 3-1	S05 2-1	J09 6-1		O17 0-0	a23 0-0	D25 3-1	M05 0-2
15 MANCHESTER U	O10 4-0	a09 3-1	N07 0-0	S26 3-1	S05 2-2	M12 3-1	J09 2-0	a23 2-0	D25 3-1	D19 4-2	J16 3-1	M26 2-0	a30 5-2	F13 2-0		N21 0-2	O24 3-1	J30 1-0
16 PRESTON N.E.	a16 1-1	a30 1-0	J16 3-1	a02 4-0	N14 3-0	S26 2-0	O03 3-1	M05 4-0	S12 2-1	D25 2-0	N28 3-0	O31 2-0	O17 4-3	D26 2-1	M19 1-1		J02 1-1	a01 0-0
17 STOCKPORT CO	M19 2-2	J23 2-1	D19 3-2	M05 2-0	O17 1-1	a23 2-2	a02 1-1	F06 1-1	a09 2-0	O03 1-4	a01 3-0	J09 1-1	S19 2-0	N28 4-0	M28 0-3	S05 1-5		J01 0-0
18 W ARSENAL	F27 3-0	S05 3-0	M26 3-0	D25 4-1	M14 2-0	F29 4-0	a25 0-0	S19 8-0	N21 6-0	J09 6-0	a04 2-1	D19 5-1	O26 8-0	N07 4-0	O03 4-0	a09 0-0	M12 5-2	

'Tim' Coleman, the former Northampton Town player who scored 23 goals for Woolwich Arsenal when they were promoted in 1903-04. Coleman later won an England cap and played for Everton, Sunderland, Fulham and Nottingham Forest. He appeared in Arsenal's FA Cup semi-final teams in 1906 and 1907.

Football League Records Season 1904-05

Top scorers: Div 1, A.Brown (Sheffield United) 22 goals; Div 2, S.Marsh (Bolton Wanderers) 27 goals.
Doncaster Rovers were elected in place of Stockport County.

LEAGUE TABLES

DIVISION 1

	P	W	D	L	F	A	W	D	L	F	A	Pts
Newcastle U	34	14	1	2	41	12	9	1	7	31	21	48
Everton	34	14	2	1	36	11	7	3	7	27	25	47
Manchester C	34	14	3	0	46	17	6	3	8	20	20	46
Aston Villa	34	11	2	4	32	15	8	2	7	31	28	42
Sunderland	34	11	3	3	37	19	5	5	7	23	25	40
Sheffield U	34	13	0	4	39	20	6	2	9	25	36	40
Small Heath	34	11	1	5	32	17	6	4	7	22	21	39
Preston NE	34	9	5	3	28	13	4	5	8	14	24	36
Sheffield W	34	10	3	4	39	22	4	2	11	22	35	33
W Arsenal	34	9	5	3	19	12	3	4	10	17	28	33
Derby Co	34	9	4	4	29	19	3	4	10	8	29	32
Stoke	34	10	3	4	26	18	3	1	13	14	40	30
Blackburn R	34	9	3	5	28	18	2	2	13	12	33	27
Wolves	34	10	2	5	30	23	1	2	14	17	50	26
Middlesbrough	34	7	3	7	21	24	2	5	10	15	32	26
Nottingham F	34	5	3	9	24	28	4	4	9	16	33	25
Bury	34	8	2	7	34	26	2	2	13	13	41	24
Notts Co	34	1	7	9	16	33	4	1	12	20	36	18

DIVISION 2

	P	W	D	L	F	A	W	D	L	F	A	Pts
Liverpool	34	14	3	0	60	12	13	1	3	33	13	58
Bolton W	34	15	0	2	53	16	12	2	3	34	16	56
Manchester U	34	16	0	1	60	10	8	5	4	21	20	53
Bristol C	34	12	3	2	40	12	7	1	9	26	33	42
Chesterfield	34	9	6	2	26	11	5	5	7	18	24	39
Gainsboro' T	34	11	4	2	32	15	3	4	10	29	43	36
Barnsley	34	11	4	2	29	13	3	1	13	9	43	33
Bradford C	34	8	5	4	31	20	4	3	10	14	29	32
Lincoln C	34	9	4	4	31	16	3	3	11	11	24	31
WBA	34	8	2	7	28	20	5	2	10	28	28	30
Burnley	34	10	1	6	31	21	2	5	10	12	31	30
Glossop	34	7	5	5	23	14	3	5	9	14	32	30
Grimsby T	34	9	3	5	22	14	2	5	10	11	32	30
Leicester F	34	8	3	6	30	25	3	4	10	10	30	29
Blackpool	34	8	5	4	26	15	1	5	11	10	33	28
Burslem PV	34	7	4	6	28	25	3	3	11	19	47	27
Burton U	34	7	2	8	20	29	1	2	14	10	55	20
Doncaster R	34	3	2	12	12	32	0	0	17	11	49	8

Newcastle United's Bill Appleyard, one of the great characters of Edwardian football, won two League Championship medals and appeared in two FA Cup Finals for the Magpies.

DIVISION 1

	ASTON VILLA	BLACKBURN R	BURY	DERBY CO	EVERTON	MANCHESTER C	MIDDLESBROUGH	NEWCASTLE U	NOTTINGHAM F	NOTTS CO	PRESTON N.E.	SHEFFIELD U	SHEFFIELD W	SMALL HEATH	STOKE	SUNDERLAND	WOLVERHAMPTON W	W ARSENAL
1 ASTON VILLA		J07 3-0	D24 2-0	O15 0-2	S12 1-0	a29 3-2	D10 0-0	N26 0-1	S17 2-0	N12 4-2	S01 1-2	M18 3-0	J21 0-2	O29 2-1	S03 3-0	O01 2-2	a27 3-0	D26 3-1
2 BLACKBURN R	S10 4-0		D31 0-2	J02 3-1	O29 1-0	N12 3-1	a15 0-2	a01 2-0	J21 0-0	M18 1-0	D10 1-1	N26 2-4	O01 0-1	M04 1-4	S17 4-0	D26 2-1	D24 3-0	O15 1-1
3 BURY	a22 2-3	S03 0-2		D26 2-0	O15 1-2	O22 2-4	a01 1-0	M18 2-4	J07 5-1	a21 2-0	N26 0-1	N12 7-1	S17 1-4	J02 1-1	D17 3-1	J21 1-0	D10 3-1	O01 1-1
4 DERBY CO	F11 0-2	O22 1-1	O08 3-2		D27 1-2	M04 0-1	S24 4-2	S10 1-1	F25 3-2	D24 1-1	J14 3-1	D31 2-3	N05 1-0	D10 3-0	N26 3-0	M11 1-0	J28 2-1	N19 0-0
5 EVERTON	O22 3-2	F25 1-0	F11 2-0	D03 0-0		D24 0-0	J28 1-0	J14 2-1	N05 5-1	D31 5-1	S24 1-0	S10 2-0	M11 5-2	a15 2-1	D10 4-1	N19 0-1	O08 2-1	a05 1-0
6 MANCHESTER C	N09 2-1	M11 2-1	F25 3-2	D17 6-0	a21 2-0		F11 3-2	J28 3-2	N19 1-1	J14 2-1	O08 6-1	S24 1-1	a15 1-1	S03 2-1	J07 1-0	D03 5-2	N14 5-1	a08 1-0
7 MIDDLESBROUGH	a08 3-1	D17 2-1	D03 2-2	J21 2-0	O01 1-0	O15 0-1		a29 0-3	M04 0-0	a24 2-5	N12 1-1	O29 0-1	S03 1-3	D24 0-1	M18 2-1	J07 1-3	M25 3-1	S17 1-0
8 NEWCASTLE U	a05 2-0	D03 1-0	N19 3-1	J07 2-0	S17 3-2	O01 2-0	N05 3-0		a08 5-1	J02 1-0	F25 1-0	O15 1-1	D17 6-2	J21 0-1	a21 4-1	a22 1-3	M11 3-0	S03 3-0
9 NOTTINGHAM F	J14 1-1	S24 5-2	S10 5-1	O29 0-1	a24 0-2	M18 2-1	D24 1-1	D10 1-3		N26 2-1	O06 0-1	a01 1-2	D26 2-1	N12 0-2	O01 0-1	O15 2-3	D31 2-2	D27 0-3
10 NOTTS CO	M11 1-2	N19 2-1	N05 0-1	F18 0-0	S03 1-2	S17 1-1	O22 0-0	O08 0-3	M25 1-2		F11 1-3	J28 1-5	D03 2-2	J07 0-0	J21 0-0	a08 2-2	F25 3-4	D17 1-5
11 PRESTON N.E.	D03 2-3	a08 0-0	M25 0-0	S17 2-0	J21 1-1	D26 0-1	M11 2-0	O29 1-0	D17 0-1	O15 3-1		a21 4-0	a22 1-0	O01 2-2	a10 2-1	S03 3-1	N19 2-2	J07 3-0
12 SHEFFIELD U	N19 0-3	M25 3-1	M11 4-0	S03 3-1	J07 1-0	J21 0-3	F25 0-1	F11 1-3	D03 4-0	O01 2-1	O22 1-0		a08 4-2	S17 2-1	D26 5-2	D17 1-0	N05 4-2	D28 4-0
13 SHEFFIELD W	S24 3-2	J28 1-2	J14 4-0	a03 1-1	N12 5-5	N26 2-1	D31 5-0	a26 1-3	O08 2-0	a01 1-0	J02 2-0	D10 1-3		M18 3-1	O15 3-0	D27 1-1	S10 4-0	O29 0-3
14 SMALL HEATH	F25 0-3	N05 2-0	O22 5-0	a08 2-0	D17 1-2	D31 3-1	O08 2-1	S24 2-1	M11 1-2	S10 1-2	J28 2-0	J14 2-0	N19 2-1		a22 0-1	M25 1-1	F11 4-1	D03 2-1
15 STOKE	D31 1-4	J14 4-0	a15 2-0	S01 1-2	a08 2-2	S10 1-0	N19 3-1	O22 1-0	J28 0-0	S24 0-2	N05 1-1	O08 2-1	F11 2-1	a29 1-0		F25 1-3	D03 2-1	M11 2-0
16 SUNDERLAND	J28 2-3	O08 2-1	S24 2-1	N12 3-0	M18 2-3	a01 0-0	S10 1-1	D24 3-1	J02 1-0	S05 5-0	D31 3-2	a24 2-1	O22 3-0	N26 1-4	O29 3-1		J14 3-0	M04 1-1
17 WOLVERHAMPTON W	D17 1-1	a22 2-0	a08 2-0	O01 2-0	D26 0-3	a24 0-3	N26 5-3	N12 1-3	S03 3-2	O29 3-1	M18 0-0	S05 4-2	J07 1-0	O15 0-1	a01 1-3	S17 1-0		J21 4-1
18 W ARSENAL	O08 1-0	F11 2-0	J28 2-1	M18 0-0	a22 2-1	D10 1-0	J14 1-1	D31 0-2	O22 0-3	a15 1-2	S10 0-0	D24 1-0	F25 3-0	a01 1-1	N12 2-1	N05 0-0	S24 2-0	

DIVISION 2

	BARNSLEY	BLACKPOOL	BOLTON W	BRADFORD C	BRISTOL C	BURNLEY	BURSLEM P.V.	BURTON U	CHESTERFIELD	DONCASTER R	GAINSBOROUGH T	GLOSSOP	GRIMSBY T	LEICESTER F	LINCOLN C	LIVERPOOL	MANCHESTER U	W.B.A.
1 BARNSLEY		S10 2-1	a24 2-1	N19 1-0	O22 1-0	D24 1-2	F11 3-0	J28 7-0	M11 1-0	a25 2-1	S24 2-1	N05 0-0	D31 2-2	D03 2-1	M25 2-1	O08 0-2	F25 0-0	a15 1-1
2 BLACKPOOL	J07 6-0		a21 0-2	D17 2-0	N19 2-4	J21 2-0	M11 3-0	F25 1-0	a08 1-1	F11 1-0	O22 2-2	D03 4-1	O01 1-1	S03 0-0	a22 1-0	N05 0-3	M25 0-1	S17 0-0
3 BOLTON W	J02 2-1	O08 3-0		F25 2-0	D31 3-1	S10 4-0	a15 3-1	N19 7-1	F11 4-3	O22 2-0	N05 5-1	J28 4-0	S24 4-1	M25 0-1	N12 4-1	D03 2-0	J03 2-4	D24 2-1
4 BRADFORD C	M18 1-2	a15 3-1	O29 2-1		J28 2-3	a01 4-1	S24 2-1	S10 3-1	O22 0-1	D24 4-1	D31 3-1	F11 1-1	D27 0-0	a24 0-0	M04 0-0	M07 2-4	O08 1-1	N26 3-1
5 BRISTOL C	M29 3-0	M18 2-0	S03 3-4	O01 1-0		M04 0-0	D24 4-2	D10 5-0	J21 2-1	N26 4-1	a01 1-1	S17 2-0	N12 5-0	O15 3-0	a25 2-0	a15 0-1	J07 1-1	O29 2-1
6 BURNLEY	a22 3-0	S24 0-1	J07 0-1	D03 2-1	N05 2-3		F25 5-0	F11 1-1	S05 2-0	J28 4-3	O08 1-3	N19 3-1	D26 1-0	D17 2-0	a08 2-1	O22 0-2	M11 2-0	S03 1-4
7 BURSLEM P.V.	O15 0-2	S05 2-2	D17 1-2	J21 1-1	a22 3-2	O29 3-1		a01 4-2	S17 0-0	M18 2-0	a21 3-2	J07 0-1	M04 2-0	a03 1-3	O01 0-1	N12 1-2	S03 2-2	F18 3-2
8 BURTON U	O01 1-2	D26 0-0	M18 0-1	J07 1-0	a08 2-0	O15 3-1	D03 2-3		S03 0-3	N02 1-0	a24 1-3	a22 2-2	F18 1-0	J21 0-3	S17 2-1	M25 2-1	D17 2-3	a21 0-6
9 CHESTERFIELD	N12 2-0	a29 2-0	O15 1-0	F18 0-0	S24 0-3	N26 1-1	a24 2-1	D31 6-0		a15 4-1	D24 3-2	O08 1-2	a01 0-0	M04 0-0	O29 0-0	S10 1-1	a21 2-0	M18 1-0
10 DONCASTER R	S17 2-0	O15 0-0	D10 0-4	a22 0-1	M25 0-2	O01 0-2	N19 2-2	N05 1-3	D17 0-2		F25 1-5	a08 2-1	a24 0-2	J07 3-0	S03 0-2	M11 1-4	D03 0-1	J21 0-1
11 GAINSBOROUGH T	J21 4-0	F18 1-1	a12 0-4	S03 3-2	D03 4-1	O26 3-1	M25 1-0	M11 2-0	a22 1-1	D26 2-0		D17 0-0	O15 2-1	S17 2-0	J07 2-0	N19 1-2	a08 0-0	O01 4-2
12 GLOSSOP	M04 5-0	a01 0-0	O01 1-2	O15 3-1	D27 0-1	M18 0-0	S10 0-0	D24 1-1	F04 0-1	J14 2-0	a15 3-1		a29 2-0	a21 0-0	F18 3-2	D31 0-2	S24 1-2	M07 2-1
13 GRIMSBY T	S03 0-0	J28 2-0	J21 2-2	a08 0-2	M11 4-0	S17 1-0	N05 0-3	O22 1-0	D03 3-1	O08 2-1	F11 0-0	M25 3-0		a22 2-0	D17 1-0	F25 0-1	N19 0-1	J07 1-3
14 LEICESTER F	a01 2-0	D31 3-1	D27 2-4	M11 1-2	F11 2-1	a05 2-2	O08 3-0	S24 2-0	N05 1-1	S10 3-2	F23 1-1	D26 0-2	D24 5-1		N19 0-1	J28 0-3	O22 0-3	D15 3-1
15 LINCOLN C	N26 2-0	D24 1-0	D26 0-2	N05 1-1	O08 1-3	a21 2-0	J28 3-3	D27 3-1	F25 0-0	D31 3-0	S10 4-1	O22 3-0	a15 0-0	M18 5-1		S24 0-2	F11 3-0	a01 0-2
16 LIVERPOOL	D26 2-1	M04 5-0	a01 1-1	S17 4-1	D17 3-1	a29 3-0	a08 8-1	S01 2-0	J07 6-1	a21 1-0	M18 6-1	S03 2-2	O29 5-0	O01 4-0	J21 1-1		a22 4-0	O15 3-2
17 MANCHESTER U	O29 4-0	a24 3-1	S17 1-2	J02 7-0	S10 4-1	N12 1-0	D31 6-1	a15 5-0	D26 3-0	a01 6-0	D10 3-1	J21 4-1	M18 2-1	F18 4-1	O15 2-0	D24 3-1		M04 2-0
18 W.B.A.	D17 4-1	N07 4-2	a22 0-1	M25 0-2	F25 0-0	D31 1-1	D26 0-1	O08 4-0	N19 0-2	S24 6-1	J28 4-3	M11 1-0	S10 0-2	a08 2-0	D03 2-0	F11 0-2	N05 0-2	

Football League Records Season 1905-06

Top scorers: Div 1, W.White (Bolton Wanderers) 26 goals; Div 2, W.Maxwell (Bristol City) 27 goals.
Doncaster Rovers failed to gain re-election. Chelsea, Hull City, Leeds City, Clapton Orient and Stockport County were elected to League. Small Heath became Birmingham.

DIVISION 1

	ASTON VILLA	BIRMINGHAM	BLACKBURN R	BOLTON W	BURY	DERBY CO	EVERTON	LIVERPOOL	MANCHESTER C	MIDDLESBROUGH	NEWCASTLE U	NOTTINGHAM F	NOTTS CO	PRESTON N.E.	SHEFFIELD U	SHEFFIELD W	STOKE	SUNDERLAND	WOLVERHAMPTON W	W ARSENAL
1 ASTON VILLA		J20 1-3	D30 0-1	D26 1-1	M03 3-3	a16 6-0	S23 4-0	S11 5-0	O21 2-1	N04 4-1	N18 0-3	F17 3-1	a21 2-1	M17 0-1	D09 4-1	O07 3-0	D23 3-0	S09 2-1	N25 6-0	D27 2-1
2 BIRMINGHAM	S16 2-0		a23 3-0	M26 2-5	a16 0-3	D02 3-1	a09 1-0	J27 1-0	a28 3-2	D26 7-0	J06 0-1	D16 5-0	F10 4-2	S02 1-1	S30 2-0	a14 5-1	O14 2-0	N11 3-0	M24 3-3	O28 2-1
3 BLACKBURN R	S02 1-1	N04 5-1		a02 4-1	D16 3-0	N18 3-0	M17 1-2	J06 0-0	a14 1-1	a28 1-1	J01 1-0	D02 1-1	J27 1-3	a13 1-2	S16 2-1	M31 1-0	S30 3-0	M03 0-3	F24 3-1	O14 2-0
4 BOLTON W	J02 4-1	O21 0-1	O07 1-0		D02 4-0	N04 5-0	M03 3-2	a16 3-2	M31 1-3	a14 2-1	a28 1-1	N18 6-0	F03 2-0	D16 1-2	S02 1-2	M17 1-0	S16 1-2	F17 6-2	J27 3-2	J01 6-1
5 BURY	O28 0-1	J01 1-0	a21 5-0	a07 2-1		D30 0-2	D25 3-2	a02 0-0	S23 2-4	F10 1-1	a13 1-4	J20 2-1	M24 0-0	O14 1-1	N11 2-5	S09 2-2	N25 3-0	D23 3-1	S30 0-1	D09 2-0
6 DERBY CO	S30 1-0	a07 0-0	M24 1-2	M10 0-1	S02 3-1		D09 0-0	F10 0-3	D25 1-2	J06 1-1	J27 2-1	D26 2-2	F24 1-1	S16 3-0	O14 1-0	a28 2-1	O28 1-0	N25 1-0	D16 2-0	N11 5-1
7 EVERTON	J27 4-2	N25 1-2	N11 3-2	O28 3-1	D26 1-2	a14 2-1		S30 4-2	a16 0-3	S02 4-1	S16 1-2	a28 4-1	O14 6-2	J06 1-0	F10 3-2	D16 2-0	a03 0-3	M24 3-1	a07 2-2	M21 0-1
8 LIVERPOOL	D02 3-0	S23 2-0	S09 1-3	D25 2-2	N04 3-1	O07 4-1	a13 1-1		M03 0-1	M17 6-1	a09 3-0	O21 4-1	D23 2-0	N18 1-1	a21 3-1	F17 2-1	J01 3-1	J20 2-0	D09 4-0	D30 3-0
9 MANCHESTER C	M14 1-4	D23 4-1	D09 1-1	N25 3-1	J27 5-2	a13 1-2	J01 1-0	O28 0-1		S30 4-0	D26 1-4	S09 5-0	N11 5-1	F10 0-0	M10 1-2	D30 2-1	M24 2-0	a21 5-1	S16 4-0	a07 1-2
10 MIDDLESBROUGH	M10 1-2	D25 1-0	D23 1-1	D09 4-4	O07 5-1	S09 0-1	D30 0-0	N11 1-5	a17 6-1		M03 1-0	S23 2-0	N25 4-1	M14 1-2	M24 0-1	J20 2-2	a07 5-0	a13 2-1	O14 3-1	a21 2-0
11 NEWCASTLE U	M24 3-1	S09 2-2	a30 3-0	D23 2-1	O21 3-1	S23 0-1	J20 4-2	N25 2-3	S06 2-2	O28 4-1		O07 3-2	D09 3-1	N04 1-0	a04 2-1	S13 0-3	a24 5-0	D30 1-1	N11 8-0	a16 1-1
12 NOTTINGHAM F	O14 2-2	a21 2-1	a07 1-2	M24 4-0	S16 3-2	a17 0-0	D23 4-3	M14 1-2	J06 0-1	J27 2-1	F10 2-1		D25 1-2	S30 1-0	O28 4-1	a16 3-4	N11 3-1	D09 1-2	S02 3-1	N25 3-1
13 NOTTS CO	D16 2-1	O07 0-0	S23 1-1	S09 3-3	N18 2-2	O21 1-0	F17 0-0	M21 3-0	M17 3-0	M31 1-1	a14 1-0	N04 1-1		D02 2-2	D26 2-3	M03 1-3	D30 1-1	D27 4-1	O05 5-2	J20 1-0
14 PRESTON N.E.	N11 2-0	D30 3-0	F03 2-1	a21 3-0	F17 1-0	J20 3-1	S09 1-1	M24 1-2	O07 2-0	O21 2-1	a26 0-0	S04 3-1	a07 4-1		N25 1-1	S23 0-1	D09 2-0	D25 1-1	O28 3-2	D23 2-2
15 SHEFFIELD U	a14 1-1	D28 3-0	J20 0-2	D30 5-2	M17 1-1	F17 1-0	O07 3-2	D16 1-2	N04 1-3	N18 1-0	D02 2-0	M03 1-4	J01 1-0	M31 0-0		O21 0-2	D25 1-1	S23 4-1	M19 4-1	S09 3-1
16 SHEFFIELD W	F10 2-2	D09 4-2	N25 0-1	N11 1-2	J06 1-1	D23 1-0	a23 3-1	O14 3-2	S02 1-0	S16 3-0	S30 1-1	D27 1-0	O28 3-1	J27 1-1	a18 1-0		a09 2-0	a07 3-3	D26 5-1	M24 4-2
17 STOKE	N13 0-1	F17 2-2	S04 3-0	J20 1-2	M26 4-2	M03 2-2	O21 2-2	D26 2-1	N18 0-0	D02 1-1	D16 1-0	M17 4-0	S02 3-0	a14 3-0	a16 2-1	N04 4-0		O07 1-0	J06 4-0	S23 2-1
18 SUNDERLAND	F28 2-0	M17 3-1	O28 3-0	O14 3-3	a28 0-3	M31 2-0	N18 2-1	S16 1-2	D16 2-0	J01 2-1	S02 3-2	a14 0-1	S30 1-3	a16 2-0	J27 2-0	D02 2-0	F10 1-0		M10 7-2	a25 2-2
19 WOLVERHAMPTON W	M31 4-1	N18 0-0	O21 2-1	S23 2-0	S11 2-2	a21 7-0	D02 2-5	a14 0-2	J20 2-3	F17 0-0	M17 0-2	D30 2-1	a16 6-1	M03 2-3	D23 1-1	S04 0-0	S09 1-2	N04 5-2		O07 0-2
20 W ARSENAL	a13 2-1	M03 5-0	F17 3-2	S30 0-0	a14 4-0	M17 1-0	N04 1-2	S02 3-1	D02 2-0	D16 2-2	D25 4-3	a02 3-1	S16 1-1	S18 2-2	J06 5-1	N18 0-2	J27 1-2	O21 2-0	F10 2-1	

DIVISION 2

	BARNSLEY	BLACKPOOL	BRADFORD C	BRISTOL C	BURNLEY	BURSLEM P.V.	BURTON U	CHELSEA	CHESTERFIELD	CLAPTON O	GAINSBOROUGH T	GLOSSOP	GRIMSBY T	HULL C	LEEDS C	LEICESTER F	LINCOLN C	MANCHESTER U	STOCKPORT CO	W.B.A.
1 BARNSLEY		a21 1-1	D23 0-1	M24 2-2	O14 1-2	S23 4-0	O28 3-0	M10 1-2	J20 8-1	F10 4-1	N11 2-1	a07 1-1	S30 2-0	a17 2-0	F24 3-0	a16 0-0	S09 4-2	N25 0-3	J01 4-0	a13 3-0
2 BLACKPOOL	D16 0-0		M03 2-2	J27 1-3	a13 0-1	a14 2-1	S02 2-0	S09 0-1	D02 2-1	a28 3-0	S16 2-2	F10 1-0	M07 2-0	M14 1-2	J01 0-3	M17 0-1	M31 2-0	S30 0-1	O14 2-0	N04 0-3
3 BRADFORD C	a28 0-0	O28 2-1		S30 1-2	F27 0-1	D16 2-0	J06 1-0	S16 1-1	a14 1-0	D26 3-0	J27 1-2	O14 2-0	a07 0-1	M31 0-2	S02 1-0	N18 3-3	D02 2-2	F10 1-5	a17 0-1	M17 0-1
4 BRISTOL C	N18 3-0	S23 2-1	S20 1-0		D02 2-0	M17 4-0	D16 4-0	a28 2-1	N04 3-1	M31 1-0	a13 2-0	S09 2-1	a17 2-0	O21 2-1	a14 2-0	F17 1-2	M03 1-0	D30 1-1	J20 7-0	O07 1-0
5 BURNLEY	F17 2-1	D25 4-1	S04 0-0	a07 2-2		O07 1-3	N11 1-0	M24 2-0	S11 1-1	O21 3-0	N25 1-0	a21 1-0	O28 0-0	J20 1-3	M10 4-3	O02 0-2	S23 2-1	D09 1-3	D23 0-1	D30 0-2
6 BURSLEM P.V.	J27 1-2	S11 1-2	a21 2-1	N11 0-1	F10 2-2		F24 4-1	O30 3-2	S09 4-3	S30 2-1	M10 1-0	N25 3-3	S16 2-2	D25 1-3	O14 2-0	a13 2-0	D30 3-1	M24 1-0	a07 0-0	D23 0-1
7 BURTON U	M03 4-1	D30 1-1	S09 0-1	a21 0-1	M17 1-3	O21 1-0		a07 2-4	F17 4-0	N04 1-0	a06 3-1	O02 1-0	N25 1-0	D26 0-3	N13 1-1	S23 0-0	O07 2-0	D23 0-2	D25 2-0	J20 2-2
8 CHELSEA	N04 6-0	J06 6-0	J20 4-2	D23 0-0	N18 1-0	M03 7-0	D02 3-0		O21 0-1	M17 6-1	a21 1-3	a16 0-0	D09 2-0	S11 5-1	M31 4-0	F05 3-3	F17 4-2	a13 1-1	D30 4-2	S23 1-0
9 CHESTERFIELD	S16 2-0	a07 2-0	D25 1-1	M10 1-2	S30 3-0	J06 2-0	O14 1-0	F24 0-2		J27 1-1	O28 0-0	M24 3-1	S02 1-4	a13 1-2	F10 0-2	D23 3-3	a16 1-2	N11 1-0	N25 3-1	a21 0-3
10 CLAPTON O	O07 0-0	D23 0-0	a13 4-2	N25 0-2	F24 3-0	F03 1-3	M10 0-1	N11 0-3	S23 3-3		M24 1-0	S11 2-0	O14 1-2	S09 0-1	M29 0-0	D30 0-2	J20 3-0	a07 0-1	a21 1-0	a16 0-2
11 GAINSBOROUGH T	M17 1-0	J20 0-1	S23 2-3	D26 1-3	M31 0-1	N04 4-0	a14 5-2	D16 0-2	M03 4-0	D04 2-1		D30 2-0	a28 1-0	F17 3-1	D02 4-1	O07 0-1	O21 2-3	O25 2-2	S09 0-0	a18 2-1
12 GLOSSOP	D02 2-2	O07 4-1	F17 2-3	J06 1-5	D16 1-1	M31 3-2	J01 2-0	D26 2-4	N18 2-0	a14 5-0	S02 1-0		J27 2-0	N04 3-1	a28 1-2	M03 0-0	M17 2-2	S16 1-2	F03 1-0	O21 1-3
13 GRIMSBY T	a05 2-1	O21 1-1	N04 1-0	D27 1-1	M03 2-0	J20 5-0	M31 1-0	a14 1-1	D30 2-0	F17 4-1	D23 2-0	S23 1-1		a21 1-0	M17 1-1	D02 1-1	a13 2-2	S09 0-1	O07 2-0	F03 3-2
14 HULL C	S02 4-1	M24 2-2	N25 5-2	F24 0-3	S16 1-1	a16 3-2	S30 1-1	F10 4-3	O11 3-0	J06 3-1	O14 2-0	M10 1-2	D16 0-1		J27 0-0	a14 0-0	a28 2-1	O28 0-1	N11 3-0	a07 4-0
15 LEEDS C	O21 3-2	a16 3-0	D30 0-2	D09 1-1	F03 1-1	F17 3-1	M24 2-1	N25 0-0	F27 3-0	M03 6-1	a07 1-0	D23 1-0	N11 3-0	S23 3-1		J20 4-1	S11 2-2	a21 1-3	a13 1-1	S09 0-2
16 LEICESTER F	D25 1-0	N11 2-0	M24 2-4	O14 1-2	J06 2-0	D26 2-1	J27 1-1	S30 0-1	D09 1-1	S02 2-1	F10 4-0	O28 2-1	F24 2-0	D07 1-2	S16 0-1		D16 3-1	M29 2-5	M10 2-0	N25 0-0
17 LINCOLN C	J06 4-1	N25 1-1	M10 5-0	O28 0-3	J27 5-0	S02 3-1	F10 5-1	O14 1-4	D26 0-1	S16 2-3	F24 3-0	N11 4-1	D25 3-1	D23 1-4	S30 1-2	a21 3-1		a25 2-3	M24 2-0	D09 1-2
18 MANCHESTER U	M31 5-1	S04 2-1	O07 0-0	S02 5-1	a14 1-0	N18 3-0	a28 6-0	D25 0-0	M17 4-1	D02 4-0	a16 2-0	J20 5-2	J06 5-0	M03 5-0	J15 0-3	O21 3-2	N04 2-1		S23 3-1	F17 0-0
19 STOCKPORT CO	a14 0-0	F17 2-1	O21 1-0	S16 2-3	a28 3-1	D02 3-0	a16 2-0	S02 1-0	M31 0-0	D16 3-3	J06 2-0	S30 5-0	F10 2-2	M17 2-1	D26 2-1	N04 1-1	N18 3-0	J27 0-1		M03 2-2
20 W.B.A.	D26 5-3	M10 5-0	N11 6-1	F10 1-3	S02 1-2	a28 4-1	S16 3-0	J27 1-1	D16 3-0	D25 1-1	S30 4-0	F24 6-0	M24 2-0	D02 1-1	J06 2-1	M31 3-0	a14 1-1	O14 1-0	O28 3-1	

LEAGUE TABLES

DIVISION 1

	P	W	D	L	F	A	W	D	L	F	A	Pts
Liverpool	38	14	3	2	49	15	9	2	8	30	31	51
Preston NE	38	12	5	2	36	15	5	8	6	18	24	47
Sheffield W	38	12	5	2	40	20	6	3	10	23	32	44
Newcastle U	38	12	4	3	49	23	6	3	10	25	25	43
Manchester C	38	11	2	6	46	23	8	3	8	27	31	43
Bolton W	38	13	1	5	51	22	4	6	9	30	45	41
Birmingham	38	14	2	3	49	20	3	5	11	16	39	41
Aston Villa	38	13	2	4	51	19	4	4	11	21	37	40
Blackburn R	38	10	5	4	34	18	6	3	10	20	34	40
Stoke	38	12	5	2	41	15	4	2	13	13	40	39
Everton	38	12	1	6	44	30	3	6	10	26	36	37
W Arsenal	38	12	4	3	43	21	3	3	13	19	43	37
Sheffield U	38	10	4	5	33	23	5	2	12	24	39	36
Sunderland	38	13	2	4	40	21	2	3	14	21	49	35
Derby Co	38	10	5	4	27	16	4	2	13	12	42	35
Notts Co	38	8	9	2	34	21	3	3	13	21	50	34
Bury	38	8	5	6	30	26	3	5	11	27	48	32
Middlesbrough	38	10	4	5	41	23	0	7	12	15	48	31
Nottingham F	38	11	2	6	40	27	2	3	14	18	52	31
Wolves	38	7	5	7	38	28	1	2	16	20	71	23

DIVISION 2

	P	W	D	L	F	A	W	D	L	F	A	Pts
Bristol C	38	17	1	1	43	8	13	5	1	40	20	66
Manchester U	38	15	3	1	55	13	13	3	3	35	15	62
Chelsea	38	13	4	2	58	16	9	5	5	32	21	53
WBA	38	13	4	2	53	16	9	4	6	26	20	52
Hull C	38	10	5	4	38	21	9	1	9	29	33	44
Leeds C	38	11	5	3	38	19	6	4	9	21	28	43
Leicester F	38	10	3	6	30	21	5	9	5	23	27	42
Grimsby T	38	11	7	1	33	13	4	3	12	13	33	40
Burnley	38	9	4	6	26	23	6	4	9	16	30	38
Stockport Co	38	11	6	2	36	16	2	3	14	8	40	35
Bradford C	38	7	4	8	21	22	6	4	9	25	38	34
Barnsley	38	11	4	4	45	17	1	5	13	15	45	33
Lincoln C	38	10	1	8	46	29	2	5	12	23	43	30
Blackpool	38	8	3	8	22	21	2	6	11	15	41	29
Gainsboro' T	38	10	2	7	35	22	2	2	15	9	35	28
Glossop	38	9	4	6	36	28	1	4	14	13	43	28
Burslem PV	38	10	4	5	34	25	2	0	17	15	57	28
Chesterfield	38	8	4	7	26	24	2	4	13	14	48	28
Burton U	38	9	4	6	26	20	1	2	16	8	47	26
Clapton O	38	6	4	9	19	22	1	3	15	16	56	21

Alex Raisbeck spent 11 seasons with Liverpool, winning two Championship medals, a Second Division winners' medal and eight Scotland caps.

Football League Records Season 1906-07

Top scorers: Div 1, A.Young (Everton) 28 goals; Div 2, F.Shinton (West Bromwich Albion) 28 goals.

LEAGUE TABLES

DIVISION 1

	P	W	D	L	F	A	W	D	L	F	A	Pts
Newcastle U	38	18	1	0	51	12	4	6	9	23	34	51
Bristol C	38	12	3	4	37	18	8	5	6	29	29	48
Everton	38	16	2	1	50	10	4	3	12	20	36	45
Sheffield U	38	13	4	2	36	17	4	7	8	21	38	45
Aston Villa	38	13	4	2	51	19	6	2	11	27	33	44
Bolton W	38	10	4	5	35	18	8	4	7	24	29	44
W Arsenal	38	15	1	3	38	15	5	3	11	28	44	44
Manchester U	38	10	6	3	33	15	7	2	10	20	41	42
Birmingham	38	13	5	1	41	17	2	3	14	11	35	38
Sunderland	38	10	4	5	42	31	4	5	10	23	35	37
Middlesbrough	38	11	2	6	33	21	4	4	11	23	42	36
Blackburn R	38	10	3	6	40	25	4	4	11	16	34	35
Sheffield W	38	8	5	6	33	26	4	6	9	16	34	35
Preston NE	38	13	4	2	35	19	1	3	15	9	38	35
Liverpool	38	9	2	8	45	32	4	5	10	19	33	33
Bury	38	9	4	6	30	23	4	2	13	28	45	32
Manchester C	38	7	7	5	29	25	3	5	11	24	52	32
Notts Co	38	6	9	4	31	18	2	6	11	15	32	31
Derby Co	38	8	6	5	29	19	1	3	15	12	40	27
Stoke	38	7	6	6	27	22	1	4	14	14	42	26

DIVISION 2

	P	W	D	L	F	A	W	D	L	F	A	Pts
Nottingham F	38	16	2	1	43	13	12	2	5	31	23	60
Chelsea	38	18	0	1	55	10	8	5	6	25	24	57
Leicester F	38	15	3	1	44	12	5	5	9	18	27	48
WBA	38	15	2	2	62	15	6	3	10	21	30	47
Bradford C	38	14	2	3	46	21	7	3	9	24	32	47
Wolves	38	13	4	2	49	16	4	3	12	17	37	41
Burnley	38	12	4	3	45	13	5	2	12	17	34	40
Barnsley	38	14	2	3	56	21	1	6	12	17	34	38
Hull C	38	11	2	6	41	20	4	5	10	24	37	37
Leeds C	38	10	5	4	38	26	3	5	11	17	37	36
Grimsby T	38	13	2	4	34	16	3	1	15	23	46	35
Stockport Co	38	8	8	3	26	12	4	3	12	16	40	35
Blackpool	38	9	4	6	25	19	2	7	10	8	32	33
Gainsboro' T	38	12	3	4	33	20	2	2	15	12	52	33
Glossop	38	10	4	5	32	21	3	2	14	21	58	32
Burslem PV	38	11	5	3	45	26	1	2	16	15	57	31
Clapton O	38	9	7	3	25	13	2	1	16	20	54	30
Chesterfield	38	10	3	6	36	26	1	4	14	14	40	29
Lincoln C	38	10	2	7	29	24	2	2	15	17	49	28
Burton U	38	7	3	9	24	23	1	4	14	10	45	23

Newcastle United's Colin Veitch, another star of Edwardian soccer, played in eight different positions for the Magpies, appeared in five FA Cup Finals and won three Championship medals.

DIVISION 1

	ASTON VILLA	BIRMINGHAM	BLACKBURN R	BOLTON W	BRISTOL C	BURY	DERBY CO	EVERTON	LIVERPOOL	MANCHESTER C	MANCHESTER U	MIDDLESBROUGH	NEWCASTLE U	NOTTS CO	PRESTON N.E.	SHEFFIELD U	SHEFFIELD W	STOKE	SUNDERLAND	W ARSENAL
1 ASTON VILLA		S15 4-1	S01 4-2	a27 0-2	D01 3-2	O13 3-1	M23 2-0	J26 2-1	M30 4-0	F23 4-1	D26 2-0	O27 2-3	N10 0-0	a13 0-0	D24 3-0	D15 5-1	F09 8-1	S10 1-0	J05 2-2	S29 2-2
2 BIRMINGHAM	J19 3-2		M16 2-0	O20 4-2	S03 2-2	D22 3-1	N24 2-1	a06 1-0	S22 2-1	M29 4-0	M02 1-1	D26 0-0	S08 2-4	O06 2-0	D29 3-0	F16 0-0	a25 1-1	N03 2-1	N17 2-0	D08 5-1
3 BLACKBURN R	D29 2-1	N10 1-0		O06 2-3	J19 0-1	D08 4-1	O27 5-1	a08 2-1	S08 1-1	a20 4-0	F16 2-4	D22 4-1	D25 4-0	S22 0-2	J01 1-1	M29 1-1	a06 0-2	O20 3-1	M09 2-1	N24 2-3
4 BOLTON W	D22 1-2	M11 2-3	F09 5-2		M29 1-2	M09 1-0	S15 1-0	O27 1-3	J01 3-0	N24 1-1	J26 0-1	a06 1-0	a20 4-2	D29 0-0	J02 3-0	S08 6-1	N10 0-0	S29 1-1	O13 1-0	M27 3-0
5 BRISTOL C	a06 2-4	S29 0-0	S15 3-0	a02 1-2		O27 2-0	D15 3-0	F09 2-1	D08 3-1	M09 2-0	S01 1-2	N10 3-0	N24 2-1	a27 1-0	M23 1-0	D24 3-3	a24 2-0	J05 4-0	J26 1-1	O13 1-3
6 BURY	F16 0-3	a27 1-0	a13 0-0	N17 2-3	M02 1-1		J05 1-0	D25 1-2	O20 1-3	J19 3-1	M30 1-2	S22 1-1	O06 3-2	N03 3-0	a01 2-0	M16 2-1	S01 0-0	D01 2-0	D15 2-3	S03 4-1
7 DERBY CO	N17 0-1	M30 1-1	M02 2-3	J19 0-1	a20 1-3	S08 2-1		a13 5-2	D01 0-1	S22 2-2	S03 2-2	O06 1-0	N03 0-0	D24 3-0	O20 3-0	D29 3-0	a01 1-0	F16 2-1	M16 1-1	D22 0-0
8 EVERTON	S22 1-2	D01 3-0	N17 2-0	M02 1-0	O06 2-0	J01 1-0	D08 2-0		M29 0-0	S03 9-1	N03 3-0	D29 5-1	J19 3-0	S17 2-2	S08 1-0	O20 4-2	D22 2-0	M16 3-0	M30 4-1	a10 2-1
9 LIVERPOOL	N24 5-2	J26 2-0	J05 0-2	D26 0-2	a13 2-4	S10 2-2	a06 2-0	S29 1-2		O27 5-4	a01 0-1	a17 2-4	M23 4-1	D15 5-1	N10 6-1	a27 2-2	O13 1-2	S01 1-0	S15 1-2	F09 4-0
10 MANCHESTER C	O20 4-2	D25 1-0	D15 0-0	M30 1-1	N03 0-1	S15 2-2	J26 2-2	D26 3-1	M02 1-0		D01 3-0	J02 3-1	F16 1-1	M16 2-1	O06 1-1	N17 0-2	J05 0-1	a13 2-2	a27 2-3	S01 1-4
11 MANCHESTER U	J01 1-0	O27 2-1	O13 1-1	S22 1-2	D29 0-0	N24 2-4	S29 1-1	a22 3-0	D25 0-0	a06 1-1		D08 3-1	D22 1-3	S08 0-0	F23 3-0	J19 2-0	a10 5-0	F09 4-1	M25 2-0	N10 1-0
12 MIDDLESBROUGH	M02 1-0	J01 1-0	a27 0-1	D01 0-0	M16 1-0	J26 3-1	F09 4-1	S01 2-2	N03 0-1	S29 2-3	a13 2-0		O20 0-3	N17 2-0	F16 2-1	M30 0-1	S15 1-3	D15 5-0	D25 2-1	J05 5-3
13 NEWCASTLE U	M16 3-2	J05 2-0	a01 3-1	D15 4-0	M30 3-0	F09 3-2	J01 2-0	S15 1-0	N17 2-0	O13 2-0	F02 5-0	F23 4-0		D01 4-3	O27 2-1	a13 0-0	S29 5-1	M29 1-0	S01 4-2	J26 1-0
14 NOTTS CO	D08 1-1	F09 2-2	J26 1-2	S01 0-0	D22 2-3	M13 1-2	M29 4-0	O13 0-1	a20 2-0	N10 0-0	J05 3-0	a10 2-2	a06 1-0		N24 0-0	a01 4-0	O27 2-2	S15 2-2	S29 0-0	a17 4-1
15 PRESTON N.E.	N03 2-0	S01 2-0	D26 1-0	D08 3-1	N17 3-1	S29 3-2	M09 1-0	J05 1-1	M16 3-1	F09 1-3	D15 2-0	O13 4-2	M02 2-2	M30 0-0		D01 2-1	J26 1-0	a27 2-2	M29 2-0	S15 0-3
16 SHEFFIELD U	a20 0-0	O13 2-0	S29 3-0	J05 2-1	D31 1-1	N10 3-0	S01 2-0	M04 4-1	D22 1-0	M23 1-4	S15 0-2	N24 1-1	D08 0-0	D26 2-1	F02 3-1		a04 2-1	J26 2-0	F09 3-2	O27 4-2
17 SHEFFIELD W	O06 2-1	D15 0-1	D01 3-1	M16 2-0	O20 3-0	D29 1-2	D25 1-1	a27 1-1	F16 2-3	S08 3-1	N17 5-2	J19 0-2	S03 2-2	M02 1-3	S22 2-1	N03 2-2		M30 0-1	a13 2-1	J01 1-1
18 STOKE	S03 0-2	M09 3-0	N12 1-1	D24 3-0	S08 0-3	a06 3-1	O13 2-1	N10 2-0	M11 1-1	D08 3-0	O06 1-2	a20 0-2	D26 1-2	J19 1-1	D22 0-2	S22 1-1	N24 1-1		O27 2-2	a15 2-0
19 SUNDERLAND	S08 2-1	M23 4-1	N03 1-0	F16 1-2	S22 3-3	a20 3-5	N10 0-2	N24 1-0	J19 5-5	D22 1-1	O20 4-1	a01 4-2	M20 2-0	a24 3-1	F13 1-0	O06 1-2	D08 1-1	M02 3-1		a06 2-3
20 W ARSENAL	a01 3-1	a13 2-1	M30 2-0	N03 2-2	F16 1-2	D26 3-1	a27 3-2	D15 3-1	O06 2-1	D29 4-1	M16 4-0	S08 2-0	S22 2-0	O20 1-0	J19 1-0	M02 0-1	M29 1-0	N17 2-1	D01 0-1	

DIVISION 2

	BARNSLEY	BLACKPOOL	BRADFORD C	BURNLEY	BURSLEM P.V.	BURTON U	CHELSEA	CHESTERFIELD	CLAPTON O	GAINSBOROUGH T	GLOSSOP	GRIMSBY T	HULL C	LEEDS C	LEICESTER F	LINCOLN C	NOTTINGHAM F	STOCKPORT CO	W.B.A.	WOLVERHAMPTON W
1 BARNSLEY		S01 3-2	J05 3-1	a18 5-0	O27 3-2	O13 6-1	M30 3-1	M23 2-1	J01 3-2	D15 6-0	D25 3-0	a11 1-1	D26 4-2	N10 3-0	J26 2-2	F09 6-2	S29 0-1	a01 3-1	S15 0-1	D01 0-1
2 BLACKPOOL	D29 2-3		M09 1-0	M29 2-0	D22 0-1	a13 1-1	S08 0-0	O27 0-0	S22 1-3	J01 1-0	O20 4-1	a20 4-3	F16 1-1	D05 1-0	M23 1-0	a06 2-0	N24 1-2	O06 0-1	N10 2-1	J19 1-2
3 BRADFORD C	S08 2-0	N03 3-0		J01 3-1	F12 3-2	a20 2-3	M19 6-3	N10 1-0	M12 5-2	O06 1-1	M02 2-1	D22 1-0	O20 1-0	D29 2-2	N24 3-1	D08 3-0	a06 1-2	F16 1-0	a23 4-0	S22 2-3
4 BURNLEY	N03 2-2	D25 2-1	S03 0-1		O13 6-0	S29 4-0	M16 1-1	F23 0-0	M30 3-0	D01 1-0	a27 1-1	F09 2-0	D15 4-2	M02 1-2	J05 5-0	J26 5-1	S15 2-1	a13 3-0	S01 0-1	N17 3-0
5 BURSLEM P.V.	M02 2-2	a27 3-0	D25 2-3	F16 4-4		J26 0-0	N03 2-0	F09 2-2	N17 3-2	M30 1-0	D15 4-1	S29 3-2	a13 2-1	O20 1-2	S01 1-2	S15 4-2	J05 4-2	D01 5-0	S10 2-1	M16 0-0
6 BURTON U	F16 1-1	O01 0-0	D15 1-0	F02 0-1	S22 2-0		O20 2-1	J05 3-1	N03 2-1	M16 0-0	D01 1-2	J19 2-3	M30 1-2	O06 0-2	M29 0-1	S01 3-4	a01 0-2	N17 0-1	a27 2-0	M02 4-1
7 CHELSEA	N24 2-1	J05 3-0	S15 5-1	N10 2-0	M09 2-1	F23 1-0		a06 7-1	D15 2-1	a27 4-1	S01 9-2	O27 2-0	M29 3-0	M23 2-0	S29 1-0	O13 2-0	F09 0-2	M04 2-0	J26 2-0	a13 4-0
8 CHESTERFIELD	N17 3-2	M02 0-1	M16 3-4	O20 0-1	O06 4-2	S08 2-0	D01 0-0		M29 2-1	D29 7-0	F16 1-3	S22 1-3	J01 3-1	N03 1-0	a13 2-1	a01 1-0	D22 1-1	J19 0-2	M30 2-2	a20 3-2
9 CLAPTON O	a13 1-0	J26 0-0	S29 1-1	N24 2-1	M23 1-1	M09 1-0	a20 0-1	D26 1-2		a01 3-1	S15 3-0	N10 1-0	J05 2-1	a06 1-1	O13 1-0	O27 1-1	F23 0-1	S01 1-1	F09 1-1	D22 4-0
10 GAINSBOROUGH T	a20 1-1	S29 2-0	F09 4-1	a06 0-2	N24 2-0	N10 2-0	D22 1-1	S01 1-0	D25 3-1		J26 2-1	N17 2-1	S15 1-1	D08 1-0	F23 1-2	M09 2-1	O27 2-3	J05 3-1	O13 2-4	O24 1-0
11 GLOSSOP	M29 2-1	F23 0-0	O27 1-2	D22 1-0	a20 4-0	a06 2-2	D29 0-1	O13 3-1	J19 3-0	S22 3-1		F12 1-0	O06 2-4	J01 2-0	N10 2-2	N24 2-1	M23 0-2	F02 2-3	a16 0-0	S08 2-1
12 GRIMSBY T	O20 1-0	D15 0-0	a27 0-2	O06 1-0	M21 2-0	S15 1-1	M02 2-1	J26 3-1	M16 1-2	D26 2-0	a13 2-1		D01 1-3	F16 4-0	a01 0-1	J05 4-0	S01 3-1	M30 3-1	M29 2-1	N03 2-1
13 HULL C	D08 2-0	O13 3-0	M14 0-3	a20 1-1	a01 4-1	N24 3-0	D25 0-1	S29 2-0	S08 2-0	J19 2-4	F09 5-0	a06 4-2		D22 2-1	M09 1-1	M23 1-2	N10 1-2	S22 3-0	O27 0-1	D29 5-1
14 LEEDS C	M16 2-1	F02 1-1	S01 1-1	O27 0-1	F23 2-0	F09 3-1	N17 0-1	M09 1-0	D01 3-2	a13 4-0	a01 1-4	O13 4-3	a27 2-2		S15 1-1	S10 1-1	J26 1-4	D15 6-1	J05 3-2	M30 2-0
15 LEICESTER F	S22 2-1	N17 5-1	M30 1-0	S08 2-0	D29 4-1	D26 3-0	F02 1-1	D08 2-0	F16 2-1	O20 3-1	M16 2-2	S03 2-0	N03 3-0	J19 2-2		D22 3-0	a20 1-2	D25 1-0	D01 3-0	O06 2-0
16 LINCOLN C	O06 1-0	D01 0-1	a13 0-2	S22 1-2	J19 4-0	D29 2-0	F16 0-5	D25 1-0	M02 3-0	N03 4-0	M30 2-1	S08 2-1	N17 0-1	S29 1-1	a27 2-2		M29 1-2	M16 3-1	D15 2-1	O20 0-4
17 NOTTINGHAM F	a02 0-0	M30 3-0	D01 3-0	J19 2-0	S08 2-2	D25 2-0	O06 3-1	O04 3-1	O20 4-0	M02 3-1	N17 2-0	D29 0-3	M16 2-1	S22 3-0	D15 2-1	a24 3-1		N03 2-1	a13 3-1	F16 1-0
18 STOCKPORT CO	D22 0-0	F09 0-0	O13 2-1	D08 2-1	a06 3-0	M23 2-0	J01 1-2	S15 1-1	D29 1-1	S08 1-2	S29 5-0	N24 3-0	J26 1-1	a20 2-2	O27 1-0	N10 1-0	M09 0-0		a08 0-1	M29 0-0
19 W.B.A.	a25 3-1	M16 3-0	N17 3-0	D29 3-2	D26 3-0	D22 5-1	S22 1-2	N24 5-2	O06 5-0	F16 5-0	N03 5-1	D25 6-1	M02 3-0	S08 5-0	a06 0-1	a20 2-1	D08 3-1	O20 1-1		a01 1-1
20 WOLVERHAMPTON W	a06 5-1	S15 1-1	J26 1-1	M23 3-0	N10 6-2	O27 3-0	D08 1-2	D15 2-1	D27 6-1	S03 1-0	J05 4-0	M09 5-0	S01 1-1	N24 3-2	F09 1-0	F23 3-0	O13 2-0	D26 1-1	S29 0-3	

Football League Records Season 1907-08

Top scorers: Div 1, E.West (Nottingham Forest) 27 goals; Div 2, J.Smith (Hull City) 30 goals.
Burslem Port Vale resigned and Burton United failed to gain re-election, Fulham and Oldham Athletic were elected in their place.

DIVISION 1

	ASTON VILLA	BIRMINGHAM	BLACKBURN R	BOLTON W	BRISTOL C	BURY	CHELSEA	EVERTON	LIVERPOOL	MANCHESTER C	MANCHESTER U	MIDDLESBROUGH	NEWCASTLE U	NOTTINGHAM F	NOTTS CO	PRESTON N.E.	SHEFFIELD U	SHEFFIELD W	SUNDERLAND	W ARSENAL
1 ASTON VILLA		J18 2-3	J04 1-1	S14 2-0	O26 4-4	N23 2-2	D28 0-0	S28 0-2	a04 5-1	N09 2-2	S02 1-4	D14 6-0	N30 3-3	D25 4-0	M02 5-1	M14 3-0	a18 1-0	F15 5-0	S09 1-0	O12 0-1
2 BIRMINGHAM	S21 2-3		M07 1-1	N16 2-1	a25 0-4	S16 0-1	O19 1-1	M28 2-1	J25 1-1	D25 2-1	N02 3-4	O05 1-4	M21 1-1	M30 1-0	D26 0-0	S07 2-0	F08 0-0	D21 2-1	D07 0-2	a11 1-2
3 BLACKBURN R	S07 2-0	N09 1-0		F29 3-2	a11 4-1	S02 1-0	O05 2-0	M14 2-0	a06 1-3	a25 0-0	O19 1-5	S21 2-0	M23 1-1	F08 3-3	D21 1-1	J01 1-1	J25 3-3	D07 2-0	N23 4-2	M28 1-1
4 BOLTON W	a17 3-1	M14 1-0	N02 3-1		D21 1-2	S07 3-6	F08 1-2	N23 3-0	S21 0-4	J01 2-0	a22 2-2	J25 1-1	a01 4-0	O19 1-0	a25 0-1	J02 2-0	O05 1-1	a11 2-1	M28 2-3	D07 3-1
5 BRISTOL C	M11 2-2	D28 0-0	D14 2-2	a18 2-0		O19 1-1	M21 0-0	S02 3-2	N02 2-0	O05 2-1	a04 1-1	M07 0-1	S21 1-1	N30 3-0	J25 2-1	F08 1-3	N16 3-2	S14 0-2	a20 3-0	J04 1-2
6 BURY	M21 2-1	S14 1-0	a17 1-1	J04 2-2	F15 1-1		a18 1-1	J18 3-0	M28 3-1	F29 0-0	J01 0-1	a04 1-4	N16 1-2	D28 0-0	O26 0-0	N09 5-1	D14 3-2	O12 0-2	S28 2-1	S09 3-2
7 CHELSEA	a25 1-3	F15 2-2	D02 1-0	O12 1-3	N23 4-1	D21 3-4		O26 2-1	a20 0-2	D07 2-2	S28 1-4	D26 1-0	S23 2-0	J18 0-4	a29 1-2	a11 0-0	S07 2-4	M14 3-1	F29 2-1	N09 2-1
8 EVERTON	J25 1-0	M18 4-1	N16 4-1	M21 2-1	D26 0-0	S21 6-1	a01 0-3		O05 2-4	S07 3-3	a08 1-3	F08 2-1	a04 2-0	N02 1-0	a20 1-0	S09 2-1	O19 2-1	a25 0-0	a11 0-3	D21 1-1
9 LIVERPOOL	D07 5-0	S28 3-4	S14 2-0	J18 1-0	F29 3-1	a27 2-1	D25 1-4	a17 0-0		M14 0-1	M25 7-4	a18 0-1	D14 1-5	J01 0-0	N09 6-0	N23 1-2	D28 3-0	O26 3-0	O12 1-0	F15 4-1
10 MANCHESTER C	M07 3-2	a17 2-1	D28 2-0	D26 1-0	a21 0-0	N02 2-2	a04 0-3	J04 4-2	N16 1-1		a18 0-0	M21 2-1	O19 1-0	D14 4-2	O12 2-1	a06 5-0	M11 0-2	S28 3-2	S14 0-0	J18 4-0
11 MANCHESTER U	a20 1-2	F29 1-0	F15 1-2	O26 2-1	D07 2-1	D25 2-1	J25 1-0	N09 4-3	S07 4-0	D21 3-1		S09 2-1	F08 1-1	O05 4-0	a11 0-1	a25 2-1	S21 2-1	M28 4-1	M14 3-0	N23 4-2
12 MIDDLESBROUGH	a11 0-1	S04 1-0	J18 3-0	S28 0-1	N09 0-2	D07 0-2	J01 3-1	O12 0-2	D21 3-1	N23 2-0	S14 2-1		a20 2-1	J04 1-1	M14 3-1	M28 1-0	F01 2-0	a08 6-1	F15 3-1	O26 0-0
13 NEWCASTLE U	a08 2-5	N23 8-0	O26 3-0	N09 3-0	J18 2-0	M14 3-0	S14 1-0	D07 2-1	a11 3-1	F15 1-1	O12 1-6	D28 1-1		S28 3-0	S04 1-1	M11 0-0	D26 2-3	J04 2-1	a18 1-3	a17 2-1
14 NOTTINGHAM F	D26 2-2	O26 1-1	O12 3-2	F15 1-0	M28 3-1	a25 1-2	S21 6-0	F29 5-2	S02 3-1	a11 3-1	a17 2-0	S07 0-3	J25 0-0		D07 2-0	D21 2-2	a20 1-1	N23 2-2	N09 4-1	M14 1-0
15 NOTTS CO	N02 0-3	D27 0-0	a18 0-2	D28 0-1	S28 3-1	O03 2-1	N30 2-0	D25 2-1	M07 2-2	F08 1-0	D14 1-1	N16 2-0	O05 0-1	a04 2-0		O19 0-1	M21 0-3	J18 1-2	J04 4-0	S14 2-0
16 PRESTON N.E.	N16 3-0	J04 1-1	D26 1-1	D25 2-0	O12 3-0	M07 3-1	D14 2-4	S14 2-2	M21 3-0	O26 2-4	D28 0-0	N30 1-1	N02 2-0	a18 0-1	F15 1-0		a04 0-0	S02 1-1	J18 3-2	S28 3-0
17 SHEFFIELD U	D21 1-1	O12 1-0	S28 4-2	D30 1-0	M14 2-0	a11 0-2	J04 0-3	F15 2-0	S10 0-0	M28 1-2	J18 2-0	D25 0-0	J01 1-1	S14 2-2	N23 0-1	D07 2-0		N09 1-3	O26 5-3	F29 2-2
18 SHEFFIELD W	O19 2-3	a18 1-4	a04 2-0	D14 5-2	S23 5-3	F08 2-0	N16 3-1	D28 1-2	M09 1-2	J25 5-1	N30 2-0	N02 3-2	S07 3-1	M21 2-1	S21 2-0	O05 1-0	M07 2-0		D26 2-3	D31 6-0
19 SUNDERLAND	O05 3-0	a04 1-0	M21 4-0	N30 1-2	D25 3-3	J25 6-2	N02 3-0	D14 1-2	F08 1-0	S02 2-5	N16 1-2	O19 0-0	D21 2-4	M07 7-2	S07 4-3	S21 4-1	F22 4-1	a17 1-2		J01 5-2
20 W ARSENAL	F08 0-1	D14 1-1	N30 2-0	a04 1-1	S07 0-4	O05 0-0	M07 0-0	a18 2-1	O19 2-1	S21 2-1	M21 1-0	F22 4-1	D25 2-2	N16 3-1	S02 1-1	J25 1-1	N02 5-1	a20 1-1	D28 4-0	

DIVISION 2

	BARNSLEY	BLACKPOOL	BRADFORD C	BURNLEY	CHESTERFIELD	CLAPTON O	DERBY CO	FULHAM	GAINSBOROUGH T	GLOSSOP	GRIMSBY T	HULL C	LEEDS C	LEICESTER F	LINCOLN C	OLDHAM A	STOCKPORT CO	STOKE	W.B.A.	WOLVERHAMPTON W
1 BARNSLEY		a18 0-0	J01 1-2	O19 2-3	F08 5-2	S05 2-2	S14 2-4	S28 6-0	M21 1-2	a21 4-1	O05 2-1	J04 4-2	M07 1-3	D14 1-3	J18 2-1	M19 2-1	N30 0-0	D28 0-1	D26 1-3	N16 5-0
2 BLACKPOOL	D21 1-1		M14 2-1	a17 1-0	a25 2-0	S07 5-0	M28 1-0	a11 2-1	J25 0-1	F08 4-0	a01 3-0	N23 1-1	S14 2-3	O19 2-2	D07 4-3	J01 1-0	O05 1-3	F29 1-0	N09 0-1	S21 0-2
3 BRADFORD C	D25 2-0	N16 3-0		a20 2-0	S07 8-1	J25 1-0	D21 3-1	D26 1-3	O19 7-1	N02 2-1	a04 1-1	a11 2-1	O05 5-0	M07 1-5	a25 2-0	S21 1-0	F22 5-0	M21 6-0	N30 0-0	F08 6-2
4 BURNLEY	F15 4-1	D25 2-1	S14 2-1		O26 1-1	N16 3-0	S28 2-2	O12 0-1	a01 2-0	a18 1-0	N02 5-1	J18 5-0	M21 1-0	D28 4-1	S16 1-2	M07 2-1	D14 4-0	S09 3-1	J04 1-1	N30 1-0
5 CHESTERFIELD	O12 1-3	D28 3-2	J04 1-1	F22 2-4		M07 1-1	J18 0-2	J01 1-1	N30 2-2	D14 3-7	O19 0-0	S14 1-2	N16 4-3	a18 2-2	S28 2-1	N02 1-2	M03 4-1	a20 2-4	a17 1-0	M21 2-0
6 CLAPTON O	F29 2-0	J04 1-1	S28 0-3	M14 0-1	N09 5-1		O12 1-0	O26 0-1	a18 2-0	a09 0-0	N30 2-1	S02 1-0	a04 0-0	a20 0-1	M26 2-0	N23 2-0	D28 4-1	S14 3-0	J18 2-2	D14 1-1
7 DERBY CO	D24 3-0	N30 2-1	a18 2-3	J25 1-0	D26 0-0	F08 4-0		S07 0-1	N02 5-2	N16 2-0	D25 4-0	D28 4-1	O19 6-1	F22 1-2	S02 4-0	O05 1-0	M07 3-0	a04 3-0	D14 2-0	a08 3-2
8 FULHAM	J25 2-0	D14 3-0	a17 0-2	F08 2-1	O05 5-0	M18 4-0	J04 0-0		N16 6-0	N30 6-1	S21 0-1	S03 0-1	N02 2-0	a04 5-1	S14 6-1	O19 1-2	M21 0-1	a18 5-1	D28 1-1	a01 2-1
9 GAINSBOROUGH T	N23 0-1	S28 2-1	F15 1-5	D07 2-0	M28 2-1	D21 0-0	F29 1-4	M14 3-3		S14 1-0	D26 3-2	O26 1-2	a22 2-1	J18 1-1	N09 5-1	a11 1-1	J04 3-2	a17 2-0	O12 1-2	O23 0-1
10 GLOSSOP	a17 3-1	O12 2-2	F29 2-2	D21 3-1	a11 3-2	D25 2-1	M14 2-3	a29 1-2	M03 1-0		J25 1-2	N09 5-1	J01 0-2	M24 2-3	F01 3-1	a25 0-0	S21 1-1	F15 2-0	O26 2-1	S07 1-1
11 GRIMSBY T	a09 4-1	O26 2-2	D07 0-1	F29 0-1	a29 4-3	M28 0-0	a20 1-0	J18 0-4	S03 1-4	S28 4-0		a18 1-1	a11 2-0	O12 1-1	J04 0-2	M14 2-0	S14 2-1	N09 1-0	N23 2-2	a17 0-1
12 HULL C	S07 2-0	M21 3-2	D14 0-2	S21 3-1	S26 2-0	O10 5-0	a25 4-0	a20 1-2	F22 0-1	M07 3-2	D21 4-2		F08 4-1	N16 3-2	D25 5-3	J25 3-2	N02 0-0	N30 2-1	a04 4-2	O19 2-0
13 LEEDS C	N09 1-1	a20 1-1	F01 0-1	N23 2-2	M14 0-0	S09 5-2	F15 5-1	F29 0-1	D28 0-0	S02 2-1	D14 4-1	O12 3-2		J04 0-0	O26 2-1	M28 1-2	a17 3-0	J18 0-1	S28 1-0	a18 3-1
14 LEICESTER F	a11 4-0	F15 2-1	N09 2-1	a25 3-1	D21 3-1	D26 0-2	N23 1-3	D07 2-3	S21 3-0	O05 3-1	F08 1-1	M14 3-2	S07 2-2		M28 1-0	D25 4-1	J25 2-1	O26 1-0	F29 3-0	S09 1-0
15 LINCOLN C	S21 0-2	a04 2-0	D28 2-4	O05 1-3	J25 4-0	F15 2-2	a17 1-0	O16 2-4	M07 2-0	M21 0-1	S07 1-0	D26 0-1	F22 5-0	N30 0-3		F08 0-2	N16 1-1	D14 1-2	a18 0-2	N02 3-1
16 OLDHAM A	O26 1-0	D26 3-2	J18 4-0	N09 1-1	F29 4-0	M21 4-1	M30 3-1	F15 3-3	D14 4-1	D28 0-0	N16 2-0	S28 3-0	N30 4-2	a21 1-1	O12 4-0		a18 5-0	J04 3-1	S14 2-1	a04 2-0
17 STOCKPORT CO	M28 2-0	S02 1-1	O26 1-1	a11 1-3	a04 1-0	a25 6-1	N09 2-1	N23 2-0	S07 1-1	J18 3-2	S09 3-0	F29 2-3	D25 2-1	S28 2-1	M14 1-1	D21 2-3		O12 1-2	F15 1-2	J01 1-3
18 STOKE	a25 4-0	N02 3-1	N23 3-0	D26 0-0	S02 1-1	N11 3-0	D07 0-3	D21 6-1	O05 5-0	O19 4-0	M19 5-0	M28 1-1	S21 2-1	a27 0-1	a11 3-0	S07 1-3	F08 1-0		M04 1-1	J25 0-0
19 W.B.A.	a20 1-1	M07 3-0	M28 3-2	S07 5-0	D25 4-0	S21 3-0	a11 1-0	a25 3-1	F08 0-1	F22 1-1	M21 1-2	D07 1-0	J25 1-0	N02 1-1	D21 5-2	N04 1-2	O19 2-0	N16 1-0		O05 1-0
20 WOLVERHAMPTON W	M14 0-1	J18 1-0	O12 0-0	M16 5-1	N23 0-0	a11 2-0	O26 2-2	N09 2-0	D25 1-0	J04 5-0	D28 5-1	F15 1-2	D21 2-0	S14 0-0	F29 3-0	a20 2-1	D26 0-1	S28 2-0	S02 1-2	

LEAGUE TABLES

DIVISION 1

	P	W	D	L	F	A	W	D	L	F	A	Pts
Manchester U	38	15	1	3	43	19	8	5	6	38	29	52
Aston Villa	38	9	6	4	47	24	8	3	8	30	35	43
Manchester C	38	12	5	2	36	19	4	6	9	26	35	43
Newcastle U	38	11	4	4	41	24	4	8	7	24	30	42
Sheffield W	38	14	0	5	50	25	5	4	10	23	39	42
Middlesbrough	38	12	2	5	32	16	5	5	9	22	29	41
Bury	38	8	7	4	29	22	6	4	9	29	39	39
Liverpool	38	11	2	6	43	24	5	4	10	25	37	38
Nottingham F	38	11	6	2	42	21	2	5	12	17	41	37
Bristol C	38	8	7	4	29	21	4	5	10	29	40	36
Everton	38	11	4	4	34	24	4	2	13	24	40	36
Preston NE	38	9	7	3	33	18	3	5	11	14	35	36
Chelsea	38	8	3	8	30	35	6	5	8	23	27	36
W Arsenal	38	9	8	2	32	18	3	4	12	19	45	*36
Blackburn R	38	10	7	2	35	23	2	5	12	16	40	*36
Sunderland	38	11	2	6	53	31	5	1	3	25	44	35
Sheffield U	38	8	6	5	27	22	4	5	10	25	36	35
Notts Co	38	9	3	7	24	19	4	5	10	15	32	34
Bolton W	38	10	3	6	35	26	4	2	13	17	32	33
Birmingham	38	6	6	7	22	28	3	6	10	18	32	30

**Woolwich Arsenal & Blackburn Rovers finished in equal 14th place*

DIVISION 2

	P	W	D	L	F	A	W	D	L	F	A	Pts
Bradford C	38	15	2	2	58	16	9	4	6	32	26	54
Leicester F	38	14	2	3	41	20	7	8	4	31	27	52
Oldham A	38	15	4	0	53	14	7	2	10	23	28	50
Fulham	38	12	2	5	50	14	10	3	6	32	35	49
WBA	38	13	3	3	38	13	6	6	7	23	26	47
Derby Co	38	15	1	3	50	13	6	3	10	27	32	46
Burnley	38	14	3	2	44	14	6	3	10	23	36	46
Hull C	38	15	1	3	50	23	6	3	10	23	39	46
Wolves	38	11	4	4	34	11	4	3	12	16	34	37
Stoke	38	11	5	3	43	13	5	0	14	14	39	37
Gainsboro' T	38	9	4	6	31	28	5	3	11	16	43	35
Leeds C	38	9	6	4	33	18	3	2	14	20	47	32
Stockport Co	38	9	4	6	35	26	3	4	12	13	41	32
Clapton O	38	10	5	4	28	13	1	5	13	12	52	32
Blackpool	38	11	3	5	33	19	0	6	13	18	39	31
Barnsley	38	8	3	8	41	31	4	3	12	13	37	30
Glossop	38	9	5	5	36	26	2	3	14	18	48	30
Grimsby T	38	8	5	6	27	24	3	3	13	16	47	30
Chesterfield	38	6	6	7	33	38	0	5	14	13	54	23
Lincoln C	38	7	2	10	27	28	2	1	16	19	55	21

'Sandy' Turnbull, one of six Manchester City players banned by the FA in 1906 over illegal payments, was Manchester United's leading scorer when they won their first League Championship in 1907-08.

Football League Records Season 1908-09

Top scorers: Div 1, B.Freeman (Everton) 38 goals; Div 2, A.Bentley (Derby County) 24 goals.
Stoke resigned and Lincoln City failed to gain re-election. Bradford and Tottenham Hotspur were elected in their place.

LEAGUE TABLES

DIVISION 1

	P	W	D	L	F	A	W	D	L	F	A	Pts
Newcastle U	38	14	1	4	32	20	10	4	5	33	21	53
Everton	38	11	3	5	51	28	7	7	5	31	29	46
Sunderland	38	14	0	5	41	23	7	2	10	37	40	44
Blackburn R	38	6	6	7	29	26	8	7	4	32	24	41
Sheffield W	38	15	0	4	48	24	2	6	11	19	37	40
W Arsenal	38	9	3	7	24	18	5	7	7	28	31	38
Aston Villa	38	8	7	4	31	22	6	3	10	27	34	38
Bristol C	38	7	7	5	24	25	6	5	8	21	33	38
Middlesbrough	38	11	2	6	38	21	3	7	9	21	32	37
Preston NE	38	8	7	4	29	17	5	4	10	19	27	37
Chelsea	38	8	7	4	33	22	6	2	11	23	39	37
Sheffield U	38	9	5	5	31	25	5	4	10	20	34	37
Manchester U	38	10	3	6	37	33	5	4	10	21	35	37
Nottingham F	38	9	2	8	39	24	5	6	8	27	33	36
Notts Co	38	9	4	6	31	23	5	4	10	20	25	36
Liverpool	38	9	5	5	36	25	6	1	12	21	40	36
Bury	38	9	6	4	35	27	5	2	12	28	50	36
Bradford C	38	7	6	6	27	20	5	4	10	20	27	34
Manchester C	38	12	3	4	50	23	3	1	15	17	46	34
Leicester F	38	6	6	7	32	41	2	3	14	22	61	25

DIVISION 2

	P	W	D	L	F	A	W	D	L	F	A	Pts
Bolton W	34	14	3	2	37	8	10	1	8	22	20	52
Tottenham H	38	12	5	2	42	12	8	6	5	25	20	51
WBA	38	13	5	1	35	9	6	8	5	21	18	51
Hull C	38	14	2	3	44	15	5	4	10	19	24	44
Derby Co	38	13	5	1	38	11	3	6	10	17	30	43
Oldham A	38	14	4	1	39	9	3	2	14	16	34	40
Wolves	38	10	6	3	32	12	4	5	10	24	36	39
Glossop	38	11	5	3	35	17	4	3	12	22	36	38
Gainsboro' T	38	12	3	4	30	20	3	5	11	19	50	38
Fulham	38	8	4	7	39	26	5	7	7	19	22	37
Birmingham	38	10	6	3	35	21	4	3	12	23	40	37
Leeds C	38	12	3	4	35	19	2	4	13	8	34	35
Grimsby T	38	9	5	5	23	14	5	2	12	18	40	35
Burnley	38	8	4	7	33	28	5	3	11	18	30	33
Clapton O	38	7	7	5	25	19	5	2	12	12	30	33
Bradford	38	9	2	8	30	25	4	4	11	21	34	32
Barnsley	38	11	3	5	36	19	0	7	12	12	38	32
Stockport Co	38	11	2	6	25	19	3	1	15	14	32	31
Chesterfield	38	10	3	6	30	28	1	5	13	7	39	30
Blackpool	38	9	6	4	30	22	0	5	14	16	46	29

Scottish international Jimmy Howie of Newcastle United, said to be the best inside-right in the game before World War One. He was a key man in Newcastle's trio of title wins and appeared in four FA Cup Finals.

DIVISION 1

	ASTON VILLA	BLACKBURN R	BRADFORD C	BRISTOL C	BURY	CHELSEA	EVERTON	LEICESTER F	LIVERPOOL	MANCHESTER C	MANCHESTER U	MIDDLESBROUGH	NEWCASTLE U	NOTTINGHAM F	NOTTS CO	PRESTON N.E.	SHEFFIELD U	SHEFFIELD W	SUNDERLAND	W ARSENAL
1 ASTON VILLA		O03 1-1	F13 1-3	N28 1-1	D26 3-0	J30 0-0	F27 3-1	O31 1-1	D25 1-1	a24 2-1	O17 3-1	D12 0-3	a26 3-0	J09 1-2	N14 1-1	a10 2-4	a09 3-0	S05 1-1	S19 2-0	M13 2-1
2 BLACKBURN R	F15 3-1		M13 1-1	S01 1-1	J23 0-1	O24 2-0	M27 0-0	N28 3-0	S12 1-0	J02 3-2	N14 1-3	D25 0-0	a24 2-4	O10 0-3	D12 0-2	J01 1-1	S26 0-1	O31 2-2	M22 8-1	a10 1-3
3 BRADFORD C	O10 1-1	N07 0-2		D25 0-1	S26 4-1	a20 3-0	N28 1-1	a10 4-1	J23 0-2	S12 0-0	a29 1-0	J02 0-2	M23 1-2	M30 1-1	a24 2-2	a12 2-0	M27 3-1	N14 0-0	O24 0-2	D12 4-1
4 BRISTOL C	a03 0-0	a13 1-4	D26 0-1		M20 4-2	D19 1-0	S05 0-2	J09 1-1	N07 1-0	a28 1-0	a12 0-0	O24 1-1	O03 3-3	D05 2-1	J30 1-0	M17 2-3	N21 1-1	F13 1-1	a17 2-4	S19 2-1
5 BURY	J01 1-2	S19 1-1	J30 2-1	N14 1-2		M31 2-1	F13 2-2	O17 2-2	D12 2-1	a10 1-0	O03 2-2	N28 2-1	M13 1-1	D25 3-2	O31 3-1	M27 0-1	S01 1-2	a24 4-2	S05 4-2	F27 1-1
6 CHELSEA	S26 0-2	F27 1-1	O31 1-1	a26 3-1	S12 4-1		N14 3-3	a29 1-0	J02 3-0	D26 1-2	M13 1-1	a09 3-0	D12 1-2	S21 2-1	a10 3-2	S01 0-0	J23 1-1	O17 2-2	O10 2-0	N28 1-2
7 EVERTON	O24 3-1	N21 4-4	a03 0-1	J02 5-2	O10 4-0	M20 3-2		a24 4-2	a09 5-0	S26 6-3	D05 3-2	J23 1-1	J01 0-1	M24 3-3	D25 0-1	S12 0-1	F20 5-1	D12 1-0	N07 4-0	S07 0-3
8 LEICESTER F	M27 4-2	a03 2-4	D05 1-4	S12 1-1	F20 2-5	N21 5-2	D19 0-2		O10 3-2	M11 3-1	a17 3-2	S26 1-1	J02 0-4	N07 0-3	a12 0-2	J23 0-0	O24 1-1	S01 1-1	M20 4-3	D25 1-1
9 LIVERPOOL	S01 3-2	J09 1-1	S19 4-0	M13 1-2	a17 2-2	S05 2-1	O03 0-1	F13 4-1		N28 1-3	J30 3-1	M27 1-2	O31 2-1	D26 1-1	F27 1-1	N14 2-1	D19 2-1	a10 1-2	a12 3-0	O17 2-2
10 MANCHESTER C	D19 2-0	S05 3-3	J09 4-3	O31 5-1	D05 6-1	D25 1-2	J30 4-0	O03 5-2	a03 4-0		S19 1-2	N14 0-0	F27 0-2	a13 2-1	O17 1-0	M13 4-1	a17 1-3	M27 4-0	S01 1-0	F13 2-2
11 MANCHESTER U	M31 0-2	M20 0-3	N21 2-0	a09 0-1	S07 2-1	N07 0-1	a10 2-2	D12 4-2	S26 3-2	J23 3-1		S12 6-3	D26 1-0	O24 2-2	J01 4-3	J02 0-2	O10 2-1	N28 3-1	M15 2-2	a27 1-4
12 MIDDLESBROUGH	a17 1-0	a12 1-0	S05 1-0	F27 4-0	a03 0-1	J01 1-4	S19 2-3	J30 6-2	N21 1-0	M20 3-0	J09 5-0		O17 0-0	D19 4-0	F13 1-2	O31 4-2	D05 1-2	M13 2-1	S09 0-3	O03 1-1
13 NEWCASTLE U	N21 0-2	D19 2-0	S02 1-0	S09 2-1	N07 3-1	a17 1-3	a12 3-0	S05 2-0	a30 0-1	O24 2-0	D25 2-1	M31 1-0		a03 1-1	S19 1-0	O10 2-0	M20 4-0	J30 1-0	D05 1-9	J09 3-1
14 NOTTINGHAM F	S12 1-2	F13 2-1	O17 2-1	a10 1-1	a12 0-2	O03 2-1	O31 1-2	a21 12-0	O01 5-1	D28 0-2	F27 2-0	a24 4-1	N28 0-4		M27 1-0	D12 1-1	J02 0-2	S19 1-2	J30 4-0	N14 0-1
15 NOTTS CO	M20 1-1	a17 2-3	D19 1-1	S26 0-1	M24 3-2	D05 3-0	D26 0-0	a09 2-3	O24 1-2	F20 5-1	a13 0-1	O10 3-2	J23 0-4	N21 3-0		M10 1-0	N07 3-1	J09 1-0	a03 0-0	S05 2-1
16 PRESTON N.E.	D05 3-2	D26 2-0	a09 0-0	O17 2-1	N21 0-2	S07 6-0	J09 3-3	S19 0-1	M20 2-0	N07 3-0	S05 0-3	M06 1-1	F13 0-1	a17 1-1	O03 0-0		a03 1-1	F27 4-1	D19 1-0	J30 0-0
17 SHEFFIELD U	F06 3-1	J30 0-0	O03 3-0	a05 3-1	M01 2-2	S19 1-3	O17 1-5	F27 2-1	S14 0-2	D12 4-0	F13 0-0	a10 2-0	N14 1-1	S05 1-2	M13 3-2	N28 2-1		D26 2-1	J09 0-2	O31 1-1
18 SHEFFIELD W	J02 4-2	a19 1-2	M20 0-2	O10 2-0	D19 4-3	M22 5-1	a17 2-0	J01 3-1	D05 2-3	N21 3-1	a03 2-0	N07 3-2	S26 2-0	J23 3-0	S12 2-0	O24 1-0	D25 1-0		M29 2-5	D28 6-2
19 SUNDERLAND	J23 4-3	O17 0-1	F27 2-1	D12 0-2	J02 3-1	F13 1-2	M13 2-0	N14 3-1	J01 1-4	a09 2-0	O31 6-1	D26 2-0	a10 3-1	S26 2-1	N28 0-1	a24 2-1	S12 3-1	O03 4-2		M27 1-0
20 W ARSENAL	N07 0-1	D05 0-1	a17 1-0	J23 1-1	O24 4-0	a03 0-0	S02 0-4	D26 2-1	F20 5-0	O10 3-0	D19 0-1	M17 1-1	S12 1-2	M20 1-2	J02 1-0	S26 1-0	a01 1-0	a12 2-0	N21 0-4	

DIVISION 2

	BARNSLEY	BIRMINGHAM	BLACKPOOL	BOLTON W	BRADFORD	BURNLEY	CHESTERFIELD	CLAPTON O	DERBY CO	FULHAM	GAINSBOROUGH T	GLOSSOP	GRIMSBY T	HULL C	LEEDS C	OLDHAM A	STOCKPORT CO	TOTTENHAM H	W.B.A.	WOLVERHAMPTON W
1 BARNSLEY		M13 3-1	O03 4-0	S05 0-1	D12 3-1	a13 1-2	F13 4-0	D26 3-0	J30 1-0	N28 1-2	N14 2-2	O17 1-3	M27 3-1	S19 2-1	J01 2-1	a09 2-0	F27 2-0	J09 1-1	O31 0-2	a24 1-1
2 BIRMINGHAM	N07 2-1		D05 2-2	S02 2-0	S07 3-1	S26 2-0	a17 3-0	O24 1-0	a03 1-1	J23 1-3	J02 2-2	D19 1-2	S12 3-1	N21 1-2	a12 1-0	F20 2-0	D25 4-2	M20 3-3	D28 0-0	O10 1-1
3 BLACKPOOL	S02 1-1	a10 2-0		O31 1-2	M31 2-1	a09 0-0	M13 2-2	J23 1-3	O24 2-2	D26 2-0	D12 3-0	N14 2-1	a24 2-2	F20 2-3	S26 1-0	S12 1-0	M27 2-1	O10 1-1	N28 0-2	J02 3-1
4 BOLTON W	J02 3-0	J01 2-1	M06 3-1		N07 0-1	O24 2-1	F20 4-0	D19 2-0	a30 1-0	O10 0-0	S12 4-0	a03 2-0	S26 2-0	S14 1-0	D25 2-0	D05 3-0	a17 4-1	J23 0-1	S15 1-1	N21 1-1
5 BRADFORD	a17 3-2	O06 1-2	J01 4-3	M13 1-2		O31 2-3	S05 1-0	a03 0-1	a09 2-0	F27 1-1	F06 4-1	D26 1-0	O17 0-2	S01 1-0	a27 2-0	D15 3-4	S19 0-1	D19 0-2	J30 0-0	M20 4-1
6 BURNLEY	D05 3-2	J30 1-1	D25 1-1	F27 1-2	M16 3-3		S01 0-1	N21 0-1	S07 2-0	O17 1-3	O03 5-2	S05 3-2	F13 2-0	D19 1-0	a03 0-0	M20 1-0	J09 5-1	a17 1-2	S19 0-2	N07 3-5
7 CHESTERFIELD	O10 1-0	D12 4-2	N07 3-1	N14 0-2	J02 2-1	a12 1-0		S26 2-0	M17 2-4	J01 2-1	a24 2-1	M27 2-1	F06 1-2	O24 0-4	O03 2-0	J23 1-1	N28 1-2	M08 1-3	a10 2-2	S12 1-1
8 CLAPTON O	D25 1-1	F27 3-2	S19 1-1	a24 0-2	N28 2-0	M27 0-1	J30 1-1		J09 2-0	N14 1-1	O31 2-2	O03 0-2	M13 2-1	J02 1-2	a13 0-0	D12 2-0	F13 5-0	a12 0-0	O17 1-0	a10 1-3
9 DERBY CO	S26 0-0	N28 1-2	F27 1-1	O17 1-0	D28 3-1	D26 1-0	O31 1-1	S12 1-0		a24 2-1	a10 5-0	a21 4-0	D12 2-1	O10 0-0	J23 5-1	J02 1-0	N14 5-0	a28 1-1	a26 2-1	S16 2-1
10 FULHAM	a03 2-2	S19 1-1	a12 3-0	F13 1-2	O24 3-1	M31 3-0	D25 0-0	M20 1-2	D19 1-2		J30 4-0	S02 2-3	O03 5-2	a17 0-3	N21 0-1	N07 3-2	S05 5-1	D05 2-3	J09 2-0	M06 1-1
11 GAINSBOROUGH T	M20 4-1	S05 1-3	a17 1-0	J09 2-1	O10 2-1	a14 1-0	D19 3-0	a28 2-0	O21 0-0	S26 1-1		D28 3-1	J23 0-3	a03 2-0	N07 1-1	O24 1-4	D26 3-2	N21 0-2	a09 2-0	F20 1-0
12 GLOSSOP	M30 3-0	a24 3-1	M20 3-0	N28 0-2	S12 1-1	J02 1-2	N21 2-0	a20 4-0	N07 3-1	a09 0-0	F23 2-2		M16 1-0	M23 2-1	O10 0-0	S26 2-1	a10 3-0	O24 1-1	D12 1-3	J23 3-2
13 GRIMSBY T	N21 0-0	J09 0-3	D19 2-1	J30 1-0	F20 1-1	O10 0-1	D26 1-0	N07 1-0	a17 2-0	M25 2-2	S19 1-2	a12 2-0		D05 0-0	M20 0-1	a20 2-0	S01 3-0	a03 1-2	S05 1-1	O24 3-0
14 HULL C	J23 4-0	M27 4-1	O17 2-0	O03 2-0	D25 2-3	a24 3-2	F27 1-0	S05 3-2	F13 4-0	D12 2-0	N28 5-1	O31 0-0	a10 0-1		J09 4-1	a29 1-0	M13 4-1	S26 1-0	N14 2-2	a12 0-1
15 LEEDS C	S14 2-0	O31 2-0	J30 1-0	D26 1-2	a10 0-3	N28 1-1	a09 3-0	S07 0-0	S19 2-5	M27 2-0	M13 0-2	F13 3-1	N14 4-1	S12 2-0		a24 3-0	O17 2-1	S05 1-0	F27 1-1	D12 5-2
16 OLDHAM A	a12 0-0	O17 2-0	J09 3-1	a10 1-1	M27 2-0	N14 4-1	S19 2-0	a17 2-0	S05 1-1	M13 1-0	F27 2-0	J30 2-1	O31 4-0	a27 2-2	D19 6-0		O03 0-1	D25 1-0	F13 2-0	N28 2-1
17 STOCKPORT CO	O24 2-1	a09 3-2	N21 1-0	D12 1-0	J23 0-1	S12 2-1	a03 2-0	O10 1-1	M20 1-0	J02 1-2	a12 0-1	D05 4-2	J01 0-1	N07 3-1	F20 1-0	M08 1-3		M06 1-3	a24 0-0	S26 1-0
18 TOTTENHAM H	S12 4-0	N14 4-0	F13 4-1	S19 2-1	a24 3-0	D12 4-2	O17 4-0	a09 0-1	O03 0-0	a10 1-0	M27 1-1	F27 3-3	N28 2-0	J30 0-0	J02 3-0	D26 3-0	O31 0-0		M13 1-3	S01 3-0
19 W.B.A.	M24 1-1	D26 1-1	a03 5-1	a12 2-0	S26 1-0	J23 0-0	N02 2-2	F20 1-0	N21 2-0	S12 1-1	D25 2-0	a17 1-0	J02 7-0	M20 1-0	O24 2-1	O10 1-0	D19 2-0	N07 3-0		S07 0-2
20 WOLVERHAMPTON W	D19 2-0	F13 2-0	S05 2-2	M27 1-2	N14 1-1	M13 2-1	J09 3-0	D05 5-1	D25 1-1	O31 0-1	O17 4-0	S19 0-0	F27 0-0	D26 3-0	a17 2-1	a03 1-1	J30 2-0	D28 1-0	O03 0-1	

Football League Records Season 1909-10

Top scorers: Div 1, J.Parkinson (Liverpool) 30 goals; Div 2, J.Smith (Hull City) 32 goals.
Chesterfield failed to gain re-election, Lincoln City were elected in their place.

DIVISION 1

	ASTON VILLA	BLACKBURN R	BOLTON W	BRADFORD C	BRISTOL C	BURY	CHELSEA	EVERTON	LIVERPOOL	MANCHESTER U	MIDDLESBROUGH	NEWCASTLE U	NOTTINGHAM F	NOTTS CO	PRESTON N.E.	SHEFFIELD U	SHEFFIELD W	SUNDERLAND	TOTTENHAM H	W ARSENAL
1 ASTON VILLA		J29 4-3	J08 3-1	O23 3-1	N06 1-0	M26 4-1	S11 4-1	O09 3-1	D18 3-1	F26 7-1	M25 4-2	a27 4-0	S25 0-0	D04 1-1	a09 3-0	D27 2-1	M12 5-0	F12 3-2	N20 3-2	S01 5-1
2 BLACKBURN R	S18 3-2		M26 4-2	a09 2-0	S13 5-2	D18 5-1	O16 1-0	a11 2-1	J22 1-1	N20 3-2	M05 1-1	S04 2-0	M12 2-2	M25 2-0	D25 2-2	a23 3-1	D04 0-0	N06 0-0	J01 2-0	O02 7-0
3 BOLTON W	S04 1-2	O09 1-2		F19 1-1	a09 4-2	D04 1-3	F12 5-2	M12 0-1	S06 1-2	N06 2-3	F05 1-1	S07 0-4	F26 2-1	J01 3-4	D18 3-1	J22 1-0	J03 0-2	O23 2-1	a23 0-2	S18 3-0
4 BRADFORD C	M05 1-2	N27 2-0	N13 1-0		S04 3-1	J22 0-0	a02 4-1	a30 2-0	O16 1-2	J01 0-2	D27 4-1	M09 3-3	a16 1-1	O02 2-1	M29 2-0	O30 2-0	M25 2-0	D11 3-1	S18 5-1	M19 0-1
5 BRISTOL C	M19 0-0	D11 2-2	N27 1-0	J08 2-0		S08 1-1	a16 1-0	D25 3-1	O30 0-1	M28 2-1	S18 4-1	a25 0-3	a30 4-0	O16 3-1	F19 2-0	N13 0-2	S11 1-1	D28 2-3	O02 0-0	a02 0-1
6 BURY	N13 0-2	a30 2-1	a16 1-2	S11 3-4	S25 1-2		D11 4-2	J01 2-2	M19 1-2	J08 1-1	O02 2-1	O30 1-2	J03 4-1	M05 1-1	O16 3-1	a02 2-0	M09 3-2	D25 0-1	a20 3-1	N27 1-2
7 CHELSEA	J22 0-0	F26 3-1	O02 3-2	N20 0-3	D04 4-1	a23 2-0		N06 0-1	S04 2-1	M26 1-1	F19 2-1	D27 2-1	O23 0-1	S01 2-2	O27 2-0	S18 2-2	a09 4-1	M12 1-4	D18 2-1	M28 0-1
8 EVERTON	M14 0-0	N13 0-2	O30 3-1	D18 1-1	D27 1-0	M28 3-0	M19 2-2		O02 2-3	a23 3-3	a16 1-1	S06 1-4	a02 0-4	S18 2-0	J22 2-1	O16 1-2	S01 1-1	N27 2-1	S04 4-2	M07 1-0
9 LIVERPOOL	a30 2-0	S11 3-1	D25 3-0	F26 1-0	M12 0-1	N06 2-2	J08 5-1	F12 0-1		O09 3-2	D11 0-0	D04 6-5	a20 7-3	a09 2-1	N20 2-0	M25 0-0	O23 3-1	S25 1-4	M26 2-0	J01 5-1
10 MANCHESTER U	O16 2-0	a02 2-0	M19 5-0	S01 1-0	M25 2-1	S04 2-0	N13 2-0	a06 3-2	F19 3-4		a30 4-1	O02 1-1	N27 2-6	S06 2-1	S18 1-1	M05 1-0	D25 0-3	a16 2-0	J22 5-0	O30 1-0
11 MIDDLESBROUGH	M28 3-2	O23 1-3	S25 1-2	D25 3-7	a20 0-0	F12 0-5	O09 0-1	D04 1-1	a23 2-2	D18 1-2		a09 1-1	N06 2-1	M26 2-0	M12 1-0	S01 0-2	J08 4-0	N20 3-2	F26 4-3	S11 5-2
12 NEWCASTLE U	D11 1-0	J08 4-1	S01 1-0	O09 1-0	O23 3-1	M12 2-2	J01 1-0	S25 1-2	a16 1-3	F12 3-4	N27 2-0		S11 1-2	N20 1-3	J03 5-2	a30 0-0	F26 3-1	a13 1-0	N06 1-0	M25 1-1
13 NOTTINGHAM F	J01 1-4	O30 0-4	O16 2-0	D04 1-1	D18 0-0	N03 3-3	M05 0-0	N20 1-0	S18 1-4	a09 2-0	M19 0-1	J22 0-1		S04 2-1	M25 0-0	O02 2-3	a23 0-6	M26 1-3	D27 2-2	M02 1-1
14 NOTTS CO	a16 2-3	D28 2-2	M28 0-0	F12 3-2	F26 0-2	O23 3-1	D25 2-1	a13 2-3	N27 3-1	S25 3-2	N13 2-1	a02 2-2	J08 4-1		N06 3-1	D11 1-2	O09 0-0	S11 1-1	M12 3-0	O07 5-1
15 PRESTON N.E.	N27 1-0	D27 3-2	a30 1-0	S25 2-2	O09 3-0	F26 2-1	J10 2-0	S11 0-1	a02 2-0	F05 1-0	O30 1-0	N13 4-0	S01 0-1	M19 4-0		a16 1-1	F12 1-0	J08 1-0	N22 4-1	D11 3-4
16 SHEFFIELD U	D25 0-1	S25 3-0	S11 2-2	M12 1-2	M26 4-0	N20 2-0	M07 0-0	F26 3-0	D28 4-2	O23 0-1	J01 2-0	D18 4-0	F12 1-4	O18 2-2	D04 5-1		N06 3-3	O09 3-0	a09 1-1	J08 2-0
17 SHEFFIELD W	O30 3-2	a16 2-1	a02 0-0	M28 2-1	J22 2-0	S18 1-4	N27 4-1	S20 1-3	M05 3-0	D27 4-1	S04 1-5	O16 3-1	D11 4-3	F19 0-0	O02 4-1	M19 1-3		a30 1-0	M14 1-1	N13 1-1
18 SUNDERLAND	O02 1-1	M19 0-0	M05 3-0	a23 3-0	J01 4-0	D27 2-3	O30 4-0	a09 0-1	M28 2-1	D04 3-0	a02 2-2	S18 0-2	N13 2-1	J22 0-3	S04 2-1	M16 1-0	D18 2-0		S01 3-1	O16 6-2
19 TOTTENHAM H	a02 1-1	M29 4-0	D11 1-1	J29 0-0	F12 3-2	O09 1-0	a30 2-1	J08 3-0	N13 1-0	S11 2-2	O16 1-3	M19 0-4	D25 2-2	O30 1-3	M05 2-1	N27 2-1	S25 3-0	M25 5-1		a16 1-1
20 W ARSENAL	a11 1-0	F12 0-1	J29 2-0	N06 0-1	N20 2-2	a09 0-0	S25 3-2	O23 1-0	D27 1-1	M12 0-0	J22 3-0	D25 0-3	O09 0-1	D18 1-2	a23 1-3	S04 0-0	M26 0-1	F26 1-2	D04 1-0	

DIVISION 2

	BARNSLEY	BIRMINGHAM	BLACKPOOL	BRADFORD	BURNLEY	CLAPTON O	DERBY CO	FULHAM	GAINSBOROUGH T	GLOSSOP	GRIMSBY T	HULL C	LEEDS C	LEICESTER F	LINCOLN C	MANCHESTER C	OLDHAM A	STOCKPORT CO	W.B.A.	WOLVERHAMPTON W
1 BARNSLEY		S11 5-1	a30 1-0	O02 4-0	O10 0-0	D11 2-1	D20 5-1	F24 2-1	M10 4-1	J08 3-0	N13 2-1	S02 1-2	M17 1-1	N27 3-1	M28 2-1	a02 1-1	S25 2-1	D27 1-0	a14 2-1	O30 7-1
2 BIRMINGHAM	J22 2-1		N27 1-2	D28 0-1	F28 2-1	a02 1-2	D11 1-3	S18 1-1	O16 5-0	S13 2-2	M05 2-4	a16 0-2	O02 1-2	M19 2-1	N13 1-0	O30 1-1	S04 2-2	a30 3-0	J01 0-1	F19 1-0
3 BLACKPOOL	D18 0-0	a09 2-0		M05 0-0	M25 2-3	O16 2-2	N06 1-1	O04 1-1	J22 0-2	N20 1-1	S18 1-0	M12 1-2	J01 3-1	O02 0-1	F19 3-0	S25 0-0	a23 1-3	M26 2-0	D04 2-1	S04 2-0
4 BRADFORD	F12 2-0	M28 5-0	O23 2-1		M12 3-1	O09 3-1	N20 1-2	F26 3-0	a23 2-0	D18 3-3	F08 6-1	N06 0-1	M26 4-2	S11 1-3	S25 4-0	D25 2-0	M08 1-6	D04 2-4	J08 1-0	a09 2-3
5 BURNLEY	F26 2-0	S25 2-0	D25 5-1	O30 1-0		J01 2-0	J08 1-2	O23 2-0	a02 2-1	a18 0-1	N27 3-1	S06 0-1	M19 3-0	D11 5-2	a30 3-0	a16 3-3	O09 1-2	S11 2-2	F12 2-3	N13 4-2
6 CLAPTON O	a07 4-0	N20 3-0	F26 2-1	F19 1-0	D27 2-1		M12 0-2	D18 0-0	S04 2-0	M26 0-0	J22 0-0	O23 0-0	M28 0-2	a25 3-0	O02 1-2	S18 3-2	D04 1-2	N06 2-0	a09 1-3	O25 1-0
7 DERBY CO	D25 2-1	a23 3-1	M19 2-1	a02 1-2	S04 5-2	O30 1-0		J01 3-1	S01 2-2	D04 2-1	O02 6-0	N13 4-0	J22 1-0	O16 0-1	M05 2-0	M16 3-1	M28 1-1	a09 1-0	D18 2-1	S18 5-0
8 FULHAM	O09 3-0	J29 0-0	S13 0-1	O16 3-1	M05 2-1	a30 0-0	M25 0-0		N13 0-1	S11 2-0	a02 3-2	D25 3-1	O30 5-1	a16 2-0	D11 1-1	N27 1-1	F12 1-1	J08 2-0	S25 0-2	M19 0-0
9 GAINSBOROUGH T	N06 0-0	F26 1-0	S11 3-1	D11 3-1	N20 2-0	J08 0-1	S25 2-4	M26 2-0		O09 1-3	a30 1-1	a20 0-1	a09 2-0	M25 0-1	J01 0-0	O27 1-3	M12 0-2	F12 1-0	O23 3-1	D04 0-2
10 GLOSSOP	S04 3-0	D25 4-1	a02 2-3	a30 3-1	S18 2-0	N13 3-1	a28 1-1	J22 0-1	F19 4-0		O16 3-0	N27 2-1	F05 2-1	O30 1-0	M19 0-1	a06 0-3	D27 6-2	D11 1-0	a26 3-2	O02 2-0
11 GRIMSBY T	a26 7-0	O23 0-2	F15 0-1	S01 0-1	a09 5-3	S11 2-0	F12 1-1	N20 0-2	D18 2-1	F26 4-0		S25 2-3	D04 3-1	M28 0-0	J08 1-2	M25 0-1	N06 0-0	O09 0-1	M12 3-0	a23 1-0
12 HULL C	O11 1-0	D04 7-0	O30 1-2	M19 2-1	M28 3-2	M05 3-0	M26 0-0	D27 3-2	S18 5-1	a09 4-2	J01 5-1		S04 3-1	a14 2-1	O16 0-0	O02 1-2	D18 4-0	N20 1-1	a23 5-1	J22 2-2
13 LEEDS C	O23 0-7	F12 2-1	D27 3-2	N13 2-3	N06 1-0	D25 2-1	S11 2-1	M12 2-2	N27 0-0	S25 1-2	a16 3-1	J08 1-1		a30 1-1	S01 5-0	D11 1-3	F26 3-5	M06 0-2	O09 0-1	a02 1-0
14 LEICESTER F	a09 1-1	N06 3-1	F12 3-2	J22 3-0	a23 1-1	S25 4-0	F26 6-0	D04 2-3	D27 9-1	M12 3-1	D25 3-1	O09 3-1	D18 6-2		J29 4-1	S04 1-3	N20 3-0	O23 1-0	M26 2-1	S01 2-1
15 LINCOLN C	a16 2-1	M26 3-2	O09 2-2	M02 1-1	D18 0-0	F12 4-0	O23 2-3	a23 2-2	D25 4-0	N06 1-2	S04 0 0	F26 1 3	D28 0 0	S18 3 1		J22 0 2	a09 0-2	M12 1-0	S29 0-3	M25 1-0
16 MANCHESTER C	M09 0-0	M12 3-0	S02 1-2	J01 3-1	D04 4-0	a13 2-1	O09 2-1	a09 3-1	M28 3-1	O23 3-3	D27 2-0	F12 3-0	a23 3-0	J08 2-0	S11 6-2		M26 0-2	F26 2-1	N06 3-2	D18 6-0
17 OLDHAM A	M14 5-0	J08 1-1	D11 2-0	S18 1-1	F19 1-0	a16 5-0	a26 4-0	O02 0-1	O30 2-0	J01 1-0	M19 4-1	a30 3-0	O16 2-1	a02 2-1	J03 6-1	N13 1-0		D25 3-0	S11 1-2	M05 3-0
18 STOCKPORT CO	J01 5-0	D18 1-1	N13 2-0	a16 2-1	J22 1-1	M19 3-0	N27 1-1	S04 0-2	O02 3-0	a23 5-0	F19 2-1	a02 1-5	S18 0-0	a06 6-2	O30 1-1	O16 1-2	M25 2-0		S01 0-2	M28 1-1
19 W.B.A.	S18 4-3	D27 3-1	a16 0-3	S04 1-0	O02 1-2	N27 3-0	a30 0-0	M29 3-2	M05 5-0	M28 0-0	O30 4-3	D11 0-2	M07 3-1	N13 1-2	a02 1-1	M19 0-0	J22 1-1	S06 0-1		D25 0-1
20 WOLVERHAMPTON W	M12 1-0	O09 4-2	J08 2-1	N27 0-2	M26 3-1	S13 3-1	J29 2-3	N06 1-1	a16 0-0	F12 3-1	D11 8-1	S11 2-2	N20 5-0	D28 4-1	D27 4-2	a30 3-2	O23 1-0	S25 2-1	O16 3-1	

LEAGUE TABLES

DIVISION 1

	P	W	D	L	F	A	W	D	L	F	A	Pts
Aston Villa	38	17	2	0	62	19	6	5	8	22	23	53
Liverpool	38	13	3	3	47	23	8	3	8	31	34	48
Blackburn R	38	13	6	0	47	17	5	3	11	26	38	45
Newcastle U	38	11	3	5	33	22	8	4	7	37	34	45
Manchester U	38	14	2	3	41	20	5	5	9	28	41	45
Sheffield U	38	10	5	4	42	19	6	5	8	20	22	42
Bradford C	38	12	3	4	38	17	5	5	9	26	30	42
Sunderland	38	12	3	4	40	18	6	2	11	26	33	41
Notts Co	38	10	5	4	41	26	5	5	9	26	33	40
Everton	38	8	6	5	30	28	8	2	9	21	28	40
Sheffield W	38	11	4	4	38	28	4	5	10	22	35	39
Preston NE	38	14	2	3	36	13	1	3	15	16	45	35
Bury	38	8	3	8	35	30	4	6	9	27	36	33
Nottingham F	38	4	7	8	19	34	7	4	8	35	38	33
Tottenham H	38	10	6	3	35	23	1	4	14	18	46	32
Bristol C	38	9	5	5	28	18	3	3	13	17	42	32
Middlesbrough	38	8	4	7	34	36	3	5	11	22	37	31
W Arsenal	38	6	5	8	17	19	5	4	10	20	48	31
Chelsea	38	10	4	5	32	24	1	3	15	15	46	29
Bolton W	38	7	2	10	31	34	2	4	13	13	37	24

DIVISION 2

	P	W	D	L	F	A	W	D	L	F	A	Pts
Manchester C	38	15	2	2	51	17	8	6	5	30	23	54
Oldham A	38	15	2	2	47	9	8	5	6	32	30	53
Hull C	38	13	4	2	52	19	10	3	6	28	27	53
Derby Co	38	15	2	2	46	15	7	7	5	26	32	53
Leicester F	38	15	2	2	60	20	5	2	12	19	38	44
Glossop	38	14	1	4	42	18	4	0	9	22	39	43
Fulham	38	9	7	3	28	13	5	6	8	23	30	41
Wolves	38	14	3	2	51	22	3	3	13	13	41	40
Barnsley	38	15	3	1	48	15	1	4	14	14	44	39
Bradford	38	12	1	6	47	28	5	3	11	17	31	38
WBA	38	8	5	6	30	23	8	0	11	28	33	37
Blackpool	38	7	7	5	24	18	7	1	11	26	34	36
Stockport Co	38	9	6	4	37	20	4	2	13	13	27	34
Burnley	38	12	2	5	43	21	2	4	13	19	40	34
Lincoln C	38	7	6	6	27	24	3	5	11	15	45	31
Clapton O	38	10	4	5	26	15	2	2	15	11	45	30
Leeds C	38	8	4	7	30	33	2	3	14	16	47	27
Gainsboro' T	38	8	3	8	22	21	2	3	14	11	54	26
Grimsby T	38	8	3	8	31	19	1	3	15	19	58	24
Birmingham	38	7	4	8	28	26	1	3	15	14	52	23

Harry Hampton, a centre-forward who terrorized defenders and made his name by charging goalkeepers. Between 1904-05 and 1919-20 he scored 242 League and Cup goals for Aston Villa.

Football League Records Season 1910-11

Top scorers: Div 1, A.Shepherd (Newcastle United) 25 goals; Div 2, R.Whittingham (Chelsea) 31 goals.
Grimsby Town failed to gain re-election, Huddersfield Town were elected in their place.

LEAGUE TABLES

DIVISION 1

	P	W	D	L	F	A	W	D	L	F	A	Pts
Manchester U	38	14	4	1	47	18	8	4	7	25	22	52
Aston Villa	38	15	3	1	50	18	7	4	8	19	23	51
Sunderland	38	10	6	3	44	22	5	9	5	23	26	45
Everton	38	12	3	4	34	17	7	4	8	16	19	45
Bradford C	38	13	1	5	33	16	7	4	8	18	26	45
Sheffield W	38	10	5	4	24	15	7	3	9	23	33	42
Oldham A	38	13	4	2	30	12	3	5	11	14	29	41
Newcastle U	38	8	7	4	37	18	7	3	9	24	25	40
Sheffield U	38	8	3	8	27	21	7	5	7	22	22	38
W Arsenal	38	9	6	4	24	14	4	6	9	17	35	38
Notts Co	38	9	6	4	21	16	5	4	10	16	29	38
Blackburn R	38	12	2	5	40	14	1	9	9	22	40	37
Liverpool	38	11	3	5	38	19	4	4	11	15	34	37
Preston NE	38	8	5	6	25	19	4	6	9	15	30	35
Tottenham H	38	10	5	4	40	23	3	1	15	12	40	32
Middlesbrough	38	9	5	5	31	21	2	5	12	18	42	32
Manchester C	38	7	5	7	26	26	2	8	9	17	32	31
Bury	38	8	9	2	27	18	1	2	16	16	53	29
Bristol C	38	8	4	7	23	21	3	1	15	20	45	27
Nottingham F	38	5	4	10	28	31	4	3	12	27	44	25

DIVISION 2

	P	W	D	L	F	A	W	D	L	F	A	Pts
WBA	38	14	2	3	40	18	8	7	4	27	23	53
Bolton W	38	17	2	0	53	12	4	7	8	16	28	51
Chelsea	38	17	2	0	48	7	3	7	9	23	28	49
Clapton O	38	14	4	1	28	7	5	3	11	16	28	45
Hull C	38	8	10	1	38	21	6	6	7	17	18	44
Derby Co	38	11	5	3	48	24	6	3	10	25	28	42
Blackpool	38	10	5	4	29	15	6	5	8	20	23	42
Burnley	38	9	9	1	31	18	4	6	9	14	27	41
Wolves	38	10	5	4	26	16	5	3	11	25	36	38
Fulham	38	12	3	4	35	15	3	4	12	17	33	37
Leeds C	38	11	4	4	35	18	4	3	12	23	38	37
Bradford	38	12	4	3	44	18	2	5	12	9	37	37
Huddersfield T	38	10	4	5	35	21	3	4	12	22	37	34
Glossop	38	11	4	4	36	21	2	4	13	12	41	34
Leicester F	38	12	3	4	37	19	2	2	15	15	43	33
Birmingham	38	10	4	5	23	18	2	4	13	19	46	32
Stockport Co	38	10	4	5	27	26	1	4	14	20	53	30
Gainsboro' T	38	9	5	5	26	16	0	6	13	11	39	29
Barnsley	38	5	7	7	36	26	2	7	10	16	36	28
Lincoln C	38	5	7	7	16	23	2	3	14	12	49	24

Enoch 'Knocker' West, who was Manchester United's leading scorer when they won the First Division title in 1910-11 but was later banned for life for allegedly helping to 'fix' a game.

DIVISION 1

	ASTON VILLA	BLACKBURN R	BRADFORD C	BRISTOL C	BURY	EVERTON	LIVERPOOL	MANCHESTER C	MANCHESTER U	MIDDLESBROUGH	NEWCASTLE U	NOTTINGHAM F	NOTTS CO	OLDHAM A	PRESTON N.E.	SHEFFIELD U	SHEFFIELD W	SUNDERLAND	TOTTENHAM H	W ARSENAL
1 ASTON VILLA		O01 2-2	J28 4-1	M11 2-0	D26 4-1	M27 2-1	D24 1-1	O15 2-1	a22 4-2	N26 5-0	N12 3-2	F11 3-1	D10 3-1	S03 1-1	a08 0-2	a14 3-0	O29 2-1	J07 2-1	F25 4-0	S17 3-0
2 BLACKBURN R	a24 0-0		O22 3-0	a08 2-0	J21 6-2	a06 0-1	S10 1-2	N12 2-0	D31 1-0	D24 5-1	D10 3-1	M27 4-1	S01 1-1	O29 1-0	J02 0-1	S24 1-2	N26 6-1	O08 0-1	a22 3-0	F18 1-0
3 BRADFORD C	S24 1-2	F28 1-0		N26 3-1	S10 2-2	N12 3-1	D31 1-3	M14 1-0	D27 1-0	a27 1-0	a08 1-0	O29 2-1	a17 0-1	O15 1-2	D24 1-0	J21 0-1	a04 5-2	a11 3-0	D10 3-0	O08 3-0
4 BRISTOL C	N05 1-2	D03 1-0	a01 0-2		O22 2-0	a29 0-1	F18 1-1	D17 2-1	O08 0-1	J21 3-2	D31 1-0	a15 5-1	F04 1-0	D27 3-2	S24 0-0	M04 0-2	D26 2-2	M18 1-1	S10 0-2	N19 0-1
5 BURY	J02 1-0	S17 2-2	J07 0-1	F25 2-1		F11 0-0	D10 3-0	O01 5-2	a08 0-3	N12 4-2	O29 1-1	J28 1-0	N26 0-0	D17 2-2	M25 1-0	a29 1-1	O15 1-1	a14 0-0	M11 2-1	S03 1-1
6 EVERTON	O22 0-1	N19 6-1	M18 0-0	D24 4-3	O08 2-1		D27 0-1	D03 1-0	S24 0-1	D31 2-0	J02 1-5	a14 2-1	J21 5-0	D10 1-0	S10 2-0	F18 1-0	a22 1-1	M04 2-2	S01 2-0	N05 2-0
7 LIVERPOOL	a29 3-1	J07 2-2	S03 1-2	O15 4-0	a15 2-0	O01 0-2		J28 1-1	N26 3-2	M11 3-0	F27 3-0	S17 2-3	M25 2-1	a08 1-0	N12 3-0	D17 2-0	F11 3-0	D26 1-2	O29 1-2	a17 1-1
8 MANCHESTER C	F18 1-1	M18 0-0	N05 1-3	a22 1-2	S01 5-1	a08 2-1	S24 1-2		J21 1-1	a14 2-1	D24 2-0	N19 1-0	S10 0-1	N26 2-0	D31 0-2	O08 0-4	D10 1-2	O22 3-3	J03 2-1	M04 1-1
9 MANCHESTER U	D17 2-0	S03 3-2	J02 1-0	F11 3-1	D03 3-2	J28 2-2	a01 2-0	S17 2-1		O29 1-2	O15 2-0	J07 4-2	N12 0-0	M25 0-0	M11 5-0	a15 1-1	O01 3-2	a29 5-1	M15 3-2	D26 5-0
10 MIDDLESBROUGH	a01 0-1	a29 2-3	D17 3-2	S17 3-0	M18 2-1	S03 1-0	N05 2-2	D26 0-0	M04 2-2		J28 0-2	J02 2-2	O22 4-1	F11 1-2	F18 2-0	N19 3-1	J07 0-1	D03 1-0	O01 2-0	a15 1-1
11 NEWCASTLE U	M18 1-0	a15 2-2	D03 6-1	S03 0-1	M04 5-1	D26 1-0	O22 6-1	a29 3-3	F18 0-1	S24 0-0		D17 4-1	O08 2-0	J07 3-0	J03 1-1	N05 1-1	a14 0-2	N19 1-1	J21 1-1	a01 0-1
12 NOTTINGHAM F	O08 3-1	N05 5-2	M04 0-2	D10 3-3	S24 1-2	N26 1-1	J21 2-0	M25 0-0	S10 2-1	D27 1-1	a05 0-1		D31 0-2	N12 4-1	O06 1-3	F04 1-2	a08 0-1	F18 1-3	D24 1-2	O22 2-3
13 NOTTS CO	a15 1-2	a14 2-0	D26 1-1	O01 2-0	a01 1-0	S17 0-0	N19 1-0	J07 0-1	M18 1-0	a18 1-0	F11 2-2	S03 1-1		M11 1-0	O29 3-3	D03 0-3	J28 2-0	D17 1-1	O15 1-0	a29 0-2
14 OLDHAM A	D31 1-1	M04 2-0	F18 1-0	a14 1-0	a22 0-0	a15 2-0	D03 3-1	a01 1-1	N19 1-3	O08 1-1	S10 0-2	M18 2-0	N05 2-1		O22 2-1	a17 3-0	D24 1-0	J21 2-1	S24 2-0	M06 3-0
15 PRESTON N.E.	D03 0-1	D26 0-0	a29 2-0	J28 4-0	N19 2-0	J07 0-2	M18 2-1	S03 1-1	N05 0-2	O15 1-1	O01 2-1	S01 0-2	M04 2-0	F25 1-1		a01 1-1	S17 1-3	a15 0-2	F11 2-0	D17 4-1
16 SHEFFIELD U	D28 2-1	J28 1-1	S17 0-1	O29 0-4	D24 3-0	O15 0-1	S19 2-0	F11 2-2	D10 2-0	M27 2-1	a03 0-0	O01 0-1	a08 0-2	D26 1-2	N26 5-0		F25 0-1	S03 1-2	N12 3-0	J07 3-2
17 SHEFFIELD W	M04 1-0	a01 1-0	N19 0-1	J02 2-1	F18 1-0	D17 0-2	O08 1-0	a15 4-1	a17 0-0	S10 1-1	D27 0-2	D03 5-2	S24 1-3	a29 2-0	J21 0-0	O22 2-0		N05 1-1	D31 2-1	M18 0-0
18 SUNDERLAND	S10 3-2	F11 2-2	O01 1-1	N12 3-1	F04 4-1	O29 4-0	J02 4-0	F25 4-0	D24 1-2	a08 3-1	S01 2-1	O15 2-2	a22 1-1	S17 2-1	D10 1-1	D31 0-2	M11 1-2		N26 4-0	J28 2-2
19 TOTTENHAM H	N19 1-2	D17 2-2	a15 2-0	J07 3-2	N05 5-0	a17 0-1	M04 1-0	D27 1-1	O22 2-2	F13 6-2	S17 1-2	D26 1-4	F18 3-0	M27 2-0	O08 1-1	M18 2-1	S03 3-1	a01 1-1		D03 3-1
20 W ARSENAL	M15 1-1	O15 4-1	F11 0-0	M25 3-0	D31 3-2	M11 1-0	a14 0-0	O29 0-1	S01 1-2	D10 0-2	N26 1-2	F25 3-2	D24 2-1	O01 0-0	a22 2-0	S10 0-0	N12 1-0	S24 0-0	a08 2-0	

DIVISION 2

	BARNSLEY	BIRMINGHAM	BLACKPOOL	BOLTON W	BRADFORD	BURNLEY	CHELSEA	CLAPTON O	DERBY CO	FULHAM	GAINSBOROUGH T	GLOSSOP	HUDDERSFIELD T	HULL C	LEEDS C	LEICESTER F	LINCOLN C	STOCKPORT CO	W.B.A.	WOLVERHAMPTON W
1 BARNSLEY		F25 2-3	J28 1-2	a17 0-0	M25 7-0	N26 0-1	J07 3-2	S17 1-2	D24 0-2	N12 4-2	a08 2-2	O01 4-0	N17 1-2	M11 0-1	D10 4-0	a14 1-1	F11 2-2	a22 1-1	O29 1-1	S03 2-2
2 BIRMINGHAM	O22 1-0		a01 2-0	a29 2-1	S10 1-0	J21 1-1	M18 2-1	N19 0-1	F18 2-0	D31 1-1	S24 1-1	D03 1-2	D17 2-1	a14 1-0	F04 2-1	M04 1-0	a15 0-1	O08 1-3	D27 1-1	N05 1-3
3 BLACKPOOL	S24 1-0	N26 3-1		O29 1-1	D24 4-1	a14 1-0	F18 0-2	O22 1-1	J21 0-1	a22 1-2	J02 1-1	M11 1-0	M25 1-1	D10 2-0	D31 1-2	M29 2-0	N12 5-1	S10 2-1	a08 0-0	O08 2-0
4 BOLTON W	J02 4-0	D24 5-1	M04 1-0		O08 1-0	O22 1-1	a26 2-0	F18 2-0	a22 2-1	S24 2-0	N05 3-0	M18 4-0	D03 3-1	S10 2-1	N19 3-0	D31 6-2	a01 3-1	S01 2-2	S05 3-1	J21 4-1
5 BRADFORD	N19 2-3	J07 2-2	a29 1-0	F11 1-1		F18 1-1	a15 2-1	D17 3-0	M18 2-1	O01 1-0	O22 5-0	D26 6-0	S03 0-1	J28 2-0	M04 0-2	a01 3-1	J02 6-0	N05 3-2	S17 3-3	D03 1-0
6 BURNLEY	a01 0-0	S17 2-2	D26 1-1	M20 1-3	O15 1-1		D17 1-1	a29 2-0	N19 2-1	F11 1-0	M04 1-1	S05 0-0	J07 2-1	O01 0-0	N05 4-1	D03 2-1	S03 3-1	M18 5-3	J28 2-0	a15 1-1
7 CHELSEA	S10 3-1	N12 2-2	O15 0-0	O01 3-0	D10 3-0	a22 3-0		F11 1-0	D31 3-2	a08 2-0	D24 3-0	M06 2-0	M20 2-0	N26 2-0	a14 4-1	J21 2-0	O29 7-0	D27 2-0	M29 2-1	S24 2-0
8 CLAPTON O	J21 3-0	M25 2-1	F25 2-1	O15 0-0	a22 1-0	D24 0-2	O08 0-0		S10 1-0	D10 1-0	D26 1-0	O29 4-0	N12 2-0	a08 1-1	a17 1-0	S24 3-1	M11 2-0	D31 1-0	N26 0-0	M20 3-1
9 DERBY CO	a29 5-1	O15 1-0	S17 1-1	D17 2-2	N12 4-2	M25 3-0	S03 1-4	J07 3-1		M15 2-2	N26 4-0	J28 2-1	O08 1-1	O29 2-3	a08 2-2	D26 3-0	O01 5-0	D10 4-1	M01 1-3	D27 2-0
10 FULHAM	M18 0-2	S03 3-0	D17 2-1	J28 2-0	F13 4-0	O08 3-0	D03 1-0	a15 1-1	N05 3-1		F18 1-0	a29 2-2	D26 2-1	S17 0-1	O22 2-1	N19 3-1	a17 0-0	M04 6-2	J07 0-1	a01 0-1
11 GAINSBOROUGH T	O26 1-1	J28 1-0	D27 2-0	M11 1-0	F25 1-2	O29 1-2	a29 3-1	a14 3-1	a01 0-0	O15 0-1		S03 3-0	S17 3-1	F11 1-1	M18 1-2	a15 2-0	J07 1-0	F04 0-0	O01 1-1	D17 1-3
12 GLOSSOP	M28 1-1	a08 2-1	N05 3-1	N12 1-2	a14 0-1	J02 1-1	O22 2-1	M04 1-3	S24 2-2	D24 2-1	D31 3-1		N26 5-2	a22 0-0	S10 2-1	O08 1-0	M25 2-0	J21 3-0	D10 0-2	F18 5-1
13 HUDDERSFIELD T	F18 2-0	a22 7-1	F04 2-2	D10 1-1	D31 0-0	S10 0-1	a18 3-1	M18 2-0	F11 0-3	F28 1-2	J21 2-1	a01 1-0		J02 2-0	S24 3-2	O22 1-2	a08 1-1	J14 4-1	D24 0-2	M04 3-1
14 HULL C	N05 5-1	D26 4-1	a15 1-1	J07 1-1	S24 2-2	D27 3-0	a01 1-1	D03 1-2	M04 2-0	J21 0-0	O08 3-2	D17 1-0	a17 2-2		F18 1-1	M18 2-2	a29 2-1	O22 4-1	S03 1-1	N19 2-2
15 LEEDS C	a15 0-0	O01 1-1	S03 1-2	M25 1-0	O29 2-0	M27 0-0	D26 3-3	D27 1-0	D03 3-2	F25 3-1	N12 4 0	J07 0-2	J28 5-2	O15 1-0		D17 2-3	S17 0-1	a01 4-0	F11 3-1	a29 1-0
16 LEICESTER F	D27 1-1	O29 2-0	O01 2-0	S03 5-0	N26 2-0	a08 1-1	S17 1-0	J28 2-1	a17 1-2	M25 3-2	D10 1-0	F11 1-1	F25 2-1	N12 0-2	a22 2-1		O15 2-0	D24 5-1	M11 2-3	J07 2-3
17 LINCOLN C	O08 1-0	D10 0-1	M18 0-1	N26 1-3	S01 0-0	D31 1-0	M04 0-0	N05 0-0	F08 0-2	a14 1-0	S10 0-0	S14 2-2	D27 2-2	D24 1-4	J21 1-1	F18 2-0		S24 2-0	a22 1-2	O22 1-5
18 STOCKPORT CO	D17 2-2	F13 3-1	J07 1-3	F25 0-1	M11 1-0	N12 4-2	J02 2-2	S03 0-3	a15 3-2	O29 1-1	M25 1-0	S17 2-1	O03 1-0	a24 1-1	N26 0-4	a29 1-0	J28 3-2		O15 0-1	a14 1-0
19 W.B.A.	M04 3-3	a17 1-0	D03 0-1	D26 2-0	J21 3-0	S24 2-1	N19 1-3	a01 3-0	O22 1-1	S10 2-1	a18 2-1	a15 3-1	a29 1-0	D31 0-2	O08 2-0	N05 5-1	D17 3-0	F18 4-2		M18 2-1
20 WOLVERHAMPTON W	D31 1-0	M11 3-1	F11 0-3	S17 3-0	a08 0-0	D10 1-0	J28 0-0	O01 1-0	S05 1-2	N26 5-1	a22 1-1	O15 2-0	O29 0-3	M25 0-0	D24 3-1	S10 1-0	a24 2-1	D26 0-0	N12 2-3	

Football League Records Season 1911-12

Top scorers: Div 1, H.Hampton (Aston Villa), G.Holley (Sunderland), D.McLean (Sheffield Wednesday) 25 goals; Div 2, B.Freeman (Burnley) 32 goals.
Lincoln City failed to gain re-election, Grimsby Town were elected in their place.

DIVISION 1

	ASTON VILLA	BLACKBURN R	BOLTON W	BRADFORD C	BURY	EVERTON	LIVERPOOL	MANCHESTER C	MANCHESTER U	MIDDLESBROUGH	NEWCASTLE U	NOTTS CO	OLDHAM A	PRESTON N.E.	SHEFFIELD U	SHEFFIELD W	SUNDERLAND	TOTTENHAM H	W.B.A.	W ARSENAL
1 ASTON VILLA		F17 0-3	a05 0-1	D30 0-0	M02 5-2	S23 3-0	D02 5-0	J20 3-1	M30 6-0	N04 2-1	a20 2-0	M16 5-1	D26 6-1	D09 1-0	D23 1-0	O21 2-3	O07 1-3	N18 2-2	S04 0-3	S09 4-1
2 BLACKBURN R	O14 3-1		N11 2-0	M23 3-1	S02 2-0	D09 2-1	F10 1-0	a06 2-0	S30 2-2	J06 2-1	a27 1-1	S16 0-0	a15 1-0	J01 3-0	O28 1-0	D25 0-0	D23 2-2	J27 0-0	a25 4-1	N25 4-0
3 BOLTON W	J01 3-0	M16 2-0		F14 2-0	M30 1-0	O21 1-2	S04 2-1	F17 2-1	a27 1-1	D02 1-0	S02 0-2	a13 3-0	S16 2-1	J27 3-0	J06 0-3	N18 4-2	N04 3-0	D16 1-0	M02 2-0	O07 2-2
4 BRADFORD C	S02 2-1	N18 1-0	S30 1-0		D02 1-0	M02 1-0	a08 0-2	O21 4-1	D26 0-1	a13 2-1	a09 1-1	D16 2-3	J27 0-0	F10 0-1	S16 1-0	M30 5-1	M16 2-1	a27 3-0	N04 4-1	F17 1-1
5 BURY	O28 1-1	D30 1-2	N25 1-3	a06 2-0		D23 1-2	F24 2-2	a20 1-2	O14 0-1	J27 0-2	M09 2-1	S30 0-1	M23 1-1	S16 0-0	F20 3-1	S09 2-2	D25 0-2	F10 2-1	J01 1-0	D09 3-1
6 EVERTON	J27 1-1	a13 1-3	F28 1-0	O28 1-0	a27 1-1		S16 2-1	N11 1-0	J06 4-0	D26 1-0	S30 2-0	a08 1-1	O16 1-1	M23 1-0	F10 3-2	D16 1-0	D02 1-0	S02 2-2	a22 3-0	M27 1-0
7 LIVERPOOL	a06 1-2	O07 1-2	D25 1-0	J01 1-0	O21 1-1	J20 1-3		S09 2-2	N18 3-2	M02 1-1	D09 0-1	N04 3-0	D23 1-0	N25 0-1	a20 2-0	F17 1-1	a05 2-1	M16 1-2	S23 1-3	D30 4-1
8 MANCHESTER C	S16 2-6	D02 3-0	O14 3-1	M28 4-0	D16 2-0	M16 4-0	J06 2-3		S02 0-0	a27 2-0	J27 1-1	D26 4-0	F10 1-3	M09 0-0	S30 0-0	a13 4-0	M30 2-0	a05 2-1	N18 0-2	O28 3-3
9 MANCHESTER U	N25 3-1	a29 3-1	D23 2-0	D25 0-1	F17 0-0	S09 2-1	M23 1-1	D30 0-0		O21 3-4	a06 0-2	M02 2-0	a20 3-1	N11 0-0	D09 1-0	O07 3-1	S23 2-2	N04 1-2	J20 1-2	J01 2-0
10 MIDDLESBROUGH	M09 1-2	S09 2-1	a06 1-0	D09 1-0	S23 1-1	D25 0-0	O28 3-2	D23 3-1	a17 3-0		N11 1-1	F10 4-0	N25 3-0	S30 4-2	M23 1-1	J20 1-1	D30 3-3	O14 2-0	a05 1-0	F24 0-2
11 NEWCASTLE U	D16 6-2	O21 4-2	D30 5-2	S09 0-2	N04 3-2	S06 2-0	a13 1-1	S23 1-0	D02 2-3	M16 0-1		N18 3-2	a05 1-1	F24 1-0	D26 2-2	M02 0-2	F17 3-1	M30 2-0	O07 0-0	J20 1-2
12 NOTTS CO	M13 2-0	J20 1-3	D09 3-2	O05 0-0	F14 2-0	a05 0-1	M09 0-0	D25 0-1	O28 0-1	O07 2-1	M23 1-4		a06 1-1	O14 1-2	N25 2-0	S23 1-0	S09 3-1	F24 2-2	D30 2-0	D23 3-1
13 OLDHAM A	a08 1-2	N04 0-1	J20 3-1	S23 3-0	N18 2-0	F17 3-0	a27 0-1	O07 4-1	D16 2-2	M30 2-0	D25 2-4	D02 1-2		J06 1-0	S02 2-3	M16 1-0	M02 0-0	a13 2-1	O21 3-1	M09 0-0
14 PRESTON N.E.	a13 4-1	D26 2-2	S23 1-2	O07 2-2	J20 1-0	N18 2-1	M30 2-1	N04 2-1	M16 0-0	a22 0-3	D23 2-1	F17 2-1	S09 0-1		a05 3-0	D30 2-3	a20 0-3	M02 0-1	D02 1-1	O21 0-1
15 SHEFFIELD U	O23 0-1	M02 1-1	S09 0-5	M04 7-3	M16 4-0	O07 2-1	D16 3-1	F26 6-2	a13 6-1	N18 1-1	J01 2-1	M30 1-3	D30 4-0	D28 4-2		N04 1-1	O21 1-2	D02 1-2	F17 1-1	S23 2-1
16 SHEFFIELD W	F24 3-0	a08 1-1	M23 0-1	N25 4-2	M18 2-1	a20 1-3	O14 2-2	D09 3-0	F10 3-0	S16 0-2	O28 1-2	J27 3-0	N11 1-0	S02 0-1	M09 1-1		D26 8-0	S30 4-0	D23 4-1	a06 3-0
17 SUNDERLAND	F10 2-2	S06 3-0	M09 0-1	N11 1-1	a08 1-0	a06 4-0	S30 1-2	N25 1-1	J27 5-0	S02 1-0	O14 1-2	J06 5-0	O28 4-2	D16 3-0	F28 0-0	J01 0-0		S16 1-1	D09 3-2	M23 1-0
18 TOTTENHAM H	M23 2-1	S23 0-2	a20 1-0	D23 2-3	O07 2-1	D30 0-1	N11 2-0	a08 0-2	a09 1-1	F17 2-1	N25 1-2	O21 2-2	D09 4-0	O28 6-2	a06 1-1	S04 3-1	J20 0-0		S09 1-0	D25 5-0
19 W.B.A.	S30 2-2	D16 2-0	O28 0-0	a26 0-0	D26 2-0	N25 1-0	J27 1-0	M23 1-1	S16 1-0	a08 3-1	F10 3-1	S02 2-1	a29 0-0	a09 0-2	O14 0-1	a27 1-5	a13 1-0	M13 2-0		N11 1-1
20 W ARSENAL	J06 2-2	a22 5-1	F10 3-0	O14 2-0	a13 1-0	N04 0-1	S02 2-2	M02 2-0	a05 2-1	D16 3-1	S16 2-0	a27 0-3	S30 1-1	a08 4-1	J27 3-1	D02 0-2	N18 3-0	D26 3-1	M16 0-2	

DIVISION 2

	BARNSLEY	BIRMINGHAM	BLACKPOOL	BRADFORD P.A.	BRISTOL C	BURNLEY	CHELSEA	CLAPTON O	DERBY CO	FULHAM	GAINSBOROUGH T	GLOSSOP	GRIMSBY T	HUDDERSFIELD T	HULL C	LEEDS C	LEICESTER F	NOTTINGHAM F	STOCKPORT CO	WOLVERHAMPTON W
1 BARNSLEY		a08 1-0	S09 1-0	F10 1-0	D25 4-1	S30 1-1	a25 0-2	D23 2-1	a22 0-2	O14 2-2	N25 4-0	a29 1-0	a06 2-2	J01 0-0	S23 1-2	a11 3-4	M23 0-0	D09 1-0	O28 2-1	N11 2-1
2 BIRMINGHAM	S11 1-3		D16 2-1	S02 2-3	N25 0-0	a06 4-0	N11 1-4	M23 4-0	S16 0-4	J06 1-3	F03 2-2	a27 2-0	O28 2-2	a13 1-0	D26 5-1	S30 4-3	O14 4-0	M09 4-2	J27 2-0	F10 3-1
3 BLACKPOOL	J06 0-0	a20 1-0		S16 0-4	D09 1-0	a05 0-0	N25 1-0	a06 1-0	S30 1-0	J27 3-1	M09 0-0	J01 2-0	N11 1-2	D23 3-1	S02 3-2	O14 3-0	O28 1-1	M23 2-0	F10 0-1	a17 1-0
4 BRADFORD	O07 1-0	D30 3-0	F06 0-0		a05 0-1	O14 2-1	D23 1-1	D25 2-1	O28 0-1	M27 0-2	a06 5-0	S23 1-1	D09 4-1	S09 3-1	M20 3-1	N11 1-1	N25 1-1	a20 2-1	M09 1-0	M23 0-2
5 BRISTOL C	D26 0-1	M30 2-1	a13 2-0	a08 1-0		M23 0-3	M09 1-1	N11 1-0	J06 1-1	S02 1-0	O14 2-0	D16 2-0	F24 3-0	D02 3-2	a27 0-0	J27 4-1	F10 0-1	O28 2-2	S16 2-1	S30 0-3
6 BURNLEY	F12 3-0	D02 1-1	D25 1-1	F17 3-1	N18 4-2		O21 2-2	N04 1-0	M16 0-0	M02 5-1	S09 2-0	D30 4-0	S23 1-1	a20 3-0	J20 5-1	S04 4-2	S11 3-0	O07 2-0	M30 4-1	D23 2-1
7 CHELSEA	D16 2-1	M16 0-2	a22 4-1	a27 1-0	N04 2-2	F24 0-2		M02 3-0	S11 1-0	D26 1-0	S30 1-0	D02 1-0	F10 4-1	N18 3-1	a13 1-0	J06 4-2	J27 2-1	O14 2-0	S02 0-0	S16 4-0
8 CLAPTON O	a27 2-0	N18 2-0	D02 2-0	D26 2-0	M16 4-0	M09 1-2	O28 1-4		S02 3-0	a08 4-0	F10 3-0	a13 2-1	O14 1-0	M30 2-1	D16 4-0	S16 2-1	S30 4-1	F24 0-2	J06 4-2	J27 1-0
9 DERBY CO	O21 0-0	F21 0-1	F24 5-1	M02 1-0	S09 3-0	D06 2-0	a08 2-0	D30 5-1		N04 6-1	a20 4-0	O07 5-0	D25 2-1	S23 4-2	F17 2-3	N25 5-2	D09 5-0	a09 1-0	M23 2-0	a06 1-1
10 FULHAM	F17 2-2	S09 2-1	S23 3-0	O21 2-0	D30 2-1	O28 3-4	D26 0-1	a06 0-2	a16 0-0		D09 7-1	a01 0-2	a20 1-3	J20 3-1	O07 0-1	M23 7-2	a06 4-1	D23 2-0	N11 3-1	N25 1-1
11 GAINSBOROUGH T	a10 1-2	O21 0-0	N04 0-0	a24 0-0	F17 2-3	J06 1-0	M20 0-2	O07 0-2	D16 1-1	a13 0-1		M16 1-1	J20 2-3	M02 5-0	O25 0-3	D26 2-1	S02 0-1	S23 1-2	a27 0-0	a05 1-0
12 GLOSSOP	S16 0-2	D23 2-0	D26 1-1	J27 0-0	a20 3-0	S02 1-3	a06 1-2	D09 3-3	F10 3-1	S30 1-1	N11 1-1		M23 5-2	a05 2-3	J06 1-1	F24 2-1	M09 6-0	N25 0-0	O14 1-1	O28 0-1
13 GRIMSBY T	S26 0-0	M02 1-0	M16 1-0	D02 0-0	O21 3-0	J27 1-0	O07 2-1	F17 2-1	D23 0-3	D16 1-0	S16 3-3	a08 0-0		N04 1-2	M30 1-0	J23 1-2	J06 4-0	M21 1-4	D26 2-2	S02 0-0
14 HUDDERSFIELD T	S02 2-1	D09 3-2	a27 4-0	J06 3-1	a06 1-2	D16 1-1	M23 1-3	N25 0-0	J27 0-0	S16 2-0	O28 2-2	D25 3-1	M09 2-0		a09 0-2	F10 1-2	F24 1-2	N11 1-2	S30 2-0	O14 1-1
15 HULL C	J27 0-0	D25 1-0	D30 3-0	S30 6-1	D23 3-0	S16 4-1	D09 1-0	a20 0-2	O14 0-0	F10 2-3	M23 1-1	S09 2-0	N25 1-0	a08 0-1		O28 1-0	N11 4-1	a06 2-1	F24 0-2	M09 3-0
16 LEEDS C	N04 3-2	a05 0-0	F17 1-0	M16 1-2	S23 3-1	D09 1-5	S09 0-0	J20 0-2	M30 0-1	N18 0-2	D25 0-0	O21 2-1	D04 1-2	O07 2-0	M02 0-0		D23 2-1	D30 3-1	a06 1-1	a20 1-1
17 LEICESTER F	N18 0-0	F17 5-2	M02 4-0	M30 3-0	O07 2-0	a08 3-2	S23 2-0	a09 2-0	a13 0-1	D02 2-5	S04 2-0	N04 1-0	S09 0-2	O21 0-2	M16 3-0	a27 2-1		F29 1-1	D16 1-1	D25 1-1
18 NOTTINGHAM F	a13 0-2	N04 0-1	N18 2-1	D16 2-1	M02 2-0	F10 0-1	F17 2-3	O21 3-0	D26 1-3	a27 1-1	J27 2-0	M30 0-1	S30 1-0	M16 3-0	D02 0-0	S02 2-1	S16 4-1		a08 1-2	J06 0-0
19 STOCKPORT CO	M02 1-1	S23 2-0	O07 1-2	N04 1-0	J20 1-0	N25 0-1	D30 0-1	S09 1-1	J01 4-0	M16 2-1	D23 0-3	F17 3-0	a05 3-0	F03 3-1	O21 1-1	a15 3-3	a20 2-3	D25 2-2		D09 1-2
20 WOLVERHAMPTON W	M16 5-0	O07 1-0	O21 3-0	N18 1-1	S04 3-1	a27 2-0	J20 3-1	S23 0-1	D02 0-1	M30 0-0	a08 1-0	M02 1-1	D30 1-2	F17 1-2	N04 8-0	D16 5-0	D26 1-0	S09 1-0	a13 4-0	

LEAGUE TABLES

DIVISION 1

	P	W	D	L	F	A	W	D	L	F	A	Pts
Blackburn R	38	13	6	0	35	10	7	3	9	25	33	49
Everton	38	13	5	1	29	12	7	1	11	17	30	46
Newcastle U	38	10	4	5	37	25	8	4	7	27	25	44
Bolton W	38	14	2	3	35	15	6	1	12	19	28	43
Sheffield W	38	11	3	5	44	17	5	6	8	25	32	41
Aston Villa	38	12	2	5	48	22	5	5	9	28	41	41
Middlesbrough	38	11	6	2	35	17	5	2	12	21	28	40
Sunderland	38	10	6	3	37	14	4	5	10	21	37	39
WBA	38	10	6	3	23	15	5	3	11	20	32	39
W Arsenal	38	12	3	4	38	19	3	5	11	17	40	38
Bradford C	38	12	3	4	31	15	3	5	11	15	35	38
Tottenham H	38	10	4	5	35	20	4	5	10	18	33	37
Manchester U	38	9	5	5	29	19	4	6	9	16	41	37
Sheffield U	38	10	4	5	47	29	3	6	10	16	27	36
Manchester C	38	10	5	4	39	20	3	4	12	17	38	35
Notts Co	38	9	4	6	26	20	5	3	11	20	43	35
Liverpool	38	8	4	7	27	23	4	6	9	22	32	34
Oldham A	38	10	3	6	32	19	2	7	10	14	35	34
Preston NE	38	8	4	7	26	25	5	3	11	14	32	33
Bury	38	6	5	8	23	25	0	4	15	9	34	21

DIVISION 2

	P	W	D	L	F	A	W	D	L	F	A	Pts
Derby Co	38	15	2	2	55	13	8	6	5	19	15	54
Chelsea	38	15	2	2	36	13	9	4	6	28	21	54
Burnley	38	14	5	0	50	14	8	3	8	27	27	52
Clapton O	38	16	0	3	44	14	5	3	11	17	30	45
Wolves	38	12	3	4	41	10	4	7	8	16	23	42
Barnsley	38	10	5	4	28	19	5	7	7	17	23	42
Hull C	38	12	3	4	36	13	5	5	9	18	38	42
Fulham	38	10	3	6	42	24	6	4	9	24	34	39
Grimsby T	38	9	6	4	24	18	6	3	10	24	37	39
Leicester F	38	11	4	4	34	18	4	3	12	15	48	37
Bradford	38	10	5	4	30	16	3	4	12	14	29	35
Birmingham	38	11	3	5	44	29	3	3	13	11	30	34
Bristol C	38	11	4	4	27	17	3	2	14	14	43	34
Blackpool	38	12	4	3	24	12	1	4	14	8	40	34
Nottingham F	38	9	3	7	26	18	4	4	11	20	30	33
Stockport Co	38	8	5	6	31	22	3	6	10	16	32	33
Huddersfield T	38	8	5	6	30	22	5	1	13	20	42	32
Glossop	38	6	8	5	33	23	2	4	13	9	33	28
Leeds C	38	7	6	6	21	22	3	2	14	29	56	28
Gainsboro' T	38	4	6	9	17	22	1	7	11	13	42	23

Cultured England full-back Bob Crompton, skipper of Blackburn Rovers in 1911-12 when they lifted their first League Championship title.

Football League Records
Season 1912-13

Top scorers: Div 1, D.McLean (Sheffield Wednesday) 30 goals; Div 2, B.Freeman (Burnley) 31 goals.
Gainsborough Trinity failed to gain re-election, Lincoln City were elected in their place.

LEAGUE TABLES

DIVISION 1

	P	W	D	L	F	A	W	D	L	F	A	Pts
Sunderland	38	14	2	3	47	17	11	2	6	39	26	54
Aston Villa	38	13	4	2	57	21	6	8	5	29	31	50
Sheffield W	38	12	4	3	44	23	9	3	7	31	32	49
Manchester U	38	13	3	3	41	14	6	5	8	28	29	46
Blackburn R	38	10	5	4	54	21	6	8	5	25	22	45
Manchester C	38	12	3	4	34	15	6	5	8	19	22	44
Derby Co	38	10	2	7	40	29	7	6	6	29	37	42
Bolton W	38	10	6	3	36	20	6	4	9	26	43	42
Oldham A	38	11	7	1	33	12	3	7	9	17	43	42
WBA	38	8	7	4	30	20	5	5	9	27	30	38
Everton	38	8	2	9	28	31	7	5	7	20	23	37
Liverpool	38	12	2	5	40	24	4	3	12	21	47	37
Bradford C	38	10	5	4	33	22	2	6	11	17	38	35
Newcastle U	38	8	5	6	30	23	5	3	11	17	24	34
Sheffield U	38	10	5	4	36	24	4	1	14	20	46	34
Middlesbrough	38	6	9	4	29	22	5	1	13	26	47	32
Tottenham H	38	9	3	7	28	25	3	3	13	17	47	30
Chelsea	38	7	2	10	29	40	4	4	11	22	33	28
Notts Co	38	6	4	9	19	20	1	5	13	9	36	23
W Arsenal	38	1	8	10	11	31	2	4	13	15	43	18

DIVISION 2

	P	W	D	L	F	A	W	D	L	F	A	Pts
Preston NE	38	13	5	1	34	12	6	10	3	22	21	53
Burnley	38	13	4	2	58	23	8	4	7	30	30	50
Birmingham	38	11	6	2	39	18	7	4	8	20	26	46
Barnsley	38	15	3	1	46	18	4	4	11	11	29	45
Huddersfield T	38	13	5	1	49	12	4	4	11	17	28	43
Leeds C	38	12	3	4	45	22	3	7	9	25	42	40
Grimsby T	38	10	8	1	32	11	5	2	12	19	39	40
Lincoln C	38	10	6	3	31	16	5	4	10	19	36	40
Fulham	38	13	5	1	47	16	4	0	15	18	39	39
Wolves	38	10	6	3	34	16	4	4	11	22	38	38
Bury	38	10	6	3	29	14	5	2	12	24	43	38
Hull C	38	12	2	5	42	19	3	4	12	18	37	36
Bradford	38	12	4	3	47	18	2	4	13	13	42	36
Clapton O	38	8	6	5	25	20	2	8	9	9	27	34
Leicester F	38	12	2	5	34	20	1	5	13	16	45	33
Bristol C	38	7	9	3	32	25	2	6	11	14	47	33
Nottingham F	38	9	3	7	35	25	3	5	11	23	34	32
Glossop	38	11	2	6	34	26	1	6	12	15	42	32
Stockport Co	38	8	4	7	32	23	0	6	13	24	55	26
Blackpool	38	8	4	7	22	22	1	4	14	17	47	26

Charlie Buchan scored 27 goals in 36 games as Sunderland won the title in 1912-13. He just missed being part of a double-winning team when Villa beat Sunderland 1-0 in that year's FA Cup Final.

DIVISION 1

	ASTON VILLA	BLACKBURN R	BOLTON W	BRADFORD C	CHELSEA	DERBY CO	EVERTON	LIVERPOOL	MANCHESTER C	MANCHESTER U	MIDDLESBROUGH	NEWCASTLE U	NOTTS CO	OLDHAM A	SHEFFIELD U	SHEFFIELD W	SUNDERLAND	TOTTENHAM H	W.B.A.	W ARSENAL
1 ASTON VILLA		F15 1-1	D07 1-1	S07 3-1	S02 1-0	O19 5-1	J25 1-1	a05 1-3	J04 2-0	N16 4-2	N02 5-1	D21 3-1	M15 1-0	D26 7-1	a28 4-2	O05 10-0	a23 1-1	M01 1-0	S21 2-4	M24 4-1
2 BLACKBURN R	O12 2-2		O26 6-0	D07 5-0	N23 1-1	D28 0-1	D26 1-2	M10 5-1	a19 2-2	F08 0-0	F10 5-2	N09 2-0	S28 2-1	M22 7-1	a07 3-1	M21 0-1	S09 4-0	S14 6-1	D21 2-4	a05 1-1
3 BOLTON W	a12 2-3	M01 1-1		S21 2-0	S07 1-0	N02 1-1	F15 0-0	D14 1-1	J25 2-2	N30 2-1	N16 3-2	S02 1-2	M29 0-0	M21 3-0	J01 4-2	O19 3-0	a26 1-3	M15 2-0	O05 2-1	J04 5-1
4 BRADFORD C	D28 1-1	a12 0-2	J18 4-1		F22 2-2	D14 2-3	M29 4-1	S14 2-0	M15 2-1	M25 1-0	F04 1-2	F08 2-0	M21 1-0	O12 0-0	S28 3-1	N30 0-0	N02 1-5	a26 3-1	N16 1-1	O26 3-1
5 CHELSEA	M21 1-2	M29 1-6	D28 2-3	O19 0-3		N30 3-1	M15 1-3	S09 1-2	M01 2-1	D25 1-4	D14 2-3	J18 1-0	a26 5-2	S28 1-1	S14 4-2	N16 0-4	O05 2-0	a12 1-0	N02 0-2	F15 1-1
6 DERBY CO	M12 0-1	S07 1-1	M08 3-3	a19 4-0	a05 3-1		S18 1-4	O26 4-2	D21 2-0	O12 2-1	S28 0-2	M22 2-1	F08 1-0	N23 1-2	N09 5-1	M24 1-4	F26 0-3	J18 5-0	D25 1-2	D07 4-1
7 EVERTON	S28 0-1	D25 2-1	O12 2-3	N23 2-1	N09 1-0	M21 2-2		F08 0-2	a05 0-0	J18 4-1	D28 1-0	O26 0-6	S14 4-0	a02 2-3	M12 0-1	a26 3-1	D14 0-4	J01 1-2	D07 1-3	M22 3-0
8 LIVERPOOL	N30 2-0	O19 4-1	a19 5-0	J04 2-1	M24 1-2	M01 2-1	O05 0-2		S21 1-2	M29 0-2	M15 4-2	D26 2-1	N16 0-0	S04 2-0	D21 2-2	F15 2-1	a12 2-5	N02 4-1	J25 2-1	S07 3-0
9 MANCHESTER C	S14 1-0	D14 3-1	S28 2-0	N09 1-3	O26 2-0	a26 1-1	N30 1-0	J18 4-1		D28 0-2	M24 3-0	O12 0-1	J02 4-0	M12 2-0	F08 3-0	a12 2-2	N16 1-0	D25 2-2	M29 2-1	M08 0-1
10 MANCHESTER U	M22 4-0	O05 1-1	a05 2-1	J01 2-0	D26 4-2	F15 4-0	S21 2-0	N23 3-1	S07 0-1		M01 2-3	a19 3-0	N02 2-1	D21 0-0	D07 4-0	J25 2-0	M15 1-3	O19 2-0	J04 1-1	M21 2-0
11 MIDDLESBROUGH	a09 1-1	S21 0-0	M22 4-0	D26 1-1	a19 0-3	J25 4-1	S07 0-0	N09 3-4	M21 0-0	O26 3-2		a05 0-0	a02 1-1	D07 2-2	N23 4-1	J04 0-2	F15 0-2	O05 1-1	J01 3-1	D21 2-0
12 NEWCASTLE U	a26 2-3	M15 0-1	S11 2-1	O05 1-1	S21 3-2	N16 2-4	M01 2-0	J01 0-0	F15 0-1	D14 1-3	N30 3-1		a12 0-0	J04 4-1	D25 1-2	N02 1-0	S07 1-1	M29 3-0	O19 1-1	J25 3-1
13 NOTTS CO	N09 1-1	J25 3-1	N23 1-0	M24 1-1	D21 0-0	O05 0-1	J04 0-1	M22 3-0	S02 0-1	M08 1-2	O19 1-3	D07 0-1		a19 2-1	a05 0-1	S21 1-2	M01 2-1	F15 0-1	S07 1-1	D26 2-1
14 OLDHAM A	S09 2-2	J01 0-0	M25 2-3	F15 0-0	J25 3-2	a15 2-2	N02 2-0	F10 3-1	O19 2-1	a26 0-0	a12 1-0	S14 1-0	D14 4-0		D28 2-0	M15 2-0	S21 3-0	N30 4-1	M01 0-0	O05 0-0
15 SHEFFIELD U	D14 3-2	N02 0-0	D26 0-2	J25 3-2	J04 3-3	M15 4-1	O19 4-1	O14 4-1	O05 1-1	a12 2-1	M31 1-0	D30 1-1	N30 2-0	S07 1-1		M01 0-2	M24 1-3	N16 4-0	F15 1-0	S21 1-3
16 SHEFFIELD W	F08 1-1	S02 2-1	F24 2-2	a05 6-0	M22 3-2	J01 3-3	D21 1-2	O12 1-0	D07 1-0	S28 3-3	S14 3-1	a14 1-2	J18 3-1	N09 5-0	O26 1-0		D25 1-2	D28 2-1	a19 3-2	N23 2-0
17 SUNDERLAND	N23 3-1	S18 2-4	D21 2-1	a30 1-0	F08 4-0	S14 0-2	a09 3-1	D07 7-0	M22 1-0	N09 3-1	O12 4-0	D28 2-0	O26 4-0	J18 1-1	M21 1-0	D26 0-2		S28 2-2	a05 3-1	J01 4-1
18 TOTTENHAM H	O26 3-3	J04 0-1	N09 0-1	D21 2-1	D07 1-0	S21 1-2	S02 0-2	M08 1-0	D26 4-0	M31 1-1	F08 5-3	N23 1-0	N04 0-3	a05 1-0	F22 1-0	S07 2-4	J25 1-2		M21 3-1	a19 1-1
19 W.B.A.	J18 2-2	a26 1-1	F08 2-2	M22 1-1	M08 0-1	D26 0-0	a12 0-0	S28 3-1	N23 0-2	S14 1-2	S04 2-0	a09 1-0	D28 2-0	O26 2-3	O12 3-1	D14 1-1	N30 3-1	M24 4-1		N09 2-1
20 W ARSENAL	S16 0-3	N30 0-1	S14 1-2	M01 1-1	O12 0-1	a12 1-2	N16 0-0	D28 1-1	N02 0-4	S02 0-0	a26 1-1	S28 1-1	D25 0-0	F08 0-0	J18 1-3	M29 2-5	O19 1-3	D14 0-3	M15 1-0	

DIVISION 2

	BARNSLEY	BIRMINGHAM	BLACKPOOL	BRADFORD	BRISTOL C	BURNLEY	BURY	CLAPTON O	FULHAM	GLOSSOP	GRIMSBY T	HUDDERSFIELD T	HULL C	LEEDS C	LEICESTER F	LINCOLN C	NOTTINGHAM F	PRESTON N.E.	STOCKPORT CO	WOLVERHAMPTON W
1 BARNSLEY		M25 1-0	F15 5-3	a03 4-0	M21 7-1	N23 1-4	J25 4-3	a19 0-0	O05 2-1	D07 2-1	S21 3-0	S07 2-0	a05 2-1	J04 2-0	M08 1-0	D21 4-0	J01 1-0	M22 1-1	N09 1-1	O26 3-2
2 BIRMINGHAM	D25 3-1		N30 3-2	D28 1-1	N23 3-0	O12 3-0	D26 1-2	M08 1-1	S09 2-1	O26 0-0	a26 2-1	a12 3-2	F22 3-1	D14 2-2	J18 5-1	N09 4-1	M22 2-0	F08 0-1	S28 1-1	S14 0-0
3 BLACKPOOL	O12 0-1	a05 2-0		N27 0-2	M22 1-1	M21 0-2	S14 2-1	F08 2-0	S28 2-0	J18 1-1	S09 2-1	a19 2-1	D28 1-2	J01 0-3	N23 2-1	F22 1-1	M08 2-1	D21 0-1	D07 1-1	N09 1-2
4 BRADFORD	O19 0-0	S07 0-0	M01 4-2		J01 4-1	a05 2-3	O05 3-1	D21 3-0	F15 2-3	a19 5-0	J25 3-0	J04 2-1	D07 2-0	S21 0-1	N09 2-2	D26 3-0	M24 3-1	N23 0-0	M22 4-2	a16 5-1
5 BRISTOL C	M24 3-0	M29 0-3	N16 0-0	S04 0-0		F08 3-3	a26 1-5	O26 1-0	D25 2-1	F22 3-3	D14 2-2	N30 0-0	O12 1-1	a12 1-1	S14 1-0	M08 2-0	N09 1-2	S28 1-1	J18 7-2	D28 3-1
6 BURNLEY	a23 0-1	F15 3-0	D25 4-0	N30 5-1	O05 2-2		M15 3-1	J04 5-0	N16 5-0	S07 2-1	N02 3-2	O19 4-0	S09 0-0	M01 2-2	D14 5-1	S21 3-1	J25 3-5	S16 2-2	a26 3-2	a12 4-2
7 BURY	S28 2-0	J01 3-0	J04 1-1	F08 2-0	D21 0-1	N09 1-1		a05 0-0	J18 1-0	N23 4-1	S07 4-2	D25 0-2	M22 3-0	M24 1-1	F22 2-2	D07 0-3	a19 2-0	M08 0-0	O26 2-0	O12 1-0
8 CLAPTON O	D14 2-2	N02 0-2	O05 1-0	a26 1-0	M01 0-0	S14 2-0	N30 1-2		a12 2-1	S28 1-0	M29 1-3	M15 1-1	J18 2-1	N16 2-0	D25 1-1	F15 1-2	O19 2-2	D28 1-2	S16 4-1	M21 0-0
9 FULHAM	F08 1-1	M24 3-2	J25 4-2	O12 3-1	a07 0-0	M22 4-2	S21 3-1	D07 1-1		a05 2-0	J04 0-1	S16 2-0	N23 2-0	S07 4-0	O26 1-1	a19 3-1	D21 0-0	N09 3-1	M08 7-0	F22 4-2
10 GLOSSOP	a12 1-0	M01 0-2	S21 2-0	F04 4-3	O19 3-1	D28 1-3	M29 1-1	J25 3-0	J02 2-0		N16 2-0	N02 1-0	S14 0-3	M15 2-1	M21 3-0	O05 0-1	F15 4-3	J01 2-3	F01 2-2	a26 1-3
11 GRIMSBY T	J18 1-1	D21 2-2	S03 1-1	S28 3-0	a19 3-0	M11 2-0	D28 4-0	N23 1-2	S14 2-1	M22 0-0		M24 0-0	N09 2-0	M21 3-2	O12 2-0	a05 0-0	D07 0-0	O26 0-0	F22 4-1	F08 2-1
12 HUDDERSFIELD T	D28 2-0	D07 0-0	D14 3-0	S14 2-0	a05 5-0	F26 1-0	S03 4-0	N09 0-0	M25 5-1	M08 6-0	D26 0-2		O26 5-2	a26 1-0	S28 3-0	M22 5-1	N23 1-1	O12 1-1	F08 3-3	M12 2-1
13 HULL C	D19 0-1	O19 1-2	S07 4-1	a12 5-0	F15 3-1	S26 0-0	N16 2-0	S21 2-1	M29 0-1	a17 2-0	M15 5-0	M01 1-3		N02 6-2	a26 2-1	J25 2-0	O05 2-1	M24 2-2	D25 3-2	D14 0-1
14 LEEDS C	S14 2-0	a19 4-0	D26 0-2	J18 2-0	D07 1-1	O26 4-1	M25 4-2	M22 3-1	D28 2-3	N09 4-0	D25 1-2	D21 0-3	M08 1-0		F08 5-1	N23 2-2	a05 1-0	F22 5-1	O12 2-1	S28 2-2
15 LEICESTER F	N02 1-0	S21 1-2	M29 5-1	M15 3-0	J04 3-1	a19 2-3	O19 3-0	M24 1-0	N30 1-0	D26 1-4	F15 1-0	J25 0-0	D21 3-2	O05 1-1		M25 1-0	S07 3-1	D07 0-3	a05 4-1	N16 0-1
16 LINCOLN C	a26 2-0	M15 0-1	O19 1-0	D25 1-1	N02 2-0	J18 1-3	a12 0-1	O12 1-1	M21 3-0	F08 0-0	F01 3-0	N16 3-1	S28 1-1	M29 3-3	S09 3-0		M01 2-1	S14 0-0	D28 3-2	M24 2-1
17 NOTTINGHAM F	O03 2-0	N16 3-1	N02 1-1	M21 1-2	M15 4-1	S28 2-1	D14 1-1	F22 0-0	a26 2-4	O12 3-2	a12 1-2	M29 0-1	F08 5-0	N30 1-2	D28 4-2	O26 1-2		F05 0-2	S14 2-1	D25 2-0
18 PRESTON N.E.	N16 4-0	O05 1-0	a26 2-1	D14 4-2	J25 5-1	a10 1-1	N02 2-0	S07 0-1	M15 1-0	D25 2-0	M01 2-0	F15 2-1	D26 1-0	O19 3-2	a12 1-0	J04 0-0	S21 1-1		S02 1-1	N30 1-1
19 STOCKPORT CO	M15 0-3	J25 0-1	a12 2-0	N16 1-0	S21 0-1	D21 0-1	M01 1-2	J01 2-0	N02 1-0	M24 1-1	O19 1-1	O05 3-1	M21 3-3	F15 6-0	N04 1-2	S07 2-4	J04 2-1	a19 1-1		M29 5-1
20 WOLVERHAMPTON W	M01 3-0	J04 2-2	M15 4-0	N02 0-0	S07 1-1	D07 0-2	F15 3-1	D26 1-1	O19 2-1	D21 3-1	O05 3-0	S21 2-0	a19 0-1	J25 2-2	M22 1-1	S02 2-0	S16 2-3	a05 2-0	N23 1-0	

Football League Records Season 1913-14

Top scorers: Div 1, G.Elliott (Middlesbrough) 32 goals; Div 2, S.Stevens (Hull City), J.Peart (Notts County) 28 goals.

DIVISION 1

	ASTON VILLA	BLACKBURN R	BOLTON W	BRADFORD C	BURNLEY	CHELSEA	DERBY CO	EVERTON	LIVERPOOL	MANCHESTER C	MANCHESTER U	MIDDLESBROUGH	NEWCASTLE U	OLDHAM A	PRESTON N.E.	SHEFFIELD U	SHEFFIELD W	SUNDERLAND	TOTTENHAM H	W.B.A.
1 ASTON VILLA		S13 1-3	F25 1-0	D27 0-1	M21 1-0	O25 1-2	a13 3-2	S27 3-1	D06 2-1	S01 1-1	N08 3-1	a25 1-3	a04 1-3	M18 0-0	N22 3-0	D26 3-0	O11 2-0	J17 5-0	D13 3-3	F07 2-0
2 BLACKBURN R	J03 0-0		a04 3-2	O18 0-0	J01 0-0	D06 3-1	O04 3-1	N08 6-0	S06 6-2	F14 2-1	D20 0-1	S20 6-0	S01 3-0	a18 2-1	D25 5-0	J24 3-2	N22 3-2	M23 3-1	F28 1-1	M21 2-0
3 BOLTON W	O18 3-0	N29 1-0		M28 3-0	S20 0-0	F11 1-1	M14 3-1	D13 0-0	F14 2-1	N15 3-0	J03 6-1	F28 1-1	O04 3-1	S06 6-2	J24 0-3	N01 3-1	S01 0-1	a11 2-1	J01 3-0	M07 1-0
4 BRADFORD C	S06 0-0	F25 0-2	N22 5-1		D20 1-1	a04 0-0	J24 0-0	M07 0-1	a13 1-0	O04 3-2	a18 1-1	J03 2-3	D26 2-0	D06 0-1	S17 0-0	S20 2-1	M21 3-1	O25 0-2	F14 2-1	N08 1-0
5 BURNLEY	N15 4-0	S08 1-2	J17 2-2	a27 2-2		S27 6-1	a11 5-1	a10 2-0	M14 5-2	D13 2-0	O11 1-2	a06 1-2	N01 1-0	F07 2-0	F28 3-4	N29 0-0	S13 3-0	D25 0-1	O18 3-1	D27 0-0
6 CHELSEA	F28 0-3	a11 2-0	a13 2-1	N29 2-1	J24 0-0		N15 2-1	a25 2-0	O18 3-0	M28 1-0	S20 0-2	N01 3-2	F14 0-1	J03 2-1	O04 2-0	M14 2-0	D25 2-1	D13 1-1	S06 1-3	S08 1-1
7 DERBY CO	D25 0-2	F07 2-3	N08 3-3	S27 3-1	D06 3-1	M21 0-1		F21 1-0	S01 1-1	J17 2-4	a04 4-2	S10 2-2	D20 2-0	N22 1-2	a18 0-1	S06 3-5	M11 1-1	O11 1-1	J03 4-0	O25 1-2
8 EVERTON	J24 1-4	M14 0-0	a18 1-1	N01 1-1	S01 1-1	D20 0-0	O18 5-0		S20 1-2	F28 1-0	D26 5-0	O04 2-0	J03 2-0	a13 0-2	S06 2-0	F14 5-0	D06 1-1	N15 1-5	M28 1-1	a04 2-0
9 LIVERPOOL	a11 0-1	D27 3-3	O11 2-1	J01 0-1	N08 1-1	M18 3-0	a10 1-0	J17 1-2		D25 4-2	a15 1-2	D13 2-1	N22 0-0	O25 0-3	M21 3-1	a27 2-1	F07 1-2	S13 1-3	N29 2-1	S27 0-0
10 MANCHESTER C	a10 3-1	O11 1-2	M21 0-1	F07 1-0	a18 4-1	N22 2-1	S20 1-2	O25 1-1	D26 1-0		D06 0-2	S06 1-1	a13 0-1	a04 2-1	D20 1-1	J03 2-1	N08 1-2	M18 3-1	J24 2-1	M25 2-3
11 MANCHESTER U	M14 0-6	a25 0-0	S13 0-1	D13 1-1	F14 0-1	J17 0-1	N29 3-3	D25 0-1	N01 3-0	a11 0-1		N15 0-1	F28 2-2	S27 4-1	O18 3-0	a22 2-1	D27 2-1	S08 3-1	O04 3-1	J01 1-0
12 MIDDLESBROUGH	D20 5-2	J17 3-0	O25 2-3	S13 1-1	N22 2-1	M07 2-0	J01 3-2	F07 2-0	a18 4-0	D27 2-0	F21 3-1		D06 3-0	N08 0-0	a04 4-1	a10 2-3	M18 5-2	S27 3-4	a13 6-0	O11 3-0
13 NEWCASTLE U	N29 2-2	a10 0-0	F07 4-3	D25 0-0	M18 3-1	O11 1-0	a25 1-1	S13 0-1	a01 1-2	J01 0-1	O25 0-1	a11 1-0		F21 0-0	N08 2-0	D13 2-1	S27 3-1	D27 2-1	N15 2-0	J17 3-3
14 OLDHAM A	N01 0-1	D13 1-1	D27 2-0	a11 3-1	O04 1-1	S13 3-2	M28 0-0	J01 2-0	F28 2-2	N29 1-3	J24 2-2	M14 3-0	O18 3-0		F14 1-0	N15 1-2	a14 2-0	a25 2-1	S20 3-0	D25 2-0
15 PRESTON N.E.	a01 3-2	D26 1-5	S27 1-1	a10 2-1	O25 2-1	F07 3-3	D13 2-0	D27 1-0	N15 0-1	a25 2-2	M05 4-2	N29 4-1	M14 4-1	O11 0-1		a11 2-4	J17 5-0	S01 2-2	N01 1-2	S13 0-2
16 SHEFFIELD U	J01 3-0	S27 1-1	a06 2-0	J17 1-1	a04 5-0	N08 3-2	D27 2-2	O11 4-1	D20 0-1	S13 1-3	N22 2-0	D25 3-1	a18 2-0	M21 2-1	D06 2-0		O25 0-1	F07 1-0	S01 1-4	M19 1-1
17 SHEFFIELD W	F14 2-3	M28 3-1	D29 1-1	N15 1-3	J03 2-6	D26 3-0	N01 1-3	a11 2-2	O04 4-1	M14 2-2	S06 1-3	O18 2-0	J24 0-0	S22 1-2	S20 2-1	F28 2-1		N29 2-1	a25 2-0	D13 1-4
18 SUNDERLAND	S20 2-0	N01 2-1	D06 3-2	F28 0-1	D26 1-1	a18 2-0	F14 1-0	M21 5-2	J03 1-2	O18 0-0	a10 2-0	J24 4-2	S06 1-2	D20 2-0	J01 3-1	O04 1-2	a04 0-1		M14 2-0	N22 0-0
19 TOTTENHAM H	a18 0-2	O25 3-3	a10 3-0	O11 0-0	F23 2-0	D27 1-2	S13 1-1	N22 4-1	a04 0-0	S27 3-1	F07 2-1	D26 0-1	M21 0-0	J17 3-1	M07 1-0	S08 2-1	D20 1-1	N08 1-4		D06 3-0
20 W.B.A.	O04 1-0	N15 2-0	D20 1-1	M14 2-1	S06 4-1	a14 3-1	F28 2-1	N29 1-1	J24 0-1	N01 0-0	a13 2-1	F14 2-1	S20 1-1	D26 2-2	J03 1-0	O18 2-1	a18 1-1	M28 2-1	a11 1-1	

DIVISION 2

	BARNSLEY	BIRMINGHAM	BLACKPOOL	BRADFORD P.A.	BRISTOL C	BURY	CLAPTON O	FULHAM	GLOSSOP	GRIMSBY T	HUDDERSFIELD T	HULL C	LEEDS C	LEICESTER F	LINCOLN C	NOTTINGHAM F	NOTTS CO	STOCKPORT CO	WOLVERHAMPTON W	W ARSENAL
1 BARNSLEY		O11 1-1	S13 2-1	N22 1-2	F21 3-0	D26 2-0	M07 2-1	a13 1-0	N08 2-0	F07 3-1	J01 2-1	D20 0-2	O25 1-4	D06 3-0	D27 1-0	J17 6-0	a04 0-1	M21 1-0	a18 2-1	S27 1-0
2 BIRMINGHAM	F14 0-0		M14 0-0	S06 1-2	a18 2-2	O18 1-0	a10 2-0	a11 0-1	D25 6-0	N29 1-2	F28 1-4	O04 1-1	D20 0-2	S20 1-0	N01 2-0	N15 2-0	J03 2-1	S03 3-2	J24 4-1	M28 2-0
3 BLACKPOOL	J03 3-1	N08 2-2		D20 2-1	M21 0-1	S20 0-1	a04 0-0	F14 1-1	a11 1-1	M07 1-1	J24 0-1	S06 2-2	N22 2-2	a10 1-0	O04 2-1	F21 2-1	a13 0-0	a18 2-2	J01 2-0	O25 1-1
4 BRADFORD	M28 1-1	D27 5-1	a25 4-1		S13 4-3	N29 3-1	S27 1-0	O18 1-0	F07 2-1	S10 3-0	a11 2-1	N15 2-0	J17 3-1	N01 3-2	D13 3-0	a10 4-0	F28 0-3	O11 0-2	M14 1-0	D25 2-3
5 BRISTOL C	O18 1-1	D13 1-2	N15 1-0	J03 2-0		F28 2-0	D26 3-0	a25 0-1	S03 4-1	a11 1-0	N01 1-0	F14 2-1	a10 1-1	J24 1-0	M14 4-1	M28 1-0	S20 1-1	S06 5-0	O04 0-0	N29 1-1
6 BURY	D25 4-0	F24 3-1	J17 1-0	a04 0-0	O25 3-1		N08 0-0	J01 1-0	M21 1-0	O11 3-1	D27 2-1	a10 2-0	M07 1-1	a18 1-1	S13 1-0	S27 1-0	D06 3-3	N24 1-0	D20 1-4	F07 1-1
7 CLAPTON O	N01 1-0	a13 2-2	N29 2-0	J24 1-0	D25 5-2	M14 1-0		S06 1-0	J03 5-1	a25 0-0	N15 0-0	F28 3-0	M02 3-1	F14 1-0	M28 5-1	a11 3-1	O04 1-0	S20 1-1	O18 2-2	D13 1-0
8 FULHAM	a10 1-2	D06 1-0	O11 0-0	F21 1-6	D20 3-1	S01 1-1	D27 2-0		J17 2-1	N22 2-2	S13 1-0	a18 0-1	D26 0-1	M21 1-2	S27 4-0	O25 2-0	M07 1-2	F07 2-0	a04 1-0	N08 6-1
9 GLOSSOP	M14 5-1	D26 4-1	D06 1-2	O04 2-1	M10 1-1	N15 2-1	S13 0-3	S20 0-1		a10 3-0	M28 2-3	N01 2-1	D27 1-1	O18 0-2	F10 4-0	D16 3-0	F14 0-1	J24 1-1	F28 1-2	a25 0-2
10 GRIMSBY T	O04 1-1	a04 0-2	N01 2-0	F24 0-0	D06 1-0	F14 1-0	D20 2-0	M28 0-3	a13 3-0		O18 2-1	J24 1-3	a18 0-1	J03 3-0	F28 1-3	M14 3-0	S06 0-0	D25 2-0	S20 1-0	N15 1-1
11 HUDDERSFIELD T	a14 3-1	O25 7-0	S27 1-0	D06 0-1	M07 1-2	S06 1-1	M21 1-0	J03 3-1	N22 2-1	F21 1-2		D25 0-3	N08 1-1	D20 1-2	J17 2-1	F07 1-1	a18 2-1	a04 0-2	S09 0-0	O11 1-2
12 HULL C	a25 0-1	F07 0-0	D27 0-0	M21 1-3	O11 0-1	a13 0-1	O25 2-0	D13 1-1	M07 3-0	S27 2-1	D26 4-1		F21 1-0	a04 0-0	O13 1-1	S13 1-0	N22 2-0	N08 3-0	D06 7-1	J17 1-2
13 LEEDS C	F28 3-0	a25 3-2	M28 2-1	S20 5-1	a13 1-0	N01 2-1	a14 0-0	D25 2-1	S06 3-0	D13 4-1	M14 5-1	O18 1-2		O04 2-1	N15 1-0	N29 8-0	J24 2-4	J03 5-1	F14 5-0	a11 0-0
14 LEICESTER F	a11 0-2	J17 0-0	D25 0-1	M07 2-3	S27 3-0	D13 0-0	O11 1-0	N15 3-0	F21 1-3	S13 2-0	a25 0-1	N29 0-4	F07 5-1		a13 2-0	S11 5-1	N08 0-2	O25 2-5	M28 2-3	D27 1-2
15 LINCOLN C	S06 2-2	M07 1-1	F07 1-2	a18 0-3	N08 2-1	J03 1-0	N22 0-0	J24 0-1	a04 1-5	O25 1-3	S20 3-0	M11 0-0	M21 1-0	D26 3-0		O11 1-0	D20 0-0	D06 0-3	a10 1-0	F21 5-2
16 NOTTINGHAM F	S20 0-2	M21 3-1	O18 3-0	a13 1-0	N22 1-1	J24 1-1	D06 1-1	F28 1-1	a18 1-2	N08 4-1	O04 1-1	J03 1-2	a04 2-1	S03 1-3	F14 2-1		D26 1-0	D20 2-2	S06 1-3	M07 0-0
17 NOTTS CO	N29 3-1	S13 5-1	S24 2-0	O25 2-3	J17 4-0	a11 2-0	F07 3-0	N01 4-0	O11 2-2	D27 4-0	D13 3-0	M28 4-1	S27 4-0	M14 4-1	O02 2-1	D25 2-2		F21 2-1	N15 2-0	J01 1-0
18 STOCKPORT CO	N15 1-1	J01 2-0	D13 0-0	F14 3-1	D27 5-1	M28 3-0	J17 0-1	O04 1-3	S27 1-1	D26 2-2	D01 0-0	M14 2-1	S13 2-1	F28 3-0	a11 2-3	a25 2-1	O18 1-2		N01 0-0	a10 2-0
19 WOLVERHAMPTON W	D13 0-1	S27 1-0	D26 1-0	N08 1-0	F07 0-2	a25 3-0	F21 2-1	N29 1-0	O25 1-0	J17 4-1	a13 2-2	a11 1-0	O11 1-3	N22 2-1	S01 1-0	D27 4-1	M21 4-1	M07 3-1		S13 1-2
20 W ARSENAL	J24 1-0	N22 1-0	F28 2-1	D26 2-0	a04 1-1	O04 0-1	a18 2-2	M14 2-0	D20 2-0	a23 2-0	F14 0-1	S20 0-0	D06 1-0	S06 2-1	O18 3-0	N01 3-2	S15 3-0	a13 4-0	J03 3-1	

LEAGUE TABLES

DIVISION 1

	P	W	D	L	F	A	W	D	L	F	A	Pts
Blackburn R	38	14	4	1	51	15	6	7	6	27	27	51
Aston Villa	38	11	3	5	36	21	8	3	8	29	29	44
Middlesbrough	38	14	2	3	55	20	5	3	11	22	40	43
Oldham A	38	11	5	3	34	16	6	4	9	21	29	43
WBA	38	11	7	1	30	16	4	6	9	16	26	43
Bolton W	38	13	4	2	41	14	3	6	10	24	38	42
Sunderland	38	11	3	5	32	17	6	3	10	31	35	40
Chelsea	38	12	3	4	28	18	4	4	11	18	37	39
Bradford C	38	8	6	5	23	17	4	8	7	17	23	38
Sheffield U	38	11	4	4	36	19	5	1	13	27	41	37
Newcastle U	38	9	6	4	27	18	4	5	10	12	30	37
Burnley	38	10	4	5	43	20	2	8	9	18	33	36
Manchester C	38	9	3	7	28	23	5	5	9	23	30	36
Manchester U	38	8	4	7	27	23	7	2	10	25	39	36
Everton	38	8	7	4	32	18	4	4	11	14	37	35
Liverpool	38	8	4	7	27	25	6	3	10	19	37	35
Tottenham H	38	9	6	4	30	19	3	4	12	20	43	34
Sheffield W	38	8	4	7	34	34	5	4	10	19	36	34
Preston NE	38	9	4	6	39	31	3	2	14	13	38	30
Derby Co	38	6	5	8	34	32	2	6	11	21	39	27

DIVISION 2

	P	W	D	L	F	A	W	D	L	F	A	Pts
Notts Co	38	16	2	1	55	13	7	5	7	22	23	53
Bradford	38	15	1	3	44	20	8	2	9	27	27	49
W Arsenal	38	14	3	2	34	10	6	6	7	20	28	49
Leeds C	38	15	2	2	54	16	5	5	9	22	30	47
Barnsley	38	14	1	4	33	15	5	6	8	18	30	45
Clapton O	38	14	5	0	38	11	2	6	11	9	24	43
Hull C	38	9	5	5	29	13	7	4	8	24	24	41
Bristol C	38	12	5	2	32	10	4	4	11	20	40	41
Wolves	38	14	1	4	33	16	4	4	11	18	36	41
Bury	38	12	6	1	30	14	3	4	12	9	26	40
Fulham	38	10	3	6	31	20	6	3	10	15	23	38
Stockport Co	38	9	6	4	32	18	4	4	11	23	39	36
Huddersfield T	38	8	4	7	28	22	5	4	10	19	31	34
Birmingham	38	10	4	5	31	18	2	6	11	17	42	34
Grimsby T	38	10	4	5	24	15	3	4	12	18	43	34
Blackpool	38	6	10	3	24	19	3	4	12	9	25	32
Glossop	38	8	3	8	32	24	3	3	13	19	43	28
Leicester F	38	7	2	10	29	28	4	2	13	16	33	26
Lincoln C	38	8	5	6	23	23	2	1	16	13	43	26
Nottingham F	38	7	7	5	27	23	0	2	17	10	53	23

Danny Shea joined Blackburn from Southern League West Ham United, for £2,000, and was their leading scorer when they won the title again in 1913-14.

Football League Records Season 1914-15

Top scorers: Div 1, R.Parker (Everton) 35 goals; Div 2, J.Lane (Blackpool) 28 goals.
Woolwich Arsenal dropped 'Woolwich' from their name.

LEAGUE TABLES

DIVISION 1

	P	W	D	L	F	A	W	D	L	F	A	Pts
Everton	38	8	5	6	44	29	11	3	5	32	18	46
Oldham A	38	11	5	3	46	25	6	6	7	24	31	45
Blackburn R	38	11	4	4	51	27	7	3	9	32	34	43
Burnley	38	12	1	6	38	18	6	6	7	23	29	43
Manchester C	38	9	7	3	29	15	6	6	7	20	24	43
Sheffield U	38	11	5	3	28	13	4	8	7	21	28	43
Sheffield W	38	10	7	2	43	23	5	6	8	18	31	43
Sunderland	38	11	3	5	46	30	7	2	10	35	42	41
Bradford	38	11	4	4	40	20	6	3	10	29	45	41
WBA	38	11	5	3	31	9	4	5	10	18	34	40
Bradford C	38	11	7	1	40	18	2	7	10	15	31	40
Middlesbrough	38	10	6	3	42	24	3	6	10	20	50	38
Liverpool	38	11	5	3	45	34	3	4	12	20	41	37
Aston Villa	38	10	5	4	39	32	3	6	10	23	40	37
Newcastle U	38	8	4	7	29	23	3	6	10	17	25	32
Notts Co	38	8	7	4	28	18	1	6	12	13	39	31
Bolton W	38	8	5	6	35	27	3	3	13	33	57	30
Manchester U	38	8	6	5	27	19	1	6	12	19	43	30
Chelsea	38	8	6	5	32	25	0	7	12	19	40	29
Tottenham H	38	7	7	5	30	29	1	5	13	27	61	28

DIVISION 2

	P	W	D	L	F	A	W	D	L	F	A	Pts
Derby Co	38	14	3	2	40	11	9	4	6	31	22	53
Preston NE	38	14	4	1	41	16	6	6	7	20	26	50
Barnsley	38	16	2	1	31	10	6	1	12	20	41	47
Wolves	38	12	4	3	47	13	7	3	9	30	39	45
Arsenal	38	15	1	3	52	13	4	4	11	17	28	43
Birmingham	38	13	3	3	44	13	4	6	9	18	26	43
Hull C	38	12	2	5	36	23	7	3	9	29	31	43
Huddersfield T	38	12	4	3	36	13	5	4	10	25	29	42
Clapton O	38	12	5	2	36	17	4	4	11	14	31	41
Blackpool	38	11	3	5	40	22	6	2	11	18	35	39
Bury	38	11	5	3	39	19	4	3	12	22	37	38
Fulham	38	12	0	7	35	20	3	7	9	18	27	37
Bristol C	38	11	2	6	38	19	4	5	10	24	37	37
Stockport Co	38	12	4	3	33	19	3	3	13	21	41	37
Leeds C	38	9	3	7	40	25	5	1	13	25	39	32
Lincoln C	38	9	4	6	29	23	2	5	12	17	42	31
Grimsby T	38	10	4	5	36	24	1	5	13	12	52	31
Nottingham F	38	9	7	3	32	24	1	2	16	11	53	29
Leicester F	38	6	4	9	31	41	4	0	15	16	47	24
Glossop	38	5	5	9	21	33	1	1	17	10	54	18

In 1914-15, former Glasgow Rangers forward Bobby Parker was the First Division's leading scorer, his 35 goals equalling Everton's club record as the Goodison club lifted the title.

DIVISION 1

	ASTON VILLA	BLACKBURN R	BOLTON W	BRADFORD	BRADFORD C	BURNLEY	CHELSEA	EVERTON	LIVERPOOL	MANCHESTER C	MANCHESTER U	MIDDLESBROUGH	NEWCASTLE U	NOTTS CO	OLDHAM A	SHEFFIELD U	SHEFFIELD W	SUNDERLAND	TOTTENHAM H	W.B.A.
1 ASTON VILLA		a02 2-1	D26 1-7	D05 1-2	F13 0-0	O17 3-3	O03 2-1	F10 1-5	a03 6-2	a21 4-1	D19 3-3	M13 5-0	O31 2-1	S02 2-1	a17 0-0	N14 1-0	J16 0-0	S05 1-3	F27 3-1	S19 2-1
2 BLACKBURN R	D25 1-2		S26 2-2	J02 2-2	M29 2-1	N28 6-0	N14 3-2	M13 2-1	S21 4-2	O03 0-1	J23 3-3	a24 4-0	D12 2-3	F13 5-1	S12 4-1	J01 1-2	F27 1-1	O17 3-1	a10 4-1	O31 2-1
3 BOLTON W	J01 2-2	S07 3-2		a02 3-2	N14 3-5	M13 3-1	a14 3-1	O31 0-0	D25 0-1	S19 2-3	S12 3-0	D12 4-0	a10 0-0	O03 1-2	J02 2-0	a26 0-1	O17 0-3	M10 1-1	N28 4-2	F27 1-1
4 BRADFORD	a10 2-2	S05 1-2	O07 1-2		a28 3-0	O31 2-2	O17 3-0	a14 1-2	D12 1-0	a24 3-1	a05 5-0	M27 2-0	N14 1-0	J16 3-1	D25 1-1	N28 2-0	M17 1-1	S19 2-1	M13 5-1	O03 1-4
5 BRADFORD C	O10 3-0	N21 3-0	M20 4-2	O24 3-2		J02 0-0	S09 2-2	D26 0-1	M10 3-2	a06 0-0	N07 4-2	S26 1-1	J23 1-1	a03 3-1	M24 1-0	F06 1-1	a17 1-0	D05 3-1	S12 2-2	D19 5-0
6 BURNLEY	F22 2-1	a03 3-2	N21 5-0	M06 2-0	S05 0-1		a05 2-0	S07 1-0	O24 3-0	J18 1-2	M20 3-0	F06 4-0	S26 2-0	D05 0-0	N07 2-3	O10 1-2	D19 2-3	a17 2-1	J23 3-1	D25 0-2
7 CHELSEA	F06 3-1	M20 1-3	N07 2-1	M01 0-1	a02 2-0	D28 1-4		D19. 2-0	O10 3-1	D25 0-0	a19 1-3	J23 2-2	S12 0-3	N21 4-1	O24 2-2	S26 1-1	D05 0-0	a03 3-0	J02 1-1	a17 4-1
8 EVERTON	S26 0-0	N07 1-3	M22 5-3	O10 4-1	D25 1-1	a02 0-2	a26 2-2		F06 1-3	D12 4-1	O24 4-2	S12 2-3	J02 3-0	M20 4-0	M17 3-4	J23 0-0	a03 0-1	N21 7-1	J01 1-1	D05 2-1
9 LIVERPOOL	N28 3-6	a05 3-0	S02 4-3	a17 2-1	O17 2-1	F27 3-0	F13 3-3	O03 0-5		M13 3-2	D26 1-1	N14 1-1	M29 2-2	S05 1-1	D19 1-2	a12 2-1	S19 2-1	J16 2-1	O31 7-2	M24 3-1
10 MANCHESTER C	N25 1-0	F06 1-3	J23 2-1	D19 2-3	S01 4-1	S12 1-0	D26 2-1	a17 0-1	D05 1-1		J02 1-1	O24 1-1	O10 1-1	F22 0-0	a05 0-0	N07 0-0	M20 4-0	M06 2-0	S26 2-1	a03 4-0
11 MANCHESTER U	a26 1-0	S19 2-0	J16 4-1	J01 1-2	M13 1-0	N14 0-2	O31 2-2	F27 1-2	a02 2-0	S05 0-0		a10 2-2	N28 1-0	J30 2-2	S02 1-3	D12 1-2	F13 2-0	O03 3-0	M27 1-1	O17 0-0
12 MIDDLESBROUGH	N07 1-1	D19 1-4	a17 0-0	N21 1-3	F03 3-0	O03 1-1	S19 3-0	J16 5-1	M20 3-0	F27 1-0	D05 1-1		O17 1-1	D25 1-0	a03 4-1	M17 2-2	a05 3-1	J01 2-3	F13 7-5	S05 2-0
13 NEWCASTLE U	a28 3-0	a17 2-1	D05 1-2	M20 1-1	S19 1-0	a14 1-2	M17 2-0	S05 0-1	N07 0-0	F13 2-1	a03 2-0	M10 1-2		D19 1-1	N21 1-2	O24 4-3	S09 0-0	D25 2-5	O03 4-0	S02 1-2
14 NOTTS CO	a05 1-1	O10 1-1	M17 0-0	S12 1-2	N28 0-0	a10 0-0	a28 2-0	N14 0-0	J02 3-1	O17 0-2	S26 4-2	D26 5-1	a24 1-0		J23 2-1	a02 3-1	O31 1-2	F27 2-1	D12 1-2	M13 1-1
15 OLDHAM A	D12 3-3	J16 3-2	S05 5-3	D26 6-2	O31 1-0	a20 1-2	F27 0-0	O17 1-1	a24 0-2	J01 0-0	a06 1-0	N28 5-1	M27 1-0	S19 2-0		a10 3-0	O03 5-2	F01 4-5	N14 4-1	M09 1-1
16 SHEFFIELD U	M20 3-0	D26 1-2	D19 3-1	a03 3-2	O03 1-1	F13 1-0	M08 1-1	S19 1-0	N21 2-1	M29 0-0	a17 3-1	O31 0-1	F27 1-0	D28 1-0	D05 3-0		S05 0-1	a05 1-1	O17 1-1	J16 2-0
17 SHEFFIELD W	S12 5-2	O24 1-1	M01 7-0	S26 6-0	D12 3-3	a24 0-0	a10 3-2	N28 1-4	J23 2-1	N14 2-1	O10 1-0	S01 3-1	J01 2-1	M06 0-0	F06 2-2	J02 1-1		N07 1-2	D25 3-2	M27 0-0
18 SUNDERLAND	J02 4-0	F20 5-1	O10 4-3	J23 3-3	a10 1-1	D12 2-1	N28 2-1	a06 0-3	S12 2-2	O31 0-2	F06 1-0	a02 4-1	D26 2-4	O24 3-1	S26 1-2	S02 3-2	M13 3-1		a24 5-0	N14 1-2
19 TOTTENHAM H	O24 0-2	D05 0-4	a03 4-2	N07 3-0	J16 0-0	S19 1-3	S05 1-1	S02 1-3	M06 1-1	M15 2-2	N21 2-0	O10 3-3	a02 0-0	F20 2-0	M20 1-0	a19 1-1	D26 6-1	D19 0-6		S28 2-0
20 W.B.A.	J23 2-0	M06 0-0	O24 3-0	F06 1-0	a24 3-0	D26 3-0	D12 2-0	a10 1-2	S26 4-0	N28 0-1	F20 0-0	J02 1-0	a05 2-0	N07 4-1	O10 0-0	S12 1-1	N21 0-0	M20 1-2	a06 3-2	

DIVISION 2

	ARSENAL	BARNSLEY	BIRMINGHAM	BLACKPOOL	BRISTOL C	BURY	CLAPTON O	DERBY CO	FULHAM	GLOSSOP	GRIMSBY T	HUDDERSFIELD T	HULL C	LEEDS C	LEICESTER F	LINCOLN C	NOTTINGHAM F	PRESTON N.E.	STOCKPORT CO	WOLVERHAMPTON W
1 ARSENAL		a05 1-0	M13 1-0	O17 2-0	N28 3-0	a10 3-1	O10 2-1	F27 1-2	S12 3-0	S01 3-0	N14 6-0	M27 0-3	S26 2-1	F06 2-0	D26 6-0	O31 1-1	a24 7-0	D12 1-2	J23 3-1	J02 5-1
2 BARNSLEY	J01 1-0		M08 2-1	M13 1-2	O03 2-1	F13 2-0	D26 1-0	a02 1-0	a03 2-2	M20 2-0	S19 0-0	J30 1-0	a17 1-0	D19 2-1	O31 1-0	S05 3-1	F27 3-0	O17 2-1	D05 2-0	N21 2-1
3 BIRMINGHAM	N07 3-0	S12 2-0		N28 3-0	a24 1-1	D25 1-0	M06 1-0	M20 0-2	M01 1-0	J23 11-1	a10 3-0	D12 1-0	M24 2-2	O24 6-3	J02 2-0	N21 2-0	D28 3-0	a05 1-1	O10 0-1	S26 1-2
4 BLACKPOOL	F20 0-2	N07 1-1	a14 3-1		J01 2-0	S12 3-4	F06 5-1	M06 2-1	D19 2-2	N21 3-0	a17 5-0	a02 3-2	J02 1-2	J23 1-0	O24 1-2	M20 0-0	O10 3-0	S26 0-2	a05 4-2	D05 1-0
5 BRISTOL C	a03 1-1	F06 3-1	D19 2-3	S02 2-1		J02 1-0	N21 3-0	D05 2-3	O24 0-0	O10 3-1	D26 7-0	a05 0-1	N07 5-2	M20 1-0	S26 1-0	a17 2-1	J23 1-2	S12 4-0	M06 0-2	F20 0-1
6 BURY	D05 3-1	O10 1-2	D26 1-3	J25 2-2	S05 2-1		a03 3-0	a17 2-0	M06 1-0	F20 5-0	a02 2-2	J01 3-1	M20 0-1	N21 0-0	F06 3-1	D14 1-1	S26 4-2	J23 0-0	N07 2-1	O24 4-1
7 CLAPTON O	F13 1-0	D25 4-2	O31 1-1	O03 2-0	M27 2-0	N28 2-2		O17 0-1	J02 2-1	a05 5-2	M13 2-1	N14 3-1	J23 0-3	S26 2-0	a24 2-0	F27 3-1	D12 0-0	a10 1-1	S12 3-0	S01 1-1
8 DERBY CO	O24 4-0	S02 7-0	N14 1-0	O31 5-0	a10 1-0	D12 2-1	F20 0-3		J23 1-1	J02 1-1	M27 1-1	N28 1-0	F06 4-1	O10 1-2	a05 1-0	M13 3-0	D26 1-0	a24 2-0	S26 1-0	S12 3-1
9 FULHAM	J16 0-1	N28 2-0	O03 2-3	a24 0-1	F27 1-2	O31 6-3	S05 4-0	S19 2-0		a10 2-0	F13 2-1	O17 2-3	a06 4-1	S09 1-0	M27 1-0	M29 3-1	N14 2-1	M13 0-2	D26 1-0	D12 0-1
10 GLOSSOP	S08 0-4	N14 0-1	S19 3-3	M27 1-3	F13 2-1	O17 3-0	a02 3-1	S05 1-1	D05 1-0		J30 0-0	O03 2-2	M16 0-5	D25 0-3	M13 2-3	J16 1-2	O31 1-0	F27 0-1	a17 1-1	a03 0-2
11 GRIMSBY T	M20 1-0	J23 2-3	D05 1-0	D12 2-0	D25 2-3	a05 1-0	N07 2-1	N21 1-2	O10 1-1	S26 1-0		a24 0-0	O24 1-1	M06 2-5	S12 1-0	a03 5-1	J02 4-0	S01 2-2	F20 6-1	F06 1-4
12 HUDDERSFIELD T	N21 3-0	S26 1-0	a17 0-0	D26 5-0	a06 5-3	S08 0-1	M20 1-1	a03 0-0	F20 2-2	F06 0-1	D19 3-1		O31 1-0	N07 1-0	S21 3-1	D05 0-1	S12 4-0	J02 3-1	O24 2-1	O10 2-0
13 HULL C	a02 1-0	D12 2-1	O17 0-0	S05 1-3	M13 1-1	N14 3-1	S19 0-1	O03 1-0	a05 2-0	a24 2-0	a29 4-1	a15 0-4		J16 2-6	a10 2-1	M11 6-1	N28 3-1	M27 0-1	S03 1-0	D25 5-1
14 LEEDS C	O03 2-2	a24 0-2	F27 2-0	S19 2-0	N14 1-1	M27 2-1	F03 0-1	F13 3-5	S02 0-1	D26 3-0	O31 5-0	M13 1-0	S12 2-3		D12 7-2	O17 3-1	a10 4-0	N28 0-0	J02 1-3	a06 2-3
15 LEICESTER F	D25 1-4	M06 0-1	S05 1-0	F27 2-2	M25 1-3	O03 1-3	J30 1-1	D28 0-6	N21 0-2	N07 3-2	J16 2-0	S19 1-2	D05 1-1	a17 5-1		S02 2-2	O17 3-1	F13 2-3	a03 5-4	M20 0-3
16 LINCOLN C	M06 1-0	J02 3-0	M27 0-1	N14 0-1	D12 3-1	a24 2-3	O24 1-0	N07 0-0	S26 3-1	S12 2-1	N28 2-1	a10 1-1	O10 0-3	F20 0-1	a02 2-3		a05 2-1	D25 3-1	F06 2-2	J23 2-2
17 NOTTINGHAM F	N18 1-1	O24 2-1	S02 1-1	F13 2-1	S19 0-1	F04 1-1	a17 0-1	D25 2-2	M20 2-2	M06 1-0	S05 4-2	J16 3-2	a03 1-0	D05 3-1	F20 1-3	O01 3-2		O03 1-1	N21 1-1	N07 3-1
18 PRESTON N.E.	a17 3-0	F20 5-2	a02 2-0	J30 1-0	F11 4-1	S19 2-0	D05 2-2	D19 1-3	N07 2-1	O24 1-0	S07 3-0	S05 1-1	N21 2-1	a03 2-0	O10 1-0	D26 0-0	F06 2-2		M20 2-0	M06 5-3
19 STOCKPORT CO	S19 1-1	a10 1-2	F13 3-1	D25 0-2	O31 2-2	M13 1-0	J16 2-0	J30 3-2	a02 0-2	D12 2-1	O17 1-1	F27 2-1	J01 3-0	S05 3-1	N28 3-0	O03 1-0	M27 1-0	N14 2-1		a24 2-2
20 WOLVERHAMPTON W	S05 1-0	M27 4-1	a19 0-0	a10 2-0	O17 2-2	F27 1-1	S07 0-0	J16 0-1	a17 2-0	N28 4-0	O03 0-1	F13 4-1	D26 1-2	a05 5-1	N14 7-0	S19 3-1	M13 5-1	O31 2-0	D19 4-1	

Football League Records Season 1919-20

Top scorers: Div 1, F.Morris (West Bromwich Albion) 37 goals; Div 2, S.Taylor (Huddersfield Town) 35 goals.
Glossop resigned after World War One. Coventry City, Gateshead, West Ham United, Stoke and Rotherham County were elected to League. Arsenal were elected to Division One. Leeds City were expelled after eight games and their fixtures taken over by Port Vale. Leicester Fosse became Leicester City.

DIVISION 1

	ARSENAL	ASTON VILLA	BLACKBURN R	BOLTON W	BRADFORD P.A.	BRADFORD C	BURNLEY	CHELSEA	DERBY CO	EVERTON	LIVERPOOL	MANCHESTER C	MANCHESTER U	MIDDLESBROUGH	NEWCASTLE U	NOTTS CO	OLDHAM A	PRESTON N.E.	SHEFFIELD U	SHEFFIELD W	SUNDERLAND	W.B.A.
1 ARSENAL		J24 0-1	O04 0-1	N08 2-2	m01 3-0	O25 1-2	a10 2-0	D06 1-1	D26 1-0	O18 1-1	S08 1-0	J03 2-2	F21 0-3	M27 2-1	A30 0-1	N22 3-1	F07 3-2	a24 0-0	M13 3-0	D20 3-1	S20 3-2	a05 1-0
2 ASTON VILLA	F11 2-1		M20 1-2	a07 3-6	O04 1-0	F28 3-1	J03 2-2	D25 5-2	S01 2-2	F14 2-2	S20 0-1	a26 0-1	D06 2-0	N01 5-3	a05 4-0	a03 3-1	D20 3-0	O18 2-4	N29 4-0	a17 3-1	S06 0-3	N15 2-4
3 BLACKBURN R	S27 2-2	a15 5-1		D20 2-2	J24 3-3	D11 4-1	S13 2-3	M11 3-1	D06 2-0	N01 3-2	F07 0-2	N15 1-4	a24 5-0	S15 0-2	M13 2-0	J01 1-1	a10 0-1	A30 4-0	m01 4-0	O18 1-0	a02 3-0	J03 1-5
4 BOLTON W	N15 2-2	M13 2-1	D27 2-1		A30 1-2	D13 1-1	S01 1-1	F07 1-2	O04 3-0	N29 0-2	J24 0-3	S20 6-2	a10 3-5	m01 2-1	F21 0-3	J03 1-0	M27 1-0	D25 4-1	a24 1-0	J01 2-0	N01 1-0	O18 1-2
5 BRADFORD	a28 0-0	S27 6-1	F23 5-2	S06 2-0		F11 0-0	N29 0-1	O25 1-0	M20 1-1	S03 0-2	N08 1-2	M22 2-1	a06 1-4	D27 1-1	O11 0-1	F14 0-1	J13 2-0	D13 3-3	D26 1-0	F28 3-0	a17 2-2	a03 0-4
6 BRADFORD C	N01 1-1	M17 3-1	N22 3-1	D06 0-1	J03 0-0		m01 2-1	J24 3-1	S20 3-1	N15 3-3	A30 1-3	a05 1-0	M27 2-1	a24 0-1	F07 1-0	D20 3-4	M13 1-1	S10 2-2	a10 1-2	D25 1-1	O18 2-0	O04 3-0
7 BURNLEY	a03 2-1	J17 0-0	S20 3-1	S10 2-1	N22 2-6	S08 1-1		O04 2-3	F28 2-0	a17 5-0	O25 1-2	F14 2-0	N08 2-1	D25 5-3	a02 1-0	S06 2-1	D13 2-1	D27 1-1	O11 2-2	F17 2-0	M20 2-1	M06 2-2
8 CHELSEA	D13 3-1	a02 2-1	F28 2-1	F14 2-3	N01 4-0	F04 1-0	S27 0-1		a17 0-0	S06 0-1	O11 1-0	a03 1-0	J17 1-0	N29 3-1	S13 0-0	M17 2-0	D26 1-0	N15 4-0	D27 1-0	M20 1-1	S01 2-0	a26 2-0
9 DERBY CO	D25 2-1	S08 1-0	D13 0-0	S27 1-2	M27 0-0	S13 3-0	F21 0-2	a24 5-0		a05 2-1	a10 3-0	N29 0-0	A30 1-1	F07 1-2	m01 1-0	O11 3-1	O25 1-1	M13 2-0	J24 5-1	N08 2-1	J03 3-1	D20 0-4
10 EVERTON	O11 2-3	F07 1-1	O25 3-0	N22 3-3	S08 2-0	N08 4-1	a24 2-2	A30 2-3	a02 4-0		D20 0-0	D26 2-0	M13 0-0	a10 5-2	J24 4-0	D06 1-2	F18 0-2	m01 0-1	M27 3-0	J03 1-1	O04 1-3	S20 2-5
11 LIVERPOOL	S01 2-3	S13 2-1	F14 3-0	F04 2-0	N15 3-3	S06 2-1	N01 0-1	O18 0-1	a03 3-0	D27 3-1		M20 1-0	J01 0-0	D13 1-0	S27 1-1	F28 3-0	a05 2-2	N29 1-2	J17 2-0	M10 1-0	D25 3-2	a17 0-0
12 MANCHESTER C	J17 4-1	m01 2-2	N08 8-2	S13 1-4	M13 4-1	J01 1-0	F07 3-1	a10 1-0	N22 3-1	D25 1-1	M27 2-1		O11 3-3	J24 1-0	a24 0-0	S27 4-1	S08 3-1	M17 1-0	A30 3-3	O25 4-2	D27 1-0	D06 2-3
13 MANCHESTER U	F28 0-1	D13 1-2	a17 1-1	a03 1-1	a02 0-1	M20 0-0	N15 0-1	J03 0-2	S06 0-2	M06 1-0	D26 0-0	O18 1-0		O04 1-1	D20 2-1	a26 0-0	F11 1-1	S20 5-1	N01 3-0	S01 0-0	F14 2-0	F25 1-2
14 MIDDLESBROUGH	M20 1-0	O25 1-4	S03 2-2	S17 1-3	D20 1-2	a17 4-0	J01 4-0	N22 0-0	F14 2-0	a03 1-1	D06 3-2	F18 0-2	S27 1-1		N08 0-1	a05 5-2	O11 1-0	J03 4-1	S13 1-0	S06 3-0	M06 0-2	F28 0-0
15 NEWCASTLE U	S06 3-1	J01 2-0	M06 0-0	F28 0-1	O18 4-0	F14 0-1	D26 0-0	S20 3-0	S24 0-0	F11 3-0	O04 3-0	a17 3-0	D27 2-1	D03 0-0		M20 2-1	J03 0-1	N01 1-0	D13 2-1	a03 1-1	N29 2-3	S03 0-2
16 NOTTS CO	N29 2-2	a10 2-1	D25 5-0	J17 2-2	F07 0-2	D27 5-2	A30 2-0	M13 0-1	O18 2-2	D13 1-1	F26 1-0	O04 4-1	m01 0-2	a02 1-1	M27 0-0		a24 2-1	J24 1-2	O02 2-2	S20 3-1	N15 2-2	N01 2-0
17 OLDHAM A	F14 3-0	D27 0-3	a03 0-0	M20 2-0	S20 2-2	M22 0-1	D06 1-0	J01 1-0	N01 3-0	F28 4-1	a02 1-1	S01 1-3	N22 0-3	O18 1-2	J17 1-0	a17 0-0		O04 4-1	N15 4-0	a26 1-0	M08 2-1	S06 2-1
18 PRESTON N.E.	a17 1-1	O11 3-0	S06 0-0	D26 1-1	D06 0-3	S01 1-5	D20 0-1	N08 3-1	M06 1-1	a26 1-1	N22 2-1	F28 1-1	S13 2-3	J17 3-1	O25 2-3	M04 2-0	S27 2-1		a02 2-0	F14 3-0	a03 5-2	M20 0-1
19 SHEFFIELD U	M06 2-0	N22 1-2	O20 2-0	a17 3-2	D25 2-2	a03 0-0	O18 1-3	D20 3-1	F09 0-0	M20 1-1	J03 3-2	S06 3-1	O25 2-2	S20 5-1	D06 2-1	S01 3-0	N08 1-0	J01 2-1		O04 3-0	F28 3-1	F14 1-0
20 SHEFFIELD W	D27 1-2	a29 0-1	O11 0-0	a05 0-2	a19 0-1	D26 1-0	J24 3-1	a06 0-2	N15 2-0	J17 1-0	M13 2-2	N01 0-0	S08 1-3	A30 0-1	M22 0-1	S13 0-0	m01 1-0	F07 0-1	S27 2-1		D13 0-2	N29 0-3
21 SUNDERLAND	S13 1-1	A30 2-1	a05 2-0	O25 2-0	a24 2-0	O11 2-0	M27 3-0	S10 3-2	J17 2-1	S27 2-3	m01 0-1	D20 2-1	F07 3-0	M13 1-1	N22 2-0	N08 3-1	J24 3-0	a10 1-0	M17 3-2	D06 2-1		J01 4-1
22 W.B.A.	a06 1-0	N10 1-2	J17 5-2	O11 4-1	a10 3-1	S27 4-1	M13 4-1	m01 4-0	D27 3-0	S13 4-3	a24 1-1	D13 2-0	J24 2-1	F21 4-1	S08 3-0	O25 8-0	A30 3-1	M27 4-1	F07 0-2	N22 1-3	D26 4-0	

DIVISION 2

	BARNSLEY	BIRMINGHAM	BLACKPOOL	BRISTOL C	BURY	CLAPTON O	COVENTRY C	FULHAM	GRIMSBY T	HUDDERSFIELD T	HULL C	LEEDS C	LEICESTER C	LINCOLN C	NOTTINGHAM F	PORT VALE	ROTHERHAM CO	SOUTH SHIELDS	STOCKPORT CO	STOKE	TOTTENHAM H	WEST HAM U	WOLVERHAMPTON W
1 BARNSLEY		F14 0-5	a17 1-1	a02 0-0	a05 1-3	J03 2-1	M20 1-0	M06 4-1	F09 0-1	a03 3-3	N08 2-3		F28 0-1	O18 5-3	S20 2-2	D26 1-0	O04 4-0	D06 0-1	O25 0-0	S06 1-2	D20 3-0	S01 7-0	N22 4-1
2 BIRMINGHAM	F07 0-0		O11 4-2	J17 1-0	M27 0-2	a24 2-1	S13 4-1	a06 2-0	D27 4-0	S27 4-2	A30 4-1		D26 0-1	M13 7-0	M10 8-0	a10 3-0	N22 2-2	S10 4-0	J24 1-1	D13 2-1	m01 0-1	O25 0-1	N08 2-0
3 BLACKPOOL	a24 0-2	O18 3-0		D27 0-0	a02 1-0	J24 3-0	N29 2-0	N15 1-1	O04 2-0	D13 0-3	M27 2-1	A30 4-2	N01 3-0	S08 6-0	m01 3-2		J01 5-1	F21 0-3	a10 1-0	S20 3-1	F07 0-1	J03 0-0	M13 1-1
4 BRISTOL C	m01 3-1	J03 1-1	D20 0-0		A30 1-0	F07 1-1	N01 1-0	O04 0-3	D06 3-1	N29 2-1	a10 2-2		a05 0-0	S20 6-0	S08 0-0	J24 1-1	O18 2-1	M13 3-1	a24 1-0	N15 1-2	F25 1-2	D26 0-0	M20 1-1
5 BURY	J01 2-0	M20 1-0	D25 1-2	S06 0-1		N22 3-0	a28 2-2	a17 2-2	M06 1-1	S01 2-0	S27 2-0		a03 1-0	D20 3-0	J17 1-1	D06 2-1	F14 4-1	O25 2-1	S13 0-2	F28 1-0	N08 2-1	F11 1-0	O11 2-0
6 CLAPTON O	J17 2-0	a17 2-1	M18 3-0	F14 1-0	N29 2-1		D27 2-2	S04 0-1	a03 3-0	S06 0-1	a02 2-2		a26 3-0	N01 1-0	D13 1-0	N15 2-1	M06 1-2	S27 4-0	D25 2-1	M20 2-1	O18 0-4	F28 1-0	S13 0-0
7 COVENTRY C	M27 1-0	S20 1-3	N22 0-0	O25 0-0	m01 2-1	D20 0-0		O11 0-1	a06 2-0	N08 0-2	F21 0-1	S11 0-4	O04 1-2	a24 2-0	a10 4-2		J03 1-1	J24 1-1	M13 1-1	D25 3-2	A30 0-5	D06 0-0	F07 1-0
8 FULHAM	M13 1-1	a05 1-2	N08 1-2	O13 1-1	a24 1-0	S15 2-1	O18 0-0		D25 2-1	O25 2-2	F07 1-0		S20 5-0	a10 3-0	M27 1-0	m01 4-0	S29 3-0	A30 1-0	F21 4-1	J03 0-0	D06 1-4	N22 1-2	J24 1-1
9 GRIMSBY T	J24 1-1	D20 0-3	S27 1-1	D13 2-2	M13 1-2	a10 2-0	J01 0-1	a02 0-2		S13 1-0	O25 2-1		J03 1-2	F21 2-2	F07 1-0	M27 2-0	N08 0-1	m01 3-1	A30 0-3	N29 2-0	a24 2-0	O11 0-1	S08 0-1
10 HUDDERSFIELD T	a10 4-1	O04 0-0	D06 1-3	N22 1-0	S09 5-0	A30 2-1	N15 5-0	N01 3-0	S20 3-0		M13 2-0		O18 0-0	m01 4-2	a28 2-1	J03 4-1	D25 7-1	F07 2-2	a12 5-0	a06 3-0	J24 1-1	D20 2-0	a14 2-0
11 HULL C	N15 3-1	S06 0-0	M20 0-1	a03 0-0	O04 4-2	O13 3-1	F28 0-1	F14 2-0	N01 4-1	M18 1-4		S20 1-1	F12 5-1	D06 5-2	O18 2-0		a26 1-0	J17 3-0	N22 4-1	S01 3-0	D26 1-3	a17 1-1	D27 10-3
12 LEEDS C			S06 1-0				S03 3-0				S13 1-2												S27 1-1
13 LEICESTER C	M04 0-0	D25 1-0	O25 2-3	a06 2-1	a10 0-5	m01 1-1	S27 1-0	S13 3-2	J17 2-0	O11 0-4	J24 3-2			M27 4-0	M13 0-0	a24 0-1	D06 1-1	N22 0-0	F07 0-2	D20 3-1	S11 2-4	N08 0-0	A30 1-2
14 LINCOLN C	O11 0-4	M06 2-2	S01 0-3	S13 0-0	D27 2-1	O25 2-1	a17 4-1	a03 0-1	F28 2-0	D31 1-3	D13 2-0		M20 0-3		D25 1-4	N22 0-0	J31 0-0	a05 1-1	N08 2-0	F14 2-1	O04 1-1	S06 1-4	J17 4-0
15 NOTTINGHAM F	S13 0-1	F28 1-2	O03 2-0	S01 1-2	J03 1-0	D06 2-1	a03 2-1	M20 0-3	F14 2-0	a17 1-2	O11 0-2		M06 0-0	D26 2-1		F18 0-1	S06 4-1	N08 0-0	S27 1-1	J28 0-2	N22 1-1	a05 2-1	O25 1-0
16 PORT VALE	D25 0-2	a03 1-3		J28 3-1	D13 2-2	N24 4-2		J01 3-4	M20 2-1	M29 0-0			a17 1-2	N20 1-0	J31 4-1		F28 4-2	N10 1-0	a08 2-0	M06 0-3	O27 0-1	F14 1-0	
17 ROTHERHAM CO	S27 1-0	N29 0-3	a05 1-2	O11 2-2	F07 1-2	M13 3-1	J17 4-3	D27 1-1	N15 3-1	D26 1-3	m01 1-2		D13 1-0	J24 3-0	A30 2-0	F21 2-2		a10 1-0	S08 1-0	N01 1-3	M27 1-1	S13 0-1	a24 2-0
18 SOUTH SHIELDS	D13 0-0	S01 1-0	F28 6-0	M10 0-2	N01 0-0	O04 2-0	J31 1-0	S06 2-0	a26 2-0	F14 1-2	J03 7-1		N29 2-0	a02 2-2	N15 5-2	O18 2-0	a03 6-2		D27 3-2	a17 2-2	S20 0-3	M20 3-0	J01 0-0
19 STOCKPORT CO	N01 1-0	M15 2-1	a03 0-0	a17 2-3	S20 1-1	D26 3-1	M06 1-1	F28 2-1	S06 1-2	M20 1-2	N29 3-1		F14 0-2	N15 3-0	O04 0-0	a02 0-4	S01 4-1	D20 1-0		O18 3-1	J03 1-2	a26 1-0	D13 4-1
20 STOKE	A30 2-0	D06 0-1	S13 2-0	N17 2-0	F21 1-1	M27 2-0	D26 6-1	J17 1-0	N22 3-0	a05 0-1	S08 3-1		D27 3-0	F07 1-3	J24 0-2	M13 0-0	O25 3-0	a24 0-0	O11 2-1		a10 1-3	S27 2-1	m01 3-0
21 TOTTENHAM H	D27 4-0	a26 0-0	F14 2-2	F28 2-0	N15 2-1	O11 2-1	S06 4-1	D13 4-0	a17 3-1	F16 2-0	D25 4-0		S01 4-0	S27 6-1	N29 5-2	N01 2-0	M20 2-0	S13 2-0	J17 2-0	a03 2-0		M22 2-0	a02 4-2
22 WEST HAM U	S08 0-2	N01 1-2	J17 1-0	D25 2-0	J24 1-0	M04 0-1	D13 2-0	N29 0-1	O18 1-0	D27 1-1	a24 2-1		N15 1-0	A30 1-1	a02 5-1	F07 3-1	S20 2-1	M27 1-0	m01 3-0	O04 1-1	M13 2-1		a10 4-0
23 WOLVERHAMPTON W	N29 2-4	N15 0-2	M06 0-3	a19 3-1	O18 0-1	S20 1-2	F14 2-0	F23 2-1	S01 6-1	F28 2-3	D20 4-2	O04 2-4	S06 1-1	J03 4-0	N01 4-0		a17 0-1	D26 0-0	D06 2-2	a26 4-0	a05 1-3	a03 1-1	

LEAGUE TABLES

DIVISION 1

	P	W	D	L	F	A	W	D	L	F	A	Pts
WBA	42	17	1	3	65	21	11	3	7	39	26	60
Burnley	42	13	5	3	43	27	8	4	9	22	32	51
Chelsea	42	15	3	3	33	10	7	2	12	23	41	49
Liverpool	42	12	5	4	35	18	7	5	9	24	26	48
Sunderland	42	17	2	2	45	16	5	2	14	27	43	48
Bolton W	42	11	3	7	35	29	8	6	7	37	36	47
Manchester C	42	14	5	2	52	27	4	4	13	19	35	45
Newcastle U	42	11	5	5	31	13	6	4	11	13	26	43
Aston Villa	42	11	3	7	49	36	7	3	11	26	37	42
Arsenal	42	11	5	5	32	21	4	7	10	24	37	42
Bradford	42	8	6	7	31	26	7	6	8	29	37	42
Manchester U	42	6	8	7	20	17	7	6	8	34	33	40
Middlesbrough	42	10	5	6	35	23	5	5	11	26	42	40
Sheffield U	42	14	5	2	43	20	2	3	16	16	49	40
Bradford C	42	10	6	5	36	25	4	5	12	18	38	39
Everton	42	8	6	7	42	29	4	8	9	27	39	38
Oldham A	42	12	4	5	33	19	3	4	14	16	33	38
Derby Co	42	12	5	4	36	18	1	7	13	11	39	38
Preston NE	42	9	6	6	35	27	5	4	12	22	46	38
Blackburn R	42	11	4	6	48	30	2	7	12	16	47	37
Notts Co	42	9	8	4	39	25	3	4	14	17	49	36
Sheffield W	42	6	4	11	14	23	1	5	15	14	41	23

DIVISION 2

	P	W	D	L	F	A	W	D	L	F	A	Pts
Tottenham H	42	19	2	0	60	11	13	4	4	42	21	70
Huddersfield T	42	16	4	1	58	13	12	4	5	39	25	64
Birmingham	42	14	3	4	54	16	10	5	6	31	18	56
Blackpool	42	13	4	4	40	18	8	6	7	25	29	52
Bury	42	14	4	3	35	15	6	4	11	25	29	48
Fulham	42	11	6	4	36	18	8	3	10	25	32	47
West Ham U	42	14	3	4	34	14	5	6	10	13	26	47
Bristol C	42	9	9	3	30	18	4	8	9	16	25	43
South Shields	42	13	5	3	47	18	2	7	12	11	30	42
Stoke	42	13	3	5	37	15	5	3	13	23	39	42
Hull C	42	13	4	4	53	23	5	2	14	25	49	42
Barnsley	42	9	5	7	41	28	6	5	10	20	27	40
Port Vale	42	11	3	7	35	27	5	5	11	24	35	*40
Leicester C	42	8	6	7	26	29	7	4	10	15	32	40
Clapton O	42	14	3	4	34	17	2	3	16	17	42	38
Stockport Co	42	11	4	6	34	24	3	5	13	18	37	37
Rotherham Co	42	10	4	7	32	27	3	4	14	19	56	34
Nottingham F	42	9	4	8	23	22	2	5	14	20	51	31
Wolves	42	8	4	9	41	32	2	6	13	14	48	30
Coventry C	42	7	7	7	20	26	2	4	15	15	47	29
Lincoln C	42	8	6	7	27	30	1	3	17	17	71	27
Grimsby T	42	8	4	9	23	24	2	1	18	11	51	25

Port Vale replaced Leeds City

West Brom's Fred Morris scored a record 37 goals when the Throstles won the League Championship in 1919-20. That form earned him two England caps.

Football League Records

Top scorers: Div 1, J.Smith (Bolton Wanderers) 38 goals; Div 2, S.Puddefoot (West Ham United) 29 goals; Div 3, J.Connor (Crystal Palace), E.Simms (Luton Town), G.Whitworth (Northampton Town) 28 goals.

Lincoln City failed to gain re-election. Cardiff City and Leeds United were elected to Division Two. Grimsby Town together with the clubs from Division One of the Southern League formed the new Division Three.

Tommy Browell joined Manchester City from Everton for £1,780 and scored 31 goals as City finished First Division runners-up in 1920-21.

Joe Lane joined Birmingham from Blackpool, for a club record fee of £3,600, and scored 15 goals as the Blues were promoted to Division One.

DIVISION 1

	ARSENAL	ASTON VILLA	BLACKBURN R	BOLTON W	BRADFORD	BRADFORD C	BURNLEY	CHELSEA	DERBY CO	EVERTON	HUDDERSFIELD T	LIVERPOOL	MANCHESTER C	MANCHESTER U	MIDDLESBROUGH	NEWCASTLE U	OLDHAM A	PRESTON N.E.	SHEFFIELD U	SUNDERLAND	TOTTENHAM H	W.B.A.
1 ARSENAL		S04 0-1	N13 2-0	O09 0-0	a09 2-1	J01 1-2	M19 1-1	D11 1-1	O30 2-0	D27 1-1	N27 2-0	m02 0-0	S11 2-1	A30 2-0	S25 2-2	a23 1-1	F19 2-2	a25 2-1	M26 2-6	J29 1-2	J22 3-2	M28 2-1
2 ASTON VILLA	A28 5-0		a16 3-0	m07 2-0	N20 4-1	F26 1-2	F09 0-0	M28 3-0	a30 1-0	J15 1-3	M12 0-0	J01 0-2	S06 3-1	D25 3-4	a02 0-1	D11 0-0	S25 3-0	O09 1-0	O23 4-0	F12 1-5	S11 4-2	N06 0-0
3 BLACKBURN R	N06 2-2	a09 0-1		N20 2-2	M05 1-0	M25 2-3	J22 1-3	m02 0-0	D04 2-0	S25 0-0	F10 1-2	M26 1-1	O23 0-2	a23 2-0	D18 3-2	M19 3-3	S20 5-1	D25 2-2	F19 1-1	S11 2-0	S04 1-1	O09 5-1
4 BOLTON W	O16 1-1	S15 5-0	N27 2-1		M26 2-0	F05 1-1	M05 1-1	S06 3-1	N13 1-0	M25 4-2	D11 3-1	a23 1-0	S25 3-0	S04 1-1	O30 6-2	a09 3-1	J22 1-1	a04 3-0	M19 2-2	D25 6-2	J01 1-0	S11 3-0
5 BRADFORD	a16 0-1	N27 4-0	F26 1-1	a02 2-1		S25 1-2	O09 1-3	J01 0-2	M12 2-1	A28 3-3	J15 1-1	N13 1-3	a30 1-2	D11 2-4	F12 3-0	O30 0-2	D27 2-1	M28 1-3	S11 2-0	S08 1-1	F05 1-1	m07 0-3
6 BRADFORD C	D18 3-1	M07 3-0	M29 3-4	F16 2-2	O02 2-1		S04 2-0	M26 1-1	D25 2-2	N06 2-2	S18 0-2	F19 0-0	D04 1-2	M19 1-1	O16 0-1	J22 1-1	a23 1-3	m02 6-2	A30 4-0	O23 2-2	a09 1-0	F09 1-1
7 BURNLEY	M12 1-0	F05 7-1	J15 4-1	F26 3-1	O16 1-0	A28 1-4		S25 4-0	F12 2-1	a30 1-1	S06 3-0	D11 1-0	a02 2-1	M25 1-0	S11 2-1	N13 3-1	N27 7-1	D18 2-0	D25 6-0	m07 2-2	O30 2-0	a16 1-1
8 CHELSEA	D04 1-2	M29 5-1	m07 1-2	S01 1-0	D18 4-1	a02 3-1	O02 1-1		S04 1-1	F26 0-1	a16 1-1	D25 1-1	J15 2-1	S18 1-2	a30 1-1	F05 2-0	O23 1-1	N06 1-1	N20 2-1	M12 3-1	O16 0-4	F12 3-0
9 DERBY CO	O23 1-1	a23 2-3	D11 0-1	N06 0-0	M19 1-0	D27 1-1	F23 0-0	A28 0-0		S11 2-4	J01 2-1	a09 0-0	O09 3-0	m02 1-1	N27 0-1	M26 0-1	F05 3-3	J22 1-1	M05 1-1	M28 0-1	A30 2-2	S25 1-1
10 EVERTON	D25 2-4	J22 1-1	O02 2-1	M28 2-3	S04 1-1	N13 2-2	a23 1-1	a06 5-1	S18 3-1		O16 0-0	O30 0-3	F05 3-0	M09 2-0	D11 2-1	S01 3-1	M26 5-2	a09 0-1	S22 3-0	N20 1-1	a27 0-0	J01 2-2
11 HUDDERSFIELD T	N20 0-4	M19 1-0	F05 0-0	D04 0-0	J22 0-0	S11 1-0	A30 1-0	a09 2-0	D18 2-0	O09 0-1		M05 1-2	N06 0-1	M26 5-2	D27 0-1	F23 1-3	m02 3-1	S04 1-0	M29 1-0	S25 0-0	a25 2-0	O23 5-1
12 LIVERPOOL	m07 3-0	D18 4-1	a02 2-0	a30 2-3	N06 0-1	F12 2-1	D04 0-0	D27 2-1	a16 1-1	O23 1-0	F26 4-1		A28 4-2	F09 2-0	M12 0-0	N27 0-1	S11 5-2	S25 6-0	O09 2-2	J15 0-0	M25 1-1	S06 0-0
13 MANCHESTER C	S18 3-1	A30 3-1	O30 0-0	O02 3-1	a23 1-0	D11 1-0	M26 3-0	J22 1-0	O16 0-0	F23 2-0	N13 3-2	S04 3-2		N27 3-0	M25 2-1	m02 3-1	M05 3-1	a20 5-1	a09 2-1	J01 3-1	M09 2-0	D25 4-0
14 MANCHESTER U	S06 1-1	D27 1-3	a30 0-1	A28 2-3	D04 5-1	M12 1-1	M28 0-3	S11 3-1	m07 3-0	F12 1-2	a02 2-0	F05 1-1	N20 1-1		a16 0-1	D18 2-0	O09 4-1	O23 1-0	N06 2-1	F26 3-0	S25 0-1	J15 1-4
15 MIDDLESBROUGH	O02 2-1	M26 1-4	J01 1-1	O23 4-1	F19 2-1	O09 2-1	S18 0-0	a23 0-0	N20 1-0	D04 3-1	D25 2-0	M19 0-1	M28 3-1	a09 2-4		M05 0-0	A28 1-2	A30 0-0	J22 2-2	N06 2-0	m02 1-0	J29 0-1
16 NEWCASTLE U	a30 1-0	D04 2-1	M12 1-2	a16 1-0	O23 2-1	J15 4-0	N06 1-2	F09 1-0	a02 0-1	S08 2-0	F12 1-0	N20 2-0	m07 1-1	J01 6-3	F26 2-0		M25 1-2	S11 4-2	S25 3-0	O09 6-1	D25 1-1	A28 1-1
17 OLDHAM A	F12 1-1	O02 1-1	A30 1-0	J15 0-0	D25 1-0	a30 2-0	N20 2-2	O30 1-2	F14 2-1	a02 0-1	m07 1-2	S18 0-0	F26 2-0	O16 2-2	S04 3-3	M28 0-0		D04 0-2	D18 0-0	a16 2-1	N13 2-5	M12 0-3
18 PRESTON N.E.	F26 0-1	O16 6-1	D27 4-2	F12 1-2	M25 3-3	m07 1-1	J01 0-3	N13 0-1	J15 2-1	a16 1-0	A28 0-1	O02 2-3	M12 0-1	O30 0-0	S06 2-0	S18 3-2	D11 4-0		F07 2-0	a30 1-1	N27 4-1	a02 2-1
19 SHEFFIELD U	a02 1-1	O30 0-0	F12 1-1	M12 2-2	S18 2-0	S06 4-1	D27 1-1	N27 0-1	F26 0-1	O04 2-0	D29 1-1	O16 0-1	a16 1-1	N13 0-0	J15 1-1	O02 0-3	J01 3-0	F05 1-0		A28 1-1	D11 1-1	a30 0-2
20 SUNDERLAND	F05 5-1	F23 0-1	S18 2-0	D27 0-0	S01 5-1	O30 0-0	m02 1-0	M19 1-0	M25 3-0	N27 0-2	O02 2-1	J22 2-1	D18 1-0	M05 2-3	N13 1-2	O16 0-2	a09 1-1	a23 2-2	S04 3-1		M26 0-1	D11 3-0
21 TOTTENHAM H	J15 2-1	S18 1-2	A28 1-2	D18 5-2	F03 2-0	a16 2-0	O23 1-2	O09 5-0	S06 2-0	M12 2-0	a30 1-0	M28 1-0	F12 2-0	O02 4-1	m07 2-2	D27 2-0	N06 5-1	N20 1-2	D04 4-1	a02 0-0		F26 1-0
22 W.B.A.	M29 3-4	N13 2-1	O16 1-1	S18 2-1	m02 0-1	N27 2-0	a09 2-0	M14 1-1	O02 3-0	D18 1-2	O30 3-0	S01 1-1	D27 2-2	J22 0-2	F05 0-1	S04 0-0	M19 0-0	M26 0-3	a23 1-1	D04 4-1	F23 3-1	

DIVISION 2

	BARNSLEY	BIRMINGHAM	BLACKPOOL	BRISTOL C	BURY	CARDIFF C	CLAPTON O	COVENTRY C	FULHAM	HULL C	LEEDS U	LEICESTER C	NOTTINGHAM F	NOTTS CO	PORT VALE	ROTHERHAM CO	SHEFFIELD W	SOUTH SHIELDS	STOCKPORT CO	STOKE	WEST HAM U	WOLVERHAMPTON W
1 BARNSLEY		a02 1-1	D27 0-1	D11 1-1	N27 5-0	F12 0-2	N13 1-0	a30 2-2	F26 3-1	O02 0-0	a16 1-1	J15 2-1	J01 0-0	S06 2-2	M28 3-0	J29 2-1	A28 0-0	S18 1-1	O30 2-0	m07 1-0	M12 1-1	O16 3-2
2 BIRMINGHAM	M26 1-3		O16 3-0	M19 0-0	M05 4-0	S18 1-1	F19 0-0	D04 3-2	M29 1-0	A30 5-1	D18 1-0	O02 5-0	a09 3-0	F05 2-1	m02 4-0	a23 3-2	O30 4-0	S04 1-1	J22 5-0	N27 3-0	D27 2-1	N13 4-1
3 BLACKPOOL	D25 1-0	O09 3-0		A30 1-2	S04 0-1	N20 2-4	S13 2-2	S11 4-0	N06 1-0	M26 1-2	S25 1-0	D04 2-0	J22 1-0	D18 0-2	M05 1-0	F19 0-1	F05 1-1	M19 3-2	a23 1-1	M25 3-1	O23 1-0	a09 3-0
4 BRISTOL C	D04 1-0	M12 0-1	S08 1-1		N13 1-0	J15 0-0	O30 2-0	a16 2-0	F12 2-0	S18 2-1	a02 0-0	J29 1-0	N20 1-0	A28 0-1	D27 3-0	J01 2-4	m07 0-1	M28 4-2	O16 5-1	a30 5-0	F26 1-0	O02 2-0
5 BURY	N20 0-0	F26 0-1	A28 2-2	N06 2-0		J01 3-1	O09 0-1	a02 2-0	J15 1-1	M25 0-0	M12 1-1	S08 4-0	O23 2-2	m07 0-1	J29 1-0	D04 1-0	a30 1-1	D25 1-0	O02 1-1	a16 3-0	F12 1-0	S18 3-1
6 CARDIFF C	M09 3-2	S11 2-1	N27 0-0	J22 1-0	D18 2-1		A30 0-0	D27 0-1	O16 3-0	a23 0-0	M28 1-0	N13 2-0	a04 3-0	O30 1-1	M26 1-2	a11 1-0	D11 1-0	a09 1-0	S04 3-0	F05 0-1	S25 0-0	m02 2-0
7 CLAPTON O	N25 3-2	F12 1-1	m07 0-0	O23 0-0	O16 1-0	S06 2-0		M12 0-0	D04 3-0	D25 1-1	F26 1-0	A28 2-0	O02 2-1	a30 3-0	a25 0-0	N20 2-0	a16 1-0	F05 1-0	S18 5-0	a02 3-2	J15 0-1	M25 0-1
8 COVENTRY C	a23 3-1	D11 0-4	S18 0-2	a09 2-1	M26 1-0	D25 2-4	M19 1-1		F05 0-2	J22 3-2	N27 1-1	M29 1-0	m02 0-0	N13 1-1	A30 0-0	S04 0-1	O02 2-3	O16 1-0	M05 1-1	O30 1-0	O04 0-1	F24 4-0
9 FULHAM	M05 1-0	M25 5-0	N13 1-2	F28 3-0	J22 0-0	O09 0-3	D11 1-0	M14 2-0		m02 3-0	D27 1-0	O30 1-1	M19 2-1	S25 3-1	a09 1-0	M26 1-0	N27 2-0	a23 0-0	A30 3-1	J01 1-3	S11 0-0	A28 2-0
10 HULL C	S25 3-0	S06 1-0	a02 2-1	S11 2-0	M28 1-1	a30 2-0	D27 3-0	J15 1-1	m07 0-0		O23 0-1	a16 1-1	D04 0-3	M12 1-1	N06 1-1	O09 1-1	F26 1-1	N27 0-2	F03 1-1	F12 1-1	S04 2-1	D18 0-1
11 LEEDS U	a09 0-0	J01 1-0	O02 2-0	M26 0-1	M19 1-0	M29 1-2	M05 2-1	D01 4-0	D25 0-0	O30 1-1		S18 3-1	a23 1-1	D11 3-0	S04 3-1	J08 1-0	O16 2-0	S01 1-2	F19 0-2	N13 0-0	J29 1-2	J22 3-0
12 LEICESTER C	J22 2-0	S25 3-0	D11 0-1	F05 0-0	S02 4-0	N06 2-0	S04 2-1	M28 0-1	O23 1-1	a09 0-0	S11 1-1		F19 2-0	N27 0-3	M19 0-0	M05 1-1	J01 2-1	M26 2-0	m02 0-0	D25 3-1	O09 1-0	a28 0-0
13 NOTTINGHAM F	D18 0-0	a16 1-1	J15 3-1	N27 0-1	O30 4-2	F26 1-2	S25 1-1	m07 0-2	M12 5-1	D11 2-0	a30 1-0	F12 1-2		S11 1-0	O09 1-4	D25 6-1	O07 4-2	N13 1-2	M25 1-1	A28 2-2	a02 1-0	F05 1-1
14 NOTTS CO	A30 1-0	F16 0-0	J01 1-2	S04 2-2	m02 2-1	O23 1-2	a23 3-1	N06 1-1	O02 2-1	M19 4-1	D04 1-2	N20 1-1	S18 2-0		F19 0-1	J22 1-0	D27 3-0	M05 2-0	a09 3-0	O16 3-0	M28 1-1	M26 2-1
15 PORT VALE	M25 1-1	m07 0-2	F26 0-1	D25 0-2	F05 3-0	a02 0-0	J01 4-0	S06 0-0	a16 0-0	N13 4-0	A28 2-0	M12 0-0	O16 0-1	F12 1-2		S11 1-1	J15 1-0	O30 0-2	D11 6-1	S25 2-1	a30 1-2	N27 2-3
16 ROTHERHAM CO	F05 1-0	a30 1-1	F12 0-2	S20 0-0	D11 0-5	M12 2-0	N27 0-0	A28 2-3	a02 2-0	O16 1-1	m07 0-2	F26 1-1	D27 0-0	J15 0-0	S18 1-1		N01 2-0	O02 5-4	N13 1-0	S06 1-1	a16 2-0	O30 1-0
17 SHEFFIELD W	S04 0-0	O23 1-2	F07 0-1	m02 2-2	a23 2-0	D04 0-1	a09 1-1	S25 3-0	N20 3-0	M21 3-0	O09 2-0	D18 0-0	A30 0-0	D25 1-1	J22 1-0	M28 2-0		F19 1-1	M26 2-1	S11 1-3	N06 0-1	a11 6-0
18 SOUTH SHIELDS	S11 3-2	A28 3-0	M12 1-0	M25 0-0	D27 2-0	a16 0-1	F02 3-0	O09 4-1	a30 3-0	N20 0-0	S08 3-0	a02 4-3	N06 0-1	F26 1-0	O23 6-1	S25 1-0	F12 2-3		J01 3-1	J15 1-1	m07 0-0	D04 1-2
19 STOCKPORT CO	O23 3-2	J15 0-3	a30 2-2	O09 0-2	S25 1-2	A28 2-5	S11 6-0	F26 3-0	S13 1-1	F05 2-2	F12 3-1	m07 0-0	M28 1-0	a16 1-0	D04 0-0	N06 0-1	a02 0-1	D18 0-0		M12 2-0	N20 2-0	D25 1-2
20 STOKE	m02 3-2	N20 1-2	M28 1-1	a23 0-0	a09 0-1	F14 0-0	M26 0-1	O23 4-1	D18 1-2	a11 1-3	N06 4-0	D27 1-1	S04 4-0	O09 1-0	O02 0-1	A30 2-0	S18 0-1	J22 0-0	M19 1-0		D04 1-0	M10 1-0
21 WEST HAM U	M19 2-1	D25 1-1	O30 1-1	M05 1-0	F19 0-1	O02 1-1	J22 1-0	J01 7-0	S18 2-0	A28 1-1	F05 3-0	O16 0-1	M26 3-0	M25 0-2	a23 1-1	a09 1-0	N13 4-0	m02 2-1	N27 5-0	D11 1-0		S06 1-0
22 WOLVERHAMPTON W	O09 1-1	N06 0-3	a16 3-1	S25 0-0	S11 2-1	m07 1-3	M28 0-2	F12 1-0	S04 1-0	J01 1-3	J15 3-0	a30 3-0	F14 2-1	a02 1-0	N20 2-2	O23 3-0	M12 1-2	D11 3-0	D27 2-0	F26 3-3	A30 1-2	

Season 1920-21

DIVISION 3

	BRENTFORD	BRIGHTON & HA	BRISTOL R	CRYSTAL P	EXETER C	GILLINGHAM	GRIMSBY T	LUTON T	MERTHYR T	MILLWALL	NEWPORT CO	NORTHAMPTON T	NORWICH C	PLYMOUTH A	PORTSMOUTH	Q.P.R.	READING	SOUTHAMPTON	SOUTHEND U	SWANSEA T	SWINDON T	WATFORD
1 BRENTFORD		S11 2-0	N13 0-0	S25 0-4	S04 0-0	J22 3-3	M28 5-0	D11 1-0	a25 0-0	A30 1-0	D18 2-2	M26 1-1	O16 3-1	m02 0-0	M05 1-2	D25 0-2	N27 3-2	O30 1-1	a09 2-2	F05 1-2	F19 0-1	M19 1-0
2 BRIGHTON & H A	S18 4-0		O02 2-0	D25 0-2	J22 1-1	M19 1-0	S29 1-3	O30 1-1	S01 0-0	F19 1-0	M05 1-0	m07 3-2	M25 2-0	N13 1-0	a09 3-0	D04 2-1	O16 2-2	F05 1-1	S04 1-0	N27 1-1	M26 0-3	a23 0-3
3 BRISTOL R	N06 2-1	S25 3-1		O09 2-1	m02 5-0	F05 2-0	S11 2-0	M29 5-0	a09 1-1	S04 1-2	S01 3-2	M19 4-2	O23 2-2	a23 2-0	F19 2-2	M25 3-0	D11 3-2	N27 1-2	M26 2-1	D25 1-2	J22 3-1	M05 2-0
4 CRYSTAL P	O02 4-2	D27 3-2	O16 3-0		N27 2-1	M05 4-1	F09 2-0	N13 2-1	S04 3-0	J22 3-2	F19 2-0	a23 5-1	S18 1-0	S01 0-0	M26 3-0	J01 0-0	O30 2-0	M29 1-1	N03 2-3	D11 0-1	M19 1-0	a09 2-2
5 EXETER C	A28 3-0	J15 1-0	m07 1-0	N20 1-1		O09 2-1	F12 1-1	a02 1-0	F05 3-3	S11 4-0	S25 0-1	D04 4-0	S01 1-1	D27 1-1	M28 0-0	F26 0-1	a30 0-1	a16 1-0	O20 0-0	M12 1-2	O23 1-0	N06 1-2
6 GILLINGHAM	J15 1-3	M12 1-0	J29 1-0	F26 0-1	O16 2-1		a02 2-1	m07 0-0	S11 0-0	O30 0-0	N13 1-4	D25 2-5	F12 0-0	O02 0-1	S15 1-1	a16 1-2	S08 1-0	A28 1-1	M25 1-1	a30 2-1	a13 1-1	M16 1-1
7 GRIMSBY T	M25 2-0	J01 2-2	S18 3-1	F05 1-0	F19 2-0	M26 2-0		O16 0-1	O30 1-1	M05 0-2	M19 1-1	A28 2-0	D25 1-1	J22 1-1	a23 0-3	N20 2-1	O02 2-0	D11 3-0	A30 1-0	N13 0-2	a09 3-0	m02 3-0
8 LUTON T	D04 2 0	O23 3 2	J01 1 2	N06 2 2	M26 3 0	D28 6 0	O09 3 1		M05 1-0	a09 0-0	a23 2-2	J22 3-1	N20 4-0	M19 1-1	A30 2-2	O02 2-1	F09 6-0	D25 1-1	m02 4-0	S11 3-0	S04 2-0	M28 1-0
9 MERTHYR T	a30 3-1	S06 4-1	a16 2-2	A28 2-1	J29 7-1	S18 0-1	O23 3-1	F26 4-1		D27 0-1	M28 1-2	N06 1-0	m07 0-0	D18 0-0	F21 2-1	J15 3-1	a02 1-0	M12 1-1	N22 2-0	F12 0-3	O02 2-2	O09 2-0
10 MILLWALL	S06 0-0	F12 0-1	A28 2-0	J15 0-1	S18 2-0	O23 4-0	F26 0-1	a16 0-0	D25 0-0		O16 1-0	J01 1-0	D11 2-0	M28 0-0	O02 1-0	M12 0-0	m07 2-0	a30 0-1	F05 4-2	a02 0-2	N06 5-0	N20 1-0
11 NEWPORT CO	J01 3-1	F26 0-4	S09 0-2	F12 0-1	O02 2-0	N06 1-0	M12 2-1	a30 2-0	M25 0-3	O09 3-1		J29 1-1	J13 2-0	S18 0-0	O23 1-0	a02 1-3	A28 0-1	m07 0-0	D25 1-1	a09 1-1	O21 0-1	D04 0-2
12 NORTHAMPTON T	a02 6-2	m02 1-0	M12 1-2	a30 2-2	D11 3-3	D27 2-0	S04 4-1	J15 1-0	N13 2-2	S13 0-2	F05 0-2		a16 1-0	N27 1-1	O09 1-0	S06 0-3	F26 1-0	F12 2-0	O30 1-0	S25 2-0	M29 1-2	S11 0-1
13 NORWICH C	O09 0-0	M28 3-0	O30 1-1	S11 0-1	S08 0-0	F19 2-1	D27 0-0	N27 3-0	m02 0-0	D04 2-0	J22 3-0	a09 3-3		S04 0-0	M19 2-2	F05 2-0	N13 2-0	S25 0-1	a23 3-1	J01 1-1	M05 3-2	M26 1-1
14 PLYMOUTH A	m07 1-0	N06 5-0	a30 2-1	S08 0-1	D25 0-0	S25 3-1	J15 0-0	M12 1-0	J01 2-1	M25 0-2	S11 5-1	N20 0-2	A28 1-1		a13 2-0	F12 1-0	a16 1-1	a02 0-0	D11 0-0	F26 1-0	O09 0-0	O23 0-2
15 PORTSMOUTH	F26 0-2	a16 3-0	F12 1-0	a02 0-0	M25 2-1	N27 2-2	a30 2-1	S08 3-0	D11 0-0	S25 0-0	O30 0-2	O16 2-0	M12 2-1	F05 1-1		m07 0-0	J15 2-2	S18 0-1	N13 3-0	A28 3-0	D18 1-1	D27 1-0
16 Q.P.R.	D27 1-0	D11 4-0	M28 2-1	D18 3-0	M05 2-1	a09 0-1	N27 2-0	S25 4-1	J22 4-2	M19 0-0	M26 2-0	S02 1-2	F17 2-0	M17 4-0	m02 0-0		S11 2-0	N13 0-0	O09 2-0	O30 1-1	a23 1-0	A28 1-2
17 READING	N20 2-1	O09 0-1	D04 2-1	O23 1-0	a23 0-1	S01 1-2	S25 4-1	F05 0-1	M26 2-0	J29 0-1	S04 4-0	M05 4-0	N06 0-1	a09 1-1	J22 1-0	S18 0-0		D18 0-4	M19 1-1	M28 1-3	D25 2-3	F19 0-0
18 SOUTHAMPTON	O23 3-0	F23 1-0	N20 4-0	M28 1-1	a09 3-0	S04 3-0	D04 0-1	D27 1-1	M19 5-0	a23 1-1	m02 0-0	M09 3-1	O02 1-0	M26 1-0	S11 2-0	N06 2-2	J01 1-2		M05 3-0	O09 3-0	A30 4-0	J22 4-1
19 SOUTHEND U	a16 4-1	A28 2-0	a02 1-0	m07 0-2	J01 0-0	M28 1-0	S06 3-1	F12 1-1	N27 0-1	a06 1-2	D27 2-1	O23 1-2	a30 3-1	D04 2-1	N06 2-1	O16 1-0	M12 1-0	F26 1-0		J15 1-2	S11 1-3	O02 4-1
20 SWANSEA T	a28 1-1	N20 0-0	D27 2-2	D04 0-0	M19 2-1	a23 2-0	N06 3-1	S18 1-1	F19 1-0	M26 0-0	a16 1-2	O02 2-2	S16 5-2	M05 3-0	S04 0-0	O23 1-3	M25 2-1	O16 1-1	J22 2-0		m02 1-1	S02 2-1
21 SWINDON T	F12 1-0	a02 2-0	J15 2-1	M12 1-3	O30 1-1	D11 1-1	a16 0-0	A28 9-1	S25 3-0	N13 4-1	N27 5-0	M28 2-1	F26 4-2	O16 1-1	J01 5-2	a30 0-1	D27 2-0	S06 3-2	S18 3-0	m07 0-0		a20 2-0
22 WATFORD	M12 1-0	a30 1-0	F26 2-1	a16 1-1	N13 0-0	J01 3-1	m07 4-2	M25 1-0	O16 1-0	N27 1-0	D11 5-1	S18 7-1	a02 2-0	O30 1-1	D25 3-2	S04 0-2	F12 1-2	J15 0-0	S25 3-0	S08 3-0	F05 0-1	

Crystal Palace, the first champions of the Third Division. Back row (left to right, players only): Harry, Nixon, King, Alderson, Irwin, Allen, Dreyer. Second row: Wood, McCracken, Jones, Kennedy, Wells, Wibley, Rhodes, Collier, Little. Front row: Bateman, Smith, Feebury, Cartwright. On ground: Conner, Storey, Menlove, Hann.

LEAGUE TABLES

DIVISION 1

	P	W	D	L	F	A	W	D	L	F	A	Pts
Burnley	42	17	3	1	56	16	6	10	5	23	20	59
Manchester C	42	19	2	0	50	13	5	4	12	20	37	54
Bolton W	42	15	6	0	53	17	4	8	9	24	36	52
Liverpool	42	11	7	3	41	17	7	8	6	22	18	51
Newcastle U	42	14	3	4	43	18	6	7	8	23	27	50
Tottenham H	42	15	2	4	46	16	4	7	10	24	32	47
Everton	42	9	8	4	40	26	8	5	8	26	29	47
Middlesbrough	42	10	6	5	29	21	7	6	8	24	32	46
Arsenal	42	9	8	4	31	25	6	6	9	28	38	44
Aston Villa	42	11	4	6	39	21	7	3	11	24	49	43
Blackburn R	42	7	9	5	36	27	6	6	9	21	32	41
Sunderland	42	11	4	6	34	19	3	9	9	23	41	41
Manchester U	42	9	4	8	34	26	6	6	9	30	42	40
WBA	42	8	7	6	31	23	5	7	9	23	35	40
Bradford C	42	7	9	5	38	28	5	6	10	23	35	39
Preston NE	42	10	4	7	38	25	5	5	11	23	40	39
Huddersfield T	42	11	4	6	26	16	4	5	12	16	33	39
Chelsea	42	9	7	5	35	24	4	6	11	13	34	39
Oldham A	42	6	9	6	23	26	3	6	12	26	60	33
Sheffield U	42	5	11	5	22	19	1	7	13	20	49	30
Derby Co	42	3	12	6	21	23	2	4	15	11	35	26
Bradford	42	6	5	10	29	35	2	3	16	14	41	24

DIVISION 2

	P	W	D	L	F	A	W	D	L	F	A	Pts
Birmingham	42	16	4	1	55	13	8	6	7	24	25	58
Cardiff C	42	13	5	3	27	9	11	5	5	32	23	58
Bristol C	42	14	3	4	35	12	5	10	6	14	17	51
Blackpool	42	12	3	6	32	19	8	7	6	22	23	50
West Ham U	42	13	5	3	38	11	6	5	10	13	19	48
Notts Co	42	12	5	4	36	17	6	6	9	19	23	47
Clapton O	42	13	6	2	31	9	3	7	11	12	33	45
South Shields	42	13	4	4	41	16	4	6	11	20	30	44
Fulham	42	14	4	3	33	12	2	6	13	10	35	42
Sheffield W	42	9	7	5	31	14	6	4	11	17	34	41
Bury	42	10	8	3	29	13	5	2	14	16	36	40
Leicester C	42	10	8	3	26	11	2	8	11	13	35	40
Hull C	42	7	10	4	24	18	3	10	8	19	35	40
Leeds U	42	11	5	5	30	14	3	5	13	10	31	38
Wolves	42	11	4	6	34	24	5	2	14	15	42	38
Barnsley	42	9	10	2	31	17	1	6	14	17	33	36
Port Vale	42	7	6	8	28	19	4	8	9	15	30	36
Nottingham F	42	9	6	6	37	26	3	6	12	11	29	36
Rotherham Co	42	8	9	4	23	21	4	3	14	14	32	36
Stoke	42	9	5	7	26	16	3	6	12	20	40	35
Coventry C	42	8	6	7	24	25	4	5	12	15	45	35
Stockport Co	42	8	6	7	30	24	1	6	14	12	51	30

DIVISION 3

	P	W	D	L	F	A	W	D	L	F	A	Pts
Crystal P	42	15	4	2	45	17	9	7	5	25	17	59
Southampton	42	14	5	2	46	10	5	11	5	18	18	54
QPR	42	14	4	3	38	11	8	5	8	23	21	53
Swindon T	42	14	5	2	51	17	7	5	9	22	32	52
Swansea T	42	9	10	2	32	19	9	5	7	24	26	51
Watford	42	14	4	3	40	15	6	4	11	19	29	48
Millwall	42	11	5	5	25	8	7	6	8	17	22	47
Merthyr T	42	13	5	3	46	20	2	10	9	14	29	45
Luton T	42	14	6	1	51	15	2	6	13	10	41	44
Bristol R	42	15	3	3	51	22	3	4	14	17	35	43
Plymouth A	42	10	7	4	25	13	1	14	6	10	21	43
Portsmouth	42	10	8	3	28	14	2	7	12	18	34	39
Grimsby T	42	12	5	4	32	16	3	4	14	17	43	39
Northampton T	42	11	4	6	32	23	4	4	13	27	52	38
Newport Co	42	8	5	8	20	23	6	4	11	23	41	37
Norwich C	42	9	10	2	31	14	1	6	14	13	39	36
Southend U	42	13	2	6	32	20	1	6	14	12	41	36
Brighton & HA	42	11	6	4	28	20	3	2	16	14	41	36
Exeter C	42	9	7	5	27	15	1	8	12	12	39	35
Reading	42	8	4	9	26	22	4	3	14	16	37	31
Brentford	42	7	9	5	27	23	2	3	16	15	44	30
Gillingham	42	6	9	6	19	24	2	3	16	15	50	28

Arthur Dominy helped Southampton from the Southern League into the Football League and proved a fine captain. He joined Everton in 1926.

Football League Records

Top scorers: Div 1, A.Wilson (Middlesbrough) 31 goals; Div 2, J.Broad (Stoke) 25 goals; Div 3(N), J.Carmichael (Grimsby Town) 37 goals; Div 3(S), F.Richardson (Plymouth Argyle) 31 goals.
The Third Division became the Southern Section and a Northern Section was formed consisting of 16 new clubs plus re-elected Chesterfield, Crewe Alexandra, Lincoln City and Walsall.

Inside-forward Dick Forshaw was an ever-present as Liverpool won the title in successive seasons.

DIVISION 1

	ARSENAL	ASTON VILLA	BIRMINGHAM	BLACKBURN R	BOLTON W	BRADFORD C	BURNLEY	CARDIFF C	CHELSEA	EVERTON	HUDDERSFIELD T	LIVERPOOL	MANCHESTER C	MANCHESTER U	MIDDLESBROUGH	NEWCASTLE U	OLDHAM A	PRESTON N.E.	SHEFFIELD U	SUNDERLAND	TOTTENHAM H	W.B.A.
1 ARSENAL		M25 2-0	N12 5-2	D10 1-1	D12 1-1	m06 1-0	J21 0-0	D26 0-0	J14 1-0	O01 1-0	O29 1-3	M22 1-0	S17 0-1	a05 3-1	a01 2-2	F04 2-1	D24 0-1	S05 1-0	A27 1-2	O15 1-2	a22 1-0	a18 2-2
2 ASTON VILLA	M18 2-0		M11 1-1	S12 1-1	a15 2-1	N12 7-1	J14 2-0	A29 2-1	a17 1-4	F08 2-1	F25 2-0	D03 1-1	S03 4-0	N19 3-1	O29 6-2	D24 1-0	a29 2-0	S17 2-0	D27 5-3	F11 2-0	O01 2-1	O15 0-1
3 BIRMINGHAM	N05 0-1	M15 1-0		N26 1-0	O22 1-1	a22 1-0	A27 2-3	D31 0-1	S05 5-1	S17 1-1	O08 0-2	F04 0-2	a18 3-1	F18 0-1	M25 4-3	J21 0-4	D10 3-0	m06 0-2	D17 2-1	O01 1-0	a01 0-3	D27 0-2
4 BLACKBURN R	D03 0-1	a01 1-2	N19 1-1		D17 1-2	S19 3-1	**F04 3-2**	J02 1-3	A27 1-1	O15 2-2	N12 2-0	M04 0-0	O01 3-1	M25 3-0	a22 2-2	M06 0-2	J14 3-2	D26 3-0	J21 2-3	O29 1-2	m06 1-1	S17 2-3
5 BOLTON W	N19 1-0	a22 1-0	O29 1-2	D24 1-1		S10 3-3	F18 0-1	O15 1-2	J21 0-2	J14 1-0	S24 3-1	M25 1-3	D10 5-0	a08 1-0	m06 4-2	M04 3-2	J02 5-1	A27 2-2	F04 3-1	a17 1-1	S05 1-0	N12 2-0
6 BRADFORD C	a29 0-2	N05 3-2	a15 1-2	A29 1-1	S17 4-3		O01 0-4	M15 1-0	N26 0-1	M11 3-1	a01 4-0	D31 0-0	F25 1-2	D03 2-1	O08 0-2	a17 2-3	S03 3-0	D17 1-0	O22 1-1	M18 0-0	D27 0-4	M08 1-1
7 BURNLEY	F20 1-0	D31 2-1	S03 3-1	F11 1-2	F25 2-0	S24 4-0		M18 1-1	O22 5-0	a29 2-0	D10 1-0	a14 1-1	a15 5-2	D27 4-2	D24 3-1	S10 2-0	M11 0-1	N05 3-3	O08 2-1	S05 2-0	N26 1-0	a08 4-2
8 CARDIFF C	D27 4-3	S05 0-4	J14 3-1	a17 1-3	O08 1-2	J21 6-3	M25 4-2		F08 2-0	N19 2-1	D17 0-0	a22 2-0	N05 0-2	m06 3-1	S24 3-1	a08 1-0	S10 0-1	F04 3-0	a26 1-1	D03 2-0	A27 0-1	O29 2-0
9 CHELSEA	D31 0-2	a14 1-0	A29 1-2	S03 1-0	J18 0-3	N19 1-0	O29 4-1	F25 1-0		a01 1-0	a10 1-0	S24 0-1	M18 0-0	S10 0-0	D27 1-1	O08 1-1	F11 1-0	D03 0-0	N05 0-2	a15 1-0	D24 1-2	M11 1-1
10 EVERTON	S24 1-1	J21 3-2	S10 2-1	O08 2-0	D31 1-0	M04 2-0	m06 2-0	N26 0-1	a08 2-3		a14 6-2	N05 1-1	D24 2-2	A27 5-0	M01 4-1	S07 2-3	O22 2-2	a10 0-0	a22 1-1	J02 3-0	M15 0-0	D03 1-2
11 HUDDERSFIELD T	O22 2-0	a05 1-0	O15 1-0	N05 3-0	O01 3-0	a08 1-2	D03 1-0	D24 0-1	m06 2-0	a18 1-2		J21 0-1	D26 2-0	F27 1-1	m01 2-1	A27 1-2	N26 1-0	a22 6-0	S06 1-1	S17 1-2	M27 1-1	J14 2-0
12 LIVERPOOL	F25 4-0	D10 2-0	F11 1-0	M11 2-0	M18 0-2	J14 2-1	a17 2-1	a15 5-1	O01 1-1	N12 1-1	D27 2-0		A31 3-2	D17 2-1	N19 4-0	D26 1-0	a01 2-0	O15 4-0	S17 1-1	S03 2-1	O29 1-1	a29 1-2
13 MANCHESTER C	S10 2-0	A27 2-1	a14 1-0	S24 1-1	D03 2-3	F22 3-2	a22 2-0	N12 1-1	M25 0-0	D17 2-1	J02 2-1	S07 1-1		O22 4-1	J21 2-2	m06 1-0	O08 2-1	a05 2-0	a08 2-2	D31 3-0	F04 3-3	N19 6-1
14 MANCHESTER U	M11 1-0	N26 1-0	F25 1-1	M18 0-1	a01 0-1	D10 1-1	D26 0-1	a29 1-1	S17 0-0	S03 2-1	F11 1-1	D24 0-0	O29 3-1		N05 3-5	J14 0-1	a15 0-3	O01 1-1	a17 3-2	J28 3-1	O15 2-1	A29 2-3
15 MIDDLESBROUGH	a08 4-2	O22 5-0	M18 1-1	a15 0-1	a29 4-2	O15 1-2	D17 4-1	O01 0-0	D26 0-1	F11 3-1	M11 5-1	N26 3-1	F01 4-1	N12 2-0		D10 1-1	A29 1-1	a17 1-0	J14 1-1	F25 3-0	S17 0-0	S03 3-2
16 NEWCASTLE U	F11 3-1	D17 1-2	F08 0-1	F25 2-0	M11 2-1	a14 1-2	S17 2-1	a01 0-0	O15 1-0	A31 3-0	S03 1-2	J02 1-1	a29 5-1	D31 3-0	D03 0-0		M18 1-1	O29 3-1	O01 2-1	N19 2-2	N12 0-2	a15 3-0
17 OLDHAM A	D17 2-1	m06 3-1	D03 0-1	D31 1-1	D26 0-0	A27 0-0	M04 0-1	S17 2-1	F04 0-3	O29 0-0	N19 1-1	a08 4-0	O15 0-1	a22 1-1	S05 0-1	M25 0-0		J21 2-0	F18 0-2	N12 3-0	a17 1-0	O01 1-0
18 PRESTON N.E.	A29 3-2	S10 1-0	m01 2-2	D27 2-1	S03 3-1	D24 2-1	N12 2-1	F11 1-1	D10 2-0	M18 1-0	a15 1-1	O08 1-1	M11 1-0	S24 3-2	a14 1-1	O22 2-0	F09 0-0		N26 3-0	a01 1-1	J14 1-2	F25 0-3
19 SHEFFIELD U	S03 4-1	D26 2-3	D24 1-2	F27 0-1	F11 1-0	O29 1-0	O15 0-1	M11 0-2	N12 1-2	a15 1-0	A29 1-1	S10 0-1	a01 1-0	J02 3-0	D31 6-1	S24 1-1	F25 1-0	N19 3-0		a29 4-1	D10 1-0	M18 0-0
20 SUNDERLAND	O08 1-0	F04 1-4	S24 2-1	O22 3-1	a14 6-2	M25 0-0	A31 3-2	D10 4-1	a22 1-2	D26 1-2	S10 2-2	A27 3-0	J14 2-3	J21 2-1	F18 1-1	N26 0-0	N05 5-1	a08 1-0	M04 1-0		a05 2-0	D24 5-0
21 TOTTENHAM H	a15 2-0	S24 3-1	a08 2-1	a29 2-1	A29 1-2	D26 1-0	N19 1-1	S03 4-1	D17 0-0	F25 2-0	M18 1-0	O22 0-1	F11 3-1	O08 2-2	S10 2-4	N05 4-0	a14 3-1	D31 5-0	D03 2-1	M11 1-0		J30 2-0
22 W.B.A.	a17 0-3	O08 0-1	D26 1-0	S10 0-2	N05 0-1	F04 1-1	a01 2-0	O22 2-2	M04 2-2	D10 1-1	D31 3-2	m06 1-4	N26 2-0	S07 0-0	A27 0-0	a22 1-2	S24 0-1	M29 2-0	M25 3-0	D17 2-1	J21 3-0	

Bill Rawlings scored 30 goals for Third Division champions Southampton and was eventually capped by England when playing in Division Two.

DIVISION 2

	BARNSLEY	BLACKPOOL	BRADFORD	BRISTOL C	BURY	CLAPTON O	COVENTRY C	CRYSTAL P	DERBY CO	FULHAM	HULL C	LEEDS U	LEICESTER C	NOTTINGHAM F	NOTTS CO	PORT VALE	ROTHERHAM CO	SHEFFIELD W	SOUTH SHIELDS	STOKE	WEST HAM U	WOLVERHAMPTON W
1 BARNSLEY		F11 3-2	F25 2-0	D26 1-1	S24 3-0	M11 4-0	O08 0-1	A29 3-1	O22 2-1	M06 2-1	a15 4-1	a01 2-2	N12 0-0	a14 2-0	a29 3-0	D24 3-2	D10 0-1	S03 2-0	F27 2-1	M18 2-2	N26 1-1	S10 2-1
2 BLACKPOOL	F04 1-0		D17 1-1	M25 2-0	S05 0-1	J14 2-0	J21 2-1	O29 1-3	A27 4-2	D03 0-2	O01 0-1	S17 1-3	D26 2-0	M04 2-1	O15 1-2	a15 0-1	N12 3-1	N19 0-2	a08 4-0	a14 3-2	m06 3-1	F18 1-3
3 BRADFORD	M22 2-3	D24 0-0		a08 2-1	S10 1-1	D26 3-1	F15 1-2	a18 0-0	J21 5-1	N19 1-2	D10 1-1	N12 0-1	A27 0-1	M25 1-0	F28 2-1	m06 2-0	S24 4-2	O29 2-1	a22 1-0	O15 2-4	S05 2-0	M04 0-0
4 BRISTOL C	D27 3-0	M18 0-1	a11 1-0		D10 2-0	a15 2-1	a17 0-2	F08 1-2	S17 1-2	M11 1-0	O29 1-0	A29 0-0	O01 1-1	D24 0-1	S03 2-2	N05 2-1	F11 1-2	F25 3-1	N26 0-1	a29 2-0	O15 0-1	D31 2-0
5 BURY	O01 1-2	A31 3-0	S17 2-2	D03 5-0		S03 0-0	O22 3-2	M18 1-2	N26 2-0	a29 1-0	F25 4-0	F11 2-1	D17 0-1	D31 1-2	M11 1-0	O08 5-2	a01 0-0	a15 1-2	N05 1-0	F08 0-1	D26 0-1	a14 2-1
6 CLAPTON O	M04 2-1	D31 3-0	D27 1-0	a22 0-1	A27 3-1		F18 4-0	N12 0-0	F04 3-2	D24 4-2	O15 0-2	O01 4-2	J21 0-0	a08 1-2	O29 2-1	S12 2-0	N19 1-2	D10 1-1	m06 0-1	S17 1-0	a17 0-0	M25 1-0
7 COVENTRY C	O15 0-1	J28 0-1	F11 2-2	a18 1-1	O29 1-2	F25 1-2		a29 1-1	N17 1-2	S03 2-0	a01 2-0	M18 1-0	N19 0-0	S10 0-1	a22 4-2	D31 4-1	A29 4-0	D24 2-2	D26 0-1	M11 0-1	O03 2-0	S24 3-1
8 CRYSTAL P	S07 0-1	O22 1-0	a17 1-1	J21 1-1	M25 4-1	N05 1-0	m06 1-1		a22 3-1	O08 2-0	J14 0-2	D24 1-2	a08 1-0	A27 4-1	D26 1-0	F18 0-0	S10 2-0	S24 2-2	F04 1-2	D10 0-2	M04 1-2	D07 1-1
9 DERBY CO	O29 1-0	S03 1-0	F18 1-3	S10 5-1	N19 1-0	F11 3-0	N05 1-0	a15 2-0		D31 1-1	M18 0-0	M11 2-0	D03 0-1	S24 1-2	a01 1-1	D27 3-2	a29 4-0	A29 0-1	a17 0-2	F25 2-4	D24 3-1	O08 2-3
10 FULHAM	J21 0-0	D10 1-0	N26 2-1	M04 0-0	m06 0-1	D17 2-0	A27 5-0	O15 1-1	J14 2-2		S17 6-0	a17 0-1	S05 0-0	F28 2-0	O01 4-0	a08 1-0	O22 4-0	N12 3-1	M25 3-0	D26 2-1	a22 2-0	F04 1-0
11 HULL C	a22 1-3	S24 2-0	D03 3-0	O22 1-0	F18 1-1	O08 2-1	a08 2-0	D31 1-0	M25 1-1	S10 2-1		N19 1-0	M04 5-2	S05 0-1	D17 2-0	J21 2-0	D26 0-1	a14 0-0	A27 1-1	N12 7-1	F04 0-0	m06 2-0
12 LEEDS U	a08 4-0	S10 0-0	N05 3-0	S05 3-0	F04 2-0	S24 2-0	M25 5-2	D17 0-0	M04 2-1	a14 2-0	N26 0-2		F20 3-0	m06 0-0	D10 1-1	A27 2-1	D31 0-2	D26 1-1	O08 0-0	O22 1-2	J21 0-0	a22 0-0
13 LEICESTER C	N05 1-0	D27 1-0	S03 2-1	S24 4-1	D24 0-0	F09 1-0	N26 1-1	a01 2-0	D10 1-1	A29 1-2	M11 0-1	F25 0-0		O08 2-2	M18 3-0	a17 3-0	a15 1-0	a29 1-1	S10 1-0	F11 3-4	J14 2-1	O22 0-1
14 NOTTINGHAM F	a17 1-1	M11 0-0	M18 4-1	D17 1-0	J14 1-2	a01 2-0	S17 1-0	S03 2-1	O01 3-0	F25 0-0	A29 3-2	a29 1-0	O15 0-0		N14 0-0	N19 1-1	F08 1-0	F11 2-0	D10 1-0	a22 3-1	O29 2-0	D26 0-0
15 NOTTS CO	O06 1-4	O08 2-1	D31 3-0	A27 0-2	a05 1-1	O22 0-0	a15 1-1	D27 3-2	a08 1-2	S24 3-0	D24 2-0	D03 4-1	a26 0-0	N05 1-1		F04 1-2	a14 2-0	S10 2-0	J21 2-0	N26 0-0	M29 1-1	S05 4-0
16 PORT VALE	D17 2-3	a22 1-0	a29 1-0	N12 3-1	O15 5-2	A29 3-0	J30 1-2	F25 3-0	D26 1-1	a01 1-1	F13 1-0	S03 0-1	a14 1-1	N26 0-2	F11 0-0		M11 1-0	M18 1-0	O22 1-1	O01 0-1	S17 2-1	D10 0-2
17 ROTHERHAM CO	N07 0-0	N05 0-1	O01 2-0	F20 0-0	a08 1-1	N26 2-0	S05 0-0	S17 1-1	m06 2-0	O29 1-0	D27 2-0	J14 1-0	a22 0-0	J21 0-1	a17 3-0	M04 0-1		O15 0-0	F18 1-1	D17 0-0	M25 0-1	A27 1-0
18 SHEFFIELD W	A27 2-3	N26 5-1	O22 2-1	F18 1-0	a22 4-1	D03 0-0	M13 3-2	O01 1-0	S05 1-1	N05 1-4	a17 0-0	D27 2-1	m06 1-0	F04 0-4	S17 0-0	a03 2-0	O08 1-0		M04 0-3	J14 0-1	a08 2-1	F13 3-1
19 SOUTH SHIELDS	D31 5-2	a01 2-1	a15 1-0	N19 2-0	N12 1-1	a29 1-1	J02 2-1	F11 1-1	a14 3-1	M18 1-0	S03 1-0	O15 0-1	S17 1-0	D03 0-0	M15 0-0	O29 0-1	J28 2-0	M11 0-0		A29 1-1	O01 1-0	D17 0-2
20 STOKE	M25 1-0	a17 1-1	O08 0-1	m06 3-0	J21 1-0	S10 0-0	M04 2-2	D03 5-1	M06 1-1	D27 3-0	N05 0-0	O29 3-0	F04 1-1	a15 1-1	N19 0-0	S24 0-0	D24 1-1	D31 1-1	S05 2-1		A27 2-0	a08 3-0
21 WEST HAM U	N19 4-0	a29 0-2	A29 1-0	O08 3-0	D27 3-2	a14 1-2	D10 3-0	M11 2-0	D17 3-1	a15 1-0	F11 1-1	J28 1-1	D31 1-0	O22 1-0	F25 2-1	S10 3-0	M18 1-2	a01 2-0	S24 1-1	S03 3-0		N05 2-0
22 WOLVERHAMPTON W	S17 2-0	F25 4-0	M11 5-0	J14 2-2	a17 1-1	M18 0-2	O01 1-0	N19 0-1	O15 0-3	F11 0-0	a29 0-2	a15 0-0	O29 1-1	D27 2-0	A29 1-2	D03 2-0	S03 3-1	J28 0-0	D24 3-2	a01 1-1	N12 0-1	

Season 1921-22

DIVISION 3 NORTH

	ACCRINGTON S	ASHINGTON	BARROW	CHESTERFIELD	CREWE A	DARLINGTON	DURHAM C	GRIMSBY T	HALIFAX T	HARTLEPOOLS U	LINCOLN C	NELSON	ROCHDALE	SOUTHPORT	STALYBRIDGE C	STOCKPORT CO	TRANMERE R	WALSALL	WIGAN B	WREXHAM
1 ACCRINGTON S		D27 3-0	N26 3-0	S24 3-1	S10 2-0	J14 1-0	N05 5-1	a22 1-0	a17 1-2	M11 4-1	D24 2-0	O08 4-1	S03 4-0	M18 1-2	F11 4-1	a08 1-3	J28 3-0	a29 3-3	F18 4-0	O22 1-0
2 ASHINGTON	J02 2-1		O15 0-2	D24 1-0	O29 0-1	a05 1-0	O01 1-0	A27 1-0	F04 3-1	a22 4-1	N12 4-2	D31 4-0	F18 7-3	a29 2-2	M18 2-3	a14 2-0	M04 1-0	J21 2-3	a08 3-1	S17 2-2
3 BARROW	J07 3-1	O08 2-0		D10 1-0	S24 1-2	N12 0-2	S17 0-1	J21 2-2	F18 1-1	m06 0-1	O22 2-0	D24 0-2	M11 1-0	D27 2-1	a08 2-1	A27 0-2	M25 2-0	F11 3-0	a22 2-0	D31 5-2
4 CHESTERFIELD	O01 0-1	M22 0-1	J02 2-0		O08 1-1	S17 0-3	D17 2-1	D27 4-1	a22 2-0	F04 2-1	J14 3-0	O22 1-2	m06 2-1	F18 2-1	S03 4-0	M04 0-1	a17 3-0	a08 1-0	J21 1-1	N12 3-0
5 CREWE A	S17 2-1	O22 1-2	O01 2-1	O15 1-2		a14 7-3	D31 3-2	a08 1-2	D17 2-1	F18 2-0	J07 0-2	N05 2-1	D26 2-0	a17 1-0	J28 5-1	M25 0-1	S03 1-1	a22 2-0	F04 2-1	m06 3-0
6 DARLINGTON	D31 3-0	J03 5-0	N05 3-0	S10 7-0	D24 0-1		O29 2-2	m06 2-0	A27 2-0	M25 0-0	N19 4-2	S24 0-1	J21 2-1	a08 3-0	F18 3-0	a15 1-0	F04 4-0	J02 5-0	M04 3-0	O15 3-0
7 DURHAM C	N12 3-1	S24 1-0	S10 2-0	N26 3-1	J14 4-2	O22 3-7		F04 1-2	M04 3-1	a18 0-1	J02 2-0	a14 2-0	M25 0-2	S03 2-0	a22 3-1	J21 0-2	a08 3-0	F18 2-0	m06 6-0	D24 3-0
8 GRIMSBY T	a15 2-1	S03 6-1	J28 4-0	D26 2-2	a01 3-0	a29 3-1	F11 5-2		D24 4-1	O08 2-0	a14 3-1	M11 3-1	N26 3-0	O29 0-0	S17 1-1	N12 2-1	J14 5-1	S06 3-1	O01 1-1	F25 2-0
9 HALIFAX T	D10 2-1	F11 2-0	F25 3-2	a15 1-2	a29 5-5	S03 5-1	M11 3-2	J16 2-0		N05 3-0	F16 1-2	a08 3-1	S17 1-1	N26 1-1	O08 2-3	D27 1-0	O01 0-2	D31 1-3	O29 1-2	M25 0-0
10 HARTLEPOOLS U	M04 2-1	a15 2-1	a29 3-1	F11 7-0	F25 1-0	M18 0-0	N19 0-1	O15 0-0	N12 4-0		a01 1-1	J28 6-1	D31 5-3	S17 1-0	J02 0-1	S24 0-0	N26 0-0	O29 1-0	D17 0-0	S03 0-1
11 LINCOLN C	D17 1-1	N05 4-1	O29 1-0	D31 2-1	N26 2-3	D26 0-2	D27 3-0	a17 0-2	J21 3-1	a08 1-1		S10 0-2	F11 1-2	a22 3-1	M04 2-1	m06 0-1	F18 4-1	A27 1-0	M25 3-0	O01 1-0
12 NELSON	O15 0-1	J14 0-2	a17 1-1	O29 2-0	N12 1-2	O01 1-1	D26 3-5	M04 3-0	a01 0-0	J21 0-4	S17 0-0		a22 4-1	F04 3-2	S12 1-0	F18 2-2	m06 0-0	a25 1-0	A27 1-2	J02 4-0
13 ROCHDALE	A27 6-3	F25 2-1	M04 0-1	a29 0-1	D27 2-0	J28 0-2	M18 1-0	N19 0-2	S10 3-3	J14 0-1	F04 0-2	a15 2-2		S24 0-1	N05 2-1	O22 0-1	O08 2-1	D24 7-0	a14 4-2	a01 3-0
14 SOUTHPORT	D26 1-1	M11 0-0	a14 1-0	F25 3-0	J02 2-0	a01 3-1	A27 1-1	O22 7-1	N19 3-0	S10 3-0	a15 0-0	F11 0-1	O01 2-1		D24 5-1	O08 2-1	D10 1-1	N05 3-0	J14 1-1	J28 1-2
15 STALYBRIDGE C	F04 3-1	M25 2-0	a01 3-0	A27 6-0	J21 2-2	F25 1-0	a15 4-3	S10 3-0	O15 2-1	D26 1-3	M11 2-0	D27 2-0	N12 1-0	F28 0-0		D31 0-4	O29 4-0	S24 2-0	N26 0-0	a29 4-1
16 STOCKPORT CO	a01 2-1	a17 3-2	S19 2-0	M11 2-1	M18 1-1	a22 1-0	J28 4-0	N05 0-1	D26 0-0	O01 1-0	a29 2-2	F25 3-0	O29 3-0	O15 2-1	J14 4-0		D24 0-0	N26 3-1	S17 3-0	F11 0-0
17 TRANMERE R	J21 2-4	D26 2-3	M18 2-2	a14 2-0	A27 4-1	F11 0-1	a01 3-3	D31 2-2	S24 2-2	D27 1-2	F25 4-0	a29 4-0	O15 7-0	a18 0-1	O22 4-1	D17 0-2		S10 0-1	N12 2-0	a15 0-0
18 WALSALL	m06 6-1	J28 6-2	F04 3-1	a01 2-1	a15 1-0	a17 0-1	F25 2-0	D10 2-1	J14 4-1	O22 3-1	S03 3-0	M18 2-0	a18 4-0	N12 4-1	O01 2-2	J16 0-2	S17 2-0		O15 4-1	D27 2-2
19 WIGAN B	F25 0-1	a01 1-1	a15 1-2	M13 1-2	F11 2-0	M29 3-3	a29 2-0	S24 1-1	O22 4-3	D24 1-0	M18 3-1	S03 1-4	D10 3-2	D31 3-2	J07 0-2	S10 0-1	N05 0-0	O08 4-2		a17 2-1
20 WREXHAM	O29 2-1	S10 2-0	J14 0-0	N05 0-1	D10 1-0	O08 1-1	J07 3-1	F18 0-1	M18 5-1	A27 0-2	S24 3-1	N26 4-2	a08 1-1	J21 2-0	a14 2-0	M08 0-0	a22 1-3	M04 4-0	D26 3-2	

DIVISION 3 SOUTH

	ABERDARE A	BRENTFORD	BRIGHTON & HA	BRISTOL R	CHARLTON A	EXETER C	GILLINGHAM	LUTON T	MERTHYR T	MILLWALL	NEWPORT CO	NORTHAMPTON T	NORWICH C	PLYMOUTH A	PORTSMOUTH	Q.P.R.	READING	SOUTHAMPTON	SOUTHEND U	SWANSEA T	SWINDON T	WATFORD
1 ABERDARE A		D27 2-0	S10 2-0	D31 2-0	O08 3-3	m06 0-2	a08 6-1	m01 2-0	a10 0-0	a22 0-0	F18 3-0	O29 4-2	M16 1-2	F04 0-0	A27 0-0	N05 4-2	D17 0-1	a18 0-1	N26 1-1	S05 2-1	M25 3-2	S24 3-0
2 BRENTFORD	D26 2-1		a14 4-0	D24 4-2	S24 0-2	a22 5-2	M25 0-1	F18 0-2	A27 0-1	a08 1-0	F04 1-0	O08 1-0	N26 2-1	J21 3-1	N05 2-2	O22 5-1	a18 2-0	J14 1-0	S05 1-0	m06 3-0	M04 3-0	S10 1-1
3 BRIGHTON & H.A.	S17 1-2	a17 2-1		D27 3-1	O29 2-0	S07 3-1	a22 0-1	M18 1-1	F04 1-3	m06 0-1	M04 3-0	N05 7-0	D24 0-2	F18 1-1	J21 3-0	N19 2-1	J14 1-1	O01 0-1	A27 0-0	D10 0-0	a08 2-1	O15 1-1
4 BRISTOL R	J14 5-1	S14 0-0	D26 1-2		S10 4-2	a08 1-3	a10 0-3	F04 2-0	O22 2-0	M25 0-0	J21 3-4	S24 2-0	N12 4-2	A27 1-3	S07 1-1	O08 1-1	N19 2-0	a14 0-0	m06 1-0	a22 0-0	F18 1-1	a18 1-1
5 CHARLTON A	O15 2-1	O01 1-1	O22 1-0	S17 2-0		A27 1-0	S05 0-0	a22 0-1	M04 1-0	J14 2-1	a08 1-1	D10 2-2	D26 2-1	M25 0-0	F18 1-2	D17 1-1	a14 0-1	N28 1-2	F04 4-0	J21 1-0	m06 4-5	N12 1-0
6 EXETER C	a29 0-1	a15 1-0	A31 0-3	a01 2-2	S03 1-0		N19 1-1	D10 0-1	a17 1-0	N12 1-0	D31 2-2	a03 2-0	M11 2-0	D26 0-2	S10 1-4	F25 0-1	M18 1-3	F11 0-0	S24 4-1	O15 1-1	O29 1-4	D24 1-3
7 GILLINGHAM	a01 3-1	M18 0-0	a15 1-0	M11 3-2	A31 2-0	M06 3-0		J14 0-1	S24 5-0	S14 0-1	a14 0-2	D26 3-2	F11 5-2	S10 1-2	O08 1-2	J28 1-2	F25 2-0	S03 2-0	O22 1-0	N12 0-0	D24 2-2	m06 1-1
8 LUTON T	M11 1-2	F25 3-0	M25 2-0	F11 1-2	a15 2-0	S14 4-0	D31 7-0		O08 3-0	D17 1-0	S10 4-0	m06 3-0	S03 2-1	S24 1-0	O22 1-0	a17 3-1	M06 0-1	A29 0-0	N05 3-0	N19 3-0	D27 2-1	a01 1-1
9 MERTHYR T	J28 0-1	S03 2-0	F11 2-1	O29 0-2	M11 1-0	a14 0-0	O01 2-0	O15 2-0		S17 3-1	N12 2-1	M18 2-1	a29 3-0	N26 0-1	D24 2-1	a15 2-0	A29 2-0	m01 0-1	J14 2-2	D26 1-0	D12 4-1	F25 1-2
10 MILLWALL	a15 0-0	a01 1-1	a29 2-0	M18 4-1	D31 0-1	N05 1-0	D10 1-0	D24 1-1	S10 4-0		D26 1-1	A27 0-0	F25 2-2	a14 1-1	S24 1-1	F11 0-0	M11 3-0	D03 0-1	O08 0-0	O29 0-0	N19 0-0	S05 0-0
11 NEWPORT CO	F25 1-0	F11 2-1	M11 0-1	J28 0-1	a27 2-1	J14 1-1	a17 1-1	S17 2-2	N05 0-2	D27 1-0		a15 2-2	O01 1-0	O22 0-0	N26 0-0	A29 0-1	S03 1-0	a29 0-1	S12 2-1	J02 2-3	O15 4-0	M18 0-0
12 NORTHAMPTON T	O22 2-0	O15 2-0	N12 2-0	O01 2-2	J19 1-0	J21 2-3	D27 3-1	a29 2-0	M25 2-0	S03 0-3	a22 2-0		a18 3-0	a08 1-3	M04 0-0	J14 1-0	S17 2-1	a24 0-0	F18 0-2	F04 0-1	S05 2-1	N19 1-0
13 NORWICH C	D10 0-0	N19 0-0	a06 1-1	N05 0-1	D27 2-0	M04 0-0	F04 2-0	A27 0-1	m06 2-0	F23 3-1	S24 2-2	a17 2-0		S08 1-1	a22 2-1	S10 0-0	O29 4-1	O08 2-2	a08 1-1	M25 3-2	J21 1-2	D31 1-1
14 PLYMOUTH A	F11 3-0	J28 4-1	F25 3-1	S03 1-0	M18 3-0	D27 0-0	S17 3-0	O01 2-0	N19 0-0	a17 2-0	O29 1-0	a01 2-0	A29 1-1		D03 0-0	a29 4-0	O15 2-0	a15 1-0	D17 4-0	D31 3-1	N12 1-0	M11 3-0
15 PORTSMOUTH	S03 2-2	N12 1-0	F08 0-0	A31 1-0	F25 1-0	S17 2-0	O15 4-1	O29 1-1	M08 2-1	O01 2-2	N19 4-3	M11 1-1	a15 0-1	D10 3-1		a01 1-0	a29 1-0	M18 0-2	D27 6-0	a14 3-0	J14 1-3	F11 2-0
16 Q.P.R.	N12 1-0	O29 1-1	N26 3-0	O15 1-2	D24 3-1	F18 2-1	J21 1-0	a14 1-0	a22 0-0	F04 6-1	S05 2-1	D31 4-0	S17 2-0	m06 2-0	a08 1-1		O01 1-1	D26 2-2	M25 1-0	M04 1-0	A27 0-0	D10 1-1
17 READING	D24 0-1	D10 0-3	D31 0-0	a05 4-0	a17 1-2	M25 0-0	F18 2-1	J21 2-1	S07 5-0	M15 1-0	A27 1-0	S10 0-0	O22 2-1	O08 0-1	m06 1-1	S24 0-1		N05 0-1	a22 4-0	a08 2-0	F04 1-1	D27 2-1
18 SOUTHAMPTON	a17 1-0	D31 0-0	S24 3-0	D10 1-0	N19 6-0	F04 2-0	A27 2-0	S05 2-1	a08 1-1	J21 4-2	m06 5-0	D24 8-0	O15 2-0	a22 0-0	M25 1-1	D27 1-1	N12 0-0		M04 5-0	F20 1-1	S10 3-1	O29 2-0
19 SOUTHEND U	N19 3-2	A29 1-1	S03 1-2	a29 3-0	F11 1-1	O01 0-1	O29 2-0	N12 0-1	D31 2-1	O15 1-1	D10 0-1	F25 1-1	a01 0-1	D24 1-0	D26 1-2	M18 1-2	a15 2-0	M11 0-0		S17 1-0	a14 1-2	a26 1-4
20 SWANSEA T	A29 1-2	a29 1-0	S12 2-1	a15 8-1	M09 0-0	O08 2-1	N05 2-0	N26 1-1	D27 3-2	O22 3-0	D24 2-2	F11 2-2	M18 1-1	J14 3-0	a17 2-2	M11 1-0	a01 0-0	F25 1-0	S10 1-1		S24 1-3	S03 3-0
21 SWINDON T	M18 2-2	M11 2-1	a01 1-0	F25 0-1	a29 0-0	O22 1-1	M20 0-0	D26 1-1	D10 3-0	N26 1-1	O08 3-2	A29 4-2	m01 6-1	N05 1-2	D31 0-0	S03 2-0	F11 4-0	S17 2-3	a17 6-1	O01 1-0		a15 0-3
22 WATFORD	O01 3-0	S17 0-0	O08 1-0	a17 1-0	N05 2-2	D17 0-0	a29 1-0	a08 4-1	F18 4-1	A31 0-1	M25 1-0	a14 2-2	J14 4-2	M04 0-1	F04 0-3	D03 2-2	D26 2-2	O22 1-1	J21 4-1	A27 0-0	a22 2-2	

LEAGUE TABLES

DIVISION 1

	P	W	D	L	F	A	W	D	L	F	A	Pts
Liverpool	42	15	4	2	43	15	7	9	5	20	21	57
Tottenham H	42	15	3	3	43	17	6	6	9	22	22	51
Burnley	42	16	3	2	49	18	6	2	13	23	36	49
Cardiff C	42	13	2	6	40	26	6	8	7	21	27	48
Aston Villa	42	16	3	2	50	19	6	0	15	24	36	47
Bolton W	42	12	4	5	40	24	8	3	10	28	35	47
Newcastle U	42	11	5	5	36	19	7	5	9	23	26	46
Middlesbrough	42	12	6	3	46	19	4	8	9	33	50	46
Chelsea	42	9	6	6	17	16	8	6	7	23	27	46
Manchester C	42	13	7	1	44	21	5	2	14	21	49	45
Sheffield U	42	11	3	7	32	17	4	7	10	27	37	40
Sunderland	42	13	4	4	46	23	3	4	14	14	39	40
WBA	42	8	6	7	26	23	7	4	10	25	40	40
Huddersfield T	42	12	3	6	33	14	3	6	12	20	40	39
Blackburn R	42	7	6	8	35	31	6	6	9	19	26	38
Preston NE	42	12	7	2	33	20	1	5	15	9	45	38
Arsenal	42	10	6	5	27	19	5	1	15	20	37	37
Birmingham	42	9	2	10	25	29	6	5	10	23	31	37
Oldham A	42	8	7	6	21	15	5	4	12	17	35	37
Everton	42	10	7	4	42	22	2	5	14	15	33	36
Bradford C	42	8	5	8	28	30	3	5	13	20	42	32
Manchester U	42	7	7	7	25	26	1	5	15	16	47	28

DIVISION 2

	P	W	D	L	F	A	W	D	L	F	A	Pts
Nottingham F	42	13	7	1	29	9	9	5	7	22	21	56
Stoke	42	9	11	1	31	11	9	5	7	29	33	52
Barnsley	42	14	5	2	43	18	8	3	10	24	34	52
West Ham U	42	15	3	3	39	13	5	5	11	13	26	48
Hull C	42	13	5	3	36	13	6	5	10	15	28	48
South Shields	42	11	7	3	25	13	6	5	10	18	25	46
Fulham	42	14	5	2	41	8	4	4	13	16	30	45
Leeds U	42	10	8	3	31	12	6	5	10	17	26	45
Leicester C	42	11	6	4	30	16	3	11	7	9	18	45
Sheffield W	42	12	4	5	31	24	3	10	8	16	26	44
Bury	42	11	3	7	35	19	4	7	10	19	36	40
Derby Co	42	11	3	7	34	22	4	6	11	26	42	39
Notts Co	42	10	7	4	34	18	2	8	11	13	33	39
Crystal P	42	9	6	6	28	20	4	7	10	17	31	39
Clapton O	42	12	4	5	33	18	3	5	13	10	32	39
Rotherham Co	42	8	9	4	17	7	6	2	13	15	36	39
Wolves	42	8	7	6	28	19	5	4	12	16	30	37
Port Vale	42	10	5	6	28	19	4	3	14	15	38	36
Blackpool	42	11	1	9	33	27	4	4	13	11	30	35
Coventry C	42	8	5	8	31	21	4	5	12	20	39	34
Bradford	42	10	5	6	32	22	2	4	15	14	40	33
Bristol C	42	10	3	8	25	18	2	6	13	12	40	33

DIVISION 3 North

	P	W	D	L	F	A	W	D	L	F	A	Pts
Stockport Co	38	13	5	1	36	10	11	3	5	24	11	56
Darlington	38	15	2	2	52	7	7	4	8	29	30	50
Grimsby T	38	15	4	0	54	15	6	4	9	18	32	50
Hartlepools U	38	10	6	3	33	11	7	2	10	19	28	42
Accrington S	38	15	1	3	50	15	4	2	13	23	42	41
Crewe A	38	13	1	5	39	21	5	4	10	21	35	41
Stalybridge	38	14	3	2	42	15	4	2	3	20	48	41
Walsall	38	15	2	2	52	17	3	1	15	14	48	39
Southport	38	11	6	2	39	12	3	4	12	16	32	38
Ashington	38	13	2	4	42	22	4	2	13	17	44	38
Durham C	38	14	0	5	43	20	3	3	13	25	47	37
Wrexham	38	12	4	3	40	17	2	5	12	11	39	37
Chesterfield	38	12	2	5	33	15	4	1	14	15	52	35
Lincoln C	38	11	2	6	32	20	3	4	12	10	39	34
Barrow	38	11	2	6	29	18	3	3	13	13	36	33
Nelson	38	7	6	6	27	23	6	1	12	21	43	33
Wigan B	38	9	4	6	32	28	2	5	12	14	44	31
Tranmere R	38	7	5	7	41	25	2	6	11	10	36	29
Halifax T	38	9	4	6	37	28	1	5	13	19	48	29
Rochdale	38	9	2	8	34	24	2	2	15	18	53	26

DIVISION 3 South

	P	W	D	L	F	A	W	D	L	F	A	Pts
Southampton	42	14	7	0	50	8	9	8	4	18	13	61
Plymouth A	42	17	4	0	43	4	8	7	6	20	20	61
Portsmouth	42	13	5	3	38	18	5	12	4	24	21	53
Luton T	42	16	2	3	47	9	6	6	9	17	26	52
QPR	42	13	7	1	36	12	5	6	10	17	32	49
Swindon T	42	10	7	4	40	21	6	6	9	32	39	45
Watford	42	9	9	3	34	21	4	9	8	20	27	44
Aberdare A	42	11	6	4	38	18	6	4	11	19	33	44
Brentford	42	15	2	4	41	17	1	9	11	11	26	43
Swansea T	42	11	8	2	40	19	2	7	12	10	28	41
Merthyr T	42	14	2	5	33	15	3	4	14	12	41	40
Millwall	42	6	13	2	22	10	4	5	12	16	32	38
Reading	42	10	5	6	28	15	4	5	12	12	32	38
Bristol R	42	8	8	5	32	24	6	2	13	20	43	38
Norwich C	42	8	10	3	29	17	4	3	14	21	45	37
Charlton A	42	10	6	5	28	19	3	5	13	15	37	37
Northampton T	42	13	3	5	30	17	0	8	13	17	54	37
Gillingham	42	11	4	6	36	20	3	4	14	11	40	36
Brighton & HA	42	9	6	6	33	19	4	3	14	12	32	35
Newport Co	42	8	7	6	22	18	3	5	13	22	43	34
Exeter C	42	7	5	9	22	29	4	7	10	16	30	34
Southend U	42	7	5	9	23	23	1	6	14	11	51	27

Football League Records

Top scorers: Div 1, C.Buchan (Sunderland) 30 goals; Div 2, H.Bedford (Blackpool) 32 goals; Div 3(N), G.Beel (Chesterfield), J.Carmichael (Grimsby Town) 23 goals; Div 3(S), F.Pagnam (Watford) 30 goals.

Goalkeeper Albert Iremonger, dropped after a 6-1 home defeat by Manchester United, he returned for the last game and helped Notts County win promotion.

Albert Fairclough scored 19 goals to help Bristol City win the Third Division South title. Later he signed for Derby County.

DIVISION 1

	ARSENAL	ASTON VILLA	BIRMINGHAM	BLACKBURN R	BOLTON W	BURNLEY	CARDIFF C	CHELSEA	EVERTON	HUDDERSFIELD T	LIVERPOOL	MANCHESTER C	MIDDLESBROUGH	NEWCASTLE U	NOTTINGHAM F	OLDHAM A	PRESTON N.E.	SHEFFIELD U	STOKE	SUNDERLAND	TOTTENHAM H	W.B.A.
1 ARSENAL		M31 2-0	D09 1-0	a02 1-1	D26 5-0	A28 1-1	S16 2-1	F24 3-1	N11 1-2	D16 1-1	S02 1-0	J20 1-0	M10 3-0	O28 1-2	F10 2-0	M17 2-0	a14 1-1	a28 2-0	D30 3-0	N25 2-3	S30 0-2	O07 3-1
2 ASTON VILLA	a07 1-1		M24 3-0	A26 2-0	O21 2-0	D26 3-1	S04 1-3	M30 1-0	a21 3-0	M03 2-1	N25 0-1	F03 2-0	S23 2-2	D16 1-1	J27 4-0	N11 3-0	D30 1-0	D09 0-1	F17 6-0	m05 1-0	O07 2-0	S09 2-0
3 BIRMINGHAM	D02 3-2	M17 1-0		O14 1-1	S30 2-0	a28 1-0	N04 0-0	S02 0-1	D16 1-1	D25 0-0	M31 0-1	S16 0-1	O28 2-0	A28 0-2	N18 2-0	F10 2-3	M10 1-0	M12 4-2	S13 2-0	J06 1-2	a14 2-1	J20 0-2
4 BLACKBURN R	J01 0-5	S02 4-2	O07 1-1		D16 1-0	O28 2-1	J20 3-1	a28 0-0	S16 5-1	N11 0-0	M12 1-0	D02 0-0	a14 2-0	M10 1-1	M17 2-0	M31 1-0	D25 1-1	S18 1-0	J22 1-5	S23 0-0	F10 1-0	D30 5-1
5 BOLTON W	D25 4-1	O28 3-0	S23 3-0	D23 3-0		F10 2-1	D30 0-0	a14 1-1	M30 0-2	O07 1-0	a18 1-1	N25 2-1	M31 1-1	M17 1-0	J02 4-2	S04 3-1	S02 1-1	J20 1-1	N04 1-1	S09 1-1	a11 0-2	D09 3-0
6 BURNLEY	S04 4-1	D25 1-1	m05 0-2	O21 3-1	M12 2-1		M30 1-5	N18 1-0	a07 0-1	M24 0-2	S30 2-0	F17 2-0	D09 3-0	O14 0-0	N04 8-2	D16 1-1	J20 2-0	J06 1-4	M03 3-2	a21 2-0	S16 0-1	A26 3-0
7 CARDIFF C	S09 4-1	A28 3-0	N11 1-1	J27 5-0	J06 1-0	a02 2-2		M10 6-1	S23 0-2	N25 0-1	O28 3-0	D16 3-1	M17 2-0	F10 5-0	a25 3-1	a28 2-0	M31 1-0	a14 1-0	D02 2-1	O07 2-4	S02 2-3	D26 3-0
8 CHELSEA	F17 0-0	a02 1-1	A26 1-1	m05 1-1	a21 3-0	N25 0-1	M03 1-1		F14 3-1	D02 2-2	D30 0-0	a07 1-1	S09 1-1	J20 3-0	D25 2-2	S23 4-0	N11 0-1	O07 0-0	S04 3-2	O21 1-3	D16 0-0	a25 2-2
9 EVERTON	N04 1-0	a14 2-1	D23 2-1	S09 2-0	a02 1-1	M31 1-0	S30 3-1	F10 3-1		D30 0-3	O14 0-1	D25 0-0	F28 5-3	S02 3-2	O28 4-2	M10 0-0	a28 1-0	M17 5-1	J20 4-0	D09 1-1	J01 3-1	N25 0-1
10 HUDDERSFIELD T	D23 4-0	M10 3-5	D26 4-0	N04 0-2	O14 0-2	M17 2-0	N18 1-0	D09 3-0	J06 1-0		a14 0-0	S30 0-0	S02 0-2	M31 2-0	A28 2-1	O28 3-0	M21 2-0	F10 2-1	S16 1-0	J27 0-1	a28 1-0	a03 4-1
11 LIVERPOOL	A26 5-2	N18 3-0	a07 0-0	F17 3-0	M03 3-0	S23 3-0	O21 3-1	J06 1-0	O07 5-1	a21 1-1		M24 2-0	J27 2-0	D02 0-2	D16 2-1	D26 2-1	S16 5-2	M30 2-1	m05 1-0	S06 5-1	N11 0-0	F07 2-0
12 MANCHESTER C	J27 0-0	F10 1-1	S09 0-1	D09 2-1	N18 2-0	F24 1-0	D23 5-1	M31 3-0	D26 2-1	S23 3-1	M17 1-0		A28 2-1	a28 0-0	a14 1-1	D30 3-2	O28 2-1	S02 3-3	O14 2-1	a02 1-0	M14 3-0	N11 1-1
13 MIDDLESBROUGH	M03 2-0	S30 2-2	O21 2-1	a21 1-2	a07 1-2	D02 4-1	M24 0-1	S16 2-1	F17 2-4	A26 2-2	J20 0-2	S04 5-0		D26 1-1	a02 4-0	O14 2-1	N25 1-1	N04 3-2	D16 3-1	a18 2-0	D30 2-0	m05 0-1
14 NEWCASTLE U	O21 1-1	D23 0-0	S06 0-0	M03 5-1	a16 1-0	O07 0-2	F28 3-1	J27 0-0	A26 2-0	a07 1-0	D09 0-1	m05 3-1	D25 1-1		J06 1-0	J01 1-0	S23 3-1	S09 3-0	a21 1-0	N04 2-1	N25 1-1	F14 2-0
15 NOTTINGHAM F	F03 2-1	J20 3-1	N25 1-1	M24 1-0	O05 1-1	N11 1-0	F17 3-2	D26 0-4	O21 2-1	S04 0-1	D23 1-3	a21 2-0	M30 2-1	D30 0-1		S16 1-0	O07 3-0	S23 1-0	a07 0-1	A26 1-0	D09 0-1	M03 0-4
16 OLDHAM A	M24 0-0	N04 0-2	F03 2-0	a07 1-0	S11 3-1	D23 1-1	m05 3-1	S30 2-0	M03 1-0	O21 0-3	D25 0-2	J06 0-3	O07 0-0	M30 0-0	S09 2-0		D09 2-1	N25 0-2	A26 4-1	F17 0-0	J20 0-3	a21 0-0
17 PRESTON N.E.	a21 1-2	J06 3-2	M03 2-3	D26 1-0	A26 3-1	J27 3-1	a07 3-0	N04 2-0	m05 2-2	F17 1-0	S09 1-3	O21 0-2	N18 1-2	S30 1-0	O14 2-2	D02 5-1		D23 2-3	F08 4-2	M24 2-0	a02 2-0	S04 0-0
18 SHEFFIELD U	O02 2-1	D02 1-1	F17 7-1	S04 1-1	J27 2-2	D30 2-1	a21 0-0	O14 0-2	a16 0-1	a09 0-2	a02 4-1	A26 2-0	N11 4-1	S16 2-0	S30 0-0	N18 2-2	D16 2-2		O21 2-0	M03 3-1	D26 2-0	a07 3-1
19 STOKE	J06 1-0	F24 1-1	a02 0-0	N18 1-1	N11 2-0	M10 0-1	D09 3-1	A28 1-2	J27 4-1	S09 2-2	a28 0-0	O07 1-1	D23 0-0	a14 1-0	M31 0-1	S02 2-2	F10 4-2	O28 4-0		D26 1-2	M17 0-0	S23 0-2
20 SUNDERLAND	N18 3-3	a28 2-0	D30 5-3	S30 4-3	S16 5-1	a14 3-1	O14 2-1	O28 1-1	D02 3-1	J20 1-1	A30 1-0	M30 2-0	F10 2-1	N11 2-0	S02 0-0	F24 2-0	M17 2-2	a11 3-5	J01 2-0		M31 2-0	D16 3-2
21 TOTTENHAM H	S23 1-2	O14 1-2	a21 2-0	F14 2-0	F17 0-1	S09 1-3	A26 1-1	D23 3-1	S04 2-0	m05 0-0	N04 2-4	M03 3-1	J06 2-0	N18 0-1	D02 2-1	J27 3-0	M30 1-1	D25 2-1	M24 3-1	a07 0-1		O21 3-1
22 W.B.A.	O14 7-0	S16 3-0	J27 1-0	J06 3-0	D02 1-1	S02 2-1	D27 3-0	M17 0-0	N18 0-0	a02 0-2	F10 0-0	N04 2-0	a28 1-0	M14 2-1	M10 0-0	a14 1-0	A28 2-2	M31 4-0	S30 0-1	D23 1-1	O28 5-1	

DIVISION 2

	BARNSLEY	BLACKPOOL	BRADFORD C	BURY	CLAPTON O	COVENTRY C	CRYSTAL P	DERBY CO	FULHAM	HULL C	LEEDS U	LEICESTER C	MANCHESTER U	NOTTS CO	PORT VALE	ROTHERHAM CO	SHEFFIELD W	SOUTHAMPTON	SOUTH SHIELDS	STOCKPORT CO	WEST HAM U	WOLVERHAMPTON W
1 BARNSLEY		J20 2-2	a02 3-1	A28 2-1	S02 2-1	M31 6-2	N25 1-2	S23 5-0	N11 0-1	D02 1-0	F10 1-0	D30 0-1	a28 2-2	O07 1-0	a14 0-1	D26 2-2	D16 2-4	S09 3-0	M10 5-0	O28 1-1	a16 2-0	M17 1-0
2 BLACKPOOL	J27 0-1		S09 3-0	a14 5-1	A28 0-0	M10 0-1	D02 4-0	O07 3-2	N25 3-0	D16 0-0	S02 1-0	D26 1-2	M31 1-0	N11 1-1	M17 0-2	a28 1-0	D30 3-0	S23 1-2	F10 3-0	M30 0-0	O28 4-1	F24 3-1
3 BRADFORD C	a03 2-0	S16 0-2		M31 4-0	a28 1-2	F24 4-0	D30 1-1	N25 0-0	D16 2-1	J20 2-1	S30 0-2	O07 2-2	M17 1-1	D09 1-2	M10 2-0	a14 0-1	D26 1-1	N11 0-0	O28 1-0	A28 2-0	S02 0-1	F10 1-1
4 BURY	S06 2-1	a21 3-0	a07 1-0		D02 5-1	O14 1-1	O21 2-1	M03 4-1	F14 0-1	A26 1-0	D25 1-1	m05 2-0	N18 2-2	F17 2-2	N11 2-0	D16 1-0	J27 4-0	M24 0-0	S16 1-0	D30 2-0	a02 2-5	S30 3-0
5 CLAPTON O	A26 0-1	S04 0-1	m05 1-0	D09 0-2		a02 0-0	F17 3-1	a07 0-0	M03 0-2	F03 2-0	O07 3-0	S09 2-0	N11 1-1	M24 2-1	S23 0-0	D30 5-1	O21 2-2	a21 1-0	D16 0-0	D26 0-2	N25 0-2	J27 4-1
6 COVENTRY C	a07 3-0	M03 1-2	F17 2-1	O07 3-0	a03 2-1		S07 2-1	O21 1-0	D11 1-0	m05 0-1	D16 1-2	M24 1-1	S23 2-0	A26 1-2	S09 1-2	N11 2-1	a21 1-1	a30 2-0	J20 0-2	N25 1-0	D30 1-3	D25 7-1
7 CRYSTAL P	N18 2-0	D09 1-1	J06 2-0	O28 1-1	F24 2-0	A30 0-0		D26 2-2	S09 0-0	O07 1-1	M17 1-0	S23 0-1	S02 2-3	M30 0-1	D23 2-0	F10 4-0	N11 2-0	J27 1-0	a14 1-1	M10 3-0	M31 1-5	a28 5-0
8 DERBY CO	S30 0-1	O14 1-0	N18 0-2	a11 1-0	M31 0-0	O28 4-0	D25 6-0		J20 2-0	M30 0-2	a28 0-1	D16 2-0	M14 1-1	D30 0-0	F10 1-2	M17 1-0	S16 1-1	D02 0-2	N11 1-0	a14 1-2	S04 2-1	S02 1-1
9 FULHAM	N04 0-1	N18 1-1	D23 0-0	F10 3-0	M10 0-0	D09 4-0	S16 2-1	J27 3-1		S30 0-0	M31 3-0	M30 2-0	O28 0-0	D26 2-1	S02 1-1	F24 1-2	O14 1-0	J06 1-1	a28 0-1	M17 3-0	a14 0-2	A28 2-0
10 HULL C	D09 2-1	D23 0-0	J27 0-0	S02 2-2	F10 2-1	a28 1-1	O14 1-1	a02 4-2	S23 1-0		M10 3-1	N11 1-3	D30 2-1	S16 0-2	A28 3-0	O28 2-3	N18 0-0	D25 1-3	M31 2-0	F24 1-0	M17 1-1	a14 0-0
11 LEEDS U	F24 1-1	A26 1-1	S23 1-0	D26 0-0	O14 0-0	D23 1-0	M24 4-1	m05 1-0	a07 1-1	M03 2-2		O21 0-0	J27 0-1	a21 3-0	J06 2-1	M30 2-0	F17 0-0	S04 1-0	N18 0-1	S09 2-0	N04 3-1	D02 1-0
12 LEICESTER C	J06 2-2	D25 1-2	O14 2-0	a28 2-0	S16 2-0	M17 2-1	S30 3-0	D23 0-1	a02 1-1	N04 0-1	O28 2-1		a14 0-1	J20 2-1	M31 3-0	A28 3-0	D02 3-1	N18 2-1	F26 3-0	S02 2-0	F15 0-6	M10 7-0
13 MANCHESTER U	J01 1-0	a07 2-1	M21 1-1	N25 0-1	N04 0-0	S30 2-1	A26 2-1	F17 0-0	O21 1-1	J06 3-2	J20 0-0	a21 0-2		F21 1-1	O07 1-2	D02 3-0	S04 1-0	M03 1-2	M30 3-0	D16 1-0	D25 1-2	S16 1-0
14 NOTTS CO	O14 1-0	N04 2-0	D02 0-0	M21 1-0	M17 3-1	S02 2-0	a02 0-4	J06 1-2	D25 1-0	S09 0-1	a14 1-0	J27 1-0	F10 1-6		O28 1-0	M10 2-0	S30 1-0	D16 1-0	A28 2-0	M31 2-0	a18 2-0	N18 4-1
15 PORT VALE	a21 1-1	F03 2-0	M03 1-2	N04 2-0	S30 3-1	S16 0-1	D16 2-0	F26 2-3	A26 0-1	S04 1-0	D30 1-2	a07 0-0	O14 1-0	O21 0-0		N25 0-0	m05 2-2	F17 0-0	D25 3-0	J13 0-2	J20 1-3	M30 1-0
16 ROTHERHAM CO	D25 1-1	m05 1-0	a21 0-2	D23 0-0	J06 0-0	N04 2-0	N06 4-1	M26 3-0	F17 1-3	O21 0-1	a02 3-1	S04 0-0	D09 1-1	M03 1-0	N18 3-1		A26 1-2	a07 0-0	S30 2-1	J27 2-1	S16 2-2	O14 3-2
17 SHEFFIELD W	D23 2-3	J06 2-3	D25 2-2	J20 2-0	O28 4-1	a14 3-0	N04 3-1	S09 0-0	O07 1-0	N25 1-0	M19 3-1	D09 2-1	A28 1-0	S23 0-1	a28 2-0	S02 1-0		J01 0-0	M17 2-0	F10 4-1	a30 0-2	M31 1-0
18 SOUTHAMPTON	S16 2-2	S30 1-1	N04 2-0	M17 0-3	a14 2-0	F10 3-0	J20 0-2	D09 0-4	D30 2-0	D26 2-1	A28 0-1	N25 0-0	a11 0-0	D23 0-1	M05 3-1	M31 4-2	a02 1-1		S02 0-2	a28 1-0	O14 2-0	O28 3-0
19 SOUTH SHIELDS	M03 2-0	M21 1-0	O21 0-0	S09 0-2	D23 3-0	J27 0-0	a21 2-0	N04 3-1	m05 2-0	a07 0-0	N25 0-2	F17 2-1	a02 0-3	S04 1-0	J01 3-1	S23 2-0	M24 1-1	A26 0-0		O07 3-0	D09 0-0	J06 1-1
20 STOCKPORT CO	O21 3-1	J01 2-2	S04 1-0	J06 1-0	D25 0-2	N18 5-1	M03 2-2	a21 2-1	M24 0-2	F17 1-1	S16 2-1	A26 4-5	D23 1-0	a07 0-0	D09 0-2	J20 1-0	M15 0-1	m05 3-0	O14 1-1		S30 2-1	N04 1-1
21 WEST HAM U	F17 0-0	O21 2-0	A26 1-2	M30 0-0	N18 1-0	J06 1-0	a07 1-1	A28 0-0	a21 1-0	a09 3-0	N11 0-0	F10 2-2	D26 0-2	m05 0-1	J27 0-0	S09 4-0	M03 2-1	O07 1-1	D02 1-0	S23 0-1		D23 1-0
22 WOLVERHAMPTON W	M24 3-3	F17 3-4	F19 4-1	S23 1-1	J20 1-3	D26 1-2	m05 1-0	A26 0-1	S04 0-0	a23 3-0	D09 0-1	M03 1-2	S09 0-1	N25 1-0	a02 3-0	O07 3-2	a07 2-0	O21 0-0	D30 1-0	N11 3-1	D16 1-4	

Season 1922-23

DIVISION 3 NORTH

	ACCRINGTON S	ASHINGTON	BARROW	BRADFORD	CHESTERFIELD	CREWE A	DARLINGTON	DURHAM C	GRIMSBY T	HALIFAX T	HARTLEPOOLS U	LINCOLN C	NELSON	ROCHDALE	SOUTHPORT	STALYBRIDGE C	TRANMERE R	WALSALL	WIGAN B	WREXHAM
1 ACCRINGTON S		D26 4-1	F17 3-4	J20 4-3	N04 0-4	J13 0-0	A26 2-1	S30 3-1	J01 4-0	D30 4-1	M10 2-1	m05 1-0	a21 0-1	F03 2-1	M24 3-1	a07 1-0	S16 4-1	D23 2-1	O07 0-0	O21 1-0
2 ASHINGTON	M03 2-5		D23 2-6	a14 2-1	O28 2-0	F10 2-4	S16 3-1	J01 0-0	F17 2-1	M31 3-2	S30 4-2	D09 0-2	O14 0-2	J06 2-0	N25 1-1	N11 0-3	a28 3-1	M17 3-0	S02 2-1	J20 1-1
3 BARROW	F24 5-2	J13 3-0		M31 1-2	S02 3-1	O28 2-0	S30 0-1	a28 2-1	F10 2-0	M24 0-1	O14 0-0	J06 1-3	N04 1-0	J27 4-1	D09 2-0	J02 0-1	a14 2-1	M10 0-0	J01 2-3	S09 1-0
4 BRADFORD	J27 5-1	a21 3-0	a07 3-0		D25 1-0	D23 3-0	F17 2-1	N04 4-1	J06 2-1	S09 2-2	M14 1-1	O21 4-1	A26 6-2	M24 3-0	m05 5-1	N18 1-0	O14 3-0	S23 2-2	a02 1-1	M03 0-1
5 CHESTERFIELD	N11 3-1	O21 2-2	A26 2-1	D09 2-2		S23 2-1	a21 0-0	D30 3-1	O14 3-2	M21 3-0	a07 1-1	a02 3-3	M03 1-2	D26 4-0	F03 3-0	F17 1-0	J01 5-0	S16 6-0	J20 3-1	m05 2-1
6 CREWE A	N25 1-1	F03 3-1	O21 1-0	D16 0-1	S30 2-0		O14 3-0	J20 4-0	N11 3-0	a02 2-1	a21 2-1	a07 3-1	M24 1-0	A26 0-1	F17 1 0	M03 4 1	D30 2-0	M30 0-0	S16 0-1	D25 0-0
7 DARLINGTON	S02 4-0	S09 1-1	S23 3-2	F24 2-0	a14 4-1	a28 5-0		M17 1-0	a02 1-3	F10 0-1	D25 4 0	J13 0 0	D09 2-3	J02 1-1	J27 2-1	J06 1-0	M10 4-0	O21 2-0	M31 2-0	N11 4-1
8 DURHAM C	S23 4-1	a02 1-1	m05 4-1	N11 0-0	J06 1-1	J27 2-0	M24 0-0		S09 0-3	O14 2-2	M03 3-2	F17 7-1	F03 0-1	a21 1-1	A26 1-1	O21 0-0	N25 1-0	D09 0-2	D23 2-2	a07 2-0
9 GRIMSBY T	D25 7-1	F24 7-4	F03 2-0	D30 0-1	O07 3-1	N04 2-3	M30 0-1	S16 1-0		D23 0-1	m05 1-0	a21 1-0	a07 0-2	O21 1-1	M03 2-1	M24 3-0	J20 0-0	N18 1-2	S23 0-0	A26 4-0
10 HALIFAX T	J06 0-0	a07 0-0	M17 3-0	S16 3-0	N25 2-0	D09 1-0	F03 2-1	O07 1-3	J22 1-0		O21 3-0	A26 3-1	D25 2-2	M03 1-0	a21 0-1	m05 2-1	S23 3-1	J20 1-2	N11 0-1	F17 1-1
11 HARTLEPOOLS U	D09 0-0	S23 3-1	O07 2-0	F10 0-1	M31 5-0	a14 1-1	J01 1-0	D26 2-1	a28 2-0	O28 3-2		J02 2-0	J06 5-1	N04 0-2	S09 1-1	J27 4-0	F24 0-1	S02 2-2	M17 0-0	N18 1-1
12 LINCOLN C	a28 0-0	M30 2-0	D30 1-1	O28 0-0	M17 0-0	M31 1-0	N25 1-1	F24 3-1	a14 1-2	S02 0-0	D23 2-1		J20 1-0	S09 0-1	N04 2-0	S23 1-1	F10 2-0	D25 0-2	M10 2-1	O14 2-0
13 NELSON	a14 2-1	O07 1-3	N11 2-1	S02 1-0	M10 4-0	M17 0-0	D23 3-0	F10 4-0	M31 1-1	S12 2-0	D30 4-1	J27 2-1		N25 1-2	S23 2-0	S09 1-0	O28 1-0	a28 3-0	F24 1-0	a24 2-0
14 ROCHDALE	F10 1-1	D30 2-0	J20 3-1	M17 0-3	M30 0-2	S02 1-1	O07 2-2	a14 2-0	O28 0-1	M10 0-1	N11 4-0	S16 1-1	J13 0-3		D23 3-2	a03 2-0	D04 0-0	F24 0-2	a28 3-2	S23 5-0
15 SOUTHPORT	M17 1-2	N18 1-0	M30 2-0	a28 0-0	F10 0-2	J01 2-0	J20 2-1	S02 1-0	M10 3-1	a14 1-3	S16 1-0	N11 3-0	S30 0-1	D25 0-1		O07 0-0	D26 0-0	M31 2-1	O21 1-0	J06 1-0
16 STALYBRIDGE C	M31 1-0	N04 2-1	N25 2-0	D26 1-0	F24 1-2	M10 0-1	D30 4-2	M30 1-0	M17 3-2	a28 4-3	J20 1-1	S30 0-1	S16 2-0	a02 0-0	O14 1-0		S02 4-1	a14 2-0	F20 0-2	D23 3-2
17 TRANMERE R	S09 4-1	D25 1-0	a21 3-0	O07 0-0	D23 2-3	J06 1-2	M03 2-2	J13 5-1	J27 3-2	S30 2-1	F17 1-1	F03 2-0	O21 0-2	a07 2-0	a02 2-0	A26 1-1		N04 2-3	M30 4-2	M24 4-0
18 WALSALL	a02 0-2	M24 2-1	M03 3-1	S30 1-0	S09 0-1	O07 1-1	O28 2-2	a03 2-0	N25 1-0	J27 2-1	A26 2-2	D26 2-0	m05 5-0	O14 0-0	a07 1-0	a21 2-1	N11 2-1		J06 3-1	F10 1-0
19 WIGAN B	O14 2-0	A26 6-1	D26 2-1	N25 3-2	J27 1-0	S09 1-1	a07 3-0	D25 0-2	S30 1-0	N04 0-1	M24 2-0	M03 9-1	F17 3-1	m05 6-0	O28 1-0	a18 3-0	D09 0-0	D30 1-0		a14 1-1
20 WREXHAM	O28 2 0	J27 0 0	S16 0-0	M10 3-0	a28 3-1	D26 2-1	N04 0-0	M31 1-0	S02 1-1	F24 2-1	N25 2-0	O07 0-2	a02 2-1	S30 3-1	D30 1-1	D09 2-1	M17 2-1	F03 1-0	a21 2-1	

DIVISION 3 SOUTH

	ABERDARE A	BRENTFORD	BRIGHTON & HA	BRISTOL C	BRISTOL R	CHARLTON A	EXETER C	GILLINGHAM	LUTON T	MERTHYR T	MILLWALL	NEWPORT CO	NORTHAMPTON T	NORWICH C	PLYMOUTH A	PORTSMOUTH	Q.P.R.	READING	SOUTHEND U	SWANSEA T	SWINDON T	WATFORD
1 ABERDARE A		F17 0-0	m01 0-1	a02 0-1	a21 0-0	M24 3-1	A26 3-1	N25 2-0	O14 2-1	D25 0 0	S30 0 1	J27 6 2	O21 0-2	F03 0-3	a07 2-2	S09 0-2	N04 0-0	m05 0-0	S11 1-1	J06 0-1	M01 3-3	M03 3-1
2 BRENTFORD	F24 0-1		O28 1-2	M31 4-0	D23 0-1	J27 0-3	O14 0-1	S02 2-0	A28 3-2	N04 3-1	a28 1-1	M17 0-0	S30 2-1	S16 1-4	J06 2-0	a14 1-0	S11 1-3	N18 1-1	M30 0-0	M10 0-1	F10 3-0	D26 2-1
3 BRIGHTON & H.A.	D09 3-1	O21 2-1		J20 2-1	M24 2 1	F17 1 0	S06 3 0	O07 3 0	S16 0-1	m05 0-0	a02 2-0	D23 2-1	J06 1-0	A26 0-0	M03 1-0	D25 7-1	S30 2-0	a07 3-1	a21 0-1	N04 1-3	N25 1-1	F21 3-0
4 BRISTOL C	M30 0-0	a07 1-1	J27 3-1		S23 0-1	m05 3-1	F17 1-1	J06 2-1	D09 1-0	F14 3-0	N18 1-1	S09 2-0	M03 1-0	M24 4-0	S04 2-0	N04 2-1	D23 3-2	A26 2-1	O21 5-0	O14 1-0	D26 3-1	a21 3-1
5 BRISTOL R	a14 1-0	a30 1-1	M17 0-0	S30 1-2		N25 1-1	D25 3-3	M10 1-0	F10 1-1	a02 3-0	O28 0-0	A28 3-1	J20 0-0	a23 3-2	N11 0-1	S02 0-1	M26 1-3	S16 1-1	O07 2-0	a28 0-0	M31 2-0	S13 1-2
6 CHARLTON A	M17 1-1	J20 1-1	a16 0-1	a28 1-0	N18 0-0		S16 0-0	F10 3-1	S02 2-1	S30 0-1	N11 0-2	a14 6-0	a02 2-0	D25 3-0	O23 1-0	A28 0-2	O28 1-1	O14 1-0	M12 5-1	M31 3-1	m03 3-1	D30 0-0
7 EXETER C	S02 1-0	O07 0-2	A30 1-0	F24 0-0	D26 0-0	S09 0-0		a28 0-1	M31 1-2	D23 2-1	M17 2-1	F10 4-0	J13 1-2	N04 2-0	a02 0-0	M10 2-3	a14 1-2	J06 4-0	D09 2-1	O28 1-0	J20 2-1	S23 1-2
8 GILLINGHAM	N18 4-0	A26 2-0	O14 2-0	D30 1-1	M03 0-1	F14 2-2	m05 2-1		M30 1-0	a21 2-0	D25 3-0	J13 3-0	S06 0-3	a25 5-0	F17 1-0	J20 4-2	S16 0-1	M24 2-1	a07 1-0	S30 2-2	N04 0-0	O21 1-4
9 LUTON T	O07 4-1	S04 4-0	S09 1-1	D02 1-1	F03 1-0	A26 2-2	a07 6-0	a02 2-0		M24 2-1	D30 2-2	N11 1-0	a21 2-1	m05 4-0	O21 2-1	D23 0-2	D26 1-0	F17 1-2	M03 2-0	J20 6-1	S23 3-2	N25 0-1
10 MERTHYR T	D26 0-2	N11 1-0	a28 2-0	F10 0-1	a03 1-1	S23 3-0	a12 3-1	a14 1-0	M17 0-1		M10 1-1	O28 1-0	M05 3-0	N18 0-1	S16 0-1	F24 3-0	M31 0-1	J20 1-1	D30 2-1	S02 2-1	A28 1-1	O07 2-3
11 MILLWALL	S23 1-0	m05 1-1	M30 2-1	N25 1-1	O21 1-0	N04 1-1	M24 3-0	D26 3-1	J06 0-0	M03 1-0		O07 0-0	a07 2-0	a21 3-0	A26 0-0	J01 1-3	J27 0-0	F10 0-0	F17 1-1	D23 0-2	S09 1-1	S04 5-1
12 NEWPORT CO	J20 0-0	M24 0-1	D16 1-0	S16 0-1	S07 4-1	a21 4-0	F03 6-2	D09 2-1	N04 0-3	O21 1-1	O14 0-0		F24 1-1	M10 1-3	m05 1-0	S30 0-0	N18 1-0	a02 3-0	A26 0-2	D27 1-2	J06 2-2	a07 0-1
13 NORTHAMPTON T	O28 3-1	S23 1-1	D30 0-0	M10 2-1	J27 1-0	a03 0-0	N25 3-0	A28 1-0	a14 2-0	D09 1-1	M31 2-1	F17 2-1		O14 1-1	D26 1-0	M17 3-0	a28 4-2	D23 5-0	N11 5-2	F10 1-3	S02 1-2	S09 1-1
14 NORWICH C	F10 1-4	S09 0-2	S02 1-0	M17 2-2	J06 0-0	D26 2-3	N11 6-0	D23 1-1	a28 1-2	N25 1-1	a14 3-2	M03 1-1	O07 1-0		J27 1-0	a07 0-2	A28 1-1	D27 2-0	S23 2-1	F24 1-4	O28 0-0	a02 2-0
15 PLYMOUTH A	M31 2-0	m02 3-0	M10 2-2	A28 5-1	N04 3-0	D09 2-0	M30 5-1	a18 2-0	O28 4-0	S09 2-0	S02 1-0	a28 1-0	D25 1-0	J20 1-1		O14 2-0	F10 2-0	S30 3-0	N25 1-1	a14 2-0	M17 2-0	D23 1-0
16 PORTSMOUTH	S16 1-0	a21 3-0	D26 1-2	N11 1-2	A26 0-0	S06 3-0	M03 3-4	J27 6-1	D16 1-2	F17 1-1	D02 2 0	S23 2 0	M24 0-0	M31 2-1	O07 1-2		J06 1-1	O21 1-0	F03 0-0	N18 0-3	M30 4-1	m05 1-0
17 Q.P.R.	N11 4-1	D09 1-1	S23 0-0	D16 1-2	F17 3 1	O21 1-2	a21 2-0	S09 2-1	D25 4-0	a07 1-1	J20 2-3	N25 1-1	m05 3-2	S04 2-0	M15 2-3	D30 0-1		M03 1-0	M24 1-0	M30 2-1	O07 0-2	A26 1-2
18 READING	a28 1-0	N25 1-0	M31 0-0	S02 0-0	S09 0-1	O07 2-1	D30 1-3	M17 1-1	F24 3-0	J27 1-0	F14 1-2	M30 2-0	D16 0-0	D09 4-1	S23 0-1	O28 0-0	M21 0-0		D26 1-1	A30 4-4	a14 1-0	N11 1-0
19 SOUTHEND U	S25 4-0	a02 1-2	a14 0-0	O28 0-3	O14 0-0	D23 0-0	D16 5-0	M31 1-1	M10 1-3	J06 1-1	F24 4-0	S02 3-1	N04 1-2	S30 3-1	a09 2-1	F10 0 0	M17 2 0	D25 3-1		S16 0-1	a28 2-0	J20 2-1
20 SWANSEA T	D30 5-1	M03 0-0	N11 0-0	O07 4-1	m05 0-1	a07 3-2	O21 5-1	S23 1-0	J27 1-0	A26 1-1	D16 0-1	D26 5-1	F03 4-0	F17 3-1	a21 1-1	N25 2-1	a02 3-0	S04 2-2	S09 1-0		O02 5-0	M24 0-0
21 SWINDON T	D23 5-4	F03 3-0	N18 3-0	D27 0-1	a07 1-0	M03 2-1	J27 2-1	N11 0-1	S30 1-1	S04 4-0	S16 0-0	D30 2-2	A26 2-0	O21 1-2	M24 2-1	a02 3-0	O14 1-0	a21 3-1	m05 3-0	D09 2-1		F17 1-1
22 WATFORD	M10 6-0	D25 2-0	F10 1-2	a14 1-1	D09 0-1	J06 2-2	S30 4-0	O28 5-2	N18 2-1	O14 1-1	A30 0-0	M31 2-1	S16 0-0	M30 2-1	D16 1-0	a28 2-3	S02 0-3	N04 1-0	J27 1-1	M17 2-1	F24 0-3	

LEAGUE TABLES

DIVISION 1

	P	W	D	L	F	A	W	D	L	F	A	Pts
Liverpool	42	17	3	1	50	13	9	5	7	20	18	60
Sunderland	42	15	5	1	50	25	7	5	9	22	29	54
Huddersfield T	42	14	2	5	35	15	7	9	5	25	17	53
Newcastle U	42	13	6	2	31	11	5	6	10	14	26	48
Everton	42	14	4	3	41	20	6	3	12	22	39	47
Aston Villa	42	15	3	3	42	11	3	7	11	22	40	46
WBA	42	12	7	2	38	10	5	4	12	20	39	45
Manchester C	42	14	6	1	38	16	3	5	13	12	33	45
Cardiff C	42	15	2	4	51	18	3	5	13	22	41	43
Sheffield U	42	11	7	3	41	20	5	3	13	27	44	42
Arsenal	42	13	4	4	38	16	3	6	12	23	46	42
Tottenham H	42	11	3	7	34	22	6	4	11	16	28	41
Bolton W	42	11	8	2	36	17	3	4	14	14	41	40
Blackburn R	42	12	7	2	32	19	2	5	14	15	43	40
Burnley	42	12	3	6	39	24	4	3	14	19	35	38
Preston NE	42	12	3	6	41	26	1	8	12	19	38	37
Birmingham	42	10	4	7	25	19	3	7	11	16	38	37
Middlesbrough	42	11	4	6	41	25	2	6	13	16	38	36
Chelsea	42	5	13	3	29	20	4	5	12	16	33	36
Nottingham F	42	12	2	7	25	23	1	6	14	16	47	34
Stoke	42	7	9	5	28	19	3	1	17	19	48	30
Oldham A	42	9	6	6	21	20	1	4	16	14	45	30

DIVISION 2

	P	W	D	L	F	A	W	D	L	F	A	Pts
Notts Co	42	16	1	4	29	15	7	6	8	17	19	53
West Ham U	42	9	8	4	21	11	11	3	7	42	27	51
Leicester C	42	14	2	5	42	19	7	7	7	23	25	51
Manchester U	42	10	6	5	25	17	7	8	6	26	19	48
Blackpool	42	12	4	5	37	14	6	7	8	23	29	47
Bury	42	14	5	2	41	16	4	6	11	14	30	47
Leeds U	42	11	8	2	26	10	7	3	11	17	26	47
Sheffield W	42	14	3	4	36	16	3	9	9	18	31	46
Barnsley	42	12	4	5	42	21	5	7	9	20	30	45
Fulham	42	10	7	4	29	12	6	5	10	14	20	44
Southampton	42	10	5	6	28	21	4	9	8	12	19	42
Hull C	42	9	8	4	29	22	5	6	10	14	23	42
South Shields	42	11	7	3	26	12	4	3	14	9	32	40
Derby Co	42	9	5	7	25	16	5	6	10	21	34	39
Bradford C	42	8	7	6	27	18	4	6	11	14	27	37
Crystal P	42	10	7	4	33	16	3	4	14	21	46	37
Port Vale	42	8	6	7	23	18	6	3	12	16	33	37
Coventry C	42	12	2	7	35	21	3	5	13	11	42	37
Clapton O	42	9	6	6	26	17	3	6	12	14	33	36
Stockport Co	42	10	6	5	32	24	4	2	15	11	34	36
Rotherham Co	42	10	7	4	30	19	3	2	16	14	44	35
Wolves	42	9	4	8	32	26	0	5	16	10	51	27

DIVISION 3 North

	P	W	D	L	F	A	W	D	L	F	A	Pts
Nelson	38	15	2	2	37	10	9	1	9	24	31	51
Bradford	38	14	4	1	51	15	5	5	9	16	23	47
Walsall	38	13	4	2	32	14	6	4	9	19	30	46
Chesterfield	38	13	5	1	49	18	6	2	11	19	34	45
Wigan B	38	14	3	2	45	11	4	5	10	19	28	44
Crewe A	38	13	3	3	32	9	4	6	9	16	29	43
Halifax T	38	11	4	4	29	14	6	3	10	24	32	41
Accrington S	38	14	2	3	40	21	3	5	11	19	44	41
Darlington	38	13	3	3	43	14	2	7	10	16	32	40
Wrexham	38	13	5	1	29	12	1	5	13	9	36	38
Stalybridge	38	13	2	4	32	18	2	4	13	10	29	36
Rochdale	38	8	5	6	29	22	5	5	9	13	31	36
Lincoln C	38	9	7	3	21	11	4	3	12	18	44	36
Grimsby T	38	10	3	6	35	18	4	2	13	20	34	33
Hartlepools U	38	10	6	3	34	14	0	6	13	14	40	32
Tranmere R	38	11	4	4	41	21	1	4	14	8	38	32
Southport	38	11	3	5	21	12	1	4	14	11	34	31
Barrow	38	11	2	6	31	17	2	2	15	19	43	30
Ashington	38	10	3	6	34	33	1	5	13	17	44	30
Durham C	38	7	9	3	31	19	2	1	16	12	40	28

DIVISION 3 South

	P	W	D	L	F	A	W	D	L	F	A	Pts
Bristol C	42	16	4	1	43	13	8	7	6	23	27	59
Plymouth A	42	18	3	0	47	6	5	4	12	14	23	53
Swansea C	42	13	6	2	46	14	9	3	9	32	31	53
Brighton & HA	42	15	3	3	39	13	5	8	8	13	21	51
Luton T	42	14	4	3	47	18	7	3	11	21	31	49
Millwall	42	9	10	2	27	13	5	8	8	18	27	46
Portsmouth	42	10	5	6	34	20	9	3	9	24	32	46
Northampton T	42	13	6	2	40	17	4	5	12	14	27	45
Swindon T	42	14	4	3	41	17	3	7	11	21	39	45
Watford	42	10	6	5	35	23	7	4	10	22	31	44
QPR	42	10	4	7	34	24	6	6	9	20	25	42
Charlton A	42	11	6	4	33	14	3	8	10	22	37	42
Bristol R	42	7	9	5	25	19	6	7	8	10	17	42
Brentford	42	9	4	8	27	23	4	8	9	14	28	38
Southend U	42	10	6	5	35	18	2	7	12	14	36	37
Gillingham	42	13	4	4	38	18	2	3	16	13	41	37
Merthyr T	42	10	4	7	27	17	1	10	10	12	31	36
Norwich C	42	8	7	6	29	26	5	3	13	22	45	36
Reading	42	9	8	4	24	15	1	6	14	12	40	34
Exeter C	42	10	4	7	27	18	3	3	15	20	66	33
Aberdare A	42	6	8	7	25	23	3	3	15	17	47	29
Newport Co	42	8	6	7	28	21	0	5	16	12	49	27

Football League Records

Top scorers: Div 1, W.Chadwick (Everton) 28 goals; Div 2, H.Bedford (Blackpool) 34 goals; Div 3(N), D.Brown (Darlington) 27 goals; Div 3(S), W.P.Haines (Portsmouth) 28 goals.
Stalybridge Celtic resigned. New Brighton, Doncaster Rovers and Bournemouth & Boscombe Athletic were elected to League.

Outside-left Billy Smith played a major role in Huddersfield Town's hat-trick of League titles and altogether scored 126 goals in 574 appearances during a 21-year playing career at Leeds Road.

DIVISION 1

	ARSENAL	ASTON VILLA	BIRMINGHAM	BLACKBURN R	BOLTON W	BURNLEY	CARDIFF C	CHELSEA	EVERTON	HUDDERSFIELD T	LIVERPOOL	MANCHESTER C	MIDDLESBROUGH	NEWCASTLE U	NOTTINGHAM F	NOTTS CO	PRESTON N.E.	SHEFFIELD U	SUNDERLAND	TOTTENHAM H	W.B.A.	WEST HAM U
1 ARSENAL		F16 0-1	S29 0-0	D01 2-2	O27 0-0	a05 2-0	J19 1-2	D29 1-0	a21 0-1	D15 1-3	M01 3-1	O13 1-2	N03 2-1	A25 1-4	M22 1-0	D27 0-0	m03 1-2	F25 1-3	a12 2-0	N17 1-1	S15 1-0	S10 4-1
2 ASTON VILLA	M12 2-1		S01 0-0	a02 1-0	J26 1-0	O13 1-1	D29 2-1	S15 0-0	S12 1-1	a30 3-1	N17 0-0	A29 2-0	D01 0-0	a21 6-1	a19 2-0	N03 0-0	S29 5-1	D22 2-2	F09 0-1	M15 0-0	O27 4-0	D25 1-1
3 BIRMINGHAM	S22 0-2	A25 3-0		O06 1-1	S10 0-3	F27 2-1	m03 0-0	M22 1-0	D08 0-1	O20 0-1	S05 2-1	D26 3-0	F16 2-1	a05 4-1	J19 0-2	N17 0-0	M01 2-0	a19 0-1	S08 0-2	J05 3-2	D22 0-0	N10 2-0
4 BLACKBURN R	D08 2-0	M01 3-1	O13 4-1		a12 3-1	N03 1-1	M20 2-1	A25 3-0	S15 2-0	D29 1-0	M22 0-0	O20 0-1	F02 2-0	S17 2-1	a05 1-1	J01 4-1	D25 2-0	F16 1-1	N24 3-2	D22 0-1	S29 4-0	J19 0-0
5 BOLTON W	O20 1-2	J19 1-0	J01 1-1	a19 3-0		M01 0-0	S01 2-2	N10 4-0	D29 2-0	N17 3-1	M12 4-1	S15 0-0	M22 2-0	a18 0-1	F16 4-0	D15 7-1	a05 0-0	S03 4-2	O13 1-0	S29 3-1	D25 2-0	D01 1-1
6 BURNLEY	a28 4-1	O06 1-2	F09 1-2	N10 1-2	a01 1-0		a19 1-2	D15 2-0	A27 2-2	a18 1-1	S22 2-0	M17 3-2	D25 0-0	D01 3-2	S08 2-4	S01 1-1	D29 1-0	O27 2-0	M15 0-3	a26 2-2	J26 4-0	N17 5-1
7 CARDIFF C	J26 4-0	J05 0-2	a26 2-0	F09 2-0	A25 3-2	a12 2-0		O13 1-1	M29 0-0	a14 0-0	D22 2-0	N24 1-1	a21 1-0	S29 1-0	D08 4-1	M15 0-2	O20 1-1	D26 3-1	A27 2-1	a07 2-1	N03 3-0	S15 1-0
8 CHELSEA	J05 0-0	S08 0-0	M15 1-1	S01 2-0	N03 0-0	D22 3-2	O06 1-2		F23 1-1	J26 0-1	a18 2-1	a30 3-1	N24 2-0	a19 1-0	D26 1-1	F09 0-6	D08 1-2	S22 1-1	a26 4-1	A27 0-1	M12 0-0	O20 0-0
9 EVERTON	a18 3-1	S19 2-0	D01 2-0	S08 0-0	J05 2-2	S03 3-3	a05 0-0	F16 2-0		S22 1-1	O06 1-0	D22 6-1	J19 1-0	M01 2-2	A25 2-1	O27 3-0	F06 1-1	N10 2-0	D26 2-3	a19 4-2	N17 2-0	M22 2-1
10 HUDDERSFIELD T	D22 6-1	a05 1-0	O27 1-0	J05 1-0	N24 1-0	a22 1-0	M01 2-0	J19 0-1	S29 2-0		N10 3-1	a12 1-1	A25 1-0	F27 1-1	m03 3-0	S15 0-0	S04 4-0	M22 1-0	D08 3-2	D26 2-1	O13 0-0	F16 1-1
11 LIVERPOOL	a02 0-0	N24 0-1	A29 6-2	M15 0-0	F09 3-1	S29 1-0	D15 0-2	J01 3-1	O13 1-2	N03 1-1		J26 0-0	a12 3-1	D25 0-1	O20 4-2	a26 1-0	S15 3-1	D08 2-3	M19 4-2	M29 1-0	S01 0-0	D29 2-0
12 MANCHESTER C	O06 1-0	S05 1-2	a18 1-0	O27 3-1	S08 1-1	F16 2-2	N17 1-1	a05 1-0	D15 2-1	a19 1-1	J19 0-1		M01 3-2	N03 1-1	F13 1-3	D01 1-0	M22 2-2	A25 2-1	S22 4-1	J01 1-0	D29 3-3	m03 2-1
13 MIDDLESBROUGH	N10 0-0	D08 0-2	F23 0-1	M08 2-0	M15 1-2	D26 3-0	J01 0-1	N17 2-0	J26 1-1	S01 2-0	a19 1-1	a02 1-1		O20 1-0	O06 5-2	A29 2-3	D22 1-2	J05 0-1	M29 1-3	S15 0-1	F09 0-1	S29 0-1
14 NEWCASTLE U	S01 1-0	J01 4-1	a09 2-1	A29 2-1	S12 1-0	D08 2-0	S22 1-1	a12 2-1	a02 3-1	F09 0-1	D26 2-1	N10 4-1	O27 3-2		J05 4-0	M19 1-2	N24 3-1	S08 2-2	D22 0-2	J26 2-2	M15 1-1	O13 0-0
15 NOTTINGHAM F	M15 2-1	a12 0-0	J26 1-1	M29 0-0	F23 1-0	S15 0-0	D01 0-1	D25 2-0	S01 1-0	a26 1-1	O27 0-1	F09 1-2	O13 3-1	D29 0-0		S29 1-0	a21 1-1	N17 1-2	M08 1-2	N03 0-0	A27 1-1	D15 2-1
16 NOTTS CO	D26 1-2	N10 0-1	N24 1-1	a18 3-0	D22 1-1	A25 2-1	M22 1-0	M05 0-0	O20 1-1	S08 1-0	m03 1-2	D08 2-0	O04 1-0	F16 1-0	S22 2-1		J19 0-0	a05 0-2	J05 1-2	O06 0-0	a19 1-0	M01 1-1
17 PRESTON N.E.	a26 0-2	S22 2-2	M08 1-0	D26 0-1	M29 0-2	J05 5-0	O27 3-1	D01 1-1	F09 0-1	A27 1-3	S08 0-1	M15 4-1	D15 4-0	N17 1-2	F02 3-1	J26 2-1		O06 1-1	N10 1-2	S01 2-2	M19 1-2	a19 2-1
18 SHEFFIELD U	F09 3-1	D15 2-1	a12 0-2	F23 4-0	A27 0-0	O20 2-1	D25 1-1	S29 1-0	N03 4-0	M15 0-1	D01 1-1	S01 3-0	D29 0-1	S15 2-1	N24 0-0	a07 3-1	O13 4-0		J26 1-1	M08 6-2	a26 2-0	J01 0-2
19 SUNDERLAND	a19 1-1	F13 2-0	S15 1-1	N17 5-1	O06 2-2	M22 0-1	S05 0-3	O17 2-0	J01 3-0	D01 2-1	F16 0-0	S29 5-2	a05 3-2	D15 3-2	M01 1-0	D29 1-1	N03 2-1	J19 2-2		O20 1-0	a18 2-0	A25 0-0
20 TOTTENHAM H	N24 3-0	M22 2-3	D29 1-1	D15 2-1	S22 0-0	m03 1-0	F16 1-1	S03 0-1	a12 2-5	D25 1-0	a05 1-1	a21 4-1	S08 2-1	J19 2-0	N10 3-0	O13 1-3	A25 2-0	M01 1-2	O27 1-1		D01 0-0	a22 0-1
21 W.B.A.	S08 4-0	O20 1-0	D15 0-0	S22 3-3	D26 0-5	J19 0-3	N10 2-4	M01 2-2	N24 5-0	O06 2-4	A25 2-0	J05 2-1	a09 1-1	M22 0-0	S03 3-2	a12 5-0	F16 1-2	m03 3-1	a21 3-1	D08 4-1		a05 0-0
22 WEST HAM U	A27 1-0	D26 1-0	N03 4-1	J26 0-1	D08 0-1	N24 0-0	S08 0-0	O27 2-0	M15 2-1	M27 2-3	J05 1-0	a26 1-2	S22 1-1	O06 1-0	D22 3-2	M08 1-1	a12 3-1	a21 2-2	S01 0-1	F09 0-0	M29 1-0	

Jack Swan was Leeds United's leading scorer in their Second Division championship season. He played for Huddersfield in the 1920 FA Cup Final.

DIVISION 2

	BARNSLEY	BLACKPOOL	BRADFORD C	BRISTOL C	BURY	CLAPTON O	COVENTRY C	CRYSTAL P	DERBY CO	FULHAM	HULL C	LEEDS U	LEICESTER C	MANCHESTER U	NELSON	OLDHAM A	PORT VALE	SHEFFIELD W	SOUTHAMPTON	SOUTH SHIELDS	STOCKPORT CO	STOKE
1 BARNSLEY		F23 3-1	D15 2-1	A27 3-1	a21 2-0	D29 1-0	S01 1-1	a26 5-2	M08 1-3	F09 2-1	M29 0-0	N24 1-3	O27 3-1	D26 1-0	M15 0-0	S29 4-1	F02 3-0	N03 0-0	J26 1-1	S15 1-0	O13 0-0	a19 0-0
2 BLACKPOOL	F16 0-2		M01 2-1	N03 2-0	J19 3-1	m03 3-0	O20 5-0	S29 2-0	D22 4-0	D08 3-0	a18 0-0	a05 1-1	a19 3-1	F06 1-0	D29 1-1	A25 2-2	M22 6-1	O13 1-0	N24 2-0	S03 1-1	D26 0-0	S15 1-1
3 BRADFORD C	D22 3-2	M08 0-2		J26 1-1	D25 2-2	M12 0-0	A27 0-0	O27 0-1	M15 1-2	F23 1-0	a12 2-1	N10 0-0	O13 2-2	D29 0-0	M29 0-2	S15 2-1	N17 2-0	S01 4-1	F09 2-1	a21 0-1	S29 0-1	a26 2-1
4 BRISTOL C	S03 1-1	N10 1-1	J19 0-1		D01 4-1	M22 0-2	S15 2-2	D25 0-0	S29 0-8	O20 0-1	D15 1-0	F16 0-1	M01 0-1	A25 1-2	N17 1-0	a19 0-0	F13 0-0	a18 2-3	O13 1-1	m03 1-0	a05 3-0	D29 1-1
5 BURY	a18 1-1	J26 2-0	J01 3-0	D08 6-0		S22 0-0	a26 5-0	M29 1-1	F09 1-0	A27 2-1	M08 1-0	D22 3-0	J02 2-0	S08 2-0	F23 2-0	O27 2-2	J05 0-0	a12 5-0	A25 1-0	O06 0-1	N03 2-1	M15 1-0
6 CLAPTON O	J05 2-1	a26 1-0	D08 1-1	M15 2-0	S29 1-0		M08 4-0	F09 1-0	S15 2-0	a19 0-0	A27 0-0	O06 0-1	D25 1-0	a18 1-0	S01 5-1	N17 1-2	N03 1-1	F23 0-0	M29 0-0	O20 3-0	D22 1-1	J26 0-2
7 COVENTRY C	A25 2-3	O27 3-1	S03 1-0	S08 1-1	F02 1-0	M01 1-1		D29 0-0	a22 0-1	O06 3-0	D17 0-2	M10 2-1	F16 2-4	N17 1-1	N10 4-0	a05 5-2	J19 1-3	D25 5-1	S22 0-0	a19 1-0	M22 0-0	D15 1-2
8 CRYSTAL P	m03 3-1	S22 3-1	O20 3-0	D26 1-0	a05 1-0	a22 2-1	J05 3-1		D08 0-1	S08 1-1	N03 0-0	S05 1-1	J19 4-3	a19 1-1	O06 1-1	M01 2-3	A25 1-2	D15 3-0	a18 0-0	M22 1-0	F16 1-1	N24 5-1
9 DERBY CO	M01 2-1	D15 2-0	M22 0-0	S22 2-3	F27 0-2	S08 1-0	a21 1-0	D01 5-0		N24 3-3	O13 4-1	a19 2-0	m03 4-0	F16 3-0	D26 6-0	S03 2-1	a05 2-0	D29 1-1	O27 1-0	J19 6-1	A25 4-1	N10 1-1
10 FULHAM	M10 3-0	D01 2-3	F16 1-1	O27 1-1	S03 0-2	a12 0-0	O13 1-1	S15 1-0	N17 3-2		D25 1-1	M22 0-2	a05 1-0	J19 3-1	D15 0-0	D29 0-0	M01 0-0	S29 4-1	N10 3-2	A25 2-3	m03 1-0	a21 3-0
11 HULL C	a05 1-2	a21 2-1	a19 2-0	D22 5-0	M01 0-1	S03 2-2	D08 3-2	N10 2-2	O06 0-1	D26 4-2		S22 1-2	A25 1-1	M22 1-1	S08 2-1	F14 0-0	m03 1-2	N24 1-1	J05 0-0	F16 1-0	J19 1-2	O20 2-0
12 LEEDS U	N17 3-1	M29 0-0	N03 1-0	M19 0-0	D15 1-2	O13 1-0	F09 3-1	A27 3-0	a12 1-1	M15 3-0	S29 5-2		S15 1-2	D01 0-0	a26 1-0	D26 5-0	O27 3-0	J26 1-0	M08 3-0	F27 2-1	a21 4-0	S01 0-0
13 LEICESTER C	O20 2-0	a12 1-2	O06 0-1	M08 5-1	N17 3-0	D26 1-2	F23 2-0	J26 1-0	a26 3-0	M29 2-1	S01 1-1	S08 2-0		N03 2-2	a22 3-1	D15 1-1	S22 2-0	F09 2-1	M15 0-1	D01 4-1	D29 1-1	A27 5-0
14 MANCHESTER U	D25 1-2	F09 0-0	J05 3-0	S01 2-1	S15 0-1	a21 2-2	J02 1-2	a12 5-1	F23 0-0	J26 0-0	M15 1-1	D08 3-1	N10 3-0		M08 0-1	O13 2-0	D22 5-0	a26 2-0	A27 1-0	S29 1-1	O20 3-0	M29 2-2
15 NELSON	M22 4-3	J05 2-3	a05 1-1	N24 2-1	F16 0-5	A25 1-1	N03 3-0	O13 4-2	D25 2-1	D22 1-1	S15 1-1	m03 3-1	a21 1-1	M01 0-2		J19 2-1	a12 1-3	O20 1-1	S11 0-0	F02 0-2	S03 1-1	S29 2-0
16 OLDHAM A	S22 1-1	S01 1-1	S08 0-0	a12 0-0	O20 0-0	D03 1-0	M29 1-1	M08 1-0	A27 2-0	J05 2-1	F09 0-0	D25 2-2	D22 0-0	O06 3-2	J26 1-0		a18 2-0	M15 2-0	a26 1-3	N03 1-0	D08 3-1	F23 0-0
17 PORT VALE	D08 4-1	M15 2-6	N24 2-2	F09 0-2	D29 2-1	N10 1-0	J26 1-1	S01 3-4	M29 2-0	M08 3-1	a26 2-2	O20 0-1	S29 2-1	D15 0-1	a19 0-0	a21 3-0		A27 2-0	M17 1-0	J21 1-1	S15 0-1	O13 2-4
18 SHEFFIELD W	N10 1-0	O06 2-2	A25 0-0	a21 1-0	a19 1-1	F16 1-0	D26 2-0	D22 6-0	J05 1-0	S22 2-1	N17 1-0	J19 0-0	F11 2-1	m03 2-0	O27 5-0	M22 1-2	S03 2-1		S08 1-1	a05 5-0	M01 3-0	D08 3-0
19 SOUTHAMPTON	J19 6-0	N17 3-2	F11 2-0	O06 1-0	S01 3-0	a05 5-0	S29 1-3	a21 1-0	O20 0-0	N03 1-0	D29 2-0	M01 0-1	M22 1-0	S03 0-0	D08 3-0	m03 3-1	F16 1-1	S15 3-0		D15 0-0	a19 0-0	O15 0-1
20 SOUTH SHIELDS	S08 2-0	A27 1-0	a18 0-0	a26 1-1	O13 1-0	O27 1-1	a12 4-2	M15 2-0	J26 3-2	S01 1-0	F23 0-1	J05 2-0	D08 1-2	S22 1-0	F09 3-0	N10 2-0	J01 3-3	M29 1-1	D22 1-2		N24 3-1	M08 1-0
21 STOCKPORT CO	O06 1-1	D25 2-1	S22 1-2	M29 0-0	N10 3-2	M31 2-0	M15 0-0	M10 2-2	S01 0-0	a26 2-1	J26 5-1	a18 1-1	J05 3-1	O27 3-2	A27 1-0	J01 0-1	S08 0-0	M08 1-0	a12 2-3	D10 3-2		F09 0-1
22 STOKE	a12 2-0	S08 2-2	D26 2-0	J05 3-0	M22 0-0	J19 0-1	D22 2-1	N17 1-1	N03 1-1	a22 0-0	O27 1-0	A25 1-1	S03 1-0	a05 3-0	S22 4-0	F16 1-1	O06 1-0	D01 1-1	S24 1-1	M01 0-0	F02 0-0	

Season 1923-24

DIVISION 3 NORTH

	ACCRINGTON S	ASHINGTON	BARROW	BRADFORD	CHESTERFIELD	CREWE A	DARLINGTON	DONCASTER R	DURHAM C	GRIMSBY T	HALIFAX T	HARTLEPOOLS U	LINCOLN C	NEW BRIGHTON	ROCHDALE	ROTHERHAM CO	SOUTHPORT	TRANMERE R	WALSALL	WIGAN B	WOLVERHAMPTON W	WREXHAM
1 ACCRINGTON S		O27 0-1	S25 3-1	F23 2-2	M08 2-0	F11 1-1	S01 2-0	a19 0-0	a30 5-4	J01 2-0	J05 1-2	M17 2-0	J26 3-1	S08 0-0	a26 0-1	M15 3-2	D26 2-0	F09 3-1	O06 0-3	N10 2-2	S22 1-0	M29 1-0
2 ASHINGTON	O20 1-1		M01 2-0	a12 1-0	a26 1-1	O13 3-0	F23 2-1	A27 3-1	S29 2-1	D08 1-0	N03 4-0	a18 0-0	M15 2-1	D22 5-0	J26 1-0	N24 1-2	F09 2-0	M29 3-3	J01 3-1	S15 3-0	J05 1-7	S01 0-2
3 BARROW	S03 0-0	M08 2-2		O13 1-1	O27 2-0	J19 1-2	D25 1-0	D08 0-0	F02 1-2	m03 3-1	a18 1-0	A25 1-2	S15 2-1	a19 2-1	D22 1-2	N10 1-2	J05 1-3	S29 1-1	M22 0-1	F23 2-1	a05 2-2	J12 0-0
4 BRADFORD	F16 1-1	a19 3-1	O06 3-0		F06 2-1	M01 1-1	D08 1-0	D26 4-2	M22 3-0	S03 2-1	J19 1-0	F02 4-0	N03 3-1	A25 1-1	S08 4-2	J05 2-0	S22 2-0	N24 2-0	m03 5-0	a05 4-0	O20 0-1	a22 2-0
5 CHESTERFIELD	M01 3-0	m03 2-0	O20 2-1	D22 2-3		M22 2-1	J05 5-1	S08 2-1	a18 1-1	J19 4-2	M26 1-1	F16 5-1	N24 2-1	S03 1-0	S22 1-1	D25 3-1	O06 4-0	D08 5-0	N10 7-0	a19 1-0	A25 0-0	J01 1-0
6 CREWE A	D08 1-2	O06 1-3	J26 2-0	M08 1-1	M15 0-1		A29 2-1	a26 0-2	N03 0-2	D26 0-0	D22 2-2	a30 2-1	F09 1-2	a18 2-0	J05 0-2	M29 1-0	S01 1-1	F16 1-1	S22 2-0	O27 0-2	S08 0-0	a12 1-1
7 DARLINGTON	A25 2-1	F16 3-2	D26 5-1	N17 3-1	D29 2-1	S05 1-1		O27 1-1	J19 3-2	a19 1-0	m03 0-0	S08 5-0	O13 1-0	a05 3-1	N24 2-2	J01 1-0	D22 3-1	N10 4-1	M01 4-2	F02 3-1	M22 1-1	S22 3-0
8 DONCASTER R	a12 1-2	S03 2-1	D01 2-2	D25 1-1	S15 0-2	m03 4-1	O20 1-0		D15 2-1	M01 2-1	M22 7-0	a05 3-1	D29 3-2	F16 2-0	N03 0-0	S29 0-1	J12 3-0	a21 4-0	J19 3-0	A25 0-0	m01 0-2	O06 1-0
9 DURHAM C	N24 3-0	a05 4-0	F09 1-2	M15 2-0	M29 1-1	N10 3-1	J26 3-2	D22 2-1		J05 0-1	D08 2-2	O20 3-0	F23 1-0	a21 2-1	S01 0-0	a12 3-2	A29 0-1	M01 1-1	S08 1-0	O13 2-2	J01 2-3	a26 4-3
10 GRIMSBY T	a18 2-0	a08 4-0	a26 5-0	A27 2-0	J26 0-0	D25 2-0	a12 3-0	M08 1-1	D29 1-0		S15 1-1	O13 0-1	S29 2-2	O27 0-0	M15 1-0	F09 1-1	M29 1-0	S01 0-0	N17 1-0	M27 1-1	N10 2-0	F23 0-0
11 HALIFAX T	D29 3-0	N10 3-0	a21 1-0	J26 0-0	F09 2-0	J01 2-0	a26 1-4	M15 0-1	M10 2-1	S08 1-3		D25 1-0	S01 1-0	S22 2-1	M29 0-1	F23 0-2	a12 1-0	A27 0-0	O27 3-0	N17 1-2	O06 2-2	M08 0-0
12 HARTLEPOOLS U	D22 3-0	a22 0-1	S01 1-0	F09 0-0	F23 2-3	a21 2-2	S15 0-1	M29 1-1	O27 0-0	O06 1-1	D26 1-3		J01 1-1	N03 0-1	a12 1-2	M08 2-5	a26 1-0	J26 2-1	J05 0-1	S29 0-0	D08 0-1	M15 4-0
13 LINCOLN C	J19 0-2	M22 2-0	S08 4-1	N10 2-3	J12 0-1	F02 0-0	O06 2-0	J05 1-1	F16 3-1	S22 1-3	A25 1-1	S05 1-1		m03 1-0	D25 0-2	D08 2-1	a21 1-1	O27 1-1	a05 2-0	M01 1-1	a12 0-0	D22 4-2
14 NEW BRIGHTON	S15 1-2	D26 1-1	a12 5-0	S01 1-0	A29 0-0	D15 2-1	M29 1-1	F23 2-0	S12 2-0	O20 0-0	S29 2-0	N10 0-0	a26 3-1		M08 1-1	J26 1-2	M15 0-0	O06 0-0	D08 1-0	D29 5-0	D01 0-1	F09 0-0
15 ROCHDALE	m03 4-1	J19 1-0	D15 3-1	S15 3-0	S29 3-0	D29 1-0	a18 0-0	N10 2-0	A25 2-0	M22 4-2	a05 3-0	J12 1-0	D26 1-0	M01 6-2		O13 1-0	J08 2-2	a22 1-0	F02 1-0	S03 1-0	F16 0-0	O27 0-0
16 ROTHERHAM CO	M22 2-0	M17 1-0	N03 2-0	M24 1-0	D26 1-2	N17 1-0	a21 2-0	S22 3-0	a19 5-1	F02 2-1	F16 3-2	M01 5-0	a22 2-0	J19 3-1	O06 0-0		O27 1-1	J12 5-1	A25 0-2	m03 4-0	S03 1-1	S08 2-1
17 SOUTHPORT	D25 1-0	F02 2-0	D29 2-0	S29 1-0	O13 1-0	A25 1-0	a29 1-0	N24 2-2	S04 1-0	a05 3-0	a19 3-0	m03 2-2	a18 3-2	J01 3-0	D08 0-1	O20 0-0		S15 1-1	F16 1-1	J26 1-1	M01 0-0	N03 1-0
18 TRANMERE R	F02 2-0	D25 2-4	S22 3-0	J01 2-1	a05 0-0	F23 1-1	N03 1-4	a18 3-0	M08 1-0	A25 2-1	S06 3-0	J19 2-0	O20 1-3	O13 1-2	a28 2-1	D22 0-1	S08 1-1		a19 3-1	M22 1-0	m03 0-0	J05 1-1
19 WALSALL	O13 2-0	a21 1-1	M15 1-1	a26 2-3	N03 0-1	S29 1-0	M08 2-1	J26 5-2	S15 1-1	N24 2-0	O20 2-0	D29 2-0	M29 0-0	J12 3-0	F09 0-1	S01 1-1	F23 0-1	a12 0-4		D25 3-0	a07 2-1	A27 1-2
20 WIGAN B	N03 2-0	S08 1-1	F16 4-0	M29 0-1	a12 3-1	O20 3-0	F09 2-2	S01 1-0	O06 0-1	D22 4-0	N24 0-1	S22 4-1	M08 0-0	J05 1-0	A27 3-0	a26 3-1	J19 1-1	M15 1-2	D26 2-1		a22 1-1	D08 3-1
21 WOLVERHAMPTON W	S29 5-1	D29 1-0	M29 3-0	O27 2-0	S01 2-1	S15 1-0	M15 2-0	F09 1-0	D26 2-1	N03 4-1	O13 4-0	F11 2-1	a19 3-0	N24 5-1	M26 0-0	A27 3-0	M08 2-1	a26 3-0	D22 0-0	a21 3-3		J26 3-0
22 WREXHAM	a05 1-0	A25 4-0	N24 2-0	a21 2-2	N17 0-0	a19 1-0	S29 0-1	O13 2-2	m03 0-0	F16 1-1	M01 0-1	M22 1-0	M12 2-1	F02 0-0	O20 1-1	S15 1-0	N10 3-0	D26 1-1	S05 0-0	S19 0-0	J19 2-2	

DIVISION 3 SOUTH

	ABERDARE A	BOURNEMOUTH	BRENTFORD	BRIGHTON & HA	BRISTOL R	CHARLTON A	EXETER C	GILLINGHAM	LUTON T	MERTHYR T	MILLWALL	NEWPORT CO	NORTHAMPTON T	NORWICH C	PLYMOUTH A	PORTSMOUTH	Q.P.R.	READING	SOUTHEND U	SWANSEA T	SWINDON T	WATFORD
1 ABERDARE A		S22 1-0	S10 1-2	N10 3-1	M31 2-0	S01 4-1	D29 0-0	M15 1-1	O20 0-1	a22 0-0	S08 1-1	a26 2-0	M08 2-2	A27 0-0	a12 1-2	M17 0-0	M29 1-1	O06 1-0	D26 5-2	F23 4-2	J26 2-2	F09 4-0
2 BOURNEMOUTH	S29 0-1		D25 2-4	D15 1-0	D29 0-1	a26 1-0	S15 1-0	F23 0-0	D08 2-3	a12 3-3	O20 2-0	a05 0-1	F09 2-1	O13 1-2	M15 0-0	a21 0-0	M08 3-1	N24 0-0	N10 0-1	J19 0-0	S01 0-0	S19 1-1
3 BRENTFORD	D08 1-1	D26 2-0		S22 1-2	O13 1-2	F23 0-0	N24 1-0	D22 3-2	S08 2-1	F09 0-0	J05 1-3	J26 0-0	a26 1-0	M08 3-0	A27 1-1	N10 1-1	S01 0-1	a21 4-1	O27 3-1	a12 2-2	M15 2-2	M29 4-1
4 BRIGHTON & H.A.	N03 5-0	D22 5-0	S29 2-0		S15 2-1	M15 3-0	O20 1-0	A29 2-2	D26 4-0	M08 0-0	D08 2-2	M26 4-0	S01 2-0	M29 3-0	F09 4-1	O13 0-4	J26 3-0	J05 4-0	a18 2-0	N24 4-1	a12 1-1	a26 3-0
5 BRISTOL R	N24 2-0	J05 3-4	O06 2-0	S08 2-0		M08 2-0	N03 0-0	S01 2-0	a21 1-1	F23 0-0	D22 4-1	F09 0-0	D08 1-1	M15 3-1	J26 1-1	O27 0-1	A27 2-1	D26 0-0	S22 3-1	a26 2-0	M29 0-1	a12 4-2
6 CHARLTON A	A25 3-1	m03 1-2	F16 3-1	M22 0-2	M01 1-3		a07 1-0	J05 0-0	a05 1-1	S08 1-0	S22 0-1	O06 2-1	D22 0-0	O20 0-0	a21 0-1	M10 1-1	D26 3-0	a19 0-0	S03 4-1	D08 1-3	N03 3-1	N24 1-1
7 EXETER C	J05 1-1	S08 0-2	a02 1-0	O27 0-1	N10 3-1	J26 0-0		a12 2-1	O06 2-1	A29 1-0	a21 2-0	S01 5-0	M29 2-1	F09 1-2	D26 0-4	S12 0-0	a26 3-0	S22 3-2	F23 2-0	M15 1-0	M19 3-1	M08 1-0
8 GILLINGHAM	M22 3-1	F16 1-0	M19 6-0	S05 1-1	A25 1-0	D29 0-1	a19 1-1		J19 0-0	M12 2-1	M01 0-2	O20 2-1	O06 1-1	D25 3-1	N17 1-0	m03 0-2	N03 0-0	F02 1-0	a05 3-2	S29 0-1	a18 1-0	S15 0-0
9 LUTON T	O27 1-0	D01 6-2	S15 2-1	D25 0-0	a18 0-0	M29 0-1	O13 1-0	J26 1-1		M15 1-1	N24 2-0	M08 2-0	A27 1-1	a12 2-1	F23 0-2	S29 4-1	F09 2-0	D15 2-0	D29 4-4	S01 1-2	a26 3-2	N03 0-0
10 MERTHYR T	a21 0-0	a19 4-2	F02 2-0	M01 2-1	F16 1-1	S15 2-1	S06 3-0	D08 0-2	M22 0-0		m03 1-0	D25 3-3	N24 0-0	S29 2-3	J05 1-0	J19 2-2	D22 2-0	a05 1-1	A25 3-2	N03 0-0	O13 2-0	O27 2-1
11 MILLWALL	S15 2-0	O27 4-2	D29 4-1	D01 0-0	D15 1-0	S29 1-0	a18 3-1	M08 5-0	N17 0-1	a26 6-0		a12 2-1	F16 4-3	S01 2-1	M29 1-0	D25 2-0	M15 3-0	N10 0-0	O13 0-0	F09 2-1	A27 1-0	J26 2-0
12 NEWPORT CO	m03 0-0	M29 2-0	a22 3-2	F16 0-0	F02 1-0	O13 0-1	A25 2-0	O27 2-1	M01 1-0	D26 4-4	a19 2-1		S22 1-1	N03 1-0	D15 1-2	S06 2-1	J01 2-1	M22 2-0	S08 5-0	a21 4-1	D01 3-0	D29 1-0
13 NORTHAMPTON T	a07 1-2	F02 3-1	m03 2-3	A25 3-0	S10 0-0	M13 1-0	a05 1-0	O13 2-0	S03 2-0	N17 3-0	F23 2-1	S29 0-0		D29 1-0	N10 1-0	a19 0-4	O20 3-0	J19 3-1	M22 8-0	S15 2-0	D27 1-1	a22 1-2
14 NORWICH C	S03 5-0	O06 1-1	M01 2-3	a05 1-0	M22 3-1	O27 2-2	F14 4-0	D26 1-0	a19 2-0	S22 2-0	A25 1-1	N10 3-1	J05 1-4		S08 0-1	F16 3-1	a21 5-0	m03 2-2	J19 3-1	a28 2-0	N17 2-0	S10 0-0
15 PLYMOUTH A	a19 2-0	M22 4-0	S03 4-1	a30 3-0	J19 2-2	a18 1-1	D25 4-0	N24 3-0	F16 0-0	D29 1-1	a05 1-1	D22 3-2	N03 0-0	S15 2-0		A25 1-2	D08 2-0	M01 2-1	m03 7-1	O20 2-0	S29 1-3	O13 1-0
16 PORTSMOUTH	D22 4-0	a18 3-0	N03 3-0	O06 1-3	O20 1-1	F09 0-0	D08 4-0	a26 3-0	S22 3-0	J26 1-0	D26 0-1	A29 5-0	a12 1-3	F23 4-0	S01 2-1		J05 7-0	S08 1-1	N24 3-0	M29 3-0	a30 4-1	M15 4-0
17 Q.P.R.	a05 3-0	M01 0-1	A25 1-0	J19 1-0	S05 1-2	D25 0-0	m03 2-0	N10 1-1	F02 0-2	D15 3-0	M22 1-1	S12 0-3	O27 3-2	a18 2-1	D01 3-2	D29 0-2		F16 1-4	a19 0-0	O13 2-2	S15 2-2	S29 2-1
18 READING	O13 0-1	N17 1-2	a18 1-0	D29 0-1	D25 3-2	a12 3-1	S29 1-0	F09 4-0	D22 0-1	M29 3-0	N03 2-0	M15 1-1	J26 1-0	a26 3-0	M08 1-2	S15 1-4	F23 4-0		J12 1-0	A29 3-4	O27 1-0	S01 1-1
19 SOUTHEND U	D25 1-1	N03 1-1	O20 3-1	a21 1-0	S29 1-0	A27 2-2	D22 0-0	M29 3-2	J05 1-1	S01 3-1	O06 0-0	S15 2-0	M15 5-1	J26 3-1	a26 0-2	S19 0-1	a12 4-2	D08 2-1		M08 0-0	F09 0-2	M19 3-0
20 SWANSEA T	F16 1-0	J26 1-0	a19 4-0	N17 1-0	m03 3-1	D01 1-0	M22 1-0	S22 3-1	A25 1-0	N10 5-1	M13 1-2	a18 2-1	S08 2-1	D22 1-0	O27 1-0	a05 0-0	O06 2-0	S03 5-1	M01 2-1		D29 1-1	D25 1-0
21 SWINDON T	J19 3-1	A25 3-1	M22 2-1	a19 4-0	a05 0-0	N10 1-1	F16 0-1	a21 4-1	m03 3-2	O06 3-0	S03 1-0	D08 3-0	D26 2-0	N24 4-2	S22 0-1	M01 0-0	S08 0-0	O20 1-0	a02 3-0	J05 1-0		D15 0-0
22 WATFORD	a18 2-0	S05 0-0	a05 0-1	m03 0-0	a19 4-0	N17 1-0	M01 4-1	S08 1-1	N10 0-0	O20 4-0	J19 1-1	J05 8-2	a21 0-2	D08 0-0	O06 0-1	M22 2-3	S22 0-2	A25 2-1	F16 4-1	D26 2-2	D22 0-0	

LEAGUE TABLES

DIVISION 1

	P	W	D	L	F	A	W	D	L	F	A	Pts
Huddersfield T	42	15	5	1	35	9	8	6	7	25	24	57
Cardiff C	42	14	5	2	35	13	8	8	5	26	21	57
Sunderland	42	12	7	2	38	20	10	2	9	33	34	53
Bolton W	42	13	6	2	45	13	5	8	8	23	21	50
Sheffield U	42	12	5	4	39	16	7	7	7	30	33	50
Aston Villa	42	10	10	1	33	11	8	3	10	19	26	49
Everton	42	13	7	1	43	18	5	6	10	19	35	49
Blackburn R	42	14	5	2	40	13	3	6	12	14	37	45
Newcastle U	42	13	5	3	40	21	4	5	12	20	33	44
Notts Co	42	9	7	5	21	15	5	7	9	23	34	42
Manchester C	42	11	7	3	34	24	4	5	12	20	47	42
Liverpool	42	11	5	5	35	20	4	6	11	14	28	41
West Ham U	42	10	6	5	26	17	3	9	9	14	26	41
Birmingham	42	10	4	7	25	19	3	9	9	16	30	39
Tottenham H	42	9	6	6	30	22	3	8	10	20	34	38
WBA	42	10	6	5	43	30	2	8	11	8	32	38
Burnley	42	10	5	6	39	27	2	7	12	16	33	36
Preston NE	42	8	4	9	34	27	4	6	11	18	40	34
Arsenal	42	8	5	8	25	24	4	4	13	15	39	33
Nottingham F	42	7	9	5	19	15	3	3	15	23	49	32
Chelsea	42	7	9	5	23	21	2	5	14	8	32	32
Middlesbrough	42	6	4	11	23	23	1	4	16	14	37	22

DIVISION 2

	P	W	D	L	F	A	W	D	L	F	A	Pts
Leeds U	42	14	5	2	41	10	7	7	7	20	25	54
Bury	42	15	5	1	42	7	6	4	11	21	28	51
Derby Co	42	15	4	2	52	15	6	5	10	23	27	51
Blackpool	42	13	7	1	43	12	5	6	10	29	35	49
Southampton	42	13	5	3	36	9	4	9	8	16	22	48
Stoke	42	9	11	1	27	10	5	7	9	17	32	46
Oldham A	42	10	10	1	24	12	4	7	10	21	40	45
Sheffield W	42	15	5	1	42	9	1	7	13	12	42	44
South Shields	42	13	5	3	34	16	4	5	12	15	34	44
Clapton O	42	11	7	3	27	10	3	8	10	13	26	43
Barnsley	42	12	7	2	34	16	4	4	13	23	45	43
Leicester C	42	13	4	4	43	16	4	4	13	21	38	42
Stockport Co	42	10	7	4	32	21	3	9	9	12	31	42
Manchester U	42	10	7	4	37	15	3	7	11	15	29	40
Crystal P	42	11	7	3	37	19	2	6	13	16	46	39
Port Vale	42	9	5	7	33	29	4	7	10	17	37	38
Hull C	42	8	7	6	32	23	2	10	9	14	28	37
Bradford C	42	8	7	6	24	21	3	8	10	11	27	37
Coventry C	42	9	6	6	34	23	2	7	12	18	45	35
Fulham	42	9	8	4	30	20	1	6	14	15	36	34
Nelson	42	8	8	5	32	31	2	5	14	8	43	33
Bristol C	42	5	8	8	19	26	2	7	12	13	39	29

DIVISION 3 North

	P	W	D	L	F	A	W	D	L	F	A	Pts
Wolves	42	18	3	0	51	10	6	12	3	25	17	63
Rochdale	42	17	4	0	40	8	8	8	5	20	18	62
Chesterfield	42	16	4	1	54	15	6	6	9	16	24	54
Rotherham Co	42	16	3	2	46	13	7	3	11	24	30	52
Bradford	42	17	3	1	50	12	4	7	10	19	31	52
Darlington	42	16	5	0	51	19	4	3	14	19	34	48
Southport	42	13	7	1	30	10	3	7	11	14	32	46
Ashington	42	14	4	3	41	21	4	4	13	18	40	44
Doncaster R	42	13	4	4	41	17	2	8	11	18	36	42
Wigan B	42	12	5	4	39	15	2	9	10	16	38	42
Grimsby T	42	11	9	1	30	7	3	4	14	19	40	41
Tranmere R	42	11	5	5	32	21	2	10	9	19	39	41
Accrington S	42	12	5	4	35	21	4	3	14	13	40	40
Halifax T	42	11	4	6	26	17	4	6	11	16	42	40
Durham C	42	12	5	4	40	23	3	4	14	19	37	39
Wrexham	42	8	11	2	24	12	2	7	12	13	32	38
Walsall	42	10	5	6	31	20	4	3	14	13	39	36
New Brighton	42	9	9	3	28	10	2	4	15	12	43	35
Lincoln C	42	8	8	5	29	22	2	4	15	19	37	32
Crewe A	42	6	7	8	20	24	1	6	14	12	34	27
Hartlepools U	42	5	7	9	22	24	2	4	15	11	46	25
Barrow	42	7	7	7	25	24	1	2	18	10	56	25

DIVISION 3 South

	P	W	D	L	F	A	W	D	L	F	A	Pts
Portsmouth	42	15	3	3	57	11	9	8	4	30	19	59
Plymouth A	42	13	6	2	46	15	10	3	8	24	19	55
Millwall	42	17	3	1	45	11	5	7	9	19	27	54
Swansea T	42	18	2	1	39	10	4	6	11	21	38	52
Brighton & HA	42	16	4	1	56	12	5	5	11	12	25	51
Swindon T	42	14	5	2	38	11	3	8	10	20	33	47
Luton T	42	11	7	3	35	19	5	7	9	15	25	46
Northampton T	42	14	3	4	40	15	3	8	10	24	32	45
Bristol R	42	11	7	3	34	15	4	6	11	18	31	43
Newport Co	42	15	4	2	39	15	2	5	14	17	49	43
Norwich C	42	13	5	3	45	18	3	3	15	15	41	40
Aberdare A	42	9	9	3	35	18	3	5	13	10	40	38
Merthyr T	42	11	8	2	33	19	0	8	13	12	46	38
Charlton A	42	8	7	6	26	20	3	8	10	12	25	37
Gillingham	42	11	6	4	27	15	1	7	13	16	43	37
Exeter C	42	14	3	4	33	17	1	4	16	4	35	37
Brentford	42	9	8	4	33	21	5	0	16	21	50	36
Reading	42	12	2	7	35	20	1	7	13	16	37	35
Southend U	42	11	7	3	35	19	1	3	17	18	65	34
Watford	42	8	8	5	35	18	1	7	13	10	36	33
Bournemouth	42	6	8	7	19	19	5	3	13	21	46	33
QPR	42	9	6	6	28	26	2	3	16	9	51	31

Football League Records

Top scorers: Div 1, F.Roberts (Manchester City) 31 goals; Div 2, A.Chandler (Leicester City) 33 goals; Div 3(N), D.Brown (Darlington) 39 goals; Div 3(S), J.Fowler (Swansea Town) 28 goals.

Future England full-back Ray Goodall skippered Huddersfield Town to their second successive League Championship win.

Former England Schoolboys winger Tommy Glidden helped West Brom into runners-up spot in 1924-5 and later skippered the Throstles in two FA Cup Finals.

DIVISION 1

	ARSENAL	ASTON VILLA	BIRMINGHAM	BLACKBURN R	BOLTON W	BURNLEY	BURY	CARDIFF C	EVERTON	HUDDERSFIELD T	LEEDS U	LIVERPOOL	MANCHESTER C	NEWCASTLE U	NOTTINGHAM F	NOTTS CO	PRESTON N.E.	SHEFFIELD U	SUNDERLAND	TOTTENHAM H	W.B.A.	WEST HAM U
1 ARSENAL		O18 1-1	D26 0-1	O04 1-0	M07 1-0	a18 5-0	O13 0-1	a04 1-1	M21 3-1	F14 0-5	D20 6-1	S06 2-0	S01 1-0	J17 0-2	D27 2-1	N08 0-1	D06 4-0	S20 2-0	N22 0-0	O25 1-0	a14 2-0	M23 1-2
2 ASTON VILLA	a01 4-0		F14 1-0	a29 4-3	N08 2-2	D20 3-0	S01 3-3	D06 1-2	N22 3-1	O04 1-1	D26 2-1	J21 1-4	a10 2-1	S06 0-0	m02 2-0	M21 0-0	a18 1-0	J17 1-1	a04 1-4	M07 0-1	O25 1-0	S20 1-1
3 BIRMINGHAM	D25 2-1	O11 1-0		N01 1-1	S08 1-0	S27 1-0	D13 0-1	S13 2-1	A30 2-2	F28 0-1	F07 0-0	N29 5-2	a25 2-1	M28 1-1	a11 1-1	S15 1-0	J24 3-0	N15 1-1	J03 2-1	S03 0-2	M16 0-0	M14 1-1
4 BLACKBURN R	F07 1-0	S27 1-1	a02 7-1		N22 0-2	J17 0-3	M19 0-1	D20 3-1	D06 3-0	J24 2-3	O25 2-3	S15 3-1	O11 3-1	S01 1-1	a13 0-0	a04 0-2	D25 0-1	D27 2-2	a18 1-1	M21 1-1	N08 1-0	S06 0-1
5 BOLTON W	N01 4-1	M14 4-0	J01 3-0	a22 6-0		F21 5-0	S06 3-3	F07 3-0	J24 1-0	N15 1-0	a10 1-0	a25 2-0	F28 4-2	D13 3-2	D25 1-0	S13 1-0	O11 6-1	a11 3-1	S27 1-2	D27 3-0	S01 1-1	N29 5-0
6 BURNLEY	D13 1-0	a25 1-1	F02 3-2	S13 3-5	O18 0-0		N29 4-0	A30 0-0	S08 0-0	D25 1-5	S20 1-1	N15 2-1	a11 1-0	M14 1-3	M28 0-0	a10 1-1	J03 1-0	N01 1-1	S29 1-2	F14 1-4	O04 0-1	F28 5-4
7 BURY	m02 2-0	S08 4-3	a18 1-4	O18 1-1	J03 1-0	a04 1-0		M21 4-1	M07 1-0	a10 0-1	D06 1-0	S20 0-0	A30 0-2	F11 0-0	J17 3-0	O25 2-1	N22 1-1	O04 1-0	N08 3-0	J01 5-2	D20 0-2	F14 4-2
8 CARDIFF C	N29 1-1	a11 2-1	J17 1-0	a15 3-0	O04 1-2	F11 4-0	N15 4-1		O18 2-1	D13 2-2	S06 3-0	D15 1-3	a01 0-2	F28 3-0	M14 2-0	F14 1-1	m02 0-0	S01 1-1	a13 2-0	M18 0-2	S20 0-1	D26 2-1
9 EVERTON	N15 2-3	M28 2-0	D27 2-1	a11 1-0	S20 2-2	J01 3-2	N01 0-0	F25 1-2		N29 0-2	m02 1-0	O04 0-1	O29 3-1	D25 0-1	F28 3-1	M18 1-0	a13 0-0	a27 1-1	O11 0-3	J17 1-0	S06 1-0	D13 1-0
10 HUDDERSFIELD T	O11 4-0	F07 4-1	O25 0-1	S20 0-0	M21 0-0	D26 2-0	a14 2-0	a18 0-0	a04 2-0		J31 2-0	m02 1-1	F21 1-1	D27 0-0	S02 3-0	N22 0-0	D20 1-0	S06 2-1	D06 4-0	N08 1-2	M11 1-1	J17 1-2
11 LEEDS U	a25 1-0	D25 6-0	O04 0-1	F28 1-1	a14 2-1	J24 0-2	a11 1-0	J03 0-0	S17 1-0	S27 1-1		M28 4-1	D13 0-3	N15 1-1	N29 1-1	S10 1-1	S13 4-0	M14 1-1	A30 1-1	O18 1-0	F14 0-1	N01 2-1
12 LIVERPOOL	J03 2-1	A30 2-4	a04 1-1	O15 0-0	D20 0-0	M21 3-0	J24 4-0	a29 1-2	F07 3-1	N12 2-3	N22 1-0		S13 5-3	F14 1-1	S27 3-0	D26 1-0	N08 3-1	O18 4-1	O25 3-1	a18 1-0	D06 1-1	a10 2-0
13 MANCHESTER C	S17 2-0	a13 1-0	D20 2-2	F14 1-3	O25 2-2	D06 3-3	J31 0-0	N22 2-2	N08 2-2	O18 1-1	a18 4-2	J17 5-0		S20 3-1	S06 4-2	M07 2-1	a04 2-1	F23 2-1	M21 1-3	m02 1-0	D25 1-2	O04 3-1
14 NEWCASTLE U	S13 2-2	J03 4-1	N22 4-0	S10 4-0	a18 0-1	N08 3-0	S27 2-2	O25 1-2	D26 1-1	A30 1-3	M21 4-1	O11 0-0	J24 2-0		F07 4-1	D20 1-0	M07 3-1	J01 0-0	F21 2-0	D06 1-1	a04 0-1	S17 4-1
15 NOTTINGHAM F	A30 0-2	O02 0-2	D06 1-1	a10 0-2	D26 1-1	N22 0-0	S13 2-0	N08 2-1	O25 0-1	S08 0-1	a04 4-0	F04 0-1	J03 0-3	O04 1-1		J24 0-0	M21 0-1	F14 2-3	M07 1-1	D20 1-0	a18 0-1	O18 2-1
16 NOTTS CO	M14 2-1	N15 0-0	m02 0-1	N29 0-0	J17 0-1	a13 2-0	F28 1-1	O11 3-0	S27 3-1	a29 1-1	S01 1-0	D25 1-2	N01 2-0	a25 2-0	S20 0-0		a01 1-0	D13 2-0	F07 4-1	S06 0-0	D27 0-2	a11 4-1
17 PRESTON N.E.	a11 2-0	D13 3-2	S20 1-0	D26 3-2	F14 1-0	S06 0-2	M28 1-1	S15 1-3	a10 1-1	a25 1-4	J17 1-4	M14 4-0	N29 2-3	N01 0-1	N15 3-1	O18 0-1		F28 0-1	N20 1-2	O04 0-3	F12 1-2	D27 3-2
18 SHEFFIELD U	J24 2-1	S13 2-2	M21 4-3	A30 2-3	D06 2-0	a06 4-0	F07 0-1	S08 1-0	D20 1-1	J03 1-1	N08 1-1	M16 0-1	S27 0-5	a13 1-2	O11 1-2	a18 2-0	O25 3-0		D26 2-1	a04 2-0	N22 2-0	S22 1-1
19 SUNDERLAND	M28 2-0	N29 1-1	S06 4-0	D13 1-0	F11 1-0	m02 1-1	M14 1-1	J01 1-0	F14 4-1	a11 1-1	D27 2-1	F28 3-0	N15 3-2	O18 1-1	N01 3-1	O04 0-1	S03 2-0	D25 0-1		S20 4-1	J17 3-0	a25 1-1
20 TOTTENHAM H	F28 2-0	N01 1-3	a10 0-1	N15 5-0	A30 3-0	O11 1-1	D25 1-1	S27 1-1	S13 0-0	M14 1-2	M09 2-1	D13 1-1	N10 1-1	a11 3-0	a25 1-0	J03 1-1	F07 2-0	N29 4-1	J24 1-0		S22 0-1	M28 1-1
21 W.B.A.	a13 2-0	F28 4-1	O18 1-1	M14 1-1	m02 0-0	F07 1-4	a25 1-1	J24 1-0	J03 3-0	N01 1-0	O11 3-1	a11 0-0	D26 3-1	N29 2-0	D13 5-1	A30 1-2	S27 1-1	M30 2-1	S13 2-1	S08 2-0		N15 4-1
22 WEST HAM U	S27 1-0	J24 2-0	N08 0-1	J03 2-0	a04 1-1	O25 2-0	O11 1-1	D25 3-2	a18 4-1	S13 0-0	M07 0-0	a13 0-1	F07 4-0	S08 0-0	a02 0-0	D06 3-0	A30 1-0	a14 6-2	D20 4-1	N22 1-1	M21 2-1	

DIVISION 2

	BARNSLEY	BLACKPOOL	BRADFORD C	CHELSEA	CLAPTON O	COVENTRY C	CRYSTAL P	DERBY CO	FULHAM	HULL C	LEICESTER C	MANCHESTER U	MIDDLESBROUGH	OLDHAM A	PORTSMOUTH	PORT VALE	SHEFFIELD W	SOUTHAMPTON	SOUTH SHIELDS	STOCKPORT CO	STOKE	WOLVERHAMPTON W
1 BARNSLEY		O04 2-4	J17 3-1	D20 3-3	a04 1-1	N08 3-1	D06 3-0	M09 3-0	a13 1-0	F14 1-2	O25 1-1	m02 0-0	D27 1-0	M21 0-0	O18 1-4	S06 1-3	N22 3-0	a18 1-1	S20 1-0	D26 0-1	M07 1-1	S01 0-0
2 BLACKPOOL	F07 1-2		a10 1-2	N08 1-2	A30 1-0	a18 3-1	O25 0-1	S15 5-1	J24 4-1	J03 0-0	a04 2-1	N22 1-1	O11 1-1	D20 1-2	S13 1-1	a22 4-1	D26 2-2	a01 1-0	S08 5-0	M21 0-1	D06 1-2	S27 2-4
3 BRADFORD C	S13 1-0	a14 1-0		a04 2-0	N08 0-0	F07 1-0	M21 0-0	O18 0-3	A30 1-1	S08 4-1	D20 1-1	a18 0-1	J24 0-1	O25 1-1	O20 2-0	S27 1-1	M07 2-0	N22 1-2	F14 1-0	D06 3-0	D26 1-0	J03 3-1
4 CHELSEA	a25 0-1	M14 3-0	N29 3-0		J24 1-1	A30 1-0	S27 2-2	N15 1-1	O11 0-0	N01 1-0	S08 4-0	a13 0-0	D13 2-0	J03 4-1	F28 2-3	a11 1-0	S13 0-0	F07 1-0	a20 1-1	O18 1-1	a27 2-1	D25 1-0
5 CLAPTON O	N29 0-0	D27 1-0	M14 0-0	S20 0-0		a10 1-2	S06 3-0	F28 0-1	D13 3-0	D25 0-0	F14 0-1	O04 0-1	M28 0-1	S01 5-1	a25 1-1	N15 3-1	O02 1-0	J17 1-0	N01 0-0	F16 1-1	O18 0-2	a11 2-1
6 COVENTRY C	M14 3-2	M09 2-1	O04 0-0	D27 0-3	a14 1-0		S01 1-4	a25 0-0	M28 0-1	a11 0-0	S20 4-2	J17 1-0	N01 2-2	O11 5-1	F12 2-1	F28 0-0	F21 1-1	S15 1-0	D25 0-1	S06 4-2	J31 3-1	N15 2-4
7 CRYSTAL P	a11 0-1	F28 1-2	N15 4-1	a01 1-0	J03 0-1	O01 0-0		N01 2-0	a25 1-2	S13 1-0	O18 0-2	F14 2-1	N29 2-2	m02 0-1	D26 1-2	M28 0-0	A30 0-1	S20 3-1	M14 0-0	O04 3-0	a10 0-1	D13 2-1
8 DERBY CO	S27 1-1	m02 2-2	F25 2-0	M21 1-0	O25 3-0	D20 5-1	M07 3-0		S13 5-1	A30 4-0	D06 0-3	a04 1-0	F07 3-1	D26 1-0	J03 6-1	O11 4-1	S08 2-1	N08 3-0	a13 0-0	N22 2-0	a18 1-2	J24 0-1
9 FULHAM	a14 1-2	S20 1-0	D27 1-1	F14 1-2	a18 0-2	N22 2-0	D20 3-1	J17 0-2		F09 4-0	N08 2-2	M07 1-0	D01 0-0	a04 1-0	O04 0-0	m02 1-1	D06 2-1	a10 1-0	S06 1-1	O25 2-0	M21 1-0	F21 1-0
10 HULL C	O11 5-2	S06 1-1	S01 0-0	M07 1-0	D26 2-1	D06 4-1	J17 5-0	D27 1-1	S27 3-0		N22 2-1	M21 0-1	M19 0-0	a18 1-0	J24 5-0	a13 2-1	D20 4-2	O25 1-1	m02 0-1	N08 3-0	a04 0-0	F07 0-1
11 LEICESTER C	F28 6-0	N29 0-2	a25 1-0	S01 4-0	O11 4-2	J24 5-1	M12 3-1	a11 0-0	M14 4-0	M28 1-0		D27 3-0	S06 0-0	S27 3-0	N15 4-0	D25 7-0	F07 6-1	a14 0-0	D13 1-1	m02 4-0	S13 0-1	N01 2-0
12 MANCHESTER U	S08 1-0	M28 0-0	D13 3-0	J01 1-0	F07 4-2	S13 5-1	O11 1-0	N29 1-1	N01 2-0	N15 2-0	A30 1-0		D26 2-0	J24 0-1	M14 2-0	a25 4-0	S27 2-0	a22 1-1	a11 1-0	a10 2-0	J03 2-0	F28 3-0
13 MIDDLESBROUGH	A30 2-0	F14 4-1	S20 1-0	a18 1-1	N22 1-1	M07 1-1	a04 0-0	O04 1-3	J01 1-3	O18 0-1	J03 1-5	D25 1-1		N08 0-0	a13 1-1	J17 0-1	M21 2-0	D06 0-0	J31 1-1	D20 1-1	O25 1-0	S10 2-0
14 OLDHAM A	N15 2-0	a25 4-1	F28 1-3	S06 0-5	S08 2-1	F14 5-0	O06 0-2	D25 0-1	N29 0-0	D13 1-0	M17 0-1	S20 0-3	M14 0-0		a11 0-2	N01 2-0	a10 1-1	D27 1-1	O18 1-0	J17 0-0	O04 2-0	M28 2-0
15 PORTSMOUTH	F21 0-0	J17 1-1	m02 5-0	O25 0-0	D20 0-2	a04 1-0	D25 0-0	S06 1-1	F07 3-0	S20 2-0	M21 1-1	N08 1-1	a10 3-1	D06 2-2		M30 2-0	a18 1-1	N29 1-1	D27 1-0	M07 1-1	N22 0-0	O11 2-2
16 PORT VALE	J03 2-0	O18 1-2	F02 1-0	D06 1-1	M21 4-2	O25 4-0	N22 3-0	F14 2-1	S08 0-1	a10 1-1	D26 1-2	D20 2-1	S13 2-1	M07 1-0	S15 0-2		N08 1-0	O13 1-1	O04 0-0	a18 4-1	J24 2-0	A30 1-3
17 SHEFFIELD W	M28 1-0	D25 2-6	N01 3-3	J17 2-1	m02 0-0	O18 2-0	D27 0-1	S01 0-1	a11 3-1	a25 5-0	O04 1-4	F23 1-1	N15 2-0	J01 1-0	D13 5-2	M14 0-1		S06 1-0	F28 0-1	S20 3-0	F14 2-1	N29 2-0
18 SOUTHAMPTON	D13 3-1	N01 2-1	a30 2-0	O04 0-0	S13 2-0	m02 3-0	J24 2-0	M14 2-0	D26 1-0	F28 2-2	a13 0-0	O18 0-2	a11 1-1	A30 0-0	S27 0-0	a04 1-0	J03 1-0		N15 1-1	F14 2-1	S08 3-0	a25 1-1
19 SOUTH SHIELDS	J24 5-2	S01 1-3	O11 1-0	N22 1-1	M07 2-0	J01 4-1	N08 1-1	a10 1-0	F25 2-1	a01 2-0	a18 1-1	D06 1-2	S27 0-1	F21 0-0	A30 0-2	F07 3-0	O25 0-1	M21 1-1		a04 0-1	D20 4-0	S13 3-3
20 STOCKPORT CO	D25 1-0	N15 1-0	a11 3-0	F21 4-0	S27 0-1	J03 1-1	F07 1-0	M28 0-0	F28 4-1	M14 0-2	S15 0-2	S01 2-1	a25 1-1	S13 2-0	N01 1-2	F25 0-2	J24 1-0	O11 1-1	N29 0-0		A30 2-0	J01 1-1
21 STOKE	N01 1-1	a11 3-1	J01 0-0	S22 1-0	F21 0-1	S27 4-1	a13 1-1	D13 1-1	N15 1-1	N29 2-0	J17 1-1	S06 0-0	F28 0-1	F07 0-1	M28 2-1	S20 0-1	O11 0-2	S01 2-0	a25 0-0	D27 3-0		M14 0-3
22 WOLVERHAMPTON W	a27 0-1	M23 2-0	S06 2-0	D26 0-1	D06 1-2	M21 3-1	a18 3-1	S20 0-4	O18 2-1	O04 2-1	M30 0-1	O25 0-0	m02 1-0	N22 2-0	F14 0-5	D27 1-0	a04 1-0	D20 3-0	J17 2-1	a13 3-0	N08 1-0	

Season 1924-25

DIVISION 3 NORTH

	ACCRINGTON S	ASHINGTON	BARROW	BRADFORD	CHESTERFIELD	CREWE A	DARLINGTON	DONCASTER R	DURHAM C	GRIMSBY T	HALIFAX T	HARTLEPOOLS U	LINCOLN C	NELSON	NEW BRIGHTON	ROCHDALE	ROTHERHAM CO	SOUTHPORT	TRANMERE R	WALSALL	WIGAN B	WREXHAM
1 ACCRINGTON S		F28 2-2	S30 1-2	S08 2-2	J03 2-2	M28 1-0	J01 2-0	M14 3-2	F23 6-0	O04 0-3	S20 2-0	F14 4-1	a25 0-2	S13 2-0	a27 0-1	O18 2-2	A30 2-0	N01 5-1	a22 2-1	a11 1-1	S17 3-1	m02 1-0
2 ASHINGTON	O25 1-2		S13 5-2	a18 1-0	A30 2-1	F21 1-1	D06 4-2	S01 2-0	a10 0-2	M21 0-2	M07 2-0	N22 0-3	J24 2-1	J03 1-1	N08 1-1	J02 4-3	J01 3-1	m02 2-0	S27 1-0	F07 6-1	F14 1-1	D20 2-0
3 BARROW	D26 3-1	J17 3-2		a04 2-1	D20 1-0	S01 2-0	N22 0-4	D27 4-0	S15 2-0	M07 3-2	J31 2-1	N08 1-1	F07 1-2	S20 3-0	O25 1-1	M21 1-0	a18 3-1	S06 1-0	O11 1-1	F21 3-2	a10 0-1	D06 2-2
4 BRADFORD	S01 3-0	D17 7-1	J01 1-1		a13 3-0	F28 6-1	F24 0-0	D25 4-1	O04 4-1	S06 0-1	N15 2-1	J17 3-0	M28 4-0	a11 1-1	D27 5-2	S20 0-0	F21 3-0	a25 1-0	M04 5-1	M14 2-0	N01 2-2	O11 3-0
5 CHESTERFIELD	S06 1-0	D27 1-1	a25 1-1	a10 1-1		J10 1-0	O18 0-1	N01 2-1	M14 6-0	a14 2-0	J17 1-3	O04 4-0	M11 2-0	D26 0-1	S20 3-0	F14 2-0	M30 3-2	F28 1-2	a11 4-1	S08 1-0	N22 3-1	J01 3-0
6 CREWE A	N22 4-2	O18 1-0	S10 3-1	O25 2-1	M21 1-1		J24 0-5	O04 1-1	J31 3-0	a18 3-1	a04 1-1	D20 3-1	S17 1-1	a10 2-1	D06 1-0	D26 2-0	N08 3-1	F14 1-1	A30 0-2	J03 1-1	S13 1-1	M07 1-2
7 DARLINGTON	a10 2-1	a11 2-1	M28 3-0	S27 2-1	F21 3-3	S20 5-1		a25 1-1	D25 0-0	D27 0-0	J02 3-0	S06 2-0	F11 0-1	N15 3-1	S03 3-1	J17 2-0	O11 4-0	D17 2-1	M14 2-1	N01 3-0	F28 5-0	F07 3-1
8 DONCASTER R	N08 4-1	S08 7-3	A30 0-0	D26 1-0	M07 0-1	F07 1-1	D20 0-2		O11 0-0	a04 2-2	M21 0-1	D06 1-0	J03 2-1	a14 1-1	N22 1-0	a18 2-1	O25 4-1	a10 0-1	S13 2-0	J24 2-1	S27 5-0	F21 1-0
9 DURHAM C	M21 2-0	S03 0-0	m02 6-0	F07 1-0	N08 1-1	S27 4-1	a13 2-1	F14 1-0		D06 6-1	N22 1-2	a18 0-1	J01 5-0	a29 3-1	a04 0-0	D20 3-2	M07 1-1	O18 0-0	M18 0-3	S13 0-2	J24 1-1	O25 1-0
10 GRIMSBY T	F07 4-0	J10 1-3	N01 2-1	J03 2-0	S27 0-0	D13 0-0	A30 0-2	J01 1-1	a11 1-1		O11 1-1	S01 2-1	F28 1-2	M14 2-0	F21 2-3	N15 1-1	J24 3-1	M28 3-1	a13 6-1	D25 2-1	a25 4-0	S13 0-1
11 HALIFAX T	J24 2-2	N01 0-0	S27 2-0	m02 1-3	S13 1-0	M12 2-2	a14 1-1	J26 2-0	M28 3-0	F14 1-0		O18 2-0	D25 1-0	F28 2-4	O04 1-2	a13 3-1	J03 4-0	M14 2-0	D20 1-3	D13 1-1	a11 1-2	A30 3-1
12 HARTLEPOOLS U	O11 3-0	M28 0-1	M14 1-0	S13 2-2	F07 1-0	a25 2-0	J03 1-1	a11 2-2	a22 1-0	S10 2-1	F21 1-1		N01 1-1	M25 2-4	a13 0-2	A30 1-1	S27 0-0	O01 1-2	F28 2-1	J01 3-1	D25 1-0	J24 1-1
13 LINCOLN C	D20 3-0	S20 5-0	O04 2-1	N22 0-4	a18 3-1	m02 4-1	M21 0-1	S06 2-0	D27 3-0	O25 0-0	D26 1-1	M07 2-1		M18 2-1	F14 2-0	N08 1-2	D06 3-1	J17 1-1	O18 3-2	a10 0-1	S01 1-0	a04 1-1
14 NELSON	J17 4-1	S06 4-0	J24 2-0	D06 2-2	D25 1-0	a13 7-0	a04 1-1	S09 3-0	S16 7-1	N08 1-0	O25 2-1	M21 2-0	S27 1-0		M07 5-0	N22 1-0	D20 4-1	a21 2-1	F07 4-1	O11 2-1	F21 1-0	a18 2-4
15 NEW BRIGHTON	S27 4-0	M14 4-4	F28 3-0	A30 0-0	J24 2-1	a11 3-0	m02 1-0	M28 0-2	D10 4-0	O18 3-2	F07 3-1	a10 2-0	O11 4-1	N01 5-0		S17 5-0	S13 3-1	J10 1-1	D26 1-0	a25 3-2	D13 3-0	J03 2-1
16 ROCHDALE	F21 0-1	a04 0-0	a28 5-1	J24 2-2	O11 2-1	D25 5-0	S13 2-1	F24 5-2	J10 3-0	m01 2-0	a10 3-1	D27 3-1	M14 3-0	M28 0-1	a14 2-0		F07 4-1	a11 1-0	N01 2-1	F28 3-0	S06 3-2	S27 3-1
17 ROTHERHAM CO	D27 1-1	D26 1-4	M16 0-1	O18 1-1	m02 1-3	M14 1-3	F14 1-1	F28 3-0	N01 1-2	S20 3-0	S06 0-0	J31 1-2	D13 1-1	a25 1-0	J17 2-1	O04 1-3		a14 1-3	S01 2-0	M28 2-0	N15 3-4	a13 0-1
18 SOUTHPORT	M07 3-1	S16 3-0	J03 5-0	D20 3-0	O25 0-2	O11 2-0	a18 1-0	a13 3-0	F21 1-1	N22 3-1	N08 3-1	a04 2-0	S13 4-0	A30 1-0	M21 2-0	D06 0-0	S09 2-0		J24 1-0	S27 1-0	O04 0-1	D25 1-0
19 TRANMERE R	a18 2-1	J31 5-4	F14 4-1	M21 2-0	D06 5-1	D27 2-2	N08 0-1	J17 1-2	S06 1-1	a10 2-3	a25 0-2	O25 4-3	F21 0-0	O04 2-0	J01 1-3	M07 3-1	a04 1-0	S20 1-0		O02 0-1	a14 2-3	N22 2-0
20 WALSALL	D06 1-1	O04 1-0	O18 1-0	N08 0-2	a04 0-0	S06 0-0	M07 2-1	S20 4-0	J17 2-2	D26 2-0	a18 0-2	m02 1-1	a13 2-0	F14 1-2	D20 2-1	O25 0-2	N22 0-1	J31 0-0	J10 2-0		D27 3-1	M21 3-0
21 WIGAN B	a04 1-2	O11 2-0	a13 2-0	M07 1-0	M28 0-0	J17 3-4	O25 1-1	J31 2-2	S20 0-0	D20 3-1	D06 2-0	D26 0-0	S08 4-0	O18 1-1	a18 0-1	J03 2-3	M21 4-1	F07 2-0	m02 4-0	A30 0-0		N08 5-0
22 WREXHAM	S24 1-0	a25 3-1	a11 3-0	F14 1-3	S17 0-0	N01 2-1	O04 0-2	O18 2-1	D13 3-1	J17 1-2	D27 0-0	S20 3-1	O01 0-1	J10 1-1	S06 0-0	J31 1-0	a10 3-1	D26 2-3	M28 4-0	N15 1-1	M14 6-2	

DIVISION 3 SOUTH

	ABERDARE A	BOURNEMOUTH	BRENTFORD	BRIGHTON & HA	BRISTOL C	BRISTOL R	CHARLTON A	EXETER C	GILLINGHAM	LUTON T	MERTHYR T	MILLWALL	NEWPORT CO	NORTHAMPTON T	NORWICH C	PLYMOUTH A	Q.P.R.	READING	SOUTHEND U	SWANSEA T	SWINDON T	WATFORD
1 ABERDARE A		a13 4-2	F16 2-1	O02 1-2	A30 1-2	M14 2-1	M09 2-0	N01 3-1	O18 2-1	F14 1-1	D25 2-0	O04 0-1	J10 1-3	a11 1-1	S20 2-1	O27 3-1	a25 1-1	S13 3-0	M28 3-0	a02 3-1	a23 1-1	N29 2-0
2 BOURNEMOUTH	a10 3-1		O22 2-0	S27 0-0	O11 1-3	a25 0-1	M14 2-1	M25 1-1	J17 3-0	S06 2-1	M28 2-0	F11 0-1	D25 0-0	N01 1-2	S03 0-0	F07 0-1	a22 0-2	J10 0-0	S20 1-0	a11 0-2	F21 0-0	F28 2-1
3 BRENTFORD	S27 2-2	m02 1-2		A30 2-4	S13 1-0	M28 1-1	D26 1-0	N15 2-5	S08 2-1	a10 3-0	F28 2-2	O18 1-0	S15 2-0	a25 1-3	F07 1-1	J03 1-0	O11 0-1	N01 0-1	J10 2-2	M14 3-1	J24 0-0	D13 0-0
4 BRIGHTON & H.A.	M25 4-1	M11 0-1	D27 4-1		F21 1-0	D26 1-0	N15 0-0	a25 2-0	S20 2-0	J17 2-1	O08 3-1	S06 3-3	O04 4-1	M14 0-1	m02 3-1	O11 2-3	M28 5-0	a11 0-1	F28 2-1	D13 0-0	a10 3-1	N01 2-0
5 BRISTOL C	D27 0-1	F14 2-1	J17 3-0	O18 2-1		F28 2-0	S24 1-1	S01 0-1	O04 2-1	M04 2-0	D13 1-0	S20 4-1	N01 2-0	M28 1-0	S06 2-0	a13 2-2	a11 5-0	a25 3-0	M14 5-0	D26 0-0	S17 0-0	N15 1-1
6 BRISTOL R	N08 1-0	D20 1-0	N22 2-0	D25 1-2	O25 0-0		S13 4-0	a10 0-1	a18 0-0	D06 1-1	A30 1-0	a04 1-1	O11 0-1	J24 0-2	M21 3-0	F21 1-1	M18 3-0	a14 1-0	F07 1-3	S08 3-0	M07 0-1	S27 2-0
7 CHARLTON A	a18 5-1	N08 2-2	D25 3-0	M21 1-0	a04 0-1	J17 1-1		S20 1-0	M07 2-0	O25 2-0	F14 3-0	a10 0-2	S06 1-0	S01 0-0	D20 3-2	N22 2-1	O18 2-0	O04 1-2	D27 0-0	F16 0-0	D06 1-0	S18 1-1
8 EXETER C	M07 3-1	a18 2-1	M21 5-1	D20 2-0	S10 0-2	a13 1-1	J24 2-1		D06 3-3	a04 0-1	J03 2-1	N22 0-0	F21 4-3	S27 0-0	N08 1-0	D26 3-0	S13 1-3	A30 1-0	O11 0-1	S24 2-0	O25 1-0	F07 4-0
9 GILLINGHAM	F21 2-0	S13 0-0	S03 1-0	J24 2-0	F07 1-1	F11 0-0	N01 2-0	a11 1-1		D27 4-1	N15 2-1	O22 1-0	a25 1-0	F28 0-1	a10 3-1	S27 0-3	M14 1-0	M28 0-0	D25 3-1	M18 0-0	O11 1-1	S06 0-0
10 LUTON T	O11 0-0	J03 0-2	a13 3-1	S13 3-1	S27 3-0	a11 1-1	F28 1-0	S08 1-1	A30 0-0		M14 6-0	S01 1-1	D13 2-2	S22 2-0	F21 0-0	J24 1-1	N01 3-0	M21 1-0	a25 4-0	M28 0-0	F07 2-2	D26 0-3
11 MERTHYR T	D26 3-1	N22 3-1	O25 4-0	a04 1-2	a18 2-3	M30 1-0	O11 2-1	S06 0-1	M21 0-0	N08 0-0		M07 2-1	S29 1-0	F21 0-2	M23 0-2	D06 1-2	F07 2-3	S20 0-0	S01 1-0	J17 0-2	D20 1-5	a14 0-1
12 MILLWALL	F07 2-1	A30 3-1	F21 3-0	J03 1-1	J24 3-1	S15 0-0	a13 1-0	M28 2-0	m02 2-0	N29 2-2	N01 3-1		a11 3-0	D25 3-1	O11 0-0	S13 0-0	F20 3-0	M14 0-1	D13 2-0	N15 1-2	S27 1-2	a25 0-1
13 NEWPORT CO	M21 1-0	D26 2-0	a04 1-0	F07 0-0	M07 0-2	F14 4-1	a14 2-1	O18 2-1	D20 2-0	a18 1-1	m02 3-0	D06 2-3		S13 1-0	N22 3-0	O25 0-0	A30 0-0	S11 1-1	S27 1-1	a10 3-0	N08 3-1	J24 3-0
14 NORTHAMPTON T	S04 5-0	M07 3-0	D20 0-2	N08 1-0	N22 1-2	S20 5-0	S08 2-1	J31 2-1	O25 1-0	S15 1-0	O18 2-0	D26 0-2	J17 0-2		a18 1-1	M21 5-2	a14 1-0	F14 2-0	S06 0-1	O04 1-3	a04 0-0	D27 1-1
15 NORWICH C	J24 1-1	O09 6-3	O04 3-0	S08 2-2	J03 0-0	N15 1-1	a25 2-1	M14 0-1	a13 0-0	O18 1-1	S27 1-0	F14 2-2	M28 2-1	a23 4-0		A30 1-1	D26 5-0	F28 0-2	a14 0-1	N01 2-0	S13 4-0	D06 2-1
16 PLYMOUTH A	D13 2-0	O04 2-0	S06 7-1	F14 1-0	a10 7-1	O18 3-2	M28 3-2	D25 1-1	J31 2-0	S20 4-0	a11 2-0	J17 1-1	F28 0-2	N15 2-1	D27 5-0		S24 1-0	a20 2-0	a29 6-0	a25 1-1	S08 2-0	M14 1-0
17 Q.P.R.	D20 4-1	M21 0-2	F14 1-0	N22 2-0	D06 3-0	S06 1-2	F21 0-0	J17 1-4	N08 1-1	M07 2-1	O04 1-1	O25 0-0	D27 4-3	a13 2-0	D25 1-2	a04 0-1		J31 1-0	m02 3-1	S20 0-0	a18 1-0	S03 0-0
18 READING	J17 2-0	a04 0-1	M07 3-1	D06 0-0	D20 0-1	m02 4-1	F07 0-0	D27 1-1	N22 0-1	O08 3-0	J24 2-1	N08 1-2	S03 0-1	O11 0-1	O25 2-0	a18 0-0	S27 2-1		a10 2-2	S06 2-0	D26 1-1	F21 3-0
19 SOUTHEND U	N22 2-1	J24 3-0	D06 6-1	O25 2-0	N08 2-0	O04 2-1	A30 0-3	F14 3-0	D26 4-0	D20 2-1	S10 2-1	a18 1-0	J31 0-1	J03 0-1	a04 0-1	M07 0-3	S17 1-0	a13 3-0		O18 1-0	M21 0-0	S13 0-4
20 SWANSEA T	O25 2-2	D06 1-0	N08 7-0	a18 1-0	D25 1-1	S01 2-2	S27 6-1	m02 2-1	a04 2-0	N22 4-1	S13 2-0	M21 2-2	a13 1-0	F07 2-1	M07 2-0	D20 2-0	J24 2-0	a30 1-0	F21 4-0		A30 2-0	O11 3-1
21 SWINDON T	S06 2-0	O18 4-0	S20 2-0	a13 3-0	m02 3-0	N01 3-0	a11 2-2	F28 1-0	F14 2-0	O04 4-1	a25 5-1	J31 1-0	M14 2-2	N29 5-0	J17 1-0	S01 1-0	N15 5-3	D25 2-1	S24 3-0	D27 0-2		M28 0-1
22 WATFORD	a04 0-0	O25 2-1	a18 3-1	M07 0-1	M21 1-0	J31 1-0	m02 0-0	O04 3-0	J03 1-2	D25 1-1	a10 3-1	D20 1-0	S20 0-5	A30 1-0	a11 0-2	N08 1-0	S10 1-0	O18 1-0	J17 0-3	F14 1-3	N22 1-0	

LEAGUE TABLES

DIVISION 1

	P	W	D	L	F	A	W	D	L	F	A	Pts
Huddersfield T	42	10	8	3	31	10	11	8	2	38	18	58
WBA	42	13	6	2	40	17	10	4	7	18	17	56
Bolton W	42	18	2	1	61	13	4	9	8	15	21	55
Liverpool	42	13	5	3	43	20	7	5	9	20	35	50
Bury	42	13	4	4	35	20	4	11	6	19	31	49
Newcastle U	42	11	6	4	43	18	5	10	6	18	24	48
Sunderland	42	13	6	2	39	14	6	4	11	25	37	48
Birmingham	42	10	8	3	27	17	7	4	10	22	36	46
Notts Co	42	11	6	4	29	12	5	7	9	13	19	45
Manchester C	42	11	7	3	44	29	6	2	13	32	39	43
Cardiff C	42	11	5	5	35	19	5	6	10	21	32	43
Tottenham H	42	9	8	4	32	16	6	4	11	20	27	42
West Ham U	42	12	7	2	37	12	3	5	13	25	48	42
Sheffield U	42	10	5	6	34	25	3	8	10	21	38	39
Aston Villa	42	10	7	4	34	25	3	6	12	24	46	39
Blackburn R	42	7	6	8	31	26	4	7	10	22	40	35
Everton	42	11	4	6	25	20	1	7	13	15	40	35
Leeds U	42	9	8	4	29	17	2	4	15	17	42	34
Burnley	42	7	8	6	28	31	4	4	13	18	44	34
Arsenal	42	12	3	6	33	17	2	2	17	13	41	33
Preston NE	42	8	2	11	29	35	2	4	15	8	39	26
Nottingham F	42	5	6	10	17	23	1	6	14	12	42	24

DIVISION 2

	P	W	D	L	F	A	W	D	L	F	A	Pts
Leicester C	42	15	4	2	58	9	9	7	5	32	23	59
Manchester U	42	17	3	1	40	6	6	8	7	17	17	57
Derby Co	42	15	3	3	49	15	7	8	6	22	21	55
Portsmouth	42	7	13	1	28	14	8	5	8	30	36	48
Chelsea	42	11	8	2	31	12	5	7	9	20	25	47
Wolves	42	14	1	6	29	19	6	5	10	26	32	46
Southampton	42	12	8	1	29	10	1	10	10	11	26	44
Port Vale	42	12	4	5	34	19	5	4	12	14	37	42
South Shields	42	9	6	6	33	21	3	11	7	9	17	41
Hull C	42	12	6	3	40	14	3	5	13	10	35	41
Clapton O	42	8	7	6	22	13	6	5	10	20	29	40
Fulham	42	11	6	4	26	15	4	4	13	15	41	40
Middlesbrough	42	6	10	5	22	21	4	9	8	14	23	39
Sheffield W	42	12	3	6	36	23	3	5	13	14	33	38
Barnsley	42	8	8	5	30	23	5	4	12	16	36	38
Bradford C	42	11	6	4	26	13	2	6	13	11	37	38
Blackpool	42	8	5	8	37	26	6	4	11	28	35	37
Oldham A	42	9	5	7	24	21	4	6	11	11	30	37
Stockport Co	42	10	6	5	26	15	3	5	13	11	42	37
Stoke	42	7	8	6	22	17	5	3	13	12	29	35
Crystal P	42	8	4	9	23	19	4	6	11	15	35	34
Coventry C	42	10	6	5	32	26	1	3	17	13	58	31

DIVISION 3 North

	P	W	D	L	F	A	W	D	L	F	A	Pts
Darlington	42	16	4	1	50	14	8	6	7	28	19	58
Nelson	42	18	2	1	58	14	5	5	11	21	36	53
New Brighton	42	17	3	1	56	16	6	4	11	19	34	53
Southport	42	17	2	2	41	7	5	5	11	18	30	51
Bradford	42	15	5	1	59	13	4	7	10	25	29	50
Rochdale	42	17	2	2	53	16	4	5	12	22	37	49
Chesterfield	42	14	3	4	42	15	3	8	10	18	29	45
Lincoln C	42	13	4	4	39	19	5	4	12	14	39	44
Halifax T	42	11	5	5	36	22	5	6	10	20	30	43
Ashington	42	13	4	4	41	24	3	6	12	27	52	42
Wigan B	42	10	7	4	39	16	5	4	12	23	49	41
Grimsby T	42	10	6	5	38	21	5	3	13	22	39	39
Durham C	42	11	6	4	38	17	2	7	12	12	51	39
Barrow	42	14	4	3	39	22	2	3	16	12	52	39
Crewe A	42	11	7	3	35	24	2	6	13	18	54	39
Wrexham	42	11	5	5	37	21	4	3	14	16	40	38
Accrington S	42	12	5	4	43	23	3	3	15	17	49	38
Doncaster R	42	12	5	4	36	17	2	5	14	18	48	38
Walsall	42	10	6	5	27	16	3	5	13	17	37	37
Hartlepools U	42	9	8	4	28	21	3	3	15	17	42	35
Tranmere R	42	11	3	7	40	29	3	1	17	19	49	32
Rotherham Co	42	6	5	10	27	31	1	2	18	15	57	21

DIVISION 3 South

	P	W	D	L	F	A	W	D	L	F	A	Pts
Swansea T	42	17	4	0	51	12	6	7	8	17	23	57
Plymouth A	42	17	3	1	55	12	6	7	8	22	26	56
Bristol C	42	14	5	2	40	10	8	4	9	20	31	53
Swindon T	42	17	2	2	51	13	3	9	9	15	25	51
Millwall	42	12	5	4	35	14	6	8	7	23	24	49
Newport Co	42	13	6	2	35	12	7	3	11	27	30	49
Exeter C	42	13	4	4	37	19	6	5	10	22	29	47
Brighton & HA	42	14	3	4	43	17	5	5	11	16	28	46
Northampton T	42	12	3	6	34	18	8	3	10	17	26	46
Southend U	42	14	1	6	34	18	5	4	12	17	43	43
Watford	42	12	3	6	22	20	5	6	10	16	27	43
Norwich C	42	10	8	3	39	18	4	5	12	14	33	41
Gillingham	42	11	8	2	25	11	2	6	13	10	33	40
Reading	42	9	6	6	28	15	5	4	12	9	23	38
Charlton A	42	12	6	3	31	13	1	6	14	15	35	38
Luton T	42	9	10	2	34	15	1	7	13	15	42	37
Bristol R	42	10	5	6	26	13	2	8	11	16	36	37
Aberdare A	42	13	4	4	40	21	1	5	15	14	46	37
QPR	42	10	6	5	28	19	4	2	15	14	44	36
Bournemouth	42	8	6	7	20	17	5	2	14	20	41	34
Brentford	42	8	7	6	28	26	1	0	20	10	65	25
Merthyr T	42	8	3	10	24	27	0	2	19	11	50	21

Football League Records

Top scorers: Div 1, E.Harper (Blackburn Rovers) 43 goals; Div 2, J.Trotter (Sheffield Wednesday) 37 goals; Div 3(N), J.Cookson (Chesterfield) 44 goals; Div 3(S), J.Cock (Plymouth Argyle) 32 goals. Rotherham County became Rotherham United; Stoke became Stoke City.

When Huddersfield Town won their third successive League Championship in 1925-6, centre-half Tommy Wilson played in all but one game.

Grimsby Town's Jimmy Carmichael was a prolific scorer but perhaps his most spectacular effort was the one he netted against New Brighton in May 1926 to give the Mariners the Third Division North title.

DIVISION 1

	ARSENAL	ASTON VILLA	BIRMINGHAM	BLACKBURN R	BOLTON W	BURNLEY	BURY	CARDIFF C	EVERTON	HUDDERSFIELD T	LEEDS U	LEICESTER C	LIVERPOOL	MANCHESTER C	MANCHESTER U	NEWCASTLE U	NOTTS CO	SHEFFIELD U	SUNDERLAND	TOTTENHAM H	W.B.A.	WEST HAM U
1 ARSENAL		a05 2-0	m01 3-0	a03 4-2	O10 2-3	F03 1-2	N14 6-1	O17 5-0	O31 4-1	a17 3-1	S26 4-1	A31 2-2	S12 1-1	M20 1-0	J16 3-2	F13 3-0	D25 3-0	M17 4-0	N28 2-0	A29 0-1	D12 1-0	S21 3-2
2 ASTON VILLA	a02 3-0		O17 3-3	D12 1-2	a26 2-2	A29 10-0	M06 1-1	O31 0-2	a03 3-1	N14 3-0	F03 3-1	M10 2-2	a06 3-0	N28 3-1	S07 2-2	S12 2-2	S26 2-1	M20 2-2	O05 4-2	a17 3-0	F13 2-1	D26 2-0
3 BIRMINGHAM	D19 1-0	F27 2-1		S05 2-0	N07 0-1	a10 1-7	J23 2-3	O10 3-2	S21 3-1	S16 1-3	D05 2-1	O24 1-1	N21 2-0	A31 1-0	a19 2-1	M13 1-1	S19 0-1	F13 2-0	J02 2-1	D25 3-1	S26 3-0	a24 1-0
4 BLACKBURN R	N21 2-3	a24 3-1	J16 4-4		F27 3-0	M13 6-3	A29 1-2	S26 6-3	D25 2-2	F11 2-1	N07 2-2	D19 0-0	D05 1-1	O10 3-3	a10 7-0	O12 1-2	O24 4-1	M01 3-1	S21 3-0	F13 4-2	S12 1-2	M27 1-0
5 BOLTON W	a28 1-1	S19 1-3	J01 5-3	O17 2-2		S16 4-2	J16 3-2	N28 0-1	m01 0-2	D12 6-1	S07 1-0	F06 2-2	a02 0-1	N14 5-1	M17 3-1	A29 2-2	J23 2-1	a17 2-1	a07 3-2	a03 1-1	O31 2-2	O03 1-0
6 BURNLEY	S19 2-2	J02 2-3	D07 3-1	O31 1-3	S09 1-1		a17 2-2	m01 4-1	O17 1-3	F20 1-1	D26 6-3	S05 4-0	O03 2-1	a06 1-2	F06 0-1	a02 1-0	S07 0-0	N14 1-1	M20 5-2	D12 1-2	a03 3-4	J23 2-2
7 BURY	M27 2-2	O24 2-3	S12 2-1	J02 3-1	S05 0-5	D16 8-1		F13 4-1	J01 1-0	a05 0-0	M13 0-2	a24 4-0	a10 0-1	D25 6-5	N21 1-3	N07 1-1	F27 3-1	S26 7-4	O28 2-2	O10 3-0	F24 2-0	D19 4-1
8 CARDIFF C	F27 0-0	M13 2-0	F20 2-0	F06 4-1	a10 0-1	D19 2-3	O03 3-2		S05 2-1	J23 1-2	M27 0-0	N07 5-2	a24 2-2	J02 2-2	O24 0-2	N21 0-0	D05 2-1	a05 0-1	S23 0-1	S21 0-1	D25 3-2	S07 0-1
9 EVERTON	M13 2-3	N21 1-1	S09 2-2	D26 3-0	D19 2-1	F27 1-1	a02 1-1	J16 1-1		O03 2-3	O24 4-2	J30 1-0	F06 3-3	F10 1-1	N07 1-3	a24 3-0	M27 3-0	A29 2-2	M17 2-1	S12 1-1	S16 4-0	D05 2-0
10 HUDDERSFIELD T	D05 2-2	M27 5-1	D28 4-1	a06 3-1	a12 3-0	O10 2-1	S08 2-1	S12 1-1	F13 3-0		F27 3-1	N21 3-0	N25 0-0	S26 2-2	M13 5-0	O24 0-1	D19 2-0	J16 4-1	D26 1-1	M03 2-1	A29 1-1	a10 2-1
11 LEEDS U	F06 4-2	S05 2-2	a17 0-0	M20 2-1	A31 2-1	D25 2-2	O31 2-3	N14 1-0	M06 1-1	O17 0-4		J23 1-0	F20 1-1	D12 3-4	O03 2-0	S16 2-0	J02 2-1	a03 2-0	a06 0-2	m01 4-1	N28 0-1	S19 5-2
12 LEICESTER C	S07 0-1	O10 1-2	M06 1-0	F20 2-1	S26 5-2	J16 3-2	D12 0-2	M20 1-2	N28 1-1	a03 2-0	S12 1-3		A29 3-1	a17 2-3	D28 1-3	F22 3-2	F13 1-0	D26 2-2	N14 4-1	O31 5-3	O17 3-0	a05 1-1
13 LIVERPOOL	J23 3-0	J01 3-1	a03 2-2	a17 2-2	a05 2-2	F13 3-2	N28 0-1	D12 0-2	S26 5-1	M20 1-2	O10 1-1	J02 0-3		O17 2-1	S19 5-0	D25 6-3	S02 2-0	m01 2-2	O31 2-2	M06 0-0	N14 2-0	S05 0-0
14 MANCHESTER C	N07 2-5	a10 4-2	a02 2-4	M17 0-1	M29 1-1	O24 8-3	D26 0-2	A29 3-2	S19 4-4	F06 1-5	a27 2-1	D05 5-1	F27 1-1		S12 1-1	D19 2-2	N21 1-1	N04 2-4	O03 4-1	J16 0-0	J01 3-1	M13 2-0
15 MANCHESTER U	S05 0-1	S02 3-0	N14 3-1	N28 2-0	D25 2-1	S26 6-1	a03 0-1	a28 1-0	M20 0-0	O31 1-1	F13 2-1	S16 3-2	M10 3-3	J23 1-6		O10 2-1	a05 0-1	D12 1-2	a21 5-1	O17 0-0	m01 3-2	J02 2-1
16 NEWCASTLE U	O03 7-0	J23 2-2	O31 1-3	S09 1-7	J02 5-1	J01 1-3	M20 4-0	a03 0-1	D12 3-3	M06 0-2	a05 3-0	S19 3-2	D26 3-0	m01 3-2	a14 4-1		S05 6-3	D09 3-1	O17 0-0	N14 3-1	a17 3-0	F06 4-1
17 NOTTS CO	D26 4-1	F06 1-0	M03 3-0	M06 1-1	S12 3-0	S21 0-1	O17 4-1	a17 2-4	N14 0-3	m01 4-2	A29 1-0	O03 2-2	O01 1-2	a03 1-0	a02 0-3	J16 1-3		O31 2-0	D12 2-0	N28 4-2	M20 0-0	M22 1-1
18 SHEFFIELD U	O24 4-0	N07 4-1	O03 4-1	S19 1-1	D05 2-0	a19 6-1	F06 3-1	J01 11-2	J02 1-1	S05 2-3	N21 2-0	D25 2-4	D19 3-1	O26 8-3	a24 2-0	a10 4-3	M13 3-0		J23 4-1	A31 2-3	F20 3-2	F27 1-1
19 SUNDERLAND	a10 2-1	D19 3-2	A29 3-1	S02 6-2	O24 2-1	N07 2-2	O14 1-0	M31 1-3	O10 7-3	J20 4-1	J01 1-3	M27 3-0	M13 3-2	F13 5-3	D05 2-1	F27 2-2	a24 3-1	S12 6-1		S26 3-0	J16 4-0	N21 4-1
20 TOTTENHAM H	J02 1-1	D05 2-2	D26 2-1	O03 4-2	N21 2-3	a24 0-2	F20 4-2	S14 1-2	J23 1-1	S19 5-5	D19 3-2	M13 1-3	O24 3-1	S05 1-0	F27 0-1	M25 1-0	a10 4-0	S07 3-2	F06 0-2		a02 3-2	N07 4-2
21 W.B.A.	a24 2-1	O03 1-1	F06 5-1	J23 1-1	M13 0-3	N21 5-3	N09 4-0	D26 3-0	S02 1-1	J02 2-2	a10 3-0	F27 3-1	M27 0-3	S23 4-1	D19 5-1	D05 4-0	N07 4-4	O10 2-0	S05 2-5	a05 1-0		O24 7-1
22 WEST HAM U	O05 0-4	D25 5-2	D12 2-2	N14 2-1	F13 6-0	S12 2-0	m01 0-2	A31 3-1	a17 1-0	N28 2-3	J30 4-2	a02 1-1	J16 1-2	O31 3-1	A29 1-0	S26 1-0	O10 1-0	O17 1-3	a03 3-2	M20 3-1	M06 3-0	

DIVISION 2

	BARNSLEY	BLACKPOOL	BRADFORD C	CHELSEA	CLAPTON O	DARLINGTON	DERBY CO	FULHAM	HULL C	MIDDLESBROUGH	NOTTINGHAM F	OLDHAM A	PORTSMOUTH	PORT VALE	PRESTON N.E.	SHEFFIELD W	SOUTHAMPTON	SOUTH SHIELDS	STOCKPORT CO	STOKE C	SWANSEA T	WOLVERHAMPTON W
1 BARNSLEY		O03 2-0	A31 0-0	J23 2-3	S05 3-1	F06 1-1	a05 0-1	O24 2-2	S19 2-1	M27 0-1	D28 4-1	J02 3-4	N21 2-2	J01 3-0	D19 2-0	M13 1-1	F20 2-0	a24 3-1	F27 1-1	N07 2-1	D05 2-0	M06 1-1
2 BLACKPOOL	F13 4-0		J30 3-0	D25 0-0	O10 3-0	S14 0-1	S12 1-2	D05 2-0	a02 2-2	S07 2-3	J16 3-0	a03 2-1	F27 2-2	S26 2-2	N07 3-1	D19 1-0	A29 2-1	M13 1-0	a10 4-1	M27 0-0	a24 0-0	O24 4-0
3 BRADFORD C	S07 4-1	S19 1-0		J02 4-2	O07 0-3	J23 2-0	F20 0-0	D19 0-0	S05 0-1	a10 2-0	O03 0-1	O24 1-1	D05 0-1	a05 2-0	N21 2-0	D25 1-4	F06 0-5	M27 1-1	a24 2-2	F27 2-1	J20 3-1	M13 1-2
4 CHELSEA	S12 3-2	D26 2-3	A29 2-0		F10 1-3	F20 5-2	a26 2-1	S26 4-0	O03 4-0	a24 0-1	S07 0-0	M13 3-0	D19 0-0	J16 3-1	O24 5-0	a10 0-0	a02 0-0	F27 0-0	N07 3-2	D05 1-1	N21 1-3	M27 3-3
5 CLAPTON O	J16 4-0	M08 2-2	a19 3-1	S19 1-2		O03 1-2	S24 0-1	F27 1-1	F06 0-0	D19 1-0	a02 0-1	N07 1-2	M27 1-1	A29 1-2	a24 1-1	D05 0-0	D25 2-1	O24 1-2	S12 2-1	M13 4-0	a10 2-0	N21 2-1
6 DARLINGTON	S26 2-2	S23 1-3	S12 1-3	O10 1-1	F13 6-0		J16 3-0	M13 1-2	D25 1-2	F27 0-2	A29 0-0	a10 1-0	O24 7-1	J30 4-0	S09 1-1	M27 5-1	S30 3-1	N07 4-1	a17 3-2	N21 1-2	D19 3-3	a24 3-4
7 DERBY CO	a06 4-0	J23 5-2	O10 0-0	D28 4-2	A31 3-1	S05 0-2		M27 3-1	J02 3-1	D05 2-0	F06 2-0	a24 1-0	M13 0-2	D26 2-0	a10 2-0	F27 4-1	S19 2-2	N21 2-0	D19 4-0	O24 7-3	O03 5-0	N07 2-0
8 FULHAM	a19 2-2	a17 1-1	m01 2-0	F06 0-3	O17 0-2	O31 4-0	N14 1-1		M20 1-1	D25 2-0	a03 0-2	J23 2-1	a05 2-3	D12 3-3	O10 2-1	J02 3-0	N28 1-1	F13 2-1	S19 1-0	S05 2-4	A31 0-1	O05 1-2
9 HULL C	J30 2-2	a05 1-2	J16 5-0	F13 0-1	S26 2-0	D26 1-1	A29 0-0	N07 1-0		O24 1-2	O12 4-1	D05 1-2	a24 1-0	S12 3-0	F27 1-1	N21 0-1	S07 4-0	O10 1-3	M13 4-0	a10 1-0	a26 4-2	D19 3-1
10 MIDDLESBROUGH	N14 5-0	S02 3-2	N28 2-5	D12 1-2	m01 1-2	O17 3-2	a17 1-2	D26 4-0	M06 3-3		O31 1-0	O03 2-1	J02 4-1	a03 3-1	S23 5-1	S19 3-0	M20 3-0	J01 1-2	F20 4-0	F06 3-0	J23 0-3	S05 4-1
11 NOTTINGHAM F	D25 4-2	S05 1-1	F13 0-0	A31 1-5	a05 1-0	J02 2-0	S26 1-2	N21 2-2	a21 4-0	M13 1-0		D19 1-1	N07 3-1	O10 2-0	D05 4-0	O24 2-0	J23 1-2	a10 4-1	M27 2-0	a24 1-2	F27 0-2	S19 1-4
12 OLDHAM A	A29 2-1	N21 3-2	M06 3-0	O31 1-1	M20 1-1	F08 0-1	D14 2-0	S12 4-0	a17 2-1	F13 4-1	m01 8-3		O10 1-3	O17 3-2	S26 3-2	S07 1-1	N14 1-0	M16 2-1	J30 3-0	S14 7-2	a02 0-0	D25 1-2
13 PORTSMOUTH	a03 1-2	O17 2-0	a17 3-1	m01 4-0	N14 3-2	M06 2-0	O31 2-2	a02 0-0	D12 2-2	A29 1-5	M20 5-1	F20 0-2		N28 3-2	S30 5-2	F06 1-2	J16 1-2	D07 4-2	D26 4-0	O03 2-0	S19 0-0	J23 3-0
14 PORT VALE	S14 3-0	F06 5-0	a02 2-0	S05 0-6	J02 4-2	S19 6-1	D25 0-1	a24 0-1	J23 3-1	N21 4-0	a12 1-1	F27 3-0	a10 1-1		M27 3-0	N07 4-3	O03 1-1	D19 2-0	O24 2-0	A31 3-0	M13 3-0	D05 3-0
15 PRESTON N.E.	m01 4-2	M20 6-4	a03 3-1	M06 3-1	D12 4-1	a02 0-0	N28 2-1	M25 2-1	O17 4-0	S14 1-0	a17 2-0	F06 2-1	A31 3-2	N14 4-0		J23 0-3	O31 2-2	D26 0-4	O03 5-3	S19 2-0	S05 4-2	J02 1-0
16 SHEFFIELD W	O31 3-0	m01 2-0	D26 5-1	N28 4-1	a17 3-0	N14 4-0	O17 1-4	A29 3-0	a03 2-0	F22 2-0	M22 2-0	D28 5-1	S26 4-2	M20 0-2	S12 5-1		D12 2-1	J16 1-0	S21 6-2	a06 2-0	O10 3-1	F13 2-1
17 SOUTHAMPTON	O10 0-0	J02 2-2	S26 1-2	a05 0-1	D26 2-0	O05 4-1	F10 2-1	a10 2-0	A31 0-2	N07 3-1	S12 2-0	M27 3-1	S05 1-3	F13 2-3	M13 2-0	a24 1-2		D05 0-1	N21 3-0	D19 1-2	O24 4-1	F27 4-2
18 SOUTH SHIELDS	D12 3-0	O31 3-4	N14 1-3	O17 0-0	M24 1-0	M20 2-4	a03 0-0	O03 5-2	M03 1-3	a02 2-2	N28 3-1	S19 0-0	O26 5-1	m01 5-2	a05 1-1	S05 1-1	M06 2-0		F06 4-2	J23 5-1	J02 3-1	S07 3-1
19 STOCKPORT CO	O17 1-1	N28 4-3	D12 1-1	M20 0-0	J23 3-2	D05 1-1	m01 3-0	F09 1-2	O31 0-1	O10 1-2	N14 3-0	S05 1-0	D25 3-3	M06 2-2	F13 1-1	A31 0-2	a03 1-2	S26 4-1		J02 2-1	J01 1-3	a02 1-0
20 STOKE C	M20 1-2	N14 1-3	O17 1-0	a17 1-3	O31 0-0	a03 6-1	M06 0-1	J16 5-0	N28 3-1	S26 4-0	D12 1-1	a26 1-0	F13 2-1	S07 0-3	F22 1-3	a05 0-1	m01 1-1	S12 0-1	A29 3-0		D26 1-1	O10 0-0
21 SWANSEA T	a17 3-0	F25 6-1	M20 1-0	a03 0-0	a12 0-0	m01 1-1	F13 2-0	S21 6-0	N14 2-0	S12 4-0	O17 3-0	a05 3-3	M18 1-0	O31 1-0	J16 4-1	M11 2-2	M29 3-1	A29 1-2	S14 4-0	D25 1-1		S26 2-4
22 WOLVERHAMPTON W	a26 7-1	D12 0-0	O31 1-1	N14 0-0	a03 3-0	M01 1-0	M20 2-0	a12 0-0	m01 3-1	J16 3-1	F08 4-0	D26 2-1	S12 4-1	a17 3-1	A29 3-0	O03 1-2	O17 4-1	S14 2-0	a05 5-1	F20 5-1	F06 2-3	

Season 1925-26

DIVISION 3 NORTH

	ACCRINGTON S	ASHINGTON	BARROW	BRADFORD	CHESTERFIELD	COVENTRY C	CREWE A	DONCASTER R	DURHAM C	GRIMSBY T	HALIFAX T	HARTLEPOOLS U	LINCOLN C	NELSON	NEW BRIGHTON	ROCHDALE	ROTHERHAM U	SOUTHPORT	TRANMERE R	WALSALL	WIGAN B	WREXHAM
1 ACCRINGTON S		O31 2-1	M20 2-0	J23 1-4	S05 2-0	O17 3-1	a03 2-0	a14 2-3	S29 3-1	S19 1-0	O03 0-1	S02 1-2	N14 3-1	F20 3-2	J20 0-2	a02 1-3	F06 2-3	m01 4-3	D25 4-3	J02 5-2	a17 4-0	M06 4-2
2 ASHINGTON	M13 3-1		D25 1-4	M27 1-1	D19 0-0	S09 2-0	S12 2-0	F13 6-1	N07 0-1	N21 4-2	D05 0-1	a02 2-0	J30 4-1	A31 5-1	J16 1-1	F27 0-1	a10 4-2	S26 1-1	O24 1-0	a24 2-0	A29 3-3	O10 2-2
3 BARROW	N07 1-2	J01 2-3		N21 0-1	M27 0-3	O10 1-4	J16 0-1	S26 0-2	S14 1-4	a10 0-3	M13 1-2	F27 1-4	S12 3-0	S28 1-0	A29 2-3	O24 1-3	D05 1-2	J30 0-3	a24 3-3	D19 5-2	a02 1-1	F13 4-3
4 BRADFORD	S12 3-0	N14 1-0	a03 3-0		A31 1-0	a17 3-0	M06 3-0	M20 2-0	J30 2-1	D26 0-1	J16 2-2	S26 4-0	O17 4-1	J09 3-0	D16 1-0	F13 3-1	A29 6-1	a06 6-1	O10 3-0	S14 8-0	m01 6-1	O31 1-1
5 CHESTERFIELD	J16 7-2	m01 6-1	N14 3-1	S07 1-1		M17 4-3	O17 4-2	O31 2-2	S12 2-0	a05 2-0	A29 1-0	J30 5-2	J01 2-0	a03 3-1	M06 3-0	S26 1-2	D26 6-1	M20 3-0	F13 4-0	O10 4-0	F24 4-0	a17 3-1
6 COVENTRY C	F27 2-1	a05 2-0	J09 2-0	D05 2-2	a10 2-4		D25 2-1	S12 4-0	O24 3-1	M13 1-1	S26 4-1	a24 5-2	A29 3-2	O03 1-0	a06 0-0	D19 2-2	N07 7-0	J16 0-0	M27 1-2	N21 2-0	S07 0-0	J30 2-0
7 CREWE A	N21 3-0	J23 2-1	S05 4-1	O24 1-2	F27 2-0	D26 2-1		S07 2-2	a10 2-0	a24 1-1	M27 0-1	D05 2-1	O10 3-1	J02 1-4	F06 4-1	M13 3-2	D19 3-1	a21 0-1	N07 1-1	O03 2-1	S19 3-1	a02 2-0
8 DONCASTER R	a24 6-2	O03 2-1	F06 0-1	N07 0-3	M13 3-0	J23 8-1	A31 5-2		D19 4-1	a22 1-4	O24 2-2	M27 2-1	a02 1-0	S19 1-1	S24 2-0	N21 2-2	F27 0-0	D26 6-1	a10 4-0	D05 1-1	F20 1-1	S05 1-1
9 DURHAM C	S09 5-1	M20 0-0	S02 2-1	S19 2-1	J23 5-2	M06 4-1	J09 1-1	m01 3-0		F06 0-0	F20 2-0	a05 0-0	a03 3-2	O17 0-2	a17 0-0	J01 0-2	O03 5-1	N14 3-2	J02 2-1	S05 4-1	O31 2-0	a28 2-1
10 GRIMSBY T	J30 5-2	a03 3-1	F25 4-0	D25 3-0	a02 1-0	O31 2-0	M25 2-0	A29 3-0	S26 3-1		S12 1-0	F13 2-0	M06 4-0	a17 3-0	m01 1-0	O10 3-0	J16 3-0	O17 3-2	S14 8-0	A31 5-1	N14 1-1	M20 1-0
11 HALIFAX T	F13 1-1	J09 0-0	O31 3-2	S05 1-2	J02 2-0	F06 1-0	N14 1-0	M06 0-3	O10 2-1	J23 0-2		S07 2-1	m01 0-2	D12 1-1	a03 1-0	S01 1-1	S19 5-1	M18 3-0	a06 1-1	D26 5-0	a15 2-0	O17 2-1
12 HARTLEPOOLS U	S16 5-1	D26 2-1	O17 2-0	F06 0-3	S19 2-1	D12 3-2	a17 0-0	N14 2-1	D25 1-1	O03 1-1	J01 1-1		J09 4-2	M06 2-0	O31 6-1	J02 4-2	F20 2-1	a03 5-0	S05 3-2	J23 9-3	M20 0-0	m01 5-0
13 LINCOLN C	M27 3-1	S19 2-0	J23 4-3	F27 1-1	S21 2-1	J02 0-3	F20 2-2	a05 3-1	N21 1-0	O24 4-1	D19 0-1	a10 2-1		S05 1-0	O03 3-1	D05 0-2	a24 0-3	S07 3-0	M13 1-3	N07 5-1	F06 2-1	D25 3-2
14 NELSON	O10 1-0	S15 2-2	S08 3-3	a10 2-2	a20 3-3	F13 4-1	A29 2-1	J30 5-3	F27 4-0	D05 1-1	N07 1-1	O24 5-2	J16 5-2		a05 1-1	a24 1-3	M13 3-0	S12 3-3	D19 7-0	M27 2-0	D25 7-0	S26 5-1
15 NEW BRIGHTON	a10 4-1	S05 1-1	J02 2-1	a24 1-1	O24 1-2	a02 5-1	S26 2-3	J01 2-1	D05 1-2	D19 1-4	N21 2-1	M13 3-2	F13 5-0	D26 0-0		N07 3-0	M27 5-1	O10 1-0	S19 3-2	F27 3-2	J23 4-2	S02 2-2
16 ROCHDALE	a05 3-2	O17 1-3	M06 2-1	O03 2-0	F06 2-4	m01 4-1	O31 2-0	a03 4-1	D26 5-0	F20 5-2	S15 2-1	A29 6-0	a17 0-1	M23 2-0	M20 2-1		S08 2-2	J25 3-1	J23 3-2	S19 2-0	J16 2-1	N14 1-2
17 ROTHERHAM U	S26 3-1	F22 5-1	a17 2-1	J02 2-3	D25 0-1	M20 2-1	m01 2-2	O17 1-1	F13 2-0	S05 2-1	J30 1-1	O10 1-0	a19 1-3	O31 1-3	N14 1-0	N02 0-4		M06 5-2	A31 2-0	a06 4-1	a03 1-0	J23 6-2
18 SOUTHPORT	D19 1-3	F06 1-1	S19 2-0	a02 2-1	N07 1-3	S05 1-2	J01 0-0	D25 3-3	M27 6-1	F27 0-1	a24 3-1	N21 1-1	S15 3-2	J23 2-1	F20 3-2	a10 1-7	O24 1-1		D05 2-1	M13 1-1	O03 3-1	J02 0-1
19 TRANMERE R	D26 2-2	M06 1-4	a05 3-0	F20 3-2	O03 0-4	N14 2-1	M20 2-0	J09 1-0	A29 2-1	O01 0-0	a02 3-1	J16 2-0	O31 2-0	m01 4-2	a12 0-1	S12 3-5	J01 3-1	a17 1-0		F06 2-1	O17 5-1	a03 4-1
20 WALSALL	A29 3-3	D12 2-0	m01 1-2	S24 3-1	F20 3-1	a03 4-1	F13 0-3	a17 2-1	J16 0-1	S07 2-2	J25 3-1	S12 1-2	M20 0-0	N14 0-2	O17 3-1	J30 1-5	a05 4-1	O31 2-2	S26 1-3		M06 0-1	J09 5-1
21 WIGAN B	D05 5-0	J02 0-2	D26 4-1	D19 1-3	a24 2-0	A31 5-1	J30 3-1	O10 0-1	M13 4-1	M27 2-2	a10 0-0	N07 1-0	S26 3-3	a06 5-0	S12 3-1	S05 2-2	N21 0-1	F13 3-1	F27 2-2	O24 2-0		J01 6-0
22 WREXHAM	O24 5-6	F20 2-3	O03 0-0	M13 4-2	D05 1-1	S19 3-1	a05 1-1	J16 0-2	a24 3-0	N07 4-1	F27 2-0	D19 2-2	D26 1-1	F06 3-2	S09 1-2	M27 1-0	S12 2-2	A29 3-2	N21 0-2	a10 0-1	S16 1-0	

DIVISION 3 SOUTH

	ABERDARE A	BOURNEMOUTH	BRENTFORD	BRIGHTON & HA	BRISTOL C	BRISTOL R	CHARLTON A	CRYSTAL P	EXETER C	GILLINGHAM	LUTON T	MERTHYR T	MILLWALL	NEWPORT CO	NORTHAMPTON T	NORWICH C	PLYMOUTH A	Q.P.R.	READING	SOUTHEND U	SWINDON T	WATFORD
1 ABERDARE A		D05 3-3	S05 3-0	D26 2-2	S19 3-3	D19 0-1	M13 3-1	a19 2-0	N21 5-0	N07 0-1	O24 2-5	a06 0-0	S07 1-2	F27 2-0	S21 1-0	F20 3-1	F06 6-1	a24 1-0	a10 2-2	O03 2-0	M27 1-1	J02 8-1
2 BOURNEMOUTH	a17 3-0		N14 3-2	F24 0-3	J13 1-1	D25 2-0	F06 4-1	m01 6-1	J16 2-1	O03 1-2	S09 2-2	F20 2-1	M20 0-0	S23 0-2	M13 4-2	a21 2-2	M06 1-2	a05 4-1	S12 1-1	O17 1-2	A29 2-0	a03 3-4
3 BRENTFORD	J16 1-0	M27 0-2		S12 1-6	F20 2-1	F27 4-1	N21 4-0	F13 3-2	a24 2-0	a10 0-0	N07 1-0	D05 1-1	D26 2-0	M13 3-3	A29 3-4	a02 5-1	a26 2-2	S26 1-2	D19 1-0	S07 1-3	O24 3-1	J30 4-3
4 BRIGHTON & H.A.	D25 6-2	a10 3-4	J23 3-2		F06 0-0	a24 2-3	D05 1-0	S19 3-2	M27 1-3	M13 1-2	F27 2-0	N07 3-1	O14 3-1	J02 2-1	a02 2-2	O28 1-1	O03 1-2	O24 2-1	N21 2-2	a21 3-2	D19 3-1	S05 3-1
5 BRISTOL C	J30 1-0	a24 5-0	O10 3-0	S26 1-0		N07 0-0	D19 4-0	O07 1-0	F27 1-0	M27 4-0	D05 5-1	N21 2-1	J16 1-1	a10 1-2	S12 1-1	A29 0-1	a05 2-1	M13 3-1	O24 0-1	D25 1-4	S09 5-1	F13 1-0
6 BRISTOL R	m01 0-3	D26 7-2	O17 1-2	D12 4-0	M20 0-1		a06 4-1	M24 3-1	A31 0-1	S05 2-0	F06 2-2	J23 0-0	a03 0-1	S19 2-2	N14 1-2	J09 2-2	O31 2-3	O03 5-0	a02 4-2	a17 2-0	D28 1-2	M06 2-1
7 CHARLTON A	O31 1-0	S26 5-0	a03 0-2	a17 1-1	m01 3-1	A29 0-1		N14 1-1	S12 1-0	F20 1-0	a05 2-1	N09 0-0	F13 1-4	S03 0-0	M20 3-3	O17 3-0	M25 0-5	D26 1-1	J30 1-2	M06 5-0	J16 2-0	F25 1-1
8 CRYSTAL P	S12 0-1	D19 3-1	O03 2-0	M10 2-1	S23 5-2	O10 0-2	M27 4-1		O24 3-2	N21 0-2	M13 3-0	a10 3-0	A29 1-2	F10 4-2	J16 1-0	D26 2-0	N28 5-5	N07 1-0	a24 3-0	a02 3-0	F27 1-0	S26 4-0
9 EXETER C	a03 4-0	S05 0-1	D28 6-1	N14 2-4	O17 1-1	S09 3-0	J23 5-3	M06 0-1		S19 2-1	F20 2-2	F06 6-2	a17 3-1	O03 2-1	a14 1-0	O31 0-1	D25 4-0	S23 3-0	J02 3-2	M20 0-1	a05 1-2	m01 6-1
10 GILLINGHAM	M20 0-1	F13 1-2	J09 1-3	O31 3-1	N14 0-1	J16 6-3	O10 0-0	a03 1-1	J30 2-0		D25 2-1	S09 3-1	O17 0-0	a02 2-0	S30 1-1	M06 2-0	m01 2-0	A29 3-0	S26 4-1	J20 3-1	S12 0-1	a17 0-1
11 LUTON T	M06 2-1	A31 4-1	M20 4-2	O17 3-3	a17 4-1	S26 1-0	a02 1-0	O31 3-2	O10 1-1	D26 5-3		J02 4-0	m01 2-2	S05 4-2	F22 3-2	N14 3-2	D28 1-1	J30 4-0	S14 0-1	a03 2-0	F13 4-1	J23 5-0
12 MERTHYR T	a05 1-1	O10 0-2	a17 6-0	M20 0-1	a03 3-2	S12 2-3	M15 0-1	J25 4-0	S26 3-1	S03 0-0	A29 2-1		M06 0-2	D25 4-1	O17 5-3	D12 3-1	N14 1-1	J16 1-0	F13 5-2	m01 5-1	F22 2-1	O31 4-1
13 MILLWALL	A31 4-2	N07 0-1	D25 2-1	M22 2-0	S05 3-0	N21 0-0	O03 1-1	J02 1-0	D05 3-0	F27 0-0	D19 7-0	O24 1-1		a24 3-3	O10 4-1	F06 3-1	J23 0-0	M27 3-0	M13 1-0	S19 8-1	a10 3-0	a02 3-0
14 NEWPORT CO	O17 0-0	O01 1-2	O31 2-3	A29 4-3	D28 1-0	J30 3-1	S17 0-0	a17 2-3	F13 3-0	a05 4-0	J16 2-1	D26 3-1	F25 1-0		M06 3-0	m01 1-1	a03 0-3	S12 4-1	O10 1-1	N14 1-0	S26 0-4	M20 3-3
15 NORTHAMPTON T	S14 3-2	O31 1-1	J02 6-1	a06 1-2	J23 1-2	M27 2-0	N07 2-1	S05 4-0	a10 2-1	D28 1-2	a24 0-1	F27 4-1	a26 3-1	O24 2-0		O03 3-2	S19 2-1	D19 3-2	D05 0-1	F06 3-3	N21 2-0	D26 2-2
16 NORWICH C	O10 2-3	S19 3-1	a05 1-0	S14 1-2	J02 1-3	a10 1-0	F27 3-0	D25 4-3	M13 3-1	O24 1-0	M27 2-0	a24 2-2	S26 1-0	D19 0-0	F13 2-1		S05 0-3	N21 1-1	N07 3-1	J23 1-2	D05 2-2	A31 1-1
17 PLYMOUTH A	S26 7-2	O24 7-2	S23 4-0	F13 5-3	a02 3-1	M13 1-2	a24 1-0	S02 6-2	D26 2-2	D19 2-1	a10 4-3	M27 3-0	S12 2-0	N21 3-0	J30 2-4	J16 6-3		D05 3-1	F27 1-3	A29 6-2	N07 1-1	O10 2-1
18 Q.P.R.	F25 1-3	a02 2-2	F06 1-1	M06 0-2	O31 0-2	F13 2-1	D25 2-2	M20 1-3	O08 0-0	J02 0-1	S19 1-0	S05 1-1	D28 3-0	J23 0-2	m01 3-2	a03 0-1	a17 0-4		S03 1-2	M04 2-2	O10 1-1	O17 2-0
19 READING	M24 2-1	J23 5-2	m01 7-1	a03 0-0	M06 1-1	a05 3-0	S19 1-1	D28 2-1	A29 3-2	F06 1-0	S30 3-0	O03 1-1	O31 2-0	F20 2-1	a17 4-2	M20 2-0	O17 1-1	S09 2-1		J16 1-0	D25 2-0	N14 4-1
20 SOUTHEND U	F13 0-1	F27 3-0	S02 3-1	O10 4-0	D26 1-2	D05 3-1	O24 1-2	a05 5-1	N07 3-1	a24 1-1	N21 2-0	D19 5-1	M17 0-2	M27 4-1	S26 6-1	S12 0-1	J02 2-0	a10 2-1	S05 2-2		M13 3-0	S16 0-1
21 SWINDON T	N14 2-1	J02 8-2	M06 2-1	m01 1-0	A31 1-3	S16 4-2	S05 3-0	O17 3-1	a02 2-1	J23 1-0	O03 2-0	S19 0-2	S23 1-1	F06 2-1	a03 1-2	a17 3-1	M20 2-0	F20 2-0	D26 1-1	O31 2-0		a21 5-3
22 WATFORD	A29 2-0	N21 0-0	S19 2-2	J16 3-3	O03 2-2	O24 2-1	a10 1-1	F06 3-0	D19 3-1	D05 3-1	S12 2-0	M13 6-1	a05 0-1	N07 5-1	D25 3-2	S09 3-1	F20 0-1	F27 3-1	M27 0-1	S23 1-4	a24 3-2	

LEAGUE TABLES

DIVISION 1

	P	W	D	L	F	A	W	D	L	F	A	Pts
Huddersfield T	42	14	6	1	50	17	9	5	7	42	43	57
Arsenal	42	16	2	3	57	19	6	6	9	30	44	52
Sunderland	42	17	2	2	67	30	4	4	13	29	50	48
Bury	42	12	4	5	55	34	8	3	10	30	43	47
Sheffield U	42	15	3	3	72	29	4	5	12	30	53	46
Aston Villa	42	12	7	2	56	25	4	5	12	30	51	44
Liverpool	42	9	8	4	43	27	5	8	8	27	36	44
Bolton W	42	11	6	4	46	31	6	4	11	29	45	44
Manchester U	42	12	4	5	40	26	7	2	12	26	47	44
Newcastle U	42	13	3	5	59	33	3	7	11	25	42	42
Everton	42	9	9	3	42	26	3	9	9	30	44	42
Blackburn R	42	11	6	4	59	33	4	5	12	32	47	41
WBA	42	13	5	3	59	29	3	3	15	20	49	40
Birmingham	42	14	2	5	35	25	2	6	13	31	56	40
Tottenham H	42	11	4	6	45	36	4	5	12	21	43	39
Cardiff C	42	8	5	8	30	25	8	2	11	31	51	39
Leicester C	42	11	3	7	42	32	3	7	11	28	48	38
West Ham U	42	14	2	5	45	27	1	5	15	18	49	37
Leeds U	42	11	5	5	38	28	3	3	15	26	48	36
Burnley	42	7	7	7	43	35	6	3	12	42	73	36
Manchester C	42	8	7	6	48	42	4	4	13	41	58	35
Notts Co	42	11	4	6	37	26	2	3	16	17	48	33

DIVISION 2

	P	W	D	L	F	A	W	D	L	F	A	Pts
Sheffield W	42	19	0	2	61	17	8	6	7	27	31	60
Derby Co	42	17	2	2	57	17	8	5	8	20	25	57
Chelsea	42	10	7	4	42	22	9	7	5	34	27	52
Wolves	42	15	4	2	55	15	6	3	12	29	45	49
Swansea T	42	13	6	2	50	16	6	5	10	27	41	49
Blackpool	42	12	6	3	41	16	5	5	11	35	53	45
Oldham A	42	14	4	3	52	24	4	4	13	22	38	44
Port Vale	42	15	3	3	53	18	4	3	14	26	51	44
South Shields	42	11	6	4	50	29	7	2	12	24	36	44
Middlesbrough	42	14	1	6	56	28	7	1	13	21	40	44
Portsmouth	42	12	4	5	48	27	5	6	10	31	47	44
Preston NE	42	17	2	2	54	28	1	5	15	17	56	43
Hull C	42	11	4	6	40	19	5	5	11	23	42	41
Southampton	42	11	2	8	39	25	4	6	11	24	38	38
Darlington	42	9	5	7	51	31	5	5	11	21	46	38
Bradford C	42	9	5	7	28	26	4	5	12	19	40	36
Nottingham F	42	11	4	6	38	25	3	4	14	13	48	36
Barnsley	42	10	7	4	38	22	2	5	14	20	62	36
Fulham	42	8	6	7	32	29	3	6	12	14	48	34
Clapton O	42	8	6	7	30	21	4	3	14	20	44	33
Stoke C	42	8	5	8	32	23	4	3	14	22	54	32
Stockport Co	42	8	7	6	34	28	0	2	19	17	69	25

DIVISION 3 North

	P	W	D	L	F	A	W	D	L	F	A	Pts
Grimsby T	42	20	1	0	61	8	6	8	7	30	32	61
Bradford	42	18	2	1	65	10	8	6	7	36	33	60
Rochdale	42	16	1	4	55	25	11	4	6	49	33	59
Chesterfield	42	18	2	1	70	19	7	3	11	30	35	55
Halifax T	42	12	5	4	34	19	5	6	10	19	31	45
Hartlepools U	42	15	5	1	59	23	3	3	15	23	50	44
Tranmere R	42	15	2	4	45	27	4	4	13	28	56	44
Nelson	42	12	8	1	67	29	4	3	14	22	42	43
Ashington	42	11	6	4	44	23	5	5	11	26	39	43
Doncaster R	42	11	7	3	52	25	5	4	12	28	47	43
Crewe A	42	14	3	4	43	23	3	6	12	20	38	43
New Brighton	42	13	4	4	51	29	4	4	13	18	38	42
Durham C	42	14	5	2	45	19	4	1	16	18	51	42
Rotherham U	42	13	3	5	44	28	4	4	13	25	64	41
Lincoln C	42	14	2	5	42	28	3	3	15	24	54	39
Coventry C	42	13	6	2	47	19	3	0	18	26	63	38
Wigan B	42	12	5	4	53	22	1	6	14	15	52	37
Accrington S	42	14	0	7	49	34	3	3	15	32	71	37
Wrexham	42	9	6	6	39	31	2	4	15	24	61	32
Southport	42	9	6	6	37	34	2	4	15	25	58	32
Walsall	42	9	4	8	40	34	1	2	18	18	73	26
Barrow	42	4	2	15	28	49	3	2	16	22	49	18

DIVISION 3 South

	P	W	D	L	F	A	W	D	L	F	A	Pts
Reading	42	16	5	0	49	16	7	6	8	28	36	57
Plymouth A	42	16	2	3	71	33	8	6	7	36	34	56
Millwall	42	14	6	1	52	12	7	5	9	21	27	53
Bristol C	42	14	3	4	42	15	7	6	8	30	36	51
Brighton & HA	42	12	4	5	47	33	7	5	9	37	40	47
Swindon T	42	16	2	3	48	22	4	4	13	21	42	46
Luton T	42	16	4	1	60	25	2	3	16	20	50	43
Bournemouth	42	10	5	6	44	30	7	4	10	31	61	43
Aberdare A	42	11	6	4	50	24	6	2	13	24	42	42
Gillingham	42	11	4	6	36	19	6	4	11	17	30	42
Southend U	42	13	2	6	50	20	6	2	13	28	53	42
Northampton T	42	13	3	5	47	26	4	4	13	35	54	41
Crystal P	42	16	1	4	50	21	3	2	16	25	58	41
Merthyr T	42	13	3	5	51	25	1	8	12	18	50	39
Watford	42	12	5	4	47	26	3	4	14	26	63	39
Norwich C	42	11	5	5	35	26	4	4	13	23	47	39
Newport Co	42	11	5	5	39	27	3	5	13	25	47	38
Brentford	42	12	4	5	44	32	4	2	15	25	62	38
Bristol R	42	9	4	8	44	28	6	2	13	22	41	36
Exeter C	42	13	2	6	54	25	2	3	16	18	45	35
Charlton A	42	9	7	5	32	23	2	6	13	16	45	35
QPR	42	5	7	9	23	32	1	2	18	14	52	21

Football League Records

Top scorers: Div 1, J.Trotter (Sheffield Wednesday) 37 goals; Div 2, G.Camsell (Middlesbrough) 59 goals; Div 3(N), A.Whitehurst (Rochdale) 44 goals; Div 3(S), D.Morris (Swindon Town) 47 goals. Coventry City transferred to Division Three South.

In his second season with Newcastle United, Hughie Gallacher scored 36 goals as the Magpies won the League Championship. He had joined them from Aidrie for £6,500, a record for a Scottish club player.

DIVISION 1

	ARSENAL	ASTON VILLA	BIRMINGHAM	BLACKBURN R	BOLTON W	BURNLEY	BURY	CARDIFF C	DERBY CO	EVERTON	HUDDERSFIELD T	LEEDS U	LEICESTER C	LIVERPOOL	MANCHESTER U	NEWCASTLE U	SHEFFIELD U	SHEFFIELD W	SUNDERLAND	TOTTENHAM H	W.B.A.	WEST HAM U
1 ARSENAL		a15 2-1	a30 3-0	N06 2-2	S01 2-1	F26 6-2	D04 1-0	J01 3-2	A28 2-1	M19 1-2	a02 0-2	F12 1-0	S11 2-2	S18 2-0	D28 1-0	O02 2-2	J22 1-1	O23 6-2	N20 2-3	D18 2-4	a16 4-1	O16 2-2
2 ASTON VILLA	a18 2-3		M19 4-2	J29 4-3	S25 3-4	S04 1-1	S18 1-2	J31 0-0	O09 3-1	D04 5-3	D18 3-0	D28 5-1	a16 2-0	A30 1-1	F19 2-0	J15 1-2	D25 4-0	N20 2-2	M05 3-1	N06 2-3	O23 2-0	a02 1-5
3 BIRMINGHAM	D11 0-0	O30 1-2		A28 3-1	a04 6-1	N13 1-0	S25 2-2	a27 1-2	O16 1-0	S20 1-0	J22 1-3	N27 2-0	J01 2-1	a23 3-0	M12 4-0	a09 2-0	m07 2-3	S13 0-0	S11 2-0	F26 1-0	F05 1-0	D27 0-2
4 BLACKBURN R	a28 1-2	D11 0-2	J15 3-2		a23 0-3	O16 1-5	O04 2-2	m07 1-0	a09 4-4	O02 3-3	D25 4-2	F26 4-1	F12 2-1	O30 2-1	N27 2-1	M12 1-2	N13 3-4	S18 2-2	S20 0-2	S04 1-0	a19 0-0	F14 4-1
5 BOLTON W	S06 2-2	F12 0-2	O02 1-0	D04 5-1		M09 3-1	O23 2-2	S18 2-0	D25 3-1	a16 5-0	a30 4-0	J15 3-0	N20 2-0	J01 2-1	O09 4-0	S04 2-1	a15 4-1	a02 3-2	D18 2-2	M19 2-2	M05 1-1	N06 2-0
6 BURNLEY	O09 2-0	J22 6-3	a02 0-2	M05 3-1	S11 4-3		N06 0-0	A28 4-3	S25 1-0	D18 5-1	O23 2-2	a15 3-2	a30 1-1	D25 4-0	F05 1-0	S06 3-3	M29 2-5	D04 1-0	O12 4-2	N20 5-0	M19 2-1	a16 2-1
7 BURY	m04 3-2	F05 0-1	F12 3-1	S15 0-2	M12 2-0	M26 3-3		O30 2-3	m07 1-2	S01 5-2	A28 2-2	a09 4-2	a15 0-0	N27 0-2	O16 0-3	N13 3-2	D11 4-4	D25 2-0	M30 1-2	O02 0-0	S11 7-3	F26 1-2
8 CARDIFF C	D27 2-0	S11 2-3	N06 1-0	D18 0-1	F05 1-0	J15 0-0	M19 2-1		M16 2-0	a30 1-0	M21 2-0	S06 3-1	D04 0-1	a18 2-0	S25 0-2	S20 1-1	O09 3-0	a16 3-2	O23 3-0	a02 1-2	S04 1-1	N20 1-2
9 DERBY CO	J15 0-2	F26 2-3	M05 4-1	N20 4-5	D27 2-0	F12 4-1	D18 2-0	O02 6-3		a02 0-0	a16 4-4	F19 1-0	N06 4-1	S04 2-1	a18 2-2	S18 1-1	S27 1-0	M19 8-0	D04 4-2	O23 4-1	a30 2-1	D28 3-0
10 EVERTON	O30 3-1	a23 2-2	a18 3-1	F19 1-0	N27 1-1	J01 3-2	S29 2-2	D11 0-1	N13 3-2		O09 0-0	M12 2-1	S18 3-4	S25 1-0	a09 0-0	O16 1-3	M26 2-0	M02 2-1	D25 5-4	J15 1-2	S15 0-0	S04 0-3
11 HUDDERSFIELD T	N13 3-3	m07 0-0	S04 0-2	D27 5-0	D11 1-0	M12 2-0	J15 3-1	O16 0-0	N27 4-2	F26 0-0		O30 4-1	O02 5-3	M26 1-0	a23 0-0	a19 1-0	a09 0-2	F12 4-3	S14 0-0	J29 2-0	A30 4-1	S18 2-1
12 LEEDS U	S25 4-1	S15 3-1	a16 2-1	O09 4-1	A28 2-5	a19 0-2	N20 4-1	A30 0-0	S11 1-0	O23 1-3	M19 1-1		M05 1-1	F23 0-0	J22 2-3	D27 1-2	F05 1-1	D18 4-1	N06 2-2	D04 1-1	a02 3-1	a30 6-3
13 LEICESTER C	F10 2-1	N27 5-1	A30 5-2	S25 4-0	a09 0-1	D11 0-3	a18 1-1	a07 3-1	M26 1-1	F05 6-2	F19 2-4	O16 3-2		M12 3-2	N13 2-3	m07 2-1	O30 2-2	S04 5-3	O09 2-1	S13 2-2	D25 5-0	J15 3-0
14 LIVERPOOL	F05 3-0	S08 2-1	D04 2-1	M19 2-2	D28 3-2	D27 2-2	a16 2-2	a15 5-0	J22 3-2	F12 1-0	N06 2-3	O02 2-4	O23 1-0		A28 4-2	F26 1-2	S11 5-1	M05 3-0	a02 1-2	a30 1-0	N20 2-1	D18 0-0
15 MANCHESTER U	S15 2-2	O02 2-1	O23 0-1	a16 2-0	F26 0-0	S18 2-1	M05 1-2	F12 1-1	a15 2-2	N20 2-1	D04 0-0	S04 2-2	a02 1-0	J15 0-1		F09 3-1	J01 5-0	N06 0-0	a30 0-0	D27 2-1	D18 2-0	M19 0-3
16 NEWCASTLE U	a06 6-1	A28 4-0	N20 5-1	O23 6-1	J22 1-0	S01 1-5	a02 3-1	D25 5-0	F05 3-0	M05 7-3	a15 1-0	J01 1-0	D18 1-1	O09 1-0	S11 4-2		S25 2-0	a30 2-1	M19 1-0	a16 3-2	N06 5-2	D04 2-0
17 SHEFFIELD U	S04 4-0	D27 3-1	D18 4-3	a02 5-3	a18 1-1	O02 2-2	m05 2-0	F26 3-1	S13 1-0	N06 3-3	N20 3-3	S18 1-0	M19 0-3	F07 1-4	A30 2-2	F12 2-1		J15 2-0	a16 2-0	M05 3-3	D04 2-1	O23 0-2
18 SHEFFIELD W	M12 4-2	a09 3-1	a19 4-4	F05 0-3	N13 2-1	a23 2-1	J01 1-3	N29 3-0	O30 2-1	S11 4-0	S25 1-1	m07 1-0	J22 2-2	O16 3-2	M26 2-0	D11 3-2	A28 2-3		F19 4-1	D28 3-1	O09 2-1	S06 1-0
19 SUNDERLAND	a09 5-1	O16 1-1	F16 4-1	J01 2-5	a19 6-2	O06 7-1	S04 3-0	M12 2-2	a23 1-2	D27 3-2	S08 1-1	M26 6-2	J29 3-0	N13 2-1	D11 6-0	O30 2-0	N27 3-0	O02 4-1		S18 3-2	J15 4-1	F12 2-3
20 TOTTENHAM H	m07 0-4	M26 0-1	O09 6-1	J22 1-1	O30 1-0	a09 4-1	F19 1-0	N13 4-1	M12 3-2	A28 2-1	S11 3-3	a23 4-1	S06 2-2	D11 1-2	D25 1-1	N27 1-3	O16 3-1	A30 7-3	F05 0-2		S25 3-0	a15 1-3
21 W.B.A.	N27 1-3	M12 6-2	S18 1-2	a18 2-0	O16 1-1	O30 4-2	J29 3-1	F21 1-2	D11 3-1	S06 3-2	J01 2-2	N13 2-4	D27 0-1	a09 0-1	m07 2-2	M26 4-2	a23 1-0	F26 2-2	A28 3-0	F12 5-0		O02 1-3
22 WEST HAM U	M07 7-0	N13 5-1	D25 1-0	S11 1-5	M26 4-4	N27 2-1	O09 1-2	a09 2-2	J01 1-2	J22 2-1	F05 3-2	D11 3-2	A28 3-3	m07 3-3	O30 4-0	a23 1-1	M12 3-0	O04 1-1	S25 1-2	a18 1-2	F19 1-2	

Goalkeeper Billy Coggins was ever present as Bristol City returned to Division Two. He later won a Second Division medal with Everton.

DIVISION 2

	BARNSLEY	BLACKPOOL	BRADFORD C	CHELSEA	CLAPTON O	DARLINGTON	FULHAM	GRIMSBY T	HULL C	MANCHESTER C	MIDDLESBROUGH	NOTTINGHAM F	NOTTS CO	OLDHAM A	PORTSMOUTH	PORT VALE	PRESTON N.E.	READING	SOUTHAMPTON	SOUTH SHIELDS	SWANSEA T	WOLVERHAMPTON W
1 BARNSLEY		J22 6-1	D11 1-0	a23 3-0	F19 4-2	D27 3-2	D28 5-0	A28 2-1	N13 1-2	F26 1-1	M12 1-1	S25 0-2	O30 4-4	A30 0-1	a18 2-0	O16 2-0	M14 3-0	S11 2-2	m07 5-1	a09 6-1	F05 1-1	M26 4-1
2 BLACKPOOL	S04 6-1		N13 3-0	M26 3-1	D11 6-0	S18 1-1	F26 0-0	D27 6-2	M12 4-0	J29 2-4	a23 2-2	J15 2-2	m07 5-0	O02 2-0	F12 2-0	N27 2-2	O30 2-3	A30 3-1	a09 3-2	a15 6-1	J01 3-1	O16 2-3
3 BRADFORD C	a30 1-1	a02 4-1		S18 0-1	S08 1-3	M05 0-1	M19 1-0	N06 2-2	F26 1-2	D18 4-3	S29 0-1	D04 1-1	a19 1-2	S11 0-1	O23 1-2	A28 1-2	F12 0-1	N20 1-1	J22 2-0	O02 3-1	a16 5-0	D27 1-2
4 CHELSEA	D04 4-2	N06 1-1	F05 5-2		J01 2-1	D18 2-2	S25 2-2	M19 2-0	D25 1-0	a30 0-0	A28 3-0	a16 2-0	S06 2-0	O23 1-0	m04 0-0	M16 2-0	O02 2-1	a02 0-0	S11 2-3	F26 4-1	N20 2-2	a18 1-0
5 CLAPTON O	O02 0-1	a30 1-0	S02 1-1	a28 3-0		N06 0-4	a16 2-3	D04 2-4	F23 1-2	M19 2-4	O09 2-3	O23 2-2	F12 2-1	N20 3-1	a02 4-5	D25 1-2	J15 1-1	D18 5-1	a15 1-0	S04 1-0	M21 1-0	S18 2-0
6 DARLINGTON	D25 3-3	F05 1-3	O16 3-0	m07 2-2	M26 2-1		J22 5-0	S11 2-3	N27 1-3	a15 2-2	O30 1-4	O09 4-2	N13 4-2	A28 0-1	N08 0-4	A30 4-3	D11 0-1	S25 4-2	M12 1-2	a23 8-2	m02 3-1	a09 3-1
7 FULHAM	S13 1-0	O09 1-0	O30 1-1	F12 1-2	N27 2-0	S04 2-1		F19 0-5	m07 3-1	J15 2-5	a09 0-3	A30 2-1	a23 3-0	S18 1-1	M14 0-0	N13 6-2	M12 0-1	D27 1-2	M28 3-0	O16 2-2	a15 4-3	D11 4-1
8 GRIMSBY T	J15 1-3	D25 2-1	M26 4-2	O30 0-0	a23 2-2	M29 2-1	O02 2-0		O16 0-1	S04 2-2	F08 4-7	J01 1-1	J29 1-4	F12 2-5	S18 0-0	a09 4-4	F26 5-2	a15 0-1	N13 0-1	M12 1-1	A30 0-1	m07 6-0
9 HULL C	a02 5-1	O23 3-0	O09 4-0	D27 0-1	S11 4-0	a16 2-1	D18 2-0	M05 2-3		N20 3-2	F05 3-3	N06 1-2	J22 2-0	a30 1-2	D04 2-1	S25 0-0	a18 3-1	S20 1-1	M14 0-0	A30 2-0	M19 2-1	A28 1-0
10 MANCHESTER C	O09 1-1	S11 2-1	m07 8-0	D11 1-0	O30 6-1	a18 7-0	A28 4-2	J22 2-0	a09 2-2		D25 3-5	F19 1-1	M26 4-1	S22 3-0	S01 4-0	M12 4-1	a23 1-0	F05 3-0	O16 3-4	N27 1-2	S25 3-1	N13 2-1
11 MIDDLESBROUGH	O23 5-1	D04 4-4	S22 4-3	J15 0-0	F26 6-0	M19 4-1	N20 6-1	a16 3-0	S18 2-0	D27 2-1		M05 1-0	O02 4-2	a02 3-1	N06 7-3	J01 5-2	S04 0-2	a30 5-0	N27 3-1	M16 5-0	D18 7-1	F12 2-0
12 NOTTINGHAM F	F12 3-1	A28 2-0	a23 3-0	N27 4-1	M12 1-1	F26 5-1	O07 2-0	S06 1-1	M26 3-1	O02 3-3	O16 4-3		F05 2-0	a15 1-1	D27 1-0	m07 0-3	a09 7-0	J22 5-1	D11 3-1	N13 4-2	S11 2-2	O30 1-1
13 NOTTS CO	M19 1-1	D18 2-3	a18 4-0	S13 5-0	S25 3-1	a02 3-1	D04 4-0	a30 3-0	S04 1-0	N06 1-0	F23 2-2	S18 1-2		a16 1-2	N20 2-3	O09 2-1	J01 1-1	M16 2-0	D25 0-1	J15 4-1	O23 1-3	F09 2-2
14 OLDHAM A	J01 0-4	F19 1-3	J29 2-1	M12 1-2	a09 5-2	J15 3-2	F05 2-3	S25 3-1	D11 1-1	S06 1-2	N13 2-1	a18 3-3	N27 5-2		S04 1-0	M26 1-3	O16 5-1	O09 3-1	O30 1-1	m07 3-2	D25 5-2	a23 2-0
15 PORTSMOUTH	a15 1-2	S25 5-0	M12 1-0	O16 2-3	N24 1-1	O25 0-0	S11 2-0	F05 5-2	a23 2-0	J01 2-1	M26 0-1	D25 0-0	a09 9-1	J22 7-2		O30 4-0	m07 5-1	M30 5-0	A28 3-1	D11 1-1	O09 1-0	N27 2-1
16 PORT VALE	M05 3-2	a16 2-4	J15 0-0	S04 0-0	D27 3-0	S20 3-2	a02 7-1	N20 6-1	F12 0-0	O23 0-2	a15 3-1	D18 0-2	F26 6-2	N06 3-0	M19 2-3		M28 2-0	D04 1-1	S27 3-1	S18 4-2	a30 1-1	O02 1-1
17 PRESTON N.E.	a16 2-1	M19 4-1	S25 3-2	M21 0-2	A28 2-2	F19 4-1	O23 2-2	O09 3-2	a15 1-0	D04 2-4	J22 2-2	N20 1-0	A30 4-1	M05 5-2	D18 1-2	S11 4-4		N06 3-1	F05 1-0	D27 4-0	a02 4-0	S27 2-0
18 READING	a06 3-2	S08 0-1	a09 2-3	N13 2-1	m07 0-1	F12 4-2	D25 2-0	a18 1-1	S15 0-1	S18 1-0	a20 2-1	S04 4-0	O16 7-1	F26 6-1	O02 1-2	a23 2-0	a27 3-0		J01 1-0	O30 2-1	J15 3-0	M12 1-2
19 SOUTHAMPTON	D18 3-1	N20 5-3	S04 0-0	a04 1-1	a18 1-2	O23 3-1	N06 4-1	a02 0-0	O02 0-1	a25 1-1	A30 2-1	a30 1-0	D27 2-0	M19 0-1	J15 0-2	S13 2-2	S18 1-1	a16 1-1		F12 6-2	D04 1-1	F26 1-0
20 SOUTH SHIELDS	N20 7-1	a18 2-2	M02 3-3	O09 5-1	J22 2-1	D04 1-0	M05 1-1	O23 3-2	J01 3-1	a16 2-2	S11 0-0	a02 1-1	A28 5-0	D18 4-1	a30 1-0	F05 3-3	D25 1-1	M19 3-0	S25 1-2		N06 0-1	m02 1-2
21 SWANSEA T	S18 5-2	S20 2-0	N27 1-0	a09 2-1	O16 3-2	O02 5-1	a18 4-2	S13 1-1	O30 1-0	F12 1-3	m07 0-1	M10 2-1	M12 0-1	D27 3-0	F26 1-1	D11 2-2	N13 0-0	A28 3-0	a23 2-2	M26 2-0		J22 4-1
22 WOLVERHAMPTON W	N06 9-1	M21 4-1	D25 7-2	A30 0-3	F05 5-0	N20 2-1	a30 2-1	D18 3-4	J15 5-2	a02 4-1	S25 1-2	M19 2-0	S11 0-1	D04 1-1	a16 0-1	a19 1-2	S13 1-2	O23 1-1	O09 2-2	a25 2-0	S04 2-2	

Season 1926-27

DIVISION 3 NORTH

	ACCRINGTON S	ASHINGTON	BARROW	BRADFORD	CHESTERFIELD	CREWE A	DONCASTER R	DURHAM C	HALIFAX T	HARTLEPOOLS U	LINCOLN C	NELSON	NEW BRIGHTON	ROCHDALE	ROTHERHAM U	SOUTHPORT	STOCKPORT CO	STOKE C	TRANMERE R	WALSALL	WIGAN B	WREXHAM
1 ACCRINGTON S		M19 3-0	F19 0-1	D18 2-3	J01 2-1	S25 3-1	a16 2-0	S20 3-0	O09 4-2	F05 7-2	S28 1-1	O23 0-5	N06 2-3	A28 0-1	a30 3-1	J22 2-2	S11 2-4	D04 0-1	D25 2-3	M05 3-5	N20 3-1	a02 1-1
2 ASHINGTON	O30 2-1		a09 3-0	F26 2-2	J03 2-1	a18 4-1	S18 1-1	J01 3-1	N13 3-0	a23 1-0	M26 1-2	M23 1-1	J15 2-3	O16 2-2	O02 4-4	m07 4-1	a11 1-1	F12 0-2	O23 4-3	a04 0-2	J29 1-1	S04 1-1
3 BARROW	O02 1-1	N20 2-2		S11 0-3	a02 1-0	J22 3-1	D18 0-1	F26 2-1	S18 1-1	J15 1-3	F12 0-3	N06 0-1	m02 0-3	S13 2-3	O23 2-2	a18 1-4	D25 1-3	M05 0-0	A30 2-1	M19 1-0	a30 2-2	D04 0-5
4 BRADFORD	m07 6-1	O09 2-0	J29 1-0		F19 5-0	O30 2-0	D25 7-3	D11 3-0	M12 2-1	M26 4-1	O16 3-1	S25 2-2	A30 1-1	J08 5-1	S04 2-2	a09 6-2	N13 3-1	J15 3-0	a23 5-3	F05 5-1	J01 2-1	a18 5-0
5 CHESTERFIELD	A30 1-1	S27 4-1	N13 8-1	O02 3-2		a09 3-0	J29 1-1	M12 7-1	M26 2-0	a19 1-0	O30 4-2	a15 1-1	D25 3-1	m07 2-3	F12 5-2	S13 5-1	a23 3-0	S18 1-1	O16 3-1	F26 2-0	S04 5-2	J15 1-3
6 CREWE A	F12 4-0	a16 2-1	S04 5-0	M19 1-1	N20 0-0		M05 1-3	O02 2-1	J29 1-2	D27 0-1	S18 3-3	a02 2-1	D04 3-2	S06 4-0	J15 2-2	a20 1-0	a15 3-2	O23 0-2	F26 4-1	N06 1-1	D18 2-4	a30 5-1
7 DONCASTER R	a25 2-0	F05 3-1	m07 7-0	D27 4-1	S11 0-3	O16 0-2		a09 5-1	a04 2-0	M12 2-0	a23 1-3	J22 6-0	S25 2-2	M26 3-2	a19 2-2	O30 3-1	S06 1-2	a15 3-1	N13 4-1	A28 2-2	O09 4-1	F19 2-2
8 DURHAM C	D27 2-0	D25 0-2	O09 1-1	a30 2-1	O23 2-1	F19 1-2	N20 2-2		S08 0-1	S25 2-1	a18 4-2	M05 3-3	M19 2-2	J22 1-3	D04 0-1	S11 4-2	F05 1-5	a16 1-2	A28 0-3	D18 3-0	a02 3-1	N06 1-0
9 HALIFAX T	F26 4-3	a02 1-1	F05 5-1	O23 2-0	N06 3-1	S11 3-1	a30 2-1	A30 1-2		J22 2-1	O02 2-1	M19 4-1	N20 2-2	J01 1-0	M05 4-2	D25 1-1	A28 4-1	D18 2-2	a19 2-0	S25 1-1	D04 0-0	a16 0-1
10 HARTLEPOOLS U	S18 3-1	D04 0-1	A28 1-1	N06 2-4	a16 1-2	D25 1-1	O23 3-0	F12 4-0	S04 0-1		J29 1-1	N20 3-2	a30 4-0	F26 3-2	M19 3-1	J01 2-0	J03 1-2	S22 1-3	O02 2-1	a02 2-2	M05 2-1	D18 4-0
11 LINCOLN C	S13 4-0	N06 4-0	S25 3-1	M05 5-1	M19 3-1	F05 3-3	D04 0-0	a15 5-0	F19 3-1	S11 1-2		O09 1-4	a02 4-1	D27 2-3	D18 1-2	A28 1-1	J22 1-3	a30 1-3	S06 1-2	O23 3-3	a16 2-0	N20 2-2
12 NELSON	M12 7-0	S13 4-0	M26 3-0	F12 1-0	a18 0-3	N13 7-1	S04 5-1	O16 1-1	O30 0-0	a09 6-2	F26 2-1		S15 2-0	a05 3-1	S18 5-3	a23 1-2	J08 6-1	J29 1-0	m07 0-2	O02 3-2	J15 4-0	J01 3-0
13 NEW BRIGHTON	M26 0-1	A28 4-0	J08 3-1	S08 3-1	D27 1-0	a23 3-0	F12 0-2	O30 3-1	a09 0-3	D11 2-1	N13 1-1	a27 7-2		M12 1-2	F26 3-0	O16 4-1	m07 1-2	O02 5-0	J22 0-0	a15 3-1	S18 3-1	J29 2-1
14 ROCHDALE	J15 2-1	M05 5-0	a19 5-1	a16 3-0	D18 8-1	A31 3-1	N06 7-2	S04 1-3	a18 2-0	O09 3-0	D25 7-3	a30 2-1	O23 1-1		N20 2-1	S25 1-0	F19 2-0	a02 4-0	J29 3-1	D04 4-4	M19 4-1	S18 3-1
15 ROTHERHAM U	J24 1-1	F19 5-0	M12 2-0	J22 1-1	S25 0-4	A28 2-1	J01 1-3	a23 3-1	O16 2-4	O30 5-3	m07 2-4	F05 2-3	O09 0-0	D11 1-1		N13 1-2	M26 1-2	D27 2-2	J08 2-2	S11 4-1	N01 2-0	A30 2-0
16 SOUTHPORT	S04 2-1	D18 4-1	a15 3-0	N20 2-1	a30 2-1	S28 2-2	M19 2-0	m03 4-5	D27 0-0	A31 1-0	J15 2-3	D04 3-4	M05 7-2	F12 1-1	a02 2-0		O09 2-2	N06 0-3	S18 1-3	a16 6-1	O02 2-2	O23 6-0
17 STOCKPORT CO	F08 3-3	a30 6-2	D27 7-0	a02 1-2	D04 4-0	J01 3-1	A30 1-0	S18 4-0	J15 1-3	a18 3-3	S04 3-3	a16 4-1	D18 1-0	O02 3-0	N06 3-1	F26 2-4		M19 2-2	F12 2-1	N20 0-2	O23 4-1	M05 3-2
18 STOKE C	a23 1-0	S25 7-0	O16 4-0	A28 0-0	F05 3-2	M12 2-1	a18 0-0	J08 4-0	m07 5-1	S13 3-1	J01 2-0	S11 4-1	F19 1-1	N13 3-1	D25 4-1	M26 4-0	O30 0-1		a09 2-0	J22 4-1	A30 2-0	O09 2-0
19 TRANMERE R	a18 2-1	D27 2-1	J01 7-2	D04 1-2	M05 3-2	O09 1-0	a02 1-1	J15 8-3	a15 0-0	F19 2-0	S20 1-1	D18 2-3	S04 4-1	S11 0-1	a16 4-0	F05 3-0	S25 0-0	N20 1-1		a30 6-0	N06 3-1	M19 3-2
20 WALSALL	O16 5-1	S06 0-0	O30 1-0	S18 1-0	O09 0-1	M26 2-3	J15 1-0	m07 1-1	F12 0-1	N13 2-2	M12 1-2	F19 4-1	a18 0-1	a23 4-1	J29 3-2	a25 1-1	a09 1-0	S04 0-1	J24 5-1		D25 3-2	S27 0-1
21 WIGAN B	a09 3-0	S11 1-4	D13 8-0	S20 1-2	M28 1-2	m07 2-2	J08 1-1	N13 3-0	J03 1-1	O16 3-0	F28 3-2	A28 2-1	F05 3-2	O30 0-3	a18 0-0	F19 3-1	M12 2-0	S06 0-3	M26 1-1	D27 5-2		S25 1-1
22 WREXHAM	N13 5-0	J22 1-1	a23 0-2	a15 1-0	A28 3-1	a06 3-1	O02 0-1	M26 3-1	J08 1-2	m07 4-0	a27 1-1	D27 2-2	S11 2-2	F05 2-2	S08 3-0	M12 3-0	O16 2-1	F26 2-6	O30 0-1	S15 1-2	M02 2-0	

DIVISION 3 SOUTH

	ABERDARE A	BOURNEMOUTH	BRENTFORD	BRIGHTON & HA	BRISTOL C	BRISTOL R	CHARLTON A	COVENTRY C	CRYSTAL P	EXETER C	GILLINGHAM	LUTON T	MERTHYR T	MILLWALL	NEWPORT CO	NORTHAMPTON T	NORWICH C	PLYMOUTH A	Q.P.R.	SOUTHEND U	SWINDON T	WATFORD
1 ABERDARE A		A28 2-1	a23 3-1	m07 2-2	D25 3-7	a09 2-1	J01 0-0	a18 0-7	F26 2-3	M26 3-1	F12 2-1	M12 0-1	O30 1-2	S06 1-3	S11 0-1	J08 6-1	O16 1-2	J22 5-6	S20 0-2	F05 1-0	D11 1-4	O02 3-2
2 BOURNEMOUTH	J15 3-0		M16 3-1	M02 1-0	a18 2-0	O30 0-1	F26 0-3	F12 1-2	S18 1-1	M12 4-3	S04 4-2	J26 2-0	O16 1-1	M26 0-1	D27 2-1	a09 3-1	a23 0-1	J01 6-2	O02 6-2	m07 3-0	S22 1-2	J29 6-0
3 BRENTFORD	D04 1-4	a02 0-0		A28 4-0	N06 3-0	F12 0-2	M19 2-0	O23 7-3	M05 3-0	F26 6-1	a30 0-0	J01 2-2	a15 1-1	S18 0-0	a16 1-1	J22 1-1	D27 3-0	N20 0-0	S11 4-2	S06 3-1	O02 2-2	D18 3-0
4 BRIGHTON & H.A.	D10 3-1	a10 0-2	J15 1-1		N20 3-0	J29 7-0	a02 3-2	M19 1-1	S01 1-1	F12 5-2	M05 3-2	a15 1-1	O02 4-0	S04 3-1	a30 1-0	D25 2-0	O06 3-2	D04 1-2	N06 4-1	F26 2-1	S18 9-3	O23 4-1
5 BRISTOL C	D27 2-1	a15 2-0	M26 1-0	a09 0-2		F26 3-1	O02 4-1	S18 3-0	J29 5-4	O16 3-2	J15 9-4	a23 6-0	m07 3-0	O30 4-1	S01 4-1	N13 4-3	F09 1-1	S22 4-2	F12 1-0	F23 5-1	M12 2-0	S04 5-0
6 BRISTOL R	N20 4-0	M19 2-1	S25 1-3	S11 0-0	O09 0-5		O23 1-1	D18 1-2	a30 4-1	D28 3-1	a16 2-1	A28 1-2	S06 2-1	a19 1-1	a02 4-0	F05 5-2	J22 1-0	N06 2-2	M05 4-1	D25 5-1	a18 3-1	D04 0-2
7 CHARLTON A	S16 5-1	O09 1-3	O30 1-1	M23 1-0	F19 0-1	M12 3-1		J29 4-2	S04 1-2	m07 1-0	D25 3-0	M03 2-2	J31 3-2	F12 1-1	a28 3-0	M26 5-2	a09 2-0	a18 1-1	S18 2-0	a23 1-0	O16 2-2	J15 2-1
8 COVENTRY C	a19 1-0	S25 6-2	M12 3-1	O30 1-2	F05 2-5	m07 2-2	S11 1-0		D25 3-1	a23 0-0	S06 0-2	N13 4-1	J08 5-1	O16 1-4	O09 3-1	A28 0-3	M26 1-0	F19 3-3	J22 1-0	a09 1-1	D28 1-3	J01 5-1
9 CRYSTAL P	O09 0-0	F05 2-2	O16 4-3	J01 2-0	S11 4-2	M16 7-4	J22 2-1	D27 1-2		F09 1-0	a18 2-2	M26 1-1	a09 1-1	m07 1-6	F19 6-2	M12 3-0	O30 7-1	S25 1-1	A28 2-1	N13 5-3	a23 5-0	S08 0-1
10 EXETER C	N06 2-1	O23 4-0	O09 3-1	S25 0-0	M05 1-1	S15 1-1	D18 1-0	D04 8-1	a16 3-1		a02 5-1	S11 1-2	A28 3-0	a18 1-1	M19 2-1	F19 3-2	F05 1-0	D27 0-2	a30 0-2	J22 2-0	J01 3-1	N20 2-0
11 GILLINGHAM	S25 2-1	J22 1-0	M30 1-2	O16 2-3	A28 1-1	M23 2-0	D27 1-1	S15 2-0	a15 2-1	N13 3-2		F19 0-0	M26 0-1	a23 2-1	J08 0-1	m07 1-2	M12 1-0	S11 4-1	S01 2-2	O30 2-3	a09 4-4	F26 3-0
12 LUTON T	O23 3-3	a30 4-0	A30 2-1	a18 4-0	D04 0-0	J15 1-1	a16 1-0	a02 4-1	N06 1-0	J29 2-2	O02 2-1		S18 2-1	D25 6-0	M05 4-1	S13 2-0	O09 2-2	D18 3-3	N20 2-0	F12 0-0	S04 1-1	M19 2-2
13 MERTHYR T	M19 2-2	M05 4-6	a19 1-0	F19 1-0	D18 1-1	A30 3-2	a30 3-0	a16 1-0	m02 1-2	J15 3-3	N06 2-0	F05 4-1		S13 1-0	S04 1-2	O09 2-0	S25 1-1	O23 5-1	D04 4-0	S11 0-1	D27 1-2	a02 1-1
14 MILLWALL	a16 1-0	N06 1-1	F05 3-0	J22 1-1	M19 0-1	O02 2-3	S25 3-0	M14 1-0	D18 1-0	a15 4-2	D04 2-0	D27 7-0	S20 3-1		N20 4-1	S11 4-2	A28 6-1	a02 1-3	O23 2-1	J01 2-0	F26 4-1	a30 3-1
15 NEWPORT CO	J29 5-2	D25 2-1	a25 0-0	M31 0-1	S09 0-0	N13 1-0	S30 2-1	F26 4-1	O02 2-1	O30 2-0	S18 1-0	O16 3-2	J22 4-3	D11 1-1		J01 1-0	m07 0-0	A28 2-1	a15 0-2	M12 3-0	M26 5-3	F12 2-1
16 NORTHAMPTON T	a30 2-1	N20 2-2	S04 2-3	D27 0-0	a02 2-0	S18 3-0	N06 0-1	J15 2-1	O23 1-1	O02 2-2	D18 2-1	D28 2-1	F26 2-0	a07 1-4	D04 1-2		S06 3-0	a16 2-1	M19 1-0	a19 2-1	F12 1-0	M05 3-2
17 NORWICH C	M05 2-2	D04 4-1	D25 2-1	O28 0-2	a16 1-1	S04 2-0	N20 2-3	N06 3-0	M19 0-1	S18 4-4	O23 0-0	F26 3-2	F12 4-0	J15 0-2	D18 1-0	S20 6-1		a30 0-2	a02 0-1	O02 1-1	J29 2-1	a18 4-0
18 PLYMOUTH A	S04 2-0	S08 1-1	a09 2-1	a23 2-0	m04 4-2	M26 3-2	a15 3-1	O02 3-0	F12 7-1	D25 2-0	J29 0-0	m07 1-0	M12 1-1	N13 1-1	J15 4-1	S01 3-0	a25 2-1		D11 2-0	O16 2-1	O30 3-1	S18 4-0
19 Q.P.R.	S30 3-0	F19 1-1	m05 1-1	M26 2-2	S25 1-2	O16 2-2	F05 2-1	S04 1-1	J15 0-2	F24 1-1	J01 1-1	a09 1-0	a23 5-1	M12 1-1	a18 2-0	O30 4-2	N13 4-0	O09 4-2		J08 3-2	m07 0-1	D25 2-4
20 SOUTHEND U	S18 5-1	D18 0-3	S15 3-1	O09 0-1	a30 0-1	D27 2-1	D04 5-0	N20 3-1	a02 3-1	S04 1-2	M19 1-0	S25 2-1	J29 3-1	A30 1-1	O23 5-0	a18 2-0	F19 3-3	M05 1-2	a16 0-3		J15 2-2	N06 2-0
21 SWINDON T	a02 3-2	S13 2-0	M09 4-2	F05 2-2	O23 2-2	a15 3-5	M05 2-0	a30 2-2	D04 6-1	A30 4-2	N20 1-0	J22 2-0	D25 3-2	O09 3-0	N06 3-1	S25 3-1	S11 3-2	M19 1-2	D18 6-2	A28 5-1		a16 4-2
22 WATFORD	F19 2-2	S11 1-2	m07 0-0	M12 1-0	J22 0-1	a23 3-3	A28 1-0	S01 1-0	S15 1-2	a09 1-0	O09 4-0	O30 2-1	N13 4-1	D28 2-4	S25 0-0	O16 4-0	a15 1-1	F05 1-4	D27 1-2	M26 4-2	J08 2-2	

LEAGUE TABLES

DIVISION 1

	P	W	D	L	F	A	W	D	L	F	A	Pts
Newcastle U	42	19	1	1	64	20	6	5	10	32	38	56
Huddersfield T	42	13	6	2	41	19	4	11	6	35	41	51
Sunderland	42	15	3	3	70	28	6	4	11	28	42	49
Bolton W	42	15	5	1	54	19	4	5	12	30	43	48
Burnley	42	15	4	2	55	30	4	5	12	36	50	47
West Ham U	42	9	6	6	50	36	10	2	9	36	34	46
Leicester C	42	13	4	4	58	33	4	8	9	27	37	46
Sheffield U	42	12	6	3	46	33	5	4	12	28	53	44
Liverpool	42	13	4	4	47	27	5	3	13	22	34	43
Aston Villa	42	11	4	6	51	34	7	3	11	30	49	43
Arsenal	42	12	5	4	47	30	5	4	12	30	56	43
Derby Co	42	14	4	3	60	28	3	3	15	26	45	41
Tottenham H	42	11	4	6	48	33	5	5	11	28	45	41
Cardiff C	42	12	3	6	31	17	4	6	11	24	48	41
Manchester U	42	9	8	4	29	19	4	6	11	23	45	40
Sheffield W	42	15	3	3	49	29	0	6	15	26	63	39
Birmingham	42	13	3	5	36	17	4	1	16	28	56	38
Blackburn R	42	9	5	7	40	40	6	3	12	37	56	38
Bury	42	8	5	8	43	38	4	7	10	25	39	36
Everton	42	10	6	5	35	30	2	4	15	29	60	34
Leeds U	42	9	7	5	43	31	2	1	18	26	57	30
WBA	42	10	4	7	47	33	1	4	16	18	53	30

DIVISION 2

	P	W	D	L	F	A	W	D	L	F	A	Pts
Middlesbrough	42	18	2	1	78	23	9	6	6	44	37	62
Portsmouth	42	14	4	3	58	17	9	4	8	29	32	54
Manchester C	42	15	3	3	65	23	7	7	7	43	38	54
Chelsea	42	13	7	1	40	17	7	5	9	22	35	52
Nottingham F	42	14	6	1	57	23	4	8	9	23	32	50
Preston NE	42	14	4	3	54	29	6	5	10	20	43	49
Hull C	42	13	4	4	43	19	7	3	11	20	33	47
Port Vale	42	11	6	4	50	26	5	7	9	38	52	45
Blackpool	42	13	5	3	65	26	5	3	13	30	54	44
Oldham A	42	12	3	6	50	37	7	3	11	24	47	44
Barnsley	42	13	5	3	56	23	4	4	13	32	64	43
Swansea C	42	13	5	3	44	21	3	6	12	24	51	43
Southampton	42	9	8	4	35	22	6	4	11	25	40	42
Reading	42	14	1	6	47	20	2	7	12	17	52	40
Wolves	42	10	4	7	54	30	4	3	14	19	45	35
Notts Co	42	11	4	6	45	24	4	1	16	25	72	35
Grimsby T	42	6	7	8	39	39	5	5	11	35	52	34
Fulham	42	11	4	6	39	31	2	4	15	19	61	34
South Shields	42	10	8	3	49	25	1	3	17	22	71	33
Clapton O	42	9	3	9	37	35	3	4	14	23	61	31
Darlington	42	10	3	8	53	42	2	3	16	26	56	30
Bradford C	42	6	4	11	30	28	1	5	15	20	60	23

DIVISION 3 North

	P	W	D	L	F	A	W	D	L	F	A	Pts
Stoke C	42	17	3	1	57	11	10	6	5	35	29	63
Rochdale	42	18	2	1	72	22	8	4	9	33	43	58
Bradford	42	18	3	0	74	21	6	4	11	27	38	55
Halifax T	42	13	6	2	46	23	8	5	8	24	30	53
Nelson	42	16	2	3	64	20	6	5	10	40	55	51
Stockport Co	42	13	4	4	60	31	9	3	9	33	38	*49
Chesterfield	42	15	4	2	65	24	6	1	14	27	44	47
Doncaster R	42	13	4	4	58	27	5	7	9	23	38	47
Tranmere R	42	13	5	3	54	22	6	3	12	31	45	46
New Brighton	42	14	2	5	49	21	4	8	9	30	46	46
Lincoln C	42	9	5	7	50	33	6	7	8	40	45	42
Southport	42	11	5	5	54	32	4	4	13	26	53	39
Wrexham	42	10	5	6	41	26	4	5	12	24	47	38
Walsall	42	10	4	7	35	22	4	6	11	33	59	38
Crewe A	42	11	5	5	46	28	3	4	14	25	53	37
Ashington	42	9	8	4	42	30	3	4	14	18	60	36
Hartlepools U	42	11	4	6	43	26	3	2	16	23	55	34
Wigan B	42	10	6	5	44	28	1	4	16	22	55	32
Rotherham U	42	8	6	7	41	35	2	6	13	29	57	32
Durham C	42	9	4	8	35	35	3	2	16	23	70	30
Ashington	42	9	3	9	45	38	1	4	16	17	60	27
Barrow	42	5	6	10	22	40	2	2	17	12	77	22

Stockport County deducted two points for fielding an ineligible player

DIVISION 3 South

	P	W	D	L	F	A	W	D	L	F	A	Pts
Bristol C	42	19	1	1	71	24	8	7	6	33	30	62
Plymouth A	42	17	4	0	52	14	8	6	7	43	47	60
Millwall	42	16	2	3	55	19	7	8	6	34	32	56
Brighton & HA	42	15	4	2	61	24	6	7	8	18	26	53
Swindon T	42	16	3	2	64	31	5	6	10	36	54	51
Crystal P	42	12	6	3	57	33	6	3	12	27	48	45
Bournemouth	42	13	2	6	49	24	5	6	10	29	42	44
Luton T	42	12	9	0	48	19	3	5	13	20	47	44
Newport Co	42	15	4	2	40	20	4	2	15	17	51	44
Bristol R	42	12	4	5	46	28	4	5	12	32	52	41
Brentford	42	10	9	2	46	20	3	5	13	24	41	40
Exeter C	42	14	4	3	46	18	1	6	14	30	55	40
Charlton A	42	13	5	3	44	22	3	3	15	16	39	40
QPR	42	9	8	4	41	27	6	1	14	24	44	39
Coventry C	42	11	4	6	44	33	4	3	14	27	53	37
Norwich C	42	10	5	6	41	25	2	6	13	18	46	35
Merthyr T	42	11	5	5	42	25	2	4	15	21	55	35
Northampton T	42	13	4	4	36	23	2	1	18	23	64	35
Southend U	42	12	3	6	44	25	2	3	16	20	52	34
Gillingham	42	10	5	6	36	26	1	5	15	18	46	32
Watford	42	9	6	6	36	27	3	2	16	21	60	32
Aberdare A	42	8	2	11	38	48	1	5	15	24	53	25

Football League Records

Top scorers: Div 1, W.Dean (Everton) 60 goals; Div 2, J.Cookson (West Bromwich Albion) 38 goals; Div 3(N), J.Smith (Stockport County) 38 goals; Div 3(S), D.Morris (Swindon Town) 38 goals.
Aberdare Athletic failed to gain re-election, Torquay United were elected in their place. Walsall transferred to Division Three South.

Dixie Dean, whose record 60 goals for Everton as they lifted the title will surely never be beaten. Dean scored a hat-trick in the last match, against Arsenal, to clinch the record.

DIVISION 1

	ARSENAL	ASTON VILLA	BIRMINGHAM	BLACKBURN R	BOLTON W	BURNLEY	BURY	CARDIFF C	DERBY CO	EVERTON	HUDDERSFIELD T	LEICESTER C	LIVERPOOL	MANCHESTER U	MIDDLESBROUGH	NEWCASTLE U	PORTSMOUTH	SHEFFIELD U	SHEFFIELD W	SUNDERLAND	TOTTENHAM H	WEST HAM U
1 ARSENAL		J21 0-3	M31 2-2	M17 3-2	O29 1-2	A31 4-1	D31 3-1	a06 3-0	F04 3-4	D24 3-2	a14 0-0	O15 2-2	M07 6-3	a28 0-1	N12 3-1	D10 4-1	M28 0-2	S03 6-1	m02 1-1	S17 2-1	J02 1-1	O01 2-2
2 ASTON VILLA	S10 2-2		M17 1-1	N26 2-0	a28 2-2	F08 3-1	S24 1-0	a14 3-1	D27 0-1	D10 2-3	m02 3-0	A27 0-3	J07 3-4	M31 3-1	O08 5-1	O29 3-0	S05 7-2	F11 1-0	D24 5-4	O15 4-2	N12 1-2	a09 1-0
3 BIRMINGHAM	N19 1-1	N05 1-1		F04 2-1	O01 1-1	M24 4-0	O22 2-2	S17 1-3	m05 2-1	J21 2-2	A29 3-1	D03 0-2	a21 2-0	S03 0-0	O15 3-2	a10 0-2	a07 2-0	M10 4-1	M07 1-0	D26 1-1	D31 3-2	D17 1-2
4 BLACKBURN R	N05 4-1	a07 0-1	S24 4-4		J07 1-6	A27 2-1	m05 0-1	S05 0-0	a26 3-2	J02 4-2	O08 1-1	O22 0-0	M10 2-1	S19 3-0	F23 3-0	F11 1-0	a24 6-0	D17 1-0	S10 3-1	D03 0-0	F25 2-1	N19 1-0
5 BOLTON W	M10 1-1	D17 3-1	F11 3-2	S03 3-1		N05 7-1	J21 2-1	D31 2-1	J02 1-3	S05 1-1	F25 0-1	M24 3-3	O22 2-1	a06 3-2	S24 0-0	O08 1-2	N19 3-1	m05 1-1	F29 2-0	a07 1-2	D26 4-1	a21 4-0
6 BURNLEY	S05 1-2	S17 4-2	N12 2-1	D31 3-1	M17 2-2		S03 2-3	D24 2-1	O01 4-2	a28 3-5	D10 0-1	D27 5-1	a06 2-2	N26 4-0	M03 1-1	M31 5-1	O15 2-0	J21 5-3	O29 3-1	F04 3-0	a14 2-2	F18 0-0
7 BURY	A27 5-1	F04 0-0	M03 2-3	D24 2-3	S10 1-0	J07 2-0		a28 3-0	F18 3-0	N26 2-3	M31 2-3	J02 2-1	S19 5-2	a14 4-3	O29 1-4	N12 1-4	D26 4-0	S17 1-0	M17 4-2	O01 5-3	D10 1-2	O15 3-1
8 CARDIFF C	a09 2-2	D03 2-1	F22 2-1	S12 1-1	A27 2-1	m05 3-2	D17 0-1		N19 4-4	D27 2-0	F11 4-0	M10 3-0	N05 1-1	F25 2-0	S10 1-1	S24 3-1	O22 3-1	a07 2-2	J07 1-1	a21 3-1	O08 2-1	M24 1-5
9 DERBY CO	S24 4-0	D26 5-0	D24 4-1	D10 6-0	a14 1-0	F11 3-4	O08 5-2	M31 7-1		N12 0-3	M17 0-0	S10 2-1	F15 2-3	M28 5-0	a28 2-1	S05 1-1	J07 2-2	F25 2-1	N26 4-6	a09 1-0	O29 1-1	A27 2-3
10 EVERTON	m05 3-3	a21 3-2	S10 5-2	a06 4-1	S14 2-2	D17 4-1	a07 1-1	D26 2-1	M24 2-2		S24 2-2	N05 7-1	O15 1-1	O08 5-2	J07 3-1	a18 3-0	M10 0-0	D03 0-0	A27 4-0	N19 0-1	F11 2-5	O22 7-0
11 HUDDERSFIELD T	D03 2-1	O22 1-1	a09 2-0	M14 3-1	O15 1-0	a25 1-2	N19 3-0	O01 8-2	N05 2-1	F04 4-1		D17 3-1	a07 2-4	S17 4-2	a10 2-4	A27 1-3	m05 4-1	a30 0-1	D26 1-0	M10 4-2	J21 4-2	J07 5-2
12 LEICESTER C	F25 3-2	D31 3-0	a14 3-0	a30 6-0	N12 4-2	D26 5-0	a09 2-2	O29 4-1	J21 4-0	M17 1-0	a28 1-2		O08 1-1	O01 1-0	D10 3-3	N26 3-0	F04 6-2	A29 3-1	M31 2-2	S03 3-3	D24 6-1	S17 2-3
13 LIVERPOOL	D27 0-2	S03 0-0	D10 2-3	O29 4-2	M03 4-2	J02 2-2	A31 5-1	M17 1-2	S17 5-2	F25 3-3	N26 4-2	a25 1-1		D24 2-0	M31 1-1	a14 0-0	O01 8-2	D31 2-1	N12 5-2	J21 2-5	a28 2-0	F04 1-3
14 MANCHESTER U	D17 4-1	N19 5-1	J07 1-1	D26 1-1	a09 2-1	a07 4-3	D03 0-1	O15 2-2	O22 5-0	M14 1-0	M07 0-0	F11 5-2	m05 6-1		A27 3-0	S10 1-7	N05 2-0	a21 2-3	S07 1-1	a25 2-1	S24 3-0	M10 1-1
15 MIDDLESBROUGH	a18 2-2	M21 0-0	F25 1-1	S17 2-0	F04 2-5	O22 2-3	M10 6-1	J21 1-2	D17 3-3	S03 4-2	J02 3-1	a21 1-1	N19 1-1	D31 1-2		D26 1-1	D03 5-1	N05 3-0	O01 3-3	m05 0-3	A31 3-1	a07 2-2
16 NEWCASTLE U	a21 1-1	M10 7-5	J02 1-1	O01 0-1	F18 2-2	N19 1-1	M24 2-3	F04 2-0	S14 4-3	S17 2-2	D31 2-3	a07 1-5	D03 1-1	J21 4-1	D27 3-3		D17 1-3	O22 1-0	O15 4-3	N05 3-1	S03 4-1	m05 3-1
17 PORTSMOUTH	O08 2-3	A31 3-1	N26 2-2	N12 2-2	M31 1-0	F25 1-0	D27 1-0	M03 3-0	S03 2-2	O29 1-3	D24 2-1	S24 2-0	F11 1-0	M17 1-0	a14 4-1	a28 0-1		a09 4-1	D10 0-0	F18 3-5	S17 3-0	J21 2-1
18 SHEFFIELD U	J07 6-4	O01 0-3	O29 3-1	a28 2-3	D24 4-3	S10 5-2	M12 3-1	N26 3-4	O15 1-0	a14 1-3	N12 1-7	S05 1-1	A27 1-1	D10 2-1	M17 4-1	a23 1-1	J02 3-1		S24 1-1	a16 5-1	M31 3-1	D26 6-2
19 SHEFFIELD W	O22 1-1	m05 2-0	O08 2-3	J21 4-1	S17 3-0	M10 5-0	N05 4-0	S03 3-3	a07 2-2	D31 1-2	D27 0-5	N19 1-2	M24 4-0	A29 0-2	F11 2-3	F25 0-0	a21 2-0	F04 3-3		D17 0-0	a10 4-2	D03 2-0
20 SUNDERLAND	M14 5-1	F25 2-3	S07 4-2	a14 1-0	N26 1-1	S24 2-3	F11 1-0	D10 0-2	a06 0-1	M31 0-2	O29 3-0	J07 2-2	S10 2-1	N12 4-1	D24 1-0	M17 1-1	A27 3-3	O08 0-1	a28 2-3		M28 0-0	J02 3-2
21 TOTTENHAM H	a07 2-0	M24 2-1	A27 1-0	O15 1-1	F06 1-2	D03 5-0	a21 1-4	M05 1-0	M10 1-2	O01 1-3	S10 2-2	S22 2-1	D17 3-1	F04 4-1	S12 4-2	J07 5-2	M19 0-3	N19 2-2	a06 1-3	O22 3-1		N05 5-3
22 WEST HAM U	F11 2-2	a06 0-0	a28 3-3	M31 4-3	D10 2-0	O08 2-0	F25 1-2	N12 2-0	D31 2-2	M03 0-0	S03 4-2	M12 4-0	S24 3-1	O29 1-2	N26 4-5	D24 5-2	S10 4-2	D27 1-1	a14 1-2	S01 2-4	M17 1-1	

Tom Johnson netted 19 goals as Manchester City won Division Two. The following season he hit 38 goals, still a City record for a First Division season.

DIVISION 2

	BARNSLEY	BLACKPOOL	BRISTOL C	CHELSEA	CLAPTON O	FULHAM	GRIMSBY T	HULL C	LEEDS U	MANCHESTER C	NOTTINGHAM F	NOTTS CO	OLDHAM A	PORT VALE	PRESTON N.E.	READING	SOUTHAMPTON	SOUTH SHIELDS	STOKE C	SWANSEA T	W.B.A.	WOLVERHAMPTON W
1 BARNSLEY		a28 2-1	O29 2-3	D24 3-1	S24 4-2	J28 8-4	a14 1-4	A27 1-1	S26 2-1	D26 0-3	a10 2-1	M31 0-0	D10 0-1	F20 4-2	J07 2-1	N26 2-0	N12 0-1	O15 0-0	M19 3-1	S10 3-3	M17 2-4	O01 2-2
2 BLACKPOOL	D17 1-3		S24 6-2	J07 2-4	S10 0-1	m05 4-0	J02 4-5	M10 2-1	N19 0-2	O22 2-2	M24 5-3	F25 3-3	A29 1-2	D03 1-6	N05 4-1	D26 3-1	O08 1-0	a21 4-1	F11 3-1	A27 2-2	J28 4-3	a07 3-0
3 BRISTOL C	M10 2-0	F04 2-2		O01 1-1	F18 5-1	O22 3-0	J21 0-0	a21 0-1	D17 1-2	D03 2-0	a07 0-0	D31 1-2	S03 2-1	A31 4-0	N19 1-3	S17 4-1	D26 3-0	m05 1-1	a06 4-0	M24 2-1	O15 0-1	N05 4-1
4 CHELSEA	m05 1-2	S03 3-0	F11 5-2		J28 1-0	J21 2-1	M14 4-0	O22 2-0	a21 2-3	M24 0-1	N19 2-1	S07 5-0	a06 2-1	a07 1-0	M10 2-1	D31 0-0	F25 0-2	D03 6-0	O08 1-0	N05 4-0	S24 1-1	D17 2-0
5 CLAPTON O	F04 2-0	J21 2-5	O08 4-2	S17 2-1		N05 3-2	D31 1-2	M24 0-0	D03 2-1	N19 0-2	a21 2-2	a09 0-1	a16 2-0	D17 0-1	O22 1-1	S03 3-0	A29 2-0	a07 2-2	F25 3-2	M10 1-1	F11 0-0	m05 0-0
6 FULHAM	S17 3-1	D24 2-2	M03 5-0	S10 1-1	M17 2-0		N26 2-2	M26 0-2	O15 1-1	a09 1-1	S15 2-0	D10 2-1	a14 1-1	O01 4-0	A27 2-2	a28 1-0	M31 1-0	F18 2-0	N12 1-5	J07 3-2	O29 3-1	F04 7-0
7 GRIMSBY T	D03 3-1	a06 3-3	S10 1-4	D26 1-1	A27 2-2	a07 1-0		F25 1-1	O22 3-2	N05 4-1	M10 2-1	F11 1-0	O08 1-2	N19 3-0	m05 4-6	A30 3-3	S24 2-2	M24 4-1	M06 1-2	D17 1-2	J07 0-6	a21 0-1
8 HULL C	D31 2-1	O29 2-2	D10 1-1	M03 0-2	N12 2-2	D27 3-2	O15 0-1		F04 3-1	a16 0-0	O01 2-0	a28 1-1	D24 2-2	J21 1-0	S05 0-0	M17 0-1	N26 1-0	S17 1-0	a14 1-0	a06 0-2	M31 1-1	S03 2-0
9 LEEDS U	A29 2-2	M31 4-0	J28 3-2	D10 5-0	a14 4-0	F25 2-1	M03 0-0	S24 2-0		a25 0-1	S10 4-0	M17 6-0	O29 1-0	D27 3-0	F11 2-4	N12 6-2	S03 2-0	D31 3-0	D24 5-1	O08 5-0	N26 1-2	a10 3-0
10 MANCHESTER C	J02 7-3	M03 4-1	a14 4-2	N12 0-1	M31 5-3	a06 2-1	M17 2-0	O08 2-1	S17 2-1		F04 3-3	D24 3-1	O01 3-1	S03 1-0	F25 2-2	O29 4-1	a28 6-1	J21 3-0	N26 4-0	A29 7-4	D10 3-1	D31 3-0
11 NOTTINGHAM F	a09 1-1	N12 4-1	N26 1-1	M31 2-2	D10 4-3	A29 7-0	O29 5-2	F11 1-1	J21 2-2	S24 4-5		S17 2-1	M17 2-1	a26 0-2	O08 3-1	M29 5-3	D24 1-1	S03 7-2	a28 0-2	F25 0-2	a14 0-2	D26 3-2
12 NOTTS CO	N19 9-0	O15 3-1	A27 1-2	O06 0-1	a06 3-0	a21 0-1	O01 3-2	D17 1-1	N05 2-2	m05 2-1	F22 1-2		F04 2-1	O22 2-4	a07 6-2	F18 1-1	S10 0-0	M10 4-1	J07 1-2	D03 2-0	D27 3-0	M24 1-2
13 OLDHAM A	a21 0-1	S05 6-0	J07 4-1	a09 2-1	D27 5-0	D03 4-2	F18 1-0	m05 5-0	M10 0-1	F11 3-2	N05 4-1	S24 0-0		M24 4-1	D17 0-0	O15 3-2	J31 3-1	O22 2-2	S10 3-1	a07 0-1	A27 3-1	N19 3-0
14 PORT VALE	O08 2-1	a14 3-0	S19 5-1	N26 1-1	a28 0-0	F11 4-1	M31 2-2	S10 1-2	D26 1-2	J07 1-2	A27 2-2	M03 3-0	N12 1-0		F06 2-0	D10 3-0	O29 4-0	a06 2-3	M17 0-0	S24 2-0	D24 4-1	F25 2-2
15 PRESTON N.E.	S03 1-2	M17 2-1	M31 5-1	O29 0-3	M03 0-0	D31 1-0	D24 3-0	A29 4-2	O01 5-1	O15 1-0	M05 5-0	N26 4-0	a28 1-1	S17 4-0		a06 4-0	a14 1-2	F04 7-2	D10 2-0	D26 4-2	N12 3-3	J21 5-4
16 READING	a07 1-1	D27 1-0	F15 3-2	A27 1-2	J07 4-0	D17 2-1	S14 2-2	N05 3-0	M24 0-1	M10 1-1	O22 0-2	O08 2-2	F25 1-0	a21 0-0	a09 2-1		F11 0-0	N19 5-1	S24 1-1	m05 0-0	S10 1-4	D03 2-1
17 SOUTHAMPTON	M24 6-1	F18 2-0	D27 3-2	O15 2-4	S05 1-3	N19 5-2	F04 5-0	a07 2-0	J07 1-4	D17 1-1	m05 2-1	J21 5-1	S17 5-2	M10 1-3	D03 0-0	O01 0-0		N05 3-5	A27 3-6	a21 0-2	a09 3-2	O22 4-1
18 SOUTH SHIELDS	F25 0-0	D10 2-2	D24 1-3	a14 2-1	N26 2-2	O08 2-1	N12 1-2	F22 1-0	A27 1-5	S10 0-1	J07 3-4	O29 2-3	M03 0-3	a09 0-1	S24 2-3	M31 0-0	M17 2-1		J02 2-3	F11 3-1	a28 2-3	S12 2-2
19 STOKE C	O22 0-0	O01 2-0	a09 1-0	F20 1-0	O15 2-0	M24 5-1	S17 0-0	D03 3-1	m05 5-1	a07 2-0	D17 1-3	S03 3-0	J21 3-0	N05 0-2	a21 3-2	F04 4-1	D31 2-1	D27 3-1		N19 1-1	S05 1-1	M10 2-2
20 SWANSEA T	J21 3-0	D31 1-0	N12 1-1	M17 0-0	O29 5-0	S03 2-1	a28 3-2	a09 2-0	F18 1-1	S05 5-3	O15 2-0	a14 1-1	N26 0-0	F04 2-0	D27 0-1	D24 0-1	D10 2-0	O01 6-3	M31 1-1		M03 3-2	S17 6-0
21 W.B.A.	N05 1-1	S17 6-3	F25 0-0	F04 3-0	O01 4-1	M10 4-0	S03 3-1	N19 1-1	a07 0-1	a21 1-1	D03 2-3	D26 2-2	D31 0-0	m05 0-0	M24 2-4	J21 5-3	a10 2-1	D17 3-0	A31 2-4	O22 5-2		F18 4-0
22 WOLVERHAMPTON W	F11 2-1	N26 2-4	M17 5-2	a28 1-2	D24 5-3	S24 3-1	D10 0-1	J07 1-1	a09 0-0	A27 2-2	D27 1-0	N12 2-2	M31 3-1	O15 2-1	S10 2-3	a14 2-1	M03 2-1	S05 2-1	O29 1-2	a30 1-1	O08 4-1	

Season 1927-28

DIVISION 3 NORTH

	ACCRINGTON S	ASHINGTON	BARROW	BRADFORD	BRADFORD C	CHESTERFIELD	CREWE A	DARLINGTON	DONCASTER R	DURHAM C	HALIFAX T	HARTLEPOOLS U	LINCOLN C	NELSON	NEW BRIGHTON	ROCHDALE	ROTHERHAM U	SOUTHPORT	STOCKPORT CO	TRANMERE R	WIGAN B	WREXHAM
1 ACCRINGTON S		F04 3-1	D24 5-1	a14 2-1	O15 1-1	D10 0-0	O01 5-0	S17 0-0	J21 1-3	N12 2-0	F18 3-2	S27 2-2	J02 1-0	D31 7-1	D26 2-1	M17 1-0	O29 3-1	M03 4-1	a28 1-0	F15 2-3	S03 2-4	M31 2-0
2 ASHINGTON	S24 1-1		D10 1-0	M03 0-3	A27 2-2	O29 0-0	A29 0-2	F25 2-3	O08 1-2	J02 2-2	S12 3-3	J28 3-1	S10 4-5	a14 5-1	J07 3-2	J14 5-1	a28 6-0	D24 1-3	M31 4-1	N12 3-0	F11 6-3	M17 2-1
3 BARROW	m05 1-0	a21 1-1		O08 0-0	O22 0-0	F11 2-0	N19 1-1	D03 2-0	a07 0-0	J28 1-2	M24 6-2	a06 2-0	N05 3-3	S29 3-1	M10 2-1	A27 1-3	J07 1-1	S10 3-1	D27 2-3	F25 2-1	D17 6-2	S24 2-2
4 BRADFORD	D03 3-3	O22 5-0	F18 1-1		J28 5-0	S10 1-0	M10 2-0	M24 6-3	N19 0-2	A27 4-0	N05 3-2	a07 3-0	D17 3-0	O15 3-2	m05 2-1	D27 4-1	a10 3-1	S05 5-3	O01 2-0	F04 6-2	a21 5-1	J07 2-0
5 BRADFORD C	F25 2-0	D31 5-0	M03 4-1	S17 2-3		D24 3-3	S03 4-1	A31 0-1	a09 1-0	J14 4-0	J21 0-0	O08 2-1	F11 3-1	N12 9-1	S24 3-1	M31 2-2	M14 3-1	a14 2-0	O29 2-2	M17 3-1	D26 3-0	a28 2-0
6 CHESTERFIELD	J14 3-1	M10 3-0	O01 6-0	J21 0-0	m05 2-0		N05 3-2	O22 1-3	M24 1-0	A29 4-2	J07 3-0	D03 1-3	a07 0-1	F18 6-0	D17 2-3	O15 1-3	D27 2-5	a09 5-2	F04 1-1	S17 2-2	N19 0-0	A27 0-1
7 CREWE A	F11 2-3	a06 3-0	M31 4-1	O29 1-3	J07 2-1	M17 4-1		D26 3-3	F25 4-1	D24 5-2	A27 1-1	S24 4-0	M21 0-0	J02 6-1	S10 1-1	a14 1-1	F08 3-2	a28 0-1	N12 3-0	M03 2-3	O08 1-2	S05 1-1
8 DARLINGTON	J28 3-0	O15 5-1	a14 1-1	N12 1-3	J02 1-2	M03 4-2	a09 1-3		F11 3-0	M17 5-0	a06 2-0	S10 5-0	J07 9-2	a16 4-1	A27 3-0	a28 1-0	D24 4-1	O08 3-1	a23 3-1	M31 3-7	S24 1-0	O29 1-3
9 DONCASTER R	S10 0-0	F18 3-2	J14 4-0	M31 2-0	a06 2-1	N12 4-0	O15 3-1	O01 5-0		O29 5-0	D26 1-1	J07 1-1	A27 3-0	a28 4-2	S05 5-1	D24 5-2	S24 2-0	M17 0-1	a14 0-2	m01 5-2	J28 4-1	M03 1-1
10 DURHAM C	M24 2-1	a18 0-0	S17 4-1	D31 0-1	a07 3-2	S07 2-0	m05 5-1	N05 3-3	M10 1-3		D17 1-1	N19 1-0	a21 0-4	F04 3-0	D03 2-1	O01 3-2	F18 1-4	O15 0-0	J21 1-2	S03 1-3	O22 3-0	a09 1-1
11 HALIFAX T	O08 3-1	S05 6-1	A29 5-2	M17 1-1	S10 2-1	S03 1-2	D31 0-0	S19 2-1	D27 0-1	a28 3-1		F11 4-1	S24 3-1	J14 5-1	a23 1-1	a10 1-1	a14 0-0	M26 1-0	M03 1-3	O29 2-2	F25 2-2	D24 4-1
12 HARTLEPOOLS U	a09 0-2	S17 4-1	J02 6-2	J14 1-1	F18 2-3	a14 1-0	F04 4-3	J21 0-1	S03 1-0	D10 2-1	O01 0-1		D26 1-2	M17 4-5	O15 3-3	O29 0-2	M03 1-3	N12 2-1	D24 2-1	a28 2-0	D31 1-1	a21 4-2
13 LINCOLN C	a06 3-1	J21 3-1	M17 5-0	a28 2-0	O01 2-2	a11 0-0	S17 5-2	S03 1-0	D31 2-0	D14 2-1	F04 5-2	D27 1-5		O29 0-0	F18 1-2	M03 3-1	N12 4-1	M31 2-0	O15 2-0	D24 1-1	A29 4-1	a14 5-0
14 NELSON	A27 1-4	D03 1-5	S12 4-0	F25 1-2	M24 0-3	O08 3-3	a21 3-3	a07 4-0	D17 0-1	S24 2-1	N19 3-2	N05 4-2	M10 1-3		O22 0-3	J07 6-3	S10 6-1	M20 1-1	a09 0-4	a24 3-5	m05 3-3	F11 4-0
15 NEW BRIGHTON	D27 3-1	S03 6-0	a18 3-3	D24 1-2	F04 1-1	a28 3-3	J21 5-1	D31 0-0	A31 3-1	a14 4-0	S17 3-1	F25 2-1	O08 2-3	M03 4-0		N12 2-1	M31 1-1	F15 0-1	M17 0-0	O01 0-1	a09 2-1	M07 0-0
16 ROCHDALE	m01 3-2	a07 2-2	D31 3-0	J03 0-4	N19 3-3	F25 5-1	D03 4-0	D17 4-1	m05 1-0	F11 1-0	a21 2-2	M10 0-1	O22 0-3	S03 1-0	M24 0-0		F28 2-1	S24 5-1	A30 2-1	a09 1-2	J21 3-0	O08 3-0
17 ROTHERHAM U	M10 2-1	D17 1-1	S03 3-0	a09 1-0	a21 0-0	D26 1-2	a07 2-0	m05 3-1	F04 2-1	O08 1-1	D03 0-0	O22 5-0	M24 2-4	J21 4-3	N19 0-0	S17 3-1		F11 1-1	D31 0-1	A29 2-1	N05 0-0	F25 0-1
18 SOUTHPORT	O22 5-0	m05 3-3	J21 4-0	A30 2-1	D03 5-1	a06 2-1	D17 3-2	F18 2-0	N05 1-2	F25 3-1	a07 3-1	M24 0-2	N19 3-1	S17 1-2	a21 4-2	F04 3-1	O01 1-1		S03 4-0	D31 0-1	M10 2-1	D26 4-1
19 STOCKPORT CO	D17 3-3	N19 3-0	D26 4-0	F11 2-2	M10 3-0	S24 3-0	M24 1-0	a21 4-0	D03 2-1	S10 2-1	O22 3-0	m05 2-2	J28 2-0	a06 8-0	N05 0-0	J02 5-1	A27 2-0	J07 6-3		O08 1-0	a07 1-1	F27 5-0
20 TRANMERE R	a07 3-2	M24 5-3	O15 5-0	S24 2-2	N05 2-1	J28 6-3	O22 3-3	N19 3-1	a21 0-0	J07 11-1	M10 2-2	D17 1-2	m05 2-2	D27 1-1	F11 4-0	a06 3-0	J02 2-0	A27 1-0	F18 5-2		D03 5-2	S10 2-1
21 WIGAN B	J07 2-0	O01 0-0	a28 1-0	F01 1-3	D27 2-2	M31 3-2	F18 2-1	F04 0-3	S17 1-1	M03 3-0	O15 1-3	A27 0-2	S07 1-3	D10 4-2	a06 2-2	S10 1-2	M17 0-0	O29 1-3	J14 1-3	a14 1-0		N12 3-0
22 WREXHAM	N19 0-1	N05 5-1	F04 5-0	S03 1-1	D17 1-0	D31 1-2	A31 2-0	M10 1-2	O22 1-2	a06 4-0	m05 2-0	S14 3-2	D03 1-0	O01 5-2	a07 0-2	F18 2-1	O15 3-2	D27 3-0	S17 1-0	J21 2-0	M24 5-1	

DIVISION 3 SOUTH

	BOURNEMOUTH	BRENTFORD	BRIGHTON & HA	BRISTOL R	CHARLTON A	COVENTRY C	CRYSTAL P	EXETER C	GILLINGHAM	LUTON T	MERTHYR T	MILLWALL	NEWPORT CO	NORTHAMPTON T	NORWICH C	PLYMOUTH A	Q.P.R.	SOUTHEND U	SWINDON T	TORQUAY U	WALSALL	WATFORD
1 BOURNEMOUTH		J07 1-0	D26 3-1	D03 4-3	a07 3-1	M10 2-3	S24 2-2	F11 2-0	O22 3-0	S10 2-2	N19 2-1	J28 5-0	N05 0-0	a09 1-1	F25 2-1	a21 2-2	S21 1-2	A31 2-3	A27 2-0	O08 1-1	M24 3-1	D17 1-0
2 BRENTFORD	S03 2-1		D31 1-3	a07 5-1	D17 1-1	O22 4-1	F11 2-1	O08 1-1	M24 2-0	J28 4-2	a21 4-0	S24 6-1	M10 3-1	A29 3-0	a06 3-1	D03 0-2	J21 0-3	a23 2-2	N05 1-4	F25 1-2	D05 3-2	m05 1-1
3 BRIGHTON & H.A.	D27 3-2	A27 5-2		a21 5-0	D03 2-2	N05 3-0	J28 4-2	S24 0-2	M10 0-0	J07 3-1	M24 5-0	S10 3-1	S14 1-4	F25 2-1	O08 1-0	N19 4-1	D17 1-3	a06 1-0	m05 4-2	F11 3-0	O22 0-0	a07 1-1
4 BRISTOL R	a14 3-0	S14 1-3	a23 1-0		F25 2-1	S10 1-1	a09 1-1	M17 1-2	J07 2-4	a28 1-2	D27 2-1	D24 1-6	J28 2-1	N12 2-2	M03 3-0	S07 3-1	F11 0-4	M31 1-3	a18 1-0	O29 5-1	A27 5-2	O08 3-1
5 CHARLTON A	a16 1-1	a28 3-2	a14 3-0	O15 2-1		J07 2-1	M17 0-4	O29 0-0	A27 1-0	D24 4-3	S19 0-0	O08 1-1	S10 3-2	M31 2-2	N12 3-2	a06 2-0	S24 1-0	M26 1-2	a30 3-1	M03 1-0	F09 1-3	F11 0-2
6 COVENTRY C	O29 3-2	M03 0-0	M17 2-2	J21 2-3	S03 3-3		F13 2-2	a14 0-0	F18 1-2	N12 4-2	F04 1-2	M31 0-3	a10 0-2	D24 2-4	a28 2-2	S17 1-1	D27 0-0	O15 6-1	S05 4-0	J14 5-1	O01 0-1	D10 2-3
7 CRYSTAL P	F04 6-1	O01 0-2	S17 1-1	a06 3-2	N05 5-0	a21 1-0		A29 2-0	D03 2-2	F18 3-2	D17 2-0	O15 0-4	N19 2-0	S03 1-0	D31 2-1	m05 0-2	O22 1-1	J21 4-1	M24 1-0	M14 3-2	a07 5-1	M10 2-1
8 EXETER C	O01 4-1	F18 0-1	F04 0-3	N05 4-1	M10 2-1	D03 0-1	S07 2-2		a07 2-2	O15 3-2	m05 2-0	a09 2-4	a21 5-1	J21 1-1	S03 2-2	D26 2-0	M24 4-0	S17 3-2	N19 0-0	D31 5-0	D17 3-0	O22 3-3
9 GILLINGHAM	M03 2-1	N12 2-1	O29 0-1	S03 3-1	D31 1-1	O08 1-2	a14 3-1	M28 1-1		M31 0-4	S17 1-1	a25 0-1	F25 4-0	O01 1-3	D24 3-0	J21 3-1	S07 1-2	M17 1-0	a06 0-1	a28 4-1	F04 2-0	D27 0-3
10 LUTON T	J21 3-3	S17 5-2	S03 2-5	D17 2-0	m05 2-1	M24 3-1	O08 6-1	F25 2-1	N19 6-1		D03 5-1	F11 1-1	O22 1-1	M19 2-0	A29 1-3	a07 1-1	N05 0-1	D31 0-0	M10 2-1	a06 5-0	a21 4-1	F04 3-2
11 MERTHYR T	M31 1-1	D10 3-1	N12 4-2	D26 2-3	A29 0-0	S24 3-2	a28 2-2	D24 0-3	M12 3-1	a14 0-0		O03 0-0	F11 0-2	O29 1-3	M17 1-1	J14 1-4	F25 0-4	M03 2-3	O08 8-2	S03 1-3	S10 3-2	a10 3-1
12 MILLWALL	S17 2-0	F04 3-0	J21 6-0	m05 1-0	F18 5-0	N19 9-1	F25 1-1	a06 2-0	a21 6-0	O01 3-2	a07 3-0		M24 5-1	D31 3-0	D27 2-1	D17 2-0	M10 6-1	S03 5-1	O22 3-3	A29 9-1	D03 7-1	N05 4-2
13 NEWPORT CO	M17 4-3	O29 3-0	S01 3-1	S17 3-1	J21 4-3	a09 3-0	a28 0-3	M22 1-0	O15 1-1	M03 7-2	O01 1-1	N12 1-3		a28 4-1	J14 2-2	F04 1-1	a06 1-6	D24 3-2	D26 1-3	a14 2-2	F18 4-1	S03 3-2
14 NORTHAMPTON T	a10 1-1	S05 3-2	O15 1-0	M24 2-0	N19 2-1	m05 2-1	J07 1-1	S10 5-0	F11 1-0	D26 6-5	M10 6-0	A27 5-2	D17 1-2		S24 4-2	O22 2-1	D03 1-0	F18 2-1	a07 3-0	J28 4-4	N05 10-0	a21 5-0
15 NORWICH C	O15 3-3	a09 1-1	F18 0-0	O22 4-2	M24 0-0	D17 0-2	A27 4-1	J07 2-2	m05 0-0	S05 3-0	N05 4-0	a30 2-0	a07 1-1	F04 3-4		M10 2-0	a21 3-1	O01 2-1	D03 1-3	S10 4-0	J28 1-4	N19 1-1
16 PLYMOUTH A	a25 3-1	a14 1-0	M31 2-0	A31 4-1	a09 2-0	J28 4-0	D24 5-1	D27 1-2	S10 2-2	m02 4-0	A27 5-0	D10 3-2	S24 2-0	M03 3-3	O29 4-2		O08 3-0	N12 3-2	F11 3-0	M17 4-1	J07 2-1	F25 0-1
17 Q.P.R.	D24 2-0	S10 2-3	a28 5-0	O01 4-2	F04 3-3	a26 1-5	M03 2-0	N12 0-1	S01 3-3	M17 3-2	O15 0-0	O29 0-1	A27 4-2	a14 0-4	m03 0-0	F18 0-1		J14 3-2	J07 0-1	M31 2-3	a09 1-1	S17 2-1
18 SOUTHEND U	S07 3-0	D26 3-2	a09 0-1	N19 2-1	a21 1-2	F25 3-2	S10 6-1	F15 1-2	N05 1-2	A27 1-0	O22 2-1	J07 0-1	m05 5-1	O08 2-0	F11 1-1	M24 3-0	a07 7-0		M14 1-1	S24 1-0	M10 2-1	D03 3-0
19 SWINDON T	M21 3-2	M17 1-1	D24 4-3	F04 2-1	S17 2-2	A29 6-0	N12 3-3	M31 3-0	a09 6-1	O29 4-2	F18 1-2	M03 3-0	D27 4-1	a25 4-0	a14 1-1	O01 2-2	S03 0-2	a28 0-1		m02 2-2	O15 5-0	J21 4-0
20 TORQUAY U	F18 2-2	O15 2-1	O01 1-1	M10 0-0	O22 1-2	a07 2-3	D27 0-2	A27 1-1	D17 1-1	a09 0-4	J07 2-2	S07 0-1	D03 1-1	S17 1-5	J21 4-2	N05 1-2	N19 1-0	F04 3-3	a21 2-1		m05 1-1	M24 1-1
21 WALSALL	N12 2-3	M31 4-2	M03 3-3	D31 1-2	D27 1-0	F11 7-0	J14 1-1	a28 5-1	S24 7-4	a23 4-1	J21 2-2	a14 2-5	O08 0-3	M17 1-1	S17 1-1	S03 2-1	a10 2-2	O29 0-1	F25 1-2	D10 4-0		A29 2-0
22 WATFORD	a28 2-0	D24 1-1	J14 3-3	F18 2-1	O01 1-2	A27 3-1	O29 2-1	M03 3-2	m02 5-3	S24 1-0	a09 1-1	M17 0-3	J07 2-3	a18 2-0	M31 2-0	O15 1-2	J28 3-3	a14 1-1	S10 2-5	N12 1-2	S07 4-0	

LEAGUE TABLES

DIVISION 1

	P	W	D	L	F	A	W	D	L	F	A	Pts
Everton	42	11	8	2	60	28	9	5	7	42	38	53
Huddersfield T	42	15	1	5	57	31	7	6	8	34	37	51
Leicester C	42	14	5	2	66	25	4	7	10	30	47	48
Derby Co	42	12	4	5	59	30	5	6	10	37	53	44
Bury	42	13	1	7	53	35	7	3	11	27	45	44
Cardiff C	42	12	7	2	44	27	5	3	13	26	53	44
Bolton W	42	12	5	4	47	26	4	6	11	34	40	43
Aston Villa	42	13	3	5	52	30	4	6	11	26	43	43
Newcastle U	42	9	7	5	49	41	6	6	9	30	40	43
Arsenal	42	10	6	5	49	33	3	9	9	33	53	41
Birmingham	42	10	7	4	36	25	3	8	10	34	50	41
Blackburn R	42	13	5	3	41	22	3	4	14	25	56	41
Sheffield U	42	12	4	5	56	42	3	6	12	23	44	40
Sheffield W	42	9	6	6	45	29	4	7	10	36	49	39
Sunderland	42	9	5	7	37	29	6	4	11	37	47	39
Liverpool	42	10	6	5	54	36	3	7	11	30	51	39
West Ham U	42	9	7	5	48	34	5	4	12	33	54	39
Manchester U	42	12	6	3	51	27	4	1	16	21	53	39
Burnley	42	12	5	4	55	31	4	2	15	27	67	39
Portsmouth	42	13	4	4	40	23	3	3	15	26	67	39
Tottenham H	42	12	3	6	47	34	3	5	13	27	52	38
Middlesbrough	42	7	9	5	46	35	4	6	11	35	53	37

DIVISION 2

	P	W	D	L	F	A	W	D	L	F	A	Pts
Manchester C	42	18	2	1	70	27	7	7	7	30	32	59
Leeds U	42	16	2	3	63	15	9	5	7	35	34	57
Chelsea	42	15	2	4	46	15	8	6	7	29	30	54
Preston NE	42	15	3	3	62	24	7	6	8	38	42	53
Stoke C	42	14	5	2	44	17	8	3	10	34	42	52
Swansea T	42	13	6	2	46	17	5	6	10	29	46	48
Oldham A	42	15	3	3	55	18	4	5	12	20	33	46
WBA	42	10	7	4	50	28	7	5	9	40	42	46
Port Vale	42	11	6	4	45	20	7	2	12	23	37	44
Nottingham F	42	10	6	5	54	37	5	4	12	29	47	40
Grimsby T	42	8	6	7	41	41	6	6	9	28	42	40
Bristol C	42	11	5	5	42	18	4	4	13	34	61	39
Barnsley	42	10	5	6	43	36	4	6	11	22	49	39
Hull C	42	9	8	4	25	19	3	7	11	16	35	39
Notts Co	42	10	4	7	47	26	3	8	10	21	48	38
Wolves	42	11	5	5	43	31	2	5	14	20	60	36
Southampton	42	11	3	7	54	40	3	4	14	14	37	35
Reading	42	9	8	4	32	22	2	5	14	21	53	35
Blackpool	42	11	3	7	55	43	2	5	14	28	58	34
Clapton O	42	9	7	5	32	25	2	5	14	23	60	34
Fulham	42	12	7	2	46	22	1	0	20	22	67	33
South Shields	42	5	5	11	30	41	2	4	15	26	70	23

DIVISION 3 North

	P	W	D	L	F	A	W	D	L	F	A	Pts
Bradford	42	18	2	1	68	22	9	7	5	33	23	63
Lincoln C	42	15	4	2	53	20	9	3	9	38	44	55
Stockport Co	42	16	5	0	62	14	7	3	11	27	37	54
Doncaster R	42	15	4	2	59	18	8	3	10	21	26	53
Tranmere R	42	14	6	1	68	28	8	3	10	37	44	53
Bradford C	42	15	4	2	59	19	3	8	10	26	41	48
Darlington	42	15	1	5	63	28	6	4	11	26	46	47
Southport	42	15	2	4	55	24	5	3	13	24	46	45
Accrington S	42	14	4	3	49	22	4	4	13	27	45	44
New Brighton	42	10	7	4	45	22	4	7	10	27	40	42
Wrexham	42	15	1	5	48	19	3	5	13	16	48	42
Halifax T	42	11	7	3	47	24	2	8	11	26	47	41
Rochdale	42	13	4	4	45	24	4	3	14	29	53	41
Rotherham U	42	11	6	4	39	19	3	5	13	26	50	39
Hartlepools U	42	10	3	8	41	35	6	3	12	28	46	38
Chesterfield	42	10	4	7	46	29	3	6	12	25	49	36
Crewe A	42	10	6	5	51	28	2	4	15	26	58	34
Ashington	42	10	5	6	54	36	1	6	14	23	67	33
Barrow	42	10	8	3	41	24	0	3	18	13	78	31
Wigan B	42	8	5	8	30	32	2	5	14	26	65	30
Durham C	42	10	5	6	37	30	1	2	18	16	70	29
Nelson	42	8	4	9	50	49	2	2	17	26	87	26

DIVISION 3 South

	P	W	D	L	F	A	W	D	L	F	A	Pts
Millwall	42	19	2	0	87	15	11	3	7	40	35	65
Northampton T	42	17	3	1	67	23	6	6	9	35	41	55
Plymouth A	42	17	2	2	60	19	6	5	10	25	35	53
Brighton & HA	42	14	4	3	51	24	5	6	10	30	45	48
Crystal P	42	15	3	3	46	23	3	9	9	33	49	48
Swindon T	42	12	6	3	60	26	7	3	11	30	43	47
Southend U	42	14	2	5	48	19	6	4	11	32	45	46
Exeter C	42	11	6	4	49	27	6	6	9	21	33	46
Newport Co	42	12	5	4	52	38	6	4	11	29	46	45
QPR	42	8	5	8	37	35	9	4	8	35	36	43
Charlton A	42	12	5	4	34	27	3	8	10	26	43	43
Brentford	42	12	4	5	49	30	4	4	13	27	44	40
Luton T	42	13	5	3	56	27	3	2	16	38	60	39
Bournemouth	42	12	6	3	44	24	1	6	14	28	55	38
Watford	42	10	5	6	42	34	4	5	12	26	44	38
Gillingham	42	10	3	8	33	26	3	8	10	29	55	37
Norwich C	42	9	8	4	41	26	1	8	12	25	44	36
Walsall	42	9	6	6	52	35	3	3	15	23	66	33
Bristol R	42	11	3	7	41	36	3	1	17	26	57	32
Coventry C	42	5	8	8	40	36	6	1	14	27	60	31
Merthyr T	42	7	6	8	38	40	2	7	12	15	51	31
Torquay U	42	4	10	7	27	36	4	4	13	26	67	30

Football League Records

Top scorers: Div 1, D.Halliday (Sunderland) 43 goals; Div 2, J.Hampson (Blackpool) 40 goals; Div 3(N), J.McConnell (Carlisle United) 43 goals; Div 3(S), A.Rennie (Luton Town) 43 goals.
Durham City failed to gain re-election, Carlisle United elected in their place.

Jimmy Seed, the man who inspired Sheffield Wednesday's 'great escape' of 1927-8, then led them to successive League Championship titles.

DIVISION 1

	ARSENAL	ASTON VILLA	BIRMINGHAM	BLACKBURN R	BOLTON W	BURNLEY	BURY	CARDIFF C	DERBY CO	EVERTON	HUDDERSFIELD T	LEEDS U	LEICESTER C	LIVERPOOL	MANCHESTER C	MANCHESTER U	NEWCASTLE U	PORTSMOUTH	SHEFFIELD U	SHEFFIELD W	SUNDERLAND	WEST HAM U
1 ARSENAL		N24 2-5	S15 0-0	M29 1-0	S01 2-0	D22 3-1	M30 7-1	M16 2-1	A29 1-3	a22 2-0	S29 2-0	a27 1-0	a13 1-1	O27 4-4	F02 0-0	D08 3-1	a02 1-2	J19 4-0	N10 2-0	D29 2-2	D26 1-1	O13 2-3
2 ASTON VILLA	a06 4-2		M09 1-2	N17 2-1	O20 3-5	F02 4-2	O13 7-1	S29 1-0	N03 2-3	D01 2-0	a20 4-1	D29 1-0	a02 4-2	S01 3-1	D19 5-1	A27 0-0	S15 1-1	D26 3-2	F20 3-2	m04 4-1	M25 3-1	J19 5-2
3 BIRMINGHAM	M13 1-1	O27 2-4		S22 4-0	D25 0-2	N24 3-6	a27 3-2	a13 0-0	O06 1-4	S08 1-3	J05 1-2	D22 5-1	S10 1-0	M16 0-0	A25 4-1	M02 1-1	M30 0-0	a01 1-0	D08 2-2	F23 4-1	F09 1-0	N10 2-2
4 BLACKBURN R	D25 5-2	M30 2-5	F02 4-1		J19 1-3	m02 1-1	N10 1-1	D22 2-0	D29 3-1	O13 2-1	a01 1-1	D08 0-1	N24 1-1	a27 2-1	S29 2-2	a13 0-3	S24 2-0	S15 4-0	M16 1-1	S01 4-1	S17 2-0	O27 2-0
5 BOLTON W	J05 1-2	a17 3-1	D26 6-2	S08 0-3		D08 0-1	O06 0-1	J01 1-0	S22 3-0	A25 2-3	S03 1-1	N10 4-1	D22 5-0	M30 0-0	a01 1-1	M16 1-1	a13 1-0	O13 4-2	O27 3-1	F09 2-2	F20 2-2	N24 4-1
6 BURNLEY	m04 3-3	S22 4-1	a06 4-0	O20 2-2	a20 3-1		F18 0-0	J05 3-0	M09 2-2	N03 2-0	a16 3-2	F23 5-0	F09 0-1	D25 3-2	N17 2-3	O06 3-4	S10 4-3	D01 4-1	S08 2-1	D15 0-2	A25 3-1	S03 3-3
7 BURY	N17 1-0	F23 2-2	M20 3-1	M23 1-0	m01 3-4	S15 2-1		F02 4-1	m04 3-3	a06 1-2	D01 2-1	J01 2-2	D25 3-1	D29 2-2	a20 1-2	M29 1-3	J19 2-0	M09 0-0	S29 4-0	O20 0-4	N03 1-3	S01 0-3
8 CARDIFF C	N03 1-1	F09 0-2	D01 1-4	m04 1-1	D15 1-1	S01 7-0	S22 4-0		J19 3-0	M23 0-2	N17 0-0	D26 2-1	O06 1-2	a01 1-2	a06 1-3	F23 2-2	D29 2-0	a20 1-1	J26 0-0	M09 3-1	O20 0-1	S10 3-2
9 DERBY CO	S26 0-0	M16 1-0	F16 2-2	A25 5-1	F02 2-1	O27 4-0	D22 3-1	S08 2-0		a02 3-0	D26 1-2	N24 3-4	N10 5-2	a13 2-5	O13 1-1	M30 6-1	a27 1-2	S29 1-0	M02 2-2	S15 6-0	J05 0-0	D08 6-0
10 EVERTON	O06 4-2	a13 0-1	J19 0-2	F23 5-2	D29 3-0	M16 2-0	N24 1-0	N10 1-0	J01 4-0		F02 0-3	O27 0-1	D08 3-1	S29 1-0	S15 2-6	a27 2-4	D22 5-2	S01 4-0	M30 1-3	A29 0-0	D25 0-0	a10 0-4
11 HUDDERSFIELD T	F09 0-1	D08 3-0	S01 0-0	O06 0-2	A27 4-1	N10 7-1	a13 0-2	M30 1-1	D25 0-0	S22 3-1		S15 6-1	a27 1-1	a10 1-3	J19 2-2	O27 1-2	M16 2-1	D29 3-1	N24 6-1	a02 0-0	F23 1-2	D22 4-0
12 LEEDS U	D15 1-1	A25 4-1	m04 0-1	a20 0-1	a29 2-2	O13 2-1	A27 3-1	D25 3-0	a06 1-1	M09 3-1	m01 1-2		J05 4-3	F02 2-2	O20 4-1	S08 3-2	F16 0-0	N03 3-2	a02 2-0	N17 0-2	D01 0-3	S29 4-1
13 LEICESTER C	D01 1-1	a01 4-1	A27 5-3	a06 2-1	m04 6-1	S29 1-1	D26 5-2	F21 2-0	M23 1-0	a20 4-1	D15 4-1	S01 4-4		J19 2-0	M09 3-2	D29 2-1	F02 1-1	O20 10-0	O13 3-1	N03 1-1	N17 1-0	S15 5-0
14 LIVERPOOL	M09 2-4	J05 4-0	N03 1-2	D15 1-1	N17 3-0	D26 8-0	A25 3-0	M29 2-0	D01 3-0	F09 1-2	O20 2-3	S22 1-1	S08 6-3		m04 1-1	F13 2-3	O13 2-1	a17 0-0	S05 1-2	a06 3-2	a20 5-2	M13 2-1
15 MANCHESTER C	S22 4-1	a27 3-0	D29 2-3	F09 1-2	M29 5-1	M30 4-1	J30 6-4	N24 1-1	F23 2-3	J26 5-1	S08 3-2	M02 3-0	O27 2-3	D22 2-3		S01 2-2	N10 2-4	O01 2-1	a13 3-1	D26 2-2	O06 5-3	M16 4-2
16 MANCHESTER U	a20 4-1	J01 2-2	O20 1-0	D01 1-4	N03 1-1	F16 1-0	a01 1-0	O13 1-1	N17 0-1	D15 1-1	M09 1-0	J19 1-2	A25 1-1	S15 2-2	J05 1-2		S29 5-0	m04 0-0	D25 1-1	M23 2-1	a06 3-0	F02 2-3
17 NEWCASTLE U	O20 0-3	M13 2-1	N17 1-0	J01 0-2	D01 4-1	A29 2-7	S08 2-1	A25 1-1	D15 4-1	m04 2-0	N03 4-1	O06 3-2	S22 1-0	F23 2-2	M23 4-0	F09 5-0		a06 0-1	J05 4-2	a20 2-1	M09 4-3	D26 1-0
18 PORTSMOUTH	S08 2-0	D25 3-2	M29 3-1	M13 2-2	F23 4-4	a13 3-1	O27 4-1	D08 0-1	F09 1-5	J05 3-0	A25 1-0	M16 0-2	a10 1-0	N10 0-1	S05 1-0	D22 3-0	N24 0-1		a29 2-3	O06 3-2	S22 4-0	M30 3-0
19 SHEFFIELD U	M23 2-2	O06 1-3	a20 3-2	N03 2-1	M09 1-1	J19 10-0	F09 6-1	S15 3-1	O20 2-1	N17 2-1	a06 1-0	a01 1-1	F23 1-4	S10 1-3	D01 1-3	D26 6-1	S01 3-1	D15 3-0		F02 1-1	m04 4-0	D29 3-3
20 SHEFFIELD W	A25 3-2	D22 4-1	O13 3-0	J05 1-0	S29 0-0	a27 1-1	M02 3-1	O27 1-0	F18 5-0	S03 1-0	J01 1-1	M30 4-2	M16 1-0	N24 3-2	D25 4-0	N10 2-1	D08 3-1	M04 2-1	S22 5-2		S08 2-1	a13 6-0
21 SUNDERLAND	J01 5-1	N10 1-3	S29 3-4	A29 3-1	S15 4-0	D29 2-1	M16 3-1	M02 1-0	S01 4-0	M29 2-2	O13 4-1	a13 2-1	M30 1-2	D08 2-1	F16 3-1	N24 5-1	O27 5-2	F02 5-0	D22 4-4	J19 4-3		a27 4-1
22 WEST HAM U	F23 3-4	S08 4-1	M23 2-1	M09 3-3	a06 3-0	M29 4-0	J05 2-3	S17 1-1	a20 2-2	O20 2-4	m04 1-1	F09 8-2	M04 2-1	O06 1-1	N03 3-0	S22 3-1	D25 1-0	N17 0-1	A25 4-0	D01 3-2	D15 3-3	

Middlesbrough's George Camsell, who scored a record 59 goals when 'Boro stormed to the Second Division title in 1926-7, hit 30 when they returned to the top flight two seasons later.

DIVISION 2

	BARNSLEY	BLACKPOOL	BRADFORD	BRISTOL C	CHELSEA	CLAPTON O	GRIMSBY T	HULL C	MIDDLESBROUGH	MILLWALL	NOTTINGHAM F	NOTTS CO	OLDHAM A	PORT VALE	PRESTON N.E.	READING	SOUTHAMPTON	STOKE C	SWANSEA T	TOTTENHAM H	W.B.A.	WOLVERHAMPTON W
1 BARNSLEY		S08 3-1	A25 1-2	S29 4-2	J30 0-1	D26 2-0	J01 0-2	N24 2-2	N10 2-2	D22 2-2	F16 1-2	M16 2-0	S22 2-1	M30 6-0	a27 4-1	D08 2-3	M02 4-1	M29 4-2	J05 2-1	a13 4-1	O13 2-0	O27 2-2
2 BLACKPOOL	J19 0-1		M29 3-0	S15 2-1	S01 0-1	F16 0-1	D26 1-1	D08 2-1	M02 3-0	N24 3-0	F02 2-2	M30 3-2	O27 4-0	a13 4-0	D29 3-2	N10 7-0	M16 3-0	O13 2-0	S03 2-2	a27 2-2	S29 0-2	D22 3-0
3 BRADFORD	D29 2-1	a01 5-2		S01 3-2	A27 1-2	F02 2-1	a29 1-0	N10 5-1	M16 3-2	D08 4-0	J19 1-1	a13 2-2	D22 2-0	a27 2-0	O27 7-2	M02 1-0	M30 4-1	S29 2-1	D25 3-1	O13 4-1	S15 4-1	N24 4-1
4 BRISTOL C	F09 3-1	J26 3-2	J05 1-0		S22 0-0	a01 1-0	A25 2-2	M30 0-0	a27 0-1	M16 5-0	O13 2-5	O27 0-4	N10 6-0	D22 2-1	D08 1-0	a13 0-0	O06 1-1	S05 1-1	S08 2-1	N24 2-1	D26 2-3	M02 3-2
5 CHELSEA	S15 1-0	J05 2-3	S05 3-1	F02 3-0		O13 2-2	a01 3-2	a13 0-0	S08 2-0	M30 0-3	S29 3-0	D22 1-1	M02 2-3	N24 3-3	N10 2-1	a27 2-1	O27 1-1	D26 3-1	A25 4-0	D08 1-1	a17 2-5	M16 0-2
6 CLAPTON O	D25 3-1	O06 2-4	S22 1-0	M29 0-1	F23 1-0		M04 3-1	O27 0-2	N24 3-0	S01 1-1	A27 1-4	N10 2-2	a13 2-0	M02 1-0	M30 1-0	D22 1-1	D08 1-1	S08 1-0	F09 1-2	M16 2-3	D29 0-2	a27 2-0
7 GRIMSBY T	A27 2-1	D25 1-4	O06 4-2	D29 3-2	M29 1-0	S15 6-1		S29 0-1	D22 1-4	a27 3-0	S01 2-2	D08 2-2	M30 1-0	N10 3-1	M16 1-0	O27 4-0	N24 2-1	F02 2-1	F23 4-1	M02 2-0	J19 3-1	a13 2-0
8 HULL C	a06 0-0	a20 1-3	M23 1-0	N17 5-1	D01 2-2	M09 0-0	F09 2-3		a01 1-1	a22 4-0	m04 0-1	S08 1-1	A27 1-0	S22 2-0	D25 5-1	O13 3-0	A25 2-2	O20 1-3	D15 1-1	a15 1-1	N03 4-1	J05 1-3
9 MIDDLESBROUGH	M23 1-0	O20 4-1	N03 5-3	D15 3-1	J19 4-5	a06 4-0	m04 3-0	S12 1-1		F23 3-0	a20 1-0	O06 3-1	F20 1-0	D25 5-1	S01 2-3	D29 0-0	S22 1-2	N17 1-0	M09 0-0	J01 3-0	D01 1-1	F09 8-3
10 MILLWALL	m04 0-2	a06 2-1	a20 1-3	N03 3-1	N17 2-1	J05 2-0	D15 4-1	S15 0-0	O13 2-3		M09 1-1	A25 0-1	D25 3-3	J19 2-1	F16 3-1	S29 5-1	M29 2-4	M23 1-3	D01 3-0	F02 5-1	O20 2-2	S03 0-5
11 NOTTINGHAM F	O06 1-3	S22 2-0	S08 3-2	F23 1-1	F09 3-0	S05 0-0	J05 0-1	D22 3-1	D08 1-1	O27 0-4		M02 1-2	a27 3-1	M16 2-2	a13 4-1	N24 1-2	N10 1-1	A25 1-5	F20 2-1	M30 2-2	M29 1-2	D26 2-1
12 NOTTS CO	N03 4-1	N17 3-1	D01 3-3	M09 2-0	M13 4-3	M23 2-0	a20 1-2	J19 6-0	F16 0-3	D29 4-5	O20 1-1		O13 2-0	S01 3-0	S29 0-1	F02 1-1	D25 1-1	D15 1-0	a06 5-1	S15 2-0	A27 3-1	a01 3-0
13 OLDHAM A	F02 1-0	M09 4-2	m04 2-1	M23 1-0	O20 1-0	D01 1-1	N17 0-3	S03 0-1	S15 1-3	D26 4-1	J01 2-0	F23 3-2		a01 1-1	J19 2-1	S01 2-1	F09 3-1	a06 1-0	N03 2-1	D29 3-1	a20 3-0	O06 0-4
14 PORT VALE	N17 3-0	D01 1-0	D15 0-1	m04 5-0	a06 1-0	O20 3-0	M23 0-3	F02 4-1	D26 2-3	S08 5-2	N03 4-2	J05 3-0	M29 2-1		O13 3-2	F25 4-0	S24 1-2	J26 1-2	a20 0-0	S29 2-1	M09 8-1	A25 1-4
15 PRESTON N.E.	D15 2-1	A25 3-1	M09 2-0	a20 2-2	M23 3-0	N17 5-2	N03 5-2	D26 1-0	J05 0-0	O06 3-4	D01 3-2	F09 0-1	S08 3-2	F23 7-1		A27 7-0	J26 0-1	m04 2-2	O20 2-2	M29 2-2	a06 1-1	S22 5-1
16 READING	a20 1-0	M23 4-1	O20 4-0	D01 2-1	D15 3-3	m04 4-2	M09 1-3	F23 3-0	A25 2-3	F09 0-2	a06 0-3	S22 1-2	J05 6-1	O06 2-1	S05 0-0		S08 0-1	N03 1-1	M29 2-0	D26 4-3	N17 5-3	M13 3-0
17 SOUTHAMPTON	O20 1-2	N03 8-2	N17 2-2	F16 2-1	M09 1-2	a20 2-0	a06 3-1	D29 3-2	F02 1-1	a01 3-0	M23 2-1	D26 4-0	S29 2-1	A27 1-2	S15 4-0	J19 2-2		D01 0-0	m04 3-0	S01 1-1	D15 1-1	F23 2-1
18 STOKE C	a01 0-0	F23 1-1	F09 2-0	A27 2-0	D25 0-1	J19 3-1	S22 1-2	M02 1-1	M30 3-2	N10 0-0	D29 1-1	a27 5-0	N24 1-1	S15 2-1	D22 1-1	M16 5-0	a13 3-0		O06 5-0	O27 2-0	S01 4-1	D08 4-3
19 SWANSEA T	S01 2-1	A27 5-5	D26 3-1	J19 0-2	D29 0-1	S29 0-1	O13 2-1	a27 0-1	O27 2-0	a13 2-0	S15 3-5	N24 1-0	M16 3-2	D08 2-0	M02 5-0	a01 0-1	D22 1-1	F16 3-3		N10 4-0	F02 6-1	M30 2-0
20 TOTTENHAM H	D01 2-0	D15 1-2	F23 3-2	a06 1-1	a20 4-1	N03 2-1	O20 2-1	O06 4-1	A27 2-5	S22 2-1	N17 2-1	J26 3-0	A25 4-1	F09 4-2	a01 2-0	D25 2-2	J05 3-2	M09 1-0	M23 1-1		m04 2-0	S08 3-2
21 W.B.A.	F23 6-2	F09 2-2	M11 1-2	D25 1-1	O06 3-0	A25 3-1	S08 1-0	M16 2-0	a13 1-1	a10 3-2	a01 3-0	S03 1-3	D08 1-0	O27 3-1	N24 1-1	M30 5-0	a27 3-1	J05 2-3	S22 5-1	D22 3-2		N10 0-2
22 WOLVERHAMPTON W	M09 3-1	m04 1-5	a06 3-1	O20 2-1	N03 1-1	D15 3-2	D01 2-2	S01 2-4	S29 3-3	A27 0-1	D25 2-3	a02 3-1	F16 0-0	D29 4-0	F02 1-2	S15 2-0	O13 1-1	a20 4-0	N17 0-0	J19 4-2	M23 0-1	

Season 1928-29

DIVISION 3 NORTH

	ACCRINGTON S	ASHINGTON	BARROW	BRADFORD C	CARLISLE U	CHESTERFIELD	CREWE A	DARLINGTON	DONCASTER R	HALIFAX T	HARTLEPOOLS U	LINCOLN C	NELSON	NEW BRIGHTON	ROCHDALE	ROTHERHAM U	SOUTHPORT	SOUTH SHIELDS	STOCKPORT CO	TRANMERE R	WIGAN B	WREXHAM
1 ACCRINGTON S		O20 0-1	N03 1-0	D25 0-1	A25 2-3	M23 0-0	J26 2-0	D15 4-0	M09 6-0	O06 1-1	S25 2-2	F23 0-1	m04 4-4	a06 3-1	D01 2-2	J05 1-3	a20 2-0	J01 2-0	F09 2-0	S22 2-0	S08 2-0	N17 4-3
2 ASHINGTON	M02 2-2		S29 1-0	O13 2-8	M16 0-4	F02 0-2	J12 0-5	A27 4-2	F16 4-7	a27 0-3	O27 3-1	D22 1-1	J01 3-2	J19 1-1	S01 2-1	N10 0-1	D29 1-3	D25 1-3	a20 0-1	a13 3-2	M30 1-1	S15 2-2
3 BARROW	M16 2-1	F09 3-0		O27 1-3	N17 1-1	J19 1-2	a29 2-4	J01 3-1	S22 2-2	S15 1-3	N10 2-1	M02 2-3	F23 7-2	D29 0-0	A27 3-3	J12 4-0	a01 1-2	O06 1-1	D22 2-4	a27 1-2	a13 1-0	S01 2-2
4 BRADFORD C	D26 4-1	F23 2-0	M09 8-0		S03 4-2	N03 6-1	S08 4-1	a20 3-0	O20 3-0	F09 2-2	a02 4-1	O06 2-3	D15 0-2	N17 5-2	a06 0-0	A25 11-1	D01 5-0	m04 3-1	S22 2-1	M06 8-0	J05 1-0	M23 5-0
5 CARLISLE U	D29 4-3	N03 5-1	M30 4-1	A30 2-2		a06 1-2	F09 1-0	J19 3-0	M23 1-2	D25 2-1	S01 8-0	J01 3-1	O20 4-0	a20 2-1	D15 4-2	J26 1-1	S13 4-2	M09 5-0	F23 0-5	O06 4-1	S22 2-1	D01 1-1
6 CHESTERFIELD	N10 4-1	S22 4-1	S08 3-0	M16 0-5	M13 1-2		a27 1-0	F23 2-1	J26 0-1	M02 3-2	M30 4-1	O27 1-1	O06 3-2	J01 0-2	M29 2-1	a13 1-2	D26 6-0	F09 3-2	S01 1-2	D22 4-1	a08 0-0	D29 3-1
7 CREWE A	S15 4-0	a06 7-0	a20 3-1	J19 0-0	S29 1-1	D15 6-1		N03 2-0	D01 1-1	D29 3-0	F02 4-2	S01 1-3	M23 1-1	D25 3-0	O20 1-1	a17 3-0	M09 1-1	N17 1-5	S03 2-0	a01 0-1	O13 0-4	m04 3-1
8 DARLINGTON	a27 0-0	S19 4-0	D26 1-2	J02 3-3	S08 0-0	O13 2-2	M16 4-2		a01 1-0	a24 2-0	D22 4-1	a13 2-1	J05 3-2	S29 3-1	F02 5-3	M02 2-1	S15 3-1	A25 2-2	M30 2-3	N10 1-2	O27 3-0	F16 0-0
9 DONCASTER R	O27 4-1	O06 2-1	F02 1-0	M02 1-1	N10 3-0	S15 2-0	D08 0-1	M29 3-1		D22 1-0	M16 4-1	S29 0-0	D26 2-2	S01 1-2	D29 4-2	M30 1-0	A27 4-2	F23 2-1	a27 0-2	a02 2-1	m01 1-2	J19 1-0
10 HALIFAX T	F16 4-2	D15 1-0	J26 2-0	S29 1-1	D26 5-2	O20 1-1	A25 2-2	a06 5-1	m04 2-2		O13 2-0	F02 4-2	D01 1-2	N03 1-1	M23 1-1	a02 3-1	N17 2-1	a20 0-2	S08 1-1	J05 2-0	S17 1-0	M09 1-2
11 HARTLEPOOLS U	a01 1-3	M09 1-3	M23 1-0	J01 1-3	J05 1-0	N17 0-2	S22 2-1	S05 2-0	N03 2-2	F23 3-1		D25 3-2	A25 2-2	D01 5-2	a20 0-2	S08 1-1	D15 4-2	O20 0-5	O06 1-1	F09 4-1	J26 1-3	a06 0-2
12 LINCOLN C	O13 3-1	a01 3-1	O20 5-0	F16 3-4	M29 3-0	M09 1-0	J05 1-0	D01 0-0	F09 2-1	S22 3-0	D26 7-1		a20 5-1	M23 4-0	N17 2-0	S03 1-1	a06 4-1	D15 5-0	J26 1-2	S08 3-1	A25 1-3	N03 1-1
13 NELSON	D22 0-2	D08 5-0	O13 3-4	a27 0-1	M02 1-0	F16 1-0	N10 4-1	S01 2-1	O02 2-4	a13 3-1	D29 1-0	S25 3-4		F02 3-0	S15 3-0	O27 4-2	J19 1-1	S12 1-0	J22 4-1	M30 4-2	M16 2-1	S29 1-3
14 NEW BRIGHTON	F06 2-1	S08 3-2	A25 1-3	M30 0-3	D12 1-0	S10 2-3	D26 2-3	F09 1-0	J05 1-1	M16 1-0	a13 1-3	N10 6-1	S22 0-1		F23 6-1	a27 0-0	O06 3-1	J26 1-0	O27 4-1	M02 1-2	D22 2-2	M29 2-0
15 ROCHDALE	a13 2-1	J05 5-0	S04 4-2	a30 1-3	J12 4-0	a01 2-1	M02 2-1	S22 5-0	A25 1-3	N10 2-2	D08 7-4	M30 0-2	J26 2-1	O13 4-2		D22 2-1	F09 1-1	S08 1-2	M16 1-3	O27 5-1	O06 0-0	D25 4-4
16 ROTHERHAM U	S01 2-1	M23 0-0	a06 2-1	D29 2-2	S15 4-0	D01 2-0	O06 1-2	O20 2-0	N17 1-2	a01 0-0	J19 3-2	A27 3-2	M09 4-0	D15 3-1	m04 5-0		F02 0-2	N03 1-1	D26 3-3	F23 0-1	F09 4-2	a20 2-1
17 SOUTHPORT	a09 3-1	A25 2-1	M29 2-2	a13 0-3	D22 4-3	D25 1-0	O27 6-2	J26 3-1	J01 3-3	M30 1-0	a27 6-2	m04 2-1	S08 5-1	F16 0-0	S29 1-1	S22 2-0		J05 5-0	N10 1-1	M16 1-2	M02 3-0	O13 1-3
18 SOUTH SHIELDS	M29 3-0	D26 0-0	a17 2-2	D22 1-1	O27 5-0	S29 6-3	M30 3-0	D29 1-3	O13 1-0	D08 2-1	M02 1-1	a27 1-0	a01 3-2	S15 0-2	J19 5-2	M16 10-1	S01 4-0		a13 0-1	J12 4-1	N10 2-2	F02 3-2
19 STOCKPORT CO	S29 6-1	S10 4-0	m04 3-2	F02 2-1	O13 2-2	J05 3-1	M29 2-2	N17 7-3	D15 4-1	J19 3-0	F16 3-0	S15 7-3	a06 3-0	M09 2-1	N03 4-0	D25 1-0	M23 2-1	D01 7-1		A25 4-1	J01 2-1	O20 6-2
20 TRANMERE R	F02 1-1	D01 3-2	D15 2-1	S15 1-0	F16 1-2	m04 3-0	J01 1-2	M23 4-0	a20 1-1	S01 2-1	S29 3-0	J19 2-1	N17 6-1	O20 1-3	M09 5-1	O13 3-0	N03 6-1	a06 4-0	D29 2-1		M29 3-2	A27 1-1
21 WIGAN B	J19 5-2	N17 5-1	D01 2-1	S01 2-0	F02 2-2	a20 5-1	F23 4-2	M09 2-0	a06 4-2	A29 1-1	S15 2-0	D29 4-0	N03 1-0	m04 1-1	F16 4-1	S29 1-0	O20 1-0	M23 4-0	a01 4-0	D25 0-1		D15 1-1
22 WREXHAM	M30 4-1	J26 4-0	J05 5-0	N10 2-1	a13 5-1	A25 4-3	D22 1-2	O06 4-3	S08 4-2	O27 2-2	J12 3-1	M16 2-1	F09 3-1	a01 1-1	D26 3-0	D08 2-0	F23 3-1	S22 1-0	M02 2-1	S05 3-1	a27 1-3	

DIVISION 3 SOUTH

	BOURNEMOUTH	BRENTFORD	BRIGHTON & HA	BRISTOL R	CHARLTON A	COVENTRY C	CRYSTAL P	EXETER C	FULHAM	GILLINGHAM	LUTON T	MERTHYR T	NEWPORT CO	NORTHAMPTON T	NORWICH C	PLYMOUTH A	Q.P.R.	SOUTHEND U	SWINDON T	TORQUAY U	WALSALL	WATFORD
1 BOURNEMOUTH		S15 1-1	a01 3-2	O27 6-2	O13 4-2	S29 2-1	a24 2-0	D25 3-1	S08 1-0	a27 4-3	F02 3-3	J05 3-0	M30 0-1	M20 2-0	S05 2-0	D22 4-1	M02 2-3	A25 2-2	a13 2-1	F06 4-3	N10 1-2	M16 3-3
2 BRENTFORD	M13 0-0		D26 5-1	M02 2-0	S03 1-0	F16 1-0	M30 2-4	A25 4-2	D22 1-2	J12 4-1	S29 0-1	S08 2-1	N10 1-3	O13 2-2	M20 4-0	a27 0-2	S22 1-1	J05 1-0	S10 2-0	a13 0-0	M16 1-0	O27 0-1
3 BRIGHTON & H.A.	M29 1-0	D25 3-2		J12 4-0	S15 2-3	S01 0-1	D22 1-5	O06 3-2	N10 2-0	O27 3-1	D29 1-0	S05 2-1	a27 2-1	J19 0-3	F02 3-0	M16 2-1	M30 2-1	F23 2-1	S29 2-2	M02 1-2	m01 2-1	a13 1-1
4 BRISTOL R	M09 1-2	O20 2-0	a06 3-0		a20 3-0	m04 1-1	D26 1-1	N17 1-1	F02 5-3	J19 2-4	F16 1-1	N03 3-0	M29 0-3	D15 1-2	D01 2-0	S15 0-1	S29 1-1	M23 4-1	D29 1-4	S01 2-1	S12 4-1	F23 1-1
5 CHARLTON A	F23 6-2	a22 1-0	J26 3-0	M14 1-2		D26 3-1	M02 1-3	S22 3-1	a17 0-0	N10 1-1	M29 4-1	O06 2-2	S01 2-2	D29 3-1	S08 1-0	M30 2-1	a13 2-2	F09 3-2	O27 4-1	M16 2-0	D22 5-0	a27 2-0
6 COVENTRY C	F09 1-2	O06 1-0	J05 3-0	D22 2-0	D25 0-1		M16 1-3	S08 1-1	J12 1-2	D08 2-0	F23 1-1	S22 6-1	O27 3-1	a01 0-2	A25 3-0	a13 1-4	a27 0-0	J26 1-1	N10 4-1	M30 2-1	M02 1-1	A27 1-1
7 CRYSTAL P	a06 1-3	N17 1-0	m04 1-0	D26 5-2	O20 0-2	N03 0-3		D15 1-0	S05 2-1	m01 3-0	M23 3-0	D01 2-0	S08 1-1	M09 1-0	M06 2-1	O13 1-4	M29 1-4	a20 3-2	F02 6-1	S29 2-0	J05 1-1	A25 3-0
8 EXETER C	D26 6-3	D29 2-3	a17 4-1	M30 2-2	F02 2-5	J19 2-3	a27 1-2		M16 1-4	M02 4-2	S01 1-1	a01 5-0	M20 6-1	S15 2-0	S29 3-1	O27 1-2	N10 1-1	S05 1-2	D22 1-1	O13 1-3	a13 1-1	a10 2-2
9 FULHAM	J19 3-0	m04 1-0	M23 3-1	S22 6-1	a06 2-5	a20 2-2	S10 2-2	N03 0-0		D29 4-3	D15 4-3	O20 1-0	F23 2-0	D01 2-1	N17 2-1	S01 5-2	J26 5-0	M09 2-4	M29 2-0	D25 2-1	O06 5-1	F09 2-3
10 GILLINGHAM	D15 2-2	J26 1-2	M09 1-1	S08 1-0	M23 1-0	a06 1-1	O06 0-1	O20 1-3	A25 2-2		D01 1-0	m04 1-0	F09 0-4	N17 2-1	N03 4-0	D26 2-0	J05 0-0	M29 0-2	F23 0-0	A29 1-1	S22 1-4	a24 0-0
11 LUTON T	S22 2-1	F09 2-1	A25 1-0	O06 4-2	a01 3-0	O13 1-1	N10 5-3	J05 4-0	a27 1-3	a13 8-0		J26 2-0	M16 5-2	S03 4-0	D25 2-1	M11 2-2	D22 3-2	S08 4-2	M30 5-3	a29 1-2	O27 3-1	M02 2-2
12 MERTHYR T	S01 1-0	J19 2-2	A27 1-0	M16 4-0	F16 2-3	F02 2-2	a13 2-2	a02 2-1	M02 4-1	D22 2-3	S15 3-4		J12 2-1	S29 2-2	O13 2-1	D29 2-2	O27 1-2	D25 2-1	a15 0-0	a27 3-0	M30 1-0	N10 2-1
13 NEWPORT CO	N17 0-2	M23 1-1	D15 1-2	a01 2-0	J05 2-0	M09 2-1	J19 1-3	a20 1-1	O13 3-3	S29 5-0	N03 1-2	a06 6-1		O20 0-3	m04 2-2	a18 1-0	S06 0-0	D01 2-2	S15 0-1	F02 4-1	A25 3-1	D25 0-2
14 NORTHAMPTON T	O06 2-0	F23 1-1	S08 1-1	a27 3-1	A25 4-1	a02 3-3	O27 8-1	J26 4-0	a13 3-3	M30 1-0	A30 2-2	F09 4-1	M02 7-0		J05 2-0	S17 3-0	D08 4-2	S22 2-3	M16 1-1	N10 6-1	D26 4-2	D22 3-0
15 NORWICH C	A27 5-1	a01 2-4	S22 3-1	a13 2-1	J19 0-1	D29 3-0	S15 0-1	F09 5-0	M30 2-2	M16 1-2	D26 3-0	F23 3-1	D22 3-1	S01 1-1		N10 0-3	a22 3-1	O06 2-5	M02 1-1	O27 3-0	a27 2-1	m02 5-2
16 PLYMOUTH A	m04 2-0	D15 4-0	N03 1-0	m01 2-0	N17 2-2	D01 3-0	F23 1-1	M09 0-0	J05 4-2	D25 3-0	a20 2-0	A25 4-0	O06 5-2	a06 1-1	M23 4-0		S08 1-2	O20 1-1	A29 3-0	M29 4-0	F09 2-2	S22 2-0
17 Q.P.R.	O20 0-0	F02 2-2	N17 3-2	F09 0-3	D01 2-2	D15 3-1	a01 1-1	M23 1-0	S15 2-1	S01 1-0	m04 1-1	M09 8-0	A30 0-0	a20 4-1	a06 3-0	J19 2-0		N03 3-1	D25 4-2	D29 5-1	F23 2-2	O06 3-2
18 SOUTHEND U	D29 4-4	S01 1-1	O13 1-1	N10 1-0	S29 1-3	S15 0-0	a10 3-0	A27 1-0	O27 0-1	a01 2-0	J19 5-0	D26 5-1	a13 4-2	F02 2-2	F16 5-3	M02 1-1	M16 0-3		a27 1-1	D22 3-0	F20 3-1	M30 1-3
19 SWINDON T	D01 3-3	a06 3-1	F09 2-2	A25 2-1	M09 1-1	M23 1-2	S22 3-2	m04 2-0	a01 1-2	O13 2-1	N17 4-2	a20 2-1	m01 5-2	N03 0-1	O20 1-2	S05 0-0	D26 2-1	D15 3-1		a24 1-1	S08 5-1	J05 5-0
20 TORQUAY U	a20 4-1	D01 4-1	O20 5-1	J05 0-1	N03 3-1	N17 0-2	F09 1-2	F23 1-3	D26 1-1	S05 2-1	a06 2-2	D15 6-2	S22 4-1	M23 0-1	M09 0-3	a01 2-2	A25 3-4	m04 2-1	O06 2-4		J26 3-2	S08 1-0
21 WALSALL	M23 2-1	N03 2-0	a20 1-2	A27 1-3	m04 0-2	O20 0-0	S01 3-1	D01 7-2	F16 2-2	F02 4-0	M09 0-0	N17 1-1	D29 3-1	D25 4-3	D15 3-3	S29 1-1	O13 3-1	a06 4-1	J19 1-1	S15 1-0		a01 4-0
22 WATFORD	N03 0-3	M09 2-0	D01 2-1	O13 1-0	D15 3-1	S05 4-2	D29 3-3	a06 3-0	S29 2-6	S15 1-0	O20 3-2	M23 4-0	D26 3-0	m04 1-1	a20 2-2	F02 6-3	F16 4-1	N17 4-1	S01 3-2	J19 0-2	M29 4-1	

LEAGUE TABLES

DIVISION 1

	P	W	D	L	F	A	W	D	L	F	A	Pts
Sheffield W	42	18	3	0	55	16	3	7	11	31	46	52
Leicester C	42	16	5	0	67	22	5	4	12	29	45	51
Aston Villa	42	16	2	3	62	30	7	2	12	36	51	50
Sunderland	42	16	2	3	67	30	4	5	12	26	45	47
Liverpool	42	11	4	6	53	28	6	8	7	37	36	46
Derby Co	42	12	5	4	56	24	6	5	10	30	47	46
Blackburn R	42	11	6	4	42	26	6	5	10	30	37	45
Manchester C	42	12	3	6	63	40	6	6	9	32	46	45
Arsenal	42	11	6	4	43	25	5	7	9	34	47	45
Newcastle U	42	15	2	4	48	29	4	4	13	22	43	44
Sheffield U	42	12	5	4	57	30	3	6	12	29	55	41
Manchester U	42	8	8	5	32	23	6	5	10	34	53	41
Leeds U	42	11	5	5	42	28	5	4	12	29	56	41
Bolton W	42	10	6	5	44	25	4	6	11	29	55	40
Birmingham	42	8	7	6	37	32	7	3	11	31	45	40
Huddersfield T	42	9	6	6	45	23	5	5	11	25	38	39
West Ham U	42	11	6	4	55	31	4	3	14	31	65	39
Everton	42	11	2	8	38	31	6	2	13	25	44	38
Burnley	42	12	5	4	55	32	3	3	15	26	71	38
Portsmouth	42	13	2	6	43	26	2	4	15	13	54	36
Bury	42	9	5	7	38	35	3	2	16	24	64	31
Cardiff C	42	7	7	7	34	26	1	6	14	9	33	29

DIVISION 2

	P	W	D	L	F	A	W	D	L	F	A	Pts
Middlesbrough	42	14	4	3	54	22	8	7	6	38	35	55
Grimsby T	42	16	2	3	49	24	8	3	10	33	37	53
Bradford	42	18	2	1	62	22	4	2	15	26	48	48
Southampton	42	12	6	3	48	22	5	8	8	26	38	48
Notts Co	42	13	4	4	51	24	6	5	10	27	41	47
Stoke C	42	12	7	2	46	16	5	5	11	28	35	46
WBA	42	13	4	4	50	25	6	4	11	30	54	46
Blackpool	42	13	4	4	49	18	6	3	12	43	58	45
Chelsea	42	10	6	5	40	30	7	4	10	24	35	44
Tottenham H	42	16	3	2	50	26	1	6	14	25	55	43
Nottingham F	42	8	6	7	34	33	7	6	8	37	37	42
Hull C	42	8	8	5	38	24	5	6	10	20	39	40
Preston NE	42	12	6	3	58	27	3	3	15	20	52	39
Millwall	42	10	4	7	43	35	6	3	12	28	51	39
Reading	42	12	3	6	48	30	3	6	12	15	56	39
Barnsley	42	12	4	5	51	28	4	2	15	18	38	38
Wolves	42	9	6	6	41	31	6	1	14	36	50	37
Oldham A	42	15	2	4	37	24	1	3	17	17	51	37
Swansea T	42	12	3	6	46	26	1	7	13	16	49	36
Bristol C	42	11	6	4	37	25	2	4	15	21	47	36
Port Vale	42	14	1	6	53	25	1	3	17	18	61	34
Clapton O	42	10	4	7	29	25	2	4	15	16	47	32

DIVISION 3 North

	P	W	D	L	F	A	W	D	L	F	A	Pts
Bradford C	42	17	2	2	82	18	10	7	4	46	25	63
Stockport Co	42	19	2	0	77	23	9	4	8	34	35	62
Wrexham	42	17	2	2	59	25	4	8	9	32	44	52
Wigan B	42	16	4	1	55	16	5	5	11	27	33	51
Doncaster R	42	14	3	4	39	20	6	7	8	37	46	50
Lincoln C	42	15	3	3	58	18	6	3	12	33	49	48
Tranmere R	42	15	3	3	55	21	7	0	14	24	56	47
Carlisle U	42	15	3	3	61	27	4	5	12	25	50	46
Crewe A	42	11	6	4	47	23	7	2	12	33	45	44
South Shields	42	13	5	3	57	24	5	3	13	26	50	44
Chesterfield	42	13	2	6	46	28	5	3	13	25	49	41
Southport C	42	13	5	3	52	27	3	3	15	23	58	40
Halifax T	42	11	7	3	42	24	2	6	13	21	38	39
New Brighton	42	11	3	7	40	28	4	6	11	24	43	39
Nelson	42	14	1	6	48	28	3	4	14	29	62	39
Rotherham U	42	12	5	4	44	23	3	4	14	16	54	30
Rochdale	42	12	4	5	55	34	1	6	14	24	62	36
Accrington S	42	11	5	5	42	22	2	3	16	26	60	34
Darlington	42	12	6	3	47	26	1	1	19	17	62	33
Barrow	42	7	6	8	42	37	3	2	16	22	56	28
Hartlepools U	42	9	4	8	35	38	1	2	18	24	74	26
Ashington	42	6	5	10	31	52	2	2	17	14	63	23

DIVISION 3 South

	P	W	D	L	F	A	W	D	L	F	A	Pts
Charlton A	42	14	5	2	51	22	9	3	9	35	38	54
Crystal P	42	14	2	5	40	25	9	6	6	41	42	54
Northampton T	42	14	6	1	68	23	6	6	9	28	34	52
Plymouth A	42	14	6	1	51	13	6	6	9	32	38	52
Fulham	42	14	3	4	60	31	7	7	7	41	40	52
QPR	42	13	7	1	50	22	6	7	8	32	39	52
Luton T	42	16	3	2	64	28	3	8	10	25	45	49
Watford	42	15	3	3	55	31	4	7	10	24	43	48
Bournemouth	42	14	4	3	54	31	5	5	11	30	46	47
Swindon T	42	12	5	4	48	27	3	8	10	27	45	43
Coventry C	42	9	6	6	35	23	5	8	8	27	34	42
Southend U	42	10	7	4	44	27	5	4	12	36	48	41
Brentford	42	11	4	6	34	21	3	6	12	22	39	38
Walsall	42	11	7	3	47	25	2	5	14	26	54	38
Brighton & HA	42	14	2	5	39	28	2	4	15	19	48	38
Newport Co	42	8	6	7	37	28	5	3	13	32	58	35
Norwich C	42	12	3	6	49	29	2	3	16	20	52	34
Torquay U	42	10	3	8	46	36	4	3	14	20	48	34
Bristol R	42	9	6	6	39	28	4	1	16	21	51	33
Merthyr T	42	11	6	4	42	28	0	2	19	13	75	30
Exeter C	42	7	6	8	49	40	2	5	14	18	48	29
Gillingham	42	7	8	6	22	24	3	1	17	21	59	29

Football League Records

Top scorers: Div 1, V.Watson (West Ham United) 41 goals; Div 2, J.Hampson (Blackpool) 45 goals; Div 3(N), F.Newton (Stockport County) 36 goals; Div 3(S), G.Goddard (Queen's Park Rangers) 37 goals. Ashington failed to gain re-election, York City elected in their place.

Derby County centre-forward Harry Bedford's 30 goals helped the Rams into runners-up spot in 1929-30. His tally equalled the club record set by Alf Bentley in 1909-10.

DIVISION 1

	ARSENAL	ASTON VILLA	BIRMINGHAM	BLACKBURN R	BOLTON W	BURNLEY	DERBY CO	EVERTON	GRIMSBY T	HUDDERSFIELD T	LEEDS U	LEICESTER C	LIVERPOOL	MANCHESTER C	MANCHESTER U	MIDDLESBROUGH	NEWCASTLE U	PORTSMOUTH	SHEFFIELD U	SHEFFIELD W	SUNDERLAND	WEST HAM U
1 ARSENAL		m03 2-4	M15 1-0	M29 4-0	S28 1-2	S14 6-1	O12 1-1	F08 4-0	O19 4-1	D14 2-0	A31 4-0	a18 1-1	a02 0-1	S11 3-2	M12 4-2	N27 1-2	N30 0-1	D26 1-2	a12 8-1	J04 2-3	a28 0-1	N02 0-1
2 ASTON VILLA	S25 5-2		A31 2-1	N30 3-0	F08 2-0	F05 1-2	S09 2-2	O12 5-2	a02 4-1	M15 5-3	J04 3-4	O19 3-0	N16 2-3	D25 0-2	N02 1-0	M29 4-2	a12 2-0	a21 0-1	D14 5-1	S14 1-3	S28 2-1	a26 2-3
3 BIRMINGHAM	N09 2-3	D28 1-1		F01 1-2	M22 3-1	M08 2-0	a05 2-4	N23 0-0	a22 0-2	S07 4-1	F22 1-0	m03 3-0	F15 1-0	D07 3-0	D26 0-1	O05 1-1	S21 5-1	a19 1-0	J18 2-1	O26 1-0	D21 3-1	S04 4-2
4 BLACKBURN R	N23 1-1	a05 2-0	S28 7-5		F22 3-1	N09 8-3	M08 0-3	O26 3-1	S14 4-1	F08 5-2	D07 2-1	J27 3-1	m03 1-0	D21 1-3	J04 5-4	J01 7-0	S16 4-2	M22 1-0	O12 0-1	a19 0-1	D25 5-3	A31 3-3
5 BOLTON W	F01 0-0	O05 3-0	N16 0-0	O19 2-1		D25 1-1	S07 1-2	D28 5-0	N30 2-3	J01 7-1	F15 4-2	M29 1-0	M15 0-2	J18 1-2	M01 4-1	S18 2-2	a09 1-1	S21 2-1	N02 2-1	S25 1-3	a18 3-0	D14 4-1
6 BURNLEY	J18 2-2	S21 1-4	N02 3-1	M15 3-2	D26 2-2		m03 6-2	S02 1-1	N16 3-1	a01 1-3	F01 0-3	F15 1-1	a12 4-1	D28 4-2	M29 4-0	D14 4-1	M11 0-3	S07 4-0	O19 5-0	O05 2-4	S10 2-0	N30 1-1
7 DERBY CO	F19 4-1	S04 4-0	N30 3-1	N02 4-3	J04 2-1	S25 1-3		S14 2-1	D14 5-4	M29 2-2	D26 3-0	a12 2-2	O19 2-2	F01 4-2	M15 1-1	M01 3-1	a26 3-1	O05 3-2	N16 2-1	a21 4-1	A31 3-0	F05 4-3
8 EVERTON	O05 1-1	M05 3-4	M29 2-4	M01 2-2	A31 3-3	a18 3-0	J18 4-0		a12 2-4	N16 0-2	S11 1-1	N30 4-5	J04 3-3	S21 2-3	D14 0-0	O19 3-2	N02 5-2	F01 1-1	a26 3-2	D25 1-4	m03 4-1	M15 1-2
9 GRIMSBY T	F22 1-1	O26 0-2	a18 2-1	J18 5-3	a05 1-1	M22 4-0	a19 2-1	D07 0-3		S24 4-2	M08 1-2	D25 1-4	F01 3-2	N09 2-2	F15 2-2	S21 0-3	S07 4-0	S04 1-1	D28 4-1	F05 0-5	N23 0-1	O05 2-2
10 HUDDERSFIELD T	a19 2-2	N09 1-1	J04 1-1	O05 0-0	D21 0-2	O26 3-0	N23 0-1	a28 1-2	m03 0-1		S14 1-0	A31 3-2	S16 3-0	a05 1-1	a22 2-2	M26 1-0	F01 2-0	D07 2-1	S21 2-2	F22 4-1	M08 0-2	D26 3-0
11 LEEDS U	D28 2-0	S07 4-1	O19 1-0	a12 4-2	O12 2-1	S28 3-0	D25 2-1	S16 2-1	N02 6-0	J18 0-1		M01 1-2	M29 1-1	a22 3-2	a26 3-1	N30 1-2	D14 5-2	S23 1-0	M15 2-2	a09 3-0	F08 5-0	N16 1-3
12 LEICESTER C	a21 6-6	F22 4-3	O17 2-1	S21 1-1	N23 5-2	D21 4-3	D07 0-0	a05 5-4	D26 1-0	D28 1-2	O26 2-2		O05 2-1	a19 3-1	S02 4-1	F01 4-1	J18 6-1	N09 0-5	S07 3-3	M08 2-1	M22 1-2	F20 1-2
13 LIVERPOOL	D21 1-0	M22 2-0	O12 1-1	O09 1-1	N09 3-0	D07 1-3	F22 2-2	S07 0-3	S28 2-0	S04 3-0	N23 1-0	F08 1-1		O26 1-6	J25 1-0	D28 5-2	a21 0-0	M08 2-0	D26 2-0	a05 1-3	a19 0-6	S14 3-1
14 MANCHESTER C	S04 3-1	D26 1-2	a12 1-4	a26 1-1	S14 2-0	A31 2-2	S28 3-0	F05 1-2	M15 3-1	N30 1-1	a21 4-1	D14 3-2	M01 4-3		F08 0-1	N02 3-1	N16 3-0	F26 5-2	M29 2-1	J01 3-3	J04 2-2	O19 4-3
15 MANCHESTER U	O26 1-0	M08 2-3	D25 0-0	S07 1-0	D07 1-1	N23 1-0	N09 3-2	a19 3-3	O12 2-5	a18 1-0	D21 3-1	S11 2-1	S21 1-2	O05 1-3		J18 0-3	D28 5-0	F22 3-0	m03 1-5	a14 2-2	a05 2-1	F01 4-2
16 MIDDLESBROUGH	a09 1-1	N23 2-3	F08 5-1	a21 2-4	m03 3-1	a19 3-1	O26 4-0	F22 1-2	M05 1-5	O12 1-3	a05 1-1	S28 0-2	A31 5-0	M08 1-0	S14 2-3		D26 2-2	D21 2-0	S04 3-1	D07 4-1	N09 3-0	J04 2-0
17 NEWCASTLE U	a05 1-1	D07 2-2	a02 1-1	S04 5-1	O26 2-3	O12 2-1	D21 2-3	M08 1-0	J04 3-1	S28 5-2	a19 2-1	S14 2-1	a18 3-1	M22 2-2	A31 4-1	D25 3-2		N23 4-1	F08 3-5	N09 1-3	F22 3-0	m03 1-0
18 PORTSMOUTH	D25 0-1	a18 1-2	D14 2-1	N16 4-0	F05 3-0	J04 7-1	F08 3-1	S28 1-4	S11 1-1	a12 0-1	m03 0-0	M15 3-0	N02 3-3	O12 2-2	O19 3-0	a26 1-1	M29 2-0		N30 3-1	A31 0-4	S14 1-1	M12 3-1
19 SHEFFIELD U	D16 4-1	a19 3-3	S14 4-2	M03 5-7	M08 2-3	F22 3-1	M22 2-0	D21 2-0	A31 2-3	F17 0-1	N09 3-2	J04 7-1	D25 4-0	N23 1-2	O07 3-1	S09 1-3	O05 1-0	a05 2-3		S28 2-2	O26 4-2	J01 4-2
20 SHEFFIELD W	S07 0-2	J18 3-0	a28 1-1	D14 4-0	S02 1-0	F08 4-1	a22 6-3	D26 4-0	a26 1-0	O19 3-1	S21 1-2	N02 4-0	N30 2-1	m03 5-1	N16 7-2	a12 1-0	M15 4-2	D28 1-1	F01 1-1		O12 1-1	M29 2-1
21 SUNDERLAND	S21 0-1	F01 4-1	a26 2-0	D26 3-1	a21 4-1	J01 3-3	D28 3-1	O02 2-2	M29 2-0	N02 1-0	O05 1-4	N16 2-1	D14 2-3	S07 5-2	N30 2-4	M15 3-2	O19 1-0	J18 1-1	M01 3-2	a30 2-4		a12 4-2
22 WEST HAM U	M08 3-2	D21 5-2	S16 0-1	D28 2-3	a19 5-3	a05 1-0	S21 2-0	N09 3-1	F08 2-0	D25 2-3	M22 3-0	O12 1-2	J18 4-1	F22 3-0	S28 2-1	S07 5-3	S09 5-1	O26 0-1	a18 1-0	N23 1-1	D07 1-1	

DIVISION 2

	BARNSLEY	BLACKPOOL	BRADFORD	BRADFORD C	BRISTOL C	BURY	CARDIFF C	CHARLTON A	CHELSEA	HULL C	MILLWALL	NOTTINGHAM F	NOTTS CO	OLDHAM A	PRESTON N.E.	READING	SOUTHAMPTON	STOKE C	SWANSEA T	TOTTENHAM H	W.B.A.	WOLVERHAMPTON W
1 BARNSLEY		O05 2-4	F05 1-1	D21 2-1	M08 3-1	F15 2-1	F22 2-2	N23 2-0	J01 1-1	a05 3-0	a21 1-2	D26 1-1	N09 2-2	m03 2-1	O26 0-0	M22 1-0	A31 3-1	D07 3-1	S28 1-0	J04 2-0	S14 2-2	a19 3-1
2 BLACKPOOL	F08 2-1		S28 1-0	a19 3-0	O26 7-1	S02 2-1	O12 3-0	M22 6-0	D25 1-1	N23 1-2	A31 4-3	S09 5-1	M08 1-2	a18 3-0	F22 5-1	N09 4-2	J04 5-1	a05 0-2	D21 3-0	S14 3-2	M05 1-0	D07 3-2
3 BRADFORD	S21 4-4	F01 5-0		S14 0-2	N09 3-1	O05 2-1	O26 2-0	a05 4-0	M12 1-3	D07 4-2	m03 6-0	S04 5-1	M22 3-3	D26 2-2	M08 5-2	N23 5-2	a22 1-1	a19 3-2	F22 3-0	A31 2-1	J04 5-1	D21 0-0
4 BRADFORD C	a26 0-1	D14 1-1	J18 1-2		O12 3-0	a12 2-1	S28 0-1	S30 4-1	N30 0-1	a21 2-1	M15 1-1	M29 1-1	S02 2-0	N16 2-4	F08 1-1	D25 1-0	N02 2-5	D28 3-0	F19 3-3	M01 0-2	O19 2-2	S07 2-2
5 BRISTOL C	N02 2-1	M01 0-1	M15 0-0	F26 1-3		O19 1-2	D25 2-0	J18 1-1	a21 2-1	S21 4-0	a12 1-0	a26 4-1	D28 0-0	D14 0-4	S18 2-2	S07 5-3	N30 3-1	F01 2-6	S11 2-1	M29 1-0	N16 2-1	O05 1-2
6 BURY	O12 2-1	J01 0-1	F08 5-1	D07 2-4	F22 2-0		D21 4-2	N09 2-2	m03 1-0	a23 2-1	J04 5-1	a18 0-0	O26 2-0	A31 0-2	D25 1-2	M08 2-4	S14 4-2	N23 2-0	a19 1-0	J25 2-1	S28 3-2	a05 3-1
7 CARDIFF C	O19 1-0	F15 4-2	M01 2-0	F01 0-1	D26 1-1	a26 5-1		D28 1-0	D14 1-0	S07 0-1	M29 3-1	a12 1-1	S16 3-1	N30 5-0	S02 2-0	a18 2-1	N16 5-2	J18 1-2	O05 0-0	M15 1-0	N02 3-2	S21 0-0
8 CHARLTON A	M29 2-0	N16 1-4	N30 2-0	m03 1-3	S14 3-1	M15 1-2	A31 4-1		N02 1-1	M17 4-0	F08 1-1	M10 5-0	a07 1-0	O19 1-1	J04 1-1	S28 0-0	a26 4-1	S09 4-4	a18 0-2	D14 1-0	a12 0-1	J01 2-0
9 CHELSEA	S11 2-0	D26 4-0	O12 1-2	a05 3-2	a18 2-1	S23 5-3	a19 1-0	M08 1-1		N09 3-0	S14 3-0	A31 2-0	F22 3-1	J04 1-1	D21 5-0	O26 1-0	J25 2-0	M22 3-2	D07 1-0	S28 3-0	F08 2-0	N23 1-1
10 HULL C	N30 2-0	M29 0-3	a12 0-2	a18 0-0	m01 0-1	N16 1-3	J04 2-2	O12 0-2	M15 1-3		O19 3-2	N02 1-2	S28 0-0	M31 1-0	S14 2-0	F08 4-2	S16 2-0	D25 3-0	A31 1-0	a26 2-0	D14 3-2	m03 2-0
11 MILLWALL	a18 2-1	D28 3-1	S16 1-2	N09 2-2	D07 1-1	S07 2-4	N23 2-0	O05 1-1	J18 0-0	F22 0-0		S21 2-2	a19 2-0	F01 2-1	a05 2-0	D21 3-1	O12 1-1	O26 2-1	M22 0-2	S02 2-5	D25 2-1	M08 4-0
12 NOTTINGHAM F	D25 4-0	m03 0-0	O03 1-1	N23 2-1	D21 5-2	a21 1-2	D07 3-1	O26 0-2	D28 0-0	M08 2-1	F05 1-1		S07 1-1	S14 1-2	a19 2-4	F22 5-0	S28 0-5	N09 2-1	a05 1-0	F08 0-0	O12 0-2	M22 5-2
13 NOTTS CO	M15 3-0	N02 0-2	N16 1-1	S09 2-0	A31 3-1	M01 1-3	S25 2-1	S21 4-0	O19 2-2	F01 4-1	D14 1-1	J04 0-0		a26 1-1	a22 0-3	J18 3-0	a12 1-2	O05 3-3	D26 0-0	N30 0-1	M29 2-1	F15 0-3
14 OLDHAM A	S16 3-2	a21 1-2	D25 5-1	M22 6-1	a19 2-2	D28 2-0	a05 4-1	F22 1-0	S07 4-2	O26 3-1	S28 2-2	J18 0-0	D21 2-2		D07 0-2	S21 0-0	F08 3-2	M08 5-0	N23 4-1	O12 2-0	J01 5-0	N09 6-0
15 PRESTON N.E.	M01 3-1	O19 4-6	N02 4-1	O05 2-2	m03 2-2	D26 1-1	S09 2-3	S07 0-3	a26 1-2	J18 1-2	N30 3-1	D14 1-2	a18 3-1	a12 0-3		D28 2-1	M29 1-1	S21 5-1	F15 0-0	N16 4-0	M15 2-2	F01 1-1
16 READING	N16 1-0	M15 1-1	M29 1-0	D26 1-1	J04 1-6	N02 0-1	a21 2-0	F01 3-1	M01 3-1	O05 1-1	a26 0-1	O19 0-1	S14 2-0	F05 1-1	A31 2-0		D14 1-1	F15 0-0	J25 3-1	a12 3-0	N30 2-2	S04 3-1
17 SOUTHAMPTON	D28 4-0	S07 4-2	a21 2-2	M08 2-1	a05 3-0	J18 0-0	M22 1-1	D21 2-0	S21 4-2	S02 2-2	M03 0-0	F01 2-0	D07 2-2	O05 2-0	N23 1-2	a19 4-3		F22 2-1	N09 2-1	D26 1-0	S09 3-2	O26 3-1
18 STOKE C	a12 3-0	N30 0-1	D14 2-1	A31 2-0	S28 6-2	M29 1-0	S14 1-1	S02 2-1	N16 1-1	D26 3-1	M01 1-0	M15 6-0	F08 1-1	N02 0-2	J25 2-3	O12 2-2	O19 4-0		J04 0-1	m03 1-0	a26 0-3	S30 3-0
19 SWANSEA T	F01 0-2	a26 3-0	O19 2-4	S21 5-0	S02 1-1	D14 2-4	F08 1-0	a21 2-0	a12 3-0	D28 2-0	N16 3-1	N30 1-1	D25 3-2	M29 3-0	O12 4-0	S16 0-1	M15 2-2	S07 2-2		N02 0-1	M01 1-0	J18 2-2
20 TOTTENHAM H	S07 2-1	J18 6-1	D28 1-1	O26 1-1	N23 2-1	S21 2-2	N09 1-2	a19 3-0	F01 3-3	D21 2-2	S23 1-1	O05 1-1	a05 2-0	F15 2-1	M22 1-0	D07 0-0	D25 3-2	O09 3-1	M08 3-0		a18 0-2	F22 4-2
21 W.B.A.	J18 4-2	S21 5-1	S07 5-0	F22 4-2	M22 2-0	F01 5-1	M08 0-2	D07 1-1	O05 2-0	a19 7-1	D26 6-1	M19 1-3	N23 4-2	S02 0-3	N09 2-0	a05 1-0	m03 5-1	D21 2-3	O26 6-2	a21 4-3		D28 7-3
22 WOLVERHAMPTON W	D14 3-0	a12 1-2	a26 4-4	J04 6-0	F08 1-0	N30 2-0	a14 4-0	D26 0-4	M29 0-1	S23 4-2	N02 1-1	N16 2-1	O12 5-1	M15 1-1	S28 4-0	S09 2-1	M01 2-0	a21 2-1	S14 4-1	O19 3-0	A31 2-4	

Sheffield Wednesday's Jack Allen was the Owls' leading scorer in their First Division title wins of 1928-9 and 1929-30. He was the scorer of Newcastle's controversial goal in the famous 'over the line' Cup Final of 1932.

Season 1929-30

DIVISION 3 NORTH

	ACCRINGTON S	BARROW	CARLISLE U	CHESTERFIELD	CREWE A	DARLINGTON	DONCASTER R	HALIFAX T	HARTLEPOOLS U	LINCOLN C	NELSON	NEW BRIGHTON	PORT VALE	ROCHDALE	ROTHERHAM U	SOUTHPORT	SOUTH SHIELDS	STOCKPORT CO	TRANMERE R	WIGAN B	WREXHAM	YORK C
1 ACCRINGTON S		N02 3-1	J01 7-2	S07 3-0	a12 0-3	D26 3-1	F24 3-3	F01 7-1	S09 3-0	J18 0-3	S24 3-0	N16 5-0	M15 0-2	F15 6-2	O05 2-0	a26 1-1	a21 1-2	M29 0-1	S21 3-3	O19 3-1	M01 1-3	M05 1-1
2 BARROW	M08 3-1		O05 0-2	a05 0-1	a21 1-0	N09 0-1	N23 1-0	D21 0-4	M22 3-0	D07 2-1	F15 0-2	A31 3-0	J04 1-1	F22 2-0	S14 5-1	m03 0-2	O26 1-3	S09 1-4	a19 1-1	F01 4-1	S21 3-3	D25 0-0
3 CARLISLE U	a18 2-1	F08 7-1		N09 6-0	A31 2-0	F22 1-4	M08 1-1	a05 2-0	O26 5-2	M22 2-4	J23 2-2	J25 2-2	S28 1-4	a19 2-0	D07 3-1	S12 4-0	D21 4-1	S14 1-5	N23 4-3	m03 5-0	O12 5-1	J04 2-2
4 CHESTERFIELD	J04 4-2	M12 2-1	M15 3-1		O19 5-1	S14 4-1	S28 2-1	a18 2-0	J25 2-0	F15 2-1	N02 3-0	a07 1-0	a12 1-1	J01 2-0	D26 2-1	M01 2-0	A31 1-2	a26 1-3	S23 1-0	N16 5-0	M29 5-0	F08 3-0
5 CREWE A	D07 2-1	a18 0-0	D28 1-2	F22 2-1		a19 1-2	S21 4-0	N09 4-1	D21 5-2	O26 1-1	S07 4-0	O12 2-3	m03 0-2	N23 6-1	M22 6-1	J18 5-4	a05 2-2	F08 1-1	M08 3-1	S02 2-1	D25 2-0	S28 2-2
6 DARLINGTON	D25 2-4	M15 4-0	O19 3-0	J18 1-4	a28 3-0		S07 6-2	O05 3-2	D28 0-0	S21 1-1	S04 6-1	M29 1-2	N16 0-1	a22 3-0	F15 8-1	D14 2-1	J01 8-3	F19 1-2	F01 7-2	M01 2-0	N02 5-1	a12 5-2
7 DONCASTER R	A31 3-1	M29 4-0	N02 1-4	F01 2-1	a10 2-1	J04 3-1		S23 1-0	S14 0-0	O05 0-0	M01 3-0	a12 1-1	m01 0-2	D26 3-1	a18 2-0	O19 3-1	S02 1-0	M20 1-1	F15 1-1	M15 4-2	N16 4-2	a26 0-3
8 HALIFAX T	S28 1-1	J11 0-1	F20 1-0	a21 3-2	M15 1-3	F08 3-1	S16 1-0		O12 0-0	D25 1-1	M29 1-1	O19 4-0	A31 1-2	S14 2-3	J04 1-1	N16 1-1	J25 0-2	M01 0-3	S09 0-1	a12 2-1	D19 2-0	N02 2-2
9 HARTLEPOOLS U	S02 2-2	N16 2-0	M01 1-0	S21 0-0	a26 5-1	A31 2-5	J18 3-0	F15 3-0		F01 4-0	O19 1-2	J11 1-1	M29 2-0	a21 2-8	J01 5-1	J04 1-1	D25 2-1	a12 0-1	O05 2-0	N02 4-0	M15 5-0	a02 3-1
10 LINCOLN C	S14 3-3	a12 3-0	N16 4-1	O12 2-1	M01 2-2	J25 2-2	F08 3-1	D26 0-1	S28 2-2		M15 4-1	a26 5-3	S16 3-2	A31 0-0	S09 1-1	N02 1-1	J04 2-2	a23 1-0	a21 8-0	M29 2-0	F19 3-0	O19 3-0
11 NELSON	D21 2-1	O12 2-0	D25 2-2	M08 0-2	J04 1-1	S11 0-1	O26 4-1	N23 1-0	F22 3-2	N09 0-0		S28 2-1	F08 2-3	J14 1-0	a05 0-1	A31 2-2	a19 0-1	J25 1-2	M22 0-1	a18 1-3	O01 4-0	S14 3-1
12 NEW BRIGHTON	M22 5-0	D28 5-0	S21 2-1	a19 1-1	F15 3-1	N23 1-3	D07 1-0	F22 4-0	a05 0-0	D21 1-4	F01 2-1		S02 0-1	M08 2-0	O26 2-2	O05 1-3	N09 4-1	a18 3-2	D26 3-0	J18 5-0	S07 2-1	J01 1-1
13 PORT VALE	N09 5-2	S07 5-0	F01 4-0	D07 4-1	S23 2-0	M22 0-2	a05 2-1	D28 3-0	N23 2-1	a19 5-2	O05 3-1	S09 5-1		O26 3-3	F22 7-1	F15 1-0	M08 3-0	D25 1-2	D21 1-0	S21 4-0	J18 3-0	a18 1-1
14 ROCHDALE	O12 4-0	O19 6-1	a29 2-0	S03 2-1	M29 3-1	S17 4-1	D25 2-4	J18 0-3	a18 1-1	a08 3-4	a12 4-1	N02 5-0	M01 0-0		S21 1-2	J11 2-2	F08 2-0	M15 3-1	S07 2-1	D14 2-1	F01 5-4	m03 4-2
15 ROTHERHAM U	F08 2-4	J18 7-0	a12 4-1	D25 1-1	N16 2-1	O12 1-4	a21 1-0	S07 2-0	m03 0-4	S02 1-0	M24 1-2	M01 2-2	O19 2-2	J25 0-4		M29 6-3	S28 0-1	N02 2-2	D28 5-0	F24 4-1	a26 1-3	M15 2-5
16 SOUTHPORT	a19 2-0	J01 0-2	S03 4-3	O26 5-1	S14 0-3	D21 3-0	F22 1-1	M22 4-0	S07 1-1	M08 3-2	D28 0-0	F08 2-1	O12 1-2	a05 2-3	N23 7-1		D07 2-1	S28 1-2	N09 4-4	D25 1-1	a18 5-3	J26 1-0
17 SOUTH SHIELDS	m03 2-2	M01 2-0	a26 5-2	D28 3-1	J11 1-0	a18 3-3	S11 2-1	S21 1-0	D26 3-5	S07 3-1	D14 2-1	M15 1-2	N02 0-0	O05 2-2	F01 5-0	a12 4-0		N16 2-3	S14 1-5	F15 2-2	O19 1-1	M29 4-1
18 STOCKPORT CO	N23 1-0	S02 5-0	J18 7-1	D21 1-0	O05 2-3	a05 4-0	a19 3-0	O26 6-0	M03 5-1	J01 1-1	S21 6-1	m03 2-0	D26 4-2	N09 4-2	M08 6-1	F01 2-2	M22 2-0		F22 3-1	S07 1-1	D28 0-1	F15 2-3
19 TRANMERE R	J25 2-2	F20 5-2	M29 3-0	a22 1-2	N02 1-2	S28 3-0	O12 2-1	S02 3-3	F08 7-1	a18 0-1	N16 2-3	D25 3-1	a26 1-5	J04 2-2	A31 5-4	M15 3-1	J18 3-0	O19 2-0		J11 3-0	a12 2-1	M01 4-4
20 WIGAN B	F22 2-1	S28 2-0	S25 8-0	M22 2-1	J01 2-2	O26 3-2	N09 3-2	D07 2-1	M08 1-3	N23 4-1	a21 2-0	S14 5-0	J25 0-3	D21 3-1	a19 1-1	D26 1-1	O12 1-1	J04 0-1	a05 0-2		F08 2-1	A31 0-2
21 WREXHAM	O26 0-1	M26 3-0	F15 3-3	N23 1-1	D26 1-0	M10 2-2	M22 0-2	a19 2-1	N09 3-5	a05 3-1	m03 5-1	J04 2-1	S14 0-2	S28 8-0	D21 1-0	a21 1-2	F22 1-3	A31 1-1	D07 2-0	O05 2-1		S11 1-1
22 YORK C	a05 2-0	D26 3-1	S07 2-2	O05 1-1	F01 4-2	D07 1-1	D21 2-2	M08 3-0	a19 4-1	F22 1-0	J18 1-0	S18 3-0	a21 0-2	M22 6-0	N09 3-0	S21 0-4	N23 2-2	O12 1-2	O20 0-0	D28 4-0	S04 0-0	

DIVISION 3 SOUTH

	BOURNEMOUTH	BRENTFORD	BRIGHTON & HA	BRISTOL R	CLAPTON O	COVENTRY C	CRYSTAL P	EXETER C	FULHAM	GILLINGHAM	LUTON T	MERTHYR T	NEWPORT CO	NORTHAMPTON T	NORWICH C	PLYMOUTH A	Q.P.R.	SOUTHEND U	SWINDON T	TORQUAY U	WALSALL	WATFORD
1 BOURNEMOUTH		M26 1-2	M12 1-1	a12 3-1	a26 5-1	F01 1-0	S18 2-1	S07 3-0	S11 5-0	D26 1-2	S21 5-1	M15 4-2	M01 1-1	F26 3-1	a21 2-3	N16 1-1	O12 0-0	J18 0-0	M29 1-3	N02 4-1	F08 1-1	O19 3-2
2 BRENTFORD	a19 1-0		D26 5-2	S25 2-1	S04 3-1	O12 3-1	M08 2-0	N23 2-0	F22 5-1	N09 2-1	D07 2-0	S14 6-0	S28 1-0	M22 2-0	O26 3-0	J04 3-0	a21 3-0	a05 2-1	A31 3-2	J25 5-0	D21 6-2	F08 5-0
3 BRIGHTON & H.A.	a05 4-3	D26 2-0		D28 1-0	S25 1-0	a18 1-1	F22 1-2	N09 1-1	D21 5-0	O26 2-0	N23 4-1	S28 4-1	O12 3-2	M08 2-1	S07 6-3	a02 0-1	a19 2-3	M22 1-0	S14 3-0	F08 5-0	D07 4-0	S04 2-1
4 BRISTOL R	a09 2-1	m03 4-1	A31 1-0		a18 0-0	S02 1-3	O26 2-3	M22 1-0	D26 4-1	M08 3-0	a05 2-2	J25 2-2	F08 2-3	N09 2-3	F22 0-1	S14 2-3	D21 4-1	N23 4-2	J04 3-2	S28 2-0	a19 3-1	O12 1-2
5 CLAPTON O	D21 0-0	S16 1-1	m03 4-1	a21 3-0		F08 3-1	N09 2-1	a05 3-0	O26 2-4	M22 2-0	a19 6-1	J04 1-0	M31 3-1	N23 0-0	M08 0-0	A31 0-2	F22 2-4	D07 1-1	D25 2-1	S14 1-1	O12 1-1	S28 1-1
6 COVENTRY C	S28 0-2	F15 2-1	a22 0-2	S09 1-0	O05 5-2		M22 1-0	D07 3-3	M08 3-1	N23 5-0	D21 5-1	A31 2-2	S14 2-0	a05 2-2	N09 3-1	D25 1-0	O26 2-3	a19 5-1	m03 1-2	J04 4-1	F22 4-0	J25 3-1
7 CRYSTAL P	m03 1-1	N02 2-1	O19 2-2	M01 3-0	M15 3-0	N16 4-3		F15 1-1	J04 4-3	F01 5-1	a21 4-1	D14 6-1	S25 1-0	O05 1-3	S14 3-2	a26 3-0	A31 1-1	S11 1-2	N30 1-0	a12 4-2	D26 5-1	M29 1-1
8 EXETER C	J04 1-2	M29 0-0	M15 1-4	N16 5-2	F05 4-0	a12 1-1	O12 6-1		S28 2-1	S04 3-0	A31 2-2	O19 1-1	a26 0-4	a21 6-4	F08 3-0	M01 1-1	J25 0-2	D26 3-1	N02 5-1	S18 0-0	S14 0-2	F19 1-0
9 FULHAM	S02 3-3	O19 2-0	a26 5-1	D25 6-2	M01 2-2	N02 2-0	S07 1-2	F01 2-2		J18 2-1	F15 1-1	F03 5-4	N16 2-1	S21 1-0	D28 3-3	a12 1-3	m03 0-2	O05 2-2	J01 4-1	M29 1-0	a21 3-2	M15 6-1
10 GILLINGHAM	D25 1-5	M15 1-3	M01 2-2	N02 3-3	N16 2-0	M29 0-3	S28 1-1	S11 2-0	S14 0-1		m03 2-0	a26 6-0	a12 5-0	F15 5-2	J25 1-2	F08 0-0	J04 3-1	a18 1-0	O19 0-0	D14 0-2	A31 2-1	J11 1-2
11 LUTON T	J25 1-0	a12 2-1	M29 1-0	M24 3-0	M10 1-2	a26 1-1	a18 2-2	D28 0-4	O12 4-1	S16 2-0		N02 4-0	O19 4-2	D25 1-0	S02 1-1	M15 5-2	F08 2-1	S07 0-3	N16 1-1	M01 3-1	S28 2-3	J18 2-0
12 MERTHYR T	N09 0-1	J18 2-3	F01 2-8	S21 1-1	S07 0-1	a14 2-2	a19 5-2	F22 0-2	a05 3-4	D21 1-1	M08 3-1		m03 5-1	S02 1-0	D07 1-5	F15 0-3	M03 1-4	O26 2-2	F08 3-3	a22 3-0	M22 2-3	D26 2-2
13 NEWPORT CO	O26 1-1	F01 1-3	M03 2-2	O05 2-2	S21 0-0	J18 4-2	a05 0-0	D21 4-1	M22 1-1	D07 5-1	F22 0-0	a10 10-0		a19 2-1	N23 4-4	a21 0-2	N09 4-5	J25 0-0	S05 2-1	D25 2-1	M08 3-2	S07 1-0
14 NORTHAMPTON T	A31 2-0	N16 1-1	N02 1-3	M15 6-1	M29 3-0	a07 2-2	F08 2-0	a22 2-2	M13 3-1	O12 3-1	D26 4-1	S09 2-0	D31 2-0		S28 4-0	O19 1-1	S14 2-1	m03 5-1	M01 3-3	a26 2-2	J04 1-0	a12 2-0
15 NORWICH C	a22 1-0	M01 2-2	J04 2-0	O19 4-2	N02 1-0	M15 10-2	J18 2-2	O05 3-1	A31 0-4	S21 2-0	S09 1-1	a12 5-1	M29 4-1	F01 4-3		a28 1-2	D25 3-0	F15 1-1	a26 1-5	J11 2-0	S16 3-0	N16 3-1
16 PLYMOUTH A	M22 2-1	S07 1-1	S21 1-1	J18 3-0	D28 3-0	D26 3-0	D21 6-1	O26 4-1	D07 3-1	O05 3-0	N09 6-1	O12 2-1	a18 3-1	F22 1-0	a19 4-1		a05 4-0	M08 1-0	M26 5-0	S11 5-0	N23 1-1	m03 2-1
17 Q.P.R	F15 3-1	a18 2-1	M27 3-1	a26 2-1	O19 1-1	M01 3-1	D28 4-1	S21 2-0	S16 0-0	S07 2-1	O05 1-0	M29 2-0	M15 4-1	J18 0-2	D26 3-2	M13 1-2		F01 2-5	a12 8-3	N16 1-1	S05 2-2	N02 0-0
18 SOUTHEND U	S14 4-1	J11 2-0	N16 0-0	M29 6-0	a12 4-1	a30 1-2	S02 3-2	D25 1-0	F08 1-2	a21 0-0	J04 1-1	M01 6-0	A31 2-1	S16 1-2	O12 1-1	N02 1-1	S28 1-0		M15 3-1	O19 1-1	F19 1-0	a26 1-3
19 SWINDON T	N23 1-1	D28 0-2	J18 0-1	S07 2-2	D26 0-0	S16 1-1	S21 3-1	M08 1-0	a19 1-1	F22 3-0	M22 1-1	O05 6-3	S09 5-1	O26 2-0	D21 2-1	S28 1-2	D07 2-2	N09 5-1		O12 2-1	a05 3-1	a18 1-3
20 TORQUAY U	M08 7-0	S21 2-1	O05 5-2	a02 2-1	J18 0-5	S07 1-3	D07 2-2	m03 2-1	N23 2-4	a19 1-1	O26 2-2	a21 4-0	D28 3-2	D21 0-1	a05 2-2	S04 3-4	M22 1-3	F22 1-1	F15 1-1		N09 5-2	D28 4-0
21 WALSALL	O05 2-2	a26 1-2	a12 2-0	a30 0-0	F15 0-1	O19 3-2	D25 0-0	J18 5-2	a22 2-2	D28 1-2	F01 1-0	N16 6-0	N02 2-1	S07 1-2	m03 1-0	M29 1-3	S09 4-0	S21 1-3	S23 4-0	a09 7-0		M01 1-2
22 WATFORD	F22 0-0	O05 1-2	S18 3-0	F15 4-3	F01 3-0	S21 1-3	N23 1-1	a19 2-1	N09 0-0	a05 4-1	S14 0-4	D26 2-3	J04 2-3	D07 1-2	M22 2-1	S25 0-2	M08 1-1	D21 2-1	a21 4-1	A31 2-0	O26 2-1	

LEAGUE TABLES

DIVISION 1

	P	W	D	L	F	A	W	D	L	F	A	Pts
Sheffield W	42	15	4	2	56	20	11	4	6	49	37	60
Derby Co	42	16	4	1	61	32	5	4	12	29	50	50
Manchester C	42	12	5	4	51	33	7	4	10	40	48	47
Aston Villa	42	13	1	7	54	33	8	4	9	38	50	47
Leeds U	42	15	2	4	52	22	5	4	12	27	41	46
Blackburn R	42	15	2	4	65	36	4	5	12	34	57	45
West Ham U	42	14	2	5	51	26	5	3	13	35	53	43
Leicester C	42	12	5	4	57	42	5	4	12	29	48	43
Sunderland	42	13	3	5	50	35	5	4	12	26	45	43
Huddersfield T	42	9	7	5	32	21	8	2	11	31	48	43
Birmingham	42	13	3	5	40	21	3	6	12	27	41	41
Liverpool	42	11	5	5	33	29	5	4	12	30	50	41
Portsmouth	42	10	6	5	43	25	5	4	12	23	37	40
Arsenal	42	10	2	9	49	26	4	9	8	29	40	39
Bolton W	42	11	5	5	46	24	4	4	13	28	50	39
Middlesbrough	42	11	3	7	48	31	5	3	13	34	53	38
Manchester U	42	11	4	6	39	34	4	4	13	28	54	38
Grimsby T	42	8	6	7	39	39	7	1	13	34	50	37
Newcastle U	42	13	4	4	52	32	2	3	16	19	60	37
Sheffield U	42	12	2	7	59	39	3	4	14	32	57	36
Burnley	42	11	5	5	53	34	3	3	15	26	63	36
Everton	42	6	7	8	48	46	6	4	11	32	46	35

DIVISION 2

	P	W	D	L	F	A	W	D	L	F	A	Pts
Blackpool	42	17	1	3	63	22	10	3	8	35	45	58
Chelsea	42	17	3	1	49	14	5	8	8	25	32	55
Oldham A	42	14	5	2	60	21	7	6	8	30	30	53
Bradford	42	14	5	2	65	28	5	7	9	26	42	50
Bury	42	14	2	5	45	27	8	3	10	33	40	49
WBA	42	16	1	4	73	31	5	4	12	32	42	47
Southampton	42	14	6	1	46	22	3	5	13	31	54	45
Cardiff C	42	14	4	3	41	16	4	4	13	20	43	44
Wolves	42	14	3	4	53	24	2	6	13	24	55	41
Nottingham F	42	9	6	6	36	28	4	9	8	19	41	41
Stoke C	42	12	4	5	41	20	4	4	13	33	52	40
Tottenham H	42	11	8	2	43	24	4	1	16	16	37	39
Charlton A	42	10	6	5	39	23	4	5	12	20	40	39
Millwall	42	10	7	4	36	26	2	8	11	21	47	39
Swansea T	42	11	5	5	42	23	3	4	14	15	38	37
Preston NE	42	7	7	7	42	36	6	4	11	23	44	37
Barnsley	42	12	7	2	39	22	2	1	18	17	49	36
Bradford C	42	7	7	7	33	30	5	5	11	27	47	36
Reading	42	10	7	4	31	20	2	4	15	23	47	35
Bristol C	42	11	4	6	36	30	2	5	14	25	53	35
Hull C	42	11	3	7	30	24	3	4	14	21	54	35
Notts Co	42	8	7	6	33	26	1	8	12	21	44	33

DIVISION 3 North

	P	W	D	L	F	A	W	D	L	F	A	Pts
Port Vale	42	17	2	2	64	18	13	5	3	39	19	67
Stockport Co	42	15	3	3	67	20	13	4	4	39	24	63
Darlington	42	14	2	5	71	29	8	4	9	37	44	50
Chesterfield	42	18	1	2	53	15	4	5	12	23	41	50
Lincoln C	42	12	8	1	54	23	5	6	10	29	38	48
York C	42	11	7	3	43	20	4	9	8	34	44	46
South Shields	42	11	6	4	49	32	7	4	10	28	42	46
Hartlepools U	42	13	4	4	50	24	4	7	10	31	50	45
Southport	42	11	5	5	49	31	4	8	9	32	43	43
Rochdale	42	14	3	4	57	30	4	4	13	32	61	43
Crewe A	42	12	5	4	55	28	5	3	13	27	43	42
Tranmere R	42	12	4	5	57	35	4	5	12	26	51	41
New Brighton	42	13	4	4	48	22	3	4	14	21	57	40
Doncaster R	42	13	5	3	39	22	2	4	15	23	47	39
Carlisle U	42	13	4	4	63	34	3	3	15	27	67	39
Accrington S	42	11	4	6	55	30	3	5	13	29	51	37
Wrexham	42	10	5	6	42	28	3	3	15	25	60	34
Wigan B	42	12	4	5	44	26	1	3	17	16	62	33
Nelson	42	9	4	8	31	25	4	3	14	20	55	33
Rotherham U	42	9	4	8	46	40	2	4	15	21	73	30
Halifax T	42	7	7	7	27	26	3	1	17	17	63	28
Barrow	42	9	4	8	31	28	2	1	18	10	70	27

DIVISION 3 South

	P	W	D	L	F	A	W	D	L	F	A	Pts
Plymouth A	42	18	3	0	63	12	12	5	4	35	26	68
Brentford	42	21	0	0	66	12	7	5	9	28	32	61
QPR	42	13	5	3	46	26	8	4	9	34	42	51
Northampton T	42	14	6	1	53	20	7	2	12	29	38	50
Brighton & HA	42	16	2	3	54	20	5	6	10	33	43	50
Coventry C	42	14	3	4	54	25	5	6	10	34	48	47
Fulham	42	12	6	3	54	33	6	5	10	33	50	47
Norwich C	42	14	4	3	55	28	4	6	11	33	49	46
Crystal P	42	14	5	2	56	26	3	7	11	25	48	46
Bournemouth	42	11	6	4	47	24	4	7	10	25	37	43
Southend U	42	11	6	4	41	19	4	7	10	28	40	43
Clapton O	42	10	8	3	38	21	4	5	12	17	41	41
Luton T	42	13	4	4	42	25	1	8	12	22	53	40
Swindon T	42	10	7	4	42	25	3	5	13	31	58	38
Watford	42	10	4	7	37	30	5	4	12	23	43	38
Exeter C	42	10	6	5	45	29	2	5	14	22	44	35
Walsall	42	10	4	7	45	24	3	4	14	26	54	34
Newport Co	42	9	9	3	48	29	3	1	17	26	56	34
Torquay U	42	9	6	6	50	38	1	5	15	14	56	31
Bristol R	42	11	3	7	45	31	0	5	16	22	62	30
Gillingham	42	9	5	7	38	28	2	3	16	13	52	30
Merthyr T	42	5	6	10	39	49	1	3	17	21	86	21

Football League Records

Top scorers: Div 1, T.Waring (Aston Villa) 49 goals; Div 2, W.Dean (Everton) 39 goals; Div 3(N), J.McConnell (Carlisle United) 37 goals; Div 3(S), P.Simpson (Crystal Palace) 46 goals.
Merthyr Town failed to gain re-election, Thames elected in their place.

Arsenal's David Jack, who scored 31 goals when Arsenal won the League Championship for the first time in 1930-31.

DIVISION 1

	ARSENAL	ASTON VILLA	BIRMINGHAM	BLACKBURN R	BLACKPOOL	BOLTON W	CHELSEA	DERBY CO	GRIMSBY T	HUDDERSFIELD T	LEEDS U	LEICESTER C	LIVERPOOL	MANCHESTER C	MANCHESTER U	MIDDLESBROUGH	NEWCASTLE U	PORTSMOUTH	SHEFFIELD U	SHEFFIELD W	SUNDERLAND	WEST HAM U
1 ARSENAL		N08 5-2	J31 1-1	S10 3-2	D27 7-1	m02 5-0	a04 2-1	F14 6-3	J28 9-1	M07 0-0	S06 3-1	S20 4-1	a18 3-1	D26 3-1	F21 4-1	N22 5-3	D20 1-2	a06 1-1	O04 1-1	M21 2-0	J17 1-3	O25 1-1
2 ASTON VILLA	M14 5-1		O18 1-1	N01 5-2	M28 4-1	J17 3-1	D26 3-3	N15 4-6	S15 2-0	O04 6-1	D13 4-3	F28 4-2	S20 4-2	a25 4-2	D27 7-0	J31 8-1	a07 4-3	D03 2-2	a11 4-0	S01 2-0	F18 4-2	S06 6-1
3 BIRMINGHAM	S27 2-4	F21 0-4		F07 4-1	O11 1-1	a04 0-2	O25 6-2	J03 1-2	N22 4-1	D06 2-0	D25 0-1	m02 2-1	D20 2-0	S13 3-2	M07 0-0	M21 1-2	S10 1-1	J28 2-1	A30 3-1	a18 2-0	a06 1-0	N08 0-2
4 BLACKBURN R	S15 2-2	M07 0-2	O04 2-1		S06 5-0	O25 2-2	N08 2-0	D25 1-0	M21 5-2	N22 5-3	J17 3-1	M02 3-0	D27 3-3	J01 0-1	D06 4-1	a18 4-5	a04 1-0	S01 1-2	F19 2-1	D20 5-2	S20 3-0	F21 1-0
5 BLACKPOOL	A30 1-4	N22 2-2	F18 0-1	J03 1-1		F21 3-3	M07 2-1	a03 1-0	D20 3-1	a18 1-1	S20 3-7	O04 5-4	O25 1-3	m02 2-2	M21 5-1	S13 3-2	N08 0-0	S10 2-2	D25 2-1	a04 0-4	J31 3-1	D06 1-3
6 BOLTON W	S01 1-4	S13 1-1	N29 2-0	F28 1-1	O18 1-0		F04 1-1	N01 1-2	O11 4-2	J03 1-0	a11 2-0	a25 4-1	J14 2-0	M28 1-1	D25 3-1	A30 3-0	S27 0-3	D13 3-1	M14 6-2	F07 2-2	N15 2-2	a06 4-2
7 CHELSEA	N29 1-5	D25 0-2	M25 1-0	M14 3-2	N01 3-0	S20 0-1		a11 1-1	D27 5-0	F18 1-2	M28 1-0	a06 1-0	J31 2-2	N15 2-0	S06 6-2	O04 4-0	m02 1-1	a25 2-0	O18 1-0	S15 0-0	D13 5-0	J17 2-1
8 DERBY CO	O11 4-2	M21 1-1	S06 0-0	D26 1-1	a06 3-2	M07 4-1	D06 6-2		S20 1-0	D20 4-1	S03 4-1	D27 1-0	N08 2-2	S27 1-1	a18 6-1	a04 1-2	F21 1-5	F07 5-1	J17 4-3	O25 2-3	S17 4-1	N22 1-1
9 GRIMSBY T	a11 0-1	S09 1-2	M28 4-1	N15 2-0	a25 6-2	F17 4-1	A30 0-1	F03 5-3		m02 2-1	N29 2-0	N01 8-2	D25 0-0	F28 3-5	J31 2-1	a03 4-1	J03 2-2	O18 0-3	D13 2-1	S13 2-3	M24 2-1	O04 4-0
10 HUDDERSFIELD T	N01 1-1	F07 1-6	a11 1-0	M28 1-1	D13 10-1	S06 3-2	O11 1-1	a25 3-0	S01 2-2		J31 3-0	O18 4-1	J17 2-1	N29 1-1	S15 3-0	S20 2-2	D26 0-3	M14 1-3	N15 1-1	a07 1-1	M16 2-0	D27 2-0
11 LEEDS U	M11 1-2	a18 0-2	D26 3-1	S13 4-2	J28 2-2	D06 3-1	N22 2-3	m02 3-1	a04 0-0	S27 1-2		F18 1-3	F21 1-2	S08 4-2	D20 5-0	O25 7-0	M07 1-0	A30 2-2	a07 4-0	N08 2-3	O04 0-3	M21 3-0
12 LEICESTER C	F05 2-7	O25 4-1	S01 2-1	S27 3-1	F07 6-0	D20 2-1	a07 2-1	A30 1-1	M07 0-1	F21 1-2	O11 4-0		M21 3-2	J03 3-2	N08 5-4	D06 0-3	a18 3-1	S13 3-1	S08 2-2	N22 2-5	D26 1-1	a04 1-1
13 LIVERPOOL	D13 1-1	J24 1-1	a15 0-0	A30 2-1	F28 5-2	S10 7-2	S27 3-1	M14 0-0	D26 1-1	S13 1-4	O18 2-0	N15 3-1		N01 0-2	a03 1-1	J03 3-1	F07 4-2	M28 3-1	N29 6-1	O11 1-2	a11 2-4	m02 2-0
14 MANCHESTER C	D25 1-4	D20 3-1	J17 4-2	a03 3-0	S03 2-4	N22 3-0	M21 2-0	J31 4-3	O25 1-0	a04 0-1	S17 1-0	S06 0-2	M07 1-1		O04 4-1	N08 4-2	D06 2-0	O11 1-3	S20 0-4	F21 2-0	D27 2-0	a18 1-1
15 MANCHESTER U	O18 1-2	A30 3-4	N01 2-0	a11 0-1	N15 0-0	D26 1-1	J03 1-0	D13 2-1	S27 0-2	S10 0-6	J01 0-0	M25 0-0	a06 4-1	F07 1-3		m02 4-4	S13 4-7	M16 0-1	M28 1-2	J28 4-1	N29 1-1	F14 1-0
16 MIDDLESBROUGH	M28 2-5	S27 3-1	N15 1-1	D13 4-1	J17 5-1	D27 3-0	F07 2-2	N29 4-1	J01 2-1	J24 2-3	F28 5-0	a11 2-2	S06 3-3	M14 4-1	S03 3-1		O11 3-1	N01 0-1	a25 4-1	D26 2-0	O18 1-0	S17 2-2
17 NEWCASTLE U	a25 1-3	J01 2-0	S17 2-2	N29 2-3	M14 0-2	J31 4-0	S03 1-0	O18 2-5	S06 1-2	a03 1-1	N01 4-1	D13 5-2	O04 0-4	a11 0-1	J17 4-3	F14 0-5		N15 4-7	F28 1-0	D27 1-2	M28 2-0	S20 4-2
18 PORTSMOUTH	a03 1-1	a04 5-0	S20 2-2	m02 3-0	S17 4-3	a18 1-0	D20 1-1	O04 2-0	F21 4-3	N08 2-2	D27 1-1	J17 2-1	N22 4-0	F18 1-1	O25 4-1	M07 1-0	M21 1-2		J31 2-3	D06 2-4	S06 1-1	D26 2-0
19 SHEFFIELD U	F07 1-1	D06 3-4	D27 3-1	O11 1-1	D26 5-1	N08 2-0	F21 4-0	S13 3-3	a18 2-1	M21 0-2	a06 1-1	S24 0-2	a04 4-1	J28 2-2	N22 3-1	D20 4-2	O25 3-1	S27 3-1		S06 1-1	S03 3-3	M07 1-2
20 SHEFFIELD W	N15 1-2	m02 3-0	D13 9-1	a25 1-3	N29 7-1	O04 1-0	S08 1-1	a20 3-2	J17 4-1	J01 2-1	M14 2-1	M28 4-0	F14 3-5	O18 1-1	S20 3-0	D29 3-2	A30 2-1	a11 2-2	J03 1-3		N01 7-2	J31 5-3
21 SUNDERLAND	S13 1-4	O11 1-1	a03 1-0	F04 8-2	S27 2-4	M21 3-1	a18 2-0	S10 1-3	N08 3-2	O25 4-2	F07 4-0	D25 2-5	D06 6-5	A30 3-3	a04 1-2	F21 1-1	N22 5-0	J03 0-0	m02 2-1	M07 5-1		D20 6-1
22 WEST HAM U	F28 2-4	J03 5-5	M16 1-2	O18 4-3	a11 3-2	a03 1-4	S13 4-1	M28 0-1	F07 3-4	A30 2-1	N15 1-1	N29 2-0	S01 7-0	D13 2-0	O11 5-1	S08 0-3	J26 3-2	D25 4-3	N01 4-1	S27 3-3	a25 0-3	

Winger Jimmy Stein, a vital member of the Everton side that won the Second and First Division titles and the FA Cup in successive seasons between 1930 and 1933.

DIVISION 2

	BARNSLEY	BRADFORD	BRADFORD C	BRISTOL C	BURNLEY	BURY	CARDIFF C	CHARLTON A	EVERTON	MILLWALL	NOTTINGHAM F	OLDHAM A	PLYMOUTH A	PORT VALE	PRESTON N.E.	READING	SOUTHAMPTON	STOKE C	SWANSEA T	TOTTENHAM H	W.B.A.	WOLVERHAMPTON W
1 BARNSLEY		D06 1-0	S06 2-1	S27 1-0	N08 0-1	a06 2-1	F07 4-0	J17 5-0	O11 1-1	O25 2-3	a18 3-1	S20 1-2	J01 0-4	D27 5-2	M07 1-1	N22 3-2	a04 3-1	F21 4-2	S01 1-0	D20 0-1	D25 0-0	M21 3-0
2 BRADFORD	a11 1-0		F28 1-2	N15 5-2	J31 4-1	M14 5-1	M28 3-0	O18 3-2	N29 4-1	D26 6-0	S06 4-1	D27 4-0	N01 7-1	S08 5-1	S20 2-2	F18 1-3	O04 1-1	m02 2-2	a25 5-1	J17 4-1	D13 3-1	a06 1-1
3 BRADFORD C	J03 1-0	D25 0-4		S13 1-1	N22 2-3	F07 3-1	F04 2-1	A30 3-2	S27 0-3	a18 0-0	M07 1-0	D20 0-0	O11 1-0	S03 2-1	a04 0-0	D06 6-1	M21 4-3	D25 2-2	a07 3-0	N08 2-0	S17 2-3	F21 4-1
4 BRISTOL C	J31 2-1	M21 2-0	J17 0-1		M07 1-1	S17 4-2	O11 1-0	S20 3-0	a03 0-1	F21 1-2	O04 1-4	O25 1-0	S03 2-1	S06 1-1	D20 1-1	a04 1-0	N08 2-1	D06 1-1	D26 2-1	a18 2-1	D27 1-1	N22 0-3
5 BURNLEY	M14 2-2	S27 3-2	M28 1-1	N01 4-2		A30 0-2	a25 1-0	N29 1-1	D13 5-2	O11 2-1	S08 5-2	a03 6-1	F28 2-2	N15 1-2	D25 1-0	S13 8-1	J03 3-2	F07 1-2	O18 2-2	m02 1-0	a11 2-1	F03 4-2
6 BURY	a03 3-1	N08 3-1	O04 3-1	S10 6-0	D27 2-1		S03 3-0	F14 0-1	D25 2-2	N22 5-0	D06 1-0	M21 1-3	S06 2-0	J31 0-3	O25 3-0	D20 2-2	a18 1-0	a04 0-3	J17 2-0	F21 2-0	S20 2-2	M07 1-0
7 CARDIFF C	O04 2-0	N22 0-3	S20 1-1	F14 0-1	D20 4-0	m02 1-3		J31 0-2	S08 1-2	D06 4-4	O25 1-1	F21 0-0	S22 4-1	J17 2-1	a18 0-0	N08 5-0	M07 0-1	M21 3-2	D27 1-0	a06 0-0	S06 3-6	a04 0-3
8 CHARLTON A	S13 1-1	F21 3-1	D27 2-1	J24 0-0	a04 2-1	O11 3-2	S27 4-1		F07 0-7	S06 2-0	D20 1-1	a18 1-1	a06 1-3	D26 3-1	N08 1-3	M21 2-1	N22 3-1	O25 1-2	S15 3-0	M07 1-0	S01 0-4	D06 1-2
9 EVERTON	F18 5-2	a04 4-2	J31 4-2	a06 1-3	a18 3-2	J01 3-2	S17 1-1	O04 7-1		M21 2-0	F21 2-0	D06 6-4	D27 9-1	S20 2-3	S03 2-1	M07 3-2	D20 2-1	N22 5-0	S06 5-1	O25 4-2	J17 2-1	N08 4-0
10 MILLWALL	F28 4-1	D25 1-1	D13 1-1	O18 2-0	F14 2-1	M28 1-0	a11 0-0	J03 6-0	N15 1-3		S20 5-1	J17 1-0	N29 4-1	a25 0-1	O04 5-7	S08 4-0	a03 1-0	A30 1-3	M14 3-1	J31 2-3	N01 2-0	m02 1-1
11 NOTTINGHAM F	D13 3-3	J03 1-0	N01 4-1	F07 6-1	S17 3-3	a11 3-0	F28 3-1	a25 4-3	O18 2-2	J24 2-1		S27 4-1	N15 1-1	M14 1-0	a06 1-4	D25 1-1	m02 3-1	S13 3-0	M28 3-0	F14 2-2	N29 1-6	A30 3-4
12 OLDHAM A	J26 0-0	A30 2-0	a25 3-0	F28 1-3	a06 3-1	N15 3-2	O18 4-2	D13 0-3	a11 3-3	S13 3-1	J31 3-1		M28 2-1	N01 3-3	F14 2-0	J01 1-1	S08 2-1	J03 3-1	N29 2-1	O04 1-2	M23 2-2	D25 2-0
13 PLYMOUTH A	S10 4-0	M07 0-0	F14 0-2	m02 5-3	O25 1-2	J03 3-6	D26 5-1	a03 1-3	A30 2-3	a04 5-0	M21 1-0	N22 1-1		O04 2-1	F21 1-2	a18 3-1	S13 2-3	N08 1-2	S20 0-0	D06 2-0	J31 5-1	D20 3-2
14 PORT VALE	A30 5-2	S22 8-2	m02 1-0	J03 1-0	M21 0-0	S27 0-1	S13 2-0	D25 1-1	J26 1-3	D20 3-2	N08 3-2	M07 2-0	F07 2-1		N22 1-0	F21 2-1	D06 1-0	a18 0-0	O11 2-0	a04 3-0	a03 1-0	O25 0-1
15 PRESTON N.E.	N01 1-1	J29 1-1	N29 4-2	a25 2-2	D26 2-0	F28 3-0	D13 7-0	M14 4-1	m02 2-1	F07 1-3	a03 2-4	O11 1-0	O18 2-1	M28 1-3		J03 3-3	A30 5-0	S27 5-1	a11 0-0	S08 2-1	N15 2-3	S13 5-4
16 READING	M28 6-1	O11 3-0	a11 0-0	N29 4-1	J17 3-1	a25 3-4	M14 3-0	N15 2-0	N01 0-2	S17 2-1	D26 5-2	S03 1-3	D13 1-2	O18 0-3	S06 1-4		S20 1-1	a03 7-3	J31 1-0	D27 1-2	a15 0-3	F07 3-0
17 SOUTHAMPTON	N29 4-0	F07 2-3	N15 4-1	M14 5-1	S06 1-1	D13 5-0	N01 0-1	M28 3-0	a25 2-1	a06 3-1	S01 0-0	S15 1-0	J17 3-3	a11 2-0	D27 2-1	J24 3-2		O11 2-1	F28 1-2	D26 0-3	O18 1-1	S27 2-0
18 STOKE C	O18 0-0	S01 1-1	D26 1-1	a11 3-1	O04 1-1	N29 3-1	N15 1-0	F28 0-0	M28 2-0	D27 2-3	J17 1-0	S06 4-0	M14 0-0	D13 1-0	F02 3-1	a06 2-1	F14 1-3		N01 5-0	S20 2-1	a30 0-1	S15 1-2
19 SWANSEA T	m02 1-0	D20 2-1	a06 1-2	D25 5-2	F21 1-1	S13 5-2	A30 3-2	S08 1-1	J03 2-5	N08 4-1	N22 3-2	a04 0-0	J24 2-0	F14 2-1	D06 2-1	S27 2-1	O25 0-1	M07 1-2		M21 1-2	O04 1-1	a18 1-1
20 TOTTENHAM H	a25 4-2	S13 3-2	M14 3-1	D13 4-1	S01 8-1	O18 3-1	a03 2-2	N01 5-0	M16 1-0	S27 4-1	O11 2-1	F07 4-0	a11 1-1	N29 5-0	S15 0-0	A30 7-1	D25 1-3	J26 3-0	N15 1-1		M28 2-2	J03 1-0
21 W.B.A.	D26 5-0	a18 1-1	S08 1-0	A30 3-0	D06 2-0	J26 2-0	J03 3-2	m02 3-2	S13 1-2	M07 0-0	a04 2-1	N08 2-0	S27 1-2	a06 4-1	M21 2-0	O25 1-0	F21 1-2	D20 4-0	F07 0-0	N22 0-2		O11 2-1
22 WOLVERHAMPTON W	N15 2-0	a07 1-1	O18 0-1	M28 0-1	S20 2-4	N01 7-0	N29 4-1	a11 1-1	M25 3-1	S01 2-0	D27 4-2	D26 3-0	a25 4-3	M11 3-0	J17 2-0	O04 3-1	J31 3-2	S08 5-1	D13 3-1	S06 3-1	F18 1-4	

Season 1930-31

DIVISION 3 NORTH

	ACCRINGTON S	BARROW	CARLISLE U	CHESTERFIELD	CREWE A	DARLINGTON	DONCASTER R	GATESHEAD	HALIFAX T	HARTLEPOOLS U	HULL C	LINCOLN C	NELSON	NEW BRIGHTON	ROCHDALE	ROTHERHAM U	SOUTHPORT	STOCKPORT CO	TRANMERE R	WIGAN B	WREXHAM	YORK C
1 ACCRINGTON S		S30 3-1	J24 3-0	O11 1-3	A30 3-1	D15 2-1	M14 2-0	N15 2-1	a11 1-1	O18 0-2	N01 1-3	a25 5-3	F28 3-1	J10 3-0	J01 2-3	F07 3-2	S10 2-0	M28 2-2	S13 5-2	D25 3-0	J03 1-3	S27 4-2
2 BARROW	S01 0-0		J03 7-2	S27 0-3	J29 2-0	J10 3-2	a25 3-1	N01 0-0	M28 3-1	F28 4-0	O18 3-0	F07 3-2	a11 2-1	N15 4-1	S08 0-0	J24 1-0	M05 1-1	M14 1-0	A30 1-3	D13 4-1	a03 2-3	S13 1-2
3 CARLISLE U	S20 7-3	S06 0-1		D27 0-0	O04 4-1	N01 2-1	J01 1-1	F28 2-2	a25 6-2	M28 3-0	a11 1-5	J15 3-6	M14 8-1	O18 2-0	J31 7-1	a03 1-2	J17 4-3	S11 5-1	m02 3-0	N15 6-1	F14 1-1	D26 2-0
4 CHESTERFIELD	F14 7-3	J31 3-1	A30 2-1		S08 2-0	M28 2-1	O18 2-1	a25 8-1	N15 7-0	D13 3-0	J24 0-4	a22 3-2	J10 2-1	M14 1-0	a06 4-1	S13 2-1	O04 2-1	N01 1-1	J01 5-1	a11 3-1	D25 4-0	J03 3-1
5 CREWE A	D27 2-1	D25 6-2	F07 3-5	S17 2-1		J17 2-2	M28 2-1	F04 6-2	M25 0-1	N01 2-1	N15 3-4	M14 2-0	O18 4-2	D17 1-3	S06 3-1	S01 2-3	a06 0-0	a11 1-0	S27 1-2	a25 3-2	J24 2-1	O11 5-1
6 DARLINGTON	a18 1-1	a04 3-2	M07 3-0	N22 5-1	S13 1-2		m02 0-0	F14 2-2	S20 4-1	a06 4-2	S10 2-4	J01 0-1	J03 2-1	J31 3-1	O25 1-1	M21 2-2	D06 2-3	O04 1-2	D20 2-0	A30 2-3	F21 1-1	N08 3-0
7 DONCASTER R	N08 6-1	D20 0-0	a18 2-0	F21 1-0	N22 2-0	S01 1-2		D27 1-1	S18 3-3	S27 1-1	S13 0-2	J24 0-1	O11 2-0	D25 0-0	M21 4-0	S06 3-3	M07 0-0	a03 2-0	D06 6-0	F07 5-1	a04 1-1	O25 0-2
8 GATESHEAD	M21 4-0	M07 4-1	O25 1-0	D20 3-3	a04 2-2	O11 1-1	A30 2-1		m02 3-1	J24 0-0	J03 1-0	S13 0-1	F07 2-0	S08 4-0	N22 0-2	F21 2-0	N08 2-3	a15 2-1	a18 3-0	S27 4-2	D06 4-3	J01 2-1
9 HALIFAX T	D06 1-1	N22 4-0	D20 1-5	M21 1-1	O25 4-0	J24 1-0	S08 0-2	S01 3-0		A30 3-1	D25 1-1	a06 3-2	S13 1-0	O04 1-0	a18 1-0	N08 0-1	a04 0-0	F14 3-0	F21 2-1	J03 0-1	S27 0-0	M07 0-0
10 HARTLEPOOLS U	F21 3-3	O25 3-2	N22 3-5	a18 1-3	M07 2-0	a03 1-1	J31 0-2	S20 2-3	D27 2-1		O04 1-3	F14 0-3	D25 4-0	S06 4-1	D20 4-0	D06 4-2	S01 0-2	J17 1-2	M21 1-2	J01 6-1	N08 2-1	a04 3-0
11 HULL C	M07 1-1	F21 1-1	D06 1-1	S20 3-1	M21 5-1	S15 1-1	J17 8-2	S06 4-0	D26 10-0	a20 5-0		S27 1-3	m02 4-0	a06 3-0	N08 3-1	O25 2-2	D20 5-1	D27 1-1	a04 1-0	O11 0-0	N22 2-3	a18 3-1
12 LINCOLN C	D20 5-2	O04 5-0	a04 5-1	O25 1-1	N08 3-1	D26 1-0	S20 1-0	J17 0-0	a03 4-1	O11 1-0	J31 3-0		S15 2-0	D27 4-0	M07 5-0	a18 1-3	F21 3-3	S06 6-1	N22 1-3	S01 2-0	M21 3-2	D06 4-1
13 NELSON	O25 4-2	D06 0-3	N08 1-2	a04 0-5	F21 1-1	S06 3-1	F14 2-0	O04 2-2	J17 3-2	D26 1-1	S02 0-2	S10 1-2		S20 2-2	D27 0-0	N22 0-0	a18 1-4	J31 1-1	M07 0-4	a03 2-1	D20 2-0	M21 2-5
14 NEW BRIGHTON	a04 0-0	M21 3-1	F21 2-0	N08 3-1	a18 3-0	S27 1-5	D26 2-1	S15 0-0	F07 3-0	J03 1-0	a03 1-1	A30 2-1	J24 2-0		D06 2-1	M07 3-1	N22 1-2	J01 0-2	O11 1-3	S13 0-2	O25 1-1	D20 5-3
15 ROCHDALE	a03 1-6	S15 4-2	S27 1-3	S01 2-3	J03 1-0	a21 1-2	N15 3-5	M28 0-1	F16 2-3	a25 1-2	M14 1-0	N01 4-2	A30 5-4	a11 2-0		O11 6-1	D26 0-4	J10 1-0	J24 1-3	O18 0-4	S13 4-3	F07 2-2
16 ROTHERHAM U	O04 8-1	S20 6-0	a06 1-0	J17 0-1	m02 1-1	N15 0-2	J03 3-0	O18 1-1	M14 2-1	a11 1-1	a27 1-1	D15 2-2	M28 3-0	N01 2-0	F14 1-3		J31 3-3	a25 3-4	D25 4-6	J10 5-2	S08 1-4	A30 2-1
17 SOUTHPORT	S16 3-3	O11 3-2	S13 1-2	F07 3-0	a03 3-1	a11 0-1	N01 2-1	M14 1-0	J13 5-2	m02 2-0	a25 1-0	O18 1-2	J01 8-1	M28 3-0	D25 4-0	S27 4-1		N15 2-0	J03 1-1	a21 3-1	A30 1-1	F17 1-0
18 STOCKPORT CO	N22 4-1	N08 6-0	S15 3-0	M07 2-1	D06 2-0	F07 0-1	a06 2-2	D25 3-1	O11 3-0	S13 3-1	A30 3-2	J03 4-2	S27 1-0	S01 2-0	a04 2-2	D20 5-2	M21 2-0		O25 1-1	J24 4-1	a18 2-2	F21 0-0
19 TRANMERE R	J17 8-0	D27 5-0	S01 2-0	a03 2-0	J31 0-0	a25 1-2	a11 1-2	a06 2-1	O18 2-2	N15 5-4	D13 4-0	M28 3-3	N01 7-1	F14 3-2	S20 7-3	D26 4-2	S06 3-1	F28 3-0		M14 5-1	O04 2-1	S18 4-1
20 WIGAN B	D26 3-2	a18 2-1	M21 1-2	D06 1-5	D20 6-0	D27 2-0	O04 3-0	J31 3-3	S06 3-0	S10 3-2	F14 3-1	m02 0-1	a06 3-1	J17 1-1	F21 3-0	a04 0-0	O25 1-0	S20 2-1	N08 4-3		M07 1-1	N22 3-1
21 WREXHAM	S06 6-1	a06 1-1	O11 2-1	D26 2-1	S20 7-0	O18 2-0	J14 4-1	a11 5-1	J31 3-2	M14 2-0	M28 2-0	N15 2-2	a25 5-1	F28 2-1	J17 1-1	S17 3-2	D27 2-4	D17 3-2	F07 2-2	N01 2-0		S03 3-2
22 YORK C	a06 3-1	J17 4-2	D25 4-0	S06 2-2	F14 4-3	M14 2-1	F28 4-2	a03 4-3	N01 4-1	F04 4-2	M18 3-2	a11 1-1	N15 3-0	a25 4-1	O04 3-0	D27 1-1	S20 3-1	O18 1-2	S10 3-1	M28 2-3	m02 0-1	

DIVISION 3 SOUTH

	BOURNEMOUTH	BRENTFORD	BRIGHTON & HA	BRISTOL R	CLAPTON O	COVENTRY C	CRYSTAL P	EXETER C	FULHAM	GILLINGHAM	LUTON T	NEWPORT CO	NORTHAMPTON T	NORWICH C	NOTTS CO	Q.P.R.	SOUTHEND U	SWINDON T	THAMES	TORQUAY U	WALSALL	WATFORD
1 BOURNEMOUTH		a18 1-0	N22 1-2	O25 4-0	S27 1-1	D26 2-0	D20 0-0	M21 3-1	a06 2-1	N08 2-1	F21 0-0	M07 4-2	D06 1-3	O11 4-1	J28 2-1	S03 2-0	S06 0-0	D27 4-1	F07 3-3	a04 2-2	S17 0-2	S13 1-1
2 BRENTFORD	D18 1-2		O04 3-2	S06 4-0	M28 3-0	O18 1-2	D25 8-2	J31 2-1	S17 4-1	S20 1-1	D27 0-1	J17 3-2	S03 0-4	M14 3-1	S24 2-2	N01 5-3	a03 3-1	a25 5-2	N15 6-1	F14 0-0	F28 6-1	a11 2-1
3 BRIGHTON & H.A.	M28 3-1	F07 1-0		D26 4-0	N01 3-1	a22 2-0	O11 1-1	S06 3-2	a11 1-1	D27 5-0	S17 2-0	a03 5-0	S27 1-1	O18 1-0	M14 1-3	J17 1-1	S03 1-2	O08 1-0	F28 2-4	J28 3-0	a25 3-3	N15 1-0
4 BRISTOL R	F20 2-5	J03 2-5	D25 3-3		a25 4-1	N15 1-0	S13 2-1	S08 1-1	M14 2-1	m02 1-0	S27 5-1	F14 2-0	A30 1-4	a11 3-0	F07 2-2	J14 3-0	J28 2-3	N04 4-1	D17 4-0	a06 3-1	M28 1-2	O18 1-5
5 CLAPTON O	J31 0-0	N22 3-0	M07 1-0	D20 3-1		S06 3-3	a04 3-2	O25 2-3	J17 2-0	F21 0-2	a18 3-2	S03 3-1	M21 2-2	D26 2-0	F14 1-4	a06 2-3	D06 3-1	S20 2-3	S18 2-1	N08 4-0	D27 2-5	O04 4-0
6 COVENTRY C	D25 3-3	F21 0-1	a18 0-0	M21 5-1	J03 4-0		O25 3-5	D06 3-1	m02 2-1	a04 1-2	N08 1-2	N22 6-4	O11 0-1	J24 3-0	A30 1-2	S27 2-0	M07 0-0	S08 4-0	S13 7-1	D20 6-1	F07 2-1	a07 2-2
7 CRYSTAL P	a25 1-0	D26 5-1	F14 0-1	J17 0-2	a20 3-1	F28 1-0		O04 7-2	O18 5-2	J31 5-0	S06 5-1	S20 7-1	S17 0-0	N15 2-1	a11 1-1	M14 4-0	D27 3-1	a03 3-1	M28 2-1	m02 5-0	N01 6-3	D17 6-1
8 EXETER C	N15 4-1	S27 4-0	J03 2-2	S17 0-3	a15 6-1	a11 2-3	F07 4-3		J14 3-2	a06 3-0	S03 1-1	D26 3-0	J28 3-3	A30 1-0	N01 3-3	a25 2-0	O11 1-1	M28 3-1	O18 4-3	S13 2-2	F18 2-5	M14 2-1
9 FULHAM	a03 1-0	S08 1-1	D06 0-1	N08 6-2	S13 2-0	S01 0-0	F21 2-0	a04 4-2		N22 1-1	M07 2-1	M21 0-1	D20 4-2	S27 1-0	J03 3-1	F07 0-2	O25 1-0	D26 6-1	J24 4-2	a18 3-0	O11 5-2	A30 3-2
10 GILLINGHAM	M14 0-0	J28 1-1	A30 0-0	S03 1-1	O18 0-0	J10 2-0	S27 6-2	a03 3-5	M28 3-2		O11 4-0	S10 4-1	S13 0-2	a25 2-1	F28 0-5	D17 2-2	F07 1-0	N15 0-1	D25 3-1	J03 2-3	a11 2-0	N01 4-2
11 LUTON T	O18 2-3	A30 1-1	S08 2-2	J31 4-1	M23 0-1	M14 2-0	J03 1-2	S29 3-1	N01 5-0	F14 4-1		O04 3-1	a06 4-0	J10 1-0	a25 3-0	M28 5-1	S13 2-1	F28 4-0	a11 8-0	D25 3-1	N15 0-0	J28 4-1
12 NEWPORT CO	N01 7-3	S13 0-2	a06 2-0	O11 1-1	m02 1-1	M28 1-1	J26 2-1	D25 4-0	N15 1-3	S15 1-3	F07 3-1		J03 5-2	D18 3-0	O18 2-3	a11 2-3	S27 3-1	M14 3-1	a25 1-1	A30 2-1	J22 1-1	F20 0-2
13 NORTHAMPTON T	a11 2-2	m02 1-2	J31 2-1	D27 1-1	N15 0-0	F14 0-3	S08 0-0	S20 1-0	a25 4-2	J17 0-1	a07 0-0	S06 1-0		N01 3-1	M28 0-0	F28 6-0	D26 4-0	D13 3-0	M14 4-1	O04 0-3	O18 3-0	J15 2-3
14 NORWICH C	F14 2-1	N08 3-0	F21 2-2	D06 1-3	D25 2-0	S20 2-2	M21 2-1	D27 1-2	J31 1-1	D20 4-0	a04 1-0	a18 4-1	M07 1-1		S08 2-2	S06 1-1	N22 0-1	O04 2-0	a06 0-0	O25 3-0	J17 3-1	m02 0-1
15 NOTTS CO	S20 2-0	a04 1-0	N08 2-2	O04 3-0	O11 5-0	D27 4-1	D06 2-2	M07 1-2	S06 0-1	O25 2-1	D20 1-0	F21 5-0	N22 2-2	O02 4-0		D26 2-0	a18 1-1	J17 2-0	S03 4-0	M21 2-0	a03 6-1	J31 1-0
16 Q.P.R.	m02 3-0	M07 3-1	S13 4-1	a04 2-0	a03 4-2	J31 2-0	N08 4-0	D20 7-2	O04 0-2	a18 1-0	N22 3-1	D06 7-1	O25 0-2	J03 3-1	D25 4-1		M21 0-2	F14 1-2	A30 3-0	F21 1-2	S20 3-0	S11 2-3
17 SOUTHEND U	D13 4-0	a06 0-1	m02 0-2	S20 4-0	a11 2-0	N01 2-0	A30 2-4	M18 5-1	F28 2-4	O04 3-2	J17 0-2	J31 6-2	D25 2-1	M28 2-0	D17 2-1	N15 2-0		O18 5-3	J10 1-0	S08 6-3	M14 2-0	a25 1-0
18 SWINDON T	A30 4-1	D20 3-2	a04 1-1	M07 3-1	J24 5-1	S17 4-0	a06 4-4	N22 2-1	D25 4-1	M21 5-2	O25 0-0	N08 4-4	a18 5-1	F07 5-2	S13 1-2	O11 4-1	F21 1-1		S27 3-0	D06 4-0	S03 4-3	J03 2-1
19 THAMES	O04 1-4	M21 2-0	O25 0-0	a18 1-2	S11 3-0	J17 1-2	N22 0-2	F21 1-0	S20 0-0	D26 2-2	D06 1-0	D20 3-1	N08 2-1	a03 2-0	m02 0-0	D27 1-0	a04 3-0	J31 3-2		M07 1-1	S06 4-1	F16 3-2
20 TORQUAY U	J21 4-4	O11 0-3	S20 3-1	S24 3-3	M14 5-2	a25 0-0	S03 3-1	J17 0-0	D17 3-1	S06 3-0	D26 1-1	D27 3-0	F07 3-0	F28 2-0	N15 1-4	O18 6-2	S17 3-1	a11 5-0	N01 5-1		J31 0-1	M28 3-1
21 WALSALL	S08 3-3	O25 1-4	D20 0-0	N22 4-2	A30 4-2	O04 1-2	M07 2-1	a18 2-1	F14 2-0	D06 2-2	M21 0-1	a04 1-0	F21 2-6	S13 7-0	a06 2-1	J24 0-2	N08 1-3	m02 2-2	J03 6-0	S27 0-4		D25 2-2
22 WATFORD	J17 2-0	D06 1-3	M21 5-0	F21 2-2	F07 1-2	a03 4-1	a18 0-2	N08 0-1	D27 2-2	M07 1-0	S20 1-0	O25 6-2	a04 1-2	S03 2-2	S27 0-1	S17 0-4	D20 1-3	S06 3-0	O11 1-0	N22 6-0	D26 2-2	

LEAGUE TABLES

DIVISION 1

	P	W	D	L	F	A	W	D	L	F	A	Pts
Arsenal	42	14	5	2	67	27	14	5	2	60	32	66
Aston Villa	42	17	3	1	86	34	8	6	7	42	44	59
Sheffield W	42	14	3	4	65	32	8	5	8	37	43	52
Portsmouth	42	11	7	3	46	26	7	6	8	38	41	49
Huddersfield T	42	10	8	3	45	27	8	4	9	36	38	48
Derby Co	42	12	6	3	56	31	6	4	11	38	48	46
Middlesbrough	42	13	5	3	57	28	6	3	12	41	62	46
Manchester C	42	13	2	6	41	29	5	8	8	34	41	46
Liverpool	42	11	6	4	48	28	4	6	11	38	57	42
Blackburn R	42	14	3	4	54	28	3	5	13	29	56	42
Sunderland	42	12	4	5	61	38	4	5	12	28	47	41
Chelsea	42	13	4	4	42	19	2	6	13	22	48	40
Grimsby T	42	13	2	6	55	31	4	3	14	27	56	39
Bolton W	42	12	6	3	45	26	3	3	15	23	55	39
Sheffield U	42	10	7	4	49	31	4	3	14	29	53	38
Leicester C	42	12	4	5	50	38	4	2	15	30	57	38
Newcastle U	42	9	2	10	41	45	6	4	11	37	42	36
West Ham U	42	11	3	7	56	44	3	5	13	23	50	36
Birmingham	42	11	3	7	37	28	2	7	12	18	42	36
Blackpool	42	8	7	6	41	44	3	3	15	30	81	32
Leeds U	42	10	3	8	49	31	2	4	15	19	50	31
Manchester U	42	6	6	9	30	37	1	2	18	23	78	22

DIVISION 2

	P	W	D	L	F	A	W	D	L	F	A	Pts
Everton	42	18	1	2	76	31	10	4	7	45	35	61
WBA	42	14	3	4	40	16	8	7	6	43	33	54
Tottenham H	42	15	5	1	64	20	7	2	12	24	35	51
Wolves	42	15	2	4	56	25	6	3	12	28	42	47
Port Vale	42	15	3	3	39	16	6	2	13	28	45	47
Bradford	42	15	4	2	71	24	3	6	12	26	42	46
Preston NE	42	12	5	4	55	31	5	6	10	28	33	45
Burnley	42	13	5	3	55	30	4	6	11	26	47	45
Southampton	42	13	4	4	46	22	6	2	13	28	40	44
Bradford C	42	12	5	4	39	26	5	5	11	22	37	44
Stoke C	42	11	6	4	34	17	6	4	11	30	54	44
Oldham A	42	13	5	3	45	28	3	5	13	16	44	42
Bury	42	14	3	4	44	20	5	0	16	31	62	41
Millwall	42	12	4	5	47	25	4	3	14	24	55	39
Charlton A	42	11	4	6	35	33	4	5	12	24	53	39
Bristol C	42	11	5	5	29	23	4	3	14	25	59	38
Nottingham F	42	12	6	3	54	35	2	3	16	26	50	37
Plymouth A	42	10	3	8	47	33	4	5	12	29	51	36
Barnsley	42	13	3	5	42	23	0	6	15	17	56	35
Swansea T	42	11	5	5	40	29	1	5	15	11	45	34
Reading	42	11	2	8	47	33	1	4	16	25	63	30
Cardiff C	42	7	6	8	32	31	1	3	17	15	56	25

DIVISION 3 North

	P	W	D	L	F	A	W	D	L	F	A	Pts
Chesterfield	42	19	1	1	66	22	7	5	9	36	35	58
Lincoln C	42	16	3	2	60	19	9	4	8	42	40	57
Wrexham	42	16	4	1	61	25	5	8	8	33	37	54
Tranmere R	42	16	3	2	73	26	8	3	10	38	48	54
Southport	42	15	3	3	52	19	7	6	8	36	37	53
Hull C	42	12	7	2	64	20	8	3	10	35	35	50
Stockport Co	42	15	5	1	54	19	5	4	12	23	42	49
Carlisle U	42	13	4	4	68	32	7	1	13	30	49	45
Gateshead	42	14	4	3	46	22	2	9	10	25	51	45
Wigan B	42	14	4	3	48	25	5	1	15	28	61	43
Darlington	42	9	6	6	44	30	7	4	10	27	29	42
York C	42	15	3	3	59	30	3	3	15	26	52	42
Accrington S	42	14	2	5	51	31	1	7	13	33	77	39
Rotherham U	42	9	6	6	50	34	4	6	11	31	49	38
Doncaster R	42	9	8	4	40	18	4	3	14	25	47	37
Barrow	42	13	4	4	45	23	2	3	16	23	66	37
Halifax T	42	11	6	4	30	16	2	3	16	25	73	35
Crewe A	42	13	2	6	52	35	1	4	16	14	58	34
New Brighton	42	12	4	5	36	25	1	3	17	13	51	33
Hartlepools U	42	10	2	9	47	37	2	4	15	20	49	30
Rochdale	42	9	1	11	42	50	3	5	13	20	57	30
Nelson	42	6	7	8	28	40	0	0	21	15	73	19

DIVISION 3 South

	P	W	D	L	F	A	W	D	L	F	A	Pts
Notts Co	42	16	4	1	58	13	8	7	6	39	33	59
Crystal P	42	17	2	2	71	20	5	5	11	36	51	51
Brentford	42	14	3	4	62	30	8	3	10	28	34	50
Brighton & HA	42	13	5	3	45	20	4	10	7	23	33	49
Southend U	42	16	0	5	53	26	6	5	10	23	34	49
Northampton T	42	10	6	5	37	20	8	6	7	40	39	48
Luton T	42	15	3	3	61	17	4	5	12	15	34	46
QPR	42	15	0	6	57	23	5	3	13	25	52	43
Fulham	42	15	3	3	49	21	3	4	14	28	54	43
Bournemouth	42	11	7	3	39	22	4	6	11	33	51	43
Torquay U	42	13	5	3	56	26	4	4	13	24	58	43
Swindon T	42	15	5	1	68	29	3	1	17	21	65	42
Exeter C	42	12	6	3	55	35	5	2	14	29	55	42
Coventry C	42	11	4	6	55	28	5	5	11	20	37	41
Bristol R	42	12	3	6	49	36	4	5	12	26	56	40
Gillingham	42	10	6	5	40	29	4	4	13	21	47	38
Walsall	42	9	5	7	44	38	5	4	12	34	57	37
Watford	42	9	4	8	41	29	5	3	13	31	46	35
Clapton O	42	12	3	6	47	33	2	4	15	16	58	35
Thames	42	12	5	4	34	20	1	3	17	20	73	34
Newport Co	42	10	5	6	45	31	1	1	19	24	80	28
Norwich C	42	10	7	4	37	20	0	1	20	10	56	28

Football League Records

Top scorers: Div 1, W.Dean (Everton) 44 goals; Div 2, C.Pearce (Swansea Town) 35 goals; Div 3(N), B.Hall (Lincoln City) 42 goals; Div 3(N), C.Bourton (Coventry City) 49 goals.
Newport County and Nelson failed to gain re-election, Mansfield Town and Chester elected in their place. Walsall transferred to Division Three North. Wigan Borough resigned on 26 October 1931.

Warney Cresswell, the cultured England full-back who missed only two games when Everton became League Champions in 1930-31.

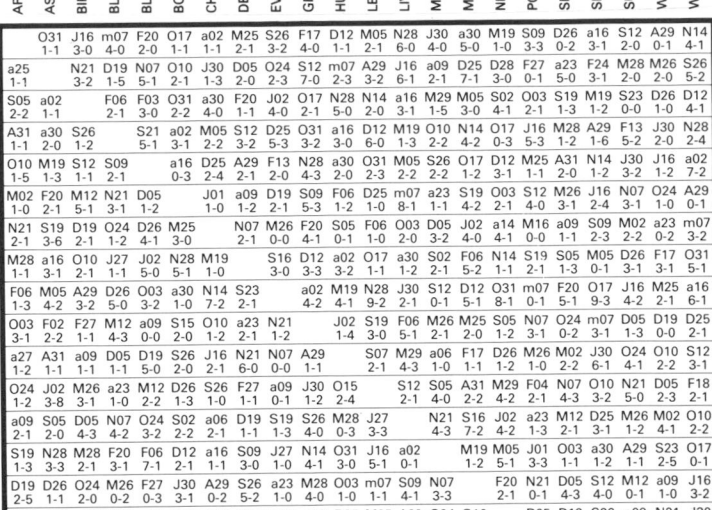

DIVISION 1

	ARSENAL	ASTON VILLA	BIRMINGHAM	BLACKBURN R	BLACKPOOL	BOLTON W	CHELSEA	DERBY CO	EVERTON	GRIMSBY T	HUDDERSFIELD T	LEICESTER C	LIVERPOOL	MANCHESTER C	MIDDLESBROUGH	NEWCASTLE U	PORTSMOUTH	SHEFFIELD U	SHEFFIELD W	SUNDERLAND	W.B.A.	WEST HAM U
1 ARSENAL		O31 1-1	J16 3-0	m07 4-0	F20 2-0	O17 1-1	a02 1-1	M25 2-1	S26 3-2	F17 4-0	D12 1-1	M05 2-1	N28 6-0	J30 4-0	a30 5-0	M19 1-0	S09 3-3	D26 0-2	a16 3-1	S12 2-0	A29 0-1	N14 4-1
2 ASTON VILLA	a25 1-1		N21 3-2	D19 1-5	N07 5-1	O10 2-1	J30 1-3	D05 2-0	O24 2-3	S12 7-0	m07 2-3	A29 3-2	J16 6-1	a09 2-1	D25 7-1	D28 3-0	F27 0-1	a23 5-0	F24 3-1	M28 2-0	M26 2-0	S26 5-2
3 BIRMINGHAM	S05 2-2	a02 1-1		F06 2-1	F03 3-0	O31 2-2	a30 4-0	F20 1-1	J02 4-0	O17 2-1	N28 5-0	N14 2-0	a16 3-1	M29 1-5	M05 3-0	S02 4-1	O03 2-1	S19 1-3	M19 1-2	S23 0-0	D26 1-0	D12 4-1
4 BLACKBURN R	A31 1-1	a30 2-0	S26 1-2		S21 5-1	a02 3-1	M05 2-2	S12 3-2	D25 5-3	O31 3-2	a16 3-0	D12 6-0	M19 1-3	O10 2-2	N14 4-2	O17 0-3	J16 5-3	M28 1-2	A29 1-6	F13 5-2	J30 2-0	N28 2-4
5 BLACKPOOL	O10 1-5	M19 1-3	S12 1-1	S09 2-1		a16 0-3	D25 2-4	A29 2-1	F13 2-0	N28 4-3	a30 2-0	O31 2-3	M05 2-2	S26 2-2	O17 1-2	D12 3-1	M25 1-1	A31 2-0	N14 1-2	J30 3-2	J16 1-2	a02 7-2
6 BOLTON W	M02 1-0	F20 2-1	M12 5-1	N21 3-1	D05 1-2		J01 1-0	a09 1-2	D19 2-1	S09 5-3	F06 1-2	D25 1-0	m07 8-1	a23 1-1	S19 4-2	O03 2-1	S12 4-0	M26 3-1	J16 2-4	N07 3-1	O24 1-0	A29 0-1
7 CHELSEA	N21 2-1	S19 3-6	D19 2-1	O24 1-2	D26 4-1	M25 3-0		N07 2-1	M26 0-0	F20 4-1	S05 0-1	F06 1-0	O03 2-0	D05 3-2	J02 4-0	a14 4-1	M16 0-0	a09 1-1	S09 2-3	M02 2-2	a23 0-2	m07 3-2
8 DERBY CO	M28 1-1	a16 3-1	O10 2-1	J27 1-1	J02 5-0	N28 5-1	M19 1-0		S16 3-0	D12 3-3	a02 3-2	O17 1-1	a30 1-2	S02 2-1	F06 5-2	N14 1-1	S19 2-1	S05 1-3	M05 0-1	D26 3-1	F17 3-1	O31 5-1
9 EVERTON	F06 1-3	M05 4-2	A29 3-2	D26 5-0	O03 3-2	a30 1-0	N14 7-2	S23 2-1		a02 4-2	M19 4-1	N28 9-2	J30 2-1	S12 0-1	D12 5-1	O31 8-1	m07 0-1	F20 5-1	O17 9-3	J16 4-2	M25 2-1	a16 6-1
10 GRIMSBY T	O03 3-1	F02 2-2	F27 1-1	M12 4-3	a09 0-0	S15 2-0	O10 1-2	a23 2-1	N21 1-2		J02 1-4	S19 3-0	F06 5-1	M26 2-1	M25 2-0	S05 1-2	N07 3-1	O24 0-2	m07 3-1	D05 1-3	D19 0-0	D25 2-1
11 HUDDERSFIELD T	a27 1-2	A31 1-1	a09 1-1	D05 1-1	D19 5-0	S26 2-0	J16 2-1	N21 6-0	N07 0-0	A29 1-1		S07 2-1	M29 4-3	a06 1-0	F17 1-1	D26 1-2	M26 1-0	M02 2-2	J30 6-1	O24 4-1	O10 2-2	S12 3-1
12 LEICESTER C	O24 1-2	J02 3-8	M26 3-1	a23 1-0	M12 2-2	D26 1-3	S26 1-0	F27 1-1	a09 0-1	J30 1-2	O15 2-4		S12 2-1	S05 4-0	A31 2-2	M29 4-2	F04 2-1	N07 4-3	O10 3-2	N21 5-0	D05 2-3	F18 2-1
13 LIVERPOOL	a09 2-1	S05 2-0	D05 4-3	N07 4-2	O24 3-2	S02 2-2	a06 2-1	D19 1-1	S19 1-3	S26 4-0	M28 0-3	J27 3-3		N21 4-3	S16 7-2	J02 4-2	a23 1-3	M12 2-1	D25 3-1	M26 1-2	M02 4-1	O10 2-2
14 MANCHESTER C	S19 1-3	N28 3-3	M28 2-1	F20 3-1	F06 7-1	D12 2-1	a16 1-1	S09 3-0	J27 1-0	N14 4-1	O31 3-0	J16 5-1	a02 0-1		M19 1-2	M05 5-1	J01 3-3	O03 1-1	a30 1-2	A29 1-1	S23 2-5	O17 0-1
15 MIDDLESBROUGH	D19 2-5	D26 1-1	O24 2-0	M26 0-2	F27 0-3	J30 3-1	A29 0-2	S26 5-2	a23 1-0	M28 4-0	O03 1-0	m07 1-1	S09 4-1	N07 3-3		F20 2-1	N21 0-1	D05 4-3	S12 4-0	M12 0-1	a09 1-0	J16 3-2
16 NEWCASTLE U	N07 3-2	J01 3-1	m07 0-3	M02 5-3	a27 2-2	F17 3-1	S12 4-1	M26 3-3	m04 0-0	J16 2-0	D25 2-1	M25 3-2	A29 0-1	O24 2-1	O10 3-1		D05 0-0	D19 5-3	S26 4-1	a09 1-2	N21 5-1	J30 2-2
17 PORTSMOUTH	S16 0-3	O17 0-3	F17 2-1	S05 2-0	M28 2-2	M09 3-2	O31 1-0	J30 2-0	S02 0-3	M19 2-0	N14 3-2	a30 0-1	D12 2-0	D26 3-2	a02 2-0	a16 6-0		J02 2-1	N28 2-0	O10 0-0	S26 0-1	M05 3-0
18 SHEFFIELD U	D25 4-1	D12 5-4	J30 1-0	J01 3-2	m07 1-3	N14 4-0	N28 4-2	J16 3-1	O10 1-5	M05 2-1	O17 0-2	M19 2-2	O31 3-0	F15 2-1	a16 2-1	a30 0-3	A29 1-2		a02 1-1	S26 1-1	S12 1-0	S07 6-0
19 SHEFFIELD W	D05 1-3	O03 1-0	N07 5-1	J02 5-1	M26 3-0	S05 7-1	S21 2-2	O24 3-1	F27 1-3	A31 4-1	S19 4-1	F20 3-1	D26 1-1	D19 1-1	J25 1-1	F06 2-0	a09 3-1	N21 2-1		a23 3-2	M12 2-5	M28 6-1
20 SUNDERLAND	a06 2-0	M25 1-1	S16 2-3	O03 2-2	S19 4-0	M19 3-0	O17 2-1	J01 0-0	S05 2-3	a16 2-0	M05 1-3	a02 4-1	N14 1-3	J02 2-5	O31 0-0	N28 1-4	F20 5-1	F06 1-0	D12 3-1		S02 2-1	a30 2-0
21 W.B.A.	J02 1-0	N14 3-0	D25 0-1	S19 4-1	S05 4-0	M05 3-0	D12 4-0	O03 4-0	M28 1-1	a30 5-6	F20 3-2	a16 1-2	O17 1-2	S14 1-1	N28 1-1	a02 2-1	F06 3-0	J25 0-1	O31 1-1	S07 1-0		M19 3-1
22 WEST HAM U	M26 1-1	F06 2-1	a23 2-4	a09 1-3	N21 1-1	J02 3-1	A31 3-1	M12 2-1	D05 4-2	D26 3-1	F01 1-1	O03 1-4	F20 1-0	M02 1-1	S05 0-2	S19 2-1	O24 2-1	S21 1-2	M25 1-2	D19 2-2	N07 1-5	

Another skilful full-back, Tom Parker skippered Arsenal into second place, two points adrift of the Merseysiders.

DIVISION 2

	BARNSLEY	BRADFORD	BRADFORD C	BRISTOL C	BURNLEY	BURY	CHARLTON A	CHESTERFIELD	LEEDS U	MANCHESTER U	MILLWALL	NOTTINGHAM F	NOTTS CO	OLDHAM A	PLYMOUTH A	PORT VALE	PRESTON N.E.	SOUTHAMPTON	STOKE C	SWANSEA T	TOTTENHAM T	WOLVERHAMPTON W
1 BARNSLEY		M05 2-2	A29 1-2	F20 1-1	a16 0-1	S07 0-1	a30 1-4	D12 3-1	J16 0-2	O07 0-0	D26 2-1	M19 3-1	F06 1-1	A31 3-1	O03 0-0	M28 3-0	N28 4-2	a02 3-3	N14 1-0	S12 2-3	J30 3-2	O31 2-2
2 BRADFORD	O24 1-0		N07 1-0	M26 2-0	S26 2-0	a09 2-1	S16 3-0	J30 1-0	D25 3-0	A29 3-1	a23 1-2	S12 4-1	M12 1-1	N21 5-0	D19 2-0	D05 2-2	F17 1-5	O10 2-1	A31 2-1	F27 2-1	J16 2-1	M29 2-1
3 BRADFORD C	J02 9-1	M19 0-0		S19 3-0	N14 1-2	O03 1-3	O17 1-1	a02 3-0	M28 4-1	D12 4-3	m07 0-0	N28 2-2	S05 0-2	F06 2-0	J27 3-3	F20 4-0	a30 0-1	O31 5-2	M05 2-2	D26 5-1	a16 2-0	S07 2-2
4 BRISTOL C	O10 4-0	N14 0-0	J30 0-1		M28 1-6	A29 1-3	N28 1-2	O17 1-1	S26 0-2	a30 2-1	S12 1-4	M05 1-1	S02 3-2	D25 1-1	S23 0-2	J16 0-2	M19 4-2	D12 0-1	a16 0-0	F13 1-1	O31 1-1	a02 0-4
5 BURNLEY	D05 5-3	F06 3-2	M26 1-1	M25 1-2		O24 2-2	J23 0-1	S07 2-2	N21 0-5	O03 2-0	D19 1-1	m07 1-0	a23 1-1	F27 1-4	N07 1-1	M12 2-2	D25 2-2	J02 1-3	S05 3-0	a09 4-1	F20 2-0	S19 1-3
6 BURY	S14 7-1	N28 4-2	F17 0-2	J02 2-1	M05 1-0		D12 6-0	O31 0-1	O10 1-4	a02 0-0	S26 2-0	a30 2-2	M25 2-1	S05 2-1	J01 2-2	J30 2-0	O17 4-1	F03 3-0	M19 0-1	A31 2-1	N14 1-1	a16 1-0
7 CHARLTON A	M07 3-1	S07 2-2	F27 1-0	a09 2-0	S12 0-1	a23 3-0		J16 0-0	O24 0-1	M28 1-0	O10 1-3	A29 3-1	M26 3-1	D05 2-2	N21 2-0	N07 2-1	J30 2-1	S26 2-3	F15 1-1	M12 3-3	D26 2-5	m07 3-2
8 CHESTERFIELD	a23 2-2	S19 3-2	N21 2-2	F27 3-1	J01 5-1	M12 4-1	S05 3-2		a09 1-1	F06 1-3	M26 1-0	F20 1-0	N07 1-4	O24 0-2	A31 1-2	D19 4-0	M28 3-1	D25 1-0	J02 1-3	D05 1-2	O03 4-2	J27 1-2
9 LEEDS U	S05 0-1	D26 3-2	M29 1-1	F06 1-0	a02 3-1	F20 1-0	M05 2-0	N28 3-3		M19 1-4	S07 0-1	a16 1-1	J23 2-2	O03 5-0	S19 0-0	m07 0-2	N14 4-1	a30 1-0	O31 2-0	J02 3-2	D12 1-0	O17 2-1
10 MANCHESTER U	F27 3-0	J02 0-2	a23 1-0	D19 0-1	F17 5-1	N21 1-2	M25 0-2	S26 3-1	N07 2-5		D05 2-0	J30 3-2	O24 3-3	M26 5-1	M12 2-1	a09 2-0	O10 3-2	S02 2-3	S16 1-1	S05 2-1	S12 1-1	D25 3-2
11 MILLWALL	D25 2-0	D12 3-0	A31 6-1	J25 1-0	a30 2-0	F06 2-1	F20 1-0	N14 5-0	S14 2-3	a16 1-1		a02 1-0	J02 4-3	S19 0-0	S05 1-3	O03 2-2	O31 4-1	M05 0-1	O17 1-0	M25 3-1	N28 1-2	M19 1-2
12 NOTTINGHAM F	N07 1-2	J27 6-1	a09 2-1	O24 3-1	O01 1-2	D19 0-2	J02 3-2	O10 4-0	D05 3-3	S19 2-1	N21 1-1		O03 2-1	M12 2-0	F27 3-2	M26 2-1	S16 2-2	M25 2-0	D26 1-1	a23 6-1	F06 1-3	S05 2-0
13 NOTTS CO	S26 2-3	O31 0-2	J16 1-1	m07 3-0	D12 5-0	M28 0-1	N14 2-2	M19 1-1	S12 1-1	M05 1-2	A29 2-0	F13 2-6		S23 1-0	F20 3-0	D25 4-2	a16 1-4	N28 5-0	a02 2-1	J30 1-2	O17 3-1	a30 3-1
14 OLDHAM A	m07 2-2	a02 2-1	S26 1-1	D26 2-1	O17 3-1	J16 1-2	a16 1-0	M05 6-1	F13 2-1	N14 1-5	J30 1-1	O31 2-4	S14 5-2		M25 1-3	S12 3-0	A29 2-2	M19 2-0	D12 1-3	O10 2-0	a30 1-2	N28 0-2
15 PLYMOUTH A	F13 3-0	a30 4-1	S12 3-3	S16 2-1	M19 4-0	D26 5-1	a02 1-1	m07 4-0	J30 3-2	O31 3-1	J16 8-1	O17 5-1	O10 3-4	M28 5-0		A29 1-3	D12 2-1	a16 1-2	N28 1-1	S26 4-2	M05 4-1	N14 3-3
16 PORT VALE	M25 3-0	a16 1-3	O10 2-0	S05 4-2	O31 1-3	S19 1-1	M19 0-1	a30 2-1	A31 1-2	N28 1-2	F13 2-2	N14 2-0	D26 2-0	J25 1-1	J02 2-0		M05 0-1	O17 0-0	F06 3-0	S21 0-4	a02 1-3	D12 1-7
17 PRESTON N.E.	a09 1-2	O03 1-0	D19 5-2	N07 1-1	D26 2-1	F29 0-2	S19 3-2	M25 2-2	M26 0-0	F20 0-0	M12 2-0	S07 1-1	D05 0-0	J02 2-3	a23 5-2	O24 1-4		S05 2-1	F25 2-0	N21 1-0	m07 2-0	F06 4-2
18 SOUTHAMPTON	N21 2-0	F20 0-3	M12 0-1	a23 1-1	A29 3-0	S12 2-1	F06 1-1	D26 1-2	D19 2-1	m07 1-1	O24 3-1	M28 4-0	a09 3-1	N07 1-1	D05 0-6	F27 5-1	J16 3-3		S19 1-2	M26 3-0	S07 2-1	O03 1-3
19 STOKE C	M26 2-0	m07 1-0	O24 3-1	D05 1-1	J16 3-0	N07 3-2	O03 4-0	A29 2-1	M12 3-4	S07 3-0	F27 0-0	D25 2-1	N21 2-2	a23 1-1	a09 3-2	S26 4-0	S12 4-1	J30 2-0		D19 0-0	M28 2-2	F20 2-1
20 SWANSEA T	J23 3-0	O17 1-0	D25 0-1	O03 2-0	N28 5-1	m07 2-0	O31 2-0	a16 1-1	A29 0-2	J16 3-1	M28 4-0	D12 4-1	S19 5-1	F20 1-0	F06 4-1	S07 2-3	a02 0-3	N14 3-4	a30 1-1		M19 1-1	M05 1-1
21 TOTTENHAM H	S19 4-2	S05 3-3	D05 1-5	M12 2-1	O10 1-1	M26 0-0	D25 0-1	F13 3-3	a23 3-1	J23 4-1	a09 1-0	S26 1-3	F27 2-0	D19 3-2	O24 0-1	N21 9-3	A31 4-0	S14 5-2	M25 3-3	N07 6-2		J02 3-3
22 WOLVERHAMPTON W	M12 2-0	M28 6-0	S14 3-1	N21 4-2	J30 3-1	D05 6-0	D28 3-1	S12 6-0	F27 1-1	D26 7-0	N07 5-0	J16 0-0	D19 0-0	a09 7-1	M26 2-0	a23 2-0	S26 3-2	F13 5-1	O10 0-1	O24 2-0	A29 4-0	

Season 1931-32

DIVISION 3 NORTH

	ACCRINGTON S	BARROW	CARLISLE U	CHESTER	CREWE A	DARLINGTON	DONCASTER R	GATESHEAD	HALIFAX T	HARTLEPOOLS U	HULL C	LINCOLN C	NEW BRIGHTON	ROCHDALE	ROTHERHAM U	SOUTHPORT	STOCKPORT CO	TRANMERE R	WALSALL	WIGAN B	WREXHAM	YORK C
1 ACCRINGTON S		a23 2-0	S02 5-3	F27 2-3	S29 2-0	N07 4-0	S05 3-2	a09 1-2	M26 4-0	O24 5-0	D19 1-1	J01 2-2	D05 4-1	J02 3-0	O03 5-2	F10 1-1	F20 2-0	F06 2-2	N21 1-0		D25 5-0	S19 2-1
2 BARROW	F18 3-0		J09 4-1	F20 4-0	a02 2-1	D25 3-4	M19 3-2	J16 3-1	S07 3-1	M28 4-1	F06 0-2	O03 0-2	S12 4-1	N14 4-1	J30 3-0	O31 1-1	a30 4-2	O17 3-1	J02 7-1		a16 1-0	M05 3-1
3 CARLISLE U	m07 3-0	a09 3-1		D19 4-3	S05 2-1	O24 0-2	S19 5-1	M26 0-0	M12 4-0	J02 3-2	D05 0-1	a23 0-3	N21 0-0	J23 4-0	M25 1-2	F06 2-2	D26 1-1	J01 1-1	N07 4-0		S10 2-2	O03 1-1
4 CHESTER	O17 1-0	O10 4-2	a30 4-1		a06 1-0	J16 3-1	J09 1-1	S26 1-1	S12 3-1	S16 2-3	M25 2-0	D25 2-1	F13 2-0	a16 7-2	O31 2-1	a02 4-0	M05 2-1	M19 3-1	J30 5-1	A29 4-0	S30 2-5	N14 3-0
5 CREWE A	S07 3-1	N21 3-2	J16 5-1	a23 1-0		F27 0-1	F06 2-0	N07 3-5	O24 4-3	D19 6-0	a09 4-3	D05 8-1	M26 3-2	S19 1-0	D25 5-0	O03 1-1	D12 2-2	M25 0-0	M12 2-1	S12 4-3	A29 3-0	F20 8-1
6 DARLINGTON	M19 4-1	S02 0-2	M05 0-1	S05 4-1	O17 1-0		a30 2-3	M25 1-2	F13 3-0	J23 6-3	S16 2-1	J02 0-6	J01 3-0	F06 3-1	a02 2-1	F24 0-1	N14 2-0	J20 1-2	O10 2-0	S19 5-0	O31 1-1	a16 4-1
7 DONCASTER R	J16 3-1	N07 0-1	J30 3-3	a09 3-0	S26 2-1	D19 3-2		O21 1-2	O10 3-1	D05 1-3	M26 2-1	N21 0-3	M12 2-1	F13 2-0	S21 2-0	M28 3-0	A29 1-1	m07 2-2	F27 2-1		S12 2-4	D25 1-0
8 GATESHEAD	J09 4-0	S05 4-0	N14 4-0	F06 1-2	M19 3-3	M28 3-2	M05 2-1		D26 1-1	O03 3-1	J23 2-1	S19 2-3	J02 4-0	O31 3-1	D16 4-1	O17 2-0	a16 2-1	F20 3-3	m07 2-0		a02 4-0	S09 8-0
9 HALIFAX T	N14 1-0	S14 1-0	O31 1-1	J23 2-1	M05 4-1	O03 0-3	F20 4-0	D25 1-2		S19 2-0	J02 2-2	S05 3-0	A31 0-0	O17 3-2	J09 1-1	a30 3-0	a02 2-2	a16 0-0	M28 1-2		M19 1-0	a28 4-1
10 HARTLEPOOLS U	M05 1-0	M25 0-2	A29 2-2	S09 2-2	J09 3-1	S12 3-3	a16 5-0	F13 1-2	J30 4-1		D26 2-3	m07 4-3	O10 1-0	D12 3-0	M19 1-4	S23 2-1	O31 2-2	N14 0-5	S26 4-3		O17 0-1	a02 7-2
11 HULL C	a30 3-0	S26 3-0	a16 2-0	M28 0-2	J14 2-4	S07 4-1	N14 4-1	S12 0-1	A29 1-0	D25 3-1		F20 4-1	J30 4-1	a02 4-1	O17 0-1	M19 1-0	F13 4-4	M05 3-0	J16 3-0		m07 5-0	O31 2-3
12 LINCOLN C	M25 5-1	F13 3-1	F24 3-1	D26 4-0	a16 5-1	A29 2-0	a02 1-2	J30 1-0	J16 9-1	A31 6-0	O10 1-0		S26 3-0	J09 3-0	M05 3-1	N14 7-0	O17 1-2	O31 4-2	S12 3-0	S14 3-0	a30 0-0	M19 1-1
13 NEW BRIGHTON	a16 2-1	J23 0-3	a02 4-1	O03 0-1	N14 0-1	D26 0-0	O31 1-0	A29 1-3	m07 2-0	F20 1-1	S19 1-2	F06 2-1		M19 1-1	a30 3-1	M05 3-1	D30 2-1	J16 1-1	S09 0-1		J09 1-1	O17 0-2
14 ROCHDALE	A29 2-2	M26 0-6	S12 4-3	D05 0-3	J30 2-3	S26 1-1	O03 3-1	M12 0-3	F27 1-4	a23 1-3	N21 3-6	a09 3-5	N07 3-2		m07 1-4	F20 0-1	S15 1-0	D26 3-6	O24 0-1		J16 2-4	M28 3-5
15 ROTHERHAM U	F13 2-3	S19 0-2	M28 4-1	M12 3-0	D26 0-2	N21 2-4	S14 6-3	a23 2-1	a09 5-0	N07 1-2	F27 2-0	O24 0-1	D19 2-2	A31 5-0		J02 2-0	S26 1-1	J23 1-0	D05 3-0		O10 0-0	S05 0-1
16 SOUTHPORT	S12 4-2	M12 3-1	S26 2-0	N21 1-1	F13 1-1	a23 3-0	M25 5-0	F27 1-1	D19 2-2	a09 1-2	N07 1-0	M26 1-1	O24 1-0	O10 3-1	A29 3-2		J16 1-0	S08 1-0	D25 5-1		J30 2-0	J01 3-0
17 STOCKPORT CO	O10 3-0	D19 2-0	D25 0-0	O24 0-0	A31 1-2	M26 1-0	J02 1-0	D05 1-1	N21 2-1	M12 3-2	O03 2-0	F27 0-1	a23 3-1	S07 3-1	F06 1-0	S05 0-1		S19 0-1	a09 0-1		M25 5-1	J23 3-2
18 TRANMERE R	S26 8-1	F27 6-1	O10 3-0	N07 2-2	M28 4-1	a09 3-1	A31 0-1	D19 4-3	D05 5-2	M26 5-0	O24 2-2	M12 1-0	S05 5-1	D25 9-1	S12 6-1	S14 2-0	J30 2-2		a23 4-1		F13 3-1	J02 2-2
19 WALSALL	a02 5-5	A29 1-2	M19 3-1	S19 1-1	O31 2-1	F20 1-0	O17 2-0	A31 1-2	M29 4-2	F06 2-3	S05 1-4	J23 0-3	S14 3-0	M05 2-1	a16 3-0	D26 2-1	J09 3-1	F18 2-1		O03 3-0	N14 2-0	D12 2-2
20 WIGAN B			O17 3-2					O10 2-1	S26 0-1	S05 1-1	S02 3-1	S09 0-3	RESIGNED									
21 WREXHAM	D26 2-1	D05 0-1	S14 1-0	S02 1-1	J02 2-4	M12 3-0	J23 2-1	N21 2-1	N07 2-3	F27 5-3	a23 2-1	D19 1-3	a09 2-1	S05 4-0	F20 1-0	S19 1-1	M28 2-1	O03 2-1	M26 5-1	O24 5-0		F06 2-1
22 YORK C	J30 1-0	O24 1-0	F13 2-4	M26 3-1	O10 3-3	D05 3-0	D26 1-2	S16 3-2	a23 7-2	N21 3-1	M12 0-0	N07 1-1	F27 4-0	M25 5-2	J16 2-0	S02 1-2	S12 1-0	A29 3-2	D19 2-0		S26 3-2	

DIVISION 3 SOUTH

	BOURNEMOUTH	BRENTFORD	BRIGHTON & HA	BRISTOL R	CARDIFF C	CLAPTON O	COVENTRY C	CRYSTAL P	EXETER C	FULHAM	GILLINGHAM	LUTON T	MANSFIELD T	NORTHAMPTON T	NORWICH C	Q.P.R.	READING	SOUTHEND U	SWINDON T	THAMES	TORQUAY U	WATFORD
1 BOURNEMOUTH		D19 1-3	F20 1-2	A29 2-2	N07 3-0	D26 0-1	F27 2-2	S19 4-1	S12 5-2	D05 0-3	O24 0-2	M12 1-1	O03 3-2	M26 1-1	S09 1-0	J16 2-2	N21 2-2	a09 0-0	M28 2-1	a23 4-2	m07 5-0	F06 3-3
2 BRENTFORD	a30 4-2		a02 2-2	O17 4-2	F13 2-3	O31 3-0	S12 4-2	a13 1-1	J16 2-2	D25 0-0	J30 1-1	S26 1-0	J13 1-1	O10 2-0	N14 0-1	A29 1-0	S24 3-0	M25 2-3	M19 2-0	m07 1-0	M05 3-0	a16 1-2
3 BRIGHTON & H.A.	O10 4-1	N21 1-2		S26 2-0	m07 0-0	S12 1-1	D05 4-1	S09 0-3	a09 1-1	N07 2-3	a23 7-0	D19 3-2	D26 4-0	F27 0-0	A29 2-1	F13 1-0	O24 2-0	M12 1-2	J16 1-0	M26 1-1	J30 0-2	M25 2-1
4 BRISTOL R	J02 4-1	F27 2-0	F06 0-4		N21 2-2	S16 2-1	M12 3-1	S05 6-1	O24 2-4	D19 2-2	N07 6-2	M26 3-1	S19 1-1	a09 3-2	O03 0-1	A31 1-1	D05 2-0	a23 0-0	F20 0-2	D26 4-1	M25 1-1	J27 3-2
5 CARDIFF C	M19 0-0	O03 3-2	A31 1-1	a02 3-1		a16 5-0	S14 6-1	O31 1-3	F20 5-2	S19 0-3	M28 1-0	D26 4-1	O17 2-0	J02 5-0	a30 0-2	N14 0-4	S05 5-1	J23 2-3	a13 3-0	F06 9-2	J13 5-2	M05 2-1
6 CLAPTON O	D25 1-2	M12 2-2	J23 2-2	S07 1-0	D05 1-1		M26 5-2	A31 1-3	N07 2-2	F27 0-1	N21 3-1	a09 0-0	S05 4-0	a23 3-2	S19 1-3	M25 3-0	D19 2-2	O03 2-4	F06 4-2	O24 1-1	O10 1-3	J02 2-2
7 COVENTRY C	O17 6-1	J28 0-1	a16 4-3	O31 1-1	S07 2-1	N14 4-2		F06 8-0	S19 4-0	J02 5-5	F13 6-4	O10 3-2	D12 5-1	M28 4-1	J09 3-0	M05 1-0	D25 5-1	A31 0-2	a02 3-2	S05 2-0	M19 3-1	a30 5-0
8 CRYSTAL P	J30 1-1	a23 1-0	S16 2-0	J16 5-0	M12 5-0	m07 0-0	S26 2-2		D19 3-0	a09 2-0	F27 1-0	O24 1-1	J09 2-1	N07 4-0	M25 3-1	S12 1-1	M26 1-1	N21 3-2	D25 0-0	D05 2-1	A29 7-0	O03 2-1
9 EXETER C	J27 1-0	S05 4-1	S30 3-1	M05 1-0	O10 3-1	M19 4-3	J30 3-0	a30 0-1		S02 0-3	S26 4-0	F13 1-1	a16 3-0	S16 0-0	a02 3-0	O17 6-2	M28 4-0	D26 3-0	N14 1-1	J02 4-1	O31 3-1	D16 2-0
10 FULHAM	a16 3-0	D26 2-1	M19 3-0	a30 3-2	J30 4-0	O17 5-1	A29 5-3	J18 4-0	m07 3-1		J16 0-2	S12 3-2	N14 2-1	S26 1-3	O31 4-0	D28 1-3	F13 3-3	O10 1-1	M05 2-2	M28 8-0	S07 10-2	a02 5-0
11 GILLINGHAM	M05 1-4	S19 0-2	a13 0-0	M19 1-0	M25 1-1	a02 0-2	O03 1-3	O17 0-0	F06 0-1	S05 2-1		S09 1-3	a30 2-0	D25 3-2	a16 3-3	O31 1-0	S02 1-1	J02 4-0	J09 2-1	J23 2-0	N14 1-1	F20 0-1
12 LUTON T	O31 1-0	F06 1-1	a30 3-2	N14 3-0	D25 2-1	J09 1-5	F20 3-1	M05 3-0	O03 6-3	J23 1-3	S14 2-0		M25 3-1	A31 1-0	M29 7-1	M19 4-1	J02 6-1	S05 1-3	a16 6-0	S19 2-0	a02 6-1	O17 0-1
13 MANSFIELD T	F13 2-1	a09 2-0	D25 3-3	J30 0-3	F27 1-2	J16 4-3	a23 3-3	O10 1-1	D05 3-1	M26 1-2	D19 3-1	M28 5-2		O24 2-0	m07 5-2	S26 2-2	M12 1-7	N07 4-4	A29 3-2	N21 4-0	S12 2-4	S07 3-2
14 NORTHAMPTON T	N14 1-1	F20 3-0	O17 0-1	D28 6-0	A29 1-0	a21 4-3	M29 3-2	M19 5-0	S07 2-1	F06 0-1	D26 1-0	S28 1-2	M05 3-0		J16 2-2	a02 6-1	J28 2-4	S19 1-2	a30 4-1	O03 0-4	a16 2-0	O31 1-1
15 NORWICH C	S14 1-2	M26 1-0	J02 2-1	F13 6-0	D19 2-0	J30 3-2	a09 6-2	M28 3-2	N21 0-1	M12 2-2	D06 1-1	a23 3-3	A31 1-1	S06 0-0		O10 2-1	F27 0-0	O24 1-1	S12 4-2	N07 7-0	S26 2-0	D26 4-1
16 Q.P.R.	S05 0-3	J02 1-2	O03 1-1	m07 2-1	M26 2-3	M28 3-2	O24 1-1	J28 2-2	F27 1-0	a23 3-1	M10 7-0	N07 3-1	F06 1-1	N21 3-2	F20 2-2		a09 2-0	D05 2-1	S10 1-2	D19 6-0	D26 3-1	S19 4-4
17 READING	a02 3-1	S09 1-2	M05 3-1	a16 3-0	J16 5-1	a30 5-0	D26 2-1	N14 3-0	M25 2-0	O03 4-2	m07 2-0	A29 2-1	O31 4-1	S12 3-2	O17 1-1	J13 3-2		F06 3-1	J30 6-2	J09 6-1	D12 4-1	M19 2-1
18 SOUTHEND U	J13 1-3	M28 1-0	O31 2-0	J09 4-1	S12 1-1	F13 1-3	m07 4-0	a02 1-0	D25 0-1	F20 4-1	A29 2-0	J16 1-1	M19 5-2	J30 0-1	M05 2-0	a16 0-0	S26 1-1		O17 3-0	S07 1-1	a30 4-2	N14 3-0
19 SWINDON T	M25 3-0	N07 1-3	S05 1-2	O10 2-1	a23 1-4	S26 2-3	N21 2-2	D26 3-2	M26 2-1	O24 2-2	a09 4-0	D05 3-2	J02 5-2	D19 3-0	J23 2-0	S16 1-2	S19 0-2	F27 1-2		M12 2-0	F13 3-0	S02 4-1
20 THAMES	D12 4-2	S03 1-1	N14 1-2	D25 0-2	S26 1-2	M05 3-3	J16 5-2	a16 1-3	A29 0-0	M25 0-0	S12 3-0	J30 2-4	a02 6-3	F13 0-2	M19 1-0	a30 3-2	O10 0-0	S17 1-3	O31 1-1		O17 1-1	J18 1-2
21 TORQUAY U	S02 1-1	O24 1-1	S19 1-1	M28 8-1	a09 2-2	F20 3-0	N07 3-3	J02 3-1	M12 2-1	S16 2-3	M26 1-0	N21 1-2	J23 2-2	D05 4-1	F06 2-4	D25 2-3	a23 1-4	D19 2-1	O03 2-1	F27 3-1		S05 3-6
22 WATFORD	S26 4-2	D05 1-4	M28 2-2	S12 5-2	O24 3-0	A29 2-1	D19 2-0	F17 1-2	a23 1-0	N21 3-1	O10 2-0	a13 3-1	S16 4-1	M12 1-2	D25 1-1	J30 2-2	N07 3-2	M26 1-1	m07 4-1	a09 3-2	J16 1-0	

LEAGUE TABLES

DIVISION 1

	P	W	D	L	F	A	W	D	L	F	A	Pts
Everton	42	18	0	3	84	30	8	4	9	32	34	56
Arsenal	42	14	5	2	52	16	8	5	8	38	32	54
Sheffield W	42	14	4	3	60	28	8	2	11	36	54	50
Huddersfield T	42	11	8	2	47	21	8	2	11	33	42	48
Aston Villa	42	15	1	5	64	28	4	7	10	40	44	46
WBA	42	12	4	5	46	21	8	2	11	31	34	46
Sheffield U	42	13	3	5	47	32	7	3	11	33	43	46
Portsmouth	42	14	2	5	37	21	5	5	11	25	41	45
Birmingham	42	13	5	3	48	22	5	3	13	30	45	44
Liverpool	42	13	4	4	56	38	6	2	13	25	55	44
Newcastle U	42	13	5	3	52	31	5	1	15	28	56	42
Chelsea	42	12	4	5	43	27	4	4	13	26	46	40
Sunderland	42	11	4	6	42	29	4	6	11	25	44	40
Manchester C	42	10	5	6	49	30	3	7	11	34	43	38
Derby Co	42	13	5	3	51	25	1	5	15	20	50	38
Blackburn R	42	12	3	6	57	41	4	3	14	32	54	38
Bolton W	42	15	1	5	51	25	2	3	16	21	55	38
Middlesbrough	42	12	3	6	41	29	3	5	13	23	60	38
Leicester C	42	11	3	7	46	39	4	4	13	28	55	37
Blackpool	42	9	4	8	42	40	3	5	13	23	62	33
Grimsby T	42	11	4	6	39	28	2	2	17	28	70	32
West Ham U	42	9	5	7	35	37	3	2	16	27	70	31

DIVISION 2

	P	W	D	L	F	A	W	D	L	F	A	Pts
Wolves	42	17	3	1	71	11	7	5	9	44	38	56
Leeds U	42	12	5	4	36	22	10	5	6	42	32	54
Stoke C	42	14	6	1	47	19	5	8	8	22	29	52
Plymouth A	42	14	4	3	69	29	6	5	10	31	37	49
Bury	42	13	4	4	44	21	8	3	10	26	37	49
Bradford	42	17	2	2	44	18	4	5	12	28	45	49
Bradford C	42	10	7	4	53	26	6	6	9	27	35	45
Tottenham H	42	11	6	4	58	37	5	5	11	29	41	43
Millwall	42	13	3	5	43	21	4	6	11	18	40	43
Charlton A	42	11	5	5	38	28	6	4	11	23	38	43
Nottingham F	42	13	4	4	49	27	3	6	12	28	45	42
Manchester U	42	12	3	6	44	31	5	5	11	27	41	42
Preston NE	42	11	6	4	37	25	5	4	12	38	52	42
Southampton	42	10	5	6	39	30	7	2	12	27	47	41
Swansea T	42	12	4	5	45	22	4	3	14	28	53	39
Notts Co	42	10	4	7	43	30	3	8	10	32	45	38
Chesterfield	42	11	3	7	43	33	2	8	11	21	53	37
Oldham A	42	10	4	7	41	34	3	6	12	21	50	36
Burnley	42	7	8	6	36	36	6	1	14	23	51	35
Port Vale	42	8	4	9	30	33	5	3	13	28	56	33
Barnsley	42	8	7	6	35	30	4	2	15	20	61	33
Bristol C	42	4	7	10	22	37	2	4	16	17	41	23

DIVISION 3 North

	P	W	D	L	F	A	W	D	L	F	A	Pts
Lincoln C	40	16	2	2	65	13	10	3	7	41	34	57
Gateshead	40	15	3	2	59	20	10	4	6	35	28	57
Chester	40	16	2	2	54	22	5	6	9	24	38	50
Tranmere R	40	15	4	1	76	23	4	7	9	31	35	49
Barrow	40	16	1	3	59	23	8	0	12	27	36	49
Crewe A	40	15	3	2	64	24	6	3	11	31	42	48
Southport	40	14	5	1	44	15	4	5	11	14	38	46
Hull C	40	14	1	5	52	21	6	4	10	30	32	45
York C	40	14	3	3	49	24	4	4	12	27	57	43
Wrexham	40	14	2	4	42	25	4	5	11	22	44	43
Darlington	40	12	1	7	41	27	5	3	12	25	42	38
Stockport	40	12	3	5	31	15	1	8	11	24	38	37
Hartlepools U	40	10	4	6	47	37	6	1	13	31	63	37
Accrington S	40	14	4	2	56	20	1	2	17	19	60	36
Doncaster R	40	12	3	5	38	27	4	1	15	21	53	36
Walsall	40	12	3	5	42	30	4	0	16	15	55	35
Halifax T	40	11	6	3	36	18	2	2	16	25	69	34
Carlisle U	40	9	7	4	40	23	2	4	14	24	56	33
Rotherham U	40	10	3	7	41	23	4	1	15	22	49	32
New Brighton	40	8	5	7	25	23	0	3	17	13	53	24
Rochdale	40	4	2	14	33	63	0	1	19	15	72	11

Wigan Borough resigned from the League

DIVISION 3 South

	P	W	D	L	F	A	W	D	L	F	A	Pts
Fulham	42	15	3	3	72	27	9	6	6	39	35	57
Reading	42	19	1	1	65	21	4	8	9	32	46	55
Southend U	42	12	5	4	41	18	9	6	6	36	35	53
Crystal P	42	14	7	0	48	12	6	4	11	26	51	51
Brentford	42	11	6	4	40	22	8	4	9	28	30	48
Luton T	42	16	1	4	62	25	4	6	11	33	45	47
Exeter C	42	16	3	2	53	16	4	4	13	24	46	47
Brighton & HA	42	12	4	5	42	21	5	8	8	31	37	46
Cardiff C	42	14	2	5	62	29	5	6	10	25	44	46
Norwich C	42	12	7	2	51	22	5	5	11	25	45	46
Watford	42	14	4	3	49	27	5	4	12	32	52	46
Coventry C	42	17	2	2	74	28	1	6	14	34	69	44
QPR	42	11	6	4	50	30	4	6	11	29	43	42
Northampton T	42	12	3	6	48	26	4	4	13	21	43	39
Bournemouth	42	8	8	5	42	32	5	4	12	28	40	38
Clapton O	42	7	8	6	41	35	5	3	13	36	55	35
Swindon T	42	12	2	7	47	31	2	4	15	23	53	34
Bristol R	42	11	6	4	46	30	2	2	17	19	62	34
Torquay U	42	9	6	6	49	39	3	3	15	23	67	33
Mansfield T	42	11	5	5	54	45	0	5	16	21	63	32
Gillingham	42	8	6	7	26	26	2	2	17	14	56	28
Thames	42	6	7	8	35	35	1	2	18	18	74	23

Football League Records

Top scorers: Div 1, J.Bowers (Derby County) 35 goals; Div 2, E.Harper (Preston North End) 37 goals; Div 3(N), W.McNaughton (Hull City) 41 goals; Div 3(S), C.Bourton (Coventry City) 40 goals.
Thames did not seek re-election. Aldershot and Newport County were elected to League. Mansfield Town transferred to Division Three North.

Cliff Bastin, who scored a record 33 goals for a winger when Arsenal regained the First Division title in 1932-3

DIVISION 1

	ARSENAL	ASTON VILLA	BIRMINGHAM	BLACKBURN R	BLACKPOOL	BOLTON W	CHELSEA	DERBY CO	EVERTON	HUDDERSFIELD T	LEEDS U	LEICESTER C	LIVERPOOL	MANCHESTER C	MIDDLESBROUGH	NEWCASTLE U	PORTSMOUTH	SHEFFIELD U	SHEFFIELD W	SUNDERLAND	W.B.A.	WOLVERHAMPTON W
1 ARSENAL		a01 5-0	D31 3-0	F25 8-0	F11 1-1	S17 3-2	D10 4-1	O08 3-3	S24 2-1	a29 2-2	D26 1-2	O29 8-2	M04 0-1	J21 2-1	N26 4-2	N12 1-0	a15 2-0	D24 9-2	a14 4-2	S03 6-1	A31 1-2	M18 1-2
2 ASTON VILLA	N19 5-3		O22 1-0	D17 4-0	N05 6-2	S03 6-1	O01 3-1	m06 2-0	M25 2-1	F18 0-3	a22 0-0	S17 4-2	J21 5-2	a08 1-1	D31 3-1	a18 3-0	F04 4-1	O15 3-0	D03 3-6	A29 1-0	M11 3-2	D26 1-3
3 BIRMINGHAM	A27 0-1	M08 3-2		S24 3-1	S10 2-1	a15 2-1	M18 0-0	F01 3-1	J07 4-0	N12 0-2	F11 2-1	a29 0-4	D10 3-0	S07 3-0	O29 1-4	D27 1-2	D24 4-0	a01 4-1	O08 2-1	a17 2-0	a26 1-1	N26 0-0
4 BLACKBURN R	O15 2-3	a29 0-5	F04 2-0		J02 6-5	M18 3-2	D31 1-3	S19 3-3	D26 3-1	M04 4-2	S03 1-1	a01 1-1	N12 2-2	F23 1-0	D24 4-2	D10 2-1	N26 3-2	O29 3-0	J21 1-1	O01 1-3	S17 4-4	a15 1-0
5 BLACKPOOL	O01 1-2	M18 6-2	J21 0-1	a14 3-0		a01 1-3	O29 4-0	D27 4-1	F22 2-1	a15 1-1	A29 2-1	O15 2-1	N26 4-1	F04 1-0	N12 3-1	D24 0-4	M04 0-2	D10 0-3	D31 3-4	S17 3-1	S03 2-4	a29 2-2
6 BOLTON W	F01 0-4	J07 0-1	D03 2-2	N05 4-2	N19 1-0		O15 2-3	M25 1-1	a08 2-4	D26 2-1	m06 5-0	O01 5-0	F04 3-3	O22 2-1	S10 4-3	A27 2-2	F22 4-1	J02 3-3	D17 3-0	M11 0-0	a22 2-2	S05 2-0
7 CHELSEA	a22 1-3	F11 0-1	N05 4-2	A27 2-2	M11 1-0	F25 1-1		O22 1-3	D03 1-0	J07 0-1	a08 6-0	a14 4-1	D27 0-2	D17 3-1	O08 2-1	S24 0-1	S07 4-4	S10 3-0	N19 0-2	m06 1-1	M25 1-2	J28 3-1
8 DERBY CO	F22 2-2	D24 0-0	S17 2-2	A31 2-1	D26 1-1	N12 4-1	M29 0-1		O15 2-0	O29 2-3	D31 5-1	N26 3-2	a01 1-1	O01 4-0	a05 2-2	a29 3-2	a17 2-0	a15 3-0	S03 2-0	F04 3-0	J21 2-2	D10 4-4
9 EVERTON	F04 1-1	N12 3-3	S03 4-1	D27 6-1	O08 2-0	N26 2-2	a15 3-2	F25 4-2		D10 2-0	a17 0-1	M08 6-3	O01 3-1	S17 2-1	a01 0-0	a05 0-0	O29 1-1	m03 1-0	A31 2-1	J21 6-1	D31 1-2	D24 5-1
10 HUDDERSFIELD T	D17 0-1	O08 0-0	M25 0-0	O22 0-3	D03 0-1	D27 2-1	S03 2-0	M11 0-0	a22 0-0		J21 2-2	A29 4-1	a18 3-1	m06 1-0	M15 0-1	F11 4-0	D31 2-2	F01 1-0	a08 4-0	N05 2-1	N19 2-1	S24 3-2
11 LEEDS U	D27 0-0	D10 1-1	O01 1-1	J07 3-1	S05 3-1	D24 4-3	N26 2-0	A27 0-2	a18 1-0	S10 1-1		N12 1-1	M18 5-0	O15 2-1	a29 0-1	a15 6-1	a01 0-1	M04 1-3	S17 3-2	F22 2-3	F04 1-1	O29 2-0
12 LEICESTER C	M11 1-1	F09 3-0	D17 2-2	N19 1-1	M30 3-0	F11 2-0	a18 1-1	a08 4-0	O22 2-2	S05 3-1	M25 3-1		O08 1-2	D03 1-2	S24 1-1	S10 0-3	D27 2-1	a27 1-1	N05 0-0	a22 4-2	m06 6-2	J07 2-2
13 LIVERPOOL	O22 2-3	S10 0-0	a22 1-0	M25 2-2	a08 4-3	S24 0-1	D26 3-0	N19 6-1	F11 7-4	a14 2-2	N05 0-1	F18 1-2		M11 1-1	F01 1-3	J07 3-0	O15 4-3	S07 2-2	m06 4-1	D03 3-3	D17 2-0	A27 5-1
14 MANCHESTER C	S10 2-3	N26 5-2	A31 1-0	O08 2-3	S24 5-1	M08 2-1	m03 1-4	F11 2-1	F01 3-0	D24 3-0	a05 0-0	a15 4-1	O29 1-1		S03 2-3	a01 1-2	D10 3-1	M22 1-0	D26 2-2	D31 2-4	a14 1-0	N12 4-1
15 MIDDLESBROUGH	a08 3-4	A27 0-2	M11 2-2	m06 4-0	M25 2-0	J21 2-1	M01 2-1	N05 0-3	N19 0-2	O15 1-1	D17 0-1	F04 1-1	S17 0-1	J07 2-0		J02 2-3	O01 5-4	D27 2-2	a22 1-1	O22 1-2	D03 3-1	a17 2-1
16 NEWCASTLE U	M25 2-1	a17 3-1	D26 2-1	a22 2-1	m06 1-2	D31 3-1	F04 2-0	D17 0-0	N05 1-2	O01 0-4	D03 3-1	J21 2-1	S03 4-3	N19 2-0	A31 5-1		S17 1-1	F18 2-0	M11 3-1	a08 0-1	O22 3-0	O15 3-2
17 PORTSMOUTH	D03 1-3	S24 2-4	m06 1-1	a08 2-0	O22 2-1	O08 2-1	A31 2-0	a14 2-0	M11 2-2	A27 1-0	N19 3-3	D26 2-1	F25 2-1	a22 1-2	F11 2-0	J28 2-0		J07 1-0	M25 3-0	D17 1-3	N05 3-0	S10 2-0
18 SHEFFIELD U	m06 3-1	a24 1-0	N19 2-1	M11 2-1	a22 1-0	a17 3-2	J21 4-1	D03 4-3	D17 3-2	S17 1-2	O22 0-0	D31 5-2	A29 6-2	N05 2-5	M27 2-0	O08 3-1	S03 2-3		F04 2-3	M25 3-0	a08 1-1	F11 0-0
19 SHEFFIELD W	J02 3-2	a15 0-2	a05 1-1	S10 1-1	A27 4-1	a29 2-0	a01 2-2	J07 0-0	S05 3-1	N26 2-1	F08 2-0	M18 4-1	D24 3-0	D27 2-1	D10 2-1	O29 2-0	N12 2-1	S24 3-3		O15 3-1	O01 3-1	M04 2-0
20 SUNDERLAND	J07 3-2	S07 1-1	a14 1-0	F11 4-2	F01 1-1	O29 7-4	D24 2-1	S24 0-2	S10 3-1	M18 1-2	O08 0-0	D10 2-1	a15 0-0	A27 3-2	M22 0-0	N26 0-2	a29 0-3	N12 2-2	F25 1-2		J02 2-2	a01 0-1
21 W.B.A.	S14 1-1	O29 3-1	O15 1-0	F08 1-3	J07 2-1	D10 4-0	N12 3-2	S10 2-0	A27 3-1	a01 2-1	S24 0-1	D24 4-3	a29 2-1	a17 4-0	a15 0-1	M04 3-2	M18 4-2	N26 0-1	F11 2-0	D26 5-1		O08 4-1
22 WOLVERHAMPTON W	N05 1-7	D27 2-4	a08 1-0	D03 5-3	D17 2-3	A29 4-1	S17 1-2	a22 3-1	m06 4-2	F04 6-4	M11 3-3	S03 1-1	D31 3-1	M25 1-2	a14 2-0	M06 1-1	J21 5-2	O01 5-1	O22 3-5	N19 0-2	F18 3-3	

George Brown led Villa's front line when 'Pongo' Waring was injured in 1932-3 and responded with 33 goals to help Villa into runners-up spot.

DIVISION 2

	BRADFORD	BRADFORD C	BURNLEY	BURY	CHARLTON A	CHESTERFIELD	FULHAM	GRIMSBY T	LINCOLN C	MANCHESTER U	MILLWALL	NOTTINGHAM F	NOTTS CO	OLDHAM A	PLYMOUTH A	PORT VALE	PRESTON N.E.	SOUTHAMPTON	STOKE C	SWANSEA T	TOTTENHAM H	WEST HAM U
1 BRADFORD		J21 2-0	S03 0-4	D03 4-0	F11 3-0	O22 5-1	M11 1-4	a17 1-1	m06 6-0	a05 1-1	N19 3-0	S24 3-1	D17 3-4	A31 1-3	F01 1-0	a22 4-2	D31 2-0	a08 2-1	O08 2-2	M25 1-0	D26 3-3	N05 3-0
2 BRADFORD C	S10 1-0		N12 2-1	D27 3-0	M18 3-0	J07 4-2	A27 2-0	a01 2-2	a18 1-1	a15 1-2	F18 1-5	O29 2-2	F04 1-2	D10 3-0	M04 2-3	O01 7-0	a29 0-0	O15 1-0	D24 1-1	S17 1-1	N26 0-1	S07 5-1
3 BURNLEY	J07 2-0	M25 0-0		m06 1-0	S24 0-1	A27 1-1	O22 3-3	D27 2-0	N05 0-0	O08 2-3	a08 3-0	J31 3-3	a22 2-1	a14 1-1	S10 1-1	N19 1-1	S05 4-0	D03 2-0	F11 1-2	D17 1-2	a24 1-1	M11 4-0
4 BURY	a15 0-0	D26 1-1	D24 5-3		D10 3-1	F25 6-0	O08 1-1	M04 4-1	S24 2-2	N12 2-2	S03 3-0	a01 5-2	A29 3-1	O29 3-3	N26 2-1	D31 0-0	M18 1-2	J21 1-0	a29 3-2	J02 3-0	S17 1-0	F11 6-1
5 CHARLTON A	O01 0-2	N05 0-0	F04 2-2	a22 1-3		m06 2-5	D03 1-2	S03 2-3	N19 4-2	A29 0-1	M25 1-4	O15 3-0	O22 3-3	J21 1-0	F18 4-1	a26 2-1	S17 0-1	D17 2-0	a14 1-0	M11 3-1	D31 0-3	a08 3-1
6 CHESTERFIELD	M04 2-1	S03 1-2	D31 6-0	O15 1-3	D24 2-3		J02 3-2	D10 1-2	D27 3-0	N26 1-1	O01 1-0	M18 0-1	S17 0-0	a29 3-1	O29 1-1	F04 2-2	N12 4-3	F22 1-0	a15 1-2	J21 1-0	a01 1-1	a14 1-0
7 FULHAM	O29 5-2	D31 1-0	M08 2-1	F18 3-3	a15 3-1	S05 2-2		a29 0-1	O15 3-2	a01 3-1	F04 1-1	D24 0-1	J21 3-4	N12 1-0	M18 3-1	S17 1-1	a14 1-0	O01 4-2	N26 1-3	S03 3-1	D10 2-2	D26 4-2
8 GRIMSBY T	a14 5-1	N19 1-1	D26 1-2	O22 1-0	J07 5-5	a22 1-1	D17 1-0		F11 3-3	J31 1-1	N05 1-1	A27 1-1	D03 1-1	F18 5-1	S06 2-3	m06 6-1	O15 5-5	M11 2-2	S10 0-1	a08 2-1	S24 3-2	M25 2-1
9 LINCOLN C	D24 2-2	a14 0-0	M18 1-4	F04 2-1	a01 1-1	D26 5-3	a05 3-0	O01 6-3		a29 3-2	J21 3-0	N26 1-1	D31 1-1	M04 1-3	a15 2-0	S03 0-1	O29 2-1	S17 1-0	D10 2-3	A29 2-0	N12 2-2	O08 6-0
10 MANCHESTER U	O15 2-1	D03 0-1	F22 2-1	M25 1-3	S07 1-1	a08 2-1	N19 4-3	S17 1-1	D17 4-1		O22 7-1	a17 2-1	N05 2-0	F04 2-0	J02 4-0	M11 1-1	O01 0-0	J07 1-2	A27 0-2	m06 1-1	J21 2-1	a22 1-2
11 MILLWALL	a01 1-1	O08 3-3	N26 4-1	J07 5-2	N12 2-1	F11 0-0	S24 2-1	M18 0-1	S10 2-0	M04 2-0		a29 1-1	D27 1-1	D24 6-1	D10 2-0	a17 0-1	a15 1-1	A27 3-0	S05 0-0	F25 3-1	O29 1-4	J31 1-0
12 NOTTINGHAM F	F04 1-1	M11 3-1	S17 1-1	N19 0-2	M16 0-1	N05 2-3	m06 1-0	D31 3-2	a08 2-2	a14 3-2	D17 0-0		F18 3-0	S03 2-3	O01 1-1	M25 1-1	J21 2-1	a22 4-2	D27 1-0	O22 2-2	A29 3-1	D03 2-2
13 NOTTS CO	a29 1-4	S24 2-0	D10 4-2	O06 2-2	M04 3-2	F01 1-1	S10 1-2	a15 1-3	A27 1-1	M18 1-0	D26 1-0	O08 2-4		N26 2-1	N12 4-1	O15 5-0	a01 0-0	a17 1-2	O29 3-4	F11 1-2	D24 3-0	J07 2-0
14 OLDHAM A	S05 1-3	a22 6-1	a17 2-2	M11 2-1	S10 0-0	D17 2-0	M25 1-3	O08 0-1	O22 5-2	S24 1-1	m06 1-0	J07 1-2	a08 5-0		A27 3-1	D03 2-1	D27 0-2	N05 2-0	J31 0-4	N19 0-0	F11 1-5	M13 3-2
15 PLYMOUTH A	S17 3-2	O22 2-1	J21 4-0	a08 1-0	O08 6-1	M11 1-0	N05 2-3	A31 4-0	D03 0-3	D26 2-3	a22 0-0	F11 1-1	M25 0-2	D31 2-1		D17 3-1	S03 5-0	N19 1-1	F25 1-0	F04 1-0	a17 2-2	m06 4-1
16 PORT VALE	D10 3-1	F11 2-0	a01 1-1	A27 1-0	D27 2-1	S24 9-1	J28 1-2	D24 4-2	J07 3-2	O29 3-3	a14 2-0	N12 0-1	M20 4-0	a15 2-4	a29 4-1		N26 0-1	S05 0-2	M04 1-3	O08 2-1	M18 1-1	S10 4-0
17 PRESTON N.E.	A27 2-3	D17 1-4	A29 6-1	N05 1-3	J28 4-2	M25 2-0	a17 1-2	M02 4-2	M11 5-0	F11 3-3	D03 0-1	S10 2-1	N19 3-0	D26 2-2	J07 3-0	a08 3-1		m06 3-1	S24 1-3	a22 1-0	O08 2-6	O22 4-1
18 SOUTHAMPTON	N26 2-0	F25 3-1	a15 3-1	S10 1-0	a29 3-0	O08 2-1	F11 2-2	O29 3-0	J28 4-0	S03 4-2	D31 2-3	D10 0-2	a14 6-2	M18 0-2	a01 2-0	A29 2-2	D24 1-0		N12 1-0	D27 2-0	M04 1-1	S24 4-3
19 STOKE C	F18 4-0	m06 4-1	O01 3-0	D17 2-3	a17 2-0	D03 2-1	a08 0-1	J21 2-0	a22 5-2	D31 0-0	A29 1-2	D26 0-1	M11 0-2	S17 4-0	O15 2-0	O22 1-0	F04 1-1	M25 3-1		N05 2-0	S03 2-0	N19 0-0
20 SWANSEA T	N12 3-1	J28 2-0	a29 2-0	a17 2-1	O29 2-0	S10 3-0	J07 3-0	N26 1-0	S05 3-1	D24 2-1	O15 1-0	M04 0-1	O01 2-0	a01 2-0	S24 0-1	F18 2-0	D10 3-1	D26 2-1	M18 0-2		a15 0-2	A27 1-0
21 TOTTENHAM H	D27 2-0	a08 1-1	O15 4-1	F01 2-1	A27 4-1	N19 4-1	a22 0-0	F04 4-3	M25 3-2	S10 6-1	M11 2-1	S05 0-0	m06 3-1	O01 1-1	a14 0-0	N05 4-0	F18 1-1	O22 5-0	J07 3-2	D03 7-0		D17 2-2
22 WEST HAM U	M20 2-1	A29 2-4	O29 4-4	O01 0-1	N26 7-3	a17 3-1	D27 1-1	N12 5-2	M27 0-0	D10 3-1	S17 3-0	a15 4-3	S03 1-1	O15 5-2	D24 2-2	J21 5-0	M06 1-1	F04 3-1	a01 1-2	D31 3-1	a29 1-0	

Season 1932-33

DIVISION 3 NORTH

	ACCRINGTON S	BARNSLEY	BARROW	CARLISLE U	CHESTER	CREWE A	DARLINGTON	DONCASTER R	GATESHEAD	HALIFAX T	HARTLEPOOLS U	HULL C	MANSFIELD T	NEW BRIGHTON	ROCHDALE	ROTHERHAM U	SOUTHPORT	STOCKPORT CO	TRANMERE R	WALSALL	WREXHAM	YORK C
1 ACCRINGTON S		M11 2-0	J28 0-0	S24 3-1	S10 1-4	O08 2-0	N19 2-0	M25 1-1	D03 0-3	A27 4-1	O22 7-1	N05 1-2	J02 6-0	J07 5-4	m03 0-3	A29 5-1	S27 1-1	a08 1-1	m06 3-0	a22 1-3	D17 5-3	F11 5-0
2 BARNSLEY	O29 4-0		a01 3-0	J02 4-1	N12 0-3	D12 7-1	F04 6-2	O01 2-3	J21 2-4	a17 1-1	D26 3-2	F18 1-0	O15 6-2	D10 1-2	a29 3-1	M04 3-1	D24 2-0	S17 2-2	A29 2-1	S03 2-1	D31 5-3	a15 1-1
3 BARROW	S17 5-0	N19 2-3		F25 2-1	O01 2-3	J14 3-0	a22 4-0	D03 3-0	m06 1-2	N05 3-3	M25 3-1	a08 0-2	S03 1-0	F04 2-1	A29 1-1	J21 2-1	D31 2-0	D17 0-3	M11 2-0	F18 1-2	O22 1-1	D27 1-0
4 CARLISLE U	F04 2-2	a08 0-1	O15 0-1		F18 1-1	S01 2-0	a27 3-0	a22 0-2	D26 1-2	M25 5-3	N19 3-1	D03 1-1	J21 3-1	O01 1-3	D31 2-2	S17 0-0	S03 0-0	S29 2-1	N05 0-1	O22 1-1	M11 2-1	a14 5-1
5 CHESTER	J21 4-2	M25 3-1	F11 2-1	O08 4-0		D26 3-1	D03 5-2	a08 2-0	D17 3-1	M11 6-3	N05 3-3	N19 1-1	D31 5-2	S17 3-0	a14 2-0	S03 1-0	A31 1-1	S14 2-2	O22 1-2	S21 1-0	F04 0-3	M29 5-0
6 CREWE A	F18 3-1	a22 2-2	a14 2-0	S05 1-0	D27 0-1		J07 2-4	m06 4-0	M11 2-0	a08 2-1	D03 6-2	D17 1-1	F04 7-0	O15 4-0	J21 3-1	O01 8-0	S17 1-1	O22 2-1	N19 2-0	N05 2-1	M25 2-0	A27 1-0
7 DARLINGTON	a01 2-2	S24 1-1	F15 1-2	a29 5-2	a15 1-1	S03 3-4		S10 2-2	A31 1-3	O08 2-1	F11 1-2	F01 3-2	M18 1-3	J18 2-1	M04 5-1	N12 4-1	O29 1-0	D31 1-1	F25 1-0	a14 1-1	J02 1-2	D24 3-0
8 DONCASTER R	N12 2-2	F11 3-1	a15 1-1	m04 4-2	a27 3-3	D24 5-1	J21 3-1		D31 3-1	M30 5-1	O08 4-1	S24 1-1	O29 2-2	a01 2-0	S17 1-0	M18 1-0	M04 2-1	S03 1-1	D26 2-2	A29 3-2	a14 1-1	a29 3-2
9 GATESHEAD	a15 1-0	S10 1-1	D24 2-3	D27 1-0	a29 3-0	O29 2-1	S07 3-0	A27 4-0		S24 3-0	J28 3-1	J07 2-3	a01 3-2	J03 2-0	M18 3-0	J25 1-1	N12 4-1	a14 0-3	F11 0-2	m03 1-1	O08 4-4	M04 2-2
10 HALIFAX T	D31 0-0	a18 2-1	M18 2-0	N12 0-1	O29 0-2	J18 1-5	F22 4-2	O15 0-0	F04 1-0		A31 4-0	D27 1-3	a29 5-1	M04 3-3	a15 2-0	D24 2-1	D12 1-0	O01 1-3	S03 4-1	S17 4-0	J21 0-0	a01 2-0
11 HARTLEPOOLS U	M04 3-1	D27 6-4	N12 0-1	a01 2-1	M18 3-1	a15 3-2	O01 2-1	F18 4-0	S17 2-2	S07 1-1		O15 0-1	D24 6-3	O29 3-2	J02 3-0	a14 2-0	a29 4-2	F04 1-1	D31 2-3	J21 2-0	S03 3-1	J14 4-2
12 HULL C	M18 4-2	O08 5-1	J19 3-0	a15 6-1	a01 2-0	a29 3-0	S17 3-1	F04 6-1	S03 1-1	D26 3-1	F25 3-0		M04 4-1	N12 5-0	D24 1-1	O29 4-2	O01 4-0	J21 3-0	a17 3-0	D31 0-0	A29 4-1	m01 2-1
13 MANSFIELD T	a17 1-3	a14 0-1	J07 2-1	S10 3-1	A27 1-0	S24 4-0	N05 3-3	M11 2-2	N19 1-2	D17 2-2	m06 7-1	O22 2-1		S05 5-0	D10 4-1	D27 9-2	O08 4-0	M25 1-2	a22 2-0	a08 2-0	D03 0-0	J28 2-0
14 NEW BRIGHTON	S03 2-2	N05 3-5	S24 1-2	F11 2-0	F08 3-1	F25 1-2	a08 7-1	N19 4-4	a22 1-1	O22 0-3	M11 5-2	M25 1-0	A31 1-0		D26 0-3	D31 5-2	a17 2-1	D03 1-1	J21 1-1	D17 2-2	m06 0-2	O08 0-1
15 ROCHDALE	O15 2-0	D17 2-3	S06 0-0	A27 0-1	a11 2-0	S10 1-4	O22 1-1	J28 2-3	N05 1-0	D03 1-0	a22 6-2	m06 3-2	O01 2-1	D27 1-0		F18 2-2	F04 1-3	M11 0-2	a08 0-3	M25 1-1	N19 3-1	J07 1-4
16 ROTHERHAM U	S05 2-3	O22 0-0	S10 1-0	J28 1-0	J07 0-5	F11 5-0	M25 3-1	N05 1-1	a08 1-2	m06 6-1	a17 1-1	M11 3-2	D26 3-0	A27 1-0	O08 2-0		a18 3-1	N19 2-1	D17 2-0	D03 4-1	a22 0-2	S24 1-0
17 SOUTHPORT	D26 2-3	m06 2-0	A27 3-0	J07 4-0	S05 2-1	J28 4-1	M11 5-1	O22 1-0	M25 4-1	J02 1-2	D17 6-3	F11 0-1	F18 5-2	a14 1-1	S24 2-0	O15 2-0		N05 2-1	D03 1-1	N19 2-1	a08 0-0	S10 5-1
18 STOCKPORT CO	J14 2-0	J28 5-4	a29 4-1	D24 0-1	m06 8-5	M04 1-0	A27 5-1	J07 5-1	a17 4-3	F11 6-0	S24 6-2	S10 3-5	N12 2-2	a15 1-1	O29 2-3	a01 1-0	M18 3-1		O08 3-0	D26 5-0	m01 1-0	S05 2-0
19 TRANMERE R	D24 4-0	S05 3-0	O29 1-3	M18 1-2	M04 2-2	a01 5-0	O15 3-1	D27 3-2	O01 4-2	J07 2-3	A27 3-3	a14 2-0	a10 3-0	S10 2-3	J18 3-1	a29 1-0	a15 2-1	F18 2-2		F04 1-3	a24 0-0	N12 2-3
20 WALSALL	D12 1-0	J07 1-1	O08 1-1	M04 5-0	D24 3-1	M18 2-1	a17 4-0	S05 2-0	O15 2-0	F09 4-0	S10 4-1	A27 1-0	J19 8-1	a29 0-0	N12 2-1	a15 1-0	a01 3-1	D27 0-0	S24 3-2		F11 2-3	O29 4-2
21 WREXHAM	a29 1-0	A27 3-0	M04 4-1	O29 2-1	S24 1-2	N12 7-0	D26 3-1	a17 3-0	F18 5-1	S10 5-2	J07 8-1	S07 3-1	a15 1-1	D24 5-0	a01 4-1	M01 5-1	J14 6-0	O15 2-0	S17 1-1	O01 3-0		M18 3-1
22 YORK C	O01 0-0	D03 3-2	a05 3-1	a17 0-1	O15 3-1	D31 4-0	m06 6-1	D17 2-3	O22 2-2	N19 5-3	a08 1-1	a22 1-2	S17 4-3	F18 3-0	S03 2-6	F04 4-3	a26 0-1	A31 2-2	M25 0-1	M11 4-2	N05 2-3	

DIVISION 3 SOUTH

	ALDERSHOT	BOURNEMOUTH	BRENTFORD	BRIGHTON & HA	BRISTOL C	BRISTOL R	CARDIFF C	CLAPTON O	COVENTRY C	CRYSTAL P	EXETER C	GILLINGHAM	LUTON T	NEWPORT CO	NORTHAMPTON T	NORWICH C	Q.P.R.	READING	SOUTHEND U	SWINDON T	TORQUAY U	WATFORD
1 ALDERSHOT		N19 1-1	m06 1-1	M29 1-1	O22 1-0	D26 1-0	S24 1-0	N05 4-0	a14 1-1	J07 3-1	a22 4-1	S10 3-0	D03 2-2	a08 2-1	M11 0-1	O08 1-3	S07 2-0	F11 4-4	A27 1-2	M25 0-1	D17 2-0	F01 2-1
2 BOURNEMOUTH	a01 1-0		F11 1-1	M18 1-1	J28 6-1	N12 2-2	S07 3-2	J07 4-2	S24 3-1	D10 3-2	F25 1-1	a29 1-0	D26 0-2	a17 1-2	S10 1-1	O29 1-1	J18 3-0	M04 0-3	a15 4-0	A27 5-1	O08 1-2	D24 2-2
3 BRENTFORD	D24 2-0	O01 1-1		a26 2-1	a17 2-1	a29 0-0	a01 7-3	O15 4-2	S08 2-1	O29 2-0	J21 0-2	M18 1-2	S17 1-0	F04 6-0	D27 1-0	a15 2-2	D31 2-0	m03 1-1	M04 3-1	F18 1-0	S03 3-1	N12 2-1
4 BRIGHTON & H.A.	O19 0-2	N05 3-0	a22 1-2		m06 7-0	M01 0-3	S10 1-0	O22 0-0	D17 1-0	S07 1-2	a08 2-1	A27 1-0	N19 2-0	M25 1-0	F11 2-1	S24 1-1	D27 4-1	F01 5-3	a14 1-2	M11 5-1	D03 1-1	J07 3-0
5 BRISTOL C	M04 2-2	S17 1-1	a14 1-2	D24 3-4		O15 3-1	a15 3-1	O01 3-0	D26 5-3	N12 3-3	D31 0-1	a01 1-1	S03 5-2	J21 3-2	F18 5-4	a29 1-1	O29 2-3	a26 4-1	M18 5-1	F04 5-1	A31 2-0	J25 2-3
6 BRISTOL R	D27 4-1	M25 1-0	D17 2-4	O08 5-3	M29 1-1		J28 0-0	M11 2-0	m06 1-0	A27 2-3	D03 1-0	J07 1-0	a08 0-0	N19 2-2	O22 4-3	F11 1-1	a17 4-1	S24 1-0	S07 3-1	N05 1-0	a22 0-2	S10 2-0
7 CARDIFF C	F04 2-1	A29 3-0	N19 2-1	J21 1-2	D03 1-1	S17 4-3		D17 6-1	a08 2-2	O15 1-1	N05 1-3	D26 1-0	M11 3-2	O22 1-3	a22 6-0	S03 4-2	O01 2-5	D31 0-1	F18 2-0	m06 3-0	M25 2-1	a14 1-1
8 CLAPTON O	M18 2-3	S03 1-1	F25 1-5	M04 2-0	F11 2-2	O29 0-3	a29 3-0		O08 2-1	J14 4-1	a14 2-2	a15 1-2	A29 0-0	D31 3-1	S24 2-2	S17 0-0	N12 2-2	D24 2-5	a01 0-0	J21 7-1	D26 1-4	D10 2-0
9 COVENTRY C	a18 3-0	F04 3-0	A29 2-3	a29 2-2	D27 6-0	D24 2-0	J14 5-0	F18 5-0		M18 6-2	S03 4-0	N12 4-2	J21 4-0	S17 3-1	O15 3-1	F02 3-5	M04 7-0	a15 3-1	O29 2-3	O01 2-1	D31 5-0	a01 1-3
10 CRYSTAL P	S03 3-0	a22 3-0	M11 2-1	A31 5-0	M25 2-2	D31 2-0	F25 4-1	a08 2-1	N05 1-3		F04 2-2	F11 5-1	m06 3-0	D17 0-0	N19 2-0	a14 4-0	J21 0-1	D26 1-1	S17 4-1	D03 4-3	O22 2-1	O08 0-3
11 EXETER C	a26 0-0	O15 2-3	S10 1-2	J18 4-1	A27 2-0	a15 1-0	M18 1-0	a17 3-0	J07 5-0	S24 1-1		M04 2-1	O01 2-0	F18 4-0	S07 3-1	a01 2-1	a29 2-0	N12 4-1	D24 3-0	D27 5-0	J28 5-0	O29 5-2
12 GILLINGHAM	J21 5-2	D17 4-0	N05 1-3	D31 2-0	N19 4-2	S03 2-0	D27 1-1	D03 3-1	M25 3-0	O01 2-0	O22 1-2		F22 1-1	m06 2-0	a08 5-1	A31 0-2	S17 4-1	a14 4-1	F04 3-2	a22 3-1	M11 1-1	F25 3-3
13 LUTON T	a15 2-1	D27 1-2	F01 5-5	a01 0-0	J07 5-4	M13 1-1	O29 8-1	S05 4-1	S10 4-1	D24 1-1	F11 4-0	O08 2-1		O15 2-2	A27 2-1	N12 1-1	a18 3-1	M18 1-1	a29 3-3	a14 6-2	S24 2-1	a26 3-2
14 NEWPORT CO	J19 2-1	J14 1-1	S24 1-6	N17 5-2	S10 1-1	a01 3-1	M04 4-2	A27 0-2	J28 2-1	a29 1-3	O08 1-1	D24 0-2	a05 3-2		J07 0-3	M18 3-4	a15 5-1	O29 3-3	F09 1-3	S05 1-2	F11 3-1	D26 2-0
15 NORTHAMPTON T	O29 5-2	J21 6-0	D26 1-0	S22 0-0	O08 2-1	M04 1-1	a10 2-0	F04 3-0	F25 5-1	a01 1-0	A29 5-3	J14 1-0	D31 1-0	S03 8-0		D24 2-2	M18 2-1	a29 1-0	N12 0-0	S17 6-0	a18 2-0	a15 0-0
16 NORWICH C	F23 3-2	M11 6-0	D03 3-0	F04 1-0	D17 3-0	O01 1-1	J07 3-1	J28 2-0	a22 2-1	a17 3-0	N19 0-0	S05 2-0	M25 2-1	N05 3-1	m06 2-0		O15 3-2	S10 2-2	D27 1-0	O22 5-2	a08 1-2	A27 1-2
17 Q.P.R.	S01 2-2	a08 3-1	A27 2-3	D26 0-1	M11 1-1	a14 1-1	F11 5-1	M25 2-1	O22 3-3	S10 2-1	D17 1-3	J28 1-1	a22 3-1	D03 6-1	N05 1-1	F25 2-2		O08 0-3	J07 6-1	N19 4-2	m06 1-1	S24 2-1
18 READING	O01 2-2	O22 6-2	a08 1-3	S17 3-0	a22 2-2	F04 3-1	A27 4-2	m06 3-1	D03 3-3	D27 2-3	M25 2-2	a17 4-0	N05 4-1	M11 4-1	D17 4-0	J21 3-2	F18 3-1		O15 1-1	J07 7-1	N19 5-2	S07 2-0
19 SOUTHEND U	D31 5-1	D03 2-1	O22 0-1	a17 2-1	N05 3-1	A29 2-2	O08 2-2	N19 3-3	M11 1-3	F01 1-2	m06 1-2	S24 2-2	D17 2-1	S14 3-0	M25 1-0	D26 2-1	S03 0-1	F25 3-1		a08 0-0	J21 2-1	F11 2-1
20 SWINDON T	N12 3-2	D31 2-0	O08 0-0	N02 5-1	S24 1-4	M18 1-1	D24 6-2	S10 3-3	F11 1-2	a15 1-0	D26 2-2	a26 1-1	a17 1-1	A31 2-0	J28 2-1	M04 2-4	a01 0-0	S03 0-1	M01 2-2		F25 0-0	a29 1-2
21 TORQUAY U	a29 1-0	F18 2-1	J07 1-1	a15 1-0	S07 0-0	a26 1-1	N12 4-1	D27 1-1	A27 3-3	M04 2-1	S17 1-3	O29 1-2	F04 3-1	O01 4-0	a17 5-1	J14 2-2	D24 3-1	a01 1-1	S10 8-1	O15 4-3		M18 3-2
22 WATFORD	S17 2-0	m06 2-1	M25 1-1	S03 0-4	a08 1-0	J21 3-1	a17 2-1	a22 1-1	N19 3-1	F18 1-0	M11 0-0	O15 2-0	O22 4-1	D27 3-2	D03 4-0	D31 1-2	F04 2-2	A31 1-1	O01 2-2	D17 2-2	N05 0-0	

LEAGUE TABLES

DIVISION 1

	P	W	D	L	F	A	W	D	L	F	A	Pts
Arsenal	42	14	3	4	70	27	11	5	5	48	34	58
Aston Villa	42	16	2	3	60	29	7	6	8	32	38	54
Sheffield W	42	15	5	1	46	20	6	4	11	34	48	51
WBA	42	16	1	4	50	23	4	8	9	33	47	49
Newcastle U	42	15	2	4	44	24	7	3	11	27	39	49
Huddersfield T	42	11	6	4	32	17	7	5	9	34	36	47
Derby Co	42	11	8	2	49	25	4	6	11	27	44	44
Leeds U	42	10	6	5	39	24	5	8	8	20	38	44
Portsmouth	42	14	3	4	39	22	4	4	13	35	54	43
Sheffield U	42	14	3	4	50	30	3	6	12	24	50	43
Everton	42	13	6	2	54	24	3	3	15	27	50	41
Sunderland	42	8	7	6	33	31	7	3	11	30	49	40
Birmingham	42	13	3	5	40	23	1	8	12	17	34	39
Liverpool	42	10	6	5	53	33	4	5	12	26	51	39
Blackburn R	42	11	6	4	48	41	3	4	14	28	61	38
Manchester C	42	12	3	6	47	30	4	2	15	21	41	37
Middlesbrough	42	8	5	8	35	33	6	4	11	28	40	37
Chelsea	42	9	4	8	38	29	5	3	13	25	44	35
Leicester C	42	9	9	3	43	25	2	4	15	32	64	35
Wolves	42	10	4	7	56	48	3	5	13	24	48	35
Bolton W	42	10	7	4	49	33	2	2	17	29	59	33
Blackpool	42	11	2	8	44	35	3	3	15	25	50	33

DIVISION 2

	P	W	D	L	F	A	W	D	L	F	A	Pts
Stoke C	42	13	3	5	40	15	12	3	6	38	24	56
Tottenham H	42	14	7	0	58	19	6	8	7	38	32	55
Fulham	42	12	5	4	46	31	8	5	8	32	34	50
Bury	42	13	7	1	55	23	7	2	12	29	36	49
Nottingham F	42	9	8	4	37	28	8	7	6	30	31	49
Manchester U	42	11	5	5	40	24	4	8	9	31	44	43
Millwall	42	11	7	3	40	20	5	4	12	19	37	43
Bradford	42	13	4	4	51	27	4	4	13	26	44	42
Preston NE	42	12	2	7	53	36	4	8	9	21	34	42
Swansea T	42	17	0	4	36	12	2	4	15	14	42	42
Bradford C	42	10	6	5	43	24	4	7	10	22	37	41
Southampton	42	15	3	3	48	22	3	2	16	18	44	41
Grimsby T	42	8	10	3	49	34	6	3	12	30	50	41
Plymouth A	42	13	4	4	45	22	3	5	13	18	45	41
Notts Co	42	10	4	7	41	31	5	6	10	26	47	40
Oldham A	42	10	4	7	38	31	5	4	12	29	49	38
Port Vale	42	12	3	6	49	27	2	7	12	17	52	38
Lincoln C	42	11	6	4	46	28	1	7	13	26	59	37
Burnley	42	8	9	4	35	20	3	5	13	32	59	36
West Ham U	42	12	6	3	56	31	1	3	17	19	62	35
Chesterfield	42	10	5	6	36	25	2	5	14	25	59	34
Charlton A	42	9	3	9	35	35	3	4	14	25	56	31

DIVISION 3 North

	P	W	D	L	F	A	W	D	L	F	A	Pts
Hull C	42	18	3	0	69	14	8	4	9	31	31	59
Wrexham	42	18	2	1	75	15	6	7	8	31	36	57
Stockport Co	42	16	2	3	69	30	5	10	6	30	28	54
Chester	42	15	4	2	57	25	7	4	10	37	41	52
Walsall	42	16	4	1	53	15	3	6	12	22	43	48
Doncaster R	42	13	8	0	52	26	4	6	11	25	53	48
Gateshead	42	12	5	4	45	25	7	4	10	33	42	47
Barnsley	42	14	3	4	60	31	5	5	11	32	49	46
Barrow	42	12	3	6	41	24	6	4	11	19	36	43
Crewe A	42	16	3	2	57	16	4	0	17	23	68	43
Tranmere R	42	11	4	6	49	31	6	4	11	21	35	42
Southport	42	15	3	3	54	20	2	4	15	16	47	41
Accrington S	42	12	4	5	55	29	3	6	12	23	47	40
Hartlepools U	42	15	3	3	56	29	1	4	16	31	87	39
Halifax T	42	12	4	5	39	23	3	4	14	32	67	38
Mansfield T	42	13	4	4	57	22	1	3	17	27	70	35
Rotherham U	42	14	3	4	42	21	0	3	18	18	63	34
Rochdale	42	9	4	8	32	33	4	3	14	26	47	33
Carlisle U	42	8	7	6	34	25	5	0	16	17	50	33
York C	42	10	4	7	51	38	3	2	16	21	54	32
New Brighton	42	8	6	7	42	36	3	4	14	21	52	32
Darlington	42	9	6	6	42	32	1	2	18	24	77	28

DIVISION 3 South

	P	W	D	L	F	A	W	D	L	F	A	Pts
Brentford	42	15	4	2	45	19	11	6	4	45	30	62
Exeter C	42	17	2	2	57	13	7	8	6	31	35	58
Norwich C	42	16	3	2	49	17	6	10	5	39	38	57
Reading	42	14	5	2	68	30	5	8	8	35	41	51
Crystal P	42	14	4	3	51	21	5	4	12	27	43	46
Coventry C	42	16	1	4	75	24	3	5	13	31	53	44
Gillingham	42	14	4	3	54	24	4	4	13	18	37	44
Northampton T	42	16	5	0	54	11	2	3	16	22	55	44
Bristol R	42	13	5	3	38	22	2	9	10	23	34	44
Torquay U	42	12	7	2	51	26	4	5	12	21	41	44
Watford	42	11	8	2	37	22	5	4	12	29	41	44
Brighton & HA	42	13	3	5	42	20	4	5	12	24	45	42
Southend U	42	11	5	5	39	27	4	6	11	26	55	41
Luton T	42	12	8	1	60	32	1	5	15	18	46	39
Bristol C	42	11	5	5	59	37	1	8	12	24	53	37
QPR	42	9	8	4	48	32	4	3	14	24	55	37
Aldershot	42	11	6	4	37	21	2	4	15	24	51	36
Bournemouth	42	10	7	4	44	27	2	5	14	16	54	36
Cardiff C	42	12	4	5	48	30	0	3	18	21	69	31
Clapton O	42	7	8	6	39	35	1	5	15	20	58	29
Newport Co	42	9	4	8	42	42	2	3	16	19	63	29
Swindon T	42	7	9	5	36	29	2	2	17	24	76	29

Football League Records

Top scorers: Div 1, J.Bowers (Derby County) 34 goals; Div 2, E.Glover (Grimsby Town) 42 goals; Div 3(N), A.Lythgoe (Stockport County) 46 goals; Div 3(S), A.Dawes (Northampton Town & Crystal Palace) 27 goals.

The legendary Alex James, who in eight seasons at Highbury helped steer Arsenal to four League titles and two FA Cup triumphs.

Grimsby Town's Pat Glover, whose 42 goals in 1933-4 saw the Mariners into Division One. It is still a club record.

DIVISION 1

	ARSENAL	ASTON VILLA	BIRMINGHAM	BLACKBURN R	CHELSEA	DERBY CO	EVERTON	HUDDERSFIELD T	LEEDS U	LEICESTER C	LIVERPOOL	MANCHESTER C	MIDDLESBROUGH	NEWCASTLE U	PORTSMOUTH	SHEFFIELD U	SHEFFIELD W	STOKE C	SUNDERLAND	TOTTENHAM H	W.B.A.	WOLVERHAMPTON W
1 ARSENAL		M10 3-2	A26 1-1	F21 2-1	D16 2-1	M30 1-0	F03 1-2	a07 3-1	D26 2-0	O21 2-0	D02 2-1	S09 1-1	S30 6-0	O14 3-0	N04 1-1	m05 2-0	J06 1-1	N18 3-0	a21 2-1	J31 1-3	S06 3-1	M24 3-2
2 ASTON VILLA	O28 2-3		a14 1-1	M31 1-1	F07 2-0	D09 0-2	D23 2-1	O07 4-3	a30 3-0	A26 2-3	S09 4-2	M07 0-0	N11 3-0	N25 2-3	F10 1-1	a02 3-0	S04 1-0	F24 1-2	S23 2-1	J06 1-5	a28 4-4	D25 6-2
3 BIRMINGHAM	D30 0-0	D02 0-0		S16 2-0	a07 0-3	F21 2-1	S02 2-2	m05 1-3	S30 4-0	M28 3-0	N04 1-2	A30 0-1	J20 0-0	F03 1-2	M24 3-1	D26 4-2	a03 3-0	M10 0-1	N18 1-1	a21 2-0	O14 0-1	O21 0-0
4 BLACKBURN R	O07 2-2	N18 2-1	J29 3-1		O21 4-2	J06 2-1	F24 1-1	D16 2-2	A26 4-2	M24 3-0	M10 3-1	F10 3-0	D25 0-0	S18 3-2	D02 3-2	a07 3-1	S23 3-1	a21 4-1	a02 0-0	J01 1-0	S09 4-0	N04 7-1
5 CHELSEA	a28 2-2	S16 1-0	N25 1-1	M03 3-0		N11 0-2	a14 2-0	S13 2-3	D23 1-1	a23 2-0	F21 2-0	D09 1-2	O14 2-3	O28 2-1	a02 4-0	J20 5-0	M17 0-1	D30 2-0	D26 4-0	S30 0-4	M31 3-2	S02 5-2
6 DERBY CO	a02 2-4	a21 1-1	O07 4-0	S02 1-1	M24 1-0		A30 1-1	O21 1-1	S16 3-1	N04 2-1	N18 3-1	D25 4-1	D30 2-0	J20 1-1	M10 0-1	D16 5-1	F24 1-1	F03 5-1	M17 0-0	a07 4-3	F10 1-1	D02 3-1
7 EVERTON	S23 3-1	m05 2-2	J06 2-0	O14 7-1	D02 2-1	J01 0-3		N04 0-1	a02 2-0	M10 1-1	F10 0-0	F07 2-0	F17 1-1	D26 3-7	a21 1-1	M24 4-0	S09 2-3	a07 2-2	D16 1-0	O21 1-1	A26 1-0	N18 1-2
8 HUDDERSFIELD T	N25 0-1	F21 2-1	D23 0-0	a28 5-3	S04 6-1	M03 2-0	a25 1-0		S09 0-0	O14 5-1	a03 0-2	M31 1-0	D09 2-1	a14 4-1	J06 4-0	S30 6-1	N11 3-2	S16 2-2	A26 2-1	D26 2-0	O28 3-1	F03 3-1
9 LEEDS U	D25 0-1	N04 2-4	F10 1-0	D30 4-0	m05 3-1	J31 0-2	M30 2-2	J20 1-1		a07 8-0	M24 5-1	F24 3-1	A28 5-2	S02 3-0	O21 1-0	a21 1-1	O07 2-1	D02 2-0	M10 3-1	N18 0-0	S23 3-0	D16 3-3
10 LEICESTER C	M08 4-1	D30 1-1	a28 3-7	N11 1-2	S23 1-1	a19 2-0	O28 3-1	F24 1-0	N25 2-2		F01 1-0	S02 0-0	D23 1-2	M31 3-2	O07 2-1	A28 4-0	a14 2-0	D26 3-1	F10 0-0	S09 1-3	D09 0-1	a03 1-1
11 LIVERPOOL	a14 2-3	J20 2-3	M17 4-1	O28 4-0	O07 3-0	M31 4-2	S30 3-2	M30 2-2	N11 4-3	S16 1-3		m02 3-2	M03 6-2	D23 1-2	D25 2-2	S02 3-2	D09 1-3	A30 1-1	F24 1-1	F03 3-1	N25 1-1	D30 1-1
12 MANCHESTER C	J20 2-1	O21 1-0	S06 1-0	S30 3-1	a21 4-2	D26 2-0	S16 2-2	N18 2-2	O14 0-1	J06 1-1	D16 2-1		F03 5-2	M21 1-1	a07 2-1	M10 4-1	A26 2-3	M24 4-2	N04 4-1	D02 2-0	J01 2-7	m05 4-0
13 MIDDLESBROUGH	F10 0-2	M24 1-2	S09 0-3	D26 3-1	F24 2-2	A26 3-1	O07 2-0	a21 3-0	J01 2-1	m05 4-1	O21 4-1	S23 2-1		a02 1-0	D16 2-0	N18 10-3	F07 2-3	N04 6-1	D02 0-4	M10 1-1	J06 3-0	a07 0-0
14 NEWCASTLE U	F24 0-1	a07 1-1	S23 0-0	S06 3-1	M10 2-2	S09 1-1	D25 1-2	D02 3-3	J06 2-0	N18 1-1	J01 9-2	O07 2-2	M30 1-1		A26 2-2	N04 3-1	F10 0-0	D16 2-2	O21 2-1	M24 1-3	J27 1-2	a21 5-1
15 PORTSMOUTH	a18 1-0	S30 3-2	N11 0-2	a14 2-0	M30 0-2	O28 1-0	D09 0-0	S02 3-0	M07 2-1	F21 3-5	D26 1-0	N25 2-0	a30 4-1	D30 2-0		F03 1-1	M31 0-2	J20 3-1	S06 0-0	O14 0-1	D23 2-2	S16 1-1
16 SHEFFIELD U	D23 1-3	J01 3-3	D25 2-1	N25 1-0	S09 4-1	A28 2-0	N11 1-1	F10 1-4	D09 2-1	S04 2-1	J06 2-2	O28 1-1	M31 3-1	M17 4-0	S23 0-1		M03 5-1	O07 1-2	J29 2-0	A26 0-0	a14 0-1	F24 3-1
17 SHEFFIELD W	S02 1-2	A28 1-2	J02 2-1	F03 4-0	N04 2-1	O14 1-1	J20 0-0	M24 1-2	F26 0-2	D02 1-1	a21 1-2	D30 1-1	S16 3-0	S30 3-1	N18 1-2	O21 0-1		m05 2-2	a07 2-0	D16 2-1	D26 3-1	M10 2-1
18 STOKE C	M31 1-1	O14 1-1	O28 1-1	D09 2-0	A26 1-0	S23 0-4	N25 1-2	J29 3-0	a14 1-2	D25 2-1	S04 1-1	N11 0-1	M17 2-0	a28 2-1	S09 2-1	F22 3-0	D23 0-1		J06 3-0	a02 2-0	M08 4-1	S30 1-1
19 SUNDERLAND	D09 3-0	F03 5-1	M31 4-1	M30 3-0	J01 0-0	D23 0-0	a28 3-2	D30 1-1	O28 4-2	S30 2-1	O14 4-1	a11 0-0	a14 2-0	M03 2-0	A30 0-2	S16 5-0	N25 4-0	S02 4-1		F21 6-0	N11 2-2	J20 3-3
20 TOTTENHAM H	S16 1-1	S02 3-2	D09 3-2	D23 4-1	F10 2-1	N25 1-2	M03 3-0	D25 1-3	M31 5-1	J20 0-1	S23 0-3	a14 5-1	O28 2-0	N11 4-0	F24 0-0	D30 4-1	a28 4-3	M30 0-0	O07 3-1		M17 2-1	A28 4-0
21 W.B.A.	S13 1-0	D16 2-1	F24 1-2	J20 0-1	N18 3-1	S30 5-1	D30 3-3	M10 2-3	F03 0-3	a21 2-0	a07 2-2	a02 4-0	S02 3-0	S16 1-1	m05 2-1	D02 3-0	D27 1-1	O21 5-1	M24 6-5	N04 1-2		F17 2-0
22 WOLVERHAMPTON W	N11 0-1	D26 4-3	M03 2-0	M17 5-3	J06 1-1	a14 3-0	M31 2-0	S23 5-2	a28 2-0	a02 1-1	A26 3-2	D23 8-0	N25 0-1	D09 2-1	F07 1-1	O14 3-2	O28 6-2	F10 0-2	S09 1-6	S04 1-0	O07 0-0	

DIVISION 2

	BLACKPOOL	BOLTON W	BRADFORD	BRADFORD C	BRENTFORD	BURNLEY	BURY	FULHAM	GRIMSBY T	HULL C	LINCOLN C	MANCHESTER U	MILLWALL	NOTTINGHAM F	NOTTS CO	OLDHAM A	PLYMOUTH A	PORT VALE	PRESTON N.E.	SOUTHAMPTON	SWANSEA T	WEST HAM U
1 BLACKPOOL		M24 1-1	m05 1-1	J06 3-2	N04 3-1	M10 1-1	F24 2-0	S04 4-3	D16 3-4	D25 0-0	O07 2-0	N18 3-1	F10 2-2	a21 2-3	F07 2-1	O21 0-0	a07 1-1	S09 1-0	A26 1-2	M30 4-2	S23 2-1	D02 1-1
2 BOLTON W	N11 1-2		J01 0-1	M31 3-0	S23 3-2	F10 4-1	S16 2-0	O28 3-1	S04 0-4	M07 3-3	D23 1-2	J20 3-1	a28 5-0	M30 1-1	a14 1-0	O07 1-0	S02 2-0	N25 3-0	F24 0-2	M17 2-0	D09 2-1	D30 5-1
3 BRADFORD	D23 1-2	D25 1-4		S09 2-1	S06 5-2	a03 5-0	N25 0-1	D09 3-1	S16 2-1	a14 3-1	M31 2-1	O14 6-1	N11 4-0	F03 6-2	O28 3-2	A26 4-2	F17 4-1	M03 2-2	J06 2-1	a28 3-1	M17 5-1	S30 0-0
4 BRADFORD C	S02 1-0	N18 5-1	J20 3-0		M24 2-1	N04 2-1	D26 2-2	a02 1-0	m05 2-1	A30 1-2	F24 3-0	a07 1-1	O07 1-0	D16 3-2	S23 3-1	M10 5-2	D02 3-4	J27 1-2	O21 1-0	D30 2-2	F10 2-1	a21 2-2
5 BRENTFORD	M17 1-0	F03 3-1	A31 2-0	N11 2-1		O07 5-2	D23 2-3	M03 1-2	a02 1-2	S30 2-2	a28 5-0	S16 3-4	D09 3-0	D30 2-1	N25 2-2	F24 2-1	J20 3-0	M31 2-0	D25 3-2	O28 2-0	a14 2-0	S02 4-1
6 BURNLEY	O28 3-2	S30 1-3	M30 1-0	M17 4-2	F17 3-1		a28 1-2	O14 2-1	D30 2-0	D23 3-1	D09 3-1	F03 1-4	a14 2-1	S02 1-0	M31 1-0	D25 0-1	S16 2-2	N11 0-0	S04 1-4	M03 2-1	N25 3-1	J20 4-2
7 BURY	O14 2-5	J02 1-1	a07 2-1	D25 1-0	m05 1-2	D16 1-1		S30 3-3	N18 1-3	F03 3-1	S09 0-2	O21 2-1	J06 5-1	M24 4-2	J01 3-1	a21 1-1	M10 4-0	S11 0-3	D02 2-1	F17 1-0	A26 4-1	N04 2-1
8 FULHAM	A28 1-0	M10 0-2	a21 0-2	M30 0-1	O21 1-1	F24 1-1	F10 2-1		D02 1-0	O07 1-1	S23 1-0	N04 0-2	J29 2-0	a07 3-1	J06 3-0	m05 1-2	M24 3-2	A26 3-0	D16 1-0	D25 1-0	S09 1-0	N18 3-1
9 GRIMSBY T	a28 7-0	A29 2-3	J30 3-2	D23 1-4	M30 2-2	A26 1-0	M31 2-0	a14 3-1		N25 4-1	N11 3-0	D26 7-3	M17 5-2	S30 2-1	M03 2-2	J06 2-1	O14 5-1	S23 1-2	S09 3-0	D09 3-1	O28 3-1	F17 1-1
10 HULL C	D26 3-0	O21 1-0	D02 1-2	S11 2-2	F10 0-1	m05 0-1	S23 3-1	F17 0-0	a07 0-1		F08 2-0	M10 4-1	S09 3-2	N18 2-2	A26 0-1	D16 2-0	N04 5-4	a02 2-1	a21 0-1	O14 1-0	J06 0-0	M24 2-0
11 LINCOLN C	F17 2-2	m05 2-2	N18 2-1	O14 0-1	D16 0-2	a21 4-0	J20 1-2	F03 5-0	M24 3-3	S16 2-1		J06 5-1	A26 0-1	N04 0-0	S04 0-1	D02 1-1	O21 1-1	D25 1-0	a07 0-1	S30 1-1	M30 1-0	M10 0-2
12 MANCHESTER U	M31 2-0	S09 1-5	F24 0-4	N25 2-1	J27 1-3	S23 5-2	M03 2-1	M17 1-0	D25 1-3	O28 4-1	S02 1-1		D23 1-1	A30 0-1	D09 1-2	F10 2-3	D30 0-3	a14 2-0	O07 1-0	N11 1-0	a28 1-1	M30 0-1
13 MILLWALL	S30 0-0	D16 2-1	M24 0-1	F17 1-1	a21 2-0	D02 0-0	S02 0-0	S16 0-1	N04 0-1	J20 2-0	D30 4-1	m05 0-2		M10 0-0	D26 3-2	a07 1-0	M30 0-0	O14 0-3	N18 1-1	a09 1-0	A28 2-1	O21 2-2
14 NOTTINGHAM F	D09 0-0	a02 2-2	S23 3-0	a28 1-2	A26 1-1	J06 0-2	N11 7-2	N25 2-0	F10 4-2	M31 0-1	M17 6-2	S07 1-1	O28 2-0		O07 2-0	S09 1-3	D26 2-1	D23 6-1	F07 2-3	a14 4-1	M03 4-2	O14 0-1
15 NOTTS CO	S16 1-1	D02 1-2	a16 1-0	F03 3-0	a07 1-2	N18 3-1	M30 2-1	S02 4-1	O21 1-2	D30 0-0	S13 2-0	a21 0-0	D25 0-1	F17 1-0		M24 1-1	D16 2-1	S30 3-2	N04 2-2	J20 2-2	F24 1-1	m05 1-2
16 OLDHAM A	M03 2-0	F20 1-3	D30 1-3	O28 4-3	O14 1-4	D26 1-0	D09 2-2	D23 2-2	S02 1-5	a28 7-0	a14 3-0	S30 2-0	N25 1-0	J20 4-1	N11 2-0		F03 1-1	M17 5-1	M30 3-1	A28 1-1	M31 0-0	S16 4-1
17 PLYMOUTH A	N25 0-3	J06 3-0	O07 4-1	a14 3-0	S09 1-1	J27 1-0	O28 3-3	N11 4-0	F24 0-2	M17 1-1	M03 3-0	A26 4-0	a02 1-0	D25 4-3	a28 1-0	S23 1-0		D09 3-0	F10 0-0	M31 0-0	D23 2-2	A30 4-4
18 PORT VALE	J20 1-0	a07 0-0	O21 3-1	S16 3-1	N18 1-0	M24 0-2	A28 4-1	D30 2-2	F05 0-1	M30 3-0	D26 1-0	D02 2-3	F24 5-1	m05 3-1	F10 0-0	N04 2-0	a21 4-0		M10 2-0	S02 2-1	O07 1-0	D16 0-0
19 PRESTON N.E.	D30 3-0	O14 1-1	S02 3-1	M07 0-1	D26 3-2	A28 3-2	a14 0-3	a28 2-0	J20 1-2	D09 5-0	N25 2-1	F21 3-2	M31 4-2	S16 4-0	M17 2-0	a02 1-0	S30 1-1	O28 0-0		D23 3-1	N11 3-0	F03 3-1
20 SOUTHAMPTON	a02 3-2	N04 1-0	D16 5-0	A26 4-1	M10 0-0	O21 2-1	O07 1-0	D26 2-0	a21 4-2	F24 1-1	F10 3-1	M24 1-0	S23 2-3	D02 2-0	S09 3-2	S04 1-0	N18 0-1	J06 1-4	m05 0-1		F05 1-0	a07 3-2
21 SWANSEA T	F03 2-2	a21 0-0	N04 5-1	S30 2-1	D02 2-3	a07 3-0	D30 1-1	J20 1-0	M10 1-1	S02 1-1	a02 1-0	D16 2-1	S04 2-0	O21 1-1	O14 1-1	N18 2-2	m05 2-1	F22 4-0	M24 1-2	S16 1-0		D26 1-1
22 WEST HAM U	a14 1-2	A26 4-2	F10 0-1	D09 1-2	J06 3-2	S09 1-2	M17 3-1	M31 5-1	O07 3-1	N11 2-1	O28 4-1	a02 2-1	M03 1-1	F24 2-1	D23 5-3	F07 1-4	S04 5-1	a28 1-0	S23 6-0	N25 0-0	D25 1-1	

Season 1933-34

DIVISION 3 NORTH

	ACCRINGTON S	BARNSLEY	BARROW	CARLISLE U	CHESTER	CHESTERFIELD	CREWE A	DARLINGTON	DONCASTER R	GATESHEAD	HALIFAX T	HARTLEPOOLS U	MANSFIELD T	NEW BRIGHTON	ROCHDALE	ROTHERHAM U	SOUTHPORT	STOCKPORT CO	TRANMERE R	WALSALL	WREXHAM	YORK C
1 ACCRINGTON S		F03 0-9	a28 0-4	D23 2-1	a14 4-1	S02 1-0	O28 0-2	J01 2-0	J03 4-1	S11 5-2	M03 1-1	F17 2-2	S30 1-1	M17 8-0	J20 1-3	N11 2-2	S26 3-2	D30 0-3	S16 2-2	M31 1-0	O14 1-1	J24 4-1
2 BARNSLEY	S23 6-0		M31 3-1	J13 1-0	M17 2-0	F10 3-2	a28 5-2	S09 4-0	N11 2-2	J27 0-0	F19 1-0	D26 5-4	a02 6-1	D23 2-0	O07 4-1	J01 5-1	J06 3-2	a14 2-0	F24 5-1	M03 1-1	A26 3-0	O28 1-0
3 BARROW	D16 2-6	N18 3-4		S04 2-0	F10 9-0	a21 2-0	A26 0-3	F24 5-2	O07 2-1	m05 12-1	D26 5-2	N04 2-2	M24 6-3	J06 3-3	D02 5-3	S09 4-1	O21 3-3	a02 2-0	a07 1-3	J27 5-5	M10 3-1	S23 2-2
4 CARLISLE U	m05 3-0	a07 1-4	A31 0-0		O07 1-0	D16 1-1	J06 6-1	O21 3-3	F24 0-1	M30 6-0	A26 1-0	M24 4-1	N18 3-2	S09 1-2	a21 3-0	J27 0-1	M10 0-0	D26 2-2	D02 2-1	S23 3-2	N04 0-0	F10 3-2
5 CHESTER	D02 7-0	N04 4-2	S30 1-3	F17 3-3		a07 3-2	a02 1-0	D16 8-0	F03 3-1	a21 4-0	S06 1-2	O21 3-3	M10 1-1	D25 0-0	N18 7-1	A26 5-1	m04 1-0	O14 1-1	M24 4-2	J06 0-1	J27 1-2	S09 1-1
6 CHESTERFIELD	J06 1-0	S30 3-0	D13 2-1	a28 4-0	J01 6-1		M03 3-2	D25 0-1	a14 1-1	A26 6-2	S09 4-2	O14 3-1	F17 3-2	O28 4-0	S16 3-0	M17 2-1	M30 2-1	D23 1-0	F03 1-0	N11 1-2	S06 4-0	M31 2-0
7 CREWE A	M10 4-2	D16 4-2	D30 1-3	S02 4-0	M30 3-5	O21 1-2		M24 2-3	D26 4-0	N04 3-2	S16 1-1	D02 1-0	a21 2-1	F10 6-2	F03 4-1	O07 0-2	M18 2-2	J20 2-2	m05 3-1	F24 1-4	a07 1-0	A30 5-3
8 DARLINGTON	a02 3-1	J20 0-4	O14 4-1	M03 1-2	a28 0-4	D26 1-1	N11 1-1		D23 4-0	S06 3-3	M17 4-2	F03 5-3	S16 1-4	M31 1-0	D30 1-1	J24 4-1	F17 4-0	O28 1-2	S02 1-3	J13 2-1	S30 2-1	D09 4-0
9 DONCASTER R	a21 5-1	M24 4-4	F17 3-2	O14 2-1	S23 3-1	D02 1-3	D25 4-0	m05 3-2		D16 5-2	M30 3-0	M10 3-0	N04 1-0	A26 1-0	a07 5-0	J06 2-1	F10 3-0	S04 0-2	N18 2-0	S09 4-0	O21 1-4	J27 3-1
10 GATESHEAD	D26 2-0	S16 1-4	D23 0-0	a02 2-3	a25 1-3	D30 2-1	M17 2-1	A30 2-2	a28 2-4		O28 4-0	S30 6-3	F03 5-3	N11 6-0	S02 2-1	M31 4-1	O14 2-2	M03 0-4	J20 1-2	J17 2-1	F17 0-3	a14 0-2
11 HALIFAX T	O21 2-1	a21 1-1	D25 4-1	D30 3-2	A30 1-0	J20 5-0	J27 3-2	N04 2-0	a02 0-1	M10 2-4		a07 6-2	D02 4-2	S23 1-1	m05 4-2	F10 3-2	M24 6-2	S02 4-2	D16 0-2	O07 2-0	N18 1-3	F24 3-0
12 HARTLEPOOLS U	O07 3-0	D25 0-2	M17 7-0	N11 3-2	M03 1-0	F24 0-3	a14 2-1	S23 6-2	O28 2-2	F10 3-3	J01 5-0		D30 3-1	F14 2-1	A30 2-1	a28 4-0	J27 1-2	M31 3-1	M30 1-1	D23 0-1	S09 4-1	S02 2-0
13 MANSFIELD T	F10 5-0	M30 1-5	N11 0-5	M31 6-0	O28 2-1	O07 0-3	D09 4-1	J27 4-0	M17 1-1	S23 1-1	a14 6-1	A26 1-1		a28 5-2	F24 5-0	D23 3-0	S09 2-2	J13 1-1	A28 0-0	D25 1-2	J06 1-1	M03 0-2
14 NEW BRIGHTON	N04 0-3	m05 0-1	S02 2-2	J20 2-1	D26 0-2	M10 0-0	S30 2-1	N18 3-2	D30 2-2	M24 3-1	F03 3-0	a21 4-1	D16 5-1		O21 0-2	F24 3-1	a07 5-2	S16 2-1	F17 1-0	A30 2-0	D02 0-1	a02 2-1
15 ROCHDALE	S09 0-1	D09 3-1	a14 1-2	F06 0-1	M31 6-0	J27 0-1	S23 2-0	A26 1-0	J13 0-2	J06 2-0	D23 1-2	S05 3-0	O14 2-2	M03 1-1		O28 0-2	D26 3-3	a28 1-1	S30 1-0	M17 3-3	M30 1-2	F20 3-6
16 ROTHERHAM U	M24 3-1	A28 0-2	J20 1-1	S16 0-1	D30 0-3	N04 1-3	F17 3-4	a07 0-0	S02 0-0	N18 3-2	S30 1-2	D16 4-2	m05 1-2	O14 2-2	M10 4-0		D02 0-1	F03 1-1	O21 2-2	a02 1-1	a21 1-3	D26 3-2
17 SOUTHPORT	A29 1-1	S02 2-2	M03 1-3	O28 1-1	D23 3-1	a02 0-0	M31 1-1	O07 3-2	S30 0-0	F24 1-1	N11 1-4	S16 0-2	J20 3-3	J13 4-0	D25 3-0	a14 4-0		M17 1-4	D30 2-2	M20 3-1	F03 1-1	J01 0-0
18 STOCKPORT CO	A26 3-0	D02 1-1	M30 4-1	D25 4-0	F24 4-2	m05 0-0	S09 1-1	M10 6-0	A28 4-3	O21 1-0	J06 13-0	N18 5-2	a07 3-1	J27 5-1	D16 4-1	S23 3-1	N04 9-2		a21 2-1	F10 3-2	M24 7-3	O07 2-1
19 TRANMERE R	F01 2-0	O14 5-2	J18 4-1	a14 3-1	N11 6-1	S23 0-1	D23 5-1	J06 2-2	M31 2-0	S09 2-1	a28 3-2	a02 3-2	S04 3-2	O07 1-0	F10 4-0	M03 1-2	A26 5-0	a23 1-1		O28 1-0	D25 1-2	M17 3-0
20 WALSALL	N18 5-0	O21 5-1	S16 2-4	F03 3-2	S02 5-0	M24 2-2	O14 5-1	D02 3-0	J20 2-0	a07 5-1	F17 2-0	m05 5-0	D26 0-0	S04 2-1	N04 2-0	M30 3-1	a21 4-1	S30 2-0	M10 5-3		D16 3-1	D30 1-0
21 WREXHAM	F24 3-2	D30 4-2	O28 3-2	M17 8-1	S16 0-3	A30 2-3	J13 5-1	F10 6-1	M03 1-1	O07 2-3	M31 0-2	J20 3-1	S02 5-0	a14 5-4	a02 4-1	M07 4-0	S23 2-1	N11 0-1	a11 5-1	a28 4-2		D23 2-3
22 YORK C	a07 3-2	M10 1-1	F03 6-1	S30 4-1	J20 3-2	N18 1-2	S06 4-1	a21 1-1	S16 1-2	D02 1-1	O14 1-0	J06 1-3	O21 1-0	M30 2-1	M24 6-1	D25 0-1	D16 1-0	F17 2-2	N04 1-0	A26 2-2	m05 2-4	

DIVISION 3 SOUTH

	ALDERSHOT	BOURNEMOUTH	BRIGHTON & HA	BRISTOL C	BRISTOL R	CARDIFF C	CHARLTON A	CLAPTON O	COVENTRY C	CRYSTAL P	EXETER C	GILLINGHAM	LUTON T	NEWPORT CO	NORTHAMPTON T	NORWICH C	Q.P.R.	READING	SOUTHEND U	SWINDON T	TORQUAY U	WATFORD
1 ALDERSHOT		D16 0-0	O14 0-1	F03 2-2	M24 0-1	a21 1-3	m05 3-2	S30 0-0	M10 1-1	N18 0-4	D02 0-2	a07 0-2	D25 0-0	J20 3-2	A30 1-1	S16 2-1	S02 3-1	O21 3-0	N04 2-0	F17 1-2	D30 3-0	M30 3-2
2 BOURNEMOUTH	a28 1-2		a18 1-1	M31 5-0	O07 2-0	S09 1-3	D30 1-2	J17 2-0	a02 3-3	F10 1-1	J27 1-3	S23 1-1	D23 4-3	M17 0-0	S02 4-0	N11 2-4	O28 3-2	D25 1-1	F24 1-4	a14 1-1	M03 3-4	A30 3-2
3 BRIGHTON & H.A.	F24 3-1	a21 6-0		S16 5-1	N04 0-2	D02 4-0	D16 1-0	F03 1-1	O21 1-1	M24 4-1	a07 2-1	N18 5-2	M30 1-1	S02 1-1	D26 3-3	J20 1-1	D30 0-1	F17 1-1	M10 1-0	S30 3-0	A30 3-1	m05 2-0
4 BRISTOL C	S23 1-1	N18 3-1	F07 5-0		A26 0-3	M24 3-0	a07 0-1	J06 3-0	D16 0-0	O21 2-2	N04 1-1	M10 1-1	F10 0-0	D26 1-1	O07 2-3	S06 0-1	a02 0-2	a21 1-2	m05 5-1	S09 2-2	F24 2-0	D02 1-0
5 BRISTOL R	N11 4-1	F17 3-0	M17 1-1	D30 5-1		O14 3-1	S30 2-5	M03 2-2	J20 4-1	A30 0-1	M30 1-1	D25 4-2	M31 0-1	a28 2-0	F28 1-1	D23 3-0	a18 4-1	S16 1-0	S02 3-1	O28 3-0	a14 2-1	F03 1-0
6 CARDIFF C	a25 1-2	J20 4-2	a14 1-4	N11 1-5	F24 1-5		S02 1-1	M31 1-2	D26 3-3	O07 4-0	S23 2-1	F10 1-3	a28 0-4	O28 1-1	D23 1-3	M17 0-2	M03 3-1	A28 2-0	M30 1-1	J17 0-1	S16 0-1	D30 4-1
7 CHARLTON A	D23 1-0	A26 4-3	a28 4-3	a23 2-1	F10 2-1	J06 2-0		a14 1-1	F24 2-0	S23 4-2	S09 4-1	J29 2-2	S04 2-0	N11 6-1	M03 1-1	M31 3-3	M17 1-2	M30 0-0	O07 1-3	m02 1-0	O28 6-0	D26 4-3
8 CLAPTON O	F10 9-2	a07 4-1	S23 2-1	S02 4-0	O21 0-0	N18 4-2	D02 1-3		m05 0-0	M10 2-0	M24 4-0	N04 2-1	O07 1-1	A28 3-0	F24 5-1	D30 3-2	D26 2-2	D16 2-3	J20 5-2	J27 1-0	M30 4-1	a21 2-3
9 COVENTRY C	O28 5-1	a03 4-1	M03 2-0	a28 9-0	S09 5-3	D25 4-1	O14 3-2	D23 3-1		J06 5-1	S04 1-3	A26 7-1	M17 2-2	a14 5-2	N11 3-1	D14 0-0	J18 0-1	S30 0-0	J27 2-0	S23 5-1	M31 3-1	F17 2-0
10 CRYSTAL P	M31 4-1	S30 4-1	N11 2-1	M03 0-1	S06 1-2	F17 3-2	F03 1-0	O28 3-2	S02 2-1		O14 0-0	M30 3-2	S13 2-2	D23 1-1	a14 1-2	D25 0-1	a28 4-1	J20 0-0	D30 1-1	M17 0-0	a25 4-1	S16 4-3
11 EXETER C	a14 0-0	S16 4-0	S13 3-0	M17 2-0	a02 0-0	F03 4-0	J20 2-0	N11 0-3	A30 1-0	F24 1-2		O07 2-0	D09 4-2	M03 1-1	a28 0-2	O28 3-4	S30 1-1	D30 4-1	D25 2-0	M31 2-2	D23 4-0	S02 3-1
12 GILLINGHAM	J17 1-2	F03 5-1	M31 3-0	O28 2-1	D26 3-2	S30 6-2	S16 1-1	M17 1-1	D30 3-7	a02 0-5	F17 1-1		a14 1-1	O14 1-0	a11 5-1	M03 1-2	D23 1-4	S02 5-1	A30 0-0	N11 3-3	a28 3-3	J20 3-3
13 LUTON T	D26 1-1	m05 2-0	a02 1-2	S30 3-0	N18 2-2	D16 3-1	A28 2-1	F17 2-0	N04 0-1	a07 2-1	a21 3-2	D02 4-2		S16 1-1	D30 3-1	F03 2-3	J20 4-2	M10 3-1	M24 3-1	O14 2-3	S02 10-2	O21 2-1
14 NEWPORT CO	S09 1-2	N04 1-1	J06 2-2	D25 2-2	D16 1-0	M10 2-2	M24 1-1	S04 1-1	D02 0-0	m05 1-0	O21 1-0	F24 3-1	J27 1-2		S23 2-0	M30 0-0	O07 1-2	a07 1-2	a21 3-0	A26 1-2	F10 0-0	N18 0-3
15 NORTHAMPTON T	S04 0-0	J06 4-1	D25 1-1	F22 2-3	a07 1-2	m05 2-0	O21 1-2	O14 3-0	M24 2-2	D02 4-2	D16 5-3	a21 1-0	A26 2-3	F03 5-3		S30 2-2	S16 2-1	N04 2-4	N18 2-0	a02 2-2	J20 1-1	M10 1-0
16 NORWICH C	J27 2-2	M24 6-1	S09 4-3	A28 7-2	m05 0-0	N04 2-0	N18 3-0	A26 3-0	a21 3-1	D26 2-0	M10 1-1	O21 4-1	S23 4-0	a02 2-1	F10 2-0		F24 1-0	D02 3-2	D16 0-0	J06 3-2	O07 0-2	a07 3-1
17 Q.P.R.	J06 2-4	M10 1-0	A26 2-0	M30 1-0	a21 1-0	O21 4-0	N04 2-1	D25 2-0	a07 0-1	D16 2-1	F10 2-0	m05 5-0	S09 2-1	F17 2-1	J31 2-1	O14 5-2		N18 0-0	D02 4-0	S07 1-0	S23 2-0	M24 0-0
18 READING	M03 3-2	D26 4-0	O07 2-0	a18 1-1	J27 2-2	S06 3-1	a02 1-0	a28 4-0	F10 1-0	S09 0-0	A26 3-1	J06 2-0	O28 4-1	J17 4-0	M17 2-2	a14 1-0	M31 5-0		S23 5-0	D23 2-0	N11 5-2	O14 6-1
19 SOUTHEND U	M17 1-0	O14 1-2	O28 0-0	D23 3-0	J06 2-2	a02 1-1	F17 1-0	S09 2-1	S16 2-1	A26 0-4	D26 3-1	S06 1-2	N11 0-1	M14 3-5	M31 2-0	a28 0-0	a14 0-2	F03 2-2		M03 4-1	J17 3-1	S30 1-1
20 SWINDON T	O07 1-0	D02 3-2	F10 1-1	J20 4-2	M10 1-0	a07 6-3	a21 1-3	S16 3-0	F03 0-1	N04 3-2	N18 1-1	M24 3-1	F24 3-1	D30 1-1	M30 1-1	S02 0-0	A30 3-1	m05 3-1	O21 1-4		D26 2-0	D16 1-0
21 TORQUAY U	A26 0-0	O21 1-0	S06 3-0	O14 2-2	D02 2-1	J27 3-1	M10 1-4	a02 2-1	N18 1-3	a21 2-1	m05 0-2	D16 2-1	J06 0-1	S30 1-2	S09 3-2	F17 1-2	F03 1-1	M24 1-1	a07 3-0	D25 2-0		N04 1-3
22 WATFORD	a02 3-0	S06 1-2	D23 2-0	a14 1-1	S23 0-0	A26 1-2	D25 0-1	D20 6-0	O07 3-3	J31 3-1	J06 2-0	S09 2-1	M03 0-1	M31 3-0	O28 2-0	J13 1-3	N11 0-0	F24 2-0	F10 2-1	a28 4-0	M17 5-0	

LEAGUE TABLES

DIVISION 1

	P	W	D	L	F	A	W	D	L	F	A	Pts
Arsenal	42	15	4	2	45	19	10	5	6	30	28	59
Huddersfield T	42	16	3	2	53	19	7	7	7	37	42	56
Tottenham H	42	14	3	4	51	24	7	4	10	28	32	49
Derby Co	42	11	8	2	45	22	6	3	12	23	32	45
Manchester C	42	14	4	3	50	29	3	7	11	15	43	45
Sunderland	42	14	6	1	57	17	2	6	13	24	39	44
WBA	42	12	4	5	49	28	5	6	10	29	42	44
Blackburn R	42	16	5	0	57	21	2	2	17	17	60	43
Leeds U	42	13	5	3	52	21	4	3	14	23	45	42
Portsmouth	42	11	5	5	31	21	4	7	10	21	34	42
Sheffield W	42	9	5	7	33	24	7	4	10	29	43	41
Stoke C	42	11	5	5	33	19	4	6	11	25	52	41
Aston Villa	42	10	5	6	45	34	4	7	10	33	41	40
Everton	42	9	7	5	38	27	3	9	9	24	36	40
Wolves	42	13	4	4	50	28	1	8	12	24	58	40
Middlesbrough	42	13	3	5	51	27	3	4	14	17	53	39
Leicester C	42	10	6	5	36	26	4	5	12	23	48	39
Liverpool	42	10	6	5	52	37	4	4	13	27	50	38
Chelsea	42	12	3	6	44	24	2	5	14	23	45	36
Birmingham	42	8	6	7	29	20	4	6	11	25	36	36
Newcastle U	42	6	11	4	42	29	4	3	14	26	48	34
Sheffield U	42	11	5	5	40	25	1	2	18	18	76	31

DIVISION 2

	P	W	D	L	F	A	W	D	L	F	A	Pts
Grimsby T	42	15	3	3	62	28	12	2	7	41	31	59
Preston NE	42	15	3	3	47	20	8	3	10	24	32	52
Bolton W	42	14	2	5	45	22	7	7	7	34	33	51
Brentford	42	15	2	4	52	24	7	5	9	33	36	51
Bradford	42	16	2	3	63	27	7	1	13	23	40	49
Bradford C	42	14	4	3	46	25	6	2	13	27	42	46
West Ham U	42	13	3	5	51	28	4	8	9	27	42	45
Port Vale	42	14	4	3	39	14	5	3	13	21	41	45
Oldham A	42	12	5	4	48	28	5	5	11	24	32	44
Plymouth A	42	12	7	2	43	20	3	6	12	26	50	43
Blackpool	42	10	8	3	39	27	5	5	11	23	37	43
Bury	42	12	4	5	43	31	5	5	11	27	42	43
Burnley	42	14	2	5	40	29	4	4	13	20	43	42
Southampton	42	15	2	4	40	21	0	6	15	14	37	38
Hull C	42	11	4	6	33	20	2	8	11	19	48	38
Fulham	42	13	3	5	29	17	2	4	15	19	50	37
Nottingham F	42	11	4	6	50	27	2	5	14	23	47	35
Notts Co	42	9	7	5	32	22	3	4	14	21	40	35
Swansea T	42	10	9	2	36	19	0	6	15	15	41	35
Manchester U	42	9	3	9	29	33	5	3	13	30	52	34
Millwall	42	8	8	5	21	17	3	3	15	18	51	33
Lincoln C	42	7	7	7	31	23	2	1	18	13	52	26

DIVISION 3 North

	P	W	D	L	F	A	W	D	L	F	A	Pts
Barnsley	42	18	3	0	64	18	9	5	7	54	43	62
Chesterfield	42	18	1	2	56	17	9	6	6	30	26	61
Stockport Co	42	18	3	0	84	23	6	8	7	31	29	59
Walsall	42	18	2	1	66	18	5	5	11	31	42	53
Doncaster R	42	17	1	3	58	24	5	8	8	25	37	53
Wrexham	42	14	1	6	68	35	9	4	8	34	38	51
Tranmere R	42	16	2	3	57	21	4	5	12	27	42	47
Barrow	42	12	5	4	78	45	7	4	10	38	49	47
Halifax T	42	15	2	4	57	30	5	2	14	23	61	44
Chester	42	11	6	4	59	26	6	0	15	30	60	40
Hartlepools U	42	14	3	4	54	24	2	4	15	35	69	39
York C	42	11	5	5	44	28	4	3	14	27	46	38
Carlisle U	42	11	6	4	43	23	4	2	15	23	58	38
Crewe A	42	12	3	6	54	38	3	3	15	27	59	36
New Brighton	42	13	3	5	41	25	1	5	15	21	62	36
Darlington	42	11	4	6	47	35	2	5	14	23	66	35
Mansfield T	42	9	7	5	49	29	2	5	14	32	59	34
Southport C	42	6	11	4	35	29	2	6	13	28	61	33
Gateshead	42	10	3	8	46	40	2	6	13	30	70	33
Accrington S	42	10	6	5	44	38	3	1	17	21	63	33
Rotherham U	42	5	7	9	31	35	5	1	15	22	56	28
Rochdale	42	7	5	9	34	30	2	1	18	19	73	24

DIVISION 3 South

	P	W	D	L	F	A	W	D	L	F	A	Pts
Norwich C	42	16	4	1	55	19	9	7	5	33	30	61
Coventry C	42	16	3	2	70	22	5	9	7	30	32	54
Reading	42	17	4	0	60	13	4	8	9	22	37	54
QPR	42	17	2	2	42	12	7	4	10	28	39	54
Charlton A	42	14	5	2	53	27	8	3	10	30	29	52
Luton T	42	14	3	4	55	28	7	7	7	28	33	52
Bristol R	42	14	4	3	49	21	6	7	8	28	26	51
Swindon T	42	13	5	3	42	25	4	6	11	22	43	45
Exeter C	42	12	5	4	43	19	4	6	11	25	38	43
Brighton & HA	42	12	7	2	47	18	3	6	12	21	42	43
Clapton O	42	14	4	3	60	25	2	6	13	15	44	42
Crystal P	42	11	6	4	40	25	5	3	13	31	42	41
Northampton T	42	10	6	5	45	32	4	6	11	26	46	40
Aldershot	42	8	6	7	28	27	5	6	10	24	44	38
Watford	42	12	4	5	43	16	3	3	15	28	47	37
Southend U	42	9	6	6	32	27	3	4	14	19	47	34
Gillingham	42	8	8	5	49	41	3	3	15	26	55	33
Newport Co	42	6	9	6	25	23	2	8	11	24	47	33
Bristol C	42	7	8	6	33	22	3	5	13	25	63	33
Torquay U	42	10	4	7	32	28	3	3	15	21	65	33
Bournemouth	42	7	7	7	41	37	2	2	17	19	65	27
Cardiff C	42	6	4	11	32	43	3	2	16	25	62	24

Football League Records

Top scorers: Div 1, E.Drake (Arsenal) 42 goals; Div 2, J.Milsom (Bolton Wanderers) 31 goals; Div 3(N), G.Alsop (Walsall) 39 goals; Div 3(S), R.Allen (Charlton Athletic) 32 goals.

Ted Drake, whose 42 goals in 1934-5 is still an Arsenal record.

DIVISION 1

	ARSENAL	ASTON VILLA	BIRMINGHAM	BLACKBURN R	CHELSEA	DERBY CO	EVERTON	GRIMSBY T	HUDDERSFIELD T	LEEDS U	LEICESTER C	LIVERPOOL	MANCHESTER C	MIDDLESBROUGH	PORTSMOUTH	PRESTON N.E.	SHEFFIELD W	STOKE C	SUNDERLAND	TOTTENHAM H	W.B.A.	WOLVERHAMPTON W
1 ARSENAL		N17 1-2	S29 5-1	S05 4-0	a06 2-2	m04 0-1	N03 2-0	M23 1-1	a20 1-0	J19 3-0	D15 8-0	S01 8-1	O13 3-0	a19 8-0	D29 1-1	D25 5-3	F02 4-1	F20 2-0	M09 0-0	O20 5-1	S15 4-3	D01 7-0
2 ASTON VILLA	M30 1-3		D29 2-2	D22 1-1	D26 0-3	S01 3-2	O13 2-2	F16 3-2	a19 1-1	D08 1-1	J19 5-0	a13 4-2	O27 4-2	a27 0-3	N26 5-4	S29 4-2	N10 4-0	M02 4-1	S15 1-1	F02 1-0	a03 2-3	A27 2-1
3 BIRMINGHAM	F09 3-0	A25 2-1		S22 1-0	O20 0-1	M23 3-2	m04 2-3	N17 3-2	D15 0-4	a22 3-1	N03 2-3	F23 1-3	S08 1-3	F06 4-2	O06 2-1	a06 3-0	D26 0-4	J05 0-0	a20 2-2	D01 2-1	S03 1-2	M09 1-1
4 BLACKBURN R	S17 2-0	m04 5-0	F02 3-1		N12 1-2	D15 2-5	a20 6-2	N03 2-2	D01 4-2	S01 1-1	M09 0-0	D29 0-2	M04 1-0	O13 3-2	D25 0-0	M23 1-0	S15 2-1	S29 0-1	O20 0-0	J01 2-0	J19 3-0	a06 4-2
5 CHELSEA	N24 2-5	D25 2-0	M06 2-2	M30 4-2		D29 1-1	F20 3-0	S29 2-0	O13 2-1	M16 7-1	S01 3-1	D08 4-1	a27 4-2	D22 2-1	a13 1-1	F02 0-0	A29 1-2	O27 0-2	J19 2-2	S15 1-3	N10 2-3	a19 4-2
6 DERBY CO	D22 3-1	J05 1-1	N10 1-1	a27 1-1	A25 3-0		a22 4-1	O13 1-4	S05 4-1	a13 1-2	S15 1-1	N24 1-2	M02 1-2	O27 2-0	M30 0-1	a10 0-3	M20 4-0	S08 0-2	F02 3-1	S29 2-1	D08 9-3	D26 2-0
7 EVERTON	M16 0-2	F23 2-2	D22 2-0	D08 5-2	O06 3-2	J01 2-2		J19 3-1	S22 4-2	M06 4-4	A29 2-1	S15 1-0	N24 1-2	a13 1-1	N10 3-2	S01 4-1	m01 2-2	M30 5-0	D25 6-2	D29 5-2	O27 4-0	F09 5-2
8 GRIMSBY T	N10 2-2	O06 5-1	M30 4-3	M16 1-2	F09 3-1	F23 1-3	S08 0-0		a02 1-1	O27 3-2	a19 3-1	M02 3-2	a13 1-1	D08 2-2	S01 3-0	D29 3-1	D22 3-1	N24 3-1	A28 0-0	D25 3-0	m01 3-0	S22 2-1
9 HUDDERSFIELD T	D08 1-1	a24 1-1	a27 2-2	a13 6-0	F23 3-0	A27 1-0	F02 1-1	S15 1-5		F09 3-1	D26 2-3	N10 8-0	M30 3-0	N24 3-1	M16 2-0	J19 3-4	O27 4-0	D22 1-4	D29 0-3	S01 0-0	M06 3-0	O06 4-1
10 LEEDS U	S08 1-1	a20 1-1	a19 1-1	J05 5-1	N03 5-2	D01 4-2	O20 2-0	M09 3-1	S29 2-0		a06 0-2	S22 0-3	D25 1-2	A25 2-4	M02 3-1	D15 3-3	O13 0-0	S03 4-2	N17 2-4	m04 4-3	F20 4-1	M23 1-1
11 LEICESTER C	a27 3-5	S08 5-0	M16 2-1	O27 0-1	J05 1-0	J31 0-1	S03 5-2	a22 2-2	D25 0-3	N24 1-0		M30 3-1	S22 1-3	M02 3-1	D22 6-3	O13 0-0	D08 0-1	N10 0-3	S29 0-2	M28 6-0	a13 0-0	A25 1-1
12 LIVERPOOL	J05 0-2	D01 3-1	O13 5-4	A25 2-0	a20 6-0	a06 1-3	M20 2-1	O20 1-1	M23 3-2	F02 4-2	N17 5-1		S05 2-1	D26 2-2	S08 0-1	M09 0-0	F20 1-2	a19 5-0	m04 2-2	D15 4-1	S29 3-2	N03 2-1
13 MANCHESTER C	F23 1-1	M09 4-1	J19 0-0	O06 3-3	D15 2-0	O20 0-1	a06 2-2	D01 1-0	N17 0-0	D26 3-0	F02 6-3	A29 3-1		F09 6-2	a19 2-4	a20 1-2	S01 4-1	S15 3-1	a10 1-0	N03 3-1	D29 3-2	m04 5-0
14 MIDDLESBROUGH	a22 0-1	D15 4-1	S15 0-1	F23 3-3	m04 2-2	M09 1-1	D01 3-2	a20 0-2	a06 2-1	D29 3-3	O20 1-0	J01 2-0	S29 1-2		A29 1-1	N03 3-3	J19 5-3	F02 2-0	F16 0-0	M23 3-1	S01 0-0	N17 2-2
15 PORTSMOUTH	A25 3-3	a06 0-1	a10 2-1	D26 3-1	D01 1-1	N17 5-1	M23 5-1	J05 1-0	N03 5-0	S15 0-0	m04 1-1	J19 1-2	a22 4-2	S05 1-0		O24 4-0	S29 2-1	O13 0-1	D15 2-4	M09 1-1	F02 0-2	a20 0-1
16 PRESTON N.E.	D26 2-1	F09 0-0	N24 0-1	N10 3-1	S22 2-0	O06 0-1	J05 2-2	A25 1-0	S08 2-0	a27 0-2	F23 2-0	O27 2-2	D08 2-4	M16 2-0	M06 1-1		M30 2-1	a13 5-2	a22 1-1	S03 1-0	D22 1-2	J28 2-1
17 SHEFFIELD W	S22 0-0	M23 2-1	D25 2-1	J28 2-2	S03 3-1	N03 1-0	D15 0-0	m04 1-0	M09 1-1	F23 1-0	a20 1-1	O06 4-1	J05 1-0	S08 3-3	F09 3-0	N17 2-1		A25 4-1	D01 2-2	a06 4-0	J01 2-1	O20 3-1
18 STOKE C	O06 2-2	O20 4-1	S01 2-0	F09 3-1	M09 0-1	J19 1-1	N17 3-2	a06 0-0	m04 2-0	A27 8-1	M23 3-0	a22 1-1	J26 2-0	S22 2-0	F23 1-2	D01 3-1	D29 1-1		N03 0-3	a20 4-1	D26 3-0	D15 1-2
19 SUNDERLAND	O27 2-1	F06 3-3	D08 5-1	M02 3-0	S08 4-0	S22 1-4	D26 7-0	S05 3-0	A25 4-1	M30 3-0	F09 2-0	D22 2-3	N10 3-2	O06 1-1	a27 4-1	a19 3-1	a13 2-2	M16 4-1		O13 1-2	N24 0-1	J05 0-0
20 TOTTENHAM H	M06 0-6	S22 0-2	a13 1-1	a19 1-0	J30 1-3	F09 2-2	A25 1-1	D26 2-1	J05 0-0	D22 1-1	O06 2-2	a27 5-1	M16 0-0	N10 3-1	O27 4-1	A27 1-2	N24 3-2	D08 3-2	F23 1-1		M30 0-1	S08 3-1
21 W.B.A.	J30 0-3	N03 2-2	A29 1-2	S08 2-2	M23 2-2	a20 4-3	M09 0-1	D15 4-2	O20 4-1	O06 6-3	D01 4-1	F09 1-1	A25 1-1	J05 6-3	S22 4-2	m04 0-0	a22 1-1	D25 3-0	a06 1-1	N17 4-0		F23 5-2
22 WOLVERHAMPTON W	a13 1-1	S03 5-2	O27 3-1	N24 2-1	a22 6-1	D25 5-1	S29 4-2	F02 0-3	F16 2-3	N10 1-2	D29 3-1	M16 5-3	D22 5-0	M30 5-3	D08 2-3	S15 2-2	M04 2-2	a27 2-1	S01 1-2	J19 6-2	O13 3-2	

Don Welsh, signed from Torquay United, began his Charlton Athletic career as they rose from Third Division South to First Division in consecutive seasons.

DIVISION 2

	BARNSLEY	BLACKPOOL	BOLTON W	BRADFORD	BRADFORD C	BRENTFORD	BURNLEY	BURY	FULHAM	HULL C	MANCHESTER U	NEWCASTLE U	NORWICH C	NOTTINGHAM F	NOTTS CO	OLDHAM A	PLYMOUTH A	PORT VALE	SHEFFIELD U	SOUTHAMPTON	SWANSEA T	WEST HAM U
1 BARNSLEY		M30 2-2	a10 1-1	D29 1-1	a22 2-0	a27 3-3	F02 0-0	N24 3-0	D22 2-0	a13 2-2	J19 0-2	M16 2-1	O27 2-1	D08 1-2	A27 1-1	S29 4-0	M02 1-4	S01 2-0	J01 0-0	O13 1-1	S15 1-0	N10 1-1
2 BLACKPOOL	N17 3-0		m04 1-1	S29 1-0	D01 2-1	S15 2-2	O20 1-0	D29 1-1	F02 1-1	S01 2-1	N03 1-2	A27 4-1	O13 2-1	J19 1-0	a20 3-1	D25 4-0	F16 4-1	M23 3-1	a06 1-0	D15 4-1	M09 2-1	a19 3-2
3 BOLTON W	O06 8-0	D22 4-2		M30 1-2	S22 3-0	m01 2-0	J02 7-0	S01 2-0	N10 4-0	M06 1-2	S03 3-1	D08 1-0	a13 4-0	O27 2-3	J30 5-1	D29 2-0	N24 3-2	F23 2-0	F09 1-1	S08 4-0	a19 1-0	a27 3-1
4 BRADFORD	A25 3-2	F09 0-0	N17 4-0		M09 2-1	a22 2-3	D01 1-1	O06 2-1	D25 0-0	F23 1-2	D15 1-2	J30 1-3	S08 1-1	S03 1-1	N03 0-0	a06 2-0	J05 2-2	m04 1-1	O20 1-3	M23 3-1	a20 3-1	S22 1-3
5 BRADFORD C	a23 1-0	a13 0-2	F02 1-1	O27 3-1		O13 3-0	J19 1-1	D08 0-0	M02 0-0	a27 3-2	D29 2-0	M30 3-3	N10 1-1	D22 4-0	F16 2-0	S15 2-0	M16 0-1	D26 3-0	A27 2-5	S29 1-1	S01 2-0	N24 0-2
6 BRENTFORD	D15 8-1	J26 2-1	N03 1-0	a19 1-0	F23 2-0		N17 6-1	S22 2-1	S05 1-0	F09 2-1	D01 3-1	J05 3-0	A25 2-1	O06 1-1	O20 4-1	M23 2-1	D25 0-0	a20 8-0	m04 3-1	M09 3-2	a06 1-0	S08 4-1
7 BURNLEY	S22 4-1	M05 1-2	D25 2-1	a13 1-2	S08 2-0	M30 0-3		O27 3-3	N24 3-1	M20 1-3	O06 1-2	D22 0-3	a27 1-0	N10 2-1	J05 4-0	a19 4-2	D08 1-2	F09 2-2	J28 0-2	A25 3-0	F23 3-0	S03 5-2
8 BURY	a06 4-1	A25 1-5	J05 2-1	F16 2-4	a20 2-1	F02 4-1	M09 0-0		S29 2-0	J19 0-1	M23 0-1	a19 0-2	S17 1-0	S15 1-0	D15 1-0	O20 2-0	O13 2-1	N17 3-1	D01 3-1	m04 4-1	N03 2-1	D25 2-4
9 FULHAM	m04 1-3	S22 4-1	M23 2-1	D26 2-2	O20 3-1	A27 2-2	a06 2-0	F09 1-2		O06 4-0	a20 3-1	S08 3-2	J05 1-3	F23 2-1	M09 7-0	N17 3-1	A25 3-0	D15 2-0	a19 7-2	N03 3-3	D01 4-1	J26 3-0
10 HULL C	D01 1-1	J05 2-2	O20 0-2	O13 2-0	D15 1-0	S29 2-1	N03 1-3	S08 0-1	F16 1-2		N17 3-2	D26 1-1	a22 1-0	F02 5-0	m04 5-1	M09 1-1	S10 1-1	a06 1-0	a20 0-3	J31 0-0	M23 0-1	S17 4-0
11 MANCHESTER U	S08 4-1	M16 3-2	S12 0-3	a27 2-0	A25 2-0	a13 0-0	M27 3-4	N10 1-0	D08 1-0	M30 3-0		M02 0-1	S22 5-0	N24 3-2	D25 2-1	O13 4-0	D22 3-1	F06 2-1	J05 3-3	J01 3-0	S29 3-1	O27 3-1
12 NEWCASTLE U	N03 4-1	S12 4-1	a20 1-3	S15 0-1	N17 4-2	S01 2-5	m04 2-0	J01 5-1	J19 1-1	D25 6-2	O20 0-1		S29 2-0	D29 2-0	a06 1-1	D15 4-2	F02 3-0	M09 1-2	M23 4-1	D01 1-0	F16 5-1	F23 3-0
13 NORWICH C	M09 0-1	F23 1-1	D01 2-3	J19 3-0	M23 6-1	D29 2-1	D15 2-3	A27 4-1	S01 0-0	a19 3-0	F02 3-2	F09 2-0		D26 3-3	N17 7-2	a20 0-0	S15 3-0	O20 0-0	N03 3-1	a06 4-0	m04 2-2	O06 1-2
14 NOTTINGHAM F	a20 4-1	S08 0-0	M09 0-1	O04 2-2	m04 2-0	F28 0-0	M23 5-0	F06 1-4	O13 1-1	S22 2-1	a06 2-2	A25 5-1	D25 5-2		F09 2-3	N03 4-0	a19 1-3	D01 2-0	D15 2-1	O20 3-1	N17 1-0	J05 2-0
15 NOTTS CO	S03 1-4	D08 3-2	S15 0-2	M16 1-1	O06 2-3	M02 0-1	S01 1-0	a27 1-2	O27 1-1	D22 1-1	D26 1-0	N24 0-1	M30 1-0	S29 3-5		J19 2-1	N10 1-3	a22 3-2	F23 0-1	F02 3-1	D29 4-0	a13 0-2
16 OLDHAM A	F09 1-4	D26 2-3	A25 1-4	N24 1-1	F05 3-1	N10 1-3	a22 1-2	M02 7-2	M30 2-1	O27 5-0	F23 3-1	a27 3-2	D08 4-2	M16 0-5	S08 1-0		a13 1-1	O06 2-0	S22 3-2	J05 0-2	S03 2-2	D22 1-2
17 PLYMOUTH A	O20 3-1	O06 1-2	a06 1-0	S01 2-2	N03 3-1	D26 1-1	a20 2-2	F23 3-0	D29 3-1	A29 6-4	m04 0-2	S22 1-3	F06 0-1	a22 5-2	M23 4-0	D01 2-0		J19 2-1	M09 2-0	N17 4-0	D15 3-2	F09 0-1
18 PORT VALE	J05 4-0	N10 2-2	O13 1-3	D22 1-1	D25 1-0	D08 2-2	S29 3-1	M30 0-1	a27 1-1	N24 1-2	S15 3-2	O27 1-3	M02 1-1	a13 2-0	a19 5-3	F16 2-0	S08 2-2		A25 2-0	S03 4-1	F02 2-1	M16 2-2
19 SHEFFIELD U	D26 2-1	N24 1-1	S29 6-2	M02 3-1	S10 1-2	D22 1-2	S15 0-0	a13 5-3	a22 1-2	D08 3-4	S01 3-2	N10 5-1	M16 1-1	a27 2-1	O13 3-0	F02 2-1	O27 1-2	D29 3-0		F16 6-1	J19 1-1	M30 1-2
20 SOUTHAMPTON	F23 0-1	a27 2-0	J19 1-2	N10 4-1	F09 1-1	O27 1-0	D29 0-0	D22 2-1	M16 1-1	S15 3-0	a22 1-0	a13 2-0	N24 1-4	M02 1-2	S22 1-1	S01 2-2	M30 1-0	A27 0-0	O06 1-1		D26 1-0	D08 2-2
21 SWANSEA T	J31 1-1	O27 2-1	a22 2-1	D08 0-0	J05 3-1	N24 2-4	O13 2-0	M16 1-0	a13 2-0	N10 2-1	F09 1-0	O06 3-4	D22 1-1	M30 3-0	A25 2-1	A27 5-1	a27 3-0	S22 1-1	S08 0-0	D25 0-1		M02 5-4
22 WEST HAM U	M23 4-3	a22 2-1	D15 4-1	F02 2-1	a06 1-0	J19 2-0	A27 1-2	D26 3-0	S15 2-1	D29 1-2	M09 0-0	O13 3-2	F18 1-0	S01 3-1	D01 4-0	m04 2-0	S29 2-1	N03 3-1	N17 2-0	a20 2-1	O20 2-0	

Season 1934-35

DIVISION 3 NORTH

	ACCRINGTON S	BARROW	CARLISLE U	CHESTER	CHESTERFIELD	CREWE A	DARLINGTON	DONCASTER R	GATESHEAD	HALIFAX T	HARTLEPOOL U	LINCOLN C	MANSFIELD T	NEW BRIGHTON	ROCHDALE	ROTHERHAM U	SOUTHPORT	STOCKPORT CO	TRANMERE R	WALSALL	WREXHAM	YORK C
1 ACCRINGTON S		D22 5-2	S25 1-0	J05 1-1	D08 1-0	F09 3-0	a22 2-1	J26 1-5	F23 4-2	M30 1-1	S22 0-4	O27 3-0	S19 2-0	A25 1-3	M02 2-5	J12 2-3	S08 1-1	O06 3-1	M16 1-0	a13 3-3	N10 2-2	D26 5-2
2 BARROW	m04 0-2		F23 2-1	a06 4-2	F02 1-1	M09 1-1	D15 4-4	M23 2-1	F16 3-2	S01 2-0	N03 2-0	a22 1-1	S29 3-0	D01 1-2	S03 1-1	J19 2-1	N17 2-1	O20 1-4	D25 1-0	S15 3-1	D29 1-3	a20 0-3
3 CARLISLE U	A30 2-0	O13 0-0		D01 1-3	S29 3-1	N03 1-3	m04 1-2	N17 1-1	O20 5-4	J19 2-4	M23 2-2	J01 2-1	a25 1-1	a20 4-1	a19 0-0	S15 2-1	a06 0-1	M09 1-2	D29 1-1	F02 1-6	S01 0-2	D15 4-0
4 CHESTER	S01 4-0	J16 6-2	a13 3-0		N10 1-1	a19 2-2	J19 3-1	F23 1-3	D29 2-2	M02 5-0	S05 4-1	a27 0-1	M30 3-2	F02 5-4	a03 1-0	O27 4-1	O06 0-2	D25 5-1	D22 0-0	M16 2-1	S29 6-2	S15 5-1
5 CHESTERFIELD	a20 0-0	S22 3-0	F09 3-0	M23 1-2		J19 1-2	D01 2-2	M09 3-2	D15 3-1	J01 4-0	O20 4-0	F23 3-1	J26 0-0	N17 1-0	O06 2-0	D29 2-1	N03 3-3	m04 5-0	A27 0-2	S01 2-0	a19 1-4	a06 3-1
6 CREWE A	S29 4-2	O27 4-3	M16 1-1	a22 1-1	S08 1-0		F16 4-1	A25 1-1	F02 2-1	D08 3-1	J05 1-1	M30 1-0	M02 1-1	S03 2-3	N10 4-1	a27 0-0	D25 2-1	S15 2-3	J12 1-2	D22 1-0	a13 2-0	O13 3-2
7 DARLINGTON	J01 5-0	J12 3-1	D22 5-0	S08 1-0	a13 2-1	O06 6-2		S22 1-1	S05 2-1	N10 0-1	F09 3-0	M02 4-1	m01 1-0	J05 1-0	D26 2-2	M30 4-0	J26 0-0	F23 0-0	O27 2-2	J16 3-2	M16 3-1	A25 2-0
8 DONCASTER R	S15 2-1	N10 2-0	M30 3-0	O13 3-0	O27 0-2	D29 2-0	F02 2-0		J19 5-0	m02 0-1	D26 3-1	a13 1-3	M16 2-1	F16 7-1	J12 1-0	a19 3-5	S03 2-0	S01 3-4	a10 2-0	M02 4-0	a27 2-1	S29 4-1
9 GATESHEAD	O13 1-1	O06 1-0	M02 3-2	A25 2-4	a27 1-4	S22 5-2	A29 3-0	S08 0-0		J12 3-1	J26 2-1	M16 0-2	D22 2-2	D25 2-1	O27 2-0	a13 1-1	J05 1-2	F09 3-2	N10 0-2	F27 1-0	M30 1-0	a19 2-1
10 HALIFAX T	N17 2-1	J05 2-1	S08 4-0	O20 1-0	D25 0-2	a20 1-0	M23 2-1	m04 1-0	a06 4-0		D15 4-1	S22 2-1	A25 2-1	M09 6-2	J26 1-1	S03 2-1	F23 4-3	D01 2-1	F09 1-2	S17 1-1	O06 3-2	N03 5-3
11 HARTLEPOOLS U	F02 4-2	M16 5-2	N10 5-2	A29 0-2	M02 1-1	S01 4-2	S29 0-1	D25 2-1	S15 1-2	a27 0-3		J12 1-5	O27 1-1	O13 2-2	M30 0-0	M06 3-1	a22 4-1	J19 4-0	a13 6-1	D29 2-1	J01 4-3	F16 3-1
12 LINCOLN C	M09 1-0	a19 6-0	D26 4-2	D15 0-0	O13 2-0	N17 1-1	O20 2-4	D01 0-2	N03 5-0	F02 2-3	a06 2-1		S03 4-0	m04 1-0	A25 3-0	S29 4-0	a20 4-1	M23 3-0	J19 2-2	F16 5-1	S15 1-3	J05 3-1
13 MANSFIELD T	D15 2-1	F09 3-2	O06 3-0	N17 1-1	S15 1-0	O20 4-1	a20 2-2	N03 2-0	m04 1-1	D29 4-0	M09 2-1	A29 3-4		a06 2-1	F23 1-0	S01 2-1	M23 2-3	F02 3-2	a19 4-2	J19 4-2	D25 4-0	D01 6-1
14 NEW BRIGHTON	D29 2-1	a13 3-1	F27 5-1	S22 0-2	M30 3-1	A29 1-1	S01 0-1	O06 1-1	D26 3-0	O27 0-0	F23 1-4	D22 0-2	J16 2-1		a27 1-0	M16 3-2	F09 0-0	a19 1-2	S15 0-1	N10 2-2	J12 0-0	J19 4-2
15 ROCHDALE	O20 2-2	A28 0-1	a22 3-1	a20 3-3	F16 0-2	M23 3-0	D25 1-3	a06 0-1	M09 6-1	S15 2-4	N17 3-2	D29 2-0	O13 1-0	D15 3-1		F02 1-3	D01 2-2	N03 0-5	S01 1-1	S29 1-0	J19 3-3	m04 2-0
16 ROTHERHAM U	a06 2-0	S08 0-0	J26 4-1	M09 6-1	A25 2-2	D15 2-2	N17 2-1	a22 1-3	D01 3-0	A27 2-2	m04 0-1	J09 5-0	J05 3-0	N03 1-2	S22 4-0		O20 4-2	a25 2-0	O06 3-1	D26 4-2	J23 2-0	M23 4-1
17 SOUTHPORT	J19 0-0	M30 0-2	J12 0-3	F16 1-1	M16 1-1	D26 2-1	S15 1-4	A28 1-2	S01 1-1	O13 1-2	a19 1-1	a02 3-3	N10 1-2	S29 2-1	a13 2-1	M02 0-3		D29 1-2	a27 4-0	O27 3-2	D22 2-1	F02 0-3
18 STOCKPORT CO	F20 5-1	M02 4-1	O27 2-0	D26 0-1	D22 4-2	F06 4-0	O13 3-0	J05 3-2	S29 5-1	a13 2-1	S08 3-2	N10 1-2	S22 0-2	a22 1-1	M16 3-1	J01 4-0	A25 6-1		M30 1-0	a27 0-3	a29 6-1	S03 0-0
19 TRANMERE R	N03 2-1	D26 2-1	A25 3-1	J01 1-1	S03 2-1	a06 5-1	M09 4-1	a20 0-2	M23 2-2	S29 1-0	D01 3-0	S08 2-1	a22 3-0	J26 0-1	J05 4-1	F16 3-3	D15 4-1	N17 3-1		O13 4-0	F02 1-1	O20 4-0
20 WALSALL	D01 6-0	J26 5-0	S22 1-0	N03 1-1	J05 2-1	m04 4-0	a06 0-0	O20 0-2	a20 5-0	a22 4-1	A25 1-2	O06 0-0	S08 2-2	M23 5-1	F09 0-0	D25 5-2	M09 2-2	D15 3-1	F23 3-0		S03 0-0	N17 2-3
21 WREXHAM	M23 2-2	A25 1-1	J05 4-2	F09 2-2	a22 2-1	D01 2-1	N03 4-0	D15 1-2	N17 3-1	F16 5-0	a20 0-2	J26 2-2	D26 1-3	O20 3-0	S08 2-0	O13 0-1	m04 3-0	a06 2-1	S22 2-2	A29 4-2		M09 2-0
22 YORK C	D25 5-2	a03 1-1	a27 7-0	J26 1-1	M27 1-1	F23 7-3	D29 2-1	F09 1-2	a22 3-0	M16 0-1	O06 3-1	S01 1-2	a13 2-1	S08 1-0	D22 0-1	N10 5-0	S22 3-1	A29 3-1	M02 0-0	M30 4-1	O27 0-0	

DIVISION 3 SOUTH

	ALDERSHOT	BOURNEMOUTH	BRIGHTON & HA	BRISTOL C	BRISTOL R	CARDIFF C	CHARLTON A	CLAPTON O	COVENTRY C	CRYSTAL P	EXETER C	GILLINGHAM	LUTON T	MILLWALL	NEWPORT CO	NORTHAMPTON T	Q.P.R.	READING	SOUTHEND U	SWINDON T	TORQUAY U	WATFORD
1 ALDERSHOT		M02 1-1	F16 1-0	M30 1-0	D25 1-2	S29 2-0	a19 3-2	m01 1-1	a13 3-1	A25 2-2	D22 0-0	M16 4-1	O13 0-1	M06 0-0	a27 3-2	S22 2-0	J05 1-0	N10 2-5	S05 3-2	J30 3-0	S08 2-0	O27 0-0
2 BOURNEMOUTH	O20 4-1		M23 1-0	a22 1-1	D01 3-0	F16 3-1	a06 2-2	J19 1-0	S01 0-2	N17 1-1	D25 3-2	S15 1-1	N03 1-3	D29 3-1	S05 3-1	S29 0-1	m04 0-2	F02 4-1	a20 2-1	M09 1-1	D15 1-2	F23 1-2
3 BRIGHTON & H.A.	O06 3-0	N10 2-0		a27 2-0	A25 3-1	F23 3-1	J05 2-1	J16 3-0	M30 2-0	S08 3-0	O27 6-0	a13 1-1	D26 4-1	D22 0-2	M02 3-1	M16 2-3	J26 6-1	M20 1-0	a19 2-2	F09 2-2	S22 0-0	S05 2-0
4 BRISTOL C	N17 2-0	a19 2-1	D15 1-0		F06 1-1	m04 4-0	M23 1-4	M13 0-0	S29 0-2	N03 0-1	S08 2-0	O13 3-1	M09 0-2	F02 4-2	J05 2-1	D25 1-1	a20 5-1	S05 1-0	O20 2-0	a06 2-0	D01 1-0	A25 3-1
5 BRISTOL R	D26 1-0	a13 4-1	D29 0-0	S15 2-2		a22 3-2	S22 0-0	a27 1-2	O27 2-1	F09 5-3	N10 5-5	D22 4-3	S01 1-1	M02 2-0	M16 5-3	J16 7-1	O06 2-0	M30 3-0	J19 2-1	A29 2-2	F23 1-0	a23 2-0
6 CARDIFF C	F09 1-1	O06 2-1	O13 0-0	D22 3-3	a19 4-1		A25 2-1	a13 3-0	J16 2-4	J05 2-0	a27 5-0	D08 0-2	A27 1-0	M30 3-1	O27 3-4	N10 2-2	S08 2-1	M16 1-1	S10 2-0	S22 1-3	J26 1-1	M02 2-1
7 CHARLTON A	a22 4-0	J12 0-1	S01 3-1	N10 4-1	F02 2-0	D29 3-1		O27 2-1	M02 3-3	O06 2-2	M16 1-0	a27 2-0	J19 4-2	S29 3-1	D08 6-0	M30 0-1	F23 3-1	D22 3-1	S15 3-0	D25 6-0	A27 3-2	a13 5-2
8 CLAPTON O	a20 3-1	S08 0-1	a06 6-0	O06 4-0	D15 5-2	D01 0-1	M09 1-2		A30 0-1	O20 2-0	F09 0-3	a19 2-2	N17 1-1	F23 2-1	S22 4-0	J05 3-2	D26 3-1	A25 2-1	m04 3-0	N03 2-0	M23 3-1	J26 1-1
9 COVENTRY C	D01 0-0	J05 4-1	N17 0-2	F09 1-1	M09 1-0	a06 2-0	O20 4-0	S03 4-0		F23 1-1	S22 1-1	D25 4-0	m04 1-0	O06 5-1	J26 5-0	A25 2-0	M23 4-1	a23 1-2	D15 6-3	a20 3-0	N03 6-0	S08 1-1
10 CRYSTAL P	D29 3-0	M30 1-0	J19 3-0	M16 3-1	S29 2-0	S01 6-1	F16 1-2	M02 1-0	O13 3-1		a20 0-1	O27 2-0	S15 2-1	N10 1-1	a13 6-0	D22 2-0	S05 2-3	a27 3-1	F02 1-0	a19 7-0	D26 2-2	J12 0-0
11 EXETER C	m04 8-1	D26 4-1	M09 3-1	J19 3-0	M23 2-2	D15 2-1	N03 3-1	S29 1-1	F02 2-0	J26 0-6		F16 2-0	O20 1-2	S15 0-1	A25 0-1	S05 3-0	D01 3-0	O13 2-3	J05 4-3	N17 3-3	a06 1-1	a22 1-1
12 GILLINGHAM	N03 1-1	J20 3-1	D01 0-0	F23 1-0	m04 1-1	a20 1-0	D15 3-6	a22 1-0	D26 2-5	M09 2-0	O06 2-1		a06 1-1	A29 1-3	F09 5-0	S08 3-1	O20 0-0	J05 1-1	N17 2-2	M23 2-0	A25 3-0	S22 1-2
13 LUTON T	F23 6-1	M16 4-0	D25 4-0	O27 1-1	J05 6-2	S03 4-0	S08 1-2	M30 3-0	D22 4-0	J30 2-2	M02 4-0	m01 2-2		N24 2-1	a22 4-1	a23 2-2	S22 1-1	a13 2-4	A25 1-1	O06 2-0	F09 3-1	N10 2-2
14 MILLWALL	a06 3-0	S10 2-0	m04 3-1	S22 0-1	O20 0-2	N17 2-2	F09 1-3	O13 1-1	F16 1-3	M23 3-2	J31 1-0	S17 3-2	D15 1-4		S08 2-0	a19 0-1	N03 2-0	D25 2-2	M09 1-0	D01 1-0	a20 4-2	J05 0-0
15 NEWPORT CO	D15 2-0	A27 6-1	O20 1-0	S01 2-0	N03 1-1	M09 4-0	a20 0-2	F02 3-3	S15 2-1	D01 2-3	D29 1-3	S29 2-2	a19 2-4	J19 1-2		O13 1-3	a06 2-1	F20 2-2	M23 0-5	m04 1-2	N17 1-4	D25 0-1
16 NORTHAMPTON T	F02 0-0	F09 0-1	N03 4-1	D26 2-2	a06 1-0	M23 3-0	N17 1-1	S01 3-1	D29 3-4	m04 3-2	A27 2-1	J19 2-1	a20 2-1	a22 1-0	F23 2-0		D15 1-0	S15 1-3	D01 1-1	O20 4-2	M09 3-0	O06 1-0
17 Q.P.R.	S01 2-0	D22 2-1	S15 2-1	J01 4-1	F16 2-0	J19 2-2	O13 0-3	D25 6-3	N10 1-1	A29 3-3	a13 1-1	M02 2-0	F02 3-0	M16 1-0	J12 4-1	a27 3-1		O27 2-0	S29 1-1	D29 1-1	a19 5-1	M30 2-1
18 READING	M23 5-4	S22 4-1	a20 4-4	A29 2-0	N17 5-1	N03 1-1	m04 2-2	D29 0-0	a19 2-0	D15 6-1	F23 2-0	S01 3-0	D01 1-0	D26 2-1	O06 6-1	J30 3-1	M09 0-0		a06 3-2	J19 2-1	O20 3-1	F09 3-2
19 SOUTHEND U	A29 2-1	a10 0-0	a22 3-2	M02 6-0	S08 5-1	D26 2-1	J26 0-3	D22 0-2	a27 1-1	S22 1-4	S01 1-2	M30 0-0	D29 3-3	O27 2-1	N10 0-1	a13 2-1	F09 2-0	m01 6-1		F23 2-0	O06 2-3	M16 0-2
20 SWINDON T	S15 3-2	O27 0-2	S29 4-4	a10 1-0	S05 1-0	F02 2-1	D26 2-2	M16 1-1	m01 0-0	a22 1-1	M30 6-1	N10 3-0	F16 0-1	a13 0-1	D22 0-0	M02 5-3	A25 3-1	S08 1-1	O13 5-0		J05 5-0	a27 2-1
21 TORQUAY U	J19 2-1	a27 1-2	F02 3-0	a13 3-1	O13 1-2	S15 5-2	S05 1-2	N10 4-2	M16 1-0	D25 7-1	J12 3-0	D29 5-0	S29 6-2	M13 1-1	M30 2-1	O27 2-0	a22 7-0	M02 1-1	F16 2-0	S01 2-1		D22 1-3
22 WATFORD	M09 0-1	O13 3-1	A29 0-1	D29 4-0	a20 3-0	O20 1-3	D01 2-0	S15 5-0	J19 2-0	a06 2-0	a19 0-1	F02 3-1	M23 2-2	S01 2-3	D26 7-0	F16 1-1	N17 2-0	S29 1-0	N03 3-1	D14 7-4	m04 3-0	

LEAGUE TABLES

DIVISION 1

	P	W	D	L	F	A	W	D	L	F	A	Pts
Arsenal	42	15	4	2	74	17	8	8	5	41	29	58
Sunderland	42	13	4	4	57	24	6	12	3	33	27	54
Sheffield W	42	14	7	0	42	17	4	6	11	28	47	49
Manchester C	42	13	5	3	53	25	7	3	11	29	42	48
Grimsby T	42	13	6	2	49	25	4	5	12	29	35	45
Derby Co	42	10	4	7	44	28	8	5	8	37	38	45
Liverpool	42	13	4	4	53	29	6	3	12	32	59	45
Everton	42	14	5	2	64	32	2	7	12	25	56	44
WBA	42	10	8	3	55	33	7	2	12	28	50	44
Stoke C	42	12	5	4	46	20	6	1	14	25	50	42
Preston NE	42	11	5	5	33	22	4	7	10	29	45	42
Chelsea	42	11	5	5	49	32	5	4	12	24	50	41
Aston Villa	42	11	6	4	50	36	3	7	11	24	52	41
Portsmouth	42	10	5	6	41	24	5	5	11	30	48	40
Blackburn R	42	12	5	4	42	23	2	6	13	24	55	39
Huddersfield T	42	11	5	5	52	27	3	5	13	24	44	38
Wolves	42	13	3	5	65	38	2	5	14	23	56	38
Leeds U	42	10	6	5	48	35	3	6	12	27	57	38
Birmingham	42	10	3	8	36	36	3	7	11	27	45	36
Middlesbrough	42	8	9	4	38	29	2	5	14	32	61	34
Leicester C	42	9	4	8	39	30	3	5	13	22	56	33
Tottenham H	42	8	8	5	34	31	2	2	17	20	62	30

DIVISION 2

	P	W	D	L	F	A	W	D	L	F	A	Pts
Brentford	42	19	2	0	59	14	7	7	7	34	34	61
Bolton W	42	17	1	3	63	15	9	3	9	33	33	56
West Ham U	42	18	1	2	46	17	8	3	10	34	46	56
Blackpool	42	16	4	1	46	18	5	7	9	33	39	53
Manchester U	42	16	2	3	50	21	7	2	12	26	34	50
Newcastle U	42	14	2	5	55	25	8	2	11	34	43	48
Fulham	42	15	3	3	62	26	2	9	10	14	30	46
Plymouth A	42	13	3	5	48	26	6	5	10	27	38	46
Nottingham F	42	12	5	4	46	23	5	3	13	30	47	42
Bury	42	14	1	6	38	26	5	3	13	24	47	42
Sheffield U	42	11	4	6	51	30	5	5	11	28	40	41
Burnley	42	11	2	8	43	32	5	7	9	20	41	41
Hull C	42	9	6	6	32	22	7	2	12	31	52	40
Norwich C	42	11	6	4	51	23	3	5	13	20	38	39
Bradford	42	7	8	6	32	28	4	8	9	23	35	38
Barnsley	42	8	10	3	32	22	5	2	14	28	61	38
Swansea T	42	13	5	3	41	22	1	3	17	15	45	36
Port Vale	42	10	7	4	42	28	1	5	15	13	46	34
Southampton	42	9	8	4	28	19	2	4	15	18	56	34
Bradford C	42	10	7	4	34	20	2	1	18	16	48	32
Oldham A	42	10	3	8	44	40	0	3	18	12	55	26
Notts Co	42	8	3	10	29	33	1	4	16	17	64	25

DIVISION 3 North

	P	W	D	L	F	A	W	D	L	F	A	Pts
Doncaster R	42	16	0	5	53	21	10	5	6	34	23	57
Halifax T	42	17	2	2	50	24	8	3	10	26	43	55
Chester	42	14	4	3	62	27	6	10	5	29	31	54
Lincoln C	42	14	3	4	55	21	8	4	9	32	37	51
Darlington	42	15	5	1	50	15	6	4	11	30	44	51
Tranmere R	42	15	4	2	53	20	5	7	9	21	35	51
Stockport Co	42	15	2	4	57	22	7	1	13	33	50	47
Mansfield T	42	16	3	2	55	25	3	6	12	20	37	47
Rotherham U	42	14	4	3	56	21	5	3	13	30	52	45
Chesterfield	42	13	4	4	46	21	4	6	11	25	31	44
Wrexham	42	12	5	4	47	25	4	6	11	29	44	43
Hartlepools U	42	12	4	5	52	34	5	3	13	28	44	41
Crewe A	42	12	6	3	41	25	2	5	14	25	61	39
Walsall	42	11	7	3	51	18	2	3	16	30	54	36
York C	42	12	5	4	50	20	3	1	17	26	62	36
New Brighton	42	9	6	6	32	25	5	2	14	27	51	36
Barrow	42	11	5	5	37	31	2	4	15	21	56	35
Accrington S	42	11	5	5	44	36	1	5	15	19	53	34
Gateshead	42	12	4	5	36	28	1	4	16	22	68	34
Rochdale	42	9	5	7	39	35	2	6	13	14	36	33
Southport	42	6	6	9	27	36	4	6	11	28	49	32
Carlisle U	42	7	6	8	34	36	1	1	19	17	66	23

DIVISION 3 South

	P	W	D	L	F	A	W	D	L	F	A	Pts
Charlton A	42	17	2	2	62	20	10	5	6	41	32	61
Reading	42	16	5	0	59	23	5	6	10	30	42	53
Coventry C	42	14	5	2	56	14	7	4	10	30	36	51
Luton T	42	12	7	2	60	23	7	5	9	32	37	50
Crystal P	42	15	3	3	51	14	4	7	10	35	50	48
Watford	42	14	2	5	53	19	5	7	9	23	30	47
Northampton T	42	14	4	3	40	21	5	4	12	25	46	46
Bristol R	42	14	6	1	54	27	3	4	14	19	50	44
Brighton & HA	42	15	4	2	51	16	2	5	14	18	46	43
Torquay U	42	15	2	4	60	22	3	4	14	21	53	42
Exeter C	42	11	5	5	48	29	5	4	12	22	46	41
Millwall	42	11	4	6	33	26	6	3	12	24	36	41
QPR	42	14	6	1	49	22	2	3	16	14	50	41
Clapton O	42	13	3	5	47	21	2	7	12	18	44	40
Bristol C	42	14	3	4	37	18	1	6	14	15	50	39
Swindon T	42	11	7	3	45	22	2	5	14	22	56	38
Bournemouth	42	10	5	6	36	26	5	2	14	18	45	37
Aldershot	42	12	6	3	35	20	1	4	16	15	55	36
Cardiff C	42	11	6	4	42	27	2	3	16	20	55	35
Gillingham	42	10	7	4	36	25	1	6	14	19	50	35
Southend U	42	10	4	7	40	29	1	5	15	25	49	31
Newport Co	42	7	4	10	36	40	3	1	17	18	72	25

Football League Records

Top scorers: Div 1, W.G.Richardson (West Bromwich Albion) 39 goals; Div 2, R.Finan (Blackpool), E.Dodds (Sheffield United) 34 goals; Div 3(N), R.Bell (Tranmere Rovers) 33 goals; Div 3(S), A.Dawes (Crystal Palace) 38 goals.

Raich Carter, Sunderland's dynamic young inside-forward who steered the Wearsiders to the League Championship and the FA Cup in consecutive years.

Jack Bowers, a prolific scorer for Derby in the past, returned after injury to help them to runners-up spot.

DIVISION 1

	ARSENAL	ASTON VILLA	BIRMINGHAM	BLACKBURN R	BOLTON W	BRENTFORD	CHELSEA	DERBY CO	EVERTON	GRIMSBY T	HUDDERSFIELD T	LEEDS U	LIVERPOOL	MANCHESTER C	MIDDLESBROUGH	PORTSMOUTH	PRESTON N.E.	SHEFFIELD W	STOKE C	SUNDERLAND	W.B.A.	WOLVERHAMPTON W
1 ARSENAL		a18 1-0	J04 1-1	O05 5-1	a01 1-1	a04 1-1	a27 1-1	N09 1-1	M25 1-1	S11 6-0	M07 1-1	m02 2-2	D26 1-2	S21 2-3	D09 2-0	F22 2-3	O26 2-1	S14 2-2	F01 1-0	A31 3-1	a10 4-0	N23 4-0
2 ASTON VILLA	D14 1-7		M28 2-1	a25 2-4	O12 1-2	J25 2-2	N16 2-2	S28 0-2	F08 1-1	N02 2-6	D25 4-1	M14 3-3	F29 3-0	a11 2-2	S09 2-7	J04 4-2	S14 5-1	A31 1-2	N30 4-0	S16 2-2	O19 0-7	a10 4-2
3 BIRMINGHAM	S07 1-1	N23 2-2		F01 4-2	M07 0-0	N09 2-1	O05 2-1	M21 2-3	D21 4-2	D26 1-1	D07 4-1	S11 2-0	F15 2-0	J18 0-1	a18 1-0	O26 4-0	a04 0-0	a22 4-1	S21 0-5	a13 2-7	m02 1-3	D28 0-0
4 BLACKBURN R	F08 0-1	D21 5-1	S28 1-2		a04 0-3	J01 1-0	S16 1-0	F22 0-0	O26 1-1	A31 1-0	N09 2-1	J04 0-3	a10 2-2	O12 4-1	M21 2-2	a18 3-1	N23 1-1	D07 3-2	D25 0-1	F15 1-1	S14 3-1	M07 1-0
5 BOLTON W	a29 2-1	F15 4-3	N30 2-0	N02 3-1		A31 0-2	M14 2-3	J04 0-2	S14 2-0	J29 4-0	F01 1-2	M28 3-0	O19 0-0	N16 3-3	O05 3-1	J01 4-0	a10 1-1	S02 1-1	F29 1-2	a11 2-1	D14 3-1	D25 0-3
6 BRENTFORD	N02 2-1	S21 1-2	F29 0-1	S05 3-1	D28 4-0		M28 2-1	m02 6-0	a13 4-1	a11 3-0	S07 1-2	N30 2-2	D14 1-2	M14 0-0	J18 1-0	M25 3-1	D25 5-2	O05 2-2	O19 0-0	N16 1-5	a25 2-2	F01 5-0
7 CHELSEA	O12 1-1	M21 1-0	F08 0-0	m02 5-1	O26 2-1	N23 2-1		a10 1-1	F22 2-2	J04 0-2	a04 1-0	S14 1-0	A31 2-2	D26 2-1	N09 2-1	a22 1-0	a18 5-2	M07 1-2	S04 3-5	S28 3-1	M11 2-2	D21 2-2
8 DERBY CO	M04 0-4	F01 1-3	N16 2-2	O19 1-0	S07 4-0	S18 2-1	a13 1-1		D28 3-3	D14 2-0	J18 2-0	a11 2-1	M28 2-2	N02 3-0	S21 3-2	D26 1-1	S11 2-0	F19 3-1	M14 0-1	a25 4-0	N30 2-0	O05 3-1
9 EVERTON	N16 0-2	O05 2-2	a25 4-3	M14 4-0	J22 3-3	a10 1-2	O19 5-1	A31 4-0		M28 4-0	S21 1-3	D14 0-0	J04 0-0	F29 2-2	F01 5-2	S11 3-0	m02 5-0	D26 4-3	N02 5-1	N30 0-3	a11 5-3	F15 4-1
10 GRIMSBY T	S03 1-0	a04 4-1	D25 1-0	D28 1-1	S21 3-1	D07 6-1	S07 1-3	a18 4-1	N23 0-4		F22 1-1	S28 0-1	J18 0-0	m02 3-1	O26 1-0	D21 1-2	M07 0-0	M24 4-0	a10 3-0	O12 4-0	F08 4-2	N09 2-1
11 HUDDERSFIELD T	N30 0-0	D26 4-1	a11 1-0	F29 1-1	S28 0-0	J04 2-2	N02 2-0	S14 1-1	J29 2-1	O19 1-0		F08 1-2	M14 1-0	a25 1-1	F19 4-1	a14 1-1	A31 1-0	m02 1-0	N16 2-1	D14 1-0	M28 2-3	S11 3-0
12 LEEDS U	S18 1-1	O26 4-2	S04 0-0	S07 1-4	N23 5-2	M07 1-2	J18 2-0	D07 1-0	a18 3-1	F01 1-2	O05 2-2		S21 1-0	a13 1-1	F22 0-1	M21 1-0	D21 0-1	N09 7-2	D28 4-1	a22 3-0	O12 1-1	a04 2-0
13 LIVERPOOL	D25 0-1	N09 3-2	O12 1-2	a13 4-1	F22 1-1	a18 0-0	D28 2-3	N23 0-0	S07 6-0	S14 7-2	O26 3-0	M18 2-1		S04 0-2	a04 2-2	M07 2-0	D07 2-1	D21 1-0	S18 2-0	F08 0-3	S28 5-0	M21 0-2
14 MANCHESTER C	M11 1-0	D07 5-0	S14 3-1	F19 2-0	M21 7-0	O26 2-1	D25 0-0	a04 1-0	N09 1-0	J01 0-3	J15 1-2	a10 1-3	S11 6-0		M07 6-0	S28 0-0	F22 1-3	N23 3-0	O05 1-2	J04 0-1	A31 1-0	a18 2-1
15 MIDDLESBROUGH	a11 2-2	S04 1-2	D14 0-2	N16 6-1	F08 0-0	S14 0-0	M04 4-1	J29 0-3	S28 6-1	M14 5-1	O12 4-2	O19 1-1	N02 2-2	N30 2-0		A31 3-2	J04 2-0	a13 5-0	a25 0-0	M28 6-0	J01 3-1	S18 4-2
16 PORTSMOUTH	O19 2-1	S07 3-0	M14 0-3	D14 3-1	m02 2-1	O12 1-3	a11 2-0	D25 3-0	S04 2-0	a25 3-2	a10 0-0	N16 2-2	N30 2-1	F01 1-2	D28 1-0		F08 1-1	S21 3-2	M28 2-0	N02 2-2	F29 3-1	J18 1-0
17 PRESTON N.E.	M14 1-0	J18 3-0	N02 3-1	M28 2-0	a13 1-0	D26 2-4	D14 2-0	S02 1-0	S18 2-2	N30 1-0	D28 4-0	a25 5-0	a11 3-1	O19 4-0	S07 0-5	O05 1-1		F01 0-1	F19 1-1	F29 3-2	N16 3-0	S21 2-0
18 SHEFFIELD W	J18 3-2	D28 5-2	O19 3-1	a11 0-0	S09 2-2	F08 3-3	N30 4-1	O12 1-0	F03 3-3	N16 3-0	S16 1-2	F29 3-0	a25 0-0	M28 1-0	a14 0-0	F12 0-1	S28 1-0		D14 0-1	M14 0-0	N02 2-5	S07 0-0
19 STOKE C	S28 0-3	M07 2-3	F03 3-1	D26 2-0	N09 1-2	F22 2-2	S09 3-0	O26 0-0	a04 2-1	a13 1-0	M21 1-0	A31 3-1	m02 2-1	F08 1-0	D21 1-1	N23 2-0	O12 2-1	a18 0-3		S14 0-2	J04 3-2	D07 4-1
20 SUNDERLAND	D28 5-4	J01 1-3	a10 2-1	S21 7-2	D07 7-2	M21 1-3	F01 3-3	D21 3-1	M07 3-3	F19 3-1	a18 4-3	D26 2-1	O05 2-0	S07 2-0	N23 2-1	a04 5-0	N09 4-2	O26 5-1	J18 1-0		S11 6-1	F22 3-1
21 W.B.A.	a13 1-0	a01 0-3	S18 0-0	J18 8-1	a18 2-2	D21 1-0	S21 1-2	M07 0-3	D07 6-1	O05 4-1	N23 1-2	F19 3-2	F01 6-1	D28 5-1	D26 5-2	N09 2-0	M21 2-4	a04 2-2	S07 2-0	S04 1-3		O26 2-1
22 WOLVERHAMPTON W	M28 2-2	a13 2-2	A31 3-1	N30 8-1	D26 3-3	S28 3-2	a25 3-3	F08 0-0	O12 4-0	M04 1-0	S02 2-2	N02 3-0	N16 3-1	D14 4-3	m02 4-0	S14 2-0	a20 4-2	J04 2-1	a11 1-1	O19 3-4	M14 2-0	

DIVISION 2

	BARNSLEY	BLACKPOOL	BRADFORD	BRADFORD C	BURNLEY	BURY	CHARLTON A	DONCASTER R	FULHAM	HULL C	LEICESTER C	MANCHESTER U	NEWCASTLE U	NORWICH C	NOTTINGHAM F	PLYMOUTH A	PORT VALE	SHEFFIELD U	SOUTHAMPTON	SWANSEA T	TOTTENHAM H	WEST HAM U
1 BARNSLEY		N02 1-2	M04 5-1	a13 0-1	S14 3-1	O19 1-1	J27 1-2	a11 2-1	J04 2-0	S28 5-1	D14 3-3	J01 0-3	S09 3-2	N16 2-3	M14 0-2	F19 1-2	A31 4-2	N30 3-2	a25 3-1	M28 0-0	m02 0-0	F08 1-2
2 BLACKPOOL	M21 3-0		F08 4-2	M07 3-3	D26 2-0	J04 2-3	F22 6-2	A31 5-2	N23 1-1	O26 4-1	S28 3-5	D07 4-1	a22 6-0	S04 2-1	S16 1-4	N09 3-1	a18 3-1	O12 3-0	a10 2-1	J29 1-1	a04 2-4	S14 4-1
3 BRADFORD	D07 3-0	O05 3-2		N23 1-1	M07 2-0	a13 1-1	D21 3-0	F26 3-1	N09 1-1	a04 2-1	J01 3-1	O26 1-0	D28 3-2	S21 1-0	F01 1-4	a18 2-2	M21 3-0	S07 3-3	J18 2-1	S16 1-1	F22 2-5	S02 2-0
4 BRADFORD C	a14 1-1	N16 2-1	M28 2-1		S28 0-0	N02 2-0	F08 2-1	M14 3-1	a29 1-0	O12 1-1	m02 2-0	J04 1-0	a01 3-2	N30 0-1	a25 0-0	S09 2-2	S14 1-1	D14 2-1	F29 2-1	O19 2-2	A31 0-1	a11 3-1
5 BURNLEY	J18 3-0	D25 3-2	N16 1-1	F01 3-0		D14 1-1	D28 0-2	M28 1-1	m02 0-2	S07 2-0	a25 2-2	a10 2-2	O05 1-2	a11 1-1	O19 1-0	S21 0-1	S09 5-1	M14 1-1	N02 2-0	N30 5-2	a20 0-0	F29 1-0
6 BURY	F22 3-0	S07 1-1	a10 1-0	M21 1-1	a18 0-4		N23 1-1	J18 5-1	D07 0-0	S21 3-1	O12 3-0	a29 2-3	N09 3-4	D25 0-1	D28 2-6	O26 2-0	a04 5-0	S09 3-2	J01 0-0	F08 2-1	M07 1-1	S28 3-0
7 CHARLTON A	S21 3-0	O19 1-1	a25 3-1	O05 2-1	A31 4-0	M28 5-2		J04 3-0	D26 2-1	J18 4-1	N30 1-0	S09 0-0	F26 4-2	N02 4-1	a11 4-0	F01 1-1	m02 1-1	N16 1-1	M14 2-0	F29 4-1	a13 2-1	D14 2-2
8 DONCASTER R	O26 1-1	D28 0-3	O12 3-2	N09 2-1	N23 1-0	S14 1-0	S07 2-0		a18 0-0	F22 6-1	F08 1-0	a04 0-0	M07 2-2	S16 3-0	D25 0-0	M21 1-2	D07 2-0	a10 0-0	S02 0-1	S28 1-1	D21 2-1	J25 0-2
9 FULHAM	S07 1-1	M28 4-2	M14 4-1	S21 5-1	S18 2-2	M04 7-0	D25 0-0	D14 1-3		D28 3-0	N16 2-0	a01 2-2	F01 3-1	O19 1-1	S02 6-0	J18 2-2	a13 7-0	N02 3-1	a11 0-2	a25 0-1	O05 1-2	N30 4-2
10 HULL C	F01 1-3	a11 0-3	N30 1-1	F20 2-5	J04 1-2	F15 2-3	S14 2-4	O19 2-3	A31 1-1		F29 3-3	m02 1-1	a13 2-3	M14 0-0	N02 2-1	O05 2-1	D26 1-2	a30 2-2	N16 2-2	D14 3-2	S09 1-0	M28 2-3
11 LEICESTER C	a18 2-0	F01 4-1	D25 5-0	S16 2-1	D21 2-0	F20 1-2	a04 4-1	O05 6-0	M07 5-2	D07 2-2		M21 1-1	M19 1-0	J18 1-1	S21 2-1	N23 2-0	N09 2-0	D28 1-3	S07 1-1	S09 4-1	O26 4-1	a13 1-1
12 MANCHESTER U	D26 1-1	F29 3-2	a11 4-0	S17 3-1	a13 4-0	a25 2-1	S04 3-0	N30 0-0	O12 1-0	S18 2-0	N02 0-1		J18 3-1	M28 2-1	D14 5-0	D28 3-2	F08 7-2	O19 3-1	F01 4-0	M14 3-0	S21 0-0	N16 2-3
13 NEWCASTLE U	S04 3-0	a25 1-0	A31 3-3	D26 3-2	F08 1-1	M14 3-0	O12 1-2	N16 2-1	S28 6-2	a10 4-1	O19 3-1	S14 0-2		F29 1-1	N30 5-1	J01 5-0	F05 2-2	M28 3-0	D14 4-1	a11 2-0	J04 1-4	N02 3-3
14 NORWICH C	M07 3-1	S11 0-1	a30 4-1	a04 1-1	O26 2-0	D26 5-3	M21 3-1	m02 2-1	F22 1-0	N09 3-0	S14 1-2	N23 3-5	D07 1-0		a13 4-0	D21 0-0	O12 4-2	S28 0-1	F08 5-1	J04 0-1	a18 1-0	A31 4-3
15 NOTTINGHAM F	N09 6-0	O03 2-2	S28 2-0	D21 1-0	F22 2-0	A31 2-2	O26 0-0	D26 6-2	S11 1-1	M21 0-0	J30 0-1	a18 1-1	a04 1-2	a10 2-2		M07 0-1	N23 9-2	F08 0-1	O12 2-0	S14 2-2	D07 4-1	J04 0-2
16 PLYMOUTH A	O12 7-1	M14 3-2	D14 2-0	S02 0-1	J29 2-0	a11 3-0	S28 4-2	N02 1-3	S14 2-0	F08 0-1	M28 2-1	A31 3-1	m02 1-0	a25 5-1	S16 3-1		J04 4-1	M11 1-1	N30 0-0	a10 1-2	D26 2-1	O19 4-1
17 PORT VALE	D28 0-4	D14 2-2	N02 3-2	J18 2-1	S02 1-1	N30 2-2	S16 2-1	F29 2-0	a10 1-0	M02 4-0	M14 1-1	O05 0-3	S21 3-0	F15 3-1	M28 2-0	S07 2-0		a11 1-1	O19 0-2	N16 0-1	F01 1-5	a25 2-3
18 SHEFFIELD U	a04 2-0	F20 1-0	J04 2-1	a18 3-0	N09 2-0	S02 3-0	M07 2-2	J01 3-0	M26 0-1	D21 7-0	A31 1-2	F22 1-1	N23 5-1	F01 3-2	O05 1-0	D07 0-0	O26 4-0		S21 2-1	D26 4-1	S14 1-1	m02 4-2
19 SOUTHAMPTON	D21 0-1	a13 1-0	S14 3-0	D07 0-0	M21 1-0	S16 0-0	N09 2-5	S09 1-0	O26 1-2	M07 1-0	J04 1-0	S28 2-1	a18 1-3	O05 1-1	F15 7-2	a04 2-0	M30 0-1	F05 0-1		A31 4-3	N23 2-0	D26 2-4
20 SWANSEA T	N23 0-0	S21 1-0	m02 1-2	F22 8-1	a04 1-3	O05 4-1	D07 1-2	F01 2-0	D21 0-2	a18 6-1	S02 2-0	N09 2-1	O26 1-2	S07 4-3	J18 2-1	a13 2-0	M07 3-2	D25 1-3	D28 0-0		M21 1-1	F15 0-1
21 TOTTENHAM H	S16 3-0	N30 3-1	O19 4-0	D28 4-0	O12 5-1	N16 4-3	a10 1-1	a25 3-1	F08 2-2	S02 3-1	a11 1-1	F05 0-0	S07 1-2	D14 2-1	M04 1-1	D25 1-2	S28 5-2	J18 1-1	M28 8-0	N02 7-2		M14 1-3
22 WEST HAM U	O05 2-0	J18 2-1	S09 1-0	O26 1-1	F03 0-0	F01 6-0	a18 1-3	S21 1-2	a04 0-0	N23 4-1	a10 3-2	M07 1-2	M21 4-1	D28 3-2	S07 5-2	F22 4-2	D21 4-0	S16 3-2	D25 0-0	O12 4-0	N09 2-2	

Season 1935-36

DIVISION 3 NORTH

	ACCRINGTON S	BARROW	CARLISLE U	CHESTER	CHESTERFIELD	CREWE A	DARLINGTON	GATESHEAD	HALIFAX T	HARTLEPOOLS U	LINCOLN C	MANSFIELD T	NEW BRIGHTON	OLDHAM A	ROCHDALE	ROTHERHAM U	SOUTHPORT	STOCKPORT CO	TRANMERE R	WALSALL	WREXHAM	YORK C
1 ACCRINGTON S		S21 2-0	M14 0-0	S02 0-3	O05 0-1	D26 2-1	M28 1-0	N16 6-1	J11 2-0	O19 3-2	D28 2-2	a13 1-1	F01 5-2	a11 1-0	S07 2-4	a22 1-1	S24 1-0	F15 1-1	F29 3-1	N02 3-1	D14 0-1	J18 7-2
2 BARROW	J25 0-1		a11 1-1	F08 2-4	A31 1-1	S14 1-1	O19 2-0	m02 3-0	M14 0-0	J23 1-1	O12 0-0	M28 2-2	S02 3-0	N02 3-0	D26 6-2	N16 3-0	S28 0-1	J04 1-0	a25 0-0	a20 1-0	F29 2-1	a13 1-1
3 CARLISLE U	O26 3-1	a30 2-2		N09 1-3	D21 2-1	F22 1-2	A31 3-0	J04 2-0	S11 0-0	O05 0-0	M21 4-1	F15 3-0	a18 3-0	S19 2-1	N23 4-3	J01 1-1	M07 4-0	S28 2-1	S14 0-1	J25 2-1	a10 5-1	a04 0-0
4 CHESTER	S11 4-0	O05 1-2	F29 3-2		D25 1-1	O02 0-1	a11 4-1	J11 4-0	a29 3-1	N02 4-0	a22 4-2	M14 4-0	F15 8-2	S25 1-1	S21 5-2	O19 0-0	A31 5-1	a10 2-0	M28 1-1	N16 2-0	J04 1-1	F01 12-0
5 CHESTERFIELD	F08 0-3	D28 6-1	a25 5-0	D26 1-0		S28 6-0	N02 5-1	M14 2-0	F29 3-1	a27 2-0	a13 0-1	a11 2-1	S07 3-1	N16 3-0	J01 2-2	J11 5-0	O12 5-0	M30 0-0	O19 0-1	J18 3-0	M28 5-0	S02 2-2
6 CREWE A	D25 4-0	J18 3-1	O19 2-0	S18 1-1	F01 5-6		N16 2-0	F29 2-4	M28 3-2	F15 3-2	S02 2-1	a25 1-1	S21 5-1	J29 2-2	D28 3-1	a27 4-1	a10 4-1	O05 0-1	N02 0-0	M14 4-3	a11 3-2	S07 2-1
7 DARLINGTON	N23 2-1	F22 4-1	D28 4-1	D07 1-1	M07 1-2	M21 2-2		J01 5-2	F15 3-2	S07 4-2	a18 1-0	J18 2-1	O26 4-1	O05 5-0	D21 4-0	S21 3-1	a04 3-2	N09 3-1	m02 1-3	S04 1-1	F01 4-2	J02 3-0
8 GATESHEAD	M21 0-0	S18 4-3	S07 1-1	a04 2-0	O26 3-3	N09 2-1	a13 1-1		D25 2-2	F12 1-0	D07 4-0	S21 3-1	F22 3-1	F15 0-0	a18 1-0	F01 1-1	N23 3-1	M07 1-0	S11 1-1	D28 2-2	O05 2-0	D21 0-0
9 HALIFAX T	a04 1-0	O26 3-2	S02 1-0	a18 2-3	N09 2-3	N23 2-4	O12 0-1	D26 1-1		D28 0-1	D21 2-1	S07 1-0	M07 3-0	F01 4-2	O05 2-0	J18 1-0	D07 1-2	M21 0-0	a13 1-0	S16 1-1	S21 4-1	F22 2-0
10 HARTLEPOOLS U	F22 2-1	a04 0-0	F08 1-1	M07 0-2	a18 2-1	O12 1-0	J04 2-1	S14 2-0	A31 1-0		N09 1-1	D25 4-1	D07 4-1	S04 0-1	M21 1-0	a10 5-1	O26 2-1	D21 1-1	J29 2-2	S28 5-0	J01 1-1	N23 4-2
11 LINCOLN C	A31 6-0	F15 2-0	N16 2-0	S14 1-1	a10 0-1	S09 6-2	a20 2-1	a11 5-0	a25 3-1	M18 1-0		N02 1-2	D26 2-0	J25 2-1	F01 5-1	M14 4-0	J04 4-0	S16 3-0	a27 5-0	M28 4-1	O19 3-1	O05 3-2
12 MANSFIELD T	a10 3-1	N23 1-3	O12 1-1	O26 0-0	D07 0-1	D21 1-1	S14 4-2	a14 3-1	J04 3-2	D26 4-0	M07 2-2		a04 2-0	A31 1-0	N09 3-0	m02 8-2	F22 5-1	a18 2-1	S28 2-3	F08 2-2	S11 3-2	M21 5-0
13 NEW BRIGHTON	S28 2-3	S11 2-3	D14 3-0	O12 3-3	J04 1-2	J25 3-1	M14 1-1	O19 1-0	N02 1-4	a11 0-0	J01 0-5	J11 1-0		F29 1-3	a10 2-0	M28 3-0	F08 2-1	S14 2-0	A31 0-0	a25 1-1	N16 0-4	m02 0-2
14 OLDHAM A	D07 3-0	M07 3-1	m02 3-0	F25 1-3	M21 0-0	a04 0-0	F08 2-0	O12 2-2	S28 3-0	S09 2-2	S21 2-3	D28 4-1	N09 6-0		F22 3-3	S07 4-1	a18 4-0	N23 1-3	D25 4-1	a13 2-1	J18 5-2	O26 6-2
15 ROCHDALE	J04 2-2	D25 1-1	M28 0-0	J25 1-1	m02 1-1	A31 2-1	a25 1-1	D14 5-0	F08 2-0	N16 0-1	S28 0-0	F29 3-1	a13 1-0	O19 2-6		N02 1-1	S14 2-1	S10 1-1	a11 0-0	M31 6-4	M14 2-1	F15 2-3
16 ROTHERHAM U	D21 1-3	M21 1-0	D26 4-0	F22 1-2	a04 0-0	a18 3-1	J25 4-0	S28 3-0	S14 2-0	a13 3-0	O26 1-1	S16 2-1	N23 5-0	J04 1-0	M07 6-0		S09 5-0	D07 1-1	F08 1-2	O12 2-0	A31 1-2	N09 5-0
17 SOUTHPORT	m02 2-1	F01 3-1	N02 0-3	D28 2-1	F15 1-0	J01 1-1	J14 4-1	M28 1-1	a11 2-0	M14 1-1	S07 0-3	O19 3-3	O05 2-1	J11 1-1	J18 1-1	S03 2-1		D25 2-3	N16 1-1	F29 1-0	a25 1-1	S21 0-1
18 STOCKPORT CO	O12 1-2	S07 2-1	F01 2-0	a13 2-0	S21 2-2	F08 0-1	F29 2-0	N02 3-1	N16 1-0	a25 2-1	m02 4-0	D14 6-1	J18 1-1	M28 2-0	S02 4-0	a11 1-2	D26 2-0		M14 2-1	O19 0-1	S23 3-2	D28 3-2
19 TRANMERE R	N09 6-0	D21 1-0	J18 4-1	N23 3-1	F22 1-3	M07 4-2	S16 2-0	S02 2-0	a10 0-2	S21 3-1	a04 1-1	F01 4-2	D28 3-1	D26 13-4	D07 5-2	O05 2-2	M21 5-2	O26 4-1		S07 3-1	F15 6-1	a18 3-1
20 WALSALL	M07 2-0	a18 5-1	S21 3-0	M21 1-0	S14 1-1	O26 4-1	S09 4-1	A31 2-0	m02 2-1	F01 6-0	N23 4-1	O05 7-0	D21 1-2	a10 1-2	a04 1-0	F15 0-1	N09 3-1	a14 0-1	J04 0-0		D25 5-0	D07 6-0
21 WREXHAM	a18 3-0	N09 2-0	a13 1-1	S07 1-0	N23 0-1	D07 0-1	S28 3-1	F08 2-4	M11 1-3	S18 1-0	F22 1-1	S04 5-1	M21 3-0	S14 0-1	O26 0-1	D28 2-0	D21 4-2	a04 4-0	O12 4-0	D26 1-1		M07 1-0
22 YORK C	S14 1-1	a10 1-2	J11 2-0	S28 1-2	S11 1-1	J04 4-1	D26 4-1	a25 2-2	O19 2-2	M28 2-2	F08 2-1	N16 7-5	S10 2-0	M14 3-1	O12 2-1	F29 2-1	M18 0-0	A31 0-4	a22 2-0	a11 0-0	N02 1-1	

DIVISION 3 SOUTH

	ALDERSHOT	BOURNEMOUTH	BRIGHTON & HA	BRISTOL C	BRISTOL R	CARDIFF C	CLAPTON O	COVENTRY C	CRYSTAL P	EXETER C	GILLINGHAM	LUTON T	MILLWALL	NEWPORT CO	NORTHAMPTON T	NOTTS CO	Q.P.R.	READING	SOUTHEND U	SWINDON T	TORQUAY U	WATFORD
1 ALDERSHOT		M21 2-0	S07 1-0	F01 0-0	D07 6-1	a18 1-1	M07 1-0	D26 1-2	F22 1-3	D28 3-0	D21 0-2	N23 0-1	O05 1-1	a10 1-1	S02 2-0	a04 3-1	J18 1-3	O26 1-0	N09 1-1	S18 1-3	F15 1-0	S21 1-1
2 BOURNEMOUTH	N16 0-0		F15 1-2	a11 3-0	D26 2-1	F01 4-4	a13 2-0	N02 1-1	J18 2-5	O19 1-1	O05 1-2	S04 2-1	J22 1-2	M14 2-0	S07 4-0	m02 0-1	F29 0-1	S21 4-1	D28 2-1	a25 1-0	M28 1-1	a22 2-2
3 BRIGHTON & H.A.	J04 2-1	O12 0-1		D25 3-0	a18 4-1	M07 1-0	D21 1-3	J25 2-1	a04 2-1	F08 3-1	N09 1-1	F22 1-1	a13 0-0	S28 7-1	N23 5-1	O26 5-1	S04 1-1	D07 4-2	M21 1-3	S14 0-2	A31 3-2	S18 2-1
4 BRISTOL C	S28 1-0	D07 1-0	D26 0-3		S07 0-2	N23 0-2	F22 2-0	O12 0-0	a29 2-0	m02 2-1	a04 2-1	M07 1-2	S14 4-1	S04 1-2	a18 3-2	N09 1-1	a13 0-0	M21 1-1	O26 2-1	F08 5-0	J25 2-0	a01 2-2
5 BRISTOL R	a11 2-2	D25 2-1	N02 5-2	J04 1-1		S11 1-1	J18 1-1	M28 3-2	O05 2-4	a25 6-1	S18 4-3	a10 2-2	F29 2-0	N16 3-0	F01 5-2	A31 0-0	M14 0-1	F15 1-4	S21 3-2	J15 2-1	a14 3-0	O19 0-1
6 CARDIFF C	N02 0-1	S28 1-1	M18 1-0	M28 1-0	S02 0-0		S16 4-1	O19 1-0	D28 1-1	F29 5-2	J25 4-0	F08 2-3	N16 3-1	J18 2-0	a10 0-0	O12 3-2	a11 3-2	S07 2-3	D26 1-1	M14 2-1	a25 1-2	J15 0-2
7 CLAPTON O	a23 0-1	a10 1-1	a25 3-1	O19 2-0	S14 2-0	m02 2-1		J16 0-1	F26 1-0	N16 1-2	D25 3-1	A31 3-0	a02 1-0	M28 4-0	O05 4-0	J04 0-2	N02 1-0	S05 1-0	F01 3-0	a11 1-2	F29 1-1	M14 0-2
8 COVENTRY C	D25 0-2	a18 2-0	S21 5-0	F15 3-1	N23 3-1	F22 5-1	a04 2-0		N09 8-1	J18 3-0	O26 4-0	a27 0-0	S09 5-0	S07 7-1	M07 4-0	M21 5-1	F01 6-1	D28 3-1	D07 3-0	a14 3-1	m02 2-1	O05 2-0
9 CRYSTAL P	O19 2-1	S14 2-0	J15 4-0	a25 6-1	F08 5-3	A31 3-2	O12 2-2	F29 3-1		a11 2-2	J04 1-1	J29 5-1	N02 5-0	D18 6-0	S23 6-1	S28 0-0	M28 0-2	a10 2-0	S11 3-0	D26 5-1	M14 1-0	N16 1-2
10 EXETER C	A31 5-1	F22 1-3	O05 3-3	S18 0-1	D21 3-1	N09 2-0	M21 2-3	S14 1-3	D07 1-0		S28 2-5	O26 1-2	D26 4-3	J25 3-3	a04 3-1	a18 0-0	F15 0-0	M07 4-5	N23 1-0	J04 0-3	a13 1-1	S04 1-3
11 GILLINGHAM	a25 4-2	F08 1-2	F29 1-2	J11 2-1	m02 1-2	S21 3-0	D26 3-0	M14 1-1	S07 0-2	F01 2-2		O12 0-1	M28 1-3	O19 3-0	D28 2-3	S11 0-0	a22 2-2	J18 2-0	a10 2-1	N02 3-1	N16 1-0	a11 0-0
12 LUTON T	M28 2-2	S09 0-0	O19 2-1	D14 1-0	a13 12-0	O05 2-2	D28 5-3	a25 1-1	S21 6-0	M14 3-1	F15 1-2		a11 0-0	N02 7-0	J18 3-3	D26 1-0	S16 2-0	F01 2-1	S07 1-2	N16 2-1	M25 1-0	F29 2-1
13 MILLWALL	F08 1-2	a04 3-0	a10 0-0	J18 1-1	N09 2-1	M21 2-4	S21 1-0	S02 2-2	a18 4-0	D25 2-2	N23 4-1	D07 0-0		S16 2-2	O26 2-1	M07 2-1	D28 2-0	D21 0-1	F22 1-2	O12 1-0	S28 1-1	S07 0-0
14 NEWPORT CO	a13 1-1	O26 0-0	F01 0-2	S09 2-0	M21 1-0	S14 0-0	N23 2-3	J04 2-1	M07 2-5	S21 2-1	M19 4-2	a18 0-2	m02 4-1		D07 5-1	F27 1-2	O05 3-4	N09 1-5	a04 3-1	A31 2-2	D25 1-6	F15 0-5
15 NORTHAMPTON T	S09 3-0	J04 2-1	M28 1-0	N02 0-2	S28 3-3	a13 2-0	F08 2-0	D14 2-4	S16 3-1	J11 1-1	A31 0-0	S14 0-0	M14 2-4	a11 3-0		J25 3-1	N16 1-4	D25 4-2	O12 2-0	F29 0-0	O19 2-1	a25 2-0
16 NOTTS CO	F12 1-2	S18 1-3	M14 1-1	F29 1-1	D28 6-0	F15 2-0	S07 2-0	N16 2-1	F01 3-1	N02 3-1	S04 3-3	D25 0-3	D18 0-0	a25 6-2	S21 3-0		O19 3-0	O05 1-3	J18 1-2	M28 0-0	a11 1-0	a13 0-2
17 Q.P.R.	S14 5-0	N09 2-0	S12 3-2	a10 4-1	O26 4-0	D07 5-1	a18 4-0	S28 0-0	N23 3-0	O12 3-1	M07 5-2	m02 0-0	A31 2-3	F08 1-1	M21 0-1	F22 2-2		a04 0-1	D21 2-1	J25 5-1	J04 2-1	D25 3-1
18 READING	M14 3-1	J25 0-2	a11 3-0	N16 5-2	O12 3-2	J04 4-1	S11 4-1	A31 2-1	a13 0-1	M18 2-0	S14 1-0	S28 2-1	a25 3-1	F29 2-1	D26 5-2	F08 3-1	J15 1-2		m02 2-1	O19 2-0	N02 2-0	M28 3-0
19 SOUTHEND U	F29 2-2	A31 3-3	N16 0-0	M14 0-1	J25 1-1	D25 3-1	S28 2-1	a11 0-0	S04 7-1	M28 4-0	a13 4-2	J04 0-1	O19 6-0	J22 1-2	a22 0-1	S14 0-0	a25 0-1	S18 1-2		a29 1-0	F08 2-1	N02 1-1
20 SWINDON T	m02 3-2	D21 2-3	J18 1-2	O05 1-1	a04 3-0	O26 2-1	D07 2-2	a13 1-2	D25 0-2	S07 1-1	a18 3-0	M21 3-0	F15 3-1	D28 1-1	N09 3-1	N23 2-1	S21 2-2	F22 4-1	M07 1-3		S04 4-1	F01 1-6
21 TORQUAY U	O12 3-1	N23 0-2	D28 1-0	S21 2-0	M07 2-0	J11 2-1	N09 1-0	S18 3-3	O26 3-2	S25 2-1	M21 4-2	a04 2-1	F01 1-3	D26 3-2	F22 3-3	D07 0-1	S07 4-2	a18 0-0	O05 1-1	S11 2-1		J18 2-1
22 WATFORD	J29 0-0	M07 4-1	m02 2-1	A31 0-2	F22 1-2	a04 4-0	O26 1-1	F08 5-0	M21 3-2	S11 1-0	D07 1-2	N09 1-3	J04 2-1	O12 2-5	D21 4-1	a10 1-2	D26 2-1	N23 4-2	a18 5-0	S28 2-1	S14 2-2	

LEAGUE TABLES

DIVISION 1

	P	W	D	L	F	A	W	D	L	F	A	Pts
Sunderland	42	17	2	2	71	33	8	4	9	38	41	56
Derby Co	42	13	5	3	43	23	5	7	9	18	29	48
Huddersfield T	42	12	7	2	32	15	6	5	10	27	41	48
Stoke C	42	13	3	5	35	24	7	4	10	22	33	47
Brentford	42	11	5	5	48	25	6	7	8	33	35	46
Arsenal	42	9	9	3	44	22	6	6	9	34	26	45
Preston NE	42	15	3	3	44	18	3	5	13	23	46	44
Chelsea	42	11	7	3	39	27	4	6	11	26	45	43
Manchester C	42	13	2	6	44	17	4	6	11	24	43	42
Portsmouth	42	14	4	3	39	22	3	4	14	15	45	42
Leeds U	42	11	5	5	41	23	4	6	11	25	41	41
Birmingham	42	10	6	5	38	31	5	5	11	23	32	41
Bolton W	42	11	4	6	41	27	3	9	9	26	49	41
Middlesbrough	42	12	6	3	56	23	3	4	14	28	47	40
Wolves	42	13	7	1	59	28	2	3	16	18	48	40
Everton	42	12	5	4	61	31	1	8	12	28	58	39
Grimsby T	42	13	4	4	44	20	4	1	16	21	53	39
WBA	42	12	3	6	54	31	4	3	14	35	57	38
Liverpool	42	11	4	6	43	23	2	8	11	17	41	38
Sheffield W	42	9	8	4	35	23	4	4	13	28	54	38
Aston Villa	42	7	6	8	47	56	6	3	12	34	54	35
Blackburn R	42	10	6	5	32	24	2	3	16	23	72	33

DIVISION 2

	P	W	D	L	F	A	W	D	L	F	A	Pts
Manchester U	42	16	3	2	55	16	6	9	6	30	27	56
Charlton A	42	15	6	0	53	17	7	5	9	32	41	55
Sheffield U	42	15	4	2	51	15	5	8	8	28	35	52
West Ham U	42	13	5	3	51	23	9	3	9	39	45	52
Tottenham H	42	12	6	3	60	25	6	7	8	31	30	49
Leicester C	42	14	5	2	53	19	5	5	11	26	38	48
Plymouth A	42	15	2	4	50	20	5	6	10	21	37	48
Newcastle U	42	13	5	3	56	27	7	1	13	32	52	46
Fulham	42	11	6	4	58	24	4	8	9	18	28	44
Blackpool	42	14	3	4	64	34	4	4	13	29	38	43
Norwich C	42	14	2	5	47	24	3	7	11	25	41	43
Bradford C	42	12	7	2	32	18	3	6	12	23	47	43
Swansea T	42	11	3	7	42	26	4	6	11	25	50	39
Bury	42	10	6	5	41	27	3	6	12	25	57	38
Burnley	42	9	8	4	35	21	3	5	13	15	38	37
Bradford	42	13	6	2	43	26	1	3	17	19	58	37
Southampton	42	11	3	7	32	24	3	6	12	15	41	37
Doncaster R	42	10	7	4	28	17	4	2	15	23	54	37
Nottingham F	42	8	8	5	43	22	4	3	14	26	54	35
Barnsley	42	9	4	8	40	32	3	5	13	14	48	33
Port Vale	42	10	5	6	34	30	2	3	16	22	76	32
Hull C	42	4	7	10	33	45	1	3	17	14	66	20

DIVISION 3 North

	P	W	D	L	F	A	W	D	L	F	A	Pts
Chesterfield	42	15	3	3	60	14	9	9	3	32	25	60
Chester	42	14	5	2	69	18	8	6	7	31	27	55
Tranmere R	42	17	2	2	75	28	5	9	7	18	30	55
Lincoln C	42	18	1	2	64	14	4	8	9	27	37	53
Stockport Co	42	15	2	4	45	18	5	6	10	20	31	48
Crewe A	42	14	4	3	55	31	5	5	11	25	45	47
Oldham A	42	13	5	3	60	25	5	4	12	26	48	45
Hartlepools U	42	13	6	2	41	18	2	6	13	16	43	42
Accrington S	42	12	5	4	43	24	5	3	13	20	48	42
Walsall	42	15	2	4	58	13	1	7	13	21	46	41
Rotherham U	42	14	3	4	52	13	2	6	13	17	53	41
Darlington	42	16	3	2	60	26	1	3	17	14	53	40
Carlisle U	42	13	5	3	44	19	1	7	13	12	43	40
Gateshead	42	11	10	0	37	18	2	4	15	19	58	40
Barrow	42	9	9	3	33	16	4	3	14	25	49	38
York C	42	10	8	3	41	28	3	4	14	21	67	38
Halifax T	42	12	3	6	34	22	3	4	14	23	39	37
Wrexham	42	12	3	6	39	18	3	4	14	27	57	37
Mansfield T	42	13	5	3	55	25	1	4	16	25	66	37
Rochdale	42	8	10	3	35	26	2	3	16	23	62	33
Southport	42	9	8	4	31	26	2	1	18	17	64	31
New Brighton	42	8	5	8	29	33	1	1	19	14	69	24

DIVISION 3 South

	P	W	D	L	F	A	W	D	L	F	A	Pts
Coventry C	42	19	1	1	75	12	5	8	8	27	33	57
Luton T	42	13	6	2	56	20	9	6	6	25	25	56
Reading	42	18	0	3	52	20	8	2	11	35	42	54
QPR	42	14	4	3	55	19	8	5	8	29	34	53
Watford	42	12	3	6	47	29	8	6	7	33	25	49
Crystal P	42	15	4	2	64	20	7	1	13	32	54	49
Brighton & HA	42	13	4	4	48	25	5	4	12	22	38	44
Bournemouth	42	9	6	6	36	26	7	5	9	24	30	43
Notts Co	42	10	5	6	40	25	5	7	9	20	32	42
Torquay U	42	14	4	3	41	27	2	5	14	21	35	41
Aldershot	42	9	6	6	29	21	5	6	10	24	40	40
Millwall	42	9	8	4	33	21	5	4	12	25	50	40
Bristol C	42	11	5	5	32	21	4	5	12	16	38	40
Clapton O	42	13	2	6	34	15	3	4	14	21	46	38
Northampton T	42	12	5	4	38	24	3	3	15	24	66	38
Gillingham	42	9	5	7	34	25	5	4	12	32	52	37
Bristol R	42	11	6	4	48	31	3	3	15	21	64	37
Southend U	42	8	7	6	38	21	5	3	13	23	41	36
Swindon T	42	10	5	6	43	33	4	3	14	21	40	36
Cardiff C	42	11	5	5	37	23	2	5	14	23	50	36
Newport Co	42	8	4	9	36	44	3	5	13	24	67	31
Exeter C	42	7	5	9	38	41	1	6	14	21	52	27

Football League Records

Top scorers: Div 1, F.Steel (Stoke City) 33 goals; Div 2, J.Bowers (Leicester City) 33 goals; Div 3(N), E.Harston (Mansfield Town) 55 goals; Div 3(S), J.Payne (Luton Town) 55 goals.
Walsall transferred to Division Three South.

Irish international Peter Doherty, who netted 30 goals when Manchester City won the League Championship. Astonishingly, City were relegated 12 months later.

DIVISION 1

	ARSENAL	BIRMINGHAM	BOLTON W	BRENTFORD	CHARLTON A	CHELSEA	DERBY CO	EVERTON	GRIMSBY T	HUDDERSFIELD T	LEEDS U	LIVERPOOL	MANCHESTER C	MANCHESTER U	MIDDLESBROUGH	PORTSMOUTH	PRESTON N.E.	SHEFFIELD W	STOKE C	SUNDERLAND	W.B.A.	WOLVERHAMPTON W
1 ARSENAL		M20 1-1	m01 0-0	S09 1-1	F24 1-1	D19 4-1	S26 2-2	A29 3-2	O24 0-0	J02 1-1	N07 4-1	M10 1-0	D05 1-3	F06 1-1	N21 5-3	a17 4-0	D25 4-1	O10 1-1	M26 0-0	S12 4-1	a03 2-0	J23 3-0
2 BIRMINGHAM	N14 1-3		O31 1-1	M13 4-0	J23 1-2	J02 0-0	D12 0-1	F27 2-0	S26 2-3	O17 4-2	O10 2-1	F06 5-0	m01 2-2	a10 2-2	M29 0-0	A29 2-1	M27 1-0	N28 1-1	S12 2-4	D25 2-0	S09 1-1	a24 1-0
3 BOLTON W	J01 0-5	M06 0-0		D26 2-2	D19 2-1	D05 2-1	O10 1-3	S12 1-2	S05 1-2	J23 2-2	O24 2-1	F24 0-1	N21 0-2	D28 0-4	N07 1-3	a03 1-0	S07 0-0	M26 1-0	a17 0-0	S26 1-1	M20 4-1	F06 1-2
4 BRENTFORD	S03 2-0	N07 2-1	A29 2-2		S17 4-2	a17 1-0	F06 6-2	J02 2-2	M03 2-3	S12 1-1	M06 4-1	O24 5-2	a03 2-6	O10 4-0	M20 4-1	D05 4-0	M26 1-1	D25 2-1	D19 2-1	J23 3-3	N21 2-1	S26 3-2
5 CHARLTON A	O17 0-2	S19 2-2	a24 1-0	m01 2-1		M29 1-0	N14 2-0	D12 2-0	D26 1-0	a10 1-0	J09 1-0	S05 1-1	F13 1-1	M13 3-0	J30 2-2	D25 0-0	F27 3-1	O31 1-0	S07 2-0	N28 3-1	O03 4-2	M27 4-0
6 CHELSEA	a24 2-0	S05 1-3	a10 0-1	D12 2-1	M26 3-0		O31 1-1	N28 4-0	S02 3-2	M27 0-0	D26 2-1	S16 2-0	F03 4-4	F27 4-2	J09 1-0	O03 1-1	F13 0-0	O17 1-1	D28 1-0	N14 1-3	S19 3-0	M13 0-1
7 DERBY CO	F03 5-4	a17 3-1	F13 3-0	O23 2-3	M20 5-0	M06 1-1		D28 3-1	N21 3-1	M29 3-3	D05 5-3	a03 4-1	F24 0-5	S05 5-4	D19 0-2	O24 1-3	S19 1-2	J09 3-2	N07 2-2	S09 3-0	D26 1-0	S23 5-1
8 EVERTON	D26 1-1	O24 3-3	J09 3-2	S05 3-0	a17 2-2	a03 0-0	D25 7-0		D19 3-0	S26 2-1	M03 7-1	S19 2-0	M20 1-1	M29 2-3	M06 2-3	N21 4-0	J01 2-2	S02 3-1	D05 1-1	F06 3-0	N07 4-2	O10 1-0
9 GRIMSBY T	F27 1-3	F02 1-1	J02 3-1	O17 2-0	A29 0-1	S08 3-0	M27 3-4	a24 1-0		D12 2-2	S19 4-1	J09 2-1	D25 5-3	N14 6-2	O03 5-1	M26 1-0	O31 6-4	M13 5-1	m01 1-3	a12 6-0	F13 2-3	N28 1-1
10 HUDDERSFIELD T	S05 0-0	F20 1-1	S19 2-0	J09 1-1	D05 1-2	N21 4-2	M30 2-0	F03 0-3	a17 0-3		O03 3-0	D19 4-0	N07 1-1	S02 3-1	O24 2-0	M20 1-2	D26 4-2	m01 1-0	a03 2-1	O10 2-1	M10 1-1	D28 4-0
11 LEEDS U	M13 3-4	F13 0-2	F27 2-2	O31 3-1	S12 2-0	A29 2-3	a10 2-0	O17 3-0	J23 2-0	F06 2-1		S26 2-0	S09 1-1	N28 2-1	D25 5-0	m01 3-1	N14 1-0	M27 1-1	J02 2-1	a24 3-0	M30 3-1	a21 0-1
12 LIVERPOOL	O31 2-1	O03 2-0	O17 0-0	F27 2-2	J02 1-2	m01 1-1	N28 3-3	J23 3-2	S12 7-1	a24 1-1	J30 3-0		M26 0-5	M27 2-0	F13 0-2	S09 0-0	M13 1-1	N14 2-2	A29 2-1	D12 4-0	D28 1-2	a10 1-0
13 MANCHESTER C	a10 2-0	S16 1-1	M27 2-2	a07 2-1	O10 1-1	S26 0-0	O17 3-2	N14 4-1	D28 1-1	M13 3-0	S02 4-0	M29 5-1		J09 1-0	D26 2-1	J23 3-1	D12 4-1	a24 4-1	F06 2-1	O31 2-4	S05 6-2	F27 4-1
14 MANCHESTER U	O03 2-0	D05 1-2	D25 1-0	F13 1-3	N07 0-0	O24 0-0	J02 2-2	M26 2-1	M20 1-1	S09 3-1	a03 0-0	N21 2-5	S12 3-2		a17 2-1	F20 0-1	F03 1-1	S19 1-1	M06 2-1	J01 2-1	D19 2-2	A29 1-1
15 MIDDLESBROUGH	M27 1-1	M26 3-1	M13 2-0	N14 3-0	S26 1-1	S12 2-0	a24 1-3	O31 2-0	F06 0-0	F27 5-0	D28 4-2	O10 3-3	A29 2-0	D12 3-2		J02 2-2	N28 2-1	a10 2-0	J23 1-0	O17 5-5	J01 4-1	S09 1-0
16 PORTSMOUTH	D12 1-5	D26 2-1	N28 1-1	a10 1-3	D28 0-1	F06 4-1	F27 1-2	M27 2-2	M29 2-1	N14 1-0	S16 3-0	S02 6-2	S19 2-1	O17 2-1	S05 2-1		a24 0-1	F03 1-0	O10 1-0	M13 3-2	J09 5-3	O31 1-1
17 PRESTON N.E.	D28 1-3	N21 2-2	A31 1-2	M29 1-1	O24 0-0	O10 1-0	J23 5-2	a14 1-0	M10 3-2	A29 1-1	M20 1-0	N07 3-1	a17 2-5	S26 3-1	a03 2-0	D19 1-1		F06 1-1	F24 0-1	J02 2-0	D05 3-2	S12 1-3
18 SHEFFIELD W	F13 0-0	a03 0-3	M29 2-0	D28 0-2	M06 3-1	F20 1-1	S12 2-3	S10 6-4	N07 2-1	S17 2-2	N21 1-2	M20 1-2	D19 5-1	J23 1-0	D05 1-0	S26 0-0	O03 0-1		O24 0-0	A29 2-0	a17 2-3	J02 1-3
19 STOKE C	M29 0-0	J09 2-0	D12 2-2	a24 5-1	A31 1-1	D25 2-0	M13 1-2	a10 2-1	S14 2-0	N28 1-1	S05 2-1	D26 1-1	O03 2-2	O31 3-0	S19 6-2	F13 2-4	O17 0-2	a05 1-0		M27 5-3	F04 10-3	N14 2-1
20 SUNDERLAND	J09 1-1	D28 4-0	F10 3-0	S19 4-1	a03 1-0	M20 2-3	S02 3-2	O03 3-1	D05 5-1	F13 3-2	D19 2-1	a17 4-2	a14 1-3	a21 1-1	F24 4-1	N07 3-2	S05 3-0	D26 2-1	N21 3-0		O24 1-0	M26 6-2
21 W.B.A.	N28 2-4	S02 3-2	N03 0-2	M27 1-0	F06 1-2	J23 2-0	A29 1-3	M13 2-1	O10 4-2	O31 2-1	M29 3-0	D25 3-1	J02 2-2	a24 1-0	m01 3-1	S12 3-1	M22 0-0	a21 2-3	S26 2-2	F27 6-4		O17 2-1
22 WOLVERHAMPTON W	S19 2-0	D19 2-1	O03 2-3	F10 4-0	N21 6-1	N07 1-2	m01 3-1	F13 7-2	a03 5-2	D25 3-1	a17 3-0	D05 2-0	O24 2-1	D26 3-1	A31 0-1	M17 1-1	J09 5-0	S05 4-3	M20 2-1	M29 1-1	a14 5-2	

Left winger Eric Brook, City's second-highest scorer behind Doherty with 20 goals.

DIVISION 2

	ASTON VILLA	BARNSLEY	BLACKBURN R	BLACKPOOL	BRADFORD	BRADFORD C	BURNLEY	BURY	CHESTERFIELD	COVENTRY C	DONCASTER R	FULHAM	LEICESTER C	NEWCASTLE U	NORWICH C	NOTTINGHAM F	PLYMOUTH A	SHEFFIELD U	SOUTHAMPTON	SWANSEA T	TOTTENHAM H	WEST HAM U
1 ASTON VILLA		O24 4-2	N21 2-2	M20 4-0	F20 4-1	S14 5-1	J09 0-0	a03 0-4	D28 6-2	O03 0-0	J30 1-1	S19 0-3	D05 1-3	M30 0-2	D19 3-0	S07 1-1	F13 5-4	M06 2-1	S05 4-0	D26 4-0	N07 1-1	a17 0-2
2 BARNSLEY	F27 0-4		O10 3-2	F26 2-1	S05 2-1	O17 1-1	D12 1-1	A31 2-2	O31 1-1	M27 3-0	N28 4-1	a10 1-0	D28 1-2	D26 1-0	S14 2-1	M13 1-0	N14 1-3	J23 1-1	a24 2-1	J09 0-1	S26 1-0	M29 0-0
3 BLACKBURN R	M27 3-4	F13 1-1		M29 2-0	O03 1-1	N14 3-0	F27 3-1	D26 2-3	N28 5-2	a24 2-5	J01 2-0	O17 0-2	S05 0-0	J30 6-1	S19 1-0	a10 9-1	D12 2-3	S21 3-1	O31 1-0	M13 2-1	D25 0-4	J09 1-2
4 BLACKPOOL	N14 2-3	O03 1-1	M26 2-0		J30 6-0	M13 4-2	O17 2-0	S14 1-2	M27 0-1	D12 3-0	a24 1-1	D28 3-1	D26 6-2	S19 3-0	J09 0-2	N28 7-1	a10 1-1	F13 1-0	F27 2-0	O31 3-2	A31 0-0	S05 1-0
5 BRADFORD	O17 3-3	J02 2-1	F06 1-2	S26 2-1		A29 2-1	a10 2-0	O10 0-1	F27 4-5	N14 1-3	M27 1-0	N28 1-1	S09 1-2	S14 0-3	M30 1-0	O31 3-2	M13 0-0	S12 0-3	D12 3-1	a24 1-1	J23 3-2	D25 2-1
6 BRADFORD C	N11 2-2	F20 3-2	M20 2-2	N07 1-4	D26 2-3		S19 1-3	N21 0-1	M29 2-2	F13 1-0	O03 0-0	J30 1-1	a03 1-2	D19 2-0	a17 2-0	D28 2-1	A31 1-1	O24 3-2	J09 2-2	S05 4-0	M10 2-2	D05 2-1
7 BURNLEY	S12 1-2	a17 3-0	O24 0-0	F24 3-0	D05 2-2	J23 3-0		M06 1-2	J02 3-1	M26 3-3	D25 3-0	S07 0-2	N07 0-0	a03 0-3	N21 3-0	A29 3-0	S14 2-0	D19 1-0	F06 1-3	S26 0-0	O10 3-1	M20 2-1
8 BURY	N28 2-1	S09 2-1	A29 1-1	J01 2-3	F13 3-1	M27 5-0	O31 3-1		a10 4-0	J02 0-4	O17 4-2	F27 1-1	J09 0-1	O03 1-2	F10 3-2	D12 1-1	a24 2-0	D28 2-0	M13 2-1	N14 2-0	M26 5-3	S19 1-1
9 CHESTERFIELD	D25 1-0	M06 2-1	a03 0-4	N21 0-4	O24 4-2	M26 7-1	S05 4-1	D05 1-1		F03 2-3	S19 5-1	J09 4-1	a17 2-5	F20 4-0	A31 3-1	F13 4-2	O03 0-1	N07 2-2	D26 3-0	J01 4-0	M20 1-3	D19 1-1
10 COVENTRY C	F06 1-0	N21 3-0	D19 0-1	a17 1-2	M20 4-0	O10 3-1	M30 0-1	S05 1-3	S26 2-1		D26 1-1	S14 1-1	F25 0-2	N07 2-2	M06 1-1	J23 2-2	S12 2-0	a03 2-0	D25 2-0	A31 2-1	D05 1-0	O24 4-0
11 DONCASTER R	S26 1-0	a03 0-1	m01 0-1	D19 0-4	N21 1-3	F06 1-1	D28 2-0	F20 1-0	J23 0-4	A29 1-1		M26 2-1	O24 0-0	M20 1-2	N07 1-2	S12 0-2	J02 2-1	D05 1-1	A31 2-0	O10 0-0	a17 1-1	M06 1-4
12 FULHAM	J23 3-2	D05 1-0	F20 1-1	D25 0-3	a03 0-0	S26 0-1	S21 2-0	O24 1-1	S12 1-0	m01 0-2	M29 1-0		M06 2-0	N21 3-4	M20 2-3	J02 5-2	A29 2-2	a17 4-0	O10 2-0	F06 5-0	D19 3-3	N07 5-0
13 LEICESTER C	a10 1-0	D25 5-1	J02 1-0	A29 1-2	A31 5-0	N28 4-1	M13 7-3	S12 0-3	D12 3-1	O17 1-0	F27 7-1	O31 2-0		F13 3-2	O03 2-2	a24 2-1	J23 3-2	M29 1-2	N14 2-2	M27 0-0	m01 4-1	F04 2-2
14 NEWCASTLE U	M26 0-2	A29 0-1	S26 2-0	J23 1-2	J01 1-1	a24 2-0	N28 3-0	F06 1-3	O17 1-2	M13 4-2	N14 7-0	M27 1-1	O10 1-0		D25 0-1	M17 3-2	O31 1-1	J02 4-0	a10 3-0	D12 5-1	S12 0-1	S09 5-3
15 NORWICH C	a24 5-1	m01 0-1	J23 0-0	S12 1-2	M29 3-1	D12 0-0	M27 2-2	S26 0-0	S09 2-0	O31 0-3	M13 2-1	N14 3-0	F06 1-2	D28 1-5		O17 4-0	F27 1-2	A29 1-1	N28 4-2	a10 3-0	J02 2-3	O10 3-3
16 NOTTINGHAM F	S02 1-1	N07 4-1	D05 2-0	a03 1-1	M06 3-2	D25 2-1	D26 1-2	a17 1-0	O10 2-2	S19 1-1	J09 2-1	S05 5-3	D19 0-3	O24 0-2	F20 3-4		F03 2-3	M20 1-1	S16 1-1	M29 6-1	a21 3-0	O03 1-0
17 PLYMOUTH A	O10 2-2	M20 1-2	a17 2-0	D05 1-3	N07 2-0	S09 4-4	m01 0-1	D19 3-0	F06 1-1	J09 1-0	S05 7-0	D26 0-3	S19 2-1	M06 1-1	O24 2-0	S26 4-1		N21 2-0	M26 3-1	D25 0-0	a03 2-2	F20 2-0
18 SHEFFIELD U	O31 5-1	S19 2-0	A31 0-1	O10 2-2	J09 3-0	F27 3-1	a24 1-1	D25 1-0	M13 5-0	N28 2-2	a10 3-1	D12 2-0	J01 3-1	S05 2-1	D26 2-0	N14 4-1	M27 2-0		F11 0-0	O17 1-0	F06 3-2	S14 2-0
19 SOUTHAMPTON	J02 2-2	D19 1-3	M06 2-2	O24 5-2	a17 0-0	S12 2-0	O03 1-1	N07 4-1	A29 3-2	D28 1-1	S07 1-0	F13 3-3	M20 1-1	D05 2-0	a03 3-1	m01 0-3	M29 0-0	S26 4-0		J23 2-1	F24 1-0	N21 0-2
20 SWANSEA T	A29 1-2	S12 3-1	N07 1-0	M06 1-1	D19 3-0	J02 3-0	F11 3-0	M20 2-0	m01 4-1	S07 2-0	F13 0-1	O03 3-0	N21 1-3	a17 1-2	D05 2-1	M26 1-0	D28 0-1	F25 2-1	S19 5-1		O24 2-1	a03 0-0
21 TOTTENHAM H	M13 2-2	F03 3-0	D28 5-1	S21 1-2	S19 5-1	O31 5-1	F13 3-0	M29 2-0	N14 5-1	a10 3-1	D12 2-0	a24 1-1	S14 4-2	J09 0-1	S05 2-3	M27 2-1	N28 1-3	O03 2-2	O17 4-0	F27 3-1		D26 2-3
22 WEST HAM U	a26 2-1	M26 0-0	S12 3-1	J02 3-0	D28 1-0	a10 4-1	N14 0-2	J23 5-1	a24 1-1	F27 4-0	O31 1-0	M13 3-3	S26 4-1	A31 0-2	F13 4-1	F06 2-2	O17 1-1	m01 1-0	M27 4-0	N28 2-0	A29 2-1	

Season 1936-37

DIVISION 3 NORTH

	ACCRINGTON S	BARROW	CARLISLE U	CHESTER	CREWE A	DARLINGTON	GATESHEAD	HALIFAX T	HARTLEPOOLS U	HULL C	LINCOLN C	MANSFIELD T	NEW BRIGHTON	OLDHAM A	PORT VALE	ROCHDALE	ROTHERHAM U	SOUTHPORT	STOCKPORT CO	TRANMERE R	WREXHAM	YORK C
1 ACCRINGTON S		D05 5-0	D19 2-1	N21 2-1	M20 4-1	S26 1-0	J23 2-1	M06 3-2	S29 1-2	S12 0-1	A29 1-2	N07 0-3	J02 5-0	M26 1-1	D25 2-3	a03 3-1	J01 3-0	F20 6-3	O10 2-1	O24 4-0	F06 2-2	a17 2-1
2 BARROW	a10 1-0		O10 5-0	J09 1-2	S05 2-2	O31 1-0	M13 3-0	A31 1-2	m01 3-1	N14 2-3	J16 0-4	D26 2-2	M27 2-1	a19 1-2	a24 3-1	S19 3-0	J30 5-1	D25 2-1	O17 0-0	M29 2-0	F27 1-1	F06 2-2
3 CARLISLE U	a24 2-0	F13 2-2		F04 1-1	S19 4-0	N14 2-0	M27 2-1	S05 1-2	M26 2-0	J21 1-1	a15 3-1	J09 1-2	a10 1-1	D25 2-1	O17 5-2	O03 1-0	F27 4-1	S03 1-1	O31 1-0	D26 3-1	M13 2-1	J01 1-1
4 CHESTER	M27 1-1	S12 6-0	S26 4-0		S02 5-0	O17 2-1	a21 6-0	D25 1-1	F06 3-0	O31 3-1	N14 7-3	M29 5-1	M13 4-1	a14 2-1	N28 0-0	J02 2-2	D12 2-1	O10 2-3	a24 1-1	S16 5-2	A29 4-1	J23 3-1
5 CREWE A	N14 2-2	J02 4-1	J23 1-2	S07 1-1		M26 1-1	O17 3-1	S16 0-1	S26 1-1	F27 2-1	M13 2-1	D28 2-1	O31 0-2	M27 1-2	J20 0-1	A29 2-2	a10 0-2	F06 3-2	a19 1-2	O10 2-2	a24 1-1	S12 2-2
6 DARLINGTON	F03 4-1	M06 2-4	M20 1-5	F20 1-3	M29 0-3		D28 0-2	a17 3-3	N21 5-5	J01 2-2	O03 2-2	D19 0-0	F13 1-2	S19 0-3	J09 1-0	O24 4-1	S05 6-3	a03 4-2	D26 1-1	D05 3-2	S09 1-1	N07 1-1
7 GATESHEAD	S19 1-1	N07 1-1	N21 1-0	O24 1-1	F20 2-0	D25 5-0		D19 0-2	a03 2-2	F13 6-3	a07 0-5	J01 3-3	O03 1-1	J09 0-3	S05 0-1	M06 3-1	D26 2-1	D05 5-4	S02 0-0	a17 4-0	M06 0-0	M20 3-2
8 HALIFAX T	O31 3-0	S07 2-1	J02 6-1	D28 1-0	m01 4-1	a19 4-1	a24 2-1		S12 2-0	F06 1-0	F27 2-3	F13 0-0	O17 0-0	a26 0-1	N14 0-1	M29 3-2	M27 4-1	J23 1-1	J16 1-1	S26 2-1	a10 1-2	A29 1-2
9 HARTLEPOOLS U	S02 1-0	J01 3-1	M29 3-0	O03 0-1	J30 4-1	M27 1-3	J16 6-1	J09 5-3		a10 2-2	a24 3-1	S19 3-0	a28 5-0	O17 1-0	F27 2-0	F13 4-1	O31 0-2	D26 2-0	M13 2-4	S05 2-1	N14 2-0	D28 2-0
10 HULL C	J09 0-3	M20 3-2	a03 1-1	M06 1-1	O24 2-0	m01 4-3	O10 3-2	O03 0-0	D05 1-0		S19 1-1	F20 3-0	J30 4-1	S05 2-0	D26 1-1	N07 1-1	A31 2-1	a17 3-2	M29 0-1	D19 5-2	D25 1-0	N21 1-0
11 LINCOLN C	D26 3-3	a03 6-0	a17 3-0	M20 3-0	N07 2-4	F06 4-3	S26 4-0	O24 4-1	D19 3-0	J23 5-0		M06 2-0	S12 1-0	A31 2-0	M29 1-0	N21 5-3	D25 3-0	S05 4-1	S14 0-2	F20 1-0	O10 6-2	D05 3-1
12 MANSFIELD T	M13 2-1	A29 2-1	S12 1-4	M26 5-0	D25 1-4	a24 3-1	m01 3-2	O10 3-0	J23 8-2	O17 5-2	O31 2-2		F27 2-3	N14 1-2	M27 7-1	S09 6-2	J16 4-1	S26 3-0	a10 0-2	F06 2-3	M30 3-0	J02 1-2
13 NEW BRIGHTON	S05 1-1	N21 1-1	D05 1-1	N07 1-0	M06 1-0	O10 2-0	F06 1-1	F20 1-1	a17 4-0	S26 1-1	J09 1-2	O24 0-0		D26 0-2	S02 2-0	M20 5-1	M26 4-0	D19 3-1	D25 1-1	S19 1-2	S16 1-0	a03 4-1
14 OLDHAM A	M29 3-1	a17 4-3	D28 2-1	a03 1-0	N21 1-1	J23 1-1	S12 4-4	N07 1-0	F20 2-0	J02 3-1	S07 1-0	M20 1-1	A29 3-1		S14 5-1	D05 3-0	O10 4-1	O24 3-3	F06 0-2	M06 3-0	S26 2-2	D19 2-2
15 PORT VALE	D28 1-1	D19 3-2	F20 1-0	D05 4-0	a03 0-0	S12 2-2	J02 4-2	M20 3-1	O24 1-0	A29 1-3	M26 1-1	N21 5-1	S07 3-1	m01 1-0		a17 1-1	F06 2-1	M06 0-2	S26 3-0	N07 2-1	J23 0-3	O10 1-1
16 ROCHDALE	a27 4-1	J23 3-1	F06 3-0	S05 0-1	D26 2-0	F27 4-0	O31 0-2	M26 3-5	O10 1-1	M13 4-0	M27 2-3	A31 1-3	N14 4-0	a10 3-0	D12 0-0		a24 1-0	S15 2-1	J09 2-2	D25 2-1	O17 0-6	S26 3-0
17 ROTHERHAM U	m01 2-2	S26 4-1	O24 0-1	a17 2-1	D05 3-2	J02 2-4	A29 3-0	N21 6-0	M06 2-4	S07 0-0	D28 3-1	a03 4-1	M29 3-0	F13 4-4	O03 2-0	D19 1-1		N07 3-0	J23 1-1	M20 3-1	S12 2-2	F20 2-2
18 SOUTHPORT	O17 3-1	M16 3-3	S08 2-1	F13 1-2	O03 1-1	J19 0-0	a10 3-0	S19 2-1	A29 1-1	J16 1-4	J02 2-1	J30 3-2	a24 3-0	F27 2-0	O31 3-3	J01 1-1	M13 4-1		N14 1-1	J09 1-0	M27 1-1	M26 1-4
19 STOCKPORT CO	F13 3-2	F20 4-1	M06 1-2	D19 4-0	a17 1-0	A29 3-3	S07 4-2	a03 0-0	N07 1-1	M26 3-1	m01 2-0	D05 3-1	D28 3-1	O03 4-1	J30 1-0	S12 3-0	S19 4-2	M20 2-1		N21 5-0	J02 2-0	O24 6-0
20 TRANMERE R	a19 1-2	M26 0-0	A29 5-1	J01 5-0	F13 6-1	a10 1-1	a26 6-1	J30 2-1	J02 1-0	D12 2-1	O17 2-2	O03 0-2	J23 3-2	O31 3-3	M13 4-2	J16 4-3	N14 1-2	S12 3-3	M27 2-2		a12 1-1	S07 0-0
21 WREXHAM	O03 1-0	O24 2-1	N07 1-0	D26 1-2	D19 5-0	A31 4-0	M29 6-0	D05 0-2	M20 0-1	a19 2-1	F13 0-3	a17 2-3	J01 4-1	J30 1-1	S19 1-0	F20 0-1	J09 4-2	N21 3-3	S05 0-0	a03 2-0		M06 2-0
22 YORK C	a14 4-2	O03 1-2	m01 5-2	S19 0-2	J09 2-3	M13 3-0	N14 2-0	D26 4-0	D25 4-1	M27 1-1	a10 0-0	S05 1-1	a21 2-1	a24 3-1	F13 1-2	F10 4-1	O17 4-3	M29 4-0	F27 2-1	S02 4-0	O31 3-4	

DIVISION 3 SOUTH

	ALDERSHOT	BOURNEMOUTH	BRIGHTON & HA	BRISTOL C	BRISTOL R	CARDIFF C	CLAPTON O	CRYSTAL P	EXETER C	GILLINGHAM	LUTON T	MILLWALL	NEWPORT CO	NORTHAMPTON T	NOTTS CO	Q.P.R.	READING	SOUTHEND U	SWINDON T	TORQUAY U	WALSALL	WATFORD
1 ALDERSHOT		A29 1-3	J02 0-1	M06 3-0	M26 4-0	a17 0-1	N21 1-1	D19 2-2	O10 1-1	F06 3-0	D05 2-3	D28 1-2	S26 2-0	S09 0-2	M20 0-1	O24 0-0	F20 0-2	J23 1-2	m01 2-1	N07 0-1	a03 4-4	S12 2-2
2 BOURNEMOUTH	D26 2-1		O10 1-0	a17 0-0	S19 3-0	N07 0-2	F20 2-1	M20 3-1	N21 0-0	S02 1-0	M06 2-1	J09 2-1	M29 5-0	a21 3-2	O03 1-0	D05 3-1	a03 2-1	D28 1-0	S05 5-2	D19 3-3	O24 3-2	m01 3-2
3 BRIGHTON & H.A.	S05 1-0	F13 1-0		D05 2-0	J30 5-2	M06 7-2	m01 1-1	N07 1-0	M20 1-0	D26 4-0	O24 2-1	S19 2-2	S02 2-0	O03 1-2	D19 2-2	a03 4-1	N21 1-1	M20 1-0	J09 2-0	a17 5-1	F20 3-0	D25 1-1
4 BRISTOL C	O31 3-0	J27 4-1	a10 1-0		J02 4-1	m01 2-1	J30 4-0	D25 1-0	M26 2-1	M13 2-0	F13 2-3	O17 2-0	N14 3-1	a24 0-1	S19 1-1	A29 3-2	S23 1-2	M27 0-1	a28 1-2	J09 4-1	O03 0-0	J16 2-2
5 BRISTOL R	M29 1-0	J23 4-0	S26 2-0	S05 3-1		N21 5-1	M06 4-0	a03 1-0	D05 4-2	D28 0-3	M20 4-0	D26 2-1	S16 1-1	S12 2-0	O24 2-3	D19 1-1	a17 2-2	O10 1-2	S02 2-1	F20 5-1	N07 3-0	F06 0-1
6 CARDIFF C	a19 4-1	M13 2-1	O31 1-2	S14 3-1	M27 3-1		A31 2-1	J23 1-1	S26 3-1	a24 2-0	S05 3-0	a12 0-1	J09 0-1	N14 2-1	M29 0-2	O10 2-0	F06 1-1	S28 1-1	a10 1-2	D28 0-2	D26 2-2	F27 2-2
7 CLAPTON O	M27 1-1	O17 2-1	S17 2-0	S26 0-0	O31 2-1	S10 0-1		A29 1-1	J02 1-0	J16 2-0	M26 0-2	M13 1-0	a10 1-2	F27 3-1	O10 1-1	J23 0-0	S12 3-2	a29 3-0	N14 1-1	F06 2-0	D28 2-2	a24 1-1
8 CRYSTAL P	a24 3-0	N14 2-2	M13 2-0	D28 1-0	J20 3-0	S19 2-2	D26 2-3		F06 8-0	J30 1-1	J09 0-4	a14 1-0	O17 6-1	M27 2-2	S02 1-2	S23 0-0	O10 3-1	F27 1-1	J16 2-0	M26 0-0	S05 3-1	O31 2-0
9 EXETER C	F13 1-2	M27 1-1	N14 0-4	M29 3-0	a10 3-2	F03 3-1	S05 0-2	O03 3-2		O17 1-1	S19 2-4	M17 1-1	F27 3-1	J20 2-5	D26 1-3	D28 0-3	m01 2-0	O31 2-2	a24 1-1	S02 2-1	J09 3-0	M13 2-1
10 GILLINGHAM	O03 1-2	S09 1-0	A29 1-0	N07 5-3	D25 1-0	D19 0-0	a03 0-2	S26 2-0	F24 2-2		a17 1-0	m01 1-0	J23 4-4	M26 2-0	N21 3-0	M06 0-0	O24 2-1	S12 1-0	F13 4-1	M20 1-0	D05 2-2	J02 2-1
11 LUTON T	a10 5-2	O31 1-0	F27 2-1	O10 4-0	N14 2-0	J02 8-1	M29 2-0	S12 5-2	J23 2-2	a07 5-2		M27 5-0	a24 5-0	M13 3-2	D25 2-1	F06 0-1	S26 4-0	A29 1-0	a21 5-1	m01 2-0	S07 2-0	O17 4-1
12 MILLWALL	D25 4-2	S12 0-2	J23 3-0	F22 3-1	A29 1-2	a03 3-1	N07 2-1	D05 3-0	a17 3-3	S21 3-0	N21 0-2		O10 7-2	J02 1-0	M08 0-0	A31 2-0	D19 0-2	F06 1-2	M26 1-1	O24 1-1	M20 3-1	S26 2-1
13 NEWPORT CO	J30 4-0	M26 4-0	S10 1-4	M20 0-0	m01 2-2	S12 2-3	D05 1-1	F20 1-1	O24 2-0	S19 0-0	D19 2-1	F13 1-2		D28 1-3	a03 2-0	N07 1-2	M06 3-0	J02 6-2	O03 1-1	N21 1-1	a17 1-2	A29 1-3
14 NORTHAMPTON T	A31 5-3	S26 0-0	F06 2-0	D19 5-1	J09 4-1	M20 2-0	O24 1-1	N21 2-0	a03 2-1	M29 5-0	N07 3-1	S05 2-2	D25 3-2		F20 1-1	a17 0-1	D05 2-1	m01 4-3	D26 4-0	S19 3-0	M06 6-3	O10 0-1
15 NOTTS CO	N14 3-0	F06 4-3	a24 0-1	J23 1-0	F27 4-3	M26 4-0	F13 0-0	S07 0-1	A29 3-1	M27 2-0	D28 2-1	O31 1-1	J16 3-1	O17 3-2		S12 1-2	J02 1-0	a10 2-1	M13 3-2	S26 2-0	O01 3-3	D12 2-1
16 Q.P.R.	F27 3-0	a10 1-2	J21 2-3	D26 5-0	a24 2-1	F13 6-0	S19 2-1	m01 1-3	D25 4-0	O31 0-1	O03 2-1	S17 0-1	M13 6-2	F18 3-2	J09 0-2		M26 0-0	N14 7-2	O17 1-1	S05 3-0	F04 2-0	M27 1-2
17 READING	O17 2-0	J20 3-2	M27 2-0	S02 2-1	F24 2-0	O03 3-0	J09 1-1	F13 1-1	S16 1-0	F27 6-2	F10 2-2	a24 3-0	O31 4-4	a10 3-1	S05 4-1	M29 2-0		M13 2-3	D25 2-2	D26 5-1	S19 0-2	N14 3-0
18 SOUTHEND U	S19 2-2	D25 0-0	M29 2-1	N21 3-0	F13 2-3	F20 8-1	a17 0-0	O24 2-1	M06 4-4	J09 0-2	D26 3-0	O03 0-0	S05 9-2	S16 2-0	D05 2-3	M20 3-2	N07 1-1		J30 2-0	a03 0-0	D19 3-0	S02 1-1
19 SWINDON T	S16 5-1	J02 3-1	S12 1-2	O24 0-1	S23 4-1	D05 4-2	M20 1-3	a17 4-0	D19 3-1	O10 3-0	a03 2-2	M29 3-0	F06 1-2	A29 2-0	N07 2-2	F20 1-1	D28 1-2	S26 4-0		M06 4-2	N21 3-0	J23 1-1
20 TORQUAY U	M13 5-1	a24 0-0	D12 0-2	S12 5-2	O17 1-0	D25 1-0	O03 4-1	M29 3-0	S09 0-1	N14 0-2	S16 2-2	F27 0-2	M27 1-2	J23 5-0	J30 2-2	J02 1-1	A29 2-2	J16 1-4	O31 2-0		F13 3-1	a10 4-7
21 WALSALL	J21 0-0	F27 1-1	O17 1-4	F06 1-5	M13 5-2	A29 1-0	D25 3-2	J02 1-0	S12 4-2	a10 2-1	A31 0-1	N14 0-3	a26 1-2	O31 2-2	m01 2-1	S26 2-4	M30 0-1	a24 3-0	M27 5-2	O10 1-0		M26 3-1
22 WATFORD	J09 5-3	S23 4-0	D28 1-0	a03 1-0	O03 3-0	O24 2-0	D19 2-1	M06 3-1	N07 1-1	S05 6-1	F20 1-3	F03 2-2	D26 3-0	F13 4-1	a17 0-2	N21 2-0	M20 6-1	S09 1-3	S19 2-2	D05 4-0	M29 0-0	

LEAGUE TABLES

DIVISION 1

	P	W	D	L	F	A	W	D	L	F	A	Pts
Manchester C	42	15	5	1	56	22	7	8	6	51	39	57
Charlton A	42	15	5	1	37	13	6	7	8	21	36	54
Arsenal	42	10	10	1	43	20	8	6	7	37	29	52
Derby Co	42	13	3	5	58	39	8	4	9	38	51	49
Wolves	42	16	2	3	63	24	5	3	13	21	43	47
Brentford	42	14	5	2	58	32	4	5	12	24	46	46
Middlesbrough	42	14	6	1	49	22	5	2	14	25	49	46
Sunderland	42	17	2	2	59	24	2	4	15	30	63	44
Portsmouth	42	13	3	5	41	29	4	7	10	21	37	44
Stoke C	42	12	6	3	52	27	3	6	12	20	30	42
Birmingham	42	9	7	5	36	24	4	8	9	28	36	41
Grimsby T	42	13	3	5	60	32	4	4	13	26	49	41
Chelsea	42	11	6	4	36	21	3	7	11	16	34	41
Preston NE	42	10	6	5	35	28	4	7	10	21	39	41
Huddersfield T	42	12	5	4	39	21	0	10	11	23	43	39
WBA	42	13	3	5	45	32	3	3	15	32	66	38
Everton	42	12	7	2	56	23	2	2	17	25	55	37
Liverpool	42	9	8	4	38	26	3	3	15	24	58	35
Leeds U	42	14	3	4	44	20	1	1	19	16	60	34
Bolton W	42	6	6	9	22	33	4	8	9	21	33	34
Manchester U	42	8	9	4	29	26	2	3	16	26	52	32
Sheffield W	42	8	5	8	32	29	1	7	13	21	40	30

DIVISION 2

	P	W	D	L	F	A	W	D	L	F	A	Pts
Leicester C	42	14	4	3	56	26	10	4	7	33	31	56
Blackpool	42	13	4	4	49	19	11	3	7	39	34	55
Bury	42	13	4	4	46	26	9	4	8	28	29	52
Newcastle U	42	11	3	7	45	23	11	2	8	35	33	49
Plymouth A	42	11	6	4	42	22	7	7	7	29	31	49
West Ham U	42	14	5	2	47	18	5	6	10	26	37	49
Sheffield U	42	16	4	1	48	14	2	6	13	18	40	46
Coventry C	42	11	5	5	35	19	6	6	9	31	35	45
Aston Villa	42	10	6	5	47	30	6	6	9	35	40	44
Tottenham H	42	13	3	5	57	26	4	6	11	31	40	43
Fulham	42	11	5	5	43	24	4	8	9	28	37	43
Blackburn R	42	11	3	7	49	32	5	7	9	21	30	42
Burnley	42	11	5	5	37	20	5	5	11	20	41	42
Barnsley	42	11	6	4	30	23	5	3	13	20	41	41
Chesterfield	42	12	3	6	54	34	4	5	12	30	55	40
Swansea T	42	14	2	5	40	16	1	5	15	10	49	37
Norwich C	42	8	6	7	38	29	6	2	13	25	42	36
Nottingham F	42	10	6	5	42	30	2	4	15	26	60	34
Southampton	42	10	8	3	38	25	1	4	16	15	52	34
Bradford	42	10	4	7	33	33	2	5	14	19	56	33
Bradford C	42	8	8	5	36	31	1	4	16	18	63	30
Doncaster R	42	6	6	9	18	29	1	4	16	12	55	24

DIVISION 3 North

	P	W	D	L	F	A	W	D	L	F	A	Pts
Stockport Co	42	17	3	1	59	18	6	11	4	25	21	60
Lincoln C	42	18	1	2	65	20	7	6	8	38	37	57
Chester	42	15	5	1	68	21	7	4	10	19	36	53
Oldham A	42	13	7	1	49	25	7	4	10	28	34	51
Hull C	42	13	6	2	39	22	4	6	11	29	47	46
Hartlepools U	42	16	1	4	53	21	3	6	12	22	48	45
Halifax T	42	12	4	5	40	20	6	5	10	28	43	45
Wrexham	42	12	3	6	41	21	4	9	8	30	36	44
Mansfield T	42	13	1	7	64	35	5	7	9	27	41	44
Carlisle U	42	13	6	2	42	19	5	2	14	23	49	44
Port Vale	42	12	6	3	39	23	5	4	12	19	41	44
York C	42	13	3	5	54	27	3	8	10	25	43	43
Accrington S	42	14	2	5	51	26	2	7	12	25	43	41
Southport	42	10	8	3	39	28	2	5	14	34	59	37
New Brighton	42	10	8	3	36	16	3	3	15	19	54	37
Barrow	42	11	5	5	42	25	2	5	14	28	61	36
Rotherham U	42	11	7	3	52	28	3	0	18	26	63	35
Rochdale	42	12	3	6	44	27	1	6	14	25	59	35
Tranmere R	42	10	8	3	52	30	2	1	18	19	58	33
Crewe A	42	6	8	7	31	31	4	4	13	24	52	32
Gateshead	42	9	8	4	40	31	2	2	17	23	67	32
Darlington	42	6	8	7	42	46	2	6	13	24	50	30

DIVISION 3 South

	P	W	D	L	F	A	W	D	L	F	A	Pts
Luton T	42	19	1	1	69	16	8	3	10	34	37	58
Notts Co	42	15	3	3	44	23	8	7	6	30	29	56
Brighton & HA	42	15	5	1	49	16	9	0	12	25	27	53
Watford	42	14	4	3	53	21	5	7	9	32	39	49
Reading	42	14	5	2	53	23	5	6	10	23	37	49
Bournemouth	42	17	3	1	45	20	3	6	12	20	39	49
Northampton T	42	15	4	2	56	22	5	2	14	29	46	46
Millwall	42	12	4	5	43	24	6	6	9	21	30	46
QPR	42	12	2	7	51	24	6	7	8	22	28	45
Southend U	42	10	8	3	49	23	7	3	11	29	44	45
Gillingham	42	14	5	2	36	18	4	3	14	16	48	44
Clapton O	42	10	8	3	29	17	4	7	10	23	35	43
Swindon T	42	12	4	5	52	24	2	7	12	23	49	39
Crystal P	42	11	7	3	45	20	2	5	14	17	41	38
Bristol R	42	14	3	4	49	20	2	1	18	22	60	36
Bristol C	42	13	3	5	42	20	2	3	16	16	50	36
Walsall	42	11	3	7	38	34	2	7	12	25	51	36
Cardiff C	42	10	5	6	35	24	4	2	15	19	63	35
Newport Co	42	7	7	7	37	28	5	3	13	30	70	34
Torquay U	42	9	5	7	42	32	2	5	14	15	48	32
Exeter C	42	9	5	7	36	37	1	7	13	23	51	32
Aldershot	42	5	6	10	29	29	2	3	16	21	60	23

Football League Records

Top scorers: Div 1, T.Lawton (Everton) 38 goals; Div 2, G.Henson (Bradford) 27 goals; Div 3(N), J.Roberts (Port Vale) 28 goals; Div 3(S), H.Crawshaw (Mansfield Town) 25 goals.
Mansfield Town transferred to Division Three South.

England full-back Eddie Hapgood, skippered Arsenal to yet another title.

Aston Villa's Frank Broome, one of the most versatile forwards in the game. His 19 goals helped Villa regain their First Division place.

DIVISION 1

	ARSENAL	BIRMINGHAM	BLACKPOOL	BOLTON W	BRENTFORD	CHARLTON A	CHELSEA	DERBY CO	EVERTON	GRIMSBY T	HUDDERSFIELD T	LEEDS U	LEICESTER C	LIVERPOOL	MANCHESTER C	MIDDLESBROUGH	PORTSMOUTH	PRESTON N.E.	STOKE C	SUNDERLAND	W.B.A.	WOLVERHAMPTON W
1 ARSENAL		a16 0-0	D27 2-1	m07 5-0	a15 0-2	a02 2-2	F19 2-0	F05 3-0	J01 2-1	M19 5-1	S01 3-1	N27 4-1	F02 3-1	a30 1-0	O02 2-1	O30 1-2	O16 1-1	D11 2-0	M05 4-0	S18 4-1	N13 1-1	S04 5-0
2 BIRMINGHAM	D04 1-2		M26 1-1	a09 2-0	D18 0-0	S18 1-1	J22 1-1	O23 1-0	a23 0-3	O02 2-2	N06 2-2	F19 3-2	S15 4-1	D27 2-2	M12 2-2	S01 3-1	S04 2-2	F05 0-2	J01 1-1	F26 2-2	a15 2-1	N20 2-0
3 BLACKPOOL	D25 2-1	N13 0-3		A30 2-2	S20 1-1	a15 1-0	O16 0-2	O02 1-1	S04 1-0	D11 2-2	J01 4-0	M19 5-2	S18 2-4	N27 0-1	F19 2-1	a16 4-2	M05 2-0	a02 1-0	O30 0-1	F05 0-0	a30 3-1	J26 0-2
4 BOLTON W	S15 1-0	N27 1-1	S06 3-0		A28 2-0	M05 1-0	O30 5-5	J22 0-2	S18 1-2	J15 3-1	J26 2-0	a02 0-0	O02 6-1	D11 0-0	a18 2-1	a30 3-1	a16 1-1	O16 1-4	N13 1-0	F19 1-1	M19 3-0	F05 1-2
5 BRENTFORD	a18 3-0	a30 1-2	S16 2-4	J01 1-1		O16 5-2	M09 1-1	F19 2-3	J26 3-0	a02 6-1	S04 2-0	D11 1-1	F05 1-1	M19 1-3	D27 2-1	N13 3-3	O30 2-0	S01 2-1	a16 0-0	O02 4-0	N27 0-2	S18 2-1
6 CHARLTON A	N20 0-3	J29 2-0	a18 4-1	O23 1-1	F26 1-0		D27 3-1	N06 1-2	D04 3-1	S06 0-0	M12 4-0	A28 1-1	D18 2-0	J15 3-0	a23 0-0	S25 1-0	O09 5-1	m07 0-0	M02 3-0	a09 2-1	S11 3-1	M26 4-1
7 CHELSEA	O09 2-2	S11 2-0	F26 1-3	M12 0-0	O23 2-1	a27 1-1		a23 3-0	M26 2-0	S15 1-0	D04 3-1	S08 4-1	a09 4-1	A28 6-1	N20 2-2	J29 0-1	F12 3-1	a15 0-2	S25 2-1	N06 0-0	J15 2-2	D18 0-2
8 DERBY CO	S25 2-0	M05 0-0	F12 3-1	D27 4-2	O09 1-3	M19 3-2	D11 4-0		S15 2-1	a30 1-2	a18 0-4	N13 2-2	J01 0-1	a16 4-1	J29 1-7	O16 1-1	a02 1-0	N27 1-1	F02 4-1	S04 2-2	O30 5-3	S01 1-2
9 EVERTON	A28 1-4	D11 1-1	J15 3-1	J29 4-1	S11 3-0	a16 3-0	N13 4-1	m07 1-1		M05 3-2	S25 1-2	O16 1-1	D27 3-0	F16 1-3	S08 4-1	M19 2-2	a30 5-2	O30 3-5	N27 3-0	a15 3-3	a02 5-3	F19 0-1
10 GRIMSBY T	N06 2-1	F12 4-0	a23 1-0	S04 0-1	N20 0-1	A31 1-1	m07 2-0	D18 0-0	O23 2-1		F26 4-2	S11 1-1	D04 2-1	J29 0-0	a09 3-1	O09 2-1	a15 1-0	J01 1-1	D25 1-5	M29 0-2	S25 1-4	M12 1-0
11 HUDDERSFIELD T	S08 2-1	M19 2-1	A28 3-1	S11 1-0	J15 0-3	O30 1-1	a16 1-2	a19 2-0	F05 1-3	O16 1-2		J29 0-3	F19 0-0	a02 1-2	m07 1-0	N27 3-0	N13 2-0	M16 1-3	m02 3-0	D27 1-1	D11 2-1	O02 1-0
12 LEEDS U	a09 0-1	O09 1-0	N06 1-1	N20 1-1	a23 4-0	J01 2-2	S01 2-0	M26 0-2	F26 4-4	J26 1-1	S18 2-1		M12 0-2	S25 2-0	D18 2-1	D25 5-3	S15 3-1	S04 0-0	a19 2-1	D04 4-3	F12 1-0	O23 1-2
13 LEICESTER C	S11 1-1	m07 1-4	J29 0-1	F12 1-1	S25 0-1	a30 1-0	N27 1-0	A28 0-0	D25 3-1	a16 1-0	O09 2-1	O30 2-4		M05 2-2	J15 1-4	a02 0-1	M19 3-3	N13 1-0	D11 2-0	A30 4-0	O16 4-1	a18 1-1
14 LIVERPOOL	D18 2-0	a06 3-2	a09 4-2	a23 2-1	N06 3-4	S04 1-2	J01 2-2	D04 3-4	O02 1-2	S18 2-1	N20 0-1	F05 1-1	O23 1-1		M26 2-0	a18 1-1	S01 3-2	F02 2-2	S15 3-0	M12 4-0	O09 0-1	F26 0-1
15 MANCHESTER C	F16 1-2	O30 2-0	O09 2-1	a15 1-2	D25 0-2	a06 5-3	a02 1-0	S18 6-1	S01 2-0	N27 3-1	S15 3-2	a30 6-2	S04 3-0	N13 1-3		M09 1-6	F05 2-1	M19 1-2	O16 0-0	F02 0-0	a16 7-1	J01 2-4
16 MIDDLESBROUGH	M12 2-1	S08 1-1	D04 2-2	D18 1-2	M26 0-1	F05 3-1	S18 4-3	F26 4-2	N06 1-2	F19 1-0	a09 0-1	D27 2-0	N20 4-2	a15 1-1	O23 4-0		J26 0-0	O02 2-1	S04 2-1	J01 2-1	m07 4-1	a23 0-3
17 PORTSMOUTH	F26 0-0	J15 1-1	O23 1-2	D04 1-1	M12 4-1	F19 2-1	O02 2-4	N20 4-0	D18 3-1	a18 3-0	M30 3-0	m07 4-0	N06 1-1	S08 1-1	S25 2-2	S11 0-2		D25 3-2	J29 2-0	a23 1-0	A28 2-3	a09 1-0
18 PRESTON N.E.	a23 1-3	S25 2-1	N20 2-0	F26 2-2	S06 1-1	S13 0-1	a18 0-0	a09 4-1	M12 2-1	A28 4-1	O23 1-1	J15 3-1	M09 0-0	S11 4-1	N06 2-2	F16 0-2	D27 1-1		O09 2-1	D18 0-0	J29 1-1	D04 2-0
19 STOKE C	O23 1-1	A28 2-2	M12 1-3	M26 3-2	D04 3-0	O02 2-0	F05 2-1	S11 8-1	a09 1-1	D27 1-1	D18 0-1	a18 0-1	a23 1-2	m07 2-0	F26 3-2	J15 3-0	S18 3-1	F19 1-1		N20 0-0	S06 4-0	N06 1-1
20 SUNDERLAND	J29 1-1	O16 1-0	S25 2-1	O09 3-1	F16 1-0	N27 1-1	M19 1-1	J15 2-0	a18 2-0	N13 2-2	D25 2-1	a16 0-0	S08 1-0	O30 2-3	S11 3-1	A28 3-1	D11 0-2	m04 0-2	a02 1-1		M09 3-0	m07 1-0
21 W.B.A.	M26 0-0	a18 4-3	D18 1-2	N06 2-4	a09 4-3	J26 0-0	S04 4-0	M12 4-2	N20 3-1	F05 2-1	a23 5-1	O02 2-1	F26 1-3	F19 5-1	M16 1-1	S13 3-1	J01 1-2	S18 1-1	A30 0-1	O23 1-6		D27 2-2
22 WOLVERHAMPTON W	J15 3-1	a02 3-2	S11 1-0	S25 1-1	J29 2-1	N13 1-1	a30 1-1	S06 2-2	O09 2-0	O30 1-1	F16 1-4	M05 1-1	a15 10-1	O16 2-0	A28 3-1	M23 0-1	N27 5-0	a16 0-0	M19 2-2	S15 4-0	m02 2-1	

DIVISION 2

	ASTON VILLA	BARNSLEY	BLACKBURN R	BRADFORD	BURNLEY	BURY	CHESTERFIELD	COVENTRY C	FULHAM	LUTON T	MANCHESTER U	NEWCASTLE U	NORWICH C	NOTTINGHAM F	PLYMOUTH A	SHEFFIELD U	SHEFFIELD W	SOUTHAMPTON	STOCKPORT CO	SWANSEA T	TOTTENHAM H	WEST HAM U
1 ASTON VILLA		D28 3-0	S11 2-1	a27 2-0	N13 0-0	M19 2-1	O09 0-2	O30 1-1	S25 2-0	S06 4-1	a02 3-0	O16 2-0	m07 2-0	M09 1-2	F23 3-0	N27 1-0	J29 4-3	J15 3-0	D11 7-1	a19 4-0	a16 2-0	A28 2-0
2 BARNSLEY	D18 0-1		M12 0-0	J01 0-1	O02 2-2	F19 2-2	a09 1-1	a18 1-1	M26 0-0	D27 3-1	F02 2-2	S06 3-0	a23 0-0	m07 2-2	D04 3-2	S18 1-1	N06 4-1	O23 0-2	S04 2-0	N20 2-0	F05 1-1	F26 1-0
3 BLACKBURN R	J27 1-0	O30 5-3		S18 0-0	D11 3-3	a02 2-1	D25 3-3	N27 1-3	S20 2-2	M19 2-2	O16 1-1	N13 2-1	S04 5-3	a16 5-1	A30 2-1	F19 2-3	a18 1-0	O02 4-0	M05 3-0	J01 3-1	a30 2-1	F05 2-1
4 BRADFORD	D27 1-2	A28 4-3	J29 7-1		a16 3-1	N13 1-1	a18 3-2	M19 0-1	F16 1-2	O16 1-1	D11 4-0	M05 2-0	S06 3-0	O30 2-2	O09 2-0	a02 5-1	S25 1-1	S11 2-0	a30 4-1	m07 0-1	N27 3-1	J15 2-1
5 BURNLEY	a05 3-0	F12 1-0	a23 3-1	D04 1-1		A28 2-0	O23 0-2	J15 2-0	D25 1-0	S25 3-2	a15 1-0	J29 2-1	N06 3-0	S11 0-0	F26 0-2	S13 2-0	D18 1-1	N20 4-0	O09 0-0	M12 2-0	S06 2-1	a09 2-0
6 BURY	N06 1-1	O09 0-2	N20 2-1	M26 5-1	J01 4-0		F26 4-0	S11 0-2	F12 4-2	F16 3-4	S13 1-2	S25 1-1	M12 3-1	J29 2-0	S04 2-0	A30 1-0	a23 2-0	a09 2-1	a15 1-3	O23 0-0	D25 1-2	D04 4-3
7 CHESTERFIELD	F19 0-1	N27 0-0	D27 3-0	a15 0-3	M05 0-1	O16 1-2		J29 4-0	J15 0-2	a02 5-2	N13 1-7	a25 2-0	O02 6-2	a30 1-0	S11 2-0	M19 1-0	A28 1-0	S06 5-0	a16 1-0	F05 4-1	O30 2-2	m07 0-1
8 COVENTRY C	M12 0-1	a19 1-0	a09 3-2	N06 0-0	S04 1-0	J27 0-2	S18 2-2		a23 0-1	O09 2-1	A30 1-0	F12 1-0	O23 2-0	S25 1-1	D18 4-0	D27 2-2	N20 0-1	J22 2-0	S13 1-0	F26 5-0	J01 2-1	M26 1-1
9 FULHAM	F05 1-1	N13 0-0	m07 3-1	O02 1-1	D27 2-1	a30 4-0	S04 1-1	D11 3-4		a16 4-1	O30 1-0	N27 1-2	S18 3-4	a02 2-0	J01 2-3	M05 1-1	S06 0-0	a15 1-0	M19 2-0	J22 8-1	O16 3-1	F19 1-1
10 LUTON T	S01 3-2	D25 4-0	N06 4-1	F26 4-2	F05 3-1	O02 0-1	N20 1-1	F19 1-4	D04 4-0		S04 1-0	m07 4-1	D18 1-1	a18 2-2	a09 1-1	F02 2-3	M26 2-2	M12 1-3	J01 6-4	a23 5-1	S18 2-4	O23 2-2
11 MANCHESTER U	N20 3-1	S11 4-1	F26 2-1	a23 3-1	a18 4-0	m07 2-0	M26 4-1	S08 2-2	M12 1-0	J15 4-2		A28 3-0	a09 0-0	D27 4-3	N06 0-0	O02 0-1	O23 1-0	S25 1-2	J29 3-1	D04 5-1	F19 0-1	F23 4-0
12 NEWCASTLE U	F26 2-0	S01 0-1	M26 2-0	O23 3-0	S18 2-2	F05 1-0	a23 3-1	O02 1-2	a09 1-2	S15 1-3	J01 2-2		a15 0-1	F19 3-1	N20 3-1	S04 6-0	D04 1-0	N06 3-0	D25 0-0	D18 1-0	F02 1-0	M12 2-2
13 NORWICH C	S16 1-0	D11 1-0	J15 3-2	S01 1-1	M19 1-0	O30 1-2	F24 2-1	M05 0-2	J29 1-2	a30 0-4	N27 2-3	a18 1-1		O16 2-0	S25 4-0	a16 2-2	S11 3-1	A28 4-3	a02 1-0	O09 1-1	N13 2-1	D27 2-2
14 NOTTINGHAM F	O23 0-2	S15 2-1	D04 3-1	M12 1-0	J26 1-1	S18 1-0	D18 4-2	F05 2-1	N20 0-1	a15 1-0	D28 2-3	O09 0-0	F26 1-2		a23 1-0	J01 2-1	a09 0-1	M26 2-1	S01 1-2	O02 2-1	S04 3-1	N06 0-0
15 PLYMOUTH A	O02 0-3	a16 2-2	S08 2-2	F19 1-0	O16 2-3	J15 2-1	J26 1-1	a30 3-1	A28 4-0	N27 2-4	M19 1-1	a02 2-1	F05 1-1	D11 1-0		O30 2-0	D25 2-4	m07 4-0	N13 2-1	S18 2-2	M09 2-2	a18 2-1
16 SHEFFIELD U	a09 0-0	J29 6-3	O09 1-1	N20 3-1	S20 2-1	S06 2-1	N06 0-2	D25 3-2	O23 2-1	S11 2-0	F17 1-2	J15 4-0	D04 4-1	A28 2-1	M12 0-0		F26 2-1	D18 5-0	S25 2-0	M28 1-1	a18 1-0	a23 3-1
17 SHEFFIELD W	S18 1-2	M19 0-1	a19 1-1	F05 1-0	a30 2-1	D11 2-0	J01 1-0	a02 2-1	S02 2-1	N13 4-0	M05 1-3	a16 3-0	J22 1-0	N27 0-2	D27 1-1	O16 0-1		F19 0-0	O30 3-3	S04 1-1	S16 0-3	O02 1-0
18 SOUTHAMPTON	S04 0-0	M05 2-0	F12 1-0	F02 2-1	a02 0-0	N27 4-1	S01 0-1	a16 0-4	a18 4-0	O30 3-6	F05 3-3	M19 1-0	J01 3-1	N13 2-0	S15 0-0	a30 2-1	O09 5-2		O16 4-1	D25 1-1	D11 2-1	S18 3-3
19 STOCKPORT CO	a23 1-3	J15 1-2	O23 0-1	D18 1-2	F19 3-1	a18 0-1	D04 1-1	m07 1-1	N06 2-0	A28 2-1	S18 1-0	M02 1-3	N20 1-1	S06 1-0	M26 1-3	F05 1-1	M12 2-1	F26 0-0		a09 1-0	O02 3-2	S11 0-0
20 SWANSEA T	a18 2-1	a02 1-0	A28 3-2	S13 0-1	O30 3-1	M05 1-0	S25 1-0	O16 3-3	S11 2-0	D11 1-1	a16 2-2	a30 2-0	F19 1-0	F12 1-0	J29 1-0	N13 3-5	J15 1-1	D27 0-0	N27 0-2		M19 3-2	S06 0-0
21 TOTTENHAM H	D04 2-1	S25 3-0	D18 3-1	a09 2-1	A30 4-0	D27 1-3	M12 2-0	A28 0-0	F26 1-1	J29 3-0	O09 0-1	S11 2-2	M26 4-0	J15 3-0	O23 3-2	a15 1-2	m07 1-2	a23 5-0	F23 2-0	N06 2-0		N20 2-0
22 WEST HAM U	J01 1-1	O16 4-1	S25 2-0	S04 3-1	N27 1-0	a16 3-1	S13 5-0	N13 0-0	O09 0-0	M05 0-0	a30 1-0	O30 1-0	D28 3-3	M19 2-1	a15 0-1	D11 0-2	F12 1-0	J29 3-1	J22 1-0	A30 2-1	a02 1-3	

Season 1937-38

DIVISION 3 NORTH

	ACCRINGTON S	BARROW	BRADFORD C	CARLISLE U	CHESTER	CREWE A	DARLINGTON	DONCASTER R	GATESHEAD	HALIFAX T	HARTLEPOOLS U	HULL C	LINCOLN C	NEW BRIGHTON	OLDHAM A	PORT VALE	ROCHDALE	ROTHERHAM U	SOUTHPORT	TRANMERE R	WREXHAM	YORK C
1 ACCRINGTON S		a23 2-0	S25 3-1	A28 1-4	S28 0-0	D04 3-2	N20 2-1	O09 0-1	N06 1-5	J15 3-4	S06 2-1	O23 0-2	F26 0-3	M12 3-1	M26 1-2	a09 2-1	D27 0-1	a15 0-0	F12 3-0	S11 0-1	J03 4-0	J29 1-2
2 BARROW	a25 0-0		M19 0-0	a16 4-2	a30 0-2	O02 1-0	S18 1-1	M05 1-1	S04 1-3	J08 2-1	a18 0-0	A30 1-0	m07 4-1	J01 3-0	J22 2-1	F05 3-0	O16 0-1	F19 1-0	O30 1-2	a02 2-2	D25 0-1	N13 1-2
3 BRADFORD C	F05 2-2	N06 1-0		O02 4-0	S18 2-2	M12 3-1	F26 2-1	J01 2-0	a25 1-1	F19 3-0	N20 4-1	D04 1-2	a09 2-0	a23 3-0	S15 1-1	O23 5-0	S04 3-1	J22 3-2	S01 1-1	D25 1-3	M26 2-2	a19 0-1
4 CARLISLE U	J01 3-1	D04 2-1	F12 2-0		S01 1-3	J08 5-1	M26 3-0	D25 2-2	M12 1-0	S11 5-2	D18 3-1	F26 0-1	S04 0-1	O23 1-1	N06 1-1	N20 3-1	a18 0-1	m07 0-1	O09 1-0	J29 0-0	a23 0-0	S25 2-1
5 CHESTER	m07 3-1	D18 3-1	J29 3-1	S08 1-0		a23 0-3	a09 3-2	F12 4-0	M26 2-1	A28 1-1	F26 6-0	M12 1-3	O23 1-1	N06 1-2	N20 3-3	D04 7-2	O09 4-1	D25 2-3	S25 2-1	J15 1-1	a15 2-1	S11 4-3
6 CREWE A	a16 3-1	F12 4-0	O30 3-1	a09 4-1	a06 1-0		J22 2-2	O16 0-0	J01 1-3	a02 4-0	D27 2-0	S15 0-1	a15 2-0	S01 1-0	S04 0-1	S18 1-2	F05 5-1	a30 3-1	M05 5-0	N13 1-0	O09 1-1	M19 4-2
7 DARLINGTON	a02 3-0	J29 0-1	O16 4-2	N13 3-1	a27 2-1	S11 0-1		a30 1-1	S15 1-2	M19 3-0	F12 2-0	D25 1-3	O09 1-4	a18 1-0	S01 1-0	J15 2-2	D11 2-4	a16 2-1	A28 1-1	O30 0-2	S25 5-3	M16 2-2
8 DONCASTER R	F19 5-1	O23 1-0	A28 4-0	D27 1-3	O02 2-1	F26 0-0	D18 4-0		D04 1-0	a15 2-2	N06 3-3	N20 2-1	M26 3-0	a09 3-0	a23 1-0	S11 3-2	S18 5-0	F05 0-1	J15 3-0	m07 1-1	M12 2-0	m02 2-1
9 GATESHEAD	M19 1-0	J15 6-0	a30 3-0	O30 2-1	N13 3-1	A28 2-0	m07 5-2	a16 2-3		M05 4-1	J29 2-1	F12 3-2	S25 1-1	O09 3-1	a18 0-0	S08 2-1	J08 3-1	a02 0-0	m02 5-0	O16 2-1	S11 2-2	D25 2-2
10 HALIFAX T	S04 1-2	a09 1-1	O09 0-2	J22 0-0	J01 1-1	N20 2-1	N06 1-0	a18 0-1	O23 2-0		a23 0-0	S18 1-0	a25 2-0	F26 2-0	M12 2-1	M26 2-1	S13 2-3	A30 1-3	D27 1-1	S25 1-0	D04 0-0	F14 2-2
11 HARTLEPOOLS U	S01 2-0	a15 1-1	a02 1-1	a30 4-1	O16 0-1	D25 2-2	O02 2-1	M19 0-0	S18 1-3	m04 2-0		S04 2-2	J01 2-0	F02 1-0	F05 2-0	F19 2-1	O30 3-3	M05 4-0	N13 1-2	a16 2-2	m07 2-0	J12 0-0
12 HULL C	M05 0-0	S06 4-0	a16 2-2	O16 2-1	O30 2-2	m07 1-1	D27 4-0	a02 2-1	O02 3-1	J29 0-1	J15 4-0		S11 1-1	F05 1-1	F19 4-1	a18 0-0	N13 4-1	M19 1-1	J13 10-1	a30 0-1	A28 3-2	a25 3-1
13 LINCOLN C	O16 2-0	S13 5-0	J26 4-0	J15 0-1	M05 1-1	a18 3-2	F19 0-0	N13 2-2	F05 3-2	a30 2-0	A28 2-1	J22 2-1		S18 4-1	O02 0-1	D27 1-0	M19 2-0	O30 5-0	a02 1-3	m02 0-1	S06 7-1	a16 2-0
14 NEW BRIGHTON	O30 2-1	A28 2-1	a11 1-1	M05 5-1	M19 4-0	S08 4-0	a15 3-0	J12 1-2	F19 4-1	O16 2-0	S11 4-1	S25 0-0	J29 0-1		m04 1-0	m07 1-1	a02 2-0	N13 2-3	a16 2-2	F12 0-1	J15 1-1	a30 2-1
15 OLDHAM A	N13 1-0	S11 0-0	m07 1-2	M19 3-0	D11 3-2	J15 0-0	S06 3-0	F01 2-1	a15 3-1	O30 2-1	S25 3-1	O09 1-1	F12 2-2	a25 2-1		A28 3-0	a16 4-2	J08 3-1	a30 2-0	M05 2-1	J29 2-0	O16 6-2
16 PORT VALE	J08 4-1	S25 4-0	M05 4-3	a02 2-2	a16 2-2	J29 1-1	S04 1-0	J22 1-1	A30 2-2	N13 0-2	O09 5-1	a15 2-4	D28 1-0	S13 3-2	J01 2-2		a30 4-1	J03 0-0	O16 1-1	M19 1-0	F12 2-0	O30 3-2
17 ROCHDALE	D25 0-1	F26 3-3	J15 2-0	a15 3-1	F19 4-0	S25 1-4	a23 1-1	J29 4-5	a09 2-2	m07 1-1	M12 2-2	M26 0-0	N06 0-1	N20 2-1	D04 1-1	D18 1-1		O02 2-0	S11 3-2	S07 0-0	O23 6-1	A28 0-0
18 ROTHERHAM U	a18 1-1	O09 3-0	S11 2-1	S13 0-1	D27 4-1	D18 1-0	D04 4-2	S25 2-2	N20 1-1	S06 4-1	O23 3-1	N06 2-2	M12 4-0	M26 1-2	a09 2-1	a23 3-2	F12 1-0		J29 1-1	A28 2-1	F26 1-1	J15 3-0
19 SOUTHPORT	O02 2-1	M12 2-0	S06 2-0	F19 1-1	F05 2-2	O23 3-1	J01 1-1	S04 1-3	a23 0-0	D25 2-2	M26 2-0	a09 2-1	N20 1-1	D04 0-0	D18 2-2	F26 1-0	J22 2-0	S18 0-3		a15 1-3	N06 1-2	S14 2-3
20 TRANMERE R	J22 5-0	N20 3-0	D27 2-1	S18 5-0	S04 0-0	M26 2-2	M12 1-1	S13 2-0	F26 4-2	F05 2-0	D04 4-0	D18 3-1	a23 2-0	O02 5-2	O23 1-1	N06 2-1	A30 3-2	J01 0-2	a18 7-2		a09 3-2	O09 1-2
21 WREXHAM	a30 2-0	D27 3-2	N13 2-1	a25 0-0	a18 3-1	F19 1-0	F05 4-0	O30 2-0	J22 0-0	a16 2-0	S13 6-3	J01 0-1	S01 1-0	S04 0-1	S18 1-0	O02 0-0	M05 2-1	O16 2-0	M19 4-1	J12 1-3		a02 1-1
22 YORK C	S18 1-1	M26 1-2	a15 3-1	F05 3-1	J26 4-0	N06 1-2	O23 1-2	S01 2-0	D27 5-1	O02 1-1	a09 1-0	a23 0-1	D04 3-1	D18 3-1	F26 0-0	F12 2-2	J01 0-5	S04 4-1	m07 1-2	F19 2-0	N20 2-1	

DIVISION 3 SOUTH

	ALDERSHOT	BOURNEMOUTH	BRIGHTON & HA	BRISTOL C	BRISTOL R	CARDIFF C	CLAPTON O	CRYSTAL P	EXETER C	GILLINGHAM	MANSFIELD T	MILLWALL	NEWPORT CO	NORTHAMPTON T	NOTTS CO	Q.P.R.	READING	SOUTHEND U	SWINDON T	TORQUAY U	WALSALL	WATFORD
1 ALDERSHOT		a16 2-0	M23 1-2	S18 1-1	M19 0-2	J12 1-1	O16 1-2	J01 1-0	F19 0-1	O02 2-0	O30 1-0	D27 2-1	J22 5-0	N13 0-2	S04 0-1	a30 1-0	S01 0-0	a15 1-0	m07 1-1	M05 1-0	a02 1-0	F05 1-0
2 BOURNEMOUTH	D04 3-0		J22 0-0	M12 0-0	m07 1-3	S25 3-0	S01 2-1	S18 1-0	N20 2-2	M26 2-0	a15 5-4	a23 0-3	O23 1-1	O09 0-0	F26 1-1	S04 1-1	D18 1-1	J01 7-1	a09 1-2	D25 0-0	F12 5-0	N06 0-0
3 BRIGHTON & H.A.	a23 2-1	S11 3-1		N06 1-1	O09 3-0	J29 2-1	D27 2-1	F26 2-1	a09 6-0	N20 1-0	S15 2-0	D18 1-0	M12 1-0	F12 1-2	O23 0-1	J01 3-1	S04 1-1	S01 3-1	D04 3-1	a15 1-1	S25 1-0	M26 1-2
4 BRISTOL C	J29 3-1	O30 2-1	M19 1-1		a30 0-0	M05 0-1	J08 2-0	O09 0-0	J15 4-1	A28 3-1	a27 2-1	S25 0-0	a15 0-0	D27 1-0	m07 3-1	N13 2-0	F12 1-0	a02 4-2	S11 1-1	a16 2-0	O16 3-1	S08 3-1
5 BRISTOL R	N06 0-1	S14 2-1	F19 0-0	D28 1-0		a18 2-1	S18 3-2	a09 1-0	O23 1-1	F26 2-1	S04 0-0	M26 0-2	a23 2-0	A31 0-0	D04 1-1	O02 1-1	N20 2-2	F05 2-1	M12 1-2	J22 2-0	D25 5-2	J01 0-2
6 CARDIFF C	a09 0-1	F05 3-0	S18 4-1	O23 0-0	a15 1-1		J01 2-0	D18 4-2	M26 1-1	N06 4-0	D27 4-1	D04 3-2	F26 3-1	S13 4-1	O02 2-2	J22 2-2	a23 4-1	S04 5-0	N20 2-2	A30 5-2	O09 3-1	M12 1-1
7 CLAPTON O	F26 2-1	S09 3-0	D28 0-3	a09 0-0	J29 1-0	A28 1-1		N06 0-2	D18 2-1	a23 3-0	S25 1-2	O23 2-1	N20 0-2	S11 1-0	M26 2-0	a15 1-1	M12 1-1	m07 1-1	O09 1-0	F12 2-0	J15 2-2	D04 1-1
8 CRYSTAL P	A28 1-1	J29 0-1	O16 3-2	F19 1-1	J19 3-2	a30 1-0	M19 1-0		D28 2-2	a15 3-0	a02 4-0	J15 0-0	O02 3-0	a16 0-1	F05 3-1	M05 4-0	S11 3-1	O30 2-1	S08 0-1	N13 4-1	M16 3-1	S15 4-1
9 EXETER C	O09 0-1	a02 3-1	J12 4-0	S04 3-2	M05 0-0	N13 2-1	a30 2-0	D27 2-2		S18 3-5	O16 4-0	m07 1-5	J01 2-0	O30 4-1	S01 0-3	a16 0-4	a18 0-2	M30 1-1	F12 0-0	F05 2-0	M19 3-2	J22 1-2
10 GILLINGHAM	F12 2-0	N13 0-2	a02 1-1	J01 1-0	O16 0-1	M19 1-0	F23 1-2	a18 2-4	J29 2-1		J22 0-0	O09 2-3	S01 1-0	M05 2-1	M16 2-1	J08 1-5	S15 1-2	a16 2-1	S25 0-0	a30 1-1	O30 3-0	S04 0-0
11 MANSFIELD T	M12 2-0	a18 3-2	m07 1-1	a23 3-5	J15 1-0	D25 3-0	F05 3-1	N20 2-0	F26 2-3	S11 3-1		N06 1-1	D04 1-1	A28 4-1	a09 1-2	F19 3-2	M26 5-1	O02 2-2	O23 2-0	S18 1-1	S08 3-1	D18 0-1
12 MILLWALL	a04 4-0	a25 4-0	a30 2-0	F05 0-3	N13 2-1	a16 1-0	M05 3-0	S04 2-2	S13 2-1	F19 5-0	M19 1-0		S18 4-0	a02 3-0	J24 5-0	A30 1-4	J01 1-1	O16 1-0	a15 0-2	O30 7-0	S20 4-0	O02 1-1
13 NEWPORT CO	S11 4-0	M05 1-1	O30 1-0	a18 0-0	m05 2-2	O16 1-1	a02 3-1	F12 0-0	A28 2-2	S09 2-0	a16 1-0	J29 3-1		a30 0-0	O09 3-0	M19 1-1	S25 2-2	N13 2-0	J15 2-0	J13 0-2	m07 1-2	D27 0-0
14 NORTHAMPTON T	M26 1-0	F19 1-3	O02 3-1	a19 1-0	S06 2-0	m07 0-0	J22 2-0	F03 1-1	M12 1-0	O23 4-1	J01 3-0	N20 0-1	D18 2-0		a23 2-0	F05 0-2	a09 2-2	S18 0-2	N06 1-0	S04 0-3	a18 1-1	F26 3-2
15 NOTTS CO	J15 1-0	O16 1-2	M05 0-3	S22 2-0	a16 1-1	F12 2-0	N13 1-0	S25 0-1	S08 0-0	D27 1-0	O07 2-0	S11 1-1	F19 1-1	D11 5-0		O30 2-2	J29 2-1	M19 0-2	A28 3-0	a02 0-0	a30 3-1	a18 1-2
16 Q.P.R.	D18 3-0	J15 1-2	A28 2-1	M26 0-2	F12 4-0	S11 2-1	a18 3-2	O23 1-0	D04 4-0	a09 2-0	O09 1-1	S09 0-2	N06 0-0	S25 1-1	M12 2-1		F26 3-0	D25 1-0	a23 3-0	m07 6-3	J29 3-1	N20 2-0
17 READING	S08 3-2	a30 4-1	J15 2-1	O02 0-1	a02 4-0	m04 0-0	O30 2-0	J22 3-2	a15 1-0	m07 2-0	N13 3-2	A28 1-0	F05 2-1	J08 4-3	S18 0-2	O16 1-0		M05 3-2	D25 2-1	M19 1-1	a16 2-1	F19 4-1
18 SOUTHEND U	a18 4-1	A28 1-0	S08 2-1	N20 5-0	S25 1-1	J15 3-1	S15 1-2	M12 2-2	a23 1-1	D04 2-0	F12 0-1	F26 1-2	M26 0-2	J29 4-2	N06 2-1	D27 2-1	O23 4-2		D18 0-0	O09 5-1	S11 1-0	a09 2-2
19 SWINDON T	S15 2-0	J26 1-0	a16 0-1	m04 2-3	O30 2-1	a02 2-0	F19 1-0	S01 4-0	O02 3-0	F05 3-0	M05 3-3	a18 1-2	S04 3-2	M19 1-0	J01 1-0	D28 1-3	D27 0-0	a30 1-1		O16 1-0	N13 1-1	S18 0-2
20 TORQUAY U	O23 1-5	D27 0-0	a18 0-1	D04 1-3	S11 4-1	S08 0-1	O02 3-1	M26 0-0	S25 2-1	D18 1-0	J29 0-1	M12 1-1	a09 0-0	J15 1-2	N20 0-3	S15 0-2	N06 3-2	F19 3-3	F26 1-0		A28 1-0	a23 0-1
21 WALSALL	N20 2-0	O02 2-0	F05 0-3	F26 2-8	D27 5-2	F19 1-0	S04 2-0	a23 1-1	N06 0-2	M12 3-1	m02 2-0	a09 1-1	S13 3-1	a15 1-1	D18 1-0	S18 0-3	D04 2-5	J22 1-5	M26 2-3	J01 0-0		O23 3-1
22 WATFORD	S25 5-1	M19 0-2	N13 1-1	S01 3-1	A28 4-0	O30 4-0	a16 2-0	m07 1-2	S11 0-0	J15 1-1	a30 2-0	F12 1-1	D25 3-0	O16 1-3	a15 2-0	a02 3-1	O09 4-0	J19 3-1	J29 4-0	D28 4-0	M05 2-1	

LEAGUE TABLES

DIVISION 1

	P	W	D	L	F	A	W	D	L	F	A	Pts
Arsenal	42	15	4	2	52	16	6	6	9	25	28	52
Wolves	42	11	8	2	47	21	9	3	9	25	28	51
Preston NE	42	9	9	3	34	21	7	8	6	30	23	49
Charlton A	42	14	5	2	43	14	2	9	10	22	37	46
Middlesbrough	42	12	4	5	40	26	7	4	10	32	39	46
Brentford	42	10	6	5	44	27	8	3	10	25	32	45
Bolton W	42	11	6	4	38	22	4	9	8	26	38	45
Sunderland	42	12	6	3	32	18	2	10	9	23	39	44
Leeds U	42	11	6	4	38	26	3	9	9	26	43	43
Chelsea	42	11	6	4	40	22	3	7	11	25	43	41
Liverpool	42	9	5	7	40	30	6	6	9	25	41	41
Blackpool	42	10	5	6	33	26	6	3	12	28	40	40
Derby Co	42	10	5	6	42	36	5	5	11	24	51	40
Everton	42	11	5	5	54	34	5	2	14	25	41	39
Huddersfield T	42	11	3	7	29	24	6	2	13	26	44	39
Leicester C	42	9	6	6	31	26	5	5	11	23	49	39
Stoke C	42	10	7	4	42	21	3	5	13	16	38	38
Birmingham	42	7	11	3	34	28	3	7	11	24	34	38
Portsmouth	42	11	6	4	41	22	2	6	13	21	46	38
Grimsby T	42	11	5	5	29	23	2	7	12	22	45	38
Manchester C	42	12	2	7	49	33	2	6	13	31	44	36
WBA	42	10	5	6	46	36	4	3	14	28	55	36

DIVISION 2

	P	W	D	L	F	A	W	D	L	F	A	Pts
Aston Villa	42	17	2	2	50	12	8	5	8	23	23	57
Manchester U	42	15	3	3	50	18	7	6	8	32	32	53
Sheffield U	42	15	4	2	46	19	7	5	9	27	37	53
Coventry C	42	12	5	4	31	15	8	7	6	35	30	52
Tottenham H	42	14	3	4	46	16	5	3	13	30	38	44
Burnley	42	15	4	2	35	11	2	6	13	19	43	44
Bradford	42	13	4	4	51	22	4	5	12	18	34	43
Fulham	42	10	7	4	44	23	6	4	11	17	34	43
West Ham U	42	13	5	3	34	16	1	9	11	19	36	42
Bury	42	12	3	6	43	26	6	2	13	20	34	41
Chesterfield	42	12	2	7	39	24	4	7	10	24	39	41
Luton T	42	10	6	5	53	36	5	4	12	36	50	40
Plymouth A	42	10	7	4	40	30	4	5	12	17	35	40
Norwich C	42	11	5	5	35	28	3	6	12	21	47	39
Southampton	42	12	6	3	42	26	3	3	15	13	51	39
Blackburn R	42	13	6	2	51	30	1	4	16	20	50	38
Sheffield W	42	10	5	6	27	21	4	5	12	22	35	38
Swansea T	42	12	6	3	31	21	1	6	14	14	52	38
Newcastle U	42	12	4	5	38	18	2	4	15	13	40	36
Nottingham F	42	12	3	6	29	21	2	5	14	18	39	36
Barnsley	42	7	11	3	30	20	4	3	14	20	44	36
Stockport Co	42	8	6	7	24	24	3	3	15	19	46	31

DIVISION 3 North

	P	W	D	L	F	A	W	D	L	F	A	Pts
Tranmere R	42	15	4	2	57	21	8	6	7	24	20	56
Doncaster R	42	15	4	2	48	16	6	8	7	26	33	54
Hull C	42	11	8	2	51	19	9	5	7	29	24	53
Oldham A	42	16	4	1	48	18	3	9	9	19	28	51
Gateshead	42	15	5	1	53	20	5	6	10	31	39	51
Rotherham U	42	13	6	2	45	21	7	4	10	23	35	50
Lincoln C	42	14	3	4	48	17	5	5	11	18	33	46
Crewe A	42	14	3	4	47	17	4	6	11	24	36	45
Chester	42	13	4	4	54	31	3	8	10	23	41	44
Wrexham	42	14	4	3	37	15	2	7	12	21	48	43
York C	42	11	4	6	40	25	5	6	10	30	43	42
Carlisle U	42	11	5	5	35	19	4	4	13	22	48	39
New Brighton	42	12	5	4	43	18	3	3	15	17	43	38
Bradford C	42	12	6	3	46	21	2	4	15	20	48	38
Port Vale	42	11	8	2	45	27	1	6	14	20	46	38
Southport	42	8	8	5	30	26	4	6	11	23	56	38
Rochdale	42	7	10	4	38	27	6	1	14	29	51	37
Halifax T	42	9	7	5	24	19	3	5	13	20	47	36
Darlington	42	10	4	7	37	31	1	6	14	17	48	32
Hartlepools U	42	10	8	3	36	20	0	4	17	17	60	32
Barrow	42	9	6	6	28	20	2	4	15	13	51	32
Accrington S	42	9	2	10	31	32	2	5	14	14	43	29

DIVISION 3 South

	P	W	D	L	F	A	W	D	L	F	A	Pts
Millwall	42	15	3	3	53	15	8	7	6	30	22	56
Bristol C	42	14	6	1	37	13	7	7	7	31	27	55
QPR	42	15	3	3	44	17	7	6	8	36	30	53
Watford	42	14	4	3	50	15	7	7	7	23	28	53
Brighton & HA	42	15	3	3	40	16	6	6	9	24	28	51
Reading	42	17	2	2	44	21	3	9	9	27	42	51
Crystal P	42	14	4	3	45	17	4	8	9	22	30	48
Swindon T	42	12	4	5	33	19	5	6	10	16	30	44
Northampton T	42	12	4	5	30	19	5	5	11	21	38	43
Cardiff C	42	13	7	1	57	22	2	5	14	10	32	42
Notts Co	42	10	6	5	29	17	6	3	12	21	33	41
Southend U	42	12	5	4	43	23	3	5	13	27	45	40
Bournemouth	42	8	10	3	36	20	6	2	13	20	37	40
Mansfield T	42	12	5	4	46	26	3	4	14	16	41	39
Bristol R	42	10	7	4	28	20	3	6	12	18	41	39
Newport Co	42	9	10	2	31	15	2	6	13	12	37	38
Exeter C	42	10	4	7	37	32	3	8	10	20	38	38
Aldershot	42	11	4	6	23	14	4	1	16	16	45	35
Clapton O	42	10	7	4	27	19	3	0	18	15	42	33
Torquay U	42	7	5	9	22	28	2	7	12	16	45	30
Walsall	42	10	4	7	34	37	1	3	17	18	51	29
Gillingham	42	9	5	7	25	25	1	1	19	11	52	26

Football League Records

Top scorers: Div 1, T.Lawton (Everton) 35 goals; Div 2, H.Billington (Luton Town) 28 goals; Div 3(N), S.Hunt (Carlisle United) 32 goals; Div 3(S), G.Morton (Swindon Town) 28 goals.
Gillingham failed to gain re-election, Ipswich Town elected in their place. Port Vale transferred to Division Three South.

Wing-half Joe Mercer, a wing-half with a superb tactical brain who played a major part in Everton's League Championship of 1938-9.

Centre-half Bob Pryde dominated Blackburn Rovers' defence as they won the Second Division title in 1938-9.

DIVISION 1

	ARSENAL	ASTON VILLA	BIRMINGHAM	BLACKPOOL	BOLTON W	BRENTFORD	CHARLTON A	CHELSEA	DERBY CO	EVERTON	GRIMSBY T	HUDDERSFIELD T	LEEDS U	LEICESTER C	LIVERPOOL	MANCHESTER U	MIDDLESBROUGH	PORTSMOUTH	PRESTON N.E.	STOKE C	SUNDERLAND	WOLVERHAMPTON W
1 ARSENAL		S24 0-0	D03 3-1	a10 2-1	M04 3-1	m06 2-0	J21 2-0	F18 1-0	S14 1-2	S10 1-2	O08 2-0	D31 1-0	N05 2-3	N19 0-0	M18 2-0	a15 2-1	a01 1-2	A27 2-0	O22 1-0	D17 4-1	F04 2-0	F01 0-0
2 ASTON VILLA	J28 1-3		M04 5-1	J14 3-1	a15 1-3	S17 5-0	D03 2-0	N19 6-2	S03 0-1	S05 0-3	D24 0-2	F15 4-0	D17 2-1	O22 1-2	F18 2-0	N05 0-2	m06 1-1	O01 2-0	a01 3-0	M18 3-0	D27 1-1	a11 2-2
3 BIRMINGHAM	a08 1-2	O29 3-0		a22 2-1	O08 0-2	D10 5-1	F04 3-4	a26 1-1	O15 3-0	N12 1-0	F25 1-1	M29 1-1	a29 4-0	S07 2-1	a10 0-0	D31 3-3	D26 2-1	N26 2-0	S24 1-3	S10 1-2	A27 1-2	M11 3-2
4 BLACKPOOL	a07 1-0	S10 2-4	D17 2-1		M18 0-0	S19 4-1	N05 0-0	O08 5-1	F04 2-2	A27 0-2	S24 3-1	D26 1-1	N19 1-2	D03 1-1	a01 1-1	F18 3-5	a15 4-0	m06 2-1	M08 2-1	O22 1-1	J25 1-1	D31 1-0
5 BOLTON W	O29 1-1	D10 1-2	F22 3-0	N12 0-1		M11 1-1	A27 2-1	S05 0-2	M25 2-1	O15 4-2	N26 1-1	F25 3-2	J14 2-2	J28 4-0	S17 3-1	a29 0-0	O01 4-1	D31 5-1	a26 0-2	J02 1-3	a08 2-1	a22 0-0
6 BRENTFORD	S08 1-0	F08 2-4	a15 0-1	a29 1-1	N05 2-2		M04 1-0	O22 1-0	O08 1-3	D31 2-0	F04 1-2	A27 2-1	M18 0-1	a01 2-0	N19 2-1	D17 2-5	D03 2-1	F22 2-0	a07 3-1	F18 1-0	S24 2-3	S10 0-1
7 CHARLTON A	D26 1-0	a08 1-0	O01 4-4	M11 3-1	D24 2-1	O29 1-1		a07 2-0	N12 1-0	a22 2-1	M29 3-1	O15 2-1	S03 2-0	S17 1-0	J14 1-3	F11 7-1	J28 3-0	F25 3-3	m06 3-1	A29 4-2	N26 3-0	D10 0-4
8 CHELSEA	O15 4-2	M25 2-1	S17 2-2	m15 1-1	m06 1-1	F25 1-3	a10 1-3		O29 0-2	a08 0-2	M11 5-1	D10 3-0	D27 2-2	S03 3-0	D24 4-1	J28 0-1	J14 4-2	a22 1-0	A31 3-1	O01 1-1	N12 4-0	N26 1-3
9 DERBY CO	a29 1-2	D31 2-1	F18 0-1	O01 2-1	N19 3-0	F11 1-2	M18 3-1	M08 0-1		D27 2-1	F01 4-1	A31 1-0	a01 1-0	a15 1-1	D03 2-2	O22 5-1	D17 1-4	a10 0-1	N05 2-0	S24 5-0	S10 1-0	A27 2-2
10 EVERTON	J14 2-0	a29 3-0	M18 4-2	D24 4-0	F18 2-1	S03 2-1	D17 1-4	D03 4-1	D26 2-2		A31 3-0	J28 3-2	O22 4-0	M08 4-0	O01 2-1	N19 3-0	N05 4-0	S17 5-1	a15 0-0	a01 1-1	a10 6-2	O08 1-0
11 GRIMSBY T	F21 2-1	A27 1-2	O22 1-0	J28 2-0	a01 1-1	O01 0-0	N19 1-1	N05 2-1	S17 1-1	m06 3-0		a07 3-3	D03 3-2	D17 6-1	a15 2-1	S10 1-0	F18 0-2	S06 2-1	M18 1-1	M07 3-1	D31 1-3	D26 2-4
12 HUDDERSFIELD T	S03 1-1	O08 1-1	N19 3-1	D27 3-0	O22 2-1	D24 1-2	F18 4-0	a15 3-1	S07 3-0	S24 3-0	a11 2-0		S17 0-1	N05 2-0	M15 1-1	a01 1-1	M18 0-1	J14 3-0	D17 3-0	D03 1-4	S14 0-1	F04 1-2
13 LEEDS U	M11 4-2	a22 2-0	A31 2-0	M25 1-0	S10 1-2	N12 3-2	D31 2-1	D26 1-1	N26 1-4	F25 1-2	a08 0-1	a19 2-1		O01 8-2	J28 1-1	a10 3-1	F11 0-1	O29 2-2	A27 2-1	m06 0-0	D10 3-3	O15 1-0
14 LEICESTER C	M25 0-2	F25 1-1	S12 2-1	a08 3-4	S24 0-0	N26 1-1	F09 1-5	D31 3-2	D10 2-3	O29 3-0	a22 0-2	M11 0-1	F04 2-0		O08 2-2	D27 1-1	a11 5-3	N21 5-0	S10 2-1	A27 2-2	O15 0-2	m04 0-2
15 LIVERPOOL	N12 2-2	O15 3-0	a07 4-0	N26 1-0	J25 1-2	M25 1-0	S10 1-0	A27 2-1	a08 2-1	F04 0-3	D10 2-2	O29 3-3	S24 3-0	M04 1-1		S07 1-0	S14 3-1	M11 4-4	D31 4-1	D27 1-0	a22 1-1	F25 0-2
16 MANCHESTER U	D10 1-0	M11 1-1	S03 4-1	O15 0-0	A31 2-2	a22 3-0	O08 0-2	S24 5-1	F25 1-1	M29 0-2	J14 3-1	N26 1-1	a07 0-0	D26 3-0	m06 2-0		D24 1-1	a08 1-1	F04 1-1	J21 0-1	O29 0-1	N12 1-3
17 MIDDLESBROUGH	N26 1-1	A31 1-1	D27 2-2	D10 9-2	F04 1-2	a08 3-1	S24 4-0	S10 1-1	a22 2-0	M11 4-4	O15 3-2	N12 4-1	O08 1-2	a10 3-2	J02 3-0	A27 3-1		M29 8-2	J25 2-2	D31 5-1	F25 3-0	O29 1-0
18 PORTSMOUTH	D24 0-0	F04 0-0	a01 2-0	A31 1-0	S03 2-1	D27 2-2	O22 0-2	D17 2-1	a07 1-3	F01 0-1	a19 2-1	S10 4-0	M08 2-0	M18 0-1	N05 1-1	D03 0-0	N19 1-1		F18 0-0	a15 2-0	O08 2-1	S24 1-0
19 PRESTON N.E.	F25 2-1	N26 3-2	J28 5-0	O29 1-1	D27 2-2	a10 2-0	S05 2-0	a29 1-1	M11 4-1	D10 0-1	N12 1-1	a22 3-0	D24 2-0	J14 2-1	S03 1-0	O01 1-1	S17 3-1	O15 2-2		F15 1-1	M25 2-1	a08 4-2
20 STOKE C	a22 1-0	N12 3-1	J14 6-3	F25 1-1	a10 4-1	O15 3-2	a29 1-0	F04 6-1	J28 3-0	N26 0-0	O29 1-2	a08 2-2	S05 1-1	D24 1-0	D26 3-1	S17 1-1	S03 1-3	D10 1-1	O08 3-1		M11 3-1	M29 5-3
21 SUNDERLAND	O01 0-0	D26 1-5	D24 1-0	S17 1-2	D03 2-2	J28 1-1	a01 1-1	M18 3-2	J14 1-0	a07 1-2	S03 1-1	a29 0-0	a15 2-1	F18 2-0	D17 2-3	M04 5-2	O22 1-2	M15 0-2	N19 1-2	N05 3-0		S07 1-1
22 WOLVERHAMPTON W	S17 0-1	a10 2-1	N05 2-1	S03 1-1	D17 1-1	J14 5-2	a15 3-1	a01 2-0	D24 0-0	F22 7-0	D27 5-0	O01 3-0	F18 4-1	A29 0-0	O22 2-2	M18 3-0	M08 6-1	J28 3-0	D03 3-0	N19 3-0	m06 0-0	

DIVISION 2

	BLACKBURN R	BRADFORD	BURNLEY	BURY	CHESTERFIELD	COVENTRY C	FULHAM	LUTON T	MANCHESTER C	MILLWALL	NEWCASTLE U	NORWICH C	NOTTINGHAM F	PLYMOUTH A	SHEFFIELD U	SHEFFIELD W	SOUTHAMPTON	SWANSEA T	TOTTENHAM H	TRANMERE R	W.B.A.	WEST HAM U
1 BLACKBURN R		J23 6-4	F18 1-0	D26 1-0	D31 3-0	N05 0-2	a10 2-1	M16 2-0	S24 3-3	F04 3-1	N19 3-0	D03 6-0	M18 3-2	D17 4-0	O08 1-2	J02 2-4	a15 3-0	S10 4-0	O22 3-1	A27 3-2	a01 3-0	S19 3-1
2 BRADFORD	S17 0-4		N05 2-2	F11 3-2	D26 0-0	a01 0-2	J28 1-5	F18 2-1	S03 4-2	J14 1-0	M04 0-1	D24 3-0	D03 1-2	O22 2-2	a15 0-3	O01 3-1	N19 2-1	A29 1-1	M18 0-0	S19 3-0	D17 4-4	a11 1-2
3 BURNLEY	O15 3-2	M11 0-0		O29 0-1	M25 1-2	D24 1-0	S05 2-0	O01 3-2	D10 1-1	F25 2-0	J14 2-0	J28 3-0	S03 2-1	F11 1-0	a07 2-3	a22 1-2	A30 2-1	N12 1-1	D26 1-0	N26 3-1	S17 0-3	a08 1-0
4 BURY	D27 2-4	O08 0-1	M04 1-0		S24 3-1	F18 5-0	A29 0-2	N19 2-5	a07 1-5	J02 1-1	a15 1-1	M18 2-3	O22 2-1	a01 3-0	D03 2-2	D24 2-3	S03 5-2	F04 4-0	D17 3-1	J21 5-0	N05 3-3	S10 1-1
5 CHESTERFIELD	S03 0-2	D27 2-2	N19 3-2	J28 2-1		M04 3-0	a24 0-1	a15 1-2	A29 0-3	D24 3-0	a07 2-0	O22 2-0	D17 7-1	N05 3-1	M18 1-0	S17 3-1	D03 6-1	m06 6-1	a01 3-1	F11 3-0	F18 3-1	O01 1-0
6 COVENTRY C	M11 0-1	N26 3-1	A27 1-1	O15 0-0	O29 2-0		D10 3-1	S05 1-0	M25 0-1	N12 2-1	O01 1-0	a11 2-0	J28 5-1	D26 1-2	a29 0-3	F25 1-0	S10 3-0	a08 3-0	D31 4-0	a22 2-0	F11 1-1	a24 0-0
7 FULHAM	a07 2-3	S24 4-0	S12 0-0	a29 1-2	S10 2-0	a15 1-0		D03 2-1	F04 2-1	O08 2-1	M18 1-1	a01 2-0	N05 2-2	M04 1-2	D17 1-2	a17 2-2	O22 1-1	J23 1-0	F18 1-0	D31 1-0	N19 3-0	A27 3-2
8 LUTON T	O29 1-1	O15 2-2	F04 1-0	M25 2-1	D10 5-0	m06 1-3	a08 2-1		J14 3-0	a22 0-0	A31 2-1	S03 2-1	D27 1-0	J21 3-4	S24 2-0	N26 1-5	a07 6-2	F25 6-3	O08 0-0	M11 3-0	D24 3-1	N12 1-2
9 MANCHESTER C	J28 3-2	D31 5-1	a15 2-0	a10 0-0	a29 3-1	N19 3-0	O01 3-5	S10 1-2		S17 1-6	D03 4-1	D17 4-1	a01 3-0	F18 1-3	O22 3-2	a26 1-1	M18 2-1	A27 5-0	N05 2-0	D27 5-2	M04 3-3	S07 2-4
10 MILLWALL	O01 4-1	S10 3-1	O22 1-1	S05 0-0	A27 3-1	M18 0-0	F11 1-1	D17 2-1	M13 3-1		a01 1-1	M04 6-0	N19 5-0	S24 3-0	F18 4-0	a07 2-0	N05 0-1	D31 1-1	a15 2-0	a29 2-1	D03 1-5	M27 0-2
11 NEWCASTLE U	M25 2-2	O29 1-0	S10 3-2	D10 6-0	J02 0-1	F04 0-4	N12 2-1	a29 2-0	a08 0-2	N26 2-2		D27 4-0	O08 4-0	A27 2-1	D31 0-0	M11 2-1	S24 1-0	a22 1-2	M01 0-1	O15 5-1	S14 5-1	F25 2-0
12 NORWICH C	a08 4-0	A27 1-3	S24 4-0	N12 3-1	F25 2-0	a10 1-1	N26 3-3	D31 2-1	a22 0-0	O29 0-2	M16 1-1		m06 1-0	S10 2-1	F02 1-2	M25 2-2	O08 2-1	O15 3-0	F04 1-2	D10 2-0	S01 2-3	M11 2-6
13 NOTTINGHAM F	N12 1-3	a08 2-0	D31 2-2	F25 1-1	a22 0-1	S24 3-0	M11 1-1	D26 2-4	N26 3-4	M25 3-0	F15 2-0	S07 1-0		a29 2-1	A27 0-2	D10 3-3	F08 0-2	O29 1-2	S10 2-1	F04 2-2	a07 2-0	O15 0-0
14 PLYMOUTH A	a22 1-0	F25 4-1	O08 1-0	N26 0-1	M11 0-0	D27 0-2	O29 0-0	S17 4-1	O15 0-0	J28 2-2	D24 0-1	m03 1-0	A31 3-0		F04 0-1	a08 1-1	m06 2-0	D10 0-0	a10 0-1	N12 3-1	S03 2-1	M25 0-0
15 SHEFFIELD U	a26 0-0	D10 3-1	J02 1-1	a08 1-1	N12 1-1	A29 0-0	a22 2-0	J28 2-2	F25 1-0	O15 2-1	S03 0-0	S17 4-0	D24 0-1	O01 0-1		O29 0-0	D26 5-1	M11 1-2	m06 6-1	M25 2-0	J14 1-1	N26 3-1
16 SHEFFIELD W	S08 3-0	F04 2-0	D17 4-1	A27 2-0	M20 0-0	O22 2-2	D27 5-1	a01 4-1	O08 3-1	a10 3-1	N05 0-2	N19 7-0	a15 1-1	D03 1-2	M04 1-0		F18 2-0	S24 1-1	a29 1-0	S10 2-0	M18 2-1	D31 1-4
17 SOUTHAMPTON	D10 1-3	M25 3-2	a29 2-1	D31 0-0	a08 2-2	J14 0-2	F25 2-1	a10 0-4	N12 1-2	M11 1-1	J28 0-0	F11 3-1	S17 2-2	S14 2-1	D27 2-2	O15 4-3		N26 4-1	A27 1-2	O29 3-1	O01 2-1	a22 0-2
18 SWANSEA T	J14 2-1	a29 2-2	M18 4-0	O01 3-3	S05 1-1	D03 2-4	S17 1-1	O22 2-3	D24 2-0	S03 1-1	D17 0-1	F18 0-1	M04 1-0	a15 2-1	N05 1-2	J28 0-1	a01 1-3		N19 1-1	a10 1-0	D27 3-2	F16 3-2
19 TOTTENHAM H	F25 4-3	N12 2-2	D27 1-0	a22 4-3	N26 2-2	S03 2-1	O15 1-0	F11 0-1	M11 2-3	D10 4-0	S17 1-0	O01 4-1	J14 4-1	a07 1-0	S12 2-2	A29 3-3	D24 1-1	M25 3-0		a08 3-1	J28 2-2	O29 2-1
20 TRANMERE R	D24 1-1	J02 2-1	a01 0-3	S17 3-0	O08 0-1	D17 1-2	S03 0-1	N05 2-3	D26 3-9	A29 2-0	F18 0-3	a15 0-1	O01 1-1	M18 2-0	N19 0-2	J14 1-4	M04 1-1	a07 2-0	D03 0-2		O22 3-1	J28 2-2
21 W.B.A.	N26 2-0	a22 0-2	F01 1-2	M11 6-0	O15 1-0	O08 3-1	M25 3-0	A27 3-0	O29 3-1	a08 0-0	S07 5-2	a29 4-2	a10 0-0	D31 4-2	S10 3-4	N12 5-1	F04 2-0	a19 0-0	S24 4-3	F25 2-0		D10 3-2
22 WEST HAM U	A29 1-2	a07 0-2	D03 1-0	J14 0-0	F04 1-1	S17 4-1	D24 1-0	M18 0-1	m06 2-1	D27 0-0	O22 1-1	N05 2-0	F18 5-0	N19 2-1	a01 0-0	S03 2-3	D17 1-2	O08 5-2	M04 0-2	S24 6-1	a15 2-1	

Season 1938-39

DIVISION 3 NORTH

	ACCRINGTON S	BARNSLEY	BARROW	BRADFORD C	CARLISLE U	CHESTER	CREWE A	DARLINGTON	DONCASTER R	GATESHEAD	HALIFAX T	HARTLEPOOLS U	HULL C	LINCOLN C	NEW BRIGHTON	OLDHAM A	ROCHDALE	ROTHERHAM U	SOUTHPORT	STOCKPORT CO	WREXHAM	YORK C
1 ACCRINGTON S		D27 0-2	J14 0-2	J28 2-3	O29 1-1	S17 2-3	F25 2-1	M11 3-0	a10 0-0	M25 1-1	D24 1-2	N12 0-0	O01 1-1	F11 3-4	S03 1-2	S27 1-3	D10 0-5	a22 2-1	O15 1-4	a29 3-2	J07 3-1	a08 3-1
2 BARNSLEY	D26 4-1		S17 4-0	O01 5-2	M11 3-0	J28 3-0	O29 5-2	N12 7-1	O15 1-1	D10 2-0	S03 1-0	M25 2-0	F11 5-1	a29 4-0	J14 1-1	D24 3-0	a22 2-0	S05 2-0	F25 3-1	a10 0-1	a08 2-1	N26 1-0
3 BARROW	S10 2-3	J21 1-2		D26 2-1	a08 5-0	a10 0-1	J07 1-2	F13 2-0	N12 4-4	a29 1-1	F04 0-0	a22 1-1	S05 3-1	A27 2-2	O08 3-0	S24 2-0	O29 3-1	D10 4-1	M25 4-0	D31 0-2	O15 4-0	F25 2-0
4 BRADFORD C	S24 2-1	F04 0-2	D27 3-0		a22 2-0	S05 1-0	M22 4-1	A27 6-2	M15 2-1	F25 1-1	S12 1-0	O15 0-1	D31 6-2	S10 3-0	a10 3-3	O08 1-4	N12 3-0	M25 5-2	a08 2-1	J25 4-0	O29 4-0	D10 6-0
5 CARLISLE U	M04 6-4	N05 3-1	D03 3-0	D17 0-2		a15 1-3	S17 1-0	D31 1-1	O01 2-3	S08 2-2	N19 1-2	A27 2-0	S10 1-2	F18 4-3	a01 1-1	M18 2-0	a29 5-1	F11 3-1	J28 1-1	O22 3-2	D27 1-1	a07 1-3
6 CHESTER	F15 1-0	S24 2-1	a07 1-2	m06 3-2	M01 6-1		a08 4-0	a22 0-0	M25 0-4	O15 2-2	O08 5-1	D27 8-2	A27 1-1	D31 0-0	A31 1-3	F04 4-2	M11 0-0	N12 1-4	a26 2-0	S10 4-3	F25 4-2	O29 5-1
7 CREWE A	O22 2-1	M04 0-0	a01 1-1	a15 0-0	J21 7-1	D03 0-2		S10 2-0	F11 1-2	A27 3-2	M18 2-2	D31 3-2	D17 0-1	S24 6-0	N19 7-1	N05 1-2	a07 4-1	a29 0-0	O01 4-2	F18 2-1	S05 1-0	D27 8-2
8 DARLINGTON	N05 3-0	M18 0-1	a15 3-1	D24 0-4	S03 2-1	D17 3-3	J14 1-0		J28 1-2	D27 5-2	a01 1-0	S07 3-0	F18 0-1	O22 3-1	D03 3-0	N19 3-3	F11 1-2	O01 3-1	S17 0-2	M04 4-3	a07 3-1	a29 1-2
9 DONCASTER R	a07 7-1	F18 1-3	M18 1-1	a20 1-2	F04 1-0	N19 4-1	O08 1-2	S24 4-1		S10 2-3	M04 0-0	J26 3-1	D03 1-0	a15 4-1	N05 4-1	O22 3-2	S12 5-0	D26 1-1	A29 0-0	D17 3-1	D31 0-0	A27 1-0
10 GATESHEAD	N19 4-1	a01 1-1	A31 2-1	O22 0-0	m06 1-1	F18 3-0	D24 0-5	D26 0-2	J14 2-0		a15 2-0	a10 2-0	M04 2-2	N05 4-0	D17 0-3	D03 2-0	J28 2-2	S17 7-1	S03 0-0	M18 4-1	F11 5-1	O01 2-3
11 HALIFAX T	A27 2-0	D31 1-4	O01 1-0	A29 2-2	M25 5-1	F11 1-1	N12 0-0	J09 1-1	O29 0-0	a24 3-3		a08 2-0	a10 1-0	D26 2-0	J28 3-1	S10 0-0	O15 2-1	F25 1-1	M11 1-1	S05 3-3	a22 0-2	J21 2-1
12 HARTLEPOOLS U	M18 2-1	N19 0-1	D17 1-2	F18 1-3	D24 2-1	D26 2-5	S03 0-1	S14 3-0	S17 1-3	a07 3-1	D03 1-0		O22 3-3	M04 2-1	a15 3-2	a01 0-0	O01 4-2	J28 1-1	J14 0-2	N05 4-2	m06 0-0	F11 3-2
13 HULL C	F04 6-1	O08 0-1	S12 4-0	S03 3-2	J14 11-1	D24 3-0	a22 2-1	O15 3-2	a08 0-0	O29 1-0	a07 1-1	F25 4-1		J21 4-2	D26 3-0	A29 0-2	M25 3-3	M09 0-2	a17 2-1	S24 4-4	M11 1-1	N12 2-0
14 LINCOLN C	O08 3-0	A29 2-4	D24 1-1	J14 4-0	O15 2-1	S03 0-3	J28 3-2	F25 3-0	m06 2-5	M11 1-0	D27 0-0	O29 2-2	S17 0-3		S12 0-0	a07 1-0	J11 2-2	a08 0-1	a22 0-1	F04 3-2	N12 8-3	M25 3-3
15 NEW BRIGHTON	D31 4-1	S10 1-2	F11 2-0	a07 2-1	D10 2-3	a29 1-3	M25 1-2	a08 3-0	M11 3-6	a22 0-1	S24 1-0	J18 5-2	D27 6-1	S07 3-2		J21 0-1	F25 3-1	O29 3-0	N12 1-1	A27 0-0	F04 2-3	O15 3-2
16 OLDHAM A	S05 2-0	A27 4-2	J28 1-0	F11 2-1	N12 6-0	O01 1-3	M11 3-0	M25 2-0	F25 0-0	a08 1-3	J14 1-0	J07 4-2	a29 4-1	a10 1-0	S17 1-0		D31 1-2	O15 2-0	O29 2-4	a17 3-1	D10 4-2	a22 6-0
17 ROCHDALE	a15 4-1	D17 2-1	M04 2-2	M18 1-1	A30 2-3	N05 5-2	a10 5-0	O08 6-1	S06 1-1	S24 5-2	F18 4-5	F04 3-4	N19 4-0	a01 4-0	O22 2-0	S03 1-2		D24 0-1	D27 5-0	D03 0-1	J21 0-0	S10 2-2
18 ROTHERHAM U	D17 2-1	S12 0-1	N05 1-2	N19 2-0	O08 4-0	M18 2-0	A29 4-1	F04 3-3	D27 0-0	J21 2-2	O22 0-1	S24 5-1	a01 0-2	D03 1-3	M04 0-0	F18 3-1	A27 7-1		a10 1-0	a15 3-2	S10 3-0	D31 2-0
19 SOUTHPORT	F18 1-0	O22 0-0	N19 4-1	D03 2-2	S24 7-1	a01 2-0	F04 1-2	J21 4-1	a29 0-4	D31 2-0	N05 1-0	S10 2-0	a15 4-0	D17 4-1	M18 1-1	M04 0-0	D26 4-1	a07 1-0		O08 3-0	A27 3-1	S06 1-1
20 STOCKPORT CO	A29 3-0	a07 1-1	S03 3-1	S17 2-0	F25 3-0	J14 0-0	O15 5-1	O29 5-2	a22 1-2	N12 3-2	m06 3-3	M11 5-0	J28 2-2	O01 3-3	D24 1-1	D27 3-1	a08 1-2	J02 5-0	F11 3-1		M25 2-1	a24 3-1
21 WREXHAM	a01 2-0	D03 1-1	F18 3-0	M04 1-1	D26 2-5	O22 3-2	S14 0-4	a10 3-1	S03 3-0	O08 2-0	D17 3-2	A29 3-0	N05 4-2	M18 1-0	O01 1-2	a15 4-1	S17 1-0	J14 2-0	D24 4-3	N19 2-1		J28 1-3
22 YORK C	D03 2-2	a15 2-3	O22 2-3	N05 0-1	a10 4-1	M04 2-2	D26 4-1	A31 1-1	D24 2-2	F04 1-1	S17 3-0	O08 2-0	M18 1-0	N19 1-3	F18 2-0	D17 4-1	J14 0-7	S03 0-1	m06 2-3	a01 1-2	S24 1-0	

DIVISION 3 SOUTH

	ALDERSHOT	BOURNEMOUTH	BRIGHTON & HA	BRISTOL C	BRISTOL R	CARDIFF C	CLAPTON O	CRYSTAL P	EXETER C	IPSWICH T	MANSFIELD T	NEWPORT CO	NORTHAMPTON T	NOTTS CO	PORT VALE	Q.P.R.	READING	SOUTHEND U	SWINDON T	TORQUAY U	WALSALL	WATFORD
1 ALDERSHOT		D17 2-1	F18 1-1	A31 0-1	S07 1-0	D03 1-1	S17 1-0	D27 2-1	a01 2-0	a15 3-1	N05 3-0	J28 1-0	O01 3-0	F11 0-3	a19 1-0	M18 2-0	O22 1-1	N19 1-0	S03 1-0	J14 1-1	M04 3-3	a07 1-1
2 BOURNEMOUTH	a22 4-0		a10 2-0	O15 4-0	M29 5-2	O08 0-0	M25 0-0	A27 1-1	F04 2-0	m06 0-0	S10 1-1	N12 0-1	M11 3-1	O29 3-2	M15 1-1	J21 4-2	A31 0-0	S24 0-4	a08 2-0	J18 2-5	D31 3-1	F25 1-1
3 BRIGHTON & H.A.	O15 0-3	a07 1-1		D27 1-0	a29 6-3	F04 1-2	N12 2-0	F25 0-0	S24 6-1	O08 2-0	D31 3-0	M11 0-0	O29 1-0	a22 2-0	a08 1-0	S10 3-1	S07 2-2	F08 3-0	J07 4-0	M25 2-0	A27 3-1	a26 0-0
4 BRISTOL C	a29 1-0	F18 2-0	D26 2-0		O22 2-1	a01 1-1	J28 3-1	a10 1-1	N19 4-1	D03 3-2	M04 2-0	O01 0-2	F11 0-0	S07 2-1	S03 5-1	N05 2-2	a15 5-1	M18 1-0	J14 1-1	S17 1-3	D17 2-1	D24 2-0
5 BRISTOL R	S12 0-0	D27 1-0	A30 0-1	F25 1-1		S24 1-1	M11 1-0	a17 1-2	J21 4-1	F04 3-3	A27 3-0	O29 0-0	a22 1-0	O15 0-0	J07 0-1	D31 0-0	O08 2-4	S10 4-1	M25 5-0	N12 0-1	a07 2-0	a08 1-1
6 CARDIFF C	a08 2-4	F11 5-0	O01 4-1	J11 2-1	J28 0-2		O15 1-2	M25 0-1	A27 1-2	J14 2-1	a29 0-0	D31 1-2	F25 2-0	a17 4-1	M11 2-4	D26 1-0	S17 0-1	a10 1-0	O29 2-1	a22 3-1	S05 2-1	N12 5-3
7 CLAPTON O	J21 2-0	N19 1-1	M18 2-0	S24 1-1	N05 2-1	F18 1-1		F04 4-0	a07 3-3	D17 1-1	D03 0-0	A27 1-3	D31 3-0	S10 1-1	S08 1-0	a15 2-1	M04 1-2	O22 5-0	a29 5-0	a17 3-0	a01 1-1	O08 0-0
8 CRYSTAL P	D26 3-0	D24 3-0	O22 1-0	a07 3-2	a15 0-0	N19 2-0	O01 4-2		M18 3-2	a01 3-0	D17 6-2	F11 1-1	S07 2-0	a29 5-1	J14 1-0	M04 0-1	D03 0-0	N05 4-3	S17 1-1	J28 1-3	F18 4-0	S03 2-0
9 EXETER C	J07 3-3	O01 0-0	J28 2-2	M25 1-1	S17 2-1	D24 1-1	a10 2-1	N12 4-4		S03 3-0	S07 2-0	F25 3-1	D10 3-2	a08 1-0	O29 1-3	a29 1-1	J14 3-2	D27 3-3	a22 0-0	O15 1-2	F15 3-2	M11 1-3
10 IPSWICH T	a26 7-2	S07 0-2	F11 0-0	a08 4-0	O01 0-0	S10 1-2	a22 3-0	J18 2-1	D31 2-2		D26 5-1	O15 1-4	J21 2-0	F25 0-2	N12 2-0	a10 1-0	m03 2-1	A27 4-2	M11 3-1	O29 1-0	a29 1-0	M25 5-1
11 MANSFIELD T	M11 1-0	J14 2-0	S03 4-2	O29 3-2	D24 1-3	A31 2-2	a08 1-0	a22 0-0	m06 4-2	D27 0-1		J11 0-2	M25 1-1	N12 2-0	J28 2-0	F04 2-2	a07 0-0	O08 3-1	F25 1-1	M08 4-0	S17 0-0	O15 0-0
12 NEWPORT CO	S24 1-0	M18 2-2	N05 2-0	F04 0-2	M04 2-0	S03 3-0	D24 2-1	O08 2-0	O22 0-0	F18 3-2	a01 0-0		S10 1-1	F02 2-1	a29 0-2	D03 2-0	D17 2-0	a15 3-0	D27 6-4	a07 1-0	N19 2-1	S08 1-0
13 NORTHAMPTON T	F04 5-0	N05 2-0	M04 1-4	O08 2-2	D17 2-1	O22 2-1	S03 3-0	m06 0-0	a15 0-0	S17 2-0	N19 3-4	J14 1-0		S24 2-1	D26 2-0	a01 1-0	F18 1-1	D03 2-2	a10 0-2	D24 4-1	M18 4-1	A29 2-0
14 NOTTS CO	O08 1-1	M04 0-1	D17 4-3	m06 0-0	F18 3-1	a15 1-1	J14 1-0	A31 0-1	D03 3-1	O22 2-1	M18 1-1	S17 2-0	J28 1-0		a10 4-0	N19 0-0	O01 2-0	a01 4-1	D24 2-0	S03 5-1	N05 0-0	D27 0-3
15 PORT VALE	A27 1-3	a15 2-0	D03 1-1	D31 4-0	a01 2-1	N05 1-1	m06 1-1	S10 2-0	M04 3-2	M18 0-0	S24 3-0	A29 2-1	D27 0-2	a07 3-1		F18 1-2	N19 0-2	D17 2-2	O01 2-0	F11 0-1	O22 5-1	J21 1-2
16 Q.P.R.	N12 7-0	S17 2-0	J14 1-2	M11 3-1	S03 1-1	D27 6-0	a24 1-1	O29 1-2	S01 6-0	a07 0-0	O01 3-0	a08 0-0	J09 3-0	M25 0-1	O15 2-2		D24 2-2	m06 1-1	F11 2-1	F25 1-1	J28 3-0	a22 1-0
17 READING	F25 5-0	a29 1-0	S14 3-0	D10 2-2	F11 2-0	F01 0-0	O29 2-2	a08 3-1	S10 1-1	S24 2-1	a10 0-0	J21 0-1	O15 5-1	F04 3-1	M25 2-1	A27 2-4		D31 3-0	N12 3-0	M11 3-5	D26 1-1	J11 3-2
18 SOUTHEND U	M25 2-1	J28 2-2	S17 1-1	N12 2-0	J14 3-2	a07 2-0	F25 1-0	M11 3-1	a12 0-1	a19 0-0	F11 2-0	m02 5-0	a08 2-0	a25 1-0	a22 0-0	S07 2-1	S03 2-0		O15 2-3	A31 1-1	O01 2-0	O29 3-0
19 SWINDON T	D31 2-1	D03 4-2	a01 3-2	S10 1-0	N19 2-1	M04 4-1	A31 2-0	J21 2-2	D17 2-1	N05 1-1	O22 1-2	D26 8-0	a07 1-0	A27 4-1	F04 1-1	O08 2-2	M18 4-2	F18 2-1		m06 3-1	a15 1-4	S24 3-0
20 TORQUAY U	S10 1-1	a01 2-0	N19 0-2	J21 3-1	M18 2-2	D17 1-3	D27 2-1	S24 1-2	F18 0-1	M04 1-1	a15 3-0	a10 1-1	A27 1-2	D31 0-2	O08 1-0	O22 2-3	N05 1-1	a29 2-0	S07 1-3		D03 0-1	F04 2-1
21 WALSALL	O29 2-2	S03 1-2	D24 0-2	a22 5-0	a10 2-2	m06 6-3	J12 5-1	O15 1-1	O08 1-2	A29 0-1	F02 0-0	M25 1-1	N12 1-0	M11 3-3	F25 4-0	S24 0-1	D27 3-0	F04 0-2	a24 5-0	a08 5-0		J14 2-0
22 WATFORD	a10 1-1	O22 1-0	a15 1-1	A27 2-2	D03 4-1	M18 1-0	F11 1-0	D31 4-1	N05 4-2	N19 0-0	F18 2-0	S14 1-1	a29 2-0	D26 0-1	S17 2-0	D17 4-1	a01 3-1	M04 3-0	J28 4-1	O01 0-0	S10 4-2	

LEAGUE TABLES

DIVISION 1

	P	W	D	L	F	A	W	D	L	F	A	Pts
Everton	42	17	3	1	60	18	10	2	9	28	34	59
Wolves	42	14	6	1	55	12	8	5	8	33	27	55
Charlton A	42	16	3	2	49	24	6	3	12	26	35	50
Middlesbrough	42	13	6	2	64	27	7	3	11	29	47	49
Arsenal	42	14	3	4	34	14	5	6	10	21	27	47
Derby Co	42	12	3	6	39	22	7	5	9	27	33	46
Stoke C	42	13	6	2	50	25	4	6	11	21	43	46
Bolton W	42	10	6	5	39	25	5	9	7	28	33	45
Preston NE	42	13	7	1	44	19	3	5	13	19	40	44
Grimsby T	42	11	6	4	38	26	5	5	11	23	43	43
Liverpool	42	12	6	3	40	24	2	8	11	22	39	42
Aston Villa	42	11	3	7	44	25	5	6	10	27	35	41
Leeds U	42	11	5	5	40	27	5	4	12	19	40	41
Manchester U	42	7	9	5	30	20	4	7	10	27	45	38
Blackpool	42	9	8	4	37	26	3	6	12	19	42	38
Sunderland	42	7	7	7	30	29	6	5	10	24	38	38
Portsmouth	42	10	7	4	25	15	2	6	13	22	55	37
Brentford	42	11	2	8	30	27	3	6	12	23	47	36
Huddersfield T	42	11	4	6	38	18	1	7	13	20	46	35
Chelsea	42	10	5	6	43	29	2	4	15	21	51	33
Birmingham	42	10	5	6	40	27	2	3	16	22	57	32
Leicester C	42	7	6	8	35	35	2	5	14	13	47	29

DIVISION 2

	P	W	D	L	F	A	W	D	L	F	A	Pts
Blackburn R	42	17	1	3	59	23	8	4	9	35	37	55
Sheffield U	42	9	9	3	35	15	11	5	5	34	26	54
Sheffield W	42	14	4	3	47	18	7	7	7	41	41	53
Coventry C	42	13	4	4	35	13	8	4	9	27	32	50
Manchester C	42	13	3	5	56	35	8	4	9	40	37	49
Chesterfield	42	16	1	4	54	20	4	8	9	15	32	49
Luton T	42	13	4	4	47	27	9	1	11	35	39	49
Tottenham H	42	13	6	2	48	27	6	3	12	19	35	47
Newcastle U	42	13	3	5	44	21	5	7	9	17	27	46
WBA	42	15	3	3	54	22	3	6	12	35	50	45
West Ham U	42	10	5	6	36	21	7	5	9	34	31	44
Fulham	42	12	5	4	35	20	5	5	11	26	35	44
Millwall	42	12	6	3	44	18	2	8	11	20	35	42
Burnley	42	13	3	5	32	20	2	6	13	18	36	39
Plymouth A	42	9	7	5	24	13	6	1	14	25	42	38
Bury	42	9	5	7	48	36	3	8	10	17	38	37
Bradford	42	8	6	7	33	35	4	5	12	28	47	35
Southampton	42	9	6	6	35	34	4	3	14	21	48	35
Swansea T	42	8	6	7	33	30	3	6	12	17	53	34
Nottingham F	42	8	6	7	33	29	2	5	14	16	53	31
Norwich C	42	10	5	6	39	29	3	0	18	11	62	31
Tranmere R	42	0	4	11	20	38	0	1	20	13	01	17

DIVISION 3 North

	P	W	D	L	F	A	W	D	L	F	A	Pts
Barnsley	42	18	2	1	60	12	12	5	4	34	22	67
Doncaster R	42	12	5	4	47	21	9	9	3	40	26	56
Bradford C	42	16	2	3	59	21	6	6	9	30	35	52
Southport	42	14	5	2	47	16	6	5	10	28	38	50
Oldham A	42	16	1	4	51	21	6	4	11	25	38	49
Chester	42	12	5	4	54	31	8	4	9	34	39	49
Hull C	42	13	5	3	57	25	5	5	11	26	49	46
Crewe A	42	12	5	4	54	23	7	1	13	28	47	44
Stockport Co	42	13	6	2	57	24	4	3	14	34	53	43
Gateshead	42	11	6	4	45	24	3	8	10	29	43	42
Rotherham U	42	12	4	5	45	21	5	4	12	19	43	42
Halifax T	42	9	10	2	33	22	4	6	11	19	32	42
Barrow	42	11	5	5	46	22	5	4	12	20	43	41
Wrexham	42	15	2	4	46	28	2	5	14	20	51	41
Rochdale	42	10	5	6	58	29	5	4	12	34	53	39
New Brighton	42	11	2	8	46	32	4	7	10	22	41	39
Lincoln C	42	9	6	6	40	33	3	3	15	26	59	33
Darlington	42	12	2	7	43	30	1	5	15	19	62	33
Carlisle U	42	10	5	6	44	33	3	2	16	22	78	33
York C	42	8	5	8	37	34	4	3	14	27	58	32
Hartlepools U	42	10	4	7	36	33	2	3	16	19	61	31
Accrington S	42	6	5	10	30	39	1	1	19	19	64	20

DIVISION 3 South

	P	W	D	L	F	A	W	D	L	F	A	Pts
Newport Co	42	15	4	2	37	16	7	7	7	21	29	55
Crystal P	42	15	4	2	49	18	5	8	8	22	34	52
Brighton & HA	42	14	5	2	43	14	5	6	10	25	35	49
Watford	42	14	6	1	44	15	3	6	12	18	36	46
Reading	42	12	6	3	46	23	4	8	9	23	36	46
QPR	42	10	8	3	44	15	5	6	10	24	34	44
Ipswich T	42	14	3	4	46	21	2	9	10	16	31	44
Bristol C	42	14	5	2	42	19	2	7	12	19	44	44
Swindon T	42	15	4	2	53	25	3	4	14	19	52	44
Aldershot	42	13	6	2	31	15	3	6	12	22	51	44
Notts Co	42	12	6	3	36	16	5	3	13	23	38	43
Southend U	42	14	5	2	38	13	2	4	15	23	51	41
Cardiff C	42	12	1	8	40	28	3	10	8	21	37	41
Exeter C	42	9	9	3	40	32	4	5	12	25	50	40
Bournemouth	42	10	8	3	38	22	3	5	13	14	36	39
Mansfield T	42	10	8	3	33	19	2	7	12	11	43	39
Northampton T	42	13	5	3	41	20	2	3	16	10	38	38
Port Vale	42	10	5	6	36	23	4	4	13	16	35	37
Torquay U	42	7	5	9	27	28	7	4	10	27	42	37
Clapton O	42	10	9	2	40	16	1	4	16	13	39	35
Walsall	42	9	6	6	47	23	2	5	14	21	46	33
Bristol R	42	8	8	5	30	17	2	5	14	25	44	33

In late September 1939, the authorities allowed football to restart with friendly games and a crowd limit of 8,000. Above: Arsenal's Reg Cumner crosses the ball against Brentford at Griffin Park. Brentford won 3-0.

Oldham Athletic full-back Tom Shipman punches the ball away at Old Trafford but Manchester United wing-half Bill McKay scored from the spot to help United to a 3-1 win.

Bristol City goalkeeper Watts punches clear during his side's 10-3 defeat at Plymouth on 3 February 1940. Regional football was now allowed but only 846 people turned up to see this South-West Division game. Indeed, it was the only match played in snowbound Britain that day.

Vic Woodley collects a high ball during Chelsea's 3-2 win at Aldershot. Sam Weaver looks on.

Season 1939-40

DIVISION 1

Saturday, 26 August 1939

Aston Villa 2 Middlesbrough 0
Chelsea 3 Bolton Wanderers 2
Everton 1 Brentford 1
Huddersfield Town 0 Blackpool 1
Manchester United 4 Grimsby Town 0
Portsmouth 2 Blackburn Rovers 1
Preston North End 0 Leeds United 0
Sheffield United 2 Liverpool 1
Stoke City 4 Charlton Athletic 0
Sunderland 3 Derby County 0
Wolverhampton Wanderers 2 Arsenal 2

Monday, 28 August 1939

Aston Villa 1 Everton 2
Blackpool 2 Brentford 1
Stoke City 1 Bolton Wanderers 2

Tuesday, 29 August 1939

Grimsby Town 0 Wolverhampton Wanderers 0

Wednesday, 30 August 1939

Arsenal 1 Blackburn Rovers 0
Chelsea 1 Manchester United 1
Derby County 2 Portsmouth 0
Leeds United 0 Charlton Athletic 1
Liverpool 4 Middlesbrough 1
Preston North End 0 Sheffield United 0
Sunderland 1 Huddersfield Town 2

Saturday, 2 September 1939

Arsenal 5 Sunderland 2
Blackburn Rovers 2 Everton 2
Blackpool 2 Wolverhampton Wanderers 1
Bolton Wanderers 2 Portsmouth 1
Brentford 1 Huddersfield Town 0
Charlton Athletic 2 Manchester United 0
Derby County 1 Aston Villa 0
Grimsby Town 2 Preston North End 0
Leeds United 0 Sheffield United 1
Liverpool 1 Chelsea 0
Middlesbrough 2 Stoke City 2

DIVISION 2

Saturday, 26 August 1939

Barnsley 4 Nottingham Forest 1
Burnley 1 Coventry City 1
Bury 3 Fulham 1
Chesterfield 2 Bradford 0
Leicester City 4 Manchester City 3
Luton Town 3 Sheffield Wednesday 0
Millwall 3 Newcastle United 0
Newport County 3 Southampton 1
Plymouth Argyle 1 West Ham United 3
Swansea Town 1 West Bromwich Albion 2
Tottenham Hotspur 1 Birmingham 1

Monday, 28 August 1939

Coventry City 3 West Bromwich Albion 3
Millwall 0 Plymouth Argyle 2
Sheffield Wednesday 3 Barnsley 1
West Ham United 2 Fulham 1

Wednesday, 30 August 1939

Birmingham 2 Leicester City 0
Bradford 0 Luton Town 3
Manchester City 1 Bury 1
Southampton 1 Swansea Town 3

Thursday, 31 August 1939

Newport County 1 Tottenham Hotspur 1
Nottingham Forest 2 Newcastle United 0

Saturday, 2 September 1939

Birmingham 2 Burnley 0
Bradford 2 Millwall 2
Coventry City 4 Barnsley 2
Fulham 1 Luton Town 1
Manchester City 2 Chesterfield 0
Newcastle United 8 Swansea Town 1
Nottingham Forest 2 Newport County 1
Sheffield Wednesday 0 Plymouth Argyle 1
Southampton 3 Bury 0
West Bromwich Albion 3 Tottenham Hotspur 4
West Ham United 0 Leicester City 2

DIVISION 3 NORTH

Saturday, 26 August 1939

Bradford City 0 Accrington Stanley 2
Darlington 1 Southport 0
Doncaster Rovers 2 Rochdale 0
Gateshead 0 Crewe Alexandra 3
Hartlepools United 1 Barrow 1
Hull City 2 Lincoln City 2
Oldham Athletic 3 Carlisle United 1
Stockport County 0 Halifax Town 3
Tranmere Rovers 3 Rotherham United 1
Wrexham 2 New Brighton 0
York City 2 Chester 2

Monday, 28 August 1939

Barrow 1 Accrington Stanley 2
Halifax Town 2 Oldham Athletic 0
Lincoln City 0 Darlington 2
Rotherham United 2 York City 1

Tuesday, 29 August 1939

Rochdale 1 Wrexham 0
Southport 3 Tranmere Rovers 3

Wednesday, 30 August 1939

Chester 1 Doncaster Rovers 0
Gateshead 3 Hartlepools United 0
New Brighton 2 Bradford City 1

Saturday, 2 September 1939

Accrington Stanley 2 Oldham Athletic 0
Barrow 2 Bradford City 2
Carlisle United 2 Stockport County 0
Chester 2 Tranmere Rovers 0
Crewe Alexandra 0 Hartlepools United 0
Halifax Town 1 Wrexham 1
Lincoln City 4 Gateshead 3
New Brighton 4 Doncaster Rovers 2
Rochdale 1 York City 0
Rotherham United 2 Darlington 2
Southport 1 Hull City 1

DIVISION 3 SOUTH

Saturday, 26 August 1939

Aldershot 0 Bristol City 1
Brighton & Hove Albion 0 Port Vale 0
Bristol Rovers 2 Reading 2
Clapton Orient 2 Ipswich Town 2
Exeter City 2 Torquay United 2
Mansfield Town 4 Crystal Palace 5
Northampton Town 1 Swindon Town 0
Norwich City 1 Cardiff City 2
Notts County 2 Bournemouth & BA 1
Queen's Park Rangers 2 Watford 2
Southend United 3 Walsall 2

Monday, 28 August 1939

Northampton Town 1 Exeter City 2

Wednesday, 30 August 1939

Bournemouth & BA 2 Queen's Park Rangers 2
Brighton & Hove Albion 2 Aldershot 1
Bristol City 1 Norwich City 2
Ipswich Town 2 Bristol Rovers 0
Reading 5 Crystal Palace 0
Swindon Town 0 Cardiff City 1
Torquay United 0 Walsall 0
Watford 1 Mansfield Town 2

Thursday, 31 August 1939

Clapton Orient 0 Southend United 0

Saturday, 2 September 1939

Bournemouth & BA 10 Northampton Town 0
Bristol City 3 Brighton & Hove Albion 3
Cardiff City 2 Notts County 4
Crystal Palace 3 Bristol Rovers 0
Ipswich Town 1 Norwich City 1
Port Vale 0 Exeter City 1
Reading 1 Southend United 0
Swindon Town 2 Aldershot 2
Torquay United 2 Mansfield Town 2
Walsall 1 Queen's Park Rangers 0
Watford 1 Clapton Orient 1

LEAGUE TABLES

DIVISION 1

	P	W	D	L	F	A	W	D	L	F	A	Pts
Blackpool	3	2	0	0	4	2	1	0	0	1	0	6
Sheffield U	3	1	0	0	2	1	1	1	0	1	0	5
Arsenal	3	2	0	0	6	2	0	1	0	2	2	5
Liverpool	3	2	0	0	5	1	0	0	1	1	2	4
Everton	3	0	1	0	1	1	1	1	0	4	3	4
Bolton W	3	1	0	0	2	1	1	0	1	4	4	4
Derby Co	3	2	0	0	3	0	0	0	1	0	3	4
Charlton A	3	1	0	0	2	0	1	0	1	1	4	4
Stoke C	3	1	0	1	5	2	0	1	0	2	2	3
Manchester U	3	1	0	0	4	0	0	1	1	1	3	3
Brentford	3	1	0	0	1	0	0	1	1	2	3	3
Chelsea	3	1	1	0	4	3	0	0	1	0	1	3
Grimsby T	3	1	1	0	2	0	0	0	1	0	4	3
Aston Villa	3	1	0	1	3	2	0	0	1	0	1	2
Sunderland	3	1	0	1	4	2	0	0	1	2	5	2
Wolves	3	0	1	0	2	2	0	1	1	1	2	2
Huddersfield T	3	0	0	1	0	1	1	0	1	2	2	2
Portsmouth	3	1	0	0	2	1	0	0	2	1	4	2
Preston NE	3	0	2	0	0	0	0	0	1	0	2	2
Blackburn R	3	0	1	0	2	2	0	0	2	1	3	1
Middlesbrough	3	0	1	0	2	2	0	0	2	1	6	1
Leeds U	3	0	0	2	0	2	0	1	0	0	0	1

DIVISION 2

	P	W	D	L	F	A	W	D	L	F	A	Pts
Luton T	3	1	0	0	3	0	1	1	0	4	1	5
Birmingham	3	2	0	0	4	0	0	1	0	1	1	5
Coventry C	3	1	1	0	7	5	0	1	0	1	1	4
Plymouth A	3	0	0	1	1	3	2	0	0	3	0	4
West Ham U	3	1	0	1	2	3	1	0	0	3	1	4
Leicester C	3	1	0	0	4	3	1	0	1	2	2	4
Tottenham H	3	0	1	0	1	1	1	1	0	5	4	4
Nottingham F	3	2	0	0	4	1	0	0	1	1	4	4
Millwall	3	1	0	1	3	2	0	1	0	2	2	3
Newport Co	3	1	1	0	4	2	0	0	1	1	2	3
Manchester C	3	1	1	0	3	1	0	0	1	3	4	3
WBA	3	0	0	1	3	4	1	1	0	5	4	3
Bury	3	1	0	0	3	1	0	1	1	1	4	3
Newcastle U	3	1	0	0	8	1	0	0	2	0	5	2
Chesterfield	2	1	0	0	2	0	0	0	1	0	2	2
Barnsley	3	1	0	0	4	1	0	0	2	3	7	2
Southampton	3	1	0	1	4	3	0	0	1	1	3	2
Sheffield W	3	1	0	1	3	2	0	0	1	0	3	2
Swansea T	3	0	0	1	1	2	1	0	1	4	9	2
Fulham	3	0	1	0	1	1	0	0	2	2	5	1
Burnley	2	0	1	0	1	1	0	0	1	0	2	1
Bradford	3	0	1	1	2	5	0	0	1	0	2	1

DIVISION 3 North

	P	W	D	L	F	A	W	D	L	F	A	Pts
Accrington S	3	1	0	0	2	0	2	0	0	4	1	6
Halifax T	3	1	1	0	3	1	1	0	0	3	0	5
Chester	3	2	0	0	3	0	0	1	0	2	2	5
Darlington	3	1	0	0	1	0	1	1	0	4	2	5
New Brighton	3	2	0	0	6	3	0	0	1	0	2	4
Rochdale	3	2	0	0	2	0	0	0	1	0	2	4
Crewe A	2	0	1	0	0	0	1	0	0	3	0	3
Wrexham	3	1	0	0	2	0	0	1	1	1	2	3
Tranmere R	3	1	0	0	3	1	0	1	1	3	5	3
Lincoln C	3	1	0	1	4	5	0	1	0	2	2	3
Rotherham U	3	1	1	0	4	3	0	0	1	1	3	3
Carlisle U	2	1	0	0	2	0	0	0	1	1	3	2
Hull C	2	0	1	0	2	2	0	1	0	1	1	2
Gateshead	3	1	0	1	3	3	0	0	1	3	4	2
Barrow	3	0	1	1	3	4	0	1	0	1	1	2
Doncaster R	3	1	0	0	2	0	0	0	2	2	6	2
Southport	3	0	2	0	4	4	0	0	1	0	1	2
Oldham A	3	1	0	0	3	1	0	0	2	0	4	2
Hartlepools U	3	0	1	0	1	1	0	1	1	0	3	2
York C	3	0	1	0	2	2	0	0	2	1	3	1
Bradford C	3	0	0	1	0	2	0	1	1	3	4	1
Stockport Co	2	0	0	1	0	3	0	0	1	0	2	0

DIVISION 3 South

	P	W	D	L	F	A	W	D	L	F	A	Pts
Reading	3	2	0	0	6	0	0	1	0	2	2	5
Exeter C	3	0	1	0	2	2	2	0	0	3	1	5
Notts Co	2	1	0	0	2	1	1	0	0	4	2	4
Ipswich T	3	1	1	0	3	1	0	1	0	2	2	4
Brighton & HA	3	1	1	0	2	1	0	1	0	3	3	4
Cardiff C	3	0	0	1	2	4	2	0	0	3	1	4
Crystal P	3	1	0	0	3	0	1	0	1	5	9	4
Bournemouth	3	1	1	0	12	2	0	0	1	1	2	3
Bristol C	3	0	1	1	4	5	1	0	0	1	0	3
Mansfield T	3	0	0	0	4	5	1	1	0	4	3	3
Norwich C	3	0	0	1	1	2	1	1	0	3	2	3
Clapton O	3	0	2	0	2	2	0	1	0	1	1	3
Southend U	3	1	0	0	3	2	0	1	1	0	1	3
Torquay U	3	0	2	0	2	2	0	1	0	2	2	3
Walsall	3	1	0	0	1	0	0	1	1	2	3	3
QPR	3	0	1	0	2	2	0	1	1	2	3	2
Watford	3	0	1	1	2	3	0	1	0	2	2	2
Northampton T	3	1	0	1	2	2	0	0	1	0	10	2
Aldershot	3	0	0	1	0	1	0	1	1	3	4	1
Swindon T	3	0	1	1	2	3	0	0	1	0	1	1
Bristol R	3	0	1	0	2	2	0	0	2	0	5	1
Port Vale	2	0	0	1	0	1	0	1	0	0	0	1

Football League Records

Top scorers: Div 1, D.Westcott (Wolverhampton Wanderers) 37 goals; Div 2, C.Wayman (Newcastle United) 30 goals; Div 3(N), C.Jordan (Doncaster Rovers) 41 goals; Div 3(S), D.Clarke (Bristol City) 36 goals.
Birmingham became Birmingham City; Clapton Orient became Leyton Orient.

Billy Liddell began his great Liverpool career as the Reds won the first post-war League Championship.

DIVISION 1

	ARSENAL	ASTON VILLA	BLACKBURN R	BLACKPOOL	BOLTON W	BRENTFORD	CHARLTON A	CHELSEA	DERBY CO	EVERTON	GRIMSBY T	HUDDERSFIELD T	LEEDS U	LIVERPOOL	MANCHESTER U	MIDDLESBROUGH	PORTSMOUTH	PRESTON N.E.	SHEFFIELD U	STOKE C	SUNDERLAND	WOLVERHAMPTON W
1 ARSENAL		J18 0-2	S04 1-3	F08 1-1	N30 2-2	O12 2-2	D14 1-0	M01 1-2	S21 0-1	m31 2-1	a26 5-3	a04 1-2	N16 4-2	m24 1-2	F01 6-2	a12 4-0	D25 2-1	M15 4-1	N02 2-3	O19 1-0	S07 2-2	D28 1-1
2 ASTON VILLA	S14 0-2		m10 2-1	J25 1-1	N16 1-1	S28 5-2	O19 4-0	M29 2-0	J04 2-0	S02 0-1	a12 3-3	D25 2-2	D14 2-1	a26 1-2	N02 0-0	A31 0-1	O12 1-1	m17 4-2	N30 2-3	m26 0-1	a08 4-0	S16 3-0
3 BLACKBURN R	S17 1-2	O05 0-1		D25 1-1	M15 2-1	J01 0-3	m26 1-0	a07 1-2	F15 1-1	S07 4-1	N30 1-1	J18 2-2	M01 1-0	N02 0-0	D14 2-1	N16 1-2	D28 0-1	a12 1-2	O19 2-0	a26 0-2	F01 1-2	S21 1-2
4 BLACKPOOL	O05 2-1	S21 1-0	D26 1-0		M01 0-1	S02 4-2	m17 0-0	N02 1-0	F01 2-1	a07 0-3	N16 2-3	D28 2-1	M29 3-0	N30 3-2	O19 3-1	D14 0-5	S23 4-3	F15 4-0	M15 4-2	a12 0-2	J18 0-5	S07 2-0
5 BOLTON W	a05 1-3	M22 2-1	N09 0-0	O26 1-1		m10 1-0	F19 0-1	D28 1-1	N23 5-1	F22 0-2	S28 1-2	D07 4-0	F03 2-0	S14 1-3	D25 2-2	O12 1-1	S07 1-0	J01 1-2	a04 3-2	S11 3-2	D21 0-1	a19 0-3
6 BRENTFORD	m26 0-1	F01 0-2	m03 0-3	S18 2-1	N02 1-0		N16 1-4	M15 0-2	O05 0-3	D28 1-1	M29 0-1	S07 2-0	N30 1-1	m17 1-1	a12 0-0	a26 0-0	a04 1-3	O19 2-3	D26 2-1	D14 1-4	S21 0-3	J18 4-1
7 CHARLTON A	a19 2-2	F22 1-1	N23 0-2	D21 0-1	O05 2-0	M22 3-0		F01 2-3	D07 2-4	O26 4-1	D26 0-0	M08 0-3	S25 5-0	m10 1-3	S07 1-3	a04 3-3	a05 0-0	J18 0-0	S21 1-2	D28 1-0	S11 5-0	N09 1-4
8 CHELSEA	O26 2-1	N23 1-3	a04 0-2	M08 1-4	A31 4-3	N09 3-2	S28 2-2		a05 3-0	D07 1-1	F08 0-0	a19 1-0	S14 3-0	J04 3-1	S04 0-3	m10 2-0	m26 0-3	D25 1-2	m03 1-4	O12 2-5	M22 2-1	D21 1-2
9 DERBY CO	m10 0-1	S07 1-2	O12 2-1	S28 1-2	M29 1-3	M01 2-1	a12 1-0	N30 3-1		D26 5-1	D14 4-1	m03 1-0	a26 2-1	N16 1-4	M15 4-3	O19 1-1	S04 2-0	N02 2-2	m17 1-2	J18 3-0	D28 5-1	a07 2-1
10 EVERTON	S11 3-2	J01 2-0	J04 1-0	a04 1-1	O19 2-1	A31 0-2	m24 1-1	a12 2-0	D25 4-1		N02 3-3	F01 1-0	m26 4-1	J29 1-0	N16 2-2	N30 2-1	S14 1-0	a26 2-0	D14 2-3	M29 2-2	F15 4-2	O05 0-2
11 GRIMSBY T	D21 0-0	D07 0-3	a05 2-1	M22 2-3	F01 2-2	N23 2-2	D25 3-1	S21 2-1	a19 2-0	M08 2-2		N09 1-0	m17 4-1	O05 1-6	D28 0-0	m03 4-0	O26 3-2	S07 2-3	J18 2-1	a04 2-5	m10 1-2	S03 0-0
12 HUDDERSFIELD T	a07 0-0	D26 1-0	S14 0-1	A31 1-3	a12 1-0	J04 3-0	N02 5-1	D14 1-4	S11 5-2	S28 1-0	M15 3-2		m10 1-0	O19 1-4	M29 2-2	m17 3-1	J29 1-2	N16 3-0	a26 1-1	N30 1-0	S25 0-0	m26 0-1
13 LEEDS U	M22 1-1	a19 1-1	O26 0-1	N23 4-2	S21 4-0	a05 1-2	S04 0-2	J18 2-1	D21 1-2	N09 2-1	O12 1-0	O05 5-0		F01 1-2	a08 0-2	D25 3-3	m24 0-1	D28 0-3	S07 2-2	m03 1-2	D07 1-1	F22 0-1
14 LIVERPOOL	N23 4-2	D21 4-1	M08 2-1	a05 2-3	J18 0-3	O26 1-0	O12 1-1	S07 7-4	M22 1-1	S21 0-0	F12 5-0	F22 1-0	S28 2-0		m03 1-0	S04 0-1	N09 3-0	a07 3-0	D28 1-2	D26 2-0	a19 1-0	D07 1-5
15 MANCHESTER U	S28 5-2	M08 2-1	a19 4-0	F22 3-0	D26 1-0	D07 4-1	J04 4-1	S18 1-1	N09 4-1	M22 3-0	A31 2-1	N23 5-2	a07 3-1	S11 5-0		S14 1-0	m17 3-0	O05 1-1	m26 6-2	F05 1-1	O26 0-3	a05 3-1
16 MIDDLESBROUGH	D07 2-0	D28 1-2	M22 0-1	a19 1-2	F15 3-1	D21 2-0	a07 1-2	O05 3-2	F22 1-0	a05 4-0	J01 3-0	O26 4-1	D26 3-0	O09 2-2	J18 2-4		N23 3-3	S21 2-0	F01 2-4	S07 5-4	N09 1-3	M08 1-1
17 PORTSMOUTH	D26 0-2	F15 3-2	A31 3-1	S11 0-1	J04 2-0	a07 3-0	N30 3-0	O19 0-2	m31 1-2	J18 2-1	M01 4-1	S21 3-1	N02 4-1	M15 1-2	a26 0-1	M29 3-1		D14 4-4	a12 0-0	N16 1-3	O05 4-1	m03 1-1
18 PRESTON N.E.	N09 2-0	O26 3-1	D07 4-0	O12 2-0	S16 0-4	F22 5-2	S14 5-1	D26 1-1	m26 1-1	D21 2-1	J04 3-0	M22 6-2	A31 3-2	a04 0-0	m10 1-1	J29 0-1	a19 1-1		S04 1-2	S28 1-3	a05 2-2	N23 2-2
19 SHEFFIELD U	j07 2-1	a05 1-2	F22 0-1	N09 4-2	a07 4-2	D25 6-1	m31 1-3	S09 2-2	O26 3-2	a19 2-0	S14 1-1	D21 2-2	J04 6-2	A31 0-1	O12 2-2	S28 2-1	m10 3-1	m24 2-3		j14 2-1	N23 4-2	M22 2-0
20 STOKE C	F22 3-1	N09 0-0	D21 0-0	D07 4-1	S02 1-2	a19 3-1	A31 2-2	F15 6-1	S14 3-2	N23 2-1	a07 3-0	a05 3-0	S16 5-2	D25 2-1	S21 3-2	J04 3-1	M22 1-1	F01 5-0	O05 3-0		m17 0-0	O26 0-3
21 SUNDERLAND	J04 1-4	a04 4-1	S28 1-0	S14 3-2	a26 3-1	m24 2-1	m03 1-1	N16 1-2	A31 3-2	O12 4-1	O19 1-2	S04 3-0	a12 1-0	D14 1-4	M01 1-1	M15 1-0	F08 0-0	N30 0-2	M29 2-1	N02 0-1		D25 0-1
22 WOLVERHAMPTON W	A31 6-1	S11 1-2	m17 3-3	J04 3-1	D14 5-0	S14 1-2	M15 2-0	a26 6-4	a08 7-2	m10 2-3	S23 2-0	O12 6-1	O19 1-0	m31 1-2	N30 3-2	N02 2-4	S28 3-1	M29 4-1	N16 3-1	M01 3-0	D26 2-1	

Manchester City goalkeeper Frank Swift, a key figure in City's promotion to Division One in 1946-7.

DIVISION 2

	BARNSLEY	BIRMINGHAM C	BRADFORD	BURNLEY	BURY	CHESTERFIELD	COVENTRY C	FULHAM	LEICESTER C	LUTON T	MANCHESTER C	MILLWALL	NEWCASTLE U	NEWPORT CO	NOTTINGHAM F	PLYMOUTH A	SHEFFIELD W	SOUTHAMPTON	SWANSEA T	TOTTENHAM H	W.B.A.	WEST HAM U
1 BARNSLEY		S14 3-1	D07 3-1	S16 1-0	O26 4-0	N23 1-2	J04 0-2	m03 4-1	M22 1-0	m10 4-0	a19 0-2	a05 4-1	S28 1-1	a04 3-1	A31 3-2	N09 1-3	S09 4-1	D25 4-4	m17 3-1	O12 1-3	m26 2-1	D21 1-2
2 BIRMINGHAM C	J18 1-2		m03 4-0	S07 0-2	D07 3-0	F22 0-0	F15 2-0	a05 2-1	S04 4-0	a19 1-0	N09 3-1	O26 4-0	a07 2-0	S21 1-1	O05 4-0	D21 6-1	N23 3-1	F01 3-1	D25 3-1	D28 1-0	S25 1-0	M22 3-0
3 BRADFORD	a12 1-3	N02 2-0		D14 0-1	S25 2-2	D28 0-0	M15 5-1	O12 1-2	D25 1-2	S04 2-1	m14 1-1	S07 0-0	O19 2-1	N30 2-1	N16 0-1	m26 3-2	M12 1-1	M29 2-3	J18 0-0	a26 2-1	m27 2-4	S28 0-1
4 BURNLEY	S30 2-2	J04 1-0	a19 1-2		m26 1-1	a05 1-1	A31 1-1	O26 2-0	N23 0-0	N09 1-1	D21 0-0	D07 3-0	J28 3-0	S09 3-2	D25 3-0	M22 2-1	F22 2-0	a04 1-0	S28 1-0	F18 0-0	S14 0-2	O12 2-1
5 BURY	M01 4-4	a12 2-0	J01 6-3	N02 2-2		O05 0-2	D14 1-0	A31 7-2	F01 2-3	J18 3-0	S18 2-2	F15 5-2	m17 2-2	O19 0-1	a26 5-0	S21 3-3	D25 4-2	J04 2-1	N16 3-3	m03 1-2	N30 4-0	a04 4-0
6 CHESTERFIELD	M29 2-1	O19 0-1	A31 1-1	N30 0-0	m31 3-1		m26 2-1	S28 1-1	m17 2-0	O12 2-1	J04 0-1	D26 2-3	a26 1-0	N16 2-0	N02 1-1	J01 4-1	j07 4-2	m03 5-0	D14 1-0	a12 0-0	a04 1-1	S14 3-1
7 COVENTRY C	S07 1-1	O12 0-0	N09 0-0	D28 0-3	a19 3-1	O26 1-1		D07 1-0	m10 2-1	D21 0-0	M22 1-1	m24 4-0	S16 1-1	J18 6-0	F01 1-1	m17 1-0	a05 5-1	S21 2-0	a08 3-2	D25 3-1	S02 3-2	N23 2-1
8 FULHAM	O19 6-1	N30 0-1	m31 0-3	m17 1-0	D28 2-0	m10 2-1	a12 2-0		S21 4-2	S07 2-1	M01 2-2	O05 3-2	N16 0-3	D26 4-1	m26 1-1	J18 3-1	a07 1-2	a26 0-0	M15 3-0	N02 1-1	M29 0-1	S09 3-2
9 LEICESTER C	N16 6-0	S12 2-1	D26 2-1	m24 1-4	S28 0-0	S19 0-1	O19 1-0	j07 2-0		m03 2-1	A31 0-3	a08 5-0	D14 2-4	M15 3-0	M01 1-1	O12 4-1	S14 3-5	N02 2-0	a12 0-1	N30 1-1	a26 1-1	J04 4-0
10 LUTON T	N02 3-1	D14 1-3	m24 3-0	M15 1-3	S14 2-0	F15 1-1	a26 1-1	J04 2-0	O05 1-2		a07 0-0	S11 3-0	N30 4-3	m31 6-3	J29 3-2	F01 3-4	A31 4-1	O19 2-2	M29 3-0	N16 3-2	a12 2-0	D26 2-1
11 MANCHESTER C	D14 5-1	M15 1-0	S21 7-2	m10 1-0	S04 3-1	S07 0-0	N16 1-0	J01 4-0	D28 1-0	a04 2-0		J18 1-0	m03 0-2	j14 5-1	M29 2-1	D25 4-3	O12 2-1	N30 1-1	O19 1-1	F01 1-0	N02 5-0	m24 2-0
12 MILLWALL	N30 3-1	m17 0-2	J04 0-1	j07 1-1	O12 1-0	D25 1-1	N02 3-5	j14 1-1	a04 1-0	O07 2-0	S14 1-3		A31 1-4	M29 3-1	M15 4-0	S02 1-1	S28 2-2	N16 3-1	a26 1-1	D14 0-3	O19 1-2	J25 0-0
13 NEWCASTLE U	F01 4-2	a04 2-2	m10 6-0	S21 1-2	N23 1-1	D21 2-1	S11 3-1	M22 1-3	a19 1-1	a05 7-2	O26 3-2	D28 0-2		O05 13-0	J01 3-0	D07 3-2	N09 4-0	F15 1-3	S07 1-1	J18 1-0	D25 2-4	m26 2-3
14 NEWPORT CO	a07 2-1	m26 0-3	m17 1-3	m03 0-3	m24 2-0	M22 3-0	S14 4-2	D25 4-2	N09 2-3	O26 1-3	D07 0-3	N23 3-1	j07 4-2		J04 2-5	m10 1-0	D21 4-3	O24 1-2	O12 2-4	S19 2-4	S28 2-7	a19 1-1
15 NOTTINGHAM F	D28 2-1	m10 1-1	j14 4-0	D26 1-0	D21 2-0	m27 1-0	S28 1-0	a19 2-1	O26 2-0	S21 4-2	N23 0-1	N09 1-2	S05 0-2	S07 6-1		m31 5-1	D07 2-2	J18 6-0	m03 1-1	a07 1-1	O12 1-1	a05 4-3
16 PLYMOUTH A	M15 3-2	a26 0-2	a07 2-4	N16 2-2	J25 3-1	S11 1-0	O05 2-2	S14 2-2	F15 4-0	S28 2-1	D26 2-3	m03 0-2	a12 0-1	N02 4-1	O19 2-0		J04 4-1	M01 2-3	N30 2-1	M29 3-4	D14 2-1	A31 3-1
17 SHEFFIELD W	S02 2-4	M29 1-0	O05 1-2	O19 1-2	D26 2-5	S21 0-1	N30 4-2	S16 1-1	J18 1-3	D28 1-1	m26 1-0	F01 3-0	m24 1-1	a26 2-1	a12 2-0	S07 2-1		D14 3-0	N02 3-0	M01 5-1	N16 2-2	J01 1-1
18 SOUTHAMPTON	D26 1-1	S28 1-0	N23 3-2	a07 0-1	S07 1-1	N09 1-1	F05 5-2	m24 2-0	m26 1-1	F22 1-3	a05 0-1	M22 1-2	O12 1-1	D28 5-1	S14 5-2	O26 5-1	a19 3-1		S04 4-0	m10 1-0	F08 0-1	D07 4-2
19 SWANSEA T	O05 2-2	D26 1-0	S14 1-6	F01 0-2	M22 1-0	a19 1-2	a07 2-3	N09 0-2	D07 3-4	N23 2-0	F22 1-2	m26 0-3	J04 1-2	F15 5-1	S09 3-2	a05 3-1	m10 2-0	O03 4-2		S21 0-2	A31 2-3	O26 2-1
20 TOTTENHAM H	j07 1-1	A31 1-2	D21 3-3	O05 1-1	N09 2-1	D07 3-4	D26 0-0	M08 1-1	a05 2-1	M22 2-1	S28 0-0	a19 2-1	S14 1-1	O07 3-1	a04 2-0	N23 2-1	O26 2-0	S09 2-1	J27 3-1		J04 2-0	m17 0-0
21 W.B.A.	S21 2-5	S18 3-0	O26 1-1	J18 1-1	a05 3-0	a07 3-2	m03 1-1	N23 6-1	D21 4-2	D07 1-2	m31 3-1	m10 2-4	D26 3-2	F01 2-2	m17 5-1	a19 2-5	M22 2-1	O05 2-0	D28 2-1	S07 3-2		N09 2-3
22 WEST HAM U	a26 4-0	N16 0-4	F01 1-1	m31 0-5	a07 3-3	J18 5-0	M29 1-2	S02 3-2	S07 0-2	D25 2-1	O05 1-0	S21 3-1	N02 0-2	F08 3-0	N30 2-2	D28 4-1	m03 2-1	a12 4-0	M01 3-0	O19 2-2	M15 3-2	

Season 1946-47

DIVISION 3 NORTH

	ACCRINGTON S	BARROW	BRADFORD C	CARLISLE U	CHESTER	CREWE A	DARLINGTON	DONCASTER R	GATESHEAD	HALIFAX T	HARTLEPOOLS U	HULL C	LINCOLN C	NEW BRIGHTON	OLDHAM A	ROCHDALE	ROTHERHAM U	SOUTHPORT	STOCKPORT CO	TRANMERE R	WREXHAM	YORK C
1 ACCRINGTON S		D14 1-3	D28 0-0	S24 4-3	N23 1-4	O26 2-3	a19 3-0	F01 0-1	D26 0-3	a04 1-1	F22 2-1	D21 0-0	m31 8-4	m10 3-1	S07 2-3	O05 2-3	M22 2-3	N09 1-0	J18 2-1	D07 2-1	S21 0-1	m14 1-2
2 BARROW	S05 1-3		S07 0-0	D26 3-1	M22 1-0	F22 0-2	D07 2-3	O05 0-1	D21 1-0	S12 3-0	D28 2-0	a19 1-0	O26 1-3	a07 0-1	J18 5-2	m10 2-2	N09 2-3	m03 2-1	S21 1-0	a05 0-1	F01 1-0	N23 0-1
3 BRADFORD C	A31 3-1	J04 5-0		m03 2-2	N09 0-0	S14 1-0	a05 2-0	m24 0-1	a19 2-2	D26 3-1	D21 1-2	D07 1-1	j14 3-0	S09 2-1	S21 1-0	a07 0-1	m31 2-0	O26 5-1	F01 0-2	N23 2-2	O05 2-1	M22 3-2
4 CARLISLE U	J01 4-2	D25 4-1	S19 4-3		a05 3-2	M08 3-3	D21 1-5	S21 2-3	F22 3-1	F15 1-0	O26 5-1	a04 0-2	N09 1-0	O05 3-2	D28 1-2	F01 1-3	N23 1-1	M22 1-1	S07 1-1	a19 4-2	m10 1-1	D07 1-2
5 CHESTER	M29 3-1	N16 3-0	m10 3-0	m31 4-0		F15 2-0	J18 1-1	S04 1-3	F01 0-1	a12 2-0	O05 2-1	S21 5-1	a04 3-0	D14 2-1	N02 2-0	a26 1-0	D25 2-2	S25 2-1	m24 3-0	S07 4-1	S18 2-0	D28 6-0
6 CREWE A	m17 5-0	O19 0-1	J18 2-2	N02 2-0	O12 0-2		D25 3-2	J22 0-3	D28 1-1	M15 2-0	S07 1-1	S09 2-0	J25 0-5	N16 3-0	a26 3-0	M29 2-2	F08 1-2	S28 2-0	m10 3-2	m03 4-3	a12 1-0	a04 2-0
7 DARLINGTON	m03 5-0	a12 0-1	J11 2-0	a26 2-1	S14 3-3	D26 4-0		N02 1-1	a04 2-0	m10 0-1	S11 2-1	F15 0-2	J01 4-3	O19 4-0	M29 1-1	M01 4-1	J04 4-3	A31 4-2	N16 1-2	S28 1-2	j07 1-1	J25 3-1
8 DONCASTER R	S28 5-0	M13 8-0	O12 4-3	J25 9-2	m03 3-0	a05 1-1	M08 5-0		M22 3-0	S14 2-0	N23 5-1	N09 4-1	a12 1-1	J04 0-0	a04 4-2	A31 2-1	D21 1-1	m10 2-0	S16 1-3	O26 2-0	D25 5-0	j07 0-0
9 GATESHEAD	D25 2-1	a26 0-5	J02 1-2	O19 1-3	S28 3-4	A31 2-1	a07 1-0	N16 1-3		m03 6-1	S04 0-1	J01 1-0	J04 3-0	N02 3-0	a12 1-0	m17 2-2	J25 2-0	S14 2-2	J15 1-2	O12 3-1	M29 3-3	m24 1-2
10 HALIFAX T	a07 2-1	S16 3-2	D25 1-2	O12 0-1	D07 1-2	N09 1-2	O05 0-2	J18 4-2	O26 2-1		m24 1-4	m17 2-0	j07 2-3	F01 0-1	S02 1-1	S21 3-0	a05 2-3	N23 1-1	D28 1-2	D21 1-3	S07 0-0	a19 0-3
11 HARTLEPOOLS U	O19 0-2	A31 1-1	a26 0-0	M01 4-1	F08 5-1	J04 5-2	S16 4-1	M29 0-2	m26 1-3	N02 1-4		D25 0-0	S14 2-0	M15 3-0	J11 1-1	N16 0-3	S28 2-1	J25 3-0	a12 1-0	a04 1-0	J01 1-3	O12 1-1
12 HULL C	a26 3-0	m31 1-0	a12 0-2	a07 2-0	M06 1-0	S02 2-2	O12 2-1	M15 0-1	S16 1-2	O19 3-0	D26 1-1		A31 0-0	j07 1-1	m24 0-1	N02 0-1	S14 0-2	J04 4-0	M29 0-3	m10 1-0	N16 1-0	S28 2-2
13 LINCOLN C	N02 1-1	m26 1-0	O19 0-1	M15 3-1	a07 2-2	S21 1-3	S04 2-0	D07 3-5	S07 4-0	N16 3-1	J18 5-2	D28 0-3		M29 5-1	F01 1-3	J22 2-3	O12 4-0	m17 4-2	a26 4-0	D26 2-1	m24 3-1	m03 2-2
14 NEW BRIGHTON	O12 4-0	a04 0-1	S04 0-0	m26 2-2	a19 0-3	M22 4-0	m24 4-1	S07 2-5	M08 2-3	S28 1-1	N09 2-1	O26 1-5	N23 4-2		D26 4-0	J18 1-2	j14 1-0	a05 1-0	J01 1-0	S21 2-1	m31 1-0	m17 0-3
15 OLDHAM A	J04 1-2	S14 0-1	J25 0-1	A31 0-2	m17 1-0	D21 3-1	N23 2-0	a07 0-1	D07 1-1	J01 6-1	a19 0-0	a05 1-2	S28 3-1	D25 2-2		S09 3-2	O26 0-1	F22 2-4	O05 0-0	M22 1-2	F15 1-5	N09 2-2
16 ROCHDALE	m24 5-1	O12 1-1	a04 0-1	S28 6-0	D21 2-1	N23 1-1	O26 3-0	D28 2-3	N09 2-3	J25 1-0	M22 1-0	M08 5-2	a05 2-0	S14 2-2	S17 1-3		a19 1-1	D07 0-0	D26 1-4	m31 3-0	S03 0-1	S07 0-1
17 ROTHERHAM U	N16 4-1	m24 4-3	N02 2-1	M29 4-0	D26 3-1	O05 5-1	S07 4-1	a26 3-2	S21 4-0	J13 6-1	F01 4-0	J18 2-0	m10 3-0	a12 3-0	m26 8-0	j07 3-3		a07 2-1	O19 2-1	D28 6-0	m03 3-2	J01 6-1
18 SOUTHPORT	M15 0-1	N02 2-2	M01 0-1	N16 0-2	S10 2-4	F01 2-2	D28 2-2	a19 0-5	J18 2-1	M29 6-1	S21 3-3	S07 3-1	O05 1-3	J11 2-0	O19 2-4	a12 0-2	a04 2-0		F15 4-1	S03 1-2	a26 1-1	D25 0-3
19 STOCKPORT CO	S14 2-0	J25 2-0	S28 4-0	J04 2-0	O26 0-3	a19 3-2	M22 1-0	S09 1-3	a05 2-0	A31 4-1	D07 1-2	N23 2-0	D21 3-2	m03 2-0	F08 4-0	D26 5-2	F22 1-2	O12 2-0		N09 4-0	a04 1-0	m31 4-2
20 TRANMERE R	a12 0-1	J11 1-1	D14 2-0	m24 1-1	J04 3-2	S18 3-2	F01 2-0	M01 3-5	F15 1-0	a26 1-1	a07 4-1	O05 1-3	D25 5-2	J25 3-3	N16 4-2	O19 2-3	A31 1-4	J01 2-0	M15 2-1		N02 0-0	S14 2-1
21 WREXHAM	J25 4-0	S28 1-1	m17 2-0	S14 2-1	m26 0-4	D07 1-0	N09 7-1	D26 0-2	N23 2-0	J04 2-0	a05 4-1	M22 0-1	a19 4-1	A31 3-2	O12 2-1	S25 2-2	S11 1-1	D21 1-1	a07 2-1	j14 0-0		O26 3-1
22 YORK C	J11 0-1	M29 0-2	N16 0-3	a12 2-2	A31 4-4	a07 2-3	S21 3-0	O19 1-4	O05 3-1	m26 2-0	m10 1-4	F01 3-0	S11 2-4	a26 1-2	m21 1-0	J04 2-3	S04 2-3	D26 1-1	N02 3-2	J18 0-1	m27 2-2	

DIVISION 3 SOUTH

	ALDERSHOT	BOURNEMOUTH	BRIGHTON & HA	BRISTOL C	BRISTOL R	CARDIFF C	CRYSTAL P	EXETER C	IPSWICH T	LEYTON O	MANSFIELD T	NORTHAMPTON T	NORWICH C	NOTTS CO	PORT VALE	Q.P.R.	READING	SOUTHEND U	SWINDON T	TORQUAY U	WALSALL	WATFORD
1 ALDERSHOT		S14 2-1	S18 1-3	A31 4-3	J11 0-2	J25 0-1	a26 0-2	m03 2-0	N02 4-1	M15 0-0	a12 1-1	O12 1-1	S28 3-1	F08 1-1	D25 0-0	N16 1-2	a04 1-3	M29 0-0	J04 2-0	M12 0-0	O19 1-2	m17 1-2
2 BOURNEMOUTH	J18 2-2		S21 1-0	F15 0-0	M01 1-3	S10 2-0	N10 4-0	m10 4-1	J01 1-1	a28 2-0	N02 3-1	S07 2-1	D25 0-1	D28 1-2	O05 3-0	S04 1-1	M29 1-0	O19 3-1	a04 5-2	M15 5-0	J15 2-3	a12 0-1
3 BRIGHTON & H.A.	S04 2-1	J25 1-1		J04 1-1	a12 1-2	S28 0-4	m03 1-0	D25 1-6	M15 0-0	N16 2-1	D14 5-0	a04 2-2	F08 3-3	O12 3-2	A31 0-0	M29 0-2	O19 1-4	J15 2-1	S14 1-4	J11 2-0	M01 2-0	N02 1-1
4 BRISTOL C	D28 9-0	O12 1-0	S07 0-0		F01 4-0	a04 2-1	N02 3-0	J18 2-2	J11 1-2	a12 3-0	O19 5-2	D26 2-3	S04 2-1	m03 1-1	S21 3-0	m10 1-1	M15 5-2	a26 2-0	F08 3-1	M01 5-0	N16 1-2	M29 1-2
5 BRISTOL R	a05 0-0	O26 0-2	D07 0-0	S28 0-3		M08 1-0	J04 2-1	a19 1-0	m10 1-1	a07 6-1	J25 1-0	N23 0-3	N09 1-2	M22 4-1	D21 0-0	F15 3-1	A31 2-2	O05 1-3	F22 3-0	S14 3-0	D25 2-2	S09 3-4
6 CARDIFF C	S21 2-1	S09 2-0	F01 4-0	a07 1-1	N02 4-0		M29 0-0	O05 5-0	a26 3-2	j07 1-0	M15 5-0	J18 6-2	D28 6-1	S07 2-1	m10 1-0	O19 2-2	J22 3-0	M01 3-1	S23 5-0	N16 1-0	a12 3-0	m03 1-0
7 CRYSTAL P	D21 0-0	M22 0-1	S11 1-0	m24 0-0	S07 2-1	N23 1-2		F22 1-0	O05 1-1	F01 2-0	D28 1-1	a19 2-2	a05 0-1	D07 2-1	O26 1-2	S21 0-0	S18 2-1	J18 0-3	N09 4-1	D25 6-1	a04 1-1	F15 2-0
8 EXETER C	S11 4-1	S28 4-1	D26 2-1	S14 1-3	D14 3-2	m17 0-2	O19 2-1		N16 0-0	M29 3-1	a26 1-0	S18 1-0	O12 3-0	a07 2-2	J04 1-1	M05 3-0	M01 1-3	a12 1-5	J25 1-1	A31 1-1	N02 2-2	M15 1-0
9 IPSWICH T	m26 1-1	a19 2-1	N09 1-2	a05 3-2	S04 0-2	D21 0-1	F08 1-1	M22 2-1		D28 0-0	a07 2-1	O26 1-2	S07 5-0	m17 1-2	N23 2-1	D26 1-1	S28 2-0	m03 1-0	D07 3-1	O12 1-1	J25 2-1	S14 2-0
10 LEYTON O	N09 1-3	m24 2-3	M22 2-1	D07 4-1	a04 3-0	D25 0-1	S28 0-1	J11 3-1	A31 2-2		O12 3-1	M08 2-1	F22 3-0	O26 1-3	a05 5-3	m03 1-1	J25 3-3	S04 1-1	a19 0-0	m10 0-1	S14 1-0	J04 3-1
11 MANSFIELD T	D07 1-3	m03 1-1	a19 0-3	m17 1-3	S21 3-1	N09 1-3	A31 3-1	D21 1-0	a04 4-3	m31 1-3		a05 3-2	M22 4-4	N23 1-0	S14 0-3	O05 0-3	D25 2-2	F01 0-1	O26 1-1	J04 1-0	S18 1-1	O09 2-0
12 NORTHAMPTON T	m29 2-2	J04 2-1	a07 6-1	D25 2-2	M29 1-2	S14 0-2	m17 1-0	S02 1-2	m31 2-2	N02 4-1	J23 3-0		J25 1-0	S28 2-1	m03 1-0	M15 4-4	a26 4-0	N16 2-3	A31 4-1	a12 0-0	a08 0-8	O19 4-1
13 NORWICH C	F01 2-3	D26 1-6	O05 2-3	S18 2-2	M15 3-3	A31 2-1	S26 2-3	F15 1-3	J04 0-1	O19 5-0	N16 3-1	S21 2-3		J18 2-2	a07 3-0	M01 0-1	a12 0-2	N02 1-5	S12 1-5	M29 2-0	m17 0-2	a26 4-2
14 NOTTS CO	O05 2-0	A31 1-0	m10 2-0	S11 0-3	N16 6-0	J04 1-1	a12 0-0	a04 0-0	O19 1-2	m26 1-2	M29 5-1	F01 1-0	S14 3-0		O03 3-2	N02 1-2	m29 1-0	m24 0-2	D25 0-0	J23 0-2	a28 3-1	J25 4-1
15 PORT VALE	D26 4-2	M10 1-0	D28 4-1	F17 2-1	a26 2-1	O12 0-4	m26 4-2	S07 1-2	M29 1-0	J16 2-1	J18 4-1	S09 1-1	a04 1-3	S23 4-1		a12 2-2	N02 5-1	m31 5-1	S28 1-1	O19 2-1	M15 2-2	N16 3-0
16 Q.P.R.	M22 4-1	S25 3-0	N23 2-0	a19 1-0	O12 0-2	m24 2-3	J25 1-2	a05 2-0	D25 1-3	S11 2-0	F08 3-1	N09 1-0	O26 1-1	M08 4-1	D07 2-0		S14 2-0	a04 1-0	D21 7-0	S28 0-0	J04 1-0	A31 2-1
17 READING	a07 1-0	N23 3-2	m17 2-0	N09 2-5	D28 1-1	a05 0-0	S04 10-2	O26 4-0	F01 1-3	S21 2-0	D26 3-0	D21 3-0	D07 4-3	a19 1-1	M08 0-2	J18 1-0		S07 7-2	M22 3-3	S11 2-2	m26 1-1	O05 2-3
18 SOUTHEND U	N23 2-1	m17 2-2	a05 0-0	D21 4-1	F08 2-3	O26 0-2	S14 2-0	D07 2-2	S12 1-1	S19 0-0	S28 1-1	M22 4-0	M08 3-0	N09 3-0	a19 1-1	a07 1-3	J04 0-2		O12 2-0	J25 0-2	A31 3-1	D26 5-0
19 SWINDON T	S07 7-0	a07 1-3	J18 2-2	O05 1-1	O19 1-0	S04 3-2	M15 1-0	S21 2-0	a12 2-1	m17 2-0	M01 6-1	D28 3-1	m03 1-1	D26 4-2	F01 2-1	a26 3-2	N16 2-2	m10 2-1		N02 2-4	M29 4-1	J11 5-0
20 TORQUAY U	a19 0-1	N09 2-2	D21 3-1	O26 2-3	J18 3-0	M22 0-0	D26 2-1	D28 2-1	F15 0-0	O05 3-2	S07 2-2	D07 2-1	N23 2-1	a05 1-2	m24 1-0	m17 0-0	m03 3-0	S21 0-1	M08 1-5		S04 2-0	a07 2-0
21 WALSALL	m10 2-0	a05 3-0	O26 1-1	M22 3-0	D26 2-0	D07 2-3	a07 3-3	m24 2-1	S21 4-2	J18 3-1	S09 0-0	O05 2-0	a19 2-2	D21 2-0	N09 4-1	S07 0-2	O12 2-2	D28 2-2	N23 0-1	m31 2-1		F01 1-3
22 WATFORD	O26 4-1	D07 0-2	m24 1-4	N23 2-3	S18 1-0	a19 2-0	O12 1-0	N09 3-1	J18 2-0	S07 3-1	S04 1-2	m10 1-1	D21 4-1	S21 2-2	M22 2-0	D28 0-2	F08 2-1	D25 4-0	a05 1-1	a04 3-3	S28 0-2	

LEAGUE TABLES

DIVISION 1

	P	W	D	L	F	A	W	D	L	F	A	Pts
Liverpool	42	13	3	5	42	24	12	4	5	42	28	57
Manchester U	42	17	3	1	61	19	5	9	7	34	35	56
Wolves	42	15	1	5	66	31	10	5	6	32	25	56
Stoke C	42	14	5	2	52	21	10	2	9	38	32	55
Blackpool	42	14	1	6	38	32	8	5	8	33	38	50
Sheffield U	42	12	4	5	51	32	9	3	9	38	43	49
Preston NE	42	10	7	4	45	27	8	4	9	31	47	47
Aston Villa	42	9	6	6	39	24	9	3	9	28	29	45
Sunderland	42	11	3	7	33	27	7	5	9	32	39	44
Everton	42	13	5	3	40	24	4	4	13	22	43	43
Middlesbrough	42	11	3	7	46	32	6	5	10	27	36	42
Portsmouth	42	11	3	7	42	27	5	6	10	24	33	41
Arsenal	42	9	5	7	43	33	7	4	10	29	37	41
Derby Co	42	13	2	6	44	28	5	3	13	29	51	41
Chelsea	42	9	3	9	33	39	7	4	10	36	45	39
Grimsby T	42	9	6	6	37	35	4	6	11	24	47	38
Blackburn R	42	6	5	10	23	27	8	3	10	22	26	36
Bolton W	42	8	5	8	30	28	5	3	13	27	41	34
Charlton A	42	6	6	9	34	32	5	6	10	23	39	34
Huddersfield T	42	11	4	6	34	24	2	3	16	19	55	33
Brentford	42	5	5	11	19	35	4	2	15	26	53	25
Leeds U	42	6	5	10	30	30	0	1	20	15	60	18

DIVISION 2

	P	W	D	L	F	A	W	D	L	F	A	Pts
Manchester C	42	17	3	1	49	14	9	7	5	29	21	62
Burnley	42	11	8	2	30	14	11	6	4	35	15	58
Birmingham C	42	17	2	2	51	11	8	3	10	23	22	55
Chesterfield	42	12	6	3	37	17	6	8	7	21	27	50
Newcastle U	42	11	4	6	60	32	8	6	7	35	30	48
Tottenham H	42	11	8	2	35	21	6	6	9	30	32	48
WBA	42	12	4	5	53	37	8	4	9	35	38	48
Coventry C	42	12	8	1	40	17	4	5	12	26	42	45
Leicester C	42	11	4	6	42	25	7	3	11	27	39	43
Barnsley	42	13	2	6	48	29	4	6	11	36	57	42
Nottingham F	42	13	5	3	47	20	2	5	14	22	54	40
West Ham U	42	12	4	5	46	31	4	4	13	24	45	40
Luton T	42	13	4	4	50	29	3	3	15	21	44	39
Southampton	42	11	5	5	45	24	4	4	13	24	52	39
Fulham	42	12	4	5	40	25	3	5	13	23	49	39
Bradford	42	7	6	8	29	28	7	5	9	36	49	39
Bury	42	11	6	4	62	34	1	6	14	18	44	36
Millwall	42	7	7	7	30	30	7	1	13	26	49	36
Plymouth A	42	11	3	7	45	34	3	2	16	34	62	33
Sheffield W	42	10	5	6	39	28	2	3	16	28	60	32
Swansea T	42	9	1	11	36	40	2	6	13	19	43	29
Newport Co	42	9	1	11	41	52	1	2	18	20	81	23

DIVISION 3 North

	P	W	D	L	F	A	W	D	L	F	A	Pts
Doncaster R	42	15	5	1	67	16	18	1	2	56	24	72
Rotherham U	42	20	1	0	81	19	9	5	7	33	34	64
Chester	42	17	2	2	53	13	8	4	9	42	38	56
Stockport Co	42	17	0	4	50	19	7	2	12	28	34	50
Bradford C	42	12	5	4	40	20	8	5	8	22	27	50
Rochdale	42	9	5	7	39	25	10	5	6	41	39	48
Wrexham	42	13	5	3	43	21	4	7	10	22	30	46
Crewe A	42	12	4	5	39	26	5	5	11	31	48	43
Barrow	42	10	2	9	28	24	7	5	9	26	38	41
Tranmere R	42	11	5	5	43	33	6	2	13	23	44	41
Hull C	42	9	5	7	25	19	7	3	11	24	34	40
Lincoln C	42	12	3	6	52	32	5	2	14	34	55	39
Hartlepools U	42	10	5	6	36	26	5	4	12	28	47	39
Gateshead	42	10	3	8	39	33	6	3	12	23	39	38
York C	42	6	4	11	35	42	8	5	8	32	39	37
Carlisle U	42	10	5	6	45	38	4	4	13	25	55	37
Darlington	42	12	4	5	48	26	3	2	16	20	54	36
New Brighton	42	11	3	7	37	30	3	5	13	20	47	36
Oldham A	42	6	5	10	29	31	6	3	12	26	49	32
Accrington S	42	8	3	10	37	38	6	1	14	19	54	32
Southport	42	6	5	10	35	41	1	6	14	18	44	25
Halifax T	42	6	3	12	28	36	2	3	16	15	56	22

DIVISION 3 South

	P	W	D	L	F	A	W	D	L	F	A	Pts
Cardiff C	42	18	3	0	60	11	12	3	6	33	19	66
QPR	42	15	2	4	42	15	8	9	4	32	25	57
Bristol C	42	13	4	4	56	20	7	7	7	38	36	51
Swindon T	42	15	4	2	56	25	4	7	10	28	48	49
Walsall	42	11	6	4	42	25	6	6	9	32	34	46
Ipswich T	42	11	5	5	33	21	5	9	7	28	32	46
Bournemouth	42	12	4	5	43	20	6	4	11	29	34	44
Southend U	42	9	7	5	38	22	8	3	10	33	38	44
Reading	42	11	6	4	53	30	5	5	11	30	44	43
Port Vale	42	14	4	3	51	28	3	5	13	17	35	43
Torquay U	42	11	5	5	33	23	4	7	10	19	38	42
Notts Co	42	11	4	6	35	19	4	6	11	28	44	40
Northampton T	42	11	5	5	46	33	4	5	12	26	42	40
Bristol R	42	9	6	6	34	26	7	2	12	25	43	40
Exeter C	42	11	6	4	37	27	4	3	14	23	42	39
Watford	42	11	4	6	39	27	6	1	14	22	49	39
Brighton & HA	42	8	7	6	31	35	5	5	11	23	37	38
Crystal P	42	9	7	5	29	19	4	4	13	20	43	37
Leyton O	42	10	5	6	40	28	2	3	16	14	47	32
Aldershot	42	6	7	8	25	26	4	5	12	23	52	32
Norwich C	42	6	3	12	38	48	4	5	12	26	52	28
Mansfield T	42	8	5	8	31	38	1	5	15	17	58	28

Football League Records

Top scorers: Div 1, R.Rooke (Arsenal) 33 goals; Div 2, E.Quigley (Sheffield Wednesday) 23 goals; Div 3(N), J.Hutchinson (Lincoln City) 32 goals; Div 3(S), C.Townsend (Bristol City) 29 goals.
Mansfield Town transferred to Division Three North.

Arsenal goalkeeper George Swindin, ever-present in another title-winning season for the Gunners.

Reg Lewis, his scheming helped Ronnie Rooke score most of Arsenal's goals but Lewis also weighed in with 14 himself.

DIVISION 1

	ARSENAL	ASTON VILLA	BLACKBURN R	BLACKPOOL	BOLTON W	BURNLEY	CHARLTON A	CHELSEA	DERBY CO	EVERTON	GRIMSBY T	HUDDERSFIELD T	LIVERPOOL	MANCHESTER C	MANCHESTER U	MIDDLESBROUGH	PORTSMOUTH	PRESTON N.E.	SHEFFIELD U	STOKE C	SUNDERLAND	WOLVERHAMPTON W
1 ARSENAL		O11 1-0	a03 2-0	N08 2-1	S10 2-0	F14 3-0	S03 6-0	M20 0-2	a17 1-2	O25 1-1	m01 8-0	N22 2-0	D27 1-2	D06 1-1	S06 2-1	M26 7-0	O04 0-0	J31 3-0	J03 3-2	S20 3-0	A23 3-1	M06 5-2
2 ASTON VILLA	F28 4-2		a14 3-2	S13 0-1	N15 3-1	N29 2-2	M30 2-1	F21 3-0	a07 2-2	S08 3-0	D20 2-2	S27 2-1	a24 2-1	A30 1-1	M22 0-1	D13 1-1	M27 2-1	N01 4-1	O18 2-0	a10 1-0	S01 2-0	D26 1-2
3 BLACKBURN R	N15 0-1	S06 0-0		S15 1-1	N01 4-0	O18 1-2	M27 0-0	J01 1-1	D25 3-4	A23 2-3	S20 4-0	M26 1-2	a10 1-2	F14 1-0	D13 1-1	N29 1-7	M13 1-0	O04 2-3	a24 4-0	F28 2-0	J31 4-3	J03 1-0
4 BLACKPOOL	M27 3-0	J31 1-0	S08 1-0		a05 1-1	a07 0-1	N29 3-1	A23 3-0	M26 2-2	J03 5-0	F14 3-1	S01 4-0	N01 2-0	O04 1-1	a28 1-0	a10 1-0	O18 1-0	D13 0-1	N15 2-1	D25 1-2	S20 0-1	S06 2-2
5 BOLTON W	J01 0-1	a03 1-0	M20 1-0	O25 1-0		J03 1-1	F21 1-0	J31 2-1	a21 0-3	m01 0-0	a17 2-0	O11 1-5	F07 3-0	N22 2-1	M29 0-1	S27 1-3	S06 4-0	S01 1-2	D27 2-3	A23 0-1	N08 3-1	D06 3-2
6 BURNLEY	S27 0-1	a17 1-0	M06 0-0	O11 1-0	A30 2-0		a20 0-2	D06 1-0	A26 0-2	a03 0-1	M20 4-1	m01 2-1	J17 3-0	O25 1-1	S08 0-0	S13 3-0	D20 3-2	D25 1-0	F21 0-0	M26 4-0	N22 4-0	N08 1-1
7 CHARLTON A	A27 2-4	M26 1-1	N08 0-1	a17 2-0	O04 2-1	S20 1-1		O25 3-1	N22 1-5	M06 2-3	D06 2-3	M20 0-0	S17 2-0	a03 0-1	J03 1-2	D25 1-0	F14 2-2	S06 1-2	A23 4-0	J31 0-1	m01 1-0	O11 5-1
8 CHELSEA	N01 0-0	O04 4-2	A27 1-0	D20 2-2	S13 1-1	a24 0-2	M13 3-0		A30 1-0	S20 3-1	D27 2-3	J17 2-4	F28 3-1	M26 2-2	N29 0-4	O18 4-2	D13 1-0	M27 2-0	a10 1-0	N15 4-1	S10 1-1	F14 1-1
9 DERBY CO	N29 1-0	S20 1-3	D27 5-0	M29 1-0	O18 2-1	S03 1-1	a10 0-3	J03 5-1		S06 1-0	O04 4-1	A23 0-0	M31 0-4	S10 0-0	N15 1-1	N01 4-2	a28 2-1	a24 2-1	M27 1-1	D13 1-1	F14 5-1	a14 1-2
10 EVERTON	M13 0-2	S17 3-0	D20 4-1	A30 1-2	D13 2-0	N15 0-3	O18 0-1	a14 2-3	J17 1-3		M29 3-1	S13 1-1	S27 0-3	A27 1-0	a10 2-0	F28 2-1	a24 0-2	N29 2-1	N01 2-0	M27 0-1	D26 3-0	O04 1-1
11 GRIMSBY T	D13 0-4	A23 3-0	F07 2-2	S27 0-1	N29 0-2	N01 1-2	a24 1-3	D25 0-0	F21 2-3	M26 3-0		S17 3-0	M27 0-2	S13 1-0	M17 1-1	N15 0-5	a10 1-0	O18 1-1	S06 0-3	M13 0-0	J03 1-2	S03 0-4
12 HUDDERSFIELD T	a10 1-1	F14 0-1	M29 1-1	A27 2-0	F28 1-2	D13 0-1	N01 0-1	S06 3-1	D20 2-1	a28 1-3	S10 5-1		O18 1-1	D27 1-1	M27 0-2	M13 2-1	A30 0-2	N15 1-0	N29 2-1	a24 0-0	O04 2-2	S20 0-1
13 LIVERPOOL	D25 1-3	D06 3-3	N22 2-1	M20 2-0	S20 0-0	S06 1-1	J01 2-3	O11 3-0	O25 2-2	a21 4-0	N08 3-1	M06 4-0		a17 1-1	S03 2-2	F21 0-1	J31 0-3	A23 3-1	M26 4-0	J03 0-0	a03 0-0	m01 2-1
14 MANCHESTER C	a24 0-0	J03 0-2	S27 1-3	F21 1-0	a10 0-2	M13 4-1	N15 4-0	M29 1-0	S17 3-2	S03 0-1	J31 3-1	D26 1-1	N29 2-0		S20 0-0	M27 2-0	N01 1-0	a21 0-3	D13 4-3	O18 3-0	S06 3-0	A23 4-3
15 MANCHESTER U	J17 1-1	O25 2-0	m01 4-1	D06 1-1	M26 0-2	J01 5-0	A30 6-2	a17 5-0	a03 1-0	N22 2-2	O11 3-4	N08 4-4	A27 2-0	a07 1-1		D20 2-1	D25 3-2	F14 1-1	S13 0-1	O04 1-1	M06 3-1	M20 3-2
16 MIDDLESBROUGH	M29 1-1	m01 1-3	a17 1-1	N22 4-0	F14 4-1	J31 1-2	D27 1-2	M06 0-0	M20 1-1	O11 0-1	a03 4-1	O25 1-0	O04 3-1	N08 2-1	A23 2-2		S20 1-2	J03 1-1	S03 3-0	S06 2-1	D06 2-2	J01 2-4
17 PORTSMOUTH	a21 0-0	N08 2-4	O25 1-1	M06 1-1	J17 2-0	A23 0-1	S27 3-1	m01 2-1	O11 0-0	D06 3-0	N22 4-0	J03 3-2	S13 1-0	M20 1-0	D27 1-3	a14 6-1		M26 1-0	S17 6-0	S03 3-0	a17 2-2	a03 2-0
18 PRESTON N.E.	S13 0-0	M20 3-0	F21 2-1	m01 0-7	A25 1-0	D26 3-2	J17 2-1	N08 2-0	D06 7-4	a17 3-0	M06 2-1	a03 0-2	D20 3-3	O11 2-1	S27 2-1	A30 2-1	M29 1-2		a07 3-3	S17 2-1	O25 2-2	N22 1-3
19 SHEFFIELD U	A30 1-2	M06 3-1	D06 4-1	a03 2-1	D25 2-1	O04 1-1	D20 1-1	N22 3-1	N08 1-2	M20 2-1	J17 4-0	a17 0-1	S08 3-1	m01 2-1	J31 2-1	A25 1-1	J01 1-2	S20 3-1		F14 3-0	O11 3-2	O25 2-2
20 STOKE C	F07 0-0	N22 1-2	O11 2-1	D27 1-1	D20 2-0	M29 3-0	S13 0-1	a03 2-0	m01 1-0	N08 1-1	O25 2-1	D06 1-1	A30 0-2	M06 3-0	F21 0-2	J17 2-4	A25 2-1	S08 0-1	S27 1-1		M20 3-1	a17 2-3
21 SUNDERLAND	D20 1-1	A27 0-0	S13 0-1	a12 1-0	J24 1-2	a10 2-0	D13 0-1	S17 2-3	S27 1-1	D25 2-0	A30 4-2	F21 2-0	N15 5-1	J17 0-1	O18 1-0	a24 3-0	N29 4-1	M13 0-2	F28 1-1	N01 1-0		M26 2-1
22 WOLVERHAMPTON W	O18 1-1	D27 4-1	A30 5-1	J17 1-1	a24 1-0	M27 1-1	F28 2-0	S27 1-0	S13 1-0	F21 2-4	A27 8-1	F07 2-1	D13 1-2	D20 1-0	N01 2-6	S10 1-3	N15 3-1	a10 4-2	M13 1-1	N29 1-2	M29 2-1	

DIVISION 2

	BARNSLEY	BIRMINGHAM C	BRADFORD	BRENTFORD	BURY	CARDIFF C	CHESTERFIELD	COVENTRY C	DONCASTER R	FULHAM	LEEDS U	LEICESTER C	LUTON T	MILLWALL	NEWCASTLE U	NOTTINGHAM F	PLYMOUTH A	SHEFFIELD W	SOUTHAMPTON	TOTTENHAM H	W.B.A.	WEST HAM U
1 BARNSLEY		D20 0-1	D06 2-2	F14 1-1	N08 2-1	m01 1-2	O25 0-3	D26 0-1	N22 2-0	S10 1-2	A27 3-0	O04 2-0	S20 3-0	M06 1-0	M29 1-1	a17 2-2	J31 2-1	J17 3-1	a03 2-1	O11 2-1	A30 0-1	M20 1-1
2 BIRMINGHAM C	A23 2-3		N22 4-3	J31 0-0	O25 2-0	a17 2-0	O11 0-0	S03 1-1	N08 3-0	O04 3-1	F14 5-1	S20 1-0	S06 2-1	D27 1-0	S10 0-0	a03 2-1	J03 1-1	D06 1-0	M20 0-0	m01 0-0	M29 4-0	M06 0-1
3 BRADFORD	a24 3-2	a10 1-2		F28 1-1	M29 5-3	F14 0-1	J03 1-3	M27 2-2	S10 4-0	N01 3-0	M13 3-1	O18 0-2	O04 2-2	S06 4-0	N15 0-3	S03 3-1	D13 3-0	S20 2-0	D26 1-3	J31 0-2	N29 3-1	A23 4-1
4 BRENTFORD	S27 3-3	S13 1-2	O11 2-1		a17 4-1	O18 0-0	a03 0-3	A30 1-4	m01 2-0	D20 0-2	M26 3-0	D25 2-2	A27 0-3	N08 2-1	J17 1-0	S10 3-1	F21 0-0	O25 1-0	D06 2-2	M20 2-0	F07 1-0	N22 1-1
5 BURY	J24 1-1	M13 1-1	M26 0-4	N29 2-2		J01 1-2	F14 2-0	F28 0-0	A30 4-2	S13 1-0	D13 1-1	a24 0-2	a10 2-2	O04 0-0	O18 3-5	D20 1-0	N15 0-0	S10 1-2	J17 3-0	A27 2-0	N01 1-2	S20 1-2
6 CARDIFF C	D13 1-0	N29 2-0	S27 1-0	M06 1-0	D26 2-2		A23 0-0	N15 1-1	A25 3-0	M27 0-0	N01 0-0	M13 3-0	O11 1-0	J03 6-0	a10 1-1	F21 4-1	S20 3-0	J31 2-1	S08 5-1	S06 0-3	a24 0-5	M26 0-3
7 CHESTERFIELD	M13 1-1	F28 0-3	A30 0-1	N15 4-0	S27 1-2	D20 2-2		D13 4-3	S13 0-3	a24 1-0	N29 3-0	a10 2-3	M27 2-0	J01 2-0	A27 0-1	J17 0-0	N01 1-1	M26 0-2	a14 0-1	D27 3-1	O18 0-2	a07 6-0
8 COVENTRY C	D25 3-2	A25 0-1	N08 5-0	J03 3-0	O11 0-0	a03 1-0	m01 3-0		O25 1-0	S20 5-2	J31 1-2	S06 0-1	A23 4-1	D06 0-1	F21 1-1	M20 1-1	M30 0-0	N22 3-1	M06 0-1	a17 1-1	S15 1-0	F14 0-1
9 DONCASTER R	a10 1-2	M27 0-0	S18 3-0	D13 0-0	J03 1-3	S04 2-2	J31 1-0	M13 0-0		O18 0-1	F28 3-0	M26 1-1	a24 0-2	S20 2-2	N01 0-3	D26 2-0	N29 2-0	O04 0-1	A23 1-1	F14 1-1	N15 2-1	S06 1-0
10 FULHAM	S17 0-1	F21 1-1	M20 0-0	A23 5-0	J31 1-1	N08 4-1	D06 0-0	a28 0-2	M06 0-0		S06 3-2	J03 3-1	M29 1-1	a17 1-0	S27 3-0	O25 0-0	D25 1-1	a03 0-2	O11 0-2	N22 0-2	S03 0-1	m01 1-1
11 LEEDS U	S03 4-1	S27 0-1	O25 2-0	M29 1-1	m01 5-1	M20 4-0	a17 3-0	S13 2-1	O11 0-0	J17 0-1		A23 3-1	D26 0-2	N22 2-1	J24 3-1	M06 2-2	S10 5-0	N08 2-2	J03 0-0	a03 1-3	F21 3-1	D06 2-1
12 LEICESTER C	a05 4-1	a19 0-0	M06 2-0	D27 1-2	D06 2-1	O25 2-1	N22 1-2	J17 2-2	M29 3-2	A30 0-2	D20 2-0		S08 3-2	a03 3-0	S13 2-2	O11 3-1	A25 2-1	M20 2-3	a28 0-0	N08 0-3	S27 1-1	a17 1-3
13 LUTON T	a14 2-1	J17 0-1	F21 3-3	S03 3-0	N22 1-1	F28 1-1	N08 2-1	D20 2-3	D06 2-1	M26 0-3	D27 6-1	S17 2-1		M20 1-2	A30 2-1	m01 2-1	S27 0-0	M06 1-1	a17 0-2	O25 0-0	S13 1-1	a03 0-0
14 MILLWALL	O18 3-3	D25 0-0	J17 0-1	M27 0-1	F21 1-7	A30 0-1	S08 0-2	a24 6-2	F07 1-0	N29 1-2	a10 1-1	N15 0-4	N01 3-1		D13 2-1	S13 2-0	M13 2-0	D20 0-0	S27 3-0	M26 0-0	F28 1-1	S01 1-1
15 NEWCASTLE U	M26 1-0	S17 1-0	a03 2-0	S06 1-0	M06 1-0	N22 4-1	S03 2-3	O04 0-0	M20 2-0	a14 1-0	S20 4-2	J31 2-0	J03 4-1	m01 1-0		N08 0-2	A23 6-1	a17 4-2	O25 5-0	D06 1-0	J01 3-1	O11 1-0
16 NOTTINGHAM F	N29 1-1	N15 0-2	A27 1-2	S17 2-0	A23 2-1	O04 1-2	S06 1-3	N01 4-0	D27 4-2	M13 0-2	O18 1-0	F28 1-0	D13 1-2	J31 5-2	M27 0-0		a24 1-1	F14 0-0	M29 1-1	S20 1-0	a10 3-1	J03 2-1
17 PLYMOUTH A	S13 1-0	A30 0-3	m01 2-2	O04 0-0	a03 0-0	F07 3-0	M20 1-2	M29 1-0	a17 2-2	D27 3-2	S17 1-0	S03 0-0	F14 1-3	O25 1-1	D20 3-0	D06 1-1		O11 0-2	N22 3-1	M06 1-1	J17 2-1	N08 1-1
18 SHEFFIELD W	S06 5-2	a24 0-0	F07 3-1	a12 1-1	S15 2-2	S13 2-1	M29 1-0	a10 1-1	a05 2-0	N15 2-0	M27 3-1	N01 1-1	O18 1-0	A23 3-2	N29 1-0	S27 2-1	F28 1-1		S01 1-2	J03 1-0	D13 1-2	D26 5-3
19 SOUTHAMPTON	N15 4-1	N01 2-0	D27 1-2	a24 2-1	S06 1-0	S17 2-2	S20 3-0	O18 3-1	D20 6-1	a21 1-0	A30 1-2	D13 3-1	N29 3-1	F14 5-1	M13 4-2	M26 2-1	a10 2-3	A27 3-1		O04 1-1	M27 1-1	J31 3-1
20 TOTTENHAM H	M15 0-3	D13 1-2	S13 3-1	N01 4-0	S01 2-2	J17 2-1	D25 3-0	N29 2-1	S27 2-0	a10 0-2	N15 3-1	M27 0-0	a05 0-1	M29 3-2	a24 1-1	a12 0-3	O18 2-0	A30 5-1	F21 0-0		D20 1-1	S15 2-2
21 W.B.A.	J03 0-2	M30 1-1	a17 6-0	S20 3-2	M20 3-3	D06 2-3	M06 1-0	S10 3-1	a03 1-3	A27 2-1	O04 3-2	F14 1-3	J31 1-0	O11 2-1	D26 0-1	N22 3-2	S06 1-1	m01 1-1	N08 1-0	A23 1-0		O25 1-2
22 WEST HAM U	N01 2-1	O18 0-0	D20 0-0	a10 0-1	F07 2-0	M29 4-2	O04 4-0	S27 1-0	J24 2-1	D13 3-0	a24 2-1	N29 1-1	N15 0-0	A25 1-1	F28 0-2	A30 2-1	M27 1-1	D27 1-4	S13 2-0	S08 1-1	M13 0-2	

Season 1947-48

DIVISION 3 NORTH

	ACCRINGTON S	BARROW	BRADFORD C	CARLISLE U	CHESTER	CREWE A	DARLINGTON	GATESHEAD	HALIFAX T	HARTLEPOOLS U	HULL C	LINCOLN C	MANSFIELD T	NEW BRIGHTON	OLDHAM A	ROCHDALE	ROTHERHAM U	SOUTHPORT	STOCKPORT CO	TRANMERE R	WREXHAM	YORK C
1 ACCRINGTON S		S20 0-1	J31 2-0	D06 1-2	N22 1-0	a17 2-1	M06 3-0	O11 1-0	O04 2-0	A23 4-2	J03 2-4	D27 2-1	a03 1-0	S30 5-3	M20 2-3	J01 1-2	m01 0-1	M29 0-0	S06 5-2	O25 1-0	F14 0-2	N08 1-0
2 BARROW	F07 3-0		S11 0-1	M06 2-0	A28 1-0	O11 2-0	a03 0-0	N08 1-2	D26 2-1	M20 1-2	S27 0-2	S13 0-1	m01 1-0	A30 1-1	a17 2-4	a13 0-1	O25 1-3	D20 2-0	F21 0-0	N22 3-0	M26 1-1	D06 1-0
3 BRADFORD C	S13 1-2	S17 1-1		O11 1-1	m01 3-2	F21 1-2	N08 4-0	M20 2-2	M30 2-1	O25 3-1	F07 2-0	J17 2-4	D06 0-1	D20 1-1	N22 0-2	D25 4-0	M06 0-1	A30 4-2	S27 1-0	a03 4-1	A27 1-0	a17 1-3
4 CARLISLE U	D13 2-3	O18 1-2	F28 1-2		F21 2-0	S27 5-2	A23 4-2	J03 1-1	N01 5-2	S06 1-1	J24 0-0	J10 2-5	J01 3-1	N15 2-1	M26 4-1	M27 5-0	J31 0-3	a10 2-3	S20 4-0	D27 4-3	M13 1-2	S04 1-1
5 CHESTER	a10 1-0	S03 0-0	a21 2-1	O04 4-1		S10 4-2	S06 1-1	J31 2-3	O18 0-0	S20 2-0	M17 4-1	N15 1-1	M26 1-2	N01 4-2	A23 2-1	M13 2-1	F14 2-3	M27 0-0	a24 2-2	J03 4-0	F28 4-1	D27 2-3
6 CREWE A	a07 0-0	F28 1-2	O04 3-2	F14 0-2	S17 1-0		J03 4-1	S06 0-1	M13 0-1	J31 2-0	a24 3-1	a10 3-0	A27 0-0	M27 4-0	D25 2-2	N01 2-1	S20 3-3	N15 4-1	a14 4-2	A23 3-2	O18 1-0	M26 1-3
7 DARLINGTON	O18 3-1	N15 2-2	M27 1-1	D20 4-3	J17 1-1	A30 0-1		S01 1-1	J10 4-1	M26 1-0	M13 2-0	F28 1-3	S13 1-2	J24 3-1	S27 0-6	a24 0-0	D25 1-1	J01 1-3	N01 0-0	F21 0-2	a10 3-1	F07 1-1
8 GATESHEAD	F28 4-2	M27 0-2	N01 2-2	A30 1-3	S13 2-1	J17 2-0	A27 1-2		a10 3-0	D25 7-0	O18 0-1	M29 3-2	F07 2-1	a24 3-1	F21 3-5	J10 5-0	D20 1-1	J24 3-2	M13 1-1	J01 3-0	N15 2-2	S27 0-0
9 HALIFAX T	F21 3-3	D25 1-1	M29 0-0	M20 2-1	M06 1-1	O25 4-1	a17 1-1	N22 0-0		a03 0-0	S15 0-2	S27 0-1	O11 1-1	S13 1-2	m01 1-5	J17 2-3	N08 2-1	F07 0-0	S01 4-0	D06 2-2	A23 0-1	J03 0-1
10 HARTLEPOOLS U	a28 4-0	N01 0-3	M13 0-2	J17 1-1	F07 2-1	S13 0-1	M29 3-0	D27 3-2	N15 1-1		F28 3-1	J24 1-2	S27 1-0	J10 1-0	J01 3-1	a10 4-1	A30 2-2	a24 2-0	O18 0-0	A27 1-1	M27 0-2	F21 2-2
11 HULL C	A30 4-2	F14 0-0	S20 2-1	m01 3-1	a17 2-1	a22 2-1	O25 0-3	M06 2-3	S11 1-2	O11 5-0		D20 0-1	N22 1-1	M29 3-0	N08 1-0	A28 0-0	J17 5-3	D26 1-0	J31 1-0	M20 3-0	O04 1-1	a03 1-1
12 LINCOLN C	D25 2-3	J31 2-1	S06 3-0	a17 3-0	a03 4-2	N22 0-0	O11 3-1	M26 3-0	F14 3-1	m01 5-0	A23 2-3		N08 0-0	S10 1-2	O25 0-2	O04 3-0	D06 3-1	S03 3-1	J03 3-0	M06 2-0	S20 2-1	M20 0-0
13 MANSFIELD T	N15 1-0	J24 1-0	a24 1-1	S08 2-3	M29 2-1	S01 3-1	J31 4-0	S20 1-2	F28 3-1	F14 3-2	a10 1-1	M27 0-2		M13 5-0	J03 1-1	O18 1-1	O04 2-1	N01 2-0	a06 1-2	S06 1-3	D27 1-0	A23 1-2
14 NEW BRIGHTON	S03 0-1	J03 1-1	A23 0-2	a03 1-3	M20 0-1	N08 1-2	m01 2-1	D06 1-2	J31 1-0	a17 1-2	M26 1-0	J01 0-1	O25 2-2		O11 2-2	S20 0-0	N22 1-2	F21 2-2	D27 1-0	F14 0-2	S06 1-1	M06 2-1
15 OLDHAM A	N01 1-0	a06 2-1	a10 3-0	M29 2-1	D20 3-1	D26 0-0	F14 3-3	O04 0-1	J24 1-1	S16 0-2	M27 0-0	M13 0-0	A30 1-1	F28 3-0		S13 1-1	A26 1-5	O18 1-1	N15 0-0	S20 0-1	a24 1-4	J17 2-2
16 ROCHDALE	S09 1-3	A23 2-2	D27 2-0	N08 2-1	O25 2-2	M20 1-2	D06 2-1	a17 2-1	S06 2-1	N22 0-2	S02 1-0	a06 1-1	M06 1-2	F07 1-0	J31 2-0		a03 1-0	S27 2-1	M26 1-2	m01 1-1	J03 2-1	O11 3-0
17 ROTHERHAM U	S22 1-0	M13 0-0	O18 4-1	S13 7-2	S27 2-1	F07 5-1	D27 0-0	A23 0-0	M27 3-0	J03 3-2	S06 0-0	a24 0-2	a12 2-1	a10 6-1	S01 4-1	N15 4-1		S15 0-2	F28 4-1	M26 2-0	N01 6-0	J01 3-2
18 SOUTHPORT	M26 1-1	S06 1-2	J03 1-2	N22 0-4	N08 3-0	a03 2-0	S08 2-0	D13 2-1	S20 2-0	a19 2-0	D25 1-2	A26 1-1	M20 1-1	O04 4-0	M06 4-0	F14 2-2	a17 1-2		A23 0-4	O11 1-4	J31 1-0	O25 2-1
19 STOCKPORT CO	J17 1-1	O04 2-3	F14 3-3	F07 2-3	D06 4-1	m01 2-1	M20 1-3	O25 1-1	A25 2-1	M06 2-0	S13 0-0	A30 1-1	a17 5-0	D25 1-2	a03 3-0	M29 4-0	O11 2-2	a26 0-3		N08 2-0	S08 0-1	N22 4-2
20 TRANMERE R	M13 0-1	a10 1-0	N15 2-1	D26 0-3	A30 2-3	D20 2-0	O04 0-1	S09 3-0	a24 0-1	S02 1-0	N01 2-1	O18 1-4	J17 0-1	S27 1-0	F07 1-0	J24 4-1	M29 0-1	F28 2-2	M27 2-3		J10 2-3	S13 4-2
21 WREXHAM	S27 1-1	M29 3-1	S03 4-2	O25 2-1	O11 2-1	M06 1-1	N22 1-2	a03 0-3	D20 6-3	N08 3-1	F21 1-0	F07 3-0	D26 2-1	J17 0-0	D06 1-2	A30 5-1	M20 1-3	S13 2-0	S17 2-0	a17 6-0		m01 3-0
22 YORK C	M27 1-2	a24 0-0	J10 3-3	A25 2-2	D26 2-0	M29 0-1	S20 0-2	F14 3-1	A30 6-0	O04 4-0	N15 2-2	N01 0-1	D20 1-2	O18 3-1	S06 1-0	F28 0-0	S10 2-0	M13 3-3	a10 3-2	J31 1-2	J24 1-1	

DIVISION 3 SOUTH

	ALDERSHOT	BOURNEMOUTH	BRIGHTON & HA	BRISTOL C	BRISTOL R	CRYSTAL P	EXETER C	IPSWICH T	LEYTON O	NEWPORT CO	NORTHAMPTON T	NORWICH C	NOTTS CO	PORT VALE	Q.P.R.	READING	SOUTHEND U	SWANSEA T	SWINDON T	TORQUAY U	WALSALL	WATFORD
1 ALDERSHOT		a10 0-3	S27 1-1	a24 1-1	M26 2-0	S03 2-0	O18 0-0	J10 0-1	F28 0-0	M13 1-2	S17 1-1	a07 2-2	M27 1-0	J17 1-1	S13 1-4	J24 1-2	N01 1-1	N15 0-3	A30 2-2	a21 1-0	D27 3-1	F07 1-1
2 BOURNEMOUTH	N22 1-1		J03 4-1	S13 2-0	D06 3-0	a03 0-0	M29 2-1	J17 4-0	F21 1-1	S17 5-0	a17 2-0	m01 1-3	S03 2-0	O25 3-0	a14 0-1	F07 2-0	D27 0-1	A23 1-0	M20 1-0	N08 6-2	S27 1-1	O11 1-1
3 BRIGHTON & H.A.	F14 1-1	A30 0-2		O18 0-2	J31 3-1	O04 1-1	N15 0-1	J24 4-1	M27 0-0	a10 3-0	S20 2-3	S06 2-0	a24 1-3	D27 2-2	A27 0-5	M13 2-0	a07 1-0	O01 0-1	S17 1-0	M26 2-1	N01 0-4	a28 1-3
4 BRISTOL C	a20 2-4	J31 0-4	M00 1-2		F14 5-2	a17 2-0	D27 1-1	S20 4-0	S17 6-0	S03 1-0	m01 1-1	O11 6-0	J03 1-0	N08 2-1	M20 2-1	F21 0-2	A23 6-0	S06 3-2	a03 2-2	N22 1-2	M26 0-0	O25 1-2
5 BRISTOL R	M29 7-1	a24 1-2	S13 4-1	S27 0-2		S08 1-1	N01 2-2	a28 2-0	M13 0-2	M27 2-3	O04 1-2	F07 2-3	a10 2-0	D20 2-1	A30 0-1	F28 2-3	N15 1-2	S22 2-2	A25 3-1	D26 0-2	O18 2-3	J17 3-0
6 CRYSTAL P	A27 1-0	N15 2-0	a12 0-0	a05 4-0	S17 0-0		F28 1-2	a10 2-1	D20 2-0	O18 2-1	D25 1-0	M29 2-0	N01 1-1	S13 2-0	M15 0-1	a24 2-1	M13 0-0	M27 4-0	J17 1-1	A30 2-1	J24 2-3	S27 1-2
7 EXETER C	M06 4-0	M26 1-1	a03 1-0	D26 3-1	M20 4-0	O11 2-0		S10 1-0	A30 1-1	J31 4-4	O25 1-1	N08 2-0	F14 0-1	a07 0-0	a17 1-2	A27 1-0	S20 0-0	O04 3-1	m01 2-1	J17 0-2	a21 0-6	N22 3-1
8 IPSWICH T	a17 2-0	S06 1-1	O11 4-0	F07 1-0	m01 0-4	N22 3-0	S17 2-0		M29 1-0	D27 3-0	a21 5-2	J31 1-2	A23 2-0	M20 2-1	O25 1-0	S27 1-0	S03 4-0	J03 3-2	N08 0-1	a03 2-1	F21 3-1	M06 1-3
9 LEYTON O	O11 0-3	O04 2-0	N08 2-1	S11 0-2	O25 2-4	A23 1-1	J03 2-4	M26 1-1		S06 2-2	M06 5-0	M20 2-1	S20 2-1	a17 0-0	N22 1-3	D27 2-2	J31 2-0	F14 1-0	D06 0-3	m01 4-1	S04 0-1	a03 0-2
10 NEWPORT CO	O25 2-2	S11 2-2	N22 1-1	A28 1-0	N08 2-2	M06 3-1	S13 3-0	D25 3-1	J17 3-2		M20 1-2	a03 1-1	O04 3-1	m01 0-0	D06 0-0	D20 2-0	F14 1-5	M29 1-1	a08 2-0	O11 0-1	A30 4-2	a17 3-4
11 NORTHAMPTON T	S11 2-1	a29 3-6	F07 4-0	J24 0-4	F21 1-3	D27 3-1	M13 3-1	a24 4-2	O18 1-1	N01 1-1		S27 1-0	N15 1-2	A30 4-1	a08 1-1	M29 1-1	M27 2-0	a10 0-1	M18 0-0	A28 1-0	F28 2-1	S13 0-1
12 NORWICH C	O04 0-1	J24 0-1	J17 2-2	F28 2-3	S20 1-5	M26 3-1	M27 3-0	S13 1-5	N01 3-0	N15 1-2	F14 2-3		a28 0-1	A27 1-2	a21 5-2	O18 2-1	a10 1-0	a24 1-2	D27 2-2	S10 1-1	M13 1-0	A30 1-0
13 NOTTS CO	N08 0-2	A28 1-2	a22 4-0	A30 3-1	N22 4-2	M20 1-0	S27 1-1	a15 0-1	F07 1-4	F21 4-1	a03 3-2	a17 1-2		O11 2-1	S11 1-1	J17 5-1	M26 2-1	D26 5-1	M06 2-1	O25 0-0	S13 1-0	m01 3-3
14 PORT VALE	S06 6-4	M13 2-1	D25 5-0	M27 1-0	A23 1-1	J31 4-1	a24 1-1	N01 4-1	J10 3-0	J24 4-1	J03 1-0	S01 2-0	F28 1-2		M26 0-2	N15 1-0	O04 2-1	O18 1-1	F14 1-0	S20 1-1	a10 0-1	S15 7-0
15 Q.P.R.	J31 0-0	O18 1-0	S04 2-0	N01 2-0	J03 5-2	S20 1-0	S25 3-1	M13 2-0	a10 1-2	a24 1-0	S06 2-0	A23 3-1	S18 4-1	M29 2-1		M27 2-0	O02 3-2	a26 0-0	O04 0-2	F14 3-3	N15 2-1	D27 5-1
16 READING	m01 0-0	S20 3-0	O25 1-0	O04 2-7	O11 0-0	a21 0-0	S03 2-1	F14 1-2	D26 6-2	A23 0-0	M26 1-1	M06 2-4	S06 3-1	a03 2-0	N08 3-2		J03 1-3	J31 4-1	N22 2-3	a17 2-0	S17 0-1	M20 2-0
17 SOUTHEND U	M20 4-0	D26 0-2	a17 2-2	D20 4-0	a03 1-0	O25 2-1	F07 2-0	A27 3-2	S13 2-1	S27 1-0	N08 3-1	N22 0-0	M29 1-2	F21 1-1	m01 0-0	A30 1-1		S10 1-1	O11 1-0	M06 1-0	J17 1-1	J24 1-1
18 SWANSEA T	a03 2-1	D20 0-2	m01 0-0	J17 6-1	a17 0-1	N08 2-0	F21 2-0	A30 1-1	S27 5-0	M26 3-0	N22 5-1	D06 3-2	D27 1-1	M06 2-0	O11 3-1	S13 1-1	S18 3-0		O25 1-0	M20 1-1	F07 1-1	A28 3-0
19 SWINDON T	J03 1-0	N01 0-1	S10 1-1	N15 2-2	S03 1-1	S06 0-0	a14 3-2	M27 0-1	a24 0-1	S20 1-2	A23 0-0	D26 3-2	O18 1-1	S27 1-0	F21 0-0	a10 1-1	F28 0-0	M13 1-0		J31 2-2	a28 0-3	M26 3-0
20 TORQUAY U	A23 2-0	M27 0-1	M29 1-2	a10 2-3	D27 1-2	J03 3-3	S06 1-2	N15 3-0	J24 0-1	F28 4-1	S03 4-2	S17 1-1	M13 2-2	F07 5-0	S27 1-1	a28 1-2	O18 4-1	N01 1-1	S13 1-1		a24 3-2	F21 0-1
21 WALSALL	D25 3-0	F14 0-0	M20 0-0	M29 2-0	M06 2-0	D06 1-1	A23 4-0	O04 1-2	A28 3-1	J03 1-1	O11 2-0	O25 3-2	J31 2-1	N22 1-2	a03 0-1	S11 0-0	S06 6-0	S20 2-1	a17 1-0	a15 1-0		N08 2-0
22 WATFORD	S20 1-2	F28 0-3	A23 2-3	M13 1-1	S06 3-2	F14 0-5	a10 3-1	O18 2-3	N15 2-1	J10 1-2	J31 1-1	J03 2-2	a07 1-3	S10 1-1	D26 0-1	N01 0-1	a24 2-2	S03 4-1	M29 1-0	O04 2-2	M27 2-0	

LEAGUE TABLES

DIVISION 1

	P	W	D	L	F	A	W	D	L	F	A	Pts
Arsenal	42	15	3	3	56	15	8	10	3	25	17	59
Manchester U	42	11	7	3	50	27	8	7	6	31	21	52
Burnley	42	12	5	4	31	12	8	7	6	25	31	52
Derby Co	42	11	6	4	38	24	8	6	7	39	33	50
Wolves	42	12	4	5	45	29	7	5	9	38	41	47
Aston Villa	42	13	5	3	42	22	6	4	11	23	35	47
Preston NE	42	13	4	4	43	35	7	3	11	24	33	47
Portsmouth	42	13	5	3	44	17	6	2	13	24	33	45
Blackpool	42	13	4	4	37	14	4	6	11	20	27	44
Manchester C	42	13	3	5	37	22	2	9	10	15	25	42
Liverpool	42	9	8	4	39	23	7	2	12	26	38	42
Sheffield U	42	13	4	4	44	24	3	6	12	21	46	42
Charlton A	42	8	4	9	33	29	9	2	10	24	37	40
Everton	42	10	2	9	30	26	7	4	10	22	40	40
Stoke C	42	9	5	7	29	23	5	5	11	12	32	38
Middlesbrough	42	8	7	6	37	27	6	2	13	34	46	37
Bolton W	42	11	2	8	29	25	5	3	13	17	33	37
Chelsea	42	11	6	4	38	27	3	3	15	15	44	37
Huddersfield T	42	7	6	8	25	24	5	6	10	26	36	36
Sunderland	42	11	4	6	33	18	2	6	13	23	49	36
Blackburn R	42	8	5	8	35	30	3	5	13	19	42	32
Grimsby T	42	5	5	11	20	35	3	1	17	25	76	22

DIVISION 2

	P	W	D	L	F	A	W	D	L	F	A	Pts
Birmingham C	42	12	7	2	34	13	10	8	3	21	11	59
Newcastle U	42	18	1	2	46	13	6	7	8	26	28	56
Southampton	42	15	3	3	53	23	6	7	8	18	30	52
Sheffield W	42	13	6	2	39	21	7	5	9	27	32	51
Cardiff C	42	12	6	3	36	18	6	5	10	25	40	47
West Ham U	42	10	7	4	29	19	6	7	8	26	34	46
WBA	42	11	4	6	37	29	7	5	9	26	29	45
Tottenham H	42	10	6	5	36	24	5	8	8	20	19	44
Leicester C	42	10	5	6	36	29	6	6	9	24	28	43
Coventry C	42	10	5	6	33	16	4	8	9	26	36	41
Fulham	42	6	9	6	24	19	9	1	11	23	27	40
Barnsley	42	10	5	6	31	22	5	5	11	31	42	40
Luton T	42	8	8	5	31	25	6	4	11	25	34	40
Bradford	42	11	3	7	45	30	5	5	11	23	42	40
Brentford	42	10	6	5	31	26	3	8	10	13	35	40
Chesterfield	42	8	4	9	32	26	8	3	10	22	29	39
Plymouth A	42	8	9	4	27	22	1	11	9	13	36	38
Leeds U	42	12	5	4	44	20	2	3	16	18	52	36
Nottingham F	42	10	5	6	32	23	2	6	13	22	37	35
Bury	42	6	8	7	27	28	3	8	10	31	40	34
Doncaster R	42	7	8	6	23	20	2	3	16	17	46	29
Millwall	42	7	7	7	27	28	2	4	15	17	46	29

DIVISION 3 North

	P	W	D	L	F	A	W	D	L	F	A	Pts
Lincoln C	42	14	3	4	47	18	12	5	4	34	22	60
Rotherham U	42	15	4	2	56	18	10	5	6	39	31	59
Wrexham	42	14	3	4	49	23	7	5	9	25	31	50
Gateshead	42	11	5	5	48	28	8	6	7	27	29	49
Hull C	42	12	5	4	38	21	6	6	9	21	27	47
Accrington S	42	13	1	7	36	24	7	5	9	26	35	46
Barrow	42	9	4	8	24	19	7	9	5	25	21	45
Mansfield T	42	11	4	6	37	24	6	7	8	20	27	45
Carlisle U	42	10	4	7	50	35	8	3	10	38	42	43
Crewe A	42	12	4	5	41	24	6	3	12	20	39	43
Oldham A	42	6	10	5	25	25	8	3	10	38	39	41
Rochdale	42	12	4	5	32	23	3	7	11	16	49	41
York C	42	8	7	6	38	25	5	7	9	27	35	40
Bradford C	42	10	4	7	38	27	5	6	10	27	39	40
Southport	42	10	4	7	34	27	4	7	10	26	36	39
Darlington	42	7	8	6	30	31	6	5	10	24	39	39
Stockport Co	42	9	6	6	42	28	4	6	11	21	39	38
Tranmere R	42	10	1	10	30	28	6	3	12	24	44	36
Hartlepools U	42	10	6	5	34	23	4	2	15	17	50	36
Chester	42	11	6	4	44	25	2	3	16	20	42	35
Halifax T	42	4	10	7	25	27	3	3	15	18	49	27
New Brighton	42	5	6	10	20	28	3	3	15	18	53	25

DIVISION 3 South

	P	W	D	L	F	A	W	D	L	F	A	Pts
QPR	42	16	3	2	44	17	10	6	5	30	20	61
Bournemouth	42	13	5	3	42	13	11	4	6	34	22	57
Walsall	42	13	5	3	37	12	8	4	9	33	28	51
Ipswich T	42	16	1	4	42	18	7	2	12	25	43	49
Swansea T	42	14	6	1	48	14	4	6	11	22	38	48
Notts Co	42	12	4	5	44	27	7	4	10	24	32	46
Bristol C	42	11	4	6	47	26	7	3	11	30	39	43
Port Vale	42	14	4	3	48	18	2	7	12	15	36	43
Southend U	42	11	8	2	32	16	4	5	12	19	42	43
Reading	42	10	5	6	37	28	5	6	10	19	30	41
Exeter C	42	11	6	4	34	22	4	5	12	21	41	41
Newport Co	42	9	8	4	38	28	5	5	11	23	45	41
Crystal P	42	12	5	4	32	14	1	8	12	17	35	39
Northampton T	42	10	5	6	35	28	4	6	11	23	44	39
Watford	42	6	6	9	31	37	8	4	9	26	42	38
Swindon T	42	6	10	5	21	20	4	6	11	20	26	36
Leyton O	42	8	5	8	31	32	5	5	11	20	41	36
Torquay U	42	7	6	8	40	29	4	7	10	23	33	35
Aldershot	42	5	10	6	22	26	5	5	11	23	41	35
Bristol R	42	7	3	11	39	34	6	5	10	32	41	34
Norwich C	42	8	3	10	33	34	5	5	11	28	42	34
Brighton & HA	42	8	4	9	26	31	3	8	10	17	42	34

Football League Records

Top scorers: Div 1, W.Moir (Bolton Wanderers) 25 goals; Div 2, C.Wayman (Southampton) 32 goals; Div 3(N), W.Ardron (Rotherham United) 29 goals; Div 3(S), D.McGibbon (Bournemouth & Boscombe Athletic) 30 goals.

Portsmouth outside-left Jack Froggatt received so much fine service from Jimmy Dickinson as Portsmouth took the title in their golden jubilee season.

DIVISION 1

	ARSENAL	ASTON VILLA	BIRMINGHAM C	BLACKPOOL	BOLTON W	BURNLEY	CHARLTON A	CHELSEA	DERBY CO	EVERTON	HUDDERSFIELD T	LIVERPOOL	MANCHESTER C	MANCHESTER U	MIDDLESBROUGH	NEWCASTLE U	PORTSMOUTH	PRESTON N.E.	SHEFFIELD U	STOKE C	SUNDERLAND	WOLVERHAMPTON W
1 ARSENAL		S11 3-1	N06 2-0	a18 2-0	F26 5-0	O09 3-1	m07 2-0	a23 1-2	D25 3-3	O23 5-0	D18 3-0	S08 1-1	D04 1-1	A28 0-1	a09 1-1	N20 0-1	m04 3-2	M12 0-0	J15 5-3	A25 3-0	F05 5-0	S25 3-1
2 ASTON VILLA	J22 1-0		D04 0-3	J01 2-5	A30 2-4	N06 3-1	O23 4-3	M26 1-1	S04 1-1	N20 0-1	S18 3-3	A21 2-1	M12 1-0	F19 2-1	m07 1-1	S13 2-4	O09 1-1	a09 2-0	O02 4-3	a23 2-1	a19 1-1	D27 5-1
3 BIRMINGHAM C	a02 1-1	a30 0-1		a16 1-1	M05 0-0	F05 0-0	F26 1-0	A28 1-0	O30 0-1	F12 0-0	N13 1-0	O16 0-1	S15 4-1	M19 1-0	A25 0-0	D25 2-0	a18 3-0	S11 1-0	N27 1-2	S25 2-1	D11 0-0	D18 0-1
4 BLACKPOOL	a15 1-1	A28 1-0	O23 1-0		F12 1-0	m07 1-1	M26 0-1	M12 2-1	S06 1-1	O09 3-0	D25 0-0	S25 1-0	N20 1-1	A23 0-3	a23 1-1	N06 1-3	a09 1-0	F26 2-2	D18 0-3	D04 2-1	J15 3-3	S11 1-3
5 BOLTON W	O02 1-0	A25 3-0	O09 0-0	S18 2-2		M26 0-1	a09 2-2	m04 1-1	F19 4-0	m07 1-0	S06 1-2	J22 0-3	N06 5-1	a15 0-1	M12 4-1	O23 1-5	a23 1-2	D04 5-3	D27 6-1	N20 2-1	D18 4-1	A28 0-5
6 BURNLEY	M05 1-1	a02 1-1	S18 2-2	D11 2-0	N27 3-0		A31 0-0	F19 3-0	a15 3-1	O02 1-0	O16 1-2	a30 0-2	A21 1-0	a16 0-2	J22 0-0	S04 0-3	J01 2-1	S06 1-0	O30 2-0	D25 1-3	N13 3-1	M19 0-0
7 CHARLTON A	D11 4-3	a16 0-2	O02 1-1	N27 0-0	N13 1-4	A25 3-1		S08 1-1	a30 1-5	a02 3-1	A28 3-1	M19 2-1	S04 3-2	M05 2-3	F19 2-0	S18 0-0	J22 0-1	D25 0-0	O16 2-1	D18 4-1	O30 4-0	a13 2-3
8 CHELSEA	O30 0-1	N27 2-1	J01 2-0	O16 3-3	S04 2-2	S25 1-0	S16 2-2		a16 0-3	S11 6-0	a02 5-0	M05 2-1	a18 1-1	N13 1-1	A21 1-0	S01 2-3	D25 1-2	F05 5-3	M19 1-0	F26 2-2	a30 0-1	D11 4-1
9 DERBY CO	D27 2-1	a27 2-2	a23 1-0	S15 3-1	S25 1-0	a18 2-0	D04 5-1	O23 2-1		M12 3-2	A25 4-1	m04 3-0	M26 2-0	D18 1-3	N06 2-0	a09 2-4	N20 1-0	O09 1-0	A28 2-1	m07 4-1	S11 2-2	F05 3-2
10 EVERTON	a16 0-0	M19 1-3	S04 0-5	M05 5-0	D11 1-0	F26 2-1	a18 1-1	J22 2-1	O16 0-1		O30 2-0	S18 1-1	D25 0-0	a27 2-0	J01 3-1	A21 3-3	S01 0-5	S25 4-1	N13 2-1	S08 2-1	N27 1-0	m04 1-0
11 HUDDERSFIELD T	A21 1-1	F12 0-1	a09 0-0	D27 1-0	S15 0-2	M12 1-0	J01 1-2	N06 3-4	S01 1-1	a23 1-1		a18 0-4	m07 1-0	a06 2-1	N20 0-0	M26 0-2	D04 0-0	O23 0-2	S11 0-0	O09 1-3	S25 2-0	m05 4-0
12 LIVERPOOL	S15 0-1	D18 1-1	M12 1-0	F19 1-1	S11 0-1	D04 1-1	N20 1-1	O09 1-1	O02 0-0	F05 0-0	a15 0-1		a09 0-1	D27 0-2	O23 4-0	a23 1-1	N06 3-1	m07 0-2	A25 3-3	M26 4-0	A28 4-0	a06 0-0
13 MANCHESTER C	a27 0-3	O16 4-1	S08 1-0	M19 1-1	a02 1-0	D18 2-2	J15 0-1	a15 1-0	N27 2-1	D27 0-0	D11 3-1	N13 2-4		S11 0-0	O02 1-0	F19 1-0	S18 1-1	A25 3-2	M05 1-0	A28 0-0	a16 1-1	O30 3-3
14 MANCHESTER U	J01 2-0	S25 3-1	N20 3-0	S01 3-4	a18 3-0	O23 1-1	O09 1-1	a09 1-1	A21 1-2	N06 2-0	S04 4-1	D25 0-0	J22 0-0		m02 1-0	D04 1-1	m07 3-2	a23 2-2	m04 3-2	M12 3-0	a21 1-2	S15 2-0
15 MIDDLESBROUGH	N13 0-1	D11 6-0	S01 1-1	O30 1-0	O16 5-0	S11 4-1	S25 2-4	D18 1-1	a02 1-0	A28 1-0	M19 1-0	a16 0-1	F26 0-1	N27 1-4		a18 3-2	S15 1-1	J15 1-0	a30 3-1	a27 1-1	D27 0-0	M05 4-4
16 NEWCASTLE U	M19 3-2	S08 2-1	D27 1-0	a02 3-1	a16 1-1	J15 1-1	F05 2-0	A25 2-2	N13 3-0	D18 1-0	N27 2-4	O30 1-0	S25 0-0	a30 0-1	a15 1-0		a06 0-5	A28 2-5	D11 3-2	S11 2-2	M05 2-1	O16 3-1
17 PORTSMOUTH	N27 4-1	M05 3-0	a15 3-1	N13 1-1	O30 0-0	A28 1-0	S11 3-1	D27 5-2	M19 1-0	A25 4-0	a30 2-0	a02 3-2	F05 3-1	D11 2-2	S08 1-0	O02 1-0		D18 3-1	S25 3-0	J15 1-0	O16 3-0	a16 5-0
18 PRESTON N.E.	O16 1-1	N13 0-1	J22 0-0	O02 1-3	a30 1-1	S15 0-3	D27 2-3	S18 3-2	M05 0-0	F19 3-1	a16 2-0	D11 3-2	S01 1-3	O30 1-6	S04 6-1	J01 2-1	A21 2-2		a02 4-1	a15 2-1	M19 1-3	N27 1-1
19 SHEFFIELD U	S04 1-1	F26 0-1	M26 4-0	A21 3-2	D25 1-1	a23 0-0	M12 2-0	N20 2-1	J01 3-1	a09 1-1	J22 0-0	A30 1-2	O09 0-2	S18 2-2	D04 1-0	m07 0-0	F19 3-1	N06 3-2		O23 2-2	S06 2-5	a18 1-1
20 STOKE C	A30 1-0	O30 4-2	F19 2-1	a30 3-2	M19 4-0	D27 2-1	A21 2-2	O02 4-3	D11 4-2	S13 1-0	M05 1-3	N27 3-0	J01 2-3	O16 2-1	S18 3-0	J22 1-1	S04 0-1	a18 2-0	a16 0-1		a02 0-0	N13 2-1
21 SUNDERLAND	S18 1-1	a15 0-0	m07 1-1	S04 2-2	A21 2-0	a09 0-0	a23 1-0	D04 3-0	J22 2-1	M26 1-1	F19 0-1	J01 0-2	O23 3-0	O02 2-1	D25 1-0	O09 1-1	M12 1-4	N20 0-0	S15 2-0	N06 1-1		S01 3-3
22 WOLVERHAMPTON W	F19 1-3	D25 4-0	A21 2-2	J22 2-1	J01 2-0	N20 3-0	N06 2-0	m07 1-1	S18 2-2	D04 1-0	O02 7-1	S04 0-0	a23 1-1	S08 3-2	O09 0-3	M12 3-0	O23 3-0	m02 2-1	a19 6-0	a09 3-1	A25 0-1	

Jimmy Dickinson, a magnificent club servant to Portsmouth and the inspiration behind their successive First Division wins. His eventual 764 League appearances were then a record for one club.

DIVISION 2

	BARNSLEY	BLACKBURN R	BRADFORD	BRENTFORD	BURY	CARDIFF C	CHESTERFIELD	COVENTRY C	FULHAM	GRIMSBY T	LEEDS U	LEICESTER C	LINCOLN C	LUTON T	NOTTINGHAM F	PLYMOUTH A	Q.P.R.	SHEFFIELD W	SOUTHAMPTON	TOTTENHAM H	W.B.A.	WEST HAM U
1 BARNSLEY		J01 1-1	F19 0-0	N06 1-2	a23 3-2	S04 1-1	m07 0-1	M12 1-1	S01 1-1	D27 2-1	O23 1-1	a06 3-1	a18 2-0	S18 1-2	S08 4-0	A21 0-0	J22 4-0	O09 4-0	O02 3-0	a09 4-1	D04 2-0	N20 2-3
2 BLACKBURN R	A28 5-3		A23 2-3	m07 2-1	M12 1-2	a15 2-1	M26 0-2	N20 2-0	F05 1-0	J15 3-3	a23 0-0	D04 2-0	N06 7-1	S20 4-1	S11 2-1	S25 2-1	D25 2-0	a09 2-1	D18 1-2	F26 1-1	O23 0-0	O09 0-0
3 BRADFORD	S25 0-2	S01 2-0		O23 3-1	a09 4-1	A21 3-0	a23 1-1	J22 2-1	D25 1-1	F26 0-1	O09 1-1	M12 3-3	m04 0-3	S04 4-1	a18 1-2	S15 2-2	J01 0-0	m07 1-1	a04 2-0	M26 1-1	N20 4-1	N06 2-3
4 BRENTFORD	a02 0-0	D11 0-1	M19 1-0		F19 8-2	D25 1-1	J22 1-1	A21 2-2	a06 0-0	N13 2-0	S01 1-3	S15 1-2	S04 2-1	O16 2-0	a16 2-1	a30 2-2	M05 0-3	J01 2-1	O30 0-0	a18 1-1	S18 0-0	O02 0-0
5 BURY	N27 4-2	O16 3-1	N13 2-1	S25 1-2		M19 0-3	A21 2-2	D25 0-2	S04 2-0	a30 5-1	a18 3-1	m04 1-2	S01 3-1	a02 3-1	D11 1-1	a27 1-1	O30 0-0	S08 2-1	a16 1-0	F05 1-1	J01 4-0	S11 2-0
6 CARDIFF C	J15 0-3	a18 1-0	D18 6-1	D27 2-0	a04 2-1		N06 3-4	a23 3-0	S25 2-1	S11 3-0	D04 2-1	m07 1-1	a09 3-1	A23 3-3	F05 1-0	F26 1-0	S13 3-0	N20 1-1	A28 2-1	O09 0-1	M26 2-2	M12 4-0
7 CHESTERFIELD	D11 3-2	O30 0-0	N27 2-3	S11 0-1	D18 4-0	a02 0-2		F26 0-0	O16 0-1	S08 0-3	S25 3-1	F05 1-1	D27 3-1	a16 1-0	M05 2-1	M19 0-0	N13 2-1	a15 1-1	a30 1-0	J15 1-0	S01 0-0	A28 0-0
8 COVENTRY C	O16 4-0	a16 0-1	S11 2-0	D18 2-1	D27 2-1	N27 0-1	O02 0-2		a02 1-0	M19 4-1	J15 4-1	A28 1-2	F19 1-0	D11 2-0	O30 1-2	N13 1-1	a30 1-1	S18 3-4	M05 2-2	A23 2-0	a19 1-0	S06 1-0
9 FULHAM	A25 1-1	S18 1-1	D27 2-0	a23 2-1	J15 7-2	F19 4-0	M12 2-1	N06 1-0		D18 3-1	a09 1-0	N20 1-0	O23 2-1	a15 4-1	A28 4-0	J22 6-1	O02 5-0	M26 1-1	S08 1-0	D04 1-1	O09 1-2	m07 2-0
10 GRIMSBY T	D25 3-0	S04 1-2	O02 0-3	a09 3-0	D04 2-3	J22 2-2	S14 3-3	O23 4-1	A21 2-3		M26 5-1	N06 1-0	O09 2-2	m03 2-1	A24 1-2	J01 2-2	S18 4-1	M12 2-0	a15 0-1	N20 1-1	m07 1-0	a23 3-0
11 LEEDS U	M19 4-1	J29 1-0	M05 4-2	A25 0-0	F12 0-1	a30 0-0	F19 1-0	S04 4-1	N13 1-1	O30 6-3		D18 3-1	S18 3-1	A28 2-0	a02 1-0	a16 1-0	D11 1-2	J22 1-1	O16 1-1	S08 0-0	O02 1-3	D27 1-3
12 LEICESTER C	O30 1-1	a21 3-1	O16 2-2	S06 0-0	O02 3-2	D11 2-2	S18 2-2	J01 3-1	a16 0-3	a02 1-1	A21 6-2		J22 5-3	M05 1-1	N13 4-2	N27 1-1	A30 2-3	S04 2-2	M19 1-3	D25 1-2	m05 0-3	a18 1-1
13 LINCOLN C	a15 0-1	a02 3-0	D04 3-6	J15 3-1	A25 1-1	N13 0-0	D25 2-2	S25 1-0	M19 0-3	M05 2-3	F05 0-0	S11 2-0		N27 4-4	O16 1-3	O30 1-2	a16 0-0	F26 3-1	D11 1-2	A28 0-0	S15 0-3	D18 4-3
14 LUTON T	F05 1-0	S06 2-0	J15 0-1	M12 2-1	N06 1-0	A30 3-0	N20 1-0	m07 2-0	a18 1-3	S25 1-1	J01 0-0	O09 1-1	a23 6-0		F26 4-3	D25 3-1	A21 0-0	D04 2-1	S11 1-1	O23 1-1	a09 0-1	M26 0-1
15 NOTTINGHAM F	S15 0-1	J22 1-0	a15 2-0	N20 1-2	m07 1-0	S18 0-0	O09 0-1	M26 3-0	J01 0-2	S01 0-0	N06 0-0	a09 2-1	M12 1-1	O02 2-0		S04 1-0	F19 0-0	O23 1-2	D25 2-1	a23 2-2	A21 0-1	D04 3-0
16 PLYMOUTH A	D18 3-1	F19 3-0	S08 3-0	D04 1-0	O09 1-0	O02 0-1	O23 2-2	a09 2-3	S11 3-1	A28 0-2	N20 2-1	a23 1-1	M26 0-0	D27 1-1	J29 1-0		a18 3-1	N06 3-2	A25 1-2	m07 0-5	M12 1-2	F05 2-0
17 Q.P.R.	S11 2-2	D27 4-2	A28 1-0	O09 2-0	M26 3-1	S09 0-0	a09 1-1	D04 0-3	F26 1-0	F05 1-2	m07 2-0	A26 4-1	N20 2-0	D18 0-3	S25 2-1	a15 2-1		a23 1-3	J29 1-3	M12 0-0	N06 0-2	O23 2-1
18 SHEFFIELD W	M05 1-1	N13 3-0	D11 2-1	A28 0-0	S13 1-2	a16 1-1	a19 0-0	F05 2-1	O30 1-2	O16 4-1	S11 3-1	a11 0-1	O02 2-2	a30 0-0	M19 2-1	a02 2-1	N27 2-0		S25 2-0	D18 3-1	D27 2-1	A23 3-0
19 SOUTHAMPTON	F26 3-0	A21 3-0	S18 2-2	M26 2-0	N20 2-0	J01 2-0	D04 1-0	O09 5-2	S15 3-0	a18 0-0	M12 2-1	O23 6-0	F12 4-0	J22 1-1	D27 2-1	S01 2-0	S04 3-0	F19 1-0		N06 3-1	a23 1-1	a09 0-1
20 TOTTENHAM H	N13 4-1	O02 4-0	O30 5-1	a15 2-0	S18 3-1	M05 0-1	S04 4-0	A30 4-0	a30 1-1	a16 5-2	S13 2-2	D27 1-1	J01 1-2	M19 2-1	F12 2-1	D11 3-0	O16 1-0	A21 3-2	a02 0-1		J22 2-0	F19 1-1
21 W.B.A.	a30 2-0	M19 2-1	a16 7-1	F05 2-0	A28 2-3	O30 2-0	A25 0-0	a18 1-0	M05 1-2	D11 5-2	a06 1-0	S25 2-1	S08 5-0	N13 2-1	D18 2-1	O16 3-0	a02 1-1	D25 1-0	N27 2-0	S11 2-2		J15 2-1
22 WEST HAM U	a16 2-0	M05 2-1	a02 4-1	a25 1-1	J22 2-1	O16 3-1	J01 1-2	S13 2-2	D11 1-0	F12 1-0	D25 3-2	a15 4-1	A21 2-2	O30 0-1	a30 0-5	S18 3-0	M19 2-0	A30 2-2	N13 1-1	S25 1-0	S04 1-0	

Season 1948-49

DIVISION 3 NORTH

	ACCRINGTON S	BARROW	BRADFORD C	CARLISLE U	CHESTER	CREWE A	DARLINGTON	DONCASTER R	GATESHEAD	HALIFAX T	HARTLEPOOLS U	HULL C	MANSFIELD T	NEW BRIGHTON	OLDHAM A	ROCHDALE	ROTHERHAM U	SOUTHPORT	STOCKPORT CO	TRANMERE R	WREXHAM	YORK C
1 ACCRINGTON S		F05 1-1	a18 6-0	J29 2-1	M19 3-1	a02 2-0	D18 3-2	D27 2-0	a30 1-2	F26 1-0	D11 1-2	S28 1-2	S11 1-1	O16 5-1	A28 1-1	a27 0-0	A25 2-3	O30 3-1	a16 2-1	J15 0-2	S25 0-1	N13 2-1
2 BARROW	S18 0-0		A21 0-0	O30 0-0	F12 1-1	a05 1-0	a16 1-1	J01 3-1	a02 3-0	A31 0-0	N13 2-0	S04 1-2	a15 1-0	a30 2-1	F19 2-1	J29 0-1	J22 0-2	D27 2-1	M19 2-1	O02 0-0	S07 1-1	O16 5-0
3 BRADFORD C	a19 2-2	J08 0-2		M05 1-2	a16 3-2	a30 1-2	O30 0-2	S18 0-1	O16 1-1	J15 2-1	M19 0-0	F19 4-2	A25 1-0	N13 1-1	D27 2-1	a02 1-0	O02 1-2	J29 4-2	S11 1-1	S08 1-3	A28 1-2	F12 2-2
4 CARLISLE U	a23 4-1	M26 2-0	O09 3-2		A21 2-1	S04 6-2	D27 0-2	F19 3-0	F26 2-1	M12 0-0	a18 0-0	m07 1-1	N06 3-1	S02 2-2	N20 2-0	S16 1-1	D04 1-8	J01 4-2	S18 2-1	a09 2-2	O23 3-2	J22 3-3
5 CHESTER	O23 3-0	m04 4-1	N20 3-0	D18 2-1		D27 1-1	S11 1-2	a09 1-2	A28 1-1	a23 0-1	J15 0-0	N06 0-2	F26 1-1	S25 2-0	M12 2-2	F05 2-1	M26 1-1	a15 2-0	A25 2-0	O09 2-2	D04 2-0	S08 4-1
6 CREWE A	N06 2-0	O09 0-1	a27 2-1	J15 3-0	D25 1-0		S25 3-1	a23 0-0	S11 2-1	m07 0-0	F05 3-0	N20 0-0	M12 3-1	a15 2-1	M26 0-4	F26 1-2	a09 0-3	S06 1-0	A28 3-3	O23 2-0	A25 1-0	J29 2-0
7 DARLINGTON	A21 3-0	N20 2-3	M26 1-5	D25 2-2	J22 3-3	F19 4-1		O23 1-5	S08 1-3	N06 2-1	A25 2-0	M12 0-1	a23 1-2	S04 0-2	m07 2-1	J01 6-1	O09 2-0	S18 0-1	a15 1-1	D04 3-2	a09 3-1	O02 3-1
8 DONCASTER R	D25 0-0	A28 0-0	F05 2-0	S25 2-0	N13 0-0	S23 0-1	M19 1-1		M05 2-1	J22 1-2	O16 0-0	O02 0-0	D18 1-1	a02 2-1	S06 3-0	O30 1-0	a15 0-0	a16 1-2	S30 3-1	A26 2-0	J15 4-2	a30 1-0
9 GATESHEAD	D04 1-1	N06 3-0	M12 6-2	O02 3-0	J01 2-1	J22 4-1	S13 1-3	O09 0-3		O23 1-2	D25 2-1	a18 0-2	a09 0-0	A21 3-0	a23 2-2	A30 2-1	m07 3-2	S04 2-2	F19 0-1	N20 3-3	M26 2-0	S18 1-1
10 HALIFAX T	O02 1-0	A23 1-0	S04 1-1	O16 3-4	J29 1-2	F12 0-0	a02 0-3	S11 1-0	M19 2-2		O30 2-0	S18 2-4	S13 2-2	a16 0-2	a18 3-1	N13 2-1	F19 2-0	a30 0-1	M05 0-1	D25 0-1	D18 2-0	A28 1-2
11 HARTLEPOOLS U	J08 1-0	a09 1-0	O23 1-0	a15 1-0	S04 2-1	S18 4-1	A30 0-1	M12 2-1	D27 1-3	M26 0-0		O09 0-2	N20 1-1	J01 3-1	D04 1-2	A21 6-1	S13 1-4	J22 2-2	O02 0-0	a23 3-0	N06 2-2	F19 2-3
12 HULL C	S09 3-1	J15 3-0	S25 2-0	M23 3-0	a02 3-2	a16 5-0	O16 0-1	m04 0-1	a15 2-0	F05 6-0	M05 2-0		A28 4-0	O30 4-1	A26 6-0	M19 1-1	D25 3-2	N13 5-1	a30 6-1	M30 2-0	S11 3-0	a06 2-3
13 MANSFIELD T	J22 2-0	a18 2-0	A30 1-0	a02 2-0	O02 1-0	O16 5-1	J29 2-2	A21 2-2	N13 1-1	S06 2-1	a16 1-0	J01 1-1		F12 2-0	S18 3-2	a30 2-0	S04 1-2	M05 1-1	O30 4-0	F19 0-0	D27 1-2	M19 3-0
14 NEW BRIGHTON	M12 1-3	a27 3-1	a09 1-0	A25 2-0	F19 1-1	a18 2-1	J15 1-0	N06 0-1	m04 2-2	N20 2-0	A28 1-1	M26 0-0	D04 1-0		O09 0-1	S11 1-2	O23 0-1	O02 0-1	S08 0-2	F05 2-1	a23 2-0	D25 3-1
15 OLDHAM A	J01 4-3	S25 2-1	D25 1-2	a16 1-0	O16 2-1	O30 3-2	F12 7-1	S14 0-2	a12 0-0	a15 2-2	a30 5-1	a26 1-1	F05 4-0	M05 4-2		S04 0-1	A21 1-3	M19 2-1	N13 5-2	S11 0-2	F26 1-1	a02 4-0
16 ROCHDALE	O09 4-1	a23 3-0	N06 1-1	S07 1-0	S18 3-1	O02 3-0	A28 3-4	M26 0-2	A24 3-0	a09 1-0	D18 0-1	O23 1-1	a04 1-0	J22 1-1	J15 1-2		M12 2-0	F19 1-0	D27 2-0	m07 2-1	N20 2-1	a18 2-0
17 ROTHERHAM U	A30 1-0	S11 2-2	F26 2-0	a30 1-1	O30 2-1	N13 6-1	M05 4-3	a18 2-0	D18 1-0	S25 4-0	S06 2-1	D27 0-0	J15 1-0	M19 1-1	a04 2-1	O16 3-1		a02 1-0	F12 2-1	A28 7-0	F05 1-3	a16 2-1
18 SOUTHPORT	M26 3-0	D25 0-0	a23 2-1	A28 2-2	a18 2-1	S14 0-0	F05 1-3	N20 0-2	J15 0-3	a26 2-3	S11 1-2	a09 0-0	O09 1-1	F26 0-1	O23 0-1	S25 3-1	N06 1-3		m02 1-0	M12 2-3	m07 3-0	A23 0-2
19 STOCKPORT CO	N20 2-1	O23 1-2	J22 5-2	F05 2-0	S01 1-1	J01 4-0	a18 2-0	m07 5-1	S25 3-1	O09 3-1	F26 4-0	D04 0-0	M26 2-0	S15 1-0	a09 1-2	D25 2-2	a23 0-1	A21 0-0		N06 4-1	M12 1-0	S04 1-1
20 TRANMERE R	S04 2-2	F26 2-0	S14 1-0	N13 2-1	m02 1-1	M19 2-2	a28 2-1	A31 2-0	a16 1-1	D27 2-2	J29 0-2	A21 1-2	S25 1-0	S18 0-1	J22 1-1	F12 0-0	J01 2-1	O16 1-0	a02 0-0		a15 0-2	O30 0-0
21 WREXHAM	F19 1-0	S15 1-0	J01 5-0	M19 4-0	J08 1-0	S01 2-2	N13 4-3	S04 2-0	O30 1-4	A21 2-1	a02 1-0	J22 0-2	m04 1-1	J29 2-1	O02 1-1	a16 2-0	S18 0-4	F12 2-0	O16 0-0	a18 0-0		M05 3-3
22 YORK C	a09 1-1	M12 2-0	m07 0-2	S11 6-0	S13 2-0	A21 1-3	F26 2-5	J08 2-3	F05 0-1	J01 2-2	S25 4-0	a23 1-3	O23 2-1	D27 2-1	N06 4-0	a15 1-1	N20 6-1	A30 1-3	J15 4-0	M26 1-0	O00 5-1	

DIVISION 3 SOUTH

	ALDERSHOT	BOURNEMOUTH	BRIGHTON & HA	BRISTOL C	BRISTOL R	CRYSTAL P	EXETER C	IPSWICH T	LEYTON O	MILLWALL	NEWPORT CO	NORTHAMPTON T	NORWICH C	NOTTS CO	PORT VALE	READING	SOUTHEND U	SWANSEA T	SWINDON T	TORQUAY U	WALSALL	WATFORD
1 ALDERSHOT		m07 0-0	F05 1-1	D25 0-0	N06 1-5	O09 3-0	S15 1-2	a06 2-0	A21 1-1	S04 5-0	a23 1-2	F26 3-1	a15 4-1	M26 0-1	J01 0-1	M12 0-6	S25 1-0	N20 1-2	S01 1-2	a09 1-3	O23 0-1	J22 0-0
2 BOURNEMOUTH	S29 1-0		S25 0-1	a02 0-0	A25 1-0	S11 2-0	S22 1-0	O02 4-2	M19 3-0	a30 2-0	D18 1-2	O16 5-2	a16 1-2	a15 2-1	O30 2-0	J15 1-3	M05 3-2	A28 1-1	N13 3-0	D25 5-0	S08 2-0	F05 2-1
3 BRIGHTON & H.A.	S18 0-4	F19 1-6		S01 0-0	a09 2-1	M12 1-1	D27 2-0	m07 6-1	J01 3-1	J22 1-2	N06 3-2	a15 0-0	S08 1-0	D04 3-2	S04 1-0	N20 2-0	F26 1-0	a23 0-2	A21 1-1	O23 3-1	M26 1-2	O09 0-0
4 BRISTOL C	D27 1-1	N06 2-1	A25 1-1		F05 1-1	O23 2-0	S11 1-0	a23 2-0	O02 3-0	S08 0-0	m07 1-1	A28 3-0	J15 1-6	N20 3-1	a18 1-1	M26 0-2	D18 2-1	a27 0-0	F19 1-3	O09 0-2	M12 2-2	a09 1-1
5 BRISTOL R	a02 0-2	A30 4-0	N13 0-0	S18 3-1		S13 1-0	F12 3-1	A21 1-6	O16 2-3	S20 2-0	S25 3-1	O30 1-0	a30 2-2	J01 3-2	a16 4-1	a15 4-1	M19 0-0	F26 1-1	M05 1-1	J22 1-0	S04 3-0	D25 3-1
6 CRYSTAL P	M05 2-1	J22 2-1	O16 0-2	M19 4-0	S08 1-0		N13 1-1	S18 1-1	a30 2-1	A28 1-1	D27 0-1	J29 2-2	a02 1-1	F19 1-5	F12 1-1	J08 0-1	a16 2-1	A25 1-1	O30 1-1	a18 0-1	O02 1-3	S04 3-1
7 EXETER C	S08 3-3	a23 2-3	D25 1-1	J22 1-1	m07 2-1	a09 3-1		N20 1-3	F19 3-1	a18 3-0	m04 1-2	A21 5-1	A28 4-1	M12 3-1	O02 2-1	O23 1-2	A25 0-0	M26 1-1	S18 3-1	J15 2-0	O09 2-1	N06 2-1
8 IPSWICH T	a30 4-1	F26 1-0	F12 2-2	J29 2-0	D18 0-1	F05 3-2	a16 2-2		N13 2-2	O30 1-0	A28 5-1	M05 4-2	O16 1-2	S15 3-2	M19 4-1	S11 3-2	a18 1-3	J15 2-0	a02 4-2	A25 5-1	D27 3-2	S25 1-2
9 LEYTON O	D18 1-2	O23 1-2	A28 0-3	F26 3-1	M12 1-1	D04 1-1	S25 5-2	a09 1-1		A26 2-2	O09 5-2	S11 0-3	F05 0-3	N06 3-1	D27 2-0	m07 0-1	J15 2-0	S16 3-1	a15 1-1	N20 3-1	a23 1-1	M26 1-0
10 MILLWALL	J15 1-1	D04 4-0	S11 6-2	S13 4-1	a23 1-1	J01 1-0	a15 2-1	M26 0-0	A30 0-0		N20 3-1	S25 3-2	F26 1-3	O23 3-2	A21 1-1	O09 1-1	F05 1-0	M12 2-0	D25 3-1	N06 1-3	a09 2-1	m07 2-2
11 NEWPORT CO	a28 0-2	A21 1-2	a02 1-1	a07 0-2	F19 2-1	D25 5-0	a30 0-2	J01 3-0	M05 3-2	a16 1-2		M19 2-0	O30 4-3	S04 3-3	O16 2-2	S16 1-1	N13 4-2	a15 2-5	O02 4-1	S18 1-2	J22 1-1	S02 1-1
12 NORTHAMPTON T	O02 2-0	M12 1-0	a18 1-1	J01 3-1	M26 0-1	a23 3-2	D18 4-0	O09 1-1	J22 4-1	F19 4-0	O23 2-1		S02 1-0	D25 1-2	S18 2-2	N06 1-2	S16 2-2	a09 0-1	S04 0-1	D04 0-0	F12 0-1	N20 1-1
13 NORWICH C	a18 0-0	N20 1-1	S15 2-1	S04 4-0	D04 3-0	N06 3-0	J01 3-0	M12 2-0	S18 0-0	O02 1-2	M26 0-0	A25 2-1		O09 3-0	F19 2-0	a09 1-2	D25 3-0	O23 1-0	J22 0-0	m07 0-0	A21 1-2	a23 0-1
14 NOTTS CO	O30 2-0	a18 2-3	a30 1-1	a16 2-1	A28 4-1	S25 5-1	O16 9-0	S09 9-2	a02 2-1	M19 1-3	J15 11-1	D27 2-0	M05 2-1		N13 2-1	F05 1-0	F12 0-0	S11 1-1	S23 1-2	D18 5-0	A26 2-0	F26 4-0
15 PORT VALE	A28 3-0	M26 0-2	J15 3-4	a15 4-2	N20 2-0	m07 0-0	F26 1-1	O23 1-2	D25 3-0	D18 1-0	M12 1-2	F05 1-0	S25 0-0	a09 1-0		A23 3-0	S11 0-2	O09 0-2	S06 2-0	a23 3-1	N06 0-2	J08 3-1
16 READING	O16 2-0	S04 4-2	a16 6-1	O30 2-1	a18 1-0	A21 5-1	M19 2-0	J22 2-1	F12 3-0	M05 2-0	S08 4-1	a02 1-0	N13 2-1	S18 1-4	S01 1-2		a27 2-1	D25 0-2	a30 0-0	O02 4-0	F19 1-0	J01 3-1
17 SOUTHEND U	F19 1-0	O09 0-0	O02 0-0	A21 1-0	O23 0-1	N20 0-1	A31 0-0	a15 1-1	S04 2-2	S18 2-1	a09 0-1	S07 0-1	D27 2-2	m07 3-2	J22 0-0	a23 0-0		N06 0-0	J01 3-4	M26 1-1	a06 2-0	M12 0-1
18 SWANSEA T	a16 2-1	J01 2-0	J29 3-0	a30 2-0	O02 5-0	S02 3-0	O30 6-0	S04 2-0	S09 3-1	O16 2-0	a18 2-1	N13 1-0	M19 2-1	J22 3-1	M05 3-1	D27 2-1	a02 2-2		S30 4-0	F19 6-1	S18 3-1	A21 2-0
19 SWINDON T	A25 3-1	a09 2-2	D18 0-0	S25 2-1	O09 1-1	M26 1-0	F05 1-1	N06 4-0	a18 1-1	D27 2-0	D04 5-2	J15 2-2	S11 3-3	a23 3-0	S15 0-2	a06 1-1	A28 2-1	m07 1-0		M12 1-1	N20 2-1	O23 1-0
20 TORQUAY U	N13 2-2	D27 1-1	M19 1-1	M05 0-2	S11 0-2	a19 2-0	S04 2-1	S01 1-1	a16 7-1	a02 2-1	M23 4-0	a30 3-0	F12 2-1	A21 3-1	M30 0-0	F26 4-2	O30 0-3	S25 0-4	O16 3-1		J01 5-1	S15 3-1
21 WALSALL	M19 0-0	S16 0-0	O30 0-0	O16 0-1	J15 0-1	F26 3-1	M05 4-3	D25 2-1	a28 2-3	N13 5-6	S11 3-1	m07 2-0	D18 4-1	S02 3-2	a02 1-1	S25 2-0	a30 0-3	F05 2-1	a16 0-1	A28 1-1		a18 0-1
22 WATFORD	S11 0-1	S18 0-1	M05 0-0	N13 1-1	D27 0-0	J15 2-0	a02 0-1	F19 1-2	O30 2-1	S29 1-1	A25 2-2	a16 0-1	J29 1-1	O02 1-1	a30 2-1	A28 4-1	O16 0-0	D18 4-2	M19 0-3	S08 1-1	a15 2-0	

LEAGUE TABLES

DIVISION 1

	P	W	D	L	F	A	W	D	L	F	A	Pts
Portsmouth	42	18	3	0	52	12	7	5	9	32	30	58
Manchester U	42	11	7	3	40	20	10	4	7	37	24	53
Derby Co	42	17	2	2	48	22	5	7	9	26	33	53
Newcastle U	42	12	5	4	35	29	8	7	6	35	27	52
Arsenal	42	13	5	3	51	18	5	8	8	23	26	49
Wolves	42	13	5	3	48	19	4	7	10	31	47	46
Manchester C	42	10	8	3	28	21	5	7	9	19	30	45
Sunderland	42	8	10	3	27	19	5	7	9	22	39	43
Charlton A	42	10	5	6	38	31	5	7	9	25	36	42
Aston Villa	42	10	6	5	40	36	6	4	11	20	40	42
Stoke C	42	14	3	4	43	24	2	6	13	23	44	41
Liverpool	42	5	10	6	25	18	8	4	9	28	25	40
Chelsea	42	10	6	5	43	27	2	8	11	26	41	38
Bolton W	42	10	4	7	43	32	4	6	11	16	36	38
Burnley	42	10	6	5	27	19	2	8	11	16	31	38
Blackpool	42	8	8	5	24	25	3	8	10	30	42	38
Birmingham C	42	9	7	5	19	10	2	8	11	17	28	37
Everton	42	12	5	4	33	25	1	6	14	8	38	37
Middlesbrough	42	10	6	5	37	23	1	6	14	9	34	34
Huddersfield T	42	6	7	8	19	24	6	3	12	21	45	34
Preston NE	42	8	6	7	36	36	3	5	13	26	39	33
Sheffield U	42	8	9	4	32	25	3	2	16	25	53	33

DIVISION 2

	P	W	D	L	F	A	W	D	L	F	A	Pts
Fulham	42	16	4	1	52	14	8	5	8	25	23	57
WBA	42	16	3	2	47	16	8	5	8	22	23	56
Southampton	42	16	4	1	48	10	7	5	9	21	26	55
Cardiff C	42	14	4	3	45	21	5	9	7	17	26	51
Tottenham H	42	14	4	3	50	18	3	12	6	22	26	50
Chesterfield	42	9	7	5	24	18	6	10	5	27	27	47
West Ham U	42	13	5	3	38	23	5	5	11	18	35	46
Sheffield W	42	12	6	3	36	17	3	7	11	27	39	43
Barnsley	42	10	7	4	40	18	4	5	12	22	43	40
Luton T	42	11	6	4	32	16	3	6	12	23	41	40
Grimsby T	42	10	5	6	44	28	5	5	11	28	48	40
Bury	42	12	5	4	41	23	5	1	15	26	53	40
QPR	42	11	4	6	31	26	3	7	11	13	36	39
Blackburn R	42	12	5	4	41	23	3	3	15	12	40	38
Leeds U	42	11	6	4	36	21	1	7	13	19	42	37
Coventry C	42	12	3	6	35	20	3	4	14	20	44	37
Bradford	42	8	8	5	37	26	5	3	13	28	52	37
Brentford	42	7	10	4	28	21	4	4	13	14	32	36
Leicester C	42	6	10	5	41	38	4	6	11	21	41	36
Plymouth A	42	11	4	6	33	25	1	8	12	16	39	36
Nottingham F	42	9	6	6	22	14	5	1	15	28	40	35
Lincoln C	42	6	7	8	31	35	2	5	14	22	56	28

DIVISION 3 North

	P	W	D	L	F	A	W	D	L	F	A	Pts
Hull C	42	17	1	3	65	14	10	10	1	28	14	65
Rotherham U	42	16	4	1	47	17	12	2	7	43	29	62
Doncaster R	42	10	8	3	26	12	10	2	9	27	28	50
Darlington	42	10	3	8	42	36	10	3	8	41	38	46
Gateshead	42	10	6	5	41	28	6	7	8	28	30	45
Oldham A	42	12	4	5	49	28	6	5	10	26	39	45
Rochdale	42	14	3	4	37	16	4	6	11	18	37	45
Stockport Co	42	13	5	3	44	16	3	6	12	17	40	43
Wrexham	42	12	6	3	35	22	5	3	13	21	40	43
Mansfield T	42	13	6	2	39	15	1	8	12	13	33	42
Tranmere R	42	8	9	4	23	19	5	6	10	23	38	41
Crewe A	42	13	4	4	31	18	3	5	13	21	56	41
Barrow	42	10	8	3	27	13	4	4	13	14	35	40
York C	42	11	3	7	49	28	4	6	11	25	46	39
Carlisle U	42	12	7	2	46	32	2	4	15	14	45	39
Hartlepools U	42	10	5	6	34	25	4	5	12	11	33	38
New Brighton	42	10	4	7	25	10	4	4	13	21	39	30
Chester	42	10	7	4	36	19	1	6	14	21	37	35
Halifax T	42	8	4	9	26	27	4	7	10	19	35	35
Accrington S	42	11	4	6	39	23	1	6	14	16	41	34
Southport	46	6	5	10	24	29	5	4	12	21	35	31
Bradford C	42	7	6	8	29	31	3	3	15	19	46	29

DIVISION 3 South

	P	W	D	L	F	A	W	D	L	F	A	Pts
Swansea T	42	20	1	0	60	11	7	7	7	27	23	62
Reading	42	17	1	3	48	18	8	4	9	29	32	55
Bournemouth	42	15	2	4	42	17	7	6	8	27	31	52
Swindon T	42	11	9	1	38	20	7	6	8	26	36	51
Bristol R	42	13	5	3	42	23	6	5	10	19	28	48
Brighton & HA	42	11	5	5	32	26	4	13	4	23	29	48
Ipswich T	42	14	3	4	53	30	4	6	11	25	47	45
Millwall	42	12	7	2	42	23	5	4	12	21	41	45
Torquay U	42	12	5	4	45	26	5	6	10	20	44	45
Norwich C	42	11	6	4	32	10	5	6	10	35	39	44
Notts Co	42	15	3	3	68	19	4	2	15	34	49	43
Exeter C	42	12	5	4	45	26	3	5	13	18	50	40
Port Vale	42	11	3	7	32	21	3	8	10	19	33	39
Walsall	42	9	5	7	34	28	6	3	12	22	36	38
Newport Co	42	8	6	7	41	35	6	3	12	27	57	37
Bristol C	42	8	9	4	28	24	3	5	13	16	38	36
Watford	42	6	9	6	24	21	4	6	11	17	33	35
Southend U	42	5	10	6	18	18	4	6	11	23	28	34
Leyton O	42	9	6	6	36	29	2	6	13	22	51	34
Northampton T	42	9	6	6	33	20	3	3	15	18	42	33
Aldershot	42	6	5	10	26	29	5	6	10	22	30	33
Crystal P	42	7	8	6	27	27	1	3	17	11	49	27

Football League Records

Top scorers: Div 1, D.Davis (Sunderland) 25 goals; Div 2, T.Briggs (Grimsby Town) 35 goals; Div 3(N), R.Phillips (Crewe Alexandra), P.Doherty (Doncaster Rovers) 26 goals; Div 3(S), T.Lawton (Notts County) 31 goals.

Peter Harris, Portsmouth's flying outside-right. Along with Jimmy Dickinson he was picked for England's summer tour. Alas, injury ruled him out, but he helped Pompey to another title.

Tottenham's Les Medley, the winger who was top scorer when the 'push and run' team lifted the Second Division title in 1949-50.

DIVISION 1

	ARSENAL	ASTON VILLA	BIRMINGHAM C	BLACKPOOL	BOLTON W	BURNLEY	CHARLTON A	CHELSEA	DERBY CO	EVERTON	FULHAM	HUDDERSFIELD T	LIVERPOOL	MANCHESTER C	MANCHESTER U	MIDDLESBROUGH	NEWCASTLE U	PORTSMOUTH	STOKE C	SUNDERLAND	W.B.A.	WOLVERHAMPTON W
1 ARSENAL		M29 1-3	S24 4-2	O22 1-0	J21 1-1	A20 0-1	N19 2-3	A31 2-3	F18 1-0	O08 5-2	N05 2-1	J14 1-0	S03 1-2	a01 4-1	D27 0-0	M08 1-1	a15 4-2	m03 2-0	a10 6-0	D24 5-0	S14 4-1	D03 1-1
2 ASTON VILLA	N26 1-1		D10 1-1	S10 0-0	a22 3-0	M25 0-1	a11 1-1	a08 4-0	A23 1-1	S24 2-2	A27 3-1	F18 2-1	M11 2-0	D17 1-0	O15 0-4	J21 4-0	D31 0-1	S05 1-0	O29 1-1	N12 2-0	F25 1-0	D27 1-4
3 BIRMINGHAM C	F04 2-1	a29 2-2		N05 0-2	O01 0-0	S03 0-1	D03 2-0	A20 0-3	D26 2-2	O22 0-0	N19 1-1	M04 2-1	S17 2-3	M18 1-0	a10 0-0	a15 0-0	a01 0-2	O08 0-3	D24 1-0	J14 1-2	A24 2-0	S14 1-1
4 BLACKPOOL	a08 2-1	J14 1-0	M25 1-1		O29 2-0	D27 2-0	S17 2-0	a22 0-0	N12 1-0	a10 0-1	O01 0-0	A20 4-1	O15 0-0	F04 0-0	N26 3-3	A22 1-1	S05 0-0	D24 2-1	D10 4-2	F25 0-1	M11 3-0	S03 1-2
5 BOLTON W	S17 2-2	D03 1-1	F18 1-0	a15 0-0		D24 0-1	M18 3-0	a10 1-0	S05 0-0	M08 1-2	a01 2-1	O08 1-2	J14 3-2	N19 3-0	A31 1-2	O22 1-2	N05 2-2	F04 1-0	A20 4-0	S03 2-1	D26 3-0	a29 2-4
6 BURNLEY	D17 0-0	N05 1-0	D31 1-1	D26 0-0	A27 2-1		a15 1-0	F18 1-2	S10 0-1	D03 5-1	M04 0-0	M18 1-0	a07 0-2	O22 0-0	S24 1-0	a29 3-2	O08 1-2	N19 2-1	S05 2-1	A23 2-2	J21 0-0	a01 0-1
7 CHARLTON A	M11 1-1	a07 1-4	a22 2-0	J21 1-2	N26 0-0	O29 1-1		O15 1-0	D10 1-3	F18 2-0	D31 2-1	S14 2-2	N12 1-3	A27 3-1	F25 1-2	S24 0-3	S10 6-3	D26 1-2	a08 2-0	M25 2-2	D17 1-2	A24 2-3
8 CHELSEA	A24 1-2	O22 1-3	D17 3-0	D03 1-1	a07 1-1	O01 0-1	M08 1-3		A27 1-2	N19 3-2	J21 0-0	a01 3-1	D26 1-1	O08 3-0	S10 1-1	M29 2-1	a29 1-3	N05 1-4	F04 2-2	S07 3-1	D31 2-1	a15 0-0
9 DERBY CO	O01 1-2	A31 3-2	D27 4-1	a01 0-0	m06 4-0	J14 1-1	a29 1-2	D24 2-2		a15 2-0	M18 2-1	O22 4-2	F04 2-2	D03 7-0	A20 0-1	N05 1-0	M29 1-1	M08 2-1	S03 2-3	S17 3-2	a07 3-1	O08 1-2
10 EVERTON	F25 0-1	F04 1-1	a08 0-0	a07 3-0	O15 0-0	a22 1-1	O01 0-1	M11 1-1	O29 1-2		D26 1-1	S03 3-0	A27 0-0	m06 3-1	N12 0-0	D17 3-1	A24 2-1	J14 1-2	N26 2-1	D10 0-2	M29 1-2	S17 1-2
11 FULHAM	M25 2-2	D24 3-0	M11 0-0	F18 1-0	N12 3-0	O15 1-0	S03 1-2	S17 1-1	N26 0-0	D27 0-0		A31 4-1	O29 0-1	J14 1-0	D10 1-0	m06 1-2	S24 2-1	a10 0-1	F25 2-2	a08 0-3	a22 0-1	A20 1-2
12 HUDDERSFIELD T	S10 2-2	O01 1-0	O15 1-0	D17 0-1	F25 2-0	N26 1-2	S07 2-1	N12 1-2	a08 2-0	D31 1-2	A24 2-2		D10 3-2	D26 1-0	M25 3-1	A27 2-2	a11 1-2	S17 0-1	M11 4-0	a22 3-1	O29 1-1	F04 1-0
13 LIVERPOOL	D31 2-0	N19 2-1	J21 2-0	M08 0-1	S10 1-1	a10 0-1	a01 1-0	D27 2-2	S24 3-1	D24 3-1	a15 1-1	m03 2-3		N05 4-0	S07 1-1	O08 2-0	O22 2-2	D03 2-2	A31 1-1	A20 4-2	F18 2-1	M18 0-2
14 MANCHESTER C	N12 0-2	A20 3-3	N26 4-0	S24 0-3	M11 1-1	a08 1-0	D24 2-0	F25 1-1	a22 2-2	S07 0-0	S10 2-0	D27 1-2	M29 1-2		D31 1-2	F18 0-1	J21 1-1	A31 1-0	O15 1-1	O29 2-1	D10 1-1	a10 2-1
15 MANCHESTER U	D26 2-0	M08 7-0	a07 0-2	M18 1-2	A24 3-0	F04 3-2	O08 3-2	J14 1-0	D17 0-1	a01 1-1	a29 3-0	N05 6-0	M15 0-0	S03 2-1		N19 2-0	D03 1-1	a15 0-2	S17 2-2	O01 1-3	A27 1-1	O22 3-0
16 MIDDLESBROUGH	O15 1-1	S17 0-2	O29 1-0	A31 2-0	a08 2-0	D10 4-1	F04 1-0	N26 2-1	M25 3-1	A20 0-1	S07 1-2	D24 3-0	F25 4-1	O01 0-0	M11 2-3		D27 1-0	S03 1-5	a22 2-0	a10 2-0	N12 3-0	J14 2-0
17 NEWCASTLE U	O29 0-3	S03 3-2	N12 3-1	m06 3-0	M25 3-1	F25 0-0	J14 1-0	D10 2-2	M11 2-1	A31 4-0	F04 3-1	a07 0-0	a08 5-1	S17 4-2	a22 2-1	D26 0-1		A20 1-3	O01 4-1	O15 2-2	N26 5-1	D24 2-0
18 PORTSMOUTH	D10 2-1	m06 5-1	F25 2-0	A27 2-3	S24 1-1	M11 2-1	D27 1-0	M25 4-0	O15 3-1	S10 7-0	a07 3-0	J21 4-0	a22 2-1	A24 1-1	O29 0-0	D31 1-1	D17 1-0		N12 0-0	N26 2-2	a08 0-1	O01 1-1
19 STOKE C	m06 2-5	a15 1-0	A27 3-1	a29 1-1	D17 3-2	S12 1-1	O22 0-3	S24 2-3	D31 1-3	M18 1-0	O08 0-2	N19 0-0	A22 0-0	M04 2-0	J21 3-1	D03 1-0	F18 1-0	a01 0-1		D27 2-1	S10 1-3	N05 2-1
20 SUNDERLAND	A27 4-2	a01 2-1	S10 1-1	O08 1-1	D31 2-0	A31 2-1	N05 2-1	m06 4-1	J21 6-1	a29 4-2	O22 2-0	D03 1-1	D17 3-2	a15 1-2	F18 2-2	a07 2-0	M04 2-2	M18 1-1	D26 3-0		S24 2-1	N19 3-1
21 W.B.A.	S07 1-2	O08 1-1	A31 3-0	a26 1-0	D27 2-1	S17 3-0	A20 1-0	S03 1-1	a10 1-0	N05 4-0	D03 4-1	a15 0-0	O01 0-1	a29 0-0	D24 1-2	a01 0-3	M18 1-1	O22 3-0	J14 0-0	F04 0-2		M04 1-1
22 WOLVERHAMPTON W	a22 3-0	D26 2-3	m06 6-1	D31 3-0	D10 1-1	N12 0-0	A29 2-1	O29 2-2	F25 4-1	J21 1-1	D17 1-1	S24 7-1	N26 1-1	a11 3-0	a08 1-1	S10 3-1	A27 2-1	F18 1-0	M25 2-1	M11 1-3	O15 1-1	

DIVISION 2

	BARNSLEY	BLACKBURN R	BRADFORD	BRENTFORD	BURY	CARDIFF C	CHESTERFIELD	COVENTRY C	GRIMSBY T	HULL C	LEEDS U	LEICESTER C	LUTON T	PLYMOUTH A	PRESTON N.E.	Q.P.R.	SHEFFIELD U	SHEFFIELD W	SOUTHAMPTON	SWANSEA T	TOTTENHAM H	WEST HAM U
1 BARNSLEY		a15 1-1	O08 3-2	N19 0-1	O22 1-0	N05 1-0	A20 1-2	S07 4-3	J14 7-2	a01 1-1	D26 1-1	M04 2-2	a10 1-0	a29 4-1	F04 0-1	S17 3-1	S03 2-2	D03 3-4	A24 2-1	O01 5-2	M18 2-0	D24 1-1
2 BLACKBURN R	N12 4-0		S17 0-1	S19 4-1	S03 2-1	A20 1-0	F04 1-1	O29 0-1	a08 3-0	A22 4-2	O15 0-1	J14 3-0	M25 0-0	O01 1-0	a07 2-3	D10 0-0	N26 0-2	D27 0-0	M11 0-0	F25 2-0	D24 1-2	a22 2-0
3 BRADFORD	F25 1-3	J21 2-2		S10 0-2	D26 1-2	S24 3-3	a11 2-0	D10 2-2	O29 4-1	D31 5-1	N26 1-2	A24 2-2	S07 1-0	D17 3-2	N12 1-2	M25 1-0	M11 1-1	A27 1-3	a08 0-0	a22 0-2	F18 1-3	O15 2-1
4 BRENTFORD	a22 3-0	S14 2-0	J14 2-0		D24 2-0	a07 1-0	S17 0-0	M25 2-0	D10 1-0	D26 3-1	M11 0-0	S03 0-1	N12 1-0	F04 0-0	F25 1-0	A31 0-2	a08 1-0	O01 1-1	O29 0-1	O15 0-0	A20 1-4	N26 0-2
5 BURY	M11 2-0	D31 3-0	D27 1-0	A27 1-2		S10 2-2	S07 2-0	F25 0-0	N12 3-1	D17 0-0	D10 2-0	O01 3-0	O15 5-2	S14 5-1	N26 1-1	a22 0-0	M25 1-5	a07 0-0	S24 1-1	a08 1-1	J21 1-2	O29 3-1
6 CARDIFF C	M25 3-0	D17 2-1	F04 1-2	a10 0-0	J14 1-0		O01 2-0	M11 1-0	N26 1-0	S05 2-0	F25 1-0	S17 2-4	O29 0-0	D27 1-0	D10 3-2	a08 4-0	a22 1-2	A22 1-0	a17 1-1	A27 1-0	S03 0-1	N12 0-1
7 CHESTERFIELD	D17 1-0	S24 2-1	a07 1-1	J21 3-1	A24 2-1	F18 0-1		a08 0-1	M11 2-1	S10 0-1	a22 3-1	S12 1-0	D10 0-1	A27 2-0	M25 2-0	O29 2-1	O15 0-1	D31 1-2	N26 0-0	N12 4-1	D27 1-1	F25 1-0
8 COVENTRY C	m06 1-1	M18 1-1	a29 3-1	N05 1-1	O08 1-2	O22 2-1	D03 3-0		D24 1-1	a15 2-0	F04 0-4	D27 1-2	A29 1-0	a01 3-0	J14 0-0	S03 0-0	A20 2-4	F11 3-0	O01 1-2	S17 1-2	M04 0-1	a11 5-1
9 GRIMSBY T	S10 2-2	D03 1-2	M18 4-0	a29 4-1	a15 4-2	a01 0-0	O22 5-2	A27 3-2		F18 1-0	a07 2-0	N05 2-1	D31 6-1	M04 2-2	A31 1-3	D26 1-1	S24 4-0	O08 4-1	D17 1-1	S07 2-1	N19 2-3	J21 2-0
10 HULL C	N26 2-0	S01 3-1	S03 3-3	D27 2-0	A20 3-2	m06 1-1	J14 1-0	N12 2-1	O01 2-2		O29 1-0	D24 4-0	a22 1-1	S17 4-2	O15 4-2	F25 1-1	D10 0-4	F04 1-1	M25 1-2	M11 0-0	a10 1-0	a08 2-2
11 LEEDS U	D27 1-0	a26 2-1	a01 0-0	O22 1-0	a29 4-1	O08 2-0	N19 0-0	S24 3-3	a10 1-0	M18 3-0		D03 1-1	F18 2-1	a15 1-1	D24 3-1	A20 1-1	S14 0-1	N05 1-1	J21 1-0	S03 1-2	J14 3-0	A31 2-2
12 LEICESTER C	O15 2-2	S10 3-3	A29 4-1	D31 1-1	F18 0-2	J21 1-0	S19 0-1	D26 1-0	M25 1-0	A27 1-2	a08 1-1		F25 3-2	F11 0-0	a22 1-0	N12 3-2	O29 1-1	D17 2-2	D10 2-2	N26 0-0	S24 1-2	M11 2-1
13 LUTON T	a07 3-1	N05 5-2	m06 3-1	a15 1-0	M04 2-1	M18 0-0	a29 1-1	A24 2-0	S03 0-0	N19 0-3	O01 1-0	O08 1-0		D03 1-1	S17 1-1	J14 1-2	D24 1-3	a01 0-0	D26 1-1	F04 1-2	O22 1-1	A20 2-2
14 PLYMOUTH A	D10 2-2	F18 0-0	A20 1-1	S24 2-0	m06 2-0	D26 0-0	D24 2-1	N26 1-2	O15 4-2	J21 1-3	N12 1-2	a10 2-1	a08 0-0		O29 1-0	M11 0-2	F25 0-1	S10 0-1	a22 0-0	M25 0-1	A31 0-2	S03 0-3
15 PRESTON N.E.	S24 1-1	a10 3-1	a15 3-0	O08 2-0	a01 3-1	a29 3-0	N05 0-0	S10 1-1	A24 2-0	M04 4-2	A27 1-1	N19 2-1	J21 0-1	M18 0-0		S14 3-2	D26 4-1	O22 0-1	D31 0-3	D17 2-1	D03 1-3	F18 2-1
16 Q.P.R.	J21 0-5	a29 2-3	N05 0-1	A24 3-3	N19 1-0	D03 0-1	M18 3-2	D31 2-0	D27 1-2	O08 1-4	D17 1-1	a15 2-0	S10 3-0	O22 0-2	S07 0-0		F18 1-3	M04 0-0	A27 1-0	a07 0-0	a01 0-2	S24 0-1
17 SHEFFIELD U	D31 1-1	a01 4-0	O22 2-1	D03 1-1	N05 4-4	N19 2-0	M04 1-0	D17 1-1	F04 3-1	a29 5-0	S05 0-1	M18 2-2	A27 2-2	O08 1-1	D27 1-0	O01 1-1		J21 2-0	F11 0-1	A22 1-1	a15 2-1	S10 0-0
18 SHEFFIELD W	a08 2-0	D26 2-0	D24 1-1	F18 3-3	a10 1-0	A29 1-1	S03 4-2	a22 1-1	a26 4-0	S24 6-2	M25 5-2	A20 3-1	N26 1-1	J14 2-4	M11 0-1	O15 1-0	S17 2-1		N12 2-2	O29 3-0	m06 0-0	D10 2-1
19 SOUTHAMPTON	A31 0-0	O22 3-1	D03 3-1	M18 2-3	F04 4-1	M04 3-1	a01 1-0	F18 1-1	A20 1-2	N05 5-0	S17 2-1	a29 5-3	D27 2-1	N19 3-3	S03 1-0	D24 1-2	a10 1-0	a15 1-0		J14 1-2	O08 1-1	m06 3-2
20 SWANSEA T	F18 4-0	O08 2-0	N19 2-0	M04 3-0	D03 1-2	D24 5-1	a15 0-2	J21 1-2	m06 2-1	O22 1-2	D31 1-2	a01 0-0	S24 0-0	N05 2-2	A20 2-1	a10 0-1	S01 1-0	M18 1-2	S10 4-0		a29 1-0	D27 1-0
21 TOTTENHAM H	O29 2-0	A27 2-3	O01 5-0	D17 1-1	S17 3-1	D31 2-0	D26 1-0	O15 3-1	a22 1-2	a07 0-0	S10 2-0	F04 0-2	M11 0-0	A22 4-1	a08 3-2	N26 3-0	N12 7-0	S05 1-0	F25 4-0	D10 3-1		M25 4-1
22 WEST HAM U	A27 2-1	N19 0-2	M04 1-0	a01 2-2	M18 4-0	a15 0-1	O08 1-1	a10 0-1	S17 4-3	D03 2-1	A22 3-1	O22 2-2	D17 0-0	D31 2-2	O01 0-3	F04 1-0	J14 0-0	a29 2-2	S05 1-2	D26 3-0	N05 0-1	

Season 1949-50

DIVISION 3 NORTH

	ACCRINGTON S	BARROW	BRADFORD C	CARLISLE U	CHESTER	CREWE A	DARLINGTON	DONCASTER R	GATESHEAD	HALIFAX T	HARTLEPOOLS U	LINCOLN C	MANSFIELD T	NEW BRIGHTON	OLDHAM A	ROCHDALE	ROTHERHAM U	SOUTHPORT	STOCKPORT CO	TRANMERE R	WREXHAM	YORK C
1 ACCRINGTON S		S10 1-0	F11 3-2	D17 1-1	a10 4-0	J21 1-1	N12 3-0	M11 2-2	O29 0-1	J28 1-0	M25 1-2	D31 2-0	A24 2-2	F25 3-0	S27 3-4	a22 1-0	A27 1-4	a08 4-0	O15 4-2	S24 2-0	D26 2-0	F18 0-0
2 BARROW	J14 2-1		M25 1-0	F04 1-3	N12 3-1	a07 0-1	a08 2-1	a22 1-1	F11 1-1	M11 4-0	D26 0-0	S06 0-0	S17 0-1	O15 1-1	D24 3-1	O29 0-1	O01 1-1	F25 1-0	a27 0-1	A30 1-2	S03 2-1	A20 3-2
3 BRADFORD C	a29 5-2	N05 3-2		M04 3-2	D27 1-0	M18 0-2	J14 4-1	A20 1-2	D24 2-1	F04 1-3	S03 1-3	a01 0-1	D03 2-1	S17 2-1	O08 1-1	O01 2-1	N19 1-2	a10 6-0	A31 0-1	O22 2-4	S14 1-0	a15 0-2
4 CARLISLE U	A20 2-1	S24 2-0	J28 3-0		a22 5-1	F18 2-2	O29 0-1	a08 0-0	O15 4-2	N12 0-2	M11 2-1	J21 0-2	D24 1-1	M25 0-0	a07 3-0	F25 2-0	S10 3-1	F11 3-3	S03 2-0	m06 0-0	S01 1-0	D27 4-3
5 CHESTER	a07 1-0	a01 1-0	D26 4-1	D03 2-4		N05 0-1	J21 4-4	D24 3-1	S03 0-3	O01 5-1	J14 3-0	N19 3-1	a29 6-3	F04 2-0	a15 1-1	S14 0-2	M04 4-2	A31 4-1	A20 0-4	M18 0-0	O08 2-1	O22 2-3
6 CREWE A	S17 2-1	a10 1-1	O29 2-2	O01 2-1	M25 1-2		A31 2-0	a19 0-2	a22 3-1	O15 6-3	F11 1-0	D26 3-2	F04 1-1	a08 1-2	S03 1-1	M11 0-1	S05 4-1	N12 1-2	F25 1-0	A20 2-0	J14 1-1	D24 3-3
7 DARLINGTON	a01 0-2	O08 1-1	S10 4-3	M18 1-1	S17 2-1	A24 1-1		S14 2-1	D26 2-3	A27 5-1	a10 1-0	a15 2-0	N05 2-2	D17 3-1	M04 1-1	D31 1-1	O22 2-1	S24 0-2	F18 1-1	a26 0-2	N19 3-1	D03 1-1
8 DONCASTER R	O22 4-1	D03 1-0	D17 1-1	O08 0-0	A27 2-0	M04 0-2	S08 2-1		F04 1-1	a07 4-0	O01 0-0	a29 1-4	a15 0-1	D27 0-0	N05 1-1	A25 0-0	J21 1-0	D31 5-1	J14 3-0	m03 1-1	M18 2-0	a01 1-1
9 GATESHEAD	M18 5-0	a29 3-1	A27 4-2	a15 2-1	D31 4-0	D03 1-1	D27 3-3	S24 1-1		A22 7-1	J02 2-0	F18 2-1	O22 0-1	a10 2-1	a01 2-0	D17 1-3	O08 2-2	S10 3-2	J21 1-0	M04 5-1	N05 0-1	N19 1-1
10 HALIFAX T	M04 1-4	O22 1-0	S24 3-1	a01 1-1	F18 2-1	a15 3-1	D24 1-3	a10 2-2	A29 5-2		A20 1-2	M18 0-1	N19 0-3	S03 3-0	a29 1-1	J21 3-2	N05 4-3	S12 0-0	D27 3-1	O08 0-1	D03 0-0	J14 1-2
11 HARTLEPOOLS U	N05 0-0	D27 2-3	D31 3-0	O22 1-5	S10 5-1	a29 1-6	a07 2-0	F18 1-1	S05 3-5	D17 3-3		O08 2-1	M18 1-3	A22 2-0	N19 0-2	A27 1-2	a15 1-2	J21 1-0	S24 1-0	D03 2-0	a01 3-1	M04 2-0
12 LINCOLN C	S03 1-0	m06 4-0	N12 2-2	S17 2-1	F25 2-0	D27 2-0	O15 2-0	F11 1-0	O01 2-0	O29 1-0	a08 6-0		J14 1-0	M11 1-2	A20 1-2	M25 2-0	F04 0-0	J28 1-1	a22 1-1	a07 0-0	D24 2-0	A24 1-0
13 MANSFIELD T	A29 2-0	J21 1-1	a22 0-2	A27 4-1	F11 0-2	S24 3-0	M25 2-1	O15 1-2	M11 1-0	F25 1-0	O29 7-1	S10 2-1		N12 2-2	D26 3-1	J28 1-1	D31 0-2	D17 1-2	a08 3-0	F18 1-1	a07 1-0	S12 1-0
14 NEW BRIGHTON	N19 3-0	a15 2-0	J21 1-0	N05 3-2	S24 3-3	O08 0-2	A20 1-0	D26 2-2	a07 0-1	D31 1-1	A31 1-0	O22 1-0	a01 1-2		D03 0-0	S10 0-4	M18 0-3	F18 1-0	S07 1-3	D24 0-0	M04 3-1	m06 3-1
15 OLDHAM A	S06 0-1	A27 1-3	a08 2-1	a10 1-1	O15 0-2	D31 2-1	J28 2-0	M25 1-4	N12 1-0	F11 2-1	F25 3-1	D17 0-2	D27 1-0	a22 3-0		S24 0-0	A23 2-2	M11 2-5	O29 3-3	S10 2-1	O01 2-3	J21 2-0
16 ROCHDALE	D03 2-0	M18 2-1	F18 2-2	N19 1-0	S05 0-1	O22 2-1	S03 2-0	A30 0-1	A20 1-3	S17 1-0	D24 4-0	N05 2-0	M04 7-1	J14 4-0	F04 1-0		a01 1-0	D26 2-0	a10 1-1	a15 3-0	a29 1-1	O08 3-1
17 ROTHERHAM U	D24 6-0	F18 1-2	F25 5-2	J14 1-1	S19 3-2	m06 0-0	M11 1-1	S17 0-2	a08 1-2	M25 2-1	O15 5-1	S24 1-3	S03 2-2	O29 3-0	A29 0-1	N12 4-3		a22 4-0	S26 2-1	D26 1-1	A20 2-2	a10 2-1
18 SOUTHPORT	O08 1-0	N19 0-1	a07 1-1	a29 1-2	A22 1-1	a01 2-2	F04 1-1	S03 3-3	J14 0-3	S05 1-1	S17 2-1	M04 1-1	A20 1-1	O01 0-2	O22 3-2	D27 3-2	D03 4-0		D24 1-0	N05 2-1	a15 0-0	M18 1-1
19 STOCKPORT CO	a15 1-0	M04 1-3	A24 1-0	D31 2-0	D17 3-0	N19 4-1	O01 2-1	S10 0-1	S17 2-1	D26 2-0	F04 1-0	D03 1-1	O08 1-0	S14 0-2	M18 1-3	a07 1-1	a29 0-2	A27 3-2		a01 2-1	O22 2-1	N05 3-1
20 TRANMERE R	F04 0-1	A23 2-1	M11 1-0	S06 0-0	O29 2-1	D17 2-2	F11 3-1	F25 2-4	J28 1-0	a08 2-1	a22 2-1	a10 2-2	O01 2-1	A27 2-1	J14 4-2	O15 1-0	D27 0-2	M25 2-0	N12 2-0		S17 2-1	S03 1-0
21 WREXHAM	D27 1-1	D31 1-0	S07 0-0	A24 1-1	a08 1-1	S10 1-2	F25 2-1	O29 0-1	M25 0-1	a22 2-3	N12 1-0	A27 4-0	a10 0-0	J28 2-2	F18 2-1	F11 3-0	D17 0-1	O15 1-0	M11 0-2	J21 0-0		S24 2-0
22 YORK C	O01 2-1	D17 2-0	O15 1-1	D26 1-1	M11 2-3	A27 1-1	a22 1-1	N12 0-3	F25 1-5	S10 3-1	J28 0-2	A29 1-2	S05 3-3	F11 2-1	S17 0-1	a08 2-2	a07 0-3	O29 0-1	M25 1-1	D31 1-0	F04 5-0	

DIVISION 3 SOUTH

	ALDERSHOT	BOURNEMOUTH	BRIGHTON & HA	BRISTOL C	BRISTOL R	CRYSTAL P	EXETER C	IPSWICH T	LEYTON O	MILLWALL	NEWPORT CO	NORTHAMPTON T	NORWICH C	NOTTINGHAM F	NOTTS CO	PORT VALE	READING	SOUTHEND U	SWINDON T	TORQUAY U	WALSALL	WATFORD
1 ALDERSHOT		N05 0-1	A24 0-1	a10 0-1	a01 3-1	M18 0-0	J21 1-2	a29 5-0	O08 2-0	A27 2-1	D27 4-1	O01 0-0	S14 2-0	F04 1-1	a15 2-0	D03 1-0	M04 2-0	m02 1-1	D31 0-0	S10 3-5	D17 1-0	O22 0-1
2 BOURNEMOUTH	M25 2-1		S24 2-2	S21 3-1	J21 0-2	O01 2-0	A24 2-0	D17 4-0	a10 4-1	O15 1-0	a22 1-1	a08 1-2	m06 2-0	N12 1-2	D31 3-0	A27 2-2	D26 2-1	S10 3-0	M11 1-1	O29 1-2	F25 1-1	S07 0-0
3 BRIGHTON & H.A.	A31 1-1	F04 1-1		S17 2-1	O08 1-2	J07 0-0	a01 0-0	N05 2-1	N19 2-2	m06 1-0	J14 5-0	A27 1-1	S03 1-3	A20 2-2	O22 2-3	M18 2-1	a15 2-1	M04 2-1	D26 0-1	a07 2-1	F18 1-1	D03 2-1
4 BRISTOL C	a07 2-0	a29 3-2	J21 1-2		J14 1-2	D03 2-0	N05 1-0	M18 4-2	a01 0-0	F18 2-1	S03 6-0	A20 3-1	D24 1-2	A30 0-2	M04 4-0	O22 2-0	N19 2-2	O08 1-1	S13 1-0	D26 0-0	S24 2-1	a15 0-1
5 BRISTOL R	N12 2-1	S17 0-0	F25 3-0	S10 2-3		F04 0-0	a10 1-0	A22 2-0	D27 3-0	M11 3-1	a24 3-0	m01 0-0	a22 5-1	a08 0-3	A27 0-3	D17 2-1	S05 2-1	D31 1-1	O29 2-0	M25 2-0	O15 1-1	O01 0-2
6 CRYSTAL P	O29 2-1	F18 1-0	F11 6-0	a22 1-1	S24 1-0		D17 5-3	A27 2-0	A24 1-1	F25 1-0	J28 1-0	N12 0-4	a08 2-0	M25 1-1	S10 1-2	D31 0-1	a07 1-1	J21 2-1	O15 2-2	M11 1-3	S07 2-0	D26 2-0
7 EXETER C	S17 1-0	A31 1-2	N12 2-3	M26 0-0	a07 2-0	A20 2-1		S24 1-1	J14 1-1	a26 2-1	O29 3-3	O15 1-3	M11 3-1	F25 0-0	m06 2-2	F18 3-1	S03 3-4	D26 1-1	a22 3-0	F11 1-1	a08 2-1	D24 3-1
8 IPSWICH T	F11 1-0	A20 1-2	M25 2-2	O29 0-0	A31 3-1	D24 4-4	F04 1-0		S17 4-4	a08 0-3	M11 1-0	F25 2-2	O15 3-0	O01 1-2	D27 0-4	m06 2-1	J14 2-0	a10 1-3	J28 3-1	a22 3-1	N12 1-5	S03 1-1
9 LEYTON O	F25 2-7	a07 2-1	a08 0-1	N12 1-0	D26 1-0	S01 2-2	S10 4-1	J21 4-0		a22 1-1	M25 2-1	M11 1-0	O29 1-2	O15 1-1	F18 1-4	S24 1-0	D24 2-1	m06 2-2	F11 1-3	S03 2-1	J28 2-2	A20 0-0
10 MILLWALL	D24 3-0	M04 1-0	S05 5-1	O01 3-1	O22 0-1	O08 2-3	a15 3-1	N19 3-1	D03 3-1		m01 1-2	J14 0-2	S17 1-2	S03 2-1	N05 1-3	a01 3-0	a29 3-1	M18 1-2	A29 1-0	A20 1-3	D27 1-1	a07 1-3
11 NEWPORT CO	D26 6-0	D03 5-0	S10 0-1	D31 6-4	a29 2-3	a15 2-2	M18 1-2	O22 1-0	N05 3-2	S24 4-3		S01 1-4	A20 3-2	a07 4-1	O08 1-1	M04 1-1	a01 1-1	M30 2-1	F18 1-2	S15 1-0	J21 2-1	N19 3-3
12 NORTHAMPTON T	F18 1-1	N19 2-3	D24 2-1	D17 4-2	a15 2-0	a01 2-2	M04 3-3	O08 1-2	O22 3-0	S10 1-0	A25 4-3		a11 3-1	S08 0-0	a29 5-1	D27 1-1	M18 2-0	D03 2-0	J21 0-1	S24 3-0	D31 2-0	N05 0-0
13 NORWICH C	S07 4-0	a15 0-1	D31 1-2	A27 3-0	D03 4-0	N19 2-0	O22 1-2	M04 1-1	M18 4-0	J21 0-2	D17 4-0	a10 2-1		D26 1-1	A24 4-3	O08 0-1	N05 1-1	a29 0-0	S24 4-0	F18 3-3	S10 3-2	a01 2-1
14 NOTTINGHAM F	S24 3-0	a01 3-0	D17 0-1	A24 3-0	N19 2-0	N05 2-0	O08 5-0	F18 2-0	M04 2-1	D31 3-1	a10 3-0	S14 0-1	D27 0-1		D03 1-2	a29 2-0	O22 1-2	a15 1-2	S10 2-1	J21 1-2	A27 1-0	M18 0-1
15 NOTTS CO	J28 3-1	S03 2-0	M11 4-2	O15 4-1	D24 2-0	J14 0-1	S08 3-3	D26 2-0	O01 7-1	M25 2-0	F25 7-0	a27 2-0	S01 5-0	a22 2-0		a07 3-1	F04 4-0	A20 2-0	N12 3-0	a08 1-1	O29 1-1	S17 1-0
16 PORT VALE	a22 0-1	D24 1-1	O29 3-0	M11 0-2	A20 1-0	S03 2-0	O01 1-0	S05 2-2	F04 2-0	N12 4-0	O15 1-0	D26 3-1	F25 2-2	F11 1-1	a10 3-1		S17 1-1	A29 0-0	a08 0-1	M27 2-0	M25 2-0	J14 2-0
17 READING	O15 1-3	D27 2-1	S14 3-0	a08 1-0	m06 0-1	a10 1-2	D31 3-2	S10 3-1	A27 5-1	S21 2-0	N12 4-1	O29 3-1	M25 4-1	M11 1-1	S24 0-1	J21 2-1		F18 5-0	D17 4-3	F25 2-0	a22 1-1	A31 1-0
18 SOUTHEND U	a08 3-0	J14 1-0	O15 3-2	F25 2-0	S03 3-1	S17 0-0	D27 1-0	a07 2-2	S06 2-0	O29 3-0	A27 6-0	a22 1-2	F11 1-0	J28 2-3	D17 2-0	A23 1-0	O01 3-2		M25 2-0	N12 2-0	M11 2-2	F04 1-1
19 SWINDON T	S03 2-1	O22 3-1	D27 4-2	m06 1-1	M18 1-0	M04 4-2	D03 7-1	a15 0-3	a29 0-1	A24 1-1	O01 1-1	S17 6-1	F04 1-1	J14 0-5	a01 1-1	N19 0-0	A20 2-0	N05 2-2		D24 1-2	a10 4-3	O08 0-1
20 TORQUAY U	J14 4-0	M18 3-1	a10 0-0	D27 3-3	N05 1-0	O22 1-0	a29 1-4	D03 2-2	D31 4-1	D17 1-0	S07 5-3	F04 1-0	O01 1-1	S17 2-0	N19 0-0	a15 0-0	O08 4-2	a01 2-4	A27 1-0		A24 2-1	M04 2-1
21 WALSALL	A20 0-0	O08 1-1	O01 4-2	F04 1-1	M04 3-1	m06 3-1	N19 3-0	a01 1-3	a15 1-2	D26 0-1	S17 2-0	S03 1-3	J14 1-1	D24 1-3	M18 3-3	N05 1-0	D03 2-0	O22 1-1	a07 0-0	S01 7-1		a29 1-1
22 WATFORD	M11 1-0	S15 4-1	a22 0-0	a20 2-0	F18 0-2	D27 0-0	A27 1-2	D31 6-0	D17 2-1	a10 0-0	a08 0-1	M25 0-0	N12 0-0	O29 1-0	J21 2-1	S10 0-2	A25 1-1	S24 1-0	F25 1-2	O15 1-0	F11 3-0	

LEAGUE TABLES

DIVISION 1

	P	W	D	L	F	A	W	D	L	F	A	Pts
Portsmouth	42	12	7	2	44	15	10	2	9	30	23	53
Wolves	42	11	8	2	47	21	9	5	7	29	28	53
Sunderland	42	14	6	1	50	23	7	4	10	33	39	52
Manchester U	42	11	5	5	42	20	7	9	5	27	24	50
Newcastle U	42	14	4	3	49	23	5	8	8	28	32	50
Arsenal	42	12	4	5	48	24	7	7	7	31	31	49
Blackpool	42	10	8	3	29	14	7	7	7	17	21	49
Liverpool	42	10	7	4	37	23	7	7	7	27	31	48
Middlesbrough	42	14	2	5	37	18	6	5	10	22	30	47
Burnley	42	9	7	5	23	17	7	6	8	17	23	45
Derby Co	42	11	5	5	46	26	6	5	10	23	35	44
Aston Villa	42	10	7	4	31	19	5	5	11	30	42	42
Chelsea	42	7	7	7	31	30	5	9	7	27	35	40
WBA	42	9	7	5	28	16	5	5	11	19	37	40
Huddersfield T	42	11	4	6	34	22	3	5	13	18	51	37
Bolton W	42	10	5	6	34	22	0	9	12	11	37	34
Fulham	42	8	6	7	24	19	2	8	11	17	35	34
Everton	42	6	8	7	24	20	4	6	11	18	46	34
Stoke C	42	10	4	7	27	28	1	8	12	18	47	34
Charlton A	42	7	5	9	33	35	6	1	14	20	30	32
Manchester C	42	7	8	6	27	24	1	5	15	9	44	29
Birmingham C	42	6	8	7	19	24	1	6	14	12	43	28

DIVISION 2

	P	W	D	L	F	A	W	D	L	F	A	Pts
Tottenham H	42	15	3	3	51	15	12	4	5	30	20	61
Sheffield W	42	12	7	2	46	23	6	9	6	21	25	52
Sheffield U	42	9	10	2	36	19	10	4	7	32	30	52
Southampton	42	13	4	4	44	25	6	10	5	20	23	52
Leeds U	42	11	8	2	33	16	6	5	10	21	29	47
Preston NE	42	12	5	4	37	21	6	4	11	23	28	45
Hull C	42	11	8	2	39	25	6	3	12	25	47	45
Swansea T	42	11	3	7	34	18	6	6	9	19	31	43
Brentford	42	11	5	5	21	12	4	8	9	23	37	43
Cardiff C	42	13	3	5	28	14	3	7	11	13	30	42
Grimsby T	42	13	5	3	53	25	3	3	15	21	48	40
Coventry C	42	8	6	7	32	24	5	7	9	23	31	39
Barnsley	42	11	6	4	45	28	2	7	12	19	39	39
Chesterfield	42	12	3	6	28	16	3	6	12	15	31	39
Leicester C	42	8	9	4	30	25	4	6	11	25	40	39
Blackburn R	42	10	5	6	30	15	4	5	12	25	45	38
Luton T	42	8	9	4	28	22	2	9	10	13	29	38
Bury	42	10	8	3	37	19	4	1	16	23	46	37
West Ham U	42	8	7	6	30	25	4	5	12	23	36	36
QPR	42	6	5	10	21	30	5	7	9	19	27	34
Plymouth A	42	6	6	9	19	24	2	10	9	25	41	32
Bradford	42	7	6	8	34	34	3	5	13	17	43	31

DIVISION 3 North

	P	W	D	L	F	A	W	D	L	F	A	Pts
Doncaster R	42	9	9	3	30	15	10	8	3	36	23	55
Gateshead	42	13	5	3	51	23	10	2	9	36	31	53
Rochdale	42	15	3	3	42	13	6	6	9	26	28	51
Lincoln C	42	14	5	2	35	9	7	4	10	25	30	51
Tranmere R	42	15	3	3	35	21	4	8	9	16	27	49
Rotherham U	42	10	6	5	46	28	9	4	8	34	31	48
Crewe A	42	10	6	5	38	27	7	8	6	30	28	48
Mansfield T	42	12	4	5	37	20	6	8	7	29	34	48
Carlisle U	42	12	6	3	39	20	4	9	8	29	31	47
Stockport Co	42	14	2	5	33	21	5	5	11	22	31	45
Oldham A	42	10	4	7	32	31	6	7	8	26	32	43
Chester	42	12	3	6	47	33	5	3	13	23	46	40
Accrington S	42	12	5	4	41	21	4	2	15	16	41	39
New Brighton	42	10	5	6	27	25	4	5	12	18	38	38
Barrow	42	9	6	6	27	20	5	3	13	20	33	37
Southport	42	7	10	4	29	26	5	3	13	22	45	37
Darlington	42	9	8	4	35	27	2	5	14	21	42	35
Hartlepools U	42	10	3	8	37	36	4	2	16	16	44	33
Bradford C	42	11	1	9	38	32	1	7	13	23	44	32
Wrexham	42	8	7	6	24	17	2	5	14	15	37	32
Halifax T	42	9	5	7	35	31	3	3	15	23	54	32
York C	42	6	7	8	29	33	3	6	12	23	37	31

DIVISION 3 South

	P	W	D	L	F	A	W	D	L	F	A	Pts
Notts Co	42	17	3	1	60	12	8	5	8	35	38	58
Northampton T	42	12	6	3	43	21	8	5	8	29	29	51
Southend U	42	15	4	2	43	15	4	9	8	23	33	51
Nottingham F	42	13	0	8	37	15	7	9	5	30	24	49
Torquay U	42	13	6	2	40	23	6	4	11	26	40	48
Watford	42	10	6	5	26	13	6	7	8	19	22	45
Crystal P	42	12	5	4	35	21	3	9	9	20	33	44
Brighton & HA	42	9	8	4	32	24	7	4	10	25	45	44
Bristol R	42	12	5	4	34	18	7	0	14	17	33	43
Reading	42	15	2	4	48	21	2	6	13	22	43	42
Norwich C	42	11	5	5	44	21	5	5	11	21	42	42
Bournemouth	42	11	6	4	38	19	5	4	12	19	37	42
Port Vale	42	12	6	3	33	13	3	5	13	14	29	41
Swindon T	42	9	7	5	41	30	6	4	11	18	32	41
Bristol C	42	12	4	5	38	19	3	6	12	22	42	40
Exeter C	42	9	8	4	37	27	5	3	13	26	48	39
Ipswich T	42	9	6	6	36	36	3	5	13	21	50	35
Leyton O	42	10	6	5	33	30	2	5	14	20	55	35
Walsall	42	8	8	5	37	25	1	8	12	24	37	34
Aldershot	42	10	5	6	30	16	3	3	15	18	44	34
Newport Co	42	11	5	5	50	34	2	3	16	17	64	34
Millwall	42	11	1	9	39	29	3	3	15	16	34	32

Football League Records

Top scorers: Div 1, S.Mortensen (Blackpool) 30 goals; Div 2, J.McCormack (Barnsley) 33 goals; Div 3(N), J.Shaw (Rotherham United) 37 goals; Div 3(S), W.Ardron (Nottingham Forest) 36 goals.
Colchester United, Gillingham, Scunthorpe & Lindsey United and Shrewsbury Town elected to League.

Alf Ramsey, a record full-back signing from Southampton who was the final piece in the jigsaw which saw Spurs win the First and Second Division titles in successive seasons.

England winger Tom Finney, who helped Preston North End to promotion from the Second Division in 1950-51.

DIVISION 1

	ARSENAL	ASTON VILLA	BLACKPOOL	BOLTON W	BURNLEY	CHARLTON A	CHELSEA	DERBY CO	EVERTON	FULHAM	HUDDERSFIELD T	LIVERPOOL	MANCHESTER U	MIDDLESBROUGH	NEWCASTLE U	PORTSMOUTH	SHEFFIELD W	STOKE C	SUNDERLAND	TOTTENHAM H	W.B.A.	WOLVERHAMPTON W
1 ARSENAL		M10 2-1	D09 4-4	a21 1-1	D16 0-1	F24 2-5	A23 0-0	O28 3-1	S06 2-1	N25 5-1	S16 6-2	a07 1-2	O14 3-0	J13 3-1	F03 0-0	M23 0-1	S02 3-0	D25 0-3	N11 5-1	A26 2-2	S30 3-0	M24 2-1
2 ASTON VILLA	O21 1-1		F03 0-3	S16 0-1	M17 3-2	D26 0-0	N18 4-2	D23 1-1	D02 3-3	J13 3-0	M03 0-1	S02 1-1	S04 1-3	N04 0-1	O07 3-0	a14 3-3	M31 2-1	m05 6-2	A21 3-1	S30 2-3	A19 2-0	M27 1-0
3 BLACKPOOL	m02 0-1	S23 1-1		M23 2-0	A21 1-2	A26 0-0	O07 3-2	F17 3-1	N04 4-0	S04 4-0	N18 3-1	D25 3-0	m05 1-1	a14 2-1	M17 2-2	M03 3-0	D02 3-2	M31 3-0	J20 2-2	D16 0-1	O21 2-1	S09 1-1
4 BOLTON W	D02 3-0	J20 1-0	M26 1-2		F10 1-1	D16 3-0	S04 1-0	S23 3-0	M03 2-0	D26 0-1	M17 4-0	F17 2-1	A26 1-0	N18 0-2	O21 0-2	O07 4-0	a14 0-1	N04 1-1	S09 1-2	A23 1-4	M31 0-2	a28 2-1
5 BURNLEY	A19 0-1	O28 2-0	A29 0-0	D09 2-0		O14 5-1	M23 2-1	a07 1-0	D26 1-1	a21 0-2	J13 0-1	N25 1-1	M24 1-2	S02 3-1	S16 1-1	S04 1-1	D23 1-0	S30 1-1	M10 1-1	F24 2-0	F03 0-1	N11 2-0
6 CHARLTON A	O07 1-3	D25 2-2	D23 2-3	A19 4-3	M03 0-0		N04 1-2	m05 1-2	O21 2-1	A30 0-0	D02 3-2	J27 1-0	J20 1-2	a28 3-0	a14 1-3	M31 0-1	J13 2-1	M17 2-0	F17 3-0	S02 1-1	N18 2-3	S23 3-2
7 CHELSEA	A30 0-1	a07 1-1	F28 0-2	m05 4-0	M26 0-2	M24 2-3		N25 1-2	S30 2-1	D09 2-0	S02 1-2	a21 1-0	N11 1-0	D23 1-1	J13 3-1	D26 1-4	A19 4-0	F03 1-1	O28 3-0	O14 0-2	S16 1-1	a25 2-1
8 DERBY CO	M17 4-2	A26 4-2	S30 4-1	F03 2-2	N18 1-1	S06 5-0	a14 1-0		a28 0-1	S16 3-2	N04 3-0	J13 1-2	M26 2-4	M31 6-0	M03 1-2	D02 2-3	O21 4-1	D30 1-1	D16 6-5	D25 1-1	O07 1-1	A23 1-2
9 EVERTON	S13 1-1	a21 1-2	M24 0-2	O14 1-1	D25 1-0	M10 0-0	F17 3-0	D09 1-2		F28 1-0	A19 3-2	S16 1-3	O28 1-4	A30 3-2	D23 3-1	S23 1-5	M26 0-0	J13 0-3	N25 3-1	N11 1-2	S02 0-3	a07 1-1
10 FULHAM	a14 3-2	S09 2-1	S13 2-2	D25 0-1	D02 4-1	A23 1-3	a28 1-2	J20 3-5	O07 1-5		O21 1-1	S23 2-1	D16 2-2	M17 2-0	M31 1-1	m02 1-4	N18 4-2	M03 2-0	D30 1-1	M23 0-1	N04 0-1	A26 2-1
11 HUDDERSFIELD T	J20 2-2	O14 4-2	a07 2-1	O28 0-4	S09 3-1	a21 1-1	a18 2-1	M24 2-0	D16 1-2	M10 1-2		N11 2-2	D09 2-3	F17 2-3	S13 0-0	A26 2-1	S23 3-4	A23 3-1	M07 3-4	N25 3-2	M27 1-2	D25 1-2
12 LIVERPOOL	N18 1-3	a25 0-0	D26 1-0	S30 3-3	a14 1-0	M23 1-0	D02 1-0	S09 1-0	J20 0-2	F03 2-0	M31 1-4		A23 2-1	O21 0-0	N04 2-4	F10 2-1	M17 2-1	O07 0-0	A26 4-0	S06 2-1	M03 1-1	D16 1-4
13 MANCHESTER U	M03 3-1	S13 0-0	S02 1-0	D23 2-3	N04 1-1	S16 3-0	M31 4-1	M23 2-0	M17 3-0	A19 1-0	a28 6-0	A30 1-0		F03 1-0	D02 1-2	O21 0-0	O07 3-1	N18 0-0	D26 3-5	J13 2-1	a14 3-0	F17 2-1
14 MIDDLESBROUGH	S09 2-1	M24 2-1	N25 4-3	a07 1-1	D30 3-3	D09 7-3	A26 3-0	N11 1-1	A23 4-0	O28 1-1	S30 8-0	M10 1-1	S23 1-2		D25 2-1	D16 3-1	J20 2-1	M23 1-0	O14 1-1	a21 1-1	S06 2-1	a11 1-2
15 NEWCASTLE U	S23 2-1	a04 0-1	O28 4-2	a18 0-1	J20 2-1	N25 3-2	S09 3-1	O14 3-1	A26 1-1	N11 1-2	S06 6-0	M24 1-1	a21 0-2	m05 1-0		a11 0-0	F17 2-0	D16 3-1	M23 2-2	a07 0-1	A23 1-1	D09 1-1
16 PORTSMOUTH	M26 1-1	N25 3-3	O14 2-0	F24 2-1	m05 2-1	N11 3-3	D25 1-3	a21 2-2	F03 6-3	S30 1-0	D23 1-0	D09 1-3	M10 0-0	A19 1-1	S02 0-0		A30 4-1	S16 5-1	a07 0-0	M24 1-1	J13 2-2	O28 1-4
17 SHEFFIELD W	D30 0-2	N11 3-2	a21 3-1	N25 3-4	A26 0-1	S09 1-2	F24 2-2	a18 4-3	m05 6-0	a07 2-2	F03 3-2	O28 4-1	F26 0-4	S16 0-1	S30 0-0	A21 2-1		S04 1-1	M24 3-0	D09 1-1	D26 3-0	O14 2-2
18 STOKE C	D26 1-0	D09 1-0	N11 1-0	M24 2-1	F17 0-0	O28 2-0	S23 2-1	S02 4-1	S09 2-0	O14 1-1	A28 0-1	F24 2-3	a07 2-0	M26 2-0	A19 1-2	J20 1-2	S11 1-1		a21 2-4	M10 0-0	D23 1-1	N25 0-1
19 SUNDERLAND	M31 0-2	A30 3-3	S16 0-2	J13 1-2	O21 1-1	S30 4-2	M17 1-1	A19 1-0	a14 4-0	S02 0-1	O07 0-0	D23 2-1	D25 2-1	M03 2-1	M26 2-1	N18 0-0	N04 5-1	D02 1-1		F03 0-0	a28 1-1	m05 0-0
20 TOTTENHAM H	D23 1-0	F17 3-2	A19 1-4	A28 4-2	O07 1-0	D30 1-0	M03 2-1	D26 2-1	M31 3-0	M26 2-1	a14 0-2	m05 3-1	S09 1-0	D02 3-3	N18 7-0	N04 5-1	a28 1-0	O21 6-1	S23 1-1		M17 5-0	J20 2-1
21 W.B.A.	F17 2-0	D16 2-0	a04 1-3	N11 0-1	S23 2-1	a07 3-0	J20 1-1	F24 1-2	D30 0-1	M24 0-0	M26 0-2	O14 1-1	N25 0-1	S13 2-3	A30 1-2	S09 5-0	D25 1-3	A26 1-1	D09 3-1	O28 1-2		a21 3-2
22 WOLVERHAMPTON W	N04 0-1	M26 2-3	J13 1-1	S02 7-1	M31 0-1	F03 2-3	O21 2-1	A28 2-3	N18 4-0	D23 1-1	D26 3-1	A19 2-0	S30 0-0	O07 3-4	m02 0-1	M17 2-3	M03 4-0	a14 2-3	S06 2-1	S16 2-1	D02 3-1	

DIVISION 2

	BARNSLEY	BIRMINGHAM C	BLACKBURN R	BRENTFORD	BURY	CARDIFF C	CHESTERFIELD	COVENTRY C	DONCASTER R	GRIMSBY T	HULL C	LEEDS U	LEICESTER C	LUTON T	MANCHESTER C	NOTTS CO	PRESTON N.E.	Q.P.R.	SHEFFIELD U	SOUTHAMPTON	SWANSEA T	WEST HAM U
1 BARNSLEY		M03 0-2	M26 3-0	S06 2-3	M31 2-3	N18 0-0	D23 0-0	a14 3-0	D26 0-1	O07 3-1	A30 4-2	J20 1-2	a28 0-0	S09 6-1	D02 1-1	M17 2-0	O21 4-1	N04 7-0	a18 1-1	A19 1-2	F17 1-0	S23 1-2
2 BIRMINGHAM C	O14 2-0		O28 3-2	a25 1-1	J20 3-3	M23 0-0	F17 2-1	S06 1-1	N11 0-2	A26 1-1	M24 2-1	a21 0-1	A23 2-0	N25 3-0	D26 1-0	D30 1-4	S09 1-0	S23 1-1	a07 3-0	F28 2-1	D16 5-0	D09 3-1
3 BLACKBURN R	M23 3-4	M17 2-3		A21 3-2	D25 2-4	O07 2-0	D02 1-1	M03 1-0	F17 4-2	O21 2-0	S23 2-2	F10 2-1	a14 1-0	A26 1-0	N18 4-1	M31 0-0	N04 2-1	a25 2-1	D16 0-2	S11 1-0	J20 3-0	S09 1-3
4 BRENTFORD	S13 0-2	O21 2-1	A30 3-2		F10 4-0	M17 4-0	a14 4-0	O07 0-4	S23 1-1	M31 5-1	J20 2-1	A26 1-2	N18 0-0	D16 1-0	M03 2-0	N04 1-3	F17 2-4	D02 2-1	M23 3-1	D26 4-0	S09 2-1	D30 1-1
5 BURY	N11 0-3	S16 4-1	J01 1-3	D09 2-1		J13 1-2	M23 2-2	S02 1-0	a21 3-1	F03 2-3	N25 0-2	F24 0-1	A19 2-3	O28 4-1	J27 2-0	S30 0-0	A30 3-1	S06 0-1	M10 1-1	M24 1-0	a07 1-1	O14 3-0
6 CARDIFF C	a07 1-1	M26 2-1	F24 1-0	O28 1-1	S09 2-2		S23 1-0	D25 2-1	M10 0-0	D16 5-2	N11 2-1	D09 1-0	F17 2-2	a21 2-1	A28 1-1	A26 2-0	D30 0-2	J20 4-2	N25 2-0	O14 2-2	M24 1-0	S04 2-1
7 CHESTERFIELD	A26 1-2	S30 1-1	a21 4-1	N25 2-2	M26 3-0	F03 0-3		S16 1-1	a07 1-4	A21 2-2	O14 0-0	M10 1-0	S02 1-0	N11 1-1	J13 1-2	D25 0-0	S11 2-0	D16 3-1	M24 0-2	D09 2-3	F24 3-1	O28 1-2
8 COVENTRY C	N25 3-3	S11 3-1	O14 6-1	F24 3-3	D30 5-2	D26 2-1	J20 1-0		O28 3-1	M27 1-0	M10 4-1	A21 1-0	S23 2-1	D09 4-1	F17 0-2	D16 1-2	A26 1-0	S09 3-0	a21 2-3	a07 2-2	N11 3-1	M24 1-0
9 DONCASTER R	D25 3-2	M31 0-1	S30 0-1	F03 0-3	D02 1-1	O21 0-0	N18 1-2	M17 2-1		N04 3-1	J13 2-4	D16 4-4	M03 2-2	M23 5-2	O07 4-3	J20 3-2	a26 2-0	a14 0-2	m05 1-1	A30 0-0	J27 1-0	A26 3-0
10 GRIMSBY T	F24 3-1	D23 1-1	M10 1-1	N11 7-2	S23 2-1	A19 0-0	A30 1-2	M23 1-2	M24 1-0		D30 1-1	N25 2-2	D25 0-2	a07 0-2	S06 4-4	S09 1-4	J20 0-4	F17 2-2	O14 2-2	O28 4-2	D09 4-2	a21 0-1
11 HULL C	A24 3-3	N04 3-2	F03 2-2	S16 3-0	a14 4-0	M31 2-0	M03 2-1	O21 0-2	S09 1-2	S02 2-1		M23 2-0	O07 1-3	m05 5-3	M17 3-3	a28 1-0	D02 0-0	N18 5-1	D26 1-1	S30 4-1	A26 2-1	D16 1-2
12 LEEDS U	S16 2-2	D02 3-0	S02 0-1	D23 1-0	O07 1-1	a28 2-0	O21 2-0	A30 1-0	A19 3-1	a14 1-0	M26 3-0		M31 2-1	S30 2-1	N04 1-1	N18 0-1	M03 0-3	M17 2-2	F03 1-0	J13 5-3	m05 2-0	D26 2-0
13 LEICESTER C	D09 1-2	A28 1-3	N25 2-0	a07 1-2	D16 4-0	S30 1-1	D30 1-0	F03 3-0	O14 2-0	D26 0-0	F24 4-0	N11 1-5		M24 3-1	S16 1-2	S04 1-1	M27 2-3	A26 6-2	S09 2-2	a21 3-1	O28 2-3	M10 1-0
14 LUTON T	J13 1-1	a14 1-1	D23 1-1	A19 2-0	M17 4-2	D02 1-1	M31 3-0	a28 1-1	M26 3-1	N18 4-0	S06 1-2	F17 2-3	N04 0-2		F03 2-2	M03 1-1	O07 1-2	O21 2-0	S16 0-0	S02 0-1	D26 3-1	A30 1-1
15 MANCHESTER C	a21 6-0	D25 3-1	a07 1-0	O14 4-0	A26 5-1	A23 2-1	S09 5-1	S30 1-0	F24 3-3	m05 2-2	O28 0-0	M24 4-1	J20 1-1	S23 1-1		M26 0-0	D16 0-3	a04 5-2	D09 5-3	N25 2-3	M14 1-2	N11 2-0
16 NOTTS CO	O28 2-1	S02 0-1	N11 1-1	M24 2-3	F17 4-2	D23 1-2	D26 1-0	A19 0-2	S16 1-2	J13 3-2	D09 2-2	a07 0-0	m05 2-3	O14 2-2	a30 0-0		S23 1-3	A31 3-3	F24 3-0	M10 2-2	a21 3-2	N25 4-1
17 PRESTON N.E.	M10 7-0	J13 1-0	M24 3-0	S30 4-2	A23 2-0	S02 1-1	S06 4-1	D23 1-1	D09 6-1	S16 2-0	a21 1-0	O14 2-0	M26 3-2	F24 1-0	A19 2-4	F03 3-1		D26 1-0	O28 1-1	N11 3-2	N25 5-1	a07 0-1
18 Q.P.R.	M24 2-1	F03 2-0	D09 3-1	J27 1-1	m05 3-2	S16 3-2	A19 1-1	J13 3-1	N25 1-2	S30 7-1	a07 3-1	O28 3-0	D23 3-0	M10 1-1	S02 1-2	A24 1-0	D25 1-4		N11 2-1	M23 2-0	O14 1-1	F24 3-3
19 SHEFFIELD U	S02 0-2	N18 3-2	A19 0-3	M26 5-1	O21 3-0	a14 1-2	N04 4-1	D02 2-0	S11 0-0	M03 4-2	D25 3-1	S23 2-2	J13 2-1	J20 2-1	a28 0-0	O07 1-2	M17 2-3	M31 2-0		D23 1-2	A28 6-1	F17 1-1
20 SOUTHAMPTON	D16 1-0	O07 0-2	S06 1-1	m05 2-1	N04 1-0	M03 1-1	a28 1-1	N18 5-4	A23 1-1	M17 5-1	F17 2-3	S09 2-0	D02 2-2	D30 1-1	a14 2-1	O21 1-0	M31 3-3	M26 2-2	A26 1-0		S23 2-1	J20 2-2
21 SWANSEA T	S30 1-0	A19 0-1	S16 1-2	J13 2-1	N18 2-0	N04 1-0	O07 2-0	M31 2-1	S02 2-2	a28 1-3	D23 1-0	S07 4-2	M17 2-1	D25 0-2	O21 2-3	D02 2-1	a14 2-1	M03 1-0	A24 1-2	F03 2-1		M26 3-2
22 WEST HAM U	F03 4-2	a28 1-2	J13 2-3	S02 1-2	M03 2-3	m05 0-0	M17 2-0	N04 3-2	D23 0-0	D02 2-1	A19 3-3	D25 3-1	O21 0-0	A24 2-1	M31 2-4	a14 4-2	N18 2-0	O07 4-1	S30 3-5	S16 3-0	M23 1-1	

Season 1950-51

DIVISION 3 NORTH

	ACCRINGTON S	BARROW	BRADFORD	BRADFORD C	CARLISLE U	CHESTER	CREWE A	DARLINGTON	GATESHEAD	HALIFAX T	HARTLEPOOLS U	LINCOLN C	MANSFIELD T	NEW BRIGHTON	OLDHAM A	ROCHDALE	ROTHERHAM U	SCUNTHORPE U	SHREWSBURY T	SOUTHPORT	STOCKPORT CO	TRANMERE R	WREXHAM	YORK C
1 ACCRINGTON S		J27 1-0	S09 3-3	N11 0-2	D26 0-4	O28 1-2	A23 1-0	a07 1-0	m05 2-2	a21 1-0	a25 2-0	O14 3-1	M26 0-2	M24 1-1	J20 1-2	M10 1-2	J01 0-2	F17 0-0	F24 2-0	A26 3-1	D09 2-3	m02 0-2	S23 1-0	S26 2-0
2 BARROW	a16 4-0		D16 2-3	F24 1-3	F10 1-2	a07 2-0	M10 0-1	D09 0-3	N11 1-1	A24 2-0	M24 3-0	a21 3-1	J20 2-3	O28 1-1	A26 2-1	O14 4-3	S23 0-2	S09 1-0	a19 0-0	S07 3-1	S30 1-0	S19 1-2	a12 2-0	M26 2-0
3 BRADFORD	J13 3-0	A19 5-0		S30 3-1	S02 0-2	M24 2-0	a21 1-1	O28 2-1	a18 2-0	O14 2-1	a07 1-1	M10 2-1	S13 1-0	a11 2-1	M26 3-1	A21 0-1	D25 0-4	J27 2-2	N11 2-4	S16 2-0	F24 3-0	F03 4-1	a30 0-1	D23 4-0
4 BRADFORD C	M31 7-0	O07 5-1	F17 4-1		O21 2-4	F10 0-1	J20 1-1	D26 0-3	S09 2-2	A26 2-0	D30 3-1	S06 0-0	N18 2-3	S23 3-0	a28 1-0	M27 2-1	M03 3-4	a14 2-0	a25 1-0	N04 3-0	D16 0-1	A23 2-2	D02 5-3	M17 5-2
5 CARLISLE U	D25 3-1	J01 1-1	D30 1-0	M10 2-1		F24 2-1	M24 2-1	a19 2-1	A24 3-0	a26 1-0	S07 1-0	a07 2-0	F17 2-0	N11 1-0	S09 1-0	O28 4-0	M23 0-0	S23 3-1	O14 2-2	D16 3-1	a21 2-2	A26 3-1	J20 0-2	m03 3-2
6 CHESTER	M17 2-2	N18 1-2	N04 2-0	m05 2-2	O07 1-1		F17 1-1	A26 3-1	S23 2-2	S09 2-1	J20 2-1	a11 2-1	D02 0-1	a25 3-1	A23 3-1	J27 1-3	a14 1-2	a28 4-1	D25 3-1	O21 0-2	a04 3-0	M31 1-3	S06 0-0	M03 3-1
7 CREWE A	A30 3-0	O21 2-0	D02 2-4	S16 1-1	N04 1-1	S30 3-0		J27 5-0	A26 0-1	D25 0-0	D16 3-1	F10 0-4	O07 2-0	J13 2-0	a14 2-1	F03 3-1	M17 1-2	M03 2-0	M23 1-2	a04 1-0	S04 0-2	a28 1-1	N18 1-1	M31 2-4
8 DARLINGTON	N18 3-0	a28 1-1	M17 1-4	a23 2-1	a14 1-0	D23 0-0	a30 2-0		J01 4-2	F17 2-0	M26 0-1	J13 1-1	A30 1-2	S13 5-3	O21 0-0	A19 0-2	J20 2-2	N04 3-2	S02 2-1	M03 1-1	S23 2-1	O07 1-1	M31 1-1	D02 0-3
9 GATESHEAD	A19 7-0	M31 1-0	a14 5-0	J13 2-0	A28 4-3	F03 2-1	D23 4-0	F10 5-2		S04 5-0	D25 0-1	M26 1-2	M17 1-3	S02 4-0	N18 3-2	S16 4-1	O21 0-3	O07 1-0	S30 3-0	a30 1-3	S18 2-0	D02 2-0	M03 0-0	N04 3-0
10 HALIFAX T	D02 2-2	A28 0-0	M03 2-2	D23 1-2	a28 1-0	J13 3-1	D26 1-0	S30 2-2	S11 1-0		J27 1-0	F03 4-1	M31 0-1	A19 0-2	O07 3-0	S02 1-1	N04 1-2	O21 3-3	S16 3-1	a14 4-0	M27 1-0	N18 0-1	M17 1 0	F10 1 3
11 HARTLEPOOLS U	a28 1-0	N04 6-1	N18 3-1	S02 1-1	S11 3-3	S16 1-2	A19 0-2	M23 6-1	D26 3-0	J06 5-2		S30 2-2	O21 1-1	D23 0-1	M03 0-1	J13 0-0	M31 3-1	M17 4-2	F03 1-0	D02 3-2	F10 2-0	a14 2-1	O07 4-1	A28 4-1
12 LINCOLN C	M03 9-1	D02 3-0	O21 1-3	S13 1 4	N18 1 1	A19 2-1	m05 4-1	S09 3-0	M23 2-1	S23 3-1	F17 1-0		D30 3-0	J27 3-0	M31 2-0	D25 4-2	a28 0-2	A23 2-1	D23 5-0	O07 1-2	J20 6-0	M17 2-1	N04 2-1	a14 2-1
13 MANSFIELD T	M23 5-0	S16 4-0	S04 3-2	a07 1-1	S30 2-1	a21 2-1	F24 4-1	A21 2-1	O28 2-1	N11 3-1	M10 1-0	S02 1-1		O14 4-0	D26 3-1	a16 1-0	J13 1-1	A26 1-1	a30 4-0	m05 2-2	M24 2-1	J10 2-1	a23 1-1	F03 3-1
14 NEW BRIGHTON	N04 1-1	M17 1-2	a28 3-3	F03 0-6	M31 0-1	m02 1-0	S09 0-2	S05 2-2	a04 0-1	D16 1-0	A26 1-0	J06 0-1	M03 0-1		D02 2-0	S30 1-5	O07 2-4	N18 1-2	F10 0-0	A22 1-0	D25 1-0	S16 1-1	a14 3-0	O21 0-0
15 OLDHAM A	S16 2-1	D23 0-1	M23 2-3	m01 2-2	J13 1-1	A29 1-0	a17 0-2	M10 2-0	a07 2-3	F24 2-0	O14 5-1	N11 0-0	D25 2-0	a21 3-1		a24 2-0	A19 4-5	S12 3-4	M24 2-1	F03 4 0	O28 1 3	S30 3-4	J27 2-2	S02 2-2
16 ROCHDALE	O21 3-1	M03 1-0	A29 1-2	M26 4-0	M17 4-1	J16 2-3	S23 1-1	m05 0-0	J20 2-0	a10 0-0	S09 3-1	a17 3-0	a14 0-0	F17 1-0	F10 0-1		N18 0-2	D02 2-0	S05 5-0	M31 1-1	A26 1-1	N04 2-3	a28 2-0	O07 0-1
17 ROTHERHAM U	F10 6-2	F03 3-0	D26 2-1	O14 1-0	M26 3-0	a16 0-0	O28 2-3	S16 0-1	M10 1-2	M24 2-0	N11 2-1	a30 3-0	S09 3-0	F24 5-0	m05 3-1	a07 3-0		D30 4-1	a21 2-0	J30 1-1	A21 0-0	S04 1-2	A26 5-0	S30 3-1
18 SCUNTHORPE U	S30 3-0	J13 1-0	J06 1-1	a18 0-0	F03 1-1	D09 2-0	O14 1-1	M24 2-0	F24 2-1	M10 2-2	O28 0-0	A30 1-1	D23 0-0	a07 6-0	S06 1-0	a21 3-0	S02 0-0		A19 0-0	M26 0-0	a30 3-0	F10 1-1	D25 2-0	S16 0-1
19 SHREWSBURY T	O07 0-1	a14 1-0	M31 1-0	J27 2-0	M03 0-3	D26 1-0	M26 0-1	D30 2-2	N25 1-0	J20 2-0	S23 1-0	A26 1-2	a28 1-1	m05 4-2	N04 2-2	S11 0-2	D02 1-2	D16 3-1		M17 1-5	S09 0-3	O21 1-2	A21 2-1	N18 1-0
20 SOUTHPORT	D23 3-0	S12 4-1	J20 2-4	M24 0-1	A19 1-0	M10 0-1	S02 2-0	O14 1-0	J27 1-0	a17 1-1	a21 3-0	F24 0-2	a10 0-1	A29 0-1	S23 1-4	N11 1-1	J09 0-1	M23 2-2	O28 1 2		a07 2-0	S09 0-1	F17 3-1	D26 1-1
21 STOCKPORT CO	a14 0-0	F17 4-1	O07 2-1	A19 3-1	D02 1-2	S02 0-3	S11 3-0	F03 1-0	J31 5-2	M26 2-1	m05 2-0	S16 2-0	N04 3-1	D26 4-0	M17 1-4	D23 2-2	A28 1-3	M31 1-2	J13 2-0	N18 3-2		M03 0-0	O21 2-1	a28 1-0
22 TRANMERE R	S02 1-1	D26 3-0	S23 2-2	A29 3-1	D23 2-2	N11 3-1	a10 3-0	F24 3-2	a21 2-2	a07 3-2	a17 1-0	O28 0-1	M07 2-1	J20 4-3	F17 1-0	M24 2-1	S12 2-1	m05 1-0	M10 0-1	J13 4-0	O14 1-1		M23 1-2	A19 7-2
23 WREXHAM	F03 1-1	S02 1-0	F10 3-1	a21 0-3	S16 2-1	S13 2-0	a07 0-2	N11 3-1	O14 0-0	O28 2-2	F24 1-0	M24 2-3	A19 2-2	a18 0-1	a04 0-2	m02 3-1	D23 0-0	D26 3-1	A30 1 0	S30 3-3	M10 2-0	M26 2-1		J13 4-3
24 YORK C	S04 3-0	M23 0-2	A26 1-3	O28 1-2	J27 1-1	O14 2-2	N11 1-2	a21 1-1	M24 1-1	m05 0-0	A21 3-0	a16 2-2	S23 1-1	M10 2-0	D30 2-2	F24 2-2	F17 3-3	J20 0-0	a07 2-0	D25 2-0	a11 0-0	a25 4-0	S09 3-0	

DIVISION 3 SOUTH

	ALDERSHOT	BOURNEMOUTH	BRIGHTON & HA	BRISTOL C	BRISTOL R	COLCHESTER U	CRYSTAL P	EXETER C	GILLINGHAM	IPSWICH T	LEYTON O	MILLWALL	NEWPORT CO	NORTHAMPTON T	NORWICH C	NOTTINGHAM F	PLYMOUTH A	PORT VALE	READING	SOUTHEND	SWINDON T	TORQUAY U	WALSALL	WATFORD
1 ALDERSHOT		a28 0-1	A26 0-0	a14 0-0	A23 1-1	a11 2-0	m02 3-0	D25 4-2	D02 2-4	O21 0-1	M17 3-1	N18 2-1	D30 3-1	J20 3-0	S09 1-1	F17 1-0	M03 2-2	S23 2-0	O07 1-1	S06 2-2	M23 0-1	m05 1-0	N04 3-0	M31 1-1
2 BOURNEMOUTH	a25 4-0		M10 2-2	A19 1-0	M14 2-0	S13 2-0	O14 5-0	M23 1-1	A23 3-1	F03 2-1	S16 5-0	D23 1-0	O28 2-0	N11 1-0	M24 0-0	F10 3-2	S30 0-2	a07 3-1	m05 1-0	D26 3-1	J27 2-1	a21 0-0	J13 3-1	S02 3-3
3 BRIGHTON & H.A.	D23 1-2	O21 2 1		O07 1-1	S16 2-2	J13 3-1	F03 1-0	M17 4-1	M03 2-2	a14 4-0	D02 3-0	S13 2-3	a18 9-1	M23 5-1	D26 1-1	A30 1-2	N18 0-6	J17 2-2	M31 1-1	N04 2-1	S02 1-0	A19 2-2	a28 1-0	F17 1-1
4 BRISTOL C	a04 1-1	D16 2-0	F24 2-0		S02 1-0	a25 0-2	S06 2-0	A23 3-1	A20 2-0	a18 2-1	S30 4-1	J13 2-1	O14 2-1	O28 1-0	M10 2-2	N11 0-3	D25 1-0	M24 3-1	M26 3-3	J17 0-3	a21 2-0	a07 0-2	F03 3-3	S16 3-0
5 BRISTOL R	A28 3-0	O07 2-0	J20 3-2	D30 2-1		D23 1-1	S09 1-1	M03 3-1	S04 3-0	M31 1 1	N18 2 1	a28 1 0	S23 1-0	m05 1-1	a30 3-3	m03 0-2	N04 3-1	D26 2-0	M17 4-0	O21 4-1	A19 1-0	J31 1-1	a14 1-1	a23 3-0
6 COLCHESTER U	J27 1-0	S07 4-1	S09 4-1	a28 1-1	A26 0-0		D30 1-0	O07 0-1	D16 4-2	N04 2-3	M31 1-0	D02 3-0	J20 1-1	F17 2-1	S23 2-3	D26 0-2	M17 3-0	m05 1-1	O21 1-1	M03 1-3	A31 4-1	M23 3-1	N18 0-1	a14 4-1
7 CRYSTAL P	A19 0-2	M03 0-1	S23 0-2	S13 1-0	J13 1-0	S02 1-3		O21 0-1	O07 4-3	N18 1-3	a14 1-1	J20 1-1	F17 1-1	D25 0-0	a18 0-5	J27 1-6	M31 0-1	M26 0-2	N04 0-3	M17 0-2	D23 2-0	A30 2-1	D02 1-0	a28 1-1
8 EXETER C	D26 3-0	M26 2-1	O28 4-2	A30 1-0	O14 0-2	F24 5-0	M10 1-2		F07 1-2	S16 2-0	J13 0-0	A19 0-1	M24 2-2	a07 1-0	N11 1-2	a21 0-5	F03 3-2	F10 0-3	S30 1-3	a18 1-0	S13 1-0	a04 0 0	S02 1 0	D23 3-3
9 GILLINGHAM	a21 3-0	A30 2-2	O14 1-1	D23 1-2	S13 1-0	A19 0-0	F24 0-0	J17 9-4		S30 0-1	F03 1-0	S02 4-3	M10 0-1	M24 3-1	O28 2-2	a07 1-4	m05 1-2	N11 1-1	D25 0-3	M23 0-0	m02 2-1	F10 2-0	S16 4-1	J13 3-1
10 IPSWICH T	M10 5-2	S23 1-0	F10 3-0	m05 2-0	N11 2-3	M24 3-0	a07 1-1	J20 1-0	F17 5-1		A23 2-2	D25 2-1	a21 2-1	A19 1-1	a11 0-1	F24 1-3	A26 2-0	S13 2-2	D30 0-2	S09 1-0	O28 4-1	O14 3-1	J06 3-1	M26 2-1
11 LEYTON O	O28 1-0	J20 2-0	a21 2-1	m03 0-2	a07 1-0	D09 1-1	F10 2-0	S09 1-3	S23 4-0	A31 2-0		a19 0-2	a12 0-3	S07 1-0	J11 3-1	O14 0-4	a26 1-2	F24 2-3	A26 2-0	D30 1-1	M24 2-1	M10 5-1	M23 2-1	D26 1-2
12 MILLWALL	a07 1-0	A26 3-0	S04 1-1	S09 5-3	a11 1-0	a21 2-0	S16 1-0	a25 5-0	D30 4-3	D26 4-0	S18 3-1		F24 2-4	M10 2-1	O14 1-1	M24 1-1	M23 1-1	O28 2-2	J10 1-3	A21 1-1	F10 1-0	N11 4-1	S30 2-0	F03 4-0
13 NEWPORT CO	S02 7-0	a30 1-0	m05 3-0	M03 0-1	F03 2-1	S16 2-0	S30 2-4	N04 0-3	O21 1-0	D02 1-2	a28 0-0	O07 2-3		S21 2-2	a25 1-1	A19 0-2	a14 2-0	A31 2-1	N18 5-0	M31 6-1	J13 2-1	D23 2-1	D26 3-0	S14 2-2
14 NORTHAMPTON T	S16 1-0	M31 0-1	M27 0-0	M17 2-2	a19 1-1	S30 2-1	D26 2-0	N18 4-1	N04 4-1	D16 2-1	S14 3-3	O21 1-2	a05 1-4		A31 1-2	S02 2-2	a28 1-3	D23 1-1	D02 1-1	a14 1-1	F03 1-2	J13 1-0	O07 1-1	M03 6-0
15 NORWICH C	J13 2-2	N04 3-0	D27 1-1	O21 0-0	S30 2-0	F03 1-1	m05 3-1	M31 3-0	M17 2-0	a28 1-3	F01 3-1	M03 2-1	M26 2-1	A23 0-0		D23 2-0	D02 1-0	A19 2-0	a14 2-1	N18 3-0	S16 2-0	S02 1-1	S13 1-0	O07 3-1
16 NOTTINGHAM F	S30 7-0	a14 1-0	A23 4-0	M31 0-0	M26 2-1	D25 0-0	J06 1-0	D02 2-2	N18 9-2	O07 0-0	M03 0-1	N04 2-0	m02 2-1	a25 2-2	A26 4-2		S06 4-1	S09 2-1	J20 1-1	a28 3-0	a18 2-1	F03 3-1	O21 4-0	M17 2-1
17 PLYMOUTH A	O14 5-1	F17 3-1	a07 3-3	D26 2-0	M24 0-0	O28 7-1	N11 4-0	S23 0-1	a18 2-0	D23 2 1	A19 2-1	M26 2-2	F10 1-1	a09 4-1	a21 2-1	S13 0-2		S02 1-0	S09 2-0	J20 2-0	M10 5-1	F24 1-0	A30 1-1	J10 3-1
18 PORT VALE	F03 3-1	N18 3-1	a23 0-1	N04 1-3	D25 0-0	a16 1-1	a26 2-2	a30 2-0	M31 4-3	S04 1-0	O07 3-1	m03 0-1	A24 1-0	A26 0-3	a02 2-1	J13 1-1	M05 2-1		a28 0-0	D02 3-1	S30 2-1	S16 1-0	M03 1-1	O21 2-1
19 READING	F24 7-1	a18 0-0	N11 7-0	M23 4-2	O28 0-0	M10 3-2	M24 1-1	F17 4-2	D26 1-1	S02 2-0	D23 4-0	m02 1-1	a07 5-0	a21 2-0	F14 3-1	S16 0-2	J13 4-0	J27 3-0		S23 0-2	O14 3-1	S13 0-0	A19 2-1	A30 1-0
20 SOUTHEND U	S12 4-2	D25 6-1	M24 3-1	J31 1-1	M10 1-1	O14 4-2	O28 5-2	m05 5-1	M26 4-0	J13 1-0	S02 0-1	A29 0-3	N11 3-0	F10 3-0	a07 0-2	a10 3-2	S16 1-0	a21 1-1	F03 3-3		F24 8-2	S30 3-0	D23 0-1	A19 5-1
21 SWINDON T	M26 4-0	J06 2-1	D30 0-0	D02 1-0	D16 1-2	A23 1-1	A26 2-0	S06 1-0	a28 2-0	M17 2-0	N04 2-0	a14 0-1	S09 2-0	S23 1-0	J20 1-0	m05 2-3	O21 1-2	F17 2-1	M03 1-1	O07 4-1		D25 2-1	M31 1-1	N18 3-2
22 TORQUAY U	S27 1-2	D02 0-2	D16 3-1	N18 4-1	J17 1-2	M26 4-1	A23 4-1	a28 2-0	a14 1-2	M03 0-1	O21 2-1	M31 2-1	A26 3-4	S09 1-1	D30 1-5	S23 3-2	O07 1-3	J20 3-2	S06 2-1	F17 2-2	D26 1-0		M17 3-2	N04 3-2
23 WALSALL	F10 3-1	S09 0-1	m03 1-0	S23 3-1	F15 1-2	a07 4-2	a21 0-0	D30 0-2	J20 2-1	J27 2-0	M26 1-1	F17 4-0	D25 0-0	F24 1-0	S07 0-1	M10 0-2	A24 1-1	O14 2-0	D16 1-2	A26 1-2	N11 1-0	O28 3-1		a19 1-0
24 WATFORD	N11 1-2	D30 2-1	S30 1-1	J20 1-2	a21 1-0	F10 2-0	D09 1-0	A26 1-2	S09 5-0	M23 0-2	D25 2-0	S23 0-0	S07 0-2	O14 0-1	F24 0-2	O28 1-1	J27 1-1	M10 2-0	A24 3-1	D16 1-3	a07 1-2	M24 2-2	m05 1-3	

LEAGUE TABLES

DIVISION 1

	P	W	D	L	F	A	W	D	L	F	A	Pts
Tottenham H	42	17	2	2	54	21	8	8	5	28	23	60
Manchester U	42	14	4	3	42	16	10	4	7	32	24	56
Blackpool	42	12	6	3	43	19	8	4	9	36	34	50
Newcastle U	42	10	6	5	36	22	8	7	6	26	31	49
Arsenal	42	11	5	5	47	28	8	4	9	26	28	47
Middlesbrough	42	12	7	2	51	25	6	4	11	25	40	47
Portsmouth	42	8	10	3	39	30	8	5	8	32	38	47
Bolton W	42	11	2	8	31	20	8	5	8	33	41	45
Liverpool	42	11	5	5	28	25	5	6	10	25	34	43
Burnley	42	9	7	5	27	16	5	7	9	21	27	42
Derby Co	42	10	5	6	53	33	6	3	12	28	42	40
Sunderland	42	8	9	4	30	21	4	7	10	33	52	40
Stoke C	42	10	5	6	28	19	3	9	9	22	40	40
Wolves	42	9	3	9	44	30	6	5	10	30	31	38
Aston Villa	42	9	6	6	39	29	3	7	11	27	39	37
WBA	42	7	4	10	30	27	6	7	8	23	34	37
Charlton A	42	9	4	8	35	31	5	5	11	28	49	37
Fulham	42	8	5	8	35	37	5	6	10	17	31	37
Huddersfield T	42	8	4	9	40	40	7	2	12	24	52	36
Chelsea	42	9	4	8	31	25	3	4	14	22	40	32
Sheffield W	42	9	6	6	43	32	3	2	16	21	51	32
Everton	42	7	5	9	26	35	5	3	13	22	51	32

DIVISION 2

	P	W	D	L	F	A	W	D	L	F	A	Pts
Preston NE	42	16	3	2	53	18	10	2	9	38	31	57
Manchester C	42	12	6	3	53	25	7	8	6	36	36	52
Cardiff C	42	13	7	1	36	20	4	9	8	17	25	50
Birmingham C	42	12	6	3	37	20	8	3	10	27	33	49
Leeds U	42	14	4	3	36	17	6	4	11	27	38	48
Blackburn R	42	13	3	5	39	27	6	5	10	26	39	46
Coventry C	42	15	3	3	51	25	4	4	13	24	34	45
Sheffield U	42	11	4	6	44	27	5	8	8	28	35	44
Brentford	42	13	3	5	44	25	5	5	11	31	49	44
Hull C	42	12	5	4	47	28	4	6	11	27	42	43
Doncaster R	42	9	6	6	37	32	6	7	8	27	36	43
Southampton	42	10	9	2	38	27	5	4	12	28	46	43
West Ham U	42	10	5	6	44	33	6	5	10	24	36	42
Leicester C	42	10	4	7	42	28	5	7	9	26	30	41
Barnsley	42	9	5	7	42	22	6	5	10	32	46	40
QPR	42	13	5	3	47	25	2	5	14	24	57	40
Notts Co	42	7	7	7	37	34	6	6	9	24	26	39
Swansea T	42	14	1	6	34	25	2	3	16	20	52	36
Luton T	42	7	9	5	34	23	2	5	14	23	47	32
Bury	42	9	4	8	33	27	3	4	14	27	59	32
Chesterfield	42	7	7	7	30	28	2	5	14	14	41	30
Grimsby T	42	6	8	7	37	38	2	4	15	24	57	28

DIVISION 3 North

	P	W	D	L	F	A	W	D	L	F	A	Pts
Rotherham U	46	16	3	4	55	16	15	6	2	48	25	71
Mansfield T	46	17	6	0	54	19	9	6	8	24	29	64
Carlisle U	46	18	4	1	44	17	7	8	8	35	33	62
Tranmere R	46	15	5	3	51	26	9	6	8	32	36	59
Lincoln C	46	18	1	4	62	23	7	7	9	27	35	58
Bradford	46	15	3	5	46	23	8	5	10	44	49	54
Bradford C	46	13	4	6	55	30	8	6	9	35	33	52
Gateshead	46	17	1	5	60	21	4	7	12	24	41	50
Crewe A	46	11	5	7	38	26	8	5	10	23	34	48
Stockport Co	46	15	3	5	45	26	5	5	13	18	37	48
Rochdale	46	11	6	6	38	18	6	5	12	31	44	45
Scunthorpe U	46	10	12	1	32	9	3	6	14	26	48	44
Chester	46	11	6	6	42	30	6	3	14	20	34	43
Wrexham	46	12	6	5	37	28	3	6	14	18	43	42
Oldham A	46	10	5	8	47	36	6	3	14	26	37	40
Hartlepools U	46	14	5	4	55	26	2	2	19	9	40	39
York C	46	7	12	4	37	24	5	3	15	29	53	39
Darlington	46	10	8	5	35	29	3	6	16	24	48	30
Barrow	46	12	3	8	38	27	4	3	16	13	49	38
Shrewsbury T	46	11	3	9	28	30	4	4	15	15	44	37
Southport	46	9	4	10	29	25	4	6	13	27	47	36
Halifax T	46	11	6	6	36	24	0	6	17	14	45	34
Accrington S	46	10	4	9	28	29	1	6	16	14	72	32
New Brighton	46	7	6	10	22	32	4	2	17	18	58	30

DIVISION 3 South

	P	W	D	L	F	A	W	D	L	F	A	Pts
Nottingham F	46	16	6	1	57	17	14	4	5	53	23	70
Norwich C	46	16	6	1	42	14	9	8	6	40	31	64
Reading	46	15	6	2	57	17	6	9	8	31	36	57
Plymouth A	46	16	5	2	54	19	8	4	11	31	36	57
Millwall	46	15	6	2	52	23	8	4	11	28	34	56
Bristol R	46	15	7	1	46	18	5	8	10	18	24	55
Southend U	46	15	4	4	64	27	6	6	11	28	42	52
Ipswich T	46	15	4	4	48	24	8	2	13	21	34	52
Bournemouth	46	17	5	1	49	16	5	2	16	16	41	51
Bristol C	46	15	4	4	41	25	5	7	11	23	34	51
Newport Co	46	13	4	6	48	25	6	5	12	29	45	47
Port Vale	46	13	6	4	35	24	3	7	13	25	41	45
Brighton & HA	46	11	8	4	51	31	2	9	12	20	48	43
Exeter C	46	11	4	8	33	30	7	2	14	29	55	42
Walsall	46	12	4	7	32	20	3	6	14	20	42	40
Colchester U	46	12	5	6	43	25	2	7	14	20	51	40
Swindon T	46	15	4	4	38	17	3	0	20	17	50	40
Aldershot	46	11	8	4	37	20	4	2	17	19	68	40
Leyton O	46	13	2	8	36	28	2	6	15	17	47	38
Torquay U	46	13	2	8	47	39	1	7	15	17	42	37
Northampton T	46	8	9	6	39	30	2	7	14	16	37	36
Gillingham	46	10	7	6	41	30	3	2	18	28	71	35
Watford	46	8	5	10	29	28	1	6	16	25	60	29
Crystal P	46	6	5	12	18	39	2	6	15	15	45	27

Football League Records

Top scorers: Div 1, G.Robledo (Newcastle United) 33 goals; Div 2, D.Dooley (Sheffield Wednesday) 46 goals; Div 3(N), A.Graver (Lincoln City) 36 goals; Div 3(S), R.Blackman (Reading) 39 goals.
New Brighton failed to gain re-election, Workington elected in their place. Shrewsbury Town transferred to Division Three South.

When Manchester United won the title in 1951-2, Jack Rowley's 30 goals included hat-tricks in the first two games and stood as a club record until beaten by Dennis Viollet eight years later.

Derek Dooley burst upon the scene in 1951-2 when his 46 goals in only 30 appearances helped Sheffield Wednesday to the Second Division title. Sadly, in February 1953, he broke a leg against Preston and had to have the limb amputated.

DIVISION 1

	ARSENAL	ASTON VILLA	BLACKPOOL	BOLTON W	BURNLEY	CHARLTON A	CHELSEA	DERBY CO	FULHAM	HUDDERSFIELD T	LIVERPOOL	MANCHESTER C	MANCHESTER U	MIDDLESBROUGH	NEWCASTLE U	PORTSMOUTH	PRESTON N.E.	STOKE C	SUNDERLAND	TOTTENHAM H	W.B.A.	WOLVERHAMPTON W
1 ARSENAL		J05 2-1	a14 4-1	N24 4-2	O13 1-0	M13 2-1	A29 2-1	S15 3-1	O27 4-3	A18 2-2	S05 0-0	J26 2-2	D08 1-3	M22 3-1	a16 1-1	D25 4-1	F16 3-3	a19 4-1	S01 3-0	S29 1-1	N10 6-3	D22 2-2
2 ASTON VILLA	S08 1-0		J19 4-0	D15 1-1	M22 4-1	N10 0-2	a15 7-1	A25 4-1	a05 4-1	S10 1-0	S22 2-0	D29 1-2	O13 2-5	N24 2-0	D08 2-2	F09 2-0	O27 3-2	F16 2-3	A27 2-1	M08 0-3	a19 2-0	D25 3-3
3 BLACKPOOL	a11 0-0	S15 0-3		a05 1-0	F16 1-0	O13 1-2	A18 1-2	J26 2-1	M08 4-2	D22 3-1	D26 2-0	S29 2-2	a19 2-2	O27 2-2	N10 6-3	A27 0-0	S10 0-3	N24 4-2	J05 3-0	D08 1-0	M22 2-0	S01 3-2
4 BOLTON W	a12 2-1	A18 5-2	N17 1-0		J26 1-4	S29 2-1	M15 3-0	F02 1-2	a14 2-1	O20 2-1	M29 1-1	D01 2-1	S01 1-0	S03 3-1	A22 0-0	N03 0-3	S15 1-1	D22 1-1	O06 1-1	J05 1-1	D25 3-2	M01 2-2
5 BURNLEY	M01 0-1	N03 2-1	O06 2-0	S22 1-3		D15 1-0	D01 1-1	M15 0-1	A25 1-0	a12 0-2	A21 0-0	O20 0-0	a11 1-1	D29 7-1	J19 2-1	a26 1-0	D25 0-2	F09 4-0	M29 0-1	S03 1-1	S08 6-1	N17 2-2
6 CHARLTON A	O20 1-3	a24 0-1	M01 2-0	F09 1-0	A18 1-0		a26 1-1	N03 3-3	D29 3-0	D01 4-0	O06 2-0	M15 0-0	S12 2-2	S08 4-3	S22 3-0	D22 0-2	A29 4-2	a14 4-0	N17 2-1	D25 0-3	J19 3-3	a12 1-0
7 CHELSEA	A22 1-3	a14 2-2	D15 2-1	O27 1-3	a19 4-1	D08 1-0		S05 0-1	S08 2-1	S15 2-1	A25 1-3	D25 0-3	N10 4-2	F16 5-0	M12 1-0	D29 1-1	N24 0-0	M22 1-0	S29 2-1	a30 0-2	O13 1-3	J26 0-1
8 DERBY CO	J19 1-2	D22 1-1	S22 1-1	D08 5-2	O27 1-0	M22 1-3	m03 1-1		N10 5-0	D26 2-1	F09 1-1	S08 1-3	F16 0-3	a05 3-1	a19 1-3	a14 1-0	M08 4-3	S01 4-2	A18 3-4	O13 4-2	N24 2-1	A29 1-3
9 FULHAM	M15 0-0	N17 2-2	O20 1-2	a11 1-2	D22 1-2	S01 3-3	J05 1-2	m01 3-0		a26 1-0	M01 1-1	N03 1-2	D26 3-3	J19 6-0	F09 1-1	O06 2-3	A18 2-3	S12 5-0	a12 0-1	A29 1-2	S22 1-0	D01 2-2
10 HUDDERSFIELD T	D15 2-3	S19 3-1	A25 1-3	M08 0-2	N24 1-3	a19 1-0	J19 1-0	D25 1-1	D08 1-0		D29 1-2	A22 5-1	M22 3-2	S22 1-0	O13 2-4	S08 0-1	a05 2-0	O27 0-2	a15 2-2	N10 1-1	F16 3-0	S29 1-7
11 LIVERPOOL	S12 0-0	J26 1-2	D25 1-1	N10 1-1	A29 3-1	F16 1-1	D22 1-1	S29 2-0	O13 4-0	S01 2-1		a14 1-2	N24 0-0	M08 1-1	M22 3-0	A18 0-2	D08 2-2	a05 2-1	S15 2-2	a19 1-1	O27 2-5	J05 1-1
12 MANCHESTER C	S22 0-2	S01 2-2	F09 0-0	a19 0-3	M12 0-1	O27 4-2	D26 3-1	J05 4-2	M22 1-1	A29 3-0	a11 1-2		S15 1-2	N10 2-1	N24 2-3	J01 0-1	O13 1-0	D08 0-1	D22 3-1	F16 1-1	a05 1-2	A18 0-0
13 MANCHESTER U	a26 6-1	M01 1-1	D01 3-1	D29 1-0	a14 6-1	S05 3-2	a21 3-0	O06 2-1	D25 3-2	N03 1-1	a12 4-0	J19 1-1		A22 4-2	A25 2-1	N17 1-3	S29 1-2	S08 4-0	O20 0-1	J26 2-0	D15 5-1	M15 2-0
14 MIDDLESBROUGH	N03 0-3	a12 2-0	M15 1-0	a23 2-0	S01 5-0	J05 2-1	O06 0-0	N17 0-0	S15 2-0	J26 2-1	O20 3-3	M29 2-2	A29 1-4		a14 2-1	M01 2-1	D22 2-5	D26 3-0	D01 0-2	A18 2-1	F09 0-1	a26 4-0
15 NEWCASTLE U	N17 2-0	a26 6-1	a07 1-3	A29 0-1	S15 7-1	J26 6-0	O20 3-1	D01 2-1	S29 0-1	M01 6-2	N03 1-1	a12 1-0	D22 2-2	a11 0-2		M15 3-3	J05 3-0	A18 6-0	D26 2-2	S01 7-2	a23 1-4	O06 3-1
16 PORTSMOUTH	D26 1-1	S29 2-0	A22 1-3	M22 3-0	D08 2-2	A25 1-0	S01 1-0	a11 3-1	F16 4-0	J05 3-1	D15 1-3	S05 1-0	a05 1-0	O13 5-4	O27 3-1		a19 1-2	N10 4-1	J26 0-2	N24 2-0	M12 1-1	S15 2-3
17 PRESTON N.E.	O06 2-0	M15 2-2	S05 3-1	J19 2-2	J01 1-2	A22 3-0	a12 1-0	O20 0-1	D15 0-1	N17 5-2	a26 4-0	M01 1-1	F09 1-2	A25 0-1	S08 1-2	D01 2-2		S22 2-0	N03 4-2	a14 1-1	D29 1-0	M29 3-0
18 STOKE C	D01 2-1	O06 4-1	a12 2-3	A25 1-2	S29 2-1	S17 1-2	N03 1-2	D29 3-1	S03 1-1	M15 0-0	N17 1-2	a26 3-1	J05 0-0	m03 3-2	D15 4-5	M29 2-0	J26 0-0		M01 1-1	S15 1-6	A20 1-1	O20 1-0
19 SUNDERLAND	D29 4-1	S05 1-3	S08 1-3	F16 0-2	N10 0-0	a05 1-1	F09 4-1	D15 3-0	N24 2-2	a11 7-1	J19 3-0	A25 3-0	M08 1-2	a19 3-1	D25 1-4	S22 3-1	M22 0-0	O13 0-1		O27 0-1	D08 3-3	J01 1-1
20 TOTTENHAM H	F09 1-2	O20 2-0	a26 2-0	S08 2-1	S10 1-1	D26 2-3	N17 3-2	M01 5-0	A20 1-0	a02 1-0	D01 2-3	O06 1-2	S22 2-0	D15 3-1	D29 2-1	a12 3-1	F23 1-0	J19 2-0	M15 2-0		A25 3-1	N03 4-2
21 W.B.A.	a21 3-1	D01 1-2	N03 1-1	D26 3-2	J05 1-1	S15 1-1	M01 0-1	a12 1-0	J26 0-2	O06 0-0	M15 3-3	N17 3-2	A18 3-3	S29 2-3	S05 3-3	O20 5-0	S01 1-1	A29 1-0	a26 1-1	D22 3-1		a14 2-1
22 WOLVERHAMPTON W	A25 2-1	D26 1-2	D29 3-0	O13 5-1	a05 1-2	N24 2-2	S22 5-3	A22 1-2	a19 2-2	F09 0-0	S08 2-1	D15 2-2	O27 0-2	D08 4-0	F16 3-0	J19 1-1	N10 1-4	M08 3-0	F23 0-3	M22 1-1	a15 1-4	

DIVISION 2

	BARNSLEY	BIRMINGHAM C	BLACKBURN R	BRENTFORD	BURY	CARDIFF C	COVENTRY C	DONCASTER R	EVERTON	HULL C	LEEDS U	LEICESTER C	LUTON T	NOTTINGHAM F	NOTTS CO	Q.P.R.	ROTHERHAM U	SHEFFIELD U	SHEFFIELD W	SOUTHAMPTON	SWANSEA T	WEST HAM U
1 BARNSLEY		M22 1-2	a14 1-2	N24 0-0	S29 3-3	O27 2-0	S15 1-0	a19 1-1	D08 1-0	D15 2-2	O13 3-1	N10 3-3	S05 1-2	a05 1-1	S12 2-1	D25 3-1	M08 0-1	S01 3-4	F16 5-4	A25 3-1	J26 2-3	J05 1-1
2 BIRMINGHAM C	N03 2-1		N17 0-1	J05 1-2	A18 2-1	a11 3-2	M01 3-1	S15 2-2	J26 1-2	M29 2-2	A22 1-1	D22 2-0	a26 3-1	S01 0-2	D01 2-0	a12 1-0	D25 4-0	M15 3-0	S12 0-0	S29 1-1	O06 1-1	O20 2-1
3 BLACKBURN R	a11 2-1	a05 1-4		D08 3-0	S15 1-2	N10 0-1	S01 0-1	A27 3-3	F16 1-0	D25 1-0	O27 2-3	N24 2-1	J26 2-1	a19 3-2	S29 2-0	J01 4-2	M22 1-1	A18 1-5	M12 0-0	O13 0-1	J05 3-1	D22 3-1
4 BRENTFORD	a12 1-1	S08 1-0	a26 1-1		O20 4-0	D29 1-1	N03 1-0	a30 1-0	A27 1-0	D01 2-1	D15 2-1	J19 1-3	M01 3-3	S22 1-1	O06 1-0	F09 0-0	A25 2-0	N17 4-1	a11 2-3	D25 1-2	M15 3-1	a21 1-1
5 BURY	F09 3-0	D15 3-0	J19 0-2	M08 1-0		D08 1-1	D25 0-2	O27 1-1	M22 1-0	S22 3-1	N24 1-2	F16 1-4	A25 0-1	O13 2-0	D29 2-1	S08 3-1	a19 3-1	J01 1-0	a05 1-2	N10 8-2	a11 4-1	A29 4-0
6 CARDIFF C	M15 3-0	a14 3-1	a21 3-1	S01 2-0	a26 3-0		O06 4-1	J05 2-1	S15 3-1	N03 1-0	m03 3-1	A18 4-0	D01 3-0	D22 4-1	a12 1-0	N17 3-1	A20 2-4	S17 1-1	S29 2-1	J26 1-0	D26 3-0	M01 1-1
7 COVENTRY C	J19 0-0	O13 1-1	D29 1-2	M22 2-1	D26 3-0	F16 2-1		N10 1-2	a05 2-1	S08 1-4	D08 4-2	M08 1-3	a15 5-2	O27 3-3	D15 0-2	A25 0-0	S03 2-1	S22 1-1	a19 0-2	N24 3-1	A20 3-2	F09 1-2
8 DONCASTER R	D01 1-2	J19 0-5	A22 1-0	S05 1-2	M15 1-1	S08 1-0	M29 1-0		D25 3-1	a26 0-1	A25 2-0	S22 2-2	O20 1-1	F09 0-1	M01 1-5	O06 4-0	D29 0-3	a12 2-1	D15 1-1	a14 0-1	N03 3-0	N17 4-1
9 EVERTON	a26 1-1	S22 1-3	O06 0-2	A22 1-0	N03 2-2	J19 3-0	N17 4-1	D26 1-1		a11 5-0	D29 2-0	F09 2-0	M15 1-3	S05 1-0	O20 1-5	M01 3-0	S08 3-3	D01 1-0	A25 3-3	D15 3-0	M29 2-1	a12 2-0
10 HULL C	A18 0-0	N10 0-1	D26 3-0	a19 4-1	J26 5-0	M22 0-0	J05 5-0	D08 2-0	a14 1-0		M08 3-2	a05 3-1	S29 1-2	N24 1-4	S20 1-3	A30 4-1	O27 3-3	D22 2-1	O13 0-1	F16 0-0	S15 5-2	S01 1-1
11 LEEDS U	M01 1-0	A29 1-1	M15 1-0	A18 1-1	a12 2-1	S12 2-1	a26 3-1	D22 0-0	S01 1-2	O20 2-0		D26 2-1	N17 1-1	a14 0-0	M29 1-0	N03 3-0	F09 3-0	O06 3-1	S15 3-2	J05 1-1	D01 1-1	J26 3-1
12 LEICESTER C	M29 1-2	A25 4-0	a12 2-1	S15 1-1	O06 1-1	D15 3-0	O20 3-1	J26 2-1	S29 1-2	N17 1-0	D25 1-2		S01 3-3	J05 3-1	a26 1-1	D01 4-0	a15 2-0	N03 5-5	A20 3-1	S03 3-0	M01 1-1	M15 3-1
13 LUTON T	m03 4-2	D08 2-4	S22 1-1	O13 0-2	D22 2-1	a19 2-2	a14 2-1	M12 1-4	O27 1-1	F09 1-1	a05 2-1	D29 1-2		F16 3-3	S08 6-0	J19 0-1	N24 1-1	A29 2-1	N10 5-3	M22 2-1	A18 2-2	D26 6-1
14 NOTTINGHAM F	N17 3-3	D29 0-1	D01 1-0	J26 2-0	M01 1-0	A25 2-3	M15 3-1	S29 1-1	S12 2-0	a12 4-0	a11 1-1	S08 2-2	O06 2-0		J19 3-2	a26 3-1	D15 4-2	M29 0-2	D26 2-1	A22 3-0	O20 2-2	N03 0-0
15 NOTTS CO	A30 4-0	a19 5-0	F09 0-1	F16 5-2	S01 2-1	N24 1-1	A18 2-1	O13 1-0	M08 0-0	S06 4-0	N10 1-2	D08 2-3	J05 5-4	S15 2-2		S22 0-0	a05 0-3	D25 3-1	M22 2-2	O27 3-4	D22 2-0	a14 1-0
16 Q.P.R.	D26 1-1	N24 0-2	S03 2-1	S29 3-1	J05 3-2	a05 1-1	D22 1-4	F16 0-2	O13 4-4	A20 1-1	M22 0-0	a19 1-0	S15 0-0	D08 4-3	J26 1-4		N10 2-3	a14 4-2	O27 2-2	M08 2-1	S01 1-1	A18 2-0
17 ROTHERHAM U	O20 4-0	D26 1-2	N03 3-0	D22 1-1	D01 4-3	A27 2-0	F23 0-1	S01 2-0	J05 1-1	M15 1-1	S29 4-2	a14 0-2	a12 0-1	A18 1-2	N17 2-0	M29 1-0		M01 3-1	J26 3-3	S15 4-1	a26 1-3	O06 2-1
18 SHEFFIELD U	D29 1-2	O27 4-2	D15 1-1	a05 1-4	S10 1-0	M12 6-1	J26 1-2	N24 2-1	a19 1-2	A25 4-1	F16 3-0	M22 5-0	A20 3-0	N10 1-4	D26 1-0	m03 1-2	O13 1-0		S08 7-3	D08 2-2	S29 5-0	S15 6-1
19 SHEFFIELD W	O06 2-1	S03 1-1	O20 2-0	a14 2-0	N17 2-1	F09 4-2	D01 3-1	A18 3-1	D22 4-0	M01 6-0	J19 1-2	A27 1-0	a02 4-0	D25 1-1	N03 6-0	M15 2-1	S22 3-5	J05 1-3		S01 3-1	a12 1-1	a26 2-2
20 SOUTHAMPTON	D22 1-1	F09 2-0	M01 2-1	D26 2-1	M29 4-2	S22 1-1	a12 2-2	S12 2-0	A18 1-0	O06 1-1	S08 0-0	F23 2-0	N03 2-3	A29 5-2	M15 4-0	O20 1-1	J19 3-1	a26 0-1	D29 1-4		N17 3-2	D01 1-2
21 SWANSEA T	S22 2-1	F16 4-0	S08 5-1	O27 1-1	a14 0-2	D25 1-1	A30 7-1	M22 1-2	N10 0-2	J19 3-0	a19 4-1	O13 1-0	D15 0-3	M08 1-2	A25 1-1	D29 2-3	D08 5-0	F09 3-1	N24 1-2	a05 1-1		S13 2-1
22 WEST HAM U	S08 2-1	M08 0-1	A25 3-1	N10 1-0	A23 1-1	O13 1-1	S29 3-1	a05 3-3	N24 3-3	D29 2-0	S22 2-0	O27 2-3	D25 3-0	M22 3-1	a11 2-1	D15 4-2	F16 2-1	J19 5-1	D08 0-6	a19 4-0	S06 2-2	

Season 1951-52

DIVISION 3 NORTH

	ACCRINGTON S	BARROW	BRADFORD	BRADFORD C	CARLISLE U	CHESTER	CHESTERFIELD	CREWE A	DARLINGTON	GATESHEAD	GRIMSBY T	HALIFAX T	HARTLEPOOLS U	LINCOLN C	MANSFIELD T	OLDHAM A	ROCHDALE	SCUNTHORPE U	SOUTHPORT	STOCKPORT CO	TRANMERE R	WORKINGTON	WREXHAM	YORK C
1 ACCRINGTON S		S15 1-1	a30 5-1	O20 0-1	D22 0-2	N03 4-2	a11 2-0	a26 2-3	D26 1-3	A18 1-2	J26 0-3	S25 2-2	M01 0-0	M29 1-3	A22 1-0	O06 1-2	a02 0-0	N17 2-2	D01 0-0	S01 0-3	a12 1-1	J05 0-0	S29 4-2	M15 2-1
2 BARROW	J19 3-1		M27 0-2	N17 1-0	S22 0-1	D01 1-0	J12 2-0	M01 2-1	M15 2-2	O20 2-1	S13 3-1	A25 0-0	M29 2-1	a26 1-2	D29 1-1	N03 0-1	S08 4-0	F23 2-1	O06 0-0	F09 1-3	D26 2-0	a11 1-0	A23 3-1	a12 0-0
3 BRADFORD	F23 1-1	A18 3-1		J19 2-1	S17 0-1	O06 3-0	J05 3-3	M29 3-2	a12 2-0	N17 2-0	D22 3-2	S22 6-1	a26 1-2	M01 1-1	F09 0-1	D01 1-0	a15 1-1	O20 2-2	N03 2-2	A27 4-2	M15 2-3	F13 2-1	S01 5-0	D26 2-1
4 BRADFORD C	M08 1-3	a05 2-2	S15 2-2		O27 1-2	D29 1-0	D08 1-0	S12 0-2	a14 3-1	m03 1-1	a23 0-2	D25 3-2	J26 0-2	A25 1-1	F16 2-1	S29 5-2	O13 3-0	M26 1-0	A22 2-1	M22 2-3	J23 2-0	N10 1-0	a19 3-2	S08 3-3
5 CARLISLE U	A25 4-1	J26 0-1	S06 1-0	M15 1-0		M29 0-0	J01 2-3	D29 2-0	O06 1-1	D26 0-0	S29 1-2	A23 2-2	O20 2-1	N17 1-4	F02 0-0	M01 3-3	M06 1-1	a12 3-0	a26 0-2	J05 2-1	D01 1-0	S15 0-1	a11 2-0	N03 2-1
6 CHESTER	M22 3-1	a19 0-0	F16 4-2	S01 1-0	N10 4-2		D26 3-0	a14 2-0	a02 2-0	S29 0-3	D08 0-3	O13 5-1	J05 3-3	F02 0-1	M08 1-5	S15 1-2	O27 4-0	A22 3-1	F23 2-1	a05 0-0	S05 4-1	a23 2-2	A18 2-1	D22 0-1
7 CHESTERFIELD	a14 2-0	F02 2-0	S08 0-0	a26 2-2	F23 3-0	D25 2-0		N03 0-0	N17 4-2	M29 1-0	A18 3-1	J19 3-1	D01 2-2	O06 2-2	S22 1-1	a12 1-0	F09 5-1	M01 3-0	M15 2-0	S10 0-1	O20 1-1	A27 3-1	D22 3-0	D29 2-1
8 CREWE A	D08 3-3	O13 1-1	N10 3-4	S03 0-1	S01 1-1	a11 1-2	M22 2-1		A18 3-0	D22 4-2	M08 1-2	a05 4-1	A29 4-2	F09 0-2	a23 1-0	J12 3-1	a19 1-0	S22 2-2	S08 1-0	D26 1-0	J19 2-1	F16 2-0	O27 2-2	F23 0-0
9 DARLINGTON	D25 4-5	O27 1-2	m03 3-0	a11 3-1	F16 1-2	S22 1-1	a05 3-0	D15 0-1		F13 3-2	M22 0-2	a19 0-2	S19 2-1	J19 1-1	D08 2-1	S05 2-2	A22 2-1	S08 2-3	A25 1-1	O13 1-2	D29 2-2	M08 2-1	N10 2-1	F09 1-0
10 GATESHEAD	M26 1-0	M08 2-0	a05 0-1	F23 2-2	D25 1-1	F09 1-0	N10 1-1	A25 1-0	J23 2-2		O27 1-1	A27 3-0	S10 2-0	S22 3-1	a19 4-1	a02 1-0	D08 1-0	J19 2-1	D29 3-0	F16 0-2	S08 4-1	O13 4-1	M22 1-1	a14 1-1
11 GRIMSBY T	S22 2-1	S05 1-0	A25 3-0	a12 2-1	F09 4-1	a26 2-1	a30 2-0	O20 0-1	N03 3-0	M15 2-0		D29 8-1	N17 2-0	A22 2-3	S08 1-1	M29 3-1	J19 4-0	D25 3-2	M01 4-1	a11 4-0	O06 1-0	m03 5-0	F02 1-0	D01 0-0
12 HALIFAX T	S03 0-4	D22 0-1	M10 0-0	D26 1-1	S10 1-2	M01 4-1	S15 0-0	N17 2-3	D01 4-1	a12 0-1	S01 3-0		F09 2-0	O20 1-3	a14 1-0	a26 1-0	a28 1-0	M15 2-1	M29 0-1	M24 1-2	N03 1-0	A18 3-1	J05 2-0	O06 1-1
13 HARTLEPOOLS U	O13 4-2	N10 3-1	D08 2-1	S22 2-1	M08 1-0	S08 2-1	a19 4-1	A20 3-0	F23 2-0	S03 1-0	a05 2-1	S29 6-1		D29 1-1	D25 2-0	a14 1-1	F16 1-1	A25 3-1	J16 3-1	O27 0-1	a30 0-1	M22 0-1	J01 1-0	J19 3-2
14 LINCOLN C	N10 2-2	D08 3-0	O13 2-0	D22 2-1	a05 2-2	J23 4-1	F16 5-1	S29 11-1	S15 7-2	J26 1-0	A29 0-2	M08 4-1	S01 4-3		O27 1-2	J05 4-0	M22 2-0	S12 4-1	a14 4-0	a23 2-1	F23 3-0	a19 7-0	D26 3-2	A18 3-1
15 MANSFIELD T	A27 3-0	S01 2-1	S29 1-0	O06 2-1	J12 1-2	O20 3-1	J26 2-1	a12 2-1	a26 3-2	D01 2-3	J05 2-2	a15 4-2	D26 0-1	M15 1-0		F23 2-1	S17 1-1	N03 4-1	N17 4-0	A18 1-0	M29 3-0	D22 3-2	S15 3-0	M01 1-1
16 OLDHAM A	F16 3-1	M22 3-1	a19 1-2	F09 2-1	O13 2-0	J19 11-2	a22 3-0	F02 5-2	S11 3-2	A21 2-0	N10 1-1	D08 2-0	a11 5-2	S08 4-1	m03 5-3		D25 1-1	D29 2-0	a29 2-1	M08 1-0	A25 3-0	O27 0-1	a05 2-1	S22 2-0
17 ROCHDALE	J15 3-1	J05 4-1	a14 1-1	M01 1-1	A18 0-4	M15 0-5	S29 2-0	D01 1-0	A28 6-2	a26 0-3	S15 0-0	F23 0-2	O06 3-0	N03 0-1	S04 1-0	D26 2-2		M29 1-2	a12 1-0	D22 0-0	N17 3-2	S01 2-0	J26 1-5	O20 0-2
18 SCUNTHORPE U	a05 3-1	m01 0-0	M08 0-0	A18 1-0	a24 1-1	A30 2-2	O13 1-1	J26 2-0	J05 5-2	S15 1-1	D26 1-3	O27 2-1	D22 2-0	S06 1-3	M22 4-1	S01 2-2	N10 3-1		S29 1-1	a19 1-1	a14 2-0	D08 3-1	F16 0-0	J17 1-1
19 SOUTHPORT	a19 0-0	F16 2-2	M22 0-0	A28 1-1	D08 2-1	m03 1-0	O27 4-1	J05 1-1	D22 3-0	S01 0-2	O13 2-0	N10 3-2	F02 2-0	a11 0-3	a05 0-1	A18 0-0	a22 1-2	F09 5-1		S15 0-1	S22 1-0	D25 4-2	M08 2-1	S11 2-1
20 STOCKPORT CO	D29 6-0	S29 2-2	A20 1-0	N03 1-2	S08 1-1	N17 0-0	S03 2-1	D25 4-2	M01 5-0	O06 0-0	a14 1-1	J12 6-2	M15 0-1	a12 1-1	D15 2-1	O20 0-0	A25 1-0	D01 1-1	J19 3-1		a26 2-0	J26 5-0	F23 0-0	M29 3-1
21 TRANMERE R	a22 3-1	D25 3-1	O27 1-2	F06 3-1	a19 3-2	S11 3-1	M08 2-0	S15 1-0	S01 3-0	J05 5-1	F16 2-3	M22 1-2	A18 4-1	J01 2-2	N10 1-1	D22 0-4	a05 4-3	a11 3-1	J26 5-1	D08 2-0		S29 3-1	O13 3-1	A28 2-0
22 WORKINGTON	S08 0-2	a14 3-1	J24 2-3	M29 0-1	J19 1-2	a12 2-2	A22 3-1	O06 3-1	O20 2-1	M01 1-2	F23 2-4	J01 2-1	N03 1-1	D01 0-3	A25 0-1	M15 0-1	D29 1-1	a26 0-0	D26 6-1	S22 0-3	F09 1-2		S05 2-0	N17 1-0
23 WREXHAM	F09 1-0	A29 2-4	D29 3-2	D01 3-0	a14 3-1	S26 3-2	A25 0-3	M15 4-0	M29 1-1	N03 2-1	J12 2-0	S08 2-1	a12 0-0	D25 4-2	J19 3-1	N17 1-0	S22 2-0	O06 1-2	O20 3-0	a30 0-0	M01 0-1	S12 0-0		a26 1-1
24 YORK C	O27 6-1	a21 2-1	D25 1-0	J05 3-1	M22 0-0	A25 4-2	S01 1-0	m03 3-0	S29 2-1	a11 1-0	a19 1-1	F16 6-2	S15 3-1	M31 1-0	O13 3-0	J26 5-0	M08 1-1	a28 0-1	S03 0-2	N10 0-1	A20 1-1	a05 5-1	D08 4-2	

DIVISION 3 SOUTH

	ALDERSHOT	BOURNEMOUTH	BRIGHTON & HA	BRISTOL C	BRISTOL R	COLCHESTER U	CRYSTAL P	EXETER C	GILLINGHAM	IPSWICH T	LEYTON O	MILLWALL	NEWPORT CO	NORTHAMPTON T	NORWICH C	PLYMOUTH A	PORT VALE	READING	SHREWSBURY T	SOUTHEND U	SWINDON T	TORQUAY U	WALSALL	WATFORD
1 ALDERSHOT		O20 1-3	N03 0-2	D01 1-0	D29 1-3	S29 1-1	a30 3-0	J26 4-1	a16 2-1	a12 1-1	S05 0-1	M15 2-1	O06 4-0	A18 0-1	S15 2-0	J05 1-2	a26 4-1	D26 0-2	F23 1-1	M01 2-2	a11 4-0	N17 1-3	A29 3-1	D22 2-0
2 BOURNEMOUTH	M08 0-2		D29 3-1	A22 0-0	M22 1-0	a19 5-0	D08 1-2	a23 0-4	A25 3-3	F23 2-2	D25 3-2	S08 0-2	S29 5-1	a14 3-0	a05 1-2	N10 1-2	S05 0-1	J16 1-2	O13 2-0	J26 2-1	S15 4-1	J12 3-1	F16 2-1	O27 0-0
3 BRIGHTON & H.A.	M22 4-2	S01 0-1		a14 1-1	a05 1-1	A18 5-1	D26 4-3	D08 2-1	F23 0-0	S12 5-1	O13 3-1	D22 0-0	S15 1-2	S29 2-0	a19 2-0	a23 2-3	D15 2-1	J26 1-0	O27 1-0	J05 5-0	F16 4-0	A29 3-4	M08 5-1	N10 4-1
4 BRISTOL C	a19 1-1	A28 1-0	a11 4-1		S15 1-1	M08 2-0	O27 2-0	O13 1-1	J12 3-2	S22 0-2	N10 1-1	S11 2-1	A18 3-1	D29 2-0	F16 2-5	D26 1-1	J05 1-0	D22 1-3	a22 3-0	F06 6-0	M22 2-1	F09 2-2	a05 2-0	D08 1-3
5 BRISTOL R	S01 5-1	N03 1-2	N17 5-0	J19 2-0		a14 6-0	S03 4-0	m01 2-2	a12 5-0	a26 1-0	F27 1-0	M29 2-1	O20 1-1	O06 2-2	S29 1-1	J26 1-2	D25 4-1	M01 1-2	A25 3-3	M15 2-0	A20 1-0	D01 5-0	a28 5-1	S08 0-1
6 COLCHESTER U	F09 0-2	D01 1-1	m01 0-0	O20 4-1	a11 2-1		A25 1-2	F02 1-0	D26 1-0	M01 1-0	S08 0-1	a26 2-2	N17 2-1	N03 2-5	A23 1-1	S13 1-0	M15 0-0	a03 4-1	S22 2-2	a12 1-0	D29 2-0	O06 0-0	J19 3-2	m03 1-0
7 CRYSTAL P	J12 0-2	a26 2-2	D25 1-2	M15 2-1	S12 0-1	D22 2-2		A18 2-1	O06 0-2	O20 3-1	J19 2-1	D29 1-1	a12 1-1	m03 3-3	F23 2-0	A29 0-1	N03 3-1	N17 1-2	F09 1-1	D01 1-0	S08 0-1	M01 1-1	S22 2-1	a14 2-0
8 EXETER C	S22 0-4	a12 2-2	a26 2-0	M01 0-0	J16 0-1	F23 0-0	M26 0-1		A22 4-2	O06 2-1	D29 6-1	D01 0-3	M29 3-4	M15 0-3	S05 2-4	a14 1-0	O20 2-0	N03 1-4	J19 4-2	N17 2-2	A25 1-2	D25 4-0	S08 1-0	F09 3-0
9 GILLINGHAM	N10 3-3	D22 0-2	F02 2-3	m03 5-0	a23 2-1	D25 1-2	F16 4-4	A29 2-1		a11 1-1	M08 1-1	A18 1-1	J05 2-3	J26 2-1	D08 1-2	a19 1-2	S29 4-2	S15 1-1	M22 0-0	S01 2-0	O13 4-0	S12 3-0	O27 4-1	a05 1-0
10 IPSWICH T	a23 2-3	F02 3-1	S05 5-0	J26 1-1	D08 1-2	O13 0-2	M08 1-1	F16 2-4	a14 1-1		M22 1-0	A29 3-0	D22 3-1	J05 3-2	D25 0-2	S29 2-2	S15 2-0	S01 4-2	a05 1-0	A18 4-1	O27 1-5	J30 2-0	N10 0-1	a19 3-0
11 LEYTON O	S12 0-1	D26 1-0	M01 2-3	m01 2-0	F07 3-3	J05 7-0	S15 0-4	S01 3-0	O20 1-0	N03 2-0		O06 0-0	a26 1-1	a12 2-1	D22 3-3	A18 1-0	N17 2-0	D01 0-4	a14 4-1	F09 1-4	J26 1-0	M15 0-1	S10 3-0	A20 0-0
12 MILLWALL	O27 3-2	J05 3-1	A25 0-3	S19 3-2	N10 1-1	D08 1-1	S01 3-1	a19 4-0	M31 3-1	A22 4-0	F16 2-0		J26 2-0	a30 2-1	a23 2-1	a05 0-2	a11 1-1	S29 3-2	M08 0-0	S15 2-0	D26 0-0	F23 4-1	O13 2-1	M22 1-0
13 NEWPORT CO	F16 4-2	F09 2-0	J19 1-1	a28 1-0	M08 2-2	a05 0-1	a24 1-0	N10 4-0	S08 1-1	A25 2-1	a03 1-0	S22 2-1		A20 2-0	M22 2-2	O27 3-3	F23 1-1	S17 3-1	D25 3-1	J17 3-0	a19 0-0	D29 1-2	a11 4-2	O13 2-5
14 NORTHAMPTON T	J24 6-2	a15 5-3	F09 3-0	S01 1-2	F16 2-0	M22 2-0	N10 5-2	O27 3-1	S22 2-1	S08 1-0	a24 4-0	J12 1-1	S06 5-0		M08 1-2	O13 3-1	S27 3-1	F23 0-3	D08 6-0	S20 4-3	a05 1-0	J19 2-4	a19 4-1	D26 1-4
15 NORWICH C	J19 1-2	N17 2-0	D01 0-1	O06 1-0	F09 1-0	A29 5-2	F02 1-0	S12 1-1	a26 5-0	D26 2-0	A25 1-0	a12 1-0	N03 1-2	O20 2-1		a30 3-0	M01 2-3	M15 2-1	S08 3-2	a02 1-0	m03 2-0	a14 7-0	D29 8-0	S22 3-0
16 PLYMOUTH A	S08 2-1	M29 4-1	a12 2-2	D25 2-2	S22 1-2	S05 3-1	A22 5-0	J12 2-1	D01 4-2	F09 2-0	M19 3-0	N17 5-0	M15 5-0	M01 2-0	J16 3-1		O06 3-0	O20 3-2	D29 6-1	N03 2-0	F13 3-0	a26 2-2	A25 3-0	J19 3-1
17 PORT VALE	D08 4-1	S10 2-2	J12 1-1	S08 1-0	D26 1-1	O27 1-1	M22 2-0	M08 3-0	F09 1-0	J19 0-0	a05 3-0	m01 2-1	M24 4-2	D22 0-0	O13 0-0	F16 1-0		A18 0-2	a19 1-0	A27 0-0	N10 2-2	S22 2-2	a21 1-0	S01 1-1
18 READING	D25 5-1	m03 5-0	S22 1-4	A25 3-0	O13 4-2	N10 4-2	a05 3-1	M22 2-1	J19 2-1	D29 4-0	a19 1-1	F09 2-0	S12 1-2	F02 2-0	O27 1-1	M08 2-0	F20 5-1		A22 6-2	a14 5-2	a23 2-0	S08 6-1	D08 3-0	F16 4-1
19 SHREWSBURY T	F02 5-1	M01 2-0	M15 1-1	a12 2-0	D22 2-1	J26 1-0	S29 2-1	S15 2-1	N03 2-2	N17 0-2	S24 3-0	O20 0-1	D26 1-4	a26 3-1	J05 0-2	S01 1-3	D01 2-0	A27 2-1		O06 0-1	J24 0-1	M29 1-1	S03 1-2	A18 2-3
20 SOUTHEND U	O13 7-1	S22 1-0	S08 2-0	F27 5-1	O27 2-1	a22 3-2	a19 4-0	a05 0-0	D29 3-1	a29 5-0	S29 1-0	J19 0-1	m03 2-1	S11 2-0	N10 2-1	M22 1-1	A21 0-0	a11 2-0	F16 2-2		D08 2-2	A25 2-2	D26 3-0	M08 5-1
21 SWINDON T	a14 1-1	J19 2-0	O06 0-2	N03 0-0	A29 0-0	S01 2-1	J05 0-2	D22 3-1	M01 2-1	M15 1-2	S22 2-0	D25 2-2	D01 1-1	N17 1-1	A18 1-1	F27 2-2	a28 2-0	a12 2-0	a30 1-2	a26 1-0		O20 2-1	F09 1-1	S12 0-1
22 TORQUAY U	a05 6-1	A18 2-2	A22 0-1	S29 1-2	a19 4-2	F16 3-1	O13 1-5	D26 5-1	S05 2-1	m03 2-0	O27 1-1	F02 2-5	S01 1-2	S15 1-2	S19 1-2	D08 3-2	J26 2-3	J05 0-3	N10 3-2	D22 1-3	M08 9-0		M22 1-1	a23 2-0
23 WALSALL	A23 1-0	O06 2-2	O20 1-1	N17 2-0	A18 1-0	S15 1-3	J26 3-0	J05 1-2	M15 1-0	M29 1-3	J24 2-4	M01 1-2	a14 0-1	D01 3-0	S01 4-0	D22 2-5	a12 3-0	a26 2-0	S13 0-4	D25 2-0	S29 0-0	N03 2-3		F02 3-1
24 WATFORD	A25 2-2	M15 1-2	a03 3-1	a26 3-1	J05 0-3	J16 0-1	a11 2-0	S29 1-1	N17 2-2	D01 1-1	A23 0-1	N03 1-2	M01 1-1	D25 2-4	J26 1-1	S15 1-3	D29 2-0	O06 3-1	J12 4-1	O20 0-0	S06 1-7	a12 1-2	F23 2-0	

LEAGUE TABLES

DIVISION 1

	P	W	D	L	F	A	W	D	L	F	A	Pts
Manchester U	42	15	3	3	55	21	8	8	5	40	31	57
Tottenham H	42	16	1	4	45	20	6	8	7	31	31	53
Arsenal	42	13	7	1	54	30	8	4	9	26	31	53
Portsmouth	42	13	3	5	42	25	7	5	9	26	33	48
Bolton W	42	11	7	3	35	26	8	3	10	30	35	48
Aston Villa	42	13	3	5	49	28	6	6	9	30	42	47
Preston NE	42	10	5	6	39	22	7	7	7	35	32	46
Newcastle U	42	12	4	5	62	28	6	5	10	36	45	45
Blackpool	42	12	5	4	40	27	6	4	11	24	37	45
Charlton A	42	12	5	4	41	24	5	5	11	27	39	44
Liverpool	42	6	11	4	31	25	6	8	7	26	36	43
Sunderland	42	8	6	7	41	28	7	6	8	29	33	42
WBA	42	8	9	4	38	29	6	4	11	36	48	41
Burnley	42	9	6	6	32	19	6	4	11	24	44	40
Manchester C	42	7	5	9	29	28	6	8	7	29	33	39
Wolves	42	8	6	7	40	33	4	8	9	33	40	38
Derby Co	42	10	4	7	43	37	5	3	13	20	43	37
Middlesbrough	42	12	4	5	37	25	3	2	16	27	63	36
Chelsea	42	10	3	8	31	29	4	5	12	21	43	36
Stoke C	42	8	6	7	34	32	4	1	16	15	56	31
Huddersfield T	42	9	3	9	32	35	1	5	15	17	47	28
Fulham	42	5	7	9	38	31	3	4	14	20	46	27

DIVISION 2

	P	W	D	L	F	A	W	D	L	F	A	Pts
Sheffield W	42	14	4	3	64	23	7	7	7	46	43	53
Cardiff C	42	18	2	1	52	15	2	9	10	20	39	51
Birmingham C	42	11	6	4	36	21	10	3	8	31	35	51
Nottingham F	42	12	6	3	41	22	6	7	8	36	40	49
Leicester C	42	12	6	3	48	24	7	3	11	30	40	47
Leeds U	42	13	7	1	35	15	5	4	12	24	42	47
Everton	42	12	5	4	42	25	5	5	11	22	33	44
Luton T	42	9	7	5	46	35	7	5	9	31	43	44
Rotherham U	42	11	4	6	40	25	6	4	11	33	46	42
Brentford	42	11	7	3	34	20	4	5	12	20	35	42
Sheffield U	42	13	2	6	57	28	5	3	13	33	48	41
West Ham U	42	13	5	3	48	29	2	6	13	19	48	41
Southampton	42	11	6	4	40	25	4	5	12	21	48	41
Blackburn R	42	11	3	7	35	30	6	3	12	19	33	40
Notts Co	42	11	5	5	45	27	5	2	14	26	41	39
Doncaster R	42	9	4	8	29	28	4	8	9	26	32	38
Bury	42	13	2	6	43	22	2	5	14	24	47	37
Hull C	42	11	5	5	44	23	2	6	13	16	47	37
Swansea T	42	10	4	7	45	26	2	8	11	27	50	36
Barnsley	42	8	7	6	39	33	3	7	11	20	39	36
Coventry C	42	9	5	7	36	33	5	1	15	23	49	34
QPR	42	8	8	5	35	35	3	4	14	17	46	34

DIVISION 3 North

	P	W	D	L	F	A	W	D	L	F	A	Pts
Lincoln C	46	19	2	2	80	23	11	7	5	41	29	69
Grimsby T	46	19	2	2	59	14	10	6	7	37	31	66
Stockport Co	46	12	9	2	47	17	11	4	8	27	23	59
Oldham A	46	19	2	2	65	22	5	7	11	25	39	57
Gateshead	46	14	7	2	41	17	7	4	12	25	32	53
Mansfield T	46	17	3	3	50	23	5	5	13	23	37	52
Carlisle U	46	10	7	6	31	24	9	6	8	31	33	51
Bradford	46	13	6	4	51	28	6	6	11	23	36	50
Hartlepools U	46	17	3	3	47	19	4	5	14	24	46	50
York C	46	16	4	3	53	19	2	9	12	20	33	49
Tranmere R	46	17	2	4	59	29	4	4	15	17	42	48
Barrow	46	13	5	5	33	19	4	7	12	24	42	46
Chesterfield	46	15	7	1	47	16	2	4	17	18	50	45
Scunthorpe U	46	10	11	2	39	23	4	5	14	26	51	44
Bradford C	46	12	5	6	40	32	4	5	14	21	36	42
Crewe A	46	12	6	5	42	28	5	2	16	21	54	42
Southport	46	12	6	5	36	22	3	5	15	17	49	41
Wrexham	46	14	5	4	41	22	1	4	18	22	51	39
Chester	46	13	4	6	46	30	2	5	16	26	55	39
Halifax T	46	11	4	8	31	23	3	3	17	30	74	35
Rochdale	46	10	5	8	32	34	1	8	14	15	45	35
Accrington S	46	6	8	9	30	34	4	4	15	31	58	32
Darlington	46	10	5	8	39	34	1	4	18	25	69	31
Workington	46	8	4	11	33	34	3	3	17	17	57	29

DIVISION 3 South

	P	W	D	L	F	A	W	D	L	F	A	Pts
Plymouth A	46	19	3	1	70	19	10	5	8	37	34	66
Reading	46	19	2	2	73	23	10	1	12	39	37	61
Norwich C	46	18	1	4	55	15	8	8	7	34	35	61
Millwall	46	16	5	2	46	21	7	7	9	28	32	58
Brighton & HA	46	15	4	4	57	24	9	6	8	30	39	58
Newport Co	46	13	7	3	45	26	8	5	10	32	50	54
Bristol R	46	14	5	4	60	20	6	7	10	29	33	52
Northampton T	46	17	1	5	65	31	5	4	14	28	43	49
Southend U	46	16	6	1	56	17	3	4	16	19	49	48
Colchester U	46	12	7	4	32	22	5	5	13	24	55	46
Torquay U	46	10	3	10	53	42	7	7	9	33	56	44
Aldershot	46	11	4	8	40	27	7	4	12	38	62	44
Port Vale	46	11	11	1	33	16	3	4	16	17	50	43
Bournemouth	46	11	4	8	42	30	5	6	12	27	45	42
Bristol C	46	13	6	4	44	26	2	6	15	14	43	42
Swindon T	46	9	9	5	29	22	5	5	13	22	46	42
Ipswich T	46	12	4	7	45	31	4	5	14	18	43	41
Leyton O	46	12	5	6	39	26	4	4	15	16	42	41
Crystal P	46	9	7	7	32	28	6	2	15	29	52	39
Shrewsbury T	46	11	3	9	35	29	2	7	14	27	57	36
Watford	46	7	7	9	34	37	6	3	14	23	44	36
Gillingham	46	10	7	6	47	31	1	6	16	24	50	35
Exeter C	46	10	4	9	40	36	3	5	15	25	50	35
Walsall	46	11	3	9	38	31	2	2	19	17	63	31

Football League Records

Top scorers: Div 1, C.Wayman (Preston North End) 24 goals; Div 2, A.Rowley (Leicester City) 39 goals; Div 3(N), J.Whitehouse (Carlisle United) 29 goals; Div 3(S), G.Bradford (Bristol Rovers) 33 goals. Port Vale transferred to Division Three North.

Peter Goring, who won an FA Cup winners' medal in 1950, was an important member of the Arsenal side which won the title in 1952-3, scoring ten goals.

DIVISION 1

	ARSENAL	ASTON VILLA	BLACKPOOL	BOLTON W	BURNLEY	CARDIFF C	CHARLTON A	CHELSEA	DERBY CO	LIVERPOOL	MANCHESTER C	MANCHESTER U	MIDDLESBROUGH	NEWCASTLE U	PORTSMOUTH	PRESTON N.E.	SHEFFIELD W	STOKE C	SUNDERLAND	TOTTENHAM H	W.B.A.	WOLVERHAMPTON W
1 ARSENAL		D20 3-1	O04 3-1	a15 4-1	m01 3-2	M07 0-1	S13 3-4	a06 2-0	F18 6-2	a04 5-3	N22 3-1	A27 2-1	N08 2-1	O25 3-0	S10 3-1	M19 1-1	O11 2-2	a18 3-1	A30 1-2	F07 4-0	M21 2-2	J17 5-3
2 ASTON VILLA	A23 1-2		S06 1-5	O04 1-1	a04 2-0	a29 2-0	D26 1-1	J24 1-1	J03 3-0	M07 4-0	O25 0-0	S20 3-3	O11 1-0	m01 0-1	F18 6-0	N08 1-0	a18 4-3	M25 1-1	S01 3-0	N22 0-3	a07 1-1	S15 0-1
3 BLACKPOOL	F21 3-2	J17 1-1		A30 3-0	O11 4-2	M25 0-1	S27 8-4	S15 3-1	a03 2-1	a18 3-1	D06 4-1	D25 0-0	N22 1-1	N08 0-2	D20 3-2	A25 1-1	O25 0-1	a15 1-1	S13 2-0	M07 2-0	a04 2-0	F07 2-0
4 BOLTON W	D25 4-6	F21 0-0	J03 4-0		N08 1-2	a18 0-1	J01 1-2	S06 1-1	A23 2-0	O11 2-2	M07 1-0	J24 2-1	F18 5-3	D06 4-2	S20 0-5	M25 0-3	N22 1-1	O25 2-1	a03 5-0	a04 2-3	a22 0-1	S01 2-1
5 BURNLEY	D13 1-1	N15 1-0	M03 0-1	M28 0-1		J24 0-0	a25 2-0	O18 1-1	O04 1-2	D25 2-0	S08 2-1	M14 2-1	A23 0-1	S06 2-1	N01 3-2	a03 2-2	S20 1-1	A26 3-2	a11 5-1	F17 3-2	J03 5-0	N29 0-0
6 CARDIFF C	a22 0-0	a25 1-2	N01 2-2	M11 1-0	S13 0-0		F28 0-1	M28 3-3	M14 2-0	a06 4-0	F21 6-0	N15 1-2	S03 1-1	D27 0-0	a11 0-1	F07 0-2	A30 4-0	S27 2-0	D13 4-1	J17 0-0	S17 1-2	D20 0-0
7 CHARLTON A	J24 2-2	M18 5-1	F23 2-0	S10 2-0	a22 0-0	O11 3-1		O04 2-2	S20 3-1	N08 3-2	a04 1-2	a03 2-2	M21 2-0	M07 0-0	A27 2-2	a18 2-1	J17 3-0	N22 5-1	D20 3-1	a30 3-2	O25 0-0	A30 2-2
8 CHELSEA	a03 1-1	S13 4-0	S10 4-0	J17 1-0	M07 0-2	N08 0-2	F21 0-1		A27 1-1	M23 3-0	a29 3-1	D20 2-3	a18 1-1	a04 1-2	A30 2-0	O11 5-3	M21 1-0	D27 0-0	F07 3-2	O25 2-1	N22 0-2	S27 1-2
9 DERBY CO	S27 2-0	A30 0-1	a06 1-1	D20 4-3	F21 1-3	O25 1-1	F07 1-1	S03 3-2		N22 3-2	a18 5-0	S10 2-3	a04 3-3	M21 0-2	D26 3-0	a29 0-1	M07 2-1	D06 4-0	J17 3-1	O11 0-0	N08 1-1	S13 2-3
10 LIVERPOOL	N15 1-5	O18 0-2	N29 2-2	M04 0-0	D26 1-1	a03 2-1	M28 1-2	a25 2-0	a11 1-1		J17 0-1	D13 1-2	S20 4-1	O04 5-3	S13 1-1	D20 2-2	A27 1-0	A30 3-2	M14 2-0	S10 2-1	F14 3-0	N01 2-1
11 MANCHESTER C	a11 2-4	M14 4-1	a25 5-0	O18 1-2	S17 0-0	O04 2-2	N15 5-1	D13 4-0	N29 1-0	S06 0-2		A30 2-1	J24 5-1	F14 2-1	F28 2-1	a22 0-2	a03 3-1	D20 2-1	N01 2-5	A27 0-1	S20 0-1	M28 3-1
12 MANCHESTER U	S03 0-0	F07 3-1	D26 2-1	S13 1-0	O25 1-3	a04 1-4	a06 3-2	A23 2-0	J01 1-0	a20 3-1	J03 1-1		D06 3-2	N22 2-2	J17 1-0	M07 5-2	N08 1-1	O11 0-2	S27 0-1	M25 3-2	a18 2-2	F21 0-3
13 MIDDLESBROUGH	M28 2-0	M04 1-0	a11 5-1	S27 1-2	D20 2-2	A27 3-0	N01 1-0	N29 4-0	N15 1-0	F07 2-3	S13 5-4	a25 5-0		a06 2-1	D13 3-2	A30 1-1	J01 2-2	J17 0-0	O18 1-2	D27 0-4	O04 4-2	M14 1-1
14 NEWCASTLE U	M14 2-2	D13 2-1	M28 0-1	a25 2-3	J17 0-0	D25 3-0	O18 3-2	N15 2-1	N01 1-0	F21 1-2	S27 2-0	a11 1-2	a03 1-0		N29 1-0	S13 4-3	D20 1-5	F07 1-2	S10 2-2	A30 1-1	J01 3-5	F28 1-1
15 PORTSMOUTH	S17 2-2	S27 1-1	A23 0-2	F07 3-1	M21 2-1	N22 0-2	S03 1-1	J03 2-0	D27 2-2	J24 3-1	O11 2-1	S06 2-0	m02 1-4	a18 5-1		O25 2-5	a04 5-2	M07 1-1	F21 5-2	N08 2-1	D06 1-2	a03 2-2
16 PRESTON N.E.	a25 2-0	M28 1-3	J01 4-2	N01 2-2	a06 2-1	S20 2-3	N29 2-1	F28 2-1	D13 3-0	A23 1-1	D26 6-2	O18 0-5	J03 3-0	J24 2-1	M14 4-0		F14 1-0	S10 3-0	N15 3-2	O04 1-0	S06 1-0	a11 1-1
17 SHEFFIELD W	M02 1-4	N29 2-2	M14 2-0	a11 1-1	F07 2-4	J03 2-0	S06 0-3	N01 1-0	O18 2-0	S03 0-2	a06 1-1	M28 0-0	S17 2-0	A23 2-2	N15 3-4	S27 1-1		F21 1-0	a25 4-0	S13 2-0	D26 4-5	D13 2-3
18 STOKE C	N29 1-1	N01 1-4	D13 4-0	M14 1-2	S01 1-3	F14 0-0	a11 1-0	D26 1-1	a25 1-2	J03 3-1	A23 2-1	F28 3-1	S06 1-0	S20 1-0	O18 2-4	S15 0-0	O04 1-3		M28 3-0	a06 2-0	J24 5-1	N15 1-2
19 SUNDERLAND	J03 3-1	J01 2-2	J24 1-1	a06 2-0	N22 2-1	a27 4-2	A23 2-1	S20 2-1	S06 2-1	O25 3-1	M21 3-3	F18 2-2	M07 1-1	S17 0-2	O04 1-1	a04 2-2	D06 2-1	N08 1-1		a18 1-1	O11 1-0	D27 5-2
20 TOTTENHAM H	S20 1-3	a11 1-1	O18 4-0	N15 1-1	S27 2-1	S06 2-1	D13 2-0	M14 2-3	M12 5-2	S15 3-1	S01 3-3	N01 1-2	D25 7-1	J03 3-2	M28 3-3	F21 4-4	J24 2-1	a03 1-0	N29 2-2		A23 3-4	a25 3-2
21 W.B.A.	N01 2-0	a06 3-2	N15 0-1	D13 0-1	A30 1-2	S10 1-0	M14 3-1	a11 0-1	M28 2-2	S27 3-0	F07 2-1	N29 3-1	F21 3-0	A27 1-0	a25 2-0	J17 2-1	D27 0-1	S13 3-2	F28 1-1	D20 2-1		O18 1-1
22 WOLVERHAMPTON W	S06 1-1	S08 2-1	S20 2-5	A25 3-1	a18 5-1	A23 1-0	J03 1-2	F18 2-2	J24 3-1	M21 3-0	N08 7-3	O04 6-2	O25 3-3	O11 2-0	a06 4-1	N22 0-2	J31 3-1	a04 3-0	D26 1-1	D06 0-0	M07 2-0	

Geoff Bradford, whose 33 goals in 1952-3 helped Bristol Rovers win promotion from the Third Division South.

DIVISION 2

	BARNSLEY	BIRMINGHAM C	BLACKBURN R	BRENTFORD	BURY	DONCASTER R	EVERTON	FULHAM	HUDDERSFIELD T	HULL C	LEEDS U	LEICESTER C	LINCOLN C	LUTON T	NOTTINGHAM F	NOTTS CO	PLYMOUTH A	ROTHERHAM U	SHEFFIELD U	SOUTHAMPTON	SWANSEA T	WEST HAM U
1 BARNSLEY		M21 1-3	a06 1-4	D26 0-2	N08 3-2	D20 2-2	S10 2-3	a29 1-1	J17 2-4	O04 5-1	M07 2-2	a18 0-3	F14 1-1	O25 2-3	A27 0-2	N22 1-2	O11 0-3	F07 2-3	S13 1-3	a04 0-1	A30 3-1	D06 2-0
2 BIRMINGHAM C	N01 3-1		a11 1-2	D13 3-1	F21 0-2	a06 2-1	a25 4-2	A30 1-4	O18 0-2	N15 4-3	S17 2-2	S13 3-1	M28 2-2	S03 2-2	N29 0-5	F07 3-2	D25 4-0	D20 4-0	M14 1-2	S27 2-0	M11 1-4	J17 2-0
3 BLACKBURN R	a03 2-0	N22 1-2		J17 3-0	a18 4-0	S13 2-1	A30 3-1	M07 2-2	S27 1-1	S08 2-0	N08 1-1	D25 2-0	S01 0-2	a04 1-1	D20 2-1	J01 3-2	M21 1-3	O25 0-1	F21 1-2	D06 3-0	F07 3-0	O11 3-0
4 BRENTFORD	D25 4-0	m01 1-2	S06 3-2		F14 2-2	F21 1-0	S20 2-4	N08 2-2	S03 1-3	J03 1-0	a18 3-3	O25 4-2	A23 1-0	a22 1-1	J24 1-1	M07 5-0	N22 1-2	a04 1-1	S17 0-0	O11 3-0	a03 0-0	M21 1-4
5 BURY	M28 5-2	O04 3-0	N29 1-0	S27 3-0		F28 2-1	D13 0-5	D20 1-1	M14 1-1	a11 2-1	A27 2-2	J17 1-4	N15 2-2	a03 1-0	a25 2-0	S13 0-1	J01 3-2	D27 2-0	N01 0-4	F07 0-0	O18 1-3	A30 1-1
6 DONCASTER R	A23 1-1	a03 1-0	J24 3-3	O04 0-2	O11 1-1		F18 3-0	J31 0-0	S09 1-1	S06 3-1	D06 0-0	M21 0-0	J03 2-0	a30 1-0	S20 1-0	a22 2-0	a18 1-1	N22 2-1	D26 0-2	M07 1-0	A27 2-3	N08 1-1
7 EVERTON	J01 2-1	D06 1-1	J03 0-3	F07 5-0	a15 3-0	S27 7-1		M25 3-3	a06 2-1	A23 0-2	N22 2-2	M07 2-2	a22 0-3	a18 1-1	S06 3-0	O11 1-0	a04 2-0	N08 0-1	S03 0-0	J24 2-2	F21 0-0	O25 2-0
8 FULHAM	D13 3-1	J03 3-1	O18 2-1	M28 5-0	A23 2-0	N15 1-3	N01 3-0		N29 0-2	F28 2-1	J24 2-1	S03 4-6	O04 4-2	S06 2-0	M14 0-1	S17 6-0	S20 2-1	F18 4-1	a25 1-2	D26 1-1	a11 3-1	a06 2-3
9 HUDDERSFIELD T	S06 6-0	M07 1-1	F14 0-3	A27 0-0	O25 2-0	S17 3-1	a07 8-2	a18 4-2		S20 1-1	A23 1-0	a04 1-0	J24 5-0	O11 3-0	O04 1-2	N08 1-0	m01 4-0	D06 1-0	J03 1-1	M21 5-0	D25 3-0	N22 0-1
10 HULL C	F21 2-2	a04 2-0	S15 3-0	A30 2-2	N22 0-2	J17 1-1	D20 1-0	O11 3-1	F07 0-2		M21 1-0	a16 1-1	a06 1-1	N08 0-2	D27 3-1	D06 6-0	O25 0-1	M07 3-2	S27 4-0	a18 1-0	S13 1-1	A25 1-0
11 LEEDS U	O18 4-1	S10 0-1	M28 0-3	N29 3-2	S03 2-0	a25 1-1	a11 2-0	S13 2-0	D20 2-1	N01 3-1		S27 0-1	M14 2-1	D27 2-2	a22 2-1	F21 3-1	A30 1-1	J17 4-0	F28 0-3	S24 1-1	D13 5-1	F07 3-2
12 LEICESTER C	N29 2-2	J24 3-4	D27 2-1	M14 2-3	S06 3-2	N01 4-2	O18 4-2	A25 6-1	N15 2-1	D13 5-0	F14 3-3		a25 3-2	S20 1-1	F28 1-1	A23 3-0	O04 2-0	a07 3-2	a11 0-0	J03 4-1	M28 2-1	S08 0-0
13 LINCOLN C	S27 1-1	N08 1-1	A27 4-1	D20 0-0	a04 4-0	A30 2-0	D26 1-1	F21 2-2	S13 2-2	a03 2-1	O25 1-1	D06 3-2		M21 1-2	S10 2-3	a18 3-0	M07 0-0	O11 1-3	F07 3-2	N22 2-2	J17 3-1	m01 3-1
14 LUTON T	M14 6-0	A27 0-1	N15 6-0	a25 0-1	a06 4-1	D13 1-2	N29 4-2	J17 2-0	F28 0-2	M28 3-2	D26 2-0	F07 2-0	N01 4-0		a11 3-0	S27 5-1	D20 1-0	A30 2-1	O18 4-1	F21 1-2	S10 3-1	S13 0-0
15 NOTTINGHAM F	S03 3-0	a18 0-2	A23 1-2	S13 3-0	D06 4-1	F07 2-2	J17 3-3	O25 0-1	F21 1-0	D26 4-1	a04 2-1	O11 1-3	S17 1-1	N22 4-3		J03 1-0	N08 3-1	M21 4-3	a06 1-1	a29 2-3	S27 6-4	M07 0-0
16 NOTTS CO	a11 1-0	S20 2-0	D13 5-0	O18 4-0	J24 2-1	M14 4-3	M05 2-2	S11 1-1	M28 1-0	a25 2-0	O04 3-2	D20 2-2	N29 1-1	F19 1-2	A30 3-2		a03 0-4	A28 2-1	N15 0-3	S06 1-2	N01 3-4	D27 1-1
17 PLYMOUTH A	F28 4-0	D27 2-1	N01 3-1	a11 1-0	S17 0-0	N29 0-0	N15 1-0	F07 3-1	D13 0-2	M14 1-2	J03 0-1	F21 2-1	O18 0-0	A23 2-1	M28 0-3	a06 2-2		S13 4-3	S06 5-2	S03 3-1	a25 3-2	S27 1-1
18 ROTHERHAM U	S20 3-1	A23 1-1	M14 0-0	N15 4-1	D26 6-1	a11 4-2	M28 2-2	S27 1-0	a25 0-0	O18 2-1	S06 3-1	a06 0-0	F28 3-2	J03 1-3	N01 2-3	S01 2-3	J24 2-3		D13 0-2	S15 2-2	N29 2-1	F21 1-1
19 SHEFFIELD U	J24 3-0	O25 2-2	O04 3-0	S08 3-2	M21 3-1	D25 2-2	A25 1-0	D06 2-1	A30 0-2	a29 0-2	O11 2-1	N22 7-2	S20 6-1	M07 1-1	S22 2-0	a04 2-1	J17 5-0	J01 1-4		N08 5-3	D20 7-1	a18 3-1
20 SOUTHAMPTON	N15 1-2	a15 1-1	a25 6-1	F28 0-2	S20 1-2	O18 3-3	S13 1-1	D27 5-3	N01 0-2	N29 5-1	a06 2-2	A30 5-2	a11 1-0	O04 1-3	D13 2-2	J17 1-1	A27 2-3	S10 2-3	M28 4-4		M14 1-4	D20 1-2
21 SWANSEA T	J03 3-0	O11 1-1	S20 1-1	a06 3-2	M07 2-0	S04 2-1	O04 2-2	N22 1-1	D27 3-3	J24 3-0	a16 3-2	N08 1-1	S06 1-1	S18 4-2	F14 2-1	M21 5-1	D06 2-2	a18 0-0	A23 1-2	O25 1-2		a04 4-1
22 WEST HAM U	a25 3-1	S06 1-2	F28 0-0	N01 3-1	J03 3-2	M28 1-3	M14 3-1	a03 1-2	a11 0-1	S01 0-0	S20 2-2	S15 4-1	D13 5-1	J24 0-1	O18 3-2	D25 2-2	F18 0-1	O04 2-4	N29 1-1	A23 1-0	N15 3-0	

Season 1952-53

DIVISION 3 NORTH

	ACCRINGTON S	BARROW	BRADFORD	BRADFORD C	CARLISLE U	CHESTER	CHESTERFIELD	CREWE A	DARLINGTON	GATESHEAD	GRIMSBY T	HALIFAX T	HARTLEPOOLS U	MANSFIELD T	OLDHAM A	PORT VALE	ROCHDALE	SCUNTHORPE U	SOUTHPORT	STOCKPORT CO	TRANMERE R	WORKINGTON	WREXHAM	YORK C
1 ACCRINGTON S		F21 1-0	J01 3-2	a11 1-1	A27 1-0	N01 1-1	J17 1-1	O18 1-1	a25 1-0	D13 1-1	S27 1-2	S10 1-1	D20 1-1	J31 2-2	a06 0-2	M14 1-1	N29 2-1	M28 2-1	F28 1-2	N15 1-4	S13 0-2	A30 0-1	D27 1-2	F07 1-0
2 BARROW	O04 2-0		S06 2-0	F28 5-1	N15 0-0	D13 3-0	J01 2-1	N29 1-2	M14 2-2	N01 2-2	S08 1-1	F19 5-1	M28 2-1	S20 3-0	J24 4-3	a25 1-2	O18 2-1	A23 2-1	a11 1-1	A25 1-0	a06 2-0	D26 3-0	J03 1-1	J31 1-0
3 BRADFORD	a22 4-0	J17 1-0		S20 2-2	N01 2-2	N29 1-0	J31 0-1	N15 1-0	F28 3-0	O18 3-0	A30 0-3	D26 1-2	M14 1-1	O04 1-1	M11 0-0	a11 2-2	A25 2-1	a25 1-1	M28 1-0	D13 1-1	S10 1-0	a06 6-1	S13 1-2	D20 2-3
4 BRADFORD C	S24 3-2	O11 2-2	F07 2-1		a07 7-2	J03 2-2	N08 2-1	S17 1-3	F21 4-3	D25 3-1	M07 1-0	a18 5-0	O01 1-1	a20 2-1	a29 0-0	A23 1-0	S27 0-3	S06 0-0	J10 2-2	J24 3-0	M21 5-3	a04 4-0	S03 3-1	O25 1-1
5 CARLISLE U	S04 4-4	a04 0-0	M21 1-3	a03 4-4		O04 1-1	a30 3-0	S20 1-2	S11 4-2	D20 2-2	S25 3-0	O11 1-2	A30 4-1	M07 1-0	O25 0-0	F14 2-0	J10 5-0	D25 8-0	J24 2-0	J01 2-1	M12 4-0	D06 3-1	N08 1-0	a18 1-1
6 CHESTER	M21 2-0	a29 2-1	a18 0-3	A30 2-0	F21 1-2		M07 2-0	a22 2-2	S13 6-3	F07 2-0	J31 0-2	N08 2-1	S27 0-1	a04 2-2	S24 0-1	a06 2-2	D06 3-0	S17 1-1	M25 0-0	D20 4-0	O11 3-2	O25 1-1	a15 1-2	A27 1-1
7 CHESTERFIELD	S06 3-0	O01 1-1	J10 1-1	M28 1-1	D13 4-2	O18 2-1		A27 1-0	a11 3-0	N29 1-1	D27 3-2	J03 2-1	a25 2-0	A23 4-1	S15 1-2	F28 1-0	N15 1-0	M14 1-1	S20 1-2	N01 2-1	S27 1-2	J24 1-1	a06 2-1	F21 1-2
8 CREWE A	M07 3-2	a18 1-1	a04 2-3	S10 1-1	F07 2-2	S29 4-1	S01 2-1		A30 0-1	J17 4-3	a29 1-2	O25 1-1	S13 2-0	M21 1-0	N08 0-1	D26 1-4	D20 4-2	a03 2-0	S27 2-0	J14 2-0	F21 1-0	O11 4-0	S24 3-3	D06 3-0
9 DARLINGTON	M25 1-0	O25 1-0	O11 1-3	O04 4-1	S17 0-0	J24 3-2	S24 3-1	J03 1-1		a03 1-0	M21 1-1	a29 0-2	J31 3-0	J01 2-1	S03 0-5	S06 0-2	D26 3-2	S20 1-0	A23 3-1	a20 1-0	a04 1-2	a18 1-0	M07 2-2	N08 0-1
10 GATESHEAD	a29 5-0	M21 3-1	M07 3-2	D27 2-2	A23 2-0	S20 4-1	a18 2-4	S06 6-1	a06 5-1		N08 2-0	F04 3-1	S08 1-1	S01 1-2	O11 1-0	J24 1-1	J01 3-1	F18 1-1	J03 1-2	O04 2-0	S22 0-1	a15 1-1	O25 1 0	a04 1-1
11 GRIMSBY T	F14 3-0	S17 2-1	J03 2-3	O18 0-0	a11 2-3	J13 5-4	D25 0-0	a25 1-0	N01 2-0	M28 0-0		S20 2-0	N15 7-0	J24 5-1	S06 1-1	D13 1-1	M14 3-2	S03 1-0	N29 1-0	F28 0-1	O01 3-1	O04 2-0	A23 2-0	a03 2-1
12 HALIFAX T	S15 3-0	S27 1-0	D27 2-4	N29 1-1	F28 2 1	M28 3-1	A30 3-1	M14 1-3	D13 3-2	J12 1-3	F07 3-2		A25 3-2	a06 1-2	S29 2-2	N01 1-2	a25 3-1	N15 2-1	O18 4-1	a11 3-0	J17 0-0	D20 5-2	F21 0-0	S13 0-0
13 HARTLEPOOLS U	A23 4-1	N08 2-0	O25 0-1	J01 0-0	J03 1-0	F14 2-2	a20 2-0	J24 2-1	J10 1-0	S15 0-0	a04 2-0	S01 0-0		O11 2-0	M07 4-1	S20 2-0	a03 2-1	O04 1-1	S06 3-0	D27 0-2	a18 4-1	a29 2-2	M21 1-2	S22 2-1
14 MANSFIELD T	a13 0-0	F07 2-2	F21 1-1	a25 3-1	O18 2-1	N15 2-2	D20 1-4	N01 3-0	S29 3-2	A25 2-0	S13 1-1	a07 2-1	F28 2-0		D27 0-2	M28 1-0	D13 2-1	a11 1-0	M14 2-2	N29 2-2	A30 1-0	S08 0-0	S27 0-2	J17 1-1
15 OLDHAM A	a03 3-0	S13 3-0	S27 2-1	D13 2-0	M14 2-4	a11 2-1	S09 1-1	M28 0-1	A26 5-0	M03 1-1	J17 1-1	a21 1-0	O18 4-2	D26 1-0		N15 0-1	O04 1-0	N29 0-1	N01 3-0	a25 1 1	D20 5 2	J13 4-1	F07 4-2	A30 2-1
16 PORT VALE	O25 0-1	a13 3-0	S22 1-0	D20 0-0	S27 0-0	a03 1-1	O11 3-0	D27 3-1	J17 2-1	S13 1-1	a30 4-0	M21 1-1	F07 3-0	N08 1-1	a04 1-1		A30 5-2	M16 4-0	F21 0-0	S08 2-0	A25 2-0	M07 2-0	a18 0-0	a20 2-0
17 ROCHDALE	a18 1-0	M07 6-2	S02 1-0	M24 2-1	J31 1-2	S06 3-1	a04 0-2	A23 0-1	D27 3-1	S30 2-3	O25 0-2	a14 1-1	a06 3-1	a29 1-0	F21 3-1	J03 1-1		J24 2-2	S16 0-0	S20 2-2	N08 3-0	S23 2-0	O11 4-1	M21 0-3
18 SCUNTHORPE U	N08 5-2	D20 1-2	M26 1-2	J17 4-0	D27 1-2	S11 1-1	O25 1-0	a06 2-0	F07 2-0	S27 0-0	A28 0-1	a04 1-1	F21 0-0	S25 0-1	a18 1-1	J31 1-2	S13 5-1		O02 3-0	A30 2-2	M07 2-0	M21 2-1	a27 1-2	O11 2-0
19 SOUTHPORT	O11 1-0	S23 3 2	N08 2-2	J31 3-0	S13 2-0	D26 2-0	F07 1-0	F14 3-0	D20 3-0	A30 3-2	a18 4-3	M07 1-1	J17 0-0	O25 1-3	M21 1-0	O04 0-0	S09 1-0	J01 2-3		a03 3-0	a21 1-2	A25 2-0	a04 1-0	a14 2-0
20 STOCKPORT CO	a04 3-1	S01 6-1	a29 2-0	S13 6-1	S29 3-0	A23 4-1	M21 4-1	J31 2-4	S27 2-2	F21 3-1	O11 2-2	S22 1-1	D25 1-1	a18 2-2	a13 1-1	S15 0-2	F07 2-0	J03 1-1	a06 3 0		O25 3-2	N08 6-0	J17 3-1	M07 1-1
21 TRANMERE R	J24 2-0	a03 2-0	S16 4-0	N01 3-1	a25 4-1	F28 4-0	F14 3-1	O04 1-0	N15 5-2	a11 2-0	J01 2-1	S06 0-0	N29 0-2	J03 1-0	A23 0-0	S02 1-1	M28 1-0	O18 0-1	D13 1-1	M14 1-0		S20 3-0	J31 4-2	a28 1-3
22 WORKINGTON	J03 3-0	D27 3-1	a03 2-2	N15 3-2	S06 1-1	M14 1-2	S13 2-3	F28 4-0	N29 3-1	a25 0-2	F21 3-1	A23 2-0	D13 1-1	S17 0-1	J31 1-1	O18 1-1	a11 1-2	N01 0-3	S03 2-4	M28 0-2	F07 2-0		a22 4-0	S27 1-3
23 WREXHAM	D26 3-1	A30 4-0	J24 0-3	A25 2-1	M28 3-0	a25 7-0	a03 2-2	a11 1-0	O18 4-2	M14 1-0	D20 3-1	O04 2-1	N01 3-2	F14 1-0	S20 2-2	N29 3-1	F28 3-0	D13 2-3	N15 3 2	S06 5-2	J21 1-0	O01 3-0		S10 1-1
24 YORK C	S20 2-0	J10 1-1	A23 3-1	M14 0-0	N29 1-0	S01 0-0	O04 0-0	D13 2-1	M28 3-0	N15 1-2	a06 2-0	J24 2-2	a11 1-0	S06 2-0	J03 1-2	S29 1-0	N01 2-0	F28 0-2	a25 3-1	O18 3-0	D26 2-0	F14 1-3	S15 2-1	

DIVISION 3 SOUTH

	ALDERSHOT	BOURNEMOUTH	BRIGHTON & HA	BRISTOL C	BRISTOL R	COLCHESTER U	COVENTRY C	CRYSTAL P	EXETER C	GILLINGHAM	IPSWICH T	LEYTON O	MILLWALL	NEWPORT CO	NORTHAMPTON T	NORWICH C	Q.P.R.	READING	SHREWSBURY T	SOUTHEND U	SWINDON T	TORQUAY U	WALSALL	WATFORD
1 ALDERSHOT		A27 1-0	M14 1-2	N15 1-2	a29 0-0	A30 0-0	D26 4-1	M28 0-1	a03 1-1	a22 3-2	D13 1-1	a25 2-0	S10 1-2	N01 2-2	N29 2-1	D20 1-2	S20 4-1	S06 2-2	F14 4-2	F28 1-1	J24 2-2	a11 0-2	O04 2-0	O18 1-2
2 BOURNEMOUTH	S03 0-3		O01 2-1	a06 4-1	N08 1-2	O11 1-0	O25 3-0	J31 4-2	M21 2-1	S24 4-2	S06 2-1	J03 4-1	a04 1-1	S17 1-2	A23 0-1	M07 0-0	m02 1-0	J24 2-0	a15 2-0	S27 5-1	F07 1-1	D27 0-1	a18 5-1	F21 4-1
3 BRIGHTON & H.A.	O25 4-2	a22 2-0		J03 0-1	a18 2-1	M21 0-0	a04 1-1	A23 4-1	S24 4-2	m02 5-0	F14 1-4	S20 3-1	a15 1-0	D27 2-2	J24 1-1	N08 2-3	O11 2-0	O04 1-1	S03 3-1	S17 2-2	M07 1-2	S06 2-1	a03 4-2	J31 1-2
4 BRISTOL C	a04 0-0	a03 1-1	A30 2-2		F07 0-0	S23 3-2	a28 1-0	S13 5-0	D06 4-1	O11 4-0	S09 4-2	a21 2-1	A20 0-0	J17 2-0	O04 2-3	a18 0-1	M21 4-4	J10 1-1	O25 3-2	D26 5-0	N08 4-2	F14 4-4	M07 6-1	D20 5-1
5 BRISTOL R	J31 4-1	M28 2-1	N29 7-0	S20 0-0		S15 3-1	F21 5-2	D13 2-0	S27 0-0	S06 3-1	M14 3-0	O18 2-1	J24 1-1	a25 3-1	F28 1-1	S29 3-1	D27 2-1	N01 4-0	A23 2-1	N15 2-1	a06 1-2	S01 3-0	J03 2-0	a11 0-3
6 COLCHESTER U	J03 1-2	F28 1-1	N01 0-0	a11 3-1	S11 0-3		a03 0-1	M19 3-0	J31 3-1	O04 1-1	A23 0-0	D13 3-1	a23 0-0	M28 3-3	a25 1-2	m02 0-4	J24 1-1	A28 2-1	S20 1-0	O18 3-3	S06 3-1	N29 4-1	F14 6-1	M14 1-1
7 COVENTRY C	D27 3-0	M14 2-3	N15 3-1	a25 2-2	O04 1-1	a06 2-2		N29 4-2	S29 1-0	S20 2-1	F28 2-0	S01 3-0	F14 4-1	a11 0-1	S15 1-1	J15 2-1	J03 2-0	O18 4-0	S06 0-0	N01 2-1	A23 1-2	D13 7-2	J24 3-1	M28 1-0
8 CRYSTAL P	N08 3-0	J10 1-0	D20 2-1	J24 1-3	m01 1-0	a04 3-1	a18 2-2		a15 2-0	A27 0-0	a22 1-1	O04 2-2	J17 0-1	A30 2-1	F14 4-3	S24 1-1	O25 4-2	S10 0-3	M07 1-2	a06 0-0	M21 3-0	S20 2-2	O11 4-1	a29 1-0
9 EXETER C	a06 2-2	N01 5-1	a11 1-5	D13 1-1	F14 0-0	J21 2-0	a22 1-0	a25 2-0		J24 0-0	O18 1-1	F28 0-1	S20 1-0	N29 3-2	A27 2-0	S10 1-0	A23 2-2	M14 2-0	J03 2-2	M28 0-2	D26 1-2	O04 4-1	S06 6-1	N15 1-1
10 GILLINGHAM	O01 2-0	a11 1-2	D13 1-2	F28 0-1	J17 0-4	F21 1-1	F07 0-0	S03 1-0	S13 1-0		M28 1-1	N01 3-2	A30 0-1	D20 1-1	M14 1-1	S27 0-3	J10 3-0	N15 2-1	a03 4-2	N29 1-1	S17 0-0	O18 2-1	D26 3-1	a25 2-1
11 IPSWICH T	m01 2-1	J17 2-1	S27 1-0	S17 1-0	O25 1-5	D20 2-2	O11 3-0	O01 2-0	M07 0-1	N08 1-1		M25 0-1	M21 1-6	F21 3-0	a06 1-1	A27 2-1.	a18 0-1	A30 1-2	S24 2-1	S13 0-0	a15 1-1	J14 2-2	a04 5-0	F07 1-1
12 LEYTON O	a16 4-1	A30 2-2	F07 3-0	O02 1-3	M07 3-3	a30 5-3	A28 1-2	F21 0-0	O11 2-0	M21 1-1	D26 3-1		O25 1-4	S27 2-1	J10 0-1	a03 3-1	S25 5-0	D20 1-1	a04 0-0	J17 3-0	a18 2-2	S08 4-1	N08 4-1	S13 2-0
13 MILLWALL	S17 0-0	N15 3-1	a25 1-1	S03 1-1	S13 3-0	a27 3-1	S27 2-0	S06 0-0	F07 0-0	J03 3-1	N01 3-2	M14 0-0		D13 3-0	O18 1-2	F21 2-3	a03 2-1	M28 1-0	D26 4-1	a11 4-1	J31 3-0	F28 3-0	A23 3-0	N29 1-1
14 NEWPORT CO	M21 2-1	S11 2 1	D25 0 3	S06 4-3	a13 2-2	N08 0-1	S25 4-4	J03 3-2	a18 1-0	A23 1-2	O04 1-3	F14 0-1	a30 1-3		S20 4-1	a04 1-1	M07 2-0	a23 1-0	O11 4-2	J15 0-1	O25 3-0	J24 3-0	S04 3-2	a03 1-1
15 NORTHAMPTON T	a18 4-0	D20 5-1	S13 5-3	F21 0-2	O11 2-2	a16 2-0	S11 3-1	S27 5-1	S04 3-1	O25 3-1	a07 2-0	J31 3-1	M07 1-1	F07 5-0		a30 3-3	a04 4-2	D26 6-1	N08 3-1	A30 4-3	S25 3-1	a23 3-3	M21 2-1	J17 4-1
16 NORWICH C	A23 5-0	O18 1-1	M28 3-2	N29 0-0	a22 0-0	D26 3-0	J31 1-1	a11 5-1	S17 2-0	F14 3-2	S03 1-0	a06 5-1	O04 2-2	N15 2-0	D13 1-2		S06 2-0	F28 3-0	J24 2-1	M14 3-1	J03 1-1	a25 3-0	S20 3-0	N01 5-2
17 Q.P.R.	F07 2-2	D13 2-1	F28 3-3	N01 2-1	D26 0-1	S13 1-0	A30 0-4	M14 1-1	D20 1-1	J31 1-1	N29 2-2	a11 0 1	a06 1-3	O18 4-2	N15 2-2	J17 3-1		a25 1-0	a20 1-0	O04 3-2	S27 1-1	M28 0-1	S08 4-2	A25 2-2
18 READING	J17 2-3	S13 1-3	F21 0-0	J31 4-0	M21 2-0	S03 2-0	M07 1-0	S17 4-1	O25 3-1	a04 3-2	J03 1-1	A23 2-0	N08 5-0	O01 2-1	a13 2-0	O11 0-1	a29 2-0		a18 5-3	F07 1-0	m01 4-1	a03 4-1	a11 0-0	S27 3-0
19 SHREWSBURY T	S27 2-1	a25 1-0	A28 0-0	M14 0-1	D20 0-1	F07 3-0	J17 1-0	O18 1-1	A30 1-3	a06 3-1	a11 2-2	N15 2-0	D27 2-4	F28 1-1	M28 2-4	S13 1-8	O02 0-3	N29 1-1		D13 7-1	F21 2-1	N01 2-1	F05 1-0	S11 3-1
20 SOUTHEND U	O11 1-1	F14 0-0	S00 1-2	a29 0-4	a04 2-1	M07 4-0	M21 1-0	a03 2-2	N08 1-1	a18 3-1	J24 2-0	S06 1-0	S23 2-1	J31 1-0	J03 3-1	O25 1-2	F21 2-0	S20 3-1	m01 2-2		S02 3-0	A23 3-1	D06 2-1	S30 1-0
21 SWINDON T	S13 3-2	S20 1-2	O18 3-0	M28 0-0	a03 1-3	J17 0-1	D20 2-3	N01 3-6	D27 5-2	S10 0-0	a25 2-0	M18 1-1	J14 1-2	M14 2-0	a11 3-0	A30 2-1	F14 1-3	D13 2-0	O04 2-2	A27 1-3		N15 2-0	O01 1-2	F28 0-0
22 TORQUAY U	S24 1-2	D26 5-1	J17 1-2	S27 1-2	A27 1-0	a18 5-1	m02 2-1	F07 1-1	F21 5-2	M07 3-2	J31 4-1	S17 5-0	O11 1-0	S13 3-3	O01 3-0	a15 4-1	N08 1-1	a06 2-0	M21 4-0	D20 4-2	a04 3-1		O25 0-3	A30 2-2
23 WALSALL	F21 0-0	a30 2-2	a06 3-0	O18 3-3	A30 3-5	S27 0-3	S13 1-1	F28 2-4	J17 2-2	D27 1-3	N15 1-3	M28 1-0	D20 0-2	A28 1-3	N01 1-5	F07 3-2	S18 1-1	S25 2-0	J15 4-4	a25 1-1	a23 1-2	M14 2-0		D13 0-0
24 WATFORD	M07 1-1	O04 3-0	J14 2-3	A23 4-1	S25 2-3	O25 2-0	N08 1-1	D26 2-0	a04 3-1	a16 0-0	S20 1-0	J24 1-0	a18 1-1	a06 0-1	S06 2-1	M21 3-2	S04 1-1	F14 2-1	S18 1-1	a23 1-1	O11 2-1	J03 1-1	J10 3-0	

LEAGUE TABLES

DIVISION 1

	P	W	D	L	F	A	W	D	L	F	A	Pts
Arsenal	42	15	3	3	60	30	6	9	6	37	34	54
Preston NE	42	15	3	3	46	25	6	9	6	39	35	54
Wolves	42	13	5	3	54	27	6	8	7	32	36	51
WBA	42	13	3	5	35	19	8	5	8	31	41	50
Charlton A	42	12	8	1	47	22	7	3	11	30	41	49
Burnley	42	11	6	4	36	20	7	6	8	31	32	48
Blackpool	42	13	5	3	45	22	6	4	11	26	48	47
Manchester U	42	11	5	5	35	30	7	5	9	34	42	46
Sunderland	42	11	9	1	42	27	4	4	13	26	55	43
Tottenham H	42	11	6	4	55	37	4	5	12	23	32	41
Aston Villa	42	9	7	5	36	23	5	6	10	27	38	41
Cardiff C	42	7	8	6	32	17	7	4	10	22	29	40
Middlesbrough	42	12	5	4	46	27	2	6	13	24	50	39
Bolton W	42	9	4	8	39	35	6	5	10	22	34	39
Portsmouth	42	10	6	5	44	34	4	4	13	30	49	38
Newcastle U	42	9	5	7	34	33	5	4	12	25	37	37
Liverpool	42	10	6	5	36	28	4	2	15	25	54	36
Sheffield W	42	8	6	7	35	32	4	5	12	27	40	35
Chelsea	42	10	4	7	35	24	2	7	12	21	42	35
Manchester C	42	12	2	7	45	28	2	5	14	27	59	35
Stoke C	42	10	4	7	35	26	2	6	13	18	40	34
Derby Co	42	9	6	6	41	29	2	4	15	18	45	32

DIVISION 2

	P	W	D	L	F	A	W	D	L	F	A	Pts
Sheffield U	42	15	3	3	60	27	10	7	4	37	28	60
Huddersfield T	42	14	4	3	51	14	10	6	5	33	19	58
Luton T	42	15	1	5	53	17	7	7	7	31	32	52
Plymouth A	42	12	5	4	37	24	8	4	9	28	36	49
Leicester C	42	13	6	2	55	29	5	6	10	34	45	48
Birmingham C	42	11	3	7	44	38	8	7	6	27	28	48
Nottingham F	42	11	5	5	46	32	7	3	11	31	35	44
Fulham	42	14	1	6	52	28	3	9	9	29	43	44
Blackburn R	42	12	4	5	40	20	6	4	11	28	45	44
Leeds U	42	13	4	4	42	24	1	11	9	29	39	43
Swansea T	42	10	9	2	45	26	5	3	13	33	55	42
Rotherham U	42	9	7	5	41	30	7	2	12	34	44	41
Doncaster R	42	9	9	3	26	17	3	7	11	32	47	40
West Ham U	42	9	5	7	38	28	4	8	9	20	32	39
Lincoln C	42	9	9	3	41	26	2	8	11	23	45	39
Everton	42	9	8	4	38	23	3	6	12	33	52	38
Brentford	42	8	8	5	38	29	5	3	13	21	47	37
Hull C	42	11	6	4	36	19	3	2	16	21	50	36
Notts Co	42	11	5	5	41	31	3	3	15	19	57	36
Bury	42	10	6	5	33	30	3	3	15	20	51	35
Southampton	42	5	7	9	45	44	5	6	10	23	41	33
Barnsley	42	4	4	13	31	46	1	4	16	16	62	18

DIVISION 3 North

	P	W	D	L	F	A	W	D	L	F	A	Pts
Oldham A	46	15	4	4	48	21	7	11	5	29	24	59
Port Vale	46	13	9	1	41	10	7	9	7	26	25	58
Wrexham	46	18	3	2	59	24	6	5	12	27	42	56
York C	46	14	5	4	35	16	6	8	9	25	29	53
Grimsby T	46	15	5	3	47	19	6	5	12	28	40	52
Southport	46	16	4	3	42	18	4	7	12	21	42	51
Bradford	46	10	8	5	37	23	9	4	10	38	38	50
Gateshead	46	13	6	4	51	24	4	9	10	25	36	49
Carlisle U	36	13	7	3	57	24	5	6	12	25	44	49
Crewe A	46	13	5	5	46	28	7	3	13	24	40	48
Stockport Co	46	13	8	2	61	26	4	5	14	21	43	47
Chesterfield	46	13	6	4	40	23	5	5	13	25	40	47*
Tranmere R	46	16	4	3	45	16	5	1	17	20	47	47*
Halifax T	46	13	5	5	47	31	3	10	10	21	37	47
Scunthorpe U	46	10	6	7	38	21	6	8	9	24	35	46
Bradford C	48	14	7	2	54	29	0	11	12	21	51	46
Hartlepools U	46	14	6	3	39	16	2	8	13	18	45	46
Mansfield T	46	11	9	3	34	25	5	5	13	21	37	46
Barrow	46	15	6	2	48	20	1	6	16	18	51	44
Chester	46	10	7	6	39	27	1	8	14	25	58	37
Darlington	46	13	4	6	33	27	1	2	20	25	69	34
Rochdale	46	12	5	6	41	27	2	0	21	21	56	33
Workington	46	9	5	9	40	33	2	5	16	15	58	32
Accrington S	46	7	9	7	25	29	1	2	20	14	60	27

DIVISION 3 South

	P	W	D	L	F	A	W	D	L	F	A	Pts
Bristol R	46	17	4	2	55	19	9	8	6	37	27	64
Millwall	46	14	7	2	46	16	10	7	6	36	28	62
Northampton T	46	18	4	1	75	30	8	6	9	34	40	62
Norwich C	46	16	6	1	56	17	9	4	10	43	38	60
Bristol C	46	13	8	2	62	28	9	7	7	33	33	59
Coventry C	46	15	5	3	52	22	4	7	12	25	40	50
Brighton & HA	46	12	6	5	48	30	7	6	10	33	45	50
Southend U	46	15	5	3	41	21	3	8	12	28	53	49
Bournemouth	46	15	3	5	49	23	4	6	13	25	46	47
Watford	46	12	8	3	39	21	3	9	11	23	42	47
Reading	46	17	3	3	53	18	2	5	16	16	46	46
Torquay U	46	15	4	4	61	28	3	5	15	26	60	45
Crystal P	46	12	7	4	40	26	3	6	14	26	56	43
Leyton O	46	12	7	4	52	28	4	3	16	16	45	42
Newport Co	46	12	4	7	43	34	4	6	13	27	48	42
Ipswich T	46	10	7	6	34	28	3	8	12	26	41	41
Exeter C	46	11	8	4	40	24	2	6	15	21	47	40
Swindon T	46	9	5	9	38	33	5	7	11	26	46	40
Aldershot	46	8	8	7	36	29	4	7	12	25	48	39
QPR	46	9	9	5	37	34	3	6	14	24	48	39
Gillingham	46	10	7	6	30	26	2	8	13	25	48	39
Colchester U	46	9	9	5	40	29	3	5	15	19	47	38
Shrewsbury T	46	11	5	7	38	35	1	7	15	30	56	36
Walsall	46	5	9	9	35	46	2	1	20	21	72	24

Football League Records

Top scorers: Div 1, J.Glazzard (Huddersfield Town) 29 goals; Div 2, J.Charles (Leeds United) 42 goals; Div 3(N), G.Ashman (Carlisle United) 30 goals; Div 3(S), J.English (Northampton Town) 28 goals.

England half-back Billy Wright, skipper of the Wolves side which lifted the First Diviision title in 1953-4.

DIVISION 1

	ARSENAL	ASTON VILLA	BLACKPOOL	BOLTON W	BURNLEY	CARDIFF C	CHARLTON A	CHELSEA	HUDDERSFIELD T	LIVERPOOL	MANCHESTER C	MANCHESTER U	MIDDLESBROUGH	NEWCASTLE U	PORTSMOUTH	PRESTON N.E.	SHEFFIELD U	SHEFFIELD W	SUNDERLAND	TOTTENHAM H	W.B.A.	WOLVERHAMPTON W
1 ARSENAL		a06 1-1	D28 1-1	N14 4-3	O17 2-5	F13 1-1	M13 3-3	S08 1-2	A22 0-0	a10 3-0	S19 2-2	M27 3-1	a24 3-1	N28 2-1	a16 3-0	O03 3-2	S01 1-1	O31 4-1	J23 1-4	F27 0-3	D12 2-2	S05 2-3
2 ASTON VILLA	A29 2-1		S12 2-1	O31 2-2	a10 5-1	D19 1-2	N28 2-1	F06 2-2	F20 2-2	F27 2-1	A24 3-0	M13 2-2	N14 5-3	O17 1-2	J16 1-1	a24 1-0	S26 4-0	M31 2-1	S14 3-1	D12 1-2	a20 6-1	D26 1-2
3 BLACKPOOL	D26 2-2	J23 3-2		N28 0-0	A31 2-0	a16 4-1	F27 3-1	A22 2-1	S05 3-1	a24 3-0	O03 2-0	a10 2-0	M13 0-0	D12 1-3	S07 1-1	M31 4-2	J02 2-2	O17 1-2	F13 3-0	N14 1-0	O31 4-1	S19 0-0
4 BOLTON W	a03 3-1	M20 3-0	a17 3-2		a16 0-0	F06 3-0	D26 3-1	N21 2-2	D05 0-0	A29 2-0	O10 3-2	S12 0-0	A26 3-2	J16 2-2	N07 6-1	F13 0-2	J01 2-1	S09 2-1	M06 3-1	O03 2-0	D19 2-1	O24 1-1
5 BURNLEY	M06 2-1	N21 3-2	A25 2-1	a19 1-1		O24 3-0	D19 2-0	a03 1-2	a17 2-1	F06 1-1	M20 3-1	F20 2-0	J16 5-0	S26 1-2	O10 1-0	D25 2-1	N07 2-1	A29 4-1	D05 5-1	S07 4-2	S12 1-4	A19 4-1
6 CARDIFF C	S26 0-3	A22 2-1	a19 0-1	S19 1-1	M13 1-0		O31 5-0	D28 0-0	S02 2-1	N28 3-1	J23 0-3	N14 1-6	D12 1-0	M27 2-1	M03 3-2	F27 2-1	S16 2-0	a24 2-2	S05 1-1	O17 1-0	a10 2-0	J02 1-3
7 CHARLTON A	O24 1-5	a17 1-1	O10 4-2	D25 1-0	A22 3-1	M20 3-2		J02 1-1	N07 2-1	S26 6-0	D05 2-1	a19 1-0	S12 8-1	F25 0-0	M06 3-1	S17 2-1	a03 3-0	J16 4-2	A19 5-3	S03 0-1	F06 1-1	N21 0-2
8 CHELSEA	S15 0-2	S19 1-2	D19 5-1	a10 2-0	N14 2-1	D26 2-0	A29 3-1		J23 2-2	O31 5-2	a16 0-1	D12 3-1	O17 1-1	a24 1-2	A25 4-3	N28 1-0	S05 1-2	F27 0-1	O03 2-2	M27 1-0	M17 5-0	F13 4-2
9 HUDDERSFIELD T	D19 2-2	O03 4-0	J16 0-0	a24 2-1	N28 3-1	A26 2-0	M27 4-1	S12 3-1		O17 2-0	S09 1-1	O31 0-0	S26 2-1	M13 3-2	A29 5-1	D12 2-2	F06 2-2	N14 2-0	D26 2-1	a10 2-5	F27 0-2	a20 2-1
10 LIVERPOOL	N21 1-2	O10 6-1	D05 5-2	J02 1-2	S19 4-0	a17 0-1	F13 2-3	M20 1-1	M06 1-3		N07 2-2	A22 4-4	a19 4-1	A26 2-2	A19 3-1	S05 1-5	O24 3-0	O03 2-2	a03 4-3	J23 2-2	D26 0-0	S16 1-1
11 MANCHESTER C	F06 0-0	S02 0-1	F24 1-4	F27 3-0	O31 3-2	S12 1-1	a24 3-0	a19 1-1	S16 0-1	a07 0-2		S05 2-0	a10 5-2	N14 0-0	S26 2-1	O17 1-4	D26 2-1	D12 3-2	J02 2-1	M17 4-1	N28 2-3	A22 0-4
12 MANCHESTER U	N07 2-2	O24 1-0	N21 4-1	J23 1-5	O03 1-2	a03 2-3	a16 2-0	A19 1-1	M20 3-1	D19 5-1	J16 1-1		S09 2-2	A29 1-1	a17 2-0	S19 1-0	D05 2-2	D25 5-2	O10 1-0	F13 2-0	A26 1-3	M06 1-0
13 MIDDLESBROUGH	D05 2-0	a03 2-1	O24 0-1	S02 3-2	S05 1-3	A19 0-0	J23 0-2	M06 3-3	F13 0-3	a16 0-1	N21 0-1	S16 1-4		D25 2-3	M20 2-2	A22 0-4	O10 2-0	S19 4-1	a17 0-0	J02 3-0	F24 1-1	N07 3-3
14 NEWCASTLE U	a17 5-2	M06 0-1	J01 2-1	S05 2-3	F13 3-1	N07 4-0	O03 0-2	D05 1-1	O24 0-2	S02 4-0	a03 4-3	J02 1-2	D26 2-3		N21 1-1	J23 0-4	M20 4-1	a16 3-0	A22 2-1	S19 1-3	S16 3-7	O10 1-2
15 PORTSMOUTH	a19 1-1	S05 2-1	S16 4-4	M27 3-2	F27 3-2	O03 1-1	O17 3-1	S02 3-2	J02 5-2	D12 5-1	F13 4-1	N28 1-1	O31 0-2	a10 2-0		N14 1-3	A22 3-4	a07 2-1	S19 4-1	D26 1-1	a24 3-0	J23 2-0
16 PRESTON N.E.	F24 0-1	D05 1-1	N07 2-3	S26 3-1	D26 2-1	O10 1-2	S09 2-0	a17 1-0	A19 1-2	J16 2-1	M06 4-0	F06 1-3	D19 1-0	S12 2-2	a03 4-0		N21 2-1	A26 6-0	O24 6-2	a16 2-1	A29 0-2	M20 0-1
17 SHEFFIELD U	A24 1-0	a26 2-1	A29 3-4	D12 3-0	M27 2-1	S07 0-1	N14 1-1	J16 1-3	S19 3-6	M13 3-1	D25 2-2	a24 1-3	F27 2-2	O31 3-1	D19 3-1	a10 1-1		S12 2-0	a19 1-3	N28 5-2	O17 1-2	O03 3-3
18 SHEFFIELD W	M20 2-1	S07 3-1	M06 1-2	S16 2-1	J02 2-0	D05 2-1	S05 1-2	O10 2-0	a03 1-4	F24 1-1	A19 2-0	D26 0-1	F06 4-2	S23 3-0	O24 4-4	S02 4-2	J23 3-2		N21 2-2	A22 2-1	S26 2-3	a17 0-0
19 SUNDERLAND	S12 7-1	J01 2-0	S26 3-2	O17 1-2	a24 2-1	J16 5-0	D12 2-1	F20 1-2	D25 1-1	N14 3-2	A29 4-5	F27 0-2	N28 0-2	D19 1-1	F06 3-1	a07 2-2	a16 2-2	a10 2-4		O31 4-3	M31 2-1	A26 3-2
20 TOTTENHAM H	O10 1-4	A19 1-0	a03 2-2	M03 3-2	S16 2-3	M06 0-1	A26 3-1	N07 2-1	N21 1-0	S12 2-1	O24 3-0	S26 1-1	A29 4-1	F06 3-0	D25 1-1	a19 2-6	a17 2-1	D19 3-1	M20 0-3		J16 0-1	D05 2-3
21 W.B.A.	A19 2-0	a19 1-1	M20 2-1	A22 1-1	J23 0-0	N21 6-1	S19 2-3	O24 5-2	O10 4-0	D25 5-2	a17 1-0	S02 2-0	O03 2-1	S09 2-2	D05 2-3	J02 3-2	M06 2-2	F13 4-2	N07 2-0	S05 5-0		a03 0-1
22 WOLVERHAMPTON W	J16 0-2	D24 1-2	F06 4-1	M24 1-1	D12 1-2	A29 3-1	a10 5-0	S26 8-1	a19 4-0	S07 2-1	D19 3-1	O17 3-1	M27 2-4	F27 3-2	S12 4-3	O31 1-0	F20 6-1	N28 4-1	A31 3-1	a24 2-0	N14 1-0	

Veteran centre-forward Tommy Lawton, a star with Everton before the war, he later played for Chelsea, Brentford and Notts County before joining Arsenal in 1953-4. His strike rate was then only moderate but he played a few games as the Gunners finished 12th.

DIVISION 2

	BIRMINGHAM C	BLACKBURN R	BRENTFORD	BRISTOL R	BURY	DERBY CO	DONCASTER R	EVERTON	FULHAM	HULL C	LEEDS U	LEICESTER C	LINCOLN C	LUTON T	NOTTINGHAM F	NOTTS CO	OLDHAM A	PLYMOUTH A	ROTHERHAM U	STOKE C	SWANSEA T	WEST HAM U
1 BIRMINGHAM C		N07 0-0	O24 5-1	M06 1-1	N21 0-0	M20 3-0	a17 0-1	D05 5-1	S19 2-2	A19 2-0	O03 3-3	S05 1-2	O10 1-0	S09 5-1	a19 2-2	D25 3-0	a03 2-1	S02 3-0	J02 2-3	J23 1-0	A22 6-0	F13 2-0
2 BLACKBURN R	a10 3-0		A31 2-2	A22 1-1	O03 4-2	J01 0-3	D25 2-0	S19 0-0	O17 5-1	J23 3-1	O31 2-2	a16 3-0	J02 6-0	M27 2-0	N14 2-0	S05 2-0	F13 4-0	N28 2-3	D12 3-0	F27 3-0	a24 1-0	M13 4-1
3 BRENTFORD	M13 2-0	A27 1-4		S05 0-3	a16 2-1	D19 0-0	S10 1-4	O03 1-0	A29 2-1	F13 2-2	O17 2-1	a24 1-3	J23 0-1	a10 0-1	O31 1-1	S19 0-0	D25 3-1	N14 1-0	N28 0-1	D12 0-0	M27 3-1	F27 3-1
4 BRISTOL R	O17 1-1	D19 1-2	J16 0-0		S07 2-0	A29 3-0	A24 0-1	D28 0-0	D12 2-1	O03 4-2	F27 1-1	N28 3-0	S19 0-1	O31 3-3	M13 1-0	F13 1-1	a16 1-0	a10 3-1	M27 1-0	a24 3-2	N14 0-1	S12 2-2
5 BURY	M27 1-1	F20 0-0	J30 1-1	S16 3-1		D25 4-0	S26 2-1	S05 2-2	O31 1-3	a07 3-0	N14 4-4	O17 2-5	S02 1-1	a24 0-1	N28 2-1	A22 3-3	J23 1-0	D12 3-0	F27 3-0	M13 0-6	S19 1-2	a10 2-0
6 DERBY CO	O31 2-4	S09 2-2	A22 4-1	J02 0-1	D26 3-1		a19 2-0	F13 2-6	F27 3-3	S19 2-0	M13 0-2	D12 2-1	S05 2-0	N14 1-2	a10 1-2	J23 0-0	O03 3-1	M27 1-4	a24 1-1	S02 1-1	N28 4-2	O17 2-1
7 DONCASTER R	N14 3-1	D26 0-2	S16 3-0	S02 1-0	F13 0-1	a16 1-3		J23 2-2	M13 2-2	S05 4-1	a10 0-0	F27 0-2	A22 1-1	N28 1-3	M27 1-3	J02 4-2	S19 1-0	a24 3-3	O03 1-2	O17 1-0	D12 1-0	O31 2-0
8 EVERTON	a24 1-0	F06 1-1	F24 6-1	D25 4-0	J16 0-0	S26 3-2	S12 4-1		N14 2-2	S02 2-0	N28 2-1	O31 1-2	a16 3-1	D19 2-1	D12 3-3	S23 3-2	A29 3-1	F27 8-4	M13 3-0	a10 1-1	O17 2-2	M27 1-2
9 FULHAM	F06 5-2	M06 2-3	J02 4-1	A20 4-4	M20 3-0	O10 5-2	O24 1-2	a17 0-0		N21 5-1	S12 1-3	S02 1-1	D05 4-1	F20 5-1	S26 3-1	a03 4-3	N07 3-1	D25 3-1	S16 2-4	A22 0-1	a19 4-3	J16 3-4
10 HULL C	D12 3-0	S12 0-2	S26 2-0	a12 4-1	A29 3-0	F06 3-0	J16 3-1	A24 1-3	M27 2-1		a24 1-1	a10 0-3	D26 3-0	F27 1-2	S07 3-0	a16 0-2	D19 8-0	O17 2-0	O31 1-0	N14 1-2	M13 4-3	N28 2-1
11 LEEDS U	F20 1-1	M20 3-2	M06 4-0	O10 3-3	a17 3-4	O24 3-1	N07 3-1	a03 3-1	J23 1-2	D05 0-0		J02 7-1	F13 5-2	a19 2-1	D26 0-2	A19 6-0	N21 2-1	S16 1-1	A22 4-2	S05 1-1	S02 3-2	S19 1-2
12 LEICESTER C	J16 3-4	a19 4-0	D05 6-0	a03 1-0	M06 2-0	A19 2-2	O10 2-0	M20 2-2	A24 2-2	N07 1-3	A29 5-0		N21 9-2	F06 2-1	S12 1-0	a17 2-2	O24 1-0	S26 4-2	D25 4-1	S07 4-0	F23 4-1	D19 2-1
13 LINCOLN C	F27 0-1	A29 8-0	S12 2-1	F06 1-2	A26 0-0	J16 2-2	D19 0-2	a19 1-1	a24 4-2	D28 3-0	S26 2-0	M27 3-1		M13 1-1	O17 2-2	O03 3-0	S09 3-1	O31 2-0	N14 4-3	N28 1-1	a10 3-1	D12 1-2
14 LUTON T	S16 2-0	N21 2-1	N07 1-1	M20 1-1	D05 3-2	a17 2-1	a03 2-0	A22 1-1	O03 1-2	O10 3-1	a16 1-1	S19 2-2	O24 1-0		A26 0-1	M06 2-1	A19 4-4	J02 2-1	J23 1-1	F13 0-1	S05 2-0	D26 3-1
15 NOTTINGHAM F	a16 1-1	a17 0-1	M20 2-1	O24 3-1	a03 2-2	N07 4-2	N21 2-2	A19 3-3	F13 4-1	S16 2-0	D25 5-2	J23 3-1	M06 4-2	S02 2-1		O10 5-0	D05 1-1	A22 3-0	S05 4-1	S19 5-4	J02 2-1	O03 4-0
16 NOTTS CO	D26 2-1	J16 0-5	F06 2-0	S26 1-5	D19 0-0	S12 0-1	A29 1-5	S10 0-2	N28 0-0	a19 1-1	D12 2-0	N14 1-1	F20 1-1	O17 1-2	F27 1-1		A27 2-0	M13 2-0	a10 1-2	M27 2-1	O31 3-0	a24 3-1
17 OLDHAM A	N28 2-3	S26 1-0	D26 2-0	a19 0-0	S12 0-0	F20 0-0	F06 2-2	a29 0-4	a10 2-3	A22 0-0	M27 4-2	a06 0-2	S14 1-0	D12 1-2	a24 1-3	S01 1-3		S05 1-1	O17 2-3	O31 1-0	F27 2-2	N14 3-1
18 PLYMOUTH A	A24 2-2	a03 1-1	a17 3-2	N07 3-3	A19 1-1	N21 3-2	D05 0-0	O10 4-0	D26 2-2	M06 2-2	S07 1-1	F13 0-3	M20 1-2	A29 2-2	D19 1-0	O24 3-3	J16 5-0		S19 0-2	O03 1-1	J23 1-1	a19 2-1
19 ROTHERHAM U	A29 1-0	A20 1-4	a03 1-1	N21 1-1	O10 1-0	D05 5-2	a29 4-0	O24 1-2	S07 3-2	M20 3-2	D19 2-4	D26 1-1	a17 4-1	S12 2-1	J16 3-0	N07 0-1	M06 7-0	F06 2-1		S21 2-2	S26 2-1	A24 5-0
20 STOKE C	S12 3-2	O10 3-0	A19 1-1	D05 3-2	O24 4-0	A24 2-2	M06 2-2	N07 2-4	D19 1-3	a17 0-1	J16 4-0	S14 2-2	a03 4-1	S26 1-1	F06 1-1	N21 0-1	M20 0-1	a26 3-2	a19 1-1		D28 5-0	A29 1-1
21 SWANSEA T	D19 1-3	D05 2-1	N21 1-0	a17 3-1	F06 2-1	a03 2-1	A19 0-1	M06 0-2	a16 2-0	O24 1-0	A27 4-3	O03 0-0	N07 4-2	J16 1-1	A29 2-1	M20 2-2	O10 4-0	S12 0-1	F13 0-2	D26 2-2		S10 1-1
22 WEST HAM U	S26 1-2	O24 2-1	O10 0-1	J23 1-1	N07 5-0	M06 0-0	M20 2-1	N21 1-1	S05 3-1	a03 1-0	F06 5-2	A22 4-1	A19 5-0	D25 1-0	F20 1-1	D05 1-2	a17 0-1	a16 2-2	A31 3-0	a12 2-2	S14 4-1	

Season 1953-54

DIVISION 3 NORTH

	ACCRINGTON S	BARNSLEY	BARROW	BRADFORD	BRADFORD C	CARLISLE U	CHESTER	CHESTERFIELD	CREWE A	DARLINGTON	GATESHEAD	GRIMSBY T	HALIFAX T	HARTLEPOOLS U	MANSFIELD T	PORT VALE	ROCHDALE	SCUNTHORPE U	SOUTHPORT	STOCKPORT CO	TRANMERE R	WORKINGTON	WREXHAM	YORK C
1 ACCRINGTON S		O24 3-0	S19 3-2	M20 0-0	F13 0-1	S28 2-2	a28 1-0	O03 2-2	a03 2-1	M06 0-0	J30 2-2	S16 3-1	D26 3-0	O10 2-0	J23 5-1	N07 2-2	a07 1-0	J01 0-1	a17 1-1	A22 2-1	a19 0-1	A26 4-2	S05 1-2	D05 2-0
2 BARNSLEY	M13 5-0		a24 3-2	A29 2-1	J09 4-2	O17 1-1	S02 3-0	S05 4-1	S16 1-1	J23 5-1	M31 0-2	O31 0-0	F27 1-2	S19 3-2	N28 2-1	D19 0-1	N14 2-1	a19 0-1	S23 2-1	M27 4-1	a21 3-0	O03 4-2	a10 3-0	D26 2-1
3 BARROW	a20 4-3	D05 0-1		J01 4-1	S14 3-0	S12 1-1	O10 2-1	D19 2-2	D28 3-1	a17 2-2	a03 0-0	S26 4-0	J16 1-1	a26 1-1	S21 4-2	A24 0-0	a19 4-2	M20 1-2	M06 2-3	F20 1-0	A29 2-1	N07 0-1	D25 1-0	O24 4-1
4 BRADFORD	O31 6-4	J02 0-2	M17 2-1		A22 4-0	M13 2-4	S30 5-0	M10 1-1	A31 1-1	S05 2-2	S19 3-1	M27 4-1	O17 4-2	J23 5-0	a24 1-0	S16 1-2	a10 2-2	O03 2-2	D28 1-1	N14 3-2	F27 1-2	F24 3-1	N28 2-0	a19 2-0
5 BRADFORD C	S26 1-0	A19 1-0	S09 1-0	D19 3-0		F06 1-0	M06 1-0	A29 2-0	O10 3-0	D05 2-0	a28 2-2	F20 3-0	S12 2-0	a17 1-1	A26 2-2	a07 1-1	D26 4-0	N07 1-3	O24 4-1	a20 1-1	J16 1-0	a03 1-1	S23 1-2	M20 1-0
6 CARLISLE U	S22 2-1	M06 2-4	J23 2-2	O24 0-1	S19 2-0		a03 1-1	F13 2-3	N07 5-0	O10 1-1	D26 1-0	S01 3-3	a16 5-0	J30 2-3	S05 5-0	M20 0-0	A22 7-0	D05 5-1	a27 3-2	S15 2-0	O03 0-2	J01 2-2	J02 0-0	a17 1-1
7 CHESTER	a10 3-0	A26 1-1	F27 1-1	S23 2-3	O17 3-0	N14 0-1		M13 2-2	a19 2-0	S16 2-2	J02 5-0	N28 1-1	M27 3-1	A22 1-1	M24 0-2	D26 0-1	D12 2-0	J23 0-0	F13 1-0	a24 1-2	O31 1-2	S05 3-0	O03 2-1	S19 3-1
8 CHESTERFIELD	F20 0-0	J16 1-1	A22 1-1	M24 5-1	J02 2-3	S26 5-0	O24 4-0		M06 0-2	A19 1-1	a17 1-1	a19 1-0	F06 1-2	D05 2-1	J01 0-0	O10 1-2	S28 2-1	a03 1-0	M20 2-0	D26 4-0	S12 2-1	a26 1-0	A31 1-0	N07 3-2
9 CREWE A	N14 0-3	S07 3-2	J30 2-0	A26 1-1	F27 1-2	M27 0-0	a16 1-0	O17 2-0		A22 1-0	S05 3-1	a10 1-1	O31 3-1	J02 3-0	D26 0-0	S28 0-0	a24 2-1	S19 1-1	O03 0-0	N28 1-5	M13 1-2	J23 2-3	a12 1-2	F13 1-1
10 DARLINGTON	O17 4-1	S12 1-1	N28 1-3	J16 2-1	a24 1-0	F27 3-2	S09 1-0	M31 3-2	D19 0-1		O03 0-2	M13 3-0	J30 1-1	M24 0-1	a10 1-2	A29 0-3	M27 0-0	D26 3-0	A26 0-1	O31 1-0	S19 2-1	a19 3-0	N14 0 2	J01 1-3
11 GATESHEAD	J09 4-0	S26 0-0	N14 1-0	a07 0-1	a10 1-0	D25 2-2	A29 2-1	N28 3-3	J16 2-0	F20 1-2		F27 7-1	D12 4-0	a19 1-3	M27 1-3	S12 1-0	M13 2-1	A24 0-0	D19 1-0	O17 4-2	a24 2-1	S21 4-1	O31 3-1	S07 3-0
12 GRIMSBY T	S09 2-0	M20 0-1	F13 1-0	N07 0-0	O03 1-0	A26 3-2	a17 0-0	a16 1-1	a28 3-1	O24 1-0	O10 2-0		S23 2 1	M06 3-0	S19 0-2	a03 2-2	S05 3-2	A22 0-1	D05 1-2	J02 1-0	D25 1-0	J30 1-0	J23 0-0	A19 3-0
13 HALIFAX T	D25 2-0	O10 1-2	S05 2-0	M06 2-2	J23 0-1	a19 2-0	N07 1-1	S19 2-1	M20 1-0	J09 0-0	A19 0-0	S28 2-0		F20 1-0	J02 2-0	O24 0-1	S14 1-1	a17 0-3	a03 1-2	A31 0-1	a29 1-1	D05 3-0	A22 0-2	a27 2-3
14 HARTLEPOOLS U	F27 0-1	F06 0-1	a10 2-2	S12 0-2	N28 1-1	a12 1-1	D19 2-0	a24 0-1	A29 0-0	S26 1-0	a16 1-0	O17 3-0	O03 2-0		N14 3-1	J16 2-1	O31 6-0	S21 3-2	S07 1-1	M13 6-0	a05 1-2	D26 2-2	M27 1-1	A24 2-2
15 MANSFIELD T	S12 1-1	a17 2-0	S28 2-3	D05 1-1	A31 0-0	J16 2-1	J09 2-1	S14 2-2	D25 6-0	D12 6-0	N07 1-1	F06 5-1	A29 3-1	a03 1-0		A19 1-2	F20 2-0	O24 2-1	O10 4-2	S26 3-1	D19 2 0	M20 0-2	a19 4-0	M06 7-2
16 PORT VALE	M30 1-0	A22 0-0	A31 4-0	S07 2-0	a01 3-0	O31 1-0	D25 1-0	F27 2-2	S21 1-0	a29 1-1	J23 0-0	N14 2-0	M15 2-0	S05 3-1	a05 1-1		N28 6-0	F13 0-0	a16 0-0	a10 7-0	O17 2-0	S19 2-0	a24 2-0	O03 5-0
17 ROCHDALE	A29 1-0	a03 1-1	a16 1-0	a27 0-1	D25 3-2	D19 2-1	D28 4-0	S22 0-1	D05 4-1	N07 3-0	O24 0-1	J16 4-1	S08 0-1	M20 2-2	O03 1-0	a17 0-0		O10 1-1	F06 2-0	S12 0-0	A25 0-1	M06 4-2	F13 6-2	J09 1-2
18 SCUNTHORPE U	M18 1-2	a16 6-0	O31 3-2	F20 4-1	M27 2-1	a24 2-1	S12 1-0	N14 2-1	F06 2-2	D25 1-1	S03 1-1	D19 2-1	N28 3-2	O01 0-0	M13 2-2	S26 0-2	F27 1-1		J16 1-1	a01 2-0	a10 3-1	S17 4-1	O17 3-1	A29 3-0
19 SOUTHPORT	N28 5-3	J01 5-2	O17 0-1	D25 1-0	M13 0-1	a10 3-0	S26 0-1	O31 2-1	F20 1-2	S01 3-0	A22 2 4	a24 2-1	N14 1-0	S15 2-1	F27 2-1	a19 0-0	S19 1-1	S05 4-3		a28 1-2	M27 0-0	J02 1-1	J30 4-0	J23 1-1
20 STOCKPORT CO	D19 1-1	N07 3-0	O03 5-1	a03 4-1	a16 5-0	S07 3-2	D05 5-0	D25 6-1	a17 1-0	M20 2-0	M06 0-1	A29 3-2	A24 1-1	O24 1-0	F13 3-2	a26 1-1	J23 1-2	M10 1-1	A19 1-1		S21 6-0	O10 2-0	S19 2-2	J16 0-1
21 TRANMERE R	a16 1-0	M03 0-1	J02 1-0	O10 1-1	S05 0-1	F20 1-2	M20 2-1	J23 1-2	O24 1-0	M10 1-0	D05 1-4	D26 2-4	S26 1-0	J01 3-2	A22 2-5	M06 1-3	S01 5-1	a27 1-1	N07 2-0	S29 2-2		a17 4-2	S15 6-1	a03 1-1
22 WORKINGTON	A31 3-1	F20 2-0	M27 1-1	S26 1-1	N14 2-2	J09 2-2	J16 2-0	a10 2-1	S12 1-2	a16 1-1	S28 2-0	M17 2-0	a24 3-1	D25 0-0	O31 1-1	F06 2-0	O17 0-1	S07 1-3	A29 0-1	F27 0-0	N28 2-1		M13 1-1	D19 5-2
23 WREXHAM	J16 4-2	a28 1-1	D26 1-2	a17 2-0	S30 0 1	A29 4-2	F20 2-1	A26 1-2	A19 1-1	a03 4-2	M20 5-1	S12 4-0	D19 5-0	N07 2-0	a16 2-0	D05 1-1	S26 2-0	M06 3-1	a07 2-1	F06 1-0	S09 3-0	O24 8-0		O10 1-1
24 YORK C	a24 1-2	D25 0-2	M13 5-2	a16 0 0	O31 3 2	N28 1-3	F06 2-1	M27 1-3	S26 0-3	S21 3-3	S14 1-1	a12 1-2	a10 1-1	A31 5-0	O17 5-1	F24 0-1	J30 1-2	J02 2-0	S12 2-1	S05 0-0	N14 0-0	A22 0-0	F27 5 2	

DIVISION 3 SOUTH

	ALDERSHOT	BOURNEMOUTH	BRIGHTON & HA	BRISTOL C	COLCHESTER U	COVENTRY C	CRYSTAL P	EXETER C	GILLINGHAM	IPSWICH T	LEYTON O	MILLWALL	NEWPORT CO	NORTHAMPTON T	NORWICH C	Q.P.R.	READING	SHREWSBURY T	SOUTHAMPTON	SOUTHEND U	SWINDON T	TORQUAY U	WALSALL	WATFORD
1 ALDERSHOT		O24 1-2	D05 2-3	F13 2-5	J23 3-0	A19 4-2	S19 1-2	D25 1-2	N07 1-2	M06 3-0	a16 1-1	O10 1-1	S30 2-0	a03 3-1	A22 0-0	J02 1-4	F20 2-2	S16 1-0	S05 1-1	a17 4-0	S02 1-0	a28 4-1	a07 3-1	M20 3-1
2 BOURNEMOUTH	a24 1-1		S19 1-1	O17 5-2	a19 4-2	S09 1-0	F27 2-0	M13 4-1	J09 4-1	S30 2-3	J02 1-2	A22 4-1	N28 1-1	A26 2-1	a10 2-0	a07 0-1	S05 1-1	N14 2-1	D25 3-1	J23 0-1	O31 4-0	O03 1-2	M27 1-1	F13 1-3
3 BRIGHTON & H.A.	a10 3-2	F06 3-0		N28 2-1	N14 1-0	S12 3-1	M13 3-0	F27 2-1	J16 3-1	S26 1-2	A26 2-1	F20 4 0	O17 4-2	A29 3-2	a24 0-0	a30 3-1	J09 3-2	a16 2-3	M27 2-1	S09 3-2	a07 1-1	D19 1-2	D26 5-3	S23 3-3
4 BRISTOL C	S26 4 0	M06 1-1	M20 1-1		S05 3-0	O24 1-0	J23 4-0	S15 5-1	A19 1-1	O10 2-3	F06 1-0	a19 2-1	D26 3-0	N07 2-1	S30 3-1	A22 1-2	a17 3-1	a29 3-1	J02 1-0	D05 4-1	F20 5-1	a03 3-0	S01 4-1	a27 2-1
5 COLCHESTER U	S12 3-0	a16 1-1	a03 1-1	J16 0-2		O10 0-3	A29 4-1	S03 0-1	M06 0-1	D19 1-2	D05 1-0	a17 3-0	J09 2-2	O24 1-1	S17 0-1	D25 5-0	M20 2-4	F20 3-1	O01 0-1	a29 0-1	F06 2-2	A20 3-1	S26 1-1	N07 2-2
6 COVENTRY C	O31 2-1	S14 2-0	J23 1-2	a24 3-0	F27 2-1		O17 0-0	N28 2-0	A31 2-1	D25 1-3	A22 4-0	S28 0-0	a10 1-2	O03 0-0	a26 1-0	a12 3-1	J02 1-1	M13 2-1	a20 2-1	S05 1-0	M27 0-0	F13 4-0	N14 2-0	S19 0-1
7 CRYSTAL P	F06 0-0	O10 3-1	a28 1-1	S12 1-2	J02 0-1	M06 3-1		J30 0-0	O24 1-2	a19 1-1	a17 2-2	J16 2-3	S16 3-0	A20 2-2	D25 1-0	S30 0-3	D05 1-0	S02 3-2	A22 4-3	M20 4-2	S26 3-2	N07 4-1	F20 1-0	a03 1-1
8 EXETER C	D26 1-3	a28 1-0	O10 0-1	S09 0-1	A26 1-2	M20 4-0	J09 7-0		D05 1-2	a03 1-2	A19 2-1	N07 4-1	J23 1-0	a17 1-0	S19 0-2	F13 0-0	O24 2-0	A29 0-1	O03 4-0	M06 1-1	S23 3-1	J16 1-2	D19 2 1	a19 2-1
9 GILLINGHAM	M27 1-3	J30 1-0	S05 0-0	O31 2-2	O17 2-0	A26 2-0	a24 3-2	a10 0-1		S16 1-1	S30 1-2	D25 2-0	D12 0-1	F13 2-1	O03 3-1	a16 1-0	A22 3-0	N28 2-0	F27 2-0	J02 3-1	N14 1-0	S19 0-4	M13 3-0	J23 2-3
10 IPSWICH T	O17 4-0	S23 2-1	F13 2-3	F27 2-1	A22 3-0	D26 4-1	a16 2-0	N14 1-1	S09 6-1		S05 3-1	J02 1-1	M13 1-2	m01 2-1	N28 1-1	a10 2-1	J23 0-1	M27 0-0	a07 2-1	S19 1-1	a24 2-0	A26 2-1	O31 3-0	O03 1-0
11 LEYTON O	a19 1-2	A29 5-0	S03 0-2	S19 4-1	a10 3-1	D19 1-0	a08 2-0	O31 3-1	S24 3-1	J16 1-2		S12 2-2	M27 3-0	D26 2-0	N14 3-1	M18 2-2	F13 2-1	a24 2-0	N28 1-4	O03 1-1	F27 1-1	S10 3-2	O17 2-1	a22 1-1
12 MILLWALL	F27 2-0	D19 2-1	O03 0-2	a16 1-0	a26 0-0	S21 1-2	S05 2-2	M27 2-1	D26 3-1	A29 1-2	J23 0-3		N14 3-1	S07 1-0	M13 1-3	N28 4-0	S19 2-0	O31 3-1	a10 2-1	F13 2-1	O17 6-1	J09 2-2	a24 3-0	A24 1-0
13 NEWPORT CO	S21 2-2	M20 4-0	M06 1-0	D25 3-2	a22 1-1	D05 2-1	S07 1-3	S12 0-3	a17 1-0	a26 1-2	N07 1-1	a03 0-0		F06 2-0	F13 4-1	O03 2-1	A20 4-1	J16 2-1	A24 0-4	O24 3-2	D19 2-0	a16 2-0	A29 4-2	O10 0-1
14 NORTHAMPTON T	N14 6-2	S03 2-1	J02 4-2	M27 3-0	a24 3-0	F20 0-1	O31 6-0	a08 2-2	S26 1-1	M25 1-0	D25 2-2	S17 4 2	S19 1-0		a20 2-0	F27 2-1	S21 1-1	a10 1-0	O17 3-0	D19 5-0	M13 2-0	J23 3-1	N28 5-1	S05 4-1
15 NORWICH C	D19 3-3	D05 1-3	O24 1-0	S23 1-1	S09 2-1	a17 2-1	D26 2-1	F06 1-2	F24 0-0	M20 1-2	a03 3-1	a28 4-3	S26 2-0	a19 4-1		A26 2-2	N07 2-3	S12 1-0	m01 1-0	A19 1-0	A29 2-2	O10 0-1	J16 3-0	M06 4-1
16 Q.P.R.	A29 0-2	a17 2-1	A19 1-2	D19 0-1	D26 0-0	J30 0-3	S21 1-1	S26 0-0	a19 3-1	D05 3-1	a26 2-1	M20 4-0	F20 5-1	O10 1-1	A31 0-2		a03 2-0	F06 0-0	S07 0-1	N07 1-0	J16 0-2	M06 5-1	S12 2-0	O24 0-4
17 READING	O03 6-1	J16 0-1	M24 2-1	a07 0-2	N28 2-0	A29 4-3	a10 4-1	a24 4-1	D19 0-1	S12 3-1	S26 1-1	M31 2-4	O31 4-1	S30 2-0	M27 4-4	N14 3 1		O17 1-1	M13 4-1	A26 2-0	a19 3-1	D25 2-4	F27 0-2	S09 4-1
18 SHREWSBURY T	S07 0-2	a03 1-1	a19 3-1	J30 4-3	O03 3-1	J09 1-1	A24 1-1	J02 1-1	M20 0-0	N07 1-1	O24 3-3	m01 3-1	S05 2-1	D05 2-4	J23 4-0	S19 1-1	M06 0-3		F13 3-2	O10 2-1	D26 1-0	a17 2-1	S21 4-1	A22 6-4
19 SOUTHAMPTON	J16 2-0	D26 2 1	N07 1-0	A29 4-2	S23 2-1	a19 2-1	D19 3-1	F20 2 0	O10 1-0	a17 1-1	M20 4-1	D05 4-2	S02 4-0	M06 1-0	M24 0-0	S16 3-1	a28 1-1	S26 4-2		a03 3-5	S12 3-1	O24 2-2	M17 0-0	A19 2-0
20 SOUTHEND U	a13 2-1	S12 2-1	S15 2-0	a10 0-1	M13 3-0	J16 2-2	N28 1 2	O17 0-1	A29 1-1	F06 3-1	F24 2-1	S26 1-2	a24 0-1	A22 2-0	O31 5-2	M27 4-1	S01 1-2	F27 3-0	N14 2-1		J30 3-1	S30 1-0	a16 3-1	D26 3-0
21 SWINDON T	A26 3-1	A19 2-1	a17 0-1	O03 5-0	S19 3-0	N07 1-1	F13 1-1	S30 2-4	a03 2-1	O24 1-2	O10 2-1	M06 2-1	A22 7-1	a28 0-0	J02 0-0	S05 0-1	a16 1-0	D25 2-1	J23 0-1	J09 3-0		M20 6-1	S16 3-0	D05 2-2
22 TORQUAY U	M13 3-0	F20 2-0	A22 2-3	N14 4-0	O31 3-1	S26 1-1	M27 1-0	S05 3-2	F06 3-3	S02 1-1	S16 2-3	J30 2-2	a19 3-2	S12 1-1	F27 2-4	O17 2-2	D26 2-2	D12 2-0	a24 1-1	S23 1-1	N28 2-1		a10 3-1	J02 2-2
23 WALSALL	J30 0-2	N07 1-0	D25 3-1	A27 0-0	F13 2-3	a03 1-0	O03 1-0	A22 1-1	a29 1-1	A19 0-2	M06 4-2	O24 0-2	J02 0-1	M20 0-1	S05 1-4	J23 2-0	O10 1-3	O01 0-0	S19 1-0	a19 2-0	S10 0-1	D05 1-3		a17 0-0
24 WATFORD	N28 6-1	S26 2-3	S29 1-1	M13 2-0	M27 3-0	F06 1-0	N14 4-1	a16 0-2	S12 6-1	M03 1-0	a30 3-1	S01 2-1	F27 1-0	J16 1-1	O17 1-3	a24 0-2	S15 3-0	D19 3-1	O31 2-0	D25 2-2	a10 2-1	A29 3-1	F24 3-1	

LEAGUE TABLES

DIVISION 1

	P	W	D	L	F	A	W	D	L	F	A	Pts
Wolves	42	16	1	4	61	25	9	6	6	35	31	57
WBA	42	13	5	3	51	24	9	4	8	35	39	53
Huddersfield T	42	13	6	2	45	24	7	5	9	33	37	51
Manchester U	52	11	6	4	41	27	7	6	8	32	31	48
Bolton W	42	14	6	1	45	20	4	6	11	30	40	48
Blackpool	42	13	6	2	43	19	6	4	11	37	50	48
Burnley	42	16	2	3	51	23	5	2	14	27	44	46
Chelsea	42	12	3	6	45	26	4	9	8	29	42	44
Charlton A	42	14	4	3	51	26	5	2	14	24	51	44
Cardiff C	42	12	4	5	32	27	6	4	11	19	44	44
Preston NE	42	12	2	7	43	24	7	3	11	44	34	43
Arsenal	42	8	8	5	42	37	7	5	9	33	36	43
Aston Villa	42	12	5	4	50	28	4	4	13	20	40	41
Portsmouth	42	13	5	3	53	31	1	6	14	28	58	39
Newcastle U	42	9	2	10	43	40	5	8	8	29	37	38
Tottenham H	42	11	3	7	38	33	5	2	14	27	43	37
Manchester C	42	10	4	7	35	31	4	5	12	27	46	37
Sunderland	42	11	4	6	50	37	3	4	14	31	52	36
Sheffield W	42	12	4	5	43	30	3	2	16	27	61	36
Sheffield U	42	9	5	7	43	38	2	6	13	26	52	33
Middlesbrough	42	6	6	9	29	35	4	4	13	31	56	30
Liverpool	42	7	8	6	49	38	2	2	17	19	59	28

DIVISION 2

	P	W	D	L	F	A	W	D	L	F	A	Pts
Leicester C	42	15	4	2	63	23	8	6	7	34	37	56
Everton	42	13	6	2	55	27	7	10	4	37	31	56
Blackburn R	42	15	4	2	54	16	8	6	8	32	34	55
Nottingham F	42	15	5	1	61	27	5	7	9	25	32	52
Rotherham U	42	13	4	4	51	26	8	3	10	29	41	49
Luton T	42	11	7	3	36	23	7	5	9	28	36	48
Birmingham C	42	12	6	3	49	18	6	5	10	29	40	47
Fulham	42	12	3	6	62	39	5	7	9	36	46	44
Bristol R	42	10	7	4	32	19	4	9	8	32	39	44
Leeds U	42	12	5	4	56	30	3	8	10	33	51	43
Stoke C	42	8	8	5	43	28	4	9	8	28	32	41
Doncaster R	42	9	5	7	32	28	7	4	10	27	35	41
West Ham U	42	11	6	4	44	20	4	3	14	23	49	39
Notts Co	42	8	6	7	26	29	5	7	9	28	45	39
Hull C	42	14	1	6	47	22	2	5	14	17	44	38
Lincoln C	42	11	6	4	46	23	3	3	15	19	60	37
Bury	42	9	7	5	39	32	2	7	12	15	40	36
Derby Co	42	9	5	7	38	35	3	6	12	26	47	35
Plymouth A	42	6	12	3	38	31	3	4	14	27	51	34
Swansea T	42	11	5	5	34	25	2	3	16	24	57	34
Brentford	42	9	5	7	25	26	1	6	14	15	52	31
Oldham A	42	6	7	8	26	31	2	2	17	14	58	25

DIVISION 3 North

	P	W	D	L	F	A	W	D	L	F	A	Pts
Port Vale	46	16	7	0	48	5	10	10	3	26	16	69
Barnsley	46	16	3	4	54	24	8	7	8	23	33	58
Scunthorpe U	46	14	7	2	49	24	7	8	8	28	32	57
Gateshead	46	15	4	4	49	22	6	9	8	25	33	55
Bradford C	46	15	6	2	40	14	7	3	13	20	41	53
Chesterfield	46	13	6	4	41	19	6	8	9	35	45	52
Mansfield T	46	15	5	3	59	22	5	6	12	29	45	51
Wrexham	46	16	4	3	59	19	5	5	13	22	49	51
Bradford	46	13	6	4	57	31	5	8	10	20	37	50
Stockport Co	46	14	6	3	57	20	4	5	14	20	47	47
Southport	46	12	5	6	41	26	5	7	11	22	34	46
Barrow	46	12	7	4	46	26	4	5	14	26	45	44
Carlisle U	46	10	8	5	53	27	4	7	12	30	44	43
Tranmere R	46	11	4	8	40	34	7	3	13	19	36	43
Accrington S	46	12	7	4	41	22	4	3	16	25	62	42
Crewe A	46	9	8	6	30	26	5	5	13	19	41	41
Grimsby T	46	14	5	4	31	15	2	4	17	20	62	41
Hartlepools U	46	10	8	5	40	21	3	6	14	19	44	40
Rochdale	46	12	5	6	40	20	3	5	15	19	57	40
Workington	46	10	9	4	36	22	3	5	15	23	58	40
Darlington	46	11	3	9	31	27	1	11	11	19	44	38
York C	46	8	7	8	39	32	4	6	13	25	54	37
Halifax T	46	9	6	8	26	21	3	4	16	18	52	34
Chester	46	10	7	6	39	22	1	3	19	9	45	32

DIVISION 3 South

	P	W	D	L	F	A	W	D	L	F	A	Pts
Ipswich T	46	15	5	3	47	19	12	5	6	35	32	64
Brighton & HA	46	17	3	3	57	31	9	6	8	29	30	61
Bristol C	46	18	3	2	59	18	7	3	13	29	48	56
Watford	46	16	3	4	52	23	5	7	11	33	46	52
Northampton T	46	18	4	1	63	18	2	7	14	19	37	51
Southampton	46	17	5	1	51	22	5	2	16	25	41	51
Norwich C	46	13	5	5	43	28	7	6	10	30	38	51
Reading	46	14	3	6	57	33	6	6	11	29	40	49
Exeter C	46	12	2	9	39	22	8	6	9	29	36	48
Gillingham	46	14	3	6	37	22	5	7	11	24	44	48
Leyton O	46	14	5	4	48	26	4	6	13	31	47	47
Millwall	46	15	3	5	44	24	4	6	13	30	53	47
Torquay U	46	10	10	3	48	33	7	2	14	33	55	46
Coventry C	46	14	5	4	36	15	4	4	15	25	41	45
Newport Co	46	14	4	5	42	28	5	2	16	19	53	44
Southend U	40	15	2	6	46	22	3	5	15	23	49	43
Aldershot	46	11	5	7	45	31	6	4	13	29	55	43
QPR	46	10	5	8	32	25	6	5	12	28	43	42
Bournemouth	46	12	5	6	47	27	4	3	16	20	43	40*
Swindon T	46	13	5	5	48	21	2	5	16	19	49	40*
Shrewsbury T	46	12	8	3	48	34	2	4	17	17	42	40
Crystal P	46	11	7	5	41	30	3	5	15	19	56	40
Colchester U	46	7	7	9	35	29	3	3	17	15	49	30
Walsall	46	8	5	10	22	27	1	3	19	18	60	26

Football League Records

Top scorers: Div 1, R.Allen (West Bromwich Albion) 27 goals; Div 2, T.Briggs (Blackburn Rovers) 33 goals; Div 3(N), D.Travis (Oldham Athletic), J.Connor (Stockport County), A.Bottom (York City) 30 goals; Div 3(S), E.Morgan (Gillingham) 31 goals.

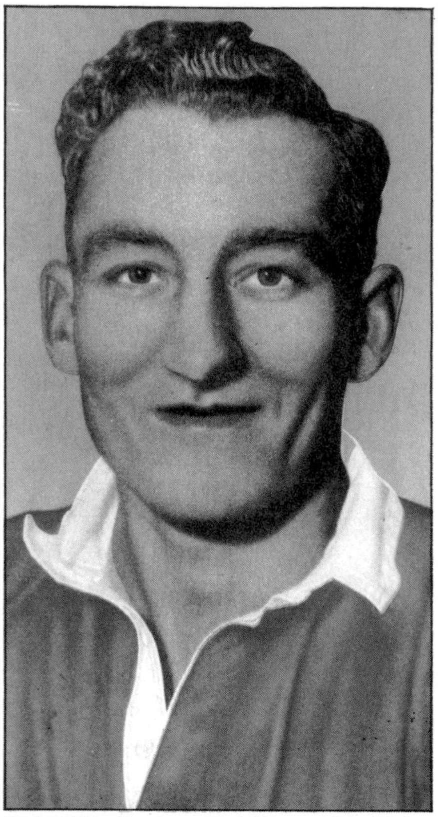

Forward Roy Bentley, one of the stars of the Chelsea side which lifted the First Division title for the first time in 1954-5.

DIVISION 1

	ARSENAL	ASTON VILLA	BLACKPOOL	BOLTON W	BURNLEY	CARDIFF C	CHARLTON A	CHELSEA	EVERTON	HUDDERSFIELD T	LEICESTER C	MANCHESTER C	MANCHESTER U	NEWCASTLE U	PORTSMOUTH	PRESTON N.E.	SHEFFIELD U	SHEFFIELD W	SUNDERLAND	TOTTENHAM H	W.B.A.	WOLVERHAMPTON W
1 ARSENAL		M12 2-0	a09 3-0	M26 3-0	S25 4-0	a08 2-0	D11 3-1	D25 1-0	A31 2-0	N13 3-5	F19 1-1	S14 2-3	a23 2-3	A21 1-3	O16 0-1	F05 2-0	S11 4-0	F26 3-2	O30 1-3	S04 2-0	J01 2-2	N27 1-1
2 ASTON VILLA	O23 2-1		J22 3-1	F12 3-0	a02 3-1	D04 0-2	S18 1-2	M05 3-2	O09 0-2	O02 0-0	N06 2-5	a30 2-0	D28 2-1	S13 1-2	S04 1-0	N20 1-3	a16 3-1	J01 0-0	A23 2-2	A21 2-4	M19 3-0	a12 4-2
3 BLACKPOOL	D04 2-2	S11 0-1		A23 2-3	a11 1-0	a16 0-0	S20 1-1	O23 1-0	a02 4-0	D18 1-1	M19 2-0	N20 1-3	A28 2-4	N06 2-0	D25 2-2	O09 1-2	a30 1-2	F19 2-1	F05 0-0	S25 5-1	M05 3-1	J15 0-2
4 BOLTON W	N06 2-2	S25 3-3	S01 3-0		a30 0-1	M19 0-0	A21 3-2	J01 2-5	a16 2-0	a27 1-0	O09 4-1	O23 2-2	S11 1-1	N20 2-1	S06 3-1	M09 2-1	M05 1-0	a08 2-2	M02 3-0	D25 1-2	a02 2-4	F05 6-1
5 BURNLEY	F12 3-0	N13 2-0	a08 0-1	O16 2-0		A21 1-0	F26 3-0	A31 1-1	S04 0-2	a09 1-1	S06 3-1	J01 2-0	D11 2-4	J22 0-1	O30 1-0	D25 2-2	O02 2-1	M12 2-0	a23 0-1	N27 1-2	S18 0-2	M26 1-0
6 CARDIFF C	a11 1-2	a09 0-1	N27 1-2	O30 2-2	D18 0-3		M12 4-3	M23 0-1	F12 4-3	S11 1-1	A28 2-1	S18 3-0	F26 3-0	O02 4-2	a23 1-1	A25 2-5	S08 1-1	N13 5-3	D11 0-1	M26 1-2	D25 3-2	a30 3-2
7 CHARLTON A	M05 1-1	F05 6-1	S16 3-3	D18 2-0	O09 3-1	O23 4-1		M19 0-2	N20 5-0	A28 2-1	A26 2-3	a16 1-1	a26 1-1	a02 1-1	a11 2-2	a30 0-4	D04 3-1	D25 3-0	S25 1-3	m05 1-2	N06 1-3	S11 1-3
8 CHELSEA	D27 1-1	D11 4-0	M12 0-0	A28 3-2	A23 1-0	S04 1-1	O30 1-2		S18 0-2	F26 4-1	D18 3-1	J22 0-2	O16 5-6	F12 4-3	N27 4-1	S06 0-1	a08 1-1	a23 3-0	M29 2-1	N13 2-1	O02 3-3	a09 1-0
9 EVERTON	A25 1-0	m04 0-1	N13 0-1	N27 0-0	J15 1-1	S25 1-1	a23 2-2	F05 1-1		M23 4-0	S11 2-2	F23 1-0	O30 4-2	a08 1-2	M26 2-3	A28 1-0	D18 2-3	D11 3-1	O16 1-0	a09 1-0	S08 1-2	D27 3-2
10 HUDDERSFIELD T	a02 0-1	F23 1-2	A21 1-3	S04 2-0	D04 0-1	m02 2-0	J01 0-0	O09 1-0	O23 2-1		a30 3-1	M19 0-0	F05 1-3	a16 2-0	A30 2-1	M05 0-4	N06 1-2	S13 3-0	D27 1-1	a12 1-0	N20 3-3	S25 2-0
11 LEICESTER C	O02 3-3	M26 4-2	O30 2-2	m04 4-0	S13 2-2	J01 2-1	A30 0-1	A21 1-1	a20 2-2	O16 1-3		S04 0-2	a09 1-0	S18 3-2	M12 4-0	a11 0-1	D27 0-1	N27 4-3	N13 1-1	a23 2-0	F12 6-3	D11 1-2
12 MANCHESTER C	S08 2-1	O16 2-4	a23 1-6	M16 4-2	A28 0-0	F05 4-1	N27 1-5	S11 1-1	O02 1-0	O30 2-4	J15 2-2		S25 3-2	D25 3-1	N13 1-2	D18 3-1	A25 5-2	M30 2-2	a09 1-0	D11 0-0	a08 4-0	a20 3-0
13 MANCHESTER U	N20 2-1	D27 0-1	J01 4-1	J22 1-1	M05 1-0	O09 5-2	S04 3-1	a30 2-1	M19 1-2	S18 1-1	D04 3-1	F12 0-5		O23 2-2	A21 1-3	N06 2-1	a02 5-0	S01 2-0	a11 2-2	S15 2-1	a16 3-0	F23 2-4
14 NEWCASTLE U	D18 5-1	S08 5-3	a25 1-1	a23 0-0	S11 2-1	a27 3-0	N13 3-1	S25 1-3	a11 4-0	N27 2-2	F05 2-0	D27 2-0	a18 2-0		D11 2-1	a20 3-3	A28 1-2	a09 5-0	F26 1-2	O16 4-4	A25 3-0	O30 2-3
15 PORTSMOUTH	a30 2-1	a27 2-2	D27 3-0	S15 1-0	M19 0-2	N20 1-3	a08 2-0	a16 0-0	N06 5-0	A25 4-2	O23 2-1	a02 1-0	D18 0-0	M05 3-1		F19 2-0	O09 6-2	S25 2-1	S11 2-2	F05 0-3	D04 6-1	A28 0-0
16 PRESTON N.E.	S18 3-1	a23 0-3	F26 3-1	a09 2-2	D27 0-1	S01 7-1	O16 1-2	S15 1-2	J01 0-0	D11 2-3	a08 2-4	A21 5-0	M26 0-2	S04 3-3	O02 1-1		F12 1-2	O30 6-0	N27 3-1	M12 1-0	J22 3-1	N13 3-3
17 SHEFFIELD U	a18 1-1	N27 1-3	O16 2-1	D11 2-0	F19 1-0	S13 1-3	a09 5-0	S20 1-2	A21 2-5	M26 2-2	D25 1-1	A30 0-2	N13 3-0	J01 6-2	m02 5-2	S25 0-5		S18 1-0	M14 1-0	O30 4-1	S04 1-2	a23 1-2
18 SHEFFIELD W	O09 1-2	A28 6-3	O02 2-1	a11 3-2	O23 1-1	a02 1-1	D27 2-2	N20 1-1	M05 2-2	S06 4-1	a16 1-0	N06 2-4	A23 2-4	D04 0-3	F12 1-3	M19 2-0	F05 1-2		J15 1-2	S11 2-2	a30 5-0	D18 2-2
19 SUNDERLAND	M19 0-1	S01 0-0	S18 2-0	O02 1-1	N20 2-2	M05 1-1	F12 1-2	N06 3-3	a30 3-0	D25 1-1	a02 1-1	D04 3-2	a08 4-3	O09 4-2	J22 2-2	a16 2-1	O23 2-2	S04 2-0		J01 1-1	A21 4-2	S15 0-0
20 TOTTENHAM H	J15 0-1	D18 1-1	F12 3-2	D27 2-0	a16 0-3	N06 0-2	O02 1-4	a02 2-4	D04 1-3	a11 1-1	N20 5-1	M05 2-2	S08 0-2	a30 2-1	S18 1-1	O23 3-1	M19 5-0	J22 7-2	A28 0-1		O09 3-1	A25 3-2
21 W.B.A.	A28 3-1	O30 2-3	D11 0-1	N13 0-0	F05 2-2	D27 1-0	M26 2-1	M09 2-4	S15 3-3	a23 2-1	S25 6-4	a11 2-1	N27 2-0	S01 4-2	a09 3-1	S11 2-0	M12 3-3	O16 1-2	D18 2-2	a27 1-2		M16 1-0
22 WOLVERHAMPTON W	a16 3-1	a11 1-0	S04 1-0	S18 1-2	N06 5-0	O16 1-1	J22 2-1	D04 3-4	D25 1-3	F12 6-4	M05 5-0	O09 2-2	O02 4-2	M19 2-2	J01 2-2	a02 1-1	N20 4-1	A21 4-2	S08 2-0	A30 4-2	O23 4-0	

Birmingham City's Peter Murphy, whose goals helped the St Andrew's club back to Division One.

DIVISION 2

	BIRMINGHAM C	BLACKBURN R	BRISTOL R	BURY	DERBY CO	DONCASTER R	FULHAM	HULL C	IPSWICH T	LEEDS U	LINCOLN C	LIVERPOOL	LUTON T	MIDDLESBROUGH	NOTTINGHAM F	NOTTS CO	PLYMOUTH A	PORT VALE	ROTHERHAM U	STOKE C	SWANSEA T	WEST HAM U
1 BIRMINGHAM C		N13 3-1	A25 2-1	S25 1-3	O30 1-1	M16 4-1	M30 3-2	S11 0-0	S08 4-0	M02 2-0	F05 3-3	D11 9-1	a20 2-1	a11 3-0	D25 0-1	a23 1-1	a09 3-1	N27 7-2	A28 3-1	D18 2-0	O16 2-0	M26 1-2
2 BLACKBURN R	a02 3-3		F05 8-3	a30 1-1	S13 5-2	D27 7-2	D18 3-1	N20 4-0	O09 4-1	D04 1-2	a08 1-0	S11 4-3	a16 0-0	N06 9-0	M05 0-1	J15 4-5	S25 2-2	F19 2-1	O23 4-1	M19 2-0	A28 4-1	A23 5-2
3 BRISTOL R	A30 1-1	S18 2-1		M19 2-1	S04 4-1	J01 1-0	F12 4-1	a02 1-0	N20 4-0	O23 5-1	N06 2-2	S06 3-0	O09 3-2	a30 2-2	a16 2-1	D27 1-4	a08 3-1	A21 1-0	M05 1-0	D04 1-1	O02 7-0	J22 2-4
4 BURY	F12 0-1	D11 2-1	O30 3-1		O16 2-2	F26 1-4	A28 1-3	a08 4-1	S18 2-1	S04 5-3	D18 3-1	M12 3-4	A24 2-1	O02 0-1	a20 1-1	N27 1-2	M26 3-1	N13 2-2	S20 2-2	D27 1-1	a09 2-1	a23 4-1
5 DERBY CO	M19 0-0	S08 0-3	F19 1-1	M05 2-3		S25 5-0	A25 3-4	a30 3-0	N06 2-0	O09 2-4	D04 3-0	A28 3-2	M02 0-0	O23 1-2	a02 1-2	D18 1-1	S11 2-2	F05 6-1	N20 2-3	a16 1-2	a08 1-4	D27 0-0
6 DONCASTER R	m04 1-5	D25 1-3	A28 2-2	O09 1-0	F12 2-0		S15 4-0	D04 2-2	M19 1-1	a02 0-1	M05 1-1	D18 4-1	a30 0-3	a16 3-1	N06 0-3	a08 4-2	J15 3-2	S27 1-0	F05 0-4	a20 1-1	A25 2-1	O02 2-1
7 FULHAM	O09 2-1	A21 5-1	S25 2-3	J01 0-0	S01 2-0	S08 5-2		a16 0-1	M05 4-1	a30 1-3	N20 3-2	F05 1-2	O23 3-1	a02 1-2	D04 1-1	S11 3-1	F19 2-3	D25 3-1	M19 1-1	N06 2-2	a20 5-1	a11 0-0
8 HULL C	a25 0-3	a09 1-4	N13 0-1	a11 1-0	D11 1-1	a23 1-1	N27 0-0		S04 4-2	A21 0-2	A30 4-0	M26 2-2	D27 0-4	S18 1-0	J01 2-3	O30 5-2	F26 0-2	O16 2-1	O02 1-2	F12 1-1	M12 4-3	S13 0-1
9 IPSWICH T	S15 1-2	F26 1-1	a09 1-0	F05 2-3	M26 2-1	O30 5-1	O16 2-4	a18 2-0		S25 1-2	S11 1-2	D27 2-0	A28 3-1	S01 6-1	M09 2-1	D11 0-1	N27 2-1	M12 1-0	D18 2-2	S22 0-1	a23 1-1	N13 0-3
10 LEEDS U	O02 1-0	a23 2-0	M12 2-0	J15 1-0	F26 1-0	N13 1-0	D11 1-1	D18 3-0	F12 4-1		A28 2-3	N27 2-2	a11 4-0	D25 1-1	S18 1-1	a09 2-0	O30 3-2	M26 3-0	A25 2-4	S08 0-1	S11 5-2	O16 2-1
11 LINCOLN C	S18 1-1	a11 2-1	M26 0-2	A21 3-2	a23 3-0	O16 5-1	a09 2-2	A25 0-1	a27 1-1	J01 2-0		O30 3-3	S08 1-2	F12 3-3	S04 2-1	M16 1-2	N13 3-2	m04 0-1	D27 2-3	O02 1-4	N27 2-2	D11 2-1
12 LIVERPOOL	a30 2-2	J22 4-1	S15 5-3	O23 1-1	J01 2-0	A21 3-2	S18 4-1	N06 2-1	D25 6-2	a16 2-2	M19 2-4		a02 4-4	D04 3-1	N20 1-0	O02 3-1	S01 3-3	a11 1-1	O09 3-1	M05 2-4	F12 1-1	S04 1-2
13 LUTON T	S04 1-0	N27 7-3	a27 2-0	S01 3-2	O02 2-0	D11 3-0	M12 3-0	D25 1-1	J01 3-2	a08 0-0	S15 2-1	N13 3-2		J22 2-0	A21 3-0	M26 3-1	O16 3-1	a23 4-2	F12 4-0	S18 3-1	O30 1-2	a09 2-0
14 MIDDLESBROUGH	a08 2-5	M26 4-3	D11 1-0	a27 1-1	M12 3-1	N27 3-1	N13 4-2	F05 1-2	A25 0-1	D27 1-0	S25 2-1	a23 1-2	S11 0-2		S08 1-4	O16 2-0	D18 4-1	a09 2-0	J15 5-1	A28 1-2	F26 4-2	O30 6-0
15 NOTTINGHAM F	D27 0-2	O16 1-2	N27 1-0	S11 2-3	N13 3-0	M26 3-1	a23 2-0	A28 0-1	O02 2-0	F05 1-1	J15 1-1	a09 3-1	D18 1-5	S15 4-2		S25 0-1	M12 2-0	O30 2-3	a08 0-2	A25 0-3	D11 0-0	m02 1-1
16 NOTTS CO	D04 3-2	S04 3-1	D25 2-0	a16 2-1	A21 2-3	a11 4-0	a27 0-0	M19 3-1	a30 2-1	N20 1-2	O23 2-1	M03 0-3	N06 3-3	M05 1-3	F12 4-1		S09 2-0	S02 1-1	a02 3-2	O09 1-0	S18 2-1	J01 5-1
17 PLYMOUTH A	N20 1-0	F12 0-2	a11 0-1	N06 2-4	J22 1-0	S04 1-2	O02 3-2	O09 1-2	a16 2-0	M19 3-1	a02 1-0	A23 1-0	M05 2-1	A21 2-2	O23 1-2	S15 1-3		J01 0-0	D04 2-1	a30 2-0	D25 2-2	S18 1-1
18 PORT VALE	a16 2-0	O02 0-3	D18 1-0	a02 1-0	S18 3-0	J22 1-1	D27 4-0	M05 3-0	O23 3-3	N06 0-1	O09 1-3	a08 4-3	D04 1-1	N20 1-1	M19 1-2	A23 1-1	A28 1-0		a30 1-0	a25 0-1	S06 1-0	F12 1-1
19 ROTHERHAM U	J01 0-2	M12 5-1	O16 6-2	S06 4-2	a09 2-1	S18 2-3	O30 2-3	F19 2-0	A21 3-2	A30 3-0	D25 3-0	m02 6-1	S25 2-0	S04 3-0	a11 3-2	N13 2-0	a23 2-0	D11 3-0		a18 2-1	a25 2-0	N27 2-2
20 STOKE C	A21 2-1	O30 1-1	a23 2-0	D25 3-2	N27 3-1	a09 3-0	M26 1-1	S25 0-0	a11 3-0	S13 0-1	F19 4-2	O16 2-0	F05 0-0	J01 1-2	A30 2-0	M28 3-0	D11 3-1	S04 0-0	S11 1-2		N13 4-1	M12 0-2
21 SWANSEA T	M05 0-3	J01 2-3	M31 1-1	N20 1-1	a11 3-0	S02 3-0	S04 2-2	O23 1-0	D04 6-1	J22 2-0	a16 3-1	S25 3-2	M19 2-1	O09 2-0	a30 3-2	F05 3-0	D27 4-2	S16 7-1	N06 2-1	a02 3-5		A21 5-2
22 WEST HAM U	N06 2-2	A30 2-5	S11 5-2	D04 3-3	D25 1-0	F24 0-1	a08 2-1	S06 1-1	a02 4-0	M05 2-1	a30 0-1	a26 0-3	N20 2-1	M19 2-1	O09 2-0	A28 3-0	F05 6-1	S25 2-0	a16 1-2	O23 3-0	D18 3-3	

Season 1954-55

DIVISION 3 NORTH

	ACCRINGTON S	BARNSLEY	BARROW	BRADFORD	BRADFORD C	CARLISLE U	CHESTER	CHESTERFIELD	CREWE A	DARLINGTON	GATESHEAD	GRIMSBY T	HALIFAX T	HARTLEPOOLS U	MANSFIELD T	OLDHAM A	ROCHDALE	SCUNTHORPE U	SOUTHPORT	STOCKPORT CO	TRANMERE R	WORKINGTON	WREXHAM	YORK C
1 ACCRINGTON S		S27 2-3	J01 6-3	M12 4-3	J29 1-0	S01 3-2	F26 3-0	J03 4-1	S18 1-0	a23 3-0	N27 6-2	O16 3-0	D27 3-1	a09 2-5	J22 3-2	S08 4-0	O30 5-4	F19 2-1	A21 1-1	N13 0-1	M26 3-1	S04 2-0	S25 2-0	a11 2-2
2 BARNSLEY	S22 1-2		S18 3-0	S01 2-1	a11 1-0	a23 3-1	m04 4-2	a09 3-0	N27 3-1	N13 4-1	M26 3-0	D27 1-3	J01 3-0	O30 0-0	O02 1-0	A21 2-2	m03 2-0	S15 1-0	a27 0-0	M12 2-0	O16 4-1	F12 3-1	J08 4-2	S04 1-0
3 BARROW	A28 1-2	F05 3-1		N13 3-1	S25 3-2	M12 2-1	O30 2-0	a21 2-0	O16 0-3	A23 1-1	D27 0-1	M26 2-0	S20 1-3	a18 0-2	D18 2-2	F19 3-1	a09 4-2	S11 1-3	S13 2-1	a23 2-0	N27 1-0	a08 2-2	J15 1-1	m05 1-5
4 BRADFORD	O23 3-2	A23 1-0	a02 3-0		D18 2-0	S06 0-2	D27 3-0	S20 1-3	J29 2-1	F19 1-1	S25 2-2	a11 2-1	D04 0-1	F05 1-0	M19 0-0	a30 0-2	A28 1-1	O09 0-0	a25 1-0	S11 2-1	M30 0-0	N06 3-1	M05 0-0	a16 1-3
5 BRADFORD C	m04 0-3	a12 0-2	F12 2-1	A21 1-1		N27 2-0	a23 0-0	N13 1-1	a09 2-0	M26 3-0	O30 1-1	a20 4-0	S04 2-0	M12 0-1	S22 1-0	J01 0-1	S01 1-0	D25 2-4	S18 0-1	O16 2-3	m02 2-1	O02 0-1	S15 2-2	a04 2-3
6 CARLISLE U	A24 1-0	D04 2-4	O23 4-0	S14 3-2	a16 1-0		S21 1-2	F05 1-2	S25 4-0	S11 0-1	m03 1-2	J29 3-1	a02 4-0	A28 3-2	O09 1-2	a26 5-2	D25 7-2	a30 1-2	M19 2-1	D18 3-3	a08 1-2	M05 0-4	F19 1-0	N06 4-5
7 CHESTER	O09 1-1	a30 0-2	M19 3-1	D25 2-0	D04 1-0	S29 1-2		S25 1-0	F19 3-1	F05 0-2	S11 1-2	S15 1-0	D11 1-3	J15 1-0	M05 1-0	a16 0-0	a08 1-2	J08 2-4	a20 0-0	A28 1-0	D18 0-1	O23 0-2	A25 1-0	a02 1-2
8 CHESTERFIELD	a30 6-1	a25 3-1	O09 4-1	S27 1-3	a02 2-1	S18 2-1	F12 5-3		a13 0-0	A28 2-0	D18 1-3	O02 1-0	M19 2-1	a08 3-0	M30 4-1	N06 1-3	m02 3-1	a16 2-0	M05 2-1	D27 3-7	S06 2-1	A30 2-0	D04 3-1	O23 0-3
9 CREWE A	F05 0-3	a16 1-2	M05 5-1	J08 2-1	a27 1-0	F12 4-1	O02 1-3	S11 2-2		M30 2-2	A28 1-1	S27 2-0	N06 0-0	D18 1-1	A25 2-1	a02 4-1	S15 2-2	D04 1-1	O23 2-3	a08 4-4	D27 3-0	O09 1-1	a30 2-2	M19 2-3
10 DARLINGTON	D04 3-3	a02 0-1	S01 3-2	O02 3-0	N06 4-0	a20 1-1	S18 4-1	J01 0-2	S04 2-1		a11 5-1	F12 1-3	O23 1-0	D27 0-1	a30 3-1	M19 0-2	S29 2-2	a27 1-1	O09 2-0	S15 0-0	J29 2-2	A21 1-2	a16 2-2	M05 1-0
11 GATESHEAD	a16 1-1	N06 0-4	D25 3-1	M09 3-2	M19 2-1	S04 0-0	M30 0-0	A21 1-3	J01 1-0	a08 1-1		S18 1-0	M05 4-0	S06 3-0	D04 4-0	O23 2-2	O02 0-1	a02 0-1	A30 1-0	M23 4-4	S27 3-1	a30 3-2	a25 0-1	O09 1-1
12 GRIMSBY T	M05 2-1	D25 1-3	N06 1-0	a08 1-0	a30 1-4	M08 2-0	S08 3-1	F19 1-2	S22 2-1	S25 0-2	F05 1-1		a16 0-1	S11 1-0	O23 3-2	D04 1-1	D18 1-1	A24 1-4	a02 0-1	J15 1-0	A28 2-2	M19 0-1	O09 1-3	a27 2-1
13 HALIFAX T	D25 1-1	A28 1-1	S29 1-2	a23 0-0	a18 0-0	N13 5-3	a09 3-1	O30 2-0	M26 3-3	M12 4-1	O16 4-0	N27 3-2		M28 1-0	S08 1-2	S11 0-0	M16 1-2	D18 3-1	O02 0-1	A25 1-2	S18 0-0	J29 2-2	a11 2-0	F12 3-3
14 HARTLEPOOLS U	a25 1-3	M19 0-3	a30 0-0	S18 0-1	O23 0-0	J01 1-0	S04 3-1	a11 2-0	A21 2-1	D25 1-0	S13 0-0	M23 3-2	O09 1-0		a16 1-2	M05 2-0	F12 3-1	N06 4-2	M30 2-1	S27 2-1	O02 4-0	D04 3-2	a02 3-0	A30 1-0
15 MANSFIELD T	S11 2-2	F19 1-1	A21 0-6	O30 2-1	S27 1-0	F26 1-1	O16 2-1	S04 2-0	A30 4-2	a18 3-1	a23 0-1	M12 3-0	S13 2-1	N27 0-2		J29 1-3	M26 3-2	S25 2-1	a11 3-0	a09 0-0	N13 3-1	J01 2-0	F05 2-1	D27 1-2
16 OLDHAM A	S13 0-1	D18 4-1	O02 3-2	a18 5-0	A28 1-1	a09 2-1	N27 2-1	M26 4-1	N13 4-0	O30 3-1	M12 1-2	a23 4-0	m02 1-2	O16 0-1	J08 1-1		S04 0-0	a08 1-1	F12 1-0	F26 1-1	A24 2-1	S21 2-1	D25 2-1	S18 3-2
17 ROCHDALE	M19 0-0	O09 3-0	a27 4-1	J01 3-2	A25 1-2	D27 1-2	a11 2-0	J29 0-0	S08 1-1	S22 2-2	F19 4-0	A21 0-3	a30 2-2	S25 2-1	N06 2-0	a20 2-1		M05 2-0	a16 0-0	F05 1-0	S11 2-0	a02 2-1	O23 2-1	D04 1-1
18 SCUNTHORPE U	O02 4-0	[illegible] 1-0	J22 3-0	m05 1-1	D27 1-0	a10 1-1	J29 1-1	N27 2-1	a23 3-1	a09 1-0	N13 0-2	S02 1-0	A21 2-2	M26 5-1	F12 2-0	a11 6-1	O16 2-2		S04 2-0	O30 3-0	M12 1-2	S18 1-1	S30 1-0	J01 1-2
19 SOUTHPORT	D18 1-1	S11 0-2	S07 2-1	a09 1-0	F05 1-0	O30 4-1	M26 1-1	O16 0-0	M12 1-0	F26 0-0	A24 1-2	N13 2-2	F19 4-0	m02 1-0	a08 1-0	S25 1-0	N27 1-0	m07 1-1		D11 1-1	a23 0-0	D27 1-2	A28 1-2	S28 2-2
20 STOCKPORT CO	a02 0-0	O23 1-0	D04 1-2	J22 6-0	M05 1-1	A21 5-2	J01 3-0	D25 3-2	a11 6-1	S06 3-0	J29 2-1	S04 0-0	A30 2-1	S20 0-2	a25 2-2	O09 3-2	S18 1-4	M19 4-2	a30 0-2		F12 2-0	a16 0-1	N06 4-0	F21 1-2
21 TRANMERE R	N06 3-1	M05 0-1	a16 0-4	S04 3-3	O09 2-0	a11 6-1	A21 1-1	S14 0-0	D25 1-2	M09 0-1	S21 1-2	J01 2-0	F05 1-2	F19 3-1	a02 2-1	A31 2-1	J22 3-1	O23 1-2	D04 2-2	S25 1-1		a26 1-1	M19 1-2	a30 1-0
22 WORKINGTON	J15 0-1	S25 1-0	a11 0-0	M26 1-3	F19 1-1	O16 1-0	M12 1-1	A25 2-3	F26 3-3	D18 6-1	a20 4-0	O30 2-2	m04 1-0	a23 0-1	A28 2-2	S29 3-0	N13 1-0	F05 1-1	D25 0-1	N27 4-1	a09 1-0		S11 2-1	S15 2-1
23 WREXHAM	F12 3-1	J29 3-0	S04 3-0	O16 1-0	S08 1-3	O02 1-1	S01 2-1	a23 0-2	a20 5-0	N27 2-2	a09 2-0	m04 5-0	a08 1-1	N13 1-4	S18 1-3	D27 2-1	M12 0-0	S22 0-1	J01 2-2	M26 1-4	O30 1-2	M30 1-1		A21 2-6
24 YORK C	a08 1-1	J15 1-3	m02 1-4	N27 1-2	S11 0-1	a13 2-1	N13 5-0	M16 3-2	O30 3-1	O16 3-1	F26 2-1	a09 0-0	S25 2-1	A23 1-0	D25 3-1	F05 2-1	a23 2-0	A28 2-3	S20 1-1	O02 4-0	a18 1-0	S06 0-0	D18 3-3	

DIVISION 3 SOUTH

	ALDERSHOT	BOURNEMOUTH	BRENTFORD	BRIGHTON & HA	BRISTOL C	COLCHESTER U	COVENTRY C	CRYSTAL P	EXETER C	GILLINGHAM	LEYTON O	MILLWALL	NEWPORT CO	NORTHAMPTON T	NORWICH C	Q.P.R.	READING	SHREWSBURY T	SOUTHAMPTON	SOUTHEND U	SWINDON T	TORQUAY U	WALSALL	WATFORD
1 ALDERSHOT		S01 1-1	N06 2-3	a30 2-2	M05 0-2	D25 2-2	a02 1-1	S18 3-0	a08 4-2	M19 0-2	D04 0-1	a16 3-0	S22 0-0	F12 3-4	D18 4-1	S15 2-0	S04 3-1	J08 2-0	a27 2-0	A28 1-0	J22 0-0	O23 2-1	O09 4-0	O02 3-0
2 BOURNEMOUTH	A25 4-0		M19 1-2	D04 1-1	a27 0-1	F05 2-0	D18 2-1	S22 4-1	S11 2-0	O23 1-2	M05 0-3	O09 0-1	J15 3-3	a11 0-1	S25 1-3	A28 2-2	a30 0-0	N06 3-1	a20 1-1	F19 2-1	S08 1-1	a16 0-2	a02 1-1	D25 1-1
3 BRENTFORD	M26 1-1	O30 1-3		J22 2-3	F12 2-2	O16 3-2	A28 2-3	a09 3-0	F26 1-0	S23 3-0	a08 2-0	D25 3-1	m02 1-0	N27 1-3	M12 1-0	S04 1-1	S16 2-2	A26 2-2	D18 0-3	m05 2-2	N13 4-2	S18 4-2	O02 0-2	a23 3-2
4 BRIGHTON & H.A.	m04 5-3	a23 1-1	S11 3-4		O02 0-1	F26 1-1	m07 2-0	N13 1-0	M23 5-3	a11 1-0	a20 1-0	D18 1-2	S18 4-1	a09 2-1	O16 0-1	O30 4-1	S22 3-2	S08 0-0	A28 1-2	M12 2-1	M26 3-1	F12 1-1	A25 3-0	N27 3-1
5 BRISTOL C	O16 6-1	a09 2-2	S25 2-1	F19 3-2		S14 4-0	F05 2-0	a19 3-0	O30 2-0	D18 1-4	A28 5-0	M09 5-1	a23 0-0	M26 5-1	J08 0-1	N27 1-1	D25 2-1	a11 4-1	S11 2-0	F26 3-2	M12 3-0	A31 1-1	S21 5-3	N13 1-0
6 COLCHESTER U	D27 1-1	S18 3-3	M05 3-2	O09 2-4	S09 0-2		O23 0-1	J01 2-0	S02 1-2	a28 2-2	a02 2-2	N06 0-2	O02 1-0	S04 4-1	S23 1-0	F12 1-0	a16 0-2	D04 2-4	a30 3-5	a08 2-0	A21 0-0	M31 0-2	M19 2-2	J22 1-3
7 COVENTRY C	N13 2-1	A21 1-0	J01 1-0	S04 2-1	S18 1-3	M12 0-0		N27 4-1	O16 1-1	S06 4-1	S20 2-2	a12 4-1	a04 3-2	a23 0-0	a18 4-0	m02 5-1	A23 2-1	O02 3-0	D25 1-1	m04 1-4	a09 1-0	J22 0-1	F12 5-3	O30 3-2
8 CRYSTAL P	F05 3-2	S29 2-1	a27 1-1	a02 1-0	a30 1-2	A28 0-0	a16 1-0		D18 1-1	J08 0-2	F19 1-1	M19 1-1	D25 2-1	S01 3-1	m04 2-0	a08 2-1	O09 1-1	M05 2-2	D04 1-2	S11 2-2	S25 0-0	N06 1-1	O23 3-1	S15 1-1
9 EXETER C	a11 0-1	J22 1-1	O09 3-2	J29 3-1	M19 0-1	A25 2-2	M05 0-0	A21 2-0		a02 1-1	N06 1-7	a30 1-4	F12 1-1	J01 3-1	S08 0-1	S18 2-1	a27 3-1	a16 1-0	O23 0-1	S29 2-1	D25 2-1	F19 1-2	D04 1-1	S04 0-0
10 GILLINGHAM	O30 0-2	M12 0-2	S29 2-1	a08 1-1	A21 1-1	a09 2-1	S15 2-1	J29 2-1	N13 1-1		S25 0-0	F19 1-1	M26 4-2	F26 2-2	N27 2-1	a20 3-1	J22 5-1	S04 3-3	A25 1-0	a23 1-1	S18 2-1	D27 3-1	J01 3-2	O16 0-1
11 LEYTON O	a23 1-5	O16 3-1	a11 0-1	D27 0-0	J01 4-1	N13 2-0	S30 1-0	O02 2-1	M26 5-0	F12 2-2		A26 1-0	M17 1-2	J29 2-1	a09 1-2	M12 3-0	S18 2-0	J22 5-0	[illegible] 4-1	N27 5-1	O30 1-0	A21 2-1	S04 1-0	F26 0-1
12 MILLWALL	N27 3-1	F26 1-1	D27 2-2	A21 2-0	S04 1-3	M26 5-2	a08 3-1	O30 5-2	m02 2-2	O02 3-2	A30 1-0		M12 1-1	S13 1-0	N13 0-0	O16 0-1	F12 2-2	S18 2-0	S20 2-0	a09 1-4	a23 1-0	J01 4-1	J22 1-0	J29 1-0
13 NEWPORT CO	S30 2-1	S04 1-1	a21 3-1	F05 1-3	D04 2-2	F19 0-0	O09 1-1	D27 0-1	S25 2-1	N06 1-3	a30 1-2	O23 2-1		A21 0-1	A26 1-1	J22 4-0	a02 3-1	a28 1-1	M05 0-1	S16 3-2	a08 2-2	M19 1-1	a16 1-0	J01 0-2
14 NORTHAMPTON T	S25 2-1	a12 5-0	a16 1-2	a27 1-0	N06 2-0	a18 6-1	D04 1-0	A26 1-1	A28 2-0	O09 4-1	J08 2-2	S09 0-1	D18 2-2		S11 1-1	D27 1-3	M05 2-6	O23 3-1	M19 2-1	F05 6-2	D11 1-0	a02 1-0	a30 1-1	S30 0-1
15 NORWICH C	A21 4-3	F12 0-1	O23 1-0	M05 0-0	J29 0-1	S29 0-2	a30 1-1	S04 2-0	S15 3-0	a16 1-2	a27 1-1	a02 2-1	S01 2-0	J22 3-2		O02 1-1	D04 0-1	M19 2-0	N06 2-0	D27 3-3	J01 2-1	O09 5-1	a11 2-1	S18 3-1
16 Q.P.R.	S07 5-0	J01 1-1	J15 1-1	M19 3-2	a16 1-1	S25 4-1	J29 3-2	a11 1-0	F05 1-2	a30 1-1	O23 2-0	M05 1-2	S11 2-0	D25 1-0	F19 2-1		N06 2-3	a02 2-0	O09 2-2	A30 1-1	S27 3-1	D04 4-2	a25 1-1	A21 2-1
17 READING	a20 2-2	M30 1-0	S08 0-0	S29 0-2	D27 0-2	N27 4-0	S01 2-2	F26 5-0	a09 0-0	S11 2-2	F05 0-2	S25 0-0	N13 2-1	O16 0-1	a23 1-1	M26 3-1		J01 1-2	F19 0-1	O30 1-1	J29 2-1	a11 3-2	A21 2-2	M12 1-1
18 SHREWSBURY T	J29 1-0	a25 3-0	A30 2-2	S13 3-0	D11 0-2	a23 2-0	F19 1-0	O16 1-1	N27 1-1	m02 1-1	S11 0-2	F05 3-2	a09 3-0	M12 4-0	O30 2-1	N13 1-0	A28 2-3		S25 3-1	D18 2-3	m06 7-0	S27 3-2	D27 2-2	a18 2-1
19 SOUTHAMPTON	a09 1-1	J29 0-0	A21 6-4	J01 3-2	J22 2-1	J08 0-1	D27 1-0	a23 2-2	M12 3-0	S01 3-1	S15 1-0	S29 3-0	O16 2-0	O30 4-0	M26 3-1	F26 2-2	O02 3-1	F12 2-1		N13 3-0	N27 1-1	S04 0-0	S18 2-1	a11 2-0
20 SOUTHEND U	J01 0-1	O02 2-2	a30 3-2	O23 4-0	O09 3-2	a11 4-2	N06 1-0	J22 3-2	S21 0-0	D04 3-1	a16 1-2	a26 1-0	S07 1-1	S18 4-1	D25 4-1	A24 2-2	M19 0-0	A21 4-1	a02 0-1		S04 4-1	M05 1-2	J29 2-1	F12 1-3
21 SWINDON T	S11 1-0	S15 0-2	a02 1-1	N06 0-2	O23 2-2	D18 1-1	a27 3-0	F12 0-0	D27 2-0	F05 2-1	M19 0-0	D04 1-1	a11 1-3	O02 0-1	A28 1-0	S22 2-0	m04 2-0	O09 2-1	a16 1-0	a20 0-1		a30 0-0	M05 2-2	S01 6-1
22 TORQUAY U	M12 2-2	N27 0-1	F05 4-2	S25 2-1	A25 2-2	m04 2-1	S11 1-2	M26 2-2	O02 1-0	D25 1-3	D18 2-7	A28 4-2	O30 2-3	N13 5-2	F26 2-0	a23 3-2	a25 3-1	S22 2-0	J15 2-2	O16 4-1	a06 1-1		S08 2-0	a09 2-2
23 WALSALL	M31 2-2	N13 6-1	F19 2-2	S02 0-2	S30 1-3	O30 3-1	S25 1-1	M12 1-4	a23 1-0	A28 0-1	m05 1-4	S11 1-1	N27 3-3	a04 6-1	a12 2-1	a09 4-1	D18 4-0	D25 4-0	F05 0-0	m02 4-1	O16 1-2	S16 2-4		M26 0-1
24 WATFORD	F19 0-0	D27 1-0	D04 2-2	a16 0-0	a02 0-2	S11 2-0	M19 1-0	S07 7-1	m06 1-1	M05 1-1	O09 1-3	M30 5-3	A28 3-2	S21 1-1	F05 2-2	D18 1-1	O23 1-3	a30 2-1	a08 2-1	S25 1-1	A24 3-0	a26 4-1	N06 4-0	

LEAGUE TABLES

DIVISION 1

	P	W	D	L	F	A	W	D	L	F	A	Pts
Chelsea	42	11	5	5	43	29	9	7	5	38	28	52
Wolves	42	13	5	3	58	30	6	5	10	31	40	48
Portsmouth	42	13	5	3	44	21	5	7	9	30	41	48
Sunderland	42	8	11	2	39	27	7	7	7	25	27	48
Manchester U	42	12	4	5	44	30	8	3	10	40	44	47
Aston Villa	42	11	3	7	38	31	9	4	8	34	42	47
Manchester C	42	11	5	5	45	36	7	5	9	31	33	46
Newcastle U	42	12	5	4	53	27	5	4	12	36	50	43
Arsenal	42	12	3	6	44	25	5	6	10	25	38	43
Burnley	42	11	3	7	29	19	6	6	9	22	29	43
Everton	42	9	6	6	32	24	7	4	10	30	44	42
Huddersfield T	42	10	4	7	28	23	4	9	8	35	45	41
Sheffield U	42	10	3	8	41	34	7	4	10	29	52	41
Preston NE	42	8	5	8	47	33	8	3	10	36	31	40
Charlton A	42	8	6	7	43	34	7	4	10	33	41	40
Tottenham H	42	9	4	8	42	35	7	4	10	30	38	40
WBA	42	11	5	5	44	33	5	3	13	32	63	40
Bolton W	42	11	6	4	45	29	2	7	12	17	40	39
Blackpool	42	8	6	7	33	26	6	4	11	27	38	38
Cardiff C	42	9	4	8	41	38	4	7	10	21	38	37
Leicester C	42	9	6	6	43	32	3	5	13	31	54	35
Sheffield W	42	7	7	7	42	38	1	3	17	21	62	26

DIVISION 2

	P	W	D	L	F	A	W	D	L	F	A	Pts
Birmingham C	42	14	4	3	56	22	8	6	7	36	25	54
Luton T	42	18	2	1	55	18	5	6	10	33	35	54
Rotherham U	42	17	1	3	59	22	8	3	10	35	42	54
Leeds U	42	14	4	3	43	19	9	3	9	27	34	53
Stoke C	42	12	5	4	38	17	9	5	7	31	29	52
Blackburn R	42	14	4	3	73	31	8	2	11	41	48	50
Notts Co	42	14	3	4	46	27	7	3	11	28	44	48
West Ham U	42	12	4	5	46	28	6	6	9	28	42	46
Bristol R	42	15	4	2	52	23	4	3	14	23	47	45
Swansea T	42	15	3	3	58	28	2	6	13	28	55	43
Liverpool	42	11	7	3	55	37	5	3	13	37	59	42
Middlesbrough	42	13	1	7	48	31	5	5	11	25	51	42
Bury	42	10	5	6	44	35	5	6	10	33	37	41
Fulham	42	10	5	6	46	29	4	6	11	30	50	39
Nottingham F	42	8	4	9	29	29	8	3	10	29	33	39
Lincoln C	42	8	6	7	39	35	5	4	12	29	44	36
Port Vale	42	10	6	5	31	21	2	5	14	17	50	35
Doncaster R	42	10	5	6	35	34	4	2	15	23	61	35
Hull C	42	7	5	9	30	35	5	5	11	14	34	34
Plymouth A	42	10	4	7	29	26	2	3	16	28	56	31
Ipswich T	42	10	3	8	37	28	1	3	17	20	64	28
Derby Co	42	6	6	9	39	34	1	3	17	14	48	23

DIVISION 3 South

	P	W	D	L	F	A	W	D	L	F	A	Pts
Bristol C	46	17	4	2	62	22	13	6	4	39	25	70
Leyton O	46	16	2	5	48	20	10	7	6	41	27	61
Southampton	46	16	6	1	49	19	8	5	10	26	32	59
Gillingham	46	12	8	3	41	28	8	7	8	36	38	55
Millwall	46	14	6	3	44	25	6	5	12	28	43	51
Brighton & HA	46	14	4	5	47	27	6	6	11	29	36	50
Watford	46	11	9	3	45	26	7	5	11	26	36	50
Torquay U	46	12	6	5	51	39	6	6	11	31	43	48
Coventry C	46	15	5	3	50	26	3	6	14	17	33	47
Southend U	46	13	5	5	48	28	4	7	12	35	52	46
Brentford	46	11	6	6	44	36	5	8	10	38	46	46*
Norwich C	46	13	5	5	40	23	5	5	13	20	37	46*
Northampton T	46	13	5	5	47	27	6	3	14	26	54	46
Aldershot	46	12	6	5	44	23	4	7	12	31	48	45
QPR	46	13	7	3	46	25	2	7	14	23	50	44
Shrewsbury T	46	14	5	4	49	24	2	5	16	21	54	42
Bournemouth	46	7	8	8	32	29	5	10	8	25	36	42
Reading	46	7	10	6	32	26	6	5	12	33	47	41
Newport Co	46	8	8	7	32	29	3	8	12	28	44	38
Crystal P	46	9	11	3	32	24	2	5	16	20	56	38
Swindon T	46	10	8	5	30	19	1	7	15	16	45	37
Exeter C	46	9	7	7	30	31	2	8	13	17	42	37
Walsall	46	9	6	8	49	36	1	8	14	26	50	34
Colchester U	46	7	6	10	33	40	2	7	14	20	51	31

DIVISION 3 North

	P	W	D	L	F	A	W	D	L	F	A	Pts
Barnsley	46	18	3	2	51	17	12	2	9	35	29	65
Accrington S	46	18	2	3	65	32	7	9	7	31	35	61
Scunthorpe U	46	14	6	3	45	18	9	6	8	36	35	58
York C	46	13	5	5	43	27	11	5	7	49	36	58
Hartlepools U	46	16	3	4	39	20	9	2	12	25	29	55
Chesterfield	46	17	1	5	54	33	7	5	11	27	37	54
Gateshead	46	11	7	5	38	26	9	5	9	27	43	52
Workington	46	11	7	5	39	23	7	7	9	29	32	50
Stockport Co	46	13	4	6	50	27	5	8	10	34	43	48
Oldham A	46	14	5	4	47	22	5	5	13	27	46	48
Southport	46	10	9	4	28	18	6	7	10	19	26	48
Rochdale	46	13	7	3	39	20	4	7	12	30	46	48
Mansfield T	46	14	4	5	40	28	4	5	14	25	43	45
Halifax T	46	9	9	5	41	27	6	4	13	22	40	43
Darlington	46	10	7	6	41	28	4	7	12	21	45	42
Bradford	46	11	7	5	29	21	4	4	15	27	49	41
Barrow	46	12	4	7	39	34	5	2	16	31	55	40
Wrexham	46	9	6	8	40	35	4	6	13	25	42	38
Tranmere R	46	9	6	8	37	30	4	5	14	18	40	37
Carlisle U	46	12	1	10	53	39	3	5	15	25	50	36
Bradford C	46	9	5	9	30	26	4	5	14	17	29	36
Crewe A	46	8	10	5	45	35	2	4	17	23	56	34
Grimsby T	46	10	4	9	28	32	3	4	16	19	46	34
Chester	46	10	3	10	23	25	2	6	15	21	52	33

Football League Records

Top scorers: Div 1, N.Lofthouse (Bolton Wanderers) 33 goals; Div 2, W.Gardiner (Leicester City) 34 goals; Div 3(N), R.Crosbie (Grimsby Town) 36 goals; Div 3(S), R.Collins (Torquay United) 40 goals.

Centre-forward Tommy Taylor, who was killed in the Munich air disaster. In 1955-6, his 25 goals were a big contribution to Manchester United winning the League Championship.

DIVISION 1

	ARSENAL	ASTON VILLA	BIRMINGHAM C	BLACKPOOL	BOLTON W	BURNLEY	CARDIFF C	CHARLTON A	CHELSEA	EVERTON	HUDDERSFIELD T	LUTON T	MANCHESTER C	MANCHESTER U	NEWCASTLE U	PORTSMOUTH	PRESTON N.E.	SHEFFIELD U	SUNDERLAND	TOTTENHAM H	W.B.A.	WOLVERHAMPTON W
1 ARSENAL		O01 1-0	a14 1-0	D17 4-1	D31 3-1	N26 0-1	A23 3-1	O29 2-4	A27 1-1	F21 3-2	a02 2-0	M31 3-0	S06 0-0	M17 1-1	O15 1-0	S17 1-3	M06 3-2	N12 2-1	F04 3-1	J14 0-1	D10 2-0	D27 2-2
2 ASTON VILLA	F11 1-1		S05 0-0	S10 1-1	S24 0-2	M19 2-0	A27 2-0	M03 1-1	J21 1-4	M31 2-0	D31 3-0	N12 1-0	D17 0-3	O15 4-4	O29 3-0	D26 1-3	D10 3-2	a14 3-2	A29 1-4	N26 0-2	a28 3-0	a03 0-0
3 BIRMINGHAM C	D03 4-0	S21 2-2		M24 1-2	a21 5-2	J14 1-2	a07 2-1	F04 4-0	N05 3-0	D26 6-2	N19 5-0	S17 0-0	O22 4-3	A20 2-2	A31 3-1	F25 3-2	S03 0-3	D24 0-2	O08 1-2	O01 3-0	a02 2-0	M10 0-0
4 BLACKPOOL	A20 3-1	J14 6-0	N12 2-0		M30 0-0	A29 1-1	O01 2-1	O15 5-0	S05 2-1	D10 4-0	D26 4-2	F18 3-2	F04 0-1	N26 0-0	M17 5-1	D24 2-3	O29 2-6	M31 1-1	S03 7-3	a14 0-2	M03 5-1	S17 2-1
5 BOLTON W	S03 4-1	F18 1-0	D10 6-0	a02 1-3		M31 0-1	S07 4-0	A27 1-3	D17 4-0	O15 1-1	J02 2-2	O29 4-0	D26 1-3	N12 3-1	a14 3-2	J14 4-0	N26 0-0	M03 2-1	S17 0-3	M21 3-2	M17 4-0	O01 2-1
6 BURNLEY	a07 0-1	N05 2-0	S10 3-2	A22 0-2	O22 2-0		F25 0-2	a02 2-1	M10 5-0	A27 0-1	O08 2-0	S05 3-1	D03 2-2	S24 0-0	D31 3-1	N19 3-0	D26 1-2	F11 1-1	M24 4-0	D17 2-0	J21 1-2	a21 1-2
7 CARDIFF C	a28 1-2	D24 1-0	N26 2-1	F11 1-0	A31 1-0	O15 2-2		D10 3-1	D26 1-1	N12 3-1	S24 1-2	a14 2-0	J14 4-1	O29 0-1	M07 1-1	a02 2-3	F18 3-1	S17 3-2	A20 3-1	a23 0-0	M31 1-3	S03 1-9
8 CHARLTON A	M10 2-0	N19 3-1	S24 2-0	F25 1-2	D24 3-1	M30 2-1	a21 0-0		O08 1-2	S10 0-2	D03 4-1	A20 2-2	N05 5-2	D27 3-0	J21 0-2	O22 6-1	S15 2-1	S01 3-2	a07 2-1	D31 1-2	F11 5-1	M24 0-2
9 CHELSEA	D24 2-0	S17 0-0	M21 1-2	a28 2-1	A20 0-2	O29 0-0	D27 2-1	F22 3-1		a14 6-1	A29 0-0	a02 0-0	O01 2-1	M03 2-4	D10 2-1	S03 1-5	M31 0-1	N26 1-0	J14 2-3	O15 2-0	N12 2-0	F04 2-3
10 EVERTON	O08 1-1	O22 2-1	D27 5-1	a21 1-0	F25 1-0	D24 1-1	M24 2-0	J14 3-2	D03 3-3		N05 5-2	S03 0-1	N19 1-1	S14 4-2	F11 0-0	F04 0-2	A20 0-4	M30 1-4	M10 1-2	S17 2-1	A31 2-0	a07 2-1
11 HUDDERSFIELD T	a03 0-1	S03 1-1	M07 1-1	D27 3-1	a28 3-1	F18 1-0	F04 1-2	a14 4-0	A24 1-3	M17 1-0		O15 0-2	S17 3-3	M31 0-2	N12 2-6	A20 1-0	O01 2-2	O29 1-2	D24 4-0	D10 1-0	N26 1-0	J14 1-3
12 LUTON T	O22 0-0	M24 2-1	J21 0-1	O08 3-1	M10 0-0	a28 2-3	D03 3-0	D17 2-1	M30 2-2	D31 2-2	F25 1-2		a21 3-2	F11 0-2	S10 4-2	a07 1-0	A31 2-1	D27 2-1	N19 8-2	A27 2-1	S24 0-2	N05 5-1
13 MANCHESTER C	A31 2-2	A20 2-2	M31 1-1	S24 2-0	D27 2-0	a14 1-3	S10 3-1	M21 0-2	F11 2-2	M07 3-0	J21 1-0	D10 3-2		S03 1-0	N26 1-2	J02 4-1	O15 0-2	a11 3-1	a02 4-2	N12 1-2	O29 2-0	D24 2-2
14 MANCHESTER U	N05 1-1	F25 1-0	D17 2-1	a07 2-1	M24 1-0	F04 2-0	M10 1-1	D26 5-1	N19 3-0	S07 2-1	O22 3-0	O01 3-1	D31 2-1		M30 5-2	a21 1-0	S17 3-2	J14 3-1	D03 2-1	A24 2-2	A27 3-1	O08 4-3
15 NEWCASTLE U	F25 2-0	M10 2-3	A24 2-2	N05 1-2	D03 3-0	S03 3-1	N19 4-0	S17 4-1	a21 1-1	O01 1-2	M24 1-1	J14 4-0	a07 3-1	a02 0-0		O08 2-1	D24 5-0	A20 4-2	D27 3-1	F04 1-2	J02 0-3	O22 3-1
16 PORTSMOUTH	J21 5-2	D27 2-2	O15 0-5	A27 3-3	S10 3-3	M03 3-1	M30 1-1	M31 4-0	D31 4-4	S24 1-0	D17 5-2	N26 0-0	a28 2-4	D10 3-2	F22 0-2		N12 0-2	M17 1-1	O01 2-1	O29 4-1	a14 1-1	A24 2-1
17 PRESTON N.E.	N19 0-1	a21 0-1	D31 1-1	M10 3-3	a07 0-1	D27 4-2	O08 1-2	S07 2-2	O22 2-3	D17 0-1	F11 1-2	A24 2-1	F25 0-3	J21 3-1	A27 4-3	M24 2-1		S24 0-2	N05 2-2	a02 3-3	S10 0-1	D03 2-0
18 SHEFFIELD U	M24 0-2	D03 2-2	A27 0-3	O22 2-1	N19 1-3	O01 1-2	J21 2-1	A22 0-0	a07 2-1	a02 1-1	M10 3-1	D26 0-4	O08 1-1	S10 1-0	D17 2-1	N05 1-3	F04 3-1		a21 2-3	S05 2-0	D31 2-2	m02 3-3
19 SUNDERLAND	S24 3-1	A24 5-1	a18 1-0	D31 0-0	J21 0-0	N12 4-4	D17 1-1	N26 3-2	S10 4-3	O29 0-0	A27 4-1	M07 1-2	M30 0-3	a14 2-2	D26 1-6	F11 4-2	M21 2-2	D10 3-2		M31 3-2	O15 2-1	J02 1-1
20 TOTTENHAM H	S10 3-1	a07 4-3	F11 0-1	D03 1-1	O08 0-3	A20 0-1	N05 1-1	S03 2-3	F25 4-0	J21 1-1	a21 1-2	D24 2-1	M24 2-1	A31 1-2	S24 3-1	M10 1-1	M30 0-4	a28 3-1	O22 2-3		D26 4-1	N19 2-1
21 W.B.A.	a21 2-1	O08 1-0	a03 0-2	N19 1-2	N05 2-0	S17 1-0	O22 2-1	O01 3-3	M24 3-0	A24 2-0	a07 1-2	F04 3-1	M10 0-4	D24 1-4	S07 1-1	D03 4-0	J14 3-2	S03 2-1	F25 3-0	D27 1-0		A20 1-1
22 WOLVERHAMPTON W	D26 3-3	a02 0-0	O29 1-0	J21 2-3	F11 4-2	D10 3-1	D31 0-2	N12 2-0	S24 2-1	N26 1-0	S10 4-0	M17 1-2	A27 7-2	F18 0-2	M31 2-1	A31 3-1	a14 2-1	O15 3-2	a28 3-1	a18 5-1	D17 3-2	

Roy Shiner, a colourful goalscorer who helped Sheffield Wednesday back into Division One.

DIVISION 2

	BARNSLEY	BLACKBURN R	BRISTOL C	BRISTOL R	BURY	DONCASTER R	FULHAM	HULL C	LEEDS U	LEICESTER C	LINCOLN C	LIVERPOOL	MIDDLESBROUGH	NOTTINGHAM F	NOTTS CO	PLYMOUTH A	PORT VALE	ROTHERHAM U	SHEFFIELD W	STOKE C	SWANSEA T	WEST HAM U
1 BARNSLEY		F25 2-1	S24 0-0	N19 4-3	S03 3-3	M24 2-2	D24 3-0	D03 2-1	A20 2-1	J14 0-1	O08 1-0	M10 0-5	J21 0-4	a21 1-1	A31 3-1	O22 1-2	D27 1-2	S14 3-2	N05 0-3	a07 1-0	a02 3-2	F11 1-1
2 BLACKBURN R	O15 5-1		O29 4-6	F04 2-0	M31 3-1	O01 1-1	A29 1-0	M30 2-0	D10 2-3	D24 2-3	A20 0-2	S03 3-3	a14 2-1	J02 2-2	M03 2-0	J14 2-1	N12 7-1	a30 3-1	D26 2-2	S17 3-0	N26 3-0	M17 4-1
3 BRISTOL C	F04 2-0	a21 2-0		O22 1-1	S17 3-1	a07 4-1	J14 2-1	N05 5-2	S03 0-1	F25 1-1	D03 5-1	O08 2-1	O01 2-0	M24 0-0	D24 1-3	D27 6-0	a02 0-0	A30 5-2	N19 3-2	M10 0-1	A20 2-1	S06 3-1
4 BRISTOL R	F18 1-1	S24 1-0	M03 0-3		N12 4-2	A27 4-2	M17 2-2	J21 4-2	O29 4-1	D26 2-1	F11 3-0	a28 1-2	N26 7-2	S10 4-1	a14 2-0	M30 2-1	D17 1-2	M31 1-4	D31 4-2	A22 4-2	O15 1-2	D10 1-1
5 BURY	D31 3-0	O08 0-4	J21 1-1	M24 0-1		N05 5-1	A20 1-5	F25 3-2	A30 1-0	M10 3-1	D24 3-3	O22 1-4	S10 1-1	D03 1-2	M30 4-0	a07 7-1	F11 2-2	D27 2-1	a21 2-5	N19 1-0	S19 2-4	S24 1-1
6 DONCASTER R	N12 1-1	F11 2-2	N26 3-2	D24 2-1	M17 2-3		O29 4-2	S24 3-0	a14 1-2	S05 6-2	D27 2-0	M30 1-0	m03 0-1	J21 1-3	O15 1-1	S01 3-1	D10 3-0	S03 1-1	S10 2-2	A20 2-4	M31 3-1	M26 2-1
7 FULHAM	A27 5-1	A24 3-0	S10 3-0	N05 3-5	D17 3-1	a21 4-0		O08 5-0	M30 1-2	O22 3-2	M10 3-0	a07 3-1	D31 4-1	m02 4-3	S07 1-1	N19 2-1	S24 1-4	F11 1-1	D03 1-2	M24 2-0	D26 4-1	J21 3-1
8 HULL C	a14 4-1	a02 0-3	M17 1-3	S17 1-2	O15 2-3	a10 1-1	M31 2-2		a28 1-4	A20 2-4	A29 2-1	D24 1-2	O29 2-2	D27 0-3	D10 2-0	S03 0-1	F18 2-1	N26 0-3	O01 2-2	m01 3-2	M03 1-4	N12 3-1
9 LEEDS U	D17 3-1	M10 1-2	D31 2-1	a21 2-1	A22 1-0	D03 3-0	a02 6-1	S05 1-0		a07 4-0	O22 1-0	N19 4-2	A27 2-0	O08 3-0	D26 1-0	M24 4-2	J21 1-1	S24 4-1	F25 2-1	N05 1-0	F11 2-2	S10 3-3
10 LEICESTER C	S10 0-0	A27 0-2	O15 2-2	D27 4-2	D10 5-0	a28 3-0	M03 2-1	D17 1-2	N26 5-2		D31 4-0	S17 3-1	M31 1-1	A22 5-2	F18 4-0	F04 5-1	O29 4-1	M17 3-1	a02 1-2	O01 3-1	N12 6-1	a14 2-1
11 LINCOLN C	M31 4-0	D17 3-0	a14 2-0	O01 2-0	A27 4-2	D26 1-1	D10 6-1	A24 2-0	M03 1-1	S03 7-1		m02 2-0	O15 1-2	a02 1-3	N26 2-0	S17 1-0	M17 1-0	N12 1-1	S07 2-2	a25 2-1	F18 3-1	O29 1-1
12 LIVERPOOL	D10 1-1	D31 1-2	M31 2-1	S07 0-2	M03 4-2	a02 1-2	N26 7-0	A27 3-0	F29 1-0	J21 3-1	S10 2-1		S24 1-1	D17 5-2	N12 2-1	O01 4-1	a14 4-1	O29 2-0	A24 0-3	D26 2-2	M17 4-1	O15 3-1
13 MIDDLESBROUGH	S17 1-1	D03 1-0	F11 2-1	a07 0-1	J14 1-3	N19 4-1	S03 1-1	a21 5-1	D24 5-3	O08 4-3	a18 4-2	F04 1-2		N05 3-2	A20 3-0	M10 1-2	J02 1-1	a02 0-1	M24 2-2	O22 1-3	A31 4-1	D26 2-0
14 NOTTINGHAM F	O29 1-0	a28 1-1	N12 0-2	J14 1-1	a14 0-2	S17 5-0	O15 1-0	D26 2-1	M31 2-0	A31 2-0	a03 2-2	A20 1-3	M17 2-4		O01 0-2	D24 3-1	N26 2-2	M03 1-0	F04 0-1	S03 2-3	D10 2-1	a18 0-0
15 NOTTS CO	A25 2-2	O22 1-2	A27 3-2	D03 5-2	a02 2-1	F25 3-2	S15 3-4	M10 0-2	D27 2-1	N19 1-1	a07 2-2	M24 2-1	D17 5-0	F11 1-3		N05 3-0	S10 0-0	J21 1-2	O08 1-1	a21 1-3	S24 1-5	D31 0-1
16 PLYMOUTH A	M03 3-0	S10 1-0	D26 5-0	a02 0-1	N26 1-4	A22 2-2	F18 0-0	D31 1-1	N12 4-3	S24 0-1	J21 1-4	F11 4-0	D10 4-0	A27 1-2	M17 1-1		O15 1-1	a14 3-1	D17 1-1	S05 0-1	O29 0-1	M31 0-1
17 PORT VALE	D26 1-2	M24 4-1	M30 2-0	A20 1-1	O01 1-1	M10 2-0	F04 2-1	N19 0-1	S17 2-0	a21 2-3	N05 1-1	D03 1-1	a28 3-2	a07 0-2	J14 3-1	F25 3-1		D24 4-1	O22 0-1	O08 1-0	S03 3-0	A22 2-1
18 ROTHERHAM U	S05 0-0	N19 3-2	A22 1-3	O08 1-0	D26 1-3	D31 3-3	O01 2-3	a07 0-2	a23 0-2	N05 3-1	M24 2-2	a21 0-1	a03 2-1	O22 2-1	S17 1-1	D03 0-0	A27 1-0		M10 2-3	a28 0-1	m03 2-3	D17 3-2
19 SHEFFIELD W	M21 3-0	D27 5-1	F18 2-1	S03 4-2	O29 3-3	J14 5-2	a14 2-3	F11 4-1	O15 4-0	S12 1-1	a28 5-3	A31 1-1	N12 3-1	S24 1-2	M31 1-0	A20 5-2	M03 4-0	D10 0-2		D24 4-0	S17 2-2	N26 1-1
20 STOKE C	N26 2-1	J21 1-2	D10 4-2	A29 1-2	a16 0-2	D17 5-2	N12 1-2	S10 4-1	M17 2-1	F11 2-0	S24 3-0	D27 3-2	M03 2-5	D31 1-1	O29 0-2	S12 4-1	M31 1-1	O15 1-0	A27 2-0		a14 5-0	a02 3-0
21 SWANSEA T	a28 3-1	a07 2-1	D17 2-1	F25 1-2	S08 5-3	O08 2-0	D27 2-0	O22 4-1	O01 1-1	M24 6-1	N19 0-2	N05 2-1	A25 2-1	M10 0-1	F04 5-1	a21 2-2	D31 0-0	S10 4-1	J21 2-1	D03 0-0		A27 4-2
22 WEST HAM U	O01 4-0	N05 2-3	a28 3-0	M10 2-1	M19 3-2	O22 6-1	S17 2-1	M24 1-1	J14 1-1	D03 1-3	a21 2-4	F25 2-0	D27 1-0	N19 1-2	S03 6-1	O08 4-0	A29 0-2	A20 1-1	a07 3-3	M30 2-0	D24 5-1	

Season 1955-56

DIVISION 3 NORTH

	ACCRINGTON S	BARROW	BRADFORD	BRADFORD C	CARLISLE U	CHESTER	CHESTERFIELD	CREWE A	DARLINGTON	DERBY CO	GATESHEAD	GRIMSBY T	HALIFAX T	HARTLEPOOLS U	MANSFIELD T	OLDHAM A	ROCHDALE	SCUNTHORPE U	SOUTHPORT	STOCKPORT CO	TRANMERE R	WORKINGTON	WREXHAM	YORK C
1 ACCRINGTON S		S10 2-0	S26 7-0	M03 2-0	S24 1-0	J21 4-0	S14 5-1	a14 5-1	D24 2-1	N26 2-0	A20 2-2	F11 0-1	J28 2-2	O15 1-0	a02 3-1	M31 2-2	A24 3-0	O29 2-0	a30 4-2	S03 3-1	a28 0-0	N12 5-1	F18 3-1	M17 1-3
2 BARROW	J14 3-1		A25 2-2	J28 3-1	F11 0-0	S24 1-2	a28 3-1	N26 5-0	S03 0-1	M17 1-2	D24 4-0	J02 0-0	F18 2-2	a14 3-2	S17 4-1	O29 4-1	S15 2-0	M03 2-2	A20 0-2	O15 2-0	D27 1-1	M31 2-0	M30 0-3	N12 0-1
3 BRADFORD	a23 1-0	A29 3-2		O15 1-1	a28 2-1	S12 1-1	S03 0-5	O29 2-0	O01 3-0	M03 2-4	F04 3-1	D27 2-1	a14 1-1	M31 1-3	M17 0-3	a03 4-1	D24 3-3	A20 2-0	S17 0-3	N12 2-0	a18 4-5	F18 4-0	N26 4-2	M14 2-1
4 BRADFORD C	O22 2-1	a21 1-1	a16 5-0		a02 0-0	O08 1-1	a07 3-5	J21 3-1	M10 3-0	S10 2-1	N05 3-1	S21 0-2	S07 2-0	S24 2-0	a25 4-2	D17 0-0	D03 2-2	D26 4-3	M24 2-0	F11 4-1	J07 5-0	A27 2-0	A24 4-3	D31 3-1
5 CARLISLE U	F04 0-4	O01 2-0	J02 4-1	M30 0-0		a24 4-1	A20 1-1	N12 4-1	S17 2-0	M31 0-3	J14 2-1	S13 1-2	A30 2-2	M17 0-3	a12 5-2	J28 3-1	D27 1-2	F18 1-2	S03 4-0	N26 4-1	D24 0-3	M03 2-4	O15 0-1	O29 3-1
6 CHESTER	S17 1-1	F04 1-0	S07 0-0	F18 1-1	S28 3-3		D27 2-1	M17 0-0	J14 2-1	N12 2-5	S03 3-0	A31 2-0	M30 1-0	N26 0-1	O15 4-3	M03 3-2	a28 0-0	m02 3-5	D24 1-3	a14 1-4	A20 0-0	O29 1-0	O01 2-1	M31 2-2
7 CHESTERFIELD	S07 0-1	S21 2-0	D31 5-1	N26 1-1	D17 2-1	D26 2-1		J28 8-0	A24 2-1	F18 2-0	J02 3-0	A27 1-0	M17 3-0	M03 2-3	M31 2-1	O15 1-0	S10 7-2	a14 2-0	O01 5-1	O29 2-3	F04 2-0	S17 2-4	N12 2-0	a02 3-1
8 CREWE A	D03 0-3	a07 0-1	M10 4-2	S17 1-4	M24 3-1	a11 0-0	a21 0-3		F25 1-1	S05 2-1	S21 1-0	N05 0-0	J14 1-4	D27 1-3	D24 2-1	O01 1-2	O22 2-0	F04 1-2	M30 1-1	A20 3-1	O08 4-0	a25 2-1	S03 1-2	A24 1-2
9 DARLINGTON	A27 2-0	D31 4-2	F11 4-1	O29 1-1	J21 3-5	S10 0-1	A31 2-1	O15 4-1		a14 1-0	D27 0-0	S24 0-1	M03 1-2	D17 0-0	F18 3-1	N12 2-1	S28 2-0	M31 1-0	a28 0-1	a02 0-0	S14 6-2	M17 2-2	J28 2-2	N26 1-4
10 DERBY CO	a07 6-2	M07 2-1	O22 4-0	J14 4-1	N05 3-0	M24 3-1	O08 3-0	S14 3-3	D03 6-2		F25 4-1	M10 1-3	S03 4-1	a28 3-2	A20 4-0	M19 2-0	a21 2-0	S17 2-2	A31 2-0	D27 2-0	a02 0-0	O01 2-2	D24 2-0	S28 3-2
11 GATESHEAD	D17 4-0	A27 3-2	S24 3-0	M31 4-1	S10 2-3	D31 1-1	S26 3-3	a28 4-1	D26 0-1	O15 2-4		J21 2-0	O29 1-1	M30 2-1	J28 3-0	M17 1-3	F11 4-1	N12 1-0	S12 2-0	F18 2-1	A22 3-3	N26 4-3	M03 2-1	a14 3-2
12 GRIMSBY T	O01 3-0	S27 3-0	D26 2-0	a28 2-0	S06 1-0	A23 6-1	D24 3-0	M31 5-1	a17 1-0	O29 2-1	S17 3-1		O15 4-0	N12 1-0	N26 2-0	F18 5-1	A20 1-1	M30 0-1	a25 2-0	M17 3-0	S03 1-0	J28 1-2	a14 1-0	M03 2-1
13 HALIFAX T	a21 2-0	O08 1-0	D03 6-0	S12 3-2	A22 2-2	a02 0-1	J07 3-0	S10 2-0	O22 3-0	D31 2-2	M10 3-3	a30 0-1		J21 0-2	F11 1-1	D26 5-1	a07 1-1	a28 0-3	N05 0-1	S24 1-0	M24 0-2	D17 2-0	S26 1-1	A27 2-4
14 HARTLEPOOLS U	m03 0-0	D03 1-0	N05 3-1	F04 1-0	a30 3-0	a07 3-1	O22 3-0	D26 6-1	A20 3-0	S19 2-0	a02 3-1	M24 1-2	S17 3-2		S03 4-2	J02 1-0	M10 1-0	O01 0-2	O08 1-0	D24 0-0	a21 4-0	A29 1-0	J14 3-2	S05 0-1
15 MANSFIELD T	M30 3-2	J21 4-0	a09 5-0	S26 0-0	D03 0-1	F25 3-0	N05 0-1	A27 1-1	O08 3-3	D17 1-1	a21 3-1	a07 0-2	O01 3-1	D31 5-1		S05 2-0	M24 6-0	A22 3-2	O22 0-1	S10 2-2	M10 6-0	S19 0-0	F04 6-1	D26 3-1
16 OLDHAM A	N05 1-3	M10 6-1	a02 5-1	A20 1-1	a21 2-2	O22 4-1	F25 2-2	F11 1-1	M24 3-3	S24 1-1	J07 1-2	O08 1-1	D27 1-3	S27 3-2	S12 1-1		D31 2-2	D24 2-1	a07 1-1	A30 3-2	D03 4-1	S10 0-1	a28 1-1	J21 2-2
17 ROCHDALE	A29 1-1	S05 5-1	A27 4-2	a14 3-1	D26 5-2	S21 4-2	a18 1-5	M03 1-0	a24 1-0	J28 0-5	O01 1-1	D17 2-0	N26 2-1	O29 1-4	N12 1-1	S03 4-4		O15 3-2	F04 1-3	M31 0-0	S17 1-3	M30 1-0	M17 1-0	F18 3-1
18 SCUNTHORPE U	M10 2-3	O22 2-0	D17 4-2	D27 2-0	O08 4-0	a21 2-1	D03 2-0	S24 1-1	N05 0-1	J21 0-2	M24 1-1	a02 0-1	S21 1-0	F11 5-1	A31 3-0	A27 2-1	M22 1-2		a18 0-1	a26 1-5	a07 2-1	D31 3-1	S07 1-1	S10 1-1
19 SOUTHPORT	D26 1-1	D17 2-1	J21 3-0	N12 3-1	D31 3-0	A27 1-0	F11 1-0	a02 5-0	S20 0-1	A23 2-5	S06 2-0	S10 2-0	M31 2-0	F18 0-0	M03 1-1	N26 1-1	S24 2-0	M17 2-2		J28 1-1	S27 1-0	a14 0-0	O29 1-1	O15 3-3
20 STOCKPORT CO	D31 1-2	F25 4-1	M24 0-0	O01 1-0	a07 8-1	D03 2-1	M10 2-1	D17 2-1	M30 2-1	D26 2-1	O08 1-2	F15 0-0	F04 3-1	A27 4-0	J14 7-2	A22 0-0	N05 0-0	S26 3-2	a21 4-0		O22 7-0	S05 4-5	S17 4-0	a28 4-1
21 TRANMERE R	S20 4-1	D26 1-1	S10 4-1	M17 1-1	A27 0-1	D17 4-0	S24 0-1	F18 2-1	S06 0-1	M30 0-1	A30 1-1	D31 0-1	N12 2-1	J28 2-2	O29 1-0	a14 0-3	J21 2-1	N26 2-1	J02 1-2	M03 2-1		O15 2-0	M31 0-2	O01 2-1
22 WORKINGTON	M24 0-0	N05 6-1	O08 4-0	D24 2-1	O22 4-0	M10 0-0	J21 0-1	S28 1-0	J07 2-0	F11 0-3	a07 6-1	a21 0-0	A20 2-0	A24 5-1	a28 2-1	J14 4-3	a02 0-1	S03 1-2	D03 2-3	S14 0-1	F25 3-0		D27 3-1	S24 0-0
23 WREXHAM	O08 1-4	a02 0-0	a07 1-0	A31 2-1	F25 5-2	F11 0-0	M24 3-0	D31 4-2	a21 2-1	A27 3-1	O22 1-1	D03 1-0	a25 1-2	S10 1-3	S24 2-0	S21 1-1	J07 0-0	S14 0-1	M10 2-1	J21 0-1	N05 3-1	D26 0-1		D17 4-5
24 YORK C	a16 0-1	M24 3-2	a21 5-0	S03 0-2	M10 3-1	N05 3-0	M30 3-1	A29 1-1	a07 4-0	a23 1-0	D03 1-0	O22 3-4	D24 5-0	S12 3-0	D27 1-1	S17 2-0	O08 1-2	a09 0-0	F25 0-1	S19 1-0	F11 2-4	F04 1-1	A20 1-3	

DIVISION 3 SOUTH

	ALDERSHOT	BOURNEMOLTH	BRENTFORD	BRIGHTON & HA	COLCHESTER U	COVENTRY C	CRYSTAL P	EXETER C	GILLINGHAM	IPSWICH T	LEYTON O	MILLWALL	NEWPORT CC	NORTHAMPTON T	NORWICH C	Q.P.R.	READING	SHREWSBURY T	SOUTHAMPTON	SOUTHEND U	SWINDON T	TORQUAY U	WALSALL	WATFORD
1 ALDERSHOT		a07 1-3	O08 4-1	D31 0-3	M24 1-0	F25 2-2	A27 1-1	M10 1-0	D03 2-2	S24 0-3	N05 1-1	a21 2-1	A24 1-0	S14 2-0	a18 0-0	D26 1-2	D17 4-4	J21 2-0	S10 3-2	O22 3-3	a28 1-1	S28 1-2	F11 2-1	a02 1-1
2 BOURNEMOUTH	N26 2-2		A27 0-0	J28 2-0	A24 3-1	D17 0-1	a14 1-0	D26 0-0	S24 1-2	F18 1-1	a28 3-1	J21 4-0	O29 0-0	M31 0-0	S28 0-1	N12 1-0	S10 2-1	M30 2-0	O01 1-3	S07 4-1	M17 4-0	M03 2-0	O15 2-0	D31 4-0
3 BRENTFORD	F18 2-0	D24 2-1		M03 4-2	J14 2-2	a23 1-1	O15 0-0	F04 2-0	A20 1-4	N12 0-2	S17 1-0	S12 2-2	a14 1-1	a02 2-1	S03 1-2	A30 2-0	D26 2-2	M17 1-1	O29 2-1	O01 2-1	M12 1-2	N26 1-3	M31 2-2	S19 0-0
4 BRIGHTON & H.A.	S03 5-2	a21 4-1	O22 3-0		a07 2-0	M10 2-1	J14 5-0	M24 1-0	J21 5-0	S28 3-0	a18 1-1	a02 2-1	D26 4-1	D24 4-0	D03 6-0	A20 1-1	O08 3-1	F11 3-2	S24 5-0	N05 4-0	S14 2-0	a28 3-2	A24 3-0	F25 2-3
5 COLCHESTER U	N12 4-0	S01 1-0	S10 0-3	N26 3-3		D31 2-0	M31 2-4	D17 5-1	S29 1-1	D26 3-3	S15 2-1	F11 1-2	O15 2-1	M17 2-0	a28 3-2	O29 4-1	S24 0-3	J28 2-0	a14 3-2	A27 3-6	M03 5-0	F18 3-2	M30 1-1	J21 4-1
6 COVENTRY C	O15 1-1	A20 3-1	S26 2-1	O29 3-2	S03 2-0		M03 1-3	S17 2-2	S12 2-0	M31 3-1	J14 3-0	D27 5-1	D10 3-0	F18 0-1	D24 5-3	a03 4-1	a28 0-0	N12 2-1	M17 2-0	M19 0-0	O01 6-0	a14 1-2	N26 1-0	A29 3-0
7 CRYSTAL P	D24 1-0	D03 1-3	F25 0-2	S10 1-2	J07 1-1	O22 3-0		N05 0-1	a21 1-3	F11 1-0	M24 1-2	D31 2-2	a28 1-0	A20 2-3	a07 2-0	S14 1-1	M30 2-3	S24 0-1	J21 0-2	M10 1-2	D27 0-2	A31 3-0	S28 2-0	O08 1-2
8 EXETER C	O29 2-1	D27 2-0	S24 2-3	N12 0-5	A20 0-0	J21 2-3	M17 6-1		a28 2-1	a14 2-2	D24 1-1	A31 3-1	a02 2-0	M03 3-1	S14 1-1	O15 2-0	S28 0-2	N26 3-0	a11 3-2	S10 0-1	F18 1-2	S03 0-0	J28 1-1	F11 1-2
9 GILLINGHAM	a14 2-0	m02 2-1	D17 1-2	S17 1-0	a25 2-1	S07 1-1	J28 1-1	S21 2-1		O15 0-0	A24 0-1	S10 4-3	M17 3-2	N26 0-2	O01 3-1	M31 0-2	D31 2-0	F18 3-1	M30 1-2	D27 2-3	N12 4-0	O29 1-3	M03 0-1	A27 3-0
10 IPSWICH T	F04 2-1	O08 1-0	M24 1-1	a25 2-1	D27 3-1	J07 1-0	O01 3-3	D03 2-2	F25 1-1		a21 2-0	O22 6-2	D24 3-2	S17 1-0	M30 4-1	J14 4-1	M10 3-3	S21 2-1	A24 4-2	a07 3-0	S03 6-2	A20 0-2	S07 5-2	N05 0-0
11 LEYTON O	M17 8-3	S22 3-0	J21 2-1	M31 0-1	S08 6-0	S10 3-1	N12 8-0	A27 1-1	S01 2-0	m03 1-2		a26 2-1	F18 3-1	O29 1-1	D26 2-2	M03 7-1	F11 1-0	a14 5-2	N26 4-0	D31 3-0	O15 4-0	M30 3-2	D17 4-0	S24 3-1
12 MILLWALL	J28 3-3	S17 4-0	S05 4-0	M30 2-4	O01 0-1	D26 0-2	S03 1-1	A22 2-0	J14 5-0	M03 0-5	a30 5-0		N12 2-4	a14 4-1	m04 1-0	N26 2-0	A27 4-0	O15 1-2	F18 3-2	a28 5-0	M31 1-1	M17 3-2	O29 3-2	D17 1-1
13 NEWPORT CO	S01 0-1	M10 1-0	D03 1-2	D27 1-0	F25 0-0	a21 4-2	S22 0-1	M30 1-2	N05 3-2	A27 2-1	O08 3-0	M24 1-4		S29 0-1	O22 2-2	O01 2-1	J07 2-3	D17 1-2	S08 1-0	a19 2-0	a12 1-0	S10 2-1	D31 2-0	a07 0-1
14 NORTHAMPTON T	S08 3-2	a12 2-1	a03 1-0	A27 3-0	N05 0-2	O08 2-1	D17 1-1	O22 3-0	a07 0-2	J21 0-5	M10 0-1	D03 4-0	a26 5-0		M24 1-1	S19 5-2	a21 1-2	S10 1-0	D31 3-1	F25 1-1	S01 2-1	F11 2-0	S24 3-1	D27 1-3
15 NORWICH C	M31 0-1	a25 0-2	D31 1-0	a14 3-3	S21 1-1	A27 1-0	N26 3-1	S07 2-1	F11 5-1	a02 3-2	D27 2-2	S24 4-1	M03 2-3	N12 4-1		M17 1-0	J21 2-1	A24 3-1	J28 1-4	D17 7-2	O29 4-1	O15 0-0	a12 3-2	S10 4-1
16 Q.P.R.	D27 2-2	M24 0-1	A22 1-1	D17 2-1	M10 6-2	M30 1-2	S05 0-3	F25 1-0	J07 2-2	S10 1-1	O22 0-1	a07 4-0	F11 0-0	a28 3-2	N05 2-3		D03 3-3	D31 1-1	A27 4-0	O08 1-2	S26 1-0	S24 3-1	J21 3-2	a21 3-2
17 READING	A20 0-5	J14 0-2	D27 5-2	F18 0-2	F27 1-3	S21 1-0	a02 1-0	a25 1-2	S03 1-2	O29 1-5	O01 0-1	D24 4-1	M31 3-0	J28 4-1	S17 2-2	a14 3-1		M03 0-1	O15 1-1	A31 4-1	N26 0-1	N12 0-3	M17 2-0	S14 6-1
18 SHREWSBURY T	S17 3-3	a02 1-1	N05 1-1	O01 2-1	a21 2-1	M24 3-0	a30 2-0	a07 2-0	O08 3-1	a28 1-1	D03 1-4	F25 3-1	A20 5-0	J14 1-1	A29 6-0	S03 1-1	O22 3-0		S26 2-0	a23 1-1	D24 1-1	S12 1-2	D26 2-1	M10 0-0
19 SOUTHAMPTON	J14 3-1	F11 3-2	M10 1-1	F04 1-2	D03 3-0	N05 3-0	S17 3-1	M31 5-0	a02 1-1	A31 2-2	a07 1-2	O08 3-0	S14 3-3	S03 2-3	a21 2-5	D24 4-0	F25 5-2	J07 1-1		M24 0-0	A20 2-1	D27 6-2	S21 4-1	O22 2-0
20 SOUTHEND U	M03 3-2	S14 4-1	F11 2-2	M17 1-2	D24 4-0	S24 3-0	O29 4-3	J14 6-0	D26 2-2	N26 2-3	S03 0-0	S21 3-1	S17 4-1	O15 2-0	A20 3-1	F18 5-1	A24 1-0	M31 1-0	N12 2-1		M30 0-0	m02 2-3	a14 3-2	a25 1-0
21 SWINDON T	S21 1-1	N05 2-2	a21 0-1	S07 0-0	O22 3-1	F11 1-1	D26 0-0	O08 0-1	M24 0-1	D31 0-1	F25 1-2	F29 1-0	S24 1-2	A24 0-1	M10 1-1	a25 0-1	a07 0-0	A27 2-1	D17 1-1	a02 1-1		J21 2-1	S10 1-2	D03 0-0
22 TORQUAY U	a25 5-0	O22 0-0	a07 3-1	S21 0-0	O08 1-2	D03 0-0	A24 1-1	D31 3-1	M10 1-1	D17 2-2	a02 1-3	N05 3-0	J14 1-1	O01 3-1	F25 1-1	F04 2-0	M24 0-0	S07 5-0	D26 3-2	a21 2-2	S17 4-0		A27 3-2	F29 4-1
23 WALSALL	O01 4-2	F25 0-0	m03 1-2	S01 2-2	a02 0-0	a07 2-0	a26 4-0	a21 3-1	O22 2-1	S15 1-3	A20 0-2	M10 2-1	S03 3-3	a16 2-0	O08 2-0	S17 2-2	N05 1-0	D27 1-0	a28 1-3	D03 3-1	J14 4-0	D24 1-4		M24 2-1
24 WATFORD	M30 1-1	S03 0-2	a28 0-2	O15 1-3	S17 1-1	A23 2-1	F18 0-2	O01 2-3	D24 0-1	M17 0-2	F04 0-4	A20 4-2	N26 1-1	D26 2-2	J14 1-1	J28 0-1	S06 1-0	O29 3-4	M03 1-0	S27 3-2	a14 2-1	M31 2-1	N12 4-2	

LEAGUE TABLES

DIVISION 1

	P	W	D	L	F	A	W	D	L	F	A	Pts
Manchester U	42	18	3	0	51	20	7	7	7	32	31	60
Blackpool	42	13	4	4	56	27	7	5	9	30	35	49
Wolves	42	15	2	4	51	27	5	7	9	38	38	49
Manchester C	42	11	5	5	40	27	7	5	9	42	42	46
Arsenal	42	13	4	4	38	22	5	6	10	22	39	46
Birmingham C	42	12	4	5	51	26	6	5	10	24	31	45
Burnley	42	11	3	7	37	20	7	5	9	27	34	44
Bolton W	42	13	3	5	50	24	5	4	12	21	34	43
Sunderland	42	10	8	3	44	36	7	1	13	36	59	43
Luton T	42	12	4	5	44	27	5	4	12	22	37	42
Newcastle U	42	12	4	5	49	24	5	3	13	36	46	41
Portsmouth	42	9	8	4	46	38	7	1	13	32	47	41
WBA	42	13	3	5	37	25	5	2	14	21	45	41
Charlton A	42	13	2	6	47	26	4	4	13	28	55	40
Everton	42	11	5	5	37	29	4	5	12	18	40	40
Chelsea	42	10	4	7	32	26	4	7	10	32	51	39
Cardiff C	42	11	4	6	36	32	4	5	12	19	37	39
Tottenham H	42	9	4	8	37	33	6	3	12	24	38	37
Preston NE	42	6	5	10	32	36	8	3	10	41	36	36
Aston Villa	42	9	6	6	32	29	2	7	12	20	40	35
Huddersfield T	42	9	4	8	32	30	5	3	13	22	53	35
Sheffield U	42	8	6	7	31	35	4	3	14	32	42	33

DIVISION 2

	P	W	D	L	F	A	W	D	L	F	A	Pts
Sheffield W	42	13	5	3	60	28	8	8	5	41	34	55
Leeds U	42	17	3	1	51	18	6	3	12	29	42	52
Liverpool	42	14	3	4	52	25	7	3	11	33	38	48
Blackburn R	42	13	4	4	55	29	8	2	11	29	36	48
Leicester C	42	15	3	3	63	23	6	3	12	31	55	48
Bristol R	42	13	3	5	53	33	8	3	10	31	37	48
Nottingham F	42	9	5	7	30	26	10	4	7	38	37	47
Lincoln C	42	14	5	2	49	17	4	5	12	30	48	46
Fulham	42	15	2	4	59	27	5	4	12	30	52	46
Swansea T	42	14	4	3	49	23	6	2	13	34	58	46
Bristol C	42	14	4	3	49	20	5	3	13	31	44	45
Port Vale	42	12	4	5	38	21	4	9	8	22	37	45
Stoke C	42	13	2	6	47	27	7	2	12	24	35	44
Middlesbrough	42	11	4	6	46	31	5	4	12	30	47	40
Bury	42	9	5	7	44	39	7	3	11	42	51	40
West Ham U	42	12	4	5	52	27	2	7	12	22	42	39
Doncaster R	42	11	5	5	45	30	1	6	14	24	66	35
Barnsley	42	10	5	6	33	35	1	7	13	14	49	34
Rotherham U	42	7	5	9	29	34	5	4	12	27	41	33
Notts Co	42	8	5	8	39	37	3	4	14	16	45	31
Plymouth A	42	7	6	8	33	25	3	2	16	21	62	28
Hull C	42	6	4	11	32	45	4	2	15	21	52	26

DIVISION 3 North

	P	W	D	L	F	A	W	D	L	F	A	Pts
Grimsby T	46	20	1	2	54	10	11	5	7	22	19	68
Derby Co	46	18	4	1	67	23	10	3	10	43	32	63
Accrington S	46	17	4	2	61	19	8	5	10	31	38	59
Hartlepools U	46	18	2	3	47	15	8	3	12	34	45	57
Southport	46	12	9	2	39	18	11	2	10	27	35	57
Chesterfield	46	18	1	4	61	21	7	3	13	33	45	54
Stockport Co	46	16	4	3	65	22	5	5	13	25	39	51
Bradford C	46	16	5	2	57	25	2	8	13	21	39	49
Scunthorpe U	46	12	4	7	40	26	8	4	11	35	37	48
Workington	46	13	4	6	47	20	6	5	12	28	43	47
York C	46	12	4	7	44	24	7	5	11	41	48	47
Rochdale	46	13	5	5	46	39	4	8	11	20	45	47
Gateshead	46	15	4	4	56	32	2	7	14	21	52	45
Wrexham	46	11	5	7	37	28	5	5	13	29	45	42
Darlington	46	11	6	6	41	28	5	3	15	19	45	41
Tranmere R	46	11	4	8	33	25	5	5	13	26	59	41
Chester	46	10	8	5	35	33	3	6	14	17	49	40
Mansfield T	46	13	6	4	59	21	1	5	17	25	60	39
Halifax T	46	10	6	7	40	27	4	5	14	26	49	39
Oldham A	46	7	12	4	48	36	3	6	14	28	50	38
Carlisle U	46	11	3	9	45	36	4	5	14	26	59	38
Barrow	46	11	6	6	44	25	1	3	19	17	58	33
Bradford	46	13	4	6	47	38	0	3	20	14	84	33
Crewe A	46	9	4	10	32	35	0	6	17	18	70	28

DIVISION 3 South

	P	W	D	L	F	A	W	D	L	F	A	Pts
Leyton O	46	18	3	2	76	20	11	5	7	30	29	66
Brighton & HA	46	20	2	1	73	16	9	5	9	39	34	65
Ipswich T	46	16	6	1	59	28	9	8	6	47	32	64
Southend U	46	16	4	3	58	25	5	7	11	30	55	53
Torquay U	46	11	10	2	48	21	9	2	12	38	42	52
Brentford	46	11	8	4	40	30	8	6	9	29	36	52
Norwich C	46	15	4	4	56	31	4	9	10	30	51	51
Coventry C	46	16	4	3	54	20	4	5	14	19	40	49
Bournemouth	46	13	6	4	39	14	6	4	13	24	37	48
Gillingham	46	12	3	8	38	28	7	7	9	31	43	48
Northampton T	46	14	3	6	44	27	6	4	13	23	44	47
Colchester C	46	14	4	5	56	37	4	7	12	20	44	47
Shrewsbury T	46	12	9	2	47	21	5	3	15	22	45	46
Southampton	46	13	6	4	60	30	5	2	16	31	51	44
Aldershot	46	9	9	5	36	33	3	7	13	34	57	40
Exeter C	46	10	6	7	39	30	5	4	14	19	47	40
Reading	46	10	2	11	40	37	5	7	11	30	42	39
QPR	46	10	7	6	44	32	4	4	15	20	54	39
Newport Co	46	12	2	9	32	26	3	7	13	26	53	39
Walsall	46	13	5	5	43	28	2	3	18	25	56	38
Watford	46	8	5	10	31	39	5	6	12	21	46	37
Millwall	46	13	4	6	56	31	2	2	19	27	69	36
Crystal P	46	7	3	13	27	32	5	7	11	27	51	34
Swindon T	46	4	10	9	18	22	4	4	15	16	56	30

Football League Records

Top scorers: Div 1, J.Charles (Leeds United) 38 goals; Div 2, A.Rowley (Leicester City) 44 goals; Div 3(N), R.Straw (Derby County) 37 goals; Div 3(S), E.Phillips (Ipswich Town) 42 goals.

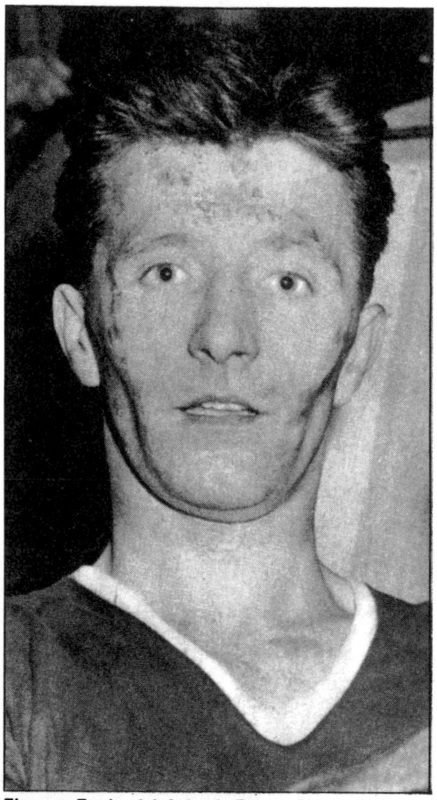

Elegant England left-back Roger Byrne skippered Manchester United to a second successive Championship. He, too, was a Munich victim.

DIVISION 1

	ARSENAL	ASTON VILLA	BIRMINGHAM C	BLACKPOOL	BOLTON W	BURNLEY	CARDIFF C	CHARLTON A	CHELSEA	EVERTON	LEEDS U	LUTON T	MANCHESTER C	MANCHESTER U	NEWCASTLE U	PORTSMOUTH	PRESTON N.E.	SHEFFIELD W	SUNDERLAND	TOTTENHAM H	W.B.A.	WOLVERHAMPTON W
1 ARSENAL		N03 2-1	D22 4-0	a19 1-1	N17 3-0	A21 2-0	A18 0-0	a20 3-1	D26 2-0	F23 2-0	a06 1-0	M09 1-3	O06 7-3	S29 1-2	S15 0-1	J12 1-1	S04 1-2	F02 6-3	D01 1-1	O20 3-1	S01 4-1	M23 0-0
2 ASTON VILLA	M16 0-0		O27 3-1	S01 3-2	S29 0-0	N10 1-0	M13 4-1	A18 3-1	N24 1-1	J12 5-1	F02 1-1	a27 1-3	F04 2-2	D08 1-3	O13 3-1	F18 2-2	M30 2-0	a13 5-0	a08 2-2	S15 2-4	A27 0-0	a22 4-0
3 BIRMINGHAM C	A25 4-2	a10 1-2		N03 2-2	O06 0-0	D29 2-0	S22 2-1	N17 4-2	J19 0-1	M09 1-3	a20 6-2	O20 3-0	a27 3-3	D15 3-1	S05 6-1	A22 3-1	S08 3-0	D25 4-0	a06 1-2	D01 0-0	a23 2-0	F09 2-2
4 BLACKPOOL	a22 2-4	D29 0-0	M16 3-1		D15 4-2	m01 1-0	D08 3-1	S22 3-2	a13 1-0	A27 5-2	D25 1-1	S08 4-0	F09 4-1	O27 2-2	N24 2-3	M30 5-0	O13 4-0	M02 3-1	J19 1-2	S03 4-1	N10 0-1	A25 3-2
5 BOLTON W	M30 2-1	F09 0-0	F20 3-1	A18 4-1		N24 3-0	S15 2-0	S12 2-0	O27 2-2	a27 1-1	J12 5-3	a19 2-2	D26 1-0	N10 2-0	D08 3-1	a13 1-1	M02 2-3	M16 3-2	S05 2-1	S01 1-0	O13 1-1	S22 0-3
6 BURNLEY	A28 3-1	a15 2-1	S01 2-0	O06 2-2	a06 1-0		D22 6-2	D01 2-1	A18 2-0	S03 2-1	O20 0-0	N03 1-1	a20 0-3	a19 1-3	F02 3-2	S15 1-1	D25 2-2	S29 4-1	M09 2-0	a29 1-0	J12 1-0	N17 3-0
7 CARDIFF C	D15 2-3	a03 1-0	F02 1-2	M09 3-4	J19 2-0	A25 3-3		M23 2-3	S08 1-1	D01 1-0	O06 4-1	a06 0-0	N03 1-1	a27 2-3	A22 5-2	a22 0-2	D29 2-3	S05 2-1	N17 1-0	a20 0-3	S29 0-0	F23 2-2
8 CHARLTON A	O13 1-3	D15 0-2	M30 1-0	F02 0-4	S20 2-1	a13 1-2	N10 0-2		M16 3-1	S29 1-2	A23 1-2	A25 1-2	S15 1-0	F18 1-5	O27 1-1	M02 1-3	D08 3-4	S08 4-4	D29 3-2	a19 1-1	N24 3-2	D25 2-1
9 CHELSEA	D25 1-1	a06 1-1	S15 1-0	D01 2-2	F23 2-2	D15 2-0	J12 1-2	N03 1-3		a20 5-1	D29 1-1	N17 4-1	M09 4-2	S05 1-2	a22 6-2	S29 3-3	A25 1-0	S19 0-0	M23 0-2	O06 2-4	F02 2-4	O20 3-3
10 EVERTON	O27 4-0	S08 0-4	D08 2-0	A22 2-3	A25 2-2	S12 1-0	a13 0-0	F09 5-0	O13 0-3		D15 2-1	J19 2-1	a22 1-1	M06 1-2	M30 2-1	N10 2-2	F27 1-4	N24 1-0	S22 2-1	D26 1-1	M16 0-1	D29 3-1
11 LEEDS U	N24 3-3	S22 1-0	O13 1-1	D26 5-0	S08 3-2	M11 1-1	F16 3-0	A29 4-0	S01 0-0	A18 5-1		F09 1-2	S12 2-0	M30 1-2	M16 0-0	D08 4-1	O27 1-2	N10 3-1	a22 3-1	M02 1-1	a13 0-0	J19 0-0
12 LUTON T	D08 1-2	S05 0-0	a03 0-0	J12 0-2	a22 1-0	M16 0-2	N24 3-0	D22 4-2	M30 0-4	S15 2-0	S29 2-2		S01 3-2	a13 0-2	F16 4-1	M20 1-0	N10 1-1	O13 2-0	A18 6-2	F02 1-3	O27 0-1	A22 1-0
13 MANCHESTER C	M20 2-3	A25 1-1	N10 3-1	S29 0-3	D25 1-3	O13 0-1	M16 4-1	J19 5-1	D08 5-4	a19 2-4	S05 1-0	D29 3-2		F02 2-4	M02 1-2	N24 5-1	a13 0-2	O27 4-2	S08 3-1	A22 2-2	M30 2-1	D15 2-3
14 MANCHESTER U	F09 6-2	M09 1-1	A18 2-2	F23 0-2	M25 0-2	a22 2-0	D26 3-1	O06 4-2	J01 3-0	O20 2-5	N17 3-2	D01 3-1	S22 2-0		J12 6-1	S01 3-0	A29 3-2	S15 4-1	a20 4-0	a06 0-0	a29 1-1	N03 3-0
15 NEWCASTLE U	J19 3-1	a20 1-2	J01 3-2	a06 2-1	M09 4-0	S22 1-1	A29 1-0	F23 3-1	a19 1-2	N17 0-0	N03 2-3	O06 2-2	O20 0-3	S08 1-1		A18 2-1	F09 1-2	D29 1-2	D22 6-2	M23 2-2	D26 5-2	D01 2-1
16 PORTSMOUTH	S08 2-3	O06 5-1	A29 3-4	N17 0-0	D01 1-1	J19 1-0	a19 1-0	O20 1-0	F09 2-2	M23 3-2	M09 2-5	M13 2-2	a06 0-1	D29 1-3	D15 2-2		S22 2-2	A25 3-1	m01 3-2	N03 2-3	a27 0-1	a20 1-0
17 PRESTON N.E.	S10 3-0	N17 3-3	J12 1-0	a20 0-0	O20 2-2	D26 1-0	S01 6-0	M09 4-3	a27 1-0	O06 0-0	F23 3-0	M23 2-0	D01 3-1	A20 1-3	S29 1-0	F02 7-1		a19 1-0	N03 6-0	A18 1-4	S15 3-2	a06 1-0
18 SHEFFIELD W	S22 2-4	D01 2-1	a29 3-0	O20 1-2	N03 1-2	F09 0-0	S12 5-3	J12 3-1	A22 4-0	a06 2-2	M26 2-3	a20 3-0	F23 2-2	J19 2-1	S01 4-0	a09 3-1	a22 3-1		O06 3-2	N17 4-1	A18 4-2	M09 2-1
19 SUNDERLAND	a13 1-0	D25 1-0	N24 0-1	S15 5-2	A22 3-0	D08 2-1	M30 1-1	S01 8-1	N10 1-3	F02 1-1	a19 2-0	D15 1-0	J12 1-1	O13 1-3	A25 1-2	O27 3-3	M16 0-0	F16 5-2		S29 0-2	M13 1-4	J01 2-3
20 TOTTENHAM H	M13 1-3	J19 3-0	a13 5-1	a27 2-1	D29 4-0	O27 2-0	O13 5-0	a22 6-2	F20 3-4	D25 6-0	A25 5-1	S22 5-0	A29 3-2	N24 2-2	N10 3-1	M16 2-0	D15 1-1	M30 1-1	F09 5-2		D08 2-2	S08 4-1
21 W.B.A.	D29 0-2	A22 2-0	a22 0-0	a03 1-3	a20 3-2	S08 2-2	F09 1-2	a06 2-2	S22 2-1	N03 3-0	D01 0-0	F23 4-0	N17 1-1	A25 2-3	D25 1-0	S05 2-1	J19 0-0	D15 1-4	O20 2-0	M09 1-1		O06 1-1
22 WOLVERHAMPTON W	N10 5-2	a23 3-0	S29 3-0	D22 4-1	F02 3-2	M30 1-2	O27 3-1	F16 7-3	M02 3-1	S01 2-1	S15 1-2	A29 5-4	A18 5-1	M16 1-1	a13 2-0	O13 6-0	N24 4-3	D08 2-1	S12 2-2	J12 3-0	a15 5-2	

Derby County centre-forward Ray Straw, whose 37 goals took the Rams out of Division Three North. Straw later signed for Coventry and was the first player to appear in all six divisions of the Football League.

DIVISION 2

	BARNSLEY	BLACKBURN R	BRISTOL C	BRISTOL R	BURY	DONCASTER R	FULHAM	GRIMSBY T	HUDDERSFIELD T	LEICESTER C	LEYTON O	LINCOLN C	LIVERPOOL	MIDDLESBROUGH	NOTTINGHAM F	NOTTS CO	PORT VALE	ROTHERHAM U	SHEFFIELD U	STOKE C	SWANSEA T	WEST HAM U
1 BARNSLEY		S15 3-3	J12 3-0	O13 0-2	M30 1-1	M02 3-1	a22 1-1	N24 2-0	N10 0-5	F27 2-0	M16 3-0	S05 5-2	O27 4-1	A25 1-3	S29 1-1	a13 1-1	D15 2-0	D26 1-1	S01 1-6	D08 2-2	A22 2-3	F02 1-2
2 BLACKBURN R	J19 2-0		F09 3-1	D08 2-0	O27 6-2	N10 2-2	D25 2-0	M16 2-0	a13 3-2	M02 1-1	O13 3-3	A25 3-4	F16 2-2	N24 1-0	J01 2-2	a19 1-1	S08 2-4	D29 3-2	S22 3-1	M30 1-0	D15 5-3	A27 0-2
3 BRISTOL C	S08 1-2	S29 3-0		S22 5-3	M16 2-0	M30 4-0	S04 0-3	N10 0-2	O27 2-1	D08 0-2	a13 4-2	D15 5-1	O13 2-1	M02 2-1	A21 1-5	F20 3-0	D29 3-3	A25 2-1	J19 5-1	N24 1-2	a27 3-1	a19 1-1
4 BRISTOL R	F23 1-1	a20 0-1	F02 0-0		D26 6-1	D22 6-1	N17 4-0	A18 1-0	S10 4-0	S15 1-2	A27 3-2	N03 0-1	a22 0-0	J12 0-2	a06 3-2	F09 3-0	D01 2-1	M09 4-2	O06 3-1	S01 4-0	M23 1-1	O20 1-1
5 BURY	N17 1-2	M09 2-2	N03 2-3	D25 7-2		S29 4-4	O06 0-1	F02 2-3	S08 1-3	S17 4-5	D29 1-3	a20 1-0	A25 0-2	A21 3-2	F23 1-2	D15 2-1	a06 1-0	O20 1-4	M23 0-1	J01 0-1	J19 1-3	D01 3-3
6 DONCASTER R	O20 5-2	M23 1-1	N17 4-1	A25 2-4	F09 1-1		D01 4-0	a22 0-1	S22 4-0	D15 0-2	J19 6-1	O06 3-1	S08 1-1	D26 2-1	M09 1-1	D29 4-2	a20 4-0	A22 1-1	a06 1-0	S10 4-0	F23 0-1	N03 3-0
7 FULHAM	a19 2-0	D26 7-2	S12 2-1	M30 3-2	F16 1-3	a13 3-0		O13 3-1	S01 1-0	N10 2-2	D08 3-1	J19 0-1	M02 1-2	M16 1-2	D22 0-1	N24 5-1	F09 6-3	S22 3-1	A29 1-2	O27 1-0	S08 7-3	A18 1-4
8 GRIMSBY T	a06 4-1	N03 1-3	M23 0-3	D15 3-2	S22 0-1	a19 4-2	F23 3-1		J19 1-2	D25 2-2	S08 0-0	F09 2-0	D29 0-0	S04 3-2	D01 0-0	A25 2-1	O20 1-0	a20 3-2	N17 1-2	A28 4-1	O06 5-0	M09 2-1
9 HUDDERSFIELD T	M23 2-0	D01 0-2	M09 2-1	S03 2-1	J12 1-2	F02 0-1	D29 1-1	S15 2-1		A20 1-2	A25 3-0	O20 0-1	D15 0-3	a23 0-1	O06 1-0	D26 3-0	N17 3-1	a06 1-0	N03 1-4	S29 2-2	a20 2-2	F23 6-2
10 LEICESTER C	O06 5-2	O20 6-0	a20 1-1	J19 7-2	S12 3-0	A18 3-1	M23 1-3	J26 4-3	A29 2-2		a22 1-4	M09 4-3	F09 3-2	S01 1-1	N17 0-0	S22 6-3	F23 2-1	D01 5-2	J12 5-0	D22 3-2	N03 1-1	a06 5-3
11 LEYTON O	N03 2-0	F23 1-1	D01 2-2	A23 1-1	S01 4-3	S15 1-1	a20 0-2	J12 1-1	D22 3-1	a19 1-5		a06 2-1	D26 0-4	S29 1-1	A18 1-4	a27 2-2	M23 3-2	N17 2-1	M09 1-2	F02 2-2	O20 3-0	O06 1-2
12 LINCOLN C	a27 4-1	D22 1-2	A18 1-1	M16 1-0	D08 2-0	F16 4-1	S15 1-0	S29 1-0	M02 1-2	O27 2-3	N24 0-2		M30 3-3	a13 1-1	J12 0-2	N10 1-0	A22 4-0	a19 3-3	D26 4-1	O13 0-1	F02 0-2	S01 0-2
13 LIVERPOOL	M09 2-1	O06 2-3	m01 2-1	a19 4-1	D22 2-0	J12 2-1	O20 4-3	S01 3-2	A18 2-3	S29 2-0	D25 1-0	N17 4-0		F02 1-2	a20 3-1	A29 3-3	N03 4-1	M23 4-1	D01 5-1	S15 0-2	a06 2-0	a27 1-0
14 MIDDLESBROUGH	D22 1-2	a06 2-1	O20 4-1	S08 3-2	A29 2-2	D25 3-2	N03 3-1	S12 2-1	a22 7-2	D29 1-3	F09 1-2	D01 3-0	S22 1-1		M23 2-2	J19 0-0	O06 3-1	F23 0-1	a20 3-1	A18 1-1	M09 6-2	N17 3-1
15 NOTTINGHAM F	F09 7-1	S06 2-1	A30 2-2	N24 1-1	O13 5-1	O27 2-1	A25 3-1	a13 2-1	F21 0-0	M30 1-2	D15 1-2	S08 1-1	D08 1-0	N10 0-4		m01 2-4	S22 4-2	J19 3-1	a22 2-1	M16 4-0	D29 4-3	a15 3-0
16 NOTTS CO	D01 3-2	a23 2-0	O06 1-1	S29 0-2	A18 2-2	S01 1-2	a06 0-0	D22 0-1	D24 1-2	F02 0-0	S13 1-3	M23 3-0	A23 1-1	S15 2-1	O20 1-2		M09 3-1	N03 1-5	F23 2-2	J12 5-0	N17 1-4	a20 4-1
17 PORT VALE	A18 0-0	J12 0-3	S01 3-1	a13 2-3	N24 3-2	D08 4-1	S29 2-1	M02 3-0	M30 1-2	O13 2-3	N10 1-2	A27 1-1	M16 1-2	F16 2-1	F02 1-7	O27 1-2		a27 2-1	M25 0-6	a29 2-2	a19 0-2	S15 0-0
18 ROTHERHAM U	D25 0-0	S01 0-2	D22 6-1	O27 0-0	M02 1-1	A27 0-1	F02 4-3	D08 2-1	N24 3-3	a13 1-1	M30 2-0	a22 3-0	N10 2-2	O13 2-3	S15 3-2	M16 0-0	J01 1-0		A18 0-4	F16 1-0	S29 6-1	J12 0-1
19 SHEFFIELD U	D29 5-0	F02 0-2	S15 1-1	F16 0-0	N10 1-1	N24 4-0	A20 5-2	M30 2-0	M16 2-0	S08 1-1	O27 2-3	D25 2-0	a13 3-0	D08 2-1	a27 0-4	O13 5-1	A25 4-2	D15 2-7		M02 1-1	J01 2-2	S29 1-0
20 STOKE C	a20 3-0	N17 4-1	a06 0-2	D29 2-1	a22 2-0	S03 1-1	M09 0-2	A20 1-0	F09 5-1	A25 3-1	S22 7-1	F23 8-0	J19 1-0	D15 3-1	N03 2-1	S08 6-0	O10 3-1	O06 6-0	O20 3-3		D01 4-1	M23 0-1
21 SWANSEA T	A30 2-3	A18 5-1	D26 5-0	N10 2-3	S15 3-0	O13 4-2	J12 4-5	F16 3-1	D08 4-2	M16 2-3	M02 1-0	S22 1-2	N24 1-1	O27 2-2	S01 1-4	M30 2-1	a22 2-2	F09 1-0	S13 4-1	a13 1-0		D22 3-1
22 WEST HAM U	S22 2-0	A20 1-3	a22 3-1	M02 1-2	a13 1-0	M16 1-1	D15 2-1	O27 0-1	O13 0-2	N24 2-1	F16 2-1	D29 2-1	S03 1-1	M30 1-1	D25 2-1	D08 2-1	J19 2-1	S08 1-1	F09 3-2	N10 1-0	A25 1-2	

Season 1956-57

DIVISION 3 NORTH

	ACCRINGTON S	BARROW	BRADFORD	BRADFORD C	CARLISLE U	CHESTER	CHESTERFIELD	CREWE A	DARLINGTON	DERBY CO	GATESHEAD	HALIFAX T	HARTLEPOOLS U	HULL C	MANSFIELD T	OLDHAM A	ROCHDALE	SCUNTHORPE U	SOUTHPORT	STOCKPORT CO	TRANMERE R	WORKINGTON	WREXHAM	YORK C
1 ACCRINGTON S		A29 4-1	M25 5-0	S24 0-2	J26 1-2	F02 4-0	S15 1-1	M23 5-0	O06 4-2	N03 0-0	D01 2-0	O20 4-0	S29 2-1	a22 0-3	S01 3-3	D22 2-2	a06 2-1	J01 0-1	J12 4-2	a08 4-0	S12 1-0	a20 2-1	M09 1-0	A18 3-0
2 BARROW	A20 3-1		F09 1-0	M02 4-0	D26 3-0	M30 3-0	N10 2-1	D29 3-0	S24 3-1	S08 2-2	S22 1-2	S03 1-0	N24 3-1	J26 1-2	O27 2-0	a13 2-1	D15 2-0	A25 1-2	M16 1-1	J01 0-3	F16 5-0	a22 5-2	J19 2-1	O13 1-2
3 BRADFORD	O13 2-0	S29 4-1		J19 2-0	F16 1-3	M02 3-1	N24 2-0	D15 4-3	F02 3-1	A25 3-2	S08 0-1	J05 2-1	a27 0-2	S17 4-1	N10 1-4	M16 2-2	a23 0-0	S03 1-2	M30 2-3	A20 3-2	a13 1-2	D26 1-3	D29 0-4	O27 0-2
4 BRADFORD C	S19 1-2	O20 0-2	S15 2-0		F09 3-2	S01 1-0	D22 3-2	D01 5-1	a20 1-2	a03 0-2	A29 3-1	M23 1-0	J12 1-1	a06 2-1	S12 4-3	a22 4-1	N03 1-1	M09 3-1	A18 3-1	S22 1-1	D25 4-1	m01 2-3	O06 2-1	J26 0-2
5 CARLISLE U	M19 2-2	D25 1-1	O06 2-1	S29 1-4		S15 3-0	J12 4-2	N03 2-1	O09 1-2	M09 1-3	F23 3-2	a06 0-0	F02 2-1	a09 1-3	D22 6-1	A18 2-2	a30 2-1	M23 0-0	S01 1-2	S25 3-3	a19 2-2	O20 1-1	D01 2-2	J01 2-0
6 CHESTER	S22 0-2	a29 2-0	O20 2-0	D29 1-2	J19 1-2		S12 3-4	O06 4-1	a06 0-3	A22 2-2	a20 4-1	M09 1-1	A25 0-1	M23 1-1	J26 6-2	a10 1-0	D01 2-2	F23 2-2	a22 2-0	S08 1-4	F09 1-1	N03 1-0	D15 0-0	S26 3-4
7 CHESTERFIELD	J19 1-0	M23 3-2	a06 4-1	A25 1-1	S08 2-2	S05 3-0		A22 2-0	m01 4-1	a19 2-2	O20 6-0	D01 2-1	D15 5-1	N03 3-1	D25 1-0	J01 1-0	F23 2-2	O06 1-0	J26 6-0	D29 1-0	S22 3-1	M09 2-2	a20 2-1	F09 3-4
8 CREWE A	N10 3-4	S01 1-1	A18 2-0	a13 1-0	M16 2-2	F16 0-0	A29 0-4		D22 1-3	J05 2-5	S03 0-3	F02 1-3	O13 1-2	J12 2-3	a27 6-4	M02 2-2	S29 1-6	S19 2-1	D25 0-0	O27 0-1	M30 0-0	S15 0-1	a22 3-0	N24 1-1
9 DARLINGTON	F16 0-0	S19 1-1	S22 0-5	a27 3-2	A22 0-1	N24 5-1	M30 4-1	A25 3-0		D29 1-1	J19 7-0	a19 0-1	M02 3-1	D25 1-1	M16 1-3	O27 1-0	J01 4-3	D15 1-2	N10 1-0	S29 3-1	O13 1-1	J26 4-2	S08 1-5	a13 2-4
10 DERBY CO	M16 2-2	J12 3-3	D22 6-1	O13 0-2	O27 3-0	A29 3-0	a22 7-1	J26 4-0	S01 1-1		A18 5-3	S29 6-0	F16 2-0	S15 1-0	M02 4-0	N24 3-2	S19 3-0	D25 4-0	a27 2-0	a13 2-0	N10 4-0	F02 2-3	S12 1-0	M30 1-0
11 GATESHEAD	a13 1-1	F02 2-2	J12 1-3	A20 1-2	O13 4-2	a27 4-1	M02 1-3	S10 1-1	S15 1-2	D15 1-1		D25 2-1	S01 4-3	S29 2-0	M30 1-1	N10 2-3	J05 2-1	a22 0-0	N24 3-1	F16 1-5	O27 3-1	S17 1-2	A25 4-2	M16 0-2
12 HALIFAX T	M02 0-1	S10 3-2	J26 3-1	N10 0-2	N24 1-3	O27 2-1	a13 2-1	S22 1-0	a22 3-2	F09 1-0	a15 0-1		M16 2-0	A18 1-0	F16 2-1	A27 1-1	S08 2-1	J19 1-0	O13 3-1	M30 3-2	a27 4-0	D22 4-2	S24 1-2	S01 0-0
13 HARTLEPOOLS U	F09 2-1	a06 2-0	a20 2-1	S08 2-0	S22 2-1	D22 2-2	A18 5-1	F23 2-0	O20 2-1	O06 2-1	D29 4-1	N03 0-1		J01 3-3	a19 2-1	J26 4-1	M09 0-0	D01 0-0	S10 5-2	J19 4-1	S24 5-1	M23 2-1	A27 2-1	D26 2-0
14 HULL C	a19 2-1	M18 3-0	S24 2-0	N24 1-0	a27 0-0	N10 2-0	M16 3-2	S08 2-0	D26 1-1	J19 3-3	F09 1-1	D15 3-1	M30 2-0		a13 1-2	O13 2-1	A25 2-0	D29 2-2	O27 2-1	M02 6-3	A20 4-1	S03 0-2	S22 1-2	F16 1-1
15 MANSFIELD T	D29 1-3	M09 1-3	M23 2-1	S03 3-1	A25 5-1	J05 1-1	a08 3-0	a20 2-1	N03 7-3	O20 1-2	D08 2-4	O06 2-0	a23 4-1	D01 2-1		S22 2-4	A20 2-3	F09 1-1	a29 1-2	D15 4-2	S08 3-0	a15 2-2	a06 3-1	J19 4-1
16 OLDHAM A	A25 2-4	D01 0-1	N03 3-1	a19 1-1	D15 2-2	D25 0-0	S18 3-3	O20 2-0	M09 3-2	a06 1-2	M23 1-2	A21 4-3	a16 0-0	F23 1-3	F02 1-1		J19 0-1	a20 1-1	S29 2-1	S10 2-0	D29 1-0	O06 1-0	a30 1-2	S08 3-1
17 ROCHDALE	N24 0-2	A18 1-0	a22 2-1	M16 4-1	M30 2-1	a13 2-1	O13 1-0	F09 1-1	S12 3-0	S26 3-1	J26 0-0	J12 1-1	O27 1-0	M05 4-3	A29 0-0	S15 0-2		S22 3-0	F16 6-1	N10 2-2	M02 1-0	S01 0-0	D26 0-2	a27 1-0
18 SCUNTHORPE U	M30 2-3	D22 1-1	S13 2-2	O27 1-1	N10 1-2	O13 3-0	F16 5-1	S27 5-1	A18 1-2	D26 1-4	a19 1-2	S15 6-1	a13 1-2	S01 1-1	S29 0-1	a27 0-0	F02 1-0		A30 1-0	M16 2-3	N24 1-4	J12 2-1	a04 4-3	M02 2-1
19 SOUTHPORT	S08 3-5	N03 0-0	J01 5-1	D15 1-5	D29 4-1	a19 1-1	M26 0-0	a24 0-1	M23 1-0	a20 3-2	a06 2-3	F23 1-1	S04 1-6	M09 1-0	S18 1-1	F09 2-0	O06 0-1	A21 2-2		A25 0-1	J19 1-0	D01 0-1	O20 1-1	S22 1-1
20 STOCKPORT CO	D25 2-1	a20 2-1	A27 4-0	F02 1-1	S17 2-0	J12 2-1	S01 2-1	M09 2-0	F09 5-2	D01 3-2	O06 1-1	a29 2-2	S15 2-4	O20 1-2	A18 2-1	S03 2-1	M23 3-1	N03 1-3	D22 2-0		J05 3-1	a06 0-1	F23 4-0	a22 3-0
21 TRANMERE R	S04 1-2	O06 0-2	D01 0-3	a15 0-0	a22 0-1	S29 3-1	F02 2-2	J01 3-0	a08 2-2	M23 0-1	M09 0-0	a20 0-2	S18 0-1	A28 2-4	J12 3-1	S01 2-1	O20 2-2	a06 4-2	S15 1-1	J26 2-2		M13 1-1	N03 2-4	D22 3-3
22 WORKINGTON	a27 4-1	a19 0-1	D25 0-1	M30 5-1	M02 2-0	M16 0-1	O27 2-1	J19 4-0	J05 6-2	S22 2-1	S26 2-1	A25 3-1	N10 1-1	S12 4-3	O13 3-3	F16 0-0	D29 5-0	S08 2-2	a13 2-0	N24 4-1	D15 3-2		F09 3-0	A29 3-2
23 WREXHAM	O27 5-2	S15 5-0	S01 2-0	F16 1-2	a13 6-4	A18 2-2	a27 1-3	a19 5-0	J12 5-0	S05 0-2	D22 4-1	S19 3-2	A22 2-2	F02 5-2	N24 0-0	M30 4-4	D25 4-1	a10 1-1	M02 1-1	O13 2-3	M16 1-0	S29 3-0		N10 1-1
24 YORK C	D15 3-1	F23 1-0	M09 1-2	J05 3-1	S03 2-0	S17 0-1	S29 1-2	a06 2-1	D01 1-0	a29 1-1	N03 1-0	D29 1-2	D25 3-3	O06 2-1	S15 2-0	J12 2-1	a20 4-0	O20 0-2	F02 9-1	a19 0-0	A25 1-0	A20 2-2	M23 1-0	

DIVISION 3 SOUTH

	ALDERSHOT	BOURNEMOUTH	BRENTFORD	BRIGHTON & HA	COLCHESTER U	COVENTRY C	CRYSTAL P	EXETER C	GILLINGHAM	IPSWICH T	MILLWALL	NEWPORT CO	NORTHAMPTON T	NORWICH C	PLYMOUTH A	Q.P.R.	READING	SHREWSBURY T	SOUTHAMPTON	SOUTHEND U	SWINDON T	TORQUAY U	WALSALL	WATFORD
1 ALDERSHOT		D26 3-2	A25 0-2	S19 1-4	D01 2-1	a27 0-1	a20 2-1	N03 1-4	A22 0-0	S29 3-1	S05 3-0	M09 3-1	a10 4-0	a06 0-0	a19 0-2	O06 4-2	D29 1-4	S15 1-1	M23 1-1	O20 5-3	D15 2-2	J26 0-1	F02 4-1	J12 3-1
2 BOURNEMOUTH	D24 3-2		F09 3-0	S08 1-1	F23 1-1	a19 1-2	D01 2-2	M09 3-1	J19 3-1	A22 1-0	D29 6-1	O20 2-1	a27 4-1	O06 1-1	N03 2-1	M23 1-0	a20 2-1	S05 6-1	D15 1-0	a06 1-1	S22 7-0	A25 0-0	S19 2-2	m03 4-0
3 BRENTFORD	D22 2-2	S29 2-2		S04 2-5	a06 1-1	M23 1-1	O20 1-1	a20 3-0	S18 3-2	F02 1-1	M04 5-0	D01 0-0	O06 2-1	a27 1-1	A18 4-1	a19 3-0	M09 1-0	J12 0-1	N03 1-0	M12 0-0	A21 4-1	D25 0-0	S15 0-1	S01 1-5
4 BRIGHTON & H.A.	S26 2-2	J12 2-2	S12 1-2		N03 0-0	O20 2-1	a22 1-1	O06 3-0	D26 3-1	S01 3-2	F02 3-2	M23 2-0	M09 5-0	a20 3-0	a06 3-1	D01 1-0	a27 8-3	A18 4-3	F23 1-0	F09 1-1	J05 2-0	S15 6-0	D22 1-3	A29 2-2
5 COLCHESTER U	a13 1-1	O13 3-0	N24 1-0	M16 0-0		J05 3-2	A27 3-3	S24 4-0	N10 0-0	F16 0-0	O27 2-1	F02 1-0	D22 5-1	D25 1-1	J12 2-1	S01 1-1	S15 3-2	S29 6-0	S10 3-1	A18 3-2	M30 1-1	M02 2-1	a19 2-1	a29 2-0
6 COVENTRY C	M30 5-1	a23 4-2	N10 1-1	M02 1-2	J26 2-4		a01 3-3	A18 1-0	O27 4-1	S24 1-1	O13 1-2	a08 2-0	J12 3-1	S10 3-2	F02 1-4	S15 5-1	S29 0-1	a13 3-3	A20 2-1	S01 2-0	M16 3-0	F16 3-2	D08 2-2	N24 0-2
7 CRYSTAL P	O27 2-1	a13 1-1	M02 0-2	a19 2-2	A22 2-4	A25 1-1		S08 0-0	F16 1-2	N24 1-3	S15 2-2	S19 2-1	S29 1-1	D15 4-1	J26 2-1	D25 2-1	S05 1-1	N10 0-1	D29 1-2	F02 2-0	O13 0-0	m01 1-1	M30 3-0	M16 0-0
8 EXETER C	M16 1-1	m01 1-2	O27 1-1	F16 1-3	S19 0-2	D15 4-2	J12 2-1		O13 4-0	a13 1-2	a22 1-1	S05 2-0	F02 0-0	A22 0-0	D26 2-1	S29 0-0	J26 1-1	M30 5-1	A25 0-4	S15 6-1	M02 3-2	S01 1-1	N24 0-1	N10 1-2
9 GILLINGHAM	A29 6-2	S15 1-0	S26 2-1	D25 0-0	M23 1-2	a20 1-2	O06 4-1	F23 2-1		J12 1-1	S29 1-3	a27 1-1	J26 1-2	N03 1-1	D01 0-3	M09 0-1	a06 0-0	D22 1-1	O20 0-0	a19 0-2	S05 3-0	F02 1-1	S01 2-1	A18 0-3
10 IPSWICH T	F09 4-1	A29 1-0	S22 4-0	D29 4-0	O06 3-1	S19 4-0	a06 4-2	D01 3-0	S08 1-1		A25 0-2	F23 5-0	M23 0-1	a22 3-1	a20 2-1	N03 4-0	O20 4-2	J26 5-1	M09 2-0	a27 3-3	J19 4-1	D15 6-0	S12 2-2	D26 4-1
11 MILLWALL	S10 1-5	S01 3-4	M18 1-1	S22 4-3	a20 3-1	F23 3-2	J19 3-0	a19 1-3	F09 2-1	D22 2-2		N03 1-0	D01 1-0	O20 5-1	a27 2-2	a06 2-0	M20 1-0	A27 0-0	O06 0-0	M09 0-0	D26 2-1	J12 7-2	A18 1-0	S24 1-1
12 NEWPORT CO	m02 3-0	M07 5-3	a13 3-0	N10 0-0	S22 1-0	M21 3-0	S27 2-2	S13 1-1	M30 4-0	O13 1-0	M16 0-0		A18 3-0	F09 3-1	S01 4-1	D22 1-1	J12 1-2	a19 2-0	a04 2-3	A30 2-1	N24 2-1	O27 3-0	F16 2-2	S15 3-0
13 NORTHAMPTON T	O13 4-2	M30 2-2	F16 5-1	a30 1-0	A25 1-0	S08 4-0	F09 1-0	S22 1-1	J05 4-1	N10 2-1	a13 2-1	D15 0-3		D29 1-1	S17 2-0	S06 3-0	A23 3-0	O27 1-1	J19 2-1	D25 2-2	a23 2-0	N24 3-0	M16 2-3	M02 1-2
14 NORWICH C	N24 1-1	F20 1-3	M30 1-1	O27 1-1	D26 1-2	S05 3-0	A18 1-0	A20 1-0	M16 1-3	a19 1-2	M02 2-0	S29 1-1	S01 2-1		S15 3-0	J12 1-2	F02 2-5	m01 3-0	N28 0-3	D22 1-2	N10 2-4	O13 1-2	J05 2-2	a13 1-2
15 PLYMOUTH A	a22 2-2	M16 2-0	D15 2-0	N24 2-0	S08 2-2	S22 0-0	M11 0-1	J05 5-0	a13 2-0	O27 1-2	M30 0-0	a10 3-2	S24 4-3	J19 3-2		A20 1-2	A25 0-6	O13 1-1	F09 2-1	S10 0-0	a29 1-0	N10 0-0	M02 2-4	F16 3-3
16 Q.P.R.	F16 0-1	N10 2-1	a22 2-2	a13 0-0	D29 1-1	J19 1-1	D26 4-2	F09 5-3	a29 5-0	M16 0-2	N24 0-0	A25 1-1	S10 1-0	S08 3-1	A27 3-0		D15 1-1	M02 2-1	S22 1-2	M25 3-0	S24 3-0	M30 0-1	O27 1-0	O13 3-1
17 READING	S01 2-1	O27 0-4	m01 2-0	M30 2-2	J19 0-3	F09 3-0	S12 1-2	M13 4-0	N24 4-0	M02 1-3	N10 3-0	S08 0-0	A29 1-1	S22 2-1	D22 3-2	A18 1-0		F16 2-2	M26 2-4	S26 3-2	a13 1-0	M16 3-1	O13 3-0	a22 1-2
18 SHREWSBURY T	J19 2-2	S10 0-0	S08 3-2	D15 4-0	F09 1-3	D01 5-0	M23 1-1	a27 1-2	A25 1-0	M28 1-1	A20 2-0	a22 2-0	a20 2-0	M09 4-5	F23 3-1	O20 0-0	O06 1-1		a06 0-0	N03 0-0	D29 7-3	S17 1-1	a29 3-2	S22 1-0
19 SOUTHAMPTON	N10 1-0	A18 3-0	M16 3-3	O13 1-0	S05 2-1	A29 1-1	S01 3-0	D22 2-2	M02 0-1	m01 0-2	F25 4-0	m04 3-0	S15 2-0	O03 2-0	S29 2-2	F02 1-2	D26 4-1	N24 4-0		J12 1-2	O27 2-1	a22 1-0	a13 3-1	M30 3-1
20 SOUTHEND U	M02 2-4	N24 2-1	O13 1-0	S29 3-1	D15 3-2	D29 1-2	S22 1-1	J19 2-0	a22 5-0	M30 2-0	m01 1-0	A22 3-3	D26 0-1	A25 0-0	S05 0-1	a15 3-0	S19 4-0	M16 1-2	S08 1-2		F16 1-0	a13 2-0	N10 2-0	O27 2-0
21 SWINDON T	A18 1-2	F02 2-1	A29 1-3	J26 3-0	a27 4-1	N03 2-2	F23 3-1	O20 3-5	S12 2-3	S15 3-1	a10 1-0	a06 1-0	a22 4-0	M23 1-1	M09 0-3	S19 1-0	D01 3-2	S01 1-2	a20 0-0	O06 3-2		S29 1-2	J12 1-2	D22 2-0
22 TORQUAY U	M13 4-2	D22 1-0	D26 2-0	J19 1-0	O20 4-2	O06 3-1	M09 3-0	D29 1-0	S22 3-3	A18 4-1	S08 7-2	a20 4-0	a06 2-0	F23 7-1	M23 1-1	a27 3-0	N03 3-1	S26 1-1	a19 2-0	D01 3-3	F09 7-0		A29 2-0	S12 3-0
23 WALSALL	S22 5-1	S27 0-0	J19 7-0	A25 3-2	a22 2-1	M09 1-1	a27 1-2	a06 2-0	D29 2-2	S06 2-0	D15 7-1	O06 0-0	N03 2-2	J26 6-3	O20 1-0	a20 0-2	F23 3-2	D25 1-1	D01 1-1	M23 0-1	S08 1-2	A23 0-1		F09 2-0
24 WATFORD	S08 3-0	M26 1-1	D29 1-1	A21 2-1	M09 0-0	a06 1-0	N03 1-4	M23 1-1	D15 2-3	D25 2-1	S18 2-0	J19 5-0	O20 2-1	D01 3-3	O06 0-1	F23 2-4	a19 1-0	F02 2-3	a27 4-2	a20 1-1	A25 3-4	S04 4-1	S29 1-0	

LEAGUE TABLES

DIVISION 1

	P	W	D	L	F	A	W	D	L	F	A	Pts
Manchester U	42	14	4	3	55	25	14	4	3	48	29	64
Tottenham H	42	15	4	2	70	24	7	8	6	34	32	56
Preston NE	42	15	4	2	50	19	8	6	7	34	37	56
Blackpool	42	14	3	4	55	26	8	6	7	38	39	53
Arsenal	42	12	5	4	45	21	9	3	9	40	48	50
Wolves	42	17	2	2	70	29	3	6	12	24	41	48
Burnley	42	14	5	2	41	21	4	5	12	15	29	46
Leeds U	42	10	8	3	42	18	5	6	10	30	45	44
Bolton W	42	13	6	2	42	23	3	6	12	23	42	44
Aston Villa	42	10	8	3	45	25	4	7	10	20	30	43
WBA	42	8	8	5	31	25	6	6	9	28	36	42
Birmingham C	42	12	5	4	52	25	3	4	14	17	44	*39
Chelsea	42	7	8	6	43	36	6	5	10	30	37	*39
Sheffield W	42	14	3	4	55	29	2	3	16	27	59	38
Everton	42	10	5	6	34	28	4	5	12	27	51	38
Luton T	42	10	4	7	32	26	4	5	12	26	50	37
Newcastle U	42	10	5	6	43	31	4	3	14	24	56	36
Manchester C	42	10	2	9	48	42	3	7	11	30	46	35
Portsmouth	42	8	6	7	37	35	2	7	12	25	57	33
Sunderland	42	9	5	7	40	30	3	3	15	27	58	32
Cardiff C	42	7	6	8	35	34	3	3	15	18	54	29
Charlton A	42	7	3	11	31	44	2	1	18	31	76	22

**Birmingham City & Chelsea finished in equal 12th position*

DIVISION 2

	P	W	D	L	F	A	W	D	L	F	A	Pts
Leicester C	42	14	5	2	68	36	11	6	4	41	31	61
Nottingham F	42	13	4	4	50	29	9	6	6	44	26	54
Liverpool	42	16	1	4	53	26	5	10	6	29	28	53
Blackburn R	42	12	6	3	49	32	9	4	8	34	43	52
Stoke C	42	16	2	3	64	18	4	6	11	19	40	48
Middlesbrough	42	12	5	4	51	29	7	5	9	33	31	48
Sheffield U	42	11	6	4	45	28	8	2	11	42	48	46
West Ham U	42	12	4	5	31	24	7	4	10	28	39	46
Bristol R	42	12	5	4	47	19	6	4	11	34	48	45
Swansea T	42	12	3	6	53	34	7	4	10	37	56	45
Fulham	42	13	1	7	53	32	6	3	12	31	44	42
Huddersfield T	42	10	3	8	33	27	8	3	10	35	47	42
Bristol C	42	13	2	6	49	32	3	7	11	25	47	41
Doncaster R	42	12	5	4	51	21	3	5	13	26	56	40
Leyton O	42	7	8	6	34	38	8	2	11	32	46	40
Grimsby T	42	12	4	5	41	26	5	1	15	20	36	39
Rotherham U	42	9	7	5	37	26	4	4	13	37	49	37
Lincoln C	42	9	4	8	34	27	5	2	14	20	53	34
Barnsley	42	8	7	6	39	35	4	3	14	20	54	34
Notts Co	42	7	6	8	34	32	2	6	13	24	54	30
Bury	42	5	3	13	37	47	3	6	12	23	49	25
Port Vale	42	7	4	10	31	42	1	2	18	26	59	22

DIVISION 3 North

	P	W	D	L	F	A	W	D	L	F	A	Pts
Derby Co	46	18	3	2	69	18	8	8	7	42	35	63
Hartlepools U	46	18	4	1	56	21	7	5	11	34	42	59
Accrington S	46	15	4	4	54	22	10	4	9	41	42	58
Workington	46	16	4	3	60	25	8	6	9	33	38	58
Stockport Co	46	16	3	4	51	26	7	5	11	40	49	54
Chesterfield	46	17	5	1	60	22	5	4	14	36	57	53
York C	46	14	4	5	43	21	7	6	10	32	40	52
Hull C	46	14	6	3	45	24	7	4	12	39	45	52
Bradford C	46	14	3	6	47	31	8	5	10	31	37	52
Barrow	46	16	2	5	51	22	5	7	11	25	40	51
Halifax T	46	16	2	5	40	24	5	5	13	25	46	49
Wrexham	46	12	7	4	63	33	7	3	13	34	41	48
Rochdale	46	14	6	3	38	19	4	6	13	27	46	48
Scunthorpe U	46	9	5	9	44	36	6	10	7	27	33	45
Carlisle U	46	9	9	5	44	36	7	4	12	32	49	45
Mansfield T	46	13	3	7	58	38	4	7	12	33	52	44
Gateshead	46	9	6	8	42	40	8	4	11	30	50	44
Darlington	46	11	5	7	47	36	6	3	14	35	59	42
Oldham A	46	9	7	7	35	31	3	8	12	31	43	39
Bradford	46	11	2	10	41	40	5	1	17	25	53	35
Chester	46	8	7	8	40	35	2	6	15	15	49	33
Southport	46	7	8	8	31	34	3	4	16	21	60	32
Tranmere R	46	5	9	9	33	38	2	4	17	18	53	27
Crewe A	46	5	7	11	31	46	1	2	20	12	64	21

DIVISION 3 South

	P	W	D	L	F	A	W	D	L	F	A	Pts
Ipswich T	46	18	3	2	72	20	7	6	10	29	34	59
Torquay U	46	19	4	0	71	18	5	7	11	18	46	59
Colchester U	46	15	8	0	49	19	7	6	10	35	37	58
Southampton	46	15	4	4	48	20	7	6	10	28	32	54
Bournemouth	46	15	7	1	57	20	4	7	12	31	42	52
Brighton & HA	46	15	6	2	59	26	4	8	11	27	39	52
Southend U	46	14	3	6	42	20	4	9	10	31	45	48
Brentford	46	12	9	2	55	29	4	7	12	23	47	48
Shrewsbury T	46	11	9	3	45	24	4	9	10	27	55	48
QPR	46	12	7	4	42	21	6	4	13	19	39	47
Watford	46	11	6	6	44	32	7	4	12	28	43	46
Newport Co	46	15	6	2	51	18	1	7	15	14	44	45
Reading	46	13	4	6	44	30	5	5	13	36	51	45
Northampton T	46	15	5	3	49	22	3	4	16	17	51	45
Walsall	46	11	7	5	49	25	5	5	13	31	49	44
Coventry C	46	12	6	6	52	36	4	7	12	22	48	44
Millwall	46	13	7	3	46	29	3	5	15	18	55	44
Plymouth A	46	10	8	5	38	31	6	3	14	30	42	43
Aldershot	46	11	5	7	43	35	4	7	12	36	57	42
Crystal P	46	7	10	6	31	28	4	8	11	31	47	40
Exeter C	46	8	8	7	37	29	4	5	14	24	50	37
Gillingham	46	7	8	8	29	29	5	5	13	25	56	37
Swindon T	46	12	3	8	43	33	3	3	17	23	63	36
Norwich C	46	7	5	11	33	37	1	10	12	28	57	31

Football League Records

Top scorers: Div 1, R.Smith (Tottenham Hotspur) 36 goals; Div 2, B.Clough (Middlesbrough) 40 goals; Div 3(N), A.Ackerman (Carlisle United) 35 goals; Div 3(S), D.Reeves (Southampton), S.McGrory (Southend United) 31 goals.

Norman Deeley, the winger who was a star of Wolves' League Championship triumph in 1957-8.

DIVISION 1

	ARSENAL	ASTON VILLA	BIRMINGHAM C	BLACKPOOL	BOLTON W	BURNLEY	CHELSEA	EVERTON	LEEDS U	LEICESTER C	LUTON T	MANCHESTER C	MANCHESTER U	NEWCASTLE U	NOTTINGHAM F	PORTSMOUTH	PRESTON N.E.	SHEFFIELD W	SUNDERLAND	TOTTENHAM H	W.B.A.	WOLVERHAMPTON W
1 ARSENAL		O02 4-0	O19 1-3	J11 2-3	F18 1-2	a19 0-0	M08 5-4	S10 2-3	S28 2-1	S14 3-1	A31 2-0	N02 2-1	F01 4-5	N30 2-3	a21 1-1	N16 3-2	D14 4-2	M22 1-0	D21 3-0	F22 4-4	A27 2-2	a07 0-2
2 ASTON VILLA	D26 3-0		D21 0-2	F01 1-1	a08 4-0	M08 3-0	F22 1-3	A31 0-1	A26 2-0	S28 5-1	S14 2-0	D14 1-2	M31 3-2	O19 4-3	a30 1-1	N02 2-1	N30 2-2	a19 2-0	J11 5-2	N16 1-1	a05 2-1	S23 2-3
3 BIRMINGHAM C	M01 4-1	A24 3-1		N23 0-0	O26 5-1	J18 2-3	D28 3-3	M29 2-1	a12 1-1	a26 0-1	M15 1-1	O05 4-0	D07 3-3	S07 1-4	S04 0-2	a07 4-1	S21 3-1	M12 1-0	N09 2-3	S11 0-0	D26 3-5	O12 1-5
4 BLACKPOOL	S07 1-0	S21 1-1	M22 4-2		D28 2-3	N16 2-4	N02 2-1	a23 0-1	A24 3-0	D25 5-1	A26 1-2	O19 2-5	S09 1-4	a05 3-2	M08 3-0	N30 2-1	a04 1-2	F22 2-2	O05 7-0	D14 0-2	a19 2-0	J18 3-2
5 BOLTON W	O05 0-1	a04 4-0	M08 1-0	A31 3-0		D14 2-1	N30 3-3	D26 1-5	F01 0-2	J11 2-3	D21 1-2	a05 0-2	S14 4-0	a19 1-1	N16 2-0	S28 1-0	a21 0-4	N02 5-4	S11 2-2	O19 3-2	F22 2-2	S04 1-1
6 BURNLEY	D07 2-1	O26 3-0	S14 3-1	M29 2-1	a26 3-1		F01 2-1	M01 0-2	N23 3-1	N09 7-3	F15 1-2	D25 2-1	M15 3-0	S28 0-2	S09 3-1	D21 3-1	A27 2-0	a04 2-0	O12 6-0	J11 2-0	A31 2-2	a12 1-1
7 CHELSEA	O26 0-0	O12 4-2	A31 5-1	M15 1-4	a12 2-2	S21 6-1		J11 3-1	D07 2-1	N23 4-0	N09 1-3	A28 2-3	a26 2-1	J18 2-1	a04 0-0	D25 7-4	F08 0-2	O05 1-0	M29 0-0	D21 2-4	S11 2-2	M11 1-2
8 EVERTON	O16 2-2	D28 1-2	N16 0-2	N20 0-0	D25 1-1	O19 1-1	S07 3-0		a04 0-1	F15 2-2	F01 0-2	a19 2-5	S04 3-3	F22 1-2	D14 1-1	M22 4-2	M08 4-2	N30 1-1	S14 3-1	a05 3-4	N02 1-1	A24 1-0
9 LEEDS U	M19 2-0	S04 4-0	N30 1-1	D21 2-1	S21 2-1	M22 1-0	a19 0-0	a07 1-0		A31 2-1	S11 0-2	N16 2-4	J11 1-1	D14 3-0	S14 1-2	F22 2-0	N02 2-3	a05 2-2	S25 2-1	M08 1-2	O19 1-1	O05 1-1
10 LEICESTER C	J18 0-1	F08 6-1	D14 2-2	D26 2-1	S07 2-3	a05 5-3	M22 3-2	O05 2-2	D28 3-0		a08 4-1	F22 8-4	A24 0-3	N02 2-1	O19 3-1	M08 2-2	N16 1-3	S18 4-1	A28 4-1	a19 1-3	N30 3-3	S21 2-3
11 LUTON T	D28 4-0	J18 3-0	N02 3-0	S04 2-0	A24 1-0	O05 3-2	a05 0-2	S21 0-1	S18 1-1	a07 2-1		M08 1-2	D26 2-2	N16 0-3	N30 3-1	a19 2-1	F22 1-3	O19 2-0	F08 7-1	M22 0-0	D14 5-1	S07 3-1
12 MANCHESTER C	M15 2-4	a26 1-2	M05 1-1	M01 4-3	N09 2-1	D26 4-1	S04 5-2	D07 6-2	M29 1-0	O12 4-3	O26 2-2		D28 2-2	a07 2-1	J11 1-1	S14 2-1	S11 2-0	O09 2-0	a12 3-1	S28 5-1	F01 4-1	N23 3-4
13 MANCHESTER U	S21 4-2	O05 4-1	a19 0-2	S18 1-2	J18 7-2	N02 1-0	D14 0-1	A28 3-0	S07 5-0	D21 4-0	D25 3-0	A31 4-1		a23 1-1	F22 1-1	O19 0-3	a05 0-0	N16 2-1	a04 2-2	N30 3-4	M08 0-4	a21 0-4
14 NEWCASTLE U	a12 3-3	M01 2-4	J11 1-2	N09 1-2	D07 1-2	a28 1-3	S14 1-3	O12 2-3	a26 1-2	M15 5-3	M29 3-2	a14 4-1	N23 1-2		D25 1-4	S11 2-0	O05 0-2	S25 0-0	F01 2-2	A31 3-1	D21 3-0	O26 1-1
15 NOTTINGHAM F	N09 4-0	N23 4-1	A28 1-1	O26 1-2	M29 0-0	S18 7-0	a07 1-1	a26 0-3	J18 1-1	M01 3-1	a12 1-0	S07 2-1	O12 1-2	D26 2-3		F01 2-0	A24 2-1	D28 5-2	D07 2-0	F15 1-2	S28 0-2	M15 1-4
16 PORTSMOUTH	M29 5-4	M15 1-0	a04 3-2	a12 1-2	F08 2-2	A24 0-0	D26 3-0	N23 3-2	O12 1-2	O26 2-0	D07 5-0	J18 2-1	a16 3-3	S18 2-2	S21 1-4		D28 0-2	S07 3-2	a26 0-2	A28 5-1	M19 2-2	N09 1-1
17 PRESTON N.E.	a26 3-0	a12 1-1	F01 8-0	a07 2-1	N23 3-0	S04 2-1	S28 5-2	O26 3-1	M15 3-0	M29 4-1	O12 1-0	S18 6-1	N09 1-1	M19 2-1	D21 2-0	A31 4-0		D26 3-0	M01 3-0	S14 3-1	J11 3-1	D07 1-2
18 SHEFFIELD W	N23 2-0	D07 2-5	S28 5-3	O12 0-3	M15 1-0	a07 1-2	F15 2-3	a12 2-1	N09 3-2	S11 2-1	M01 2-1	D21 4-5	M29 1-0	S04 1-0	A31 1-2	J11 4-2	D25 4-4		O26 3-3	F01 2-0	S14 1-2	a26 2-1
19 SUNDERLAND	A24 0-1	S07 1-1	a05 1-6	F15 1-4	S18 1-2	F22 2-3	N16 2-2	J18 1-1	D26 2-1	S04 3-2	S28 3-0	N30 2-1	a07 1-2	S21 2-0	a19 3-0	D14 1-1	O19 0-0	M08 3-3		N02 1-1	M22 2-0	D28 0-2
20 TOTTENHAM H	O12 3-1	M29 6-2	S18 7-1	a26 2-1	M12 4-1	S07 3-1	A24 1-1	N09 3-1	O26 2-0	D07 1-4	N23 3-1	F08 5-1	a12 1-0	D28 3-3	O05 3-4	S04 3-5	J18 3-3	S21 4-2	M15 0-1		a04 0-0	D26 1-0
21 W.B.A.	S04 1-2	N09 3-2	O01 0-0	D07 1-1	O12 2-2	D28 5-1	S18 1-1	M15 4-0	M12 1-0	a12 6-2	a26 4-2	S21 9-2	O26 4-3	A24 2-1	F08 3-2	O05 3-1	S07 4-1	J18 3-1	N23 3-0	a07 0-2		M29 0-3
22 WOLVERHAMPTON W	a08 1-2	S16 2-1	F22 5-1	S14 3-1	A28 6-1	N30 2-1	O19 2-1	D21 2-0	F19 3-2	F01 5-1	J11 1-1	M22 3-3	S28 3-1	M08 3-1	N02 2-0	a05 1-0	a19 2-0	D14 4-3	A31 5-0	O02 4-0	N16 1-1	

John Dick netted 21 goals as West Ham returned to Division One. Only three players have scored more than his 166 goals for the Hammers overall.

DIVISION 2

	BARNSLEY	BLACKBURN R	BRISTOL C	BRISTOL R	CARDIFF C	CHARLTON A	DERBY CO	DONCASTER R	FULHAM	GRIMSBY T	HUDDERSFIELD T	IPSWICH T	LEYTON O	LINCOLN C	LIVERPOOL	MIDDLESBROUGH	NOTTS CO	ROTHERHAM U	SHEFFIELD U	STOKE C	SWANSEA T	WEST HAM U
1 BARNSLEY		S18 0-2	N30 4-1	A24 2-2	a19 1-1	O19 4-1	D28 3-0	M08 1-1	J18 1-0	N16 3-3	M22 2-3	S04 5-1	a05 3-0	a08 1-3	D14 2-1	S21 1-1	D26 1-1	N02 3-0	a23 0-2	F22 1-2	S07 1-0	S28 1-0
2 BLACKBURN R	S09 3-1		M24 5-0	J18 2-0	N16 4-0	D14 1-1	S21 3-1	a07 3-2	O05 1-1	M08 3-0	O19 1-1	A24 0-0	a19 4-1	S07 0-1	F22 3-3	N30 3-3	D28 3-0	a05 5-0	D25 1-0	N02 1-0	F08 2-2	A26 2-1
3 BRISTOL C	a12 5-0	N09 0-0		O12 3-2	a07 2-0	J18 1-2	D25 2-1	S21 2-2	D07 0-5	S10 3-2	O05 1-3	M15 1-0	S07 2-2	M01 4-0	A24 1-2	D28 0-0	O26 3-1	F08 0-1	M29 1-4	S03 2-1	a26 1-2	N23 1-1
4 BRISTOL R	D21 1-1	S14 4-0	a05 3-3		O19 0-2	N16 1-0	A26 5-2	F22 2-1	a04 2-2	D14 0-7	a19 1-1	F01 3-1	M22 4-0	F19 3-0	M08 3-1	N02 5-0	S28 5-2	N30 1-3	J11 2-2	S16 2-0	D26 3-0	A31 2-3
5 CARDIFF C	D07 7-0	M29 4-3	a04 2-3	M26 0-2		S21 0-3	O12 3-2	F08 3-1	a26 3-0	S04 1-3	S11 1-0	N09 1-1	J18 1-1	O26 3-2	D28 6-1	S07 0-2	M15 2-0	O05 2-2	N23 0-0	D26 5-2	A24 0-0	a12 0-3
6 CHARLTON A	M01 4-2	a26 3-4	S14 1-0	M29 2-3	F01 3-1		N09 2-2	D25 2-0	O26 2-2	A31 2-0	D21 7-6	D07 4-1	S12 3-2	N23 4-1	S28 5-1	F15 6-2	a12 4-1	a04 4-0	A29 3-1	J11 3-0	M15 1-1	O12 0-3
7 DERBY CO	A31 1-4	F01 0-3	D26 5-2	S04 2-1	a05 0-2	M22 1-3		N16 1-0	D21 3-3	a19 1-0	N30 2-4	S28 2-2	N02 2-0	S18 3-2	O19 2-1	M08 2-1	F15 2-1	F22 3-4	S14 2-0	D14 0-0	a07 1-0	J11 2-3
8 DONCASTER R	O28 1-1	a04 1-5	F01 2-1	N23 3-2	S28 0-1	D26 1-2	M29 1-2		M15 1-6	J11 3-3	A31 0-3	a26 1-1	A28 2-0	a12 1-3	F19 1-1	S18 3-2	D07 4-0	D21 3-2	O12 2-2	S14 0-1	N09 3-0	M01 1-2
9 FULHAM	S14 1-1	a23 1-1	a19 3-4	a07 3-0	D14 2-0	M08 3-1	A24 2-0	N02 4-1		F22 6-0	N16 2-1	S18 0-0	O19 3-1	D26 4-1	S07 2-2	a21 0-1	S04 1-0	m01 3-1	S28 6-3	N30 3-4	D28 2-0	F01 2-2
10 GRIMSBY T	M29 2-1	O26 3-4	S17 1-1	a26 3-2	A27 1-1	D28 4-2	D07 3-2	S07 3-1	N23 3-1		S21 4-1	M01 0-2	A24 7-2	F08 4-0	D25 3-1	a04 4-1	O12 2-0	J18 3-1	M15 1-3	a22 0-0	a12 2-2	N09 1-2
11 HUDDERSFIELD T	N09 0-5	M05 2-1	F19 0-0	D07 0-0	S18 1-1	A24 3-3	a12 0-0	D28 2-2	M29 0-3	F01 1-0		O12 3-0	a08 2-0	a26 0-1	S04 2-1	D25 1-0	J18 3-0	S07 1-3	O26 1-1	S28 1-0	N23 2-2	M15 3-1
12 IPSWICH T	A28 3-0	D21 2-1	N02 4-2	S21 3-2	M22 3-1	a19 1-4	F08 2-2	D14 2-0	S11 1-1	O19 3-2	a05 4-0		N30 5-3	J18 1-1	N16 3-1	F22 1-1	S07 2-1	A31 1-2	a07 1-0	M08 1-3	O05 0-1	D26 2-1
13 LEYTON O	O12 2-1	D07 5-1	J11 4-0	N09 1-3	S14 4-2	S19 3-2	M15 1-1	S05 2-0	M13 1-3	D21 5-1	a04 3-1	a12 2-0		M29 1-0	F01 1-0	S28 4-0	N23 2-2	D25 6-2	a26 0-1	A31 0-2	O26 5-1	F20 1-4
14 LINCOLN C	a07 1-3	J11 1-1	a23 4-0	O05 0-1	a30 3-1	F22 2-3	S11 1-1	N30 1-1	D25 0-1	S28 1-4	D14 1-1	S14 2-1	N16 2-0		N02 0-1	M22 2-3	F01 2-2	a19 2-0	A31 2-2	a05 1-3	S04 4-0	D21 1-6
15 LIVERPOOL	a26 1-1	N23 2-0	D21 4-3	O26 2-0	A31 3-0	F08 3-1	M05 2-0	O05 5-0	J11 2-1	D26 3-2	A28 1-1	M29 3-1	S21 3-0	M15 1-0		J18 0-2	N09 4-0	N27 2-0	a12 1-0	a07 3-0	O12 4-0	D07 1-1
16 MIDDLESBROUGH	F01 3-1	a12 2-3	A31 0-0	M15 4-3	J11 4-1	O05 2-0	O26 3-2	S11 5-0	O12 2-0	a07 5-1	D26 0-1	N23 5-2	M19 2-0	N09 3-1	S14 2-2		M29 3-1	A28 2-2	D07 1-2	D21 1-3	M01 2-1	a26 1-3
17 NOTTS CO	D25 2-3	A31 1-1	M08 0-1	a23 0-0	N02 5-2	N30 2-1	O05 1-0	a19 0-5	A29 1-5	a05 2-0	S14 1-1	J11 0-3	F22 0-1	S21 1-0	M22 0-2	N16 2-0		D14 1-0	D21 1-0	O19 1-2	S12 2-4	a08 1-0
18 ROTHERHAM U	M15 4-1	O12 1-2	S28 4-1	a12 2-0	a21 3-1	a07 1-5	N23 0-2	A24 2-1	N09 3-1	F15 2-0	J11 1-1	D28 1-4	D26 2-2	D07 1-2	S19 2-2	S05 1-4	a26 1-3		M01 1-6	F01 0-2	M29 5-2	O26 1-2
19 SHEFFIELD U	O05 0-0	D26 4-2	N16 0-3	S07 2-0	F22 3-0	S02 0-3	J18 0-1	a05 3-0	a28 1-1	N02 3-1	M08 3-2	a08 1-1	D14 0-2	D28 4-0	N30 1-1	a19 3-2	A24 1-0	O19 2-0		M22 3-0	S21 2-2	S16 2-1
20 STOKE C	N23 3-1	M15 2-4	A26 3-0	S09 3-5	N04 3-0	S07 2-2	a26 2-1	J18 0-0	a12 1-2	O05 4-1	F08 1-1	O26 5-1	D28 1-3	O12 1-1	S23 1-2	A24 4-1	M01 0-1	S21 4-1	N09 2-3		D09 6-2	M29 1-4
21 SWANSEA T	J11 4-2	S28 0-4	D14 5-1	D25 6-4	D21 0-1	N02 1-3	a08 7-0	M22 4-3	A31 4-4	N30 0-2	F22 1-1	F15 0-0	M08 1-2	A29 5-1	a05 0-2	O19 1-4	S19 1-3	N16 1-3	F01 0-2	a19 4-1		S14 3-2
22 WEST HAM U	F08 1-1	S02 1-1	F22 3-2	D28 6-1	N30 1-1	a05 0-0	S07 2-1	O19 1-1	S21 3-2	M22 2-0	N02 5-2	D25 1-1	O05 3-2	A24 2-2	a19 1-1	D14 2-1	a04 3-1	M08 8-0	S09 0-3	N16 5-0	J18 6-2	

Season 1957-58

DIVISION 3 NORTH

	ACCRINGTON S	BARROW	BRADFORD	BRADFORD C	BURY	CARLISLE U	CHESTER	CHESTERFIELD	CREWE A	DARLINGTON	GATESHEAD	HALIFAX T	HARTLEPOOLS U	HULL C	MANSFIELD T	OLDHAM A	ROCHDALE	SCUNTHORPE U	SOUTHPORT	STOCKPORT CO	TRANMERE R	WORKINGTON	WREXHAM	YORK C
1 ACCRINGTON S		a24 3-2	D28 5-2	M15 2-2	M05 3-0	S07 3-2	S30 1-2	S16 0-4	D26 2-0	a12 0-0	N23 3-0	a14 2-1	A24 1-2	O26 3-0	M29 4-1	O05 1-1	S02 3-2	O12 2-1	J18 2-2	M01 3-2	a04 2-1	N09 3-0	D14 2-1	S21 3-0
2 BARROW	S28 3-1		S16 0-0	a21 1-2	F01 4-2	a07 2-3	F15 4-1	J01 4-1	a12 0-1	N09 2-1	D07 1-2	a26 0-3	S30 3-3	S02 0-0	O26 2-1	S14 2-2	O12 2-1	M29 0-1	A24 1-0	J11 1-1	D25 1-4	M01 0-0	N23 2-2	D28 1-0
3 BRADFORD	A31 1-3	S09 1-1		O12 0-0	D21 1-4	J04 4-1	J11 3-0	S14 2-0	M15 3-1	a14 4-1	A26 2-2	D07 0-2	S28 2-3	a12 4-4	F15 0-2	a07 1-3	N09 2-2	M01 1-2	D25 3-5	N23 1-0	F01 1-0	a26 3-3	O26 2-0	S25 0-2
4 BRADFORD C	N02 1-1	a05 4-1	M22 2-1		M08 3-3	D14 1-1	a19 5-0	a29 0-0	J18 2-1	O05 3-1	M11 0-1	D28 3-0	N30 0-1	a08 1-0	D26 1-1	O19 0-0	S07 1-0	a24 2-3	S18 2-0	A24 2-1	F22 3-0	O01 0-0	S21 3-1	S04 3-2
5 BURY	J01 1-1	S21 4-1	A24 1-0	O26 1-0		D28 3-0	D25 1-2	S23 1-0	a26 2-0	N23 5-0	M29 4-1	S02 1-0	a07 3-3	M01 1-1	N09 0-2	F08 4-0	F15 4-1	a12 2-1	S07 4-1	F12 1-1	S16 8-2	M15 3-0	O12 3-0	J18 4-1
6 CARLISLE U	J11 6-1	a14 2-1	J01 2-3	a26 0-3	A31 0-2		S14 3-2	F01 2-2	N09 2-0	M01 5-2	F18 5-1	N23 2-1	F15 1-2	O12 0-1	A27 3-4	D21 1-1	M29 1-0	O26 3-4	O01 4-0	a12 3-1	S28 3-1	D25 2-2	M15 4-0	S10 2-1
7 CHESTER	a30 5-1	O05 2-2	S07 1-2	N09 0-0	D26 0-0	J18 0-0		a07 0-0	A28 3-2	O12 0-1	a12 1-1	M01 1-1	D28 2-1	M15 1-1	N23 1-2	J04 0-0	a16 2-0	D14 1-2	S21 1-1	O26 3-0	A24 1-3	M29 4-3	S18 0-1	F08 9-2
8 CHESTERFIELD	S11 1-0	J04 4-3	J18 1-1	M29 0-1	a23 1-1	S21 1-3	a04 2-1		D07 1-1	a26 2-0	O12 5-3	O26 1-1	S07 2-1	N09 0-0	a12 1-4	D26 2-1	M01 2-2	A24 1-1	a16 0-0	M15 2-1	D28 2-1	N23 3-0	S04 3-2	O05 2-0
9 CREWE A	D25 4-1	N30 1-4	N02 3-0	S14 2-2	D14 0-1	a19 0-0	S02 0-3	a05 1-2		a04 2-2	D21 2-2	F15 1-2	M08 2-1	F01 1-2	A31 1-0	M22 0-2	a21 0-0	S18 0-2	a23 3-2	S28 1-2	O19 0-4	J11 0-3	O02 2-0	F22 3-4
10 DARLINGTON	N30 0-2	a19 3-0	a05 4-0	F19 4-0	F22 3-2	O19 1-2	M22 2-3	D14 2-0	a07 3-0		S14 2-2	O02 5-0	S04 1-3	a23 2-2	F01 2-0	a28 3-1	S18 4-2	D28 1-1	M19 1-2	D26 1-0	S07 2-1	S28 3-1	A24 2-1	N02 2-0
11 GATESHEAD	F22 1-3	N02 0-2	S02 2-4	J01 0-0	J04 1-2	a05 3-2	N30 3-2	M22 3-0	A24 3-1	J18 4-0		S16 0-0	S21 0-0	D26 3-1	a14 2-1	a19 1-0	a07 3-2	S07 1-2	O19 2-1	O14 3-0	D14 2-3	F15 3-0	D28 1-1	M24 0-0
12 HALIFAX T	a05 0-2	D14 3-1	M29 2-0	A31 3-2	A26 1-2	F22 5-0	O19 2-1	M08 3-2	O05 2-0	S23 1-0	S09 4-1		a19 3-0	J11 2-2	a08 4-0	S21 4-0	a29 4-1	D26 0-1	N30 4-1	S14 0-0	N02 1-1	D21 2-2	a21 0-0	M22 2-1
13 HARTLEPOOLS U	D21 1-1	S23 4-1	F08 0-0	a12 2-0	a04 2-1	O05 0-1	A31 2-1	J11 0-2	O26 1-1	A26 5-1	F01 2-2	N09 5-0		N23 5-1	a26 2-0	S09 4-1	M15 1-3	a28 1-2	J01 2-1	M29 1-2	S14 1-1	O12 1-0	M01 1-2	D25 2-2
14 HULL C	M25 1-0	A26 1-1	N30 3-3	a07 1-3	O19 2-1	M22 4-0	N02 3-0	a19 1-0	S21 1-0	M10 2-1	D25 1-1	S07 5-2	F22 1-1		S30 1-1	a05 9-0	J18 2-1	O05 2-0	D14 3-2	D28 1-0	M17 0-0	S09 3-2	F08 2-0	A24 0-1
15 MANSFIELD T	J25 0-2	M08 4-2	O05 2-1	D25 5-2	a19 6-4	S02 2-0	F22 3-1	N30 1-1	D28 2-1	S21 4-2	a28 3-0	a07 2-1	D14 5-1	S23 1-3		N02 4-4	A24 2-4	J18 3-5	a05 3-0	S09 2-2	M22 4-1	M10 6-3	S07 2-1	O19 2-1
16 OLDHAM A	F15 0-3	J18 1-1	a04 4-2	M01 1-1	S28 1-3	A24 1-0	a22 5-1	D25 2-1	O12 1-0	M29 2-2	N09 0-0	F01 2-4	S17 4-0	a15 1-1	M15 1-1		a26 0-0	N23 2-1	D28 3-2	S03 2-4	O01 1-0	O26 4-1	a12 4-1	S07 2-3
17 ROCHDALE	A28 3-0	M22 1-1	a19 1-2	J11 0-2	O05 1-1	M11 1-0	a05 1-1	O19 3-4	J04 3-0	S11 5-4	a04 0-0	S28 5-1	N02 7-0	S14 2-1	D21 3-0	D14 1-3		S25 1-4	F22 2-0	F01 3-0	M08 2-0	A31 1-0	D25 2-0	N30 2-1
18 SCUNTHORPE U	M22 1-0	a17 1-0	O19 6-2	S28 0-2	N30 1-0	m01 3-1	a26 2-1	D21 1-1	S12 3-2	A31 5-0	J11 2-1	O31 1-1	a05 2-0	F20 2-0	S14 3-3	F22 1-1	O03 2-0		N02 1-0	M13 4-0	S05 1-0	F01 2-2	a07 1-0	a19 1-2
19 SOUTHPORT	S14 3-3	D21 0-4	D26 2-1	S10 0-2	J11 2-2	S24 2-0	F01 2-4	S28 5-2	M29 2-0	O26 0-3	M01 1-0	a12 0-3	J04 0-0	a26 1-2	M31 4-1	A31 2-1	N23 0-2	M15 1-2		O12 1-0	F15 0-3	A27 0-1	N09 1-3	a04 0-1
20 STOCKPORT CO	O19 0-0	S07 2-0	F22 3-0	D21 0-4	a05 4-0	N30 4-1	M08 2-2	N02 4-1	F08 5-1	D25 4-1	S23 5-1	J18 4-2	a14 2-1	A31 1-0	S16 3-3	A26 3-0	S21 0-3	a21 2-1	M22 1-2		a19 2-1	a04 0-2	O05 1-1	D14 2-1
21 TRANMERE R	a07 0-1	D26 1-1	S21 5-0	N23 4-1	S09 1-1	F08 0-1	D21 2-2	A31 1-2	M01 5-2	J11 2-1	a26 2-1	M15 2-0	J18 3-2	M29 4-4	O12 1-2	S23 1-1	O26 3-1	A26 1-4	O05 2-1	N09 2-2		a12 1-0	a30 2-1	J01 6-1
22 WORKINGTON	a19 0-1	O19 0-1	D14 1-2	S25 1-1	N02 3-0	D26 2-1	J25 5-3	F22 0-2	S07 3-2	F08 2-2	O05 1-1	A24 4-4	M22 1-0	S18 3-2	a23 4-0	M08 4-2	D28 1-2	S21 3-2	S04 2-0	a07 1-1	N30 1-2		J18 4-2	a05 0-0
23 WREXHAM	a26 1-0	F22 0-0	M08 1-1	F01 1-1	M22 2-0	N02 1-0	S11 1-0	A28 2-2	S25 0-1	D21 2-0	A31 1-2	J04 2-1	O19 3-1	S28 6-0	J11 4-2	N30 2-2	D26 2-0	a04 1-0	a19 1-0	F15 1-0	a05 2-2	S14 1-1		a16 2-2
24 YORK C	F01 0-3	A31 0-0	S30 3-0	A26 2-0	S14 2-1	S16 0-5	S28 1-2	F15 3-3	N23 3-1	m01 3-0	O26 2-2	O12 1-1	D26 2-2	D21 3-1	M01 3-1	J11 2-2	a12 1-0	N09 0-0	a07 1-0	a26 0-0	a23 4-0	a28 3-0	M29 1-2	

DIVISION 3 SOUTH

	ALDERSHOT	BOURNEMOUTH	BRENTFORD	BRIGHTON & HA	COLCHESTER U	COVENTRY C	CRYSTAL P	EXETER C	GILLINGHAM	MILLWALL	NEWPORT CO	NORTHAMPTON T	NORWICH C	PLYMOUTH A	PORT VALE	Q.P.R.	READING	SHREWSBURY T	SOUTHAMPTON	SOUTHEND U	SWINDON T	TORQUAY U	WALSALL	WATFORD
1 ALDERSHOT		M22 0-0	N02 0-2	O02 2-3	a16 2-1	a19 1-1	O19 4-1	F15 2-2	S28 2-0	F01 2-2	a04 2-1	S04 0-0	J25 2-1	D28 3-3	A24 0-1	a23 1-1	J11 1-0	D14 0-1	D25 1-5	S18 0-2	S14 2-1	M08 1-1	N30 1-3	F22 2-2
2 BOURNEMOUTH	N23 5-1		J18 1-0	S04 1-3	S21 1-1	S18 0-0	D28 3-1	O26 2-1	M15 2-1	N09 4-0	M29 4-3	a04 1-1	F08 3-1	a12 0-0	a30 3-1	M01 4-1	D25 4-1	O02 3-1	F15 5-2	O12 2-1	a26 1-1	S07 2-0	J04 1-2	A24 2-1
3 BRENTFORD	M15 4-2	S14 4-2		a28 1-0	A31 3-3	S28 1-3	D25 0-3	A27 1-0	O12 1-0	M01 4-1	N23 2-1	S10 7-1	J11 7-1	N09 2-0	a26 4-1	D21 1-1	M11 2-1	F15 2-0	a12 0-0	M29 4-2	O26 0-0	a07 0-1	F01 2-1	O01 0-0
4 BRIGHTON & H.A.	S26 0-1	A28 2-1	a10 1-1		D14 5-2	O19 3-0	M22 3-2	A31 2-2	D21 5-2	a07 4-2	O05 5-3	a05 1-4	S21 0-1	S11 3-2	J04 0-0	J11 1-1	N02 1-2	M08 2-1	F08 1-1	S14 3-1	D26 1-0	N30 1-1	F22 2-0	a30 6-0
5 COLCHESTER U	N09 1-1	F01 3-2	D28 1-1	M29 1-2		F15 4-1	a07 1-1	O12 3-0	M01 3-3	O26 3-1	a12 1-1	S30 1-0	S14 1-2	a26 1-2	N23 2-1	S02 2-1	S09 1-3	a21 3-0	m01 4-2	J11 1-0	M15 1-3	A24 3-0	S28 1-1	D26 4-0
6 COVENTRY C	M17 6-0	S09 0-3	F08 0-0	M01 2-2	O05 1-0		J18 2-2	N09 6-1	a26 1-1	N23 1-4	S02 1-2	D28 1-1	a21 2-1	M29 1-1	D25 1-0	M15 1-1	A24 1-0	a08 5-0	O12 0-0	O26 1-0	a12 0-1	S21 2-1	M24 4-1	S07 2-2
7 CRYSTAL P	M01 1-1	A31 3-0	D26 2-1	N23 2-4	a04 1-1	S14 2-0		M29 2-0	S11 3-0	A28 0-1	N09 2-2	F15 1-3	D21 0-3	O26 3-0	M15 1-0	a16 2-3	S28 2-2	F01 3-0	a26 1-4	a12 2-0	O12 4-1	O02 1-1	J11 4-1	a23 4-2
8 EXETER C	O05 3-0	M08 1-2	S04 3-5	D28 2-0	F22 4-3	a05 1-0	D14 0-1		S25 1-3	S11 2-0	J18 0-2	N30 0-1	O19 2-2	F08 4-2	S21 1-0	a07 0-0	M22 1-1	a16 2-1	S07 2-2	A24 0-5	a23 0-1	D26 5-1	N02 2-1	a19 1-2
9 GILLINGHAM	F08 1-1	a16 1-1	F22 3-2	A24 0-1	O19 2-3	a30 3-2	S18 3-0	O02 1-1		a23 1-0	S07 0-1	a19 1-2	M08 1-0	S21 1-0	J18 0-2	D25 1-1	N30 2-1	M22 1-3	D28 2-1	a04 2-0	O05 2-1	S04 1-0	a05 3-0	D14 1-1
10 MILLWALL	S21 3-3	a05 0-2	O19 0-1	a04 2-2	M08 1-4	J04 4-1	S02 3-0	S16 3-0	M17 3-1		D28 1-2	D14 0-0	N02 2-2	J18 0-1	S07 2-1	S30 5-0	a19 0-0	N30 1-3	A24 1-2	D26 1-2	F08 1-1	F22 1-2	J25 1-3	O05 2-3
11 NEWPORT CO	a07 3-2	D14 3-1	M22 1-2	F15 1-2	N30 2-2	A29 2-2	a05 0-0	S14 0-0	J11 5-0	A31 1-2		M08 0-1	a19 1-0	D25 0-2	N11 2-1	F01 4-2	O28 0-0	F22 2-0	J04 1-1	S28 1-0	D21 4-1	M06 3-2	S12 2-0	N02 2-1
12 NORTHAMPTON T	A29 0-0	a08 4-0	S16 3-1	N09 2-4	S26 4-1	A31 4-0	O05 1-2	a12 9-0	M27 3-1	M29 7-2	O26 0-3		D26 0-1	O12 5-0	M01 3-2	N23 1-5	S14 1-2	J11 2-0	M15 1-3	a26 1-3	F01 3-0	a24 1-0	D21 3-0	F08 2-3
13 NORWICH C	a26 1-3	S28 2-2	S07 3-2	F01 0-0	J18 1-1	M05 1-1	A24 3-2	M01 3-2	O26 2-0	M15 1-1	a16 5-2	O09 2-2		N23 1-0	a12 3-0	O12 2-0	O23 2-2	S18 2-0	M29 0-2	S04 0-2	N09 1-1	D28 3-1	F15 2-1	a07 1-1
14 PLYMOUTH A	A31 4-2	N30 3-1	a05 0-0	S16 2-1	O09 1-1	D14 4-0	M08 1-0	S28 1-0	F01 2-1	S14 1-0	D26 1-0	F22 3-0	M22 0-1		a04 1-0	F15 3-1	A26 1-0	D21 2-2	S30 4-0	a21 2-3	J11 2-2	N02 1-0	a19 2-1	O19 2-1
15 PORT VALE	D21 6-1	a19 2-3	M24 0-1	a23 2-2	M22 2-0	D26 0-1	N02 4-0	F01 3-2	S14 2-0	J11 1-1	S30 2-2	O19 3-0	N30 2-2	a07 0-0		S28 2-1	F22 1-2	S02 0-0	S16 4-0	F15 1-3	A31 3-1	a05 2-1	D14 2-1	M08 5-0
16 Q.P.R.	M03 0-1	O19 3-0	A24 1-0	S07 0-1	A26 1-0	N02 3-0	a19 4-2	a04 1-1	D26 1-1	S23 3-0	S21 1-1	M22 1-0	F22 1-1	O05 1-0	F08 2-1		M17 3-0	a28 3-0	J18 3-2	D28 1-1	S16 2-1	D14 1-1	M08 1-0	N30 3-0
17 READING	S07 3-0	D26 2-0	a23 1-2	M15 1-1	S18 7-0	D21 3-1	F08 2-2	N23 2-0	a12 4-0	F19 4-1	M01 1-0	J18 5-2	O02 1-2	S04 1-3	O12 3-0	J25 3-0		A31 2-2	O26 1-0	N09 1-1	M29 0-4	O05 1-0	a04 3-1	S21 1-1
18 SHREWSBURY T	M29 5-1	S23 0-4	O05 0-2	O26 2-0	J04 0-0	a07 1-3	S21 0-0	a26 1-0	N23 2-1	a12 0-1	O12 1-1	S07 3-1	S09 0-0	A24 2-0	A26 1-0	N09 2-1	D28 0-2		M01 1-3	M15 1-1	D07 1-3	F08 3-0	D26 2-0	J18 1-1
19 SOUTHAMPTON	D26 2-2	O05 7-0	N30 4-2	S28 5-0	a19 3-2	F22 7-1	J25 2-1	J11 6-0	A31 5-1	D21 3-2	a23 2-1	N02 2-1	D14 7-3	S25 0-1	S11 0-3	S14 5-0	M08 0-1	O19 2-2		F01 2-2	O09 1-3	M22 4-2	A28 4-1	a05 5-0
20 SOUTHEND U	S11 1-2	F22 2-0	D14 0-0	J18 0-2	S07 2-3	M08 5-1	N30 1-1	D21 2-0	a07 2-0	D25 2-0	F08 1-1	m02 6-3	A28 5-2	a16 2-1	O05 1-1	A31 6-0	a05 2-1	N02 5-1	S21 3-2		S25 2-3	a19 0-0	O19 4-1	M22 2-1
21 SWINDON T	J18 3-0	J25 1-0	M08 4-1	D25 2-2	N02 4-0	N30 2-1	F22 0-0	J04 5-1	F15 1-1	S28 3-0	A24 4-0	S21 5-1	a05 1-2	S07 1-0	D28 0-0	S11 1-1	D14 1-1	a19 1-0	a07 1-0	O02 2-1		O19 3-1	M22 2-3	S04 0-0
22 TORQUAY U	O26 2-1	J11 3-1	a04 0-1	a12 2-0	D21 1-3	F01 1-0	S26 1-1	D26 1-3	A28 3-2	O12 2-3	a26 2-2	a16 1-0	A31 1-1	M15 0-2	N09 1-1	M29 3-1	F15 1-4	S28 0-2	N23 1-1	a29 2-2	M01 2-2		S14 2-1	S11 1-0
23 WALSALL	a12 0-0	a24 3-1	S21 0-2	O12 2-3	F08 3-0	M10 4-1	S07 2-1	M15 3-0	N09 1-1	a26 4-2	S19 3-0	A24 2-1	O05 2-1	M03 0-2	M29 3-0	O26 1-2	a07 0-0	D25 0-1	S05 1-1	M01 1-1	N23 1-1	J18 0-0		D28 1-3
24 WATFORD	O12 1-3	D21 1-1	S24 4-1	a26 0-1	O15 1-1	J11 1-0	M25 2-1	D07 5-4	M29 3-0	F15 3-0	M15 2-2	S28 0-2	a04 1-4	M01 0-2	O26 0-2	a12 0-0	F01 1-1	S14 3-0	N09 3-0	N23 1-1	A27 0-0	S17 1-0	A31 1-1	

LEAGUE TABLES

DIVISION 1

	P	W	D	L	F	A	W	D	L	F	A	Pts
Wolves	42	17	3	1	60	21	11	5	5	43	26	64
Preston NE	42	18	2	1	63	14	8	5	8	37	37	59
Tottenham H	42	13	4	4	58	33	8	5	8	35	44	51
WBA	42	14	4	3	59	29	4	10	7	33	41	50
Manchester C	42	14	4	3	58	33	8	1	12	46	67	49
Burnley	42	16	2	3	52	21	5	3	13	28	53	47
Blackpool	42	11	2	8	47	35	8	4	9	33	32	44
Luton T	42	13	3	5	45	22	6	3	12	24	41	44
Manchester U	42	10	4	7	45	31	6	7	8	40	44	43
Nottingham F	42	10	4	7	41	27	6	6	9	28	36	42
Chelsea	42	10	5	6	47	34	5	7	9	36	45	42
Arsenal	42	10	4	7	48	39	6	3	12	25	46	39
Birmingham C	42	8	6	7	43	37	6	5	10	33	52	39
Aston Villa	42	12	4	5	46	26	4	3	14	27	60	39
Bolton W	42	9	5	7	38	35	5	5	11	27	52	38
Everton	42	5	9	7	34	35	8	2	11	31	40	37
Leeds U	42	10	6	5	33	23	4	3	14	18	40	37
Leicester C	42	11	4	6	59	41	3	1	17	32	71	33
Newcastle U	42	6	4	11	38	42	6	4	11	35	39	32
Portsmouth	42	10	6	5	45	34	2	2	17	28	54	32
Sunderland	42	7	7	7	32	33	3	5	13	22	64	32
Sheffield W	42	12	2	7	45	40	0	5	16	24	52	31

DIVISION 2

	P	W	D	L	F	A	W	D	L	F	A	Pts
West Ham U	42	12	8	1	56	25	11	3	7	45	29	57
Blackburn R	42	13	7	1	50	18	9	5	7	43	39	56
Charlton A	42	15	3	3	65	33	9	4	8	42	36	55
Liverpool	42	17	3	1	50	13	5	7	9	29	41	54
Fulham	42	13	5	3	53	24	7	7	7	44	35	52
Sheffield U	42	12	5	4	38	22	9	5	7	37	28	52
Middlesbrough	42	13	3	5	52	29	6	4	11	31	45	45
Ipswich T	42	13	4	4	45	29	3	8	19	23	40	44
Huddersfield T	42	9	8	4	28	24	5	8	8	35	42	44
Bristol R	42	12	5	4	52	31	5	3	13	33	49	42
Stoke C	42	9	4	8	49	36	9	2	10	26	37	42
Leyton O	42	14	2	5	53	27	4	3	14	24	52	41
Grimsby T	42	13	4	4	54	30	4	2	15	32	53	40
Barnsley	42	10	6	5	40	25	4	6	11	30	49	40
Cardiff C	42	10	5	6	44	31	4	4	13	19	46	37
Derby Co	42	11	3	7	37	36	3	5	13	23	45	36
Bristol C	42	9	5	7	35	31	4	4	13	28	57	35
Rotherham U	42	8	3	10	38	44	6	2	13	27	57	33
Swansea T	42	8	3	10	48	45	3	6	12	24	54	31
Lincoln C	42	6	6	9	33	35	5	3	13	22	47	31
Notts Co	42	9	3	9	24	31	3	3	15	20	49	30
Doncaster R	42	7	5	9	34	40	1	6	14	22	48	27

DIVISION 3 North

	P	W	D	L	F	A	W	D	L	F	A	Pts
Scunthorpe U	46	16	5	2	46	19	13	3	7	42	31	66
Accrington S	46	16	4	3	53	28	9	5	9	30	33	59
Bradford C	46	13	7	3	42	19	8	8	7	31	30	57
Bury	46	17	4	2	61	18	6	6	11	33	44	56
Hull C	46	15	6	2	49	20	4	9	10	29	47	53
Mansfield T	46	16	3	4	68	42	6	5	12	32	50	52
Halifax T	46	15	5	3	52	20	5	6	12	31	49	51
Chesterfield	46	12	8	3	39	28	6	7	10	32	41	51
Stockport Co	46	15	4	4	54	28	3	7	13	20	39	47
Rochdale	46	14	4	5	50	25	5	4	14	29	42	46
Tranmere R	46	12	6	5	51	32	6	4	13	31	44	46
Wrexham	46	13	8	2	39	18	4	4	15	22	45	46
York C	46	11	8	4	40	26	6	4	13	28	50	46
Gateshead	46	12	5	6	41	27	3	10	10	27	49	45
Oldham A	46	11	7	5	44	32	3	10	10	28	52	45
Carlisle U	46	13	3	7	56	35	6	3	14	24	43	44
Hartlepools U	46	11	6	6	45	26	5	6	12	28	50	44
Barrow	46	9	7	7	36	32	4	8	11	30	42	41
Workington	46	11	6	6	46	33	3	7	13	26	48	41
Darlington	46	15	3	5	53	25	2	4	17	25	64	41
Chester	46	7	10	6	38	26	6	3	14	35	55	39
Bradford	46	8	6	9	41	41	5	5	13	27	54	37
Southport	46	8	3	12	29	40	3	3	17	23	48	28
Crewe A	46	6	5	12	29	41	2	2	19	18	52	23

DIVISION 3 South

	P	W	D	L	F	A	W	D	L	F	A	Pts
Brighton & HA	46	13	6	4	52	30	11	6	6	36	34	60
Brentford	46	15	5	3	52	24	9	5	9	30	32	58
Plymouth A	46	17	4	2	43	17	8	4	11	24	31	58
Swindon T	46	14	7	2	47	16	7	8	8	32	34	57
Reading	46	14	5	4	52	23	7	8	8	27	28	55
Southampton	46	16	3	4	78	31	6	7	10	34	41	54
Southend U	46	14	5	4	56	26	7	7	9	34	32	54
Norwich C	46	11	9	3	41	28	8	6	9	34	42	53
Bournemouth	46	16	5	2	54	24	5	4	14	27	50	51
QPR	46	15	6	2	40	14	3	8	12	24	51	50
Newport Co	46	12	6	5	40	24	5	8	10	33	43	48
Colchester U	46	13	5	5	45	27	4	8	11	32	52	47
Northampton T	46	13	1	9	60	33	6	5	12	27	46	44
Crystal P	46	12	5	6	46	30	3	8	12	24	42	43
Port Vale	46	12	6	5	49	24	4	4	15	18	34	42
Watford	46	9	8	6	34	27	4	8	11	25	50	42
Shrewsbury T	46	10	6	7	29	25	5	4	14	20	46	40
Aldershot	46	7	9	7	31	34	5	7	11	28	55	40
Coventry C	46	10	9	4	41	24	3	4	16	20	57	39
Walsall	46	10	7	6	37	24	4	2	17	24	51	37
Torquay U	46	9	7	7	33	34	2	6	15	16	40	35
Gillingham	46	12	5	6	33	24	1	4	18	19	57	35
Millwall	46	6	6	11	37	36	5	3	15	26	55	31
Exeter C	46	10	4	9	37	35	1	5	17	20	64	31

Football League Records

Top scorers: Div 1, J.Greaves (Chelsea) 33 goals; Div 2, B.Clough (Middlesbrough) 42 goals; Div 3, E.Towers (Brentford) 32 goals; Div 4, A.Rowley (Shrewsbury Town) 37 goals.
The two sections of Division Three formed the new Third and Fourth Divisions. Scunthorpe & Lindsey United dropped '& Lindsey' from their name.

Ron Flowers, another England half-back who skippered Wolverhampton Wanderers to the First Division title.

DIVISION 1

	ARSENAL	ASTON VILLA	BIRMINGHAM C	BLACKBURN R	BLACKPOOL	BOLTON W	BURNLEY	CHELSEA	EVERTON	LEEDS U	LEICESTER C	LUTON T	MANCHESTER C	MANCHESTER U	NEWCASTLE U	NOTTINGHAM F	PORTSMOUTH	PRESTON N.E.	TOTTENHAM H	W.B.A.	WEST HAM U	WOLVERHAMPTON W
1 ARSENAL		D13 1-2	m04 2-1	M14 1-1	N29 1-4	S09 6-1	A26 3-0	a11 1-1	J17 3-1	F24 1-0	A30 5-1	D27 1-0	S20 4-1	F28 3-2	N01 3-2	N15 3-1	a25 5-2	D20 1-2	S13 3-1	O04 4-3	M28 1-2	O18 1-1
2 ASTON VILLA	O22 1-2		A23 1-1	F18 1-0	S20 1-1	O25 2-1	a18 0-0	J31 3-1	N08 2-4	M07 2-1	a04 1-2	M21 3-1	D06 1-1	D27 0-2	O04 2-1	S06 2-3	A25 3-2	N22 2-0	M30 1-1	O11 1-4	J03 1-2	S08 1-3
3 BIRMINGHAM C	a14 4-1	D20 4-1		a22 3-0	D13 4-2	a08 1-3	S13 2-1	a25 4-1	F21 2-1	S17 4-1	S27 4-2	A30 0-1	D26 6-1	N29 0-4	N15 1-0	O18 0-3	N01 2-2	F07 5-1	a11 5-1	S03 0-6	F28 3-0	M14 0-3
4 BLACKBURN R	O25 4-2	S27 2-3	N08 3-2		S15 0-0	D06 1-1	M07 4-1	D25 0-3	M21 2-1	N22 2-4	A25 5-0	a20 3-1	a18 2-1	M02 1-3	D20 3-0	M27 3-0	F07 2-1	O11 4-1	A30 5-0	a04 0-0	F21 1-2	S13 1-2
5 BLACKPOOL	a18 1-2	F07 2-1	a20 2-0	S08 1-1		M07 4-0	O11 1-1	M27 5-0	O25 1-1	a04 3-0	M21 2-1	D06 3-0	N22 0-0	A30 2-1	A25 3-0	F21 1-0	S13 1-1	D25 4-2	D20 0-0	N08 1-1	S27 2-0	a13 0-1
6 BOLTON W	S17 2-1	M18 1-3	S06 2-0	a25 3-1	O18 4-0		S27 1-2	M04 6-0	D27 0-3	A23 4-0	M27 3-3	J31 4-2	S03 4-1	N15 6-3	D13 1-1	S20 3-2	N29 2-1	F21 2-1	M28 4-1	J03 2-1	N01 0-2	a11 2-2
7 BURNLEY	S02 3-1	N29 3-1	J31 0-1	O18 0-0	M17 3-1	a14 0-1		O04 4-0	S09 3-1	J03 3-1	D27 3-3	S20 2-2	A23 3-4	M28 4-2	a25 2-2	N01 0-2	a11 2-1	M27 1-0	D13 3-1	S06 1-3	M14 1-0	N15 0-2
8 CHELSEA	N22 0-3	S13 2-1	D06 1-0	D27 0-2	M30 3-1	O11 0-1	F21 1-3		a18 3-1	N08 2-0	O25 5-2	M07 3-3	a04 2-0	D20 2-3	S10 6-5	S27 4-1	J17 2-2	M21 3-1	A27 4-2	a22 0-2	F07 3-2	A30 6-2
9 EVERTON	S06 1-6	M28 2-1	O04 3-1	N01 2-2	M14 3-1	D26 1-0	S17 1-2	N29 3-1		S20 3-2	D20 0-1	M30 3-1	J31 3-1	O18 3-2	A30 0-2	a11 1-3	D13 2-1	A27 1-4	F28 2-1	F18 3-3	N15 2-2	a25 0-1
10 LEEDS U	S27 2-1	O18 0-0	S10 0-0	a11 2-1	N15 1-1	D20 3-4	A30 1-1	M28 4-0	F07 1-0		S13 1-1	A26 1-1	F21 0-4	N01 1-2	N29 3-2	D13 1-0	F28 1-1	J17 1-3	M14 3-1	D27 0-1	a25 1-0	M31 1-3
11 LEICESTER C	J03 2-3	N15 6-3	M18 2-4	S03 1-1	N01 0-3	M30 0-0	D26 1-1	M14 0-3	A23 2-0	J31 0-1		O04 3-1	S06 3-1	a25 2-1	F28 0-1	N29 0-3	M28 3-1	S17 2-2	O18 3-4	S20 2-2	a11 1-1	D13 1-0
12 LUTON T	D26 6-3	N01 2-1	J03 0-1	D13 1-1	a25 1-1	S13 0-0	F07 6-2	O18 2-1	M27 0-1	S03 1-1	F21 4-3		S17 5-1	a11 0-0	M28 4-2	a09 5-1	a22 3-1	S27 4-1	N15 1-2	A23 1-1	S06 4-1	N29 0-1
13 MANCHESTER C	F07 0-0	a25 0-0	D27 4-1	N29 0-1	a11 0-2	A27 3-3	D20 1-4	N15 5-1	S13 1-3	O04 2-1	a29 3-1	S10 1-1		S27 1-1	M14 5-1	M28 1-1	O18 3-2	A30 1-1	N01 5-1	M30 0-2	D13 3-1	F28 1-4
14 MANCHESTER U	O11 1-1	D26 2-1	a18 1-0	S06 6-1	J03 3-1	a04 3-0	N08 1-3	A23 5-2	M07 2-1	M21 4-0	D06 4-1	N22 2-1	F14 4-1		J31 4-4	S03 1-1	M27 6-1	O08 0-2	S20 2-2	O25 1-2	S17 4-1	F21 2-1
15 NEWCASTLE U	M21 1-0	F21 1-0	a29 1-1	A23 1-5	S03 1-0	a22 2-0	D06 5-2	S17 1-2	J03 4-0	a18 2-2	O11 3-1	N08 1-0	O25 4-1	S13 1-1		D26 1-3	S27 2-0	M07 1-2	J17 1-2	N22 1-2	M30 3-1	F07 3-4
16 NOTTINGHAM F	a04 1-1	a20 2-0	M07 1-7	M31 1-1	O04 2-0	F07 3-0	M21 1-2	a15 1-3	N22 2-1	a22 0-3	a18 1-4	O11 3-1	N08 4-0	A27 0-3	D27 3-0		A30 5-0	O25 0-1	S10 1-1	D06 1-1	S13 4-0	D20 1-3
17 PORTSMOUTH	D06 0-1	S03 5-2	M21 1-1	S20 2-1	J31 1-2	a18 0-1	N22 4-2	S06 2-2	a15 2-3	O11 2-0	N08 4-1	O25 2-2	M07 3-4	M30 1-3	M11 1-5	J03 0-1		a04 1-2	O04 1-1	S17 2-6	A23 1-2	D26 3-5
18 PRESTON N.E.	A23 2-1	a11 4-2	S20 3-0	F28 1-2	D26 0-3	O04 0-0	M30 0-4	N01 2-0	S01 3-1	S06 1-2	S22 3-1	a06 0-0	J03 2-0	D13 3-4	O18 3-4	M16 3-5	N15 3-1		a25 2-2	J31 2-4	N29 2-1	M28 1-2
19 TOTTENHAM H	J31 1-4	M27 3-2	N22 0-4	J03 3-1	A23 2-3	N08 1-1	a08 2-2	S03 4-0	O11 10-4	O25 2-3	M07 6-0	a04 3-0	M21 3-1	F07 1-3	S06 1-3	S17 1-0	F21 4-4	D06 1-2		a18 5-0	D26 1-4	S27 2-1
20 W.B.A.	F21 1-1	a29 1-1	A27 2-2	N15 2-3	M28 3-1	A30 1-1	M11 2-4	D13 4-0	S27 2-3	D26 1-2	F07 2-2	a15 2-0	M31 3-0	M14 1-3	a11 2-2	a25 2-0	S10 1-2	S13 1-1	N29 4-3		O18 2-1	N01 2-1
21 WEST HAM U	N08 0-0	A30 7-2	O11 1-2	O04 6-3	F16 1-0	M21 4-3	O25 1-0	S20 4-2	a04 3-2	D06 2-3	N22 0-3	a13 0-0	a20 5-1	S08 3-2	M27 3-0	J31 5-3	D20 6-0	a18 1-1	D25 2-1	M07 3-1		A25 2-0
22 WOLVERHAMPTON W	M07 6-1	S17 4-0	O25 3-1	J31 5-0	S06 2-0	N22 1-2	a04 3-3	J03 1-2	D06 1-0	F14 6-2	a22 3-0	a18 5-0	O11 2-0	O04 4-0	S20 1-3	A23 5-1	D27 7-0	N08 2-0	M02 1-1	M21 5-2	S03 1-1	

Sheffield Wednesday's Alan Finney helped the Owls win Division Two in 1958-9. Altogether, Finney made 503 League and Cup appearances for Wednesday, scoring 90 goals.

DIVISION 2

	BARNSLEY	BRIGHTON & HA	BRISTOL C	BRISTOL R	CARDIFF C	CHARLTON A	DERBY CO	FULHAM	GRIMSBY T	HUDDERSFIELD T	IPSWICH T	LEYTON O	LINCOLN C	LIVERPOOL	MIDDLESBROUGH	ROTHERHAM U	SCUNTHORPE U	SHEFFIELD U	SHEFFIELD W	STOKE C	SUNDERLAND	SWANSEA T
1 BARNSLEY		F14 0-2	A27 4-7	M07 0-0	D20 3-2	S10 7-1	O11 0-0	a18 2-4	O04 3-1	A30 1-0	O25 3-0	a29 1-3	N22 2-2	M30 0-2	D27 1-0	J31 1-1	M21 0-1	S20 1-3	D06 0-1	N08 2-1	a04 0-2	a20 3-1
2 BRIGHTON & H.A.	S27 1-1		J17 2-2	N08 1-1	S13 2-2	A30 2-2	a22 3-1	D27 3-0	S10 2-0	F07 2-0	a04 4-1	O25 2-2	M21 2-1	S24 2-2	D20 4-6	F21 3-0	M07 2-1	M30 2-0	O11 1-3	a18 2-2	D06 2-0	N22 2-2
3 BRISTOL C	S02 3-1	S06 3-0		M21 1-1	D26 2-3	O04 2-4	D06 1-3	N08 1-1	F24 1-0	S16 2-1	M27 3-0	a18 0-1	a21 1-0	S20 1-3	F14 2-2	A23 6-1	N22 0-1	J03 3-1	a04 1-2	M07 2-1	O25 4-1	O11 4-0
4 BRISTOL R	O18 0-2	F28 2-0	N01 1-2		S08 2-0	a25 2-1	S22 2-1	S13 0-0	N15 7-3	M28 1-1	D27 1-1	D20 1-3	F07 3-0	a11 3-0	N29 3-1	M14 4-1	A30 4-0	D13 1-1	a30 2-1	F21 1-0	S27 2-1	M30 4-4
5 CARDIFF C	A23 0-1	J31 3-1	D27 1-0	S17 2-4		M31 1-2	M21 0-0	a04 1-2	S20 4-1	S03 3-2	O11 1-2	D06 2-1	N08 3-0	F14 3-0	O04 3-2	J03 1-0	a18 0-2	S06 3-1	N22 2-2	O25 2-1	a22 2-1	M07 0-1
6 CHARLTON A	S18 4-0	J03 2-3	F21 4-1	D06 4-3	M30 0-0		a18 1-2	a23 2-1	S06 2-1	D27 2-1	M21 5-1	N22 4-1	O25 3-2	J31 2-3	S20 1-0	S04 5-2	a04 2-3	A23 1-1	N08 3-3	O11 1-2	M07 3-2	F14 2-1
7 DERBY CO	M28 3-0	D13 1-3	a25 4-1	S03 3-2	N01 1-3	N29 3-2		F07 2-0	F28 3-0	D20 3-1	S17 3-2	A30 1-2	S27 1-0	N15 3-2	a11 0-3	O18 1-1	J17 3-1	M14 2-1	S13 1-4	M30 3-0	F21 2-0	D26 3-1
8 FULHAM	N29 5-2	D26 3-1	F28 1-0	J31 1-0	N15 2-1	D13 2-1	S20 4-2		M28 3-0	a11 1-0	S06 3-2	F14 5-2	S17 4-2	O18 0-1	M14 3-2	a25 4-0	O04 1-1	N01 4-2	M27 6-2	A23 6-1	S03 6-2	J03 1-2
9 GRIMSBY T	F21 3-3	S16 1-1	S13 2-0	a04 1-2	F07 5-1	a14 1-5	N08 3-0	O11 2-2		S27 2-1	N22 2-3	a21 4-1	A26 4-2	D20 2-3	A30 3-2	M27 1-1	O25 1-1	D25 1-2	M07 0-2	D06 2-2	M21 1-1	a18 0-1
10 HUDDERSFIELD T	J03 2-1	S20 3-2	S09 0-1	O11 1-2	A27 3-0	D25 1-0	A23 1-1	N22 2-1	F14 2-0		M07 3-0	M21 0-0	a04 2-1	O04 5-0	M30 5-1	S06 3-0	D06 0-1	J31 0-2	a18 1-2	a22 1-2	N08 1-1	O25 3-2
11 IPSWICH T	M14 3-1	N15 5-3	M30 1-1	D26 0-2	M28 3-3	N01 3-1	S10 1-1	J17 1-2	a11 2-1	O18 0-0		A27 2-1	S13 4-1	N29 2-0	a25 2-1	D13 1-0	D20 3-1	a30 1-0	A30 0-2	S27 0-2	F07 0-2	F21 3-2
12 LEYTON O	S06 5-1	M14 2-2	N29 4-2	A23 1-3	a25 3-0	a11 6-1	J03 1-3	S27 0-2	D13 0-1	N01 2-5	S04 2-0		F21 0-0	F28 1-3	N15 5-2	M28 2-0	S13 2-1	O18 1-1	F07 0-2	D26 0-1	M30 6-0	S18 0-0
13 LINCOLN C	a11 2-1	N01 4-2	D13 0-2	S20 4-1	F28 4-2	M14 3-3	F14 1-4	S10 2-4	S03 4-4	N15 1-1	J31 3-1	O04 2-0		M28 2-1	O18 1-1	N29 1-0	M27 3-3	a25 1-2	D27 0-1	J03 3-1	A23 3-1	S06 1-2
14 LIVERPOOL	M27 3-2	S03 5-0	F07 3-2	N22 2-1	S27 1-2	S13 3-0	a04 3-0	M07 0-0	A23 3-3	F21 2-2	a18 3-1	N08 3-0	O11 3-2		a08 1-2	D27 4-0	a22 3-0	S10 2-1	O25 3-2	M20 3-4	J03 3-1	D06 4-0
15 MIDDLESBROUGH	D26 3-1	A23 9-0	S27 0-0	a18 2-2	F21 1-1	F07 1-3	N22 5-0	O25 2-3	M11 1-0	J01 3-1	D06 2-3	a04 4-2	M07 1-2	S06 2-1		S17 1-2	N08 6-1	S03 0-0	a22 2-2	J31 0-0	O11 0-0	M21 6-2
16 ROTHERHAM U	S13 3-0	O04 0-1	D20 1-2	O25 3-3	A30 1-0	A28 4-3	M07 3-0	D06 4-0	M30 2-1	a30 0-1	a23 1-2	O11 1-1	a18 1-0	D26 0-1	S11 1-4		F07 1-0	a15 2-2	M21 1-0	a04 0-0	N22 0-4	N08 3-3
17 SCUNTHORPE U	N01 1-0	O18 2-3	a11 3-3	J03 0-0	D18 1-0	N15 3-3	S06 2-2	F21 1-2	M14 1-3	a25 0-3	A23 1-1	J31 2-0	M30 3-1	D13 1-2	F28 0-3	S20 2-0		M28 1-3	S27 1-4	S18 1-1	D26 3-2	S04 3-1
18 SHEFFIELD U	F07 5-0	M31 3-1	A30 4-0	a20 5-2	a27 1-1	D20 5-0	O25 1-2	M21 2-0	D27 2-1	S13 0-0	N08 2-0	M07 2-3	D06 6-1	S15 2-0	A25 0-1	S27 2-0	O11 4-1		F21 1-0	N22 2-1	a18 3-1	a04 2-0
19 SHEFFIELD W	a25 5-0	M28 2-0	N15 2-3	S06 3-1	a11 3-1	F27 4-1	J31 1-1	M30 2-2	O18 6-0	N29 4-1	J03 3-1	S20 2-0	D26 7-0	a14 1-0	D13 2-0	N01 5-0	F14 2-0	O04 2-0		S03 4-1	S17 6-0	A23 2-1
20 STOKE C	F28 2-1	N29 3-0	O18 2-1	O04 2-2	M14 0-1	M28 2-1	O22 2-1	D20 4-1	a25 4-0	D13 5-1	F16 1-0	D27 3-2	A30 1-0	N01 0-2	S13 3-1	N15 3-0	S10 4-3	a11 1-2	A27 3-0		a06 0-0	S20 3-0
21 SUNDERLAND	N15 2-2	a25 4-1	M14 3-1	F14 3-1	D13 0-2	O18 0-3	O04 3-0	A27 1-2	N01 1-0	F28 1-0	S20 0-2	J01 4-0	D20 2-0	A30 2-1	M28 0-0	a11 1-1	D27 3-1	N29 4-1	S10 3-3	S06 3-1		J31 2-1
22 SWANSEA T	D13 2-1	a11 4-2	M28 1-0	M27 2-1	a15 1-3	S27 2-2	D27 4-4	A30 1-2	N29 1-1	M14 0-1	O04 4-2	S11 3-3	J17 3-1	a25 3-3	N01 5-2	F28 3-0	A28 3-0	N15 0-2	D20 4-0	F07 1-0	S13 5-0	

Season 1958-59

DIVISION 3

	ACCRINGTON S	BOURNEMOUTH	BRADFORD C	BRENTFORD	BURY	CHESTERFIELD	COLCHESTER U	DONCASTER R	HALIFAX T	HULL C	MANSFIELD T	NEWPORT CO	NORWICH C	NOTTS CO	PLYMOUTH A	Q.P.R.	READING	ROCHDALE	SOUTHAMPTON	SOUTHEND U	STOCKPORT CO	SWINDON T	TRANMERE R	WREXHAM
1 ACCRINGTON S		M26 3-2	S27 1-3	S12 1-1	M14 0-2	S29 3-1	S17 1-1	M11 2-0	D26 4-2	F07 0-1	A30 2-0	A27 2-2	M23 0-2	D20 3-0	a25 1-1	N01 2-4	D13 4-3	M28 4-2	O08 0-0	O17 3-0	a11 2-2	F18 0-0	N29 3-1	F21 1-1
2 BOURNEMOUTH	M30 5-2		O25 4-0	N08 0-0	J03 2-0	N22 2-1	D27 1-1	S20 1-0	A27 3-0	D06 1-0	J24 3-3	a29 1-1	S24 2-0	a18 0-0	F14 1-1	S06 2-0	S10 0-1	J31 0-0	O11 2-1	A23 1-4	a22 2-0	a04 3-3	O04 4-0	M07 0-0
3 BRADFORD C	F14 0-0	M14 0-1		D20 3-0	M10 1-0	S10 1-0	O18 1-3	a11 3-0	O04 1-3	A30 2-1	A27 1-1	a22 1-0	N01 2-2	D27 4-1	D13 0-0	a25 1-0	F28 1-2	N29 7-1	S20 2-3	M28 6-1	M31 4-2	O01 1-2	S06 2-0	J31 3-2
4 BRENTFORD	J31 2-1	M28 1-1	A23 4-0		N29 0-0	O04 1-1	N01 2-1	S02 0-1	S20 2-0	S30 1-1	S09 2-0	F14 3-0	a30 0-4	a21 4-0	M27 3-0	a11 1-0	M14 3-1	D13 2-1	S06 2-0	a25 6-1	O18 1-4	D25 2-2	F28 5-2	J03 2-1
5 BURY	O25 3-1	A30 5-1	a04 2-2	a18 1-1		M30 1-0	D20 0-0	J01 5-0	M07 3-1	J24 2-1	a28 2-2	O11 0-0	a14 3-2	F07 0-1	S08 1-1	F14 3-1	S22 1-1	O04 6-1	M21 1-0	S13 2-3	A26 3-3	N22 0-0	D26 4-2	N08 3-0
6 CHESTERFIELD	S22 0-1	a11 1-0	S15 2-0	F21 1-2	M27 3-0		N29 2-2	O25 2-0	A23 2-3	J01 2-1	F07 3-1	J03 3-1	D13 1-1	S13 1-0	N01 1-2	F28 2-3	a25 1-0	O18 0-0	A25 3-3	S06 4-0	a13 1-0	S27 1-3	M28 3-2	D26 1-1
7 COLCHESTER U	S08 1-0	D26 3-1	M07 3-2	M21 0-4	A23 1-3	a18 1-0		J31 1-0	a27 3-1	O25 1-3	a04 1-3	N22 3-2	A25 2-1	F23 4-1	S20 2-0	J03 3-0	a20 3-1	S06 2-1	M27 1-3	S29 0-1	O04 8-2	N08 1-0	F14 1-1	O11 1-1
8 DONCASTER R	a04 3-0	F07 5-1	N22 0-3	A28 1-0	O09 0-1	M14 2-1	O16 2-1		N08 1-2	a23 0-2	O11 0-2	M21 1-0	S27 0-1	M07 2-1	O02 4-6	S09 2-0	F24 2-5	D27 1-1	J24 3-2	F21 2-1	A30 4-1	M27 2-0	D20 2-0	a18 1-1
9 HALIFAX T	D27 0-2	S01 0-1	F21 3-3	F07 0-0	O18 4-2	D20 3-2	a30 4-1	M28 5-1		S27 1-2	J17 0-0	S22 3-1	M31 1-1	A30 1-1	a20 0-1	M14 2-1	a11 4-1	N01 2-1	S08 2-0	F28 1-0	N29 4-3	S13 1-0	a25 3-0	a15 4-1
10 HULL C	S20 4-2	N01 5-3	J03 4-0	S22 3-1	a25 2-0	O06 3-1	M14 3-0	D13 5-1	F14 4-0		D26 5-2	O04 2-3	M28 3-3	S15 5-0	A23 1-1	N29 1-0	O18 2-0	a11 2-1	J31 3-0	J10 3-2	F28 3-1	S01 0-0	M30 1-0	S06 1-0
11 MANSFIELD T	J03 3-2	a25 1-4	S01 2-1	S15 1-1	D13 0-2	S20 2-1	F02 3-2	F28 3-1	S06 4-3	D27 1-1		J31 2-1	a06 1-1	F14 3-0	O18 1-4	O04 3-4	M20 1-0	M30 0-0	A23 1-6	a11 1-4	N01 2-1	a13 0-0	M14 0-2	S22 3-1
12 NEWPORT CO	S04 2-1	D13 4-1	O09 3-2	S27 0-1	F28 1-1	A30 0-1	m04 0-1	N01 3-1	O02 0-2	F21 1-3	S13 1-0		D20 2-2	M16 3-1	M28 0-1	O20 3-1	N29 2-1	M14 1-0	D25 4-2	a13 3-1	a25 2-0	F07 3-0	M09 3-0	S18 2-1
13 NORWICH C	O11 2-4	O01 2-2	M21 4-2	a04 4-1	S06 3-2	a29 2-1	S03 1-2	F04 3-0	M30 3-1	N08 0-1	a18 1-0	A23 3-0		N22 3-3	O04 1-1	J31 5-1	D26 1-0	S20 2-1	M07 3-1	J03 4-0	S17 1-3	a08 1-1	a22 0-0	O25 2-2
14 NOTTS CO	A23 1-1	N29 4-3	D26 1-3	O09 0-0	S20 1-1	J31 3-1	a25 0-1	O18 2-2	J03 4-4	S11 1-1	S27 3-4	S06 1-1	a11 1-3		M14 1-2	M30 0-1	J10 3-1	F28 1-1	S25 1-2	D13 1-4	M28 0-2	F21 1-0	N01 1-1	S04 2-0
15 PLYMOUTH A	M04 2-4	S27 3-1	a29 1-1	M30 1-1	S18 3-0	M21 2-0	F07 1-1	S22 4-0	a04 1-1	D20 1-1	M07 8-3	N08 3-2	F21 0-1	O25 3-0		D26 3-2	S13 2-2	S04 2-1	a18 1-0	O08 3-1	J17 2-1	O11 3-2	A30 4-0	N22 2-2
16 Q.P.R.	M21 3-1	J17 0-4	M18 3-0	N22 1-2	S27 2-1	O11 2-2	A30 4-2	S15 3-1	O25 3-1	a18 1-1	F21 1-1	M07 4-2	S13 2-1	M27 2-1	D27 2-1		D20 2-0	a20 3-0	N08 2-2	F07 1-3	S29 0-0	a27 2-1	A25 1-1	a04 5-0
17 READING	a29 5-0	S17 2-0	O11 3-2	O25 3-1	S29 1-0	J24 1-2	O08 0-0	S06 2-0	N22 3-0	a15 2-0	N08 3-3	a18 1-3	D27 3-1	a04 3-1	J31 0-2	A23 2-2		J03 3-0	F21 4-1	S03 3-0	F14 2-1	M21 3-1	S20 0-0	M30 2-1
18 ROCHDALE	N08 1-0	S13 2-1	a18 0-3	a27 0-0	F21 1-0	M07 0-0	M16 0-1	D26 1-0	M21 1-0	N22 0-1	M27 2-2	O25 1-1	F07 1-2	O11 1-2	A25 0-2	O07 2-2	A30 1-0		a04 1-0	S27 1-1	D20 0-2	S10 1-1	S23 1-4	J24 3-1
19 SOUTHAMPTON	a22 3-1	F28 0-0	F07 1-2	M09 0-6	N01 4-2	S01 0-0	M30 3-0	a25 1-1	S17 5-0	S13 6-1	D20 3-2	D27 3-3	O18 1-1	O01 3-0	N29 5-1	M28 1-0	O04 3-3	F02 6-1		M14 3-2	D13 2-1	A30 1-1	a11 2-3	S27 1-2
20 SOUTHEND U	M07 4-2	D20 2-0	N08 1-1	a08 2-0	J31 1-0	J17 2-5	S24 1-1	O04 5-0	O11 3-2	a04 1-1	N22 5-1	M30 1-0	A30 1-0	a29 5-2	J24 0-0	S20 4-0	A27 2-2	F14 3-1	O25 1-1		D27 3-1	a18 0-2	S10 1-3	M21 4-1
21 STOCKPORT CO	N22 0-0	O06 3-1	M27 1-1	M07 1-1	S01 0-1	a04 1-1	F21 0-1	J03 2-0	a18 0-1	O11 2-1	M21 4-1	M02 2-1	S08 2-3	N08 1-1	S06 2-2	S22 2-3	S27 0-1	A23 1-0	a27 4-0	O20 0-1		O25 2-0	J31 1-0	F07 2-2
22 SWINDON T	S06 1-2	J10 0-1	S24 2-2	D26 1-1	a11 0-0	F14 1-2	M28 2-0	M30 0-0	J31 0-2	A27 2-0	a22 2-1	S20 2-1	a25 4-3	O04 3-1	F28 3-4	D13 2-0	N01 2-0	S17 2-1	J03 3-1	N29 2-1	M14 3-0		O18 1-2	A23 1-0
23 TRANMERE R	a18 9 0	F21 4-0	F23 3-1	O11 1-2	D27 4-0	N08 2-0	S27 3-3	A23 3-0	J24 1-2	M27 1-0	O25 2-2	a04 2-1	O06 0-1	M21 0-3	M16 2-0	S01 2-0	F07 2-1	S29 2-1	N22 2-0	S15 1-1	S13 3-1	M07 3-1		J01 1-2
24 WREXHAM	O04 2-2	O18 1-0	S13 3-3	A30 2-1	M28 0-0	D27 3-4	F28 2-0	N29 2-1	a22 1-1	a29 5-1	O01 2-1	S10 0-0	a13 1-2	A27 3-2	a11 1-1	a08 1-0	M27 0-1	a25 1-0	F14 1-3	N01 3-1	S20 3-1	D20 1-0	D13 2-5	

DIVISION 4

	ALDERSHOT	BARROW	BRADFORD	CARLISLE U	CHESTER	COVENTRY C	CREWE A	CRYSTAL P	DARLINGTON	EXETER C	GATESHEAD	GILLINGHAM	HARTLEPOOLS U	MILLWALL	NORTHAMPTON T	OLDHAM A	PORT VALE	SHREWSBURY T	SOUTHPORT	TORQUAY U	WALSALL	WATFORD	WORKINGTON	YORK C
1 ALDERSHOT		A30 0-1	D13 3-3	D20 4-0	F28 1-0	O01 0-4	J10 0-0	D26 1-2	S04 1-4	a22 1-0	S13 8-1	M30 4-2	M14 2-4	F14 4-2	a11 1-3	J17 1-3	S20 0-4	S17 0-0	N01 3-2	M28 1-4	O04 0-5	O18 0-0	N29 2-0	a25 0-1
2 BARROW	J03 3-4		F28 2-3	S29 1-3	N01 1-2	O04 0-3	a25 0-2	M14 1-0	S20 2-1	S01 1-0	A23 0-3	S15 2-2	a21 1-1	S06 3-1	D13 2-2	M30 2-1	O18 1-2	F14 3-4	a11 3-0	N29 2-2	J31 0-0	M28 0-4	J01 2-2	D27 2-3
3 BRADFORD	a27 5-1	O11 0-2		M07 0-3	S27 3-0	N08 2-0	J01 0-2	F07 5-0	N22 1-2	M21 0-3	J17 4-1	O25 2-0	S01 4-1	J24 4-1	M27 1-2	D26 2-1	S13 0-2	a04 3-1	S15 3-0	S29 3-1	a18 3-2	F21 1-1	A23 3-2	J03 2-1
4 CARLISLE U	A23 1-0	S23 1-0	O18 1-1		M28 4-3	F14 1-6	D13 2-0	N01 3-3	M11 1-1	O04 1-2	M30 4-2	A26 1-2	a11 1-0	J03 0-2	S09 2-1	M03 3-0	M14 0-3	S20 0-0	N29 5-0	a25 0-1	S08 1-1	M16 2-0	D26 3-2	F28 0-0
5 CHESTER	O11 2-2	M21 2-0	F14 2-0	N08 2-1		a18 1-1	a22 0-1	S03 3-2	a29 1-0	N22 4-2	M07 0-1	a04 1-2	O08 1-1	D27 0-0	S06 2-3	O25 5-2	O04 1-2	J24 3-5	M30 2-1	A23 0-2	S17 2-0	O01 2-1	J31 1-2	S20 2-2
6 COVENTRY C	S22 7-1	F21 2-0	M28 0-0	S27 1-2	N29 5-1		F28 3-2	a11 2-0	A23 0-0	S13 2-0	S15 4-1	F07 1-1	D13 4-1	O06 1-0	O18 2-0	S01 1-0	M10 1-0	J03 3-2	S06 1-0	D26 3-0	M31 0-0	a25 1-0	M14 4-0	N01 2-0
7 CREWE A	a04 5-0	J24 5-0	O08 4-1	F17 3-1	A30 2-4	O11 1-1		D20 4-1	O25 2-1	M05 0-0	N22 0-0	F21 0-2	S13 0-2	N08 4-1	S01 1-2	a18 5-0	M27 2-0	M07 2-4	F07 1-1	S27 1-1	M21 5-3	J17 1-3	S18 2-0	O01 2-4
8 CRYSTAL P	D27 4-1	O25 2-2	S20 2-0	M21 0-2	A27 3-3	N22 1-1	A23 6-2		J24 4-1	a04 1-1	O11 3-1	N08 4-1	O01 1-2	F21 4-0	J03 1-1	M07 4-0	F14 1-1	a18 4-3	O08 1-0	M27 3-1	a29 1-3	S17 3-0	S06 1-1	J31 0-0
9 DARLINGTON	A25 2-3	F07 5-2	a11 1-1	S13 0-1	D13 0-0	D20 1-4	M14 1-1	a25 1-4		A30 1-1	F21 3-2	a16 1-2	D27 3-1	S18 0-2	N01 2-2	S27 1-1	N29 2-0	J01 2-1	F28 4-0	O18 3-2	O01 2-3	O08 1-1	M28 1-1	M18 0-1
10 EXETER C	O08 2-0	A28 4-0	N01 4-0	F21 2-1	a11 1-1	J31 2-1	D27 3-0	a15 3-1	J03 2-2		a06 1-1	S27 3-0	a25 3-0	M30 3-1	F28 3-4	S10 3-2	M28 3-4	S06 1-0	D13 3-2	S20 2-2	A23 3-0	N29 3-0	O18 1-0	M14 0-2
11 GATESHEAD	J31 1-0	D20 4-0	S06 1-4	M27 4-1	O18 0-1	S08 1-1	a11 0-0	F28 1-3	O04 1-3	O27 1-2		a20 2-0	N01 3-0	S20 1-2	N29 4-1	A30 2-1	J01 0-4	A25 1-2	M28 1-1	a13 1-0	F14 2-1	M14 1-0	a25 0-3	D13 1-0
12 GILLINGHAM	M27 3-0	S10 4-2	M14 1-1	S01 1-1	J17 3-3	S20 2-0	O04 3-0	M28 1-1	S06 0-0	F14 0-2	O08 3-0		N29 4-1	A23 1-2	D26 4-1	O01 3-2	N01 0-2	J31 2-1	a25 2-0	a08 3-2	J03 4-2	a11 2-1	F28 5-1	O18 2-2
13 HARTLEPOOLS U	O25 0-3	a04 10-1	A25 3-0	N22 1-2	J01 1-3	a27 2-1	J31 2-1	S22 4-1	D26 1-0	J24 3-3	M21 0-0	a18 3-1		M07 3-1	S20 3-0	N08 4-0	S08 1-5	A23 0-2	J03 1-1	S06 2-4	O11 1-1	M27 4-3	F14 0-3	O04 1-5
14 MILLWALL	S27 4-0	J17 3-0	a25 1-1	A30 1-0	D25 0-1	a20 1-1	M28 2-0	O04 2-1	S08 1-2	M27 1-1	F07 0-2	D20 2-0	O18 3-2		J10 3-0	S13 4-2	D13 4-2	S22 0-0	M14 1-1	N01 2-0	S01 1-3	F28 4-1	a11 1-1	N29 5-2
15 NORTHAMPTON T	N22 1-0	a30 2-0	M31 4-1	a06 0-0	a13 4-0	M07 4-0	A28 3-0	A30 3-0	M21 1-3	O11 1-1	a18 1-0	D27 4-2	F07 2-1	a04 0-1		J24 2-1	D20 2-4	O25 3-3	S27 3-1	F21 1-1	N08 3-2	S13 2-1	S25 1-1	O09 1-2
16 OLDHAM A	S06 0-1	M27 2-0	D27 1-0	a28 2-0	M14 3-5	A26 2-0	N29 2-1	O18 3-0	F14 1-3	S15 2-1	J03 3-0	S22 3-1	M28 1-0	J31 1-3	a25 2-1		F28 0-2	O04 3-1	a20 2-0	a11 1-0	S20 1-4	N01 3-5	D13 1-0	A23 0-1
17 PORT VALE	F07 3-2	M07 4-1	J31 4-2	O25 1-1	F21 4-0	a04 3-0	M30 1-1	S27 2-3	a18 1-1	N08 5-3	D26 8-0	M21 3-1	S15 1-1	a27 5-2	A23 1-4	O11 0-0		N22 2-0	S29 4-1	O06 3-1	J23 2-1	S01 1-3	M02 2-0	S06 2-2
18 SHREWSBURY T	S08 3-1	S27 1-2	J10 0-1	F07 4-1	a25 3-0	A30 4-1	O18 2-2	N29 2-1	M30 1-0	a30 3-0	S01 1-1	S13 3-2	D20 3-0	S29 1-2	M14 4-0	F21 0-0	a11 4-3		D26 6-2	F28 5-0	a20 2-0	D13 4-2	N01 1-1	M28 2-2
19 SOUTHPORT	M21 0-1	N22 0-0	S09 1-0	a18 0-1	M27 1-1	a14 1-2	S20 3-0	J01 0-2	O11 2-0	a28 0-1	N08 2-2	J24 2-1	A30 1-1	O25 2-1	F14 1-2	a04 1-1	S23 2-2	D25 0-1		J31 2-2	M07 1-1	D20 0-3	O04 3-0	S02 1-0
20 TORQUAY U	N08 1-1	a18 1-0	S22 2-1	F25 0-0	D20 4-0	D27 1-1	F14 6-2	M30 0-2	M07 4-1	F07 3-4	a04 0-1	a29 3-1	J17 1-3	M21 2-0	O04 4-2	N22 2-1	a22 1-1	O11 1-4	S13 1-0		O25 1-2	A30 2-3	S04 4-1	S17 1-1
21 WALSALL	F21 2-4	S13 3-1	N29 3-2	a14 5-0	S11 2-2	M30 3-0	O31 6-0	D13 0-2	S25 0-0	M17 3-0	S27 0-1	A30 1-2	F28 0-0	A28 2-1	M28 2-1	F07 3-0	a25 1-1	O09 2-3	O18 5-1	M14 2-2		D26 3-2	a09 3-0	a11 5-0
22 WATFORD	M07 2-1	N08 1-1	O04 2-1	a04 2-2	O14 4-2	J24 1-4	S06 0-1	S09 2-2	a21 0-0	a18 2-1	O25 5-1	N22 2-2	M30 4-1	O11 1-1	J31 3-1	M21 2-1	A26 0-2	m07 1-4	A23 5-1	J03 1-2	D27 1-2		S20 3-0	F14 2-3
23 WORKINGTON	a18 1-0	O08 2-2	D20 2-1	D27 0-1	S13 1-0	O25 2-2	S10 1-0	M16 0-4	N08 3-3	M07 2-2	D05 4-2	O11 0-1	S27 3-0	N22 1-1	O01 3-3	a22 2-0	A30 2-2	M21 1-1	F21 2-0	A25 3-3	a04 0-1	F07 3-1		M30 2-2
24 YORK C	J24 0-0	D26 1-0	A30 4-0	O11 1-1	F07 1-1	M21 0-0	S22 4-0	S13 1-1	a04 2-1	O25 0-2	a27 1-0	M07 3-1	F21 1-1	a18 3-3	a20 2-1	D20 3-1	a15 0-0	N08 2-0	A25 2-0	S08 1-0	N22 3-2	S27 0-0	M27 2-2	

LEAGUE TABLES

DIVISION 1

	P	W	D	L	F	A	W	D	L	F	A	Pts
Wolves	42	15	3	3	68	19	13	2	6	42	30	61
Manchester U	42	14	4	3	58	27	10	3	8	45	39	55
Arsenal	42	14	3	4	53	29	7	5	9	35	39	50
Bolton W	42	14	3	4	56	30	6	7	8	23	36	50
WBA	42	8	7	6	41	33	10	6	5	47	35	49
West Ham U	42	15	3	3	59	29	6	3	12	26	41	48
Burnley	42	11	4	6	41	29	8	6	7	40	41	48
Blackpool	42	12	7	2	39	13	6	4	11	27	36	47
Birmingham C	42	14	1	6	54	35	6	5	10	30	33	46
Blackburn R	42	12	3	6	48	28	5	7	9	28	42	44
Newcastle U	42	11	3	7	40	29	6	4	11	40	51	41
Preston NE	42	9	3	9	40	39	8	4	9	30	38	41
Nottingham F	42	9	4	8	37	32	8	2	11	34	42	40
Chelsea	42	13	2	6	52	37	5	2	14	25	61	40
Leeds U	42	8	7	6	28	27	7	2	12	29	47	39
Everton	42	11	3	7	39	38	6	1	14	32	49	38
Luton T	42	11	6	4	50	26	1	7	13	18	45	37
Tottenham H	42	10	3	8	56	42	3	7	11	29	53	36
Leicester C	42	7	6	8	34	36	4	4	13	33	62	32
Manchester C	42	8	7	6	40	32	3	2	16	24	63	31
Aston Villa	42	8	5	8	31	33	3	3	15	27	54	30
Portsmouth	42	5	4	12	38	47	1	5	15	26	65	21

DIVISION 2

	P	W	D	L	F	A	W	D	L	F	A	Pts
Sheffield W	42	18	2	1	68	13	10	4	7	38	35	62
Fulham	42	18	1	2	65	26	9	5	7	31	35	60
Sheffield U	42	16	2	3	54	15	7	5	9	28	33	53
Liverpool	42	15	3	3	57	25	9	2	10	30	37	53
Stoke C	42	16	2	3	48	19	5	5	11	24	39	49
Bristol R	42	13	5	3	46	23	5	7	9	34	41	48
Derby Co	42	15	1	5	46	29	5	7	9	28	42	48
Charlton A	42	13	3	5	53	33	5	4	12	39	57	43
Cardiff C	42	12	2	7	37	26	6	5	10	28	39	43
Bristol C	42	11	3	7	43	27	6	4	11	31	43	41
Swansea T	42	12	5	4	52	30	4	4	13	27	51	41
Brighton & HA	42	10	9	2	46	29	5	2	14	28	61	41
Middlesbrough	42	9	7	5	51	26	6	3	12	36	45	40
Huddersfield T	42	12	3	6	39	20	4	5	12	23	35	40
Sunderland	42	13	4	4	42	23	3	4	14	22	52	40
Ipswich T	42	12	4	5	37	27	5	2	14	25	50	40
Leyton O	42	9	4	8	43	30	5	4	12	28	48	36
Scunthorpe U	42	7	6	8	32	37	5	3	13	23	47	33
Lincoln C	42	10	5	6	45	37	1	2	18	18	56	29
Rotherham U	42	9	5	7	32	28	1	4	16	10	54	29
Grimsby T	42	7	7	7	41	36	2	3	16	21	54	28
Barnsley	42	8	4	9	34	34	2	3	16	21	57	27

DIVISION 3

	P	W	D	L	F	A	W	D	L	F	A	Pts
Plymouth A	46	14	7	2	55	27	9	9	5	34	32	62
Hull C	46	19	3	1	65	21	7	6	10	25	34	61
Brentford	46	15	5	3	49	22	6	10	7	27	27	57
Norwich C	46	13	6	4	51	29	9	7	7	38	33	57
Colchester U	46	15	2	6	46	31	6	8	9	25	36	52
Reading	46	16	4	3	15	21	5	4	14	27	42	50
Tranmere R	46	15	3	5	53	22	6	5	12	29	45	50
Southend U	46	14	6	3	52	26	7	2	14	33	54	50
Halifax T	46	14	5	4	48	25	7	3	13	32	52	50
Bury	46	12	9	2	51	24	5	5	13	18	34	48
Bradford C	46	13	4	6	47	25	5	7	11	37	51	47
Bournemouth	46	12	9	2	40	18	5	3	15	29	51	46
QPR	46	14	6	3	49	28	5	2	16	25	49	46
Southampton	46	12	7	4	57	33	5	4	14	31	47	45
Swindon T	46	13	4	6	39	25	3	9	11	20	32	45
Chesterfield	46	12	5	6	40	26	5	5	13	27	38	44
Newport Co	46	15	2	6	43	24	2	7	14	26	44	43
Wrexham	46	12	6	5	40	30	2	8	13	23	47	42
Accrington S	46	10	8	5	42	31	5	4	14	29	56	42
Mansfield T	46	11	5	7	38	42	3	8	12	35	56	41
Stockport Co	46	9	7	7	33	23	4	3	16	32	55	36
Doncaster R	46	13	2	8	40	32	1	3	19	10	58	33
Notts Co	46	5	9	9	33	39	3	4	16	22	57	29
Rochdale	46	8	7	8	21	26	0	5	18	16	53	28

DIVISION 4

	P	W	D	L	F	A	W	D	L	F	A	Pts
Port Vale	46	14	6	3	62	30	12	6	5	48	28	64
Coventry C	46	18	4	1	50	11	6	8	9	34	36	60
York C	46	12	10	1	37	17	9	8	6	36	35	60
Shrewsbury T	46	15	5	3	59	24	9	5	9	42	39	58
Exeter C	46	16	4	3	55	24	7	7	9	32	37	57
Walsall	46	13	5	5	56	25	8	5	10	39	39	52
Crystal P	46	12	8	3	54	27	8	4	11	36	44	52
Northampton T	46	14	5	4	48	25	7	4	12	37	53	51
Millwall	46	13	6	4	46	23	7	4	12	30	46	50
Carlisle U	46	11	6	6	37	30	8	6	9	25	35	50
Gillingham	46	14	6	3	53	27	6	3	14	29	50	49
Torquay U	46	11	5	7	45	32	5	7	11	33	45	44
Chester	46	10	5	8	39	33	6	7	10	33	51	44
Bradford	46	15	1	7	51	29	3	6	14	24	48	43
Watford	46	10	6	7	46	36	6	4	13	35	43	42
Darlington	46	7	8	8	37	36	6	8	9	29	32	42
Workington	46	9	10	4	40	32	3	7	13	23	46	41
Crewe A	46	11	5	7	52	32	4	5	14	18	50	40
Hartlepools U	46	11	4	8	50	41	4	6	13	24	47	40
Gateshead	46	11	3	9	33	30	5	5	13	23	55	40
Oldham A	46	15	0	8	39	29	1	4	18	20	55	36
Aldershot	46	8	4	11	37	45	6	3	14	26	52	35
Barrow	46	6	6	11	34	45	3	4	16	17	59	28
Southport	46	7	8	8	26	25	0	4	19	15	61	26

Football League Records

Top scorers: Div 1, D.Viollet (Manchester United) 32 goals; Div 2, B.Clough (Middlesbrough) 39 goals; Div 3, D.Reeves (Southampton) 39 goals; Div 4, C.Holton (Watford) 42 goals.

Irish international inside-forward Jimmy McIlroy guided Burnley to the title in 1959-60.

DIVISION 1

	ARSENAL	BIRMINGHAM C	BLACKBURN R	BLACKPOOL	BOLTON W	BURNLEY	CHELSEA	EVERTON	FULHAM	LEEDS U	LEICESTER C	LUTON T	MANCHESTER C	MANCHESTER U	NEWCASTLE U	NOTTINGHAM F	PRESTON N.E.	SHEFFIELD W	TOTTENHAM H	W.B.A.	WEST HAM U	WOLVERHAMPTON W
1 ARSENAL		O31 3-0	F06 5-2	S26 2-1	S15 2-1	D12 2-4	a09 1-4	F20 2-1	a15 2-0	M26 1-1	M15 1-1	D26 0-3	S12 3-1	a23 5-2	F27 1-0	S01 1-1	O17 0-3	A22 0-1	S05 1-1	N28 2-4	N14 1-3	J02 4-4
2 BIRMINGHAM C	a16 3-0		a30 1-0	N21 2-1	M19 2-5	a27 0-1	S09 1-1	a02 2-2	O24 2-4	O03 2-0	S19 3-4	N07 1-1	D05 4-2	S05 1-1	A26 4-3	M05 4-1	J23 2-1	O10 0-0	J02 0-1	a18 1-7	D26 2-0	A22 0-1
3 BLACKBURN R	S19 1-1	N28 2-1		D25 1-0	A31 1-0	O17 3-2	M30 1-0	S21 3-1	A22 4-0	a27 3-2	a23 0-1	a15 0-2	F13 2-1	O31 1-1	a09 1-1	J02 1-2	O03 1-4	S05 3-1	F27 1-4	N14 3-2	D12 6-2	J23 0-1
4 BLACKPOOL	F13 2-1	a09 0-1	D26 1-0		A22 3-2	a23 1-1	D12 3-1	a18 0-0	J02 3-1	O17 3-3	S14 3-3	A31 0-0	O03 1-3	F27 0-6	N14 2-0	S05 0-1	O31 0-2	J23 0-2	N28 2-2	M26 2-0	M12 3-2	S19 3-1
5 BOLTON W	S09 0-1	D12 4-1	A26 0-3	D19 0-3		F27 2-1	a23 2-0	A29 2-1	S19 3-2	O31 1-1	N28 3-1	M09 2-2	a18 3-1	N14 1-1	M12 1-4	F13 1-1	a09 2-1	O03 1-0	M26 2-1	O17 0-0	S12 5-1	D26 2-1
6 BURNLEY	M19 3-2	S26 3-1	M05 1-0	O10 1-4	D05 4-0		J16 2-1	A25 5-2	a30 0-0	D19 0-1	a15 1-0	a16 3-0	O24 4-3	D28 1-4	F06 2-1	N21 8-0	S08 2-1	a02 3-3	M01 2-0	S12 2-1	A29 1-3	N07 4-1
7 CHELSEA	N21 1-3	S16 4-2	N07 3-1	M19 2-3	O10 0-2	S05 4-1		O24 1-0	F13 4-2	J23 1-3	J02 2-2	M05 3-0	a02 3-0	S02 3-6	D26 2-2	a16 1-1	A22 4-4	D05 0-4	a15 1-3	F24 2-2	S19 2-4	a30 1-5
8 EVERTON	O03 3-1	N14 4-0	S16 2-0	a15 4-0	J02 0-1	S02 1-2	M12 6-1		S05 0-0	a23 1-0	O31 6-1	A22 2-2	D26 2-1	N28 2-1	M25 1-2	J23 6-1	F27 4-0	S19 2-1	a09 2-1	D12 2-2	O17 0-1	F13 0-2
9 FULHAM	a18 3-0	M12 2-2	D19 0-1	A29 1-0	F06 1-1	N28 1-0	S26 1-3	J16 2-0		F27 5-0	a09 1-1	S12 4-2	A26 5-2	M26 0-5	O17 4-3	O03 3-1	N14 1-2	D28 1-2	D12 1-1	a23 2-1	O31 1-0	S09 3-1
10 LEEDS U	N07 3-2	M09 3-3	O24 0-1	M05 2-4	a16 1-0	A22 2-3	S12 2-1	O10 3-3	D05 1-4		S02 1-1	J02 1-1	M19 4-3	S16 2-2	S26 2-3	a30 1-0	a19 2-1	N21 1-3	D26 2-4	F06 1-4	J16 3-0	a02 0-3
11 LEICESTER C	O24 2-2	F06 1-3	O10 2-3	S09 1-1	a30 1-2	a18 2-1	A29 3-1	a16 3-3	N21 0-1	A26 3-2		D05 3-3	M05 5-0	F24 3-1	S12 0-2	a02 0-1	D26 2-2	N07 2-0	S26 1-1	J16 0-1	D19 2-1	M19 2-1
12 LUTON T	D28 0-1	M26 1-1	a18 1-1	A26 0-1	S05 0-0	O31 1-1	O17 1-2	D19 2-1	J23 4-1	A29 0-1	F27 2-0		S09 1-2	a09 2-3	D12 3-4	S19 1-0	N28 1-3	F13 0-1	N14 1-0	M12 0-0	a23 3-1	O03 1-5
13 MANCHESTER C	J23 1-2	F27 3-0	S26 2-1	M09 2-3	a15 1-0	m02 1-2	N14 1-1	D28 4-0	S02 3-1	D12 3-3	O17 3-2	S16 1-2		S19 3-0	N28 3-4	A22 2-1	a23 2-1	J02 4-1	O31 1-2	a09 0-1	M30 3-1	S05 4-6
14 MANCHESTER U	O10 4-2	J16 2-1	a16 1-0	D05 3-1	a02 2-0	D26 1-2	A26 0-1	a30 5-0	N07 3-3	S09 6-0	O03 4-1	N21 4-1	F06 0-0		A29 3-2	M19 3-1	F13 1-1	O24 3-1	S12 1-5	D19 2-3	a18 5-3	M05 0-2
15 NEWCASTLE U	D05 4-1	S02 1-0	N21 3-1	a02 1-1	O24 0-2	S19 1-3	D28 1-1	N07 8-2	M05 3-1	F13 2-1	J23 0-2	M19 3-2	a30 0-1	J02 7-3		O10 2-1	S05 1-2	a15 3-3	A22 1-5	S16 0-0	O03 0-0	a16 1-0
16 NOTTINGHAM F	A26 0-3	O17 0-2	A29 2-2	J16 0-0	S26 2-0	a09 0-1	O31 3-1	S12 1-1	F20 2-2	N28 4-1	N14 1-0	F06 2-0	D19 1-2	D12 1-5	a23 3-0		M26 1-1	S09 2-1	M12 1-3	D28 1-2	F27 3-1	a19 0-0
17 PRESTON N.E.	M05 0-3	S12 3-2	M01 5-3	a16 4-1	N21 1-0	S15 1-0	D19 4-5	D05 0-0	a02 4-1	a18 1-1	D28 1-1	a30 2-0	O10 1-5	S26 4-0	J16 1-2	N07 1-0		M19 3-4	F06 1-1	A29 1-1	A25 1-1	O24 4-3
18 SHEFFIELD W	D19 5-1	a23 2-4	J16 3-0	S12 5-0	F24 1-0	N14 1-1	F27 1-1	F06 2-2	D26 1-1	a09 1-0	a06 2-2	S26 2-0	A29 1-0	M30 4-2	a18 2-0	S16 0-1	D12 2-2		O17 2-1	O31 2-0	N28 7-0	S02 2-2
19 TOTTENHAM H	J16 3-0	A29 0-0	D05 2-1	a30 4-1	N07 0-2	O03 1-1	a18 0-1	N21 3-0	M19 1-1	D28 1-4	F13 1-2	a02 1-1	a16 0-1	J23 2-1	D19 4-0	O24 2-1	S19 5-1	M05 4-1		A26 2-2	S09 2-2	O10 5-1
20 W.B.A.	a30 1-0	a19 1-1	a02 2-0	N07 2-1	M05 1-1	J23 0-0	O03 1-3	M19 6-2	O10 2-4	S19 3-0	S05 5-0	O24 4-0	N21 2-0	A22 3-2	S09 2-2	D26 2-3	J02 4-0	a16 3-1	S02 1-2		M09 3-2	D05 0-1
21 WEST HAM U	a02 0-0	D28 3-1	M19 2-1	O24 1-0	J23 1-2	J02 2-5	F06 4-2	M05 2-2	a16 1-2	S05 1-2	A22 3-0	O10 3-1	N07 4-1	a15 2-1	F20 3-5	D05 4-1	A31 2-1	a30 1-1	S14 1-2	S26 4-1		N21 3-2
22 WOLVERHAMPTON W	A29 3-3	D19 2-0	S12 3-1	F06 1-1	D28 0-1	M30 6-1	N28 3-1	S26 2-0	S16 9-0	N14 4-2	D12 0-3	F23 3-2	J16 4-2	O17 3-2	O31 2-0	a18 3-1	M16 3-3	A26 3-1	a23 1-3	F27 3-1	a11 5-0	

Peter McParland, another Irish international star. His performances at outside-left helped Aston Villa back to Division One.

DIVISION 2

	ASTON VILLA	BRIGHTON & HA	BRISTOL C	BRISTOL R	CARDIFF C	CHARLTON A	DERBY CO	HUDDERSFIELD T	HULL C	IPSWICH T	LEYTON O	LINCOLN C	LIVERPOOL	MIDDLESBROUGH	PLYMOUTH A	PORTSMOUTH	ROTHERHAM U	SCUNTHORPE U	SHEFFIELD U	STOKE C	SUNDERLAND	SWANSEA T
1 ASTON VILLA		D19 3-1	a09 2-1	J16 4-1	D12 2-0	N14 11-1	M15 3-2	F06 4-0	D28 1-1	S12 3-1	S26 1-0	M01 1-1	M30 4-4	O17 1-0	O31 2-0	S14 5-2	a23 3-0	N28 5-0	F27 1-3	a18 2-1	A31 3-0	A29 1-0
2 BRIGHTON & H.A.	A22 1-2		M12 5-1	M02 2-2	N14 2-2	O17 1-1	D12 2-0	S02 3-2	a09 1-1	D28 1-4	S16 1-1	a18 3-3	F27 1-2	a23 3-2	S19 2-2	S05 3-1	M26 0-0	O31 0-1	N28 0-2	J23 1-0	J02 2-1	S26 1-2
3 BRISTOL C	N21 0-5	O24 0-1		O10 2-1	J16 0-3	S15 1-2	F20 0-1	a16 2-3	S12 0-1	a18 5-1	D05 1-1	M19 1-0	S01 1-0	S26 2-0	D28 2-1	N07 2-0	A29 2-3	D19 0-2	F06 2-2	a30 1-2	a02 1-0	M05 2-2
4 BRISTOL R	S05 1-1	O03 4-5	F27 2-1		O31 1-1	S21 2-2	N28 2-1	a15 2-0	M26 1-0	S07 2-1	A22 2-2	J02 3-3	D12 0-2	a09 0-2	a23 2-0	S19 2-0	M12 3-1	O17 1-1	N14 3-2	F13 3-1	J23 3-1	D26 3-1
5 CARDIFF C	a16 1-0	a02 1-4	S05 4-2	a30 2-2		J02 5-1	S16 2-0	M05 2-1	F20 3-2	O24 3-2	O10 5-1	F13 6-2	A22 3-2	A26 2-0	a19 0-1	M19 1-4	S19 1-4	J23 4-2	D26 2-0	N21 4-4	D05 2-1	N07 2-1
6 CHARLTON A	a02 2-0	M05 3-1	S09 4-2	A26 2-2	A29 2-1		S26 6-1	D05 1-1	J16 3-2	a16 1-3	M19 0-0	N21 2-2	D26 3-0	F06 1-0	F20 5-2	a30 6-1	D19 2-2	a18 5-2	S12 1-1	O24 1-2	N07 3-1	O10 2-2
7 DERBY CO	O24 2-2	a16 0-1	O03 3-0	M19 1-0	S09 1-2	F24 1-2		a02 3-2	a18 1-3	N21 3-0	N07 1-1	a30 3-1	S19 1-2	A29 1-7	J23 1-0	O10 1-0	A26 1-1	D28 3-0	D19 1-1	J16 2-0	M05 0-1	D05 1-2
8 HUDDERSFIELD T	S19 0-1	A26 2-0	D12 6-1	a18 0-1	O17 0-1	a23 4-0	N14 2-2		M12 1-0	D19 3-1	S05 1-1	J23 3-0	N28 1-0	M26 2-0	a09 2-0	O03 6-3	F27 2-1	A29 2-0	O31 0-1	D28 2-3	F13 1-1	S09 4-3
9 HULL C	D26 0-1	N21 3-1	J23 1-1	N07 3-1	O03 0-0	S05 0-4	a15 1-1	O24 1-1		a30 2-0	M05 1-2	O10 0-5	J02 0-1	S14 3-3	A22 3-1	D05 1-3	F13 1-0	S19 0-2	A31 0-2	M17 4-0	a16 0-0	a02 3-1
10 IPSWICH T	J23 2-1	D26 3-0	a15 1-3	S16 3-0	M12 1-1	D12 1-1	a09 1-1	A22 1-4	O31 2-0		J02 6-3	S05 3-0	a23 0-1	N14 1-0	N28 3-3	F13 1-1	O17 2-3	F27 1-0	M26 2-0	O03 4-0	S19 6-1	A26 4-1
11 LEYTON O	F13 0-0	S10 3-2	a23 3-1	D19 1-2	F27 3-4	N28 2-0	M26 3-0	J16 2-1	O17 3-1	A29 4-1		S19 4-0	a09 2-0	O31 5-0	N14 2-3	D26 1-2	S12 2-3	D12 1-1	M17 1-1	A27 2-1	O03 1-1	a15 2-1
12 LINCOLN C	O03 0-0	a15 2-1	N28 3-1	A29 0-1	S26 2-3	a09 5-3	O31 6-2	S12 0-2	F27 3-0	J16 0-1	F06 2-2		N14 4-2	M12 5-2	M26 0-1	A26 0-2	D12 0-1	a23 2-1	O17 2-0	S09 3-0	D28 0-0	D19 2-0
13 LIVERPOOL	N07 2-1	O10 2-2	A26 4-2	a16 4-0	D19 0-4	D28 2-0	a06 4-1	M19 2-2	A29 5-3	D05 3-1	N21 4-3	a02 1-3		S12 1-2	S26 4-1	O24 1-1	a18 3-0	S09 2-0	J16 3-0	M05 5-1	a30 3-0	F20 4-1
14 MIDDLESBROUGH	M05 0-1	D05 4-1	F13 6-3	N21 5-1	S02 1-1	S19 3-0	J02 3-0	N07 1-0	S09 4-0	a02 4-1	a30 2-2	O24 3-2	J23 3-3		S05 6-2	A22 0-0	D28 3-0	O03 3-1	a18 1-2	a16 1-0	O10 1-1	M19 2-0
15 PLYMOUTH A	a30 3-0	F06 3-2	D26 1-4	D05 5-3	J30 1-1	O03 6-4	S12 0-5	N21 1-3	D19 3-2	M19 3-1	a02 1-0	N07 0-2	F13 1-1	J16 2-2		M05 1-1	S07 1-0	A24 4-0	A29 1-1	O10 2-3	O24 0-0	a16 3-1
16 PORTSMOUTH	S09 1-2	J16 2-2	M26 2-0	F06 4-5	N28 1-1	O31 2-2	F27 2-3	F20 0-2	a23 1-1	S26 0-2	D28 1-1	S02 1-2	M12 2-1	D19 6-3	O17 1-0		a09 2-0	N14 4-0	D12 0-2	A29 2-2	a18 1-2	S12 1-3
17 ROTHERHAM U	D05 2-1	N07 1-0	J02 3-1	O24 3-0	F06 2-2	A22 3-3	A31 1-2	O10 1-1	S26 1-0	M05 1-4	J23 1-1	a16 1-0	a19 2-2	D26 0-2	S16 1-1	N21 2-1		S05 1-1	M02 0-0	a02 3-0	M19 1-0	a30 1-1
18 SCUNTHORPE U	M19 1-2	a30 1-2	A22 1-1	M05 3-4	S12 1-2	a15 1-1	D26 3-2	J02 0-2	F06 3-0	O10 2-2	a16 2-1	D05 5-0	S17 1-1	F20 1-1	S03 2-0	a02 1-0	J16 2-1		S26 1-1	N07 1-1	N21 3-1	O24 3-1
19 SHEFFIELD U	O10 1-1	M19 4-1	S19 5-2	a02 1-1	D28 2-1	J23 2-0	A22 2-1	a30 2-0	A24 6-0	N07 1-0	O24 0-2	M05 3-2	S05 2-1	a19 0-0	J02 4-0	a16 0-0	O03 2-3	F13 2-1		D05 0-1	S07 1-2	N21 3-3
20 STOKE C	S30 3-3	S12 1-3	O31 1-3	S26 0-1	a09 0-1	M12 1-3	S05 2-1	D26 1-1	N28 3-1	M30 1-2	S02 2-1	S16 6-1	O17 1-1	D12 2-5	F27 1-0	J02 4-0	N14 2-3	M26 1-3	a23 1-2		A22 3-1	F06 4-2
21 SUNDERLAND	A26 1-0	A29 0-0	N14 3-2	S12 2-2	a23 1-1	M26 1-3	O17 3-1	S26 0-0	D12 1-3	F06 0-1	F20 1-4	D26 2-4	O31 1-1	F27 2-2	M12 4-0	a15 2-0	N28 1-2	a09 1-0	S16 5-1	D19 0-2		J16 4-0
22 SWANSEA T	J02 1-3	F13 2-2	a26 6-1	D28 3-0	M26 3-3	F27 5-2	a23 1-3	S17 3-1	N14 0-0	S03 2-1	a18 1-0	A22 2-1	O03 5-4	N28 3-1	D12 6-1	J23 1-1	O31 2-2	M12 3-1	a09 2-1	S19 2-2	S05 1-2	

Season 1959-60

DIVISION 3

	ACCRINGTON S	BARNSLEY	BOURNEMOUTH	BRADFORD C	BRENTFORD	BURY	CHESTERFIELD	COLCHESTER U	COVENTRY C	GRIMSBY T	HALIFAX T	MANSFIELD T	NEWPORT CO	NORWICH C	PORT VALE	Q.P.R.	READING	SHREWSBURY T	SOUTHAMPTON	SOUTHEND U	SWINDON T	TRANMERE R	WREXHAM	YORK C
1 ACCRINGTON S		J09 2-1	S07 2-1	F06 0-4	M11 3-4	N28 1-3	D05 1-3	D12 1-2	S26 0-2	J16 2-4	a09 0-5	M21 0-1	a18 0-0	O17 3-4	F27 1-3	S12 1-2	S28 0-0	A24 2-2	O31 2-2	M26 0-4	O12 3-1	D19 1-3	A29 2-2	M30 4-0
2 BARNSLEY	a23 5-0		M19 1-0	O24 2-0	A22 1-2	F13 2-2	F20 3-1	J02 2-1	M05 1-0	N07 3-3	S19 1-2	J23 2-2	a16 0-2	S16 2-0	S30 1-0	D12 2-1	D26 3-3	a19 0-0	O07 1-0	S05 4-1	S02 0-3	N21 2-0	a02 6-1	O10 1-1
3 BOURNEMOUTH	S16 3-1	N28 1-1		S26 3-2	O17 1-2	a09 2-1	a18 1-1	M12 3-2	F20 2-2	S12 4-2	m04 1-0	M26 6-0	S23 4-1	F27 0-0	S02 3-0	F06 1-1	O31 1-1	D19 2-2	a23 1-3	D12 0-0	D26 3-1	A29 2-1	J16 1-3	O07 2-0
4 BRADFORD C	S19 4-5	M12 0-0	F13 0-0		a23 0-2	O17 0-0	S05 1-0	O31 0-0	S15 1-3	D28 2-2	F27 1-2	S01 4-1	J23 6-2	N28 1-1	a09 3-1	a18 3-1	M26 0-2	M15 2-3	D12 2-0	S29 3-1	J02 1-0	O03 1-0	O13 2-2	A22 2-0
5 BRENTFORD	O24 3-0	D19 3-0	M05 1-0	m03 4-0		S08 1-1	M08 3-0	O06 2-0	M19 3-1	F20 0-2	S22 1-1	a15 1-1	a30 1-2	S26 3-4	F06 2-0	a16 1-1	J16 2-2	S12 2-1	A29 2-2	D28 3-1	a02 2-1	O10 2-1	A25 3-1	N21 1-2
6 BURY	M19 0-1	S26 0-2	N21 0-2	M05 0-0	S15 1-0		a16 1-1	A22 3-1	O10 2-1	a30 1-1	J23 2-2	S05 4-1	J30 0-1	S29 1-0	a15 3-1	O24 2-0	O06 1-0	D28 2-1	F20 1-2	J02 3-0	F06 0-3	a02 4-1	N07 3-2	S01 2-0
7 CHESTERFIELD	D26 0-3	O03 4-1	a15 4-0	J16 1-2	M26 1-0	O31 0-2		J09 1-1	S12 0-3	D19 2-2	a23 2-1	N28 0-1	J01 2-0	D12 2-1	M12 4-1	A29 0-4	F27 2-1	O17 2-2	A24 3-2	a09 1-0	S26 1-3	S21 2-0	S07 5-1	F06 2-0
8 COLCHESTER U	a30 5-1	A29 2-2	O24 1-2	a16 2-1	O12 2-1	D19 3-0	a02 1-0		J30 0-0	A24 2-2	S07 1-0	S21 3-0	N07 2-1	F20 3-0	S26 3-1	D28 2-0	S12 4-2	F06 3-2	M21 1-1	a15 2-3	N21 0-0	M05 4-0	O10 3-1	M19 2-2
9 COVENTRY C	F13 2-1	O17 2-1	O03 4-0	S07 2-2	N28 2-1	F27 0-1	J23 1-0	a23 3-1		a19 0-2	A24 0-1	A22 2-0	S19 1-1	a09 2-1	M07 1-1	S21 0-0	a30 1-1	M26 1-1	M12 4-1	O31 2-0	S05 3-1	O05 1-0	D25 5-3	J02 5-2
10 GRIMSBY T	S05 4-0	M26 2-0	J23 1-1	D26 1-3	O03 1-3	D12 2-2	A22 5-1	S01 4-1	a15 3-0		M12 3-2	O17 2-1	J02 0-1	O31 1-1	a23 1-1	O13 3-1	a09 0-1	N28 2-1	a26 3-2	F27 1-1	S15 3-0	S19 1-1	F13 3-1	S29 2-2
11 HALIFAX T	N21 0-2	F06 5-0	a02 1-0	O10 4-0	S28 1-0	S12 1-0	a28 0-1	S14 3-2	A31 2-2	O24 1-2		J02 4-2	M19 2-1	J09 0-1	D26 1-1	M05 3-1	a11 2-2	O05 1-2	S26 3-1	A22 2-1	a16 3-1	N07 0-3	a30 2-0	J16 1-2
12 MANSFIELD T	a02 4-1	S12 1-4	N07 3-4	A24 0-0	a18 0-1	J16 1-5	M19 4-1	S28 1-3	a04 2-4	M05 3-2	A29 1-1		N21 3-1	D26 3-2	a25 6-3	O10 4-3	S26 4-4	F20 1-0	F06 4-2	S14 1-1	M28 1-2	a30 0-2	O24 6-2	a16 2-0
13 NEWPORT CO	a15 1-3	O31 4-0	S28 5-2	S12 2-0	D12 4-2	a23 3-1	O12 3-1	M26 3-2	F15 2-0	A29 0-2	N28 5-1	a09 0-1		M12 1-1	O19 4-3	J16 2-3	A24 3-2	F27 1-3	M07 5-1	M21 1-1	F20 1-3	S07 2-1	F29 4-1	S26 3-2
14 NORWICH C	M05 4-0	S09 0-0	O10 2-3	M19 0-0	F13 2-1	S23 2-0	a30 3-0	O03 3-2	N21 1-4	a16 1-1	a18 3-0	D28 5-1	O24 1-0		S12 5-1	J30 1-0	A29 4-2	M30 1-1	D19 1-2	a27 4-3	N07 3-2	A26 3-0	F06 3-1	a02 1-0
15 PORT VALE	O10 2-0	S21 1-0	A24 1-0	N21 0-2	S19 3-1	a18 3-0	O24 3-1	F13 1-1	a02 0-1	F10 2-1	D28 7-0	O12 4-1	M05 2-1	J23 2-1		M19 0-0	D19 4-1	A29 0-3	S07 1-1	O03 3-1	a30 6-1	J16 1-1	a16 3-1	N07 2-0
16 Q.P.R.	J23 5-1	a30 1-0	S19 3-0	a15 5-0	O31 2-4	M12 2-0	M28 3-3	D26 3-1	S28 2-1	O05 0-0	O17 3-0	F27 2-0	S05 3-0	a23 0-0	N28 2-2		M07 2-0	a09 1-1	M26 0-1	A31 0-0	A22 2-0	F13 2-1	O03 2-1	S14 0-0
17 READING	S23 2-0	D30 3-2	a16 2-2	a27 1-0	S05 3-3	O14 0-1	O10 6-3	J23 2-1	D12 4-2	N21 1-2	O03 1-1	F13 3-2	S02 0-1	J02 0-2	A22 2-3	a02 2-0		S09 2-3	a15 2-0	S19 4-1	M05 3-0	J30 5-4	M19 0-1	O24 1-0
18 SHREWSBURY T	A31 5-0	a18 2-2	A22 0-0	a02 3-0	J23 1-1	D26 0-2	M05 2-4	S19 4-1	N07 3-2	M19 5-2	a25 2-2	O03 6-3	O10 6-2	S05 1-3	J02 2-1	N21 1-1	S14 3-2		S28 1-1	F13 1-3	O24 3-0	a16 0-0	J30 3-2	D12 4-0
19 SOUTHAMPTON	a16 5-1	O14 2-1	F24 4-3	a30 2-0	J02 2-0	O03 0-2	S02 4-3	S05 4-2	O24 5-1	a02 1-1	F13 3-2	S19 5-2	D26 2-0	A22 2-2	S16 3-2	N07 2-1	a18 1-0	S23 6-3		J23 3-1	O10 5-1	M19 1-1	N21 3-0	M05 3-1
20 SOUTHEND U	N07 6-1	F29 2-2	a30 3-0	S21 2-1	D26 2-0	A29 0-4	N21 1-2	a18 1-0	a16 1-0	O10 3-0	D19 3-0	S07 0-2	a02 3-2	O05 1-0	F22 2-1	A24 3-2	F06 2-0	S26 2-1	S12 2-4		M19 1-3	O24 7-1	M05 1-1	J30 1-1
21 SWINDON T	O07 0-1	A26 1-1	D28 2-0	A29 5-3	J09 0-0	S19 1-0	F13 1-1	a09 4-3	m04 2-0	S09 3-2	O31 1-1	a23 2-1	O03 1-0	M26 0-1	D12 2-3	D19 2-1	O17 0-4	M12 4-2	F27 0-3	N28 2-0		a18 1-1	S23 4-1	S12 1-1
22 TRANMERE R	A22 5-1	a09 2-0	J02 1-1	F29 2-3	F27 2-1	a25 2-0	S28 3-0	O17 1-1	O12 3-1	F22 2-0	M28 1-1	D12 4-2	S14 2-2	A31 0-0	S05 6-0	S26 0-3	a23 0-1	O31 3-3	N28 2-4	M12 1-0	a15 2-2		S12 4-1	D26 2-2
23 WREXHAM	J02 2-3	M09 1-0	S05 1-2	O07 4-3	S02 3-2	M26 1-1	O28 2-3	F27 1-1	D26 1-3	S26 2-1	D12 2-1	M12 3-0	A22 0-0	S19 1-2	O31 1-0	m04 1-1	N28 2-1	a23 1-1	a09 2-1	O17 3-1	S30 1-2	J23 1-0		a18 3-1
24 YORK C	O03 3-0	F27 0-0	O12 3-2	D19 1-1	a09 0-1	A24 1-0	S19 1-0	N28 2-3	A29 1-1	S21 3-3	S05 1-2	O31 2-1	F12 2-0	M16 1-2	M26 2-0	S07 2-1	M12 2-3	a30 0-1	O17 2-2	a23 2-3	J23 1-0	D28 3-0	a15 3-0	

DIVISION 4

	ALDERSHOT	BARROW	BRADFORD	CARLISLE U	CHESTER	CREWE A	CRYSTAL P	DARLINGTON	DONCASTER R	EXETER C	GATESHEAD	GILLINGHAM	HARTLEPOOLS U	MILLWALL	NORTHAMPTON T	NOTTS CO	OLDHAM A	ROCHDALE	SOUTHPORT	STOCKPORT CO	TORQUAY U	WALSALL	WATFORD	WORKINGTON
1 ALDERSHOT		A29 6-1	M12 6-1	N28 0-2	F27 3-2	D28 6-1	O17 1-0	S02 3-0	O07 1-1	M26 1-0	S21 3-2	J16 3-1	D19 3-0	F06 1-2	F20 3-0	a23 1-1	a09 2-0	J09 0-0	S12 0-0	O31 1-0	S26 1-3	a30 0-2	M16 2-2	S16 3-1
2 BARROW	J02 3-0		O17 3-3	a09 5-1	D26 3-0	S05 0-0	F27 0-1	A22 4-1	S14 1-1	O31 3-3	A31 2-2	S12 0-1	D12 2-2	S26 2-2	a25 0-1	N28 4-3	J09 2-0	S28 3-0	F06 3-1	M12 5-1	m02 1-1	a23 2-3	M26 2-1	a18 2-1
3 BRADFORD	O24 3-2	M05 2-0		A29 1-1	F20 1-1	S26 2-2	O07 3-1	M19 1-0	a16 3-3	S21 1-0	N07 4-2	O10 3-0	F06 6-2	S07 1-1	a07 3-0	J16 1-1	D19 2-0	a02 0-0	D26 3-0	a19 1-1	a30 2-2	S12 1-3	A24 1-1	N21 3-2
4 CARLISLE U	a19 0-0	N21 0-1	J02 1-3		S01 2-1	S29 4-2	A22 2-2	J30 1-0	O10 2-0	J23 0-4	a30 4-0	a02 0-1	a15 1-1	M19 3-3	M05 0-2	O06 2-0	F13 0-1	M29 1-1	N07 1-0	S05 0-4	O24 2-0	S15 1-1	S19 1-0	D26 0-1
5 CHESTER	O10 5-1	D28 3-2	O03 1-1	A26 0-1		S12 0-0	F13 0-1	M05 1-1	a02 2-0	S07 1-0	O24 4-2	F06 4-2	J16 1-1	J30 2-1	N21 1-1	D19 2-1	S23 0-0	M19 2-1	a30 2-2	O14 1-2	a16 1-1	A29 1-3	a16 0-1	N07 3-1
6 CREWE A	D26 3-2	J16 3-2	F13 4-1	S23 3-0	J23 2-1		S19 1-1	O10 5-0	N07 2-0	O14 1-1	M05 4-1	a30 1-2	A29 1-0	a16 2-0	a02 0-1	A26 2-1	a18 2-2	O24 1-3	M16 5-1	O03 4-2	N21 1-2	D19 1-5	S09 1-3	M19 2-0
7 CRYSTAL P	M05 1-1	O10 9-0	a27 1-0	D19 2-1	S26 3-4	F06 4-0		O24 2-0	N21 4-0	a15 1-0	M19 2-2	D28 3-3	S12 5-2	O28 1-2	a16 0-1	A29 1-1	S02 3-2	N07 4-0	F20 2-2	S16 3-1	J30 1-1	J16 1-2	S23 8-1	a02 0-1
8 DARLINGTON	A24 4-0	D19 3-1	O31 4-3	a23 2-1	O17 0-0	F27 1-1	M12 1-1		m04 2-2	a25 0-1	a15 2-1	A29 2-1	D28 2-0	S12 1-1	S26 3-2	D12 5-2	N28 1-3	S16 0-0	J16 5-0	M26 1-2	F06 1-0	S30 0-2	a09 0-3	O07 0-3
9 DONCASTER R	O15 1-2	S08 1-4	N28 2-0	F27 4-1	M08 2-0	M26 4-0	a09 1-2	O03 0-1		D12 0-1	F13 1-0	a15 3-0	O31 5-1	A27 0-0	A29 3-2	O17 0-4	D28 0-0	S19 2-1	S24 5-0	a23 1-0	D19 1-3	M12 1-1	S05 1-0	J23 2-0
10 EXETER C	N07 3-1	M19 2-2	S30 3-1	S12 1-3	S17 2-0	O07 2-4	a18 2-2	a02 0-0	a30 4-2		N21 2-1	O24 2-0	F20 5-0	O10 2-2	A22 1-1	F06 3-3	J16 4-3	a16 4-1	M05 1-1	S02 2-1	D28 1-0	S26 1-2	A29 2-0	J30 1-0
11 GATESHEAD	S28 4-1	A24 3-1	M26 1-2	D12 1-0	M12 0-1	O17 4-2	O31 0-2	a18 1-3	S26 5-0	a09 1-0		D19 2-2	F27 1-1	J16 1-0	F06 1-3	S07 0-0	a23 2-0	O05 1-2	A29 1-0	J09 2-1	S12 0-2	a25 3-0	N28 1-3	M28 2-1
12 GILLINGHAM	S05 3-1	J23 1-0	F27 2-0	m06 3-1	S19 3-1	D12 1-1	m04 0-0	J02 2-0	a18 2-1	M12 2-1	A22 5-4		a23 3-1	F20 3-1	S16 2-1	a09 0-1	M26 2-2	S03 2-0	S26 4-1	O17 0-2	O07 1-0	N28 2-0	O31 2-0	S30 2-2
13 HARTLEPOOLS U	A22 3-0	a30 0-1	S19 3-0	a18 1-2	S05 2-3	J02 2-0	J23 0-1	D26 1-2	M19 2-6	O03 4-3	O10 3-0	J30 3-1		N21 0-2	N07 1-4	S21 2-4	S07 2-2	M05 0-1	a16 3-2	F13 2-1	a02 4-0	A31 1-2	M23 0-0	O24 1-4
14 MILLWALL	S19 2-0	F13 3-3	S14 2-0	O31 1-1	a23 7-1	N28 1-4	D12 1-0	J23 5-2	A31 1-1	F27 2-3	S05 4-0	O03 3-3	a09 4-0		S28 2-1	M26 1-1	M12 0-1	J02 2-0	O05 2-2	M07 3-2	a15 2-0	J09 1-1	O17 2-2	A22 3-0
15 NORTHAMPTON T	O30 2-0	a11 6-0	a23 3-1	O17 2-2	a09 1-0	a28 0-0	N28 0-2	F13 3-1	J02 3-1	D19 1-1	S19 2-0	S10 2-1	M26 3-0	S21 0-3		M12 4-2	F27 8-1	J23 3-1	a19 2-2	D12 1-1	A27 3-0	O31 0-1	D28 1-2	S05 0-0
16 NOTTS CO	J30 5-3	a16 1-2	S05 0-1	O15 2-1	A22 2-1	S03 4-1	J02 7-1	a30 5-4	M05 3-4	S19 3-0	S17 4-0	N21 3-1	O01 4-0	N07 2-1	O24 2-1		O03 3-1	D26 2-1	a02 4-1	J23 3-0	M19 1-1	a18 2-1	F13 2-1	O10 2-0
17 OLDHAM A	N21 0-1	a02 1-0	A22 2-0	S26 0-1	S29 0-0	a15 2-4	A24 1-0	a16 1-3	D26 1-1	S05 1-2	J30 1-1	N07 3-1	S15 1-2	O24 1-1	O10 0-1	m03 0-3		a30 1-0	M19 0-1	J02 0-0	M05 0-2	a12 2-4	J23 0-0	F06 2-2
18 ROCHDALE	a18 2-0	S22 4-1	M15 0-1	O03 3-0	O31 0-0	M12 4-2	M26 4-0	S08 2-0	F06 2-0	N28 3-0	O13 2-0	A27 1-0	O17 2-0	A29 0-1	S12 2-2	D28 1-4	D12 2-0		D19 1-0	a09 3-0	J16 4-2	F27 0-2	a23 3-3	S26 1-1
19 SOUTHPORT	J23 0-4	S19 1-0	D28 1-1	M26 1-1	D12 3-1	a23 0-1	O03 3-1	S05 0-1	m02 1-1	O17 3-2	J02 1-0	F13 1-1	N28 2-1	a25 1-0	a15 0-4	J09 1-2	O31 1-0	A22 2-2		F27 3-0	S15 1-2	a09 1-4	M12 1-1	S01 2-2
20 STOCKPORT CO	M19 1-1	O24 1-0	a15 0-0	J16 0-0	O05 3-0	F29 1-0	S07 0-1	N07 1-0	J30 2-0	A24 1-0	a02 0-0	M05 1-1	S26 2-1	D28 2-2	a30 3-0	S12 3-1	A29 3-1	N21 2-1	O10 1-0		S21 0-1	F06 2-0	D19 4-0	a16 2-0
21 TORQUAY U	F13 2-1	O03 3-2	D12 1-1	M12 2-1	N28 1-2	a09 5-2	a23 2-1	S19 1-2	A22 2-1	D26 2-3	J23 1-0	a27 2-0	J09 3-0	a18 2-2	S02 5-3	O31 3-1	O17 4-1	S05 1-1	S09 4-0	S30 4-0		M26 2-1	F27 2-1	J02 2-1
22 WALSALL	D12 1-0	J29 2-1	J23 2-1	S10 0-1	J02 2-1	A22 3-1	S05 3-0	S22 1-0	O24 5-2	M22 2-2	D26 2-2	a16 2-3	A25 2-2	a02 2-1	M19 1-2	a19 2-2	O13 2-1	O10 4-2	N21 8-0	S19 3-1	N07 3-2		O03 3-4	M05 2-2
23 WATFORD	a02 1-3	N07 2-0	S01 1-0	F06 3-1	a15 4-2	S15 2-0	S29 4-2	N21 2-1	J16 1-2	J02 5-2	a16 5-0	M19 3-1	O13 7-2	M05 0-2	M01 3-1	S26 4-2	S12 6-0	a26 2-1	O24 2-1	A22 0-0	O10 0-1	m03 2-2		D12 3-2
24 WORKINGTON	S10 3-3	a15 1-1	a09 0-1	D29 1-0	M26 5-0	O31 5-0	F25 1-1	O15 1-1	S12 2-0	a23 2-1	O03 1-1	S24 1-1	M12 3-0	D19 4-0	J16 5-1	F27 0-1	S19 2-0	F13 2-0	A27 1-1	N28 1-1	A29 0-2	O17 0-3	a30 0-1	

LEAGUE TABLES

DIVISION 1

	P	W	D	L	F	A	W	D	L	F	A	Pts
Burnley	42	15	2	4	52	28	9	5	7	33	33	55
Wolves	42	15	3	3	63	28	9	3	9	43	39	54
Tottenham H	42	10	6	5	43	24	11	5	5	43	26	53
WBA	42	12	4	5	48	25	7	7	7	35	32	49
Sheffield W	42	12	7	2	48	20	7	4	10	32	39	49
Bolton W	42	12	5	4	37	27	8	3	10	22	24	48
Manchester U	42	13	3	5	53	30	6	4	11	49	50	45
Newcastle U	42	10	5	6	42	32	8	3	10	40	46	44
Preston NE	42	10	6	5	43	34	6	6	9	36	42	44
Fulham	42	12	4	5	42	28	5	6	10	31	52	44
Blackpool	42	9	6	6	32	32	6	4	11	27	39	40
Leicester C	42	8	6	7	38	32	5	7	9	28	43	39
Arsenal	42	9	5	7	39	38	6	4	11	29	42	39
West Ham U	42	12	3	6	47	33	4	3	14	28	58	38
Everton	42	13	3	5	50	20	0	8	13	23	58	37
Manchester C	42	11	2	8	47	34	6	1	14	31	50	37
Blackburn	42	12	3	6	38	29	4	2	15	22	41	37
Chelsea	42	7	5	9	44	50	7	4	10	32	41	37
Birmingham C	42	9	5	7	37	36	4	5	12	26	44	36
Nottingham F	42	8	6	7	30	28	5	3	13	20	46	35
Leeds U	42	7	5	9	37	46	5	5	11	28	46	34
Luton T	42	6	5	10	25	29	3	7	11	25	44	30

DIVISION 2

	P	W	D	L	F	A	W	D	L	F	A	Pts
Aston Villa	42	17	3	1	62	19	8	6	7	27	24	59
Cardiff C	42	15	2	4	55	36	8	10	3	35	26	58
Liverpool	42	15	3	3	59	28	5	7	9	31	38	50
Sheffield U	42	12	5	4	43	22	7	7	7	25	29	50
Middlesbrough	42	14	5	2	56	21	5	5	11	34	43	48
Huddersfield T	42	13	3	5	44	20	6	6	9	29	32	47
Charlton A	42	12	7	2	55	28	5	6	10	35	59	47
Rotherham U	42	9	9	3	31	23	8	4	9	30	37	47
Bristol R	42	12	6	3	42	28	6	5	10	30	50	47
Leyton O	42	12	4	5	47	25	3	10	8	29	36	44
Ipswich T	42	12	5	4	48	24	7	1	13	30	44	44
Swansea T	42	12	6	3	54	32	3	4	14	28	52	40
Lincoln C	42	11	3	7	41	25	5	4	12	34	53	39
Brighton & HA	42	7	8	6	35	32	6	4	11	32	44	38
Scunthorpe U	42	9	7	5	38	26	4	3	14	19	45	36
Sunderland	42	8	6	7	35	29	4	6	11	17	36	36
Stoke C	42	8	3	10	40	38	6	4	11	26	45	35
Derby Co	42	9	4	8	31	28	5	3	13	30	49	35
Plymouth A	42	10	6	5	42	36	3	3	15	19	53	35
Portsmouth	42	6	6	9	36	36	4	6	11	23	41	32
Hull C	42	7	6	8	27	30	3	4	14	21	46	30
Bristol C	42	8	3	10	27	31	3	2	16	33	66	27

DIVISION 3

	P	W	D	L	F	A	W	D	L	F	A	Pts
Southampton	46	19	3	1	68	30	7	6	10	38	45	61
Norwich C	46	16	4	3	53	24	8	7	8	29	30	59
Shrewsbury T	46	12	7	4	58	34	6	9	8	39	41	52
Grimsby T	46	12	7	4	48	27	6	9	8	39	43	52
Coventry C	46	14	6	3	44	22	7	4	12	34	41	52
Brentford	46	13	6	4	46	24	8	3	12	32	37	51
Bury	46	13	4	6	26	23	8	5	10	28	28	51
QPR	46	14	7	2	45	16	4	6	13	28	38	49
Colchester U	46	15	6	2	51	22	3	5	15	32	52	47
Bournemouth	46	12	8	3	47	27	5	5	13	25	45	47
Reading	46	13	3	7	49	34	5	7	11	35	43	46
Southend U	46	15	3	5	49	28	4	5	14	27	46	46
Newport Co	46	15	2	6	59	36	5	4	14	21	43	46*
Port Vale	46	16	4	3	51	19	3	4	16	29	60	46*
Halifax T	46	13	3	7	42	27	5	7	11	28	45	46
Swindon T	46	12	6	5	39	30	7	2	14	30	48	46
Barnsley	46	13	6	4	45	25	2	8	13	20	41	44
Chesterfield	46	13	3	7	41	31	5	4	14	30	53	43
Bradford C	46	10	7	6	39	28	5	5	13	27	46	42
Tranmere R	46	11	8	4	50	29	3	5	15	22	46	41
York C	46	11	5	7	38	26	2	7	14	19	47	38
Mansfield T	46	11	4	8	55	48	4	2	17	26	64	36
Wrexham	46	12	5	6	39	30	2	3	18	29	71	36
Accrington S	46	4	5	14	31	53	7	0	16	26	70	27

DIVISION 4

	P	W	D	L	F	A	W	D	L	F	A	Pts
Walsall	46	14	5	4	57	33	14	4	5	45	27	65
Notts Co	46	19	1	3	66	27	7	7	9	41	42	60
Torquay U	46	17	3	3	56	27	9	5	9	28	31	60
Watford	46	17	2	4	62	28	7	7	9	30	39	57
Millwall	46	12	8	3	54	28	6	9	8	30	33	53
Northampton T	46	13	6	4	50	22	9	3	11	35	41	53
Gillingham	46	17	4	2	47	21	4	6	13	27	48	52
Crystal P	46	12	6	5	61	27	7	6	10	23	37	50
Exeter C	46	13	7	3	50	30	6	4	13	30	40	49
Stockport Co	46	15	6	2	35	10	4	5	14	23	44	49
Bradford	46	12	10	1	48	25	5	5	13	22	43	49
Rochdale	46	15	4	4	46	19	3	6	14	19	41	46
Aldershot	46	14	5	4	50	22	4	4	15	27	52	45
Crewe A	46	14	3	6	51	31	4	6	13	28	57	45
Darlington	46	11	6	6	40	30	6	3	14	23	43	43
Workington	46	10	8	5	41	20	4	6	13	27	40	42
Doncaster R	46	13	3	7	40	23	3	7	13	29	53	42
Barrow	46	11	8	4	52	29	4	3	16	25	58	41
Carlisle U	46	9	6	8	28	28	6	5	12	23	38	41
Chester	46	10	8	5	37	26	4	4	15	22	51	40
Southport	46	9	7	7	30	32	1	7	15	18	60	34
Gateshead	46	12	3	8	37	27	0	6	17	21	59	33
Oldham A	46	5	7	11	20	30	3	5	15	21	53	28
Hartlepools U	46	9	2	12	40	41	1	5	17	19	68	27

Football League Records

Top scorers: Div 1, J.Greaves (Chelsea) 41 goals; Div 2, R.Crawford (Ipswich Town) 39 goals; Div 3, A.Richards (Walsall) 36 goals; Div 4, T.Bly (Peterborough United) 52 goals.
Gateshead failed to gain re-election, Peterborough United were elected in their place.

Danny Blanchflower, creative right-half for Spurs and Northern Ireland. Blanchflower skippered Tottenham to their historic League and Cup double in 1960-61.

Terry Bly, the prolific scorer who helped former Midland League club Peterborough United make such a great impression as members of the Football League.

DIVISION 1

	ARSENAL	ASTON VILLA	BIRMINGHAM C	BLACKBURN R	BLACKPOOL	BOLTON W	BURNLEY	CARDIFF C	CHELSEA	EVERTON	FULHAM	LEICESTER C	MANCHESTER C	MANCHESTER U	NEWCASTLE U	NOTTINGHAM F	PRESTON N.E.	SHEFFIELD W	TOTTENHAM H	W.B.A.	WEST HAM U	WOLVERHAMPTON W
1 ARSENAL		O15 2-1	S06 2-0	M11 0-0	a08 1-0	D10 5-1	D17 2-5	F11 2-3	N12 1-4	N26 3-2	a03 4-2	F25 1-3	J14 5-4	O29 2-1	S17 5-0	A27 3-0	A23 1-0	D26 1-1	S10 2-3	O01 1-0	M25 0-0	a22 1-5
2 ASTON VILLA	M04 2-2		O22 6-2	J21 2-2	D31 2-2	a04 4-0	N05 2-0	S12 2-1	A20 3-2	S03 3-2	N19 2-1	O01 1-3	D03 5-1	S17 3-1	O08 2-0	a01 1-2	a15 1-0	a29 4-1	F11 1-2	M28 0-1	A29 2-1	D24 0-2
3 BIRMINGHAM C	S14 2-0	M11 1-1		M25 1-1	a22 0-2	D17 2-2	a27 0-1	a03 2-1	O15 1-0	D10 2-4	J14 1-0	N26 0-2	M22 3-2	N12 3-1	D26 2-1	S24 3-1	S10 1-3	A27 1-1	a08 2-3	A31 3-1	F25 4-2	O29 1-2
4 BLACKBURN R	O22 2-4	S10 4-1	N05 2-0		D27 2-0	S24 3-1	O08 1-4	N19 2-2	S19 3-1	M31 1-3	D03 5-1	J14 1-1	M18 4-1	D17 1-2	a29 2-4	A24 4-1	M04 1-0	a01 1-1	A27 1-4	a15 2-1	M20 4-1	F04 2-1
5 BLACKPOOL	N19 1-1	A27 5-3	D03 1-2	D24 2-0		S10 0-1	M21 0-0	N05 6-1	S24 1-4	S05 1-4	O08 2-5	D17 5-1	a29 3-3	M31 2-0	a15 2-1	O22 4-0	F18 0-1	M15 0-1	A22 1-3	a01 0-1	F04 3-0	M04 5-2
6 BOLTON W	a01 1-1	a03 3-0	A20 2-2	F11 0-0	J21 3-1		N19 3-5	M04 3-0	S03 4-1	S17 3-4	O22 0-3	D24 2-0	N05 3-1	O01 1-1	D03 2-1	a15 3-1	a29 1-1	M18 0-1	S07 1-2	O08 0-1	D31 3-1	A24 0-2
7 BURNLEY	A20 3-2	M25 1-1	S17 2-1	F25 1-1	O29 1-2	a08 2-0		S03 1-2	M11 4-4	D26 1-3	O01 5-0	D10 3-2	A30 1-3	O15 5-3	D31 5-3	M31 4-1	S06 5-0	F11 3-4	a22 4-2	J21 0-1	a18 2-2	N12 5-3
8 CARDIFF C	S24 1-0	S07 1-1	M31 0-2	a08 1-1	M24 0-2	O15 0-1	J14 2-1		D10 2-1	N12 1-1	D17 2-0	O28 2-1	F04 3-3	N26 3-0	F22 3-2	S10 1-3	A27 2-0	A24 0-1	M11 3-2	D26 3-1	a22 1-1	F25 3-2
9 CHELSEA	a15 3-1	D17 2-4	M04 3-2	S07 5-2	F11 2-2	J14 1-1	O22 2-6	a01 6-1		O01 3-3	F04 2-1	A24 1-3	N19 6-3	D24 1-2	N05 4-2	a29 4-3	M18 1-1	a26 0-2	a03 2-3	D03 7-1	S10 3-2	A27 3-3
10 EVERTON	a29 4-1	M22 1-2	a01 1-0	a03 2-2	S14 1-0	F04 1-2	D27 0-3	a15 5-1	F18 1-1		M04 1-0	A27 3-1	O24 4-2	A24 4-0	N19 5-0	M18 1-0	O08 0-0	D03 4-2	D17 1-3	N05 1-1	S24 4-1	S10 3-1
11 FULHAM	M31 2-2	a08 1-1	S03 2-1	a22 1-1	F25 4-3	M11 2-2	F22 0-1	A20 2-2	S17 3-2	O15 2-3		N12 4-2	D26 1-0	D10 4-4	A31 4-3	S13 1-0	S24 2-0	J21 1-6	M25 0-0	D31 1-2	O29 1-1	N26 1-3
12 LEICESTER C	O08 2-1	a19 3-1	a29 3-2	S03 2-4	A20 1-1	D26 2-0	a01 2-2	a10 3-0	A31 1-3	D31 4-1	a15 1-2		a26 1-2	J21 6-0	F11 5-3	D03 1-1	N04 5-2	N19 2-1	S17 1-2	O22 2-2	a03 5-1	S14 2-0
13 MANCHESTER C	S03 0-0	a22 4-1	O01 2-1	O29 4-0	a19 1-1	M25 0-0	A24 2-1	S17 4-2	a08 2-1	M11 2-1	D24 3-2	O15 3-1		M04 1-3	J21 3-3	D17 1-2	M31 2-3	S07 1-1	F25 0-1	F11 3-0	N12 1-2	D10 2-4
14 MANCHESTER U	M18 1-1	F04 1-1	a15 4-1	A20 1-3	a03 2-0	F18 3-1	a12 6-0	a29 3-3	D26 6-0	A31 4-0	a01 3-1	S10 1-1	D31 5-1		O22 3-2	O24 2-1	D03 1-0	N05 0-0	J16 2-0	N19 3-0	S14 6-1	S24 1-3
15 NEWCASTLE U	F04 3-3	F25 2-1	D24 2-2	N26 3-1	N12 4-3	a22 4-1	A27 0-1	O01 5-0	M25 1-6	a08 0-4	A24 7-2	S24 1-3	S10 1-3	M11 1-1		J14 2-2	D17 0-0	M31 0-1	O29 3-4	S14 3-2	D10 5-5	O15 4-4
16 NOTTINGHAM F	D31 3-5	D10 2-0	F11 1-0	A31 1-1	M11 0-0	N12 2-2	a03 3-1	J21 2-1	N26 2-1	O29 1-2	S21 4-2	a22 2-2	A20 2-2	F25 3-2	S03 0-2		D24 2-0	O01 1-2	O15 0-4	S17 1-2	a08 1-1	M25 1-1
17 PRESTON N.E.	A30 2-0	N12 1-1	J21 2-3	O15 2-0	O01 1-0	a18 0-0	S13 2-3	D31 1-1	O29 0-2	F25 1-0	F11 2-0	M25 0-0	a03 1-1	a22 2-4	A20 2-3	D26 0-1		S17 2-2	D10 0-1	S03 2-1	M11 4-0	a08 1-2
18 SHEFFIELD W	D23 1-1	N26 1-2	D31 2-0	D10 5-4	O15 4-0	O29 2-0	S24 3-1	A31 2-0	F25 1-0	a22 1-2	S10 2-0	a08 2-2	S14 3-1	M25 5-1	a03 1-1	F21 1-0	F04 5-1		N12 2-1	A20 1-0	S03 1-0	M11 0-0
19 TOTTENHAM H	J21 4-2	S24 6-2	N19 6-0	D31 5-2	A31 3-1	S14 3-1	D03 4-4	N02 3-2	M31 4-2	A20 2-0	N05 5-1	F04 2-3	O10 1-1	S03 4-1	M22 1-2	a26 1-0	a01 5-0	a17 2-1		a29 1-2	D24 2-0	F22 1-1
20 W.B.A.	F18 2-3	O29 0-2	A24 1-2	N12 1-2	D10 3-1	F25 3-2	S10 0-2	D27 1-1	a22 3-0	M25 3-0	A27 2-4	M11 1-0	S24 6-3	a08 1-1	S05 6-0	F04 1-2	J14 3-1	D17 2-2	N26 1-3		O15 1-0	a03 2-1
21 WEST HAM U	N05 6-0	A22 5-2	O08 4-3	O01 3-2	S17 3-3	A27 2-1	a29 1-2	D03 2-0	J21 3-1	F11 4-0	M18 1-2	M31 1-0	a15 1-1	S05 2-1	a01 1-1	N19 2-4	O22 5-2	J14 1-1	D26 0-3	M04 1-2		D17 5-0
22 WOLVERHAMPTON W	D03 5-3	D26 3-2	M18 5-1	S17 0-0	S03 1-0	A31 3-1	a15 2-1	O08 2-2	D31 6-1	J21 4-1	a29 2-4	S07 3-2	a01 1-0	F11 2-1	M08 2-1	N05 5-3	N19 3-0	O22 4-1	O01 0-4	J28 4-2	A20 4-2	

DIVISION 2

	BRIGHTON & HA	BRISTOL R	CHARLTON A	DERBY CO	HUDDERSFIELD T	IPSWICH T	LEEDS U	LEYTON O	LINCOLN C	LIVERPOOL	LUTON T	MIDDLESBROUGH	NORWICH C	PLYMOUTH A	PORTSMOUTH	ROTHERHAM U	SCUNTHORPE U	SHEFFIELD U	SOUTHAMPTON	STOKE C	SUNDERLAND	SWANSEA T
1 BRIGHTON & H.A.		A27 6-1	O15 3-5	D17 3-2	a22 2-1	S07 2-4	S24 2-1	A24 1-1	a08 1-0	J14 3-1	N12 1-0	F18 0-1	F25 2-2	M31 2-0	N26 2-2	S10 1-0	D27 1-1	M11 0-0	F04 0-1	O29 0-1	D10 1-2	M25 0-0
2 BRISTOL R	D31 0-1		N26 3-1	F11 1-1	O29 1-2	S03 1-1	A29 4-4	S17 4-2	O15 3-1	a04 4-3	F25 4-1	A20 2-3	a08 3-1	N12 2-5	M11 2-0	S12 2-1	J21 3-3	a22 3-1	M20 4-2	D10 1-0	M25 1-0	O01 4-2
3 CHARLTON A	M04 3-1	a01 2-1		D03 3-1	M31 2-3	O08 0-2	a29 2-0	M18 2-0	F11 3-0	N19 1-3	S17 4-1	O22 6-6	A31 0-1	D26 6-4	O01 7-4	a15 4-3	A20 1-1	D31 2-3	N05 1-3	S03 3-1	S07 2-2	J21 6-2
4 DERBY CO	A20 4-1	S24 1-1	a22 2-3		M25 1-1	a24 1-4	D24 2-3	J21 3-1	M11 3-1	F18 1-4	O15 4-1	A31 1-0	N26 0-0	a08 4-1	O29 6-2	a03 3-0	S03 2-5	D10 2-0	S14 2-2	S17 1-1	N12 1-1	F25 2-3
5 HUDDERSFIELD T	D03 0-1	a29 4-0	a03 2-2	N05 1-3		a01 1-3	J21 0-1	a15 1-0	D31 4-1	O22 2-4	A20 1-1	M18 1-0	F21 1-1	S24 1-5	S03 3-3	M04 0-1	N19 1-2	S14 0-1	O08 3-1	D26 0-0	F04 4-2	A31 3-1
6 IPSWICH T	S13 4-0	J14 3-2	F25 2-1	A27 4-1	N26 4-2		F18 4-0	D17 6-2	N12 3-1	S10 1-0	M25 0-1	M31 3-1	D27 4-1	D10 3-1	a08 2-2	F04 1-1	A30 2-0	O15 0-1	S24 3-3	M11 2-1	a22 4-0	O29 0-3
7 LEEDS U	F10 3-2	A24 1-1	O29 1-0	D27 3-3	S10 1-4	O01 2-5		S07 1-3	a22 7-0	D17 2-2	M08 1-2	S17 4-4	M11 1-0	O15 2-1	D10 0-0	A27 2-0	a25 2-2	M25 1-2	J14 3-0	N12 0-1	F25 2-4	a08 2-2
8 LEYTON O	A31 2-1	F04 3-2	D10 1-1	S10 2-1	M21 2-0	A20 1-3	S14 0-1		O29 1-2	S24 1-3	M11 2-1	M14 1-1	a22 1-0	M07 1-1	M25 2-1	F20 2-1	D31 2-1	S03 1-4	M29 1-1	a10 3-1	a08 0-1	O15 2-2
9 LINCOLN C	N19 2-1	M04 1-2	S24 2-2	O22 3-4	A27 0-0	a15 1-4	D03 2-3	a29 2-0		O08 1-2	D27 1-1	a01 5-2	F04 1-4	S10 3-1	D17 2-3	A24 0-1	N05 0-2	F22 0-5	M18 0-3	M31 1-1	J14 1-2	S14 2-0
10 LIVERPOOL	S03 2-0	M31 3-0	a08 2-1	O01 1-0	M11 3-1	J21 1-1	A20 2-0	F11 5-0	F25 2-0		S07 2-2	D31 3-4	N12 2-1	M24 1-1	O15 3-3	D26 2-1	S17 3-2	N26 4-2	A31 0-1	a22 3-0	O29 1-1	D10 4-0
11 LUTON T	a15 3-1	O08 4-2	a26 4-1	M04 1-1	D17 1-0	N05 3-2	a01 1-1	O22 0-1	D26 3-0	S14 2-1		N19 6-1	S10 0-2	J14 3-2	A24 1-0	M18 2-1	a29 0-0	S24 1-4	D03 4-1	F23 4-1	A27 3-3	M31 2-2
12 MIDDLESBROUGH	O01 2-2	D17 1-1	M11 2-2	A24 1-2	D10 2-1	a03 3-1	F04 3-0	D26 2-0	N26 1-1	A27 1-1	a08 2-1		O15 2-0	F25 3-1	a22 3-0	J14 2-2	S21 1-3	O29 3-1	S10 5-0	M25 1-0	S24 1-0	N12 3-1
13 NORWICH C	O08 2-2	N19 2-1	A24 4-0	a01 0-2	O01 2-0	D26 0-3	O22 3-2	D03 3-2	S17 5-1	a15 2-1	J21 2-1	M04 4-1		S07 1-0	F11 3-1	N05 3-1	M18 0-1	A20 1-1	a29 5-0	D31 1-0	a03 3-0	S03 0-0
14 PLYMOUTH A	a03 1-2	a15 5-0	D27 6-4	N19 4-2	F11 2-1	M18 1-2	M04 3-1	a01 3-2	J21 1-1	N05 0-4	S03 1-1	O08 3-3	S14 3-0		S17 5-1	a29 3-3	D03 3-1	A31 2-0	O22 1-3	A20 3-1	O01 1-0	D31 1-0
15 PORTSMOUTH	a01 4-0	a19 3-0	F18 1-1	a29 3-2	J14 1-3	N19 1-0	M18 3-1	N05 1-2	A20 3-0	M04 2-2	A31 3-2	J28 0-3	S24 3-0	F04 0-2		O08 2-2	a15 2-2	a03 1-2	D31 1-1	S07 1-0	S10 2-1	D27 1-1
16 ROTHERHAM U	a18 5-2	S07 4-0	N12 2-3	a04 1-1	O15 2-2	S17 1-1	D31 1-3	O01 2-1	A29 2-0	D27 1-0	D10 5-2	S03 1-2	M25 0-2	O29 0-0	F25 1-0		F11 4-0	a08 1-2	A20 1-0	N26 0-0	M11 0-0	a22 3-3
17 SCUNTHORPE U	D23 2-2	S10 2-1	a11 0-0	J14 1-2	a08 0-1	A25 4-0	a03 3-2	A27 2-2	M25 3-1	F04 2-3	O29 1-0	S15 1-1	D10 2-1	a22 2-0	N12 5-1	S24 1-1		F25 1-1	F18 2-0	O15 1-1	N26 3-3	M11 1-2
18 SHEFFIELD U	O22 2-1	D03 2-3	A27 1-0	a19 3-1	S06 3-1	M07 1-3	N05 3-2	J14 4-1	O01 2-1	a01 1-1	F11 2-1	a29 4-1	D17 1-1	A23 3-0	S20 3-1	N19 3-1	O08 2-0		a15 2-1	J21 4-1	D27 0-1	S17 3-0
19 SOUTHAMPTON	S17 4-2	D26 4-2	M25 1-2	S07 5-1	F25 4-2	F11 1-1	S03 2-4	a03 1-1	D10 2-3	A24 4-1	a22 3-2	J21 3-2	O29 2-2	M11 1-1	A27 5-1	D17 3-2	O01 4-2	N12 0-1		a08 0-1	O15 3-2	N26 5-0
20 STOKE C	a29 0-2	M18 2-0	J16 5-3	M20 2-1	D24 2-2	O22 2-4	a15 0-0	O08 1-2	a03 0-0	m03 3-1	O01 3-0	N05 1-1	A27 1-1	D17 9-0	S12 1-0	a01 1-4	M04 2-0	S10 2-0	N19 1-2		A22 0-0	F11 1-3
21 SUNDERLAND	M18 2-1	N05 2-0	S14 2-2	a15 1-2	S17 1-2	D03 2-0	O08 2-3	N19 4-1	S03 2-2	a29 1-1	D31 7-1	F11 2-0	M31 0-3	F22 2-1	J21 4-1	O22 1-1	a01 2-0	D26 1-1	a17 3-1	A31 4-0		A20 2-1
22 SWANSEA T	N05 2-3	F28 2-1	S10 3-3	O08 2-1	A23 2-0	a29 2-1	N19 3-2	M04 1-0	S06 1-2	M18 2-0	a03 3-1	a15 3-2	J14 4-1	A27 1-2	D26 4-0	M14 2-1	O24 2-2	F04 3-0	a01 4-1	S24 0-0	D17 3-3	

Season 1960-61

DIVISION 3

	BARNSLEY	BOURNEMOUTH	BRADFORD C	BRENTFORD	BRISTOL C	BURY	CHESTERFIELD	COLCHESTER U	COVENTRY C	GRIMSBY T	HALIFAX T	HULL C	NEWPORT CO	NOTTS CO	PORT VALE	Q.P.R.	READING	SHREWSBURY T	SOUTHEND U	SWINDON T	TORQUAY U	TRANMERE R	WALSALL	WATFORD
1 BARNSLEY		S17 2-3	F11 5-2	O22 1-1	D31 2-0	D03 3-1	a15 3-1	S14 3-0	A20 4-1	D26 3-2	a03 1-1	S28 1-0	a24 1-3	J21 5-2	a01 5-1	S03 3-3	A31 1-1	m03 4-2	N19 2-1	M18 2-1	a12 1-0	O08 2-1	a29 2-2	M22 0-1
2 BOURNEMOUTH	F04 1-2		S10 2-2	O08 0-1	A31 2-2	N19 0-3	a01 1-0	F18 4-4	S28 2-1	O05 2-1	a29 1-2	S12 2-2	S24 2-2	D31 1-3	M18 1-1	A20 1-0	D27 2-0	D03 2-2	J28 3-2	M04 2-1	O22 1-3	J14 2-1	a15 0-3	M31 0-1
3 BRADFORD C	S24 1-4	F14 3-1		M04 3-1	A20 2-0	a15 0-1	N19 3-2	M07 0-1	A30 4-1	S13 1-3	F04 2-2	D26 0-0	F18 1-2	S03 2-2	F28 3-3	D31 1-1	M23 2-1	a29 1-1	a01 2-1	O22 2-1	M18 0-3	a03 1-1	M14 1-2	O08 2-2
4 BRENTFORD	M11 0-0	a22 2-2	O15 2-2		D10 2-0	S17 1-5	F11 2-2	M25 0-0	F25 1-1	N12 0-1	D31 2-0	a08 2-2	O29 2-4	a03 3-0	a25 0-0	S27 2-0	m02 2-1	S03 4-0	O01 1-1	D23 2-1	S06 2-3	A20 4-1	J21 3-1	A23 2-1
5 BRISTOL C	A27 4-0	A23 1-0	D17 1-2	a29 3-0		M18 1-2	O22 3-0	S10 5-0	O04 2-0	F04 2-1	N19 3-2	S24 1-2	J14 3-0	S20 2-1	O08 3-4	D26 1-1	F18 2-0	a01 0-0	M04 2-0	S06 1-1	M31 2-2	a15 2-0	F21 2-0	M14 4-1
6 BURY	F25 2-1	a08 1-1	J07 2-2	F04 1-0	O29 1-0		A30 3-3	S20 4-0	M11 1-0	a04 2-0	O04 4-1	a22 3-0	D10 4-1	N12 7-0	A27 3-1	M25 1-0	O15 3-0	J02 3-1	M21 2-0	S10 3-0	F14 6-0	F18 3-0	D26 3-4	S24 0-2
7 CHESTERFIELD	M27 5-1	N12 0-1	a08 4-1	S24 1-1	M11 3-0	A22 2-2		D10 2-3	O15 4-1	D17 2-3	S05 3-0	M31 1-2	F25 1-0	M25 3-1	J14 0-0	O29 0-1	a22 2-2	D26 2-3	A27 0-3	F04 1-1	S10 2-0	J02 1-1	S26 1-2	F18 2-0
8 COLCHESTER U	S05 4-2	O01 0-1	a24 2-4	J28 2-4	J21 0-1	S26 0-2	a29 4-3		S03 4-3	A22 1-1	M04 3-1	A20 4-0	D26 1-1	F11 1-2	a15 2-0	S17 0-1	D31 2-2	O08 1-1	D03 2-0	a01 3-1	N19 3-3	O22 0-3	M31 0-4	M18 1-4
9 COVENTRY C	D17 5-2	S19 1-0	A22 2-2	D02 2-0	a24 2-1	O22 1-2	M03 3-1	J14 2-0		S10 0-0	a01 2-0	F04 4-0	A27 4-1	D26 2-2	a04 1-1	S05 4-4	S24 2-1	J30 3-2	O08 3-0	a28 1-1	F20 5-1	N19 4-1	M18 1-2	a14 0-1
10 GRIMSBY T	D20 3-2	a25 0-1	S06 1-0	a01 0-0	S17 5-2	M31 2-2	A20 0-0	A30 2-1	a18 2-3		O22 6-1	D31 2-0	S20 2-1	O01 1-1	D03 0-5	F11 3-1	S03 3-1	M04 0-2	a29 1-0	N28 3-2	a15 4-2	M18 4-1	O08 3-1	J28 1-3
11 HALIFAX T	a10 1-0	D10 2-1	S17 3-2	A27 1-0	a08 2-1	a24 0-2	S12 2-1	O15 2-1	N12 2-2	M11 0-0		O29 3-0	a22 2-1	F25 0-1	S26 3-3	a17 1-1	M25 1-0	F11 1-1	D24 6-2	D17 1-1	A22 3-2	S10 5-0	O01 1-0	J14 0-0
12 HULL C	S19 2-0	S05 2-0	D27 3-0	N19 3-0	F13 3-3	O08 0-1	a03 2-2	D17 1-1	S17 1-1	A27 2-3	M18 4-2		A22 5-1	O03 3-1	a29 2-2	O01 3-1	a20 1-0	O22 3-1	J14 0-1	a15 0-0	D03 2-3	J28 4-2	M04 2-1	a01 3-2
13 NEWPORT CO	M13 2-3	F11 2-0	O01 1-0	M18 0-1	S03 4-1	a29 0-0	D05 5-1	D22 3-2	M20 3-3	S26 1-1	O08 1-1	A29 3-1		S17 2-2	F13 2-1	J23 1-3	A20 5-2	a03 1-1	a15 1-2	J28 2-0	a01 2-2	M04 1-0	S15 4-2	M06 5-1
14 NOTTS CO	S10 5-1	A27 3-2	J14 2-1	a04 0-0	S29 3-0	a01 0-3	J28 1-0	S24 4-2	D27 3-0	F18 0-1	M23 1-1	a27 2-1	F04 6-0		O22 2-2	A25 2-1	S08 4-2	a15 2-1	M18 1-2	O08 1-0	M04 0-1	a29 4-1	N19 3-1	D17 3-1
15 PORT VALE	N12 2-0	O29 3-0	M25 2-4	O03 3-2	a22 1-1	D31 4-3	S03 7-1	F06 3-0	M31 3-1	F25 3-2	S19 2-3	D10 4-1	a08 3-1	M11 1-3		O15 0-1	S17 1-1	A29 4-1	J21 4-0	F18 4-1	S24 0-3	D26 5-0	A20 1-1	S05 3-0
16 Q.P.R.	J14 4-2	D17 3-1	A27 1-0	S19 0-0	D27 1-1	J28 3-1	M18 1-2	F04 3-2	S12 2-1	S24 2-0	a15 5-1	F18 2-1	S10 2-0	A29 2-0	M04 1-0		O03 5-2	N19 1-1	O22 2-1	M31 3-1	O08 3-3	D03 9-2	a01 1-0	a29 2-1
17 READING	A24 0-1	D26 4-3	S21 3-1	a14 4-0	O01 1-1	M04 1-3	O08 2-0	A27 2-1	F11 0-0	J14 3-1	J28 1-1	S10 2-4	D17 2-3	S14 2-0	F04 2-1	a26 3-1		M18 2-1	a03 3-0	D03 1-1	a29 5-1	a01 1-2	O22 3-2	N19 1-1
18 SHREWSBURY T	O01 1-2	F25 2-1	a12 2-0	J14 3-0	N12 4-2	S07 2-1	D27 4-2	a22 2-2	M25 2-1	O15 2-1	S24 1-1	M11 0-0	a17 5-0	M08 4-0	A24 1-1	a08 4-1	O29 6-1		S21 2-2	A27 1-1	D17 2-1	F04 1-2	a26 1-2	S10 2-2
19 SOUTHEND U	a08 2-0	M25 0-0	N12 0-0	F18 1-1	O15 1-0	A20 0-3	D31 1-1	F25 2-1	a22 4-1	D10 1-1	D26 2-2	S03 3-1	J07 4-2	O29 3-1	S10 2-1	M11 0-0	a04 0-1	S26 1-1		S24 0-2	F04 3-2	S12 1-2	A29 1-2	O03 6-1
20 SWINDON T	a19 1-0	O15 0-1	M11 4-0	J07 1-1	O19 3-1	J21 4-0	S17 2-0	N12 0-2	D10 1-2	a08 3-0	A20 1-1	a12 1-1	M25 2-0	a22 1-0	O01 6-0	a03 1-0	F25 1-1	D31 2-2	F11 1-1		a26 3-1	A31 1-0	S03 1-0	S28 1-2
21 TORQUAY U	M25 1-1	M11 0-1	O29 2-1	S14 1-1	a03 0-0	S03 1-1	J21 3-0	a08 1-1	O01 3-0	F06 0-0	S01 1-1	F25 1-2	N12 0-0	O15 2-2	F11 1-1	a22 1-6	D10 4-2	A20 2-0	S17 2-1	O05 1-1		S22 5-2	D31 3-0	D23 2-2
22 TRANMERE R	a22 2-1	S03 4-3	M31 1-0	D19 2-0	F27 3-2	O01 1-7	a24 1-1	M11 7-2	a08 2-0	O29 3-6	J21 6-2	M24 1-0	O15 2-4	D10 2-3	D27 3-3	F25 1-2	N12 1-1	S17 4-2	S05 2-1	A22 2-2	S26 2-2		F11 1-4	A27 0-2
23 WALSALL	D10 1-0	J09 2-0	F25 4-0	S10 4-0	M25 4-0	D23 1-0	S20 2-1	a03 3-0	O28 1-1	a22 2-1	F18 0-0	O15 1-0	S06 2-2	a08 2-1	D17 6-2	N12 4-3	M11 2-2	O03 3-2	A23 5-1	M21 2-1	A27 3-0	S24 3-1		F04 5-2
24 WATFORD	O15 1-2	a03 0-1	a22 2-2	A30 6-1	F25 0-1	F11 1-1	O01 3-1	O29 2-2	a11 7-2	M25 2-0	S03 4-3	N12 2-2	M11 4-1	A20 2-2	S13 0-0	D10 0-3	a08 2-0	J21 3-1	a25 3-0	S20 1-0	D27 3-0	D31 2-2	S17 2-0	

DIVISION 4

	ACCRINGTON S	ALDERSHOT	BARROW	BRADFORD	CARLISLE U	CHESTER	CREWE A	CRYSTAL P	DARLINGTON	DONCASTER R	EXETER C	GILLINGHAM	HARTLEPOOLS U	MANSFIELD T	MILLWALL	NORTHAMPTON T	OLDHAM A	PETERBOROUGH U	ROCHDALE	SOUTHPORT	STOCKPORT CO	WORKINGTON	WREXHAM	YORK C
1 ACCRINGTON S		F18 1-0	S26 0-0	D24 1-2	M11 1-0	S10 2-0	J14 1-3	D17 2-3	D10 2-2	a03 2-2	a08 0-1	S12 3-0	F25 3-0	M25 1-4	A29 3-3	O03 3-2	S24 5-1	a11 3-2	O29 2-0	a22 2-1	N12 4-1	F04 1-2	O14 0-3	a19 2-0
2 ALDERSHOT	O01 3-1		S17 2-1	S03 3-0	a22 2-1	S07 3-2	D27 5-0	M25 2-1	O29 1-3	N12 5-0	F25 3-1	J21 0-1	a08 4-0	A20 2-0	F11 0-2	D31 2-2	A31 4-0	O15 1-1	D10 3-0	M11 1-0	a03 3-2	S28 0-0	M27 0-0	a26 6-1
3 BARROW	S19 1-1	F04 2-0		N26 5-0	M25 0-2	A27 3-0	D17 3-4	F25 0-3	a03 1-1	O15 2-1	a22 1-1	a17 0-1	M11 2-1	J07 1-1	S05 2-1	S24 1-0	S10 1-2	D10 2-1	N12 1-0	D27 0-1	m01 3-1	J14 0-4	O29 1-1	A22 1-1
4 BRADFORD	m01 2-2	J14 1-0	O01 4-0		a08 0-0	A22 1-0	S19 2-0	M11 3-1	O15 1-0	O29 1-1	S17 5-2	F11 0-0	M25 1-3	a22 2-1	a24 2-1	S10 1-3	A27 5-1	a20 1-0	J07 2-1	F25 1-0	D10 4-2	D17 4-0	N12 3-1	S05 3-3
5 CARLISLE U	O22 3-1	D03 2-2	J28 1-0	N19 2-2		M31 3-1	O08 0-1	F04 2-0	S10 4-4	S24 2-1	D17 2-2	J02 1-3	F18 2-2	S27 3-1	M18 1-2	a15 2-1	a29 3-0	A27 3-3	S06 1-2	J14 1-0	A23 1-4	D27 2-4	a11 1-0	M04 1-1
6 CHESTER	J21 2-3	S14 2-0	D31 0-0	A31 3-1	a03 3-2		F11 0-0	J07 3-0	a08 0-3	a22 1-2	O29 4-4	A20 2-2	D10 1-2	O15 3-3	S03 1-4	M08 0-2	D26 3-1	M25 1-2	F25 3-1	N12 1-0	M11 0-0	N26 2-2	O01 1-0	S17 2-1
7 CREWE A	S03 0-1	D26 2-1	A20 0-1	S28 1-1	F25 3-0	S24 5-2		a22 1-2	a19 1-1	D10 1-1	M25 2-0	A31 2-1	S17 3-0	M11 1-2	D31 2-2	S07 0-2	O05 2-1	N12 3-1	O15 3-0	a08 0-1	O29 4-1	F18 1-2	M31 2-1	J21 1-5
8 CRYSTAL P	A20 9-2	a19 2-1	O08 4-2	O22 4-1	S17 1-1	J28 5-1	D03 0-0		A24 3-2	D31 5-1	D27 0-0	M04 2-0	S03 2-2	O01 4-1	M31 0-2	M18 2-3	a01 2-1	S07 0-2	F11 4-1	S28 5-0	a26 2-1	N19 4-2	J21 3-2	a29 1-0
9 DARLINGTON	a29 3-2	M18 2-2	M31 2-3	M04 0-0	J21 0-0	N19 5-1	a15 0-1	A31 0-1		A20 1-0	a24 3-0	O08 2-2	D31 4-0	F11 3-2	S19 5-2	O22 1-1	J28 0-1	D26 2-2	S17 1-0	S14 1-0	O01 2-0	a01 1-1	S03 1-2	D03 2-1
10 DONCASTER R	M31 1-0	a01 3-1	M04 3-0	M18 2-0	F11 1-0	D03 2-1	a29 6-0	A27 1-5	D17 4-0		S06 2-1	O22 2-3	J21 5-3	a25 2-3	O08 3-0	J28 0-2	N19 2-1	S20 1-2	O01 3-2	A23 0-1	D26 3-1	a15 3-4	S17 3-1	J14 0-2
11 EXETER C	N19 2-4	O08 1-0	D03 2-2	F04 4-2	A20 0-0	M18 4-1	M16 0-1	D26 2-3	O05 1-3	S14 2-0		a29 2-0	S26 2-1	S03 0-2	a15 2-3	a03 1-3	M04 3-0	S24 3-4	D31 1-0	F18 2-1	J21 2-1	O22 0-0	A31 1-0	a01 2-1
12 GILLINGHAM	S07 2-1	S10 5-2	a27 2-2	S24 3-4	N12 1-1	D17 3-0	A24 0-0	O15 1-2	F25 0-1	M11 2-0	D10 4-2		O29 5-1	m03 0-0	D27 1-2	a12 0-1	J14 2-3	O01 4-4	a08 0-0	a03 2-0	a22 1-1	A27 4-2	M25 0-3	S21 3-2
13 HARTLEPOOLS U	O08 4-1	N19 3-1	O22 0-2	J28 2-4	O01 0-1	a29 4-4	F04 1-2	J14 2-4	A27 5-0	S10 2-1	S19 0-0	M18 1-0		D27 3-2	M04 2-2	a01 4-2	a15 5-1	A22 0-2	a24 2-0	D17 1-5	S05 0-2	D03 4-1	F11 0-0	J02 1-3
14 MANSFIELD T	M22 0-0	D17 2-0	N19 5-1	a12 1-2	S19 1-3	M04 3-1	O22 1-1	F18 1-2	S24 2-1	a17 1-2	J14 2-3	a15 1-0	D26 2-1		a01 5-1	a29 4-2	a03 1-2	S10 1-0	A22 0-2	F04 1-2	A27 2-2	O08 2-0	S12 0-3	M18 1-3
15 MILLWALL	A22 2-2	S24 2-2	S12 3-0	O03 5-1	O29 4-2	J14 5-1	A27 2-3	a03 0-2	S26 0-1	F25 0-1	J07 2-2	D26 1-2	O15 5-2	N12 3-0		F18 3-1	F04 0-1	a22 4-3	M25 4-1	D10 3-1	a08 3-0	S10 0-3	M11 2-0	D17 3-2
16 NORTHAMPTON T	a25 2-1	A27 2-1	F11 3-0	J21 0-1	M21 0-0	S19 3-2	S13 4-1	O29 1-2	M11 1-1	M25 3-0	a04 3-1	S17 3-1	N12 3-3	D10 1-0	O01 2-2		D17 1-0	F25 0-3	a22 5-1	O15 3-1	S03 4-2	A29 3-2	a08 3-0	D27 3-0
17 OLDHAM A	F11 5-2	A23 0-2	J21 3-1	D31 4-0	D10 5-2	D27 4-1	a25 1-0	N12 4-3	M25 3-3	a08 1-1	O15 5-2	S03 1-1	J07 2-1	M31 3-1	S17 2-3	A20 1-2		M11 1-1	S27 0-2	O29 3-2	F25 3-0	S12 3-5	a22 0-2	O01 3-1
18 PETERBOROUGH U	a15 3-0	M04 7-1	a29 6-2	a03 3-1	D31 5-0	M13 6-0	a01 4-1	S12 4-1	D24 5-1	S26 6-2	F11 7-1	F18 2-0	A29 3-2	J21 2-1	D03 4-2	O08 3-3	O22 2-2		S03 4-3	O03 3-4	S17 0-1	M18 2-1	A20 3-0	N19 1-1
19 ROCHDALE	M18 3-2	a29 1-1	a01 0-0	a15 2-3	S13 2-1	O08 2-0	M04 3-0	S24 2-2	F04 1-0	F18 2-1	A27 3-1	N19 2-0	O03 4-0	A30 1-2	J28 4-0	D03 1-1	S20 3-0	a18 2-2		S10 0-1	a10 1-1	a03 2-0	D26 2-1	O22 0-0
20 SOUTHPORT	D03 3-0	O22 1-1	D26 4-1	O08 2-3	S03 3-0	a01 1-2	N19 2-0	S20 3-3	S06 1-4	A30 1-1	O01 2-0	M31 1-2	A20 2-0	S17 2-1	a29 4-1	M04 2-0	M18 2-0	a25 3-3	J21 0-1		F11 1-0	J28 3-0	D31 2-2	a15 2-2
21 STOCKPORT CO	a01 0-3	M31 2-0	a15 1-0	a29 2-3	A29 2-0	O22 1-1	M18 0-1	O03 5-2	F18 2-1	D27 1-0	S10 0-0	M06 2-0	S12 1-1	D31 1-0	N19 3-1	a17 1-1	O08 0-1	F04 0-6	A20 1-0	S24 2-0		M04 1-0	S26 1-0	M13 2-0
22 WORKINGTON	S17 2-1	S21 0-4	S03 3-1	A20 1-3	D26 2-1	O05 1-0	O01 0-0	a08 1-0	N12 1-3	J07 1-3	M11 3-1	D31 2-0	a22 2-0	F24 1-3	J21 2-2	A24 3-0	S07 1-1	O29 0-3	M31 3-0	M25 3-1	O15 1-0		D10 3-1	F10 2-0
23 WREXHAM	M04 3-0	a15 3-1	M18 1-0	a01 0-1	O05 2-1	F18 1-2	a03 0-1	S10 1-2	M15 3-1	F04 2-2	A25 3-1	M08 0-0	S24 1-0	S07 2-0	O22 0-1	N19 2-2	D03 2-2	D17 0-1	D27 2-0	A27 3-0	S21 1-3	a29 2-1		O08 4-0
24 YORK C	D31 1-0	O03 4-1	A29 2-0	S12 2-0	O15 4-0	F04 2-0	S10 3-1	D10 0-2	a22 4-1	S03 1-1	N12 6-1	S26 0-0	M31 4-0	O29 3-2	A20 3-2	D26 0-1	F18 1-0	a08 0-1	M11 2-0	M20 2-0	M25 0-0	S24 4-0	F25 2-1	

LEAGUE TABLES

DIVISION 1

	P	W	D	L	F	A	W	D	L	F	A	Pts
Tottenham H	42	15	3	3	65	28	16	1	4	50	27	66
Sheffield W	42	15	4	2	45	17	8	8	5	33	30	58
Wolves	42	17	2	2	61	32	8	5	8	42	43	57
Burnley	42	11	4	6	58	40	11	3	7	44	37	51
Everton	42	13	4	4	47	23	9	2	10	40	46	50
Leicester C	42	12	4	5	54	31	6	5	10	33	39	45
Manchester U	42	14	5	2	58	20	4	4	13	30	56	45
Blackburn R	42	12	3	6	48	34	3	10	8	29	42	43
Aston Villa	42	13	3	5	48	28	4	6	11	30	49	43
WBA	42	10	3	8	43	32	8	2	11	24	39	41
Arsenal	42	12	3	6	44	35	3	8	10	33	50	41
Chelsea	42	10	5	6	61	48	5	2	14	37	52	37
Manchester C	42	10	5	6	41	30	3	6	12	38	60	37
Nottingham F	42	8	7	6	34	33	6	2	13	28	45	37
Cardiff C	42	11	5	5	34	26	2	6	13	26	59	37
West Ham U	42	12	4	5	53	31	1	6	14	24	57	36
Fulham	42	8	8	5	39	39	6	0	15	33	56	36
Bolton W	42	9	5	7	38	29	3	6	12	20	44	35
Birmingham C	42	10	4	7	35	31	4	2	15	27	53	34
Blackpool	42	9	3	9	44	34	3	6	12	24	39	33
Newcastle U	42	7	7	7	51	49	4	3	14	35	60	32
Preston NE	42	7	6	8	28	25	3	4	14	15	46	30

DIVISION 2

	P	W	D	L	F	A	W	D	L	F	A	Pts
Ipswich T	42	15	3	3	55	24	11	4	6	45	31	59
Sheffield U	42	16	2	3	49	22	10	4	7	32	29	58
Liverpool	42	14	5	2	49	21	7	5	9	38	37	52
Norwich C	42	15	3	3	46	20	5	6	10	24	33	49
Middlesbrough	42	13	6	2	44	20	5	6	10	39	54	48
Sunderland	42	12	5	4	47	24	5	8	8	28	36	47
Swansea T	42	14	4	3	49	26	4	7	10	28	47	47
Southampton	42	12	4	5	57	35	6	4	11	27	46	44
Scunthorpe U	42	9	8	4	39	25	5	7	9	30	39	43
Charlton A	42	12	3	6	60	42	4	8	9	37	49	43
Plymouth A	42	13	4	4	52	32	4	4	13	29	50	42
Derby Co	42	9	6	6	46	35	6	4	11	34	45	40
Luton T	42	13	5	3	48	27	2	4	15	23	52	39
Leeds U	42	7	7	7	41	38	7	3	11	34	45	38
Rotherham U	42	9	7	5	37	24	3	6	12	28	40	37
Brighton & HA	42	9	6	6	33	26	5	3	13	28	49	37
Bristol R	42	13	4	4	52	35	2	3	16	21	57	37
Stoke C	42	9	6	6	39	26	3	6	12	12	33	36
Leyton O	42	10	5	6	31	29	4	3	14	24	49	36
Huddersfield T	42	7	5	9	33	33	6	4	11	29	38	35
Portsmouth	42	10	6	5	38	27	1	5	15	26	64	33
Lincoln C	42	5	4	12	30	43	3	4	14	18	52	24

DIVISION 3

	P	W	D	L	F	A	W	D	L	F	A	Pts
Bury	46	18	3	2	62	17	12	5	6	46	28	68
Walsall	46	19	4	0	62	20	9	2	12	36	40	62
QPR	46	18	4	1	58	23	7	6	10	35	37	60
Watford	46	12	7	4	52	27	8	5	10	33	45	52
Notts Co	46	16	3	4	52	24	5	6	12	30	53	51
Grimsby T	46	14	4	5	48	32	6	6	11	29	37	50
Port Vale	46	15	3	5	63	30	2	12	9	33	49	49
Barnsley	46	15	5	3	56	30	6	2	15	27	50	49
Halifax T	46	14	7	2	42	22	2	10	11	29	56	49
Shrewsbury T	46	13	7	3	54	26	2	9	12	29	49	46
Hull C	46	13	6	4	51	28	4	6	13	22	45	46
Torquay U	46	8	12	3	37	26	6	5	12	38	57	45
Newport Co	46	12	7	4	51	30	5	4	14	30	60	45
Bristol C	46	15	4	4	50	19	2	6	15	20	49	44
Coventry C	46	14	6	3	54	25	2	6	15	26	58	44
Swindon T	46	13	6	4	41	16	1	9	13	21	39	43
Brentford	46	10	9	4	41	28	3	8	12	15	42	43
Reading	46	13	5	5	48	29	1	7	15	24	54	40
Bournemouth	46	8	7	8	34	39	7	3	13	24	37	40
Southend U	46	10	8	5	38	26	4	3	16	22	50	39
Tranmere R	46	11	5	7	53	50	4	3	16	26	65	38
Bradford C	46	8	8	7	37	36	3	6	14	28	51	36
Colchester U	46	8	5	10	40	44	3	6	14	28	57	33
Chesterfield	46	9	6	8	42	29	1	6	16	25	58	32

DIVISION 4

	P	W	D	L	F	A	W	D	L	F	A	Pts
Peterboro' U	46	18	3	2	85	30	10	7	6	49	35	66
Crystal P	46	16	4	3	64	28	13	2	8	46	41	64
Northampton T	46	16	4	3	53	25	9	6	8	37	37	60
Bradford	46	16	5	2	49	22	10	3	10	35	52	60
York C	46	17	3	3	50	14	4	6	13	30	46	51
Millwall	46	13	3	7	56	33	8	5	10	41	53	50
Darlington	46	11	7	5	41	24	7	6	10	37	46	49
Workington	46	14	3	6	38	28	7	4	12	36	48	49
Crewe A	46	11	4	8	40	29	9	5	9	21	38	49
Aldershot	46	16	4	3	55	19	2	5	16	24	50	45
Doncaster R	46	15	0	8	52	23	4	7	12	24	45	45
Oldham A	46	13	4	6	57	38	6	3	14	22	50	45
Stockport Co	46	14	4	5	31	21	4	5	14	26	45	45
Southport	46	12	6	5	47	27	7	0	16	22	40	44
Gillingham	46	9	7	7	45	34	6	6	11	19	32	43
Wrexham	46	12	4	7	38	22	5	4	14	24	34	42
Rochdale	46	13	7	3	43	19	4	1	18	17	47	42
Accrington S	46	12	4	7	44	32	4	4	15	30	56	40
Carlisle U	46	10	7	6	43	37	3	6	14	18	42	39
Mansfield T	46	10	3	10	39	34	6	3	14	32	44	38
Exeter C	46	12	3	8	39	32	2	7	14	27	62	38
Barrow	46	10	6	7	33	28	3	5	15	19	51	37
Hartlepools U	46	10	4	9	46	40	2	4	17	25	63	32
Chester	46	9	7	7	38	35	2	2	19	23	69	31

Football League Records

Top scorers: Div 1, R.Crawford (Ipswich Town), D.Kevan (West Bromwich Albion) 33 goals; Div 2, R.Hunt (Liverpool) 41 goals; Div 3, C.Holton (Watford & Northampton Town) 37 goals; Div 4, R.R.Hunt (Colchester) 37 goals.

Ray Crawford, one of the architects of Ipswich Town's remarkable climb from the Second Division to League Championship winners.

Roger Hunt, whose 41 goals in Liverpool's Second Division promotion season of 1961-2 is still a club record.

DIVISION 1

	ARSENAL	ASTON VILLA	BIRMINGHAM C	BLACKBURN R	BLACKPOOL	BOLTON W	BURNLEY	CARDIFF C	CHELSEA	EVERTON	FULHAM	IPSWICH T	LEICESTER C	MANCHESTER C	MANCHESTER U	NOTTINGHAM F	SHEFFIELD U	SHEFFIELD W	TOTTENHAM H	W.B.A.	WEST HAM U	WOLVERHAMPTON W
1 ARSENAL		M31 4-5	S23 1-1	M03 0-0	O07 3-0	J13 1-2	A19 2-2	M17 1-1	N04 0-3	m01 2-3	D26 1-0	a23 0-3	A29 4-4	S09 3-0	O21 5-1	N18 2-1	a28 2-0	N14 1-0	D23 2-1	F03 0-1	D02 2-2	a14 3-1
2 ASTON VILLA	N11 3-1		O28 1-3	F03 1-0	S23 5-0	a07 3-0	M24 0-2	m01 2-2	A26 3-1	D16 1-1	F24 2-0	D09 3-0	a21 8-3	N25 2-1	S18 1-1	a23 5-1	J13 0-0	O16 1-0	F21 0-0	M14 1-0	S09 2-4	O02 1-0
3 BIRMINGHAM C	F10 1-0	M17 0-2		M30 2-1	N04 1-1	S30 2-1	S16 2-6	D02 3-0	O21 3-2	a24 0-0	A19 2-1	J20 3-1	S02 1-5	D26 1-1	M03 1-1	A30 1-1	a14 3-0	D23 1-1	a28 2-3	S20 1-2	N18 4-0	O07 3-6
4 BLACKBURN R	O14 0-0	S16 4-2	N11 2-0		A28 1-1	a21 2-3	F24 2-1	A19 0-0	F10 3-0	a07 1-1	N25 0-2	S18 2-2	O28 2-1	D09 4-1	a10 3-0	J20 2-1	S30 1-2	a26 0-2	a23 0-1	M24 1-1	M28 1-0	S02 2-1
5 BLACKPOOL	F24 0-1	F10 1-2	M24 1-0	A21 2-1		O14 2-1	a23 1-1	D23 3-0	S30 4-0	N11 1-1	a07 2-1	O28 1-1	M10 2-1	a21 3-1	S02 2-3	S16 1-3	a03 2-4	N25 1-3	A19 1-2	D09 2-2	S04 2-0	J20 7-2
6 BOLTON W	S02 2-1	N18 1-1	F17 3-2	D02 1-1	M03 0-0		a11 0-0	J20 1-1	M31 4-2	a04 1-1	S20 2-3	A19 0-0	a23 1-0	F03 0-2	M17 1-0	a14 6-1	N04 2-0	A30 4-3	O09 1-2	S23 3-2	a28 1-0	O21 1-0
7 BURNLEY	D16 0-2	N04 3-0	F03 7-1	a17 0-1	a20 2-0	A26 3-1		O21 2-1	a28 1-1	S23 2-1	F20 2-1	A22 4-3	S05 2-0	J13 6-3	a14 1-3	a03 0-0	D02 4-2	D26 4-0	M17 2-2	S09 3-1	M03 6-0	N18 3-3
8 CARDIFF C	O28 1-1	D26 1-0	a21 3-2	D16 1-1	A26 3-2	S09 1-2	M14 1-1		S06 5-2	D09 0-0	M23 0-3	N25 0-3	a07 0-4	F24 0-0	S16 1-2	S30 2-2	A23 1-1	N11 2-1	J13 1-1	O18 2-2	a23 3-0	F09 2-3
9 CHELSEA	M24 2-3	D23 1-0	M09 1-1	S23 1-1	F16 1-0	N11 1-0	D09 1-2	S20 2-3		O28 1-1	S02 0-0	a21 2-2	O14 1-3	a07 1-1	A30 2-0	A19 2-2	S09 6-1	F24 1-0	D26 0-2	N25 4-1	F03 0-1	a20 4-5
10 EVERTON	S30 4-1	A19 2-0	a20 4-1	N18 1-0	M30 2-2	D26 1-0	F10 2-2	a28 8-3	M17 4-0		D23 3-0	S16 5-2	J20 3-2	S06 0-2	D02 5-1	O07 6-0	O21 1-0	S02 0-4	N04 3-0	A30 3-1	a14 3-0	M03 4-0
11 FULHAM	a11 5-2	O07 3-1	D16 0-1	a14 2-0	N18 0-1	S06 2-2	S30 3-5	N04 0-1	J13 3-4	A26 2-1		F10 1-2	S16 2-1	A23 3-4	a28 2-0	M03 1-1	M17 5-2	J20 0-2	a17 1-1	a23 1-2	O21 2-0	D02 0-1
12 IPSWICH T	a20 2-2	a28 2-0	S09 4-1	S05 2-1	M17 1-1	D16 2-1	A29 6-2	a14 1-0	D02 5-2	F03 4-2	S23 2-4		D26 1-0	A26 2-4	N18 4-1	N04 1-0	M03 4-0	M09 2-1	O21 3-2	J13 3-0	O07 4-2	M31 3-2
13 LEICESTER C	A23 0-1	D02 0-2	J13 1-2	M17 2-0	O21 0-2	a24 1-1	S20 2-6	N18 3-0	a11 2-0	S09 2-0	F03 4-1	M28 0-2		D16 2-0	a04 4-3	a28 2-1	O07 4-1	S23 1-0	a30 2-3	A26 1-0	F17 2-2	N04 3-0
14 MANCHESTER C	J20 3-2	a14 1-0	a11 1-4	a28 3-1	D02 2-4	S16 2-1	S02 1-3	O07 1-2	N18 2-2	S20 1-3	A30 2-1	D23 3-0	A19 3-1		F10 0-2	O21 3-0	M31 1-1	a20 3-1	M03 6-2	F21 3-1	N04 3-5	M17 2-2
15 MANCHESTER U	a16 2-3	J15 2-0	O14 0-2	A26 6-1	J13 0-1	O28 0-3	N25 1-4	F03 3-0	A23 3-2	a21 1-1	D09 3-0	a07 5-0	N11 2-2	S23 3-2		D26 6-3	a23 0-1	M24 1-1	S09 1-0	F24 4-1	D16 1-2	S30 0-2
16 NOTTINGHAM F	a07 0-1	a24 2-0	A22 2-1	S09 1-2	F03 3-4	N25 0-1	N11 3-2	F17 2-1	D16 3-0	F24 2-1	O14 1-1	M24 1-1	D09 0-0	M10 1-2	M20 1-0		A26 2-0	a21 3-1	S23 2-0	O28 4-4	J13 3-0	S19 3-1
17 SHEFFIELD U	D09 2-1	S02 0-2	N25 3-1	F20 0-0	D26 2-1	M24 3-1	a21 2-0	A28 1-0	J20 3-1	M14 1-1	O28 2-2	O14 2-1	F24 3-1	N11 3-1	a24 2-3	D22 2-0		S16 1-0	S04 1-1	a07 1-1	S23 1-4	A19 2-1
18 SHEFFIELD W	S20 1-1	M03 3-0	A26 5-1	O21 1-0	a14 3-2	A23 4-2	a30 4-0	a03 2-0	O07 5-3	J13 3-1	S09 1-1	S30 1-4	F10 1-2	a23 1-0	N04 3-1	D02 3-0	F03 1-2		N18 0-0	D16 2-1	M17 0-0	a28 3-2
19 TOTTENHAM H	A26 4-3	S30 1-0	D09 3-1	a20 4-1	D16 5-2	F24 2-2	O28 4-2	S02 3-2	D30 5-2	M24 3-1	N11 4-2	M14 1-3	N25 1-2	O14 2-0	J20 2-2	F10 4-2	a09 3-3	a07 4-0		a21 1-2	A23 2-2	S16 1-0
20 W.B.A.	S16 4-0	O21 1-1	S06 0-0	N04 4-0	a28 7-1	F10 6-2	J20 1-1	M03 5-1	a14 4-0	A23 2-0	a24 2-0	S02 1-3	D23 2-0	S30 2-2	O07 1-1	M17 2-2	N18 3-1	A19 0-2	D02 2-4		M31 0-1	D26 1-1
21 WEST HAM U	a21 3-3	J20 2-0	a06 2-2	D26 2-3	S18 2-2	D09 1-0	O14 2-1	a20 4-1	S16 2-1	N25 3-1	a30 4-2	F24 2-2	S30 4-1	M24 0-4	A19 1-1	S02 3-2	F10 1-2	O28 2-3	A28 2-1	N11 3-3		D18 4-2
22 WOLVERHAMPTON W	N25 2-3	A28 2-2	F24 2-1	J13 0-2	S09 2-2	M10 5-1	a07 1-1	S23 1-1	a23 1-1	O14 0-3	a21 1-3	N11 2-0	M24 1-1	O28 4-1	F28 2-2	S27 2-1	D16 0-1	D09 3-0	F03 3-1	M28 1-5	A26 3-2	

DIVISION 2

	BRIGHTON & HA	BRISTOL R	BURY	CHARLTON A	DERBY CO	HUDDERSFIELD T	LEEDS U	LEYTON O	LIVERPOOL	LUTON T	MIDDLESBROUGH	NEWCASTLE U	NORWICH C	PLYMOUTH A	PRESTON N.E.	ROTHERHAM U	SCUNTHORPE U	SOUTHAMPTON	STOKE C	SUNDERLAND	SWANSEA T	WALSALL
1 BRIGHTON & H.A.		D30 1-0	S02 0-2	a10 2-2	D09 1-2	N11 2-2	A22 1-3	a07 0-1	S16 0-0	O14 2-1	O28 2-0	M10 0-4	a20 2-1	a21 3-2	N25 0-0	F10 0-3	D16 0-3	F24 0-0	S05 2-1	S30 1-1	A26 2-2	M24 3-2
2 BRISTOL R	D26 0-1		A28 0-1	a20 2-2	N11 1-4	M10 1-1	S23 4-0	S16 2-1	A19 0-2	D09 1-0	N25 0-2	a07 2-1	F27 2-1	O14 4-3	F24 2-1	D22 4-2	S18 2-1	M24 1-0	J20 0-2	S02 2-3	O28 4-1	a21 2-2
3 BURY	J13 2-1	A22 2-0		S15 1-2	M24 2-2	a21 1-2	a20 1-1	M13 0-1	F10 0-3	F24 2-1	M10 2-1	O14 2-7	D16 2-3	N25 1-1	a07 2-1	S30 2-1	A26 4-1	S09 0-2	D26 0-2	S19 3-2	N11 1-1	O24 2-1
4 CHARLTON A	S09 2-3	a23 2-1	F03 1-0		O28 4-0	N25 0-2	D16 3-1	M24 1-2	S30 0-4	S23 0-1	O14 1-0	F24 1-1	A26 2-2	a07 3-1	D09 4-0	S20 0-2	J13 3-3	M06 1-0	A22 2-2	D26 2-0	a21 3-2	M10 3-3
5 DERBY CO	a28 2-0	M31 4-1	N04 3-0	M17 0-1		S30 1-0	D02 3-3	J20 1-2	O21 2-0	A23 2-0	D16 3-2	a23 1-2	a14 1-1	F10 2-2	S16 3-2	M03 1-1	N18 2-2	D26 1-1	J13 2-0	O07 1-1	S06 6-3	A26 1-3
6 HUDDERSFIELD T	M31 2-0	O21 4-1	D02 2-0	a14 0-2	a09 4-0		M03 2-1	S27 1-1	N18 1-2	J13 1-2	F03 0-0	S09 2-1	O07 1-1	A23 5-1	a02 2-2	a28 0-3	a23 1-2	A26 1-0	M17 3-0	N04 0-0	M26 3-1	S23 4-2
7 LEEDS U	A30 1-1	F10 0-0	a24 0-0	A19 1-0	a21 0-0	O14 1-0		N11 0-0	D23 1-0	M24 2-1	a07 2-0	J27 0-1	S20 0-1	F24 2-3	S30 1-2	S02 1-3	D26 1-4	O28 1-1	S16 3-1	J20 1-0	M10 2-0	N25 4-1
8 LEYTON O	N18 4-1	F03 2-3	a28 2-0	N04 2-1	S09 2-0	S20 3-0	M31 0-0		M17 2-2	a20 0-0	A26 2-0	D16 2-0	D02 2-0	S29 1-2	F09 0-2	O21 1-1	a14 0-1	A21 1-3	O07 3-0	M03 1-1	D26 1-0	J13 3-0
9 LIVERPOOL	F03 3-1	D16 2-0	S23 5-0	a30 2-1	M10 4-1	a07 1-1	A26 5-0	O28 3-3		N11 1-1	F24 5-1	O04 2-0	J13 5-4	D09 2-1	M24 4-1	M28 4-1	S09 2-1	a21 2-0	a23 2-1	A23 3-0	N25 5-0	O14 6-1
10 LUTON T	M03 2-1	a28 2-0	O07 4-0	F10 1-6	A30 4-2	S02 3-4	N04 3-2	a23 1-3	M31 1-0		S27 3-2	F17 1-0	M17 1-2	D23 0-2	A19 4-1	D02 4-3	O21 1-2	S16 1-4	N18 0-0	a14 1-2	J20 5-1	a11 2-0
11 MIDDLESBROUGH	M16 4-0	a14 5-0	O21 2-1	M03 3-2	A19 3-4	S16 1-0	N18 1-3	D23 2-3	O07 2-0	S20 2-4		M07 3-0	a28 2-1	J20 1-1	S02 1-0	A30 5-1	N04 1-2	S30 1-1	D02 2-2	M31 0-1	F10 1-3	a24 3-0
12 NEWCASTLE U	O21 5-0	N18 5-2	M03 1-2	O07 4-1	a20 3-0	J20 1-1	a28 0-3	A19 0-0	S20 1-2	S30 4-1	D26 3-4		N04 0-0	S02 0-2	D23 0-2	M31 1-0	M17 2-1	F10 3-2	a14 2-0	D02 2-2	S16 2-2	A23 1-0
13 NORWICH C	a23 3-0	S30 2-2	A19 3-1	D23 2-2	N25 3-2	F24 1-2	S06 2-0	a21 0-0	S02 1-2	O28 0-4	D09 5-4	M24 0-0		D26 0-2	N11 2-0	J20 0-1	A23 2-2	M10 1-1	F10 1-0	S16 3-1	O14 2-1	a07 3-1
14 PLYMOUTH A	D02 5-0	M03 3-1	a14 1-2	N18 2-1	S23 2-3	A30 4-2	O07 1-1	F17 2-1	a28 2-3	A26 0-3	S09 1-1	J13 1-1	D30 3-1		S20 1-0	N04 2-5	M31 3-1	D16 4-0	O21 3-1	M17 3-2	a23 0-0	F03 2-1
15 PRESTON N.E.	a14 3-1	O07 1-0	N18 1-2	a28 2-0	F03 1-0	D26 1-0	a09 1-1	S23 3-2	N04 1-3	D16 2-0	J13 4-3	A26 0-1	M30 2-0	S26 1-1		M17 2-0	D02 4-1	a23 1-1	M03 1-2	O21 0-1	A22 1-1	S09 2-3
16 ROTHERHAM U	S23 2-1	A26 4-0	F17 2-0	S26 3-2	O14 2-2	D08 3-3	J12 2-1	M09 2-1	D26 1-0	a21 1-1	a03 0-1	N11 0-0	S09 3-1	M24 1-3	O28 2-2		F02 0-1	N25 4-2	D16 1-2	a24 0-3	a07 1-2	F24 2-2
17 SCUNTHORPE U	A19 3-3	S05 2-1	D22 1-2	S01 6-1	a06 2-0	a24 1-3	F20 2-1	N24 0-2	J20 1-1	M10 2-0	M23 1-1	O27 3-2	A29 2-0	N11 5-1	a20 2-1	S15 5-2		O13 5-1	S29 2-2	F10 3-1	F23 2-0	M06 2-1
18 SOUTHAMPTON	O07 6-1	N04 0-2	J20 5-3	M31 1-2	D30 2-1	D23 3-1	M17 4-1	A30 1-2	D02 2-0	F03 3-0	F21 1-3	S23 1-0	O21 2-2	A19 1-2	O18 0-0	a14 2-1	M03 6-4		a28 5-1	N18 2-0	S02 5-1	S06 1-1
19 STOKE C	S18 0-1	S09 2-1	a11 1-3	A28 4-0	S02 1-1	O28 3-0	F03 2-1	F24 0-1	a24 0-0	a07 2-1	a21 2-0	N25 3-1	S23 3-1	M10 2-0	O14 1-1	A19 1-2	F17 1-0	D09 3-2		D23 1-0	M24 0-0	N11 2-1
20 SUNDERLAND	F17 0-0	J13 6-1	S27 3-0	M14 4-1	F24 2-1	M24 3-1	S09 2-1	O14 2-1	A30 1-4	N25 2-2	N11 2-1	a21 3-0	F03 2-0	O28 5-0	M21 0-0	a23 4-0	S23 4-0	a07 3-0	A26 2-1		D09 7-2	D16 3-0
21 SWANSEA T	D23 3-0	M17 1-1	M31 0-1	D02 1-0	S19 3-1	A19 1-1	O21 2-1	D30 1-3	m04 4-2	S09 3-2	S23 3-3	F02 3-2	M03 0-3	a24 5-0	A29 1-2	N18 2-2	O07 2-1	J13 0-1	N04 1-0	a28 1-1		F17 1-3
22 WALSALL	N04 2-2	D02 0-0	M17 3-0	O21 2-2	D23 2-0	F10 2-2	a14 1-1	S02 1-5	M03 1-1	D26 2-0	a23 1-2	A29 1-0	N18 5-0	S16 1-0	J20 2-1	O07 5-0	a28 4-1	S19 0-2	M30 3-1	A19 4-3	S30 0-0	

Season 1961-62

DIVISION 3

	BARNSLEY	BOURNEMOUTH	BRADFORD	BRENTFORD	BRISTOL C	COVENTRY C	CRYSTAL P	GRIMSBY T	HALIFAX T	HULL C	LINCOLN C	NEWPORT CO	NORTHAMPTON T	NOTTS CO	PETERBOROUGH U	PORTSMOUTH	PORT VALE	Q.P.R.	READING	SHREWSBURY T	SOUTHEND U	SWINDON T	TORQUAY U	WATFORD
1 BARNSLEY		F09 2-2	a07 1-2	O28 2-2	N11 7-3	M09 2-1	S16 0-3	J27 0-3	M27 1-2	a23 1-0	D26 0-1	A30 1-1	O11 3-2	O14 2-0	D09 0-3	J20 2-2	M24 2-1	A26 2-4	S02 2-3	a21 1-1	F24 1-1	S27 6-2	m02 4-2	S30 3-0
2 BOURNEMOUTH	S23 5-0		D09 2-2	a07 1-1	a21 2-1	N11 1-1	a20 1-0	M24 2-3	S09 2-1	S06 1-1	D16 0-0	M10 2-1	S27 3-2	O04 2-1	F24 1-1	F17 2-0	O14 1-0	F03 3-1	J27 1-0	A23 0-0	O28 3-0	J13 0-0	A26 3-1	D30 4-1
3 BRADFORD	N18 3-2	a28 1-2		a04 1-2	S23 2-0	O16 0-0	M07 2-0	a24 0-1	O21 2-0	M03 1-0	A23 2-0	O25 4-1	O07 1-2	A26 3-2	S09 6-2	M31 2-1	F03 2-1	a14 3-3	S06 1-3	J13 1-1	M14 4-0	M17 2-2	F17 3-1	D02 1-1
4 BRENTFORD	M17 1-1	N18 2-2	D26 2-0		O10 0-2	S19 2-1	a13 4-2	m01 0-2	A22 0-2	m03 0-2	D02 1-0	J13 3-1	a27 3-0	F02 0-1	F17 2-0	O21 3-2	a20 1-2	D16 1-4	A26 1-2	S23 4-0	S09 0-0	O07 1-0	M03 0-2	M30 3-1
5 BRISTOL C	M31 0-0	D02 2-1	F10 6-1	O03 3-0		a24 3-2	a28 2-2	S29 3-0	a14 4-3	O07 1-1	F03 2-0	S05 1-2	A22 1-0	D16 6-0	J13 1-2	M06 0-4	S09 0-1	N18 2-0	F06 5-0	A26 0-1	S26 3-2	O21 5-3	M17 4-1	M03 2-1
6 COVENTRY C	O20 1-1	M30 0-1	O09 3-0	S25 2-0	a23 1-1		N17 0-2	D26 2-0	S04 3-1	a28 0-2	M02 2-2	A25 3-0	D02 1-0	S09 2-2	S23 1-3	a14 2-0	a16 0-1	M16 2-3	D16 1-0	F03 4-1	J13 3-3	A21 2-1	O06 2-2	M12 1-0
7 CRYSTAL P	F03 1-3	a23 0-0	M24 0-0	J27 2-2	D09 2-3	a07 2-2		N11 4-1	J13 4-3	M21 1-2	S20 1-3	O28 2-0	S06 1-4	A23 4-1	O14 5-2	S23 1-2	a21 0-0	S09 2-2	M10 3-4	F24 2-1	S30 2-2	A26 3-1	D16 7-2	O11 1-1
8 GRIMSBY T	a14 4-0	J06 3-0	a23 3-2	S05 1-0	F17 1-0	a10 2-0	M30 0-0		M17 3-0	D02 1-0	O07 4-1	D16 1-0	M03 3-2	J13 2-1	F03 2-1	N18 1-0	S23 1-1	O21 1-1	S26 4-0	S09 2-1	A26 3-1	O10 0-1	A22 2-3	a28 5-3
9 HALIFAX T	A19 3-1	J20 3-1	a18 2-3	A28 1-0	J27 3-4	a30 0-2	S02 1-1	O28 3-3		F10 2-1	a24 0-3	O14 0-0	S30 1-3	a09 1-2	N11 2-1	D23 0-1	a07 3-3	m03 1-1	F23 2-1	M24 1-2	a21 0-2	M19 2-0	F19 1-0	S16 2-0
10 HULL C	a20 4-0	a12 2-1	O14 0-1	M24 3-0	F24 3-2	D09 3-1	D26 2-4	a21 2-1	S23 1-2		J13 1-0	a07 4-0	A26 1-0	M10 2-1	D16 1-1	J06 0-1	A31 3-1	F16 3-1	N11 0-1	O28 3-1	J27 0-0	F03 0-1	S09 4-0	S21 1-0
11 LINCOLN C	J31 2-2	A19 0-2	A30 3-2	a21 3-3	S16 1-1	O14 1-2	S27 3-2	F23 1-1	a23 0-1	S02 0-3		M23 3-2	J20 0-0	a06 2-2	M10 1-2	m02 2-2	O28 1-1	a30 0-5	D09 2-3	F07 1-2	N11 2-0	F16 2-2	S23 1-3	D23 0-0
12 NEWPORT CO	A21 0-2	O21 0-1	S18 1-2	S02 6-1	O16 3-1	D23 1-2	M17 2-1	A19 0-2	M05 0-1	N18 0-2	M26 4-0		M31 0-0	F17 2-0	O02 2-3	F05 0-5	M12 1-1	O07 2-4	M19 0-0	a16 3-2	S23 0-3	D02 2-2	a28 0-3	a14 0-0
13 NORTHAMPTON T	O03 3-1	S18 0-3	F24 2-0	D09 5-0	A29 0-1	a21 4-1	O17 1-1	O14 7-0	F17 3-1	D23 2-0	S09 2-2	N11 5-0		J27 1-2	O28 2-2	M20 2-2	S02 1-1	a24 1-1	M24 1-0	M10 3-1	a07 3-1	S23 1-2	F03 1-2	D16 2-0
14 NOTTS CO	M03 0-2	O12 3-2	D23 4-2	S16 3-1	A19 1-0	J20 2-0	A31 0-0	S02 2-0	a28 0-0	a03 3-0	N18 1-0	S30 8-1	a14 1-4		S07 2-2	O07 2-1	S21 2-3	D02 0-0	F10 2-2	D26 3-2	a23 2-0	a12 0-1	M31 2-0	M17 1-0
15 PETERBOROUGH U	a28 4-2	O07 1-2	M19 1-0	S30 6-0	S02 3-4	F10 2-3	M03 4-1	S16 2-1	M31 5-1	A19 3-2	O21 5-4	O09 2-1	M17 0-2	a30 2-0		D02 0-1	D23 1-3	F19 5-1	a23 1-0	S25 0-3	D26 4-1	N18 3-2	a14 2-1	A28 4-3
16 PORTSMOUTH	S09 3-2	S30 1-1	N11 4-2	M10 4-0	M24 5-0	J27 3-2	F10 2-1	a07 0-2	A26 1-1	O11 2-1	S06 0-0	S16 2-2	D26 4-1	F24 0-0	a21 0-3		D09 1-0	J13 4-1	O28 2-0	O14 3-1	A23 1-0	D16 2-2	S27 2-0	a23 2-1
17 PORT VALE	M05 2-0	M19 1-0	S16 3-2	a23 3-0	J20 0-2	S30 2-0	D02 0-1	F10 0-2	N18 1-1	A21 4-0	M17 4-0	D26 3-0	J13 1-1	S25 1-0	A26 0-1	a28 2-3		M31 2-3	O09 2-1	D16 4-1	S04 0-0	a14 1-1	O21 4-1	O07 1-3
18 Q.P.R.	M19 3-0	S16 1-1	a11 1-2	A19 3-0	a07 4-1	O28 4-1	J20 1-0	M10 3-2	S25 6-2	S30 1-1	O09 1-3	F24 4-0	a23 2-0	a21 2-0	M24 3-3	S02 0-1	N11 2-1		A21 3-6	D09 3-1	O14 5-3	S04 6-1	D30 6-0	F10 1-2
19 READING	J12 0-0	a14 0-1	m02 3-1	D23 4-0	D26 2-2	A19 4-0	O20 2-1	S20 1-2	O06 3-2	M30 1-1	a27 4-0	S08 2-1	a11 2-0	S23 4-2	a20 3-2	M16 0-3	O04 0-0	A30 0-2		F17 3-0	F02 3-1	M02 1-1	D02 1-0	N17 3-2
20 SHREWSBURY T	D02 4-1	A30 2-2	S02 4-1	F10 1-3	D23 2-2	S16 1-1	O07 1-5	J20 1-2	M14 0-0	M17 2-0	a14 0-0	a23 4-1	O21 1-3	M28 3-0	S20 3-4	M03 0-1	A19 4-2	a28 1-2	S30 4-1		O25 1-1	M30 1-3	N18 1-1	O18 5-1
21 SOUTHEND U	O07 1-2	M17 0-0	A19 2-1	J20 0-0	S18 1-0	S02 2-0	F17 2-2	D23 2-0	D02 2-1	a14 2-1	M31 0-0	F10 1-0	N18 1-3	a20 3-2	D30 1-1	A28 2-2	O16 4-1	M03 2-3	S16 0-2	O02 1-1		a28 0-2	J06 2-1	O21 0-1
22 SWINDON T	S19 1-1	S02 1-1	O28 3-2	F23 5-2	M10 0-4	A29 3-3	D23 5-0	O03 0-0	a16 6-0	S16 1-1	S30 4-0	a21 3-0	F10 2-2	M23 1-0	a07 3-2	A19 1-3	a30 1-0	O17 0-0	O13 4-1	N11 1-2	D09 0-0		a20 0-1	J20 3-1
23 TORQUAY U	S07 0-2	D22 2-1	S30 1-3	O14 3-1	O28 1-3	F24 1-0	A19 1-2	A30 1-2	O11 2-3	J20 4-2	F10 3-4	D09 3-2	S16 1-2	N11 3-3	a02 1-3	S20 0-2	M10 2-0	D26 2-2	a21 0-0	a07 3-1	M24 2-2	a23 3-0		S02 3-4
24 WATFORD	F17 3-1	D26 0-0	a21 0-2	N11 2-1	O14 1-1	M23 0-1	O03 3-2	D09 2-1	F03 0-0	S26 1-1	A26 3-3	J27 3-1	A19 0-0	O28 3-1	A22 2-3	a20 0-0	F24 2-0	S23 3-2	a06 1-1	S05 1-1	M09 1-3	S09 2-0	J13 4-1	

DIVISION 4

	ACCRINGTON S	ALDERSHOT	BARROW	BRADFORD C	CARLISLE U	CHESTER	CHESTERFIELD	COLCHESTER U	CREWE A	DARLINGTON	DONCASTER R	EXETER C	GILLINGHAM	HARTLEPOOLS U	MANSFIELD T	MILLWALL	OLDHAM A	ROCHDALE	SOUTHPORT	STOCKPORT CO	TRANMERE R	WORKINGTON	WREXHAM	YORK C
1 ACCRINGTON S		S23 0-2	S25 2-2	F03 0-2	S09 1-0	A26 0-1	J27 0-0	J13 0-4	O14 1-0	A21 3-1					S04 0-0	D09 0-2	O02 1-0	F24 0-2		F16 1-2	D16 1-1	N11 0-4	O28 0-2	
2 ALDERSHOT	F09 2-2		M09 3-1	A26 2-2	D16 0-1	a04 6-2	S02 1-1	a23 1-0	M24 1-0	S30 6-1	J26 3-1	N11 1-1	S27 4-0	O09 1-1	O14 4-2	F24 0-2	S16 3-1	O28 3-0	S06 2-0	J20 4-1	A23 3-1	a21 3-1	a07 3-1	D09 2-0
3 BARROW	S18 3-1	O21 2-2		M17 1-1	M26 0-3	N18 3-2	S30 1-0	M31 4-0	A19 3-0	a09 3-0	J01 4-1	D23 3-0	O09 7-0	a28 5-1	A28 1-1	a30 2-2	O07 3-1	a20 0-1	D02 1-1	M03 3-1	a14 2-0	S16 1-1	S02 0-2	F10 0-0
4 BRADFORD C	S16 0-1	M14 2-1	O28 1-1		a23 3-2	A30 2-0	O18 0-2	D26 4-1	N11 3-3	F10 3-2	a25 2-0	a07 5-1	F24 5-2	S30 5-1	M10 6-1	O14 2-4	M20 1-1	M23 1-0	O11 1-0	S02 1-3	a11 3-1	D09 1-1	m02 5-3	A19 2-2
5 CARLISLE U	J20 2-0	A19 2-1	M24 0-0	a20 2-4		m01 2-0	F24 3-1	A29 1-1	a06 3-0	S16 1-0	D09 1-0	J27 2-1	O14 1-2	F10 1-0	O28 1-0	M10 3-2	S02 2-0	N11 2-2	S30 2-1	D23 1-0	O10 0-3	D26 1-2	M13 1-0	S27 3-2
6 CHESTER	D23 0-0	D26 2-3	a07 2-3	A23 1-2	S06 1-1		M10 4-1	O11 2-2	a21 1-0	S02 2-2	S27 2-3	D09 1-1	O28 1-1	J20 4-4	N11 0-1	M24 2-4	A19 1-0	J27 2-3	S16 2-0	a23 2-0	F09 1-1	F24 1-3	S30 1-1	O14 1-1
7 CHESTERFIELD		J13 2-3	F17 2-2	S18 2-1	O07 1-3	O21 4-1		M03 4-1	a30 3-1	N18 1-1	a20 3-0	A28 2-0	S09 3-2	M31 2-0	S23 0-4	F03 2-3	D02 2-3	a16 1-0	a09 3-2	a28 3-2	M17 1-2	A19 0-1	D26 1-5	D23 1-1
8 COLCHESTER U	S02 3-2	a20 3-0	N11 1-1	D30 9-1	A21 2-0	O02 5-2	O14 3-3		J27 5-3	J20 2-0	a30 5-3	a21 2-0	M10 6-0	S16 6-1	M23 2-0	O28 2-2	D23 5-1	a07 1-1	F10 2-0	A19 3-0	S30 3-0	S25 6-1	D09 2-4	F24 3-1
9 CREWE A	M02 4-0	M07 2-0	D16 1-1	M31 1-2	N18 3-0	D02 1-1	S06 2-1	a14 4-0		O07 5-1	F10 2-0	J20 3-1	A23 5-2	S20 3-0	a20 3-2	F14 2-1	O21 3-5	A26 2-1	J13 3-1	M17 3-2	a28 3-0	S30 2-0	S16 0-3	O11 0-0
10 DARLINGTON	A28 1-1	F17 2-0	D26 1-0	S23 3-3	F03 2-1	J13 2-0	a07 4-4	S09 0-2	F24 2-1		O28 1-0	O14 1-0	J27 1-1	a23 1-2	M19 3-1	a21 1-5	S04 3-0	S18 2-0	D16 1-2	O02 3-0	A26 2-1	M24 1-1	M10 1-0	N11 0-0
11 DONCASTER R	F27 1-1	a13 2-1	J20 3-2	D02 2-0	a28 1-2	S19 2-0	a23 0-0	S05 1-4	S23 3-0	M17 1-2		F16 3-1	D16 2-1	M10 2-2	J12 0-1	A26 1-2	M30 0-0	F03 1-2	M03 1-2	N18 1-1	O07 6-1	A22 1-1	O10 0-2	D26 1-2
12 EXETER C	O21 3-0	M31 2-1	A26 3-0	N18 1-2	a14 4-0	a28 5-0	A23 4-1	D02 0-2	S09 2-1	M03 0-1	S30 1-5		D26 1-3	O07 1-1	D16 2-1	a23 1-1	M17 3-3	J13 1-3	S19 1-1	J06 4-3	F03 1-0	O11 3-1	F10 1-1	a11 2-1
13 GILLINGHAM	D02 5-1	S20 0-1	O04 3-2	O07 3-1	M03 4-1	M17 0-0	J20 5-1	O21 2-1	A30 0-1	a14 2-2	A19 2-2	D30 2-2		N18 4-0	F17 2-2	S23 3-1	a28 0-2	m03 4-2	M31 4-0	F03 1-1	J06 0-1	D23 4-2	a23 2-3	S02 1-2
14 HARTLEPOOLS U		O02 0-2	D09 2-3	F17 1-3	S23 0-3	S09 1-3	N11 1-2	F03 1-1	S25 2-1	a20 2-0	O21 3-0	F24 0-0	a07 1-3		a21 0-1	J27 2-0	A21 1-1	D16 3-1	A26 4-2	S04 2-2	J13 0-0	O28 0-1	O14 1-4	M24 0-2
15 MANSFIELD T		M02 4-1	A21 0-1	O21 0-1	M17 5-2	M30 3-0	F10 2-2	J15 4-0	a23 1-1	a28 3-0	S02 4-0	A19 3-1	S30 3-1	D02 3-1		O16 0-0	M26 2-0	D26 0-1	a14 3-1	O07 2-0	N18 1-2	J20 4-1	D23 1-2	S16 3-1
16 MILLWALL		O07 2-1	S04 1-0	M03 1-2	O21 3-0	J06 2-0	S16 2-1	M17 2-0	D30 4-3	D02 4-2	M05 2-0	a20 2-0	F10 0-0	a14 3-2	O02 4-0		F17 2-0	A28 1-1	N18 1-1	S18 1-3	M31 3-0	S02 5-0	A19 0-1	J20 2-1
17 OLDHAM A	O11 5-0	F03 2-1	F24 3-2	S09 2-2	J13 5-0	D16 4-1	a21 3-1	A26 2-2	M10 2-0	m02 0-1	N11 3-1	O28 1-1	D09 1-1	A30 5-2	N15 2-3	S30 4-2		O14 2-2	D26 2-1	S23 0-0	a23 2-0	a07 0-2	M24 1-1	M13 1-0
18 ROCHDALE	O07 1-0	M17 1-0	a23 0-2	J31 4-1	M31 1-1	a14 3-2	O11 1-1	N18 0-1	M13 3-0	O18 1-3	S16 2-3	S02 3-0	S06 3-1	A19 3-1	a11 3-2	A23 4-1	M03 3-1		a28 2-0	O21 3-3	D02 1-0	F10 1-3	J20 2-1	S30 3-1
19 SOUTHPORT		m01 2-1	a21 0-0	O03 2-1	F16 0-0	F03 1-0	M24 0-2	S23 3-0	S02 2-0	A19 1-4	O14 3-1	S25 1-1	N11 1-1	D23 0-1	M05 2-1	a07 3-1	D30 0-5	D09 3-0		A22 2-1	S09 2-1	M10 1-1	F24 4-2	O28 3-1
20 STOCKPORT CO	S29 2-0	S08 3-1	O14 3-0	J13 3-1	A26 1-2	a20 0-1	M12 2-1	D16 1-4	O28 0-1	O09 3-0	a06 2-1	M23 1-0	S16 3-1	a09 1-1	F23 2-1	S25 1-1	F10 1-1	M09 5-2	A28 1-4		D26 3-0	M19 3-1	N11 1-2	a21 2-1
21 TRANMERE R	A19 2-0	A28 1-2	N24 2-1	S04 3-2	O02 0-3	S23 4-1	O28 1-0	F17 5-2	D09 1-6	M12 0-0	F23 3-2	S16 3-4	M24 4-2	S01 3-2	a07 2-0	N11 5-1	a20 3-1	a21 2-0	J19 3-1	M26 1-3		O14 3-2	S25 2-0	M09 2-2
22 WORKINGTON		D02 2-1	F03 1-2	a28 5-3	M07 2-1	O07 4-1	D16 2-0	S21 1-2	F17 0-1	a04 2-1	A30 0-0	O04 3-1	A26 5-1	M17 1-1	S09 1-1	J13 2-2	N18 0-2	S23 2-1	O21 3-0	a14 1-1	M03 2-1		a11 1-0	a23 0-0
23 WREXHAM		N18 2-1	J13 1-1	a14 2-1	D02 2-2	F17 0-0	M28 4-2	a28 0-0	F03 1-1	O21 5-0	O18 3-1	S23 1-2	a20 3-0	M03 10-1	A26 5-0	D16 2-2	a04 2-1	S09 3-0	O07 2-3	M30 0-1	S20 4-0	S04 2-3		A30 2-1
24 YORK C	N18 1-0	a28 0-1	S23 5-0	D16 4-0	S18 1-1	M03 5-1	A26 4-0	O07 5-0	O02 4-2	M31 2-1	a02 5-2	S04 2-1	J13 4-0	M19 2-0	F03 2-1	S09 0-1	a14 4-1	F17 2-1	M16 2-2	D02 1-0	O21 1-2	a20 4-0	A21 3-2	

LEAGUE TABLES

DIVISION 1

	P	W	D	L	F	A	W	D	L	F	A	Pts
Ipswich T	42	17	2	2	58	28	7	6	8	35	39	56
Burnley	42	14	4	3	57	26	7	7	7	44	41	53
Tottenham H	42	14	4	3	59	34	7	6	8	29	35	52
Everton	42	17	2	2	64	21	3	9	9	24	33	51
Sheffield U	42	13	5	3	37	23	6	4	11	24	46	47
Sheffield W	42	14	4	3	47	23	6	2	13	25	35	46
Aston Villa	42	13	5	3	45	20	5	3	13	20	36	44
West Ham U	42	11	6	4	49	37	6	4	11	27	45	44
WBA	42	10	7	4	50	23	5	6	10	33	44	43
Arsenal	42	9	6	6	39	31	7	5	9	32	41	43
Bolton W	42	11	7	3	35	22	5	3	13	27	44	42
Manchester C	42	11	3	7	46	38	6	4	11	32	43	41
Blackpool	42	10	4	7	41	30	5	7	9	29	45	41
Leicester C	42	12	2	7	38	27	5	4	12	34	44	40
Manchester U	42	10	3	8	44	31	5	6	10	28	44	39
Blackburn R	42	10	6	5	33	22	4	5	12	17	36	39
Birmingham C	42	9	6	6	37	35	5	4	12	28	46	38
Wolves	42	8	7	6	38	34	5	3	13	35	52	36
Nottingham F	42	12	4	5	39	23	1	6	14	24	56	36
Fulham	42	8	3	10	38	34	5	4	12	28	40	33
Cardiff C	42	6	9	6	30	33	3	5	13	20	48	32
Chelsea	42	7	7	7	34	29	2	3	16	29	65	28

DIVISION 2

	P	W	D	L	F	A	W	D	L	F	A	Pts
Liverpool	42	18	3	0	68	19	9	5	7	31	24	62
Leyton O	42	11	5	5	34	17	11	5	5	35	23	54
Sunderland	42	17	3	1	60	16	5	6	10	25	34	53
Scunthorpe U	42	14	4	3	52	26	7	3	11	34	45	49
Plymouth A	42	12	4	5	45	30	7	4	10	30	45	46
Southampton	42	13	3	5	53	28	5	6	10	24	34	45
Huddersfield T	42	11	5	5	39	22	5	7	9	28	37	44
Stoke C	42	13	4	4	34	17	4	4	13	21	40	42
Rotherham U	42	9	6	6	36	30	7	3	11	34	46	41
Preston NE	42	11	4	6	34	23	4	6	11	21	34	40
Newcastle U	42	10	5	6	40	27	5	4	12	24	31	39
Middlesbrough	42	11	3	7	45	29	5	4	12	31	43	39
Luton T	42	12	1	8	44	37	5	4	12	25	34	39
Walsall	42	11	7	3	42	23	3	4	14	28	52	39
Charlton A	42	10	5	6	38	30	5	4	12	31	45	39
Derby Co	42	10	7	4	42	27	4	4	13	26	48	39
Norwich C	42	10	6	5	36	28	4	5	12	25	42	39
Bury	42	9	4	8	32	36	8	1	12	20	40	39
Leeds U	42	9	6	6	24	19	3	6	12	26	42	36
Swansea T	42	10	5	6	38	30	2	7	12	23	53	36
Bristol R	42	11	3	7	36	31	2	4	15	17	50	33
Brighton & HA	42	7	7	7	24	32	3	4	14	18	54	31

DIVISION 3

	P	W	D	L	F	A	W	D	L	F	A	Pts
Portsmouth	46	15	6	2	48	23	12	5	6	39	24	65
Grimsby T	46	18	3	2	49	18	10	3	10	31	38	62
Bournemouth	46	14	8	1	42	18	7	9	7	27	27	59
QPR	46	15	3	5	65	31	9	8	6	46	42	59
Peterboro' U	46	16	0	7	60	38	10	6	7	47	44	58
Bristol C	46	15	3	5	56	27	8	5	10	38	45	54
Reading	46	14	5	4	46	24	8	4	11	31	42	53
Northampton T	46	12	6	5	52	24	8	5	10	33	33	51
Swindon T	46	11	8	4	48	26	6	7	10	30	45	49
Hull C	46	15	2	6	43	20	5	6	12	24	34	48
Bradford	46	13	5	5	47	27	7	2	14	33	51	47
Port Vale	46	12	4	7	41	23	5	7	11	24	35	45
Notts Co	46	14	5	4	44	23	3	4	16	23	51	43
Coventry C	46	11	6	6	38	26	5	5	13	26	45	43
Crystal P	46	8	8	7	50	41	6	6	11	33	39	42
Southend U	46	10	7	6	31	26	3	9	11	26	43	42
Watford	46	10	9	4	37	26	4	4	15	26	48	41
Halifax T	46	9	5	9	34	35	6	5	12	28	49	40
Shrewsbury T	46	8	7	8	46	37	5	5	13	27	47	38
Barnsley	46	9	6	8	45	41	4	6	13	26	54	38
Torquay U	46	9	4	10	48	44	6	2	15	28	56	36
Lincoln C	46	4	10	9	31	43	5	7	11	26	44	35
Brentford	46	11	3	9	34	29	2	5	16	19	64	34
Newport Co	46	6	5	12	29	38	1	3	19	17	64	22

DIVISION 4

	P	W	D	L	F	A	W	D	L	F	A	Pts
Millwall	44	16	3	3	47	18	7	7	8	40	44	56
Colchester U	44	17	4	1	78	24	6	5	11	26	47	55
Wrexham	44	12	6	4	56	23	10	3	9	40	33	53
Carlisle U	44	15	3	4	35	22	7	5	10	29	41	52
Bradford C	44	14	5	3	58	32	7	4	11	36	54	51
York C	44	17	2	3	62	19	3	8	11	22	34	50
Aldershot	44	16	4	2	56	20	6	1	15	25	40	49
Workington	44	12	6	4	40	23	7	5	10	29	47	49
Barrow	44	12	7	3	49	20	5	7	10	25	38	48
Crewe A	44	16	3	3	53	24	4	3	15	26	46	46
Oldham A	44	12	7	3	47	26	5	5	12	30	44	46
Rochdale	44	14	3	5	47	28	5	4	13	24	43	45
Darlington	44	13	5	4	37	24	5	4	13	24	49	45
Mansfield T	44	14	3	5	51	19	5	3	14	26	47	44
Tranmere R	44	15	2	5	53	37	5	2	15	17	44	44
Stockport Co	44	13	3	6	42	27	4	6	12	28	42	43
Southport	44	13	5	4	36	25	4	4	14	25	46	43
Exeter C	44	11	5	6	43	32	2	6	14	19	45	37
Chesterfield	44	11	3	8	43	38	3	6	13	27	49	37
Gillingham	44	10	6	6	48	30	3	5	14	25	64	37
Doncaster R	44	8	5	9	34	29	3	2	17	26	56	29
Hartlepools U	44	6	5	11	27	35	2	6	14	25	66	27
Chester	44	5	9	8	36	37	2	3	17	18	59	26

Accrington Stanley resigned from the League

Football League Records

Top scorers: Div 1, J.Greaves (Tottenham Hotspur) 37 goals; Div 2, R.Tambling (Chelsea) 35 goals; Div 3, G.Hudson (Coventry City) 30 goals; Div 4, K.Wagstaff (Mansfield Town) 34 goals.
Accrington Stanley resigned, Oxford United were elected in their place.

Everton's Alex Young, the Scottish international inside-forward who became such a hero at Goodison. His vision steered the Merseysiders to the First Division title in 1962-3.

DIVISION 1

	ARSENAL	ASTON VILLA	BIRMINGHAM C	BLACKBURN R	BLACKPOOL	BOLTON W	BURNLEY	EVERTON	FULHAM	IPSWICH T	LEICESTER C	LEYTON O	LIVERPOOL	MANCHESTER C	MANCHESTER U	NOTTINGHAM F	SHEFFIELD U	SHEFFIELD W	TOTTENHAM H	W.B.A.	WEST HAM U	WOLVERHAMPTON W
1 ARSENAL		S04 1-2	A21 2-0	M23 3-1	D08 2-0	F16 3-2	m11 2-3	M26 4-3	m14 3-0	N24 3-1	S22 1-1	D15 2-0	M09 2-2	a20 2-3	A25 1-3	a06 0-0	N10 1-0	S08 1-2	F23 2-3	a12 3-2	O13 1-1	O27 5-4
2 ASTON VILLA	S10 3-1		M16 4-0	J19 0-0	S01 1-1	D01 5-0	N17 2-1	a01 0-2	N03 1-2	S29 4-2	m15 3-1	O20 1-0	m18 2-0	m08 3-1	a09 1-2	m04 0-2	S15 1-2	a13 0-2	A20 2-1	O06 2-0	A18 3-1	a16 0-2
3 BIRMINGHAM C	A29 2-2	O27 3-2		D08 3-3	a20 3-6	a03 2-2	S08 5-1	a16 0-1	S22 4-1	a06 0-1	m18 3-2	A25 2-2	N24 0-2	O13 2-2	m10 2-1	N10 2-2	M23 0-1	M30 1-1	D15 0-2	S19 0-0	m01 3-2	M09 3-4
4 BLACKBURN R	N03 5-5	S08 4-1	a27 6-1		M25 3-3	M29 5-0	O06 2-3	N17 3-2	M16 0-1	D15 0-1	O20 2-0	D01 1-1	A25 1-0	m01 4-1	M02 2-2	A20 2-5	S17 1-2	a12 3-0	m20 3-0	a13 3-1	S22 0-4	m13 5-1
5 BLACKPOOL	a27 3-2	M29 4-0	D01 1-1	a23 4-1		N17 3-1	M20 0-0	a13 1-2	O20 0-0	A20 1-0	a08 1-1	M02 3-2	D15 1-2	S22 2-2	O06 2-2	S03 2-1	a15 3-1	M16 2-3	S08 1-2	N03 0-2	m13 0-0	A25 0-2
6 BOLTON W	S29 3-0	a20 4-1	a24 0-0	N24 0-0	a06 3-0		A22 2-2	S15 0-2	A25 1-0	S08 1-3	m11 2-0	a15 0-1	m13 1-0	N10 3-1	S05 3-0	O27 1-0	M09 3-2	m06 0-4	D08 1-0	M25 1-2	M23 3-0	O13 3-0
7 BURNLEY	S01 2-1	a06 3-1	m14 3-1	a02 1-0	S29 2-0	A28 2-1		A18 1-3	a12 4-0	D08 3-1	S04 1-1	S15 2-0	M23 1-3	O27 0-0	m04 0-1	a20 0-0	O13 5-1	D29 4-0	N24 2-1	a30 2-1	M09 1-1	N10 2-0
8 EVERTON	a24 1-1	O13 1-1	a15 2-2	a06 0-0	N10 5-0	m04 1-0	D15 3-1		m11 4-1	O27 3-1	S08 3-2	S05 3-0	S22 2-2	M23 2-1	A22 3-1	M09 2-0	N24 3-0	A25 4-1	a20 1-0	S29 4-2	D08 1-1	F23 0-0
9 FULHAM	S15 1-3	M23 1-0	m04 3-3	O27 0-0	M09 2-0	m01 2-1	a15 1-1	S01 1-0		O13 1-1	A18 2-1	S29 0-2	a20 0-0	N24 2-4	D26 0-1	F23 3-1	A29 2-2	S19 4-1	N10 0-2	m18 1-2	a06 2-0	D08 0-5
10 IPSWICH T	M30 1-1	m21 1-1	N17 1-5	A18 3-3	A28 5-2	m17 4-1	a27 2-1	M19 0-3	M02 0-1		O06 0-1	a13 1-1	M05 2-2	S11 0-0	N03 3-5	S01 1-1	D21 1-0	D01 2-0	M16 2-4	O20 1-1	a15 2-3	S22 2-3
11 LEICESTER C	F09 2-0	D08 3-3	S29 3-0	M09 2-0	N24 0-0	S01 4-1	S19 3-3	F12 3-1	D15 2-3	F23 3-0		D26 5-1	O13 3-0	a06 2-0	a16 4-3	A25 2-1	O27 3-1	A22 3-3	M23 2-2	S15 1-0	N10 2-0	a20 1-1
12 LEYTON O	A18 1-2	M09 0-2	D22 2-2	a20 1-1	O13 0-2	a12 0-1	m07 0-1	S12 3-0	F16 1-1	N10 1-2	a03 0-2		m02 2-1	F23 1-1	S08 1-0	M23 0-1	D08 2-2	S22 2-4	O27 1-5	A29 2-3	S01 2-0	N24 0-4
13 LIVERPOOL	N14 2-1	F13 4-0	m08 5-1	D22 3-1	A18 1-2	O06 1-0	N03 1-2	a08 0-0	D01 2-1	S15 1-1	M02 0-2	N17 5-0		A29 4-1	a13 1-0	a18 0-2	S01 2-0	a29 0-2	a12 5-2	M20 2-2	S12 2-1	F16 4-1
14 MANCHESTER C	D01 2-4	A25 0-2	M02 2-1	S29 0-1	m04 0-3	a13 2-1	M26 2-5	N03 1-1	M29 2-3	S05 2-1	N17 1-1	O06 2-0	A22 2-2		m15 1-1	a12 1-0	a24 1-3	O20 3-2	m11 1-0	a27 1-5	S08 1-6	D15 3-3
15 MANCHESTER U	m06 2-3	N24 2-2	S01 2-0	O13 0-3	F23 1-1	S12 3-0	S22 2-5	A29 0-1	a01 0-2	M23 0-1	a15 2-2	m18 3-1	N10 3-3	S15 2-3		D08 5-1	a20 1-1	m01 1-3	M09 0-2	A18 2-2	O27 3-1	a22 2-1
16 NOTTINGHAM F	N17 3-0	S22 3-1	a13 0-2	A28 2-0	S11 2-0	M16 1-0	D01 2-1	N13 3-4	O06 3-1	m10 2-1	F19 0-2	N03 1-1	S08 3-1	a15 1-1	m20 3-2		A18 2-1	M02 0-3	m18 1-1	m14 2-2	D29 3-4	a30 2-0
17 SHEFFIELD U	a13 3-3	m01 2-1	N03 0-2	S05 1-1	a16 0-0	O20 4-1	M02 1-0	M30 2-1	A22 2-0	A25 2-1	M26 0-0	a26 2-0	m11 0-0	a03 3-1	D01 1-1	D15 3-1		O06 2-2	S22 3-1	N17 1-0	F16 0-2	S08 1-2
18 SHEFFIELD W	m18 2-3	N10 0-0	S15 5-0	a15 4-0	O27 0-0	A18 1-1	a23 0-1	D22 2-2	S12 1-0	a20 0-3	A29 0-3	m04 3-1	D08 0-2	M09 4-1	S29 1-0	O13 2-2	m15 3-1		a08 3-1	S01 3-1	N24 1-3	M23 3-1
19 TOTTENHAM H	O06 4-4	A29 4-2	A18 3-0	S15 4-1	J19 2-0	a27 4-1	M30 1-1	D01 0-0	a13 1-1	D26 5-0	N03 4-0	M27 2-0	a15 7-2	S01 4-2	O24 6-2	S29 9-2	m04 4-2	N17 1-1		M02 2-1	D22 4-4	S12 1-2
20 W.B.A.	a15 1-2	m11 1-0	S12 1-0	N10 2-5	M23 1-2	S22 5-4	A25 1-2	m07 0-4	S08 6-1	M09 6-1	m04 2-1	A22 2-1	O27 1-0	D08 2-1	D15 3-0	N24 1-4	a06 1-2	J12 0-3	O13 1-2		a20 1-0	a03 2-2
21 WEST HAM U	M02 0-4	D15 1-1	O06 5-0	m04 0-1	S14 2-2	N03 1-2	O22 1-1	a27 1-2	N17 2-2	a12 1-3	a13 2-0	m11 2-0	S03 1-0	m18 6-1	M18 3-1	a22 4-1	S29 1-1	a02 2-0	A25 1-6	D01 2-2		A20 1-4
22 WOLVERHAMPTON W	a08 1-0	a15 3-1	O24 0-2	S01 4-2	m09 2-0	M20 4-0	a13 7-2	O06 0-2	a27 2-1	m04 0-0	D01 1-3	M30 2-1	S29 3-2	A18 8-1	N17 2-3	S15 1-1	J19 0-0	N03 2-2	S19 2-2	M16 7-0	A29 0-0	

DIVISION 2

	BURY	CARDIFF C	CHARLTON A	CHELSEA	DERBY CO	GRIMSBY T	HUDDERSFIELD T	LEEDS U	LUTON T	MIDDLESBROUGH	NEWCASTLE U	NORWICH C	PLYMOUTH A	PORTSMOUTH	PRESTON N.E.	ROTHERHAM U	SCUNTHORPE U	SOUTHAMPTON	STOKE C	SUNDERLAND	SWANSEA T	WALSALL
1 BURY		N03 1-0	S22 3-1	a16 2-0	a13 3-3	O06 2-0	M30 1-1	S18 3-1	A18 1-0	N17 1-0	D01 0-0	J19 0-3	M02 1-2	a02 2-0	O20 0-0	M19 0-5	S01 0-2	m07 1-1	m14 2-1	D29 3-0	A30 2-0	a27 0-0
2 CARDIFF C	M23 3-1		a06 1-2	F23 1-0	D22 1-0	S12 5-3	m18 3-0	D08 0-0	O13 1-0	S01 1-2	A18 4-4	A29 2-4	m01 2-1	S22 1-2	m06 1-1	N10 4-1	O27 4-0	M09 3-1	N24 1-1	a20 5-2	S15 5-2	a15 2-2
3 CHARLTON A	F09 0-0	N17 2-4		D22 1-4	a27 0-0	O20 0-3	a13 1-0	a15 1-2	S01 2-0	D01 3-4	a23 1-2	M02 0-2	M16 6-3	M30 2-0	N03 2-1	S29 2-3	S15 1-0	m18 2-1	S18 0-3	A28 2-2	A18 2-2	O06 3-2
4 CHELSEA	a12 2-0	O06 6-0	A25 5-0		M27 3-1	a13 2-1	M02 1-2	a30 2-2	a01 3-1	O20 3-2	N03 4-2	N17 2-0	D01 1-1	m21 7-0	a27 2-0	D15 3-0	A22 3-0	S10 2-0	m11 0-1	S08 1-0	S22 2-2	M30 0-1
5 DERBY CO	N24 0-0	A25 1-2	D08 2-3	O27 1-3		S22 2-4	D15 2-1	O13 0-0	M23 1-0	a15 3-3	S19 0-1	m06 3-0	M20 3-2	m10 4-0	S08 1-0	a20 3-2	a06 6-2	N10 3-1	A22 1-1	F23 2-2	M09 0-2	a24 2-0
6 GRIMSBY T	m18 5-1	S18 1-2	M09 2-1	N24 0-3	m04 0-0		D29 1-1	N10 1-1	a20 3-1	S29 3-4	S15 0-1	S01 0-2	D15 1-1	A21 1-1	a12 2-0	O13 1-2	A25 3-0	D08 4-1	O27 1-1	M23 1-2	a06 1-0	a30 3-1
7 HUDDERSFIELD T	N10 0-1	S08 1-0	N24 2-0	O13 1-0	A18 3-3	a24 0-0		S01 1-1	M09 2-0	a29 0-0	a16 2-1	S12 0-0	a01 4-2	m13 1-3	S22 1-0	a06 1-0	M23 2-0	O27 2-3	a20 3-3	D08 0-3	m06 4-1	A29 4-0
8 LEEDS U	S05 1-2	a27 3-0	a16 4-1	S15 2-0	M02 3-1	M30 3-0	m11 0-1		m04 3-0	O06 2-3	O20 1-0	N03 3-0	N17 6-1	D01 3-3	a13 4-1	A22 3-4	a03 1-0	S29 1-1	D15 3-1	A25 1-0	m18 5-0	M13 3-0
9 LUTON T	D15 2-1	a24 2-3	m11 4-1	D26 0-2	N03 1-2	D01 2-2	M16 3-2	S22 2-2		M25 4-3	M30 2-3	a13 4-2	a27 3-0	O06 3-3	S05 0-2	A25 2-3	a15 1-0	A29 3-2	S08 0-0	m13 0-3	m01 3-1	N17 4-3
10 MIDDLESBROUGH	a06 0-0	m11 3-2	a20 2-1	M09 1-0	a12 5-1	F16 0-1	A25 0-5	m06 2-1	O27 0-2		A22 4-2	m21 6-2	S22 3-0	S07 4-2	m15 2-0	N24 2-1	N10 4-3	M23 1-2	D08 2-2	D15 3-3	O13 2-2	S12 2-3
11 NEWCASTLE U	a20 1-3	D15 2-1	a03 3-2	M23 2-0	S12 0-0	M27 0-0	a12 1-1	M09 1-1	N10 3-1	A29 6-1		S22 2-1	S08 3-1	A25 1-1	m11 2-2	D08 4-1	N24 1-1	a06 4-1	m01 5-2	O13 1-1	O27 6-0	m08 0-2
12 NORWICH C	S08 1-1	A22 0-0	O13 1-4	a06 4-1	S29 2-0	m11 0-0	S05 2-3	M23 3-2	N24 3-3	D29 3-4	m04 1-2		A25 2-1	a16 5-3	D15 1-1	F23 4-2	D08 3-3	a20 1-0	M09 6-0	O27 4-2	N10 5-0	S15 2-1
13 PLYMOUTH A	O13 0-0	D26 4-2	O27 6-1	a20 2-1	S15 2-1	A18 2-0	S29 1-1	a06 3-1	D08 3-1	F09 4-5	J19 0-2	D22 1-0		S19 2-0	A22 7-1	M09 2-2	F23 2-3	a12 2-1	M23 0-1	N10 1-1	N24 1-0	S01 3-0
14 PORTSMOUTH	O27 2-1	m04 2-0	N10 3-3	S29 0-2	S01 1-0	A29 2-1	S15 1-1	a20 3-0	F23 3-1	m18 1-1	D22 3-1	a15 0-2	S12 1-2		m01 1-2	M23 1-2	M09 1-2	O13 1-1	a06 0-3	N24 3-1	D08 0-0	A18 4-1
15 PRESTON N.E.	M09 0-2	S29 2-6	M23 4-1	D08 1-3	m18 1-0	a15 0-0	m04 2-0	N24 4-1	S11 3-1	S15 0-1	S01 2-1	A18 2-2	A28 0-0	D26 4-2		O27 2-2	O13 3-1	F23 1-0	N10 1-1	a06 1-1	a20 6-3	M19 4-2
16 ROTHERHAM U	S15 1-5	M29 2-1	a30 1-2	A18 0-1	N30 2-2	m07 0-0	N17 0-2	A28 2-1	D21 2-1	a13 4-1	a27 3-1	O05 0-3	O20 3-2	N03 0-0	M16 3-1		m17 1-0	S01 2-0	D26 1-2	S11 4-2	a15 2-1	m04 1-2
17 SCUNTHORPE U	m10 1-0	M15 2-2	m07 2-0	A28 3-0	N16 2-1	D21 1-1	N02 2-2	a23 0-2	a12 2-0	M29 1-1	S04 2-1	a26 3-1	O06 2-2	O19 1-2	M26 4-1	S08 1-0		A18 2-1	S22 0-0	a30 1-1	S11 1-0	N30 2-0
18 SOUTHAMPTON	A25 0-3	O31 3-5	S08 1-0	S19 2-1	m01 5-0	m13 4-1	M20 3-1	m15 3-1	A22 2-2	N03 6-0	N17 3-0	D01 3-1	a15 1-1	M02 4-2	O06 1-0	m11 1-0	D15 1-1		m22 2-0	S22 2-4	a22 3-0	a13 2-0
19 STOKE C	S29 2-0	a13 1-0	S12 6-3	S01 0-0	A29 3-3	M16 4-1	D01 2-1	A18 0-1	m18 2-0	a27 0-1	O06 3-1	O20 3-0	N03 2-2	N17 3-1	M30 3-0	a01 3-1	m04 2-3	S15 3-1		a15 2-1	M27 2-0	M02 3-0
20 SUNDERLAND	D26 0-1	D01 2-1	A22 1-0	m18 0-1	O06 3-0	N03 6-2	a27 1-1	D22 2-1	S15 3-1	A18 3-1	M02 0-0	M20 7-1	M30 1-1	a13 1-0	N17 2-1	S05 2-0	S29 0-0	m04 4-0	a12 0-0		S01 3-1	O20 5-0
21 SWANSEA T	A23 3-0	S04 2-1	D15 2-1	F09 2-0	O19 2-0	N17 1-0	O06 1-2	S08 0-2	S29 1-0	M02 1-1	M16 1-0	a09 2-0	a13 2-1	a27 0-0	D01 1-1	a16 2-2	S18 1-0	D26 1-1	A25 2-1	m11 3-4		N03 3-0
22 WALSALL	D08 3-1	a16 2-1	m24 1-2	N10 1-5	M16 1-3	S08 4-1	A21 1-1	O27 1-1	a06 1-1	S04 1-0	S29 0-6	m14 3-1	M26 2-2	D15 3-5	A25 4-1	S22 1-0	a20 1-1	N24 1-1	O13 0-0	M09 2-3	M23 0-1	

Dennis Viollet, the former Manchester United star who helped lift Stoke City back to Division One.

Season 1962-63

DIVISION 3

	BARNSLEY	BOURNEMOUTH	BRADFORD	BRIGHTON & HA	BRISTOL C	BRISTOL R	CARLISLE U	COLCHESTER U	COVENTRY C	CRYSTAL P	HALIFAX T	HULL C	MILLWALL	NORTHAMPTON T	NOTTS CO	PETERBOROUGH U	PORT VALE	Q.P.R.	READING	SHREWSBURY T	SOUTHEND U	SWINDON T	WATFORD	WREXHAM
1 BARNSLEY		a02 2-2	a30 1-4	A28 2-0	M16 1-1	N27 4-0	a16 2-0	a27 2-3	O05 2-1	m22 0-4	S04 1-0	S22 1-2	a13 4-1	S08 1-1	J12 3-1	D21 0-2	M29 2-1	m10 0-0	m13 1-0	N17 1-0	D01 2-2	A18 1-1	O20 4-1	O02 2-1
2 BOURNEMOUTH	M20 1-1		A22 2-2	m08 1-0	S05 1-1	a06 1-1	a20 5-1	S01 1-1	a12 1-1	O27 3-0	N10 1-1	M09 3-0	S15 1-1	F23 3-0	D22 3-1	A18 3-3	S29 2-0	O13 2-1	N24 1-0	m04 0-0	m18 0-0	D08 0-0	S19 1-0	M23 3-1
3 BRADFORD	O13 1-1	A29 1-1		D08 1-5	S29 2-5	a20 2-2	S12 3-1	A18 1-1	S24 0-0	N10 2-1	J04 1-1	M23 3-1	S01 2-2	M09 2-3	a16 5-0	M06 2-2	S15 2-1	O27 0-3	m04 3-2	M26 2-1	M19 2-2	D26 2-0	O10 1-0	a06 3-1
4 BRIGHTON & H.A.	A21 2-0	a13 0-1	a27 3-1		M19 1-0	S22 1-1	O09 1-0	M30 3-0	D01 2-2	J12 1-2	F02 0-1	A25 2-1	M16 0-2	a12 0-5	N17 1-3	S18 0-3	M02 3-1	D15 2-2	O06 2-4	O20 1-1	J26 0-0	S04 1-1	m04 1-4	S08 1-3
5 BRISTOL C	O27 5-2	S11 1-0	F16 4-2	D26 1-2		a23 4-1	F23 2-2	A28 1-2	O02 1-1	m07 1-1	D08 2-2	a06 3-1	A18 2-2	M23 3-1	a30 1-1	M09 1-1	S01 2-0	N10 2-4	m18 4-2	D22 3-1	a16 6-3	O13 2-2	S22 3-3	m03 0-2
6 BRISTOL R	S18 3-2	N17 1-2	D01 3-3	F09 4-1	S15 1-2		S29 1-1	m14 2-0	a13 2-2	A25 2-0	S08 5-2	D15 2-5	O20 2-0	A21 2-2	M30 1-1	S04 3-1	O06 1-1	a15 0-0	F26 1-0	M02 2-0	M16 1-2	O09 2-0	a27 3-1	m11 1-1
7 CARLISLE U	a12 2-1	N30 0-3	a23 3-0	O02 1-0	O05 2-5	a02 4-0		N17 3-1	a27 0-1	S08 2-2	S22 1-0	m11 2-1	m14 4-3	D15 1-2	M12 4-2	A21 1-4	O20 1-1	A24 2-5	m06 1-1	M16 2-1	M30 1-2	S18 0-0	D26 2-1	m23 2-1
8 COLCHESTER U	D08 1-1	m11 3-1	D15 1-4	N10 4-1	A20 1-0	M22 1-0	a06 2-1		A25 0-0	O13 1-2	O27 1-1	M04 2-3	S29 2-5	S15 2-2	S08 2-2	a20 2-0	S10 0-1	a22 2-1	S24 4-2	O08 3-2	m04 3-1	m06 0-2	a16 3-2	M08 1-1
9 COVENTRY C	F23 2-0	a16 1-2	S18 3-1	a20 1-1	O23 4-2	a29 5-0	D08 3-2	F26 2-2		M23 1-0	a06 5-4	O27 2-2	a08 2-0	O13 1-1	A18 2-0	D29 3-3	m04 0-1	M09 4-1	S29 2-1	S15 0-0	S01 3-4	A28 2-0	S04 3-1	N10 3-0
10 CRYSTAL P	S29 1-2	M16 1-0	M30 6-0	S01 2-2	a13 3-2	M20 2-1	m18 3-0	M27 0-1	m15 0-0		A18 0-0	m01 1-1	D26 3-0	O10 1-2	O20 1-1	a24 0-2	a27 2-1	S12 1-0	D01 2-1	A29 2-2	O06 2-3	S15 0-0	N17 0-1	a15 5-0
11 HALIFAX T	S11 2-0	M30 3-1	a13 4-4	S15 2-1	a27 2-5	m18 2-3	M26 2-4	M15 1-2	N17 2-4	D15 2-2		a15 0-2	m21 3-0	S24 1-3	m07 2-1	O08 2-0	a03 0-4	A27 1-4	m11 1-2	O06 2-2	O19 0-1	S29 4-3	D01 1-3	A25 2-0
12 HULL C	m04 0-2	O20 1-1	M13 1-0	D22 2-1	N17 4-0	A18 3-0	A31 3-1	O06 2-2	m07 2-0	S20 0-0	a12 2-0		S13 4-1	S29 2-0	m20 1-1	S15 3-2	D01 0-1	a25 4-1	a13 0-1	a27 2-2	D29 1-2	m18 1-1	M30 1-0	A23 1-3
13 MILLWALL	m18 4-1	M11 1-0	m11 3-1	O27 2-2	D15 4-2	M09 2-1	M23 2-0	F16 2-1	S08 3-3	a01 1-1	O13 1-1	S03 5-1		a20 1-3	S22 0-2	a06 0-1	A27 0-0	D08 0-0	a12 4-1	S17 1-2	O01 3-1	N10 3-4	A25 6-0	F23 2-4
14 NORTHAMPTON T	a23 4-2	O06 2-2	O20 3-1	a16 3-0	a08 5-1	A28 2-0	m09 2-0	M12 3-1	M02 0-0	O02 3-1	S17 7-1	m24 3-0	D01 1-1		a02 2-2	S01 2-3	N17 0-0	S22 1-0	M30 5-0	a13 1-0	a27 5-3	M26 1-1	M16 1-0	S11 8-0
15 NOTTS CO	S01 2-0	A25 2-0	a12 3-2	a06 0-1	S20 3-2	N10 1-3	M21 1-0	m17 6-0	D15 1-1	M09 0-2	M23 5-0	O13 1-1	m04 3-3	D26 2-1		D08 2-0	O11 1-0	F23 3-2	S06 1-0	S29 1-5	S15 2-1	a20 2-0	A23 1-3	O27 3-2
16 PETERBOROUGH U	A25 4-2	D15 3-0	O06 2-0	O15 3-1	O20 3-1	S10 1-0	A27 2-2	D01 6-2	D26 0-3	S22 0-0	O01 1-1	M25 1-3	N17 6-0	m11 0-4	a27 0-0		M18 3-1	S08 1-2	M16 1-1	a02 2-3	a13 1-3	a15 3-1	M02 4-0	F16 1-3
17 PORT VALE	N09 1-0	m13 0-3	m06 2-1	O13 1-2	m11 3-1	m20 2-0	M09 2-0	S03 4-2	S22 2-1	D08 4-1	a22 2-0	a20 1-0	A20 1-1	a06 3-1	O01 1-1	M23 3-2		a29 3-2	A25 2-0	a12 0-0	S24 5-1	O27 2-1	S08 1-3	D15 2-2
18 Q.P.R.	S15 2-1	M02 1-0	M16 1-2	A18 2-2	M30 3-1	a12 3-5	D22 2-2	a01 1-2	m22 1-3	S03 4-1	A20 5-0	O22 4-1	a27 2-3	F09 1-3	O06 0-1	m18 0-0	a13 3-1		N17 3-2	D01 0-0	a08 1-0	S01 2-2	m13 2-2	S17 1-2
19 READING	M22 4-1	O03 2-1	S21 4-1	F23 4-5	S08 0-3	m08 1-0	O12 2-0	S19 4-1	m01 4-1	a19 0-1	A31 4-2	M20 2-2	a16 2-0	N10 2-1	S12 1-1	O26 0-1	D22 4-3	a05 1-1		A18 5-0	A29 1-3	M08 1-2	a03 0-0	M11 3-0
20 SHREWSBURY T	a06 1-3	S22 2-1	S07 1-2	M09 2-1	A25 3-3	O13 7-2	O27 1-1	O03 1-2	m20 2-1	A22 3-1	F23 4-2	D08 1-4	S26 3-3	m01 1-0	a24 2-2	N10 5-4	a15 2-1	a20 0-3	D15 2-1		S12 6-0	M23 1-2	m11 3-0	D26 4-2
21 SOUTHEND U	a20 0-0	S08 0-1	A25 3-1	M23 1-1	a15 2-2	O27 3-2	N10 2-0	S22 2-3	m11 1-1	m20 1-0	M09 1-1	D26 0-1	a22 2-1	D08 5-1	m13 1-2	m06 2-1	S17 2-0	S29 1-3	A20 2-0	S03 3-1		a06 1-1	D15 1-1	O13 2-0
22 SWINDON T	D15 2-1	a27 2-1	a02 2-1	S11 5-1	M02 3-2	O02 3-0	a30 2-0	a13 6-1	A21 4-1	F02 1-0	m04 1-1	S08 2-0	M30 1-0	A25 2-3	D01 3-1	a12 2-3	M16 2-3	J12 5-0	O20 1-1	m14 1-0	N17 4-1		O06 3-1	S22 3-0
23 WATFORD	M12 0-0	S25 0-1	O02 3-2	S29 2-0	M26 1-4	D08 0-1	D29 5-1	a15 1-1	S11 6-1	a06 1-4	a20 2-1	N10 4-2	a30 0-2	O27 4-2	A28 4-0	O13 2-3	m18 1-2	M23 2-5	S15 4-0	S01 4-3	A18 3-1	F23 3-3		a09 3-1
24 WREXHAM	m08 2-1	m15 1-0	N17 3-1	m18 0-0	D01 2-1	S01 5-2	S15 2-1	O20 4-1	a01 6-1	a12 3-4	m01 3-1	A29 2-0	O06 6-1	O24 1-4	M16 5-1	S29 4-4	A18 0-1	O10 3-1	a27 1-1	M20 2-0	M02 1-1	F27 0-0	a13 0-0	

DIVISION 4

	ALDERSHOT	BARROW	BRADFORD C	BRENTFORD	CHESTER	CHESTERFIELD	CREWE A	DARLINGTON	DONCASTER R	EXETER C	GILLINGHAM	HARTLEPOOLS U	LINCOLN C	MANSFIELD T	NEWPORT CO	OLDHAM A	OXFORD U	ROCHDALE	SOUTHPORT	STOCKPORT CO	TORQUAY U	TRANMERE R	WORKINGTON	YORK C
1 ALDERSHOT		A22 2-1	M20 3-1	O20 0-0	O06 2-2	M06 1-0	O10 2-2	D15 2-3	D01 3-1	a13 1-1	m11 0-1	S19 3-2	a03 1-2	M30 2-3	m18 2-1	O24 1-1	S15 0-0	M16 2-0	A25 4-2	a27 2-2	a12 1-1	S29 2-3	N17 2-2	a08 4-1
2 BARROW	A27 1-1		D22 1-1	F16 1-1	D01 4-3	O06 2-0	M30 2-3	D26 4-1	m06 4-0	M02 0-2	N17 1-1	a15 2-0	S15 2-1	M16 3-2	m13 3-0	a29 3-2	A18 3-2	a22 1-1	S10 6-2	a13 1-0	m04 0-0	S01 1-1	O20 5-1	a27 2-1
3 BRADFORD C	S22 0-2	A25 3-0		a13 2-1	M16 2-0	M30 1-1	O20 1-0	S08 3-0	O03 2-3	D01 2-3	m08 1-1	m11 1-1	M13 2-2	a03 1-3	m01 3-4	D15 1-3	a15 1-4	N17 1-2	M27 0-2	O06 3-2	A22 2-1	O24 2-1	a27 2-2	m15 1-2
4 BRENTFORD	M09 4-2	S29 2-1	N10 5-2		D26 2-1	m04 2-1	a30 3-1	F23 1-3	D15 1-0	S08 3-1	A21 1-2	O02 4-0	a20 3-2	A25 1-3	O27 3-1	D08 2-1	M23 4-0	S22 1-0	O13 3-3	S18 2-1	M12 2-2	a06 4-0	m23 4-3	a15 2-1
5 CHESTER	F23 0-2	a19 1-0	O27 2-0	a03 1-2		m22 0-2	S19 1-2	A29 1-2	m11 1-1	S22 3-1	D15 1-0	D07 1-0	a06 3-2	S08 0-2	O13 2-2	M13 1-0	M09 2-1	a15 1-0	O03 6-1	A25 0-1	N10 3-1	M23 0-0	m08 1-1	S12 0-0
6 CHESTERFIELD	M23 3-1	m20 1-1	m06 0-1	S15 1-1	S29 1-1		a12 1-2	M09 6-1	A20 3-1	A25 1-1	a29 0-2	O13 2-2	S01 2-2	S17 4-4	N10 1-2	a22 0-0	a06 1-0	m17 1-3	O27 6-0	S03 1-2	D08 2-0	a20 4-0	D15 1-1	a01 1-1
7 CREWE A	O03 2-1	a03 2-1	M09 5-0	S12 3-0	a22 3-0	a17 2-0		D08 2-1	S08 3-0	m22 1-0	A25 2-2	a20 4-1	N10 1-1	m08 3-0	M13 4-1	a06 2-3	O13 3-2	M27 1-2	D15 2-2	m11 1-2	M23 1-1	O27 2-0	S22 0-1	A29 1-0
8 DARLINGTON	A18 1-1	M18 2-1	m17 2-1	O06 1-3	A20 2-1	O20 2-1	a27 1-4		N17 5-1	M16 0-1	D01 2-0	S10 0-2	S29 0-0	a13 2-1	D22 4-2	a15 1-1	S01 2-1	a08 3-0	N24 1-3	M29 5-1	m06 1-3	S15 2-3	m13 3-1	M11 2-1
9 DONCASTER R	a20 2-1	M23 2-2	O09 1-1	A18 0-2	S01 1-2	A28 0-0	m18 1-1	a06 2-0		a02 1-1	S15 1-0	N10 2-3	M09 3-0	a15 1-1	D08 2-2	O27 1-1	S29 4-2	O30 2-2	m04 0-0	F09 1-2	O13 2-0	a25 2-1	D26 2-0	D22 3-2
10 EXETER C	N10 4-2	O13 0-2	a20 0-2	m17 2-2	m04 2-1	D22 2-2	S29 1-1	O27 1-3	S12 0-1		a15 0-0	M09 3-1	O03 1-1	A22 0-3	a06 1-0	F23 2-1	m08 1-1	S01 0-2	M23 2-1	D26 0-1	A18 0-3	D08 2-1	S20 1-0	S15 2-1
11 GILLINGHAM	S01 1-0	a06 2-3	O13 2-1	A29 1-4	A18 2-1	D26 2-1	D22 4-0	a20 1-0	m01 1-0	a12 4-0		M30 5-1	M23 3-0	S22 0-1	a24 3-1	N10 4-3	m20 2-1	S12 2-1	D08 3-1	S08 1-0	O27 4-2	M09 0-0	F16 2-2	S26 0-0
12 HARTLEPOOLS U	S24 1-2	a12 1-1	S01 2-2	a22 2-1	a27 0-3	a08 1-1	D01 1-5	S03 0-2	a13 1-1	O20 0-2	a01 1-1		m04 3-0	m13 3-4	A18 2-3	S29 0-1	D22 1-2	O06 4-0	A27 4-0	N17 3-0	S15 0-3	m18 0-2	M16 2-2	a29 1-1
13 LINCOLN C	D26 2-4	m18 1-2	S26 3-2	D01 1-3	N17 1-3	m11 1-3	a13 1-2	m01 2-1	O19 1-2	O10 4-1	m15 2-1	S22 4-1		M27 2-6	S12 6-3	S08 1-2	A29 1-0	a27 3-0	a15 0-2	M16 0-0	D21 3-0	A18 4-2	O06 3-2	M29 2-4
14 MANSFIELD T	M18 2-2	O27 5-0	a29 3-1	D22 1-2	m18 4-0	O22 3-0	S15 2-2	N10 6-0	a16 4-2	A27 1-0	m04 0-0	M23 3-1	O13 2-0		a20 2-1	M09 4-2	D08 3-2	A18 1-0	a06 6-1	S29 0-1	a08 1-2	O01 6-1	S10 0-0	S01 2-0
15 NEWPORT CO	S08 2-2	S17 6-0	S29 2-0	M16 1-4	M04 0-1	O01 2-3	O06 5-1	A25 2-2	a27 2-4	N17 4-0	a13 2-0	D15 2-1	S03 2-1	D01 1-1		A20 0-0	m23 1-0	m20 1-1	M11 1-0	m04 3-1	M18 1-0	D10 1-2	a01 2-2	O18 1-3
16 OLDHAM A	S12 2-0	S22 2-1	A18 2-1	a27 2-1	M30 2-0	a13 2-1	N17 2-2	a12 1-0	M16 4-0	O06 1-2	O10 2-1	m08 6-1	J19 4-1	O20 3-2	A29 3-2		S26 2-0	F02 5-1	D26 11-0	J26 2-1	S01 1-1	F27 1-1	M02 2-2	D01 3-2
17 OXFORD U	m01 1-1	D15 4-1	a12 2-1	m11 2-1	O20 3-0	N17 0-0	m15 0-0	m04 4-2	M20 3-3	M30 0-3	O06 2-3	A25 6-2	A22 2-1	a27 3-0	S22 5-1	S19 1-1		a13 0-0	S08 0-0	O03 1-1	S05 1-1	a04 2-2	D01 2-1	M16 0-2
18 ROCHDALE	O27 1-1	O02 6-0	a06 2-1	M20 3-5	a16 0-0	S08 3-2	D29 2-0	O13 1-1	O23 3-1	m11 3-0	M05 1-1	M12 2-1	m07 1-0	D15 3-1	M23 3-3	S15 1-1	N10 2-1		M09 1-0	O16 1-0	a20 3-0	m23 2-0	A25 3-2	S29 1-0
19 SOUTHPORT	a22 1-1	S03 3-3	S15 3-3	M02 1-0	O08 4-1	M16 0-2	A18 1-3	M04 4-2	M30 2-1	a29 1-3	a27 0-0	A20 1-1	a12 0-0	N17 3-2	S01 2-1	a02 2-1	m18 4-2	O20 1-1		D01 2-0	S28 4-4	m07 0-0	a13 6-3	O06 2-1
20 STOCKPORT CO	D08 3-0	N10 1-3	a22 3-1	N24 2-1	M18 1-0	S10 0-1	S01 1-1	a01 0-1	S22 2-1	D29 4-3	m18 0-0	a06 4-1	O27 1-2	m20 1-1	S15 1-1	M23 2-1	O08 1-1	A27 1-0	a20 0-2		M09 1-2	O13 2-2	a12 2-3	A18 1-1
21 TORQUAY U	a15 3-1	S08 2-1	A29 4-1	M29 1-1	a13 1-0	a27 2-1	M06 1-2	S22 1-1	M02 2-2	D15 3-0	M16 0-0	F02 2-0	A25 0-0	O06 3-3	F27 3-1	F20 2-0	S12 2-2	D01 2-1	F16 5-1	O20 2-2		m01 1-0	O04 2-0	N17 1-0
22 TRANMERE R	m04 1-3	m11 2-0	S10 1-1	M04 1-2	m13 3-0	D01 4-1	M16 2-1	M25 3-1	O06 2-3	a27 2-1	O20 2-1	S08 6-1	D15 3-0	a22 5-1	a12 0-0	A25 1-2	M11 3-0	M30 3-2	S21 7-1	M02 3-1	S17 1-1		A20 0-1	a13 2-1
23 WORKINGTON	a06 0-1	M09 3-5	D08 2-3	S01 3-1	S15 3-0	A18 0-0	m04 0-1	M23 2-0	M28 1-0	S24 3-1	S29 5-2	O27 0-0	F23 1-1	M14 3-2	m11 4-0	O13 0-1	a19 0-0	D22 1-0	N10 2-0	a15 4-0	a22 1-2	A28 1-0		m18 3-0
24 YORK C	O13 0-0	D08 1-1	M22 3-0	a12 1-1	N12 0-0	S22 3-4	A20 2-0	O01 5-1	A25 1-0	M18 3-3	S17 0-3	M25 2-0	a22 3-1	m11 2-1	M08 2-0	a20 5-2	O26 1-2	m04 1-0	m20 1-1	D15 3-1	a05 1-0	N10 1-2	S08 1-2	

LEAGUE TABLES

DIVISION 1

	P	W	D	L	F	A	W	D	L	F	A	Pts
Everton	42	14	7	0	48	17	11	4	6	36	25	61
Tottenham H	42	14	6	1	72	28	9	3	9	39	34	55
Burnley	42	14	4	3	41	17	8	6	7	37	40	54
Leicester C	42	14	6	1	53	23	6	6	9	26	30	52
Wolves	42	11	6	4	51	25	9	4	8	42	40	50
Sheffield W	42	10	5	6	38	26	9	5	7	39	37	48
Arsenal	42	11	4	6	44	33	7	6	8	42	44	46
Liverpool	42	13	3	5	45	22	4	7	10	26	37	44
Nottingham F	42	12	4	5	39	28	5	6	10	28	41	44
Sheffield U	42	11	7	3	33	20	5	5	11	25	40	44
Blackburn R	42	11	4	6	55	34	4	8	9	24	37	42
West Ham U	42	8	6	7	39	34	6	6	9	34	35	40
Blackpool	42	8	7	6	34	27	5	7	9	24	37	40
WBA	42	11	1	9	40	37	5	6	10	31	42	39
Aston Villa	42	12	2	7	38	23	3	6	12	24	45	38
Fulham	42	8	6	7	28	30	6	4	11	22	41	38
Ipswich T	42	5	8	8	34	39	7	3	11	25	39	35
Bolton W	42	13	3	5	35	18	2	2	17	20	57	35
Manchester U	42	6	6	9	36	38	6	4	11	31	43	34
Birmingham C	42	6	8	7	40	40	4	5	12	23	50	33
Manchester C	42	7	5	9	30	45	3	6	12	28	57	31
Leyton O	42	4	5	12	22	37	2	4	15	15	44	21

DIVISION 2

	P	W	D	L	F	A	W	D	L	F	A	Pts
Stoke C	42	15	3	3	49	20	5	10	6	24	30	53
Chelsea	42	15	3	3	54	16	9	1	11	27	26	52
Sunderland	42	14	5	2	46	13	6	7	8	38	42	52
Middlesbrough	42	12	4	5	48	35	8	5	8	38	50	49
Leeds U	42	15	2	4	55	19	4	8	9	24	34	48
Huddersfield T	42	11	6	4	34	21	6	8	7	29	29	48
Newcastle U	42	11	8	2	48	23	7	3	11	31	36	47
Bury	42	11	6	4	28	20	7	5	9	23	27	47
Scunthorpe U	42	12	7	2	35	18	4	5	12	22	41	44
Cardiff C	42	12	5	4	50	29	6	2	13	33	44	43
Southampton	42	15	3	3	52	23	2	5	14	20	44	42
Plymouth A	42	13	4	4	48	24	2	8	11	28	49	42
Norwich C	42	11	6	4	53	33	6	2	13	27	46	42
Rotherham U	42	11	3	7	34	30	6	3	12	33	44	40
Swansea T	42	13	5	3	33	17	2	4	15	18	55	39
Portsmouth	42	9	5	7	33	27	4	6	11	30	52	37
Preston NE	42	11	6	4	43	30	2	5	14	16	44	37
Derby Co	42	10	5	6	40	29	2	7	12	21	43	36
Grimsby T	42	8	6	7	34	26	3	7	11	21	40	35
Charlton A	42	8	4	9	33	38	5	1	15	29	56	31
Walsall	42	7	7	7	33	37	4	2	15	20	52	31
Luton T	42	10	4	7	45	40	1	3	17	16	44	29

DIVISION 3

	P	W	D	L	F	A	W	D	L	F	A	Pts
Northampton T	46	16	6	1	64	19	10	4	9	45	41	62
Swindon T	46	18	2	3	60	22	4	12	7	27	34	58
Port Vale	46	16	4	3	47	25	7	4	12	25	33	54
Coventry C	46	14	6	3	54	28	4	11	8	29	41	53
Bournemouth	46	11	12	0	39	16	7	4	12	24	30	52
Peterboro' U	46	11	5	7	48	33	9	6	8	45	42	51
Notts Co	46	15	3	5	46	29	4	10	9	27	45	51
Southend U	46	11	7	5	38	24	8	5	10	37	53	50
Wrexham	46	14	6	3	54	27	6	3	14	30	56	49
Hull C	46	12	6	5	40	22	7	4	12	34	47	48
Crystal P	46	10	7	6	38	22	7	6	10	30	36	47
Colchester U	46	11	6	6	41	35	7	5	11	32	58	47
QPR	46	9	6	8	44	36	8	5	10	41	40	45
Bristol C	46	10	9	4	54	38	6	4	13	46	54	45
Shrewsbury T	46	13	4	6	57	41	3	8	12	26	40	44
Millwall	46	11	6	6	50	32	4	7	12	32	55	43
Watford	46	12	3	8	55	40	5	5	13	27	45	42
Barnsley	46	12	6	5	39	28	3	5	15	24	46	41
Bristol R	46	11	8	4	45	29	4	3	16	25	59	41
Reading	46	13	4	6	51	30	3	4	16	23	48	40
Bradford	46	10	9	4	43	36	4	3	16	36	61	40
Brighton & HA	46	7	6	10	28	38	5	6	12	30	46	36
Carlisle U	46	12	4	7	41	37	1	5	17	20	52	35
Halifax T	46	8	3	12	41	51	1	9	13	23	55	30

DIVISION 4

	P	W	D	L	F	A	W	D	L	F	A	Pts
Brentford	46	18	2	3	59	31	9	6	8	39	33	62
Oldham A	46	18	4	1	65	23	6	7	10	30	37	59
Crewe A	46	15	4	4	50	21	9	7	7	36	37	59
Mansfield T	46	16	4	3	61	20	8	5	10	47	49	57
Gillingham	46	17	3	3	49	23	5	10	8	22	26	57
Torquay U	46	14	8	1	45	20	6	8	9	30	36	56
Rochdale	46	16	6	1	48	21	4	5	14	19	38	51
Tranmere R	46	15	3	5	57	25	5	7	11	24	42	50
Barrow	46	14	7	2	52	26	5	5	13	30	54	50
Workington	46	13	4	6	42	20	4	9	10	34	48	47
Aldershot	46	9	9	5	42	32	6	8	9	31	37	47
Darlington	46	13	3	7	44	33	6	3	14	28	54	44
Southport	46	11	9	3	47	35	4	5	14	25	71	44
York C	46	12	6	5	42	25	4	5	14	25	37	43
Chesterfield	46	7	10	6	43	29	6	6	11	27	35	42
Doncaster R	46	9	10	4	36	26	5	4	14	28	51	42
Exeter C	46	9	6	8	27	32	7	4	12	30	45	42
Oxford U	46	10	10	3	44	27	3	5	15	26	44	41
Stockport Co	46	9	7	7	34	29	6	4	13	22	41	41
Newport Co	46	11	6	6	44	29	3	5	15	32	61	39
Chester	46	11	5	7	31	23	4	4	15	20	43	39
Lincoln C	46	11	1	11	48	46	2	8	13	20	43	35
Bradford C	46	8	5	10	37	40	3	5	15	27	53	32
Hartlepools U	46	5	7	11	33	39	2	4	17	23	65	25

Football League Records

Top scorers: Div 1, J.Greaves (Tottenham Hotspur) 35 goals; Div 2, R.Saunders (Portsmouth) 33 goals; Div 3, A.Biggs (Bristol Rovers) 30 goals; Div 4, H.McIlmoyle (Carlisle United) 39 goals.

Scottish international forward Ian St John scored 21 goals when Liverpool won the League Championship in 1963-4. The following year his glorious headed goal won the FA Cup for the Merseysiders.

Bobby Collins, the great Scottish midfield general on whose talent Don Revie launched his great sides. Collins missed only one game as Leeds were promoted from Division Two in 1963-4.

DIVISION 1

	ARSENAL	ASTON VILLA	BIRMINGHAM C	BLACKBURN R	BLACKPOOL	BOLTON W	BURNLEY	CHELSEA	EVERTON	FULHAM	IPSWICH T	LEICESTER C	LIVERPOOL	MANCHESTER U	NOTTINGHAM F	SHEFFIELD U	SHEFFIELD W	STOKE C	TOTTENHAM H	W.B.A.	WEST HAM U	WOLVERHAMPTON W
1 ARSENAL		S10 3-0	N05 4-1	a11 0-0	N23 5-3	S07 4-3	F08 3-2	M14 2-4	D10 6-0	J18 2-2	O05 6-0	D21 0-1	D07 1-1	S21 2-1	O26 4-2	M28 1-3	M24 1-1	F29 1-1	O15 4-4	A27 3-2	N09 3-3	A24 1-3
2 ASTON VILLA	O19 2-1		M30 0-3	A31 1-2	J11 3-1	N02 3-0	a04 2-0	S14 2-0	O07 0-1	M21 2-2	N30 0-0	a18 1-3	F19 2-2	N16 4-0	D14 3-0	S28 0-1	M07 2-2	A26 1-3	S16 2-4	F22 1-0	F01 2-2	D28 2-2
3 BIRMINGHAM C	D28 1-4	M31 3-3		M13 2-2	N09 3-2	A24 2-1	J18 0-0	M28 3-4	O05 0-2	D21 0-0	S21 1-0	S04 2-0	a22 3-1	S07 1-1	N23 3-3	a25 3-0	F08 1-2	a11 0-1	F29 1-2	S11 0-1	D07 2-1	O26 2-2
4 BLACKBURN R	N30 4-1	D21 2-0	N16 3-0		M27 1-2	O09 3-0	O19 1-2	S16 2-2	M21 1-2	O05 2-0	a18 3-1	M07 5-2	A24 1-2	F22 1-3	F08 2-0	S04 2-2	N02 1-1	S21 1-0	S07 7-2	a04 0-2	D28 1-3	J18 1-1
5 BLACKPOOL	a04 0-1	S07 0-4	M20 3-0	M30 3-2		M07 2-0	F22 1-1	D26 1-5	N02 1-1	S30 1-0	O19 2-2	N30 3-3	D21 0-1	S16 1-0	O05 1-0	A24 2-2	a18 2-2	F08 1-0	J18 0-2	N16 1-0	S02 0-1	S21 1-2
6 BOLTON W	J11 1-1	M28 1-1	D14 0-2	F29 0-5	O26 1-1		M30 2-1	a11 1-0	S04 1-3	F08 2-1	S18 6-0	S14 0-0	N09 1-2	O05 0-1	F01 2-3	a08 3-0	D28 3-0	O12 3-4	D07 1-3	A31 1-2	N23 1-1	a24 0-4
7 BURNLEY	S28 0-3	N23 2-0	S14 2-1	O01 3-0	O12 1-0	M31 1-1		A27 0-0	J11 2-3	S10 4-1	D14 3-1	M10 2-0	a14 0-3	D26 6-1	D07 1-1	O26 1-2	A31 3-1	M28 1-0	a21 7-2	F01 3-2	M03 3-1	N09 1-0
8 CHELSEA	N16 3-1	J18 1-0	N02 2-3	S11 1-0	D28 1-0	N30 4-0	S04 2-0		a18 1-0	M07 1-2	F22 4-0	a06 1-0	S07 1-3	O02 1-1	M30 1-0	D21 3-2	O19 1-2	O05 3-3	S21 0-3	M21 3-1	A24 0-0	F08 2-3
9 EVERTON	O02 2-1	F28 4-2	F18 3-0	N09 2-4	M28 3-1	S11 2-0	S07 3-4	D07 1-1		A24 3-0	J18 1-1	D28 0-3	F08 3-1	D21 4-0	M14 6-1	O15 4-1	S21 3-2	N23 2-0	O26 1-0	M27 1-1	a25 2-0	a11 3-3
10 FULHAM	S14 1-4	N09 2-0	A31 2-1	F19 1-1	F29 1-1	S28 3-1	S18 2-1	O26 0-1	D14 2-2		D26 10-1	F01 2-1	M14 1-0	M27 2-2	O12 0-0	N23 3-1	A28 2-0	a25 3-3	M28 1-1	J11 1-1	a11 2-0	D07 4-1
11 IPSWICH T	F18 1-2	a11 4-3	F01 3-2	D07 0-0	a25 4-3	O01 1-3	A24 3-1	O12 1-3	S14 0-0	D28 4-2		M30 1-1	O26 1-2	S03 2-7	M28 4-3	F29 1-0	J11 1-4	N09 0-2	N23 2-3	S28 1-2	D20 3-2	a14 1-0
12 LEICESTER C	A31 7-2	D07 0-0	A28 3-0	O26 4-3	a11 2-3	J18 1-0	O05 0-0	N23 2-4	D26 2-0	S21 0-1	M31 2-1		M28 0-2	F08 3-2	F29 1-1	N09 0-1	S11 2-0	J11 2-1	a25 0-1	D14 0-2	M18 2-2	O14 0-1
13 LIVERPOOL	a18 5-0	O05 5-2	F22 2-1	D14 1-2	A31 1-2	M20 2-0	N30 2-0	J11 2-1	S28 2-1	N16 2-0	M07 6-0	N02 0-1		a04 3-0	A28 1-2	F01 6-1	O09 3-1	D26 6-1	M30 3-1	O19 1-0	S14 1-2	S16 6-0
14 MANCHESTER U	F01 3-1	a06 1-0	J11 1-2	O28 2-2	S11 3-0	F19 5-0	D28 5-1	M23 1-1	A31 5-1	M30 3-0	A28 2-0	S28 3-1	N23 0-1		a25 3-1	a13 2-1	D14 3-1	D07 5-2	N09 4-1	S14 1-0	O26 0-1	M28 2-2
15 NOTTINGHAM F	M07 2-0	A24 0-1	a04 4-0	S28 1-1	F15 0-1	S21 3-1	a18 1-3	M31 0-1	N16 2-2	F22 2-0	N02 3-1	O08 2-0	S03 0-0	O19 1-2		D26 3-3	M21 3-2	J18 0-0	D21 1-2	N30 0-3	S17 3-1	S07 3-0
16 SHEFFIELD U	N02 2-2	F08 1-1	O19 3-0	A28 0-1	D14 1-0	N16 0-1	M07 2-0	A31 1-1	F22 0-0	a04 1-0	O09 3-1	M21 0-1	S21 3-0	N30 1-2	D28 1-2		S14 1-1	S11 4-1	O05 3-3	a18 2-1	J11 2-1	M31 4-3
17 SHEFFIELD W	M30 0-4	O26 1-0	S28 2-1	M28 5-2	D07 1-0	D26 3-0	D21 3-1	F29 3-2	F01 0-3	S04 3-0	S07 3-1	O02 1-2	M04 2-2	A24 3-3	N09 3-1	J18 3-0		a08 2-0	a13 2-0	F15 2-2	O12 3-0	N23 5-0
18 STOKE C	O09 1-2	S04 2-2	N30 4-1	F01 3-1	S28 1-2	F22 0-1	N02 4-4	M04 2-0	a04 3-2	O19 1-1	M21 9-1	S07 3-3	a29 3-1	a18 3-1	S14 0-1	S18 0-2	N16 4-4		A24 2-1	M07 1-1	M31 3-0	D21 0-2
19 TOTTENHAM H	F22 3-1	J25 3-1	O02 6-1	J11 4-1	S14 6-1	a18 1-0	N16 3-2	F01 1-2	M07 2-4	N02 1-0	a04 6-3	O19 1-1	M27 1-3	M21 2-3	A31 4-1	F15 0-0	N30 1-1	D14 2-1		D28 0-2	S28 3-0	S04 4-3
20 W.B.A.	S04 4-0	O12 4-3	S18 3-1	N23 1-3	M13 2-1	D21 1-1	S21 0-0	N09 1-1	M31 4-2	S07 3-0	F08 2-1	A24 1-1	a25 2-2	J18 1-4	a11 2-3	D07 2-0	O05 1-3	O26 2-3	D26 4-4		M28 0-1	F29 3-1
21 WEST HAM U	M21 1-1	S21 0-1	a17 5-0	D26 2-8	A26 3-1	a04 2-3	O07 1-1	D14 2-2	O19 4-2	N30 1-1	A30 2-2	N16 2-2	J18 1-0	M07 0-2	S09 0-2	S07 2-3	F22 4-3	M27 4-1	F08 4-0	N02 4-2		O05 1-1
22 WOLVERHAMPTON W	D14 2-2	D26 3-3	M07 5-1	S14 1-5	F01 1-1	O19 2-2	M21 1-1	S28 4-1	N30 0-0	a18 4-0	N16 2-1	F22 1-2	S09 1-3	N02 2-0	J11 2-3	M30 1-1	a04 1-1	A31 2-1	A28 1-4	O02 0-0	F17 0-2	

DIVISION 2

	BURY	CARDIFF C	CHARLTON A	DERBY CO	GRIMSBY T	HUDDERSFIELD T	LEEDS U	LEYTON O	MANCHESTER C	MIDDLESBROUGH	NEWCASTLE U	NORTHAMPTON T	NORWICH C	PLYMOUTH A	PORTSMOUTH	PRESTON N.E.	ROTHERHAM U	SCUNTHORPE U	SOUTHAMPTON	SUNDERLAND	SWANSEA T	SWINDON T
1 BURY		S17 4-1	F22 0-2	O08 1-2	O19 1-1	M07 0-2	D21 1-2	N02 1-2	S28 1-1	a04 1-1	N30 1-2	J18 1-1	S03 4-2	S21 2-2	a13 3-2	a18 2-1	A24 4-2	M31 3-2	a21 1-5	S07 0-1	M21 3-2	F18 1-0
2 CARDIFF C	S11 2-1		M07 1-1	a04 2-1	O02 0-0	N16 2-1	S21 0-0	F22 2-1	A28 2-2	N02 1-1	M20 2-2	O05 1-0	A24 3-1	N30 3-1	S07 1-2	D26 0-4	J17 2-1	a08 3-1	a18 2-4	F08 0-2	O19 1-1	M30 1-0
3 CHARLTON A	O12 3-0	O26 5-2		F01 2-0	S17 2-1	S14 5-2	a25 0-2	M30 1-2	F15 4-3	A31 2-4	J11 1-2	M28 1-1	a11 3-1	S28 1-0	F29 0-1	S03 3-0	N09 4-3	N23 0-1	D14 2-2	D07 0-0	D28 3-1	M14 2-2
4 DERBY CO	M14 2-1	N23 2-1	S21 1-1		F08 0-0	A31 2-0	M28 1-1	S11 1-0	O26 1-3	D28 2-2	D14 1-2	J11 0-0	F29 2-1	J18 3-1	a25 3-1	O05 1-2	D07 1-4	J25 2-2	M30 3-2	O16 0-3	A28 3-0	a11 3-0
5 GRIMSBY T	M28 1-0	a15 0-2	S10 0-2	S28 1-3		F01 2-2	N09 0-2	D26 1-1	O12 1-1	J11 3-1	S14 2-1	D07 4-1	O26 3-1	F15 1-1	N23 0-3	M27 0-3	F29 1-3	a11 2-0	A31 2-2	a25 2-2	D13 1-1	A28 1-2
6 HUDDERSFIELD T	O26 2-1	F29 2-1	a07 2-1	D21 0-0	S21 1-2		O12 0-2	O05 2-1	a11 0-2	M31 1-0	D28 3-0	a13 0-1	N09 1-1	S07 4-3	D07 1-1	F08 2-2	M28 0-3	a25 3-2	S03 4-0	A24 0-2	S10 1-0	N23 2-0
7 LEEDS U	A31 3-0	F01 1-1	N02 1-1	O19 2-2	M21 3-1	F22 1-1		a04 2-1	J11 1-0	O09 2-0	M30 2-1	D14 0-0	S28 4-2	a18 1-1	S11 3-1	N16 1-1	A28 1-0	F15 1-0	M07 3-1	D26 1-1	N30 2-1	S14 0-0
8 LEYTON O	a25 1-1	a13 4-0	M26 0-3	S18 3-0	D28 0-0	F24 2-3	N23 0-2		D07 0-2	F01 3-2	S28 1-0	N09 0-0	D21 1-1	S03 1-0	O26 3-6	A24 2-2	a11 0-2	M14 2-2	S14 1-0	a06 2-5	J11 4-0	M28 2-1
9 MANCHESTER C	F08 1-1	S04 4-0	O05 1-3	M07 3-2	F22 0-4	N30 5-2	S07 3-2	a18 2-0		M17 1-0	a04 3-1	S21 3-0	M27 5-0	O09 1-1	A24 0-2	O19 2-3	D21 6-1	D26 8-1	M21 1-1	J18 0-3	N02 1-0	S18 0-0
10 MIDDLESBROUGH	N23 2-0	a24 3-1	D21 2-3	D26 3-0	S07 6-0	M30 1-1	M14 1-3	S21 2-0	F29 2-2		A26 3-0	a10 1-0	D07 0-1	A24 5-0	O12 3-1	J18 3-0	S09 2-2	M28 2-0	O05 1-0	O26 2-0	F08 2-1	N09 1-1
11 NEWCASTLE U	a11 0-4	N09 0-4	S07 5-0	A24 3-1	J18 4-0	D26 2-0	M27 0-1	F08 3-0	N23 3-1	S04 2-0		O26 2-3	a25 2-0	D21 1-1	O02 1-0	S21 2-4	a08 5-2	D07 3-1	S11 2-2	M14 1-0	O05 4-1	F29 4-1
12 NORTHAMPTON T	S13 1-2	F15 2-1	O19 1-2	S07 0-1	a18 1-2	O08 1-0	O01 0-3	M21 1-2	F01 2-1	N30 3-2	M07 2-2		S16 3-2	F18 0-0	M31 2-1	N02 0-3	D26 1-3	S03 2-0	a04 2-0	D21 5-1	N16 2-3	S28 4-0
13 NORWICH C	A28 0-1	D14 5-1	N30 1-3	N16 3-0	M07 2-0	M21 2-2	F08 2-2	A31 1-2	M30 1-2	a18 1-1	N02 3-1	S11 3-3		a04 1-1	J18 3-1	O02 2-1	S21 2-2	S07 2-1	O19 1-1	O05 2-3	F22 3-0	D26 3-2
14 PLYMOUTH A	F01 1-0	a11 1-1	F08 1-1	S14 0-0	O05 3-2	J11 0-0	D07 0-1	A28 2-2	M14 2-1	D14 2-0	A31 3-4	O12 0-3	N23 1-2		N09 0-4	S18 0-2	a25 0-0	F29 3-1	D28 1-1	O02 1-1	M30 3-2	O26 2-4
15 PORTSMOUTH	D28 3-3	J11 5-0	N16 4-1	N02 1-1	a04 2-2	a18 2-1	S18 1-1	M07 4-3	D14 2-2	F22 1-0	O19 5-2	M30 3-0	S14 1-1	M21 1-2		N30 1-2	O05 2-1	F01 3-4	S28 2-0	S04 2-4	O09 0-0	A31 1-4
16 PRESTON N.E.	D07 3-0	D28 4-0	A27 3-1	F17 0-2	M30 1-0	S28 2-1	M03 2-0	D14 0-0	M28 2-0	S14 2-2	F01 3-0	a25 2-1	M17 3-0	S09 0-0	a11 0-0		N23 2-2	O26 1-0	J11 2-1	N09 1-1	A31 3-3	O12 1-0
17 ROTHERHAM U	D14 6-2	S13 1-0	M20 5-0	a18 2-0	N16 1-0	O19 3-1	S03 2-2	N30 2-4	A31 1-2	S17 2-1	F22 2-3	D28 1-0	F01 4-0	N02 3-1	F15 4-2	a04 4-2		S28 2-1	O01 2-3	M30 2-2	M07 3-0	J11 0-0
18 SCUNTHORPE U	M26 0-0	A30 1-2	a04 1-1	M20 3-2	N30 2-2	N02 1-0	O05 0-1	O01 0-0	D28 2-4	O19 1-0	a18 2-0	A27 1-2	J11 2-2	N16 1-0	S21 1-1	M07 1-0	F08 4-3		F22 1-2	S09 1-1	S12 2-2	D14 3-0
19 SOUTHAMPTON	F29 0-1	D07 3-2	A24 6-1	a01 6-4	D21 6-0	A28 1-1	O26 1-4	J18 3-0	N09 4-2	F15 2-2	S18 2-0	N23 3-1	M28 3-0	D26 1-2	F08 2-3	S07 4-5	a27 6-1	J29 7-2		a11 0-0	S21 4-0	a25 5-1
20 SUNDERLAND	J11 4-1	S28 3-3	a18 2-1	F22 3-0	N02 3-0	D14 3-2	D28 2-0	N16 4-1	S14 2-0	M07 0-0	O09 2-1	A31 0-2	F19 0-0	O19 1-0	A28 3-0	M21 4-0	M27 2-0	S18 1-0	N30 1-2		a04 1-0	F01 6-0
21 SWANSEA T	N09 0-2	M28 3-0	D26 1-2	S03 2-1	A24 1-1	S17 1-2	a11 0-3	S07 1-0	a25 3-3	S28 2-1	M17 0-1	a07 1-1	O15 3-1	M31 2-1	a21 1-1	D20 5-1	O26 4-2	J16 4-1	M03 6-0	N23 1-2		D07 3-0
22 SWINDON T	O05 2-1	M27 1-2	O01 2-2	N30 0-0	S03 2-1	a04 1-2	J18 2-2	O19 5-0	S10 3-0	M21 2-0	N16 0-0	F08 2-3	D28 2-2	M07 2-1	D21 2-0	F22 1-4	S07 3-1	A24 3-0	N02 1-2	S21 1-0	a18 2-1	

Season 1963-64

DIVISION 3

	BARNSLEY	BOURNEMOUTH	BRENTFORD	BRISTOL C	BRISTOL R	COLCHESTER U	COVENTRY C	CREWE A	CRYSTAL P	HULL C	LUTON T	MANSFIELD T	MILLWALL	NOTTS CO	OLDHAM A	PETERBOROUGH U	PORT VALE	Q.P.R.	READING	SHREWSBURY T	SOUTHEND U	WALSALL	WATFORD	WREXHAM
1 BARNSLEY		S21 2-1	O19 1-1	N02 2-4	O29 1-2	D14 1-1	D26 1-1	a04 1-0	N30 2-0	J17 2-2	S06 3-1	a18 1-1	A31 1-1	M03 2-1	O08 2-2	M31 3-2	a20 0-0	O04 3-1	M20 0-3	M07 2-1	A27 0-1	F22 1-3	S17 0-0	F08 3-0
2 BOURNEMOUTH	F01 4-1		D28 2-0	O19 0-1	M27 1-0	J11 2-2	M21 2-1	a22 3-0	J04 4-3	S28 1-0	F22 3-1	O05 0-0	S14 4-0	N02 1-1	A28 1-0	S18 3-0	M07 3-0	O16 4-2	N30 1-2	a18 2-0	D14 1-0	a04 1-1	A31 2-0	O30 2-0
3 BRENTFORD	a25 1-1	a13 2-0		A27 1-2	O12 2-5	M14 3-1	O05 2-3	D21 2-2	S07 2-1	a28 1-3	F08 2-6	O29 4-0	O26 3-1	A24 4-1	a11 2-0	N23 2-0	O01 1-2	F29 2-2	S21 4-2	M30 0-1	M28 3-0	J18 1-1	N09 1-2	O15 9-0
4 BRISTOL C	M14 5-2	a25 3-1	S10 3-3		A24 3-0	M28 3-1	O15 0-1	J18 1-1	S21 1-1	O26 1-0	O29 5-1	M27 2-3	N09 0-0	S07 2-0	F29 3-1	O11 3-1	D21 0-0	M10 2-1	O05 0-2	O01 2-2	a11 2-2	F08 5-1	N23 2-0	F11 4-0
5 BRISTOL R	O22 1-1	M31 2-3	F22 3-1	D14 4-0		S28 3-1	a04 0-1	O19 1-2	M07 1-3	O08 4-0	a13 1-2	N30 3-2	F15 2-2	a18 4-0	A31 0-1	J11 2-2	D28 4-4	S17 0-0	a21 2-5	M21 7-0	S14 3-1	N02 3-0	F01 1-2	A27 1-1
6 COLCHESTER U	A24 4-1	S07 1-2	N02 1-2	F24 1-1	F08 2-3		O19 2-1	F22 4-0	a15 1-1	D21 1-1	a18 1-1	M07 1-1	S30 2-0	N30 4-0	O05 2-3	O28 4-1	a04 1-2	S21 2-0	D26 2-1	a20 1-0	O14 3-3	S09 0-0	M31 1-1	J18 4-1
7 COVENTRY C	D28 3-1	F29 2-2	F15 2-2	O08 2-1	N23 4-2	a25 1-0		S17 5-1	A24 5-1	F01 2-2	J18 3-3	S28 0-3	J03 3-0	S10 2-0	M28 4-1	N09 3-2	M31 1-1	a11 4-2	S07 0-0	O22 8-1	M13 2-5	D21 1-0	O26 2-2	O12 3-0
8 CREWE A	N23 1-2	N09 1-0	A31 1-1	S14 2-0	a25 4-1	O12 1-1	O02 2-2		O23 0-2	M28 1-4	A28 1-0	D14 3-2	a11 1-0	S28 0-1	J25 1-0	D26 0-0	J31 1-0	O26 2-0	M27 2-2	J11 3-2	F14 1-2	O08 0-1	F29 0-1	M14 1-2
9 CRYSTAL P	a11 1-2	M28 2-1	J11 1-0	F01 1-0	O26 1-0	F29 0-0	D14 1-1	O30 1-0		N23 2-2	O02 1-1	A31 3-1	O12 2-1	F15 2-0	a25 1-3	J25 1-0	S28 2-0	M14 1-0	S11 4-1	S14 3-0	D28 3-0	M18 1-0	O09 2-0	N09 2-1
10 HULL C	S14 2-2	F08 3-4	a18 0-0	M07 4-4	F26 0-2	A31 0-0	S21 2-1	M11 2-1	a04 1-1		M21 2-0	D26 3-1	J11 0-0	a22 4-1	M27 0-1	A28 0-0	N02 4-1	O30 3-0	F22 1-1	O19 4-2	O02 1-0	N30 3-1	D14 2-2	O05 4-2
11 LUTON T	J11 2-3	O12 1-0	S28 0-2	O23 1-4	M28 4-2	J25 3-1	S14 1-3	S11 3-3	S18 0-4	F29 2-1		F01 0-2	D28 1-3	M30 2-0	N09 1-2	M14 2-3	O09 1-0	N23 4-4	D21 2-1	F15 2-0	O26 4-1	A24 1-0	a25 2-1	a11 3-1
12 MANSFIELD T	M09 2-1	F15 1-1	O21 2-2	M30 4-0	a11 2-0	O26 1-1	F08 3-2	A24 2-1	D21 1-1	D28 2-0	S21 1-1		a25 4-1	S16 4-0	N23 1-1	M28 4-1	S09 1-1	O12 1-0	J18 2-1	O07 3-1	N09 4-1	S07 2-1	a06 1-1	F29 3-1
13 MILLWALL	a13 4-2	J18 3-0	M07 1-3	a20 0-1	O05 0-1	S16 0-1	a18 0-0	N30 1-0	F22 0-1	S07 0-1	D26 3-0	O19 0-1		a04 6-1	O28 2-1	O14 0-2	M16 3-1	F08 2-2	A24 2-0	N02 2-2	M27 1-1	M21 2-1	A26 0-3	S21 1-4
14 NOTTS CO	M28 1-1	M14 1-3	D14 2-0	J11 1-1	a09 3-4	a11 3-1	A29 0-3	F08 0-0	O05 1-1	J25 0-1	M26 1-1	O03 1-0	N23 2-0		D28 4-2	F01 0-0	S14 2-0	a25 2-2	O17 0-1	A31 0-1	F29 1-1	O24 0-1	O12 1-2	O26 3-0
15 OLDHAM A	O16 2-0	S11 2-4	N30 4-1	M21 1-2	D21 2-2	F15 2-2	J22 2-0	a18 3-2	O19 3-1	M30 1-1	a22 0-1	a04 1-0	O23 1-2	D26 2-0		S14 4-2	S07 1-0	A24 2-1	N02 3-1	F22 2-4	F01 0-3	M07 2-4	S28 1-0	O02 3-2
16 PETERBOROUGH U	M30 3-2	S30 2-1	a04 3-0	F22 4-2	S07 2-2	O21 4-0	a20 2-0	D28 3-2	a18 1-1	S09 5-1	N02 0-0	J04 1-3	O07 2-3	S21 5-1	J18 0-0		M23 1-1	D21 2-1	M07 1-0	N30 2-2	S28 3-0	O19 1-2	F15 0-1	A24 5-2
17 PORT VALE	N09 1-0	O26 0-0	S16 3-0	A31 4-1	D26 1-0	N23 0-2	M30 1-1	S21 4-0	F08 1-2	a13 1-0	O14 1-0	A26 1-0	M28 1-0	J18 0-1	J11 1-0	F29 1-2		a06 2-0	O28 0-0	D14 1-1	O12 4-1	O05 2-2	a11 0-0	a25 5-0
18 Q.P.R.	a27 2-2	O07 1-0	M20 2-2	D28 0-2	S30 1-0	F01 0-0	N30 3-6	M07 2-0	N02 3-4	O21 0-2	a29 1-1	F22 2-0	S28 2-0	O19 3-2	D14 3-2	A31 3-0	a10 3-0		a14 4-2	S09 3-4	J11 4-5	m01 3-0	S14 1-0	M27 1-0
19 READING	F29 6-1	a11 2-0	F01 4-3	F15 1-1	N09 3-1	D28 5-3	J11 2-2	M30 2-2	A28 0-0	O12 2-0	A31 1-1	S14 4-3	D14 1-0	O09 3-2	M14 0-1	O26 1-0	O23 1-0	M28 1-2		S28 2-0	a25 4-2	S18 0-1	J25 2-0	N23 2-1
20 SHREWSBURY T	O26 3-1	J25 5-2	M31 1-1	S18 2-0	F29 0-1	N09 1-1	O30 0-0	S07 3-0	J18 1-1	a25 5-1	O05 1-0	O16 2-0	M14 0-1	D21 5-2	O12 2-0	a11 0-0	A24 1-0	A26 1-2	F08 2-1		N23 2-2	S21 2-1	M28 3-0	D28 1-2
21 SOUTHEND U	S09 4-1	A24 1-1	M16 2-1	N30 1-1	J18 3-4	O07 0-0	N02 1-2	O05 1-1	D26 2-1	S16 1-1	M07 0-1	a20 2-1	M30 1-1	M20 3-1	S21 2-2	F08 2-0	F22 1-1	S07 1-3	O19 2-0	a04 7-1		a18 1-1	O21 3-0	D21 1-1
22 WALSALL	O11 4-4	N23 0-2	S14 2-2	S28 1-1	M14 2-3	A27 1-1	A31 0-3	O14 2-1	M30 2-2	a11 1-1	D14 4-0	J11 3-1	F28 0-2	O29 2-1	O26 1-1	a25 2-0	F15 2-1	N09 0-2	O01 1-1	F01 1-1	D07 2-0		D28 1-3	M28 0-2
23 WATFORD	O01 2-1	D21 3-0	a21 2-2	a04 2-2	S21 3-2	M27 3-1	M07 1-1	M21 4-1	O15 3-1	A24 3-3	O19 2-0	N02 3-0	S10 2-2	F22 2-0	F08 2-1	O05 1-2	N30 1-1	J18 3-1	a18 1-0	J04 2-1	O29 3-1	D26 5-3		S07 4-2
24 WREXHAM	S27 7-2	O23 3-4	O09 2-4	a18 1-1	S11 1-2	S14 5-4	F22 1-1	N02 1-1	a22 2-2	F15 0-1	N30 2-0	M20 2-0	F01 3-0	M07 1-0	S18 0-1	D14 2-3	O19 1-2	M30 0-1	a03 0-3	D26 2-3	A31 1-3	J04 4-0	J11 3-1	

DIVISION 4

	ALDERSHOT	BARROW	BRADFORD	BRADFORD C	BRIGHTON & HA	CARLISLE U	CHESTER	CHESTERFIELD	DARLINGTON	DONCASTER R	EXETER C	GILLINGHAM	HALIFAX T	HARTLEPOOLS U	LINCOLN C	NEWPORT CO	OXFORD U	ROCHDALE	SOUTHPORT	STOCKPORT CO	TORQUAY U	TRANMERE R	WORKINGTON	YORK C
1 ALDERSHOT		N30 8-2	O19 0-3	O23 2-3	M21 1-0	F08 3-2	M09 2-1	M07 0-2	D21 1-2	N02 4-2	S18 0-1	M30 1-1	J18 0-0	A24 4-1	O09 2-0	D26 2-0	a22 2-0	a18 1-1	S11 3-1	F22 7-0	S21 1-0	S07 5-4	O05 4-0	a04 5-2
2 BARROW	a11 0-2		O05 2-2	J25 2-3	M30 1-1	M16 2-2	S09 2-2	J01 5-2	O12 3-1	O14 0-2	O26 1-1	N09 0-3	A24 0-0	F28 1-2	a25 2-0	S21 1-1	S07 1-1	D20 1-2	M14 1-3	F07 1-2	a13 1-0	D28 1-1	J18 1-1	S30 1-2
3 BRADFORD	F29 2-1	F15 1-0		O12 1-3	S14 2-1	O26 1-1	F01 4-0	A31 0-1	N23 4-1	J11 3-1	J25 3-2	D14 1-0	N09 4-4	a11 3-1	D28 0-1	A26 2-5	O08 5-2	O23 2-2	M28 3-0	S17 2-2	a27 1-1	a25 4-2	M30 1-0	S28 1-3
4 BRADFORD C	O30 3-0	a04 7-1	F22 1-0		N02 3-1	O05 2-2	M21 1-1	O19 4-2	S07 1-2	M07 2-1	A24 1-2	S11 0-2	S21 0-0	D21 2-0	M31 4-0	O16 2-1	a18 2-1	N30 2-0	O02 2-0	J29 1-0	F08 2-1	J18 0-3	a22 0-2	J04 3-2
5 BRIGHTON & H.A.	N09 3-1	M27 2-0	J18 0-1	M14 1-2		a25 1-3	O29 0-0	S21 1-1	D07 2-0	F08 4-0	D26 1-2	F29 2-1	a11 3-0	F15 4-1	O26 5-1	D21 1-2	O01 2-1	S10 3-1	O12 1-0	S07 1-2	N23 3-0	J25 1-1	A24 1-2	O17 0-0
6 CARLISLE U	S27 4-0	a17 4-1	M07 4-0	F04 1-2	F24 0-1		a04 3-1	N02 1-0	A24 3-3	M21 6-0	A26 3-0	O15 3-1	S07 3-0	O01 7-1	O22 5-0	F22 3-3	S20 2-1	a21 1-0	M27 5-2	O18 0-0	J18 0-1	D21 5-2	D28 3-1	N30 4-0
7 CHESTER	a25 2-0	A28 2-0	S21 1-0	N09 3-0	O23 0-0	N23 4-2		F08 4-2	O16 0-1	O05 1-1	O12 2-0	O26 1-0	J25 5-2	D28 2-1	M13 3-1	S07 3-0	A24 0-2	O02 2-0	F29 5-0	J18 2-1	a11 2-1	M28 0-2	D21 2-1	M30 1-1
8 CHESTERFIELD	O26 4-0	M28 1-1	D21 1-2	F29 3-2	F01 1-0	M14 2-0	S28 1-0		a11 2-1	S14 3-3	a13 0-1	D26 0-3	a25 2-2	J25 0-2	O12 1-3	S16 0-1	M27 0-0	a06 1-1	J11 1-0	A24 1-1	N09 1-1	N23 1-1	S09 2-2	F15 1-0
9 DARLINGTON	A31 0-1	F22 3-3	a04 2-2	J11 1-2	a20 1-2	D14 1-6	O07 1-0	N30 3-2		a18 2-0	F15 1-1	F01 1-1	S09 0-0	O21 0-0	S14 1-1	M23 3-1	M07 3-0	O19 3-2	S28 2-2	J04 2-3	S16 2-0	M30 3-5	N02 1-1	D28 4-2
10 DONCASTER R	M14 1-1	O08 3-1	S07 3-2	O25 2-1	S28 1-1	N09 1-1	F15 3-2	J18 1-1	J25 10-0		F01 1-0	O12 1-2	N23 3-1	M28 2-2	F29 0-0	A24 1-1	S10 0-1	M24 2-0	D28 3-0	D21 4-1	a25 1-0	a11 1-2	S17 2-3	O22 0-0
11 EXETER C	O02 0-0	M07 0-0	a18 2-3	D14 4-1	D28 0-0	S11 1-0	F22 3-0	a21 6-1	O05 1-1	S21 3-1		J11 0-0	O09 0-0	F08 2-1	A31 0-0	a04 3-1	M21 3-2	N02 0-1	S14 1-1	N29 2-0	M27 0-0	O23 5-0	J04 2-1	O19 1-0
12 GILLINGHAM	M27 2-0	a08 3-1	A24 2-0	A28 0-0	O19 1-0	O09 2-0	M07 2-1	D28 1-0	S21 2-1	F22 1-1	S07 0-0		O05 2-1	J18 2-0	S18 1-0	a18 1-1	a15 2-0	J04 0-0	D21 5-1	a22 0-0	O23 2-0	F08 2-2	N30 3-1	N02 1-0
13 HALIFAX T	S14 3-3	D14 1-0	M21 2-1	F01 0-1	N30 2-2	J11 1-2	a18 1-0	M04 3-2	A26 2-2	a04 0-2	O14 2-0	F15 0-0		M30 4-1	S28 0-2	M07 2-0	F22 3-1	M11 3-2	O28 4-1	N02 4-2	A31 5-1	S16 2-0	O19 1-3	a20 2-0
14 HARTLEPOOLS U	D14 1-4	O19 0-0	N30 4-2	A31 1-0	O05 2-2	S16 0-6	D26 2-0	a17 1-0	J01 0-2	a20 2-1	S28 1-1	S14 0-0	M27 1-1		J11 1-2	a06 1-1	N02 2-1	M07 1-1	F01 2-3	a04 3-0	A26 1-4	M23 3-2	M21 1-2	F22 0-1
15 LINCOLN C	O16 3-3	a29 3-0	D26 3-0	M30 1-2	M07 0-2	O30 0-2	N02 3-2	F22 5-2	J18 3-1	O19 3-1	D21 1-1	O02 0-3	F08 4-0	S07 4-2		a22 2-1	N30 3-2	a04 2-0	A24 2-0	S11 1-0	O05 3-2	S21 0-1	a18 0-2	M20 3-2
16 NEWPORT CO	D28 2-1	F03 3-0	S09 4-0	O07 3-1	A31 2-0	O12 1-4	J11 0-1	S30 0-1	N09 1-2	D14 1-0	N23 0-1	a30 0-1	O26 4-2	a25 2-1	M28 4-2		M02 1-0	S28 1-1	a11 3-0	M30 3-1	F29 0-3	M14 0-2	O21 0-0	S14 0-0
17 OXFORD U	M28 1-1	J11 0-0	O16 2-1	M11 1-1	S18 1-3	F01 1-2	D14 2-1	M30 1-2	O26 5-0	A28 0-1	N09 0-2	N23 3-1	O12 2-2	M14 5-1	a11 2-0	O05 2-1		S14 1-1	a25 0-0	O30 1-0	D26 1-0	a29 0-2	F08 2-1	A31 4-4
18 ROCHDALE	F25 2-2	A31 1-3	O30 0-0	a11 1-2	A28 1-1	M28 1-1	M04 1-0	O16 0-1	F29 2-1	M31 2-2	M14 1-3	a25 2-1	D28 4-1	O26 2-0	N23 2-2	F08 0-1	J18 0-0		N09 4-0	O05 1-0	J11 1-2	O12 1-1	S21 5-0	D14 2-0
19 SOUTHPORT	A27 4-1	N02 3-3	a21 0-1	S17 3-3	F22 3-3	M30 3-0	O19 0-2	S07 0-1	F08 3-1	D26 3-0	J18 1-1	A31 1-1	O22 3-1	S21 2-1	D14 1-0	N30 4-2	a13 1-1	M20 2-1		a18 2-0	O07 1-0	O05 2-0	a04 0-3	M07 0-3
20 STOCKPORT CO	O12 2-2	S28 5-0	S30 2-1	D28 2-1	J11 1-1	F29 0-3	S14 1-0	D14 2-1	a25 2-0	A31 1-3	a11 0-0	M28 2-0	M14 1-2	N23 1-0	A26 4-0	M27 1-0	O21 0-0	F15 1-0	J25 1-4		O26 0-0	N09 1-1	O14 0-0	F01 2-0
21 TORQUAY U	F01 3-0	a22 1-1	N02 6-2	S28 4-0	a03 3-0	S14 3-1	N30 5-0	M20 1-1	O03 3-1	a08 1-0	M30 1-1	O30 1-0	D21 3-2	S11 4-2	F15 2-2	O19 8-3	D28 0-0	S07 1-0	O14 3-1	M06 4-0		A24 1-1	F21 2-1	a17 0-1
22 TRANMERE R	J10 3-0	D26 1-1	J03 3-1	S13 0-1	a17 1-2	A30 6-1	J01 3-3	a03 2-1	M27 0-2	N29 3-0	O28 2-1	S27 0-0	S30 2-2	O07 2-3	J31 3-0	N02 2-3	O18 1-3	F21 2-1	F14 2-0	M20 4-2	D14 3-1		M06 0-2	A26 1-0
23 WORKINGTON	F14 4-0	S13 4-1	M27 1-1	M28 1-0	D14 1-0	D26 2-2	A31 1-1	A27 1-2	M14 3-0	O01 4-1	a25 0-0	a11 1-0	F28 2-4	N09 2-0	J25 1-1	F24 2-0	S27 3-1	F01 3-0	N23 2-1	O08 1-1	O11 2-1	O25 4-2		J10 1-0
24 YORK C	N23 1-2	S16 1-2	F08 2-0	a25 1-0	O07 2-3	a11 0-0	M27 1-0	O05 2-0	a06 3-1	O28 3-1	F28 1-2	a27 0-1	M28 1-3	O12 0-1	N09 0-0	J18 3-0	D21 0-2	A24 0-3	O25 4-1	S20 2-0	J25 1-1	S09 1-2	S07 0-1	

LEAGUE TABLES

DIVISION 1

	P	W	D	L	F	A	W	D	L	F	A	Pts
Liverpool	42	16	0	5	60	18	10	5	6	32	27	57
Manchester U	42	15	3	3	54	19	8	4	9	36	43	53
Everton	42	14	4	3	53	26	7	6	8	31	38	52
Tottenham H	42	13	3	5	54	31	9	4	8	43	50	51
Chelsea	42	12	3	6	36	24	8	7	6	36	32	50
Sheffield W	42	15	3	3	50	24	4	8	9	34	43	49
Blackburn R	42	10	4	7	44	28	8	6	7	45	37	46
Arsenal	42	10	7	4	56	37	7	4	10	34	45	45
Burnley	42	14	3	4	46	23	3	7	11	25	41	44
WBA	42	9	6	6	43	35	7	5	9	27	26	43
Leicester C	42	9	4	8	33	27	7	7	7	28	31	43
Sheffield U	42	10	6	5	35	22	6	5	10	26	42	43
Nottingham F	42	9	5	7	34	24	7	4	10	30	44	41
West Ham U	42	8	7	6	45	38	6	5	10	24	36	40
Fulham	42	11	8	2	45	23	2	5	14	13	42	39
Wolves	42	6	9	6	36	34	6	6	9	34	46	39
Stoke C	42	9	6	6	49	33	5	4	12	28	45	38
Blackpool	42	8	6	7	26	29	5	3	13	26	44	35
Aston Villa	42	8	6	7	35	29	3	6	12	27	42	34
Birmingham C	42	7	7	7	33	32	4	0	17	21	60	29
Bolton W	42	6	5	10	30	35	4	3	14	18	45	28
Ipswich T	42	9	3	9	38	45	0	4	17	18	76	25

DIVISION 2

	P	W	D	L	F	A	W	D	L	F	A	Pts
Leeds U	42	12	9	0	35	16	12	6	3	36	18	63
Sunderland	42	16	3	2	47	13	9	8	4	34	24	61
Preston NE	42	13	7	1	37	14	10	3	8	42	40	56
Charlton A	42	11	4	6	44	30	8	6	7	32	40	48
Southampton	42	13	3	5	69	32	6	6	9	31	41	47
Manchester C	42	12	4	5	50	27	6	6	9	34	39	46
Rotherham U	42	14	3	4	52	26	5	4	12	38	52	45
Newcastle U	42	14	2	5	49	26	6	3	12	25	43	45
Portsmouth	42	9	7	5	46	34	7	4	10	33	36	43
Middlesbrough	42	14	4	3	47	16	1	7	13	20	36	41
Northampton T	42	10	2	9	35	31	6	7	8	23	29	41
Huddersfield T	42	11	4	6	31	25	4	6	11	26	39	40
Derby Co	42	10	6	5	34	27	4	5	12	22	40	39
Swindon T	42	11	5	5	39	24	3	5	13	18	45	38
Cardiff C	42	10	7	4	31	27	4	3	14	25	54	38
Leyton O	42	8	6	7	32	32	5	4	12	22	40	36
Norwich C	42	9	7	5	43	30	2	6	13	21	50	35
Bury	42	8	5	8	35	36	5	4	12	22	37	35
Swansea T	42	11	4	6	44	26	1	5	15	19	48	33
Plymouth A	42	6	8	7	26	32	2	8	11	19	35	32
Grimsby T	42	6	7	8	28	34	3	7	11	19	41	32
Scunthorpe U	42	8	8	5	30	25	2	2	17	22	57	30

DIVISION 3

	P	W	D	L	F	A	W	D	L	F	A	Pts
Coventry C	46	14	7	2	62	32	8	9	6	36	29	60
Crystal P	46	17	4	2	38	14	6	10	7	35	37	60
Watford	46	16	6	1	57	28	7	6	10	22	31	58
Bournemouth	46	17	4	2	47	15	7	4	12	32	43	56
Bristol C	46	13	7	3	52	24	7	8	8	32	40	55
Reading	46	15	5	3	49	26	6	5	12	30	36	52
Mansfield T	46	15	8	0	51	20	5	3	15	25	42	51
Hull C	46	11	9	3	45	27	5	8	10	28	41	49
Oldham A	46	13	3	7	44	35	7	5	11	29	35	48
Peterboro' U	46	13	6	4	52	27	5	5	13	23	43	47
Shrewsbury T	46	13	6	4	43	19	5	5	13	30	61	47
Bristol R	46	9	6	8	52	34	10	2	11	39	45	46
Port Vale	46	13	6	4	35	13	3	8	12	18	36	46
Southend U	46	9	10	4	42	26	6	5	12	35	52	45
QPR	46	13	4	6	47	34	5	5	13	29	44	45
Brentford	46	11	4	8	54	36	4	10	9	33	44	44
Colchester U	46	10	8	5	45	26	2	11	10	25	42	43
Luton T	46	12	2	9	42	41	4	8	11	22	39	42
Walsall	46	7	9	7	34	35	6	5	12	26	41	40
Barnsley	46	9	9	5	34	29	3	6	14	34	65	39
Millwall	46	9	4	10	33	29	5	6	12	20	38	38
Crewe A	46	10	5	8	29	26	1	7	15	21	51	34
Wrexham	46	9	4	10	50	42	4	2	17	25	65	32
Notts Co	46	7	8	8	29	26	2	1	20	16	66	27

DIVISION 4

	P	W	D	L	F	A	W	D	L	F	A	Pts
Gillingham	46	16	7	0	37	10	7	7	9	22	20	60
Carlisle U	46	17	3	3	70	20	8	7	8	43	38	60
Workington	46	15	6	2	46	19	9	5	9	30	33	59
Exeter C	46	12	9	2	39	14	8	9	6	23	23	58
Bradford C	46	15	3	5	45	24	10	3	10	31	38	56
Torquay U	46	16	6	1	60	20	4	5	14	20	34	51
Tranmere R	46	12	4	7	46	30	8	7	8	39	43	51
Brighton & HA	46	13	3	7	45	22	6	9	8	26	30	50
Aldershot	46	15	3	5	58	28	4	7	12	25	50	48
Halifax T	46	14	4	5	47	28	3	10	10	30	49	48
Lincoln C	46	15	2	6	49	31	4	7	12	18	44	47
Chester	46	17	3	3	47	18	2	5	16	18	42	46
Bradford	46	13	5	5	50	34	5	4	14	25	47	45
Doncaster R	46	11	8	4	46	23	4	4	15	24	52	42
Newport Co	46	12	3	8	35	24	5	5	13	29	49	42
Chesterfield	46	8	9	6	29	27	7	3	13	28	44	42
Stockport Co	46	12	7	4	32	19	3	5	15	18	49	42
Oxford U	46	10	7	6	37	27	4	6	13	22	36	41
Darlington	46	8	9	6	40	37	6	3	14	26	56	40
Rochdale	46	9	8	6	36	24	3	7	13	20	35	39
Southport	46	12	6	5	42	29	3	3	17	21	59	39
York C	46	9	3	11	29	26	5	4	14	23	40	35
Hartlepools U	46	8	7	8	30	36	4	2	17	24	57	33
Barrow	46	4	10	9	30	36	2	8	13	21	57	30

Football League Records

Top scorers: Div 1, A.McEvoy (Blackburn Rovers), J.Greaves (Tottenham Hotspur) 29 goals; Div 2, G.O'Brien (Southampton) 34 goals; Div 3, K.Wagstaff (Mansfield Town & Hull City) 34 goals; Div 4, A.Jeffrey (Doncaster Rovers) 36 goals.

George Best, the wayward genius whose skills lit up Manchester United's title-winning season of 1964-5.

DIVISION 1

	ARSENAL	ASTON VILLA	BIRMINGHAM C	BLACKBURN R	BLACKPOOL	BURNLEY	CHELSEA	EVERTON	FULHAM	LEEDS U	LEICESTER C	LIVERPOOL	MANCHESTER U	NOTTINGHAM F	SHEFFIELD U	SHEFFIELD W	STOKE C	SUNDERLAND	TOTTENHAM H	W.B.A.	WEST HAM U	WOLVERHAMPTON W
1 ARSENAL		A29 3-1	a06 3-0	S08 1-1	a19 3-1	O17 3-2	S26 1-3	O31 3-1	F20 2-0	F13 1-2	J23 4-3	D12 0-0	N28 2-3	O06 0-3	M06 1-1	A25 1-1	D26 3-2	S12 3-1	F23 3-1	a03 1-1	N14 0-3	J02 4-1
2 ASTON VILLA	D19 3-1		a12 3-0	S05 0-4	J16 3-2	N28 1-0	A31 2-2	O05 1-2	O31 2-0	A22 1-2	a20 1-0	F06 0-1	a28 2-1	M20 2-1	a17 2-1	S19 2-0	N14 3-0	S14 2-1	a03 1-0	O17 0-1	M31 2-3	M22 3-2
3 BIRMINGHAM C	N07 2-3	F13 0-1		a24 5-5	O24 3-0	S12 2-1	N21 1-6	S26 3-5	A26 2-2	a26 3-3	a10 2-0	O10 0-0	a19 2-4	D12 1-1	J23 1-1	F27 0-0	A29 1-2	D05 4-3	J02 1-0	S09 1-1	D26 2-1	M13 0-1
4 BLACKBURN R	S16 1-2	J02 5-1	O31 3-1		S02 4-1	F24 1-4	F13 0-3	M06 0-2	N28 2-0	D28 0-2	S26 3-1	A29 3-2	a03 0-5	a27 1-1	O17 4-0	J29 0-1	O07 1-1	M23 3-2	a19 3-1	N14 4-2	M20 4-0	S12 4-1
5 BLACKPOOL	a16 1-1	S12 3-1	M06 3-1	A24 4-2		D12 2-4	a26 3-2	O17 1-1	a03 3-0	S07 4-0	F13 1-1	J02 2-3	N14 1-2	N28 0-2	F20 2-2	A29 1-0	a17 1-1	S26 3-1	S28 1-1	M20 3-0	O31 1-2	J23 1-1
6 BURNLEY	F27 2-1	a10 2-2	J16 2-0	O10 1-1	A22 2-2		a24 6-2	S05 1-1	D26 4-0	O24 0-1	N07 2-1	D05 1-5	O06 0-0	S08 2-2	D19 3-1	M13 4-1	a20 1-0	M27 0-0	A25 2-2	F06 0-1	S19 3-2	N21 1-1
7 CHELSEA	F06 2-1	A26 2-1	a03 3-1	O03 5-1	D26 2-0	O31 0-1		N14 5-1	S12 1-0	S19 2-0	J02 4-1	a16 4-0	S30 0-2	F22 0-1	M22 3-0	S09 1-1	O17 4-0	A29 3-1	M10 3-1	a17 2-2	N28 0-3	D12 2-1
8 EVERTON	a24 1-0	M13 3-1	F06 1-1	O24 2-3	F27 0-0	J02 2-1	M31 1-1		a16 2-0	N07 0-1	N21 2-2	a12 2-1	S08 3-3	A25 1-0	S12 1-1	O10 1-1	D12 1-1	a10 1-1	A29 4-1	D26 3-2	O03 1-1	D05 5-0
9 FULHAM	D05 3-4	a24 1-1	S02 3-1	a09 3-2	N21 3-3	D28 0-1	J16 1-2	a19 1-1		M13 2-2	O10 5-2	N07 1-1	S05 2-1	J23 4-1	S16 1-2	M27 2-0	S26 1-4	F27 1-0	F13 4-1	D19 3-1	A22 1-2	O24 2-0
10 LEEDS U	N11 3-1	D12 1-0	N14 4-1	D26 1-1	S16 3-0	M15 5-1	J23 2-2	M20 4-1	S30 2-2		S12 3-2	A26 4-2	a17 0-1	S26 1-2	O31 4-1	a20 2-0	a05 3-1	J02 2-1	O17 3-1	N28 1-0	a03 2-1	A29 3-2
11 LEICESTER C	S19 2-3	a19 1-1	N28 4-4	F06 2-3	O05 3-2	M20 0-2	S05 1-1	a03 2-1	F24 5-1	J16 2-2		S09 2-0	A29 2-2	O17 3-2	N14 0-2	D26 2-2	a26 0-1	D12 0-1	O31 4-2	S30 4-2	a17 1-0	A26 3-2
12 LIVERPOOL	A22 3-2	S26 5-1	F24 4-3	D19 3-2	S05 2-2	a17 1-1	a19 2-0	S19 0-4	M20 3-2	S02 2-1	O13 0-1		O31 0-2	N14 2-0	O07 3-1	J16 4-2	a03 3-2	D28 0-0	N28 1-1	a06 0-3	O17 2-2	F13 2-1
13 MANCHESTER U	a26 3-1	O24 7-0	D16 1-1	N21 3-0	M22 2-0	F13 3-2	M13 4-0	S16 2-1	M15 4-1	D05 0-1	a12 1-0	a24 3-0		S12 3-0	D28 1-1	N07 1-0	J23 1-1	O10 1-0	S26 4-1	A22 2-2	S02 3-1	F27 3-0
14 NOTTINGHAM F	M13 3-0	N07 4-2	A22 4-3	D05 2-5	a10 2-0	S15 3-1	O10 2-2	S01 3-1	S19 2-3	F06 0-0	F27 2-1	a01 2-2	J16 2-2		a19 0-0	N21 2-2	F13 3-1	O24 5-2	D26 1-2	S05 0-0	D19 3-2	a24 0-2
15 SHEFFIELD U	O24 4-0	D05 4-2	S19 3-1	F27 1-1	O10 1-3	A29 2-0	N07 0-2	J16 0-0	S09 1-1	a24 0-3	M26 0-2	M13 3-0	D26 0-1	a20 0-2		J02 2-3	A26 0-1	N21 3-0	D12 3-3	O03 1-1	F06 2-1	a10 0-2
16 SHEFFIELD W	S02 2-1	M15 3-1	O17 5-2	A22 1-0	D19 4-1	S23 5-1	S16 2-3	F20 0-1	N14 1-1	a19 3-0	D28 0-0	S12 1-0	M20 1-0	a03 0-0	S05 0-2		N28 1-1	F13 2-0	a17 1-0	O31 1-1	M06 2-0	S26 2-0
17 STOKE C	D28 4-1	M27 2-1	M17 2-1	M13 1-1	D05 4-2	a19 2-0	F27 0-2	A22 0-2	F06 3-1	O10 2-3	O24 3-3	N21 1-1	S19 1-2	O03 1-1	S02 0-1	a10 4-1		a24 3-1	S09 2-0	J16 2-0	S05 3-1	N07 0-2
18 SUNDERLAND	J16 0-2	S09 2-2	a17 2-1	S19 1-0	F06 1-0	N14 3-2	D19 3-0	N28 4-0	O17 0-0	S05 3-3	A22 3-3	D26 2-3	F24 1-0	M06 4-0	a03 3-1	a28 3-0	O31 2-2		M20 2-1	S02 2-2	F20 3-2	a16 1-2
19 TOTTENHAM H	O10 3-1	N21 4-0	S05 4-1	a16 5-2	M13 4-1	S02 4-1	O24 1-1	D19 2-2	O05 3-0	F27 0-0	a24 6-2	a09 3-0	F06 1-0	D28 4-0	A22 2-0	D05 3-2	S16 2-1	N07 3-0		S19 1-0	J16 3-2	M27 7-4
20 W.B.A.	N21 0-0	F27 3-1	S16 0-2	M26 0-0	N07 1-3	S26 1-2	D05 0-2	M23 4-0	A29 2-2	a12 1-2	M13 6-0	O24 3-0	D12 1-1	J02 2-2	F13 0-1	a24 1-0	S12 5-3	A26 4-1	J23 2-0		a19 4-2	O10 5-1
21 WEST HAM U	M27 2-1	O10 3-0	D28 2-1	N07 1-1	a23 2-1	J23 3-2	a12 3-2	F13 0-1	D12 2-0	N21 3-1	D05 0-0	F27 2-1	A24 3-1	A28 2-3	S26 3-1	O24 1-2	J02 0-1	M13 2-3	S12 3-2	a16 6-1		S07 5-0
22 WOLVERHAMPTON W	S05 0-1	D26 0-1	S30 0-2	J16 4-2	S19 1-2	a03 1-2	A22 0-3	a17 2-4	M30 0-0	D19 0-1	S02 1-1	a26 1-3	O17 2-4	O31 1-2	N28 1-0	F06 3-1	M20 3-1	a20 3-0	N14 3-1	M15 3-2	S14 4-3	

Midfielder Dave Hilley was outstanding in Newcastle's promotion season. Hugely creative, he also scored 12 goals as the Magpies topped Division Two.

DIVISION 2

	BOLTON W	BURY	CARDIFF C	CHARLTON A	COVENTRY C	CRYSTAL P	DERBY CO	HUDDERSFIELD T	IPSWICH T	LEYTON O	MANCHESTER C	MIDDLESBROUGH	NEWCASTLE U	NORTHAMPTON T	NORWICH C	PLYMOUTH A	PORTSMOUTH	PRESTON N.E.	ROTHERHAM U	SOUTHAMPTON	SWANSEA T	SWINDON T
1 BOLTON W		F13 0-1	a28 1-0	M29 1-1	A29 1-3	O10 3-0	N07 3-1	D15 1-0	J23 0-0	a24 0-0	a10 4-0	S16 4-2	a19 1-1	D26 0-0	F27 5-2	S26 6-1	N21 3-2	S12 5-1	O24 2-0	S02 3-0	M13 2-1	M26 1-1
2 BURY	O02 2-1		a03 1-2	a20 2-0	N13 5-0	F06 3-1	D19 2-1	M19 0-2	M05 0-1	S08 2-1	D28 0-2	F23 3-2	O17 1-2	a17 1-4	S19 1-0	O06 0-2	S01 1-1	N27 1-1	a27 0-1	O30 3-3	S04 2-2	A22 6-1
3 CARDIFF C	S05 1-3	N21 4-0		N07 2-1	a19 3-1	a10 0-0	O10 2-1	S16 1-1	A22 0-0	M27 0-2	M12 2-2	J15 6-1	S19 1-1	F06 0-2	D05 1-3	D19 4-0	O24 1-0	A26 3-3	a24 3-2	M24 2-2	a06 5-0	F27 2-0
4 CHARLTON A	M06 1-3	a19 1-2	M22 2-2		O31 3-0	S15 1-2	J16 1-3	a17 0-0	a03 4-0	D28 2-0	A22 2-1	O06 0-2	S01 0-1	F20 1-1	O03 2-1	N28 3-2	D19 3-3	N14 2-3	F06 1-1	O17 2-5	S19 1-0	S05 3-2
5 COVENTRY C	D19 0-0	M27 2-1	a20 0-2	M13 2-0		N21 0-0	S15 0-2	O03 2-3	S01 5-3	N07 1-1	O24 2-2	S05 3-0	J16 5-4	S19 0-1	a10 3-0	A22 2-0	F27 1-2	D28 3-0	D05 3-5	F06 1-1	a24 3-0	O10 3-2
6 CRYSTAL P	a07 2-0	S26 0-2	N28 0-0	S30 3-1	a03 2-2		A22 2-3	N14 3-0	O07 1-1	F13 1-0	a19 1-1	O17 3-1	a17 1-1	O31 1-2	J16 2-0	S19 2-1	D26 4-2	M17 1-0	S05 2-1	M20 0-2	D19 3-3	S02 3-1
7 DERBY CO	M20 2-3	A29 3-1	F20 1-0	S12 4-4	S09 2-1	D12 3-3		O07 2-0	a17 2-3	J02 1-0	J30 2-0	N14 3-3	a03 0-3	N28 2-2	A26 0-1	O31 3-2	S26 4-0	O17 3-1	M24 2-2	M06 2-1	a19 3-4	F13 4-1
8 HUDDERSFIELD T	A22 1-1	N07 0-2	S29 3-1	O24 0-1	F13 2-1	M27 2-0	a24 3-1		D28 0-0	M13 0-0	F27 1-0	M30 1-0	S05 0-1	J16 2-0	N21 0-0	S02 1-2	O10 2-1	a19 3-0	a10 1-0	S19 0-3	D05 4-0	F06 2-1
9 IPSWICH T	S19 1-4	D05 1-0	D12 1-1	N21 1-1	A25 1-3	a24 3-2	O24 2-1	D26 3-2		a10 1-1	M27 4-1	F06 5-2	O03 3-1	S15 0-0	J02 3-0	J16 2-2	N07 7-0	A29 1-5	O10 4-4	a19 2-0	F27 3-0	M13 0-0
10 LEYTON O	S28 3-1	S14 1-0	N14 1-3	D26 4-2	a28 1-3	O03 0-1	S05 1-4	O31 1-0	N28 0-0		A31 4-3	a16 1-1	F20 2-1	O17 2-2	F06 2-3	M31 2-0	A22 5-2	a03 2-1	S19 2-1	a17 0-0	J16 2-3	D19 0-3
11 MANCHESTER C	N28 2-4	D26 0-0	O31 2-0	a28 2-1	a17 1-1	a16 0-2	S19 2-0	O17 2-3	N14 4-0	A26 6-0		M06 1-1	O14 3-0	A29 0-2	S09 0-2	a03 2-1	S05 2-0	M20 4-3	O03 2-1	F20 3-1	F06 1-0	J16 1-2
12 MIDDLESBROUGH	S07 5-2	O10 3-3	S12 0-0	a24 1-2	J02 2-3	F27 0-0	M27 1-2	A29 0-0	S26 2-4	a19 2-0	D05 0-1		D26 0-2	A24 1-0	O24 2-0	F13 1-3	a09 4-1	J23 1-1	M13 3-5	D12 4-1	N07 4-0	N21 4-1
13 NEWCASTLE U	a16 2-0	F27 2-3	J23 2-0	A24 1-1	S12 2-0	O24 2-0	N21 2-2	J02 2-1	F13 2-2	O10 5-0	a24 0-0	D28 2-1		D12 5-0	M13 2-0	S16 2-1	D05 3-0	S26 5-2	N07 3-1	A29 2-1	M27 3-1	a10 1-0
14 NORTHAMPTON T	M02 4-0	O24 2-0	S26 1-0	O10 1-0	J23 1-1	M13 1-1	a10 2-2	S11 3-2	S29 3-2	F27 2-0	D19 2-0	S01 1-1	S08 1-0		N07 0-0	a20 3-1	a24 1-1	F13 2-1	M27 1-0	J02 2-2	N21 2-1	D05 2-1
15 NORWICH C	O17 3-2	J23 1-1	M06 2-1	F13 2-0	N28 1-0	S12 1-2	S02 5-2	a03 0-2	S05 2-1	S26 2-0	S16 4-1	a17 2-0	O31 1-1	M20 1-1		F20 3-0	a20 3-1	O07 4-2	D19 3-0	N14 2-2	A22 2-1	J30 3-1
16 PLYMOUTH A	F06 1-3	a24 2-2	A29 3-1	a10 1-5	D12 2-3	J23 1-1	M13 1-1	A26 0-0	S12 1-1	D05 1-1	N21 3-2	O03 1-0	S30 2-1	a19 5-2	O10 1-0		M27 2-1	J02 0-1	F27 1-1	F17 4-0	O24 2-1	N07 2-1
17 PORTSMOUTH	a03 3-0	A26 2-1	a17 1-0	A29 2-3	O17 0-2	D28 1-1	F06 3-1	F20 3-0	M20 0-2	D12 1-1	J02 1-1	N28 2-1	M06 1-2	O07 3-3	a19 4-0	N14 0-1		O31 1-0	S30 2-0	S12 0-3	O03 1-0	S19 5-0
18 PRESTON N.E.	J16 2-2	a10 2-2	A31 1-1	M26 2-1	D26 3-2	D05 1-0	F27 2-2	a20 2-0	D19 4-1	N21 3-0	N07 2-5	S19 4-3	F06 2-0	O03 2-2	a24 3-1	S05 1-3	M13 6-1		A22 0-0	N02 0-0	O10 2-2	O24 2-1
19 ROTHERHAM U	a17 0-0	S12 3-0	O06 3-1	S26 3-2	M06 0-2	J02 1-0	D28 1-1	N28 2-3	F20 2-2	a06 3-0	F13 0-0	O31 2-3	M20 1-1	N14 1-1	A29 4-0	O17 4-2	S15 1-0	D12 2-2		a03 1-3	A25 4-2	a19 1-0
20 SOUTHAMPTON	A26 3-2	M13 3-1	F13 1-1	F27 4-0	S26 4-1	N07 0-1	D05 3-3	J23 3-3	a21 1-1	O24 2-2	O10 1-0	A22 0-3	D19 0-1	S05 2-0	M27 1-0	D26 5-0	J16 2-2	S16 3-1	N21 6-1		a10 3-1	a24 2-1
21 SWANSEA T	O31 2-0	J02 2-2	D26 3-2	J23 1-3	S29 1-1	A29 2-1	a20 2-1	M06 2-2	O17 1-1	S12 2-5	S26 3-0	M20 1-2	N14 3-1	a03 1-2	D12 0-0	a17 3-0	F13 0-0	M23 4-0	S01 0-3	N28 3-3		S15 4-0
22 SWINDON T	N14 1-3	D12 2-0	O17 3-3	J02 2-0	F20 4-1	A25 2-0	O03 4-2	S26 4-1	O31 3-1	A29 1-0	S12 0-1	a03 0-1	N28 1-6	M23 4-2	D26 0-1	M20 2-3	J23 0-0	a17 2-2	a16 3-2	O13 2-1	S08 3-0	

Season 1964-65

DIVISION 3

	BARNSLEY	BOURNEMOUTH	BRENTFORD	BRISTOL C	BRISTOL R	CARLISLE U	COLCHESTER U	EXETER C	GILLINGHAM	GRIMSBY T	HULL C	LUTON T	MANSFIELD T	OLDHAM A	PETERBOROUGH U	PORT VALE	Q.P.R.	READING	SCUNTHORPE U	SHREWSBURY T	SOUTHEND U	WALSALL	WATFORD	WORKINGTON
1 BARNSLEY		O10 2-2	N07 3-1	N03 1-2	M13 0-2	a10 1-2	M26 1-2	F27 0-0	S15 1-0	M30 1-0	S30 1-1	J30 3-0	a24 2-3	O24 0-1	D28 3-2	N21 0-2	A22 0-0	S04 1-1	S25 2-0	D18 6-2	J16 1-4	F13 0-1	O20 4-0	a20 0-3
2 BOURNEMOUTH	F20 1-0		a19 0-1	N28 1-2	S30 1-1	F06 0-4	O14 3-1	A26 2-2	a03 1-2	S05 1-2	J09 2-3	S19 4-0	J16 2-0	S09 0-0	D19 0-1	O03 3-0	M06 2-0	A22 3-2	O17 2-1	O28 2-1	D26 2-1	a17 4-0	O31 0-0	M20 4-0
3 BRENTFORD	M20 1-0	a16 2-1		D26 2-1	S26 1-1	D19 6-1	J16 1-0	O20 2-1	S19 2-0	S15 2-0	O27 1-3	A22 2-2	A31 1-0	F13 2-2	O06 3-1	S05 4-0	F20 5-2	a17 2-1	a27 4-0	O17 2-0	O31 2-1	a03 0-0	N28 5-1	a07 3-0
4 BRISTOL C	A25 5-1	a09 0-0	M02 3-2		F13 2-1	O23 1-2	O10 1-1	J30 1-1	S26 1-2	M26 4-0	J23 1-2	M13 1-0	N07 1-1	a24 2-0	N21 3-1	F27 3-0	O13 2-0	S29 2-0	D12 2-2	a20 3-0	S08 4-0	A29 5-1	J02 1-1	S12 5-0
5 BRISTOL R	O31 1-0	O06 4-2	F06 1-2	O03 1-1		S05 5-2	S19 2-2	a16 1-1	O27 3-0	S01 5-3	M06 1-1	D19 3-2	A22 4-1	O20 0-0	S15 4-0	J16 4-0	D26 3-1	O17 1-0	M20 2-0	F23 0-0	a17 2-2	M16 0-1	a03 1-0	N28 4-0
6 CARLISLE U	N28 4-0	S26 3-4	A28 0-1	a16 1-1	J02 1-2		D12 4-1	M09 2-1	O17 3-1	J09 3-1	F20 0-0	O07 1-1	a20 3-0	S12 2-0	F13 2-1	A24 1-1	O30 2-0	M16 1-2	M06 3-1	M19 2-1	a02 4-3	O27 2-1	S08 1-1	D26 1-0
7 COLCHESTER U	J09 4-1	O19 4-3	S12 0-3	F20 2-3	J23 1-1	A22 0-1		F13 1-1	D28 2-1	O05 0-1	S05 1-2	A31 0-1	S14 0-1	S26 2-2	a16 0-1	D19 2-0	O17 1-2	O31 2-2	a03 2-1	a17 0-4	M20 3-1	N28 2-1	M06 0-0	O26 1-1
8 EXETER C	O17 3-0	a28 1-3	O14 0-0	M06 0-1	a19 0-1	S19 0-0	O03 2-0		N28 1-1	D19 4-1	a03 0-2	J16 5-1	S05 2-3	O08 2-1	A22 4-2	F06 2-1	M31 2-2	D26 2-2	J08 1-3	S16 0-1	F20 1-1	O31 0-1	M20 1-0	M22 0-0
9 GILLINGHAM	S09 1-0	N21 1-1	J23 1-0	F06 2-0	a24 1-3	F27 1-0	D26 2-1	a10 0-1		N07 0-0	S12 1-0	O24 5-0	M13 0-0	J30 2-1	M26 2-0	O10 2-0	O03 2-2	a16 2-1	A26 0-0	O21 5-0	S30 1-0	D12 4-0	A29 5-2	J02 5-1
10 GRIMSBY T	S19 3-2	J02 2-2	S09 2-1	M09 0-2	A25 1-1	O21 1-1	S30 2-0	A29 2-1	M20 1-1		O31 3-0	O03 2-2	F06 1-1	D12 3-1	S12 2-0	a16 2-0	a03 0-0	M06 1-1	a06 3-0	N28 2-2	O28 1-0	F20 2-2	O17 1-0	a17 0-1
11 HULL C	O07 7-0	M27 2-1	a24 2-1	S19 3-2	J30 3-2	O09 1-0	J02 5-1	N21 3-1	J16 1-1	M13 3-3		F27 3-1	O24 1-1	a10 2-1	N07 0-2	D28 4-0	F06 3-1	O12 1-0	S09 1-2	O03 1-2	a19 0-0	A26 2-0	D12 1-1	A29 2-2
12 LUTON T	a07 5-1	F17 0-1	D12 4-2	O31 0-0	A29 0-2	O01 1-1	A26 3-1	S12 1-2	a17 0-2	F13 1-1	O17 1-3		O21 1-1	J02 2-0	S26 1-1	S09 1-1	M20 2-0	a03 3-1	O28 1-1	M10 2-7	N28 0-1	a16 1-3	D26 2-4	a29 0-0
13 MANSFIELD T	O26 4-3	S12 0-0	A24 4-1	M20 3-0	D12 3-0	a19 2-0	S07 0-1	J02 2-1	O31 3-1	S26 2-2	a17 2-1	O12 2-0		A29 4-1	M29 0-0	S28 2-2	M15 8-1	N28 2-1	O03 3-2	a03 1-0	a05 6-1	D28 2-0	F20 3-0	O17 3-5
14 OLDHAM A	a17 1-1	S15 1-1	O03 1-1	O28 7-3	O14 1-2	J16 2-3	F06 3-1	S28 2-0	M06 2-0	A22 1-5	N28 2-1	S05 0-2	D19 2-1		S01 3-1	S19 0-1	a16 5-3	F20 1-2	O31 2-1	D28 1-3	O17 0-2	M20 1-3	J27 2-0	a03 0-2
15 PETERBOROUGH U	D26 4-1	A29 4-3	S28 3-1	a03 0-1	S07 3-1	O03 1-2	a19 4-1	D12 0-0	a28 1-0	J16 3-1	M20 2-1	F06 2-0	S19 4-5	A24 5-0		O12 2-2	N28 6-1	O26 2-1	M08 2-2	M15 4-1	S05 4-2	O17 3-2	a17 2-1	O31 0-4
16 PORT VALE	a03 2-0	F13 1-2	J02 2-1	O17 1-2	S12 1-1	A31 1-3	A29 1-2	S26 0-1	F20 0-4	a20 2-3	D26 0-3	S14 1-0	O05 2-2	M15 2-1	O19 0-1		a17 0-0	M20 2-0	N28 0-1	O31 1-1	J08 2-2	a26 2-1	O26 2-2	M29 2-0
17 Q.P.R.	D11 3-2	J29 1-1	O09 1-3	O19 1-0	D28 3-1	M12 1-2	F26 5-0	a23 0-0	F13 3-1	N21 1-1	S25 2-1	N06 7-1	M26 2-0	a19 1-1	a10 3-2	O23 3-1		S07 0-1	A28 2-1	O05 2-1	A24 2-0	J01 1-0	S11 2-2	a05 2-1
18 READING	J02 1-1	D12 1-0	O24 1-1	O07 1-1	F27 1-1	M27 1-2	M13 1-1	a07 2-2	a19 3-0	M24 2-0	O21 3-3	N21 1-2	a10 2-1	O10 1-0	a24 4-2	N07 1-1	S16 5-3		S12 2-0	A26 3-1	A29 2-0	J23 0-2	S26 6-2	F13 1-0
19 SCUNTHORPE U	F05 2-3	F26 3-1	M26 2-0	A22 5-2	N07 1-1	J29 0-1	N20 0-0	O24 0-0	N03 2-3	D26 2-1	S15 1-1	a24 8-1	F12 0-1	M12 1-1	O10 2-3	a09 0-0	D18 2-1	J15 1-1		S04 3-2	S18 2-1	O13 4-0	a20 0-2	S29 1-1
20 SHREWSBURY T	A29 3-3	a24 1-2	F27 1-0	a19 1-5	O10 2-1	N07 2-2	O24 3-0	S08 1-0	O13 2-0	a10 1-3	F13 0-4	M26 0-2	N03 1-1	D26 1-3	a07 1-1	M13 0-0	a12 3-2	S01 4-0	J02 3-2		D12 1-3	S11 3-1	J23 2-2	S26 6-1
21 SOUTHEND U	S12 2-0	D28 2-1	M13 0-1	S14 0-4	O24 6-3	N21 1-0	N07 6-3	O10 0-0	O05 3-1	a24 4-0	a16 2-1	a10 5-0	J30 1-4	F27 6-1	J02 2-0	M26 2-1	A31 0-0	D19 2-2	J23 0-1	A22 1-0		S26 0-0	F13 0-1	O12 3-0
22 WALSALL	O03 1-1	O24 0-1	N21 4-3	D19 2-4	M27 2-0	D05 1-0	a10 2-1	M13 2-1	A22 0-1	O10 1-0	a06 3-3	a19 0-1	D26 2-1	N07 1-2	F27 0-1	J30 0-0	S05 4-1	S19 4-1	O20 1-2	J16 1-1	F06 2-3		O06 0-4	S15 1-4
23 WATFORD	M16 1-1	M13 2-0	a10 1-1	S05 2-2	N21 1-1	S17 0-0	J30 3-0	N07 1-0	D19 1-2	F27 1-1	A22 2-1	D28 2-0	O10 3-1	M27 3-2	O24 1-1	a24 1-0	J16 0-2	F06 5-1	a16 5-0	S19 2-2	O03 2-1	S29 3-0		M08 3-2
24 WORKINGTON	a16 0-0	N07 2-0	M17 1-1	J15 1-0	a09 2-1	D28 0-1	a23 1-0	M26 0-1	S05 1-1	O24 2-2	D19 1-3	O09 1-0	F26 1-5	N21 0-0	M12 1-0	A22 4-1	S18 0-0	O02 0-2	O06 2-0	F05 2-2	O19 3-1	O28 3-1	A26 2-0	

DIVISION 4

	ALDERSHOT	BARROW	BRADFORD	BRADFORD C	BRIGHTON & HA	CHESTER	CHESTERFIELD	CREWE A	DARLINGTON	DONCASTER R	HALIFAX T	HARTLEPOOLS U	LINCOLN C	MILLWALL	NEWPORT CO	NOTTS CO	OXFORD U	ROCHDALE	SOUTHPORT	STOCKPORT CO	TORQUAY U	TRANMERE R	WREXHAM	YORK C
1 ALDERSHOT		J30 2-1	A26 1-1	O28 1-1	O31 0-2	A22 3-1	S05 2-0	O03 5-2	a19 0-1	D19 3-0	S19 2-0	a03 3-0	M30 3-2	a17 0-0	F06 2-1	J16 1-2	M20 4-1	N28 1-2	S09 0-3	F20 2-0	M17 2-5	S30 3-0	O19 5-0	O17 1-0
2 BARROW	M27 2-0		N21 2-1	O03 1-0	D12 1-4	a16 2-1	M13 1-2	D28 1-2	J02 3-1	N07 1-2	F27 1-0	J16 4-2	A24 2-2	F06 0-5	O10 1-4	O24 2-0	A29 1-1	S19 2-2	a10 1-1	O19 0-1	S28 2-1	a24 0-2	J11 0-2	S07 0-2
3 BRADFORD	A31 3-1	a03 3-2		S15 3-3	M20 2-0	D28 3-1	D22 1-0	F06 2-3	O03 3-1	A22 5-2	D05 5-1	N28 4-0	O31 3-1	O27 4-0	S19 2-2	S05 2-2	J30 1-0	a17 0-0	O13 0-0	O17 1-0	F20 4-2	a21 1-1	S29 0-0	M06 0-0
4 BRADFORD C	a24 2-0	F13 1-3	S09 0-2		a06 4-1	A25 1-3	a10 0-0	M13 5-2	O24 2-3	F03 0-3	M27 3-1	a19 4-0	S12 0-1	O21 1-2	N07 1-0	N21 0-2	S26 2-1	O07 0-2	D26 2-1	A29 1-1	D12 2-3	F27 1-2	O10 4-1	J02 1-2
5 BRIGHTON & H.A.	M13 2-0	A22 3-1	N07 2-2	S19 3-3		F06 4-4	F27 5-0	J09 3-1	a26 3-1	O24 1-1	D26 2-1	D19 5-0	O20 4-0	J16 2-0	S15 1-0	O10 6-0	A25 0-0	S05 3-0	M26 3-1	a19 3-1	O03 3-1	a10 2-1	N21 5-1	O06 3-1
6 CHESTER	D12 0-2	a19 4-1	D26 3-0	F10 3-1	S26 3-1		F24 4-0	N07 2-2	M13 4-5	a24 3-0	N21 1-0	O07 4-0	J23 5-1	S16 3-1	M26 4-3	a10 4-1	F13 2-1	M10 0-1	O10 3-1	J02 4-0	A29 0-1	O24 3-2	F27 6-1	S12 4-1
7 CHESTERFIELD	J02 0-1	O31 2-0	A29 2-4	N28 3-1	O17 1-1	a17 1-3		S28 2-1	M29 3-0	S12 1-0	O03 3-0	M20 3-1	F20 1-0	a03 2-3	a16 2-1	F06 0-0	M06 2-1	J30 1-1	D12 1-2	S19 2-0	a05 2-1	S07 1-0	A24 0-0	D28 1-1
8 CREWE A	F13 4-1	D26 6-2	S26 1-1	O31 2-1	O28 3-2	M20 5-1	O07 0-2		A29 1-2	a16 4-4	S08 2-2	F20 2-3	a17 5-0	M06 1-1	A26 1-1	M10 2-1	D12 2-2	O17 1-1	J23 4-1	a03 3-2	J29 2-0	J02 1-1	S12 1-0	N28 2-3
9 DARLINGTON	J01 4-1	S05 1-2	F13 1-2	M22 3-1	a17 2-0	O31 2-0	O19 2-2	D19 0-2		O05 2-2	A31 5-1	F22 2-3	N28 3-1	O17 1-3	A22 0-1	S14 5-1	O26 2-0	F20 2-0	S26 3-2	M15 3-2	M20 1-2	S12 2-1	a05 5-1	a03 1-0
10 DONCASTER R	A29 1-0	M20 4-2	D12 1-1	a17 0-0	M06 2-1	a06 1-4	J16 2-0	a19 3-1	S29 6-3		F06 4-0	J30 0-1	O17 1-2	N28 4-0	O03 1-0	S18 0-0	O31 2-2	a03 2-2	A25 1-2	D26 3-0	S05 2-0	a27 1-0	S08 1-1	F20 4-3
11 HALIFAX T	J23 3-3	O17 3-2	S12 2-3	J30 0-3	D28 1-1	a03 3-4	F13 2-1	S15 2-0	A25 4-0	S26 2-4		M16 2-1	O06 2-1	M20 1-2	O19 2-0	a19 1-1	F20 1-3	O31 1-2	J02 2-1	a17 0-1	N28 0-1	D12 0-1	A29 2-1	O27 1-1
12 HARTLEPOOLS U	N21 1-1	S12 3-0	a10 2-0	a16 2-2	A29 1-1	S28 1-1	N07 1-1	O10 2-4	D26 4-3	M29 1-1	O24 4-0		D12 3-0	O03 1-0	F27 2-4	M13 2-2	J02 1-1	F06 1-1	a05 2-1	S07 4-3	S21 1-0	J23 2-0	a24 1-0	A24 2-2
13 LINCOLN C	O24 3-1	S23 1-0	M12 2-2	J16 0-2	O14 0-1	S19 2-2	O10 0-2	F17 1-2	a10 2-0	F27 0-2	S30 2-3	A22 4-2		S05 2-2	a24 4-3	D26 1-0	S09 0-2	D18 1-1	N07 3-0	O03 6-0	F06 0-1	N20 1-2	M26 0-2	a16 0-1
14 MILLWALL	a05 5-0	S26 3-1	a24 1-0	O12 3-0	S12 2-0	S07 1-0	N21 4-2	O24 0-0	F27 1-1	a10 1-1	N07 5-1	F13 0-0	J02 2-1		M13 4-0	M27 4-1	J23 2-2	a16 0-0	S29 0-0	D12 1-0	A24 2-2	O10 1-0	D26 2-2	A29 1-1
15 NEWPORT CO	S26 2-1	F20 2-2	J23 4-3	M19 4-2	S07 1-1	J30 0-1	a19 4-1	A31 2-2	D12 2-1	F13 1-0	O12 0-2	O17 2-0	O26 7-0	O31 2-2		S28 3-1	D26 0-3	M29 2-3	S12 5-0	N28 2-0	a03 4-0	A29 1-1	J02 2-0	a17 2-0
16 NOTTS CO	S12 0-0	M06 4-1	J02 3-3	a03 1-0	F20 1-2	N28 1-1	S26 5-1	O22 2-0	S10 4-2	J23 5-2	a20 4-0	O31 1-0	D28 2-1	a29 1-2	O08 1-0		O17 0-0	M20 0-0	A29 0-0	O29 2-0	a17 0-0	A27 2-4	D12 1-3	O03 3-1
17 OXFORD U	N07 0-0	D19 7-0	M27 3-0	F06 3-1	M31 2-2	O03 3-2	O24 1-0	A22 4-2	a24 1-0	M13 1-0	O10 1-0	S05 3-0	S16 2-0	S19 0-2	F17 4-1	F27 4-0		J16 2-2	N21 1-1	O07 2-0	a19 3-0	J09 1-0	a09 4-0	O21 2-0
18 ROCHDALE	a10 3-1	J23 3-0	J09 4-3	S30 3-1	M22 2-2	O14 2-1	M26 1-2	F27 1-0	O10 1-1	N21 2-1	M13 3-0	S26 3-0	A29 2-0	a21 0-2	O24 2-0	N07 1-1	S12 3-3		a24 2-0	A26 4-0	S07 1-0	D28 0-1	F13 2-1	D12 1-2
19 SOUTHPORT	S21 3-1	N28 0-4	O19 1-1	D28 0-4	J30 1-2	F20 2-2	A22 1-0	S18 2-3	F06 3-3	A31 3-5	S05 5-2	a17 1-1	M20 4-4	O05 0-0	J16 5-3	D19 0-0	a03 0-3	O26 1-0		M06 1-1	O17 0-1	O03 2-2	a19 0-2	O31 0-1
20 STOCKPORT CO	O10 2-1	O12 1-0	F27 0-2	M08 2-0	a16 1-4	S04 4-5	J23 0-1	N20 1-1	M26 0-0	D28 2-0	M22 2-0	S14 0-1	F13 3-1	A22 1-4	a10 2-0	a23 0-1	S20 0-0	F15 1-2	O23 2-2		J16 0-2	N06 2-3	M12 3-2	S25 1-2
21 TORQUAY U	D26 5-2	O07 6-2	O10 1-1	A22 2-2	F13 0-1	D19 3-2	a24 0-2	M27 0-1	N07 2-0	J02 2-4	a10 2-0	O19 2-1	S26 0-2	M31 0-0	N21 2-2	F24 2-1	a21 1-1	S16 2-1	F27 2-0	S12 1-0		M13 2-1	O24 3-4	J23 1-3
22 TRANMERE R	O05 3-1	O26 3-0	a16 0-0	O16 5-1	N27 4-2	M29 4-1	S14 4-0	S04 1-0	J15 2-1	O19 3-0	A22 5-2	S18 5-1	a02 4-0	F19 1-0	D18 3-2	A31 4-0	a17 2-4	D26 4-1	F12 3-1	M19 1-1	O30 3-1		S25 6-0	J29 2-1
23 WREXHAM	O12 4-0	a17 3-3	O07 4-1	F20 3-2	a03 1-2	O17 4-2	M17 1-2	J16 3-3	S19 4-2	S16 0-2	D19 1-1	O28 3-0	J30 5-3	a27 0-1	S05 4-2	A22 4-0	N28 1-1	O03 2-3	a16 1-1	O31 4-1	a28 2-3	F06 3-2		M20 2-0
24 YORK C	F27 1-0	S14 2-0	O24 0-1	S05 5-2	S28 2-1	J16 3-2	D26 7-1	a09 3-1	N21 2-1	O09 4-2	a24 4-0	A31 0-0	a19 3-0	D19 3-1	M01 5-1	F13 2-1	O12 2-1	A22 2-1	M12 3-2	F06 3-0	S18 1-2	M26 4-0	N07 2-1	

LEAGUE TABLES

DIVISION 1

	P	W	D	L	F	A	W	D	L	F	A	Pts
Manchester U	42	16	4	1	52	13	10	5	6	37	26	61
Leeds U	42	16	3	2	53	23	10	6	5	30	29	61
Chelsea	42	15	2	4	48	19	9	6	6	41	35	56
Everton	42	9	10	2	37	22	8	5	8	32	38	49
Nottingham F	42	10	7	4	45	33	7	6	8	26	34	47
Tottenham H	42	18	3	0	65	20	1	4	16	22	51	45
Liverpool	42	12	5	4	42	33	5	5	11	25	40	44
Sheffield W	42	13	5	3	37	15	3	6	12	20	40	43
West Ham U	42	14	2	5	48	25	5	2	14	34	46	42
Blackburn R	42	12	2	7	46	33	4	8	9	37	46	42
Stoke C	42	11	4	6	40	27	5	6	10	27	39	42
Burnley	42	9	9	3	39	26	7	1	13	31	44	42
Arsenal	42	11	5	5	42	31	6	2	13	27	44	41
WBA	42	10	5	6	45	25	3	8	10	25	40	39
Sunderland	42	12	6	3	45	26	2	3	16	19	48	37
Aston Villa	42	14	1	6	36	24	2	4	15	21	58	37
Blackpool	42	9	7	5	41	28	3	4	14	26	50	35
Leicester C	42	9	6	6	43	36	2	7	12	26	49	35
Sheffield U	42	7	5	9	30	29	5	6	10	20	35	35
Fulham	42	10	5	6	44	32	1	7	13	16	46	34
Wolves	42	8	2	11	33	36	5	2	14	26	53	30
Birmingham C	42	6	8	7	36	40	2	3	16	28	56	27

DIVISION 2

	P	W	D	L	F	A	W	D	L	F	A	Pts
Newcastle U	42	16	4	1	50	16	8	5	8	31	29	57
Northampton T	42	14	7	0	37	16	6	9	6	29	34	56
Bolton W	42	13	6	2	46	17	7	4	10	34	41	50
Southampton	42	12	6	3	49	25	5	8	8	34	38	48
Ipswich T	42	11	7	3	48	30	4	10	7	26	37	47
Norwich C	42	15	4	2	47	21	5	3	13	14	36	47
Crystal P	42	11	6	4	37	24	5	7	9	18	27	45
Huddersfield T	42	12	4	5	28	15	5	6	10	25	36	44
Derby Co	42	11	5	5	48	35	5	6	10	36	44	43
Coventry C	42	10	5	6	41	29	7	4	10	31	41	43
Manchester C	42	12	3	6	40	24	4	6	11	23	38	41
Preston NE	42	11	8	2	46	29	3	5	13	30	52	41
Cardiff C	42	10	7	4	43	25	3	7	11	21	32	40
Rotherham U	42	10	7	4	39	25	4	5	12	31	44	40
Plymouth A	42	10	7	4	36	28	6	1	14	27	51	40
Bury	42	9	4	8	36	30	5	6	10	24	36	38
Middlesbrough	42	8	5	8	40	31	5	4	12	30	45	35
Charlton A	42	8	5	8	35	34	5	4	12	29	41	35
Leyton O	42	10	4	7	36	34	2	7	12	14	38	35
Portsmouth	42	11	4	6	36	22	1	6	14	20	55	34
Swindon T	42	12	3	6	43	30	2	2	17	20	51	33
Swansea T	42	9	7	5	40	29	2	3	16	22	55	32

DIVISION 3

	P	W	D	L	F	A	W	D	L	F	A	Pts
Carlisle U	40	14	5	4	46	24	11	5	7	30	29	60
Bristol C	46	14	6	3	53	18	10	5	8	39	37	59
Mansfield T	46	17	4	2	61	23	7	7	9	34	38	59
Hull C	46	14	6	3	51	25	9	6	8	40	32	58
Brentford	46	18	4	1	55	18	6	5	12	28	37	57
Bristol R	46	14	7	2	52	21	6	8	9	30	37	55
Gillingham	46	16	5	2	45	13	7	4	12	25	37	55
Peterboro' U	46	16	3	4	61	33	6	4	13	24	41	51
Watford	46	13	8	2	45	21	4	8	11	26	43	50
Grimsby T	46	11	10	2	37	21	5	7	11	31	46	49
Bournemouth	46	12	4	7	40	24	6	7	10	32	39	47
Southend U	46	14	4	5	48	24	5	4	14	30	47	46
Reading	46	12	8	3	45	26	4	6	13	25	44	46
QPR	46	15	5	3	48	23	2	7	14	24	57	46
Workington	46	11	7	5	30	22	6	5	12	28	47	46
Shrewsbury T	46	10	6	7	42	38	6	6	12	34	46	42
Exeter C	46	8	7	8	33	27	4	10	9	18	25	41
Scunthorpe U	46	9	8	6	42	27	5	4	14	23	45	40
Walsall	46	9	4	10	34	36	6	3	14	21	44	37
Oldham A	46	10	3	10	40	39	3	7	13	21	44	36
Luton T	46	6	8	9	32	36	5	3	15	19	58	33
Port Vale	46	7	6	10	27	33	2	8	13	14	43	32
Colchester U	46	7	6	10	30	34	3	4	16	20	55	30
Barnsley	46	8	5	10	33	31	1	6	16	21	59	29

DIVISION 4

	P	W	D	L	F	A	W	D	L	F	A	Pts
Brighton & HA	46	18	5	0	68	20	8	6	9	34	37	63
Millwall	40	13	10	0	45	15	10	6	7	33	30	62
York C	46	20	1	2	63	21	8	5	10	28	35	62
Oxford U	46	18	4	1	54	13	5	11	7	33	31	61
Tranmere R	46	20	2	1	72	20	7	4	12	27	36	60
Rochdale	46	15	4	4	46	22	7	10	6	28	31	58
Bradford	46	14	8	1	52	22	6	9	8	34	40	57
Chester	46	19	1	3	75	26	6	5	12	44	55	56
Doncaster R	46	13	6	4	46	25	7	5	11	38	47	51
Crewe A	46	11	8	4	55	34	7	5	11	35	47	49
Torquay U	46	11	5	7	41	33	10	2	11	29	37	49
Chesterfield	46	13	5	5	36	22	7	3	13	22	48	48
Notts Co	46	12	7	4	43	23	3	7	13	18	50	44
Wrexham	46	12	5	6	59	37	5	4	14	25	55	43
Hartlepools U	46	11	10	2	44	28	4	3	16	17	67	43
Newport Co	46	14	5	4	54	26	3	3	17	31	55	42
Darlington	46	14	2	7	52	30	4	4	15	32	57	42
Aldershot	46	14	3	6	46	25	1	4	18	18	59	37
Bradford C	46	9	2	12	37	36	3	6	14	33	52	32
Southport	46	5	9	9	35	45	3	7	13	23	44	32
Barrow	46	9	4	10	30	38	3	2	18	29	67	30
Lincoln C	46	8	4	11	35	33	3	2	18	23	66	28
Halifax T	46	9	4	10	37	37	2	2	19	17	66	28
Stockport Co	46	8	4	11	30	34	2	3	18	14	53	27

Football League Records

Top scorers: W.Irvine (Burnley) 29 goals; Div 2, M.Chivers (Southampton) 30 goals; Div 3, L.Allen (Queen's Park Rangers) 30 goals; Div 4, K.Hector (Bradford) 44 goals.

Ron Yeats, Liverpool's giant centre-half and one of the dominant figures in yet another Championship success.

Mike Summerbee was Joe Mercer's first signing when he took over at Maine Road in 1965. Summerbee helped City back to Division One and then shared in all City's domestic and European triumphs.

DIVISION 1

	ARSENAL	ASTON VILLA	BLACKBURN R	BLACKPOOL	BURNLEY	CHELSEA	EVERTON	FULHAM	LEEDS U	LEICESTER C	LIVERPOOL	MANCHESTER U	NEWCASTLE U	NORTHAMPTON T	NOTTINGHAM F	SHEFFIELD U	SHEFFIELD W	STOKE C	SUNDERLAND	TOTTENHAM H	W.B.A.	WEST HAM U
1 ARSENAL		D04 3-3	O23 2-2	M05 0-0	F05 1-1	S04 1-3	M12 0-1	O09 2-1	m05 0-3	m07 1-0	J08 0-1	S25 4-2	M26 1-3	S28 1-1	S14 1-0	N06 6-2	D28 5-2	A21 2-1	a23 1-1	M08 1-1	a05 1-1	N20 3-2
2 ASTON VILLA	a30 3-0		F19 3-1	S11 3-0	a16 2-1	N27 2-4	D11 3-2	M12 2-5	A23 0-2	A28 2-2	M26 0-3	a06 1-1	J01 4-2	a02 1-2	J15 3-0	J29 0-2	O30 2-0	N13 0-1	S06 3-1	S25 3-2	O16 1-1	F07 1-2
3 BLACKBURN R	J15 2-1	S04 0-2		m02 1-3	J01 0-2	O16 0-1	O30 1-2	S01 3-2	M19 2-3	a08 0-2	F05 1-4	m07 1-4	N13 4-2	D11 6-1	N27 5-0	O02 0-0	a30 1-2	S15 0-1	F26 2-0	m09 0-1	a16 0-1	S18 1-2
4 BLACKPOOL	O16 5-3	F26 0-1	D25 4-2		A30 1-3	J01 1-2	J15 2-0	A21 2-2	M28 1-0	S06 4-0	S04 2-3	O30 1-2	a20 1-1	a30 3-0	a16 0-3	a08 2-1	N27 2-1	D11 1-1	S18 1-2	F05 0-0	N13 1-1	M19 2-1
5 BURNLEY	A28 2-2	N20 3-1	O09 1-4	A24 3-1		J29 1-2	F19 1-1	J08 1-0	m07 0-1	D18 4-2	a23 2-0	S11 3-0	M12 1-0	S07 4-1	M26 4-1	O23 2-0	a11 2-1	D28 4-1	a09 1-0	D04 1-1	S25 2-0	N06 3-1
6 CHELSEA	F19 0-0	m16 0-2	m04 1-0	O09 0-1	A21 1-1		S11 3-1	F05 2-1	N06 1-0	O23 0-2	D04 0-1	M12 2-0	S25 1-1	D28 1-0	a11 1-0	m07 2-0	S15 1-1	S01 1-2	F22 3-2	J08 2-1	a25 2-3	a09 6-2
7 EVERTON	S18 3-1	J08 2-0	O05 2-2	O23 0-0	S04 1-0	F26 2-1		D18 2-0	N20 0-0	N06 1-2	M19 0-0	a25 0-0	a11 1-0	A21 5-2	M15 3-0	a09 1-3	A31 5-1	F05 2-1	D04 2-0	O09 3-1	S07 2-3	J11 2-2
8 FULHAM	J01 1-0	S18 3-6	A25 5-2	J29 0-0	D11 2-5	A28 0-3	O16 3-2		a08 1-3	a18 0-4	F26 2-0	J15 0-1	O30 2-0	N27 1-4	N13 1-1	S08 0-0	a16 4-2	a30 1-1	M19 3-0	S04 0-2	a02 2-1	O02 3-0
9 LEEDS U	N13 2-0	S01 2-0	S25 3-0	M26 1-2	O30 1-1	a04 2-0	a16 4-1	a12 0-1		M12 3-2	D28 0-1	J12 1-1	a30 3-0	O16 6-1	S04 2-1	S11 2-2	J01 3-0	J15 2-2	A21 1-0	S15 2-0	D11 4-0	F05 5-0
10 LEICESTER C	O30 3-1	F05 2-1	a12 2-0	S14 0-3	O16 0-1	M21 1-1	m04 3-0	D28 5-0	S18 3-3		A21 1-3	N13 0-5	a16 1-2	O02 1-1	a30 2-1	M19 1-0	D11 4-1	J01 1-0	S04 4-1	S01 2-2	N27 2-1	m09 2-1
11 LIVERPOOL	D11 4-2	O02 3-1	N17 5-2	F19 4-1	N27 2-1	a30 2-1	S25 5-0	S11 2-1	D27 0-1	J29 1-0		J01 2-1	O16 2-0	N13 5-0	O30 4-0	A25 0-1	a06 1-0	a16 2-0	F12 4-0	M12 1-0	J15 2-2	S15 1-1
12 MANCHESTER U	M19 2-1	m09 6-1	N06 2-2	a27 2-1	F26 4-2	S18 4-1	D15 3-0	O23 4-1	m19 1-1	a09 1-2	O09 2-0		S15 1-1	F05 6-2	S01 0-0	N20 3-1	A21 1-0	S04 1-1	J08 1-1	D18 5-1	D27 1-1	D04 0-0
13 NEWCASTLE U	O02 0-1	O09 1-0	a09 2-1	N06 2-0	S18 3-2	M19 0-1	a08 0-0	m07 1-1	m16 2-0	N20 1-5	D18 0-0	S08 1-2		S04 2-0	A21 2-2	a23 0-2	F05 2-0	F26 3-1	M05 2-0	O23 0-0	A25 0-1	J08 2-1
14 NORTHAMPTON T	A25 1-1	N06 2-1	J08 2-1	D04 2-1	S15 1-2	D27 2-3	J29 0-2	a23 2-4	M05 2-1	M26 2-2	a09 0-0	A28 1-1	F19 3-1		M12 3-3	O09 0-1	S25 0-0	a12 1-0	a25 2-1	N20 0-2	S10 3-4	O23 2-1
15 NOTTINGHAM F	S07 0-1	O23 1-2	a23 0-3	N20 2-1	M08 1-0	a12 1-2	D27 1-0	a26 1-2	F19 0-4	D04 2-0	m10 1-1	A24 4-2	J29 1-2	S18 1-1		J08 1-0	m07 1-0	M19 4-3	D18 0-0	N06 1-0	A28 3-2	O09 5-0
16 SHEFFIELD U	a25 3-0	A21 1-0	M29 2-0	a11 0-1	J15 2-1	O30 1-2	N13 2-0	S15 2-0	F26 1-1	S25 2-2	S01 0-0	a16 3-1	N27 3-2	J01 2-2	D11 1-1		S18 1-0	O16 3-2	F05 2-2	D28 1-3	a30 0-2	S04 5-3
17 SHEFFIELD W	D27 4-0	a27 2-0	D04 2-1	a04 3-0	m09 0-2	m02 1-1	A25 3-1	N20 1-0	O09 0-0	J08 1-2	N06 0-2	J29 0-0	A28 1-0	M19 3-1	S11 3-1	M12 2-2		M30 4-1	O23 3-1	a09 1-1	F19 1-2	D18 0-0
18 STOKE C	J29 1-3	a09 2-0	S08 3-2	J08 4-1	D27 3-1	A25 2-2	A28 1-1	D04 3-2	O23 1-2	O09 1-0	N20 0-0	F19 2-2	S11 4-0	F12 6-2	S25 1-0	M25 2-0	m04 3-1		N06 1-1	a23 0-1	M12 1-1	m07 1-0
19 SUNDERLAND	a20 0-2	S15 2-0	S11 1-0	M12 2-1	N13 0-4	a16 2-0	a30 2-0	S25 2-2	J29 2-0	F19 0-3	a11 2-2	D11 2-3	J03 2-0	O30 3-0	O16 3-2	A28 4-1	J26 0-2	a02 2-0		M26 2-0	J01 1-5	S01 2-1
20 TOTTENHAM H	S11 2-2	M19 5-5	J29 4-0	A27 4-0	a30 0-1	D11 4-2	J01 2-2	F19 4-3	S08 3-2	A25 4-2	S18 2-1	O16 5-1	J15 2-2	a16 1-1	a02 2-3	D27 1-0	N13 2-3	N27 2-2	O06 3-0		O30 2-1	a08 1-4
21 W.B.A.	a11 4-4	F11 2-2	N20 2-1	a09 2-1	M19 1-2	O02 1-2	S15 1-1	N06 6-2	J08 1-2	a22 5-1	O23 3-0	m04 3-3	S01 1-2	F26 1-1	F05 5-3	D04 1-1	S04 4-2	S18 6-2	O09 4-1	m07 2-1		A21 3-0
22 WEST HAM U	a16 2-1	M05 4-2	M12 4-1	S25 1-1	a02 1-1	N13 2-1	N27 3-0	M26 1-3	A28 2-1	S11 2-5	S06 1-5	a30 3-2	D11 4-3	J15 1-1	J01 0-3	F19 4-0	O16 4-2	O30 0-0	A23 1-1	a25 2-0	J29 4-0	

DIVISION 2

	BIRMINGHAM C	BOLTON W	BRISTOL C	BURY	CARDIFF C	CARLISLE U	CHARLTON A	COVENTRY C	CRYSTAL P	DERBY CO	HUDDERSFIELD T	IPSWICH T	LEYTON O	MANCHESTER C	MIDDLESBROUGH	NORWICH C	PLYMOUTH A	PORTSMOUTH	PRESTON N.E.	ROTHERHAM U	SOUTHAMPTON	WOLVERHAMPTON W
1 BIRMINGHAM C		M19 0-1	a22 1-3	D18 4-0	N06 4-2	J08 2-1	S04 2-2	N20 0-1	A21 2-1	a09 5-5	D28 2-1	m03 4-1	S08 2-2	D04 3-1	A25 1-1	O09 1-0	F26 1-0	S18 1-3	F05 1-1	m07 3-0	O23 0-1	a11 2-2
2 BOLTON W	S25 1-2		J08 1-2	F26 2-1	O23 2-1	m04 4-0	A21 4-2	N06 4-2	S01 3-0	D18 0-1	S15 1-1	M12 3-1	M26 2-0	N20 1-0	a11 6-0	m07 1-1	F05 0-1	S04 2-0	M16 1-3	a25 1-3	O09 2-3	D04 2-1
3 BRISTOL C	N27 2-0	N13 2-2		F11 2-1	S25 1-1	M12 2-0	m03 0-0	S11 1-1	J01 1-1	M25 1-1	S04 2-1	m10 4-1	a30 2-0	F05 1-1	D11 2-2	A31 0-0	O30 0-0	a02 1-0	O16 1-0	A21 2-1	a08 0-1	D28 0-1
4 BURY	O16 5-1	N16 1-1	S07 1-2		J29 1-1	m10 2-1	M05 3-0	A24 1-1	N13 2-2	A28 4-1	a19 0-4	J01 1-1	J15 3-0	a12 2-1	O30 2-0	S18 2-5	a30 1-0	D11 1-0	a16 5-0	O02 6-1	F19 1-3	M19 1-0
5 CARDIFF C	a02 1-3	M05 1-1	M18 2-1	A21 1-0		a08 1-1	N10 3-1	O06 1-2	a30 1-0	A25 2-1	N27 0-1	O30 1-0	N13 3-1	S18 4-3	m03 5-3	m10 0-2	J01 5-1	O16 1-2	D11 1-3	F26 0-0	D27 3-5	S04 1-4
6 CARLISLE U	N13 1-0	O30 1-1	S17 5-0	D27 4-1	a12 2-0		J01 3-1	M18 2-2	D11 3-1	S07 2-1	a30 2-0	a02 3-1	a15 1-0	F26 1-2	M08 2-1	A21 4-1	O16 1-3	J15 2-1	O02 0-2	S03 1-0	A31 1-0	F05 2-1
7 CHARLTON A	F19 2-1	J29 0-1	O23 1-4	a23 0-1	S14 5-2	O09 3-2		a26 2-0	M26 1-0	m07 2-2	S25 0-2	A28 2-0	S11 3-0	m13 2-3	M12 1-0	m18 2-1	A31 1-1	D27 2-2	a08 5-2	N06 2-2	D04 2-2	J08 1-1
8 COVENTRY C	a16 4-3	a02 2-2	F26 2-2	A31 1-0	M26 3-1	S25 3-2	O16 3-1		S18 0-1	a12 3-2	D11 0-3	N13 3-1	N27 1-1	S04 3-3	a30 2-1	D28 2-0	J15 5-1	O30 3-2	J01 5-1	F05 2-2	S14 5-1	A21 2-1
9 CRYSTAL P	J29 1-0	A25 1-1	O09 2-1	J08 1-0	D04 0-0	m07 2-0	O02 2-0	M12 0-1		a23 1-1	S11 2-1	D27 3-1	A28 2-1	D18 0-2	F19 1-1	N06 0-0	a08 3-1	S08 4-1	M19 1-1	O23 2-2	N20 1-0	a09 0-1
10 DERBY CO	O30 5-3	O16 2-0	O02 2-1	F05 4-1	S01 1-5	S15 3-1	D11 2-0	a11 1-0	N27 4-0		a16 4-1	J15 2-2	a02 1-3	M19 1-2	N13 5-0	S04 3-1	M05 1-2	J01 3-1	a30 1-0	S18 1-3	A21 0-3	F26 2-2
11 HUDDERSFIELD T	M15 2-0	S07 1-0	F19 3-0	N06 2-0	a23 1-1	D04 2-0	M19 1-1	m07 0-2	F26 1-1	N20 1-3		A24 1-0	J29 1-1	O09 0-0	A28 6-0	a09 0-0	O02 2-1	a11 2-0	S18 2-1	D18 4-0	J08 2-0	O23 1-1
12 IPSWICH T	M26 0-1	S18 2-0	N20 0-0	O09 3-4	a09 2-1	N06 1-0	F05 1-4	J08 1-0	F11 2-2	O23 2-2	A31 2-2		a11 3-2	a23 1-1	S07 2-1	M19 2-0	S04 4-1	F26 1-0	A21 1-0	D04 0-0	D18 3-0	m07 5-2
13 LEYTON O	S13 2-1	O02 1-0	D04 0-4	O23 2-2	J08 1-1	N20 2-1	F26 1-2	a23 1-1	F05 0-2	N06 0-0	A21 0-2	a08 1-4		m07 2-2	a18 2-3	M28 0-0	S18 0-1	M19 0-0	S04 2-2	A30 1-4	m09 1-1	O09 0-3
14 MANCHESTER C	a30 3-1	a16 4-1	A28 2-2	a08 1-0	M12 2-2	S11 2-1	O30 0-0	F19 1-0	O16 3-1	S25 1-0	J01 2-0	N27 2-1	D11 5-0		J29 3-1	O27 0-0	a02 1-1	N13 3-1	J15 0-0	J12 3-1	m18 0-0	A25 2-1
15 MIDDLESBROUGH	A31 1-1	a12 1-1	M05 4-2	a09 1-0	N20 3-4	a23 0-2	S18 2-2	D04 1-1	S04 2-2	J08 0-0	F05 1-3	S14 3-2	D27 2-1	A21 1-1		O22 0-1	M19 0-1	O26 5-2	F26 2-1	O09 4-0	N06 0-0	D18 3-1
16 NORWICH C	J01 2-2	D11 3-0	A25 0-0	M12 4-0	A28 3-2	J29 2-0	a16 2-0	D27 1-1	a02 2-1	F19 0-1	O30 1-1	S25 1-0	O16 2-1	S15 3-3	a27 1-2		N27 0-0	a30 1-3	N13 1-1	a11 1-2	S11 3-4	O02 0-3
17 PLYMOUTH A	S11 6-1	A28 1-3	a09 0-2	D04 2-2	O09 2-2	M14 0-0	A25 3-0	O23 1-2	a11 1-2	D27 0-0	M25 0-0	F19 3-0	M12 1-1	N06 1-0	S25 2-2	a23 2-0		J29 3-1	S08 0-1	J08 5-2	m07 2-3	N20 2-2
18 PORTSMOUTH	M12 0-1	F19 1-0	N06 2-4	m07 4-0	D18 3-1	O23 4-1	D28 3-1	a09 2-0	S15 1-1	O09 1-1	a06 2-1	S11 1-0	S25 4-1	J08 2-2	M25 4-1	D04 0-3	A21 4-1		S01 4-1	N20 1-1	F05 2-5	a23 2-0
19 PRESTON N.E.	A28 3-3	a19 0-1	D18 1-1	N20 2-1	m07 9-0	a25 2-1	a11 3-3	O09 0-0	S25 2-0	D04 2-0	M12 1-1	J29 0-1	F19 1-2	O23 0-3	S11 1-1	J08 0-0	S13 2-0	A23 4-1		a09 1-1	a23 1-1	N06 2-2
20 ROTHERHAM U	D11 3-4	N27 2-1	J29 1-2	M25 2-1	S11 6-4	m12 3-3	m09 0-0	A28 1-1	J15 3-0	M12 3-0	O16 0-0	a30 0-0	A24 2-1	m04 0-1	J01 4-1	a12 2-1	N13 2-0	a16 3-3	O30 6-3		S25 1-0	S07 4-3
21 SOUTHAMPTON	M05 0-1	J01 5-1	a11 2-2	S04 6-2	a20 3-2	A25 1-0	a30 1-0	S08 1-0	a16 1-0	J29 3-1	N13 0-1	O16 1-2	O30 1-0	O02 0-1	a02 3-1	F26 2-2	D11 4-1	A28 2-2	N27 5-2	M19 1-1		S18 9-3
22 WOLVERHAMPTON W	a12 2-0	a30 3-1	D27 1-1	S25 3-0	F19 2-1	A28 3-0	N13 2-2	J29 0-1	O30 1-0	S11 4-0	J15 2-1	D11 4-1	J01 2-1	A30 2-4	O16 3-0	M26 2-1	a16 0-0	N27 8-2	a02 3-0	S13 4-1	M12 1-1	

Season 1965-66

DIVISION 3

	BOURNEMOUTH	BRENTFORD	BRIGHTON & HA	BRISTOL R	EXETER C	GILLINGHAM	GRIMSBY T	HULL C	MANSFIELD T	MILLWALL	OLDHAM A	OXFORD U	PETERBOROUGH U	Q.P.R.	READING	SCUNTHORPE U	SHREWSBURY T	SOUTHEND U	SWANSEA T	SWINDON T	WALSALL	WATFORD	WORKINGTON	YORK C
1 BOURNEMOUTH		a26 0-1	N20 0-1	D28 1-0	D17 0-1	F19 1-1	M26 1-0	m10 1-1	N06 2-2	a08 0-0	m07 1-0	S14 1-1	O09 2-3	J08 1-1	O23 3-2	a23 1-2	S25 2-0	S11 0-0	A24 2-1	M12 1-0	A21 0-1	a09 2-0	F05 1-1	M05 1-0
2 BRENTFORD	m17 1-0		a11 2-0	F05 0-5	N20 1-2	m28 0-2	N23 3-2	a09 2-4	m07 0-3	N06 1-2	O23 0-0	F26 5-1	J08 1-0	A21 6-1	a23 1-1	O09 0-1	S14 4-0	M01 2-0	S18 2-0	M05 0-1	M19 2-2	m10 1-1	O02 0-1	S04 0-1
3 BRIGHTON & H.A.	a16 1-2	a08 2-0		J01 4-3	S11 2-1	M26 0-1	O05 1-2	A28 1-2	J29 6-4	S25 2-2	m13 3-1	M08 2-0	M12 1-0	N23 0-2	F19 1-1	F12 0-1	D11 1-1	N27 9-1	O30 1-1	a30 1-0	a02 2-1	D27 2-0	m20 3-1	O15 3-1
4 BRISTOL R	D27 0-0	A28 1-1	O09 0-0		a23 2-0	N06 0-0	J29 2-1	m06 1-2	F19 6-0	J08 1-1	O19 4-0	S18 3-1	N20 1-1	a12 1-0	a09 0-0	M29 2-0	A24 3-2	M05 3-1	M19 2-1	S07 0-1	O02 3-0	O23 1-1	N09 2-2	F26 0-0
5 EXETER C	O16 1-0	a16 5-0	m03 2-0	N27 1-0		D04 3-1	m21 2-0	O02 1-4	M19 2-2	O06 1-2	A21 4-0	D11 1-2	M05 2-5	S18 0-0	a27 1-2	S04 4-0	a02 0-0	J15 1-1	D27 1-1	O30 1-1	a13 0-2	F05 1-2	J01 2-1	a30 0-2
6 GILLINGHAM	S04 2-0	O30 1-0	O02 3-1	a02 2-0	A25 1-1		M05 3-2	F23 0-3	m03 2-0	A28 1-0	a27 3-0	a16 1-2	J29 1-1	m18 3-1	M23 2-4	M19 0-1	O16 0-1	a11 1-0	N27 2-0	J01 1-0	a30 1-0	S18 2-2	D11 1-0	m21 0-0
7 GRIMSBY T	O02 2-0	A24 3-2	S15 3-1	A21 1-1	J08 1-1	O23 3-1		a23 1-0	a09 0-1	m28 2-0	D18 3-1	S04 1-1	N06 3-0	m07 4-2	N20 3-3	a08 1-3	m04 2-1	m17 1-0	F26 2-2	D27 2-2	S18 3-1	O09 2-1	M19 1-0	F05 3-1
8 HULL C	O30 3-0	a30 4-1	F05 1-0	D11 6-1	a20 6-1	M09 1-0	N27 1-1		F26 4-0	D27 1-0	O06 5-1	a11 2-1	m17 2-1	S04 1-3	S25 3-3	A21 3-2	a16 2-1	m20 1-0	J01 4-1	S01 1-0	O16 3-2	N24 3-1	J15 6-0	S18 1-4
9 MANSFIELD T	m23 1-0	D11 2-0	A21 3-1	S04 2-0	S25 0-0	M14 0-0	a30 2-1	S11 1-2		a25 1-1	F21 1-0	J01 1-4	M26 1-7	F05 2-1	M12 0-2	M07 2-2	M21 0-3	m09 2-0	O16 3-0	a16 1-5	J15 0-3	O04 2-2	O30 0-1	a11 4-1
10 MILLWALL	a12 1-0	a02 1-0	M19 3-2	O25 3-3	S13 3-0	F05 2-0	O30 2-1	D28 3-0	m16 2-0		S04 1-0	N27 2-0	N22 4-1	O02 2-1	M05 3-0	S18 2-2	J15 4-2	J01 2-0	a30 1-0	O16 1-0	D11 1-1	F26 0-0	A21 2-0	a16 2-0
11 OLDHAM A	D11 2-2	J15 1-1	m18 1-0	O30 2-0	J29 3-1	S11 5-3	O16 1-4	O13 2-2	M05 1-1	M01 0-2		m21 3-0	A28 2-4	m25 0-2	A25 2-2	O02 1-3	J01 0-1	S17 1-0	a16 1-0	a12 1-1	M15 1-2	M18 0-1	a30 1-1	m10 3-0
12 OXFORD U	N03 2-1	S11 2-0	O23 0-0	M12 1-0	m07 0-1	N20 0-4	F19 2-0	a08 0-2	O09 4-1	a23 3-1	J08 3-3		a09 1-0	D18 1-3	M26 2 0	m28 0-3	A28 0-1	A25 3-2	a27 2-2	J29 0-3	D27 7-1	N06 1-2	M05 0-2	S25 4-1
13 PETERBOROUGH U	J01 1-0	m21 3-0	S18 2-2	a16 5-2	m09 2-0	A21 1-0	a02 1-1	a25 4-1	O02 3-2	A23 0-2	F05 0-1	a30 2-3		M19 1-1	M28 0-0	F26 3-1	O30 4-1	O16 4-0	D11 5-2	J15 2-3	O04 3-1	S04 2-2	a11 1-1	N27 1-0
14 Q.P.R.	m21 5-0	J29 1-0	A23 4-1	a08 4-1	M12 1-0	a25 1-3	D11 3-0	F19 3-3	A28 1-2	M26 6-1	m02 1-1	O16 2-3	S25 2-1		S11 0-2	O04 1-0	a30 2-1	a16 2-1	J15 6-2	N27 3-2	O30 2-1	F15 1-1	a02 4-1	J01 7-2
15 READING	M07 1-0	N27 2-0	S03 0-0	a29 0-1	m18 4-1	S15 2-2	m23 0-0	M18 0-1	S17 2-1	F12 1-1	M30 3-2	O01 0-1	D27 2-1	m13 2-1		F05 2-0	m20 4-1	O29 1-0	a13 2-1	a01 0-2	J01 3-0	A21 1-2	O15 1-1	D11 3-0
16 SCUNTHORPE U	N27 3-0	J01 3-2	M05 2-2	O16 3-0	F19 2-1	S25 0-1	a12 2-2	J29 2-4	A25 0-1	M12 4-4	M26 1-1	O30 1-2	S11 1-1	S14 1-2	A28 2-0		D28 1-4	a30 0-0	a02 1-1	D11 2-1	m21 4-2	m17 1-1	a16 4-1	J15 4-1
17 SHREWSBURY T	M19 0-2	O06 0-0	m06 3-1	N01 1-0	N06 4-0	M30 2-1	m02 3-1	N20 2-2	a22 2-1	O22 2-0	O09 3-1	F05 4-0	m12 3-1	a09 0-0	J08 3-3	D27 1-4		O01 3-0	S03 5-0	m18 1-1	M24 1-2	a11 0-0	S17 1-1	A21 4-1
18 SOUTHEND U	F26 1-2	M07 1-0	a22 0-0	F12 2-0	O23 4-2	a08 5-2	a25 3 1	N06 0-2	J08 1-0	O08 0-2	M11 0-2	N22 2-1	D18 2-0	N20 1-3	m27 2-1	m13 0-1	M14 2-0		A21 2-0	S24 4-2	F05 5-3	m06 1-0	O25 3-1	S13 2-3
19 SWANSEA T	N23 5-0	M12 1-1	m28 2-2	S25 3-0	J22 1-0	a23 0-3	S11 1-0	O09 4-2	M01 1-2	a09 0-2	N20 4 1	m17 3-2	m07 1-1	O23 4-2	a11 5-4	N06 3-4	F19 4-0	J29 5-0		A28 1-1	m24 1-0	J08 4-2	S14 1-6	M25 7-2
20 SWINDON T	S18 0-0	F12 2-1	a09 3-2	O05 4-3	m28 2-2	O09 0-1	m10 0-0	J08 3-1	N20 6 2	M15 1-0	a11 0-1	A21 0-0	O23 3-0	a23 2-1	N06 5-0	m07 0-0	a26 0-0	M19 4-0	F05 2-2		S04 0-0	M26 0-1	m03 0-1	O19 6-0
21 WALSALL	J29 2-1	S25 1-1	N06 2-1	M26 1-1	a11 1-1	a09 6-1	M12 1-0	D17 2-4	O23 2-1	m07 1-4	a23 2-2	m04 1-1	S14 2-0	m28 0-1	O09 3-0	J08 3-0	S11 3-0	A28 3-0	M05 1-1	F19 5-0		N20 3-0	A24 1-1	m17 2-0
22 WATFORD	a30 1-0	O16 1-1	M22 0-1	J15 2-0	A28 3-0	M12 1-0	J01 1-1	A24 1-1	S14 2-1	S11 0-1	S25 4-0	a02 1-1	F19 1-0	M05 1-2	J29 1-2	a26 2-1	a08 1-0	D11 4-1	m13 0-1	O02 2-0	a16 0-1		N27 1-2	O30 3-2
23 WORKINGTON	A28 2 2	M26 1-1	J07 1-0	a26 0-0	O09 6-1	m07 1-0	S25 1-0	O22 3-0	m27 2-0	J28 0-0	a09 0-1	F11 2-1	a21 1-1	N05 1-1	m09 1-0	N19 1-2	M11 1-3	F19 3-1	O04 7-0	S11 0-3	M30 1-0	a23 1-0		M15 2-1
24 YORK C	F12 0-2	M28 1-1	D17 0-1	S10 1-5	a09 2-0	J08 1-2	A27 1-1	M12 1-2	a08 2-1	N19 2-1	N05 2-2	M18 1-4	a23 1-1	O09 2-2	m06 1-2	D04 1-3	J29 2-2	O04 0-3	O01 5-1	A23 0-2	a25 0-3	J21 1-0	D27 3-3	

DIVISION 4

	ALDERSHOT	BARNSLEY	BARROW	BRADFORD	BRADFORD C	CHESTER	CHESTERFIELD	COLCHESTER U	CREWE A	DARLINGTON	DONCASTER R	HALIFAX T	HARTLEPOOLS U	LINCOLN C	LUTON T	NEWPORT CO	NOTTS CO	PORT VALE	ROCHDALE	SOUTHPORT	STOCKPORT CO	TORQUAY U	TRANMERE R	WREXHAM
1 ALDERSHOT		a23 1-1	F19 3-1	a27 5-1	a09 5-2	O09 2-2	S15 1-3	N20 1-3	m07 1-0	M23 0-1	M12 1-1	a08 0-0	S11 5-0	O23 2-0	A28 3-1	O06 2-1	M09 0-0	F12 3-0	J29 2-3	S25 3-0	N06 1-0	F16 3-2	J08 1-3	M26 2-2
2 BARNSLEY	M15 2-1		O15 3-0	a15 1-1	A28 4-2	N23 0-2	S03 0-0	F26 1-1	J29 0-1	O01 3-1	O29 1-5	D27 1-2	J15 2-2	a26 0-1	J01 3-0	a29 2-2	F12 1-1	A24 1-0	M08 5-0	m13 4-0	M18 1-2	D11 1-0	S17 4-0	m10 3-0
3 BARROW	S04 2-2	D18 1-5		F05 5-2	O23 2-0	N20 4-1	M19 3-2	O09 3-0	a18 1-1	m07 1-1	D27 2-1	J08 3-0	O04 2-0	m12 2-2	a25 0-1	F26 2-2	a23 2-1	N06 2-2	O02 0-2	S13 3-3	M05 1-0	S18 2-0	a11 1 1	A21 4-2
4 BRADFORD	N01 5-1	N20 7-2	A28 2-3		a23 5-1	a12 0-1	J04 3-1	J08 1-0	a09 2-1	O23 0-2	S11 0-1	M26 2-1	a19 4-1	D18 4-2	J29 1-3	F12 6-1	O09 4-0	m07 1-2	A24 1-2	M12 2-1	m24 3-1	O04 1-1	N06 1-1	S25 4-2
5 BRADFORD C	a30 1-1	F05 1-0	J15 0-0	F16 3-0		M05 1-2	a11 1-1	S04 1-2	A25 0-1	M19 2-0	m16 1-1	M16 0-1	O30 1-3	O02 2-0	O16 2-2	D11 3-2	a27 0-4	J12 2-0	J01 2-1	a20 3-0	S18 1-7	A21 4-1	F26 2-4	m12 4-1
6 CHESTER	J01 3-2	O06 3-3	a16 0-0	a08 2-4	F12 4-0		O30 3-0	D28 2-1	O27 3-0	F05 3-2	a30 1-4	S26 1-0	N27 2-0	S04 4-2	m20 1-1	O10 6-1	F20 1-1	M26 2-0	a02 1-2	D11 1-0	A21 1-0	J15 1-1	S15 3-1	S18 4-2
7 CHESTERFIELD	A23 1-1	F19 3-1	S25 2-2	D27 0-3	a08 1-1	M28 2-2		m07 2-4	O09 3-1	N20 1-2	a26 1-1	O23 3-2	M25 1-3	J08 1-0	M12 1-3	A21 1-2	N06 0-0	D18 3-1	S11 4-1	m02 3-2	a23 2-1	F05 1-1	a09 0-0	S06 1-1
8 COLCHESTER U	a16 0-0	S11 4-0	J01 2-2	F28 6-3	F19 0-1	D27 1-1	D11 3-0		A28 1-1	a25 0-1	J15 2-1	A23 1-0	O16 2-0	M05 3-0	a08 2-2	N27 3-2	N22 4-1	J29 3-0	S18 2-0	O30 0-0	O02 3-2	a30 0-2	M19 2-1	a02 1-1
9 CREWE A	D11 2-0	A21 0-1	O20 2-1	a30 2-5	S15 7-1	m18 1-1	J01 1-0	F05 0-2		S17 0-1	m11 0-1	F23 3-0	a01 3-1	M18 7-0	J15 2-0	M02 2-2	O01 1-0	M09 0-0	O16 3-1	a15 2-1	m04 1-1	a08 2-1	S04 1-2	N27 0-1
10 DARLINGTON	O30 4-3	M26 2-1	D11 1-0	M14 4-1	S25 3-0	A28 0-1	a16 4-1	m16 2-0	M12 1-1		a11 3-2	M28 2-0	D28 1-1	A23 0-2	a30 1-0	m09 0-1	J29 1-0	S11 2-1	F28 3-1	J01 2-0	O04 3-0	m21 0-0	M07 0-1	O16 2-0
11 DONCASTER R	S17 3-2	m03 2-1	D28 1-1	F25 6-2	N06 1-1	a09 1-1	F15 1-0	D04 2-0	J08 4-1	a12 6-3		a22 2-2	A24 4-0	A21 4-0	N23 1-1	M19 1-0	m06 0-0	N19 1-0	M04 2-0	F05 1-1	O09 1-0	O02 0-1	D18 3-1	S04 2-0
12 HALIFAX T	a12 3-4	D28 2-2	J22 2-1	O01 1-0	O05 3-2	M18 2-0	F12 4-1	S14 1-1	M05 1-0	S03 2-2	M08 2-3		a15 1-0	F26 2-2	m16 3-0	D31 4-4	S18 0-1	m10 2-0	O29 4-1	a29 1-2	F05 0-1	O16 0-2	A21 2-2	D10 4-0
13 HARTLEPOOLS U	F26 3-0	O23 1-2	m09 3-0	S04 2-3	m21 1-1	a23 2-0	O02 1-2	D18 0-1	N06 4-1	D27 1-1	S13 2-0	N20 1-2		m07 3-1	M05 2-0	S18 5-2	a09 2-0	J08 2-0	m16 0-0	A21 3-1	a08 2-1	M19 0-2	O09 0-0	F05 4-2
14 LINCOLN C	J15 2-1	M22 4-1	a30 4-0	O15 1-1	M25 1-0	F19 2-2	M09 0-2	F12 0-2	S24 1-1	S15 4-1	J28 0-3	S11 3-3	D11 2-1		N27 2-2	O30 1-1	A28 1-2	M12 0-1	a16 2-0	a08 4-0	M15 1-2	a02 1-1	O06 1-0	J01 0-2
15 LUTON T	F05 3-1	O09 5-4	m19 3-2	A21 3-1	D18 2-3	J08 5-2	S18 1-2	a11 1-1	O23 4-0	a09 2-0	O07 4-3	N06 4-1	F12 2-1	a23 0-0		S04 2-1	N20 5-1	m14 5-0	M19 4-1	D28 2-0	m07 2-0	F26 3-2	M26 2-1	S16 1-0
16 NEWPORT CO	N22 3-1	a09 1-0	S11 3-2	M07 3-1	m07 2-2	m23 3-2	J31 3-4	m28 2-1	M21 1-0	N08 3-0	S25 4-0	O09 3-1	M12 3-0	m02 0-0	m25 3-1		O25 1-2	a11 0-1	A28 1-1	M25 1-1	J08 1-0	S13 3-2	N19 0-0	m16 2-2
17 NOTTS CO	O16 2-0	M05 0-1	N27 0-2	J01 2-0	m18 2-1	S11 3-3	a02 2-0	O07 1-0	M26 0-1	A21 0-0	D11 1-2	M12 1-1	a30 1-0	F05 2-1	a16 1-1	J15 1-1		S25 3-1	m21 3 3	S04 1 2	S16 1-1	O30 1-1	m13 1-2	a11 3-1
18 PORT VALE	M05 2-1	S13 1-1	m02 0-0	D11 3-3	a04 0-0	O02 5-2	O16 1-1	A21 1-0	O04 2-0	F26 3-1	a16 0-1	a27 2-0	M21 0-0	S18 3-0	O30 1-2	a12 3-0	M19 0-1		J15 2-1	N27 4-1	S04 2-0	J01 0-0	F05 2-3	a30 1-0
19 ROCHDALE	A21 1-0	a11 2-1	M25 4-0	S14 2-3	O08 5-1	N05 3 0	F26 1-1	M11 0-1	D18 2-1	a22 1-2	F12 0-1	a19 0-1	a26 3-1	N20 0-1	S24 1-2	F05 2-1	J08 0-2	O22 1-0		O05 3-0	a09 4-0	S04 2-3	m06 3-5	D27 6-0
20 SOUTHPORT	M18 0-2	a04 3-1	A23 1-1	S17 2-1	J08 4-0	m07 2-0	M21 1-0	m10 0-1	N20 1-1	O08 1-1	A28 2-1	a09 1-0	J29 4-1	a11 5-1	D27 3-2	O02 2-0	F19 1-0	a23 2-1	N22 4-0		D17 2-0	a25 3-3	O23 1-1	F26 2-2
21 STOCKPORT CO	m16 1-2	S24 1-0	F11 5-2	O29 2-3	M21 1-1	J28 0-1	N26 2-1	M25 1-0	S10 2-0	N22 1-1	J01 1-1	A27 3-0	a11 1-2	F21 2-1	D10 4-1	m20 2-1	A23 1-3	F18 3-0	a29 3-1	O15 2-2		a15 1-0	S06 1-2	J14 2-4
22 TORQUAY U	D27 5-1	O20 3-0	M12 0-1	N23 2-1	J29 4-3	O23 1-0	A28 2-0	a09 0-1	a11 2-1	J08 0-4	M26 0-0	m02 1-0	S25 2-0	N06 4-1	S11 2-0	A25 1-0	m09 2-0	O09 1-0	F19 4-0	S22 1-1	N20 1-4		a23 2-1	F12 3-1
23 TRANMERE R	O18 5-2	M11 1-0	a08 1-2	a01 1-2	S10 2-2	A23 1-0	a29 3-2	S24 2-0	F18 3-1	M04 1-2	O15 1-0	J28 5-2	J01 6-1	N22 3-2	N03 2-0	a15 0-1	D27 0-3	A27 1-0	D10 6-2	J14 0-2	a25 6-2	N26 0-1		O29 6-3
24 WREXHAM	O02 4-0	J08 6-3	J29 3-1	M19 3-2	N20 1-1	M12 2-1	O25 2-1	N06 2-3	a23 1-4	D18 1-2	F19 4-3	m07 2-2	A28 1-1	O09 0-1	A23 2-0	a25 0-1	a08 1-3	m04 1-0	M30 2-2	S11 3-1	O23 1-4	M05 0-2	S29 1-5	

LEAGUE TABLES

DIVISION 1

	P	W	D	L	F	A	W	D	L	F	A	Pts
Liverpool	42	17	2	2	52	15	9	7	5	27	19	61
Leeds U	42	14	4	3	49	15	9	5	7	30	23	55
Burnley	42	15	3	3	45	20	9	4	8	34	27	55
Manchester U	42	12	8	1	50	20	6	7	8	34	39	51
Chelsea	42	11	4	6	30	21	11	3	7	35	32	51
WBA	42	11	6	4	58	34	8	6	7	33	35	50
Leicester C	42	12	4	5	40	28	9	3	9	40	37	49
Tottenham H	42	11	6	4	55	37	5	6	10	20	29	44
Sheffield U	42	11	6	4	37	25	5	5	11	19	34	43
Stoke C	42	12	6	3	42	22	3	6	12	23	42	42
Everton	42	12	6	3	39	19	3	5	13	17	43	41
West Ham U	42	12	5	4	46	33	3	4	14	24	50	39
Blackpool	42	9	5	7	36	29	5	4	12	19	36	37
Arsenal	42	8	8	5	36	31	4	5	12	26	44	37
Newcastle U	42	10	5	6	26	20	4	4	13	24	43	37
Aston Villa	42	10	3	8	39	34	5	3	13	30	46	36
Sheffield W	42	11	6	4	35	18	3	2	16	21	48	36
Nottingham F	42	11	3	7	31	26	3	5	13	25	46	36
Sunderland	42	13	2	6	36	28	1	6	14	15	44	36
Fulham	42	9	4	8	34	37	5	3	13	33	48	35
Northampton T	42	8	6	7	31	32	2	7	12	24	60	33
Blackburn R	42	6	1	14	30	36	2	3	16	27	52	20

DIVISION 2

	P	W	D	L	F	A	W	D	L	F	A	Pts
Manchester C	42	14	7	0	40	14	8	8	5	36	30	59
Southampton	42	13	4	4	51	25	9	6	6	34	31	54
Coventry C	42	14	5	2	54	31	6	8	7	19	22	53
Huddersfield T	42	12	7	2	35	12	7	6	8	27	24	51
Bristol C	42	9	10	2	27	15	8	7	6	36	33	51
Wolves	42	15	4	2	52	18	5	6	10	35	43	50
Rotherham U	42	12	6	3	48	29	4	8	9	27	45	46
Derby Co	42	13	2	6	48	31	3	9	9	23	37	43
Bolton W	42	12	2	7	43	25	4	7	10	19	34	41
Birmingham C	42	10	6	5	41	29	6	3	12	29	46	41
Crystal P	42	11	7	3	29	16	3	6	12	18	36	41
Portsmouth	42	13	4	4	47	26	3	4	14	27	52	40
Norwich C	42	8	7	6	33	27	4	8	9	19	25	39
Carlisle U	42	16	2	3	43	19	1	3	17	17	44	39
Ipswich T	42	12	6	3	38	23	3	3	15	20	43	39
Charlton A	42	10	6	5	39	29	2	8	11	22	41	38
Preston NE	42	7	10	4	37	23	4	5	12	25	47	37
Plymouth A	42	7	8	6	37	26	5	5	11	17	37	37
Bury	42	12	5	4	45	25	2	2	17	17	51	35
Cardiff C	42	10	3	8	37	35	2	7	12	34	56	34
Middlesbrough	42	8	8	5	36	28	2	5	14	22	58	33
Leyton O	42	3	9	9	19	36	2	4	15	19	44	23

DIVISION 3

	P	W	D	L	F	A	W	D	L	F	A	Pts
Hull C	46	19	2	2	64	24	12	5	6	45	38	69
Millwall	46	19	4	0	47	13	8	7	8	29	30	65
QPR	46	16	3	4	62	29	8	6	9	33	36	57
Scunthorpe U	46	9	8	6	44	34	12	3	8	36	33	53
Workington	46	13	6	4	38	18	6	8	9	29	39	52
Gillingham	46	14	4	5	33	19	8	4	11	29	35	52
Swindon T	46	11	8	4	43	18	8	5	10	31	30	51
Reading	46	13	5	5	36	19	6	8	9	34	44	51
Walsall	46	13	7	3	48	21	7	3	13	29	43	50
Shrewsbury T	46	13	7	3	48	22	6	4	13	25	42	49
Grimsby T	46	15	6	2	47	25	2	7	14	21	37	47
Watford	46	12	4	7	33	19	5	9	9	22	32	47
Peterboro' U	46	13	6	4	50	26	4	6	13	30	40	46
Oxford U	46	11	3	9	38	33	8	5	10	32	41	46
Brighton & HA	46	13	4	6	48	28	3	7	13	19	37	43
Bristol R	46	11	10	2	38	15	3	4	16	26	49	42
Swansea T	46	14	4	5	61	37	1	7	15	20	59	41
Bournemouth	46	9	8	6	24	19	4	4	15	14	37	38
Mansfield T	46	10	5	8	31	36	5	3	15	28	53	38
Oldham A	46	8	7	8	34	33	4	6	13	21	48	37
Southend U	46	15	1	7	43	28	1	3	19	11	55	36
Exeter C	46	9	6	8	36	28	3	5	15	17	51	35
Brentford	46	9	4	10	34	30	1	8	14	14	39	32
York C	46	5	7	11	30	44	4	2	17	23	62	27

DIVISION 4

	P	W	D	L	F	A	W	D	L	F	A	Pts
Doncaster R	46	15	6	2	49	21	9	5	9	36	33	59
Darlington	46	16	3	4	41	17	9	6	8	31	36	59
Torquay U	46	17	2	4	43	20	7	8	8	29	29	58
Colchester U	46	13	7	3	45	21	10	3	10	25	26	56
Tranmere R	46	15	1	7	56	32	9	7	7	37	34	56
Luton T	46	19	2	2	65	27	5	6	12	25	43	56
Chester	46	15	5	3	52	27	5	7	11	27	43	52
Notts Co	46	9	8	6	32	25	10	4	9	29	28	50
Newport Co	46	14	6	3	46	24	4	6	13	29	51	48
Southport	46	15	6	2	47	20	3	6	14	21	49	48
Bradford	46	14	2	7	59	31	7	3	13	43	61	47
Barrow	46	12	8	3	48	31	4	7	12	24	45	47
Stockport Co	46	12	4	7	42	29	6	2	15	29	41	42
Crewe A	46	12	4	7	42	23	4	5	14	19	40	41
Halifax T	46	11	6	6	46	31	4	5	14	21	44	41
Barnsley	46	11	6	6	43	24	4	4	15	31	54	40
Aldershot	46	12	6	5	47	27	3	4	16	28	57	40
Hartlepools U	46	13	4	6	44	22	3	4	16	19	53	40
Port Vale	46	12	7	4	38	18	3	2	18	10	41	39
Chesterfield	46	8	9	6	37	35	5	4	14	25	43	39
Rochdale	46	12	1	10	46	27	4	4	15	25	60	37
Lincoln C	46	9	7	7	37	29	4	4	15	20	53	37
Bradford C	46	10	5	8	37	34	2	8	13	26	60	37
Wrexham	46	10	4	9	43	43	3	5	15	29	61	35

Football League Records

Top scorers: Div 1, R.Davies (Southampton) 37 goals; Div 2, R.Gould (Coventry City) 24 goals; Div 3, R.Marsh (Queen's Park Rangers) 30 goals; Div 4, E.Phythian (Hartlepools United) 23 goals.

The legendary Bobby Charlton, a key figure in another Manchester United success he went on to help United to European Cup glory.

DIVISION 1

	ARSENAL	ASTON VILLA	BLACKPOOL	BURNLEY	CHELSEA	EVERTON	FULHAM	LEEDS U	LEICESTER C	LIVERPOOL	MANCHESTER C	MANCHESTER U	NEWCASTLE U	NOTTINGHAM F	SHEFFIELD U	SHEFFIELD W	SOUTHAMPTON	STOKE C	SUNDERLAND	TOTTENHAM H	W.B.A.	WEST HAM U
1 ARSENAL		A27 1-0	S17 1-1	D03 0-0	F04 2-1	a25 3-1	N19 1-0	N05 0-1	O01 2-4	M28 1-1	J14 1-0	M03 1-1	O08 2-0	a22 1-1	M25 2-0	S06 1-1	D26 4-1	m06 3-1	D17 2-0	J07 0-2	O22 2-3	A23 2-1
2 ASTON VILLA	D31 0-1		J14 3-2	a22 0-1	S17 2-6	m06 2-4	a08 1-1	O08 3-0	F04 0-1	O01 2-3	S03 3-0	D03 2-1	A20 1-1	N19 1-1	O22 0-0	A22 0-1	S05 0-1	M25 2-1	D27 2-1	M04 3-3	N05 3-2	M28 0-2
3 BLACKPOOL	J21 0-3	S10 0-2		F11 0-2	M27 0-2	a22 0-1	D03 0-1	M25 0-2	A22 1-1	S05 1-2	S24 0-1	O08 1-2	O22 6-0	M04 1-1	a08 0-1	D17 1-1	A27 2-3	N19 0-1	J07 1-1	N05 2-2	m06 1-3	D26 1-4
4 BURNLEY	a29 1-4	N26 4-2	O01 1-0		F25 1-2	m13 1-1	A23 3-0	S03 1-1	O15 5-2	M18 1-0	O29 2-3	F04 1-1	J14 0-2	M28 0-2	A20 4-0	a01 2-0	N12 4-1	D26 0-2	a15 1-0	S17 2-2	D31 5-1	D10 4-2
5 CHELSEA	S24 3-1	J21 3-1	M24 0-2	O08 1-3		D03 1-1	M04 0-0	m06 2-2	S07 2-2	D24 1-2	F11 0-0	N05 1-3	M25 2-1	A24 2-1	N19 1-1	A27 0-0	J07 4-1	a22 1-0	S10 1-1	O26 3-0	a10 0-2	D17 5-5
6 EVERTON	N12 0-0	a01 3-1	N26 0-1	S06 1-1	a19 3-1		D17 3-2	F04 2-0	O29 2-0	A27 3-1	a29 1-1	A23 1-2	O01 1-1	D23 0-1	J14 4-1	O15 2-1	M18 0-1	S03 0-1	m16 4-1	M22 0-1	S17 5-4	F25 4-0
7 FULHAM	a19 0-0	N12 5-1	a29 2-2	A29 0-0	O29 1-3	A20 0-1		S17 2-2	D27 4-2	F25 2-2	N26 4-1	M27 2-2	F04 5-1	m13 2-3	S03 0-1	M18 1-2	D10 3-1	D31 4-1	a01 3-1	O01 3-4	J14 2-2	O15 4-2
8 LEEDS U	O15 3-1	F25 0-2	D10 1-1	J07 3-1	a01 1-0	S24 1-1	J21 3-1		N12 3-1	m03 2-1	M18 0-0	A27 3-1	D26 5-0	S10 1-1	M28 2-0	m15 1-0	O29 0-1	F11 3-0	S07 2-1	D17 3-2	A24 2-1	N26 2-1
9 LEICESTER C	F11 2-1	S24 5-0	A31 3-0	N05 5-1	m09 3-2	M04 2-2	D26 0-2	a10 0-0		J18 2-1	M28 2-1	N30 1-2	m06 4-2	O08 3-0	a22 2-2	J07 0-1	S10 1-1	D03 4-2	J21 1-2	M25 0-1	N19 2-1	A27 5-4
10 LIVERPOOL	M27 0-0	F11 1-0	m13 1-3	N09 2-0	D26 2-1	D31 0-0	O08 2-2	N19 5-0	A20 3-2		A30 3-2	M25 0-0	a07 3-1	N05 4-0	D03 1-0	S10 1-1	J21 2-1	M04 2-1	S24 2-2	m06 0-0	a22 0-1	J07 2-0
11 MANCHESTER C	S10 1-1	a19 1-1	F04 1-0	M04 1-0	O01 1-4	N19 1-0	a22 3-0	m08 2-1	M24 1-3	A24 2-1		J21 1-1	N05 1-1	D03 1-1	m06 1-1	J02 0-0	D17 1-1	a12 3-1	A27 1-0	O08 1-2	M25 2-2	S07 1-4
12 MANCHESTER U	O29 1-0	a29 3-1	F25 4-0	S24 4-1	O15 1-1	A31 3-0	M28 2-1	D31 0-0	M18 5-2	D10 2-2	S17 1-0		S03 3-2	F11 1-0	D27 2-0	N12 2-0	a18 3-0	m13 0-0	N26 5-0	J14 1-0	A20 5-3	a01 3-0
13 NEWCASTLE U	F25 2-1	D17 0-3	M18 2-1	S10 1-1	D10 2-2	F11 0-3	S24 1-1	D24 1-2	a01 1-0	N12 0-2	O15 2-0	M11 0-0		J21 0-0	A31 1-0	N26 3-1	a29 3-1	M24 3-1	O29 0-3	A27 0-2	S07 1-3	a26 1-0
14 NOTTINGHAM F	N26 2-1	a15 3-0	O29 2-0	M27 4-1	A30 0-0	D26 1-0	S06 2-1	J14 1-0	F25 1-0	O15 1-1	m02 2-0	O01 4-1	S17 3-0		D31 3-1	D10 1-1	a01 3-1	A20 1-2	N12 3-1	F04 1-1	S03 2-1	M18 1-0
15 SHEFFIELD U	D10 1-1	M18 3-3	N12 1-1	D17 1-1	a17 3-0	S10 0-0	J07 4-0	M27 1-4	N26 0-1	a28 0-1	a01 1-0	D26 2-1	A23 0-1	A27 1-2		F04 1-0	F25 2-0	J21 2-1	O15 2-0	S06 2-1	O01 4-3	O29 3-1
16 SHEFFIELD W	m13 1-1	A31 2-0	A20 3-0	m06 7-0	D31 6-1	N05 1-2	O22 1-1	D03 0-0	S03 1-1	J14 0-1	D27 1-0	a10 2-2	a22 0-0	M25 0-2	S24 2-2		F11 4-1	O08 1-3	M28 5-0	N19 1-0	a19 1-0	S17 0-2
17 SOUTHAMPTON	D27 2-1	m13 6-2	D31 1-5	a08 4-0	S03 0-3	O25 1-3	M25 4-2	M04 0-2	J14 4-4	S17 1-2	A20 1-1	N19 1-2	D03 2-0	m06 2-1	O08 2-3	O01 4-2		N05 3-2	A31 3-1	a22 0-1	M29 2-2	F04 6-2
18 STOKE C	a01 2-2	D10 6-1	a15 2-0	D27 4-3	N26 1-1	J07 2-1	A27 1-2	O01 0-0	a29 3-1	O29 2-0	N12 0-1	S07 3-0	M27 0-1	D17 1-2	S17 3-0	F25 0-2	O15 3-2		M18 3-0	A24 2-0	F04 1-1	S10 1-1
19 SUNDERLAND	A20 1-3	D26 2-1	S03 4-0	N19 4-3	J14 2-0	M25 0-2	m06 3-1	m13 0-2	S17 2-3	F04 2-2	D31 1-0	a22 0-0	M04 3-0	a19 1-0	N05 4-1	M24 2-0	A24 2-0	O25 2-1		D03 0-1	O08 2-2	O01 2-4
20 TOTTENHAM H	S03 3-1	O29 0-1	O15 1-3	J21 2-0	M18 1-1	M27 2-0	F11 4-2	A20 3-1	D10 2-0	a01 2-1	F25 1-1	S10 2-1	D31 4-0	S24 2-1	m13 2-0	a15 2-1	N26 5-3	A31 2-0	m03 1-0		D27 0-0	N12 3-4
21 W.B.A.	M18 0-1	O15 2-1	a01 3-1	A27 1-2	N12 0-1	J21 1-0	S10 5-1	A31 2-0	a15 1-0	N26 2-1	D10 0-3	D17 3-4	m13 6-1	J07 1-2	F11 1-2	O29 1-2	M27 3-2	S24 0-1	F25 2-2	D26 3-0		a28 3-1
22 WEST HAM U	A29 2-2	M24 2-1	D27 4-0	M25 3-2	A20 1-2	O08 2-3	N05 6-1	a22 0-1	D31 0-1	S03 1-1	m13 1-1	m06 1-6	N19 3-0	O26 3-1	a04 0-2	J21 3-0	S24 2-2	J14 1-1	F11 2-2	m09 0-2	D03 3-0	

Coventry City goalkeeper Bill Glazier, part of manager Jimmy Hill's Sky Blue revolution at Highfield Road.

DIVISION 2

	BIRMINGHAM C	BLACKBURN R	BOLTON W	BRISTOL C	BURY	CARDIFF C	CARLISLE U	CHARLTON A	COVENTRY C	CRYSTAL P	DERBY CO	HUDDERSFIELD T	HULL C	IPSWICH T	MILLWALL	NORTHAMPTON T	NORWICH C	PLYMOUTH A	PORTSMOUTH	PRESTON N.E.	ROTHERHAM U	WOLVERHAMPTON W
1 BIRMINGHAM C		O29 1-1	a01 2-2	O15 4-0	S10 1-3	D10 1-2	M18 1-2	N12 4-0	J07 1-1	N26 3-1	a15 2-0	a28 0-1	M27 2-1	F25 2-2	F11 2-0	D26 3-0	A27 2-1	S27 0-0	A30 3-0	J21 3-1	S24 2-3	D17 3-2
2 BLACKBURN R	M04 1-0		a25 0-0	F11 1-0	O08 2-1	S10 4-1	D27 2-0	A24 2-1	M25 0-1	A27 2-1	D17 0-0	F18 2-0	a08 4-1	S24 1-2	D03 1-0	a22 3-0	O22 0-0	N19 3-0	N05 2-2	S07 2-0	m06 1-1	J21 0-0
3 BOLTON W	N05 3-1	M27 0-1		a19 0-0	M25 3-1	J21 3-1	S07 3-0	D17 2-1	O22 1-1	M11 0-0	A27 3-1	S10 1-0	N19 2-1	F11 1-1	m06 5-0	D03 1-2	M04 1-1	a22 1-2	a08 0-1	O08 4-2	A24 2-2	S24 0-0
4 BRISTOL C	M25 3-1	O01 2-2	D26 1-1		m06 3-3	A27 1-2	F04 3-0	S06 4-0	J21 2-2	A23 0-1	M28 4-1	D17 1-1	M04 2-1	S10 1-1	N19 1-1	a07 1-0	O08 1-0	N05 1-0	O21 3-3	D03 2-0	a22 1-2	J07 1-0
5 BURY	J14 0-2	F25 1-2	O14 2-1	D10 2-1		a15 2-0	O01 0-2	M18 2-1	F04 0-1	a01 1-1	O29 2-2	N12 0-0	D31 3-2	a28 1-2	M28 0-1	S20 1-2	S17 2-0	A20 1-0	S03 1-3	D27 3-4	S06 5-2	N26 2-1
6 CARDIFF C	m06 3-0	J14 1-1	S17 2-5	D31 5-1	N19 3-0		S03 4-2	F03 4-1	a22 1-1	D26 1-2	O01 1-1	S07 1-1	O08 2-4	A20 0-2	M04 1-1	D14 4-2	D03 2-0	M25 4-1	M22 0-0	a08 4-0	N04 0-0	A31 0-3
7 CARLISLE U	O22 2-0	D26 1-2	m13 6-1	S24 2-1	F11 2-0	J07 3-0		M28 1-0	O08 2-1	D17 3-0	A23 0-0	A27 2-1	N05 2-0	J21 2-1	a22 2-1	N19 2-0	S27 1-0	a08 0-0	M04 5-1	m06 1-1	D03 2-3	S10 1-3
8 CHARLTON A	m12 1-0	A30 0-0	A20 0-1	S27 5-0	O22 4-0	S24 5-0	M24 1-0		F18 1-2	S10 1-1	J07 3-1	J21 1-2	a22 1-3	D20 2-1	D31 0-0	m06 3-0	N05 0-0	D03 1-0	N19 0-2	M11 2-0	O08 2-0	F11 1-3
9 COVENTRY C	S03 1-1	O15 2-0	M18 1-1	S17 1-0	S24 3-0	N26 3-2	F25 2-1	O29 1-0		N12 1-2	a01 2-2	a15 1-0	A20 1-0	D09 5-0	m13 3-1	M28 2-0	J14 2-1	A30 1-0	D31 5-1	F11 2-1	D26 4-2	a29 3-1
10 CRYSTAL P	a22 2-1	D31 2-1	S03 3-2	A31 2-1	N05 3-1	D27 3-1	A20 4-2	J14 1-0	a08 1-1		S17 2-1	F11 1-1	m06 4-1	M27 0-2	M25 1-2	O08 5-1	N19 0-0	F04 2-1	D03 0-2	M07 1-0	O22 1-1	m13 4-1
11 DERBY CO	N19 1-2	A20 2-3	D31 2-2	M27 2-0	M04 3-1	F11 1-1	A31 0-1	S03 0-2	N05 1-2	J21 2-0		S24 4-3	D03 2-3	S28 2-2	O08 5-1	J14 4-3	a08 1-1	m06 1-1	a22 0-0	O22 5-1	M25 2-0	D26 0-3
12 HUDDERSFIELD T	D03 3-1	S03 3-1	J14 2-1	A20 2-0	a08 4-2	m13 3-1	D31 1-1	S17 4-1	N19 3-1	O01 0-2	F04 1-0		D27 1-0	A30 1-0	O22 2-0	M25 0-2	a22 0-1	O08 1-1	m06 1-1	N05 1-0	M04 3-0	M27 0-1
13 HULL C	M28 0-2	N12 2-3	a15 1-1	O29 0-2	A27 2-0	F25 1-0	a01 1-2	N26 2-2	D17 2-2	D10 6-1	a27 1-3	D26 2-0		M18 1-1	J21 2-0	S23 6-1	S20 5-0	F11 4-2	S28 2-0	J07 2-2	S10 1-0	O15 3-1
14 IPSWICH T	O08 3-2	F04 1-1	O01 2-2	J14 0-0	D03 2-0	D17 0-0	S17 1-2	D26 0-0	m06 1-1	M28 2-0	S06 4-3	A23 3-0	O22 5-4		a08 4-1	N05 6-1	a18 0-2	M04 1-1	M25 4-2	a22 0-0	N19 3-2	A27 3-1
15 MILLWALL	O01 3-1	a29 1-1	D10 2-0	a15 3-2	M24 2-0	O29 1-0	N26 2-1	A27 0-0	S05 1-0	O15 1-1	F25 3-2	M18 1-3	S17 2-1	N12 1-0		S03 1-0	D26 2-1	J14 1-2	F04 1-1	S19 2-0	D17 2-0	a01 1-1
16 NORTHAMPTON T	D27 2-1	N26 2-1	a29 2-1	N12 2-1	A30 0-0	M18 2-0	a15 3-3	J17 1-1	M11 0-0	F25 1-0	S10 0-2	O15 0-1	F04 2-2	a01 1-1	J07 1-2		S06 1-2	S17 2-1	O01 2-4	D17 1-5	A27 3-1	O29 0-4
17 NORWICH C	D31 3-3	M18 0-1	O29 1-0	F25 1-0	J21 2-0	a29 3-2	O15 2-0	a01 1-1	S10 1-1	a15 4-3	N12 4-1	N26 0-0	A31 0-2	S03 1-2	D27 1-1	m13 1-0		M27 3-1	A20 0-0	S24 1-1	F11 1-0	D10 1-2
18 PLYMOUTH A	S07 1-1	a15 4-0	N26 2-0	a01 1-2	D17 4-1	O15 7-1	N12 1-2	a29 2-1	A24 4-2	S24 1-0	D10 1-2	F25 2-3	O01 3-1	O29 1-1	S10 3-1	J21 1-0	M24 2-2		D27 0-0	A27 1-0	J07 1-0	M18 0-1
19 PORTSMOUTH	A24 4-5	a01 1-1	N12 2-1	M18 1-1	J07 1-2	M27 1-2	O29 2-1	a15 1-2	A27 0-2	a29 1-1	N26 0-3	D10 1-1	S07 0-1	O15 4-2	S24 0-1	F11 3-2	D17 3-3	D26 2-1		S10 2-0	J21 3-2	F25 2-3
20 PRESTON N.E.	S17 3-0	S26 3-0	F25 1-3	a29 2-2	D24 2-2	N12 4-0	D10 2-3	O15 2-1	O01 3-2	O29 1-0	M18 2-0	a01 1-2	S03 4-2	N26 2-0	O24 2-1	A20 2-1	F04 3-1	D31 2-0	J14 1-0		M28 1-1	a15 1-2
21 ROTHERHAM U	F04 3-2	D10 2-1	A30 0-1	N26 3-3	m13 3-0	a01 4-1	a29 2-3	F25 2-0	D27 1-1	M18 0-1	O15 0-0	O29 4-2	J14 1-1	a15 0-2	A20 3-1	D31 1-2	O01 2-1	S03 4-2	S17 0-1	M27 2-1		N12 2-2
22 WOLVERHAMPTON W	A20 1-2	S17 4-0	F04 5-2	S03 1-1	a22 4-1	S21 7-1	J14 1-1	O01 1-0	D03 1-3	S07 1-1	D24 5-3	M28 1-0	M25 4-0	D31 0-0	N05 2-0	M04 1-0	m06 4-1	O22 2-1	O08 3-1	N19 3-2	a08 2-0	

Season 1966-67

DIVISION 3

	BOURNEMOUTH	BRIGHTON & HA	BRISTOL R	COLCHESTER U	DARLINGTON	DONCASTER R	GILLINGHAM	GRIMSBY T	LEYTON O	MANSFIELD T	MIDDLESBROUGH	OLDHAM A	OXFORD U	PETERBOROUGH U	Q.P.R.	READING	SCUNTHORPE U	SHREWSBURY T	SWANSEA T	SWINDON T	TORQUAY U	WALSALL	WATFORD	WORKINGTON
1 BOURNEMOUTH		S28 2-1	M27 0-0	D26 1-1	F25 1-1	N12 4-1	J21 1-0	m13 0-0	S24 1-0	a15 1-3	F18 1-1	A27 2-1	D17 0-0	D10 1-1	O15 1-3	a01 2-2	J28 0-0	N16 0-3	a26 1-0	O29 1-4	O01 1-0	a29 3-0	M18 0-0	S10 0-2
2 BRIGHTON & H.A.	S07 0-3		N19 3-2	a22 1-1	O19 5-0	S03 0-0	M04 2-2	S17 0-2	O08 1-0	J14 1-0	m06 1-1	N05 2-0	a08 2-0	O01 5-2	D27 2-2	D31 0-1	M25 2-2	D03 2-1	M08 3-2	A20 2-2	a12 0-1	F04 2-3	M27 1-0	O22 0-0
3 BRISTOL R	M24 1-1	a15 2-2		J14 4-1	O04 3-0	F25 4-2	O18 4-1	M18 0-0	D27 1-0	O15 4-4	D31 2-2	F11 2-1	S24 2-1	a01 1-1	a29 2-1	S27 2-1	O24 1-1	S03 1-0	A20 3-3	S17 3-0	N12 1-0	O29 4-2	D10 0-3	M11 0-1
4 COLCHESTER U	D27 2-0	m13 3-2	S10 3-1		a29 2-3	O15 5-0	M11 0-0	O29 4-0	O17 2-2	M18 3-0	A20 2-3	S24 3-2	J21 1-2	N12 1-4	D10 1-3	F25 2-0	F11 0-1	D31 3-1	M24 3-1	S26 2-1	a15 1-0	a01 5-1	S03 2-1	a10 2-2
5 DARLINGTON	O08 1-2	N14 3-1	a22 0-3	D03 0-4		J14 3-2	O22 1-1	F04 1-0	M04 0-0	S17 1-1	D26 0-3	a08 2-3	N19 1-2	a10 5-0	M27 0-0	S03 0-1	N05 2-1	m06 1-1	S05 1-0	D31 2-1	F18 0-0	O01 0-1	A20 1-0	M25 1-1
6 DONCASTER R	a08 1-1	m16 1-1	O07 3-2	M03 1-4	S09 0-4		a21 2-3	D23 3-2	N18 2-2	N15 4-6	M25 0-4	M10 1-1	S06 2-1	D17 3-1	J21 1-1	a25 0-2	m05 3-0	O21 2-1	N05 4-1	F11 1-0	A27 2-1	M28 2-1	S23 0-0	D03 2-1
7 GILLINGHAM	S17 0-0	O15 2-0	N16 1-0	F18 2-1	M18 1-2	m13 3-1		D10 2-0	J14 0-0	a29 5-2	O01 5-1	M27 1-0	D27 3-1	O05 2-2	O29 2-2	a15 0-2	D17 0-1	a26 1-1	F04 0-0	N12 1-0	F25 0-0	S03 0-0	a01 4-1	A27 1-1
8 GRIMSBY T	a22 1-0	J21 2-3	O22 0-0	M25 0-0	S24 4-1	D26 4-1	m06 4-0		D03 1-2	M24 1-2	a08 2-1	O08 1-0	M04 1-0	m02 1-1	F11 1-1	O19 2-0	S07 7-1	N05 1-1	N19 2-1	a05 3-4	S10 1-0	A27 3-1	a12 0-2	D17 4-1
9 LEYTON O	F04 1-0	F25 3-2	D26 0-2	N14 3-3	O15 1-2	a15 4-1	S09 0-1	a29 1-1		m12 4-2	a10 2-0	D17 2-2	M27 2-1	S17 1-1	M18 0-0	N11 3-2	A27 3-1	F18 2-2	O01 1-0	a01 0-0	S05 0-0	m19 0-2	O29 1-1	m27 2-1
10 MANSFIELD T	N19 1-0	S10 2-1	M04 2-0	O22 2-0	J21 2-2	O17 3-1	D03 4-1	M28 4-0	a22 1-1		N05 4-5	S05 2-4	O08 1-1	A27 0-0	S24 1-7	F22 4-2	D27 3-1	M25 0-1	a08 1-2	a24 1-3	O31 4-2	D17 4-1	F11 2-1	m06 0-1
11 MIDDLESBROUGH	M11 3-1	D10 1-0	A27 1-2	D17 4-0	D27 4-0	O29 2-0	F11 1-1	N12 0-1	a24 3-1	a01 1-0		S10 0-2	m16 4-1	m13 2-1	S26 2-2	M18 2-2	J21 2-1	M27 1-0	O17 4-1	O15 4-0	a29 4-0	a15 0-2	F25 3-0	S24 3-2
12 OLDHAM A	D31 1-1	a01 4-1	O01 3-0	F04 4-0	N12 4-0	F18 1-0	M29 2-1	F24 0-1	A20 3-1	S27 0-0	J14 0-1		a25 1-1	M18 1-0	a15 0-1	D10 1-3	O18 2-0	S17 4-1	S03 4-1	a28 1-0	O29 5-0	O15 6-2	m13 1-1	D27 3-0
13 OXFORD U	A20 1-1	N12 1-2	F04 4-1	S17 1-1	a15 3-2	S28 6-1	D26 1-1	O15 3-1	M24 0-0	F25 2-1	S03 1-1	a12 3-1		O29 0-3	m13 2-1	O01 1-3	F18 2-1	J14 2-1	D31 2-3	D10 0-0	a01 2-2	M18 1-2	a29 0-0	O19 3-0
14 PETERBOROUGH U	m06 2-0	F11 2-1	N05 1-1	a08 2-1	a24 2-0	A20 3-3	S05 2-0	S03 2-1	J21 0-2	D31 3-1	a22 1-2	O22 3-1	M25 2-3		F20 0-2	M28 2-1	M04 1-0	N19 0-2	D03 4-4	D23 1-2	S24 0-1	J14 2-1	O17 2-2	O08 3-0
15 Q.P.R.	M07 4-0	D26 3-0	D03 3-0	m06 2-1	M24 4-0	S17 6-0	M25 2-0	O01 5-1	O22 4-1	F04 0-0	S06 4-0	N19 0-1	a22 3-1	M11 0-0		J14 2-1	a08 5-1	A20 2-2	O08 4-2	S03 3-1	N15 2-1	a25 0-0	D31 4-1	N05 4-1
16 READING	N05 0-0	A27 1-1	S07 1-2	O08 2-3	S21 1-0	a12 4-0	N19 2-1	N16 6-0	a08 1-0	M11 2-2	O22 0-0	m06 2-1	F11 1-2	M27 2-2	S10 2-2		D03 4-0	M03 2-0	M25 2-0	S24 2-1	D17 2-1	D27 3-1	J21 1-1	a22 2-0
17 SCUNTHORPE U	S03 0-1	O28 0-1	a24 3-1	S30 3-1	M31 2-0	D09 2-1	A20 1-2	S27 0-0	D30 2-2	D23 2-1	S17 3-2	N15 1-1	M10 2-2	O14 1-0	N12 0-2	a28 0-2		F04 2-0	J14 4-3	m12 1-2	M17 3-1	F24 2-0	a14 1-0	M27 4-1
18 SHREWSBURY T	O19 4-1	a29 0-0	N02 3-4	A27 2-1	D10 3-0	M18 2-1	a12 3-1	a01 0-1	M11 6-1	O29 1-0	M29 1-0	J21 3-1	S10 1-0	a15 1-1	D17 0-0	O15 1-0	S24 4-3		D27 2-2	F25 3-1	S21 3-2	N12 1-2	S26 1-1	F11 3-1
19 SWANSEA T	a04 0-1	M11 1-1	D17 2-2	M27 1-0	S27 1-1	a01 6-0	S24 1-1	a15 2-0	F11 2-0	N12 0-1	N15 4-4	A29 3-0	A27 0-1	a29 3-3	F25 1-3	O29 5-2	S10 0-1	D26 5-2		M18 2-2	D10 0-0	m13 4-1	O15 2-2	J21 5-2
20 SWINDON T	M25 1-0	D17 1-1	J21 0-1	S06 1-1	A27 4-0	O01 0-1	a08 2-0	F28 3-1	N05 5-1	a11 3-1	M04 4-1	D03 6-3	m06 3-0	D26 4-1	m02 1-1	F04 0-1	a22 2-1	O08 2-2	O22 4-0		M28 0-0	a18 3-2	S10 1-2	N19 3-0
21 TORQUAY U	F11 3-2	a26 5-0	a08 2-1	N19 5-0	M11 2-0	D31 4-0	O08 4-1	J14 3-1	S28 1-1	S03 1-2	D03 2-1	M25 4-0	N05 1-0	F04 1-0	O19 1-1	A20 3-0	O22 1-1	a22 0-2	m06 2-4	M27 1-0		S17 5-2	D14 1-0	M04 5-1
22 WALSALL	D03 3-0	S24 2-1	M25 1-1	N04 1-0	F11 1-1	M27 4-0	O11 3-0	D31 1-0	m06 1-1	A20 1-2	N19 2-1	M03 1-1	O22 2-0	S10 1-1	a11 2-0	D26 3-1	O08 2-0	a08 2-2	a22 1-1	O18 1-1	J21 0-1		M11 0-1	S06 2-0
23 WATFORD	O22 3-0	M24 1-1	m06 3-1	m09 0-0	D17 2-0	F04 4-1	N05 1-1	a25 3-1	M25 1-3	O01 0-1	O08 2-0	a22 2-2	D03 2-0	N15 3-1	A27 1-0	S17 1-0	N19 0-1	S06 1-0	M03 1-1	J14 2-0	D26 2-1	F18 2-1		a08 2-1
24 WORKINGTON	J14 0-0	M17 2-1	F18 0-2	J28 1-0	O28 1-2	a20 3-1	D31 1-3	A20 2-1	S02 3-1	D10 2-4	F04 1-2	D26 1-1	N16 0-0	F25 1-0	a01 0-2	m13 1-2	M28 1-0	m17 2-3	S16 6-3	a15 1-3	O14 1-2	S28 4-0	N12 1-2	

DIVISION 4

	ALDERSHOT	BARNSLEY	BARROW	BRADFORD	BRADFORD C	BRENTFORD	CHESTER	CHESTERFIELD	CREWE A	EXETER C	HALIFAX T	HARTLEPOOLS U	LINCOLN C	LUTON T	NEWPORT CO	NOTTS CO	PORT VALE	ROCHDALE	SOUTHEND U	SOUTHPORT	STOCKPORT CO	TRANMERE R	WREXHAM	YORK C
1 ALDERSHOT		S17 3-2	N11 0-1	M18 1-2	F18 0-3	S03 3-1	O15 3-0	a29 4-0	a01 1-0	M24 1-0	D31 0-1	A20 1-1	O26 1-0	F04 4-1	J14 5-0	F25 4-1	O29 0-1	O01 4-0	D26 5-2	S28 4-1	D10 1-1	N14 1-1	a26 2-0	a15 0-0
2 BARNSLEY	J21 1-1		A30 2-3	a01 2-0	D26 1-1	A20 0-1	O29 1-2	S02 0-3	a15 1-0	O24 2-1	M27 4-1	M11 1-2	D10 2-1	S10 2-1	D31 1-1	M18 0-0	N12 1-0	F25 3-1	F11 1-2	O15 0-0	S27 1-2	a11 2-2	S23 2-2	a28 0-1
3 BARROW	a08 1-1	M25 2-0		F04 1-0	M04 0-1	m06 1-0	S16 1-1	M24 2-1	a24 3-2	O08 5-0	J02 1-0	S26 2-3	F18 2-1	N19 3-0	M06 1-0	J14 0-1	O01 2-2	D31 2-0	a22 1-0	S03 2-2	A20 1-1	O22 0-0	N05 1-1	O17 1-1
4 BRADFORD	O22 1-1	F15 1-3	S24 0-1		N05 2-0	N19 2-2	D31 2-3	F08 2-0	J21 1-4	m06 2-2	M25 1-0	D03 1-2	a11 2-1	a22 0-0	a08 3-1	A20 4-1	S10 1-1	F18 0-3	O08 1-2	M28 0-0	O18 0-1	S06 2-3	M04 1-3	F11 1-0
5 BRADFORD C	M11 4-1	D27 1-1	O15 5-2	S03 2-3		O01 2-0	D10 2-3	a01 3-1	F25 0-3	J14 1-1	F04 1-2	S17 3-0	O29 2-1	N16 2-1	a26 1-2	a29 3-1	S28 2-0	a15 4-1	D17 2-1	M08 3-3	N12 0-1	A27 1-0	M27 3-3	M18 1-0
6 BRENTFORD	O11 1-0	D17 3-1	D10 0-3	a15 1-1	F11 2-0		N12 4-0	F25 1-0	a29 0-2	a11 3-1	O18 1-0	D27 1-2	S27 2-2	A27 1-0	M27 1-1	a01 1-0	m13 2-0	M18 4-0	J21 1-1	O29 2-1	O15 2-1	S24 1-1	S10 1-1	F18 1-1
7 CHESTER	M04 0-0	a22 1-0	J21 1-1	A27 0-3	m06 1-0	a08 1-2		a12 2-1	S10 0-3	D03 0-2	N19 0-2	M25 1-0	F11 0-1	O22 0-0	N05 4-2	M24 1-2	J28 1-3	O19 3-2	S07 1-1	F18 2-1	D26 1-1	D17 0-1	O08 1-3	S24 3-1
8 CHESTERFIELD	D03 1-1	N05 1-0	M27 1-2	D27 4-1	J28 0-1	O08 3-0	a24 0-2		F18 0-0	a22 1-0	M04 1-1	O22 1-0	A27 3-1	m06 0-0	S05 0-1	O01 1-1	m08 2-1	S17 0-0	N19 2-1	F04 2-1	J14 2-1	a08 3-1	M25 4-0	D17 1-0
9 CREWE A	N05 2-1	N19 2-2	a12 3-2	S16 1-3	O08 1-0	m10 1-0	J14 3-1	M11 2-1		S05 2-2	m06 1-1	F11 1-2	a05 3-0	a08 3-1	M25 3-2	S03 4-1	F03 1-0	A20 2-1	O22 1-0	D31 1-1	M24 1-1	M04 1-2	a22 1-2	D26 2-0
10 EXETER C	M27 1-1	N16 0-3	F25 1-2	D10 4-1	S10 2-2	a25 1-0	a29 2-0	O29 1-1	S27 2-0		O01 3-2	F04 1-0	M18 1-0	F18 2-1	D26 0-0	m13 1-0	S17 0-1	N12 0-0	A27 0-1	a15 0-0	a01 0-3	J28 1-4	D17 4-1	O15 3-1
11 HALIFAX T	A27 2-2	M28 1-1	D26 1-4	m13 0-0	S23 2-2	N15 3-2	a15 2-1	O15 1-0	D10 1-0	F11 0-0		a11 2-1	F25 0-0	D17 1-1	M11 2-2	N12 5-2	a29 2-2	O29 1-1	S09 2-2	a01 2-0	M18 0-1	J21 2-1	m10 3-1	O27 2-1
12 HARTLEPOOLS U	D17 3-2	F18 1-1	S05 2-1	a29 2-0	J21 1-0	D26 2-2	J30 3-2	M18 3-2	O01 1-2	S24 3-1	a24 1-3		O15 5-0	M24 2-1	S19 0-1	a15 2-1	D10 2-1	a01 2-1	J06 1-2	N12 1-1	O29 1-0	S10 0-2	A27 2-1	F25 4-2
13 LINCOLN C	M25 0-4	m06 0-1	M11 2-1	a26 2-2	a22 1-4	S07 3-1	O01 2-3	D31 2-1	N16 1-1	O22 1-1	O07 3-3	M04 3-0		D03 8-1	A20 2-2	F04 2-1	D27 0-1	J14 0-2	a08 2-2	S17 0-4	S02 0-1	N05 2-0	N19 1-1	M24 2-2
14 LUTON T	S24 4-0	J14 1-1	a15 3-1	O29 2-2	O20 0-0	D31 3-0	M18 1-0	D10 3-2	N12 2-1	M11 4-0	A20 2-0	M27 0-2	a29 2-1		S03 3-1	O15 2-5	a01 1-1	S29 3-1	a12 1-0	F25 0-0	S17 0-3	D27 2-0	F11 3-1	m13 5-1
15 NEWPORT CO	S10 1-2	A27 2-0	a29 0-1	N12 0-0	a10 1-1	M28 1-1	a03 2-3	S26 4-1	m13 2-1	D27 3-2	m01 3-0	O17 0-2	M13 0-0	O24 2-0		O29 1-0	a17 1-1	O15 2-2	S24 3-0	M18 0-0	F25 1-1	F13 1-2	J21 1-1	D10 4-2
16 NOTTS CO	O08 3-0	O22 0-3	S10 2-2	D17 2-1	D03 1-3	N05 3-2	M28 3-0	F11 0-2	N01 1-1	M25 0-1	a08 2-1	N19 0-0	S24 2-1	M04 1-2	a22 2-1		A27 0-0	D27 2-0	M10 1-0	O19 0-1	a26 2-2	m06 0-0	S07 2-2	J21 2-0
17 PORT VALE	a22 0-2	a08 3-1	F11 2-1	J14 0-0	S05 3-2	M25 1-3	S03 1-1	O17 2-3	S24 1-1	J21 2-0	D03 0-1	m06 0-0	m03 2-2	N05 1-0	N19 2-0	D31 0-0		M28 5-0	M04 1-3	A20 2-1	M11 0-2	O08 1-1	O22 0-2	a24 4-1
18 ROCHDALE	F11 2-1	O08 1-1	A27 1-3	M11 1-0	N19 0-1	O22 1-3	M01 0-1	J21 2-1	D17 0-1	a08 1-0	a22 3-0	N05 3-2	S10 1-0	S06 3-0	M04 2-0	J27 1-1	M27 1-2		D03 1-2	a10 1-1	S24 1-0	M25 1-2	m06 1-3	m02 2-2
19 SOUTHEND U	D27 4-0	S30 3-0	O28 1-3	F25 4-0	A20 2-1	S17 3-0	S26 5-1	a15 4-1	M17 1-1	D31 0-0	J14 1-0	S02 2-0	N12 3-0	a24 2-0	F04 1-0	F18 1-0	O14 4-1	a29 0-0		D10 0-1	m13 0-1	M27 0-0	N14 1-1	M31 2-1
20 SOUTHPORT	S05 1-0	M04 3-0	O10 4-1	M27 1-0	M25 2-1	a22 2-0	M11 4-3	S24 1-2	A26 4-1	N19 1-1	N05 2-0	a08 3-1	J21 2-1	O08 4-1	O22 1-0	S19 2-1	D17 0-0	a24 1-2	m06 1-0		F11 4-0	D03 1-0	D26 1-0	S10 2-0
21 STOCKPORT CO	m05 1-0	S05 2-1	D16 2-1	N14 4-0	a07 1-0	M03 1-2	D23 1-1	S09 3-1	M27 1-1	N04 1-0	O21 2-1	a21 2-0	m26 4-5	J20 1-0	O07 0-0	a10 2-0	F17 1-1	F03 2-2	M25 4-1	S30 1-0		N18 1-0	D02 1-0	A26 3-1
22 TRANMERE R	O17 2-2	a24 3-3	M17 1-2	S26 2-2	D30 3-1	F03 0-0	A20 0-0	N11 1-0	O14 5-0	S03 1-1	S16 1-0	J13 2-0	M31 1-0	D26 1-0	S30 2-1	m17 3-0	F24 2-1	m12 3-1	M24 1-2	a28 1-2	a14 3-0		F17 2-1	O28 2-1
23 WREXHAM	a10 2-0	F04 2-2	a01 1-1	O15 6-0	M24 1-1	J14 0-0	F25 3-1	m13 3-2	O29 1-1	A20 0-0	S03 4-0	D31 4-1	a15 0-0	O01 2-0	S17 2-2	S26 3-2	M18 2-1	D10 4-2	O17 2-0	a03 1-1	a29 2-2	M11 0-0		N12 1-1
24 YORK C	N19 1-2	D03 0-3	N14 1-2	S30 3-1	O22 4-1	M11 0-0	F04 1-1	A20 1-1	D27 0-2	M03 2-4	S05 4-3	O07 1-1	M27 3-1	M25 5-1	m05 2-1	S16 4-1	a10 3-1	S02 1-1	N04 2-1	J14 2-0	D31 1-2	a21 0-1	a07 4-0	

LEAGUE TABLES

DIVISION 1

	P	W	D	L	F	A	W	D	L	F	A	Pts
Manchester U	42	17	4	0	51	13	7	8	6	33	32	60
Nottingham F	42	16	4	1	41	13	7	6	8	23	28	56
Tottenham H	42	15	3	3	44	21	9	5	7	27	27	56
Leeds U	42	15	4	2	41	17	7	7	7	21	25	55
Liverpool	42	12	7	2	36	17	7	6	8	28	30	51
Everton	42	11	4	6	39	22	8	6	7	26	24	48
Arsenal	42	11	6	4	32	20	5	8	8	26	27	46
Leicester C	42	12	4	5	47	28	6	4	11	31	43	44
Chelsea	42	7	9	5	33	29	8	5	8	34	33	44
Sheffield U	42	11	5	5	34	22	5	5	11	18	37	42
Sheffield W	42	9	7	5	39	19	5	6	10	17	28	41
Stoke C	42	11	5	5	40	21	6	2	13	23	37	41
WBA	42	11	1	9	40	28	5	6	10	37	45	39
Burnley	42	11	4	6	43	28	4	5	12	23	48	39
Manchester C	42	8	9	4	27	25	4	6	11	16	27	39
West Ham U	42	8	6	7	40	31	6	2	13	40	53	36
Sunderland	42	12	3	6	39	26	2	5	14	19	46	36
Fulham	42	8	7	6	49	34	3	5	13	22	49	34
Southampton	42	10	3	8	49	41	4	3	14	25	51	34
Newcastle U	42	9	5	7	24	27	3	4	14	15	54	33
Aston Villa	42	7	5	9	30	33	4	2	15	24	52	29
Blackpool	42	1	5	15	18	36	5	4	12	23	40	21

DIVISION 2

	P	W	D	L	F	A	W	D	L	F	A	Pts
Coventry C	42	17	3	1	46	16	6	10	5	28	27	59
Wolves	42	15	4	2	53	20	10	4	7	35	28	58
Carlisle U	42	15	3	3	42	16	8	3	10	29	38	52
Blackburn R	42	13	6	2	33	11	6	7	8	23	35	51
Ipswich T	42	11	8	2	45	25	6	8	7	25	29	50
Huddersfield T	42	14	3	4	36	17	6	6	9	22	29	49
Crystal P	42	14	4	3	42	23	5	6	10	19	32	48
Millwall	42	14	5	2	33	17	4	4	13	16	41	45
Bolton W	42	10	7	4	36	19	4	7	10	28	39	42
Birmingham C	42	11	5	5	42	23	5	3	13	28	43	40
Norwich C	42	10	7	4	31	21	3	7	11	18	34	40
Hull C	42	11	5	5	46	25	5	2	14	31	47	39
Preston NE	42	14	3	4	44	23	2	4	15	21	44	39
Portsmouth	42	7	5	9	34	37	6	8	7	25	33	39
Bristol C	42	10	8	3	38	22	2	6	13	18	40	38
Plymouth A	42	12	4	5	42	21	2	5	14	17	37	37
Derby Co	42	8	6	7	40	32	4	6	11	28	40	36
Rotherham U	42	10	5	6	39	28	3	5	13	22	42	36
Charlton A	42	11	4	6	34	16	2	5	14	15	37	35
Cardiff C	42	9	7	5	43	28	3	2	16	18	59	33
Northampton T	42	8	6	7	28	33	4	0	17	19	51	30
Bury	42	9	3	9	31	30	2	3	16	18	53	28

DIVISION 3

	P	W	D	L	F	A	W	D	L	F	A	Pts
QPR	46	18	4	1	66	15	8	11	4	37	23	67
Middlesbrough	46	16	3	4	51	20	7	6	10	36	44	55
Watford	46	15	5	3	39	17	5	9	9	22	29	54
Reading	46	13	7	3	45	20	9	2	12	31	37	53
Bristol R	46	13	8	2	47	28	7	5	11	29	39	53
Shrewsbury T	46	15	5	3	48	24	5	7	11	29	38	52
Torquay U	46	17	3	3	57	20	4	6	13	16	34	51
Swindon T	46	14	5	4	53	21	6	5	12	28	38	50
Mansfield T	46	12	4	7	48	37	8	5	10	36	42	49
Oldham A	46	15	4	4	51	16	4	6	13	29	47	48
Gillingham	46	11	9	3	36	18	4	7	12	22	44	46
Walsall	46	12	8	3	37	16	6	2	15	28	56	46
Colchester U	46	14	3	6	52	30	3	7	13	24	43	44
Leyton O	46	10	9	4	36	27	3	9	11	22	41	44
Peterboro' U	46	12	4	7	40	31	2	11	10	26	40	43
Oxford U	46	10	8	5	41	29	5	5	13	20	37	43
Grimsby T	46	13	5	5	46	23	4	4	15	15	45	43
Scunthorpe U	46	13	4	6	39	26	4	4	15	19	47	42
Brighton & HA	46	10	8	5	37	27	3	7	13	24	44	41
Bournemouth	46	8	10	5	24	24	4	7	12	15	33	41
Swansea T	46	9	9	5	50	30	3	6	14	35	59	39
Darlington	46	8	7	8	26	28	5	4	14	21	53	37
Doncaster R	46	11	6	6	40	40	1	2	20	18	77	32
Workington	46	9	3	11	35	35	3	4	16	20	54	31

DIVISION 4

	P	W	D	L	F	A	W	D	L	F	A	Pts
Stockport Co	46	16	5	2	41	18	10	7	6	28	24	64
Southport	46	19	2	2	47	15	4	11	8	22	27	59
Barrow	46	12	8	3	35	18	12	3	8	41	36	59
Tranmere R	46	14	6	3	42	20	8	8	7	24	23	58
Crewe A	46	14	5	4	42	26	7	7	9	28	29	54
Southend U	46	15	5	3	44	12	7	4	12	26	37	53
Wrexham	46	11	12	0	46	20	5	8	10	30	42	52
Hartlepools U	46	15	3	5	44	29	7	4	12	22	35	51
Brentford	46	13	7	3	36	19	5	6	12	22	37	49
Aldershot	46	14	4	5	48	19	4	8	11	24	38	48
Bradford C	46	13	4	6	48	31	6	6	11	26	31	48
Halifax T	46	10	11	2	37	27	5	3	15	22	41	44
Port Vale	46	9	7	7	33	27	5	8	10	22	31	43
Exeter C	46	11	6	6	30	24	3	9	11	20	36	43
Chesterfield	46	13	6	4	33	16	4	2	17	27	47	42
Barnsley	46	8	7	8	30	28	5	8	10	30	36	41
Luton T	46	15	5	3	47	23	1	4	18	12	50	41
Newport Co	46	9	9	5	35	23	3	7	13	21	40	40
Chester	46	8	5	10	24	32	7	5	11	30	46	40
Notts Co	46	10	7	6	31	25	3	4	16	22	47	37
Rochdale	46	10	4	9	30	27	3	7	13	23	48	37
York C	46	11	5	7	45	31	1	6	16	20	48	35
Bradford	46	7	6	10	30	34	4	7	12	22	45	35
Lincoln C	46	7	8	8	39	39	2	5	16	19	43	31

Football League Records

Top scorers: Div 1, G.Best (Manchester United), R.Davies (Southampton) 28 goals; Div 2, J.Hickton (Middlesbrough) 24 goals; Div 3, D.Rogers (Swindon Town) 25 goals; Div 4, L.Massie (Halifax Town), R.Chapman (Port Vale) 25 goals.
Leyton Orient dropped 'Leyton' from their name.

Francis Lee joined Manchester City from Bolton for £60,000 in October 1967 and at the end of the season had won a League Championship medal.

DIVISION 1

	ARSENAL	BURNLEY	CHELSEA	COVENTRY C	EVERTON	FULHAM	LEEDS U	LEICESTER C	LIVERPOOL	MANCHESTER C	MANCHESTER U	NEWCASTLE U	NOTTINGHAM F	SHEFFIELD U	SHEFFIELD W	SOUTHAMPTON	STOKE C	SUNDERLAND	TOTTENHAM H	W.B.A.	WEST HAM U	WOLVERHAMPTON W
1 ARSENAL		a27 2-0	D30 1-1	S02 1-1	N11 2-2	O28 5-3	m07 4-3	a13 2-1	A28 2-0	S23 1-0	F24 0-2	F10 0-0	D23 3-0	J13 1-1	a30 3-2	a15 0-3	A19 2-0	O14 2-1	S16 4-0	m11 2-1	N25 0-0	M16 0-2
2 BURNLEY	D02 1-0		N04 1-1	A19 2-1	D30 2-1	S30 2-0	m11 3-0	a15 1-1	O24 1-1	M02 0-1	F17 2-1	N18 2-0	O07 1-1	m04 0-2	D23 2-1	M23 2-0	a20 4-0	S16 3-0	S02 5-1	a06 0-0	A29 3-3	F03 1-1
3 CHELSEA	D26 2-1	a22 2-1		S30 1-1	O14 1-1	A26 1-1	M20 0-0	M16 4-1	F12 3-1	a16 1-0	N25 1-1	A23 1-1	F03 1-0	S06 4-2	N11 3-0	S02 2-6	S16 2-2	a27 1-0	a13 2-0	D16 0-3	O28 1-3	a29 1-0
4 COVENTRY C	J06 1-1	D16 5-1	F10 2-1		N25 0-2	N11 0-3	a13 0-1	a27 0-1	D26 1-1	S09 0-3	M16 2-0	J20 1-4	A29 1-3	A26 2-2	F24 3-0	S05 2-1	a15 2-0	O28 2-2	O14 2-3	S23 4-2	D08 1-1	M30 1-0
5 EVERTON	a06 2-0	D26 2-0	a20 2-1	M02 3-1		m21 5-1	S16 0-1	a09 2-1	F03 1-0	N04 1-1	A19 3-1	M23 1-0	D02 1-0	N18 1-0	a15 1-0	O07 4-2	m04 3-0	D23 3-0	A29 0-1	O24 2-1	S05 2-0	S02 4-2
6 FULHAM	M23 1-3	F10 4-3	D23 2-2	a06 1-1	S09 2-1		J06 0-5	J20 0-1	D02 1-1	O21 2-4	a12 0-4	a20 2-0	N18 2-0	M13 0-1	F28 2-0	m04 2-2	m01 0-2	A28 3-2	D30 1-2	O07 1-2	S23 0-3	A19 1-2
7 LEEDS U	N04 3-1	S20 2-1	O07 7-0	N18 1-1	J20 2-0	S02 2-0		S23 3-2	m04 1-2	M23 2-0	N08 1-0	O25 2-0	M13 1-1	a06 3-0	D30 3-2	J13 5-0	D02 2-0	A19 1-1	a17 1-0	a20 3-1	F10 2-1	D23 2-1
8 LEICESTER C	N18 2-2	a16 0-2	O25 2-2	D02 0-0	S30 0-2	S16 1-2	F03 2-2		O07 2-1	a06 1-0	D23 2-2	N04 2-2	m04 4-2	M02 3-1	A30 3-0	a20 4-1	m11 0-0	S02 0-2	A19 2-3	M23 2-3	D30 2-4	J13 3-1
9 LIVERPOOL	A22 2-0	M16 3-2	S09 3-1	D30 1-0	S23 1-0	a27 4-1	D09 2-0	F24 3-1		D16 1-1	N11 1-2	A26 6-0	m11 6-1	a12 1-2	O28 1-0	J20 2-0	S30 2-1	a13 2-1	a29 1-1	J06 4-1	O14 3-1	N25 2-1
10 MANCHESTER C	F03 1-1	N25 4-2	a12 1-0	M09 3-1	a29 2-0	M16 5-1	O28 1-0	N11 6-0	A19 0-0		S30 1-2	S06 2-0	S02 2-0	S16 5-2	a25 1-0	A30 4-2	D23 4-2	F24 1-0	D09 4-1	D30 0-2	a13 3-0	O14 2-0
11 MANCHESTER U	O07 1-0	S09 2-2	M02 1-3	O25 4-0	D16 3-1	a15 3-0	A23 1-0	A26 1-1	a06 1-2	M27 1-3		m04 6-0	M23 3-0	a20 1-0	J20 4-2	N18 3-2	N04 1-0	m11 1-2	S23 3-1	D02 2-1	J06 3-1	D26 4-0
12 NEWCASTLE U	S30 2-1	a13 1-0	A30 5-1	S16 3-2	O28 1-0	O14 2-1	M16 1-1	a03 0-0	D23 1-1	m11 3-4	D09 2-2		J13 0-0	F03 1-0	N25 4-0	A19 3-0	S02 1-1	D26 2-1	a27 1-3	a12 2-2	N11 1-0	F24 2-0
13 NOTTINGHAM F	A26 2-0	F24 1-0	S23 3-0	A22 3-3	a22 1-0	a13 2-2	N25 0-2	M19 2-1	S05 0-1	J06 0-3	O28 3-1	S09 4-0		D16 1-0	O14 0-0	F10 2-2	D26 3-0	M30 0-3	M16 0-0	J20 3-2	a16 1-1	N11 3-1
14 SHEFFIELD U	S09 2-4	D09 1-0	m11 1-2	D23 2-0	a13 0-1	a23 2-3	N11 1-0	N25 0-0	a15 1-1	J20 0-3	O14 0-3	S23 2-1	A19 1-3		S02 0-1	D30 4-1	A29 1-0	M16 1-2	F26 3-2	F10 1-1	a27 1-2	O28 1-1
15 SHEFFIELD W	m04 1-2	A26 2-1	a06 2-2	O07 4-0	a16 0-0	S06 4-2	D26 0-1	A23 2-1	M23 1-2	D02 1-1	S16 1-1	M02 1-1	a20 0-0	J06 1-1		N04 2-0	O23 1-1	F03 0-1	J17 1-2	N18 2-2	D16 4-1	S30 2-2
16 SOUTHAMPTON	a10 2-0	O28 2-2	J06 3-5	m11 0-0	F26 3-2	M08 2-1	S09 1-1	O14 1-5	S16 1-0	A23 3-2	a13 2-2	D16 0-0	S30 2-1	D26 3-3	M30 2-0		F03 1-2	N25 3-2	N11 1-2	A26 4-0	M16 0-0	a27 1-1
17 STOKE C	D16 0-1	O14 0-2	J20 0-1	a16 3-3	D09 1-0	N25 0-1	a23 3-2	S06 3-2	m15 2-1	A26 3-0	M30 2-4	J06 2-1	D30 1-3	A23 1-1	M16 0-1	S23 3-2		N11 2-1	O28 2-1	S09 0-0	F26 2-0	a13 0-2
18 SUNDERLAND	a20 2-0	J20 2-2	D02 2-3	M23 1-1	A26 1-0	A23 3-0	D16 2-2	J06 0-2	N18 1-1	O07 1-0	S06 1-1	D30 3-3	N04 1-0	O25 2-1	S23 0-2	M02 0-3	a06 3-1		F10 0-1	m04 0-0	S09 1-5	a15 2-0
19 TOTTENHAM H	J20 1-0	M30 5-0	N18 2-0	a20 4-2	A23 1-1	D26 2-2	a12 2-1	D16 0-1	N04 1-1	m04 1-3	F03 1-2	D02 1-1	O25 1-1	O07 1-1	S09 2-1	a06 6-1	M23 3-0	S30 3-0		M01 0-0	A26 5-1	S06 2-1
20 W.B.A.	S06 1-3	N11 8-1	A19 0-1	F03 0-1	M16 2-6	F24 2-1	O14 2-0	O28 0-0	S02 0-2	D26 3-2	a29 6-3	a15 2-0	S16 2-1	S30 4-1	a13 1-1	D23 0-0	M13 3-0	a02 0-0	N25 2-0		m01 3-1	A30 4-1
21 WEST HAM U	M29 1-1	A21 4-2	M23 0-1	m04 0-0	m11 1-1	F03 7-2	S30 0-0	D26 4-2	a20 1-0	N18 2-3	S02 1-3	a06 5-0	a12 3-0	D02 3-0	A19 2-3	O23 0-1	O07 3-4	a24 1-1	D23 2-1	D11 2-3		S16 1-2
22 WOLVERHAMPTON W	O23 3-2	S23 3-2	m04 3-0	N04 2-0	J06 1-3	D16 3-2	A26 2-0	S09 1-3	M02 1-1	a20 0-0	D30 2-3	O07 2-2	a06 6-1	M23 1-3	M19 2-3	D02 2-0	N18 3-4	M09 2-1	m11 2-1	A23 3-3	J20 1-2	

Brian Kidd made his senior Manchester United debut in 1967-8 and ended the campaign with a European Cup winners' medal as well as helping United to runners-up spot in Division One.

DIVISION 2

	ASTON VILLA	BIRMINGHAM C	BLACKBURN R	BLACKPOOL	BOLTON W	BRISTOL C	CARDIFF C	CARLISLE U	CHARLTON A	CRYSTAL P	DERBY CO	HUDDERSFIELD T	HULL C	IPSWICH T	MIDDLESBROUGH	MILLWALL	NORWICH C	PLYMOUTH A	PORTSMOUTH	PRESTON N.E.	Q.P.R.	ROTHERHAM U
1 ASTON VILLA		O07 2-4	M23 1-2	O21 3-2	a20 1-1	m04 2-4	D30 2-1	N04 1-0	J20 4-1	S23 0-1	J06 2-1	D02 0-0	N18 2-3	a06 2-2	F10 0-1	M02 3-1	D16 4-2	A28 0-1	a16 1-0	S09 1-0	m11 1-2	A26 3-1
2 BIRMINGHAM C	F24 2-1		S16 1-1	F03 1-2	A19 4-0	D26 4-1	a13 0-0	J13 1-3	m07 4-0	N25 1-0	a02 3-1	D23 6-1	S04 6-2	S02 0-0	S26 6-1	S30 2-3	M16 0-0	a16 2-2	O14 2-2	N11 3-0	D09 2-0	O28 4-1
3 BLACKBURN R	M13 2-1	J20 1-2		a03 2-1	S23 2-1	S09 2-0	a27 1-1	A23 1-0	M09 3-2	M16 2-1	D26 3-0	F14 0-0	A26 2-0	S06 2-1	J06 3-0	D16 2-0	F24 0-0	a24 1-1	N25 2-2	a13 0-1	M30 0-1	D09 3-1
4 BLACKPOOL	M16 1-0	S23 1-0	a15 2-1		F10 1-1	J20 1-1	N11 3-1	D26 1-1	a13 2-0	O14 2-0	D09 1-1	S04 2-0	J06 3-1	A21 0-0	S09 3-0	A26 1-4	N25 0-2	M30 2-0	a27 2-0	D16 4-1	O28 0-1	F24 1-1
5 BOLTON W	N25 2-3	D16 1-1	F03 2-1	S30 1-2		a17 1-0	A26 1-1	S16 2-3	N22 2-0	a27 2-2	O28 5-3	S02 3-1	A23 6-1	M09 1-2	D26 2-0	S06 1-1	O14 2-0	D09 1-2	a13 1-2	M30 0-0	F24 1-1	M16 0-2
6 BRISTOL C	F27 0-0	D30 3-1	J13 0-0	S16 2-4	a02 1-1		O14 1-1	S02 1-0	N25 0-2	F24 2-1	N10 1-0	A19 2-3	S30 3-3	D22 1-1	S05 0-0	F03 0-2	D05 0-2	a13 2-0	M16 3-0	a27 4-1	A22 0-2	M29 0-1
7 CARDIFF C	D26 3-0	N18 1-3	D02 3-2	a06 1-3	D23 1-3	M02 0-1		a20 1-0	m11 0-0	A30 4-2	S23 1-5	m04 0-0	M22 2-3	O07 1-1	O24 3-0	D05 2-2	S09 3-1	A19 1-1	J06 3-0	F10 2-0	a16 1-0	J20 2-2
8 CARLISLE U	M30 1-2	S09 1-1	A29 1-0	D30 1-3	J20 3-0	J06 0-0	N25 1-3		M16 0-0	O28 3-0	a13 1-1	S23 2-1	D16 1-1	F10 4-1	A26 2-2	a16 1-1	D09 2-2	a27 2-0	F23 1-1	O14 4-1	N11 3-1	S05 4-1
9 CHARLTON A	S16 3-0	D02 3-1	M01 3-0	N18 0-2	a06 2-0	a20 1-2	S05 1-1	O21 2-2		M05 0-1	D16 1-2	F17 4-2	m04 5-1	M23 0-1	O07 2-2	J06 1-0	D26 3-3	S30 1-0	O03 4-1	A26 0-0	F03 3-3	a12 4-1
10 CRYSTAL P	F03 0-1	a20 0-0	O23 1-0	M02 3-1	D02 0-3	O07 2-0	S27 2-1	M23 1-1	S09 3-0		A26 1-0	a06 0-1	J20 0-1	m01 1-3	m04 1-3	N18 2-2	a16 6-0	S06 5-0	D26 2-2	m15 2-0	S30 1-0	D16 1-0
11 DERBY CO	S02 3-1	N04 2-2	D30 2-2	m04 1-3	M23 2-1	a06 3-1	F03 3-4	N18 0-1	A19 3-2	D23 1-1		O21 1-0	a20 1-2	M02 2-3	D02 2-4	O07 3-3	M09 1-1	S16 1-0	S30 0-1	a15 1-2	F17 4-0	S27 4-1
12 HUDDERSFIELD T	a27 0-0	A26 2-3	S30 2-1	m11 1-3	J06 1-1	D16 0-3	D09 1-0	F03 1-1	M30 4-1	N11 1-1	M16 3-1		D26 2-0	S16 1-4	a16 1-0	A22 1-0	a13 2-0	F24 0-1	S09 2-2	O28 1-1	N25 1-0	O14 2-0
13 HULL C	a13 3-0	m11 0-1	D22 1-1	S02 0-1	A30 1-2	F10 4-2	O27 1-2	A19 1-0	D09 1-1	S16 1-1	N25 3-0	D30 1-1		a15 1-1	S23 0-2	J13 1-1	N11 0-2	M16 0-2	M30 1-1	F24 1-1	O14 2-0	a25 2-1
14 IPSWICH T	N11 2-1	J06 2-1	m11 1-1	A29 1-1	S09 1-1	A26 5-0	F24 4-2	S30 3-1	O28 3-2	M30 2-2	O14 4-0	J20 2-0	a16 2-0		D16 1-2	D26 2-1	S23 0-0	N25 1-1	D09 1-2	M16 4-0	a27 2-2	a13 2-0
15 MIDDLESBROUGH	S30 1-1	A29 1-1	S02 0-0	J13 0-0	D30 1-2	m11 2-1	M09 2-3	D23 4-0	F24 1-1	D09 3-0	a27 2-2	a15 3-2	F03 2-1	A19 0-2		S16 0-1	M30 2-0	O14 5-0	O28 1-0	N25 5-0	a13 3-1	N11 1-1
16 MILLWALL	O14 1-2	F10 1-1	A19 1-2	O24 1-1	F16 3-0	S23 1-1	M30 3-1	a15 1-0	S02 0-0	a13 5-1	F24 1-1	A29 1-1	S09 1-1	D30 1-1	J20 4-0		a27 1-0	O28 3-0	N11 3-2	D09 2-0	M16 1-1	N25 0-0
17 NORWICH C	A19 1-0	O21 4-2	O07 1-0	a20 1-2	M02 3-1	M23 3-2	m08 1-0	m04 2-1	D30 1-1	a15 2-1	S06 3-2	N18 0-1	a06 2-2	F03 3-4	N04 2-1	D02 5-2		S02 2-0	S16 1-3	A23 1-3	D23 0-0	F10 2-2
18 PLYMOUTH A	A23 2-1	a15 1-2	F17 2-1	M09 2-2	m04 1-2	N18 0-1	D16 0-0	D02 3-1	F10 1-4	m11 2-1	J20 3-4	O07 1-1	O21 2-5	a20 0-1	M02 0-1	M23 2-1	J10 2-2		A26 1-2	S23 1-2	D26 0-1	S09 0-1
19 PORTSMOUTH	a15 2-2	M02 1-2	a20 2-1	D02 3-1	N18 3-0	O21 2-0	S02 3-1	O07 2-1	S27 4-0	D30 2-2	F10 3-2	J13 3-1	N04 3-0	m04 1-2	M23 2-0	a06 0-0	J20 3-0	D23 0-0		S06 2-1	A19 1-1	S23 1-1
20 PRESTON N.E.	M18 2-1	a06 0-0	N18 3-5	A19 0-2	N04 1-1	D02 0-1	S30 3-0	M02 0-2	D23 4-1	S02 0-0	a16 1-1	M23 3-1	O07 3-2	O21 1-1	a20 0-0	m04 0-1	A28 1-0	F03 2-0	m11 3-1		S16 0-2	D26 2-2
21 Q.P.R.	S05 3-0	m04 2-0	D12 3-1	M23 2-0	O07 1-0	A29 3-1	a12 1-0	a06 1-0	S23 2-1	F10 2-1	S09 0-1	a20 3-0	M09 1-1	D02 1-0	N18 1-1	O21 3-1	A26 2-0	D30 4-1	D16 2-0	J20 2-0		J06 6-0
22 ROTHERHAM U	D23 0-2	M23 1-1	m04 1-0	O07 1-2	O21 2-2	N04 1-0	S16 3-2	m11 1-2	a16 1-1	A19 0-3	A28 1-3	M02 1-0	D02 1-3	N18 1-3	a06 0-1	a20 2-0	S30 1-3	M19 1-0	F03 1-1	D30 1-0	S02 1-3	

Season 1967-68

DIVISION 3

	BARROW	BOURNEMOUTH	BRIGHTON & HA	BRISTOL R	BURY	COLCHESTER U	GILLINGHAM	GRIMSBY T	ORIENT	MANSFIELD T	NORTHAMPTON T	OLDHAM A	OXFORD U	PETERBOROUGH U	READING	SCUNTHORPE U	SHREWSBURY T	SOUTHPORT	STOCKPORT CO	SWINDON T	TORQUAY U	TRANMERE R	WALSALL	WATFORD
1 BARROW		A26 1-1	D02 1-1	O02 1-0	D16 1-1	N13 5-0	O21 0-1	M02 2-0	a06 1-0	J20 0-1	N04 4-0	D30 4-1	M09 3-0	S09 1-2	a15 1-0	m11 2-1	m04 3-0	F10 3-1	a20 3-0	S04 1-1	O07 3-0	N18 2-1	M23 1-1	S23 0-0
2 BOURNEMOUTH	D23 3-0		a12 2-2	A19 3-1	J13 1-0	S23 1-2	a06 4-0	N04 1-0	D02 0-0	m11 3-0	a20 0-2	M09 0-0	S02 2-1	F10 3-3	O21 2-0	S04 1-0	O07 1-1	O04 4-1	J20 1-0	M02 2-1	M23 1-1	m04 3-0	N18 1-1	D26 0-1
3 BRIGHTON & H.A.	a27 1-1	a15 2-3		N25 1-1	S02 1-0	F24 0-0	D26 3-0	O23 3-1	F03 1-1	M16 3-0	S30 0-2	a13 0-1	J27 0-0	O14 1-1	M20 1-1	N11 3-1	A26 3-0	M30 1-0	m01 3-0	D16 0-0	S25 0-1	S16 2-0	F28 1-0	O28 1-0
4 BRISTOL R	O24 1-0	D16 2-0	a20 3-1		M09 3-1	A26 1-1	M02 1-1	O07 3-0	a30 0-2	S09 2-0	M23 2-0	F17 4-3	S26 1-1	N14 2-1	D26 1-0	F10 4-0	D02 4-1	S23 1-3	N18 0-2	m04 1-2	a12 1-0	a06 3-1	O21 2-3	J20 0-2
5 BURY	A19 1-2	S09 4-0	J17 4-0	F27 4-2		J20 2-0	N04 3-2	M23 2-0	a19 1-0	F10 3-1	N18 3-1	S05 3-1	D23 1-1	S23 4-0	M02 2-0	O03 4-3	a12 2-0	D30 3-2	m04 5-3	O07 1-1	O21 5-1	D02 3-3	a06 2-1	m11 2-0
6 COLCHESTER U	S02 3-2	F03 0-1	O07 0-0	D23 2-0	S16 0-0		N18 2-2	a06 1-3	m04 1-1	D30 1-2	D02 2-1	A19 0-0	M25 1-2	m11 1-5	M23 2-5	F26 1-0	M02 0-3	S25 1-1	a12 1-1	O21 2-1	N04 3-5	F10 1-2	a20 2-2	O02 2-1
7 GILLINGHAM	M16 3-0	N11 0-0	D30 1-1	O14 0-0	M30 2-0	a13 1-0		S09 1-0	M09 2-3	a27 2-1	A19 2-0	F24 1-0	O28 2-1	N25 3-2	S23 3-0	a15 3-1	m11 0-1	S02 1-4	O04 3-1	F10 3-1	J20 1-1	S27 1-1	D23 0-1	a24 0-0
8 GRIMSBY T	O14 0-1	M30 2-1	O04 4-2	F24 3-2	O28 3-1	N11 1-2	M13 1-1		A19 0-0	N25 0-0	D23 0-0	a12 0-1	M16 0-1	a13 1-1	F10 1-1	S16 2-1	D30 0-1	a24 2-0	S06 3-1	m11 3-2	S23 1-1	M20 3-0	S02 3-0	a27 0-1
9 ORIENT	N11 4-2	a27 1-0	S23 1-2	M30 2-2	N25 1-0	a22 1-1	m07 0-4	D16 1-0		a15 0-0	O24 1-3	O28 0-2	a13 1-0	D30 3-0	N13 1-0	M16 2-1	J20 1-1	O14 3-0	F10 2-2	S09 0-0	A26 0-2	m11 0-1	S25 2-0	F24 0-1
10 MANSFIELD T	S16 1-2	F17 1-1	O21 1-3	M11 3-0	S30 1-1	D26 2-1	D02 0-1	a20 1-1	a16 0-0		S25 3-2	S02 1-1	F03 1-0	O23 2-3	a06 2-2	D23 3-0	M23 0-1	A19 4-2	M02 1-0	N04 2-2	N18 2-0	O07 0-3	m04 0-3	M09 1-2
11 NORTHAMPTON T	M30 3-0	N25 1-0	F10 2-2	O28 4-5	a13 0-1	a27 2-2	D16 1-1	A26 3-0	O03 2-1	S05 1-1		M16 1-2	N11 1-1	a23 3-1	S09 1-2	O14 1-0	S23 2-2	F24 1-1	M19 4-1	J20 2-0	N14 1-0	D26 0-1	M09 3-0	a16 1-1
12 OLDHAM A	D26 3-1	M12 1-1	N18 3-0	m11 3-5	S26 1-2	D16 2-1	O07 0-1	a16 2-1	M23 2-2	N14 1-0	O21 2-0		O24 3-1	A26 0-2	m04 1-3	S23 3-4	a20 0-0	J20 2-0	a06 4-1	D02 0-2	F10 0-1	N04 2-1	M02 0-3	S09 2-0
13 OXFORD U	a03 3-1	N15 3-2	m04 2-0	S06 0-2	A26 5-4	S09 3-1	M23 3-0	O21 2-1	N18 2-0	S23 2-0	a06 1-0	O04 3-1		J20 3-1	O07 2-0	D30 2-3	D16 2-2	m11 1-0	D02 2-2	a12 0-0	M02 2-0	a20 1-0	N04 4-0	F10 1-0
14 PETERBOROUGH U	J13 0-1	S30 2-0	M02 2-3	S02 4-1	F03 0-2	F17 3-1	a20 3-0	N18 3-2	D26 3-2	O02 2-0	m04 4-0	D23 2-1	S16 1-1		N04 2-3	A19 1-1	O21 0-1	M09 1-0	O07 2-0	M23 1-1	a06 2-0	a15 1-1	D02 2-1	S04 6-1
15 READING	a12 3-0	M16 1-0	M09 1-0	D30 2-1	O14 3-4	O28 1-0	F03 3-1	S30 3-0	S02 4-2	N11 2-1	F14 0-0	a24 0-1	F24 1-1	M30 0-1		a27 2-1	S27 0-0	N25 1-1	A19 3-0	O04 2-1	m11 4-0	D23 3-0	S16 2-2	a13 2-0
16 SCUNTHORPE U	F17 2-4	S26 1-1	a06 1-3	S30 1-1	O24 3-1	M09 5-1	J26 2-1	J20 0-3	O21 1-1	A25 3-3	M02 1-1	F03 2-0	D26 1-1	D15 2-1	D01 1-2		N17 0-0	S09 1-0	N03 0-2	a19 3-1	m03 2-0	M22 1-1	O07 2-5	N14 1-1
17 SHREWSBURY T	a24 1-0	F24 1-0	D23 0-0	a27 0-0	a15 1-0	O14 4-0	F17 1-2	D26 3-2	S16 2-2	O28 2-1	F03 2-0	N25 4-2	A19 2-0	M16 1-1	S06 2-1	a13 4-0		N11 3-2	S02 0-0	M09 0-1	O25 5-0	M05 1-1	S30 0-1	M30 3-1
18 SOUTHPORT	S29 1-0	O23 1-1	N04 1-0	F03 2-1	D26 2-2	S04 2-3	N13 4-1	m03 0-1	M01 0-0	D16 3-1	O07 1-3	S15 1-0	F16 1-0	a01 2-1	a19 2-1	m06 1-1	a05 0-0		M22 4-3	N18 1-1	D02 0-2	O20 2-0	a15 2-0	A26 2-0
19 STOCKPORT CO	N24 1-0	S15 3-1	S08 2-0	a13 3-1	a22 4-2	a15 1-0	O23 1-1	S25 1-1	S29 2-0	O13 1-0	F17 4-0	N10 0-2	a26 0-4	F23 2-2	D15 3-0	M29 4-1	N13 4-2	O30 4-3		A25 2-0	J26 0-0	F02 5-2	D29 0-0	M15 2-0
20 SWINDON T	S26 0-1	O14 4-0	A19 2-1	a23 4-1	F24 2-3	M16 1-1	S30 2-2	F27 5-0	M12 4-0	M30 1-1	S16 4-0	a27 0-0	a16 1-1	O28 0-0	O24 5-1	N25 2-0	M19 0-0	a13 3-3	D19 2-0		D30 1-0	S02 3-1	F03 3-0	N11 2-0
21 TORQUAY U	F24 0-2	O28 2-1	S06 1-1	a15 2-0	M16 3-0	M30 3-0	S16 2-1	F03 1-0	a01 1-1	a13 0-2	S02 0-0	S30 2-1	O14 1-1	N11 3-1	F17 2-1	a25 2-1	O04 3-0	a27 2-2	M09 3-0	D26 1-1		A19 1-0	J13 4-1	N25 1-0
22 TRANMERE R	a13 0-0	a22 0-0	J19 2-2	N10 3-3	a26 2-0	S29 4-2	S04 2-1	a29 1-2	M25 3-0	F23 1-1	D30 2-2	M29 1-0	N24 1-1	a12 0-1	A25 1-2	O27 2-0	S08 4-1	M15 0-2	S22 2-1	N13 3-2	D15 2-3		O23 2-0	O13 1-2
23 WALSALL	O28 4-0	a13 1-1	m11 1-2	M16 2-1	N11 2-1	N25 1-1	A26 3-0	N14 2-0	S05 5-0	a23 2-1	a02 4-0	O14 3-1	M29 0-1	a27 3-2	J20 2-2	F24 0-0	F10 1-2	a16 1-1	D26 0-1	S23 3-2	S09 1-1	O03 5-1		D16 1-1
24 WATFORD	F03 3-2	D30 0-2	M23 4-0	S16 4-0	F17 1-1	O24 1-1	m04 3-0	D02 7-1	O07 1-1	M19 1-2	a12 5-1	J16 1-2	S30 2-0	S26 4-1	N18 3-0	S02 4-0	N04 2-0	D23 0-1	O21 5-0	a06 2-0	a20 2-1	M01 3-2	A19 1-2	

DIVISION 4

	ALDERSHOT	BARNSLEY	BRADFORD	BRADFORD C	BRENTFORD	CHESTER	CHESTERFIELD	CREWE A	DARLINGTON	DONCASTER R	EXETER C	HALIFAX T	HARTLEPOOLS U	LINCOLN C	LUTON T	NEWPORT CO	NOTTS CO	PORT VALE	ROCHDALE	SOUTHEND U	SWANSEA T	WORKINGTON	WREXHAM	YORK C
1 ALDERSHOT		M02 1-1	N18 1-1	N15 3-3	a20 0-0	F10 2-1	M13 3-0	S09 2-0	O04 0-0	a06 2-1	D26 0-0	A26 1-1	J27 2-0	D16 3-2	M20 0-1	a12 0-0	J20 0-0	S23 2-0	D02 2-1	M23 1-3	O07 1-1	S06 5-0	O21 3-1	m04 2-2
2 BARNSLEY	O14 1-0		S26 2-0	N11 1-0	a15 3-0	a23 2-1	S15 0-0	F24 3-1	a13 1-0	A19 1-0	J27 2-1	M30 0-0	F10 4-0	O28 2-1	D23 2-2	m11 4-2	N25 3-1	a26 2-0	O03 1-1	S02 1-1	S23 3-0	M16 2-1	M05 2-2	D30 1-0
3 BRADFORD	F24 1-1	S04 1-1		S30 1-2	S23 1-0	M16 0-2	O28 2-1	J27 1-2	N11 1-2	F17 1-1	M30 0-1	a22 0-1	A26 0-1	a27 1-5	D30 2-1	N13 0-2	a13 1-4	O14 2-2	J20 0-0	O23 0-1	D16 1-2	N25 1-1	a16 0-1	S09 1-1
4 BRADFORD C	S02 1-3	a06 1-0	F10 1-2		M09 2-3	a15 2-2	S27 3-1	O18 2-1	D23 1-0	m04 1-1	A19 2-1	F03 0-1	M23 1-1	S16 2-1	D02 2-0	O21 3-0	D26 5-1	O04 2-1	O07 0-0	a20 2-1	N04 4-1	J24 1-0	N18 3-1	M02 0-0
5 BRENTFORD	N25 1-1	J06 0-1	F03 2-1	J27 0-1		O28 3-1	M30 1-1	a13 2-1	F24 2-0	S30 4-2	N11 5-1	S16 0-0	D16 0-1	a23 1-3	F17 0-2	A26 3-1	O14 2-1	M16 3-1	S09 4-0	D26 1-2	S26 2-1	a27 2-1	O24 0-0	N14 3-1
6 CHESTER	S30 2-5	m04 1-1	O21 0-0	a16 2-3	M23 3-0		a03 3-0	S06 0-4	F03 0-1	M02 2-3	S16 3-1	O25 3-2	a20 0-2	D30 6-0	O07 1-3	N18 2-1	D16 1-3	A26 1-1	N04 0-1	J27 0-0	D02 2-3	F17 1-2	N15 1-1	a06 1-1
7 CHESTERFIELD	F17 1-2	J20 2-3	M23 2-0	S04 2-1	N04 2-1	S09 3-1		D16 4-1	S30 3-1	O21 2-0	F03 1-1	a16 0-0	D02 3-1	O23 2-0	M02 0-0	a20 1-2	A26 4-0	N13 3-0	a06 0-2	O07 3-1	m04 3-1	D26 0-0	M09 3-1	N18 3-1
8 CREWE A	M27 1-1	N18 3-3	M09 4-0	F17 1-1	O07 2-0	S27 2-0	A19 1-1		S02 1-1	D30 2-2	D23 2-0	S30 5-1	N04 2-1	F03 2-1	m04 2-1	M23 1-1	O25 4-0	a12 1-1	M02 2-1	D02 1-0	a06 2-0	S16 3-2	a20 0-0	O21 0-0
9 DARLINGTON	O23 6-2	O07 0-2	a06 0-0	A26 2-2	N18 2-3	S23 0-2	F10 1-1	a01 0-0		N04 1-1	F17 0-1	D16 0-0	D30 2-3	S25 1-1	M23 1-2	m04 1-0	S09 2-2	J20 2-2	a20 2-0	O21 1-1	M04 2-0	a12 1-0	M02 1-1	D02 3-1
10 DONCASTER R	N11 3-0	D15 1-2	m10 2-0	a23 2-2	F10 2-0	O14 0-0	M15 1-0	D26 2-2	M29 2-1		O28 3-1	a26 0-0	N14 0-1	N25 0-0	O03 2-0	S09 1-1	M08 3-1	a13 0-0	S23 2-0	a16 2-1	A26 1-2	F24 3-0	S05 2-2	J19 2-0
11 EXETER C	D30 3-0	M09 2-0	m01 0-0	D16 4-1	a06 0-3	J20 1-0	S23 1-1	A26 1-4	m11 0-0	M23 0-1		S27 0-0	m04 0-0	a12 0-1	O21 0-5	D02 2-1	N15 3-3	S09 3-1	N18 3-1	M02 0-2	F10 1-3	O25 1-0	O07 2-2	a20 3-1
12 HALIFAX T	D23 2-2	N04 1-1	m04 1-0	S23 1-0	J20 3-0	O31 2-2	a15 0-2	M05 0-1	A19 2-0	D02 2-3	S04 1-1		O21 3-0	J13 1-0	a20 0-1	M02 4-1	m10 0-1	D30 0-1	M09 2-0	N18 1-2	a02 2-2	S02 2-1	a06 2-2	O07 2-1
13 HARTLEPOOLS U	M09 1-0	S29 2-1	D22 2-0	O27 1-0	A19 2-0	N24 0-0	a26 2-1	M30 1-1	D26 1-0	S01 0-0	a01 3-1	M15 0-0		O13 1-1	J13 2-1	O23 2-0	N10 3-1	F24 2-2	S04 1-1	S16 0-1	m11 2-0	a13 2-1	F03 3-0	a12 1-0
14 LINCOLN C	A19 1-1	M23 0-1	D02 5-1	J20 2-0	m04 1-0	D26 3-0	O04 2-2	S23 2-4	S06 1-2	a20 2-0	a15 1-1	S09 1-0	M02 1-2		N18 2-3	O07 2-1	F10 1-3	m11 0-1	J06 3-2	a06 4-2	O21 3-0	D23 3-0	N04 0-2	J27 1-3
15 LUTON T	M30 3-1	A26 2-0	D26 2-0	a27 1-3	m11 2-1	a13 0-0	O14 1-0	a24 4-0	F26 3-1	O25 5-3	M16 0-0	N25 2-0	S09 1-0	F24 4-2		J20 1-1	a12 2-0	M09 2-0	F10 4-1	S27 3-1	N15 4-0	N11 4-0	D16 2-1	S23 3-1
16 NEWPORT CO	a15 0-2	F17 3-0	S02 4-0	M16 0-3	D23 2-2	F24 1-1	N25 0-3	O31 0-0	a23 1-0	F27 2-1	a27 1-1	O14 0-1	O03 2-0	a13 0-1	S16 1-1		M30 1-0	N21 1-1	A19 1-1	F06 2-0	D30 3-0	a29 2-1	S30 3-2	S05 2-1
17 NOTTS CO	S16 0-1	a20 1-4	O07 0-0	D30 1-0	M02 2-1	A19 1-2	D23 1-0	O04 1-0	J13 0-0	m01 0-2	S02 1-0	F17 1-3	a06 0-3	S30 0-0	a15 2-2	N04 3-1		S06 0-0	O21 2-0	m04 4-3	N18 3-2	F03 2-1	D02 1-1	M23 1-1
18 PORT VALE	F03 0-3	D02 2-0	M02 4-0	O23 1-2	O21 4-1	D23 4-4	S02 0-1	a15 0-2	S16 0-1	O07 4-2	M25 1-0	D26 2-1	N18 2-3	F16 1-1	J26 0-0	a06 0-1	S25 4-1		M23 1-1	A19 1-2	a20 4-2	S30 4-2	m04 1-1	N04 1-0
19 ROCHDALE	a27 0-2	O23 1-0	S16 1-1	a13 3-2	M18 1-1	M30 1-1	N11 1-4	O14 1-1	N25 1-0	F03 2-0	F24 2-2	a29 2-1	S25 1-1	S02 1-2	S30 2-2	D16 4-3	M16 0-0	O28 3-1		F17 0-1	a15 1-2	J27 1-3	D30 3-0	A26 3-2
20 SOUTHEND U	O27 1-1	N13 4-1	O02 2-1	N25 1-1	D30 1-0	M08 5-1	a13 1-1	a26 0-0	M15 2-2	a08 1-2	O14 1-0	F24 2-2	J20 2-1	N11 2-1	S04 3-0	S22 2-2	a22 0-1	D15 1-1	m10 3-1		S08 1-0	M29 7-0	A25 3-1	F10 0-1
21 SWANSEA T	a13 1-0	F03 1-1	A19 1-1	M30 0-0	S05 2-1	a27 1-0	a23 0-1	N11 1-2	M09 0-1	D23 3-1	S30 1-1	O28 2-1	m06 0-2	M16 2-2	S02 2-2	D26 4-2	F24 2-0	N25 4-2	a16 1-0	M19 2-2		O14 5-2	S16 2-0	O03 1-1
22 WORKINGTON	S28 3-2	O21 0-1	a20 2-2	S09 0-1	D02 2-0	m11 1-0	D30 3-1	J20 2-2	a15 0-1	N17 2-2	O04 1-0	N15 1-1	O07 2-1	A26 2-4	a06 0-1	M09 1-1	S23 5-1	F10 1-1	m04 0-1	N04 2-2	M02 3-1		M23 1-2	D16 1-1
23 WREXHAM	M16 2-1	S09 2-0	a12 3-0	F24 0-2	O02 1-2	S02 2-0	M18 3-0	N25 1-0	O14 3-1	S25 0-0	a13 0-0	N11 2-0	S23 6-0	M30 2-1	A19 1-1	F10 0-1	a27 2-0	a22 1-0	D26 2-0	O16 4-1	J20 2-1	O28 5-0		m11 3-1
24 YORK C	a22 2-3	D26 1-1	M25 6-2	O14 0-1	S02 0-1	N11 4-1	F24 0-2	M16 1-1	a27 1-1	S16 1-2	N25 4-0	a13 1-2	a15 0-2	M09 1-0	F03 1-1	S25 0-1	O28 4-2	M30 5-1	D23 4-1	S30 2-2	O23 2-1	A19 1-1	F17 3-1	

LEAGUE TABLES

DIVISION 1

	P	W	D	L	F	A	W	D	L	F	A	Pts
Manchester C	42	17	2	2	52	16	9	4	8	34	27	58
Manchester U	42	15	2	4	49	21	9	6	6	40	34	56
Liverpool	42	17	2	2	51	17	5	9	7	20	23	55
Leeds U	42	17	3	1	49	14	5	6	10	22	27	53
Everton	42	18	1	2	43	13	5	5	11	24	27	52
Chelsea	42	11	7	3	34	25	7	5	9	28	43	48
Tottenham H	42	11	7	3	44	20	8	2	11	26	39	47
WBA	42	12	4	5	45	25	5	8	8	30	37	46
Arsenal	42	12	6	3	37	23	5	4	12	23	33	44
Newcastle U	42	12	7	2	38	20	1	8	12	16	47	41
Nottingham F	42	11	6	4	34	22	3	5	13	18	42	39
West Ham U	42	8	5	8	43	30	6	5	10	30	39	38
Leicester C	42	7	7	7	37	34	6	5	10	27	35	38
Burnley	42	12	7	2	38	16	2	3	16	26	55	38
Sunderland	42	8	7	6	28	28	5	4	12	23	33	37
Southampton	42	9	8	4	37	31	4	3	14	29	52	37
Wolves	42	10	4	7	45	36	4	4	13	21	39	36
Stoke C	42	10	3	8	30	29	4	4	13	20	44	35
Sheffield W	42	6	10	5	32	24	5	2	14	19	39	34
Coventry C	42	8	5	8	32	32	1	10	10	19	39	33
Sheffield U	42	7	4	10	25	31	4	6	11	24	39	32
Fulham	42	6	4	11	27	41	4	3	14	29	57	27

DIVISION 2

	P	W	D	L	F	A	W	D	L	F	A	Pts
Ipswich T	42	12	7	2	45	20	10	8	3	34	24	59
QPR	42	18	2	1	45	9	7	6	8	22	27	58
Blackpool	42	12	6	3	33	16	12	4	5	38	27	58
Birmingham C	42	12	6	3	54	21	7	8	6	29	30	52
Portsmouth	42	13	6	2	43	18	5	7	9	25	37	49
Middlesbrough	42	10	7	4	39	19	7	5	9	21	35	46
Millwall	42	9	10	2	35	16	5	7	9	27	34	45
Blackburn R	42	13	5	3	34	16	3	6	12	22	33	43
Norwich C	42	12	4	5	40	30	4	7	10	20	35	43
Carlisle U	42	9	9	3	38	22	5	4	12	20	30	41
Crystal P	42	11	4	6	34	19	3	7	11	22	37	39
Bolton W	42	8	6	7	37	28	5	7	9	23	35	39
Cardiff C	42	9	6	6	35	29	4	6	11	25	37	38
Huddersfield T	42	10	6	5	29	23	3	6	12	17	38	38
Charlton A	42	10	6	5	43	25	2	7	12	20	43	37
Aston Villa	42	10	3	8	35	30	5	4	12	19	34	37
Hull C	42	6	8	7	25	23	6	5	10	33	50	37
Derby Co	42	8	5	8	40	35	5	5	11	31	43	36
Bristol C	42	7	7	7	26	25	6	3	12	22	37	36
Preston NE	42	8	7	6	29	24	4	4	13	14	41	35
Rotherham U	42	7	4	10	22	32	3	7	11	20	44	31
Plymouth A	42	5	4	12	26	36	4	5	12	12	36	27

DIVISION 3

	P	W	D	L	F	A	W	D	L	F	A	Pts
Oxford U	46	18	3	2	49	20	4	10	9	20	27	57
Bury	46	19	3	1	64	24	5	5	13	27	42	56
Shrewsbury T	46	14	6	3	42	17	6	9	8	19	32	55
Torquay U	46	15	6	2	40	17	6	5	12	20	39	53
Reading	46	15	5	3	43	17	6	4	13	27	43	51
Watford	46	15	3	5	59	20	6	5	12	15	30	50
Walsall	46	12	7	4	47	22	7	5	11	27	39	50
Barrow	46	14	6	3	43	13	7	2	14	22	41	50
Peterboro' U	46	14	4	5	46	23	6	6	11	33	44	*50
Swindon T	46	13	8	2	51	16	3	9	11	23	35	49
Brighton & HA	46	11	8	4	31	14	5	8	10	26	41	48
Gillingham	46	13	6	4	35	19	5	6	12	24	44	48
Bournemouth	46	13	7	3	39	17	3	8	12	17	34	47
Stockport Co	46	16	5	2	49	22	3	4	16	21	53	47
Southport	46	13	6	4	35	22	4	6	13	30	43	46
Bristol R	46	14	3	6	42	25	3	6	14	30	53	43
Oldham A	46	11	3	9	37	32	7	4	12	23	33	43
Northampton T	46	10	8	5	40	25	4	5	14	18	47	41
Orient	46	10	6	7	27	24	2	11	10	19	38	41
Tranmere R	46	10	7	6	39	28	4	5	14	23	46	40
Mansfield T	46	8	7	8	32	31	4	6	13	19	36	37
Grimsby T	46	10	7	6	33	21	4	2	17	19	48	37
Colchester U	46	6	8	9	29	40	3	7	13	21	47	33
Scunthorpe U	46	8	9	6	36	34	2	3	18	20	53	32

**Peterborough United deducted 19 points for irregular bonuses — automatically demoted to the Fourth Division*

DIVISION 4

	P	W	D	L	F	A	W	D	L	F	A	Pts
Luton T	46	19	3	1	55	16	8	9	6	32	28	66
Barnsley	46	17	6	0	43	14	7	7	9	25	32	61
Hartlepools U	46	15	7	1	34	12	10	3	10	26	34	60
Crewe A	46	13	10	0	44	18	7	8	8	30	31	58
Bradford C	46	14	5	4	41	22	9	6	8	31	29	57
Southend U	46	12	8	3	45	21	8	6	9	32	37	54
Chesterfield	46	15	4	4	47	20	6	7	10	24	30	53
Wrexham	46	17	3	3	47	12	3	10	10	25	41	53
Aldershot	46	10	11	2	36	19	8	6	9	34	36	53
Doncaster R	46	12	8	3	36	16	6	7	10	30	40	51
Halifax T	46	10	6	7	34	24	5	10	8	18	25	46
Newport Co	46	11	7	5	32	22	5	6	12	26	41	45
Lincoln C	46	11	3	9	41	31	6	6	11	30	37	43
Brentford	46	13	4	6	41	24	5	3	15	20	40	43
Swansea T	46	11	8	4	38	25	5	2	16	25	52	42
Darlington	46	6	11	6	31	27	6	6	11	16	26	41
Notts Co	46	10	7	6	27	27	5	4	14	26	52	41
Port Vale	46	10	5	8	41	31	2	10	11	20	41	39
Rochdale	46	9	8	6	35	32	3	6	14	16	40	38
Exeter C	46	9	7	7	30	30	2	9	12	15	35	38
York C	46	9	6	8	44	30	2	8	13	21	38	36
Chester	46	6	6	11	35	38	3	8	12	22	40	32
Workington	46	8	8	7	35	29	2	3	18	19	58	31
Bradford	46	3	7	13	18	35	1	8	14	12	47	23

Football League Records

Top scorers: Div 1, J.Greaves (Tottenham Hotspur) 27 goals; Div 2, J.Toshack (Cardiff City) 22 goals; Div 3, D.Rogers (Swindon Town) 22 goals; Div 4, G.Talbot (Chester) 22 goals.
Hartlepools United became Hartlepool.

Mick Jones, Leeds' first £100,000 signing, was their leading scorer when they won the First Division in 1968-9.

Kevin Hector, the king of the Baseball Ground as his goals helped Brian Clough's Derby County back to Division One.

DIVISION 1

	ARSENAL	BURNLEY	CHELSEA	COVENTRY C	EVERTON	IPSWICH T	LEEDS U	LEICESTER C	LIVERPOOL	MANCHESTER C	MANCHESTER U	NEWCASTLE U	NOTTINGHAM F	Q.P.R.	SHEFFIELD W	SOUTHAMPTON	STOKE C	SUNDERLAND	TOTTENHAM H	W.B.A.	WEST HAM U	WOLVERHAMPTON W
1 ARSENAL		F15 2-0	N23 0-1	O12 2-1	D07 3-1	F18 0-2	a12 1-2	A13 3-0	A17 1-1	A27 4-1	D26 3-0	N09 0-0	F01 1-1	A31 2-1	J11 2-0	M29 0-0	S14 1-0	S28 0-0	M24 1-0	D21 2-0	O26 0-0	a07 3-1
2 BURNLEY	N30 0-1		S28 2-1	A31 1-1	a08 1-2	N02 1-0	O19 5-1	D28 2-1	O05 0-4	M04 2-1	S14 1-0	A17 1-0	M01 3-1	J18 2-2	a12 2-0	A20 3-1	D14 1-1	a23 1-2	M29 2-2	M15 2-2	O08 3-1	N16 1-1
3 CHELSEA	a14 2-1	a05 2-3		M10 2-1	S07 1-1	O05 3-1	N30 1-1	O19 3-0	J18 1-2	N02 2-0	M15 3-2	a04 1-1	A14 1-1	a19 2-1	A28 1-0	N16 2-3	M05 1-0	F22 5-1	A31 2-2	A17 3-1	S21 1-1	D14 1-1
4 COVENTRY C	D14 0-1	M22 4-1	S10 0-1		S21 2-2	N30 0-2	N16 0-1	a01 1-0	a22 0-0	O19 1-1	a08 2-1	S07 2-1	a19 1-1	F25 5-0	M08 3-0	N02 1-1	M18 1-1	M04 3-1	S17 1-2	A27 4-2	A24 1-2	O05 0-1
5 EVERTON	a29 1-0	A13 3-0	M29 1-2	a12 3-0		J18 2-2	a22 0-0	N30 7-1	A27 0-0	O05 2-0	M10 0-0	a14 1-1	A31 2-1	N16 4-0	S14 3-0	D14 1-0	O19 2-1	N02 2-0	A17 0-2	S28 4-0	a01 1-0	J28 4-0
6 IPSWICH T	A24 1-2	J11 2-0	D26 1-3	M25 0-0	N09 2-2		A20 2-3	m03 2-1	S14 0-2	M11 2-1	F01 1-0	O12 1-4	D21 2-3	A27 3-0	a25 2-0	a12 0-0	S28 3-1	a04 1-0	O26 0-1	D07 4-1	N23 2-2	A10 1-0
7 LEEDS U	S21 2-0	D21 6-1	F15 1-0	F01 3-0	N23 2-1	F12 2-0		a19 2-0	A31 1-0	a05 1-0	J11 2-1	D26 2-1	a30 1-0	A14 4-1	D07 2-0	M01 3-2	A17 2-0	A28 1-1	N09 0-0	O26 0-0	O12 2-0	S07 2-1
8 LEICESTER C	a08 0-0	O26 0-2	D21 1-4	S28 1-1	m14 1-1	A17 1-3	S14 1-1		a12 1-2	A21 3-0	D07 2-1	J11 2-1	N09 2-2	M12 2-0	N23 1-1	A31 3-1	M15 0-0	m05 2-1	a29 1-0	O12 0-2	F01 1-1	O09 2-0
9 LIVERPOOL	M31 1-1	D26 1-1	N09 2-1	N23 2-0	O08 1-1	a19 4-0	a28 0-0	S21 4-0		A10 2-1	O12 2-0	O26 2-1	F15 0-2	S07 2-0	F01 1-0	D03 1-0	A20 2-1	A24 4-1	D21 1-0	J11 1-0	D07 2-0	a05 1-0
10 MANCHESTER C	O09 1-1	D07 7-0	J11 4-1	D21 4-2	D26 1-3	A31 1-1	S28 3-1	a04 2-0	m12 1-0		A17 0-0	m05 1-0	O26 3-3	M15 3-1	N09 0-1	S14 1-1	M29 3-1	a12 1-0	O12 4-0	N23 5-1	a30 1-1	A14 3-2
11 MANCHESTER U	O05 0-0	a19 2-0	A24 0-4	A21 1-0	A10 2-1	N16 0-0	N02 0-0	m17 3-2	D14 1-0	M08 0-1		S21 3-1	a05 3-1	M19 8-1	M22 1-0	O19 1-2	M24 1-1	J18 4-1	A28 3-1	a02 2-1	S07 1-1	N30 2-0
12 NEWCASTLE U	J18 2-1	M08 1-0	A21 3-2	M29 2-0	A24 0-0	D14 2-1	O05 0-1	N02 0-0	m17 1-1	N16 1-0	a12 2-0		A28 1-1	O19 3-2	a09 3-2	N30 4-1	a30 5-0	M22 1-1	S28 2-2	S14 2-3	A10 1-1	a21 4-1
13 NOTTINGHAM F	N16 0-2	A10 2-2	a08 1-2	S14 0-0	a25 1-0	O19 1-2	F25 0-2	J18 0-0	N30 0-1	M24 1-0	M31 0-1	O08 2-4		M04 1-0	A20 0-0	M11 1-0	O05 3-3	D14 1-0	a12 0-2	M22 3-0	M08 0-1	N02 0-0
14 Q.P.R.	M22 0-1	N09 0-2	S14 0-4	D07 0-1	F01 0-1	O08 2-1	J24 0-1	A10 1-1	M29 1-2	A24 1-1	O26 2-3	D21 1-1	N23 2-1		O12 3-2	S28 1-1	a12 2-1	A20 2-2	F15 1-1	D26 0-4	J11 1-1	M08 0-1
15 SHEFFIELD W	M01 0-5	S21 1-0	O09 1-1	A17 3-0	a19 2-2	S07 2-1	a01 0-0	a14 1-3	N16 1-2	J18 1-1	A31 5-4	A14 1-1	a07 0-1	D14 4-0		D28 0-0	N30 2-1	O05 1-1	m12 0-0	M05 1-0	a05 1-1	O19 0-2
16 SOUTHAMPTON	S07 1-2	a07 5-1	F01 5-0	J11 1-0	O12 2-5	S21 2-2	A10 1-3	M22 1-0	A14 2-0	a19 3-0	D21 2-0	F15 0-0	D07 1-1	a05 3-2	O26 1-1		A28 2-0	M08 1-0	N23 2-1	N09 2-0	D26 2-2	A24 2-1
17 STOKE C	a19 1-3	O12 1-3	O26 2-0	N09 0-3	D21 0-0	a05 2-1	M08 1-5	A24 1-0	a07 0-0	S07 1-0	N23 0-0	D07 1-0	D26 3-1	S21 1-1	a22 1-1	O09 1-0		A10 2-1	J11 1-1	F01 1-1	A14 0-2	M22 4-1
18 SUNDERLAND	a05 0-0	N23 2-0	D07 3-2	O26 3-0	J11 1-3	A14 3-0	O09 0-1	S07 2-0	M15 0-2	S21 0-4	N09 1-1	A31 1-1	O12 3-1	a07 0-0	D26 0-0	A17 1-0	M01 4-1		F01 0-0	M10 0-1	D21 2-1	a19 2-0
19 TOTTENHAM H	A10 1-2	S07 7-0	M22 1-0	a04 2-0	M08 1-1	M18 2-2	J18 0-0	O05 3-2	O19 2-1	D14 1-1	O09 2-2	a02 0-1	S21 2-1	J29 3-2	A24 1-2	a22 2-1	N02 1-1	N16 5-1		A21 1-1	a19 1-0	F22 1-1
20 W.B.A.	O19 1-0	A24 3-2	M08 0-3	O09 6-1	a05 1-1	a23 2-2	a09 1-1	D14 1-1	N02 0-0	a16 2-0	A14 3-1	a19 5-1	S07 2-5	O05 3-1	A10 0-0	J18 1-2	N16 2-1	N30 3-0	a07 4-3		a14 3-1	S21 0-0
21 WEST HAM U	a21 1-2	A26 5-0	a12 0-0	M14 5-2	A19 1-4	M21 1-3	D14 1-1	N16 4-0	F22 1-1	N30 2-1	M29 0-0	M01 3-1	A17 1-0	N02 4-3	S28 1-1	O05 0-0	a08 0-0	O19 8-0	S14 2-2	A31 4-0		M24 3-1
22 WOLVERHAMPTON W	A21 0-0	F01 1-1	O12 1-1	a15 1-1	O26 1-2	M01 1-1	M29 0-0	A28 1-0	S28 0-6	a08 3-1	F15 2-2	N23 5-0	J11 1-0	A17 3-1	D21 0-3	M15 0-0	A31 1-1	S14 1-1	D07 2-0	a12 0-1	N09 2-0	

DIVISION 2

	ASTON VILLA	BIRMINGHAM C	BLACKBURN R	BLACKPOOL	BOLTON W	BRISTOL C	BURY	CARDIFF C	CARLISLE U	CHARLTON A	CRYSTAL P	DERBY CO	FULHAM	HUDDERSFIELD T	HULL C	MIDDLESBROUGH	MILLWALL	NORWICH C	OXFORD U	PORTSMOUTH	PRESTON N.E.	SHEFFIELD U
1 ASTON VILLA		a12 1-0	M15 1-1	A31 0-1	a08 1-1	A26 1-0	F15 1-0	D26 2-0	O26 0-0	D07 0-0	O12 1-1	M29 0-1	A17 1-1	J11 1-0	S14 1-1	N23 1-0	A19 1-1	D21 2-1	S28 2-0	F01 2-0	N09 0-1	M01 3-1
2 BIRMINGHAM C	S21 4-0		J18 3-1	N16 1-0	M25 5-0	D14 2-0	S17 1-3	O08 2-0	a05 3-0	a07 0-0	M08 0-1	J14 1-1	O05 5-4	S07 5-1	N30 5-2	a19 3-1	O19 1-2	A10 1-2	N02 0-1	A24 5-2	M21 3-1	M04 2-2
3 BLACKBURN R	A24 2-0	N09 3-2		A28 1-1	a19 2-3	M22 1-3	D21 3-0	J11 1-0	O12 0-2	N23 0-1	a28 1-2	A10 1-1	a05 2-2	D07 0-0	M08 1-1	M25 1-1	S07 2-4	O26 3-0	S18 1-0	a07 3-1	D26 1-0	S21 1-0
4 BLACKPOOL	M22 1-1	F01 2-1	O07 0-1		S07 1-0	A24 2-2	N23 6-0	N09 1-2	D21 1-0	J11 2-3	O26 3-0	M08 2-3	S21 2-2	D26 0-0	A10 2-0	D07 1-1	a19 1-0	M19 2-1	a07 1-0	O12 1-1	S16 1-1	a05 1-1
5 BOLTON W	S18 4-1	N23 0-0	S14 1-1	M29 1-4		a07 1-0	A17 2-0	D21 1-2	D26 0-1	O12 3-0	J11 2-2	S28 1-2	M15 3-2	O26 2-3	a12 1-0	F01 0-0	O09 0-4	D04 1-1	M01 1-1	D07 1-0	a16 0-0	A31 4-2
6 BRISTOL C	O08 1-0	O12 0-0	A31 1-0	M15 1-1	A20 2-2		D07 2-1	S28 0-3	F15 3-0	D26 2-0	F25 1-1	S14 0-0	M01 6-0	N09 0-1	M29 1-1	J11 3-0	a08 0-0	N23 0-1	a12 2-0	O26 2-2	F01 2-1	A17 1-1
7 BURY	N30 3-2	a08 1-2	O19 1-3	M26 2-0	M07 2-1	a15 1-2		A21 3-3	A10 3-2	A27 2-3	A24 2-1	J25 0-1	D28 5-1	a05 1-1	J18 0-0	S21 2-3	O05 0-0	M22 1-2	D14 3-1	a18 3-2	S07 0-1	N16 0-2
8 CARDIFF C	O05 1-1	A28 4-0	N02 2-1	F12 1-0	O19 0-2	J25 3-0	a07 2-0		S21 2-1	A14 0-1	A10 0-4	N16 1-1	M24 0-2	a19 0-2	D28 3-0	S07 2-0	D14 2-0	M07 3-1	F08 5-0	M21 2-2	A24 1-0	N30 4-1
9 CARLISLE U	D28 0-1	S28 2-3	D14 4-1	O19 1-0	O05 1-1	N30 3-0	M01 2-0	a12 1-0		A17 1-1	M29 1-2	M11 1-1	N16 2-0	A31 0-0	N04 1-0	M15 3-0	F22 1-0	S14 0-4	A27 0-2	A13 0-0	a07 1-0	J18 0-1
10 CHARLTON A	F22 1-1	A20 3-1	a15 4-0	N02 0-0	D14 2-2	O05 0-0	O08 2-2	a04 4-1	M08 1-1		M22 1-1	J18 2-0	N30 5-3	S21 1-0	N16 1-1	a05 2-0	A10 3-4	A24 2-1	O19 1-0	S07 2-1	a19 0-1	M25 2-1
11 CRYSTAL P	D14 4-2	A17 3-2	N16 1-0	J25 1-2	N02 2-1	O19 2-1	M15 1-0	M01 3-1	S07 5-0	A31 3-3		N30 1-2	a19 3-2	A14 2-1	F22 2-0	a04 0-0	M19 4-2	A28 2-0	M26 1-1	a05 3-1	S21 1-2	O05 1-1
12 DERBY CO	S07 3-1	O26 1-0	M01 4-2	A17 1-1	a05 5-1	a19 5-0	J11 2-0	F01 2-0	N23 3-3	N09 2-1	M05 0-1		S18 1-0	M15 1-0	A28 2-2	D26 3-2	S21 1-0	D07 1-1	A31 2-0	D21 2-1	O12 1-0	a07 1-0
13 FULHAM	M08 1-1	D26 2-0	S28 1-1	a12 0-0	A24 0-2	A10 1-0	O26 0-0	D07 1-5	F01 0-2	F15 0-1	S13 1-0	a02 0-1		N23 4-3	A21 0-0	D21 0-3	M22 2-0	O12 1-3	M29 0-1	N09 2-2	F26 2-1	O09 2-2
14 HUDDERSFIELD T	N02 3-1	M29 0-0	a30 2-1	O05 2-1	M04 3-0	J18 4-1	S28 4-1	S14 3-0	M22 2-0	a12 0-0	a08 0-0	A24 2-0	a15 3-0		D14 0-3	O08 3-0	N16 0-2	A20 2-2	N30 2-1	A10 0-0	M08 1-1	O19 1-0
15 HULL C	a19 1-0	a15 1-2	A17 1-3	M01 2-2	S21 1-0	S07 1-1	N08 3-0	O26 3-3	J11 1-2	F01 5-2	D07 2-0	O09 1-0	a07 4-0	O12 3-0		A31 3-0	a05 2-0	D26 0-1	M14 0-0	N23 2-2	D20 1-1	S18 1-1
16 MIDDLESBROUGH	M04 0-0	S14 3-1	N30 2-0	F22 2-1	N16 0-0	D03 4-1	a12 2-3	M29 0-0	A24 1-0	S28 1-0	A20 4-0	O05 0-0	O19 2-0	A27 1-1	M22 5-3		J18 1-1	a08 0-0	J24 2-0	M08 1-0	A10 2-1	J28 3-1
17 MILLWALL	a04 0-1	D21 1-3	M28 2-2	S14 1-2	A26 3-1	S16 2-2	D26 1-0	O12 2-0	D07 1-1	M01 3-2	N23 0-2	a12 0-1	A31 2-0	F01 5-1	S28 2-3	N09 2-0		J11 3-1	A17 2-1	F15 0-0	O26 0-0	M14 1-0
18 NORWICH C	O19 1-1	M01 1-1	a23 3-1	N30 0-1	J18 2-0	M26 1-1	A31 2-2	A17 3-1	a19 2-1	M15 0-1	O09 0-1	a16 1-4	D14 2-0	a07 1-0	O05 1-2	A14 0-2	N02 0-3		N16 1-1	S21 0-1	a05 1-1	S07 2-0
19 OXFORD U	a05 1-0	J11 1-2	a04 2-1	A21 0-0	A10 1-1	S21 0-0	O12 2-2	N23 0-2	O09 0-1	D21 0-1	N09 0-2	M22 0-2	S07 1-0	F15 3-0	A24 1-1	O26 2-4	M08 1-0	F01 0-2		M05 3-1	D07 2-1	a19 1-0
20 PORTSMOUTH	N16 2-0	M15 0-0	A21 0-1	D14 1-0	F22 2-2	D28 1-1	S13 1-2	A31 1-3	a09 2-1	M29 4-1	S28 3-3	O19 0-1	J18 3-1	M01 1-2	F08 1-0	A17 3-0	N30 3-0	a12 5-2	O05 3-0		O09 1-1	N02 2-1
21 PRESTON N.E.	J18 1-0	A31 4-1	O05 1-1	a08 1-0	N30 1-4	N16 1-0	M29 3-0	M15 0-1	S30 2-2	S14 1-1	a12 0-0	D14 0-0	N25 0-0	A17 1-0	O19 1-0	M01 1-2	M03 0-1	S28 1-3	F22 2-1	A26 0-0		M17 2-2
22 SHEFFIELD U	A10 3-1	D07 2-0	a12 3-0	S28 2-1	M22 5-2	M08 2-1	F01 5-0	M11 2-2	N09 0-1	O26 2-0	D26 1-1	A20 2-0	A27 1-0	D21 0-0	a08 1-1	O12 1-3	A24 1-0	M29 1-0	S14 1-2	J11 2-0	N23 4-0	

Season 1968-69

DIVISION 3

	BARNSLEY	BARROW	BOURNEMOUTH	BRIGHTON & HA	BRISTOL R	CREWE A	GILLINGHAM	HARTLEPOOL	ORIENT	LUTON T	MANSFIELD T	NORTHAMPTON T	OLDHAM A	PLYMOUTH A	READING	ROTHERHAM U	SHREWSBURY T	SOUTHPORT	STOCKPORT CO	SWINDON T	TORQUAY U	TRANMERE R	WALSALL	WATFORD
1 BARNSLEY		A10 2-3	J11 1-0	S28 4-0	M04 4-2	N09 2-2	A24 0-1	D21 2-1	S14 2-2	O08 3-1	a08 2-0	a25 2-1	M08 0-1	N23 0-0	O26 1-0	M21 0-1	D26 1-0	S17 2-1	a29 2-0	F01 1-1	a12 1-0	M29 2-2	O12 0-0	a22 3-2
2 BARROW	M01 0-1		F01 0-2	A31 1-1	a21 3-0	O26 2-0	S16 2-1	J11 1-2	S28 3-1	A17 0-0	S14 3-0	M03 0-2	O07 2-1	N09 1-0	M17 0-0	a04 2-0	O12 2-1	M29 0-0	D26 3-3	F15 0-3	M15 2-0	a12 1-0	N23 1-1	D21 1-4
3 BOURNEMOUTH	N02 3-0	a28 1-0		O05 2-0	M15 0-0	A28 4-0	N30 2-0	M01 4-0	a25 0-1	F08 0-2	D14 2-1	M29 3-2	J18 3-1	A17 0-1	a04 1-1	D28 1-0	A31 2-0	O19 2-1	S14 1-0	S18 2-0	N06 3-0	J04 3-4	S28 1-0	a12 1-3
4 BRIGHTON & H.A.	a05 4-1	M22 4-1	D26 4-1		N09 3-1	J25 3-1	a19 0-2	M19 1-1	a04 2-0	S21 1-0	A10 1-2	N23 1-1	A24 6-0	M05 0-0	D20 2-0	S07 2-2	F01 3-0	M08 4-0	J11 1-1	O12 1-3	A28 1-1	a16 2-2	F15 3-0	O26 0-1
5 BRISTOL R	F18 4-2	N04 4-2	A24 3-2	J18 1-1		M21 1-0	O19 5-1	S06 2-1	F24 0-1	M31 0-0	M25 6-2	a04 2-1	O05 1-0	a19 1-1	a05 1-3	D13 1-1	A27 1-2	N30 2-1	a15 2-0	S21 2-1	M11 1-1	N02 0-2	M08 0-1	A10 1-1
6 CREWE A	J18 1-4	D28 1-1	O07 0-2	N06 1-0	A31 6-1		a30 4-2	A17 1-0	J04 2-0	J29 2-0	O18 2-1	S14 2-2	M12 3-0	M01 2-1	S18 1-2	N30 1-0	M14 0-1	a21 3-3	M29 1-1	a04 1-2	D14 2-1	O05 2-3	a11 0-1	S28 2-3
7 GILLINGHAM	M14 1-1	a07 2-0	a22 0-0	S14 5-0	D21 0-2	M26 1-0		F01 2-2	A17 2-2	A31 1-3	S28 1-1	J25 2-0	a16 2-0	O26 1-0	D26 2-2	O09 2-0	N23 4-1	a12 0-0	O12 0-0	M05 2-0	M29 0-0	M01 1-1	N09 4-0	J11 0-5
8 HARTLEPOOL	O18 2-1	N01 1-4	A10 1-1	F22 2-5	M28 1-0	m05 0-0	M10 1-1		a21 0-0	D14 1-0	O04 1-1	a11 3-0	F24 0-2	O14 1-1	M22 2-0	J18 0-3	S13 0-0	N06 2-2	S28 0-0	A24 0-0	J04 2-2	N29 2-4	a04 1-1	S16 2-1
9 ORIENT	a19 1-1	a05 1-2	M17 1-0	O21 3-2	N23 2-1	M03 2-0	M08 1-1	O26 0-1		S07 0-0	A24 1-0	D09 0-0	S21 3-0	F15 1-2	J25 4-2	A10 3-3	a28 4-0	M22 0-2	M26 2-0	D26 1-0	a09 0-1	S09 0-0	F01 0-0	N09 1-1
10 LUTON T	A28 5-1	M26 5-1	N23 1-1	a12 3-0	M19 3-0	F26 2-0	M22 1-1	O12 3-0	M29 2-1		S18 4-2	O26 2-1	A10 4-0	D21 2-0	F01 2-1	A24 3-1	M05 2-1	a08 0-0	a25 4-1	N09 2-0	S28 1-0	S14 3-1	J25 1-0	a30 2-1
11 MANSFIELD T	a14 0-0	a19 4-2	O12 3-1	M01 3-2	O26 0-0	D21 2-1	a05 2-0	D26 2-0	M15 0-2	a07 1-0		N09 0-2	S07 4-0	a28 1-0	J11 1-1	S21 0-1	m09 1-2	A26 3-1	F01 0-0	N23 2-0	A17 2-1	A31 1-1	a25 2-1	m05 3-0
12 NORTHAMPTON T	N30 3-1	J28 4-0	S07 1-3	F25 1-1	S17 2-2	a19 0-1	N05 0-1	S21 0-0	D14 4-1	D28 0-2	J18 0-0		F22 1-1	a05 1-1	M08 4-2	O05 1-0	a08 3-4	M11 1-0	A27 1-1	N26 2-6	N02 1-1	O19 2-1	M22 3-1	S10 2-0
13 OLDHAM A	A17 1-1	A27 0-1	M25 2-0	M15 2-0	D26 2-1	F01 3-0	a04 1-0	N23 1-2	a12 3-1	M01 0-1	M28 2-2	a29 1-1		J11 0-2	F18 1-1	S17 0-0	J25 2-2	S14 0-1	M04 5-2	O26 2-3	A31 3-1	S28 1-2	D20 1-0	O12 0-3
14 PLYMOUTH A	S23 0-0	J18 4-1	M08 1-1	J04 1-1	S14 3-1	A10 2-2	D28 1-1	O09 3-0	N30 2-1	O19 2-0	N06 1-0	S28 0-1	N02 1-1		A24 3-1	M12 1-2	M29 1-1	D14 0-4	a12 2-2	M22 2-1	O05 1-2	F22 1-0	S18 1-0	a08 1-2
15 READING	J29 3-2	a23 0-1	a16 0-1	O18 1-0	S27 2-1	a07 3-1	O04 3-2	A30 7-0	N06 0-1	M12 1-1	N02 2-1	A16 1-0	N30 4-1	M14 1-2		M24 1-0	a11 2-4	J18 1-0	F28 4-2	O09 0-1	M31 1-1	D14 2-0	M28 2-2	S13 0-1
16 ROTHERHAM U	A31 0-0	a15 3-1	O26 1-1	M29 1-1	O12 3-2	a25 3-0	A27 1-0	N09 1-1	M01 3-1	M15 2-2	a12 3-0	J21 0-1	a08 1-2	F01 0-1	M04 4-1		D21 1-0	S28 3-1	J25 4-1	m02 1-1	S14 1-0	A17 4-1	J11 0-1	N23 0-2
17 SHREWSBURY T	O05 0-0	D14 1-0	M22 1-0	M12 1-2	O09 1-0	A24 1-1	m05 1-1	a19 1-1	N02 1-0	J08 3-1	N30 1-1	a16 1-0	N05 0-1	S07 1-0	S21 3-3	O19 1-0		m02 5-1	a07 2-1	a05 1-1	a23 1-0	J18 0-1	A10 0-1	M08 1-1
18 SOUTHPORT	a07 1-0	S06 1-0	D20 2-1	A17 2-3	a23 3-0	N22 4-0	S20 4-2	J24 3-0	A30 2-2	a14 1-1	O07 3-2	M26 2-0	a18 3-1	O11 2-0	N08 1-1	a05 0-0	M17 5-0		O25 5-0	J11 1-1	m06 2-2	M14 2-2	D26 2-1	M03 1-1
19 STOCKPORT CO	M31 1-1	O04 4-1	a18 0-1	N01 3-1	a08 0-1	S06 2-1	D13 5-0	a05 1-0	O18 5-2	N29 2-0	M10 1-1	O07 1-0	J06 0-0	S20 2-3	A10 2-2	N04 3-1	S16 4-3	D28 3-0		M08 2-1	J17 1-2	a21 1-0	A23 2-2	M21 4-2
20 SWINDON T	M25 2-0	m05 2-0	a08 3-0	D14 1-0	a12 2-2	a15 1-0	F25 1-0	F04 1-1	O05 1-0	J18 0-0	a22 1-0	M01 1-0	J28 5-1	A31 3-0	A27 0-0	F22 1-0	S28 3-0	N02 5-1	A17 1-0		O19 2-1	F18 1-0	S14 1-0	M29 0-1
21 TORQUAY U	S21 3-1	A24 3-1	J25 0-0	O09 1-1	F01 0-1	O12 2-0	S07 2-0	M03 3-0	a16 0-0	a04 1-1	a30 0-1	J11 2-0	M22 3-1	F05 0-1	N23 1-0	a19 1-0	O26 2-0	A10 3-0	N09 0-1	D21 0-1		a07 2-5	S30 4-2	F15 2-1
22 TRANMERE R	S06 3-1	S20 0-3	M03 2-1	O14 0-2	J10 1-2	D26 0-1	A10 2-0	a24 1-0	O07 3-0	a18 0-2	M21 2-1	D20 2-1	a05 6-2	M17 2-2	O11 2-1	M07 0-0	N08 3-1	A23 1-0	N22 1-1	J24 3-5	S16 0-1		O25 2-1	J31 0-3
23 WALSALL	D14 3-0	F25 1-1	a05 0-0	N30 4-0	A17 2-2	S20 1-1	J28 2-1	a15 1-2	M11 2-1	N05 2-0	a01 3-1	A31 0-1	O19 2-1	a07 1-1	S07 2-2	N02 0-0	M01 2-0	O05 3-0	M15 2-0	a19 0-2	F22 0-1	M25 1-1		O08 0-0
24 WATFORD	N04 1-2	O19 4-0	S21 1-0	D28 1-0	M01 1-0	a05 4-0	N02 2-1	a07 0-0	J18 0-0	O05 1-0	F22 2-1	M14 3-0	D14 2-0	a15 1-0	a19 1-0	F08 5-1	A17 2-0	a01 1-0	A31 0-1	S07 0-0	N30 0-0	M11 3-1	A27 0-0	

DIVISION 4

	ALDERSHOT	BRADFORD	BRADFORD C	BRENTFORD	CHESTER	CHESTERFIELD	COLCHESTER U	DARLINGTON	DONCASTER R	EXETER C	GRIMSBY T	HALIFAX T	LINCOLN C	NEWPORT CO	NOTTS CO	PETERBOROUGH U	PORT VALE	ROCHDALE	SCUNTHORPE U	SOUTHEND U	SWANSEA T	WORKINGTON	WREXHAM	YORK C
1 ALDERSHOT		O09 4-1	O12 2-1	J11 1-2	D21 4-0	F15 2-0	F01 1-2	S20 0-0	N23 1-2	D26 2-0	a19 3-1	A24 0-2	a04 0-1	J04 4-0	M22 0-0	M19 1-4	M05 3-0	N09 0-0	O26 3-2	S18 2-1	M08 5-2	S07 0-1	A10 2-1	J25 2-0
2 BRADFORD	A26 0-1		J25 0-0	N23 0-2	O12 1-1	O26 0-1	N09 2-1	a05 1-3	D21 2-1	S09 2-1	S07 1-1	m12 0-0	S16 1-1	S21 1-5	A24 1-1	a02 0-2	m05 0-1	J11 1-4	F01 2-2	a08 0-3	A10 1-1	a19 1-0	M08 1-2	M26 1-0
3 BRADFORD C	D14 1-1	N06 1-0		S28 3-0	A17 2-0	A31 2-1	S14 1-1	a25 0-0	M01 1-1	a07 1-0	M12 1-1	J18 1-1	O19 2-0	N30 1-1	D07 1-1	a29 2-1	a16 2-2	a12 1-1	M29 3-0	m02 3-2	F12 1-0	D28 0-1	O05 1-3	O09 5-0
4 BRENTFORD	N02 2-4	a21 3-0	m05 2-1		a30 2-1	S07 1-0	A10 4-0	N04 0-1	a14 1-0	M22 0-1	F22 4-2	N30 1-1	J18 2-2	O05 1-1	M26 0-0	a19 2-0	A24 3-1	A26 1-1	M08 2-1	M10 1-1	D14 2-1	J04 0-3	O19 1-1	S21 5-1
5 CHESTER	O19 3-1	D14 4-1	M08 0-0	S18 2-2		S21 2-0	A24 5-1	J04 1-2	S03 2-1	a19 0-1	M26 0-1	M12 2-2	a23 2-0	F22 4-0	J18 3-1	a05 2-3	S06 2-0	a08 2-1	M22 0-2	N02 1-2	O05 3-0	N30 0-2	N06 1-1	A10 2-0
6 CHESTERFIELD	N30 1-2	D28 1-1	M22 0-1	M29 1-2	a12 2-0		S16 0-2	N02 2-2	S28 0-1	M08 2-0	D14 0-0	N04 2-0	M17 1-1	a21 2-1	O05 0-2	A28 2-0	A10 3-1	S14 1-1	a08 1-2	a25 0-0	J18 2-0	O19 0-1	M10 0-1	A24 1-1
7 COLCHESTER U	M10 2-0	J18 3-0	a18 1-1	F28 2-1	M14 1-1	a04 1-0		O19 0-0	A31 1-2	a05 1-0	O04 2-1	a21 0-0	M24 1-1	D14 2-1	F22 1-1	a14 2-2	S20 1-0	A17 0-0	A26 0-4	N29 4-0	a25 0-1	N04 3-0	N02 2-1	S07 1-0
8 DARLINGTON	a12 1-0	S28 2-0	m09 1-3	J25 3-1	M03 2-2	J11 1-3	a28 1-1		D26 0-0	O26 1-2	A17 0-0	M29 0-1	A31 5-0	O07 1-0	S14 3-2	N09 3-3	F01 1-0	O12 0-0	N23 0-1	m05 2-3	a08 3-0	M01 6-2	S16 1-0	a21 3-2
9 DONCASTER R	F25 7-0	O18 4-1	A10 1-1	a08 5-0	O08 4-3	a05 0-0	M22 1-0	O04 0-1		S07 3-1	N29 2-1	J14 0-0	N02 0-2	F04 2-2	M11 0-0	S20 1-0	a19 2-0	S17 2-0	A23 4-3	J18 2-0	N06 0-0	a22 0-0	D14 0-0	M07 2-1
10 EXETER C	O05 0-0	F24 4-2	S18 2-3	A31 2-2	S14 2-2	A17 3-0	S28 1-1	M24 2-0	M29 0-0		N02 2-2	a24 2-1	N06 3-0	M12 2-0	O19 0-0	M01 0-1	O08 3-1	M15 2-2	a12 3-1	D14 1-2	N30 0-1	M31 1-0	M18 5-3	a09 5-0
11 GRIMSBY T	S14 0-2	M29 2-0	F01 1-5	m03 0-2	O26 0-0	O12 1-2	D26 2-4	M08 1-1	m05 1-3	J11 1-2		a04 0-1	a12 1-1	A10 3-0	S17 2-0	D21 2-2	N23 1-1	D07 2-0	J25 0-1	S28 0-0	A24 1-2	A27 0-1	M22 1-1	N09 3-0
12 HALIFAX T	m03 1-0	A31 3-0	N09 1-1	a28 2-0	F01 0-0	M25 0-0	M04 2-1	S07 0-4	O26 4-1	N23 2-1	a15 0-0		A17 0-1	a19 3-0	O08 3-1	O12 2-1	D21 2-1	m08 1-0	D26 2-0	M01 1-1	a05 2-1	a07 3-0	S21 2-0	J11 0-4
13 LINCOLN C	a16 2-1	a07 3-2	D21 2-0	N09 1-0	N23 2-0	O16 2-2	O26 0-3	M22 2-1	J11 1-1	J25 3-2	S21 3-0	M08 0-0		A24 1-0	A10 5-0	M05 1-1	D26 0-1	F01 0-0	F15 1-2	A28 2-1	S07 0-1	a05 4-1	a19 0-0	O12 3-0
14 NEWPORT CO	S28 3-4	a12 1-0	F15 1-3	D26 1-1	M17 2-5	N23 1-2	O12 1-0	A26 0-0	M03 0-0	F01 2-1	F28 2-0	S14 2-0	M15 2-1		M29 0-0	J11 4-2	N08 0-0	F10 1-1	F24 1-1	A31 4-1	S16 2-1	A17 0-0	a08 0-2	O26 1-1
15 NOTTS CO	A31 0-2	M15 5-0	J11 0-2	O26 0-2	N09 3-2	D26 2-1	m02 2-0	a19 0-0	F01 1-1	D21 3-1	a07 2-1	A28 1-2	M01 0-0	S07 3-1		J25 2-1	O12 0-0	a28 1-1	M05 1-0	A17 2-2	S21 0-3	a16 0-0	a05 5-0	N23 0-0
16 PETERBOROUGH U	a21 2-0	N30 6-1	A24 2-2	S14 2-1	S28 1-2	O07 3-0	a08 0-1	J29 1-1	a12 0-1	A10 1-1	O19 1-1	F05 0-0	J13 0-0	N02 1-1	N04 1-0		M08 0-1	M29 0-1	S16 3-2	O05 1-0	M10 2-2	F24 1-1	J04 2-3	M22 2-1
17 PORT VALE	M24 0-0	a25 1-1	a08 1-1	M15 4-1	M29 2-1	M01 0-1	a12 0-0	M10 1-0	S14 0-2	S30 1-0	a21 1-0	O19 1-1	O05 1-1	J18 5-0	D14 0-2	A17 1-0		A31 1-1	S28 4-1	N04 1-1	D28 1-0	N02 3-1	N30 1-0	S16 3-0
18 ROCHDALE	J18 3-0	N02 6-0	S21 6-0	O07 0-0	a14 4-1	a19 0-0	M08 4-0	F24 2-0	a07 0-0	A24 1-1	J04 6-1	a30 1-0	M10 2-1	N04 0-1	N30 0-0	S07 1-1	M22 1-0		A10 3-2	m10 3-0	O19 0-1	O05 0-0	a23 2-1	a05 2-1
19 SCUNTHORPE U	a29 4-1	D06 1-0	S06 1-0	A17 1-1	A30 2-2	a15 0-1	O08 2-3	m02 0-0	M14 0-2	S21 2-1	N06 1-2	O04 0-1	N30 0-0	O18 1-0	J04 2-1	a07 1-2	a05 0-1	M01 0-0		m12 4-1	N01 3-1	J28 0-1	M25 1-0	a18 2-1
20 SOUTHEND U	a07 4-2	a14 5-0	N22 2-0	J31 4-0	J10 1-2	M03 2-2	F14 3-1	A23 1-1	N09 2-0	O11 6-1	a05 0-1	A10 2-1	O07 3-0	a28 1-0	M07 4-0	D26 2-1	F24 1-1	O26 1-3	M17 0-3		a18 4-0	S20 1-0	S06 1-0	D20 1-2
21 SWANSEA T	A17 2-2	M01 3-0	M04 0-2	O12 2-3	D26 0-5	N09 0-0	N23 2-0	a15 1-1	J25 0-1	m05 2-0	M15 1-1	S28 1-0	M29 5-0	a07 3-2	a12 3-0	F01 0-0	O26 1-0	D21 3-0	J11 2-0	S14 2-2		A31 0-0	A27 0-0	M18 2-1
22 WORKINGTON	M28 1-0	S14 3-1	O26 0-0	M05 1-0	F15 0-0	D21 1-1	J24 0-1	A10 1-2	M19 1-1	N09 3-0	O09 2-0	S18 1-1	S28 1-1	m08 3-2	a08 1-1	N23 1-0	J11 0-0	D26 1-2	O12 1-1	a12 0-0	M22 0-3		A24 0-0	a30 2-0
23 WREXHAM	M01 2-0	A17 3-0	M31 1-1	D21 2-0	J25 1-1	F01 1-1	J11 0-3	a04 2-1	O12 3-1	a21 2-2	A31 2-0	a12 2-2	S14 0-1	a14 4-0	S28 3-2	O26 0-0	a28 2-0	N23 3-2	N09 0-1	M28 3-3	O07 2-0	m05 1-0		a16 2-1
24 YORK C	N04 2-1	O05 4-2	A26 1-1	a12 2-1	a28 4-2	M15 3-1	M29 2-0	N30 1-1	A17 1-1	O28 0-2	J18 2-5	m05 0-0	D14 1-1	D28 0-0	a23 2-0	A31 2-1	a04 3-1	S28 0-0	S14 2-1	O19 1-1	m02 0-2	M10 2-1	F24 1-0	

LEAGUE TABLES

DIVISION 1

	P	W	D	L	F	A	W	D	L	F	A	Pts
Leeds U	42	18	3	0	41	9	9	10	2	25	17	67
Liverpool	42	16	4	1	36	10	9	7	5	27	14	61
Everton	42	14	5	2	43	10	7	10	4	34	26	57
Arsenal	42	12	6	3	31	12	10	6	5	25	15	56
Chelsea	42	11	7	3	40	24	9	3	9	33	29	50
Tottenham H	42	10	8	3	39	22	4	9	8	22	29	45
Southampton	42	13	5	3	41	21	3	8	10	16	27	45
West Ham U	42	10	8	3	47	22	3	10	8	19	28	44
Newcastle U	42	12	7	2	40	20	3	7	11	21	35	44
WBA	42	11	7	3	43	26	5	4	12	21	41	43
Manchester U	42	13	5	3	38	18	2	7	12	19	35	42
Ipswich T	42	10	4	7	32	26	5	7	9	27	34	41
Manchester C	42	13	6	2	49	20	2	4	15	15	35	40
Burnley	42	11	6	4	36	25	4	3	14	19	57	39
Sheffield W	42	7	9	5	27	26	3	7	11	14	28	36
Wolves	42	7	10	4	26	22	3	5	13	15	36	35
Sunderland	42	10	6	5	28	18	1	6	14	15	49	34
Nottingham F	42	6	6	9	17	22	4	7	10	28	35	33
Stoke C	42	9	7	5	24	24	0	8	13	16	39	33
Coventry C	42	8	6	7	32	22	2	5	14	14	42	31
Leicester C	42	8	8	5	27	24	1	4	16	12	44	30
QPR	42	4	7	10	20	33	0	3	18	19	62	18

DIVISION 2

	P	W	D	L	F	A	W	D	L	F	A	Pts
Derby Co	42	16	4	1	43	16	10	7	4	22	16	63
Crystal P	42	14	4	3	45	24	8	8	5	25	23	56
Charlton A	42	11	8	2	39	21	7	6	8	22	31	50
Middlesbrough	42	13	7	1	36	13	6	4	11	22	36	49
Cardiff C	42	13	3	5	38	19	7	4	10	29	35	47
Huddersfield T	42	13	6	2	37	14	4	6	11	16	32	46
Birmingham C	42	13	3	5	52	24	5	5	11	21	35	44
Blackpool	42	9	8	4	33	20	5	7	9	18	21	43
Sheffield U	42	14	4	3	41	15	2	7	12	20	35	43
Millwall	42	10	5	6	33	23	7	4	10	24	26	43
Hull C	42	10	7	4	38	20	3	9	9	21	32	42
Carlisle U	42	10	5	6	25	17	6	5	10	21	32	42
Norwich C	42	7	6	8	24	25	8	4	9	29	31	40
Preston NE	42	8	8	5	23	19	4	7	10	15	25	39
Portsmouth	42	11	5	5	39	22	1	9	11	19	36	38
Bristol C	42	9	9	3	30	15	2	7	12	16	38	38
Bolton W	42	8	7	6	29	26	4	7	10	26	41	38
Aston Villa	42	10	8	3	22	11	2	6	13	15	37	38
Blackburn R	42	9	6	6	30	24	4	5	12	22	39	37
Oxford U	42	8	5	8	21	23	4	4	13	13	32	33
Bury	42	8	4	9	35	33	3	4	14	16	47	30
Fulham	42	6	7	8	20	28	1	4	16	20	53	25

DIVISION 3

	P	W	D	L	F	A	W	D	L	F	A	Pts
Watford	46	16	5	2	35	7	11	5	7	39	27	64
Swindon T	46	18	4	1	38	7	9	6	8	33	28	64
Luton T	46	20	3	0	57	14	5	8	10	17	24	61
Bournemouth	46	16	2	5	41	17	5	7	11	19	28	51
Plymouth A	46	10	8	5	34	25	7	7	9	19	24	49
Torquay U	46	13	4	6	35	18	5	8	10	19	28	48
Tranmere R	46	12	3	8	36	31	7	7	9	34	37	48
Southport	46	14	8	1	52	20	3	5	15	19	44	47
Stockport Co	46	14	5	4	49	25	2	9	12	18	43	46
Barnsley	46	13	6	4	37	21	3	8	12	21	42	46
Rotherham U	46	12	6	5	40	21	4	7	12	16	29	45
Brighton & HA	46	12	7	4	49	21	4	6	13	23	44	45
Walsall	46	10	9	4	34	18	4	7	12	16	31	44
Reading	46	13	3	7	41	25	2	10	11	26	41	43
Mansfield T	46	14	5	4	37	18	2	6	15	21	44	43
Bristol R	46	12	6	5	41	27	4	5	14	22	44	43
Shrewsbury T	46	11	8	4	28	17	5	3	15	23	50	43
Orient	46	10	8	5	31	19	4	6	13	20	39	42
Barrow	46	11	6	6	30	23	6	2	15	26	52	42
Gillingham	46	10	10	3	35	20	3	5	15	19	43	41
Northampton T	46	9	8	6	37	30	5	4	14	17	31	40
Hartlepool	46	6	12	5	25	29	4	7	12	15	41	39
Crewe A	46	11	4	8	40	31	2	5	16	12	45	35
Oldham A	46	9	6	8	33	27	4	3	16	17	56	35

DIVISION 4

	P	W	D	L	F	A	W	D	L	F	A	Pts
Doncaster R	46	13	8	2	42	16	8	9	6	23	22	59
Halifax T	46	15	5	3	36	18	5	12	6	17	19	57
Rochdale	46	14	7	2	47	11	4	13	6	21	24	56
Bradford C	46	11	10	2	36	18	7	10	6	29	28	56
Darlington	46	11	6	6	40	26	6	12	5	22	19	52
Colchester U	46	12	8	3	31	17	8	4	11	26	36	52
Southend U	46	15	3	5	51	21	4	10	9	27	40	51
Lincoln C	46	13	6	4	38	19	4	11	8	16	33	51
Wrexham	46	13	7	3	41	22	5	7	11	20	30	50
Swansea T	46	11	8	4	35	20	8	3	12	23	34	49
Brentford	46	12	7	4	40	24	6	5	12	24	41	48
Workington	46	8	11	4	24	17	7	6	10	16	26	47
Port Vale	46	12	8	3	33	15	4	6	13	13	31	46
Chester	46	12	4	7	43	24	4	9	10	33	42	45
Aldershot	46	13	3	7	42	23	6	4	13	24	43	45
Scunthorpe U	46	10	5	8	28	22	8	3	12	33	38	44
Exeter C	46	11	8	4	45	24	5	3	15	21	41	43
Peterboro' U	46	8	9	6	32	23	5	7	11	28	34	42
Notts Co	46	10	8	5	33	22	2	10	11	15	35	42
Chesterfield	46	7	7	9	24	22	6	8	9	19	28	41
York C	46	12	8	3	36	25	2	3	18	17	50	39
Newport Co	46	9	9	5	31	26	2	5	16	18	48	36
Grimsby T	46	5	7	11	25	31	4	8	11	22	38	33
Bradford	46	5	8	10	19	34	0	2	21	13	72	20

Football League Records

Top scorers: Div 1, J.Astle (West Bromwich Albion) 25 goals; Div 2, J.Hickton (Middlesbrough) 24 goals; Div 3, G.Jones (Bury) 26 goals; Div 4, A.Kinsey (Wrexham) 27 goals.

Joe Royle, whose 23 goals were a vital factor in Everton's League Championship win of 1969-70.

DIVISION 1

	ARSENAL	BURNLEY	CHELSEA	COVENTRY C	CRYSTAL P	DERBY CO	EVERTON	IPSWICH T	LEEDS U	LIVERPOOL	MANCHESTER C	MANCHESTER U	NEWCASTLE U	NOTTINGHAM F	SHEFFIELD W	SOUTHAMPTON	STOKE C	SUNDERLAND	TOTTENHAM H	W.B.A.	WEST HAM U	WOLVERHAMPTON W
1 ARSENAL		D13 3-2	J17 0-3	O04 0-1	M30 2-0	N08 4-0	A09 0-1	O25 0-0	A19 1-1	M14 2-1	N22 1-1	S20 2-2	D27 0-0	A23 2-1	S06 0-0	D06 2-2	F07 0-0	F28 3-1	S16 2-3	O07 1-1	a04 2-1	M28 2-2
2 BURNLEY	S13 0-1		a15 3-1	N15 0-0	O11 4-2	F14 1-1	M07 1-2	S27 0-1	A26 1-1	D26 1-5	A30 1-1	N29 1-1	N01 0-1	F21 5-0	O18 4-2	M24 1-1	M27 1-1	A16 3-0	A19 0-2	M21 2-1	J31 3-2	J10 1-3
3 CHELSEA	S27 3-0	S17 2-0		N01 1-0	A30 1-1	O11 2-2	N15 1-1	A16 1-0	J10 2-5	a18 2-1	D20 3-1	M21 2-1	F25 0-0	M07 1-1	M25 3-1	D26 3-1	M17 1-0	J31 3-1	a04 1-0	O18 2-0	A20 0-0	S13 2-2
4 COVENTRY C	J31 2-0	M28 1-1	F28 0-3		S13 2-2	A16 1-1	O25 0-1	D26 3-1	S27 1-2	M03 2-3	J10 3-0	N08 1-2	N22 1-0	S16 3-2	M14 1-1	M31 4-0	a04 0-3	M24 1-1	D06 3-2	A12 3-1	O11 2-2	A30 1-0
5 CRYSTAL P	N01 1-5	F11 1-2	D27 1-5	D13 0-3		D06 0-1	O08 0-0	M28 1-1	O18 1-1	A27 1-3	a06 1-0	A09 2-2	O04 0-3	J17 1-1	F21 0-2	M14 2-0	S06 3-1	A13 2-0	A23 0-2	S20 1-3	M24 0-0	N22 2-1
6 DERBY CO	F21 3-2	A09 0-0	F11 2-2	O08 1-3	M21 3-1		S06 2-1	A20 3-1	M30 4-1	N01 4-0	O18 0-1	O04 2-0	D13 2-0	N29 0-2	J17 1-0	S10 3-0	A23 0-0	N15 3-0	S20 5-0	D27 2-0	M07 3-0	a04 2-0
7 EVERTON	F14 2-2	N22 2-1	M28 5-2	F21 0-0	A16 2-1	D20 1-0		J10 3-0	A30 3-2	D06 0-3	D23 1-0	A19 3-0	J24 0-0	N01 1-0	A26 2-1	S27 4-2	O18 6-2	O11 3-1	M14 3-2	a01 2-0	S13 2-0	J31 1-0
8 IPSWICH T	M31 2-1	J17 0-1	N18 1-4	A23 0-1	N15 2-0	A12 0-1	S20 0-3		a21 3-2	O18 2-2	N01 1-1	F10 0-1	S06 2-0	A09 0-0	O04 1-0	a04 2-0	M07 1-1	M21 2-0	D27 2-0	D13 0-1	N29 1-0	S16 1-1
9 LEEDS U	A13 0-0	a04 2-1	S20 2-0	J17 3-1	F28 2-0	O25 2-0	D27 2-1	N08 4-0		N22 1-1	a18 1-3	S06 2-2	A23 1-1	O29 6-1	D13 2-0	M28 1-3	O04 2-1	N19 2-0	A09 3-1	F10 5-1	D17 4-1	D06 3-1
10 LIVERPOOL	N29 0-1	A23 3-3	A09 4-1	S06 2-1	a03 3-0	F28 0-2	M21 0-2	M24 2-0	M07 0-0		A12 3-2	D13 1-4	F16 0-0	O04 1-1	M16 3-0	O25 4-1	S20 3-1	S09 2-0	O07 0-0	J17 1-1	N15 2-0	N08 0-0
11 MANCHESTER C	F18 1-1	J06 1-1	S06 0-0	S20 3-1	M11 0-1	M27 0-1	A23 1-1	F28 1-0	N29 1-2	A20 0-2		N15 4-0	O08 2-1	F07 1-1	A09 4-1	N08 1-0	J17 0-1	a04 0-1	D13 1-1	O04 2-1	M21 1-5	O25 1-0
12 MANCHESTER U	J10 2-1	M17 3-3	D06 0-2	M30 1-1	F14 1-1	J31 1-0	A13 0-2	O11 2-1	J26 2-2	S13 1-0	M28 1-2		A27 0-0	O18 1-1	a15 2-2	A16 1-4	N01 1-1	A30 3-1	N22 3-1	a08 7-0	S27 5-2	D26 0-0
13 NEWCASTLE U	A30 3-1	M30 0-1	O25 0-1	a14 4-0	J31 0-0	S13 0-1	S17 1-2	D20 4-0	D26 2-1	O11 1-0	A16 1-0	a04 5-1		N15 3-1	A13 3-1	F11 2-1	M21 3-1	N08 3-0	F28 1-2	F06 1-0	M02 4-1	S27 1-1
14 NOTTINGHAM F	D26 1-1	O25 1-1	N22 1-1	a07 1-4	S27 0-0	M14 1-3	F28 1-1	a10 1-0	A16 1-4	J31 1-0	O11 2-2	M31 1-2	M28 2-2		D06 2-1	S13 2-1	A12 0-0	J24 2-1	N08 2-2	A26 1-0	A30 1-0	D20 4-2
15 SHEFFIELD W	D20 1-1	F28 2-0	N08 1-3	J28 0-1	O25 0-0	S27 1-0	a04 0-1	J31 2-2	S13 1-2	A30 1-1	a22 1-2	S17 1-3	A20 1-0	M21 2-1		O11 1-1	N15 0-2	D26 2-0	M30 0-1	M10 2-0	J10 2-3	A16 2-3
16 SOUTHAMPTON	M21 0-2	S06 1-1	A23 2-2	O18 0-0	N29 1-1	a15 1-1	J17 2-1	A27 4-2	N15 1-1	M11 0-1	a08 0-0	O08 0-3	S20 1-1	D13 1-2	F07 4-0		D27 0-0	M07 1-1	O04 2-2	A09 0-2	N01 1-1	A20 2-3
17 STOKE C	O11 0-0	N08 2-1	a13 1-2	A27 2-0	D20 1-0	D26 1-0	M30 0-1	N22 3-3	J31 1-1	J10 0-2	S27 2-0	F28 2-2	D06 0-1	A20 1-1	M28 2-1	A30 2-1		S13 4-2	O25 1-1	a15 3-2	A16 2-1	F14 1-1
18 SUNDERLAND	O18 1-1	O08 0-1	O04 0-0	A09 0-0	A20 0-0	M28 1-1	a08 0-0	D06 2-1	N01 0-0	a15 0-1	A27 0-4	D27 1-1	M27 1-1	S20 2-1	A23 1-2	N22 2-2	D13 0-3		J17 2-1	S06 2-2	F21 0-1	M14 2-1
19 TOTTENHAM H	m02 1-0	A13 4-0	A27 1-1	M21 1-2	D26 2-0	J10 2-1	M11 0-1	A30 3-2	F14 1-1	A16 0-2	S13 0-3	a13 2-1	O18 2-1	M27 4-1	N01 1-0	J31 0-1	F21 1-0	S27 0-1		N15 2-0	D20 0-2	O11 0-1
20 W.B.A.	A16 0-1	D06 0-1	M30 3-1	A20 0-1	J10 3-2	A30 0-2	N08 2-0	S13 2-2	O11 1-1	S27 2-2	J31 3-0	O25 2-1	M14 2-2	a04 4-0	N22 3-0	F20 1-0	S17 1-3	J27 3-1	M28 1-1		D26 3-1	F28 3-3
21 WEST HAM U	A25 1-1	O04 3-1	A11 2-0	F11 1-2	N08 2-1	N22 3-0	D13 0-1	M14 0-0	a02 2-2	M28 1-0	D06 0-4	J17 0-0	A09 1-0	D27 1-1	S20 3-0	F28 0-0	O06 3-3	O25 1-1	S06 0-1	A23 1-3		M31 3-0
22 WOLVERHAMPTON W	N15 2-0	S20 1-1	D13 3-0	a10 0-1	M18 1-1	A27 1-1	O04 2-3	J24 2-0	M21 1-2	M30 0-1	F21 1-3	A23 0-0	J17 1-1	S06 3-3	O08 2-2	A13 2-1	A09 3-1	N29 1-0	F07 2-2	N01 1-0	O18 1-0	

The much-travelled Frank Worthington had a particularly happy time at Huddersfield Town, where he scored 18 goals when Town won the Second Division title in 1969-70.

DIVISION 2

	ASTON VILLA	BIRMINGHAM C	BLACKBURN R	BLACKPOOL	BOLTON W	BRISTOL C	CARDIFF C	CARLISLE U	CHARLTON A	HUDDERSFIELD T	HULL C	LEICESTER C	MIDDLESBROUGH	MILLWALL	NORWICH C	OXFORD U	PORTSMOUTH	PRESTON N.E.	Q.P.R.	SHEFFIELD U	SWINDON T	WATFORD
1 ASTON VILLA		O18 0-0	M21 1-1	N15 0-0	N19 3-0	F21 0-2	F07 1-1	N12 1-0	F25 1-0	O08 4-1	S20 3-2	A27 0-1	a08 2-0	S06 2-2	A09 0-1	M31 0-0	J17 3-5	O04 0-0	N01 1-1	a13 1-0	A23 0-2	D13 0-2
2 BIRMINGHAM C	M30 0-2		O11 3-0	D26 2-3	F24 2-0	J31 2-2	O25 1-1	S27 1-1	J10 3-0	D06 2-2	a04 2-4	F14 0-1	M14 0-0	N22 2-0	S16 3-1	A16 1-3	A19 1-1	M28 1-0	A30 3-0	S13 2-1	N08 2-0	F28 0-0
3 BLACKBURN R	D06 2-0	M04 1-1		N12 2-1	N08 3-1	N22 3-3	O08 1-0	M28 1-0	a08 3-0	a04 0-2	A23 2-1	O25 3-1	S06 4-0	S20 4-0	O04 3-1	M14 2-0	D27 0-3	D13 4-2	S17 0-1	F28 1-2	A09 2-0	J17 1-0
4 BLACKPOOL	M28 2-1	A23 2-0	A18 0-0		O25 1-1	M14 1-0	O04 3-2	D06 1-1	F28 2-0	D13 2-0	M18 0-1	N08 1-1	J17 1-1	F07 1-1	O06 0-0	N22 1-0	A09 2-1	S15 0-0	a04 1-1	M30 1-0	S06 3-2	S20 0-3
5 BOLTON W	S17 2-1	S06 2-0	M30 1-0	F21 0-2		N01 3-1	M18 0-1	a04 0-0	M21 1-1	J17 1-1	D13 2-1	N12 2-3	F11 2-1	A09 4-1	a09 0-0	O18 1-1	S20 0-1	A23 2-0	N29 6-4	N15 0-0	O04 0-1	O08 2-3
6 BRISTOL C	N08 1-0	O04 2-0	M07 4-0	N29 2-1	M27 2-2		A23 0-2	O25 0-0	S23 6-0	D27 1-2	O07 3-1	F28 0-0	D13 0-0	J17 1-1	S20 4-0	N11 2-0	F07 3-0	S06 0-0	N15 2-0	a04 0-1	M21 3-3	A09 1-0
7 CARDIFF C	O11 4-0	F21 3-1	A16 0-0	J31 2-2	A30 2-1	D29 1-0		F14 1-1	D20 1-0	M14 0-1	N01 6-0	S13 1-1	A27 1-0	a15 0-0	O18 0-1	M28 0-0	M25 2-0	N22 2-1	S27 4-2	J10 3-0	A13 2-2	D06 3-1
8 CARLISLE U	A19 1-1	J17 4-3	N15 0-1	M21 1-2	A26 2-1	M31 2-1	A09 2-3		M07 1-1	O04 0-2	S06 2-1	a14 2-2	A23 1-0	D13 4-0	D27 2-1	F21 1-1	N01 3-3	S20 1-0	O18 3-2	N29 0-1	O07 2-2	F10 5-0
9 CHARLTON A	M14 1-0	S20 0-1	O18 0-0	N01 0-2	D06 1-1	a14 2-1	S06 0-0	N22 2-1		F07 1-2	J17 1-4	M28 0-5	M03 0-2	O07 2-2	D13 3-0	A26 1-0	O04 2-2	A09 2-1	M31 1-1	A19 3-2	D27 1-1	A23 0-0
10 HUDDERSFIELD T	A16 2-0	M21 2-0	A26 0-1	S13 2-0	S27 1-0	A30 3-0	J24 1-0	J31 1-0	O11 4-0		M30 2-2	M10 1-1	O18 0-0	N01 0-0	F21 1-1	F24 1-0	N15 4-0	A19 3-2	J20 2-0	D26 2-1	M24 1-1	a14 3-1
11 HULL C	M10 3-1	A27 0-0	D26 3-0	A29 1-0	S13 4-2	A16 2-0	M31 1-1	D20 2-4	S27 1-1	O25 2-3		M14 4-1	M28 3-2	J24 2-1	A13 1-0	O11 3-1	a15 3-3	N08 3-1	F14 1-2	J31 2-3	F28 1-1	N22 1-1
12 LEICESTER C	a04 1-0	A09 3-1	M17 2-1	M31 0-0	A20 2-2	O18 2-0	D13 1-2	S17 1-2	N15 2-2	S20 1-1	D17 2-2		O08 2-1	D27 1-1	A23 3-0	N01 2-1	S06 2-1	F25 3-0	a18 2-1	M21 2-1	J17 0-2	O04 3-1
13 MIDDLESBROUGH	A30 1-0	D16 4-2	J13 4-1	S27 0-2	O11 4-0	S13 2-0	a04 2-1	D26 0-2	N08 2-0	M31 1-1	N15 1-0	A16 2-1		A12 3-1	M21 0-0	J10 2-0	M07 2-1	F28 1-1	J31 1-0	M17 1-0	S16 0-0	O25 3-1
14 MILLWALL	M16 2-0	M11 6-2	J20 3-1	O11 1-3	F14 2-0	S27 1-1	D15 1-2	S13 4-2	A16 1-1	F28 1-0	M21 2-1	A30 0-1	A18 1-1		N15 1-0	J31 0-0	D08 3-1	M30 2-1	D26 2-0	O25 1-0	a04 3-1	N08 1-0
15 NORWICH C	F14 3-1	a15 6-0	J31 0-1	A16 3-1	N22 1-0	J10 4-1	F28 1-1	A30 1-0	S13 1-1	N08 1-2	A20 2-1	D26 3-0	M11 2-0	M28 2-1		S27 2-0	A27 0-0	O25 1-2	O11 1-0	D20 1-1	M30 1-0	a18 1-1
16 OXFORD U	O25 2-2	O08 2-0	N29 1-0	a18 2-0	F28 3-1	M18 2-0	N15 1-1	N08 1-0	a04 1-1	A09 1-2	F07 0-0	M27 0-1	S20 1-1	O04 0-0	J17 1-0		A23 0-2	F18 3-1	M21 0-0	S17 0-0	D13 0-0	S06 2-1
17 PORTSMOUTH	S27 0-0	N12 1-1	A30 2-0	F14 2-3	J10 1-1	O11 0-0	N08 3-0	F28 4-0	J31 5-1	M28 1-3	S17 1-4	D20 2-3	N22 2-3	M14 0-1	a04 1-4	J24 2-1		D06 4-0	S13 1-3	A16 1-5	O25 3-1	a01 3-1
18 PRESTON N.E.	J31 1-1	N15 4-1	S13 0-0	a13 0-3	D26 1-3	J24 0-1	a20 1-2	J10 3-1	M16 4-1	N10 1-3	F21 3-3	O11 2-1	N01 0-1	O18 1-1	M31 1-1	A30 0-1	M21 1-2		A16 0-0	S27 2-1	N29 3-1	A25 3-0
19 Q.P.R.	F28 4-2	D27 2-1	a14 2-3	A26 6-1	M14 0-4	M28 2-2	J17 2-1	M27 0-0	O25 1-1	S06 4-2	A09 3-0	N22 1-1	O04 4-0	A23 3-2	F17 4-0	D06 1-2	D13 2-0	O07 0-0		N08 2-1	S20 2-0	N11 2-1
20 SHEFFIELD U	N22 5-0	D13 6-0	N01 4-0	O18 2-3	M28 0-1	A26 2-1	S20 1-0	M13 1-0	A12 2-0	A23 0-0	O04 3-0	D06 1-0	A09 3-0	M31 3-1	S06 1-0	a15 5-1	O07 5-0	J17 2-0	F24 2-0		F09 1-2	D27 1-1
21 SWINDON T	D26 1-1	M31 4-1	a20 1-0	a07 1-1	J31 3-2	D06 1-1	A19 2-1	A16 2-2	A30 5-0	N22 2-1	O18 1-0	S27 1-1	a14 0-3	S30 2-1	N01 2-0	S13 0-0	M03 3-1	M14 1-0	J10 0-0	O11 2-1		M28 1-0
22 WATFORD	S13 3-0	N01 2-3	S27 0-2	J10 0-1	A16 0-0	F14 2-0	M21 2-1	O11 1-2	D26 1-1	S17 1-1	M06 1-1	J31 2-1	M27 2-3	F24 1-1	a07 1-1	D20 2-0	O18 4-0	a04 0-0	A20 0-1	A30 1-2	N15 0-0	

Season 1969-70

DIVISION 3

	BARNSLEY	BARROW	BOURNEMOUTH	BRADFORD C	BRIGHTON & HA	BRISTOL R	BURY	DONCASTER R	FULHAM	GILLINGHAM	HALIFAX T	LUTON T	MANSFIELD T	ORIENT	PLYMOUTH A	READING	ROCHDALE	ROTHERHAM U	SHREWSBURY T	SOUTHPORT	STOCKPORT CO	TORQUAY U	TRANMERE R	WALSALL
1 BARNSLEY		O04 2-1	A09 1-0	F07 3-2	N22 1-2	O07 2-0	D13 3-3	D27 2-1	F21 3-3	J17 5-1	N01 2-0	M31 2-1	M28 1-1	S20 1-2	F09 0-1	A26 4-3	M03 1-0	M13 1-0	M17 1-1	O18 1-1	A23 1-0	a07 3-0	a14 1-1	S06 2-0
2 BARROW	J31 1-1		M21 1-1	D01 0-1	F16 1-1	N29 1-1	F21 3-1	M09 1-1	A30 3-1	O18 1-1	S29 0-1	F14 2-1	S13 0-1	A25 1-1	N01 1-1	J24 2-2	D20 2-0	S27 1-2	M27 2-0	D26 1-0	M07 4-1	O11 0-4	A16 0-3	F23 0-1
3 BOURNEMOUTH	F14 3-1	M04 0-0		M28 0-0	D26 0-0	O25 2-2	a04 2-0	N26 3-1	O11 2-2	N22 2-1	S27 0-0	A16 0-1	a18 1-0	F28 0-2	M14 1-3	J10 1-2	S29 0-3	A30 1-0	S17 3-3	J31 1-0	N08 1-0	S13 1-2	D20 2-2	M27 2-2
4 BRADFORD C	O11 1-1	a08 3-3	J24 8-1		S27 1-0	M07 2-4	M30 0-1	M21 3-0	F14 0-0	N01 1-0	D26 2-1	S13 1-1	a22 0-1	a15 0-1	O18 1-0	O01 4-0	F04 0-3	J31 0-1	F21 2-2	A30 1-0	N29 1-0	A16 2-1	F25 1-1	A27 3-0
5 BRIGHTON & H.A.	M07 2-0	S20 2-0	A23 1-1	J17 2-1		O04 0-3	D27 2-0	J03 1-0	N01 2-1	S06 3-1	M11 4-0	O18 1-2	a15 1-2	D13 0-0	O07 2-0	M27 2-1	A27 2-0	a08 2-1	F07 1-0	M21 1-0	M18 1-0	N29 2-2	F21 2-0	A09 1-1
6 BRISTOL R	A16 3-3	M14 2-1	F21 5-2	N22 1-1	J31 0-2		O18 2-1	M31 1-1	S13 3-2	a14 1-2	A30 2-0	F10 3-0	J10 4-1	M28 1-0	A26 3-1	D26 1-1	S27 3-3	O11 3-0	N01 1-3	F14 2-0	a07 1-0	J24 3-1	S30 3-0	M03 3-1
7 BURY	S13 1-2	O25 4-0	A26 1-0	N08 0-2	A30 1-2	F28 2-2		a14 1-1	A16 1-0	M03 1-3	J31 1-1	J24 1-3	S30 1-0	M14 0-1	M28 3-1	S27 2-1	D06 2-1	F14 2-1	a07 2-2	O11 4-3	J03 4-1	F16 1-0	J10 8-0	N22 4-2
8 DONCASTER R	A30 1-0	M28 3-2	a07 2-1	M03 1-1	S30 2-0	N08 3-1	S16 1-1		J31 0-1	M14 1-0	J10 0-1	O11 2-0	A16 2-0	M30 0-1	N21 1-1	J20 2-3	J23 3-1	D26 1-2	a04 2-1	S27 1-0	O24 0-1	a09 1-0	S13 2-1	F28 0-0
9 FULHAM	O25 0-0	D27 2-1	F06 1-1	A09 0-0	M30 4-1	D13 3-1	O08 2-4	O04 1-1		A23 2-1	a15 2-1	a08 0-1	N22 1-1	J02 1-1	S20 4-3	a20 2-1	M14 2-0	F28 3-2	S06 3-1	A27 3-2	J17 1-1	N08 1-1	M28 1-1	M18 4-0
10 GILLINGHAM	S27 1-3	F28 0-1	a25 0-0	M27 1-1	D20 0-1	S17 1-0	M21 1-0	F18 2-1	D26 2-0		a22 2-0	A30 0-2	a10 3-3	O25 0-1	N26 4-0	A16 1-3	S13 2-2	J10 1-1	M11 2-1	O01 2-4	a04 0-2	J31 2-4	O11 0-0	N08 1-3
11 HALIFAX T	F28 0-2	J27 3-0	J17 4-1	A23 0-0	M28 1-0	D27 1-1	O04 2-0	S20 1-1	S16 0-8	M17 1-1		a04 0-0	O25 1-2	O07 1-1	D13 2-0	M14 1-1	N08 3-1	M03 4-2	A09 1-0	D06 1-0	S06 1-0	M31 1-1	N22 2-2	a24 0-1
12 LUTON T	N08 1-1	A09 3-0	O07 0-0	D13 5-0	F28 1-1	S06 4-0	M17 0-0	F07 4-0	N25 1-0	D27 1-2	A26 1-1		M14 2-2	A23 3-2	J17 0-2	M28 5-0	N22 2-0	M27 2-1	S20 2-2	a14 1-0	O04 2-0	O25 1-1	M03 2-0	a11 3-0
13 MANSFIELD T	M09 2-0	D13 4-2	M16 2-0	S06 2-1	S15 1-0	S20 1-1	F23 3-1	O06 1-2	a06 2-3	A09 1-0	F21 3-3	a20 0-0		D27 4-1	O04 1-2	O18 2-1	N03 1-2	a04 2-0	J17 2-0	a01 5-0	M23 4-1	M21 2-0	N01 1-2	A23 0-0
14 ORIENT	F16 4-2	a04 2-0	N01 3-0	S15 2-1	S13 1-1	M09 0-0	J26 3-0	O18 2-0	S29 3-1	a27 1-2	A16 1-0	D26 1-0	A30 1-0		M27 4-1	O11 0-1	a11 2-2	D20 1-1	a25 1-0	a20 3-2	M21 3-0	S27 1-1	J31 2-0	N24 2-0
15 PLYMOUTH A	S29 0-0	M31 1-0	N29 0-1	F28 0-1	A16 0-1	a04 2-2	M11 2-2	M07 0-0	J10 2-0	F25 2-2	S13 1-0	S27 1-3	J31 1-0	N08 1-0		F14 1-1	O11 2-3	J24 0-3	M21 4-2	D20 1-1	S17 2-0	D26 6-0	A30 2-1	O25 1-0
16 READING	a04 6-2	M18 6-3	S20 2-0	J14 1-0	N08 1-0	A23 1-5	J17 3-2	S06 1-0	M21 0-4	O08 1-0	F11 4-1	M11 0-1	M30 1-0	F07 3-2	A09 2-1		F28 1-0	O25 1-1	D27 3-1	a22 8-0	D13 3-1	S17 1-1	a08 1-1	O04 2-3
17 ROCHDALE	M21 1-1	S06 1-0	J26 0-1	S20 1-2	a04 2-1	J17 0-0	A23 3-3	M16 2-0	a18 0-1	D13 0-0	M30 5-0	a25 1-2	N24 2-1	A09 0-3	F07 2-1	N01 3-2		S15 4-2	O04 3-0	F21 1-1	O06 2-0	M09 1-1	O18 4-0	a09 1-2
18 ROTHERHAM U	D02 2-0	J17 5-0	D27 3-0	O04 2-3	N25 2-0	F07 0-0	A09 4-3	A23 0-1	O18 0-0	S20 0-1	M21 1-1	N01 1-1	A26 2-2	S06 0-0	M17 1-0	F21 1-1	a14 3-1		O07 1-2	M10 2-0	J13 0-0	M23 2-1	M31 0-1	D13 4-1
19 SHREWSBURY T	J24 1-1	N08 1-1	a15 2-0	O25 1-0	O11 2-2	M30 0-0	N26 3-3	A27 0-0	D20 1-1	M28 2-2	F14 3-1	J10 5-1	S27 0-0	N22 1-1	a18 3-0	A30 0-0	J31 1-0	A16 1-0		S13 1-2	F28 3-1	O01 1-0	D26 2-0	M14 1-1
20 SOUTHPORT	M27 0-1	A23 1-0	O04 3-0	a24 1-0	M03 2-0	A09 0-0	F06 4-0	J17 2-2	a03 0-2	a17 1-1	a07 1-0	S16 0-3	N08 0-1	M17 1-0	S06 0-0	N22 6-2	O25 0-3	M28 2-1	D13 0-2		S20 1-1	F28 4-2	M14 2-0	O08 0-1
21 STOCKPORT CO	D26 1-0	N22 2-2	M30 0-2	M14 0-2	J23 0-1	N24 0-1	N01 1-0	F21 3-1	S27 1-4	A25 1-0	F02 0-1	J31 1-1	O11 1-3	M02 0-2	a13 0-1	S13 2-2	A16 0-1	O13 1-1	O18 1-1	J10 0-0		A30 0-1	a24 0-1	M28 2-2
22 TORQUAY U	N26 1-1	F07 1-1	D13 2-2	O08 2-1	M14 2-1	M18 1-2	S06 3-0	A09 2-1	M27 1-1	O04 3-2	O18 0-1	F21 2-2	M04 0-2	J17 0-1	A23 1-2	D05 1-1	M28 3-0	N22 0-0	a22 3-0	N01 0-0	S10 3-0		A27 5-1	S20 0-0
23 TRANMERE R	S15 0-1	O06 5-0	S06 1-5	M16 1-0	O25 2-0	a17 5-2	S20 3-2	D13 1-3	a27 1-0	a20 0-0	M06 1-1	M21 3-2	F28 1-1	O04 1-1	a06 3-1	N24 1-5	M27 0-0	N08 2-2	A23 3-1	N29 0-1	A09 3-0	a03 1-1		J17 0-0
24 WALSALL	D20 3-2	S16 1-0	O18 2-1	a04 2-0	F25 0-3	M21 2-1	M24 1-1	O31 1-3	J27 1-3	M31 0-1	O11 2-1	S30 1-3	D26 1-0	a07 2-0	a17 2-2	a14 4-1	A30 1-4	S13 0-2	N29 3-2	A16 4-0	a22 0-0	J10 0-1	S27 0-0	

DIVISION 4

	ALDERSHOT	BRADFORD	BRENTFORD	CHESTER	CHESTERFIELD	COLCHESTER U	CREWE A	DARLINGTON	EXETER C	GRIMSBY T	HARTLEPOOL	LINCOLN C	NEWPORT CO	NORTHAMPTON T	NOTTS CO	OLDHAM A	PETERBOROUGH U	PORT VALE	SCUNTHORPE U	SOUTHEND U	SWANSEA T	WORKINGTON	WREXHAM	YORK C
1 ALDERSHOT		a20 4-2	a24 1-2	N22 3-1	A27 1-0	N01 1-1	A16 4-1	F25 4-0	a15 1-0	M28 2-2	O01 4-1	O11 1-1	A30 1-1	O18 5-2	S27 2-0	M30 1-0	F21 1-0	J31 2-0	J10 3-1	M14 2-1	D26 2-2	D20 3-1	S13 0-2	N26 4-1
2 BRADFORD	A09 2-0		S20 0-1	J19 1-2	S06 1-1	F07 0-1	M02 0-0	F28 0-1	D27 2-1	A23 1-1	M31 3-0	M28 0-3	M13 1-1	O04 1-2	O25 1-3	M16 0-0	O06 2-3	N08 1-2	a04 0-5	J17 1-0	N22 0-2	S15 2-0	N24 2-3	D13 2-0
3 BRENTFORD	M21 0-0	J10 1-1		a04 2-0	F21 0-1	a18 2-0	D26 1-1	A30 1-1	M27 2-0	N24 3-0	F23 3-0	S29 2-1	D20 1-0	M07 1-0	A16 1-0	O18 1-1	N01 5-2	J24 1-0	O11 3-0	S15 3-1	S13 2-2	J31 1-0	S27 0-0	M09 0-0
4 CHESTER	a30 2-1	O01 1-0	A27 1-2		O18 1-2	a01 1-0	S27 2-1	J31 1-3	N01 2-0	a15 3-1	O11 2-1	J10 1-2	F25 2-0	F21 2-1	S13 0-1	M11 2-1	M21 2-3	D20 1-1	F14 1-1	N26 2-0	A16 2-2	A30 3-0	D26 2-0	N29 3-0
5 CHESTERFIELD	a04 4-2	a17 4-0	O25 1-0	F28 0-1		M21 2-0	S29 1-0	D26 2-0	N24 2-1	N08 1-2	A30 3-0	J24 4-0	S13 4-0	M09 2-1	O11 5-0	N29 3-1	a27 3-1	A16 0-1	J31 2-1	M31 3-0	a21 0-0	S27 4-0	F25 2-0	S15 3-1
6 COLCHESTER U	M27 3-1	O11 2-1	M14 1-1	O25 0-1	M02 4-1		S13 1-0	D20 2-1	M28 2-1	N22 3-2	J10 1-1	a22 2-0	J31 1-1	a06 0-3	D26 2-1	a13 3-1	A25 2-1	A30 0-0	S29 0-2	N08 0-2	S27 1-1	J24 3-0	A16 2-0	F28 3-0
7 CREWE A	O08 1-0	M21 0-0	A23 1-2	J17 3-0	a24 2-1	D13 0-1		N29 2-0	F07 1-1	O04 3-0	a10 3-0	N26 3-1	F21 1-1	A09 2-0	A27 1-1	S20 1-1	S06 2-0	a15 0-0	N01 0-2	J27 5-3	M27 0-1	O18 1-0	M11 2-3	M18 3-0
8 DARLINGTON	M16 0-2	N01 1-1	D27 1-2	O04 1-2	A23 0-1	S06 3-2	M14 2-0		O06 4-0	F07 0-0	a22 4-0	N22 0-3	A25 0-0	D13 2-2	M28 1-2	J17 1-1	S20 1-2	M02 2-2	M30 2-0	A09 0-2	a13 2-1	F23 1-1	O18 2-1	a27 1-0
9 EXETER C	S17 2-1	A30 3-0	N08 2-2	M30 1-0	a07 1-1	M11 2-1	O11 3-0	A16 1-2		O25 0-1	J24 6-0	J31 1-2	D26 1-1	M21 1-0	J10 1-1	M07 0-2	N29 1-1	S27 1-2	D20 4-1	F28 3-0	O01 6-0	S13 5-1	F14 1-0	a04 2-1
10 GRIMSBY T	M10 2-2	D26 2-2	a07 2-1	S16 4-1	M27 1-0	a28 5-3	J31 0-2	O11 0-1	F21 2-0		A16 2-0	S27 0-2	S30 1-1	a18 0-1	J03 2-1	N01 4-1	O18 0-0	J10 2-0	S13 1-1	a04 2-2	J24 0-2	F14 1-1	A30 0-0	M21 0-0
11 HARTLEPOOL	F02 1-3	O18 5-2	A09 0-0	F07 1-2	D27 0-0	S20 0-0	N22 1-1	N24 1-3	M16 2-0	O06 0-1		M14 0-3	a13 0-1	S06 1-1	M02 4-0	O04 1-1	J17 4-2	M28 0-2	F20 1-2	D13 2-1	A25 3-0	M27 1-0	N01 1-3	A23 2-2
12 LINCOLN C	F07 1-1	M23 5-2	J03 1-0	S20 2-0	M18 0-2	A09 3-3	a08 2-1	a25 1-0	O04 1-0	J17 2-0	a18 3-0		M27 3-0	D27 0-0	a15 2-4	S06 0-1	D13 3-0	A27 0-0	O18 1-2	A23 3-3	F21 0-0	N01 1-1	M21 0-0	O08 4-0
13 NEWPORT CO	D27 3-4	N29 5-1	S06 1-0	M16 3-1	D13 0-2	O04 4-1	O25 0-0	a04 2-1	A23 2-0	a25 1-0	S15 1-1	N08 3-1		J17 0-2	F28 1-0	O06 2-1	F07 0-1	M30 1-1	M09 3-0	S20 4-0	a06 1-2	M21 0-1	M07 1-2	A09 1-2
14 NORTHAMPTON T	F28 4-0	J31 3-0	N22 1-1	N08 0-1	M28 0-1	N25 1-1	F23 1-2	S13 1-1	M02 2-0	M14 3-1	D20 0-1	A30 1-1	S27 4-1		S30 3-1	A26 0-0	a14 2-2	D26 2-0	F18 2-1	O25 2-0	a10 4-1	O28 3-0	O11 0-1	M31 2-2
15 NOTTS CO	J17 3-0	M30 5-2	O08 1-0	D13 3-0	F07 1-1	A23 1-1	a04 0-1	M11 4-1	S20 4-0	S06 2-1	M21 1-0	S17 2-0	O18 4-1	a24 2-0		A09 0-0	D27 2-2	a08 1-2	N29 3-1	M18 2-0	N01 0-1	a21 0-3	F21 3-2	O04 0-2
16 OLDHAM A	O25 4-2	J24 0-0	M31 4-1	M28 5-0	M14 1-0	S16 1-2	a21 2-1	S27 1-1	N22 1-1	F28 0-2	J31 1-0	F10 1-1	A16 3-0	a04 0-2	F14 5-0		a07 4-2	S13 2-3	A30 1-3	M03 3-0	O11 0-1	D26 1-2	O01 2-3	N08 3-1
17 PETERBOROUGH U	N08 4-1	A16 2-1	F28 0-0	a18 0-0	N22 1-2	a04 1-1	F25 3-0	J10 3-2	M14 1-1	M30 1-0	S27 4-0	S13 2-1	O11 4-0	S17 1-0	A30 1-0	N26 8-1		a22 0-0	D26 2-2	M28 3-4	J31 1-1	S30 1-1	a10 5-2	O25 3-1
18 PORT VALE	O04 0-0	F21 4-1	M16 0-0	S06 3-0	O06 1-1	a25 1-1	S15 2-0	M21 4-0	J17 2-0	S20 1-0	M09 3-0	a04 0-0	N01 3-1	A23 4-1	a18 1-1	D13 1-0	A09 0-0		M23 1-2	F23 3-0	O18 0-0	N29 3-1	a01 1-0	F07 1-1
19 SCUNTHORPE U	S20 0-0	A26 2-0	F10 1-1	A09 2-3	O04 1-2	J27 1-1	M31 0-1	N08 2-0	S06 0-0	D13 1-1	O25 3-1	F28 2-1	M28 4-0	M17 1-0	M14 2-3	D27 2-1	A23 2-1	N22 2-1		O07 2-0	M03 1-2	N25 1-0	a14 1-3	J17 1-1
20 SOUTHEND U	N29 2-2	S27 1-1	a13 2-2	a06 4-2	N01 0-0	F21 2-1	A30 2-0	a10 2-0	O18 1-1	A25 1-3	S13 0-2	D26 2-2	J10 3-2	M27 2-2	J24 2-5	M21 1-0	M09 2-0	S29 1-1	A15 3-0		D20 2-1	O11 3-1	J31 1-0	m01 1-0
21 SWANSEA T	A23 1-1	M07 5-0	D13 1-0	O07 2-1	A09 0-0	J17 1-0	N08 3-0	S16 3-1	F24 0-0	M17 2-0	a04 3-0	O25 2-2	N25 1-1	S20 3-2	M31 1-1	F07 4-0	O04 4-1	F28 0-0	M21 2-1	S06 2-0		M23 0-0	F17 1-2	D27 2-1
22 WORKINGTON	S06 1-2	a15 1-0	O04 1-2	F18 1-1	J17 1-1	M18 1-1	F28 1-0	O25 1-0	D13 1-2	A09 0-0	N08 1-3	M30 1-1	M04 3-0	O08 2-0	N22 0-2	A23 1-0	J15 1-1	M14 3-2	a08 2-2	F06 5-0	M28 0-0		A27 2-0	S20 1-1
23 WREXHAM	D13 1-1	a06 4-0	J17 1-0	A23 2-0	S20 2-1	O06 4-2	M28 2-2	M27 6-2	A09 3-0	a20 3-2	F28 1-0	M02 0-0	N22 3-0	a27 3-0	N08 2-0	a18 1-1	M16 2-1	O25 1-1	S15 2-1	O04 4-0	M14 1-1	a04 4-1		S06 4-0
24 YORK C	a07 2-0	S13 4-1	M28 4-2	M13 0-0	a13 1-1	O18 4-2	a17 0-0	S29 2-1	A25 1-0	M02 1-1	D26 0-0	A16 2-0	a21 2-1	N01 1-1	J31 1-2	F21 0-0	M27 3-0	O11 0-1	S27 3-2	N22 1-0	A30 3-0	F09 1-0	a24 2-1	

LEAGUE TABLES

DIVISION 1

	P	W	D	L	F	A	W	D	L	F	A	Pts
Everton	42	17	3	1	46	19	12	5	4	26	15	66
Leeds U	42	15	4	2	50	19	6	11	4	34	30	57
Chelsea	42	13	7	1	36	18	8	6	7	34	32	55
Derby Co	42	15	3	3	45	14	7	6	8	19	23	53
Liverpool	42	10	7	4	34	20	10	4	7	31	22	51
Coventry C	42	9	6	6	35	28	10	5	6	23	20	49
Newcastle U	42	14	2	5	42	16	3	11	7	15	19	47
Manchester U	42	8	9	4	37	27	6	8	7	29	34	45
Stoke C	42	10	7	4	31	23	5	8	8	25	29	45
Manchester C	42	8	6	7	25	22	8	5	8	30	26	43
Tottenham H	42	11	2	8	27	21	6	7	8	27	34	43
Arsenal	42	7	10	4	29	23	5	8	8	22	26	42
Wolves	42	8	8	5	30	23	4	8	9	25	34	40
Burnley	42	7	7	7	33	29	5	8	8	23	32	39
Nottingham F	42	8	9	4	28	28	2	9	10	22	43	38
WBA	42	10	6	5	39	25	4	3	14	19	41	37
West Ham U	42	8	8	5	28	21	4	4	13	23	39	36
Ipswich T	42	9	5	7	23	20	1	6	14	17	43	31
Southampton	42	3	12	6	24	27	3	5	13	22	40	29
Crystal P	42	5	6	10	20	36	1	9	11	14	32	27
Sunderland	42	4	11	6	17	24	2	3	16	13	44	26
Sheffield W	42	6	5	10	23	27	2	4	15	17	44	25

DIVISION 2

	P	W	D	L	F	A	W	D	L	F	A	Pts
Huddersfield T	42	14	6	1	36	10	10	6	5	32	27	60
Blackpool	42	10	9	2	25	16	10	4	7	31	29	53
Leicester C	42	12	6	3	37	22	7	7	7	27	28	51
Middlesbrough	42	15	4	2	36	14	5	6	10	19	31	50
Swindon T	42	13	7	1	35	17	4	9	8	22	30	50
Sheffield U	42	16	2	3	50	10	6	3	12	23	28	49
Cardiff C	42	12	7	2	38	14	6	6	9	23	27	49
Blackburn R	42	15	2	4	42	19	5	5	11	12	31	47
QPR	42	13	5	3	47	24	4	6	11	19	33	45
Millwall	42	14	4	3	38	18	1	10	10	18	38	44
Norwich C	42	13	5	3	37	14	3	6	12	12	32	43
Carlisle U	42	10	6	5	39	28	4	7	10	19	28	41
Hull C	42	11	6	4	43	28	4	5	12	29	42	41
Bristol C	42	11	7	3	37	13	2	6	13	17	37	39
Oxford U	42	9	9	3	23	13	3	6	12	12	29	39
Bolton W	42	9	6	6	31	23	3	6	12	23	38	36
Portsmouth	42	8	4	9	39	35	5	5	11	27	45	35
Birmingham C	42	9	7	5	33	22	2	4	15	18	56	33
Watford	42	6	8	7	26	21	3	5	13	18	36	31
Charlton A	42	7	8	6	23	28	0	9	12	12	48	31
Aston Villa	42	7	8	6	23	21	1	5	15	13	41	29
Preston NE	42	7	6	8	31	28	1	6	14	12	35	28

DIVISION 3

	P	W	D	L	F	A	W	D	L	F	A	Pto
Orient	46	16	5	2	43	15	9	7	7	24	21	62
Luton T	46	13	8	2	46	15	10	6	7	31	28	60
Bristol R	46	15	5	3	51	26	5	11	7	29	33	56
Fulham	46	12	9	2	43	26	8	6	9	38	29	55
Brighton & HA	46	16	4	3	37	16	7	5	11	20	27	55
Mansfield T	46	14	4	5	46	22	7	7	9	24	27	53
Barnsley	46	14	6	3	43	24	5	9	9	25	35	53
Reading	46	16	3	4	52	29	5	8	10	35	48	53
Rochdale	46	11	6	6	39	24	7	4	12	30	36	46
Bradford C	46	11	6	6	37	22	6	6	11	20	28	46
Doncaster R	46	13	4	6	31	19	4	8	11	21	35	46
Walsall	46	11	4	8	33	31	6	8	9	21	36	46
Torquay U	46	9	9	5	36	22	5	8	10	26	37	45
Rotherham U	46	10	8	5	36	19	5	6	12	26	35	44
Shrewsbury T	46	10	12	1	35	17	3	6	14	27	46	44
Tranmere R	46	10	8	5	38	29	4	8	11	18	43	44
Plymouth A	46	10	7	6	32	23	6	4	13	24	41	43
Halifax T	46	10	9	4	31	25	4	6	13	16	30	43
Bury	46	13	4	6	47	29	2	7	14	28	51	41
Gillingham	46	7	6	10	28	33	6	7	10	24	31	39
Bournemouth	46	8	9	6	28	27	4	6	13	20	44	39
Southport	46	11	5	7	31	22	3	5	15	17	44	38
Barrow	46	7	9	7	28	27	1	5	17	18	54	30
Stockport Co	46	4	7	12	17	30	2	4	17	10	41	23

DIVISION 4

	P	W	D	L	F	A	W	D	L	F	A	Pts
Chesterfield	46	19	1	3	55	12	8	9	6	22	20	64
Wrexham	46	17	6	0	56	16	9	3	11	28	33	61
Swansea T	46	14	8	1	43	14	7	10	6	23	31	60
Port Vale	46	13	9	1	39	10	7	10	6	22	23	59
Brentford	46	14	8	1	36	11	6	8	9	22	28	56
Aldershot	46	16	5	2	52	22	4	8	11	26	43	53
Notts Co	46	14	4	5	44	21	8	4	11	29	41	52
Lincoln C	46	11	8	4	38	20	6	8	9	28	32	50
Peterboro' U	46	13	8	2	51	21	4	6	13	26	48	48
Colchester U	46	14	5	4	38	22	3	9	11	26	41	48
Chester	46	14	3	6	39	23	7	3	13	19	43	48
Scunthorpe U	46	11	6	6	34	23	7	4	12	33	42	46
York C	46	14	7	2	38	16	2	7	14	17	46	46
Northampton T	46	11	7	5	41	19	5	5	13	23	36	44
Crewe A	46	12	6	5	37	18	4	6	13	14	33	44
Grimsby T	46	9	9	5	33	24	5	6	12	21	34	43
Southend U	46	12	8	3	40	28	3	2	18	19	57	40
Exeter C	46	13	5	5	48	20	1	6	16	9	39	39
Oldham A	46	11	4	8	45	28	2	9	12	15	37	39
Workington	46	9	9	5	31	21	3	5	15	15	43	38
Newport Co	46	12	3	8	39	24	1	8	14	14	50	37
Darlington	46	8	7	8	31	27	5	3	15	22	46	36
Hartlepool	46	7	7	9	31	30	3	3	17	11	52	30
Bradford	46	6	5	12	23	32	0	6	17	18	64	23

Football League Records

Top scorers: Div 1, A.Brown (West Bromwich Albion) 28 goals; Div 2, J.Hickton (Middlesbrough) 25 goals; Div 3, G.Ingram (Preston North End), D.Roberts (Mansfield Town) 22 goals; Div 4, E.MacDougall (Bournemouth & Boscombe Athletic) 42 goals.
Bradford failed to gain re-election, Cambridge United were elected in their place. Swansea Town became Swansea City.

John Radford, who netted 15 League goals in Arsenal's double-winning season of 1970-71.

Tony Hateley, another much-travelled goalscorer, who played in Notts County's Fourth Division championship side of 1970-71.

DIVISION 1

	ARSENAL	BLACKPOOL	BURNLEY	CHELSEA	COVENTRY C	CRYSTAL P	DERBY CO	EVERTON	HUDDERSFIELD T	IPSWICH T	LEEDS U	LIVERPOOL	MANCHESTER C	MANCHESTER U	NEWCASTLE U	NOTTINGHAM F	SOUTHAMPTON	STOKE C	TOTTENHAM H	W.B.A.	WEST HAM U	WOLVERHAMPTON W
1 ARSENAL		M20 1-0	a20 1-0	a03 2-0	a06 1-0	N14 1-1	O31 2-0	O17 4-0	A25 1-0	F20 3-2	S01 0-0	N28 2-0	F06 1-0	A22 4-0	a17 1-0	O03 4-0	D27 0-0	m01 1-0	S05 2-0	S19 6-2	J09 2-0	D12 2-1
2 BLACKPOOL	N07 0-1		D26 1-1	O24 3-4	D12 1-0	a26 3-1	F20 0-1	S19 0-2	O17 2-2	N28 0-2	M13 1-1	A17 0-0	J16 3-3	m01 1-1	a03 0-1	a17 2-3	S05 0-3	O03 1-1	a12 0-0	A22 3-1	F27 1-1	F06 0-2
3 BURNLEY	S12 1-2	a10 1-0		S01 0-0	O10 0-0	O31 2-1	a24 1-2	J09 2-2	N14 2-3	M27 2-2	A29 0-3	A15 1-2	D19 0-4	A25 0-2	J30 1-1	N21 2-1	M06 0-1	F23 1-1	M20 0-0	D05 1-1	a13 1-0	S26 2-3
4 CHELSEA	A29 2-1	M06 2-0	a26 0-1		a24 2-1	a10 1-1	A15 2-1	A26 2-2	M20 0-0	S26 2-1	M27 3-1	a12 1-0	O10 1-1	J09 1-2	D05 1-0	F17 2-0	O31 2-2	N21 2-1	N14 0-2	J30 4-1	D19 2-1	S12 2-2
5 COVENTRY C	O24 1-3	F13 2-0	a17 3-0	S19 0-1		N21 2-1	a27 0-0	O03 3-1	S05 0-0	J09 1-0	F26 0-1	M13 1-0	N07 2-1	a13 2-1	m01 2-0	O17 2-0	A22 1-0	D05 1-0	a03 0-0	D26 1-1	F08 0-1	A25 0-1
6 CRYSTAL P	M13 0-2	S02 1-0	F27 0-2	J13 0-0	F20 1-2		D12 0-0	m01 2-0	M24 0-3	F06 1-0	N07 1-1	J16 1-0	A19 0-1	a17 3-5	A22 1-0	S05 2-0	O03 3-1	a03 3-2	S19 0-3	O17 3-0	O24 1-1	N29 1-1
7 DERBY CO	F27 2-0	N21 2-0	S19 1-0	O17 1-2	S02 3-4	F17 1-0		a17 3-1	a03 3-2	A26 2-0	O24 0-2	N07 0-0	M13 0-0	D26 4-4	S05 1-2	M31 1-2	a12 0-0	A22 2-0	O03 1-1	m01 2-0	D05 2-4	J09 1-2
8 EVERTON	A15 2-2	a24 0-0	A18 1-1	J16 3-0	a12 3-0	S26 3-1	O10 1-1		F06 2-1	S12 2-0	D19 0-1	F20 0-0	A29 0-1	F23 1-0	O24 3-1	N07 1-0	D12 4-1	M13 2-0	N28 0-0	F27 3-3	M30 0-1	a10 1-2
9 HUDDERSFIELD T	J16 2-1	A15 3-0	M13 0-1	N07 0-1	M27 1-0	S12 0-2	A29 0-0	D05 1-1		O10 1-0	a12 0-0	D19 0-0	a10 1-0	J30 1-2	F13 1-1	O24 0-0	A18 3-1	F27 0-1	S01 1-1	N21 2-1	S26 1-1	a24 1-2
10 IPSWICH T	N21 0-1	J30 2-1	S05 3-0	m01 0-0	A18 0-2	D05 1-2	J16 0-1	a06 0-0	a17 2-0		F23 2-4	O24 1-0	F26 2-0	S19 4-0	M13 1-0	A22 0-0	a03 1-3	O17 2-0	M23 1-2	O03 2-2	N07 2-1	S01 2-3
11 LEEDS U	a26 1-0	N14 3-1	a03 4-0	S05 1-0	O31 2-0	M20 2-1	M06 1-0	A22 3-2	O03 2-0	D12 0-0		F06 0-1	N28 1-0	O17 2-2	D26 3-0	m01 2-0	S19 1-0	N18 4-1	J09 1-2	a17 1-2	A26 3-0	F20 3-0
12 LIVERPOOL	J30 2-0	J09 2-2	O17 2-0	O03 1-0	N14 0-0	A25 1-1	M20 2-0	N21 3-2	A22 4-0	M29 2-1	D05 1-1		J12 0-0	S05 1-1	a06 1-1	S19 3-0	m01 1-0	D26 0-0	a17 0-0	a02 1-1	F16 1-0	O31 2-0
13 MANCHESTER C	D05 0-2	A26 2-0	A22 0-0	a17 1-1	M20 1-1	J09 1-0	N14 1-1	a03 3-0	D26 1-1	O31 2-0	J30 0-2	a26 2-2		m05 3-4	O03 1-1	a09 1-3	O17 1-1	S19 4-1	m01 0-1	S05 4-1	N21 2-0	M06 0-0
14 MANCHESTER U	D19 1-3	S26 1-1	J16 1-1	A19 0-0	S12 2-0	O10 0-1	a10 1-2	S02 2-0	N28 1-1	a24 3-2	A15 0-1	a19 0-2	D12 1-4		F27 1-0	M13 2-0	F20 5-1	N07 2-2	F06 2-1	O24 2-1	A29 1-1	a12 1-0
15 NEWCASTLE U	O10 1-1	A29 1-2	N28 3-1	F06 0-1	S26 0-0	D19 2-0	M27 3-1	M18 2-1	D12 2-0	N14 0-0	a10 1-1	S12 0-0	a12 0-0	O31 1-0		A26 1-1	M20 2-2	J09 0-2	F20 1-0	a28 3-0	a21 1-1	A15 3-2
16 NOTTINGHAM F	a13 0-3	O10 3-1	F20 1-0	D12 1-1	A15 2-0	M27 3-1	N28 2-4	M20 3-2	M06 1-3	D19 0-1	S26 0-0	a24 0-1	S12 0-1	N14 1-2	J16 2-1		F06 2-0	a27 0-0	O31 0-1	A18 3-3	a10 1-0	A29 4-1
17 SOUTHAMPTON	a10 1-2	M27 1-1	O24 2-0	F27 0-0	D19 3-0	m04 6-0	S12 4-0	F16 2-2	J09 1-0	A29 1-0	a24 0-3	S26 1-0	A15 1-1	N21 1-0	N07 2-0	D05 4-1		J30 2-1	A25 0-0	M13 1-0	a27 1-2	O10 1-2
18 STOKE C	S26 5-0	a13 1-1	D12 0-0	F20 1-2	F06 2-1	A29 0-0	D19 1-0	N14 1-1	O31 3-1	A15 0-0	S12 3-0	a10 0-1	a24 2-0	M20 1-2	A19 3-0	S02 0-0	N28 0-0		m05 0-1	J16 2-0	O10 2-1	a07 1-0
19 TOTTENHAM H	m03 0-1	S12 3-0	N07 4-0	M13 2-1	A29 1-0	a24 2-0	a07 2-1	J30 2-1	a28 1-1	a10 2-0	A19 0-2	O10 1-0	S26 2-0	D05 2-2	N21 1-2	M10 0-1	J16 1-3	O24 3-0		F17 2-2	A15 2-2	D19 0-0
20 W.B.A.	a24 2-2	D19 1-1	F06 1-0	N28 2-2	a10 0-0	A15 0-0	S26 2-1	O31 3-0	F20 2-1	a12 0-1	O10 2-2	A29 1-1	M27 0-0	M06 4-3	S02 1-2	J09 0-1	N14 1-0	A26 5-2	D12 3-1		S12 2-1	M20 2-4
21 WEST HAM U	A17 0-0	O31 2-1	O03 3-1	A22 2-2	N28 1-2	M06 0-0	F06 1-4	S05 1-2	m01 0-1	M20 2-2	J16 2-3	D12 1-2	F20 0-0	a03 2-1	S19 0-2	F24 2-0	A31 1-1	a17 1-0	O17 2-2	a09 2-1		N14 3-3
22 WOLVERHAMPTON W	M02 0-3	D05 1-0	m01 1-0	F13 1-0	J16 0-0	J30 2-1	A19 2-4	D26 2-0	S19 3-1	a28 0-0	N21 2-3	F27 1-0	O24 3-0	O03 3-2	O17 3-2	a03 4-0	a17 0-1	S05 1-1	A22 0-3	N07 2-1	M13 2-0	

DIVISION 2

	BIRMINGHAM C	BLACKBURN R	BOLTON W	BRISTOL C	CARDIFF C	CARLISLE U	CHARLTON A	HULL C	LEICESTER C	LUTON T	MIDDLESBROUGH	MILLWALL	NORWICH C	ORIENT	OXFORD U	PORTSMOUTH	Q.P.R.	SHEFFIELD U	SHEFFIELD W	SUNDERLAND	SWINDON T	WATFORD
1 BIRMINGHAM C		a10 1-0	F20 4-0	J09 2-0	M27 2-0	D19 1-0	S26 1-1	a13 0-0	O20 0-0	A29 1-1	S01 0-1	F06 3-1	N28 2-2	N14 1-0	S12 1-1	a24 1-1	A15 2-1	O10 0-1	D12 1-0	M20 3-1	O31 2-1	M06 2-0
2 BLACKBURN R	D26 2-2		S19 0-2	m01 2-2	M13 1-1	F20 0-2	F06 1-0	D12 0-1	O03 2-2	J16 1-0	a09 1-1	a17 0-2	O24 2-1	A22 0-0	S21 0-0	F27 1-1	S02 0-2	N07 1-3	a03 3-2	N28 0-1	S05 1-0	O17 2-3
3 BOLTON W	N21 3-0	a24 1-1		O24 1-0	S12 0-2	a10 0-3	O10 4-0	M27 0-0	F27 0-3	A15 4-2	F13 0-3	M13 1-1	N07 0-1	S30 0-1	S26 0-2	D19 1-1	A29 2-2	J16 2-1	A19 2-1	a12 1-3	D05 0-3	J30 0-1
4 BRISTOL C	S29 2-1	S26 1-1	M06 1-1		A29 1-0	N28 2-1	D19 2-2	S12 3-3	a27 0-1	a09 3-2	J16 0-2	F20 3-2	D12 0-1	F06 0-0	O10 0-4	a10 2-0	a24 0-0	M27 0-1	O31 1-2	A15 4-3	M20 2-1	N14 3-0
5 CARDIFF C	S05 2-0	N14 4-1	a07 1-0	a03 1-0		M06 4-0	F20 1-1	O31 5-1	O17 2-2	N28 0-0	O03 3-4	A22 2-2	S19 1-1	m01 1-0	F06 1-0	O28 1-0	M20 1-0	S02 1-1	J09 4-0	D12 3-1	D26 1-1	a17 0-1
6 CARLISLE U	A22 0-3	N21 1-0	D26 1-0	J30 2-1	O24 1-1		J09 1-1	S01 2-0	a03 0-1	M13 1-0	O17 1-0	O02 3-0	a17 4-2	S05 2-0	N07 3-2	D05 6-0	F13 3-0	F27 1-0	m01 3-0	O20 0-0	S19 2-1	a13 2-1
7 CHARLTON A	m01 1-1	D05 2-4	a17 4-1	A22 1-1	N21 2-1	S29 1-1		J16 0-1	S19 0-1	O24 1-1	M13 1-0	S05 1-3	a09 2-1	a03 2-0	F26 2-0	N07 2-2	a20 0-3	F13 0-2	O17 2-3	a27 1-1	O03 2-1	M02 1-2
8 HULL C	O03 0-1	F23 0-0	S05 1-0	a12 1-0	F27 1-1	a28 1-2	O21 2-0		D05 3-0	N07 0-2	A22 1-0	S19 2-0	m01 1-0	a17 5-2	M13 0-1	J30 0-1	N21 1-1	O24 1-1	D26 4-4	J09 4-0	O16 2-0	a03 1-0
9 LEICESTER C	J16 1-4	a13 1-1	O31 1-0	S02 4-0	A15 0-1	A29 2-2	a24 1-0	F06 0-0		S12 1-0	S30 3-2	D12 2-1	F20 2-1	N28 4-0	M27 0-0	S26 2-0	D19 0-0	a10 0-0	M10 1-0	O10 1-0	N14 3-1	M20 1-1
10 LUTON T	a03 3-2	O20 2-0	O17 2-0	O03 3-0	m04 3-0	N14 3-3	M06 1-1	M20 3-1	a12 1-3		S05 1-0	M30 1-1	A22 0-0	S19 4-0	S01 4-0	N21 2-1	J09 0-0	D05 2-1	a17 2-2	O31 1-2	m01 1-1	F13 1-0
11 MIDDLESBROUGH	a27 0-0	S12 1-1	D12 1-0	O20 1-0	a13 1-1	A15 2-1	N14 3-0	D19 1-0	J09 1-0	M27 2-1		N28 1-0	F06 5-0	M20 0-1	A29 0-2	O10 3-2	S26 6-2	a24 1-1	F20 1-0	a10 2-2	M06 3-0	O31 2-2
12 MILLWALL	D05 2-1	O10 2-0	N14 2-0	N21 2-0	D19 2-1	a05 2-1	M27 2-0	a24 4-0	M01 0-0	a10 4-0	J30 1-0		J23 2-2	M06 0-1	A15 1-2	A29 0-0	O31 3-0	S14 1-2	M20 1-0	S26 0-0	J09 2-2	O19 3-0
13 NORWICH C	J30 2-2	M06 2-1	M20 2-1	F13 3-2	a24 1-2	O10 1-1	S12 2-0	S26 0-2	N21 2-2	D19 1-1	D05 1-1	S02 1-0		O31 4-2	a12 1-1	A15 1-1	a10 3-0	A29 1-0	N14 0-0	M27 3-0	O21 1-0	J09 2-1
14 ORIENT	M13 0-2	D19 1-1	J09 3-1	D05 1-1	S26 0-0	M27 1-1	A29 0-0	O10 0-1	M29 0-1	a24 1-2	N07 0-0	O24 0-0	F26 1-0		a10 0-0	a26 1-1	a12 0-1	A15 3-1	O19 1-1	S12 1-0	F13 1-0	N21 1-1
15 OXFORD U	a09 1-0	J09 2-1	m01 1-1	a17 1-0	D05 1-0	M20 1-1	O31 2-1	N14 0-3	S05 1-0	a28 2-1	a03 2-2	O17 2-3	O03 1-1	M10 0-1		M24 1-1	O21 1-3	J30 1-2	A22 1-1	M06 0-0	N21 0-0	S19 2-1
16 PORTSMOUTH	S19 1-0	O31 4-1	A22 4-0	M10 1-1	J16 1-3	F06 1-4	M20 2-0	N28 2-2	m01 1-2	F20 0-1	a17 1-1	a03 0-2	O17 0-2	S02 1-1	D12 1-0		M06 2-0	S30 1-5	S05 2-0	N14 2-1	a12 0-2	O03 5-0
17 Q.P.R.	O17 5-2	a27 2-0	a03 4-0	S19 2-1	N07 0-1	D12 1-1	N28 1-4	F20 1-1	A22 1-3	S29 0-1	m01 1-1	F27 2-0	M23 0-1	O03 5-1	J16 2-0	O24 2-0		M13 2-2	a06 1-0	F06 2-0	a17 4-2	S05 1-1
18 SHEFFIELD U	a17 3-0	M20 5-0	O20 2-2	S05 3-3	a27 5-1	O31 2-2	D12 3-0	M09 1-2	D26 2-1	F06 2-1	S19 1-1	a13 2-0	a03 0-0	O17 3-1	N28 3-0	J09 2-0	N14 1-1		O03 3-2	F20 1-0	A22 2-1	m01 3-0
19 SHEFFIELD W	F13 3-3	A29 1-1	S02 1-1	F27 2-0	A26 1-2	S26 3-0	A15 1-0	a10 1-1	O24 0-3	O10 1-5	N21 3-2	N07 1-0	M13 2-1	J16 2-1	D19 1-1	M30 3-1	S12 1-0	a12 0-0		a24 1-2	J30 2-2	D05 2-1
20 SUNDERLAND	N07 2-1	J30 3-2	O03 4-1	O17 1-0	F13 0-4	J16 2-0	S02 3-0	O07 0-1	a17 0-0	F27 0-0	D26 2-2	m01 0-1	S05 2-1	a09 1-0	O24 0-1	M13 0-0	D05 3-1	N21 0-0	S19 3-1		a03 5-2	A22 3-3
21 SWINDON T	F27 1-2	M27 3-0	F06 3-1	N07 2-1	a10 2-2	a24 0-0	a13 1-1	A15 1-1	M13 0-1	S26 0-0	O24 3-0	S29 3-0	J16 3-2	D12 1-1	F20 3-0	S12 2-1	O10 1-0	D19 3-0	N28 3-0	A29 2-0		S01 1-1
22 WATFORD	O24 2-1	A15 2-1	N28 1-1	M13 0-3	O10 0-1	S12 0-0	a10 1-1	A29 1-2	N07 0-1	D12 0-1	F26 1-0	J16 0-4	S30 2-0	F20 0-0	a24 2-1	a09 0-0	M27 1-2	S26 0-0	F06 3-0	D19 1-1	a28 1-2	

Season 1970-71

DIVISION 3

	ASTON VILLA	BARNSLEY	BRADFORD C	BRIGHTON & HA	BRISTOL R	BURY	CHESTERFIELD	DONCASTER R	FULHAM	GILLINGHAM	HALIFAX T	MANSFIELD T	PLYMOUTH A	PORT VALE	PRESTON N.E.	READING	ROCHDALE	ROTHERHAM U	SHREWSBURY T	SWANSEA C	TORQUAY U	TRANMERE R	WALSALL	WREXHAM
1 ASTON VILLA		a12 0-0	D05 1-0	O03 0-0	S30 1-1	N11 1-0	O17 0-0	S05 3-2	J30 1-0	S23 2-1	M13 1-1	A31 0-1	A22 1-1	J16 1-0	S19 2-0	m04 2-1	a17 1-0	F13 1-0	D26 2-0	a03 3-0	N07 0-1	O24 1-0	M17 0-0	m01 3-4
2 BARNSLEY	S12 1-1		D19 2-0	F06 1-0	J02 0-4	A28 1-1	J16 1-0	O31 0-1	A15 0-1	S29 3-1	S26 2-2	a10 1-0	N28 2-0	a13 1-0	F20 0-1	a24 3-0	M06 2-2	O10 2-1	M20 2-1	N14 0-0	M09 2-0	M26 0-0	a27 1-2	J23 3-1
3 BRADFORD C	F06 1-0	A22 1-0		a12 2-3	F20 1-1	M13 1-3	m01 1-0	D26 3-0	a28 2-3	M17 0-1	F27 0-1	N20 1-1	S19 0-1	J23 1-1	O02 0-2	S30 0-1	a03 3-0	N07 1-1	S05 1-0	a17 0-2	O24 2-0	J16 1-1	O17 0-0	S23 1-3
4 BRIGHTON & H.A.	a09 1-0	D05 1-2	S12 1-2		S26 0-0	M27 1-0	N07 1-2	J09 3-0	M10 3-2	M13 3-1	a24 0-2	D19 2-0	a28 1-1	O10 0-0	F27 0-0	a10 2-0	O21 1-1	A29 1-1	F13 1-2	N25 2-2	A15 0-0	M31 0-0	J30 2-2	O24 2-0
5 BRISTOL R	J09 1-2	M16 3-0	N10 4-2	m01 1-3		O24 0-1	O03 3-2	S22 2-0	F13 0-1	a17 2-0	D05 1-0	O20 2-0	a13 1-3	S01 3-0	a03 0-0	N07 4-0	O17 2-2	F27 0-2	A22 2-2	D26 0-0	M23 1-1	M13 0-1	S19 3-0	S05 3-2
6 BURY	F20 3-1	a03 0-0	N14 1-1	S05 0-2	M06 3-0		a06 1-1	O03 2-3	M20 2-0	A22 2-1	O20 1-1	J23 0-0	a17 3-0	O31 2-3	S22 0-1	F06 5-1	M16 0-2	a27 0-1	S19 1-1	m01 1-1	J09 1-0	N28 0-0	D26 1-1	O17 1-2
7 CHESTERFIELD	A15 2-3	O21 4-2	S26 0-1	M20 2-1	a12 2-0	S12 0-0		F20 4-0	M26 0-0	S02 2-0	O10 5-0	J02 2-2	N14 2-0	M10 3-0	N28 0-0	A29 4-0	F10 1-1	a10 1-1	M06 2-0	O31 0-0	a24 5-0	D19 2-0	J09 1-1	F06 1-0
8 DONCASTER R	M26 2-1	F26 1-0	a10 3-1	S29 2-0	M09 0-1	a13 2-0	N10 2-1		a24 0-1	F13 2-2	S11 1-2	A15 1-2	J16 0-0	J02 1-2	N06 1-1	O10 2-0	a27 1-2	D19 0-2	J30 1-1	D05 1-2	S26 0-1	A29 2-2	O23 1-2	M13 2-1
9 FULHAM	N28 0-2	O17 1-1	S02 5-0	S23 1-0	M02 2-1	N07 2-1	S05 2-0	S19 1-1		D28 1-0	O24 3-1	F06 0-0	O03 1-1	F20 4-1	m01 0-1	J16 1-1	a07 2-0	M13 1-0	a17 0-0	A22 4-1	F26 4-0	S28 2-0	a03 1-0	M17 1-0
10 GILLINGHAM	M10 0-0	J09 2-1	J12 2-1	N14 1-1	O10 1-4	D19 1-2	a28 1-1	J23 0-1	a10 1-3		A29 2-1	S26 2-2	M20 0-2	a24 1-1	F06 2-1	A15 0-0	F20 0-0	M27 2-1	O31 0-2	M06 0-0	S12 1-2	a12 0-0	O21 2-1	N28 1-2
11 HALIFAX T	N14 2-1	m01 4-1	O31 1-2	S19 0-1	F06 0-0	J16 3-0	a17 1-0	D12 4-0	M06 2-1	a03 2-1		M20 0-1	S22 4-1	N28 2-0	O17 1-0	J23 4-0	D26 1-4	S29 1-3	O03 2-0	M15 2-2	J11 2-0	F20 4-3	S05 2-1	A22 2-0
12 MANSFIELD T	a26 2-0	D26 1-2	J30 3-5	A22 1-0	J16 4-1	F13 1-0	M15 2-2	O17 2-1	D05 1-0	m01 2-0	N07 3-2		S04 1-5	S28 2-0	a17 3-1	O24 0-0	O03 3-2	N09 1-1	a03 1-1	a13 2-0	M13 0-0	F27 6-2	O14 2-2	S19 1-1
13 PLYMOUTH A	D19 1-1	F01 2-1	a24 1-3	S02 1-1	S12 0-0	O10 3-4	M13 1-1	O21 1-1	a12 1-1	N07 2-1	J02 1-1	M27 0-0		A29 2-1	O24 1-1	M24 4-0	J09 2-2	S26 4-1	N11 4-4	F13 2-3	a10 1-2	A15 0-1	D05 3-1	F27 2-2
14 PORT VALE	O19 2-0	O03 1-1	F12 0-0	a17 2-1	a26 2-0	F27 0-0	S21 0-2	M15 1-0	N09 0-1	S19 1-1	J30 0-1	J09 2-0	a03 2-1		S05 1-0	M13 3-1	A22 4-1	O24 1-0	a12 0-1	O17 4-0	D05 0-1	N07 2-2	m01 1-1	D26 0-3
15 PRESTON N E	a24 0-0	N09 3-1	a13 1-1	O31 1-1	A29 3-2	M08 2-0	J30 1-0	M20 4-0	S26 1-1	D05 1-0	A15 1-1	O10 2-1	M06 1-0	M27 1-0		S12 4-1	N14 3-1	m04 3-0	J09 2-0	O19 1-1	D19 2-2	a10 1-1	F13 1-0	A31 3-2
16 READING	O31 3-5	S19 2-0	J09 1-1	a21 0-3	M20 0-2	D05 1-5	a03 1-1	a17 1-0	O21 1-1	O17 3-2	F13 1-1	M06 1-0	M17 0-2	N14 2-1	a12 1-0		m01 1-1	J30 4-2	S23 2-1	S05 3-1	N11 2-1	S02 1-1	A22 1-2	O03 0-0
17 ROCHDALE	O10 1-1	O24 1-0	A29 0-0	J16 3-3	A15 1-1	F22 2-0	F13 2-0	A31 1-0	S12 1-2	N10 0-1	a10 0-3	a12 1-1	N02 1-1	D19 0-3	M13 1-2	S26 1-2		a24 4-3	D05 1-2	J30 0-0	M27 2-0	M08 0-0	F27 2-0	N07 4-1
18 ROTHERHAM U	J23 1-1	a17 1-0	M20 1-1	a03 2-0	O31 1-1	S01 3-2	D26 1-2	A22 2-0	N14 1-1	S05 0-0	J09 2-2	F20 2-1	m01 1-1	M06 2-1	M16 1-1	N28 2-1	S19 5-1		O17 1-1	S22 2-0	O20 3-1	F06 2-0	O03 1-0	a12 1-1
19 SHREWSBURY T	a10 2-1	N06 1-0	M27 1-1	M24 0-1	D18 1-4	a23 2-0	O24 1-1	N27 0-3	O10 0-1	F26 0-0	a14 2-2	A28 5-2	F20 1-1	S12 7-3	S30 0-1	M10 3-1	F06 0-2	A15 4-2		a28 1-0	a20 1-0	S25 3-1	M13 1-1	J16 1-0
20 SWANSEA C	A29 1-2	M12 0-2	O10 2-0	F20 1-0	a10 1-3	S26 3-0	F27 1-0	F05 1-1	D19 4-1	O24 1-0	m04 3-1	S12 2-4	M30 0-2	A15 0-2	J15 2-2	M27 5-0	N28 4-2	M09 1-1	S01 5-0		a12 0-1	a24 0-0	N07 1-1	S29 3-0
21 TORQUAY U	M20 1-1	S21 0-1	M06 1-1	O16 1-0	N28 1-1	S30 2-1	S18 1-1	m01 2-1	O31 3-1	a13 2-3	a28 2-0	N14 0-0	D26 2-1	F05 1-1	A22 3-1	F19 0-4	S04 3-0	J15 3-1	m06 1-0	O03 2-1		F01 4-2	a16 1-2	a02 1-2
22 TRANMERE R	M05 1-1	S04 2-2	O19 3-1	M15 3-0	N13 0-2	J29 0-0	A21 0-0	a02 1-0	J08 0-3	O02 1-0	N09 0-1	O30 4-1	O16 1-0	M22 1-1	D26 3-3	a26 0-0	a19 0-2	D04 5-0	a30 1-0	S18 0-0	F12 0-0		a09 0-0	D12 1-1
23 WALSALL	J02 3-0	S01 1-2	A15 1-2	N28 1-0	a24 1-2	a10 3-0	S29 2-1	M06 1-2	A29 3-2	J16 3-0	M27 0-0	M09 0-1	F06 1-0	S26 3-1	J27 0-1	D19 1-2	O31 0-3	a13 0-1	N14 0-1	M19 0-1	O10 1-4	S12 2-0		F20 3-1
24 WREXHAM	S26 2-0	F13 1-0	F22 2-0	m07 1-1	M27 1-0	A15 3-2	D05 0-3	N14 0-0	J02 2-2	M01 3-4	D19 2-2	a24 4-0	O31 4-0	a10 1-1	a26 1-1	a09 2-0	M20 3-1	S12 1-1	O19 2-1	J09 1-1	A29 1-0	O10 4-1	N09 2-1	

DIVISION 4

	ALDERSHOT	BARROW	BOURNEMOUTH	BRENTFORD	CAMBRIDGE U	CHESTER	COLCHESTER U	CREWE A	DARLINGTON	EXETER C	GRIMSBY T	HARTLEPOOL	LINCOLN C	NEWPORT CO	NORTHAMPTON T	NOTTS CO	OLDHAM A	PETERBOROUGH U	SCUNTHORPE U	SOUTHEND U	SOUTHPORT	STOCKPORT CO	WORKINGTON	YORK C
1 ALDERSHOT		O24 3-0	A15 2-0	J16 1-0	S30 2-2	a09 1-0	F26 0-1	M27 0-0	O10 2-2	F20 2-2	N28 3-2	a24 1-0	S26 0-2	F06 1-1	a10 1-1	A29 0-1	M10 1-1	D19 2-2	S11 0-1	M29 2-2	F22 2-1	a28 5-0	N07 1-1	M13 0-1
2 BARROW	M06 1-1		J02 1-2	F06 0-1	N28 2-1	O10 1-4	A31 0-2	A29 0-1	A15 1-1	N14 1-1	F20 0-1	M27 3-0	S12 1-4	J23 3-1	a24 2-1	D19 1-2	a10 1-1	S26 2-3	M08 1-2	M20 2-0	a12 0-2	O31 2-2	O19 0-3	J09 0-2
3 BOURNEMOUTH	O17 1-1	M17 0-0		a17 1-0	O03 3-0	M06 3-1	S18 4-1	N28 2-2	M20 1-0	J27 4-1	A22 2-1	N14 3-0	O31 3-0	a03 2-2	J23 4-2	F06 1-1	J16 5-0	A31 1-0	S30 0-2	a09 4-0	F20 0-1	S05 2-0	S23 1-0	m01 4-0
4 BRENTFORD	O19 2-3	D05 2-1	O10 1-2		a26 1-2	A15 1-2	M29 1-0	M08 3-1	S26 1-0	O31 5-0	N14 2-0	F24 1-0	D19 2-1	M20 0-3	a09 3-0	a24 2-2	M27 1-1	S12 1-1	a10 0-1	M06 4-2	A29 0-1	J09 3-0	m07 3-0	N09 6-4
5 CAMBRIDGE U	J09 1-1	J30 3-3	a13 0-2	A31 1-0		M08 1-1	D05 2-1	a24 1-0	J02 2-0	M06 2-0	M20 2-3	S26 2-0	A15 1-1	N14 3-2	D19 0-2	a10 2-1	A29 3-1	O10 1-1	M27 1-1	O31 0-3	S12 0-0	O19 1-1	N09 1-2	F13 1-1
6 CHESTER	O03 1-2	a17 2-1	O24 4-2	O17 1-2	S23 2-1		A22 2-1	F20 1-0	F06 2-1	S19 3-1	O07 5-0	N28 0-1	S02 1-0	m01 2-1	J16 2-2	J23 2-1	N07 0-1	F27 2-0	M13 2-0	M17 2-0	S30 1-0	D26 3-0	a03 1-0	a12 1-1
7 COLCHESTER U	O30 5-2	a26 4-1	a23 1-1	N28 4-0	F05 2-1	D18 0-1		S25 3-0	M08 2-0	M20 1-1	F22 1-0	A15 1-0	a10 1-1	F20 4-2	A29 1-1	S12 2-3	O09 1-2	a09 3-0	M22 2-0	N13 1-1	M27 1-0	m07 1-1	J08 2-1	O19 1-0
8 CREWE A	S05 0-3	a03 1-0	J30 3-3	S23 5-3	S19 1-2	N11 0-3	m01 0-3		J09 3-0	a09 4-1	M17 4-0	O21 1-0	F13 3-1	D26 2-0	M13 3-0	a28 1-2	F27 0-1	D05 1-3	O24 3-1	a17 1-2	N07 1-0	O03 2-3	O17 1-0	A22 3-4
9 DARLINGTON	a17 1-2	O17 3-1	N07 1-0	m01 2-1	M15 2-0	D05 5-1	S21 0-0	S28 0-1		S05 3-2	D26 5-1	a26 2-0	J30 3-2	S19 2-1	O24 0-0	J16 2-3	F13 3-1	M13 1-0	N09 3-0	a03 0-4	F27 1-1	A22 1-0	a12 0-1	O03 2-0
10 EXETER C	N11 4-1	M13 4-2	a10 0-0	F27 1-0	O24 1-0	a24 3-1	N07 2-2	S12 6-2	M27 2-1		O21 4-0	O10 1-1	a12 0-0	J09 1-1	F09 1-1	S26 0-1	D19 0-2	A29 3-2	A15 1-1	S02 2-0	D12 2-1	F13 2-1	F16 0-1	D05 0-2
11 GRIMSBY T	J30 0-2	N10 3-1	D19 1-0	M13 1-5	N07 2-0	M27 2-2	a30 3-1	m04 2-0	a10 1-1	J16 1-2		A30 1-1	M09 1-1	a27 2-0	S12 0-2	O10 2-1	A15 4-1	a24 2-1	a09 1-0	S20 2-0	S26 1-2	D05 1-2	F27 1-0	O24 3-1
12 HARTLEPOOL	S19 1-1	S05 2-1	M13 2-1	M15 0-0	m01 0-0	J30 0-2	O17 1-2	J16 0-2	A31 2-2	a17 3-0	a03 2-2		D05 0-0	O03 2-2	F27 2-2	S30 2-1	N09 0-1	N07 1-2	F13 1-1	S21 0-1	O24 1-2	a09 3-0	A22 1-1	D26 2-1
13 LINCOLN C	m01 4-4	a09 0-3	F27 1-2	A22 2-0	O17 0-1	a28 2-0	D26 1-2	J23 2-2	N28 2-1	O03 4-1	S23 3-0	F06 2-0		M17 1-1	N18 1-3	F20 0-1	M13 2-1	O24 2-1	N07 4-1	S19 1-2	J16 3-0	a17 1-1	S05 3-1	a03 4-5
14 NEWPORT CO	D05 1-2	F12 3-2	A29 0-2	N07 0-1	M12 2-0	S26 0-1	N10 1-3	a10 1-3	a24 3-1	S29 0-1	S01 0-1	a13 2-0	a20 2-2		A15 0-1	M09 2-1	S12 1-4	M27 2-0	O10 2-3	J15 3-0	D19 2-2	M02 3-1	O24 2-2	F26 0-3
15 NORTHAMPTON T	D26 2-0	S19 1-0	F13 2-3	O03 1-0	A22 2-1	O20 3-1	a03 2-1	N14 1-1	M05 2-0	M16 2-2	a13 0-4	O31 2-0	J09 2-1	O17 1-0		M20 1-1	D05 1-3	N10 2-0	J30 1-0	m01 0-2	S01 2-1	S22 1-1	a17 5-0	S05 3-2
16 NOTTS CO	a03 3-0	A22 3-1	D05 2-1	S19 0-0	D26 4-1	F13 2-1	a12 4-0	S02 5-1	O21 3-0	m01 1-1	a17 1-0	J09 3-0	N11 0-0	S23 2-0	N07 1-0		O24 2-0	J30 6-0	F27 3-0	S05 2-1	M13 3-1	M17 5-1	O03 2-2	O17 2-1
17 OLDHAM A	S22 5-2	D26 2-1	O20 2-2	S05 5-1	a03 4-1	M20 1-1	a17 4-0	O31 5-3	J23 3-1	A22 2-1	O17 1-0	M30 2-0	N14 4-2	D12 4-0	F06 1-1	M06 1-3		J09 3-0	O06 1-1	O03 2-0	N28 2-4	m09 1-1	S19 1-3	M15 1-1
18 PETERBOROUGH U	A22 1-0	m01 4-0	a28 3-1	a12 1-2	a17 2-3	O31 1-0	O03 1-2	F06 3-1	N14 0-1	a03 1-3	S19 1-1	M20 5-0	M06 1-1	S05 2-1	F20 1-0	N28 1-1	S30 2-1		J16 1-2	D26 4-0	J23 1-0	O17 5-1	M17 3-1	S23 2-1
19 SCUNTHORPE U	a13 2-1	S22 1-1	J09 1-1	D26 1-1	S05 0-0	N14 0-2	M16 2-0	M06 1-1	F20 0-0	O17 3-0	O03 1-2	J23 2-1	M20 3-1	a17 0-1	N28 2-2	O03 0-1	S01 2-3	O20 5-2		A22 3-0	F06 2-0	a03 1-2	m01 4-0	S19 0-1
20 SOUTHEND U	F12 2-2	N06 2-3	S11 1-2	O24 4-3	F26 1-1	F22 1-1	M12 1-1	O09 0-2	A28 0-0	a28 0-0	J08 1-1	M10 2-0	m03 1-1	O21 3-0	S25 1-0	M26 1-0	a12 3-0	a05 1-2	D18 2-2		A15 1-1	N09 2-1	D04 1-1	J29 1-0
21 SOUTHPORT	M17 3-3	O02 1-0	N10 0-1	a03 2-0	a09 0-1	J09 2-0	S04 2-1	M19 1-0	O30 0-3	S21 0-2	S08 1-0	M05 5-0	O20 1-0	A21 6-1	a26 2-1	N14 0-2	J29 1-4	F12 3-2	D04 5-1	O16 3-0		S18 1-0	D26 1-0	a16 2-2
22 STOCKPORT CO	A31 1-0	F26 2-0	M26 1-1	S28 1-0	J15 0-1	a10 0-1	O23 0-0	a12 2-2	D18 1-1	J22 0-3	F05 1-0	S11 2-1	O09 4-3	N27 3-2	D12 1-1	F22 1-0	S25 1-1	A15 0-0	A28 2-0	F19 0-0	a23 3-0		M12 1-0	N06 1-0
23 WORKINGTON	M20 4-0	J16 2-1	M10 1-0	M24 1-1	F20 3-1	A29 1-0	S30 1-1	A15 1-1	S12 0-0	N28 1-0	O31 1-0	D19 0-1	M27 2-1	M06 2-1	O10 2-0	a08 0-1	a24 0-0	M31 2-1	S26 0-0	F06 1-1	a10 2-1	N13 0-1		a27 1-0
24 YORK C	N13 3-1	O12 4-3	S26 1-1	F20 0-0	M01 3-0	S12 1-1	J16 1-1	D19 1-0	a09 2-0	F06 2-2	M05 4-1	a10 4-0	A29 2-0	O30 1-0	M27 4-1	A15 0-0	a19 0-1	M08 2-1	a24 2-0	N27 3-0	O09 2-0	M19 2-1	A31 1-0	

LEAGUE TABLES

DIVISION 1

	P	W	D	L	F	A	W	D	L	F	A	Pts
Arsenal	42	18	3	0	41	6	11	4	6	30	23	65
Leeds U	42	16	2	3	40	12	11	8	2	32	18	64
Tottenham H	42	11	5	5	33	19	8	9	4	21	14	52
Wolves	42	13	3	5	33	22	9	5	7	31	32	52
Liverpool	42	11	10	0	30	10	6	7	8	12	14	51
Chelsea	42	12	6	3	34	21	6	9	6	18	21	51
Southampton	42	12	5	4	35	15	5	7	9	21	29	46
Manchester U	42	9	6	6	29	24	7	5	9	36	42	43
Derby Co	42	9	5	7	32	26	7	5	9	24	28	42
Coventry C	42	12	4	5	24	12	4	6	11	13	26	42
Manchester C	42	7	9	5	30	22	5	8	8	17	20	41
Newcastle U	42	9	9	3	27	16	5	4	12	17	30	41
Stoke C	42	10	7	4	28	11	2	6	13	16	37	37
Everton	42	10	7	4	32	16	2	6	13	22	44	37
Huddersfield T	42	7	8	6	19	16	4	6	11	21	33	36
Nottingham F	42	9	4	8	29	26	5	4	12	13	35	36
WBA	42	9	8	4	34	25	1	7	13	24	50	35
Crystal P	42	9	5	7	24	24	3	6	12	15	33	35
Ipswich T	42	9	4	8	28	22	3	6	12	14	26	34
West Ham U	42	6	8	7	28	30	4	6	11	19	30	34
Burnley	42	4	8	9	20	31	3	5	13	9	32	27
Blackpool	42	3	9	9	22	31	1	6	14	12	35	23

DIVISION 2

	P	W	D	L	F	A	W	D	L	F	A	Pts
Leicester C	42	12	7	2	30	14	11	6	4	27	16	59
Sheffield U	42	14	6	1	49	18	7	8	6	24	21	56
Cardiff C	42	12	7	2	39	16	8	6	7	25	25	53
Carlisle U	42	16	3	2	39	13	4	10	7	26	30	53
Hull C	42	11	5	5	31	16	8	8	5	23	25	51
Luton T	42	12	7	2	40	18	6	6	9	22	25	49
Middlesbrough	42	13	6	2	37	16	4	8	9	23	27	48
Millwall	42	13	5	3	36	12	6	4	11	23	30	47
Birmingham	42	12	7	2	30	12	5	5	11	28	36	46
Norwich C	42	11	8	2	34	20	4	6	11	20	32	44
QPR	42	11	5	5	39	22	5	6	10	19	31	43
Swindon T	42	12	7	2	38	14	3	5	13	23	37	42
Sunderland	42	11	6	4	34	21	4	6	11	18	33	42
Oxford U	42	8	8	5	23	23	6	6	9	18	25	42
Sheffield W	42	10	7	4	32	27	2	5	14	19	42	36
Portsmouth	42	9	4	8	32	28	1	10	10	14	33	34
Orient	42	5	11	5	16	15	4	5	12	13	36	34
Watford	42	6	7	8	18	22	4	6	11	20	38	33
Bristol C	42	9	6	6	30	28	1	5	15	16	36	31
Charlton A	42	7	6	8	28	30	1	8	12	13	35	30
Blackburn R	42	5	8	8	20	28	1	7	13	17	41	27
Bolton W	42	6	5	10	22	31	1	5	15	13	43	24

DIVISION 3

	P	W	D	L	F	A	W	D	L	F	A	Pts
Preston NE	46	15	8	0	42	16	7	9	7	21	23	61
Fulham	46	15	6	2	39	12	9	6	8	29	29	60
Halifax T	46	16	2	5	46	22	6	10	7	28	33	56
Aston Villa	46	13	7	3	27	13	6	8	9	27	33	53
Chesterfield	46	13	8	2	45	12	4	9	10	21	26	51
Bristol R	46	11	5	7	38	24	8	8	7	31	26	51
Mansfield T	46	13	7	3	44	28	5	8	10	20	34	51
Rotherham U	46	12	10	1	38	19	5	6	12	26	41	50
Wrexham	46	12	8	3	43	25	6	5	12	29	40	49
Torquay U	46	12	6	5	37	26	7	5	11	17	31	49
Swansea C	46	11	5	7	41	25	4	11	8	18	31	46
Barnsley	46	12	6	5	30	19	5	5	13	19	33	45
Shrewsbury T	46	11	6	6	37	28	5	7	11	21	34	45
Brighton & HA	46	8	10	5	28	20	6	6	11	22	27	44
Plymouth A	46	6	12	5	39	33	6	7	10	24	30	43
Rochdale	46	8	8	7	29	26	6	7	10	32	42	43
Port Vale	46	11	6	6	29	18	4	6	13	23	41	42
Tranmere R	46	8	11	4	27	18	2	11	10	18	37	42
Bradford C	46	7	6	10	23	25	6	8	9	26	37	40
Walsall	46	10	1	12	30	27	4	10	9	21	30	39
Reading	46	10	7	6	32	33	4	4	15	16	52	39
Bury	46	7	9	7	30	23	5	4	14	22	37	37
Doncaster R	46	8	5	10	28	27	5	4	14	17	39	35
Gillingham	46	6	9	8	22	29	4	4	15	20	38	33

DIVISION 4

	P	W	D	L	F	A	W	D	L	F	A	Pts
Notts Co	46	19	4	0	59	12	11	5	7	30	24	69
Bournemouth	46	16	5	2	51	15	8	7	8	30	31	60
Oldham A	46	14	6	3	57	29	10	5	8	31	34	59
York C	46	16	6	1	45	14	7	4	12	33	40	56
Chester	46	17	2	4	42	18	7	5	11	27	37	55
Colchester U	46	14	6	3	44	19	7	6	10	26	35	54
Northampton T	46	15	4	4	39	24	4	9	10	24	35	51
Southport	46	15	2	6	42	24	6	4	13	21	33	48
Exeter C	46	12	7	4	40	23	5	7	11	27	45	48
Workington	46	13	7	3	28	13	5	5	13	20	36	48
Stockport Co	46	12	8	3	28	17	4	6	13	21	48	46
Darlington	46	15	3	5	42	22	2	8	13	16	35	45
Aldershot	46	8	10	5	32	23	6	7	10	34	48	45
Brentford	46	13	3	7	45	27	5	5	13	21	35	44
Crewe A	46	13	1	9	49	35	5	7	11	26	41	44
Peterboro' U	46	14	3	6	46	23	4	4	15	24	48	43
Scunthorpe U	46	9	7	7	36	23	6	6	11	20	38	43
Southend U	46	8	11	4	32	24	6	4	13	21	42	43
Grimsby T	46	13	4	6	37	26	5	3	15	20	45	43
Cambridge U	46	9	9	5	31	27	6	4	13	20	39	43
Lincoln C	46	11	4	8	45	33	2	9	12	25	38	39
Newport Co	46	8	3	12	32	36	2	5	16	23	49	28
Hartlepool	46	6	10	7	28	27	2	2	19	6	47	28
Barrow	46	5	5	13	25	38	2	3	18	26	52	22

Football League Records

Top scorers: Div 1, F.Lee (Manchester City) 33 goals; Div 2, R.Latchford (Birmingham City) 23 goals; Div 3, E.MacDougall (AFC Bournemouth) 35 goals; Div 4, P.Price (Peterborough United) 28 goals. Bournemouth & Boscombe Athletic became AFC Bournemouth.

Derby County skipper Roy McFarland missed only four games as the Rams won the League Championship for the first time in their history.

DIVISION 1

	ARSENAL	CHELSEA	COVENTRY C	CRYSTAL P	DERBY CO	EVERTON	HUDDERSFIELD T	IPSWICH T	LEEDS U	LEICESTER C	LIVERPOOL	MANCHESTER C	MANCHESTER U	NEWCASTLE U	NOTTINGHAM F	SHEFFIELD U	SOUTHAMPTON	STOKE C	TOTTENHAM H	W.B.A.	WEST HAM U	WOLVERHAMPTON W
1 ARSENAL		A14 3-0	D11 2-0	N27 2-1	F12 2-0	J01 1-1	J22 1-0	O30 2-1	S11 2-0	S25 3-0	m08 0-0	N13 1-2	a25 3-0	O09 4-2	a01 3-0	A24 0-1	M28 1-0	A28 0-1	m11 0-2	D18 2-0	a22 2-1	a08 2-1
2 CHELSEA	O16 1-2		S04 3-3	a08 2-1	S18 1-1	J29 4-0	J08 2-2	D27 2-0	D11 0-0	F19 2-1	M11 0-0	A21 2-2	A18 2-3	a22 3-3	N06 2-0	M29 2-0	O23 3-0	a24 2-0	N27 1-0	S01 1-0	M25 3-1	O02 3-1
3 COVENTRY C	m01 0-1	D17 1-1		O22 1-1	A24 2-2	a04 4-1	N06 2-1	J22 1-1	O09 3-1	D04 1-1	N20 0-2	a15 1-1	a01 2-3	A28 1-0	S11 1-1	a18 3-2	J01 1-0	A14 1-1	S25 1-0	M17 0-2	M21 1-1	F19 0-0
4 CRYSTAL P	a11 2-2	N20 2-3	F12 2-2		M28 0-1	S25 2-1	a29 0-0	N13 1-1	D18 1-1	a03 1-1	A24 0-1	J22 1-2	S11 1-3	A14 2-0	A28 1-1	D04 5-1	a01 2-3	a26 2-0	J01 1-1	O09 0-2	O30 0-3	M18 0-2
5 DERBY CO	O23 2-1	J01 1-0	J29 1-0	N06 3-0		D18 2-0	a15 3-0	M22 1-0	a01 2-0	M18 3-0	m01 1-0	D04 3-1	A14 2-2	a03 0-1	F19 4-0	N20 3-0	A28 2-2	S11 4-0	O09 2-2	S25 0-0	A18 2-0	M04 2-1
6 EVERTON	S18 2-1	A24 2-0	O02 1-2	M21 0-0	S04 0-2		D27 2-2	O16 1-1	F12 0-0	a15 0-0	N13 1-0	M11 1-2	A31 1-0	O30 1-0	m02 1-1	A21 0-1	N20 8-0	D04 0-0	M01 1-1	J22 2-1	J08 2-1	M25 2-2
7 HUDDERSFIELD T	A17 0-1	A28 1-2	a11 0-1	D11 0-1	N27 2-1	a01 0-0		a08 1-3	S25 2-1	A14 2-2	F12 0-1	O30 1-1	O09 0-3	J29 0-0	O26 0-1	M21 0-0	D18 0-2	J01 0-0	M28 1-1	S11 1-0	N13 1-0	a22 0-1
8 IPSWICH T	F19 0-1	a01 1-2	A17 3-1	M04 0-2	A31 0-0	A14 0-0	N20 1-0		A28 0-2	S11 1-2	D04 0-0	a18 2-1	D18 0-0	S25 0-0	O09 1-1	a15 0-0	M18 1-1	O23 2-1	a03 2-1	J01 2-3	J29 1-0	N06 2-1
9 LEEDS U	M25 3-0	m01 2-0	M11 1-0	S04 2-0	D27 3-0	O23 3-2	a05 3-1	J08 2-2		N06 2-1	S18 1-0	O16 3-0	F19 5-1	S01 5-1	M27 6-1	J22 1-0	M04 7-0	N20 1-0	A25 1-1	D04 3-0	O02 0-0	A21 0-0
10 LEICESTER C	a04 0-0	O30 1-1	a22 1-0	O02 0-0	A21 0-2	N27 0-0	O16 2-0	M25 1-0	M22 0-0		J08 1-0	S04 0-0	a08 2-0	N13 3-0	A18 2-1	S18 0-1	S01 0-1	J29 2-1	D11 0-1	F12 0-1	M11 2-0	D27 1-2
11 LIVERPOOL	N06 3-2	O09 0-0	a08 3-1	J29 4-1	D11 3-2	M04 4-0	O23 2-0	a22 2-0	J01 0-2	A28 3-2		F26 3-0	S25 2-2	M18 5-0	A14 3-1	F19 2-0	S11 1-0	M28 2-1	D18 0-0	a01 2-0	N27 1-0	A17 3-2
12 MANCHESTER C	M04 2-0	M18 1-0	N27 4-0	A18 4-0	a22 2-0	O09 1-0	F19 1-0	D11 4-0	A14 0-1	D18 1-1	S01 1-0		N06 3-3	S11 2-1	J01 2-2	O23 2-1	S25 3-0	a01 1-2	A28 4-0	M01 2-1	a08 3-1	J29 5-2
13 MANCHESTER U	A20 3-1	J22 0-1	D27 2-2	M25 4-0	O16 1-0	M08 0-0	M11 2-0	S04 1-0	O30 0-1	N20 3-2	a03 0-3	a12 1-3		F12 0-2	D04 3-2	O02 2-0	a15 3-2	a29 3-0	N13 3-1	A23 3-1	S18 4-2	J08 1-3
14 NEWCASTLE U	M11 2-0	D04 0-0	J08 4-2	O16 1-2	O02 0-1	F19 0-0	A25 0-0	a05 0-1	a19 1-0	M04 2-0	A21 3-2	M25 0-0	O23 0-1		N20 2-1	D27 1-2	N06 3-1	m08 0-0	J22 3-1	m03 4-2	S04 2-2	S18 2-0
15 NOTTINGHAM F	D27 1-1	M14 2-1	M25 4-0	J08 0-1	O30 0-2	D11 1-0	O02 1-2	M11 0-2	N27 0-2	J22 1-2	O16 2-3	S18 2-2	a22 0-0	a08 1-0		S04 2-3	A24 2-3	A31 0-0	F12 0-1	N13 4-1	A21 1-0	a25 1-3
16 SHEFFIELD U	J29 0-5	S25 1-0	N13 2-0	a22 1-0	a08 0-4	M18 1-1	A31 3-1	N27 7-0	A17 3-0	J01 1-1	O30 1-1	F12 3-3	a04 1-1	a01 1-0	D18 2-1		A14 3-1	O09 2-3	S11 2-2	A28 0-0	F29 3-0	D11 2-2
17 SOUTHAMPTON	O02 0-1	a18 2-2	S18 3-1	D27 1-0	J08 1-2	a08 0-1	S04 1-2	A21 0-0	N13 2-1	a11 1-0	M25 0-1	a04 2-0	N27 2-5	F26 1-2	J29 4-1	O16 3-2		A17 3-1	a22 0-0	O30 1-1	D11 3-3	M11 1-2
18 STOKE C	J08 0-0	N13 0-1	O16 1-0	A21 3-1	M25 1-1	a22 1-1	S18 1-0	F12 3-3	a08 0-3	A25 3-1	O02 0-0	D27 1-3	D11 1-1	N27 3-3	a10 0-2	M11 2-2	J22 3-1		O30 2-0	m05 1-1	a04 0-0	S04 0-1
19 TOTTENHAM H	N24 1-1	a15 3-0	M31 1-0	S18 3-0	M11 0-1	N06 3-0	A21 4-1	O02 2-1	J29 1-0	a29 4-3	S04 2-0	J08 1-1	M04 2-0	A18 0-0	O23 6-1	M25 2-0	D04 1-0	F19 2-0		N20 3-2	D27 0-1	O16 4-1
20 W.B.A.	S04 0-1	a27 4-0	A21 1-1	M11 1-1	a05 0-0	A18 2-0	M25 1-1	S18 1-2	a22 0-1	O23 0-1	D27 1-0	O02 0-2	J29 2-1	D11 0-3	M04 1-0	J08 2-2	F19 3-2	N06 0-1	a08 1-1		O16 0-0	N27 2-3
21 WEST HAM U	D04 0-0	S11 2-1	A30 4-0	F19 1-1	J22 3-3	A28 1-0	M04 3-0	A23 0-0	M31 2-2	O09 1-1	a15 0-2	N20 0-2	J01 3-0	D18 0-1	M18 4-2	N06 1-2	m01 1-0	S25 2-1	a01 2-0	A14 0-1		O23 1-0
22 WOLVERHAMPTON W	N20 5-1	a12 0-2	O30 1-1	A31 1-0	N13 2-1	S11 1-1	D04 2-2	F26 2-2	m08 2-1	a01 0-1	J22 0-0	A24 2-1	A28 1-1	J01 2-0	S25 4-2	a28 1-2	O09 4-2	D18 2-0	A14 2-2	a15 0-1	F12 1-0	

Charlie Aitken, one of Aston Villa's all-time greats. Altogether he made 656 full League and Cup appearances for them and was a great inspiration when they returned from the Third Division in 1971-2.

DIVISION 2

	BIRMINGHAM C	BLACKPOOL	BRISTOL C	BURNLEY	CARDIFF C	CARLISLE U	CHARLTON A	FULHAM	HULL C	LUTON T	MIDDLESBROUGH	MILLWALL	NORWICH C	ORIENT	OXFORD U	PORTSMOUTH	PRESTON N.E.	Q.P.R.	SHEFFIELD W	SUNDERLAND	SWINDON T	WATFORD
1 BIRMINGHAM C		a04 2-1	S18 1-0	F19 2-0	D27 3-0	A21 3-2	S04 4-1	N27 3-1	a25 2-0	M25 1-0	a22 1-1	a08 1-0	M04 4-0	N06 2-0	O02 0-0	J08 6-3	O23 2-2	M11 0-0	D11 0-0	O16 1-1	J29 4-1	S28 4-1
2 BLACKPOOL	S25 1-1		J22 1-0	a01 4-2	A16 3-0	N06 2-0	a29 5-0	F19 2-1	D18 1-1	N20 0-1	a03 3-1	M18 0-0	S11 1-2	O09 4-1	a15 2-0	a24 1-2	D04 1-1	O23 1-1	A28 1-0	M04 1-1	A14 4-1	J01 5-0
3 BRISTOL C	J01 1-0	S28 4-0		D18 0-2	A31 2-0	N19 1-4	F19 2-0	N06 1-2	S11 4-0	D04 0-0	A28 2-1	A14 3-3	S25 0-1	O23 5-3	a29 4-2	J29 1-1	a01 4-1	M04 2-0	M18 1-0	a15 3-1	M31 1-0	O09 2-1
4 BURNLEY	O30 1-1	D27 2-1	S04 1-1		O16 3-0	M11 3-1	a04 3-1	M25 1-1	F12 0-2	A21 2-1	N13 5-2	a22 2-0	J29 1-0	S28 6-1	J08 1-1	D11 1-3	a25 1-0	S18 1-0	F26 5-3	O02 0-1	N27 1-2	a08 3-0
5 CARDIFF C	a01 0-0	J29 3-4	a26 2-3	A14 2-2		a15 3-1	O23 6-1	M04 1-0	A28 1-1	a29 1-1	J01 1-0	O09 1-2	F19 0-0	a12 1-0	M21 1-1	D01 3-2	M29 5-2	N06 0-0	S11 3-2	N20 1-2	S25 0-1	D18 2-0
6 CARLISLE U	M21 2-2	F26 2-0	a08 2-0	O09 0-3	N27 2-1		S28 5-2	a22 3-1	S25 2-1	F12 0-0	M14 3-0	a04 3-3	D18 3-0	J01 2-0	O30 2-1	N13 1-0	A14 0-0	D11 1-4	J29 2-2	a25 1-2	A28 0-0	S11 2-0
7 CHARLTON A	D18 1-1	D11 2-3	O30 2-0	S25 2-0	F12 2-2	J22 1-1		a08 2-2	A14 1-0	F26 2-0	S11 0-2	a25 0-2	a01 0-2	M31 1-2	N13 3-0	a22 1-1	J01 2-1	N27 2-1	O09 2-2	O19 2-2	M18 3-1	A28 2-0
8 FULHAM	a18 0-0	O30 2-1	F26 2-0	S11 0-2	N13 4-3	D04 0-1	N20 1-0		O09 1-0	J22 3-1	D18 2-2	a01 1-0	A28 0-0	S25 2-1	O12 1-1	F12 1-1	M18 0-0	A31 0-3	M28 4-0	a29 0-0	J01 2-4	A14 3-0
9 HULL C	S01 1-0	S04 1-0	M25 1-1	O23 1-2	J08 0-0	a03 2-0	O16 2-3	M11 4-0		O02 0-0	D11 4-3	N27 0-0	N06 1-2	M04 1-1	A21 1-0	S18 1-3	F19 3-2	a08 1-1	a22 1-0	D27 2-3	S29 2-0	J29 4-0
10 LUTON T	S11 0-0	a08 1-4	a22 0-0	M18 1-0	D11 2-2	O23 0-2	N06 1-2	S28 2-0	a04 0-1		S25 3-2	J01 2-1	A14 1-1	D18 2-0	F05 1-2	N27 3-2	A28 1-1	J29 1-1	a01 3-1	F19 1-2	O09 0-0	M04 0-0
11 MIDDLESBROUGH	D04 0-0	O02 1-0	J08 1-0	M04 1-0	S18 1-0	D27 2-2	M25 2-2	S04 2-0	a29 3-0	M31 0-0		O19 1-0	a15 1-0	N20 1-0	M11 2-1	O16 2-1	N06 0-1	A21 3-2	A31 2-1	J22 2-0	F19 2-0	O23 2-1
12 MILLWALL	N20 3-0	A21 1-0	O16 3-1	D04 1-1	M11 1-1	O02 2-1	A30 2-1	D27 4-1	a15 2-1	S18 2-2	J29 1-0		O23 2-1	F19 2-1	M25 2-0	M31 1-0	a29 2-0	J08 0-0	S27 1-1	S04 1-1	M04 2-2	N06 3-2
13 NORWICH C	N13 2-2	M25 5-1	a04 2-2	O13 3-0	O30 2-1	S04 1-0	D27 3-0	J08 2-1	M15 2-0	O16 3-1	N27 2-0	F12 2-2		S01 0-0	S18 3-2	A21 3-1	J22 1-1	O02 0-0	a08 1-0	M11 1-1	a22 1-0	D11 1-1
14 ORIENT	m02 0-1	M11 0-1	F12 2-0	J22 1-0	A21 4-1	S18 2-1	O02 3-2	a03 1-0	N13 1-0	S04 0-0	a08 1-1	O30 2-2	a24 1-2		O16 1-1	M24 2-1	O18 3-2	D27 2-0	N27 0-3	J08 5-0	D11 0-1	a22 1-0
15 OXFORD U	M31 0-1	N27 3-1	D11 0-0	A28 2-1	a22 1-0	F19 3-1	M04 2-1	J29 1-0	M18 2-2	S01 1-1	O09 0-0	S11 1-2	J01 0-2	A14 1-1		a08 2-2	D18 2-0	S29 3-1	S25 1-0	O23 2-0	N06 1-1	a01 0-0
16 PORTSMOUTH	A28 1-0	S01 1-3	O20 1-1	a29 1-2	J22 2-0	M04 1-0	D04 0-0	O23 6-3	J01 0-0	a15 0-3	A14 2-1	S25 1-1	M18 2-1	S11 3-2	N20 2-0		O09 1-1	F19 1-0	D18 1-2	N06 2-2	a01 1-2	a03 2-2
17 PRESTON N.E.	F12 0-0	a22 1-4	D27 1-0	A30 1-3	O02 1-2	O16 3-0	S18 2-1	A21 2-0	O30 3-1	J08 0-1	a17 1-0	D11 4-0	S28 0-2	J29 1-1	S04 1-0	M11 4-0		M25 1-1	N13 1-0	a04 1-3	m01 2-2	N27 2-0
18 Q.P.R.	O09 1-0	F12 0-1	N13 3-0	J01 3-1	m02 3-0	a29 3-0	a15 2-0	a25 0-0	N20 2-1	O19 1-0	M18 1-0	A28 1-1	a03 0-0	a01 1-0	J22 4-2	O30 1-1	S11 2-1		A14 3-0	D04 2-1	D18 3-0	S25 3-0
19 SHEFFIELD W	a29 1-2	J08 1-2	A21 1-5	N06 2-1	M25 2-2	O20 2-1	a10 2-1	O02 4-0	D04 2-1	D27 2-2	a26 1-0	J22 1-1	N20 1-1	a17 3-1	a03 0-0	S04 1-1	M04 1-0	O16 0-0		S18 3-0	O23 1-0	F19 2-1
20 SUNDERLAND	A14 1-1	N13 0-0	N27 1-1	a03 4-3	a08 1-1	S01 0-3	J29 3-0	D11 2-1	a01 0-1	O30 2-2	S29 4-1	D18 3-3	O09 1-1	A28 2-0	F12 3-0	M01 3-2	S25 4-3	a22 0-1	J01 2-0		S11 1-0	a17 5-0
21 SWINDON T	O19 1-1	O16 1-0	O02 0-1	a15 0-1	a04 3-1	J08 0-0	A21 2-1	S18 4-0	J22 2-1	a18 2-1	O30 0-1	N13 0-2	D04 0-1	a29 2-2	F26 4-0	D27 3-1	N20 1-1	S04 0-0	F12 1-0	M25 1-1		a25 2-0
22 WATFORD	J22 0-1	S18 1-0	M11 0-2	N20 2-1	S04 2-2	M25 1-2	J08 0-3	O16 1-2	O20 1-2	N13 2-1	F12 0-1	F26 0-1	a29 1-1	D04 0-1	D27 0-1	O02 1-0	a15 1-0	M31 0-2	O30 1-1	A21 1-1	S01 0-0	

Season 1971-72

DIVISION 3

	ASTON VILLA	BARNSLEY	BLACKBURN R	BOLTON W	BOURNEMOUTH	BRADFORD C	BRIGHTON & HA	BRISTOL R	CHESTERFIELD	HALIFAX T	MANSFIELD T	NOTTS CO	OLDHAM A	PLYMOUTH A	PORT VALE	ROCHDALE	ROTHERHAM U	SHREWSBURY T	SWANSEA C	TORQUAY U	TRANMERE R	WALSALL	WREXHAM	YORK C
1 ASTON VILLA		J22 2-0	O30 4-1	D18 3-2	F12 2-1	D04 3-0	S11 2-0	a03 2-1	m05 1-0	J01 1-0	S22 0-1	N13 1-0	a10 1-0	A14 3-1	F26 2-0	A28 2-0	O09 1-2	J19 3-0	a01 2-0	a29 5-1	O20 2-0	M18 0-0	S25 2-0	F05 1-0
2 BARNSLEY	S28 0-4		a08 0-0	a01 1-0	N27 0-0	O23 0-2	a04 0-1	J01 0-0	O09 1-4	S11 1-2	J29 1-1	a22 2-1	N06 2-1	J15 2-2	M21 0-0	S25 3-3	M18 1-1	A28 1-3	D18 0-1	F19 0-0	A31 0-0	A14 4-2	M08 2-1	M04 2-1
3 BLACKBURN R	F19 1-1	F05 4-0		S11 0-3	a26 2-1	N06 1-0	a12 2-2	M27 1-2	D18 1-0	m08 2-0	O23 1-1	O20 0-2	D04 0-1	M18 3-2	J22 3-1	O09 3-0	A14 2-1	M31 1-0	S25 1-2	M04 1-0	a15 4-1	J01 1-1	A28 2-1	J15 3-0
4 BOLTON W	S04 2-0	D27 0-0	M25 1-0		A21 0-0	M15 0-0	D04 1-1	F19 0-0	M04 1-0	S29 1-1	O02 2-0	J08 1-2	O16 2-1	J29 2-1	M11 3-0	a12 2-1	a29 2-2	a15 2-0	O23 0-0	a19 2-0	a03 1-0	M22 0-1	N06 0-2	S18 0-1
5 BOURNEMOUTH	O23 3-0	a15 0-0	A31 1-0	M18 1-2		M04 3-0	a01 1-1	M08 2-0	S25 1-0	D18 3-1	F19 1-1	J22 2-0	a29 2-0	F05 1-0	O19 3-2	S11 4-1	A28 3-1	A14 3-1	O09 2-1	N06 1-0	m03 0-0	F23 0-0	J01 4-0	D04 2-2
6 BRADFORD C	a22 0-1	F12 0-2	F26 1-2	m10 0-3	N13 2-2		M18 2-1	D18 1-1	S11 2-2	A28 2-1	J15 2-2	N27 2-3	J29 2-2	M20 0-1	a08 0-0	a01 1-1	J01 1-0	S25 2-1	A14 0-2	a26 0-1	O30 1-1	O09 3-0	a03 0-2	S29 3-1
7 BRIGHTON & H.A.	M25 2-1	O02 0-0	a19 3-0	a22 1-1	D27 2-0	A21 3-1		S29 3-1	N27 2-1	N13 2-1	J08 1-0	S18 1-1	M15 0-1	F26 3-0	O16 1-1	m03 1-1	a26 2-1	O30 2-0	J29 1-0	M31 3-1	M11 2-0	F12 1-2	a08 3-2	S04 0-2
8 BRISTOL R	O02 0-1	S18 3-0	M14 3-0	O30 2-0	a18 1-2	S04 7-1	J22 2-2		m02 3-1	a08 1-0	M11 2-1	a04 0-2	M25 1-0	N27 2-2	D27 2-1	F12 5-2	N09 1-2	N13 3-1	a25 2-1	J08 2-0	A21 2-1	F26 2-1	a22 3-1	O16 5-4
9 CHESTERFIELD	a19 0-4	M11 0-0	S04 2-0	N13 2-1	a05 0-0	M25 0-1	a15 0-1	a29 1-3		F12 2-1	S18 2-0	A21 1-2	O02 0-1	O30 2-1	J08 2-1	F26 2-0	a12 0-1	O20 0-0	D04 1-2	O16 2-0	M15 2-2	J22 1-1	O06 1-0	D27 2-1
10 HALIFAX T	S18 0-1	M25 2-0	D27 0-1	J22 0-1	S04 1-0	J08 2-1	M04 0-5	F05 2-1	O23 2-0		O16 1-1	a18 3-1	M11 0-0	N15 0-1	a04 2-0	O19 2-2	N06 1-1	a29 0-0	a15 0-1	M14 0-0	O02 3-2	D04 3-1	F19 4-1	A21 3-1
11 MANSFIELD T	a24 1-1	O18 0-0	F12 1-0	M27 1-0	O29 0-5	a29 1-1	A28 0-3	O09 0-0	J01 2-1	A14 0-0		F26 1-1	F05 2-1	D18 2-3	N13 0-1	M18 3-1	S25 0-1	M20 2-2	S11 0-2	D04 0-0	J22 1-1	a01 1-1	m01 1-1	a15 0-0
12 NOTTS CO	M04 0-3	D04 3-0	J29 1-0	A28 1-2	S29 1-1	a15 2-0	J01 1-0	S25 2-3	M18 1-4	a12 3-1	N06 2-0		O23 2-0	O09 1-0	a26 2-1	A14 4-0	M22 1-1	S11 1-0	a03 5-0	m03 2-1	a29 1-0	D18 3-0	a01 1-0	F19 2-2
13 OLDHAM A	N27 0-6	F26 6-0	D11 1-1	A14 2-2	M21 3-1	O19 0-2	J15 2-4	S11 3-2	M31 1-1	O09 0-0	a08 2-1	F12 0-1		S25 0-1	O30 1-0	J01 3-2	m05 5-1	D18 1-4	M28 1-0	J22 1-0	N13 3-1	A28 1-3	M18 0-2	A31 1-0
14 PLYMOUTH A	O16 3-2	M14 2-1	A21 1-0	O12 2-0	O02 1-1	a18 1-4	N06 1-2	a15 2-1	F19 1-0	a25 1-1	S04 3-1	M11 1-1	a03 0-0		M25 0-0	J22 4-1	M04 2-1	D04 1-2	m02 4-1	D27 3-1	S18 2-2	S13 3-2	O23 1-2	J08 4-0
15 PORT VALE	N06 4-4	a29 1-0	S27 0-0	O09 1-1	J29 1-1	F05 1-0	A14 1-1	a01 0-0	A28 0-2	S25 1-0	M04 1-0	A30 0-3	F19 1-0	S11 0-0		m12 1-1	m08 1-2	J01 2-1	M18 3-0	a15 0-0	D04 2-1	a03 1-1	D18 1-0	O23 4-3
16 ROCHDALE	J08 1-0	a03 0-2	M11 2-1	a24 2-2	M25 1-1	D27 0-1	a29 1-2	O23 3-1	N06 0-2	J29 3-2	A21 2-1	O16 1-1	S18 1-1	S27 3-2	M13 3-2		D04 2-1	F05 0-0	F19 1-1	O02 5-0	S03 2-1	a15 0-0	M04 1-0	a17 1-2
17 ROTHERHAM U	M11 0-2	A21 3-0	O16 2-1	m02 2-0	J08 0-0	S18 2-0	A31 2-4	J29 0-0	a08 0-1	F26 3-2	a03 3-1	M14 2-2	D27 3-1	N13 4-3	a18 3-0	a22 5-1		F12 2-1	S28 4-0	S04 2-2	M25 0-0	O30 1-1	N27 2-2	O02 1-1
18 SHREWSBURY T	M15 1-1	J07 1-0	O02 7-1	N26 1-0	O15 3-2	a04 3-0	F19 3-5	M04 2-2	J28 3-4	m03 3-0	a19 4-2	M25 1-1	S04 2-4	a22 1-2	S18 0-0	a08 2-1	O23 0-1		N05 3-0	A21 2-0	D27 0-0	S01 4-1	S29 2-1	M10 2-1
19 SWANSEA C	D27 1-2	S04 2-0	a04 0-1	F12 3-2	M11 1-2	O16 2-0	O19 2-1	A31 2-0	a22 1-3	N27 3-0	M24 1-1	O02 1-1	a18 0-0	a08 1-1	A21 0-1	O30 1-0	J22 0-2	F26 1-0		S18 0-0	J08 1-1	N13 2-0	a11 0-2	M14 2-1
20 TORQUAY U	a12 2-1	O30 1-2	N13 3-1	m05 1-1	F26 0-2	S01 2-1	S25 2-2	A28 1-1	A14 3-2	M22 2-0	a22 0-1	a08 1-1	S29 0-2	a01 2-1	N27 3-0	S13 1-1	D18 0-1	M18 2-0	J01 1-4		F12 0-1	S11 2-2	O09 2-3	J29 0-1
21 TRANMERE R	J28 0-1	a24 0-0	N26 1-3	S24 0-0	a07 1-2	F19 4-1	O08 2-0	M17 0-1	m15 1-2	M31 2-3	S27 2-2	m08 2-1	M04 2-2	J01 3-2	a21 3-2	D17 2-0	S10 0-0	m10 0-4	A27 0-0	O22 2-0		M27 3-3	A14 2-1	N05 2-0
22 WALSALL	A21 1-1	O16 1-1	S18 0-0	a08 1-1	M14 1-1	M11 3-0	O23 0-1	N06 2-0	S28 1-1	a21 0-0	D27 2-1	S04 1-2	J08 2-3	a11 1-0	O02 2-0	N26 3-0	F19 0-0	a25 4-1	M04 4-0	M25 1-0	a18 4-1		J29 2-1	a04 2-1
23 WREXHAM	M31 0-2	a17 2-0	J08 1-1	F26 1-2	S18 1-3	O02 2-1	F05 1-2	D04 1-1	M20 2-0	O30 2-0	M13 1-1	D27 1-1	A21 3-1	F12 0-2	S04 1-2	N13 1-3	a15 0-0	J22 2-1	a29 2-0	M11 1-2	O16 3-0	O18 3-1		M25 2-0
24 YORK C	a08 0-1	N13 1-1	a29 0-1	J01 0-0	a22 0-2	J21 3-1	D18 1-2	A14 0-0	a01 4-1	M18 1-1	N27 1-2	O30 0-2	a24 0-0	A28 2-3	F12 2-1	M20 2-0	M31 2-0	O09 1-1	J24 1-1	O18 3-1	F26 5-0	S25 2-0	S11 1-1	

DIVISION 4

	ALDERSHOT	BARROW	BRENTFORD	BURY	CAMBRIDGE U	CHESTER	COLCHESTER U	CREWE A	DARLINGTON	DONCASTER R	EXETER C	GILLINGHAM	GRIMSBY T	HARTLEPOOL	LINCOLN C	NEWPORT CO	NORTHAMPTON T	PETERBOROUGH U	READING	SCUNTHORPE U	SOUTHEND U	SOUTHPORT	STOCKPORT CO	WORKINGTON
1 ALDERSHOT		J15 1-1	M18 1-2	M04 2-2	M31 1-1	S01 0-0	O09 0-2	a12 0-0	O23 3-0	a08 3-0	a01 0-0	D18 0-2	N27 1-1	F19 2-0	a22 0-0	J01 3-0	J29 0-2	N06 1-1	A28 1-2	S25 1-1	S11 0-0	S29 1-1	m03 4-0	A14 2-2
2 BARROW	M13 1-1		a24 0-3	D27 1-1	N27 1-1	M25 2-0	N06 2-2	A21 2-1	a17 0-4	J08 1-2	M20 0-0	a08 1-0	S04 0-0	a03 2-0	O02 2-2	M04 1-0	A14 0-1	M11 0-2	S27 0-0	O23 0-1	F19 2-1	S18 0-2	J28 3-2	a22 2-0
3 BRENTFORD	A21 1-1	A30 4-0		O16 2-0	a08 2-1	M31 1-1	M04 0-2	D27 1-0	J08 6-2	a17 2-1	a22 1-0	N27 1-3	M25 2-0	S04 0-0	M13 2-0	N06 3-1	O02 0-1	S18 5-1	J29 1-2	F19 0-3	O23 1-2	D11 1-0	S27 2-0	M27 2-0
4 BURY	N13 3-1	a01 4-0	A14 0-2		S11 0-1	F26 3-1	A28 3-0	F12 2-0	J22 3-2	a11 3-3	S25 4-3	M21 5-0	a22 1-1	O19 1-1	O30 0-1	M31 3-0	N27 4-2	a25 1-1	J01 2-1	O09 3-1	D18 2-0	a08 2-1	M18 4-0	M09 2-0
5 CAMBRIDGE U	O02 1-1	a15 1-0	F05 1-1	M25 0-2		O16 2-0	O23 4-2	S04 3-2	S18 0-0	M11 1-1	S29 0-1	a26 2-1	D27 3-1	M15 2-1	a03 0-0	F19 0-1	A21 1-1	a19 2-5	N06 4-1	a29 2-0	D04 1-1	J08 0-0	M04 2-0	M20 0-0
6 CHESTER	a26 0-0	S11 0-0	S25 0-0	N06 2-0	A14 1-1		a03 2-1	a22 0-0	F19 2-1	N27 1-1	J01 1-2	A28 5-1	a08 1-2	O23 4-0	M21 2-1	a01 3-0	S29 3-2	M04 1-1	M18 2-0	a19 0-0	O09 1-1	J29 1-1	J15 0-0	D18 2-1
7 COLCHESTER U	M11 1-0	F26 0-1	N13 1-1	J08 0-0	F12 1-1	O01 1-0		S17 4-2	M24 4-3	M13 1-2	N26 3-0	O29 2-2	a17 0-1	A20 1-0	O15 5-2	a24 2-3	M31 2-0	D27 1-1	a10 2-1	J21 1-1	O18 1-0	S03 1-0	a21 3-2	a07 1-0
8 CREWE A	a29 2-1	M18 1-0	a01 2-1	O23 0-0	D18 1-1	D04 3-1	J01 2-4		F05 1-1	S29 0-1	M31 0-1	S11 0-1	J29 0-1	a15 1-2	S01 3-1	m03 1-2	M04 0-1	F19 2-0	S25 2-0	A28 0-2	J15 1-2	N06 2-1	A14 3-1	O09 0-0
9 DARLINGTON	F12 4-2	M27 0-1	A28 0-0	S27 0-0	J01 2-1	O30 1-1	S11 2-0	a08 1-1		F26 4-1	J15 2-1	m01 0-0	N13 3-2	a24 1-2	N27 3-3	S25 0-0	M20 5-2	J29 1-1	D18 1-0	M31 0-1	M18 2-3	a22 0-0	O09 1-2	a01 4-0
10 DONCASTER R	F05 2-1	A28 0-1	M21 0-3	a29 4-1	O09 1-1	a15 0-0	J15 2-0	J21 0-0	N06 4-0		S11 2-1	a04 1-1	a25 2-1	M04 2-1	O19 2-0	A14 4-2	O22 1-1	D04 3-2	a01 1-1	D18 0-2	S25 0-2	F19 2-1	J01 2-2	M18 0-0
11 EXETER C	D27 1-0	a29 7-1	D04 0-1	a03 3-2	J22 3-4	S18 1-1	a15 3-3	O02 3-1	M15 3-0	M25 1-0		O20 1-1	A21 3-4	a19 1-0	M11 1-2	F05 1-0	J08 1-3	S04 3-2	F19 0-0	N06 1-0	M04 0-0	O16 1-3	O23 2-0	a26 0-2
12 GILLINGHAM	S04 0-1	F05 1-1	a15 0-1	M15 2-0	S01 2-0	J08 1-0	F19 0-2	M25 2-1	O16 4-2	O02 2-0	J29 0-2		M11 0-1	S18 1-0	a19 3-3	O23 1-2	D27 4-1	a03 1-1	M04 4-2	D04 0-1	a29 0-0	A21 2-1	N06 3-2	S29 0-0
13 GRIMSBY T	a15 3-3	D18 2-0	S11 3-1	D04 4-1	a01 2-1	F05 1-0	M21 3-0	O19 2-3	M04 2-0	A31 3-1	m02 3-0	O09 2-1		N06 3-2	J22 2-2	J15 4-2	F19 4-2	a29 3-2	M31 2-0	A14 4-1	J01 4-1	O23 0-1	S25 4-1	A28 1-1
14 HARTLEPOOL	O30 0-1	S25 4-3	D18 1-2	J29 3-1	J15 1-2	F12 2-1	M18 3-2	N27 1-0	A30 2-3	N13 0-0	M27 1-0	J01 3-1	F26 0-1		a08 2-1	O09 0-1	a22 2-0	S27 1-0	A14 3-1	a01 1-0	A28 2-2	a10 1-0	M31 5-0	S11 1-3
15 LINCOLN C	D04 2-2	a12 3-2	J15 4-1	F19 2-0	S25 3-1	a29 4-0	A14 2-0	a26 0-0	a15 0-1	J29 2-0	O09 4-1	M09 1-1	S29 3-0	F05 2-1		A28 3-1	N06 2-0	O23 3-2	S11 0-0	M18 1-0	a01 0-0	M04 2-1	D18 2-1	J01 1-0
16 NEWPORT CO	S18 2-3	N13 2-1	F26 0-0	O02 2-1	O30 3-0	D27 1-0	A31 2-1	a18 2-0	a04 4-0	O16 1-3	a08 0-0	F12 1-2	M13 2-1	M10 0-2	D11 2-0		S04 1-1	A21 1-1	a22 2-1	m01 1-0	J22 2-0	M24 2-2	a11 1-0	N27 0-1
17 NORTHAMPTON T	O19 2-3	O15 2-0	a03 0-0	a15 2-2	M18 1-2	J22 4-2	S25 1-1	N12 4-1	a29 1-2	F12 1-1	A28 1-1	a01 6-1	O30 3-0	D04 2-1	F26 2-3	D18 1-1		F05 1-1	O09 5-0	J01 0-2	a11 1-1	a25 0-0	S10 2-0	J15 1-2
18 PETERBOROUGH U	F26 0-0	O09 7-0	J01 2-2	A30 2-0	M09 2-0	N13 2-0	a01 4-0	O30 2-0	O18 1-3	a22 2-0	D18 3-3	S25 2-1	M27 0-2	J22 2-2	F12 4-4	M18 3-1	a08 1-0		m01 3-2	S11 0-1	A14 2-0	N27 2-0	A28 4-2	a04 1-1
19 READING	J08 2-0	J22 1-0	O20 2-1	S18 0-2	F26 1-0	A21 1-0	a29 2-4	a03 1-0	S04 2-0	D27 3-1	O30 3-1	N13 1-2	O02 1-3	O16 3-0	M25 0-1	D04 4-2	M11 2-1	M15 2-1		a15 2-0	M22 1-4	a19 1-1	a26 2-2	F12 0-0
20 SCUNTHORPE U	a04 1-0	F12 2-1	O30 0-0	M11 3-0	a11 2-1	D11 2-0	S28 2-0	J08 2-0	O02 3-1	S04 0-0	F26 3-0	a22 3-3	O16 1-2	D27 2-2	A21 2-1	J29 1-0	S17 0-0	M25 0-0	N27 1-1		a25 1-1	M14 1-0	a08 0-2	N13 2-0
21 SOUTHEND U	M24 1-0	O29 1-0	F12 3-1	S04 0-0	a21 1-2	M10 4-2	J28 1-4	M13 4-1	A20 3-0	M31 2-1	N12 3-0	m03 2-2	S17 3-1	J07 3-1	D27 2-1	S27 3-1	a17 4-1	O15 2-1	a07 4-1	A30 2-3		O01 2-1	N26 4-2	F26 2-0
22 SOUTHPORT	J22 0-0	J01 1-0	O08 0-0	F05 0-1	A27 4-1	O18 4-3	D18 3-0	F26 4-2	D04 2-1	O30 3-0	A14 4-0	M18 1-0	F12 1-0	a28 1-0	N12 1-1	S10 4-2	A30 4-0	a15 2-4	m04 5-2	J15 1-1	a03 0-1		a01 1-0	S24 2-2
23 STOCKPORT CO	a17 0-0	O18 1-3	J21 0-1	A20 2-2	N12 3-0	M13 0-0	D03 2-2	O15 3-1	M10 2-1	S17 1-2	F12 0-4	F26 2-1	a03 0-2	O01 2-1	S03 4-2	a28 4-4	M24 3-1	J07 0-0	A30 0-1	F05 0-0	a14 2-2	D27 1-1		O29 1-1
24 WORKINGTON	O16 5-0	D04 0-1	a29 3-0	a19 1-0	O20 0-1	S04 0-0	F05 1-0	M11 1-0	D27 0-0	A21 2-0	S01 0-0	J22 1-1	J08 0-0	M25 0-0	S18 0-0	a15 3-0	M15 2-0	O02 4-1	O23 5-0	M04 2-1	N06 3-1	M31 0-0	F19 1-1	

LEAGUE TABLES

DIVISION 1

	P	W	D	L	F	A	W	D	L	F	A	Pts
Derby Co	42	16	4	1	43	10	8	6	7	26	23	58
Leeds U	42	17	4	0	54	10	7	5	9	19	21	57
Liverpool	42	17	3	1	48	16	7	6	8	16	14	57
Manchester C	42	16	3	2	48	15	7	8	6	29	30	57
Arsenal	42	15	2	4	36	13	7	6	8	22	27	52
Tottenham H	42	16	3	2	45	13	3	10	8	18	29	51
Chelsea	42	12	7	2	41	20	6	5	10	17	29	48
Manchester U	42	13	2	6	39	26	6	8	7	30	35	48
Wolves	42	10	7	4	35	23	8	4	9	30	34	47
Sheffield U	42	10	8	3	39	26	7	4	10	22	34	46
Newcastle U	42	10	6	5	30	18	5	5	11	19	34	41
Leicester C	42	9	6	6	18	11	4	7	10	23	35	39
Ipswich T	42	7	8	6	19	19	4	8	9	20	34	38
West Ham U	42	10	6	5	31	19	2	6	13	16	32	36
Everton	42	8	9	4	28	17	1	9	11	9	31	36
WBA	42	6	7	8	22	23	6	4	11	20	31	35
Stoke C	42	6	10	5	26	25	4	5	12	13	31	35
Coventry C	42	7	10	4	27	23	2	5	14	17	44	33
Southampton	42	8	5	8	31	28	4	2	15	21	52	31
Crystal P	42	4	8	9	26	31	4	5	12	13	34	29
Nottingham F	42	6	4	11	25	29	2	5	14	22	52	25
Huddersfield T	42	4	7	10	12	22	2	6	13	15	37	25

DIVISION 2

	P	W	D	L	F	A	W	D	L	F	A	Pts
Norwich C	42	13	8	0	40	16	8	7	6	20	20	57
Birmingham	42	15	6	0	46	14	4	12	5	14	17	56
Millwall	42	14	7	0	38	17	5	10	6	26	29	55
QPR	42	16	4	1	39	9	4	10	7	18	19	54
Sunderland	42	11	7	3	42	24	6	9	6	25	33	50
Blackpool	42	12	6	3	43	16	8	1	12	27	34	47
Burnley	42	13	4	4	43	22	7	2	12	27	33	46
Bristol C	42	14	3	4	43	22	4	7	10	18	27	46
Middlesbrough	42	16	4	1	31	11	3	4	14	19	37	46
Carlisle U	42	12	6	3	38	22	5	3	13	23	35	43
Swindon T	42	10	6	5	29	16	5	6	10	18	31	42
Hull C	42	10	6	5	33	21	4	4	13	16	32	38
Luton T	42	7	8	6	25	24	3	10	8	18	24	38
Sheffield W	42	11	7	3	33	22	2	5	14	18	36	38
Oxford U	42	10	8	3	28	17	2	6	13	15	38	38
Portsmouth	42	9	7	5	31	26	3	6	12	28	42	37
Orient	42	12	4	5	32	19	2	5	14	18	42	37
Preston NE	42	11	4	6	32	21	1	8	12	20	37	36
Cardiff C	42	9	7	5	37	25	1	7	13	19	44	34
Fulham	42	10	7	4	29	20	2	3	16	16	48	34
Charlton A	42	9	7	5	33	25	3	2	16	22	52	33
Watford	42	5	5	11	15	25	0	4	17	9	50	19

DIVISION 3

	P	W	D	L	F	A	W	D	L	F	A	Pts
Aston Villa	46	20	1	2	45	10	12	5	6	40	22	70
Brighton & HA	46	15	5	3	39	18	12	6	5	43	29	65
Bournemouth	46	16	6	1	43	13	7	10	6	30	24	62
Notts Co	46	16	3	4	42	19	9	9	5	32	25	62
Rotherham U	46	12	8	3	46	25	8	7	8	23	27	55
Bristol R	46	17	2	4	54	26	4	10	9	21	30	54
Bolton W	46	11	8	4	25	13	6	8	9	26	28	50
Plymouth A	46	13	6	4	43	26	7	4	12	31	38	50
Walsall	46	12	8	3	38	16	3	10	10	24	41	48
Blackburn R	46	14	4	5	39	22	5	5	13	15	35	47
Oldham A	46	11	4	8	37	35	6	7	10	22	28	45
Shrewsbury T	46	13	5	5	50	29	4	5	14	23	36	44
Chesterfield	46	10	5	8	25	23	8	3	12	32	34	44
Swansea C	46	10	6	7	27	21	7	4	12	19	38	44
Port Vale	46	10	10	3	27	21	3	5	15	16	38	41
Wrexham	46	10	5	8	33	26	6	3	14	26	37	40
Halifax T	46	11	6	6	31	22	2	6	15	17	39	38
Rochdale	46	11	7	5	35	26	1	6	16	22	57	37
York C	46	8	8	7	32	22	4	4	15	25	44	36
Tranmere R	46	9	7	7	34	30	1	9	13	16	41	36
Mansfield T	46	5	12	6	19	26	3	8	12	22	37	36
Barnsley	46	6	10	7	23	30	3	8	12	9	34	36
Torquay U	46	8	6	9	31	31	2	6	15	10	38	32
Bradford C	46	6	8	9	27	32	5	2	16	18	45	32

DIVISION 4

	P	W	D	L	F	A	W	D	L	F	A	Pts
Grimsby T	46	18	3	2	61	26	10	4	9	27	30	63
Southend U	46	18	2	3	56	26	6	10	7	25	29	60
Brentford	46	16	2	5	52	21	8	9	6	24	23	59
Scunthorpe U	46	13	8	2	34	15	9	5	9	22	22	57
Lincoln C	46	17	5	1	46	15	4	9	10	31	44	56
Workington	46	12	9	2	34	7	4	10	9	16	27	51
Southport	46	15	5	3	48	21	3	9	11	18	25	50
Peterboro' U	46	14	6	3	51	24	3	10	10	31	40	50
Bury	46	16	4	3	55	22	3	8	12	18	37	50
Cambridge U	46	11	8	4	38	22	6	6	11	24	38	48
Colchester U	46	13	6	4	38	23	6	4	13	32	46	48
Doncaster R	46	11	8	4	35	24	5	6	12	21	39	46
Gillingham	46	11	5	7	33	24	5	8	10	28	43	45
Newport Co	46	13	5	5	34	20	5	3	15	26	52	44
Exeter C	46	11	5	7	40	30	5	6	12	21	38	43
Reading	46	14	3	6	37	26	3	5	15	19	50	42
Aldershot	46	5	13	5	27	20	4	9	10	21	34	40
Hartlepool	46	14	2	7	39	25	3	4	16	19	44	40
Darlington	46	9	9	5	37	24	5	2	16	27	58	39
Chester	46	10	11	2	34	16	0	7	16	13	40	38
Northampton T	46	8	9	6	43	27	4	4	15	23	52	37
Barrow	46	8	8	7	23	26	5	3	15	17	45	37
Stockport Co	46	7	10	6	33	32	2	4	17	22	55	32
Crewe A	46	9	4	10	27	25	1	5	17	16	44	29

Football League Records

Top scorers: B.Robson (West Ham United) 28 goals; Div 2, D.Givens (Queen's Park Rangers) 23 goals; Div 3, A.Horsfield (Charlton Athletic) 26 goals; Div 4, F.Binney (Exeter City) 27 goals. Barrow failed to gain re-election, Hereford United were elected in their place.

Despite missing several games through injury, John Toshack still managed 13 goals for Liverpool in their 1972-3 Championship season.

Burnley's Martin Dobson, a long-serving midfielder who played a major part in getting the Clarets back into the First Division.

DIVISION 1

	ARSENAL	BIRMINGHAM C	CHELSEA	COVENTRY C	CRYSTAL P	DERBY CO	EVERTON	IPSWICH T	LEEDS U	LEICESTER C	LIVERPOOL	MANCHESTER C	MANCHESTER U	NEWCASTLE U	NORWICH C	SHEFFIELD U	SOUTHAMPTON	STOKE C	TOTTENHAM H	W.B.A.	WEST HAM U	WOLVERHAMPTON W
1 ARSENAL		S26 2-0	S02 1-1	N04 0-2	M26 1-0	M31 0-1	N18 1-0	O14 1-0	D02 2-1	F17 1-0	S16 0-0	O28 0-0	J06 3-1	J27 2-2	D26 2-0	M03 3-2	S30 1-0	A19 2-0	a14 1-1	D16 2-1	A29 1-0	A15 5-2
2 BIRMINGHAM C	D23 1-1		O07 2-2	M24 3-0	A26 1-1	F10 2-0	S23 2-1	D30 1-2	a30 2-1	D09 1-1	a07 2-1	S09 4-1	M10 3-1	A15 3-2	N25 4-1	A12 1-2	O21 1-1	a21 3-1	N04 0-0	a28 3-2	a23 0-0	F27 0-1
3 CHELSEA	J20 0-1	M03 0-0		a23 2-0	N25 0-0	D30 1-1	D23 1-1	S23 2-0	A12 4-0	N11 1-1	A23 1-2	A26 2-1	a28 1-0	O28 1-1	D09 3-1	F10 4-2	a21 2-1	a07 1-3	a03 0-1	O14 3-1	S09 1-3	M06 0-2
4 COVENTRY C	A22 1-1	O28 0-0	S30 1-3		M02 2-0	a14 0-2	D02 1-0	M31 2-1	a02 0-1	J06 3-2	a17 1-2	O14 3-2	J27 1-1	S16 0-3	D16 3-1	N18 3-0	A19 1-1	S02 2-1	F17 0-1	D26 0-0	N11 3-1	A29 0-1
5 CRYSTAL P	O21 2-3	M06 0-0	M31 2-0	O07 0-1		A15 0-0	N04 1-0	a14 1-1	N18 2-2	a20 0-1	A19 1-1	A29 1-0	D16 5-0	S02 2-1	S30 0-2	M13 0-1	D26 3-0	F17 3-2	J27 0-0	S16 0-2	M24 1-3	M10 1-1
6 DERBY CO	N25 5-0	S16 1-0	A19 1-2	D09 2-0	N11 2-2		a28 3-1	a30 3-0	M03 2-3	O14 2-1	S02 2-1	A23 1-0	D26 3-1	D16 1-1	J06 1-0	O28 2-1	F17 4-0	F14 0-3	S30 2-1	J27 2-0	a21 1-1	m04 3-0
7 EVERTON	a21 0-0	D26 1-1	a17 1-0	a07 2-0	A22 1-1	A29 1-0		O28 2-2	O14 1-2	J27 0-1	M03 0-2	N11 2-3	A19 2-0	S30 3-1	a03 2-2	M17 2-1	S16 0-1	J06 2-0	D16 3-1	S02 1-0	N25 1-2	D09 0-1
8 IPSWICH T	M10 1-2	A19 2-0	D26 3-0	D05 2-0	D09 2-1	O21 3-1	M24 0-1		N04 2-2	S30 0-2	D16 1-1	a07 1-1	F17 4-1	J06 1-0	A15 1-2	a28 1-1	J27 2-2	S16 2-0	S02 1-1	M17 2-0	O07 1-1	a21 2-1
9 LEEDS U	m09 6-1	D16 4-0	F17 1-1	O21 1-1	a21 4-0	O07 5-0	M10 2-1	A23 3-3		S16 3-1	S30 1-2	N25 3-0	a18 0-1	D26 1-0	S02 2-0	N11 2-1	A30 1-0	J27 1-0	J06 2-1	A19 2-0	D09 1-0	M24 0-0
10 LEICESTER C	A12 0-1	a14 0-1	A16 1-1	A26 0-0	D23 2-1	M10 0-0	S09 1-2	a24 1-1	F10 2-0		A30 3-2	J20 1-1	N04 2-2	M31 0-0	O21 1-2	F24 0-0	O07 1-0	M24 2-0	N18 0-1	D02 3-1	D30 2-1	S23 1-1
11 LIVERPOOL	F10 0-2	D02 4-3	N04 3-1	D23 2-0	D30 1-0	J20 1-1	O07 1-0	F24 2-1	a23 2-0	a28 0-0		A12 2-0	A15 2-0	N18 3-2	M24 3-1	S23 5-0	M10 3-2	O21 2-1	M31 1-1	a14 1-0	A26 3-2	S09 4-2
12 MANCHESTER C	M24 1-2	J27 1-0	M27 0-1	M10 1-2	a28 2-3	N04 4-0	A16 0-1	D02 1-1	M31 1-0	S02 1-0	F17 1-1		N18 3-0	a18 2-0	A19 3-0	a14 3-1	D16 2-1	D26 1-1	S16 2-1	S30 2-1	O21 4-3	O07 1-1
13 MANCHESTER U	A26 0-0	O14 1-0	A30 0-0	S09 0-1	a11 2-0	S23 3-0	J24 0-0	A12 1-2	D23 1-1	A23 1-1	N11 2-0	a21 0-0		M17 2-1	a07 1-0	a23 1-2	N25 2-1	D09 0-2	O28 1-4	M03 2-1	J20 2-2	F10 2-1
14 NEWCASTLE U	S09 2-1	N11 3-0	M24 1-1	F10 1-1	J20 2-0	F28 2-0	a25 0-0	A26 1-2	S23 3-2	J01 2-2	a21 2-1	D23 2-1	O21 2-1		O07 3-1	D30 4-1	D09 0-0	M10 1-0	A30 0-1	A23 1-1	a07 1-2	A12 2-1
15 NORWICH C	S23 3-2	M31 1-2	a14 1-0	M07 1-1	a24 2-1	A26 1-0	A12 1-1	N11 0-0	J20 1-2	M17 1-1	O28 1-1	D30 1-1	D02 0-2	F24 0-1		S09 1-1	A23 0-0	A30 2-0	O14 2-1	N18 2-0	F10 0-1	D23 1-1
16 SHEFFIELD U	O07 1-0	F17 0-1	S16 2-1	a21 3-1	a07 2-0	M24 3-1	O21 0-1	A29 0-0	A15 0-2	D16 2-0	D26 0-3	D09 1-1	S30 1-0	A19 1-2	J27 2-0		S02 3-1	N04 0-0	m02 3-2	J06 3-0	M10 0-0	N25 1-2
17 SOUTHAMPTON	a23 2-2	M17 2-0	N18 3-1	D30 2-1	S23 2-0	A12 1-1	F10 0-0	S09 1-2	a28 3-1	M03 0-0	O14 1-1	M06 1-1	M31 0-2	a14 1-1	N04 1-0	J20 1-1		A15 1-0	D02 1-1	O28 2-1	D23 0-0	A26 1-1
18 STOKE C	D30 0-0	N18 1-2	D02 1-1	M26 2-1	A12 2-0	D23 4-0	A26 1-1	a04 1-0	S09 2-2	O28 1-0	M17 0-1	S23 5-1	a14 2-2	O14 2-0	a28 2-0	A23 2-2	N11 3-3		M14 1-1	M31 2-0	F24 2-0	a24 2-0
19 TOTTENHAM H	D09 1-2	A23 2-0	O21 0-1	A12 2-1	S09 2-1	a18 1-0	F24 3-0	J20 0-1	A26 0-0	a21 1-1	N25 1-2	F10 2-3	M24 1-1	a28 3-2	M10 3-0	D23 2-0	a07 1-2	O07 4-3		N11 1-1	S23 1-0	a30 2-2
20 W.B.A.	F28 1-0	A30 2-2	M10 1-1	S23 1-0	F10 0-4	S09 2-1	a11 4-1	D23 2-0	M28 1-1	a07 1-0	D09 1-1	a25 1-2	O07 2-2	N04 2-3	a21 0-1	A26 0-2	M24 1-1	N25 2-1	A16 0-1		A12 0-0	O21 1-0
21 WEST HAM U	a28 1-2	S30 2-0	J27 3-1	A14 1-0	O28 4-0	N18 1-2	M31 2-0	M02 0-1	a14 1-1	A19 5-2	J06 0-1	M17 2-1	S02 2-2	D02 1-1	S16 4-0	O14 3-1	a20 4-3	D16 3-2	D26 2-2	F17 2-1		N04 2-2
22 WOLVERHAMPTON W	N11 1-3	S02 3-2	D16 1-0	a28 3-0	O14 1-1	D02 1-2	a14 4-2	N18 0-1	O28 0-2	D26 2-0	J27 2-1	M03 5-1	S16 2-0	F17 1-1	a23 3-0	M31 1-1	J06 0-1	S30 5-3	A19 3-2	M20 2-0	A22 3-0	

DIVISION 2

	ASTON VILLA	BLACKPOOL	BRIGHTON & HA	BRISTOL C	BURNLEY	CARDIFF C	CARLISLE U	FULHAM	HUDDERSFIELD T	HULL C	LUTON T	MIDDLESBROUGH	MILLWALL	NOTTINGHAM F	ORIENT	OXFORD U	PORTSMOUTH	PRESTON N.E.	Q.P.R.	SHEFFIELD W	SUNDERLAND	SWINDON T
1 ASTON VILLA		N11 0-0	S02 1-1	a14 1-0	J06 0-3	J27 2-0	A29 1-0	M03 2-3	A19 2-0	D02 2-0	N18 0-2	O28 1-1	S30 1-0	D26 2-2	D16 1-0	M31 2-1	M17 2-0	F17 1-1	O14 0-1	a24 2-1	S27 2-0	S16 2-1
2 BLACKPOOL	O17 1-1		A19 6-2	N18 3-0	D26 1-2	M07 1-0	N04 0-0	M17 2-0	F17 1-1	M31 4-3	M03 1-1	S30 0-1	S02 2-1	a23 2-0	S16 1-1	O14 2-1	D02 3-1	a14 2-0	O28 2-0	D16 1-2	A28 0-0	J27 2-0
3 BRIGHTON & H.A.	J20 1-3	D30 1-2		A12 1-1	N18 0-1	N04 2-2	M21 1-0	S09 2-1	M10 2-1	O07 1-1	F10 2-0	D02 0-2	S20 1-3	a28 2-2	a14 2-1	S23 2-2	a23 1-1	M31 2-0	D23 1-2	O21 3-3	A26 2-2	M24 3-1
4 BRISTOL C	M27 3-0	a21 3-0	F17 3-1		D16 0-1	D26 1-0	a07 4-1	S26 1-1	S30 0-0	a28 2-1	O28 0-1	S16 1-1	A19 2-2	O14 1-1	J27 2-2	M17 0-0	M03 3-1	a23 2-1	N11 1-2	S02 1-2	N25 1-0	J06 3-0
5 BURNLEY	A26 4-1	S23 4-3	a21 3-0	F24 1-1		O21 3-0	A12 2-2	D30 2-2	F03 2-1	F10 4-1	a24 3-0	S26 0-0	M24 2-1	N25 1-0	N11 1-2	D23 1-1	M20 4-0	A29 2-0	S09 1-1	M10 0-1	a16 2-0	O07 2-1
6 CARDIFF C	S09 0-2	A26 1-2	S27 1-1	S23 1-3	M17 0-1		F10 1-0	N25 3-1	a21 4-1	m09 0-2	A12 2-1	O14 2-0	A30 1-0	N11 2-1	M03 3-1	J19 2-0	D29 0-2	O28 3-0	a18 0-0	D09 4-1	m07 1-1	a07 1-1
7 CARLISLE U	a28 2-2	S26 2-3	D16 5-1	D02 1-2	F17 1-1	S16 4-0		O14 2-1	J06 0-0	a14 0-1	M31 2-0	J27 1-1	a24 0-1	S02 1-2	M17 1-0	N18 2-1	O28 1-0	D26 6-1	M03 1-3	S30 1-1	N11 4-3	A19 3-0
8 FULHAM	O07 2-0	O21 2-0	J27 5-1	N04 5-1	A19 1-1	M31 1-1	M10 1-0		S16 1-1	S20 2-0	M27 0-1	J06 2-1	D26 1-0	D16 3-1	S30 1-1	a14 2-0	N18 0-0	S02 1-3	O17 0-2	F17 1-0	M24 1-2	a20 0-0
9 HUDDERSFIELD T	D30 1-1	A12 1-0	O14 0-2	N14 0-1	a14 0-2	N18 2-1	A26 1-1	F10 1-0		D23 1-3	J20 1-2	M17 1-1	M31 1-0	M03 1-1	O28 1-1	S09 2-0	a28 2-0	D02 0-0	M06 2-2	N04 1-0	S23 1-1	S19 1-1
10 HULL C	a07 1-2	N25 1-2	M02 2-0	A29 2-0	S16 1-1	D16 1-1	D09 1-1	N11 2-2	a23 0-0		a10 4-0	D26 3-1	F17 0-2	A19 0-0	S02 2-0	O27 0-1	O14 5-1	J27 6-2	S26 4-1	J06 1-1	a21 0-2	S30 3-2
11 LUTON T	a21 0-0	O07 2-2	S16 2-1	M24 1-3	S30 2-2	F17 1-1	N25 0-1	a07 1-0	S02 4-1	O21 1-2		a23 0-1	D16 2-2	J27 1-0	J06 1-1	A30 0-1	O18 2-2	A19 1-0	D09 2-2	D26 0-0	M10 1-0	N04 0-1
12 MIDDLESBROUGH	M24 1-1	F02 2-0	a07 1-1	F10 2-1	N04 3-3	M10 2-0	S09 1-0	A26 1-2	O21 2-1	S23 1-0	D23 0-1		O07 1-0	D09 0-0	a28 3-2	D30 1-0	F24 3-0	S19 0-0	J20 0-0	a21 3-0	A12 2-1	N25 0-2
13 MILLWALL	a23 1-1	J20 1-1	N11 3-0	D30 3-0	O28 1-1	a28 1-1	D23 1-0	S23 1-3	N25 1-0	A12 2-0	F26 3-2	M02 1-0		S25 2-1	O14 2-0	F10 3-1	A26 0-2	M17 4-1	a21 0-1	a07 2-1	S09 0-1	D09 1-1
14 NOTTINGHAM F	S23 1-1	D23 4-0	A29 1-0	M10 1-0	M31 3-0	S19 2-1	J20 2-1	F24 2-1	O07 1-1	M13 1-2	S09 0-1	a14 1-3	N04 3-2		D02 2-1	A26 2-1	A12 0-0	N18 0-1	F10 0-0	M24 3-0	a24 1-0	O21 2-2
15 ORIENT	F24 4-0	F10 2-0	D09 1-0	S09 0-2	S18 1-1	O07 0-0	O21 2-1	a23 3-2	M24 3-1	J20 0-0	A26 0-1	A28 2-0	M10 3-1	a07 3-0		A12 1-1	D23 0-1	N03 1-2	S23 2-2	N25 3-2	a30 1-1	a21 1-0
16 OXFORD U	N25 2-0	M10 0-1	D26 3-0	O21 0-2	a20 0-2	S02 2-1	a21 1-1	D09 0-0	J27 2-0	M23 5-2	a28 2-1	A19 4-0	S16 2-1	J06 1-0	F17 2-1		N04 1-3	S30 0-2	a07 2-0	S20 1-0	O07 5-1	D16 1-0
17 PORTSMOUTH	O21 0-1	a07 1-0	S30 2-0	O07 0-3	S02 0-2	A19 3-1	M24 0-0	a21 1-2	A30 1-2	M10 2-2	N11 2-2	D16 0-0	J06 1-1	F17 2-0	a20 1-0	S27 1-0		S16 0-1	N25 0-1	J27 1-0	D09 2-3	D26 1-1
18 PRESTON N.E.	A12 0-1	D09 0-3	N25 4-0	D23 3-3	a28 1-1	M24 0-0	S23 1-0	J20 0-3	a07 0-0	S09 1-0	D30 2-0	N11 0-1	O21 1-0	a21 2-1	S25 0-0	a24 0-1	F10 0-5		A26 1-1	O07 1-1	M19 1-3	M10 1-1
19 Q.P.R.	M10 1-0	M24 4-0	a24 2-0	S19 1-1	J27 2-0	S30 3-0	O07 4-0	a28 2-0	F06 3-1	N04 1-1	a14 2-0	S02 2-2	N18 1-3	S16 3-0	D26 3-1	D02 0-0	M31 5-0	J06 3-0		A19 4-2	O21 3-2	F17 5-0
20 SHEFFIELD W	D23 2-2	F28 2-0	M17 1-1	M14 3-2	O14 0-1	a14 1-0	a23 0-0	A12 3-0	S27 3-2	A26 4-2	S23 4-0	N18 2-1	D02 2-2	O28 1-2	M31 2-0	N11 0-1	S09 2-1	M03 2-1	D30 3-1		F10 1-0	A16 2-1
21 SUNDERLAND	N04 2-2	a28 1-0	J06 4-0	M31 2-2	D02 0-1	a23 2-1	M27 2-1	O28 0-0	a10 3-0	N18 1-1	O14 0-2	F17 4-0	J27 2-0	S30 4-1	A19 1-0	M03 1-0	a14 2-0	D16 0-0	m09 0-3	S16 1-1		S02 3-2
22 SWINDON T	F10 1-3	S09 0-0	O28 2-2	A26 2-1	M02 0-1	F27 3-0	M12 2-0	D23 2-2	N11 1-1	a24 2-1	S26 0-2	M31 1-0	a14 0-0	M17 0-0	N18 3-1	F24 1-3	S23 1-1	O14 3-2	A12 2-2	A29 1-0	J20 1-1	

Season 1972-73

DIVISION 3

	BLACKBURN R	BOLTON W	BOURNEMOUTH	BRENTFORD	BRISTOL R	CHARLTON A	CHESTERFIELD	GRIMSBY T	HALIFAX T	NOTTS CO	OLDHAM A	PLYMOUTH A	PORT VALE	ROCHDALE	ROTHERHAM U	SCUNTHORPE U	SHREWSBURY T	SOUTHEND U	SWANSEA C	TRANMERE R	WALSALL	WATFORD	WREXHAM	YORK C
1 BLACKBURN R		S02 0-3	a14 2-1	J06 2-1	F17 0-0	O28 3-1	M14 0-1	N04 0-0	D02 3-0	M07 2-0	a28 1-1	S20 3-1	O14 0-1	A19 1-1	a20 2-1	S30 3-0	J27 0-0	D16 2-1	M17 3-0	M31 2-2	O25 2-0	S16 0-0	M03 1-1	F03 2-0
2 BOLTON W	M28 0-1		A12 3-0	a28 2-0	N11 2-0	F20 3-0	S27 1-0	F10 2-0	a16 3-0	D30 2-2	A26 2-1	S09 2-0	D23 2-0	M17 2-1	N25 2-1	O14 0-0	M21 2-0	O28 1-1	O11 3-0	S23 2-0	M03 3-1	a07 1-1	J30 1-0	a21 3-0
3 BOURNEMOUTH	M20 3-0	F17 2-0		D26 3-2	D16 0-0	N25 3-1	A19 2-2	M24 1-1	A29 1-0	M10 1-1	a07 2-0	O21 0-1	S26 4-0	O24 4-2	F03 4-0	S02 1-1	S30 2-0	S16 2-0	a21 2-0	O07 1-1	a20 0-1	J06 3-0	N11 1-0	J27 2-3
4 BRENTFORD	A26 4-0	A28 2-1	S23 1-1		S25 2-1	F26 1-0	N11 3-1	F24 0-1	A12 0-1	a20 1-1	D30 1-1	J20 0-2	F10 5-0	O28 1-0	J13 1-1	M03 1-0	a07 1-2	M17 1-2	S09 0-2	O09 2-0	O14 2-0	M19 1-1	D23 1-0	N25 2-0
5 BRISTOL R	A12 3-0	S19 1-1	F24 2-0	N04 3-1		D23 2-1	A29 2-2	A26 2-1	D30 4-1	N07 1-0	F10 3-3	S23 2-0	J30 4-1	M06 0-0	M10 3-0	D02 5-1	O21 5-1	M31 1-2	a20 3-1	J13 2-0	a14 2-1	M24 2-1	S09 2-0	O07 1-2
6 CHARLTON A	M24 1-2	D16 2-3	M31 1-1	N28 2-1	a24 3-3		F03 2-2	M10 1-1	M06 1-0	S19 6-1	O21 4-2	O07 3-0	D02 2-0	J06 1-0	J27 1-2	S16 2-0	A19 1-2	D26 0-0	A29 6-0	N04 1-1	F16 1-1	S30 2-1	a14 2-1	S02 1-0
7 CHESTERFIELD	S23 3-1	N04 0-1	D30 1-1	S20 3-0	a28 0-1	O18 1-0		D23 2-1	F07 2-0	F24 0-2	A12 4-1	A26 2-2	S09 1-2	M31 2-1	O07 3-2	a14 2-1	M24 2-0	M07 2-4	J13 1-0	a24 2-0	D02 3-0	O21 0-0	F10 1-2	M10 0-0
8 GRIMSBY T	S26 2-0	S16 2-0	O28 0-1	D16 4-0	J06 2-0	O14 0-2	a20 2-1		M17 0-0	D02 3-1	N11 6-2	a28 1-1	M06 0-1	S30 1-0	A19 2-1	D26 1-0	F13 3-2	O24 3-1	M03 2-0	a14 2-0	J27 6-2	S02 2-0	M31 0-1	F17 1-2
9 HALIFAX T	a07 2-2	S30 1-1	a28 2-0	a04 3-2	A19 3-0	a21 3-0	S02 0-1	O21 1-1		O07 0-1	J13 0-3	M24 2-1	N11 2-2	F03 0-0	D26 0-1	J27 1-0	F27 0-1	a24 2-1	N25 1-1	M10 2-1	S16 0-1	O24 1-1	A22 2-2	M13 1-0
10 NOTTS CO	a21 0-0	A19 1-0	O14 0-2	S30 1-0	F03 2-0	N11 3-1	D16 2-0	a07 4-0	M03 3-0		N25 2-4	M21 2-0	O28 1-1	S16 2-2	O25 2 0	a23 2 0	F17 1-0	J27 2-0	S27 2-0	a28 4-1	S02 1-1	D26 1-0	M17 1-0	J06 1-0
11 OLDHAM A	A29 1-2	J06 2-0	D02 1-1	A19 1-1	S16 3 0	M17 0-1	M27 3-0	S19 1-2	a14 1-1	M31 1-1		N04 7-1	M03 1-0	a20 0-0	S30 1-0	O24 3-0	S02 2-1	F03 0-1	O28 2-0	M07 3-1	D16 2-1	J27 2-1	O14 2-2	D26 1-1
12 PLYMOUTH A	N11 1-2	J27 1-0	M17 1-0	S02 0-1	D26 3-2	M03 5 0	F20 2-2	A29 3-1	O28 2-1	a14 1-4	S26 1-3		M31 2-1	m01 3-2	F17 4-1	F06 3-0	S16 3-0	A19 2-0	O14 3-1	D02 0-1	S30 0-2	a23 1-1	M06 1-0	O24 1-1
13 PORT VALE	M10 2-1	a23 2-2	N04 2-1	S16 1-0	S02 2-1	a07 3-1	J27 2-1	a21 3-0	S18 2-1	M24 1-1	O07 0-2	N25 1-1		a09 0-0	F26 4-1	D16 2-0	O23 1-1	S30 3-1	M19 3-1	O21 0-0	D26 1-2	F03 1-0	A28 3-2	A19 2-1
14 ROCHDALE	D30 0-1	O21 2-2	J29 1-0	M24 0-1	D09 0-0	A26 0-2	N25 1-2	a23 3-2	O09 0-0	F10 4-1	D23 0-0	F24 0-6	A12 0-0		a07 0-1	N11 0-2	M10 1-1	a28 3-2	M12 1-1	S09 1-1	S25 2-1	O07 1-0	S23 1-0	M19 1-0
15 ROTHERHAM U	D23 1-1	M31 1-0	O10 2-7	M06 2-1	O14 1-1	S09 2-1	M03 1-0	D30 2-0	S23 0 1	J30 1 4	a23 2-3	A12 1-0	A26 7-0	D02 0-0		O28 2-1	S19 2-0	a14 1-0	F10 0-2	F24 1-2	M17 2-0	N04 1-0	J20 1-1	a28 1-2
16 SCUNTHORPE U	a24 1-1	M10 1-1	J20 1-1	O07 1-0	a07 0-2	F10 0-2	M20 0-1	S23 1-2	S08 0-3	D23 1-0	M13 0-0	O10 1-1	F24 0-1	S19 1-2	M24 2-1		N25 1-0	N04 0-0	A12 1-0	D30 1-5	A29 2-1	a21 1-0	A26 1-1	O21 1-0
17 SHREWSBURY T	S09 2-0	a13 0-2	a24 0-0	D02 2-0	M16 4-2	D30 0-2	O27 2-0	O10 3-2	A25 0-0	A12 0-0	J19 2-2	F09 1-1	M27 2-3	O14 3-2	N11 1-1	M30 4-2		M02 1-0	S23 2-1	D22 0-0	M06 1-1	A29 0-0	F23 0-0	S26 1-0
18 SOUTHEND U	F24 0-1	M24 1-1	F09 2-2	O21 4-0	N24 0-0	S22 1-1	a21 5-1	M12 2-0	D22 1-1	S09 2-1	O09 0-1	D29 3-1	a20 5-0	A28 1-2	M19 1-0	S25 1-0	O06 2-0		A25 3-1	J20 1-0	N10 2-0	M09 0-0	A12 0-1	a06 3-0
19 SWANSEA C	O21 2-2	a04 2-3	M06 1-0	J26 2-1	S30 0-2	a28 2-1	O24 2-1	O07 6-2	M31 2-0	N04 3-0	M24 0-0	M09 1-1	a14 0-1	S02 2-3	S16 0-1	F03 2-1	D26 0-2	J06 1-1		S19 1-1	A19 2-1	F27 2-1	D01 3-1	J29 1-3
20 TRANMERE R	N24 1-1	D26 1-1	M02 0-0	F02 6-2	O23 1-1	S25 4-0	S29 1-0	M19 1 1	O13 1 1	A28 0-2	a21 0-1	a06 2-2	M16 2-0	F06 0-1	D15 2-0	A18 2-1	a20 1-0	S01 3-1	N10 1-1		J05 3-1	F16 1-0	O27 4-0	S15 1-0
21 WALSALL	J13 0-2	O07 3-2	D23 1-0	M10 3-0	M19 4-3	A12 3-2	a07 3-2	S09 1-0	m01 0-1	J23 1-3	F24 3-0	a25 1-3	S23 2-0	N04 0-2	O21 1-0	a28 1-1	a21 1-0	S19 3-1	F19 1-1	A26 2-0		N25 1-3	O10 2-0	M24 0-0
22 WATFORD	F10 1-3	D02 2-1	A26 3-2	a14 2-2	O28 2-1	a20 1-1	M17 0-0	J20 1-2	M28 2-1	S23 1-0	S09 2-1	D23 3-2	O10 1-1	M02 0-0	S27 1-1	M06 5-1	a28 0-1	O14 1-0	F24 0-1	A12 1-0	M31 1-0		M14 0-0	N11 2-2
23 WREXHAM	O07 0-0	O30 1-3	O02 1-1	a23 4-1	J27 2-2	M19 2-2	S16 1 0	N25 3-2	N04 0-0	O21 2-0	M10 1-1	a21 1-2	a27 5-0	D26 3-3	S02 1-0	J06 1-2	D16 0-0	F17 4-2	a07 1-0	M23 0-0	F03 2-1	A19 1-0		S30 3-1
24 YORK C	O09 1-0	M05 0-1	S09 0-0	M31 0-1	M03 0-0	J20 1-1	O14 2-0	A12 0-0	F24 2-1	A26 1-1	S23 0-0	M26 1-2	D30 0-0	a14 1-2	A28 0-1	M17 3 1	N04 2 1	D02 2 0	D23 3-0	F10 4-1	O28 0-0	S18 0-0	a20 1-1	

DIVISION 4

	ALDERSHOT	BARNSLEY	BRADFORD C	BURY	CAMBRIDGE U	CHESTER	COLCHESTER U	CREWE A	DARLINGTON	DONCASTER R	EXETER C	GILLINGHAM	HARTLEPOOL	HEREFORD U	LINCOLN C	MANSFIELD T	NEWPORT CO	NORTHAMPTON T	PETERBOROUGH U	READING	SOUTHPORT	STOCKPORT CO	TORQUAY U	WORKINGTON
1 ALDERSHOT		O28 0-2	D16 2-1	O14 2-0	a24 1-1	J27 1-1	F03 2-0	M07 3-0	J13 3-1	M17 1-0	N11 0-0	D26 0-0	S27 2-1	M31 2-0	J06 0-0	S16 0-1	M02 0-2	J17 3-0	a14 2-1	S30 1-0	S02 2-2	O25 2-0	F17 2-1	A19 2-0
2 BARNSLEY	M24 0-2		F17 1-2	a21 0-1	A19 3-1	S30 0-0	S16 4-0	S26 2-2	O21 0-2	A29 4-2	a06 1-1	S02 1-1	D08 2-1	N11 0-0	a24 4-1	D26 1-1	N25 2-1	M10 2-0	O07 3-2	D16 0-0	J27 0-1	J06 1-3	O24 0-0	F06 1-0
3 BRADFORD C	F24 1-0	A12 3-1		M28 0-0	M02 0-1	O04 0-1	N04 3-0	F10 2-2	D23 7-0	a23 4-3	D30 4-0	M31 3-1	S23 0-2	A26 1-1	D02 3-1	O14 1-1	O11 2-1	S09 2-1	J20 1-4	O28 1-1	a28 0-2	M07 1-0	M17 1-0	a14 2-2
4 BURY	M10 1-2	M06 2-1	O24 0-0		D16 1-1	F17 1-1	a23 4-0	D02 0-1	O07 1-0	M31 5-0	O21 2-1	A19 2-1	M24 1-1	a14 3-0	S16 0-4	J27 1-0	A29 0-0	S19 2-2	N04 3-1	a10 4-0	F03 0-1	D26 1-2	S02 0-0	S30 3-0
5 CAMBRIDGE U	D23 2-2	D30 1-1	O07 2-1	F24 2-2		M24 1-0	O20 3-0	J31 1-0	A12 0-3	A26 3-1	J20 1-3	N04 3-1	S09 1-1	O11 1-0	M07 2-1	a28 3-2	F10 3-1	D09 3-1	S23 3-1	a14 1-0	M10 2-2	S20 1-0	D02 0-0	M31 1-0
6 CHESTER	S09 0-0	a20 0-0	N11 1-1	A12 2-0	O28 1-1		A30 4-0	S23 2-1	F10 5-0	F20 1-2	D23 0-1	a14 1-0	O11 2-0	F24 0-1	O14 2-1	M17 2-2	D30 0-2	M28 3-0	A26 8-2	M07 2-0	S26 0-0	D01 2-0	M31 1-2	M03 1-3
7 COLCHESTER U	O09 2-3	F10 1-2	S25 0-0	D23 2-1	M16 0-1	a27 2-3		S08 5-1	J19 1-0	F24 1-1	a16 1-2	a30 4-0	D29 1-1	A12 1-0	M03 0-2	O28 1-1	A26 1-3	S22 2-2	a09 1-0	M30 2-2	N10 3-1	a13 3-0	M05 1-1	O13 1-1
8 CREWE A	a21 0-2	N04 1-0	S16 1-2	a07 2-1	O25 1-1	D26 1-1	J27 1-2		N25 0-0	S20 0-1	O07 1 0	S30 1 1	M10 2 0	A30 2 1	S02 1-1	D16 0-4	M21 0-0	M24 1-0	O21 0-2	m02 0-0	a18 0-2	F03 0-1	A19 1-1	J06 2-0
9 DARLINGTON	A28 1-4	M17 0-0	a20 1-0	M03 1-1	F17 3-3	S16 1-1	S02 2-1	M31 3-1		O28 0-1	S25 0-0	F03 2-3	N11 1-2	M05 2-2	A19 1-1	S30 2-3	O14 2-3	a14 0-0	D02 2-2	O23 0-2	J06 0-7	J27 2-0	D16 0-3	a09 2-1
10 DONCASTER R	O21 1-0	a27 0-0	S29 1-0	N25 4-1	J06 0-0	O24 0-0	D16 1-0	N11 0-2	M23 2-0		M20 5-1	J26 0-1	a07 2-1	S26 0-0	D26 1-1	A19 0-1	a21 1-5	O06 3-0	M09 1-1	a24 0-2	S15 2-0	S01 2-2	F03 1-0	F16 1-1
11 EXETER C	S20 1-0	D02 2-1	A19 5-1	M17 1-1	S02 3-1	a23 0-0	S30 1-0	M03 0-0	N04 1-1	a14 0-1		D16 3-2	A28 1-1	O14 1-0	N06 2-0	J06 4-2	O28 0-0	M31 4-1	F12 1-1	a03 0-0	F17 0-1	S16 3-0	D26 3-2	J27 4-2
12 GILLINGHAM	S23 1-2	J20 5-1	N25 4-2	D30 2-2	S26 1-2	D09 1-0	a06 2-1	a23 3-2	O10 4-0	S08 3-0	F24 1-0		J13 2-0	F10 2-0	M17 1-1	N11 2-1	A12 0-0	A25 1-3	D23 2-0	O14 1-0	a21 2-0	a28 3-0	M02 1-1	O28 0-2
13 HARTLEPOOL	N04 1-1	a14 1-4	D26 1-0	O28 1-1	J27 0-0	F03 0-0	A19 2-1	O14 1-1	S18 0-0	D02 0-0	a28 0-0	O23 2-0		M03 0-1	F17 1-0	a20 1-1	M16 1-0	M05 2-0	M31 0-1	S02 1-2	S30 0-2	D16 0-0	J06 1-0	S16 1-0
14 HEREFORD U	N25 1-0	S19 1-2	J06 1-0	D09 1-0	F03 2-1	J17 3-1	F17 4-1	a28 1-0	M12 1-0	N04 3-2	M10 1-0	S16 0-0	O07 0-0		J27 2-1	O25 3-1	a07 2-0	O21 2-0	M24 3-0	A19 3-0	D26 2-2	a18 1-0	S30 2-1	S02 0-0
15 LINCOLN C	A26 0-2	D23 1-2	a07 2-1	F10 2-2	a21 2-1	M10 1-0	O07 3-2	J20 1-1	F28 1-0	S23 2-1	J13 2-2	O21 1-0	A12 1-2	S09 4-1		N25 1-1	F24 0-2	O11 1-1	a20 1-0	N11 0-0	M21 3-1	M24 5-3	S27 3-1	a28 1-1
16 MANSFIELD T	F10 2-0	S23 3-1	M10 4-1	S09 1-1	A30 3-1	O21 4-1	M24 1-1	F24 5-1	a24 5-0	D30 0-0	A26 3-0	S18 2-0	D23 2-0	J13 1-1	M31 0-2		M26 0-0	A12 1-0	O09 4-2	D02 1-1	O07 3-3	N04 1-0	a14 2-1	M05 4-0
17 NEWPORT CO	O07 2-1	M31 1-1	F06 0-0	a28 4-3	S16 0-2	A19 3-2	J06 1-0	a14 0-0	M09 0-0	M06 1-0	M24 2-0	F17 5-1	O21 5-1	N28 0-1	D16 2-2	S02 0-1		N04 1-0	S19 1-1	D26 1-0	O24 3-1	S30 1-0	J23 2-1	a24 2-0
18 NORTHAMPTON T	a07 0-2	O14 2-2	J27 1-2	N11 0-1	S30 2-2	S01 1-0	D26 4-0	O28 1-0	M20 2-2	M02 0-2	N25 1-2	J06 2-1	a21 3-1	M17 0-4	F03 0-0	F16 1-0	S26 0-1		a28 1-3	S16 1-1	D15 0-1	F13 1-1	a23 0-2	O24 1-0
19 PETERBOROUGH U	M19 1-0	M02 6-3	S02 3-0	S25 1-1	D26 1-1	J06 2-2	O23 2-2	M17 4-3	a07 1-1	O14 3-1	a21 1-1	a24 0-1	N25 3-0	O28 1-1	S30 2-2	F03 1-0	N11 1-0	A28 1-2		J27 4-2	A19 0-1	F17 2-3	S16 0-1	D16 2-1
20 READING	a23 0-0	F24 0-0	M24 2-0	A26 0-0	M21 1-0	a21 2-1	N25 0-1	A12 1-1	F21 1-0	D23 1-0	O11 2-0	M10 3-1	J20 1-0	D30 0-1	S20 1-1	a07 2-0	S23 5-0	F10 3-0	S09 2-0		O21 1-1	O07 0-0	F28 3-0	N04 2-0
21 SOUTHPORT	J20 3-1	S09 1-0	S11 3-1	O11 2-1	O13 1-1	N03 3-2	S20 1-0	D22 2-0	A26 2-1	F09 2-2	A12 1-0	M06 0-0	a23 1-1	S22 2-0	a14 1-0	M02 3-1	J30 0-2	F23 1-2	D30 2-1	M16 4-1		M30 1-0	O27 2-1	D01 2-1
22 STOCKPORT CO	m04 1-1	A25 2-0	a21 3-1	S22 0-0	N10 2-2	a06 2-1	M19 2-0	O09 0-0	S08 3-1	J19 2-1	F09 1-0	S11 2-3	F23 0-1	D22 1-1	O28 2-1	S25 2-1	a23 1-0	D29 0-0	A12 3-2	M02 2-2	N24 2-0		O13 2-0	M16 3-0
23 TORQUAY U	A12 1-1	J13 0-0	O21 1-2	J20 0-1	a07 1-2	N25 1-2	a20 0-0	D30 0-0	F24 2-1	O11 1-0	S23 0-2	O07 0-0	A26 1-0	a24 0-0	N04 2-0	M21 1-1	S09 2-2	D23 2-1	F10 1-0	a28 2-2	M24 2-0	M10 0-0		S20 3-0
24 WORKINGTON	D30 2-1	O11 3-2	M21 1-1	a20 2-0	N25 5-1	O07 3-1	M10 1-0	A26 1-1	S23 2-1	A12 2-0	S09 3-1	M24 1-1	F10 0-0	J20 2-1	A30 0-3	D09 2-0	D23 3-2	J13 3-0	F23 2-2	S27 0-0	a07 2-0	O21 2-0	N11 2-2	

LEAGUE TABLES

DIVISION 1

	P	W	D	L	F	A	W	D	L	F	A	Pts
Liverpool	42	17	3	1	45	19	8	7	6	27	23	60
Arsenal	42	14	5	2	31	14	9	6	6	26	29	57
Leeds U	42	15	4	2	45	13	6	7	8	26	32	53
Ipswich T	42	10	7	4	34	20	7	7	7	21	25	48
Wolves	42	13	3	5	43	23	5	8	8	23	31	47
West Ham U	42	12	5	4	45	25	5	7	9	22	28	46
Derby Co	42	15	3	3	43	18	4	5	12	13	36	46
Tottenham H	42	10	5	6	33	23	6	8	7	25	25	45
Newcastle U	42	12	6	3	35	19	4	7	10	25	32	45
Birmingham	42	11	7	3	39	22	4	5	12	14	32	42
Manchester C	42	12	4	5	36	20	3	7	11	21	40	41
Chelsea	42	9	6	6	30	22	4	8	9	19	29	40
Southampton	42	8	11	2	26	17	3	7	11	21	35	40
Sheffield U	42	11	4	6	28	18	4	6	11	23	41	40
Stoke C	42	11	8	2	38	17	3	2	16	23	39	38
Leicester C	42	7	9	5	23	18	3	8	10	17	28	37
Everton	42	9	5	7	27	21	4	6	11	14	28	37
Manchester U	42	9	7	5	24	19	3	6	12	20	41	37
Coventry C	42	9	5	7	27	24	4	4	13	13	31	35
Norwich C	42	7	9	5	22	19	4	1	16	14	44	32
Crystal P	42	7	7	7	25	21	2	5	14	16	37	30
WBA	42	8	7	6	25	24	1	3	17	13	38	28

DIVISION 2

	P	W	D	L	F	A	W	D	L	F	A	Pts
Burnley	42	13	6	2	44	18	11	8	2	28	17	62
QPR	42	16	4	1	54	13	8	9	4	27	24	61
Aston Villa	42	12	5	4	27	17	6	9	6	24	30	50
Middlesbrough	42	12	6	3	29	15	5	7	9	17	28	47
Bristol C	42	10	7	4	34	18	7	5	9	29	33	46
Sunderland	42	12	6	3	35	17	5	6	10	24	32	46
Blackpool	42	12	6	3	37	17	6	4	11	19	34	46
Oxford U	42	14	2	5	36	18	5	5	11	16	25	45
Fulham	42	11	6	4	32	16	5	6	10	26	33	44
Sheffield W	42	14	4	3	40	20	3	6	12	19	35	44
Millwall	42	12	5	4	33	18	4	5	12	22	29	42
Luton T	42	6	9	6	24	23	9	2	10	20	30	41
Hull C	42	9	7	5	39	22	5	5	11	25	37	40
Nottingham F	42	12	5	4	32	18	2	7	12	15	34	40
Orient	42	11	6	4	33	18	1	6	14	16	35	36
Swindon T	42	8	9	4	28	23	2	7	12	18	37	36
Portsmouth	42	7	6	8	21	22	5	5	11	21	37	35
Carlisle U	42	10	5	6	30	24	1	7	13	10	28	34
Preston NE	42	6	8	7	19	25	5	4	12	18	39	34
Cardiff C	42	11	4	6	32	21	0	7	14	11	37	33
Huddersfield T	42	7	9	5	21	20	1	8	12	15	36	33
Brighton & HA	42	7	8	6	32	31	1	5	15	14	52	29

DIVISION 3

	P	W	D	L	F	A	W	D	L	F	A	Pts
Bolton W	46	18	4	1	44	9	7	7	9	29	30	61
Notts Co	46	17	4	2	40	12	6	7	10	27	35	57
Blackburn R	46	12	8	3	34	16	8	7	8	23	31	55
Oldham A	46	12	7	4	40	18	7	9	7	32	36	54
Bristol R	46	17	4	2	55	20	3	9	11	22	36	53
Port Vale	46	15	6	2	41	21	6	5	12	15	48	53
Bournemouth	46	14	6	3	44	16	3	10	10	22	28	50
Plymouth A	46	14	3	6	43	26	6	7	10	31	40	50
Grimsby T	46	16	2	5	45	18	4	6	13	22	43	48
Tranmere R	46	12	8	3	38	17	3	8	12	18	35	46
Charlton A	46	12	7	4	46	24	5	4	14	23	43	45
Wrexham	46	11	9	3	39	23	3	8	12	16	31	45
Rochdale	46	8	8	7	22	26	6	9	8	26	28	45
Southend U	46	13	6	4	40	14	4	4	15	21	40	44
Shrewsbury T	46	10	10	3	31	21	5	4	14	15	33	44
Chesterfield	46	13	4	6	37	22	4	5	14	20	39	43
Walsall	46	14	3	6	37	26	4	4	15	19	40	43
York C	46	8	10	5	24	14	5	5	13	18	32	41
Watford	46	11	8	4	32	23	1	9	13	11	25	41
Halifax T	46	9	8	6	29	23	4	7	12	14	30	41
Rotherham U	46	12	4	7	34	27	5	3	15	17	38	41
Brentford	46	12	5	6	33	18	3	2	18	18	51	37
Swansea C	46	11	5	7	37	29	3	4	16	14	44	37
Scunthorpe U	46	8	7	8	18	25	2	3	18	15	47	30

DIVISION 4

	P	W	D	L	F	A	W	D	L	F	A	Pts
Southport	46	17	4	2	40	19	9	6	8	31	29	62
Hereford U	46	18	4	1	39	12	5	8	10	17	26	58
Cambridge U	46	15	6	2	40	23	5	11	7	27	34	57
Aldershot	46	14	6	3	33	14	8	6	9	27	24	56
Newport Co	46	14	6	3	37	18	8	6	9	27	26	56
Mansfield T	46	15	7	1	52	17	5	7	11	26	34	54
Reading	46	14	7	2	33	7	3	11	9	18	31	52
Exeter C	46	13	8	2	40	18	5	6	12	17	33	50
Gillingham	46	15	4	4	44	20	4	7	12	19	38	49
Lincoln C	46	12	7	4	38	27	4	9	10	26	30	48
Stockport Co	46	14	7	2	38	18	4	5	14	15	35	48
Bury	46	11	7	5	37	19	3	11	9	21	32	46
Workington	46	15	7	1	44	20	2	5	16	15	41	46
Barnsley	46	9	8	6	32	24	5	8	10	26	36	44
Chester	46	11	6	6	40	19	3	9	11	21	33	43
Bradford C	46	12	6	5	42	25	4	5	14	19	40	43
Doncaster R	46	10	8	5	28	19	5	4	14	21	39	42
Torquay U	46	8	10	5	23	17	4	7	12	21	30	41
Peterboro' U	46	10	8	5	42	29	4	5	14	29	47	41
Hartlepool	46	8	10	5	17	15	4	7	12	17	34	41
Crewe A	46	7	8	8	18	23	2	10	11	20	38	36
Colchester U	46	8	8	7	36	28	2	3	18	12	48	31
Northampton T	46	7	6	10	24	30	3	5	15	16	43	31
Darlington	46	5	9	9	28	41	2	6	15	14	44	29

Football League Records

Top scorers: Div 1, M.Channon (Southampton) 21 goals; Div 2, D.McKenzie (Nottingham Forest) 26 goals; Div 3, W.Jennings (Watford) 26 goals; Div 4, B.Yeo (Gillingham) 31 goals.

Billy Bremner, the tenacious Scottish midfielder and skipper of Leeds' 1973-4 Championship team.

DIVISION 1

	ARSENAL	BIRMINGHAM C	BURNLEY	CHELSEA	COVENTRY C	DERBY CO	EVERTON	IPSWICH T	LEEDS U	LEICESTER C	LIVERPOOL	MANCHESTER C	MANCHESTER U	NEWCASTLE U	NORWICH C	Q.P.R.	SHEFFIELD U	SOUTHAMPTON	STOKE C	TOTTENHAM H	WEST HAM U	WOLVERHAMPTON W
1 ARSENAL		O06 1-0	F02 1-1	N17 0-0	D01 2-2	a20 2-0	D22 1-0	O20 1-1	A28 1-2	S08 0-2	N03 0-2	M23 2-0	A25 3-0	J01 0-1	J12 2-0	a30 1-1	S11 1-0	M02 1-0	S22 2-1	F16 0-1	a06 0-0	D04 2-2
2 BIRMINGHAM C	F23 3-1		a16 2-2	S11 2-4	D26 1-0	S01 0-0	O27 0-2	S29 0-3	D29 1-1	N24 3-0	S15 1-1	J19 1-1	M16 1-0	D08 1-0	a27 2-1	a23 4-0	M30 1-0	N10 1-1	a13 0-0	A28 1-2	D15 3-1	O13 2-1
3 BURNLEY	D15 2-1	a12 2-1		A28 1-0	S01 2-2	S15 1-1	M16 3-1	F09 0-1	N10 0-0	a13 0-0	D26 2-1	S29 3-0	O27 0-0	a27 1-1	D08 1-0	O13 2-1	J19 1-2	a22 3-0	N24 1-0	S11 2-2	F23 1-1	D29 1-1
4 CHELSEA	a13 1-3	S05 3-1	M13 3-0		S15 1-0	J19 1-1	N10 3-1	O13 2-3	D15 1-2	D08 3-2	D29 0-1	F09 1-0	M30 1-3	M16 1-0	O26 3-0	F23 3-3	S01 1-2	N24 4-0	a27 0-1	a15 0-0	D26 2-4	S29 2-2
5 COVENTRY C	a27 3-3	M02 0-1	J01 1-1	J12 2-2		S18 1-0	O06 1-2	N03 0-1	a13 0-0	D22 1-2	A28 1-0	S11 2-1	F02 1-0	S22 2-2	F26 1-0	M23 0-1	N24 3-1	S08 2-0	M09 2-0	A25 1-0	O20 0-1	D08 1-0
6 DERBY CO	D08 1-1	J01 1-1	J12 5-1	A25 1-0	a15 1-0		S08 2-1	M23 2-0	N24 0-0	O20 2-1	S12 3-1	A29 1-0	F16 2-2	F02 1-0	O06 1-1	N03 1-2	a13 4-1	S22 6-2	M02 1-1	D22 2-0	M09 1-1	a27 2-0
7 EVERTON	S29 1-0	M09 4-1	O20 1-0	M23 1-1	F23 1-0	D29 2-1		S01 3-0	J19 0-0	A28 1-1	D08 0-1	D26 2-0	a23 1-0	N24 1-1	a13 4-1	S15 1-0	D15 1-1	a27 0-3	S11 1-1	N03 1-1	O13 1-0	F09 2-1
8 IPSWICH T	M16 2-2	D22 3-0	S22 3-2	F26 1-1	M30 3-0	N10 3-0	J01 3-0		D08 0-3	A25 1-1	a13 1-1	N24 2-1	S08 2-1	S04 1-3	M02 1-1	a15 1-0	a27 0-1	F02 7-0	J12 1-1	O06 0-0	F05 1-3	O27 2-0
9 LEEDS U	F05 3-1	S08 3-0	M23 1-4	F02 1-1	N17 3-0	a06 2-0	A25 3-1	a20 3-2		F26 1-1	O20 1-0	M09 1-0	S22 0-0	M02 1-1	D22 1-0	D01 2-2	a15 0-0	J12 2-1	O06 1-1	J01 1-1	N03 4-1	S05 4-1
10 LEICESTER C	D29 2-0	a06 3-3	N17 2-0	a20 3-0	S29 0-2	M16 0-1	M02 2-1	J19 5-0	O13 2-2		S01 1-1	S15 1-1	S05 1-0	N10 1-0	a29 3-0	D15 2-0	F23 1-1	O27 0-1	a16 1-1	D01 3-0	F09 0-1	D26 2-2
11 LIVERPOOL	a24 0-1	J12 3-2	M02 1-0	S08 1-0	F05 2-1	S04 2-0	a20 0-0	N17 4-2	M16 1-0	J01 1-1		a16 4-0	D22 2-0	O06 2-1	F02 1-0	a06 2-1	O27 1-0	F26 1-0	A25 1-0	S22 3-2	D01 1-0	N10 1-0
12 MANCHESTER C	N10 1-2	A25 3-1	D22 2-0	S22 3-2	S05 1-0	F06 1-0	a02 1-1	a06 1-3	O27 0-1	J12 2-0	a12 1-1		M13 0-0	M27 2-1	S08 2-1	N17 1-0	M16 0-1	O06 1-1	J01 0-0	F02 0-0	a20 2-1	M30 1-1
13 MANCHESTER U	J19 1-1	O20 1-0	a03 3-3	N03 2-2	D15 2-3	O13 0-1	a15 3-0	D29 2-0	F09 0-2	S12 1-2	S29 0-0	a27 0-1		a13 1-0	N24 0-0	S01 2-1	D26 1-2	D08 0-0	A29 1-0	M23 0-1	S15 3-1	F23 0-0
14 NEWCASTLE U	S01 1-1	a20 1-1	a10 1-2	O20 2-0	F09 5-1	D15 0-2	a06 2-1	S12 3-1	D26 0-1	M23 1-1	F23 0-0	O13 1-0	N17 3-2		a15 0-0	S29 2-3	D29 1-0	A29 0-1	N03 2-1	m11 0-2	J19 1-1	S15 2-0
15 NORWICH C	S15 0-4	M20 2-1	a20 1-0	M09 2-2	O13 0-0	F23 2-4	N17 1-3	D26 1-2	S29 0-1	N03 1-0	D15 1-1	D29 1-1	a06 0-2	a17 1-1		A29 0-0	F09 2-1	S12 2-0	M23 4-0	O20 1-1	S01 2-2	J19 1-1
16 Q.P.R.	O27 2-0	S22 2-2	F27 2-1	O06 1-1	N10 3-0	M30 0-0	J12 1-0	a12 0-1	a27 0-1	F02 0-0	N24 2-2	a09 3-0	J01 3-0	D22 3-2	F05 1-2		D08 0-0	A25 1-1	S08 3-3	M02 3-1	S04 0-0	M16 0-0
17 SHEFFIELD U	S04 5-0	N03 1-1	A25 0-2	J01 1-2	a06 0-1	N17 3-0	F02 1-1	M12 0-3	a16 0-2	O06 1-1	a08 1-0	O20 1-2	M02 0-1	S08 1-1	S22 1-0	a20 1-1		D22 4-2	F16 0-0	J12 2-2	M23 1-0	F05 1-0
18 SOUTHAMPTON	D26 1-1	M23 0-2	N03 2-2	a06 0-0	D29 1-1	M05 1-1	D01 2-0	D15 2-0	S15 1-2	M18 1-0	O13 1-0	F23 0-2	a20 1-1	F05 3-1	S04 2-2	J19 2-2	S29 3-0		O20 3-0	N17 1-1	a15 1-1	S01 2-1
19 STOKE C	M30 0-0	N17 5-2	a06 4-0	J27 1-0	O27 3-0	D26 0-0	S05 0-0	S15 1-1	F23 3-2	a15 1-0	J19 1-1	S01 1-1	a29 1-0	a03 2-1	N10 2-0	D29 4-1	O13 1-2	M16 4-1		a20 1-0	S29 2-0	D15 2-3
20 TOTTENHAM H	O13 2-0	F06 4-2	S05 2-3	a03 1-2	J19 2-1	S29 1-0	M30 0-2	F23 1-1	S01 0-3	a27 1-0	m08 1-1	D15 0-2	N10 2-1	O27 0-2	M16 0-0	D26 0-0	S15 1-2	a13 3-1	D08 2-1		D29 2-0	N24 1-3
21 WEST HAM U	N24 1-3	F02 0-0	O06 0-1	M02 3-0	M16 2-3	O27 0-0	F16 4-3	A27 3-3	M30 3-1	S22 1-1	a27 2-2	D08 2-1	J12 2-1	A25 1-2	J01 4-2	S10 2-3	N10 2-2	a12 4-1	D22 0-2	S08 0-1		a13 0-0
22 WOLVERHAMPTON W	a15 3-1	F16 1-0	S08 0-2	D22 2-0	a20 1-1	a09 4-0	S22 1-1	M09 3-1	S11 0-2	a23 1-0	M23 0-1	N03 0-0	O06 2-1	J12 1-0	A25 3-1	O20 2-4	A28 2-0	J01 2-1	F02 1-1	a06 1-1	N17 0-0	

New Middlesbrough manager Jack Charlton appointed Stuart Boam captain and Boam led 'Boro to the Second Division championship in 1973-4.

DIVISION 2

	ASTON VILLA	BLACKPOOL	BOLTON W	BRISTOL C	CARDIFF C	CARLISLE U	CRYSTAL P	FULHAM	HULL C	LUTON T	MIDDLESBROUGH	MILLWALL	NOTTINGHAM F	NOTTS CO	ORIENT	OXFORD U	PORTSMOUTH	PRESTON N.E.	SHEFFIELD W	SUNDERLAND	SWINDON T	W.B.A.
1 ASTON VILLA		a15 0-1	F27 1-1	O20 2-2	O06 5-0	M13 2-1	O23 2-1	S19 1-1	N17 1-1	F02 0-1	J12 1-1	J01 0-0	a24 3-1	D22 1-1	S22 2-2	S08 2-0	M23 4-1	A25 2-0	N03 1-0	a20 1-2	a06 1-1	M02 1-3
2 BLACKPOOL	a16 2-1		M02 0-2	M19 2-2	F16 2-1	a20 4-0	S17 1-0	O22 2-0	a06 1-2	D22 3-0	S22 0-0	S08 1-0	O20 2-2	O06 0-1	J12 1-1	F02 2-0	N03 5-0	M23 3-0	J01 0-0	D01 0-2	N17 2-0	A25 2-3
3 BOLTON W	O13 1-2	D26 1-1		J20 2-1	a06 1-1	F23 2-0	S15 2-0	a02 0-0	S01 1-0	M23 1-0	a15 2-1	O20 0-1	S29 1-0	N17 1-3	S11 1-1	N03 2-1	D29 4-0	a20 0-2	F16 4-2	D05 1-0	D15 2-0	M09 1-1
4 BRISTOL C	M16 0-1	O27 0-1	A25 1-0		F02 3-2	a06 2-0	N10 0-1	M30 0-1	S18 3-1	S08 1-3	D22 1-1	F26 5-2	a12 1-0	D01 2-2	J01 0-2	M02 0-0	a20 0-2	J12 0-0	S22 2-0	N17 2-0	O23 1-0	O06 1-1
5 CARDIFF C	F23 0-1	O13 1-0	N24 1-0	D15 0-1		J19 2-2	a30 1-1	S15 0-0	S29 1-3	N14 0-0	a13 3-2	M23 1-3	D08 1-1	J26 1-0	a27 1-1	S12 5-0	S01 1-1	M09 2-0	O20 0-1	D29 4-1	D26 2-1	N03 0-1
6 CARLISLE U	a27 2-0	D08 2-3	O06 1-0	N24 2-1	A25 1-1		M16 1-0	O27 3-0	N10 4-0	J01 2-0	O23 1-1	D22 1-1	a13 2-1	S08 3-0	F02 3-0	S22 2-1	S18 0-2	M02 2-2	J12 2-2	a16 1-0	M30 5-1	F25 0-1
7 CRYSTAL P	S11 0-0	O02 1-2	J12 0-0	M23 3-1	S22 3-3	O20 0-1		a16 0-2	a20 0-2	O06 1-2	S08 2-3	N17 1-1	N03 0-1	A25 1-4	M03 0-0	F17 2-0	a06 0-0	F03 2-0	D22 0-0	M09 3-0	D01 4-2	J01 1-0
8 FULHAM	O02 1-0	S12 0-0	S22 1-0	N03 2-1	J12 0-1	M09 0-2	a12 1-3		D01 0-0	M05 2-1	M19 0-4	A25 2-0	M23 2-0	F16 2-0	S08 0-3	D22 3-1	N17 2-0	O06 0-0	F02 4-1	O20 0-2	a20 4-1	a06 0-0
9 HULL C	a13 1-1	N24 1-0	J01 0-0	O02 2-1	D22 1-1	M23 1-1	D08 3-0	a27 2-0		M09 1-3	F16 1-3	J12 1-1	S11 0-0	F02 1-0	O06 1-1	A25 0-0	O20 4-1	S08 1-0	M02 2-1	N03 2-0	a15 0-1	S22 0-0
10 LUTON T	D15 1-0	S29 3-0	N10 2-1	D29 1-0	D12 1-0	S01 6-1	F23 2-1	D26 1-1	O27 2-2		M30 0-1	a20 3-0	J19 2-2	F05 1-1	M16 3-1	a16 0-1	S15 3-3	a06 4-2	N17 2-1	m01 3-4	O13 2-1	D01 0-2
11 MIDDLESBROUGH	S15 0-0	F09 0-0	a09 0-0	S29 2-0	N17 3-0	S11 1-0	D29 2-0	S01 0-2	O13 1-0	N03 2-1		M09 2-1	D15 1-0	a06 4-0	O02 3-2	M23 1-0	J19 3-0	D11 3-0	a20 8-0	D26 2-1	F23 2-1	O20 0-0
12 MILLWALL	S01 1-1	D29 2-2	M16 2-1	O13 0-2	N10 2-0	S29 1-2	a13 3-2	J20 1-0	S15 3-0	D08 0-1	O27 0-1		F23 0-0	M30 0-0	N24 0-1	a27 0-0	D26 1-1	O22 5-1	S17 1-0	D15 2-1	F16 3-0	a12 1-0
13 NOTTINGHAM F	O27 1-2	M16 2-0	D22 3-2	a16 1-1	a20 2-1	N17 2-0	M30 1-2	N10 3-0	O23 0-0	A25 4-0	F02 5-1	O06 3-0		M03 0-0	F26 2-1	J01 1-1	M26 2-0	S22 1-1	S08 2-1	a06 2-2	S18 2-0	J12 1-4
14 NOTTS CO	S29 2-0	F23 0-3	a13 0-0	a27 2-1	a15 1-1	D29 0-3	J20 1-3	O13 2-1	D15 3-2	S11 1-1	N24 2-2	N03 3-3	D26 0-1		D08 2-4	O02 0-0	F09 4-0	O20 2-1	M09 1-5	S01 1-4	S15 2-0	M23 1-0
15 ORIENT	m03 1-1	S15 3-2	O22 3-0	S01 0-1	D01 1-2	D15 0-1	D26 3-0	D29 1-0	F23 1-1	O20 2-0	S17 0-0	a06 1-1	O13 2-1	a20 1-1		M10 1-1	a15 2-1	N03 2-2	M23 0-1	J19 2-1	S29 0-0	N17 2-0
16 OXFORD U	D29 2-1	D15 2-2	M30 0-2	D26 5-0	O24 4-2	a23 0-1	O13 1-1	S26 0-0	J19 1-1	a12 1-1	N10 0-2	J26 0-3	S01 1-0	S19 2-1	O27 1-1		F23 3-0	N17 1-1	a06 1-0	S15 0-1	M17 1-1	a20 1-0
17 PORTSMOUTH	N10 2-0	M30 0-0	S08 0-2	D08 1-0	J01 1-0	O02 2-1	N24 2-2	a13 3-0	M16 3-1	J12 0-0	A25 0-1	M02 0-0	a27 0-2	S22 1-2	a12 0-0	O06 2-1		D22 3-0	F20 1-1	S11 1-1	O27 3-1	F03 1-1
18 PRESTON N.E.	J19 0-0	N10 1-3	D08 2-1	S15 1-1	O27 2-2	D26 0-1	D15 1-1	F23 0-1	D29 2-0	N24 2-2	a27 2-4	S11 2-0	F10 2-1	M16 0-2	M30 0-1	a13 0-0	S29 2-1		a12 0-0	O13 1-0	S01 1-1	O01 3-1
19 SHEFFIELD W	a01 2-4	S01 0-0	a27 1-0	F10 3-1	M16 5-0	S15 1-0	S29 4-0	D15 0-3	D26 1-1	a13 2-2	D08 2-2	O03 3-2	D29 1-1	O27 0-0	N10 1-2	N24 0-1	O13 1-2	a15 1-0		F23 0-1	J19 2-1	S12 3-1
20 SUNDERLAND	D08 2-0	a27 2-1	N13 3-0	a13 1-2	S08 1-1	a12 2-1	O27 0-0	M16 1-0	M30 1-0	S22 0-1	M02 0-2	F02 4-0	N24 0-0	J01 1-2	A25 1-1	J12 0-0	M05 3-0	F16 2-1	O06 3-1		N10 4-1	D22 1-1
21 SWINDON T	N24 1-0	a13 1-0	F03 2-2	S11 0-1	M02 1-1	N03 2-2	a27 0-1	D08 1-1	J26 1-1	F26 0-2	O06 0-1	S22 1-3	O02 0-0	F19 1-4	D22 2-2	O20 1-0	M09 1-2	J01 3-1	A25 3-1	M23 0-2		S08 1-0
22 W.B.A.	D26 2-0	J19 1-1	O27 0-0	F23 2-2	M30 2-2	O13 1-1	S01 1-0	N24 2-0	M19 2-3	a27 1-1	M16 0-4	a17 1-1	S15 3-3	N10 2-1	a13 1-0	D08 1-0	D15 1-2	S18 0-2	O24 2-0	S29 1-1	D29 2-0	

Season 1973-74

DIVISION 3

	ALDERSHOT	BLACKBURN R	BOURNEMOUTH	BRIGHTON & HA	BRISTOL R	CAMBRIDGE U	CHARLTON A	CHESTERFIELD	GRIMSBY T	HALIFAX T	HEREFORD U	HUDDERSFIELD T	OLDHAM A	PLYMOUTH A	PORT VALE	ROCHDALE	SHREWSBURY T	SOUTHEND U	SOUTHPORT	TRANMERE R	WALSALL	WATFORD	WREXHAM	YORK C
1 ALDERSHOT		a27 4-0	O24 1-3	M03 0-1	J27 2-3	a13 6-0	O27 2-1	M27 2-2	M16 1-0	D08 2-1	F03 1-0	J12 1-0	O06 0-1	S19 3-2	N10 0-0	M13 4-0	S22 2-2	F17 3-3	J01 4-0	A25 0-0	S08 1-0	M30 1-0	N14 5-1	D22 2-2
2 BLACKBURN R	a24 1-2		M23 4-3	O06 3-1	S22 0-2	O20 2-0	O24 1-1	J12 2-1	S19 1-0	a15 1-1	J01 1-2	M27 1-0	M02 0-1	N03 2-0	a06 1-1	a20 3-1	J27 2-0	A25 1-0	F03 2-1	F17 0-0	D22 0-2	N17 5-0	m01 1-2	S08 4-0
3 BOURNEMOUTH	S12 3-0	N10 1-2		J01 0-0	A25 0-3	D08 1-0	N14 1-0	S08 0-1	a13 1-1	a24 1-1	M02 3-2	D22 1-0	F02 0-3	a12 0-0	M16 2-2	O03 2-0	F16 1-0	J25 1-3	O06 2-0	S22 2-1	J12 1-0	O27 1-0	a27 0-1	M27 1-3
4 BRIGHTON & H.A.	D26 0-1	F23 3-0	S01 0-2		D01 2-8	a03 4-1	S15 1-2	N17 0-0	F09 1-1	O13 0-1	M10 2-1	M23 1-2	S19 1-2	D29 1-0	M20 2-1	J20 2-1	O20 2-0	a15 0-2	O24 4-0	a20 1-3	a06 2-1	S29 0-1	F27 2-1	N03 0-0
5 BRISTOL R	a02 2-1	M12 3-0	J19 3-0	a27 1-1		S29 1-0	S01 2-1	N03 1-0	D29 1-1	S15 2-0	S11 1-1	M08 2-1	a13 1-2	D26 4-2	O13 1-1	M05 1-1	O02 1-0	D08 4-0	N13 3-1	a16 1-0	M23 0-2	F23 1-0	M19 1-0	O20 0-0
6 CAMBRIDGE U	N17 1-2	M16 0-2	a20 2-1	J27 1-1	D22 2-2		N10 1-0	F02 1-2	M30 0-1	O27 0-1	F17 2-0	J01 2-2	S22 1-1	m01 3-1	O24 4-2	a06 3-3	S08 2-1	J12 3-2	A25 2-0	M27 1-0	M03 0-0	S19 3-2	a16 2-1	O06 0-0
7 CHARLTON A	m03 2-0	S11 4-3	a06 0-0	J12 0-4	J01 1-1	M23 2-0		S22 3-3	a15 2-1	O02 5-2	S08 2-0	J26 2-1	M26 4-1	N17 2-0	D01 2-0	O20 3-0	F03 3-3	M03 2-1	D22 0-1	O06 1-0	F17 0-1	a20 1-3	N03 0-0	A25 2-4
8 CHESTERFIELD	J05 0-0	S15 3-0	D29 2-1	a13 1-0	M30 0-0	M13 3-0	F09 3-1		S01 1-0	F23 1-1	D08 1-1	O24 0-2	M16 1-0	J19 1-0	S29 2-1	D26 1-0	a27 0-2	N14 0-0	O27 4-2	N10 1-0	a17 1-0	O13 3-1	a03 2-2	S19 0-2
9 GRIMSBY T	O20 1-0	O02 4-2	N17 1-1	S22 0-0	S08 1-1	N03 1-0	a12 5-0	J01 1-1		S11 4-1	A25 1-3	F02 2-1	a24 2-1	a06 3-0	a20 2-0	J26 5-1	D22 1-2	M26 2-1	F16 2-1	J12 5-0	N06 1-0	a29 2-2	M23 1-1	M02 1-2
10 HALIFAX T	a20 0-0	a16 1-1	N03 1-1	F16 2-2	J12 0-0	M10 0-1	S18 2-1	O06 2-0	a09 1-2		S22 1-1	M02 0-0	A25 0-0	M23 1-0	N17 1-0	a22 1-0	M26 1-0	S08 0-0	J27 1-1	D22 2-1	F03 3-1	a06 0-0	O20 1-2	a30 2-1
11 HEREFORD U	M20 0-2	S01 1-0	D26 0-2	O27 3-0	O24 0-0	O13 0-0	D29 2-3	a20 2-1	J19 2-1	M13 3-1		N17 0-1	N10 3-4	F20 0-1	F23 2-1	a03 2-1	a15 1-1	M16 1-2	M30 3-0	S19 0-2	D01 3-1	S15 1-1	S29 2-0	a06 0-0
12 HUDDERSFIELD T	S15 1-0	J29 1-0	S29 1-1	N10 2-2	O27 1-2	S01 2-1	a02 2-0	S11 1-0	M20 1-0	D26 4-0	a13 0-0		D08 2-1	O13 2-1	D29 3-0	F23 5-0	N13 1-0	M30 0-1	a27 3-1	M16 0-0	O09 2-2	J19 1-2	a24 2-1	a16 0-1
13 OLDHAM A	F23 2-0	D26 2-3	M19 4-2	O02 0-1	N17 1-1	M05 6-1	a30 0-2	O20 0-0	a02 3-1	J19 3-2	M23 1-1	a20 6-0		S29 1-0	S01 1-1	O13 3-1	N03 3-0	S11 2-0	a12 6-0	a06 2-2	M09 2-1	D29 0-3	S15 0-0	M12 2-1
14 PLYMOUTH A	O02 2-1	M30 2-1	a15 2-0	S08 0-1	M02 1-0	a27 4-1	a16 1-0	A25 1-1	N13 1-0	N10 1-1	M26 0-1	F16 1-1	m03 0-0		O27 2-0	S11 5-0	O06 2-2	F02 1-1	J12 4-1	J01 2-0	S22 2-1	M16 2-0	D08 1-2	m06 0-2
15 PORT VALE	M23 0-1	N12 1-2	O20 0-0	F02 2-1	F17 3-1	S10 2-1	a27 3-1	D22 0-1	D08 1-1	a13 1-1	O06 1-3	S08 4-2	J01 3-0	M10 2-1		N03 3-1	A25 3-0	S22 0-0	M02 2-1	J26 1-0	M25 1-1	a16 1-2	O01 1-0	J12 2-2
16 ROCHDALE	a15 2-2	D08 1-2	S17 3-3	A25 1-1	M25 0-1	F05 0-2	M16 1-1	M02 1-2	O27 1-1	a27 1-1	F26 1-1	O06 1-1	F16 1-3	O22 1-3	M30 1-1		J12 3-2	D22 1-1	S22 2-2	S08 0-1	J01 0-1	N10 1-3	a13 0-0	F03 1-3
17 SHREWSBURY T	F10 0-0	a02 3-0	O13 1-1	M16 1-0	S18 0-2	D29 2-0	M19 3-3	D01 0-1	S29 1-1	J05 0-2	a16 1-1	a06 3-0	M30 0-2	F23 0-0	J19 0-1	S15 2-0		O27 1-2	N10 2-0	O23 1-3	a20 0-0	D26 3-2	S01 0-1	N17 0-2
18 SOUTHEND U	O13 2-1	J19 1-1	a01 2-2	a12 0-2	a19 0-0	S14 3-1	D26 2-0	a05 1-3	a22 4-1	D29 1-2	O19 2-1	N03 5-2	O22 2-2	M18 2-0	F09 1-0	S29 1-2	M10 2-0		S17 0-1	D01 1-1	N17 2-1	A31 2-3	F24 1-1	M24 3-3
19 SOUTHPORT	S01 3-0	a08 2-2	F24 1-0	S10 1-1	a05 1-0	J19 0-0	S29 1-2	M09 1-1	O12 0-1	a01 1-1	N02 1-1	D01 0-0	a15 0-2	S15 1-1	D26 0-1	M10 0-0	M23 1-0	O01 0-0		N17 2-2	O19 1-1	J05 1-1	D29 0-2	a19 1-1
20 TRANMERE R	J20 0-1	O12 1-1	F10 1-1	D08 4-1	a12 0-0	a22 5-2	F24 2-0	M23 1-2	S14 0-0	S28 0-1	O08 0-0	O19 1-1	F04 0-2	S01 2-0	a01 3-0	D29 1-1	S10 1-0	a26 2-0	a13 3-1		N02 3-0	a08 1-0	D26 0-1	M09 0-0
21 WALSALL	D29 3-2	S29 2-0	S15 1-2	N13 0-1	N10 0-0	D26 3-0	O13 4-0	a15 2-0	F23 3-1	M19 2-2	a27 3-1	S17 3-0	O27 1-1	F10 0-4	a30 0-0	S01 0-0	D08 2-0	a13 1-2	M17 2-0	M30 0-1		a02 2-2	J20 3-0	O16 0-0
22 WATFORD	N03 2-1	a13 0-0	M09 1-1	D22 1-0	O06 0-0	O03 3-0	D08 1-3	F16 2-1	a27 1-2	N12 0-0	J12 2-1	A25 1-1	S08 0-1	O20 0-3	a24 2-1	M23 4-0	M02 1-0	J01 1-0	M27 4-0	F02 4-2	J26 1-3		S12 2-0	S22 1-1
23 WREXHAM	a06 0-0	O27 2-2	D01 0-1	M25 1-0	F02 1-0	a12 2-1	M30 4-0	M04 2-1	N10 1-1	M16 2-1	D22 5-0	S22 0-0	J12 1-2	a20 5-2	S17 0-0	N17 3-0	J01 3-1	O06 5-1	S08 3-2	M02 0-0	A25 2-0	O22 1-0		F20 1-0
24 YORK C	S29 3-1	D29 1-0	M06 4-1	M30 3-0	M16 2-1	F24 2-0	J19 0-1	O01 0-0	D26 1-1	S01 1-1	N12 0-0	a12 2-1	a27 1-1	a03 1-1	S15 3-1	J05 2-1	a13 0-1	N10 1-0	D08 4-0	O27 2-0	S10 1-1	F10 2-2	O12 1-0	

DIVISION 4

	BARNSLEY	BRADFORD C	BRENTFORD	BURY	CHESTER	COLCHESTER U	CREWE A	DARLINGTON	DONCASTER R	EXETER C	GILLINGHAM	HARTLEPOOL	LINCOLN C	MANSFIELD T	NEWPORT CO	NORTHAMPTON T	PETERBOROUGH U	READING	ROTHERHAM U	SCUNTHORPE U	STOCKPORT CO	SWANSEA C	TORQUAY U	WORKINGTON
1 BARNSLEY		O06 2-2	D22 2-1	N03 3-2	J27 1-1	A25 0-1	N17 2-1	F24 1-0	O23 2-0	M23 3-0	M26 3-1	a20 2-0	S18 0-1	S08 1-1	O20 1-1	a06 0-2	a16 0-0	F03 3-2	M03 1-0	J01 5-0	S22 4-0	M10 1-0	J12 1-0	F17 4-0
2 BRADFORD C	F23 3-0		D08 1-1	D29 4-2	O27 1-1	a27 1-1	S29 0-1	D26 3-0	S01 1-1	J20 1-0	O31 0-0	M06 2-0	F10 4-0	N14 3-1	a03 3-0	O13 1-1	S15 1-1	N10 4-3	S12 2-1	O03 2-1	M17 0-1	M20 3-1	M30 2-1	a13 3-2
3 BRENTFORD	S29 5-1	a20 2-0		F09 1-2	N17 3-0	a16 0-0	a01 3-0	D15 0-0	S15 2-0	S01 0-1	D01 0-3	J19 1-2	F23 2-1	N03 4-1	D26 1-1	M18 3-1	O13 0-1	S17 0-1	O20 1-1	M09 2-1	a06 0-0	J05 0-2	S10 0-0	M23 1-1
4 BURY	M30 2-0	S08 3-0	S22 3-0		O06 3-1	F03 2-0	M17 2-0	O02 5-1	a13 3-1	a12 0-0	F17 3-2	S11 1-0	N13 2-1	J27 2-0	a27 5-0	O27 3-1	N10 0-2	J12 1-0	D22 3-1	M26 0-0	M03 1-1	D08 0-2	A25 4-0	J01 3-1
5 CHESTER	a03 3-1	M10 1-0	a13 0-0	F24 1-1		N14 0-4	D26 1-0	F10 1-0	O13 3-0	S15 0-1	O20 2-4	A31 3-1	S29 2-3	O03 1-1	D29 3-0	m01 0-0	M20 2-1	a27 0-0	N03 1-0	M23 2-0	a16 2-1	J19 1-0	D08 1-1	S12 1-0
6 COLCHESTER U	J19 2-0	D01 4-0	a12 2-1	M19 1-1	a05 1-1		S01 3-2	O12 3-0	a02 3-0	S28 1-0	a20 0-2	F22 3-0	J05 4-1	M22 1-0	S15 4-1	D29 1-0	D26 1-1	S11 0-0	M08 0-1	O19 2-0	N17 3-1	F08 2-0	O02 2-2	N02 3-0
7 CREWE A	a13 0-1	D22 1-0	J26 0-0	O20 1-0	M03 1-0	J01 1-2		N03 1-1	D08 4-0	M10 2-5	A25 1-0	M23 1-3	a27 2-1	S22 1-1	O03 4-1	a16 0-2	N14 2-1	M27 2-1	S08 1-8	J12 1-0	O06 1-3	S12 0-0	F17 0-0	F03 1-0
8 DARLINGTON	a27 4-2	M03 2-1	S08 1-2	S17 0-0	S22 1-2	F16 1-0	M30 3-0		O27 1-0	O22 1-0	J12 1-3	a16 1-1	M17 0-3	D22 1-0	a13 0-1	N10 2-3	D08 2-2	J01 2-1	O06 1-1	F03 3-0	J26 1-1	N12 1-1	J27 0-0	A25 0-0
9 DONCASTER R	S11 1-0	J01 2-2	J12 1-2	N17 1-1	F17 1-2	J27 2-0	a20 0-2	M10 0-0		a06 1-0	D22 1-2	O20 2-2	a16 2-0	M26 0-0	M22 2-0	a23 2-1	O02 3-1	O06 0-0	F03 1-2	M02 1-0	A25 1-1	N03 3-1	S07 0-1	S22 5-2
10 EXETER C	N10 6-1	A25 0-0	J01 2-1	a15 0-3	J12 2-1	D22 1-0	O27 2-0	S12 3-0	N14 1-2		O06 2-1	O03 2-0	a13 0-1	M09 1-1	D08 0-1	M16 1-1	M30 1-2	S22 0-1	a30 0-0	a22 4-0	M27 2-1	a27 2-0	M02 4-2	S08 1-1
11 GILLINGHAM	J05 1-1	a15 2-0	a27 1-0	O13 3-0	M17 1-0	D08 4-1	J20 3-0	S15 0-1	S29 5-1	F23 2-1		F10 3-0	a24 2-0	a13 2-2	S01 1-1	D26 3-1	a03 1-0	M30 0-1	O03 1-1	S12 7-2	O27 2-1	D29 1-1	N10 2-1	N14 4-0
12 HARTLEPOOL	D08 1-2	M27 1-0	A25 1-0	O22 1-1	J01 0-0	O06 0-0	N10 1-0	a12 1-2	M17 3-0	S17 1-3	S22 2-1		O27 0-2	F17 4-0	N12 0-1	J05 1-0	a27 0-1	S08 1-2	J12 2-0	D22 3-0	F03 3-0	a13 0-1	J26 0-0	M03 3-0
13 LINCOLN C	O03 1-1	S22 0-1	O06 3-2	a06 4-3	D22 2-2	M27 0-1	D01 4-2	O20 2-1	a15 3-3	N17 2-1	F03 2-3	M09 0-1		M03 1-1	N03 3-0	a20 1-1	S12 1-1	F17 0-2	J27 2-1	A25 1-0	S08 1-1	M23 2-2	J01 3-0	J12 2-0
14 MANSFIELD T	D29 2-2	a06 0-0	M30 1-1	a01 1-2	S17 3-0	N10 2-2	F10 1-2	S29 1-0	a29 2-0	M18 3-3	N17 2-2	O13 2-0	D26 4-3		F24 2-1	S01 2-0	J20 2-1	M16 1-1	D01 3-0	a20 2-2	O22 5-0	S15 2-1	O27 2-1	a17 2-0
15 NEWPORT CO	M17 1-0	a22 2-2	M02 1-1	D01 1-0	S08 0-2	J12 1-3	S18 4-2	N17 2-0	N09 3-1	J27 2-1	J01 3-3	a06 0-0	M30 0-1	O09 2-0		O23 3-1	O27 0-1	A25 0-0	S22 1-0	F17 2-1	D22 3-1	a16 2-1	F03 2-2	M25 4-0
16 NORTHAMPTON T	N13 2-1	F17 3-0	F02 0-0	M09 3-1	M26 3-3	S07 0-0	a15 1-1	M24 5-0	a27 3-1	O20 1-2	M03 0-0	N03 1-0	D08 1-0	J01 2-0	S11 1-0		a13 0-1	J27 3-3	A25 3-1	S21 2-0	J12 2-0	O02 2-0	O05 0-0	D22 1-0
17 PETERBOROUGH U	a15 3-0	J12 1-1	F16 1-0	M23 2-2	F02 0-0	M02 2-0	a06 4-0	a20 1-0	S17 5-1	N03 2-0	m01 4-2	D01 2-0	O22 1-0	A25 2-1	M09 2-0	N17 3-0		D22 2-0	M26 2-0	S08 1-0	J01 3-2	O20 3-0	S22 1-1	O06 2-0
18 READING	M20 1-0	M24 0-0	O03 1-0	S15 2-2	a22 3-0	O24 1-1	J05 2-0	S01 2-0	F24 5-0	F10 4-1	N03 0-1	D29 1-1	O13 0-0	O20 3-0	J19 1-1	a03 1-2	S29 1-1		N17 1-0	a06 0-0	a20 1-1	D26 1-2	a12 4-0	M10 2-0
19 ROTHERHAM U	D26 2-1	O23 2-1	M16 1-1	S29 1-0	M30 3-2	O27 0-0	D29 1-1	F23 0-1	M19 1-2	O13 4-0	S18 1-1	S15 2-2	a02 2-0	a27 2-1	F10 1-1	J20 1-2	m11 3-1	a13 1-1		a15 1-1	N10 1-2	S01 1-0	N13 1-0	D08 1-1
20 SCUNTHORPE U	S01 3-0	S18 2-1	O27 4-1	a30 1-2	N10 2-1	M16 1-0	S14 0-0	M19 1-0	D26 2-1		O23 1-1	S29 1-1	J19 1-1	D08 5-3	O13 0-0	F10 1-2	D29 2-1	N13 1-0	a16 3-0		M30 2-1	F23 0-0	a13 0-0	a27 0-1
21 STOCKPORT CO	F10 1-1	O20 0-1	N12 1-1	D26 3-2	a15 0-1	D15 0-3	F24 0-0	a01 1-2	J20 0-0	J05 0-1	M10 2-0	a22 1-1	D29 2-2	S10 1-1	S28 1-1	S14 2-2	S01 1-1	D08 0-0	M23 0-1	N02 3-1		O13 0-1	a26 2-1	O01 1-1
22 SWANSEA C	O27 2-0	F03 0-1	M26 0-0	a20 0-1	A25 2-0	S22 2-0	O23 2-0	a06 0-0	M30 0-0	D01 2-0	S08 0-3	N17 0-0	N10 3-0	J12 2-0	a15 1-1	S18 1-1	M16 0-2	M03 2-1	J01 4-2	O06 1-2	F17 3-0		D22 0-1	J27 1-0
23 TORQUAY U	S15 1-1	N03 1-0	O24 3-0	J19 1-2	a20 2-2	S19 0-4	O13 2-1	J05 0-0	D29 3-0	D26 0-0	M23 0-1	a03 0-2	S01 2-1	M10 4-0	D15 3-2	F24 1-0	m07 1-2	a15 1-1	a06 3-0	N17 1-1	D01 2-2	S29 3-1		O20 3-0
24 WORKINGTON	O13 1-0	N17 1-0	N10 0-2	S01 0-0	O24 1-1	M30 1-4	a24 0-0	J20 5-2	F10 3-1	D15 3-1	a06 3-3	D26 0-2	S15 1-1	a15 0-0	J05 3-2	S29 1-0	F24 4-1	O27 0-0	a20 0-2	a10 1-2	S19 1-1	a03 1-0	M17 3-1	

LEAGUE TABLES

DIVISION 1

	P	W	D	L	F	A	W	D	L	F	A	Pts
Leeds U	42	12	8	1	38	18	12	6	3	28	13	62
Liverpool	42	18	2	1	34	11	4	11	6	18	20	57
Derby Co	42	13	7	1	40	16	4	7	10	12	26	48
Ipswich T	42	10	7	4	38	21	8	4	9	29	37	47
Stoke C	42	13	6	2	39	15	2	10	9	15	27	46
Burnley	42	10	9	2	29	16	6	5	10	27	37	46
Everton	42	12	7	2	29	14	4	5	12	21	34	44
QPR	42	8	10	3	30	17	5	7	9	26	35	43
Leicester C	42	10	7	4	35	17	3	9	9	16	24	42
Arsenal	42	9	7	5	23	16	5	7	9	26	35	42
Tottenham H	42	9	4	8	26	27	5	10	6	19	23	42
Wolves	42	11	6	4	30	18	2	9	10	19	31	41
Sheffield U	42	7	7	7	25	22	7	5	9	19	27	40
Manchester C	42	10	7	4	25	17	4	5	12	14	29	40
Newcastle U	42	9	6	6	28	21	4	6	11	21	27	38
Coventry C	42	10	5	6	25	18	4	5	12	18	36	38
Chelsea	42	9	4	8	36	29	3	9	9	20	31	37
West Ham U	42	7	7	7	36	32	4	8	9	19	28	37
Birmingham C	42	10	7	4	30	21	2	6	13	22	43	37
Southampton	42	8	10	3	30	20	3	4	14	17	48	36
Manchester U	42	7	7	7	23	20	3	5	13	15	28	32
Norwich C	42	6	9	6	25	27	1	6	14	12	35	29

DIVISION 2

	P	W	D	L	F	A	W	D	L	F	A	Pts
Middlesbrough	42	16	4	1	40	8	11	7	3	37	22	65
Luton T	42	12	5	4	42	25	7	7	7	22	26	50
Carlisle U	42	13	5	3	40	17	7	4	10	21	31	49
Orient	42	9	8	4	28	17	6	10	5	27	25	48
Blackpool	42	11	5	5	35	17	6	8	7	22	23	47
Sunderland	42	11	6	4	32	15	8	3	10	26	29	47
Nottingham F	42	12	6	3	40	19	3	9	9	17	24	45
WBA	42	8	9	4	28	24	6	7	8	20	21	44
Hull C	42	9	9	3	25	15	4	8	9	21	32	43
Notts Co	42	8	6	7	30	35	7	7	7	25	25	43
Bolton W	42	12	5	4	30	17	3	7	11	14	23	42
Millwall	42	10	6	5	28	16	4	8	9	23	25	42
Fulham	42	11	4	6	26	20	5	6	10	13	23	42
Aston Villa	42	8	9	4	33	21	5	6	10	15	24	41
Portsmouth	42	9	8	4	26	16	5	4	12	19	46	40
Bristol C	42	9	5	7	25	20	5	5	11	22	34	38
Cardiff C	42	8	7	6	27	20	2	9	10	22	42	36
Oxford U	42	8	8	5	27	21	2	8	11	8	25	36
Sheffield W	42	9	6	6	33	24	3	5	13	18	39	35
Crystal P	42	6	7	8	24	24	5	5	11	19	32	34
Preston NE	42	7	8	6	24	23	2	6	13	16	39	*31
Swindon T	42	6	7	8	22	27	1	4	16	14	45	25

**Preston North End had one point deducted for fielding an ineligible player*

DIVISION 3

	P	W	D	L	F	A	W	D	L	F	A	Pts
Oldham A	46	13	6	4	50	23	12	6	5	33	24	62
Bristol R	46	15	6	2	37	15	7	11	5	28	18	61
York C	46	13	8	2	37	15	8	11	4	30	23	61
Wrexham	46	15	6	2	44	15	7	6	10	19	28	56
Chesterfield	46	14	6	3	31	16	7	8	8	24	26	56
Grimsby T	46	14	6	3	48	21	4	9	10	19	29	51
Watford	46	12	6	5	34	21	7	6	10	30	35	50
Aldershot	46	13	6	4	47	22	6	5	12	18	30	49
Halifax T	46	9	11	3	23	15	5	10	8	25	36	49
Huddersfield T	46	14	5	4	37	16	3	8	12	19	39	47
Bournemouth	46	11	5	7	25	23	5	10	8	29	35	47
Southend U	46	10	7	6	40	30	6	7	10	22	32	46
Blackburn R	46	13	4	6	38	21	5	6	12	24	43	46
Charlton A	46	13	5	5	43	29	6	3	14	23	44	46
Walsall	46	11	7	5	37	19	5	6	12	20	29	45
Tranmere R	46	10	8	5	31	15	5	7	11	19	29	45
Plymouth A	46	13	6	4	37	17	4	4	15	22	37	44
Hereford U	46	10	5	8	31	25	4	10	9	22	32	43
Brighton & HA	46	10	3	10	31	31	6	8	9	21	27	43
Port Vale	46	12	6	5	37	23	2	8	13	15	35	42
Cambridge U	46	11	7	5	36	27	2	2	19	12	54	35
Shrewsbury T	46	7	7	9	24	24	3	4	16	17	38	31
Southport	46	4	14	5	19	20	2	2	19	16	62	28
Rochdale	46	1	12	10	24	38	1	5	17	14	56	21

DIVISION 4

	P	W	D	L	F	A	W	D	L	F	A	Pts
Peterboro' U	46	19	4	0	49	10	8	7	8	26	28	65
Gillingham	46	16	5	2	51	16	9	7	7	39	33	62
Colchester U	46	16	5	2	46	14	8	7	8	27	22	60
Bury	46	18	3	2	51	14	6	8	9	30	35	59
Northampton T	46	14	7	2	39	14	6	6	11	24	34	53
Reading	46	11	9	3	37	13	5	10	8	21	24	51
Chester	46	13	6	4	31	19	4	9	10	23	36	49
Bradford C	46	14	7	2	45	20	3	7	13	13	32	48
Newport Co	46	13	6	4	39	23	3	8	12	17	42	*45
Exeter C	45	12	5	6	37	20	6	3	13	21	35	†44
Hartlepool	46	11	4	8	29	16	5	8	10	19	31	44
Lincoln C	46	10	8	5	40	30	6	4	13	23	37	44
Barnsley	46	15	5	3	42	16	2	5	16	16	48	44
Swansea C	46	11	6	6	28	15	5	5	13	17	31	43
Rotherham U	46	10	9	4	33	22	5	4	14	23	36	43
Torquay U	46	11	7	5	37	23	2	10	11	15	34	43
Mansfield T	46	13	8	2	47	24	0	9	14	15	45	43
Scunthorpe U	45	12	7	3	33	17	2	5	16	14	47	†42
Brentford	46	9	7	7	31	20	3	9	11	17	30	40
Darlington	46	9	8	6	29	24	4	5	14	11	38	39
Crewe A	46	11	5	7	28	30	3	5	15	15	41	38
Doncaster R	46	10	7	6	32	22	2	4	17	15	58	35
Workington	46	10	8	5	33	26	1	5	17	10	48	35
Stockport Co	46	4	12	7	22	25	3	8	12	22	44	34

**Newport County had one point deducted for fielding an ineligible player. †Scunthorpe United awarded points after Exeter City failed to turn up.*

Football League Records

Top scorers: Div 1, M.Macdonald (Newcastle United) 21 goals; Div 2, B.Little (Aston Villa) 20 goals; Div 3, R.McNeil (Hereford United) 31 goals; Div 4, R.Clarke (Mansfield Town) 28 goals.

Archie Gemmill, Derby's Scottish midfield dynamo, who in the absence of the injured Roy McFarland, proved an inspirational captain as the Rams lifted the League Championship for the second time.

DIVISION 1

	ARSENAL	BIRMINGHAM C	BURNLEY	CARLISLE U	CHELSEA	COVENTRY C	DERBY CO	EVERTON	IPSWICH T	LEEDS U	LEICESTER C	LIVERPOOL	LUTON T	MANCHESTER C	MIDDLESBROUGH	NEWCASTLE U	Q.P.R.	SHEFFIELD U	STOKE C	TOTTENHAM H	WEST HAM U	WOLVERHAMPTON W
1 ARSENAL		M15 1-1	S07 0-1	J11 2-1	D26 1-2	a08 2-0	N16 3-1	M01 0-2	A20 0-1	a12 1-2	D14 0-0	F01 2-0	S21 2-2	A24 4-0	N30 2-0	M18 3-0	O12 2-2	M31 1-0	M29 1-1	a26 1-0	O26 3-0	N02 0-0
2 BIRMINGHAM C	S28 3-1		F01 1-1	M25 2-0	N02 2-0	O05 1-2	S14 3-2	J18 0-3	D28 0-1	O15 1-0	A20 3-4	D21 3-1	a19 1-4	N16 4-0	A17 0-3	O19 3-0	M22 4-1	a29 0-0	D07 0-3	F18 1-0	M18 1-1	A31 1-1
3 BURNLEY	M22 3-3	N09 2-2		D28 2-1	A27 1-2	A31 3-0	M31 2-5	O26 1-1	O15 1-0	S14 2-1	F08 2-0	M08 1-1	J18 1-0	O12 2-1	D21 1-1	N23 4-1	D07 3-0	F22 2-1	a26 0-0	a12 3-2	S28 3-5	A17 1-2
4 CARLISLE U	D07 2-1	S21 1-0	a01 4-2		D14 1-2	a05 0-0	O19 3-0	M29 3-0	J18 2-1	N23 1-2	M01 0-1	O05 0-1	M15 1-2	S24 0-0	A27 0-1	D26 1-2	F22 1-2	F08 0-1	S07 0-2	A24 1-0	N09 0-1	a19 1-0
5 CHELSEA	S14 0-0	F08 2-1	A21 3-3	A17 0-2		N13 3-3	M08 1-2	a26 1-1	M31 0-0	J18 0-2	N09 0-0	A31 0-3	D07 2-0	a12 0-1	M22 1-2	F22 3-2	D28 0-3	a23 1-1	O26 3-3	O12 1-0	D21 1-1	S28 0-1
6 COVENTRY C	N23 3-0	a12 1-0	M01 0-3	O26 2-1	A24 1-3		A27 1-1	S21 1-1	F22 3-1	N09 1-3	M15 2-2	N30 1-1	S24 2-1	S07 2-2	a26 0-2	D14 2-0	F08 1-1	M28 2-2	D26 2-0	F15 1-1	O12 1-1	J11 2-1
7 DERBY CO	F22 2-1	D26 2-1	S21 3-2	a26 0-0	S25 4-1	A21 1-1		D14 0-1	N23 2-0	F08 0-0	O12 1-0	J11 2-0	M29 5-0	a01 2-1	O26 2-3	S07 2-2	N09 5-2	A24 2-0	M15 1-2	M01 3-1	a12 1-0	a09 1-0
8 EVERTON	A31 2-1	N30 4-1	a04 1-1	D21 2-3	O19 1-1	M31 1-0	A17 0-0		M22 1-1	S28 3-2	J11 3-0	N16 0-0	F25 3-1	N02 2-0	D28 1-1	O05 1-1	M08 2-1	a19 2-3	A20 2-1	F01 1-0	O15 1-1	S14 0-0
9 IPSWICH T	A27 3-0	a01 3-2	A24 2-0	N30 3-1	S21 2-0	N16 4-0	F25 3-0	S07 1-0		O12 0-0	M29 2-1	N02 1-0	D26 0-1	O26 1-1	J11 2-0	M15 5-4	a12 2-1	M01 0-1	S24 3-1	D14 4-0	a26 4-1	F01 2-0
10 LEEDS U	O05 2-0	A24 1-0	D26 2-2	F25 3-1	N30 2-0	F01 0-0	N02 0-1	M15 0-0	a19 2-1		M31 2-2	a05 0-2	S07 1-1	M01 2-2	N16 2-2	M29 1-1	A21 0-1	S21 5-1	D14 3-1	D04 2-1	J11 2-1	O19 2-0
11 LEICESTER C	A17 0-1	A28 1-1	N02 1-0	A31 1-1	F01 1-1	S28 0-1	a19 0-0	D07 0-2	D20 0-1	D28 0-2		M19 1-1	O05 0-0	M08 1-0	a09 1-0	a05 4-0	S14 3-1	O19 3-0	J18 1-1	N16 1-2	a01 3-0	M22 3-2
12 LIVERPOOL	N09 1-3	M29 1-0	S24 0-1	a12 2-0	M01 2-2	J18 2-1	D07 2-2	F22 0-0	F08 5-2	O26 1-0	A24 2-1		D14 2-0	D26 4-1	O12 2-0	M25 4-0	a26 3-1	M15 0-0	S21 3-0	S07 5-2	N23 1-1	A27 2-0
13 LUTON T	M25 2-0	O12 1-3	N30 2-3	S28 3-1	J11 1-1	M08 1-3	D21 1-0	a09 2-1	S14 1-4	M22 2-1	a12 3-0	A17 1-2		a26 1-1	O16 0-1	F08 1-0	A31 1-1	N09 0-1	F22 0-0	O26 1-1	A28 0-0	D28 3-2
14 MANCHESTER C	O16 2-1	F22 3-1	a19 2-0	M19 1-2	O05 1-1	M22 1-0	D28 1-2	F08 2-1	a23 1-1	A31 2-1	N23 4-1	S14 2-0	O19 1-0		M28 2-1	J18 5-1	S28 1-0	D07 3-2	N09 1-0	A21 1-0	A17 4-0	D21 0-0
15 MIDDLESBROUGH	J18 0-0	D14 3-0	M29 2-0	A20 0-2	S07 1-1	O19 4-4	a05 1-1	M18 2-0	D07 3-0	F22 0-1	D10 3-0	a19 1-0	A24 1-1	S21 3-0		N09 0-0	N23 1-3	D26 1-0	M01 2-0	M15 3-0	F08 0-0	O05 2-1
16 NEWCASTLE U	a23 3-1	a26 1-2	F15 3-0	S14 1-0	N16 5-0	A17 3-2	M22 0-2	a12 0-1	S28 1-0	D21 3-0	O26 0-1	F12 4-1	N02 1-0	N30 2-1	F01 2-1		M31 2-2	A21 2-2	O12 2-2	J11 2-5	A31 2-0	O16 0-0
17 Q.P.R.	a19 0-0	S07 0-1	J11 0-1	N16 2-1	M18 1-0	N02 2-0	F01 4-1	S24 2-2	O05 1-0	A27 1-1	D26 4-2	O19 0-1	M01 2-1	M15 2-0	F25 0-0	S21 1-2		D14 1-0	A24 0-1	M29 0-1	N30 0-2	a05 2-0
18 SHEFFIELD U	D28 1-1	O26 3-2	N16 2-2	N02 2-1	F15 2-1	D20 1-0	O15 1-2	O12 2-2	A31 3-1	a01 1-1	a26 4-0	S28 1-0	F01 1-1	J11 1-1	S14 1-0	A27 2-1	A17 1-1		a12 2-0	N30 0-1	M22 3-2	M08 1-0
19 STOKE C	D21 0-2	J11 0-0	O19 2-0	M22 5-2	a05 3-0	S14 2-0	S28 1-1	A28 1-1	M18 1-2	A17 3-0	N30 1-0	M31 2-0	N16 4-2	F01 4-0	A31 1-1	a19 0-0	N27 1-0	O05 3-2		N02 2-2	D28 2-1	F15 2-2
20 TOTTENHAM H	O19 2-0	N23 0-0	O05 2-3	O16 1-1	a19 2-0	D28 1-1	A31 2-0	N09 1-1	A17 0-1	a28 4-2	F22 0-3	M22 0-2	a05 2-1	A28 1-2	S28 1-2	D07 3-0	D21 1-2	J18 1-3	F08 0-2		S14 2-1	M28 3-0
21 WEST HAM U	a28 1-0	S25 3-0	M15 2-1	F01 2-0	M29 0-1	a19 1-2	O05 2-2	A24 2-3	O19 1-0	D07 2-1	S21 6-2	F19 0-0	A19 2-0	D14 0-0	N02 3-0	F28 0-1	J18 2-2	S07 1-2	M28 2-2	D26 1-1		N16 5-2
22 WOLVERHAMPTON W	F08 1-0	M01 0-1	D14 4-2	O12 2-0	M15 7-1	D07 2-0	J18 0-1	D26 2-0	N09 2-1	a26 1-1	S07 1-1	A20 0-0	M31 5-2	M29 1-0	a12 2-0	A24 4-2	O26 1-2	S24 1-1	N23 2-2	S21 2-3	F22 3-1	

Manchester United's Stuart Pearson, signed by Tommy Docherty from Hull for £200,000. His 17 goals in 1974-5 helped United straight back to Division One.

DIVISION 2

	ASTON VILLA	BLACKPOOL	BOLTON W	BRISTOL C	BRISTOL R	CARDIFF C	FULHAM	HULL C	MANCHESTER U	MILLWALL	NORWICH C	NOTTINGHAM F	NOTTS CO	OLDHAM A	ORIENT	OXFORD U	PORTSMOUTH	SHEFFIELD W	SOUTHAMPTON	SUNDERLAND	W.B.A.	YORK C
1 ASTON VILLA		O12 1-0	M05 0-0	J11 2-0	D26 1-0	a09 2-0	F08 1-1	A28 6-0	F22 2-0	S21 3-0	A24 1-1	O02 3-0	N09 0-1	a12 5-0	S07 3-1	N29 0-0	N23 2-0	O26 3-1	M15 3-0	a26 2-0	M29 3-1	D14 4-0
2 BLACKPOOL	a19 0-3		A24 2-1	F15 2-0	M15 0-0	S24 4-0	J18 1-0	O05 1-2	O19 0-3	S07 1-0	D14 2-1	M29 0-0	D07 3-1	D26 1-0	A20 0-0	N16 0-0	a05 2-2	N02 3-1	M01 3-0	F01 3-2	M31 2-0	S21 1-1
3 BOLTON W	A31 1-0	O22 0-0		M22 0-2	J18 5-1	O19 2-1	D28 0-0	a19 1-1	M08 0-1	F01 2-0	F15 0-0	N02 2-0	S28 1-1	N12 1-1	O05 2-0	D21 3-1	A17 3-0	S14 0-1	N16 3-2	M31 0-2	D07 0-1	a05 1-1
4 BRISTOL C	D07 1-0	N23 0-1	S07 2-1		a01 1-1	D26 0-0	a26 3-1	J18 2-0	N09 1-0	M15 2-1	M29 0-1	D14 1-0	O26 3-0	M01 3-1	A24 0-0	N05 3-0	F08 3-1	a12 1-0	S21 2-0	O12 1-1	F22 2-1	S24 0-0
5 BRISTOL R	S14 2-0	S28 1-3	N30 1-0	D28 1-4		O05 1-0	M11 1-2	A31 2-0	M28 1-1	O19 2-0	F01 0-2	a05 4-2	A17 0-0	J11 2-1	N16 0-0	F15 1-0	D21 0-1	S17 1-1	N02 0-1	M22 2-1	O22 2-1	a19 1-3
6 CARDIFF C	D28 3-1	M08 1-1	a26 1-2	S14 0-1	a12 2-2		D11 0-0	S28 1-2	A31 0-1	F14 0-1	J11 2-1	N16 2-1	D21 0-0	O26 3-1	F01 0-0	A17 1-1	a02 1-0	M22 0-0	N29 2-2	N02 2-0	O12 0-2	O16 3-2
7 FULHAM	N02 3-1	N30 1-0	M28 2-1	O19 1-1	S25 0-0	A24 4-0		F01 1-1	O05 1-2	M04 0-0	S21 4-0	J11 0-1	A28 3-0	M15 0-0	D26 0-0	a22 0-0	a19 2-2	F25 2-1	M24 3-2	N16 1-3	D14 1-0	S07 0-2
8 HULL C	A20 1-1	a12 1-0	O12 2-0	N30 1-0	M01 2-0	M15 1-1	N09 2-1		N23 2-0	S24 1-1	S07 0-0	D26 1-3	F08 1-0	S21 1-1	M29 0-0	J11 1-0	F22 0-0	a26 1-0	D14 1-1	O26 3-1	A24 1-0	M31 2-0
9 MANCHESTER U	N16 2-1	a26 4-0	S25 3-0	F01 0-1	S21 2-0	M01 4-0	a12 1-0	F15 2-0		A24 4-0	M15 1-1	S07 2-2	O12 1-0	M31 3-2	D14 0-0	N02 4-0	A28 2-1	J11 2-0	O26 1-0	N30 3-2	D26 2-1	M29 2-1
10 MILLWALL	a01 1-3	M22 0-0	N09 1-1	S28 1-0	a26 1-1	J25 5-1	A31 2-0	M08 2-0	S16 0-1		a12 1-1	A19 3-0	J18 3-0	F08 0-0	D07 1-1	S14 0-0	D28 0-0	D21 2-1	O12 4-0	A17 1-4	O26 2-2	F22 1-3
11 NORWICH C	a30 1-4	A17 2-1	N23 2-0	D21 3-2	N09 0-1	D07 1-1	M31 1-2	M22 1-0	S28 2-0	O05 2-0		a19 3-0	S14 3-0	F22 1-0	a05 2-0	D28 1-0	O19 2-0	A31 1-1	A21 1-0	M08 0-0	F08 3-2	J18 2-3
12 NOTTINGHAM F	M08 2-3	D21 0-0	F08 2-3	A17 0-0	O26 1-0	F22 0-0	D07 1-1	S14 4-0	M22 0-1	A27 2-1	O12 1-3		D28 0-2	N09 1-0	J18 2-2	A31 1-2	S17 1-2	a01 1-0	a12 0-0	S28 1-1	a26 2-1	N23 2-1
13 NOTTS CO	F01 1-3	J11 0-0	M15 1-1	a05 1-2	D14 3-2	M29 0-2	A20 1-1	N02 5-0	a19 2-2	N30 2-1	D26 1-1	M25 2-2		A24 1-0	S24 1-1	O19 4-1	O05 1-1	N16 3-3	S07 3-2	F15 0-0	S21 0-0	M01 2-1
14 OLDHAM A	O05 1-2	S14 1-0	F04 1-0	A31 2-0	D07 3-4	a05 4-0	S28 1-0	M28 0-1	D28 1-0	N02 1-1	N16 2-2	F01 2-0	O15 1-0		a19 0-0	M22 1-1	M08 2-0	A17 2-1	F15 1-1	D21 0-0	J18 0-0	O19 2-3
15 ORIENT	M22 1-0	A27 0-0	a12 0-0	a15 1-0	F22 1-0	N09 1-1	S14 0-0	D21 0-0	A17 0-2	J11 2-1	O26 0-3	N30 1-1	M08 0-1	O12 3-1		M31 1-1	A31 1-1	S28 1-0	a26 2-1	D28 1-1	N23 0-2	F08 1-0
16 OXFORD U	J18 1-2	F22 0-0	M29 2-1	O23 2-0	N23 2-1	D14 1-0	O26 2-1	D07 3-1	F08 1-0	D26 3-1	J25 2-1	F28 1-1	a26 1-2	S07 1-0	S21 1-2		N09 1-0	O12 1-0	S25 0-4	a12 1-0	M15 1-1	A24 3-1
17 PORTSMOUTH	F18 2-3	O26 0-0	D14 2-0	N02 0-1	M29 3-0	S21 2-2	O12 0-0	N16 1-1	O15 0-0	M31 1-0	a26 0-3	A24 2-0	a12 1-1	S24 1-1	F28 3-0	F01 2-1		N30 1-0	D26 1-2	J11 4-2	S07 1-3	M15 1-0
18 SHEFFIELD W	a23 0-4	F08 0-0	D26 0-2	O05 1-1	A24 1-1	S07 1-2	N23 1-0	O19 2-1	D07 4-4	M29 0-1	a08 0-1	S21 2-3	F22 0-1	D14 1-1	M15 0-1	a19 1-1	J18 0-2		M31 0-1	O02 0-2	S25 0-0	N09 3-0
19 SOUTHAMPTON	S28 0-0	A31 1-1	F22 0-1	M28 0-1	F08 3-0	a22 2-0	D21 0-0	A17 3-3	a05 0-1	a18 3-2	A27 1-1	O05 0-1	M22 3-2	J25 1-0	O19 4-2	M18 2-1	S14 2-1	D28 0-1		J14 1-1	N09 1-0	D07 2-1
20 SUNDERLAND	O19 0-0	N09 1-0	S21 0-0	a19 3-0	S07 5-1	F08 3-1	F22 1-2	a05 1-0	J18 0-0	D14 2-0	S24 0-0	M15 0-0	N23 3-0	M25 2-2	M28 3-0	O05 2-0	D07 4-1	O15 3-0	A24 3-1		M01 3-0	D26 2-0
21 W.B.A.	D21 2-0	D28 2-0	a08 0-1	N16 1-0	N06 2-2	a19 2-0	A17 0-1	S18 2-2	S14 1-1	a05 2-1	N02 1-1	O19 0-1	a02 4-1	N30 1-0	F15 1-0	S28 3-0	M22 2-1	M08 4-0	F01 0-3	A31 1-0		O05 2-0
22 YORK C	A17 1-1	a01 0-0	O26 1-3	M08 1-0	O12 3-0	A27 1-0	M22 3-2	D28 3-0	D21 0-1	N16 2-1	N30 1-0	F14 1-1	A31 2-2	a26 0-0	N01 0-1	S17 1-1	S28 3-0	J31 3-0	J10 1-1	S14 0-1	a12 1-3	

Season 1974-75

DIVISION 3

	ALDERSHOT	BLACKBURN R	BOURNEMOUTH	BRIGHTON & HA	BURY	CHARLTON A	CHESTERFIELD	COLCHESTER U	CRYSTAL P	GILLINGHAM	GRIMSBY T	HALIFAX T	HEREFORD U	HUDDERSFIELD T	PETERBOROUGH U	PLYMOUTH A	PORT VALE	PRESTON N.E.	SOUTHEND U	SWINDON T	TRANMERE R	WALSALL	WATFORD	WREXHAM
1 ALDERSHOT		F22 1-1	J18 1-2	M31 2-1	O19 1-1	N09 3-0	D07 1-0	S21 0-1	J25 2-1	D26 2-1	M15 0-0	O02 3-1	M19 2-2	A24 1-0	a05 5-0	S04 4-3	O05 2-1	S07 1-2	M29 3-0	F12 0-1	F28 2-0	a19 0-0	F08 3-1	S25 1-2
2 BLACKBURN R	N16 2-0		O05 1-0	S07 1-0	N02 1-0	J11 3-1	a19 2-0	A24 3-2	N06 1-1	O02 4-1	M19 1-1	S21 1-0	M29 1-0	M28 1-1	F01 0-1	F15 5-2	O19 2-2	D26 3-0	S25 1-0	M01 2-0	M15 2-1	a05 3-3	N30 0-0	a28 0-0
3 BOURNEMOUTH	N30 1-0	a12 0-0		S21 2-0	N16 2-1	O26 1-2	F25 0-0	M01 0-2	O12 4-0	A24 2-0	O23 0-1	M29 0-1	D26 2-1	J04 1-1	m05 2-1	J11 3-7	N02 1-2	M15 1-0	S07 0-0	M31 1-1	M18 0-0	F01 0-1	a26 4-2	O02 0-2
4 BRIGHTON & H.A.	D28 2-0	M22 0-1	M26 2-1		S28 0-0	M08 1-1	A31 2-1	J25 2-0	A17 1-0	a05 4-3	O16 3-1	a16 0-0	F22 2-1	a19 2-0	a23 2-0	D21 2-2	S18 1-1	O19 0-4	D07 2-0	N09 1-1	F08 3-1	a09 1-0	S14 2-0	O05 3-3
5 BURY	a26 2-1	F08 1-2	F22 1-0	M15 2-1		O12 2-1	F04 1-1	S24 0-0	N09 2-2	F11 0-1	S07 1-1	D26 4-1	M28 3-0	S21 3-0	N05 3-0	O26 0-1	J11 3-1	O01 2-0	A24 0-1	M18 0-0	M29 3-1	N30 2-0	a12 1-0	M01 2-2
6 CHARLTON A	F01 3-1	D07 2-1	a05 2-3	S24 2-1	a19 0-1		O19 3-2	J01 4-1	J17 1-0	F28 2-1	M29 1-1	M18 3-1	A24 2-0	S07 1-0	O05 3-0	N02 0-2	F15 2-2	a29 3-1	M15 2-1	S21 3-3	O01 3-3	N16 4-2	O22 4-1	J04 1-1
7 CHESTERFIELD	J11 0-2	O12 1-2	O16 0-0	M01 2-4	F15 2-0	a26 2-0		S07 1-1	a12 2-1	M29 2-1	S21 2-0	F19 1-1	M15 4-1	D26 3-0	N16 2-0	N30 1-2	F01 1-0	M31 0-0	M19 1-1	O02 0-2	S25 1-0	N02 2-2	O26 4-4	A24 3-1
8 COLCHESTER U	J04 0-0	a22 2-0	A31 1-0	F15 2-2	m02 3-2	S14 3-0	M22 1-2		D20 1-1	O05 4-2	N15 5-0	a04 2-0	N06 1-2	F01 3-2	D28 4-1	S17 1-0	O15 2-0	a19 2-2	O29 1-1	M04 2-0	D06 2-1	S28 1-2	A17 1-1	N02 1-1
9 CRYSTAL P	F15 3-0	O22 1-0	a19 4-1	M18 3-0	F01 2-2	N30 2-1	O05 1-4	M25 2-1		a29 4-0	O01 3-0	F28 1-1	J04 2-2	M15 1-1	N02 1-1	N16 3-3	a05 1-1	S24 1-0	D26 1-1	S07 6-2	A24 2-1	O19 1-0	J11 1-0	S21 2-0
10 GILLINGHAM	S14 0-0	a09 1-1	a23 1-0	O26 2-1	S18 1-0	A31 0-1	D21 4-0	a12 2-1	D28 3-1		a26 2-0	N09 4-0	O12 2 3	J11 3-2	S28 1-1	M31 2-2	M22 0-0	N06 2-1	F08 2-1	F22 3-1	J25 2-3	A17 2-2	M08 2-1	N30 2-1
11 GRIMSBY T	S28 2-0	A17 1-2	M08 0-0	O08 3-2	M22 2-0	D21 1-1	M28 2-0	F22 1-1	a08 2-1	O19 2-1		D07 2-1	M04 0-0	O05 1-2	S14 1-2	a22 1-1	A31 3-0	a05 2-1	J18 0-0	F08 2-0	N09 3-2	D28 0-0	S17 2-2	a19 2-0
12 HALIFAX T	a08 1-0	a01 1-1	D21 3-2	N30 1-0	S14 0-1	A17 2-2	S17 1-3	O26 1-1	A31 3-1	F01 1-1	J11 1-1		a26 2-2	N16 2-1	M08 2-1	D28 1-1	S28 1-1	N02 3-0	O15 3-1	O12 0-0	a12 0-0	a22 1-0	M22 2-0	F15 1-0
13 HEREFORD U	A17 2-0	D21 6-3	S14 0-1	N16 2-0	D28 1-1	a23 2-2	S28 5-0	O23 3-1	S18 2-0	a19 1-1	F15 3-2	O19 0-0		N02 1-1	A31 2-0	M08 1-5	M31 1-0	O05 2-2	a05 1-0	D07 2-1	J18 2-0	M22 2-0	S04 0-1	F01 1-0
14 HUDDERSFIELD T	a22 2-2	D28 1-2	D03 2-2	O12 1-0	a01 0-0	M22 1-3	S14 2-0	N09 3-2	S28 0-1	D07 0-2	a12 1-0	F22 1-2	F08 2-1		A17 1-2	a08 0-2	M08 3-1	J18 0-1	M04 4-1	O26 2-2	a26 0-0	D21 3-2	A31 3-1	O22 0-0
15 PETERBOROUGH U	O26 1-1	N09 1-0	a16 3-0	A24 2-0	O16 3-1	a12 1-1	F22 0-2	M28 1 0	F08 1 1	M15 0-0	D26 1-3	S25 1-1	M01 1-1	M19 2-1		a26 1-0	N30 0-2	S21 0-0	O02 1-0	M29 0-0	a30 1-2	J11 0-0	O12 1-0	S07 2-1
16 PLYMOUTH A	O15 1-0	F04 2-1	D07 1-0	M29 2-2	a05 2-1	F08 1-1	J18 3-0	a15 1-0	F22 0-1	S21 1-1	A24 2-1	M28 2-0	S24 1-0	O01 2-0	O19 2-0		a19 1-1	M18 2-1	F28 1-0	D26 4-3	S07 4-1	O05 2-1	N09 1-1	M15 0-3
17 PORT VALE	a12 3-1	a26 1-4	F08 0-0	a28 1-0	D07 1-0	M03 1-0	N09 3-2	S30 2-2	O26 2-1	S07 2-1	M01 1-0	M15 2-1	S21 3-0	D14 4-0	J18 1-3	O12 2-0		M29 2-1	a01 0-0	A24 2-2	D26 1-0	N04 1-1	F22 0-0	M17 2-0
18 PRESTON N.E.	M22 3-1	S14 0-0	S28 5-2	a26 1-0	S03 3-0	S17 2-0	D28 2-1	O12 0-2	M08 1-1	O22 1-0	O20 2-0	F08 1-0	a12 2-2	N30 4-0	a01 1-1	A17 1-0	D21 1-0		N09 1-4	F18 2-0	F22 1-0	A31 3-2	a22 2-2	J11 3-1
19 SOUTHEND U	D23 1-1	M08 2-2	M21 0-0	J11 1-0	a21 1-0	S27 2-1	A17 2-1	a25 1-1	S13 0-1	N01 2-2	N29 3-0	S02 4-0	O25 0-0	F15 1-0	O07 1-2	A30 2-1	D28 1-3	F01 1-1		a11 2-0	O11 1-0	S16 3-0	M28 0-0	N16 1-1
20 SWINDON T	S17 3-2	A31 2-0	D28 2-1	F04 1-0	A17 0-2	a01 2-0	N05 1 0	N30 4 1	M22 1-1	N16 1-0	N02 3-2	a19 3-1	J11 1-0	a05 4-1	D21 0-1	S14 2-0	a22 3-2	F15 1-0	O05 2-0		S03 0-0	M08 3-0	S28 2-2	O19 2-1
21 TRANMERE R	A31 2-0	S27 1-1	A17 0-1	N02 1-2	D21 0-0	a07 0-1	M07 1-2	J10 2-0	m07 2-0	F14 1-1	J31 3-1	O04 3-1	N29 6-1	O19 1-2	a09 1-0	M21 1-3	S13 1-0	N15 3-1	a18 2-1	O21 3-0		M28 3-0	D28 2-2	a03 0-1
22 WALSALL	O11 3-0	O26 1-3	N09 2-0	O01 6-0	J18 3-0	F22 0-1	F08 2-2	M15 5-2	a25 3-0	M18 1-1	J14 2-0	A24 1-1	S07 3-1	M29 2-0	D07 0-1	a12 0-0	O08 0-0	F28 2-0	F04 3-0	S24 2-0	S21 1-0		F19 2-0	D26 2-1
23 WATFORD	N02 1-1	J18 0-0	O19 1-0	D26 1-1	O05 2-1	N06 0-2	a05 2-2	M19 1-2	D07 1-2	S25 0-0	J04 3-2	S07 2-2	O02 1-1	F28 1-0	a19 0-3	F01 1-3	N16 3-2	A24 3-2	S21 2-0	M15 1-0	a14 1-0	a29 2-3		M29 1-2
24 WREXHAM	M08 4-0	N25 1-1	a07 1-1	a12 2-1	A31 3-1	D28 0-3	a21 0-0	F08 2-1	M31 0-0	J18 0-1	O12 2 3	F04 4 0	N09 2 1	N04 3 0	M22 1-2	S28 5-1	A17 2-2	D07 1-1	F22 1-1	a26 1-2	O26 1-0	S14 0-0	D21 5-1	

DIVISION 4

	BARNSLEY	BRADFORD C	BRENTFORD	CAMBRIDGE U	CHESTER	CREWE A	DARLINGTON	DONCASTER R	EXETER C	HARTLEPOOL	LINCOLN C	MANSFIELD T	NEWPORT CO	NORTHAMPTON T	READING	ROCHDALE	ROTHERHAM U	SCUNTHORPE U	SHREWSBURY T	SOUTHPORT	STOCKPORT CO	SWANSEA C	TORQUAY U	WORKINGTON
1 BARNSLEY		F01 2-2	N02 1-1	S17 1-1	A31 0-1	M08 1-1	a19 1-1	F15 0-1	A17 1-0	O19 2-1	N16 0-2	O15 1-3	S28 2-1	D21 5-1	a05 2-0	M22 5-3	F25 1-1	S03 2-2	J18 1-0	J04 3-0	S13 2-0	a22 1-0	D07 0-1	O05 0-1
2 BRADFORD C	N09 2-0		O23 1-0	M22 1-1	S14 2-0	A17 1-2	J18 1-1	O12 2-0	S04 0-1	J29 3-0	a12 1-2	F08 1-1	S18 0-1	a23 2-1	F22 1-3	D28 1-0	a16 1-1	A31 3-0	O26 1-2	D21 1-2	S28 2-0	M31 1-2	D14 3-0	D07 1-1
3 BRENTFORD	F08 3-0	N04 0-0		S14 1-0	M22 1-1	S28 1-0	D07 3-0	a12 1-1	D28 2-0	F22 1-0	O12 1-1	N09 2-3	a01 0-0	A17 1-0	J25 1-0	M08 3-0	S16 3-4	D21 2-0	a26 2-1	a21 1-0	a07 3-0	A31 1-0	O26 3-1	J18 2-2
4 CAMBRIDGE U	J14 2-0	S06 0-1	D26 2-0		S03 3-0	a04 2-0	M14 1-0	M28 4-1	O18 1-1	O01 3-2	S21 5-0	S24 2-2	N16 1-1	N01 3-4	M18 1-0	F01 1-1	N30 0-0	a19 2-0	O15 0-2	O04 1-0	J11 1-0	F15 2-0	F28 3-1	A23 3-0
5 CHESTER	M01 2-1	D26 1-0	S07 2-0	O23 1-1		O19 2-0	a16 1-0	O02 3-0	a05 1-1	A24 3-0	M19 4-1	M15 0-0	F15 4-1	F01 4-1	S25 2-0	N02 4-0	J11 0-1	O05 1-0	J04 1-1	a19 3-0	N30 3-1	N16 3-0	S21 3-0	M29 0 0
6 CREWE A	S25 1-1	M19 0-0	M15 1-1	O26 0-0	a26 0-1		M29 2-1	S21 2-1	O23 2-1	S07 2-0	A24 1-0	D26 0-2	O12 1-2	J18 3-1	J04 1-0	D07 0-1	M05 1-0	F08 1-1	F28 0-0	N09 0-0	F22 2-0	a12 2-2	O02 0-1	D14 0-0
7 DARLINGTON	O12 0-0	N30 0-3	J11 2-1	S28 6-0	D28 1-1	D21 1-0		a26 4-1	M08 2-0	N09 1-2	O26 1-4	a12 2-1	a21 3-0	M22 2-0	F08 0-1	S16 1-2	a01 0-1	S14 3-1	J25 1-2	S02 1-1	A31 0-2	A17 3-2	O14 2-2	O21 2-0
8 DONCASTER R	J24 1-1	a19 4-1	O05 2-1	D21 0-1	N05 1-1	a01 2-1	O19 1-3		a22 3 3	D07 3 0	O15 2 2	F22 4-3	A31 0-2	M08 2-0	J18 1-1	S13 4-1	S28 0-0	S17 1-1	N08 1-3	D28 1-1	A17 2-1	M21 3-2	F08 3-0	a05 0-0
9 EXETER C	D14 4-2	O02 1-0	M31 1-0	a26 1-4	O26 1-0	N06 2-0	S25 4-1	A24 2-1		J04 1-0	M01 1-2	S07 0-1	a12 3-1	D07 2-2	S21 0-2	J18 2-1	F22 0-4	N09 0-0	M29 1-0	F08 1-0	J24 4-1	O12 1-2	D26 0-0	M15 1-0
10 HARTLEPOOL	a26 4-3	F15 1-2	N16 3-2	a07 1-1	a21 1-0	M22 1-1	F01 2-0	J11 2-1	M10 0-3		F12 2-0	O26 2-1	A17 2-0	J01 2-0	N06 2-3	D21 5-0	S14 3-2	M28 1-0	a12 1-1	A31 1-1	M08 1-1	S28 0-2	O12 0-0	N02 3-0
11 LINCOLN C	F22 3-0	O05 2-1	a19 1-1	M31 0-0	A17 2-1	a23 0-0	a05 1-1	N13 4-0	A31 5-0	J17 2-0		F25 0-0	a09 5-2	S14 2-2	D06 1-1	S28 3-0	M22 2-0	D28 1-0	F08 3-0	S18 1-1	J20 2-0	M08 1-3	N08 3-1	O19 3-0
12 MANSFIELD T	O21 2-1	N02 3-0	F01 1-1	M07 2-1	S27 0-0	S14 0-0	O05 4-2	N16 5-2	M21 3-2	a05 2-0	a14 3-1		D28 3-0	O28 3-0	O19 1-1	A30 2-0	D21 1-1	a21 7-0	D07 3-1	A17 2-1	a01 1-1	O07 3-0	J18 3-0	a19 1-0
13 NEWPORT CO	M15 3-4	J04 2-1	S21 1-0	F22 1-2	J25 3-0	a19 1-1	A24 2-1	F28 0-2	O05 1-2	M17 2-0	M03 1-1	M31 2-1		O18 2-1	a15 2-2	a05 3-2	F08 1-1	D07 2-0	S07 2-4	J17 1-0	N09 3-3	S03 3-0	M29 2-1	S24 3-1
14 NORTHAMPTON T	M28 2-1	A24 1-2	J04 0-0	F08 1-2	N09 2-0	N29 3-0	S06 3-0	S24 2-0	J11 1-1	a01 3-0	D26 1-0	M25 0-2	a25 3-2		F20 0-3	N05 0-1	a12 1-1	F11 3-0	S21 3-3	F22 1-1	O11 4-1	O26 5-1	a15 1-1	O01 3-0
15 READING	O26 0-3	N16 1-1	F15 1-0	A17 2-0	M08 2-1	S18 1-1	N02 3-0	N30 2-0	a02 3-0	F24 0-0	J11 1-0	a26 1-1	S14 3-0	A31 3-2		a09 2-1	a23 1-1	M22 1-1	O12 1-2	S28 4-1	D28 1-3	D21 1-2	a12 1-0	F01 3-0
16 ROCHDALE	S07 3-1	F17 1-1	S23 0-0	N09 0-0	F08 0-1	J11 3-0	J04 2-0	D26 2-0	N30 1-1	M29 3-0	M15 1-1	M01 0-1	O26 2-4	O21 2-2	S30 0-2		O12 1-2	F22 4-2	M17 0-0	M11 3-3	a12 3-0	a26 1-0	A24 1-1	S21 2-0
17 ROTHERHAM U	M31 2-0	S24 4-0	F04 3-0	J18 0-0	D07 1-2	F15 1-1	S21 1-1	M15 1-0	N16 1-1	D26 1-2	S07 2-2	M29 2-1	N02 1-1	O05 1-3	A24 2-1	a19 3-1		a05 3-2	O01 0-0	O19 3-0	N06 3-0	F01 1-0	M18 3-1	M01 1-0
18 SCUNTHORPE U	O01 1-0	M01 1-2	a15 1-2	O12 2-0	a12 1-3	N02 1-1	D26 1-1	J04 0-0	F01 2-1	S21 1-1	a01 1-1	A24 0-1	J11 4-1	F15 2-1	S07 0-1	N16 2-2	O26 0-3		M15 1-0	O15 3-3	a26 0-0	N30 1-2	S24 0-2	M18 2-1
19 SHREWSBURY T	N30 3-1	a05 3-2	O19 1-0	D28 1-0	S17 2-0	A31 0-1	F15 2-0	F01 7-4	D21 2-2	O05 0-1	N02 0-4	J11 0-1	M22 1-0	M31 6-0	a19 2-0	A17 1-1	a08 3-1	S28 5-0		M08 1-0	a22 0-0	S14 2-0	N05 2-0	N16 2-0
20 SOUTHPORT	S20 1-0	M28 1-2	A24 3-0	a11 2-2	O11 2-1	J31 1-1	O01 1-0	M31 2-1	N02 3-0	F28 0-0	a28 3-2	M18 1-1	N30 1-3	N15 0-0	D13 2-0	F14 1-0	a26 2-0	a08 1-0	S25 1-2		O25 2-1	J10 3-0	S06 1-1	D26 2-2
21 STOCKPORT CO	D26 0-3	M14 1-1	S30 1-1	D06 1-0	J17 1-1	N15 1-0	F28 2-1	M17 0-2	F15 3-2	O28 1-1	J20 0-0	S20 3-2	J31 1-1	a18 1-0	M31 1-0	O04 2-3	O21 1-0	O19 3-2	A24 0-3	a04 0-0		N01 2-1	J03 0-0	S06 1-3
22 SWANSEA C	A24 0-3	S21 1-1	F28 0-1	M04 2-1	F22 0-1	O05 2-1	A27 1-0	S07 3-3	a19 0-2	M15 1-0	S24 2-1	O01 1-2	O15 2-0	a05 1-0	M29 1-2	O18 3-3	N08 0-2	J18 1-0	D26 1-4	D06 2-2	F08 1-0		M28 0-1	J04 0-1
23 TORQUAY U	J11 1-1	O19 0-1	a05 3-2	A31 1-0	M31 3-0	S04 1-0	N16 0-0	N02 2-0	S14 2-2	a19 2-1	F01 1-3	N30 0-2	D21 0-1	S28 0-1	O05 2-1	a23 3-0	A17 0-3	M08 1-1	O23 1-1	M22 3-2	S18 2-2	D28 0-0		F15 2-1
24 WORKINGTON	a12 1-2	J11 0-0	N30 0-1	a23 1-2	D21 0-0	D28 3-0	N06 1-2	O26 0-3	S28 0-1	a15 1-1	a26 0-2	O12 1-3	M08 3-1	a09 2-2	N08 2-1	M31 2-1	A31 0-2	A17 1-1	F22 0-2	S14 0-1	M22 1-0	S18 2-0	J25 2-1	

LEAGUE TABLES

DIVISION 1

	P	W	D	L	F	A	W	D	L	F	A	Pts
Derby Co	42	14	4	3	41	18	7	7	7	26	31	53
Liverpool	42	14	5	2	44	17	6	6	9	16	22	51
Ipswich T	42	17	2	2	47	14	6	3	12	19	30	51
Everton	42	10	9	2	33	19	6	9	6	23	23	50
Stoke C	42	12	7	2	40	18	5	8	8	24	30	49
Sheffield U	42	12	7	2	35	20	6	6	9	23	31	49
Middlesbrough	42	11	7	3	33	14	7	5	9	21	26	48
Manchester C	42	16	3	2	40	15	2	7	12	14	39	46
Leeds U	42	10	8	3	34	20	6	5	10	23	29	45
Burnley	42	11	6	4	40	29	6	5	10	28	38	45
QPR	42	10	4	7	25	17	6	6	9	29	37	42
Wolves	42	12	5	4	43	21	2	6	13	14	33	39
West Ham U	42	10	6	5	38	22	3	7	11	20	37	39
Coventry C	42	8	9	4	31	27	4	6	11	20	35	39
Newcastle U	42	12	4	5	39	23	3	5	13	20	49	39
Arsenal	42	10	6	5	31	16	3	5	13	16	33	37
Birmingham C	42	10	4	7	34	28	4	5	12	19	33	37
Leicester C	42	8	7	6	25	17	4	5	12	21	43	36
Tottenham H	42	8	4	9	29	27	5	4	12	23	36	34
Luton T	42	8	6	7	27	26	3	5	13	20	39	33
Chelsea	42	4	9	8	22	31	5	6	10	20	41	33
Carlisle U	42	8	2	11	22	21	4	3	14	21	38	29

DIVISION 2

	P	W	D	L	F	A	W	D	L	F	A	Pts
Manchester U	42	17	3	1	45	12	9	6	6	21	18	61
Aston Villa	42	16	4	1	47	6	9	4	8	32	26	58
Norwich C	42	14	3	4	34	17	6	10	5	24	20	53
Sunderland	42	14	6	1	41	8	5	7	9	24	27	51
Bristol C	42	14	5	2	31	10	7	3	11	16	23	50
WBA	42	13	4	4	33	15	5	5	11	21	27	45
Blackpool	42	12	6	3	31	17	2	11	8	7	16	45
Hull C	42	12	8	1	25	10	3	6	12	15	43	44
Fulham	42	9	8	4	29	17	4	8	9	15	22	42
Bolton W	42	9	7	5	27	16	6	5	10	18	25	42
Oxford U	42	14	3	4	30	19	1	9	11	11	32	42
Orient	42	8	9	4	17	16	3	11	7	11	23	42
Southampton	42	10	6	5	29	20	5	5	11	24	34	41
Notts Co	42	7	11	3	34	26	5	5	11	15	33	40
York C	42	9	7	5	28	18	5	3	13	23	37	38
Nottingham F	42	7	7	7	24	23	5	7	9	19	32	38
Portsmouth	42	9	7	5	28	20	3	6	12	16	34	37
Oldham A	42	10	7	4	28	16	0	8	13	12	32	35
Bristol R	42	10	4	7	25	23	2	7	12	17	41	35
Millwall	42	8	9	4	31	19	2	3	16	13	37	32
Cardiff C	42	7	8	6	24	21	2	6	13	12	41	32
Sheffield W	42	3	7	11	17	29	2	4	15	12	35	21

DIVISION 3

	P	W	D	L	F	A	W	D	L	F	A	Pts
Blackburn R	46	15	7	1	40	16	7	9	7	28	29	60
Plymouth A	46	16	5	2	38	19	8	6	9	41	39	59
Charlton A	46	15	5	3	51	29	7	6	10	25	32	55
Swindon T	46	18	3	2	43	17	3	8	12	21	41	53
Crystal P	46	14	8	1	48	22	4	7	12	18	35	51
Port Vale	46	15	6	2	37	19	3	9	11	24	35	51
Peterboro' U	46	10	9	4	24	17	9	3	11	23	36	50
Walsall	46	15	5	3	46	13	3	8	12	21	39	49
Preston NE	46	16	5	2	42	19	3	6	14	21	37	49
Gillingham	46	14	6	3	43	23	3	8	12	22	37	48
Colchester U	46	13	7	3	45	22	4	6	13	25	41	47
Hereford U	46	14	6	3	42	21	2	8	13	22	45	46
Wrexham	46	10	8	5	41	23	5	7	11	24	32	45
Bury	46	13	6	4	38	17	3	6	14	15	33	44
Chesterfield	46	11	7	5	37	25	5	5	13	25	41	44
Grimsby T	46	12	8	3	35	19	3	5	15	20	45	43
Halifax T	46	11	10	2	33	20	2	7	14	16	45	43
Southend U	46	11	9	3	32	17	2	7	14	14	34	42
Brighton & HA	46	14	7	2	38	21	2	3	18	18	43	42
Aldershot	46	13	5	5	40	21	1	6	16	13	42	*38
Bournemouth	46	9	6	8	27	25	4	6	13	17	33	38
Tranmere R	46	12	4	7	39	21	2	5	16	16	36	37
Watford	46	9	7	7	30	31	1	10	12	22	44	37
Huddersfield T	46	9	6	8	32	29	2	4	17	15	47	32

Aldershot had one point deducted for fielding an unregistered player

DIVISION 4

	P	W	D	L	F	A	W	D	L	F	A	Pts
Mansfield T	46	17	6	0	55	15	11	6	6	35	25	68
Shrewsbury T	46	16	3	4	46	18	10	7	6	34	25	62
Rotherham U	46	13	7	3	40	19	9	8	6	31	22	59
Chester	46	17	5	1	48	9	6	6	11	16	29	57
Lincoln C	46	14	8	1	47	14	7	7	9	32	34	57
Cambridge U	46	15	5	3	43	16	5	9	9	19	28	54
Reading	46	13	6	4	38	20	8	4	11	25	27	52
Brentford	46	15	6	2	38	14	3	7	13	15	31	49
Exeter C	46	14	3	6	33	24	5	8	10	27	39	49
Bradford C	46	10	5	8	32	21	7	8	8	24	30	47
Southport	46	13	7	3	36	19	2	10	11	20	37	47
Newport Co	46	13	5	5	43	30	6	4	13	25	45	47
Hartlepool	46	13	6	4	40	24	3	5	15	12	38	43
Torquay U	46	10	7	6	30	25	4	7	12	16	36	42
Barnsley	46	10	7	6	34	24	5	4	14	28	41	41
Northampton T	46	12	6	5	43	22	3	5	15	24	51	41
Doncaster R	46	10	9	4	41	29	4	3	16	24	50	40
Crewe A	46	9	9	5	22	16	2	9	12	12	31	40
Rochdale	46	9	9	5	35	22	4	4	15	24	53	39
Stockport Co	46	10	8	5	26	27	2	6	15	17	43	38
Darlington	46	11	4	8	38	27	2	6	15	16	40	36
Swansea C	46	9	4	10	25	31	6	2	15	21	42	36
Workington	46	7	5	11	23	29	3	6	14	13	37	31
Scunthorpe U	46	7	8	8	27	29	0	7	16	14	49	29

Football League Records

Top scorers: Div 1, E.MacDougall (Norwich City) 23 goals; Div 2, D.Hales (Charlton Athletic) 28 goals; Div 3, R.McNeil (Hereford United) 35 goals; Div 4, R.Moore (Tranmere Rovers) 34 goals.

Liverpool and England goalkeeper Ray Clemence was in the middle of a remarkably consistent run as the Reds gained another Championship trophy. Clemence did not miss a League game for four seasons.

DIVISION 1

	ARSENAL	ASTON VILLA	BIRMINGHAM C	BURNLEY	COVENTRY C	DERBY CO	EVERTON	IPSWICH T	LEEDS U	LEICESTER C	LIVERPOOL	MANCHESTER C	MANCHESTER U	MIDDLESBROUGH	NEWCASTLE U	NORWICH C	Q.P.R.	SHEFFIELD U	STOKE C	TOTTENHAM H	WEST HAM U	WOLVERHAMPTON W
1 ARSENAL		J10 0-0	F21 1-0	D20 1-0	O11 5-0	N08 0-1	S20 2-2	a17 1-2	D06 1-2	S06 1-1	F24 1-0	O04 2-3	N22 3-1	O25 2-1	M16 0-0	A26 2-1	D27 2-0	J31 1-0	A23 0-1	a03 0-2	M20 6-1	a13 2-1
2 ASTON VILLA	S13 2-0		S27 2-1	O25 1-1	A30 1-0	a19 1-0	N22 3-1	M06 0-0	A16 1-2	N29 1-1	a10 0-0	A27 1-0	F21 2-1	a24 2-1	J17 1-1	D13 3-2	J31 0-2	N08 5-1	M27 0-0	O11 1-1	D26 4-1	F24 1-1
3 BIRMINGHAM C	N15 3-1	a03 3-2		S20 4-0	M20 1-1	D06 2-1	A23 0-1	a13 3-0	O18 2-2	D20 2-1	M13 0-1	F14 2-1	A19 0-2	F07 2-1	S23 3-2	F28 1-1	S06 1-1	O04 2-0	D27 1-1	a17 3-1	N01 1-5	J10 0-1
4 BURNLEY	A16 0-0	F28 2-2	a10 1-0		a24 1-3	J17 1-2	A19 1-1	F07 0-1	S27 0-1	F17 1-0	D06 0-0	M13 0-0	a19 0-1	A30 4-1	D26 0-1	S13 4-4	O18 1-0	F24 3-1	N01 0-1	M20 1-2	D13 2-0	N15 1-5
5 COVENTRY C	M13 1-1	a13 1-1	N29 3-2	O04 1-2		A19 1-1	D19 1-2	S06 0-0	F28 0-1	a03 0-2	O18 0-0	A23 2-0	F07 1-1	S23 0-1	M27 1-1	N15 1-0	N01 1-1	J10 1-0	S20 0-3	D27 2-2	F14 2-0	a17 3-1
6 DERBY CO	F18 2-0	D27 2-0	M27 4-2	S06 3-0	J31 2-0		a21 1-3	O04 1-0	N01 3-2	a17 2-2	F28 1-1	S20 1-0	S24 2-1	N29 3-2	A27 3-2	M13 3-1	A23 1-5	D20 3-2	M24 1-1	J10 2-3	N15 2-1	O18 3-2
7 EVERTON	a10 0-0	O18 2-1	D13 5-2	J31 2-3	A16 1-4	A30 2-0		D06 3-3	M20 1-3	N01 1-1	S27 0-0	N15 1-1	D23 1-1	a19 3-1	S13 3-0	J17 1-1	M13 0-2	A26 3-0	a07 2-1	F24 1-0	a24 2-0	F28 3-0
8 IPSWICH T	D26 2-0	N01 3-0	A30 4-2	A26 0-0	J17 1-1	a24 2-6	M27 1-0		D13 2-1	O18 1-1	S13 2-0	a07 2-1	a10 3-0	S27 0-3	A16 0-3	S23 2-0	N15 1-1	N29 1-1	M13 1-1	J31 1-2	a19 4-0	F17 3-0
9 LEEDS U	M27 3-0	D20 1-0	N22 3-0	a03 2-1	O25 2-0	M02 1-1	N29 5-2	A23 1-0		D27 4-0	A26 0-3	a17 2-1	O11 1-2	F21 0-2	N08 3-0	J31 0-3	O04 2-1	a14 0-1	J10 2-0	S20 1-1	M09 1-1	S06 3-0
10 LEICESTER C	J17 2-1	M20 2-2	A16 3-3	N08 3-2	S27 0-3	D26 2-1	M06 1-0	N22 0-0	a20 2-1		A30 1-1	J31 1-0	a24 2-1	O11 0-0	D13 1-0	a10 0-0	F25 0-1	F21 1-1	A27 1-1	O25 2-3	S13 3-3	D06 2-0
11 LIVERPOOL	D02 2-2	S20 3-0	O11 3-1	M27 2-0	N22 1-1	O25 1-1	a03 1-0	J10 3-3	F07 2-0	a06 1-0		D27 1-0	N08 3-1	M06 0-2	F21 2-0	N29 1-3	D20 2-0	S06 1-0	a17 5-3	A23 3-2	A19 2-2	O04 2-0
12 MANCHESTER C	a24 3-1	F07 2-1	N08 2-0	O11 0-0	D13 4-2	a10 4-3	F21 3-0	O25 1-1	D26 0-1	A20 1-1	a19 0-3		S27 2-2	S13 4-0	A30 4-0	A16 3-0	D06 0-0	M06 4-0	S24 1-0	N22 2-1	J17 3-0	M20 3-2
13 MANCHESTER U	O18 3-1	N15 2-0	J31 3-1	D27 2-1	A27 1-1	F25 1-1	a17 2-1	S20 1-0	M13 3-2	O04 0-0	F18 0-0	m04 2-0		M27 3-0	N29 1-0	N01 1-0	J10 2-1	A23 5-1	a21 0-1	S06 3-2	F28 4-0	D20 1-0
14 MIDDLESBROUGH	F28 0-1	O04 0-0	A26 2-0	F14 1-1	F24 2-0	M20 0-2	D27 1-1	a03 2-0	N15 0-0	M13 0-1	N01 0-1	J10 1-0	D06 0-0		J31 3-3	a06 0-1	S20 0-0	a17 3-0	S06 3-0	D20 1-0	O18 3-0	A23 1-0
15 NEWCASTLE U	N01 2-0	S06 3-0	a07 4-0	a17 0-1	D06 4-0	F07 4-3	J10 5-0	D20 1-1	M31 2-3	A23 3-0	N15 1-2	a14 2-1	M20 3-4	A20 1-1		O18 5-2	a03 1-2	D27 1-1	M03 0-1	O04 2-2	M13 2-1	S20 5-1
16 NORWICH C	F07 3-1	A23 5-3	O25 1-0	J10 3-1	F21 0-3	O11 0-0	S06 4-2	M31 1-0	A20 1-1	S20 2-0	M20 0-1	D20 2-2	M17 1-1	N08 0-1	N22 1-2		a17 3-2	a03 1-3	O04 0-1	M06 3-1	D06 1-0	D27 1-1
17 Q.P.R.	a19 2-1	A19 1-1	J17 2-1	N22 1-0	M06 4-1	D13 1-1	O11 5-0	F21 3-1	a24 2-0	S23 1-0	A16 2-0	M27 1-0	S13 1-0	a10 4-2	S27 1-0	D26 2-0		O25 1-0	N29 3-2	N08 0-0	A30 1-1	F07 4-2
18 SHEFFIELD U	A19 1-3	F14 2-1	m04 1-1	S23 2-1	S13 0-1	A16 1-1	F07 0-0	M20 1-2	A30 0-2	N15 1-2	J17 0-0	N01 2-2	D13 1-4	D26 1-1	a19 1-0	S27 0-1	F28 0-0		O18 0-2	D06 1-2	a10 3-2	M13 1-4
19 STOKE C	D13 2-1	D06 1-1	a19 1-0	M06 4-1	a10 0-1	S27 1-0	N08 3-2	O11 0-1	S13 3-2	F07 1-2	D26 1-1	a02 0-0	A30 0-1	J17 1-0	O25 1-1	a24 0-2	M20 0-1	N22 2-1		F21 1-2	A16 1-2	A20 2-2
20 TOTTENHAM H	S27 0-0	M13 5-2	D26 1-3	N29 2-1	a19 4-1	S13 2-3	D10 2-2	A20 1-1	a10 0-0	F28 1-1	D13 0-4	O18 2-2	J17 1-1	A16 1-0	a24 0-3	A30 2-2	F14 0-3	M27 5-0	N15 1-1		F07 1-1	N01 2-1
21 WEST HAM U	N29 1-0	a17 2-2	M06 1-2	A23 3-2	N08 1-1	F21 1-2	O04 0-1	D27 1-2	F23 1-1	J10 1-1	J31 0-4	S06 1-0	O25 2-1	N22 2-1	O11 2-1	M27 0-1	J24 1-0	S20 2-0	D20 3-1	A25 1-0		a03 0-0
22 WOLVERHAMPTON W	A30 0-0	S23 0-0	S13 2-0	F21 3-2	D26 0-1	N22 0-0	O25 1-2	N08 1-0	J17 1-1	M27 2-2	m04 1-3	N29 0-4	A16 0-2	D13 1-2	a10 5-0	a19 1-0	A26 2-2	O11 5-1	J31 2-1	M16 0-1	S27 0-1	

Sunderland's Bryan 'Pop' Robson, who played a major role in the Wearsiders' winning the Second Division title in 1975-6, when he scored 13 goals.

DIVISION 2

	BLACKBURN R	BLACKPOOL	BOLTON W	BRISTOL C	BRISTOL R	CARLISLE U	CHARLTON A	CHELSEA	FULHAM	HULL C	LUTON T	NOTTINGHAM F	NOTTS CO	OLDHAM A	ORIENT	OXFORD U	PLYMOUTH A	PORTSMOUTH	SOUTHAMPTON	SUNDERLAND	W.B.A.	YORK C
1 BLACKBURN R		S24 0-2	N08 1-1	S06 1-2	M06 1-2	a16 1-0	N29 2-0	O25 1-1	O04 0-1	N04 1-0	a03 3-0	D27 1-4	M27 2-1	A23 4-1	D20 1-1	N22 0-0	J31 3-1	F21 0-3	J28 1-1	S20 0-1	O11 0-0	a17 4-0
2 BLACKPOOL	F24 1-1		M06 1-1	a03 2-1	O25 1-4	a17 2-1	J10 2-1	N22 0-2	D20 1-1	J31 2-2	O04 3-2	N04 1-1	N29 1-0	S06 1-1	A23 1-0	F21 2-0	M27 0-0	O11 0-0	S20 4-3	a20 1-0	N08 0-1	D27 0-0
3 BOLTON W	M23 0-1	N01 1-0		D20 1-0	a28 3-1	N15 0-0	O04 5-0	M27 2-1	A23 2-2	F28 1-0	J27 3-0	a03 0-0	O18 2-1	a17 4-0	S20 1-1	M02 0-1	M13 0-0	N04 4-1	S06 3-0	D27 2-1	N29 1-2	a13 1-2
4 BRISTOL C	J17 1-0	S27 2-0	A16 1-0		A30 1-1	D06 0-0	O11 4-0	a10 2-2	M20 0-0	D13 3-0	M06 3-0	F21 0-2	a24 1-2	F24 1-0	N07 0-0	S12 4-1	D26 2-2	a20 1-0	F07 1-1	A19 3-0	O25 0-2	N22 4-1
5 BRISTOL R	N01 1-1	F28 1-1	S23 2-2	a16 0-0		S20 0-1	S06 0-0	N29 1-2	J10 1-0	M13 0-1	D27 0-1	O04 4-2	F14 0-0	D20 1-0	a03 1-1	M27 0-1	N15 0-0	J31 2-0	a17 2-0	O18 1-0	N04 1-1	A23 2-1
6 CARLISLE U	A30 0-1	D26 1-0	F21 3-2	M27 0-1	a10 4-2		O25 1-1	D13 2-1	J31 2-2	a20 0-0	O11 1-1	M06 1-1	J17 1-2	N04 2-1	N22 1-2	A16 1-1	a24 2-0	S13 2-1	N29 1-0	F24 2-2	S27 1-1	N08 1-0
7 CHARLTON A	M20 2-1	S13 1-1	a24 0-4	M12 2-2	J17 3-0	F27 4-2		a19 1-1	F17 3-2	S26 1-0	D03 1-5	F24 2-2	A16 1-2	O18 3-1	M23 1-1	A29 2-1	D12 2-0	D26 1-3	O31 4-1	N15 1-2	a09 2-1	J31 3-2
8 CHELSEA	F28 3-1	O18 2-0	D06 0-1	S20 1-1	M20 0-0	A23 3-1	D27 2-3		a06 0-0	F18 0-0	a16 2-2	S06 0-0	N15 2-0	J10 0-3	a17 0-2	A27 3-1	N01 2-2	F25 2-0	M13 1-1	D20 1-0	J31 1-2	O04 0-0
9 FULHAM	a24 1-1	A16 0-0	D13 1-2	N29 1-2	S13 0-2	A20 3-0	N08 1-1	S27 2-0		a10 1-1	N22 2-0	O11 0-0	D26 3-2	M27 1-0	O25 1-1	J17 1-1	a19 0-0	M06 0-1	M09 1-0	F07 2-0	A30 4-0	F21 2-0
10 HULL C	F06 0-1	A19 1-0	O25 2-2	A23 3-1	O11 0-0	D27 2-3	a03 2-2	N08 1-2	S20 1-2		D20 1-2	J10 1-0	S23 0-2	a16 3-0	S06 1-0	M06 2-0	N29 4-0	N22 1-0	O04 0-0	a17 1-4	F21 2-1	M27 1-1
11 LUTON T	S27 1-1	a24 3-0	S13 0-2	N01 0-0	a19 3-1	M13 3-0	M27 1-1	A30 3-0	O18 1-0	A16 2-0		J31 1-1	a10 1-1	N15 2-3	N29 1-0	D26 3-2	S24 1-1	J17 3-1	M02 1-0	F28 2-0	D13 2-1	N04 4-0
12 NOTTINGHAM F	a20 1-0	F07 3-0	S27 1-2	N15 1-0	a24 3-0	N01 4-0	S24 1-2	J17 1-3	M13 1-0	S13 1-2	O21 0-0		A30 0-1	F28 4-3	M27 1-0	a10 4-0	A16 2-0	D13 0-1	O18 3-1	M17 2-1	D26 0-2	N29 1-0
13 NOTTS CO	D06 3-0	M20 1-2	N22 1-1	O04 1-1	N08 1-1	S06 1-0	D20 2-0	F21 3-2	a17 4-0	F24 1-2	S20 1-0	a13 0-0		D27 5-1	a27 2-0	O11 0-1	N04 1-0	O25 2-0	A23 0-0	a03 0-0	M06 0-2	J10 4-0
14 OLDHAM A	D13 2-1	J17 1-0	D26 2-1	O07 2-4	A16 2-0	F07 2-2	N22 2-0	S13 2-1	D06 2-2	A30 1-0	F21 1-1	O25 0-0	a19 2-2		M06 1-1	N08 1-1	S27 3-2	a10 5-2	O21 3-2	M20 1-1	a24 0-1	O11 2-0
15 ORIENT	A16 1-1	D12 0-1	a10 0-0	F14 0-1	S26 0-0	O18 1-0	M02 0-1	D26 3-1	F28 2-0	J17 1-0	M20 3-0	D06 1-1	A19 1-1	N01 2-0		a24 2-1	S13 1-0	A29 0-1	N15 2-1	M13 0-2	a20 0-0	S23 1-0
16 OXFORD U	O18 0-0	N15 1-3	A20 2-0	J10 1-1	D06 2-1	D20 0-0	a16 1-0	F07 1-1	S06 1-3	N01 2-3	a17 1-3	S20 0-1	M13 2-1	F14 1-1	O04 2-1		F28 2-2	M20 1-0	D27 1-2	A23 1-1	N12 0-1	a03 1-0
17 PLYMOUTH A	O21 2-2	D06 1-2	O11 2-3	J24 0-0	F21 3-0	O04 2-1	A23 1-0	M06 0-3	D27 4-0	M20 1-1	F24 3-0	D20 1-0	F07 1-3	a03 2-1	J10 3-0	O25 2-1		N08 3-1	a16 1-0	S06 1-0	N22 2-1	S20 1-1
18 PORTSMOUTH	N15 0-1	M13 2-0	F07 0-1	D27 0-1	O21 1-2	J10 1-0	a17 2-2	S23 1-1	N01 0-1	O18 1-1	S06 0-2	A23 1-1	F28 1-3	S20 1-1	a13 2-1	N29 0-2	F14 2-0		a06 0-1	O04 0-0	M27 0-1	D20 0-1
19 SOUTHAMPTON	S13 2-1	a10 3-1	J17 0-0	A26 3-1	D26 3-0	M20 1-1	a12 3-2	O11 4-1	F24 2-1	a24 1-0	N08 3-1	N22 0-3	D13 2-1	J31 3-2	F21 3-0	a19 2-1	A29 1-0	S27 4-0		D06 4-0	A16 3-0	O25 2-0
20 SUNDERLAND	a10 3-0	A30 2-0	a19 2-1	M23 1-1	N22 1-1	S23 3-2	F21 4-1	A16 2-1	A26 2-0	D26 3-1	O25 2-0	N08 3-0	S27 4-0	N29 2-0	O11 3-1	D13 1-0	J17 2-1	a24 2-0	M27 3-0		S13 2-0	M30 1-0
21 W.B.A.	M13 2-2	M31 0-0	M20 2-0	M17 0-1	F07 3-0	a03 3-0	S20 1-1	A20 0-0	a14 3-1	N15 2-0	A23 1-0	a17 2-0	N01 0-0	O04 1-1	D27 1-1	F25 2-0	O18 1-0	D06 3-1	D19 0-2	J10 0-0		S06 2-2
22 YORK C	D26 2-1	a19 1-1	A30 1-2	O18 1-4	D13 0-0	F14 1-2	O21 1-3	a24 2-2	N15 1-0	D06 1-2	F07 2-3	M20 3-2	S13 1-2	M13 1-0	F24 0-2	S27 2-0	a10 3-1	A16 2-1	F28 2-1	N01 1-4	J17 0-1	

Season 1975-76

DIVISION 3

	ALDERSHOT	BRIGHTON & HA	BURY	CARDIFF C	CHESTER	CHESTERFIELD	COLCHESTER U	CRYSTAL P	GILLINGHAM	GRIMSBY T	HALIFAX T	HEREFORD U	MANSFIELD T	MILLWALL	PETERBOROUGH U	PORT VALE	PRESTON N.E.	ROTHERHAM U	SHEFFIELD W	SHREWSBURY T	SOUTHEND U	SWINDON T	WALSALL	WREXHAM
1 ALDERSHOT		a17 1-1	J10 1-1	O22 2-1	M13 1-1	F14 3-1	O18 2-2	D27 1-0	N01 3-0	a07 0-3	A23 1-2	D20 0-2	S06 2-1	S24 1-1	M24 1-0	F07 2-0	S20 1-1	F28 3-0	N15 1-1	M27 1-1	O04 2-1	a14 0-1	N29 3-2	a03 2-3
2 BRIGHTON & H.A.	D30 4-1		N04 2-1	A30 0-1	S13 6-0	S27 3-0	J17 6-0	F24 2-0	a19 1-1	M17 4-2	F21 1-0	D06 4-2	J31 1-0	F03 1-0	M06 5-0	a10 3-0	O11 1-0	A16 3-0	a24 1-1	M10 2-2	N08 2-0	M20 2-0	S10 1-2	O25 3-2
3 BURY	A30 1-1	F07 1-1		m04 0-1	a27 1-0	S13 3-1	a12 0-0	D06 0-1	A16 2-0	M06 1-1	O25 0-0	M20 2-3	S23 2-1	S27 2-0	M16 2-1	a19 1-2	F21 2-0	a10 4-0	D26 0-0	M30 2-1	O11 1-0	O21 5-0	J17 1-1	N08 0-1
4 CARDIFF C	J31 1-0	J10 0-1	A23 1-1		F28 2-0	O31 4-3	N15 2-0	S06 0-1	F14 4-1	a03 2-1	S20 0-0	a14 2-0	J20 1-0	M27 0-0	D27 5-2	F25 1-1	a07 1-0	M13 1 1	O18 2 0	N29 3-0	D22 3-1	a17 0-0	N04 0-0	O04 3-0
5 CHESTER	O11 1-0	J24 3-0	a16 0-0	O25 1-1		M20 2-1	S24 1-0	m04 2-1	D06 2-2	S06 1-2	a07 2-1	O04 0-1	J10 1-1	N08 3-1	S20 1-1	F21 1-0	D27 3-0	F07 3-1	O21 1-0	M06 1-0	A23 1-1	D20 2-1	M16 1-1	a17 1-3
6 CHESTERFIELD	N08 5-2	a07 2-1	F11 3-2	M06 1-1	N29 1-1		N05 6-1	A23 1-2	J31 0-1	a16 4-3	D20 1-2	S20 2-3	a17 1-2	O25 2-2	S06 1-1	J24 0-1	O04 3-0	M27 1-0	S24 1-0	O11 2-1	D27 1-2	a03 4-0	F21 2-1	J10 1-1
7 COLCHESTER U	M16 2-0	S20 2-0	O04 0-0	F21 3-2	F24 1-0	F07 2-3		J10 0-3	M20 2-2	D27 1-0	S06 0-1	J24 1-4	A23 0-2	M23 0-1	a16 1-1	O25 1-0	a03 1-1	O21 0-0	D06 2-1	N08 1-1	a17 2-1	a06 1-2	O11 2-0	D20 0-2
8 CRYSTAL P	a20 0-0	S23 0-1	M27 1-0	a10 0-1	A16 2-0	a28 0-0	A30 3-2		D30 0-1	O11 3-0	a13 1-1	O21 2-2	N29 4-1	M30 0-0	N08 1-1	M09 2-2	M16 2-0	S13 2-0	S27 1-1	J17 1-1	O25 1-1	F07 3-3	J06 0-1	F21 1-1
9 GILLINGHAM	M06 1-1	D27 1-0	a03 2-0	N08 2-2	M27 2-0	O21 2-2	N29 0-1	a17 1-2		A23 3-0	O04 1-1	a06 3-4	S20 3-1	F21 3-1	D20 2-2	O11 2-1	S06 1-0	S23 0-0	F07 0-0	M16 2-1	a13 1-2	J10 3-2	O25 2-3	J24 1-1
10 GRIMSBY T	S27 1-0	O18 2-1	N01 0-0	A16 2-0	a10 2-0	J03 3-0	a19 0-1	M13 1-2	a24 2-1		S23 2-2	F14 1-0	N15 4-1	S13 2-1	F07 1-1	M30 1-1	N29 0-0	D26 4-1	J17 1-1	A30 3-2	M27 2-2	F28 1-0	M09 1-2	N11 3 2
11 HALIFAX T	a24 1-3	N15 1 3	F28 0-2	J17 1-1	S27 5-2	M30 1-0	a26 1-1	N01 1-3	M09 1-1	F24 2-1		O18 0-1	F14 1-2	A16 1-2	D06 0-1	D26 1-3	N04 2-1	a19 0-1	M02 0-0	S13 0-0	M23 1-0	M13 0-2	A30 2-1	M20 0-1
12 HEREFORD U	M31 2-1	M27 1-1	N29 2-0	F04 4-1	M10 5-0	J17 4-2	S13 0-0	J31 1-1	S27 1-1	N08 3-2	M17 1-2		F11 1-0	a10 0-0	O25 2-4	A16 0-0	a28 3-1	a24 3-2	A30 3-1	a19 3-1	F21 2-1	S24 1-0	D26 1-3	O11 2-0
13 MANSFIELD T	a10 1-0	M01 1-0	F23 1-1	S13 1-4	A30 1-1	D26 0-1	a24 0-0	M20 1-1	J17 1-1	F21 1-0	N08 1-1	F07 2-2		M08 1-1	O11 1-1	J03 3-1	O25 0-1	M29 1-1	a19 3-0	A16 1-2	M15 3-1	D06 3-1	S27 4-1	M06 0-0
14 MILLWALL	F25 4-1	a16 3-1	a07 0-0	D06 1-3	F14 1-0	F28 2-0	N01 1-1	D20 2-1	N15 2-2	J24 1-1	a03 1-0	S06 1-0	O04 1-0		a17 2-0	M20 1-0	J10 2-0	O18 3 1	M13 1 0	N04 0 0	S20 2-1	D27 0-0	J31 2-1	A23 2-1
15 PETERBOROUGH U	S13 1-1	N01 1-0	O18 4-0	a19 0-0	J17 3-0	a10 0 1	J14 3-1	F18 2-0	M31 1-1	N04 4-2	M27 1-0	F27 0-3	M13 0-3	D26 1-1		A30 0-0	J31 2-0	S27 1-3	M10 2-2	a24 3-2	N29 3-2	N15 3-1	A16 0-0	S24 2-0
16 PORT VALE	N03 0-1	S06 1-1	D27 2-1	S22 2-1	N15 0-1	O18 1-1	F28 3-2	O04 0-0	M13 1-1	D20 4-3	a17 1-1	a03 1-1	a20 2-2	N29 2-0	J10 2-0		A23 1-1	N01 1-0	F16 1-0	J31 0-0	F09 1-1	S20 3-0	M27 1-2	a05 3-1
17 PRESTON N.E.	J17 1-0	M13 1-0	N15 0-0	S27 3-1	a19 0-0	M09 3-1	A16 2-1	O18 0-0	a10 4-0	M20 0-0	F07 2-1	N01 3-4	F28 0-2	A30 2-1	O21 2-1	a24 3-0		J13 3-2	M30 4-2	F03 0-2	F24 5-1	F14 4-2	S13 3-1	D06 0-1
18 ROTHERHAM U	O25 2-2	a03 1-1	S06 3-3	O11 1-0	N04 0-1	D06 2-0	J31 2-0	F03 4-1	F24 2-0	a17 3-0	D27 0-1	A23 1-1	D20 2-1	M16 1-2	a06 1-1	M06 1-2	a20 1-1		M20 1-0	F21 0-1	J10 2-0	O04 0-2	N08 3-1	S20 2-1
19 SHEFFIELD W	F21 3-1	A23 3-3	a17 1-0	M17 1-3	J31 2-0	M24 1-3	M27 1-0	a07 1-0	N06 1-0	S20 4-0	a20 1-0	J10 1-2	D27 0-0	O11 4-1	O04 2-2	N08 0-3	D20 2-2	N29 0-0		O25 1-1	a29 2-1	J24 0-2	M06 2-1	S06 1-0
20 SHREWSBURY T	D06 5-3	O04 1-2	D20 1-3	M20 3-1	N01 2-0	M13 0-2	F14 1-0	S20 2-4	O18 1-0	J10 1-0	J24 2-0	D27 2-1	a02 1-2	F07 1-0	A23 3-1	O21 1-0	a17 1-0	N15 0-2	a13 0-0		a06 3-1	S06 3-0	F24 1-1	a21 1-2
21 SOUTHEND U	M08 0-2	F17 4-0	M13 2-0	M29 0-2	a23 2-0	a19 1-1	D26 2-0	F27 1-2	M01 2-2	D05 5-2	O20 4-1	J26 1-3	O17 2-2	J16 0-0	M19 0-0	S13 3-3	S22 0-2	A30 1-2	A16 2-1	S27 1-3		O31 3-0	a09 2-2	F06 2-1
22 SWINDON T	F10 6-3	N29 3-2	J31 2-1	D26 4-0	M30 2-1	A16 0-1	S27 0-1	N04 1-2	A30 2-2	O25 3-0	O11 3-1	F24 0-1	M27 0-2	a20 0-2	F21 0-3	J17 2-1	N08 1-3	M09 1-1	S13 2-1	a10 3-0	M06 0-0		a24 5-1	a29 2-2
23 WALSALL	M20 4-1	D20 2-0	S20 0-1	F07 2-3	O18 1-0	N15 1-0	M13 1-1	S16 1-1	F27 4-0	O04 2-0	J10 2-0	a17 0-0	a06 0-1	O21 1-1	a03 2-2	D06 3-1	J24 3-1	F13 5-1	D02 2-2	S22 2-0	S06 2-3	A23 1-1		D27 2-2
24 WREXHAM	A10 3-1	F28 3-0	F14 2-1	M08 1-1	D26 1-1	A30 1-0	D13 1-1	N15 1-3	S13 2-0	J31 1-0	N29 1-1	M13 2-1	N01 1-0	J03 1-1	F23 3-0	S27 1-0	M27 1-2	J17 3-0	a10 3-0	F09 2-3	a27 2-2	O18 2-0	a19 0-3	

DIVISION 4

	BARNSLEY	BOURNEMOUTH	BRADFORD C	BRENTFORD	CAMBRIDGE U	CREWE A	DARLINGTON	DONCASTER R	EXETER C	HARTLEPOOL	HUDDERSFIELD T	LINCOLN C	NEWPORT CO	NORTHAMPTON T	READING	ROCHDALE	SCUNTHORPE U	SOUTHPORT	STOCKPORT CO	SWANSEA C	TORQUAY U	TRANMERE R	WATFORD	WORKINGTON
1 BARNSLEY		M09 2-0	M27 1-1	a10 1-1	M30 4-0	S12 1-1	F14 1-0	S24 0-1	O21 0-0	F28 3-1	N29 2-3	a19 0-1	M13 3-1	A30 3-1	O18 4-2	D26 2-1	J03 1-0	a24 2-0	N15 2-2	N01 0-0	F07 0-0	J17 1-0	A16 1-0	S27 0-0
2 BOURNEMOUTH	O04 1-1		J10 2-1	S24 3-0	N01 3-0	F07 1-0	A23 1-2	S06 0-1	a16 1-0	a03 4-2	D20 1-0	a26 1-1	S20 2-0	N29 0-0	a07 0-1	O22 2-1	N15 1-0	M13 3-3	J24 2-0	D27 2-0	a17 0-0	O18 4-2	F14 4-1	M27 1-0
3 BRADFORD C	D06 2-1	A30 0-1		A16 1-1	a24 1-2	a19 4-1	N01 2-0	O22 3-4	F07 0-0	N15 1-2	S24 2-2	M31 1-5	m03 3-0	a10 1-2	M13 1-1	J17 3-0	D26 0-0	M10 1-1	O18 1-2	F28 0 0	M20 3 1	S13 3 0	S27 1-0	J14 1-0
4 BRENTFORD	S06 1-0	F23 1-2	a03 2-2		F28 0-0	M20 0-0	D20 3-0	J24 0-1	a17 5-1	A23 1-1	a05 0-0	M13 1-0	O04 1-3	J31 2-1	D27 2-2	D06 3-0	N01 5-2	O18 1-0	S20 2-1	a16 1-0	J10 1-1	F14 0-1	N15 1-0	N03 4-0
5 CAMBRIDGE U	D20 1-1	M06 0-1	A23 0-0	O25 2-1		O11 1-1	O04 1-0	a03 3-3	J24 0-1	a16 4-0	S20 0-0	O21 2-4	a06 0-1	N08 0-1	a21 2-2	F21 0-0	F07 2 2	M20 2 2	S06 0 1	J10 3-1	D27 2-1	D06 3-3	S23 4-1	M16 4-1
6 CREWE A	J23 1-1	N05 1-0	D27 1-3	N29 1-0	M13 1-2		S20 2-0	J10 1-2	a07 0-0	O04 0-0	a14 0-2	N01 2-3	a17 4-0	M27 0-1	A23 3-3	S24 0-0	O18 1-0	F13 4-0	a03 3-1	D20 2-1	S06 6-0	N15 1-0	M03 2-2	J31 0-0
7 DARLINGTON	N08 2-0	a24 2-0	M22 2-2	M29 2-0	D13 1-1	J17 0-0		O25 2-2	O11 0-0	N03 1-2	F21 0-3	S27 0-0	M27 4-0	S13 0-1	N29 0-1	a20 4-0	A16 2-0	J03 2-0	F23 0-1	a28 1-1	M15 1-0	a10 2-0	A30 1-0	D26 1-0
8 DONCASTER R	F24 2-2	a10 1 1	J30 1 1	S15 1 1	A16 0-2	A30 3-1	F27 3-2		M20 0-0	F14 3-0	N04 4-1	D26 2-4	N15 5-1	M09 0-4	N01 1-1	J20 1-2	a19 0-1	S27 5-2	M13 3-1	O18 2-1	D06 0-1	D13 3-0	J17 1-2	M30 1-0
9 EXETER C	J31 2-0	J02 1-0	N04 0-0	D26 0-0	S13 1-2	S27 2-2	M13 1-1	N28 1-0		O18 3-1	M27 4-1	J17 0-0	F28 3-0	D13 0-0	F13 4-1	M09 1-0	a23 5-4	A16 2-0	O31 2-0	N14 3-0	F25 0-0	A29 0-2	a19 1-3	a10 1-0
10 HARTLEPOOL	O25 1-0	A16 1-1	F21 2-2	a24 1-0	F18 2-2	M10 1-3	F07 2-3	N08 2-1	O13 2-1		M06 1-1	A30 2-2	N29 4-1	D26 3-0	S22 2-4	M31 3-0	S13 1-2	J17 0-0	O22 3-0	M27 1-0	O11 0-1	S27 1-2	a10 2-1	a20 0-2
11 HUDDERSFIELD T	M20 1-2	M30 0-0	a29 0-0	S27 2-1	J17 2-0	J27 1-0	N15 1-0	F07 1-2	D06 0-1	N01 2-0		S13 0-1	O18 2-1	A16 1-1	F28 3-0	A30 0-0	a10 1-1	a19 1-2	F14 2-2	M13 2-0	O21 2-3	D26 1-0	a24 1-0	M09 2-0
12 LINCOLN C	D27 2-1	O25 1-0	D20 4-2	O11 3-1	J31 3-0	M06 2-0	a07 2-1	a17 5-0	S20 4-1	J10 3-0	M23 0-0		a03 4-1	M17 3-1	S06 3-1	N08 2-0	N28 3-0	F25 6-0	a16 2-0	O04 4-0	A23 4-2	N04 2-2	M26 5-1	F21 4-1
13 NEWPORT CO	O11 1-0	J17 3-1	N08 3-1	M08 1-0	S27 2-0	D26 2-2	D06 4-1	F21 2-3	O25 3-3	M20 0-1	M17 1-2	A16 3-1		a20 1-1	O20 0-0	a10 1-1	A30 0-0	S13 2-0	F07 2-2	F23 1-2	M05 0-2	J03 1-5	M31 0-2	a24 2-3
14 NORTHAMPTON T	J10 5-0	M20 6-0	S06 4-2	O21 3-1	F14 4-2	D06 2-1	J24 3-2	O03 2-1	D20 3-1	a17 5-2	a03 1-1	O18 1-0	D27 3-0		a16 4-1	F07 1-1	F27 2-1	N15 1-0	a23 4-0	S19 0-0	a06 2-2	M12 1-1	N01 3-0	S23 2-1
15 READING	M17 0-0	S27 2-1	O11 2-1	a19 1-0	D26 1-0	a24 3-1	M20 4-1	M06 0-1	N08 4-3	F25 1-0	O25 2-0	a10 1-1	M02 1-0	J03 1-0		A16 2-0	D13 1-0	A30 1-0	D06 5-0	N05 1-0	F21 0-0	M31 5-0	S13 3-0	J17 1-0
16 ROCHDALE	a17 0-0	F10 2-2	S20 0-0	M27 1-2	N14 1-1	M22 0-1	D27 1-0	a16 1-0	O04 0-1	D20 1-1	M01 0-0	F14 0-0	S06 4-3	N03 0-2	a03 0-0		M12 1-1	F28 2-0	a05 2-3	A23 2-1	J24 2-2	N01 4-1	O18 2-1	N29 1-1
17 SCUNTHORPE U	a20 1-0	F21 2-0	a17 2-0	M06 2-1	N04 0-1	M16 1-0	a03 2-1	D27 2-1	A23 0-1	M02 5-1	S06 0-1	M20 0-2	J10 1-2	O25 0-2	O04 2-1	O11 1-3		D06 1-2	D20 0-0	a08 1-1	S20 3-1	F24 2-2	F10 0-1	N08 3-0
18 SOUTHPORT	A23 0-0	O10 0-2	O03 1-2	M16 2-0	N29 2-4	N07 2-2	a16 2-0	a06 1-1	a02 1-0	S19 2-4	D27 1-2	S24 1-2	J24 3-0	F21 0-1	J10 1-2	O25 0-1	M26 1-1		a17 2-0	S05 1-1	D19 1-3	J31 0-0	N04 1-2	M05 2-1
19 STOCKPORT CO	F20 1-1	S12 0-0	M15 2-1	J16 2-0	J01 0-1	A16 0-0	S22 0-0	O10 1-2	M05 2-1	J30 2-0	N08 0-1	a12 0-3	N03 0-1	A22 1-3	M26 1 1	S26 0 1	M29 0 0	D26 1-0		N28 3-2	O24 1-0	a19 0-2	D12 2-2	A30 4-1
20 SWANSEA C	M05 3-1	a20 1-1	O25 3-1	a26 2-2	A30 1-0	J03 4-0	O21 2-0	M16 2-1	F20 0-3	D06 3-1	O11 1-1	M09 2-2	S23 2-2	J16 1-1	F06 5-1	a23 1-1	S27 2-0	a10 2-0	M19 5-0		N08 3-0	A16 1-1	D26 4-2	S13 1-0
21 TORQUAY U	N05 2-0	D30 2-1	N29 1-0	A30 2-3	a19 0-0	a10 2-1	O18 2-4	M27 2-2	S24 1-0	M13 1-1	F17 1-3	a24 2-2	N01 1-1	S27 0-1	N15 0-0	S13 1-0	J17 1-0	M31 2-1	F28 4-1	F14 0-2		M10 2-1	J03 1-0	A16 1-0
22 TRANMERE R	S19 1-0	M15 2-0	a26 3-3	N07 5-1	M26 3-2	F20 2-1	S05 2-0	A22 2-2	J09 1-1	a06 1-2	a17 3-0	F06 2-0	a14 3-1	O10 2-0	D19 2-0	M06 0-1	S22 2-1	O20 1-0	D27 5-0	a02 3-0	O03 7-1		N28 3-0	O24 6-0
23 WATFORD	a03 1-0	N08 1-1	a06 3-0	F21 3-2	F24 1-0	O25 2-1	J10 2-0	S20 2-1	D27 2-0	S06 2-1	A23 0-2	D06 1-3	D20 3-1	M06 0-1	J24 2-1	M16 3-0	O21 1-0	F07 2-0	O04 1-1	a17 2-1	a16 0-0	M20 2-2		O11 2-0
24 WORKINGTON	a07 1-7	D06 1-3	a16 0-3	F07 1-1	O18 1-0	O22 0-3	a17 0-0	D20 3-1	S06 1-0	D27 1-2	O04 0-2	N15 0-3	A23 1-2	F25 1-0	S20 0-2	M20 0-0	F14 2-3	J09 2-1	J10 1-2	J24 1-1	a03 1-3	F28 0-1	M13 1-3	

LEAGUE TABLES

DIVISION 1

	P	W	D	L	F	A	W	D	L	F	A	Pts
Liverpool	42	14	5	2	41	21	9	9	3	25	10	60
QPR	42	17	4	0	42	13	7	7	7	25	20	59
Manchester U	42	16	4	1	40	13	7	6	8	28	29	56
Derby Co	42	15	3	3	45	30	6	8	7	30	28	53
Leeds U	42	13	3	5	37	19	8	6	7	28	27	51
Ipswich T	42	11	6	4	36	23	5	8	8	18	25	46
Leicester C	42	9	9	3	29	24	4	10	7	19	27	45
Manchester C	42	14	5	2	46	18	2	6	13	18	28	43
Tottenham H	42	6	10	5	33	32	8	5	8	30	31	43
Norwich C	42	10	5	6	33	26	6	5	10	25	32	42
Everton	42	10	7	4	37	24	5	5	11	23	42	42
Stoke C	42	8	5	8	25	24	7	6	8	23	26	41
Middlesbrough	42	9	7	5	23	11	6	3	12	23	34	40
Coventry C	42	6	9	6	22	22	7	5	9	25	35	40
Newcastle U	42	11	4	6	51	26	4	5	12	20	36	39
Aston Villa	42	11	8	2	32	17	0	9	12	19	42	39
Arsenal	42	11	4	6	33	19	2	6	13	14	34	36
West Ham U	42	10	5	6	26	23	3	5	13	22	48	36
Birmingham C	42	11	5	5	36	26	2	2	17	21	49	33
Wolves	42	7	6	8	27	25	3	4	14	24	43	30
Burnley	42	6	6	9	23	26	3	4	14	20	40	28
Sheffield U	42	4	7	10	19	32	2	3	16	14	50	22

DIVISION 2

	P	W	D	L	F	A	W	D	L	F	A	Pts
Sunderland	42	19	2	0	48	10	5	6	10	19	26	56
Bristol C	42	11	7	3	34	14	8	8	5	25	21	53
WBA	42	10	9	2	29	12	10	4	7	21	21	53
Bolton W	42	12	5	4	36	14	8	7	6	28	24	52
Notts Co	42	11	6	4	33	13	8	5	8	27	28	49
Southampton	42	18	2	1	49	16	3	5	13	17	34	49
Luton T	42	13	6	2	38	15	6	4	11	23	36	48
Nottingham F	42	13	1	7	34	18	4	11	6	21	22	46
Charlton A	42	11	5	5	40	34	4	7	10	21	38	42
Blackpool	42	9	9	3	26	22	5	5	11	14	27	42
Chelsea	42	7	9	5	25	20	5	7	9	28	34	40
Fulham	42	9	8	4	27	14	4	6	11	18	33	40
Orient	42	10	6	5	21	12	3	8	10	16	27	40
Hull C	42	9	5	7	29	23	5	6	10	16	26	39
Blackburn R	42	8	6	7	27	22	4	8	9	18	28	38
Plymouth A	42	13	4	4	36	20	0	8	13	12	34	38
Oldham A	42	11	8	2	37	24	2	4	15	20	44	38
Bristol R	42	7	9	5	20	15	4	7	10	18	35	38
Carlisle U	42	9	8	4	29	22	3	5	13	16	37	37
Oxford U	42	7	7	7	23	25	4	4	13	16	34	33
York C	42	8	3	10	28	34	2	5	14	11	37	28
Portsmouth	42	4	6	11	15	23	5	1	15	17	38	25

DIVISION 3

	P	W	D	L	F	A	W	D	L	F	A	Pts
Hereford U	46	14	6	3	45	24	12	5	6	41	31	63
Cardiff C	46	14	7	2	38	13	8	6	9	31	35	57
Millwall	46	16	6	1	35	14	4	10	9	19	29	56
Brighton & HA	46	18	3	2	58	15	4	6	13	20	38	53
Crystal P	46	7	12	4	30	20	11	5	7	31	26	53
Wrexham	46	13	6	4	38	21	7	6	10	28	34	52
Walsall	46	11	8	4	43	22	7	6	10	31	39	50
Preston NE	46	15	4	4	45	23	4	6	13	17	34	48
Shrewsbury T	46	14	2	7	36	25	5	8	10	25	34	48
Peterboro' U	46	12	7	4	37	23	3	11	9	26	40	48
Mansfield T	46	8	11	4	31	22	8	4	11	27	30	47
Port Vale	46	10	10	3	33	21	5	6	12	22	33	46
Bury	46	11	7	5	33	16	3	9	11	18	30	44
Chesterfield	46	11	5	7	45	30	6	4	13	24	39	43
Gillingham	46	10	8	5	38	27	2	11	10	20	41	43
Rotherham U	46	11	6	6	35	22	4	6	13	19	43	42
Chester	46	13	7	3	34	19	2	5	16	9	43	42
Grimsby T	46	13	7	3	39	21	2	3	18	23	53	40
Swindon T	46	11	4	8	42	31	5	4	14	20	44	40
Sheffield W	46	12	6	5	34	25	0	10	13	14	34	40
Aldershot	46	10	8	5	34	26	3	5	15	25	49	39
Colchester U	46	9	6	8	25	27	3	8	12	16	38	38
Southend U	46	9	7	7	40	31	3	6	14	25	44	37
Halifax T	46	6	5	12	22	32	5	8	10	19	29	35

DIVISION 4

	P	W	D	L	F	A	W	D	L	F	A	Pts
Lincoln C	46	21	2	0	71	15	11	8	4	40	24	74
Northampton T	46	18	5	0	62	20	11	5	7	25	20	68
Reading	46	19	3	1	42	9	5	9	9	28	42	60
Tranmere R	46	18	3	2	61	16	6	7	10	28	39	58
Huddersfield T	46	11	6	6	28	17	10	8	5	28	24	56
Bournemouth	46	15	5	3	39	16	5	7	11	18	32	52
Exeter C	46	13	7	3	37	17	5	7	11	19	30	50
Watford	46	16	4	3	38	18	6	2	15	24	44	50
Torquay U	46	12	6	5	31	24	6	8	9	24	39	50
Doncaster R	46	10	6	7	42	31	9	5	9	33	38	49
Swansea C	46	14	8	1	51	21	2	7	14	15	36	47
Barnsley	46	12	8	3	34	16	2	8	13	18	32	44
Cambridge U	46	7	10	6	36	28	7	5	11	22	34	43
Hartlepool	46	10	6	7	37	29	6	4	13	25	49	42
Rochdale	46	7	11	5	27	23	5	7	11	13	31	42
Crewe A	46	10	7	6	36	21	3	8	12	22	36	41
Bradford C	46	9	7	7	35	26	3	10	10	28	39	41
Brentford	46	12	7	4	37	18	2	6	15	19	42	41
Scunthorpe U	46	11	3	9	31	24	3	7	13	19	35	38
Darlington	46	11	7	5	30	14	3	3	17	18	43	38
Stockport Co	46	8	7	8	23	23	5	5	13	20	53	38
Newport Co	46	8	7	8	35	33	5	2	16	22	57	35
Southport	46	6	6	11	27	31	2	4	17	14	46	26
Workington	46	5	4	14	19	43	2	3	18	11	44	21

Football League Records

Top scorers: Div 1, M.Macdonald (Arsenal), A.Gray (Aston Villa) 25 goals; Div 2, M.Walsh (Blackpool) 26 goals; Div 3, P.Ward (Brighton & Hove Albion) 32 goals; Div 4, B.Joicey (Barnsley) 25 goals.

Emlyn Hughes, the powerful, adaptable footballer who captained Liverpool to another Championship and also led them to their first European Cup Final victory in 1977.

Wolves centre-forward John Richards scored 15 times as the Molineux club topped Division Two.

DIVISION 1

	ARSENAL	ASTON VILLA	BIRMINGHAM C	BRISTOL C	COVENTRY C	DERBY CO	EVERTON	IPSWICH T	LEEDS U	LEICESTER C	LIVERPOOL	MANCHESTER C	MANCHESTER U	MIDDLESBROUGH	NEWCASTLE U	NORWICH C	Q.P.R.	STOKE C	SUNDERLAND	TOTTENHAM H	W.B.A.	WEST HAM U
1 ARSENAL		a25 3-0	N06 4-0	A21 0-1	a23 2-0	m03 0-0	S18 3-1	M05 1-4	J03 1-1	a02 3-0	N20 1-1	S04 0-0	D18 3-1	m07 1-1	D04 5-3	J15 1-0	O02 3-2	O16 2-0	F05 0-0	a11 1-0	M08 1-2	F19 2-3
2 ASTON VILLA	O20 5-1		S18 1-2	O23 3-1	N20 2-2	M02 4-0	F05 2-0	S04 5-2	m07 2-1	S25 2-0	D15 5-1	m04 1-1	N06 3-2	a05 1-0	D18 2-1	a23 1-0	m20 1-1	m16 1-0	M23 4-1	a20 2-1	m23 4-0	A21 4-0
3 BIRMINGHAM C	J18 3-3	m10 2-1		a09 3-0	M05 3-1	O02 5-1	m14 1-1	D07 2-4	A24 0-0	a30 1-1	A28 2-1	N27 0-0	J22 2-3	O16 3-1	a02 1-2	F12 3-2	O30 2-1	a16 2-0	D11 2-0	M19 1-2	S11 0-1	D27 0-0
4 BRISTOL C	J22 2-0	a02 0-0	O26 0-1		N06 0-0	M15 2-2	M05 1-2	O02 1-2	m10 1-0	O16 0-1	m16 2-1	F19 1-0	m07 1-1	D18 1-2	F05 1-1	N20 3-1	M19 1-0	A24 1-1	S04 4-1	a12 1-0	a05 1-2	S18 1-1
5 COVENTRY C	N27 1-2	a16 2-3	S25 2-1	m19 2-2		a25 2-0	D11 4-2	D27 1-1	A28 4-2	O02 1-1	m10 0-0	m14 0-1	A24 0-2	J22 1-1	O16 1-1	S11 2-0	N09 2-0	a30 5-2	O30 1-2	a02 1-1	a19 1-1	a09 1-1
6 DERBY CO	D15 0-0	a09 2-1	M12 0-0	O30 2-0	M09 1-1		a16 2-3	m14 0-0	F12 0-1	D27 1-0	S11 2-3	a30 4-0	A28 0-0	A25 0-0	J22 4-2	a06 2-2	m11 2-0	a02 2-0	N27 1-0	O16 8-2	S25 2-2	a20 1-1
7 EVERTON	M01 2-1	A28 0-2	D18 2-2	S25 2-0	m07 1-1	N20 2-0		A24 1-1	N06 0-2	F12 1-2	M22 0-0	O05 2-2	a05 1-2	D29 2-2	m24 2-0	a19 3-1	J22 1-3	S11 3-0	m19 2-0	M26 4-0	m16 1-1	O23 3-2
8 IPSWICH T	S25 3-1	F12 1-0	a11 1-0	M12 1-0	a05 2-1	D18 0-0	J15 2-0		N20 1-1	S11 0-0	D04 1-0	O23 1-0	J03 2-1	a23 0-1	m07 2-0	F15 5-0	A28 2-2	F26 0-1	N23 3-1	A21 3-1	N06 7-0	M22 4-1
9 LEEDS U	O30 2-1	D11 1-3	F02 1-0	a30 2-0	F05 1-2	S04 2-0	m04 0-0	a16 2-1		N27 2-2	O23 1-1	D27 0-2	O02 0-2	M05 2-1	S18 2-2	M23 3-2	m14 0-1	N10 1-1	a09 1-1	F19 2-1	A21 2-2	a26 1-1
10 LEICESTER C	O23 4-1	M05 1-1	D04 2-6	M26 0-0	M12 3-1	a12 1-1	S04 1-1	F19 1-0	m16 0-1		O27 0-1	A21 2-2	N20 1-1	M15 3-3	m04 1-0	N06 1-1	S18 2-2	S29 1-0	J15 2-0	D18 2-1	m07 0-5	F05 2-0
11 LIVERPOOL	a16 2-0	O30 3-0	F05 4-1	N27 2-1	S04 3-1	F19 3-1	O16 3-1	a30 2-1	a02 3-1	N09 5-1		a09 2-1	m03 1-0	O02 0-0	M05 1-0	A21 1-0	D11 3-1	D27 4-0	J01 2-0	S18 2-0	J15 1-1	m14 0-0
12 MANCHESTER C	F12 1-0	A25 2-0	a19 2-1	S11 2-1	D18 2-0	D04 3-2	m10 1-1	a02 2-1	a08 2-1	J22 5-0	D29 1-1		S25 1-3	a11 1-0	N06 0-0	M01 2-0	O16 0-0	A28 0-0	M09 1-0	m07 5-0	N20 1-0	O02 4-2
13 MANCHESTER U	m14 3-2	J01 2-0	A21 2-2	J19 2-1	J15 2-0	F05 3-1	D27 4-0	O30 0-1	M12 1-0	a16 1-1	F16 0-0	M05 3-1		S18 2-0	F19 3-1	O23 2-2	a30 1-0	a09 3-0	N10 3-3	S04 2-3	M23 2-2	N27 0-2
14 MIDDLESBROUGH	F15 3-0	D27 3-2	M22 2-2	m14 0-0	A21 1-0	J15 2-0	a09 2-2	N27 0-2	S25 1-0	O30 0-1	M12 0-1	D07 0-0	a26 3-0		S04 1-0	O09 1-0	a16 0-2	J01 0-0	S11 2-1	F05 2-0	O23 1-0	a29 1-1
15 NEWCASTLE U	a30 0-2	m14 3-2	O23 3-2	A28 0-0	M23 1-0	A21 2-2	N24 4-1	M09 1-1	M02 3-0	a09 0-0	S25 1-0	F16 2-2	S11 2-2	M26 1-0		M12 5-1	N27 2-0	O30 1-0	D27 2-0	F26 2-0	O06 2-0	a16 3-0
16 NORWICH C	A25 1-3	N27 1-1	S04 1-0	a16 2-1	F19 3-0	S18 0-0	a30 2-1	a09 0-1	O16 1-2	J01 3-2	J22 2-1	O30 0-2	a02 2-1	M09 1-0	O02 3-2		D27 2-0	J29 1-1	m14 2-2	M05 1-3	F05 1-0	N10 1-0
17 Q.P.R.	M12 2-1	S11 2-1	m23 2-2	a26 0-1	a11 1-1	N06 1-1	A21 0-4	m16 1-0	M08 0-0	F26 3-2	m07 1-1	M22 0-0	a19 4-0	N20 3-0	a23 1-2	O05 2-3		S25 2-0	O23 2-0	J11 2-1	S04 1-0	a04 1-1
18 STOKE C	M23 1-1	O02 1-0	N20 1-0	a20 2-2	F16 2-0	O23 1-0	F19 0-1	S18 2-1	a12 2-1	M19 0-1	a11 0-0	F05 0-2	m11 3-3	N06 3-1	M15 0-0	m07 0-0	M05 1-0		A21 0-0	a23 0-0	D18 0-2	S04 2-1
19 SUNDERLAND	A28 2-2	O16 0-1	m07 1-0	F11 1-0	J03 0-1	a23 1-1	O02 0-1	M19 1-0	D29 0-1	A24 0-0	N06 0-1	S18 0-2	a11 2-1	F19 4-0	a08 2-2	D18 0-1	a02 1-0	J22 0-0		N20 2-1	F22 6-1	M05 6-0
20 TOTTENHAM H	D27 2-2	a30 3-1	O20 1-0	N13 0-1	O23 0-1	M23 0-0	O30 3-3	J22 1-0	S11 1-0	m14 2-0	M09 1-0	D11 2-2	F12 1-3	A28 0-0	A25 0-2	S25 1-1	a09 3-0	N27 2-0	a16 1-1		M12 0-2	J01 2-1
21 W.B.A.	a09 0-2	N10 1-1	F28 2-1	D27 1-1	S17 1-1	M05 1-0	N27 3-0	M16 4-0	J22 1-2	D11 2-2	A25 0-1	a16 0-2	O16 4-0	a02 2-1	M19 1-1	A28 2-0	F12 1-1	m14 3-1	a30 2-3	O02 4-2		O30 3-0
22 WEST HAM U	S11 0-2	J22 0-1	a08 2-2	F26 2-0	m04 2-0	m07 2-2	a02 2-2	O16 0-2	O06 1-3	A28 0-0	D18 2-0	M12 1-0	m16 4-2	D04 0-1	N20 1-2	a11 1-0	A23 1-0	F12 1-0	S25 1-1	N06 5-3	J03 0-0	

DIVISION 2

	BLACKBURN R	BLACKPOOL	BOLTON W	BRISTOL R	BURNLEY	CARDIFF C	CARLISLE U	CHARLTON A	CHELSEA	FULHAM	HEREFORD U	HULL C	LUTON T	MILLWALL	NOTTINGHAM F	NOTTS CO	OLDHAM A	ORIENT	PLYMOUTH A	SHEFFIELD U	SOUTHAMPTON	WOLVERHAMPTON W
1 BLACKBURN R		S04 0-1	A21 3-1	S18 0-0	D27 2-2	F05 2-1	a06 1-3	a30 0-0	O23 0-2	m14 1-0	N27 1-0	N13 1-0	O30 1-0	M26 2-0	J01 1-3	O09 6-1	F19 2-0	M12 2-2	M02 2-0	M05 1-0	a20 3-0	a16 0-2
2 BLACKPOOL	F12 1-1		M12 1-0	J22 4-0	a09 1-1	a02 1-0	D27 0-0	a16 2-2	S25 0-1	N27 3-2	F14 2-1	J01 0-0	a30 1-0	S11 4-2	O16 1-0	F26 1-1	A24 0-2	A28 3-0	O09 0-2	N13 1-0	m14 1-0	O30 2-2
3 BOLTON W	J22 3-1	O02 0-3		O16 1-0	N09 2-1	m10 2-1	M22 3-4	N27 1-0	F26 2-2	O30 2-1	a30 3-1	S11 5-1	D21 2-1	A28 3-1	D27 1-1	F12 4-0	a02 3-0	A24 2-0	M05 3-0	a09 1-2	a16 3-0	m14 0-1
4 BRISTOL R	M08 0-0	A21 1-4	m17 2-2		a16 1-1	J15 1-1	D11 2-1	O30 1-1	O05 2-1	F12 2-1	N13 2-3	N27 3-0	J01 1-0	M12 0-0	a30 1-1	S25 5-1	A28 0-0	S11 1-0	O23 1-1	m14 3-1	a09 2-3	D27 1-5
5 BURNLEY	a08 3-1	D28 0-0	a12 0-0	N20 1-1		D04 0-0	F26 2-0	O16 4-4	a23 1-0	A24 3-1	F12 1-1	S25 0-0	A28 1-2	D18 1-3	a02 0-1	m07 3-1	N06 1-0	O09 3-3	J03 0-2	M12 1-0	S11 2-0	J22 0-0
6 CARDIFF C	A28 2-1	O23 2-2	O09 3-2	A25 1-2	a30 0-1		m14 1-1	J22 1-1	M12 1-3	J01 3-0	D27 3-1	D11 1-1	a16 4-2	S24 0-0	N27 0-3	S11 2-3	F12 3-1	M02 0-1	M26 0-1	O30 0-2	N10 1-0	a09 2-2
7 CARLISLE U	D29 1-1	O12 1-1	N06 0-1	m07 2-3	S18 2-1	D18 4-3		O02 4-2	F05 0-1	M19 1-2	S14 2-2	S04 1-1	O16 1-1	N20 0-1	M05 1-1	J03 0-2	a12 1-1	D04 1-0	a23 3-1	F19 4-1	J22 0-6	a19 2-1
8 CHARLTON A	D04 4-0	N20 1-2	a22 1-1	J03 4-3	a26 5-2	A21 0-2	M11 1-0		a11 4-0	A28 1-1	F25 1-1	O09 3-1	S10 4-3	a08 3-2	J14 2-1	J29 1-1	m07 2-1	F15 2-0	N05 3-1	O23 3-2	S24 6-2	F12 1-1
9 CHELSEA	a02 3-1	M05 2-2	S18 2-1	M19 2-0	N27 2-1	O02 2-1	A28 2-1	N10 2-1		D27 2-0	J01 5-1	m14 4-0	a09 2-0	F12 1-1	a16 2-1	A25 1-1	O16 4-3	J22 1-1	F19 2-2	a30 4-0	O30 3-1	D11 3-3
10 FULHAM	D14 2-0	a23 0-0	J03 0-2	S04 1-0	J15 2-2	N06 1-2	N16 2-0	F05 1-1	a08 3-1		S25 4-1	O23 0-0	F26 1-2	D28 2-3	A21 2-2	N20 1-5	D04 5-0	m07 6-1	a11 2-0	M26 3-2	M11 1-1	S11 0-0
11 HEREFORD U	a23 1-0	m07 1-1	D15 3-3	a11 1-1	S04 3-0	a06 2-2	m04 0-0	S18 1-2	N06 2-2	M05 1-0		A21 1-0	M19 0-1	a20 3-1	M02 0-1	O23 1-4	N20 0-0	D18 2-3	F09 1-1	M23 2-2	m11 2-0	O02 1-6
12 HULL C	a12 1-0	N06 2-2	F19 2-2	a23 0-1	M05 4-1	m07 1-2	F12 3-1	M19 0-0	D18 1-1	a02 1-0	J22 1-1		A24 3-1	F15 0-0	O02 1-0	a08 0-1	D28 0-1	a19 1-1	N20 3-1	S17 1-1	A28 4-0	O16 2-0
13 LUTON T	F15 2-0	D04 0-0	m07 1-1	N06 4-2	F05 2-0	N20 2-1	M26 5-0	F19 2-0	D29 4-0	S18 0-2	O09 2-0	J24 2-1		a12 1-2	S04 1-1	a23 4-2	M08 1-0	a11 0-0	M12 1-1	A21 2-0	O23 1-4	M05 2-0
14 MILLWALL	O16 0-1	F19 1-1	F05 3-0	O02 2-0	m14 2-0	M05 0-2	a16 1-1	D27 1-1	S04 3-0	a09 0-0	O30 4-2	a30 2-1	N13 4-2		D11 0-2	J22 2-5	M19 2-1	a02 0-1	S18 3-0	N27 0-1	A25 0-0	J01 1-1
15 NOTTINGHAM F	N06 3-0	M26 3-0	a06 3-1	D04 4-2	O23 5-2	a23 0-1	S25 5-1	A25 1-1	N20 1-1	J22 3-0	S11 4-3	M12 2-0	F12 1-2	m07 1-0		M08 1-2	a27 3-0	M29 3-0	D18 1-1	O09 6-1	M22 2-1	A28 1-3
16 NOTTS CO	M19 0-0	S18 2-0	S04 0-1	M05 2-1	M02 5-1	F19 1-0	O30 2-1	m14 0-1	F15 2-1	a16 0-0	a01 3-2	D27 1-1	N27 0-4	A21 1-2	a09 1-1		O02 1-0	O16 0-1	F05 2-0	M28 2-1	a30 3-1	N13 1-1
17 OLDHAM A	S11 2-0	J15 1-0	O23 2-2	F05 4-0	F15 3-1	S04 3-2	N13 4-1	M22 1-1	a19 0-0	a30 1-0	a16 3-5	a09 3-0	m14 1-2	O09 2-1	O30 1-0	M12 1-1		S25 0-0	A21 2-2	D27 1-2	N27 2-1	M15 0-2
18 ORIENT	O02 0-1	m10 0-1	M15 2-2	F19 2-0	M19 0-1	S18 3-0	a30 0-0	a09 0-0	A21 0-1	D11 0-0	m14 1-1	m17 1-1	D27 1-0	M08 1-1	N13 0-1	M26 1-0	M05 0-2		S04 2-2	a16 0-2	a26 2-3	N27 2-4
19 PLYMOUTH A	A24 4-0	M19 2-0	S25 1-1	a02 1-1	O30 0-1	O16 2-2	N27 0-1	J01 1-0	S11 2-3	N13 2-2	a09 2-1	a16 1-2	O02 1-0	F26 2-2	m02 1-2	A28 1-2	J22 2-2	F12 1-2		D11 0-0	D27 1-1	a30 0-0
20 SHEFFIELD U	S25 1-1	a12 1-5	D28 2-3	D18 2-3	O02 1-0	M08 3-0	S11 3-0	a02 3-0	D03 1-0	O16 1-1	A28 1-1	F26 1-1	J22 0-3	m03 1-1	M19 2-0	N06 1-0	a05 2-1	N20 1-1	m07 1-0		F12 2-2	A24 2-2
21 SOUTHAMPTON	m07 2-0	D18 3-3	N20 1-3	D29 2-1	F19 2-0	a11 3-2	A21 1-2	M05 2-1	D07 1-1	O02 4-1	O16 1-0	F05 2-2	a02 1-0	J15 0-2	S18 1-1	D04 2-1	a23 4-0	N06 2-2	a08 4-1	S04 1-1		m03 1-0
22 WOLVERHAMPTON W	N20 1-2	M01 2-1	D18 1-0	a05 1-0	A21 0-0	a26 4-1	O23 4-0	S04 3-0	m07 1-1	F19 5-1	M12 2-1	M26 2-1	S25 1-2	N06 3-1	F05 2-1	a11 2-2	S18 5-0	a23 1-0	D04 4-0	F09 2-1	O05 2-6	

Season 1976-77

DIVISION 3

	BRIGHTON & HA	BURY	CHESTER	CHESTERFIELD	CRYSTAL P	GILLINGHAM	GRIMSBY T	LINCOLN C	MANSFIELD T	NORTHAMPTON T	OXFORD U	PETERBOROUGH U	PORTSMOUTH	PORT VALE	PRESTON N.E.	READING	ROTHERHAM U	SHEFFIELD W	SHREWSBURY T	SWINDON T	TRANMERE R	WALSALL	WREXHAM	YORK C
1 BRIGHTON & H.A.		M19 1-1	J15 3-0	D18 2-1	O02 1-1	D29 2-0	F19 3-0	J29 4-0	a02 3-1	J03 2-0	A21 3-2	O16 1-0	a06 4-0	a23 1-0	F05 2-0	a12 2-0	S04 3-1	m03 3-2	M15 4-0	N06 4-0	M05 1-1	O05 7-0	N27 0-2	S18 7-2
2 BURY	O09 3-0		S18 2-0	m07 3-1	F19 0-1	N26 3-1	A21 2-0	a11 3-0	M12 2-0	F15 1-1	M26 2-1	S25 4-1	a23 1-0	a08 3-0	O23 3-2	J29 1-0	J15 1-1	N06 1-3	m03 0-1	O26 0-1	S04 2-1	D18 0-2	M01 0-2	F05 4-2
3 CHESTER	A24 0-1	M08 1-0		a23 1-2	F12 2-1	F22 1-0	M19 2-0	m03 1-0	O16 1-0	N27 2-1	A28 1-3	O02 2-1	a11 1-1	m07 1-1	S11 0-0	F01 3-1	M05 1-3	F15 1-0	D28 1-2	D18 2-1	J22 1-0	N06 1-0	a08 1-2	a02 1-0
4 CHESTERFIELD	m14 1-1	D04 7-0	N10 1-0		a30 0-2	M12 1-0	F16 0-1	S25 1-4	D27 0-1	A21 0-0	m04 2-0	a16 0-0	F05 1-2	M30 4-0	J29 1-1	O09 4-0	a09 1-0	F26 2-0	M26 1-1	S04 0-1	N03 0-0	O23 1-0	S11 0 6	O30 2-0
5 CRYSTAL P	M12 3-1	S11 2-1	S04 1-2	N27 0-0		a05 3-1	J15 2-1	m07 4-1	S25 2-0	D18 1-1	O09 2-2	F26 0-0	F22 2-1	F01 2-0	M22 1-0	N06 1-1	O23 2-1	a23 4-0	O26 2-1	a12 5-0	F05 1-0	J03 3-0	m03 2-1	A21 1-0
6 GILLINGHAM	a09 0-1	a30 1-0	a16 1-0	O02 2-1	D27 0-3		N02 1-1	O16 0-1	N13 3-1	S04 1-1	J29 1-1	M22 1-1	S18 2-1	F19 1-1	O30 1-1	A21 2-2	D04 1-2	M19 1-0	F15 2-1	M05 2-2	m14 3-0	F05 1-0	a02 2-0	m03 2-0
7 GRIMSBY T	S11 2-0	J22 2-0	O09 0-0	N06 1-2	A24 0-1	a11 1-1		a08 1-2	F12 0-1	J29 0-1	F26 1-2	A28 2-2	N27 1-0	J03 2-4	S25 1-0	D18 2-1	M12 1-1	D28 1-1	a23 2-1	m07 2-0	a02 1-0	m03 2-2	N30 3-0	O16 1-0
8 LINCOLN C	a20 2-2	N03 2-3	M29 3-3	M05 3-2	M02 3-2	M26 4-0	D27 2-0		F15 3-2	F05 5-4	a16 0-1	m11 1-1	M15 2-1	S04 2-0	a30 2-0	O23 3-1	O29 2-2	O02 1-1	A21 1-1	S18 0-0	N13 2-2	J18 4-1	M18 1-1	a09 2-0
9 MANSFIELD T	O23 1-1	O02 5-0	M26 1-1	a11 2-1	M05 1-0	a23 2-2	S04 3-0	N06 3-1		m07 3-0	F07 3-0	M19 1-1	m02 2-0	D28 2-1	A21 3-1	N08 4-0	F05 3-1	J11 1-0	a12 1-0	N27 1-1	S18 1-1	F28 3-0	D18 2-0	F19 4-1
10 NORTHAMPTON T	O30 0-2	a09 3-0	a29 0-0	J22 2-1	M15 3-0	F12 1-2	a19 0-0	A28 1-0	M08 0-1		N13 1-0	N02 2-2	O15 3-1	M19 3-0	J01 0-1	S11 1-2	D27 1-4	J15 0-2	F26 5-3	a01 1-1	J07 3-4	S25 0-1	O01 0-2	a16 3-0
11 OXFORD U	J22 1-0	O16 2-2	F05 2-0	J08 3-2	M19 0-1	D11 3-1	S18 5-2	O26 1-2	S07 0-3	a23 1-0		a02 2-3	N06 2-1	N27 0-0	S04 2-2	D29 1-0	F19 1-2	D18 1-1	M01 4-2	a08 0-0	O02 1-1	a12 0-0	m07 2-2	M05 0-2
12 PETERBOROUGH U	M26 2-0	M05 0-1	M11 3-2	O06 0-3	S18 0-0	N06 0-1	F05 3-1	a26 1-2	O09 2-1	a12 3-1	O23 2-0		J03 4-2	m04 1-1	J15 0-0	S14 2-1	A21 0-2	N27 1-2	J29 2-1	S29 1-0	F19 0-0	m07 3-5	a23 0-2	S04 3-0
13 PORTSMOUTH	D27 1-0	N13 1-1	N02 2-1	A28 0-1	a09 0-0	F26 3-2	a30 1-2	S11 1-1	J18 2-2	M26 2-1	J01 1-1	O30 0-0		O23 1-1	D04 0-0	S25 0-2	a16 5-1	F12 0-3	M12 2-0	A24 2-1	a19 0-3	O09 1-1	J22 0-1	m14 3-1
14 PORT VALE	N13 2-2	D27 0-1	M14 1-0	A23 1-1	a26 4-1	S11 1-2	O30 2-0	M21 1-0	a09 1-4	O08 2-1	a30 2-1	M07 1-1	a02 1-0		N01 0-0	F28 1-0	m14 1-4	A28 2-0	S25 1-2	J22 2-2	a16 1-1	M11 0-0	O16 2-3	F07 0-2
15 PRESTON N.E.	A28 1-1	a02 0-1	F19 3-4	a19 2-2	O16 2-1	a26 1-0	M05 2-1	N27 3-0	J22 1-2	N06 3-0	F12 2-1	O12 6-2	m07 0-0	S14 4 0		a23 3-0	S18 0-0	M29 4-1	D17 2-1	F08 2-0	M19 1-0	a11 0-1	M15 2-1	O02 4-2
16 READING	N03 2-3	F26 1-3	O30 2-0	M19 2-0	J01 0-0	J22 1-2	m14 2-0	a02 1-2	a16 1-0	F19 2-4	a09 2-0	D27 1-0	M05 2-0	S18 1-1	N13 0-2		m11 0-3	O16 0-1	F05 0-0	O02 4-1	a30 0-0	S04 2-1	S08 2-0	F16 1-1
17 ROTHERHAM U	F12 0-0	A24 3-0	S25 1-1	D28 1-0	a02 1-1	m07 1-0	O02 3-2	M08 1-0	A28 3-0	a11 2-0	S11 1-1	J22 0-0	O26 2-2	D18 1-1	F26 2-0	m03 1-2		a12 0-1	N06 1-0	a23 1-1	O16 1-2	N27 1-0	F15 2-0	M19 1-1
18 SHEFFIELD W	J08 0-0	J25 1-0	O05 3-0	S18 4-1	N09 1-0	O09 2-0	a09 1-0	M12 1-1	O30 0-2	A25 2-1	m14 2-0	a30 4-0	S04 1-1	F05 1-2	a16 1-0	M26 2-1	N02 1-3		O23 0-1	F19 3-1	D04 3-1	A21 0-0	M05 3-1	D27 3-2
19 SHREWSBURY T	D04 1-0	J11 0-1	a09 2-0	O16 3-0	a16 1-1	A24 4-2	N13 2-1	J22 2-1	N02 0-0	S18 3-0	O30 1-0	a19 2-1	O02 4-1	M05 1-1	m14 1-2	A28 2-0	F01 0-0	a02 1-1		M19 2-2	D27 2-2	F19 1-2	F12 3-2	a30 2-1
20 SWINDON T	m10 2-1	a16 0-1	m14 2-1	F12 3-0	N02 1-1	S25 2-2	M08 4-1	F26 2-2	a30 0-1	O23 5-1	D27 1-0	a09 0-4	m17 4-3	A21 1-0	m03 0-1	M11 2-2	N13 2-4	S11 5-2	O09 1-0		O30 1-1	M26 2-2	A28 3-2	M29 5-1
21 TRANMERE R	S25 1-3	M28 1-2	A21 0-1	a12 2-1	A27 1-0	D17 2-0	O22 2-0	a23 2-2	M21 4-0	m02 2-1	M11 1-1	S11 2-0	J28 1-3	O25 1-1	O08 0-0	N26 2-1	M25 0-1	m06 1-0	a08 2-1	F21 0-1		D28 0-0	N05 0-0	J31 4-4
22 WALSALL	a16 1-0	m14 3-3	M22 1-0	a02 2-2	O30 0-0	A28 1-2	F01 1-0	S14 1-3	a19 1-2	M05 0-3	N02 2-2	D03 1-1	M19 1-1	O02 3-1	D27 0-1	F12 6-1	a30 0-1	J22 5-1	S11 3-3	O16 2-0	a09 2-0		F26 2-3	N13 1-2
23 WREXHAM	a30 0-0	O30 0-0	D27 4-2	F19 3-1	m11 2-4	O23 2-1	a16 3-2	O09 3-0	m14 0-1	M12 3-1	D04 1-1	N10 2-0	A21 2-0	M24 6-2	a09 2-0	J15 3-1	a18 2-1	S25 2-2	S04 1-0	F05 2-2	M07 2-0	S18 1-0		N01 1-1
24 YORK C	F26 0-1	A28 2-2	O23 0-2	J25 2-1	J22 2-1	J08 2-2	M26 1-1	F22 2-2	S11 0-1	O20 1-4	S25 2-1	F12 2-1	D18 1-4	N06 1-0	M12 0-2	m07 1-1	O09 1 1	a11 0 2	N27 0-3	a19 4-2	S07 1-0	a23 0-0	a12 0-0	

DIVISION 4

	ALDERSHOT	BARNSLEY	BOURNEMOUTH	BRADFORD C	BRENTFORD	CAMBRIDGE U	COLCHESTER U	CREWE A	DARLINGTON	DONCASTER R	EXETER C	HALIFAX T	HARTLEPOOL	HUDDERSFIELD T	NEWPORT CO	ROCHDALE	SCUNTHORPE U	SOUTHEND U	SOUTHPORT	STOCKPORT CO	SWANSEA C	TORQUAY U	WATFORD	WORKINGTON
1 ALDERSHOT		M26 0-1	J03 1-0	A21 2-1	S10 1-1	m18 1-3	a05 1-1	J29 1-1	M12 1-2	J15 1-0	M02 2-2	m04 0-0	N27 3-0	O23 1-0	F26 4-0	O27 0-2	a23 1-1	N06 0-0	A28 1-0	O09 2-0	S25 2-2	F12 0-1	a12 2-1	m07 2-0
2 BARNSLEY	O16 1-0		J29 3-1	S25 2-2	J22 2-0	a22 2-1	N27 0-1	O19 2-2	S11 1-1	M19 1-1	m03 3-4	D29 1-0	D18 3-0	O02 2-1	A28 2-0	m07 2-0	N06 5-1	O26 3-1	a02 1-0	F26 1-0	F12 1-0	N09 2-1	M09 1-1	a11 4-0
3 BOURNEMOUTH	O30 4-1	a19 1-0		D04 1-1	J01 3-1	F26 0-1	S25 0-0	O23 0-0	a16 0-1	m14 3-1	O09 2-0	J22 3-0	F12 2-0	J08 1-0	N02 1-0	M12 1-1	S11 2-2	A28 2-0	N13 5-0	a30 3-0	D27 1-1	a09 1-1	M26 2-1	A24 1-1
4 BRADFORD C	F09 3-1	M06 0-0	m07 1-1		O02 3-2	N08 0-0	D18 1-0	a11 1-0	A28 3-1	a02 3-1	J29 1-1	O27 3-0	D22 2-2	M19 3-1	O16 3-1	a06 3-0	m04 4-0	a23 2-0	F12 1-0	S11 3-3	A25 4-1	F26 3-2	N27 0-0	J03 4-1
5 BRENTFORD	F19 0-1	A21 0-1	N06 3-2	M12 4-0		N27 0 2	J03 1 1	m02 0 0	O23 0 0	S04 2-2	a12 1-0	J29 2-1	a23 3-1	F05 1-3	O09 1-1	F22 3-2	m07 4-2	a08 1-0	S18 3-0	J15 4-0	M26 4-0	M05 3-2	M23 3-0	O25 5-0
6 CAMBRIDGE U	a09 4-1	N13 0-0	S18 2-0	J01 2-1	a30 3-2		A21 2-0	F19 2-0	J29 4-0	m03 3-0	F05 1-1	a01 4-0	M19 2-0	N02 1-1	D27 3-1	J15 0-0	O15 1-0	O02 2-3	a16 5-1	D04 2-2	m14 2-3	O29 4-1	S04 4-0	M05 4-1
7 COLCHESTER U	D27 1-0	a29 1-0	M04 1-0	m14 2-1	O30 2-1	J21 0-1		S18 3-2	D04 4-0	a15 1-0	S04 3-1	A24 3-0	O16 6-2	a19 3-1	J01 5-0	F05 1-0	a02 1-1	M19 0-1	J18 4-1	N12 1-0	a08 1-1	N01 4-0	F19 1-0	O01 3-1
8 CREWE A	a20 1-0	D27 1-0	a02 2-1	N03 1-0	J08 3-2	S11 1-0	F26 1-0		M16 1-1	a30 1-2	M11 2-0	O16 3-1	A28 3-1	m14 0-0	M23 2-0	S25 1-1	F12 2 1	A25 1 1	a09 0-0	a06 2-1	O30 3-1	a16 2-1	O09 2-0	J22 1-1
9 DARLINGTON	O02 2-1	F19 2-1	O25 4-0	F05 0-0	a02 2-2	a18 0-2	m07 2-0	a23 4-0		M05 1-3	N27 2-1	N06 0-0	a08 3-1	S18 2-0	A23 1-0	a12 0-2	M07 5-2	F21 0-0	M19 2-1	S03 0-2	J22 0-4	O16 2-1	D18 0-0	D28 3-2
10 DONCASTER R	S14 1-2	O09 2-1	D18 0-0	O22 2-3	F12 5-0	J08 1-1	O25 3-2	N27 3-0	S25 4-0		m07 0-3	a12 3-0	N05 2-1	M25 2-0	S10 1-0	J11 2-0	a11 3-0	D28 0-3	J22 3-1	M11 1-0	F26 2-1	A28 0-4	a23 1-0	a19 6-3
11 EXETER C	m14 3-0	J08 1-0	M19 1-1	a20 0-0	N03 3-2	A28 1-1	F12 1-0	O02 3-0	a30 1-0	D04 0-2		F26 1-0	J22 3-1	N12 2-0	a09 1-0	S11 2-1	S29 2-0	a02 3-1	O30 3-1	a16 2-1	J01 2-0	D27 3-0	M05 2-2	O16 0-0
12 HALIFAX T	M22 2-0	a09 0-1	A21 2-3	a16 2-1	a19 0-0	O23 0-2	M08 1-2	M26 3-0	F14 2-1	N02 6-0	S18 1-2		S24 1-0	D27 0-0	a30 0-0	S04 0-0	O09 0-1	F19 3-1	m14 1-1	O30 2-1	N09 1-0	F08 2-0	M12 1-1	F05 6-1
13 HARTLEPOOL	a30 0-2	m14 0-2	S04 0-1	a09 0-1	N13 2-0	O09 2-2	M26 2-2	F05 3-0	D27 1-1	J01 0-0	A21 2-2	M05 1-0		O30 0-1	a16 0-1	O23 2-0	M12 3-0	S18 1-1	M28 1-1	N01 1-1	a18 2-2	J08 4-0	J15 1-0	F19 2-0
14 HUDDERSFIELD T	a02 2-0	M12 1-0	m03 0-0	O09 3-0	A28 1-0	a12 1-2	M21 0-0	D18 0-1	F26 3-1	O16 2-1	a23 0-1	a05 1-0	F15 4-1		F12 3-0	N26 2-1	D28 1-0	m07 1-1	S14 1-0	S25 2-0	S11 2-2	J22 2-1	O26 2-2	N06 2-1
15 NEWPORT CO	S18 2-1	M28 1-1	a12 1-0	M26 2-0	M18 3-1	a05 4-2	F22 1-2	m07 2-1	J14 0-1	M01 1-2	a26 0-3	N27 1-1	O26 1-1	S04 1-1		a23 3-0	J28 0-0	m10 3-0	M04 3-1	A21 0-1	O22 0-2	O02 0-0	m03 3-0	m17 1-0
16 ROCHDALE	a16 2-1	J25 2-3	O02 0-0	D27 0-1	m14 2-3	A23 2-2	A28 1-0	M05 0-1	N01 2-2	O30 1-0	F19 1-2	F12 4-1	a02 0-1	a30 2-2	N13 0-0		J22 5-0	O16 0-0	M01 3-0	a09 1-1	J08 1-0	a26 0-1	S18 3-1	M19 0-3
17 SCUNTHORPE U	N13 1-3	F08 1-2	F19 0-0	J08 2-1	J25 2-1	M26 0 2	O23 2-0	S03 4-0	O30 3-0	D27 1-1	M15 4-1	M19 2-1	O02 2-0	a09 0-4	a19 1-0	A21 0-1		M05 1-0	N02 1-1	m14 2-2	a16 0-3	a30 0-0	F05 0-0	S18 3-1
18 SOUTHEND U	J01 5-0	a15 1-1	F04 2-2	N12 4-1	D27 2-1	M11 0-1	O08 0-0	J15 1-0	m02 0-0	a09 2-1	O23 2-0	S10 1-1	F25 1-0	D04 1-1	O29 1-1	M25 3-0	S24 1-1		a29 3-2	J28 0-0	M15 1-2	m13 0-3	A21 2-1	S03 2-0
19 SOUTHPORT	F05 0-1	O22 1-0	a22 0-0	S03 0-4	M08 1-2	O26 0-0	m03 1-3	D29 0-0	O08 0-0	A21 2-2	J03 1-1	D18 0-0	m07 1-2	J15 2-2	S25 0-1	N06 1-1	a12 2-1	N27 0-0		M26 1-0	M11 1-3	S11 1-1	J29 1-3	a08 1-1
20 STOCKPORT CO	M10 0-0	S17 2-1	N26 1-0	M28 1-1	A23 2-0	m06 0-0	a22 1-1	N05 1-2	F11 2-2	O01 2-1	O25 0-0	J31 1-1	M07 1-0	M04 2-3	J21 2-1	D29 0-1	D17 1-0	a18 0-0	O15 2-2		A27 3-0	a01 2-1	a11 2-2	J07 1-0
21 SWANSEA C	M05 4-2	S04 2-1	a11 3-0	M01 2-3	O15 5-3	D18 3-1	D29 2-1	J04 3-0	A21 2-1	S18 1-1	N06 0-0	a23 2-1	J29 4-2	a26 2-1	a02 3-1	m03 3-2	D11 2-0	a12 2-0	O02 2-1	M22 4-4		M18 4-1	m07 1-4	N27 4-0
22 TORQUAY U	S04 0-1	J15 1-0	F16 2-1	S18 0-3	S25 1-1	J03 2-2	a11 2-2	O27 5-0	M26 2-0	F05 0-1	a08 0-1	m07 3-2	m04 1-0	A21 1-0	M12 1-0	J29 2-0	N27 1-3	D18 0-0	M23 0-0	O23 1-2	O09 2-1		N06 3-1	a23 3-1
23 WATFORD	N02 1-1	O30 1-0	O16 1-1	a30 1-1	a09 0-1	F12 2-0	S11 2-1	M19 3-1	m14 1-1	M29 5-1	S25 4-1	O02 0-0	A24 4-0	a16 2-0	J11 2-0	F26 3-1	A28 2-1	J22 1-1	a19 2-0	D27 1-1	D04 2-0	J01 4-0		a02 2-0
24 WORKINGTON	F16 1-1	N03 0-1	M09 1-1	O29 0-1	a16 1-3	S25 0-2	M12 2-4	A21 1-0	a09 2-3	J29 1-1	M26 1-3	A28 1-1	S11 1-1	J01 3-2	m14 0-1	O09 0-2	F26 1-0	F12 0-3	D27 2-2	m04 2-2	a30 1-3	N13 2-4	O23 0-1	

LEAGUE TABLES

DIVISION 1

	P	W	D	L	F	A	W	D	L	F	A	Pts
Liverpool	42	18	3	0	47	11	5	8	8	15	22	57
Manchester C	42	15	5	1	38	13	6	9	6	22	21	56
Ipswich T	42	15	4	2	41	11	7	4	10	25	28	52
Aston Villa	42	17	3	1	55	17	5	4	12	21	33	51
Newcastle U	42	14	6	1	40	15	4	7	10	24	34	49
Manchester U	42	12	6	3	41	22	6	5	10	30	40	47
WBA	42	10	6	5	38	22	6	7	8	24	34	45
Arsenal	42	11	6	4	37	20	5	5	11	27	39	43
Everton	42	9	7	5	35	24	5	7	9	27	40	42
Leeds U	42	8	8	5	28	26	7	4	10	20	25	42
Leicester C	42	8	9	4	30	28	4	9	8	17	32	42
Middlesbrough	42	11	6	4	25	14	3	7	11	15	31	41
Birmingham C	42	10	6	5	38	25	3	6	12	25	36	38
QPR	42	10	7	4	31	21	3	5	13	16	31	38
Derby Co	42	9	9	3	36	18	0	10	11	14	37	37
Norwich C	42	12	4	5	30	23	2	5	14	17	41	37
West Ham U	42	9	6	6	28	23	2	8	11	18	42	36
Bristol C	42	8	7	6	25	19	3	6	12	13	29	35
Coventry C	42	7	9	5	34	26	3	6	12	14	33	35
Sunderland	42	9	5	7	29	16	2	7	12	17	38	34
Stoke C	42	9	8	4	21	16	1	6	14	7	35	34
Tottenham H	42	9	7	5	26	20	3	2	16	22	52	33

DIVISION 2

	P	W	D	L	F	A	W	D	L	F	A	Pts
Wolves	42	15	3	3	48	21	7	10	4	36	24	57
Chelsea	42	15	6	0	51-	22	6	7	8	22	31	55
Nottingham F	42	14	3	4	53	22	7	7	7	24	21	52
Bolton W	42	15	2	4	46	21	5	9	7	29	33	51
Blackpool	42	11	7	3	29	17	6	10	5	29	25	51
Luton T	42	13	5	3	39	17	8	1	12	28	31	48
Charlton A	42	14	5	2	52	27	2	11	8	19	31	48
Notts Co	42	11	5	5	29	20	8	5	8	36	40	48
Southampton	42	12	6	3	40	24	5	4	12	32	43	44
Millwall	42	9	6	6	31	22	6	7	8	26	31	43
Sheffield U	42	9	8	4	32	25	5	4	12	22	38	40
Blackburn R	42	12	4	5	31	18	3	5	13	11	36	39
Oldham A	42	11	6	4	37	23	3	4	14	15	41	38
Hull C	42	9	8	4	31	17	1	9	11	14	36	37
Bristol R	42	8	9	4	32	27	4	4	13	21	41	37
Burnley	42	8	9	4	27	20	3	5	13	19	44	36
Fulham	42	9	7	5	39	25	2	6	13	15	36	35
Cardiff C	42	7	6	8	30	30	5	4	12	26	37	34
Orient	42	4	8	9	18	23	5	8	8	19	32	34
Carlisle U	42	7	7	7	31	33	4	5	12	18	42	34
Plymouth A	42	5	9	7	27	25	3	7	11	19	40	32
Hereford U	42	6	9	6	28	30	2	6	13	29	48	31

DIVISION 3

	P	W	D	L	F	A	W	D	L	F	A	Pts
Mansfield T	46	17	6	0	52	13	11	2	10	26	29	64
Brighton & HA	46	19	3	1	63	14	6	8	9	20	26	61
Crystal P	46	17	5	1	46	15	6	8	9	22	25	59
Rotherham U	46	11	9	3	30	15	11	6	6	39	29	59
Wrexham	46	15	6	2	47	22	9	4	10	33	32	58
Preston NE	46	15	4	4	48	21	6	8	9	16	22	54
Bury	46	15	2	6	41	21	8	6	9	23	38	54
Sheffield W	46	15	4	4	39	18	7	5	11	26	37	53
Lincoln C	46	12	9	2	50	30	7	5	11	27	40	52
Shrewsbury T	46	13	7	3	40	21	5	4	14	25	38	47
Swindon T	46	12	6	5	48	33	3	9	11	20	42	45
Gillingham	46	11	8	4	31	21	5	4	14	24	43	44
Chester	46	14	3	6	28	20	4	5	14	20	38	44
Tranmere R	46	10	7	6	31	23	3	10	10	20	30	43
Walsall	46	8	7	8	39	32	5	8	10	18	33	41
Peterboro' U	46	11	4	8	33	28	2	11	10	22	37	41
Oxford U	46	9	8	6	34	29	3	7	13	21	36	39
Chesterfield	46	10	6	7	30	20	4	4	15	20	44	38
Port Vale	46	9	7	7	29	28	2	9	12	18	43	38
Portsmouth	46	8	9	6	28	26	3	5	15	25	44	36
Reading	46	10	5	8	29	24	3	4	16	20	49	35
Northampton T	46	9	4	10	33	29	4	4	15	27	46	34
Grimsby T	46	10	6	7	29	22	2	3	18	16	47	33
York C	46	7	8	8	25	34	3	4	16	25	55	32

DIVISION 4

	P	W	D	L	F	A	W	D	L	F	A	Pts
Cambridge U	46	16	5	2	57	18	10	8	5	30	22	65
Exeter C	46	17	5	1	40	13	8	7	8	30	33	62
Colchester U	46	19	2	2	51	14	6	7	10	26	29	59
Bradford C	46	16	7	0	51	18	7	6	10	27	33	59
Swansea C	46	18	3	2	60	30	7	5	11	32	38	58
Barnsley	46	16	5	2	45	18	7	4	12	17	21	55
Watford	46	15	7	1	46	13	3	8	12	21	37	51
Doncaster R	46	16	2	5	47	25	5	7	11	24	40	51
Huddersfield T	46	15	5	3	36	15	4	7	12	24	34	50
Southend U	46	11	9	3	35	19	4	10	9	17	26	49
Darlington	46	13	5	5	37	25	5	8	10	22	39	49
Crewe A	46	16	6	1	36	15	3	5	15	11	45	49
Bournemouth	46	13	8	2	39	13	2	10	11	15	31	48
Stockport Co	46	10	10	3	29	19	3	9	11	24	38	45
Brentford	46	14	3	6	48	27	4	4	15	29	49	43
Torquay U	46	12	5	6	33	22	5	4	14	26	45	43
Aldershot	46	10	8	5	29	19	6	3	14	20	40	43
Rochdale	46	8	7	8	32	25	5	5	13	18	34	38
Newport Co	46	11	6	6	33	21	3	4	16	9	37	38
Scunthorpe U	46	11	6	6	32	24	2	5	16	17	49	37
Halifax T	46	11	6	6	36	18	0	8	15	11	40	36
Hartlepool	46	8	9	6	30	20	2	3	18	17	53	32
Southport	46	3	12	8	17	28	0	7	16	16	49	25
Workington	46	3	7	13	23	42	1	4	18	18	60	19

Football League Records

Top scorers: Div 1, R.Latchford (Everton) 30 goals; Div 2, R.Hatton (Blackpool) 22 goals; Div 3, A.Bruce (Preston North End) 27 goals; Div 4, S.Phillips (Brentford), A.Curtis (Swansea City) 32 goals. Workington failed to gain re-election, Wimbledon were elected in their place. Hartlepool became Hartlepool United.

Peter Withe, a key member of the Nottingham Forest side that won the League Championship for the first time. Three years later, Withe helped Villa to the title.

Bolton's Neil Whatmore netted 19 goals when the Trotters won the Second Division title in 1977-8. Altogether he scored 121 goals in 338 games for them.

DIVISION 1

	ARSENAL	ASTON VILLA	BIRMINGHAM C	BRISTOL C	CHELSEA	COVENTRY C	DERBY CO	EVERTON	IPSWICH T	LEEDS U	LEICESTER C	LIVERPOOL	MANCHESTER C	MANCHESTER U	MIDDLESBROUGH	NEWCASTLE U	NORWICH C	NOTTINGHAM F	Q.P.R.	W.B.A.	WEST HAM U	WOLVERHAMPTON W
1 ARSENAL		F04 0-1	O29 1-1	M18 4-1	D26 3-0	N12 1-1	N26 1-3	A23 1-0	J02 1-0	D10 1-1	S17 2-1	O04 0-0	M04 3-0	a01 3-1	a29 1-0	a15 2-1	F28 0-0	S03 3-0	O15 1-0	M25 4-0	O01 3-0	J14 3-1
2 ASTON VILLA	S10 1-0		O01 0-1	J28 1-0	a15 2-0	D26 1-1	M25 0-0	A27 1-2	a29 6-1	a26 3-1	M04 0-0	a01 0-3	A24 1-4	O29 2-1	N12 0-1	a17 2-0	O15 3-0	a05 0-1	J02 1-1	D10 3-0	M18 4-1	S23 2-0
3 BIRMINGHAM C	M21 1-1	F25 1-0		D27 3-0	D31 4-5	O08 1-1	O22 3-1	D17 0-0	a11 0-0	J14 2-3	N19 1-1	S03 0-1	a22 1-4	A20 1-4	F04 1-2	S17 3-0	a08 2-1	D03 0-2	O04 2-1	F28 1-2	M28 3-0	N05 2-1
4 BRISTOL C	O22 0-2	S03 1-1	M25 0-1		M21 3-0	a29 1-1	N12 3-1	M11 0-1	D10 2-0	O08 3-2	J14 0-0	a15 1-1	F17 2-2	a25 0-1	N26 4-1	a01 3-1	F04 3-0	D31 1-3	O01 2-2	D26 3-1	S17 3-2	A20 2-3
5 CHELSEA	M27 0-0	N19 0-0	A24 2-0	O29 1-0		A27 1-2	S10 1-1	D03 0-1	J21 5-3	O01 1-2	O05 0-0	M04 3-1	m05 0-0	F11 2-2	O15 0-0	M18 2-2	D17 1-1	N05 1-0	m02 3-1	J02 2-2	D27 2-1	a22 1-1
6 COVENTRY C	D17 1-2	M21 2-3	M04 4-0	D03 1-1	J14 5-1		A20 3-1	a08 3-2	O22 1-1	S03 2-2	M11 1-0	F04 1-0	O04 4-2	D31 3-0	S17 2-1	a04 0-0	D27 5-4	a22 0-0	N19 4-1	O01 1-2	N05 1-0	M28 4-0
7 DERBY CO	m09 3-0	D27 0-3	M18 1-3	D17 1-0	M11 1-1	J02 4-2		N05 0-1	A24 0-0	S17 2-2	a22 4-1	M08 4-2	D03 2-1	S03 0-1	O01 4-1	M04 1-1	O29 2-2	J14 0-0	M27 2-0	O15 1-1	N19 2-1	a08 3-1
8 EVERTON	D31 2-0	J14 1-0	N12 2-1	O15 1-0	a29 6-0	N26 6-0	a01 2-1		a15 1-0	M25 2-0	F04 2-0	a05 0-1	O01 1-1	D26 2-6	D10 3-0	O29 4-4	S17 3-0	A20 1-3	M04 3-3	O04 3-1	F18 2-1	S03 0-0
9 IPSWICH T	A20 1-0	D03 2-0	O15 5-2	a22 1-0	S03 1-0	M18 1-1	D31 1-2	N19 3-3		F04 0-1	D17 1-0	S17 1-1	N05 1-0	J14 1-2	M21 1-1	O01 2-1	M27 4-0	a25 0-2	D27 3-2	M04 2-2	O29 0-2	m09 1-2
10 LEEDS U	a22 1-3	O05 1-1	A27 1-0	M04 0-2	F25 2-0	J21 2-0	a12 2-0	D27 3-1	S10 2-1		M28 5-1	O15 1-2	D17 2-0	S24 1-1	M18 5-0	J02 0-2	N05 2-2	N19 1-0	D03 3-0	A24 2-2	a08 1-2	M27 2-1
11 LEICESTER C	F11 1-1	O08 0-2	a15 1-4	A27 0-0	a26 0-2	O15 1-2	D10 1-1	S10 1-5	N12 2-1	O29 0-0		N26 0-4	J02 0-1	M25 2-3	D26 0-0	a29 3-0	M18 2-2	S24 0-3	J21 0-0	a01 0-1	A24 1-0	F25 1-0
12 LIVERPOOL	M25 1-0	N05 1-2	J21 2-3	N19 1-1	O08 2-0	S10 2-0	S24 1-0	O22 0-0	a18 2-2	M11 1-0	a08 3-2		m01 4-0	F25 3-1	J02 2-0	A23 2-0	a22 3-0	m04 0-0	D17 1-0	A27 3-0	D03 2-0	D27 1-0
13 MANCHESTER C	O08 2-1	D31 2-0	D10 3-0	S24 2-0	N26 6-2	a25 3-1	a29 1-1	F25 1-0	a01 2-1	N12 2-3	A20 0-0	O29 3-1		S10 3-1	M25 2-2	D26 4-0	S03 4-0	a11 0-0	F11 2-1	a15 1-3	J14 3-2	O22 0-2
14 MANCHESTER U	N05 1-2	M29 1-1	J02 1-2	F08 1-1	S17 0-1	A24 2-1	J21 4-0	M27 1-2	A27 0-0	M01 0-1	D27 3-1	O01 2-0	M15 2-2		M04 0-0	O15 3-2	N19 1-0	D17 0-4	a08 3-1	M18 1-1	a22 3-0	D03 3-1
15 MIDDLESBROUGH	D03 0-1	D17 1-0	S10 1-2	a08 2-0	a04 2-0	a11 1-1	F25 3-1	a22 0-0	S24 1-1	O22 2-1	M27 0-1	A20 1-1	D27 0-2	O08 2-1		A27 2-0	D31 2-2	M29 2-2	N05 1-1	J21 1-0	a25 1-2	N19 0-0
16 NEWCASTLE U	N19 1-2	a08 1-1	M15 1-1	N05 1-1	O22 1-0	S24 1-2	O08 1-2	M24 0-2	F25 0-1	A20 3-2	D03 2-0	D31 0-2	M29 2-2	M11 2-2	J14 2-4		a26 2-2	D28 0-2	a22 0-3	S10 0-3	S03 2-3	D17 4-0
17 NORWICH C	S24 1-0	M11 2-1	N26 1-0	S10 1-0	N12 0-0	M25 1-2	M29 0-0	M15 0-0	D26 1-0	a01 3-0	O22 2-0	D10 2-1	J21 1-3	a15 1-3	A24 1-1	O05 2-1		F25 3-3	A27 1-1	a29 1-1	J02 2-2	O08 2-1
18 NOTTINGHAM F	J21 2-0	S17 2-0	a29 0-0	A23 1-0	a01 3-1	D10 2-1	A27 3-0	J02 1-1	O04 4-0	a15 1-1	M14 1-0	D26 1-1	O15 2-1	N12 2-1	O29 4-0	M25 2-0	O01 1-1		a18 1-0	N26 0-0	M04 2-0	F04 2-0
19 Q.P.R.	a11 2-1	A20 1-2	a25 0-0	F25 2-2	S24 1-1	a15 2-1	D26 0-0	O08 1-5	M25 3-3	a29 0-0	S03 3-0	N12 2-0	S17 1-1	N26 2-2	a01 1-0	D10 0-1	J14 2-1	O22 0-2		O29 2-1	M14 1-0	D31 1-3
20 W.B.A.	D27 1-3	a22 0-3	S24 3-1	M27 2-1	A20 3-0	F25 3-3	a18 1-0	a25 3-1	O08 1-0	D31 1-0	N05 2-0	J14 0-1	N19 0-0	O22 4-0	S03 2-1	a12 2-0	D03 0-0	m02 2-2	M22 2-0		D17 1-0	S17 2-2
21 WEST HAM U	F25 2-2	O22 2-2	D26 1-0	F11 1-2	M25 3-1	a01 2-1	a15 3-0	S24 1-1	M24 3-0	N26 0-1	D31 3-2	a29 0-2	A27 0-1	D10 2-1	O03 0-2	J21 1-0	A20 1-3	O08 0-0	S10 2-2	N12 3-3		M11 1-2
22 WOLVERHAMPTON W	A27 1-1	m02 3-1	a01 0-1	J02 0-0	D10 1-3	O29 1-3	O04 1-2	J21 3-1	N26 0-0	D26 3-1	O01 3-0	M25 1-3	M18 1-1	a29 2-1	a15 0-0	N12 1-0	M04 3-3	S10 2-3	A23 1-0	M14 1-1	O15 2-2	

DIVISION 2

	BLACKBURN R	BLACKPOOL	BOLTON W	BRIGHTON & HA	BRISTOL R	BURNLEY	CARDIFF C	CHARLTON A	CRYSTAL P	FULHAM	HULL C	LUTON T	MANSFIELD T	MILLWALL	NOTTS CO	OLDHAM A	ORIENT	SHEFFIELD U	SOUTHAMPTON	STOKE C	SUNDERLAND	TOTTENHAM H
1 BLACKBURN R		S10 1-2	a26 0-1	a08 0-1	M11 0-1	M27 0-1	A27 3-0	O08 2-1	D03 3-0	M15 4-0	M24 1-1	F11 2-0	N19 3-1	D17 2-1	J02 1-0	F25 4-2	S24 1-0	a22 1-1	N05 2-1	O22 2-1	D27 1-1	A24 0-0
2 BLACKPOOL	F04 5-2		D27 0-2	D03 0-1	S03 3-1	M28 1-1	O01 3-0	J14 5-1	O04 3-1	a18 1-2	M11 3-0	O22 2-1	a22 1-2	N19 2-2	M07 2-2	A20 1-1	D31 0-0	N05 1-1	D17 0-1	a08 1-1	M27 1-1	S17 0-2
3 BOLTON W	O03 4-2	M25 2-1		M04 1-1	a15 3-0	J02 1-2	D10 6-3	N12 2-1	a18 2-0	a29 0-0	J21 1-0	O29 2-1	O15 2-0	A23 2-1	D26 2-0	S10 1-0	a01 2-0	A27 2-1	M18 0-0	O01 1-1	M07 2-0	N26 1-0
4 BRIGHTON & H.A.	N26 2-2	a29 2-1	O08 1-2		D26 1-1	F11 2-1	O29 4-0	a25 1-0	O22 1-1	M25 2-0	S10 2-1	S27 3-2	J21 5-1	A27 3-2	a01 2-1	D10 1-1	N12 1-0	S24 2-1	J02 1-1	M11 2-1	F25 2-1	a15 3-1
5 BRISTOL R	O15 4-1	J21 2-0	N19 0-1	a18 0-4		M04 2-2	J02 3-2	F25 2-2	D27 3-0	A27 0-0	D03 1-1	S10 1-2	O04 3-1	N05 2-0	A23 2-2	S24 0-0	F11 2-1	a08 4-1	O29 0-0	a22 4-1	D17 3-2	M18 2-3
6 BURNLEY	D26 2-3	O29 0-1	A20 0-1	S17 0-0	O08 3-1		a15 4-2	D10 1-0	S03 1-1	a25 2-0	O22 1-1	a29 2-1	M14 2-0	O01 0-2	N12 3-1	M25 4-1	N26 0-0	M11 4-1	F04 3-3	J14 1-0	D31 0-0	a01 2-1
7 CARDIFF C	J14 1-1	F25 2-1	a22 1-0	M24 1-0	A20 1-1	N19 2-1		D31 1-0	a08 2-2	S24 3-1	D17 0-0	O08 1-4	S17 1-1	D28 4-1	m03 2-1	O22 1-0	m09 0-1	D03 1-6	M29 1-0	N05 2-0	J28 5-2	S03 0-0
8 CHARLTON A	M04 2-2	A27 3-1	D17 2-1	O04 4-3	S30 3-1	a22 3-2	a04 0-0		M24 1-0	J02 0-1	a08 0-1	J21 0-0	N05 2-2	F28 0-2	M17 0-0	F10 2-2	S10 2-1	N19 3-0	D27 1-3	M28 3-2	D03 3-2	O15 4-1
9 CRYSTAL P	a29 5-0	a25 2-2	S24 2-1	M18 0-0	M25 1-0	J21 1-1	N26 2-0	O29 1-1		O01 2-3	A27 0-1	D26 3-3	A23 3-1	J02 1-0	D10 2-0	a01 0-0	a15 1-0	F11 1-0	O15 1-2	M04 0-1	S10 2-2	N12 1-2
10 FULHAM	S03 0-0	O08 1-1	D03 2-0	D28 2-1	J14 1-1	O04 4-1	M07 1-0	A20 1-1	F25 1-1		N19 2-0	M10 1-0	M27 0-2	a22 0-1	S17 5-1	D30 0-2	O22 1-2	M24 2-0	a07 1-1	D17 3-0	N05 3-3	F04 1-1
11 HULL C	O29 0-1	O15 2-0	S03 0-0	F04 1-1	a29 0-1	M18 1-3	N12 4-1	N26 0-2	J14 1-0	a15 0-1		a01 1-1	O01 0-2	M04 3-2	M25 1-1	D26 0-1	D10 2-2	D31 2-3	a11 0-3	S17 0-0	A20 3-0	O04 2-0
12 LUTON T	S17 0-0	M18 4-0	M21 2-1	D31 1-0	F08 1-1	D03 1-2	M04 3-1	S03 7-1	M27 1-0	O15 1-0	N05 1-1		D17 1-1	O04 1-0	O01 2-0	J14 0-1	A20 1-0	D27 4-0	a22 1-2	N19 1-2	a08 1-3	F22 1-4
13 MANSFIELD T	a15 2-2	D10 1-3	M11 0-1	S03 1-2	a24 3-0	S24 4-1	F11 2-2	a01 0-3	D31 1-3	D26 2-1	F25 1-0	N12 3-1		S10 0-0	O29 1-3	N26 0-2	a29 1-1	O08 1-1	J14 1-2	A20 2-1	O22 1-2	M25 3-3
14 MILLWALL	N12 1-1	a15 2-0	D31 1-0	J14 0-1	a01 1-3	F25 1-1	M25 1-1	S24 1-1	A20 0-3	D10 0-3	O08 1-1	a25 1-0	m02 1-0		N26 0-0	a29 2-0	M21 2-0	O22 1-1	S17 3-0	S03 0-0	a18 3-1	D26 1-3
15 NOTTS CO	A20 1-1	S24 1-1	M27 1-1	N05 1-0	D31 3-2	D17 3-0	S10 1-1	O22 2-0	a22 2-0	a04 1-1	D27 2-1	F25 2-0	M21 1-0	a08 1-1		M11 3-2	O08 1-1	a25 1-2	S03 2-3	D03 2-0	N19 2-2	J14 3-3
16 OLDHAM A	O01 0-2	J02 2-1	F18 2-2	a22 1-1	a04 4-1	D27 2-0	M18 1-1	S17 1-1	N05 1-1	A23 2-0	M27 2-1	A27 1-0	a08 0-1	D03 2-2	O15 2-1		J21 2-1	D17 3-0	N19 1-1	O04 1-1	M24 1-1	M04 1-1
17 ORIENT	a04 0-0	A23 1-4	N05 1-1	D17 0-1	S17 2-1	a18 3-0	O15 2-1	m03 0-0	N19 0-0	M17 1-1	a22 2-1	J02 0-0	D03 4-2	O29 0-0	M04 0-0	S03 5-3		M27 3-1	a25 1-1	D27 2-0	J14 2-2	O01 1-1
18 SHEFFIELD U	D10 2-0	a01 0-0	J14 1-5	a04 2-0	N26 1-1	O15 2-1	a29 0-1	a15 1-0	S17 0-2	O29 2-1	A23 2-0	M25 4-1	M04 2-0	M18 5-2	O04 4-1	N12 1-0	D26 2-0		O01 3-2	M14 1-2	S03 1-1	J02 2-2
19 SOUTHAMPTON	a01 5-0	N12 2-0	O22 2-2	A20 1-1	M27 3-1	S10 3-0	D26 3-1	M25 4-1	M11 2-0	N26 2-0	S24 1-0	D10 0-1	A27 1-0	F11 2-3	J21 3-1	a15 2-2	O04 1-0	F25 2-1		D31 1-0	O08 4-2	a29 0-0
20 STOKE C	M18 4-2	N26 1-2	F25 0-0	O15 1-0	D10 3-2	A27 2-1	a01 2-0	D26 4-0	O08 0-2	N12 2-0	M08 1-0	a15 0-0	J02 1-1	a12 2-1	a29 1-1	a26 3-0	M25 5-1	S10 4-0	A24 1-0		S24 0-0	O29 1-3
21 SUNDERLAND	M25 0-1	D26 2-1	S17 0-2	O01 0-2	N12 5-1	A23 3-0	O04 1-1	a29 3-0	M14 0-0	a01 2-2	J02 2-0	N26 1-1	M18 1-0	O15 2-0	a15 3-1	O29 3-1	A27 1-1	J21 5-1	M04 0-0	a04 1-0		D10 1-2
22 TOTTENHAM H	D31 4-0	F11 2-2	a08 1-0	N19 0-0	O22 9-0	N05 3-0	J21 2-1	M11 2-1	D17 2-2	S10 1-0	a26 1-0	S24 2-0	D27 1-1	M27 3-3	A27 2-1	O08 5-1	F25 1-1	A20 4-2	D03 0-0	M22 3-1	a22 2-3	

Season 1977-78

DIVISION 3

	BRADFORD C	BURY	CAMBRIDGE U	CARLISLE U	CHESTER	CHESTERFIELD	COLCHESTER U	EXETER C	GILLINGHAM	HEREFORD U	LINCOLN C	OXFORD U	PETERBOROUGH U	PLYMOUTH A	PORTSMOUTH	PORT VALE	PRESTON N.E.	ROTHERHAM U	SHEFFIELD W	SHREWSBURY T	SWINDON T	TRANMERE R	WALSALL	WREXHAM
1 BRADFORD C		N12 2-1	A20 4-0	M11 2-2	S10 2-2	D31 1-3	J07 1-2	a15 1-2	M01 2-1	O22 0-0	D03 2-2	A27 2-3	S28 2-1	S24 0-1	a01 1-0	M08 1-1	O08 1-1	F25 3-0	O29 3-2	S27 2-0	a26 2-1	M14 2-0	a29 2-3	D26 2-1
2 BURY	a08 2-2		J07 5-2	D31 1-1	N19 1-1	O22 0-0	D27 1-1	J21 5-0	S13 2-2	a25 1-1	A20 1-0	D10 3-2	O08 0-0	a22 1-1	M11 0-0	F25 3-0	M27 1-1	N05 1-1	S03 3-0	S24 0-3	J28 0-0	S27 1-0	M14 0-1	M24 2-3
3 CAMBRIDGE U	J14 4-1	N08 3-0		O08 2-0	J28 0-0	a15 2-0	O22 2-0	a29 2-1	A27 2-3	M11 2-0	N12 5-0	O29 2-1	J02 1-0	F11 3-0	M25 1-0	D26 2-0	F25 1-1	S24 1-1	D03 3-0	M07 2-0	S27 5-2	S10 1-0	a01 2-1	a25 1-0
4 CARLISLE U	O15 1-1	a01 0-3	M04 1-1		S20 0-0	O29 2-1	O01 1-3	a03 2-0	M18 1-0	a11 2-0	O04 2-3	S17 2-2	M07 0-0	A27 0-0	N12 3-1	D03 1-1	S10 3-1	F07 2-1	J02 1-0	a15 1-0	a29 2-2	J14 2-2	D26 2-0	M27 1-4
5 CHESTER	F04 3-2	a15 1-0	S02 0-0	M01 2-2		D03 2-1	J21 2-1	a01 2-1	S17 2-2	A20 4-1	D31 2-2	a12 3-1	a29 4-3	O08 1-1	a26 2-0	N12 2-1	M24 1-2	M11 2-1	S14 2-1	D26 1-0	O22 1-0	F25 0-0	M27 1-1	S28 1-1
6 CHESTERFIELD	N05 2-0	M18 2-1	N19 2-1	M28 2-1	a22 1-2		O05 0-0	O01 0-0	a26 5-2	S14 2-1	M01 0-0	J02 3-0	A27 2-0	a08 4-1	J28 3-0	J14 2-0	D27 0-1	M27 0-0	M04 2-2	S07 3-1	m03 3-1	D10 1-1	O15 0-1	S17 1-0
7 COLCHESTER U	A23 3-0	M25 1-0	M17 2-1	F25 2-2	A27 2-0	a04 2-0		D09 3-1	J13 1-1	O08 0-0	D26 1-1	O14 1-1	O28 3-0	S09 3-1	M07 4-0	S27 2-3	S24 0-0	m03 0-0	a29 1-1	a01 1-2	N11 2-0	J27 0-0	J02 1-1	a15 1-1
8 EXETER C	N19 1-0	A27 2-2	D03 2-4	S26 0-1	J02 1-1	a18 0-0	a22 0-0		a08 2-1	D27 1-0	M11 3-0	N05 2-1	F11 1-0	M28 0-0	S24 0-1	S10 4-1	O22 2-0	M08 1-0	O12 2-1	J28 1-1	M22 0-0	a26 4-2	J14 1-1	O08 0-1
9 GILLINGHAM	S03 4-1	M07 1-4	J21 3-1	O22 1-1	F21 1-0	S27 3-0	A20 1-3	N12 1-0		J07 4-0	a29 0-0	S10 2-1	M25 0-0	F25 1-1	D26 0-0	a04 1-1	M11 2-1	O08 2-1	a15 2-1	O29 1-1	D31 2-2	S24 1-1	D03 3-1	a01 0-0
10 HEREFORD U	M18 2-1	O05 1-0	O15 0-0	S24 1-0	J14 2-2	M08 2-1	M04 1-0	M25 4-0	S07 2-0		a05 1-1	O01 2-1	D26 0-0	J28 1-3	a15 0-2	O29 1-1	F11 0-0	S10 2-3	a01 0-1	J02 1-1	D03 1-1	A27 0-1	N12 3-2	a29 1-1
11 LINCOLN C	a22 3-2	J14 0-0	a08 4-1	a26 2-1	N05 2-1	S23 1-0	M27 0-0	O15 1-2	D10 0-2	S28 0-0		M08 1-0	S10 0-1	J02 2-2	F11 1-0	M28 3-0	N19 2-2	M24 3-3	M18 3-1	A26 1-3	O08 3-1	D27 1-1	A24 2-2	F24 0-1
12 OXFORD U	J21 3-1	a29 0-0	J11 2-3	F11 0-0	S24 4-1	a01 1-1	M11 3-0	D31 0-0	F04 1-1	F25 3-0	S14 1-0		a26 3-3	O22 2-1	S28 0-0	M25 1-1	S03 1-0	A20 2-3	N12 1-0	D03 1-1	D26 3-3	O08 1-0	a15 3-1	M01 2-1
13 PETERBOROUGH U	a04 5-0	M04 2-1	N05 2-0	S13 2-1	D10 0-0	a11 2-0	M14 1-0	S17 1-1	D27 1-1	M28 2-1	F04 0-1	O04 1-0		N19 1-0	A20 0-0	M17 1-1	D31 1-0	a08 1-0	F22 2-1	O15 2-1	a18 2-0	a22 1-0	O01 0-0	S03 2-2
14 PLYMOUTH A	m01 6-0	D03 0-1	S17 0-1	J21 0-1	M04 2-2	N12 2-0	F04 1-1	D26 2-2	O01 1-3	S03 2-0	M13 1-2	M18 2-1	a15 1-0		O29 3-1	a29 3-2	A20 0-0	a11 1-1	a04 1-1	O04 2-2	M25 0-2	O15 0-1	O13 3-3	D31 0-1
15 PORTSMOUTH	J02 3-1	O15 1-1	D27 2-2	a08 3-3	O04 0-0	S03 3-0	S13 0-0	F28 1-1	M27 1-1	N19 2-0	S17 0-2	a04 0-2	J14 2-2	M21 1-5		N15 1-1	a22 0-2	D10 3-3	O01 2-2	M18 2-0	J20 1-2	N05 2-5	M04 1-2	F04 0-1
16 PORT VALE	S12 1-0	O01 1-2	M28 1-1	a22 0-1	a08 0-0	A20 1-3	a24 0-3	F08 4-0	O10 2-2	M22 1-0	S03 2-1	D27 1-1	O22 0-0	D09 3-3	J07 2-0		N05 0-0	D31 3-0	S17 0-0	M04 1-2	M11 1-0	N19 1-1	F28 2-2	a11 1-1
17 PRESTON N.E.	M04 3-1	D26 4-0	O01 2-0	F04 2-1	O29 2-1	M25 0-0	F28 4-0	M18 0-0	O15 2-0	S17 0-0	a15 4-0	F21 3-2	a01 0-1	J14 5-2	D03 3-1	J02 2-0		A27 3-2	O04 2-1	a29 2-2	S13 1-1	O25 2-1	a04 1-0	N12 1-3
18 ROTHERHAM U	O01 2-1	J02 0-3	M14 1-0	S03 0-0	O15 1-1	D26 1-2	S17 1-0	S13 1-0	M04 2-0	a18 1-0	O29 0-0	J14 2-0	N12 0-1	O11 1-2	a29 0-1	a01 2-0	a25 2-1		M25 1-2	a04 0-0	a15 1-3	M18 2-0	O04 3-0	D03 2-2
19 SHEFFIELD W	M21 2-0	J28 3-2	a22 0-0	N05 3-1	M07 1-1	O08 1-0	D03 1-2	J17 2-1	N19 0-0	D31 1-0	O22 2-0	a08 2-1	S24 0-1	S27 1-1	F25 0-0	F11 3-1	a18 1-0	D27 1-0		S10 0-1	A20 1-1	M27 1-0	A27 0-0	m03 2-1
20 SHREWSBURY T	D27 4-0	a18 5-3	S13 3-3	N19 0-3	M25 0-0	J31 1-1	D31 1-0	S03 0-2	D06 1-2	N05 3-0	J21 0-1	a22 1-0	M11 0-0	a25 3-1	O22 6-1	O08 3-0	D10 0-0	S27 4-1	F28 0-0		J25 2-3	a08 3-1	S17 0-0	A20 2-1
21 SWINDON T	O04 0-1	S16 1-1	a04 0-0	D10 2-2	M17 1-1	S10 2-1	a08 0-0	O29 4-0	N05 3-2	a22 1-0	M04 1-0	M27 3-2	A23 2-0	D27 3-1	A27 3-1	O15 1-1	M07 0-2	N19 2-0	J14 2-2	S30 5-0		J02 1-0	a11 2-3	M14 1-2
22 TRANMERE R	S16 0-0	a03 0-0	F03 0-1	A20 3-2	S30 5-0	a28 1-1	S02 1-0	O03 2-1	a11 1-1	J20 2-1	M25 3-1	D16 4-1	D02 0-2	M10 1-1	D30 2-0	a14 2-1	J06 1-0	O21 2-2	D26 3-1	N12 2-0	M31 1-1		O28 0-1	S12 3-1
23 WALSALL	D10 1-1	S10 1-2	D31 0-0	M25 0-0	D27 3-0	M11 2-2	N05 4-2	A20 1-3	a22 2-1	a08 2-0	F07 3-1	N19 2-1	F25 1-0	M07 1-0	O08 1-1	S24 2-0	S27 0-0	m01 3-1	a25 1-1	F11 3-0	S03 2-0	J17 0-0		O22 0-1
24 WREXHAM	M25 2-0	O29 3-1	O03 4-1	D27 3-1	a03 1-2	F11 1-1	N19 2-1	M04 2-1	J02 3-3	D10 2-1	O01 1-0	A22 2-2	m01 0-0	N05 2-0	S10 2-0	A27 1-1	a08 0-0	a22 7-1	O15 1-1	J14 0-0	S24 2-1	M06 6-1	M18 1-0	

DIVISION 4

	ALDERSHOT	BARNSLEY	BOURNEMOUTH	BRENTFORD	CREWE A	DARLINGTON	DONCASTER R	GRIMSBY T	HALIFAX T	HARTLEPOOL U	HUDDERSFIELD T	NEWPORT CO	NORTHAMPTON T	READING	ROCHDALE	SCUNTHORPE U	SOUTHEND U	SOUTHPORT	STOCKPORT CO	SWANSEA C	TORQUAY U	WATFORD	WIMBLEDON	YORK C
1 ALDERSHOT		S10 0-0	O29 2-0	D26 1-0	S28 2-0	F28 3-2	A27 1-0	M17 4-2	a15 0-0	a29 3-0	J28 3-3	O08 2-2	a01 2-1	a04 1-1	S24 2-0	D03 4-0	M25 3-0	J02 0-0	A24 2-1	F25 2-2	N12 3-0	O15 1-0	M08 3-1	J14 1-1
2 BARNSLEY	F07 2-0		M31 3-0	N12 0-0	D26 4-0	J07 2-1	M04 0-0	O14 1-2	a04 3-2	O29 3-2	M18 1-1	S03 1-0	a15 2-3	D03 4-1	A20 4-0	S13 3-0	D31 1-1	M25 2-1	F18 0-1	a11 0-2	O04 2-0	S17 1-0	a29 3-2	O01 2-1
3 BOURNEMOUTH	M24 0-0	J02 2-2		F04 3-2	J14 1-0	N19 2-0	O05 0-1	a22 1-0	S17 0-0	M04 1-0	D10 1-0	M28 4-2	M17 1-1	O25 1-0	a08 1-0	J21 1-1	S03 0-3	O01 3-1	N05 1-0	D27 0-1	M14 1-1	a04 1-2	O15 1-2	S13 2-1
4 BRENTFORD	M27 2-0	a08 2-0	S10 1-1		J28 5-1	a22 2-0	a18 2-2	D10 3-1	O01 4-1	M18 2-0	J02 1-1	D27 3-3	A20 3-0	A27 1-1	M06 4-0	S24 2-0	O29 1-0	O15 0-0	a03 4-0	N19 0-2	M04 3-0	O03 0-3	A22 4-1	N05 1-0
5 CREWE A	a25 0-2	M27 2-1	A20 3-1	S03 4-6		D31 2-2	a22 2-0	N19 0-2	F22 0-0	O01 1-0	D27 1-1	S14 2-0	O14 3-2	M17 1-1	N05 2-1	J07 1-1	F01 0-1	a11 2-0	D09 1-1	a08 2-1	S17 2-0	M24 2-2	M04 0-0	O05 1-0
6 DARLINGTON	S17 1-1	S06 0-2	a15 1-0	D02 1-3	a01 2-0		M18 1-1	J14 1-2	S13 2-1	M25 1-2	O15 2-2	F04 2-1	O04 2-0	J02 2-0	J24 1-0	a29 1-1	N12 2-0	D26 3-0	O01 2-2	S03 1-1	a03 0-0	a18 0-0	O29 3-1	M04 0-2
7 DONCASTER R	a11 4-3	O08 2-1	a25 0-0	S17 3-1	D03 2-0	O21 1-2		F28 0-1	D31 1-1	a15 2-0	F25 4-3	A20 2-2	N12 4-2	a29 2-2	M10 1-1	D26 1-1	S27 2-0	S20 2-1	F04 1-0	J10 1-1	a01 1-0	S03 0-1	M25 0-2	M28 1-1
8 GRIMSBY T	O22 1-0	M11 1-0	D03 0-2	a29 2-1	a15 2-2	A20 2-0	S24 0-0		D26 0-0	S13 2-1	M24 1-0	F25 1-0	M25 0-1	N12 0-1	S03 2-1	O08 0-0	a01 2-0	a25 2-0	J21 0-0	a18 2-1	D31 3-1	a11 1-1	O04 3-1	F04 3-2
9 HALIFAX T	N19 2-1	S27 1-1	F28 0-0	F25 1-1	S10 1-1	M07 0-2	N05 0-1	M27 0-0		A23 3-0	O08 0-0	a08 3-1	A27 0-1	a18 2-4	D17 3-1	M28 2-2	S24 0-1	M18 2-1	D27 1-1	D10 3-1	O15 0-0	a22 1-1	J14 1-2	J02 2-0
10 HARTLEPOOL U	D10 2-2	M24 1-2	O08 0-1	O22 3-1	F25 1-1	D27 2-1	N19 0-2	M07 3-1	F07 1-1		a25 3-2	a22 1-1	a11 0-2	S24 2-1	S27 1-0	S03 1-0	M11 1-0	F28 2-1	a08 2-0	D31 0-4	A20 1-2	N05 1-2	S10 2-0	M14 4-2
11 HUDDERSFIELD T	S03 1-1	O22 2-0	a29 2-0	a01 1-3	M25 3-0	M11 2-1	O01 4-1	O29 1-3	M04 2-2	O04 3-1		J21 2-0	a04 0-1	a15 0-2	J07 3-1	D31 4-1	D26 2-0	D02 3-1	S17 0-0	A20 0-0	S13 1-1	M14 1-0	D17 3-0	a11 1-2
12 NEWPORT CO	M04 2-1	F28 3-1	D26 3-2	M25 1-2	M07 1-0	S10 1-1	J14 1-0	O01 3-0	N12 2-0	D03 4-2	A27 2-0		J02 5-3	a01 0-0	F11 3-0	O04 3-1	a29 1-2	a15 1-1	O15 2-2	S24 1-0	S29 0-0	M17 2-2	a25 0-1	S06 2-1
13 NORTHAMPTON T	D31 1-1	N19 1-1	O22 1-0	J14 2-2	M11 0-0	a25 2-2	a08 0-0	D27 2-1	M14 1-2	S17 5-3	S27 3-1	N05 2-4		O08 0-2	O11 3-1	F25 1-2	M21 0-0	F04 1-0	S13 2-1	a22 3-1	S03 1-0	M28 0-2	F28 0-3	D10 1-1
14 READING	O05 1-0	a22 0-0	J07 0-0	a12 0-0	O22 2-0	N05 2-1	D10 3-0	a08 0-0	S03 2-1	F18 2-3	N19 1-0	D31 2-0	M04 0-0		D28 4-3	M11 1-0	A20 0-1	S17 3-1	M27 2-1	M24 1-4	F08 3-3	S14 1-3	O01 2-2	a26 1-0
15 ROCHDALE	m01 0-0	J14 1-1	N12 1-1	S13 1-2	J02 0-2	A27 2-0	O15 3-1	M20 1-3	O04 3-1	a04 0-1	O17 0-0	S17 0-1	O29 1-1	a24 1-0		a15 1-1	D03 1-2	a01 2-1	M04 2-1	F27 2-1	a29 1-3	O01 2-3	D26 3-0	M18 1-2
16 SCUNTHORPE U	a22 1-1	M07 1-0	A26 0-0	M14 1-1	A23 3-0	D10 3-0	M27 0-0	M03 2-1	O29 2-0	a18 2-0	N05 1-1	a04 2-0	O01 2-2	O15 0-1	N19 1-0		S10 1-2	J14 0-2	J02 3-0	S27 1-0	M18 0-1	a08 0-1	S17 3-0	D27 2-1
17 SOUTHEND U	D27 3-1	N04 0-0	J27 5-1	M24 2-1	A26 1-0	a07 2-0	a03 4-0	J02 1-1	F17 5-0	O14 1-1	M27 1-3	D09 4-2	A22 0-0	J13 0-2	a21 3-1	F03 2-0		M04 4-2	O03 0-2	S12 2-1	S30 4-0	N19 1-0	M17 1-0	S16 0-0
18 SOUTHPORT	N05 1-1	D27 1-1	F25 0-0	M11 1-3	S23 1-2	M27 1-0	M07 1-1	S27 2-2	O21 1-2	A27 1-1	a22 1-1	N19 3-3	S09 3-1	M14 1-1	D31 3-1	A20 1-1	O07 0-0		M24 2-0	a04 0-3	J07 0-0	D10 2-2	a17 0-5	a07 4-1
19 STOCKPORT CO	J06 2-1	S23 3-0	D30 2-1	S26 1-1	a28 1-2	F24 1-0	S09 1-1	A26 2-0	M25 1-3	N11 6-0	F27 0-1	M10 2-0	M06 1-2	D26 2-0	O07 2-0	M31 1-1	a24 1-0	O28 2-1		O22 2-0	a14 3-0	A20 1-3	D02 2-2	J27 2-0
20 SWANSEA C	O01 1-0	A27 2-1	M25 1-0	a15 2-1	N12 5-0	J28 1-2	A23 3-0	S16 2-0	a29 2-0	a01 8-0	J14 1-0	F17 4-0	D03 2-4	O29 2-1	S10 3-0	a25 3-1	M07 0-0	O04 1-1	M17 3-1		D26 1-1	M03 3-3	J02 3-0	O15 1-1
21 TORQUAY U	a08 1-2	a26 3-1	S24 1-1	O08 2-1	M01 1-2	S26 0-0	J02 2-0	N05 3-1	M11 2-2	J14 0-0	M08 2-1	M22 2-0	J28 2-1	S10 3-0	D10 3-0	O22 4-2	a18 0-1	O12 2-2	N19 2-0	M27 2-4		D27 2-3	A27 1-1	a22 3-0
22 WATFORD	M11 1-0	F11 0-0	S27 2-1	a25 1-1	O29 5-2	S24 2-1	J28 6-0	S06 1-0	D03 1-1	J02 1-0	S10 2-0	O22 2-0	D26 3-0	M07 1-0	F25 1-0	N12 4-1	a15 1-1	a29 3-2	J13 1-0	O08 2-1	M25 1-0		a01 2-0	A27 1-3
23 WIMBLEDON	S13 1-2	D10 0-0	M11 3-1	J07 1-1	O08 0-0	N07 1-1	D28 3-3	a04 2-2	A20 3-3	F20 3-0	a08 2-0	S27 3-0	S24 2-0	F24 1-1	M27 5-1	F11 0-0	O22 1-3	S03 2-2	a22 2-0	N05 1-1	J21 0-1	D31 1-3		N19 2-1
24 YORK C	A20 1-2	F24 1-2	M07 0-0	D31 3-2	a04 1-1	O07 1-2	O28 2-1	S10 1-2	M31 1-1	D26 1-0	S24 1-1	J07 2-0	a29 0-3	S27 2-0	O21 2-2	M24 0-2	F28 1-2	N12 2-1	S02 2-1	M11 2-1	D03 0-0	J21 0-4	a15 1-1	

LEAGUE TABLES

DIVISION 1

	P	W	D	L	F	A	W	D	L	F	A	Pts
Nottingham F	42	15	6	0	37	8	10	8	3	32	16	64
Liverpool	42	15	4	2	37	11	9	5	7	28	23	57
Everton	42	14	4	3	47	22	8	7	6	29	23	55
Manchester C	42	14	4	3	46	21	6	8	7	28	30	52
Arsenal	42	14	5	2	38	12	7	5	9	22	25	52
WBA	42	13	5	3	35	18	5	9	7	27	35	50
Coventry C	42	13	5	3	48	23	5	7	9	27	39	48
Aston Villa	42	11	4	6	33	18	7	6	8	24	24	46
Leeds U	42	12	4	5	39	21	6	6	9	24	32	46
Manchester U	42	9	6	6	32	23	7	4	10	35	40	42
Birmingham C	42	8	5	8	32	30	8	4	9	23	30	41
Derby Co	42	10	7	4	37	24	4	6	11	17	35	41
Norwich C	42	10	8	3	28	20	1	10	10	24	46	40
Middlesbrough	42	8	8	5	25	19	4	7	10	17	35	39
Wolves	42	7	8	6	30	27	5	4	12	21	37	36
Chelsea	42	7	11	3	28	20	4	3	14	18	49	36
Bristol C	42	9	6	6	37	26	2	7	12	12	27	35
Ipswich T	42	10	5	6	32	24	1	8	12	15	37	35
QPR	42	8	8	5	27	26	1	7	13	20	38	33
West Ham U	42	8	6	7	31	28	4	2	15	21	41	32
Newcastle U	42	4	6	11	26	37	2	4	15	16	41	22
Leicester C	42	4	7	10	16	32	1	5	15	10	38	22

DIVISION 2

	P	W	D	L	F	A	W	D	L	F	A	Pts
Bolton W	42	16	4	1	39	14	8	6	7	24	19	58
Southampton	42	15	4	2	44	16	7	9	5	26	23	57
Tottenham H	42	13	7	1	50	19	7	9	5	33	30	56
Brighton & HA	42	15	5	1	43	21	7	7	7	20	17	56
Blackburn R	42	12	4	5	33	16	4	9	8	23	44	45
Sunderland	42	11	6	4	36	17	3	10	8	31	42	44
Stoke C	42	13	5	3	38	16	3	5	13	15	33	42
Oldham A	42	9	10	2	32	20	4	6	11	22	38	42
Crystal P	42	9	7	5	31	20	4	8	9	19	27	41
Fulham	42	9	8	4	32	19	5	5	11	17	30	41
Burnley	42	11	6	4	35	20	4	4	13	21	44	40
Sheffield U	42	13	4	4	38	22	3	4	14	24	51	40
Luton T	42	11	4	6	35	20	3	6	12	19	32	38
Orient	42	8	11	2	30	20	2	7	12	13	29	38
Notts Co	42	10	9	2	36	22	1	7	13	18	40	38
Millwall	42	8	8	5	23	20	4	6	11	26	37	38
Charlton A	42	11	6	4	38	27	2	6	13	17	41	38
Bristol R	42	10	7	4	40	26	3	5	13	21	51	38
Cardiff C	42	12	6	3	32	23	1	6	14	19	48	38
Blackpool	42	7	8	6	35	25	5	5	11	24	35	37
Mansfield T	42	6	6	9	30	34	4	5	12	19	35	31
Hull C	42	6	6	9	23	25	2	6	13	11	27	28

DIVISION 3

	P	W	D	L	F	A	W	D	L	F	A	Pts
Wrexham	46	14	8	1	48	19	9	7	7	30	26	61
Cambridge U	46	19	3	1	49	11	4	9	10	23	40	58
Preston NE	46	16	5	2	48	19	4	11	8	15	19	56
Peterboro' U	46	15	7	1	32	11	5	9	9	15	22	56
Chester	46	14	8	1	41	24	2	14	7	18	32	54
Walsall	42	12	8	3	35	17	6	9	8	26	33	53
Gillingham	46	11	10	2	36	21	4	10	9	31	39	50
Colchester U	46	10	11	2	36	16	5	7	11	19	28	48
Chesterfield	46	14	6	3	40	16	3	8	12	18	33	48
Swindon T	46	12	7	4	40	22	4	9	10	27	38	48
Shrewsbury T	46	11	7	5	42	23	5	8	10	21	34	47
Tranmere R	46	13	7	3	39	19	3	8	12	18	33	47
Carlisle U	46	10	9	4	32	26	4	10	9	27	33	47
Sheffield W	46	13	7	3	28	14	2	9	12	22	38	46
Bury	46	7	13	3	34	22	6	6	11	28	34	45
Lincoln C	46	10	8	5	35	26	5	7	11	18	35	45
Exeter C	46	11	8	4	30	18	4	6	13	19	41	44
Oxford U	46	11	10	2	38	21	2	4	17	26	46	40
Plymouth A	46	7	8	8	33	28	4	9	10	28	40	39
Rotherham U	46	11	5	7	26	19	2	8	13	25	49	39
Port Vale	46	7	11	5	28	23	1	9	13	18	44	36
Bradford C	46	11	6	6	40	29	1	4	18	16	57	34
Hereford U	46	9	9	5	28	22	0	5	18	6	38	32
Portsmouth	46	4	11	8	31	38	3	6	14	10	37	31

DIVISION 4

	P	W	D	L	F	A	W	D	L	F	A	Pts
Watford	46	18	4	1	44	14	12	7	4	41	24	71
Southend U	46	15	5	3	46	18	10	5	8	20	21	60
Swansea C	46	16	5	2	54	17	7	5	11	33	30	56
Brentford	46	15	6	2	50	17	6	8	9	36	37	56
Aldershot	46	15	8	0	45	16	4	8	11	22	31	54
Grimsby T	46	14	6	3	30	15	7	5	11	27	36	53
Barnsley	46	15	4	4	44	20	3	10	10	17	29	50
Reading	46	12	7	4	33	23	6	7	10	22	29	50
Torquay U	46	12	6	5	43	25	4	9	10	14	31	47
Northampton T	46	9	8	6	32	30	8	5	10	31	38	47
Huddersfield T	46	13	5	5	41	21	2	10	11	22	34	45
Doncaster R	46	11	8	4	37	26	3	9	11	15	39	45
Wimbledon	46	8	11	4	39	26	6	5	12	27	41	44
Scunthorpe U	46	12	6	5	31	14	2	10	11	19	41	44
Crewe A	46	11	8	4	34	25	4	6	13	16	44	44
Newport Co	46	14	6	3	43	22	2	5	16	22	51	43
Bournemouth	46	12	6	5	28	20	2	9	12	13	31	43
Stockport	46	14	4	5	41	19	2	6	15	15	37	42
Darlington	46	10	8	5	31	22	4	5	14	21	37	41
Halifax T	46	7	10	6	28	23	3	11	9	24	39	41
Hartlepool U	46	12	4	7	34	29	3	3	17	17	55	37
York C	46	8	7	8	27	31	4	5	14	23	38	36
Southport	46	5	13	5	30	32	1	6	16	22	44	31
Rochdale	46	8	6	9	29	28	0	2	21	14	57	24

Football League Records

Top scorers: Div 1, F.Worthington (Bolton Wanderers) 24 goals; Div 2, B.Robson (West Ham United) 24 goals; Div 3, R.Jenkins (Watford) 29 goals; Div 4, J.Dungworth (Aldershot) 26 goals. Southport failed to gain re-election, Wigan Athletic were elected in their place.

Kenny Dalglish, a £440,000 signing from Celtic, he was top scorer for Liverpool in 1978-9 and went on to share in many Anfield triumphs as a player and manager.

Dave Swindlehurst of Crystal Palace, top scorer with 14 goals when the Selhurst Park club inched their way to the Second Division championship.

DIVISION 1

	ARSENAL	ASTON VILLA	BIRMINGHAM C	BOLTON W	BRISTOL C	CHELSEA	COVENTRY C	DERBY CO	EVERTON	IPSWICH T	LEEDS U	LIVERPOOL	MANCHESTER C	MANCHESTER U	MIDDLESBROUGH	NORWICH C	NOTTINGHAM F	Q.P.R.	SOUTHAMPTON	TOTTENHAM H	W.B.A.	WOLVERHAMPTON W
1 ARSENAL		O07 1-1	D30 3-1	S16 1-0	M10 2-0	a16 5-2	a03 1-1	D16 2-0	N18 2-2	N04 4-1	A19 2-2	D02 1-0	M24 1-1	S23 1-1	F10 0-0	a28 1-1	J13 2-1	S02 5-1	O21 1-0	a10 1-0	D26 1-2	F24 0-1
2 ASTON VILLA	a25 5-1		M03 1-0	M07 3-0	N18 2-0	a28 2-1	M28 1-1	a11 3-3	S16 1-1	m02 2-2	D26 2-2	a16 3-1	N04 1-1	O14 2-2	O27 0-2	D16 1-1	S30 1-2	M20 3-1	S02 1-1	M24 2-3	m11 0-1	A19 1-0
3 BIRMINGHAM C	m05 0-0	O21 0-1		N21 3-0	N25 1-1	S23 1-1	M10 0-0	A26 1-1	D09 1-3	a03 1-1	F10 0-1	S09 0-3	O07 1-2	N11 5-1	A22 1-3	M27 1-0	a21 0-2	M06 3-1	a07 2-2	F24 1-0	a24 1-1	a14 1-1
4 BOLTON W	M26 4-2	m05 0-0	S02 2-2		A19 1-2	F24 2-1	N04 0-0	S09 2-1	a03 3-1	a21 2-3	O07 3-1	m01 1-4	O21 2-2	D22 3-0	a14 0-0	S23 3-2	N25 0-1	a07 2-1	M24 2-0	m08 1-3	N18 0-1	D09 3-1
5 BRISTOL C	O28 1-3	A26 1-0	M31 2-1	N11 4-1		a10 3-1	D26 5-0	D02 1-0	S30 2-2	F03 3-1	a28 0-0	D16 1-0	D30 1-1	M03 1-2	M17 1-1	A22 1-1	O14 1-3	a03 2-0	S16 3-1	J13 0-0	a17 1-0	N21 0-1
6 CHELSEA	m14 1-1	D09 0-1	F03 2-1	O14 4-3	D23 0-0		F21 1-3	a04 1-1	A19 0-1	m05 2-3	S02 0-3	M03 0-0	S16 1-4	N25 0-1	a21 2-1	O28 3-3	a07 1-3	M17 1-3	a14 1-2	N18 1-3	S30 1-3	M24 1-2
7 COVENTRY C	N25 1-1	a07 1-1	O28 2-1	M17 2-2	a14 3-2	S09 3-2		N21 4-2	D23 3-2	O07 2-2	S23 0-0	M06 0-0	F24 0-3	M20 4-3	N11 2-1	A26 4-1	A22 0-0	D09 1-0	a21 4-0	F10 1-3	M03 1-3	m05 3-0
8 DERBY CO	a21 2-0	D23 0-0	N18 2-1	M21 3-0	a07 0-1	O07 1-0	S02 0-2		M24 0-0	F28 0-1	M10 0-1	F24 0-2	A19 1-1	D09 1-3	m05 0-3	F10 1-1	a14 1-2	N25 2-1	S23 2-1	O21 2-2	S16 3-2	N04 4-1
9 EVERTON	A26 1-0	J31 1-1	a28 1-0	a16 1-0	F10 4-1	N11 3-2	a10 3-3	A22 2-1		F24 0-1	D16 1-1	O28 1-0	D26 1-0	N21 3-0	S09 2-0	M30 2-2	M10 1-1	M03 2-1	O07 0-0	D30 1-1	m01 0-2	S23 2-0
10 IPSWICH T	M17 2-0	S09 0-2	a17 3-0	D16 3-0	S23 0-1	D30 5-1	M13 1-1	a16 2-1	O14 0-1		D02 2-3	A22 0-3	M31 2-1	A26 3-0	N21 2-1	D26 1-1	M03 1-1	O28 2-1	F10 0-0	a28 2-1	N11 0-1	J20 3-1
11 LEEDS U	N11 0-1	a14 1-0	S30 3-0	a25 5-1	D09 1-1	N22 2-1	F03 1-0	O28 4-0	a21 1-0	a07 1-1		m17 0-3	J13 1-1	A23 2-3	D23 3-1	M03 2-2	m15 1-2	m04 4-3	N25 4-0	S16 1-2	O14 1-3	A26 3-0
12 LIVERPOOL	a07 3-0	m08 3-0	F13 1-0	S30 3-0	a21 1-0	O21 2-0	S16 1-0	O14 5-0	M13 1-1	M24 2-0	N04 1-1		N18 1-0	a14 2-0	N25 2-0	F21 6-0	D09 2-0	A19 2-1	m05 2-0	S02 7-0	F03 2-1	M20 2-0
13 MANCHESTER C	A22 1-1	m15 2-3	m01 3-1	M03 2-1	m05 2-0	J20 2-3	O14 2-0	N11 1-2	a14 0-0	N25 1-2	S09 3-0	A26 1-4		F10 0-3	a24 1-0	F27 2-2	D23 0-0	a21 3-1	D09 1-2	S23 2-0	O28 2-2	a07 3-1
14 MANCHESTER U	F03 0-2	F24 1-1	A19 1-0	a11 1-2	O21 1-3	m16 1-1	a16 0-0	a28 0-0	S02 1-1	N18 2-0	M24 4-1	D26 0-3	S30 1-0		O07 3-2	a25 1-0	S16 1-1	F28 2-0	N04 1-1	D16 2-0	D30 3-5	m07 3-2
15 MIDDLESBROUGH	S30 2-3	M10 2-0	M24 2-1	D26 1-1	N04 0-0	D16 7-2	A19 1-2	M13 3-1	M06 1-2	S02 0-0	a10 1-0	m11 0-1	a17 2-0	M27 2-2		O14 2-0	F03 1-3	S16 0-2	N18 2-0	M31 1-0	a28 1-1	O21 2-0
16 NORWICH C	D09 0-0	a21 1-2	S16 4-0	F03 0-0	M24 3-0	M10 2-0	N18 1-0	S30 3-0	N25 0-1	a14 0-1	O21 2-2	O07 1-4	S02 1-1	a07 2-2	F24 1-0		m05 1-1	J31 1-1	A19 3-1	N04 2-2	J13 1-1	M07 0-0
17 NOTTINGHAM F	S09 2-1	a04 4-0	D16 1-0	M31 1-1	F24 2-0	M28 6-0	M24 3-0	D26 1-1	N04 0-0	O21 1-0	a16 0-0	a28 0-0	m09 3-1	a18 1-1	S23 2-2	M14 2-1		N18 0-0	m02 1-0	A19 1-1	S02 0-0	O07 3-1
18 Q.P.R.	F13 1-2	S23 1-0	m07 1-3	D02 1-3	O07 1-0	N04 0-0	a28 5-1	M31 2-2	O21 1-1	m11 0-4	D30 1-4	N11 1-3	D16 2-1	S09 1-1	J20 1-1	a13 0-0	A26 0-0		F24 0-1	D26 2-2	A22 0-1	F10 3-3
19 SOUTHAMPTON	M03 2-0	N21 2-0	D02 1-0	A22 2-2	F20 2-0	D26 0-0	D16 4-0	F03 1-2	F17 3-0	S30 1-2	M31 2-2	a24 1-1	a28 1-0	a30 1-1	A26 2-1	N11 2-2	O28 0-0	O14 1-1		a16 3-3	a13 1-1	S09 3-2
20 TOTTENHAM H	D23 0-5	A23 1-4	O14 1-0	O28 2-0	S09 1-0	A26 2-2	S30 1-1	M03 2-0	m05 1-1	D09 1-0	J20 1-2	N22 0-0	F03 0-3	a21 1-1	a07 1-2	M17 0-0	N11 1-3	a14 1-1	M28 0-0		m14 1-0	N25 1-0
21 W.B.A.	a14 1-1	N25 1-1	N04 1-0	A26 4-0	J01 3-1	M14 1-0	O21 7-1	M26 2-1	a07 1-0	A19 2-1	F24 1-2	S23 1-1	a04 4-0	m05 1-0	D09 2-0	S09 2-2	m18 0-1	M24 2-1	m08 1-0	O07 0-1		a21 1-1
22 WOLVERHAMPTON W	O14 1-0	N11 0-4	D26 2-1	a28 1-1	S02 2-0	A22 0-1	D30 1-1	a24 4-0	F03 1-0	S16 1-3	N18 1-1	a10 0-1	M27 1-1	O28 2-4	M03 1-3	a16 1-0	a30 1-0	S30 1-0	J17 2-0	a03 3-2	D16 0-3	

DIVISION 2

	BLACKBURN R	BRIGHTON & HA	BRISTOL R	BURNLEY	CAMBRIDGE U	CARDIFF C	CHARLTON A	CRYSTAL P	FULHAM	LEICESTER C	LUTON T	MILLWALL	NEWCASTLE U	NOTTS CO	OLDHAM A	ORIENT	PRESTON N.E.	SHEFFIELD U	STOKE C	SUNDERLAND	WEST HAM U	WREXHAM
1 BLACKBURN R		D09 1-1	a04 0-2	a14 1-2	M28 1-0	F28 1-4	S30 1-2	A19 1-1	m09 2-1	S16 1-1	O14 0-0	a21 1-1	a25 1-3	N18 3-4	M14 0-2	S02 3-0	M24 0-1	a07 2-0	N25 2-2	J17 1-1	m05 1-0	O28 1-1
2 BRIGHTON & H.A.	a28 2-1		a16 3-0	M03 2-1	A22 0-2	D26 5-0	a13 2-0	F17 0-0	O14 3-0	F03 3-1	D16 3-1	N21 3-0	D30 2-0	M31 0-0	S09 1-0	D02 2-0	S30 5-1	M17 2-0	J20 1-1	A26 2-0	O28 1-2	N11 2-1
3 BRISTOL R	O07 4-1	M20 1-2		a21 2-0	F10 2-0	S02 4-2	N18 5-5	a14 0-1	A19 3-1	M10 1-1	S09 2-0	D09 0-3	N04 2-0	F24 2-2	M24 0-0	O21 2-1	m05 0-1	N25 2-1	D23 0-0	a07 0-0	J20 0-1	S23 2-1
4 BURNLEY	D26 2-1	O21 3-0	D16 2-0		M31 1-1	D30 0-0	M24 2-1	N04 2-1	N18 5-3	A19 2-2	M13 2-1	m08 0-1	a10 1-0	S02 2-1	O07 1-0	a28 0-1	M10 1-1	M06 1-1	F24 0-3	S23 1-2	S09 3-2	a16 0-0
5 CAMBRIDGE U	O21 0-1	M24 0-0	S30 1-1	N25 2-2		J13 5-0	S16 1-1	D23 0-0	a14 1-0	N18 1-1	F03 0-0	M20 2-1	S02 0-0	M10 0-1	D09 3-3	N04 3-1	O07 1-0	m05 1-0	A19 0-1	a21 0-2	a07 0-0	F24 1-0
6 CARDIFF C	S23 2-0	a14 3-1	m07 2-0	m05 1-1	S09 1-0		N04 1-4	N25 2-2	D23 2-0	O21 1-0	a25 2-1	a07 2-1	M10 2-1	O07 2-3	A26 1-3	F24 1-0	A19 2-2	a21 4-0	M24 1-3	D09 1-1	m11 0-0	m14 1-0
7 CHARLTON A	F10 2-0	D23 0-3	A26 3-0	A22 1-1	M06 2-3	M17 1-1		M27 1-1	N25 0-0	F24 1-0	N21 1-2	M10 2-4	O21 4-1	S22 1-1	m05 2-0	O06 0-2	a07 1-1	D09 3-1	a14 1-4	N11 1-2	a21 0-0	S09 1-1
8 CRYSTAL P	N11 3-0	O07 3-1	D26 0-1	m11 2-0	a10 1-1	M31 2-0	a17 1-0		O28 0-1	D16 3-1	A22 3-1	J20 0-0	D02 1-0	a28 2-0	S23 1-0	D30 1-1	F24 0-0	N21 3-1	F10 1-1	S09 1-1	A26 1-1	M03 1-0
9 FULHAM	N03 1-2	F24 0-1	N10 3-0	A26 0-0	D26 5-1	a11 2-2	M31 3-1	M10 0-0		a28 3-0	D30 1-0	S23 1-0	D16 1-3	D02 1-1	F10 1-0	a16 2-2	O21 5-3	S09 2-0	O07 2-0	J20 2-2	N21 0-0	A22 0-1
10 LEICESTER C	J20 1-1	S23 4-1	O28 0-0	N11 2-1	A26 1-1	M03 1-2	O14 0-3	a20 1-1	M21 1-0		M28 3-0	m05 0-0	M17 2-1	S09 0-1	J01 2-0	F10 5-3	D23 1-1	A23 0-1	a07 1-1	a14 1-2	N25 1-2	N22 1-1
11 LUTON T	F24 2-1	a21 1-1	J16 3-2	a07 4-1	S23 1-1	S16 7-1	S02 3-0	M24 0-1	m05 2-0	N04 0-1		a14 2-2	N18 2-0	O21 6-0	A19 6-1	M10 2-1	D09 1-2	F10 1-1	F06 0-0	N25 0-3	F26 1-4	O07 2-1
12 MILLWALL	D16 1-1	S02 1-4	a28 0-3	S30 0-2	a17 2-0	D02 2-0	O28 0-2	S16 0-3	a24 0-0	a04 2-0	D26 0-2		A19 2-1	M24 0-1	N04 2-3	a10 2-0	a22 0-2	O14 1-1	N18 3-0	M03 0-1	m14 2-1	m17 2-2
13 NEWCASTLE U	S09 3-1	m05 1-3	m02 3-0	D23 3-1	N22 1-0	O28 3-0	M03 5-3	a07 1-0	a21 0-0	O07 1-0	A26 1-0	N11 1-0		a18 1-2	N25 1-1	S23 0-0	a04 4-3	a14 1-3	D09 2-0	F24 1-4	A23 0-3	m08 2-0
14 NOTTS CO	A26 2-1	N25 1-0	O14 2-1	N21 1-1	O28 1-1	M27 1-0	F03 1-1	D09 0-0	a07 1-1	a24 0-1	M03 3-1	A22 1-1	S30 1-2		a14 0-0	S16 1-0	a21 0-0	M13 4-1	m05 0-1	D23 1-1	N11 1-0	m01 1-1
15 OLDHAM A	a13 5-0	M06 1-3	A22 3-1	m14 2-0	a28 4-1	N18 2-1	D30 0-3	a03 0-0	S30 0-2	a16 2-1	N11 2-0	m11 4-1	M31 1-3	D26 3-3		D16 0-0	S16 2-0	M03 1-1	S02 1-1	O28 0-0	O14 2-2	a24 1-0
16 ORIENT	N21 2-0	a07 3-3	M03 1-1	D09 2-1	M17 3-0	O14 2-2	M20 2-1	m05 0-1	M27 1-0	S30 0-1	O28 3-2	D23 2-1	F03 2-0	J20 3-0	a21 0-0		N25 2-0	N11 1-1	S09 0-1	A22 3-0	a14 0-2	A26 0-1
17 PRESTON N.E.	A22 4-1	F10 1-0	D30 1-1	O28 2-2	a24 0-2	N11 2-1	D12 6-1	O14 2-3	M03 2-2	a17 4-0	a28 2-2	S09 0-0	a16 0-0	D16 1-1	M20 1-1	M31 1-1		A26 2-2	S23 0-1	N21 3-1	M17 0-0	D26 2-1
18 SHEFFIELD U	m02 0-1	N04 0-1	M31 1-0	S16 4-0	D30 3-3	D16 2-1	a28 2-1	S02 0-2	F06 1-1	m08 2-2	S30 1-1	F24 0-2	D26 1-0	a10 5-1	O21 4-2	A19 1-2	N18 0-1		M10 0-0	O07 3-2	a02 3-0	a17 1-1
19 STOKE C	M31 1-2	S27 2-2	a17 2-0	O14 3-1	N11 1-3	A23 2-0	D26 2-2	S30 1-1	a04 2-0	D02 0-0	a16 0-0	A26 2-0	a28 0-0	D30 2-0	N22 4-0	M14 3-1	F28 1-1	O28 2-1		M27 0-1	M03 2-0	D16 3-0
20 SUNDERLAND	a16 0-1	N18 2-1	D02 5-0	F03 3-1	D16 0-2	a28 1-2	A19 1-0	M14 1-2	S16 1-1	D26 1-1	M31 1-0	O21 3-2	O14 1-1	a13 3-0	M10 3-0	M24 1-0	S02 3-1	a25 6-2	N04 0-1		S30 2-1	M07 1-0
21 WEST HAM U	D30 4-0	M10 0-0	S16 2-0	a24 3-1	D02 5-0	a16 1-1	D16 2-0	N18 1-1	S02 0-1	M31 1-1	a09 1-0	O07 3-0	M24 5-0	A19 5-2	F24 3-0	D26 0-2	N04 3-1	S23 2-0	O21 1-1	F10 3-3		a28 1-1
22 WREXHAM	M10 2-1	A19 0-0	m10 0-1	M21 0-1	O14 2-0	S30 1-2	a02 1-1	O21 0-0	M24 1-1	S02 0-0	m07 2-0	N25 3-0	S16 0-0	N04 3-1	a07 2-0	N18 3-1	a14 2-1	F28 4-0	a21 0-1	m05 1-2	D09 4-3	

Season 1978-79

DIVISION 3

	BLACKPOOL	BRENTFORD	BURY	CARLISLE U	CHESTER	CHESTERFIELD	COLCHESTER U	EXETER C	GILLINGHAM	HULL C	LINCOLN C	MANSFIELD T	OXFORD U	PETERBOROUGH U	PLYMOUTH A	ROTHERHAM U	SHEFFIELD W	SHREWSBURY T	SOUTHEND U	SWANSEA C	SWINDON T	TRANMERE R	WALSALL	WATFORD
1 BLACKPOOL		m05 0-1	a07 1-2	S02 3-1	D23 3-0	S12 0-0	F10 2-1	a24 1-1	S26 2-0	F20 3-1	O07 2-0	O21 2-0	A19 1-0	D09 0-0	M10 0-0	N18 1-2	N04 0-1	M20 5-0	F24 1-2	a21 1-3	m15 5-2	a14 2-0	S16 2-1	M24 1-1
2 BRENTFORD	M31 3-2		O07 0-1	D30 0-0	M10 6-0	A26 0-3	A21 1-0	N11 0-0	S23 0-2	S09 1-0	S25 2-1	a28 1-0	N04 3-0	J20 0-0	D26 2-1	a23 1-0	a17 2-1	M26 2-3	a13 3-0	F10 1-0	m08 1-2	O21 2-0	D02 1-0	F24 3-3
3 BURY	M06 1-3	m15 2-3		a13 2-2	S30 1-1	O14 3-1	a28 2-2	M03 4-2	A26 2-2	O28 1-1	a16 2-2	D30 0-0	M20 1-1	m19 1-0	S12 1-2	D26 3-2	m01 0-0	M31 3-0	A22 3-3	N11 0-1	M27 0-1	F27 1-0	O17 1-1	S16 1-2
4 CARLISLE U	N11 1-1	a21 1-0	F13 1-2		a14 1-1	A22 1-1	S08 4-0	D09 1-1	a07 1-0	M27 2-2	J20 2-0	F10 1-0	m05 0-1	M20 4-1	O07 1-1	O21 1 1	F24 0-0	M17 1-1	S23 0-0	S25 2-0	O28 2-0	M06 2-0	A26 1-0	a24 1-0
5 CHESTER	a13 4-2	O28 3-1	F10 1-1	D26 1-2		M28 3-0	J17 2-2	A26 3-0	F21 1-1	N11 2-1	M07 5-1	M31 1-1	M03 4-1	S08 1-1	O18 0-0	M14 0-1	a28 2-2	a16 0-0	M21 0-1	S23 2-0	S27 2-0	F24 1-1	A23 2-1	O07 2-1
6 CHESTERFIELD	M14 1-3	N18 0-0	F24 2-1	M24 2-3	N04 3-1		O18 2-1	S09 0-1	m19 0-2	a04 1-2	a17 1-3	a16 1-0	S02 1-1	S23 3-1	A19 1-3	a28 1-0	D26 3-3	M07 2-1	S27 3-2	O07 2-1	F28 1-1	M10 5-2	M31 0-0	O21 0-2
7 COLCHESTER U	S30 3-1	M24 1-1	D09 0-0	a02 2-1	S12 2-1	a24 0-0		F02 2-2	m07 2-2	a21 2-1	J23 2-0	M09 1-0	a14 1-1	m04 4-2	N03 2-1	S02 0-0	N18 1-0	S15 1-0	O20 1-1	A19 2-2	O06 3-2	a06 1-0	F27 2-0	D23 0-1
8 EXETER C	O18 3-0	S02 2-2	O21 2-1	a28 3-2	N18 0-1	J13 3-1	S27 2-1		O07 0-0	S23 3-1	D30 3-2	A19 0-0	J20 2-0	F10 1-0	a17 1-0	M31 2-0	M24 2-2	S13 0-1	D02 0-0	F24 2-1	a11 1-2	N04 3-0	D26 3-1	M10 0-0
9 GILLINGHAM	F03 2-0	J27 0-0	N18 3-3	D02 0-0	S16 1-0	S30 2-1	a16 3-0	m14 2-0		O14 2-0	O17 4-2	M24 0-0	M10 2-1	M03 1-0	D30 2-0	A19 0-0	S12 0-0	a28 2-0	D26 1-0	N04 2-0	M31 2-2	J13 3-2	a10 3-1	S02 2-3
10 HULL C	a16 0-0	M06 1-0	M10 4 1	A19 1-1	S02 3-0	S16 1-1	M13 1-0	m07 1-0	F24 0-1		M31 0-0	D26 3 0	S30 0-1	O07 1-1	m01 2-1	M24 1-0	a13 1-1	F03 1-1	a24 2 0	O21 2-2	a28 1-1	N18 2-1	S12 4-1	N04 4-0
11 LINCOLN C	m07 1-2	M21 1-0	m09 1-4	S16 1-1	a07 0-0	D23 0-1	O13 0-0	a21 0-1	a25 2-4	m05 4-2		N04 0-1	D09 2-2	a14 0-1	N18 3-3	a04 3-0	S02 1-2	m02 1-2	M10 1-1	M24 2-1	O21 0-3	A19 2-1	S29 1-1	S13 0-5
12 MANSFIELD T	M03 1 1	D09 2-1	a21 3-0	S30 1-0	m05 2-0	m21 2-1	O28 1-1	M26 1-1	A21 1-1	a14 0-2	m11 2-0		m14 1-1	D23 1-1	M12 5-0	m19 0-1	S16 1-1	m07 2-2	A26 1-1	a23 2-2	N11 0-1	N13 0-0	O14 1-3	a07 0-3
13 OXFORD U	M28 1-0	a04 0-1	S09 0-0	M31 5-1	O21 0-0	N11 1-1	D26 2-0	S16 3-2	O28 1-1	F10 1-0	a28 2-1	S27 3-2		F24 0-2	a11 3-2	D02 1-0	a25 1-1	A23 0-1	M07 0-0	A26 0-2	a16 0-1	O07 0-0	D30 2-1	J27 1-1
14 PETERBOROUGH U	a28 1-2	S16 3-1	N04 2-2	S12 0-0	J13 2-1	m08 0-0	M31 1-2	S30 1-1	O21 1-1	m11 3-0	D26 0-1	a17 1-2	O14 1-1		M24 2-1	a16 1-1	A19 2-0	D06 0-2	D30 0-1	M10 2-0	a24 2-1	S02 1-0	F03 0-3	N18 0-1
15 PLYMOUTH A	O28 0-0	a14 2-1	a03 3-0	F17 2-0	a24 2-2	D16 1-1	M17 1-1	F27 4-2	a21 2-1	a07 3 4	A26 2-1	S09 1-4	F20 0-1	N14 3-2		S30 2-0	J27 2-0	O14 1-1	N11 1-1	m05 2-2	S16 2-0	F03 2-2	M03 1-0	D09 1-1
16 ROTHERHAM U	A26 2-1	O17 1-0	a14 2-1	M03 1-3	a21 0-1	D09 1-0	N11 1-0	m05 2-1	M27 1-1	S05 0-2	S09 2-0	S23 2-0	a07 0-0	m01 1-1	F10 1-0		O07 0-1	O28 1-2	F06 2-1	M06 0-1	F24 1-3	D23 3-2	m14 4-1	S26 2-1
17 SHEFFIELD W	m17 2-0	M13 1-0	S26 0-0	O14 0-0	D09 0-0	a14 4-0	A26 0-0	O24 2-1	M06 2-1	m19 2-3	N11 0-0	a03 1-2	O17 1-1	M27 3-0	S23 2-3	m07 2-1		M03 0-0	S09 3-2	a07 0-0	m11 2-1	a21 1-2	O28 0-2	m05 2-3
18 SHREWSBURY T	S09 2-0	A19 1-0	m05 1-0	N04 0-0	J30 1-0	a21 1-1	J19 2-0	m17 4-1	D09 1-1	S20 1-0	S23 2-0	O07 2-2	M24 0-0	a07 2-0	F24 2-0	m10 3-1	O21 2-2		F09 2-0	D23 3-0	A26 0-0	a24 2-1	N10 1-1	a14 1-1
19 SOUTHEND U	O14 4-0	D23 1-1	M24 0-0	M12 1-1	A19 0-1	F02 2-0	M02 1-1	a06 0-1	a14 0-1	O23 3-0	O27 2-0	N17 1-1	S11 2-0	a21 0-0	S01 2-1	S15 2-1	F13 2-1	S29 0-1		D08 0-2	M16 5-3	m04 0-1	a30 1-0	a02 1-0
20 SWANSEA C	D30 1-0	S30 2-1	S02 2-0	F02 0-0	F27 2-2	m11 2-1	M27 4-1	O14 1-0	M16 3-1	M02 5-3	A22 3-0	O17 3-2	N18 1-1	O28 4-1	M31 2-1	S12 4-4	D02 4-2	a10 1-1	a28 3-2		D26 1-2	S16 4-3	a17 2-2	M20 3-2
21 SWINDON T	S23 0-1	S12 2-0	A19 2-1	M10 0-0	F03 2-0	a07 1-0	M20 1-2	a03 1-1	m05 3-1	D09 2-0	M03 6-0	S02 1-0	m02 2-0	O17 3-1	J20 1-3	O14 1-0	S30 3-0	N18 2-1	N04 1-0	a14 0-1		M24 4-1	J16 4-1	a21 2-0
22 TRANMERE R	D26 0-2	M03 0-1	S22 0-0	a16 1-1	O13 6-2	O27 1-1	m09 1-5	M16 2-2	D09 1-1	A26 1-3	M26 0-0	a30 1-2	F16 1-0	N10 1-0	S25 2-1	a18 1-1	F19 1-1	O16 2-2	M30 1-2	a03 1-2	A21 1-1		a27 0-0	F10 1-1
23 WALSALL	F06 2-1	a07 2-3	a24 0-1	N18 1-2	M24 2-1	m05 0-1	S23 2-2	a14 2-2	M20 0-1	J06 1-2	M13 4-1	F24 1-1	a21 0-1	S26 4-1	O21 2-1	N04 0-1	M10 0-2	S02 1-1	O07 1-1	F20 1-1	S09 4-1	D09 2-0		A19 2-4
24 WATFORD	A22 5-1	O14 2-0	J20 3-3	O17 2-1	m02 1-0	M03 2-0	a13 0-3	O28 1-0	N11 1-0	m14 4-0	J06 2 0	D02 1 1	S23 4-2	A26 1-2	a28 2-2	F03 2-2	M31 1-0	D26 2-2	a17 2-0	S09 0-2	D30 2-0	S30 4-0	M27 3-1	

DIVISION 4

	ALDERSHOT	BARNSLEY	BOURNEMOUTH	BRADFORD C	CREWE A	DARLINGTON	DONCASTER R	GRIMSBY T	HALIFAX T	HARTLEPOOL U	HEREFORD U	HUDDERSFIELD T	NEWPORT CO	NORTHAMPTON T	PORTSMOUTH	PORT VALE	READING	ROCHDALE	SCUNTHORPE U	STOCKPORT CO	TORQUAY U	WIGAN A	WIMBLEDON	YORK C
1 ALDERSHOT		O17 1-0	M20 1-0	S12 6-0	M10 3-0	S30 1-1	D09 2-1	N04 2-0	S02 1-0	O14 1-1	M03 2-0	a07 1-0	M24 2-3	a14 2-0	S23 0-2	J13 1-1	F06 2-2	N18 1-0	F03 2-0	D23 3-2	J20 1-0	a21 1-0	A19 1-1	m05 1-0
2 BARNSLEY	a24 2-0		M06 1-0	N18 0-1	M24 3-1	a30 1-1	a03 3-0	m08 2-1	A19 4-2	a12 1-0	a16 2-1	S16 1-0	M10 1-0	O07 1-1	M30 1-1	D26 6-2	S30 3-1	a28 0-3	M13 4-1	F24 4-4	S12 1-2	O21 0-0	N04 3-1	S02 3-0
3 BOURNEMOUTH	O07 0-1	a07 0-2		a21 1-0	J13 0-1	N18 2-2	F03 7-1	O21 0 0	M10 1-0	S02 0-1	F24 1-1	S12 2-0	A19 3-1	F21 0-0	S29 3-1	F06 3-1	a14 0-0	S16 3-1	M24 0-0	a23 3-1	N04 1-0	m05 2-1	D23 1 2	D09 1-2
4 BRADFORD C	M07 0-2	A26 1-2	D30 2-1		a20 6-0	M31 0-0	a30 1-0	a16 1-3	S27 3-0	m02 1-2	A23 2-1	O28 1-1	S23 1-3	N11 3-0	M28 2-0	O18 2-3	M13 2-3	D26 1-0	M03 1-1	S09 1-1	a11 3-1	m07 1-1	a04 1-0	O14 2-1
5 CREWE A	O27 1-1	A23 0-2	S09 1-0	D09 1-2		F23 1-1	F13 2-4	S23 0-3	F10 1-0	O21 0-1	F06 0-0	M28 3-3	M13 0-1	a10 2-4	N11 0-0	A25 1-5	a07 0-2	m18 1-2	m05 0-2	S27 2-2	O07 6-2	a14 1-1	a25 1-2	a21 0-1
6 DARLINGTON	a03 2-1	S26 0-0	A26 0-0	m05 1-1	O13 1-1		a14 3-2	S09 0-1	F27 2-1	m07 0-1	N11 2-1	A22 1-0	a07 1-0	m14 0-0	m11 2-0	O28 4-0	O17 1-2	M03 0-2	D23 2-2	M27 0 1	S23 1-2	D09 1-1	a21 1-1	M06 0-1
7 DONCASTER R	a28 1-1	S23 2-2	S26 1-1	N04 2-0	a16 2-0	D26 2-3		M31 0-1	a17 1-1	M23 0-0	J30 1-0	F27 0-2	O21 0-0	F10 2-0	O17 2-3	S12 1-3	M20 2-2	D02 1-0	S01 0-0	O07 2-0	O10 1-0	F24 0-1	M09 1-0	N18 1-2
8 GRIMSBY T	M17 0-0	a21 2-0	M03 1-0	J09 5-1	F27 2-2	J16 7-2	m05 3-4		N18 2-1	S16 0-1	O28 1-1	F03 2-1	D09 1-0	O17 4 3	O14 1-0	a03 1-0	A19 1-2	S30 4-0	a14 1-1	a07 2-1	S02 3-0	M24 3-1	S12 2-2	D23 3-0
9 HALIFAX T	N11 1-1	M27 0-2	O28 0-2	a26 2-0	S30 0-0	S16 0-2	M06 0-0	A26 1-2		m14 2-4	m09 1-0	a14 2-3	m05 1-2	a21 2-2	M03 2-0	O14 0-3	D09 0-0	m07 2-1	m18 2-3	A22 2-1	a03 1-0	D16 1-2	a07 2-1	S12 0-1
10 HARTLEPOOL U	F24 2-2	D23 1-1	N11 0-0	a07 2-2	M03 2-2	O07 0-2	A19 3-4	J20 1-0	S23 3-1		S09 2-1	m05 2-0	S25 0-0	m17 2-0	A25 1-1	m10 1-2	a21 0-0	O28 5-1	O17 1-1	M13 1-3	F10 3-2	a03 1-1	D09 1-1	a14 1-1
11 HEREFORD U	O21 1-1	F28 1 1	O14 0 0	M24 0 1	S16 0-1	S02 1-0	a21 2-0	M10 0-1	N04 2-2	M07 1-0		a25 3-0	D22 0-3	D09 4-3	m07 0-1	[illegible] 1-0	[illegible] 0-0	M21 2-2	a07 3-1	a14 1-0	N18 3-1	A19 0-0	m05 0-0	F03 1-0
12 HUDDERSFIELD T	D02 0-0	m02 1-0	M13 2-1	M10 0-0	A19 0-0	M24 2-2	S09 2-1	S26 2-0	D26 2-0	M31 2-0	O17 2-3		F24 0-1	S23 1-0	a28 2-0	a16 3-2	S02 1-1	a17 1-0	N18 3-2	a04 0-0	a30 1-1	O07 1-1	O21 3-0	N04 1-0
13 NEWPORT CO	A22 1-2	O28 1-1	m01 2-0	F27 2-4	S12 1-2	D02 2-1	M03 3-0	a28 1-1	M31 2-0	F02 3-2	a11 4-1	O14 2-1		M16 2-1	a16 1-2	D30 1-0	J13 3-2	O17 0-0	a18 2-0	A26 1-2	D26 1-1	N10 2-1	S16 1-3	S30 1-1
14 NORTHAMPTON T	D26 2 3	a26 0-1	a16 4-2	S02 1-0	a17 3-1	S12 4-1	S30 3-0	a24 1-2	D30 2-1	A23 1-1	a28 2-1	M06 2-3	N04 3-1		D02 0-2	M13 1-0	O14 2-2	M31 1-0	S15 1-0	O21 2-2	M24 1-2	M10 2-4	N18 1-1	a03 1-0
15 PORTSMOUTH	m15 1-1	m05 0-1	F10 1-1	A19 0-1	S02 3-0	N04 3-0	a24 4-0	F24 1-3	O21 3-1	N18 3-0	O07 1-0	D09 1-0	F20 2-1	a07 1-0		S16 2-0	D23 4-0	J13 1-1	S12 0-0	a21 1-1	M10 1-0	S26 1-0	a14 0-0	M24 1-1
16 PORT VALE	S09 1-1	a14 3-2	S23 1-2	a24 2-1	N18 2-2	M10 2-1	J16 1-3	O07 1-1	F24 0-1	N04 2-0	m01 1-1	J01 1-0	a21 1-1	S26 2-2	M21 0-0		m05 0-3	S02 1-1	A19 2-2	D09 2-1	O21 1-2	J09 2-1	M24 1-0	a07 0-0
17 READING	a16 4-0	F10 1-0	D26 1-0	O07 3-0	D06 3-0	a25 1 0	S16 3-0	M28 4-0	a28 1-0	F26 3-1	F21 3-0	N11 1-1	S09 2-1	F24 5-1	a13 2-0	M31 0-0		A23 2-0	M16 0-1	O28 3-3	S27 1-0	A26 2-0	m02 1-0	O21 3-0
18 ROCHDALE	A26 1-1	D09 0-3	a03 2-1	a14 1-0	N04 2-1	O21 2-1	a07 2-0	M13 2-5	O07 1-1	M10 1-1	S23 0-2	a11 0-2	a23 1-0	m05 4-1	S09 0-2	N11 0-1	M24 1-0		a21 1-0	m01 2-0	m09 1-0	M19 0-2	S25 0 0	A19 1-2
19 SCUNTHORPE U	S26 2-0	S09 0-1	A22 1-0	O21 3-2	M31 0-1	a10 1-0	N11 0-0	D26 2-1	a16 1 0	a24 3-1	D16 4-2	A25 3-1	O07 2-3	M20 0-3	a03 2-2	M27 2-0	N04 0-3	D30 0-4		S23 1-0	a28 2 2	m01 0-1	m08 2-0	M10 2-3
20 STOCKPORT CO	a09 2-2	O13 0-0	O16 1-0	J12 1-0	M05 4-3	A19 3-0	F21 0-1	D04 2-1	M23 1-2	S11 4-0	D26 0-2	S29 3-1	N17 1-1	M02 2-1	D29 4-2	a27 0-0	M09 0-0	a16 3-0	F26 0-2		M30 0-1	N03 0-1	S01 0-1	S15 2-0
21 TORQUAY U	S16 2-1	J31 3-2	M17 0-1	F14 1-2	F20 3-0	J27 1-0	M28 2-1	N11 3-1	S09 2-0	S30 4-1	A26 1-0	a21 2-1	a14 2-0	A19 0-1	O28 2-1	M03 2-2	F03 1-1	O14 1-1	D09 0-1	m05 1-0		a07 1-1	F28 1-6	a25 3-0
22 WIGAN A	D30 3-2	M03 1-1	M31 1-0	S16 1-3	D26 1-0	a28 2-2	O14 1-0	A23 0-3	O18 1-0	a16 2-2	M28 0-0	F17 2-1	S02 2-3	O28 2-0	F03 2-0	a13 5-3	N18 3-0	S13 3-0	S30 1-0	M17 2-0	M14 3-1		F14 1-2	F28 1-1
23 WIMBLEDON	M27 3-1	m14 1-1	a10 4-0	S30 2-1	O17 1-1	m17 2-0	O28 3-2	M20 0-1	D02 2-1	a28 3-1	M31 2-0	M03 2-1	M06 0-0	A26 4-1	D26 2-4	A22 1-0	S23 1-0	F03 3-2	O14 3-1	N11 2-0	a16 5-0	S09 2-1		m11 2-1
24 YORK C	M31 1-1	N11 0-1	a28 2-1	F24 2-2	m01 1-0	a16 5-2	A26 1-1	a13 0-0	M13 2-0	D26 1-1	S26 1-0	m19 1-3	M20 1-2	S09 1-0	A22 5-3	m07 4-0	M03 0-1	M27 2-1	O28 1-0	m14 1-0	O17 0-0	S23 0-1	O07 1-4	

LEAGUE TABLES

DIVISION 1

	P	W	D	L	F	A	W	D	L	F	A	Pts
Liverpool	42	19	2	0	51	4	11	6	4	34	12	68
Nottingham F	42	11	10	0	34	10	10	8	3	27	16	60
WBA	42	13	5	3	38	15	11	6	4	34	20	59
Everton	42	12	7	2	32	17	5	10	6	20	23	51
Leeds U	42	11	4	6	41	25	7	10	4	29	27	50
Ipswich T	42	11	4	6	34	21	9	5	7	29	28	49
Arsenal	42	11	8	2	37	18	6	6	9	24	30	48
Aston Villa	42	8	9	4	37	26	7	7	7	22	23	46
Manchester U	42	9	7	5	29	25	6	8	7	31	38	45
Coventry C	42	11	7	3	41	29	3	9	9	17	39	44
Tottenham H	42	7	8	6	19	25	6	7	8	29	36	41
Middlesbrough	42	10	5	6	33	21	5	5	11	24	29	40
Bristol C	42	11	6	4	34	19	4	4	13	13	32	40
Southampton	42	9	10	2	35	20	3	6	12	12	33	40
Manchester C	42	9	5	7	34	28	4	8	9	24	28	39
Norwich C	42	7	10	4	29	19	0	13	8	22	38	37
Bolton W	42	10	5	6	36	28	2	6	13	18	47	35
Wolves	42	10	4	7	26	26	3	4	14	18	42	34
Derby Co	42	8	5	8	25	25	2	6	13	19	46	31
QPR	42	4	9	8	24	33	2	4	15	21	40	25
Birmingham C	42	5	9	7	24	25	1	1	19	13	39	22
Chelsea	42	3	5	13	23	42	2	5	14	21	50	20

DIVISION 2

	P	W	D	L	F	A	W	D	L	F	A	Pts
Crystal P	42	12	7	2	30	11	7	12	2	21	13	57
Brighton & HA	42	16	3	2	44	11	7	7	7	28	28	56
Stoke C	42	11	7	3	35	15	9	9	3	23	16	56
Sunderland	42	13	3	5	39	19	9	8	4	31	25	55
West Ham U	42	12	7	2	46	15	6	7	8	24	24	50
Notts Co	42	8	10	3	23	15	6	6	9	25	45	44
Preston NE	42	7	11	3	36	23	5	7	9	23	34	42
Newcastle U	42	13	3	5	35	24	4	5	12	16	31	42
Cardiff C	42	12	5	4	34	23	4	5	12	22	47	42
Fulham	42	10	7	4	35	19	3	8	10	15	28	41
Orient	42	11	5	5	32	18	4	5	12	19	33	40
Cambridge U	42	7	10	4	22	15	5	6	10	22	37	40
Burnley	42	11	6	4	31	22	3	6	12	20	40	40
Oldham A	42	10	7	4	36	23	3	6	12	16	38	39
Wrexham	42	10	6	5	31	16	2	8	11	14	26	38
Bristol R	42	10	6	5	34	23	4	4	13	14	37	38
Leicester C	42	7	8	6	28	23	3	9	9	15	29	37
Luton T	42	11	5	5	46	24	2	5	14	14	33	36
Charlton A	42	6	8	7	28	28	5	5	11	32	41	35
Sheffield U	42	9	6	6	34	24	2	6	13	18	45	34
Millwall	42	7	4	10	22	29	4	6	11	20	32	32
Blackburn R	42	5	8	8	24	29	5	2	14	17	43	30

DIVISION 3

	P	W	D	L	F	A	W	D	L	F	A	Pts
Shrewsbury T	46	14	9	0	36	11	7	10	6	25	30	61
Watford	46	15	5	3	47	22	9	7	7	36	30	60
Swansea C	46	16	6	1	57	32	8	6	9	26	29	60
Gillingham	46	15	7	1	39	15	6	10	7	26	27	59
Swindon T	46	17	2	4	44	14	8	5	10	30	38	57
Carlisle U	46	11	10	2	31	13	4	12	7	22	29	52
Colchester C	46	13	9	1	35	19	4	8	11	25	36	51
Hull C	46	12	9	2	36	14	7	2	14	30	47	49
Exeter C	46	14	6	3	38	18	3	9	11	23	38	49
Brentford	46	14	4	5	35	19	5	5	13	18	30	47
Oxford U	46	10	8	5	27	20	4	10	9	17	30	46
Blackpool	46	12	5	6	38	19	6	4	13	23	40	45
Southend U	46	11	6	6	30	17	4	9	10	21	32	45
Sheffield W	46	9	8	6	30	22	4	11	8	23	31	45
Plymouth A	46	11	9	3	40	27	4	5	14	27	41	44
Chester	46	11	9	3	42	21	3	7	13	15	40	44
Rotherham U	46	13	3	7	30	23	4	7	12	19	32	44
Mansfield T	46	7	11	5	30	24	5	8	10	21	28	43
Bury	46	6	11	6	35	32	5	9	9	24	33	42
Chesterfield	46	10	5	8	35	34	3	9	11	16	31	40
Peterboro' U	46	8	7	8	26	24	3	7	13	18	39	36
Walsall	46	7	6	10	34	32	3	6	14	22	39	32
Tranmere R	46	4	12	7	26	31	2	4	17	19	47	28
Lincoln C	46	5	7	11	26	38	2	4	17	15	50	25

DIVISION 4

	P	W	D	L	F	A	W	D	L	F	A	Pts
Reading	46	19	3	1	49	8	7	10	6	27	27	65
Grimsby T	46	15	5	3	51	23	11	4	8	31	26	61
Wimbledon	46	18	3	2	50	20	7	8	8	28	26	61
Barnsley	46	15	5	3	47	23	9	8	6	26	19	61
Aldershot	46	16	5	2	38	14	4	12	7	25	33	57
Wigan A	46	14	5	4	40	24	7	8	8	23	24	55
Portsmouth	46	13	7	3	35	12	7	5	11	27	36	52
Newport Co	46	12	5	6	39	28	9	5	9	27	27	52
Huddersfield T	46	13	8	2	32	15	5	3	15	25	38	47
York C	46	11	6	6	33	24	7	5	11	18	31	47
Torquay U	46	14	4	5	38	24	5	4	14	20	41	46
Scunthorpe U	46	12	3	8	33	30	5	8	10	21	30	45
Hartlepool U	46	7	12	4	35	28	6	6	11	22	38	44
Hereford U	46	12	8	3	35	18	3	5	15	18	35	43
Bradford C	46	11	5	7	38	26	6	4	13	24	42	43
Port Vale	46	8	10	5	29	28	6	4	13	28	42	42
Stockport Co	46	11	5	7	33	21	3	7	13	25	39	40
Bournemouth	46	11	6	6	34	19	3	5	15	13	29	39
Northampton	46	12	4	7	40	30	3	5	15	24	46	39
Rochdale	46	11	4	8	25	26	4	5	14	22	38	39
Darlington	46	8	8	7	25	21	3	7	13	24	45	37
Doncaster	46	8	8	7	25	22	5	3	15	25	51	37
Halifax T	46	7	5	11	24	32	2	3	18	15	40	26
Crewe A	46	3	7	13	24	41	3	7	13	19	49	26

Football League Records

Top scorers: Div 1, P.Boyer (Southampton) 23 goals; Div 2, C.Allen (Queen's Park Rangers) 28 goals; Div 3, T.Curran (Sheffield Wednesday) 22 goals; Div 4, C.Garwood (Aldershot & Portsmouth) 27 goals.

Alan Hansen, the tall, elegant defender who made 38 appearances in yet another Liverpool Championship-winning season.

DIVISION 1

	ARSENAL	ASTON VILLA	BOLTON W	BRIGHTON & HA	BRISTOL C	COVENTRY C	CRYSTAL P	DERBY CO	EVERTON	IPSWICH T	LEEDS U	LIVERPOOL	MANCHESTER C	MANCHESTER U	MIDDLESBROUGH	NORWICH C	NOTTINGHAM F	SOUTHAMPTON	STOKE C	TOTTENHAM H	W.B.A.	WOLVERHAMPTON W
1 ARSENAL		F09 3-1	F23 2-0	N03 3-0	M11 0-0	D08 3-1	M22 1-1	J19 2-0	N17 2-0	A21 0-2	J12 0-1	N24 0-0	O06 0-0	A25 0-0	S15 2-0	D21 1-1	m05 0-0	a05 1-1	O20 0-0	D26 1-0	a26 1-1	S29 2-3
2 ASTON VILLA	S22 0-0		N03 3-1	A22 2-1	A25 0-2	D19 3-0	F02 2-0	M01 1-0	J12 2-1	M22 1-1	N24 0-0	D08 1-3	F27 2-2	S08 0-3	M19 0-2	M26 2-0	a05 3-2	O06 3-0	N17 2-1	a26 1-0	O13 0-0	M10 1-3
3 BOLTON W	O13 0-0	A18 1-1		J12 0-2	D01 1-1	a15 1-1	O27 1-1	M15 1-2	D26 1-1	D15 0-1	S22 1-1	O09 1-1	N17 0-1	a07 1-3	a08 2-2	M11 1-0	M01 1-0	A25 2-1	a19 2-1	M22 2-1	S08 0-0	m03 0-0
4 BRIGHTON & H.A.	A18 0-4	M03 1-1	S01 3-1		a07 0-1	M01 1-1	D26 3-0	D01 2-0	m03 0-0	S15 2-0	O13 0-0	N10 1-4	D29 4-1	M15 0-0	a19 2-1	O27 2-4	M29 1-0	S22 0-0	D15 0-0	J19 0-2	F16 0-0	a08 3-0
5 BRISTOL C	O27 0-1	D29 1-3	a12 2-1	J01 2-2		O09 1-0	M01 0-2	N10 0-2	F19 2-1	J19 0-3	A18 2-2	M15 1-3	N24 1-0	O13 1-1	a22 3-1	a26 2-3	S22 1-1	D21 0-1	S15 0-0	D08 1-3	a05 0-0	S01 2-0
6 COVENTRY C	m03 0-1	a29 1-2	S15 3-1	O20 2-1	A21 3-1		a19 2-1	a07 2-1	O06 2-1	D01 4-1	N10 3-0	J19 1-0	F09 0-0	D15 1-2	J01 2-0	S01 2-0	D29 0-3	F23 3-0	N03 1-3	S29 1-1	M08 0-2	M29 1-3
7 CRYSTAL P	N10 1-0	S15 2-0	M08 3-1	a05 1-1	O20 1-1	N24 0-0		S01 4-0	F23 1-1	S29 4-1	a12 1-0	a26 0-0	N03 2-0	M29 0-2	D29 1-2	J01 0-0	D08 1-0	A21 0-0	F09 0-1	O06 1-1	J26 2-2	J19 1-0
8 DERBY CO	S08 3-2	O20 1-3	O06 4-0	a12 3-0	M22 3-3	D26 1-2	J12 1-2		A25 0-1	N17 0-1	a05 2-0	D22 1-3	a26 3-1	F02 1-3	S22 1-0	D08 0-0	N24 4-1	F16 2-2	M08 2-2	F23 2-1	N03 2-1	A22 0-1
9 EVERTON	M28 0-1	S01 1-1	a05 3-1	D08 2-0	S29 0-0	M15 1-1	O13 3-1	D29 1-1		F09 0-4	N13 5-1	M01 1-2	D22 1-2	O27 0-0	N10 0-2	A18 2-4	J01 1-0	a26 2-0	M18 2-0	N24 1-1	a28 0-0	S15 2-3
10 IPSWICH T	O09 1-2	N10 0-0	a26 1-0	F02 1-1	S08 1-0	a12 3-0	F19 3-0	M29 1-1	S22 1-1		M14 1-0	O13 1-2	D08 4-0	M01 6-0	O27 1-0	a05 4-2	A18 0-1	N24 3-1	S01 3-1	D21 3-1	J01 4-0	D29 1-0
11 LEEDS U	S01 1-1	a19 0-0	F09 2-2	F23 1-1	N03 1-3	M22 0-0	D01 1-0	J01 1-0	A22 2-0	O06 2-1		S15 1-1	S29 1-2	m03 2-0	a02 2-0	D29 2-2	J19 1-2	M08 2-0	a08 3-0	O20 1-2	N17 1-0	D15 3-0
12 LIVERPOOL	a19 1-1	m03 4-1	A21 0-0	M22 1-0	O06 4-0	S08 4-0	D15 3-0	a08 3-0	O20 2-2	F23 1-1	M19 3-0		M11 2-0	D26 2-0	D01 4-0	S22 0-0	F19 2-0	J12 1-1	a01 1-0	N17 2-1	A25 3-1	N03 3-0
13 MANCHESTER C	M15 0-3	a07 1-1	M29 2-2	A25 3-2	a19 3-1	S22 3-0	A18 0-0	D15 3-0	a02 1-1	m03 2-1	F16 1-1	O27 0-4		N10 2-0	O10 1-0	M01 0-0	O13 1-0	S08 0-1	D26 1-1	J12 1-1	F02 1-3	D01 2-3
14 MANCHESTER U	D29 3-0	a23 2-1	F27 2-0	O06 2-0	F23 4-0	a26 2-1	N17 1-1	S15 1-0	M12 0-0	O20 1-0	D08 1-1	a05 2-1	M22 1-0		S01 2-1	N24 5-0	D22 3-0	N03 1-0	S29 4-0	a12 4-1	A22 2-0	F09 0-1
15 MIDDLESBROUGH	m19 5-0	S29 0-0	D21 3-1	N24 1-1	N17 1-0	a05 1-2	A25 1-1	F09 3-0	M22 2-1	M11 1-1	D26 3-1	m06 1-0	A21 3-0	J12 1-1		S08 1-0	a26 0-0	D08 0-1	F23 1-3	N03 0-0	O06 2-1	O20 1-0
16 NORWICH C	a02 2-1	D01 1-1	S29 2-1	M08 2-2	D15 2-0	J12 1-0	a07 2-1	m03 4-2	N03 0-0	D26 3-3	A25 2-1	F09 3-5	O20 2-2	a19 0-2	F27 0-0		S15 3-1	N17 2-1	O06 2-2	A22 4-0	M22 1-1	F23 0-4
17 NOTTINGHAM F	D01 1-1	D26 2-1	O20 5-2	N17 0-1	F09 0-0	A25 4-1	m03 4-0	a19 1-0	m09 1-0	N03 2-0	S08 0-0	S29 1-0	F23 4-0	a02 2-0	F16 2-2	a30 2-0		M22 2-0	A22 1-0	M11 4-0	J12 3-1	O06 3-2
18 SOUTHAMPTON	J01 0-1	M15 2-0	D29 2-0	F09 5-1	a29 5-2	O13 2-3	O09 4-1	S29 4-0	D15 1-0	a19 0-1	O27 1-2	S01 3-2	J19 4-1	A18 1-1	m03 4-1	M29 2-0	N10 4-1		D01 3-1	S15 5-2	M01 1-1	a07 0-3
19 STOKE C	M01 2-3	M29 2-0	N24 1-0	a26 1-0	F02 1-0	A18 3-2	S22 1-2	O27 3-2	S08 2-3	J12 0-1	D21 0-2	a23 0-2	a05 0-0	F16 1-1	O13 0-0	M15 2-1	O10 1-1	a12 1-2		A25 3-1	D08 3-2	N10 0-1
20 TOTTENHAM H	a07 1-2	D15 1-2	N10 2-0	S08 2-1	m03 0-0	F27 4-3	M15 0-0	O13 1-0	a19 3-0	a02 0-2	M01 2-1	M29 2-0	S01 2-1	D01 1-2	A18 1-3	O10 3-2	O27 1-0	F02 0-0	D29 1-0		S22 1-1	a23 2-2
21 W.B.A.	D15 2-2	F23 1-2	M18 4-4	S29 2-2	D26 3-0	O27 4-1	a01 3-0	A18 0-0	D01 1-1	a07 0-0	M29 2-1	D29 0-2	S15 4-0	O10 2-0	M14 0-0	N10 2-1	S01 1-5	O20 4-0	m03 0-1	F09 2-1		a19 0-0
22 WOLVERHAMPTON W	m16 1-2	O27 1-1	D08 3-1	D21 1-3	J12 3-0	N17 0-3	S08 1-1	O09 0-0	F02 0-0	A25 3-0	a26 3-1	F26 1-0	a12 1-2	S22 3-1	M01 0-2	O13 1-0	m12 3-1	D26 0-0	M22 3-0	a05 1-2	N24 0-0	

Kevin Drinkell, the local boy made good who scored 16 goals when Grimsby Town won the Third Division title in 1979-80.

DIVISION 2

	BIRMINGHAM C	BRISTOL R	BURNLEY	CAMBRIDGE U	CARDIFF C	CHARLTON A	CHELSEA	FULHAM	LEICESTER C	LUTON T	NEWCASTLE U	NOTTS CO	OLDHAM A	ORIENT	PRESTON N.E.	Q.P.R.	SHREWSBURY T	SUNDERLAND	SWANSEA C	WATFORD	WEST HAM U	WREXHAM
1 BIRMINGHAM C		S01 1-1	D15 2-0	N10 1-0	D29 2-1	S15 1-0	M11 5-1	A18 3-4	D01 1-2	a19 1-0	S29 0-0	m03 3-3	a01 2-0	F09 3-1	M15 2-2	J01 2-1	O27 1-0	O09 1-0	O20 2-0	M29 2-0	a07 0-0	F23 2-0
2 BRISTOL R	J12 1-0		D01 0-0	F02 0-0	S29 1-1	O20 3-0	F23 3-0	a04 1-0	a23 1-1	A21 3-2	N17 1-1	O06 2-3	D15 2-0	M08 1-2	M11 3-3	N03 1-3	A25 2-1	a19 2-2	D26 4-1	S08 1-1	m03 0-2	M22 1-0
3 BURNLEY	a26 0-0	a12 1-1		N24 5-3	O13 0-2	A21 1-1	O06 0-1	F02 2-1	M22 1-2	N17 0-0	D26 3-2	A25 0-1	S08 1-1	N03 1-2	M01 1-1	M08 0-3	a05 0-0	S22 1-1	J12 0-0	D08 1-0	F19 0-1	D21 1-0
4 CAMBRIDGE U	M22 2-1	S15 4-1	a19 3-1		F09 2-0	F23 1-0	S29 0-1	D15 4-0	A21 1-1	N03 1-2	M08 0-0	a08 2-3	D26 3-3	O22 1-1	m03 3-2	D01 2-1	J12 2-0	J19 3-3	O06 0-1	A25 2-2	a01 2-0	N17 2-0
5 CARDIFF C	A25 1-2	F16 0-1	F23 2-1	S22 0-0		M08 3-1	O20 1-2	D26 1-0	a08 0-1	O06 2-1	M22 1-1	N03 3-2	D01 1-0	N17 0-0	D15 0-2	A22 1-0	S08 1-0	m03 1-1	a07 1-0	F02 1-0	a19 0-1	J12 1-0
6 CHARLTON A	F02 0-1	M01 4-0	O09 3-3	O13 1-1	O27 3-2		M29 1-2	a08 0-1	D15 2-0	a04 1-4	A25 1-1	D26 0-0	N09 2-1	J12 0-1	A18 0-3	a19 2-2	S22 2-1	M15 0-4	m03 1-2	F26 0-0	D01 1-0	S08 1-2
7 CHELSEA	S08 1-2	O13 1-0	M15 2-1	F16 1-1	M01 1-0	N17 3-1		O27 0-2	D26 1-0	a07 1-1	J12 4-0	a19 1-0	m03 3-0	M22 1-0	D01 2-0	a02 0-2	F02 2-4	A18 0-0	D15 3-0	S22 2-0	N14 2-1	A25 3-1
8 FULHAM	N03 2-4	F26 1-1	S15 3-1	a26 1-2	a15 2-1	a22 1-0	M08 1-2		F09 0-0	S29 1-3	a12 1-0	O20 1-3	M28 0-1	A22 0-0	S01 1-0	J19 0-2	D08 2-1	D29 0-1	F23 1-2	N24 0-0	N10 1-2	O06 0-2
9 LEICESTER C	a12 2-1	J01 3-0	N10 1-1	O10 2-1	D21 0-0	a26 2-1	a05 1-0	S22 3-3		S01 1-3	F02 1-0	S08 1-0	M01 0-1	D08 2-2	M29 1-2	D29 2-0	M15 2-0	O27 2-1	F20 1-1	A18 2-0	O13 1-2	N24 2-0
10 LUTON T	N24 2-3	O09 3-1	M29 1-1	A18 1-1	M14 1-2	D21 3-0	J01 3-3	F16 4-0	J12 0-0		D08 1-1	F02 2-1	S22 0-0	A25 2-1	O27 1-1	N10 1-1	a12 0-0	O13 2-0	S08 5-0	a05 1-0	M01 1-1	a26 2-0
11 NEWCASTLE U	F20 0-0	M29 3-1	a07 1-1	O27 2-0	N10 1-0	D29 2-0	S01 2-1	D01 2-0	S15 3-2	m03 2-2		a02 2-2	A18 3-2	N19 2-0	O10 0-0	D15 4-2	O13 1-0	J01 3-1	a19 1-3	M01 0-2	M15 0-0	S22 1-0
12 NOTTS CO	D08 1-1	M15 0-0	D29 2-3	J01 0-0	A18 4-1	a05 0-0	N24 2-3	M01 1-1	J19 0-1	S15 0-0	D22 2-2		O13 1-1	a26 1-1	N10 2-1	S01 1-0	O09 5-2	M29 0-1	S22 0-0	a12 1-2	O27 0-1	F26 1-1
13 OLDHAM A	D21 1-0	a26 2-1	M04 2-1	a05 1-1	a12 0-3	M22 4-3	D08 1-0	N17 0-1	O20 1-1	F09 2-1	N03 1-0	F23 1-0		O06 1-0	S15 3-2	S29 0-0	N24 0-2	S01 3-0	M08 4-1	F19 1-1	a29 0-0	A21 2-3
14 ORIENT	S22 2-2	O27 2-1	A18 2-2	M01 2-0	M29 1-1	S01 1-1	N10 3-7	O09 1-0	m03 0-1	D29 2-2	S08 1-4	D15 1-0	M14 1-1		a19 2-2	a08 1-1	F16 0-1	D01 2-1	a30 0-0	O13 1-0	J01 0-4	F02 4-0
15 PRESTON N.E.	O06 0-0	S22 3-2	O20 3-2	D08 2-2	a26 2-0	N03 1-1	a12 1-1	J12 3-2	N17 1-1	M08 1-1	A21 1-0	M22 2-0	F02 0-1	N24 2-2		F23 0-3	D26 3-0	F16 2-1	A25 1-1	D21 1-2	S08 1-1	a05 0-0
16 Q.P.R.	a05 1-1	A18 2-0	O27 7-0	a12 2-2	O09 3-0	N24 4-0	D18 2-2	S08 3-0	A25 1-4	M22 2-2	a26 2-1	J12 1-3	F16 4-3	F12 0-0	O13 1-1		N17 2-1	M01 0-0	F02 3-2	M14 1-1	S22 3-0	D08 2-2
17 SHREWSBURY T	M08 1-0	D29 3-1	J01 2-0	S01 1-2	J19 1-2	F09 3-1	S15 3-0	m03 5-2	O06 2-2	D01 1-2	F23 3-1	A21 1-1	a19 0-1	S29 1-0	a01 1-3	M29 3-0		a08 1-2	N03 2-2	N10 1-0	D15 3-0	O20 3-1
18 SUNDERLAND	A22 2-0	N24 3-2	F09 5-0	S08 2-0	D08 2-1	O06 4-0	N03 2-1	A25 2-1	M08 0-0	F23 1-0	a05 1-0	N17 3-1	J12 4-2	a12 1-1	S29 1-1	O20 3-0	D21 2-1		M22 1-1	a26 5-0	m12 2-0	D26 1-1
19 SWANSEA C	F29 0-1	a05 2-0	S01 2-1	M14 2-4	J01 2-1	D08 1-0	a26 1-1	O13 4-1	S29 0-2	M04 2-0	N24 2-3	F09 0-1	O27 2-0	D21 0-1	D29 1-0	S15 1-2	A18 2-0	N10 3-1		O09 1-0	M29 2-1	a12 1-0
20 WATFORD	N17 1-0	J19 0-0	m03 4-0	D29 0-0	S15 1-1	S29 2-1	F09 2-3	a19 4-0	N03 1-3	D26 0-1	O20 2-0	D01 2-1	a07 1-0	F23 0-3	a09 0-0	O06 1-2	M22 0-1	D15 1-1	A21 0-0		S01 2-0	M18 3-1
21 WEST HAM U	a22 1-2	D08 2-1	S29 2-1	D21 3-1	N24 3-0	m05 4-1	A20 0-1	M22 2-3	F23 3-1	O20 1-2	O06 1-1	M11 1-2	A25 1-0	a05 2-0	J19 2-0	F09 2-1	a26 1-3	S15 2-0	N17 2-0	J12 1-1		N03 1-0
22 WREXHAM	O13 1-0	N10 1-2	a04 1-0	M29 1-0	S01 0-1	J19 3-2	D29 2-0	M15 1-1	a19 0-1	D15 3-1	F09 1-0	S29 1-0	O08 1-1	S15 2-1	J01 2-0	m03 1-3	M01 0-1	a07 0-1	D01 1-0	O27 3-0	A18 1-0	

Season 1979-80

DIVISION 3

	BARNSLEY	BLACKBURN R	BLACKPOOL	BRENTFORD	BURY	CARLISLE U	CHESTER	CHESTERFIELD	COLCHESTER U	EXETER C	GILLINGHAM	GRIMSBY T	HULL C	MANSFIELD T	MILLWALL	OXFORD U	PLYMOUTH A	READING	ROTHERHAM U	SHEFFIELD U	SHEFFIELD W	SOUTHEND U	SWINDON T	WIMBLEDON
1 BARNSLEY		O02 1-1	D21 2-1	M15 1-0	N06 2-1	M01 1-1	O27 1-1	O09 0-1	F16 1-2	N10 2-2	O13 2-0	a05 0-1	a22 3-1	S08 1-0	S22 2-1	J26 2-0	a26 0-0	A25 2-0	M04 0-0	M25 0-0	A18 0-3	D01 1-2	J12 1-2	a11 4-0
2 BLACKBURN R	S19 0-1		F09 2-0	M01 3-0	m03 1-2	O10 1-2	N07 2-0	N14 1-0	O27 3-0	F27 1-1	M14 3-1	S01 0-0	a04 1-0	D26 0-0	A18 1-1	D08 2-1	O13 1-0	a19 4-2	S29 0-3	a07 1-0	a22 1-2	S15 1-1	M29 2-0	J19 3-0
3 BLACKPOOL	a04 1-1	S22 2-1		O13 5-4	O10 1-2	a07 2-1	m03 0-0	N07 2-2	F29 1-0	M15 1-0	A18 2-1	J26 0-3	D26 2-2	a19 1-1	M29 2-2	J05 1-2	F16 1-3	D08 5-2	S15 3-2	O02 2-3	N10 1-1	J18 1-0	O27 0-1	S01 3-0
4 BRENTFORD	O06 3-1	O20 2-0	F23 2-1		a08 0-0	a19 0-3	D26 2-2	S01 3-1	N10 1-0	S17 0-2	J05 0-2	S15 1-0	D08 7-2	a07 2-0	m03 1-0	D15 1-1	M08 0-0	N03 2-2	M29 0-1	O22 1-2	J19 2-2	S29 2-0	D29 1-3	F09 0-1
5 BURY	O23 2-2	a29 1-2	A21 3-0	D21 4-2		M04 0-2	S01 2-0	D01 2-0	J29 0-1	J19 3-0	M29 0-2	S18 1-1	S15 0-1	F23 0-2	N10 3-0	F09 1-2	N03 2-1	M08 1-0	a05 1-0	O20 1-2	a12 1-0	O06 1-1	a26 0-0	S29 1-2
6 CARLISLE U	O20 3-1	A21 1-1	M18 2-0	D01 3-1	A25 1-0		S29 2-2	a05 0-2	a26 2-0	F09 4-1	S08 1-2	D21 0-2	F23 3-2	O23 1-1	J12 4-0	M08 2-2	M22 2-1	a15 3-3	S18 3-1	N17 1-0	F26 0-2	N03 4-0	a12 2-1	O06 1-1
7 CHESTER	M08 0-0	O24 0-0	D29 1-0	a05 1-1	J12 1-0	F20 1-0		a23 1-0	a12 2-1	M26 1-3	a30 0-2	A22 3-1	O20 2-1	N17 1-0	S08 1-1	M22 1-0	O06 1-0	S22 0-2	D21 3-1	A25 1-1	D01 2-2	a26 2-1	M19 1-0	N03 3-1
8 CHESTERFIELD	A21 2-0	M22 0-1	O23 0-0	J12 1-0	a19 2-0	D26 3-2	a07 2-0		S08 3-0	m03 3-0	a01 0-0	F23 2-3	S18 1-1	N03 2-0	D08 3-2	O06 2-2	A25 3-1	N17 7-1	F09 3-0	J05 2-1	S29 2-1	M08 1-0	M25 2-1	O20 0-0
9 COLCHESTER U	S29 0-0	M08 0-1	O19 3-1	M22 6-1	a07 2-1	D07 1-1	J08 1-1	J18 0-1		a02 0-0	D26 2-2	F08 2-1	N02 1-1	S18 2-1	a19 0-0	m02 3-0	N16 5-2	O05 1-1	D29 1-1	A21 1-0	S15 0-0	F22 2-1	A31 2-3	O23 4-0
10 EXETER C	M22 2-1	a12 2-0	O06 1-0	O03 0-0	S08 1-0	S22 1-2	O13 1-0	J26 1-2	D21 3-1		F16 3-1	N03 1-2	M08 2-2	A25 2-1	F02 2-1	N17 0-0	J01 2-2	M01 1-0	D01 1-1	J12 3-1	a26 1-0	O24 4-2	a05 4-1	A22 0-2
11 GILLINGHAM	F23 1-1	O06 1-2	N03 1-1	a12 0-1	N17 2-1	J19 1-1	S15 2-2	F26 0-1	a05 2-2	S29 1-0		O20 0-1	M04 1-0	M08 2-0	A25 1-1	O23 4-0	m03 0-1	J12 1-1	a26 0-1	M22 3-0	M18 1-1	N13 1-0	D01 0-0	S18 1-0
12 GRIMSBY T	D26 3-0	J12 1-2	A25 4-3	F02 5-1	O02 1-0	a04 2-0	O09 0-2	O13 1-1	S22 1-2	A18 4-1	M01 1-0		a07 1-1	D08 2-1	M15 2-0	a19 2-0	S08 1-0	J15 2-1	O27 2-0	m03 4-0	N06 3-1	M22 1-0	F16 2-0	N17 1-0
13 HULL C	N17 0-2	D21 0-1	a05 3-1	a26 2-1	m05 0-1	O13 2-0	M01 1-0	O02 2-1	A18 0-2	O27 2-2	S22 0-0	M25 2-2		J12 3-1	F16 1-0	A25 2-2	a12 1-0	M22 0-1	N06 1-1	S08 3-1	O09 1-1	m03 1-0	M14 1-0	D01 1-1
14 MANSFIELD T	a14 1-4	a05 0-1	D01 1-1	M10 0-0	O13 1-0	N06 2-1	M29 2-1	A18 3-2	O01 0-1	D29 0-1	O27 2-0	a26 0-0	S01 1-1		M01 1-0	S15 1-0	D21 0-0	F16 2-2	O08 5-1	S22 3-4	M15 1-1	a12 3-1	N10 1-1	J26 1-1
15 MILLWALL	F09 2-2	N03 1-0	N17 2-0	M18 3-1	M22 0-1	S01 1-0	J19 3-1	a26 2-0	D01 1-2	S15 5-1	D29 2-0	O06 2-0	S29 3-2	O20 2-2		F23 3-0	A21 2-1	O23 2-0	a12 0-0	M08 1-1	S18 3-3	F12 1-2	M04 6-2	a05 2-2
16 OXFORD U	S01 1-0	a26 0-1	a12 0-2	O10 0-2	S22 3-1	O27 1-0	N10 0-1	M14 1-2	J12 0-2	M29 2-0	N07 1-1	D01 0-1	D29 3-0	F02 3-1	O13 1-2		O31 1-1	S08 4-0	A18 5-1	F16 1-1	M01 0-2	a05 1-0	F06 2-2	M19 4-1
17 PLYMOUTH A	D08 2-1	F23 0-1	S29 2-2	O27 0-1	A18 2-0	N10 4-2	M15 1-0	D29 1-0	M29 2-0	a07 2-0	J26 2-2	J19 1-1	J05 5-1	a01 0-0	O09 1-1	S18 1-1		D26 2-0	O20 1-0	a19 4-1	S01 1-3	a22 0-0	N06 2-0	S15 3-0
18 READING	D29 7-0	D01 1-1	a26 0-1	A18 2-2	O27 3-1	S15 2-0	F09 2-1	M29 2-2	M14 2-0	O20 2-1	S01 1-3	a12 1-1	N10 3-0	S29 1-0	N07 2-0	M26 2-0	a05 1-0		F20 1-1	F23 2-1	D21 0-2	S19 1-1	O10 2-1	M05 3-0
19 ROTHERHAM U	a07 1-1	F05 1-3	m06 0-2	N17 4-2	D26 0-2	O02 4-1	a01 2-0	S22 2-0	A25 3-0	a19 2-0	D08 2-1	M08 0-0	O23 2-1	A21 2-1	M25 2-1	N03 0-2	M01 3-1	m03 1-1		O06 1-2	O13 1-2	J12 2-1	S08 3-0	M22 0-0
20 SHEFFIELD U	S15 2-0	J01 2-1	S18 3-1	N06 0-2	M01 0-0	M29 0-2	F26 1-1	a29 0-2	O09 1-2	S01 3-1	N10 4-0	D29 1-1	J19 1-1	F09 1-0	O27 0-1	S29 3-1	D01 3-2	O13 2-0	M15 1-0		a05 1-1	D21 2-0	A18 2-1	a26 2-1
21 SHEFFIELD W	N03 0-2	A25 0-3	M22 4-1	S08 0-2	F05 5-1	m03 0-0	a19 3-0	F16 3-3	F02 3-0	D08 0-1	a07 1-0	O23 2-0	A21 0-0	O06 0-0	O02 2-0	O20 2-2	J12 0-1	a01 1-1	F23 5-0	D26 4-0		N17 2-0	S22 4-2	M08 3-1
22 SOUTHEND U	a19 2-1	F02 0-1	S07 1-2	F16 3-2	M14 0-0	A18 1-0	D07 4-1	O26 0-0	O12 0-1	N05 4-0	O29 0-3	N09 1-0	J25 3-0	M17 1-1	a07 1-0	D26 1-1	S21 4-1	F25 2-2	S01 0-2	a04 2-1	M29 1-1		F29 1-0	D29 1-3
23 SWINDON T	m03 0-1	N17 2-0	M08 2-1	A25 4-0	D08 8-0	M11 0-0	S18 3-1	S15 2-1	a22 2-3	D26 2-3	a19 3-0	S29 3-0	O06 0-0	M22 2-1	a29 1-0	a07 1-1	O23 2-1	A21 0-0	a15 6-2	N03 3-2	F09 1-2	O20 1-0		F23 2-1
24 WIMBLEDON	M11 1-2	S08 1-0	J12 1-2	S22 0-0	F26 0-1	M14 0-0	A18 2-3	M01 1-1	N06 3-3	O09 2-2	F12 1-0	M29 3-6	a19 3-2	m03 3-2	a22 2-2	a15 1-3	F19 3-1	a07 1-1	N10 0-1	D08 1-1	O27 3-4	A25 0-1	O13 2-0	

DIVISION 4

	ALDERSHOT	BOURNEMOUTH	BRADFORD C	CREWE A	DARLINGTON	DONCASTER R	HALIFAX T	HARTLEPOOL U	HEREFORD U	HUDDERSFIELD T	LINCOLN C	NEWPORT CO	NORTHAMPTON T	PETERBOROUGH U	PORTSMOUTH	PORT VALE	ROCHDALE	SCUNTHORPE U	STOCKPORT CO	TORQUAY U	TRANMERE R	WALSALL	WIGAN A	YORK C
1 ALDERSHOT		D26 0-1	O06 3-1	S22 3-0	F02 1-1	a19 1-1	N17 3-1	J12 0-2	M08 3-3	N03 0-2	O23 2-0	A21 0-1	O13 2-0	O30 2-0	a07 1-2	A25 3-1	M22 3-0	S08 2-0	J26 2-0	M01 1-1	m06 0-0	F16 1-1	m03 0-3	D08 2-2
2 BOURNEMOUTH	a05 3-1		M08 1-1	a26 0-1	D29 1-0	N17 0-0	S22 0-1	O06 2-1	O23 2-2	O20 1-3	M22 0-0	A25 3-2	D21 2-2	D01 0-0	O02 0-1	a12 3-1	N03 4-0	M25 3-3	F02 2-0	J01 1-2	F16 2-1	A21 1-1	S08 1-2	F23 0-0
3 BRADFORD C	M15 2-0	O27 2-2		A18 4-0	a05 3-0	J26 3-1	N07 2-0	D21 2-0	a26 1-0	N10 0-0	S08 1-1	a22 3-0	O10 3-1	J12 1-1	M01 0-0	O02 2-0	J01 1-2	S22 2-0	O13 6-1	a12 1-1	A25 2-0	D01 0-1	F16 2-1	M29 1-2
4 CREWE A	F09 1-0	D07 0-0	N03 2-0		N17 0-0	O06 1-2	J12 2-1	M08 2-1	F23 1-0	S19 1-3	A22 0-2	M22 0-3	S29 2-1	F01 1-4	F12 1-1	S07 0-2	O20 2-1	a07 1-1	a19 1-0	A24 2-2	D26 0-0	O24 1-2	a04 2-1	m03 2-0
5 DARLINGTON	S15 0-0	m03 0-1	F26 3-4	M29 0-0		a04 2-1	O13 1-1	J19 0-1	J26 1-1	a08 2-3	M04 1-1	a19 1-1	N10 0-0	O27 1-1	M15 1-1	M01 1-1	A31 3-1	N06 3-1	O02 3-0	F16 2-0	D08 3-1	S22 1-3	A18 2-2	O09 2-1
6 DONCASTER R	D01 1-1	M29 1-0	S01 0-3	a22 1-1	D21 0-1		O09 2-1	M11 0-2	a11 1-0	D29 1-2	F02 1-1	S22 1-3	A18 2-1	D09 2-1	O26 2-0	J12 2-3	a26 2-0	F16 5-0	M01 1-1	S11 5-3	O02 1-1	a05 1-1	O13 3-1	N06 2-0
7 HALIFAX T	M29 1-0	F09 2-0	O23 0-1	S01 3-1	F23 1-1	A21 1-1		S29 2-1	S15 1-0	D26 2-1	D08 1-0	O06 2-1	M04 2-1	D29 0-0	a19 1-2	N10 0-0	S18 1-0	a08 2-2	a22 1-3	a29 3-3	N03 0-0	O20 2-1	M19 0-0	a07 1-1
8 HARTLEPOOL U	S01 1-0	M15 3-1	a04 0-1	O27 3-1	S08 3-1	a08 1-2	F16 1-2		N10 3-0	J26 1-1	a19 0-0	D08 0-0	M29 2-1	M01 1-2	A18 0-3	O13 2-1	D29 1-1	O09 3-2	N06 1-2	S22 2-2	J05 2-1	F02 2-2	a15 1-1	D26 3-1
9 HEREFORD U	O27 0-1	N07 2-1	D08 0-2	O13 2-0	A25 1-0	J05 2-2	F02 2-0	M22 2-1		a19 1-3	a02 0-0	a07 0-2	M01 0-1	F16 0-1	D26 0-0	O10 0-0	N17 1-1	m03 1-1	M15 2-0	O03 0-0	S08 1-2	J12 0-1	S22 2-1	A18 3-1
10 HUDDERSFIELD T	A18 2-0	M01 2-0	M22 0-0	O02 3-0	J01 2-1	A25 3-0	a05 5-0	m03 2-1	D01 0-1		J12 3-2	S08 2-1	N06 5-0	M15 0-0	O13 1-3	S22 7-1	D21 5-1	a15 2-1	F16 5-0	a26 4-2	N17 1-1	a12 1-1	O09 4-0	O27 2-2
11 LINCOLN C	M19 1-1	N10 1-1	J30 1-0	O10 3-0	a12 2-1	S15 1-1	a25 4-0	N30 3-3	F06 2-0	S01 2-0		F16 2-1	F13 0-0	A18 0-1	M29 1-0	M15 3-0	a05 0-0	O13 4-0	O27 1-0	J26 2-0	S22 3-0	O03 2-2	F29 4-0	D29 1-1
12 NEWPORT CO	O09 4-2	J26 0-0	S15 1-2	N10 1-1	D01 4-0	F26 2-1	M14 5-2	a26 1-0	J01 1-0	J18 2-2	S29 1-1		S18 2-1	D21 1-1	N06 4-3	A18 2-1	a12 1-0	D15 2-1	M29 3-1	a05 3-0	O13 2-0	D29 0-1	O27 3-2	S01 2-0
13 NORTHAMPTON T	F23 2-1	a08 0-1	A22 1-2	F16 1-0	M22 2-0	N03 1-0	S07 0-0	N17 2-1	O20 2-0	O23 4-2	a07 0-0	O02 3-2		S22 1-0	m03 0-2	F02 3-1	M08 0-0	D08 0-0	D26 2-0	M18 3-0	O06 2-1	A25 1-2	a19 1-1	J05 2-0
14 PETERBOROUGH U	S19 1-3	a19 2-0	m03 1-0	S15 3-0	M08 3-0	M22 3-2	A25 2-1	O20 2-0	S29 2-0	O06 1-3	N03 3-1	a08 0-1	F09 0-0		D08 0-0	J26 3-0	F23 2-0	J05 3-1	a07 1-1	O24 2-1	A22 1-2	N17 1-3	D26 1-2	M05 2-1
15 PORTSMOUTH	J01 1-3	S18 4-0	O20 4-1	a12 1-1	O06 4-3	M08 2-0	D01 3-1	N03 2-1	a05 0-0	F23 4-1	N17 4-0	O23 0-2	D29 6-1	a26 4-0		D21 2-2	F09 3-0	A25 6-1	S08 1-0	A21 3-0	F02 1-1	M22 1-2	J12 1-1	S29 5-2
16 PORT VALE	D29 0-2	J05 1-1	S17 1-2	F20 2-0	O20 2-0	m03 3-0	M22 1-0	F23 1-1	A20 0-1	F09 1-1	O06 1-2	N03 2-0	S15 5-0	S01 0-1	a01 2-3		S29 5-1	D26 1-0	D07 1-2	N17 1-1	O22 0-1	M08 2-2	a07 1-1	a19 1-2
17 ROCHDALE	D04 2-1	A18 0-2	a07 0-1	M01 0-0	N11 2-2	F12 3-2	O02 2-2	A24 1-0	m06 0-2	a01 0-2	M11 1-1	a29 2-0	O26 3-2	O12 0-0	S22 1-2	F15 0-2		a18 0-1	O09 0-1	a15 0-0	m02 2-0	S08 1-1	N06 0-2	M14 0-2
18 SCUNTHORPE U	a22 1-1	S01 2-1	F09 3-3	M04 1-1	O23 3-0	S28 0-0	D21 1-0	A21 1-3	D29 1-0	S14 1-1	F23 1-0	O20 1-3	a25 3-0	a12 1-0	J26 1-0	a05 1-0	N30 2-0		N10 1-1	N03 1-1	M08 2-2	O06 2-2	M29 1-3	S18 6-1
19 STOCKPORT CO	a11 0-4	S14 1-1	F22 2-2	N30 2-1	S17 1-1	O19 0-3	m02 4-1	O22 0-0	O05 2-1	S28 1-2	M08 2-1	N17 0-5	a04 2-0	J21 1-0	M10 1-1	a25 0-1	A20 1-1	M21 1-2		D21 4-0	J11 2-2	N02 1-0	A25 1-2	F08 1-0
20 TORQUAY U	O20 2-1	a07 0-0	M05 2-3	D29 1-0	S29 4-0	J19 2-2	O27 3-0	a23 3-1	S19 1-1	D08 3-1	m03 2-5	D26 2-0	S01 2-2	N07 2-0	O10 2-1	M29 1-1	S15 3-0	A18 3-0	a02 0-0		a19 3-1	F23 0-1	M14 2-2	N10 4-3
21 TRANMERE R	D21 1-2	S28 0-5	D28 4-0	a05 2-0	a26 1-2	S17 1-0	A18 2-0	a11 1-0	M25 0-0	M29 0-0	F09 1-0	F22 0-2	M14 1-1	O08 3-0	S14 4-1	N12 1-1	J25 5-1	O26 1-2	A31 0-1	N30 2-0		M04 0-1	M10 1-3	O19 1-2
22 WALSALL	S29 1-1	O09 0-0	a19 1-1	N06 1-0	F09 1-1	D26 3-1	M01 2-0	S15 3-1	S01 3-2	J05 1-1	S18 3-0	m03 2-4	J26 5-1	M29 2-3	N10 1-1	O27 2-1	F19 2-0	M15 1-1	A18 2-1	O13 1-1	a07 2-0		D08 1-1	a01 3-1
23 WIGAN A	M05 2-1	F06 2-1	S29 4-1	D21 2-0	N03 4-1	a30 0-0	a12 3-1	S19 2-1	F09 1-1	A22 1-2	O20 2-1	M08 0-1	D01 0-0	a05 2-1	S01 1-2	M26 3-1	O24 1-1	N17 4-1	D29 3-1	O06 0-3	M22 0-0	a26 3-0		S15 2-5
24 YORK C	a26 1-1	O12 1-1	N17 2-2	J26 2-2	A21 3-1	O23 1-3	F12 2-2	a05 2-1	N03 3-1	M08 0-4	A25 0-2	J12 2-1	a12 1-2	S08 0-2	F16 1-0	D01 5-1	O06 3-2	O02 2-0	S22 2-2	M22 1-0	M01 0-1	D21 0-1	F02 1-2	

LEAGUE TABLES

DIVISION 1

	P	W	D	L	F	A	W	D	L	F	A	Pts
Liverpool	42	15	6	0	46	8	10	4	7	35	22	60
Manchester U	42	17	3	1	43	8	7	7	7	22	27	58
Ipswich T	42	14	4	3	43	13	8	5	8	25	26	53
Arsenal	42	8	10	3	24	12	10	6	5	28	24	52
Nottingham F	42	16	4	1	44	11	4	4	13	19	32	48
Wolves	42	9	6	6	29	20	10	3	8	29	27	47
Aston Villa	42	11	5	5	29	22	5	9	7	22	28	46
Southampton	42	14	2	5	53	24	4	7	10	12	29	45
Middlesbrough	42	11	7	3	31	14	5	5	11	19	30	44
WBA	42	9	8	4	37	23	2	11	8	17	27	41
Leeds U	42	10	7	4	30	17	3	7	11	16	33	40
Norwich C	42	10	8	3	38	30	3	6	12	20	36	40
Crystal P	42	9	9	3	26	13	3	7	11	15	37	40
Tottenham H	42	11	5	5	30	22	4	5	12	22	40	40
Coventry C	42	12	2	7	34	24	4	5	12	22	42	39
Brighton & HA	42	8	8	5	25	20	3	7	11	22	37	37
Manchester C	42	8	8	5	28	25	4	5	12	15	41	37
Stoke C	42	9	4	8	27	26	4	6	11	17	32	36
Everton	42	7	7	7	28	25	2	10	9	15	26	35
Bristol C	42	6	6	9	22	30	3	7	11	15	36	31
Derby Co	42	9	4	8	36	29	2	4	15	11	38	30
Bolton W	42	5	11	5	19	21	0	4	17	19	52	25

DIVISION 2

	P	W	D	L	F	A	W	D	L	F	A	Pts
Leicester C	42	12	5	4	32	19	9	8	4	26	19	55
Sunderland	42	16	5	0	47	13	5	7	9	22	29	54
Birmingham C	42	14	5	2	37	16	7	6	8	21	22	53
Chelsea	42	14	3	4	34	16	9	4	8	32	36	53
QPR	42	10	9	2	46	25	8	4	9	29	28	49
Luton T	42	9	10	2	36	17	7	7	7	30	28	49
West Ham U	42	13	2	6	37	21	7	5	9	17	22	47
Cambridge U	42	11	6	4	40	23	3	10	8	21	30	44
Newcastle U	42	13	6	2	35	19	2	8	11	18	30	44
Preston NE	42	8	10	3	30	23	4	9	8	26	29	43
Oldham A	42	12	5	4	30	21	4	6	11	19	32	43
Swansea C	42	13	1	7	31	20	4	8	9	17	33	43
Shrewsbury T	42	12	3	6	41	23	6	2	13	19	30	41
Orient	42	7	9	5	29	31	5	8	8	19	23	41
Cardiff C	42	11	4	6	21	16	5	4	12	20	32	40
Wrexham	42	13	2	6	26	15	3	4	14	14	34	38
Notts Co	42	4	11	6	24	22	7	4	10	27	30	37
Watford	42	9	6	6	27	18	3	7	11	12	28	37
Bristol R	42	9	8	4	33	23	2	5	14	17	41	35
Fulham	42	6	4	11	19	28	5	3	13	23	46	29
Burnley	42	5	9	7	19	23	1	6	14	20	50	27
Charlton A	42	6	6	9	25	31	0	4	17	14	47	22

DIVISION 3

	P	W	D	I	F	A	W	D	I	F	A	Pts
Grimsby T	46	18	2	3	46	16	8	8	7	27	26	62
Blackburn R	46	13	5	5	34	17	12	4	7	24	19	59
Sheffield W	46	12	6	5	44	20	9	10	4	37	27	58
Chesterfield	46	16	5	2	46	16	7	6	10	25	30	57
Colchester U	46	10	10	3	39	20	10	2	11	25	36	52
Carlisle U	46	13	6	4	45	26	5	6	12	21	30	48
Reading	46	14	6	3	43	19	2	10	11	23	46	48
Exeter C	46	14	5	4	38	22	5	5	13	22	46	48
Chester	46	14	6	3	29	18	3	7	13	20	39	47
Swindon T	46	15	4	4	50	20	4	4	15	21	43	46
Barnsley	46	10	7	6	29	20	6	7	10	24	36	46
Sheffield U	46	13	5	5	35	21	5	5	13	25	45	46
Rotherham U	46	13	4	6	38	24	5	6	12	20	42	46
Millwall	46	14	6	3	49	23	2	7	14	16	36	45
Plymouth A	46	13	7	3	39	17	3	5	15	20	38	44
Gillingham	46	8	9	6	26	18	6	5	12	23	33	42
Oxford U	46	10	4	9	34	24	4	9	10	23	38	41
Blackpool	46	10	7	6	39	34	5	4	14	23	40	41
Brentford	46	10	6	7	33	26	5	5	13	26	47	41
Hull C	46	11	7	5	29	21	1	9	13	22	48	40
Bury	46	10	4	9	30	23	6	3	14	15	36	39
Southend U	46	11	6	6	33	23	3	4	16	14	35	38
Mansfield T	46	9	9	5	31	24	1	7	15	16	34	36
Wimbledon	46	6	8	9	34	38	4	6	13	18	43	34

DIVISION 4

	P	W	D	L	F	A	W	D	L	F	A	Pts
Huddersfield T	46	16	5	2	61	18	11	7	5	40	30	66
Walsall	46	12	9	2	43	23	11	9	3	32	24	64
Newport Co	46	16	5	2	47	22	11	2	10	36	28	61
Portsmouth	46	15	5	3	62	23	9	7	7	29	26	60
Bradford C	46	14	6	3	44	14	10	6	7	33	36	60
Wigan A	46	13	5	5	42	26	8	8	7	34	35	55
Lincoln C	46	14	8	1	43	12	4	9	10	21	30	53
Peterboro' U	46	14	3	6	39	22	7	7	9	19	25	52
Torquay U	46	13	7	3	47	25	2	10	11	23	44	47
Aldershot	46	10	7	6	35	23	6	6	11	27	30	45
Bournemouth	46	8	9	6	32	25	5	9	9	20	26	44
Doncaster R	46	11	6	6	37	27	4	8	11	25	36	44
Northampton T	46	14	5	4	33	16	2	7	14	18	50	44
Scunthorpe	46	11	9	3	37	23	3	6	14	21	52	43
Tranmere R	46	10	4	9	32	24	4	9	10	18	32	41
Stockport Co	46	9	7	7	30	31	5	5	13	18	41	40
York C	46	9	6	8	35	34	5	5	13	30	48	39
Halifax T	46	11	9	3	29	20	2	4	17	17	52	39
Hartlepool U	46	10	7	6	36	28	4	3	16	23	36	38
Port Vale	46	8	6	9	34	24	4	6	13	22	46	36
Hereford U	46	8	7	8	22	21	3	7	13	16	31	36
Darlington	46	7	11	5	33	26	2	6	15	17	48	35
Crewe A	46	10	6	7	25	27	1	7	15	10	41	35
Rochdale	46	6	7	10	20	28	1	6	16	13	51	27

Football League Records

Top scorers: Div 1, P.Withe (Aston Villa), S.Archibald (Tottenham Hotspur) 20 goals; Div 2, D.Cross (West Ham United) 22 goals; Div 3, A.Kellow (Exeter City) 25 goals; Div 4, A.Cork (Wimbledon) 23 goals.

Gary Shaw, the only Birmingham-born player in Aston Villa's 1980-81 Championship side. He scored 18 goals that season.

DIVISION 1

	ARSENAL	ASTON VILLA	BIRMINGHAM C	BRIGHTON & HA	COVENTRY C	CRYSTAL P	EVERTON	IPSWICH T	LEEDS U	LEICESTER C	LIVERPOOL	MANCHESTER C	MANCHESTER U	MIDDLESBROUGH	NORWICH C	NOTTINGHAM F	SOUTHAMPTON	STOKE C	SUNDERLAND	TOTTENHAM H	W.B.A.	WOLVERHAMPTON W
1 ARSENAL		m02 2-0	M31 2-1	N01 2-0	J31 2-2	a20 3-2	N22 2-1	D27 1-1	a11 0-0	O04 1-0	M28 1-0	F24 2-0	D20 2-1	F28 2-2	O21 3-1	S27 1-0	A19 1-1	S13 2-0	O18 2-2	A30 2-0	N15 2-2	D06 1-1
2 ASTON VILLA	N29 1-1		D13 3-0	O22 4-1	A30 1-0	F21 2-1	S13 0-2	a14 1-2	N15 1-1	N01 2-0	J10 2-0	J31 1-0	M14 3-3	a25 3-0	A20 1-0	a18 2-0	M28 2-1	D26 1-0	O04 4-0	N18 3-0	a08 1-0	S20 2-1
3 BIRMINGHAM C	O07 3-1	O11 1-2		F07 2-1	A16 3-1	N08 1-0	m02 1-1	D20 1-3	a21 0-2	D06 1-2	S06 1-1	M21 2-0	A23 0-0	a04 2-1	F20 4-0	N11 2-0	J17 0-3	O25 1-1	D27 3-2	N22 2-1	S20 1-1	M17 1-0
4 BRIGHTON & H.A.	a04 0-1	D20 1-0	S13 2-2		M07 4-1	D27 3-2	O07 1-3	N11 1-0	m02 2-0	a20 2-1	F21 2-2	O25 1-2	N22 1-4	N08 0-1	S20 2-0	O11 0-1	F24 2-0	M21 1-1	D06 2-1	J31 0-2	A30 1-2	A16 2-0
5 COVENTRY C	A23 3-1	J17 1-2	N15 2-1	O04 3-3		S06 3-1	S27 0-5	F28 0-4	N01 2-1	M14 4-1	A19 0-0	J10 1-1	a11 0-2	D26 1-0	O18 0-1	N29 1-1	a25 1-0	a18 2-2	O21 2-1	M28 0-1	D13 3-0	F07 2-2
6 CRYSTAL P	D26 2-2	S27 0-1	a11 3-1	a18 0-3	F17 0-3		F28 2-3	S13 1-2	M28 0-1	O18 2-1	N15 2-2	N29 2-3	N01 1-0	A23 5-2	D13 4-1	a25 1-3	O21 3-2	J10 1-1	M14 0-1	A19 3-4	O04 0-1	J17 0-0
7 EVERTON	J10 1-2	F07 1-3	N29 1-1	D13 4-3	F21 3-0	S20 5-0		J17 0-0	M14 1-2	A19 1-0	O18 2-2	D26 0-2	M28 0-1	a18 4-1	a11 0-2	A23 0-0	O04 2-1	a25 0-1	N15 2-1	N01 2-2	O21 1-1	S06 2-0
8 IPSWICH T	a18 0-2	S06 1-0	J13 5-1	A19 2-0	S20 2-0	F07 3-2	A30 4-0		O04 1-1	N15 3-1	D13 1-1	a25 1-0	O18 1-1	F17 1-0	D26 2-0	J10 2-0	m13 2-3	J31 4-0	M28 4-1	M14 3-0	N01 0-0	F21 3-1
9 LEEDS U	N08 0-5	A16 1-2	D26 0-0	N29 1-0	a04 3-0	O25 1-0	O11 1-0	M31 3-0		A30 1-2	a18 0-0	O08 1-0	S20 0-0	N12 2-1	J31 1-0	D13 1-0	J10 0-3	F14 1-3	F21 1-0	S13 0-0	m06 0-0	M21 1-3
10 LEICESTER C	M07 1-0	a04 2-4	a25 1-0	D26 0-1	O11 1-3	M21 1-1	N12 0-1	A16 0-1	J17 0-1		A23 2-0	N08 1-1	F07 1-0	D13 1-0	N29 1-2	F28 1-1	a18 2-2	O08 1-1	S06 0-1	S27 2-1	J10 0-2	O25 2-0
11 LIVERPOOL	O25 1-1	N22 2-1	F14 2-2	S27 4-1	N11 2-1	A16 3-0	M21 1-0	O11 1-1	D27 0-0	J31 1-2		m19 1-0	a14 0-1	O07 4-2	A30 4-1	N08 0-0	F28 2-0	a03 3-0	m02 0-1	D06 2-1	S13 4-0	D20 1-0
12 MANCHESTER C	S06 1-1	A23 2-2	O18 0-1	M28 1-1	N22 3-0	m02 1-1	a20 3-1	D06 1-1	D20 1-0	M31 3-3	O04 0-3		F21 1-0	J17 3-2	N01 1-0	F07 1-1	N15 3-0	S20 1-2	A20 0-4	O22 3-1	M14 2-1	D27 4-0
13 MANCHESTER U	O11 0-0	O08 3-3	J31 2-0	J10 2-1	N08 0-0	a04 1-0	O25 2-0	M21 2-1	F28 0-1	S13 5-0	D26 0-0	S27 2-2		A16 3-0	a25 1-0	M18 1-1	N29 1-1	D13 2-2	A30 1-1	F17 0-0	a18 2-1	N12 0-0
14 MIDDLESBROUGH	S20 2-1	D06 2-1	N01 1-2	a11 1-0	a21 0-1	D31 2-0	D27 1-0	m02 2-1	A19 3-0	O21 1-0	m05 1-2	A30 2-2	N15 1-1		O04 6-1	S06 0-0	O18 1-1	F21 3-1	F07 1-0	D20 4-1	M28 2-1	N22 2-0
15 NORWICH C	M21 1-1	N12 1-3	S27 2-2	F28 3-1	D20 2-0	O29 1-1	N08 2-1	a20 1-0	A23 2-3	m02 2-3	J17 0-1	a04 2-0	D06 2-2	M17 2-0		O25 1-1	S13 1-0	A16 5-1	N22 1-0	D27 2-2	F14 0-2	O11 1-1
16 NOTTINGHAM F	F21 3-1	D27 2-2	A20 2-1	M14 4-1	m02 1-1	D06 3-0	J31 1-0	N22 1-2	O22 2-1	S20 5-0	a11 0-0	S13 3-2	O04 1-2	M03 1-0	M28 2-1		N01 2-1	A30 5-0	D20 3-1	N15 0-3	O18 2-1	a20 1-0
17 SOUTHAMPTON	N11 3-1	O25 1-2	A30 3-1	S06 3-1	D06 1-0	D20 4-2	M17 3-0	N08 3-3	N22 2-1	D27 4-0	S20 2-2	A16 2-0	M07 1-0	M21 1-0	F07 2-1	a04 2-0		O11 1-2	J31 2-1	a20 1-1	F21 2-2	O07 4-2
18 STOKE C	F07 1-1	a20 1-1	M28 0-0	O18 0-0	D27 2-2	N22 1-0	D06 2-2	A23 2-2	S06 3-0	D20 1-0	N01 2-2	M18 2-1	O22 1-2	S27 1-0	N15 3-1	F18 1-2	M14 1-2		a11 2-0	O04 2-3	A20 0-0	m02 3-2
19 SUNDERLAND	D13 2-0	M07 1-2	a18 3-0	a25 1-2	M21 3-0	O11 1-0	A16 3-1	O25 0-2	S27 4-1	F14 1-0	N29 2-4	N12 2-0	J28 2-0	S13 0-1	J10 3-0	O08 2-2	A23 1-2	N08 0-0		F28 1-1	D26 0-0	a04 0-1
20 TOTTENHAM H	J17 2-0	M21 2-0	J10 1-0	A23 2-2	O25 4-1	N12 4-2	a04 2-2	D17 5-3	F07 1-1	F21 1-2	a25 1-1	D13 2-1	S06 0-0	O11 3-2	a18 2-3	A16 2-0	D26 4-4	M11 2-2	S20 0-0		N29 2-3	N08 2-2
21 W.B.A.	A16 0-1	N08 0-0	F28 2-2	J17 2-0	O08 1-0	M07 1-0	M31 2-0	a04 3-1	D06 1-2	N22 3-1	F07 2-0	O11 3-1	D27 3-1	O25 3-0	S06 3-0	M21 2-1	S27 2-1	N25 0-0	a20 2-1	m02 4-2		A23 1-1
22 WOLVERHAMPTON W	a25 1-2	F28 0-1	O04 1-0	N15 0-2	S13 0-1	A30 2-0	m04 0-0	S27 0-2	O18 2-1	M28 0-1	N25 4-1	a18 1-3	A19 1-0	J10 3-0	M14 3-0	D26 1-4	D13 1-1	N29 1-0	N01 2-1	a30 1-0	J31 2-0	

West Ham United and England midfielder Trevor Brooking, who was probably at the peak of his career when the Hammers won the Second Division title in 1980-81.

DIVISION 2

	BLACKBURN R	BOLTON W	BRISTOL C	BRISTOL R	CAMBRIDGE U	CARDIFF C	CHELSEA	DERBY CO	GRIMSBY T	LUTON T	NEWCASTLE U	NOTTS CO	OLDHAM A	ORIENT	PRESTON N.E.	Q.P.R.	SHEFFIELD W	SHREWSBURY T	SWANSEA C	WATFORD	WEST HAM U	WREXHAM
1 BLACKBURN R		a18 0-0	a11 1-0	N29 2-0	O22 2-0	N15 2-3	O18 1-1	F14 1-0	S20 2-0	S13 3-0	a25 3-0	M28 0-0	A20 1-0	J31 2-0	D26 0-0	O04 2-1	M14 3-1	A30 2-0	N01 0-0	J10 0-0	D13 0-0	F21 1-1
2 BOLTON W	D27 1-2		O18 1-1	S06 2-0	N01 6-1	F07 4-2	O04 2-3	J24 3-1	N22 1-1	m02 0-3	A23 4-0	N25 3-0	F24 2-0	D06 3-1	O21 2-1	D19 1-2	A19 0-0	M14 0-2	S20 1-4	a11 2-1	M28 1-1	a20 1-1
3 BRISTOL C	N08 2-0	D13 3-1		A23 0-0	J10 0-1	D26 0-0	a18 0-0	O25 2-2	M10 1-1	O07 2-1	O11 2-0	S20 0-1	N29 1-1	a04 3-1	N15 0-0	F21 0-1	F07 1-0	a25 1-1	S06 0-1	J17 0-0	A19 1-1	M21 0-2
4 BRISTOL R	m02 0-1	F14 2-1	J31 0-0		O04 0-1	F28 0-1	M14 1-0	N22 1-1	A30 2-2	D27 2-4	S27 0-0	D19 1-1	S13 0-0	A16 1-1	M28 2-0	N11 1-2	O18 3-3	a11 1-1	a21 1-2	N04 3-1	N01 0-1	D06 0-1
5 CAMBRIDGE U	D20 0-0	a04 2-3	N22 2-1	M07 1-3		M21 2-0	S13 0-1	A16 3-0	m02 5-1	O25 1-3	N08 2-1	a20 1-2	O11 3-1	N11 1-0	F14 1-0	D06 1-0	J24 0-2	F28 3-1	J17 3-1	A23 3-1	S27 1-2	O07 1-0
6 CARDIFF C	A16 1-2	S13 1-1	a20 2-3	S20 2-1	O17 1-2		O31 0-1	m02 0-0	D06 1-1	N22 1-0	F25 1-0	F20 0-1	J31 0-2	A30 4-2	a11 1-3	O22 1-0	M04 0-0	M28 2-2	D27 3-3	O04 1-0	m06 0-0	N12 1-0
7 CHELSEA	M21 0-0	M07 2-0	D27 0-0	O08 2-0	F07 3-0	a04 0-1		N12 1-3	O11 3-0	a20 0-2	O25 6-0	m02 0-2	N08 1-0	D20 0-1	S20 1-1	A30 1-1	N22 2-0	J31 3-0	D06 0-0	F21 0-1	S06 0-1	A16 2-2
8 DERBY CO	S06 2-2	A30 1-0	M28 1-0	J10 2-1	N15 0-3	N29 1-1	A20 3-2		F07 2-1	D31 2-2	a18 2-0	a11 2-2	D26 4-1	F21 1-1	m06 1-2	O18 3-3	O04 3-1	N01 1-1	M31 0-1	D13 1-1	N26 2-0	S20 0-1
9 GRIMSBY T	F28 0-0	J10 4-0	O04 1-0	J17 2-0	N29 3-1	a25 0-1	D13 2-0	S13 0-1		S27 0-0	D26 0-0	M14 2-1	a18 0-0	F14 2-0	A19 0-0	N01 0-0	O21 0-0	N15 1-0	M28 1-0	O18 1-1	a11 1-5	A23 1-0
10 LUTON T	F07 3-1	N29 2-2	M14 3-1	a18 1-0	M28 0-0	J10 2-2	D26 2-0	A23 1-2	F21 0-2		J17 0-1	O04 0-1	a25 1-2	S20 2-1	D13 4-2	a11 3-0	N01 3-0	O18 1-1	O21 2-2	A19 1-0	N15 3-2	S06 1-1
11 NEWCASTLE U	a15 0-0	J31 2-1	D20 0-0	F21 0-0	a11 2-1	S06 2-1	M28 1-0	D27 0-2	a20 1-1	A30 2-1		A20 1-1	S20 0-0	m02 3-1	M14 2-0	F07 1-0	N15 1-0	O22 1-0	O18 1-2	N01 2-1	O04 0-0	N22 0-1
12 NOTTS CO	O25 2-0	A16 2-1	F28 2-1	O11 3-1	m05 2-0	S27 4-2	N29 1-1	N08 0-0	O07 0-0	M07 0-1	N11 0-0		D13 0-2	M21 1-0	a18 0-0	S06 2-1	A23 2-0	J10 0-0	F07 2-1	a25 1-2	J17 1-1	a05 1-1
13 OLDHAM A	N11 1-0	S27 1-1	m02 2-0	F07 1-0	M15 2-2	A23 2-0	a11 0-0	a20 0-2	D27 1-2	D06 0-0	F28 0-0	O21 0-1		N22 0-1	N01 1-1	A16 1-0	S06 2-0	O04 0-0	D20 2-2	M28 2-1	O18 0-0	F17 1-3
14 ORIENT	A23 1-1	a26 2-2	N01 3-1	N15 2-2	A19 3-0	J17 2-2	O21 0-1	S27 1-0	S06 2-0	M01 0-0	N29 1-1	O18 0-2	J10 2-3		O04 4-0	M31 4-0	M28 2-0	D13 1-0	a11 1-1	D26 1-1	a18 0-2	F07 2-1
15 PRESTON N.E.	a21 0-0	M24 1-2	A16 1-1	O25 0-0	S06 2-0	N08 3-1	F28 1-0	D06 0-3	D02 2-4	O11 1-0	O07 2-3	D27 2-2	a04 1-2	M07 3-0		N22 3-2	a14 2-1	S27 0-0	m02 1-3	F07 2-1	A23 0-0	D20 1-1
16 Q.P.R.	M07 1-1	O11 3-1	S27 4-0	A19 4-0	a25 5-0	F03 2-0	J17 1-0	M21 3-1	a04 1-0	N08 3-2	S13 1-2	F14 1-1	N15 2-0	O07 0-0	J10 1-1		F28 1-2	N29 0-0	A23 0-0	a18 0-0	D26 3-0	O25 0-1
17 SHEFFIELD W	O07 2-1	N11 2-0	S13 2-1	D13 4-1	a18 4-1	O11 2-0	J10 0-0	M07 0-0	a28 1-2	a04 3-1	A16 2-0	J31 1-2	F14 3-0	O25 2-2	A30 3-0	S20 1-0		D26 1-1	F21 2-0	N29 1-0	m08 0-1	N08 2-1
18 SHREWSBURY T	J17 1-1	O07 1-2	D06 4-0	N08 3-1	S20 2-1	O25 2-0	A23 2-2	a04 1-0	A16 1-1	D19 0-1	M21 1-0	N22 1-1	M07 2-2	O11 1-2	F21 3-0	m02 3-3	a21 2-0		N11 0-0	S06 2-1	F07 0-2	D27 1-2
19 SWANSEA C	a04 2-0	F28 3-0	M17 0-0	D26 2-1	A30 1-1	a18 1-1	a25 3-0	O11 3-1	O24 1-0	a27 2-2	D13 4-0	S13 1-1	O07 3-0	N08 0-2	N28 3-0	J31 1-2	S27 2-3	A19 2-1		D16 1-0	J10 1-3	M06 3-1
20 WATFORD	N22 1-1	N08 3-1	A30 1-0	M21 3-1	J31 0-0	M07 4-2	S27 2-3	O07 1-1	D20 3-1	N11 0-1	a04 0-0	D06 2-0	O25 2-1	a17 2-0	S13 2-1	D27 1-1	m02 2-1	F14 1-0	A16 2-1		F28 1-2	O11 1-0
21 WEST HAM U	O11 2-0	O25 2-1	N11 5-0	a04 2-0	F21 4-2	O07 1-0	F14 4-0	D20 3-1	N08 2-1	A16 1-2	M07 1-0	A30 4-0	M21 1-1	D27 2-1	J31 5-0	a21 3-0	D06 2-1	S13 3-0	N22 2-0	S20 3-2		m02 1-0
22 WREXHAM	S27 0-1	D26 0-1	O21 1-0	a25 3-1	D13 0-0	A19 0-1	N15 0-4	F28 2-2	J31 0-2	M31 0-0	J10 0-0	N01 1-1	A30 3-2	S13 3-1	O18 0-1	M28 1-1	a11 4-0	a18 1-2	O04 1-1	m04 0-1	N29 2-2	

Season 1980-81

DIVISION 3

	BARNSLEY	BLACKPOOL	BRENTFORD	BURNLEY	CARLISLE U	CHARLTON A	CHESTER	CHESTERFIELD	COLCHESTER U	EXETER C	FULHAM	GILLINGHAM	HUDDERSFIELD T	HULL C	MILLWALL	NEWPORT CO	OXFORD U	PLYMOUTH A	PORTSMOUTH	READING	ROTHERHAM U	SHEFFIELD U	SWINDON T	WALSALL
1 BARNSLEY		D20 2-0	S30 0-1	M28 3-2	N04 3-1	O04 0-0	N01 2-0	a20 1-1	a07 3-0	a10 1-0	N29 2-2	J31 3-3	S13 1-0	N11 5-0	O18 2-0	m02 4-1	O21 1-1	J10 2-1	A16 1-2	F21 2-3	a28 1-0	A30 2-1	S20 2-0	D27 3-0
2 BLACKPOOL	a25 1-0		S20 0-3	a18 0-0	M28 0-1	M25 0-2	D26 2-3	O22 0-3	O18 1-1	D06 0-0	F14 0-2	O04 4-0	J31 1-2	S13 2-2	M04 0-0	N01 2-4	a12 1-1	M14 1-0	A30 0-2	J17 0-0	A20 0-0	O01 2-1	N15 1-1	F21 1-0
3 BRENTFORD	S15 1-1	F28 2-0		J03 0-0	M14 1-1	N15 0-1	O18 0-1	a11 3-2	D26 2-1	N03 0-1	S13 1-3	O20 3-3	J17 0-0	S27 2-2	A18 1-0	O04 0-1	N01 3-0	M28 0-1	F14 2-2	A23 1-2	a25 2-1	a18 1-1	D06 1-1	J24 4-0
4 BURNLEY	D02 0-1	D27 4-1	O25 2-0		a21 0-3	F17 0-1	F28 1-0	A23 1-0	S06 1-0	F07 1-0	M07 3-0	N29 3-2	a14 4-2	S16 2-0	S27 5-0	A16 1-1	m02 1-1	D20 2-1	J27 1-3	N08 1-2	O11 1-1	O07 3-2	a04 0-0	N11 0-0
5 CARLISLE U	O07 2-2	O28 2-0	O11 1-2	D26 3-2		a25 1-2	J31 3-0	S27 2-6	D06 4-0	M31 1-1	N08 2-2	S13 0-0	N11 1-1	M21 2-0	S16 2-1	A30 1-4	F28 0-0	F14 2-0	a04 0-0	F10 0-0	a18 0-1	A16 0-3	M17 2-1	M07 1-1
6 CHARLTON A	M07 1-1	O25 2-1	A16 3-1	A30 2-0	D20 2-1		S13 1-0	N29 1-0	S20 1-2	F21 1-0	D27 1-1	m02 2-1	a04 1-2	J10 3-2	M17 0-0	N11 3-0	a21 0-0	J31 1-1	a14 1-2	O28 4-2	N08 2-0	O11 2-0	M21 0-0	O07 2-0
7 CHESTER	a04 2-2	a17 2-1	J10 0-0	S20 0-0	A23 1-0	F07 4-0		D27 2-1	F21 0-0	S06 1-0	O25 0-1	D20 1-2	O29 0-2	O08 4-1	J24 0-1	D03 1-1	A16 0-1	N12 1-0	m02 0-1	O11 1-0	M21 0-1	N08 3-2	M07 1-0	D06 1-0
8 CHESTERFIELD	D26 0-0	M21 3-2	N08 2-1	J31 3-0	F21 1-0	J17 0-1	a18 2-0		S30 3-0	m08 1-0	a04 0-0	A30 2-0	A16 2-1	O11 1-0	D06 3-0	S20 3-2	F14 2-1	S13 2-2	M07 3-0	m05 3-2	O07 2-0	N11 1-0	a07 2-2	O25 1-2
9 COLCHESTER U	O11 2-2	J10 3-2	a20 0-2	F14 2-1	m02 1-0	F28 2-0	S27 1-1	S16 1-1		F03 1-2	N11 3-2	D27 2-1	M07 1-2	O28 2-0	S13 3-0	D20 1-0	N29 3-0	A16 2-2	O07 1-0	M22 1-2	O25 0-0	a04 1-1	N08 1-0	A23 1-1
10 EXETER C	N08 0-1	m02 0-0	O08 0-0	S13 0-0	N29 2-0	S27 4-3	a29 2-2	D20 2-2	A30 4-0		S17 1-0	A16 2-1	O11 1-4	J31 1-3	F28 2-0	D27 2-2	N12 1-1	a21 1-1	J14 2-0	a04 3-1	M18 2-1	M21 1-1	O25 3-4	J10 0-3
11 FULHAM	J16 2-3	S05 1-2	F07 1-1	O04 0-2	a11 2-3	a18 1-0	M17 0-1	N01 1-1	A20 1-0	O01 0-1		M14 3-2	D06 2-2	A29 0-0	O22 1-1	M28 2-1	O18 0-4	N04 0-0	F21 3-0	a25 1-2	N15 1-1	D26 2-1	J31 2-0	S20 2-1
12 GILLINGHAM	A23 1-1	M07 3-1	M21 2-0	a07 0-0	F07 0-1	D06 0-1	a25 2-1	J24 1-0	a18 0-0	N15 1-5	O11 1-0		S16 0-0	O25 2-0	D26 1-2	S06 3-2	S27 1-1	F28 0-1	N08 0-1	A19 2-0	J03 0-0	O28 2-2	O07 0-0	a03 1-0
13 HUDDERSFIELD T	F07 1-0	A23 1-1	N29 3-0	O21 0-0	A19 1-1	N01 0-1	M28 0-0	N15 2-0	O04 2-0	a07 5-0	m02 4-2	S30 1-0		D27 5-0	a11 0-1	J10 4-1	N04 2-0	O18 2-0	D20 0-0	S06 4-1	J24 1-0	S20 1-0	F21 0-2	a21 1-1
14 HULL C	A19 1-2	F07 2-1	F21 0-0	S30 0-0	O21 0-1	O18 0-2	N04 0-0	M14 0-0	M17 0-1	A23 3-3	a07 0-1	M28 2-2	a18 2-1		N15 3-1	m07 3-1	O04 0-1	N01 1-0	S20 2-1	D06 2-0	D26 1-2	a25 1-1	a14 0-0	S06 0-1
15 MILLWALL	M21 1-1	O07 0-0	N11 2-2	F21 2-2	S30 3-0	S06 2-0	A30 1-0	m02 0-2	F07 3-1	S20 1-0	J10 3-1	a20 0-0	N08 2-1	A16 1-1		J31 0-0	D20 2-1	N29 1-1	D27 0-0	M08 2-1	a04 0-1	O25 1-4	O11 3-1	O28 0-1
16 NEWPORT CO	D06 0-0	a04 3-1	M07 1-1	N15 1-2	m05 4-0	A19 1-2	D13 1-1	F28 5-1	a25 1-0	a18 2-1	O28 2-1	F14 1-1	O25 3-2	N08 4-0	A23 2-1		S13 0-1	S27 0-2	O11 2-1	O07 0-0	J16 0-1	J03 4-0	D26 0-2	a07 1-1
17 OXFORD U	M24 1-1	N08 0-2	a04 1-1	D06 0-2	S20 1-2	D26 1-0	N15 1-0	S06 0-3	J17 2-1	A20 1-2	M21 2-0	F21 1-1	O08 0-2	M07 1-1	a29 1-0	F07 0-1		A30 0-0	O25 1-2	a18 2-1	O29 1-1	J31 2-0	O01 0-0	O11 1-1
18 PLYMOUTH A	O25 1-3	O11 0-2	O28 0-1	a25 2-1	S06 4-1	A23 1-1	A19 2-0	F07 1-0	N15 1-1	D26 0-2	O07 2-1	S20 4-1	M17 0-0	a04 0-0	J17 2-0	F21 3-2	J24 3-0		M21 1-0	S30 2-1	D00 3-1	a14 1-0	a18 0-0	N08 2-0
19 PORTSMOUTH	N15 0-1	J24 3-3	S06 0-2	O18 4-2	N01 2-1	S16 1-0	N29 2-0	O04 1-0	N04 2-1	F10 5-0	S27 1-0	a11 0-0	a25 1-2	F28 2-1	a18 2-1	M14 0-0	M29 1-1	O21 1-3		D26 0-0	A23 3-1	J10 1-0	A19 1-0	F07 2-0
20 READING	S27 3-2	N29 3-0	J31 0-0	a11 1-3	J10 3-1	M28 1-3	J02 3-0	O18 2-3	O22 1-0	N01 2-1	D20 0-0	N12 0-1	F14 2-1	m02 2-0	O04 4-1	F18 1-1	D27 0-1	S17 1-1	a20 2-1		F28 1-1	S13 1-0	A30 4-1	A16 2-0
21 ROTHERHAM U	S06 2-0	N11 4-0	D20 4-1	M31 1-0	D27 3-0	a11 3-0	O21 0-0	N04 0-0	M28 2-0	O04 3-1	A16 2-2	O18 2-0	A30 0-0	a20 1-1	N01 3-0	N29 1-0	J10 0-0	m02 2-1	J31 3-0	S20 2-0		F21 2-1	F07 1-0	S30 2-1
22 SHEFFIELD U	M31 1-1	S16 4-2	D27 0-0	N04 0-0	N15 2-2	M14 3-2	a07 2-0	A19 2-0	N01 3-0	O18 3-1	a21 1-2	J17 0-1	F28 2-2	D20 3-1	M28 2-3	O14 2-0	A23 1-0	O04 0-0	D06 1-0	F07 2-0	S27 1-2		S06 3-0	m02 0-1
23 SWINDON T	F28 2-0	A16 1-2	m02 0-0	N01 0-3	O18 1-1	O21 0-3	O04 1-2	J10 0-1	a11 3-0	M28 2-2	A23 3-4	N04 0-0	S27 1-0	N29 3-1	M14 0-0	a20 1-1	S16 1-0	D27 3-0	N11 0-2	J24 3-1	S13 2-1	F14 5-2		D19 3-1
24 WALSALL	a10 1-1	S27 2-2	A30 2-3	A20 3-1	O04 4-3	N04 2-2	J17 2-1	M28 4-3	J31 3-1	O21 1-3	M01 1-2	N01 3-3	D26 2-2	F14 1-1	J03 0-0	O18 1-0	M14 0-3	a11 1-3	S13 3-0	N15 2-2	S16 0-2	N29 4-4	a25 2-1	

DIVISION 4

	ALDERSHOT	BOURNEMOUTH	BRADFORD C	BURY	CREWE A	DARLINGTON	DONCASTER R	HALIFAX T	HARTLEPOOL U	HEREFORD U	LINCOLN C	MANSFIELD T	NORTHAMPTON T	PETERBOROUGH U	PORT VALE	ROCHDALE	SCUNTHORPE U	SOUTHEND U	STOCKPORT CO	TORQUAY U	TRANMERE R	WIGAN A	WIMBLEDON	YORK C
1 ALDERSHOT		O07 0-0	a04 1-1	S05 1-0	A23 2-0	F21 2-1	O25 1-0	D06 2-1	M07 2-1	D26 4-0	S30 0-0	S20 1-0	J03 0-0	N08 0-0	F07 0-0	O11 0-0	N15 0-0	a18 1-2	J17 3-0	O28 2-1	M22 3-2	J24 0-1	A19 2-0	a25 1-1
2 BOURNEMOUTH	N04 0-2		F14 4-0	a11 2-2	O21 0-0	M14 3-3	D06 1-2	J17 2-1	S16 1-0	A19 1-0	a25 0-1	O18 0-1	A23 0-0	F28 4-1	M28 0-0	S27 2-1	O04 2-2	D26 2-1	J03 0-1	J24 1-1	S13 1-0	N01 3-0	a18 0-1	N15 1-1
3 BRADFORD C	N01 1-0	S06 1-1		M28 0-2	O04 2-2	N04 3-0	D26 1-1	F11 0-0	a19 2-0	m15 0-1	O22 1-2	M14 0-2	S17 3-1	J28 1-1	O18 2-1	M08 2-1	A23 0-0	M04 2-1	A20 1-1	F07 2-0	S27 0-3	a11 3-3	N16 2-0	D06 1-1
4 BURY	F14 0-0	N08 3-0	O25 2-2		S16 1-3	A30 1-2	M31 2-0	J31 0-0	N11 0-0	O28 2-1	m04 1-1	S13 4-1	O07 1-2	M07 1-1	S27 2-1	M21 3-1	a18 6-1	A16 1-2	a25 0-1	O11 3-0	a04 2-2	F28 0-0	N29 1-0	D26 2-0
5 CREWE A	J31 0-0	J10 0-2	M07 1-0	O01 2-2		D20 1-1	O11 0-0	S20 2-1	a03 2-0	O07 5-0	A30 0-3	N29 1-2	M21 3-1	D27 1-0	m01 0-0	O25 1-0	F14 1-0	O29 1-1	F21 2-0	A16 0-1	N12 3-0	D13 1-2	S13 0-3	N08 1-1
6 DARLINGTON	S27 1-2	O11 1-2	O07 2-1	J24 2-1	a25 2-1		N11 5-0	a18 3-1	D26 3-0	M08 2-1	M10 0-0	F15 2-2	A16 1-0	M21 2-0	m05 1-1	O28 4-4	S16 0-1	O25 0-2	A23 2-2	a05 1-0	N08 2-0	S13 3-1	M17 4-1	J03 0-0
7 DONCASTER R	J10 3-1	m02 2-1	a21 2-0	O21 1-0	M13 1-1	A19 2-0		O18 0-0	J24 1-2	S06 5-1	O04 0-1	D19 2-1	F06 1-1	A23 0-4	N15 2-0	N29 1-2	M27 1-0	S19 1-0	a10 2-1	S30 2-0	D27 1-0	N04 1-1	N01 2-1	F20 3-2
8 HALIFAX T	m02 1-0	N29 1-2	O28 2-0	A23 4-2	M24 1-0	D27 1-2	M21 0-3		N08 1-2	O25 0-0	F14 1-3	A16 0-2	a04 0-1	N11 2-3	D20 2-2	a20 2-0	S13 1-0	O11 1-6	J24 2-0	M07 2-1	J10 1-1	S16 0-1	S27 0-1	O07 3-1
9 HARTLEPOOL U	O04 1-0	S30 1-0	D27 2-2	A19 1-2	N01 6-2	a17 2-0	A30 1-0	a11 3-0		S20 2-0	O18 2-0	O21 0-1	S06 2-3	D20 1-1	J10 3-0	J31 2-2	N04 2-0	F21 1-3	M28 1-0	N29 0-2	m02 3-0	N15 3-1	M14 2-3	F07 1-0
10 HEREFORD U	a20 0-0	N12 1-0	D20 4-0	J10 0-1	N05 0-0	O04 0-1	F14 1-3	M28 0-1	F28 3-0		N01 0-2	J31 2-1	S27 4-1	m02 1-1	O22 2-3	S17 3-0	a11 2-1	S13 0-0	m06 2-0	D27 0-1	A16 1-1	N29 1-1	O18 1-1	A30 1-1
11 LINCOLN C	S17 0-1	D20 2-0	J10 1-1	D06 2-1	J24 2-1	m02 1-0	M07 1-1	S06 3-0	M21 2-0	a04 1-0		D27 1-1	O25 8-0	A16 1-1	a20 1-0	O08 3-0	S27 2-2	N08 2-1	F07 1-0	N12 5-0	O29 2-0	A23 2-0	F28 0-0	O11 1-1
12 MANSFIELD T	a06 1-2	M21 1-1	O11 1-0	F07 2-0	J17 4-1	S06 1-0	m06 1-1	N15 0-1	M16 0-1	A23 4-0	a18 2-0		O27 2-0	O25 2-1	J24 5-0	a04 2-2	D26 1-0	M07 0-1	D06 1-0	N08 1-1	O06 1-1	S27 3-1	S15 1-0	A18 0-1
13 NORTHAMPTON T	O21 2-0	J31 0-1	S30 0-1	N04 5-3	O17 4-1	N15 2-2	S13 0-2	O31 2-1	F14 3-1	a14 0-0	M28 1-1	J10 0-1		a21 2-2	D27 5-1	D20 3-2	M13 3-3	S23 2-0	O03 0-1	m01 1-0	N29 3-1	F03 1-1	a11 1-1	S19 2-0
14 PETERBOROUGH U	a11 0-0	S20 1-0	A30 2-2	O04 2-0	a18 2-1	O18 1-0	J31 0-1	A20 2-2	a25 1-1	D06 3-0	N15 1-0	M28 1-0	D26 3-0		N01 1-1	S13 2-2	O22 0-2	O01 5-2	N04 1-2	F21 1-3	M18 4-1	M13 0-0	M04 1-1	J17 3-0
15 PORT VALE	S13 0-1	O27 0-2	a14 2-1	F21 1-3	D05 2-2	S20 4-2	A16 3-0	a26 0-0	O25 1-1	M16 4-0	D20 0-1	A30 0-0	a18 1-1	a04 1-1		N08 1-1	M03 2-2	N10 1-0	S29 2-0	O06 3-1	O11 5-1	F14 3-0	J31 2-3	M07 2-0
16 ROCHDALE	M14 0-2	F21 0-0	S20 0-2	O18 2-1	J03 2-0	M28 0-0	J17 2-2	D26 1-1	A23 1-1	S30 0-0	N04 1-0	N01 1-4	m03 0-1	F07 2-3	a12 2-1		A19 4-0	D06 0-2	J12 2-1	S06 2-1	J24 3-1	O04 3-0	O21 2-0	a18 3-2
17 SCUNTHORPE U	A16 2-2	M06 1-1	J31 1-0	D27 2-2	S06 1-1	S30 3-0	O28 1-1	F07 2-2	O07 3-3	N08 3-1	F21 2-2	a20 2-0	O11 0-2	J10 1-1	F24 1-1	N11 1-1		M22 2-1	S19 2-0	O25 0-2	D20 2-0	m02 4-4	A30 1-2	a04 3-2
18 SOUTHEND U	D27 3-0	a17 2-1	D12 3-1	N15 1-0	M27 3-0	J09 1-0	F27 0-0	M13 5-1	S26 4-0	F06 2-0	a11 0-0	O03 2-0	J23 0-0	S15 1-0	A18 5-1	m01 1-1	O17 2-0		O31 2-0	D19 3-1	A20 2-0	O20 1-0	N03 1-0	S05 3-0
19 STOCKPORT CO	N29 1-0	O24 2-1	N10 1-2	D19 1-2	S26 1-3	J30 0-1	N07 2-1	A29 1-1	O27 0-2	O10 0-0	S13 0-0	m01 2-1	M06 1-2	O06 3-4	S15 2-1	A10 2-2	F27 2-0	a03 1-0		F16 4-1	a20 1-0	D27 0-1	F13 0-0	M20 2-0
20 TORQUAY U	M29 2-0	A30 2-0	S13 2-0	M14 3-1	N15 1-0	N01 0-2	S16 2-3	O04 1-0	J17 2-1	a18 0-1	A20 1-2	a12 1-1	D06 3-3	S27 2-0	N05 4-0	F14 2-0	F04 2-1	a25 0-3	O22 1-2		M01 2-1	O18 2-0	D26 2-3	a08 1-2
21 TRANMERE R	O17 3-1	F06 0-1	M10 1-1	O31 3-1	A18 0-1	a10 3-1	a17 1-1	O20 2-0	D05 2-2	a29 2-1	M03 0-0	N03 1-0	J16 3-2	S05 1-2	M24 1-2	A29 3-1	a24 1-2	J30 2-2	D26 1-0	S19 1-0		M29 2-3	O03 3-0	S29 5-0
22 WIGAN A	A30 1-0	a04 0-1	N08 0-1	S20 2-1	D26 0-0	F07 3-1	O08 3-0	O01 4-1	A16 0-3	F11 1-0	J31 0-2	F21 2-0	N12 3-0	O11 1-1	S06 1-0	M07 0-1	D06 1-1	J03 0-1	a18 2-1	M21 2-0	O25 1-1		a25 1-0	O29 1-0
23 WIMBLEDON	N11 4-0	D27 2-0	A16 2-2	m02 2-4	F07 2-0	D06 1-1	a04 1-0	F21 3-0	O11 5-0	M22 0-0	S20 0-1	S30 2-1	N08 1-0	O28 2-1	A23 1-0	a28 4-1	J19 2-2	O07 0-1	S06 1-2	a20 1-0	M07 2-1	M31 1-0		O25 3-0
24 YORK C	D20 4-1	A16 4-0	m02 0-3	a14 0-1	a11 2-0	O21 1-2	S27 0-1	N04 1-1	S13 0-1	J24 1-2	M14 1-0	N11 2-0	m05 1-2	M24 1-2	O04 4-1	D27 1-2	N01 1-0	F14 0-1	O18 1-0	A23 0-0	S23 4-1	J10 2-1	M28 0-1	

LEAGUE TABLES

DIVISION 1

	P	W	D	L	F	A	W	D	L	F	A	Pts
Aston Villa	42	16	3	2	40	13	10	5	6	32	27	60
Ipswich T	42	15	4	2	45	14	8	6	7	32	29	56
Arsenal	42	13	8	0	36	17	6	7	8	25	28	53
WBA	42	15	4	2	40	15	5	8	8	20	27	52
Liverpool	42	13	5	3	38	15	4	12	5	24	27	51
Southampton	42	15	4	2	47	22	5	6	10	29	34	50
Nottingham F	42	15	3	3	44	20	4	9	8	18	24	50
Manchester U	42	9	11	1	30	14	6	7	8	21	22	48
Leeds U	42	10	5	6	19	19	7	5	9	20	28	44
Tottenham H	42	9	9	3	44	31	5	6	10	26	37	43
Stoke C	42	8	9	4	31	23	4	9	8	20	37	42
Manchester C	42	10	7	4	35	25	4	4	13	21	34	39
Birmingham C	42	11	5	5	32	23	2	7	12	18	38	38
Middlesbrough	42	14	4	3	38	16	2	1	18	15	45	37
Everton	42	8	6	7	32	25	5	4	12	23	33	36
Coventry C	42	9	6	6	31	30	4	4	13	17	38	36
Sunderland	42	10	4	7	32	19	4	3	14	20	34	35
Wolves	42	11	2	8	26	20	2	7	12	17	35	35
Brighton & HA	42	10	3	8	30	26	4	4	13	24	41	35
Norwich C	42	9	7	5	34	25	4	0	17	15	48	33
Leicester C	42	7	5	9	20	23	6	1	14	20	44	32
Crystal P	42	6	4	11	32	37	0	3	18	15	46	19

DIVISION 2

	P	W	D	L	F	A	W	D	L	F	A	Pts
West Ham U	42	19	1	1	53	12	9	9	3	26	17	66
Notts Co	42	10	8	3	26	15	8	9	4	23	23	53
Swansea C	42	12	5	4	39	19	6	9	6	25	25	50
Blackburn R	42	12	8	1	28	7	4	10	7	14	22	50
Luton T	42	10	6	5	35	23	8	6	7	26	23	48
Derby Co	42	9	8	4	34	26	6	7	8	23	26	45
Grimsby T	42	10	8	3	21	10	5	7	9	23	32	45
QPR	42	11	7	3	36	12	4	6	11	20	34	43
Watford	42	13	5	3	34	18	3	6	12	16	27	43
Sheffield W	42	14	4	3	38	14	3	4	14	15	37	42
Newcastle U	42	11	7	3	22	13	3	7	11	8	32	42
Chelsea	42	8	6	7	27	15	6	6	9	19	26	40
Cambridge U	42	13	1	7	36	23	4	5	12	17	42	40
Shrewsbury T	42	9	7	5	33	22	2	10	9	13	25	39
Oldham A	42	7	9	5	19	16	5	6	10	20	32	39
Wrexham	42	5	8	8	22	24	7	6	8	21	21	38
Orient	42	9	8	4	34	20	4	4	13	18	36	38
Bolton W	42	10	5	6	40	27	4	5	12	21	39	38
Cardiff C	42	7	7	7	23	24	5	5	11	21	36	36
Preston NE	42	8	7	6	28	26	3	7	11	13	36	36
Bristol C	42	6	10	5	19	15	1	6	14	10	36	30
Bristol R	42	4	9	8	21	24	1	4	16	13	41	23

DIVISION 3

	P	W	D	L	F	A	W	D	L	F	A	Pts
Rotherham U	46	17	6	0	43	8	7	7	9	19	24	61
Barnsley	46	15	5	3	46	19	6	12	5	26	26	59
Charlton A	46	14	6	3	36	17	11	3	9	27	27	59
Huddersfield T	46	14	6	3	40	11	7	8	8	31	29	56
Chesterfield	46	17	4	2	42	16	6	6	11	30	32	56
Portsmouth	46	14	5	4	35	19	8	4	11	20	28	53
Plymouth A	46	14	5	4	35	18	5	9	9	21	26	52
Burnley	46	13	5	5	37	21	5	9	9	23	27	50
Brentford	46	7	9	7	30	25	7	10	6	22	24	47
Reading	46	13	5	5	39	22	5	5	13	23	40	46
Exeter C	46	9	9	5	36	30	7	4	12	26	36	45
Newport Co	46	11	6	6	38	22	4	7	12	26	39	43
Fulham	46	8	7	8	28	29	7	6	10	29	35	43
Oxford U	46	7	8	8	20	24	6	9	8	19	23	43
Gillingham	46	9	8	6	23	19	3	10	10	25	39	42
Millwall	46	10	9	4	30	21	4	5	14	13	39	42
Swindon T	46	10	6	7	35	27	3	9	11	16	29	41
Chester	46	11	5	7	25	17	4	6	13	13	31	41
Carlisle U	46	8	9	6	32	29	6	4	13	24	41	41
Walsall	46	8	9	6	43	43	5	6	12	16	31	41
Sheffield U	46	12	6	5	38	20	2	6	15	27	43	40
Colchester U	46	12	7	4	35	22	2	4	17	10	43	39
Blackpool	46	5	9	9	19	28	4	5	14	26	47	32
Hull C	46	7	8	8	23	22	1	8	14	17	49	32

DIVISION 4

	P	W	D	L	F	A	W	D	L	F	A	Pts
Southend U	46	19	4	0	47	6	11	3	9	32	25	67
Lincoln C	46	15	7	1	44	11	10	8	5	22	14	65
Doncaster R	46	15	4	4	36	20	7	8	8	23	29	56
Wimbledon	46	15	4	4	42	17	8	5	10	22	29	55
Peterboro' U	46	11	8	4	37	21	6	10	7	31	33	52
Aldershot	46	12	9	2	28	11	6	5	12	15	30	50
Mansfield T	46	13	5	5	36	15	7	4	12	22	29	49
Darlington	46	13	6	4	43	23	6	5	12	22	36	49
Hartlepool U	46	14	3	6	42	22	6	6	11	22	39	49
Northampton T	46	11	7	5	42	26	7	6	10	23	41	49
Wigan A	46	13	4	6	29	16	5	7	11	22	39	47
Bury	46	10	8	5	38	21	7	3	13	32	41	45
Bournemouth	46	9	8	6	30	21	7	5	11	17	27	45
Bradford C	46	9	9	5	30	24	5	7	11	23	36	44
Rochdale	46	11	6	6	33	25	3	9	11	27	45	43
Scunthorpe U	46	8	12	3	40	31	3	8	12	20	38	42
Torquay U	46	13	2	8	38	26	5	3	15	17	37	41
Crewe A	46	10	7	6	28	20	3	7	13	20	41	40
Port Vale	46	10	8	5	40	23	2	7	14	17	47	39
Stockport Co	46	10	5	8	29	25	6	2	15	15	32	39
Tranmere R	46	12	5	6	41	24	1	5	17	18	49	36
Hereford U	46	8	8	7	29	20	3	5	15	9	42	35
Halifax T	46	9	3	11	28	32	2	9	12	16	39	34
York C	46	10	2	11	31	23	2	7	14	16	43	33

Football League Records

Top scorers: Div 1, K.Keegan (Southampton) 26 goals; Div 2, R.Moore (Rotherham United) 22 goals; Div 3, G.Davies (Fulham) 24 goals; Div 4, K.Edwards (Sheffield United & Hull City) 36 goals.
From this season three points were awarded for a win.

Liverpool's goalscoring sensation Ian Rush. In his first full season with the Reds he hit 17 goals in another Championship-winning campaign.

DIVISION 1

	ARSENAL	ASTON VILLA	BIRMINGHAM C	BRIGHTON & HA	COVENTRY C	EVERTON	IPSWICH T	LEEDS U	LIVERPOOL	MANCHESTER C	MANCHESTER U	MIDDLESBROUGH	NOTTINGHAM F	NOTTS CO	SOUTHAMPTON	STOKE C	SUNDERLAND	SWANSEA C	TOTTENHAM H	W.B.A.	WEST HAM U	WOLVERHAMPTON W
1 ARSENAL		M27 4-3	S22 1-0	J26 0-0	O31 1-0	N28 1-0	M13 1-0	J30 1-0	m11 1-1	O17 1-0	S26 0-0	F16 1-0	a17 2-0	F13 1-0	m15 4-1	A29 0-1	S12 1-1	F27 0-2	a12 1-3	M16 2-2	m01 2-0	F02 2-1
2 ASTON VILLA	N07 0-2		S26 0-0	a12 3-0	F27 2-1	m15 1-2	O31 0-1	a28 1-4	J30 0-3	m01 0-0	S12 1-1	a17 1-0	N28 3-1	A29 0-1	F10 1-1	S23 2-2	F02 1-0	m21 3-0	F17 1-1	M30 2-1	O17 3-2	M13 3-1
3 BIRMINGHAM C	m04 0-1	F20 0-1		M27 1-0	J26 3-3	a06 0-2	S01 1-1	a10 0-1	m08 0-1	S19 3-0	M06 0-1	F06 0-0	S05 4-3	D05 2-1	O10 4-0	M13 2-1	F16 2-0	a24 2-1	M23 0-0	O31 3-3	O03 2-2	N21 0-3
4 BRIGHTON & H.A.	a10 2-1	D28 0-1	N07 1-1		S19 2-2	F06 3-1	m08 0-1	M02 1-0	O17 3-3	O03 4-1	a24 0-1	S05 2-0	F20 0-1	N21 2-2	a03 1-1	O31 0-0	D05 2-1	S01 1-2	M09 1-3	F27 2-2	J16 1-0	m04 2-0
5 COVENTRY C	M20 1-0	O10 1-1	m15 0-1	J30 0-1		a13 1-0	J16 2-4	S12 4-0	S22 1-2	D12 0-1	A29 2-1	N28 1-1	M09 0-1	F16 1-5	S26 4-2	N24 3-0	a27 6-1	O24 3-1	m01 0-0	D26 0-2	a17 1-0	M27 0-0
6 EVERTON	a24 2-1	D19 2-0	A29 3-1	S12 1-1	D28 3-2		O17 2-1	m04 1-0	M27 1-3	O31 0-1	a10 3-3	M13 2-0	a20 2-1	S22 3-1	J19 1-1	F13 0-0	N21 1-2	D05 3-1	J30 1-1	S26 1-0	F27 0-0	m08 1-1
7 IPSWICH T	O24 2-1	M20 3-1	J05 3-2	M30 3-1	a03 1-0	M06 3-0		S26 2-1	S12 2-0	N28 2-0	a20 2-1	m01 3-1	m15 1-3	J30 1-3	F16 5-2	a17 2-0	A29 3-3	N07 2-3	m17 2-1	S22 1-0	a13 3-2	O10 1-0
8 LEEDS U	S19 0-0	O03 1-1	m12 3-3	m15 2-1	F06 0-0	S02 1-1	F20 0-2		F27 0-2	M10 0-1	a03 0-0	a13 1-1	M20 1-1	N07 1-0	a17 1-3	m01 0-0	O24 1-0	J16 2-0	D12 0-0	O17 3-1	N28 3-3	S05 3-0
9 LIVERPOOL	S05 2-0	S19 0-0	M30 3-1	M06 0-1	F20 4-0	N07 3-1	F06 4-0	O10 3-0		D26 1-3	O24 1-2	S01 1-1	m01 2-0	a02 1-0	N28 0-1	a13 2-0	M20 1-0	O03 2-2	m15 3-1	a17 1-0	J05 3-0	J16 2-1
10 MANCHESTER C	M06 0-0	D05 1-0	J30 4-2	F13 4-0	m08 1-3	M20 1-1	a24 1-1	S23 4-0	a10 0-5		O10 0-0	N07 3-2	O24 0-0	m05 1-0	S12 1-1	J09 1-1	D19 2-3	N21 4-0	S26 0-1	A29 2-1	a03 0-1	D28 2-1
11 MANCHESTER U	F20 0-0	F06 4-1	O17 1-1	N28 2-0	M17 0-1	J06 1-1	S05 1-2	S30 1-0	a07 0-1	F27 1-1		O21 1-0	A31 0-0	O31 2-1	m01 1-0	m15 2-0	M27 0-0	S19 1-0	a17 2-0	a12 1-0	J27 1-0	O03 5-0
12 MIDDLESBROUGH	m08 1-3	N21 3-3	S12 2-1	a20 2-1	a24 0-0	O24 0-2	D05 0-1	a06 0-0	m18 0-0	M27 0-0	S22 0-2		O10 1-1	a10 3-0	J30 0-1	S26 3-2	N14 0-0	F13 1-1	A29 1-3	M09 1-0	M20 2-3	M06 0-0
13 NOTTINGHAM F	N21 1-2	a24 1-1	J09 2-1	S26 2-1	O17 2-1	a03 0-1	M17 1-1	O31 2-1	D05 0-2	M13 1-1	m05 0-1	F27 1-1		J23 0-2	A29 2-1	J30 0-0	S23 2-0	m08 0-2	m12 2-0	S12 0-0	N07 0-0	a10 0-1
14 NOTTS CO	O03 2-1	J16 1-0	m01 1-4	a17 4-1	S05 2-1	N24 2-2	S19 1-4	M27 2-1	J26 0-4	S01 1-1	M20 1-3	m11 0-1	a12 1-2		M06 1-1	a26 3-1	O10 2-0	F06 0-1	N28 2-2	m15 1-2	O24 1-1	F20 4-0
15 SOUTHAMPTON	J23 3-1	a10 0-3	F27 3-1	D08 0-2	m04 5-5	S05 1-0	O03 4-3	N21 4-0	a24 2-3	F06 2-1	D05 3-2	S19 2-0	F13 2-0	O17 3-1		M27 4-3	m08 1-0	D28 3-1	O31 1-2	M13 0-0	F20 2-1	S01 4-1
16 STOKE C	J20 0-1	m05 1-0	O24 1-0	M20 0-0	S02 4-0	O03 3-1	N21 2-0	D05 1-2	M09 1-5	S05 1-3	J23 0-3	F20 2-0	S19 1-2	m08 2-2	N07 0-2		a10 0-1	O17 1-2	F27 0-2	m20 3-0	F06 2-1	a24 2-1
17 SUNDERLAND	F06 0-0	S02 2-1	a12 2-0	m01 3-0	O03 0-0	a17 3-1	a07 1-1	M13 0-1	O31 0-2	m15 1-0	N07 1-5	a03 0-2	N25 2-3	F27 1-1	M10 2-0	F10 0-2		F20 0-1	O17 0-2	N28 1-2	S05 0-2	S19 0-0
18 SWANSEA C	O10 2-0	D15 2-1	N28 1-0	N24 0-0	M13 0-0	m01 1-3	M27 1-2	A29 5-1	F16 2-0	a17 2-0	J30 2-0	m15 1-2	D12 1-2	S12 3-2	a13 1-0	M06 3-0	S26 2-0		S22 2-1	a06 3-1	M30 0-1	O31 0-0
19 TOTTENHAM H	M29 2-2	S05 1-3	a28 1-1	O24 0-1	D05 1-2	S19 3-0	a10 1-0	m08 2-1	m03 2-2	F20 2-0	N21 3-1	J27 1-0	O03 3-0	a24 3-1	M20 3-2	O10 2-0	a14 2-2	m05 2-1		N07 1-2	S02 0-4	F06 6-1
20 W.B.A.	S02 0-2	m08 0-1	M20 1-1	O10 0-0	a10 1-2	F20 0-0	m05 1-2	m18 2-0	N21 1-1	a21 0-1	m12 0-3	O03 2-0	F06 2-1	M24 2-4	O24 1-1	N14 1-2	a24 2-3	S05 4-1	M27 1-0		S19 0-0	D05 3-0
21 WEST HAM U	D05 1-2	M06 2-2	F13 2-2	A29 1-1	N21 5-2	O10 1-1	M02 2-0	a24 4-3	S26 1-1	F02 1-1	m08 1-1	O31 3-2	M27 0-1	M13 1-0	S22 4-2	S12 3-2	m04 1-1	a10 1-1	m10 2-2	J30 3-1		a06 3-1
22 WOLVERHAMPTON W	a03 1-1	O24 0-3	a17 1-1	S22 0-1	N07 1-0	J23 0-3	F27 2-1	M16 1-0	A29 1-0	a12 4-1	F13 0-1	O17 0-0	F16 0-0	S26 3-2	N24 0-0	N28 2-0	J30 0-1	M20 0-1	S12 0-1	m01 1-2	m15 2-1	

Burnley's Welsh international Bryan Flynn, a great servant who sadly missed much of the Clarets' Third Division title-winning season of 1980-81.

DIVISION 2

	BARNSLEY	BLACKBURN R	BOLTON W	CAMBRIDGE U	CARDIFF C	CHARLTON A	CHELSEA	CRYSTAL P	DERBY CO	GRIMSBY T	LEICESTER C	LUTON T	NEWCASTLE U	NORWICH C	OLDHAM A	ORIENT	Q.P.R.	ROTHERHAM U	SHEFFIELD W	SHREWSBURY T	WATFORD	WREXHAM
1 BARNSLEY		F27 0-1	S12 3-0	J30 0-0	S26 0-1	a24 1-0	M12 2-1	D05 2-0	a10 0-0	M23 3-2	m04 0-2	M16 4-3	O17 1-0	F24 0-1	N07 3-1	O31 1-0	m08 3-0	a02 3-0	S22 1-0	A29 4-0	F09 0-0	N21 2-2
2 BLACKBURN R	O10 2-1		a12 0-2	S23 1-0	J30 1-0	J13 0-2	m15 1-1	M27 1-0	M06 4-1	M13 2-0	S26 0-2	N14 0-1	m01 4-1	N28 3-0	a09 0-0	S12 2-0	F16 2-1	J23 2-0	A29 0-1	N25 0-0	a17 1-2	O31 0-0
3 BOLTON W	F06 2-1	D28 2-2		O24 3-4	M06 1-0	D19 2-0	J16 2-2	a24 0-0	m04 3-2	O03 1-2	O10 0-3	S05 1-2	S29 1-0	M20 0-1	S19 0-2	N21 1-0	D05 1-0	F20 0-1	m08 3-1	a03 1-1	N07 2-0	a10 2-0
4 CAMBRIDGE U	S19 2-1	m04 1-0	M13 2-1		O31 2-1	m08 4-0	O03 1-0	J26 0-0	S01 1-2	F27 2-2	a24 1-2	a10 1-1	F06 1-0	a03 1-2	F20 0-0	a20 2-0	F09 1-0	S05 3-0	S21 1-2	N07 2-0	O17 1-2	D05 2-3
5 CARDIFF C	F20 0-0	S19 1-3	O17 2-1	M20 5-4		D28 0-1	S05 1-2	m08 0-1	D04 1-0	M30 2-1	N21 3-1	m17 2-3	O03 0-4	N07 1-0	J20 0-1	a10 2-1	a24 1-2	F06 1-2	F27 0-2	O24 1-1	a03 2-0	N04 3-2
6 CHARLTON A	N28 2-1	S05 2-0	a28 1-0	J23 0-0	a13 2-2		N24 3-4	F06 2-1	O03 2-1	S19 2-0	N07 1-4	J19 0-0	a03 0-1	D30 0-0	O20 3-1	M12 5-2	O31 1-2	a17 1-2	O17 3-0	F27 1-0	m01 1-1	F20 1-0
7 CHELSEA	O24 1-2	D19 1-1	A29 2-0	a07 4-1	F17 1-0	S23 2-2		M17 1-2	a24 0-2	N21 1-1	M09 4-1	m08 1-2	N07 2-1	S26 2-1	a03 2-2	m05 2-2	a10 2-1	M20 1-4	D05 2-1	J30 3-1	S12 1-3	O10 2-0
8 CRYSTAL P	m01 1-2	N07 1-2	N28 1-0	A29 2-1	M09 1-0	S12 2-0	a12 0-1		O24 0-1	a03 0-3	M23 0-2	M20 3-3	m15 1-2	N24 2-1	a17 4-0	S22 1-0	J30 0-0	O10 3-1	J19 1-2	S26 0-1	a27 0-3	m11 2-1
9 DERBY CO	a28 0-1	O17 1-1	S23 0-2	N25 2-1	m01 0-0	F13 1-1	N28 1-1	M13 4-1		O31 1-1	S12 3-1	M27 0-0	F27 2-2	a17 0-2	J23 1-0	A29 1-2	S26 3-1	a12 3-1	J30 3-1	M10 1-1	m15 3-2	N14 2-1
10 GRIMSBY T	a09 3-2	O24 1-1	M02 1-1	O10 1-2	m15 0-1	J30 3-3	a17 3-3	a20 0-1	M20 1-0		A29 2-2	M06 0-0	N28 1-1	S22 1-2	m01 2-1	J09 1-2	S12 2-1	F09 1-2	S26 0-1	a27 5-1	M16 0-2	M27 1-1
11 LEICESTER C	S08 1-0	F20 1-0	F27 1-0	N28 4-1	a17 3-1	M27 3-1	O16 1-1	O03 1-1	F06 2-1	m12 1-2		S19 1-2	M02 3-0	m01 1-4	a13 2-1	N14 0-1	M13 3-2	M17 1-0	O31 0-0	m15 0-0	D12 1-1	S05 1-0
12 LUTON T	m15 1-1	a03 2-0	N24 2-0	M02 1-0	S22 2-3	A29 3-0	a20 2-2	O31 1-0	N07 3-2	O17 6-0	J30 2-1		a17 3-2	a12 2-0	F27 2-0	M30 2-0	m11 3-2	N28 3-1	S12 0-3	a30 4-1	S26 4-1	M12 0-0
13 NEWCASTLE U	M06 1-0	D05 0-0	F03 2-0	S12 1-0	F13 2-1	N14 4-1	M27 1-0	M31 0-0	O10 3-0	a24 0-1	a10 0-0	N21 3-2		J30 2-1	M20 2-0	S26 1-0	m05 0-4	O24 1-1	F24 1-0	S23 2-0	A29 0-1	m08 4-2
14 NORWICH C	S05 1-1	a24 2-0	O31 0-0	N14 2-1	M27 2-1	a10 5-0	F20 2-1	S02 1-0	N21 4-1	m05 2-1	D05 0-0	D28 1-3	S19 2-1		O03 1-2	m08 2-0	F27 0-1	J16 2-0	F03 2-3	O17 2-1	M13 4-2	F06 4-0
15 OLDHAM A	M27 1-1	D26 0-3	J30 1-1	S26 2-0	A29 2-2	m04 1-0	N16 1-0	N21 0-0	m08 1-1	D05 3-1	D28 1-1	O10 1-1	O31 3-1	F16 2-0		D19 3-2	S22 2-0	M06 0-3	M13 0-3	S12 1-1	J09 1-1	a24 2-1
16 ORIENT	J23 1-3	F06 0-0	a17 3-0	a12 0-0	a28 1-1	O25 1-1	S28 0-2	F21 0-0	J16 3-2	S05 1-2	m18 3-0	O03 0-3	N24 1-0	M16 1-1	m15 0-3		O18 1-1	m01 1-2	N07 3-0	N28 2-0	F27 1-3	S19 0-0
17 Q.P.R.	D12 1-0	O03 2-0	m01 7-1	m15 2-1	N28 2-0	M20 4-0	D26 0-2	S19 1-0	F20 3-0	F06 1-0	O24 2-0	S01 1-2	S05 3-0	O10 2-0	N24 0-0	a06 3-0		N07 1-1	M29 2-0	a17 2-1	a12 0-0	J16 1-1
18 ROTHERHAM U	N14 2-4	m08 4-1	S26 2-0	F13 1-0	S12 1-0	N21 2-1	O31 6-0	F27 2-0	F02 2-1	a10 2-2	S22 1-1	a24 2-2	M13 0-0	A29 4-1	O17 1-2	D05 1-0	M27 1-0		m04 2-2	F16 3-0	J30 1-2	F23 2-0
19 SHEFFIELD W	N24 2-2	J16 2-2	F16 0-1	a17 2-1	O10 2-1	M06 1-1	m01 0-0	S05 1-0	S19 1-1	F20 1-1	M20 2-0	F06 3-3	a12 2-1	m15 2-1	O24 2-1	M27 2-0	N14 1-3	S08 2-0		M02 0-0	N28 3-1	O03 0-3
20 SHREWSBURY T	F02 0-2	S01 1-2	N14 2-0	M27 1-0	M13 1-1	O10 1-1	S19 1-0	m04 1-0	S05 4-1	m08 2-0	M30 1-1	D05 2-2	F20 0-0	a20 0-2	F06 2-1	a24 2-0	N21 2-1	O03 2-1	a10 0-1		O31 0-2	M16 1-1
21 WATFORD	O03 3-1	N21 3-2	M27 3-0	M06 0-0	N14 0-0	D05 2-2	F06 1-0	a09 1-1	J26 6-1	S01 0-2	m08 3-1	F20 1-1	J16 2-3	O24 3-0	S05 1-1	O10 3-0	M09 4-0	S19 1-0	a24 4-0	M20 3-1		m04 2-0
22 WREXHAM	a17 0-0	M20 1-0	M09 2-1	m01 0-0	N24 3-1	S26 1-0	F27 1-0	O17 0-1	a03 1-1	N07 2-0	a20 0-0	O24 0-2	a06 4-2	S12 2-3	N28 0-3	J30 0-1	A29 1-3	m15 3-2	F13 0-1	a12 1-0	S22 0-1	

Season 1981-82

DIVISION 3

	BRENTFORD	BRISTOL C	BRISTOL R	BURNLEY	CARLISLE U	CHESTER	CHESTERFIELD	DONCASTER R	EXETER C	FULHAM	GILLINGHAM	HUDDERSFIELD T	LINCOLN C	MILLWALL	NEWPORT CO	OXFORD U	PLYMOUTH A	PORTSMOUTH	PRESTON N.E.	READING	SOUTHEND U	SWINDON T	WALSALL	WIMBLEDON
1 BRENTFORD		N07 0-1	M22 1-0	O31 0-0	O03 1-2	N28 1-0	M13 2-0	m01 2-2	F27 2-0	J23 0-1	S21 0-1	J02 0-1	O17 3-1	a09 4-1	F20 2-0	a03 1-2	S19 0-0	F06 2-2	a17 0-0	m15 1-2	O19 0-1	a19 4-2	S05 0-0	a26 2-3
2 BRISTOL C	M27 0-1		a12 1-2	N28 2-3	a06 1-1	m15 1-0	O31 0-0	S05 2-2	F23 3-2	F06 0-0	m01 2-1	J16 0-0	M13 0-1	m12 4-1	S19 2-1	M06 0-2	S22 3-2	F20 0-1	O10 0-0	O20 2-0	N14 0-2	a17 0-3	O03 0-1	J02 1-3
3 BRISTOL R	m03 1-2	D29 1-0		S12 2-1	D19 0-1	A29 2-2	J19 1-0	M20 3-0	F09 3-2	D05 1-2	N07 2-0	O24 3-2	S26 0-2	a03 0-1	N03 2-0	m11 1-0	m08 2-3	a10 1-1	F13 2-0	J30 1-1	F27 2-1	O17 1-4	a24 2-1	S29 2-2
4 BURNLEY	M20 0-0	a24 2-0	F06 4-0		m04 1-0	N03 1-0	m18 1-1	S22 0-1	O17 3-3	O24 2-2	F02 1-0	S19 0-0	a10 1-0	F20 1-1	J16 2-1	D05 2-1	S05 1-0	F27 3-0	m11 2-0	a03 3-0	a20 3-5	O03 0-2	m08 2-1	N07 2-2
5 CARLISLE U	F13 1-0	A29 2-2	m15 1-2	S29 1-0		a13 3-0	F09 3-0	N03 2-0	a20 3-2	N07 1-2	N28 2-0	M09 2-2	J30 1-0	a17 2-1	M20 2-2	S26 2-1	O17 3-1	a03 2-0	F02 1-0	M23 2-1	S12 3-2	F27 1-1	O24 2-1	m01 2-1
6 CHESTER	a24 1-2	a21 0-0	J23 1-1	M17 0-1	m19 0-1		O21 0-2	D02 1-1	N14 0-2	m05 0-2	F06 0-0	F20 3-1	m08 1-2	S19 0-0	a10 0-2	O10 2-2	M13 0-3	J19 3-2	M27 0-1	O31 2-3	D05 1-1	S05 0-0	S23 0-0	M31 1-1
7 CHESTERFIELD	O24 0-2	M20 1-0	S05 2-0	a12 1-2	S22 1-0	M09 3-5		F02 3-1	a17 2-1	S19 3-0	m15 1-3	N03 1-0	a03 0-2	a27 0-1	J23 1-0	N07 2-2	F20 2-2	O03 2-2	J05 0-0	F27 2-1	O17 1-2	m01 2-1	F06 1-0	N28 2-0
8 DONCASTER R	S26 1-0	m18 2-2	O31 4-2	F09 0-1	M16 1-1	F13 4-3	a10 0-0		S11 3-0	m08 2-1	a03 1-1	N06 1-2	O20 4-1	O07 1-0	F27 0-2	M23 1-1	a24 2-2	D05 0-0	S29 1-0	A29 0-1	m04 1-1	M12 0-0	a20 1-0	J29 1-3
9 EXETER C	O10 3-1	a10 4-0	S23 1-3	M06 2-1	S05 2-1	a03 3-0	D05 0-3	F06 2-1		M10 1-0	F20 1-1	m12 1-0	M24 1-2	O03 5-4	a24 1-0	N04 1-2	D28 1-1	m05 3-3	O24 4-3	N07 4-3	m08 1-1	S19 1-2	J16 2-0	M20 2-1
10 FULHAM	A29 1-2	S12 2-1	a17 4-2	M13 1-1	M27 4-1	S26 2-0	J30 1-0	a06 3-1	O20 4-1		m11 0-0	F27 2-2	m18 1-1	N28 0-0	O17 3-1	F23 0-0	M16 1-3	O31 1-1	m15 3-0	m01 2-2	S29 2-1	a13 2-0	N14 1-1	F09 4-1
11 GILLINGHAM	F09 1-1	S29 1-1	M27 2-0	A29 3-1	a24 0-0	S12 0-1	a06 3-2	N14 3-0	S26 2-3	a10 2-0		O17 3-2	m04 1-0	M12 1-1	D28 1-1	m08 2-1	F27 3-2	O20 4-2	J30 0-2	m18 2-1	M16 2-0	O31 1-0	D05 1-4	F13 6-1
12 HUDDERSFIELD T	m08 1-1	m04 5-0	M13 0-2	J30 1-2	O20 2-1	S29 1-2	M23 1-1	M27 1-2	A29 1-1	O10 1-0	M06 2-0		M02 0-2	O31 1-2	M30 2-0	J09 2-0	D05 0-0	a24 0-1	F09 2-3	F13 6-1	S26 3-2	N14 3-0	a10 2-1	S12 1-1
13 LINCOLN C	M06 1-0	O24 1-2	m01 1-0	M31 1-1	S19 0-0	F03 3-0	N14 2-1	M10 5-0	m15 2-0	S05 1-1	J16 2-0	a12 2-0		S23 0-1	O03 2-2	M20 2-1	F06 2-0	J23 1-1	N04 1-2	a17 2-1	M27 1-1	N28 2-0	F20 1-1	O10 5-1
14 MILLWALL	D28 0-1	N03 2-0	N14 0-0	S26 4-3	D05 1-2	J30 2-1	m04 3-2	M06 0-2	F14 5-1	a25 4-3	O24 1-2	a06 1-3	F09 1-1		M09 1-0	S29 1-2	a20 2-1	m08 1-0	A29 2-1	S13 0-1	a12 1-1	M28 0-0	O11 2-0	F24 2-1
15 NEWPORT CO	S29 0-1	J30 1-1	M16 1-1	m01 0-0	O31 2-0	D26 0-1	A29 1-0	O10 1-0	N28 1-1	M07 1-3	a12 4-2	m15 1-0	F13 0-0	O20 1-1		S12 3-2	N14 0-1	M13 1-1	S26 1-1	J02 3-1	m11 3-2	m18 1-0	M27 2-2	a17 0-0
16 OXFORD U	N14 1-2	O17 1-0	O21 1-1	a17 0-0	F20 2-1	F27 3-1	M27 1-1	a12 3-1	M17 0-0	O03 2-0	M31 1-1	S05 1-0	O31 1-1	m01 0-0	F06 1-1		a28 1-0	S23 0-2	N28 3-0	F03 1-0	M13 0-2	a07 5-0	S19 0-1	m15 0-3
17 PLYMOUTH A	J30 1-0	F09 2-1	J02 4-0	J09 1-1	M06 1-0	O24 5-1	S26 0-2	N28 4-2	a09 2-1	N03 3-1	O10 1-2	a17 1-1	S12 0-2	m15 2-1	a02 1-2	A29 0-1		N07 0-0	m01 0-3	S29 1-1	F13 0-0	D26 2-1	M20 4-1	a14 2-0
18 PORTSMOUTH	S12 2-2	S26 2-0	D26 0-0	O10 1-2	N14 1-2	m01 2-0	F13 5-1	a17 0-0	S29 2-0	M20 1-1	M09 1-0	N28 2-1	A29 1-1	m21 2-2	O24 0-0	F09 1-1	M27 1-0		a06 1-1	a12 3-0	J30 0-0	m15 3-0	M06 1-0	N03 1-0
19 PRESTON N.E.	D05 1-3	F27 1-3	O03 0-1	O20 1-1	a10 0-1	N07 0-1	m08 2-0	F20 3-1	M13 1-0	a20 1-3	S19 1-1	S22 1-1	M16 1-1	J23 1-0	m04 2-1	a24 2-2	J16 1-0	S05 1-0		O17 0-0	O31 1-0	F06 0-0	a27 1-0	a03 3-2
20 READING	J27 4-1	M10 3-1	S19 0-3	N14 1-1	m08 2-2	M20 4-1	O10 0-2	F17 3-3	M27 4-0	J20 0-3	S05 3-2	O03 1-2	D05 3-2	F06 4-0	S23 2-1	a10 0-3	J23 2-2	J06 2-1	M06 2-1		a24 0-2	F20 1-1	N04 0-0	O24 2-1
21 SOUTHEND U	M08 1-1	a03 3-0	O09 1-0	m14 1-4	F06 1-1	a17 2-0	M05 0-2	J16 1-1	J01 2-1	F19 0-0	N02 3-0	m01 4-0	N07 0-2	F01 2-2	S04 0-4	O24 0-1	O03 3-0	S19 2-0	M19 2-2	N27 2-0		S21 0-0	J23 3-2	a09 2-0
22 SWINDON T	N03 0-3	D05 0-0	M06 5-2	F13 1-2	O10 2-1	a27 3-0	S29 1-2	O24 2-2	J31 3-2	D30 1-4	M20 0-1	a03 1-5	a24 1-0	N07 1-2	m08 1-1	m04 3-2	a10 0-2	F23 2-0	S12 4-0	S26 0-2	F09 0-0		M09 2-2	A29 4-1
23 WALSALL	J19 3-0	F13 0-1	N28 2-1	M02 1-1	M13 1-1	F09 2-1	S12 1-1	m15 0-0	m01 2-1	a03 1-1	a17 1-0	F16 1-1	S29 2-1	F27 1-1	N07 3-1	J30 1-3	O31 0-1	O17 3-1	a13 0-3	M16 1-2	A29 0-1	O20 5-0		S26 1-0
24 WIMBLEDON	a12 1-2	m08 0-0	F20 1-0	M27 0-0	m11 3-1	O17 1-0	a24 3-1	S19 0-1	O31 1-1	S22 1-3	O03 0-2	F06 2-0	F27 1-1	S05 1-3	D05 2-3	a20 2-3	O20 2-1	m18 3-2	N14 3-2	M13 0-0	M23 3-0	J23 1-1	m04 2-0	

DIVISION 4

	ALDERSHOT	BLACKPOOL	BOURNEMOUTH	BRADFORD C	BURY	COLCHESTER U	CREWE A	DARLINGTON	HALIFAX T	HARTLEPOOL U	HEREFORD U	HULL C	MANSFIELD T	NORTHAMPTON T	PETERBOROUGH U	PORT VALE	ROCHDALE	SCUNTHORPE U	SHEFFIELD U	STOCKPORT CO	TORQUAY U	TRANMERE R	WIGAN A	YORK C
1 ALDERSHOT		O17 3-2	O20 2-0	F28 0-2	N07 1-2	F09 1-1	J31 3-0	A29 0-0	S12 3-1	O31 1-2	a12 2-2	M12 0-3	S26 2-3	F23 2-1	M16 0-1	a03 1-2	F14 2-2	m01 4-0	a17 1-1	a06 1-1	J03 1-1	N28 2-1	m15 2-0	S29 0-1
2 BLACKPOOL	M06 0-2		N14 0-3	M03 1-0	N04 1-1	a17 0-0	S12 5-0	J30 1-0	S30 7-1	m15 2-2	m01 1-0	S26 3-1	F13 2-3	F17 1-0	M27 2-2	N11 2-3	F10 1-1	J09 2-0	M20 0-1	A29 2-0	O10 2-1	J13 1-2	a09 1-2	M10 3-1
3 BOURNEMOUTH	M09 2-2	a03 1-0		F02 0-2	O24 3-2	D26 1-1	A29 2-0	S12 2-0	J30 1-1	a17 5-1	m15 1-1	m01 1-0	F23 1-0	O10 1-1	M06 1-1	N07 1-1	S26 1-0	N03 2-0	N28 0-0	F13 1-0	a13 4-0	M20 1-1	S29 0-0	F09 5-1
4 BRADFORD C	O11 4-1	a24 1-0	m08 2-2		F24 1-1	S28 2-1	m05 4-1	J03 3-0	a10 5-2	N08 1-0	J30 0-0	J09 1-1	J20 3-4	M07 2-1	D05 2-0	N04 1-0	S30 2-0	F14 0-0	O24 0-2	M10 5-1	M21 3-0	a03 1-1	A29 3-3	S12 6-2
5 BURY	M27 1-1	m18 0-1	M13 2-2	a12 1-1		m01 4-3	F09 2-1	S26 2-0	F13 1-1	J19 1-1	a06 1-1	N28 0-2	J30 3-2	O31 7-1	N14 3-1	O17 3-2	A29 3-0	S29 4-0	a27 1-1	S12 2-0	a17 0-1	F27 4-0	O20 5-3	m15 3-1
6 COLCHESTER U	S22 1-1	D04 2-1	a10 1-2	F19 1-2	J16 1-1		M30 1-1	a24 1-0	M12 1-1	J23 3-3	O20 4-0	M26 2-0	M16 0-1	O02 5-1	a27 1-1	m03 1-0	F26 3-2	N13 2-1	F06 5-2	m07 0-1	S18 3-0	S04 4-0	O30 1-2	O16 4-0
7 CREWE A	S18 2-3	F05 1-1	J23 0-0	a26 0-1	S23 1-2	m15 1-3		N04 1-0	O31 0-1	M16 1-2	M23 1-0	a17 1-1	M13 0-2	M27 2-2	F19 0-1	O06 0-2	O21 1-2	O10 3-0	m01 2-3	M06 0-2	S06 0-1	a12 1-1	J26 0-1	N28 1-1
8 DARLINGTON	J23 0-1	S19 2-2	F06 0-1	S22 1-5	F20 2-3	N28 1-2	a04 1-0		O20 1-1	a12 5-2	M14 0-1	M23 2-1	O17 1-0	a17 3-0	O03 0-0	S05 1-1	O31 2-0	F17 4-1	m15 0-2	N07 2-0	m18 1-1	a30 1-2	M16 3-1	F28 3-1
9 HALIFAX T	F06 2-2	F20 0-0	S19 1-1	M23 0-0	O03 2-1	O24 0-2	M20 2-1	M09 3-3		m01 2-0	F27 1-2	a14 2-2	N07 2-1	m04 2-1	S05 1-1	J22 1-1	O17 0-0	N28 1-2	a12 1-5	a02 4-1	N03 1-2	S22 0-2	a17 0-0	m11 0-0
10 HARTLEPOOL U	M20 2-2	a28 2-2	D05 1-1	M27 0-2	m08 1-0	A29 1-3	N04 1-2	F03 1-2	S26 3-2		F13 2-1	S30 3-2	m05 3-0	N14 3-1	O10 0-1	a24 3-1	M31 1-1	F10 3-3	M06 2-3	a10 2-2	O24 0-0	M10 0-0	S12 2-1	J30 3-2
11 HEREFORD U	F03 0-1	a21 2-1	M31 1-2	S19 1-2	S05 3-0	M10 2-2	m08 4-1	O24 1-1	O10 2-2	O03 1-1		N14 2-2	a24 3-1	F20 2-1	m05 2-1	a10 1-0	D05 0-0	M06 2-1	F17 1-1	N04 0-0	S23 0-3	F06 1-1	M27 3-0	M20 2-1
12 HULL C	O24 1-2	m04 1-0	m11 0-0	S05 2-1	a24 3-2	N07 2-3	D05 1-0	a10 1-3	M02 2-0	F20 5-2	a03 2-1		F27 2-0	F06 0-1	S22 1-1	M20 3-1	m08 2-1	M09 2-0	S19 2-1	a20 0-0	J23 1-0	O03 1-2	O17 0-2	N03 2-0
13 MANSFIELD T	F20 1-0	O03 2-2	S05 0-1	m15 0-2	S19 1-1	N02 1-3	O24 0-1	M06 2-3	M27 3-2	J16 3-2	N28 2-1	O10 3-3		S21 4-1	J23 1-2	F06 1-3	N14 4-3	a13 1-1	M08 1-1	M20 2-2	m01 3-1	a17 3-0	J02 1-2	a05 0-2
14 NORTHAMPTON T	a10 0-0	O13 0-1	F27 1-0	O17 0-2	M20 1-0	F14 1-2	N08 3-0	D05 0-1	a20 0-1	a03 2-1	S26 2-3	S12 1-1	F09 1-1		a24 1-0	F02 3-5	M02 2-1	A29 1-1	N03 1-2	S29 0-0	M09 2-0	O24 3-2	J30 2-3	M23 5-0
15 PETERBOROUGH U	N04 7-1	N07 3-1	O17 1-0	a17 2-0	a03 1-0	a13 2-2	S26 3-0	F13 3-1	J26 0-0	F27 4-4	O28 3-1	F10 3-0	A29 1-0	N28 1-0		M10 1-0	S12 5-1	M20 2-1	a21 0-4	J30 2-0	M24 1-0	m15 1-2	m01 0-3	O24 0-1
16 PORT VALE	N14 1-0	M13 2-0	M27 1-1	M15 1-1	M06 0-0	S28 2-1	F13 0-0	J20 2-2	A29 0-0	N28 5-2	a26 1-1	O31 2-1	S12 0-0	a12 1-0	O19 1-3		J30 1-1	a17 2-1	O10 0-2	S26 1-0	m15 2-0	J25 0-0	F08 1-1	m01 0-0
17 ROCHDALE	O04 0-0	S22 0-0	F20 0-1	m01 1-1	J23 1-1	O11 1-2	M09 1-0	M20 3-2	J13 0-1	S05 2-1	a17 0-1	a06 0-1	a03 1-1	m15 5-3	F06 1-1	S19 1-2		a20 1-1	J16 0-1	O24 4-1	N08 1-0	N03 0-0	N28 1-1	a12 2-0
18 SCUNTHORPE U	M23 1-1	S05 1-1	M16 0-2	O03 1-3	m04 2-2	a02 2-1	F28 0-1	m08 1-1	a24 0-0	S22 2-1	O17 2-2	O20 4-4	F02 1-0	J23 2-1	O31 0-1	D05 0-0	a10 1-0		F20 2-1	M30 0-0	F06 0-2	S19 2-1	M12 2-7	N07 0-3
19 SHEFFIELD U	D05 2-0	O31 3-1	a24 0-0	M30 1-1	a10 1-1	S12 1-0	S29 4-0	J26 0-0	J02 2-2	O17 1-1	A29 2-2	J30 0-0	O20 4-1	M16 7-3	m08 4-0	F27 2-1	m04 3-1	S26 1-0		F09 4-0	a03 4-1	N07 2-0	M23 1-0	F13 4-0
20 STOCKPORT CO	S04 4-2	F01 2-3	O03 1-2	O19 2-3	F06 2-1	M22 0-0	O16 2-0	M26 1-0	N13 2-1	J25 0-2	M15 1-1	a12 1-2	O30 3-0	a30 0-0	S18 3-0	F19 1-2	M12 0-4	m14 1-1	S21 1-0		N28 2-1	F15 1-1	F26 0-1	a16 4-1
21 TORQUAY U	m08 2-1	F27 1-1	D28 1-2	O31 2-0	D05 1-1	J30 1-0	F24 1-1	m05 1-2	a27 2-2	M13 1-1	F10 1-2	A29 2-1	S30 2-0	O21 2-2	a10 1-2	D19 0-1	M27 2-1	S12 1-0	N14 1-1	a24 1-0		O17 1-2	F13 0-0	S26 3-2
22 TRANMERE R	a24 1-0	a10 3-1	O31 0-1	N14 1-1	O10 1-3	M02 2-1	J19 3-0	S29 1-1	F09 1-1	O20 1-0	S12 0-0	F13 2-2	D05 2-2	M13 0-2	F23 1-2	m08 1-2	M16 2-0	J30 0-1	M27 2-2	m04 2-0	M06 1-1		S26 0-0	A29 0-2
23 WIGAN A	F17 1-0	M30 2-1	m04 0-0	J23 4-1	M09 3-2	M20 3-2	a10 3-0	N04 2-1	D05 2-0	F06 1-1	N07 1-1	M06 2-1	m08 3-1	S19 3-1	J19 5-0	S23 2-0	a24 1-1	O24 2-1	S05 0-1	O10 2-1	O03 1-0	J05 0-0		a02 4-2
24 YORK C	m04 4-0	O20 0-4	S22 0-1	F06 0-3	F02 0-0	M05 3-0	a23 6-0	O09 2-2	m07 4-0	S18 1-2	O31 3-4	M16 1-3	a10 2-1	S04 2-1	M13 4-3	F22 2-0	a27 1-2	M26 3-1	O03 3-4	D05 2-2	F19 1-1	J23 1-3	N14 0-0	

LEAGUE TABLES

DIVISION 1

	P	W	D	L	F	A	W	D	L	F	A	Pts
Liverpool	42	14	3	4	39	14	12	6	3	41	18	87
Ipswich T	42	17	1	3	47	25	9	4	8	28	28	83
Manchester U	42	12	6	3	27	9	10	6	5	32	20	78
Tottenham H	42	12	4	5	41	26	8	7	6	26	22	71
Arsenal	42	13	5	3	27	15	7	6	8	21	22	71
Swansea C	42	13	3	5	34	16	8	3	10	24	35	69
Southampton	42	15	2	4	49	30	4	7	10	23	37	66
Everton	42	11	7	3	33	21	6	6	9	23	29	64
West Ham U	42	9	10	2	42	29	5	6	10	24	28	58
Manchester C	42	9	7	5	32	23	6	6	9	17	27	58
Aston Villa	42	9	6	6	28	24	6	6	9	27	29	57
Nottingham F	42	7	7	7	19	20	8	5	8	23	28	57
Brighton & HA	42	8	7	6	30	24	5	6	10	13	28	52
Coventry C	42	9	4	8	31	24	4	7	10	25	38	50
Notts Co	42	8	5	8	32	33	5	3	13	29	36	47
Birmingham C	42	8	6	7	29	25	2	8	11	24	36	44
WBA	42	6	6	9	24	25	5	5	11	22	32	44
Stoke C	42	9	2	10	27	28	3	6	12	17	35	44
Sunderland	42	6	5	10	19	26	5	6	10	19	32	44
Leeds U	42	6	11	4	23	20	4	1	16	16	41	42
Wolves	42	8	5	8	19	20	2	5	14	13	43	40
Middlesbrough	42	5	9	7	20	24	3	6	12	14	28	39

DIVISION 2

	P	W	D	L	F	A	W	D	L	F	A	Pts
Luton T	42	16	3	2	48	19	9	10	2	38	27	88
Watford	42	13	6	2	46	16	10	5	6	30	26	80
Norwich C	42	14	3	4	41	19	8	2	11	23	31	71
Sheffield W	42	10	8	3	31	23	10	2	9	24	28	70
QPR	42	15	4	2	40	9	6	2	13	25	34	69
Barnsley	42	13	4	4	33	14	6	6	9	26	27	67
Rotherham U	42	13	5	3	42	19	7	2	12	24	35	67
Leicester C	42	12	5	4	31	19	6	7	8	25	29	66
Newcastle U	42	14	4	3	30	14	4	4	13	22	36	62
Blackburn R	42	11	4	6	26	15	5	7	9	21	28	59
Oldham A	42	9	9	3	28	23	6	5	10	22	28	59
Chelsea	42	10	5	6	37	30	5	7	9	23	30	57
Charlton A	42	11	5	5	33	22	2	7	12	17	43	51
Cambridge U	42	11	4	6	31	19	2	5	14	17	34	48
Crystal P	42	9	2	10	25	26	4	7	10	9	19	48
Derby Co	42	9	8	4	32	23	3	4	14	21	45	48
Grimsby T	42	5	8	8	29	30	6	5	10	24	35	46
Shrewsbury T	42	10	6	5	26	19	1	7	13	11	38	46
Bolton W	42	10	4	7	28	24	3	3	15	11	37	46
Cardiff C	42	9	2	10	28	32	3	6	12	17	29	44
Wrexham	42	9	4	8	22	22	2	7	12	18	34	44
Orient	42	6	8	7	23	24	4	1	16	13	37	39

DIVISION 3

	P	W	D	L	F	A	W	D	L	F	A	Pts
Burnley	46	13	7	3	37	20	8	10	5	29	25	80
Carlisle U	46	17	4	2	44	21	6	7	10	21	29	80
Fulham	46	12	9	2	44	22	9	6	8	33	29	78
Lincoln C	46	13	7	3	40	16	8	7	8	26	24	77
Oxford U	46	10	8	5	28	18	9	6	8	35	31	71
Gillingham	46	14	5	4	44	26	6	6	11	20	30	71
Southend U	46	11	7	5	35	23	7	8	8	28	28	69
Brentford	46	8	6	9	28	22	11	5	7	28	25	68
Millwall	46	12	4	7	36	28	6	9	8	26	34	67
Plymouth A	46	12	5	6	37	24	6	6	11	27	32	66
Chesterfield	46	12	4	7	33	27	6	6	11	24	31	64
Reading	46	11	6	6	43	35	6	5	12	24	40	62
Portsmouth	46	11	10	2	33	14	3	9	11	23	37	61
Preston NE	46	10	7	6	25	22	6	6	11	25	34	61
Bristol R	46	12	4	7	35	28	6	5	12	23	37	61*
Newport Co	46	9	10	4	28	21	5	6	12	26	33	58
Huddersfield T	46	10	5	8	38	25	5	7	11	26	34	57
Exeter C	46	14	4	5	46	33	2	5	16	25	51	57
Doncaster R	46	9	9	5	31	24	4	8	11	24	44	56
Walsall	46	10	7	6	32	23	3	7	13	19	32	53
Wimbledon	46	10	6	7	33	27	4	5	14	28	48	53
Swindon T	46	9	5	9	37	36	4	8	11	18	35	52
Bristol C	46	7	6	10	24	29	4	7	12	16	36	46
Chester	46	2	10	11	16	30	5	1	17	20	48	32

* Bristol Rovers had two points deducted for fielding an unregistered player.

DIVISION 4

	P	W	D	L	F	A	W	D	L	F	A	Pts
Sheffield U	46	15	8	0	53	15	12	7	4	41	26	96
Bradford C	46	14	7	2	52	23	12	6	5	36	22	91
Wigan A	46	17	5	1	47	18	9	8	6	33	28	91
Bournmouth	46	12	10	1	37	15	11	9	3	25	15	88
Peterboro' U	46	16	3	4	46	22	8	7	8	25	35	82
Colchester U	46	12	6	5	47	23	8	6	9	35	34	72
Port Vale	46	9	12	2	26	17	9	4	10	30	32	70
Hull C	46	14	3	6	36	23	5	9	9	34	38	69
Bury	46	13	7	3	53	26	4	10	9	27	33	68
Hereford U	46	10	9	4	36	25	6	10	7	28	33	67
Tranmere R	46	7	9	7	27	25	7	9	7	24	31	60
Blackpool	46	11	5	7	40	26	4	8	11	26	34	58
Darlington	46	10	5	8	36	28	5	8	10	25	34	58
Hartlepool U	46	9	8	6	39	34	4	8	11	34	50	55
Torquay U	46	9	8	6	30	25	5	5	13	17	34	55
Aldershot	46	8	7	8	34	29	5	8	10	23	39	54
York C	46	9	5	9	45	37	5	3	15	24	54	50
Stockport Co	46	10	5	8	34	28	2	8	13	14	39	49
Halifax T	46	6	11	6	28	30	3	11	9	23	42	49
Mansfield T	46	8	6	9	39	39	5	4	14	24	42	47*
Rochdale	46	7	9	7	26	22	3	7	13	24	40	46
Northampton	46	9	5	9	32	27	2	4	17	25	57	42
Scunthorpe U	46	7	9	7	26	35	2	6	15	17	44	42
Crewe A	46	3	6	14	19	32	3	3	17	10	52	27

* Mansfield Town had two points deducted for fielding an ineligible player.

Football League Records

Top scorers: Div 1, L.Blissett (Watford) 27 goals; Div 2, G.Lineker (Leicester City) 26 goals; Div 3, K.Dixon (Reading) 26 goals; Div 4, S.Cammack (Scunthorpe United) 25 goals.

Graeme Souness, a strong, intelligent midfielder who played a great part in many of Liverpool's triumphs of the 1980s. In 1991 he returned to Anfield as manager.

Queen's Park Rangers' striker Tony Sealy top-scored with 16 goals when Rangers won the Second Division title in 1982-3.

DIVISION 1

	ARSENAL	ASTON VILLA	BIRMINGHAM C	BRIGHTON & HA	COVENTRY C	EVERTON	IPSWICH T	LIVERPOOL	LUTON T	MANCHESTER C	MANCHESTER U	NORWICH C	NOTTINGHAM F	NOTTS CO	SOUTHAMPTON	STOKE C	SUNDERLAND	SWANSEA C	TOTTENHAM H	WATFORD	W.B.A.	WEST HAM U
1 ARSENAL		D07 2-1	O30 0-0	F05 3-1	a09 2-1	N13 1-1	M22 2-2	S04 0-2	M19 4-1	a23 3-0	m02 3-0	A31 1-1	M05 0-0	S18 2-0	a02 0-0	J15 3-0	m07 0-1	J01 2-1	D27 2-0	N27 2-4	O16 2-0	O02 2-3
2 ASTON VILLA	m14 2-1		a04 1-0	N13 1-0	M19 4-0	F12 2-0	D29 1-1	D18 2-4	S08 4-1	J22 1-1	N20 2-1	M05 3-2	S11 4-1	M08 2-0	J03 2-0	a30 4-0	A28 1-3	S25 2-0	O30 4-0	O16 3-0	a19 1-0	D04 1-0
3 BIRMINGHAM C	M15 2-1	D27 3-0		m02 1-1	S18 1-0	a23 1-0	O23 0-0	A31 0-0	O09 2-3	J01 2-2	J15 1-2	a09 0-4	F26 1-1	M26 3-0	D11 0-2	S04 1-4	N27 2-1	a02 1-1	m07 2-0	O02 1-1	N06 2-1	F05 3-0
4 BRIGHTON & H.A.	S07 1-0	M26 0-0	S25 1-0		a23 1-0	a09 1-2	A28 1-1	M22 2-2	J22 2-4	m07 0-1	N06 1-0	D11 3-0	J03 1-1	N27 0-2	D27 0-1	F26 1-2	S11 3-2	O09 1-1	a02 2-1	J01 1-1	F12 0-0	O23 3-1
5 COVENTRY C	S11 0-2	N06 0-0	a16 0-1	D04 2-0		S25 4-2	N23 1-1	a12 0-0	N20 4-2	F12 4-0	D28 3-0	O30 2-0	a05 1-2	O16 1-0	A28 1-0	D18 2-0	S07 1-0	J22 0-0	M12 1-1	M05 0-1	a30 0-1	m14 2-4
6 EVERTON	M26 2-3	A31 5-0	D04 0-0	O02 2-2	m02 1-0		m14 1-1	N06 0-5	D18 5-0	O09 2-1	a19 2-0	S18 1-1	D28 3-1	F05 3-0	M15 2-0	a04 3-1	O23 3-1	F26 2-2	S04 3-1	J15 1-0	N20 0-0	a30 2-0
7 IPSWICH T	O09 0-1	a02 1-2	M05 3-1	J15 2-0	S04 1-1	D11 0-2		O02 1-0	F26 3-0	N13 1-0	F05 1-1	D27 2-3	M19 2-0	a09 0-0	J01 2-1	S18 2-3	a23 4-1	N27 3-1	A31 1-2	m07 3-1	O30 6-1	m03 1-2
8 LIVERPOOL	J03 3-1	m07 1-1	J22 1-0	O30 3-1	N13 4-0	M19 0-0	F12 1-0		S11 3-3	D27 5-2	O16 0-0	F23 0-2	S07 4-3	J01 5-1	S25 5-0	M05 5-1	a02 1-0	a09 3-0	N27 3-0	D11 3-1	A28 2-0	M12 3-0
9 LUTON T	N06 2-2	a09 2-1	a12 3-1	S18 5-0	J01 1-2	m07 1-5	O16 1-1	F05 1-3		D11 3-1	O02 1-1	a02 0-1	O30 0-2	S04 5-3	N27 3-3	m02 0-0	M26 1-3	a23 3-1	J15 1-1	D27 1-0	M05 0-0	A31 0-2
10 MANCHESTER C	D04 2-1	S18 0-1	N20 0-0	D18 1-1	O02 3-2	M02 0-0	M26 0-1	a04 0-4	m14 0-1		M05 1-2	J15 4-1	a30 1-2	F19 0-1	N06 2-0	S01 1-0	O16 2-2	O30 2-1	F05 2-2	S04 1-0	D28 2-1	a16 2-0
11 MANCHESTER U	S25 0-0	J01 3-1	A28 3-0	M19 1-1	a02 3-0	S08 2-1	S11 3-1	F26 1-1	m09 3-0	O23 2-2		N27 3-0	J22 2-0	D11 4-0	a09 1-1	O09 1-0	D27 0-0	m07 2-1	N13 1-0	a23 2-0	J03 0-0	M22 2-1
12 NORWICH C	a20 3-1	O23 1-0	S08 5-1	m14 2-1	M23 1-1	J22 0-1	a04 0-0	D04 1-0	D28 1-0	A28 1-2	a30 1-1		D18 0-1	N06 1-2	S11 1-1	N20 4-2	a16 2-0	J03 1-0	O16 0-0	M02 3-0	S25 1-3	M26 1-1
13 NOTTINGHAM F	O23 3-0	F05 1-2	O16 1-1	S04 4-0	D27 4-2	a02 2-0	N06 2-1	m02 1-0	M12 0-1	N27 3-0	S01 0-3	m07 2-2		a23 2-1	M26 1-2	O02 1-0	J01 0-0	D11 2-1	a09 2-2	S18 2-0	F19 0-0	J15 1-0
14 NOTTS CO	J22 1-0	O09 4-1	N13 0-0	a30 1-0	F26 5-1	S11 1-0	S25 0-6	N20 1-2	a16 1-1	S07 1-0	m14 3-2	M19 2-2	D04 3-2		F15 1-2	D28 4-0	J03 0-1	A28 0-0	M05 3-0	O30 3-2	a04 2-1	D18 1-2
15 SOUTHAMPTON	F28 2-2	S04 1-0	m14 0-1	a05 0-0	J15 1-1	O30 3-2	N20 0-1	a16 3-2	a30 2-2	M19 4-1	S18 0-1	F05 4-0	N13 1-1	O02 1-0		D04 1-0	F19 2-0	M05 2-1	m03 1-2	A31 1-4	D18 4-1	O16 3-0
16 STOKE C	A28 2-1	N27 0-3	J03 1-1	O16 3-0	m07 0-3	D27 1-0	J22 1-0	O23 1-1	S25 4-4	a09 1-0	M02 1-0	J01 1-0	M16 1-0	a02 1-0	a23 1-1		M12 0-1	S11 4-1	D11 2-0	M26 4-0	S08 0-3	N06 5-2
17 SUNDERLAND	D18 3-0	J15 2-0	a30 1-2	a19 1-1	F05 2-1	M05 2-1	D04 2-3	D28 0-0	N13 1-1	F26 3-2	a04 0-0	O02 4-1	N20 0-1	S01 1-1	O09 1-1	O30 2-2		M19 1-1	S18 0-1	m02 2-2	m14 1-1	S04 1-0
18 SWANSEA C	N20 1-2	m02 2-1	D29 0-0	M01 1-2	A31 2-1	O16 0-3	a30 1-1	S18 0-3	D04 2-0	M12 4-1	D18 0-0	S04 4-0	m14 0-3	J15 2-0	O23 3-2	a16 1-1	N06 3-0		O02 2-0	F06 1-3	M26 2-1	a05 1-5
19 TOTTENHAM H	a04 5-0	M23 2-0	D18 2-1	D28 2-0	O09 4-0	J03 2-1	a16 3-1	a30 2-0	A28 2-2	S11 1-2	m11 2-0	F26 0-0	S25 4-1	O23 4-2	S08 6-0	m14 4-1	J22 1-1	F12 1-0		N06 0-1	D04 1-1	N20 2-1
20 WATFORD	a30 2-1	F26 2-1	M22 2-1	N20 4-1	O23 0-0	A28 2-0	D18 2-1	m14 2-1	a04 5-2	J03 2-0	D04 0-1	O09 2-2	a16 1-3	M12 5-3	J22 2-0	N13 1-0	S25 8-0	S07 2-1	M19 0-1		S11 3-0	D29 2-1
21 W.B.A.	F26 0-0	O02 1-0	M19 2-0	S01 5-0	N27 2-0	J01 2-2	M12 4-1	J15 0-1	O23 1-0	a02 0-2	S04 3-1	m02 1-0	O09 2-1	D27 2-2	m07 1-0	F05 1-1	D11 3-0	N13 3-3	a23 0-1	a09 1-3		S18 1-2
22 WEST HAM U	m10 1-3	a23 2-0	S11 5-0	M05 2-1	D11 0-3	N27 2-0	S07 1-1	O09 3-1	J04 2-3	S25 4-1	O30 3-1	N13 1-0	A28 1-2	m07 2-0	F26 1-1	M19 1-1	a09 2-1	D27 3-2	J01 3-0	a02 2-1	J22 0-1	

DIVISION 2

	BARNSLEY	BLACKBURN R	BOLTON W	BURNLEY	CAMBRIDGE U	CARLISLE U	CHARLTON A	CHELSEA	CRYSTAL P	DERBY CO	FULHAM	GRIMSBY T	LEEDS U	LEICESTER C	MIDDLESBROUGH	NEWCASTLE U	OLDHAM A	Q.P.R.	ROTHERHAM U	SHEFFIELD W	SHREWSBURY T	WOLVERHAMPTON W
1 BARNSLEY		a23 2-2	M05 3-1	S18 3-0	a09 2-3	D11 2-2	m07 0-0	N13 1-1	J15 3-1	O19 1-1	O02 4-3	J01 4-0	N27 2-1	a02 1-2	M19 2-0	m04 0-5	S04 1-1	O09 0-1	F26 2-1	D27 0-0	O30 2-2	F05 2-1
2 BLACKBURN R	D04 1-1		N20 1-1	a04 2-1	S04 3-1	N06 3-2	M13 2-0	O16 3-0	a16 3-0	m02 2-0	F19 0-0	F05 2-1	O23 0-0	S18 3-1	a30 1-1	S01 1-2	D29 2-2	M26 1-3	D18 3-0	O02 2-3	m14 1-0	J15 2-2
3 BOLTON W	O23 0-2	J01 1-0		J15 3-0	a23 2-0	D27 1-0	D11 4-1	m07 0-1	O02 1-0	M26 0-2	F05 0-1	m02 0-0	a02 1-2	N27 3-1	F26 3-1	S04 3-1	S28 2-3	M12 3-2	O09 2-2	a09 0-2	N06 1-4	S18 0-1
4 BURNLEY	J22 3-1	D27 0-1	A28 0-0		N13 2-1	S07 4-1	F26 7-1	a23 3-0	O09 2-1	N27 1-1	M05 1-0	m07 1-1	a09 1-2	D11 2-4	J03 1-1	M19 1-0	O30 1-2	m10 2-1	S11 1-2	J01 4-1	S25 1-2	a02 0-1
5 CAMBRIDGE U	S07 1-1	J03 2-0	D04 0-0	M26 2-0		S25 1-1	S11 3-2	A28 0-1	D28 1-0	M15 0-0	a05 1-0	M12 1-0	F12 0-0	N06 3-1	D17 2-0	a30 1-0	m14 1-4	N20 1-4	J22 2-0	O16 2-2	a16 0-0	N02 2-1
6 CARLISLE U	m14 1-1	M19 3-1	a05 5-0	a16 1-1	m03 2-2		O09 4-1	O30 2-1	S18 4-1	J15 3-0	D18 3-2	S04 2-3	F26 2-2	F05 0-1	D28 1-3	N20 2-0	M05 0-0	a30 1-0	N13 2-2	S28 4-2	D04 2-3	O02 0-2
7 CHARLTON A	D18 3-2	O30 3-0	m14 4-1	O16 2-1	F05 2-1	F19 0-0		M05 5-2	a04 2-1	O02 1-1	S28 3-0	S18 0-1	M19 0-1	J15 2-1	N13 2-3	D04 2-0	a17 4-1	D29 1-3	N20 1-5	S04 0-3	a29 0-1	m02 3-3
8 CHELSEA	M26 0-3	F26 2-0	D18 2-1	D04 2-1	J15 6-0	M12 4-2	O23 3-1		N06 0-0	F05 1-3	D28 0-0	O02 5-2	O09 0-0	S04 1-1	m14 0-0	a16 0-2	S18 2-0	a04 0-2	a30 1-1	m02 1-1	N20 1-2	A31 0-0
9 CRYSTAL P	A28 1-1	S11 2-0	F22 3-0	m17 1-0	a02 0-0	a09 2-1	D27 1-1	M19 0-0		m07 4-1	O30 1-1	a23 2-0	N13 1-1	J01 1-0	S25 3-0	M05 0-2	O16 1-0	J22 0-3	J03 1-1	D11 2-0	S07 2-1	N27 3-4
10 DERBY CO	a16 1-1	S25 1-2	N13 0-0	a30 2-0	O09 1-1	A28 0-3	a13 1-1	S08 1-0	D18 1-1		m14 1-0	F26 2-0	J22 3-3	O23 0-4	S11 1-1	a04 2-1	N20 2-2	J03 2-0	D04 3-0	M19 0-0	D29 2-3	M12 1-1
11 FULHAM	a19 1-0	O09 3-1	S11 4-0	O23 3-1	D27 1-1	m07 2-0	a09 2-1	a02 1-1	M12 1-0	D11 2-1		M26 4-0	S25 3-2	a23 0-1	J22 1-0	F26 2-2	N06 0-3	S07 1-1	A28 1-1	N27 1-0	J03 2-1	J01 1-3
12 GRIMSBY T	N20 1-2	S07 5-0	S25 1-0	D18 3-2	O30 1-0	J03 2-1	J22 1-1	F12 2-1	D04 4-1	O16 1-1	N13 0-4		A28 1-1	F19 2-0	a16 0-3	D28 2-2	a30 0-2	m14 1-1	a04 1-2	M05 1-1	S11 2-0	M19 1-1
13 LEEDS U	a30 0-0	M05 2-1	D28 1-1	O20 3-1	O02 2-1	O16 1-1	N06 1-2	F19 3-3	M26 2-1	S18 2-1	a16 1-1	J15 1-0		m02 2-2	N20 0-0	O30 3-1	a05 0-0	D04 0-1	m14 2-2	a27 1-2	D18 1-1	S04 0-0
14 LEICESTER C	D28 1-0	J22 0-1	a30 0-0	m14 0-0	M19 4-0	S11 6-0	A28 1-2	J03 3-0	N20 0-1	M05 1-1	D04 2-0	O09 2-0	S08 0-1		a05 1-0	N13 2-2	D18 2-1	S25 0-1	a16 3-1	O30 0-2	F22 3-2	F26 5-0
15 MIDDLESBROUGH	N06 2-0	N27 1-5	O16 1-0	S04 1-4	m07 0-1	a02 1-0	M26 3-0	D11 3-1	m10 2-0	a09 2-3	S18 1-4	S28 1-4	J01 0-0	D27 1-1		F05 1-1	O02 1-1	O23 2-1	M12 1-1	J15 1-1	M08 2-1	a23 0-0
16 NEWCASTLE U	S25 1-2	a09 3-2	J03 2-2	N06 3-0	N27 2-0	J01 2-2	a23 4-2	S11 1-1	O23 1-0	D27 1-0	O16 1-4	a02 4-0	M12 2-1	M26 2-2	S08 1-1		F19 1-0	A28 1-0	a20 4-0	m07 2-1	J22 4-0	D11 1-1
17 OLDHAM A	J03 1-1	a01 0-0	J22 2-3	a12 3-0	D11 3-0	O23 4-3	S25 2-2	a09 2-2	F26 2-0	J01 2-2	M19 1-0	N27 1-1	D26 2-2	m07 1-2	F12 3-0	O09 2-2		S11 0-1	S07 1-1	a23 1-1	A28 1-0	N13 4-1
18 Q.P.R.	F19 3-0	N13 2-2	O30 1-0	O02 3-2	A31 2-1	N27 1-0	M22 5-1	D27 1-2	S28 0-0	S04 4-1	m02 3-1	D11 4-0	a23 1-0	a09 2-2	M05 6-1	J15 2-0	F05 1-0		M19 4-0	S18 0-2	O16 4-0	m07 2-1
19 ROTHERHAM U	O16 1-0	a07 3-1	F19 1-1	F05 1-1	S18 2-0	M26 1-2	J01 1-0	N27 1-0	S04 2-2	a23 1-1	J15 0-1	D27 3-0	D11 0-1	A31 1-3	O30 1-1	O02 1-5	J29 1-3	N06 0-0		a02 0-3	M05 0-3	a09 1-1
20 SHEFFIELD W	a04 0-1	F15 0-0	S07 3-1	N20 1-1	F26 3-1	J22 1-1	J03 5-4	S25 3-2	m14 2-1	N06 2-0	a30 2-1	O23 2-0	S11 2-3	M22 2-2	A28 3-1	D18 1-1	D04 1-1	a19 0-1	D28 0-1		M26 0-0	O09 0-0
21 SHREWSBURY T	M12 3-1	D11 0-0	M19 1-0	m03 1-2	S28 2-1	a23 2-1	N27 0-0	J01 2-0	F05 1-1	a02 1-1	S04 0-1	a08 0-0	m07 0-0	O02 0-2	O09 2-2	S18 2-1	J15 0-0	F26 0-0	O23 2-0	N13 1-0		D27 0-2
22 WOLVERHAMPTON W	S11 2-0	A28 2-1	a16 0-0	D28 2-0	M05 1-1	F12 2-1	S07 5-0	J22 2-1	a30 1-0	O30 2-1	N20 2-4	N06 3-0	J03 3-0	O16 0-3	D04 4-0	m14 2-2	M26 0-0	D18 4-0	S25 2-0	M01 1-0	a04 2-2	

Season 1982-83

DIVISION 3

	BOURNEMOUTH	BRADFORD C	BRENTFORD	BRISTOL R	CARDIFF C	CHESTERFIELD	DONCASTER R	EXETER C	GILLINGHAM	HUDDERSFIELD T	LINCOLN C	MILLWALL	NEWPORT CO	ORIENT	OXFORD U	PLYMOUTH A	PORTSMOUTH	PRESTON N.E.	READING	SHEFFIELD U	SOUTHEND U	WALSALL	WIGAN A	WREXHAM
1 BOURNEMOUTH		N27 2-2	J01 4-3	N02 0-0	O09 3-1	a09 2-1	m02 2-2	S25 2-0	O23 0-1	N06 0-1	a23 1-0	J22 3-0	M26 0-1	a02 2-0	F01 2-0	M15 1-0	F26 0-2	M12 4-0	D27 1-1	S11 0-0	S28 0-2	A28 3-0	m07 2-2	F12 1-1
2 BRADFORD C	a30 2-3		M19 0-1	F12 2-0	F16 4-2	F26 1-0	O23 1-0	N13 3-3	J03 1-1	m14 3-1	M12 1-1	a16 0-0	S11 4-2	J12 2-3	N03 3-2	O09 4-0	D04 2-2	a04 1-2	A28 3-2	m08 2-0	S25 1-0	S29 1-1	J22 0-1	D28 0-0
3 BRENTFORD	m14 2-1	N06 0-2		A28 5-1	J03 1-3	O09 4-2	F26 1-0	D18 4-0	D28 1-1	M26 1-0	O23 2-0	S25 1-1	S28 2-0	J22 5-2	M22 1-1	M11 2-0	a01 1-1	N02 3-1	F12 1-2	a30 2-1	S11 4-2	a16 2-3	J08 1-3	D04 4-1
4 BRISTOL R	N30 1-1	O02 4-1	J15 2-0		m14 1-1	J29 3-0	S04 2-0	D29 4-4	S07 2-1	a30 1-0	S18 1-2	O19 4-0	F19 1-3	M05 2-1	a05 0-1	F05 2-0	N13 6-1	a16 3-2	O30 3-0	M29 2-1	M19 2-2	D04 2-0	O16 4-0	D18 4-0
5 CARDIFF C	F19 1-1	O19 1-0	m02 3-1	J01 3-1		D07 1-1	a09 3-0	S28 2-0	O16 1-0	M15 1-1	M26 1-0	F01 3-0	D27 3-2	m07 2-0	F12 3-0	a02 0-0	O30 1-0	N06 3-1	M01 0-0	S25 2-0	a23 4-1	J22 3-1	S11 3-2	A28 1-2
6 CHESTERFIELD	D04 0-0	O16 3-0	F19 2-1	S11 0-0	a30 0-1		M12 3-3	a16 1-3	N02 1-2	a04 0-1	N06 1-3	m14 0-1	F01 3-1	A28 1-2	S28 1-2	O23 1-2	D18 0-1	M26 1-1	J22 0-0	D28 3-1	M15 0-2	M01 0-0	S25 2-0	J03 5-1
7 DONCASTER R	J03 2-1	M05 1-2	O16 4-4	J08 1-2	D04 2-2	O30 0-0		S10 6-1	M25 0-2	M01 0-4	F19 2-2	D18 2-1	A28 0-0	a12 0-3	a16 0-1	N08 2-2	a30 0-2	D28 2-0	S25 7-5	a05 2-0	J22 0-0	m14 1-3	S28 3-6	O19 1-1
8 EXETER C	F05 4-2	M26 2-1	a23 1-7	a02 0-1	J29 0-2	O02 2-3	m07 3-0		S04 2-2	J15 3-4	M02 3-1	O16 2-1	J01 0-1	N27 2-0	M12 3-1	D27 1-0	S08 1-1	S18 5-1	D11 2-2	O23 0-3	m02 4-3	N06 4-3	N03 2-1	F19 3-3
9 GILLINGHAM	M05 2-5	m03 3-0	a02 2-2	m07 1-0	F26 2-3	F15 3-1	N13 1-1	J08 4-4		O30 1-3	J01 0-2	S11 1-0	a09 2-0	O19 4-0	A28 0-1	a23 2-1	M19 1-0	O09 2-1	S28 1-0	M15 0-2	D27 1-0	S25 3-0	N27 0-2	J22 1-1
10 HUDDERSFIELD T	M19 0-0	J01 6-3	N13 2-0	N27 3-1	O23 4-0	D27 3-1	N02 3-0	A28 1-1	M12 3-2		a02 1-1	F12 5-1	m07 1-0	S28 6-0	S25 2-0	a09 2-0	O09 1-1	F26 1-1	a23 3-1	J22 0-0	O19 2-1	S11 2-2	m10 1-1	M29 4-1
11 LINCOLN C	D18 0-0	O30 1-0	M05 2-1	J22 2-1	N13 2-1	M19 2-0	O09 5-1	O20 4-1	m14 3-1	D28 1-2		D04 3-1	M23 1-4	S25 2-0	a30 1-1	F26 1-2	F16 0-3	J03 3-0	S11 4-0	S29 3-0	F23 0-1	a04 2-1	A28 2-1	a16 2-0
12 MILLWALL	S08 2-0	S18 1-1	m08 1-0	a12 1-1	S05 0-4	J01 1-1	a23 3-0	F26 5-2	J30 4-1	O02 3-0	a09 2-1		m02 3-0	D26 0-1	O09 2-1	N02 2-2	F06 0-2	J15 1-0	N28 1-1	M12 1-2	a02 3-1	O23 2-2	M27 2-0	N06 1-1
13 NEWPORT CO	N13 5-1	J29 1-1	F06 0-0	O09 2-0	a04 1-0	S04 1-0	J15 1-2	m14 1-1	D04 2-1	S18 2-1	O02 1-0	J03 2-2		F26 4-1	D28 1-2	S07 2-2	a16 0-3	F15 3-0	M19 1-0	N02 3-1	O23 1-1	D18 1-1	M12 1-0	a30 4-0
14 ORIENT	D28 5-0	S04 0-1	S18 3-3	O23 1-5	S08 4-0	J15 2-0	O02 1-0	a30 5-1	M01 2-0	a16 1-3	F05 1-1	a04 2-3	O16 1-5		D04 1-5	J29 0-2	J18 2-1	D17 2-1	F20 3-3	m14 4-1	M13 1-1	N02 2-1	N06 1-1	M25 0-0
15 OXFORD U	S04 2-0	M02 5-1	O20 2-2	D27 4-2	O02 2-2	m07 1-0	S08 3-0	O30 1-1	J15 1-1	F05 1-1	M16 1-0	a27 1-0	a02 0-3	a09 2-2		M26 1-1	S18 1-1	J29 3-2	m02 1-2	N06 0-0	J01 1-0	O16 4-2	a20 2-0	M05 2-0
16 PLYMOUTH A	O19 2-0	F19 3-1	O30 2-0	S28 0-4	D28 3-2	M05 2-0	M19 1-2	a01 1-0	D18 2-0	D04 2-1	O16 0-2	M01 3-1	J22 2-4	S11 2-0	N13 2-1		m14 0-1	a30 1-1	F01 3-0	a16 3-1	A28 1-0	F08 0-0	a19 0-2	S25 2-0
17 PORTSMOUTH	O16 0-2	a09 0-1	D27 2-1	M26 1-0	M12 0-0	a23 4-0	N27 2-1	F12 3-2	N06 1-0	F22 3-2	N02 4-1	S28 2-0	S25 1-2	m02 2-2	J22 1-0	J01 2-1		O23 3-1	a02 2-2	A28 4-1	m07 2-0	m10 1-0	M01 0-0	S11 3-0
18 PRESTON N.E.	O30 0-1	D27 0-0	M01 3-0	S25 2-2	M19 2-1	N13 1-1	a02 4-1	J22 2-2	F19 0-0	O16 0-0	m02 1-0	A28 3-2	O19 0-0	a23 2-1	S11 1-2	N27 2-2	M05 0-0		m07 2-0	a12 1-0	a08 1-1	M29 1-0	J01 4-1	S28 3-0
19 READING	a04 2-1	J15 2-1	S08 1-1	M12 1-2	N03 1-2	S18 0-0	F06 2-0	D04 3-1	a16 0-0	D18 1-1	J29 1-1	a30 3-3	N06 4-2	O09 3-0	J03 0-3	S04 3-2	D28 1-2	O02 2-3		F23 2-0	F26 1-1	M25 1-1	O23 2-1	m14 1-0
20 SHEFFIELD U	J29 2-2	a23 2-1	N27 1-2	m02 2-1	F05 2-0	a02 3-1	D27 3-1	M05 3-0	O02 0-2	S07 2-0	m07 0-1	O30 1-1	M01 2-0	J01 3-0	M19 3-2	S18 3-1	J15 2-1	S04 2-1	O19 1-1		N13 0-1	F19 3-1	a09 2-0	O16 2-0
21 SOUTHEND U	a16 0-0	F05 1-1	J29 4-2	N05 1-0	D17 1-2	S06 2-0	S18 3-2	J03 1-1	a01 1-1	F14 0-1	S04 2-0	D28 1-1	M04 1-4	O29 1-1	m13 1-2	J14 3-1	O01 4-0	D03 2-3	O15 4-2	M26 3-1		a29 1-1	F18 2-0	F28 2-2
22 WALSALL	J15 3-1	m07 1-1	O02 2-1	a09 5-0	S18 1-2	O19 0-1	J01 1-0	M19 3-2	F05 0-0	J29 2-0	D27 1-1	M05 4-0	a23 2-1	F15 2-0	F26 1-0	m02 2-0	S04 0-3	S07 2-1	N13 2-1	O09 0-0	N27 1-3		a02 2-0	O30 1-1
23 WIGAN A	S18 1-2	S07 3-2	S04 3-2	F26 0-5	a16 0-0	F05 2-2	J29 0-3	F15 1-0	a30 2-2	J03 2-0	J15 2-1	N13 3-1	O30 0-1	M19 0-1	D18 0-1	O02 3-0	O19 0-1	m14 0-1	M05 2-2	D04 3-2	O09 4-0	D29 1-3		a04 3-1
24 WREXHAM	O02 1-0	a02 0-4	a08 3-4	a22 0-0	J15 0-0	m02 0-0	F15 5-0	O09 1-2	S18 1-0	S04 1-1	S07 0-1	M19 4-3	N27 1-0	N13 1-0	O23 1-1	m07 2-3	J29 0-2	F05 3-1	J01 4-0	F26 4-1	N02 3-2	M12 4-0	D27 1-1	

DIVISION 4

	ALDERSHOT	BLACKPOOL	BRISTOL C	BURY	CHESTER	COLCHESTER U	CREWE A	DARLINGTON	HALIFAX T	HARTLEPOOL U	HEREFORD U	HULL C	MANSFIELD T	NORTHAMPTON T	PETERBOROUGH U	PORT VALE	ROCHDALE	SCUNTHORPE U	STOCKPORT CO	SWINDON T	TORQUAY U	TRANMERE R	WIMBLEDON	YORK C
1 ALDERSHOT		N27 2-1	O30 0-0	a09 1-1	N13 1-2	a02 0-1	O19 2-1	M01 1-6	m07 6-1	M05 0-2	m02 2-1	S25 1-2	J01 2-1	F12 3-0	S11 2-0	S28 1-4	a23 6-4	M15 1-1	O16 2-1	D27 1-1	J22 2-1	A28 1-0	F19 1-1	M19 2-3
2 BLACKPOOL	a30 4-1		a16 1-4	S07 1-1	J29 1-1	F05 1-2	N06 2-0	O02 2-0	O09 0-0	m14 1-2	O23 5-1	D04 1-1	J15 2-1	M26 0-0	J03 0-3	M12 2-0	F26 1-0	D18 3-1	a01 0-0	S04 2-1	N02 1-0	D28 0-2	S18 1-1	O19 1-1
3 BRISTOL C	M12 2-0	S11 0-0		a23 2-1	N02 0-0	N27 0-2	m07 2-1	m02 2-2	F15 3-0	F26 2-0	a02 1-1	A28 2-1	M26 3-1	J22 1-3	F12 1-0	D27 1-3	a09 0-0	S25 0-2	N06 2-2	J01 1-1	S28 0-1	J18 1-0	O23 4-2	O09 2-2
4 BURY	D04 3-1	J22 4-1	D18 2-2		M19 3-2	O30 1-0	S11 0-1	M05 3-0	S25 2-0	D28 4-0	A28 3-2	M01 2-3	F19 1-0	J03 1-1	a16 1-0	J08 0-1	F12 0-0	a30 1-0	O19 3-2	O16 0-0	N13 3-0	S28 3-0	m14 1-3	a04 2-1
5 CHESTER	M26 1-1	S29 1-2	D11 1-0	N06 0-1		M05 1-1	A28 1-0	F19 2-3	F12 2-0	D04 2-1	S25 5-0	a30 0-0	O16 1-3	a16 2-1	O20 1-1	J22 1-0	J08 5-2	m14 1-2	D28 0-2	O30 0-1	S11 0-0	a01 0-0	J04 1-2	D10 0-1
6 COLCHESTER U	D28 0-0	S25 4-1	a29 3-1	M12 2-1	N09 1-0		J21 4-3	O15 2-2	A28 1-0	J03 4-1	J07 3-2	S28 0-0	N05 2-0	M01 3-1	a01 1-0	a12 1-2	S10 4-1	a15 5-1	D17 3-0	F18 1-0	m13 1-0	M25 3-3	N02 3-0	D03 0-0
7 CREWE A	F15 0-0	M19 3-1	S07 4-1	J29 3-3	J15 3-2	S17 0-1		S03 2-5	M11 1-1	a15 3-0	F26 3-1	D17 0-3	O01 1-2	a04 1-0	D28 0-3	O22 1-2	O08 1-1	N12 0-1	J03 3-0	F05 3-0	D03 1-1	m13 0-1	a30 0-2	N02 2-1
8 DARLINGTON	N02 1-1	a12 0-1	J03 2-2	O23 1-2	O09 0-2	F26 1-3	J08 1-1		J22 1-2	a04 2-1	S11 2-1	D28 1-2	M12 0-0	a30 2-0	m17 4-3	S25 0-0	A28 3-0	S28 0-1	M26 3-1	N06 1-0	a16 0-2	F15 1-0	D04 0-2	m14 1-3
9 HALIFAX T	S18 1-3	F18 2-0	O19 2-2	F05 1-0	O01 0-0	J14 4-0	O30 0-3	S07 2-0		a29 1-1	N05 2-2	a04 1-2	S03 0-0	F01 2-0	M01 1-2	O15 0-2	M04 0-0	D28 3-1	m13 1-0	M15 1-0	J03 3-0	D17 1-2	m10 1-1	a15 2-2
10 HARTLEPOOL U	O23 1-1	J01 2-1	O16 3-1	a02 0-1	a09 1-0	m02 1-4	S29 1-0	D27 2-0	N27 1-2		M26 0-1	J22 0-0	N03 0-4	S11 2-1	J12 0-0	M02 2-2	m07 3-0	A28 0-0	F19 3-2	a23 1-2	F12 0-2	S25 4-0	N06 1-0	M12 2-0
11 HEREFORD U	J03 2-1	M05 0-0	D28 1-3	J15 0-2	F05 5-2	S04 0-0	O16 1-0	J29 0-0	M19 2-0	N13 1-0		O20 2-0	S18 0-2	D18 1-1	m14 0-1	F19 0-2	O30 1-0	D04 0-2	M02 0-0	S08 1-2	a05 0-1	a30 1-0	a16 1-4	O02 0-0
12 HULL C	F05 2-2	a09 3-1	J15 1-0	N02 2-1	N27 2-0	D11 3-0	a23 1-0	a02 0-0	D27 1-1	S18 1-1	F15 2-0		m02 2-2	O23 4-0	N06 4-1	M26 1-0	J01 2-1	F26 1-1	J29 7-0	O02 0-0	O09 4-1	M12 0-1	S04 1-1	S07 4-0
13 MANSFIELD T	m14 4-1	A28 2-1	N13 1-1	O09 1-4	F26 2-1	M19 1-1	M28 1-0	O30 0-2	J08 1-2	M14 3-0	J22 0-1	J03 3-1		D28 2-0	S27 0-0	S11 0-2	S25 2-1	O18 0-2	D04 1-0	M05 1-0	D17 2-1	a16 1-1	a05 2-2	a30 2-2
14 NORTHAMPTON T	O02 1-1	N13 2-1	S19 7-1	S21 0-3	S07 1-1	O19 2-1	D27 4-0	N28 3-3	a10 3-1	J29 3-1	a23 2-1	M06 1-2	a02 1-2		O30 0-0	J01 2-2	a19 1-1	M20 2-1	F05 2-3	S28 0-1	F26 2-0	O10 1-0	J15 2-2	S04 1-1
15 PETERBOROUGH U	J29 0-0	m04 3-1	O02 3-0	S18 1-1	F16 0-1	D27 2-1	a02 2-1	a23 1-1	N03 2-1	S04 2-1	J01 4-0	M19 1-1	m07 3-2	M12 2-0		N27 0-0	N13 1-0	O09 0-1	J15 1-0	a09 4-3	O23 1-3	F26 3-0	S08 0-3	F05 2-2
16 PORT VALE	a16 2-1	O30 1-0	a04 1-1	S04 0-0	S18 2-1	S06 0-0	M05 1-1	F05 2-1	F26 2-1	O18 3-0	O09 2-0	N13 1-0	J29 4-1	m14 1-2	a29 2-1		M19 4-0	m09 0-1	O02 2-3	J15 3-0	D28 1-0	D04 0-1	D18 1-0	J03 2-1
17 ROCHDALE	D18 3-1	O16 3-1	D04 1-0	O02 0-0	S04 0-1	a26 2-1	M15 2-0	J15 1-1	O23 2-2	S07 2-0	M12 4-1	F14 1-3	F05 2-2	N02 2-0	M26 1-1	N06 3-3		a04 0-1	a16 1-0	S18 1-1	a30 2-2	J03 4-2	D11 0-2	D28 1-0
18 SCUNTHORPE U	S04 1-1	a23 4-3	F05 1-1	N27 0-1	J01 2-0	O02 2-1	M25 2-0	m07 2-2	a01 2-0	J16 3-0	a08 1-2	O15 0-1	M01 2-2	N06 5-1	a26 3-0	N02 1-0	D27 1-1		S07 3-0	m02 2-0	M12 2-0	O23 2-1	J29 0-0	S19 0-0
19 STOCKPORT CO	F26 2-1	D27 3-0	M18 2-2	F14 2-1	a02 3-3	a22 3-0	D10 3-2	N12 2-1	J01 4-2	O08 1-1	N01 2-1	S10 1-1	a08 1-1	S24 0-1	A28 1-1	m06 0-2	S27 2-2	F12 1-1		N26 1-2	a17 1-0	J21 3-2	M11 1-3	O22 2-1
20 SWINDON T	a04 2-0	a19 3-3	m14 2-0	F26 1-1	M12 2-3	O10 3-0	S25 1-0	M19 1-2	S11 0-1	D18 3-0	F12 3-2	a16 0-1	O23 4-0	m08 1-5	D04 1-0	A28 1-0	J22 4-1	J03 2-2	a30 2-0		a26 2-1	N02 4-2	D28 0-1	N13 3-2
21 TORQUAY U	S08 4-2	M02 1-3	M20 0-2	M26 2-3	m07 0-1	J01 2-0	a09 2-1	S18 1-0	m02 1-3	O02 3-2	D27 2-1	F19 0-0	a23 3-1	O16 3-1	M05 2-1	a02 0-1	N27 3-2	O30 1-1	S04 3-0	O20 1-1		N06 3-0	F05 0-1	J15 1-3
22 TRANMERE R	J25 1-1	a02 1-1	S04 2-2	m07 1-1	D27 2-4	N13 2-4	J01 1-1	O18 2-0	a23 1-2	F05 1-1	N27 2-1	O30 0-1	S06 3-0	F19 2-1	O16 1-0	a08 0-2	m16 0-0	M05 0-4	S18 1-1	F28 2-0	M18 2-0		O02 0-2	J29 3-0
23 WIMBLEDON	O09 6-1	m07 5-0	M05 2-1	J01 2-1	m02 4-0	F15 2-1	a19 3-2	a09 3-1	N13 2-4	M19 2-0	S28 1-0	J08 1-2	D27 1-1	A28 1-1	J22 2-1	a23 1-0	O19 3-0	S11 2-2	O30 2-1	a01 0-0	S25 4-1	M15 4-0		F26 4-3
24 YORK C	N06 4-0	F15 2-0	F19 3-0	D27 3-1	a23 1-0	a09 3-0	M01 2-0	J01 5-2	S28 3-2	O30 5-1	m07 5-1	a19 1-0	N27 6-1	M15 5-2	S25 1-1	m02 0-0	a02 1-0	J23 2-1	M05 3-1	M26 0-0	A28 1-1	S11 2-1	O16 1-4	

LEAGUE TABLES

DIVISION 1

	P	W	D	L	F	A	W	D	L	F	A	Pts
Liverpool	42	16	4	1	55	16	8	6	7	32	21	82
Walford	42	16	2	3	49	20	6	3	12	25	37	71
Manchester U	42	14	7	0	39	10	5	6	10	17	28	70
Tottenham H	42	15	4	2	50	15	5	5	11	15	35	69
Nottingham F	42	12	5	4	34	18	8	4	9	28	32	69
Aston Villa	42	17	2	2	47	15	4	3	14	15	35	68
Everton	42	13	6	2	43	19	5	4	12	23	29	64
West Ham U	42	13	3	5	41	23	7	1	13	27	39	64
Ipswich T	42	11	3	7	39	23	4	10	7	25	27	58
Arsenal	42	11	6	4	36	19	5	4	12	22	37	58
WBA	42	11	5	5	35	20	4	7	10	16	29	57
Southampton	42	11	5	5	36	22	4	7	10	18	36	57
Stoke C	42	13	4	4	34	21	3	5	13	19	43	57
Norwich C	42	10	6	5	30	18	4	6	11	22	40	54
Notts Co	42	12	4	5	37	25	3	3	15	18	46	52
Sunderland	42	7	10	4	30	22	5	4	12	18	39	50
Birmingham C	42	9	7	5	29	24	3	7	11	11	31	50
Luton T	42	7	7	7	34	33	5	6	10	31	51	49
Coventry C	42	10	5	6	29	17	3	4	14	19	42	48
Manchester C	42	9	5	7	26	23	4	3	14	21	47	47
Swansea C	42	10	4	7	32	29	0	7	14	19	40	41
Brighton & HA	42	8	7	6	25	22	1	6	14	13	46	40

DIVISION 2

	P	W	D	L	F	A	W	D	L	F	A	Pts
QPR	42	16	3	2	51	16	10	4	7	26	20	85
Wolves	42	14	5	2	42	16	6	10	5	26	28	75
Leicester C	42	11	4	6	36	15	9	6	6	36	29	70
Fulham	42	13	5	3	36	20	7	4	10	28	27	69
Newcastle U	42	13	6	2	43	21	5	7	9	32	32	67
Sheffield W	42	9	8	4	33	23	7	7	7	27	24	63
Oldham A	42	8	10	3	38	24	6	9	6	26	23	61
Leeds U	42	7	11	3	28	22	6	10	5	23	24	60
Shrewsbury T	42	8	9	4	20	15	7	5	9	28	33	59
Barnsley	42	9	8	4	37	28	5	7	9	20	27	57
Blackburn R	42	11	7	3	38	21	4	5	12	20	37	57
Cambridge U	42	11	7	3	26	17	2	5	14	16	43	51
Derby Co	42	7	10	4	27	24	3	9	9	22	34	49
Carlisle U	42	10	6	5	44	28	2	6	13	24	42	48
Crystal P	42	11	7	3	31	17	1	5	15	12	35	48
Middlesbrough	42	8	7	6	27	29	3	8	10	19	38	48
Charlton A	42	11	3	7	40	31	2	6	13	23	55	48
Chelsea	42	8	8	5	31	22	3	6	12	20	39	47
Grimsby T	42	9	7	5	32	26	3	4	14	13	44	47
Rotherham	42	6	7	8	22	29	4	8	9	23	39	45
Burnley	42	10	4	7	38	24	2	4	15	18	42	44
Bolton W	42	10	2	9	30	26	1	9	11	12	35	44

DIVISION 3

	P	W	D	L	F	A	W	D	L	F	A	Pts
Portsmouth	46	16	4	3	43	19	11	6	6	31	22	91
Cardiff C	46	17	5	1	45	14	8	6	9	31	36	86
Huddersfield T	46	15	8	0	56	18	8	5	10	28	31	82
Newport Co	46	13	7	3	40	20	10	2	11	36	34	78
Oxford U	46	12	9	2	41	23	10	3	10	30	30	78
Lincoln C	46	17	1	5	55	22	6	6	11	22	29	76
Bristol R	46	16	4	3	55	21	6	5	12	29	37	75
Plymouth A	46	15	2	6	37	23	4	6	13	24	43	65
Brentford	46	14	4	5	50	28	4	6	13	38	49	64
Walsall	46	14	5	4	38	19	3	8	12	26	44	64
Sheffield U	46	16	3	4	44	20	3	4	16	18	44	64
Bradford C	46	11	7	5	41	27	5	6	12	27	42	61
Gillingham	46	12	4	7	37	29	4	9	10	21	30	61
Bournemouth	46	11	7	5	35	20	5	6	12	24	48	61
Southend U	46	10	8	5	41	28	5	6	12	25	37	59
Preston NE	46	11	10	2	35	17	4	3	16	25	52	58
Millwall	46	12	7	4	41	24	2	6	15	23	53	55
Wigan A	46	10	4	9	35	33	5	5	13	25	39	54
Exeter C	46	12	4	7	49	43	2	8	13	32	61	54
Orient	46	10	6	7	44	38	5	3	15	20	50	54
Reading	46	10	8	5	37	28	2	9	12	27	51	53
Wrexham	46	11	6	6	40	26	1	9	13	16	50	51
Doncaster R	46	6	8	9	38	44	3	3	17	19	53	38
Chesterfield	46	6	6	11	28	28	2	7	14	15	40	37

DIVISION 4

	P	W	D	L	F	A	W	D	L	F	A	Pts
Wimbledon	46	17	4	2	57	23	12	7	4	39	22	98
Hull C	46	14	8	1	48	14	11	7	5	27	20	90
Port Vale	46	15	4	4	37	16	11	6	6	30	18	88
Scunthorpe U	46	13	7	3	41	17	10	7	6	30	25	83
Bury	46	15	4	4	43	20	8	8	7	31	26	81
Colchester U	46	17	5	1	51	19	7	4	12	24	36	81
York C	46	18	4	1	59	19	4	9	10	29	39	79
Swindon T	46	14	3	6	45	27	5	8	10	16	27	68
Peterboro' U	46	13	6	4	38	23	4	7	12	20	29	64
Mansfield T	46	11	6	6	32	26	5	7	11	29	44	61
Halifax T	46	9	8	6	31	23	7	4	12	28	43	60
Torquay U	46	12	3	8	38	30	5	4	14	18	35	58
Chester	46	8	6	9	28	24	7	5	11	27	36	56
Bristol C	46	10	8	5	32	25	3	9	11	27	45	56
Northampton T	46	10	8	5	43	29	4	4	15	22	46	54
Stockport	46	11	8	4	41	31	3	4	16	19	48	54
Darlington	46	8	5	10	27	30	5	8	10	34	41	52
Aldershot	40	11	5	7	40	35	1	10	12	21	47	51
Tranmere R	46	8	8	7	30	29	5	3	15	19	42	50
Rochdale	46	11	8	4	38	25	0	8	15	17	48	49
Blackpool	46	10	8	5	32	23	3	4	16	23	51	*49
Hartlepool U	46	11	5	7	30	24	2	4	17	16	52	48
Crewe A	46	9	5	9	35	32	2	3	18	18	39	41
Hereford U	46	8	6	9	19	23	3	2	18	23	56	41

**Blackpool had two points deducted for fielding an ineligible player*

Football League Records

Top scorers: Div 1, I.Rush (Liverpool) 32 goals; Div 2, K.Dixon (Chelsea) 28 goals; Div 3, K.Edwards (Sheffield United) 33 goals; Div 4, T.Senior (Reading) 36 goals.
Chester became Chester City.

Liverpool's brilliantly eccentric goalkeeper Bruce Grobbelaar, who took over from Ray Clemence at Anfield.

DIVISION 1

	ARSENAL	ASTON VILLA	BIRMINGHAM C	COVENTRY C	EVERTON	IPSWICH T	LEICESTER C	LIVERPOOL	LUTON T	MANCHESTER U	NORWICH C	NOTTINGHAM F	NOTTS CO	Q.P.R.	SOUTHAMPTON	STOKE C	SUNDERLAND	TOTTENHAM H	WATFORD	W.B.A.	WEST HAM U	WOLVERHAMPTON W
1 ARSENAL		F18 1-1	D27 1-1	O15 0-1	N19 2-1	M10 4-1	a28 2-1	S10 0-2	A27 2-1	S06 2-3	S24 3-0	O22 4-1	J21 1-1	F04 0-2	D31 2-2	a07 3-1	N05 1-2	a21 3-2	D17 3-1	D03 0-1	m07 3-3	M24 4-1
2 ASTON VILLA	O29 2-6		O15 1-0	a07 2-0	m07 0-2	D17 4-0	N19 3-1	J20 1-3	F04 0-0	M03 0-3	S10 1-0	M17 1-0	a28 3-1	D31 2-1	S24 1-0	N12 1-1	A29 1-0	D27 0-0	a21 2-1	A27 4-3	D03 1-0	F25 4-0
3 BIRMINGHAM C	a23 1-1	M31 2-1		N05 1-2	J02 0-2	S17 1-0	O01 2-1	m05 0-0	M20 1-1	F07 2-2	D10 0-1	D26 1-2	M24 0-0	a14 0-2	m12 0-0	S06 1-0	N26 0-1	O22 0-1	S03 2-0	F28 2-1	J14 3-0	F11 0-0
4 COVENTRY C	M31 1-4	M13 3-3	M03 0-1		S03 1-1	O01 1-2	S17 2-1	D10 4-0	m05 2-2	D26 1-1	m12 2-1	a17 2-1	S06 2-1	N12 1-0	N26 0-0	F18 2-3	J02 2-1	M24 2-4	J14 1-2	O22 1-2	F11 1-2	a14 2-1
5 EVERTON	a09 0-0	D10 1-1	S24 1-1	D31 0-0		M17 1-0	M20 1-1	M03 1-1	O15 0-1	m05 1-1	N26 0-2	N12 1-0	F04 4-1	m12 3-1	M31 1-0	A27 1-0	D26 0-0	J21 2-1	O22 1-0	S10 0-0	A29 0-1	a23 2-0
6 IPSWICH T	N12 1-0	m12 2-1	J21 1-2	F04 3-1	S06 3-0		O22 0-0	N26 1-1	M31 3-0	D10 0-2	a23 2-0	a14 2-2	D31 1-0	O15 0-2	F21 0-3	S10 5-0	m05 1-0	A27 3-1	M14 0-0	S24 3-4	M03 0-3	D26 3-1
7 LEICESTER C	N26 3-0	a14 2-0	F04 2-3	J21 1-1	O29 2-0	F25 2-0		a18 3-3	A31 0-3	N12 1-1	M31 2-1	m05 2-1	A27 0-4	D26 2-1	N30 2-1	S24 2-2	m12 0-2	S10 0-3	M03 4-1	D31 1-1	M17 4-1	D10 5-1
8 LIVERPOOL	F11 2-1	S17 2-1	D03 1-0	m07 5-0	N06 3-0	a28 2-2	D27 2-2		O29 6-0	J02 1-1	m15 1-1	S03 1-0	D17 5-0	F25 2-0	S06 1-1	N19 1-0	O01 0-1	M10 3-1	F01 3-0	a21 3-0	a07 6-0	J14 0-1
9 LUTON T	J14 1-2	O01 1-0	N12 1-1	D03 2-4	a07 0-3	M13 2-1	M24 0-0	F18 0-0		F12 0-5	S06 2-2	J02 2-3	a21 3-2	M03 0-0	O22 3-1	m07 0-1	S03 4-1	N19 2-4	a28 1-2	D18 2-0	D27 0-1	S17 4-0
10 MANCHESTER U	M17 4-0	N05 1-2	a07 1-0	a21 4-1	D03 0-1	m07 1-2	M10 2-0	S24 1-0	S10 2-0		F04 0-0	A29 1-2	D27 3-3	A27 3-1	J21 3-2	D31 1-0	F25 2-1	D16 4-2	N19 4-1	O15 3-0	a28 0-0	O29 3-0
11 NORWICH C	J02 1-1	F11 3-1	m07 1-1	D17 0-0	a28 1-1	D27 0-0	O19 3-1	A31 0-1	M17 0-0	O01 3-3		S17 2-3	M13 0-1	O29 0-3	N05 1-0	a21 2-2	J14 3-0	D03 2-1	a07 6-1	N19 2-0	F25 1-0	S03 3-0
12 NOTTINGHAM F	F25 0-1	S07 2-2	a21 5-1	D28 3-0	M13 1-0	N19 2-1	D04 3-2	D31 0-1	S24 1-0	m16 2-0	J21 3-0		O16 3-1	S10 3-2	A27 0-1	a28 0-0	O29 1-1	F04 2-2	m07 5-1	a07 3-1	D17 3-0	N05 5-0
13 NOTTS CO	S17 0-4	N26 5-2	A30 2-1	M17 2-1	O01 0-1	S03 0-2	J14 2-5	m12 0-0	D26 0-3	a14 1-0	N12 1-1	M31 0-0		m05 0-3	m17 1-3	O22 1-1	D10 6-1	F21 0-0	F11 3-5	M03 1-1	J02 2-2	m01 4-0
14 Q.P.R.	O01 2-0	S03 2-1	N19 2-1	M10 2-1	D17 2-0	a07 1-0	a21 2-0	O22 0-1	N05 0-1	J13 1-1	F14 2-0	F11 0-1	D03 1-0		M24 4-0	J17 6-0	S17 3-0	a28 2-1	S06 1-1	m07 1-1	F07 1-1	J02 2-1
15 SOUTHAMPTON	S03 1-0	J02 2-2	D17 2-1	a28 8-2	a17 3-1	O29 3-2	a07 2-2	M16 2-0	F25 2-1	S17 3-0	M03 2-1	J23 0-1	N19 0-2	A29 0-0		D03 3-1	F11 1-1	m07 5-0	D27 1-0	N12 1-0	a21 2-0	O01 1-0
16 STOKE C	J28 1-0	M10 1-0	M17 2-1	O29 1-3	J14 1-1	F11 1-0	J02 0-1	a14 2-0	D10 2-4	S03 0-1	D26 2-0	N26 1-1	F25 1-0	a23 1-2	m05 1-1		M31 2-1	N05 1-1	S17 0-4	A29 3-1	O01 3-1	m12 4-0
17 SUNDERLAND	M03 2-2	M24 0-1	a28 2-1	S24 1-0	a21 2-1	D03 1-1	D18 1-1	F04 0-0	D31 2-0	O22 0-1	A27 1-1	F18 1-1	m07 0-0	M07 1-0	S10 0-2	O15 2-2		a07 1-1	N12 3-0	D27 3-0	N19 0-1	S07 3-2
18 TOTTENHAM H	D26 2-4	a18 2-1	F25 0-1	A29 1-1	S17 1-2	J14 2-0	F11 3-2	N12 2-2	a14 2-1	m12 1-1	m05 2-0	O02 2-1	O29 1-0	N26 3-2	D10 0-0	M03 1-0	F08 3-0		J02 2-3	M17 0-1	S03 0-2	M31 1-0
19 WATFORD	m12 2-1	D26 3-2	D31 1-0	A27 2-3	F25 4-4	A30 2-2	N05 3-3	M31 0-2	N26 1-2	a17 0-0	O15 1-3	D10 3-2	S10 3-1	M17 1-0	a24 1-1	J21 2-0	M20 2-1	S24 2-3		F04 3-1	O28 0-0	m05 0-0
20 W.B.A.	m05 1-3	F14 3-1	O29 1-2	F25 1-1	F11 1-1	J02 2-1	S03 1-0	D26 1-2	m12 3-0	M31 2-0	a14 0-0	F08 0-5	N05 2-0	D10 1-2	m14 0-2	M24 3-0	a23 3-1	S07 1-1	O01 2-0		S17 1-0	N26 1-3
21 WEST HAM U	D10 3-1	m05 0-1	A27 4-0	S10 5-2	m14 0-1	N05 2-1	S06 3-1	O15 1-3	a17 3-1	N27 1-1	O22 0-0	m12 1-2	S24 3-0	M31 2-2	D26 0-1	F04 3-0	a14 0-1	D31 4-1	F21 2-4	J21 1-0		M10 1-1
22 WOLVERHAMPTON W	A29 1-2	O23 1-1	S10 1-1	N19 0-0	D27 3-0	a21 0-3	m07 1-0	A27 1-1	J21 1-2	F18 1-1	D31 2-0	M03 1-0	a07 0-1	S24 0-4	F04 0-1	D17 0-0	M17 0-0	O15 2-3	D03 0-5	a28 0-0	N12 0-3	

Former Liverpool idol Kevin Keegan was the toast of Tyneside as Newcastle United clinched the last promotion place to Division One in 1983-4.

DIVISION 2

	BARNSLEY	BLACKBURN R	BRIGHTON & HA	CAMBRIDGE U	CARDIFF C	CARLISLE U	CHARLTON A	CHELSEA	CRYSTAL P	DERBY CO	FULHAM	GRIMSBY T	HUDDERSFIELD T	LEEDS U	MANCHESTER C	MIDDLESBROUGH	NEWCASTLE U	OLDHAM A	PORTSMOUTH	SHEFFIELD W	SHREWSBURY T	SWANSEA C
1 BARNSLEY		a23 0-0	N26 3-1	D26 2-0	F04 2-3	m12 2-1	a14 2-0	D10 0-0	F18 1-1	M31 5-1	A27 3-0	S27 3-1	O15 2-2	O22 0-2	D31 1-1	S10 0-2	S24 1-1	m05 0-1	M17 0-3	M03 0-1	M13 3-0	N12 3-2
2 BLACKBURN R	D28 1-1		S24 2-2	D31 1-0	m07 1-1	M24 4-1	M21 1-1	S07 0-0	D17 2-1	S10 5-1	a29 0-1	D04 1-1	A27 2-2	N12 1-1	J21 2-1	a07 1-0	a20 1-1	O22 3-1	N19 2-1	F04 0-0	O16 1-1	M07 4-1
3 BRIGHTON & H.A.	a28 1-0	J02 1-1		F28 3-0	D03 3-1	S17 1-1	O01 7-0	S03 1-2	a21 3-1	S06 1-0	D27 1-1	a07 2-0	N05 3-1	M24 3-0	M10 1-1	m07 3-0	D17 0-1	J14 4-0	O08 0-1	O22 1-3	N19 2-2	F11 1-1
4 CAMBRIDGE U	a21 0-3	S03 2-0	O29 3-4		M10 0-2	J14 0-2	S17 2-2	F11 0-1	O08 1-3	N05 0-1	D03 1-1	D28 2-2	O18 0-3	a07 2-2	D17 0-0	N19 0-0	a28 1-0	O01 2-1	F25 1-3	M17 1-2	m07 1-0	J02 1-1
5 CARDIFF C	O01 0-3	A29 0-1	m05 2-2	N12 5-0		O08 2-0	J31 2-1	M31 3-3	a17 0-2	a23 1-0	F19 0-4	S03 3-1	N26 3-1	F11 0-1	A29 2-1	M03 2-1	O19 0-2	a14 2-0	S17 0-0	m12 0-2	M17 2-0	D26 3-2
6 CARLISLE U	D17 4-2	D10 0-1	J21 1-2	A27 0-0	a07 1-1		M17 3-0	O22 0-0	m07 2-2	F04 2-1	O15 2-0	a28 1-1	S24 0-0	D03 1-0	N19 2-0	a20 1-1	D27 3-1	F18 2-0	N12 0-0	D31 1-1	S10 1-0	M03 2-0
7 CHARLTON A	N19 3-2	N05 2-0	F04 2-0	J21 5-2	A27 2-0	S06 1-0		N15 1-1	D27 1-0	S24 1-0	m07 3-4	M10 3-3	D31 1-2	D15 2-0	O15 1-0	D03 2-0	a07 1-3	M24 2-1	a21 2-1	S10 1-1	a28 2-4	O22 2-2
8 CHELSEA	m07 3-1	M16 2-1	D31 1-0	S10 2-1	O15 2-0	F25 0-0	O29 3-2		N19 2-2	A27 5-0	a07 4-0	D17 2-3	F04 3-1	a28 5-0	D03 0-1	S24 0-0	N12 4-0	M03 3-0	D27 2-2	J21 3-2	a21 3-0	D06 6-1
9 CRYSTAL P	O29 0-1	m12 0-2	D26 0-2	a01 1-1	N08 1-0	D11 1-2	a23 2-0	a14 0-1		O15 0-1	S11 1-1	F25 0-1	M17 0-0	M03 0-0	A27 0-2	F04 1-0	J21 3-1	N12 2-1	S27 2-1	N26 1-0	D31 1-1	m05 2-0
10 DERBY CO	O08 0-2	F11 1-1	M17 0-3	M03 1-0	D27 2-3	O01 1-4	J02 0-1	J14 1-2	a07 3-0		a21 1-0	O29 1-2	F25 1-1	N19 1-1	a28 1-0	N12 1-0	D03 3-2	S17 2-2	m09 2-0	A29 1-1	D17 1-0	S03 2-1
11 FULHAM	J14 1-0	N26 0-1	a23 3-1	m05 1-0	O31 0-2	M31 0-0	D10 0-1	O08 3-5	F11 1-1	D26 2-2		J02 1-1	a14 0-2	S17 2-1	M17 5-1	S27 2-1	M03 2-2	m12 3-0	S03 0-2	N11 1-1	F25 3-0	O01 5-0
12 GRIMSBY T	a10 1-0	m05 3-2	O15 5-0	a23 0-0	D31 1-0	N26 1-1	N12 2-1	m12 0-1	O22 2-0	F21 2-1	S24 2-1		M31 2-1	S06 2-0	F04 1-1	J21 0-0	S10 1-1	D13 3-0	M03 3-4	D26 1-0	A27 1-1	a14 3-0
13 HUDDERSFIELD T	a07 0-1	J14 0-2	M03 0-1	M24 3-0	a28 4-0	J02 0-0	S03 0-0	O01 2-3	S06 2-1	O22 3-0	N19 2-0	O08 0-0		a21 2-2	D27 1-3	D17 2-2	m07 2-2	F11 0-1	D03 2-1	m01 0-1	N12 1-0	S17 1-0
14 LEEDS U	F25 1-2	M10 1-0	A29 3-2	O14 3-1	S10 1-0	m05 3-0	m12 1-0	N26 1-1	N05 1-1	a14 0-0	J21 1-0	M17 2-1	D26 1-2		S24 1-2	D31 4-1	A27 0-1	a24 2-0	O29 2-1	M31 1-1	F04 3-0	F15 1-0
15 MANCHESTER C	S03 3-2	S17 6-0	N12 4-0	m12 5-0	M24 2-1	a14 3-1	M31 0-1	m04 0-2	J14 3-1	N26 1-1	S07 0-0	O01 2-1	a23 2-3	J02 1-1		O22 2-1	F18 1-2	D26 2-0	F11 2-1	D10 1-2	M03 1-0	O08 2-1
16 MIDDLESBROUGH	F11 2-1	O08 1-2	D10 0-0	a14 1-1	N05 2-0	D26 0-1	m05 1-0	J02 2-1	O01 1-3	M20 0-0	M24 0-2	S17 1-1	m12 0-0	S03 2-2	F25 0-0		S06 3-2	M31 3-2	J14 0-0	a25 2-0	O29 4-0	N26 1-0
17 NEWCASTLE U	J02 1-0	D26 1-1	m12 3-1	N26 2-1	F25 3-1	a23 5-1	O08 2-1	M10 1-1	S17 3-1	m05 4-0	N05 3-2	F11 0-1	D10 5-2	M28 1-0	O29 5-0	M17 3-1		S03 3-0	O01 4-2	a14 0-1	A29 0-1	M31 2-0
18 OLDHAM A	D03 1-0	F25 0-0	A27 1-0	F04 0-0	N19 2-1	O29 2-3	S27 0-0	N05 1-1	M10 3-2	J21 3-0	D17 3-0	m07 2-1	S10 0-3	D27 3-2	a20 2-2	O15 2-1	D31 1-2		a28 3-2	S24 1-3	a07 0-1	M17 3-3
19 PORTSMOUTH	S06 2-1	a14 2-4	M31 5-1	N01 5-0	J21 1-1	M10 0-1	D26 4-0	a24 2-2	M24 0-1	D10 3-0	D31 1-4	N05 4-0	m05 1-1	F18 2-3	S10 1-2	A27 0-1	F04 1-4	N26 3-4		O15 0-1	S24 4-1	m12 5-0
20 SHEFFIELD W	N05 2-0	O01 4-2	F25 2-1	S06 1-0	D17 5-2	S03 2-0	F11 4-1	S17 2-1	a28 1-0	a10 3-1	M07 1-1	a21 1-0	O29 0-0	O08 3-1	m07 0-0	D27 0-2	N19 4-2	J02 3-0	a07 2-0		D03 1-1	J14 6-1
21 SHREWSBURY T	S17 3-2	M30 1-0	a14 2-1	D10 1-0	S06 1-0	F11 0-0	N26 1-1	D26 2-4	S03 1-1	m12 3-0	O22 0-0	J14 1-2	M10 1-0	O01 5-1	N05 1-3	F28 1-0	M24 2-2	O08 2-0	J02 2-0	m05 2-1		a24 2-0
22 SWANSEA C	M10 1-0	O29 0-1	S10 1-3	S24 2-1	a21 3-2	N05 0-0	F25 1-0	N22 1-3	D03 1-0	D31 2-0	F05 0-3	N19 0-1	J18 2-2	m07 2-2	a07 0-2	a27 2-1	O16 1-2	S06 0-0	D17 1-2	A27 0-1	D27 0-2	

Season 1983-84

DIVISION 3

	BOLTON W	BOURNEMOUTH	BRADFORD C	BRENTFORD	BRISTOL R	BURNLEY	EXETER C	GILLINGHAM	HULL C	LINCOLN C	MILLWALL	NEWPORT CO	ORIENT	OXFORD U	PLYMOUTH A	PORT VALE	PRESTON N.E.	ROTHERHAM U	SCUNTHORPE U	SHEFFIELD U	SOUTHEND U	WALSALL	WIGAN A	WIMBLEDON
1 BOLTON W		a28 0-1	M27 0-2	D03 1-0	F04 3-0	S27 0-0	M17 1-0	a07 0-1	O18 0-0	F14 0-2	J02 2-0	O15 2-3	N05 3-2	D27 1-0	a16 2-1	F25 2-0	D17 2-2	S24 2-0	J21 0-0	m07 3-1	O29 2-0	S10 8-1	a21 0-1	A27 2-0
2 BOURNEMOUTH	N26 2-2		m12 4-1	F18 0-3	S27 0-1	a09 1-0	D31 3-1	S24 2-0	N05 2-3	F04 3-0	J21 1-1	D26 1-1	a24 3-2	O22 2-1	O08 2-1	m05 1-1	A27 0-1	N01 4-2	a14 1-1	M24 0-1	M10 1-0	M03 3-0	S10 0-1	M31 2-3
3 BRADFORD C	S03 0-2	D17 5-2		a28 1-1	m02 0-1	a21 2-1	O01 1-3	a11 3-2	S07 0-0	m07 0-0	N12 3-3	a25 1-0	J14 4-1	M03 2-2	D03 2-0	F11 2-2	J02 3-2	F18 1-0	O08 2-2	a07 2-1	S17 1-1	O22 0-0	D27 6-2	J07 5-2
4 BRENTFORD	a14 3-0	O29 1-1	N26 1-4		M31 2-2	S24 0-0	a20 3-0	F04 2-3	O15 1-1	S10 3-0	A27 2-2	D31 2-0	M10 1-1	M17 1-2	N05 2-2	O18 3-1	a03 4-1	M20 2-1	m05 3-0	F25 1-3	F14 0-0	m12 1-1	J21 0-1	D24 3-4
5 BRISTOL R	O01 2-1	a07 1-3	O15 1-0	S06 3-1		N12 2-1	S17 2-0	D27 3-0	D17 1-3	a28 3-1	m08 3-2	J14 4-0	F11 0-0	a21 1-1	M03 2-0	J28 0-0	N01 3-1	M06 2-0	O22 4-1	D03 1-1	S03 2-1	F18 4-2	M27 2-1	M17 1-1
6 BURNLEY	M31 2-2	S03 5-1	D26 1-2	F11 2-2	M10 0-0		F14 4-0	O15 2-3	m15 0-2	F25 4-0	M17 1-0	S06 2-0	m05 2-3	M27 1-1	O01 2-1	N26 7-0	N05 2-1	a14 2-2	D31 5-0	N08 2-1	O18 3-0	a23 0-2	O29 3-0	m12 0-2
7 EXETER C	O08 2-2	m07 0-2	F03 0-2	D27 1-2	J21 1-2	N02 1-1		M03 0-0	D03 2-1	S28 0-3	D17 3-2	O22 1-2	F18 3-4	J02 3-1	a21 1-1	N05 1-1	a28 2-1	S10 0-1	a11 1-1	M10 1-2	M23 3-3	A27 0-1	a07 1-1	S24 0-3
8 GILLINGHAM	S06 2-0	F11 2-1	F14 0-0	O01 4-2	a23 1-2	M24 0-1	O18 3-1		S03 1-2	N05 2-0	O29 3-3	m05 4-1	M31 3-1	S17 2-3	m01 2-1	a14 1-1	O08 2-0	N26 4-2	m12 1-1	J14 4-2	D26 5-1	M10 1-3	F25 3-0	D31 0-1
9 HULL C	M03 1-1	M06 3-1	M31 1-0	M24 2-0	m12 0-0	A27 4-1	a14 1-0	a17 0-0		S24 2-0	S10 5-0	N12 0-0	N26 2-1	F28 0-1	O22 1-2	D31 1-0	a10 3-0	a23 5-0	D26 1-0	O08 4-1	m05 2-1	N01 2-2	F04 1-0	S27 1-0
10 LINCOLN C	N02 0-0	O01 3-0	D31 2-3	F01 2-0	N26 4-0	O22 3-1	M31 1-1	M07 4-0	F11 1-3		O15 2-2	M03 2-3	S07 2-0	J14 2-2	S17 3-1	m12 3-2	F18 2-1	m05 0-1	N12 2-1	S03 0-2	a23 1-2	D26 2-1	M17 0-1	a14 1-2
11 MILLWALL	m05 3-0	S17 3-1	M10 0-0	J15 1-2	D30 1-0	O09 2-0	m12 3-0	F19 2-2	J28 1-0	m01 0-2		N01 1-1	D26 4-3	F11 2-1	S03 1-0	S06 3-2	O21 1-0	M03 2-0	N26 2-1	O01 1-2	a18 4-0	a14 2-0	N05 2-0	a23 1-1
12 NEWPORT CO	M24 2-3	a21 2-1	S10 4-3	m07 1-1	A27 2-1	a07 1-0	F25 1-0	M27 1-0	M10 1-1	O18 1-0	F14 1-1		O08 0-0	a28 1-1	D27 2-0	O29 2-1	S27 1-1	F04 1-4	S24 1-1	D17 0-2	N05 1-1	J22 3-1	D03 5-3	M06 1-1
13 ORIENT	M06 2-1	D27 2-0	A27 2-0	N12 2-0	S23 0-1	J02 1-2	O29 2-2	O24 1-1	a28 3-1	a07 1-1	a21 5-3	M17 2-2		m07 1-2	D17 3-2	O14 3-0	D03 2-1	J22 2-1	S09 1-0	O18 2-0	F26 1-0	J07 0-1	J27 0-0	F04 2-6
14 OXFORD U	a20 5-0	F25 3-2	O19 2-0	O08 2-1	D26 3-2	S10 2-2	m05 1-1	M13 0-1	O29 1-1	A27 3-0	S24 4-2	N26 2-0	D31 5-2		M24 5-0	M10 2-0	F04 2-0	m12 3-2	M31 1-0	N05 2-2	a14 2-1	S28 6-3	m02 0-0	F15 2-0
15 PLYMOUTH A	N12 2-0	M17 1-0	m09 3-0	M06 1-1	O18 1-1	F04 1-1	D26 2-2	S10 1-1	F25 2-0	J21 2-2	M20 0-1	a20 0-1	m12 3-1	O15 2-1		F14 3-0	S24 1-0	M30 1-1	S27 4-0	O29 0-1	D31 4-0	m05 3-1	A27 0-0	a10 1-2
16 PORT VALE	O22 1-2	J02 2-1	S24 1-2	M03 4-3	S10 2-0	a28 2-3	M05 2-2	D03 0-1	m07 1-0	D17 0-1	m14 1-0	F18 4-2	a09 2-0	N12 1-3	O31 0-1		a21 1-1	a02 2-3	A27 0-0	D27 2-0	J30 2-1	F04 0-2	S26 1-1	J21 2-0
17 PRESTON N.E.	m12 2-1	J14 2-0	m05 1-2	S03 3-3	F14 1-0	M06 4-2	N26 2-1	M17 2-2	S17 0-0	O29 1-2	F25 0-0	M30 2-0	a14 3-1	O01 1-2	F11 2-1	D26 4-0		N12 1-0	a24 1-0	J31 2-2	S06 4-1	D31 0-1	O15 2-3	O18 2-3
18 ROTHERHAM U	F11 1-1	a17 1-0	O29 1-0	a07 4-0	N05 2-2	D03 1-1	m01 1-0	a28 3-0	D27 0-1	J02 1-1	O18 1-0	O01 0-1	S17 0-1	D17 1-2	S06 2-0	S03 2-1	M10 0-1		m15 3-0	a21 0-1	a10 0-0	O08 0-1	m07 4-1	F25 1-2
19 SCUNTHORPE U	S16 1-0	D03 1-2	M17 2-1	J02 4-4	F25 2-2	m07 4-0	S03 3-1	D17 2-0	a21 2-0	M10 0-0	a27 0-1	F10 3-3	m01 3-1	S07 0-0	a07 3-0	a17 1-1	D27 1-5	O15 1-2		M27 1-1	S30 1-6	N05 0-0	O18 0-0	O29 5-1
20 SHEFFIELD U	D31 5-0	O15 2-0	S27 2-0	O22 0-0	a14 4-0	J21 0-0	N12 2-2	A27 4-0	M17 2-2	F07 0-0	F04 2-0	m12 2-0	M03 6-3	M06 1-2	F28 2-0	a24 3-1	S10 1-1	D26 3-0	N01 5-3		N26 5-0	M31 2-0	S24 2-2	m05 1-2
21 SOUTHEND U	F06 0-1	N11 0-0	a16 2-1	O31 6-0	J09 1-2	M02 2-2	O15 0-3	a20 3-1	J02 2-2	D27 2-0	S19 3-2	a30 3-1	O21 3-0	D02 0-1	m07 1-1	M19 1-2	a06 1-1	A27 2-2	F03 0-0	a28 0-1		S24 0-0	D17 1-0	S10 1-1
22 WALSALL	J28 1-0	O18 3-1	F25 1-2	D17 1-0	O29 2-1	D27 1-1	J14 4-1	N12 3-1	M27 2-1	a21 0-1	D03 1-1	S17 3-2	S03 0-1	a07 0-1	J02 3-2	O01 2-0	m07 2-1	M17 2-2	M06 1-1	S06 1-2	F11 4-0		a28 3-0	O15 4-0
23 WIGAN A	D26 0-1	M20 1-3	a23 0-1	S17 2-1	a17 0-0	F18 1-0	S06 1-1	O22 1-2	O01 1-1	O08 2-0	M06 0-0	a14 1-0	N01 0-1	S03 0-2	a03 1-1	M31 3-0	M24 1-0	D31 2-1	M03 2-0	F11 3-0	m12 1-0	N26 0-1		N12 3-2
24 WIMBLEDON	J14 4-0	S06 3-2	N05 4-1	a21 2-1	O08 1-1	D17 1-4	F11 2-1	m07 1-3	a07 1-4	D03 3-1	D27 4-3	S03 0-0	O01 2-2	N01 3-1	a28 1-0	S17 4-2	M03 2-2	O22 3-1	F18 1-1	J02 3-1	J28 3-2	M24 2-0	M10 2-2	

DIVISION 4

	ALDERSHOT	BLACKPOOL	BRISTOL C	BURY	CHESTER C	CHESTERFIELD	COLCHESTER U	CREWE A	DARLINGTON	DONCASTER R	HALIFAX T	HARTLEPOOL U	HEREFORD U	MANSFIELD T	NORTHAMPTON T	PETERBOROUGH U	READING	ROCHDALE	STOCKPORT CO	SWINDON T	TORQUAY U	TRANMERE R	WREXHAM	YORK C
1 ALDERSHOT		m05 3-2	O22 1-0	S10 1-2	M10 5-2	D31 2-1	a23 5-1	M31 0-0	m12 0-0	M24 2-1	F18 5-2	J07 2-1	A27 1-4	F04 7-1	N01 1-0	N05 3-2	D26 0-0	N26 2-1	D10 1-1	S27 2-1	J21 3-1	O08 1-1	S24 1-1	a14 1-4
2 BLACKPOOL	J02 5-0		N01 1-0	a07 1-1	M24 3-3	O22 1-0	m01 3-2	S24 3-0	N05 3-1	M10 3-1	m07 4-0	D27 1-0	a28 3-1	S27 2-0	S10 2-3	D03 1-2	A27 1-0	O08 0-2	a10 1-1	J21 1-1	D17 1-0	a21 0-1	M03 4-0	F04 3-0
3 BRISTOL C	F25 2-1	F14 1-1		J31 3-2	D31 4-2	N26 2-0	M31 4-1	a17 2-1	M10 1-0	N05 1-2	O08 3-0	S10 2-0	F04 1-0	A27 4-0	a14 4-1	O29 0-1	S27 3-1	M13 1-1	D26 3-1	m05 1-0	S24 5-0	M24 1-1	J21 2-1	O18 1-0
4 BURY	m01 0-3	S06 0-0	S03 2-1		a14 2-1	a23 2-0	M03 1-1	N13 1-1	a01 0-3	F11 2-3	S18 3-0	F18 3-0	M24 1-4	O08 2-2	m05 1-2	N29 2-2	N26 2-3	D26 3-1	N01 2-1	m12 2-1	M06 0-0	F07 0-0	O22 2-0	D31 1-3
5 CHESTER C	N12 1-2	N09 0-2	m07 1-2	D03 2-1		M07 0-2	F04 1-4	S10 0-1	M17 2-1	a28 1-0	N02 1-1	M03 4-1	a07 0-1	D27 0-4	A27 1-1	D17 1-1	S24 2-1	F18 1-0	O22 2-4	F08 0-3	S28 1-2	J02 0-0	a21 1-0	a18 1-1
6 CHESTERFIELD	m07 3-1	F25 1-1	a28 1-1	D27 1-5	N05 1-1		S24 1-1	J07 1-3	O29 1-1	O18 0-0	J02 0-0	a07 4-1	S27 0-0	a21 0-0	F04 2-1	M10 1-0	J21 2-1	M24 3-0	O08 2-0	A27 1-0	M18 3-2	D03 3-3	D17 1-1	S10 2-1
7 COLCHESTER U	D27 4-1	S03 2-1	S06 0-0	O18 1-0	O01 1-0	F11 2-0		O29 2-0	J14 2-1	F14 1-1	D17 4-1	D03 6-0	m07 3-0	M10 1-0	O15 2-2	a21 1-1	N05 3-0	S17 4-0	J28 1-1	F25 0-0	a28 3-0	a07 0-1	J02 1-1	M17 1-3
8 CREWE A	S06 0-0	F11 2-1	D28 2-2	M10 2-1	J28 1-1	S03 2-1	F18 1-1		S17 2-1	D18 1-1	M03 0-1	N01 2-0	a21 1-1	m07 1-3	O22 3-2	a07 0-1	M23 1-1	J14 0-1	S30 0-3	O08 2-0	J02 2-1	a28 3-0	m15 1-1	N05 0-3
9 DARLINGTON	D17 0-1	m15 2-0	N12 0-1	S27 1-2	O08 2-1	F18 2-1	A27 0-2	M27 2-0		D27 1-2	a28 3-2	a21 2-0	M03 0-0	D03 3-0	F28 5-3	J02 1-0	F04 1-1	O22 1-0	m02 1-0	S10 1-0	a07 0-1	N01 1-0	m08 2-2	S24 0-0
10 DONCASTER R	O15 3-1	N12 2-1	M06 1-0	S24 3-1	N26 0-0	M03 2-1	N01 3-3	m12 1-0	a24 3-2		O21 3-2	m15 0-1	S11 3-0	J07 3-1	D26 1-0	M17 1-1	m01 2-3	m05 3-0	D31 2-1	a14 3-0	F04 1-1	F18 1-1	A27 3-0	S27 2-2
11 HALIFAX T	O29 1-0	D31 1-0	M17 1-2	J21 0-0	F14 2-2	m04 2-1	m11 4-1	O18 1-0	N25 0-2	F25 1-2		S23 3-2	J07 2-1	S09 0-0	S27 2-2	O15 2-1	a13 0-1	a23 5-0	M09 2-0	M30 2-1	A27 2-2	N04 1-2	F04 1-1	D26 1-2
12 HARTLEPOOL U	S03 0-1	a20 0-1	J28 2-2	O29 1-3	O19 1-1	S07 2-2	a14 0-0	F15 2-1	D26 2-1	S17 1-0	F11 3-0		N05 0-0	F25 4-1	D31 2-0	M27 1-1	m12 3-3	M31 1-2	m05 1-2	M10 0-1	M17 2-1	O01 0-1	O15 1-1	N26 2-3
13 HEREFORD U	J14 2-1	N26 1-2	O01 0-2	J18 1-2	S07 2-1	M31 3-1	a04 1-1	D26 0-1	O19 1-0	J28 0-3	S03 0-0	M07 5-0		O29 0-0	N12 0-0	S17 2-1	m05 1-1	a14 2-1	a23 2-0	F15 2-1	F25 1-1	F11 0-1	M17 3-0	m12 2-1
14 MANSFIELD T	O01 5-2	M31 1-1	M27 0-1	M17 1-1	a24 3-1	D26 0-1	N12 0-0	D31 3-3	a14 1-0	S03 1-2	a10 7-1	O22 5-0	F18 1-1		m12 3-1	F11 0-0	M03 2-0	N01 3-0	S06 1-2	N26 2-2	O15 1-3	S17 1-0	M06 3-4	m05 0-1
15 NORTHAMPTON T	F14 1-4	M20 1-5	D03 1-0	J02 1-0	J14 2-1	O01 1-1	M24 3-1	F25 2-0	S03 2-0	a21 1-4	a07 1-1	a10 1-1	M10 0-3	D18 2-1		D27 2-1	O09 2-2	F11 1-1	S18 0-0	N05 2-0	O18 2-1	S06 0-0	a28 3-3	O29 1-2
16 PETERBOROUGH U	M07 1-2	a14 4-0	F18 4-1	F04 2-1	m12 1-0	N12 2-0	D26 2-0	S28 1-0	m05 2-2	O08 1-1	M24 4-0	A27 3-1	J21 1-1	S24 3-0	a24 6-0		N02 3-3	M03 2-0	N26 2-0	D31 1-1	S10 5-0	O22 2-0	J07 0-1	a01 0-2
17 READING	a21 1-0	J14 2-0	a07 2-0	a28 1-1	F11 1-0	S17 1-1	M07 1-0	O14 5-0	O01 1-0	S07 3-2	D02 1-0	D17 5-1	J02 3-1	O19 4-0	M17 3-0	F15 1-1		J28 0-0	S03 6-2	O29 2-2	D27 2-2	m07 1-0	N12 4-1	F25 1-0
18 ROCHDALE	a28 3-1	M17 1-0	D17 0-1	a21 0-2	O29 1-1	O15 2-4	a17 0-0	A27 1-0	F25 2-0	J02 3-3	D27 1-1	S27 2-0	D03 3-3	F14 0-0	S24 1-1	O18 2-1	S10 4-1		N05 2-2	F04 3-3	m07 1-0	M10 2-3	a07 1-2	M27 0-2
19 STOCKPORT CO	O17 2-2	O29 1-2	a21 0-0	F13 1-1	F24 2-1	M16 2-0	S09 0-0	F03 2-3	O15 2-0	m07 0-2	N11 4-0	J02 1-0	D27 1-0	a06 0-4	J20 1-0	a27 4-1	J06 3-0	M05 2-1		S23 1-3	D02 2-1	D16 2-1	S26 1-1	A27 0-2
20 SWINDON T	a07 0-2	S17 0-0	J24 1-1	D17 0-0	S03 4-0	J14 1-2	O22 2-1	M18 1-0	a17 1-0	D03 2-1	S06 2-3	N12 3-2	N01 3-0	a29 1-1	M06 0-0	m07 2-0	F18 1-1	O01 2-1	F11 2-1		a21 2-3	M03 1-1	D27 0-1	O15 3-2
21 TORQUAY U	S17 0-1	m12 1-0	F11 1-0	N05 2-0	m02 1-0	N02 1-1	N26 2-1	m05 3-1	S07 0-1	O01 4-1	J14 1-1	O08 0-0	O22 1-1	M24 1-0	M03 2-1	J28 1-0	a23 2-2	D31 4-2	a14 1-1	D26 1-0		S03 1-1	F18 1-0	M10 1-3
22 TRANMERE R	M17 3-0	D26 3-2	O14 2-0	A27 1-1	m05 2-2	a14 0-3	S26 2-1	N26 2-3	F13 0-1	O29 1-1	M05 3-2	F03 0-1	S23 0-1	J30 1-0	M30 1-0	F24 0-0	D30 2-3	N12 2-2	m12 1-0	O17 2-1	J07 3-0		S10 2-1	a23 0-1
23 WREXHAM	F11 1-1	O18 0-1	S16 3-1	F25 3-0	D26 2-0	m12 4-2	m05 0-2	a14 0-1	D31 1-1	J14 1-2	O01 1-0	M24 1-4	O08 0-0	N05 2-3	N26 0-1	S03 2-2	M10 0-3	S06 5-1	M30 1-2	a20 0-3	O29 2-2	m21 5-1		F28 0-0
24 YORK C	D03 2-0	O01 4-0	M03 1-1	m07 3-0	S17 4-1	J31 1-0	O07 3-0	M06 5-2	F11 2-0	a08 1-1	a20 4-1	a28 2-0	D17 4-0	J02 2-1	F18 3-0	S06 2-0	O22 2-2	S03 2-0	J14 3-1	M24 2-0	N12 2-3	D27 1-1	N01 3-2	

LEAGUE TABLES

DIVISION 1

	P	W	D	L	F	A	W	D	L	F	A	Pts
Liverpool	42	14	5	2	50	12	8	9	4	23	20	80
Southampton	42	15	4	2	44	17	7	7	7	22	21	77
Nottingham F	42	14	4	3	47	17	8	4	9	29	28	74
Manchester U	42	14	3	4	43	18	6	11	4	28	23	74
QPR	42	14	4	3	37	12	8	3	10	30	25	73
Arsenal	42	10	5	6	41	29	8	4	9	33	31	63
Everton	42	9	9	3	21	12	7	5	9	23	30	62
Tottenham H	42	11	4	6	31	24	6	6	9	33	41	61
West Ham U	42	10	4	7	39	24	7	5	9	21	31	60
Aston Villa	42	14	3	4	34	22	3	6	12	25	39	60
Watford	42	9	7	5	36	31	7	2	12	32	46	57
Ipswich T	42	11	4	6	34	23	4	4	13	21	34	53
Sunderland	42	8	9	4	26	18	5	4	12	16	35	52
Norwich C	42	9	8	4	34	20	3	7	11	14	29	51
Leicester C	42	11	5	5	40	30	2	7	12	25	38	51
Luton T	42	7	5	9	30	33	7	4	10	23	33	51
WBA	42	10	4	7	30	25	4	5	12	18	37	51
Stoke C	42	11	4	6	30	23	2	7	12	14	40	50
Coventry C	42	8	5	8	33	33	5	6	10	24	44	50
Birmingham C	42	7	7	7	19	18	5	5	11	20	32	48
Notts Co	42	6	7	8	31	36	4	4	13	19	36	41
Wolves	42	4	8	9	15	28	2	3	16	12	52	29

DIVISION 2

	P	W	D	L	F	A	W	D	L	F	A	Pts
Chelsea	42	15	4	2	55	17	10	9	2	35	23	88
Sheffield W	42	16	4	1	47	16	10	6	5	25	18	88
Newcastle U	42	16	2	3	51	18	8	6	7	34	35	80
Manchester C	42	13	3	5	43	21	7	7	7	23	27	70
Grimsby T	42	13	6	2	36	15	6	7	8	24	32	70
Blackburn R	42	9	11	1	35	19	8	5	8	22	27	67
Carlisle U	42	10	9	2	29	13	6	7	8	19	28	64
Shrewsbury T	42	13	5	3	34	18	4	5	12	15	35	61
Brighton & HA	42	11	6	4	42	17	6	3	12	27	43	60
Leeds U	42	13	4	4	33	16	3	8	10	22	40	60
Fulham	42	9	6	6	35	24	6	6	9	25	29	57
Huddersfield T	42	8	6	7	27	20	6	9	6	29	29	57
Charlton A	42	13	4	4	40	26	3	5	13	13	38	57
Barnsley	42	9	6	6	33	23	6	1	14	24	30	52
Cardiff C	42	11	3	7	32	27	4	3	14	21	39	51
Portsmouth	42	8	3	10	46	32	6	4	11	27	32	49
Middlesbrough	42	9	8	4	26	18	3	5	13	15	29	49
Crystal P	42	8	5	8	18	18	4	6	11	24	34	47
Oldham A	42	10	6	5	33	27	3	2	16	14	46	47
Derby Co	42	9	5	7	26	26	2	4	15	10	46	42
Swansea C	42	7	4	10	20	28	0	4	17	16	57	29
Cambridge U	42	4	7	10	20	33	0	5	16	8	44	24

DIVISION 3

	P	W	D	L	F	A	W	D	L	F	A	Pts
Oxford U	46	17	5	1	58	22	11	6	6	33	28	95
Wimbledon	46	15	5	3	58	35	11	4	8	39	41	87
Sheffield U	46	14	7	2	56	18	10	4	9	30	35	83
Hull C	46	16	5	2	42	11	7	9	7	29	27	83
Bristol R	46	16	5	2	47	21	6	8	9	21	33	79
Walsall	46	14	4	5	44	22	8	5	10	24	39	75
Bradford C	46	11	9	3	46	30	9	2	12	27	35	71
Gillingham	46	13	4	6	50	29	7	6	10	24	40	70
Millwall	46	16	4	3	42	18	2	9	12	29	47	67
Bolton W	46	13	4	6	36	17	5	6	12	20	43	64
Orient	46	13	5	5	40	27	5	4	14	31	54	63
Burnley	46	12	5	6	52	25	4	9	10	24	36	62
Newport Co	46	11	9	3	35	27	5	5	13	23	48	62
Lincoln C	46	11	4	8	42	29	6	6	11	17	33	61
Wigan A	46	11	5	7	26	18	5	8	10	20	38	61
Preston NE	46	12	5	6	42	27	3	6	14	24	39	56
Bournemouth	46	11	5	7	38	27	5	2	16	25	46	55
Rotherham U	46	10	5	8	29	17	5	4	14	28	47	54
Plymouth A	46	11	8	4	38	17	2	4	17	18	45	51
Brentford	46	8	9	6	41	30	3	7	13	28	49	49
Scunthorpe U	46	9	9	5	40	31	0	10	13	14	42	46
Southend U	46	8	9	6	34	24	2	5	16	21	52	44
Port Vale	46	10	4	9	33	29	1	6	16	18	54	43
Exeter C	46	4	8	11	27	39	2	7	14	23	45	33

DIVISION 4

	P	W	D	L	F	A	W	D	L	F	A	Pts
York C	46	18	4	1	58	16	13	4	6	38	23	101
Doncaster R	46	15	6	2	46	22	9	7	7	36	32	85
Reading	46	17	6	0	51	14	5	10	8	33	42	82
Bristol C	46	18	3	2	51	17	6	7	10	19	27	82
Aldershot	46	14	6	3	49	29	8	3	12	27	40	75
Blackpool	46	15	4	4	47	19	6	5	12	23	33	72
Peterboro' U	46	15	5	3	52	16	3	9	11	20	32	68
Colchester U	46	14	7	2	45	14	3	9	11	24	39	67
Torquay U	46	13	7	3	32	18	5	6	12	27	46	67
Tranmere R	46	11	5	7	33	26	6	10	7	20	27	66
Hereford U	46	11	6	6	31	21	5	9	9	23	32	63
Stockport Co	46	12	5	6	34	25	5	6	12	26	39	62
Chesterfield	46	10	11	2	34	24	5	4	14	25	37	60
Darlington	46	13	4	6	31	19	4	4	15	18	31	59
Bury	46	9	7	7	34	32	6	7	10	27	32	59
Crewe A	46	10	8	5	35	27	6	3	14	21	40	59
Swindon T	46	11	7	5	34	23	4	6	13	24	33	58
Northampton T	46	10	8	5	32	32	3	6	14	21	46	53
Mansfield T	46	9	7	7	44	27	4	6	13	22	43	52
Wrexham	46	7	6	10	34	33	4	9	10	25	41	48
Halifax T	46	11	6	6	36	25	1	6	16	19	64	48
Rochdale	46	8	9	6	35	31	3	4	16	17	49	46
Hartlepool U	46	7	8	8	31	28	3	2	18	16	57	40
Chester C	46	7	5	11	23	35	0	8	15	22	47	34

Football League Records

Top scorers: Div 1, K.Dixon (Chelsea), G.Lineker (Leicester City) 24 goals; Div 2, J.Aldridge (Oxford United) 30 goals; Div 3, T.Tynan (Plymouth Argyle) 31 goals; Div 4, J.Clayton (Tranmere Rovers) 31 goals.

Everton's Graeme Sharp netted 21 times when the League Championship trophy moved across Stanley Park in 1985.

DIVISION 1

	ARSENAL	ASTON VILLA	CHELSEA	COVENTRY C	EVERTON	IPSWICH T	LEICESTER C	LIVERPOOL	LUTON T	MANCHESTER U	NEWCASTLE U	NORWICH C	NOTTINGHAM F	Q.P.R.	SHEFFIELD W	SOUTHAMPTON	STOKE C	SUNDERLAND	TOTTENHAM H	WATFORD	W.B.A.	WEST HAM U
1 ARSENAL		N10 1-1	A25 1-1	F02 2-1	O06 1-0	M19 1-1	M16 2-0	S08 3-1	D01 3-1	F23 0-1	S04 2-0	a06 2-0	a13 1-1	N17 1-0	a27 1-0	m06 1-0	S22 4-0	O20 3-2	J01 1-2	D22 1-1	D15 4-0	M02 2-1
2 ASTON VILLA	M13 0-0		S08 4-2	A25 1-0	M16 1-1	F02 2-1	M02 0-1	D15 0-0	m06 0-1	O06 3-0	D22 4-0	O20 2-2	S05 0-5	a27 5-2	a06 3-0	N17 2-2	M27 2-0	D01 1-0	S22 0-1	a24 1-1	J01 3-1	N03 0-0
3 CHELSEA	J19 1-1	a16 3-1		N03 6-2	A31 0-1	O27 2-0	S29 3-0	D01 3-1	m08 2-0	D29 1-3	F16 1-0	m14 1-2	J01 1-0	a06 1-0	m06 2-1	M09 0-2	D15 1-1	A27 1-0	a27 1-1	O13 2-3	N17 3-1	S15 3-0
4 COVENTRY C	S29 1-2	J19 0-3	F23 1-0		m26 4-1	N10 1-0	S01 2-0	m06 0-2	m23 1-0	S15 0-3	O13 1-1	A28 0-0	N17 1-3	M09 3-0	O27 1-0	D15 2-1	J01 4-0	a13 0-1	D01 1-1	M23 3-1	a27 2-1	D29 1-2
5 EVERTON	M23 2-0	O13 2-1	D22 3-4	S08 2-1		S04 1-1	N03 3-0	m23 1-0	J01 2-1	O27 5-0	J12 4-0	a27 3-0	D15 5-0	m06 2-0	D01 1-1	S22 2-2	N17 4-0	a06 4-1	A25 1-4	F02 4-0	a16 4-1	m08 3-0
6 IPSWICH T	S15 2-1	S29 3-0	M02 2-0	m14 0-0	D29 0-2		a23 2-0	a27 0-0	A28 1-1	S01 1-1	M23 1-1	J01 2-0	a06 1-0	O13 1-1	a13 1-2	D01 0-1	m06 5-1	D15 0-2	N17 0-3	N03 3-3	O20 2-0	m17 0-1
7 LEICESTER C	O13 1-4	O27 5-0	F02 1-1	D23 5-1	F23 1-2	S08 2-1		a06 0-1	D15 2-2	N10 2-3	A25 2-3	N17 2-0	a27 1-0	D01 4-0	M09 3-1	J01 1-2	J12 0-0	m06 2-0	a13 1-2	S05 1-1	S22 2-1	M23 1-0
8 LIVERPOOL	F12 3-0	m11 2-1	m04 4-3	D04 3-1	O20 0-1	N24 2-0	D26 1-2		D29 1-0	M31 0-1	a20 3-1	J19 4-0	M02 1-0	S01 1-1	S29 0-2	N10 1-1	F23 2-0	S15 1-1	M16 0-1	m17 4-3	O06 0-0	A27 3-0
9 LUTON T	m04 3-1	D08 1-0	S22 0-0	D26 2-0	m28 2-0	M30 3-1	m11 4-0	S04 1-2		a21 2-1	N03 2-2	a16 3-1	a24 1-2	M23 2-0	O13 1-2	S08 1-1	A25 2-0	M02 2-1	F02 2-2	O20 3-2	D18 1-2	N24 2-2
10 MANCHESTER U	N02 4-2	M23 4-0	S05 1-1	J12 0-1	M02 1-1	D22 3-0	a03 2-1	S22 1-1	N17 2-0		S08 5-0	D01 2-0	m06 2-0	D15 3-0	J01 1-2	a24 0-0	a06 5-0	a27 2-2	O20 1-0	A25 1-1	F02 2-0	O13 5-1
11 NEWCASTLE U	D29 1-3	S01 3-0	N10 2-1	a17 0-1	S15 2-3	O06 3-0	M20 1-4	N18 0-2	F23 1-0	F09 1-1		D15 1-1	O20 1-1	a13 1-0	A27 2-1	a27 2-1	D01 2-1	J01 3-1	m06 2-3	M02 3-1	a06 1-0	S29 1-1
12 NORWICH C	D26 1-0	M09 2-2	O06 0-0	M30 2-1	N24 4-2	a08 0-2	a20 1-3	A25 3-3	N10 3-0	m04 0-1	m11 0-0		F02 0-1	O27 2-0	a03 1-1	J12 1-0	S19 0-0	M16 1-3	D22 1-2	S22 3-2	S05 2-1	D08 1-0
13 NOTTINGHAM F	A29 2-0	D29 3-2	a10 2-0	a20 2-0	m11 1-0	D26 2-0	N25 2-1	O28 0-2	S16 3-1	D08 3-2	M09 0-0	S29 3-1		F09 2-0	M20 0-0	F23 2-0	O06 1-1	S01 3-1	N10 1-2	m04 1-1	M16 1-2	M30 1-2
14 Q.P.R.	a20 1-0	N24 2-0	D26 2-2	O20 2-1	D08 0-0	M16 3-0	m04 4-3	D21 0-2	O06 2-3	m11 1-3	S22 5-5	M02 2-2	S08 3-0		N10 0-0	F02 0-4	D04 2-0	F23 1-0	J12 2-2	M30 2-0	A25 3-1	a08 4-2
15 SHEFFIELD W	N25 2-1	D26 1-1	D08 1-1	M02 1-0	m04 0-1	S22 2-2	O20 5-0	F02 1-1	M16 1-1	a09 1-0	M30 4-2	N03 1-2	A25 3-1	a23 3-1		S04 2-1	D22 2-1	O06 2-2	S08 2-1	F24 1-1	J12 2-0	m11 2-1
16 SOUTHAMPTON	D08 1-0	a20 2-0	O20 1-0	m11 2-1	M30 1-2	m04 3-0	a09 3-1	m14 1-1	a02 1-0	A28 0-0	N24 1-0	S15 2-1	N03 1-0	S29 1-1	D29 0-3		M16 0-0	J29 1-0	O06 1-0	D26 1-2	M02 4-3	S01 2-3
17 STOKE C	M30 2-0	A27 1-3	m11 0-1	m17 0-1	a20 0-2	D08 0-2	S15 2-2	N03 0-1	a08 0-4	D26 2-1	m04 0-1	a24 2-3	M23 1-4	D29 0-2	S01 2-1	O13 1-3		S29 2-2	M02 0-1	N24 1-3	M12 0-0	O20 2-4
18 SUNDERLAND	M09 0-0	m04 0-4	M30 0-2	S22 0-0	D26 1-2	m11 1-2	D08 0-4	a03 0-3	O27 3-0	N24 3-2	a08 0-0	O13 2-1	D23 0-2	N03 3-0	a16 0-0	A25 3-1	F02 1-0		S04 1-0	M12 1-1	S08 1-1	a20 0-1
19 TOTTENHAM H	a17 0-2	M30 0-2	N24 1-1	m04 4-2	a03 1-2	a20 2-3	A27 2-2	O12 1-0	S29 4-2	M12 1-2	D08 3-1	S01 3-1	m17 1-0	S15 5-0	m14 2-0	M23 5-1	O27 4-0	D29 2-0		m11 1-5	N03 2-3	D26 2-2
20 WATFORD	S01 3-4	S15 3-3	M16 1-3	O06 0-1	S29 4-5	a16 3-1	D29 4-1	J01 1-1	M19 3-0	m13 5-1	O27 3-3	a13 2-0	D01 2-0	A28 1-1	N17 1-0	a06 1-1	a27 2-0	N10 3-1	D15 1-2		m07 0-2	a02 5-0
21 W.B.A.	m11 2-2	a08 1-0	a20 0-1	N24 5-2	A27 2-1	a03 1-2	M30 2-0	M23 0-5	S01 4-0	S29 1-2	D26 2-1	D29 0-1	O13 4-1	J26 0-0	S15 2-2	O27 0-0	N10 2-0	a24 1-0	F23 0-1	D08 2-1		m04 5-1
22 WEST HAM U	O27 3-1	F23 1-2	a13 1-1	S04 3-1	N10 0-1	A25 0-0	O06 3-1	m20 0-3	a27 0-0	M15 2-2	F02 1-1	m06 1-0	S22 0-0	J01 1-3	D15 0-0	D22 2-3	m14 5-1	N17 1-0	a06 1-1	S08 2-0	D01 0-2	

Oxford United's John Aldridge was a key man in their promotion to the First Division. Soon, however, Aldridge was sharing in Liverpool's continuing glory.

DIVISION 2

	BARNSLEY	BIRMINGHAM C	BLACKBURN R	BRIGHTON & HA	CARDIFF C	CARLISLE U	CHARLTON A	CRYSTAL P	FULHAM	GRIMSBY T	HUDDERSFIELD T	LEEDS U	MANCHESTER C	MIDDLESBROUGH	NOTTS CO	OLDHAM A	OXFORD U	PORTSMOUTH	SHEFFIELD U	SHREWSBURY T	WIMBLEDON	WOLVERHAMPTON W
1 BARNSLEY		a27 0-1	J01 1-1	M13 0-0	S15 2-0	A27 1-3	O27 1-0	M23 3-1	D01 1-0	a30 0-0	a13 2-1	O13 1-0	a06 0-0	F26 1-0	D29 0-0	S01 0-1	a02 3-0	F09 2-2	N13 1-0	N17 3-1	m06 0-0	S29 5-1
2 BIRMINGHAM C	N24 0-0		O13 0-2	M23 1-1	m04 2-0	S15 2-0	a20 2-1	a16 3-0	D29 2-2	D26 2-1	S29 1-0	m11 1-0	M19 0-0	D08 3-2	M09 2-1	M05 0-1	O27 0-0	S18 0-1	a08 4-1	N03 0-0	S01 4-2	M30 1-0
3 BLACKBURN R	a08 0-0	M16 2-1		N10 2-0	S18 2-1	S01 4-0	N24 3-0	a23 0-1	F09 2-1	S15 3-1	D29 1-3	D26 2-1	M02 0-1	a20 3-0	M30 1-0	O20 1-1	F23 1-1	m04 0-1	D08 3-1	O06 3-1	S29 2-0	m11 3-0
4 BRIGHTON & H.A.	O20 0-0	O06 2-0	M06 3-1		F09 1-0	F05 4-1	a08 2-1	S15 1-0	S29 2-0	D08 0-0	S01 0-1	a20 1-1	N03 0-0	N24 1-2	A28 2-1	M29 2-0	M16 0-0	D26 1-1	m11 1-0	M02 1-0	D29 2-1	m04 5-1
5 CARDIFF C	a23 3-0	D01 1-2	a13 1-2	S08 2-4		N17 2-1	A25 0-3	m06 0-3	M09 0-2	O27 2-4	a27 3-0	S12 2-1	S22 0-3	F02 2-1	M17 1-4	N10 2-2	a06 0-2	O06 1-2	D22 1-3	J01 0-0	D15 1-3	F23 0-0
6 CARLISLE U	M30 2-0	M12 2-1	D23 0-1	A25 0-3	a20 0-1		m03 1-1	O13 1-0	N20 3-0	M09 1-1	O27 0-1	F26 2-2	S08 0-0	D26 0-3	N24 1-0	m11 2-5	F02 0-1	D08 3-0	S22 1-1	S04 2-0	M23 6-1	a08 0-1
7 CHARLTON A	M02 5-3	N17 2-1	a27 1-0	J01 0-1	M05 1-4	N30 1-1		a06 1-1	O13 1-2	D29 4-1	A28 2-2	N03 2-3	D15 1-3	M22 1-0	S01 3-0	S15 2-1	m07 3-3	S29 2-2	a16 0-0	O20 1-1	a13 0-1	M12 1-0
8 CRYSTAL P	O07 0-1	S08 0-2	A25 1-1	a02 1-1	D09 1-1	M17 2-1	D26 2-1		O27 2-2	m11 0-2	N10 1-1	S22 3-1	F02 1-2	m04 1-0	a08 1-0	N25 3-0	F05 1-0	a20 2-1	M30 1-3	N06 2-2	F24 0-5	M09 0-0
9 FULHAM	m04 1-1	S04 0-1	S08 3-2	F02 2-0	O20 3-2	F23 3-2	M16 0-0	M02 2-2		a20 2-1	O06 2-1	M30 0-2	D22 3-2	S22 2-1	m11 1-0	D07 3-1	F19 1-0	a08 1-3	D26 1-0	A25 1-2	N10 3-1	N24 1-2
10 GRIMSBY T	A25 1-0	a05 1-0	J12 1-1	m07 2-4	M02 6-3	O20 1-0	S04 2-1	D15 1-3	N17 2-4		J01 5-1	S08 0-2	a13 4-1	D22 3-1	F23 2-0	O06 4-1	S22 1-2	M16 2-3	F02 0-2	D01 2-1	a27 2-1	N10 5-1
11 HUDDERSFIELD T	S22 1-1	F02 0-1	S04 1-1	D22 1-2	N24 2-1	M02 2-0	M30 2-1	F16 2-0	M23 2-2	a09 0-0		O20 1-0	J12 0-2	N03 3-1	a20 1-2	D26 2-1	A25 0-3	m11 0-2	m13 2-2	S08 1-5	O13 2-1	D08 3-1
12 LEEDS U	M16 2-0	D15 0-1	a06 0-0	N17 1-0	D29 1-1	N10 1-1	F23 1-0	a13 4-1	A27 2-0	F09 0-0	M09 0-0		J01 1-1	O27 2-0	J19 5-0	S29 6-0	a27 1-0	S15 0-1	O06 1-1	m06 1-0	D01 5-2	S01 3-2
13 MANCHESTER C	D26 1-1	N10 1-0	O27 2-1	F23 2-0	M30 2-2	F09 1-3	m11 5-1	S29 2-1	S01 2-3	A27 3-0	S15 1-0	a08 1-2		M09 1-0	D08 2-0	m04 0-0	O06 1-0	N24 2-2	a20 2-0	M16 4-0	J19 3-0	D29 4-0
14 MIDDLESBROUGH	N10 0-0	m06 0-0	N17 1-2	a27 2-1	S29 3-2	a06 1-2	O06 1-0	D01 1-1	a13 2-0	S01 1-5	F23 2-2	M02 0-0	O20 2-1		F09 0-1	F05 1-2	J01 0-1	J19 0-0	M16 1-0	D14 1-1	S18 2-4	S15 1-1
15 NOTTS CO	S04 0-2	O20 1-3	S22 0-3	a14 1-2	O14 0-2	a27 3-0	J19 0-0	J01 0-0	D16 2-1	N03 1-1	N17 0-2	A25 1-2	m06 3-2	S08 3-2		M02 0-0	D01 2-0	a02 1-3	J12 0-0	F02 1-3	a06 2-3	M23 4-1
16 OLDHAM A	D23 2-1	A25 0-1	M09 2-0	S22 1-0	F16 0-1	D15 2-3	J12 2-1	a27 1-0	m06 2-1	M23 2-0	a06 2-2	F02 1-1	D01 0-2	O02 2-0	O27 3-2		N17 0-0	N03 0-2	S08 2-2	a13 0-1	J01 0-1	O13 3-2
17 OXFORD U	m11 4-0	M02 0-3	N03 2-1	O13 2-1	D26 4-0	S29 4-0	D08 5-0	D29 5-0	S15 3-2	M30 1-0	a17 3-0	N24 5-2	M23 3-0	a08 1-0	m04 1-1	a20 5-2		S01 1-1	O20 5-1	a24 1-0	M13 4-0	S19 3-1
18 PORTSMOUTH	S08 0-0	a13 1-3	D01 2-2	a06 1-1	M23 0-0	m06 3-1	F02 0-1	N17 1-1	J01 4-4	O13 3-2	D15 3-2	M12 3-1	a27 1-2	A25 1-0	N10 3-1	F23 5-1	D22 2-1		O02 2-1	S22 3-0	M09 1-0	O27 0-1
19 SHEFFIELD U	F23 3-1	J01 3-4	m06 1-3	D15 1-1	S01 2-1	a13 0-0	N10 1-1	S18 1-2	a06 0-1	S29 2-3	D01 0-2	M23 2-1	N17 0-0	O13 0-3	S15 3-0	F12 2-0	M09 1-1	D29 4-1		a27 0-1	O27 3-0	J26 2-2
20 SHREWSBURY T	a20 2-0	F23 1-0	M23 3-0	O27 0-0	a09 0-0	D29 4-2	M09 1-1	S01 4-1	J26 3-1	m04 4-1	M12 5-1	D08 2-3	O13 1-0	m11 0-2	S29 4-2	S18 3-0	N10 2-2	M30 0-0	N24 3-3		S15 1-2	D26 2-1
21 WIMBLEDON	D08 3-3	D22 1-2	F02 1-1	O02 1-0	m11 2-1	O06 3-0	S22 1-3	N04 3-2	a16 1-1	N24 1-1	a30 0-1	m04 2-2	A25 2-2	M30 1-1	D26 3-2	a09 1-0	S08 1-3	O20 3-2	M02 5-0	M27 4-1		a20 1-1
22 WOLVERHAMPTON W	F02 0-1	S22 0-2	D15 0-3	D01 0-1	N03 3-0	J01 0-2	S08 1-0	O20 2-1	a27 0-4	M05 0-1	m06 2-1	D22 0-2	S04 2-0	J12 0-0	O06 2-3	M16 0-3	a13 1-2	M02 0-0	A25 2-2	a06 0-1	N17 3-3	

Season 1984-85

DIVISION 3

	BOLTON W	BOURNEMOUTH	BRADFORD C	BRENTFORD	BRISTOL C	BRISTOL R	BURNLEY	CAMBRIDGE U	DERBY CO	DONCASTER R	GILLINGHAM	HULL C	LINCOLN C	MILLWALL	NEWPORT CO	ORIENT	PLYMOUTH A	PRESTON N.E.	READING	ROTHERHAM U	SWANSEA C	WALSALL	WIGAN A	YORK C
1 BOLTON W		O13 2-1	m06 0-2	a27 1-1	M05 1-4	A25 0-1	M02 1-3	D22 0-0	J12 3-0	F02 3-1	N24 1-2	S08 0-0	N03 1-0	D15 2-0	a13 3-1	J01 0-0	S22 7-2	O20 4-0	M23 1-2	D26 2-0	F16 0-0	O02 3-1	a06 1-0	N06 2-1
2 BOURNEMOUTH	M16 4-0		a26 4-1	N24 1-0	D15 2-1	F02 1-0	O06 1-1	a06 0-0	A25 1-0	S22 1-3	J01 2-0	J12 1-1	M09 3-1	m08 1-2	m13 3-0	D21 1-0	J26 1-0	O27 2-0	F23 0-3	S08 3-0	O02 1-2	a13 4-1	N06 1-0	O23 4-0
3 BRADFORD C	D29 2-1	D01 1-0		M23 5-4	O20 1-1	F13 2-0	a20 3-2	A25 2-0	N10 3-1	D26 0-1	M02 1-1	O03 2-0	m11 0-0	N28 3-1	S22 1-0	F02 4-1	M30 1-0	M06 3-0	m04 2-5	a08 1-1	J26 1-1	S08 1-1	J12 4-2	O13 1-0
4 BRENTFORD	D01 2-1	a20 0-0	O06 0-1		F23 1-2	D26 0-3	M05 2-1	F02 2-0	M30 1-1	O02 1-1	O20 5-2	m11 2-1	N10 2-2	m19 1-1	J26 2-5	A25 0-1	a08 3-1	m04 3-1	D29 2-1	a23 3-0	S22 3-0	M27 3-1	S08 2-0	O27 2-1
5 BRISTOL C	O23 3-2	m04 2-0	M09 2-0	N03 1-1		N10 3-0	D29 1-0	J26 3-0	F26 3-0	M30 1-0	O13 2-0	a08 2-0	D01 2-1	M02 0-1	a30 2-1	S22 3-2	D26 4-3	a20 4-0	m11 2-3	O02 0-1	S08 2-2	F02 1-2	A25 2-0	M23 1-0
6 BRISTOL R	J29 1-2	S29 1-0	S18 2-0	a06 3-0	a13 1-0		a16 4-0	J01 2-1	O06 2-1	O20 1-1	m07 3-2	O27 1-1	a02 0-0	N24 1-1	D15 2-0	a27 0-1	F23 1-0	S01 3-0	S15 1-0	M16 1-0	D22 4-2	a23 0-0	M05 2-0	m14 1-1
7 BURNLEY	O27 3-2	M23 1-1	N24 1-2	O23 3-1	m06 0-1	S08 0-0		a13 2-0	a23 0-1	M12 0-1	N06 0-1	S22 1-1	O13 1-2	a27 1-1	O02 2-0	F16 1-1	A25 1-1	F23 2-0	M09 0-2	F02 7-0	D15 1-1	D22 1-2	J01 1-2	a06 1-1
8 CAMBRIDGE U	m11 2-3	D26 1-0	a23 0-4	S29 1-2	S15 2-3	a08 0-2	N10 2-3		D01 0-2	M05 1-1	a02 1-2	M30 1-3	a30 0-2	S01 1-0	F23 1-2	M16 2-3	m04 1-1	S18 0-3	a20 0-2	D29 0-2	O27 0-2	O06 0-1	O19 1-1	F09 0-4
9 DERBY CO	S01 3-2	J30 2-3	a13 0-0	N07 1-0	S19 1-0	M23 0-0	S15 2-2	a27 1-0		N28 3-1	a06 1-0	O20 3-1	S29 2-0	a03 1-2	D22 3-3	D15 1-0	O13 3-1	M13 2-0	a17 4-1	M02 1-1	m06 1-1	M06 2-0	N24 2-2	J01 1-0
10 DONCASTER R	S29 2-0	F09 3-0	a06 0-3	F16 2-2	N06 1-1	M08 2-2	A31 2-0	O23 3-2	F22 2-1		D22 0-1	M16 1-2	S14 3-2	S18 0-1	a27 3-2	m06 1-1	O26 4-3	M26 1-2	J19 0-4	O07 0-1	N24 4-1	J01 4-1	D14 1-1	a14 3-0
11 GILLINGHAM	a20 2-3	a09 3-2	O27 2-2	M09 2-0	M16 1-3	D29 4-1	M29 1-1	S08 3-0	F26 3-2	m11 2-1		F26 1-0	m04 3-2	O06 1-4	A25 1-1	J12 2-0	O02 3-3	D01 4-0	O23 4-1	N10 2-1	F02 1-1	S22 3-0	m17 5-1	F23 1-0
12 HULL C	a02 2-2	S01 3-0	F16 0-2	D22 4-0	J01 2-1	M02 2-0	F09 2-0	N06 2-1	M09 3-2	O13 3-2	S18 2-0		M19 1-0	a06 2-1	N24 2-0	a13 5-1	M23 2-2	S15 1-2	S29 0-0	N03 0-0	O23 4-1	D15 1-0	a27 3-1	m06 0-2
13 LINCOLN C	F23 2-0	O20 0-0	D22 1-2	a13 1-1	a27 1-1	S22 1-2	M16 3-1	N27 1-1	F02 0-0	a24 0-2	D15 2-0	A25 0-0		M06 0-1	N07 2-2	a06 0-0	S08 2-2	O06 4-0	O27 5-1	M13 3-3	J01 1-0	m06 0-0	F16 1-0	N24 2-1
14 MILLWALL	m04 5-2	D29 2-1	F23 4-0	O13 2-0	O27 1-1	a20 1-0	D01 2-1	a16 2-1	O02 2-1	a30 2-1	M23 2-1	D18 2-2	O23 2-0		F02 2-0	S09 1-0	m11 2-0	N10 3-0	a09 0-0	M29 0-0	A25 2-0	J26 0-0	S22 4-1	M09 1-0
15 NEWPORT CO	N10 3-2	S18 1-1	a16 0-1	N27 2-0	S01 0-0	m04 1-1	a02 2-1	N03 1-2	m11 1-3	D01 2-1	M12 0-3	a20 0-1	M30 2-1	S29 3-2		O20 2-0	D29 1-0	a08 3-3	D26 1-2	D08 0-2	O13 2-0	M02 1-2	M23 1-1	M20 1-1
16 ORIENT	a09 4-3	m11 0-0	S29 1-0	a16 0-1	F09 0-1	N30 1-4	S18 0-2	O13 2-2	m04 2-2	D29 2-1	S01 2-4	N10 4-5	D26 1-0	J29 1-0	M09 1-1		O23 3-0	a30 0-0	M30 0-0	a20 0-1	M23 4-2	N03 0-3	M02 1-1	S15 1-3
17 PLYMOUTH A	F09 2-0	S15 0-0	N06 0-0	J01 1-1	a05 1-0	N03 3-2	M26 2-2	D15 2-0	M16 0-1	M02 2-1	M19 1-1	O06 0-1	a16 2-0	D22 3-1	m06 1-0	M05 1-1		S29 6-4	S01 1-2	O20 1-0	a27 1-2	N24 1-3	a13 1-0	S19 1-1
18 PRESTON N.E.	M09 1-0	M02 2-1	O23 1-4	D15 1-1	N24 3-2	J12 2-2	N03 3-3	F26 3-1	S08 2-1	A25 2-0	a27 0-0	a23 1-4	M23 0-1	a13 2-1	J01 1-1	O02 0-1	F02 1-2		O13 0-2	S22 0-3	N06 3-2	a06 1-0	m06 2-5	D19 2-4
19 READING	O06 3-1	N03 0-2	D15 0-3	m06 0-0	D22 1-0	J26 3-2	O20 5-1	N24 3-1	S22 0-0	S08 1-4	m14 0-2	F02 4-2	M02 1-1	J01 2-2	a06 0-1	N07 1-1	a24 1-1	M16 3-0		A25 1-0	a13 0-1	m01 1-1	O03 0-1	a27 1-2
20 ROTHERHAM U	S15 3-1	J19 1-0	J01 1-2	S18 1-1	F16 2-1	O13 3-3	S29 3-2	m06 0-1	O27 2-0	M23 2-3	a13 1-0	F23 1-1	S01 0-0	M16 0-0	O23 1-0	N24 2-1	M09 0-2	F09 3-0	M26 3-0		a06 0-1	a27 0-1	D22 3-3	D15 4-1
21 SWANSEA C	S18 2-1	F12 0-0	S15 1-2	F09 3-2	m17 0-0	m11 3-2	m04 0-1	M01 2-2	D29 1-5	a19 3-1	S29 0-1	M05 0-2	a09 2-2	M26 1-2	M17 0-3	O06 3-1	D01 0-2	M30 4-1	N10 1-2	D26 1-0		O20 1-2	N03 2-2	S01 1-3
22 WALSALL	M19 1-0	N10 0-0	a02 0-0	S01 0-1	S29 4-1	M30 1-2	m11 2-3	M23 5-0	O23 0-0	a08 1-0	a16 0-1	m04 0-1	D29 0-0	S15 3-3	O27 1-1	F23 4-2	a20 0-3	D26 2-1	S18 3-1	D01 0-2	M09 3-0		O13 0-0	F26 3-0
23 WIGAN A	D26 1-0	M30 1-2	S01 1-0	J19 1-1	a23 2-2	O23 1-0	a08 2-0	M09 3-3	a20 2-0	m03 5-2	S15 0-1	D01 1-1	S18 1-0	F09 0-1	O06 1-1	O27 4-2	N10 1-0	D29 2-0	m13 1-1	m11 2-1	a30 2-0	M17 1-2		S29 1-2
24 YORK C	M29 0-3	M05 4-1	M17 1-2	M02 1-0	O06 0-2	O02 1-0	D26 4-0	S22 3-2	a08 1-1	N11 3-1	N03 7-1	D29 1-2	a20 2-1	O20 1-1	S08 2-0	a02 2-1	F12 0-0	m11 0-1	D01 2-2	m03 3-0	J12 1-0	A25 1-1	F02 2-0	

DIVISION 4

	ALDERSHOT	BLACKPOOL	BURY	CHESTER C	CHESTERFIELD	COLCHESTER U	CREWE A	DARLINGTON	EXETER C	HALIFAX T	HARTLEPOOL U	HEREFORD U	MANSFIELD T	NORTHAMPTON T	PETERBOROUGH U	PORT VALE	ROCHDALE	SCUNTHORPE U	SOUTHEND U	STOCKPORT CO	SWINDON T	TORQUAY U	TRANMERE R	WREXHAM
1 ALDERSHOT		M23 1-0	O13 0-1	S01 1-2	J05 1-1	a23 1-0	D26 1-1	S29 3-4	S15 1-1	a02 2-0	D01 1-0	m11 0-1	O23 0-0	M09 0-0	S18 0-0	N10 1-0	m17 5-0	F23 1-2	O27 6-2	M30 2-1	a20 0-1	a09 1-0	m04 3-2	D29 2-1
2 BLACKPOOL	O06 1-0		O20 0-0	S29 3-1	a02 1-0	M26 1-1	a09 6-1	S15 0-0	S01 3-0	J05 1-1	D29 2-1	a20 2-0	D01 1-0	O27 2-1	M30 4-2	S18 1-1	D26 3-0	M16 1-0	F23 1-0	N10 4-1	F19 1-0	m04 3-3	M05 1-2	m11 0-0
3 BURY	a30 2-1	M09 1-0		a23 4-1	S29 0-0	S15 4-3	N10 2-2	M19 1-0	F09 2-2	S01 3-0	a08 1-0	O23 2-1	a20 0-0	F23 3-1	m11 1-1	D26 4-0	M29 2-2	O27 0-1	O06 2-0	M26 2-1	S18 2-0	D01 3-1	D29 3-0	m04 2-3
4 CHESTER C	M27 2-0	F12 0-0	S08 2-3		O27 1-1	O20 1-2	M06 0-2	F23 5-2	M16 1-3	O06 2-0	m11 1-0	m01 2-1	M30 0-3	S22 1-0	a09 1-3	a20 2-0	D11 0-1	A25 1-1	J26 5-1	m04 2-1	J30 2-0	N10 0-1	O03 2-4	D26 2-1
5 CHESTERFIELD	A25 2-1	S22 2-1	F02 0-1	M02 3-1		N03 1-1	m04 3-1	O06 0-0	O20 5-1	M16 3-0	F12 0-0	O02 3-1	D26 0-0	J12 2-1	D29 2-0	M05 0-0	m11 0-0	J26 1-0	S08 2-1	D01 3-0	a09 1-0	a20 1-0	N10 4-2	M30 2-1
6 COLCHESTER U	S22 2-0	S08 1-1	J26 1-0	M08 1-1	F22 3-1		m10 4-1	M15 1-2	O16 3-4	O26 1-3	N09 1-0	D26 2-2	F26 2-1	F01 4-1	D01 3-1	D28 3-2	a19 1-1	a02 1-1	A25 3-3	O23 3-0	m03 1-1	O02 2-1	M29 2-1	a08 4-1
7 CREWE A	a06 1-1	J01 0-2	a13 1-0	O23 2-0	D15 1-1	D21 1-4		m06 2-2	a27 0-0	N23 0-1	F01 2-0	S08 0-3	J26 1-1	N06 3-2	F23 2-1	M22 0-0	O27 3-1	F16 1-1	O02 0-2	M09 2-1	O13 3-2	A25 3-0	F26 1-3	S22 3-0
8 DARLINGTON	F02 1-1	m01 0-4	A25 1-1	N03 2-1	M23 1-3	O13 4-0	M12 2-1		M02 2-1	M09 2-0	O02 0-1	M29 1-1	a08 3-1	S08 4-0	a20 2-1	m04 1-1	O23 1-0	S22 2-1	a02 3-1	m11 3-1	D02 1-0	m14 1-0	D26 2-1	N10 2-1
9 EXETER C	J26 3-0	a17 1-1	S22 0-2	O13 1-1	M09 0-1	M23 1-5	D01 0-2	O27 1-1		F23 1-0	M30 3-2	D29 0-0	O03 0-0	A25 5-0	D15 0-1	a08 2-1	N10 1-1	S08 2-1	F01 2-1	a20 0-2	O24 1-1	D26 4-3	m11 0-1	F13 2-0
10 HALIFAX T	S08 1-2	A25 0-2	J12 4-1	M22 0-4	O13 1-3	M01 0-0	a19 1-1	O19 0-1	M26 2-3		D26 2-3	m03 2-1	N10 1-0	F26 1-0	M05 0-0	N30 2-1	a08 0-2	F01 1-2	S21 1-0	a23 2-1	m10 2-1	M30 0-1	F12 2-1	F16 1-2
11 HARTLEPOOL U	a27 1-0	m06 0-2	J02 0-1	D22 2-1	S19 1-0	a13 2-1	S29 3-0	F17 1-2	N05 1-1	a06 0-1		O13 2-2	O27 0-0	D15 0-0	F09 0-3	J19 2-2	S15 0-2	N24 3-2	O24 2-1	a03 5-1	S01 2-2	M09 3-1	M23 2-4	F23 2-0
12 HEREFORD U	D23 2-1	N24 2-1	M06 5-3	S19 0-0	M20 0-1	a06 2-1	a24 3-2	N07 0-1	m06 1-2	D15 3-0	M16 2-1		O06 3-0	a27 1-1	S01 1-0	S29 1-0	a03 1-2	a13 1-0	J01 3-0	S15 2-0	a17 0-3	F23 1-0	O20 2-1	O27 2-1
13 MANSFIELD T	M06 1-2	a27 1-1	N24 0-2	N07 2-0	a06 0-0	S19 0-1	S15 0-2	J01 2-0	a03 2-2	a13 2-1	M02 2-0	M23 1-1		D22 2-0	M27 0-0	M13 1-1	S01 5-1	a24 0-1	m06 1-0	a17 1-0	S29 0-0	O13 1-0	N03 0-0	O20 1-0
14 NORTHAMPTON T	O20 4-0	M02 0-1	N03 0-1	M19 0-2	S01 1-3	S29 1-3	M30 1-3	a23 2-1	J05 5-2	S15 0-1	a15 2-0	D01 0-3	a30 1-0		D26 0-3	a17 1-0	S18 0-0	O06 0-2	M17 1-2	a09 4-0	N10 4-0	D29 3-1	a20 2-0	M05 0-4
15 PETERBOROUGH U	a17 1-2	N07 2-0	D19 1-4	J01 3-1	m06 0-0	a27 0-1	N03 2-1	N24 1-1	m04 0-0	O24 2-0	S22 3-1	J12 1-1	S08 1-0	a02 0-0		M02 0-0	M09 1-1	O03 3-1	a13 1-4	O13 3-1	M23 0-1	F02 1-0	A25 1-0	J26 2-1
16 PORT VALE	a13 1-2	a22 1-1	a06 0-0	N23 0-0	O22 0-0	m06 3-2	O06 2-0	D15 0-2	J01 5-1	a27 3-1	S08 1-1	F02 3-1	A25 0-1	O01 0-3	O27 3-1		M16 3-1	D22 1-1	N05 4-1	F22 3-2	M09 2-0	J26 2-2	S22 2-1	M25 0-0
17 ROCHDALE	O02 1-2	a06 1-1	N06 1-1	a27 1-2	D21 3-1	N24 1-1	M02 1-3	M05 1-2	a13 2-0	J01 2-0	a30 4-3	A25 0-1	m14 2-1	F16 3-0	O20 2-1	O13 1-2		m06 3-3	D15 2-2	m08 0-0	N03 0-1	S22 0-0	F02 2-1	S08 0-2
18 SCUNTHORPE U	N03 2-1	O13 1-1	M02 2-2	M12 2-1	S15 2-4	A31 2-2	S18 2-3	F08 0-1	M19 7-1	S28 4-0	a19 2-0	N09 1-1	m04 2-2	M22 2-1	F12 2-1	m10 3-3	F26 4-2		M08 2-1	D26 1-0	M29 6-2	O23 2-0	a09 5-2	N30 5-2
19 SOUTHEND U	M02 1-0	N03 1-4	M23 3-3	S14 1-1	a23 0-1	J29 2-5	D08 3-1	S10 1-1	S28 1-0	F08 2-1	M04 1-1	a08 0-0	D29 1-3	O13 2-1	N10 2-1	M29 1-1	m03 0-2	O19 1-1		S17 1-1	D26 3-2	m11 1-0	D01 2-3	a19 0-1
20 STOCKPORT CO	F25 6-0	D07 1-3	O01 2-0	D14 5-1	a27 0-1	M04 1-0	O19 0-1	D21 0-0	N24 1-0	m06 0-3	A25 4-1	M11 2-1	S22 1-1	J01 4-2	M16 1-1	N03 3-1	O05 1-1	a06 2-0	F15 1-2		M01 2-1	a01 1-2	S07 0-2	F01 2-2
21 SWINDON T	N24 2-1	O02 4-1	M12 1-0	m06 4-4	J01 4-0	D15 2-1	M16 1-1	a28 1-0	M05 2-0	D22 2-1	M31 2-1	S22 0-3	F02 1-0	a13 2-0	O07 1-1	O20 0-1	F23 2-1	N06 0-0	a06 2-0	O27 4-0		S08 1-3	J26 2-1	A25 2-1
22 TORQUAY U	J01 1-3	D15 0-2	a27 0-2	a13 2-0	N24 0-1	a16 1-1	J05 0-0	S18 1-1	a06 1-1	N06 1-1	O20 0-1	N03 1-0	M19 1-0	m06 0-2	S29 0-0	S15 1-3	F09 1-0	M05 0-0	D22 2-2	S01 0-0	F26 0-0		M02 1-1	O06 4-3
23 TRANMERE R	D15 4-3	O23 3-0	m06 3-2	a16 1-0	a13 0-1	N06 3-1	S01 3-1	a06 3-0	D21 3-2	S17 1-0	O06 1-2	M08 0-1	F22 0-0	N23 1-2	J05 4-0	a01 4-1	S29 3-1	J01 2-0	a26 2-0	a29 3-0	S14 0-2	O27 3-1		M16 3-1
24 WREXHAM	m06 1-0	D22 1-2	D15 3-0	a06 2-0	a16 2-0	J01 2-2	a02 1-3	a13 1-1	S11 2-0	M12 0-1	N03 1-1	M02 1-1	M09 2-2	O16 0-3	S15 1-3	S01 1-1	a23 2-0	a27 2-1	N24 1-2	S29 3-4	J05 4-0	M23 2-0	O13 4-0	

LEAGUE TABLES

DIVISION 1

	P	W	D	L	F	A	W	D	L	F	A	Pts
Everton	42	16	3	2	58	17	12	3	6	30	26	90
Liverpool	42	12	4	5	36	19	10	7	4	32	16	77
Tottenham H	42	11	3	7	46	31	12	5	4	32	20	77
Manchester U	42	13	6	2	47	13	9	4	8	30	34	76
Southampton	42	13	4	4	29	18	6	7	8	27	29	68
Chelsea	42	13	3	5	38	20	5	9	7	25	28	66
Arsenal	42	14	5	2	37	14	5	4	12	24	35	66
Sheffield W	42	12	7	2	39	21	5	7	9	19	24	65
Nottingham F	42	13	4	4	35	18	6	3	12	21	30	64
Aston Villa	42	10	7	4	34	20	5	4	12	26	40	56
Watford	42	10	5	6	48	30	4	8	9	33	41	55
WBA	42	11	4	6	36	23	5	3	13	22	39	55
Luton T	42	12	5	4	40	22	3	4	14	17	39	54
Newcastle U	42	11	4	6	33	26	2	9	10	22	44	52
Leicester C	42	10	4	7	39	25	5	2	14	26	48	51
West Ham U	42	7	8	6	27	23	6	4	11	24	45	51
Ipswich T	42	8	7	6	27	20	5	4	12	19	37	50
Coventry C	42	11	3	7	29	22	4	2	15	18	42	50
QPR	42	11	6	4	41	30	2	5	14	12	42	50
Norwich C	42	9	6	6	28	24	4	4	13	18	40	49
Sunderland	42	7	6	8	20	26	3	4	14	20	36	40
Stoke C	42	3	3	15	18	41	0	5	16	6	50	17

DIVISION 2

	P	W	D	L	F	A	W	D	L	F	A	Pts
Oxford U	42	18	2	1	62	15	7	7	7	22	21	84
Birmingham C	42	12	6	3	30	15	13	1	7	29	18	82
Manchester C	42	14	4	3	42	16	7	7	7	24	24	74
Portsmouth	42	11	6	4	39	25	9	8	4	30	25	74
Blackburn R	42	14	3	4	38	15	7	7	7	28	26	73
Brighton & HA	42	13	6	2	31	11	7	6	8	23	23	72
Leeds U	42	12	7	2	37	11	7	5	9	29	32	69
Shrewsbury T	42	12	6	3	45	22	6	5	10	21	31	65
Fulham	42	13	3	5	35	26	6	5	10	33	38	65
Grimsby T	42	13	1	7	47	32	5	7	9	25	32	62
Barnsley	42	11	7	3	27	12	3	9	9	15	30	58
Wimbledon	42	9	8	4	40	29	7	2	12	31	46	58
Huddersfield T	42	9	5	7	28	29	6	5	10	24	35	55
Oldham A	42	10	4	7	27	23	5	4	12	22	44	53
Crystal P	42	8	7	6	25	27	4	5	12	21	38	48
Carlisle U	42	8	5	8	27	23	5	3	13	23	44	47
Charlton A	42	8	7	6	34	30	3	5	13	17	33	45
Sheffield U	42	7	6	8	31	28	3	8	10	23	38	44
Middlesbrough	42	6	8	7	22	26	4	2	15	19	31	40
Notts Co	42	6	5	10	25	32	4	2	15	20	41	37
Cardiff C	42	5	3	13	24	42	4	5	12	23	37	35
Wolves	42	5	4	12	18	32	3	5	13	19	47	33

DIVISION 3

	P	W	D	L	F	A	W	D	L	F	A	Pts
Bradford C	46	15	6*	2	44	23	13	4	6	33	22	94
Millwall	46	18	5	0	44	12	8	7	8	29	30	90
Hull C	46	16	4	3	46	20	9	8	6	32	29	87
Gillingham	46	15	5	3	54	29	10	3	10	26	33	83
Bristol C	46	17	2	4	46	19	7	7	9	28	28	81
Bristol R	46	15	6	2	37	13	6	6	11	29	35	75
Derby Co	46	14	7	2	40	20	5	6	12	25	34	70
York C	46	13	5	5	42	22	7	4	12	28	35	69
Reading	46	8	7	8	31	29	11	5	7	37	33	69
Bournemouth	46	16	3	4	42	16	3	8	12	15	30	68
Walsall	46	9	7	7	33	22	9	6	8	25	30	67
Rotherham U	46	11	6	6	36	24	7	5	11	19	31	65
Brentford	46	13	5	5	42	27	3	9	11	20	37	62
Doncaster R	46	11	5	7	42	33	6	3	14	30	41	59
Plymouth A	46	11	7	5	33	23	4	7	12	29	42	59
Wigan A	46	12	6	5	36	22	3	8	12	24	42	59
Bolton W	46	12	5	6	38	22	4	1	18	31	53	54
Newport Co	46	9	6	8	30	30	4	7	12	25	37	52
Lincoln C	46	8	11	4	32	20	3	7*	13	18	31	51
Swansea C	46	7	5	11	31	39	5	6	12	22	41	47
Burnley	46	6	8	9	30	24	5	5	13	30	49	46
Orient	46	7	7	9	30	36	4	6	13	21	40	46
Preston NE	46	9	5	9	33	41	4	2	17	18	59	46
Cambridge U	46	2	3	18	17	48	2	6	15	20	47	21

* Includes one match abandoned at 0-0 after 40 minutes. Result stands.

DIVISION 4

	P	W	D	L	F	A	W	D	L	F	A	Pts
Chesterfield	46	16	6	1	40	13	10	7	6	24	22	91
Blackpool	46	15	7	1	42	15	9	7	7	31	24	86
Darlington	46	16	4	3	41	22	8	9	6	25	27	85
Bury	46	15	6	2	46	20	9	6	8	30	30	84
Hereford U	46	16	2	5	38	21	6	9	8	27	26	77
Tranmere R	46	17	1	5	50	21	7	2	14	33	45	75
Colchester U	46	13	7	3	49	29	7	7	9	38	36	74
Swindon T	46	16	4	3	42	21	5	5	13	20	37	72
Scunthorpe U	46	14	6	3	61	33	5	8	10	22	29	71
Crewe A	46	10	7	6	32	28	8	5	10	33	41	66
Peterboro' U	46	11	7	5	29	21	5	7	11	25	32	62
Port Vale	46	11	8	4	39	24	3	10	10	22	35	60
Aldershot	46	11	6	6	33	20	6	2	15	23	43	59
Mansfield T	46	10	8	5	25	15	3	10	10	16	23	57
Wrexham	46	10	6	7	39	27	5	3	15	28	43	54
Chester C	46	11	3	9	35	30	4	6	13	25	42	54
Rochdale	46	8	7	8	33	30	5	7	11	22	39	53
Exeter C	46	9	7	7	30	27	4	7	12	27	52	53
Hartlepool U	46	10	6	7	34	29	4	4	15	20	38	52
Southend U	46	8	8	7	30	34	5	3	15	28	49	50
Halifax T	46	9	3	11	26	32	6	2	15	16	37	50
Stockport C	46	11	5	7	40	26	2	3	18	18	53	47
Northampton T	46	10	1	12	32	32	4	4	15	21	42	47
Torquay U	46	5	11	7	18	24	4	3	16	20	39	41

Football League Records

Top scorers: Div 1, G.Lineker (Everton) 30 goals; Div 2, K.Drinkell (Norwich City) 22 goals; Div 3, T.Senior (Reading) 27 goals; Div 4, S.Taylor (Rochdale), R.Cadette (Southend United) 25 goals.

South African-born Craig Johnston, signed from Australian soccer, was an individualist whose style was harnessed to the Reds' team by manager Kenny Dalglish.

DIVISION 1

	ARSENAL	ASTON VILLA	BIRMINGHAM C	CHELSEA	COVENTRY C	EVERTON	IPSWICH T	LEICESTER C	LIVERPOOL	LUTON T	MANCHESTER C	MANCHESTER U	NEWCASTLE U	NOTTINGHAM F	OXFORD U	Q.P.R.	SHEFFIELD W	SOUTHAMPTON	TOTTENHAM H	WATFORD	W.B.A.	WEST HAM U
1 ARSENAL		O05 3-2	N30 0-0	a29 2-0	M23 3-0	a12 0-1	O19 1-0	A31 1-0	D14 2-0	F01 2-1	N02 1-0	A24 1-2	S28 0-0	a08 1-1	N16 2-1	D28 3-1	S14 1-0	A20 3-2	J01 0-0	M31 0-2	a26 2-2	M15 1-0
2 ASTON VILLA	M08 1-4		M22 0-3	a26 3-1	S14 1-1	S28 0-0	a16 1-0	M31 1-0	A21 2-2	A31 3-1	J01 0-1	D14 1-3	O26 1-2	O12 1-2	N02 2-0	A24 1-2	N16 1-1	F01 0-0	N30 1-2	a12 4-1	D28 1-1	M19 2-1
3 BIRMINGHAM C	m03 0-1	S07 0-0		D21 1-2	O26 0-1	J18 0-2	J11 0-1	S21 2-1	N23 0-2	a06 0-2	S03 1-0	M29 1-1	N09 0-1	D26 0-1	A26 3-1	M01 2-0	O05 0-2	a19 0-2	M15 1-2	D07 1-2	F08 0-1	A17 1-0
4 CHELSEA	S21 2-1	N23 2-1	A24 2-0		A20 1-0	O12 2-1	a05 1-1	F02 2-2	m03 0-1	J11 1-0	M08 1-0	O26 1-2	a19 1-1	N09 4-2	F08 1-4	M19 1-1	D14 2-1	S14 2-0	D28 2-0	m05 1-5	A31 3-0	M29 0-4
5 COVENTRY C	S07 0-2	J11 3-3	F16 4-4	D07 1-1		D21 1-3	D26 0-1	O06 3-0	N09 0-3	a19 1-0	A17 1-1	a05 1-3	A26 1-2	M29 0-0	S03 5-2	m03 2-1	M15 0-1	F22 3-2	O20 2-3	J18 0-2	S28 3-0	N23 0-1
6 EVERTON	N09 6-1	M01 2-0	A31 4-1	M16 1-1	A24 1-1		a19 1-0	D14 1-2	S21 2-3	S14 2-0	F11 4-0	D26 3-1	M29 1-0	N23 1-1	O05 2-0	J11 4-3	D28 3-1	m03 6-1	F01 1-0	O19 4-1	A20 2-0	m05 3-1
7 IPSWICH T	M11 1-2	S21 0-3	S14 0-1	N02 0-2	M31 1-0	N16 3-4		a08 0-2	F01 2-1	D28 1-1	a12 0-0	A20 0-1	O12 2-2	M08 1-0	a26 3-2	D14 1-0	N30 2-1	A31 1-1	A24 1-0	J01 0-0	M22 1-0	O26 0-1
8 LEICESTER C	J18 2-2	D26 3-1	M12 4-2	A28 0-0	M08 2-1	A17 3-1	S28 1-0		a30 0-2	M29 0-0	D07 1-1	N23 3-0	m03 2-0	S08 0-3	O02 4-4	a14 1-4	O19 2-3	N09 2-2	a05 1-4	S04 2-2	O12 2-2	J11 0-1
9 LIVERPOOL	A17 2-0	D07 3-0	a26 5-0	N30 1-1	a12 5-0	F22 0-2	A26 5-0	N02 1-0		O26 3-2	M31 2-0	F09 1-1	D21 1-1	S03 2-0	M22 6-0	M08 4-1	J01 2-2	O12 1-0	S28 4-1	S07 3-1	N16 4-1	J18 3-1
10 LUTON T	A27 2-2	J18 2-0	N02 2-0	S07 1-1	N16 0-1	M22 2-1	O01 1-0	J01 3-1	a16 0-1		N30 2-1	O05 1-1	D07 2-0	A17 1-1	M15 1-2	S21 2-0	M01 1-0	O19 7-0	a12 1-1	a26 3-2	a01 3-0	D21 0-0
11 MANCHESTER C	a05 0-1	M29 2-2	D28 1-1	O05 0-1	D14 5-1	O26 1-1	N09 1-1	A21 1-1	D26 1-0	m03 1-1		S14 0-3	N23 1-0	a19 1-2	M01 0-3	F08 2-0	A24 1-3	J11 1-0	A31 2-1	M15 0-1	F01 2-1	S21 2-2
12 MANCHESTER U	D21 0-1	A17 4-0	J01 1-0	a09 1-2	N02 2-0	M31 0-0	D07 1-0	a26 4-0	O19 1-1	M19 2-0	M22 2-2		S04 3-0	J18 2-3	S07 3-0	O12 2-0	a13 0-2	S28 1-0	N16 0-0	N30 1-1	F22 3-0	A26 2-0
13 NEWCASTLE U	M01 1-0	a09 2-2	a12 4-1	N16 1-3	F01 3-2	J01 2-2	M15 3-1	N30 2-1	A24 1-0	A21 2-2	a26 3-1	a16 2-4		O19 0-3	S21 3-0	A31 3-1	M31 4-1	D14 2-1	M22 2-2	N02 1-1	S14 4-1	O05 1-2
14 NOTTINGHAM F	O26 3-2	M15 1-1	M31 3-0	a12 0-0	J01 5-2	a26 0-0	O05 3-1	M22 4-3	D28 1-1	D14 2-0	N16 0-2	A31 1-3	F08 1-2		D01 1-1	F01 4-0	A21 0-1	A24 2-1	S14 0-1	S21 3-2	N03 2-1	a02 2-1
15 OXFORD U	m05 3-0	a05 1-1	F01 0-1	O19 2-1	J25 0-1	a30 1-0	N23 4-3	A24 5-0	S14 2-2	O12 1-1	S28 1-0	J11 1-3	M19 1-2	m03 1-2		M29 3-3	A31 0-1	D26 3-0	A21 1-1	a09 1-1	D14 2-2	N09 1-2
16 Q.P.R.	S03 0-1	D17 0-1	S28 3-1	M31 6-0	N30 0-2	S07 3-0	A17 1-0	N16 2-0	O05 2-1	F22 1-1	O19 0-0	M15 1-0	J18 3-1	A27 2-1	J01 3-1		N02 1-1	M11 0-2	a26 2-5	M22 2-1	a12 1-0	D07 0-1
17 SHEFFIELD W	a16 2-0	a19 2-0	M08 5-1	A17 1-1	O12 2-2	S03 1-5	m03 1-0	M18 1-0	M29 0-0	S28 3-2	D21 3-2	N09 1-0	D26 2-2	D07 2-1	J18 2-1	a08 0-0		N23 2-1	F22 1-2	A26 2-1	O26 1-0	S07 2-2
18 SOUTHAMPTON	D07 3-0	A27 0-0	N16 1-0	M22 0-1	S21 1-1	N30 2-3	J18 1-0	a12 0-0	M15 1-2	F08 1-2	S07 3-0	M01 1-0	A17 1-1	D20 3-1	a01 1-1	O26 3-0	a26 2-3		N02 1-0	O05 3-1	J01 3-1	S03 1-1
19 TOTTENHAM H	M29 1-0	m03 4-2	a16 2-0	S04 4-1	F08 0-1	A26 0-1	D21 2-0	O26 1-3	M02 1-2	N09 1-3	J18 0-2	a19 0-0	S07 5-1	J11 0-3	D07 5-1	N23 1-1	S21 5-1	m05 5-3		A17 4-0	M08 5-0	D26 1-0
20 WATFORD	a01 3-0	N09 1-1	A20 3-0	S28 3-1	A31 3-0	a15 0-2	M29 0-0	D28 2-1	J12 2-3	N23 1-2	O12 3-2	m03 1-1	a05 4-1	a21 1-1	O26 2-2	S14 2-0	F01 2-1	a29 1-1	D14 1-0		A24 5-1	a19 0-2
21 W.B.A.	N23 0-0	S04 0-3	O19 2-1	J18 0-3	M19 0-0	D07 0-3	S07 1-2	M15 2-2	a19 1-2	D26 1-2	A26 2-3	S21 1-5	J11 1-1	a05 1-1	A17 1-1	N09 0-1	a22 1-1	M29 1-0	O05 1-1	D22 3-1		m03 2-3
22 WEST HAM U	O12 0-0	O19 4-1	D14 2-0	a15 1-2	a26 1-0	N02 2-1	a30 2-1	S14 3-0	A31 2-2	A24 0-1	a28 1-0	F02 2-1	a21 8-1	S28 4-2	a12 3-1	A20 3-1	M22 1-0	a08 1-0	M31 2-1	N16 2-1	N30 4-0	

Goalkeeper Chris Woods was ever-present when Norwich City won the Second Division in 1985-6. He later signed for Glasgow Rangers and became regarded as England's number-one after the retirement of Peter Shilton.

DIVISION 2

	BARNSLEY	BLACKBURN R	BRADFORD C	BRIGHTON & HA	CARLISLE U	CHARLTON A	CRYSTAL P	FULHAM	GRIMSBY T	HUDDERSFIELD T	HULL C	LEEDS U	MIDDLESBROUGH	MILLWALL	NORWICH C	OLDHAM A	PORTSMOUTH	SHEFFIELD U	SHREWSBURY T	STOKE C	SUNDERLAND	WIMBLEDON
1 BARNSLEY		a12 1-1	M15 2-2	A20 3-2	M22 1-2	D14 2-1	a26 2-4	A31 2-0	S21 1-0	M31 1-3	J01 1-4	O27 3-0	M25 0-0	N30 2-1	F01 2-2	N02 1-0	O05 0-1	a08 2-1	S14 2-0	A24 0-0	N16 1-1	D28 0-1
2 BLACKBURN R	N09 0-3		O05 3-0	M18 1-4	A31 2-0	N23 0-0	F15 1-2	S21 1-0	m05 3-1	a15 0-1	F01 2-2	D26 2-0	a05 0-1	M15 1-2	A20 2-1	O19 0-0	M01 1-0	a19 6-1	A24 1-1	M29 0-1	D14 2-0	S14 2-0
3 BRADFORD C	O12 2-0	M08 3-2		D20 3-2	D13 1-0	M19 1-2	N02 1-0	a02 3-1	M01 0-1	M22 3-0	S14 4-2	a09 0-1	a23 2-1	a30 0-2	a12 0-2	M04 1-0	D03 2-1	O26 1-4	a26 3-1	S01 3-1	J01 2-0	m08 1-1
4 BRIGHTON & H.A.	D07 0-1	S07 3-1	A24 2-1		O05 6-1	O19 3-5	J01 2-0	a16 2-3	A17 2-2	N16 4-3	N30 3-1	S04 0-1	J18 3-3	M22 1-0	N02 1-1	a02 1-1	M31 2-3	A27 0-0	a12 0-2	M15 2-0	a26 3-1	S21 2-0
5 CARLISLE U	S07 1-1	J18 2-1	A17 1-2	a29 2-0		m03 2-3	A27 2-2	a19 2-1	J11 1-2	M18 2-0	M11 2-1	N23 1-2	D26 1-0	D07 1-0	O12 0-4	S17 3-1	D22 0-1	M29 1-0	S28 0-2	N09 3-0	O19 1-2	a06 2-3
6 CHARLTON A	A17 2-1	a26 3-0	O15 1-1	F04 2-2	N30 3-0		S07 3-1	a29 2-0	D21 2-0	a12 3-0	N16 1-2	J18 4-0	A27 2-0	a15 3-3	M31 1-0	M22 1-1	M15 1-2	D07 2-0	N02 4-1	S21 2-0	O05 2-1	m06 0-0
7 CRYSTAL P	N23 1-0	O26 2-0	a05 2-1	M29 1-0	F01 1-1	J11 2-1		S14 0-0	N09 2-1	A31 2-3	O01 0-2	a19 3-0	M08 2-1	S21 2-1	J25 1-2	O12 3-2	a08 2-1	m03 1-1	D15 0-1	M18 0-1	A24 1-0	D26 1-3
8 FULHAM	J18 2-0	M11 3-3	D07 4-1	S28 1-0	a08 0-1	a22 0-3	M22 2-3		A26 2-1	a26 2-1	a12 1-1	A17 3-1	D21 0-3	M31 1-2	J01 0-1	N30 2-2	S07 0-1	S17 2-3	O05 2-1	O19 1-0	N02 1-2	M15 0-2
9 GRIMSBY T	a22 1-2	N30 5-2	S28 2-0	D14 0-2	S13 1-0	A24 2-2	a12 3-0	F01 1-0		A20 1-1	a01 0-1	F08 1-0	O26 3-2	N02 5-1	a26 1-0	M08 1-4	N16 1-0	O12 0-1	J01 3-1	J25 3-3	M22 1-1	A31 0-1
10 HUDDERSFIELD T	D26 1-1	S03 0-0	S07 2-0	a19 1-0	O26 3-3	N09 0-2	J18 0-0	N23 1-3	D07 2-2		F25 2-1	O05 3-1	M29 0-3	A17 4-3	S21 0-0	D21 2-0	A26 1-2	J11 3-1	M15 1-0	a05 2-0	M01 2-0	m03 0-1
11 HULL C	M29 0-1	A26 2-2	J11 1-0	m02 2-0	S21 4-0	a19 1-1	D07 1-2	N09 5-0	D26 2-0	O19 3-1		D22 2-1	S07 0-0	S17 3-0	a29 1-0	J18 4-2	A17 2-2	a05 0-0	M04 4-3	O05 0-2	M15 1-1	N23 1-1
12 LEEDS U	F15 0-2	M31 1-1	S21 2-1	D28 2-3	a26 2-0	A31 1-2	N16 1-3	D14 1-0	O19 1-1	M08 2-0	A24 1-1		O12 1-0	a12 3-1	N30 0-2	J01 3-1	N02 2-1	S28 1-1	M22 1-1	F01 4-0	S14 1-1	A21 0-0
13 MIDDLESBROUGH	S28 0-0	N02 0-0	O19 1-1	A31 0-1	M31 1-3	F01 1-3	O05 0-2	A24 1-0	M04 3-1	J01 0-1	M22 1-2	M15 2-2		a26 3-0	S14 1-1	N16 3-2	a12 1-0	M18 1-2	N30 3-1	S10 1-1	D28 2-0	D14 1-0
14 MILLWALL	m03 2-2	O12 0-1	a19 2-1	S14 0-1	O22 3-1	M29 2-2	a22 3-2	M18 1-1	a05 1-0	D14 2-1	D28 5-0	N09 3-1	N23 3-0		A24 4-2	S28 0-1	O26 0-4	M08 3-0	F01 2-0	J11 2-3	A31 1-0	M11 0-1
15 NORWICH C	A26 1-1	D07 3-0	N09 0-0	a05 3-0	M15 2-1	D26 3-1	S18 4-3	M29 2-1	N23 3-2	M12 4-1	S28 2-0	m03 4-0	J11 2-0	D21 6-1		A17 1-0	J18 2-0	S07 4-0	O19 3-1	a19 1-1	a09 0-0	O05 1-2
16 OLDHAM A	a06 1-1	F08 3-1	D26 0-1	O26 4-0	m05 2-1	S13 2-1	M15 2-0	m03 2-1	O05 2-1	A24 1-1	A31 3-1	M28 3-1	a19 1-0	M01 0-0	D14 1-3		S21 2-0	N09 1-5	A20 4-3	N23 2-4	F01 2-2	J11 2-1
17 PORTSMOUTH	M08 1-1	S28 3-0	m03 4-0	D26 1-2	A24 4-0	O12 1-0	O19 1-0	J11 1-1	a19 3-1	F01 4-1	D14 1-1	a05 2-3	J25 1-0	M25 2-1	A31 2-0	F22 1-2		N23 0-3	D28 4-0	S14 3-0	A20 3-0	M29 1-1
18 SHEFFIELD U	O19 3-1	N16 3-3	M11 3-1	F01 3-0	J01 1-0	O01 1-1	N30 0-0	D28 2-1	M15 1-1	S14 1-1	N02 3-1	a22 3-2	S21 0-1	O05 1-3	M22 2-5	a12 2-0	a26 0-0		A31 1-1	D14 1-2	M31 1-0	A24 4-0
19 SHREWSBURY T	J11 3-0	D20 2-0	N23 2-0	N09 2-1	M01 0-0	a05 2-1	A18 0-2	M08 2-1	M29 0-2	O12 3-0	O26 0-0	S07 1-3	m03 2-1	A27 1-1	F08 0-3	D07 2-0	S03 1-1	J18 3-1		D26 1-0	S21 1-2	a19 1-1
20 STOKE C	D21 0-0	J01 2-2	J18 3-1	O12 1-1	a12 0-0	F22 0-0	S28 0-0	F18 1-0	S04 1-1	N02 3-0	M08 0-1	A26 6-2	D07 3-2	S07 0-0	N16 1-1	a26 2-0	a22 2-0	A17 1-3	M31 2-2		N30 1-0	O25 0-0
21 SUNDERLAND	a19 2-0	A17 0-2	M29 1-1	N23 2-1	F08 2-2	M08 1-2	D22 1-1	a05 4-2	S07 3-3	S28 1-0	O12 1-1	J11 4-2	O22 1-0	J18 1-2	O26 0-2	A26 0-3	D07 1-3	D26 2-1	a29 2-0	m03 2-0		N09 2-1
22 WIMBLEDON	S03 1-0	M22 1-1	A26 1-0	F22 0-0	N03 4-1	S28 3-1	a01 1-1	O12 1-0	J18 3-0	N30 2-2	a26 3-1	D07 0-3	A17 3-0	O19 1-1	M08 2-1	S07 0-0	J01 1-3	D21 5-0	N16 2-1	a29 1-0	a12 3-0	

Season 1985-86

DIVISION 3

	BLACKPOOL	BOLTON W	BOURNEMOUTH	BRENTFORD	BRISTOL C	BRISTOL R	BURY	CARDIFF C	CHESTERFIELD	DARLINGTON	DERBY CO	DONCASTER R	GILLINGHAM	LINCOLN C	NEWPORT CO	NOTTS CO	PLYMOUTH A	READING	ROTHERHAM U	SWANSEA C	WALSALL	WIGAN A	WOLVERHAMPTON W	YORK C
1 BLACKPOOL		D26 1-1	a29 2-0	O26 4-0	M01 2-1	N09 4-2	O19 5-0	S21 3-0	F04 0-1	D28 0-0	F01 0-1	O01 4-0	O05 2-2	F25 2-0	m03 0-0	A24 1-3	N30 1-1	J18 0-0	M29 2-1	A31 2-0	a19 2-1	M15 1-2	a05 0-1	S14 0-2
2 BOLTON W	M31 1-3		N02 1-0	O12 1-2	a26 0-4	F04 0-2	A26 1-4	M22 5-0	D14 2-1	N05 0-3	N23 0-1	D21 2-0	J11 0-1	S17 1-1	F22 4-0	a12 1-0	S28 3-1	M08 2-0	A17 1-1	O19 1-1	J25 3-1	J01 1-2	S07 4-1	M04 1-1
3 BOURNEMOUTH	S17 1-4	M18 2-1		D28 0-0	A24 5-0	O26 6-1	O12 2-1	M08 1-1	J31 3-2	S28 4-2	J18 1-1	a19 1-1	O19 2-3	M04 2-2	A31 0-1	S14 0-0	a05 1-3	D26 0-1	D17 1-2	M29 4-0	m03 0-1	F22 0-2	N09 3-2	F04 2-0
4 BRENTFORD	M22 1-1	M14 1-1	A26 1-0		a13 1-2	D22 1-0	D14 1-0	N02 3-0	N23 1-0	m05 2-1	N06 3-3	J24 1-3	M31 1-2	a22 0-1	O19 0-0	J21 1-1	S07 1-1	S17 1-2	S28 1-1	O05 1-0	F04 1-3	J11 1-3	A17 2-1	a26 3-3
5 BRISTOL C	S28 2-1	N30 2-0	D21 1-3	N09 0-0		M29 2-0	F04 4-1	J25 2-1	O05 0-0	O19 1-0	S17 1-1	J07 4-1	A26 1-2	a05 1-1	M04 3-1	M15 3-0	D26 2-0	m03 3-0	J11 3-1	a19 0-1	A17 2-3	S07 1-0	O26 3-0	F22 2-2
6 BRISTOL R	a12 1-0	O22 2-1	M22 2-3	A24 0-1	a22 1-1		N05 2-1	N23 2-1	a26 1-1	J18 3-1	A31 0-0	F08 1-0	D14 1-0	S14 0-0	F01 2-0	O01 1-1	M08 1-2	D28 0-2	O12 5-2	M01 0-0	S21 0-1	a01 1-1	M25 1-1	N02 0-1
7 BURY	a22 4-1	F25 2-1	M15 3-0	m03 0-0	O22 6-3	a05 1-1		a08 3-0	J18 1-1	F01 0-1	S14 1-1	M29 1-2	S21 1-2	A31 4-0	D26 1-1	M01 2-4	N09 0-1	O26 3-1	a19 2-0	M25 2-2	N30 2-1	O05 0-0	O01 3-1	A24 4-2
8 CARDIFF C	F22 1-0	O26 0-1	O05 0-1	J04 1-0	S14 1-3	a19 2-0	S17 0-0		A24 0-2	F04 0-1	S28 0-2	N08 0-1	M15 1-1	m03 2-1	D28 1-1	J18 1-3	M28 1-2	A31 1-3	M25 2-3	D26 1-0	a05 1-1	O19 3-1	N30 1-1	J31 2-1
9 CHESTERFIELD	O22 1-2	m03 3-0	S07 0-1	a19 1-3	M08 0-0	a15 2-0	A17 4-3	D20 3-4		S17 1-0	F22 1-0	O26 0-0	J25 1-1	D26 2-2	N09 3-1	F08 2-2	M18 1-2	M04 3-4	A27 2-0	a05 4-1	M25 2-3	S28 1-1	M29 3-0	O12 1-0
10 DARLINGTON	A26 2-1	a24 0-1	M01 0-0	O01 3-5	m15 1-1	A18 3-3	O30 1-1	O22 4-1	a22 2-1		m12 2-1	D08 0-2	D20 3-2	M29 1-0	M18 3-2	S22 2-3	m03 0-2	a19 0-0	D26 2-2	N09 6-0	O27 0-3	a29 1-1	a02 2-1	M09 1-0
11 DERBY CO	S07 1-2	a19 2-1	A17 3-0	a05 1-1	M19 2-0	a09 0-2	a30 1-1	M01 2-1	S21 0-0	M15 1-1		m03 1-1	a07 2-0	N09 7-0	M29 1-1	O05 2-0	O26 1-2	N30 1-1	m09 2-1	O02 5-1	M12 3-1	D22 1-0	A26 4-2	O19 2-1
12 DONCASTER R	M04 0-0	A24 1-1	N23 1-1	S13 1-0	N02 1-1	O19 0-2	J01 1-0	a12 0-2	M21 2-0	A31 2-0	D15 0-3		a25 2-3	F01 1-1	J18 1-1	D28 2-1	S17 1-0	S28 0-1	a15 0-0	F04 0-0	O05 1-0	N05 2-2	M15 0-1	M31 1-1
13 GILLINGHAM	M08 2-2	A31 2-1	F08 2-0	M18 1-2	D28 1-1	m03 2-0	F22 1-0	O12 2-0	S14 1-1	A24 1-1	O22 1-2	N30 4-0		J18 2-0	a29 0-1	F01 4-0	M04 1-1	M29 3-0	a04 3-0	O26 5-1	N09 5-2	S17 2-0	a19 2-0	S28 1-2
14 LINCOLN C	N02 0-3	M25 1-1	O02 3-2	S21 3-0	N06 1-1	a30 2-2	J11 2-0	D14 0-4	M31 2-1	J01 1-1	a12 0-1	S08 3-3	A17 1-0		O05 1-1	M22 0-2	a16 1-1	O19 0-1	D22 0-0	M16 4-1	A26 3-2	a26 0-0	m05 2-3	N24 3-4
15 NEWPORT CO	D14 1-1	S21 0-1	J11 2-1	M11 1-2	O01 1-1	S07 3-0	M31 1-0	A26 1-2	a12 3-3	a26 3-0	a22 1-1	A17 2-2	N02 1-1	M08 1-2		N23 1-2	J25 3-1	O12 0-2	O22 0-0	F16 2-0	F28 1-5	M22 3-4	D21 3-1	N06 1-1
16 NOTTS CO	D22 1-2	N09 1-0	a15 3-1	M29 0-4	O12 4-0	M04 0-0	S28 2-2	A17 1-4	O19 2-1	m06 5-0	M08 0-3	A26 1-1	S07 1-1	O27 3-2	a19 1-2		J11 2-0	a05 0-0	m03 1-0	N30 3-0	a08 3-1	F04 1-1	D26 4-0	S17 3-1
17 PLYMOUTH A	a26 3-1	a22 4-1	N05 2-1	F01 2-0	a29 4-0	O05 4-2	a12 3-0	J01 4-4	N02 0-0	D14 4-2	M22 4-1	F15 0-1	O01 3-0	O22 2-1	S14 2-0	A31 0-1		A24 0-1	a08 4-0	D28 2-0	M15 2-0	N23 2-1	S21 3-1	J18 2-2
18 READING	A17 1-0	O05 1-0	M31 1-2	a16 3-1	D14 1-0	A26 3-2	M22 2-0	J11 1-1	O02 4-2	N23 0-2	a26 1-0	m05 2-0	J01 1-2	M12 0-2	M15 2-0	N06 3-1	D21 4-3		M19 2-1	S21 2-0	S07 2-1	N02 1-0	O23 2-2	a12 0-0
19 ROTHERHAM U	J01 4-1	J18 4-0	a26 4-1	M01 1-2	A31 2-0	M15 2-0	N23 2-0	O01 3-0	D28 1-2	M31 1-2	N02 1-1	S21 2-1	N06 1-1	A24 1-0	F04 0-0	D14 1-0	O19 1-1	S14 1-2		F01 4-1	F15 3-0	a12 0-0	O05 1-2	M22 4-1
20 SWANSEA C	J11 2-0	F08 3-1	J01 1-1	M08 2-0	N23 1-3	S28 0-1	N02 1-0	M31 2-0	N05 1-1	a12 2-2	m06 0-3	O22 0-2	M22 2-2	O11 3-1	S17 1-1	a26 0-0	A26 0-2	F22 2-3	S07 1-0		J07 2-1	A17 0-1	J25 0-2	D14 1-0
21 WALSALL	N23 1-1	S14 2-0	D14 4-2	O22 1-2	J18 2-1	M18 6-0	a26 3-2	N05 6-3	A31 3-0	M22 0-0	M31 1-1	M08 1-0	a12 4-1	D28 2-1	S28 2-0	N02 0-0	O12 2-2	F01 6-0	S17 3-1	A24 3-1		a15 3-3	F09 1-1	J01 3-1
22 WIGAN A	O12 1-1	M29 1-3	S21 3-0	A31 4-0	F01 1-1	D26 4-0	M11 1-0	F08 2-0	M01 2-0	S14 5-1	A24 2-1	a05 0-1	F15 3-3	N30 3-2	O26 0-0	O22 3-1	a19 3-0	a22 1-0	N09 2-0	J18 5-0	O01 2-0		m03 5-3	M18 1-0
23 WOLVERHAMPTON W	N05 2-1	F01 0-2	a12 0-3	J18 1-4	M22 2-1	S17 3-4	M18 1-1	a26 3-1	J01 1-0	N02 2-1	D28 0-4	O12 1-2	N23 1-3	S28 1-1	A24 1-2	M31 2-2	M11 0-3	a08 2-3	M08 0-0	S14 1-5	O19 0-0	D14 2-2		A31 3-2
24 YORK C	m06 3-0	O01 3-0	O22 2-1	N30 1-0	S21 1-1	M12 4-0	D20 0-0	S07 1-1	M15 2-0	O05 7-0	F08 1-3	D26 0-1	M01 2-0	a19 2-1	a05 3-1	a22 2-2	A17 3-1	N09 0-1	O26 2-1	m03 3-1	M29 1-0	A26 4-1	J11 2-1	

DIVISION 4

	ALDERSHOT	BURNLEY	CAMBRIDGE U	CHESTER C	COLCHESTER U	CREWE A	EXETER C	HALIFAX T	HARTLEPOOL U	HEREFORD U	MANSFIELD T	NORTHAMPTON T	ORIENT	PETERBOROUGH U	PORT VALE	PRESTON N.E.	ROCHDALE	SCUNTHORPE U	SOUTHEND U	STOCKPORT CO	SWINDON T	TORQUAY U	TRANMERE R	WREXHAM
1 ALDERSHOT		A31 0-2	F01 2-1	D07 1-1	D28 1-1	O26 3-2	A24 4-0	M08 1-2	a05 0-1	a29 2-0	S14 1-2	N09 1-0	F04 1-1	N30 1-0	S17 0-0	m03 4-0	J18 2-1	S28 2-1	O12 1-3	a19 6-1	a22 2-4	M29 1-1	a15 3-1	O19 6-0
2 BURNLEY	M11 1-2		a12 1-1	M08 1-0	O01 0-2	a15 0-1	N23 3-1	M22 1-3	S07 2-0	J25 3-2	N05 2-1	A17 3-2	D14 1-0	M01 1-1	A26 1-2	a22 1-1	S21 1-0	a26 1-2	N02 1-3	A23 0-1	O12 0-2	O22 3-0	M31 3-1	J01 5-2
3 CAMBRIDGE U	S07 0-2	N09 0-4		D26 3-2	a29 1-3	a19 1-0	S20 1-1	a08 4-0	A17 4-2	J11 4-0	O05 4-2	N30 2-5	O19 1-2	O26 3-1	J25 1-3	O02 2-0	M28 1-0	M15 0-1	A27 1-2	D06 1-2	a05 1-1	m03 3-0	D20 3-2	F04 4-3
4 CHESTER C	N02 1-0	O05 4-0	M31 1-1		N06 4-0	S21 4-0	a12 2-1	A17 1-1	A26 1-1	S07 1-0	O02 1-0	F05 2-3	N23 3-0	D21 2-1	J01 4-1	M15 2-0	F15 1-1	D14 1-1	a26 2-0	M01 1-2	O19 0-1	J25 3-1	J11 1-0	M22 2-1
5 COLCHESTER U	A27 4-0	m06 2-2	S17 4-1	a04 2-3		M25 1-2	O04 1-1	S06 3-1	m02 3-1	J03 4-1	M14 0-0	O26 0-2	a08 4-0	a22 5-0	S27 1-0	a18 4-0	N08 0-1	O18 1-1	F04 2-0	A17 3-1	M28 1-1	J11 0-0	J24 1-2	D20 5-2
6 CREWE A	M22 2-0	O19 3-1	N23 0-1	F22 2-2	a26 0-2		D13 0-1	N02 2-2	D20 0-0	A27 2-0	a11 2-1	J25 0-1	N05 1-3	F04 1-1	M31 0-1	O05 3-3	M15 4-2	M04 4-0	A17 1-1	S06 0-1	S17 2-0	S28 1-0	M18 2-1	J11 3-2
7 EXETER C	D21 2-0	a19 0-2	F21 0-0	N09 1-3	M08 2-2	m03 1-2		O23 1-0	O26 1-2	M29 3-2	F08 0-1	A26 1-2	O12 1-1	M19 1-0	A17 1-0	N30 3-0	a04 2-0	S18 2-0	S07 0-2	J11 1-0	M04 0-3	M26 2-2	S28 1-0	J25 0-1
8 HALIFAX T	O05 1-1	O26 2-2	S27 1-1	J17 1-2	J31 2-2	J04 1-0	F04 1-0		M28 3-2	D03 1-0	m05 1-2	a18 2-0	S13 2-1	N09 1-1	a29 2-0	A30 2-1	D20 1-1	A23 2-1	S17 2-3	a04 0-0	m02 1-3	a14 0-0	O18 1-2	M14 5-2
9 HARTLEPOOL U	N06 2-1	F01 3-1	J18 2-1	J08 1-1	D14 4-1	A24 4-1	M22 0-0	J01 3-0		O19 2-1	N02 1-1	S18 2-1	A31 1-2	O05 2-1	M05 1-1	F05 1-0	S13 2-0	a01 0-1	a12 3-2	M14 1-1	S28 1-0	a15 1-0	N23 1-0	a26 3-3
10 HEREFORD U	O02 4-1	S14 2-2	A31 1-0	F01 0-2	N02 2-0	D28 4-1	J01 4-1	a26 2-1	a09 2-2		J18 4-2	M08 3-0	M31 3-2	S21 2-1	N06 1-1	M01 1-1	O23 2-2	M22 1-1	M19 2-1	a16 3-2	A24 4-1	O12 4-1	D14 1-4	a12 3-1
11 MANSFIELD T	J25 2-0	a05 0-0	M08 2-0	M04 0-0	O12 2-1	N09 2-2	O19 2-1	A27 2-0	a22 4-0	A17 4-0		J11 1-0	S18 1-1	m03 0-1	D22 2-1	M29 2-3	N30 3-2	M25 1-1	S28 3-0	D26 4-2	a19 1-1	O26 4-0	a29 0-0	S07 1-1
12 NORTHAMPTON T	a12 2-3	J18 2-0	a26 0-2	O22 2-2	M22 1-0	S14 0-1	a08 2-2	N23 4-0	M11 3-0	O05 1-3	A31 1-0		a15 2-3	M15 2-2	D14 2-2	S10 6-0	M01 1-0	N02 2-2	M31 0-0	S21 3-1	F01 0-1	a29 5-1	N05 2-2	O01 1-2
13 ORIENT	O22 1-1	m03 3-0	F08 3-1	a19 0-0	S21 1-2	a05 0-1	M15 2-2	a22 1-0	J11 1-1	D26 2-2	F15 0-1	M29 0-1		A27 2-2	S07 1-0	N09 2-0	O01 5-0	O05 3-0	D21 3-0	O26 0-1	N30 1-0	M18 4-2	A17 3-1	M01 1-3
14 PETERBOROUGH U	a26 3-0	S28 0-0	M22 0-0	A24 3-0	M31 1-2	O23 0-0	N02 1-1	a12 1-1	M08 3-1	M26 0-0	D14 4-2	O12 0-5	D28 2-2		N23 1-0	J18 1-1	m07 1-1	A31 1-0	J01 1-1	a08 2-0	S14 3-0	S18 2-0	M05 0-1	N06 1-1
15 PORT VALE	M18 3-1	F24 1-1	S14 4-1	M29 1-1	M01 1-1	D26 3-0	J17 0-0	S21 3-2	S30 4-0	a05 1-0	A24 0-0	m03 0-0	F01 2-0	a19 2-0		J04 0-1	A31 1-1	F03 3-1	O19 4-0	N09 1-1	O26 3-0	D17 1-0	M15 0-0	O05 4-0
16 PRESTON N.E.	D14 1-3	S17 1-0	M18 1-2	O12 3-6	N23 3-2	M08 1-2	a26 2-2	J11 0-1	O22 2-1	S28 2-0	J01 0-2	D21 1-1	a12 1-3	A17 2-4	N02 0-1		F08 1-1	N05 0-1	M22 3-2	S13 1-2	F22 0-3	S07 4-0	A26 2-2	M31 1-0
17 ROCHDALE	A17 2-0	M18 1-0	J01 2-1	a29 1-2	a12 3-3	O12 1-0	N05 1-1	M31 1-0	J25 0-2	F04 1-1	a26 1-1	S28 3-2	m05 1-4	S07 2-1	J11 3-3	O19 1-1		N23 1-0	a21 2-1	A26 4-1	M08 1-2	D21 5-0	M22 1-1	N02 3-2
18 SCUNTHORPE U	M01 1-0	N30 1-1	O11 0-0	m03 2-0	a15 1-1	O01 3-1	a22 1-0	D22 3-3	D26 1-0	O25 2-1	S21 0-3	M18 1-0	M08 2-2	J11 2-0	O22 0-0	a04 1-3	a18 3-1		J24 2-0	M28 2-3	N09 0-2	A17 4-0	S06 0-1	A26 1-1
19 SOUTHEND U	M15 2-0	J03 2-3	D28 1-0	N29 1-1	O22 2-4	J18 0-1	J31 2-0	M05 2-1	N09 3-2	a18 3-1	a15 3-1	D06 0-4	A23 5-1	M29 0-1	m05 2-1	O25 2-1	m02 5-0	S14 2-1		O01 0-0	A30 0-0	a04 1-2	O04 2-2	S20 3-0
20 STOCKPORT CO	N23 3-2	D20 1-1	N01 3-1	S28 2-2	J17 1-1	J31 3-0	F24 1-1	N04 2-1	O11 1-3	S16 1-1	M31 0-2	F21 1-0	M21 2-3	O18 2-2	a11 1-2	J24 2-1	D28 3-0	J01 0-0	M03 2-1		F03 0-2	M07 1-1	a25 1-1	D13 2-0
21 SWINDON T	M31 4-1	M15 3-1	N06 1-0	a08 4-2	J01 2-1	m05 1-0	O01 2-1	D14 3-2	M25 3-1	D22 1-0	N23 2-1	S06 3-2	a27 4-1	a15 3-0	M23 0-0	D07 4-1	O05 4-0	a12 1-1	J12 2-1	O22 1-0		A26 2-1	N02 2-1	A17 0-1
22 TORQUAY U	a08 1-2	F04 2-0	D14 1-1	S14 0-3	A31 2-1	M01 0-0	a01 1-2	O01 2-0	S21 1-3	M15 2-1	M22 1-2	O19 1-1	N02 2-2	M11 2-0	a26 0-1	F01 1-0	A24 1-2	J18 1-0	N06 2-2	O05 4-3	D28 0-1		a12 1-2	N23 1-3
23 TRANMERE R	S21 3-0	D26 2-1	A23 6-2	A31 2-3	S14 3-4	M29 0-1	F28 0-1	F07 0-3	a18 4-2	m02 1-2	O22 1-2	a04 1-3	J17 0-3	O29 7-0	O12 1-2	M25 2-3	O26 2-0	J31 2-1	M07 1-1	N29 2-3	J04 3-1	N09 2-0		F15 1-3
24 WREXHAM	M25 4-1	M29 0-1	O15 6-2	O26 1-1	A24 2-1	A31 2-1	S14 1-1	O12 2-1	F25 1-0	N09 0-1	F01 1-2	M04 1-0	S28 1-3	a05 0-1	M08 1-3	D26 1-1	M11 2-0	a29 1-0	a08 0-0	m03 3-0	J18 0-1	a19 3-2	S17 1-1	

LEAGUE TABLES

DIVISION 1

	P	W	D	L	F	A	W	D	L	F	A	Pts
Liverpool	42	16	4	1	58	14	10	6	5	31	23	88
Everton	42	16	3	2	54	18	10	5	6	33	23	86
West Ham U	42	17	2	2	48	16	9	4	8	26	24	84
Manchester U	42	12	5	4	35	12	10	5	6	35	24	76
Sheffield W	42	13	6	2	36	23	8	4	9	27	31	73
Chelsea	42	12	4	5	32	27	8	7	6	25	29	71
Arsenal	42	13	5	3	29	15	7	4	10	20	32	69
Nottingham F	42	11	5	5	38	25	8	6	7	31	28	68
Luton T	42	12	6	3	37	15	6	6	9	24	29	66
Tottenham H	42	12	2	7	47	25	7	6	8	27	27	65
Newcastle U	42	12	5	4	46	31	5	7	9	21	41	63
Watford	42	11	6	4	40	22	5	5	11	29	40	59
QPR	42	12	3	6	33	20	3	4	14	20	44	52
Southampton	42	10	6	5	32	18	2	4	15	19	44	46
Manchester C	42	7	7	7	25	26	4	5	12	18	31	45
Aston Villa	42	7	6	8	27	28	3	8	10	24	39	44
Coventry C	42	6	5	10	31	35	5	5	11	17	36	43
Oxford U	42	7	7	7	34	27	3	5	13	28	53	42
Leicester C	42	7	8	6	35	35	3	4	14	19	41	42
Ipswich T	42	8	5	8	20	24	3	3	15	12	31	41
Birmingham C	42	5	2	14	13	25	3	3	15	17	48	29
WBA	42	3	8	10	21	36	1	4	16	14	53	24

DIVISION 2

	P	W	D	L	F	A	W	D	L	F	A	Pts
Norwich C	42	16	4	1	51	15	9	5	7	33	22	84
Charlton A	42	14	5	2	44	15	8	6	7	34	30	77
Wimbledon	42	13	6	2	38	16	8	7	6	20	21	76
Portsmouth	42	13	4	4	43	17	9	3	9	26	24	73
Crystal P	42	12	3	6	29	22	7	6	8	28	30	66
Hull C	42	11	7	3	39	19	6	6	9	26	36	64
Sheffield U	42	10	7	4	36	24	7	4	10	28	39	62
Oldham A	42	13	4	4	40	28	4	5	12	22	33	60
Millwall	42	12	3	6	39	24	5	5	11	25	41	59
Stoke C	42	8	11	2	29	16	6	4	11	19	34	57
Brighton & HA	42	10	5	6	42	30	6	3	12	22	34	56
Barnsley	42	9	6	6	29	26	5	8	8	18	24	56
Bradford C	42	14	1	6	36	24	2	5	14	15	39	54
Leeds U	42	9	7	5	30	22	6	1	14	26	50	53
Grimsby T	42	11	4	6	35	24	3	6	12	23	38	52
Huddersfield T	42	10	6	5	30	23	4	4	13	21	44	52
Shrewsbury T	42	11	5	5	29	20	3	4	14	23	44	51
Sunderland	42	10	5	6	33	29	3	6	12	14	32	50
Blackburn R	42	10	4	7	30	20	2	9	10	23	42	49
Carlisle U	42	10	2	9	30	28	3	5	13	17	43	46
Middlesbrough	42	8	6	7	26	23	4	3	14	18	30	45
Fulham	42	8	3	10	29	32	2	3	16	16	37	36

DIVISION 3

	P	W	D	L	F	A	W	D	L	F	A	Pts
Reading	46	16	3	4	39	22	13	4	6	28	29	94
Plymouth A	46	17	3	3	56	20	9	6	8	32	33	87
Derby Co	46	13	7	3	45	20	10	8	5	35	21	84
Wigan A	46	17	4	2	54	17	6	10	7	28	31	83
Gillingham	46	14	5	4	48	17	8	8	7	33	37	79
Walsall	46	15	7	1	59	23	7	2	14	31	41	75
York C	46	16	4	3	49	17	4	7	12	28	41	71
Notts Co	46	12	6	5	42	26	7	8	8	29	34	71
Bristol C	46	14	5	4	43	19	4	9	10	26	41	68
Brentford	46	8	8	7	29	29	10	4	9	29	32	66
Doncaster R	46	7	10	6	20	21	9	6	8	25	31	64
Blackpool	46	11	6	6	38	19	6	6	11	28	36	63
Darlington	46	10	7	6	39	33	5	6	12	22	45	58
Rotherham U	46	13	5	5	44	18	2	7	14	17	41	57
Bournemouth	46	9	6	8	41	31	6	3	14	24	41	54
Bristol R	46	9	8	6	27	21	5	4	14	24	54	54
Chesterfield	46	10	6	7	41	30	3	8	12	20	34	53
Bolton W	46	10	4	9	35	30	5	4	14	19	38	53
Newport Co	46	7	8	8	35	33	4	10	9	17	32	51
Bury	46	11	7	5	46	26	1	6	16	17	41	49
Lincoln C	46	7	9	7	33	34	3	7	13	22	43	46
Cardiff C	46	7	5	11	22	29	5	4	14	31	54	45
Wolves	46	6	6	11	29	47	5	4	14	28	51	43
Swansea C	46	9	6	8	27	27	2	4	17	16	60	43

DIVISION 4

	P	W	D	L	F	A	W	D	L	F	A	Pts
Swindon T	46	20	2	1	52	19	12	4	7	30	24	102
Chester C	46	15	5	3	44	16	8	10	5	39	34	84
Mansfield T	46	13	8	2	43	17	10	4	9	31	30	81
Port Vale	46	13	9	1	42	11	8	7	8	25	26	79
Orient	46	11	6	6	39	21	9	6	8	40	43	72
Colchester U	46	12	6	5	51	22	7	7	9	37	41	70
Hartlepool U	46	15	6	2	41	20	5	4	14	27	47	70
Northampton T	46	9	7	7	44	29	9	3	11	35	29	64
Southend U	46	13	4	6	43	27	5	6	12	26	40	64
Hereford U	46	15	6	2	55	30	3	4	16	19	43	64
Stockport U	46	9	9	5	35	28	8	4	11	28	43	64
Crewe A	46	10	6	7	35	26	8	3	12	19	35	63
Wrexham	46	11	5	7	34	24	6	4	13	34	56	60
Burnley	46	11	3	9	35	30	5	8	10	25	35	59
Scunthorpe U	46	11	7	5	33	23	4	7	12	17	32	59
Aldershot	46	12	5	6	45	25	5	2	16	21	49	58
Peterboro' U	46	9	11	3	31	19	4	6	13	21	45	56
Rochdale	46	12	7	4	41	29	2	6	15	16	48	55
Tranmere R	46	9	1	13	46	41	6	8	9	28	32	54
Halifax T	46	10	8	5	35	27	4	4	15	25	44	54
Exeter C	46	10	4	9	26	25	3	11	9	21	34	54
Cambridge U	46	12	2	9	45	38	3	7	13	20	42	54
Preston NE	46	7	4	12	32	41	4	6	13	22	48	43
Torquay U	46	8	5	10	29	32	1	5	17	14	56	37

Football League Records

Top scorers: Div 1, C.Allen (Tottenham Hotspur) 33 goals; Div 2, M.Quinn (Portsmouth) 22 goals; Div 3, A.Jones (Port Vale) 29 goals; Div 4, R.Hill (Northampton Town) 29 goals.
Play-offs: Div 1, Ipswich Town v Charlton Athletic 0-0, 1-2; Leeds United v Oldham Athletic 1-0, 1-2; Charlton Athletic v Leeds United 1-0, 0-1, 2-1; Div 2, Gillingham v Sunderland 3-2, 3-4; Wigan Athletic v Swindon Town 2-3, 0-0; Gillingham v Swindon Town 1-0, 1-2, 0-2; Div 3, Aldershot v Bolton Wanderers 1-0, 2-2; Colchester United v Wolverhampton Wanderers 0-2, 0-0; Aldershot v Wolverhampton Wanderers 2-0, 1-0. Aston Villa, Leicester City and Manchester City relegated from Div 1; Derby County and Portsmouth promoted to Div 1. Brighton & Hove Albion, Grimsby Town and Sunderland relegated from Div 2; AFC Bournemouth, Middlesbrough and Swindon Town promoted to Div 2; Bolton Wanderers, Carlisle United, Darlington and Newport County relegated from Div 3; Preston North End, Northampton Town, Southend United and Aldershot promoted to Div 3; Lincoln City were relegated from Division Four and replaced by Scarborough.

Everton skipper and Welsh international Kevin Ratcliffe holds aloft the League Championship trophy at Goodison Park in 1987.

Derby County's Bobby Davison was the Rams' spearhead in successive promotions from the Third Division to the First.

DIVISION 1

	ARSENAL	ASTON VILLA	CHARLTON A	CHELSEA	COVENTRY C	EVERTON	LEICESTER C	LIVERPOOL	LUTON T	MANCHESTER C	MANCHESTER U	NEWCASTLE U	NORWICH C	NOTTINGHAM F	OXFORD U	Q.P.R.	SHEFFIELD W	SOUTHAMPTON	TOTTENHAM H	WATFORD	WEST HAM U	WIMBLEDON
1 ARSENAL		m02 2-1	a11 2-1	O25 3-1	J18 0-0	M28 0-1	a20 4-1	M10 0-1	D20 3-0	N22 3-0	A23 1-0	a14 0-1	m09 1-2	M17 0-0	S20 0-0	D06 3-1	S02 2-0	D27 1-0	S06 0-0	O11 3-1	N08 0-0	J01 3-1
2 ASTON VILLA	N29 0-4		D26 2-0	N15 0-0	M28 1-0	a18 0-1	N01 2-0	F21 2-2	S03 2-1	a04 0-0	D13 3-3	O25 2-0	S20 1-4	J03 0-0	S06 1-2	F07 0-1	m04 1-2	O11 3-1	A23 0-3	M25 1-1	a25 4-0	M04 0-0
3 CHARLTON A	N01 0-2	a20 3-0		a07 0-0	S20 1-1	O11 3-2	O18 2-0	D20 0-0	m02 0-1	D28 5-0	F07 0-0	D06 1-1	S06 1-2	J31 0-1	M24 0-0	m09 2-1	A23 1-1	N22 1-3	J01 0-2	a04 4-3	M07 2-1	S02 0-1
4 CHELSEA	M07 1-0	D27 4-1	O04 0-1		S02 0-0	a04 1-2	m02 3-1	m09 3-3	S06 1-3	O18 2-1	F21 1-1	N22 1-3	A23 0-0	S20 2-6	F10 4-0	J01 3-1	F07 2-0	a20 1-1	D20 0-2	N01 0-0	M21 1-0	D06 0-4
5 COVENTRY C	A26 2-1	O04 0-1	F28 2-1	F14 3-0		A30 1-1	D06 1-0	m02 1-0	J01 0-1	D21 2-2	m06 1-1	S13 3-0	N22 2-1	N08 1-0	M20 3-0	a20 4-1	M07 1-0	m09 1-1	D27 4-3	S27 1-0	J24 1-3	O19 1-0
6 EVERTON	O04 0-1	J01 3-0	M21 2-1	N08 2-2	F07 3-1		D28 5-1	N23 0-0	m09 3-1	m02 0-0	S21 3-1	a20 3-0	D06 4-0	A23 2-0	S02 3-1	S06 0-0	J17 2-0	M14 3-0	m11 1-0	O25 3-2	a11 4-0	D20 3-0
7 LEICESTER C	D26 1-1	a11 1-1	M14 1-0	N29 2-2	m04 1-1	N15 0-2		S03 2-1	A23 1-1	M28 4-0	S06 1-1	N08 1-1	F21 0-2	O11 3-1	D14 2-0	M25 4-1	J03 6-1	O25 2-3	S20 1-2	a25 1-2	a18 2-0	F07 3-1
8 LIVERPOOL	A30 2-1	S27 3-3	S13 2-0	D14 3-0	N29 2-0	a25 3-1	F14 4-3		M07 2-0	A25 0-0	D26 0-1	J24 2-0	N01 6-2	a18 3-0	O18 4-0	M18 2-1	N16 1-1	F28 1-0	O11 0-1	m04 1-0	J03 1-0	M28 1-2
9 LUTON T	S13 0-0	F14 2-1	N29 1-0	J03 1-0	a18 2-0	D13 1-0	J24 1-0	O25 4-1		S27 1-0	M14 2-1	A30 0-0	O11 0-0	N15 4-2	m05 2-3	N01 1-0	a25 0-0	A26 2-1	M28 3-1	D26 0-2	F28 2-1	a04 0-0
10 MANCHESTER C	a25 3-0	N08 3-1	N15 2-1	M14 1-2	S06 0-1	N29 1-3	O04 1-2	J17 0-1	F21 1-1		O26 1-1	M21 0-0	S03 2-2	m04 1-0	J03 1-0	S20 0-0	D26 1-0	a11 2-4	a15 1-1	a18 1-2	D13 3-1	A23 3-1
11 MANCHESTER U	J24 2-0	m09 3-1	A30 0-1	S28 0-1	N01 1-1	F28 0-0	D20 2-0	a20 1-0	O18 1-0	M07 2-0		J01 4-1	D27 0-1	M28 2-0	a04 3-2	N22 1-0	O11 3-1	S13 5-1	D07 3-3	F14 3-1	A25 2-3	m02 0-1
12 NEWCASTLE U	O18 1-2	M07 2-1	m04 0-3	a25 1-0	J03 1-2	D26 0-4	a04 2-0	A23 0-2	F07 2-2	O11 3-1	a18 2-1		a08 4-1	D13 3-2	N01 0-0	S03 0-2	S06 2-3	M28 2-0	M25 1-1	N15 2-2	N30 4-0	S20 1-0
13 NORWICH C	D13 1-1	F28 1-1	J03 1-1	J24 2-2	a25 1-1	m04 0-1	S17 2-1	a11 2-1	M21 0-0	F14 1-1	N15 0-0	S27 2-0		D26 2-1	N29 2-1	O04 1-0	a18 1-0	A30 4-3	N08 2-1	S13 1-3	O18 1-1	M07 0-0
14 NOTTINGHAM F	S27 1-0	S13 6-0	A27 4-0	F28 0-1	a04 0-0	J25 1-0	M22 2-1	J01 1-1	D28 2-2	D06 2-0	O04 1-1	m09 2-1	a20 1-1		M07 2-0	O18 1-0	N01 3-2	D20 0-0	m02 2-0	A30 1-1	F14 1-1	N22 3-2
15 OXFORD U	F25 0-0	D20 2-2	S27 3-2	A25 1-1	O11 2-0	F14 1-1	m09 0-0	M14 1-3	D06 4-2	S13 0-0	N08 2-0	a11 1-1	m02 0-1	O25 2-1		D27 0-1	M28 2-1	J01 3-1	N22 2-4	J24 1-3	A30 0-0	a20 3-1
16 Q.P.R.	m04 1-4	A30 1-0	D13 0-0	a18 1-1	D26 3-1	J03 0-1	S27 0-1	N08 1-3	a11 2-2	F28 1-0	a25 1-1	F14 2-1	M28 1-1	M14 3-1	N15 1-1		N29 2-2	J24 2-1	O25 2-0	A26 3-2	S13 2-3	O11 2-1
17 SHEFFIELD W	F14 1-1	D06 2-1	J24 1-1	A30 2-0	O25 2-2	A25 2-2	S13 2-2	D27 0-1	N22 1-0	a20 2-1	M21 1-0	D21 2-0	J01 1-1	a14 2-3	O04 6-1	m02 7-1		N08 3-1	a07 0-1	F28 0-1	S27 2-2	m09 0-2
18 SOUTHAMPTON	N15 0-4	M21 5-0	a25 2-2	D26 1-2	F03 2-0	O18 0-2	M07 4-0	S20 2-1	M24 3-0	N01 1-1	J03 1-1	O04 4-1	F07 1-2	S06 1-3	a18 3-0	A23 5-1	a22 1-1		S02 2-0	N29 3-1	m04 1-0	a07 2-2
19 TOTTENHAM H	J04 1-2	J24 3-0	a18 1-0	S13 1-3	N15 1-0	S27 2-0	F25 5-0	M22 1-0	O04 0-0	A30 1-0	m04 4-0	A25 1-1	a04 3-0	N29 2-3	a25 3-1	M07 1-0	O18 1-1	F14 2-0		D13 2-1	D26 4-0	N01 1-2
20 WATFORD	M21 2-0	O18 4-2	N08 4-1	a14 3-1	a30 2-3	M08 2-1	N22 5-1	D06 2-0	a21 2-0	J01 1-1	S16 1-0	D27 1-0	D19 1-1	F07 1-1	A23 3-0	a06 0-3	S20 0-1	m02 1-1	m09 1-0		O04 2-2	S06 0-1
21 WEST HAM U	a08 3-1	N22 1-1	O25 1-3	O11 5-3	A23 1-0	N02 1-0	J01 4-1	S06 2-5	S20 2-0	m09 2-0	a14 0-0	m02 1-1	M14 0-2	S02 1-2	F07 0-1	D20 1-1	M24 0-2	D06 3-1	a20 2-1	M28 1-0		D27 2-3
22 WIMBLEDON	a18 1-2	A26 3-2	F15 2-0	m05 2-1	M24 2-1	S13 1-2	A30 1-0	O04 1-3	N08 0-1	J24 0-0	N29 1-0	F28 3-1	O25 2-0	a25 2-1	D26 1-1	M21 1-1	D13 3-0	S27 2-2	a22 2-2	J03 2-1	N15 0-1	

DIVISION 2

	BARNSLEY	BIRMINGHAM C	BLACKBURN R	BRADFORD C	BRIGHTON & HA	CRYSTAL P	DERBY CO	GRIMSBY T	HUDDERSFIELD T	HULL C	IPSWICH T	LEEDS U	MILLWALL	OLDHAM A	PLYMOUTH A	PORTSMOUTH	READING	SHEFFIELD U	SHREWSBURY T	STOKE C	SUNDERLAND	W.B.A.
1 BARNSLEY		M28 2-2	N01 1-1	O11 2-0	M14 3-1	A23 2-3	N15 0-1	F24 1-0	m04 0-1	a18 1-1	a25 2-1	S02 0-1	F07 1-0	J03 1-1	S20 1-1	S06 0-2	a04 2-0	O25 2-2	M03 2-1	D26 0-2	D13 1-0	N29 2-2
2 BIRMINGHAM C	O04 1-1		D06 1-1	A25 2-1	F14 2-0	O18 4-1	A30 1-1	m02 1-0	S13 1-1	F28 0-0	S27 2-2	N21 2-1	D29 1-1	N08 1-3	J01 3-2	M21 0-1	a20 1-1	D19 2-1	m09 0-2	J24 0-0	M31 2-0	a12 0-1
3 BLACKBURN R	a11 4-2	m05 1-0		M24 2-1	a25 1-1	S20 0-2	a17 3-1	J17 2-2	D26 1-2	N15 0-2	N29 0-0	A23 2-1	F21 1-0	J31 1-0	S30 1-2	J03 1-0	a14 0-0	N08 0-2	F07 2-1	M14 2-1	S06 6-1	O11 0-1
4 BRADFORD C	M21 0-0	J03 0-0	M07 2-0		m04 2-0	S03 1-2	D26 0-1	F07 4-2	N15 4-3	a25 2-0	O18 3-4	S20 2-0	J17 4-0	S06 0-3	A23 2-2	a04 1-0	N01 3-0	O04 1-1	F21 0-0	N29 1-4	a18 3-2	D12 1-3
5 BRIGHTON & H.A.	O18 1-1	S03 2-0	N22 0-2	D06 2-2		a20 2-0	M07 0-1	S06 0-1	a03 1-1	N01 2-1	M21 1-2	m09 0-1	J01 0-1	F21 1-2	a07 1-1	A23 0-0	D27 1-1	m02 2-0	D21 3-0	O04 1-0	F07 0-3	S20 2-0
6 CRYSTAL P	J24 0-1	M14 6-0	F28 2-0	F14 1-1	D26 2-0		J03 1-0	N08 0-3	S09 1-0	D13 5-1	N15 3-3	M21 1-0	O04 2-1	a25 2-1	a11 0-0	m04 1-0	S27 1-3	S13 1-2	O25 2-3	A30 1-0	N29 2-0	a18 1-1
7 DERBY CO	D27 3-2	F07 2-2	M18 3-2	a20 1-0	O25 4-1	S06 1-0		D21 4-0	a08 2-0	O11 1-1	N08 2-1	m02 2-1	S20 1-1	A23 0-1	m09 4-2	M04 0-0	D06 3-0	N22 2-0	M14 3-1	a11 0-0	O01 3-2	F21 1-1
8 GRIMSBY T	S27 0-1	N29 0-1	D02 1-0	A30 0-0	J03 1-2	a04 0-1	S13 0-1		a18 0-1	m05 2-2	J24 1-1	O25 0-0	N01 1-0	D26 2-2	O11 1-1	a25 0-2	F14 3-2	F28 1-0	M28 0-1	D13 1-1	N15 1-1	M14 3-1
9 HUDDERSFIELD T	M31 2-2	M03 2-2	a20 1-2	D27 5-2	N08 2-1	D20 1-2	O04 2-0	J01 0-0		O25 1-3	a11 1-2	S06 1-1	m09 3-0	S20 5-4	N22 1-2	F21 2-0	m02 2-0	M14 1-1	O21 2-1	M21 2-2	A23 0-2	F07 2-1
10 HULL C	J01 3-4	S20 3-2	D27 0-0	N22 2-1	a28 1-0	m09 3-0	M21 1-1	D06 1-1	M07 0-0		O04 2-1	a08 0-0	a14 2-1	F07 1-0	S06 0-3	S02 0-2	O18 0-2	a20 0-0	m02 3-0	N08 0-4	M03 1-0	A23 2-0
11 IPSWICH T	N22 1-0	F21 3-0	m02 3-1	M14 1-0	O11 1-0	D27 3-0	a04 0-2	A23 1-1	N01 3-0	M28 0-0		J01 2-0	a21 0-0	S02 0-1	D19 3-0	F07 0-1	m09 1-1	D06 2-2	S06 1-0	O25 2-0	S20 1-1	M03 1-0
12 LEEDS U	F14 2-2	a25 4-0	J24 0-0	F28 1-0	D13 3-1	O11 3-0	N29 2-0	M07 2-0	J03 1-1	S27 3-0	a18 3-2		a04 2-0	N15 0-2	M28 4-0	O18 3-1	S13 3-2	A30 0-1	N01 1-0	A25 2-1	D26 1-1	m04 3-2
13 MILLWALL	A30 1-0	N15 0-2	S27 2-2	S13 1-2	a18 3-1	M28 0-1	F28 0-1	a11 1-0	N13 4-0	A26 0-1	D26 1-0	N08 1-0		M14 0-0	O25 3-1	N29 1-1	J24 2-1	F14 1-0	O11 4-0	J03 1-1	m05 1-1	a25 0-1
14 OLDHAM A	A25 2-0	a04 2-2	m09 3-0	D21 2-1	S27 1-1	N22 1-0	J24 1-4	a21 1-1	F28 2-0	A30 0-0	F14 2-1	D27 0-1	O17 2-1		m02 2-1	N01 0-0	M06 4-0	J01 3-1	D06 3-0	S13 2-0	O11 1-1	M28 2-1
15 PLYMOUTH A	F28 2-0	a18 0-0	F14 1-1	J24 3-2	S13 2-2	N01 3-1	D13 1-1	M21 5-0	a25 1-1	J03 4-0	O21 2-0	O04 1-1	M07 1-0	N29 3-2		D26 2-3	A30 1-0	O14 1-0	a04 3-2	m04 1-3	O18 2-4	N15 1-0
16 PORTSMOUTH	D20 2-1	O11 2-0	S13 1-0	N08 2-1	J24 1-0	D06 2-0	O21 3-1	N27 2-1	S27 1-0	F14 1-0	A30 1-1	M10 1-1	m02 2-0	a11 3-0	a20 0-1		J01 1-0	m09 1-2	D29 3-0	F28 3-0	M28 3-1	O25 2-1
17 READING	N08 0-0	D26 2-2	O04 4-0	a11 0-1	N15 2-1	F21 1-0	m04 2-0	O01 2-3	F17 3-2	M14 1-0	D13 1-4	a22 2-1	A23 0-1	O25 2-3	F07 2-0	a18 2-2		M21 2-0	S20 3-1	a25 0-1	J31 1-0	S06 1-1
18 SHEFFIELD U	M07 1-0	S06 1-1	a04 4-1	M28 2-2	N29 0-1	M17 1-0	a25 0-1	S20 1-2	O18 0-0	D26 4-2	m04 0-0	F07 0-0	S02 2-1	a18 2-0	F21 2-1	D13 1-0	O11 3-3		A23 1-1	N15 3-1	N01 2-1	J03 1-1
19 SHREWSBURY T	S13 1-0	D13 1-0	A30 0-1	S27 0-1	S16 1-0	M24 0-0	O18 0-1	O04 4-1	F14 1-2	N29 3-0	J03 2-1	a14 0-2	M21 1-2	m05 2-0	N08 1-1	N15 1-0	F28 0-0	J24 1-0		a18 4-1	a25 0-1	D26 1-0
20 STOKE C	a20 1-2	A23 0-2	O18 1-0	m02 2-3	M28 1-1	F07 3-1	N01 0-2	m09 5-1	O11 2-0	a04 1-1	M25 0-0	D21 7-2	S06 2-0	a28 0-2	D06 1-0	S20 1-1	N22 3-0	D27 5-2	J01 1-0		M17 3-0	S02 1-1
21 SUNDERLAND	m09 2-3	O25 2-0	D21 3-0	a28 2-3	A30 1-1	m02 1-0	F14 1-2	D27 0-1	J24 2-1	S13 1-0	F28 1-0	a20 1-1	D06 1-1	M21 0-2	M14 2-1	O04 0-0	O21 1-1	a11 1-2	N22 1-1	S27 2-0		N08 0-3
22 W.B.A.	m02 0-1	N01 3-2	M21 0-1	m09 2-2	F28 0-0	J01 1-2	S27 2-0	O18 1-1	A30 1-0	J24 1-1	S13 3-4	D06 3-0	N22 0-1	O04 2-0	D27 0-0	a29 1-0	D19 1-2	A25 1-0	a20 1-2	F14 4-1	a04 2-2	

Season 1986-87

DIVISION 3

	BLACKPOOL	BOLTON W	BOURNEMOUTH	BRENTFORD	BRISTOL C	BRISTOL R	BURY	CARLISLE U	CHESTER C	CHESTERFIELD	DARLINGTON	DONCASTER R	FULHAM	GILLINGHAM	MANSFIELD T	MIDDLESBROUGH	NEWPORT CO	NOTTS CO	PORT VALE	ROTHERHAM U	SWINDON T	WALSALL	WIGAN A	YORK C
1 BLACKPOOL		M17 1-1	a25 1-3	J03 2-0	N01 1-0	F21 6-1	D13 1-1	S06 1-2	m04 1-0	A23 0-0	a18 2-1	a28 1-1	a07 1-0	a11 0-1	M07 1-2	M21 0-1	N29 1-1	O18 3-1	S30 2-0	N08 1-0	F07 1-1	O04 1-1	S20 5-1	D26 2-1
2 BOLTON W	O21 1-0		J31 0-1	M03 0-2	a25 0-0	J17 2-2	D26 2-3	a18 2-0	O25 1-1	S30 1-2	S06 4-3	m04 0-1	F07 3-2	D13 3-0	J03 0-1	a11 0-1	N08 0-1	O04 1-1	S20 3-0	M14 0-0	A23 1-2	M21 1-0	a07 1-2	N29 3-1
3 BOURNEMOUTH	F03 1-1	S13 2-1		J10 1-1	S27 2-0	a20 2-0	M14 1-0	N08 2-1	S16 2-0	N22 2-0	M28 1-0	O21 3-2	D27 3-2	D02 0-2	F14 4-1	M03 3-1	A30 2-1	J24 3-0	m02 0-0	m09 2-0	J01 1-0	a11 1-0	O25 3-1	F28 3-0
4 BRENTFORD	N22 1-1	N01 1-2	A23 1-1		M17 1-1	D28 1-2	S30 0-2	F07 3-1	a04 3-1	J01 2-2	S20 5-3	a14 1-1	F01 3-3	F21 3-2	M21 3-1	D21 0-1	O04 2-0	N04 1-0	S06 0-2	m02 2-0	a20 1-1	M07 0-1	m09 2-3	O18 3-1
5 BRISTOL C	M03 3-1	D20 4-1	F21 2-0	a28 0-2		J01 0-1	A23 2-2	S20 3-0	M28 1-0	J31 1-0	S30 1-1	F07 5-0	a04 0-0	a22 2-0	N04 0-0	O25 2-2	M14 4-0	m02 3-1	a20 1-0	N22 0-1	m09 1-1	D27 2-1	S06 2-1	O11 3-0
6 BRISTOL R	S27 2-2	A30 1-0	D26 0-3	m04 0-1	a18 0-0		N08 1-1	a22 4-0	a28 3-2	O04 3-2	a30 2-1	m06 2-3	M18 0-0	a25 0-1	S13 0-0	S17 1-2	D14 2-2	F28 0-0	O18 0-0	F14 0-2	a11 3-4	M11 0-3	M21 1-0	J23 1-0
7 BURY	m09 4-1	a20 0-0	O18 0-1	F28 1-1	M31 1-2	a04 1-0		M17 0-0	A30 1-1	m02 1-1	F03 2-0	O11 2-0	M07 2-1	M28 1-0	S16 1-1	J24 0-3	S27 4-3	D27 0-2	N01 2-2	S13 0-2	N22 1-2	D20 4-0	J01 1-3	F14 1-0
8 CARLISLE U	J24 3-1	F03 0-0	a04 0-0	S15 0-0	F14 1-2	O25 2-0	O21 2-1		m06 0-2	m09 3-0	O11 1-0	M28 1-0	N22 1-3	M14 2-4	S27 1-2	a20 0-1	F28 2-2	D21 0-2	N04 2-0	D27 3-5	m02 0-3	S13 0-3	M03 0-2	A30 2-2
9 CHESTER C	D27 1-4	M07 0-0	F07 2-2	N08 1-1	O04 0-3	N22 3-1	M25 0-1	A23 2-2		D19 1-1	F21 6-0	O01 1-0	S06 2-2	O15 1-1	O18 1-1	m02 1-2	M21 2-0	F17 1-2	m09 1-2	a11 1-0	a01 2-0	N01 0-0	a20 1-2	M18 2-1
10 CHESTERFIELD	F17 1-1	F28 0-0	J03 1-1	a18 1-2	S13 0-3	M28 1-1	N29 1-1	D13 3-2	a25 0-1		m04 1-0	D26 4-1	N04 3-1	M03 1-0	J25 0-1	F14 2-1	O25 3-2	S27 1-2	O11 2-4	S16 2-1	M14 1-3	A30 3-2	O21 4-3	a04 1-0
11 DARLINGTON	M10 1-1	F18 0-1	O04 0-3	F15 1-1	F28 0-0	M03 1-1	a11 4-1	M21 0-1	S27 1-0	D27 1-1		M14 2-2	m02 0-1	O21 1-1	A30 2-1	N08 0-1	S16 1-3	S13 2-1	D19 3-2	a20 1-1	O25 0-0	m09 1-3	N22 1-0	F24 2-2
12 DONCASTER R	S14 2-2	D27 3-0	M17 0-3	A30 2-0	S17 1-0	m02 2-0	M21 0-0	O14 2-0	F27 1-1	a20 1-1	O18 0-0		N01 2-1	N07 2-0	F17 1-0	m09 0-2	F14 0-1	M07 1-2	N22 2-1	J01 3-0	D21 2-2	J24 1-1	a22 1-1	S27 3-1
13 FULHAM	A30 0-1	S16 4-2	m04 1-3	S13 1-3	N08 0-3	O21 2-2	O25 2-1	J03 3-0	J24 0-5	a11 3-1	O29 3-1	M03 0-0		D26 2-2	D13 1-1	S27 2-2	a18 2-0	F14 3-1	M28 0-6	F17 1-1	O11 0-2	F28 2-2	a28 2-2	a25 1-0
14 GILLINGHAM	N04 2-1	m09 1-0	M21 2-1	S27 2-0	A30 1-1	D19 4-1	O04 1-0	O18 1-0	F14 1-2	N01 3-0	M17 4-1	a04 2-1	a20 4-1		F28 2-0	S13 0-0	F17 1-1	N22 3-1	M07 0-0	F03 1-0	D27 1-3	J01 4-0	m02 0-0	S16 2-0
15 MANSFIELD T	D06 1-1	N22 2-2	S20 1-1	O11 1-0	a11 2-0	J31 5-0	F07 1-3	F21 2-0	M14 2-3	S07 1-1	a28 1-0	A23 2-1	m09 1-1	S30 1-0		D27 1-1	N25 1-0	a21 1-2	J01 0-1	M03 0-0	N08 0-0	m02 2-0	D21 1-5	M28 1-1
16 MIDDLESBROUGH	O11 1-3	N04 0-0	N01 4-0	a25 2-0	M07 1-0	F07 1-0	S06 3-1	D26 1-0	N29 1-2	S20 2-0	a05 1-1	D13 1-0	F21 3-0	a28 3-0	m04 1-0		J03 2-0	M17 2-0	A23 2-2	M28 0-0	S30 1-0	O18 3-1	m06 0-0	a18 3-1
17 NEWPORT CO	m02 1-1	a04 2-1	F24 0-1	a07 2-2	D02 0-1	m09 0-1	F21 2-2	O28 1-1	O11 2-2	M08 1-0	a14 3-0	S20 3-2	J01 0-0	A23 1-2	M17 0-3	N22 0-1		N01 1-1	D27 0-2	D20 1-2	S06 2-2	a20 2-4	M31 1-2	N04 1-1
18 NOTTS CO	M14 3-2	M28 0-0	S06 1-1	a11 1-1	N29 2-0	S30 3-0	m04 1-2	a26 2-1	a18 1-1	F21 2-1	J31 2-2	O25 3-1	S20 2-3	J03 3-1	D26 0-0	O21 1-0	M03 5-2		F07 4-1	O11 5-0	a28 2-3	N08 2-1	A23 2-0	D13 5-1
19 PORT VALE	F28 1-6	F14 1-1	M31 1-2	J24 4-1	D26 0-0	M14 4-1	M03 2-0	a11 0-1	D14 2-1	M31 2-2	a25 1-2	F03 4-2	O04 0-1	O25 1-2	a18 3-2	F17 0-0	m04 6-1	S16 1-1		A30 1-1	O21 3-4	S27 4-1	N08 0-1	S13 2-3
20 ROTHERHAM U	a04 1-0	O18 1-0	D13 4-2	N30 2-3	J03 2-0	S20 0-1	J31 2-1	m04 2-1	N04 3-0	F07 0-1	D26 0-0	a18 2-0	A23 0-0	S06 0-1	N01 2-2	O04 1-4	a25 3-1	M21 1-1	J27 1-1		F21 1-2	M17 1-0	S30 0-2	M07 0-0
21 SWINDON T	S16 2-6	M24 2-0	a18 1-1	D26 2-0	D14 1-2	N04 1-2	J03 1-0	N29 2-0	S13 1-1	O18 2-1	a22 1-0	a25 1-1	M21 2-0	m04 1-1	a03 3-0	F28 1-0	J25 3-0	A31 1-2	M17 1-0	S27 2-0		m06 0-0	O05 3-1	N01 3-1
22 WALSALL	M28 2-1	O11 3-3	N04 2-0	O25 5-2	m04 1-1	A23 0-3	a25 3-1	a07 3-0	a22 1-0	a14 2-1	D13 4-2	S06 1-3	S30 1-1	a18 1-0	N29 2-0	M14 1-0	D26 2-0	a04 1-1	a28 5-2	O21 4-1	N25 1-0		F07 2-3	M24 3-2
23 WIGAN A	F13 4-1	S26 2-1	a14 0-2	D13 1-1	J24 3-1	O11 4-3	a17 1-0	N01 2-0	D26 2-2	M17 1-1	J03 1-1	N04 1-1	O18 2-0	N29 3-1	a25 3-0	A30 0-2	S13 1-2	M24 1-0	a04 2-1	F28 2-1	M28 3-2	S16 5-1		m04 3-2
24 YORK C	a20 1-1	m02 2-1	S30 2-0	M14 2-1	M21 1-1	S06 1-0	S20 1-0	M31 2-0	O21 1-1	N08 1-1	A23 3-1	F21 1-1	D20 1-1	F07 2-1	O04 1-3	J01 3-1	a11 3-0	m09 1-1	a14 1-4	O25 2-1	M03 0-3	N22 1-5	D27 1-1	

DIVISION 4

	ALDERSHOT	BURNLEY	CAMBRIDGE U	CARDIFF C	COLCHESTER U	CREWE A	EXETER C	HALIFAX T	HARTLEPOOL U	HEREFORD U	LINCOLN C	NORTHAMPTON T	ORIENT	PETERBOROUGH U	PRESTON N.E.	ROCHDALE	SCUNTHORPE U	SOUTHEND U	STOCKPORT CO	SWANSEA C	TORQUAY U	TRANMERE R	WOLVERHAMPTON W	WREXHAM
1 ALDERSHOT		O11 2-0	O21 4-1	m09 1-2	D27 1-0	D20 1-0	m02 2-1	M24 4-1	O25 1-1	M03 1-0	S13 4-0	m06 3-3	a20 1-2	J24 1-1	M14 0-0	N22 2-1	S16 2-1	J01 0-1	N09 3-1	F28 4-1	F14 1-1	S27 0-2	A30 1-2	a11 1-0
2 BURNLEY	M21 0-1		a04 0-2	D19 1-3	N04 2-1	D27 4-0	M07 0-0	S27 3-0	S13 1-1	J24 0-6	N22 3-1	M17 2-1	m09 2-1	N01 0-0	O04 1-4	J01 0-3	A30 1-0	m02 2-1	O18 2-0	S16 1-1	a14 2-2	F28 2-2	F14 2-5	a20 0-0
3 CAMBRIDGE U	M17 0-3	N08 3-1		m01 2-1	a21 0-1	O31 0-3	S13 2-2	A30 1-0	J24 3-0	m09 2-1	S27 1-1	O17 2-3	M10 2-0	N22 1-1	M11 2-0	D20 3-0	F28 1-0	D28 1-2	O03 5-0	a11 1-0	S16 3-3	F14 1-1	J10 0-0	M07 1-0
4 CARDIFF C	D13 2-0	a25 1-0	N29 3-0		M14 0-2	O04 1-1	M31 0-0	M03 0-0	m07 4-0	S27 4-1	S16 1-1	m04 1-1	M24 1-1	F28 0-1	a11 1-1	A30 0-0	O25 1-1	N08 0-2	J03 1-1	D26 0-0	a18 3-1	S13 0-2	J24 0-2	M21 0-0
5 COLCHESTER U	m04 0-1	a10 1-0	D26 1-2	O17 3-1		M17 2-1	A29 1-1	N28 3-1	S16 2-1	F27 2-0	J10 2-0	a17 3-1	N07 0-0	S27 1-3	D13 0-2	F13 2-0	J03 1-0	M20 1-2	M06 5-1	a24 2-1	S12 3-0	J23 1-1	O31 3-0	O03 2-1
6 CREWE A	a25 1-3	m04 1-0	M03 0-0	M28 1-2	O21 1-1		S16 2-2	O25 2-2	F28 1-0	A30 1-2	a11 1-2	N28 0-5	O10 3-2	F14 1-3	D26 2-2	M31 5-1	J24 2-2	M13 2-1	a17 5-0	S27 1-1	D13 1-0	J03 3-2	S13 1-1	N08 1-1
7 EXETER C	N29 4-0	O25 3-0	J31 1-1	S20 0-0	J17 2-0	F07 1-0		a11 2-2	O22 2-0	M14 1-0	O11 2-0	J03 1-1	A23 1-0	N08 1-1	M04 1-2	M28 1-1	a25 0-0	O01 0-0	S06 4-0	a18 2-2	D26 2-2	D13 1-0	m04 1-3	F21 4-2
8 HALIFAX T	A23 1-0	F21 2-2	a14 1-0	O31 1-1	a29 0-0	M07 0-3	N04 2-0		a20 1-0	D19 2-1	F24 1-2	S30 3-6	N21 4-0	m09 1-0	F07 1-3	D27 3-1	a03 1-1	S05 0-1	S19 0-2	O04 1-0	M21 2-4	O17 0-0	M17 3-4	J31 2-1
9 HARTLEPOOL U	M07 1-1	J31 2-2	S06 2-2	A23 1-1	F06 1-0	O01 0-5	M18 1-0	D26 0-0		O11 0-0	M29 2-1	N01 3-3	F21 1-3	O18 1-2	m04 2-2	a04 1-1	a17 0-2	a14 1-0	N28 1-0	J03 1-1	N04 2-1	a24 1-1	D13 0-1	S21 0-1
10 HEREFORD U	N01 1-0	S06 2-0	F13 2-3	F21 0-2	O01 2-3	J28 2-0	O18 1-1	a26 1-0	M21 4-0		N08 0-0	a08 3-2	S20 1-1	O04 2-0	F25 2-3	M18 0-1	N29 2-2	F07 0-1	a11 1-2	m04 2-0	J03 2-2	a18 1-0	D26 2-0	A23 0-0
11 LINCOLN C	M31 0-2	J03 2-1	F22 0-3	F07 0-1	A23 3-1	N04 2-1	M21 1-1	a18 0-0	O05 1-4	a04 0-0		a26 3-1	S30 2-0	M08 1-2	S06 1-1	O18 1-1	m04 1-2	S20 1-3	D26 0-0	D13 4-0	M17 1-1	N01 3-1	N29 3-0	a14 0-1
12 NORTHAMPTON T	O04 4-2	O22 4-2	M14 3-0	D28 4-1	J01 3-2	a29 2-1	D02 4-0	F27 1-0	M04 1-1	O25 3-2	D21 3-1		a12 2-0	S14 2-1	N08 3-1	J24 5-0	M11 1-0	a20 2-1	M21 2-1	F14 0-1	A31 1-0	S17 2-0	S27 2-1	D13 2-2
13 ORIENT	D26 1-3	D13 2-0	a18 3-0	M17 2-0	a03 1-0	M21 1-1	a07 2-0	J03 1-3	S27 2-0	F14 2-0	F28 2-1	N04 0-1		A30 1-0	a25 1-2	S16 3-0	S13 3-1	O04 1-0	O31 1-0	J24 1-4	m04 3-2	N29 2-2	M07 3-1	O18 2-4
14 PETERBOROUGH U	S06 1-1	M04 1-1	J04 2-1	O01 1-2	F21 2-0	S20 1-2	a04 2-2	D13 2-0	M14 3-1	M28 2-1	O25 0-1	J31 0-1	J17 0-1		N29 2-1	O11 1-1	D26 1-1	A23 2-0	m04 0-0	O22 1-1	a25 2-1	N05 2-1	a18 0-1	F07 1-0
15 PRESTON N.E.	O18 1-2	M28 2-1	O11 1-0	N04 0-1	m09 1-0	a20 2-1	N01 2-1	S16 3-2	D27 0-0	S13 2-1	J24 3-0	a03 1-0	D20 1-0	m02 0-0		a14 2-4	F14 2-1	N22 2-0	M17 3-0	A30 2-1	S27 1-1	a28 2-0	F28 2-2	J01 1-0
16 ROCHDALE	F24 3-1	a18 0-2	a25 2-0	M10 0-0	S20 1-0	A23 1-1	O04 0-0	m04 5-3	N08 0-2	O21 2-0	M14 1-1	S06 1-2	F07 0-0	M21 3-2	a07 0-2		D13 1-1	F21 1-2	m06 2-1	a29 2-0	N29 3-3	D26 0-1	a11 0-3	M25 3-3
17 SCUNTHORPE U	F07 2-0	a28 2-1	S30 1-1	M07 1-3	N21 5-2	S07 2-1	D19 3-1	N09 2-1	J01 1-2	m01 3-1	D27 2-1	A23 2-2	F10 0-2	a20 2-0	S19 4-0	m09 2-0		a11 3-0	F21 1-2	M21 3-2	O17 2-0	J31 6-0	O05 0-2	N01 3-3
18 SOUTHEND U	a18 2-0	N28 2-1	m05 3-1	a03 2-0	O10 1-1	O18 3-1	F27 2-1	F03 2-3	A29 1-1	S16 2-0	F14 1-0	D26 0-4	M27 2-1	J10 2-2	J03 1-2	S26 5-3	N04 3-1		D13 0-0	S12 1-2	O31 4-0	M06 3-0	a24 1-0	M17 0-3
19 STOCKPORT CO	a03 0-0	M13 0-1	M27 3-2	N22 2-0	O24 1-1	J01 2-1	J23 0-0	F14 2-0	m01 0-2	N03 1-2	a20 1-0	O27 0-3	M02 2-2	D27 3-1	O20 1-3	S12 1-1	a13 1-0	m08 0-2		a27 3-1	F27 0-0	A29 0-2	S15 0-2	D19 2-1
20 SWANSEA C	S30 2-1	F06 2-2	N04 2-0	a20 2-0	D20 1-2	F21 1-1	J01 1-0	M29 0-2	N22 1-0	D27 1-3	m09 2-0	S20 2-1	S06 4-1	M17 0-1	J17 1-1	N01 1-0	O11 1-2	J31 1-0	A23 3-0		a07 0-1	a03 2-0	O18 1-0	m02 0-3
21 TORQUAY U	S20 2-2	A23 1-1	F07 1-0	a28 1-0	J31 3-1	m09 2-2	a20 1-1	O11 1-0	a11 0-1	N22 1-1	O21 0-1	F24 0-1	D27 2-2	M31 1-0	F21 0-2	m02 2-1	M14 2-2	M03 2-1	S30 0-0	O25 3-5		M28 0-2	N08 1-2	S06 2-1
22 TRANMERE R	F21 1-1	S30 2-1	S20 1-1	F24 2-1	S05 3-4	N22 3-2	m08 1-0	M13 3-4	J10 1-1	J01 3-3	M03 2-0	F06 1-1	m01 1-3	a11 1-1	A23 1-1	a20 1-1	O21 1-0	O24 1-3	a07 0-3	N08 1-1	O03 2-2		M21 0-1	D27 0-2
23 WOLVERHAMPTON W	F17 3-0	S20 0-1	A23 1-2	S06 0-1	M03 2-0	J31 2-3	D27 2-2	O21 1-2	m09 4-1	a20 1-0	m02 3-0	F21 1-1	O25 3-1	J01 0-3	S30 1-0	N04 0-0	M28 1-0	D20 1-2	F07 3-1	M14 4-0	a04 1-0	O11 2-1		N22 0-3
24 WREXHAM	O28 3-0	D26 2-2	D10 2-1	O11 5-1	M28 0-1	a04 2-1	S27 0-0	S12 3-1	F14 1-1	m06 2-2	A30 1-1	m09 1-3	M14 1-1	O14 4-3	a18 1-1	F28 2-2	M03 1-1	a30 4-0	a25 0-0	N29 0-0	J24 2-1	m04 1-1	J03 0-0	

LEAGUE TABLES

DIVISION 1

	P	W	D	L	F	A	W	D	L	F	A	Pts
Everton	42	16	4	1	49	11	10	4	7	27	20	86
Liverpool	42	15	3	3	43	16	8	5	8	29	26	77
Tottenham H	42	14	3	4	40	14	7	5	9	28	29	71
Arsenal	42	12	5	4	31	12	8	5	8	27	23	70
Norwich C	42	9	10	2	27	20	8	7	6	26	31	68
Wimbledon	42	11	5	5	32	22	8	4	9	25	28	66
Luton T	42	14	5	2	29	13	4	7	10	18	32	66
Nottingham F	42	12	8	1	36	14	6	3	12	28	37	65
Watford	42	12	5	4	38	20	6	4	11	29	34	63
Coventry C	42	14	4	3	35	17	3	8	10	15	28	63
Manchester U	42	13	3	5	38	18	1	11	9	14	27	56
Southampton	42	11	5	5	44	24	3	5	13	25	44	52
Sheffield W	42	9	7	5	39	24	4	6	11	19	35	52
Chelsea	42	8	6	7	30	30	5	7	9	23	34	52
West Ham U	42	10	4	7	33	28	4	6	11	19	39	52
QPR	42	9	7	5	31	27	4	4	13	17	37	50
Newcastle U	42	10	4	7	33	29	2	7	12	14	36	47
Oxford U	42	8	8	5	30	25	3	5	13	14	44	46
Charlton A	42	7	7	7	26	22	4	4	13	19	33	44
Leicester C	42	9	7	5	39	24	2	2	17	15	52	42
Manchester C	42	8	6	7	28	24	0	9	12	8	33	39
Aston Villa	42	7	7	7	25	25	1	5	15	20	54	36

DIVISION 2

	P	W	D	L	F	A	W	D	L	F	A	Pts
Derby Co	42	14	6	1	42	18	11	3	7	22	20	84
Portsmouth	42	17	2	2	37	11	6	7	8	16	17	78
Oldham A	42	13	6	2	36	16	9	3	9	29	28	75
Leeds U	42	15	4	2	43	16	4	7	10	15	28	68
Ipswich T	42	12	6	3	29	10	5	7	9	30	33	64
Crystal P	42	12	4	5	35	20	7	1	13	16	33	62
Plymouth A	42	12	6	3	40	23	4	7	10	22	34	61
Stoke C	42	11	5	5	40	21	5	5	11	23	32	58
Sheffield U	42	10	8	3	31	19	5	5	11	19	30	58
Bradford C	42	10	5	6	36	27	5	5	11	26	35	55
Barnsley	42	8	7	6	26	23	6	6	9	23	29	55
Blackburn R	42	11	4	6	30	22	4	6	11	15	33	55
Reading	42	11	4	6	33	23	3	7	11	19	36	53
Hull C	42	10	6	5	25	22	3	8	10	16	33	53
WBA	42	8	6	7	29	22	5	6	10	22	27	51
Millwall	42	10	5	6	27	16	4	4	13	12	29	51
Huddersfield T	42	9	6	6	38	30	4	6	11	16	31	51
Shrewsbury T	42	11	3	7	24	14	4	3	14	17	39	51
Birmingham C	42	8	9	4	27	21	3	8	10	20	38	50
Sunderland	42	8	6	7	25	23	4	6	11	24	36	48
Grimsby T	42	5	8	8	18	21	5	6	10	21	38	44
Brighton & HA	42	7	6	8	22	20	2	6	13	15	34	39

DIVISION 3

	P	W	D	L	F	A	W	D	L	F	A	Pts
Bournemouth	46	19	3	1	44	14	10	7	6	32	26	97
Middlesbrough	46	16	5	2	38	11	12	5	6	29	19	94
Swindon T	46	14	5	4	37	19	11	7	5	40	28	87
Wigan A	46	15	5	3	47	26	10	5	8	36	34	85
Gillingham	46	16	5	2	42	14	7	4	12	23	34	78
Bristol C	46	14	6	3	42	15	7	8	8	21	21	77
Notts Co	46	14	6	3	52	24	7	7	9	25	32	76
Wallsall	46	16	4	3	50	27	6	5	12	30	40	75
Blackpool	46	11	7	5	35	20	5	9	9	39	39	64
Mansfield T	46	9	9	5	30	23	6	7	10	22	32	61
Brentford T	46	9	7	7	39	32	6	8	9	25	34	60
Port Vale	46	8	6	9	43	36	7	6	10	33	34	57
Doncaster R	46	11	8	4	32	19	3	7	13	24	43	57
Rotherham U	46	10	6	7	29	23	5	6	12	19	34	57
Chester C	46	7	9	7	32	28	6	8	9	29	31	56
Bury	46	9	7	7	30	26	5	6	12	24	34	55
Chesterfield	46	11	5	7	36	33	2	10	11	20	36	54
Fulham	46	8	8	7	35	41	4	9	10	24	36	53
Bristol R	46	7	8	8	26	29	6	4	13	23	46	51
York C	46	11	8	4	34	29	1	5	17	21	50	49
Bolton W	46	8	5	10	29	26	2	10	11	17	32	45
Carlisle U	46	7	5	11	26	35	3	3	17	13	43	38
Darlington	46	6	10	7	25	28	1	6	16	20	49	37
Newport Co	46	4	9	10	26	34	4	4	15	23	52	37

DIVISION 4

	P	W	D	L	F	A	W	D	L	F	A	Pts
Northampton T	46	20	2	1	56	20	10	7	6	47	33	99
Preston NE	46	16	4	3	36	18	10	8	5	36	29	90
Southend U	46	14	4	5	43	27	11	1	11	25	28	80
Wolves	46	12	3	8	36	24	12	4	7	33	26	79
Colchester U	46	15	3	5	41	20	6	4	13	23	36	70
Aldershot	46	13	5	5	40	22	7	5	11	24	35	70
Orient	46	15	2	6	40	25	5	7	11	24	36	69
Scunthorpe U	46	15	3	5	52	27	3	9	11	21	30	66
Wrexham	46	8	13	2	38	24	7	7	9	32	27	65
Peterboro' U	46	10	7	6	29	21	7	7	9	28	29	65
Cambridge U	46	12	6	5	37	23	5	5	13	23	39	62
Swansea C	46	13	3	7	31	21	4	8	11	25	40	62
Cardiff C	46	6	12	5	24	18	9	4	10	24	32	61
Exeter C	46	11	10	2	37	17	0	13	10	16	32	56
Halifax T	46	10	5	8	32	32	5	5	13	27	42	55
Hereford U	46	10	6	7	33	23	4	5	14	27	38	53
Crewe A	46	8	9	6	38	35	5	5	13	32	37	53
Hartlepool U	46	6	11	6	24	30	5	7	11	20	35	51
Stockport Co	46	9	6	8	25	27	4	6	13	15	42	51
Tranmere R	46	6	10	7	32	37	5	7	11	22	35	50
Rochdale	46	8	8	7	31	30	3	9	11	23	43	50
Burnley	46	9	7	7	31	35	3	6	14	22	39	49
Torquay U	46	8	8	7	28	29	2	10	11	28	43	48
Lincoln C	46	8	7	8	30	27	4	5	14	15	38	48

Football League Records

Top scorers: Div 1, J.Aldridge (Liverpool) 26 goals; Div 2, D.Currie (Barnsley) 28 goals; Div 3, D.Crown (Southend United) 26 goals; Div 4, S.Bull (Wolverhampton Wanderers) 34 goals. Play-offs: Div 1, Blackburn Rovers v Chelsea 0-2, 1-4; Bradford City v Middlesbrough 2-1, 0-2; Middlesbrough v Chelsea 2-0, 1-0; Div 2, Bristol City v Sheffield United 1-0, 1-1; Notts County v Walsall 1-3, 1-1; Bristol City v Walsall 1-3, 2-0, 0-4; Div 3, Swansea City v Rotherham United 1-0, 1-1; Torquay United v Scunthorpe United 2-1, 1-1; Swansea City v Torquay United 2-1, 3-3.

Aston Villa, Millwall and Middlesbrough promoted to Div 1; Chelsea, Oxford United, Portsmouth and Watford relegated to Div 2; Brighton & Hove Albion, Sunderland and Walsall promoted to Div 2; Huddersfield Town, Reading and Sheffield United relegated to Div 3; Bolton Wanderers, Cardiff City, Swansea City and Wolverhampton Wanderers promoted to Div 3; Doncaster Rovers, Grimsby Town, Rotherham United and York City relegated to Div 4; Newport County were relegated from Division Four and replaced by Lincoln City. Orient became Leyton Orient.

Peter Beardsley, signed from Newcastle United for £1.9 million, he took a little time to settle at Anfield but eventually proved his worth.

DIVISION 1

	ARSENAL	CHARLTON A	CHELSEA	COVENTRY C	DERBY CO	EVERTON	LIVERPOOL	LUTON T	MANCHESTER U	NEWCASTLE U	NORWICH C	NOTTINGHAM F	OXFORD U	PORTSMOUTH	Q.P.R.	SHEFFIELD W	SOUTHAMPTON	TOTTENHAM H	WATFORD	WEST HAM U	WIMBLEDON
1 ARSENAL		F27 4-0	N03 3-1	m02 1-1	O24 2-1	D19 1-1	A15 1-2	F13 2-1	J24 1-2	M19 1-1	a04 2-0	D26 0-2	O10 2-0	A29 6-0	J02 0-0	D05 3-1	N21 0-1	M06 2-1	a15 0-1	S26 1-0	S19 3-0
2 CHARLTON A	O03 0-3		D20 2-2	N21 2-2	O17 0-1	D05 0-0	J23 0-2	S19 1-0	A29 1-3	a23 2-0	N07 2-0	A15 1-2	M26 0-0	D26 2-1	S05 0-1	F20 3-1	O31 1-1	m02 1-1	a04 1-0	M12 3-0	F13 1-1
3 CHELSEA	a02 1-1	m07 1-1		O17 1-0	a09 1-0	M12 0-0	a30 1-1	A29 3-0	F13 1-2	O03 2-2	S19 1-0	S05 4-3	O31 2-1	J23 0-0	D26 1-1	A15 2-1	M26 0-1	J02 0-0	M29 1-1	D12 1-1	N28 1-1
4 COVENTRY C	D13 0-0	a09 0-0	M05 3-3		M19 0-3	a19 1-2	A29 1-4	M15 4-0	S05 0-0	O24 1-3	F20 0-0	S19 0-3	a02 1-0	a30 1-0	m07 0-0	F13 3-0	O20 2-3	A15 2-1	O03 1-0	N28 0-0	N14 3-3
5 DERBY CO	M26 0-0	M05 1-1	N22 2-0	O31 2-0		m02 0-0	M16 1-1	A15 1-0	F10 1-2	a04 2-1	D26 1-2	O10 0-1	S26 0-1	S05 0-0	a13 0-2	S19 2-2	a23 2-0	D20 1-2	D05 1-1	F27 1-0	A29 0-1
6 EVERTON	m07 1-2	a30 1-1	O10 4-1	S26 1-2	D12 3-0		M20 1-0	D26 2-0	S19 2-1	M05 1-0	A15 1-0	J03 1-0	N28 0-0	a09 2-1	F13 2-0	A29 4-0	F27 1-0	S05 0-0	O24 2-0	N14 3-1	M29 2-2
7 LIVERPOOL	J16 2-0	S15 3-2	D06 2-1	J01 4-0	S29 4-0	N01 2-0		m09 1-1	a04 3-3	D28 4-0	N21 0-0	a13 5-0	S12 2-0	O03 4-0	O17 4-0	D19 1-0	m02 1-1	a23 1-0	N24 4-0	F06 0-0	M26 2-1
8 LUTON T	A31 1-1	D28 1-0	J01 3-0	A18 0-1	J16 1-0	S12 2-1	O24 0-1		O03 1-1	N07 4-0	D05 1-2	m13 1-1	F06 7-4	M29 4-1	a19 2-1	a05 2-2	D18 2-2	N21 2-0	m02 2-1	A22 2-2	O17 2-0
9 MANCHESTER U	A19 0-0	J01 0-0	A31 3-1	F06 1-0	a02 4-1	D28 2-1	N15 1-1	a12 3-0		S12 2-2	O17 2-1	O31 2-2	D12 3-1	m07 4-1	a30 2-1	M12 4-1	J16 0-2	S26 1-0	A22 2-0	M26 3-1	m09 2-1
10 NEWCASTLE U	O31 0-1	N28 2-1	F27 3-1	M26 2-2	N14 0-0	O17 1-1	S20 1-4	a02 4-0	D26 1-0		F13 1-3	A29 0-1	a30 3-1	D12 1-1	a09 1-1	J02 2-2	S26 2-1	J23 2-0	a12 3-0	m07 2-1	S05 1-2
11 NORWICH C	N14 2-4	a02 2-0	D28 3-0	A22 3-1	S12 1-2	J16 0-3	a20 0-0	a30 2-2	M05 1-0	S01 1-1		S26 0-2	M16 4-2	N28 0-1	O31 1-1	M26 0-3	A19 0-1	O10 2-1	F06 0-0	J01 4-1	m07 0-1
12 NOTTINGHAM F	S12 0-1	J16 2-2	F06 3-2	D28 4-1	M30 2-1	A22 0-0	a02 2-1	m15 1-1	M19 0-0	J01 0-2	m04 2-0		m07 5-3	N14 5-0	D13 4-0	O17 3-0	S02 3-3	O24 3-0	A19 1-0	a20 0-0	a30 0-0
13 OXFORD U	M30 0-0	O24 2-1	M19 4-4	N07 1-0	F20 0-0	a23 1-1	D26 0-3	S05 2-5	m02 0-2	D05 1-3	O03 3-0	D19 0-2		A15 4-2	S19 2-0	a13 0-3	a04 0-0	F13 0-0	N21 1-1	O17 1-2	J02 2-5
14 PORTSMOUTH	J01 1-1	S12 1-1	A18 0-3	D05 0-0	F06 2-1	N21 0-1	F27 0-2	O10 3-1	D19 1-2	m02 1-2	a23 2-2	a04 0-1	J16 2-2		M26 0-1	O31 1-2	A22 2-2	N04 0-0	D28 1-1	A31 2-1	S26 2-1
15 Q.P.R.	A22 2-0	F06 2-0	S12 3-1	D18 1-2	A19 1-1	S02 1-0	M05 0-1	S26 2-0	D05 0-2	N21 1-1	M19 3-0	M16 2-1	D28 3-2	O24 2-1		a23 1-1	J01 3-0	a04 2-0	N07 0-0	J16 0-1	F27 1-0
16 SHEFFIELD W	a30 3-3	S26 2-0	J16 3-0	A31 0-3	D28 2-1	J01 1-0	m07 1-5	N14 0-2	O10 2-4	A22 0-1	O24 1-0	M05 0-1	A18 1-1	M19 1-0	N28 3-1		F06 2-1	F27 0-3	S12 2-3	a02 2-1	D12 1-0
17 SOUTHAMPTON	a09 4-2	M19 0-1	O24 3-0	M12 1-2	N28 1-2	O03 0-4	D12 2-2	m07 1-1	A15 2-2	M01 1-1	J23 0-0	F13 1-1	N14 3-0	J03 0-2	A29 0-1	S05 1-1		D26 2-1	O17 1-0	a30 2-1	a02 2-2
18 TOTTENHAM H	O18 1-2	D13 0-1	A22 1-0	J16 2-2	M01 0-0	M09 2-1	N28 0-2	m04 2-1	F23 1-1	A19 3-1	M12 1-3	M26 1-1	S01 3-0	a04 0-1	N14 1-1	O03 2-0	S12 2-1		J01 2-1	D28 2-1	O31 0-3
19 WATFORD	N28 2-0	N14 2-1	S26 0-3	F27 0-1	a30 1-1	M26 1-2	F13 1-4	D12 0-1	J02 0-1	a19 1-1	S05 0-1	J23 0-0	a09 3-0	S19 0-0	a01 0-1	D26 1-3	M05 0-1	A29 1-1		O31 1-2	A15 1-0
20 WEST HAM U	a12 0-1	O10 1-1	m02 4-1	a23 1-1	O03 1-1	a04 0-0	S05 1-1	J02 1-1	O25 1-1	D19 2-1	A29 2-0	N21 3-2	M05 1-1	F13 1-1	A15 0-3	N07 0-1	D05 2-1	S19 0-1	F19 1-0		D26 1-2
21 WIMBLEDON	D28 3-1	S01 4-1	a23 2-2	a05 1-2	J01 2-1	A18 1-1	N04 1-1	M05 2-0	N21 2-1	F06 0-0	D18 1-0	D05 1-1	A22 1-1	a19 2-2	O03 1-2	m03 1-1	N07 2-0	M19 3-0	J16 1-2	S12 1-1	

Teddy Sheringham was Millwall's leading scorer with 22 goals as the Lions won promotion to Division One for the first time.

DIVISION 2

	ASTON VILLA	BARNSLEY	BIRMINGHAM C	BLACKBURN R	BOURNEMOUTH	BRADFORD C	CRYSTAL P	HUDDERSFIELD T	HULL C	IPSWICH T	LEEDS U	LEICESTER C	MANCHESTER C	MIDDLESBROUGH	MILLWALL	OLDHAM A	PLYMOUTH A	READING	SHEFFIELD U	SHREWSBURY T	STOKE C	SWINDON T	W.B.A.
1 ASTON VILLA		S12 0-0	A22 0-2	S30 1-1	O17 1-1	m02 1-0	O21 4-1	D28 1-1	J01 5-0	J16 1-0	M12 1-2	F06 2-1	A31 1-1	S08 0-1	N07 1-2	a04 1-2	F27 5-2	O31 2-1	S26 1-1	a23 1-0	M26 0-1	D05 2-1	D18 0-0
2 BARNSLEY	J02 1-3		a23 2-2	F13 0-1	M08 2-1	N07 3-0	A29 2-1	a04 1-0	O17 1-3	F27 2-3	A16 1-1	M12 1-1	M26 3-1	m02 0-3	D19 4-1	D26 1-1	S05 2-1	O20 5-2	S29 1-2	N21 2-1	O31 5-2	S15 0-1	D05 3-1
3 BIRMINGHAM C	D12 1-2	N03 2-0		S15 1-0	A29 1-1	M05 1-1	S05 0-6	O03 2-0	a02 1-1	N28 1-0	m06 0-0	N14 2-2	a30 0-3	O24 0-0	F09 1-0	M19 1-3	D26 0-1	O10 2-2	a09 1-0	S19 0-0	A15 2-0	J02 1-1	M08 0-1
4 BLACKBURN R	F20 3-2	A18 0-1	D19 2-0		M12 3-1	D28 1-1	N21 2-0	S12 2-2	J16 2-1	S01 1-0	O03 1-1	M19 3-3	F06 2-1	S26 0-2	D05 2-1	N07 1-0	O24 1-1	m02 1-1	J01 4-1	a04 2-2	O17 2-0	a25 0-0	A22 3-1
5 BOURNEMOUTH	M05 1-2	A31 1-2	J01 4-2	O10 1-1		A22 2-0	N07 2-3	N21 0-2	F06 6-2	O31 1-1	M26 0-0	S26 2-3	D01 0-2	D19 0-0	a19 1-2	D05 2-2	S29 2-2	S12 3-0	J16 1-2	O20 2-0	F27 0-0	m02 2-0	D28 3-2
6 BRADFORD C	N28 2-4	a02 1-1	O17 4-0	S19 2-1	D12 2-0		O31 2-0	M01 0-1	a09 2-0	m07 2-3	A29 0-0	a30 4-1	O21 2-4	O03 2-0	S05 3-1	F13 5-3	S16 3-1	a20 3-0	N14 2-0	D26 1-1	J02 1-4	A15 2-0	M12 4-1
7 CRYSTAL P	a09 1-1	J01 3-2	F06 3-0	a30 2-0	a02 3-0	M19 1-1		J16 2-1	A22 2-2	S26 1-2	N28 3-0	S12 2-1	m07 2-0	S01 3-1	O10 1-0	M05 3-1	N03 5-1	D28 2-3	D13 2-1	F27 1-2	N14 2-0	O24 2-1	S08 4-1
8 HUDDERSFIELD T	S19 0-1	N14 2-2	F27 2-2	J02 1-2	a30 1-2	S29 1-2	A15 2-2		O20 0-2	a08 1-2	S15 0-0	N28 1-0	a02 1-0	O10 1-4	O31 2-1	a19 2-2	D12 2-1	M05 0-2	m07 0-2	A29 0-0	D26 0-3	F13 0-3	M26 1-3
9 HULL C	A29 2-1	M05 1-2	N07 2-0	A15 2-2	S05 2-1	N03 0-0	D19 2-1	a23 4-0		O10 1-0	J03 3-1	O24 2-2	S29 3-1	a04 0-0	m02 0-1	S19 1-0	M19 1-1	D05 2-2	F27 1-2	S15 1-1	F13 0-0	a12 1-4	N21 1-0
10 IPSWICH T	A15 1-1	O03 1-0	m02 1-0	J30 0-2	M19 1-2	D05 4-0	D26 2-3	N03 3-0	M12 2-0		S05 1-0	F20 0-2	O17 3-0	a23 4-0	J02 1-1	N21 2-0	F13 1-2	N07 2-1	O24 1-0	D18 2-0	A29 2-0	S19 3-2	a04 1-1
11 LEEDS U	O10 1-3	J16 0-2	D05 4-1	F27 2-2	O24 3-2	J01 2-0	m02 1-0	D19 3-0	S12 0-2	F06 1-0		A19 1-0	S26 2-0	D28 2-0	a06 1-2	a23 1-1	M05 1-0	A22 0-0	M19 5-0	N07 2-1	S30 0-0	N21 4-2	A31 1-0
12 LEICESTER C	S05 0-2	O10 0-0	a05 2-0	O31 1-2	D26 0-1	N21 0-2	J02 4-4	m02 3-0	M26 2-1	S30 1-1	F13 3-2		F27 1-0	D05 0-0	A29 1-0	S16 4-1	S19 4-0	a23 1-0	M05 1-0	A15 0-1	M16 1-1	N07 3-2	O21 3-0
13 MANCHESTER C	J23 0-2	O24 1-1	N21 3-0	S05 1-2	F13 2-0	a23 2-2	D05 1-3	N07 10-1	M02 2-0	M05 2-0	D26 1-2	O03 4-2		N04 1-1	S16 4-0	D19 1-2	A15 2-1	a04 2-0	O10 2-3	J02 1-3	S19 3-0	M19 1-1	M02 4-2
14 MIDDLESBROUGH	F14 2-1	N28 2-0	M26 1-1	D26 1-1	S15 3-0	F27 1-2	J23 2-1	M12 2-0	N14 1-0	O20 3-1	S19 2-0	m07 1-2	a09 2-1		A15 1-1	A29 1-0	a30 3-1	S29 0-0	a02 6-0	O31 4-0	D12 2-0	S05 2-3	O17 2-1
15 MILLWALL	a02 2-1	A22 3-1	S01 3-1	m07 1-4	N03 1-2	F06 0-1	M12 1-1	M19 4-1	N28 2-0	S12 2-1	N14 3-1	J01 1-0	D12 0-1	J16 2-1		F20 1-1	a09 3-2	D01 3-0	D28 3-1	O17 4-1	a30 2-0	O03 2-2	S26 2-0
16 OLDHAM A	N14 0-1	S26 1-0	O31 1-2	a01 4-2	m07 2-0	A18 0-2	J29 1-0	A31 3-2	D28 1-2	a30 3-1	O20 1-1	D12 2-0	A22 1-1	J01 3-1	S29 0-0		N28 0-1	F06 4-2	S12 3-2	M26 2-2	a09 5-1	M12 4-3	J16 2-1
17 PLYMOUTH A	O03 1-3	a15 0-0	S26 1-1	M26 3-0	a26 1-2	D20 2-1	a23 1-3	A22 6-1	O31 3-1	A18 0-0	O17 6-3	D28 4-0	J16 3-2	N21 0-1	O20 1-2	m02 1-0		J01 1-3	A31 1-0	D05 2-0	M12 3-0	a04 1-0	S12 3-3
18 READING	M19 0-2	a09 2-1	M12 1-1	N28 0-0	a13 0-0	O24 1-1	S19 2-3	O17 3-2	m07 0-0	a02 1-1	D12 0-1	J30 1-2	N14 0-2	F20 0-0	F13 2-3	S05 3-0	A29 0-1		a30 2-1	J23 1-0	S16 0-1	D26 0-1	O03 1-2
19 SHEFFIELD U	D26 1-1	F20 1-0	O20 0-2	A29 3-1	A15 0-1	a04 1-2	S15 1-1	D05 2-2	O03 2-1	M26 4-1	O31 2-2	O17 2-1	M08 1-2	N07 0-2	S19 1-2	J02 0-5	a19 1-0	N21 4-1		F13 0-1	S05 0-0	D20 1-0	a23 0-0
20 SHREWSBURY T	N03 1-2	a30 1-1	D28 0-0	N14 1-2	a08 2-1	S26 2-2	O03 2-0	J01 3-1	D12 2-2	A22 0-0	a02 1-0	J16 0-0	S12 0-0	M19 0-1	M05 0-0	O24 2-3	m07 2-1	S01 0-1	N17 2-0		N28 0-3	F20 2-1	F06 0-1
21 STOKE C	O24 0-0	M19 3-1	J16 3-1	M05 2-1	O03 1-0	S12 1-2	a04 1-1	S26 1-1	A18 1-1	J01 1-2	F23 2-1	A31 2-1	D28 1-3	A22 1-0	N21 1-2	D08 2-2	O10 1-0	D19 4-2	F06 1-0	m02 1-1		a23 1-0	N07 3-0
22 SWINDON T	m07 0-0	M15 3-0	S12 0-2	a09 1-2	N28 4-2	M30 2-2	M27 2-2	D01 4-1	A31 0-0	D28 4-2	a30 1-2	a02 3-2	O31 3-4	F06 1-1	F27 0-1	O10 2-0	N14 1-1	S26 4-0	A22 2-0	S29 1-1	O20 3-0		J01 2-0
23 W.B.A.	S16 0-2	m07 2-2	S30 3-1	D12 0-1	S19 3-0	O10 0-1	F13 1-0	O24 3-2	a30 1-1	N14 2-2	J30 1-4	a09 1-1	N28 1-1	M05 0-0	D26 1-4	A15 0-0	J02 1-0	F27 0-1	N04 4-0	S05 2-1	a02 2-0	A29 1-2	

Season 1987-88

DIVISION 3

	ALDERSHOT	BLACKPOOL	BRENTFORD	BRIGHTON & HA	BRISTOL C	BRISTOL R	BURY	CHESTER C	CHESTERFIELD	DONCASTER R	FULHAM	GILLINGHAM	GRIMSBY T	MANSFIELD T	NORTHAMPTON T	NOTTS CO	PORT VALE	PRESTON N.E.	ROTHERHAM U	SOUTHEND U	SUNDERLAND	WALSALL	WIGAN A	YORK C
1 ALDERSHOT		M29 0-0	S26 4-1	S12 1-4	N07 2-1	J01 3-0	J16 0-2	F06 4-1	O20 2-0	A31 2-1	M26 0-3	D28 6-0	D19 3-2	a19 3-0	O31 4-4	F23 0-2	a15 3-0	m02 0-0	N28 1-3	a04 0-1	F27 3-2	J09 0-1	S29 3-2	M05 1-2
2 BLACKPOOL	M12 3-2		J16 0-1	F06 1-3	N03 4-2	A31 2-1	J01 5-1	S12 0-1	m02 1-0	a15 4-2	O03 2-1	F20 3-3	a23 3-0	M19 2-0	N28 3-1	D28 1-1	a04 1-2	S26 3-0	N07 3-0	D19 1-1	O17 0-2	A22 1-2	O24 0-0	M01 2-1
3 BRENTFORD	D26 3-0	S19 2-1		M26 1-1	A29 0-2	O31 1-1	M12 0-3	O20 1-1	S15 2-0	a30 1-1	F14 3-1	a09 2-2	F23 0-2	D12 2-2	J09 0-1	a02 1-0	O03 1-0	M01 2-0	S05 1-1	J02 1-0	A15 0-1	O17 0-0	N21 2-1	m07 1-2
4 BRIGHTON & H.A.	J02 1-1	S05 1-3	O24 2-1		F13 3-2	m07 2-1	O03 2-1	D12 1-0	F17 2-2	N04 2-0	A29 2-0	a02 2-0	M19 0-0	a30 3-1	a15 3-0	N28 1-1	M02 2-0	O17 0-0	S16 1-1	D26 0-0	S19 3-1	M12 2-1	a09 1-0	A15 1-0
5 BRISTOL C	a02 2-0	a09 2-1	J01 2-3	D28 5-2		S12 3-3	F06 3-2	N21 2-2	S29 2-1	m07 1-0	D15 4-0	S26 3-3	M05 1-1	F20 1-2	F27 2-2	J16 2-1	A31 1-0	A22 3-1	M26 2-0	O10 3-2	O20 0-1	F09 0-0	a30 4-1	D12 3-2
6 BRISTOL R	A29 3-1	a27 2-0	M19 0-0	D19 1-2	a12 1-0		a04 0-0	O17 2-2	N07 2-0	O24 4-0	D26 3-1	M12 2-0	N28 4-2	O03 2-1	S19 0-2	M02 1-1	a23 1-0	N04 1-2	A15 3-1	F13 0-0	F24 4-0	m02 3-0	S05 2-3	S16 2-1
7 BURY	S19 1-0	A29 3-1	O10 2-2	F27 2-1	S05 1-1	N21 4-1		m07 0-1	J30 2-0	M19 2-1	D12 1-1	a30 2-1	S15 0-2	N03 1-0	F13 0-0	a09 0-1	M05 0-1	O24 4-0	J09 2-2	A15 2-2	J02 2-3	S29 2-2	D26 0-2	a02 0-1
8 CHESTER C	S05 4-1	J02 1-1	a23 1-1	m02 2-2	a04 1-0	M05 0-3	D18 4-4		N28 1-1	D05 1-1	S16 1-2	M02 3-1	S19 1-0	O24 0-2	A15 0-5	O03 1-2	N04 1-0	M19 1-0	J30 1-0	J09 1-1	D26 1-2	N07 1-1	F13 1-0	A29 1-0
9 CHESTERFIELD	a09 1-0	D12 1-1	a19 2-1	A22 0-0	M01 1-4	a02 0-1	A31 1-0	a30 0-0		J16 0-1	m07 1-0	F06 1-4	O10 0-3	J01 3-1	M05 0-2	S26 2-0	S12 1-3	F20 0-0	O03 3-2	O24 3-1	N21 1-1	D28 2-1	N03 0-1	M19 2-1
10 DONCASTER R	J31 0-0	S15 2-1	N28 0-1	a23 0-2	D19 1-2	M25 0-1	O31 1-2	M11 2-2	S18 1-0		J09 2-2	O03 4-2	A15 1-0	M01 0-2	S05 0-2	O17 0-1	N07 1-1	a04 3-2	F13 2-2	m02 0-1	A29 0-2	O20 0-4	J01 3-4	D26 2-0
11 FULHAM	O24 1-2	F27 3-1	D28 2-2	J01 1-2	M19 0-0	S26 3-1	m02 0-1	a15 1-0	D19 1-3	A22 4-0		S12 0-2	N03 5-0	F06 0-0	N07 0-0	S01 0-0	J16 1-2	N28 0-1	a04 3-1	a23 3-1	S29 0-2	F20 2-0	M05 3-2	O10 3-1
12 GILLINGHAM	F13 2-1	A15 0-0	N03 0-1	N07 1-1	D26 1-1	O10 3-0	N28 3-3	S29 0-1	S05 10-0	F27 3-1	J02 2-2		F02 1-1	M05 0-0	a04 1-2	O24 3-1	M19 0-0	a23 4-0	m02 0-2	A29 8-1	S15 0-0	D18 0-1	J23 0-1	S19 3-1
13 GRIMSBY T	m07 1-1	O20 1-1	A31 0-1	O31 0-1	O17 1-4	a30 0-0	J26 2-0	J16 2-1	M12 1-1	F20 0-0	a09 0-2	A22 2-0		S12 2-3	M26 2-2	J01 0-0	D28 3-1	F06 0-1	M08 2-1	O03 1-3	a02 0-1	S26 0-2	D12 0-2	N21 5-1
14 MANSFIELD T	M22 1-0	O31 0-0	m02 2-1	N21 1-1	A15 2-0	F27 1-0	a23 0-0	M26 1-2	A29 0-1	S29 2-0	S04 0-2	O17 2-2	J02 1-0		O20 3-1	M12 1-1	D20 4-0	N07 0-0	D26 0-1	S19 1-0	a26 0-4	a05 1-3	S15 0-1	F13 2-1
15 NORTHAMPTON T	M19 1-1	a30 3-3	S09 2-1	A31 1-1	O03 3-0	J16 2-1	D28 0-0	F20 2-0	O17 4-0	F06 1-0	a02 3-2	N21 2-1	O24 2-1	a10 2-0		S12 0-1	S26 1-0	J27 0-1	M11 0-0	M02 4-0	D12 0-2	J01 2-2	J30 1-1	N04 0-0
16 NOTTS CO	S15 2-1	F13 2-3	N07 3-0	a04 1-2	S19 0-1	S29 1-1	O20 3-0	F27 1-0	D26 2-0	M05 2-0	J30 5-1	M26 0-1	A29 0-0	O11 1-1	J02 3-1		m02 1-2	D19 4-2	a23 4-0	S05 6-2	O31 2-1	N21 3-1	A15 4-4	J09 3-0
17 PORT VALE	A15 4-2	N22 0-0	F27 1-0	S28 2-0	a18 1-1	O19 2-1	O17 1-0	a09 1-1	J02 0-1	a02 5-0	S19 1-1	O31 0-0	F13 2-0	m07 1-1	D26 1-1	D12 1-3		M12 3-2	A29 0-0	S14 4-1	a30 0-1	M26 2-1	a25 2-1	S05 2-1
18 PRESTON N.E.	D12 0-2	D26 2-1	S29 1-2	M05 3-0	J09 2-0	a08 3-1	M26 1-0	O31 1-1	A15 0-1	N21 1-2	a30 2-1	O20 1-1	S05 1-3	a02 1-0	S15 0-0	m07 1-2	O10 3-2		S19 0-0	J30 1-1	F13 2-2	F27 1-0	A29 0-1	J02 3-0
19 ROTHERHAM U	a30 1-0	a02 0-1	F17 2-0	M16 1-0	O24 4-1	F20 1-1	A22 0-1	A31 5-2	F27 1-1	D28 1-0	N21 0-2	D12 1-2	S29 0-0	S26 2-1	O11 2-2	N03 1-1	J01 1-0	J16 2-2		M05 1-1	m07 1-4	S12 0-1	M19 1-1	a08 0-1
20 SOUTHEND U	N21 0-1	m07 4-0	S12 2-3	S26 2-1	M11 2-0	D28 4-2	F20 1-0	A22 2-2	M25 3-0	D11 4-1	O20 0-2	J01 1-3	F26 0-0	J15 2-1	S29 1-1	F05 1-2	J22 3-3	S01 1-2	O16 1-1		a09 1-4	O30 1-1	a01 3-2	a29 3-1
21 SUNDERLAND	O03 3-1	M05 2-2	F20 2-0	J16 1-0	a23 0-1	A22 1-1	S12 1-1	S26 0-2	a04 3-2	J01 3-1	M01 2-0	J30 2-1	N07 1-1	A31 4-1	m02 3-1	M19 1-1	N28 2-1	D28 1-1	D20 3-0	N03 7-0		F06 1-1	O10 4-1	O24 4-2
22 WALSALL	N03 2-0	F23 3-2	M05 4-2	O10 1-1	S15 1-1	D12 0-0	M01 2-1	a02 1-0	F13 0-0	a09 2-1	A15 0-1	m07 0-0	D26 3-2	N28 2-1	A29 1-0	a30 2-1	O24 2-1	O03 1-0	J02 5-2	M19 2-1	S05 2-2		S19 1-2	J30 2-1
23 WIGAN A	M01 4-0	M25 0-0	a04 1-1	O20 3-3	N28 1-1	F06 1-0	S26 0-2	D28 1-0	a23 1-2	S12 2-1	O17 1-3	A31 1-1	m02 0-1	M28 2-1	D19 2-2	F20 2-1	a12 2-0	J01 2-0	O31 3-0	N07 1-0	M12 2-2	J16 3-1		O03 1-1
24 YORK C	O17 2-2	S29 1-3	D18 1-1	F20 0-2	m02 0-1	a15 0-4	N07 1-1	J01 2-0	O31 1-0	S26 1-1	M12 1-3	J16 0-2	a04 0-2	D28 2-2	a23 2-2	A22 3-5	F06 2-3	S12 1-1	O20 1-2	N28 0-3	M26 2-1	A31 1-3	F27 3-1	

DIVISION 4

	BOLTON W	BURNLEY	CAMBRIDGE U	CARDIFF C	CARLISLE U	COLCHESTER U	CREWE A	DARLINGTON	EXETER C	HALIFAX T	HARTLEPOOL U	HEREFORD U	LEYTON O	NEWPORT CO	PETERBOROUGH U	ROCHDALE	SCARBOROUGH	SCUNTHORPE U	STOCKPORT CO	SWANSEA C	TORQUAY U	TRANMERE R	WOLVERHAMPTON W	WREXHAM
1 BOLTON W		a04 2-1	N28 2-2	A22 1-0	O17 5-0	m02 4-0	A15 1-1	M11 1-1	O20 1-0	S12 2-0	S26 1-2	F06 1-0	N07 1-0	a23 6-0	A31 2-0	M26 0-0	J01 3-1	a19 0-0	D28 2-1	O31 1-1	J16 1-2	M01 2-0	O03 1-0	D19 2-0
2 BURNLEY	N21 2-1		S19 0-2	m07 1-2	A29 4-3	A15 0-3	S29 0-0	F13 2-1	M05 3-0	a08 3-1	O10 1-0	D12 0-0	M22 2-0	J09 2-0	a30 1-2	D26 4-0	F27 0-1	O20 1-1	O31 1-1	S05 1-0	m04 1-0	J02 1-1	a02 0-3	S15 1-0
3 CAMBRIDGE U	a29 2-2	J16 2-0		S01 0-0	m07 1-2	O24 0-1	A22 4-1	a01 1-0	F19 2-1	S26 2-1	a19 1-1	N03 0-1	M05 2-0	O10 4-0	J01 1-3	N21 1-2	D28 1-0	S12 3-3	D11 2-0	F27 0-3	F06 1-0	M19 1-1	a10 1-1	S29 0-1
4 CARDIFF C	a15 1-0	D19 2-1	J30 4-0		S19 4-2	F13 1-0	m02 2-0	S15 3-1	N07 3-2	S29 0-0	N28 1-1	O10 0-1	A15 1-1	a04 4-0	M04 0-0	O31 1-0	a23 2-0	M26 0-1	F27 0-0	A29 1-0	O20 2-1	D26 3-0	S05 3-2	M16 1-1
5 CARLISLE U	M05 0-2	J01 3-4	D18 2-1	J16 0-0		a23 4-0	M19 0-1	S29 3-3	J23 0-0	a19 1-1	S12 1-3	A31 3-1	N03 1-2	N07 3-1	F20 0-2	F27 2-0	S26 4-0	A22 3-1	F06 2-0	m02 0-1	N28 3-3	O24 3-2	O10 0-1	a04 0-4
6 COLCHESTER U	D11 3-0	F19 0-1	M25 0-0	D28 2-1	O20 1-0		F05 1-4	O30 2-1	S25 0-2	a01 2-1	J15 0-0	a19 1-0	O09 0-0	F26 0-0	S12 4-1	a08 1-0	A31 1-3	J01 0-3	a29 2-0	S29 2-1	A21 0-1	m07 0-0	N21 0-1	M04 1-2
7 CREWE A	F20 2-1	M01 0-1	a15 0-0	D12 0-0	O31 4-1	S04 0-0		a09 3-1	M26 0-0	a29 0-0	O03 1-1	a01 0-0	S18 3-3	F13 2-1	m07 0-1	J29 0-1	O17 1-0	N21 2-2	O20 3-1	D26 2-2	M11 0-1	S15 0-0	J02 0-2	A29 2-0
8 DARLINGTON	O10 1-0	D20 4-2	N00 0-1	F02 0-0	J09 2-1	M19 2-0	N03 1-0		D08 4-1	F20 4-1	J01 1-1	J17 3-1	a04 2-2	m02 0-2	M15 2-1	M05 2-1	S12 2-1	S26 1-4	A22 1-2	D10 2-0	A31 1-1	O03 0-0	O24 2-2	a23 2-1
9 EXETER C	a09 1-1	O17 1-2	A15 3-0	a02 0-2	S16 1-1	D26 0-2	O24 3-1	a30 4-1		m07 1-2	M02 1-0	M19 2-2	J02 2-3	A29 3-0	M09 0-1	S19 1-1	M12 1-0	D12 1-1	N21 2-1	J09 3-1	O03 0-1	J30 0-1	F13 2-4	S05 1-1
10 HALIFAX T	J12 0-0	N03 2-1	D26 1-1	M01 0-1	a26 1-1	N06 1-2	N27 1-2	A15 2-2	D18 2-0		a23 3-1	O03 2-1	a14 1-0	S05 3-1	O24 0-0	A28 1-2	a04 2-2	M12 2-2	O16 2-0	S16 3-1	m02 2-3	S18 2-1	F16 2-1	F23 2-0
11 HARTLEPOOL U	D26 0-0	M12 2-1	S16 2-1	a30 0-1	J02 0-0	S19 3-1	F27 2-1	A29 2-5	S30 3-1	O21 2-1		m07 1-2	S05 2-2	A15 0-0	a02 0-1	F13 1-1	M26 1-0	O31 1-0	a09 1-3	J30 0-2	O17 0-0	N21 1-2	D12 0-0	J26 1-0
12 HEREFORD U	S05 0-3	m02 2-1	a23 1-0	M13 1-2	J30 2-0	S16 1-0	N07 1-1	S19 1-0	O31 1-1	F27 2-1	D19 4-2		N28 0-3	D26 4-2	S30 0-1	A15 0-0	O21 1-1	O17 2-3	M26 0-1	J02 0-0	a04 0-0	J09 1-1	A29 1-2	F13 0-2
13 LEYTON O	a02 1-2	S01 4-1	O17 0-2	F20 4-1	a09 4-1	M12 0-0	J16 1-1	N20 4-3	S12 2-3	O31 4-1	F06 0-2	a30 4-0		S29 4-1	S26 2-0	O20 8-0	A22 3-1	D28 1-1	J23 1-1	M26 3-0	J01 0-2	D12 3-1	m07 0-2	F27 2-1
14 NEWPORT CO	N03 0-1	A22 0-1	M12 0-0	N21 1-2	a02 1-2	O03 1-2	D28 1-2	J12 2-1	J01 1-1	F05 1-0	F19 2-3	S27 0-0	M01 0-0		a09 0-4	m07 0-1	a12 0-4	J16 1-1	A31 1-2	M05 1-2	S12 3-1	a30 0-3	a26 1-3	O24 2-0
15 PETERBOROUGH U	J30 0-4	N28 5-0	A29 1-0	O17 4-3	A15 1-0	J02 2-0	D18 0-4	S05 1-2	a23 2-1	M26 1-0	N07 0-1	F24 1-2	D26 1-2	O21 3-0		J09 1-1	m02 0-0	O03 1-1	M12 0-0	a04 0-1	O31 0-2	F13 2-1	S16 1-1	S19 1-0
16 ROCHDALE	O24 2-2	S26 2-1	a04 2-1	M29 2-2	O03 1-2	N03 1-4	A31 2-2	O17 1-3	J16 0-0	J01 0-0	D28 0-2	F20 3-1	a23 1-3	D19 3-0	A22 1-1		N28 1-1	F06 2-1	S12 0-1	N07 2-3	J26 1-1	M12 0-0	M01 0-1	m02 1-2
17 SCARBOROUGH	A29 4-0	O03 1-0	F13 0-0	N04 1-1	D26 3-1	J30 3-1	M05 2-0	J02 0-1	O10 3-1	N21 1-1	O24 1-1	a09 2-1	F24 3-1	S16 3-1	D12 1-1	a30 2-1		a02 0-0	m07 1-1	S19 2-0	M02 1-2	S05 2-0	A15 2-2	M19 0-2
18 SCUNTHORPE U	S15 1-1	a23 1-1	J02 3-2	O24 2-1	a12 1-0	A29 2-2	a04 2-1	D26 1-0	m02 1-1	O10 1-0	M19 3-0	M05 3-0	F13 3-2	S19 3-1	F27 5-0	S05 1-0	N07 0-1		S29 0-0	N28 1-2	D18 2-3	A15 3-0	J30 0-1	N03 3-1
19 STOCKPORT CO	F12 1-2	M18 2-0	m02 0-2	O02 0-1	S04 3-0	N27 1-1	a22 1-1	a19 1-1	a04 2-1	M04 1-0	N03 1-0	O23 0-2	S15 1-2	J29 5-1	O10 0-1	J02 1-1	D19 1-1	M01 1-1		A15 0-2	N06 2-1	A28 1-2	S19 0-2	D26 1-1
20 SWANSEA C	M18 1-0	F06 0-0	O03 1-1	J01 2-2	D12 3-1	M01 1-2	S26 2-4	m07 3-0	A22 0-2	J23 1-1	A31 2-1	S12 3-0	O24 3-0	O17 1-2	N21 2-1	a02 0-3	J16 3-0	a30 1-1	F19 1-1		D28 1-1	a09 1-2	N03 1-2	O10 2-1
21 TORQUAY U	S19 2-1	O24 1-3	S05 0-1	a09 2-0	a30 1-0	a15 0-0	O10 1-0	a27 0-0	F27 1-1	D12 1-2	M05 1-1	N21 1-0	A29 1-1	a19 6-1	M19 0-0	S15 5-0	S29 0-1	m07 1-2	a02 3-0	M29 0-1		N03 1-0	F23 0-0	A15 6-1
22 TRANMERE R	D15 2-0	S11 0-1	O30 0-1	S25 0-1	M25 3-0	D18 0-2	a25 2-2	F26 2-1	A31 2-1	J15 2-0	a04 3-1	A21 0-1	m02 2-1	N27 4-0	D28 3-1	O09 6-1	F06 1-0	F20 1-3	J01 4-0	O20 1-2	a22 1-1		M04 3-0	N06 1-0
23 WOLVERHAMPTON W	F27 4-0	N07 3-0	O20 3-0	F06 1-4	M12 3-1	a04 2-0	S12 2-2	M26 5-3	D28 3-0	A22 0-1	m02 2-0	J01 2-0	D19 2-0	O31 2-1	M22 0-1	S29 2-0	F19 0-0	A31 4-1	J16 1-1	a23 2-0	S26 1-2	O17 3-0		N28 0-2
24 WREXHAM	m07 0-1	F02 1-3	M01 3-0	S12 3-0	N21 4-0	O17 0-1	J01 2-1	O20 0-1	M22 3-0	A31 2-2	A22 2-1	D28 0-0	O03 2-2	M26 4-1	J16 3-1	D12 2-3	O31 1-0	a09 2-1	S26 2-1	M12 1-2	F20 2-3	a02 3-0	a30 4-2	

LEAGUE TABLES

DIVISION 1

	P	W	D	L	F	A	W	D	L	F	A	Pts
Liverpool	40	15	5	0	49	9	11	7	2	38	15	90
Manchester U	40	14	5	1	41	17	9	7	4	30	21	81
Nottingham F	40	11	7	2	40	17	9	6	5	27	22	73
Everton	40	14	4	2	34	11	5	9	6	19	16	70
QPR	40	12	4	4	30	14	7	6	7	18	24	67
Arsenal	40	11	4	5	35	16	7	8	5	23	23	66
Wimbledon	40	8	9	3	32	20	6	6	8	26	27	57
Newcastle U	40	9	6	5	32	23	5	8	7	23	30	56
Luton T	40	11	6	3	40	21	3	5	12	17	37	53
Coventry C	40	6	8	6	23	25	7	6	7	23	28	53
Sheffield W	40	10	2	8	27	30	5	6	9	25	36	53
Southampton	40	6	8	6	27	26	6	6	8	22	27	50
Tottenham H	40	9	5	6	26	23	3	6	11	12	25	47
Norwich C	40	7	5	8	26	26	5	4	11	14	26	45
Derby Co	40	6	7	7	18	17	4	6	10	17	28	43
West Ham U	40	6	9	5	23	21	3	6	11	17	31	42
Charlton A	40	7	7	6	23	21	2	8	10	15	31	42
Chelsea	40	7	11	2	24	17	2	4	14	26	51	42
Portsmouth	40	4	8	8	21	27	3	6	11	15	39	35
Watford	40	4	5	11	15	24	3	6	11	12	27	32
Oxford U	40	5	7	8	24	34	1	6	13	20	46	31

DIVISION 2

	P	W	D	L	F	A	W	D	L	F	A	Pts
Millwall	44	15	3	4	45	23	10	4	8	27	29	82
Aston Villa	44	9	7	6	31	21	13	5	4	37	20	78
Middlesbrough	44	15	4	3	44	16	7	8	7	19	20	78
Bradford C	44	14	3	5	49	26	8	8	6	25	28	77
Blackburn R	44	12	8	2	38	22	9	6	7	30	30	77
Crystal P	44	16	3	3	50	21	6	6	10	36	38	75
Leeds U	44	14	4	4	37	18	5	8	9	24	33	69
Ipswich T	44	14	3	5	38	17	5	6	11	23	35	66
Manchester C	44	11	4	7	50	28	8	4	10	30	32	65
Oldham A	44	13	4	5	43	27	5	7	10	29	37	65
Stoke C	44	12	6	4	34	22	5	5	12	16	35	62
Swindon T	44	10	7	5	43	25	6	4	12	30	35	59
Leicester C	44	12	5	5	35	20	4	6	12	27	41	59
Barnsley	44	11	4	7	42	32	4	8	10	19	30	57
Hull C	44	10	8	4	32	22	4	7	11	22	38	57
Plymouth A	44	12	4	6	44	26	4	4	14	21	41	56
Bournemouth	44	7	7	8	36	30	6	3	13	20	38	49
Shrewsbury T	44	7	8	7	23	22	4	8	10	19	32	49
Birmingham C	44	7	9	6	20	24	4	6	12	21	42	48
WBA	44	8	7	7	29	26	4	4	14	21	43	47
Sheffield U	44	8	6	8	27	28	5	1	16	18	46	46
Reading	44	5	7	10	20	25	5	5	12	24	45	42
Huddersfield T	44	4	6	12	20	38	2	4	16	21	62	28

DIVISION 3

	P	W	D	L	F	A	W	D	L	F	A	Pts
Sunderland	46	14	7	2	51	22	13	5	5	41	26	93
Brighton & HA	46	15	7	1	37	16	8	8	7	32	31	84
Walsall	46	15	6	2	39	22	8	7	8	29	28	82
Notts Co	46	14	4	5	53	24	9	8	6	29	25	81
Bristol C	46	14	6	3	51	30	7	6	10	26	32	75
Northampton T	46	12	8	3	36	18	6	11	6	34	33	73
Wigan A	46	11	8	4	36	23	9	4	10	34	38	72
Bristol R	46	14	5	4	43	19	4	7	12	25	37	66
Fulham	46	10	5	8	36	24	9	4	10	33	36	66
Blackpool	46	13	4	6	45	27	4	10	9	26	35	65
Port Vale	46	12	8	3	36	19	6	3	14	22	37	65
Brentford	46	9	8	6	27	23	7	6	10	26	36	62
Gillingham	46	8	9	6	45	21	6	8	9	32	40	59
Bury	46	9	7	7	33	26	6	7	10	25	31	59
Chester C	46	9	8	6	29	30	5	8	10	22	32	58
Preston NE	46	10	6	7	30	23	5	7	11	18	36	58
Southend U	46	10	6	7	42	33	4	7	12	23	50	55
Chesterfield	46	10	5	8	25	28	5	5	13	16	42	55
Mansfield T	46	10	6	7	25	21	4	6	13	23	38	54
Aldershot	46	12	3	8	45	32	3	5	15	19	42	53
Rotherham U	46	8	8	7	28	25	4	8	11	22	41	52
Grimsby T	46	6	7	10	25	29	6	7	10	23	29	50
York C	46	4	7	12	27	45	4	2	17	21	46	33
Doncaster R	46	6	5	12	25	36	2	4	17	15	48	33

DIVISION 4

	P	W	D	L	F	A	W	D	L	F	A	Pts
Wolves	46	15	3	5	47	19	12	6	5	35	24	90
Cardiff C	46	15	6	2	39	14	9	7	7	27	27	85
Bolton W	46	16	5	2	42	12	7	6	10	24	30	78
Scunthorpe U	46	14	5	4	42	20	6	12	5	34	31	77
Torquay U	46	10	7	6	34	16	11	7	5	32	25	77
Swansea C	46	9	7	7	35	28	11	3	9	27	28	70
Peterboro' U	46	10	5	8	28	26	10	5	8	24	27	70
Leyton Orient	46	13	4	6	55	27	6	8	9	30	36	69
Colchester U	46	10	5	8	23	22	9	5	9	24	29	67
Burnley	46	12	5	6	31	22	8	2	13	26	40	67
Wrexham	46	13	3	7	46	26	7	3	13	23	32	66
Scarborough	46	12	8	3	38	19	5	6	12	18	29	65
Darlington	46	13	6	4	39	25	5	5	13	32	44	65
Tranmere R*	46	14	2	7	43	20	5	7	11	18	33	64
Cambridge U	46	10	6	7	32	24	6	7	10	18	28	61
Hartlepool U	46	9	7	7	25	25	6	7	10	25	32	59
Crewe A	46	7	11	5	25	19	6	8	9	32	34	58
Halifax T†	46	11	7	5	37	25	3	7	13	17	34	55
Hereford U	46	8	7	8	25	27	6	5	12	16	32	54
Stockport Co	46	7	7	9	26	26	5	8	10	18	32	51
Rochdale	46	5	9	9	28	34	6	6	11	19	42	48
Exeter C	46	8	6	9	33	29	3	7	13	20	39	46
Carlisle U	46	9	5	9	38	33	3	3	17	19	53	44
Newport Co	46	4	5	14	19	36	2	2	19	16	69	25

*Two points deducted for failing to meet a fixture. †One point deducted for fielding an unregistered player.

Football League Records

Top scorers: Div 1, A.Smith (Arsenal) 23 goals; Div 2, K.Edwards (Hull City) 26 goals; Div 3, S.Bull (Wolverhampton Wanderers) 37 goals; Div 4, P.Stant (Hereford United) 28 goals.
Play-offs: Div 1, Blackburn Rovers v Watford 0-0, 1-1; Swindon Town v Crystal Palace 1-0, 0-2; Blackburn Rovers v Crystal Palace 3-1, 0-3; Div 2, Bristol Rovers v Fulham 1-0, 4-0; Preston North End v Port Vale 1-1, 1-3; Bristol Rovers v Port Vale 1-1, 0-1; Div 3, Leyton Orient v Scarborough 2-0, 0-1; Wrexham v Scunthorpe United 3-1, 2-0; Wrexham v Leyton Orient 0-0, 1-2.

Chelsea, Crystal Palace and Manchester City promoted to Div 1; Middlesbrough, Newcastle United and West Ham United relegated to Div 2; Port Vale, Sheffield United and Wolverhampton Wanderers promoted to Div 2; Birmingham City, Shrewsbury Town and Walsall relegated to Div 3; Crewe Alexandra, Leyton Orient, Rotherham United and Tranmere Rovers promoted to Div 3; Darlington were relegated from Division Four and replaced by Maidstone United.

Alan Smith was Arsenal's top scorer with 23 goals when the Gunners won the Championship from Liverpool in the most dramatic fashion in 1988-9.

DIVISION 1

	ARSENAL	ASTON VILLA	CHARLTON A	COVENTRY C	DERBY CO	EVERTON	LIVERPOOL	LUTON T	MANCHESTER U	MIDDLESBROUGH	MILLWALL	NEWCASTLE U	NORWICH C	NOTTINGHAM F	Q.P.R.	SHEFFIELD W	SOUTHAMPTON	TOTTENHAM H	WEST HAM U	WIMBLEDON
1 ARSENAL		S03 2-3	M21 2-2	O29 2-0	m13 1-2	a08 2-0	D04 1-1	F25 2-0	D17 2-1	N19 3-0	F28 0-0	a15 1-0	m01 5-0	M11 1-3	O22 2-1	J21 1-1	S17 2-2	J02 2-0	F04 2-1	m17 2-2
2 ASTON VILLA	D31 0-3		F25 1-2	m13 1-1	N19 1-2	O22 2-0	S10 1-1	a01 2-1	M12 0-0	a29 1-1	A27 2-2	J14 3-1	D03 3-1	S24 1-1	D26 2-1	F04 2-0	m02 1-2	O29 2-1	M25 0-1	O08 0-1
3 CHARLTON A	D26 2-3	O15 2-2		M25 0-0	m10 3-0	N12 1-2	A27 0-3	J14 3-0	a22 1-0	a01 2-0	S10 0-3	S24 2-2	F04 1-2	N26 0-1	D10 1-1	O29 2-1	M11 2-2	O08 2-2	D31 0-0	m06 1-0
4 COVENTRY C	F21 1-0	N26 2-1	S17 3-0		D17 0-2	S03 0-1	M22 1-3	N12 1-0	D10 1-0	O01 3-4	O15 0-0	F11 1-2	a08 2-1	m15 2-2	a22 0-3	J02 5-0	M27 2-1	M18 1-1	N05 1-1	J21 2-1
5 DERBY CO	N26 2-1	m06 2-1	O22 0-0	a01 1-0		F25 3-2	D26 0-1	D10 0-1	N12 2-2	A27 1-0	D31 0-1	S10 2-0	O08 0-1	M25 0-2	S24 0-1	a22 1-0	F04 3-1	M11 1-1	J14 1-2	O29 4-1
6 EVERTON	J14 1-3	F14 1-1	a10 3-2	D31 3-1	m15 1-0		m03 0-0	S24 0-2	O30 1-1	D26 2-1	M25 1-1	A27 4-0	N19 1-1	S10 1-1	a01 4-1	M11 1-0	O08 4-1	D03 1-0	m13 3-1	F04 1-1
7 LIVERPOOL	m26 0-2	J03 1-0	M01 2-0	O22 0-0	M29 1-0	D11 1-1		M14 5-0	S03 1-0	N05 3-0	N12 1-1	O01 1-2	D17 0-1	m10 1-0	m16 2-0	a08 5-1	J21 2-0	S17 1-1	m23 5-1	N26 1-1
8 LUTON T	O25 1-1	D17 1-1	m02 5-2	a15 2-2	a29 3-0	J21 1-0	O08 1-0		S17 0-2	F18 1-0	M11 1-2	D03 0-0	m13 1-0	F04 2-3	O29 0-0	M18 0-1	J02 6-1	M28 1-3	N19 4-1	S03 2-2
9 MANCHESTER U	a02 1-1	N05 1-1	D03 3-0	a29 0-1	a15 0-2	m10 1-2	J01 3-1	M25 2-0		S10 1-0	J14 3-0	m13 2-0	O26 1-2	D26 2-0	A27 0-0	N23 1-1	N19 2-2	F05 1-0	S24 2-0	m02 1-0
10 MIDDLESBROUGH	m06 0-1	D10 3-3	D17 0-0	F04 1-1	M18 0-1	M27 3-3	M11 0-4	O22 2-1	J02 1-0		O29 4-2	F26 1-1	S03 2-3	a22 3-4	N12 1-0	N26 0-1	a08 3-3	J21 2-2	O08 1-0	S17 1-0
11 MILLWALL	F11 1-2	M18 2-0	J02 1-0	F25 1-0	S03 1-0	S17 2-1	a11 1-2	N05 3-1	a08 0-0	F21 2-0		N19 4-0	J22 2-3	O22 2-2	O01 3-2	D17 1-0	m13 1-1	a29 0-5	D03 0-1	M27 0-1
12 NEWCASTLE U	N12 0-1	a08 1-2	J21 0-2	O08 0-3	J02 0-1	M22 2-0	F04 2-2	a22 0-0	N27 0-0	O26 3-0	m06 1-1		S17 0-2	O29 0-1	M11 1-2	M27 1-3	D17 3-3	S03 2-2	m03 1-2	D10 2-1
13 NORWICH C	D10 0-0	a22 2-2	O01 1-3	J14 1-2	F11 1-0	m06 1-0	a01 0-1	N26 2-2	F25 2-1	D31 0-0	S24 2-2	M25 0-2		A27 2-1	S10 1-0	N12 1-1	O29 1-1	O22 3-1	D27 2-1	M11 1-0
14 NOTTINGHAM F	N06 1-4	J21 4-0	m13 4-0	N19 0-0	S17 1-1	J02 2-0	O26 2-1	O01 0-0	M27 2-0	D03 2-2	m03 4-1	M15 1-1	a05 2-0		F11 0-0	S03 1-1	a12 3-0	M22 1-2	m18 1-2	D18 0-1
15 Q.P.R.	F18 0-0	M17 1-0	a29 1-0	D03 2-1	J21 0-1	D17 0-0	N19 0-1	M21 1-1	m08 3-2	a15 0-0	F04 1-2	N05 3-0	J02 1-1	O08 1-2		S17 2-0	S03 0-1	m13 1-0	O15 2-1	a06 4-3
16 SHEFFIELD W	S24 2-1	O01 1-0	M04 3-1	S10 1-2	D03 1-1	N05 1-1	J14 2-2	A27 1-0	F11 0-2	m13 1-0	a01 3-0	D26 1-2	m17 2-2	D31 0-3	M25 0-2		F18 1-1	N20 0-2	m09 0-2	a05 1-1
17 SOUTHAMPTON	M25 1-3	N12 3-1	N05 2-0	D26 2-2	O01 0-0	F11 1-1	S24 1-3	S10 2-1	m06 2-1	J14 1-3	N26 2-2	a01 1-0	a19 0-0	D10 1-1	D31 1-4	O22 1-2		F25 0-2	A27 4-0	a22 0-0
18 TOTTENHAM H	S10 2-3	M01 2-0	F11 1-1	N23 1-1	N05 1-3	a22 2-1	M26 1-2	D26 0-0	O01 2-2	S24 3-2	D10 2-0	D31 2-0	F21 2-1	J15 1-2	N26 2-2	a12 0-0	O25 1-2		a01 3-0	N12 3-2
19 WEST HAM U	O01 1-4	S17 2-2	S03 1-3	M11 1-1	a08 1-1	N26 0-1	O29 0-2	m06 1-0	J21 1-3	a11 1-2	a22 3-0	O22 2-0	M27 0-2	N12 3-3	F25 0-0	D10 0-0	a15 1-2	D17 0-2		J02 1-2
20 WIMBLEDON	A27 1-5	F11 1-0	N19 1-1	S24 0-1	M01 4-0	O01 2-1	m13 1-2	D31 4-0	O22 1-1	M25 1-1	D26 1-0	a29 4-0	N05 0-2	a01 4-1	J14 1-0	F25 1-0	D03 2-1	a15 1-2	S10 0-1	

Kerry Dixon, the former Reading striker who helped Chelsea back to Division One in 1988-9.

DIVISION 2

	BARNSLEY	BIRMINGHAM C	BLACKBURN R	BOURNEMOUTH	BRADFORD C	BRIGHTON & HA	CHELSEA	CRYSTAL P	HULL C	IPSWICH T	LEEDS U	LEICESTER C	MANCHESTER C	OLDHAM A	OXFORD U	PLYMOUTH A	PORTSMOUTH	SHREWSBURY T	STOKE C	SUNDERLAND	SWINDON T	WALSALL	WATFORD	W.B.A.
1 BARNSLEY		a15 0-0	F25 0-1	N26 5-2	N12 0-0	F04 2-2	S17 1-1	M11 1-1	J02 0-2	O22 2-0	M19 2-2	D17 3-0	S24 1-2	J21 4-3	m01 1-0	O29 3-1	m06 1-0	a08 1-0	S03 1-0	M27 3-0	A29 1-1	D10 1-0	F28 2-2	O08 2-1
2 BIRMINGHAM C	O01 3-5		a22 2-0	F11 0-1	m01 1-0	a08 1-2	D16 1-4	D10 0-1	m06 1-0	N26 1-0	N22 0-0	S03 2-3	F18 0-2	J02 0-0	M04 0-0	O04 0-1	N05 0-0	M27 1-2	O25 0-1	S17 3-2	a18 1-2	M18 1-0	J21 2-3	O15 1-4
3 BLACKBURN R	O15 2-1	S24 3-0		m01 2-0	F04 2-1	N12 2-1	J21 1-1	O08 5-4	M18 4-0	D10 1-0	M27 2-0	a08 0-0	a15 4-0	S03 3-1	F21 3-1	M11 1-2	N26 3-1	N22 0-1	J02 4-3	F28 2-2	S17 0-0	m06 3-0	D17 2-1	O29 1-2
4 BOURNEMOUTH	a29 3-2	O08 0-1	D03 2-1		M11 3-0	J02 2-1	S03 1-0	N12 2-0	N29 5-1	O29 1-0	S17 0-0	M27 2-1	N19 0-1	F28 2-2	S24 2-1	m13 0-0	F25 1-0	O21 0-1	a15 0-1	J21 0-1	M18 2-3	D17 2-1	a08 0-1	F04 2-1
5 BRADFORD C	M04 1-2	D03 2-2	O05 1-1	N15 0-1		J21 0-1	N19 2-2	O15 0-1	M27 1-1	a15 2-2	O26 1-1	a29 2-1	m13 1-1	S17 2-0	M15 0-0	F11 1-1	O01 2-1	S03 1-0	A29 0-0	J02 1-0	D17 2-2	a08 3-1	M18 2-1	F18 2-0
6 BRIGHTON & H.A.	O05 0-1	D31 4-0	M04 3-0	S10 1-2	A27 1-3		M15 0-1	D26 3-1	m01 1-1	m06 0-1	O01 2-1	F11 1-1	a01 2-1	O22 2-0	M25 2-1	J14 2-2	a05 2-1	N05 3-1	D10 1-1	N26 3-0	a22 0-2	O26 2-2	F25 1-0	S21 0-1
7 CHELSEA	a01 5-3	a04 3-1	A27 1-2	M25 2-0	m06 3-1	O29 2-0		J14 1-0	F28 2-1	D26 3-0	a22 1-0	O01 2-1	S20 1-3	F25 2-2	S10 1-1	O22 5-0	D10 3-3	N26 2-0	m01 2-1	N12 1-1	F11 3-2	O04 2-0	M11 2-2	D31 1-1
8 CRYSTAL P	N05 1-1	m13 4-1	F11 2-2	M04 2-3	F25 2-0	M27 2-1	A30 1-1		O22 3-1	O04 2-0	D17 0-0	N19 4-2	D03 0-0	a08 2-0	O25 1-0	O01 4-1	a15 2-0	S17 1-1	m09 1-0	M18 1-0	J21 2-1	J02 4-0	S03 0-2	a29 1-0
9 HULL C	S10 0-0	N19 1-1	S20 1-3	J14 4-0	D26 1-1	D03 5-2	O25 3-0	a11 0-1		D31 1-1	M14 1-2	O04 2-2	A27 1-0	a22 1-1	a04 1-2	M25 3-0	a01 1-1	F11 3-0	M04 1-4	O15 0-0	N05 1-0	O01 0-0	a29 0-3	m13 0-1
10 IPSWICH T	F21 2-0	a29 4-0	m13 2-0	M14 3-1	S24 1-1	N19 2-3	M28 0-1	F04 1-2	a08 1-1		N05 0-1	J02 2-0	O08 1-0	D16 2-1	O15 1-2	D03 2-2	O25 0-1	M18 2-0	J21 5-1	S03 2-0	M04 1-2	N08 3-1	S17 3-2	a22 2-1
11 LEEDS U	S21 2-0	J14 1-0	D26 2-0	a01 3-0	M01 3-3	a15 1-0	S24 0-2	a05 1-2	O29 2-1	M11 2-4		O22 1-1	S10 1-1	m06 0-0	A27 1-1	D31 2-0	M25 1-0	D10 2-3	N26 4-0	F04 2-0	F25 0-0	m01 1-0	O08 0-1	N12 2-1
12 LEICESTER C	a11 0-1	M25 2-0	D31 4-0	D26 0-1	N26 1-0	O08 1-0	a15 2-0	m06 2-2	F04 0-2	S10 0-1	F18 1-2		N05 0-0	m01 1-2	a01 1-0	S21 1-0	J14 2-1	M15 1-1	O15 2-0	D10 3-1	O26 3-3	M04 1-0	S24 2-2	A27 1-1
13 MANCHESTER C	a22 1-2	O22 0-0	O01 1-0	m06 3-3	D10 4-0	S17 2-1	M18 2-3	m01 1-1	J21 4-1	F11 4-0	J02 0-0	M11 4-2		A29 1-4	N26 2-1	F25 2-0	O05 4-1	D17 2-2	M27 2-1	O29 1-1	a08 2-1	S03 2-2	N12 3-1	M01 1-1
14 OLDHAM A	A27 1-1	S10 4-0	M24 1-1	O25 2-0	a01 1-1	F18 2-1	O15 1-4	D30 2-3	S24 2-2	a04 4-0	N19 2-2	D03 1-1	J14 0-1		S20 3-0	a29 2-2	M14 5-3	M03 3-0	O08 2-2	a15 2-2	m13 2-2	N05 3-0	F04 3-1	D26 1-3
15 OXFORD U	D03 2-0	N12 3-0	O22 1-1	a22 3-1	O29 3-4	S03 3-2	J02 2-3	M01 1-0	A29 1-0	F25 1-1	J21 3-2	S17 1-1	a29 2-4	M18 1-1		N19 0-1	F11 1-0	O01 4-1	a08 3-2	N02 2-4	O05 1-1	M27 1-0	m13 0-4	M11 1-1
16 PLYMOUTH A	a25 1-2	F04 0-1	N05 4-3	D10 1-1	O08 3-1	D06 3-0	F18 0-1	a22 0-2	S03 2-0	m01 0-1	a09 1-0	M18 1-1	O15 0-1	N26 3-0	m06 3-1		M04 0-1	O25 0-0	S17 4-0	D18 1-4	M27 4-1	J21 2-0	J02 1-0	S24 1-1
17 PORTSMOUTH	N19 3-0	M11 1-0	a29 1-2	O15 2-1	a22 1-2	D17 2-0	m13 2-3	S24 1-1	S17 1-3	F28 0-1	S03 4-0	A29 3-0	F04 0-1	O29 1-1	O08 2-1	N12 2-0		J21 2-0	M18 0-0	a08 2-0	J02 0-2	F18 1-1	M27 2-2	D03 0-0
18 SHREWSBURY T	D31 2-3	D26 0-0	J14 1-1	a11 1-0	M25 1-3	M11 1-1	a29 1-1	a01 2-1	O08 1-3	S20 1-5	m13 3-3	O29 3-0	a04 0-1	N11 0-0	a15 2-2	F28 2-0	A27 1-2		F04 1-2	S24 0-0	D03 0-1	O15 0-0	N19 1-1	S10 1-1
19 STOKE C	M25 1-1	F28 1-0	S10 0-1	O01 2-1	J14 2-1	m13 2-2	D03 0-3	O29 2-1	N13 4-0	A27 1-1	a29 2-3	F25 2-2	D26 3-1	F11 0-0	D31 1-0	a01 2-2	S20 2-2	O04 0-0		M11 2-0	N19 2-1	a22 0-3	O22 2-0	a04 0-0
20 SUNDERLAND	D26 1-0	a01 2-2	O25 2-0	A27 1-1	S10 0-0	a29 1-0	M21 1-2	S20 1-1	F25 2-0	M25 4-0	O04 2-1	m13 2-2	M14 2-4	O01 3-2	J14 1-0	a04 2-1	D31 4-0	a22 2-1	N05 1-1		O22 4-0	F11 0-3	D03 1-1	N19 1-1
21 SWINDON T	J14 0-0	O29 2-1	a01 1-1	S20 3-1	a04 1-0	S24 3-0	O09 1-1	a25 1-0	M11 1-0	N12 2-3	O16 0-0	F28 2-1	D31 1-2	D10 2-2	F05 3-0	D26 1-0	S11 1-1	m01 1-0	m06 3-0	F18 4-1		N26 1-0	a15 1-1	M25 0-0
22 WALSALL	m13 1-3	S20 5-0	N19 1-2	a04 1-1	D31 0-1	F28 1-0	F04 0-7	S10 0-0	a15 1-1	J14 2-4	D03 0-3	N12 0-1	M25 3-3	M11 2-2	D26 1-5	A27 2-2	O22 1-1	F25 1-1	S24 1-2	O08 2-0	a29 2-2		O29 0-1	a01 0-0
23 WATFORD	O25 4-0	A27 1-0	a04 2-2	D31 1-0	S20 2-0	O15 1-1	N05 1-2	M24 0-1	N26 2-0	a01 3-2	F11 1-1	a22 2-1	M04 1-0	O04 3-1	D10 1-1	S10 3-0	D26 1-0	m06 0-0	a11 3-2	m01 0-1	O01 2-3	a18 5-0		J14 2-0
24 W.B.A.	F11 1-1	F25 0-0	M15 2-0	O05 0-0	O22 1-0	M18 1-0	a08 2-3	N26 5-3	D10 2-0	O01 1-2	M05 2-1	J21 1-1	O26 1-0	M27 3-1	N05 3-2	a15 2-2	m01 3-0	J02 4-0	D18 6-0	m06 0-0	S03 3-1	S17 0-0	A29 0-1	

Season 1988-89

DIVISION 3

	ALDERSHOT	BLACKPOOL	BOLTON W	BRENTFORD	BRISTOL C	BRISTOL R	BURY	CARDIFF C	CHESTER C	CHESTERFIELD	FULHAM	GILLINGHAM	HUDDERSFIELD T	MANSFIELD T	NORTHAMPTON T	NOTTS CO	PORT VALE	PRESTON N.E.	READING	SHEFFIELD U	SOUTHEND U	SWANSEA C	WIGAN A	WOLVERHAMPTON W
1 ALDERSHOT		a29 1-0	S24 0-3	D18 0-0	F21 0-1	J21 1-3	a08 4-1	J02 0-1	O29 1-1	M18 2-0	a25 1-2	S03 0-2	O22 0-1	m13 0-0	F04 5-1	D03 2-3	M11 2-2	J07 2-1	M27 1-1	N08 1-0	S17 2-2	O09 0-1	O04 3-1	a15 1-2
2 BLACKPOOL	N12 4-0		F18 2-0	M27 0-3	S20 2-2	D17 1-1	J02 2-2	O29 1-0	M18 1-1	a22 1-2	M11 0-1	m01 4-1	m06 2-1	S17 1-1	O04 3-1	S03 0-1	O22 3-2	J21 1-0	a08 2-4	O15 1-2	m09 3-2	N26 0-0	F04 2-0	F28 0-2
3 BOLTON W	a22 1-0	O08 2-2		m06 4-2	M11 2-0	S17 1-1	N12 2-4	S03 4-0	D17 0-1	O29 5-0	S20 3-2	J06 2-1	m01 3-1	J02 0-0	N26 2-1	a08 3-3	a25 1-1	M27 1-0	J21 1-1	O01 2-0	M18 0-0	F11 1-0	m09 1-1	O22 1-2
4 BRENTFORD	a01 2-1	D26 1-0	D03 3-0		a04 3-0	a15 2-1	F25 2-2	m13 1-1	F11 0-1	F28 1-0	M24 0-1	O01 1-0	A27 1-0	a29 1-0	J14 2-0	N08 2-1	O29 2-1	O22 0-2	M11 3-2	S24 1-4	O09 4-0	m09 1-1	S10 1-1	D31 2-2
5 BRISTOL C	O25 1-1	a15 1-2	N05 1-1	a11 0-1		J02 0-1	M27 3-0	D17 2-0	J21 0-1	S03 4-0	O08 1-5	F11 1-0	a18 6-1	M21 2-0	M04 3-1	M18 0-4	S24 0-1	S17 1-1	D03 2-1	m13 2-0	a08 0-2	O01 2-0	a29 0-1	N08 0-1
6 BRISTOL R	S10 2-2	a01 1-0	J28 2-0	S21 1-2	M25 1-1		N26 1-3	F04 0-1	O22 4-1	M11 2-1	m06 0-0	N12 2-0	O29 5-1	F18 0-0	a22 1-1	O15 2-0	a05 2-2	O05 1-0	M01 1-1	J14 1-1	m01 1-1	D31 1-1	A27 3-2	D26 0-0
7 BURY	D31 0-1	M25 0-0	a29 0-0	O15 3-1	D26 2-1	m13 0-0		a15 1-0	N08 2-1	F04 2-1	J28 3-1	M04 1-0	a01 0-6	S24 0-1	a04 0-1	N05 1-1	S10 0-0	F18 1-1	O04 2-1	M14 1-2	O25 3-1	J14 1-0	D03 1-1	A27 3-1
8 CARDIFF C	M25 3-2	m16 0-0	J14 1-0	N25 1-0	a01 1-1	O01 2-2	N01 3-0		m09 2-0	m01 0-1	A27 1-2	N05 1-0	S10 3-0	M04 0-0	N12 1-0	a18 0-1	J28 3-0	m05 0-0	O08 1-2	F11 0-0	a22 2-0	D26 2-2	D30 2-2	a04 1-1
9 CHESTER C	M15 1-1	A27 1-1	a01 0-0	O05 3-2	S10 2-0	M04 0-2	m01 2-0	O15 0-0		N12 3-1	a05 7-0	m06 2-0	S24 3-0	O26 0-0	D31 2-1	F18 1-0	J14 1-2	a22 0-1	F04 3-0	a19 0-1	N26 2-4	N05 3-1	D26 1-0	M25 1-1
10 CHESTERFIELD	A27 2-1	S24 0-2	M14 1-1	O25 2-2	J14 1-0	N05 0-3	O01 1-2	M21 4-0	a29 1-2		D31 4-1	F18 3-1	D26 1-1	D03 1-3	J28 1-1	F11 3-0	a15 1-2	O15 0-3	m13 2-4	M25 2-1	M04 2-1	a01 2-0	a04 1-1	S10 0-3
11 FULHAM	O15 5-1	N05 1-1	a15 1-1	J02 3-3	F18 3-1	D03 0-2	S17 1-0	M18 2-0	J07 4-1	a08 2-1		M27 1-2	F04 1-2	J21 1-1	O25 3-2	M14 2-1	m13 1-2	D17 2-1	N08 2-1	a29 2-2	S03 1-0	M04 1-0	S24 1-1	O05 2-2
12 GILLINGHAM	J14 1-1	N08 1-0	a04 0-1	F04 0-0	O04 0-1	a28 2-3	O22 3-4	M11 1-2	D03 0-2	O08 0-1	D26 0-1		J28 1-2	a15 3-0	a01 1-0	m13 2-1	D30 1-0	F28 1-3	S24 0-1	S10 2-1	F25 1-1	A27 2-3	M24 2-1	O29 1-3
13 HUDDERSFIELD T	M04 2-1	D03 1-1	N08 0-1	a25 1-2	O15 0-1	M14 2-3	D17 3-2	J21 1-0	a15 3-1	M27 1-1	O01 2-0	S17 1-1		a08 2-0	F18 1-2	S20 3-1	F11 0-0	S03 2-0	M07 2-2	N05 3-2	J02 3-2	O25 1-1	m13 1-1	a29 0-0
14 MANSFIELD T	N26 1-1	J28 0-1	M25 1-1	N12 1-0	O29 2-2	O08 2-1	a22 1-1	O22 2-2	F28 2-0	m06 3-1	S10 3-1	S20 2-1	D31 1-0		A27 1-1	O01 1-1	D26 0-1	M11 0-3	F25 2-1	a04 0-1	F11 4-0	m02 0-0	J14 0-1	a01 3-1
15 NORTHAMPTON T	O01 6-0	F11 4-2	m13 2-3	S03 1-0	O22 1-3	S24 1-2	J07 2-0	a29 3-0	a08 0-2	S17 3-0	F28 2-1	D18 1-2	O08 1-3	M18 2-1		J21 1-3	N08 1-3	J02 1-0	O29 1-3	a15 1-2	M27 2-2	F26 1-0	M11 1-1	D04 3-1
16 NOTTS CO	m06 4-1	J14 1-1	D31 2-0	m01 3-0	A27 0-0	F25 1-0	M11 3-0	F28 2-0	O09 2-2	O04 4-0	O29 0-1	N26 1-2	a22 3-0	F04 2-1	S10 0-1		M25 1-4	S24 0-0	O22 3-3	D26 1-4	N12 1-1	a04 1-0	a01 1-0	J29 1-1
17 PORT VALE	F13 3-0	M04 1-0	O15 2-1	M13 3-2	a21 0-1	m09 1-0	J21 1-3	S17 6-1	S03 1-2	S19 5-0	N26 3-0	a08 2-1	O03 2-0	M27 1-2	m01 1-2	J02 1-0		M18 1-1	D17 3-0	O24 3-3	m06 2-0	N12 2-1	F18 2-1	F04 0-0
18 PRESTON N.E.	a04 2-2	S10 1-0	D26 3-1	M04 5-3	J28 2-0	F11 1-1	O08 1-0	D03 3-3	S20 3-3	F25 6-0	a01 1-4	O25 5-0	J14 1-0	N05 2-0	M25 3-2	a15 3-0	A27 1-3		a29 2-1	D31 2-0	O01 3-2	M14 1-1	N08 2-2	m13 3-3
19 READING	D28 3-1	D30 2-1	S10 1-1	N05 2-2	m05 1-2	O26 3-1	F11 1-1	F18 3-1	O01 3-1	N26 0-0	m01 0-1	a22 1-2	a05 2-1	O15 1-0	M15 1-1	M04 1-3	a01 3-0	N12 2-2		A27 1-3	S21 4-0	M25 2-0	a19 0-3	J14 0-2
20 SHEFFIELD U	m01 1-0	F25 4-1	F04 4-0	a22 2-2	N26 3-0	S03 4-1	O29 2-1	a11 0-1	S17 6-1	J02 1-3	N12 1-0	J21 4-2	M11 5-1	a25 1-2	S20 4-0	M27 1-1	F28 0-0	a08 3-1	M18 1-0		D17 1-2	m06 5-1	O22 2-1	O08 2-0
21 SOUTHEND U	J28 1-1	a04 2-1	A27 2-0	a18 1-1	D31 1-2	N08 2-2	F28 1-1	S23 0-0	m13 1-0	O22 3-1	J13 0-0	O15 2-1	M25 2-4	O04 1-1	D26 2-1	a28 1-1	D02 1-1	F03 2-1	a14 2-1	M31 2-1		S10 0-2	O28 1-2	M10 3-1
22 SWANSEA C	F17 1-0	m13 1-2	O04 1-0	S17 1-1	F03 1-1	a08 1-2	S03 1-1	M27 1-1	M11 1-1	D17 2-0	O22 2-0	M19 3-2	M22 1-0	N08 3-1	O15 1-0	J07 2-0	a29 0-0	O29 1-1	J02 2-0	D03 2-2	J21 2-0		a15 1-2	S24 2-5
23 WIGAN A	F11 2-1	S30 2-1	O25 1-1	J21 1-1	N12 0-1	m03 3-0	m06 1-0	a07 1-0	M27 3-0	J07 0-2	a22 0-1	J02 3-0	N26 0-2	S03 0-0	N05 1-3	D18 0-1	O08 0-2	m01 1-1	S17 3-0	M04 1-2	D10 3-0	N01 1-2		m16 1-1
24 WOLVERHAMPTON W	S20 1-0	O25 2-1	M04 1-0	a08 2-0	m01 2-0	M27 0-1	M18 4-0	J10 2-0	J02 3-1	J21 1-0	F11 5-2	M14 6-1	N12 4-1	D17 6-2	m06 3-2	S17 0-0	O01 3-3	N26 6-0	S03 2-1	m09 2-2	N05 3-0	a22 1-1	O15 2-1	

DIVISION 4

	BURNLEY	CAMBRIDGE U	CARLISLE U	COLCHESTER U	CREWE A	DARLINGTON	DONCASTER R	EXETER C	GRIMSBY T	HALIFAX T	HARTLEPOOL U	HEREFORD U	LEYTON O	LINCOLN C	PETERBOROUGH U	ROCHDALE	ROTHERHAM U	SCARBOROUGH	SCUNTHORPE U	STOCKPORT CO	TORQUAY U	TRANMERE R	WREXHAM	YORK C
1 BURNLEY		O29 2-0	M21 0-0	S24 2-0	a04 1-0	a15 0-1	a29 3-0	O08 3-0	D31 1-0	J14 2-1	D03 0-0	a01 3-3	O22 2-2	N08 1-4	F25 1-1	A27 2-1	O04 1-0	m13 0-1	M11 0-1	J28 1-0	F04 1-0	M25 2-2	D26 1-3	S10 6-0
2 CAMBRIDGE U	M14 2-1		S30 3-2	M05 3-1	a22 1-1	m02 1-3	D26 0-0	N04 2-0	A27 4-1	O08 2-1	F11 6-0	J14 2-1	N26 2-2	S20 2-3	M25 2-1	D30 2-0	N12 1-1	O25 2-2	F25 0-3	S10 1-0	m06 3-0	J28 1-1	M31 2-0	a04 1-1
3 CARLISLE U	O25 0-0	a15 1-1		O04 1-2	M25 0-1	N12 1-2	a04 0-1	M04 1-0	N26 2-1	J28 3-1	a01 2-1	F18 3-0	m01 2-1	M14 2-1	A27 2-2	D26 1-0	S24 0-2	N05 0-1	F04 0-3	D31 1-1	O15 2-1	S10 1-1	m06 1-2	J14 0-0
4 COLCHESTER U	F10 2-2	O21 1-2	a21 1-1		M10 2-1	N25 1-2	S09 0-1	m05 4-0	M24 0-0	m01 3-2	D30 1-2	a04 1-1	F24 1-0	O01 1-3	D26 1-2	M31 3-0	F28 1-1	S20 3-1	O08 1-2	O28 1-1	N11 2-2	J13 2-3	a25 2-1	A27 1-0
5 CREWE A	m09 4-0	O04 2-0	J02 1-0	N04 3-1		S17 2-0	O15 0-2	M14 2-1	O25 2-2	m05 2-2	M04 3-0	F04 2-1	J21 2-1	M18 2-0	N25 1-1	a14 3-1	M27 1-3	a08 1-1	S03 3-2	S23 1-1	D16 0-0	N12 2-1	F17 2-2	m01 1-2
6 DARLINGTON	O01 1-1	N08 1-1	m13 2-3	a29 1-2	J28 1-1		N05 1-3	S20 2-2	a04 1-1	D26 0-2	J14 0-0	D31 0-0	F11 1-3	M04 2-1	S10 2-2	M14 1-2	O08 1-1	a22 2-1	D03 3-3	A27 1-4	O25 0-0	a01 1-2	M25 2-1	F25 2-2
7 DONCASTER R	N26 1-0	M27 1-1	J10 1-3	M18 3-1	F24 0-1	M10 1-0		S03 2-1	m01 2-3	O21 1-4	O08 1-0	O04 3-2	O29 1-0	a08 0-1	N12 2-3	F04 1-1	J21 1-0	J02 3-1	D17 2-2	a14 2-2	S16 1-2	m06 0-0	S24 2-2	F28 1-2
8 EXETER C	F18 3-0	M11 0-3	O22 3-0	D03 4-2	O29 1-2	F04 2-1	J14 3-0		O15 2-1	S10 4-1	a29 2-1	D26 3-1	M01 1-1	m13 0-1	a01 3-1	J28 5-1	a15 0-0	N09 1-0	S24 2-2	M25 2-2	O05 3-0	a05 0-1	A27 0-2	D31 2-0
9 GRIMSBY T	a08 1-0	J21 4-0	a29 0-0	J02 2-2	F28 0-0	F14 0-0	N08 5-0	F25 2-1		O29 3-2	m13 3-0	a15 1-1	D17 2-2	M27 1-0	O08 0-0	S24 1-3	S17 0-4	D03 2-1	M18 1-1	M11 2-0	S03 1-0	O04 0-0	F04 0-1	O22 2-0
10 HALIFAX T	S03 1-2	F17 0-0	S16 3-3	N08 3-2	D02 0-1	M27 1-0	M03 2-0	M17 0-3	M14 2-1		N04 1-0	m13 2-2	F14 2-2	a29 0-1	O25 5-0	O14 4-1	a07 1-1	D17 0-2	J02 5-1	F04 2-2	J20 2-0	S23 2-3	O04 4-0	a14 0-0
11 HARTLEPOOL U	m06 2-2	S24 3-2	D17 0-2	a08 2-1	O22 0-3	S03 2-1	F18 2-1	N26 2-2	N12 2-1	M11 2-0		O29 1-1	S17 1-0	J21 3-2	m01 2-1	O04 0-1	J02 1-1	a11 3-1	M27 0-2	F28 2-2	M18 0-1	a15 2-2	O15 1-3	F04 0-1
12 HEREFORD U	D17 0-0	S03 4-2	O08 2-1	a12 1-1	S21 0-1	a08 1-1	a22 3-1	M27 1-0	O01 2-1	N12 3-1	M15 2-0		M18 1-1	F11 3-2	M04 4-0	O26 4-4	N26 1-1	S17 1-3	J21 1-2	F25 2-1	J02 1-1	m01 2-1	N05 0-0	m06 1-2
13 LEYTON O	M04 3-0	a29 1-1	N08 2-0	O15 8-0	A27 0-0	S23 1-0	M14 4-0	O25 4-0	a01 5-0	a04 2-0	M21 4-3	S10 1-3		D03 3-1	N05 1-2	M25 3-0	F04 3-1	F18 2-3	m13 4-1	J14 1-2	a15 3-1	D26 2-0	D31 0-1	O04 4-0
14 LINCOLN C	m01 2-3	F04 3-0	O29 0-2	a15 1-1	S10 2-2	O22 3-2	D28 3-1	N12 2-0	D26 2-2	N26 2-1	A27 0-1	S24 2-0	m06 0-1		J28 1-1	a05 4-1	M11 0-1	O15 2-2	O05 1-0	a01 0-0	F18 1-0	M01 2-1	J14 4-3	M25 2-1
15 PETERBOROUGH U	O15 3-0	J03 1-5	J21 1-4	M27 3-0	a29 3-2	M18 1-1	m13 2-0	D17 0-1	a25 1-2	M01 2-1	N09 0-1	O22 2-1	M11 0-1	S17 1-1		D03 1-0	J07 0-3	S03 1-4	O29 1-2	O05 1-0	a08 3-1	F04 1-1	a15 1-0	S24 0-1
16 ROCHDALE	J21 2-1	a08 2-1	M27 0-0	D16 1-1	O01 2-1	O29 2-2	S20 2-0	S17 2-1	F11 0-2	a25 1-1	a22 0-0	F28 2-2	J02 0-3	J07 2-2	m06 0-0		S03 0-2	M18 2-1	O22 1-0	O08 1-1	m01 2-1	M11 3-1	N12 3-3	N26 2-0
17 ROTHERHAM U	a22 3-1	m13 0-0	F11 2-1	O25 2-0	D26 1-2	F18 1-2	A27 3-0	O01 0-1	M07 1-0	D31 2-0	M25 4-0	a29 6-0	S20 4-1	N05 2-0	a04 1-1	J14 3-1		M14 1-1	N08 3-3	D03 2-1	M04 1-0	O15 0-0	S10 2-2	a01 0-1
18 SCARBOROUGH	N12 1-0	M01 2-1	M11 0-1	F04 0-0	D31 2-1	O05 3-2	M25 2-0	m01 2-1	m06 2-3	a01 3-1	a05 2-0	J28 0-2	O08 0-0	F25 1-1	J14 2-1	S10 3-3	O29 1-0		a15 1-0	O22 1-1	S24 5-2	A27 0-0	N26 0-3	D26 0-0
19 SCUNTHORPE U	N05 2-1	O15 1-0	S20 1-1	F18 2-3	J14 2-2	m06 5-1	a01 2-1	F11 2-0	S10 1-1	M25 0-0	D26 1-1	A27 3-1	N12 2-2	a22 0-0	M14 3-0	M04 4-0	m01 0-0	O01 0-3		a04 1-1	N26 1-0	D31 0-1	O25 3-1	J28 4-2
20 STOCKPORT CO	S16 0-0	M17 0-0	a07 1-1	M13 1-0	F10 0-1	J20 0-0	O01 2-0	J02 4-0	N05 3-1	S19 1-1	O24 3-0	O15 1-2	S03 0-0	D17 1-0	a21 1-2	F17 3-0	m06 1-3	M04 2-2	J07 1-2		M27 0-0	N25 1-1	m01 2-2	N11 3-2
21 TORQUAY U	S20 2-0	D02 3-1	m03 1-0	m13 1-3	M31 2-1	F28 1-0	J28 3-2	a22 0-4	J14 2-2	A27 0-2	S10 2-0	M25 1-0	O01 3-0	O08 1-0	D31 1-0	N08 1-0	O22 1-2	F11 0-1	a28 0-2	D26 2-1		O29 3-2	a04 0-0	a25 2-0
22 TRANMERE R	J02 2-1	S16 1-2	M17 0-0	S02 0-0	m13 1-1	D16 2-0	D02 2-2	M20 2-0	m09 3-2	F10 2-0	S30 2-1	N07 1-0	M27 3-0	O24 1-0	S19 1-0	N04 2-0	F25 0-0	J21 1-1	a07 2-1	a28 1-0	M13 3-0		M03 2-1	O07 0-1
23 WREXHAM	M27 4-2	D16 3-1	D03 2-1	S16 2-2	O08 0-0	J02 3-3	F11 1-1	J21 3-0	S20 1-2	a21 3-0	M07 4-3	M11 1-1	a08 0-1	S03 3-0	O01 1-1	m13 2-1	M18 1-4	a29 0-1	F28 2-0	N08 2-0	m09 1-0	O22 3-3		O29 2-1
24 YORK C	M18 0-0	m09 1-2	S03 1-1	J21 2-0	N08 3-0	O15 4-1	O25 1-1	a08 3-1	M04 0-3	O01 5-3	S20 2-3	D03 4-1	a22 1-1	J02 2-1	F11 5-1	a29 3-3	D16 1-1	M27 0-0	S17 1-2	m13 2-0	N05 1-1	F18 0-1	M14 1-0	

LEAGUE TABLES

DIVISION 1

	P	W	D	L	F	A	W	D	L	F	A	Pts
Arsenal	38	10	6	3	35	19	12	4	3	38	17	76
Liverpool	38	11	5	3	33	11	11	5	3	32	17	76
Nottingham F	38	8	7	4	31	16	9	6	4	33	26	64
Norwich C	38	8	7	4	23	20	9	4	6	25	25	62
Derby Co	38	9	3	7	23	18	8	4	7	17	20	58
Tottenham H	38	8	6	5	31	24	7	6	6	29	22	57
Coventry C	38	9	4	6	28	23	5	9	5	19	19	55
Everton	38	10	7	2	33	18	4	5	10	17	27	54
QPR	38	9	5	5	23	16	5	6	8	20	21	53
Millwall	38	10	3	6	27	21	4	8	7	20	31	53
Manchester U	38	10	5	4	27	13	3	7	9	18	22	51
Wimbledon	38	10	3	6	30	19	4	6	9	20	27	51
Southampton	38	6	7	6	25	26	4	8	7	27	40	45
Charlton A	38	6	7	6	25	24	4	5	10	19	34	42
Sheffield W	38	6	6	7	21	25	4	6	9	13	26	42
Luton T	38	8	6	5	32	21	2	5	12	10	31	41
Aston Villa	38	7	6	6	25	22	2	7	10	20	34	40
Middlesbrough	38	6	7	6	28	30	3	5	11	16	31	39
West Ham U	38	3	6	10	19	30	7	2	10	18	32	38
Newcastle U	38	3	6	10	19	28	4	4	11	13	35	31

DIVISION 2

	P	W	D	L	F	A	W	D	L	F	A	Pts
Chelsea	46	15	6	2	50	25	14	6	3	46	25	99
Manchester C	46	12	8	3	48	28	11	5	7	29	25	82
Crystal P	46	15	6	2	42	17	8	6	9	29	32	81
Watford	46	14	5	4	41	18	8	7	8	33	30	78
Blackburn R	46	16	4	3	50	22	6	7	10	24	37	77
Swindon T	46	13	8	2	35	15	7	8	8	33	38	76
Barnsley	46	12	8	3	37	21	8	6	9	29	37	74
Ipswich T	46	13	3	7	42	23	9	4	10	29	38	73
WBA	46	13	7	3	43	18	5	11	7	22	23	72
Leeds U	46	12	6	5	34	20	5	10	8	25	30	67
Sunderland	46	12	8	3	40	23	4	7	12	20	37	63
Bournemouth	46	13	3	7	32	20	5	5	13	21	42	62
Stoke C	46	10	9	4	33	25	5	5	13	24	47	59
Bradford C	46	8	11	4	29	22	5	6	12	23	37	56
Leicester C	46	11	6	6	31	20	2	10	11	25	43	55
Oldham A	46	9	10	4	49	32	2	11	10	26	40	54
Oxford U	46	11	6	6	40	34	3	6	14	22	36	54
Plymouth A	46	11	4	8	35	22	3	8	12	20	44	54
Brighton & HA	46	11	5	7	36	24	3	4	16	21	42	51
Portsmouth	46	10	6	7	33	21	3	6	14	20	41	51
Hull C	46	7	9	7	31	25	4	5	14	21	43	47
Shrewsbury	46	4	11	8	25	31	4	7	12	15	36	42
Birmingham C	46	6	4	13	21	33	2	7	14	10	43	35
Walsall	46	3	10	10	27	42	2	6	15	14	38	31

DIVISION 3

	P	W	D	L	F	A	W	D	L	F	A	Pts
Wolves	46	18	4	1	61	19	8	10	5	35	30	92
Sheffield U	46	16	3	4	57	21	9	6	8	36	33	84
Port Vale	46	15	3	5	46	21	9	9	5	32	27	84
Fulham	46	12	7	4	42	28	10	2	11	27	39	75
Bristol R	46	9	11	3	34	21	10	6	7	33	30	74
Preston NE	46	14	7	2	56	31	5	8	10	23	29	72
Brentford	46	14	5	4	36	21	4	9	10	30	40	68
Chester C	46	12	6	5	38	18	7	5	11	26	43	68
Notts Co	46	11	7	5	37	22	7	6	10	27	32	67
Bolton W	46	12	8	3	42	23	4	8	11	16	31	64
Bristol C	46	10	3	10	32	25	8	6	9	21	30	63
Swansea C	46	11	8	4	33	22	4	8	11	18	31	61
Bury	46	11	7	5	27	22	5	6	12	28	45	61
Huddersfield T	46	10	8	5	35	25	7	1	15	28	48	60
Mansfield T	46	10	8	5	32	22	4	9	10	16	30	59
Cardiff C	46	10	9	4	30	16	4	6	13	14	40	57
Wigan A	46	9	5	9	28	22	5	9	9	27	31	56
Reading	46	10	6	7	37	29	5	5	13	31	43	56
Blackpool	46	10	6	7	36	29	4	7	12	20	30	55
Northampton T	46	11	2	10	41	34	5	4	14	25	42	54
Southend U	46	10	9	4	33	26	3	6	14	23	49	54
Chesterfield	46	9	5	9	35	35	5	2	16	16	51	49
Gillingham	46	7	3	13	25	32	5	1	17	22	49	40
Aldershot	46	7	6	10	29	29	1	7	15	19	49	37

DIVISION 4

	P	W	D	L	F	A	W	D	L	F	A	Pts
Rotherham U	46	13	6	4	44	18	9	10	4	32	17	82
Tranmere R	46	13	6	2	34	13	6	11	6	28	30	80
Crewe A	46	13	7	3	42	24	8	8	7	25	24	78
Scunthorpe U	46	11	9	3	40	22	10	5	8	37	35	77
Scarborough	46	12	7	4	33	23	9	7	7	34	39	77
Leyton Orient	46	16	2	5	61	19	5	10	8	25	31	75
Wrexham	46	12	7	4	44	28	7	7	9	33	35	71
Cambridge U	46	13	7	3	45	25	5	7	11	26	37	68
Grimsby T	46	11	9	3	33	18	6	6	11	32	41	66
Lincoln C	46	12	6	5	39	26	6	4	13	25	34	64
York C	46	10	8	5	43	27	7	5	11	19	36	64
Carlisle U	46	9	6	8	26	25	6	9	8	27	27	60
Exeter C	46	14	4	5	46	23	4	2	17	19	45	60
Torquay U	46	15	2	6	32	23	2	6	15	13	37	59
Hereford U	46	11	8	4	40	27	3	8	12	26	45	58
Burnley	46	12	6	5	35	20	2	7	14	17	41	55
Peterboro' U	46	10	3	10	29	32	4	9	10	23	42	54
Rochdale	46	10	10	3	32	26	3	4	16	24	56	53
Hartlepool U	46	10	6	7	33	33	4	4	15	17	45	52
Stockport Co	46	8	10	5	31	20	2	11	10	23	32	51
Halifax T	46	10	7	6	42	27	3	4	16	27	48	50
Colchester U	46	8	7	8	35	30	4	7	12	25	48	50
Doncaster R	46	9	6	8	32	32	4	4	15	17	46	49
Darlington	46	3	12	8	28	38	5	6	12	25	38	42

Football League Records

Top scorers: Div, G.Lineker (Tottenham Hotspur) 24 goals; Div 2, M.Quinn (Newcastle United) 32 goals; Div 3, R.Taylor (Bristol City) 27 goals; Div 4, B.Angell (Stockport County) 23 goals.
Play-offs: Div 1, Blackburn Rovers v Swindon Town 1-2, 2-1; Sunderland v Newcastle United 0-0, 2-0; Sunderland v Swindon Town (Wembley) 0-1; Div 2, Bolton Wanderers v Notts County 1-1, 0-2; Bury v Tranmere Rovers 0-0, 0-2; Notts County v Tranmere Rovers (Wembley) 2-0; Div 3, Cambridge United v Maidstone United 1-1, 2-0; Chesterfield v Stockport County 4-0, 2-0; Cambridge United v Chesterfield (Wembley) 1-0.

Leeds United, Sheffield United and Sunderland promoted to Div 1; Charlton Athletic, Millwall and Sheffield Wednesday relegated to Div 2; Bristol City, Bristol Rovers and Notts County promoted to Div 2; AFC Bournemouth, Bradford City and Stoke City relegated to Div 3; Exeter City, Grimsby Town, Cambridge United and Southend United promoted to Div 3; Blackpool, Cardiff City, Northampton Town and Walsall relegated to Div 4; Swindon Town demoted to Div 2, Sunderland took their place in Div 1; Colchester United were relegated from Division Four and replaced by Darlington.

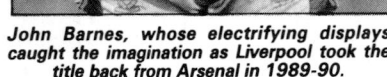

John Barnes, whose electrifying displays caught the imagination as Liverpool took the title back from Arsenal in 1989-90.

DIVISION 1

	ARSENAL	ASTON VILLA	CHARLTON A	CHELSEA	COVENTRY C	CRYSTAL P	DERBY CO	EVERTON	LIVERPOOL	LUTON T	MANCHESTER C	MANCHESTER U	MILLWALL	NORWICH C	NOTTINGHAM F	Q.P.R.	SHEFFIELD W	SOUTHAMPTON	TOTENHAM H	WIMBLEDON
1 ARSENAL		a11 0-1	S23 1-0	M17 0-1	A22 2-0	J01 4-1	O28 1-1	M31 1-0	a18 1-1	D16 3-2	O14 4-0	D03 1-0	a28 2-0	N04 4-3	M07 3-0	N18 3-0	S09 5-0	m02 2-1	J20 1-0	A26 0-0
2 ASTON VILLA	D30 2-1		A26 1-1	a14 1-0	N18 4-1	O28 2-1	S30 1-0	N05 6-2	A23 1-1	M10 2-0	a01 1-2	D26 3-0	a21 1-0	a28 3-3	D02 2-1	S23 1-3	F10 1-0	J20 2-1	S09 2-0	F24 0-3
3 CHARLTON A	F27 0-0	J13 0-2		A29 3-0	O28 1-1	D16 1-2	A19 0-0	S16 0-1	a11 0-4	F19 2-0	N25 1-1	N04 2-0	D09 1-1	M03 0-1	M17 1-1	M31 1-0	a28 1-2	J01 2-4	O14 1-3	a17 1-2
4 CHELSEA	S30 0-0	J01 0-3	J20 3-1		S23 1-0	a16 3-0	M31 1-1	a28 2-1	D16 2-5	a07 1-0	O28 1-1	F24 1-0	N04 4-0	M10 0-0	S09 2-2	A22 1-1	A26 4-0	N18 2-2	F10 1-2	D02 2-5
5 COVENTRY C	D09 0-1	M04 2-0	M24 1-2	F03 3-2		J13 1-0	a07 1-0	A19 2-0	m05 1-6	S16 1-0	A30 2-1	O21 1-4	F17 3-1	N25 1-0	O14 0-2	a16 1-1	M17 1-4	N11 1-0	J01 0-0	D16 2-1
6 CRYSTAL P	a14 1-1	M24 1-0	a21 2-0	D26 2-2	A26 0-1		M20 1-1	S30 2-1	J20 0-2	N11 1-1	m05 2-2	A22 1-1	O21 4-3	D30 1-0	S23 1-0	D02 0-3	F24 1-1	F10 3-1	N18 2-3	S09 2-0
7 DERBY CO	M24 1-3	M17 0-1	D02 2-0	O21 0-1	D30 4-1	O14 3-1		D26 0-1	S09 0-3	m05 2-3	N11 6-0	A26 2-0	a14 2-0	a21 0-2	J20 0-2	F10 2-0	N18 2-0	S23 0-1	F24 2-1	A23 1-1
8 EVERTON	O21 3-0	m05 3-3	F10 2-1	N11 0-1	D02 2-0	M17 4-0	a16 2-1		S23 1-3	J01 2-1	D17 0-0	S09 3-2	O14 2-1	M24 3-1	a04 4-0	a07 1-0	J20 2-0	A26 3-0	A22 2-1	N18 1-1
9 LIVERPOOL	N26 2-1	D09 1-1	D30 1-0	a21 4-1	N04 0-1	S12 9-0	m01 1-0	F03 2-1		J13 2-2	A19 3-1	D23 0-0	M03 1-0	S16 0-0	a14 2-2	a28 2-1	D26 2-1	M31 3-2	O29 1-0	a03 2-1
10 LUTON T	a21 2-0	O14 0-1	S09 1-0	D30 0-3	M07 3-2	a28 1-0	N04 1-0	a14 2-2	A26 0-0		M17 1-1	N18 1-3	M24 2-1	O21 4-1	D26 1-1	J20 1-1	A22 2-0	F24 1-1	D02 0-0	S23 1-1
11 MANCHESTER C	M10 1-1	O22 0-2	F24 1-2	M21 1-1	J20 1-0	N04 3-0	a28 0-1	a21 1-0	D02 1-4	S30 3-1		S23 5-1	D30 2-0	D26 1-0	N18 0-3	S09 1-0	a14 2-1	A23 1-2	A26 1-1	F10 1-1
12 MANCHESTER U	A19 4-1	a17 2-0	m05 1-0	N25 0-0	M31 3-0	D09 1-2	J13 1-2	M14 0-0	M18 1-2	M03 4-1	F03 1-1		S16 5-1	A30 0-2	N12 1-0	J01 0-0	O14 0-0	O28 2-1	D16 0-1	a30 0-0
13 MILLWALL	N11 1-2	D16 2-0	A22 2-2	m05 1-3	S09 4-1	M31 1-2	J01 1-1	M21 1-2	N19 1-2	O28 1-1	a07 1-1	F10 1-2		S30 0-1	A26 1-0	F24 1-2	S23 2-0	D02 2-2	a16 0-1	J20 0-0
14 NORWICH C	m05 2-2	N11 2-0	N18 0-0	O14 2-0	M14 0-0	a04 2-0	D16 1-0	O28 1-1	F10 0-0	M31 2-0	a16 0-1	J21 2-0	M17 1-1		A23 1-1	A26 0-0	D02 2-1	S09 4-4	S23 2-2	J01 0-1
15 NOTTINGHAM F	S16 1-2	A19 1-1	S30 2-0	F17 1-1	M10 2-4	F03 3-1	A30 2-1	N25 1-0	J01 2-2	a16 3-0	M03 1-0	m02 4-0	J13 3-1	D09 0-1		O28 2-2	N04 0-1	D17 2-0	a07 1-3	M31 0-1
16 Q.P.R.	M03 2-0	M20 1-1	O21 0-1	D09 4-2	D26 1-1	A19 2-0	S16 0-1	D30 1-0	N11 3-2	A30 0-0	a11 1-3	a14 1-2	N25 0-0	J13 2-1	M24 2-0		a21 1-0	O14 1-4	M17 3-1	m05 2-3
17 SHEFFIELD W	F17 1-0	S16 1-0	N11 3-0	J14 1-1	S30 0-0	N25 2-2	M03 1-0	A30 1-1	N29 2-0	D09 1-1	J01 2-0	M21 1-0	F03 1-1	A19 0-2	m05 0-3	D16 2-0		a07 0-1	M31 2-4	O28 0-1
18 SOUTHAMPTON	D26 1-0	A29 2-1	a14 3-2	M03 2-3	a28 3-0	S16 1-1	M10 2-1	J13 2-2	O21 4-1	N25 6-3	D09 2-1	M24 0-2	A19 1-2	F27 4-1	a21 2-0	a03 0-2	D30 2-2		N04 1-1	S30 2-2
19 TOTTENHAM H	O18 2-1	F21 0-2	M10 3-0	S16 1-4	a14 3-2	M03 0-1	N25 1-2	D09 2-1	M21 1-0	A19 2-1	J13 1-1	a21 2-1	D26 3-1	F04 4-0	D30 2-3	S30 3-2	O21 3-0	m05 2-1		N11 0-1
20 WIMBLEDON	J13 1-0	N25 0-2	D26 3-1	A19 0-1	a21 0-0	m02 0-1	D09 1-1	M03 3-1	O14 1-2	F14 1-2	S16 1-0	D30 2-2	A29 2-2	a14 1-1	O21 1-3	N04 0-0	M24 1-1	M17 3-3	a28 1-0	

Leeds United spent around £5 million to win back their First Division place. Lee Chapman was one signing and his goals helped achieve promotion.

DIVISION 2

	BARNSLEY	BLACKBURN R	BOURNEMOUTH	BRADFORD C	BRIGHTON & HA	HULL C	IPSWICH T	LEEDS U	LEICESTER C	MIDDLESBROUGH	NEWCASTLE U	OLDHAM A	OXFORD U	PLYMOUTH A	PORTSMOUTH	PORT VALE	SHEFFIELD U	STOKE C	SUNDERLAND	SWINDON T	WATFORD	W.B.A.	WEST HAM U	WOLVERHAMPTON W
1 BARNSLEY		a03 0-0	a21 0-1	S23 2-0	A26 1-0	F24 1-1	D02 0-1	D30 1-0	O28 2-2	S09 1-1	N18 1-1	M17 1-0	M31 1-0	J20 1-1	N04 0-1	O14 0-3	O17 1-2	S05 3-2	a10 1-0	F10 0-1	D26 0-1	a28 2-2	a14 1-1	S26 2-2
2 BLACKBURN R	S30 5-0		F03 1-1	J01 2-2	m05 1-1	O31 0-0	N11 2-2	J13 1-2	D09 2-4	N21 2-4	M24 2-0	A19 1-0	S02 2-2	a07 2-0	M20 2-0	F17 1-0	m01 0-0	J27 3-0	S16 1-1	a16 2-1	O21 2-2	M10 2-1	N25 5-4	M03 2-3
3 BOURNEMOUTH	D16 2-1	S23 2-4		F24 1-0	D02 0-2	A26 5-4	J20 3-1	m05 0-1	a17 2-3	F10 2-2	S09 2-1	O14 2-0	M06 0-1	J01 2-2	O21 0-1	S26 1-0	N11 0-1	N18 2-1	M17 0-1	a07 1-2	M24 0-0	A22 1-1	N01 1-1	a03 1-1
4 BRADFORD C	F03 0-0	a14 0-1	N25 1-0		O07 2-0	N11 2-3	O18 1-0	O28 0-1	S16 2-0	D26 0-1	M21 3-2	m07 1-1	F17 1-2	m05 0-1	S02 1-1	A19 2-2	M03 1-4	M10 1-0	M31 0-1	S30 1-1	a21 2-1	D30 2-0	D09 2-1	J13 1-1
5 BRIGHTON & H.A.	J13 1-1	N04 1-2	A19 2-1	M17 2-1		a06 2-0	S27 1-0	a21 2-2	F17 1-0	F28 1-0	O21 0-3	M03 1-1	D30 0-1	M07 2-1	D26 0-0	S02 2-0	M14 2-2	a28 1-4	N25 1-2	N01 1-2	O14 1-0	a14 0-3	S16 3-0	D09 1-1
6 HULL C	N25 1-2	a10 2-0	J13 1-4	a28 2-1	O28 0-2		m01 4-3	S16 0-1	A19 1-1	M10 0-0	S30 1-3	O17 0-0	M03 1-0	a24 3-3	F17 1-2	D09 2-1	F03 0-0	M20 0-0	J01 3-2	O07 2-3	N04 0-0	M31 0-2	S02 1-1	a16 2-0
7 IPSWICH T	A19 3-1	a28 3-1	S02 1-1	M24 1-0	M10 2-1	M21 0-1		F17 2-2	M03 2-2	D30 3-0	O07 2-1	N25 1-1	M13 1-0	O21 3-0	a10 0-1	a14 3-2	J13 1-1	S30 2-2	D09 1-1	M20 1-0	O31 1-0	N04 3-1	D26 1-0	S16 1-3
8 LEEDS U	a25 1-2	A26 1-1	N04 3-0	a07 1-1	D16 3-0	F10 4-3	S09 1-1		a28 2-1	A23 2-1	D02 1-0	J01 1-1	S27 2-1	N01 2-1	M24 2-0	M07 0-0	a16 4-0	J20 2-0	O14 2-0	S23 4-0	N18 2-1	F24 2-2	M17 3-2	O21 1-0
9 LEICESTER C	a07 2-2	A23 0-1	D26 2-1	F10 1-1	S23 1-0	D02 2-1	N18 0-1	N11 4-3		a21 2-1	A26 2-2	a03 3-0	O14 0-0	M24 1-1	a14 1-1	M17 2-0	m05 2-5	F24 2-1	S27 2-3	O21 2-1	J20 1-1	S09 1-3	D30 1-0	N01 0-0
10 MIDDLESBROUGH	m02 0-1	M17 0-3	S16 2-1	a16 2-0	O18 2-2	S27 1-0	a25 1-2	D09 0-2	D16 4-1		m05 4-1	M31 1-0	N25 1-0	O14 0-2	F03 2-0	a11 2-3	S02 3-3	J01 0-1	J14 3-0	N11 0-2	M07 1-2	O28 0-0	M03 0-1	A19 4-2
11 NEWCASTLE U	M03 4-1	O18 2-1	F28 3-0	O14 1-0	M31 2-0	M07 2-0	M17 2-1	A19 5-2	J13 5-4	N04 2-2		S02 2-1	D09 2-3	a03 3-1	S16 1-0	O28 2-2	N25 2-0	a16 3-0	F04 1-1	a25 0-0	S27 2-1	a11 2-1	a28 2-1	J01 1-4
12 OLDHAM A	O07 2-0	D01 2-0	M20 4-0	O31 2-2	N18 1-1	M24 3-2	F24 4-1	a13 3-1	S30 1-0	O21 2-0	J20 1-1		m01 4-1	S09 3-2	D30 3-3	D26 2-1	M28 0-2	F10 2-0	N04 2-1	A26 2-2	A22 1-1	S23 2-1	a21 3-0	m03 1-1
13 OXFORD U	O21 2-3	J20 1-1	S30 1-2	S09 2-1	a25 0-1	N18 0-0	S23 2-2	M10 2-4	M21 4-2	F24 3-1	S13 2-1	N11 0-1		D02 3-2	O07 2-1	m05 0-0	J01 3-0	N01 3-0	a16 0-1	M24 2-2	A26 1-1	F10 0-1	a07 0-2	D16 2-2
14 PLYMOUTH A	S02 2-1	O28 2-2	a14 1-0	N04 1-1	S30 2-1	D29 1-2	M31 1-0	a10 1-1	O17 3-1	M20 1-2	a21 1-1	a18 2-0	A19 2-0		D10 0-2	N25 1-2	S16 0-0	O07 3-0	M03 3-0	M10 0-3	a28 0-0	D26 2-2	J13 1-1	F03 0-1
15 PORTSMOUTH	m05 2-1	O14 1-1	M31 2-1	J20 3-0	a16 3-0	S09 2-2	O28 2-3	O17 3-3	J01 2-3	S23 3-1	F10 1-1	a21 2-1	M17 2-1	S12 0-3		N11 2-0	a07 3-2	A26 0-0	D16 3-3	F24 1-1	D02 1-2	N18 1-1	S26 0-1	M06 1-3
16 PORT VALE	M19 2-1	S09 0-0	M10 1-1	D02 3-2	J20 2-1	S12 1-1	J01 5-0	S30 0-0	O07 2-1	O30 1-1	a07 1-2	a16 2-0	N04 1-2	F24 3-0	a28 1-1		D16 1-1	F03 0-0	m01 1-2	N18 2-0	F10 1-0	A26 2-1	O21 2-2	M24 3-1
17 SHEFFIELD U	M24 1-2	D30 1-2	a28 4-2	N18 1-1	S09 5-4	S23 0-0	A26 2-0	D26 2-2	N04 1-1	J20 1-0	F24 1-1	S26 2-1	a14 2-1	F10 1-0	O31 2-1	a21 2-1		O21 2-1	a03 1-3	S12 2-0	a10 4-1	D02 3-1	O14 0-2	M17 3-0
18 STOKE C	D09 0-1	a21 0-1	M03 0-0	S26 1-1	N11 3-2	O14 1-1	M06 0-0	S02 1-1	N25 0-1	a14 0-0	D26 2-1	S16 1-2	a10 1-2	M17 0-0	J13 1-2	S23 1-1	M31 0-1		O28 0-2	m05 1-1	D30 2-2	O17 2-1	A19 1-1	F17 2-0
19 SUNDERLAND	O31 4-2	F10 0-1	O07 3-2	O21 1-0	F24 2-1	a14 0-1	A22 2-4	M20 0-1	M10 2-2	A27 2-1	S24 0-0	m05 2-3	D26 1-0	N18 3-1	a21 2-2	D30 2-2	S30 1-1	a07 2-1		D02 2-2	S09 4-0	J20 1-1	A24 4-3	N11 1-1
20 SWINDON T	S16 0-0	D26 4-3	D05 2-3	M06 3-1	a10 1-2	M17 1-3	O14 3-0	F04 3-2	M31 1-1	a28 1-1	D30 1-1	J13 3-2	O17 3-0	S26 3-0	N26 2-2	M03 3-0	D10 0-2	N04 6-0	A19 0-2		a14 2-0	a21 2-1	F18 2-2	S03 3-1
21 WATFORD	a17 2-2	M31 3-1	O17 2-2	D16 7-2	M20 4-2	m05 3-1	a07 3-3	M03 1-0	S02 3-1	S30 1-0	M10 0-0	D09 3-0	J13 0-1	N11 1-2	A19 1-0	S16 1-0	O28 1-3	a24 1-1	F17 1-1	J01 0-2		O07 0-2	M13 0-1	N25 3-1
22 W.B.A.	N11 7-0	S27 2-2	D09 2-2	M14 2-0	J01 3-0	O21 1-1	m05 1-3	N25 2-1	F21 0-1	a07 0-0	N01 1-5	F03 2-2	S16 3-2	a16 0-3	M03 0-0	J13 2-3	A19 0-3	M24 1-1	S02 1-1	D17 1-2	M17 2-0		a04 1-3	O15 1-2
23 WEST HAM U	J01 4-2	F24 1-1	a11 4-1	A23 2-0	F10 3-1	J20 1-2	a17 2-0	O07 0-1	m02 3-1	N18 2-0	N11 0-0	D16 0-2	O28 3-2	A26 3-2	M10 2-1	M31 2-2	M21 5-0	D02 0-0	O18 5-0	S09 1-1	S23 1-0	S30 2-3		m05 4-0
24 WOLVERHAMPTON W	M10 1-1	N18 1-2	D30 3-1	A26 1-1	S12 2-4	D26 1-2	F10 2-1	M31 1-0	a10 5-0	D02 2-0	a14 0-1	O28 1-1	a21 2-0	S23 1-0	S30 5-0	O17 2-0	O07 1-2	S09 0-0	a28 0-1	J20 2-1	F24 1-1	M20 2-1	N04 1-0	

Season 1989-90

DIVISION 3

	BIRMINGHAM C	BLACKPOOL	BOLTON W	BRENTFORD	BRISTOL C	BRISTOL R	BURY	CARDIFF C	CHESTER C	CREWE A	FULHAM	HUDDERSFIELD T	LEYTON O	MANSFIELD T	NORTHAMPTON T	NOTTS CO	PRESTON N.E.	READING	ROTHERHAM U	SHREWSBURY T	SWANSEA C	TRANMERE R	WALSALL	WIGAN A
1 BIRMINGHAM C		M06 3-1	N25 1-0	M13 0-1	J13 0-4	a16 2-2	a07 0-0	O31 1-1	M24 0-0	A19 3-0	J01 1-1	O21 0-1	N11 0-0	M03 4-1	O14 4-0	a24 1-2	D16 3-1	m05 0-1	M17 4-1	J27 0-1	S02 2-0	S16 2-1	S26 2-0	F17 0-0
2 BLACKPOOL	S30 3-2		a16 2-1	N11 4-0	J13 1-3	m05 0-3	O31 0-1	O21 1-0	a24 1-3	S16 1-3	D16 0-1	J01 2-2	M20 1-0	F03 3-1	M24 1-0	J13 0-0	M10 2-2	O06 0-0	a07 1-2	S02 0-1	a30 2-2	N25 0-3	M03 4-3	A19 0-0
3 BOLTON W	F24 3-1	D26 2-0		M24 0-1	a28 1-0	S09 1-0	D30 3-1	J20 3-1	O21 1-0	M20 0-0	A26 0-0	m01 2-2	S23 2-1	S30 1-1	D02 0-3	M10 3-0	a07 2-1	a03 3-0	F10 0-2	a21 0-1	N04 0-0	a14 1-1	O31 1-1	O07 3-2
4 BRENTFORD	S23 0-1	a28 5-0	O17 1-2		O07 0-2	J20 2-1	S09 0-1	F21 0-1	A26 1-1	M10 0-2	O28 2-0	F10 2-1	D03 4-3	D17 2-1	F25 3-2	a07 0-1	M20 2-2	a16 1-1	J06 4-2	M31 1-1	m02 2-1	N04 2-4	J01 4-0	S30 3-1
5 BRISTOL C	A26 1-0	S09 2-0	N11 1-1	M17 2-0		S23 0-0	J20 1-0	F10 1-0	J30 1-0	a10 4-1	a16 5-1	a24 1-1	D16 2-1	M31 1-1	M27 3-1	O17 2-0	J01 2-1	F24 0-1	D02 0-0	S26 2-1	O14 1-3	M06 1-3	m05 4-0	O28 3-0
6 BRISTOL R	D26 0-0	N04 1-1	J28 1-1	A19 1-0	m02 3-0		M21 2-1	M24 2-1	a07 2-1	a21 1-1	O07 2-0	N01 2-2	M11 0-0	J13 1-1	O21 4-2	S02 3-2	S16 3-0	S30 0-0	a14 2-0	a28 1-0	N25 2-0	D30 2-0	F18 2-0	M03 6-1
7 BURY	O28 0-0	a10 2-0	a24 2-0	J27 0-2	A19 1-1	O14 0-0		m05 2-0	M17 1-0	N25 0-3	M31 0-0	a16 6-0	J01 2-0	S16 3-0	M06 1-0	M03 3-2	J13 1-2	N11 4-0	S26 1-1	F03 0-0	O17 3-2	F17 1-2	D16 0-2	S02 2-2
8 CARDIFF C	a10 0-1	M31 2-2	A19 0-2	S02 2-2	S16 0-3	O17 1-1	N03 3-1		O13 1-1	F17 0-0	a28 3-3	M17 1-5	O28 1-1	M27 1-0	S26 2-3	D16 1-3	N25 3-0	m01 3-2	M06 2-0	M02 0-1	a16 0-2	J13 0-0	a24 3-1	F03 1-1
9 CHESTER C	O17 4-0	D30 2-0	M31 2-0	J12 1-1	J03 0-3	O28 0-0	O07 1-4	M20 1-0		S02 2-1	S30 0-2	N04 2-1	J06 1-0	A19 0-2	a14 0-1	S15 3-3	F03 3-1	M09 1-1	a28 2-0	F17 1-0	J26 1-0	a20 2-2	N24 1-1	D26 0-0
10 CREWE A	J20 0-2	F10 2-0	O14 2-2	S26 2-3	O31 0-1	D15 1-0	F24 2-1	D02 1-1	F13 0-0		S09 2-3	M13 3-0	a24 0-1	N10 2-1	S23 2-1	J01 1-0	M24 1-0	A25 1-1	O21 0-0	M06 1-1	M17 1-1	a06 2-2	a16 3-1	m05 3-2
11 FULHAM	a14 1-2	a21 0-0	J13 2-2	a10 1-0	D26 0-1	M17 1-2	O21 2-2	N11 2-5	M06 1-0	J27 1-1		S26 0-0	m05 1-2	S02 1-0	O31 1-1	F17 5-2	M03 3-1	M24 1-2	O14 1-1	D30 2-1	S16 2-0	A19 1-2	a04 0-0	N25 4-0
12 HUDDERSFIELD T	M31 1-2	a14 2-2	S02 1-1	S16 1-0	D30 2-1	a10 1-1	D26 2-1	O07 2-3	m05 4-1	M03 0-1	M10 0-1		S30 2-0	F17 1-0	N11 2-2	N25 1-2	a03 0-2	M20 0-1	a21 2-1	O28 1-1	A19 1-0	F03 1-0	J13 1-0	O17 2-0
13 LEYTON O	a28 1-2	O14 2-0	M27 0-0	F18 0-1	a21 1-1	S26 0-1	a14 2-3	a07 3-1	O31 0-3	D30 2-1	N05 1-1	M06 1-0		N25 3-1	D26 1-1	A19 0-1	S02 3-1	O21 4-1	M24 1-1	J13 1-0	M03 0-2	M17 0-1	J27 1-1	S16 1-0
14 MANSFIELD T	a03 5-2	S23 0-3	M06 0-1	a21 2-3	O21 1-0	A26 0-1	F10 1-0	S09 1-0	J20 1-0	a28 2-1	F13 3-0	D02 1-2	F24 1-0		D30 1-2	N04 1-3	O31 2-2	a07 1-1	D26 3-1	M17 2-1	O24 4-0	M24 1-0	O14 0-2	a14 1-0
15 NORTHAMPTON T	M20 2-2	O17 4-2	F17 0-2	N25 0-2	S02 2-0	M31 1-2	S30 0-1	M10 1-1	J01 1-0	a30 3-1	a07 2-2	a28 1-0	a16 0-1	a24 1-2		O28 0-0	O07 1-2	D17 2-1	N04 1-2	S16 2-1	J13 1-1	M03 0-4	F20 1-1	M13 1-1
16 NOTTS CO	D30 3-2	A26 0-1	S26 2-1	O31 3-1	M24 0-0	a26 3-1	J06 0-4	a21 2-1	F10 0-0	a14 2-0	D02 2-0	F24 1-0	J20 1-0	m05 4-2	a10 3-2		O21 2-1	S09 0-0	S23 2-0	D26 4-0	M06 2-1	O14 1-0	M17 2-0	N11 1-1
17 PRESTON N.E.	a21 2-2	S26 2-1	O28 1-4	O14 4-2	a14 2-2	F10 0-1	A26 2-3	F24 4-0	S23 5-0	O17 0-0	J06 1-0	S09 3-3	F13 0-3	a10 4-0	M17 0-0	M31 2-4		D02 1-0	J20 0-1	N04 2-1	a28 2-0	D26 2-2	M06 2-0	D30 1-1
18 READING	N04 0-2	M17 1-1	M03 2-0	D26 1-0	N25 1-1	M06 0-1	a28 1-0	a14 0-1	S26 1-1	J13 1-1	O17 3-2	O14 0-0	M31 1-1	O28 1-0	a21 3-2	m03 1-1	F17 6-0		D30 3-2	A19 3-3	F20 1-1	S02 1-0	S16 0-1	a10 2-0
19 ROTHERHAM U	O07 5-1	O28 1-1	S16 1-0	M03 2-1	a03 1-2	J01 3-2	M10 1-3	S30 4-0	N11 5-0	M31 1-3	M20 2-1	D16 0-0	O17 5-2	a16 0-0	m05 2-0	F03 1-2	A19 3-1	a24 1-1		N25 4-2	F17 3-2	J27 0-0	S02 2-2	J13 1-2
20 SHREWSBURY T	S09 2-0	F13 1-1	D16 3-3	O21 1-0	J10 0-1	N11 2-3	S23 3-1	M13 0-0	D02 2-0	S30 0-0	a24 2-0	a07 3-3	A26 4-2	O07 0-1	a03 2-0	a17 2-2	m05 2-0	J20 1-1	F24 1-1		J01 1-1	O31 3-1	M24 2-0	M20 1-3
21 SWANSEA C	F13 1-1	D02 0-0	m05 0-0	D30 2-1	M20 0-5	F24 0-0	M23 0-1	D26 0-1	S09 2-1	O07 3-2	F10 4-2	J21 1-3	a03 0-1	M10 1-0	A26 1-1	S30 0-0	N11 2-1	S23 1-6	O31 1-0	a14 0-1		O20 1-0	a07 2-0	a21 3-0
22 TRANMERE R	F09 5-1	F23 4-2	J06 1-3	m05 2-2	S29 6-0	a23 1-2	D02 2-4	A26 3-0	D15 0-0	O27 1-1	J19 2-1	S22 4-0	O06 3-0	O16 1-1	m02 0-0	M19 2-0	a16 2-1	F12 3-1	S09 2-1	a09 3-1	M30 3-0		N10 2-1	M09 2-0
23 WALSALL	M10 0-1	M27 1-1	a10 2-1	a14 2-1	N04 0-2	D02 1-2	a21 2-2	D30 0-2	F24 1-1	D26 1-1	S23 0-0	A26 2-3	S09 1-3	M20 1-0	A19 1-0	O07 2-2	S30 1-0	F10 1-1	m01 1-1	O17 0-2	O28 0-1	a28 2-1		M31 1-2
24 WIGAN A	D01 1-0	J20 1-1	M16 2-0	M06 2-1	a07 2-3	a04 1-2	F13 0-0	S23 1-1	a16 1-0	N04 1-0	F24 2-1	M24 1-2	F10 0-2	J01 4-0	S09 0-0	a28 1-1	a24 0-1	O31 3-1	A26 0-3	O14 0-0	D16 2-0	S26 1-3	O21 3-0	

DIVISION 4

	ALDERSHOT	BURNLEY	CAMBRIDGE U	CARLISLE U	CHESTERFIELD	COLCHESTER U	DONCASTER R	EXETER C	GILLINGHAM	GRIMSBY T	HALIFAX T	HARTLEPOOL U	HEREFORD U	LINCOLN C	MAIDSTONE U	PETERBOROUGH U	ROCHDALE	SCARBOROUGH	SCUNTHORPE U	SOUTHEND U	STOCKPORT CO	TORQUAY U	WREXHAM	YORK C
1 ALDERSHOT		a06 1-1	m05 0-2	O31 1-0	F10 0-0	O07 4-0	M10 1-1	D26 0-1	J20 1-0	F24 0-0	D02 2-0	N11 6-1	m01 0-2	A26 0-1	a14 0-2	F27 0-1	D30 1-1	a21 1-1	S30 4-2	S09 0-5	S23 2-1	O21 1-2	M27 1-0	M24 2-2
2 BURNLEY	O28 0-0		a14 1-3	D26 2-1	a03 0-0	N04 0-0	M31 0-1	S09 1-0	F10 1-2	D02 1-1	D30 1-0	O14 0-0	S23 3-1	F24 0-0	M17 1-1	O17 1-2	J20 0-1	J09 3-0	a28 0-1	a10 0-0	A26 0-0	M06 1-0	a21 2-3	S26 1-1
3 CAMBRIDGE U	N04 2-2	J01 0-1		S26 1-2	S09 0-1	a29 4-0	O17 1-0	F10 3-2	m01 2-1	J20 2-0	S22 1-0	a10 2-1	A26 0-1	a17 2-1	M06 2-0	D17 3-2	D02 0-3	a02 5-2	O28 5-3	F25 2-1	a23 0-2	O13 5-2	M30 1-1	M16 2-2
4 CARLISLE U	a10 1-3	a16 1-1	a04 3-1		A26 4-3	S30 1-0	M20 1-0	F13 1-0	S23 3-0	S09 1-1	F10 1-1	O28 1-0	J20 2-1	a24 1-2	N04 3-2	D02 0-0	F24 0-1	M31 3-1	O17 0-1	J06 3-0	D17 3-1	a28 2-0	O07 1-0	J01 2-1
5 CHESTERFIELD	S16 2-0	S02 0-1	a25 1-1	J13 3-0		A19 1-1	J01 0-1	M20 2-1	M31 2-0	m05 2-0	O17 4-3	N25 3-1	M10 2-1	O07 0-0	F03 3-1	a16 1-1	S30 2-1	a10 2-2	m01 1-1	O28 1-1	N11 1-1	M03 5-1	F17 3-0	D16 0-0
6 COLCHESTER U	M17 1-0	m05 1-2	N10 1-2	M06 4-0	J20 1-0		a24 2-0	a10 0-1	F23 2-0	F20 1-0	A26 2-2	J01 3-1	S08 1-1	D02 0-1	S26 4-1	O28 0-1	F10 1-2	S23 0-0	M31 1-0	a16 0-2	J05 0-1	D16 0-3	O17 1-3	O13 0-2
7 DONCASTER R	S26 0-1	O21 2-3	M25 2-1	O14 1-1	a14 1-0	D30 2-0		J20 2-1	A26 0-0	J16 0-0	a21 3-4	M06 2-2	F25 0-1	F13 0-1	O31 1-1	S09 0-3	a28 4-0	F10 1-1	N04 1-2	S22 0-1	D02 2-1	M17 2-1	D26 2-2	a07 1-2
8 EXETER C	a16 2-0	m01 2-1	S16 3-2	S02 0-0	O14 2-1	N01 2-1	A19 1-0		D16 3-1	S27 2-1	M07 2-0	J13 3-1	O21 2-0	N04 3-0	F17 2-0	M17 2-0	M24 5-0	a28 3-2	M28 1-0	a25 2-1	a07 1-1	J01 3-0	N25 1-1	M03 3-1
9 GILLINGHAM	A19 0-0	S16 0-0	M03 1-0	F27 2-1	O21 3-0	N24 3-3	J13 3-1	a21 1-1		M24 1-2	M16 3-1	J27 0-0	a14 0-1	a28 1-1	D26 1-2	M06 0-0	O31 1-0	N04 2-0	S02 0-3	S26 5-0	O14 0-3	a07 0-2	D30 1-0	F17 0-0
10 GRIMSBY T	N25 2-1	F17 4-2	A19 0-0	J27 1-0	N04 0-1	S02 4-1	M03 2-1	M10 1-0	O17 2-0		O28 1-1	a24 0-0	S30 0-2	M31 1-0	S16 2-3	a10 1-2	O07 1-2	M20 3-0	a17 2-1	D19 2-0	J01 4-2	J13 0-0	a28 5-1	F03 3-0
11 HALIFAX T	F17 4-1	a24 0-0	F02 0-0	S15 1-1	M24 1-1	J12 1-1	D15 0-2	S30 1-2	O06 0-1	a07 2-2		A19 4-0	O31 1-1	M20 0-1	N25 1-2	J01 2-2	O21 1-0	M10 1-2	M03 0-1	N10 1-2	m05 1-2	S02 3-1	J26 4-2	a16 2-2
12 HARTLEPOOL U	a28 2-0	M20 3-0	O31 1-2	a07 1-0	F24 3-1	a14 0-2	S30 0-6	A26 0-3	S09 1-2	D30 4-2	J20 2-0		D02 1-2	J06 1-1	a21 4-2	S23 2-2	M10 2-1	D26 4-1	O07 3-2	F13 1-1	F10 5-0	M24 1-1	N04 3-0	O21 1-2
13 HEREFORD U	M03 4-1	M28 0-1	J13 0-2	A19 2-2	S27 3-2	M14 2-0	N25 0-1	M31 2-1	J01 1-2	M07 0-1	a11 0-1	F17 4-1		O28 2-2	S02 3-0	a28 1-2	N04 1-3	O18 3-1	D16 1-2	O14 0-3	M17 1-2	a16 0-0	S16 0-0	a25 1-2
14 LINCOLN C	J13 0-1	N25 1-0	D26 4-3	D30 1-3	M17 1-1	F17 2-1	S02 2-1	m05 1-5	N11 1-3	O21 1-1	O14 2-1	M03 4-1	a07 1-0		M25 1-2	S27 1-0	a21 1-2	a14 0-0	A19 1-0	M07 2-0	N01 0-0	a04 2-2	F03 1-0	S16 0-0
15 MAIDSTONE U	J01 5-1	O07 1-2	S30 2-2	m05 5-2	S23 0-1	M10 4-1	a11 1-0	D02 1-0	a16 0-1	F10 2-2	F24 1-2	D16 4-2	F14 2-0	O18 2-0		J20 1-1	a04 2-0	A26 4-1	M21 1-1	M31 3-0	S09 0-1	a25 5-1	O28 2-0	N11 1-0
16 PETERBOROUGH U	S02 1-1	M24 4-1	a21 1-2	F17 3-0	D26 1-1	a07 1-0	J27 2-1	O07 4-3	S30 1-1	N01 1-1	a14 3-0	F07 0-2	N11 1-1	M13 1-0	A19 1-0		M21 0-1	D30 1-2	S16 1-1	m05 1-2	O21 2-0	N25 1-1	M03 3-1	J13 1-1
17 ROCHDALE	a24 2-0	A19 2-1	M27 2-0	N25 1-2	M06 1-0	S16 2-2	N11 1-3	O17 1-0	a10 1-0	M17 0-1	M31 0-2	S26 0-0	m05 5-2	D16 1-0	M03 3-2	O14 1-2		O28 1-0	J13 3-0	J01 0-1	a16 1-1	F03 0-0	S02 0-3	F06 0-1
18 SCARBOROUGH	J06 1-0	M03 4-2	S02 1-1	O21 2-1	N01 2-3	F03 2-2	S16 1-2	N11 1-2	m05 0-1	O14 3-1	S27 2-3	a16 4-1	M24 0-1	J01 2-0	J13 0-1	a25 2-1	a07 2-1		J27 0-0	M17 1-1	D09 2-0	F17 0-0	A19 2-1	N24 1-3
19 SCUNTHORPE U	M06 3-2	N11 3-0	a07 1-1	M24 2-3	D30 0-1	O21 4-0	m05 4-1	S23 5-4	F13 0-0	D26 2-2	J06 1-1	M17 0-1	a21 3-3	J20 1-1	O14 1-0	F10 0-0	A26 0-1	S09 0-1		D02 1-1	F24 5-0	S26 2-0	a14 3-1	O31 1-1
20 SOUTHEND U	J27 5-0	O31 3-2	N24 0-0	M03 2-0	a07 0-2	D26 0-2	F02 2-0	D30 1-2	M09 2-0	a20 0-2	a27 2-0	S01 3-0	M20 2-0	S30 2-0	O21 0-1	N04 0-0	a14 3-2	O07 1-0	F16 0-0		M23 2-0	S15 1-0	J12 2-1	A19 2-0
21 STOCKPORT CO	F03 1-1	J13 3-1	D29 3-1	a20 3-1	a28 3-1	M02 1-1	F16 3-1	O28 2-1	M19 1-0	a14 2-4	N03 0-1	S15 6-0	O07 2-1	a09 1-1	J27 1-2	M30 0-0	D26 2-1	S30 3-2	N25 4-2	O16 1-0		A19 1-1	M09 0-2	S01 2-2
22 TORQUAY U	M31 1-2	S30 0-1	M20 3-0	N11 1-2	M13 1-0	a21 4-1	O07 2-0	a14 0-2	N14 0-2	A26 0-3	M27 1-0	O17 4-3	D26 1-1	S09 0-3	D30 2-1	F24 2-1	S23 1-0	D02 3-2	M10 0-3	F06 3-0	J20 3-0		a10 0-1	m05 1-1
23 WREXHAM	O14 2-2	M13 1-0	O21 2-3	M17 1-0	D02 0-2	M24 3-2	a16 0-0	F24 1-1	a24 2-1	N11 0-1	S09 2-1	m05 1-2	F10 0-0	S23 0-2	a07 4-2	J06 2-1	F13 1-1	J20 0-2	J01 0-0	A26 3-3	S05 0-1	O31 1-1		M06 2-0
24 YORK C	O17 2-2	M10 1-3	O07 4-2	a14 0-1	a21 4-0	J27 3-1	O28 2-1	a02 3-0	D09 1-0	S23 0-1	D26 0-2	M31 1-1	D30 1-2	F10 0-0	a28 0-0	A26 1-0	S09 1-0	F24 1-2	a10 0-1	J20 2-1	F13 0-3	N04 1-1	S30 1-0	

LEAGUE TABLES

DIVISION 1

	P	W	D	L	F	A	W	D	L	F	A	Pts
Liverpool	38	13	5	1	38	15	10	5	4	40	22	79
Aston Villa	38	13	3	3	36	20	8	4	7	21	18	70
Tottenham H	38	12	1	6	35	24	7	5	7	24	23	63
Arsenal	38	14	3	2	38	11	4	5	10	16	27	62
Chelsea	38	8	7	4	31	24	8	5	6	27	26	60
Everton	38	14	3	2	40	16	3	5	11	17	30	59
Southampton	38	10	5	4	40	27	5	5	9	31	36	55
Wimbledon	38	5	8	6	22	23	8	8	3	25	17	55
Nottingham F	38	9	4	6	31	21	6	5	8	24	26	54
Norwich C	38	7	10	2	24	14	6	4	9	20	28	53
QPR	38	9	4	6	27	22	4	7	8	18	22	50
Coventry C	38	11	2	6	24	25	3	5	11	15	34	49
Manchester U	38	8	6	5	26	14	5	3	11	20	33	48
Manchester C	38	9	4	6	26	21	3	8	8	17	31	48
Crystal P	38	8	7	4	27	23	5	2	12	15	43	48
Derby Co	38	9	1	9	29	21	4	6	9	14	19	46
Luton T	38	8	8	3	24	18	2	5	12	19	39	43
Sheffield W	38	8	6	5	21	17	3	4	12	14	34	43
Charlton A	38	4	6	9	18	25	3	3	13	13	32	30
Millwall	38	4	6	9	23	25	1	5	13	16	40	26

DIVISION 2

	P	W	D	L	F	A	W	D	L	F	A	Pts
Leeds U	46	16	6	1	46	18	8	7	8	33	34	85
Sheffield U	46	14	5	4	43	27	10	8	5	35	31	85
Newcastle U	46	17	4	2	51	26	5	10	8	29	29	80
Swindon T	46	12	6	5	49	29	8	8	7	30	30	74
Blackburn R	46	10	9	4	43	30	9	8	6	31	29	74
Sunderland	46	10	8	5	41	32	10	6	7	29	32	74
West Ham U	46	14	5	4	50	22	6	7	10	30	35	72
Oldham A	46	15	7	1	50	23	4	7	12	20	34	71
Ipswich T	46	13	7	3	38	22	6	5	12	29	44	69
Wolves	46	12	5	6	37	20	6	8	9	30	40	67
Port Vale	46	11	9	3	37	20	4	7	12	25	37	61
Portsmouth	46	9	8	6	40	34	6	8	9	22	31	61
Leicester C	46	10	8	5	34	29	5	6	12	33	50	59
Hull C	46	7	8	8	27	31	7	8	8	31	34	58
Watford	46	11	6	6	41	28	3	9	11	17	32	57
Plymouth A	46	9	8	6	30	23	5	5	13	28	40	55
Oxford U	46	8	7	8	35	31	7	2	14	22	35	54
Brighton & HA	46	10	6	7	28	27	5	3	15	28	45	54
Barnsley	46	7	9	7	22	23	6	6	11	27	48	54
WBA	46	6	8	9	35	37	6	7	10	32	34	51
Middlesbrough	46	10	3	10	33	29	3	8	12	19	34	50
Bournemouth	46	8	6	9	30	31	4	6	13	27	45	48
Bradford C	46	9	6	8	26	24	0	8	15	18	44	41
Stoke C	46	4	11	8	20	24	2	8	13	15	39	37

DIVISION 3

	P	W	D	L	F	A	W	D	L	F	A	Pts
Bristol R	46	15	8	0	43	14	11	7	5	28	21	93
Bristol C	46	15	5	3	40	16	12	5	6	36	24	91
Notts Co	46	17	4	2	40	18	8	8	7	33	35	87
Tranmere R	46	15	5	3	54	22	8	6	9	32	27	80
Bury	46	11	7	5	35	19	10	4	9	35	30	74
Bolton W	46	12	7	4	32	19	6	8	9	27	29	69
Birmingham C	46	19	7	6	33	19	8	5	10	27	40	66
Huddersfield T	46	11	5	7	30	23	6	9	8	31	39	65
Rotherham U	46	12	6	5	48	28	5	7	11	23	34	64
Reading	46	10	9	4	33	21	5	10	8	24	32	64
Shrewsbury T	46	10	9	4	38	24	6	6	11	21	30	63
Crewe A	46	10	8	5	32	24	5	9	9	24	29	62
Brentford	46	11	4	8	41	31	7	3	13	25	35	61
Leyton Orient	46	9	6	8	28	24	7	4	12	24	32	58
Mansfield T	46	13	2	8	34	25	3	5	15	16	40	55
Chester C	46	11	7	5	30	23	2	8	13	13	32	54
Swansea C	46	10	6	7	25	27	4	6	13	20	36	54
Wigan A	46	10	6	7	29	22	3	8	12	19	42	53
Preston NE	46	10	7	6	42	30	4	3	16	23	49	52
Fulham	46	8	8	7	33	27	4	7	12	22	39	51
Cardiff C	46	6	9	8	30	35	6	5	12	21	35	50
Northampton T	46	7	7	9	27	31	4	7	12	24	37	47
Blackpool	46	8	6	9	29	33	2	10	11	20	40	46
Walsall	46	6	8	9	23	30	3	6	14	17	42	41

DIVISION 4

	P	W	D	L	F	A	W	D	L	F	A	Pts
Exeter C	46	20	3	0	50	14	8	2	13	33	34	89
Grimsby T	46	14	4	5	41	20	8	9	6	29	27	79
Southend U	46	15	3	5	35	14	7	6	10	26	34	75
Stockport Co	46	13	6	4	45	27	8	5	10	23	35	74
Maidstone U	46	14	4	5	49	21	8	3	12	28	40	73
Cambridge U	46	14	3	6	45	30	7	7	9	31	36	73
Chesterfield	46	12	9	2	41	19	7	5	11	22	31	71
Carlisle U	46	15	4	4	38	20	6	4	13	23	40	71
Peterboro' U	46	10	8	5	35	23	7	9	7	24	23	68
Lincoln C	46	11	6	6	30	27	7	8	8	18	21	68
Scunthorpe U	46	9	9	5	42	25	8	6	9	27	29	66
Rochdale	46	11	4	8	28	23	9	2	12	24	32	66
York C	46	10	5	8	29	24	6	11	6	26	29	64
Gillingham	46	9	8	6	28	21	8	3	12	18	27	62
Torquay U	46	12	2	9	33	29	3	10	10	20	37	57
Burnley	46	6	10	7	19	18	8	4	11	26	37	56
Hereford U	46	7	4	12	31	32	8	6	9	25	30	55
Scarborough	46	10	5	8	35	28	5	5	13	25	45	55
Hartlepool U	46	12	4	7	45	33	3	6	14	21	55	55
Doncaster R	46	7	7	9	29	29	7	2	14	24	31	51
Wrexham	46	8	8	7	28	28	5	4	14	23	39	51
Aldershot	46	8	7	8	28	26	4	7	12	21	43	50
Halifax T	46	5	9	9	31	29	7	4	12	26	36	49
Colchester U	46	9	3	11	26	25	2	7	14	22	50	43

Football League Records

Top scorers: Div 1, L.Chapman (Leeds United) 31 goals; Div 2, E.Sheringham (Millwall) 38 goals; Div 3, B.Angell (Southend United), A.Philliskirk (Bolton Wanderers) 26 goals; Div 4, J.Allon (Hartlepool United), S.Norris (Halifax Town) 35 goals.

Play-offs: Div 1, Brighton & Hove Albion v Millwall 4-1, 2-1; Middlesbrough v Notts County 1-1, 0-1; Brighton & Hove Albion v Notts County (Wembley) 1-3; Div 2, Brentford v Tranmere Rovers 2-2, 0-1; Bury v Bolton Wanderers 1-1, 0-1; Bolton Wanderers v Tranmere Rovers (Wembley) 0-1; Div 3, Scunthorpe United v Blackpool 1-1, 1-2; Torquay United v Burnley 2-0, 0-1; Blackpool v Torquay United (Wembley) 2-2 (4-5 penalties).

Oldham Athletic, West Ham United, Sheffield Wednesday and Notts County promoted to Div 1; Sunderland and Derby County relegated to Div 2; Cambridge United, Southend United, Grimsby Town and Tranmere Rovers promoted to Div 2; West Bromwich Albion and Hull City relegated to Div 3; Darlington, Stockport County, Hartlepool United, Peterborough United and Torquay United promoted to Div 3; Crewe Alexandra, Rotherham United and Mansfield Town relegated to Div 4.

Arsenal's Swedish international midfielder Anders Limpar, scored 11 goals in 34 appearances for the Gunners in their latest title-winning campaign.

DIVISION 1

	ARSENAL	ASTON VILLA	CHELSEA	COVENTRY C	CRYSTAL P	DERBY CO	EVERTON	LEEDS U	LIVERPOOL	LUTON T	MANCHESTER C	MANCHESTER U	NORWICH C	NOTTINGHAM F	Q.P.R.	SHEFFIELD U	SOUTHAMPTON	SUNDERLAND	TOTTENHAM H	WIMBLEDON
1 ARSENAL		a03 5-0	S15 4-1	m11 6-1	F23 4-0	D26 3-0	J19 1-0	M17 2-0	D02 3-0	A29 2-1	a17 2-2	m06 3-1	O06 2-0	M20 1-1	a23 2-0	D29 4-1	N17 4-0	O27 1-0	S01 0-0	D15 2-2
2 ASTON VILLA	D23 0-0		m11 2-2	S08 2-1	J01 2-0	F02 3-2	M30 2-2	O27 0-0	J12 0-0	M09 1-2	a23 1-5	a06 1-1	m08 2-1	N10 1-1	S22 2-2	D01 2-1	A25 1-1	O06 3-0	M16 3-2	a20 1-2
3 CHELSEA	F02 2-1	N03 1-0		D22 2-1	D08 2-1	A25 2-1	J01 1-2	M30 1-2	m04 4-2	a06 3-3	S22 1-1	M09 3-2	N10 1-1	O20 0-0	J12 2-0	S29 2-2	M23 0-2	S08 3-2	D01 3-2	F16 0-0
4 COVENTRY C	N03 0-2	J19 2-1	a01 1-0		M02 3-1	a13 3-0	A29 3-1	N24 1-1	N17 0-1	M13 2-1	M23 3-1	D15 2-2	D29 2-0	S01 2-2	S29 3-1	m04 0-0	O20 1-2	F23 0-0	D26 2-0	S15 0-0
5 CRYSTAL P	N10 0-0	a13 0-0	A28 2-1	D01 2-1		M16 2-1	a20 0-0	O06 1-1	D30 1-0	D16 1-0	a01 1-3	m11 3-0	J19 1-3	S15 2-2	F16 0-0	S01 1-0	M09 2-1	D26 2-1	a17 1-0	O27 4-3
6 DERBY CO	M30 0-2	S15 0-2	D15 4-6	J01 1-1	S29 0-2		m08 2-3	a23 0-1	M23 1-7	N03 2-1	O20 1-1	N10 0-0	F23 0-0	N24 2-1	D23 1-1	A29 1-1	m04 6-2	M02 3-3	J20 0-1	S01 1-1
7 EVERTON	S08 1-1	D26 1-0	a13 2-2	D08 1-0	O20 0-0	D29 2-0		A25 2-3	S22 2-3	m04 1-0	J13 2-0	D01 0-1	a01 1-0	M23 0-0	N03 3-0	F23 1-2	S29 3-0	F02 2-0	N18 1-1	a10 1-2
8 LEEDS U	S29 2-2	m04 5-2	D26 4-1	M09 2-0	M23 1-2	N17 3-0	D16 2-0		a13 4-5	J19 2-1	a10 1-2	A28 0-0	S01 3-0	N03 3-1	O20 2-3	m08 2-1	D01 2-1	a02 5-0	S15 0-2	D29 3-0
9 LIVERPOOL	M03 0-1	S01 2-1	O27 2-0	a09 1-1	a23 3-0	O06 2-0	F09 3-1	J01 3-0		N10 4-0	N24 2-2	S16 4-0	a20 3-0	A28 2-0	M30 1-3	D15 2-0	D22 3-2	M16 2-1	m11 2-0	J19 1-1
10 LUTON T	D08 1-1	N24 2-0	D29 2-0	S22 1-0	A25 1-1	m11 2-0	O27 1-1	S08 1-0	F23 3-1		N17 2-2	S04 0-1	M16 0-1	M02 1-0	F02 1-2	D26 0-1	J12 3-4	a20 1-2	a01 0-0	a13 0-1
11 MANCHESTER C	J01 0-1	S05 2-1	F09 2-1	O06 2-0	D22 0-2	a20 2-1	S01 1-0	N11 2-3	M09 0-3	M05 3-0		O27 3-3	S15 2-1	a06 3-1	D01 2-1	J19 2-0	M30 3-3	m11 3-2	D15 2-1	M16 1-1
12 MANCHESTER U	O20 0-1	D29 1-1	N25 2-3	A25 2-0	N03 2-0	a16 3-1	M02 0-2	D08 1-1	F03 1-1	M23 4-1	m04 1-0		D26 3-0	S29 0-1	S08 3-1	N17 2-0	S22 3-2	J12 3-0	m20 1-1	a02 2-1
13 NORWICH C	M23 0-0	N17 2-0	a17 1-3	a06 2-2	S08 0-3	S22 2-1	D22 1-0	J12 2-0	O20 1-1	S29 1-3	F02 1-2	M30 0-3		J02 2-6	m04 1-0	N03 3-0	D08 3-1	A25 3-2	a10 2-1	D01 0-4
14 NOTTINGHAM F	S22 0-2	F23 2-2	a20 7-0	J12 3-0	F02 0-1	a10 1-0	O07 3-1	m11 4-3	m06 2-1	D01 2-2	D29 1-3	M16 1-1	a24 5-0		A25 1-1	a01 2-0	S08 3-1	N17 2-0	O27 1-2	D26 2-1
15 Q.P.R.	N24 1-3	a10 2-1	S01 1-0	M16 1-0	N17 1-2	a01 1-1	m11 1-1	a17 2-0	D26 1-1	S15 6-1	M02 1-0	J19 1-1	O27 1-3	D15 1-2		a13 1-2	F23 2-1	D29 3-2	O06 0-0	A29 0-1
16 SHEFFIELD U	a06 0-2	M02 2-1	M16 1-0	O27 0-1	J12 0-1	J26 1-0	N10 0-0	S23 0-2	A25 1-3	M30 2-1	S08 1-1	F26 2-1	m11 2-1	D22 3-2	J01 1-0		F02 4-1	N24 0-2	a20 2-2	O06 1-2
17 SOUTHAMPTON	a09 1-1	D15 1-1	O06 3-3	a20 2-1	N24 2-3	O27 0-1	M16 3-4	M02 2-0	a01 1-0	S01 1-2	D26 2-1	M13 1-1	A28 1-0	J19 1-1	N10 3-1	S15 2-0		a13 3-1	D29 3-0	m11 1-1
18 SUNDERLAND	m04 0-0	M23 1-3	J19 1-0	N10 0-0	M30 2-1	D01 1-2	S15 2-2	D23 0-1	S29 0-1	O20 2-0	N03 1-1	S01 2-1	D15 1-2	F16 1-0	a06 0-1	M09 0-1	J01 1-0		A28 0-0	a23 0-0
19 TOTTENHAM H	J12 0-0	S29 2-1	M02 1-1	M30 2-2	S22 1-1	S08 3-0	a24 3-3	F02 0-0	N04 1-3	D22 2-1	A25 3-1	J01 1-2	N24 2-1	m04 1-1	M23 0-0	O20 4-0	a06 2-0	D08 3-3		N10 4-2
20 WIMBLEDON	A25 0-3	O20 0-0	N17 2-1	F02 1-0	m04 0-3	J12 3-1	N24 2-1	a06 0-1	S08 1-2	J01 2-0	S29 1-1	D22 1-3	M02 0-0	M30 3-1	D08 3-0	M23 1-1	N03 1-1	S22 2-2	F23 5-1	

Andy Ritchie, whose goalscoring helped Oldham Athletic into Division One after an absence of 68 years.

DIVISION 2

	BARNSLEY	BLACKBURN R	BRIGHTON & HA	BRISTOL C	BRISTOL R	CHARLTON A	HULL C	IPSWICH T	LEICESTER C	MIDDLESBROUGH	MILLWALL	NEWCASTLE U	NOTTS CO	OLDHAM A	OXFORD U	PLYMOUTH A	PORTSMOUTH	PORT VALE	SHEFFIELD W	SWINDON T	WATFORD	W.B.A.	WEST HAM U	WOLVERHAMPTON W
1 BARNSLEY		a23 0-1	A25 2-1	J01 2-0	F26 1-0	M16 1-1	a06 3-1	O02 5-1	N10 1-1	m11 1-0	J12 1-2	m07 1-1	a09 1-0	S08 0-1	O06 3-0	M30 1-0	M19 4-0	S22 1-1	O23 1-1	O27 5-1	M02 2-1	a20 1-1	D22 1-0	N24 1-1
2 BLACKBURN R	S15 1-2		S29 1-2	D15 0-1	M12 2-2	a13 2-2	A28 2-1	J19 0-1	S18 4-1	a01 1-0	N03 1-0	S01 0-1	D26 0-1	M23 2-0	D29 1-3	O20 0-0	F09 1-1	N23 1-1	N10 1-0	M02 2-1	O13 0-2	F16 0-3	a27 3-1	m04 1-1
3 BRIGHTON & HA	D15 1-0	M16 1-0		a23 0-1	D26 0-1	S15 3-2	O24 3-1	m11 2-1	F20 3-0	O27 2-4	N24 0-0	J16 4-2	a13 0-0	M02 1-2	a20 0-3	N10 3-2	S19 3-2	a03 1-2	O03 0-4	O06 3-3	J19 3-0	M20 2-0	a10 1-0	S01 1-1
4 BRISTOL C	a13 1-0	A25 4-2	S22 3-1		M05 1-0	D01 0-1	N17 4-1	M09 4-2	M12 1-0	D29 3-0	a27 1-4	S29 1-0	a01 3-2	O20 1-2	F23 3-1	S08 1-1	D26 4-1	m04 1-1	D08 1-1	J12 0-4	N03 3-2	F02 2-0	O13 1-1	M23 1-1
5 BRISTOL R	N07 2-1	O03 1-2	M30 1-3	J26 3-2		S01 2-1	S15 1-1	a10 1-0	D15 0-0	a20 2-0	M02 1-0	D22 1-1	M16 1-1	N24 2-0	O24 1-0	a06 0-0	O27 1-2	N10 2-0	O06 0-1	M20 2-1	F16 3-1	m11 1-1	J01 0-1	J19 1-1
6 CHARLTON A	S29 2-1	J01 0-0	F02 1-2	M02 2-1	J12 2-2		D22 2-1	a06 1-1	O13 1-2	F23 0-1	S22 0-0	a27 1-0	J22 3-1	a16 1-1	N17 3-3	N03 0-1	N24 2-1	M23 0-1	S08 0-1	A25 1-2	O20 1-2	M30 2-0	m04 1-1	M12 1-0
7 HULL C	D29 1-2	D08 3-1	a27 0-1	F16 1-2	F02 2-0	a01 2-2		N10 3-3	N23 5-2	M02 0-0	a16 1-1	N03 2-1	A25 1-2	O13 2-2	D26 3-3	m04 2-0	a13 0-2	S29 3-2	J12 0-1	S08 1-1	M12 1-1	S22 1-1	M23 0-0	O20 1-2
8 IPSWICH T	a25 2-0	S08 2-1	N03 1-3	N24 1-1	S22 2-1	D29 4-4	F23 2-0		m04 3-2	D26 0-1	F02 0-3	O20 2-1	N17 0-0	a27 1-2	a13 1-1	M22 3-1	a02 2-2	O13 3-0	A25 0-2	D08 1-1	S29 1-1	J12 1-0	a17 0-1	M02 0-0
9 LEICESTER C	F23 2-1	J26 1-3	a06 3-0	O03 3-0	A25 3-2	M20 1-2	M09 0-1	O27 1-2		M16 4-3	M30 1-2	D01 5-4	O06 2-1	a10 0-0	m11 1-0	F02 3-1	a20 2-1	J12 1-1	S22 2-4	O24 2-2	D23 0-0	J01 2-1	S08 1-2	N17 1-0
10 MIDDLESBROUGH	N03 1-0	D22 0-1	m04 2-0	a06 2-1	O20 1-2	N10 1-2	D01 3-0	M30 1-1	S29 6-0		O13 2-1	M12 3-0	S08 1-0	S22 0-1	M09 0-0	J12 0-0	F26 1-2	a09 4-0	J01 0-2	F02 2-0	M23 1-2	F19 3-2	A25 0-0	a27 2-0
11 MILLWALL	S01 4-1	m11 2-1	M09 3-0	O24 1-2	D01 1-1	a10 3-1	S19 3-3	S15 1-1	D26 2-1	M20 2-2		J19 0-1	a20 1-2	D29 0-0	N07 1-2	F16 4-1	O03 2-0	a13 1-2	O27 4-2	M16 1-0	D15 0-2	O06 4-1	N10 1-1	a03 2-1
12 NEWCASTLE U	N17 0-0	J12 1-0	F27 0-0	M16 0-0	a01 0-2	O24 1-3	m11 1-2	a20 2-2	M02 2-1	O03 0-0	S08 1-2		D29 0-2	a13 3-2	a10 2-2	A25 2-0	O06 2-1	F02 2-0	a17 1-0	D26 1-1	N24 1-0	O27 1-1	S22 1-1	F23 0-0
13 NOTTS CO	S18 2-3	M30 4-1	J01 2-1	D22 3-2	S29 3-2	O30 2-2	D15 2-1	m07 3-1	M23 0-2	J19 3-2	O20 0-1	a06 3-0		m04 2-0	S01 3-1	a27 4-0	S15 2-1	M12 1-1	M02 0-2	N24 0-0	a16 1-0	N10 4-3	N03 0-1	O13 1-1
14 OLDHAM A	J19 2-0	O06 1-1	D01 6-1	a20 2-1	M09 2-0	S18 1-1	M20 1-2	O23 2-0	A28 2-0	m07 2-0	a06 1-1	J01 1-1	O27 2-1		S15 3-0	D21 5-3	S01 3-1	F16 2-0	m11 3-2	O02 3-2	N10 4-1	M16 2-1	M29 1-1	D15 4-1
15 OXFORD U	M23 2-0	a06 0-0	O20 3-0	N10 3-1	a27 3-1	F16 1-1	M30 1-0	J01 2-1	N03 2-2	N24 2-5	F27 0-0	O13 0-0	J12 3-3	F02 5-1		a17 0-0	M02 1-0	A25 5-2	D22 2-2	S22 2-4	m04 0-1	S08 1-3	M13 2-1	S29 1-1
16 PLYMOUTH A	D26 1-1	a20 4-1	F23 2-0	J19 1-0	D29 2-2	m11 2-0	O27 4-1	O06 0-0	S15 2-0	S01 1-1	N17 3-2	D16 0-1	O23 0-0	a01 1-2	S18 2-2		M16 1-1	M02 2-0	M19 1-1	a13 3-3	A28 1-1	O02 2-0	N24 0-1	a09 1-0
17 PORTSMOUTH	O13 0-0	S22 3-2	a16 1-0	M30 4-1	m04 3-1	M09 0-1	J01 5-1	D21 1-1	O20 3-1	N17 0-3	M12 0-0	M23 0-1	F02 2-1	J12 1-4	D01 1-1	S29 3-1		S08 2-4	a06 2-0	F23 2-1	a27 0-1	A25 1-1	D08 0-1	N03 0-0
18 PORT VALE	a15 0-1	M09 3-0	D22 0-1	O27 3-2	F23 3-2	O06 1-1	M16 0-0	M18 1-2	S01 2-0	S17 3-1	J01 0-2	S15 0-1	O01 0-1	N17 1-0	D15 1-0	D01 5-1	J19 3-2		m06 1-1	m11 3-1	M30 0-0	O22 1-2	a06 0-1	A28 1-2
19 SHEFFIELD W	a27 3-1	a10 3-1	M13 1-1	m08 3-1	M23 2-1	J19 0-0	S01 5-1	D15 2-2	a24 0-0	a13 2-0	m04 2-1	S18 2-2	D01 2-2	N03 2-2	a01 0-2	O13 3-0	D29 2-1	O20 1-1		N17 2-1	S15 2-0	M09 1-0	S29 1-1	D26 2-2
20 SWINDON T	m04 1-2	D01 1-1	M23 1-3	S02 0-1	O13 0-2	D15 1-1	J19 3-1	A28 1-0	a27 5-2	S15 1-3	S30 0-0	M30 3-2	a23 1-2	M12 2-2	M05 0-0	J01 1-1	N10 3-0	N03 1-2	F19 2-1		a06 1-2	D22 2-1	O20 0-1	S18 1-0
21 WATFORD	D01 0-0	M19 0-3	S08 0-1	m11 2-3	N17 1-1	a20 2-1	O02 0-1	M16 1-1	a01 1-0	O06 0-3	A25 1-2	M09 1-2	S22 1-3	F23 1-1	O27 1-1	D08 2-0	O23 0-1	D26 2-1	F02 2-2	D29 2-2		a23 1-1	J12 0-1	a13 3-1
22 W.B.A.	O20 1-1	N17 2-0	O13 1-1	S15 2-1	N03 3-1	D26 1-0	a10 1-1	S01 1-2	a13 2-1	N06 0-1	M23 0-1	m04 1-1	F23 2-2	S29 0-0	J19 2-0	M13 1-2	D15 0-0	a27 1-1	N24 1-2	a01 2-1	D05 1-1		M02 0-0	D29 1-1
23 WEST HAM U	a01 3-2	O24 1-0	N17 2-1	M20 1-0	m08 1-0	O27 2-1	O06 7-1	S19 3-1	J19 1-0	D15 0-0	F24 3-1	a24 1-1	m11 1-2	D26 2-0	O03 2-0	M05 2-2	A29 1-1	D29 0-0	M16 1-3	a20 2-0	S01 1-0	D01 3-1		S15 1-1
24 WOLVERHAMPTON W	M09 0-5	O27 2-3	J12 2-3	O06 4-0	S08 1-1	O02 3-0	a20 0-0	D01 2-2	M05 2-1	O23 1-0	D22 4-1	N10 2-1	M19 0-2	A25 2-3	M16 3-3	S22 3-1	m11 3-1	F26 3-1	M30 3-2	a16 1-2	J01 0-0	a06 2-2	F02 2-1	

Season 1990-91

DIVISION 3

	BIRMINGHAM C	BOLTON W	BOURNEMOUTH	BRADFORD C	BRENTFORD	BURY	CAMBRIDGE U	CHESTER C	CREWE A	EXETER C	FULHAM	GRIMSBY T	HUDDERSFIELD T	LEYTON O	MANSFIELD T	PRESTON N.E.	READING	ROTHERHAM U	SHREWSBURY T	SOUTHEND U	STOKE C	SWANSEA C	TRANMERE R	WIGAN A
1 BIRMINGHAM C		D29 1-3	N24 0-0	J05 1-1	D26 0-2	S15 1-0	J19 0-3	F23 1-0	a27 0-2	S18 1-1	M12 2-0	O20 0-0	N03 1-2	S01 3-1	a13 0-0	S29 1-1	M23 1-1	D15 2-1	m04 0-1	O13 1-1	a16 2-1	M02 2-0	a02 1-0	F05 0-0
2 BOLTON W	a07 3-1		J01 4-1	S01 0-1	F05 1-0	M19 1-3	D22 2-2	m11 1-0	S15 3-2	F13 1-0	M09 3-0	F16 0-0	F09 1-1	a20 1-0	O02 1-1	S18 1-2	N10 3-1	O23 0-0	J19 1-0	M30 1-0	O06 0-1	O27 1-0	D01 2-1	M16 2-1
3 BOURNEMOUTH	F16 1-2	a13 1-0		S18 3-1	J19 2-0	S01 1-1	a16 0-1	M02 1-0	O20 1-1	F05 2-1	S29 3-0	a02 2-1	a27 3-1	D29 2-2	D26 0-0	m02 0-0	M12 2-0	N10 4-2	N03 3-2	M23 3-1	S15 1-1	D14 1-0	O30 1-0	M05 0-3
4 BRADFORD C	F13 2-0	J12 1-1	F02 3-0		O06 0-1	J01 3-1	D15 0-1	O03 2-1	M26 2-0	M20 3-0	M30 0-0	J26 0-2	M03 2-2	M16 4-0	a20 1-0	N10 2-1	S08 2-1	m11 1-0	D22 2-4	a06 2-1	O24 1-2	S22 0-1	A25 1-2	O27 2-1
5 BRENTFORD	M30 2-2	S22 4-2	A25 0-0	M23 6-1		N10 2-2	O14 0-3	S08 0-1	a06 1-0	F16 1-0	a16 1-2	S29 1-0	O20 1-0	D02 1-0	J12 0-0	M12 2-0	a27 1-0	F02 1-2	J01 3-0	N04 0-1	M09 0-4	J26 2-0	m04 0-2	D23 1-0
6 BURY	J26 0-1	O13 2-2	J12 2-4	a13 0-0	F23 1-1		M23 3-1	A25 2-1	S29 1-3	D15 3-1	a27 1-1	a09 3-2	a01 2-1	F19 1-0	S22 1-0	D29 3-1	O20 2-1	S08 3-1	M12 2-1	m04 0-1	N24 1-1	F02 1-0	N03 3-0	M02 2-2
7 CAMBRIDGE U	A25 0-1	a02 2-1	a24 4-0	m07 2-1	M19 0-0	O06 2-2		S21 1-1	N30 3-4	M16 1-0	J12 1-0	D29 1-0	F23 0-0	O02 1-0	F01 2-1	a13 1-1	a09 3-0	O27 4-1	N24 3-1	S09 1-4	a20 3-0	m11 2-0	D26 3-1	O23 2-3
8 CHESTER C	N10 0-1	N03 0-2	D01 0-0	M12 4-2	a30 1-2	J19 1-0	M25 0-2		m04 3-1	S01 1-2	a06 1-0	O13 1-2	S29 1-2	S15 2-0	M09 1-0	a27 1-1	M05 1-0	M30 1-2	O20 3-2	D22 1-0	S18 1-1	a23 2-1	M23 0-2	F26 1-2
9 CREWE A	O23 1-1	a16 1-3	a20 0-2	N24 0-0	D29 3-3	M16 2-2	M01 3-1	O27 1-3		a13 1-1	A25 1-1	S08 1-2	D15 1-1	a01 3-3	m11 3-0	D26 2-2	F01 1-0	a30 3-1	F22 1-2	J12 0-2	O02 1-2	M19 3-0	S21 2-3	O06 1-0
10 EXETER C	F02 0-2	M26 2-1	S22 2-0	O13 2-2	N24 1-1	M09 2-0	S29 0-1	J12 1-1	J01 3-0		m04 0-1	N03 0-0	M13 2-2	F23 2-0	J26 2-0	M23 4-0	A25 1-3	D22 2-0	a30 3-0	a27 1-2	D01 2-0	S08 2-0	O20 0-0	M30 1-0
11 FULHAM	O02 2-2	D15 0-1	M16 1-1	D26 0-0	a23 0-1	O23 2-0	S01 0-2	D29 4-1	J19 2-1	O27 3-2		a13 0-0	S16 0-0	m11 1-1	a01 1-0	F05 1-0	M02 1-1	O06 2-0	a09 4-0	F23 0-3	M19 0-1	a20 1-1	N24 1-2	S18 1-2
12 GRIMSBY T	a20 0-0	N24 0-1	D22 5-0	S15 1-1	M16 2-0	J05 0-1	a06 1-0	M20 2-0	a23 0-1	m11 2-1	J01 3-0		S18 4-0	O23 2-2	D01 2-0	J19 4-1	M30 3-0	O02 2-1	F05 1-0	M09 1-0	O27 2-0	O06 1-0	F23 0-1	S01 4-3
13 HUDDERSFIELD T	m11 0-1	S08 4-0	O23 1-3	D02 1-2	a20 1-2	D22 2-1	N10 3-1	M16 1-1	M09 3-1	O02 1-0	J26 1-0	F02 1-1		O06 1-0	O27 2-2	F16 1-0	S22 0-2	M19 4-0	M30 2-1	A25 1-2	a06 3-0	J12 1-2	F26 2-1	J01 1-0
14 LEYTON O	J12 1-1	O20 0-1	a06 2-0	S29 2-1	M03 1-2	M30 1-0	M12 0-3	J26 1-0	D22 3-2	N10 1-0	N04 1-0	a27 0-2	M23 1-0		S08 2-1	D15 1-0	m04 4-0	S22 3-0	O13 3-2	a09 0-1	J01 0-2	A25 3-0	F02 4-0	a23 1-1
15 MANSFIELD T	J01 1-2	M12 4-0	M30 1-1	O20 0-1	S01 0-2	F05 0-1	S18 2-2	D15 1-0	N03 1-3	S15 0-2	D22 1-1	M02 1-1	m04 0-0	a16 3-3		O13 0-1	a06 2-0	a23 1-2	M23 2-1	S29 0-1	M05 0-0	N10 2-0	a27 0-2	J19 1-1
16 PRESTON N.E.	M16 2-0	F02 1-2	O27 0-0	F23 0-3	O02 1-1	a06 1-1	J01 0-2	O23 0-0	M30 5-1	O06 1-0	S22 1-0	A25 1-3	N24 1-1	M09 2-1	M19 3-1		J12 1-2	a20 1-2	D01 4-3	J26 2-1	D22 2-0	M26 2-0	S08 0-4	m11 2-1
17 READING	O06 2-2	F23 0-1	O02 2-1	a30 1-2	O23 1-2	a20 1-0	S15 2-2	a13 2-2	S18 2-1	J19 1-0	D01 1-0	D26 2-0	M26 1-2	O27 1-2	D29 2-1	S01 3-3		M16 2-0	a23 1-2	N24 2-4	m11 1-0	a01 0-0	M09 1-0	J26 3-1
18 ROTHERHAM U	M09 1-1	a27 2-2	F23 1-1	N03 0-2	S18 2-2	M05 0-3	m04 3-2	D26 2-1	a09 1-1	a01 2-4	M23 3-1	M12 1-4	O13 1-3	F05 0-0	N24 1-1	O20 1-0	S29 0-2		S01 2-2	D01 0-1	J19 0-0	a13 2-3	D29 1-1	S15 5-1
19 SHREWSBURY T	O27 4-1	A25 0-1	m11 3-1	a02 1-0	a13 1-1	O02 1-1	a18 1-2	a20 1-0	N09 1-0	D29 2-2	S08 2-2	S22 1-2	F19 0-0	M19 3-0	O06 0-3	M02 0-1	m07 5-1	J12 0-0		F02 0-1	M16 2-0	O23 1-2	M26 0-1	D15 0-0
20 SOUTHEND U	M18 2-1	D26 1-1	O05 2-1	D28 1-1	m11 0-1	O27 2-1	a30 0-0	a02 1-1	S01 3-2	O23 2-1	N10 1-1	D15 2-0	J19 0-1	m07 1-1	M15 2-1	S14 3-2	F19 1-2	M01 2-1	S18 2-1		F05 1-0	O02 4-1	a12 1-0	a19 0-2
21 STOKE C	S08 0-1	M23 2-2	F27 1-3	a27 2-1	D16 2-2	F16 2-2	O20 1-1	F02 2-3	M13 1-0	M02 2-1	O13 2-1	m04 0-0	D29 2-0	a13 1-2	M26 3-1	a01 0-1	N03 0-1	A25 3-1	S29 1-3	S22 4-0		D26 2-2	J12 1-1	N10 2-0
22 SWANSEA C	D01 2-0	m04 1-2	M09 1-2	m09 0-2	S15 2-2	S18 1-2	N03 0-0	N24 1-0	O13 3-1	F26 0-3	O20 2-2	M23 0-0	S01 1-0	a30 0-0	F23 1-2	a16 3-1	D22 3-1	J01 5-0	a27 0-1	M12 1-4	M30 2-1		S28 1-1	a06 1-6
23 TRANMERE R	D21 1-0	M01 1-1	M18 1-0	J18 2-1	O26 2-1	m11 1-2	M29 2-0	O06 1-2	F04 2-0	a20 1-0	F16 1-1	N10 1-2	J05 2-0	S17 3-0	O22 6-2	m07 2-1	D14 0-0	a05 1-2	S14 1-1	J01 3-1	A31 1-2	M15 2-1		O01 1-1
24 WIGAN A	S22 1-1	S28 2-1	S08 2-0	m04 3-0	a01 1-0	D01 1-2	a27 0-1	a16 2-0	M23 1-0	D26 4-1	F02 2-0	J12 2-0	a13 1-1	N24 1-2	A25 0-2	N03 2-1	O13 1-0	M26 2-0	M09 2-2	O20 4-1	F23 4-0	D29 2-4	M12 0-1	

DIVISION 4

	ALDERSHOT	BLACKPOOL	BURNLEY	CARDIFF C	CARLISLE U	CHESTERFIELD	DARLINGTON	DONCASTER R	GILLINGHAM	HALIFAX T	HARTLEPOOL U	HEREFORD U	LINCOLN C	MAIDSTONE U	NORTHAMPTON T	PETERBOROUGH U	ROCHDALE	SCARBOROUGH	SCUNTHORPE U	STOCKPORT CO	TORQUAY U	WALSALL	WREXHAM	YORK C
1 ALDERSHOT		F23 1-4	a16 1-2	S18 0-0	a13 3-0	a23 1-0	F19 0-2	M02 1-1	a27 1-0	N02 2-2	M12 1-5	D15 1-0	M23 0-3	N24 4-3	S14 3-3	D29 5-0	J19 2-2	S29 2-2	S01 3-2	O19 2-2	O12 2-3	m04 0-4	M05 3-2	a01 0-1
2 BLACKPOOL	N10 4-2		S18 1-2	a17 3-0	a02 6-0	F05 3-0	O13 1-2	F16 2-0	O20 2-0	a30 2-0	S29 2-0	M02 3-0	D29 5-0	D15 2-2	m07 2-1	D26 1-1	S01 0-0	M12 3-1	J19 3-1	a27 3-2	M23 1-0	N03 1-2	S15 4-1	a13 1-0
3 BURNLEY	S22 3-0	a23 2-0		D01 2-0	M16 2-1	M30 0-1	J12 3-1	a30 1-0	M09 2-2	N24 2-1	D22 4-0	M19 2-1	A25 2-2	O23 2-1	O02 3-0	a20 4-1	O27 1-0	S08 2-1	J01 1-1	J26 3-2	a06 1-1	F23 2-0	m11 2-0	O06 0-0
4 CARDIFF C	F01 1-3	m02 1-1	M01 3-0		D26 3-1	N10 2-1	a13 0-1	O23 0-2	F15 2-0	D29 1-0	J12 1-0	a20 0-2	J26 0-1	m11 0-0	a01 1-0	O27 1-1	O02 0-1	A25 0-0	M16 1-0	S22 3-3	S08 3-3	D15 0-2	O05 1-0	M19 2-1
5 CARLISLE U	J01 1-2	D23 1-0	S28 1-1	M30 3-2		O20 1-0	F26 0-2	A25 2-3	M12 0-4	O13 0-3	S22 1-0	J26 0-1	N03 0-0	S08 1-0	D15 4-1	J12 3-2	F16 1-1	a27 4-1	a06 0-3	F02 1-0	m04 3-1	M23 0-3	M02 2-0	N10 1-0
6 CHESTERFIELD	a30 1-0	S22 2-2	M05 2-1	F23 0-0	a20 4-1		a01 2-2	O27 2-1	D01 1-1	M09 2-1	A25 2-3	S08 1-0	F02 1-1	a13 1-2	O06 0-0	m11 2-2	M19 1-1	J12 0-1	O23 1-0	D29 1-1	J26 1-1	N25 2-2	M16 2-1	O02 2-2
7 DARLINGTON	M30 3-1	M19 1-1	S01 3-1	J01 4-1	J05 3-1	D22 1-0		M16 1-1	J29 1-1	S15 3-0	N10 0-1	O06 3-1	a09 1-1	a20 1-1	O23 1-1	O02 0-1	m11 2-0	a06 2-1	O27 0-0	M02 1-0	D15 3-0	M05 1-0	F05 1-0	S18 0-0
8 DONCASTER R	D01 3-0	N24 1-0	F26 2-1	a27 1-1	J19 4-0	m04 0-1	S29 0-1		N03 1-1	a23 1-2	O13 2-2	D29 3-1	O20 1-0	D26 3-0	a13 2-1	F22 0-2	J25 1-0	M24 0-2	M08 2-3	a01 1-0	m07 1-1	S18 2-0	S01 3-1	F05 2-2
9 GILLINGHAM	O23 1-1	a20 2-2	D15 3-2	N24 4-0	O02 2-1	M02 0-1	A25 1-0	m11 2-0		F22 1-0	S08 3-0	F02 2-1	a01 2-2	S22 0-2	D29 0-0	F26 2-3	O06 2-2	J25 1-1	M19 1-1	a13 1-3	J11 2-2	D26 1-0	O27 2-3	M16 0-0
10 HALIFAX T	m11 3-0	O27 5-3	F16 1-2	a06 1-2	M19 1-1	D15 2-1	J26 0-0	S08 0-1	N09 1-2		J01 1-2	O23 0-4	J12 1-1	a16 3-2	M15 2-1	F01 1-1	D21 2-0	M30 1-2	O06 0-0	A25 0-0	S21 0-1	M02 5-2	M26 2-0	a19 2-1
11 HARTLEPOOL U	O02 1-0	M16 1-2	a01 0-0	S01 0-2	F05 4-1	J19 2-0	F23 0-0	a16 1-1	a30 1-0	a13 2-1		O27 2-1	D15 2-0	O06 1-0	m11 3-1	O23 2-0	S18 2-2	N24 2-0	a09 2-0	J29 3-1	M02 0-0	M26 2-1	a20 2-1	O16 0-1
12 HEREFORD U	M09 1-0	D01 1-1	O13 3-0	O20 1-1	S15 4-2	a17 2-3	M23 1-1	a06 1-1	S19 1-1	a27 1-0	m04 1-3		M13 0-1	F23 4-0	A25 1-2	N24 0-0	J30 2-0	N03 3-3	D22 2-0	S29 0-0	J01 0-0	F06 0-0	M30 1-0	S01 2-0
13 LINCOLN C	O06 2-2	a06 0-1	J19 1-0	S15 0-0	m11 6-2	S19 1-1	N24 0-3	a20 0-0	D22 1-1	S01 1-0	M09 3-1	O03 1-1		M16 2-1	O27 3-1	M20 0-2	O24 1-2	D01 2-0	a17 1-2	F23 0-3	M30 3-2	J05 2-1	J01 0-0	M26 2-1
14 MAIDSTONE U	m08 1-1	M09 1-1	a27 1-0	N03 3-0	m01 0-0	J01 1-0	O20 2-3	M30 0-1	a24 3-1	F27 5-1	M23 1-4	N10 1-1	S29 4-1		S01 1-3	D01 2-0	a06 0-1	m04 0-1	S15 6-1	M13 2-3	D22 2-2	O13 1-3	O31 0-2	J19 5-4
15 NORTHAMPTON T	J26 2-1	S08 1-0	M12 0-0	D21 0-0	M09 1-1	M23 2-0	a27 0-3	J01 0-0	a06 2-1	S29 1-0	N03 3-2	J19 3-0	a30 1-1	J12 2-0		S22 1-2	D01 3-2	F01 0-2	M30 2-1	O13 1-0	a16 1-4	O19 5-0	N09 1-0	F15 2-1
16 PETERBOROUGH U	a06 3-2	M30 2-0	O20 3-2	m04 3-0	S01 1-1	N03 2-1	M12 2-2	N10 1-1	a16 2-0	S18 2-0	a27 1-1	m07 3-0	O13 2-0	M02 2-0	F05 1-0		J02 1-1	D21 2-0	a23 0-0	M23 0-0	S29 1-2	S15 0-0	J19 2-2	D15 2-0
17 ROCHDALE	A25 4-0	J12 2-1	m04 0-0	M12 0-0	N24 0-1	O13 3-0	N03 1-1	S15 0-3	M23 1-3	a01 1-1	a23 0-0	a30 2-1	a27 0-0	D29 3-2	M02 1-1	a13 0-3		S22 1-1	F23 2-1	S08 1-0	O20 0-0	S29 3-2	D15 2-0	a16 2-1
18 SCARBOROUGH	M16 2-0	O03 0-1	M26 0-1	F19 1-2	O24 1-1	S01 1-0	D29 1-1	O07 2-1	S15 2-1	D26 4-1	F16 2-0	m11 2-1	M02 3-0	O27 0-2	S18 1-1	a03 3-1	F06 0-0		a20 3-1	D16 0-2	N09 1-0	a13 1-0	D07 4-2	J05 2-2
19 SCUNTHORPE U	J12 6-2	A25 2-0	a13 1-3	S29 0-2	D29 2-0	a27 3-0	m04 2-1	D15 1-1	O13 1-0	M23 4-4	F26 2-1	a01 3-0	S22 2-1	J26 2-2	M05 3-0	S08 1-1	N10 2-1	O20 3-0		N03 3-0	F02 3-0	M12 1-0	m07 2-0	M02 2-1
20 STOCKPORT CO	a19 3-2	O22 0-0	S14 2-2	F26 1-1	S17 3-1	a06 3-1	D01 3-1	D21 0-0	J01 1-1	J18 5-1	M29 1-3	M16 4-2	N10 4-0	O01 1-0	a09 2-0	O06 2-1	M26 3-0	M08 2-2	m11 5-0		a23 2-1	S01 3-0	J04 2-0	O26 2-0
21 TORQUAY U	a08 5-0	O06 2-1	D29 2-0	a10 2-1	O27 3-0	S15 2-0	M09 2-1	O02 1-0	A31 3-1	F05 3-1	D01 0-1	a13 1-1	M05 0-1	a02 1-1	M26 0-0	M15 0-0	a20 3-1	a30 2-0	S18 1-1	D07 1-1		J19 0-0	O16 1-0	m11 2-1
22 WALSALL	O27 2-2	m11 2-0	N10 1-0	M09 0-0	O06 1-1	F16 3-0	S08 2-2	F02 1-0	M30 0-0	D01 3-1	a06 0-1	S22 0-0	F19 0-0	M20 0-0	a20 3-3	J26 0-1	M16 0-1	J01 0-0	O02 3-0	J12 0-2	A25 2-2		D21 1-0	O23 1-1
23 WREXHAM	S08 4-2	J26 0-1	N03 2-4	M22 1-0	D01 3-0	S29 1-1	S22 1-1	J12 2-1	m04 3-0	M12 1-2	O20 2-2	D26 1-2	a13 2-2	a09 2-2	F23 0-2	A25 0-0	M09 2-1	O13 1-2	N24 1-0	a16 1-3	a27 2-1	a01 1-1		D29 0-4
24 YORK C	D21 2-0	J01 0-1	M23 2-0	O13 1-2	F23 2-0	M12 0-2	F02 0-1	S22 3-1	S29 1-1	O20 3-3	J26 0-0	J12 1-0	F26 1-0	A25 0-1	N24 0-1	M09 0-4	M30 0-2	a23 2-0	D01 2-2	m04 0-2	N03 0-0	a26 1-0	a06 0-0	

LEAGUE TABLES

DIVISION 1

	P	W	D	L	F	A	W	D	L	F	A	Pts
Arsenal	38	15	4	0	51	10	9	9	1	23	8	*83
Liverpool	38	14	3	2	42	13	9	4	6	35	27	76
Crystal P	38	11	6	2	26	17	9	3	7	24	24	69
Leeds U	38	12	2	5	46	23	7	5	7	19	24	64
Manchester C	38	12	3	4	35	25	5	8	6	29	28	62
Manchester U	38	11	4	4	34	17	5	8	6	24	28	†59
Wimbledon	38	8	6	5	28	22	6	8	5	25	24	56
Nottingham F	38	11	4	4	42	21	3	8	8	23	29	54
Everton	38	9	5	5	26	15	4	7	8	24	31	51
Tottenham H	38	8	9	2	35	22	3	7	9	16	28	49
Chelsea	38	10	6	3	33	25	3	4	12	25	44	49
QPR	38	8	5	6	27	22	4	5	10	17	31	46
Sheffield U	38	9	3	7	23	23	4	4	11	13	32	46
Southampton	38	9	6	4	33	22	3	3	13	25	47	45
Norwich C	38	9	3	7	27	32	4	3	12	14	32	45
Coventry C	38	10	6	3	30	16	1	5	13	12	33	44
Aston Villa	38	7	9	3	29	25	2	5	12	17	33	41
Luton T	38	7	5	7	22	18	3	2	14	20	43	37
Sunderland	38	6	6	7	15	16	2	4	13	23	44	34
Derby Co	38	3	8	8	25	36	2	1	16	12	39	24

Arsenal had two points deducted for disciplinary reasons.
†Manchester United had one point deducted for disciplinary reasons.

DIVISION 2

	P	W	D	L	F	A	W	D	L	F	A	Pts
Oldham A	46	17	5	1	55	21	8	8	7	28	32	88
West Ham U	46	15	6	2	41	18	9	9	5	19	16	87
Sheffield W	46	12	10	1	43	23	10	6	7	37	28	82
Notts Co	46	14	4	5	45	28	9	7	7	31	27	80
Millwall	46	11	6	6	43	28	9	7	7	27	23	73
Brighton & HA	46	12	4	7	37	31	9	3	11	26	38	70
Middlesbrough	46	12	4	7	36	17	8	5	10	30	30	69
Barnsley	46	13	7	3	39	16	6	5	12	24	32	69
Bristol C	46	14	5	4	44	28	6	2	15	24	43	67
Oxford U	46	10	9	4	41	29	4	10	9	28	37	61
Newcastle U	46	8	10	5	24	22	6	7	10	25	34	59
Wolves	46	11	6	6	45	35	2	13	8	18	28	58
Bristol R	46	11	7	5	29	20	4	6	13	27	39	58
Ipswich T	46	9	8	6	32	28	4	10	9	28	40	57
Port Vale	46	10	4	9	32	24	5	8	10	24	40	57
Charlton A	46	8	7	8	27	25	5	10	8	30	36	56
Portsmouth	46	10	6	7	34	27	4	5	14	24	43	53
Plymouth A	46	10	10	3	36	20	2	7	14	18	48	53
Blackburn R	46	8	6	9	26	27	6	4	13	25	39	52
Watford	46	5	8	10	24	32	7	7	9	21	27	51
Swindon T	46	8	6	9	31	30	4	8	11	34	43	50
Leicester C	46	12	4	7	41	33	2	4	17	19	50	50
WBA	46	7	11	5	26	21	3	7	13	26	40	48
Hull C	46	6	10	7	35	32	4	5	14	22	53	45

DIVISION 3

	P	W	D	L	F	A	W	D	L	F	A	Pts
Cambridge U	46	14	5	4	42	22	11	6	6	33	23	86
Southend U	46	13	6	4	34	23	13	1	9	33	28	85
Grimsby T	46	16	3	4	42	13	8	8	7	24	21	83
Bolton W	46	14	5	4	33	18	10	6	7	31	32	83
Tranmere R	46	13	5	5	38	21	10	4	9	26	25	78
Brentford	46	12	4	7	30	22	9	9	5	29	25	76
Bury	46	13	6	4	39	26	7	7	9	28	30	73
Bradford C	46	13	3	7	36	22	7	7	9	26	32	70
Bournemouth	46	14	6	3	37	20	5	7	11	21	38	70
Wigan A	46	14	3	6	40	20	6	6	11	31	34	69
Huddersfield T	46	13	3	7	37	23	5	10	8	20	28	67
Birmingham C	46	8	9	6	21	21	8	8	7	24	28	65
Leyton Orient	46	15	2	6	35	19	3	8	12	20	39	64
Stoke C	46	9	7	7	36	29	7	5	11	19	30	60
Reading	46	11	5	7	34	28	6	3	14	19	38	59
Exeter C	46	12	6	5	35	16	4	3	16	23	36	57
Preston NE	46	11	5	7	33	29	4	6	13	21	38	56
Shrewsbury T	46	8	7	8	29	22	6	3	14	32	46	52
Chester C	46	10	3	10	27	27	4	6	13	19	31	51
Swansea C	46	8	6	9	31	33	5	3	15	18	39	48
Fulham	46	8	8	7	27	22	2	8	13	14	34	46
Crewe A	46	6	9	8	35	35	5	2	16	27	45	44
Rotherham U	46	5	10	8	31	38	5	2	16	19	49	42
Mansfield T	46	5	8	10	23	27	3	6	14	19	36	38

DIVISION 4

	P	W	D	L	F	A	W	D	L	F	A	Pts
Darlington	46	13	8	2	36	14	9	9	5	32	24	83
Stockport Co	46	16	6	1	54	19	7	7	9	30	28	82
Hartlepool U	46	15	5	3	35	15	9	5	9	32	33	82
Peterboro' U	46	13	9	1	38	15	8	8	7	29	30	80
Blackpool	46	17	3	3	55	17	6	7	10	23	30	79
Burnley	46	17	5	1	46	16	6	5	12	24	35	79
Torquay U	46	14	7	2	37	13	4	11	8	27	34	72
Scunthorpe U	46	17	4	2	51	20	3	7	13	20	42	71
Scarborough	46	13	5	5	36	21	6	7	10	23	35	69
Northampton T	46	14	5	4	34	21	4	8	11	23	37	67
Doncaster R	46	12	5	6	36	22	5	9	9	20	24	65
Rochdale	46	10	9	4	29	22	5	8	10	21	31	62
Cardiff C	46	10	6	7	26	23	5	9	9	17	31	60
Lincoln C	46	10	7	6	32	27	4	10	9	18	34	59
Gillingham	46	9	9	5	35	27	3	9	11	22	33	54
Walsall	46	7	12	4	25	17	5	5	13	23	34	53
Hereford U	46	9	10	4	32	19	4	4	15	21	39	53
Chesterfield	46	8	12	3	33	26	5	2	16	14	36	53
Maidstone U	46	9	5	9	42	34	4	7	12	24	37	51
Carlisle U	46	12	3	8	30	30	1	6	16	17	59	48
York C	46	8	6	9	21	23	3	7	13	24	34	46
Halifax T	46	9	6	8	34	29	3	4	16	25	50	46
Aldershot	46	8	7	8	38	43	2	4	17	23	58	41
Wrexham	46	8	7	8	33	34	2	3	18	15	40	40

Football League Records

Top scorers: Div 1, I.Wright (Arsenal) 29 goals (5 for Crystal Palace); Div 2, A.Shearer, D.Speedie (both Blackburn Rovers) 23 goals; Div 3, D.Holdsworth (Brentford), I.Roberts (Huddersfield Town) 24 goals; Div 4, D.Bamber (Blackpool), P.Stant (Mansfield Town) 28 goals.
Play-offs: Prem Lge, Blackburn Rovers v Derby County 4-2, 1-2; Cambridge United v Leicester City 1-1, 0-5; Blackburn Rovers v Leicester City (Wembley) 1-0; Div 1, Stockport County v Stoke City 1-0, 1-1; Peterborough United v Huddersfield Town 2-2, 2-1; Peterborough United v Stockport County (Wembley) 2-1; Div 2, Barnet v Blackpool 1-0, 0-2; Crewe Alexandra v Scunthorpe United 2-2, 0-2; Blackpool v Scunthorpe United (Wembley) 1-1 (4-3 penalties).
From 1992-93 Division 1 became Premier League and Divisions 2, 3 and 4 became Divisions 1, 2 and 3.
Ipswich Town, Middlesbrough and Blackburn Rovers promoted to Prem Lge; Luton Town, Notts County and West Ham United relegated to Div 1; Brentford, Birmingham City and Peterborough United promoted to Div 1; Plymouth Argyle, Brighton & Hove Albion and Port Vale relegated to Div 2; Burnley, Rotherham United, Mansfield Town and Blackpool promoted to Div 2; Bury, Shrewsbury Town, Torquay United and Darlington relegated to Div 3.

Gordon Strachan with the League Championship trophy won by Leeds United.

Gary Lineker, top-scored for Tottenham before leaving for a new challenge in Japan.

DIVISION 1

	ARSENAL	ASTON VILLA	CHELSEA	COVENTRY C	CRYSTAL P	EVERTON	LEEDS U	LIVERPOOL	LUTON T	MANCHESTER C	MANCHESTER U	NORWICH C	NOTTINGHAM F	NOTTS CO	OLDHAM A	Q.P.R.	SHEFFIELD U	SHEFFIELD W	SOUTHAMPTON	TOTTENHAM H	WEST HAM U	WIMBLEDON
1 ARSENAL		J11 0-0	O05 3-2	S07 1-2	a11 4-1	D21 4-2	M22 1-1	a20 4-0	A27 2-0	A31 2-1	F01 1-1	F11 1-1	M31 3-3	O26 2-0	M10 2-1	A17 1-1	S21 5-2	F15 7-1	m02 5-1	D01 2-0	N02 0-1	J01 1-1
2 ASTON VILLA	A24 3-1		a20 3-1	m02 2-0	S04 0-1	F02 0-0	N24 1-4	a11 1-0	O05 4-0	D07 3-1	A21 0-1	M28 1-0	S21 3-1	N16 1-0	F22 1-0	M14 0-1	M31 1-1	J18 0-1	D28 2-1	S07 0-0	D26 3-1	O26 2-1
3 CHELSEA	a25 1-1	S18 2-0		M14 0-1	F08 1-1	S28 2-2	S14 0-1	O19 2-2	A31 4-1	J01 1-1	D15 1-3	N16 0-3	N30 1-0	A28 2-2	D21 4-2	a18 2-1	M21 1-2	F29 0-3	F12 1-1	J11 2-0	a04 2-1	A17 2-2
4 COVENTRY C	a04 0-1	S28 1-0	N02 0-1		O19 1-2	a18 0-1	S18 0-0	F08 0-0	A21 5-0	A17 0-1	F29 0-0	M04 0-0	M11 0-2	S14 1-0	M21 1-1	J11 2-2	A28 3-1	a08 0-0	N30 2-0	J01 1-2	a25 1-0	A31 0-1
5 CRYSTAL P	S14 1-4	M21 0-0	O26 0-0	F01 0-1		a04 2-0	O01 1-0	M14 1-0	F25 1-1	J11 1-1	N30 1-3	F29 3-4	M03 0-0	J01 1-0	a18 0-0	S28 2-2	A31 2-1	a25 1-1	N16 1-0	D22 1-2	S17 2-3	A27 3-2
6 EVERTON	A20 3-1	O19 0-2	m02 2-1	S21 3-0	S07 2-2		F23 1-1	D28 1-1	M14 1-1	a20 1-2	A24 0-0	S03 1-1	J19 1-1	N23 1-0	M07 2-1	F08 0-0	a11 0-2	D26 0-1	a01 0-1	O05 3-1	D07 4-0	N16 2-0
7 LEEDS U	S03 2-2	M03 0-0	a11 3-0	a20 2-0	J18 1-1	N30 1-0		S21 1-0	F29 2-0	S07 3-0	D29 1-1	M02 1-0	A20 1-0	F01 3-0	O26 1-0	N16 2-0	O05 4-3	A24 1-1	D26 3-3	D14 1-1	M28 0-0	M14 5-1
8 LIVERPOOL	J29 2-0	S14 1-1	F01 1-2	O26 1-0	N02 1-2	A31 3-1	a18 0-0		J11 2-1	D21 2-2	a26 2-0	N30 2-1	D14 2-0	M31 4-0	A17 2-1	A27 1-0	J01 2-1	S28 1-1	F29 0-0	M21 2-1	M11 1-0	a08 2-3
9 LUTON T	D26 1-0	a25 2-0	D28 2-0	D20 1-0	M07 1-1	N02 0-1	D07 0-2	A24 0-0		N23 2-2	a18 1-1	F08 2-0	a14 2-1	S28 1-1	S14 2-1	S17 0-1	F22 2-1	O19 2-2	S04 2-1	M11 0-0	J18 0-1	a04 2-1
10 MANCHESTER C	D28 1-0	F29 2-0	M28 0-0	J18 1-0	A24 3-2	S17 0-1	a04 4-0	A21 2-1	F15 4-0		N16 0-0	D26 2-1	S04 2-1	a25 2-0	S28 1-2	D14 2-2	O26 3-2	S14 0-1	M15 0-1	F01 1-0	a18 2-0	N30 0-0
11 MANCHESTER U	O19 1-1	J22 1-0	F26 1-1	D07 4-0	F22 2-0	J11 1-0	A31 1-1	O06 0-0	S21 5-0	a07 1-1		S07 3-0	a20 1-2	A17 2-0	A28 1-0	J01 1-4	N02 2-0	F08 1-1	a16 1-0	m02 3-1	N23 2-1	M21 0-0
12 NORWICH C	a08 1-3	J01 2-1	M11 0-1	N23 3-2	D07 3-3	M21 4-3	S28 2-2	F22 3-0	O26 1-0	A28 0-0	M31 1-3		N02 0-0	a18 0-1	J11 1-2	D21 0-1	A17 2-2	S18 1-0	F01 2-1	A31 0-1	S14 2-1	a25 1-1
13 NOTTINGHAM F	D08 3-2	a18 2-0	F22 1-1	N16 1-0	N23 5-1	A17 2-1	D22 0-0	a22 1-1	J01 1-1	M21 2-0	M18 1-0	M14 2-0		J11 1-1	A31 3-1	a25 1-1	F01 2-5	a04 0-2	O26 1-3	A28 1-3	S28 2-2	S14 4-2
14 NOTTS CO	F08 0-1	M10 0-0	D26 2-0	a11 1-0	M28 2-3	M17 0-0	O19 2-4	S07 1-2	m02 2-1	O06 1-3	J18 1-1	S21 2-2	A24 0-4		N02 2-0	N30 0-1	a20 1-3	S03 2-1	A20 1-0	a07 0-2	D28 3-0	F25 1-1
15 OLDHAM A	N16 1-1	N30 3-2	A21 3-0	S03 2-1	S21 2-3	D14 2-2	F08 2-0	J18 2-3	a11 5-1	m02 2-5	D26 3-6	A24 2-2	D28 2-1	M14 4-3		F15 2-1	S07 2-1	M28 3-0	O05 1-1	a20 1-0	O19 2-2	F29 0-1
16 Q.P.R.	J18 0-0	N02 0-1	S21 2-2	A24 1-1	m02 1-0	O26 3-1	M11 4-1	D26 0-0	a20 2-1	M07 4-0	M28 0-0	A21 0-2	O05 0-2	F22 1-1	N23 1-3		D07 1-0	D28 1-1	S07 2-2	a11 1-2	S04 0-0	F01 1-1
17 SHEFFIELD U	a18 1-1	D14 2-0	S03 0-1	D26 0-3	D28 1-1	S14 2-1	a26 2-3	M28 2-0	N30 1-1	F08 4-2	M14 1-2	J18 1-0	O19 4-2	S17 1-3	a04 2-0	F29 0-0		N17 2-0	A24 0-2	a14 2-0	A20 1-1	S28 0-0
18 SHEFFIELD W	N23 1-1	A17 2-3	D07 3-0	M07 1-1	O05 4-1	A28 2-1	J12 1-6	m02 0-0	F01 3-2	a11 2-0	O26 3-2	a20 2-0	S07 2-1	M21 1-0	J01 1-1	A31 4-1	M11 1-3		S21 2-0	N02 0-0	F22 2-1	D21 2-0
19 SOUTHAMPTON	S28 0-4	A31 1-1	N23 1-0	F22 0-0	M11 1-0	J01 1-2	A28 0-4	D07 1-1	M21 2-1	N02 0-3	S14 0-1	O19 0-0	A08 0-1	D20 1-1	a25 1-0	a04 2-1	J11 2-4	a18 0-1		A17 2-3	M03 1-0	S18 1-0
20 TOTTENHAM H	F22 1-1	a04 2-5	A24 1-3	M28 4-3	F16 0-1	a25 3-3	M07 1-3	D18 1-2	N16 4-1	O19 0-1	S28 1-2	D28 3-0	D26 1-2	D07 2-1	J25 0-0	S14 2-0	N23 0-1	M14 0-2	J18 1-2		a01 3-0	a18 3-2
21 WEST HAM U	M14 0-2	A28 3-1	S07 1-1	O05 0-1	a20 0-2	F29 0-2	J01 1-3	N17 0-0	A17 0-0	S21 1-2	a22 1-0	a11 4-0	m02 3-0	A31 0-2	F01 1-0	M21 2-2	D21 1-1	N30 1-2	a14 0-1	O26 2-1		J11 1-1
22 WIMBLEDON	M28 1-3	F08 2-0	J18 1-2	D28 1-1	D26 1-1	M10 0-0	N02 0-0	N23 0-0	S07 3-0	F22 2-1	S03 1-2	O05 3-1	a02 3-0	M07 2-0	D07 2-1	O19 0-1	m02 3-0	O02 2-1	a20 0-1	S21 3-5	A24 2-0	

DIVISION 2

	BARNSLEY	BLACKBURN R	BRIGHTON & HA	BRISTOL C	BRISTOL R	CAMBRIDGE U	CHARLTON A	DERBY CO	GRIMSBY T	IPSWICH T	LEICESTER C	MIDDLESBROUGH	MILLWALL	NEWCASTLE U	OXFORD U	PLYMOUTH A	PORTSMOUTH	PORT VALE	SOUTHEND U	SUNDERLAND	SWINDON T	TRANMERE R	WATFORD	WOLVERHAMPTON W
1 BARNSLEY		M28 2-1	A24 1-2	O19 1-2	N09 0-1	F08 0-0	F29 1-0	a04 0-3	D14 4-1	S14 1-0	S17 3-1	N05 2-1	S28 0-2	N30 3-0	M14 1-0	J18 1-3	O12 2-0	D26 0-0	F15 1-0	A20 0-3	D28 1-1	a18 1-1	S03 0-3	a25 2-0
2 BLACKBURN R	N16 3-0		N02 1-0	J11 4-0	D14 3-0	J01 2-1	M21 0-2	F11 2-0	O26 2-1	A31 1-2	a18 0-1	N30 2-1	a25 2-1	F15 3-1	F29 1-1	O12 5-2	A17 1-1	S14 1-0	M10 2-2	a29 2-2	F01 2-1	S28 0-0	S17 1-0	a14 1-2
3 BRIGHTON & HA	J11 3-1	M14 0-3		J01 0-0	S28 3-1	M28 1-1	F01 1-2	a15 1-2	N06 3-0	O12 2-2	O30 1-2	N09 1-1	D21 3-4	D14 2-2	F15 1-2	N30 1-0	a29 2-1	S18 3-1	F29 3-2	a25 2-2	O26 0-2	A17 0-2	S14 0-1	A31 3-3
4 BRISTOL C	F01 0-2	A24 1-0	A20 2-1		S04 1-0	M14 1-2	N30 0-2	a25 1-2	F29 1-1	a18 2-1	a04 2-1	a07 1-1	S17 2-2	O26 1-1	M28 1-1	N05 2-0	S28 0-2	D28 3-0	J18 2-2	N09 1-0	D26 1-1	S14 2-2	O12 1-0	M17 2-0
5 BRISTOL R	M21 0-0	M07 3-0	a20 4-1	D21 3-2		D07 2-2	m02 1-0	N23 2-3	S07 2-3	A17 3-3	J01 1-1	O05 2-1	F22 3-2	A31 1-2	S21 2-1	O19 0-0	J29 1-0	N02 3-3	a01 4-1	F08 2-1	a12 1-1	J11 1-0	N16 1-1	M11 1-1
6 CAMBRIDGE U	O26 2-1	F25 2-1	N16 0-0	N02 0-0	F28 6-1		F15 1-0	S13 0-0	J18 0-1	M21 1-1	S29 5-1	M17 0-0	a04 1-0	M10 0-2	N30 1-1	D26 1-1	a17 2-2	a25 4-2	S03 0-1	O12 3-0	A24 3-2	J31 0-0	D29 0-1	S17 2-1
7 CHARLTON A	D07 1-1	N09 0-2	O19 2-0	F22 2-1	O12 1-0	N23 1-2		S01 0-2	M03 1-3	O30 1-1	a25 2-0	M28 0-0	M07 1-0	A18 2-1	J08 2-2	a04 0-0	S14 3-0	S28 2-0	F08 2-0	S17 1-4	N06 0-0	a28 0-1	a18 1-1	J15 0-2
8 DERBY CO	S07 1-1	S04 0-2	S21 3-1	O05 4-1	F15 1-0	a01 0-0	D28 1-2		D26 0-0	N16 1-0	N30 1-2	A21 2-0	F08 0-2	a20 4-1	a11 2-2	M25 2-0	O19 2-0	M11 3-1	A24 1-2	J18 1-2	m02 2-1	N02 0-1	F29 3-1	M21 1-2
9 GRIMSBY T	M07 0-1	F08 2-3	M10 0-1	D07 3-1	a04 0-1	A17 3-4	N02 1-0	a07 0-1		S28 1-2	M17 0-1	O19 1-0	N23 1-1	M21 1-1	J11 1-0	S14 2-1	S17 1-1	O12 1-2	F18 3-2	a18 2-0	F22 0-0	A31 2-2	a25 0-1	J01 0-2
10 IPSWICH T	M31 2-0	D28 2-1	m02 3-1	S21 4-2	J18 1-0	N09 1-2	D26 2-0	M28 2-1	a21 0-0		M14 0-0	A24 2-1	O19 0-0	a11 3-2	O05 2-1	F29 2-0	F08 5-2	A20 2-1	S07 1-0	N05 0-1	S03 1-4	N30 4-0	M17 1-2	a07 2-1
11 LEICESTER C	a11 3-1	S21 3-0	D26 2-1	S07 2-1	N20 1-1	a21 2-1	O05 0-2	F22 1-2	S04 2-0	N02 2-2		a01 2-1	D07 1-1	m02 1-2	F08 2-1	A24 2-0	M11 2-2	N23 0-1	D28 2-0	a08 3-2	J18 3-1	a15 1-0	M21 1-2	O19 3-0
12 MIDDLESBROUGH	a13 0-1	F22 0-0	M21 4-0	N23 3-1	a25 2-1	M07 1-1	N16 2-0	J01 1-1	a28 2-0	J11 1-0	S14 3-0		A17 1-0	A27 3-0	a15 2-1	a18 2-1	A31 2-0	O26 1-0	N02 1-1	S28 2-1	D07 2-2	S17 1-0	a04 1-2	O12 0-0
13 MILLWALL	a22 1-1	O05 1-3	S04 1-2	a11 2-3	N30 0-1	S07 1-2	F26 1-0	O26 1-2	F15 1-1	F01 2-3	F29 2-0	J18 2-0		S21 2-1	a01 2-1	D28 2-1	N02 1-1	M21 1-0	m02 2-0	A24 4-1	a08 1-1	M11 0-3	D26 0-4	N16 2-1
14 NEWCASTLE U	F22 1-1	N23 0-0	M07 0-1	F08 3-0	D28 2-1	N06 1-1	J18 3-4	S28 2-2	N09 2-0	S17 1-1	O12 2-0	D26 0-1	a18 0-1		O19 4-3	S04 2-2	a25 1-0	D07 2-2	N20 3-2	M29 1-0	M14 3-1	a04 2-3	A24 2-2	S14 1-2
15 OXFORD U	N02 0-1	D07 1-3	N23 3-1	N16 1-1	a18 2-2	F22 1-0	O23 1-2	S18 2-0	A24 1-2	a25 1-1	O26 1-2	S04 1-2	S14 2-2	F01 5-2		S28 3-2	M21 2-1	J18 2-2	D26 0-1	D28 3-0	M07 5-3	O12 1-0	M11 0-0	a04 1-0
16 PLYMOUTH A	A17 2-1	m02 1-3	F22 1-1	M10 1-0	F01 0-0	F11 0-1	S07 0-2	M07 1-1	M31 1-2	D07 1-0	J11 2-2	S21 1-1	A31 3-2	D20 2-0	a20 3-1		J01 3-2	N16 1-0	a11 0-2	N23 1-0	O05 0-4	M21 1-0	O26 0-1	N02 1-0
17 PORTSMOUTH	m02 2-0	J18 2-2	S07 0-0	a20 1-0	D26 2-0	S21 3-0	M31 1-2	F01 0-1	a11 2-0	O26 1-1	N05 1-0	D28 4-0	M14 6-1	O05 3-1	N09 2-1	F04 4-1		A24 1-0	D14 1-1	S03 1-0	M28 1-1	F29 2-0	a22 0-0	N30 1-0
18 PORT VALE	A27 0-0	M31 2-0	a11 2-1	A31 1-1	M14 0-1	O05 1-0	a21 1-1	N06 1-0	m02 0-1	J01 1-2	F15 1-2	F08 1-2	N09 0-2	F29 0-1	A17 2-1	M28 1-0	J11 0-2		S21 0-0	O19 3-3	S07 2-2	D13 1-1	N30 2-1	D21 1-1
19 SOUTHEND U	N23 2-1	N05 3-0	D07 2-1	A17 1-1	S14 2-0	D22 1-1	O26 1-1	J11 1-0	M28 3-1	a04 1-2	A31 1-2	M14 0-1	O12 2-3	J01 4-0	O30 2-3	S17 2-1	M17 2-3	a15 0-0		F22 2-0	N09 3-2	a25 1-1	F01 1-0	S28 0-2
20 SUNDERLAND	J01 2-0	S07 1-1	O05 4-2	M21 1-3	O26 1-1	m02 2-2	a11 1-2	A17 1-1	S21 1-2	a14 3-0	D14 1-0	a20 1-0	J11 6-2	N17 1-1	A31 2-0	a16 0-1	D21 1-0	F01 1-1	N30 1-2		a27 0-0	F11 1-1	N02 3-1	F29 1-0
21 SWINDON T	A31 3-1	O19 2-1	F08 2-1	F04 2-0	S17 1-0	J11 0-2	M10 1-2	O12 1-2	N30 1-1	D20 0-0	A17 0-0	F29 0-1	J01 3-1	N02 2-1	J28 2-1	a25 1-0	N16 2-3	a04 1-0	M21 3-1	S14 5-3		M17 2-0	S28 3-1	a18 1-0
22 TRANMERE R	S21 2-1	a20 2-2	J17 1-1	M31 2-2	A23 2-2	O18 1-2	S03 2-2	M14 4-3	D28 1-1	F21 0-1	M27 1-2	a10 1-2	N05 2-1	S07 3-2	m02 1-2	N08 1-0	a07 2-0	M06 2-1	O04 1-1	D26 1-0	N22 0-0		J24 1-1	F08 4-3
23 WATFORD	D22 1-1	a11 2-1	M31 0-1	m02 5-2	M28 1-0	A31 1-3	S21 2-0	D07 1-2	O05 2-0	M07 0-1	N09 0-1	S07 1-2	O29 0-2	J11 2-2	N06 2-0	F08 1-0	N23 2-1	F22 0-0	O19 1-2	M14 1-0	a20 0-0	J01 0-0		A17 0-2
24 WOLVERHAMPTON W	O05 1-2	D26 0-0	D28 2-0	M07 1-1	N05 2-3	a11 2-1	A24 1-1	N09 2-3	N26 2-1	N23 1-2	F01 0-1	m02 1-2	M28 0-0	M31 6-2	S07 3-1	M14 1-0	F22 0-0	S03 0-2	a20 3-1	D07 1-0	S21 2-1	O26 1-1	J18 3-0	

Season 1991-92

DIVISION 3

	BIRMINGHAM C	BOLTON W	BOURNEMOUTH	BRADFORD C	BRENTFORD	BURY	CHESTER C	DARLINGTON	EXETER C	FULHAM	HARTLEPOOL U	HUDDERSFIELD T	HULL C	LEYTON O	PETERBOROUGH U	PRESTON N.E.	READING	SHREWSBURY T	STOCKPORT CO	STOKE C	SWANSEA C	TORQUAY U	W.B.A.	WIGAN A
1 BIRMINGHAM C		a14 2-1	F15 0-1	N30 2-0	M10 1-0	A17 3-2	S17 3-2	A31 1-0	N23 1-0	D21 3-1	a18 2-1	M21 2-0	J01 2-2	J11 2-2	S14 1-1	S28 3-1	a04 2-0	a25 1-0	O12 3-0	F29 1-1	M03 1-1	N02 3-0	F08 0-3	O19 3-3
2 BOLTON W	M17 1-1		M31 0-2	a11 1-1	a20 1-2	M21 2-1	F08 0-0	J01 2-0	F22 1-2	O19 0-3	J18 2-2	A17 1-1	D14 1-0	A31 1-0	M24 2-1	N23 1-0	N02 1-1	F11 1-0	M10 0-0	m02 3-1	a07 0-0	O05 1-0	S07 3-0	S21 1-1
3 BOURNEMOUTH	D14 2-1	S14 1-2		O26 1-3	N22 0-0	F11 4-0	a03 2-0	A17 1-2	M24 1-0	S27 0-0	O12 2-0	a14 1-1	A31 0-0	F01 0-1	M07 1-2	J01 1-0	a25 3-2	S17 1-0	N01 1-0	D21 1-2	M20 3-0	M10 2-1	F22 2-1	J18 3-0
4 BRADFORD C	F11 1-2	S17 4-4	F08 3-1		N02 0-1	J04 1-1	S14 1-1	M07 0-1	M10 1-1	O12 3-4	A31 1-1	D22 1-1	J18 2-1	J01 1-1	M21 2-1	a04 1-1	a18 1-0	S28 3-0	a25 1-0	A17 1-0	N23 4-6	O19 2-0	D14 1-1	F22 1-1
5 BRENTFORD	N06 2-2	S28 3-2	M29 2-2	M14 3-4		F08 0-3	M03 2-0	a17 4-1	D22 3-0	a26 4-0	J01 1-0	A31 2-3	S17 4-1	A17 4-3	O12 2-1	J25 1-0	S14 1-0	a04 2-0	F29 2-1	J11 2-0	N30 3-2	F15 3-2	O19 1-2	N09 4-0
6 BURY	D28 1-0	N09 1-1	N30 0-1	F29 0-1	O26 0-3		F25 1-2	a25 1-0	a14 3-1	S17 3-1	S28 1-1	S14 4-4	a04 3-2	F15 4-2	S03 3-0	O12 2-3	D26 0-1	A24 0-0	a18 0-0	N05 1-3	J11 1-0	M03 0-0	M14 1-1	M28 1-4
7 CHESTER C	a11 0-1	O26 0-1	S07 0-1	M31 0-0	J18 1-1	M07 3-1		J04 2-5	F11 5-2	A17 2-0	F22 2-0	J01 0-0	M21 1-1	m02 1-0	M10 2-4	N02 3-2	N23 2-2	D14 1-4	M24 3-2	O05 0-0	A31 2-0	a20 2-0	S21 1-2	F18 1-0
8 DARLINGTON	D26 1-1	S03 3-2	D28 0-0	a07 1-3	S21 1-2	O05 0-2	F29 1-1		m02 5-2	N30 3-1	N02 4-0	F15 1-3	F08 0-1	M31 0-1	N23 1-2	M21 0-2	M10 2-4	O19 3-3	M03 1-3	S07 0-1	a11 1-1	J11 3-2	A24 0-1	a20 0-1
9 EXETER C	M28 2-1	J11 2-2	F29 0-3	N06 1-0	A24 1-2	O19 5-2	N30 0-0	O12 4-1		J25 1-1	S14 1-1	a04 0-1	a25 0-3	M14 2-0	a18 2-2	M03 4-1	S28 2-1	D26 1-0	S17 2-1	N09 0-0	F15 2-1	S04 1-0	D28 1-1	F08 0-1
10 FULHAM	A24 0-1	F01 1-1	a20 2-0	m02 2-1	O05 0-1	a11 4-2	D28 2-2	F11 4-0	M07 0-0		M20 1-0	M10 1-0	N02 0-0	S21 2-1	F22 0-1	O26 1-0	a07 1-0	J18 0-1	N23 1-2	M31 1-1	S07 3-0	D26 2-1	S03 0-0	J28 1-1
11 HARTLEPOOL U	S21 1-0	M03 0-4	m02 1-0	D26 1-0	S03 1-0	a20 0-0	J11 1-0	M14 2-0	M31 3-1	N09 2-0		N30 0-0	O19 2-3	S07 2-3	F08 0-1	F15 2-0	A24 2-0	M28 4-2	F18 0-1	a11 1-1	F29 0-1	D28 1-1	N05 0-0	O05 4-3
12 HUDDERSFIELD T	N09 3-2	D28 1-0	S21 0-0	A25 1-0	D26 2-1	M31 3-0	S04 2-0	D14 2-1	S07 0-0	N06 3-1	F11 1-0		F25 1-1	a20 1-0	J18 0-0	F01 1-2	F22 1-2	M07 2-1	O25 0-1	M14 1-2	O05 1-0	m02 4-0	M28 3-0	a11 3-1
13 HULL C	S03 1-2	a29 2-0	D26 0-1	M03 0-0	a11 0-3	S07 0-1	N09 1-0	O26 5-2	O05 1-2	M14 0-0	F01 0-2	F29 1-0		M28 1-0	A24 1-2	N30 2-2	D28 0-1	N05 4-0	J11 0-2	J25 0-1	m02 3-0	S21 4-1	a20 1-0	M31 1-1
14 LEYTON O	F22 0-0	D26 2-1	O19 1-1	S03 1-1	D28 4-2	M24 4-0	O12 1-0	S14 2-1	N02 1-0	a18 0-1	a04 4-0	S28 1-0	N23 1-0		a25 1-2	S17 0-0	M07 1-1	J28 2-0	A24 3-3	F08 0-1	M10 1-2	M21 2-0	J18 1-1	F11 3-1
15 PETERBOROUGH U	M31 2-3	F29 1-0	a08 2-0	N09 2-1	m02 0-1	J01 0-0	N05 2-0	M28 1-1	S21 1-1	J11 4-1	O26 3-2	M03 2-0	D20 3-0	O05 0-2		A17 1-0	F01 5-3	M14 1-0	F15 3-2	A31 1-1	a21 3-1	N30 1-1	a11 0-0	S07 0-0
16 PRESTON N.E.	a21 3-2	M28 2-1	S03 2-2	S07 1-1	M07 3-2	m02 2-0	M14 0-3	N09 2-1	J18 1-3	F08 1-2	D14 1-4	O19 1-0	F11 3-1	a11 2-1	D28 1-1		a14 1-1	F22 2-2	D26 3-2	S21 2-2	M31 1-1	A24 3-0	O01 2-0	N05 3-0
17 READING	S07 1-1	M14 1-0	O05 0-0	S21 1-2	a01 0-0	A31 3-2	M28 0-0	N05 2-2	a20 1-0	F15 0-2	D20 0-1	J11 1-0	A17 0-1	a29 3-2	O19 1-1	F29 2-2		F08 2-1	N30 1-1	M04 3-4	J01 1-0	a11 6-1	N09 1-2	m02 3-2
18 SHREWSBURY T	O05 1-1	N30 1-3	a11 1-2	a21 3-2	S07 1-0	D21 1-1	F15 2-2	F01 0-2	A31 6-1	M03 0-0	N23 1-4	J25 1-1	M10 2-3	F29 0-1	N02 2-0	J11 2-0	O26 1-2		M20 0-1	J01 1-0	S21 0-0	M31 2-2	m02 1-3	A18 1-0
19 STOCKPORT CO	m02 2-0	N05 2-2	M13 5-0	O05 4-1	J04 2-1	S21 2-0	O18 0-4	J18 2-0	a10 4-1	M27 2-0	M06 0-1	F07 0-0	F22 1-1	D20 1-0	D14 3-0	A30 2-0	F11 1-0	N26 1-4		a20 0-0	A17 5-0	S06 2-1	M31 3-0	J01 3-3
20 STOKE C	J04 2-1	O12 2-0	A24 1-1	D28 0-0	D22 2-1	M11 1-2	a25 0-1	a03 3-0	M21 5-2	S14 2-2	S17 3-2	N02 0-2	M07 2-3	O26 2-0	D26 3-3	a18 2-1	J18 3-0	S04 1-0	S28 2-2		F01 2-1	N23 3-0	F12 1-0	D14 3-0
21 SWANSEA C	J18 0-2	A24 1-1	N08 3-1	M28 2-2	F11 1-1	F22 2-1	D26 3-0	J28 4-2	D14 1-0	a04 2-2	a28 1-1	a25 0-1	O11 0-0	N05 2-2	S28 1-0	S14 2-2	S03 1-2	a17 1-2	D28 2-1	O19 2-1		F08 1-0	M06 0-0	M14 3-0
22 TORQUAY U	M24 1-2	a25 2-0	N06 1-0	F01 1-1	D14 1-1	J18 0-2	S28 3-2	F22 3-0	J01 1-0	A31 0-1	A17 3-1	O12 0-1	a14 2-1	N09 1-0	a28 2-2	D20 1-0	S17 1-2	S14 1-2	a04 2-0	M28 1-0	O26 1-0		J04 1-0	M07 0-1
23 W.B.A.	O26 0-1	a04 2-2	J11 4-0	F15 1-1	F01 2-0	N02 1-1	a18 1-1	D22 3-1	A17 6-3	J01 2-3	M11 1-2	N23 2-1	S28 1-0	M03 1-3	S17 4-0	a25 3-0	M21 2-0	O12 2-0	S14 1-0	N30 2-2	J25 2-3	F29 1-0		A31 1-1
24 WIGAN A	a28 3-0	a18 1-1	M03 2-0	J11 2-1	M20 2-1	N22 2-0	A23 2-1	S20 1-2	O26 4-1	F28 0-2	a24 1-1	S17 1-3	S14 0-1	N30 1-1	a03 3-0	M10 3-0	O11 1-1	D28 1-1	S03 1-3	F15 1-0	N01 1-0	a07 0-0	D26 0-1	

DIVISION 4

	ALDERSHOT	BARNET	BLACKPOOL	BURNLEY	CARDIFF C	CARLISLE U	CHESTERFIELD	CREWE A	DONCASTER R	GILLINGHAM	HALIFAX T	HEREFORD U	LINCOLN C	MAIDSTONE U	MANSFIELD T	NORTHAMPTON T	ROCHDALE	ROTHERHAM U	SCARBOROUGH	SCUNTHORPE U	WALSALL	WREXHAM	YORK C
1 ALDERSHOT		J17 0-1	N05 2-5	D21 1-2	N08 1-2	S06 2-2		J01 0-2	D14 0-0	F11 0-0	S20 1-3		M14 0-3	A31 3-0	F21 1-3	M07 1-4	O04 1-1	O18 0-1		J03 0-0	F08 1-1		
2 BARNET	M03 5-0		O19 3-0	M24 0-0	S28 3-1	N05 4-2	N30 1-2	A17 4-7	S14 1-0	a18 2-0	N09 3-0	A31 1-0	J01 1-0	F15 3-2	D21 2-0	a04 3-0	M28 3-0	J11 2-5	F08 5-1	S17 3-2	a25 0-1	M14 2-0	O12 2-0
3 BLACKPOOL	M10 1-0	F18 4-2		J11 5-2	S14 1-1	D21 1-0	M21 3-1	N23 0-2	a14 1-0	S17 2-0	N30 3-0	M03 2-0	O13 3-0	F29 1-1	a04 2-1	a25 1-0	F15 3-0	S28 3-0	N02 1-1	A31 2-1	A17 3-0	N19 4-0	J01 3-1
4 BURNLEY	A24 2-0	M07 3-0	F22 1-1		a22 3-1	O05 2-0	S03 3-0	S07 1-1	D28 2-1	J18 4-1	M14 1-0	M31 2-0	F08 1-0	M28 2-1	N09 3-2	F11 5-0	S21 0-1	D26 1-2	a20 1-1	D14 1-1	O19 2-0	m02 1-2	N05 3-1
5 CARDIFF C	M20 2-0	a20 3-1	M31 1-1	F29 0-2		A31 1-0	J25 4-0	a28 1-1	O26 2-1	M10 2-3	a11 4-0	J11 1-0	A17 1-2	J01 0-5	J31 3-2	N23 3-2	S07 1-2	N30 1-0	S21 2-1	N02 2-2	M03 2-1	O05 5-0	F15 3-0
6 CARLISLE U		M10 1-3	A24 1-2	a25 1-1	D28 2-2		F29 1-2	O26 2-1	D26 1-0	N02 0-0	J25 1-1	N23 1-0	S14 0-2	N30 3-0	S17 1-2	a18 2-1	J11 0-0	S03 1-3	M21 2-2	O12 0-0	S28 3-3	M24 0-1	M03 1-1
7 CHESTERFIELD	S28 2-1	F11 3-2	N09 1-1	J01 0-2	M07 2-2	J04 0-0		M24 2-1	J18 0-0	a25 3-3	a07 4-0	O26 2-0	a18 1-5	A17 3-0	A31 0-2	D21 1-2	M14 0-1	O12 1-1	F22 1-0	S14 0-1	S17 0-1	M28 1-1	a04 1-3
8 CREWE A	S03 4-0	D26 3-0	M28 1-0	a04 1-0	A24 1-1	F07 2-1	F15 3-1		a24 1-0	S28 2-1	F28 3-2	N30 4-2	J11 1-0	N05 1-1	S13 1-2	S17 1-1	M03 1-1	D28 0-1	O19 3-3	a18 1-1	O11 0-1	N09 2-1	F25 1-0
9 DONCASTER R	F15 1-0	M31 1-0	S20 0-2	A31 1-4	F08 1-2	A17 0-3	M03 0-1	O05 1-3		O19 1-1	J11 0-2	F18 2-0	N30 1-5	m02 3-0	M14 0-1	J01 0-3	a20 2-0	N06 1-1	a11 3-2	D20 1-2	F29 0-1	S07 3-1	N08 0-1
10 GILLINGHAM	N30 3-1	S21 3-3	a11 3-2	M03 3-0	N05 0-0	M14 1-2	O05 0-1	a20 0-1	F01 2-1		m02 2-0	J01 2-1	F29 1-3	N09 1-1	M28 2-0	O26 3-1	M17 0-0	F15 5-1	S07 2-0	A17 4-0	J11 4-0	M31 2-1	D21 1-1
11 HALIFAX T		M21 3-1	F12 1-2	N02 0-2	S17 1-1	M06 3-2	O19 2-0	a14 2-1	F22 0-0	O12 0-3		M11 0-2	a25 1-4	D21 1-1	S27 1-3	A17 0-1	F08 1-1	S13 0-4	N22 1-0	J18 1-4	a03 1-0	D13 4-3	A30 0-0
12 HEREFORD U	O12 1-0	D28 2-2	J18 1-2	S14 2-0	F22 2-2	M28 1-0	F08 1-0	F12 1-2	M07 0-1	S04 2-0	N06 0-2		S28 3-0	M14 2-2	F25 0-1	a28 1-2	N09 1-1	a04 1-0	A24 4-1	a25 1-2	a18 1-2	D26 3-1	S17 2-1
13 LINCOLN C	N02 0-0	S04 0-6	m02 2-0	O26 0-3	D26 0-0	a01 1-0	S21 1-2	F22 2-2	F12 2-0	J04 1-0	O05 0-0	a20 3-0		a11 1-0	M07 2-0	M21 1-2	D28 0-3	A24 0-2	D17 0-2	N23 4-2	M11 1-0	J18 0-0	M18 0-0
14 MAIDSTONE U	D28 1-2	J08 1-1	J04 0-0	N23 0-1	S04 1-1	F12 5-1	D26 0-1	M11 2-0	O12 2-2	M21 1-1	A24 0-1	N02 3-2	S17 0-2		a25 0-0	J18 1-1	O19 1-1	a18 0-0	M07 2-1	a04 0-1	S14 2-1	F22 2-4	S28 1-0
15 MANSFIELD T	J11 3-0	A24 1-2	S07 1-1	M21 0-1	O19 3-0	a11 2-1	D28 2-1	M31 4-3	N02 2-2	N23 4-3	a21 3-2	F15 1-1	M24 0-0	O05 2-0		M10 2-0	m02 2-1	M03 1-0	D26 1-2	F08 1-3	N30 3-1	S03 3-0	F29 5-2
16 NORTHAMPTON T	F04 1-0	S07 1-1	O06 1-1	N30 1-2	M28 0-0	S21 2-2	O15 1-1	a11 0-1	S03 3-1	F08 0-0	D26 4-0	F29 0-1	N09 1-0	M03 1-0	N05 1-2		M31 2-2	M14 1-2	D07 3-2	O19 0-1	F15 0-1	D28 1-1	J11 2-2
17 ROCHDALE		N23 1-0	D14 4-2	m05 1-3	a04 2-0	F22 3-1	N02 3-3	J18 1-0	S28 1-1	M07 2-1	O26 1-0	M21 3-1	A31 1-0	a07 1-2	O12 0-2	S14 1-0		S17 1-1	F11 2-2	M10 2-0	J01 1-1	a22 2-1	A17 1-1
18 ROTHERHAM U	F01 2-0	F22 3-0	a20 2-0	A17 2-1	F11 1-2	J01 1-0	m02 1-1	A31 1-2	M10 3-1	D14 1-1	M31 1-0	S07 0-0	D21 1-1	S21 3-3	J18 1-1	N02 1-0	a11 2-0		J04 0-2	M21 5-0	N22 2-1	M07 3-0	O25 4-0
19 SCARBOROUGH	S14 0-2	O26 0-4	M14 1-2	S28 3-1	a14 2-2	N09 2-2	M17 3-2	F18 2-1	S19 1-0	a04 2-1	M28 3-0	a07 1-1	F15 1-1	a29 2-0	A17 0-0	O12 2-1	N30 3-2	F29 0-3		J01 4-1	A31 2-3	N05 4-1	a25 1-0
20 SCUNTHORPE U	F29 1-0	a11 1-1	D28 2-1	F15 2-2	M14 1-0	m02 4-0	M31 2-0	S21 1-0	A24 3-2	D26 2-0	M03 1-0	O05 1-1	M28 0-2	S07 2-0	O26 1-4	a14 3-0	N05 6-2	N09 1-0	S03 1-1		J25 1-1	a20 3-1	N30 1-0
21 WALSALL	O26 3-1	O05 2-0	D26 4-2	F01 2-2	J18 0-0	a21 0-0	a11 2-2	m02 2-3	J04 1-3	F22 0-1	S07 3-0	S21 3-0	N05 0-0	M31 1-1	F11 3-3	J28 1-2	S03 1-3	M28 0-2	D28 0-0	M07 2-1		A24 0-0	M14 1-1
22 WREXHAM	S17 0-0	N02 1-0	F08 1-1	O12 2-6	a25 0-3	O19 3-0	N23 0-1	M21 1-0	a03 1-2	S14 2-1	F15 2-0	A17 0-1	M03 1-1	J11 0-0	J01 3-2	A31 2-2	F29 2-1	a28 0-3	M10 2-0	S28 4-0	D20 2-1		a18 2-1
23 YORK C	N23 1-0	m02 1-4	S03 1-0	a28 1-2	D14 1-3	J18 2-0	S07 0-1	M07 1-1	M21 1-1	A24 1-1	D28 1-1	a11 1-0	O19 1-1	a20 1-1	J04 1-2	F22 0-0	D26 0-1	F08 1-1	O05 4-1	F11 3-0	N02 2-0	S21 2-2	

LEAGUE TABLES

DIVISION 1

	P	W	D	L	F	A	W	D	L	F	A	Pts
Leeds U	42	13	8	0	38	13	9	8	4	36	24	82
Manchester U	42	12	7	2	34	13	9	8	4	29	20	78
Sheffield W	42	13	5	3	39	24	8	7	6	23	25	75
Arsenal	42	12	7	2	51	22	7	8	6	30	24	72
Manchester C	42	13	4	4	32	14	7	6	8	29	34	70
Liverpool	42	13	5	3	34	17	3	11	7	13	23	64
Aston Villa	42	13	3	5	31	16	4	6	11	17	28	60
Nottingham F	42	10	7	4	36	27	6	4	11	24	31	59
Sheffield U	42	9	6	6	29	23	7	3	11	36	40	57
Crystal P	42	7	8	6	24	25	7	7	7	29	36	57
QPR	42	6	10	5	25	21	6	8	7	23	26	54
Everton	42	8	8	5	28	19	5	6	10	24	32	53
Wimbledon	42	10	5	6	32	20	3	9	9	21	33	53
Chelsea	42	7	8	6	31	30	6	6	9	19	30	53
Tottenham H	42	7	3	11	33	35	8	4	9	25	28	52
Southampton	42	7	5	9	17	28	7	5	9	22	27	52
Oldham A	42	11	5	5	46	36	3	4	14	17	31	51
Norwich C	42	8	6	7	29	28	3	6	12	18	35	45
Coventry C	42	6	7	8	18	15	5	4	12	17	29	44
Luton T	42	10	7	4	25	17	0	5	16	13	54	42
Notts Co	42	7	5	9	24	29	3	5	13	16	33	40
West Ham U	42	6	6	9	22	24	3	5	13	15	35	38

DIVISION 2

	P	W	D	L	F	A	W	D	L	F	A	Pts
Ipswich T	46	16	3	4	42	22	8	9	6	28	28	84
Middlesbrough	46	15	6	2	37	13	8	5	10	21	28	80
Derby Co	46	11	4	8	35	24	12	5	6	34	27	78
Leicester C	46	14	4	5	41	24	9	4	10	21	31	77
Cambridge U	46	10	9	4	34	19	9	8	6	31	28	74
Blackburn R	46	14	5	4	41	21	7	6	10	29	32	74
Charlton A	46	9	7	7	25	23	11	4	8	29	25	71
Swindon T	46	15	3	5	38	22	3	12	8	31	33	69
Portsmouth	46	15	6	2	41	12	4	6	13	24	39	69
Watford	46	9	5	9	25	23	9	6	8	26	25	65
Wolves	46	11	6	6	36	24	7	4	12	25	30	64
Southend U	46	11	5	7	37	26	6	6	11	26	37	62
Bristol R	46	11	9	3	43	29	5	5	13	17	34	62
Tranmere R	46	9	9	5	37	32	5	10	8	19	24	61
Millwall	46	10	4	9	32	32	7	6	10	32	39	61
Barnsley	46	11	4	8	27	25	5	7	11	19	32	59
Bristol C	46	10	8	5	30	24	3	7	13	25	47	54
Sunderland	46	10	8	5	36	23	4	3	16	25	42	53
Grimsby T	46	7	5	11	25	28	7	6	10	22	34	53
Newcastle U	46	9	8	6	38	30	4	5	14	28	54	52
Oxford U	46	10	6	7	39	30	3	5	15	27	43	50
Plymouth A	46	11	5	7	26	26	2	4	17	16	38	48
Brighton & HA	46	7	7	9	36	37	5	4	14	20	40	47
Port Vale	46	7	8	8	23	25	3	7	13	19	34	45

DIVISION 3

	P	W	D	L	F	A	W	D	L	F	A	Pts
Brentford	46	17	2	4	55	29	8	5	10	26	26	82
Birmingham C	46	15	6	2	42	22	8	6	9	27	30	81
Huddersfield T	46	15	4	4	36	15	7	8	8	23	23	78
Stoke C	46	14	5	4	45	24	7	9	7	24	25	77
Stockport Co	46	15	5	3	47	19	7	5	11	28	32	76
Peterboro' U	46	13	7	3	38	20	7	7	9	27	38	74
WBA	46	12	6	5	45	25	7	8	8	19	24	71
Bournemouth	46	13	4	6	33	18	7	7	9	19	30	71
Fulham	46	11	7	5	29	16	8	6	9	28	37	70
Leyton Orient	46	12	7	4	36	18	6	4	13	26	34	65
Hartlepool U	46	12	5	6	30	21	6	6	11	27	36	65
Reading	46	9	8	6	33	27	7	5	11	26	35	61
Bolton W	46	10	9	4	26	19	4	8	11	31	37	59
Hull C	46	9	4	10	28	23	7	7	9	26	31	59
Wigan A	46	11	6	6	33	21	4	8	11	25	43	59
Bradford C	46	8	10	5	36	30	5	9	9	26	31	58
Preston NE	46	12	7	4	42	32	3	5	15	19	40	57
Chester C	46	10	6	7	34	29	4	8	11	22	30	56
Swansea C	46	10	9	4	35	24	4	5	14	20	41	56
Exeter C	46	11	7	5	34	25	3	4	16	23	55	53
Bury	46	8	7	8	31	31	5	5	13	24	43	51
Shrewsbury T	46	7	7	9	30	31	5	4	14	23	37	47
Torquay U	46	13	3	7	29	19	0	5	18	13	49	47
Darlington	46	5	5	13	31	39	5	2	16	25	51	37

DIVISION 4

	P	W	D	L	F	A	W	D	L	F	A	Pts
Burnley	42	14	4	3	42	16	11	4	6	37	27	83
Rotherham U	42	12	6	3	38	16	10	5	6	32	21	77
Mansfield T	42	13	4	4	43	26	10	4	7	32	27	77
Blackpool	42	17	3	1	48	13	5	7	9	23	32	76
Scunthorpe U	42	14	5	2	39	18	7	4	10	25	41	72
Crewe A	42	12	6	3	33	20	8	4	9	33	31	70
Barnet	42	16	1	4	48	23	5	5	11	33	38	69
Rochdale	42	12	6	3	34	22	6	7	8	23	31	67
Cardiff C	42	13	3	5	42	26	4	12	5	24	27	66
Lincoln C	42	9	5	7	21	24	8	6	7	29	20	62
Gillingham	42	12	5	4	41	19	3	7	11	22	34	57
Scarborough	42	12	5	4	39	28	3	7	11	25	40	57
Chesterfield	42	6	7	8	26	28	8	4	9	23	33	53
Wrexham	42	11	4	6	31	26	3	5	13	21	47	51
Walsall	42	5	10	6	28	26	7	3	11	20	32	49
Northampton T	42	5	9	7	25	23	6	4	11	21	34	46
Hereford U	42	9	4	8	31	24	3	4	14	13	33	44
Maidstone U	42	6	9	6	24	22	2	9	10	21	34	42
York C	42	6	9	6	26	23	2	7	12	16	35	40
Halifax T	42	7	5	9	23	35	3	3	15	11	40	38
Doncaster R	42	6	2	13	21	35	3	6	12	19	30	35
Carlisle U	42	5	9	7	24	27	2	4	15	17	40	34

Aldershot resigned from the League

The Football Association Cup

1871-72

First Round
WANDERERS v Harrow Chequers† .... wo
Clapham R v Upton Park 3-0
Crystal Palace v Hitchin 0-0
Maidenhead v Great Marlow 2-0
Queen's Park, Glasgow .... bye
Donington School (Spalding) .... bye
ROYAL ENGINEERS v Reigate Priory† .... wo
Hampstead Heathens .... bye
Barnes v Civil Service 2-0

Second Round
WANDERERS v Clapham R 3-1
Crystal Palace v Maidenhead 3-0
Queen's Park v Donington School† .... wo
ROYAL ENGINEERS v Hitchin 5-0
Hampstead Heathens v Barnes 1-1, 1-0

Third Round
WANDERERS v Crystal Palace* .... draw
Queen's Park .... bye
ROYAL ENGINEERS v Hampstead Heathens 2-0

Semi-final
WANDERERS v Queen's Park† .... wo
ROYAL ENGINEERS v Crystal Palace 3-0

FINAL (Kennington Oval)
WANDERERS 1
ROYAL ENGINEERS 0
Wanderers: R.de C.Welch; C.W.Alcock, M.P.Betts, A.G.Bonsor, E.E.Bowen, W.P.Crake, T.C.Hooman, E.Lubbock, A.C.Thompson, R.W.S.Vidal, C.H.R.Wollaston.
Goalscorer: M.P.Betts‡
Royal Engineers: Capt Merriman; Capt Marindin, Lt Addison, Lt Creswell, Lt Mitchell, Lt Renny-Tailyour, Lt Rich, Lt Goodwyn, Lt Muirhead, Lt Cotter, Lt Bogle.
Referee: A.Stair (Upton Park) Attendance: 2,000
*Clubs drawing were permitted to either replay or proceed to next round. ‡M.P.Betts played under the pseudonym of A.H.Chequer, a loose reference to him representing another club 'a Harrow Chequer'.
wo = walk-over. † = scratched.

1872-73

First Round
Clapham R v Hitchin† .... wo
OXFORD UNIVERSITY v Crystal Palace 3-2
Royal Engineers v Civil Service 3-0
1st Surrey Rifles v Upton Park 2-0
Maidenhead v Marlow 1-0
South Norwood v Barnes 1-0
Windsor Home Park v Reigate Priory 4-2
Queen's Park, Glasgow* .... bye
WANDERERS‡ Cup holders.

Second Round
Clapham R v OXFORD UNIVERSITY 0-3
Royal Engineers .... bye
1st Surrey Rifles v Maidenhead 0-3
South Norwood v Windsor Home Park 0-3

Third Round
OXFORD UNIVERSITY v Royal Engineers 1-0
Maidenhead v Windsor Home Park 1-0

Fourth Round
OXFORD UNIVERSITY v Maidenhead 4-0

Semi-final
OXFORD UNIVERSITY v Queen's Park† .... wo

FINAL (Amateur Athletic Club, Lillie Bridge)
WANDERERS 2
OXFORD UNIVERSITY 0
Wanderers: E.E.Bowen; C.M.Thompson, R.de C.Welch, Hon A.F.Kinnaird, L.S.Howell, C.H.R.Wollaston, J.R.Sturgiss, Revd H.H.Stewart, W.S.Kenyon-Slaney, R.K.Kingsford, A.G.Bonsor.
Goalscorers: Wollaston, Kinnaird
Oxford University: A.Kirke-Smith; A.J.Leach, C.C.Mackarness, F.H.Birley, C.J.Longman, F.B.Chappell-Maddison, H.B.Dixon, W.B.Paton, R.W.S.Vidal, W.E.Sumner, C.J.Ottaway.
Referee: A.Stair (Upton Park) Attendance: 3,000

*Queen's Park, Glasgow, because of travelling involved, were excused until the semi-final where they scratched to Oxford University. ‡This was the only occasion when the Cup holders were excused from taking part until the Final. Excercising their right allowed by Rule 14 the Wanderers, as Cup holders, had choice of ground.
wo = walk-over. † = scratched.

1873-74

First Round
OXFORD UNIVERSITY v Upton Park 4-0
Barnes v 1st Surrey Rifles 0-0, 1-0
Wanderers v Southall† .... wo
Trojans v Farningham† .... wo
Clapham R v AAC† .... wo
Cambridge University v South Norwood 1-0
Sheffield v Shropshire W .... 0-0, wo
Pilgrims v Great Marlow 1-0
ROYAL ENGINEERS v Brondesbury 5-0
Uxbridge v Gitanos 3-0
Maidenhead v Civil Service† .... wo
High Wycombe v Old Etonians† .... wo
Swifts v Crystal Palace 1-0
Woodford Wells v Reigate Priory 3-2

Second Round
OXFORD UNIVERSITY v Barnes 2-0
Wanderers v Trojans† .... wo
Clapham R v Cambridge University 1-1, 1-1, 4-1
Sheffield v Pilgrims 1-0
ROYAL ENGINEERS v Uxbridge 2-1
Maidenhead v High Wycombe 1-0
Swifts v Woodford Wells 2-1

Third Round
OXFORD UNIVERSITY v Wanderers 1-1, 1-0
Clapham R v Sheffield 2-1
ROYAL ENGINEERS v Maidenhead 7-0
Swifts .... bye

Semi-final
OXFORD UNIVERSITY v Clapham R 1-0
ROYAL ENGINEERS v Swifts 2-0

FINAL (Kennington Oval)
OXFORD UNIVERSITY 2
ROYAL ENGINEERS 0
Oxford University: C.E.B.Neapean; C.C.Mackarness, F.H.Birley, F.T.Green, R.W.S.Vidal, C.J.Ottaway, R.H.Benson, F.J.Patton, W.S.Rawson, F.B.Chappell-Maddison, Revd A.H.Johnson.
Goalscorers: Mackarness, Patton
Royal Engineers: Capt Merriman; Maj Marindin, Lt G.W.Addison, Lt G.C.Onslow, LT H.G.Oliver, Lt T.Digby, Lt H.W.Renny-Tailyour, Lt H.E.Rawson, Lt J.E.Blackman, Lt A.K.Wood, Lt P.G.von Donop.
Referee: A.Stair (Upton Park) Attendance: 2,000
wo = walk-over. † = scratched.

1874-75

First Round
ROYAL ENGINEERS v Great Marlow 3-0
Cambridge University v Crystal Palace 0-0, 2-1
Clapham R v Panthers 3-0
Pilgrims v South Norwood 3-1
Oxford University v Brondesbury 6-0
Windsor Home Park v Uxbridge† .... wo
Wanderers v Farningham 16-0
Barnes v Upton Park 3-0
OLD ETONIANS v Swifts 0-0, 1-1, 3-0
Maidenhead v Hitchin 1-0
Reigate Priory .... bye
Shropshire W v Sheffield† .... wo
Civil Service v Harrow Chequers† .... wo
Woodford Wells v High Wycombe 1-0
Southall v Leyton 0-0, 5-0

Second Round
ROYAL ENGINEERS v Cambridge University 5-0
Clapham R v Pilgrims 2-0
Oxford University v Windsor Home Park† .... wo
Wanderers v Barnes 5-0
OLD ETONIANS .... bye
Maidenhead v Reigate Priory 2-1
Shropshire W v Civil Service 1-0
Woodford Wells v Southall 3-0

Third Round
ROYAL ENGINEERS v Clapham R 3-2
Oxford University v Wanderers 2-1
OLD ETONIANS v Maidenhead 1-0
Shropshire W v Woodford Wells 1-1, 2-0

Semi-final
ROYAL ENGINEERS v Oxford University 1-1, 1-0
OLD ETONIANS v Shropshire W 1-0

FINAL (Kennington Oval)
ROYAL ENGINEERS 2
OLD ETONIANS 0
(following a 1-1 draw after extra-time)
Royal Engineers: Maj Merriman; Lt G.H.Sim, Lt G.C.Onslow; Lt R.M.Ruck, Lt P.G.von Donop, Lt C.K.Wood; Lt H.E.Rawson, Lt R.H.Stafford, Capt H.W.Renny-Tailyour, Lt Mein, Lt C.Wingfield-Stratford.
Goalscorers: Renny-Tailyour, Stafford
Old Etonians: Capt E.H.Drummond-Moray; M.Farrer, E.Lubbock, F.H.Wilson, Hon A.F.Kinnaird, J.H.Stronge, F.J.Patton, C.E.Farmer, A.G.Bonsor, A.Lubbock, T.Hammond.
(C.J.Ottaway, W.S.Kenyon-Slaney, R.H.Benson and A.G.Thompson took part in the first match in place of A.Lubbock, T.Hammond, M.Farrer and Capt E.H.Drummond-Moray). C.E.Farmer was the goalkeeper in the first game.
Referee: C.W.Alcock (Wanderers) Attendance: 3,000
The venue and referee were the same for the first game, Renny-Tailyour scoring for Royal Engineers and Bonsor for Old Etonians.
wo = walk-over. † = scratched.

The Royal Engineers team in 1875, showing nine of the side which lifted the FA Cup. Back row (left to right): Lt H.L.Mulholland, Lt G.C.Onslow, Lt H.E.Rawson, unknown, Lt A.L.Mein, Lt C.V.Wingfield-Stratford. Middle row: Lt R.M.Ruck, Maj W.Merriman (captain), Capt H.W.Renny-Tailyour, Lt P.G.von Donop. Front row: Lt G.H.Sim, Lt G.T.Jones.

1875-76

First Round
WANDERERS v 1st Surrey Rifles ... 5-0
Crystal Palace v 105th Regiment ... 0-0, 3-0
Sheffield Club v Shropshire W† ... wo
Upton Park v Southall ... 1-0
Swifts v Great Marlow ... 2-0
South Norwood v Clydesdale† ... wo
Royal Engineers v High Wycombe ... 15-0
Panthers v Woodford Wells ... 1-0
Reigate Priory v Barnes ... 1-0
Cambridge University v Civil Service† ... wo
Oxford University v Forest School ... 6-0
Herts Rgrs v Rochester ... 4-0
OLD ETONIANS v Pilgrims ... 4-1
Maidenhead v Ramblers ... 2-0
Clapham R v Hitchin† ... wo
Leyton v Harrow Chequers† ... wo

Second Round
WANDERERS v Crystal Palace ... 3-0
Sheffield Club v Upton Park† ... wo
Swifts v South Norwood ... 5-0
Royal Engineers v Panthers† ... wo
Reigate Priory v Cambridge University ... 0-8
Oxford University v Herts Rgrs ... 8-2
OLD ETONIANS v Maidenhead ... 8-0
Clapham R v Leyton ... 12-0

Third Round
WANDERERS v Sheffield Club ... 2-0
Swifts v Royal Engineers ... 3-1
Cambridge University v Oxford University ... 0-4
OLD ETONIANS v Clapton R ... 1-0

Semi-final
WANDERERS v Swifts ... 2-1
Oxford University v OLD ETONIANS ... 0-1

FINAL (Kennington Oval)
WANDERERS ... 3
OLD ETONIANS ... 0
(after a 1-1 draw)

Wanderers: W.D.O.Greig; A.Stratford, W.Lindsay, F.B.C.Maddison, F.H.Birley, C.H.R.Wollaston, H.Heron, F.Heron, J.H.Edwards, J.Kenrick, T.Hughes.
Goalscorers: Wollaston, Hughes 2
Old Etonians: Q.Hogg; E.Lubbock, Hon E.Lyttelton, M.G.Faner, Hon A.F.Kinnaird, J.H.Stronge, W.S.Kenyon-Slaney, Hon A.Lyttelton, J.R.Sturgis, A.G.Bonsor, H.P.Allene. (C.Meysey, A.C.Thompson and J.E.C.Welldon took part in the first match in place of J.H.Stronge, M.G.Faner and E.Lubbock).
Referee: R.A.Ogilvie (Clapham Rovers) Attendance: 1,500

Final referee Ogilvie was also a linesman in the first game at the same venue when the referee was W.S.Buchanan, also of Clapham Rovers. Edwards scored for Wanderers in the 1-1 draw with Bonsor netting for Old Etonians.
wo = walk-over. † = scratched.

1876-77

First Round
WANDERERS v Saffron Walden† ... wo
Southall v Old Wykehamists† ... wo
Pilgrims v Ramblers ... 4-1
Panthers v Wood Grange ... 3-0
Cambridge University v High Wycombe† ... wo
Clapham R v Reigate Priory ... 5-0
Rochester v Highbury Union ... 5-0
Swifts v Reading Hornets ... 2-0
Royal Engineers v Old Harrovians ... 2-1
Shropshire W v Druids† ... wo
Sheffield v Trojans† ... wo
South Norwood v Saxons ... 4-1
OXFORD UNIVERSITY v Old Salopians† ... wo
105th Regiment v 1st Surrey Rifles ... 3-0
Queen's Park, Glasgow ... bye
Upton Park v Leyton ... 7-0
Barnes v Old Etonians† ... wo
Great Marlow v Herts Rgrs ... 2-1
Forest School v Gresham ... 4-1

Second Round
WANDERERS v Southall ... 6-0
Pilgrims v Panthers ... 1-0
Cambridge University v Clapham R ... 2-1
Rochester v Swifts ... 1-0
Royal Engineers v Shropshire W ... 3-0
Sheffield v South Norwood ... 7-0
OXFORD UNIVERSITY v 105th Regiment ... 6-1
Queen's Park ... bye
Upton Park v Barnes ... 1-0
Great Marlow v Forest School ... 1-0

Third Round
WANDERERS v Pilgrims ... 3-0
Cambridge University v Rochester ... 4-0
Royal Engineers v Sheffield ... 1-0
OXFORD UNIVERSITY v Queen's Park† ... wo
Upton Park v Great Marlow ... 2-2, 1-0

Fourth Round
WANDERERS ... bye
Cambridge University v Royal Engineers ... 1-0
OXFORD UNIVERSITY v Upton Park ... 0-0, 1-0

Semi-final
WANDERERS v Cambridge University ... 1-0
OXFORD UNIVERSITY ... bye

FINAL (Kennington Oval)
WANDERERS ... 2
OXFORD UNIVERSITY ... 1
(after extra-time)

Wanderers: Hon A.F.Kinnaird; W.Lindsay, A.Stratford, F.H.Birley, C.A.Denton, F.T.Green, H.Heron, T.Hughes, J.Kenrick, H.Wace, C.H.R.Wollaston.
Goalscorers: Kenrick, Lindsay
Oxford University: E.H.Allington; J.Bain, O.R.Dunnell, J.H.Savory, A.H.Todd, E.W.Waddington, P.H.Fernandez, A.F.Hills, H.S.Otter, E.H.Parry, W.S.rawson.
Goalscorer: Kinnaird (own-goal)
Referee: S.H.Wright (Marlow) Attendance: 3,000
wo = walk-over. † = scratched.

1877-78

First Round
WANDERERS v Panthers ... 9-1
High Wycombe v Wood Grange ... 4-0
Barnes v St Marks† ... wo
Great Marlow v Hendon ... 2-0
Sheffield v Nottingham ... 1-1, 3-0
Darwen v Manchester ... 3-0
ROYAL ENGINEERS v Highbury Union† ... wo
Pilgrims v Ramblers ... 0-0, 1-0
Druids (Wales) v Shropshire W ... 1-0
Oxford University v Herts Rgrs ... 5-2
Old Foresters v Old Wykehamists† ... wo
Clapham R v Grantham ... 2-0
Swifts v Leyton ... 3-2
Old Harrovians v 105th Regiment ... 2-0
1st Surrey Rifles v Forest School ... 1-0
Cambridge University v Southall Park ... 3-1
Maidenhead v Reading Hornets ... 10-0
Upton Park v Rochester ... 3-0
Reading v South Norwood ... 2-0
Remnants v St Stephens ... 4-0
Hawks v Minerva ... 5-2
Queen's Park, Glasgow ... bye (later withdrew)

Second Round
WANDERERS v High Wycombe ... 9-0
Barnes v Great Marlow ... 3-1
Sheffield v Darwen ... 1-0
ROYAL ENGINEERS v Pilgrims ... 6-0
Druids ... bye
Oxford University v Old Foresters ... 1-0
Clapham R v Swifts ... 4-0
Old Harrovians v 1st Surrey Rifles ... 6-0
Cambridge University v Maidenhead ... 4-2
Upton Park v Reading ... 1-0
Remnants v Hawks ... 2-0

Third Round
WANDERERS v Barnes ... 1-1, 4-1
Sheffield ... bye
ROYAL ENGINEERS v Druids ... 8-0
Oxford University v Clapham R ... 2-2, 3-2
Old Harrovians v Cambridge University ... 2-2, 2-0
Upton Park v Remnants ... 3-0

Fourth Round
WANDERERS v Sheffield ... 3-0
ROYAL ENGINEERS v Oxford University ... 3-3, 2-2, 4-2
Old Harrovians v Upton Park ... 3-1

Semi-final
WANDERERS ... bye
ROYAL ENGINEERS v Old Harrovians ... 2-1

FINAL (Kennington Oval)
WANDERERS ... 3
ROYAL ENGINEERS ... 1

Wanderers: J.Kirkpatrick; A.Stratford, W.Lindsay, Hon A.F.Kinnaird, F.T.Green, C.H.R.Wollaston, H.Heron, J.G.Wylie, H.Wace, C.A.Denton, J.Kenrick.
Goalscorers: Kenrick 2, Kinnaird
Royal Engineers: L.B.Friend; J.H.Cowan, W.J.Morris, C.B.Mayne, F.C.Heath, C.E.Haynes, M.Lindsay, R.B.Hedley, F.G.Bond, H.H.Barnett, O.E.Ruck.
Goalscorer: Unknown
Referee: S.R.Bastard (Upton Park) Attendance: 4,500

Wanderers won outright but the trophy was restored to the Football Association.
wo = walk-over. † = scratched.

1878-79

First Round
OLD ETONIANS v Wanderers ... 7-2
Reading v Hendon ... 1-0
Minerva v 105th Regiment† ... wo
Grey Friars v Great Marlow ... 2-1
Darwen v Birch, Manchester† ... wo
Eagley, Bolton ... bye
Remnants v Unity† ... wo
Pilgrims v Brentwood ... 3-1
Nottingham F v Nottingham ... 3-1
Sheffield v Grantham ... 1-1, 3-1
Old Harrovians v Southill Park ... 8-0
Panthers v Runnymede† ... wo
Oxford University v Wednesbury Strollers ... 7-0
Royal Engineers v Old Foresters ... 3-0
Barnes v Maidenhead ... 1-1, 4-0
Upton Park v Saffron Walden ... 5-0
CLAPHAM R v Finchley† ... wo
Forest School v Rochester ... 4-2
Cambridge University v Herts Rgrs ... 2-0
South Norwood v Leyton† ... wo
Swifts v Hawks ... 2-1
Romford v Ramblers ... 3-1

Second Round
OLD ETONIANS v Reading ... 1-0
Minerva v Grey Friars ... 3-0
Darwen v Eagley ... 0-0, 4-1
Remnants v Pilgrims ... 6-2
Nottingham F v Sheffield ... 2-0
Old Harrovians v Panthers ... 3-0
Oxford University v Royal Engineers ... 4-0
Barnes v Upton Park ... 3-2
CLAPHAM R v Forest School ... 10-1
Cambridge University v South Norwood ... 3-0
Swifts v Romford ... 3-1

Third Round
OLD ETONIANS v Minerva ... 5-2
Darwen v Remnants ... 3-2
Nottingham F v Old Harrovians ... 2-0
Oxford University v Barnes ... 2-1
CLAPHAM R v Cambridge University ... 1-0
Swifts ... bye

Fourth Round
OLD ETONIANS v Darwen ... 5-5, 2-2, 6-2
Nottingham F v Oxford University ... 2-1
CLAPHAM R v Swifts ... 8-1

Semi-final
OLD ETONIANS v Nottingham F ... 2-1
CLAPHAM R ... bye

FINAL (Kennington Oval)
OLD ETONIANS ... 1
CLAPHAM ROVERS ... 0

Old Etonians: J.P.Hawtrey; E.Christian, L.Bury, Hon A.F.Kinnaird, E.Lubbock, C.J.Clerke, N.Pares, H.C.Goodhart, H.Whitfield, J.B.T.Chevallier, H.Beaufoy.
Goalscorer: Clerke
Clapham Rovers: R.H.Birkett; R.A.Ogilvie, E.Field, N.C.Bailey, J.F.M.Prinsep, F.L.Rawson, A.J.Stanley, S.W.Scott, H.S.Bevington, E.F.Growse, C.Keith-Falconer.
Referee: C.W.Alcock (Wanderers) Attendance: 5,000
wo = walk-over. † = scratched.

1879-80

First Round
Blackburn R v Tyne Association ... 5-1
Turton v Brigg ... 7-0
Darwen v Eagley ... 1-0
Nottingham F v Notts Club ... 4-0
Sheffield v Queen's Park, Glasgow† ... wo
Providence, Sheffield ... bye
Maidenhead v Calthorpe, Birmingham ... 3-1
Stafford Road* v Wednesbury Strollers ... 2-0
OXFORD UNIVERSITY v Great Marlow ... 1-1, 1-0
Birmingham v Panthers† ... wo
Henley v Reading† ... wo
Aston Villa ... bye
Old Carthusians v Acton ... 4-0
Hotspurs v Argonauts ... 1-1, 1-0
Old Etonians v Barnes† ... wo
Wanderers v Rochester ... 6-0
West End v Swifts† ... wo

Royal Engineers v Cambridge University 2-0
Grey Friars v Hanover Ath 2-1
Old Harrovians v Finchley 2-0
Gresham v Kildare 3-0
Upton Park v Remnants 1-1, 5-2
Hendon v Old Foresters 1-1, 2-2, 3-1
CLAPHAM R v Romford 7-0
Pilgrims v Clarence 5-2
South Norwood v Brentwood 4-2
Mosquitoes v St Peter's Institute 3-1
Herts Rgrs v Minerva 2-1

Second Round
CLAPHAM R v South Norwood 4-0
Pilgrims v Herts Rgrs† wo
Hendon v Mosquitoes 7-1
Old Etonians bye
Wanderers v Old Carthusians 1-0
West End v Hotspurs 1-0
OXFORD UNIVERSITY v Birmingham 6-0
Aston Villa v Stafford Road* 1-1, 3-1
Maidenhead v Henley 3-1
Royal Engineers v Upton Park 4-1
Old Harrovians bye
Grey Friars v Gresham 9-0
Nottingham F v Turton 6-0
Blackburn R v Darwen 3-1
Sheffield v Sheffield Providence 3-3, 3-0

Third Round
CLAPHAM R v Pilgrims 7-0
Hendon bye
Old Etonians v Wanderers 3-1
West End bye
OXFORD UNIVERSITY v Aston Villa† wo
Maidenhead bye
Royal Engineers v Old Harrovians 2-0
Grey Friars bye
Nottingham F v Blackburn R 6-0
Sheffield bye

Fourth Round
CLAPHAM R v Hendon 2-0
Old Etonians v West End 5-1
OXFORD UNIVERSITY v Maidenhead 1-0
Royal Engineers v Grey Friars 1-0
Nottingham F v Sheffield ‡2-2

Fifth Round
CLAPHAM R v Old Etonians 1-0
OXFORD UNIVERSITY v Royal Engineers 1-1, 1-0
Nottingham F bye

Semi-final
CLAPHAM R bye
OXFORD UNIVERSITY v Nottingham F 1-0

FINAL (Kennington Oval)
CLAPHAM ROVERS 1
OXFORD UNIVERSITY 0
Clapham Rovers: R.H.Birkett; R.A.Ogilvie, E.Field, A.Weston, N.C.Bailey, H.Brougham, A.J.Stanley, F.Barry, F.J.Sparks, C.A.Lloyd-Jones, E.A.Ram.
Goalscorer: Lloyd-Jones
Oxford University: P.C.Parr; C.W.Wilson, C.J.S.King, F.A.H.Phillips, B.Rogers, R.T.Heygate, G.B.Childs, J.Eyre, F.D.Crowdy, E.H.Hill, J.B.Lubbock.
Referee: Major Marindin (Royal Engineers)
Attendance: 6,000

Oxford won the Cup without conceding a goal in any round.
‡Sheffield disqualified. *Wolverhampton. wo = walk-over. † = scratched.

1880-81

First Round
Astley Bridge v Eagley 4-0
Blackburn R v Sheffield Providence 6-2
Turton v Britannia Recreation, Brigg 5-0
Sheffield Wed v Queen's Park, Glasgow† wo
Sheffield Club v Blackburn Olympic 5-4
Darwen v Brigg 8-0
Aston Villa v Wednesbury Strollers 5-3
Stafford Road* v Spilsby 7-0
Nottingham v Derby 4-4, 4-2
Grantham v Birmingham Calthorpe 2-1
Nottingham F v Caius College, Cambridge† wo
Reading v Hotspurs 5-1
Weybridge Swallows v Henley 3-0
Clapham R v Finchley 15-0
Upton Park v Mosquitoes 8-1
Swifts v Old Foresters 1-1, 2-1
Herts Rgrs v Barnes 6-0
OLD ETONIANS v Brentwood 10-0
Hendon v St Peter's Institute 8-1
Maidenhead v Old Harrovians 1-1, 1-0
Grey Friars v Windsor Home Park 0-0, 3-1
Dreadnought v Rochester 2-1
OLD CARTHUSIANS v Saffron Walden 7-0
Royal Engineers v Remnants 0-0, 1-0
Rangers v Wanderers† wo
Pilgrims v Old Philberdians† wo
Great Marlow v Clarence 6-0
West End v Hanover Utd 1-0
Reading Abbey v St Albans 1-0
Romford v Reading Minster† 1-1, wo
Acton v Kildare 1-1, 5-0

Second Round
OLD CARTHUSIANS v Dreadnought 5-1
Royal Engineers v Pilgrims 1-0
Rangers bye
Clapham R bye
Swifts v Reading 1-0
Upton Park v Weybridge 3-0
Darwen v Sheffield 5-1
Sheffield Wed v Blackburn R 4-0
Turton v Astley Bridge 3-0
Romford bye
Reading Abbey v Acton 2-1
Great Marlow v West End 4-0
OLD ETONIANS v Hendon 2-0
Herts Rgrs bye
Grey Friars v Maidenhead 1-0
Stafford Road* v Grantham 1-1, 7-1
Aston Villa v Nottingham F 2-1
Nottingham bye

Third Round
OLD CARTHUSIANS bye
Royal Engineers v Rangers 6-0
Clapham R v Swifts 2-1
Upton Park bye
Darwen bye
Sheffield Wed v Turton 2-0
Romford v Reading Abbey 2-0
Marlow bye
OLD ETONIANS v Herts Rgrs 3-0
Grey Friars bye
Stafford Road* bye
Aston Villa v Nottingham 3-1

Fourth Round
OLD CARTHUSIANS v Royal Engineers 2-1
Clapham R v Upton Park 5-4
Darwen v Sheffield Wed 5-2
Romford v Great Marlow 2-1
OLD ETONIANS v Grey Friars 4-0
Stafford Road* v Aston Villa 3-2

Fifth Round
OLD CARTHUSIANS v Clapham R 3-1
Darwen v Romford 15-0
OLD ETONIANS v Stafford Road* 2-1

Semi-final
OLD CARTHUSIANS v Darwen 4-1
OLD ETONIANS bye

FINAL (Kennington Oval)
OLD CARTHUSIANS 3
OLD ETONIANS 0
Old Carthusians: L.F.Gillett; W.H.Norris, E..G.Colvin, J.F.M.Prinsep, A.J.Vintcent, W.E.Hensell, L.M.Richards, W.R.Page, E.G.Wynyard, E.H.Parry, A.H.Todd.
Goalscorers: Wyngard, Parry, Todd
Old Etonians: J.F.P.Rawlinson; C.W.Foley, C.H.French, Hon A.F.Kinnaird, R.B.Farrer, J.B.T.Chevallier, W.J.Anderson, H.C.Goodhart, R..H.Macaulay, H.Whitfield, P.C.Novelli.
Referee: W.Pierce-Dix (Sheffield) *Attendance: 4,500*

*Wolverhampton. wo = walk-over. † = scratched.

1881-82

First Round
Bootle v Blackburn Law 2-1
Turton v Astley Bridge 2-2, 1-1, 3-3, 2-0
Darwen v Blackburn Olympic 3-1
Bolton W v Eagley 5-5, 1-0
BLACKBURN R v Park Road 9-1
Accrington v Queen's Park, Glasgow† wo
Aston Villa v Nottingham F 4-1
Nottingham v Calthorpe† wo
Wednesbury Old Ath v St George's 9-1
Small Heath Alliance v Derby 4-1
Wednesbury Strollers v Stafford Road* 3-1
Staveley v Spilsby 5-1
Grantham v Brigg 6-0
Sheffield v Britannia Recreation, Brigg 8-0
Heeley v Lockwood Bros 5-1
Sheffield Wed v Providence 2-0
Great Marlow v Brentwood 3-1
Reading v Hendon 5-0
West End v Remnants 3-2
St Bartholomew's Hospital v Wanderers† wo
Dreadnought v Caius College† wo
Pilgrims v Mosquitoes 1-1, 5-0
Barnes v Rochester 3-1
Old Foresters v Morton Rgrs 3-0
Royal Engineers v Kildare 6-0
Old Carthusians v Esher Leopold 5-0
Swifts v Herts Rgrs 4-0
Acton v Finchley 0-0, 4-0
OLD ETONIANS v Clapham R 2-2, 1-0
Maidenhead v Henley 2-0
Old Harrovians v Olympic 4-2
Romford v Rangers† wo
Upton Park v St Albans 3-0
Hotspur v Union 1-0
Reading Abbey v Woodford Bridge 1-1, 2-1
Reading Minster v Windsor Home Park 1-0
Hanover Utd bye

Second Round
BLACKBURN R v Bolton W 6-2
Darwen v Accrington 3-1
Turton v Bootle 4-0
Wednesbury Old Ath v Small Heath Alliance 6-0
Aston Villa bye
Nottingham v Wednesbury Strollers 11-1
Sheffield Wed bye
Staveley v Grantham 3-1
Heeley v Sheffield 4-0
Upton Park v Hanover Utd 3-1
Hotspur v Reading Abbey 4-1
Reading Minster v Romford 3-1
OLD ETONIANS bye
Swifts v Old Harrovians 7-1
Maidenhead v Acton 2-1
Great Marlow v St Bart's Hospital 2-0
Dreadnought bye
Reading v West End† wo
Old Foresters v Pilgrims 3-1
Royal Engineers bye
Old Carthusians v Barnes 7-1

Third Round
BLACKBURN R bye
Darwen v Turton 4-2
Wednesbury Old Ath bye
Aston Villa v Nottingham 2-2, 2-2, 4-1
Sheffield Wed v Staveley 2-2, 0-0, 5-1
Heeley bye
Upton Park bye
Hotspur v Reading Minster 0-0, 2-0
OLD ETONIANS v Swifts 3-0
Maidenhead bye
Great Marlow v Dreadnought 2-1
Reading bye
Old Foresters bye
Royal Engineers v Old Carthusians 2-0

Fourth Round
BLACKBURN R v Darwen 5-1
Wednesbury Old Ath v Aston Villa 4-2
Sheffield Wed v Heeley 3-1
Upton Park v Hotspur 5-0
OLD ETONIANS v Maidenhead 6-3
Great Marlow v Reading† wo
Old Foresters v Royal Engineers 2-1

Fifth Round
BLACKBURN R v Wednesbury Old Ath 3-1
Sheffield Wed v Upton Park 6-0
OLD ETONIANS bye
Great Marlow v Old Foresters 0-0, 1-0

Semi-final
BLACKBURN R v Sheffield Wed 0-0, 5-1
OLD ETONIANS v Great Marlow 5-0

FINAL (Kennington Oval)
OLD ETONIANS 1
BLACKBURN ROVERS 0
Old Etonians: J.F.P.Rawlinson; T.H.French, P.J.de Paravicini, Hon A.F.Kinnaird, C.W.Foley, P.C.Novelli, A.T.R.Dunn, R.H.Macaulay, H.C.Goodhart, J.B.T.Chevallier, W.J.Anderson.
Goalscorer: Macaulay
Blackburn Rovers: R.Howarth; H.McIntyre, F.Suter, F.Hargreaves, H.Sharples, J.Hargreaves, G.Avery, J.Brown, T.Strachan, J.Douglas, J.Duckworth.
Referee: J.C.Clegg (Sheffield) *Attendance: 6,500*

*Wolverhampton. wo = walk-over. † = scratched.

1882-83

First Round
Grimsby T v Queen's Park, Glasgow† wo
Lockwood Bros v Macclesfield T 4-3
Nottingham v Sheffield 6-1
Phoenix Bessemer v Grantham† wo
Sheffield Wed v Spilsby 12-2
Nottingham F v Brigg Britannia† wo

Heeley ... bye
Birmingham St George's v Calthorpe ... 4-1
Walsall T v Staveley ... 4-1
Stafford Road* v Small Heath Alliance ... 3-3, 6-2
Aston Villa v Walsall Swifts ... 4-1
Wednesbury Old Ath v Spital ... 7-1
Aston Unity ... bye
Blackburn R v Blackpool ... 11-1
Darwen Ramblers v South Shore ... 5-2
BLACKBURN OLYMPIC v Accrington ... 6-3
Darwen v Blackburn Park Road ... 4-1
Church v Clitheroe ... 5-0
Lower Darwen v Irwell Springs ... 5-2
Haslingden ... bye
Northwich Vic v Astley Bridge ... 3-2
Liverpool Ramblers v Southport ... 1-1, 4-0
Eagley v Bolton Olympic ... 7-4
Bolton W v Bootle ... 6-1
Druids v Oswestry ... 1-1, 2-0
Halliwell v Great Lever ... 3-2
United Hospitals v London Olympic ... 3-0
Hanover Utd v Mosquitoes ... 1-0
Clapham R v Kildare ... 3-0
Windsor v Acton ... 3-0
Brentwood v Barnes ... 4-2
Rochester v Hotspur ... 2-0
OLD ETONIANS v Old Foresters ... 1-1, 3-1
Swifts v Union ... 4-1
Upton Park ... bye
Etonian Ramblers v Romford ... 6-2
Old Carthusians v Pilgrims ... 6-0
Old Westminsters v Maidenhead ... 2-0
Royal Engineers v Woodford Bridge ... 3-1
Reading ... bye
Great Marlow v Hornchurch ... 2-0
Hendon v West End ... 3-1
South Reading v Dreadnought ... 2-1
Reading Minster v Remnants† ... wo
Chatham ... bye

Second Round
BLACKBURN OLYMPIC v Lower Darwen ... 8-1
Darwen Ramblers v Haslingden ... 3-2
Church ... bye
Darwen v Blackburn R ... 1-0
Druids v Northwich Vic ... 5-0
Bolton W v Liverpool Ramblers ... 3-0
Eagley v Halliwell ... 3-1
Old Carthusians v Etonian Ramblers ... 7-0
Old Westminsters ... bye
Royal Engineers v Reading ... 8-0
Clapham R v Hanover Utd ... 7-1
Windsor v United Hospitals ... 3-1
OLD ETONIANS v Brentwood ... 2-1
Rochester ... bye
Swifts v Upton Park ... 2-2, 3-2
Hendon v Chatham ... 2-1
South Reading ... bye
Great Marlow v Reading Minster† ... wo
Notts Co ... bye
Phoenix Bessemer v Grimsby T ... 8-1
Sheffield Wed v Lockwood Bros ... 6-0
Nottingham F v Heeley ... 7-2
Aston Villa v Wednesbury Old Ath ... 4-1
Aston Unity v Birmingham St George's ... 3-1
Walsall T v Stafford Road* ... 4-1

Third Round
BLACKBURN OLYMPIC v Darwen Ramblers ... 8-0
Church v Darwen ... 2-2, 2-0
Druids v Bolton W ... 0-0, 1-1, 1-0
Eagley ... bye
Old Carthusians v Old Westminsters ... 3-2
Royal Engineers ... bye
Clapham R v Windsor ... 3-0
OLD ETONIANS v Rochester ... 7-0
Swifts ... bye
Hendon v South Reading ... 11-1
Great Marlow ... bye
Notts Co v Phoenix Bessemer ... 4-1
Sheffield Wed v Nottingham F ... 2-2, 3-2
Aston Villa v Aston Unity ... 3-1
Walsall T ... bye

Fourth Round
BLACKBURN OLYMPIC v Church ... 2-0
Druids v Eagley ... 2-1
Old Carthusians v Royal Engineers ... 6-2
Clapham R ... bye
OLD ETONIANS v Swifts ... 2-0
Hendon v Great Marlow ... 3-0
Notts Co v Sheffield Wed ... 4-1
Aston Villa v Walsall T ... 2-1

Fifth Round
BLACKBURN OLYMPIC v Druids ... 4-1
Old Carthusians v Clapham R ... 5-3
OLD ETONIANS v Hendon ... 4-2
Notts Co v Aston Villa ... 4-3

Semi-final
BLACKBURN OLYMPIC v Old Carthusians ... 4-0
OLD ETONIANS v Notts Co ... 2-1

Blackburn Olympic, the first team to wrest the FA Cup from the grasp of the 'privileged' south. The* Eton Chronicle *hinted darkly that they were professionals.

FINAL (Kennington Oval)
BLACKBURN OLYMPIC ... 2
OLD ETONIANS ... 1
(after extra-time)

Blackburn Olympic: T.Hacking; S.A.Warburton, J.T.Ward, W.Astley, J.Hunter, T.G.Gibson, T.Dewhurst, A.Matthews, G.Wilson, J.Yates, W.Crossley.
Goalscorers: Matthews, Crossley
Old Etonians: J.F.P.Rawlinson; P.J.de Paravicini, T.H.French, Hon A.F.Kinnaird, C.W.Foley, A.T.B.Dunn, H.W.Bainbridge, J.B.T.Chevallier, W.J.Anderson, H.C.Goodhart, R.H.Macaulay.
Goalscorer: Goodhart

Referee: C.Crump (Wolverhampton)
Attendance: 8,000

From the beginning of season 1882-83 instead of tossing for choice of ground, the FA decided that the first-named club drawn out of the hat in each tie should have choice of ground.
*Wolverhampton. wo = walk-over. † = scratched.

1883-84

First Round
Grantham v Spilsby ... 3-2
Rotherham v Spital ... 1-1, 7-2
Notts Co v Heeley ... 3-1
Staveley v Middlesbrough ... 5-1
Lockwood Brothers v Sheffield Club ... 4-1
Grimsby v Hull T ... 3-1
Nottingham F v Redcar & Coatham† ... wo
Sheffield Wed ... bye
Walsall T v Calthorpe ... 9-0
Birmingham Excelsior v Small Heath All ... 1-1, 3-2
Stafford Road* v Aston Unity ... 5-1
Wednesbury Old Ath v St George's ... 5-0
Wednesbury T v West Bromwich A ... 2-0
Aston Villa v Walsall Swifts ... 5-1
Wolves v Long Eaton Rgrs ... 4-1
Derby Midland ... bye
Blackburn Olympic v Darwen Ramblers ... 5-1
Blackburn Park Road v Low Moor ... 6-0
Accrington v Blackpool ... 4-0
Padiham v Lower Darwen ... 3-1
Darwen v Church ... 2-2, 1-0
South Shore v Clitheroe ... 3-3, 3-2
BLACKBURN R v Southport ... 7-0
Eagley v Halliwell ... 5-2
Bolton W v Bolton Olympic ... 9-0
Great Lever v Astley Bridge ... 4-1
Hurst v Turton ... 3-1
Rossendale v Irwell Springs ... 6-2
Bolton v Bradshaw ... 5-1
Preston NE ... bye
Druids v Northwich Vic ... 0-1
Oswestry v Hartford St John's ... 7-0
Davenham v Macclesfield T ... 2-0
Manchester v Stoke-on-Trent ... 2-1
QUEEN'S PARK, GLASGOW v Crewe Alex ... 10-0
Wrexham v Liverpool Ramblers† ... wo
Brentwood v Hanover Utd ... 6-1
Hendon v Old Etonians ... 3-2
Mosquitoes v Pilgrims ... 3-2
Old Westminsters v Chatham ... 3-0
Romford v Woodford Bridge ... 3-0
Reading v South Reading ... 2-2, 4-0
Upton Park v Acton ... 2-0
Old Carthusians v Reading Minster ... 10-1
Old Foresters v Dreadnought ... 2-1
West End v Maidenhead ... 1-0
Clapham R v Kildare† ... wo
Great Marlow v Hornchurch ... 9-0
Windsor v Royal Engineers ... 5-3
Old Wykehamists v Upton Rgrs ... 7-0
Rochester v Uxbridge ... 2-1
Swifts ... bye

Second Round
Staveley v Sheffield Wed ... 3-1
Notts Co v Nottingham F ... 3-0
Lockwood Brothers v Rotherham ... 3-1
Grantham v Grimsby T ... 4-0
Derby Midland v Birmingham Excelsior ... 1-1, 2-1
Wednesbury T v Walsall T ... 2-2, 6-0
Aston Villa v Stafford Road* ... 5-0
Wednesbury Old Ath v Wolves ... 4-2
BLACKBURN R v South Shore ... 7-0
Accrington v Park Road ... 3-2
(Accrington disqualified)
Blackburn Olympic v Darwen ... 2-1
Padiham ... bye
Preston NE v Great Lever ... 4-1
Hurst v Irwell Springs ... 3-2
Bolton W v Bolton ... 3-0
Eagley ... bye
Oswestry v Wrexham ... 4-3
QUEEN'S PARK v Manchester ... 15-0
Northwich Vic v Davenham ... 5-1
Romford v Mosquitoes ... 3-1
Old Westminsters v Hendon ... 2-1
Brentwood ... bye
Reading v West End ... 1-0
Old Foresters v Old Carthusians ... 7-2
Upton Park ... bye
Swifts v Great Marlow ... 2-0
Clapham R v Rochester ... 7-0
Old Wykehamists v Windsor ... 1-0

Third Round
Notts Co v Grantham ... 4-1
Staveley v Lockwood Brothers ... 1-0
Wednesbury T v Derby Midland ... 1-0
Aston Villa v Wednesbury Old Ath ... 7-4
BLACKBURN R v Padiham ... 3-0
Blackburn Olympic ... bye
Preston NE v Eagley ... 9-1
Bolton W v Irwell Springs ... 8-1
QUEEN'S PARK v Oswestry ... 7-1
Northwich Vic ... bye
Brentwood v Romford ... 4-1
Old Westminsters ... bye
Upton Park v Reading ... 6-1
Old Foresters ... bye
Swifts v Clapham R ... 2-1
Old Wykehamists ... bye

Fourth Round
Upton Park v Preston NE ... 1-1
(Preston NE disqualified, professionalism)

Blackburn Rovers with the FA Cup in 1884, on the road to a hat-trick of Cup Final victories. Back row (left to right): Lofthouse, McIntyre, Beverley, Arthur, Suter, Forrest, Mr R.Birtwistle. Front row: Douglas, Sowerbutts, Brown, Avery, J.Hargreaves.

QUEEN'S PARK v Aston Villa 6-1
Northwich Vic v Brentwood 3-0
Notts Co v Bolton W 2-2, 2-1
BLACKBURN R v Staveley 5-1
Blackburn Olympic v Old Wykehamists 6-0
Swifts v Old Foresters 2-1
Old Westminsters v Wednesbury T 5-0

Fifth Round
QUEEN'S PARK v Old Westminsters 1-0
BLACKBURN R v Upton Park 3-0
Notts Co v Swifts 1-1, 1-0
Blackburn Olympic v Northwich Vic 9-1

Semi-final
QUEEN'S PARK v Blackburn Olympic 4-0
BLACKBURN R v Notts Co 1-0

FINAL (Kennington Oval)
BLACKBURN ROVERS 2
QUEEN'S PARK 1
Blackburn Rovers: H.J.Arthur; J.Berverley, F.Suter, H.McIntyre, J.Hargreaves, J.H.Forrest, J.M.Lofthouse, J.Douglas, J.Sowerbutts, J.Inglis, J.Brown.
Goalscorers: Sowerbutts, Forrest
Queen's Park: G.Gillespie; W.Arnott, J.Macdonald, C.Campbell, J.J.Gow, W.Anderson, W.W.Watt, Dr J.Smith, W.Harrower, D.S.Allan, R.M.Christie.
Goalscorer: Gillespie
Referee: Major Marindin (Royal Engineers)
Attendance: 14,000
*Wolverhampton. wo = walk-over. † = scratched.

1884-85

First Round
Wednesbury Old Ath v Derby Midland 2-1
St George's Birmingham v Aston Unity 5-0
Aston Villa v Wednesbury T 4-1
Walsall Swifts v Stafford Road Works* 0-0, 2-1
Walsall T v Derby Co 7-0
Derby St Luke's v Wolves 0-0, 4-2
Birmingham Excelsior v Small Heath Alliance 2-0
West Bromwich A v Junction Street School‡ 7-1
Nottingham F v Rotherham 5-0
Sheffield v Lockwood Brothers 3-0
Staveley v Notts Rgrs 4-1
Sheffield Wed v Long Eaton Rgrs 1-0
Heeley v Notts Wand 1-0
Notts Co v Notts Olympic 2-0
Spital bye
Bolton Association v Astley Bridge† wo
Darwen Old W v Higher Walton 1-1, 4-1
Lower Darwen v Halliwell 4-1
Darwen v Bradshaw 11-0
Bolton W v Preston Zingari (not played)
Fishwick Ramblers v Darwen Ramblers 2-1
Chirk v Davenham 4-2
Druids v Liverpool Ramblers 6-1
Crewe Alex v Oswestry 2-1
Leek T v Northwich Vic 4-3
Wrexham Olympic v Goldenhill 1-0
Macclesfield T v Hartford St John's 9-0
QUEEN'S PARK, GLASGOW v Stoke-on-Trent† wo
Newtown v Stafford Rgrs† wo
Lincoln C v Hull T 5-1
Grimsby T v Grantham 1-0
Redcar v Sunderland 3-1
Middlesbrough v Grimsby District† wo
Newark v Spilsby 7-3
Blackburn Olympic v Oswaldtwistle R 12-0
Accrington § v Southport 3-0
Low Moor v Park Road† wo
Church v Hurst 3-2
BLACKBURN R v Rossendale 11-0
South Shore v Rawtenstall† wo
Witton v Clitheroe† wo
Old Carthusians v Acton 7-1
Upton Park v West End† 3-3, wo
Reading v Rochester 2-0
Great Marlow v Royal Engineers 10-1
Hotspur v Uxbridge 3-1
Old Wykehamists v Maidenhead 3-0
Dulwich v Pilgrims 3-2
Old Foresters v Hoddesdon 8-0
Hanover Utd v Reading Minster 1-0
Hendon v Clapham R 3-3, 6-0
Chatham v Windsor† wo
Romford v Clapton 3-2
Swifts v Old Brightonians 3-0
Brentwood v Barnes 2-0
South Reading v Casuals 4-1
Old Westminsters v Bournemouth R 6-0
Old Etonians v Luton W 3-1
Henley bye

Second Round
Walsall Swifts v Derby St Luke's 1-0
St George's, Birmingham v Birmingham Excelsior 2-2, 2-0
Aston Villa v Walsall T 2-0
West Bromwich A v Wednesbury Old Ath 4-2
Sheffield v Spital Chesterfield 4-1
Nottingham F v Heeley 4-1
Notts Co v Staveley 2-0
Sheffield Wed bye
Darwen v Fishwick Ramblers 2-0
Darwen Old Wand v Bolton Association 7-2
Lower Darwen bye
Druids v Newtown 1-1, 6-0
Chirk v Wrexham Olympic 4-1
QUEEN'S PARK v Crewe Alex 2-1
Leek T v Macclesfield T 5-1
Middlesbrough v Newark 4-1
Grimsby T v Redcar 3-1
Lincoln C bye
Church v South Shore 3-2
Southport v Low Moor 3-1
BLACKBURN R v Blackburn Olympic 3-2
Witton bye
Old Wykehamists v Hotspur 2-1
Upton Park v Reading 3-1
Old Carthusians v Great Marlow 5-3
Chatham v Hendon 1-0
Hanover Utd v Old Foresters 2-1
Romford v Dulwich 3-0
Old Westminsters v Henley 7-0
Swifts v South Reading 3-2
Old Etonians v Brentwood 2-2, 6-1

Third Round
West Bromwich A v Aston Villa 0-0, 3-0
Walsall Swifts v St George's 3-2
Nottingham F v Sheffield Wed 2-1
Notts Co v Sheffield 5-0
Lower Darwen v Darwen Old Wand 4-2
Darwen bye
QUEEN'S PARK v Leek T 3-2
Druids v Chirk 4-1
Grimsby T v Lincoln C 1-0
Middlesbrough bye
BLACKBURN R v Witton 5-1
Church v Southport 10-0
Old Wykehamists v Upton Park 2-1
Old Carthusians bye
Chatham v Hanover Utd 2-0
Romford bye
Swifts v Old Westminsters 1-1, 2-2, 2-1
Old Etonians bye

Fourth Round
Old Carthians v Grimsby T 3-0
Nottingham F v Swifts 1-0
West Bromwich A v Druids 1-0
QUEEN'S PARK v Old Wykehamists 7-0
Church v Darwen 3-0
Chatham v Lower Darwen 1-0
Notts Co v Walsall Swifts 4-1
BLACKBURN R v Romford 8-0
Old Etonians v Middlesbrough 5-2

Fifth Round
Old Carthusians v Chatham 3-0
Old Etonians bye
Nottingham F bye
QUEEN'S PARK bye
West Bromwich A bye
Notts Co bye
BLACKBURN R bye
Church bye

Sixth Round
Nottingham F v Old Etonians 2-0
QUEEN'S PARK v Notts Club 2-2, 2-1
BLACKBURN R v West Bromwich A 2-0
Old Carthusians v Church 1-0

Semi-final
QUEEN'S PARK v Nottingham F 1-1, 3-0
BLACKBURN R v Old Carthusians 5-1

FINAL (Kennington Oval)
BLACKBURN ROVERS 2
QUEEN'S PARK 0
Blackburn Rovers: H.J.Arthur; R.G.Turner, F.Suter, H.McIntyre, G.Haworth, J.H.Forrest, J.M.Lofthouse, J.Douglas, J.Brown, H.E.Fecitt, J.Sowerbutts.
Goalscorers: Forrest, Brown
Queen's Park: G.Gillespie; W.Arnott, W.MacLeod, C.Campbell, J.Macdonald, A.Hamilton, W.Anderson, W.Sellar, W.Gray, N.McWhannel, D.S.Allan.
Referee: Major Marindin (Royal Engineers)
Attendance: 12,500
*Wolverhampton. ‡Derby. wo = walk-over. † = scratched.

1885-86

First Round
Preston NE v Great Lever† wo
Queen's Park, Glasgow v Partick Thistle 5-1
South Shore v Higher Walton 4-3
Hurst v Bradshaw 3-1
Rawtenstall v Glasgow Rgrs† wo
Halliwell v Fishwick Ramblers 2-1
Astley Bridge v Southport 3-2
Bolton W v Eagley 6-0
BLACKBURN R v Clitheroe 2-0
Church v Blackburn Olympic 3-1
Accrington v Witton 5-4
3rd Lanark RV v Blackburn Park Road 4-2
Rossendale v Low Moor 6-2
Padiham v Heart of Midlothian† wo
Darwen Old W v Burnley 11-0
Oswaldtwistle R v Lower Darwen 3-1
Derby Midland v Birmingham Excelsior 2-1
Wolves v Derby St Luke's 7-0
Aston Villa v Walsall T 5-0
WEST BROMWICH A v Aston Unity 4-1
Stafford Road* v Matlock 7-0
Derby Co v St George's, Birmingham 3-0
Small Heath Alliance v Burton W 9-2
Wednesbury Old Ath v Burton Swifts 5-1
Darwen v Junction Street School‡ 2-2, 4-0
Walsall Swifts bye
Sheffield v Newark 3-0
Notts Olympic v Notts W 2-2, 4-1
Nottingham F v Mellors 6-2
Notts Rgrs v Lockwood Brothers 2-2, 4-0
Sheffield Heeley v Eckington Works 2-1
Staveley v Mexborough† 1-1, wo

Long Eaton Rgrs v Sheffield Wed 2-0
Notts Co v Rotherham 15-0
Burslem Port Vale v Chirk 3-1
Oswestry v Bollington 5-0
Macclesfield T v Northwich Vic 4-1
Crewe Alex v Stoke-on-Trent 2-2, 1-0
Leek T v Wrexham Olympic 6-3
Davenham v Goldenhill 2-1
Newtown v Hartford St John's 3-1
Druids v Stafford Rgrs 4-1
Middlesbrough v Horncastle† wo
Grimsby T v Lincoln C 2-0
Redcar v Sunderland 3-0
Lincoln Lindum v Grimsby & District 4-0
Gainsboro' Trin v Grantham 4-1
Darlington bye
Luton W v Chesham 3-2
Great Marlow v Luton T 3-0
Upton Park v United London Scottish 4-2
Old Westminsters v Hotspur 3-1
Romford v Hanover Utd 1-1, 3-0
Old Brightonians v Acton 2-1
Old Wykehamists v Uxbridge 5-0
Old Carthusians v Chatham 2-0
Old Etonians v Bournemouth R† wo
Rochester v Reading 6-1
Brentford v Maidenhead 3-0
Lancing Old Boys v Barnes 7-1
Clapton v Hendon 4-0
Old Harrovians v St James' Forest Gate† wo
Swifts v Casuals 7-1
Clapham R v 1st Surrey Rifles 12-0
South Reading v Dulwich 2-1
Old Foresters v Royal Engineers 5-1

Second Round
Bolton W v Rawtenstall § 3-3, wo
Preston NE v Astley Bridge 11-3
Halliwell v Hurst† wo
South Shore v Queen's Park† wo
Rossendale v Padiham 9-1
BLACKBURN R v Oswaldtwistle R 1-0
Darwen Old W v Accrington 2-1
Church v 3rd Lanark RV† wo
Walsall Swifts v Derby Midland 3-1
WEST BROMWICH A v Wednesbury Old Ath 3-2
Derby Co v Aston Villa 2-0
Wolves v Stafford Road* 4-2
Small Heath Alliance v Darwen 3-1
Staveley v Long Eaton Rgrs 4-1
Notts Rgrs v Sheffield Heeley 6-1
Nottingham F v Notts Olympic 4-1
Notts Co v Sheffield 8-0
Leek T v Newton† wo
Burslem Port Vale v Druids 2-2, 5-1
Davenham v Macclesfield T 8-1
Crewe Alex v Oswestry § 1-1, wo
Grimsby T v Darlington 8-0
Redcar v Lincoln Lindum 2-0
Middlesbrough v Gainsboro' Trin 2-1
Old Wykehamists v Luton W 10-0
Old Westminsters v Old Brightonians 3-0
Great Marlow v Old Etonians 6-1
Old Carthusians v Upton Park 8-0
Romford bye
South Reading v Clapton § 1-1, wo
Brentford v Lancing Old Boys 6-1
Swifts v Rochester 5-1
Old Harrovians v Old Foresters 2-1
Clapham R bye

Third Round
South Shore v Halliwell 6-1
Preston NE v Bolton W 3-2
Church v Rossendale 5-1
BLACKBURN R v Darwen Old Wand 6-1
Wolves v Walsall Swifts 2-1
Small Heath Alliance v Derby Co 4-2
WEST BROMWICH A bye
Staveley v Nottingham F 2-1
Notts Co v Notts Rgrs 3-0
Davenham v Crewe Alex 2-1
Burslem Port Vale v Leek T 3-2
Middlesbrough v Grimsby T 2-1
Redcar bye
Old Westminsters v Romford 5-1
Old Wykehamists v Great Marlow† wo
Old Carthusians bye
South Reading v Clapham R† wo
Swifts v Old Harrovians† wo
Brentwood bye

Fourth Round
Bolton W bye
South Shore bye
Church bye
BLACKBURN R bye
WEST BROMWICH A v Wolves 3-1
Small Heath Alliance bye
Staveley bye
Notts Co bye
Davenham bye
Burslem Port Vale bye
Middlesbrough bye
Redcar bye
Old Carthusians bye
Old Westminsters bye
Brentwood v South Reading 3-0
Swifts bye

Fifth Round
South Shore v Notts Co 2-1
Swifts v Church 6-2
WEST BROMWICH A v Old Carthusians 1-0
Redcar v Middlesbrough 2-1
BLACKBURN R v Staveley 7-1
Small Heath Alliance v Davenham 2-1
Brentwood v Burslem Port Vale 1-2
(Burslem Port Vale disqualified)
Old Westminsters v Bolton W wo

Sixth Round
Small Heath Alliance v Redcar 2-0
WEST BROMWICH A v Old Westminsters 6-0
Swifts v South Shore 2-1
BLACKBURN R v Brentwood 3-1

Semi-final
BLACKBURN R v Swifts 2-1
WEST BROMWICH A v Small Heath Alliance 4-0

FINAL (County Ground, Derby)
BLACKBURN ROVERS 2
WEST BROMWICH ALBION 0
(after a 0-0 draw)
Blackburn Rovers: H.J.Arthur; R.G.Turner, F.Suter, J.Douglas, J.H.Forrest, H.McIntyre, N.Walton, T.Strachan, J.Brown, H.E.Fecitt, J.Sowerbutts. J.Heyes played in the first game and was replaced by Walton.
Goalscorers: Sowerbutts, Brown
West Bromwich Albion: Roberts; H.Green, H.Bell, Horton, Perry, Timmins, Woodhall, T.Green, Bayliss, Loach, G.Bell.
Referee: Major Marindin (Royal Engineers)
Attendance: 15,000

A special trophy was awarded for Blackburn's third consecutive win. The first game was played at the Kennington Oval so the replay was the first time the Final was fought outside London. The referee was the same.
§Disqualified. *Wolverhampton. ‡Derby. wo = walk-over. † = scratched.

1886-87

First Round
Blackburn R v Halliwell† wo
Astley Bridge v Burnley 0-0, 2-2
(both disqualified)
Bolton W v South Shore 5-3
Witton v Oswaldtwistle R 3-2
3rd Lanark RV v Higher Walton 5-0
Darwen v Heart of Midlothian 7-1
Renton v Accrington 1-0
Preston NE v Queen's Park, Glasgow 3-0
Glasgow Rgrs v Everton† wo
Cowlairs v Darwen Old Wand 4-1
Fleetwood Rgrs v Newton Heath § 2-2
Cliftonville, Belfast v Blackburn Park Road 2-2, 7-2
Partick Thistle v Blackburn Olympic 3-1
Church v Rawtenstall 1-1, 7-1
Great Lever v Bootle 4-2
Rossendale bye
Crosswell's Brewery, Oldbury v Burton Swifts 1-0
Wolves v Matlock 6-0
Derby Junction v St George's Wellington 1-0
WEST BROMWICH A v Burton W 6-0
Mitchell's St George v Small Heath Alliance 3-1
ASTON VILLA v Wednesbury Old Ath 13-0
Derby Co v Aston Unity 4-1
Derby Midland v Birmingham Excelsior 3-3, 2-1
Walsall T v Derby St Luke's 3-3, 6-1
Lockwood Brothers v Long Eaton Rgrs 1-0
Notts Rgrs v Sheffield Club 3-0
Cleethorpe T v Mellors Limited 2-1
Notts Co v Basford R 13-0
Grimsby T v Sheffield Heeley 4-1
Staveley v Attercliffe 7-0
Nottingham F v Notts Olympic 3-0
Rotherham bye
Crewe Alex v Wrexham Olympic 4-1
Leek T v Druids 2-1
Goldenhill v Macclesfield T 3-2
Chirk v Hartford St John's 8-1
Burslem Port Vale v Davenham 1-1, 3-0
Oswestry v Bollington 8-2
Northwich Vic v Furness Vale R 10-0
Stoke-on-Trent v Caernarfon W 10-1
Chester bye
Gainsboro' Trin v South Bank 4-0
Newcastle West End v Sunderland 1-0
Redcar v Tyne 4-0
Grantham v Lincoln Lindum 1-0
Middlesbrough v Bishop Auckland Church Institute 1-0
Horncastle v Darlington 3-1
Lincoln C bye
Chatham v Bournemouth R† wo
Crusaders v Clapton 5-0
Old Wykehamists v Hanover Utd 3-0
Hotspur v Luton T 3-1
Caledonians v Hendon 2-1
Old Carthusians v Reading 2-1
Swifts v Luton Wand 13-0
Old Foresters v Cannon† wo
Swindon T v Watford R 1-0
Maidenhead v South Reading 2-0
Chesham v Lyndhurst 4-2
Great Marlow v Rochester 2-0
Upton Park v 1st Surrey Rifles 9-0
Dulwich v Casuals 4-2
Old Brightonians v Clapham R 6-0
Old Etonians v Royal Engineers 1-0
Old Westminsters v Old Harrovians 4-0

Second Round
Darwen bye
Bolton W v 3rd Lanark RV 3-2
Renton v Blackburn R 2-2, 2-0
Preston NE v Witton 6-0
Cowlairs v Rossendale 10-2
Cliftonville v Great Lever 3-1
Partick Thistle v Fleetwood Rgrs 7-0
Glasgow Rgrs v Church 2-1
WEST BROMWICH A v Derby Junction 2-1
Wolves v Crosswell's Brewery 14-0
ASTON VILLA v Derby Midland 6-1
Mitchell's St George's v Derby Co 2-1
Walsall T bye
Staveley v Rotherham 4-0
Notts Co v Notts Rgrs 3-3, 5-0
Lockwood Brothers v Cleethorpes T 4-1
Nottingham F v Grimsby T 2-2, 1-0
Goldenhill v Chester § 0-1
Leek T v Oswestry 4-2
Crewe Alex v Stoke-on-Trent 6-4
Chirk v Northwich Vic 0-0, 3-0
Burslem Port Vale bye
Lincoln C v Middlesbrough 1-1, 2-0
Grantham v Redcar 3-2
Gainsboro' Trin v West End 5-2
Horncastle bye
Old Carthusians v Crusaders 4-2
Caledonians v Old Wykehamists 1-0
Swifts v Swindon T 7-1
Chatham v Hotspur 1-0
Old Foresters bye
Old Westminsters v Old Brightonians 1-1, 3-1
Dulwich v Maidenhead 3-2
Great Marlow v Upton Park 4-0
Old Etonians v Chesham 7-1

Third Round
Preston NE v Renton 2-0
Darwen v Bolton W 4-3
Partick Thistle v Cliftonville 11-1
Glasgow Rgrs v Cowlairs 3-2
Mitchell's St George's v Walsall T 7-2
WEST BROMWICH A bye
ASTON VILLA v Wolves 2-2, 1-1, 3-3, 2-0
Lockwood Brothers v Nottingham F 2-1
Notts Co v Staveley 3-0
Chirk v Goldenhill[1] wo
Crewe Alex bye
Leek T v Burslem Port Vale 2-2, 3-1
Lincoln C v Gainsboro' Trin 2-2, 1-0
Horncastle v Grantham 2-0
Old Foresters v Chatham 4-1
Old Carthusians v Caledonians† wo
Swifts bye
Old Westminsters v Old Etonians 3-0
Great Marlow v Dulwich 2-0

Fourth Round
Preston NE bye
Darwen bye
Partick Thistle bye
Glasgow Rgrs bye
WEST BROMWICH A v Mitchell's St George's 1-0
ASTON VILLA bye
Lockwood Brothers bye
Notts Co bye
Chirk bye
Leek T v Crewe Alex 1-0
Lincoln C bye
Horncastle bye
Old Foresters v Swifts 2-0
Old Carthusians bye
Old Westminsters bye
Great Marlow bye

Fifth Round
Preston NE v Old Foresters 3-0

The earliest known action photograph of a Cup Final, albeit heavily retouched. West Brom's Jem Bayliss heads towards the Aston Villa goal in the 1887 game at The Oval. Note the taped crossbar.

Notts Co v Great Marlow 5-2
Darwen v Chirk 2-1
Old Westminsters v Partick Thistle 1-0
Glasgow Rgrs v Lincoln C 3-0
Old Carthusians v Leek T 2-0
ASTON VILLA v Horncastle 5-0
WEST BROMWICH A v Lockwood Bros ... *1-0, 2-1

Sixth Round
WEST BROMWICH A v Notts Co 4-1
Preston NE v Old Carthusians 2-1
ASTON VILLA v Darwen 3-2
Glasgow Rgrs v Old Westminsters 5-1

Semi-final
ASTON VILLA v Glasgow Rgrs 3-1
WEST BROMWICH ALBION v Preston NE 3-1

FINAL (Kennington Oval)
ASTON VILLA 2
WEST BROMWICH ALBION 0
Aston Villa: Warner; Coulton, Simmonds, Yates, Dawson, Burton, Davis, Brown, Hunter, Vaughton, Hodgetts.
Goalscorers: Hodgetts, Hunter
West Bromwich Albion: Roberts; H.Green, Aldridge, Horton, Perry, Timmins, Woodhall, T.Green, Bayliss, Paddock, Pearson.
Referee: Major Marindin (Royal Engineers)
Attendance: 15,500

§Disqualified. *Replayed following a dispute over the goal in the first game. wo = walk-over. † = scratched.

1887-88

First Round
Scarborough v Shankhouse 3-5
South Bank v Newcastle East End 3-2
Elswick Rgrs v Church Institute 3-3, 2-0
Whitburn v Middlesbrough 0-4
Sunderland v Morpeth Harriers 4-2
West End, Newcastle v Redcar 5-1
Gateshead v Darlington 0-3
Church v Cliftonville, Belfast† .... wo
Oswaldtwistle R v Witton 1-4
Rawtenstall v Darwen 1-3
Blackburn R v Bury 10-0
Accrington v Rossendale 11-0
Blackburn Park Road† v Belfast Distillery 2-1
Burnley v Darwen Old W 4-0
Blackburn Olympic .... bye
Liverpool Stanley v Halliwell 1-5
Higher Walton v Heywood Central 8-1
Bootle v Workington 6-0
Hurst § v Astley Bridge 5-3
PRESTON NE v Hyde 26-0
South Shore v Denton .... wo
Bolton W v Everton § .... 1-2‡, 2-2, 1-1, 1-2
Fleetwood Rgrs v West Manchester 4-1
Stoke v Burslem Port Vale 1-0
Leek T v Northwich Vic 2-2, 2-4
Chirk v St Oswald's, Chester 4-1
Crewe Alex v Druids 5-0
Vale of Llangollen v Oswestry .... 1-3‡, 0-2
Chester v Davenham 2-3
Macclesfield T v Shrewsbury T 1-3
Over W v Wellington St George's 3-1
Wrexham Olympic .... bye
Aston Shakespeare v Burton W § 2-3
Walsall Swifts v Wolves 1-2
Walsall T v Mitchell's St George's 1-2
Warwick Co v Excelsior .... 1-4‡, 0-5
Small Heath Alliance v Aston Unity 6-1
Stafford Road*† v Great Bridge Unity 1-1, 2-1
WEST BROMWICH A v Wednesbury Old Ath ... 7-1
Burton Swifts v Birmingham Southfield 7-0
Oldbury T v Aston Villa 0-4
Staveley v Derby Co 1-2
Ecclesfield v Derby Midland 4-1
Sheffield v Lockwood Brothers 1-3
Long Eaton Rgrs v Park Grange 6-3
Belper T v Sheffield Wed 2-3
Owlerton v Eckington Works 2-1
Derby St Luke's v Derby Junction 2-3
Heeley v Attercliffe 9-0
Matlock T v Rotherham 2-3
Basford R v Lincoln Albion 3-2
Notts Rgrs v Jardines 10-1
Lincoln Lindum v Grantham 0-4
Notts Swifts v Nottingham F 1-2
Gainsboro' Trin v Boston 7-0
Mellor's Limited v Notts Olympic .... 6-3‡, 2-1
Lincoln C v Horncastle 4-1
Cleethorpes v Grimsby T 0-4
Lincoln Ramblers v Notts Co 0-9
Chatham v Luton T 5-1
Rochester v Royal Engineers 0-3
Hitchin v Old Wykehamists 2-5
Millwall R v Casuals† .... wo
Crusaders, Belfast v Lyndhurst 9-0
Lancing Old Boys v Old Etonians 2-4
Clapton v Old Westminsters 1-4
Old St Mark's v East Sheen 7-2
Reading v Dulwich 0-2
Great Marlow v South Reading 4-1
Old Brightonians v Swindon T 1-0
Old Carthusians v Hanover Limited 5-0
Chesham v Watford R .... 4-2‡, 1-3
Swifts v Maidenhead 3-1
London Caledonians v Old Foresters 1-6
Hendon v Old Harrovians 2-4
Hotspur .... bye

Second Round
Darlington v Elswick Rgrs 4-3
Sunderland v Belfast Distillery 3-1
Middlesbrough v South Bank 4-1
Shankhouse .... bye
Blackburn Olympic v Blackburn R 1-5
Newcastle West End v Witton 2-4
Accrington v Darwen Old W 3-2
Darwen v Church 2-0
Astley Bridge v Halliwell 0-4
Fleetwood Rgrs v Higher Walton 1-3
Bootle v South Shore 1-1, 3-0
PRESTON NE v Bolton W 9-1
Wrexham Olympic v Davenham 1-2
Chirk v Shrewsbury T 10-2
Northwich Vic v Crewe Alex 0-1
Over W v Stoke-on-Trent 0-3
Oswestry .... bye
Burton Swifts v Great Bridge Unity 2-5
Lockwood Brothers .... bye
Small Heath Alliance v Aston Villa 0-4
Wolves v Aston Shakespeare 3-0
Mitchell's St George's v WEST BROMWICH A 0-1
Birmingham Excelsior .... bye
Owlerton v Sheffield Heeley 1-0
Derby Junction v Rotherham 3-2
Long Eaton Rgrs v Sheffield Wed 1-2
Derby Co v Ecclesfield 6-0
Lincoln C v Gainsboro' Trin 2-1
Grantham v Notts Rgrs 0-4
Notts Co v Basford R† .... wo
Nottingham F v Mellors Limited 2-0
Grimsby T .... bye
Old Etonians v Old St Mark's 3-2
Chatham v Royal Engineers 3-1
Old Wykehamists v Crusaders 2-3
Old Westminsters v Millwall R 8-1
Dulwich v Hotspur 2-1
Great Marlow v Old Foresters 2-3
Old Harrovians v Old Brightonians 0-4
Watford R v Old Carthusians 1-3
Swifts .... bye

Third Round
Darlington v Shankhouse 0-2
Middlesbrough v Sunderland★ 2-2, 2-4
Accrington v Blackburn R 1-3
Darwen v Witton 1-1, 2-0
Higher Walton v Bootle 1-6
PRESTON NE v Halliwell 4-0
Stoke-on-Trent v Oswestry 3-0
Davenham v Chirk 2-2, 1-6
Crewe Alex .... bye
Birmingham Excelsior v Great Bridge Unity 1-2
WEST BROMWICH A v Wolves 2-0
Aston Villa .... Bye
Derby Junction v Lockwood Brothers 2-1
Derby Co v Owlerton 6-2
Sheffield Wed .... bye
Grimsby T v Lincoln C 2-0
Nottingham F v Notts Co 2-1
Notts Rgrs .... bye
Crusaders v Chatham 4-0
Old Etonians v Old Westminsters 7-2
Dulwich v Swifts 1-3
Old Brightonians v Old Carthusians 0-5
Old Foresters .... bye

Fourth Round
Great Bridge Unity v Bootle 2-1
Nottingham F v Old Etonians 6-0
Old Foresters v Grimsby T 4-2
Crewe Alex v Swifts § .... 2-2, 2-3‡, 2-1
Crusaders v Sheffield Wed 0-1
Shankhouse v Aston Villa 0-9
Darwen v Notts Rgrs 3-1
Chirk .... bye
Derby Junction .... bye
Derby Co .... bye
WEST BROMWICH A .... bye
Middlesbrough .... bye
Blackburn R .... bye
Old Carthusians .... bye
PRESTON NORTH END .... bye
Stoke-on-Trent .... bye

Fifth Round
Old Carthusians v Great Bridge Unity 2-0
Darwen v Blackburn R 0-3
WEST BROMWICH A v Stoke-on-Trent 4-1
Crewe Alex v Derby Co 1-0
Aston Villa v PRESTON NE 1-3
Middlesbrough v Old Foresters .... ☆4-0
Derby Junction v Chirk 1-1, 1-0
Nottingham Forest v Sheffield Wed 2-4

Sixth Round
WEST BROMWICH A v Old Carthusians 4-2
Middlesbrough v Crewe Alex 0-2
Derby Junction v Blackburn R 2-1
Sheffield Wed v PRESTON NE 1-3

Semi-final
WEST BROMWICH A v Derby Junction 3-0
PRESTON NE v Crewe Alex 4-0

FINAL (Kennington Oval)
WEST BROMWICH ALBION 2
PRESTON NORTH END 1
West Bromwich Albion: Roberts; Aldridge, Green, Horton, Perry, Timmins, Bassett, Woodhall, Bayliss, Wilson, Pearson.
Goalscorers: Bayliss, Woodhall
Preston North End: Dr R.H.Mills-Roberts; Howarth, N.J.Ross, Holmes, Russell, Graham, Gordon, J.Ross, J.Goodall, F.Dewhurst, Drummond.
Goalscorer: Dewhurst
Referee: Major Marindin (Royal Engineers)
Attendance: 19,000

§Disqualified. ‡Replay after protest. ★Sunderland disqualified for veiled professionalism.☆FA ordered replay at Middlesbrough after Old Foresters protested at the state of the ground. Old Foresters scratched. *Wolverhampton. wo = walk-over. † = scratched.

1888-89

First Round
Grimsby T v Sunderland Alb ... 3-1
Bootle v PRESTON NE ... 0-3
Halliwell v Crewe Alex ... 2-2, 5-1
Birmingham St George's v Long Eaton Rgrs ... 3-2
Chatham v South Shore ... 2-1
Nottingham F v Linfield A† ... wo
Small Heath v West Bromwich A ... 2-3
Burnley v Old Westminsters ... 4-3
WOLVES v Old Carthusians ... 4-3
Walsall T Swifts v Sheffield Heeley ... 5-1
Sheffield Wed v Notts Rgrs ... 1-1, 3-0
Notts Co v Old Brightonians ... 2-0
Blackburn R v Accrington ... 1-1, 5-0
Swifts v Wrexham ... 3-1
Aston Villa v Witton ... 3-2
Derby Co v Derby Junction ... 1-0

Second Round
Grimsby T v PRESTON NE ... 0-2
Halliwell v Birmingham St George's ... 2-3
Chatham v Nottingham F ... 1-1, 2-2, 3-2
West Bromwich A v Burnley ... 5-1
WOLVES v Walsall T Swifts ... 6-1
Sheffield Wed v Notts Co ... 3-2
Blackburn R v Swifts† ... wo
Aston Villa v Derby Co ... 5-3

Third Round
PRESTON NE v Birmingham St George's ... 2-0
Chatham v West Bromwich A ... 1-10
WOLVES v Sheffield Wed ... 3-0
Blackburn R v Aston Villa ... 8-1

Semi-final
PRESTON NE v West Bromwich A ... 1-0
WOLVES v Blackburn R ... 1-1, 3-1

FINAL (Kennington Oval)
PRESTON NORTH END ... 3
WOLVERHAMPTON WANDERERS ... 0
Preston North End: Dr R.H.Mills-Roberts; Howarth, Holmes, Drummond, Russell, Graham, Gordon, Ross, J.Goodall, F.Dewhurst, Thomson.
Goalscorers: Dewhurst, Ross, Thomson
Wolverhampton Wanderers: Baynton; Baugh, Mason, Fletcher, Allen, Lowder, Hunter, Wykes, Brodie, Wood, Knight.
Referee: Major Marindin (Royal Engineers) Attendance: 22,000

wo = walk-over. † = scratched.

1889-90

First Round
Preston NE v Newton Heath ... 6-1
Lincoln C v Chester ... 2-0
Bolton W v Belfast Distillery ... 10-1
Sheffield Utd v Burnley ... 2-1
SHEFFIELD WED v Swifts ... 4-1
Accrington v West Bromwich A ... 3-1‡, 3-0
Notts Co v Birmingham St George's ... 4-4, 6-2
South Shore v Aston Villa ... 2-4
Bootle v Sunderland Alb ... 1-3
Derby Midland v Nottingham F ... 3-0
BLACKBURN R v Sunderland ... 4-2
Newcastle West End v Grimsby T ... 1-2
Wolves v Old Carthusians ... 4-0
Small Heath v Clapton ... 3-1
Stoke v Old Westminsters ... 3-0
Everton v Derby Co ... 11-2

Second Round
Preston NE v Lincoln C ... 4-0
Bolton W v Sheffield Utd ... 13-0
SHEFFIELD WED v Accrington ... 2-1
Notts Co v Aston Villa ... 4-1
Bootle v Derby Midland ... 2-1
BLACKBURN R v Grimsby T ... 3-0
Wolves v Small Heath ... 2-1
Stoke v Everton ... 4-2

Third Round
Preston NE v Bolton W ... 2-3
SHEFFIELD WED v Notts Co ... 5-0, 2-3‡, 2-1
Bootle v BLACKBURN R ... 0-7
Wolves v Stoke ... 4-0‡, 8-0

Semi-final
Bolton W v SHEFFIELD WED ... 1-2
BLACKBURN R v Wolves ... 1-0

Blackburn Rovers' 1891 winning side. Back row (left to right): Brandon, Pennington, Barton, John Southworth, Dewar, Forrest, E.Murray (trainer). Front row: Lofthouse, Walton, Forbes, Hall, Townley. The previous year, Walter Townley had become the first man to score an FA Cup Final hat-trick.

FINAL (Kennington Oval)
BLACKBURN ROVERS ... 6
SHEFFIELD WEDNESDAY ... 1
Blackburn Rovers: J.K.Horne; James Southworth, Forbes, Barton, Dewar, Forrest, Lofthouse, Campbell, John Southworth, Walton, Townley.
Goalscorers: Townley 3, Walton, John Southworth, Lofthouse
Sheffield Wednesday: J.Smith; H.Morley, Brayshaw, Dungworth, Betts, Waller, Ingram, Woodhouse, Mumford, Cawley, Bennett.
Goalscorer: Bennett
Referee: Major Marindin (Royal Engineers) Attendance: 20,000

One of the linesmen for this Final, M.P.Betts, was the scorer of the first FA Cup Final goal in 1872.
‡Replay after protest.

1890-91

First Round
Middlesbrough Iron v BLACKBURN R ... 1-2‡, 0-3
Chester v Lincoln C ... 1-0
Accrington v Bolton W ... 2-2, 5-1
Long Eaton Rgrs v Wolves ... 1-2
Royal Arsenal v Derby Co ... 1-2
Sheffield Wed v Halliwell ... 12-0
Crusdaders, Belfast v Birmingham St George's 0-2
West Bromwich A v Old Westminsters† ... wo
Darwen v Kidderminster H ... 3-1‡, 13-0
Sunderland v Everton ... 1-0
Clapton v Nottingham F ... 0-14
Sunderland Alb v 93rd Highlanders ... 2-0
Sheffield Utd v NOTTS CO ... 1-9
Burnley v Crewe Alex ... 4-2
Stoke v Preston NE ... 3-0
Aston Villa v Casuals ... 13-1

Second Round
BLACKBURN R v Chester ... 7-0
Accrington v Wolves ... 2-3
Derby C v Sheffield Wed ... 2-3
Birmingham St George's v West Bromwich A 0-3
Darwen v Sunderland ... 0-2
Nottingham F v Sunderland Alb ... 1-1, 3-3, 5-0
NOTTS CO v Burnley ... 2-1
Stoke v Aston Villa ... 3-0

Third Round
BLACKBURN R v Wolves ... 2-0
Sheffield Wed v West Bromwich A ... 0-2
Sunderland v Nottingham F ... 4-0
NOTTS CO v Stoke ... 1-0

Semi-final
BLACKBURN R v West Bromwich A ... 3-2
Sunderland v NOTTS CO ... 3-3, 0-2

FINAL (Kennington Oval)
BLACKBURN ROVERS ... 3
NOTTS COUNTY ... 1
Blackburn Rovers: Pennington; Brandon, J.Forbes, Barton, Dewar, Forrest, Lofthouse, Walton, John Southworth, Hall, Townley.
Goalscorers: Dewar, Southworth, Townley
Notts County: Thraves; Ferguson, Hendry, H.Osborne, Calderhead, Shelton, A.McGregor, McInnes, Oswald, Locker, H.B.Daft.
Goalscorer: Oswald
Referee: C.J.Hughes (Northwich) Attendance: 23,000

*Replay after protest. wo = walk-over. † = scratched.

1891-92

First Round
Old Westminsters v WEST BROMWICH A ... 2-3
Blackburn R v Derby Co ... 4-1
Sheffield Wed v Bolton W ... 2-1‡, 4-1
Small Heath v Royal Arsenal ... 5-1
Sunderland Alb v Birmingham St George's ... 4-0
Nottingham F v Newcastle East End ... 2-1
Luton T v Middlesbrough ... 0-3
Preston NE v Middlesbrough Iron ... 2-2, 6-0
Crewe Alex v Wolves ... 2-2, 1-4
Blackpool v Sheffield Utd ... 0-3
ASTON VILLA v Heanor T ... 4-1
Bootle v Darwen ... 0-2
Crusaders, Belfast v Accrington ... 1-4
Sunderland v Notts Co ... 3-0‡, 4-0
Everton v Burnley ... 2-4‡, 1-3
Stoke v Casuals ... 3-0‡, 3-0

Second Round
WEST BROMWICH A v Blackburn R ... 3-1
Sheffield Wed v Small Heath ... 2-0
Sunderland Alb v Nottingham F ... 0-1
Middlesbrough v Preston NE ... 1-2
Wolves v Sheffield Utd ... 3-1
ASTON VILLA v Darwen ... 2-0
Accrington v Sunderland ... 1-0‡, 1-3
Burnley v Stoke ... 1-3

Third Round
WEST BROMWICH A v Sheffield Wed ... 2-1
Nottingham F v Preston NE ... 2-0
Wolves v ASTON VILLA ... 1-3
Sunderland v Stoke ... 2-2, 4-0

Semi-final
WEST BROMWICH A v Nottingham F ... 1-1, 1-1, 6-2
ASTON VILLA v Sunderland ... 4-1

FINAL (Kennington Oval)
WEST BROMWICH ALBION ... 3
ASTON VILLA ... 0
West Bromwich Albion: Reader; Nicholson, McCulloch, Reynolds, Perry, Groves, Bassett, McLeod, Nicholls, Pearson, Geddes.
Goalscorers: Geddes, Nicholls, Reynolds
Aston Villa: Warner; Evans, Cox, H.Devey, Cowan, Baird, Athersmith, J.Devey, Dickson, Campbell, Hodgetts.
Referee: J.C.Clegg (Sheffield) Attendance: 32,810
‡Replay after protest.

1892-93

First Round

EVERTON v West Bromwich A	4-1
Nottingham F v Casuals	4-0
Sheffield Wed v Derby Co	3-2
Burnley v Small Heath	2-0
Accrington v Stoke	2-1
Preston NE v Burton Swifts	9-2
Marlow v Middlesbrough Iron	1-3
Notts Co v Shankhouse	4-0
WOLVES v Bolton W	1-1, 2-1
Newcastle Utd v Middlesbrough	2-3
Darwen v Aston Villa	5-4
Grimsby T v Stockton	5-0
Blackburn R v Newton Heath	4-0
Loughborough v Northwich Vic	1-2
Blackpool v Sheffield Utd	1-3
Sunderland v Royal Arsenal	6-0

Second Round

EVERTON v Nottingham F	4-2
Sheffield Wed v Burnley	1-0
Accrington v Preston NE	1-4
Middlesbrough Iron v Notts Co	3-2
WOLVES v Middlesbrough	2-1
Darwen v Grimsby T	2-0
Blackburn R v Northwich Vic	4-1
Sheffield Utd v Sunderland	1-3

Third Round

EVERTON V Sheffield Wed	3-0
Preston NE v Middlesbrough Iron	2-2, 7-0
WOLVES v Darwen	5-0
Blackburn R v Sunderland	3-0

Semi-final

EVERTON v Preston NE	2-2, 0-0, 2-1
WOLVES v Blackburn R	2-1

FINAL (Manchester Athletic Club, Fallowfield)

WOLVERHAMPTON WANDERERS	1
EVERTON	0

Wolverhampton Wanderers: Rose; Baugh, Swift, Malpass, Allen, Kinsey, R.Topham, Wykes, Butcher, Wood, Griffin.
Goalscorer: Allen
Everton: Williams; Kelso, Howarth, Boyle, Holt, Stewart, Latta, Gordon, Maxwell, Chadwick, Milward.
Referee: C.J.Hughes (Northwich)
Attendance: 45,000

1893-94

First Round

Middlesbrough Iron v Luton T	2-1
Nottingham F v Heanor T	1-0
NOTTS CO v Burnley	1-0
Stockport Co v Burton W	0-1
Leicester Fosse v South Shore	2-1
Derby Co v Darwen	2-0
Newton Heath v Middlesbrough	4-0
West Bromwich A v Blackburn R	2-3
Newcastle Utd v Sheffield Utd	2-0
Small Heath v BOLTON W	3-4
Liverpool v Grimsby T	3-0
Preston NE v Reading	18-0
Woolwich Arsenal v Sheffield Wed	1-2
Stoke v Everton	1-0
Sunderland v Accrington	3-0
Aston Villa v Wolves	4-2

Second Round

Middlesbrough Iron v Nottingham F	0-2
Burton W v NOTTS CO	1-2
Leicester Fosse v Derby Co	0-0, 0-3
Newton Heath v Blackburn R	0-0, 1-5
Newcastle Utd v BOLTON W	1-2
Liverpool v Preston NE	3-2
Sheffield Wed v Stoke	1-0
Sunderland v Aston Villa	2-2, 1-3

Third Round

Nottingham F v NOTTS CO	1-1, 1-4
Derby Co v Blackburn R	1-4
BOLTON W v Liverpool	3-0
Sheffield Wed v Aston Villa	3-2

Semi-final

NOTTS CO v Blackburn R	1-0
BOLTON W v Sheffield Wed	2-1

FINAL (Goodison Park, Liverpool)

NOTTS COUNTY	4
BOLTON WANDERERS	1

Notts County: Toone; Harper, Hendrey, Bramley, Calderhead, Shelton, Watson, Donnelly, Logan, Bruce, Daft.
Goalscorers: Watson, Logan 3

Bolton Wanderers: Sutcliffe; Somerville, Jones, Gardiner, Paton, Hughes, Tannahill, Wilson, Cassidy, Bentley, Dickenson.
Goalscorer: Cassidy
Referee: C.J.Hughes (Northwich)
Attendance: 37,000

1894-95

First Round

ASTON VILLA v Derby Co	2-1
Newcastle Utd v Burnley	2-1
Barnsley St Peter's v Liverpool	1-2‡, 0-4
Southampton St Mary's v Nottingham F	1-4
Sunderland v Fairfield	11-1
Luton T v Preston NE	0-2
Bolton W v Woolwich Arsenal	1-0
Bury v Leicester Fosse	4-1
Sheffield Utd v Millwall A	3-1
Small Heath v WEST BROMWICH A	1-2
Darwen v Wolves	0-0, 0-2
Newton Heath v Stoke C	2-3
Sheffield Wed v Notts Co	5-1
Middlesbrough v Chesterfield	4-0
Southport Central v Everton	0-3
Burton W v Blackburn R	1-2

Second Round

ASTON VILLA v Newcastle Utd	7-1
Liverpool v Nottingham F	0-2
Sunderland v Preston NE	2-0
Bolton W v Bury	1-0
Sheffield Utd v WEST BROMWICH A	1-1, 1-2
Wolves v Stoke	2-0
Sheffield Wed v Middlesbrough	6-1
Everton v Blackburn R	1-1, 3-2

Third Round

ASTON VILLA v Nottingham F	6-2
Sunderland v Bolton W	2-1
WEST BROMWICH A v Wolves	1-0
Sheffield Wed v Everton	2-0

Semi-final

ASTON VILLA v Sunderland	2-1
WEST BROMWICH A v Sheffield Wed	2-0

FINAL (The Crystal Palace)

ASTON VILLA	1
WEST BROMWICH ALBION	0

Aston Villa: Wilkes; Spencer, Walford, Reynolds, Cowan, Russell, Athersmith, Chatt, Devey, Hodgetts, Smith.
Goalscorer: Devey
West Bromwich Albion: Reader; Williams, Horton, Perry, Higgins, Taggart, Bassett, McLeod, Richards, Hutchinson, Banks.
Referee: J.Lewis (Blackburn) *Attendance: 42,560*

In September 1895 the FA Cup was stolen from the shop window of William Shillcock, football and boot manufacturer of Newtown Row, Birmingham. The £25 Villa were fined paid for a new trophy for 1896.
‡Replay after protest.

1895-96

First Round

WOLVES v Notts Co	2-2, 4-3
Liverpool v Millwall	4-1
Burnley v Woolwich Arsenal	6-1
Stoke v Tottenham H	5-0
Derby Co v Aston Villa	4-2
Newton Heath v Kettering T	2-1
Darwen v Grimsby T	0-2
Blackburn R v West Bromwich A	1-2
Southampton St Mary's v SHEFFIELD WED	2-3
Sunderland v Preston NE	4-1
Nottingham F v Everton	0-2
Burton W v Sheffield Utd	1-1, 0-1
Blackpool v Burton Swifts	4-1
Crewe Alex v Bolton W	0-4
Chesterfield v Newcastle Utd	0-4
Small Heath v Bury	1-4

Second Round

WOLVES v Liverpool	2-0
Burnley v Stoke	1-1, 1-7
Newton Heath v Derby Co	1-1, 1-5
Grimsby T v West Bromwich A	1-1, 0-3
SHEFFIELD WED v Sunderland	2-1
Everton v Sheffield Utd	3-0
Blackpool v Bolton W	0-2
Newcastle Utd v Bury	1-3

Third Round

WOLVES v Stoke	3-0
Derby Co v West Bromwich A	1-0
SHEFFIELD WED v Everton	4-0
Bolton W v Bury	2-0

Semi-final

WOLVES v Derby Co	2-1
SHEFFIELD WED v Bolton W	1-1, 3-1

FINAL (The Crystal Palace)

SHEFFIELD WEDNESDAY	2
WOLVERHAMPTON WANDERERS	1

Sheffield Wednesday: Massey; Earp, Langley, Brandon, Crawshaw, Petrie, Brash, Brady, Bell, Davis, Spiksley.
Goalscorer: Spiksley 2
Wolverhampton Wanderers: Tennant; Baugh, Dunn, Owen, Malpass, Griffiths, Tonks, Henderson, Beats, Wood, Black.
Goalscorer: Black
Referee: Lt W.Simpson (Hon Sec FA)
Attendance: 48,836

1896-97

First Round

ASTON VILLA v Newcastle Utd	5-0
Small Heath v Notts Co	1-2
Preston NE v Manchester C	6-0
Stoke v Glossop NE	5-2
Burnley v Sunderland	0-1
Sheffield Wed v Nottingham F	0-1
Luton T v West Bromwich A	0-1

The Aston Villa attack which led to John Devey's goal in the 1895 FA Cup Final at the Crystal Palace.

Liverpool v Burton Swifts....4-3
EVERTON v Burton W....5-2
Stockton v Bury....0-0, 1-12
Blackburn R v Sheffield Utd....2-1
Millwall A v Wolves....1-2
Derby Co v Barnsley St Peter's....8-1
Grimsby T v Bolton W....0-0, 3-3, 2-3
Southampton St Mary's v Heanor T....1-1, 1-0
Newton Heath v Kettering T....5-1

Second Round
ASTON VILLA v Notts Co....2-1
Preston NE v Stoke....2-1
Sunderland v Nottingham F....1-3
West Bromwich A v Liverpool....1-2
EVERTON v Bury....3-0
Blackburn R v Wolves....2-1
Derby Co v Bolton W....4-1
Southampton St Mary's v Newton Heath 1-1, 1-3

Third Round
Preston NE v ASTON VILLA....1-1, 0-0, 2-3
Liverpool v Nottingham F....1-1, 1-0
EVERTON v Blackburn R....2-0
Derby Co v Newton Heath....2-0

Semi-final
ASTON VILLA v Liverpool....3-0
EVERTON v Derby Co....3-2

FINAL (The Crystal Palace)
ASTON VILLA....3
EVERTON....2
Aston Villa: Whitehouse; Spencer, Evans, Reynolds, James Cowan, Crabtree, Athersmith, Devey, Campbell, Wheldon, John Cowan.
Goalscorers: Campbell, Wheldon, Crabtree
Everton: Menham; Meecham, Storrier, Boyle, Holt, Stewart, Taylor, Bell, Hartley, Chadwick, Milward.
Goalscorers: Bell, Boyle
Referee: J.Lewis (Blackburn) Attendance: 65,891

1897-98

First Round
Southampton v Leicester Fosse....2-1
Preston NE v Newcastle Utd....1-2
Luton T v Bolton W....0-1
Manchester C v Wigan C....1-0
West Bromwich A v New Brighton Tower....2-0
Sunderland v Sheffield Wed....0-1
NOTTINGHAM F v Grimsby T....4-0
Long Eaton Rgrs v Gainsboro' Trin....0-1
Liverpool v Hucknall St John's....2-0
Newton Heath v Walsall....1-0
Nott Co v Wolves....0-1
DERBY CO v Aston Villa....1-0
Burnley v Woolwich Arsenal....3-1
Sheffield Utd v Burslem Port Vale....1-1, 1-2
Everton v Blackburn R....1-0
Bury v Stoke....1-2

Second Round
Southampton v Newcastle Utd....1-0
Bolton W v Manchester C....1-0
West Bromwich A v Sheffield Wed....1-0
NOTTINGHAM F v Gainsboro' Trin....4-0
Newton Heath v Liverpool....0-0, 1-2
Wolves v DERBY CO....0-1
Burnley v Burslem Port Vale....3-0
Stoke v Everton....0-0, 1-5

Third Round
Bolton W v Southampton....0-0, 0-4
West Bromwich A v NOTTINGHAM F....2-3
DERBY CO v Liverpool....1-1, 5-1
Burnley v Everton....1-3

Semi-final
Southampton v NOTTINGHAM F....1-1, 0-2
DERBY CO v Everton....3-1

FINAL (The Crystal Palace)
NOTTINGHAM FOREST....3
DERBY COUNTY....1
Nottingham Forest: Allsop; Ritchie, Scott, Forman, McPherson, Wragg, McInnes, Richards, Benbow, Capes, Spouncer.
Goalscorers: Capes 2, McPherson
Derby County: Fryer; Methven, Leiper, Cox, A.Goodall, Turner, J.Goodall, Bloomer, Boag, Stevenson, McQueen.
Goalscorer: Bloomer
Referee: J.Lewis (Blackburn) Attendance: 62,017

1898-99

First Round
Everton v Jarrow....3-1
Nottingham F v Aston Villa....2-1
Burnley v SHEFFIELD UTD....2-2, 1-2
Preston NE v Grimsby T....7-0
West Bromwich A v South Shore....8-0
Heanor T v Bury....0-3
Liverpool v Blackburn R....2-0
Glossop v Newcastle Utd....0-1
Notts Co v Kettering T....2-0
New Brompton v Southampton....0-1
Woolwich Arsenal v DERBY CO....0-6
Wolves v Bolton W....0-0, 1-0
Small Heath v Manchester C....3-2
Sheffield Wed v Stoke....2-2, 0-2
Tottenham H v Newton Heath....1-1, 5-3
Bristol C v Sunderland....2-4

Second Round
Everton v Nottingham F....0-1
Preston NE v SHEFFIELD UTD....2-2, 1-2
West Bromwich A v Bury....2-1
Liverpool v Newcastle Utd....3-1
Notts Co v Southampton....0-1
DERBY Co v Wolves....2-1
Stoke v Small Heath....2-2, 2-1
Tottenham H v Sunderland....2-1

Third Round
Nottingham F v SHEFFIELD UTD....0-1
West Bromwich A v Liverpool....0-2
Southampton v DERBY CO....1-2
Stoke v Tottenham H....4-1

Semi-final
SHEFFIELD UTD v Liverpool....2-2, 4-4, *0-1, 1-0
DERBY CO v Stoke....3-1

FINAL (The Crystal Palace)
SHEFFIELD UNITED....4
DERBY COUNTY....1
Sheffield United: Foulke; Thickett, Boyle, Johnson, Morren, Needham, Bennett, Beers, Hedley, Almond, Priest.
Goalscorers: Bennett, Beers, Almond, Priest
Derby County: Fryer; Methven, Staley, Cox, Paterson, May, Arkesden, Bloomer, Boag, McDonald, Allen.
Goalscorer: Boag
Referee: A.Scragg (Crewe) Attendance: 73,833
*Match abandoned after the crowd encroached on the field.

1899-1900

First Round
Preston NE v Tottenham H....1-0
Portsmouth v Blackburn R....0-0, 1-1, 0-5
Nottingham F v Grimsby T....3-0
Derby Co v Sunderland....2-2, 0-3
Sheffield Wed v Bolton W....1-0
Sheffield Utd v Leicester Fosse....1-0
Notts Co v Chorley....6-0
Burnley v BURY....0-1
SOUTHAMPTON v Everton....3-0
Newcastle Utd v Reading....2-1
Walsall v West Bromwich A....1-1, 1-6
Stoke v Liverpool....0-0, 0-1
Queen's Park R v Wolves....1-1, 1-0
Jarrow v Millwall A....0-2
Manchester C v Aston Villa....1-1, 0-3
Bristol C v Stalybridge R....2-1

Second Round
Preston NE v Blackburn R....1-0
Nottingham F v Sunderland....3-0
Sheffield Utd v Sheffield Wed....1-1, 2-0
Notts Co v BURY....0-0, 0-2
SOUTHAMPTON v Newcastle Utd....4-1
Liverpool v West Bromwich A....1-1, 1-2
Queen's Park R v Millwall A....0-2
Aston Villa v Bristol C....5-1

Third Round
Preston NE v Nottingham F....0-0, 0-1
Sheffield Utd v BURY....2-2, 0-2
SOUTHAMPTON v West Bromwich A....2-1
Millwall A v Aston Villa....1-1, 0-0, 2-1

Semi-final
Nottingham F v BURY....1-1, 2-3
SOUTHAMPTON v Millwall A....0-0, 3-0

FINAL (The Crystal Palace)
BURY....4
SOUTHAMPTON....0
Bury: Thompson; Darroch, Davidson, Pray, Leeming, Ross, Richards, Wood, McLuckie, Sagar, Plant.
Goalscorers: McLuckie 2, Wood, Plant
Southampton: Robinson; Meehan, Durber, Meston, Chadwick, Petrie, Turner, Yates, Farrell, Wood, Milward.
Referee: A.G.Kingscott (Derby) Attendance: 68,945

1900-01

First Round
Bolton W v Derby Co....1-0
Reading v Bristol R....2-0
TOTTENHAM H v Preston NE....1-1, 4-2
Sheffield Wed v Bury....0-1
Middlesbrough v Newcastle Utd....3-1
Kettering T v Chesterfield....1-1, 2-1
Woolwich Arsenal v Blackburn R....2-0
West Bromwich A v Manchester C....1-0
Notts C v Liverpool....2-0
Wolves v New Brighton Tower....5-1
Sunderland v SHEFFIELD UTD....1-2
Southampton v Everton....1-3
Stoke v Small Heath....1-1, 1-2
Newton Heath v Burnley....0-0, 1-7
Aston Villa v Millwall A....5-0
Nottingham F v Leicester Fosse....5-1

Second Round
Bolton W v Reading....0-1
TOTTENHAM H v Bury....2-1
Middlesbrough v Kettering T....5-0
Woolwich Arsenal v West Bromwich A....0-1
Notts Co v Wolves....2-3
SHEFFIELD UTD v Everton....2-0
Small Heath v Burnley....1-0
Aston Villa v Nottingham F....0-0, 3-1

Third Round
Reading v TOTTENHAM H....1-1, 0-3
Middlesbrough v West Bromwich A....0-1
Wolves v SHEFFIELD UTD....0-4
Small Heath v Aston Villa....0-0, 0-1

Semi-final
TOTTENHAM H v West Bromwich A....4-0
SHEFFIELD UTD v Aston Villa....2-2, 3-0

FINAL (Burnden Park, Bolton)
TOTTENHAM HOTSPUR....3
SHEFFIELD UNITED....1
(after a 2-2 draw at The Crystal Palace)

Bury's skipper with the Cup after their victory over Southampton in the 1900 Final. The game was played in a 'terrible heatwave'.

Tottenham's Sandy Brown, hidden behind the giant figure of Willie Foulke, about to score in the 1901 Final.

Tottenham Hotspur: Clawley; Erentz, Tait, Morris, Hughes, James, Smith, Cameron, Brown, Copeland, Kirwan.
Goalscorers: Cameron, Smith, Brown
Sheffield United: Foulke; Thickett, Boyle, Johnson, Morren, Needham, Bennett, Field, Hedley, Priest, Lipsham.
Goalscorer: Priest

Referee: A.G.Kingscott (Derby) Attendance: 20,470

The venue and referee were the same for the first game but with an attendance of 114,815. Brown scored twice for Tottenham with Priest and Bennett for Sheffield United. There were no team changes.

1901-02

First Round
Tottenham H v SOUTHAMPTON 1-1, 2-2, 1-2
Liverpool v Everton 2-2, 2-0
Bury v West Bromwich A 5-1
Walsall v Burnley 1-0
Glossop v Nottingham F 1-3
Preston NE v Manchester C 1-1, 0-0, 2-4
Stoke v Aston Villa 2-2, 2-1
Middlesbrough v Bristol R 1-1, 0-1
Northampton T v SHEFFIELD UTD 0-2
Wolves v Bolton W 0-2
Woolwich Arsenal v Newcastle Utd 0-2
Sheffield Wed v Sunderland 0-1
Blackburn R v Derby C 0-2
Oxford C v Lincoln C 0-0, 0-4
Grimsby T v Portsmouth 1-1, 0-2
Notts Co v Reading 1-2

Second Round
SOUTHAMPTON v Liverpool 4-1
Walsall v Bury 0-5
Manchester C v Nottingham F 0-2
Bristol R v Stoke 0-1
SHEFFIELD UTD v Bolton W 2-1
Newcastle Utd v Sunderland 1-0
Lincoln C v Derby C 1-3
Reading v Portsmouth 0-1

Third Round
Bury v SOUTHAMPTON 2-3
Nottingham F v Stoke 2-0
Newcastle Utd v SHEFFIELD UTD 1-1, 1-2
Portsmouth v Derby Co 0-0, 3-6

Semi-final
SOUTHAMPTON v Nottingham F 3-1
SHEFFIELD UTD v Derby Co 1-1, 1-1, 1-0

FINAL (The Crystal Palace)
SHEFFIELD UNITED 2
SOUTHAMPTON 1
(after a 1-1 draw)
Sheffield United: Foulke; Thickett, Boyle, Johnson, Wilkinson, Needham, Barnes, Common, Hedley, Priest, Lipsham. (Bennett played in the place of Barnes in the first game)
Goalscorers: Hedley, Barnes
Southampton: Robinson; C.B.Fry, Molyneux, Meston, Bowman, Lee, A.Turner, Wood, Brown, Chadwick, J.Turner.
Goalscorer: Brown

Referee: T.Kirkham (Burslem) Attendance: 33,068

The venue and referee were the same for the first game but with an attendance of 76,914. Common scored for Sheffield United and Wood for Southampton.

1902-03

First Round
Tottenham H v West Bromwich A 0-0, 2-0
Bolton W v Bristol C 0-5
Aston Villa v Sunderland 4-1
Barnsley v Lincoln C 2-0
Woolwich Arsenal v Sheffield Utd 1-3
BURY v Wolves 1-0
Grimsby T v Newcastle Utd 2-1
Notts Co v Southampton 0-0, 2-2, 2-1
DERBY CO v Small Heath 2-1
Blackburn R v Sheffield Wed 0-0, 1-0
Nottingham F v Reading 0-0, 6-3
Glossop v Stoke 2-3
Millwall A v Luton T 3-0
Preston NE v Manchester C 3-1
Everton v Portsmouth 5-0
Manchester Utd v Liverpool 2-1

Second Round
Tottenham H v Bristol C 1-0
Aston Villa v Barnsley 4-1
Sheffield Utd v BURY 0-1
Grimsby T v Notts Co 0-2
DERBY CO v Blackburn R 2-0
Nottingham F v Stoke 0-0, 0-2
Millwall A v Preston NE 4-1
Everton v Manchester Utd 3-1

Third Round
Tottenham H v Aston Villa 2-3
BURY v Notts Co 1-0
DERBY CO v Stoke 3-0
Millwall A v Everton 1-0

Semi-final
Aston Villa v BURY 0-3
DERBY CO v Millwall A 3-0

FINAL (The Crystal Palace)
BURY 6
DERBY COUNTY 0
Bury: Monteith; Lindsey, McEwen, Johnstone, Thorpe, Ross, W.Richards, Wood, Sagar, Leeming, Plant.
Goalscorers: Ross, Sagar, Leeming 2, Wood, Plant
Derby County: Fryer; Methven, Morris, Warren, Goodall, May, Warrington, York, Boag, G.Richards, Davis.

Referee: J.Adams (Birmingham) Attendance: 63,102

This remains the record Final score, Bury winning the Cup without conceding a goal in any round. Derby used three goalkeepers during the game, Fryer, Morris and Methven.

1903-04

First Round
MANCHESTER C v Sunderland 3-2
Woolwich Arsenal v Fulham 1-0
Millwall v Middlesbrough 0-2
Preston NE v Grimsby T 1-0
Plymouth Arg v Sheffield Wed 2-2, 0-2
Notts Co v Manchester Utd 3-3, 1-2
Everton v Tottenham H 1-2
Stoke v Aston Villa 2-3
Reading v BOLTON W 1-1, 2-3
Southampton v Burslem Port Vale 3-0
Bristol C v Sheffield Utd 1-3
Bury v Newcastle Utd 2-1
Portsmouth v Derby Co 2-5
Stockton v Wolves 1-4
Blackburn R v Liverpool 3-1
West Bromwich A v Nottingham F 1-1, 1-3

Second Round
Woolwich Arsenal v MANCHESTER C 0-2
Preston NE v Middlesbrough 0-3
Sheffield Wed v Manchester Utd 6-0
Tottenham H v Aston Villa 1-0
BOLTON W v Southampton 4-1
Bury v Sheffield Utd 1-2
Derby Co v Wolves 2-2, 2-2, 1-0
Blackburn R v Nottingham F 3-1

Third Round
MANCHESTER C v Middlesbrough 0-0, 3-1
Tottenham H v Sheffield Wed 1-1, 0-2
Sheffield Utd v BOLTON W 0-2
Derby Co v Blackburn R 2-1

Semi-final
MANCHESTER C v Sheffield Wed 3-0
BOLTON W v Derby Co 1-0

FINAL (The Crystal Palace)
MANCHESTER CITY 1
BOLTON WANDERERS 0
Manchester City: Hillman; McMahon, Burgess, Frost, Hynds, Ashworth, Meredith, Livingstone, Gillespie, A.Turnbull, Booth.
Goalscorer: Meredith
Bolton Wanderers: Davies; Brown, Struthers, Clifford, Greenhalgh, Freebairn, Stokes, Marsh, Yenson, White, Taylor.

Referee: A.J.Barker (Hanley) Attendance: 61,374

1904-05

First Round
Lincoln C v Manchester C 1-2
Bolton W v Bristol R 1-1, 3-0
Middlesbrough v Tottenham H 1-1, 0-1
NEWCASTLE UTD v Plymouth Arg 1-1, 1-1, 2-0
Woolwich Arsenal v Bristol C 0-0, 0-1
Derby Co v Preston NE 0-2
Blackburn R v Sheffield Wed 1-2
Small Heath v Portsmouth 0-2
Stoke v Grimsby T 2-0
Liverpool v Everton 1-1, 1-2
Sunderland v Wolves 1-1, 0-1
Southampton v Millwall 3-1
ASTON VILLA v Leicester Fosse 5-1
Bury v Notts Co 1-0
Fulham v Reading 0-0, 0-0, 1-0
Nottingham F v Sheffield Utd 2-0

Second Round
Manchester C v Bolton W 1-2
Tottenham H v NEWCASTLE UTD 1-1, 0-4
Bristol C v Preston NE 0-0, 0-1
Sheffield Wed v Portsmouth 2-1
Stoke v Everton 0-4
Wolves v Southampton 2-3
ASTON VILLA v Bury 3-2
Fulham v Nottingham F 1-0

Third Round
Bolton W v NEWCASTLE UTD 0-2
Preston NE v Sheffield Wed 1-1, 0-3
Everton v Southampton 4-0
ASTON VILLA v Fulham 5-0

Semi-final
NEWCASTLE UTD v Sheffield Wed 1-0
Everton v ASTON VILLA 1-1, 1-2

FINAL (The Crystal Palace)
ASTON VILLA 2
NEWCASTLE UNITED 0
Aston Villa: George; Spencer, Miles, Pearson, Leake, Windmill, Brown, Garratty, Hampton, Bache, Hall.
Goalscorer: Hampton
Newcastle United: Lawrence; McCombie, Carr, Gardner, Aitken, McWilliam, Rutherford, Howie, Appleyard, Veitch, Gosnell.

Referee: P.R.Harrower (London) Attendance: 101,117

1905-06

First Round
Woolwich Arsenal v West Ham Utd 1-1, 3-2
Worcester C v Watford 0-6
Sunderland v Notts Co 1-0

Burslem Port Vale v Gainsboro' Trin 0-3
Manchester Utd v Staple Hill............................7-2
Norwich C v Tonbridge WR.......................1-1, 5-0
Aston Villa v King's Lynn.................................11-0
New Crusaders v Plymouth Arg.........................3-6
NEWCASTLE UTD v Grimsby T............................6-0
Derby Co v Kettering T......................................4-0
Blackpool v Crystal Palace.................1-1, 1-1, 1-0
Sheffield Utd v Manchester C...........................4-1
Tottenham H v Burnley.......................................2-0
Hull C v Reading 0-1
Birmingham v Preston NE 1-0
Stoke v Blackburn R...1-0
EVERTON v West Bromwich A 3-1
Clapton O v Chesterfield 0-0, 0-3
Bradford C v Barrow 3-2
Bishop Auckland v Wolves 0-3
Sheffield Wed v Bristol R....................................1-0
Millwall v Burton W...1-0
Bury v Nottingham F 1-1, 2-6
Fulham v Queen's Park R 1-0
Liverpool v Leicester Fosse................................2-1
Crewe Alex v Barnsley..............................1-1, 0-4
Brentford v Bristol C 2-1
Lincoln C v Stockport Co....................................4-2
Southampton v Portsmouth................................5-1
New Brompton v Northampton T.......................2-1
Middlesbrough v Bolton W.................................3-0
Brighton & HA v Swindon T...............................3-0

Second Round
Woolwich Arsenal v Watford...............................3-0
Sunderland v Gainsboro' Trin 1-1, 3-0
Manchester Utd v Norwich C..............................3-0
Aston Villa v Plymouth Arg......................0-0, 5-1
Derby Co v NEWCASTLE UTD 0-0, 1-2
Blackpool v Sheffield Utd....................................2-1
Tottenham H v Reading 3-2
Stoke v Birmingham 0-1
EVERTON v Chesterfield.....................................3-0
Bradford C v Wolves 5-0
Sheffield Wed v Millwall 1-1, 3-0
Fulham v Nottingham F 1-3
Liverpool v Barnsley...1-0
Brentford v Lincoln C 3-0
New Brompton v Southampton.................0-0, 0-1
Brighton & HA v Middlesbrough.........1-1, 1-1, 1-3

Third Round
Woolwich Arsenal v Sunderland 5-0
Manchester Utd v Aston Villa.............................5-1
NEWCASTLE UTD v Blackpool 5-0
Tottenham H v Birmingham 1-1, 0-2
EVERTON v Bradford C 1-0
Sheffield Wed v Nottingham F...........................4-1
Liverpool v Brentford 2-0
Southampton v Middlesbrough 6-1

Fourth Round
Manchester Utd v Woolwich Arsenal.................2-3
Birmingham v NEWCASTLE UTD..............2-2, 0-3
EVERTON v Sheffield Wed 4-3
Liverpool v Southampton 3-0

Semi-final
Woolwich Arsenal v NEWCASTLE UTD.............0-2
EVERTON v Liverpool..2-0

FINAL (The Crystal Palace)
EVERTON 1
NEWCASTLE UNITED...0
Everton: Scott; Crelley, W.Balmer, Makepeace, Taylor, Abbott, Sharp, Bolton, Young, Settle, H.P.Hardman.
Goalscorer: Young
Newcastle United: Lawrence; McCombie, Carr, Gardner, Aitken, McWilliam, Rutherford, Howie, Orr, Veitch, Gosnell.
Referee: F.Kirkham (Preston) Attendance: 75,609

Everton attacking the Newcastle goal in the 1906 Final. Note that the Newcastle goalkeeper Jimmy Lawrence is still not wearing a distinguishing jersey.

1906-07

First Round
Burslem Port Vale v Irthlingboro 7-1
Notts Co v Preston NE..1-0
Blackburn R v Manchester C...................2-2, 1-0
Tottenham H v Hull C.......................0-0, 0-0, 1-0
West Bromwich A v Stoke...................1-1, 2-2, 2-1
Norwich C v Hastings 3-1
Derby Co v Chesterfield............................1-1, 4-0
Lincoln C v Chelsea...................................2-2, 1-0
Fulham v Stockport Co 0-0, 2-1
Newcastle Utd v Crystal Palace 0-1
Brentford v Glossop 2-1
Middlesbrough v Northampton T 4-2
West Ham Utd v Blackpool 2-1
EVERTON v Sheffield Utd 1-0
Burnley v Aston Villa 1-3
Bolton W v Brighton & HA.................................3-1
Grimsby T v Woolwich Arsenal.................1-1, 0-3
Bristol C v Leeds C...4-1
Bristol R v Queen's Park R 0-0, 1-0
Millwall v Plymouth Arg 2-0
Nottingham F v Barnsley...........................1-1, 1-2
Portsmouth v Manchester Utd 2-2, 2-1
Oxford C v Bury..0-3
Burton Utd v New Brompton 0-0, 0-2
Oldham Ath v Kidderminster H.........................5-0
Liverpool v Birmingham.....................................2-1
Bradford C v Reading 2-0
Crewe Alex v Accrington S 1-1, 0-1
Southampton v Watford......................................2-1
SHEFFIELD WED v Wolves 3-2
Gainsboro' Trin v Luton T.........................0-0, 1-2
Sunderland v Leicester Fosse.............................4-1

Second Round
Burslem Port Vale v Notts Co....................2-2, 0-5
Blackburn R v Tottenham H................1-1, 1-1, 1-2
West Bromwich A v Norwich C 1-0
Derby Co v Lincoln C..1-0
Fulham v Crystal Palace 0-0, 0-1
Brentford v Middlesbrough.................................1-0
West Ham Utd v EVERTON 1-2
Bolton W v Aston Villa..2-0
Woolwich Arsenal v Bristol C 2-1
Bristol R v Millwall...3-0
Barnsley v Portsmouth 1-0
Bury v New Brompton...1-0
Oldham Ath v Liverpool 0-1
Bradford C v Accrington S 1-0
Southampton v SHEFFIELD WED.............1-1, 1-3
Luton T v Sunderland 0-0, 0-1

Third Round
Notts Co v Tottenham H.....................................4-0
West Bromwich A v Derby Co 2-0
Crystal Palace v Brentford.........................1-1, 1-0
EVERTON v Bolton W................................0-0, 3-0
Woolwich Arsenal v Bristol R 1-0
Barnsley v Bury..1-0
Liverpool v Bradford C 1-0
SHEFFIELD WED v Sunderland................0-0, 1-0

Fourth Round
West Bromwich A v Notts Co 3-1
Crystal Palace v EVERTON 1-1, 0-4
Barnsley v Woolwich Arsenal..............................1-2
SHEFFIELD WED v Liverpool 1-0

Semi-final
West Bromwich A v EVERTON 1-2
Woolwich Arsenal v SHEFFIELD WED 1-3

FINAL (The Crystal Palace)
SHEFFIELD WEDNESDAY 2
EVERTON 1
Sheffield Wednesday: Lyall; Layton, Burton, Brittleton, Crawshaw, Bartlett, Chapman, Bradshaw, Wilson, Stewart, Simpson.
Goalscorers: Stewart, Simpson
Everton: Scott; W.Balmer, R.Balmer, Makepeace, Taylor, Abbott, Sharp, Bolton, Young, Settle, H.P.Hardman.
Goalscorer: Sharp
Referee: N.Whittaker (London) Attendance: 84,594

1907-08

First Round
Bradford C v WOLVES...............................1-1, 0-1
Bury v Millwall 2-1
Swindon T v Sheffield Utd.......................0-0, 3-2
Queen's Park R v Reading 1-0
Stoke v Lincoln C 5-0
Gainsboro' Trin v Watford 1-0
Hastings v Portsmouth 0-1
Leicester Fosse v Blackburn R 2-0
Notts Co v Middlesbrough 2-0
Bolton W v Woking 5-0
Oldham Ath v Leeds C 2-1
Everton v Tottenham H 1-0
Burnley v Southampton 1-2
West Bromwich A v Birmingham..............1-1, 2-1
Northampton T v Bristol R 0-1
Chesterfield v Stockton......................................4-0
NEWCASTLE UTD v Nottingham F 2-0
West Ham Utd v Rotherham T...........................1-0
Liverpool v Derby Co...4-2
Brighton & HA v Preston NE.............1-1, 1-1, 1-0
Bristol C v Grimsby T...............................0-0, 1-2
Carlisle Utd v Brentford............................2-2, 3-1
Coventry C v Crystal Palace 2-4
Plymouth Arg v Barnsley 1-0
Glossop v Manchester C 0-0, 0-6
New Brompton v Sunderland 3-1
Luton T v Fulham...3-8
Norwich C v Sheffield Wed 2-0
Manchester Utd v Blackpool 3-1
Chelsea v Worksop 9-1
Aston Villa v Stockport Co 3-0
Woolwich Arsenal v Hull C 0-0, 1-4

Second Round
WOLVES v Bury...2-0
Swindon T v Queen's Park R 2-1
Stoke v Gainsboro' Trin 1-1, 2-2, 3-1
Portsmouth v Leicester Fosse............................1-0
Notts Co v Bolton W 1-1, 1-2
Oldham Ath v Everton 0-0, 1-6
Southampton v West Bromwich A 1-0
Bristol R v Chesterfield 2-0
NEWCASTLE UTD v West Ham Utd...................2-0
Liverpool v Brighton & HA........................1-1, 3-0
Grimsby T v Carlisle Utd 6-2
Plymouth Arg v Crystal Palace...........................2-3
Manchester C v New Brompton..................1-1, 2-1
Fulham v Norwich C 2-1
Manchester Utd v Chelsea 1-0
Aston Villa v Hull C..3-0

Third Round
WOLVES v Swindon T 2-0
Portsmouth v Stoke 0-1
Bolton W v Everton..................................3-3, 1-3
Southampton v Bristol R....................................2-0
NEWCASTLE UTD v Liverpool 3-1
Grimsby T v Crystal Palace 1-0
Manchester C v Fulham 1-1, 1-3
Aston Villa v Manchester Utd.............................0-2

Fourth Round
Stoke v WOLVES 0-1
Everton v Southampton.............................0-0, 2-3
NEWCASTLE UTD v Grimsby T..........................5-1
Fulham v Manchester Utd 2-1

Semi-final
WOLVES v Southampton....................................2-0
NEWCASTLE UTD v Fulham 6-0

FINAL (The Crystal Palace)
WOLVERHAMPTON WANDERERS.......................3
NEWCASTLE UNITED...1
Wolverhampton Wanderers: Lunn; Jones, Collins, Revd K.R.G.Hunt, Wooldridge, Bishop, Harrison, Shelton, Hedley, Radford, Pedley.
Goalscorers: Hunt, Hedley, Harrison
Newcastle United: Lawrence; McCracken, Pudan, Gardner, Veitch, McWilliam, Rutherford, Howie, Appleyard, Speedie, Wilson.
Goalscorer: Howie
Referee: T.P.Campbell (Blackburn) Attendance: 74,697

1908-09

First Round
MANCHESTER UTD v Brighton & HA...................1-0
Everton v Barnsley...3-1
Notts Co v Blackburn R 0-1
Hull C v Chelsea.......................................1-1, 0-1
Manchester C v Tottenham H 3-4
Fulham v Carlisle Utd 4-1
Wolves v Crystal Palace 2-2, 2-4
Bristol R v Burnley...1-4
Newcastle Utd v Clapton Orient 5-0

Blackpool v Hastings 2-0
Oldham Ath v Leeds C 1-1, 0-2
Queen's Park R v West Ham Utd 0-0, 0-1
Sheffield Utd v Sunderland 2-3
Preston NE v Middlesbrough 1-0
Bradford C v Workington †0-0, 2-0
West Bromwich A v Bolton W 3-1
BRISTOL C v Southampton 1-1, 2-0
Bury v Kettering T 8-0
Norwich C v Reading 0-0, 1-1, 3-2
Liverpool v Lincoln C 5-1
Grimsby T v Stockport Co †2-2, 0-2
Chesterfield v Glossop 0-2
Birmingham v Portsmouth 2-5
Sheffield Wed v Stoke 5-0
Northampton T v Derby Co 1-1, 2-4
Watford v Leicester Fosse 1-1, 1-3
Plymouth Arg v Swindon T 1-0
Wrexham v Exeter C 1-1, 1-2
Nottingham F v Aston Villa 2-0
Brentford v Gainsboro' Trin 2-0
Luton T v Millwall Ath 1-2
Croydon Com v Woolwich Arsenal 1-1, 0-2

Second Round
MANCHESTER UTD v Everton 1-0
Blackburn R v Chelsea 2-1
Tottenham H v Fulham 1-0
Crystal Palace v Burnley 0-0, 0-9
Newcastle Utd v Blackpool 2-1
Leeds C v West Ham Utd 1-1, 1-2
Preston NE v Sunderland 1-2
West Bromwich A v Bradford C 1-2
BRISTOL C v Bury 2-2, 1-0
Liverpool v Norwich C 2-3
Stockport Co v Glossop 1-1, 0-1
Portsmouth v Sheffield Wed 2-2, 0-3
Leicester Fosse v Derby Co 0-2
Plymouth Arg v Exeter C 2-0
Nottingham F v Brentford 1-0
Woolwich Arsenal v Millwall Ath 1-1, 0-1

Third Round
MANCHESTER UTD v Blackburn R 6-1
Tottenham H v Burnley 0-0, 1-3
West Ham Utd v Newcastle Utd 0-0, 1-2
Bradford C v Sunderland 0-1
BRISTOL C v Norwich C 2-0
Sheffield Wed v Glossop 0-1
Derby Co v Plymouth Arg 1-0
Nottingham F v Millwall Ath 3-1

Fourth Round
Burnley v MANCHESTER UTD ‡1-0, 2-3
Newcastle Utd v Sunderland 2-2, 3-0
Glossop v BRISTOL C 0-0, 0-1
Derby Co v Nottingham F 3-0

Semi-final
MANCHESTER UTD v Newcastle Utd 1-0
BRISTOL C v Derby Co 1-1, 2-1

FINAL (The Crystal Palace)
MANCHESTER UNITED 1
BRISTOL CITY 0
Manchester United: Moger; Stacey, Hayes, Duckworth, Roberts, Bell, Meredith, Halse, J.Turnbull, A.Turnbull, Wall.
Goalscorer: A.Turnbull
Bristol City: Clay; Annan, Cottle, Hanlin, Wedlock, Spear, Staniforth, Hardy, Gilligan, Burton, Hilton.
Referee: J.Mason (Burslem) Attendance: 71,401
†Abandoned because of blizzards. ‡Abandoned after 72 minutes.

1909-10

First Round
Stoke v NEWCASTLE UTD 1-1, 1-2
Chesterfield v Fulham 0-0, 1-2
Blackburn R v Accrington S 7-1
Bradford C v Notts Co 4-2
Birmingham v Leicester Fosse 1-4
Bury v Glossop 2-1
Leyton v New Brompton 0-0, 2-2, 1-0
Stockport Co v Bolton W 4-1
Crystal Palace v Swindon T 1-3
Burnley v Manchester Utd 2-0
Plymouth Arg v Tottenham H 1-1, 1-7
Chelsea v Hull C 2-1
Workington v Manchester C 1-2
Brighton & HA v Southampton 0-1
Oldham Ath v Aston Villa 1-2
Derby Co v Millwall Ath 5-0
Blackpool v BARNSLEY 1-1, 0-6
Grimsby T v Bristol R 0-2
West Bromwich A v Clapton Orient 2-0
Bristol C v Liverpool 2-0
Norwich C v Queen's Park R 0-0, 0-3
Gainsboro' Trin v Southend Utd 1-1, 0-1
West Ham Utd v Carlisle Utd 1-1, 5-0
Reading v Wolves 0-5
Middlesbrough v Everton 1-1, 3-5
Woolwich Arsenal v Watford 3-0
Sunderland v Leeds C 1-0
Bradford v Bishop Auckland 8-0
Preston NE v Coventry C 1-2
Portsmouth v Shrewsbury T 3-0
Nottingham F v Sheffield Utd 3-2
Northampton T v Sheffield Wed 0-0, 1-0

Second Round
NEWCASTLE UTD v Fulham 4-0
Bradford C v Blackburn R 1-2
Leicester Fosse v Bury 3-2
Stockport Co v Leyton 0-2
Swindon T v Burnley 2-0
Chelsea v Tottenham H 0-1
Southampton v Manchester C 0-5
Aston Villa v Derby Co 6-1
BARNSLEY v Bristol R 4-0
Bristol C v West Bromwich A 1-1, 2-4
Southend Utd v Queen's Park R 0-0, 2-3
Wolves v West Ham Utd 1-5
Everton v Woolwich Arsenal 5-0
Sunderland v Bradford 3-1
Portsmouth v Coventry C 0-1
Northampton T v Nottingham F 0-0, 0-1

Third Round
NEWCASTLE UTD v Blackburn R 3-1
Leicester Fosse v Leyton 1-0
Swindon T v Tottenham H 3-2
Aston Villa v Manchester C 1-2
BARNSLEY v West Bromwich A 1-0
Queen's Park R v West Ham Utd 1-1, 1-0
Everton v Sunderland 2-0
Coventry C v Nottingham F 3-1

Fourth Round
NEWCASTLE UTD v Leicester Fosse 3-0
Swindon T v Manchester C 2-0
BARNSLEY v Queen's Park R 1-0
Coventry C v Everton 0-2

Semi-final
NEWCASTLE UTD v Swindon T 2-0
BARNSLEY v Everton 0-0, 3-0

FINAL (Goodison Park, Liverpool)
NEWCASTLE UNITED 2
BARNSLEY 0
(after a 1-1 draw)
Newcastle United: Lawrence; McCracken, Carr, Veitch, Low, McWilliam, Rutherford, Howie, Shepherd, Wilson, Higgins. (Whitson played in place of Carr in the first game)
Goalscorers: Shepherd 2 (1 pen)
Barnsley: Mearns; Downs, Ness, Glendinning, Boyle, Utley, Tuffnell, Lillycrop, Gadsby, Forman, Bartrop.
Referee: J.T.Ibbotson (Derby) Attendance: 69,000
The first game was played at the Crystal Palace and the referee was the same. The attendance was 77,747 with Rutherford scoring for Newcastle and Tuffnell for Barnsley.

1910-11

First Round
New Brompton v BRADFORD C 0-1
Norwich C v Sunderland 3-1
Grimsby T v Croydon Com 3-0
Bristol C v Crewe Alex 0-3
Burnley v Exeter C 2-0
Watford v Barnsley 0-2
Sheffield Wed v Coventry C 1-2
Leeds C v Brighton & HA 1-3
Blackburn R v Southend Utd 5-1
Tottenham H v Millwall Ath 2-1
Middlesbrough v Glossop 1-0
Leicester Fosse v Southampton 3-1
West Ham Utd v Nottingham F 2-1
Brentford v Preston NE 0-1
Manchester Utd v Blackpool 2-1
Portsmouth v Aston Villa 1-4
NEWCASTLE UTD v Bury 6-1
Northampton T v Luton T 5-1
Bristol R v Hull C 0-0, 0-1
Birmingham v Oldham Ath 1-1, 2-0
Derby Co v Plymouth Arg 2-1
West Bromwich A v Fulham 4-1
Crystal Palace v Everton 0-4
Liverpool v Gainsboro' Trin 3-2
Chelsea v Leyton 0-0, 2-0
Bolton W v Chesterfield 0-2
Wolves v Accrington S 2-0
Stoke v Manchester C 1-2
Swindon T v Notts Co 3-1
Clapton Orient v Woolwich Arsenal *0-1, 1-2
Sheffield Utd v Darlington 0-1
Bradford v Queen's Park R 5-3

Second Round
BRADFORD C v Norwich C 2-1
Crewe Alex v Grimsby T 1-5
Burnley v Barnsley 2-0
Brighton & HA v Coventry C 0-0, 0-2
Blackburn R v Tottenham H 0-0, 2-0
Middlesbrough v Leicester Fosse 0-0, 2-1
West Ham Utd v Preston NE 3-0
Manchester Utd v Aston Villa 2-1
NEWCASTLE UTD v Northampton T 1-1, 1-0
Hull C v Oldham Ath 1-0
Derby Co v West Bromwich A 2-0
Everton v Liverpool 2-1
Chelsea v Chesterfield 4-1
Wolves v Manchester C 1-0
Swindon T v Woolwich Arsenal 1-0
Darlington v Bradford 2-1

Third Round
BRADFORD C v Grimsby T 1-0
Burnley v Coventry C 5-0
Middlesbrough v Blackburn R 0-3
West Ham Utd v Manchester Utd 2-1
NEWCASTLE UTD v Hull C 3-2
Derby Co v Everton 5-0
Wolves v Chelsea 0-2
Darlington v Swindon T 0-3

Fourth Round
BRADFORD C v Burnley 1-0
West Ham Utd v Blackburn R 2-3
NEWCASTLE UTD v Derby Co 4-0
Chelsea v Swindon T 3-1

General view of the 1911 Final between Bradford City and Newcastle United at the Crystal Palace.

Semi-final
BRADFORD C v Blackburn R 3-0
NEWCASTLE UTD v Chelsea 3-0

FINAL (Old Trafford, Manchester)
BRADFORD CITY 1
NEWCASTLE UNITED 0
(after a 0-0 draw)

Bradford City: Mellors; Campbell, Taylor, Robinson, Torrance, McDonald, Logan, Speirs, O'Rourke, Devine, Thompson.
Goalscorer: Speirs
Newcastle United: Lawrence; McCracken, Whitson, Veitch, Low, Willis, Rutherford, Jobey, Stewart, Higgins, Wilson.
Referee: J.H.Pearson (Crewe) Attendance: 58,000

The first game was played at the Crystal Palace when the referee was the same. The attendance was 69,098. After the FA Cup's design had been duplicated for another competition it was withdrawn and presented to Lord Kinnaird on his completion of 21 years as FA President. This was the first year the present trophy was awarded.
*Abandoned because of fog.

1911-12

First Round
Manchester Utd v Huddersfield T 3-1
Southampton v Coventry C 0-2
Aston Villa v Walsall 6-0
Southport v Reading 0-2
Blackburn R v Norwich C 4-1
Derby Co v Newcastle Utd 3-0
Watford v Wolves 0-0, 0-10
Lincoln C v Stockport Co 2-0
WEST BROMWICH A v Tottenham H 3-0
Leeds C v Glossop 1-0
Sunderland v Plymouth Arg 3-1
Brentford v Crystal Palace 0-0, 0-4
Fulham v Burnley 2-1
Liverpool v Leyton 1-0
Northampton T v Bristol C 1-0
Darlington v Brighton & HA 2-1
Swindon T v Sutton Junction 5-0
Luton T v Notts Co 2-4
West Ham Utd v Gainsboro' Trin 2-1
Middlesbrough v Sheffield Wed 0-0, 2-1
Clapton Orient v Everton 1-2
Bury v Millwall Ath 2-1
Oldham Ath v Hull C 1-1, 1-0
Preston NE v Manchester C 0-1
Queen's Park R v Bradford C 0-0, 0-4
Chelsea v Sheffield Utd 1-0
Nottingham F v Bradford 0-1
Bristol R v Portsmouth 1-2
Birmingham v BARNSLEY 0-0, 0-3
Croydon Com v Leicester Fosse 2-2, 1-6
Bolton W v Woolwich Arsenal 1-0
Crewe Alex v Blackpool 1-1, 2-2, 1-2

Second Round
Coventry C v Manchester Utd 1-5
Aston Villa v Reading 1-1, 0-1
Derby Co v Blackburn R 1-2
Wolves v Lincoln C 2-1
Leeds C v WEST BROMWICH A 0-1
Crystal Palace v Sunderland 0-0, 0-1
Fulham v Liverpool 3-0
Darlington v Northampton T 1-1, 0-2
Swindon T v Notts Co 2-0
Middlesbrough v West Ham Utd 1-1, 1-2
Everton v Bury 1-1, 6-0
Manchester C v Oldham Ath 0-1
Bradford C v Chelsea 2-0
Bradford v Portsmouth 2-0
BARNSLEY v Leicester Fosse 1-0
Bolton W v Blackpool 1-0

Third Round
Reading v Manchester Utd 1-1, 0-3
Blackburn R v Wolves 3-2
Sunderland v WEST BROMWICH A 1-2
Fulham v Northampton T 2-1
West Ham Utd v Swindon T 1-1, 0-4
Oldham Ath v Everton 0-2
Bradford v Bradford C 0-1
Bolton W v BARNSLEY 1-2

Fourth Round
Manchester Utd v Blackburn R 1-1, 2-4
WEST BROMWICH A v Fulham 3-0
Swindon T v Everton 2-1
BARNSLEY v Bradford C 0-0, 0-0, †0-0, 3-2

Semi-final
Blackburn R v WEST BROMWICH A 0-0, 0-1
Swindon T v BARNSLEY 0-0, 0-1

Tommy Barber's winner for Aston Villa against Newcastle in 1913.

FINAL (Bramall Lane, Sheffield)
BARNSLEY 1
WEST BROMWICH ALBION 0
(after extra-time)
(following a 0-0 draw)

Barnsley: Copper; Downs, Taylor, Glendinning, Bratley, Utley, Bartrop, Tuffnell, Lillycrop, Travers, Moore.
Goalscorer: Tuffnell
West Bromwich Albion: Pearson; Cook, Pennington, Baddeley, Buck, McNeal, Jephcott, Wright, Pailor, Bowser, Shearman.
Referee: J.R.Schumacher (London)
Attendance: 38,555

The first game was played at the Crystal Palace with the referee and teams unchanged. The attendance was 54,556.
†Abandoned after 86 minutes when the crowd were continually spilling over the touch-lines.

1912-13

First Round
Derby Co v ASTON VILLA 1-3
West Bromwich A v West Ham Utd 1-1, 2-2, 0-3
Crystal Palace v Glossop 2-0
Southampton v Bury 1-1, 1-2
Bradford v Barrow 1-1, 1-0
Wolves v London Caledonian 3-1
Sheffield Wed v Grimsby T 5-1
Chelsea v Southend Utd 5-2
Oldham Ath v Bolton W 2-0
Chesterfield v Nottingham F 1-4
Manchester Utd v Coventry C 1-1, 2-1
Plymouth Arg v Preston NE 2-0
Everton v Stockport Co 5-1
Portsmouth v Brighton & HA 1-2
Bristol R v Notts Co 2-0
Leicester Fosse v Norwich C 1-4
SUNDERLAND v Clapton Orient 6-0
Manchester C v Birmingham 4-0
Rochdale v Swindon T 0-2
Huddersfield T v Sheffield Utd 3-1
Newcastle Utd v Bradford C 1-0
Fulham v Hull C 0-2
Liverpool v Bristol C 3-0
Croydon Com v Woolwich Arsenal 0-0, 1-2
Leeds C v Burnley 2-3
South Shields v Gainsboro' Trin 0-1
Millwall Ath v Middlesbrough 0-0, 1-4
Queen's Park R v Halifax T 4-2
Blackburn R v Northampton T 7-2
Gillingham v Barnsley 0-0, 1-3
Stoke v Reading 2-2, 0-3
Tottenham H v Blackpool 1-1, 6-1

Second Round
ASTON VILLA v West Ham Utd 5-0
Crystal Palace v Bury 2-0
Bradford v Wolves 3-0
Chelsea v Sheffield Wed 1-1, 0-6
Oldham Ath v Nottingham F 5-1
Plymouth Arg v Manchester Utd 0-2
Brighton & HA v Everton 0-0, 0-1
Bristol R v Norwich C 1-1, 2-2, 1-0
SUNDERLAND v Manchester C 2-0
Huddersfield T v Swindon T 1-2
Hull C v Newcastle Utd 0-0, 0-3
Woolwich Arsenal v Liverpool 1-4
Burnley v Gainsboro' Trin 4-1
Middlesbrough v Queen's Park R 3-2
Barnsley v Blackburn R 2-3
Reading v Tottenham H 1-0

Third Round
ASTON VILLA v Crystal Palace 5-0
Bradford v Sheffield Wed 2-1
Oldham Ath v Manchester Utd 0-0, 2-1
Bristol R v Everton 0-4
SUNDERLAND v Swindon T 4-2
Liverpool v Newcastle Utd 1-1, 0-1
Burnley v Middlesbrough 3-1
Reading v Blackburn R 1-2

Fourth Round
Bradford v ASTON VILLA 0-5
Everton v Oldham Ath 0-1
SUNDERLAND v Newcastle Utd 0-0, 2-2, 3-0
Blackburn R v Burnley 0-1

Semi-final
ASTON VILLA v Oldham Ath 1-0
SUNDERLAND v Burnley 0-0, 3-2

FINAL (The Crystal Palace)
ASTON VILLA 1
SUNDERLAND 0

Aston Villa: Hardy; Lyons, Weston, Barber, Harrop, Leach, Wallace, Halse, Hampton, Stephenson, Bache.
Goalscorer: Barber
Sunderland: Butler; Gladwin, Ness, Cuggy, Thomson, Low, Mordue, Buchan, Richardson, Holley, Martin.
Referee: A.Adams (Nottingham) Attendance: 121,919

1913-14

First Round
Newcastle Utd v Sheffield Utd 0-5
Bradford v Reading 5-1
Millwall Ath v Chelsea 0-0, 1-0
Bradford C v Woolwich Arsenal 2-0
Manchester C v Fulham 2-0
Leicester Fosse v Tottenham H 5-5, 0-2
Blackburn R v Middlesbrough 3-0
Hull C v Bury 0-0, 1-2
BURNLEY v South Shields 3-1
Derby Co v Northampton T 1-0
Bolton W v Port Vale 3-0
Swindon T v Manchester Utd 1-0
Sunderland v Chatham 9-0
Plymouth Arg v Lincoln C 4-1
Preston NE v Bristol R 5-2
Glossop v Everton 2-1
Aston Villa v Stoke 4-0
Portsmouth v Exeter C 0-4
West Bromwich A v Grimsby T 2-0
Gainsboro' Trin v Leeds C 2-4
Sheffield Wed v Notts Co 3-2
Wolves v Southampton 3-0
Oldham Ath v Brighton & HA 1-1, 0-1
Clapton Orient v Nottingham F 2-2, 1-0
LIVERPOOL v Barnsley 1-1, 1-0
Gillingham v Blackpool 1-0
West Ham Utd v Chesterfield 8-1
Crystal Palace v Norwich C 2-1
Queen's Park R v Bristol C 2-2, 2-0
Swansea T v Merthyr Tydfil 2-0
Birmingham v Southend Utd 2-1
Huddersfield T v London Caledonian 3-0

Second Round
Sheffield Utd v Bradford 3-1

Burnley v Liverpool at the Crystal Palace in 1914.

Millwall Ath v Bradford C 1-0
Manchester C v Tottenham H 2-1
Blackburn R v Bury 2-0
BURNLEY v Derby Co 3-2
Bolton W v Swindon T 4-2
Sunderland v Plymouth Arg 2-1
Glossop v Preston NE 0-1
Exeter C v Aston Villa 1-2
Leeds C v West Bromwich A 0-2
Wolves v Sheffield Wed 1-1, 0-1
Brighton & HA v Clapton Orient 3-1
LIVERPOOL v Gillingham 2-0
West Ham Utd v Crystal Palace 2-0
Swansea T v Queen's Park R 1-2
Birmingham v Huddersfield T 1-0

Third Round
Millwall Ath v Sheffield Utd 0-4
Blackburn R v Manchester C 1-2
BURNLEY v Bolton W 3-0
Sunderland v Preston NE 2-0
Aston Villa v West Bromwich A 2-1
Sheffield Wed v Brighton & HA 3-0
West Ham Utd v LIVERPOOL 1-1, 1-5
Birmingham v Queen's Park R 1-2

Fourth Round
Manchester C v Sheffield Utd 0-0, 0-0, 0-1
Sunderland v BURNLEY 0-0, 1-2
Sheffield Wed v Aston Villa 0-1
LIVERPOOL v Queen's Park R 2-1

Semi-final
Sheffield Utd v BURNLEY 0-0, 0-1
Aston Villa v LIVERPOOL 0-2

FINAL (The Crystal Palace)
BURNLEY 1
LIVERPOOL 0
Burnley: Sewell; Bamford, Taylor, Halley, Boyle, Watson, Nesbitt, Lindley, Freeman, Hodgson, Mosscrop.
Goalscorer: Freeman
Liverpool: Campbell; Longworth, Pursell, Fairfoul, Ferguson, MacKinlay, Sheldon, Metcalfe, Miller, Lacey, Nicholl.
Referee: H.S.Bamlett (Gateshead) *Attendance: 72,778*

1914-15

First Round
Blackpool v SHEFFIELD UTD 1-2
Liverpool v Stockport Co 3-0
Bradford v Portsmouth 1-0
Bury v Plymouth Arg 1-1, 2-1
Croydon Com v Oldham Ath 0-3
Rochdale v Gillingham 2-0
Birmingham v Crystal Palace 2-2, 3-0
Brighton & HA v Lincoln C 2-1
Bolton W v Notts Co 2-1
Millwall Ath v Clapton Orient 2-1
Burnley v Huddersfield T 3-1
Bristol R v Southend Utd 0-0, 0-3
Hull C v West Bromwich A 1-0
Grimsby T v Northampton T 0-3
Southampton v Luton T 3-0
South Shields v Fulham 1-2
CHELSEA v Swindon T 1-1, 5-2
Arsenal v Merthyr Tydfil 3-0
Preston NE v Manchester C 0-0, 0-3
Aston Villa v Exeter C 2-0
West Ham Utd v Newcastle Utd 2-2, 2-3
Swansea T v Blackburn R 1-0
Sheffield Wed v Manchester Utd 1-0
Reading v Wolves 0-1
Everton v Barnsley 3-0
Bristol C v Cardiff C 2-0
Queen's Park R v Glossop 2-1
Derby Co v Leeds C 1-2
Darlington v Bradford C 0-1
Middlesbrough v Goole T 9-3
Nottingham F v Norwich C 1-4
Tottenham H v Sunderland 2-1

Second Round
SHEFFIELD UTD v Liverpool 1-0
Bury v Bradford 0-1
Oldham Ath v Rochdale 3-0
Brighton & HA v Birmingham 0-0, 0-3
Bolton W v Millwall Ath 0-0, 2-2, 4-1
Burnley v Southend Utd 6-0
Hull C v Northampton T 2-1
Fulham v Southampton 2-3
CHELSEA v Arsenal 1-0
Manchester C v Aston Villa 1-0
Newcastle Utd v Swansea T 1-1, 2-0
Sheffield Wed v Wolves 2-0
Everton v Bristol C 4-0
Queen's Park R v Leeds C 1-0
Bradford C v Middlesbrough 1-0
Norwich C v Tottenham H 3-2

Third Round
SHEFFIELD UTD v Bradford 1-0
Birmingham v Oldham Ath 2-3
Bolton W v Burnley 2-1
Southampton v Hull C 2-2, 0-4
Manchester C v CHELSEA 0-1
Sheffield Wed v Newcastle Utd 1-2
Queen's Park R v Everton 1-2
Bradford C v Norwich C 1-1, 0-0, †2-0

Fourth Round
Oldham Ath v SHEFFIELD UTD 0-0, 0-3
Bolton W v Hull C 4-2
CHELSEA v Newcastle Utd 1-1, 1-0
Bradford C v Everton 0-2

Semi-final
SHEFFIELD UTD v Bolton W 2-1
CHELSEA v Everton 2-0

FINAL (Old Trafford, Manchester)
SHEFFIELD UNITED 3
CHELSEA 0
Sheffield United: Gough; Cook, English, Sturgess, Brelsford, Utley, Simmons, Fazackerley, Kitchen, Masterman, Evans.
Goalscorers: Simmons, Fazackerley, Kitchen
Chelsea: Molyneux; Bettridge, Harrow, Taylor, Logan, Walker, Ford, Halse, Thomson, Croal, McNeil.
Referee: H.H.Taylor (Altrincham) *Attendance: 49,557*

†Second replay at Lincoln behind closed doors.

1919-20

First Round
ASTON VILLA v Queen's Park R 2-1
Port Vale v Manchester Utd 0-1
Sunderland v Hull C 6-2
Thorneycroft's (W) v Burnley 0-0, 0-5
Bristol R v Tottenham H 1-4
West Stanley v Gillingham 3-1
Southampton v West Ham Utd 0-0, 1-3
Bury v Stoke 2-0
Bolton W v Chelsea 0-1
Fulham v Swindon T 1-2
Newport Co v Leicester C 0-0, 0-2
Manchester C v Clapton Orient 4-1
Bradford v Nottingham F 3-0
Castleford T v Hednesford T 2-0
Notts Co v Millwall Ath 2-0
Middlesbrough v Lincoln C 4-1
Grimsby T v Bristol C 1-2
Arsenal v Rochdale 4-2
Cardiff C v Oldham Ath 2-0
Blackburn R v Wolves 2-2, 0-1
Bradford C v Portsmouth †2-2, 2-0
Sheffield Utd v Southend Utd 3-0
Preston NE v Stockport Co 3-1
Blackpool v Derby Co 0-0, 4-1
HUDDERSFIELD T v Brentford 5-1
Newcastle Utd v Crystal Palace 2-0
Plymouth Arg v Reading 2-0
West Bromwich A v Barnsley 0-1
South Shields v Liverpool 1-1, 0-2
Luton T v Coventry C 2-2, 1-0
Birmingham v Everton 2-0
Darlington v Sheffield Wed 0-0, 2-0

Second Round
Manchester Utd v ASTON VILLA 1-2
Burnley v Sunderland 1-1, 0-2
Tottenham H v West Stanley 4-0
West Ham Utd v Bury 6-0
Chelsea v Swindon T 4-0
Leicester C v Manchester C 3-0
Bradford v Castleford T 3-2
Notts Co v Middlesbrough 1-0
Bristol C v Arsenal 1-0
Wolves v Cardiff C 1-2
Bradford C v Sheffield Utd 2-1
Preston NE v Blackpool 2-1
Newcastle Utd v HUDDERSFIELD T 0-1
Plymouth Arg v Barnsley 4-1
Luton T v Liverpool 0-2
Birmingham v Darlington 4-0

Third Round
ASTON VILLA v Sunderland 1-0
Tottenham H v West Ham Utd 3-0
Chelsea v Leicester C 3-0
Notts Co v Bradford 3-4
Bristol C v Cardiff C 2-1
Preston NE v Bradford C 0-3
HUDDERSFIELD T v Plymouth Arg 3-1
Liverpool v Birmingham 2-0

Fourth Round
Tottenham H v ASTON VILLA 0-1
Chelsea v Bradford 4-1
Bristol C v Bradford C 2-0
HUDDERSFIELD T v Liverpool 2-1

Semi-final
ASTON VILLA v Chelsea 3-1
Bristol C v HUDDERSFIELD T 1-2

Aston Villa and Huddersfield Town skippers look down at the coin before the 1920 FA Cup Final at Stamford Bridge.

FINAL (Stamford Bridge, London)
ASTON VILLA 1
HUDDERSFIELD TOWN 0
(after extra-time)
Aston Villa: Hardy; Smart, Weston, Ducat, Barson, Moss, Wallace, Kirton, Walker, Stephenson, Dorrell.
Goalscorer: Kirton
Huddersfield Town: Mutch; Wood, Bullock, Slade, Wilson, Watson, Richardson, Mann, Taylor, Swann, Islip.
Referee: J.T.Howcroft (Bolton) *Attendance: 50,018*

†Abandoned at half-time because of flooded ground.

1920-21

First Round
Southend Utd v Eccles 5-1
Darlington v Blackpool 2-2, 1-2
TOTTENHAM H v Bristol R 6-2
Bradford C v Barnsley 3-1
Notts Co v West Bromwich A 3-0
Aston Villa v Bristol C 2-0
Bradford v Clapton Orient 1-0
Brentford v Huddersfield T 1-2
Crystal Palace v Manchester C 2-0
Hull C v Bath C 3-0
Leicester C v Burnley 3-7
Queen's Park R v Arsenal 2-0
South Shields v Portsmouth 3-0
Luton T v Birmingham 2-1
Preston NE v Bolton W 2-0
Watford v Exeter C 3-0
Everton v Stockport Co 1-0
Sheffield Wed v West Ham Utd 1-0
Newcastle Utd v Nottingham F 1-1, 2-0
Liverpool v Manchester Utd 1-1, 2-1
Millwall Ath v Lincoln C 0-3
Blackburn R v Fulham 1-1, 0-1
Derby Co v Middlesbrough 2-0
WOLVES v Stoke 3-2
Grimsby T v Norwich C 1-0
Northampton T v Southampton 0-0, 1-4
Brighton & HA v Oldham Ath 4-1
Sunderland v Cardiff C 0-1
Swansea T v Bury 3-0
Plymouth Arg v Rochdale 2-0
Swindon T v Sheffield Utd 1-0
Reading v Chelsea 0-0, 2-2, 1-3

Second Round
Southend Utd v Blackpool 1-0
TOTTENHAM H v Bradford C 4-0
Notts Co v Aston Villa 0-0, 0-1
Bradford v Huddersfield T 0-1
Crystal Palace v Hull C 0-2
Burnley v Queen's Park R 4-2
South Shields v Luton T 0-4
Preston NE v Watford 4-1
Everton v Sheffield Wed 1-1, 1-0
Newcastle Utd v Liverpool 1-0
Lincoln C v Fulham 0-0, 0-1
Derby Co v WOLVES 1-1, 0-1
Grimsby T v Southampton 1-3
Brighton & HA v Cardiff C 0-0, 0-1
Swansea T v Plymouth Arg 1-2
Swindon T v Chelsea 0-2

Third Round
Southend Utd v TOTTENHAM H 1-4
Aston Villa v Huddersfield T 2-0
Hull C v Burnley 3-0
Luton T v Preston NE 2-3
Everton v Newcastle Utd 3-0
Fulham v WOLVES 0-1
Southampton v Cardiff C 0-1
Plymouth Arg v Chelsea 0-0, 0-0, 1-2

Fourth Round
TOTTENHAM H v Aston Villa 1-0
Hull C v Preston NE 0-0, 0-1
Everton v WOLVES 0-1
Cardiff C v Chelsea 1-0

Semi-final
TOTTENHAM H v Preston NE 2-1
WOLVES v Cardiff C 0-0, 3-1

FINAL (Stamford Bridge, London)
TOTTENHAM HOTSPUR 1
WOLVERHAMPTON WANDERERS 0
Tottenham Hotspur: Hunter; Clay, McDonald, Smith, Walters, Grimsdell, Banks, Seed, Cantrell, Bliss, Dimmock.
Goalscorer: Dimmock
Wolverhampton Wanderers: George; Woodward, Marshall, Gregory, Hodnett, Riley, Lea, Burrill, Edmonds, Potts, Brooks.
Referee: S.Davies (Rainhill) *Attendance: 72,805*

King George V presents Tottenham's Arthur Grimsdell with the FA Cup in 1921.

1921-22

First Round
Everton v Crystal Palace 0-6
Millwall Ath v Ashington 4-2
Worksop T v Southend Utd 1-2
Swansea T v West Ham Utd 0-0, 1-1, 1-0
Blackburn R v Southport 1-1, 2-0
Swindon T v Leeds Utd 2-1
Brighton & HA v Sheffield Utd 1-0
Burnley v HUDDERSFIELD T 2-2, 2-3
Aston Villa v Derby Co 6-1
Portsmouth v Luton T 1-1, 1-2
Port Vale v Stoke 2-4
Northampton T v Reading 3-0
Chelsea v West Bromwich A 2-4
Sunderland v Liverpool 1-1, 0-5
Walsall v Bradford C 3-3, 0-4
Grimsby T v Notts Co 1-1, 0-3
Bradford v Sheffield Wed 1-0
Arsenal v Queen's Park R 0-0, 2-1
Plymouth Arg v Fulham 1-1, 0-1
Leicester C v Clapton Orient 2-0
Barnsley v Norwich C 1-1, 2-1
Gillingham v Oldham Ath 1-3
Newcastle Utd v Newport Co 6-0
PRESTON NE v Wolves 3-0
Manchester Utd v Cardiff C 1-4
Southampton v South Shields 3-1
Hull C v Middlesbrough 5-0
Bristol C v Nottingham F 0-0, 1-3
Manchester C v Darlington 3-1
Bolton W v Bury 1-0
Blackpool v Watford 1-2
Brentford v Tottenham H 0-2

Second Round
Crystal Palace v Millwall Ath 0-0, 0-2
Southend Utd v Swansea T 0-1
Swindon T v Blackburn R 0-1
Brighton & HA v HUDDERSFIELD T 0-0, 0-2
Aston Villa v Luton T 1-0
Northampton T v Stoke 2-2, 0-3
Liverpool v West Bromwich A 0-1
Bradford C v Notts Co 1-1, 1-1, 0-1
Bradford v Arsenal 2-3
Leicester C v Fulham 2-0
Barnsley v Oldham Ath 3-1
PRESTON NE v Newcastle Utd 3-1
Southampton v Cardiff C 1-1, 0-2
Nottingham F v Hull C 3-0
Bolton W v Manchester C 1-3
Tottenham H v Watford 1-0

Third Round
Millwall Ath v Swansea T 4-0
Blackburn R v HUDDERSFIELD T 1-1, 0-5
Stoke v Aston Villa 0-0, 0-4
West Bromwich A v Notts Co 1-1, 0-2
Arsenal v Leicester C 3-0
Barnsley v PRESTON NE 1-1, 0-3
Cardiff C v Nottingham F 4-1
Tottenham H v Manchester C 2-1

Fourth Round
HUDDERSFIELD T v Millwall Ath 3-0
Notts Co v Aston Villa 2-2, 4-3
Arsenal v PRESTON NE 1-1, 1-2
Cardiff C v Tottenham H 1-1, 1-2

Semi-final
HUDDERSFIELD T v Notts Co 3-1
PRESTON NE v Tottenham H 2-1

FINAL (Stamford Bridge, London)
HUDDERSFIELD TOWN 1
PRESTON NORTH END 0
Huddersfield Town: Mutch; Wood, Wadsworth, Slade, Wilson, Watson, Richardson, Mann, Islip, Stephenson, W.H.Smith.
Goalscorer: Smith
Preston North End: J.F.Mitchell; Hamilton, Doolan, Duxbury, McCall, Williamson, Rawlings, Jefferis, Roberts, Woodhouse, Quinn.
Referee: J.W.P.Fowler (Sunderland)
Attendance: 53,000

1922-23

First Round
Norwich C v BOLTON W 0-2
Portsmouth v Leeds Utd 0-0, 1-3
Clapton Orient v Millwall Ath 0-2
Huddersfield T v Birmingham 2-1
Manchester C v Charlton Ath 1-2
Aberdare Ath v Preston NE 1-3
West Bromwich A v Stalybridge Cel 0-0, 2-0
Sunderland v Burnley 3-1
Oldham Ath v Middlesbrough 0-1
Nottingham F v Sheffield Utd 0-0, 0-0, 1-1, 0-1
Liverpool v Arsenal 0-0, 4-1
Merthyr Tydfil v Wolves 0-1
Queen's Park R v Crystal Palace 1-0
Wigan Bor v Bath C 4-1
South Shields v Halifax T 3-1
Aston Villa v Blackburn R 0-1
Bury v Luton T 2-1
Blyth Spartans v Stoke 0-3
Chelsea v Rotherham Co 1-0
Newcastle Utd v Southampton 0-0, 1-3
Brighton & HA v Corinthians 1-1, 1-1, 1-0
Hull C v WEST HAM UTD 2-3
Plymouth Arg v Notts Co 0-0, 1-0
Everton v Bradford 1-1, 0-1
Derby Co v Blackpool 2-0
Bristol C v Wrexham 5-1
Sheffield Wed v New Brighton 3-0
Swindon T v Barnsley 0-0, 0-2
Tottenham H v Worksop T 0-0 9-0
Bradford C v Manchester Utd 1-1, 0-2
Cardiff C v Watford 1-1, 2-2, 2-1
Leicester C v Fulham 4-0

Second Round
BOLTON W v Leeds Utd 3-1
Millwall Ath v Huddersfield T 0-0, 0-3
Charlton Ath v Preston NE 2-0
West Bromwich A v Sunderland 2-1
Middlesbrough v Sheffield Utd 1-1, 0-3
Wolves v Liverpool 0-2

Jimmy Dimmock's goal for Spurs against Wolves in the 54th minute of the 1921 Final at Stamford Bridge.

Wigan Bor v Queen's Park R 2-4
South Shields v Blackburn R 0-0, 1-0
Bury v Stoke 3-1
Chelsea v Southampton 0-0, 0-1
Brighton & HA v WEST HAM UTD 1-1, 0-1
Plymouth Arg v Bradford 4-1
Bristol C v Derby Co 0-3
Sheffield Wed v Barnsley 2-1
Tottenham H v Manchester Utd 4-0
Leicester C v Cardiff C 0-1

Third Round
Huddersfield T v BOLTON W 1-1, 0-1
Charlton Ath v West Bromwich A 1-0
Liverpool v Sheffield Utd 1-2
Queen's Park R v South Shields 3-0
Bury v Southampton 0-0, 0-1
WEST HAM UTD v Plymouth Arg 2-0
Derby Co v Sheffield Wed 1-0
Cardiff C v Tottenham H 2-3

Fourth Round
Charlton Ath v BOLTON W 0-1
Queen's Park R v Sheffield Utd 0-1
Southampton v WEST HAM UTD 1-1, 1-1, 0-1
Tottenham H v Derby Co 0-1

Semi-final
BOLTON W v Sheffield Utd 1-0
WEST HAM UTD v Derby Co 5-2

Above and below: Sections of the huge crowd at the first Wembley FA Cup Final of 1923, trying desperately to gain a vantage point.

FINAL (Wembley Stadium)
BOLTON WANDERERS 2
WEST HAM UNITED 0
Bolton Wanderers: Pym; Haworth, Finney, Nuttall, Seddon, Jennings, Butler, Jack, J.R.Smith, J.Smith, Vizard.
Goalscorers: Jack, J.R.Smith
West Ham United: Hufton; Henderson, Young, Bishop, Kay, Tresadern, Richards, Brown, Watson, Moore, Ruffell.
Referee: D.H.Asson (West Bromwich)
Attendance: 126,047

The start of the Final was delayed for 40 minutes when the crowd, estimated at between 70-100,000 more than the official attendance, had to be cleared from the playing area.

1923-24

First Round
Derby Co v Bury 2-1
Portsmouth v NEWCASTLE UTD 2-4
Exeter C v Grimsby T 1-0
Middlesbrough v Watford 0-1
Chelsea v Southampton 1-1, 0-2
Blackpool v Sheffield Utd 1-0
Liverpool v Bradford C 2-1
Hull C v Bolton W 2-2, 0-4
Manchester C v Nottingham F 2-0
Northampton T v Halifax T 1-1, 1-1, 2-4
Barnsley v Brighton & HA 0-0, 0-1
Everton v Preston NE 3-1
Cardiff C v Gillingham 0-0, 2-0
Arsenal v Luton T 4-1
Sheffield Wed v Leicester C 4-1
Norwich C v Bristol C 0-1
Ashington v ASTON VILLA 1-5
Swansea T v Clapton Orient 1-1, 1-1, 2-1
West Ham Utd v Aberdare Ath 5-0
Leeds Utd v Stoke 1-0
Millwall Ath v West Bromwich A 0-1
Corinthians v Blackburn R 1-0
Accrington S v Charlton Ath 0-0, 0-1
Wolves v Darlington 3-1
Swindon T v Bradford 4-0
Oldham Ath v Sunderland 2-1
Crystal Palace v Tottenham H 2-0
Queen's Park R v Notts Co 1-2
Burnley v South Shields 3-2
Fulham v Llanelly 2-0
Huddersfield T v Birmingham 1-0
Manchester Utd v Plymouth Arg 1-0

Second Round
Derby Co v NEWCASTLE UTD 2-2, 2-2, 2-2, 3-5
Exeter C v Watford 0-0, 0-1
Southampton v Blackpool 3-1
Bolton W v Liverpool 1-4
Manchester C v Halifax T 2-2, 0-0, 3-0
Brighton & HA v Everton 5-2
Cardiff C v Arsenal 1-0
Sheffield Wed v Bristol C 1-1, 0-2
Swansea T v ASTON VILLA 0-2
West Ham Utd v Leeds Utd 1-1, 0-1
West Bromwich A v Corinthians 5-0
Charlton Ath v Wolves 0-0, 0-1
Swindon T v Oldham Ath 2-0
Crystal Palace v Notts Co 0-0, 0-0, 0-0, 2-1
Burnley v Fulham 0-0, 1-0
Manchester Utd v Huddersfield T 0-3

Third Round
Watford v NEWCASTLE UTD 0-1
Southampton v Liverpool 0-0, 0-2
Brighton & HA v Manchester C 1-5
Cardiff C v Bristol C 3-0
ASTON VILLA v Leeds Utd 3-0
West Bromwich A v Wolves 1-1, 2-0
Crystal Palace v Swindon T 1-2
Burnley v Huddersfield T 1-0

Fourth Round
NEWCASTLE UTD v Liverpool 1-0
Manchester C v Cardiff C 0-0, 1-0
West Bromwich A v ASTON VILLA 0-2
Swindon T v Burnley 1-1, 1-3

Semi-final
NEWCASTLE UTD v Manchester C 2-0
ASTON VILLA v Burnley 3-0

FINAL (Wembley Stadium)
NEWCASTLE UNITED 2
ASTON VILLA 0
Newcastle United: Bradley; Hampson, Hudspeth, Mooney, Spencer, Gibson, Low, Cowan, Harris, McDonald, Seymour.
Goalscorers: Harris, Seymour
Aston Villa: Jackson; Smart, Mort, Moss, Dr V.E.Milne, Blackburn, York, Kirton, Capewell, Walker, Dorrell.
Referee: W.E.Russell (Swindon) *Attendance: 91,695*

1924-25

First Round
CARDIFF C v Darlington 0-0, 0-0, 2-0
Swindon T v Fulham 1-2
Doncaster R v Norwich C 1-2
Coventry C v Notts Co 0-2
Hull C v Wolves 1-1, 1-0
Crystal Palace v South Shields 2-1
Newcastle Utd v Hartlepools Utd 4-1
Leicester C v Stoke 3-0
Blackpool v Barrow 0-0, 2-0
Bradford v Middlesbrough 1-0
Nottingham F v Clapton Orient 1-0
West Ham Utd v Arsenal 0-0, 2-2, 1-0
Tottenham H v Northampton T 3-0
Bolton W v Huddersfield T 3-0
Accrington S v Portsmouth 2-5
Blackburn R v Oldham Ath 1-0
Southampton v Exeter C †5-0, 3-1
Watford v Brighton & HA 1-1, 3-4
Millwall Ath v Barnsley 0-0, 1-2
Derby Co v Bradford C 0-1
Birmingham v Chelsea 2-0
Queen's Park R v Stockport Co 1-3
Bristol R v Bristol C 0-1
Liverpool v Leeds Utd 3-0
West Bromwich A v Luton T 4-0
Preston NE v Manchester C 4-1
Swansea T v Plymouth Arg 3-0
Aston Villa v Port Vale 7-2
Everton v Burnley 2-1
Bury v Sunderland 0-3
Sheffield Wed v Manchester Utd 2-0
SHEFFIELD UTD v Corinthians 5-0

Second Round
CARDIFF C v Fulham 1-0
Notts Co v Norwich C 4-0
Hull C v Crystal Palace 3-2
Newcastle Utd v Leicester C 2-2, 0-1
Bradford v Blackpool 1-1, 1-2
Nottingham F v West Ham Utd 0-2

Jimmy Seed equalizes for Spurs against Bolton in the 1924-5 second round.

Tottenham H v Bolton W 1-1, 1-0
Blackburn R v Portsmouth 0-0, 0-0, 1-0
Southampton v Brighton & HA 1-0
Barnsley v Bradford C 0-3
Birmingham v Stockport Co 1-0
Bristol C v Liverpool 0-1
West Bromwich A v Preston NE 2-0
Swansea T v Aston Villa 1-3
Sunderland v Everton 0-0, 1-2
SHEFFIELD UTD v Sheffield Wed 3-2

Third Round
Notts Co v CARDIFF C 0-2
Hull C v Leicester C 1-1, 1-3
West Ham Utd v Blackpool 1-1, 0-3
Tottenham H v Blackburn R 2-2, 1-3
Southampton v Bradford C 2-0
Liverpool v Birmingham 2-1
West Bromwich A v Aston Villa 1-1, 2-1
SHEFFIELD UTD v Everton 1-0

Fourth Round
CARDIFF C v Leicester C 2-1
Blackburn R v Blackpool 1-0
Southampton v Liverpool 1-0
SHEFFIELD UTD v West Bromwich A 2-0

Semi-final
CARDIFF C v Blackburn R 3-1
SHEFFIELD UTD v Southampton 2-0

FINAL (Wembley Stadium)
SHEFFIELD UNITED 1
CARDIFF CITY 0

Sheffield United: Sutcliffe; Cook, Mitton, Pantling, King, Green, Mercer, Boyle, Johnson, Gillespie, Tunstall.
Goalscorer: Tunstall
Cardiff City: Farquharson; Nelson, Blair, Wake, Keenor, Hardy, W.Davies, Gill, Nicholson, Beadles, J.Evans.
Referee: G.N.Watson (Nottingham) Attendance: 91,763

†Abandoned after 77 minutes because of fog.

1925-26

First Round

Aberdare Ath v Bristol R 4-1
Accrington S v Wrexham 4-0
Blyth Spartans v Hartlepools Utd 2-2, 1-1, 2-1
Bournemouth & Bos Ath v Merthyr Tydfil 3-0
Boston T v Mansfield T 5-2
Bradford v Lincoln C 2-2, 1-1, 2-1
Brentford v Barnet 3-1
Brighton & HA v Watford 1-1, 0-2
Carlisle Utd v Chilton Coll 0-2
Clapton Orient v Norwich C 3-1
Charlton Ath v Windsor & Eton 4-2
Chatham v Sittingbourne 0-3
Doncaster R v Wellington T 2-0
Exeter C v Swansea T 1-3
Farnham United Breweries v Swindon T 1-10
Gillingham v Southall 6-0
Halifax T v Rotherham Utd 0-3
Horden Ath v Darlington 2-3
Leyton v St Albans C 1-0
London Caledonians v Ilford Utd 1-2
Luton T v Folkestone 3-0
New Brighton v Barrow 2-0
Northampton T v Barnsley 3-1
Northfleet v Queen's Park R 2-2, 0-2
Oldham Ath v Lytham 10-1
Rochdale v West Stanley 4-0
Southend Utd v Dulwich Hamlet 5-1
Southport v Mold 1-0
Torquay Utd v Reading 1-1, 1-1, 0-2
Tranmere R v Crewe Alex 0-0, 1-2
Walsall v Grimsby T 0-1
Wath Ath v Chesterfield 0-5
Weymouth v Newport Co 0-1
Worksop T v Coventry C 1-0
Durham C v Ashington 4-1
Wigan Bor v Nelson 3-0
South Bank v Stockton 1-4
Worcester C v Kettering T 0-0, 0-0, 0-2

Second Round

Aberdare Ath v Luton T 1-0
Accrington S v Blyth Spartans 5-0
Brentford v Bournemouth & Bos Ath 1-2
Crewe Alex v Wigan Bor 2-2, 1-2
Stockton v Oldham Ath 4-6
Boston T v Bradford 1-0
Swindon T v Sittingbourne 7-0
Reading v Leyton 6-0
Swansea T v Watford 3-2
Southend Utd v Gillingham 1-0
Clapton Orient v Ilford Utd 1-0
Queen's Park R v Charlton Ath 1-1, 0-1
Chilton Coll v Rochdale 1-1, 2-1
Kettering T v Grimsby T 1-1, 1-3
New Brighton v Darlington 2-0
Doncaster R v Rotherham Utd 0-2
Worksop T v Chesterfield 1-2
Durham C v Southport 0-3
Northampton T v Newport Co 3-1

Third Round

BOLTON W v Accrington S 1-0
Bournemouth & Bos Ath v Reading 2-0
South Shields v Chilton Coll 3-0
Birmingham v Grimsby T 2-0
Nottingham F v Bradford C 1-0
Clapton v Swindon T 2-3
Southend Utd v Southport 5-2
Derby Co v Portsmouth 0-0, 1-1, 2-0
Blackpool v Swansea T 0-2
Wigan Bor v Stoke C 2-5
Millwall v Oldham Ath 1-1, 1-0
Rotherham Utd v Bury 2-3
Wolves v Arsenal 1-1, 0-1
Blackburn R v Preston NE 1-1, 4-1
Hull C v Aston Villa 0-3
West Bromwich A v Bristol C 4-1
Corinthians v MANCHESTER C 3-3, 0-4
Charlton Ath v Huddersfield T 0-1
Northampton T v Crystal Palace 3-3, 1-2
Plymouth Arg v Chelsea 1-2
Chesterfield v Clapton Orient 0-1
Middlesborough v Leeds Utd 5-1
Newcastle Utd v Aberdare Ath 4-1
Cardiff C v Burnley 2-2, 2-0
Port Vale v Manchester Utd 2-3
Tottenham H v West Ham Utd 5-0
Sunderland v Boston T 8-1
Sheffield Utd v Stockport Co 2-0
Everton v Fulham 1-1, 0-1
Southampton v Liverpool 0-0, 0-1
Notts Co v Leicester C 2-0
New Brighton v Sheffield Wed 2-1

Fourth Round

Bournemouth & Bos Ath v BOLTON W 2-2, 2-6
South Shields v Birmingham 2-1
Nottingham F v Swindon T 2-0
Southend Utd v Derby Co 4-1
Swansea T v Stoke C 6-3
Bury v Millwall 3-3, 0-2
Arsenal v Blackburn R 3-1
West Bromwich A v Aston Villa 1-2
MANCHESTER C v Huddersfield T 4-0
Crystal Palace v Chelsea 2-1
Clapton Orient v Middlesbrough 4-2
Cardiff C v Newcastle Utd 0-2
Tottenham H v Manchester Utd 2-2, 0-2
Sheffield Utd v Sunderland 1-2
Fulham v Liverpool 3-1
Notts Co v New Brighton 2-0

Fifth Round

BOLTON W v South Shields 3-0
Southend Utd v Nottingham F 0-1
Millwall v Swansea T 0-1
Aston Villa v Arsenal 1-1, 0-2
MANCHESTER C v Crystal Palace 11-4
Clapton Orient v Newcastle Utd 2-0
Sunderland v Manchester Utd 3-3, 1-2
Notts Co v Fulham 0-1

Sixth Round

Nottingham F v BOLTON W 2-2, 0-0, 0-1
Swansea T v Arsenal 2-1
Clapton Orient v MANCHESTER C 1-6
Fulham v Manchester Utd 1-2

Semi-final

BOLTON W v Swansea T 3-0
MANCHESTER C v Manchester Utd 3-0

FINAL (Wembley Stadium)

BOLTON WANDERERS 1
MANCHESTER CITY 0

Bolton Wanderers: Pym; Haworth, Greenhalgh, Nuttall, Seddon, Jennings, Butler, Jack, J.R.Smith, J.Smith, Vizard.
Goalscorer: Jack
Manchester City: Goodchild; Cookson, McCloy, Pringle, Cowan, McMullan, Austin, Browell, Roberts, Johnson, Hicks.
Referee: I.Baker (Crewe) Attendance: 91,447

Starting this season, clubs playing in the First and Second Divisions of the Football League were exempted to the third round.

Bolton's David Jack, who scored the first Wembley FA Cup Final goal in 1923, here nets the only goal of the 1926 Final against Manchester City. Above: Bolton, with the trophy, come down from the Royal Box.

1926-27

First Round

Accrington S v Rochdale 4-3
Annfield Plain v Chilton Coll 2-4
Barking T v Gillingham 0-0, 0-2
Bishop Auckland v Bedlington Utd 0-1
Boston T v Northampton T 1-1, 1-2
Bournemouth & Bos Ath v Swindon T 1-1, 4-3
Brighton & HA v Barnet 3-0
Carlisle Utd v Hartlepools Utd 6-2
Chatham v St Albans C 3-1
Chesterfield v Mexborough *0-0, 2-1
Clapton Orient v Brentford 1-1, 3-7
Crewe Alex v Northern Nomads 4-1
Crystal Palace v Norwich C 0-0, 0-1
Doncaster R v Desborough *0-0, 3-0
Dulwich Hamlet v Southend Utd 1-4
Exeter C v Aberdare Ath 3-0
Grimsby T v Halifax T 3-2
Kettering T v Coventry C 2-3
Lincoln C v Rotherham Utd 2-0
Luton T v London Caledonians 4-2
Merthyr Tydfil v Bristol C 0-2
Nelson v Stockport Co 4-1
Nunhead v Kingstonian 9-0
Poole v Newport Co 1-0
Reading v Weymouth 4-4, 5-0
Rhyl Ath v Stoke C 1-1, 1-1, 2-1
Sittingbourne v Northfleet Utd 1-3
Southport v Tranmere R 1-1, 2-1
Stockton v Ashington 1-2
Torquay Utd v Bristol R 1-1, 0-1
Watford v Lowestoft 10-1
Walsall v Bradford 1-0
Wellington T v Mansfield T 1-2
Wigan Bor v Barrow 2-2, 1-0
Woking v Charlton Ath 1-3
Workington v Crook T 1-2
Wrexham v New Brighton 1-1, 2-2, 3-1
York C v Worksop T *1-1, 4-1

Second Round

Ashington v Nelson 2-1
Bristol C v Bournemouth & Bos Ath 1-1, 0-2
Bristol R v Charlton Ath 4-1
Carlisle Utd v Bedlington Utd 4-0
Crewe Alex v Wigan Bor 4-1
Coventry C v Lincoln C 1-1, 1-2
Doncaster R v Chesterfield 0-1
Chilton Coll v Accrington S 0-3
Exeter C v Northampton T 1-0
Gillingham v Brentford 1-1, 0-1
Grimsby T v York C 2-1
Luton T v Northfleet Utd 6-2
Norwich C v Chatham 5-0
Nunhead v Poole 1-2
Reading v Southend Utd 3-2
Rhyl Ath v Wrexham 3-1
Southport v Crook T 2-0
Walsall v Mansfield T 2-0
Watford v Brighton & HA 0-1

Third Round

Chelsea v Luton T 4-0
Exeter C v Accrington S 0-2
Fulham v Chesterfield 4-3
Burnley v Grimsby T 3-1
Leeds Utd v Sunderland 3-2
Blackpool v Bolton W 1-3
Darlington v Rhyl Ath 2-1

CARDIFF C v Aston Villa 2-1
Sheffield Wed v Brighton & HA 2-0
South Shields v Plymouth Arg 3-1
Barnsley v Crewe Alex 6-1
Swansea T v Bury 4-1
Reading v Manchester Utd 1-1, 2-2, 2-1
Bristol R v Portsmouth 3-3, 0-4
West Ham Utd v Tottenham H 3-2
Oldham Ath† v Brentford †2-1, 2-4
Clapton Orient v Port Vale 1-1, 1-5
Sheffield Utd v ARSENAL 2-3
Bournemouth & Bos Ath v Liverpool 1-1, 1-4
Southport v Blackburn R 2-0
Carlisle Utd v Wolves 0-2
Ashington v Nottingham F 0-2
Hull C v West Bromwich A 2-1
Everton v Poole 3-1
Bradford C v Derby C 2-6
Millwall v Huddersfield T 3-1
Lincoln C v Preston NE 2-4
Middlesbrough v Leicester C 5-3
Southampton v Norwich C 3-0
Birmingham v Manchester C 4-1
Walsall v Corinthians 0-4
Newcastle Utd v Notts Co 8-1

Fourth Round
Chelsea v Accrington S 7-2
Fulham v Burnley 0-4
Leeds Utd v Bolton W 0-0, 0-3
Darlington v CARDIFF C 0-2
Sheffield Wed v South Shields 1-1, 0-1
Barnsley v Swansea T 1-3
Reading v Portsmouth 3-1
West Ham Utd v Brentford 1-1, 0-2
Port Vale v ARSENAL 2-2, 0-1
Liverpool v Southport 3-1
Wolves v Nottingham F 2-0
Hull C v Everton 1-1, 2-2, 3-2
Derby Co v Millwall 0-2
Preston NE v Middlesbrough 0-3
Southampton v Birmingham 4-1
Corinthians v Newcastle Utd 1-3

Fifth Round
Chelsea v Burnley 2-1
Bolton W v CARDIFF C 0-2
South Shields v Swansea T 2-2, 1-2
Reading v Brentford 1-0
ARSENAL v Liverpool 2-0
Wolves v Hull C 1-0
Millwall v Middlesbrough 3-2
Southampton v Newcastle Utd 2-1

Sixth Round
Chelsea v CARDIFF C 0-0, 2-3
Swansea T v Reading 1-3
ARSENAL v Wolves 2-1
Millwall v Southampton 0-0, 0-2

Semi-final
CARDIFF C v Reading 3-0
ARSENAL v Southampton 2-1

FINAL (Wembley Stadium)
CARDIFF CITY 1
ARSENAL 0
Cardiff City: Farquharson; Nelson, Watson, Keenor, Sloan, Hardy, Curtis, Irving, Ferguson, L.Davies, McLachlan.
Goalscorer: Ferguson
Arsenal: Lewis; Parker, Kennedy, Baker, Butler, John, Hulme, Buchan, Brain, Blythe, Hoar.
Referee: W.F.Bunnell (Preston) *Attendance: 91,206*

†Abandoned after 71 minutes because of fog.
*Abandoned.

1927-28

First Round
Aldershot v Queen's Park R 2-1
Bath C v Southall 2-0
Nelson v Bradford 0-3
Bradford C v Workington 6-0
Watford v Brighton & HA 1-2
Bristol R v Walsall 4-2
Carlisle Utd v Doncaster R 2-1
Coventry C v Bournemouth & Bos Ath 2-2, 0-2
Crewe Alex v Ashington 2-2, 2-0
Dartford v Crystal Palace 1-3
Darlington v Chesterfield 4-1
Durham C v Wrexham 1-1, 0-4
Exeter C v Aberdare Ath 9-1
Gainsboro' Trin v Stockton 6-0
Gillingham v Plymouth Arg 2-1
Halifax T v Hartlepools Utd 3-0
Ilford v Dulwich Hamlet 4-0
Kettering T v Chatham 2-0
Accrington S v Lincoln C 2-5
Northfleet Utd v London Caledonians 0-1
Luton T v Clapton Orient 9-0
Merthyr T v Charlton Ath 0-0, 1-2
Shildon v New Brighton 1-3
Northampton T v Leyton 8-0
Poole v Norwich C 1-1, 0-5
Botwell Mission v Peterborough & Fletton Utd 3-4
Rhyl Ath v Wigan Bor 4-3
Rochdale v Crook T 8-2
Southend Utd v Wellington T 1-0
Denaby Utd v Southport 2-3
Spennymoor Utd v Rotherham Utd 1-1, 2-4
Stockport Co v Oswestry T 5-2
Newport Co v Swindon T 0-1
Shirebrook v Tranmere R 1-3

Second Round
Bournemouth & Bos Ath v Bristol R 6-1
Charlton Ath v Kettering T 1-1, 2-1
Crewe Alex v Stockport Co 2-0
Darlington v Rochdale 2-1
Exeter C v Ilford 5-3
Gillingham v Southend Utd 2-0
Gainsboro' Trin v Lincoln C 0-2
London Caledonians v Bath C 1-0
Luton T v Norwich C 6-0
New Brighton v Rhyl Ath 7-2
Northampton T v Brighton & HA 1-0
Peterborough & Fletton Utd v Aldershot 2-1
Bradford C v Rotherham Utd 2-3
Bradford v Southport 0-2
Swindon T v Crystal Palace 0-0, 2-1
Tranmere R v Halifax T 3-1
Wrexham v Carlisle Utd 1-0

Third Round
BLACKBURN R v Newcastle Utd 4-1
Rotherham Utd v Exeter C 3-3, 1-3
Port Vale v Barnsley 3-0
New Brighton v Corinthians 2-1
Manchester Utd v Brentford 7-1
Charlton Ath v Bury 1-1, 3-4
Wrexham v Swansea T 2-1
Birmingham v Peterborough & Fletton Utd 4-3
Arsenal v West Bromwich A 2-0
Preston NE v Everton 0-3
Burnley v Aston Villa 0-2
London Caledonians v Crewe Alex 2-3
Sunderland v Northampton T 3-3, 3-0
Manchester C v Leeds Utd 1-0
Stoke C v Gillingham 6-1
Bolton W v Luton T 2-1
HUDDERSFIELD T v Lincoln C 4-2
Portsmouth v West Ham Utd 0-2
Southport v Fulham 3-0
Middlesbrough v South Shields 3-0
Reading v Grimsby T 4-0
Hull C v Leicester C 0-1
Bristol C v Tottenham H 1-2
Blackpool v Oldham Ath 1-4
Notts Co v Sheffield Utd 2-3
Wolves v Chelsea 2-1
Swindon T v Clapton Orient 2-1
Sheffield Wed v Bournemouth & Bos Ath 3-0
Nottingham F v Tranmere R 1-0
Millwall v Derby Co 1-2
Cardiff C v Southampton 2-1
Liverpool v Darlington 1-0

Fourth Round
Exeter C v BLACKBURN R 2-2, 1-3
Port Vale v New Brighton 3-0
Bury v Manchester Utd 1-1, 0-1
Wrexham v Birmingham 1-3
Arsenal v Everton 4-3
Aston Villa v Crewe Alex 3-0
Sunderland v Manchester C 1-2
Stoke C v Bolton W 4-2
HUDDERSFIELD T v West Ham Utd 2-1
Southport v Middlesbrough 0-3
Reading v Leicester C 0-1
Tottenham H v Oldham Ath 3-0
Sheffield Utd v Wolves 3-1
Swindon T v Sheffield Wed 1-2
Derby Co v Nottingham F 0-0, 0-2
Cardiff C v Liverpool 2-1

Fifth Round
BLACKBURN R v Port Vale 2-1
Manchester Utd v Birmingham 1-0
Arsenal v Aston Villa 4-1
Manchester C v Stoke C 0-1
HUDDERSFIELD T v Middlesbrough 4-0
Leicester C v Tottenham H 0-3
Sheffield Wed v Sheffield Utd 1-1, 1-4
Nottingham F v Cardiff C 2-1

Sixth Round
BLACKBURN R v Manchester Utd 2-0
Arsenal v Stoke C 4-1
HUDDERSFIELD T v Tottenham H 6-1
Sheffield Utd v Nottingham F 3-0

Semi-final
BLACKBURN R v Arsenal 1-0
HUDDERSFIELD T v Sheffield Utd 2-2, 0-0, 1-0

FINAL (Wembley Stadium)
BLACKBURN ROVERS 3
HUDDERSFIELD TOWN 1
Blackburn Rovers: Crawford; Hutton, Jones, Healless, Rankin, Campbell, Thornewell, Puddefoot, Roscamp, McLean, Rigby.
Goalscorers: Roscamp 2, McLean
Huddersfield Town: Mercer; Goodall, Barkas, Redfern, Wilson, Steele, A.Jackson, Kelly, Brown, Stephenson, W.H.Smith.
Goalscorer: Jackson
Referee: T.G.Bryan (Willenhall) *Attendance: 92,041*

Blackburn Rovers skipper Harry Healless with the Cup after Rovers beat Huddersfield in the 1928 Final.

Roscamp's first goal, scored within 30 seconds of the start of the Final, is recorded as the fastest in an FA Cup Final.

Cardiff City's goal under seige in the 1927 Final against Arsenal. But the Bluebirds took the Cup out of England for the first time.

1928-29

First Round
Accrington S v South Shields 2-1
York C v Barrow 0-1
Poole v Bournemouth & Bos Ath 1-4
Bradford C v Doncaster R 4-1
Brentford v Brighton & HA 4-1
Bristol R v Wellingborough T 2-1
Wrexham v Carlisle Utd 0-1
Peterborough & Fletton Utd v Charlton Ath 0-2
Chesterfield v Rochdale 3-2
Crystal Palace v Kettering T 2-0
Darlington v New Brighton 3-0
Exeter C v Barking T 6-0
Coventry C v Fulham 1-4
Gainsboro' Trin v Crewe Alex 3-1
Grantham v Rhyl Ath 1-0
Guildford C v Queen's Park R 4-2
Lancaster T v Lincoln C 1-3
Luton T v Southend Utd 5-1
Shirebrook v Mansfield T 2-4
Merthyr Tydfil v Dulwich Hamlet 4-2
Newport Co v Woking 7-0
Northfleet Utd v Ilford 5-2
Norwich C v Chatham 6-1
Yeovil & Petters Utd v Plymouth Arg 1-4
Horwich RMI v Scarborough T 1-2
Sittingbourne v Southall 2-1
Annfield Plain v Southport 1-4
Spennymoor Utd v Hartlepools Utd 5-2
Stockport Co v Halifax T 1-0
Gillingham v Torquay Utd 0-0, 1-5
Tranmere R v Rotherham Utd 2-1
Walsall v Worcester C 3-1
Leyton v Watford 0-2
Wigan Bor v Ashington 2-0

Second Round
Accrington S v Spennymoor Utd 7-0
Tranmere R v Bradford C 0-1
Guildford C v Bournemouth & Bos Ath 1-5
Northfleet Utd v Charlton Ath 1-5
Gainsboro' Trin v Chesterfield 2-3
Crystal Palace v Bristol R 3-1
Scarborough T v Darlington 2-2, 1-2
Torquay Utd v Exeter C 0-1
Carlisle Utd v Lincoln C 0-1
Fulham v Luton T 0-0, 1-4
Barrow v Mansfield T 1-2
Norwich C v Newport Co 6-0
Brentford v Plymouth Arg 0-1
Stockport Co v Southport 3-0
Walsall v Sittingbourne 2-1
Watford v Merthyr T 2-0
Wigan Bor v Grantham 2-1

Third Round
Blackburn R v Barnsley 1-0
Derby Co v Notts Co 4-3
Port Vale v Manchester Utd 0-3
Darlington v Bury 2-6
Lincoln C v Leicester C 0-1
Nottingham F v Swansea T 1-2
Bristol C v Liverpool 0-2
BOLTON W v Oldham Ath 2-0
Grimsby T v West Bromwich A 1-1, 0-2
Walsall v Middlesbrough 1-1, 1-5
Plymouth Arg v Blackpool 3-0
Hull C v Bradford 1-1, 1-3
Chesterfield v Huddersfield T 1-7
Exeter C v Leeds Utd 2-2, 1-5
Millwall v Northampton T 1-1, 2-2, 2-0
Luton T v Crystal Palace 0-0, 0-7
Chelsea v Everton 2-0
Birmingham v Manchester C 3-1
PORTSMOUTH v Charlton Ath 2-1
Bradford C v Stockport Co 2-0
Accrington S v Bournemouth & Bos Ath 1-1, 0-2
Watford v Preston NE 1-0
West Ham Utd v Sunderland 1-0
Norwich C v Corinthians 0-5
Reading v Tottenham H 2-0
Wigan Bor v Sheffield Wed 1-3
Aston Villa v Cardiff C 6-1
Southampton v Clapton Orient 0-0, 1-2
Burnley v Sheffield Utd 2-1
Swindon T v Newcastle Utd 2-0
Arsenal v Stoke C 2-1
Wolves v Mansfield T 0-1

Fourth Round
Blackburn R v Derby Co 1-1, 3-0
Manchester Utd v Bury 0-1
Leicester C v Swansea T 1-0
Liverpool v BOLTON W 0-0, 2-5
West Bromwich A v Middlesbrough 1-0
Plymouth Arg v Bradford 0-1
Huddersfield T v Leeds Utd 3-0
Millwall v Crystal Palace 0-0, 3-5
Chelsea v Birmingham 1-0

Portsmouth's goalkeeper Gilfillan can only look on as right-back Mackie helps Harold Blackmore's shot over the line to seal the 1929 FA Cup Final for Bolton Wanderers.

PORTSMOUTH v Bradford C 2-0
Bournemouth & Bos Ath v Watford 6-4
West Ham Utd v Corinthians 3-0
Reading v Sheffield Wed 1-0
Aston Villa v Clapton Orient 0-0 8-0
Burnley v Swindon T 3-3, 2-3
Arsenal v Mansfield T 2-0

Fifth Round
Blackburn R v Bury 1-0
Leicester C v BOLTON W 1-2
West Bromwich A v Bradford 6-0
Huddersfield T v Crystal Palace 5-2
Chelsea v PORTSMOUTH 1-1, 0-1
Bournemouth & Bos Ath v West Ham Utd 1-1, 1-3
Reading v Aston Villa 1-3
Swindon T v Arsenal 0-0, 0-1

Sixth Round
Blackburn R v BOLTON W 1-1, 1-2
West Bromwich A v Huddersfield T 1-1, 1-2
PORTSMOUTH v West Ham Utd 3-2
Aston Villa v Arsenal 1-0

Semi-final
BOLTON W v Huddersfield T 3-1
PORTSMOUTH v Aston Villa 1-0

FINAL (Wembley Stadium)
BOLTON WANDERERS 2
PORTSMOUTH 0

Bolton Wanderers: Pym; Haworth, Finney, Kean, Seddon, Nuttall, Butler, McClelland, Blackmore, Gibson, W.Cook.
Goalscorers: Butler, Blackmore
Portsmouth: Gilfillan; Mackie, Bell, Nichol, McIlwane, Thackeray, Forward, Smith, Weddle, Watson, F.Cook.
Referee: A.Josephs (South Shields)
Attendance: 92,576

1929-30

First Round
Accrington S v Rochdale 3-1
Barrow v Newark 1-0
Barry T v Dagenham 0-0, 1-0
Tunbridge Wells v Bath C 1-3
Bournemouth & Bos Ath v Torquay U 2-0
Brighton & HA v Peterborough & Fletton Utd 4-0
Nunhead v Bristol R 0-2
Caernarfon v Darlington 4-2
Carlisle Utd v Halifax T 2-0
Southport v Chesterfield 0-0, 2-3
Clapton Orient v Folkestone 0-0, 2-2, 4-1
Norwich C v Coventry C 3-3, 0-2
Nelson v Crewe Alex 0-3
Doncaster R v Shildon 0-0, 1-1, 3-0
Fulham v Thames 4-0
Leyton v Merthyr T 4-1
Lincoln C v Wigan Bor 3-1
Mansfield T v Manchester Central 0-2
Gillingham v Margate 0-2
New Brighton v Lancaster T 4-1
Newport Co v Kettering T 3-2
Aldershot v Northampton T 0-1
Wimbledon v Northfleet Utd 1-4
Dulwich Hamlet v Plymouth Arg 0-3
Gainsboro' Trin v Port Vale 0-0, 0-5
Rotherham Utd v Ashington 3-0
Luton T v Queen's Park R 2-3
Scunthorpe Utd v Hartlepools Utd 1-0
Southend Utd v Brentford 1-0
Wellington T v Stockport Co 1-4
Walsall v Exeter C 1-0
Ilford v Watford 0-3
South Shields v Wrexham 2-4
York C v Tranmere R 2-2, 1-0

Second Round
Caernarfon v Bournemouth & Bos Ath 1-1, 2-5
Brighton & HA v Barry T 4-1
Bristol R v Accrington S 4-1
Carlisle Utd v Crewe Alex 4-2
Clapton Orient v Northfleet Utd 2-0
Coventry C v Bath C 7-1
Doncaster R v New Brighton 1-0
Leyton v Fulham 1-4
Northampton T v Margate 6-0
Queen's Park R v Lincoln C 2-1
Watford v Plymouth Arg 1-1, 0-3
Scunthorpe Utd v Rotherham Utd 3-3, 4-5
Stockport Co v Barrow 4-0
Newport Co v Walsall 2-3
Manchester Central v Wrexham 0-1
Southend Utd v York C 1-4
Chesterfield v Port Vale 2-0

Third Round
West Ham Utd v Notts Co 4-0
Leeds Utd v Crystal Palace 8-1
Corinthians v Millwall 2-2, 1-1, 1-5
Doncaster R v Stoke C 1-0
ARSENAL v Chelsea 2-0
Birmingham v Bolton W 1-0
Chesterfield v Middlesbrough 1-1, 3-4
Charlton Ath v Queen's Park R 1-1, 3-0
Plymouth Arg v Hull C 3-4
Blackpool v Stockport Co 2-1
Tottenham H v Manchester C 2-2, 1-4
Manchester Utd v Swindon T 0-2
Newcastle Utd v York C 1-1, 2-1
Clapton Orient v Bristol R 1-0
Brighton & HA v Grimsby T 1-1, 1-0
Portsmouth v Preston NE 2-0
Aston Villa v Reading 5-1
Walsall v Swansea T 2-0
Blackburn R v Northampton T 4-1
Carlisle Utd v Everton 2-4
Bury v HUDDERSFIELD T 0-0, 1-3
Sheffield Utd v Leicester C 2-1
Bradford C v Southampton 4-1
Wrexham v West Bromwich A 1-0
Rotherham Utd v Nottingham F 0-5
Fulham v Bournemouth & Bos Ath 1-1, 2-0
Coventry C v Sunderland 1-2
Liverpool v Cardiff C 1-2
Sheffield Wed v Burnley 1-0
Oldham Ath v Wolves 1-0
Barnsley v Bradford 0-1
Derby Co v Bristol C 5-1

Fourth Round
West Ham Utd v Leeds Utd 4-1
Millwall v Doncaster R 4-0
ARSENAL v Birmingham 2-2, 1-0
Middlesbrough v Charlton Ath 1-1, 1-1, 1-0
Hull C v Blackpool 3-1
Swindon T v Manchester C 1-1, 1-10
Newcastle Utd v Clapton Orient 3-1
Portsmouth v Brighton & HA 0-1
Aston Villa v Walsall 3-1
Blackburn R v Everton 4-1
HUDDERSFIELD T v Sheffield Utd 2-1
Wrexham v Bradford C 0-0, 1-2
Nottingham F v Fulham 2-1
Sunderland v Cardiff C 2-1
Oldham Ath v Sheffield Wed 3-4
Derby Co v Bradford 1-1, 1-2

Fifth Round
West Ham Utd v Millwall 4-1
Middlesbrough v ARSENAL 0-2
Manchester C v Hull C 1-2
Newcastle Utd v Brighton & HA 3-0
Aston Villa v Blackburn R 4-1
HUDDERSFIELD T v Bradford C 2-1
Sunderland v Nottingham F 2-2, 1-3
Sheffield Wed v Bradford 5-1

Sixth Round
West Ham Utd v ARSENAL 0-3
Newcastle Utd v Hull C 1-1, 0-1
Aston Villa v HUDDERSFIELD T 1-2
Nottingham F v Sheffield Wed 2-2, 1-3

Semi-final
ARSENAL v Hull C 2-2, 1-0
HUDDERSFIELD T v Sheffield Wed 2-1

FINAL (Wembley Stadium)
ARSENAL 2
HUDDERSFIELD TOWN 0

Arsenal skipper Tom Parker with the Cup after the Gunners' 1930 win over Huddersfield Town.

Arsenal: Preedy; Parker, Hapgood, Baker, Seddon, John, Hulme, Jack, Lambert, James, Bastin.
Goalscorers: James, Lambert
Huddersfield Town: Turner; Goodall, Spence, Naylor, Wilson, Campbell, Jackson, Kelly, Davies, Raw, Smith.
Referee: T.Crewe (Leicester) *Attendance: 92,488*

1930-31

First Round
Accrington S v Lancaster T 3-1
Aldershot T v Peterborough & Fletton Utd 4-1
Ilford v Brentford 1-6
Bristol R v Merthyr Tydfil 4-1
Carlisle Utd v New Brighton 3-1
Northampton T v Coventry C 1-2
Crewe Alex v Jarrow 1-0
Crystal Palace v Taunton T 6-0
Rochdale v Doncaster R 1-2
Northfleet Utd v Exeter C 0-3
Folkestone v Sittingbourne 5-3
Fulham v Wimbledon 1-1 6-0
Gainsboro' Trin v Scunthorpe Utd 1-0
Tranmere R v Gateshead 4-4, 2-3
Gillingham v Guildford C 7-2
Halifax T v Mansfield T 2-2, 2-1
Lincoln C v Barrow 8-3
Luton T v Clapton Orient 2-2, 4-2
Nelson v Workington 4-0
Dulwich Hamlet v Newport Co 2-2, 1-4
Newark v Rotherham Utd 2-1
Norwich C v Swindon T 2-0
Chesterfield v Notts Co 1-2
Queen's Park R v Thames 5-0
Scarborough v Rhyl Ath 6-0
Southport v Darlington 4-2
Hartlepools Utd v Stockport Co 2-3
Southend Utd v Torquay Utd 0-1
Tunbridge Wells R v Kingstonians 3-0
Watford v Walthamstow Ave 5-1
Walsall v Bournemouth & Bos Ath 1-0
Wellington T v Wombwell 0-0, 3-0
Wrexham v Wigan Bor 2-0
York C v Gresley R 3-1

Second Round
Gillingham v Aldershot T 1-3
Brentford v Norwich C 1-0
Bristol R v Stockport Co 4-2
Carlisle Utd v Tunbridge Wells 4-2
Crystal Palace v Newark 6-0
Exeter C v Coventry C 1-1, 2-1
Fulham v Halifax T 4-0
Gateshead v Folkestone 3-2
Doncaster R v Notts Co 0-1
Queen's Park R v Crewe Alex 4-2
Scarborough T v Lincoln C 6-4
Gainsboro' Trin v Southport 0-4
Accrington S v Torquay Utd 0-1
Walsall v Newport Co 4-0
Watford v Luton T 3-1
Wellington T v Wrexham 2-4
Nelson v York C 1-1, 2-3

Third Round
Liverpool v BIRMINGHAM 0-2
Corinthians v Port Vale 1-3
Oldham Ath v Watford 1-3
Leicester C v Brighton & HA 1-2
West Ham Utd v Chelsea 1-3
Arsenal v Aston Villa 2-2, 3-1
Blackburn R v Walsall 1-1, 3-0
Bristol R v Queen's Park R 3-1
Bolton W v Carlisle Utd 1-0
Sunderland v Southampton 2-0
Sheffield Utd v York C 1-1, 2-0
Notts Co v Swansea T 3-1
Bury v Torquay Utd 1-1, 2-1
Exeter C v Derby Co 3-2
Leeds Utd v Huddersfield T 2-0
Newcastle Utd v Nottingham F 4-0
Crystal Palace v Reading 1-1, 1-1, 2-0
Plymouth Arg v Everton 0-2
Scarborough v Grimsby T 1-2
Stoke C v Manchester Utd 3-3, 0-0, 2-4
Southport v Millwall 3-1
Hull C v Blackpool 1-2
Aldershot T v Bradford 0-1
Burnley v Manchester C 3-0
Brentford v Cardiff C 2-2, 2-1
Fulham v Portsmouth 0-2
WEST BROMWICH A v Charlton Ath 2-2, 1-1, 3-1
Tottenham H v Preston NE 3-1
Barnsley v Bristol C 4-1
Gateshead v Sheffield Wed 2-6
Middlesbrough v Bradford C 1-1, 1-2
Wolves v Wrexham 9-1

Fourth Round
BIRMINGHAM v Port Vale 2-0
Watford v Brighton & HA 2-0
Chelsea v Arsenal 2-1
Blackburn R v Bristol R 5-1
Bolton W v Sunderland 1-1, 1-3
Sheffield Utd v Notts Co 4-1
Bury v Exeter C 1-2
Leeds Utd v Newcastle Utd 4-1
Crystal Palace v Everton 0-6
Grimsby T v Manchester Utd 1-0
Southport v Blackpool 2-1
Bradford v Burnley 2-0
Brentford v Portsmouth 0-1
WEST BROMWICH A v Tottenham H 1-0
Barnsley v Sheffield Wed 2-1
Bradford v Wolves 0-0, 2-4

Fifth Round
BIRMINGHAM C v Watford 3-0
Chelsea v Blackburn R 3-0
Sunderland v Sheffield Utd 2-1
Exeter C v Leeds Utd 3-1
Everton v Grimsby T 5-3
Southport v Bradford 1-0
Portsmouth v WEST BROMWICH A 0-1
Barnsley v Wolves 1-3

Sixth Round
BIRMINGHAM v Chelsea 2-2, 3-0
Sunderland v Exeter C 1-1, 4-2
Everton v Southport 9-1
WEST BROMWICH A v Wolves 1-1, 2-1

Semi-final
BIRMINGHAM v Sunderland 2-0
Everton v WEST BROMWICH A 0-1

FINAL (Wembley Stadium)
WEST BROMWICH ALBION 2
BIRMINGHAM 1

West Bromwich Albion: Pearson; Shaw, Trentham, Magee, W.Richardson, Edwards, Glidden, Carter, W.G.Richardson, Sandford, Wood.
Goalscorer: W.G.Richardson 2
Birmingham: Hibbs; Liddell, Barkas, Cringan, Morrall, Leslie, Briggs, Crosbie, Bradford, Gregg, Curtis.
Goalscorer: Bradford
Referee: A.H.Kingscott (Long Eaton)
Attendance: 92,406

Jubilant West Brom players after their 2-1 win over close rivals Birmingham City in the 1931 Final.

1931-32

First Round
Aldershot v Chelmsford 7-0
Barnet v Queen's Park R 3-7
Bath C v Nunhead 9-0
Bournemouth & Bos Ath v Northfleet Utd 1-1, 1-0
Bristol R v Gillingham 5-1
Cardiff C v Enfield 8-0
Chester v Hartlepools Utd 4-1
Coventry C v Clapton Orient 2-2, 0-2
Crewe Alex v Gainsboro' Trin 2-2, 0-1
Crook T v Stockport Co 3-1
Darlington v Walsall 1-0
Darwen v Peterborough & Fletton Utd 4-1
Folkestone v Brighton & HA 2-5
Fulham v Guildford C 2-0
Gateshead v Wrexham 3-2
Lancaster T v Blyth Spartans 0-3
Hull C v Mansfield T 4-1
Manchester Central v Lincoln C 0-3
Newark T v Halifax T 1-1, 1-2
New Brighton v York C 3-1
Northampton T v Metropolitan Police 9-0
Reading v Crystal Palace 0-1
Rotherham Utd v Accrington S 0-0, 0-5
Scunthorpe Utd v Rochdale 2-1
Swindon T v Luton T 0-5
Thames v Watford 2-2, 2-3
Tunbridge Wells Rgrs v Brentford 1-1, 1-2
Torquay Utd v Southend Utd 1-3
Tranmere R v West Stanley 3-0
Wimbledon v Norwich C 1-3
Yeovil & Petters Utd v Hayes 3-1
Yorks Amateurs v Carlisle Utd 1-3
Barrow v Doncaster R 3-3, 1-1, 1-1, 0-1
Burton T v Wigan Bor wo

Second Round
Gainsboro' Trin v Watford 2-5
Brighton & HA v Doncaster R 5-0
Brentford v Norwich C 4-1
Burton T v Gateshead 4-1
Scunthorpe Utd v Queen's Park R 1-4
Cardiff C v Clapton Orient 4-0
New Brighton v Hull C 0-4
Lincoln C v Luton T 2-2, 1-4
Halifax T v Accrington S 3-0
Northampton T v Southampton 3-0
Bath C v Crystal Palace 2-1
Darwen v Chester 2-1
Carlisle Utd v Darlington 0-2
Tranmere R v Bristol R 2-0
Aldershot v Crook T 1-1, 0-1
Bournemouth & Bos Ath v Blyth Spartans 1-0
Fulham v Yeovil & Petters Utd 0-0, 5-2

Third Round
Oldham Ath v Huddersfield T 1-1, 0-6
Queen's Park R v Leeds Utd 3-1
Preston NE v Bolton W 0-0, 5-2
Luton T v Wolves 1-2
Middlesbrough v Portsmouth 1-1, 0-3
West Bromwich A v Aston Villa 1-2
ARSENAL v Darwen 11-1
Plymouth Arg v Manchester Utd 4-1
Bury v Swansea T 2-1
Sheffield Utd v Corinthians 2-1
Sunderland v Southampton 0-0, 4-2
Stoke C v Hull C 3-0
Millwall v Manchester C 2-3
Brentford v Bath C 2-0
Burnley v Derby Co 0-4
Burton T v Blackburn R 0-4
Chesterfield v Nottingham F 5-2
Everton v Liverpool 1-2
Grimsby T v Exeter C 4-1
Birmingham v Bradford C 1-0
Tottenham H v Sheffield Wed 2-2, 1-3

Arsenal and Newcastle players emerge for the 1932 Final. Newcastle won with the help of the hugely controversial 'over the line' goal from Jack Allen.

Halifax v Bournemouth & Bos Ath ... 1-3
Tranmere R v Chelsea ... 2-2, 3-5
Charlton Ath v West Ham Utd ... 1-2
Blackpool v NEWCASTLE UTD ... 1-1, 0-1
Barnsley v Southport ... 0-0, 1-4
Brighton & HA v Port Vale ... 1-2
Leicester C v Crook T ... 7-0
Watford v Fulham ... 1-1, 3-0
Notts Co v Bristol C ... 2-2, 2-3
Bradford v Cardiff C ... 2-0
Darlington v Northampton T ... 1-1, 0-2

Fourth Round
Huddersfield T v Queen's Park R ... 5-0
Preston NE v Wolves ... 2-0
Portsmouth v Aston Villa ... 1-1, 1-0
ARSENAL v Plymouth Arg ... 4-2
Bury v Sheffield Utd ... 3-1
Sunderland v Stoke C ... 1-1, 1-1, 1-2
Manchester C v Brentford ... 6-1
Derby Co v Blackburn R ... 3-2
Chesterfield v Liverpool ... 2-4
Grimsby T v Birmingham ... 2-1
Sheffield Wed v Bournemouth & Bos Ath ... 7-0
Chelsea v West Ham Utd ... 3-1
NEWCASTLE UTD v Southport ... 1-1, 1-1, 9-0
Port Vale v Leicester C ... 1-2
Watford v Bristol C ... 2-1
Bradford v Northampton T ... 4-2

Fifth Round
Huddersfield T v Preston NE ... 4-0
Portsmouth v ARSENAL ... 0-2
Bury v Stoke C ... 3-0
Manchester C v Derby Co ... 3-0
Liverpool v Grimsby T ... 1-0
Sheffield Wed v Chelsea ... 1-1, 0-2
NEWCASTLE UTD v Leicester C ... 3-1
Watford v Bradford ... 1-0

Sixth Round
Huddersfield T v ARSENAL ... 0-1
Bury v Manchester C ... 3-4
Liverpool v Chelsea ... 0-2
NEWCASTLE UTD v Watford ... 5-0

Semi-final
ARSENAL v Manchester C ... 1-0
Chelsea v NEWCASTLE UTD ... 1-2

FINAL (Wembley Stadium)
NEWCASTLE UNITED ... 2
ARSENAL ... 1
Newcastle United: McInroy; Nelson, Fairhurst, McKenzie, Davidson, Weaver, Boyd, Richardson, Allen, McMenemy, Lang.
Goalscorer: Allen 2
Arsenal: Moss; Parker, Hapgood, Jones, Roberts, Male, Hulme, Jack, Lambert, Bastin, John.
Goalscorer: John
Referee: W.P.Harper (Stourbridge)
Attendance: 92,298

1932-33

First Round
Accrington S v Hereford Utd ... 2-1
Barrow v Gateshead ... 0-1
Carlisle Utd v Denaby Utd ... 1-0
Chester v Rotherham Utd ... 4-0
Crewe Alex v Crook T ... 4-0
Darlington v Boston T ... 1-0
Doncaster R v Gainsboro' Trin ... 4-1
Halifax T v Darwen ... 2-0
Marine, Liverpool v Hartlepools Utd ... 2-5
Rochdale v Stockport Co ... 0-2
Southport v Nelson ... 3-3, 4-0
Stalybridge Cel v Hull C ... 2-8
Tranmere R v New Brighton ... 3-0
Walsall v Mansfield T ... 4-1
Workington v Scunthorpe Utd ... 5-1
Wrexham v Spennymoor Utd ... 3-0
York C v Scarborough ... 1-3
Bristol C v Romford ... 4-0
Cardiff C v Bristol R ... 1-1, 1-4
Clapton Orient v Aldershot ... 0-1
Crystal Palace v Brighton & HA ... 1-2
Dartford v Yeovil & Petters Utd ... 0-0, 2-4
Folkestone v Norwich C ... 1-0
Gillingham v Wycombe W ... 1-1, 4-2
Guildford C v Coventry C ... 1-2
Luton T v Kingstonians ... 2-2, 3-2
Margate v Ryde Sports ... 5-0
Merthyr Tydfil v Queen's Park R ... 1-1, 1-5
Newport Co v Ilford ... 4-2
Northampton T v Lloyds ... 8-1
Reading v Brentford ... 3-2
Southend Utd v Exeter C ... 1-1, 1-0
Swindon T v Dulwich Hamlet ... 4-1
Torquay Utd v Bournemouth & Bos Ath ... 0-0, 2-2, 3-2

Second Round
Gateshead v Margate ... 5-2
Southend Utd v Scarborough ... 4-1
Stockport Co v Luton T ... 2-3
Reading v Coventry C ... 2-2, 3-3, 1-0
Bristol C v Tranmere R ... 2-2, 2-3
Accrington S v Aldershot ... 1-2
Southport v Swindon T ... 1-2
Walsall v Hartlepools Utd ... 2-1
Chester v Yeovil & Petters Utd ... 2-1
Halifax T v Workington ... 2-1
Folkestone v Newport Co ... 2-1
Crewe Alex v Darlington ... 0-2
Carlisle Utd v Hull C ... 1-1, 1-2
Bristol R v Gillingham ... 1-1, 3-1
Torquay Utd v Queen's Park R ... 1-1, 1-3
Northampton T v Doncaster R ... 0-1
Brighton & HA v Wrexham ... 0-0, 3-2

Third Round
Swindon T v Burnley ... 1-2
Swansea T v Sheffield Utd ... 2-3
Darlington v Queen's Park R ... 2-0
Sheffield Wed v Chesterfield ... 2-2, 2-4
Charlton Ath v Bolton W ... 1-5
Grimsby T v Portsmouth ... 3-2
Gateshead v MANCHESTER C ... 1-1, 0-9
Walsall v Arsenal ... 2-0
Watford v Southend Utd ... 1-1, 0-2
Wolves v Derby Co ... 3-6
Aldershot v Bristol R ... 1-0
Millwall v Reading ... †2-2, 1-1, 2-0
Bradford C v Aston Villa ... 2-2, 1-2
Hull C v Sunderland ... 0-2
Blackpool v Port Vale ... 2-1
Huddersfield T v Folkestone ... 2-0
Leicester C v EVERTON ... 2-3
Bury v Nottingham F ... 2-2, 2-1
Tranmere R v Notts Co ... 2-1
Newcastle Utd v Leeds Utd ... 0-3
Chester v Fulham ... 5-0
Doncaster R v Halifax T ... 0-3
Barnsley v Luton T ... 0-0, 0-2
Oldham Ath v Tottenham H ... 0-6
Brighton & HA v Chelsea ... 2-1
Bradford v Plymouth Arg ... 5-1
Corinthians v West Ham Utd ... 0-2
West Bromwich A v Liverpool ... 2-0
Manchester Utd v Middlesbrough ... 1-4
Stoke C v Southampton ... 1-0
Birmingham v Preston NE ... 2-1
Lincoln C v Blackburn R ... 1-5

Fourth Round
Burnley v Sheffield Utd ... 3-1
Darlington v Chesterfield ... 0-2
Bolton W v Grimsby T ... 2-1
MANCHESTER C v Walsall ... 2-0
Southend Utd v Derby Co ... 2-3
Aldershot v Millwall ... 1-0
Aston Villa v Sunderland ... 0-3
Blackpool v Huddersfield T ... 2-0
EVERTON v Bury ... 3-1
Tranmere R v Leeds Utd ... 0-0, 0-4
Chester v Halifax T ... 0-0, 2-3
Luton T v Tottenham H ... 2-0
Brighton & HA v Bradford ... 2-1
West Ham Utd v West Bromwich A ... 2-0
Middlesbrough v Stoke C ... 4-1
Birmingham v Blackburn R ... 3-0

Fifth Round
Burnley v Chesterfield ... 1-0
Bolton W v MANCHESTER C ... 2-4
Derby Co v Aldershot ... 2-0
Sunderland v Blackpool ... 1-0
EVERTON v Leeds Utd ... 2-0
Halifax T v Luton T ... 0-2
Brighton & HA v West Ham Utd ... 2-2, 0-1
Middlesbrough v Birmingham ... 0-0, 0-3

Sixth Round
Burnley v MANCHESTER C ... 0-1
Derby Co v Sunderland ... 4-4, 1-0
EVERTON v Luton T ... 6-0
West Ham Utd v Birmingham ... 4-0

Semi-final
MANCHESTER C v Derby Co ... 3-2
EVERTON v West Ham Utd ... 2-1

FINAL (Wembley Stadium)
EVERTON ... 3
MANCHESTER CITY ... 0
Everton: Sagar; Cook, Cresswell, Britton, White, Thomson, Geldard, Dunn, Dean, Johnson, Stein.
Goalscorers: Stein, Dean, Dunn
Manchester City: Langford; Cann, Dale, Busby, Cowan, Bray, Toseland, Marshall, Herd, McMullen, Brook.
Referee: E.Wood (Sheffield) *Attendance: 92,950*
†Abandoned because of fog.

1933-34

First Round
Barrow v Doncaster R ... 4-2
Bath C v Charlton Ath ... 0-0, 1-3
Bournemouth & Bos Ath v Hayes ... 3-0
Cardiff C v Aldershot ... 0-0, 1-3
Carlisle Utd v Wrexham ... 2-1
Cheltenham T v Barnet ... 5-1
Chester v Darlington ... 6-1
Clapton Orient v Epsom T ... 4-2
Coventry C v Crewe Alex ... 3-0
Crystal Palace v Norwich C ... 3-0
Dulwich Hamlet v Newport Co ... 2-2, 2-6
Folkestone v Bristol R ... 0-0, 1-3
Gainsboro' Trin v Altrincham ... 1-0
Gateshead v Darwen ... 5-2
Halifax T v Barnsley ... 3-2
Ilford v Swindon T ... 2-4
Kingstonian v Bristol C ... 1-7
Lancaster T v Stockport Co ... 0-1
London PM v Southend Utd ... 0-1
New Brighton v Mansfield T ... 0-0, 4-3
Northampton T v Exeter C ... 2-0
Northfleet Utd v Dartford ... 0-2
North Shields v Scarborough ... 3-0
Oxford C v Gillingham ... 1-5
Queen's Park R v Kettering T ... 6-0
Rotherham Utd v South Bank St Peters ... 3-2
Scunthorpe Utd v Accrington S ... 1-1, 0-3
Sutton T v Rochdale ... 2-1
Torquay Utd v Margate ... 1-1, 2-0
Tranmere R v Newark T ... 7-0
Walsall v Spennymoor Utd ... 4-0
Watford v Reading ... 0-3
Workington v Southport ... 1-0
York C v Hartlepools Utd ... 2-3

Second Round
Bournemouth & Bos Ath v Tranmere R ... 2-4
Workington v Newport Co ... 3-1
Northampton T v Torquay Utd ... 3-0
Bristol C v Barrow ... 2-1
Rotherham Utd v Coventry C ... 2-1
Southend Utd v Chester ... 2-1
Stockport Co v Crystal Palace ... 1-2
Carlisle Utd v Cheltenham T ... 1-2
Sutton T v Reading ... 1-2
Gainsboro' Trin v Aldershot ... 0-2
Halifax T v Hartlepools Utd ... 1-1, 2-1
Queen's Park R v New Brighton ... 1-1, 4-0
Charlton Ath v Gillingham ... 1-0
Accrington S v Bristol R ... 1-0

Gateshead v North Shields 1-0
Swindon T v Dartford 1-0
Walsall v Clapton Orient 0-0, 0-2

Third Round
Manchester Utd v PORTSMOUTH 1-1, 1-4
Grimsby T v Clapton Orient 1-0
Burnley v Bury 0-0, 2-3
Swansea T v Notts Co 1-0
Liverpool v Fulham 1-1, 3-2
Tranmere R v Southend Utd 3-0
Brighton & HA v Swindon T 3-1
Bolton W v Halifax T 3-1
Leeds Utd v Preston NE 0-1
Workington v Gateshead 4-1
Southampton v Northampton T 1-1, 0-1
Plymouth Arg v Huddersfield T 1-1, 2-6
Birmingham v Sheffield Utd 2-1
Charlton Ath v Port Vale 2-0
Millwall v Accrington S 3-0
Leicester C v Lincoln C 3-0
Chesterfield v Aston Villa 2-2, 0-2
Sunderland v Middlesbrough 1-1, 2-1
West Ham Utd v Bradford C 3-2
Tottenham H v Everton 3-0
Bristol C v Derby Co 1-1, 0-1
Wolves v Newcastle Utd 1-0
Crystal Palace v Aldershot 1-0
Luton T v Arsenal 0-1
Stoke C v Bradford 3-0
Cheltenham T v Blackpool 1-3
Nottingham F v Queen's Park R 4-0
Chelsea v West Bromwich A 1-1, 1-0
Rotherham Utd v Sheffield Wed 0-3
Reading v Oldham Ath 1-2
Hull C v Brentford 1-0
MANCHESTER C v Blackburn R 3-1

Fourth Round
PORTSMOUTH v Grimsby T 2-0
Bury v Swansea T 1-1, 0-3
Liverpool v Tranmere R 3-1
Brighton & HA v Bolton W 1-1, 1-6
Workington v Preston NE 1-2
Huddersfield T v Northampton T 0-2
Birmingham v Charlton Ath 1-0
Millwall v Leicester C 3-6
Aston Villa v Sunderland 7-2
Tottenham H v West Ham Utd 4-1
Derby Co v Wolves 3-0
Arsenal v Crystal Palace 7-0
Stoke C v Blackpool 3-0
Chelsea v Nottingham F 1-1, 3-0
Oldham Ath v Sheffield Wed 1-1, 1-6
Hull C v MANCHESTER C 2-2, 1-4

Fifth Round
Swansea T v PORTSMOUTH 0-1
Liverpool v Bolton W 0-3
Preston NE v Northampton T 4-0
Birmingham v Leicester C 1-2
Tottenham H v Aston Villa 0-1
Arsenal v Derby Co 1-0
Stoke C v Chelsea 3-1
Sheffield Wed v MANCHESTER C 2-2, 0-2

Sixth Round
Bolton W v PORTSMOUTH 0-3
Preston NE v Leicester C 0-1
Arsenal v Aston Villa 1-2
MANCHESTER C v Stoke C 1-0

Semi-final
PORTSMOUTH v Leicester C 4-1
MANCHESTER C v Aston Villa 6-1

FINAL (Wembley Stadium)
MANCHESTER CITY 2
PORTSMOUTH 0
Manchester City: Swift; Barnett, Dale, Busby, Cowan, Bray, Toseland, Marshall, Tilson, Herd, Brook.
Goalscorer: Tilson
Portsmouth: Gilfillan; Mackie, W.Smith, Nichol, Allen, Thackeray, Worrall, J.Smith, Weddle, Easson, Rutherford.
Goalscorer: Rutherford
Referee: S.F.Rous (Herts) *Attendance: 93,258*

King George V presents the FA Cup to Manchester City skipper Sam Cowan after the 1934 Final. At the end of their 2-0 win over Portsmouth, City's 19-year-old goalkeeper Frank Swift fainted.

1934-35

First Round
Southend Utd v Golders Green 10-1
Coventry C v Scunthorpe Utd 7-0
Mansfield T v Accrington S 6-1
Carlisle Utd v Wigan Ath 1-6
Ashford v Clapton Orient 1-4
Gateshead v Darlington 1-4
Wrexham v Rochdale 4-1
Bedford T v Dartford 2-3
Burton T v York C 2-3
Swindon T v Newport Co 4-0
Aldershot v Bournemouth & Bos Ath 4-0
Brighton & HA v Folkestone 3-1
Chester v Dinnington Ath 3-1
Tranmere R v Stalybridge Cel 3-1
Charlton Ath v Exeter C 2-2, 2-5
Shildon Coll v Lincoln C 2-2, 0-4
Yeovil & Petters Utd v Crystal Palace 3-0
Bristol R v Harwich & Parkeston 3-0
Crewe Alex v Walsall 1-2
Darwen v Boston Utd 1-2
Dulwich Hamlet v Torquay Utd 1-2
Guildford C v Bath C 1-2
Cardiff C v Reading 1-2
Queen's Park R v Walthamstow Ave 2-0
Rotherham Utd v Spennymoor Utd 2-0
Watford v Corinthians 2-0
Workington v Birmingham Corporation Trams 2-0
Bristol C v Gillingham 2-0
Doncaster R v Barrow 0-2
Halifax T v Hartlepools Utd 1-1, 0-2
Southport v New Brighton 1-1, 1-1, 1-2
Wimbledon v Leyton 1-1, 1-0
Blyth Spartans v Stockport Co 1-1, 1-4
Barry v Northampton T 0-1

Second Round
Swindon T v Lincoln C 4-3
Wimbledon v Southend Utd 1-5
Mansfield T v Tranmere R 4-2
Yeovil & Petters Utd v Exeter C 4-1
Wigan Ath v Torquay Utd 3-2
Stockport Co v Darlington 3-2
Hartlepools Utd v Coventry C 0-4
Clapton Orient v Chester 1-3
Reading v Wrexham 3-0
Bath C v Boston Utd 2-1
Queen's Park R v Brighton & HA 1-2
Rotherham Utd v Bristol C 1-2
Barrow v Aldershot 0-2
Watford v Walsall 1-1, 1-0
York C v New Brighton 1-0
Dartford v Bristol R 0-1
Northampton T v Workington 0-0, 1-0

Third Round
SHEFFIELD WED v Oldham Ath 3-1
Wolves v Notts Co 4-0
Norwich C v Bath C 2-0
Leeds Utd v Bradford 4-1
Aldershot v Reading 0-0, 1-3
Wigan Ath v Millwall 1-4
Leicester C v Blackpool 2-1
Brighton & HA v Arsenal 0-2
Birmingham v Coventry C 5-1
Walsall v Southampton 1-2
Yeovil & Petters Utd v Liverpool 2-6
Middlesbrough v Blackburn R 1-1, 0-1
Chester v Nottingham F 0-4
Bristol R v Manchester Utd 1-3
Chelsea v Luton T 1-1, 0-2
Burnley v Mansfield T 4-2
Northampton T v Bolton W 0-2
Brentford v Plymouth Arg 0-1
Hull C v Newcastle Utd 1-5
Tottenham H v Manchester C 1-0
York C v Derby Co 0-1
Swansea T v Stoke C 4-1
Sunderland v Fulham 3-2
Everton v Grimsby T 6-3
Preston NE v Barnsley 0-0, 1-0
Swindon T v Chesterfield 2-1
Portsmouth v Huddersfield T 1-1, 3-2
Bristol C v Bury 1-1, 2-2, 2-1
West Ham Utd v Stockport Co 1-1, 0-1
Aston Villa v Bradford C 1-3
Southend Utd v Sheffield Utd 0-4
WEST BROMWICH A v Port Vale 2-1

Fourth Round
Wolves v SHEFFIELD WED 1-2
Norwich C v Leeds Utd 3-3, 2-1
Reading v Millwall 1-0
Leicester C v Arsenal 0-1
Southampton v Birmingham 0-3
Blackburn R v Liverpool 1-0
Nottingham F v Manchester Utd 0-0, 3-0
Burnley v Luton T 3-1

Plymouth Arg v Bolton W 1-4
Tottenham H v Newcastle Utd 2-0
Derby Co v Swansea T 3-0
Sunderland v Everton 1-1, 4-6
Swindon T v Preston NE 0-2
Portsmouth v Bristol C 0-0, 0-2
Bradford C v Stockport C 0-0, 2-3
WEST BROMWICH A v Sheffield Utd 7-1

Fifth Round
Norwich C v SHEFFIELD WED 0-1
Reading v Arsenal 0-1
Blackburn R v Birmingham 1-2
Nottingham F v Burnley 0-0, 0-3
Tottenham H v Bolton W 1-1, 1-1, 0-2
Everton v Derby Co 3-1
Bristol C v Preston NE 0-0, 0-5
WEST BROMWICH A v Stockport Co 5-0

Sixth Round
SHEFFIELD WED v Arsenal 2-1
Burnley v Birmingham 3-2
Everton v Bolton W 1-2
WEST BROMWICH A v Preston NE 1-0

Semi-final
SHEFFIELD WED v Burnley 3-0
Bolton W v WEST BROMWICH A 1-1, 0-2

FINAL (Wembley Stadium)
SHEFFIELD WEDNESDAY 4
WEST BROMWICH ALBION 2
Sheffield Wednesday: Brown; Nibloe, Catlin, Sharp, Millership, Burrows, Hooper, Surtees, Palethorpe, Starling, Rimmer.
Goalscorers: Palethorpe, Hooper, Rimmer 2
West Bromwich Albion: Pearson; Shaw, Trentham, Murphy, W.Richardson, Edwards, Glidden, Carter, W.G.Richardson, Sandford, Boyes.
Goalscorers: Boyes, Sandford
Referee: A.E.Fogg (Bolton) *Attendance: 93,204*

1935-36

First Round
Barrow v Wrexham 4-1
Brighton & HA v Cheltenham 0-0 6-0
Bristol C v Crystal Palace 0-1
Cardiff C v Dartford 0-3
Chester v Gateshead 1-0
Chesterfield v Southport 3-0
Clapton Orient v Aldershot 0-0, 1-0
Coventry C v Scunthorpe Utd 1-1, 2-4
Crewe Alex v Boston Utd 4-2
Darlington v Accrington S 4-2
Dulwich Hamlet v Torquay Utd 2-3
Exeter C v Gillingham 0-4
Gainsboro' Trin v Blyth Spartans 3-1
Grantham v Notts Co 0-2
Halifax T v Rochdale 4-0
Kidderminster H v Bishop Auckland 4-1
Mansfield T v Hartlepools Utd 2-3
Margate v Queen's Park R 3-1
New Brighton v Workington 1-3
Newport Co v Southend Utd 0-1
Northampton T v Bristol R 0-0, 1-3
Nunhead v Watford 2-4
Oldham Ath v Ferryhill Ath 6-1
Reading v Corinthians 8-3
Romford v Folkestone 3-3, 1-2
Scarborough v Darwen 2-0
Southall v Swindon T 3-1
Stalybridge Cel v Kells Utd 4-0
Tranmere R v Carlisle Utd 3-0
Walsall v Lincoln C 2-0
Walthamstow Ave v Bournemouth & Bos Ath 1-1, 1-8
Wigan Ath v Rotherham Utd 1-2
Yeovil & Petters Utd v Newport (IoW) 0-1
York C v Burton T 1-5

Second Round
Southall v Newport (IoW) 8-0
Tranmere R v Scunthorpe Utd 6-2
Bournemouth & Bos Ath v Barrow 5-2
Workington v Kidderminster H 5-1
Chester v Reading 3-3, 0-3
Southend Utd v Burton T 5-0
Dartford v Gainsboro' Trin 4-0
Margate v Crystal Palace 3-1
Notts Co v Torquay Utd 3-0
Crewe Alex v Gillingham 2-1
Folkestone v Clapton Orient 1-2
Halifax T v Hartlepools Utd 1-1, 0-0, 1-4
Oldham Ath v Bristol R 1-1, 1-4
Rotherham Utd v Watford 1-1, 0-1
Scarborough v Brighton & HA 1-1, 0-3
Stalybridge Cel v Darlington 0-1
Chesterfield v Walsall 0-0, 1-2

Third Round
Bristol R v ARSENAL 1-5
Liverpool v Swansea T 1-0
Crewe Alex v Sheffield Wed 1-1, 1-3
Walsall v Newcastle Utd 0-2
Barnsley v Birmingham 3-3, 2-0
Notts Co v Tranmere R 0-0, 3-4
Millwall v Stoke C 0-0, 0-4
Reading v Manchester Utd 1-3
Hartlepools Utd v Grimsby T 0-0, 1-4
Sunderland v Port Vale 2-2, 0-2
Manchester C v Portsmouth 3-1
West Ham Utd v Luton T 2-2, 0-4
Middlesbrough v Southampton 1-0
Clapton Orient v Charlton Ath 3-0
Leicester C v Brentford 1-0
Southall v Watford 1-4
Fulham v Brighton & HA 2-1
Blackpool v Margate 3-1
Norwich C v Chelsea 1-1, 1-3
Stockport Co v Plymouth Arg 2-3
Bradford C v Bournemouth & Bos Ath 1-0
Blackburn R v Bolton W 1-1, 1-0
Derby Co v Dartford 3-2
Doncaster R v Nottingham F 1-2
Everton v Preston NE 1-3
Burnley v SHEFFIELD UTD 0-0, 1-2
Wolves v Leeds Utd 1-1, 1-3
Darlington v Bury 2-3
Tottenham H v Southend Utd 4-4, 2-1
Aston Villa v Huddersfield T 0-1
Bradford v Workington 3-2
West Bromwich A v Hull C 2-0

Fourth Round
Liverpool v ARSENAL 0-2
Sheffield Wed v Newcastle Utd 1-1, 1-3
Tranmere R v Barnsley 2-4
Stoke C v Manchester Utd 0-0, 2-0
Port Vale v Grimsby T 0-4
Manchester C v Luton T 2-1
Middlesbrough v Clapton Orient 3-0
Leicester C v Watford 6-3
Fulham v Blackpool 5-2
Chelsea v Plymouth Arg 4-1
Bradford C v Blackburn R 3-1
Derby C v Nottingham F 2-0
Preston NE v SHEFFIELD UTD 0-0, 0-2
Leeds Utd v Bury †2-1, 3-2
Tottenham H v Huddersfield T 1-0
Bradford v West Bromwich A 1-1, 1-1, 2-0

Fifth Round
Newcastle Utd v ARSENAL 3-3, 0-3
Barnsley v Stoke C 2-1
Grimsby T v Manchester C 3-2
Middlesbrough v Leicester C 2-1
Chelsea v Fulham 0-0, 2-3
Bradford C v Derby Co 0-1
SHEFFIELD UTD v Leeds Utd 3-1
Bradford v Tottenham H 0-0, 1-2

Sixth Round
ARSENAL v Barnsley 4-1
Grimsby T v Middlesbrough 3-1
Fulham v Derby Co 3-0
SHEFFIELD UTD v Tottenham H 3-1

Semi-final
ARSENAL v Grimsby T 1-0
Fulham v SHEFFIELD UTD 1-2

FINAL (Wembley Stadium)
ARSENAL 1
SHEFFIELD UNITED 0
Arsenal: Wilson; Male, Hapgood, Crayston, Roberts, Copping, Hulme, Bowden, Drake, James, Bastin.
Goalscorer: Drake
Sheffield United: Smith; Hooper, Wilkinson, Jackson, Johnson, McPherson, Barton, Barclay, Dodds, Pickering, Williams.
Referee: H.Nattrass (New Seaham)
Attendance: 93,384

†Abandoned after 75 minutes because of fog.

1936-37

First Round
Accrington S v Wellington T 3-1
Aldershot v Millwall 1-6
Barrow v Mansfield T 0-4
Bath C v Tunbridge Wells Rgrs 1-2
Blyth Spartans v Wrexham 0-2
Boston Utd v Spennymoor Utd 1-1, 0-2
Bournemouth & Bos Ath v Harwich & Parkeston 5-1
Burton T v Wigan Ath 5-1
Cardiff C v Southall 3-1
Carlisle Utd v Stockport Co 2-1
Clapton Orient v Torquay Utd 2-1
Corinthians v Bristol R 0-2
Crewe Alex v Rochdale 5-1
Crystal Palace v Southend Utd 1-1, 0-2
Dartford v Peterborough Utd 3-0
Exeter C v Folkestone 3-0
Frickley Coll v Southport 0-2
Gateshead v Notts Co 2-0
Halifax T v Darlington 1-2
Ilford v Reading 2-4
Ipswich T v Watford 2-1
Lincoln C v New Brighton 1-1, 3-2
Newport Co v Bristol C 3-0
Oldham Ath v Tranmere R 1-0
Queen's Park R v Brighton & HA 5-1
Rotherham Utd v Hartlepools Utd 4-4, 0-2
Rhyde Sports v Gillingham 1-5
Shildon v Stalybridge Cel 4-2
South Liverpool v Morecambe 1-0
Swindon T v Dulwich Hamlet 6-0
Walsall v Scunthorpe Utd 3-0
Walthamstow Ave v Northampton T 6-1
Yeovil & Petters Utd v Worthing 4-3
York C v Hull C 5-2

Second Round
Reading v Newport Co 7-2
Millwall v Gateshead 7-0
Southend Utd v York C 3-3, 1-2
Carlisle Utd v Clapton Orient 4-1
Lincoln C v Oldham Ath 2-3
Bristol R v Southport 2-1
Cardiff C v Swindon T 2-1
Burton T v Darlington 1-2
Ipswich T v Spennymoor Utd 1-2
Mansfield T v Bournemouth & Bos Ath 0-3
Shildon v Dartford 0-3
Wrexham v Gillingham 2-0
Crewe Alex v Hartlepools Utd 1-1, 2-1
Walsall v Yeovil & Petters Utd 1-1, 1-0
Walthamstow Ave v Exeter C *1-1, 2-3
Accrington S v Tunbridge Wells Rgrs 1-0
South Liverpool v Queen's Park R 0-1

Third Round
Southampton v SUNDERLAND 2-3
Luton T v Blackpool 3-3, 2-1
Swansea T v Carlisle Utd 1-0
Bradford C v York C 2-2, 0-1
Cardiff C v Grimsby T 1-3
Walsall v Barnsley 3-1
Wolves v Middlesbrough 6-1
Nottingham F v Sheffield Utd 2-4
Millwall v Fulham 2-0
Chelsea v Leeds Utd 4-0
Bradford v Derby Co 0-4
Brentford v Huddersfield T 5-0
West Ham Utd v Bolton W 0-0, 0-1
Norwich C v Liverpool 3-0
Wrexham v Manchester C 1-3
Blackburn R v Accrington S 2-2, 1-3
Portsmouth v Tottenham H 0-5
Crewe Alex v Plymouth Arg 0-2
Everton v Bournemouth & Bos Ath 5-0
Sheffield Wed v Port Vale 2-0
PRESTON NE v Newcastle Utd 2-0
Stoke C v Birmingham 4-1
Exeter C v Oldham Ath 3-0
Bristol R v Leicester C 2-5
Coventry C v Charlton Ath 2-0
Chester v Doncaster R 4-0
West Bromwich A v Spennymoor Utd 7-1
Dartford v Darlington 0-1
Aston Villa v Burnley 2-3
Bury v Queen's Park R 1-0
Chesterfield v Arsenal 1-5
Manchester Utd v Reading 1-0

Fourth Round
Luton T v SUNDERLAND 2-2, 1-3
Swansea T v York C 0-0, 3-1
Grimsby T v Walsall 5-1
Wolves v Sheffield Utd 2-2, 2-1
Millwall v Chelsea 3-0
Derby Co v Brentford 3-0
Bolton W v Norwich C 1-1, 2-1
Manchester C v Accrington S 2-0
Tottenham H v Plymouth Arg 1-0
Everton v Sheffield Wed 3-0
PRESTON NE v Stoke C 5-1
Exeter C v Leicester C 3-1
Coventry C v Chester 2-0
West Bromwich A v Darlington 3-2
Burnley v Bury 4-1
Arsenal v Manchester Utd 5-0

Fifth Round
SUNDERLAND v Swansea T 3-0
Grimsby T v Wolves 1-1, 2-6
Millwall v Derby Co 2-1
Bolton W v Manchester C 0-5
Everton v Tottenham H 1-1, 3-4

Sunderland's young skipper Raich Carter is carried aloft after the Wearsiders' victory over Preston North End in 1937.

PRESTON NE v Exeter C 5-3
Coventry C v West Bromwich A 2-3
Burnley v Arsenal 1-7

Sixth Round
Wolves v SUNDERLAND 1-1, 2-2, 0-4
Millwall v Manchester C 2-0
Tottenham H v PRESTON NE 1-3
West Bromwich A v Arsenal 3-1

Semi-final
SUNDERLAND v Millwall 2-1
PRESTON NE v West Bromwich A 4-1

FINAL (Wembley Stadium)
SUNDERLAND 3
PRESTON NORTH END 1
Sunderland: Mapson; Gorman, Hall, Thomson, Johnson, McNab, Duns, Carter, Gurney, Gallacher, Burbanks.
Goalscorers: Gurney, Carter, Burbanks
Preston North End: Burns; Gallimore, A.Beattie, Shankly, Tremelling, Milne, Dougal, Beresford, F.O'Donnell, Fagan, H.O'Donnell.
Goalscorer: F.O'Donnell
Referee: R.G.Rudd (Kenton) *Attendance: 93,495*
*Abandoned

1937-38

First Round
Accrington S v Lancaster T 1-1, 1-1, 4-0
Barrow v Crewe Alex 0-1
Bournemouth & Bos Ath v Dartford 0-0 6-0
Brighton & HA v Tunbridge Wells Rgrs 5-1
Bristol C v Enfield 3-0
Bristol R v Queen's Park R 1-8
Burton T v Rotherham Utd 1-1, 0-3
Corinthians v Southend Utd 0-2
Crystal Palace v Kettering T 2-2, 4-0
Darlington v Scarborough 0-2
Doncaster R v Blyth Spartans 7-0
Dulwich Hamlet v Aldershot 1-2
Exeter C v Folkestone 1-0
Gillingham v Swindon T 3-4
Guildford C v Reading 1-0
Hartlepools Utd v Southport 3-1
Hull C v Scunthorpe Utd 4-0
Kidderminster H v Newport Co 2-2, 1-4
King's Lynn v Bromley 0-4
New Brighton v Workington 5-0
Northampton T v Cardiff C 1-2
Port Vale v Gainsboro' Trin 1-1, 1-2
Rochdale v Lincoln C 1-1, 0-2
Torquay Utd v Clapton Orient 1-2
Tranmere Rovers v Carlisle Utd 2-1
Walker Celtic v Bradford C 1-1, 3-11
Walsall v Gateshead 4-0
Watford v Cheltenham T 3-0
Wellington T v Mansfield T 1-2
Westbury Utd v Walthamstow Ave 1-3
Wigan Ath v South Liverpool 1-4
Wrexham v Oldham Ath 2-1
Yeovil & Petters Utd v Ipswich T 2-1
York C v Halifax T 1-1, 1-0

Second Round
Accrington S v Crystal Palace 0-1
Cardiff C v Bristol C 1-1, 2-0
Clapton Orient v York C 2-2, 0-1
Crewe Alex v New Brighton 2-2, 1-4
Doncaster R v Guildford C 4-0
Exeter C v Hull C 1-2
Mansfield T v Lincoln C 2-1
Newport Co v Bournemouth & Bos Ath 2-1
Rotherham Utd v Aldershot 1-3
Scarborough v Bromley 4-1
South Liverpool v Brighton & HA 1-1, 0-6
Swindon T v Queen's Park R 2-1
Tranmere R v Hartlepools Utd 3-1
Walthamstow Ave v Southend Utd 0-1
Watford v Walsall 3-0
Wrexham v Bradford C 1-2
Yeovil & Petters Utd v Gainsboro' Trin 2-1

Third Round
PRESTON NE v West Ham Utd 3-0
Mansfield T v Leicester C 1-2
Swansea T v Wolves 0-4
Arsenal v Bolton W 3-1
Manchester Utd v Yeovil & Petters Utd 3-0
Southend Utd v Barnsley 2-2, 1-2
Tranmere R v Portsmouth 1-2
Brentford v Fulham 3-1
Millwall v Manchester C 2-2, 1-3
Bury v Brighton & HA 2-0
Grimsby T v Swindon T 1-1, 1-2
Scarborough v Luton T 1-1, 1-5
Charlton Ath v Cardiff C 5-0
Leeds Utd v Chester 3-1
Birmingham v Blackpool 0-1
Norwich C v Aston Villa 2-3
Sunderland v Watford 1-0
Chelsea v Everton 0-1
Derby Co v Stoke C 1-2
Bradford v Newport Co 7-4
Bradford C v Chesterfield 1-1, 1-1, 0-2
Sheffield Wed v Burnley 1-1, 1-3
New Brighton v Plymouth Arg 1-0
Tottenham H v Blackburn R 3-2
York C v Coventry C 3-2
West Bromwich A v Newcastle Utd 1-0
Nottingham F v Southampton 3-1
Middlesbrough v Stockport Co 2-0
Crystal Palace v Liverpool 0-0, 1-3
Doncaster R v Sheffield Utd 0-2
Aldershot v Notts Co 1-3
HUDDERSFIELD T v Hull C 3-1

Fourth Round
PRESTON NE v Leicester C 2-0
Wolves v Arsenal 1-2
Barnsley v Manchester Utd 2-2, 0-1
Brentford v Portsmouth 2-1
Manchester C v Bury 3-1
Luton T v Swindon T 2-1
Charlton Ath v Leeds Utd 2-1
Aston Villa v Blackpool 4-0
Everton v Sunderland 0-1
Bradford v Stoke C 1-1, 2-1
Chesterfield v Burnley 3-2
New Brighton v Tottenham H 0-0, 2-5
York C v West Bromwich A 3-2
Nottingham F v Middlesbrough 1-3
Sheffield Utd v Liverpool 1-1, 0-1
HUDDERSFIELD T v Notts Co 1-0

Fifth Round
Arsenal v PRESTON NE 0-1
Brentford v Manchester Utd 2-0
Luton T v Manchester C 1-3
Charlton Ath v Aston Villa 1-1, 2-2, 1-4
Sunderland v Bradford 1-0
Chesterfield v Tottenham H 2-2, 1-2
York C v Middlesbrough 1-0
Liverpool v HUDDERSFIELD T 0-1

Sixth Round
Brentford v PRESTON NE 0-3
Aston Villa v Manchester C 3-2
Tottenham H v Sunderland 0-1
York C v HUDDERSFIELD T 0-0, 1-2

Semi-final
PRESTON NE v Aston Villa 2-1
Sunderland v HUDDERSFIELD T 1-3

FINAL (Wembley Stadium)
PRESTON NORTH END 1
HUDDERSFIELD TOWN 0
(after extra-time)
Preston North End: Holdcroft; Gallimore, A.Beattie, Shankly, Smith, Batey, Watmough, Mutch, Maxwell, R.Beattie, H.O'Donnell.
Goalscorer: Mutch (pen)
Huddersfield Town: Hesford; Craig, Mountford, Willingham, Young, Boot, Hulme, Isaac, MacFadyen, Barclay, Beasley.
Referee: A.J.Jewell (London) *Attendance: 93,357*

Preston's George Mutch scores from the penalty-spot to give his side the Cup with an extra-time victory over Huddersfield Town in the dramatic 1938 Final.

1938-39

First Round

Aldershot v Guildford 1-1, 4-3
Bournemouth & Bos Ath v Bristol C 2-1
Bristol R v Peterborough Utd 4-1
Bromley v Apsley 2-1
Chester v Bradford C 3-1
Chelmsford C v Kidderminster H 4-0
Cheltenham T v Cardiff C 1-1, 0-1
Clapton Orient v Hayes 3-1
Crystal Palace v Queen's Park R 1-1, 0-3
Darlington v Stalybridge Cel 4-0
Doncaster R v New Brighton 4-2
Folkestone v Colchester Utd 2-1
Gainsboro' Trin v Gateshead 2-1
Halifax T v Rochdale 7-3
Hartlepools Utd v Accrington S 2-1
Horden Welfare v Chorley 1-1, 2-1
Hull C v Rotherham Utd 4-1
Ipswich T v Street 7-0
Lincoln C v Barrow 4-1
North Shields v Stockport Co 1-4
Oldham Ath v Crewe Alex 2-2, 0-1
Reading v Newport Co 3-3, 1-3
Runcorn v Wellington T 3-0
Scarborough v Southport 0-0, 3-5
Scunthorpe Utd v Lancaster C 4-2
Southend Utd v Corinthians 3-0
Swindon T v Lowestoft T 6-0
Torquay Utd v Exeter C 3-1
Walthamstow Ave v Tunbridge Wells Rgrs 4-1
Walsall v Carlisle Utd 4-1
Watford v Northampton T 4-1
Workington v Mansfield T 1-1, 1-2
Wrexham v Port Vale 1-2
Yeovil & Petters Utd v Brighton & HA 2-1

Second Round

Bristol R v Bournemouth & Bos Ath 0-3
Cardiff C v Crewe Alex 1-0
Chelmsford C v Darlington 3-1
Chester v Hull C 2-2, 1-0
Folkestone v Yeovil & Petters Utd 1-1, 0-1
Gainsboro' Trin v Doncaster R 0-1
Halifax T v Mansfield T 1-1, 3-3, 0-0, 2-1
Hartlepools Utd v Queen's Park R 0-2
Horden Welfare v Newport Co 2-3
Ipswich T v Torquay Utd 4-1
Lincoln C v Bromley 8-1
Port Vale v Southend Utd 0-1
Runcorn v Aldershot 3-1
Scunthorpe Utd v Watford 1-2
Southport v Swindon T 2-0
Stockport Co v Walthamstow Ave 0-0, 3-1
Walsall v Clapton Orient 4-2

Third Round

PORTSMOUTH v Lincoln C 4-0
West Bromwich A v Manchester Utd 0-0, 5-1
Queen's Park R v West Ham Utd 1-2
Tottenham H v Watford 7-1
Runcorn v Preston NE 2-4
Aston Villa v Ipswich T 1-1, 2-1
Cardiff C v Charlton Ath 1-0
Brentford v Newcastle Utd 0-2
Leeds Utd v Bournemouth & Bos Ath 3-1
Huddersfield T v Nottingham F 0-0, 3-0
Notts Co v Burnley 3-1
Newport Co v Walsall 0-2
Middlesbrough v Bolton W 0-0, 0-0, 1-0
Sunderland v Plymouth Arg 3-0
Blackburn R v Swansea T 2-0
Chesterfield v Southend Utd †1-1, 1-1, 3-4
WOLVES v Bradford 3-1
Leicester C v Stoke C 1-1, 2-1
Liverpool v Luton T 3-0
Barnsley v Stockport Co 1-2
Derby Co v Everton 0-1
Southport v Doncaster R 1-1, 1-2
Birmingham v Halifax T 2-0
Chelmsford C v Southampton 4-1
Chelsea v Arsenal 2-1
Fulham v Bury 6-0
Sheffield Wed v Yeovil & Petters Utd 1-1, 2-1
Chester v Coventry C 1-0
Blackpool v Sheffield Utd 1-2
Norwich C v Manchester C 0-5
York C v Millwall 0-5
Grimsby T v Tranmere R 6-0

Fourth Round

PORTSMOUTH v West Bromwich A 2-0
West Ham Utd v Tottenham H 3-3, 1-1, 2-1
Preston NE v Aston Villa 2-0
Cardiff C v Newcastle Utd 0-0, 1-4
Leeds Utd v Huddersfield T 2-4
Notts Co v Walsall 0-0, 0-4
Middlesbrough v Sunderland 0-2
Blackburn R v Southend Utd 4-2
WOLVES v Leicester C 5-1
Liverpool v Stockport Co 5-1
Everton v Doncaster R 8-0
Birmingham v Chelmsford C 6-0
Chelsea v Fulham 3-0
Sheffield Wed v Chester 1-1, 1-1, 2-0
Sheffield Utd v Manchester C 2-0
Millwall v Grimsby T 2-2, 2-3

Fifth Round

PORTSMOUTH v West Ham Utd 2-0
Newcastle Utd v Preston NE 1-2
Huddersfield T v Walsall 3-0
Sunderland v Blackburn R 1-1, 0-0, 0-1
WOLVES v Liverpool 4-1
Birmingham v Everton 2-2, 1-2
Chelsea v Sheffield Wed 1-1, 0-0, 3-1
Sheffield Utd v Grimsby T 0-0, 0-1

Sixth Round

PORTSMOUTH v Preston NE 1-0
Huddersfield T v Blackburn R 1-1, 2-1
WOLVES v Everton 2-0
Chelsea v Grimsby T 0-1

Semi-final

PORTSMOUTH v Huddersfield T 2-1
WOLVES v Grimsby T 5-0

FINAL (Wembley Stadium)

PORTSMOUTH 4
WOLVERHAMPTON WANDERERS 1

Portsmouth: Walker; Morgan, Rochford, Guthrie, Rowe, Wharton, Worrall, McAlinden, Anderson, Barlow, Parker.
Goalscorers: Barlow 2, Anderson, Parker
Wolverhampton Wanderers: Scott; Morris, Taylor, Galley, Cullis, Gardiner, Burton, McIntosh, Westcott, Dorsett, Maguire.
Goalscorer: Dorsett

Referee: T.Thompson (Lemington-on-Tyne)
Attendance: 99,370

†Abandoned after 73 minutes.

Bert Barlow, a former Wolves favourite, scores Portsmouth's first goal against the Molineux club in the 1939 Final.

1945-46

First Round (agg)

Barnet v Queen's Park R 2-6, 1-2 (3-8)
Barrow v Netherfield 1-0, 2-2 (3-2)
Bath C v Cheltenham T 3-2, 2-0 (5-2)
Brighton & HA v Romford 3-1, 1-1 (4-2)
Bromley v Slough Utd 6-1, 0-1 (6-2)
Carlisle Utd v South Shields 5-1, 3-2 (8-3)
Chorley v Accrington S 2-1, 0-2 (2-3)
Clapton Orient v Newport (IoW) 2-1, 0-2 (2-3)
Crewe Alex v Wrexham 4-2, 0-3 (4-5)
Darlington v Stockton 2-0, 4-1 (6-1)
Doncaster R v Rotherham Utd 0-1, 1-2 (1-3)
Halifax T v York C 1-0, 2-4 (3-4)
Hartlepools Utd v Gateshead 1-2, 2-6 (3-8)
Kettering T v Grantham 1-5, 2-2 (3-7)
Lovell's Ath v Bournemouth & Bos Ath 4-1, 2-3 (6-4)
Mansfield T v Gainsboro' Trin 3-0, 2-4 (5-4)
Marine (Crosby) v Stalybridge Cel 4-0, 3-3 (7-3)
Northampton T v Chelmsford 5-1, 5-0 (10-1)
Notts Co v Bradford C 2-2, 2-1 (4-3)
Port Vale v Wellington T 4-0, 2-0 (6-0)
Reading v Aldershot 3-1, 3-7 (6-8)
Shrewsbury T v Walsall 5-0, 1-4 (6-4)
South Liverpool v Tranmere R 1-1, 1-6 (2-7)
Southport v Oldham Ath 1-2, 1-3 (2-5)
Stockport Co v Rochdale 1-2, 1-1 (2-3)
Sutton Utd v Walthamstow Ave 1-4, 2-7 (3-11)
Swindon T v Bristol R 1-0, 1-4 (2-4)
Torquay Utd v Newport Co 0-1, 1-1 (1-2)
Trowbridge v Exeter C 1-3, 2-7 (3-10)
Watford v Southend Utd 1-1, 3-0 (4-1)
Willington v Bishop Auckland 0-5, 2-0 (2-5)
Wisbech v Ipswich T 0-3, 0-5 (0-8)
Yeovil & Petters Utd v Bristol C 2-2, 0-3 (2-5)
Yorkshire Amateurs v Lincoln C 1-0, 1-5 (2-5)

Second Round (agg)

Aldershot v Newport (IoW) 7-0, 5-0 (12-0)
Barrow v Carlisle Utd 4-2, 4-3 (8-5)
Bishop Auckland v York C 1-2, 0-3 (1-5)
Bristol C v Bristol R 4-2, 2-0 (6-2)
Bromley v Watford 1-3, 1-1 (2-4)
Darlington v Gateshead 2-4, 2-1 (4-5)
Grantham v Mansfield T 1-2, 1-2 (2-4)
Lovell's Ath v Bath C 2-1, 5-2 (7-3)
Newport Co v Exeter C 5-1, 3-1 (8-2)
Northampton T v Notts Co 3-1, 0-1 (3-2)
Oldham Ath v Accrington S 2-1, 1-3 (3-4)
Port Vale v Marine (Crosby) 3-1, 1-1 (4-2)
Queen's Park R v Ipswich T 4-0, 2-0 (6-0)
Rotherham Utd v Lincoln C 2-1, 1-1 (3-2)
Shrewsbury T v Wrexham 0-1, 1-1 (1-2)
Tranmere R v Rochdale 3-1, 0-3 (3-4)
Walthamstow Ave v Brighton & HA 1-1, 2-4 (3-5)

Third Round (agg)

Accrington S v Manchester Utd 2-2, 1-5 (3-7)
Aldershot v Plymouth Arg 2-0, 1-0 (3-0)
Birmingham C v Portsmouth 1-0, 0-0 (1-0)
Bolton W v Blackburn R 1-0, 3-1 (4-1)
Bradford v Port Vale 2-1, 1-1 (3-2)
Bristol C v Swansea T 5-1, 2-2 (7-3)
Bury v Rochdale 3-3, 4-2 (7-5)
Cardiff C v West Bromwich A 1-1, 0-4 (1-5)
CHARLTON ATH v Fulham 3-1, 1-2 (4-3)
Chelsea v Leicester C 1-1, 2-0 (3-1)
Chester v Liverpool 0-2, 1-2 (1-4)
Chesterfield v York C 1-1, 2-3 (3-4)
Coventry C v Aston Villa 2-1, 0-2 (2-3)
Grimsby T v Sunderland 1-3, 1-2 (2-5)
Huddersfield T v Sheffield Utd 1-1, 0-2 (1-3)
Leeds Utd v Middlesbrough 4-4, 2-7 (6-11)

Lovell's Ath v Wolves 2-4, 1-8 (3-12)
Luton T v DERBY CO 0-6 0-3 (0-9)
Manchester C v Barrow 6-2, 2-2 (8-4)
Mansfield T v Sheffield Wed 0-0, 0-5 (0-5)
Newcastle Utd v Barnsley 4-2, 0-3 (4-5)
Northampton T v Millwall 2-2, 0-3 (2-5)
Norwich C v Brighton & HA 1-2, 1-4 (2-6)
Nottingham F v Watford 1-1, 1-1, 0-1 (2-3)
Preston NE v Everton 2-1, 2-2 (4-3)
Queen's Park R v Crystal Palace 0-0, 0-0, 1-0 (1-0)
Rotherham Utd v Gateshead 2-2, 2-0 (4-2)
Southampton v Newport Co 4-3, 2-1 (6-4)
Stoke C v Burnley 3-1, 1-2 (4-3)
Tottenham H v Brentford 2-2, 0-2 (2-4)
West Ham Utd v Arsenal 6-0, 0-1 (6-1)
Wrexham v Blackpool 1-4, 1-4 (2-8)

Fourth Round (agg)
Barnsley v Rotherham Utd 3-0, 1-2 (4-2)
Birmingham C v Watford 5-0, 1-1 (6-1)
Blackpool v Middlesbrough 3-2, 2-3, 0-1 (5-6)
Bolton W v Liverpool 5-0, 0-2 (5-2)
Bradford v Manchester C 1-3 8-2 (9-5)
Brighton & HA v Aldershot 3-0, 4-1 (7-1)
Bristol C v Brentford 2-1, 0-5 (2-6)
CHARLTON ATH v Wolves 5-2, 1-1 (6-3)
Chelsea v West Ham Utd 2-0, 0-1 (2-1)
DERBY CO v West Bromwich A 1-0, 3-1 (4-1)
Manchester Utd v Preston NE 1-0, 1-3 (2-3)
Millwall v Aston Villa 2-4, 1-9 (3-13)
Sheffield Wed v York C 5-1, 6-1 (11-2)
Southampton v Queen's Park R 0-1, 3-4 (3-5)
Stoke C v Sheffield Utd 2-0, 2-3 (4-3)
Sunderland v Bury 3-1, 4-5 (7-6)

Fifth Round (agg)
Barnsley v Bradford 0-1, 1-1 (1-2)
Bolton W v Middlesbrough 1-0, 1-1 (2-1)
Brighton & HA v DERBY CO 1-4, 0-6 (1-10)
Chelsea v Aston Villa 0-1, 0-1 (0-2)
Preston NE v CHARLTON ATH 1-1, 0-6 (1-7)
Queen's Park R v Brentford 1-3, 0-0 (1-3)
Stoke C v Sheffield Wed 2-0, 0-0 (2-0)
Sunderland v Birmingham C 1-0, 1-3 (2-3)

Sixth Round (agg)
Aston Villa v DERBY CO 3-4, 1-1 (4-5)
Bradford v Birmingham C 2-2, 0-6 (2-8)
CHARLTON ATH v Brentford 6-3, 3-1 (9-4)
Stoke C v Bolton W 0-2, 0-0 (0-2)

Semi-final
Bolton W v CHARLTON ATH 0-2
DERBY CO v Birmingham C 1-1, 4-0

FINAL (Wembley Stadium)
DERBY COUNTY 4
CHARLTON ATHLETIC 1
(after extra-time)

Derby County: Woodley; Nicholas, Howe, Bullions, Leuty, Musson, Harrison, Carter, Stamps, Doherty, Duncan.
Goalscorers: H.Turner (og), Doherty, Stamps 2
Charlton Athletic: Bartram; Phipps, Shreeve, H.Turner, Oakes, Johnson, Fell, Brown, A.A.Turner, Welsh, Duffy.
Goalscorer: H.Turner
Referee: E.D.Smith (Whitehaven) *Attendance: 98,215*

Derby County skipper Jack Nicholas on full-back Jack Howe's shoulders after the Rams won the first post-war FA Cup Final, beating Charlton Athletic 4-1 after extra-time.

For this season only all ties up to the semi-final stage were played on a home and away basis, ties being decided on aggregate of goals. The first-named team played at home in the first tie.

1946-47

First Round
Aldershot v Cheltenham T 4-2
Barnet v Sutton Utd 3-0
Barrow v Halifax T 0-0, 0-1
Bournemouth & Bos Ath v Exeter C 4-2
Bristol C v Hayes 9-3
Brush Sports v Southend Utd 1-6
Carlisle Utd v Runcorn 4-0
Doncaster R v Accrington S 2-2, 5-0
Gainsboro' Trin v Darlington 1-2
Gateshead v Bradford C 3-1
Gillingham v Gravesend & Northfleet 4-1
Hartlepools Utd v North Shields 6-0
Hull C v New Brighton 0-0, 2-1
Ipswich T v Torquay Utd 2-0
Lancaster C v Spennymoor Utd 1-0
Leyton Orient v Notts Co 1-2
Leytonstone v Walsall 1-6
Merthyr Tydfil v Bristol R 3-1
Northampton T v Mansfield T 2-0
Norwich C v Brighton & HA 7-2
Oldham Ath v Tranmere R 1-0
Port Vale v Finchley 5-0
Queen's Park R v Poole T 2-2, 6-0
Reading v Colchester Utd 5-0
Rochdale v Bishop Auckland 6-1
Rotherham Utd v Crewe Alex 2-0
South Liverpool v Workington 2-1
Stockport Co v Southport 2-0
Stockton v Lincoln C 2-4
Swindon T v Cambridge T 4-1
Wellington T v Watford 1-1, 0-1
Wrexham v Marine (Crosby) 5-0
Yeovil T v Peterborough Utd 2-2, 0-1
York C v Scunthorpe Utd 0-1

Second Round
Barnet v Southend Utd 2-9
Bournemouth & Bos Ath v Aldershot 4-2
Bristol C v Gillingham 1-2
Darlington v Hull C 1-2
Gateshead v Lancaster C 4-0
Halifax T v Stockport Co 1-1, 1-2
Lincoln C v Wrexham 1-1, 3-3, 2-1
Merthyr Tydfil v Reading 1-3
Norwich C v Queen's Park R 4-4, 0-2
Notts Co v Swindon T 2-1
Oldham Ath v Doncaster R 1-2
Peterborough Utd v Northampton T 1-1, 1-1, 1-8
Rochdale v Hartlepools Utd 6-1
Rotherham Utd v Scunthorpe Utd 4-1
South Liverpool v Carlisle Utd 2-3
Walsall v Ipswich T 0-0, 1-0
Watford v Port Vale 1-1, 1-2

Third Round
CHARLTON ATH v Rochdale 3-1
West Bromwich A v Leeds Utd 2-1
Blackburn R v Hull C 1-1, 3-0
Millwall v Port Vale 0-3
Northampton T v Preston NE 1-2
Huddersfield T v Barnsley 3-4
Sheffield Wednesday v Blackpool 4-1
Everton v Southend Utd 4-2
Newcastle Utd v Crystal Palace 6-2
Southampton v Bury 5-1
West Ham Utd v Leicester C 1-2
Brentford v Cardiff C 1-0
Sheffield Utd v Carlisle Utd 3-0
Wolves v Rotherham Utd 3-0
Tottenham H v Stoke C 2-2, 0-1
Chester v Plymouth Arg 2-0
BURNLEY v Aston Villa 5-1
Coventry C v Newport Co 5-2
Luton T v Notts Co 6-0
Swansea T v Gillingham 4-1
Queen's Park R v Middlesbrough 1-1, 1-3
Chesterfield v Sunderland 2-1
Lincoln C v Nottingham F 0-1
Bradford v Manchester Utd 0-3
Walsall v Liverpool 2-5
Reading v Grimsby T 2-2, 1-3
Bournemouth & Bos Ath v Derby Co 0-2
Chelsea v Arsenal 1-1, 1-1, 2-0
Fulham v Birmingham C 1-2
Doncaster R v Portsmouth 2-3
Manchester C v Gateshead 3-0
Bolton W v Stockport Co 5-1

Fourth Round
West Bromwich A v CHARLTON ATH 1-2
Blackburn R v Port Vale 2-0
Preston NE v Barnsley 6-0
Sheffield Wednesday v Everton 2-1
Newcastle Utd v Southampton 3-1
Brentford v Leicester C 0-0, 0-0, 1-4
Wolves v Sheffield Utd 0-0, 0-2
Chester v Stoke C 0-0, 2-3
BURNLEY v Coventry C 2-0
Luton T v Swansea T 2-0
Middlesbrough v Chesterfield 2-1
Manchester Utd v Nottingham F 0-2
Liverpool v Grimsby T 2-0
Chelsea v Derby Co 2-2, 0-1
Birmingham C v Portsmouth 1-0
Bolton W v Manchester C 3-3, 0-1

Fifth Round
CHARLTON ATH v Blackburn R 1-0
Sheffield Wednesday v Preston NE 0-2
Newcastle Utd v Leicester C 1-1, 2-1
Stoke C v Sheffield Utd 0-1
Luton T v BURNLEY 0-0, 0-3
Nottingham F v Middlesbrough 2-2, 2-6
Liverpool v Derby Co 1-0
Birmingham C v Manchester C 5-0

Sixth Round
CHARLTON ATH v Preston NE 2-1
Sheffield Utd v Newcastle Utd 0-2
Middlesbrough v BURNLEY 1-1, 0-1
Liverpool v Birmingham C 4-1

Semi-final
CHARLTON ATH v Newcastle Utd 4-0
Liverpool v BURNLEY 0-0, 0-1

FINAL (Wembley Stadium)
CHARLTON ATHLETIC 1
BURNLEY 0
(after extra-time)

Charlton Athletic: Bartram; Croker, Shreeve, Johnson, Phipps, Whittaker, Hurst, Dawson, W.Robinson, Welsh, Duffy.
Goalscorer: Duffy
Burnley: Strong; Woodruff, Mather, Attwell, Brown, Bray, Chew, Morris, Harrison, Potts, Kippax.
Referee: J.M.Wiltshire (Sherbourne)
Attendance: 99,000

Now it is Charlton's turn. Skipper Don Welsh with the Cup in 1947.

1947-48

First Round
Aldershot v Bromsgrove R 2-1
Barrow v Carlisle Utd 3-2
Bournemouth & Bos Ath v Guildford C 2-0
Bristol R v Leytonstone 3-2
Bromley v Reading 3-3, 0-3
Cheltenham T v Street 5-0
Chester v Bishop Auckland 3-1
Colchester Utd v Banbury Spencer 2-1
Crewe Alex v South Shields 4-1
Crystal Palace v Port Vale 2-1
Dartford v Bristol C 0-0, 2-9
Exeter C v Northampton T 1-1, 0-2
Gateshead v Bradford C 1-3
Gillingham v Leyton Orient 1-0
Great Yarmouth v Shrewsbury T 1-4
Hartlepools Utd v Darlington 1-0
Hull C v Southport 1-1, 3-2
Lincoln C v Workington 0-2
New Brighton v Marine (Crosby) 4-0
Newport Co v Southend Utd 3-2
Norwich C v Merthyr Tydfil 3-0
Notts Co v Horsham 9-1
Oldham Ath v Lancaster C 6-0
Runcorn v Scunthorpe Utd 4-2
Stockport Co v Accrington S 3-1
Stockton v Grantham T 2-1
Swindon T v Ipswich T 4-2
Tranmere R v Stalybridge Cel 2-0

Trowbridge T v Brighton & HA 1-1, 0-5
Vauxhall Motors (Luton) v Walsall 1-2
Watford v Torquay Utd 1-1, 0-3
Wimbledon v Mansfield T 0-1
Wrexham v Halifax T 5-0
York C v Rochdale 0-1

Second Round
Aldershot v Swindon T 0-0, 0-2
Bournemouth & Bos Ath v Bradford C 1-0
Bristol C v Crystal Palace 0-1
Bristol R v New Brighton 4-0
Colchester Utd v Wrexham 1-0
Hartlepools Utd v Brighton & HA 1-1, 1-2
Hull C v Cheltenham T 4-2
Northampton T v Torquay Utd 1-1, 0-2
Norwich C v Walsall 2-2, 2-3
Notts Co v Stockton 1-1, 4-1
Oldham Ath v Mansfield T 0-1
Reading v Newport Co 3-0
Rochdale v Gillingham 1-1, 0-3
Runcorn v Barrow 0-1
Stockport Co v Shrewsbury T 1-1, 2-2, 3-2
Tranmere R v Chester 0-1
Workington v Crewe Alex 1-2

Third Round
Gillingham v Queen's Park R 1-1, 1-3
Mansfield T v Stoke C 2-4
Plymouth Arg v Luton T 2-4
Coventry C v Walsall 2-1
Rotherham Utd v Brentford 0-3
Hull C v Middlesbrough 1-3
Crewe Alex v Sheffield Utd 3-1
Derby Co v Chesterfield 2-0
Aston Villa v MANCHESTER UTD 4-6
Liverpool v Nottingham F 4-1
Charlton Ath v Newcastle Utd 2-1
Stockport Co v Torquay Utd 3-0
Manchester C v Barnsley 2-1
Chelsea v Barrow 5-0
Portsmouth v Brighton & HA 4-1
Millwall v Preston NE 1-2
Fulham v Doncaster R 2-0
Bristol R v Swansea T 3-0
Bournemouth & Bos Ath v Wolves 1-2
Grimsby T v Everton 1-4
BLACKPOOL v Leeds Utd 4-0
Crystal Palace v Chester 0-1
Colchester Utd v Huddersfield T 1-0
Arsenal v Bradford 0-1
Southampton v Sunderland 1-0
Blackburn R v West Ham Utd 0-0, 4-2
Burnley v Swindon T 0-2
Birmingham C v Notts Co 0-2
Bolton W v Tottenham H 0-2
West Bromwich A v Reading 2-0
Leicester C v Bury 1-0
Cardiff C v Sheffield Wednesday 1-2

Fourth Round
Queen's Park R v Stoke C 3-0
Luton T v Coventry C 3-2
Brentford v Middlesbrough 1-2
Crewe Alex v Derby Co 0-3
MANCHESTER UTD v Liverpool 3-0
Charlton Ath v Stockport Co 3-0
Manchester C v Chelsea 2-0
Portsmouth v Preston NE 1-3
Fulham v Bristol R 5-2
Wolves v Everton 1-1, 2-3
BLACKPOOL v Chester 4-0
Colchester Utd v Bradford 3-2
Southampton v Blackburn R 3-2
Swindon T v Notts Co 1-0
Tottenham H v West Bromwich A 3-1
Leicester C v Sheffield Wednesday 2-1

Fifth Round
Queen's Park R v Luton T 3-1
Middlesbrough v Derby Co 1-2
MANCHESTER UTD v Charlton Ath 2-0
Manchester C v Preston NE 0-1
Fulham v Everton 1-1, 1-0
BLACKPOOL v Colchester Utd 5-0
Southampton v Swindon T 3-0
Tottenham H v Leicester C 5-2

Sixth Round
Queen's Park R v Derby Co 1-1, 0-5
MANCHESTER UTD v Preston NE 4-1
Fulham v BLACKPOOL 0-2
Southampton v Tottenham H 0-1

Semi-final
Derby Co v MANCHESTER UTD 1-3
BLACKPOOL v Tottenham H 3-1

Final (Wembley Stadium)
MANCHESTER UNITED 4
BLACKPOOL 2

Eddie Shimwell gives Blackpool the lead from the penalty-spot in 1948. But Manchester United went on to win a classic Final 4-2.

Manchester United: Crompton; Carey, Aston, Anderson, Chilton, Cockburn, Delaney, Morris, Rowley, Pearson, Mitten.
Goalscorers: Rowley 2, Pearson, Anderson.
Blackpool: Robinson; Shimwell, Crosland, Johnston, Hayward, Kelly, Matthews, Munro, Mortensen, Dick, Rickett.
Goalscorers: Shimwell (pen), Mortensen
Referee: C.J.Barrick (Northampton)
Attendance: 99,000

1948-49

First Round
Barnet v Exeter C 2-6
Bradford C v Doncaster R 4-3
Colchester Utd v Reading 2-4
Crewe Alex v Billingham Synthonia Rec 5-0
Crystal Palace v Bristol C 0-1
Dartford v Leyton Orient 2-3
Gainsboro' Trin v Witton Albion 1-0
Gateshead v Netherfield 3-0
Halifax T v Scunthorpe Utd 0-0, 0-1
Hartlepools Utd v Chester 1-3
Hull C v Accrington S 3-1
Ipswich T v Aldershot 0-3
Kidderminster H v Hereford Utd 0-3
Leytonstone v Watford 2-1
Mansfield T v Gloucester C 4-0
Millwall v Tooting & Mitcham 1-0
New Brighton v Carlisle Utd 1-0
Newport Co v Brighton & HA 3-1
Northampton T v Dulwich Hamlet 2-1
Norwich C v Wellington T 1-0
Notts Co v Port Vale 2-1
Peterborough Utd v Torquay Utd 0-1
Rochdale v Barrow 1-1, 0-2
Rhyl Ath v Scarborough 0-2
Southend Utd v Swansea T 1-2
Southport v Horden Coll Welfare 2-1
Tranmere R v Darlington 1-3
Walsall v Bristol R 2-1
Walthamstow Ave v Cambridge T 3-2
Weymouth v Chelmsford C 2-1
Workington v Stockport Co 0-3
Wrexham v Oldham Ath 0-3
Yeovil T v Romford 4-0
York C v Runcorn 2-1

Second Round
Aldershot v Chester 1-0
Bradford C v New Brighton 0-0, 0-1
Bristol C v Swansea T 3-1
Crewe Alex v Millwall 3-2
Darlington v Leyton Orient 1-0
Exeter C v Hereford Utd 2-1
Gateshead v Scarborough 3-0
Hull C v Reading 0-0, 2-1
Leytonstone v Newport Co 3-4
Mansfield T v Northampton T 2-1
Notts Co v Barrow 3-2
Scunthorpe Utd v Stockport Co 0-1
Southport v York C 2-2, 2-0
Torquay Utd v Norwich C 3-1
Walsall v Gainsboro' Trin 4-3
Walthamstow Ave v Oldham Ath 2-2, 1-3
Weymouth v Yeovil T 0-4

Third Round
Manchester Utd v Bournemouth & Bos Ath 6-0
Newcastle Utd v Bradford 0-2
Yeovil T v Bury 3-1
Crewe Alex v Sunderland 0-2
Blackburn R v Hull C 1-2
Grimsby T v Exeter C 2-1
Swindon T v Stoke C 1-3
Barnsley v Blackpool 0-1
WOLVES v Chesterfield 6-0
Sheffield Utd v New Brighton 5-2
Nottingham F v Liverpool 2-2, 0-4
Plymouth Arg v Notts Co 0-1
Lincoln C v West Bromwich A 0-1
Gateshead v Aldershot 3-1
Bristol C v Chelsea 1-3
Everton v Manchester C 1-0
LEICESTER C v Birmingham C 1-1, 1-1, 2-1
Preston NE v Mansfield T 2-1
Luton T v West Ham Utd 3-1
Fulham v Walsall 0-1
Brentford v Middlesbrough 3-2
Torquay Utd v Coventry C 1-0
Burnley v Charlton Ath 2-1
Rotherham Utd v Darlington 4-2
Portsmouth v Stockport Co 7-0
Sheffield Wednesday v Southampton 2-1
Leeds Utd v Newport Co 1-3
Queen's Park R v Huddersfield T 0-0, 0-5
Derby Co v Southport 4-1
Arsenal v Tottenham H 3-0
Oldham Ath v Cardiff C 2-3
Aston Villa v Bolton W 1-1, 0-0, 2-1

Fourth Round
Manchester Utd v Bradford 1-1, 1-1, 5-0
Yeovil T v Sunderland 2-1
Grimsby T v Hull C 2-3
Stoke C v Blackpool 1-1, 1-0
Sheffield Utd v WOLVES 0-3
Liverpool v Notts Co 1-0
Gateshead v West Bromwich A 1-3
Chelsea v Everton 2-0
LEICESTER C v Preston NE 2-0
Luton T v Walsall 4-0
Brentford v Torquay Utd 1-0
Rotherham Utd v Burnley 0-1
Portsmouth v Sheffield Wed 2-1
Newport Co v Huddersfield T 3-3, 3-1
Derby Co v Arsenal 1-0
Aston Villa v Cardiff C 1-2

Fifth Round
Manchester Utd v Yeovil T 8-0
Stoke C v Hull C 0-2
WOLVES v Liverpool 3-1
West Bromwich A v Chelsea 3-0
Luton T v LEICESTER C 5-5, 3-5
Brentford v Burnley 4-2
Portsmouth v Newport Co 3-2
Derby Co v Cardiff C 2-1

Sixth Round
Hull C v Manchester Utd 0-1
WOLVES v West Bromwich A 1-0
Brentford v LEICESTER C 0-2
Portsmouth v Derby Co 2-1

Semi-final
Manchester Utd v WOLVES 1-1, 0-1
LEICESTER C v Portsmouth 3-1

FINAL (Wembley Stadium)
WOLVERHAMPTON WANDERERS 3
LEICESTER CITY 1
Wolverhampton Wanderers: Williams; Pritchard,

Billy Wright and his teammates after Wolves' Wembley win over Leicester City in 1949.

Springthorpe, Crook, Shorthouse, Wright, Hancocks, Smyth, Pye, Dunn, Mullen.
Goalscorers: Pye 2, Smyth
Leicester City: Bradley; Jelly, Scott, W.Harrison, Plummer, King, Griffiths, Lee, J.Harrison, Chisholm, Adam.
Goalscorer: Griffiths

Referee: R.A.Mortimer (Huddersfield)
Attendance: 99,500

1949-50

First Round

Accrington S v Hartlepools Utd 0-1
Bradford C v Fleetwood 9-0
Bromley v Watford 1-2
Carlisle Utd v Lincoln C 1-0
Chester v Goole T 4-1
Crystal Palace v Newport Co 0-3
Darlington v Crewe Alex 2-2, 0-1
Doncaster R v New Brighton 5-1
Gateshead v York C 3-1
Gloucester C v Norwich C 2-3
Gravesend & Northfleet Utd v Torquay Utd 1-3
Hastings Utd v Gillingham 1-3
Hereford Utd v Bromsgrove R 3-0
Ipswich T v Brighton & HA 2-1
Leyton Orient v Southend Utd 0-2
Leytonstone v Chelmsford C 1-2
Mansfield T v Walsall 4-1
Millwall v Exeter C 3-5
Netherfield v North Shields 4-3
Northampton T v Walthamstow Ave 4-1
Notts Co v Tilbury 4-0
Nottingham F v Bristol C 1-0
Nuneaton Bor v King's Lynn 2-1
Oldham Ath v Stockton 4-0
Port Vale v Wealdstone 1-0
Rhyl v Rochdale 0-3
Southport v Barrow 1-1, 1-0
Stockport Co v Billingham Synthonia Rec 3-0
Swindon T v Bristol R 1-0
Tranmere R v Halifax T 2-1
Weymouth v Aldershot 2-2, 3-2
Witton Albion v Mossley 0-1
Wrexham v Grantham 4-1
Yeovil T v Romford 4-1

Second Round

Carlisle Utd v Swindon T 2-0
Chelmsford C v Ipswich T 1-1, 0-1
Crewe Alex v Oldham Ath 1-1, 0-0, 0-3
Doncaster R v Mansfield T 1-0
Exeter C v Chester 2-0
Hartlepools Utd v Norwich C 1-1, 1-5
Newport Co v Gateshead 1-1, 2-1
Northampton T v Torquay Utd 4-2
Nottingham F v Stockport Co 0-2
Nuneaton Bor v Mossley 0-0, 3-0
Port Vale v Tranmere R 1-0
Rochdale v Notts Co 1-2
Southport v Bradford C 2-1
Watford v Netherfield 6-0
Weymouth v Hereford Utd 2-1
Wrexham v Southend Utd 2-2, 0-2
Yeovil T v Gillingham 3-1

Third Round

ARSENAL v Sheffield Wed 1-0
Swansea T v Birmingham C 3-0
Notts Co v Burnley 1-4
Newport Co v Port Vale 1-2
Carlisle Utd v Leeds Utd 2-5
Coventry C v Bolton W 1-2
Cardiff C v West Bromwich A 2-2, 1-0
Charlton Ath v Fulham 2-2, 2-1
Brentford v Chelsea 0-1
Oldham Ath v Newcastle Utd 2-7
Chesterfield v Yeovil T 3-1
Aston Villa v Middlesbrough 2-2, 0-0, 0-3
Manchester Utd v Weymouth 4-0
Watford v Preston NE 2-2, 1-0
Portsmouth v Norwich C 1-1, 2-0
Luton T v Grimsby T 3-4
Blackburn R v LIVERPOOL 0-0, 1-2
Exeter C v Nuneaton Bor 3-0
Stockport Co v Barnsley 4-2
Southport v Hull C 0-0, 0-5
Blackpool v Southend Utd 4-0
Reading v Doncaster R 2-3
Plymouth Arg v Wolves 1-1, 0-3
Sheffield Utd v Leicester C 3-1
Queen's Park R v Everton 0-2
West Ham Utd v Ipswich T 5-1
Stoke C v Tottenham H 0-1
Sunderland v Huddersfield T 6-0
Manchester C v Derby Co 3-5
Bury v Rotherham Utd 5-4
Northampton T v Southampton 1-1, 3-2
Bradford v Bournemouth & Bos Ath 0-1

Fourth Round

ARSENAL v Swansea T 2-1
Burnley v Port Vale 2-1
Leeds Utd v Bolton W 1-1, 3-2
Charlton Ath v Cardiff C 1-1, 0-2
Chelsea v Newcastle Utd 3-0
Chesterfield v Middlesbrough 3-2
Watford v Manchester Utd 0-1
Portsmouth v Grimsby T 5-0
LIVERPOOL v Exeter C 3-1
Stockport Co v Hull C 0-0, 2-0
Blackpool v Doncaster R 2-1
Wolves v Sheffield Utd 0-0, 4-3
West Ham Utd v Everton 1-2
Tottenham H v Sunderland 5-1
Bury v Derby Co 2-2, 2-5
Bournemouth & Bos Ath v Northampton T 1-1, 1-2

Fifth Round

ARSENAL v Burnley 2-0
Leeds Utd v Cardiff C 3-1
Chesterfield v Chelsea 1-1, 0-3
Manchester Utd v Portsmouth 3-3, 3-1
Stockport Co v LIVERPOOL 1-2
Wolves v Blackpool 0-0, 0-1
Everton v Tottenham H 1-0
Derby Co v Northampton T 4-2

Sixth Round

ARSENAL v Leeds Utd 1-0
Chelsea v Manchester Utd 2-0
LIVERPOOL v Blackpool 2-1
Derby Co v Everton 1-2

Semi-final

ARSENAL v Chelsea 2-2, 1-0
LIVERPOOL v Everton 2-0

FINAL (Wembley Stadium)
ARSENAL 2
LIVERPOOL 0
Arsenal: Swindin; Scott, Barnes, Forbes, L.Compton, Mercer, Cox, Logie, Goring, Lewis, D.Compton.
Goalscorer: Lewis 2
Liverpool: Sidlow; Lambert, Spicer, Taylor, Hughes, Jones, Payne, Barron, Stubbins, Fagan, Liddell.
Referee: H.Pearce (Luton) *Attendance: 100,000*

Veteran Joe Mercer and his Arsenal men after the Gunners' 1950 win over Liverpool.

1950-51

First Round

Aldershot v Bromley 2-2, 1-0
Bishop Auckland v York C 2-2, 1-2
Bournemouth & Bos Ath v Colchester Utd 1-0
Bradford C v Oldham Ath 2-2, 1-2
Bristol C v Gloucester C 4-0
Bristol R v Llanelly 1-1, 1-1, 3-1
Bromsgrove R v Hereford Utd 1-3
Carlisle Utd v Barrow 2-1
Chelmsford C v Tonbridge 2-2, 1-0
Chester v Bradford 1-2
Cleator Moor Celtic v Tranmere R 0-5
Crewe Alex v North Shields 4-0
Crystal Palace v Millwall 1-4
Darlington v Rotherham Utd 2-7
Gainsboro' Trin v Plymouth Arg 0-3
Glastonbury v Exeter C 1-2
Guildford C v Dartford 1-5
Halifax T v Ashington 2-3
Leyton Orient v Ipswich T 1-2
Linby Coll v Gillingham 1-4
Lincoln C v Southport 1-1, 2-3
Mansfield T v Walthamstow Ave 1-0
Newport Co v Walsall 4-2
Norwich C v Watford 2-0
Nottingham F v Torquay Utd 6-1
Port Vale v New Brighton 3-2
Reading v Cheltenham T 3-1
Rochdale v Willington 3-1
Scarborough v Rhyl 1-2
Tooting & Mitcham v Brighton & HA 2-3
Witton Albion v Nelson 1-2
Southend Utd v Swindon T 0-3
Worcester C v Hartlepools Utd 1-4
Wrexham v Accrington S 1-0

Second Round

Aldershot v Bournemouth & Bos Ath 3-0
Ashington v Rochdale 1-2
Brighton & HA v Ipswich T 2-0
Bristol C v Wrexham 2-1
Bristol R v Gillingham 2-2, 1-1, 2-1
Chelmsford C v Mansfield T 1-4
Crewe Alex v Plymouth Arg 2-2, 0-3
Exeter C v Swindon T 3-0
Hartlepools Utd v Oldham Ath 1-2
Hereford Utd v Newport Co 0-3
Millwall v Bradford 1-1, 1-0
Port Vale v Nelson 3-2
Reading v Dartford 4-0
Rhyl v Norwich C 0-1
Rotherham Utd v Nottingham F 3-1
Southport v Carlisle Utd 1-3
York C v Tranmere R 2-1

Third Round

NEWCASTLE UTD v Bury 4-1
Bolton W v York C 2-0
Stoke C v Port Vale 2-2, 1-0
West Ham Utd v Cardiff C 2-1
Luton T v Portsmouth 2-0
Bristol R v Aldershot 5-1
Hull C v Everton 2-0
Rotherham Utd v Doncaster R 2-1
Plymouth Arg v Wolves 1-2
Aston Villa v Burnley 2-0
Leicester C v Preston NE 0-3
Huddersfield T v Tottenham H 2-0
Sunderland v Coventry C 2-0
Notts Co v Southampton 3-4
Newport Co v Reading 3-2

Norwich C v Liverpool 3-1
Charlton Ath v BLACKPOOL 2-2, 0-3
Stockport Co v Brentford 2-1
Mansfield T v Swansea T 2-0
Sheffield Utd v Gateshead 1-0
Grimsby T v Exeter C 3-3, 2-4
Rochdale v Chelsea 2-3
Queen's Park R v Millwall 3-4
Fulham v Sheffield Wed 1-0
Derby Co v West Bromwich A 2-2, 1-0
Birmingham C v Manchester C 2-0
Bristol C v Blackburn R 2-1
Brighton & HA v Chesterfield 2-1
Manchester Utd v Oldham Ath 4-1
Leeds Utd v Middlesbrough 1-0
Arsenal v Carlisle Utd 0-0, 4-1
Northampton T v Barnsley 3-1

Fourth Round
NEWCASTLE UTD v Bolton W 3-2
Stoke C v West Ham Utd 1-0
Luton T v Bristol R 1-2
Hull C v Rotherham Utd 2-0
Wolves v Aston Villa 3-1
Preston NE v Huddersfield T 0-2
Sunderland v Southampton 2-0
Newport Co v Norwich C 0-2
BLACKPOOL v Stockport Co 2-1
Sheffield Utd v Mansfield T 0-0, 1-2
Exeter C v Chelsea 1-1, 0-2
Millwall v Fulham 0-1
Derby Co v Birmingham C 1-3
Bristol C v Brighton & HA 1-0
Manchester Utd v Leeds Utd 4-0
Arsenal v Northampton T 3-2

Fifth Round
Stoke C v NEWCASTLE UTD 2-4
Bristol R v Hull C 3-0
Wolves v Huddersfield T 2-0
Sunderland v Norwich C 3-1
BLACKPOOL v Mansfield T 2-0
Chelsea v Fulham 1-1, 0-3
Birmingham C v Bristol C 2-0
Manchester Utd v Arsenal 1-0

Sixth Round
NEWCASTLE UTD v Bristol R 0-0, 3-1
Sunderland v Wolves 1-1, 1-3
BLACKPOOL v Fulham 1-0
Birmingham C v Manchester Utd 1-0

Semi-final
NEWCASTLE UTD v Wolves 0-0, 2-1
BLACKPOOL v Birmingham C 0-0, 2-1

FINAL (Wembley Stadium)
NEWCASTLE UNITED 2
BLACKPOOL 0
Newcastle United: Fairbrother; Cowell, Corbett, Harvey, Brennan, Crowe, Walker, Taylor, Milburn, G.Robledo, Mitchell.
Goalscorer: Milburn 2
Blackpool: Farm; Shimwell, Garrett, Johnston, Hayward, Kelly, Matthews, Mudie, Mortensen, Slater, Perry.
Referee: W.Ling (Cambridge)
Attendance: 100,000

1951-52

First Round
Accrington S v Chester 1-2
Aylesbury Utd v Watford 0-5
Bangor C v Southport 2-2, 0-3
Barnstaple T v Folkestone T 2-2, 2-5
Barrow v Chesterfield 0-2
Blackhall Coll Welfare v Workington 2-5
Blyth Spartans v Bishop Auckland 2-1
Bradford C v Carlisle Utd 6-1
Brighton & HA v Bristol C 1-2
Bristol R v Kettering T 3-0
Brush Sports v Weymouth 2-3
Colchester Utd v Port Vale 3-1
Crewe Alex v Lincoln C 2-4
Crystal Palace v Gillingham 0-1
Grimsby T v Darlington 4-0
Guildford C v Hereford Utd 4-1
Hartlepools Utd v Rhyl 2-0
Ilkeston T v Rochdale 0-2
King's Lynn v Exeter C 1-3
Leyton v Chippenham T 3-0
Leyton Orient v Gorleston T 2-2, 0-0, 5-4
Leytonstone v Shrewsbury T 2-0
Merthyr Tydfil v Ipswich T 2-2, 0-1
Millwall v Plymouth Arg 1-0
Nelson v Oldham Ath 0-4
Newport Co v Barry T 4-0
Norwich C v Northampton T 3-2
Rawmarsh Welfare v Buxton T 1-4
Reading v Walsall 1-0
Scunthorpe Utd v Billingham Synthonia Rec 5-0
Southend Utd v Bournemouth & Bos Ath 6-1
Stockport Co v Gateshead 2-2, 1-1, 1-2
Stockton v Mansfield T 1-1, 2-0
Swindon T v Bedford T 2-0
Tonbridge v Aldershot 0-0, 2-3
Torquay Utd v Bromley 3-2
Tranmere R v Goole T 4-2
Witton Albion v Gainsboro' Trin 2-1
Wrexham v Halifax T 3-0
York C v Bradford 1-1, 1-1, 0-4

Second Round
Bradford v Bradford C 3-2
Bristol R v Weymouth 2-0
Buxton T v Aldershot 4-3
Chester v Leyton 5-2
Colchester Utd v Bristol C 2-1
Gateshead v Guildford C 2-0
Gillingham v Rochdale 0-3
Ipswich T v Exeter C 4-0
Leytonstone v Newport Co 2-2, 0-3
Lincoln C v Grimsby T 3-1
Millwall v Scunthorpe Utd 0-0, 0-3
Norwich C v Chesterfield 3-1
Reading v Southport 1-1, 1-1, 2-0
Southend Utd v Oldham Ath 5-0
Stockton v Folkestone T 2-1
Swindon T v Torquay Utd 3-3, 1-1, 3-1
Tranmere R v Blyth Spartans 1-1, 1-1, 2-2, 5-1
Watford v Hartlepools Utd 1-2
Witton Albion v Workington 3-3, 0-1
Wrexham v Leyton Orient 1-1, 2-3

Third Round
NEWCASTLE UTD v Aston Villa 4-2
Scunthorpe Utd v Tottenham H 0-3
Reading v Swansea T 0-3
Rotherham Utd v Bury 2-1
Portsmouth v Lincoln C 4-0
Notts Co v Stockton 4-0
Doncaster R v Buxton T 2-0
Middlesbrough v Derby Co 2-2, 2-0
Nottingham F v Blackburn R 2-2, 0-2
Manchester Utd v Hull C 0-2
West Bromwich A v Bolton W 4-0
Ipswich T v Gateshead 2-2, 3-3, 1-2
Burnley v Hartlepools Utd 1-0
Leicester C v Coventry C 1-1, 1-4
Liverpool v Workington 1-0
Manchester C v Wolves 2-2, 1-4
Norwich C v ARSENAL 0-5
Barnsley v Colchester Utd 3-0
Leyton Orient v Everton 0-0, 3-1
Fulham v Birmingham C 0-1
Luton T v Charlton Ath 1-0
Brentford v Queen's Park R 3-1
Cardiff C v Swindon T 1-1, 0-1
Sunderland v Stoke C 0-0, 1-3
Chelsea v Chester 2-2, 3-2
Huddersfield T v Tranmere R 1-2
Rochdale v Leeds Utd 0-2

Bradford v Sheffield Wed 2-1
Sheffield Utd v Newport Co 2-0
West Ham Utd v Blackpool 2-1
Southend Utd v Southampton 3-0
Bristol R v Preston NE 2-0

Fourth Round
Tottenham H v NEWCASTLE UTD 0-3
Swansea T v Rotherham Utd 3-0
Notts Co v Portsmouth 1-3
Middlesbrough v Doncaster R 1-4
Blackburn R v Hull C 2-0
Gateshead v West Bromwich A 0-2
Burnley v Coventry C 2-0
Liverpool v Wolves 2-1
ARSENAL v Barnsley 4-0
Birmingham C v Leyton Orient 0-1
Luton T v Brentford 2-2, 0-0, 3-2
Swindon T v Stoke C 1-1, 1-0
Chelsea v Tranmere R 4-0
Leeds Utd v Bradford 2-0
West Ham Utd v Sheffield Utd 0-0, 2-4
Southend Utd v Bristol R 2-1

Fifth Round
Swansea T v NEWCASTLE UTD 0-1
Portsmouth v Doncaster R 4-0
Blackburn R v West Bromwich A 1-0
Burnley v Liverpool 2-0
Leyton Orient v ARSENAL 0-3
Luton T v Swindon T 3-1
Leeds Utd v Chelsea 1-1, 1-1, 1-5
Southend Utd v Sheffield Utd 1-2

Sixth Round
Portsmouth v NEWCASTLE UTD 2-4
Blackburn R v Burnley 3-1
Luton T v ARSENAL 2-3
Sheffield Utd v Chelsea 0-1

Semi-final
NEWCASTLE UTD v Blackburn 0-0, 2-1
ARSENAL v Chelsea 1-1, 3-0

FINAL (Wembley Stadium)
NEWCASTLE UNITED 1
ARSENAL 0
Newcastle United: Simpson; Cowell, McMichael, Harvey, Brennan, E.Robledo, Walker, Foulkes, Milburn, G.Robledo, Mitchell.
Goalscorer: G.Robledo
Arsenal: Swindin; Barnes, L.Smith, Forbes, Daniel, Mercer, Cox, Logie, Holton, Lishman, Roper.
Referee: A.E.Ellis (Halifax) *Attendance: 100,000*

1952-53

First Round
Aldershot v Millwall 0-0, 1-7
Bath C v Southend Utd 3-1
Beighton Miners' Welfare v Wrexham 0-3
Boston Utd v Oldham Ath 1-2
Bradford v Rochdale 2-1
Bradford C v Rhyl 4-0

Newcastle United goalkeeper Ronnie Simpson keeps his eye on the ball during the 1952 Final against Arsenal. Newcastle were great Cup fighters in that decade.

Chester v Hartlepools Utd 0-1
Chesterfield v Workington 1-0
Coventry C v Bristol C 2-0
Crystal Palace v Reading 1-1, 3-1
Darlington v Grimsby T 2-3
Gainsboro' Trin v Netherfield 1-1, 3-0
Gateshead v Crewe Alex 2-0
Grays' Ath v Llanelly 0-5
Guildford C v Great Yarmouth 2-2, 0-1
Halifax T v Ashton Utd 1-1, 2-1
Hendon v Northampton T 0-0, 0-2
Horden Coll Welfare v Accrington S 1-2
Ipswich T v Bournemouth & Bos Ath 2-2, 2-2, 3-2
Kidderminster H v Finchley 0-1
Leyton v Hereford Utd 0-0, 2-3
Leyton Orient v Bristol R 1-1, 0-1
Leytonstone v Watford 0-2
Newport Co v Walsall 2-1
North Shields v Stockport Co 3-6
Peterborough Utd v Torquay Utd 2-1
Port Vale v Exeter C 2-1
Queen's Park R v Shrewsbury T 2-2, 2-2, 1-4
Scarborough v Mansfield T 0-8
Scunthorpe Utd v Carlisle Utd 1-0
Selby T v Bishop Auckland 1-5
Southport v Bangor C 3-1
Swindon T v Newport (IoW) 5-0
Tonbridge v Norwich C 2-2, 0-1
Tranmere R v Ashington 8-1
Walthamstow Ave v Wimbledon 2-2, 3-0
Wellington v Gillingham 1-1, 0-3
Weymouth v Colchester Utd 1-1, 0-4
Yeovil T v Brighton & HA 1-4
York C v Barrow 1-2

Second Round
Accrington S v Mansfield T 0-2
Barrow v Millwall 2-2, 1-4
Bishop Auckland v Coventry C 1-4
Bradford v Gateshead 1-2
Bradford C v Ipswich T 1-1, 1-5
Brighton & HA v Norwich C 2-0
Colchester Utd v Llanelly 3-2
Finchley v Crystal Palace 3-1
Great Yarmouth v Wrexham 1-2
Grimsby T v Bath C 1-0
Halifax T v Southport 4-2
Hereford Utd v Scunthorpe Utd 0-0, 1-2
Newport Co v Gainsboro' Trin 2-1
Peterborough Utd v Bristol R 0-1
Port Vale v Oldham Ath 0-3
Shrewsbury T v Chesterfield 0-0, 4-2
Stockport Co v Gillingham 3-1
Swindon T v Northampton T 2-0
Tranmere R v Hartlepools Utd 2-1
Walthamstow Ave v Watford 1-1, 2-1

Third Round
Sheffield Wed v BLACKPOOL 1-2
Huddersfield T v Bristol R 2-0
Lincoln C v Southampton 1-1, 1-2
Shrewsbury T v Finchley 2-0
Arsenal v Doncaster R 4-0
Grimsby T v Bury 1-3
Portsmouth v Burnley 1-1, 1-3
Sunderland v Scunthorpe Utd 1-1, 2-1
Tranmere R v Tottenham H 1-1, 1-9
Preston NE v Wolves 5-2
Halifax T v Cardiff C 3-1
Stoke C v Wrexham 2-1
Oldham Ath v Birmingham C 1-3
Newport Co v Sheffield Utd 1-4
Derby Co v Chelsea 4-4, 0-1
West Ham Utd v West Bromwich A 1-4
BOLTON W v Fulham 3-1
Leicester C v Notts Co 2-4
Luton T v Blackburn R 6-1
Manchester C v Swindon T 7-0
Gateshead v Liverpool 1-0
Hull C v Charlton Ath 3-1
Plymouth Arg v Coventry C 4-1
Barnsley v Brighton & HA 4-3
Everton v Ipswich T 3-2
Mansfield T v Nottingham F 0-1
Millwall v Manchester Utd 0-1
Walthamstow Ave v Stockport Co 2-1
Aston Villa v Middlesbrough 3-1
Brentford v Leeds Utd 2-1
Rotherham Utd v Colchester Utd 2-2, 2-0
Newcastle Utd v Swansea T 3-0

Fourth Round
BLACKPOOL v Huddersfield T 1-0
Shrewsbury T v Southampton 1-4
Arsenal v Bury 6-2
Burnley v Sunderland 2-0
Preston NE v Tottenham H 2-2, 0-1
Halifax T v Stoke C 1-0
Sheffield Utd v Birmingham C 1-1, 1-3
Chelsea v West Bromwich A 1-1, 0-0, 1-1, 4-0
BOLTON W v Notts Co 1-1, 2-2, 1-0
Manchester C v Luton T 1-1, 1-5
Hull C v Gateshead 1-2
Plymouth Arg v Barnsley 1-0
Everton v Nottingham F 4-1
Manchester Utd v Walthamstow Ave 1-1, 5-2
Aston Villa v Brentford 0-0, 2-1
Newcastle Utd v Rotherham Utd 1-3

Fifth Round
BLACKPOOL v Southampton 1-1, 2-1
Burnley v Arsenal 0-2
Halifax T v Tottenham H 0-3
Chelsea v Birmingham C 0-4
Luton T v BOLTON W 0-1
Plymouth Arg v Gateshead 0-1
Everton v Manchester Utd 2-1
Rotherham Utd v Aston Villa 1-3

Sixth Round
Arsenal v BLACKPOOL 1-2
Birmingham C v Tottenham H 1-1, 2-2, 0-1
Gateshead v BOLTON W 0-1
Aston Villa v Everton 0-1

Semi-final
BLACKPOOL v Tottenham H 2-1
BOLTON W v Everton 4-3

FINAL (Wembley Stadium)
BLACKPOOL 4
BOLTON WANDERERS 3
Blackpool: Farm; Shimwell, Garrett, Fenton, Johnston, Robinson, Matthews, Taylor, Mortensen, Mudie, Perry.
Goalscorers: Mortensen 3, Perry
Bolton Wanderers: Hanson; Ball, R.Banks, Wheeler, Barrass, Bell, Holden, Moir, Lofthouse, Hassall, Langton.
Goalscorers: Lofthouse, Moir, Bell
Referee: B.M.Griffiths (Newport) *Attendance: 100,000*

Harry Johnstone and Stanley Matthews after the historic 'Matthews Final' of 1953 when the Seasiders came from 3-1 down to beat Bolton Wanderers.

1953-54

First Round
Aldershot v Wellington T 5-3
Barnsley v York C 5-2
Bath C v Walsall 0-3
Blyth Spartans v Accrington S 0-1
Brighton & HA v Coventry C 5-1
Cambridge Utd v Newport Co 2-2, 2-1
Colchester Utd v Millwall 1-1, 0-4
Crewe Alex v Bradford C 0-0, 1-0
Darlington v Port Vale 1-3
Exeter C v Hereford Utd 1-1, 0-2
Finchley v Southend Utd 1-3
Gainsboro' Trin v Chesterfield 1-4
Gateshead v Tranmere R 1-2
Great Yarmouth v Crystal Palace 1-0
Grimsby T v Rochdale 2-0
Halifax T v Rhyl 0-0, 3-4
Hartlepools Utd v Mansfield T 1-1, 3-0
Harwich & Parkeston v Headington Utd 2-3
Hastings Utd v Guildford C 1-0
Hitchin T v Peterborough Utd 1-3
Horden Coll Welfare v Wrexham 0-1
Ipswich T v Reading 4-1
Leyton Orient v Kettering T 3-0
Northampton T v Llanelly 3-0
Nuneaton Bor v Watford 3-0
Queen's Park R v Shrewsbury T 2-0
Scunthorpe Utd v Boston Utd 9-0
Selby T v Bradford 0-2
Southampton v Bournemouth & Bos Ath 1-1, 1-3
Southport v Carlisle Utd 1-0
Spennymoor Utd v Barrow 0-3
Stockport Co v Chester 4-2
Swindon T v Newport (IoW) 2-1
Torquay Utd v Bristol C 1-3
Walthamstow Ave v Gillingham 1-0
Weymouth v Bedford T 2-0
Wigan Ath v Scarborough 4-0
Witton Alb v Nelson 4-1
Workington v Ferryhill Ath 3-0
Yeovil T v Norwich C 0-2

Second Round
Accrington S v Tranmere R 2-2, 1-5
Barrow v Great Yarmouth 5-2
Cambridge Utd v Bradford 1-2
Hastings Utd v Swindon T 4-1
Ipswich T v Walthamstow Ave 2-2, 1-0
Leyton Orient v Weymouth 4-0
Millwall v Headington Utd 3-3, 0-1
Northampton T v Hartlepools Utd 1-1, 0-1
Norwich C v Barnsley 2-1
Peterborough Utd v Aldershot 2-1
Queen's Park R v Nuneaton Bor 1-1, 2-1
Rhyl v Bristol C 0-3
Scunthorpe Utd v Bournemouth & Bos Ath 1-0
Southend Utd v Chesterfield 1-2
Southport v Port Vale 1-1, 0-2
Stockport Co v Workington 2-1
Walsall v Crewe Alex 3-0
Wigan Ath v Hereford Utd 4-1
Witton Alb v Grimsby T 1-1, 1-6
Wrexham v Brighton & HA 1-1, 1-1, 3-1

Third Round
WEST BROMWICH A v Chelsea 1-0
Bristol C v Rotherham Utd 1-3
Newcastle Utd v Wigan Ath 2-2, 3-2
Burnley v Manchester Utd 5-3
Leeds Utd v Tottenham H 3-3, 0-1
Bradford v Manchester C 2-5
Brentford v Hull C 0-0, 2-2, 2-5
Bristol R v Blackburn R 0-1
Queen's Park R v Port Vale 0-1
Cardiff C v Peterborough Utd 3-1
Blackpool v Luton T 1-1, 0-0, 1-1, 2-0
West Ham Utd v Huddersfield T 4-0
Tranmere R v Leyton Orient 2-2, 1-4
Grimsby T v Fulham 5-5, 1-3
Sunderland v Doncaster R 0-2
Plymouth Arg v Nottingham F 2-0
Derby Co v PRESTON NE 0-2
Lincoln C v Walsall 1-1, 1-1, 2-1
Ipswich T v Oldham Ath 3-3, 1-0
Wolves v Birmingham C 1-2
Middlesbrough v Leicester C 0-0, 2-3
Stoke C v Hartlepools Utd 6-2
Hastings Utd v Norwich C 3-3, 0-3
Arsenal v Aston Villa 5-1
Sheffield Wed v Sheffield Utd 1-1, 3-1
Chesterfield v Bury 2-0
Everton v Notts Co 2-1
Barrow v Swansea T 2-2, 2-4
Bolton W v Liverpool 1-0
Stockport Co v Headington Utd 0-0, 0-1
Portsmouth v Charlton Ath 3-3, 3-2
Wrexham v Scunthorpe Utd 3-3, 1-3

West Brom's Len Millard receives the FA Cup from the Queen Mother in 1954. FA secretary Stanley Rous looks on.

Fourth Round
WEST BROMWICH A v Rotherham Utd 4-0
Burnley v Newcastle Utd 1-1, 0-1
Manchester C v Tottenham H 0-1
Blackburn R v Hull C 2-2, 1-2
Cardiff C v Port Vale 0-2
West Ham Utd v Blackpool 1-1, 1-3
Leyton Orient v Fulham 2-1
Plymouth Arg v Doncaster R 0-2
Lincoln C v PRESTON NE 0-2
Ipswich T v Birmingham C 1-0
Stoke C v Leicester C 0-0, 1-3
Arsenal v Norwich C 1-2
Sheffield Wed v Chesterfield 0-0, 4-2
Everton v Swansea T 3-0
Headington Utd v Bolton W 2-4
Scunthorpe Utd v Portsmouth 1-1, 2-2, 0-4

Fifth Round
WEST BROMWICH A v Newcastle Utd 3-2
Hull C v Tottenham H 1-1, 0-2
Port Vale v Blackpool 2-0
Leyton Orient v Doncaster R 3-1
PRESTON NE v Ipswich T 6-1
Norwich C v Leicester C 1-2
Sheffield Wed v Everton 3-1
Bolton W v Portsmouth 0-0, 2-1

Sixth Round
WEST BROMWICH A v Tottenham H 3-0
Leyton Orient v Port Vale 0-1
Leicester C v PRESTON NE 1-1, 2-2, 1-3
Sheffield Wed v Bolton W 1-1, 2-0

Semi-final
WEST BROMWICH A v Port Vale 2-1
PRESTON NE v Sheffield Wed 2-0

FINAL (Wembley Stadium)
WEST BROMWICH ALBION 3
PRESTON NORTH END 2
West Bromwich Albion: Sanders; Kennedy, Millard, Dudley, Dugdale, Barlow, Griffin, Ryan, Allen, Nicholls, Lee.
Goalscorers: Allen 2 (1 pen), Griffin
Preston North End: Thompson; Cunningham, Walton, Docherty, Marston, Forbes, Finney, Foster, Wayman, Baxter, Morrison.
Goalscorers: Morrison, Wayman
Referee: A.W.Luty (Leeds) *Attendance: 100,000*

1954-55

First Round
Accrington S v Cresswell Coll 7-1
Aldershot v Chelmsford 3-1
Barnet v Southampton 1-4
Barnsley v Wigan Ath 3-2
Barnstaple v Bournemouth & Bos Ath 1-4
Barrow v Darlington 1-1, 1-2
Bishop Auckland v Kettering T 5-1
Boston Utd v Blyth Spartans 1-1, 4-5
Bradford v Southport 2-0
Bradford C v Mansfield T 3-1
Brentford v Nuneaton Bor 2-1
Brighton & HA v Tunbridge Wells 5-0
Bristol C v Southend Utd 1-2
Corby T v Watford 0-2
Crook T v Stanley 5-3
Dorchester v Bedford T 2-0
Frome v Leyton Orient 0-3
Gateshead v Chester 6-0
Gillingham v Newport Co 2-0
Grimsby T v Halifax T 2-1
Hartlepools Utd v Chesterfield 1-0
Hinckley v Newport (IoW) 4-3
Horden Coll Welfare v Scunthorpe Utd 0-1
Hounslow T v Hastings Utd 2-4
Merthyr Tydfil v Wellington 1-1 6-1
Millwall v Exeter C 3-2
Netherfield v Wrexham 3-3, 0-4
Northampton T v Coventry C 0-1
Norwich C v Headington Utd 4-2
Oldham Ath v Crewe Alex 1-0
Queen's Park R v Walthamstow Ave 2-2, 2-2, 0-4
Reading v Colchester Utd 3-3, 2-1
Selby T v Rhyl 2-1
Stockport Co v Carlisle Utd 0-1
Swindon T v Crystal Palace 0-2
Torquay Utd v Cambridge Utd 4-0
Tranmere R v Rochdale 3-3, 0-1
Walsall v Shrewsbury T 5-2
Workington v Hyde 5-1
York C v Scarborough 3-2

Second Round
Blyth Spartans v Torquay Utd 1-3
Bournemouth & Bos Ath v Oldham Ath 1-0
Bradford v Southend Utd 2-3
Bradford C v Merthyr Tydfil 7-1
Brentford v Crook T 4-1
Carlisle Utd v Watford 2-2, 1-4
Coventry C v Scunthorpe Utd 4-0
Crystal Palace v Bishop Auckland 2-4
Dorchester v York C 2-5
Gateshead v Barnsley 3-3, 1-0
Gillingham v Reading 1-1, 3-5
Grimsby T v Southampton 4-1
Hartlepools Utd v Aldershot 4-0
Leyton Orient v Workington 0-1
Millwall v Accrington S 3-2
Norwich C v Brighton & HA 0-0, 1-5
Rochdale v Hinckley 2-1
Selby T v Hastings Utd 0-2
Walthamstow Ave v Darlington 0-3
Wrexham v Walsall 1-2

Third Round
Plymouth Arg v NEWCASTLE UTD 0-1
Brentford v Bradford C 1-1, 2-2, 1-0
Sheffield Utd v Nottingham F 1-3
Hartlepools Utd v Darlington 1-1, 2-2, 2-0
Huddersfield T v Coventry C 3-3, 2-1
Leeds Utd v Torquay Utd 2-2, 0-4
Lincoln C v Liverpool 1-1, 0-1
Everton v Southend Utd 3-1
Blackpool v York C 0-2
Ipswich T v Bishop Auckland 2-2, 0-3
Gateshead v Tottenham H 0-2
West Ham Utd v Port Vale 2-2, 1-3
Middlesbrough v Notts Co 1-4
Sheffield Wed v Hastings Utd 2-1
Chelsea v Walsall 2-0
Bristol R v Portsmouth 2-1
Derby Co v MANCHESTER C 1-3
Reading v Manchester Utd 1-1, 1-4
Luton T v Workington 5-0
Rotherham Utd v Leicester C 1-0
Hull C v Birmingham C 0-2
Bolton W v Millwall 3-1
Watford v Doncaster R 1-2
Brighton & HA v Aston Villa 2-2, 2-4
Sunderland v Burnley 1-0
Fulham v Preston NE 2-3
Blackburn R v Swansea T 0-2
Bury v Stoke C 1-1, 3-3, 2-2, 2-3
Grimsby T v Wolves 2-5
Arsenal v Cardiff C 1-0
Rochdale v Charlton Ath 1-3
Bournemouth & Bos Ath v West Bromwich A 0-1

Fourth Round
NEWCASTLE UTD v Brentford 3-2
Hartlepools Utd v Nottingham F 1-1, 1-2
Torquay Utd v Huddersfield T 0-1
Everton v Liverpool 0-4
Bishop Auckland v York C 1-3
Tottenham H v Port Vale 4-2
Sheffield Wed v Notts Co 1-1, 0-1
Bristol R v Chelsea 1-3
MANCHESTER C v Manchester Utd 2-0
Rotherham Utd v Luton T 1-5
Birmingham C v Bolton W 2-1
Doncaster R v Aston Villa 0-0, 2-2, 1-1, 0-0, 3-1
Preston NE v Sunderland 3-3, 0-2
Swansea T v Stoke C 3-1
Wolves v Arsenal 1-0
West Bromwich A v Charlton Ath 2-4

Fifth Round
Nottingham F v NEWCASTLE UTD 1-1, 2-2, 1-2
Liverpool v Huddersfield T 0-2
York C v Tottenham H 3-1
Notts Co v Chelsea 1-0
Luton T v MANCHESTER C 0-2
Birmingham C v Doncaster R 2-1
Swansea T v Sunderland 2-2, 0-1
Wolves v Charlton Ath 4-1

Sixth Round
Huddersfield v NEWCASTLE UTD 1-1, 0-2
Notts Co v York C 0-1
Birmingham C v MANCHESTER C 0-1
Sunderland v Wolves 2-0

Semi-final
NEWCASTLE UTD v York C 1-1, 2-0
MANCHESTER C v Sunderland 1-0

Newcastle trio Bobby Mitchell, George Hannah and Jackie Milburn after the Magpies' 1955 win over Manchester City.

FINAL (Wembley Stadium)
NEWCASTLE UNITED 3
MANCESTER CITY 1
Newcastle United: Simpson; Cowell, Batty, Scoular, Stokoe, Casey, White, Milburn, Keeble, Hannah, Mitchell.
Goalscorers: Milburn, Mitchell, Hannah
Manchester City: Trautmann; Meadows, Little, Barnes, Ewing, Paul, Spurdle, Hayes, Revie, Johnstone, Fagan.
Goalscorer: Johnstone
Referee: R.J.Leafe (Nottingham) *Attendance: 100,000*

1955-56

First Round
Accrington S v Wrexham 3-1
Barrow v Crewe Alex 0-0, 3-2
Bedford T v Leyton 3-0
Bishop Auckland v Durham C 3-1
Boston Utd v Northwich Vic 3-2
Bradford C v Oldham Ath 3-1
Brentford v March T Utd 4-0
Brighton & HA v Newport Co 8-1
Chesterfield v Chester 1-0
Coventry C v Exeter C 0-1
Crook T v Derby Co 2-2, 1-5
Crystal Palace v Southampton 0-0, 0-2
Darlington v Carlisle Utd 0-0, 0-0, 3-1
Easington Coll Welfare v Tranmere R 0-2
Gillingham v Shrewsbury T 1-1, 1-4
Goole T v Halifax T 1-2
Halesowen v Hendon 2-4
Hartlepools Utd v Gateshead 3-0
Hastings Utd v Southall 6-1
Leyton Orient v Lovell's Ath 7-1
Mansfield T v Stockport Co 2-0
Margate v Walsall 2-2, 1-6
Netherfield v Grimsby T 1-5
Northampton T v Millwall 4-1
Norwich C v Dorchester T 4-0
Peterborough Utd v Ipswich T 3-1
Reading v Bournemouth & Bos Ath 1-0
Rhyl v Bradford 0-3
Rochdale v York C 0-1
Scunthorpe Utd v Shildon 3-0
Skegness T v Worksop T 0-4
Southend Utd v Queen's Park R 2-0
Southport v Ashton Utd 6-1
Swindon T v Hereford Utd 4-0
Torquay Utd v Colchester Utd 2-0
Watford v Ramsgate Ath 5-3
Weymouth v Salisbury 3-2
Workington v Scarborough 4-2
Wycombe W v Burton Alb 1-3
Yeovil T v Aldershot 1-1, 1-1, 0-3

Second Round
Bedford T v Watford 3-2
Bishop Auckland v Scunthorpe Utd 0-0, 0-2
Bradford v Workington 4-3
Bradford C v Worksop T 2-2, 0-1
Brighton & HA v Norwich C 1-2
Chesterfield v Hartlepools Utd 1-2
Darlington v Accrington S 0-1
Derby Co v Boston Utd 1-6
Exeter C v Hendon 6-2
Halifax T v Burton Alb 0-0, 0-1
Leyton Orient v Brentford 4-1
Northampton T v Hastings Utd 4-1
Reading v Aldershot 2-2, 0-3
Shrewsbury T v Torquay Utd 0-0, 1-5
Southport v Grimsby T 0-0, 2-3
Swindon T v Peterborough Utd 1-1, 2-1
Tranmere R v Barrow 0-3
Walsall v Southampton 2-1
Weymouth v Southend Utd 0-1
York C v Mansfield T 2-1

Third Round
Torquay Utd v BIRMINGHAM C 1-7
Leyton Orient v Plymouth Arg 1-0
Wolves v West Bromwich A 1-2
Portsmouth v Grimsby T 3-1
Arsenal v Bedford T 2-2, 2-1
Aston Villa v Hull C 1-1, 2-1
Charlton Ath v Burton Alb 7-0
Swindon T v Worksop T 1-0
Sunderland v Norwich C 4-2
Swansea T v York C 1-2
Sheffield Utd v Barrow 5-0
Bolton W v Huddersfield T 3-0
Sheffield Wed v Newcastle Utd 1-3
Notts Co v Fulham 0-1
Exeter C v Stoke C 0-0, 0-3
Luton T v Leicester C 0-4
MANCHESTER C v Blackpool 2-1
Lincoln C v Southend Utd 2-3
Liverpool v Accrington S 2-0
Rotherham Utd v Scunthorpe Utd 1-1, 2-4
Everton v Bristol C 3-1
Walsall v Port Vale 0-1
Hartlepools Utd v Chelsea 0-1
Bury v Burnley 0-1
Tottenham H v Boston Utd 4-0
Bradford v Middlesbrough 0-4
Doncaster R v Nottingham F 3-0
Bristol R v Manchester Utd 4-0
West Ham Utd v Preston NE 5-2
Leeds Utd v Cardiff C 1-2
Northampton T v Blackburn R 1-2
Aldershot v Barnsley 1-2

Fourth Round
Leyton Orient v BIRMINGHAM C 0-4
West Bromwich A v Portsmouth 2-0
Arsenal v Aston Villa 4-1
Charlton Ath v Swindon T 2-1
York C v Sunderland 0-0, 1-2
Bolton W v Sheffield Utd 1-2
Fulham v Newcastle Utd 4-5
Leicester C v Stoke C 3-3, 1-2
Southend Utd v MANCHESTER C 0-1
Liverpool v Scunthorpe Utd 3-3, 2-1
Port Vale v Everton 2-3
Burnley v Chelsea 1-1, 1-1, 2-2, 0-0, 0-2
Tottenham H v Middlesbrough 3-1
Bristol R v Doncaster R 1-1, 0-1
West Ham Utd v Cardiff C 2-1
Barnsley v Blackburn R 0-1

Fifth Round
West Bromwich A v BIRMINGHAM C 0-1
Charlton Ath v Arsenal 0-2
Sheffield Utd v Sunderland 0-0, 0-1
Newcastle Utd v Stoke C 2-1
MANCHESTER C v Liverpool 0-0, 2-1
Everton v Chelsea 1-0
Doncaster R v Tottenham H 0-2
West Ham Utd v Blackburn R 0-0, 3-2

Sixth Round
Arsenal v BIRMINGHAM C 1-3
Newcastle Utd v Sunderland 0-2
MANCHESTER C v Everton 2-1
Tottenham H v West Ham Utd 3-3, 2-1

Semi-final
BIRMINGHAM C v Sunderland 3-0
MANCHESTER C v Tottenham H 1-0

FINAL (Wembley Stadium)
MANCHESTER CITY 3
BIRMINGHAM CITY 1
Manchester City: Trautmann; Leivers, Little, Barnes, Ewing, Paul, Johnstone, Hayes, Revie, Dyson, Clarke.
Goalscorers: Hayes, Dyson, Johnstone
Birmingham City: Merrick; Hall, Green, Newman, Smith, Boyd, Astall, Kinsey, Brown, Murphy, Govan.
Goalscorer: Kinsey
Referee: A.Bond (Fulham) *Attendance: 100,000*

Roy Paul and son after Manchester City went back to Wembley 12 months later to win the Cup against Birmingham City.

1956-57

First Round
Accrington S v Morecambe 4-1
Bishop Auckland v Tranmere R 2-1
Boston Utd v Bradford 0-2
Bournemouth & Bos Ath v Burton Alb 8-0
Brentford v Guildford C 3-0
Brighton & HA v Millwall 1-1, 1-3
Carlisle Utd v Billingham Synthonia Rec 6-1
Cheltenham T v Reading 1-2
Chester v Barrow 0-0, 1-3
Colchester Utd v Southend Utd 1-4
Crewe Alex v Wrexham 2-2, 1-2
Crystal Palace v Walthamstow Ave 2-0
Darlington v Evenwood T 7-2
Derby Co v Bradford C 2-1
Ely C v Torquay U 2-6
Exeter C v Plymouth Arg 0-2
Halifax T v Oldham Ath 2-3
Hartlepools Utd v Selby T 3-1
Hereford Utd v Aldershot 3-2
Hull C v Gateshead 4-0
Ilkeston T v Blyth Spartans 1-5
Ipswich T v Hastings Utd 4-0
Mansfield T v Workington 1-1, 1-2
Margate v Dunstable T 3-1
New Brighton v Stockport Co 3-3, 3-2
Newport (IoW) v Watford 0-6
Norwich C v Bedford T 2-4
Queen's Park R v Dorchester T 4-0
Rhyl v Scarborough 3-2
Scunthorpe Utd v Rochdale 1-0
Southampton v Northampton T 2-0
Southport v York C 0-0, 1-2
South Shields v Chesterfield 2-2, 0-4
Swindon T v Coventry C 2-1
Tooting & Mitcham v Bromsgrove 2-1
Walsall v Newport Co 0-1
Weymouth v Shrewsbury T 1-0
Wigan Ath v Goole T 1-2
Yeovil T v Peterborough Utd 1-3
Yiewsley v Gillingham 2-2, 0-2

Second Round
Accrington S v Oldham Ath 2-1
Blyth Spartans v Hartlepools Utd 0-1
Brentford v Crystal Palace 1-1, 2-3
Carlisle Utd v Darlington 2-1
Chesterfield v Barrow 4-1
Derby Cov New Brighton 1-3
Gillingham v Newport Co 1-2
Goole T v Workington 2-2, 1-0
Hereford Utd v Southend Utd 2-3
Hull C v York C 2-1
Millwall v Margate 4-0
Peterborough Utd v Bradford 3-0
Reading v Bedford T 1-0
Rhyl v Bishop Auckland 3-1
Scunthorpe Utd v Wrexham 0-0, 2-6
Southampton v Weymouth 3-2
Swindon T v Bournemouth & Bos Ath 0-1
Tooting & Mitcham v Queen's Park R 0-2
Torquay Utd v Plymouth Arg 1-0
Watford v Ipswich T 1-3

Third Round
Luton T v ASTON VILLA 2-2, 0-2
Middlesbrough v Charlton Ath 1-1, 3-2
Bristol C v Rotherham Utd 4-1
Notts Co v Rhyl 1-3
Burnley v Chesterfield 7-0
New Brighton v Torquay Utd 2-1
Huddersfield T v Sheffield Utd 0-0, 1-1, 2-1
Peterborough Utd v Lincoln C 2-2, 5-4
Arsenal v Stoke C 4-2
Newport Co v Southampton 3-3, 1-0
Preston NE v Sheffield Wed 0-0, 2-2, 5-1
Hull C v Bristol R 3-4
Bolton W v Blackpool 2-3
Ipswich T v Fulham 2-3
Sunderland v Queen's Park R 4-0
Doncaster R v West Bromwich A 1-1, 0-2
Hartlepools Utd v MANCHESTER UTD 3-4
Wrexham v Reading 1-1, 2-1
Everton v Blackburn R 1-0
West Ham Utd v Grimsby T 5-3
Bournemouth & Bos Ath v Accrington S 2-0
Wolves v Swansea T 5-3
Tottenham H v Leicester C 2-0
Leyton Orient v Chelsea 0-2
Carlisle Utd v Birmingham C 3-3, 0-4
Southend Utd v Liverpool 2-1
Millwall v Crystal Palace 2-0
Newcastle Utd v Manchester C 1-1, 5-4
Barnsley v Port Vale 3-3, 1-0
Leeds Utd v Cardiff C 1-2
Bury v Portsmouth 1-3
Nottingham F v Goole T 6-0

Fourth Round
Middlesbrough v ASTON VILLA 2-3
Bristol C v Rhyl 3-0
Burnley v New Brighton 9-0
Huddersfield T v Peterborough Utd 3-1
Newport Co v Arsenal 0-2
Bristol R v Preston NE 1-4
Blackpool v Fulham 6-2
West Bromwich A v Sunderland 4-2

Wrexham v MANCHESTER UTD 0-5
Everton v West Ham Utd 2-1
Wolves v Bournemouth & Bos Ath 0-1
Tottenham H v Chelsea 4-0
Southend Utd v Birmingham C 1-6
Millwall v Newcastle Utd 2-1
Cardiff C v Barnsley 0-1
Portsmouth v Nottingham F 1-3

Fifth Round
ASTON VILLA v Bristol C 2-1
Huddersfield T v Burnley 1-2
Preston NE v Arsenal 3-3, 1-2
Blackpool v West Bromwich A 0-0, 1-2
MANCHESTER UTD v Everton 1-0
Bournemouth & Bos Ath v Tottenham H 3-1
Millwall v Birmingham C 1-4
Barnsley v Nottingham F 1-2

Sixth Round
Burnley v ASTON VILLA 1-1, 0-2
West Bromwich A v Arsenal 2-2, 2-1
Bournemouth & Bos Ath v MANCHESTER UTD 1-2
Birmingham C v Nottingham F 0-0, 1-0

Semi-final
ASTON VILLA v West Bromwich A 2-2, 1-0
MANCHESTER UTD v Birmingham C 2-0

Aston Villa's victorious skipper Johnny Dixon after Villa's win over Manchester United in 1957. United lost goalkeeper Ray Wood with a fractured cheekbone.

FINAL (Wembley Stadium)
ASTON VILLA 2
MANCHESTER UNITED 1
Aston Villa: Sims; Lynn, Aldis, Crowther, Dugdale, Saward, Smith, Sewell, Myerscough, Dixon, McParland.
Goalscorer: McParland 2
Manchester United: Wood; Foulkes, Byrne, Colman, Blanchflower, Edwards, Berry, Whelan, Taylor, Charlton, Pegg.
Goalscorer: Taylor
Referee: F.Coultas (Hull) *Attendance: 100,000*

1957-58

First Round
Aldershot v Worcester C 0-0, 2-2, 3-2
Bath C v Exeter C 2-1
Bishop Auckland v Bury 0-0, 1-4
Boston Utd v Billingham Synthonia Rec 5-2
Bradford C v Scarborough 6-0
Brighton & HA v Walsall 2-1
Carlisle Utd v Rhyl 5-1
Chester v Gateshead 4-3
Clapton v Queen's Park R 1-1, 1-3
Coventry C v Walthamstow Ave 1-0
Dorchester T v Wycombe W 3-2
Durham C v Spalding Utd 3-1
Gillingham v Gorleston 10-1
Guildford C v Yeovil T 2-2, 0-1
Hartlepools Utd v Prescot Cables 5-0
Hull C v Crewe Alex 2-1
Mansfield T v Halifax T 2-0
Margate v Crystal Palace 2-3
Millwall v Brentford 1-0
Newport (IoW) v Hereford Utd 0-3
Northampton T v Newport Co 3-0
Norwich C v Redhill 6-1
Oldham Ath v Bradford 2-0
Oswestry T v Bournemouth & Bos Ath 1-5
Peterborough Utd v Torquay Utd 3-3, 0-1
Plymouth Arg v Watford 6-2
Port Vale v Shrewsbury T 2-1
Reading v Swindon T 1-0
Rochdale v Darlington 0-2
Scunthorpe Utd v Goole T 2-1
Southport v Wigan Ath 1-2
South Shields v Frickley Coll 3-2
Stockport Co v Barrow 2-1
Tranmere R v Witton Alb 2-1
Trowbridge T v Southend Utd 0-2
Walton & Hersham v Southampton 1-6
Wisbech T v Colchester Utd 1-0
Workington v Crook T 8-1
Wrexham v Accrington S 0-1
York C v Chesterfield 1-0

Second Round
Aldershot v Coventry C 4-1
Carlisle Utd v Accrington S 1-1, 2-3
Chester v Bradford C 3-3, 1-3
Crystal Palace v Southampton 1-0
Darlington v Boston Utd 5-3
Durham C v Tranmere R 0-3
Hereford Utd v Queen's Park R 6-1
Millwall v Gillingham 1-1, 1-6
Northampton T v Bournemouth & Bos Ath 4-1
Norwich C v Brighton & HA 1-1, 2-1
Oldham Ath v Workington 1-5
Plymouth Arg v Dorchester T 5-2
Port Vale v Hull C 2-2, 3-4
Reading v Wisbech T 2-1
Scunthorpe Utd v Bury 2-0
South Shields v York C 1-3
Stockport Co v Hartlepools Utd 2-1
Torquay Utd v Southend Utd 1-1, 1-2
Wigan Ath v Mansfield T 1-1, 1-3
Yeovil T v Bath C 2-0

Third Round
Rotherham Utd v Blackburn R 1-4
Sunderland v Everton 2-2, 1-3
Leyton Orient v Reading 1-0
Leeds Utd v Cardiff C 1-2
Liverpool v Southend Utd 1-1, 3-2
Northampton T v Arsenal 3-1
Plymouth Arg v Newcastle Utd 1-6
Scunthorpe Utd v Bradford C 1-0
Lincoln C v Wolves 0-1
Portsmouth v Aldershot 5-1
Norwich C v Darlington 1-2
Doncaster R v Chelsea 0-2
Stoke C v Aston Villa 1-1, 3-3, 2-0
Middlesbrough v Derby Co 5-0
York C v Birmingham C 3-0
Preston NE v BOLTON W 0-3
Workington v MANCHESTER UTD 1-3
Crystal Palace v Ipswich T 0-1
Hull C v Barnsley 1-1, 2-0
Hereford Utd v Sheffield Wed 0-3
West Bromwich A v Manchester C 5-1
Nottingham F v Gillingham 2-0
Tottenham H v Leicester C 4-0
Sheffield Utd v Grimsby T 5-1
Bristol R v Mansfield T 5-0
Burnley v Swansea T 4-2
Notts Co v Tranmere R 2-0
Accrington S v Bristol C 2-2, 1-3
West Ham Utd v Blackpool 5-1
Stockport Co v Luton T 3-0
Huddersfield T v Charlton Ath 2-2, 0-1
Fulham v Yeovil T 4-0

Fourth Round
Everton v Blackburn R 1-2
Cardiff C v Leyton Orient 4-1
Liverpool v Northampton T 3-1
Newcastle Utd v Scunthorpe Utd 1-3
Wolves v Portsmouth 5-1
Chelsea v Darlington 3-3, 1-4
Stoke C v Middlesbrough 3-1
York C v BOLTON W 0-0, 0-3
MANCHESTER UTD v Ipswich T 2-0
Sheffield Wed v Hull C 4-3
West Bromwich A v Nottingham F 3-3, 5-1
Tottenham H v Sheffield Utd 0-3
Bristol R v Burnley 2-2, 3-2
Notts Co v Bristol C 1-2
West Ham Utd v Stockport Co 3-2
Fulham v Charlton Ath 1-1, 2-0

Fifth Round
Cardiff C v Blackburn R 0-0, 1-2
Scunthorpe Utd v Liverpool 0-1
Wolves v Darlington 6-1
BOLTON W v Stoke C 3-1
MANCHESTER UTD v Sheffield Wed 3-0
Sheffield Utd v West Bromwich A 1-1, 1-4
Bristol C v Bristol R 3-4
West Ham Utd v Fulham 2-3

Sixth Round
Blackburn R v Liverpool 2-1
BOLTON W v Wolves 2-1
West Bromwich A v MANCHESTER UTD 2-2, 0-1
Fulham v Bristol R 3-1

Semi-final
Blackburn R v BOLTON W 1-2
MANCHESTER UTD v Fulham 2-2, 5-3

FINAL (Wembley Stadium)
BOLTON WANDERERS 2
MANCHESTER UNITED 0

Bolton centre-forward Nat Lofthouse and manager Bill Riddings after the Trotters' 1958 win over post-Munich Manchester United. Billy Foulkes of United is in the background.

Bolton Wanderers: Hopkinson; Hartle, Banks, Hennin, Higgins, Edwards, Birch, Stevens, Lofthouse, Parry, Holden.
Goalscorer: Lofthouse 2
Manchester United: Gregg; Foulkes, Greaves, Goodwin, Cope, Crowther, Dawson, Taylor, Charlton, Viollet, Webster.
Referee: J.U.Sherlock (Sheffield) *Attendance: 100,000*

1958-59

First Round
Accrington S v Workington 5-1
Ashford v Crystal Palace 0-1
Brentford v Exeter C 3-2
Bury v York C *0-0, 1-0
Buxton v Crook T 4-1
Chelmsford C v Worcester C 0-0, 1-3
Chester v Boston Utd 3-2
Chesterfield v Rhyl 3-0
Colchester Utd v Bath C 2-0
Crewe Alex v South Shields 2-2, 0-5
Denaby Utd v Oldham Ath 0-2
Doncaster R v Consett 5-0
Gateshead v Bradford 1-4
Guildford C v Hereford Utd 1-2
Hartlepools Utd v Rochdale 1-1, 3-3, 2-1
Headington Utd v Margate 3-2
Heanor T v Carlisle Utd 1-5
Hitchin T v Millwall 1-1, 1-2
Hull C v Stockport Co 0-1
King's Lynn v Merthyr T 2-1
Mansfield T v Bradford C 3-4
Morecambe v Blyth Spartans 1-2
Newport (IoW) v Shrewsbury T 0-0, 0-5
Northampton T v Wycombe W 2-0
Norwich C v Ilford 3-1
Notts Co v Barrow 1-2
Peterborough Utd v Kettering T 2-2, 3-2
Plymouth Arg v Gillingham 2-2, 4-1
Southampton v Woking 4-1
Southend Utd v Yeovil T 0-0, 0-1
Southport v Halifax T 0-2
Swindon T v Aldershot 5-0

Tooting & Mitcham v Bournemouth & Bos Ath 3-1
Torquay Utd v Port Vale 1-0
Tranmere R v Bishop Auckland 8-1
Walsall v Queen's Park R 0-1
Watford v Reading 1-1, 2-0
Weymouth v Coventry C 2-5
Wisbech T v Newport Co 2-2, 1-4
Wrexham v Darlington 1-2

Second Round
Accrington S v Buxton 6-1
Barrow v Hartlepools Utd 2-0
Blyth Spartans v Stockport Co 3-4
Bradford v Bradford C 0-2
Brentford v King's Lynn 3-1
Carlisle Utd v Chesterfield 0-0, 0-1
Chester v Bury 1-1, 1-2
Colchester Utd v Yeovil T 1-1 7-1
Coventry C v Plymouth Arg 1-3
Crystal Palace v Shrewsbury T 2-2, 2-2, 4-1
Halifax T v Darlington 1-1, 0-3
Hereford Utd v Newport Co 0-2
Oldham Ath v South Shields 2-0
Peterborough Utd v Headington Utd 4-2
Queen's Park R v Southampton 0-1
Swindon T v Norwich C 1-1, 0-1
Tooting & Mitcham v Northampton T 2-1
Torquay Utd v Watford 2-0
Tranmere R v Doncaster R 1-2
Worcester C v Millwall 5-2

Third Round
LUTON T v Leeds Utd 5-1
Leicester C v Lincoln C 1-1, 2-0
Stoke C v Oldham Ath 5-1
Ipswich T v Huddersfield T 1-0
Southampton v Blackpool 1-2
Doncaster R v Bristol C 0-2
Sheffield Wed v West Bromwich A 0-2
Brentford v Barnsley 2-0
Colchester Utd v Chesterfield 2-0
Bury v Arsenal 0-1
Worcester C v Liverpool 2-1
Sheffield Utd v Crystal Palace 2-0
Tottenham H v West Ham Utd 2-0
Newport Co v Torquay Utd 0-0, 1-0
Norwich C v Manchester Utd 3-0
Plymouth Arg v Cardiff C 0-3
Bristol R v Charlton Ath 0-4
Everton v Sunderland 4-0
Newcastle Utd v Chelsea 1-4
Aston Villa v Rotherham Utd 2-1
Blackburn R v Leyton Orient 4-2
Stockport Co v Burnley 1-3
Accrington S v Darlington 3-0
Portsmouth v Swansea T 3-1
Barrow v Wolves 2-4
Scunthorpe Utd v Bolton W 0-2
Derby Co v Preston NE 2-2, 2-4
Brighton & HA v Bradford C 0-2
Middlesbrough v Birmingham C 0-1
Fulham v Peterborough Utd 0-0, 1-0
Grimsby T v Manchester C 2-2, 2-1
Tooting & Mitcham v NOTTINGHAM F 2-2, 0-3

Fourth Round
Leicester C v LUTON T 1-1, 1-4
Stoke C v Ipswich T 0-1
Bristol C v Blackpool 1-1, 0-1
West Bromwich A v Brentford 2-0
Colchester Utd v Arsenal 2-2, 0-4
Worcester C v Sheffield Utd 0-2
Tottenham H v Newport Co 4-1
Norwich C v Cardiff C 3-2
Charlton Ath v Everton 2-2, 1-4
Chelsea v Aston Villa 1-2
Blackburn R v Burnley 1-2
Accrington S v Portsmouth 0-0, 1-4
Wolves v Bolton W 1-2
Preston NE v Bradford C 3-2
Birmingham C v Fulham 1-1, 3-2
NOTTINGHAM F v Grimsby T 4-1

Fifth Round
Ipswich T v LUTON T 2-5
Blackpool v West Bromwich A 3-1
Arsenal v Sheffield Utd 2-2, 0-3
Tottenham H v Norwich C 1-1, 0-1
Everton v Aston Villa 1-4
Burnley v Portsmouth 1-0
Bolton W v Preston NE 2-2, 1-1, 1-0
Birmingham C v NOTTINGHAM F 1-1, 1-1, 0-5

Sixth Round
Blackpool v LUTON T 1-1, 0-1
Sheffield Utd v Norwich C 1-1, 2-3
Aston Villa v Burnley 0-0, 2-0
NOTTINGHAM F v Bolton W 2-1

Semi-final
LUTON T v Norwich C 1-1, 1-0
Aston Villa v NOTTINGHAM F 0-1

Jack Burkitt after ten-man Nottingham Forest's 1959 win over Luton Town, when Forest lost Roy Dwight with a broken leg.

FINAL (Wembley Stadium)
NOTTINGHAM FOREST 2
LUTON TOWN 1
Nottingham Forest: Thomson; Whare, McDonald, Whitefoot, McKinlay, Burkitt, Dwight, Quigley, Wilson, Gray, Imlach.
Goalscorers: Dwight, Wilson
Luton Town: Baynham; McNally, Hawkes, Groves, Owen, Pacey, Bingham, Brown, Morton, Cummins, Gregory.
Goalscorer: Pacey
Referee: J.H.Clough (Bolton) *Attendance: 100,000*
*Abandoned

1959-60

First Round
Accrington S v Mansfield T 1-2
Barnsley v Bradford C 3-3, 1-2
Bath C v Millwall 3-1
Bedford T v Gillingham 0-4
Bradford v Scarborough 6-1
Brentford v Ashford 5-0
Burscough R v Crewe Alex 1-3
Bury v Hartlepools Utd 5-0
Cheltenham T v Watford 0-0, 0-3
Colchester Utd v Queen's Park R 2-3
Coventry C v Southampton 1-1, 1-5
Crook T v Matlock T 2-2, 1-0
Crystal Palace v Chelmsford C 5-1
Darlington v Prescot Cables 4-0
Doncaster R v Gainsboro' Trin 3-3, 1-0
Dorchester T v Port Vale 1-2
Enfield T v Headington Utd 4-3
Exeter C v Barnstaple 4-0
Gateshead v Halifax T 3-4
Hastings Utd v Notts Co 1-2
Kettering T v Margate 1-1, 2-3
King's Lynn v Aldershot 3-1
Newport Co v Hereford Utd 4-2
Norwich C v Reading 1-1, 1-2
Peterborough Utd v Shrewsbury T 4-3
Rhyl v Grimsby T 1-2
Rochdale v Carlisle Utd 2-2, 3-1
Salisbury v Barnet 1-0
Shildon v Oldham Ath 1-1, 0-3
Southend Utd v Oswestry 6-0
Southport v Workington 2-2, 0-3
South Shields v Chesterfield 2-1
Swindon T v Walsall 2-3
Torquay Utd v Northampton T 7-1
Tranmere R v Chester 0-1
Walthamstow Ave v Bournemouth & Bos Ath 2-3
West Auckland T v Stockport Co 2-6
Wrexham v Blyth Spartans 2-1
Wycombe W v Wisbech T 4-2
York C v Barrow 3-1

Second Round
Bury v Oldham Ath 2-1
Crook T v York C 0-1
Doncaster R v Darlington 3-2
Enfield T v Bournemouth & Bos Ath 1-5
Exeter C v Brentford 3-1
Gillingham v Torquay Utd 2-2, 2-1
Grimsby T v Wrexham 2-3
Mansfield T v Chester 2-0
Margate v Crystal Palace 0-0, 0-3
Notts Co v Bath C 0-1
Queen's Park R v Port Vale 3-3, 1-2
Reading v King's Lynn 4-2
Rochdale v Bradford C 1-1, 1-2
Salisbury v Newport Co 0-1
Southampton v Southend Utd 3-0
South Shields v Bradford 1-5
Stockport Co v Crewe Alex 0-0, 0-2
Walsall v Peterborough Utd 2-3
Watford v Wycombe W 5-1
Workington v Halifax T 1-0

Third Round
Sunderland v BLACKBURN R 1-1, 1-4
Blackpool v Mansfield T 3-0
Crewe Alex v Workington 2-0
Newport Co v Tottenham H 0-4
Bradford C v Everton 3-0
Bournemouth & Bos Ath v York C 1-0
Gillingham v Swansea T 1-4
Lincoln C v Burnley 1-1, 0-2
Sheffield Utd v Portsmouth 3-0
Nottingham F v Reading 1-0
Manchester C v Southampton 1-5
Watford v Birmingham C 2-1
Liverpool v Leyton Orient 2-1
Derby Co v Manchester Utd 2-4
Sheffield Wed v Middlesbrough 2-1
Ipswich T v Peterborough Utd 2-3
Scunthorpe Utd v Crystal Palace 1-0
Cardiff C v Port Vale 0-2
Chelsea v Bradford 5-1
Aston Villa v Leeds Utd 2-1
Bristol R v Doncaster R 0-0, 2-1
Stoke C v Preston NE 1-1, 1-3
Rotherham Utd v Arsenal 2-2, 1-1, 2-0
Bath C v Brighton & HA 0-1
Wrexham v Leicester C 1-2
Fulham v Hull C 5-0
West Bromwich A v Plymouth Arg 3-2
Bury v Bolton W 1-1, 2-4
Huddersfield T v West Ham Utd 1-1, 5-1
Exeter C v Luton T 1-2
Newcastle Utd v WOLVES 2-2, 2-4
Bristol C v Charlton Ath 2-3

Fourth Round
BLACKBURN R v Blackpool 1-1, 3-0
Crewe Alex v Tottenham H 2-2, 2-13
Bradford C v Bournemouth & Bos Ath 3-1
Swansea T v Burnley 0-0, 1-2
Sheffield Utd v Nottingham F 3-0
Southampton v Watford 2-2, 0-1
Liverpool v Manchester Utd 1-3
Sheffield Wed v Peterborough Utd 2-0
Scunthorpe Utd v Port Vale 0-1
Chelsea v Aston Villa 1-2
Bristol R v Preston NE 3-3, 1-5
Rotherham Utd v Brighton & HA 1-1, 1-1, 0-6
Leicester C v Fulham 2-1
West Bromwich A v Bolton W 2-0
Huddersfield T v Luton T 0-1
WOLVES v Charlton Ath 2-1

Fifth Round
Tottenham H v BLACKBURN R 1-3
Bradford C v Burnley 2-2, 0-5
Sheffield Utd v Watford 3-2
Manchester Utd v Sheffield Wed 0-1
Port Vale v Aston Villa 1-2
Preston NE v Brighton & HA 2-1
Leicester C v West Bromwich A 2-1
Luton T v WOLVES 1-4

Sixth Round
Burnley v BLACKBURN R 3-3, 0-2
Sheffield Utd v Sheffield Wed 0-2
Aston Villa v Preston NE 2-0
Leicester C v WOLVES 1-2

Semi-final
BLACKBURN R v Sheffield Wed 2-1
Aston Villa v WOLVES 0-1

FINAL (Wembley Stadium)
WOLVERHAMPTON WANDERERS 3
BLACKBURN ROVERS 0
Wolverhampton Wanderers: Finlayson; Showell, Harris, Clamp, Slater, Flowers, Deeley, Stobart, Murray, Broadbent, Horne.
Goalscorers: McGrath (og), Deeley 2
Blackburn Rovers: Leyland; Bray, Whelan, Clayton, Woods, McGrath, Bimpson, Dobing, Dougan, Douglas, MacLeod.
Referee: K.Howley (Middlesbrough)
Attendance: 100,000

Wolves skipper Bill Slater holds up the Cup after victory over yet another side to suffer the Wembley 'jinx'. Victim in the 1960 Final was Blackburn's Dave Whelan, who also suffered a broken leg.

1960-61

First Round
Accrington S v Barrow 2-1
Aldershot v Notts Co 2-0
Ashford v Gillingham 1-2
Bangor C v Wrexham 1-0
Bishop Auckland v Bridlington 3-2
Bradford C v Scarborough 0-0, 3-1
Bridgwater T v Hereford Utd 3-0
Bristol C v Chichester 11-0
Chelmsford C v Port Vale 2-3
Chester v Carlisle Utd 0-1
Chesterfield v Doncaster R 3-3, 1-0
Clacton v Southend Utd 1-3
Colchester Utd v Maidenhead Utd 5-0
Crewe Alex v Rochdale 1-1, 2-1
Crystal Palace v Hitchin T 6-2
Darlington v Grimsby T 2-0
Dover v Peterborough Utd 1-4
Exeter C v Bournemouth & Bos Ath 1-1, 1-3
Gateshead v Barnsley 0-0, 0-2
Halifax T v Hartlepools Utd 5-1
Hendon v Oxford Utd 2-2, 2-3
Hull C v Sutton T 3-0
Loughborough v King's Lynn 0-0, 0-3
Mansfield T v Blyth Spartans 3-1
Northampton T v Hastings Utd 2-1
Queen's Park R v Walthamstow Ave 3-2
Reading v Millwall 6-2
Rhyl v Oldham Ath 0-1
Shrewsbury T v Newport Co 4-1
Southport v Macclesfield T 7-2
Stockport Co v Workington 1-0
Swindon T v Bath C 2-2 6-4
Sutton Utd v Romford 2-2, 0-5
Tranmere R v Bury 1-0
Walsall v Yeovil T 0-1
Watford v Brentford 2-2, 2-0
Weymouth v Torquay Utd 1-3
Worcester C v Coventry C 1-4
Wycombe W v Kettering T 1-2
York C v Bradford 0-0, 2-0

Second Round
Accrington S v Mansfield T 3-0
Aldershot v Colchester Utd 3-1
Bangor C v Southport 1-1, 1-3
Bournemouth & Bos Ath v Yeovil T 3-1
Bradford C v Barnsley 1-2
Chesterfield v Oldham Ath 4-4, 3-0
Crystal Palace v Watford 0-0, 0-1
Darlington v Hull C 1-1, 1-1, 1-1, 0-0, 0-3
Gillingham v Southend Utd 3-2
Halifax T v Crewe Alex 2-2, 0-3
King's Lynn v Bristol C 2-2, 0-3
Oxford Utd v Bridgwater T 2-1
Port Vale v Carlisle Utd 2-1
Queen's Park R v Coventry C 1-2
Reading v Kettering T 4-2
Romford v Northampton T 1-5
Stockport Co v Bishop Auckland 2-0
Swindon T v Shrewsbury T 0-1
Torquay Utd v Peterborough Utd 1-3
Tranmere R v York C 1-1, 1-2

Third Round
LEICESTER C v Oxford Utd 3-1
Plymouth Arg v Bristol C 0-1
Nottingham F v Birmingham C 0-2
Rotherham Utd v Watford 1-0
Wolves v Huddersfield T 1-1, 1-2
Reading v Barnsley 1-1, 1-3
Luton T v Northampton T 4-0
Cardiff C v Manchester C 1-1, 0-0, 0-2
Newcastle Utd v Fulham 5-0
Stockport C v Southport 3-1
West Ham Utd v Stoke C 2-2, 0-1
Aldershot v Shrewsbury T 1-1, 2-2, 2-0
Everton v Sheffield Utd 0-1
Lincoln C v West Bromwich A 3-1
Hull C v Bolton W 0-1
Chesterfield v Blackburn R 0-0, 0-3
Southampton v Ipswich T 7-1
Gillingham v Leyton Orient 2-6
Sheffield Wed v Leeds Utd 2-0
Manchester Utd v Middlesbrough 3-0
Brighton & HA v Derby Co 3-1
Burnley v Bournemouth & Bos Ath 1-0
Swansea T v Port Vale 3-0
Preston NE v Accrington S 1-1, 4-0
Scunthorpe Utd v Blackpool 6-2
York C v Norwich C 1-1, 0-1
Liverpool v Coventry C 3-2
Sunderland v Arsenal 2-1
Portsmouth v Peterborough Utd 1-2
Bristol R v Aston Villa 1-1, 0-4
Chelsea v Crewe Alex 1-2
TOTTENHAM H v Charlton Ath 3-2

Fourth Round
LEICESTER C v Bristol C 5-1
Birmingham C v Rotherham Utd 4-0
Huddersfield T v Barnsley 1-1, 0-1
Luton T v Manchester C 3-1
Newcastle Utd v Stockport Co 4-0
Stoke C v Aldershot 0-0, 0-0, 3-0
Sheffield Utd v Lincoln C 3-1
Bolton W v Blackburn R 3-3, 0-4
Southampton v Leyton Orient 0-1
Sheffield Wed v Manchester Utd 1-1 7-2
Brighton & HA v Burnley 3-3, 0-2
Swansea T v Preston NE 2-1
Scunthorpe Utd v Norwich C 1-4
Liverpool v Sunderland 0-2
Peterborough Utd v Aston Villa 1-1, 1-2
TOTTENHAM H v Crewe Alex 5-1

Fifth Round
Birmingham C v LEICESTER C 1-1, 1-2
Barnsley v Luton T 1-0
Newcastle Utd v Stoke C 3-1
Sheffield Utd v Blackburn R 2-1
Leyton Orient v Sheffield Wed 0-2
Burnley v Swansea T 4-0
Norwich C v Sunderland 0-1
Aston Villa v TOTTENHAM H 0-2

Sixth Round
LEICESTER C v Barnsley 0-0, 2-1
Newcastle Utd v Sheffield Utd 1-3
Sheffield Wed v Burnley 0-0, 0-2
Sunderland v TOTTENHAM H 1-1, 0-5

Semi-final
LEICESTER C v Sheffield Utd 0-0, 0-0, 2-0
Burnley v TOTTENHAM H 0-3

FINAL (Wembley Stadium)
TOTTENHAM HOTSPUR 2
LEICESTER CITY 0

Tottenham Hotspur: Brown; Baker, Henry, Blanchflower, M.Norman, Mackay, Jones, White, Smith, Allen, Dyson.
Goalscorers: Smith, Dyson
Leicester City: Banks; Chalmers, R.Norman, McLintock, King, Appleton, Riley, Walsh, McIlmoyle, Keyworth, Cheesebrough.
Referee: J.Kelly (Chorley) *Attendance: 100,000*

Danny Blanchflower and Bobby Smith each have a hand on the Cup after Spurs completed the first modern League and Cup double with victory over Leicester City in 1961.

1961-62

First Round

Aldershot v Tunbridge Wells Utd 3-1
Barry T v Queen's Park R 1-1, 0-7
Bournemouth & Bos Ath v Margate 0-3
Bradford v Port Vale 0-1
Bradford C v York C 1-0
Brentford v Oxford Utd 3-0
Bridgwater T v Weston-super-Mare 0-0, 1-0
Brierley Hill v Grantham 3-0
Bristol C v Hereford Utd 1-1, 5-2
Chelmsford C v King's Lynn 1-2
Chester v Ashington 4-1
Coventry C v Gillingham 2-0
Crewe Alex v Lincoln C 2-0
Crystal Palace v Portsmouth 3-0
Darlington v Carlisle Utd 0-4
Doncaster R v Chesterfield 0-4
Exeter C v Dartford 3-3, 1-2
Hartlepools Utd v Blyth Spartans 5-1
Hull C v Rhyl 5-0
Mansfield T v Grimsby T 3-2
Morecambe v South Shields 2-1
Northampton T v Millwall 2-0
Notts Co v Yeovil T 4-2
Oldham Ath v Shilton 5-2
Peterborough Utd v Colchester Utd 3-3, 2-2, 3-0
Reading v Newport Co 1-1, 0-1
Rochdale v Halifax T 2-0
Shrewsbury T v Banbury Utd 7-1
Southend Utd v Watford 0-2
Southport v Northwich Vic 1-0
Stockport Co v Accrington S 0-1
Swindon T v Kettering T 2-2, 0-3
Torquay Utd v Harwich & Parkeston 5-1
Tranmere R v Gateshead 2-3
Walthamstow Ave v Romford 2-3
West Auckland T v Barnsley 3-3, 0-2
Weymouth v Barnet 1-0
Workington v Worksop 2-0
Wrexham v Barrow 3-2
Wycombe W v Ashford 0-0, 0-3

Second Round

Aldershot v Brentford 2-2, 0-2
Ashford v Queen's Park R 0-3
Barnsley v Carlisle Utd 1-2
Bridgwater T v Crystal Palace 0-3
Bristol C v Dartford 8-2
Chester v Morecambe 0-1
Chesterfield v Oldham Ath 2-2, 2-4
Coventry C v King's Lynn 1-2
Crewe Alex v Port Vale 1-1, 0-3
Gateshead v Workington 0-2
Hartlepools Utd v Accrington S 2-1
Hull C v Bradford C 0-2
Margate v Notts Co 1-1, 1-3
Northampton T v Kettering T 3-0
Rochdale v Wrexham 1-2
Romford v Watford 1-3
Shrewsbury T v Brierley Hill 3-0
Southport v Mansfield T 4-2
Torquay Utd v Peterborough Utd 1-4
Weymouth v Newport Co 1-0

Third Round

BURNLEY v Queen's Park R 6-1
Brentford v Leyton Orient 1-1, 1-2
Everton v King's Lynn 4-0
Notts Co v Manchester C 0-1
Newcastle Utd v Peterborough Utd 0-1
Bury v Sheffield Utd 0-0, 2-2, 0-2
Norwich C v Wrexham 3-1
Ipswich T v Luton T 1-1, 1-1, 5-1
Fulham v Hartlepools Utd 3-1
Bristol C v Walsall 0-0, 1-4
Southampton v Sunderland 2-2, 0-3
Port Vale v Northampton T 3-1
Leicester C v Stoke C 1-1, 2-5
Brighton & HA v Blackburn R 0-3
Southport v Shrewsbury T 1-3
Middlesbrough v Cardiff C 1-0
Bristol R v Oldham Ath 1-1, 0-2
Liverpool v Chelsea 4-3
Preston NE v Watford 3-2
Morecambe v Weymouth 0-1
Manchester Utd v Bolton W 2-1
Arsenal v Bradford C 3-0
Workington v Nottingham F 1-2
Sheffield Wed v Swansea T 1-0
Aston Villa v Crystal Palace 4-3
Huddersfield T v Rotherham Utd 4-3
Charlton Ath v Scunthorpe Utd 1-0
Leeds Utd v Derby Co 2-2, 1-3
Wolves v Carlisle Utd 3-1
Blackpool v West Bromwich A 0-0, 1-2
Plymouth Arg v West Ham Utd 3-0
Birmingham C v TOTTENHAM H 3-3, 2-4

Fourth Round

BURNLEY v Leyton Orient 1-1, 1-0
Everton v Manchester C 2-0
Peterborough Utd v Sheffield Utd 1-3
Norwich C v Ipswich T 1-1, 2-1
Fulham v Walsall 2-2, 2-0
Sunderland v Port Vale 0-0, 1-3
Stoke C v Blackburn R 0-1
Shrewsbury T v Middlesbrough 2-2, 1-5
Oldham Ath v Liverpool 1-2
Preston NE v Weymouth 2-0
Manchester Utd v Arsenal 1-0
Nottingham F v Sheffield Wed 0-2
Aston Villa v Huddersfield T 2-1
Charlton Ath v Derby Co 2-1
Wolves v West Bromwich A 1-2
Plymouth v TOTTENHAM H 1-5

Fifth Round

BURNLEY v Everton 3-1
Sheffield Utd v Norwich C 3-1
Fulham v Port Vale 1-0
Blackburn R v Middlesbrough 2-1
Liverpool v Preston NE 0-0, 0-0, 0-1
Manchester Utd v Sheffield Wed 0-0, 2-0
Aston Villa v Charlton Ath 2-1
West Bromwich A v TOTTENHAM H 2-4

Sixth Round

Sheffield Utd v BURNLEY 0-1
Fulham v Blackburn R 2-2, 1-0
Preston NE v Manchester Utd 0-0, 1-2
TOTTENHAM H v Aston Villa 2-0

Semi-final

BURNLEY v Fulham 1-1, 2-1
Manchester Utd v TOTTENHAM H 1-3

FINAL (Wembley Stadium)

TOTTENHAM HOTSPUR 3
BURNLEY 1

Danny Blanchflower skippered Tottenham to another Wembley win, over Burnley in 1962.

Tottenham Hotspur: Brown; Baker, Henry, Blanchflower, Norman, Mackay, Medwin, White, Smith, Greaves, Jones.
Goalscorers: Greaves, Smith, Blanchflower (pen)
Burnley: Blacklaw; Angus, Elder, Adamson, Cummings, Miller, Connelly, McIlroy, Pointer, Robson, Harris.
Goalscorer: Robson

Referee: J.Finney (Hereford)   Attendance: 100,000

1962-63

First Round

Aldershot v Brentford 1-0
Andover v Gillingham 0-1
Barnsley v Rhyl 4-0
Bedford T v Cambridge Utd 2-1
Blyth Spartans v Morecambe 2-1
Boston Utd v King's Lynn 1-2
Bristol C v Wellington T 4-2
Bristol R v Port Vale 0-2
Buxton v Barrow 2-2, 1-3
Carlisle Utd v Hartlepools Utd 2-1
Chelmsford C v Shrewsbury T 2-6
Cheltenham T v Enfield 3-6
Chester v Tranmere R 0-2
Chesterfield v Stockport Co 4-1
Coventry C v Bournemouth & Bos Ath 1-0
Crewe Alex v Scarborough 1-1, 3-2
Crystal Palace v Hereford Utd 2-0
Falmouth v Oxford Utd 1-2
Gateshead v Wigan Ath 2-1
Gravesend & Northfleet v Exeter C 3-2
Halifax T v Bradford 1-0
Hinckley Ath v Sittingbourne 3-0
Hounslow v Mansfield T 3-3, 2-9
Hull C v Crook T 5-4
Lincoln C v Darlington 1-1, 2-1
Maidenhead Utd v Wycombe W 0-3
Millwall v Margate 3-1
Northampton T v Torquay Utd 1-2
North Shields v Workington 2-2, 2-7
Notts Co v Peterborough Utd 0-3
Oldham Ath v Bradford C 2-5
Queen's Park R v Newport C 3-2
Southend Utd v Brighton & HA 2-1
Southport v Wrexham 1-1, 2-3
South Shields v Doncaster R 0-0, 1-2
Swindon T v Reading 4-2
Watford v Poole T 2-2, 2-1
Wimbledon v Colchester Utd 2-1
Yeovil T v Dartford 3-2
York C v Rochdale 0-0, 2-1

Second Round

Barnsley v Chesterfield 2-1
Blyth Spartans v Carlisle Utd 0-2
Bradford C v Gateshead 3-2
Bristol C v Wimbledon 2-1
Crystal Palace v Mansfield T 2-2, 2-7
Doncaster R v Tranmere R 1-4
Gillingham v Bedford T 3-0
Gravesend & Northfleet v Wycombe W 3-1
Hull C v Workington 2-0
King's Lynn v Oxford Utd 1-2
Lincoln C v Halifax T 1-0
Millwall v Coventry C 0-0, 1-2
Peterborough Utd v Enfield 1-0
Port Vale v Aldershot 2-0
Queen's Park R v Hinckley Ath 7-2
Shrewsbury T v Torquay Utd 2-1
Southend Utd v Watford 0-2
Wrexham v Barrow 5-2
Yeovil T v Swindon T 0-2
York C v Crewe Alex 2-1

Third Round

Grimsby T v LEICESTER C 1-3
Mansfield T v Ipswich T 2-3
Leyton Orient v Hull C 1-1, 2-0
Derby Co v Peterborough Utd 2-0
Walsall v Manchester C 0-1
Birmingham C v Bury 3-3, 0-2
Norwich C v Blackpool 1-1, 3-1
Bradford C v Newcastle Utd 1-6
Arsenal v Oxford Utd 5-1
Shrewsbury T v Sheffield Wed 1-1, 1-2
Tottenham H v Burnley 0-3
Wrexham v Liverpool 0-3
West Ham Utd v Fulham 0-0, 2-1
Swansea T v Queen's Park R 2-0
Luton T v Swindon T 0-2
Barnsley v Everton 0-3
Plymouth Arg v West Bromwich A 1-5
Nottingham F v Wolves 4-3
Blackburn R v Middlesbrough 1-1, 1-3
Leeds Utd v Stoke C 3-1
Southampton v York C 5-0
Watford v Rotherham Utd 2-0
Gillingham v Port Vale 2-4
Sheffield Utd v Bolton W 3-1
Portsmouth v Scunthorpe Utd 1-1, 2-1
Lincoln C v Coventry C 1-5
Carlisle Utd v Gravesend & Northfleet 0-1
Preston NE v Sunderland 1-4
Charlton Ath v Cardiff C 1-0
Tranmere R v Chelsea 2-2, 1-3
Bristol C v Aston Villa 1-1, 2-3
MANCHESTER UTD v Huddersfield T 5-0

Fourth Round

LEICESTER C v Ipswich T 3-1
Leyton Orient v Derby Co 3-0
Manchester C v Bury 1-0
Norwich C v Newcastle Utd 5-0
Arsenal v Sheffield Wed 2-0
Burnley v Liverpool 1-1, 1-2
West Ham Utd v Swansea T 1-0
Swindon T v Everton 1-5
West Bromwich A v Nottingham F 0-0, 1-2
Middlesbrough v Leeds Utd 0-2
Southampton v Watford 3-1
Port Vale v Sheffield Utd 1-2
Portsmouth v Coventry C 1-1, 2-2, 1-2
Gravesend & Northfleet v Sunderland 1-1, 2-5
Charlton Ath v Chelsea 0-3
MANCHESTER UTD v Aston Villa 1-0

Maurice Setters, Noel Cantwell and Paddy Crerand after Manchester United's victory over Leicester City in 1963.

Fifth Round
Leyton Orient v LEICESTER C 0-1
Manchester C v Norwich C 1-2
Arsenal v Liverpool 1-2
West Ham Utd v Everton 1-0
Nottingham F v Leeds Utd 3-0
Southampton v Sheffield Utd 1-0
Coventry C v Sunderland 2-1
MANCHESTER UTD v Chelsea 2-1

Sixth Round
Norwich C v LEICESTER C 0-2
Liverpool v West Ham Utd 1-0
Nottingham F v Southampton 1-1, 3-3, 0-5
Coventry C v MANCHESTER UTD 1-3

Semi-final
LEICESTER C v Liverpool 1-0
Southampton v MANCHESTER UTD 0-1

FINAL (Wembley Stadium)
MANCHESTER UNITED 3
LEICESTER CITY 1
Manchester United: Gaskell; Dunne, Cantwell, Crerand, Foulkes, Setters, Giles, Quixall, Herd, Law, Charlton.
Goalscorers: Law, Herd 2
Leicester City: Banks; Sjoberg, Norman, McLintock, King, Appleton, Riley, Cross, Keyworth, Gibson, Stringfellow.
Goalscorer: Keyworth
Referee: K.G.Aston (Ilford) *Attendance: 100,000*

1963-64

First Round
Altrincham v Wrexham 0-0, 0-0
Barnsley v Stockport Co 1-0
Barrow v Bangor C 3-2
Bexley Utd v Wimbledon 1-5
Bournemouth & Bos Ath v Bristol R 1-3
Bradford v Heanor T 3-1
Bradford C v Port Vale 1-2
Brentford v Margate 2-2, 2-0
Bridgwater T v Luton T 0-3
Brighton & HA v Colchester Utd 0-1
Cambridge Utd v Chelmsford C 0-1
Chester v Blyth Spartans 3-2
Corby T v Bristol C 1-3
Crook T v Chesterfield 1-2
Crystal Palace v Harwich & Parkeston 8-2
Darlington v Gateshead 1-4
Doncaster R v Tranmere R 3-0
Exeter C v Shrewsbury T 2-1
Hartlepools Utd v Lincoln C 0-1
Hereford Utd v Newport Co 1-1, 0-4
Hull C v Crewe Alex 2-2, 3-0
Kettering T v Millwall 1-1, 3-2
Maidenhead Utd v Bath C 0-2
Netherfield v Loughborough Utd 6-1
Notts Co v Frickley Coll 2-1
Oldham Ath v Mansfield T 3-2
Oxford Utd v Folkestone T 2-0
Peterborough Utd v Watford 1-1, 1-2
Queen's Park R v Gillingham 4-1
Reading v Enfield 2-2, 4-2
Rochdale v Chorley 2-1
Southport v Walsall 2-1
Sutton Utd v Aldershot 0-4
Tooting & Mitcham v Gravesend & Northfleet 1-2
Torquay Utd v Barnet 6-2
Trowbridge T v Coventry C 1-6
Weymouth v Bedford T 1-1, 0-1
Workington v Halifax T 4-1
Yeovil T v Southend Utd 1-0
York C v Carlisle Utd 2-5

Second Round
Barnsley v Rochdale 3-1
Brentford v Gravesend & Northfleet 1-0
Carlisle Utd v Gateshead 4-3
Chelmsford C v Bedford T 0-1
Chester v Barrow 0-2
Colchester Utd v Queen's Park R 0-1
Coventry C v Bristol R 1-2
Doncaster R v Notts Co 1-1, 2-1
Exeter C v Bristol C 0-2
Lincoln C v Southport 2-0
Luton T v Reading 2-1
Netherfield v Chesterfield 1-1, 1-4
Newport Co v Watford 2-0
Oldham Ath v Bradford 2-0
Oxford Utd v Kettering T 2-1
Port Vale v Workington 2-1
Torquay Utd v Aldershot 2-3
Wimbledon v Bath C 2-2, 0-4
Wrexham v Hull C 0-2
Yeovil T v Crystal Palace 3-1

Third Round
WEST HAM UTD v Charlton Ath 3-0
Leicester C v Leyton Orient 2-3
Aston Villa v Aldershot 0-0, 1-2
Swindon T v Manchester C 2-1
Burnley v Rotherham Utd 1-1, 3-2
Newport Co v Sheffield Wed 3-2
Tottenham H v Chelsea 1-1, 0-2
Plymouth Arg v Huddersfield T 0-1
Sunderland v Northampton T 2-0
Doncaster R v Bristol C 2-2, 0-2
Cardiff C v Leeds Utd 0-1
Hull C v Everton 1-1, 1-2
Scunthorpe Utd v Barnsley 2-2, 2-3
Yeovil T v Bury 0-2
Southampton v Manchester Utd 2-3
Bristol R v Norwich C 2-1
Ipswich T v Oldham Ath 6-3
Stoke C v Portsmouth 4-1
Lincoln C v Sheffield Utd 0-4
Swansea T v Barrow 4-1
West Bromwich A v Blackpool 2-2, 1-0
Arsenal v Wolves 2-1
Liverpool v Derby Co 5-0
Birmingham C v Port Vale 1-2
Oxford Utd v Chesterfield 1-0
Brentford v Middlesbrough 2-1
Blackburn R v Grimsby T 4-0
Fulham v Luton T 4-1
Newcastle Utd v Bedford T 1-2
Carlisle Utd v Queen's Park R 2-0
Bath C v Bolton W 1-1, 0-3
Nottingham F v PRESTON NE 0-0, 0-1

Fourth Round
Leyton Orient v WEST HAM UTD 1-1, 0-3
Aldershot v Swindon T 1-2
Burnley v Newport Co 2-1
Chelsea v Huddersfield T 1-2
Sunderland v Bristol C 6-1
Leeds Utd v Everton 1-1, 0-2
Barnsley v Bury 2-1
Manchester Utd v Bristol R 4-1
Ipswich T v Stoke C 1-1, 0-1
Sheffield Utd v Swansea T 1-1, 0-4
West Bromwich A v Arsenal 3-3, 0-2
Liverpool v Port Vale 0-0, 2-1
Oxford Utd v Brentford 2-2, 2-1
Blackburn R v Fulham 2-0
Bedford T v Carlisle Utd 0-3
Bolton W v PRESTON NE 2-2, 1-2

Fifth Round
Swindon T v WEST HAM UTD 1-3
Burnley v Huddersfield T 3-0
Sunderland v Everton 3-1
Barnsley v Manchester Utd 0-4
Stoke C v Swansea T 2-2, 0-2
Arsenal v Liverpool 0-1
Oxford Utd v Blackburn R 3-1
PRESTON NE v Carlisle Utd 1-0

Sixth Round
WEST HAM UTD v Burnley 3-2
Manchester Utd v Sunderland 3-3, 2-2, 5-1
Liverpool v Swansea T 1-2
Oxford Utd v PRESTON NE 1-2

Semi-final
WEST HAM UTD v Manchester Utd 3-1
Swansea T v PRESTON NE 1-2

West Ham manager Ron Greenwood looks a happy man, holding the Cup after the Hammers beat Preston 3-2 in 1964. Bobby Moore manages to get one hand on the trophy.

FINAL (Wembley Stadium)
WEST HAM UNITED 3
PRESTON NORTH END 2
West Ham United: Standen; Bond, Burkett, Bovington, Brown, Moore, Brabrook, Boyce, Byrne, Hurst, Sissons.
Goalscorers: Sissons, Hurst, Boyce
Preston North End: Kelly; Ross, Lawton, Smith, Singleton, Kendall, Wilson, Ashworth, Dawson, Spavin, Holden.
Goalscorers: Holden, Dawson
Referee: A.Holland (Barnsley) *Attendance: 100,000*

1964-65

First Round
Barnet v Cambridge Utd 2-1
Barrow v Grimsby T 1-1, 2-2, 0-2
Bournemouth & Bos Ath v Gravesend & Northfleet 7-0
Bradford v Doncaster R 2-3
Bristol C v Brighton & HA 1-0
Canterbury C v Torquay Utd 0-6
Chester v Crewe Alex 5-0
Chesterfield v South Shields 2-0
Colchester Utd v Bideford 3-3, 2-1
Corby T v Hartlepools Utd 1-3
Crook T v Carlisle Utd 1-0
Dartford v Aldershot 1-1, 0-1
Exeter C v Hayes 1-0
Cuildford C v Gillingham 2-2, 0-1
Halifax T v South Liverpool 2-2, 2-4
Kidderminster H v Hull C 1-4
King's Lynn v Shrewsbury T 0-1
Luton T v Southend Utd 1-0
Macclesfield T v Wrexham 1-2
Millwall v Kettering T 2-0
Netherfield v Barnsley 1-3
Newport Co v Spalding Utd 5-3
Notts Co v Chelmsford C 2-0
Oldham Ath v Hereford Utd 4-0
Oxford Utd v Mansfield T 0-1
Peterborough Utd v Salisbury 5-1
Port Vale v Hendon 2-1
Queen's Park R v Bath C 2-0
Reading v Watford 3-1
Romford v Enfield 0-0, 0-0, 2-4
Scarborough v Bradford C 1-0
Scunthorpe Utd v Darlington 1-2
Southport v Annfield Plain 6-1
Stockport Co v Wigan Ath 2-1
Tranmere R v Lincoln C 0-0, 0-1
Walsall v Bristol R 0-2
Welton R v Weymouth 1-1, 3-4
Wisbech T v Brentford 0-2
Workington v Rochdale 2-0
York C v Bangor C 5-1

Second Round
Aldershot v Reading 1-3
Barnsley v Chester 2-5
Bournemouth & Bos Ath v Bristol C 0-3
Brentford v Notts Co 4-0
Bristol R v Weymouth 4-1
Chesterfield v York C 2-1
Crook T v Oldham Ath 0-1
Doncaster R v Scarborough 0-0, 2-1
Enfield v Barnet 4-4, 0-3
Exeter C v Shrewsbury T 1-2
Hartlepools Utd v Darlington 0-0, 1-4
Hull C v Lincoln C 1-1, 1-3
Luton T v Gillingham 1-0
Millwall v Port Vale 4-0
Newport Co v Mansfield T 3-0
Queen's Park R v Peterborough Utd 3-3, 1-2
South Liverpool v Workington 0-2
Stockport Co v Grimsby T *0-0, 1-0
Torquay Utd v Colchester Utd 2-0
Wrexham v Southport 2-3

Third Round
West Bromwich A v LIVERPOOL 1-2
Bristol R v Stockport Co 0-0, 2-3
Bolton W v Workington 4-1
Barnet v Preston NE 2-3
Leicester C v Blackburn R 2-2, 2-1
Plymouth Arg v Derby Co 4-2
Middlesbrough v Oldham Ath 6-2
Cardiff C v Charlton Ath 1-2
Chelsea v Northampton T 4-1
West Ham Utd v Birmingham C 4-2
Torquay Utd v Tottenham H 3-3, 1-5
Swindon T v Ipswich T 1-2
Chesterfield v Peterborough Utd 0-3
Darlington v Arsenal 0-2
Swansea T v Newcastle Utd 1-0
Doncaster R v Huddersfield T 0-1
Portsmouth v Wolves 0-0, 2-3
Rotherham Utd v Lincoln C 5-1
Bristol C v Sheffield Utd 1-1, 0-3
Aston Villa v Coventry C 3-0
Stoke C v Blackpool 4-1
Manchester Utd v Chester 2-1
Reading v Newport Co 2-2, 1-0
Burnley v Brentford 1-1, 2-0
Southampton v Leyton Orient 3-1
Crystal Palace v Bury 5-1
Luton T v Sunderland 0-3
Nottingham F v Norwich C 1-0
Fulham v Millwall 3-3, 0-2
Manchester C v Shrewsbury T 1-1, 1-3
Everton v Sheffield Wed 2-2, 3-0
LEEDS UTD v Southport 3-0

Ian St John scores Liverpool's second goal against Leeds United in the 1965 Final.

Fourth Round
LIVERPOOL v Stockport Co 1-1, 2-0
Preston NE v Bolton W 1-2
Leicester C v Plymouth Arg 5-0
Charlton Ath v Middlesbrough 1-1, 1-2
West Ham Utd v Chelsea 0-1
Tottenham H v Ipswich T 5-0
Peterborough Utd v Arsenal 2-1
Swansea T v Huddersfield T 1-0
Wolves v Rotherham Utd 2-2, 3-0
Sheffield Utd v Aston Villa 0-2
Stoke C v Manchester Utd 0-0, 0-1
Reading v Burnley 1-1, 0-1
Southampton v Crystal Palace 1-2
Sunderland v Nottingham F 1-3
Millwall v Shrewsbury T 1-2
LEEDS UTD v Everton 1-1, 2-1

Fifth Round
Bolton W v LIVERPOOL 0-1
Middlesbrough v Leicester C 0-3
Chelsea v Tottenham H 1-0
Peterborough Utd v Swansea T 0-0, 2-0
Aston Villa v Wolves 1-1, 0-0, 1-3
Manchester Utd v Burnley 2-1
Crystal Palace v Nottingham F 3-1
LEEDS UTD v Shrewsbury T 2-0

Sixth Round
Leicester C v LIVERPOOL 0-0, 0-1
Chelsea v Peterborough Utd 5-1
Wolves v Manchester Utd 3-5
Crystal Palace v LEEDS UTD 0-3

Semi-final
LIVERPOOL v Chelsea 2-0
Manchester Utd v LEEDS UTD 0-0, 0-1

FINAL (Wembley Stadium)
LIVERPOOL 2
LEEDS UNITED 1
(after extra-time)

Liverpool: Lawrence; Lawler, Byrne, Strong, Yeats, Stevenson, Callaghan, Hunt, St John, Smith, Thompson.
Goalscorers: Hunt, St John
Leeds United: Sprake; Reaney, Bell, Bremner, Charlton, Hunter, Giles, Storrie, Peacock, Collins, Johanneson.
Goalscorer: Bremner
Referee: W.Clements (West Bromwich)
Attendance: 100,000

*Abandoned

1965-66

First Round
Aldershot v Wellingborough T 2-1
Altrincham v Scarborough 6-0
Barrow v Grimsby T 1-2
Barnet v Dartford 0-2
Bath v Newport Co 2-0
Bournemouth & Bos Ath v Weymouth 0-0, 4-1
Bradford v Hull C 2-3
Brentford v Yeovil T 2-1
Brighton & HA v Wisbech T 10-1
Chesterfield v Chester 0-2
Colchester Utd v Queen's Park R 3-3, 0-4
Corby T v Burton Alb 6-3
Corinthian Casuals v Watford 1-5
Crewe Alex v Scunthorpe Utd 3-0
Darlington v Bradford C 3-2
Doncaster R v Wigan Ath 2-2, 1-3
Exeter C v Bedford T 1-2
Fleetwood v Rochdale 2-2, 0-5
Gateshead v Crook T 4-2
Gillingham v Folkestone T 1-2
Grantham v Hendon 4-1
Guildford C v Wycombe W 2-2, 1-0
Hartlepools Utd v Workington 3-1
Leytonstone v Hereford Utd 0-1
Lincoln C v Barnsley 1-3
Mansfield T v Oldham Ath 1-3
Millwall v Wealdstone 3-1
Oxford Utd v Port Vale 2-2, 2-3
Peterborough Utd v Kidderminster H 2-1
Reading v Bristol R 3-2
Romford v Luton T 1-1, 0-1
Shrewsbury T v Torquay Utd 2-1
Southend Utd v Notts Co 3-1
Southport v Halifax T 2-0
South Shields v York C 3-1
Swindon T v Merthyr Tydfil T 5-1
Tranmere R v Stockport Co 0-1
Walsall v Swansea T 6-3
Wimbledon v Gravesend & Northfleet 4-1
Wrexham v South Liverpool 4-1

Second Round
Aldershot v Walsall 0-2
Barnsley v Grimsby T 1-1, 0-2
Bournemouth & Bos Ath v Bath C 5-3
Brighton & HA v Bedford T 1-1, 1-2
Chester v Wigan Ath 2-1
Corby T v Luton T 2-2, 1-0
Crewe Alex v South Shields 3-1
Darlington v Oldham Ath 0-1
Gateshead v Hull C 0-4
Grantham v Swindon T 1-6
Hartlepools Utd v Wrexham 2-0

Hereford Utd v Millwall 1-0
Port Vale v Dartford 1-0
Queen's Park R v Guildford C 3-0
Reading v Brentford 5-0
Rochdale v Altrincham 1-3
Shrewsbury T v Peterborough Utd 3-2
Southend Utd v Watford 2-1
Southport v Stockport Co 3-3, 2-0
Wimbledon v Folkestone T 0-1

Third Round
EVERTON v Sunderland 3-0
Bedford T v Hereford Utd 2-1
Swindon T v Coventry C 1-2
Folkestone T v Crewe Alex 1-5
Blackpool v Manchester C 1-1, 1-3
Grimsby T v Portsmouth 0-0, 3-1
Birmingham C v Bristol C 3-2
Aston Villa v Leicester C 1-2
Derby Co v Manchester Utd 2-5
Rotherham Utd v Southend Utd 3-2
Wolves v Altrincham 5-0
Sheffield Utd v Fulham 3-1
Bolton W v West Bromwich A 3-0
Charlton Ath v Preston NE 2-3
Tottenham H v Middlesbrough 4-0
Bournemouth & Bos Ath v Burnley 1-1, 0-7
Liverpool v Chelsea 1-2
Leeds Utd v Bury 6-0
Queen's Park R v Shrewsbury T 0-0, 0-1
Carlisle Utd v Crystal Palace 3-0
Hull C v Southampton 1-0
Northampton T v Nottingham F 1-2
Southport v Ipswich T 0-0, 3-2
Cardiff C v Port Vale 2-1
Leyton Orient v Norwich C 1-3
Stoke C v Walsall 0-2
Oldham Ath v West Ham Utd 2-2, 1-2
Blackburn R v Arsenal 3-0
Plymouth Arg v Corby T 6-0
Huddersfield T v Hartlepools Utd 3-1
Chester v Newcastle Utd 1-3
Reading v SHEFFIELD WED 2-3

Fourth Round
Bedford T v EVERTON 0-3
Crewe Alex v Coventry C 1-1, 1-4
Manchester C v Grimsby T 2-0
Birmingham C v Leicester C 1-2
Manchester Utd v Rotherham Utd 0-0, 1-0
Wolves v Sheffield Utd 3-0
Bolton W v Preston NE 1-1, 2-3
Tottenham H v Burnley 4-3
Chelsea v Leeds Utd 1-0
Shrewsbury T v Carlisle Utd 0-0, 1-1, 4-3
Hull C v Nottingham F 2-0
Southport v Cardiff C 2-0
Norwich C v Walsall 3-2
West Ham Utd v Blackburn R 3-3, 1-4
Plymouth Arg v Huddersfield T 0-2
Newcastle Utd v SHEFFIELD WED 1-2

Fifth Round
EVERTON v Coventry C 3-0
Manchester C v Leicester C 2-2, 1-0
Wolves v Manchester Utd 2-4
Preston NE v Tottenham H 2-1
Chelsea v Shrewsbury T 3-2
Hull C v Southport 2-0
Norwich C v Blackburn R 2-2, 2-3
Huddersfield T v SHEFFIELD WED 1-2

Sixth Round
Manchester C v EVERTON 0-0, 0-0, 0-2
Preston NE v Manchester Utd 1-1, 1-3
Chelsea v Hull C 2-2, 3-1
Blackburn R v SHEFFIELD WED 1-2

Brian Labone and Brian Harris parade the Cup after Everton's great fight-back against Sheffield Wednesday in 1966.

Semi-final
EVERTON v Manchester Utd 1-0
Chelsea v SHEFFIELD WED 0-2

FINAL (Wembley Stadium)
EVERTON 3
SHEFFIELD WEDNESDAY 2
Everton: West; Wright, Wilson, Gabriel, Labone, Harris, Scott, Trebilcock, A.Young, Harvey, Temple.
Goalscorers: Trebilcock 2, Temple
Sheffield Wednesday: Springett; Smith, Megson, Eustace, Ellis, G.Young, Pugh, Fantham, McCalliog, Ford, Quinn.
Goalscorers: McCalliog, Ford
Referee: J.K.Taylor (Wolverhampton)
Attendance: 100,000

1966-67

First Round
Aldershot v Torquay Utd 2-1
Ashford v Cambridge C 4-1
Barnsley v Southport 3-1
Bath C v Sutton Utd 1-0
Bishop Auckland v Blyth Spartans 1-1, 0-0, 3-3, 4-1
Bournemouth & Bos Ath v Welton R 3-0
Bradford v Witton Alb 3-2
Bradford C v Port Vale 1-2
Brentford v Chelmsford C 1-0
Chester v Middlesbrough 2-5
Crewe Alex v Grimsby T 1-1, 1-0
Darlington v Stockport Co 0-0, 1-1, 4-2
Enfield v Chesham Utd 6-0
Exeter C v Luton T 1-1, 0-2
Folkestone T v Swansea T 2-2, 2-7
Gainsboro' Trin v Colchester Utd 0-1
Gillingham v Tamworth 4-1
Grantham v Wimbledon 2-1
Halifax T v Doncaster R 2-2, 3-1
Hendon v Reading 1-3
Horsham v Swindon T 0-3
Leyton Orient v Lowestoft 2-1
Lincoln C v Scunthorpe Utd 3-4
Mansfield T v Bangor C 4-1
Newport Co v Brighton & HA 1-2
Oldham Ath v Notts Co 3-1
Oxford C v Bristol R 2-2, 0-4
Peterborough Utd v Hereford Utd 4-1
Queen's Park R v Poole T 3-2
Rochdale v Barrow 1-3
South Shields v Workington 1-4
Shrewsbury T v Hartlepools Utd 5-2
Tranmere R v Wigan Ath 1-1, 1-0
Walsall v St Neots T 2-0
Watford v Southend Utd 1-0
Wealdstone v Nuneaton Bor 0-2
Wrexham v Chesterfield 3-2
Wycombe W v Bedford T 1-1, 3-3, 1-1, 2-3
Yeovil T v Oxford Utd 1-3
York C v Morecambe 0-0, 1-1, 1-0

Second Round
Aldershot v Reading 1-0
Barnsley v Port Vale 1-1, 3-0
Barrow v Tranmere R 2-1
Bath C v Brighton & HA 0-5
Bishop Auckland v Halifax T 0-0, 0-7
Bradford v Workington 3-0
Bristol R v Luton T 3-2
Colchester Utd v Peterborough Utd 0-3
Crewe Alex v Darlington 2-1
Enfield v Watford 2-4
Grantham v Oldham Ath 0-4
Leyton Orient v Brentford 0-0, 1-3
Mansfield T v Scunthorpe Utd 2-1
Middlesbrough v York C 1-1, 0-0, 4-1
Nuneaton Bor v Swansea T 2-0
Oxford Utd v Bedford T 1-1, 0-1
Queen's Park R v Bournemouth & Bos Ath 2-0
Shrewsbury T v Wrexham 5-1
Swindon T v Ashford 5-0
Walsall v Gillingham 3-1

Third Round
Huddersfield T v CHELSEA 1-2
Aldershot v Brighton & HA 0-0, 1-3
Bradford v Fulham 1-3
Charlton Ath v Sheffield Utd 0-1
Manchester Utd v Stoke C 2-0
Norwich C v Derby Co 3-0
Sheffield Wed v Queen's Park R 3-0
Mansfield T v Middlesbrough 2-0
Sunderland v Brentford 5-2
Bedford T v Peterborough Utd 2-6
Leeds Utd v Crystal Palace 3-0
Northampton T v West Bromwich A 1-3
Barnsley v Cardiff C 1-1, 1-2
Manchester C v Leicester C 2-1
Ipswich T v Shrewsbury T 4-1

Blackburn R v Carlisle Utd 1-2
Nottingham F v Plymouth Arg 2-1
Coventry C v Newcastle Utd 3-4
West Ham Utd v Swindon T 3-3, 1-3
Bury v Walsall 2-0
Oldham Ath v Wolves 2-2, 1-4
Burnley v Everton 0-0, 1-2
Watford v Liverpool 0-0, 1-3
Preston NE v Aston Villa 0-1
Nuneaton Bor v Rotherham Utd 1-1, 0-1
Birmingham C v Blackpool 2-1
Bolton W v Crewe Alex 1-0
Bristol R v Arsenal 0-3
Halifax T v Bristol C 1-1, 1-4
Barrow v Southampton 2-2, 0-3
Hull C v Portsmouth 1-1, 2-2, 1-3
Millwall v TOTTENHAM H 0-0, 0-1

Fourth Round
Brighton & HA v CHELSEA 1-1, 0-4
Fulham v Sheffield Utd 1-1, 1-3
Manchester Utd v Norwich C 1-2
Sheffield Wed v Mansfield T 4-0
Sunderland v Peterborough Utd 7-1
Leeds Utd v West Bromwich A 5-0
Cardiff C v Manchester C 1-1, 1-3
Ipswich T v Carlisle Utd 2-0
Nottingham F v Newcastle Utd 3-0
Swindon T v Bury 2-1
Wolves v Everton 1-1, 1-3
Liverpool v Aston Villa 1-0
Rotherham Utd v Birmingham C 0-0, 1-2
Bolton W v Arsenal 0-0, 0-3
Bristol C v Southampton 1-0
TOTTENHAM H v Portsmouth 3-1

Fifth Round
CHELSEA v Sheffield Utd 2-0
Norwich C v Sheffield Wed 1-3
Sunderland v Leeds Utd 1-1, 1-1, 1-2
Manchester C v Ipswich T 1-1, 3-0
Nottingham F v Swindon T 0-0, 1-1, 3-0
Everton v Liverpool 1-0
Birmingham C v Arsenal 1-0
TOTTENHAM H v Bristol C 2-0

Sixth Round
CHELSEA v Sheffield Wed 1-0
Leeds Utd v Manchester C 1-0
Nottingham F v Everton 3-2
Birmingham C v TOTTENHAM H 0-0, 0-6

Semi-final
CHELSEA v Leeds Utd 1-0
Nottingham F v TOTTENHAM H 1-2

FINAL (Wembley Stadium)
TOTTENHAM HOTSPUR 2
CHELSEA 1
Tottenham Hotspur: Jennings; Kinnear, Knowles, Mullery, England, Mackay, Robertson, Greaves, Gilzean, Venables, Saul.
Goalscorers: Robertson, Saul
Chelsea: Bonetti; A.Harris, McCreadie, Hollins, Hinton, R.Harris, Cooke, Baldwin, Hateley, Tambling, Boyle.
Goalscorer: Tambling
Referee: K.Dagnall (Bolton) *Attendance: 100,000*

Terry Venables and Jimmy Robertson after Tottenham's 2-1 win against Chelsea in 1967.

1967-68

First Round
Arnold v Bristol R 0-3
Barrow v Oldham Ath 2-0
Bournemouth & Bos Ath v Northampton T 2-0
Bradford C v Wrexham 7-1

Brentford v Guildford C 2-2, 1-2
Brighton & HA v Southend Utd 1-0
Chelmsford C v Oxford Utd 3-3, 3-3, 1-0
Chesterfield v Barnsley 2-0
Corby T v Boston Utd 0-3
Dagenham v Tonbridge 1-0
Goole T v Spennymoor Utd 0-0, 1-3
Grantham v Altrincham 0-3
Grimsby T v Bradford 1-1, 1-4
Halifax T v Crewe Alex 3-2
Hartlepools Utd v Bury 2-3
Hereford Utd v Barnet 3-2
Leytonstone v Walsall 0-1
Lowestoft T v Watford 0-1
Newport Co v Gillingham 3-0
Nuneaton Bor v Exeter C 0-0, 0-0, 0-1
Peterborough Utd v Falmouth 5-2
Oxford C v Luton T 1-2
Port Vale v Chester 1-2
Reading v Aldershot 6-2
Runcorn v Notts Co 1-0
Ryhope CW v Workington 0-1
Scunthorpe Utd v Skelmersdale Utd 2-0
Shrewsbury T v Darlington 3-0
Southport v Lincoln C 3-1
Stockport Co v Macclesfield T 1-1, 1-2
Swansea T v Enfield 2-0
Swindon T v Salisbury 4-0
Torquay Utd v Colchester Utd 1-1, 1-2
Tow Law T v Mansfield T 5-1
Tranmere R v Rochdale 5-1
Walthamstow Ave v Kidderminster H 2-1
Weymouth v Leyton Orient 0-2
Wimbledon v Romford 3-0
Yeovil T v Margate 1-3
York C v Doncaster R 0-1

Second Round
Altrincham v Barrow 1-2
Boston Utd v Leyton Orient 1-1, 1-2
Bradford v Tranmere R 2-3
Bradford C v Bury 2-3
Chelmsford C v Colchester Utd 0-2
Chester v Chesterfield 0-1
Doncaster R v Workington 1-1, 2-1
Exeter C v Walsall 1-3
Guildford C v Newport Co 0-1
Halifax T v Scunthorpe Utd 1-0
Macclesfield T v Spennymoor Utd 2-0
Margate v Peterborough Utd 0-4
Reading v Dagenham 1-1, 1-0
Southport v Runcorn 4-2
Swansea T v Brighton & HA 2-1
Swindon T v Luton T 3-2
Tow Law T v Shrewsbury T 1-1, 2-6
Walthamstow Ave v Bournemouth & Bos Ath 1-3
Watford v Hereford Utd 3-0
Wimbledon v Bristol R 0-4

Third Round
Southport v EVERTON 0-1
Newcastle Utd v Carlisle Utd 0-1
Coventry C v Charlton Ath 3-0
Tranmere R v Huddersfield T 2-1
Aston Villa v Millwall 3-0
Rotherham Utd v Wolves 1-0
Manchester C v Reading 0-0, 7-0
Barrow v Leicester C 1-2
Leeds Utd v Derby Co 2-0
Nottingham F v Bolton W 4-2
Middlesbrough v Hull C 1-1, 2-2, 1-0
Bristol C v Bristol R 0-0, 2-1
Stoke C v Cardiff C 4-1
Burnley v West Ham Utd 1-3
Watford v Sheffield Utd 0-1
Blackpool v Chesterfield 2-1
Doncaster R v Swansea T 0-2
Shrewsbury T v Arsenal 1-1, 0-2
Halifax T v Birmingham C 2-4
Leyton Orient v Bury 1-0
Sheffield Wed v Plymouth Arg 3-0
Swindon T v Blackburn R 1-0
Chelsea v Ipswich T 3-0
Norwich C v Sunderland 1-1, 1-0
Manchester Utd v Tottenham H 2-2, 0-1
Queen's Park R v Preston NE 1-3
Walsall v Crystal Palace 1-1, 2-1
Bournemouth & Bos Ath v Liverpool 0-0, 1-4
Fulham v Macclesfield T 4-2
Peterborough Utd v Portsmouth 0-1
Southampton v Newport Co 1-1, 3-2
Colchester Utd v WEST BROMWICH A 1-1, 0-4

Fourth Round
Carlisle Utd v EVERTON 0-2
Coventry C v Tranmere R 1-1, 0-2
Aston Villa v Rotherham Utd 0-1
Manchester C v Leicester C 0-0, 3-4
Leeds Utd v Nottingham F 2-1
Middlesbrough v Bristol C 1-1, 1-2
Stoke C v West Ham Utd 0-3
Sheffield Utd v Blackpool 2-1
Swansea T v Arsenal 0-1
Birmingham C v Leyton Orient 3-0
Sheffield Wed v Swindon T 2-1
Chelsea v Norwich C 1-0
Tottenham H v Preston NE 3-1
Walsall v Liverpool 0-0, 2-5
Fulham v Portsmouth 0-0, 0-1
WEST BROMWICH A v Southampton 1-1, 3-2

Fifth Round
EVERTON v Tranmere R 2-0
Rotherham Utd v Leicester C 1-1, 0-2
Leeds Utd v Bristol C 2-0
West Ham Utd v Sheffield Utd 1-2
Arsenal v Birmingham C 1-1, 1-2
Sheffield Wed v Chelsea 2-2, 0-2
Tottenham H v Liverpool 1-1, 1-2
Portsmouth v WEST BROMWICH A 1-2

Sixth Round
Leicester C v EVERTON 1-3
Leeds Utd v Sheffield Utd 1-0
Birmingham C v Chelsea 1-0
WEST BROMWICH A v Liverpool 0-0, 1-1, 2-1

Semi-final
EVERTON v Leeds Utd 1-0
Birmingham C v WEST BROMWICH A 0-2

FINAL (Wembley Stadium)
WEST BROMWICH ALBION 1
EVERTON 0
(after extra-time)
West Bromwich Albion: Osborne; Fraser, Williams, Brown, Talbot, Kaye(Clarke), Lovett, Collard, Astle, Hope, Clark.
Goalscorer: Astle
Everton: West; Wright, Wilson, Kendall, Labone, Harvey, Husband, Ball, Royle, Hurst, Morrissey.

Referee: L.Callaghan (Merthyr Tydfil)
Attendance: 100,000

West Brom striker Jeff Astle examines his medal after scoring the only goal of the 1968 Cup Final against Everton.

1968-69

First Round
Altrincham v Crewe Alex 0-1
Bangor C v Morecambe 2-3
Barnet v Brentwood T 1-1, 0-1
Barnsley v Rochdale 0-0, 1-0
Bilston v Halifax T 1-3
Bradford C v Chester 1-2
Brentford v Woking 2-0
Brighton & HA v Kidderminster H 2-2, 1-0
Bristol R v Peterborough Utd 3-1
Bury T v Bournemouth & Bos Ath 0-0, 0-3
Canterbury C v Swindon T 0-1
Cheltenham T v Watford 0-4
Chesterfield v Skelmersdale Utd 2-0
Colchester Utd v Chesham Utd 5-0
Darlington v Grimsby T 2-0
Dartford v Aldershot 3-1
Doncaster R v Notts Co 1-0
Exeter C v Newport Co 0-0, 3-1
Goole T v Barrow 1-3
Grantham v Chelmsford C 2-1
Hartlepool v Rotherham Utd 1-1, 0-3
Hereford Utd v Torquay Utd 0-0, 2-4
Leytonstone v Walsall 0-1
Luton T v Ware 6-1
Macclesfield T v Lincoln C 1-3
Mansfield T v Tow Law T 4-1
Northampton T v Margate 3-1
Orient v Gillingham 1-1, 0-2
Oxford C v Swansea T 2-3
Reading v Plymouth Arg 1-0
Shrewsbury T v Port Vale 1-1, 1-3
Southend Utd v King's Lynn 9-0
South Shields v York C 0-6
Stockport Co v Bradford 3-0
Tranmere R v Southport 0-1
Waterlooville v Kettering T 1-2
Wealdstone v St Albans C 1-1, 0-1
Weymouth v Yeovil T 2-1
Workington v Scunthorpe Utd 2-0
Wrexham v Oldham Ath 4-2

Second Round
Bournemouth & Bos Ath v Bristol R 0-0, 0-1
Brighton & HA v Northampton T 1-2
Chester v Lincoln C 1-1, 1-2
Chesterfield v Wrexham 2-1
Colchester Utd v Exeter C 0-1
Darlington v Barnsley 0-0, 0-1
Doncaster R v Southport 2-1
Grantham v Swindon T 0-2
Halifax T v Crewe Alex 1-1, 3-1
Kettering T v Dartford 5-0
Luton T v Gillingham 3-1
Port Vale v Workington 0-0, 2-1
Reading v Torquay Utd 0-0, 2-1
Rotherham Utd v Mansfield T 2-2, 0-1
St Albans C v Walsall 1-1, 1-3
Southend Utd v Brentwood T 10-1
Stockport Co v Barrow 2-0
Watford v Brentford 1-0
Weymouth v Swansea T 1-1, 0-2
York C v Morecambe 2-0

Third Round
MANCHESTER C v Luton T 1-0
Newcastle Utd v Reading 4-0
Blackburn R v Stockport Co 2-0
Portsmouth v Chesterfield 3-0
Walsall v Tottenham H 0-1
Hull C v Wolves 1-3
Oxford Utd v Southampton 1-1, 0-2
Aston Villa v Queen's Park R 2-1
Sheffield Wed v Leeds Utd 1-1, 3-1
Birmingham C v Lincoln C 2-1
Exeter C v Manchester Utd 1-3
Watford v Port Vale 2-0
Everton v Ipswich T 2-1
Coventry C v Blackpool 3-1
Bolton W v Northampton T 2-1
Bristol R v Kettering T 1-1, 2-1
Preston NE v Nottingham F 3-0
Chelsea v Carlisle Utd 2-0
York C v Stoke C 0-2
Swansea T v Halifax T 0-1
Sunderland v Fulham 1-4
West Bromwich A v Norwich C 3-0
Cardiff C v Arsenal 0-0, 0-2
Charlton Ath v Crystal Palace 0-0, 2-0
Mansfield T v Sheffield Utd 2-1
Swindon T v Southend Utd 0-2
Bury v Huddersfield T 1-2
West Ham Utd v Bristol C 3-2
Liverpool v Doncaster R 2-0
Burnley v Derby Co 3-1
Middlesbrough v Millwall 1-1, 0-1
Barnsley v LEICESTER C 1-1, 1-2

Fourth Round
Newcastle Utd v MANCHESTER C 0-0, 0-2
Blackburn R v Portsmouth 4-0
Tottenham H v Wolves 2-1
Southampton v Aston Villa 2-2, 1-2
Sheffield Wed v Birmingham C 2-2, 1-2
Manchester Utd v Watford 1-1, 2-0
Everton v Coventry C 2-0
Bolton W v Bristol R 1-2
Preston NE v Chelsea 0-0, 1-2
Stoke C v Halifax T 1-1, 3-0

Fulham v West Bromwich A 1-2
Arsenal v Charlton Ath 2-0
Mansfield T v Southend Utd 2-1
Huddersfield T v West Ham Utd 0-2
Liverpool v Burnley 2-1
Millwall v LEICESTER C 0-1

Fifth Round
Blackburn R v MANCHESTER C 1-4
Tottenham H v Aston Villa 3-2
Birmingham C v Manchester Utd 2-2, 2-6
Everton v Bristol R 1-0
Chelsea v Stoke C 3-2
West Bromwich A v Arsenal 1-0
Mansfield T v West Ham Utd 3-0
LEICESTER C v Liverpool 0-0, 1-0

Sixth Round
MANCHESTER C v Tottenham H 1-0
Manchester Utd v Everton 0-1
Chelsea v West Bromwich A 1-2
Mansfield T v LEICESTER C 0-1

Semi-final
MANCHESTER C v Everton 1-0
West Bromwich A v LEICESTER C 0-1

FINAL (Wembley Stadium)
MANCHESTER CITY 1
LEICESTER CITY 0

Manchester City manager Joe Mercer shows off the Cup to ecstatic City fans at Wembley in 1969.

Manchester City: Dowd; Book, Pardoe, Doyle, Booth, Oakes, Summerbee, Bell, Lee, Young, Coleman.
Goalscorer: Young
Leicester City: Shilton; Rodrigues, Nish, Roberts, Woollett, Cross, Fern, Gibson, Lochhead, Clarke, Glover(Manley).
Referee: G.McCabe (Sheffield) *Attendance: 100,000*

1969-70

First Round
Alfreton T v Barrow 1-1, 0-0, 2-2, 0-2
Bangor C v Kirkby T 6-0
Bournemouth & Bos Ath v Luton T 1-1, 1-3
Bradford C v Grimsby T 2-1
Brentford v Plymouth Arg 0-0, 0-2
Brentwood T v Reading 1-0
Brighton & HA v Enfield 2-1
Bury v Mansfield T 2-2, 0-2
Chelmsford T v Hereford Utd 1-2
Cheltenham T v Oxford C 0-2
Dagenham v Sutton Utd 0-1
Darlington v Barnsley 0-0, 0-2
Doncaster R v Crewe Alex 1-1, 1-0
Exeter C v Fulham 2-0
Falmouth v Peterborough Utd 1-4
Halifax T v Chester 3-3, 0-1
Hartlepool v North Shields 3-0
Hendon v Carshalton Ath 5-3
Hillindon Bor v Wimbledon 2-0
Kettering T v Swansea T 0-2
Lincoln C v Southport 2-0
Macclesfield T v Scunthorpe Utd 1-1, 2-4
Margate v Aldershot 2-7
Newport Co v Colchester Utd 2-1
Northampton T v Weymouth 0-0, 3-1
Notts Co v Rotherham Utd 0-3
Oldham Ath v Grantham 3-1
Southend Utd v Gillingham 0-0, 0-2
South Shields v Bradford 2-1
Spennymoor Utd v Wrexham 1-4
Stockport Co v Mossley 1-1, 1-0
Tamworth v Torquay Utd 2-1
Telford Utd v Bristol R 0-3
Tranmere R v Chesterfield 3-0
Walton & Hersham v Barnet 0-1
Walsall v Orient 0-0, 2-0
Wigan Ath v Port Vale 1-1, 2-2, 0-1
Workington v Rochdale 2-1
Yeovil T v Shrewsbury T 2-3
York C v Whitby T 2-0

Second Round
Aldershot v Bristol R 3-1
Bangor C v York C 0-0, 0-2
Barnet v Sutton Utd 0-2
Barnsley v Barrow 3-0
Bradford C v Lincoln C 3-0
Brighton & HA v Walsall 1-1, 1-1, 0-0, 1-2
Chester v Doncaster R 1-1, 2-0
Gillingham v Tamworth 6-0
Hartlepool v Wrexham 0-1
Hendon v Brentford T 0-2
Hillingdon Bor v Luton T 2-1
Newport Co v Hereford Utd 2-1
Northampton T v Exeter C 1-1, 0-0, 2-1
Oxford C v Swansea T 1-5
Peterborough Utd v Plymouth Arg 2-0
Port Vale v Tranmere R 2-2, 1-3
Rotherham Utd v Workington 3-0
Shrewsbury T v Mansfield T 1-2
South Shields v Oldham Ath 0-0, 2-1
Stockport Co v Scunthorpe Utd 0-0, 0-4

Third Round
CHELSEA v Birmingham C 3-0
Burnley v Wolves 3-0
Bradford C v Tottenham H 2-2, 0-5
Crystal Palace v Walsall 2-0
Aston Villa v Charlton Ath 1-1, 0-1
Queen's Park R v South Shields 4-1
Preston NE v Derby Co 1-1, 1-4
Sheffield Utd v Everton 2-1
Bolton W v Watford 1-2
Oxford Utd v Stoke C 0-0, 2-3
Gillingham v Newport Co 1-0
Rotherham Utd v Peterborough Utd 0-1
Coventry C v Liverpool 1-1, 0-3
Norwich C v Wrexham 1-2
Southampton v Newcastle Utd 3-0
Leicester C v Sunderland 1-0
Portsmouth v Tranmere R 1-2
Brentwood T v Northampton T 0-1
Ipswich T v Manchester Utd 0-1
Hull C v Manchester C 0-1
Nottingham F v Carlisle Utd 0-0, 1-2
Huddersfield T v Aldershot 1-1, 1-3
Middlesbrough v West Ham Utd 2-1
York C v Cardiff C 1-1, 1-1, 3-1
Blackburn R v Swindon T 0-4
Chester v Bristol C 2-1
Sheffield Wed v West Bromwich A 2-1
Scunthorpe Utd v Millwall 2-1
Arsenal v Blackpool 1-1, 2-3
Mansfield T v Barnsley 3-2
Hillingdon Bor v Sutton Utd 0-0, 1-4
LEEDS UTD v Swansea T 2-1

Fourth Round
CHELSEA v Burnley 2-2, 3-1
Tottenham H v Crystal Palace 0-0, 0-1
Charlton Ath v Queen's Park R 2-3
Derby Co v Sheffield Utd 3-0
Watford v Stoke C 1-0
Gillingham v Peterborough Utd 5-1
Liverpool v Wrexham 3-1
Southampton v Leicester C 1-1, 2-4
Tranmere R v Northampton T 0-0, 1-2
Manchester Utd v Manchester C 3-0
Carlisle Utd v Aldershot 2-2, 4-1
Middlesbrough v York C 4-1
Swindon T v Chester 4-2
Sheffield Wed v Scunthorpe Utd 1-2
Blackpool v Mansfield T 0-2
Sutton Utd v LEEDS UTD 0-6

Fifth Round
Crystal Palace v CHELSEA 1-4
Queen's Park R v Derby Co 1-0
Watford v Gillingham 2-1
Liverpool v Leicester C 0-0, 2-0
Northampton T v Manchester Utd 2-8
Carlisle Utd v Middlesbrough 1-2
Swindon T v Scunthorpe Utd 3-1
LEEDS UTD v Mansfield T 2-0

Sixth Round
Queen's Park R v CHELSEA 2-4
Watford v Liverpool 1-0
Middlesbrough v Manchester Utd 1-1, 1-2
Swindon T v LEEDS UTD 0-2

Semi-final
CHELSEA v Watford 5-1
Manchester Utd v LEEDS UTD 0-0, 0-0, 0-1

Chelsea's Ron Harris, Peter Houseman and Marvin Hinton after the dramatic 1970 Cup Final replay against Leeds United.

FINAL (Old Trafford, Manchester)
CHELSEA 2
LEEDS UNITED 1
(after extra-time)
(following a 2-2 draw after extra-time)

Chelsea: Bonetti; Harris, McCreadie, Hollins, Dempsey, Webb, Baldwin, Cooke, Osgood(Hinton), Hutchinson, Houseman. (Webb and Harris' positions were switched for the first game as were Houseman's and Cooke's, with Harris being substituted by Hinton)
Goalscorers: Osgood, Webb
Leeds United: Harvey; Madeley, Cooper, Bremner, Charlton, Hunter, Lorimer, Clarke, Jones, Giles, Gray. (Sprake played in place of Harvey in the first game)
Goalscorer: Jones
Referee: E.Jennings (Stourbridge)
Attendance: 62,078

The first game was played at Wembley Stadium and the referee was the same but with an attendance of 100,000. Houseman and Hutchinson scored for Chelsea with Charlton and Jones for Leeds United.

Third-place Final
Manchester Utd v Watford 2-0 (at Highbury)

1970-71

First Round
Bradford C v Macclesfield T 3-2
Great Harwood v Rotherham Utd 2-6
Lincoln C v Barrow 2-1
Grimsby T v Bury 0-1
Grantham v Stockport Co 2-1
Scarborough v Workington 2-3
Barnsley v Bradford 1-0
Mansfield T v Wrexham 2-0
Preston NE v Chester 1-1, 0-1
Chesterfield v Halifax T 2-0
Southport v Boston Utd 0-2
Tamworth v York C 0-0, 0-5
Rhyl v Hartlepool 1-0
Crewe Alex v Doncaster R 0-0, 3-1
Darlington v Bangor C 5-1
South Shields v Wigan Ath 1-1, 0-2
Rochdale v Oldham Ath 2-0
Notts Co v Port Vale 1-0
Tranmere R v Scunthorpe Utd 1-1, 0-0, 0-1
Peterborough Utd v Wimbledon 3-1
Fulham v Bristol R 1-2
Dagenham v Margate 2-0
Yeovil T v Aveley 1-0
Brighton & HA v Cheltenham T 4-0
Colchester Utd v Ringmer 3-0
Swansea C v Exeter C 4-1
Hereford Utd v Northampton T 2-2, 2-1
Walsall v Plymouth Arg 3-0
Torquay Utd v Aston Villa 3-1
Crawley T v Chelmsford C 1-1, 1-6
Oxford C v Bournemouth & Bos Ath 1-1, 1-8
Southend Utd v Weymouth 7-0
Minehead v Shrewsbury T 1-2
Enfield v Cambridge Utd 0-1
Hendon v Aldershot 0-2
Wycombe W v Slough T 1-1, 0-1
Brentford v Gillingham 2-1
Walton & Hersham v Telford Utd 2-5

Barnet v Newport Co ... 6-1
Reading v Bishop's Stortford ... 6-1

Second Round
Rhyl v Barnsley ... 0-0, 1-1, 2-0
Lincoln C v Bradford C ... 2-2, 2-2, 4-1
Chester v Crewe Alex ... 1-0
Grantham v Rotherham Utd ... 1-4
Wigan Ath v Peterborough Utd ... 2-1
Boston Utd v York C ... 1-2
Bury v Notts Co ... 1-1, 0-3
Chesterfield v Workington ... 0-0, 2-3
Scunthorpe Utd v Mansfield T ... 3-0
Darlington v Rochdale ... 0-2
Hereford Utd v Brighton & HA ... 1-2
Chelmsford C v Torquay Utd ... 0-1
Southend Utd v Dagenham ... 1-0
Shrewsbury T v Reading ... 2-2, 0-1
Slough T v Barnet ... 0-1
Aldershot v Bristol R ... 1-1, 3-1
Swansea C v Telford Utd ... 6-2
Bournemouth & Bos Ath v Yeovil T ... 0-1
Colchester Utd v Cambridge Utd ... 3-0
Brentford v Walsall ... 1-0

Third Round
Yeovil T v ARSENAL ... 0-3
Portsmouth v Sheffield Utd ... 2-0
Crystal Palace v Chelsea ... 2-2, 0-2
Manchester C v Wigan Ath ... 1-0
Leicester C v Notts Co ... 2-0
Torquay Utd v Lincoln C ... 4-3
Oxford Utd v Burnley ... 3-0
Watford v Reading ... 5-0
Hull C v Charlton Ath ... 3-0
Blackpool v West Ham Utd ... 4-0
Cardiff C v Brighton & HA ... 1-0
Workington v Brentford ... 0-1
Stoke C v Millwall ... 2-1
Huddersfield T v Birmingham C ... 1-1, 2-0
West Bromwich A v Scunthorpe Utd ... 0-0, 3-1
Newcastle Utd v Ipswich T ... 1-1, 1-2
Everton v Blackburn R ... 2-0
Manchester Utd v Middlesbrough ... 0-0, 1-2
Chester v Derby Co ... 1-2
Wolves v Norwich C ... 5-1
Rochdale v Coventry C ... 2-1
Barnet v Colchester Utd ... 0-1
Rotherham Utd v Leeds Utd ... 0-0, 2-3
Queen's Park R v Swindon T ... 1-2
Southend Utd v Carlisle Utd ... 0-3
Tottenham H v Sheffield Wed ... 4-1
Nottingham F v Luton T ... 1-1, 4-3
Sunderland v Orient ... 0-3
York C v Bolton W ... 2-0
Southampton v Bristol C ... 3-0
Swansea C v Rhyl ... 6-1
LIVERPOOL v Aldershot ... 1-0

Fourth Round
Portsmouth v ARSENAL ... 1-1, 2-3
Chelsea v Manchester C ... 0-3
Leicester C v Torquay Utd ... 3-0
Oxford Utd v Watford ... 1-1, 2-1
Hull C v Blackpool ... 2-0
Cardiff C v Brentford ... 0-2
Stoke C v Huddersfield T ... 3-3, 0-0, 1-0
West Bromwich A v Ipswich T ... 1-1, 0-3
Everton v Middlesbrough ... 3-0
Derby Co v Wolves ... 2-1
Rochdale v Colchester Utd ... 3-3, 0-5
Leeds Utd v Swindon T ... 4-0
Carlisle Utd v Tottenham H ... 2-3
Nottingham F v Orient ... 1-1, 1-0
York C v Southampton ... 3-3, 2-3
LIVERPOOL v Swansea C ... 3-0

Fifth Round
Manchester C v ARSENAL ... 1-2
Leicester C v Oxford Utd ... 1-1, 3-1
Hull C v Brentford ... 2-1
Stoke C v Ipswich T ... 0-0, 1-0
Everton v Derby Co ... 1-0
Colchester Utd v Leeds Utd ... 3-2
Tottenham H v Nottingham F ... 2-1
LIVERPOOL v Southampton ... 1-0

Sixth Round
Leicester C v ARSENAL ... 0-0, 0-1
Hull C v Stoke C ... 2-3
Everton v Colchester Utd ... 5-0
LIVERPOOL v Tottenham H ... 0-0, 1-0

Semi-final
ARSENAL v Stoke C ... 2-2, 2-0
Everton v LIVERPOOL ... 1-2

FINAL (Wembley Stadium)
ARSENAL ... 2
LIVERPOOL ... 1
(after extra-time)

Charlie George's extra-time winner against Liverpool in 1971 gives Arsenal the double.

Arsenal: Wilson; Rice, McNab, Storey(Kelly), McLintock, Simpson, Armstrong, Graham, Radford, Kennedy, George.
Goalscorers: Kelly, George
Liverpool: Clemence; Lawler, Lindsay, Smith, Lloyd, Hughes, Callaghan, Evans(Thompson), Heighway, Toshack, Hall.
Goalscorer: Heighway
Referee: N.Burtenshaw (Great Yarmouth)
Attendance: 100,000

In equalizing for Arsenal, Eddie Kelly became the first substitute to score in an FA Cup Final.

Third-place Final
Stoke C v Everton ... 3-2 (at Crystal Palace)

1971-72

First Round
Barrow v Darlington ... 0-2
Bolton W v Bangor C ... 3-0
Chesterfield v Oldham Ath ... 3-0
Crewe Alex v Blyth Spartans ... 0-1
Hartlepool v Scarborough ... 6-1
Frickley Coll v Rotherham Utd ... 2-2, 0-4
Ellesmere Port T v Boston Utd ... 0-3
Lincoln C v Bury ... 1-2
Blackburn R v Port Vale ... 1-1, 1-3
Wigan Ath v Halifax T ... 2-1
Southport v Workington ... 1-3
South Shields v Scunthorpe Utd ... 3-3, 3-2
Rochdale v Barnsley ... 1-3
Rossendale Utd v Altrincham ... 1-0
Chester v Mansfield T ... 1-1, 3-4
Doncaster R v Stockport Co ... 1-2
Wrexham v Bradford C ... 5-1
York C v Grimsby T ... 4-2
Skelmersdale Utd v Tranmere R ... 0-4
Basingstoke T v Northampton T ... 1-5
Enfield v Maidenhead Utd ... 2-0
Crawley T v Exeter C ... 0-0, 0-2
AFC Bournemouth v Margate ... 11-0
Colchester Utd v Shrewsbury T ... 1-4
Redditch Utd v Peterborough Utd ... 1-1, 0-6
Swansea C v Brentford ... 1-1, 3-2
Witney T v Romford ... 0-3
Notts Co v Newport Co ... 6-0
King's Lynn v Hereford Utd ... 0-0, 0-1
Kettering T v Barnet ... 2-4
Gillingham v Plymouth Arg ... 3-2
Walsall v Dagenham ... 4-1
Aldershot v Alvechurch ... 4-2
Cambridge Utd v Weymouth ... 2-1
Bridgwater T v Reading ... 0-3
Torquay Utd v Nuneaton Bor ... 1-0
Guildford C v Dover ... 0-0, 2-0
Southend Utd v Aston Villa ... 1-0
Brighton & HA v Hillingdon Bor ... 7-1
Bristol R v Telford Utd ... 3-0

Second Round
Boston Utd v Hartlepool ... 2-1
Rotherham Utd v York C ... 1-1, 3-2
Barnsley v Chesterfield ... 0-0, 0-1
Port Vale v Darlington ... 1-0
Workington v Bury ... 1-3
South Shields v Notts Co ... 1-3
Mansfield T v Tranmere R ... 2-2, 2-4
Blyth Spartans v Stockport Co ... 1-0
Wrexham v Wigan Ath ... 4-0
Rossendale Utd v Bolton W ... 1-4
Brighton & HA v Walsall ... 1-1, 1-2
Barnet v Torquay Utd ... 1-4
Peterborough Utd v Enfield ... 4-0
Hereford Utd v Northampton T ... 0-0, 2-2, 2-1
Shrewsbury T v Guildford C ... 2-1
Bristol R v Cambridge Utd ... 3-0
Swansea C v Exeter C ... 0-0, 1-0
Romford v Gillingham ... 0-1
Reading v Aldershot ... 1-0
AFC Bournemouth v Southend Utd ... 2-0

Third Round
LEEDS UTD v Bristol R ... 4-1
Oxford Utd v Liverpool ... 0-3
Sheffield Utd v Cardiff C ... 1-3
Sunderland v Sheffield Wed ... 3-0
Crystal Palace v Everton ... 2-2, 2-3
Walsall v AFC Bournemouth ... 1-0
Tottenham H v Carlisle Utd ... 1-1, 3-1
Bury v Rotherham Utd ... 1-1, 1-2
Birmingham C v Port Vale ... 3-0
Peterborough Utd v Ipswich T ... 0-2
Boston Utd v Portsmouth ... 0-1
Swansea C v Gillingham ... 1-0
Burnley v Huddersfield T ... 0-1
Queen's Park R v Fulham ... 1-1, 1-2
Newcastle Utd v Hereford Utd ... 2-2, 1-2
West Ham Utd v Luton T ... 2-1
Preston NE v Bristol C ... 4-2
Southampton v Manchester Utd ... 1-1, 1-4
Millwall v Nottingham F ... 3-1
Manchester C v Middlesbrough ... 1-1, 0-1
Charlton Ath v Tranmere R ... 0-0, 2-4
Stoke C v Chesterfield ... 2-1
West Bromwich A v Coventry C ... 1-2
Norwich C v Hull C ... 0-3
Wolves v Leicester C ... 1-1, 0-2
Orient v Wrexham ... 3-0
Blackpool v Chelsea ... 0-1
Bolton W v Torquay Utd ... 2-1
Derby Co v Shrewsbury T ... 2-0
Watford v Notts Co ... 1-4
Blyth Spartans v Reading ... 2-2, 1-6
Swindon T v ARSENAL ... 0-2

Fourth Round
Liverpool v LEEDS UTD ... 0-0, 0-2
Cardiff C v Sunderland ... 1-1, 1-1, 3-1
Everton v Walsall ... 2-1
Tottenham H v Rotherham Utd ... 2-0
Birmingham C v Ipswich T ... 1-0

Leeds win the FA Cup at last. Billy Bremner on his teammates' shoulders after their win against Arsenal in the 1972 Centenary Final.

Portsmouth v Swansea C 2-0
Huddersfield T v Fulham 3-0
Hereford Utd v West Ham Utd 0-0, 1-3
Preston NE v Manchester Utd 0-2
Millwall v Middlesbrough 2-2, 1-2
Tranmere R v Stoke C 2-2, 0-2
Coventry C v Hull C 0-1
Leicester C v Orient 0-2
Chelsea v Bolton W 3-0
Derby Co v Notts Co 6-0
Reading v ARSENAL 1-2

Fifth Round
Cardiff C v LEEDS UTD 0-2
Everton v Tottenham H 0-2
Birmingham C v Portsmouth 3-1
Huddersfield T v West Ham Utd 4-2
Manchester Utd v Middlesbrough 0-0, 3-0
Stoke C v Hull C 4-1
Orient v Chelsea 3-2
Derby C v ARSENAL 2-2, 0-0, 0-1

Sixth Round
LEEDS UTD v Tottenham H 2-1
Birmingham C v Huddersfield T 3-1
Manchester Utd v Stoke C 1-1, 1-2
Orient v ARSENAL 0-1

Semi-final
LEEDS UTD v Birmingham C 3-0
Stoke C v ARSENAL 1-1, 1-2

FINAL (Wembley Stadium)
LEEDS UNITED 1
ARSENAL 0
Leeds United: Harvey; Reaney, Madeley, Bremner, Charlton, Hunter, Lorimer, Clarke, Jones, Giles, Gray.
Goalscorer: Clarke
Arsenal: Barnett; Rice, McNab, Storey, McLintock, Simpson, Armstrong, Ball, George, Radford(Kennedy), Graham.
Referee: D.Smith (Gloucester) *Attendance: 100,000*

1972-73

First Round
Doncaster R v Bury 3-1
South Liverpool v Tranmere R 0-2
Hartlepool v Scunthorpe Utd 0-0, 0-0, 1-2
Stockport Co v Workington 1-0
Spennymoor Utd v Shrewsbury T 1-1, 1-3
Chesterfield v Rhyl 4-2
Altrincham v Notts Co 0-1
Port Vale v Southport 2-1
Rochdale v Bangor C 1-2
Boston Utd v Lancaster C 1-2
Bolton W v Chester 1-1, 1-0
Crewe Alex v Stafford Rgrs 1-0
Darlington v Wrexham 1-1, 0-5
Lincoln C v Blackburn R 2-2, 1-4
Barnsley v Halifax T 1-1, 1-2
Bradford C v Grantham 3-0
Oldham Ath v Scarborough 1-1, 1-2
Grimsby T v Wigan Ath 2-1
York C v Mansfield T 2-1
Rotherham Utd v South Shields 4-0
Yeovil T v Brentford 2-1
Margate v Swansea C 1-0
Peterborough Utd v Northampton T 1-0
Banbury Utd v Barnet 0-2
Walton & Hersham v Exeter C 2-1
Tonbridge v Charlton Ath 0-5
Walsall v Kettering T 3-3, 2-1
Newport Co v Alton T 5-1
Hayes v Bristol R 1-0
Watford v Guildford C 4-2
Torquay Utd v Hereford Utd 3-0
Barnstaple T v Bilston 0-2
AFC Bournemouth v Cambridge Utd 5-1
Colchester Utd v Bognor Regis T 6-0
Southend Utd v Aldershot 0-2
Enfield v Bishop's Stortford 1-1, 0-1
Telford Utd v Nuneaton Bor 3-2
Chelmsford C v Hillingdon Bor 2-0
Plymouth Arg v Hendon 1-0
Gillingham v Reading 1-2

Second Round
Bolton W v Shrewsbury T 3-0
Grimsby T v Chesterfield 2-2, 1-0
Blackburn R v Crewe Alex 0-1
Rotherham Utd v Stockport Co 0-1
Scarborough v Doncaster R 1-2
Port Vale v Wrexham 1-0
Bradford C v Tranmere R 2-1
Bangor C v York C 2-3
Notts Co v Lancaster C 2-1
Scunthorpe Utd v Halifax T 3-2
Barnet v Bilston 1-1, 1-0
Walsall v Charlton Ath 1-2
AFC Bournemouth v Colchester Utd 0-0, 2-0
Walton & Hersham v Margate 0-1
Reading v Hayes 0-0, 1-0
Watford v Aldershot 2-0
Chelmsford C v Telford Utd 5-0
Yeovil T v Plymouth Arg 0-2
Torquay Utd v Newport Co 0-1
Bishop's Stortford v Peterborough U 2-2, 1-3

Third Round
Notts Co v SUNDERLAND 1-1, 0-2
Reading v Doncaster R 2-0
Burnley v Liverpool 0-0, 0-3
Manchester C v Stoke C 3-2
Charlton Ath v Bolton W 1-1, 0-4
Scunthorpe Utd v Cardiff C 2-3
Newcastle Utd v AFC Bournemouth 2-0
Luton T v Crewe Alex 2-0
Sheffield Wed v Fulham 2-0
Crystal Palace v Southampton 2-0
Brighton & HA v Chelsea 0-2
Chelmsford C v Ipswich T 1-3
Carlisle Utd v Huddersfield T 2-2, 1-0
Watford v Sheffield Utd 0-1
Arsenal v Leicester C 2-2, 2-1
Bradford C v Blackpool 2-1
Wolves v Manchester Utd 1-0
Portsmouth v Bristol C 1-1, 1-4
Everton v Aston Villa 3-2
Millwall v Newport Co 3-0
Orient v Coventry C 1-4
Grimsby T v Preston NE 0-0, 1-0
Stockport Co v Hull C 0-0, 0-2
Port Vale v West Ham Utd 0-1
Peterborough Utd v Derby Co 0-1
Margate v Tottenham H 0-6
York C v Oxford Utd 0-1
Queen's Park R v Barnet 0-0, 3-0
West Bromwich A v Nottingham F 1-1, 0-0, 3-1
Swindon T v Birmingham C 2-0
Plymouth Arg v Middlesbrough 1-0
Norwich C v LEEDS UTD 1-1, 1-1, 0-5

Fourth Round
SUNDERLAND v Reading 1-1, 3-1
Liverpool v Manchester C 0-0, 0-2
Bolton W v Cardiff C 2-2, 1-1, 1-0
Newcastle Utd v Luton T 0-2
Sheffield Wed v Crystal Palace 1-1, 1-1, 3-2
Chelsea v Ipswich T 2-0
Carlisle Utd v Sheffield Utd 2-1
Arsenal v Bradford C 2-0
Wolves v Bristol C 1-0
Everton v Millwall 0-2
Coventry C v Grimsby T 1-0
Hull C v West Ham Utd 1-0
Derby Co v Tottenham H 1-1, 5-3
Oxford Utd v Queen's Park R 0-2
West Bromwich A v Swindon T 2-0
LEEDS UTD v Plymouth Arg 2-1

Fifth Round
Manchester C v SUNDERLAND 2-2, 1-3
Bolton W v Luton T 0-1
Sheffield Wed v Chelsea 1-2
Carlisle Utd v Arsenal 1-2
Wolves v Millwall 1-0
Coventry C v Hull C 3-0
Derby Co v Queen's Park R 4-2
LEEDS UTD v West Bromwich A 2-0

Sixth Round
SUNDERLAND v Luton T 2-0
Chelsea v Arsenal 2-2, 1-2
Wolves v Coventry C 2-0
Derby Co v LEEDS UTD 0-1

Semi-final
SUNDERLAND v Arsenal 2-1
Wolves v LEEDS UTD 0-1

FINAL (Wembley Stadium)
SUNDERLAND 1
LEEDS UNITED 0
Sunderland: Montgomery; Malone, Watson, Pitt, Guthrie, Horswill, Kerr, Porterfield, Hughes, Halom, Tueart.
Goalscorer: Porterfield
Leeds United: Harvey; Reaney, Madeley, Hunter, Cherry, Bremner, Giles, Lorimer, Gray(Yorath), Jones, Clarke.
Referee: K.Burns (Stourbridge) *Attendance: 100,000*

Sunderland's Ian Porterfield smashes home the only goal of the 1973 Final to give the Second Division side a sensational victory over Leeds.

1973-74

First Round

Crewe Alex v Scarborough ... 0-0, 1-2
Chesterfield v Barnsley ... 0-0, 1-2
Bradford C v Workington ... 2-0
Runcorn v Grimsby T ... 0-1
Rochdale v South Shields ... 2-0
Stockport Co v Port Vale ... 0-1
Huddersfield T v Wigan Ath ... 2-0
Alfreton T v Blyth Spartans ... 0-0, 1-2
Altrincham v Hartlepool ... 2-0
Formby v Oldham Ath ... 0-2
York C v Mansfield T ... 0-0, 3-5
Rotherham Utd v Southport ... 2-1
Chester v Telford Utd ... 1-0
Halifax T v Frickley Coll ... 6-1
Tranmere R v Bury ... 2-1
Willington v Blackburn R ... 0-0, 1-6
Doncaster R v Lincoln C ... 1-0
Scunthorpe Utd v Darlington ... 1-0
Wrexham v Shrewsbury T ... 1-1, 1-0
King's Lynn v Wimbledon ... 1-0
Wycombe W v Newport Co ... 3-1
Walsall v Swansea C ... 1-0
Hitchin T v Guildford C ... 1-1, 4-1
Plymouth Arg v Brentford ... 2-1
Weymouth v Merthyr Tydfil ... 0-1
AFC Bournemouth v Charlton Ath ... 1-0
Hillingdon Bor v Grantham ... 0-4
Reading v Slough T ... 3-0
Banbury Utd v Northampton T ... 0-0, 2-3
Hereford Utd v Torquay Utd ... 3-1
Dagenham v Aldershot ... 0-4
Exeter C v Alvechurch ... 0-1
Cambridge Utd v Gillingham ... 3-2
Boston Utd v Hayes ... 0-0, 2-1
Colchester Utd v Peterborough Utd ... 2-3
Watford v Chelmsford C ... 1-0
Bideford v Bristol R ... 0-2
Hendon v Leytonstone ... 3-0
Southend Utd v Boreham Wood ... 3-0
Walton & Hersham v Brighton & HA ... 0-0, 4-0

Second Round

Halifax T v Oldham Ath ... 0-1
Grantham v Rochdale ... 1-1, 5-3
Port Vale v Scarborough ... 2-1
Barnsley v Bradford C ... 1-1, 1-2
Chester v Huddersfield T ... 3-2
Mansfield T v Scunthorpe Utd ... 1-1, 0-1
Blackburn R v Altrincham ... 0-0, 2-0
Grimsby T v Blyth Spartans ... 1-1, 2-0
Doncaster R v Tranmere R ... 3-0
Wrexham v Rotherham Utd ... 3-0
Northampton T v Bristol R ... 1-2
Wycombe W v Peterborough Utd ... 1-3
Aldershot v Cambridge Utd ... 1-2
Hereford Utd v Walton & Hersham ... 3-0
Boston Utd v Hitchin T ... 1-0
Alvechurch v King's Lynn ... 6-1
Merthyr Tydfil v Hendon ... 0-3
Watford v AFC Bournemouth ... 0-1
Plymouth Arg v Walsall ... 1-0
Southend Utd v Reading ... 2-0

Third Round

LIVERPOOL v Doncaster R ... 2-2, 2-0
Carlisle Utd v Sunderland ... 0-0, 1-0
Manchester Utd v Plymouth Arg ... 1-0
Ipswich T v Sheffield Utd ... 3-2
West Ham Utd v Hereford Utd ... 1-1, 1-2
Bristol C v Hull C ... 1-1, 1-0
Peterborough Utd v Southend Utd ... 3-1
Wolves v Leeds Utd ... 1-1, 0-1
Sheffield Wed v Coventry C ... 0-0, 1-3
Derby Co v Boston Utd ... 0-0, 6-1
Chelsea v Queen's Park R ... 0-0, 0-1
Birmingham C v Cardiff C ... 5-2
Port Vale v Luton T ... 1-1, 2-4
Bradford C v Alvechurch ... 4-2
Fulham v Preston NE ... 1-0
Leicester C v Tottenham H ... 1-0
Cambridge Utd v Oldham Ath ... 2-2, 3-3, 1-2
Grimsby T v Burnley ... 0-2
Norwich C v Arsenal ... 0-1
Aston Villa v Chester ... 3-1
Southampton v Blackpool ... 2-1
Bolton W v Stoke C ... 3-2
Crystal Palace v Wrexham ... 0-2
Grantham v Middlesbrough ... 0-2
Nottingham F v Bristol R ... 4-3
Oxford Utd v Manchester C ... 2-5
Portsmouth v Swindon T ... 3-3, 1-0
Orient v AFC Bournemouth ... 2-1
Everton v Blackburn R ... 3-0
West Bromwich A v Notts Co ... 4-0
Millwall v Scunthorpe Utd ... 1-1, 0-1
NEWCASTLE UTD v Hendon ... 1-1, 4-0

Fourth Round

LIVERPOOL v Carlisle Utd ... 0-0, 2-0
Manchester Utd v Ipswich T ... 0-1
Hereford Utd v Bristol C ... 0-1
Peterborough Utd v Leeds Utd ... 1-4
Coventry C v Derby Co ... 0-0, 1-0
Queen's Park R v Birmingham C ... 2-0
Luton T v Bradford C ... 3-0
Fulham v Leicester C ... 1-1, 1-2
Oldham Ath v Burnley ... 1-4
Arsenal v Aston Villa ... 1-1, 0-2
Southampton v Bolton W ... 3-3, 2-0
Wrexham v Middlesbrough ... 1-0
Nottingham F v Manchester C ... 4-1
Portsmouth v Orient ... 0-0, 1-1, 2-0
Everton v West Bromwich A ... 0-0, 0-1
NEWCASTLE UTD v Scunthorpe Utd ... 1-1, 3-0

Fifth Round

LIVERPOOL v Ipswich T ... 2-0
Bristol C v Leeds Utd ... 1-1, 1-0
Coventry C v Queen's Park R ... 0-0, 2-3
Luton T v Leicester C ... 0-4
Burnley v Aston Villa ... 1-0
Southampton v Wrexham ... 0-1
Nottingham F v Portsmouth ... 1-0
West Bromwich A v NEWCASTLE UTD ... 0-3

Sixth Round

Bristol C v LIVERPOOL ... 0-1
Queen's Park R v Leicester C ... 0-2
Burnley v Wrexham ... 1-0
NEWCASTLE UTD v Nottingham F ... *4-3, 0-0, 1-0

Semi-final

LIVERPOOL v Leicester C ... 0-0, 3-1
Burnley v NEWCASTLE UTD ... 0-2

FINAL (Wembley Stadium)

LIVERPOOL ... 3
NEWCASTLE UNITED ... 0

Liverpool: Clemence; Smith, Thompson, Hughes, Lindsay, Hall, Callaghan, Cormack, Keegan, Toshack, Heighway.
Goalscorers: Keegan 2, Heighway
Newcastle United: McFaul; Clark, Howard, Moncur, Kennedy, Smith(Gibb), McDermott, Cassidy, Macdonald, Tudor, Hibbitt.
Referee: C.G.Kew (Amersham) *Attendance: 100,000*

*This match declared void by order of the FA.

Liverpool skipper Emlyn Hughes in triumphant mood after the 1975 Cup Final win over Newcastle.

1974-75

First Round

Crewe Alex v Gateshead Utd ... 2-2, 0-1
Matlock T v Blackburn R ... 1-4
Hartlepool v Bradford C ... 1-0
Stockport Co v Stafford Rgrs ... 0-0, 0-1
Farsley Celtic v Tranmere R ... 0-2
Mansfield T v Wrexham ... 3-1
Rochdale v Marine ... 0-0, 2-1
Blyth Spartans v Preston NE ... 1-1, 1-5
Bury v Southport ... 4-2
Chesterfield v Boston Utd ... 3-1
Oswestry T v Doncaster R ... 1-3
Bishop Auckland v Morecambe ... 5-0
Grimsby T v Huddersfield T ... 1-0
Barnsley v Halifax T ... 1-2
Shrewsbury T v Wigan Ath ... 1-1, 1-2
Darlington v Workington ... 1-0
Rotherham Utd v Chester ... 1-0
Port Vale v Lincoln C ... 2-2, 0-2
Scunthorpe Utd v Altrincham ... 1-1, 1-3
Hereford Utd v Gillingham ... 1-0
Wimbledon v Bath C ... 1-0
AP Leamington v Southend Utd ... 1-2
Romford v Ilford ... 0-2
Wycombe W v Cheltenham T ... 3-1
Hitchin T v Cambridge Utd ... 0-0, 0-3
Torquay Utd v Northampton T ... 0-1
Ashford T v Walsall ... 1-3
Slough T v Brentford ... 1-4
Swindon T v Reading ... 4-0
Bishop's Stortford v Leatherhead ... 0-0, 0-2
Tooting & Mitcham v Crystal Palace ... 1-2
Exeter C v Newport Co ... 1-2
Swansea C v Kettering T ... 1-1, 1-3
Brighton & HA v Aldershot ... 3-1
Chelmsford C v Charlton Ath ... 0-1
Nuneaton Bor v Maidstone Utd ... 2-2, 0-2
AFC Bournemouth v Southwick ... 5-0
Dartford v Plymouth Arg ... 2-3
Peterborough Utd v Weymouth ... 0-0, 3-3, 3-0
Watford v Colchester Utd ... 0-1

Second Round

Chesterfield v Doncaster R ... 1-0
Rotherham Utd v Northampton T ... 2-1
Grimsby T v Bury ... 1-1, 1-2
Hartlepool v Lincoln C ... 0-0, 0-1
Stafford Rgrs v Halifax T ... 2-1
Altrincham v Gateshead Utd ... 3-0
Bishop Auckland v Preston NE ... 0-2
Wigan Ath v Mansfield T ... 1-1, 1-3
Blackburn R v Darlington ... 1-0
Rochdale v Tranmere R ... 1-1, 0-1
Cambridge Utd v Hereford Utd ... 2-0
Leatherhead v Colchester Utd ... 1-0
Brighton & HA v Brentford ... 1-0
Ilford v Southend Utd ... 0-2
Wimbledon v Kettering T ... 2-0
Plymouth Arg v Crystal Palace ... 2-1
Swindon T v Maidstone Utd ... 3-1
Newport Co v Walsall ... 1-3
Peterborough Utd v Charlton Ath ... 3-0
Wycombe W v AFC Bournemouth ... 0-0, 2-1

Third Round

Southampton v WEST HAM UTD ... 1-2
Swindon T v Lincoln C ... 2-0
Southend v Queen's Park R ... 2-2, 0-2
Notts Co v Portsmouth ... 3-1
Coventry C v Norwich C ... 2-0
Arsenal v York C ... 1-1, 3-1
Leicester C v Oxford Utd ... 3-1
Brighton & HA v Leatherhead ... 0-1
Wolves v Ipswich T ... 1-2
Liverpool v Stoke C ... 2-0
Oldham Ath v Aston Villa ... 0-3
Sheffield Utd v Bristol C ... 2-0
Orient v Derby Co ... 2-2, 1-2
Blackburn R v Bristol R ... 1-2
Leeds Utd v Cardiff C ... 4-1
Burnley v Wimbledon ... 0-1
Chelsea v Sheffield Wed ... 3-2
Luton T v Birmingham C ... 0-1
Manchester Utd v Walsall ... 0-0, 2-3
Manchester C v Newcastle Utd ... 0-2
Stafford Rgrs v Rotherham Utd ... 0-0, 2-0
Peterborough Utd v Tranmere R ... 1-0
Wycombe W v Middlesbrough ... 0-0, 0-1
Sunderland v Chesterfield ... 2-0
Bury v Millwall ... 2-2, 1-1, 2-0
Mansfield T v Cambridge Utd ... 1-0
Preston NE v Carlisle Utd ... 0-1
Bolton W v West Bromwich A ... 0-0, 0-4
Plymouth Arg v Blackpool ... 2-0
Everton v Altrincham ... 1-1, 2-0
Nottingham F v Tottenham H ... 1-1, 1-0
FULHAM v Hull C ... 1-1, 2-2, 1-0

Fourth Round

WEST HAM UTD v Swindon T ... 1-1, 2-1
Queen's Park R v Notts Co ... 3-0
Coventry C v Arsenal ... 1-1, 0-3
Leatherhead v Leicester C ... 2-3
Ipswich T v Liverpool ... 1-0
Aston Villa v Sheffield Utd ... 4-1
Derby Co v Bristol R ... 2-0
Leeds Utd v Wimbledon ... 0-0, 1-0
Chelsea v Birmingham C ... 0-1
Walsall v Newcastle Utd ... 1-0
Stafford Rgrs v Peterborough Utd ... 1-2
Middlesbrough v Sunderland ... 3-1
Bury v Mansfield T ... 1-2
Carlisle Utd v West Bromwich A ... 3-2
Plymouth Arg v Everton ... 1-3
FULHAM v Nottingham F ... 0-0, 1-1, 1-1, 2-1

West Ham's Alan Taylor (not in picture) scores his second goal against Fulham in the 1975 Final.

Fifth Round
WEST HAM UTD v Queen's Park R 2-1
Arsenal v Leicester C 0-0, 1-1, 1-0
Ipswich T v Aston Villa 3-2
Derby Co v Leeds Utd 0-1
Birmingham C v Walsall 2-1
Peterborough Utd v Middlesbrough 1-1, 0-2
Mansfield T v Carlisle Utd 0-1
Everton v FULHAM 1-2

Sixth Round
Arsenal v WEST HAM UTD 0-2
Ipswich T v Leeds Utd 0-0, 1-1, 0-0, 3-2
Birmingham C v Middlesbrough 1-0
Carlisle Utd v FULHAM 0-1

Semi-final
WEST HAM UTD v Ipswich T 0-0, 2-1
Birmingham C v FULHAM 1-1, 0-1

FINAL (Wembley Stadium)
WEST HAM UNITED 2
FULHAM 0
West Ham United: Day; McDowell, Lampard, T.Taylor, Lock, Bonds, Paddon, Brooking, A.Taylor, Jennings, Holland.
Goalscorer: A.Taylor 2
Fulham: Mellor; Cutbush, Fraser, Lacy, Moore, Mullery, Conway, Slough, Mitchell, Busby, Barrett.
Referee: P.Partridge (Bishop Auckland) *Attendance: 100,000*

1975-76

First Round
Wigan Ath v Matlock T 4-1
Preston NE v Scunthorpe Utd 2-1
Sheffield Wed v Macclesfield T 3-1
Bury v Doncaster R 4-2
Bradford C v Chesterfield 1-0
Rotherham Utd v Crewe Alex 2-1
Workington v Rochdale 1-1, 1-2
Darlington v Chester 0-0, 0-2
Spennymoor Utd v Southport 4-1
Halifax T v Altrincham 3-1
Rossendale Utd v Shrewsbury T 0-1
Hartlepool v Stockport Co 3-0
Scarborough v Morecambe 2-0
Grantham v Port Vale 2-2, 1-4
Peterborough Utd v Winsford Utd 4-1
Mansfield T v Wrexham 1-1, 1-1, 2-1
AP Leamington v Stafford Rgrs 2-3
Marine v Barnsley 3-1
Walsall v Huddersfield T 0-1
Grimsby T v Gateshead Utd 1-3
Boston Utd v Lincoln C 0-1
Coventry Sporting v Tranmere R 2-0
Sutton Utd v AFC Bournemouth 1-1, 0-1
Crystal Palace v Walton & Hersham 1-0
Aldershot v Wealdstone 4-3
Nuneaton Bor v Wimbledon 0-1
Yeovil T v Millwall 1-1, 2-2, 0-1
Colchester Utd v Dover 3-3, 1-4
Weymouth v Gillingham 0-2
Watford v Brighton & HA 0-3
Brentford v Northampton T 2-0
Hereford Utd v Torquay Utd 2-0
Wycombe W v Bedford T 0-0, 2-2, 2-1
Cardiff C v Exeter C 6-2
Southend Utd v Swansea C 2-0
Dartford v Bishop's Stortford 1-4
Leatherhead v Cambridge Utd 2-0
Newport Co v Swindon T 2-2, 0-3
Romford v Tooting & Mitcham 0-1
Hendon v Reading 1-0

Second Round
Mansfield T v Lincoln C 1-2
Huddersfield T v Port Vale 2-1
Marine v Hartlepool 1-1, 3-6
Stafford Rgrs v Halifax T 1-3
Coventry Sporting v Peterborough Utd 0-4
Shrewsbury T v Chester 3-1
Bury v Spennymoor Utd 3-0
Scarborough v Preston NE 3-2
Gateshead Utd v Rochdale 1-1, 1-3
Sheffield Wed v Wigan Ath 2-0
Rotherham Utd v Bradford C 0-3
Southend Utd v Dover 4-1
Cardiff C v Wycombe W 1-0
Wimbledon v Brentford 0-2
Gillingham v Brighton & HA 0-1
Millwall v Crystal Palace 1-1, 1-2
Aldershot v Bishop's Stortford 2-0
AFC Bournemouth v Hereford Utd 2-2, 0-2
Leatherhead v Tooting & Mitcham 0-0, 1-2
Hendon v Swindon T 0-1

Third Round
SOUTHAMPTON v Aston Villa 1-1, 2-1
Blackpool v Burnley 1-0
West Bromwich A v Carlisle Utd 3-1
Aldershot v Lincoln C 1-2
Norwich C v Rochdale 1-1, 0-0, 2-1
Luton T v Blackburn R 2-0
Shrewsbury T v Bradford C 1-2
Swindon T v Tooting & Mitcham 2-2, 1-2
Tottenham H v Stoke C 1-1, 1-2
Manchester C v Hartlepool 6-0
Sunderland v Oldham Ath 2-0
Hull C v Plymouth Arg 1-1, 4-1
York C v Hereford Utd 2-1
Chelsea v Bristol R 1-1, 1-0
Notts Co v Leeds Utd 0-1
Scarborough v Crystal Palace 1-2
Derby Co v Everton 2-1
West Ham Utd v Liverpool 0-2
Southend Utd v Brighton & HA 2-1
Orient v Cardiff C 0-1
Fulham v Huddersfield T 2-3
Brentford v Bolton W 0-0, 0-2
Coventry C v Bristol C 2-1
Queen's Park R v Newcastle Utd 0-0, 1-2
Ipswich T v Halifax T 3-1
Wolves v Arsenal 3-0
Charlton Ath v Sheffield Wed 2-1
Portsmouth v Birmingham C 1-1, 1-0
Leicester C v Sheffield Utd 3-0
Middlesbrough v Bury 0-0, 2-3
Nottingham F v Peterborough Utd 0-0, 0-1
MANCHESTER UTD v Oxford Utd 2-1

Fourth Round
SOUTHAMPTON v Blackpool 3-1
West Bromwich A v Lincoln C 3-2
Norwich C v Luton T 2-0
Bradford C v Tooting & Mitcham 3-1
Stoke C v Manchester C 1-0
Sunderland v Hull C 1-0
York C v Chelsea 0-2
Leeds Utd v Crystal Palace 0-1
Derby Co v Liverpool 1-0
Southend Utd v Cardiff C 2-1
Huddersfield T v Bolton W 0-1
Coventry C v Newcastle Utd 1-1, 0-5
Ipswich T v Wolves 0-0, 0-1
Charlton Ath v Portsmouth 1-1, 3-0
Leicester C v Bury 1-0
MANCHESTER UTD v Peterborough Utd 3-1

Fifth Round
West Bromwich A v SOUTHAMPTON 1-1, 0-4
Norwich C v Bradford C 1-2
Stoke C v Sunderland 0-0, 1-2
Chelsea v Crystal Palace 2-3
Derby Co v Southend Utd 1-0
Bolton W v Newcastle Utd 3-3, 0-0, 1-2
Wolves v Charlton Ath 3-0
Leicester C v MANCHESTER UTD 1-2

Sixth Round
Bradford C v SOUTHAMPTON 0-1
Sunderland v Crystal Palace 0-1
Derby Co v Newcastle Utd 4-2
MANCHESTER UTD v Wolves 1-1, 3-2

Semi-final
SOUTHAMPTON v Crystal Palace 2-0
Derby Co v MANCHESTER UTD 0-2

FINAL (Wembley Stadium)
SOUTHAMPTON 1
MANCHESTER UNITED 0
Southampton: Turner; Rodrigues, Blyth, Steele, Peach, Holmes, Gilchrist, McCalliog, Channon, Osgood, Stokes.
Goalscorer: Stokes
Manchester United: Stepney; Forsyth, Greenhoff, Buchan, Houston, Daly, Macari, Coppell, McIlroy, Pearson, Hill(McCreery).
Referee: C.Thomas (Treorchy) *Attendance: 100,000*

Southampton's Mick Channon after the Saints' 1-0 win over Manchester United in 1976.

1976-77

First Round
Huddersfield T v Mansfield T 0-0, 1-2
Crook T v Nuneaton Bor 1-4
Rotherham Utd v Altrincham 5-0
Droylsden v Grimsby T 0-0, 3-5
Barnsley v Boston 3-1
Rochdale v Northwich Vic 1-1, 0-0, 1-2
Barrow v Goole T 0-2
Scarborough v Darlington 0-0, 1-4
Scunthorpe Utd v Chesterfield 1-2
Walsall v Bradford C 0-0, 2-0
Bury v Workington 6-0
Lincoln C v Morecambe 1-0
Doncaster R v Shrewsbury T 2-2, 3-4
Chester v Hartlepool 1-0
Matlock T v Wigan Ath 2-0
Dudley T v York C 1-1, 1-4
Stafford Rgrs v Halifax T 0-0, 0-1
Wrexham v Gateshead Utd 6-0
Tranmere R v Peterborough Utd 0-4
Sheffield Wed v Stockport Co 2-0
Southport v Port Vale 1-2
Crewe Alex v Preston NE 1-1, 2-2, 0-3
Waterlooville v Wycombe W 1-2
Aldershot v Portsmouth 1-1, 1-2
Brentford v Chesham Utd 2-0
Reading v Wealdstone 1-0
Gillingham v Watford 0-1
Torquay Utd v Hillingdon Bor 1-2
Swansea C v Minehead 0-1
Tooting & Mitcham Utd v Dartford 4-2
Weymouth v Hitchin T 1-1, 2-2, 3-3, 1-3
AFC Bournemouth v Newport Co 0-0, 0-3
Brighton & HA v Crystal Palace 2-2, 1-1, 0-1
Cambridge Utd v Colchester Utd 1-1, 0-2
Wimbledon v Woking 1-0
Swindon T v Bromley 7-0
Exeter C v Southend Utd 1-1, 1-2
Leatherhead v Northampton T 2-0
Enfield v Harwich & Parkeston 0-0, 3-0
Kettering T v Oxford Utd 1-1, 1-0

Second Round
Bury v Shrewsbury T 0-0, 1-2
Chesterfield v Walsall 1-1, 0-0, 0-1
Darlington v Sheffield Wed 1-0
Port Vale v Barnsley 3-0
Northwich Vic v Peterborough Utd 4-0
Wrexham v Goole T 1-1, 1-0
Halifax T v Preston NE 1-0
Mansfield T v Matlock T 2-5
Lincoln C v Nuneaton Bor 6-0
Rotherham Utd v York C 0-0, 1-1, 2-1
Grimsby T v Chester 0-1
Hillingdon Bor v Watford 2-3
Leatherhead v Wimbledon 1-3
Colchester Utd v Brentford 3-2
Southend Utd v Newport Co 3-0
Portsmouth v Minehead 2-1
Kettering T v Tooting & Mitcham Utd 1-0
Wycombe W v Reading 1-2
Hitchin T v Swindon T 1-1, 1-3
Enfield v Crystal Palace 0-4

Third Round
MANCHESTER UTD v Walsall 1-0
Queen's Park R v Shrewsbury T 2-1
Nottingham F v Bristol R 1-1, 1-1 6-0
Southampton v Chelsea 1-1, 3-0
Leicester C v Aston Villa 0-1
West Ham Utd v Bolton W 2-1
Hull C v Port Vale 1-1, 1-3
Burnley v Lincoln C 2-2, 1-0
Ipswich T v Bristol C 4-1
Wolves v Rotherham Utd 3-2
Southend Utd v Chester 0-4
Halifax T v Luton T 0-1
Birmingham C v Portsmouth 1-0
Leeds Utd v Norwich C 5-2
Sheffield Utd v Newcastle Utd 0-0, 1-3
Manchester C v West Bromwich A 1-1, 1-0
Cardiff C v Tottenham H 1-0
Sunderland v Wrexham 2-2, 0-1
Fulham v Swindon T 3-3, 0-5
Everton v Stoke C 2-0
Kettering T v Colchester Utd 2-3
Blackpool v Derby Co 0-0, 2-3
Charlton Ath v Blackburn R 1-1, 0-2
Darlington v Orient 2-2, 0-0, 0-3
Wimbledon v Middlesbrough 0-0, 0-1
Hereford Utd v Reading 1-0
Notts Co v Arsenal 0-1
Coventry C v Millwall 1-0
Northwich Vic v Watford 3-2
Oldham Ath v Plymouth Arg 3-0
Carlisle Utd v Matlock T 5-1
LIVERPOOL v Crystal Palace 0-0, 3-2

Stuart Pearson nets Manchester United's first goal against Liverpool in 1977.

Fourth Round
MANCHESTER UTD v Queen's Park R 1-0
Nottingham F v Southampton 3-3, 1-2
Aston Villa v West Ham Utd 3-0
Port Vale v Burnley 2-1
Ipswich T v Wolves 2-2, 0-1
Chester v Luton T 1-0
Birmingham C v Leeds Utd 1-2
Newcastle Utd v Manchester C 1-3
Cardiff C v Wrexham 3-2
Swindon T v Everton 2-2, 1-2
Colchester Utd v Derby Co 1-1, 0-1
Blackburn R v Orient 3-0
Middlesbrough v Hereford Utd 4-0
Arsenal v Coventry C 3-1
Northwich Vic v Oldham Ath 1-3
LIVERPOOL v Carlisle Utd 3-0

Fifth Round
Southampton v MANCHESTER UTD 2-2, 1-2
Aston Villa v Port Vale 3-0
Wolves v Chester 1-0
Leeds Utd v Manchester C 1-0
Cardiff C v Everton 1-2
Derby Co v Blackburn R 3-1
Middlesbrough v Arsenal 4-1
LIVERPOOL v Oldham Ath 3-1

Sixth Round
MANCHESTER UTD v Aston Villa 2-1
Wolves v Leeds Utd 0-1
Everton v Derby Co 2-0
LIVERPOOL v Middlesbrough 2-0

Semi-final
MANCHESTER UTD v Leeds Utd 2-1
Everton v LIVERPOOL 2-2, 0-3

FINAL (Wembley Stadium)
MANCHESTER UNITED 2
LIVERPOOL 1
Manchester United: Stepney; Nicholl, B.Greenhoff, Buchan, Albiston, McIlroy, Macari, Coppell, Pearson, J.Greenhoff, Hill(McCreery).
Goalscorers: Pearson, J.Greenhoff
Liverpool: Clemence; Neal, Smith, Hughes, Jones, Kennedy, Case, McDermott, Keegan, Johnson(Callaghan), Heighway.
Goalscorer: Case
Referee: R.Matthewson (Bolton) *Attendance: 100,000*

1977-78

First Round
Chesterfield v Halifax T 1-0
Wigan Ath v York C 1-0
Workington v Grimsby T 0-2
Chester v Darlington 4-1
Scarborough v Rochdale 4-2
Tranmere R v Hartlepool Utd 1-1, 1-3
Blyth Spartans v Burscough 1-0
Barnsley v Huddersfield T 1-0
Rotherham Utd v Mossley 3-0
Spennymoor Utd v Goole T 3-1
Southport v Runcorn 2-2, 0-1
Preston NE v Lincoln C 3-2
Sheffield Wed v Bury 1-0
Doncaster R v Shrewsbury T 0-1
Stockport Co v Scunthorpe Utd 3-0
Arnold v Port Vale 0-0, 2-5
Wrexham v Burton Alb 2-0
Carlisle Utd v Stafford Rgrs 2-0
Bradford C v Crewe Alex 0-1
Nuneaton Bor v Oxford Utd 2-0
Wealdstone v Hereford Utd 0-0, 3-2
Gillingham v Weymouth 1-1, 1-0
Tooting & Mitcham Utd v Northampton T 1-2
Barnet v Peterborough Utd 1-2
Lowestoft T v Cambridge Utd 0-2
Walsall v Dagenham 1-0
Minehead v Wycombe W 2-0
Brentford v Folkestone & Shepway 2-0
Reading v Aldershot 3-1
Torquay Utd v Southend Utd 1-2
Bath C v Plymouth Arg 0-0, 0-2
Enfield v Wimbledon 3-0
Portsmouth v Bideford 3-1
AP Leamington v Enderby T 6-1
Colchester Utd v AFC Bournemouth 1-1, 0-0, 4-1
Tilbury v Kettering T 2-2, 3-2
Borehamwood v Swindon T 0-0, 0-2
Newport Co v Exeter C 1-1, 2-4
Leatherhead v Swansea C 0-0, 1-2
Watford v Hendon 2-0

Second Round
Wigan Ath v Sheffield Wed 1-0
Grimsby T v Barnsley 2-0
Shrewsbury T v Stockport Co 1-1, 2-1
Crewe Alex v Scarborough 0-0, 0-2
Carlisle Utd v Chester 3-1
Blyth Spartans v Chesterfield 1-0
Hartlepool Utd v Runcorn 4-2
Walsall v Port Vale 1-1, 3-1
Rotherham Utd v Spennymoor Utd 6-0
Preston NE v Wrexham 0-2
Gillingham v Peterborough Utd 1-1, 0-2
AP Leamington v Southend Utd 0-0, 0-4
Wealdstone v Reading 2-1
Nuneaton Bor v Tilbury 1-2
Swindon T v Brentford 2-1
Plymouth Arg v Cambridge Utd 1-0
Minehead v Exeter C 0-3
Portsmouth v Swansea C 2-2, 1-2
Northampton T v Enfield 0-2
Watford v Colchester Utd 2-0

Third Round
Cardiff C v IPSWICH T 0-2
Hartlepool Utd v Crystal Palace 2-1
Sunderland v Bristol R 0-1
Grimsby T v Southampton 0-0, 0-0, 1-4
Rotherham Utd v Millwall 1-1, 0-2
Luton T v Oldham Ath 1-1, 2-1
Brighton & HA v Scarborough 3-0
Charlton Ath v Notts Co 0-2
Derby Co v Southend Utd 3-2
Birmingham C v Wigan Ath 4-0
Carlisle Utd v Manchester Utd 1-1, 2-4

West Bromwich A v Blackpool 4-1
Nottingham F v Swindon T 4-1
Leeds Utd v Manchester C 1-2
West Ham v Watford 1-0
Queen's Park R v Wealdstone 4-0
Middlesbrough v Coventry C 3-0
Everton v Aston Villa 4-1
Tottenham H v Bolton W 2-2, 1-2
Mansfield T v Plymouth Arg 1-0
Orient v Norwich C 1-1, 1-0
Blackburn R v Shrewsbury T 2-1
Chelsea v Liverpool 4-2
Burnley v Fulham 1-0
Peterborough Utd v Newcastle Utd 1-1, 0-2
Bristol C v Wrexham 4-4, 0-3
Stoke C v Tilbury 4-0
Blyth Spartans v Enfield 1-0
Walall v Swansea C 4-1
Hull C v Leicester C 0-1
Exeter C v Wolves 2-2, 1-3
Sheffield Utd v ARSENAL 0-5

Fourth Round
IPSWICH T v Hartlepool Utd 4-1
Bristol R v Southampton 2-0
Millwall v Luton T 4-0
Brighton & HA v Notts Co 1-2
Derby Co v Birmingham C 2-1
Manchester Utd v West Bromwich A 1-1, 2-3
Nottingham F v Manchester C 2-1
West Ham Utd v Queen's Park R 1-1, 1-6
Middlesbrough v Everton 3-2
Bolton W v Mansfield T 1-0
Orient v Blackburn R 3-1
Chelsea v Burnley 6-2
Newcastle Utd v Wrexham 2-2, 1-4
Stoke C v Blyth Spartans 2-3
Walsall v Leicester C 1-0
ARSENAL v Wolves 2-1

Fifth Round
Bristol R v IPSWICH T 2-2, 0-3
Millwall v Notts Co 2-1
Derby Co v West Bromwich A 2-3
Queen's Park R v Nottingham F 1-1, 1-1, 1-3
Middlesbrough v Bolton W 2-0
Orient v Chelsea 0-0, 2-1
Wrexham v Blyth Spartans 1-1, 2-1
ARSENAL v Walsall 4-1

Sixth Round
Millwall v IPSWICH T 1-6
West Bromwich A v Nottingham F 2-0
Middlesbrough v Orient 0-0, 1-2
Wrexham v ARSENAL 2-3

Semi-final
IPSWICH T v West Bromwich A 3-1
Orient v ARSENAL 0-3

FINAL (Wembley Stadium)
IPSWICH TOWN 1
ARSENAL 0

Ipswich Town: Cooper; Burley, Hunter, Beattie, Mills, Osborne(Lambert), Talbot, Wark, Mariner, Geddis, Woods.
Goalscorer: Osborne
Arsenal: Jennings; Rice, O'Leary, Young, Nelson, Price, Hudson, Brady(Rix), Sunderland, Macdonald, Stapleton.
Referee: D.R.G.Nippard (Christchurch)
Attendance: 100,000

1978-79

First Round
Barnsley v Worksop T 5-1
Stockport Co v Morecambe 5-1
Altrincham v Southport 4-3
Scunthorpe Utd v Sheffield Wed 1-1, 0-1
Blackpool v Lincoln C 2-1
Carlisle Utd v Halifax T 1-0
Chester v Runcorn 1-1, 5-0
Bradford C v Port Vale 1-0
Hartlepool Utd v Grimsby T 1-0
Tranmere R v Boston Utd 2-1
Rochdale v Droylsden 0-1
Hull C v Stafford Rgrs 2-1
Darlington v Chesterfield 1-1, 1-0
Doncaster R v Huddersfield T 2-1
Rotherham Utd v Workington 3-0
Mansfield T v Shrewsbury T 0-2
Wigan Ath v Bury 2-2, 1-4
York C v Blyth Spartans 1-1, 5-3
Chorley v Scarborough 0-1
Nuneaton Bor v Crewe Alex 0-2
Portsmouth v Northampton T 2-0
Yeovil T v Barking 0-1
Colchester Utd v Oxford Utd 4-2
Gravesend & Northfleet v Wimbledon 0-0, 0-1
Exeter C v Brentford 1-0
Reading v Gillingham 0-0, 2-1
Swindon T v March T Utd 2-0
Southend Utd v Peterborough Utd 3-2
Walsall v Torquay Utd 0-2
Hereford Utd v Newport Co 0-1
Wealdstone v Enfield 0-5
AFC Bournemouth v Hitchin T 2-1
Barnet v Woking 3-3, 3-3, 0-3
Aldershot v Weymouth 1-1, 2-0
Leatherhead v Merthyr Tydfil 2-1
Worcester C v Plymouth Arg 2-0
Maidstone Utd v Wycombe W 1-0
Watford v Dagenham 3-0
Dartford v AP Leamington 1-2
Swansea C v Hillingdon Bor 4-1

Second Round
Droylsden v Altrincham 0-2
Barnsley v Rotherham Utd 1-1, 1-2
Doncaster R v Shrewsbury T 0-3
York C v Scarborough 3-0
Darlington v Chester 2-1
Tranmere R v Sheffield Wed 1-1, 0-4
Crewe Alex v Hartlepool Utd 0-1
Bury v Blackpool 3-1
Stockport Co v Bradford C 4-2
Carlisle Utd v Hull C 3-0
Barking v Aldershot 1-2
Watford v Southend Utd 1-1, 0-1
Maidstone Utd v Exeter C 1-0
Portsmouth v Reading 0-1
Wimbledon v AFC Bournemouth 1-1, 2-1
Swindon T v Enfield 3-0
Newport Co v Worcester C 0-0, 2-1
Swansea C v Woking 2-2, 5-3
AP Leamington v Torquay Utd 0-1
Leatherhead v Colchester Utd 1-1, 0-4

Third Round
Sheffield Wed v ARSENAL 1-1, 1-1, 2-2, 3-3, 0-2
Notts Co v Reading 4-2
Nottingham F v Aston Villa 2-0
York C v Luton T 2-0
Hartlepool Utd v Leeds Utd 2-6
Coventry C v West Bromwich A 2-2, 0-4
Preston NE v Derby Co 3-0
Wimbledon v Southampton 0-2
Middlesbrough v Crystal Palace 1-1, 0-1
Bristol C v Bolton W 3-1
Newcastle Utd v Torquay Utd 3-1
Brighton & HA v Wolves 2-3
Sheffield Utd v Aldershot 0-0, 0-1
Swindon T v Cardiff C 3-0
Shrewsbury T v Cambridge Utd 3-1
Manchester C v Rotherham Utd 0-0, 4-2
Ipswich T v Carlisle Utd 3-2
Orient v Bury 3-2
Swansea C v Bristol R 0-1
Charlton Ath v Maidstone Utd 1-1, 2-1
Southend Utd v Liverpool 0-0, 0-3
Millwall v Blackburn R 1-2
Birmingham C v Burnley 0-2
Sunderland v Everton 2-1
Stoke C v Oldham Ath 0-1
Leicester C v Norwich C 3-0
Tottenham H v Altrincham 1-1, 3-0
Wrexham v Stockport Co 6-2
Newport Co v West Ham Utd 2-1
Darlington v Colchester Utd 0-1
Fulham v Queen's Park R 2-0
MANCHESTER UTD v Chelsea 3-0

Fourth Round
ARSENAL v Notts Co 2-0
Nottingham F v York C 3-1
Leeds Utd v West Bromwich A 3-3, 0-2
Preston NE v Southampton 0-1
Crystal Palace v Bristol C 3-0
Newcastle Utd v Wolves 1-1, 0-1
Aldershot v Swindon T 2-1
Shrewsbury T v Manchester C 2-0
Ipswich T v Orient 0-0, 2-0
Bristol R v Charlton Ath 1-0
Liverpool v Blackburn R 1-0
Burnley v Sunderland 1-1, 3-0
Oldham Ath v Leicester C 3-1
Tottenham H v Wrexham 3-3, 3-2
Newport Co v Colchester Utd 0-0, 0-1
Fulham v MANCHESTER UTD 1-1, 0-1

Fifth Round
Nottingham F v ARSENAL 0-1
West Bromwich A v Southampton 1-1, 1-2
Crystal Palace v Wolves 0-1
Aldershot v Shrewsbury T 2-2, 1-3
Ipswich T v Bristol R 6-1
Liverpool v Burnley 3-0
Oldham Ath v Tottenham H 0-1
Colchester Utd v MANCHESTER UTD 0-1

Sixth Round
Southampton v ARSENAL 1-1, 0-2
Wolves v Shrewsbury T 1-1, 3-1
Ipswich T v Liverpool 0-1
Tottenham H v MANCHESTER UTD 1-1, 0-2

Semi-final
ARSENAL v Wolves 2-0
Liverpool v MANCHESTER UTD 2-2, 0-1

FINAL (Wembley Stadium)
ARSENAL 3
MANCHESTER UNITED 2

Arsenal: Jennings; Rice, Nelson, Talbot, O'Leary, Young, Brady, Sunderland, Stapleton, Price(Walford), Rix.
Goalscorers: Talbot, Stapleton, Sunderland
Manchester United: Bailey; Nicholl, Albiston, McIlroy, McQueen, Buchan, Coppell, J.Greenhoff, Jordan, Macari, Thomas.
Goalscorers: McQueen, McIlroy
Referee: R.Challis (Tonbridge) *Attendance: 100,000*

Roger Osborne's winner against Arsenal in the 1978 Final. Moments later Osborne left the field, physically and emotionally drained.

Frank Stapleton heads a 43rd-minute goal for Arsenal against Manchester United in 1978 but the game did not come to life until the dying stages.

1979-80

First Round

Carlisle Utd v Hull C	3-3, 2-0
Kidderminster H v Blackburn R	0-2
Morecambe v Rotherham Utd	1-1, 0-2
Altrincham v Crewe Alex	3-0
Barnsley v Hartlepool Utd	5-2
Darlington v Huddersfield T	1-1, 1-0
Grimsby T v Chesterfield	1-1, 3-2
Rochdale v Scunthorpe Utd	2-1
Tranmere R v AP Leamington	9-0
Brandon Utd v Bradford C	0-3
Stafford Rgrs v Moor Green	3-2
Sheffield Utd v Burscough	3-0
Blyth Spartans v Mansfield T	0-2
York C v Mossley	5-2
Sheffield Wed v Lincoln C	3-0
Port Vale v Doncaster R	1-3
Nuneaton Bor v Northwich Vic	3-3, 0-3
Chester v Workington	5-1
Blackpool v Wigan Ath	1-1, 0-2
Halifax T v Scarborough	2-0
Walsall v Stockport Co	2-0
Burton Alb v Bury	0-2
Portsmouth v Newport Co	1-0
Fareham T v Merthyr Tydfil	2-3
Peterborough Utd v AFC Bournemouth	1-2
Enfield v Yeovil T	0-1
Aldershot v Exeter C	4-1
Barking v Oxford Utd	1-0
Wealdstone v Southend Utd	0-1
Reading v Kettering T	4-2
Wycombe W v Croydon	0-3
Swindon T v Brentford	4-1
Hereford Utd v Northampton T	1-0
Gillingham v Wimbledon	0-0, 2-4
Salisbury v Millwall	1-2
Gravesend & Northfleet v Torquay Utd	0-1
Colchester Utd v Plymouth Arg	1-1, 1-0
Minehead v Chesham Utd	1-2
Slough T v Hungerford T	3-1
Harlow T v Leytonstone & Ilford	2-1

Second Round

Grimsby T v Sheffield Utd	2-0
Bury v York C	0-0, 2-0
Chester v Barnsley	1-0
Rotherham Utd v Altrincham	0-2
Darlington v Bradford C	0-1
Doncaster R v Mansfield T	1-2
Northwich Vic v Wigan Ath	2-2, 0-1
Walsall v Halifax T	1-1, 1-1, 0-2
Carlisle Utd v Sheffield Wed	3-0
Blackburn R v Stafford Rgrs	2-0
Tranmere R v Rochdale	2-2, 1-2
Colchester Utd v AFC Bournemouth	1-0
Torquay Utd v Swindon T	3-3, 2-3
Yeovil T v Slough T	1-0
Reading v Barking	3-1
Croydon v Millwall	1-1, 2-3
Hereford Utd v Aldershot	1-2
Chesham Utd v Merthyr Tydfil	1-1, 3-1
Wimbledon v Portsmouth	0-0, 3-3, 0-1
Southend Utd v Harlow T	1-1, 0-1

Third Round

Cardiff C v ARSENAL	0-0, 1-2
Mansfield T v Brighton & HA	0-2
Sunderland v Bolton W	0-1
Halifax T v Manchester C	1-0
Notts Co v Wolves	0-3
Yeovil T v Norwich C	0-3
Queen's Park R v Watford	1-2
Leicester C v Harlow T	1-1, 0-1
Luton T v Swindon T	0-2
Tottenham H v Manchester Utd	1-1, 1-0
Birmingham C v Southampton	2-1
Portsmouth v Middlesbrough	1-1, 0-3
Leeds Utd v Nottingham F	1-4
Liverpool v Grimsby T	5-0
Rochdale v Bury	1-1, 2-3
Burnley v Stoke C	1-0
Everton v Aldershot	4-1
Chelsea v Wigan Ath	0-1
Carlisle Utd v Bradford C	3-2
Wrexham v Charlton Ath	6-0
Bristol C v Derby Co	6-2
Preston NE v Ipswich T	0-3
Newcastle Utd v Chester	0-2
Millwall v Shrewsbury T	5-1
Blackburn R v Fulham	1-1, 1-0
Oldham Ath v Coventry C	0-1
Chesham Utd v Cambridge Utd	0-2
Bristol R v Aston Villa	1-2
Swansea C v Crystal Palace	2-2, 3-3, 2-1
Reading v Colchester Utd	2-0
Altrincham v Orient	1-1, 1-2
West Bromwich A v WEST HAM UTD	1-1, 1-2

Fourth Round

ARSENAL v Brighton & HA	2-0
Bolton W v Halifax T	2-0
Wolves v Norwich C	1-1, 3-2
Watford v Harlow T	4-3
Swindon T v Tottenham H	0-0, 1-2
Birmingham C v Middlesbrough	2-1
Nottingham F v Liverpool	0-2
Bury v Burnley	1-0
Everton v Wigan Ath	3-0
Carlisle Utd v Wrexham	0-0, 1-3
Bristol C v Ipswich T	1-2
Chester v Millwall	2-0
Blackburn R v Coventry C	1-0
Cambridge Utd v Aston Villa	1-1, 1-4
Swansea C v Reading	4-1
Orient v WEST HAM UTD	2-3

Fifth Round

Bolton W v ARSENAL	1-1, 0-3
Wolves v Watford	0-3
Tottenham H v Birmingham C	3-1
Liverpool v Bury	2-0
Everton v Wrexham	5-2
Ipswich T v Chester	2-1
Blackburn R v Aston Villa	1-1, 0-1
WEST HAM UTD v Swansea C	2-0

Sixth Round

Watford v ARSENAL	1-2
Tottenham H v Liverpool	0-1
Everton v Ipswich T	2-1
WEST HAM UTD v Aston Villa	1-0

Semi-final

ARSENAL v Liverpool	0-0, 1-1, 1-1, 1-0
Everton v WEST HAM UTD	1-1, 1-2

FINAL (Wembley Stadium)

WEST HAM UNITED	1
ARSENAL	0

Trevor Brooking celebrates a rare headed goal, the winner against Arsenal in the 1980 Final.

West Ham United: Parkes; Stewart, Lampard, Bonds, Martin, Devonshire, Pike, Brooking, Cross, Pearson, Allen.
Goalscorer: Brooking
Arsenal: Jennings; Rice, Devine(Nelson), Talbot, O'Leary, Young, Price, Rix, Brady, Stapleton, Sunderland.
Referee: G.Courtney (Spennymoor)
Attendance: 100,000

1980-81

First Round

Addlestone v Brentford	2-2, 0-2
Barnet v Minehead	2-2, 2-1
Blyth Spartans v Burton Alb	2-1
Boston Utd v Rotherham Utd	0-4
Burnley v Scarborough	1-0
Burscough v Altrincham	1-2
Chester v Barnsley	1-2
Colchester Utd v Portsmouth	3-0
Darlington v Bury	0-2
Enfield v Wembley	3-0
Exeter C v Leatherhead	5-0
Fleetwood v Blackpool	0-4
Gillingham v Dagenham	2-1
Gravesend v St Albans	1-2
Harlow v Charlton Ath	0-2
Hull C v Halifax T	2-1
Kettering T v Maidstone Utd	1-1, 0-0, 1-3
Kidderminster H v Millwall	1-1, 0-1
Lincoln C v Gateshead	1-0
Mansfield T v Rochdale	3-1
Mossley v Crewe Alex	1-0
Northampton T v Peterborough Utd	1-4
Northwich Vic v Huddersfield T	1-1, 0-6
Oxford U v Aldershot	1-0
Plymouth Arg v Newport Co	2-0
Port Vale v Bradford C	4-2
Reading v Fulham	1-2
Scunthorpe Utd v Hartlepool Utd	3-1
Southend Utd v Hereford Utd	0-1
Stockport Co v Sheffield Utd	0-0, 2-3
Sutton Coldfield v Doncaster R	0-2
Swindon T v Weymouth	3-2
Torquay Utd v Barton R	2-0
Tranmere R v York C	0-0, 2-1
Walsall v Stafford Rgrs	3-0
Wigan Ath v Chesterfield	2-2, 0-2
Wimbledon v Windsor	7-2
Workington v Carlisle Utd	0-0, 1-4
Wycombe W v AFC Bournemouth	0-3
Yeovil T v Farnborough	2-1

Second Round

Barnet v Peterborough Utd	0-1
Burnley v Port Vale	1-1, 0-2
Bury v Lincoln C	2-0
Charlton Ath v AFC Bournemouth	2-1
Colchester Utd v Yeovil T	1-1, 2-0
Doncaster R v Blackpool	2-1
Enfield v Hereford Utd	2-0
Fulham v Brentford	1-0
Gillingham v Maidstone Utd	0-0, 0-0, 0-2
Hull C v Blyth Spartans	1-1, 2-2, 2-1
Millwall v Exeter C	0-1
Mossley v Mansfield T	1-3
Plymouth Arg v Oxford Utd	3-0
Rotherham Utd v Barnsley	0-1
St Albans v Torquay Utd	1-1, 1-4
Scunthorpe Utd v Altrincham	0-0, 0-1
Sheffield Utd v Chesterfield	1-1, 0-1
Tranmere R v Huddersfield T	0-3
Wimbledon v Swindon T	2-0
Carlisle Utd v Walsall	3-0

Third Round

Queen's Park R v TOTTENHAM H	0-0, 1-3
Hull C v Doncaster R	1-0
Leeds Utd v Coventry C	1-1, 0-1
Birmingham C v Sunderland	1-1, 2-1
Newcastle Utd v Sheffield Wed	2-1
Orient v Luton T	1-3
Leicester C v Cardiff C	3-0
Maidstone Utd v Exeter C	2-4
Swansea C v Middlesbrough	0-5
West Bromwich A v Grimsby T	3-0
Barnsley v Torquay Utd	2-1
Port Vale v Enfield	1-1, 0-3
Colchester Utd v Watford	0-1
Stoke C v Wolves	2-2, 1-2
West Ham Utd v Wrexham	1-1, 0-0, 0-1
Wimbledon v Oldham Ath	0-0, 1-0
Southampton v Chelsea	3-1
Preston NE v Bristol R	3-4
Everton v Arsenal	2-0
Liverpool v Altrincham	4-1
Notts Co v Blackburn R	2-1
Peterborough Utd v Chesterfield	1-1, 2-1
MANCHESTER C v Crystal Palace	4-0
Norwich C v Cambridge U	1-0
Nottingham F v Bolton W	3-3, 1-0
Manchester Utd v Brighton & HA	2-2, 2-0
Mansfield T v Carlisle Utd	2-2, 1-2
Derby Co v Bristol C	0-0, 0-2
Huddersfield T v Shrewsbury T	0-3
Ipswich T v Aston Villa	1-0
Bury v Fulham	1-1, 0-0, 0-1
Plymouth Arg v Charlton Ath	1-2

Fourth Round

TOTTENHAM H v Hull C	2-0
Coventry C v Birmingham C	3-2
Newcastle Utd v Luton T	2-1
Leicester C v Exeter C	1-1, 1-3
Middlesbrough v West Bromwich A	1-0
Barnsley v Enfield	1-1, 3-0
Watford v Wolves	1-1, 1-2
Wrexham v Wimbledon	2-1
Southampton v Bristol R	3-1
Everton v Liverpool	2-1
Notts Co v Peterborough Utd	0-1
MANCHESTER C v Norwich C	6-0
Nottingham F v Manchester Utd	1-0
Carlisle Utd v Bristol C	1-1, 0-5
Shrewsbury T v Ipswich T	0-0, 0-3
Fulham v Charlton Ath	1-2

Fifth Round

TOTTENHAM H v Coventry C	3-1
Newcastle Utd v Exeter C	1-1, 0-4
Middlesbrough v Barnsley	2-1
Wolves v Wrexham	3-1

Spurs' Ricky Villa scores a stunning individual Wembley goal in the 1981 replay against Manchester City.

Southampton v Everton 0-0, 0-1
Peterborough Utd v MANCHESTER C 0-1
Nottingham F v Bristol C 2-1
Ipswich T v Charlton Ath 2-0

Sixth Round
TOTTENHAM H v Exeter C 2-0
Middlesbrough v Wolves 1-1, 1-3
Everton v MANCHESTER C 2-2, 1-3
Nottingham F v Ipswich T 3-3, 0-1

Semi-final
TOTTENHAM H v Wolves 2-2, 3-0
MANCHESTER C v Ipswich T 1-0

FINAL (Wembley Stadium)
TOTTENHAM HOTSPUR 3
MANCHESTER CITY 2
(following a 1-1 draw after extra-time)
Tottenham Hotspur: Aleksic; Hughton, Miller, Roberts, Perryman, Villa, Ardiles, Archibald, Galvin, Hoddle, Crooks. (Brooke replaced Villa in the first game)
Goalscorers: Villa 2, Crooks
Manchester City: Corrigan; Ranson, McDonald(Tueart), Caton, Reid, Gow, Power, MacKenzie, Reeves, Bennett, Hutchison. (Henry replaced Hutchison in the first game)
Goalscorers: MacKenzie, Reeves (pen)
Referee: K.Hackett (Sheffield) *Attendance: 92,000*

The first game was played at Wembley Stadium in front of 100,000 spectators when Hutchison scored for both sides.

1981-82

First Round
Aldershot v Leytonstone & Ilford 2-0
Bedford T v Wimbledon 0-2
Bideford v Barking 1-2
Bishop Auckland v Nuneaton Bor 4-1
Bishop's Stortford v Sutton Utd 2-2, 1-2
Blyth Spartans v Walsall 1-2
Boston Utd v Kettering T 0-1
AFC Bournemouth v Reading 1-0
Brentford v Exeter C 2-0
Bristol C v Torquay Utd 0-0, 2-1
Bristol R v Fulham 1-2
Burnley v Runcorn 0-0, 2-1
Chesterfield v Preston NE 4-1
Colchester Utd v Newport Co 2-0
Dagenham v Yeovil T 2-2, 1-0
Darlington v Carlisle Utd 2-2, 1-3
Dorchester v Minehead 3-3, 4-0
Dover v Oxford Utd 0-2
Enfield v Hastings 2-0
Halifax T v Peterborough Utd 0-3
Harlow v Barnet 0-0, 0-1
Hendon v Wycombe W 1-1, 0-2
Hereford Utd v Southend Utd 3-1
Horden CW v Blackpool 0-1
Lincoln C v Port Vale 2-2, 0-0, 0-2
Mansfield T v Doncaster R 0-1
Penrith v Chester 1-0
Plymouth Arg v Gillingham 0-0, 0-1
Portsmouth v Millwall 1-1, 2-3
Rochdale v Hull C 2-2, 2-2, 0-1
Scunthorpe Utd v Bradford C 1-0
Sheffield Utd v Altrincham 2-2, 0-3
Stafford Rgrs v York C 1-2
Stockport Co v Mossley 3-1
Swindon T v Taunton 2-1
Tranmere R v Bury 1-1, 1-3
Weymouth v Northampton T 0-0, 2-6
Wigan Ath v Hartlepool Utd 2-2, 0-1
Willenhall v Crewe Alex 0-1
Workington v Huddersfield T 1-1, 0-5

Second Round
Aldershot v Oxford Utd 2-2, 2-4
Barnet v Wycombe W 2-0
Brentford v Colchester Utd 1-1, 0-1
Bristol C v Northampton T 3-0
Bury v Burnley 1-1, 1-2
Carlisle Utd v Bishop Auckland 1-0
Chesterfield v Huddersfield T 0-1
Crewe Alex v Scunthorpe Utd 1-3
Dagenham v Millwall 1-2
Doncaster R v Penrith 3-0
Dorchester v AFC Bournemouth 1-1, 1-2
Enfield v Wimbledon 4-1
Gillingham v Barking 1-1, 3-1
Hereford Utd v Fulham 1-0
Hull C v Hartlepool Utd 2-0
Kettering T v Blackpool 0-3
Peterborough Utd v Walsall 2-1
Port Vale v Stockport Co 4-1
Swindon T v Sutton 2-1
York C v Altrincham 0-0, 3-4

Third Round
Barnsley v Blackpool 0-2
QUEEN'S PARK R v Middlesbrough 1-1, 3-2
Newcastle Utd v Colchester Utd 1-1, 4-3
Millwall v Grimsby T 1-6
Enfield v Crystal Palace 2-3
Bolton W v Derby Co 3-1
Carlisle Utd v Huddersfield T 2-3
Orient v Charlton Ath 1-0
Gillingham v Oldham Ath 2-1
West Bromwich A v Blackburn R 3-2
Stoke C v Norwich C 0-1
Doncaster R v Cambridge Utd 2-1
Manchester C v Cardiff C 3-1
Coventry C v Sheffield Wed 3-1
Barnet v Brighton & HA 0-0, 1-3
AFC Bournemouth v Oxford Utd 0-2
Chelsea v Hull C 0-0, 2-0
Nottingham F v Wrexham 1-3
Rotherham Utd v Sunderland 1-1, 0-1
Swansea C v Liverpool 0-4
TOTTENHAM H v Arsenal 1-0
Wolves v Leeds Utd 1-3
Peterborough Utd v Bristol C 0-1
Notts Co v Aston Villa 0-6
Scunthorpe Utd v Hereford Utd 1-1, 1-4
Leicester C v Southampton 3-1
Watford v Manchester Utd 1-0
West Ham Utd v Everton 2-1
Shrewsbury T v Port Vale 1-0
Burnley v Altrincham 6-1
Luton T v Swindon T 2-1
Birmingham C v Ipswich T 2-3

Fourth Round
Blackpool v QUEEN'S PARK R 0-0, 1-5
Newcastle Utd v Grimsby T 1-2
Crystal Palace v Bolton W 1-0
Huddersfield T v Orient 1-1, 0-2
Gillingham v West Bromwich A 0-1
Norwich C v Doncaster R 2-1
Manchester C v Coventry C 1-3
Brighton & HA v Oxford Utd 0-3
Chelsea v Wrexham 0-0, 1-1, 2-1
Sunderland v Liverpool 0-3
TOTTENHAM H v Leeds Utd 1-0
Bristol C v Aston Villa 0-1
Hereford Utd v Leicester C 0-1
Watford v West Ham Utd 2-0
Shrewsbury T v Burnley 1-0
Luton T v Ipswich T 0-3

Fifth Round
QUEEN'S PARK R v Grimsby T 3-1
Crystal Palace v Orient 0-0, 1-0
West Bromwich A v Norwich C 1-0
Coventry C v Oxford Utd 4-0
Chelsea v Liverpool 2-0
TOTTENHAM H v Aston Villa 1-0
Leicester C v Watford 2-0
Shrewsbury T v Ipswich T 2-1

Sixth Round
QUEEN'S PARK R v Crystal Palace 1-0
West Bromwich A v Coventry C 2-0
Chelsea v TOTTENHAM H 2-3
Leicester C v Shrewsbury T 5-2

Semi-final
QUEEN'S PARK R v West Bromwich A 1-0
TOTTENHAM H v Leicester C 2-0

FINAL (Wembley Stadium)
TOTTENHAM HOTSPUR 1
QUEEN'S PARK RANGERS 0
(following a 1-1 draw after extra-time)
Tottenham Hotspur: Clemence; Hughton, Miller, Price, Hazard(Brooke), Perryman, Roberts, Archibald, Galvin, Hoddle, Crooks.
Goalscorer: Hoddle (pen)
Queen's Park Rangers: Hucker; Fenwick, Gillard, Waddock, Hazell, Neill, Currie, Flanagan, Micklewhite(Burke), Stainrod, Gregory. (Roeder played in place of Neill, Allen in place of Micklewhite who replaced Allen in the first game)
Referee: C.White (Harrow) *Attendance: 90,000*

The first game was played at Wembley Stadium in front of 100,000 spectators. Hoddle scored for Tottenham and Fenwick for Queen's Park Rangers.

Another replay for Tottenham and Glenn Hoddle scores from the penalty-spot against QPR in 1982.

1982-83

First Round

Aldershot v Wimborne 4-0
Altrincham v Rochdale 2-1
Blackpool v Horwich RMI 3-0
Boston Utd v Crewe Alex 3-1
AFC Bournemouth v Southend Utd 0-2
Bristol R v Wycombe W 1-0
Carshalton v Barnet 4-0
Chesham v Yeovil T 0-1
Chester v Northwich Vic 1-1, 1-3
Chesterfield v Peterborough Utd 2-2, 1-2
Colchester Utd v Torquay Utd 0-2
Darlington v Scunthorpe Utd 0-1
Enfield v Newport Co 0-0, 2-4
Gillingham v Dagenham 1-0
Halifax T v North Shields 0-1
Hartlepool Utd v Lincoln C 3-0
Holbeach v Wrexham 0-4
Huddersfield T v Mossley 1-0
Hull C v Sheffield Utd 1-1, 0-2
Macclesfield T v Worcester C 1-5
Mansfield T v Stockport Co 3-2
Northampton T v Wimbledon 2-2, 2-0
Orient v Bristol C 4-1
Oxford Utd v Folkestone 5-2
Plymouth Arg v Exeter C 2-0
Portsmouth v Hereford Utd 4-1
Port Vale v Bradford C 0-1
Preston NE v Shepshed Charterhouse 5-1
Reading v Bishop's Stortford 1-2
Slough v Millwall 1-0
Swindon T v Wealdstone 2-0
Tranmere R v Scarborough 4-2
Walsall v Kettering T 3-0
Weymouth v Maidstone Utd 4-3
Wigan Ath v Telford Utd 0-0, 1-2
Windsor & Eton v Brentford 0-7
Wokingham v Cardiff C 1-1, 0-3
Workington v Doncaster R 1-2
Worthing v Dartford 2-1
York C v Bury 3-1

Second Round

Altrincham v Huddersfield T 0-1
Boston Utd v Sheffield Utd 1-1, 1-5
Bristol R v Plymouth Arg 2-2, 0-1
Cardiff C v Weymouth 2-3
Gillingham v Northampton T 1-1, 2-3
Hartlepool Utd v York C 1-1, 0-4
Mansfield T v Bradford C 1-1, 2-3
Newport Co v Orient 1-0
North Shields v Walsall 0-3
Oxford Utd v Worthing 4-0
Peterborough Utd v Doncaster R 5-2
Portsmouth v Aldershot 1-3
Preston NE v Blackpool 2-1
Scunthorpe Utd v Northwich Vic 2-1
Slough v Bishop's Stortford 1-4
Southend Utd v Yeovil T 3-0
Swindon T v Brentford 2-2, 3-1
Telford Utd v Tranmere R 1-1, 1-2
Torquay Utd v Carshalton 4-1
Worcester C v Wrexham 2-1

Third Round

Derby Co v Nottingham F 2-0
Huddersfield T v Chelsea 1-1, 0-2
Luton T v Peterborough Utd 3-0
MANCHESTER UTD v West Ham Utd 2-0
Newport Co v Everton 1-1, 1-2
Shrewsbury T v Rotherham Utd 2-1
Tottenham H v Southampton 1-0
West Bromwich A v Queen's Park R 3-2
Middlesbrough v Bishop's Stortford 2-2, 2-1
Leicester C v Notts Co 2-3
Arsenal v Bolton W 2-1
Leeds Utd v Preston NE 3-0
Northampton T v Aston Villa 0-1
Tranmere R v Wolves 0-1
Watford v Plymouth Arg 2-0
Oldham Ath v Fulham 0-2
Crystal Palace v York C 2-1
Walsall v Birmingham C 0-0, 0-1
Carlisle Utd v Burnley 2-2, 1-3
Swindon T v Aldershot 7-0
Cambridge Utd v Weymouth 1-0
Bradford C v Barnsley 0-1
Oxford Utd v Torquay Utd 1-1, 1-2
Southend Utd v Sheffield Wed 0-0, 2-2, 1-2
Blackburn R v Liverpool 1-2
Sheffield Utd v Stoke C 0-0, 2-3
BRIGHTON & HA v Newcastle Utd 1-1, 1-0
Sunderland v Manchester C 0-0, 1-2
Coventry C v Worcester C 3-1
Norwich C v Swansea C 2-1
Charlton Ath v Ipswich T 2-3
Scunthorpe Utd v Grimsby T 0-0, 0-2

Fourth Round

Derby Co v Chelsea 2-1
Luton T v MANCHESTER UTD 0-2
Everton v Shrewsbury T 2-1
Tottenham H v West Bromwich A 2-1
Middlesbrough v Notts Co 2-0
Arsenal v Leeds Utd 1-1, 1-1, 2-1
Aston Villa v Wolves 1-0
Watford v Fulham 1-1, 2-1
Crystal Palace v Birmingham C 1-0
Burnley v Swindon T 3-1
Cambridge Utd v Barnsley 1-0
Torquay Utd v Sheffield Wed 2-3
Liverpool v Stoke C 2-0
BRIGHTON & HA v Manchester C 4-0
Coventry C v Norwich C 2-2, 1-2
Ipswich T v Grimsby T 2-0

Fifth Round

Derby Co v MANCHESTER UTD 0-1
Everton v Tottenham H 2-0
Middlesbrough v Arsenal 1-1, 2-3
Aston Villa v Watford 4-1
Crystal Palace v Burnley 0-0, 0-1
Cambridge Utd v Sheffield Wed 1-2
Liverpool v BRIGHTON & HA 1-2
Norwich C v Ipswich T 1-0

Sixth Round

MANCHESTER UTD v Everton 1-0
Arsenal v Aston Villa 2-0
Burnley v Sheffield Wed 1-1, 0-5
BRIGHTON & HA v Norwich C 1-0

Semi-final

MANCHESTER UTD v Arsenal 2-1
Sheffield Wed v BRIGHTON & HA 1-2

FINAL (Wembley Stadium)

MANCHESTER UNITED 4
BRIGHTON & HOVE ALBION 0
(following a 2-2 draw after extra-time)

Manchester United: Bailey; Duxbury, Albiston, Wilkins, Moran, McQueen, Robson, Muhren, Stapleton, Whiteside, Davies.
(Changes from the first game were only positional)
Goalscorers: Robson 2, Whiteside, Muhren (pen)
Brighton & Hove Albion: Moseley; Gatting, Pearce, Grealish, Foster, Stevens, Case, Howlett, Robinson, Smith, Smillie. (Ramsey, who was substituted by Ryan, played in place of Foster in the first game with some positional changes)
Referee: A.W.Grey (Great Yarmouth)
Attendance: 92,000

The first game was played at Wembley Stadium in front of 100,000 spectators. Smith and Stevens scored for Brighton with Stapleton and Wilkins for Manchester United.

Manchester United are all smiles after their replay victory over Brighton in 1983.

1983-84

First Round

Aldershot v Worcester C 1-1, 1-2
AP Leamington v Gillingham 0-1
Barking v Farnborough T 2-1
Barnet v Bristol R 0-0, 1-3
Boston Utd v Bury 0-3
AFC Bournemouth v Walsall 4-0
Bradford C v Wigan Ath 0-0, 2-4
Burton A v Windsor 1-2
Chelmsford v Wycombe W 0-0, 2-1
Chester C v Chesterfield 1-2
Corinthian Casuals v Bristol C 0-0, 0-4
Dagenham v Brentford 2-2, 1-2
Darlington v Mossley 5-0
Exeter C v Maidstone Utd 1-1, 1-2
Frickley Ath v Altrincham 0-1
Gainsborough Tr v Blackpool 0-2
Halifax T v Whitby 2-3
Hyde v Burnley 0-2
Kettering T v Swindon T 0-7
Macclesfield T v York C 0-0, 0-2
Mansfield T v Doncaster R 3-0
Millwall v Dartford 2-1
Northampton T v Waterlooville 1-1, 1-1, 2-0
Northwich Vic v Bangor C 1-1, 0-1
Oxford Utd v Peterborough Utd 2-0
Penrith v Hull C 0-2
Poole T v Newport Co 0-0, 1-3
Port Vale v Lincoln C 1-2
Reading v Hereford Utd 2-0
Rochdale v Crew Alex 1-0
Rotherham Utd v Harlepool Utd 0-0, 1-0
Scunthorpe Utd v Preston NE 1-0
Southend Utd v Plymouth Arg 0-0, 0-2
Telford Utd v Stockport Co 3-0
Torquay Utd v Colchester Utd 1-2
Tranmere R v Bolton W 2-2, 1-4
Wealdstone v Enfield 1-1, 2-2, 2-0
Wimbledon v Orient 2-1
Wrexham v Sheffield Utd 1-5
Yeovil T v Harrow 0-1

Second Round

Bangor C v Blackpool 1-1, 1-2
Bolton W v Mansfield T 2-0
Brentford v Wimbledon 3-2
Bristol R v Bristol C 1-2
Chesterfield v Burnley 2-2, 2-3
Colchester Utd v Wealdstone 4-0
Darlington v Altrincham 0-0, 2-0
Gillingham v Chelmsford 6-1
Harrow v Newport Co 1-3
Lincoln C v Sheffield Utd 0-0, 0-1
Maidstone Utd v Worcester C 3-2
Millwall v Swindon T 2-3
Northampton T v Telford Utd 1-1, 2-3
Plymouth Arg v Barking 2-1
Reading v Oxford Utd 1-1, 0-3
Rotherham Utd v Hull C 2-1
Scunthorpe Utd v Bury 2-0
Wigan Ath v Whitby 1-0
Windsor v AFC Bournemouth 0-0, 0-2
York C v Rochdale 0-2

Third Round

Burnley v Oxford Utd 0-0, 1-2
Blackpool v Manchester C 2-1
Sheffield Wed v Barnsley 1-0
Coventry C v Wolves 1-1, 1-1, 3-0
Carlisle Utd v Swindon T 1-1, 1-3
Blackburn R v Chelsea 1-0
Portsmouth v Grimsby T 2-1
Nottingham F v Southampton 1-2
Huddersfield T v Queen's Park R 2-1
Notts Co v Bristol C 2-2, 2-0
Middlesbrough v Arsenal 3-2
AFC Bournemouth v Manchester Utd 2-0
Stoke C v EVERTON 0-2
Gillingham v Brentford 5-3
Shrewsbury T v Oldham Ath 3-0
Cardiff C v Ipswich T 0-3
Rotherham Utd v West Bromwich A 0-0, 0-3
Leeds Utd v Scunthorpe Utd 1-1, 1-1, 2-4
Plymouth Arg v Newport Co 2-2, 1-0
Darlington v Maidstone Utd 4-1
Cambridge Utd v Derby Co 0-3
Rochdale v Telford Utd 1-4
Fulham v Tottenham H 0-0, 0-2
Aston Villa v Norwich C 1-1, 0-3
Bolton W v Sunderland 0-3
Sheffield Utd v Birmingham C 1-1, 0-2
Crystal Palace v Leicester C 1-0
West Ham Utd v Wigan Ath 1-0
Colchester Utd v Charlton Ath 0-1
Luton T v WATFORD 2-2, 3-4
Brighton & HA v Swansea C 2-0
Liverpool v Newcastle Utd 4-0

Fourth Round
Oxford Utd v Blackpool 2-1
Sheffield Wed v Coventry C 3-2
Swindon T v Blackburn R 1-2
Portsmouth v Southampton 0-1
Huddersfield T v Notts Co 1-2
Middlesbrough v AFC Bournemouth 2-0
EVERTON v Gillingham 0-0, 0-0, 3-0
Shrewsbury T v Ipswich T 2-0
West Bromwich A v Scunthorpe Utd 1-0
Plymouth Arg v Darlington 2-1
Derby Co v Telford Utd 3-2
Tottenham H v Norwich C 0-0, 1-2
Sunderland v Birmingham C 1-2
Crystal Palace v West Ham Utd 1-1, 0-2
Charlton Ath v WATFORD 0-2
Brighton & HA v Liverpool 2-0

Fifth Round
Oxford Utd v Sheffield Wed 0-3
Blackburn R v Southampton 0-1
Notts Co v Middlesbrough 1-0
EVERTON v Shrewsbury T 3-0
West Bromwich A v Plymouth Arg 0-1
Derby Co v Norwich C 2-1
Birmingham C v West Ham Utd 3-0
WATFORD v Brighton & HA 3-1

Sixth Round
Sheffield Wed v Southampton 0-0, 1-5
Notts Co v EVERTON 1-2
Plymouth Arg v Derby Co 0-0, 1-0
Birmingham C v WATFORD 1-3

Semi-final
Southampton v EVERTON 0-1
Plymouth Arg v WATFORD 0-1

FINAL (Wembley Stadium)
EVERTON 2
WATFORD 0
Everton: Southall; Stevens, Bailey, Ratcliffe, Mouthfield, Reid, Steven, Heath, Sharp, Gray, Richardson.
Goalscorers: Sharp, Gray
Watford: Sherwood; Bardsley, Price(Atkinson), Taylor, Terry, Sinnott, Callaghan, Johnston, Reilly, Jackett, Barnes.
Referee: J.Hunting (Leicester) *Attendance: 100,000*

Everton's Kevin Ratcliffe led his side to victory over Watford in 1984.

1984-85

First Round
Bangor C v Tranmere R 1-1, 0-7
Barry v Reading 1-2
Blackpool v Altrincham 0-1
Bradford C v Tow Law 7-2
Brentford v Bishop's Stortford 4-0
Bristol R v King's Lynn 2-1
Buckingham v Orient 0-2
Burton A v Staines 2-0
Cambridge Utd v Peterborough Utd 0-2
Dagenham v Swindon T 0-0, 2-1
Darlington v Chester C 3-2
Exeter C v Enfield 2-2, 0-3
Fisher A v Bristol C 0-1
Frickley Ath v Stalybridge Cel 2-1
Gillingham v Windsor & Eton 2-1
Halifax T v Goole 2-0
Hartlepool Utd v Derby Co 2-1
Hereford Utd v Farnborough T 3-0
Hull C v Bolton W 2-1
Kettering T v AFC Bournemouth 0-0, 2-3
Lincoln C v Telford Utd 1-1, 1-2
Macclesfield T v Port Vale 1-2
Mansfield T v Rotherham Utd 2-1
Met Police v Dartford 0-3
Newport Co v Aldershot 1-1, 0-4
Northampton T v VS Rugby 2-2, 1-0
Northwich Vic v Crewe Alex 3-1
Nuneaton Bor v Scunthorpe Utd 1-1, 1-2
Penrith v Burnley 0-9
Preston NE v Bury 4-3
Plymouth Arg v Barnet 3-0
Rochdale v Doncaster R 1-2
Southend Utd v Colchester Utd 2-2, 2-3
Stockport Co v Walsall 1-2
Swansea C v Bognor 1-1, 1-3
Torquay Utd v Yeovil T 2-0
Weymouth v Millwall 0-3
Whitby v Chesterfield 1-3
Wrexham v Wigan Ath 0-2
York C v Blue Star 2-0

Second Round
Aldershot v Burton A 0-2
Altrincham v Doncaster R 1-3
Bradford C v Mansfield T 2-1
Brentford v Northampton T 2-2, 2-0
Bristol C v Bristol R 1-3
Burnley v Halifax T 3-1
Colchester Utd v Gillingham 0-5
Dagenham v Peterborough Utd 1-0
Darlington v Frickley Ath 1-0
Dartford v AFC Bournemouth 1-1, 1-4
Hartepool Utd v York C 0-2
Millwall v Enfield 1-0
Orient v Torquay Utd 3-0
Plymouth Arg v Hereford Utd 0-0, 0-2
Port Vale v Scunthorpe Utd 4-1
Preston NE v Telford Utd 1-4
Reading v Bognor 6-2
Tranmere R v Hull C 0-3
Walsall v Chesterfield 1-0
Wigan Ath v Northwich Vic 2-1

Third Round
Barnsley v Reading 4-3
Birmingham C v Norwich C 0-0, 1-1, 1-1, 0-1
Brighton & HA v Hull C 1-0
Bristol R v Ipswich T 1-2
Burton A v Leicester C‡ 0-1
Carlisle Utd v Dagenham 1-0
Chelsea v Wigan Ath 2-2, 5-0
Coventry C v Manchester C 2-1
Doncaster R v Queen's Park R 1-0
Fulham v Sheffield Wed 2-3
Gillingham v Cardiff C 2-1
Hereford Utd v Arsenal 1-1, 2-7
Leeds Utd v EVERTON 0-2
Liverpool v Aston Villa 3-0
Luton T v Stoke C 1-1, 3-2
MANCHESTER UTD v AFC Bournemouth 3-0
Middlesbrough v Darlington 0-0, 1-2
Millwall v Crystal Palace 1-1, 2-1
Nottingham F v Newcastle Utd 1-1, 3-1
Notts Co v Grimsby T 2-2, 2-4
Oldham Ath v Brentford 2-1
Orient v West Bromwich A 2-1
Portsmouth v Blackburn R 0-0,1-2
Shrewsbury T v Oxford Utd 0-2
Southampton v Sunderland 4-0
Telford Utd v Bradford C 2-1
Tottenham H v Charlton Ath 1-1, 2-1
Watford v Sheffield Utd 5-0
West Ham Utd v Port Vale 4-1
Wimbledon v Burnley 3-1
Wolves v Huddersfield T 1-1, 1-3
York C v Walsall 3-0

Fourth Round
Barnsley v Brighton & HA 2-1
Chelsea v Millwall 2-3
Darlington v Telford Utd 1-1, 0-3
EVERTON v Doncaster R 2-0
Grimsby T v Watford 1-3
Ipswich T v Gillingham 3-2
Leicester C v Carlisle Utd 1-0
Liverpool v Tottenham H 1-0
Luton T v Huddersfield T 2-0
MANCHESTER UTD v Coventry C 2-1
Nottingham F v Wimbledon 0-0, 0-1
Orient v Southampton 0-2
Oxford Utd v Blackburn R 0-1
Sheffield Wed v Oldham Ath 5-1
West Ham Utd v Norwich C 2-1
York C v Arsenal 1-0

Fifth Round
Blackburn R v MANCHESTER UTD 0-2
EVERTON v Telford Utd 3-0
Ipswich T v Sheffield Wed 3-2
Luton T v Watford 0-0, 2-2, 1-0
Millwall v Leicester C 2-0
Southampton v Barnsley 1-2
Wimbledon v West Ham Utd 1-1, 1-5
York C v Liverpool 1-1, 0-7

Sixth Round
Barnsley v Liverpool 0-4
EVERTON v Ipswich T 2-2, 1-0
Luton T v Millwall 1-0
MANCHESTER UTD v West Ham Utd 4-2

Semi-final
EVERTON v Luton T 2-1
Liverpool v MANCHESTER UTD 2-2, 1-2

FINAL (Wembley Stadium)
MANCHESTER UNITED 1
EVERTON 0
(after extra-time)
Manchester United: Bailey; Gidman, Albiston(Duxbury), Whiteside, McGrath, Moran, Robson, Strachan, Hughes, Stapleton, Olsen.
Goalscorer: Whiteside
Everton: Southall; Stevens, Van den Hauwe, Ratcliffe, Mountfield, Reid, Steven, Gray, Sharp, Bracewell, Sheedy.
Referee: P.N.Willis (Meadowfield) *Attendance: 100,000*

‡Leicester won the first game 6-1 at the Baseball Ground, Derby, but the FA ordered the game to be replayed behind closed doors at Highfield Road, Coventry.

Manchester United's Kevin Moran and Norman Whiteside (scorer of the only goal) after United's extra-time win over Everton in 1985.

1985-86

First Round

Bishop's Stortford v Peterborough Utd 2-2, 1-3
AFC Bournemouth v Dartford 0-0, 2-0
Brentford v Bristol R 1-3
Bury v Chester C 2-0
Chelmsford C v Weymouth 1-0
Chorley v Altrincham 0-2
Dagenham v Cambridge Utd 2-1
Derby Co v Crewe Alex 5-1
Enfield v Bognor Regis 0-2
Exeter C v Cardiff C 2-1
Fareham T v Maidstone Utd 0-3
Farnborough T v Bath C 0-4
Frickley Ath v Halesowen 1-1, 3-1
Gillingham v Northampton T 3-0
Halifax T v Scunthorpe Utd 1-3
Lincoln C v Blackpool 0-1
Macclesfield T v Hartlepool Utd 1-2
Mansfield T v Port Vale 1-1, 0-1
Notts Co v Scarborough 6-1
Nuneaton Bor v Burnley 2-3
Plymouth Arg v Aldershot 1-0
Reading v Wealdstone 1-0
Rochdale v Darlington 2-1
Rotherham Utd v Wolves 6-0
Runcorn v Boston Utd 2-2, 1-1, 4-1
Slouth T v Aylesbury 2-2, 5-2
Southend Utd v Newport Co 0-1
Stockport Co v Telford Utd 0-1
Swansea C v Leyton Wingate 2-0
Swindon T v Bristol C 0-0, 2-4
Tranmere R v Chesterfield 2-2, 1-0
VS Rugby v Orient 2-2, 1-4
Walsall v Preston NE 7-3
Whitby T v South Liverpool 1-0
Wigan Ath v Doncaster R 4-1
Windsor & Eton v Torquay Utd 1-1, 0-3
Wrexham v Bolton W 3-1
Wycombe W v Colchester Utd 2-0
Yeovil T v Hereford Utd 2-4
York C v Morecambe 0-0, 2-0

Second Round

Bristol C v Exeter C 1-2
AFC Bournemouth v Dagenham 4-1
Blackpool v Altrincham 1-2
Derby Co v Telford Utd 6-1
Gillingham v Bognor Regis 6-1
Hartlepool Utd v Frickley Ath 0-1
Newport Co v Torquay Utd 1-1, 3-2
Notts Co v Wrexham 2-2, 3-0
Orient v Slough T 2-2, 3-2
Peterborough Utd v Bath C 1-0
Plymouth Arg v Maidstone Utd 3-0
Port Vale v Walsall 0-0, 1-2
Reading v Hereford Utd 2-0
Rotherham Utd v Burnley 4-1
Runcorn v Wigan Ath 1-1, 0-4
Scunthorpe Utd v Rochdale 2-2, 1-2
Swansea C v Bristol R 1-2
Tranmere R v Bury 1-1, 1-2
Wycombe W v Chelmsford C 2-0
York C v Whitby T 3-1

Third Round

Birmingham C v Altrincham 1-2
Bristol R v Leicester C 3-1
Bury v Barnsley 2-0
Carlisle Utd v Queen's Park R 1-0
Charlton Ath v West Ham Utd 0-1
Coventry C v Watford 1-3
Crystal Palace v Luton T 1-2
EVERTON v Exeter C 1-0
Frickley Ath v Rotherham Utd 1-3
Gillingham v Derby Co 1-1, 1-3
Grimsby T v Arsenal 3-4
Huddersfield T v Reading 0-0, 1-2
Hull C v Plymouth Arg 2-2, 1-0
Ipswich T v Bradford C 4-4, 1-0
LIVERPOOL v Norwich C 5-0
Manchester Utd v Rochdale 2-0
Middlesbrough v Southampton 1-3
Millwall v Wimbledon 3-1
Newcastle Utd v Brighton & HA 0-2
Nottingham F v Blackburn R 1-1, 2-3
Oldham A v Orient 1-2
Oxford Utd v Tottenham H 1-1, 1-2
Peterborough Utd v Leeds Utd 1-0
Portsmouth v Aston Villa 2-2, 2-3
Sheffield Utd v Fulham 2-0
Sheffield Wed v West Bromwich A 2-2, 3-2
Shrewsbury T v Chelsea 0-1
Stoke C v Notts Co 0-2
Sunderland v Newport Co 2-0
Walsall v Manchester C 1-3
Wigan Ath v AFC Bournemouth 3-0
York C v Wycombe W 2-0

Fourth Round

Arsenal v Rotherham Utd 5-1
Aston Villa v Millwall 1-1, 0-1
Chelsea v LIVERPOOL 1-2
EVERTON v Blackburn R 3-1
Hull C v Brighton & HA 2-3
Luton T v Bristol R 4-0
Manchester C v Watford 1-1, 0-0, 1-3
Notts Co v Tottenham H 1-1, 0-5
Peterborough Utd v Carlisle Utd 1-0
Reading v Bury 1-1, 0-3
Sheffield Utd v Derby Co 0-1
Sheffield Wed v Orient 5-0
Sunderland v Manchester Utd 0-0, 0-3
Southampton v Wigan Ath 3-0
West Ham Utd v Ipswich T 0-0, 1-1, 1-0
York C v Altrincham 2-0

Fifth Round

Derby Co v Sheffield Wed 1-1, 0-2
Luton T v Arsenal 2-2, 0-0, 3-0
Peterborough Utd v Brighton & HA 2-2, 0-1
Southampton v Millwall 0-0, 1-0
Tottenham H v EVERTON 1-2
Watford v Bury 1-1, 3-0
West Ham Utd v Manchester Utd 1-1, 2-0
York C v LIVERPOOL 1-1, 1-3

Sixth Round

Brighton & HA v Southampton 0-2
LIVERPOOL v Watford 0-0, 2-1
Luton T v EVERTON 2-2, 0-1
Sheffield Wed v West Ham Utd 2-1

Semi-final

EVERTON v Sheffield W 2-1
LIVERPOOL v Southampton 2-0

FINAL (Wembley Stadium)

LIVERPOOL 3
EVERTON 1

Liverpool: Grobbelaar; Lawrenson, Beglin, Nicol, Whelan, Hansen, Dalglish, Johnston, Rush, Molby, MacDonald.
Goalscorers: Rush 2, Johnston
Everton: Mimms; Stevens(Heath), Van den Hauwe, Ratcliffe, Mountfield, Reid, Steven, Lineker, Sharp, Bracewell, Sheedy.
Goalscorer: Lineker
Referee: A.Robinson (Waterlooville)
Attendance: 98,000

Craig Johnston of Liverpool leaps high as Ian Rush joins in the celebrations. Liverpool won the Cup in 1986, beating Everton in the first all-Merseyside FA Cup Final.

1986-87

First Round

Aldershot v Torquay Utd 1-0
Bath C v Aylesbury 3-2
Bishop's Stortford v Colchester Utd 1-1, 0-2
AFC Bournemouth v Fareham T 7-2
Bristol C v VS Rugby 3-1
Bristol R v Brentford 0-0, 0-2
Bromsgrove v Newport Co 0-1
Caernarfon T v Stockport Co 1-0
Chester C v Rotherham Utd 1-1, 1-1, 1-0
Chorley v Wolves 1-1, 1-1, 3-0
Darlington v Mansfield T 2-1
Dartford v Enfield 1-1, 0-3
Exeter C v Cambridge Utd 1-1, 0-2
Farnborough T v Swindon T 0-4
Frickley Ath v Altrincham 0-0, 0-4
Halifax T v Bolton W 1-1, 1-1, 1-3
Hereford Utd v Fulham 3-3, 0-4
Kettering T v Gillingham 0-3
Middlesbrough v Blackpool 3-0
Northampton T v Peterborough Utd 3-0
Notts Co v Carlisle Utd 1-1, 3-0
Nuneaton Bor v Rochdale 0-3
Port Vale v Stafford Rgrs 1-0
Preston NE v Bury 5-1
Runcorn v Boston Utd 1-1, 2-1
Scunthorpe Utd v Southport 2-0
Slough T v Bognor T 1-1, 1-0
Southend Utd v Halesowen 4-1
Spennymoor v Tranmere R 2-3
Telford Utd v Burnley 3-0
Ton Pentre v Cardiff C 1-4
Walsall v Chesterfield 2-0
Wealdstone v Swansea C 1-1, 1-4
Welling Utd v Maidstone Utd 1-1, 1-4
Whitby v Doncaster R 2-2, 2-3
Wigan Ath v Lincoln C 3-1
Woking v Chelmsford 1-1, 1-2
Woodford V Orient 0-1
Wrexham v Hartlepool Utd 2-1
York C v Crewe Alex 3-1

Second Round

Aldershot v Colchester Utd 3-2
Bolton W v Tranmere R 2-0
AFC Bournemouth v Orient 0-1
Bristol C v Bath C 1-1, 3-0
Caernarfon T v York C 0-0, 2-1
Cardiff C v Brentford 2-0
Chester C v Doncaster R 3-1
Chorley v Preston NE 0-0, 0-5
Darlington v Wigan Ath 0-5
Fulham v Newport Co 2-0
Gillingham v Chelmsford 2-0
Maidstone Utd v Cambridge Utd 1-0
Notts Co v Middlesbrough 0-1
Rochdale v Wrexham 1-4
Scunthorpe Utd v Runcorn 1-0
Southend Utd v Northampton T 4-4, 2-3
Swansea C v Slough T 3-0
Swindon T v Enfield 3-0
Telford Utd v Altrincham 1-0
Walsall v Port Vale 5-0

Third Round

Aldershot v Oxford Utd 3-0
Aston Villa v Chelsea 2-2, 1-2
Bristol C v Plymouth Arg 1-1, 1-3
Caernarfon T v Barnsley 0-0, 0-1
Charlton Ath v Walsall 1-2
COVENTRY C v Bolton W 3-0
Crystal Palace v Nottingham F 1-0
Everton v Southampton 2-1
Fulham v Swindon T 0-1
Grimsby T v Stoke C 1-1, 1-1, 0-6
Ipswich T v Birmingham C 0-1
Luton T v Liverpool 0-0, 0-0, 3-0
Manchester Utd v Manchester C 1-0
Middlesbrough v Preston NE 0-1
Millwall v Cardiff C 0-0, 2-2, 0-1
Newcastle Utd v Northampton T 2-1
Norwich C v Huddersfield T 1-1, 4-2
Oldham Ath v Bradford C 1-1, 1-5
Orient v West Ham Utd 1-1, 1-4
Portsmouth v Blackburn R 2-0
Queen's Park R v Leicester C 5-2
Reading v Arsenal 1-3
Sheffield Utd v Brighton & HA 0-0, 2-1
Sheffield Wed v Derby Co 1-0
Shrewsbury T v Hull C 1-2
Swansea C v West Bromwich A 3-2
Telford Utd v Leeds Utd 1-2
TOTTENHAM H v Scunthorpe Utd 3-2
Watford v Maidstone Utd 3-1
Wigan Ath v Gillingham 2-1
Wimbledon v Sunderland 2-1
Wrexham v Chester C 1-2

Fourth Round

Aldershot v Barnsley 1-1, 0-3
Arsenal v Plymouth Arg 6-1
Bradford C v Everton 0-1
Chester C v Sheffield Wed 1-1, 1-3
Luton T v Queen's Park R 1-1, 1-2
Manchester Utd v COVENTRY C 0-1
Newcastle Utd v Preston NE 2-0
Stoke C v Cardiff C 2-1
Swansea C v Hull C 0-1
Swindon T v Leeds Utd 1-2
TOTTENHAM H v Crystal Palace 4-0
Walsall v Birmingham C 1-0

Coventry City, surprise winners over Tottenham Hotspur in the 1987 FA Cup Final.

Watford v Chelsea 1-0
West Ham Utd v Sheffield Utd 4-0
Wigan Ath v Norwich C 1-0
Wimbledon v Portsmouth 4-0

Fifth Round
Arsenal v Barnsley 2-0
Leeds Utd v Queen's Park R 2-1
Sheffield Wed v West Ham Utd 1-1, 2-0
Stoke C v COVENTRY C 0-1
TOTTENHAM H v Newcastle Utd 1-0
Walsall v Watford 1-1, 4-4, 0-1
Wigan Ath v Hull C 3-0
Wimbledon v Everton 3-1

Sixth Round
Arsenal v Watford 1-3
Sheffield Wed v COVENTRY C 0-3
Wigan Ath v Leeds Utd 0-2
Wimbledon v TOTTENHAM H 0-2

Semi-final
TOTTENHAM H v Watford 4-1
COVENTRY C v Leeds Utd 3-2

FINAL (Wembley Stadium)
COVENTRY CITY 3
TOTTENHAM HOTSPUR 2
(after extra-time)

Coventry City: Ogrizovic; Phillips, Downs, McGrath, Kilcline(Rodger), Peake, Bennett, Gynn, Regis, Houchen, Pickering. Sub: Sedgley.
Goalscorers: Bennett, Houchen, Mabbutt(og)
Tottenham Hotspur: Clemence; Hughton(Claesen), M.Thomas, Hodge, Gough, Mabbutt, C.Allen, P.Allen, Waddle, Hoddle, Ardiles(Stevens).
Goalscorers: C.Allen, Mabbutt
Referee: N.Midgley (Salford) Attendance: 98,000

1987-88

First Round
Altrincham v Wigan Ath 0-2
Barnet v Hereford Utd 0-1
Billingham v Halifax T 2-4
Bishop Auckland v Blackpool 1-4
Bognor v Torquay Utd 0-3
Brentford v Brighton & HA 0-2
Bristol C v Aylesbury 1-0
Bristol R v Merthyr Tydfil 6-0
Burnley v Bolton W 0-1
Cambridge Utd v Farnborough T 2-1
Chelmsford C v Bath C 1-2
Chester C v Runcorn 0-1
Chorley T v Hartlepool Utd 0-2
Colchester Utd v Tamworth 3-0
Dagenham v Maidstone Utd 0-2
Doncaster R v Rotherham Utd 1-1, 0-2
Gillingham v Fulham 2-1
Halesowen T v Kidderminster H 2-2, 0-4
Hayes v Swansea C 0-1
Leyton Orient v Exeter C 2-0
Lincoln C v Crewe Alex 2-1
Macclesfield T v Carlisle Utd 4-2
Northampton T v Newport Co 2-1
Northwich Vic v Colwyn Bay 1-0
Notts Co v Chesterfield 3-3, 1-0
Peterborough Utd v Cardiff C 2-1
Preston NE v Mansfield T 1-1, 2-4
Rochdale v Wrexham 0-2
Scarborough v Grimsby T 1-2
Scunthorpe Utd v Bury 3-1
Southend Utd v Walsall 0-0, 1-2
Sunderland v Darlington 2-0
Sutton Utd v Aldershot 3-0
Telford Utd v Stockport Co 1-1, 0-2
Tranmere R v Port Vale 2-2, 1-3
VS Rugby v Atherstone 0-0, 2-0
Welling v Carshalton 3-2
Wolves v Cheltenham T 5-1
Worcester C v Yeovil T 1-1, 0-1
York C v Burton A 0-0, 2-1

Second Round
Bristol C v Torquay Utd 0-1
Cambridge Utd v Yeovil T 0-1
Colchester Utd v Hereford Utd 3-2
Gillingham v Walsall 2-1
Grimsby T v Halifax T 0-0, 0-2
Leyton Orient v Swansea C 2-0
Macclesfield T v Rotherham Utd 4-0
Maidstone Utd v Kidderminster H 1-1, 2-2, 0-0, 2-1
Mansfield T v Lincoln C 4-3
Northampton T v Brighton & HA 1-2
Northwich Vic v Blackpool 0-2
Peterborough Utd v Sutton Utd 1-3
Port Vale v Notts Co 2-0
Runcorn v Stockport Co 0-1
Scunthorpe Utd v Sunderland 2-1
VS Rugby v Bristol R 1-1, 0-4
Welling v Bath 0-1
Wigan Ath v Wolves 1-3
Wrexham v Bolton W 1-2
York C v Hartlepool Utd 1-1, 1-3

Third Round
Stoke C v LIVERPOOL 0-0, 0-1
Leeds Utd v Aston Villa 1-2
Sutton Utd v Middlesbrough 1-1, 0-1
Sheffield Wed v Everton 1-1, 1-1, 1-1, 0-5
Plymouth Arg v Colchester Utd 2-0
Shrewsbury T v Bristol R 2-1
Scunthorpe Utd v Blackpool 0-0, 0-1
Huddersfield T v Manchester C 2-2, 0-0, 0-3
Arsenal v Millwall 2-0
Brighton & HA v AFC Bournemouth 2-0
Derby Co v Chelsea 1-3
Ipswich T v Manchester Utd 1-2
Gillingham v Birmingham C 0-3
Barnsley v Bolton W 3-1
Stockport Co v Leyton Orient 1-2
Halifax T v Nottingham F 0-4
Hartlepool Utd v Luton T 1-2
Reading v Southampton 0-1
West Ham Utd v Charlton Ath 2-0
Yeovil T v Queen's Park R 0-3
Bradford C v Wolves 2-1
Oxford Utd v Leicester C 2-0
Sheffield Utd v Maidstone Utd 1-0
Blackburn R v Portsmouth 1-2
Watford v Hull C 1-1, 2-2, 1-0
Coventry C v Torquay Utd 2-0
Oldham Ath v Tottenham H 2-4
Port Vale v Macclesfield T 1-0
Newcastle Utd v Crystal Palace 1-0
Swindon T v Norwich C 0-0, 2-0
Mansfield T v Bath C 4-0
WIMBLEDON v West Bromwich A 4-1

Fourth Round
Aston Villa v LIVERPOOL 0-2
Everton v Middlesbrough 1-1, 2-2, 2-1
Plymouth Arg v Shrewsbury T 1-0
Blackpool v Manchester C 1-1, 1-2
Brighton & HA v Arsenal 1-2
Manchester Utd v Chelsea 2-0
Barnsley v Birmingham C 0-2
Leyton Orient v Nottingham F 1-2
Luton T v Southampton 2-1
Queen's Park R v West Ham Utd 3-1
Bradford C v Oxford Utd 4-2
Portsmouth v Sheffield Utd 2-1
Coventry C v Watford 0-1
Port Vale v Tottenham H 2-1
Newcastle Utd v Swindon T 5-0
Mansfield T v WIMBLEDON 1-2

Fifth Round
Everton v LIVERPOOL 0-1
Manchester C v Plymouth Arg 3-1
Arsenal v Manchester Utd 2-1
Birmingham C v Nottingham F 0-1
Queen's Park R v Luton T 1-1, 0-1
Portsmouth v Bradford C 3-0
Port Vale v Watford 0-0, 0-2
Newcastle Utd v WIMBLEDON 1-3

Sixth Round
Manchester C v LIVERPOOL 0-4
Arsenal v Nottingham F 1-2
Luton T v Portsmouth 3-1
WIMBLEDON v Watford 2-1

Semi-final
LIVERPOOL v Nottingham F 2-1
Luton T v WIMBLEDON 1-2

FINAL (Wembley Stadium)
WIMBLEDON 1
LIVERPOOL 0

Wimbledon: Beasant; Goodyear, Phelan, Jones, Young, Thorn, Gibson(Scales), Cork(Cunningham), Fashanu, Sanchez, Wise.
Goalscorer: Sanchez
Liverpool: Grobbelaar; Gillespie, Ablett, Nicol, Spackman(Molby), Hansen, Beardsley, Aldridge(Johnston), Houghton, Barnes, McMahon.
Referee: B.Hill (Kettering) Attendance: 98,203

Dave Beasant dives to save John Aldridge's penalty in the 1988 Final. Wimbledon, a Southern League club until quite recently, were about to complete a fairy-tale victory.

1988-89

First Round
Aldershot v Hayes 1-0
Altrincham v Lincoln C 3-2
Bath C v Grays Ath 2-0
Blackpool v Scunthorpe Utd 2-1
Bognor Regis T v Exeter C 2-1
Bolton W v Chesterfield 0-0, 3-2
Brentford v Halesowen T 2-0
Bristol C v Southend Utd 3-1
Bristol R v Fisher Ath 3-0
Burnley v Chester C 0-2
Cardiff C v Hereford Utd 3-0
Dagenham v Sutton Utd 0-4
Darlington v Notts Co 1-2
Doncaster R v Brandon Utd 0-0, 2-1
Enfield v Leyton Orient 1-1, 2-2, 1-0
Frickley Ath v Northwich Vic 0-2
Fulham v Colchester Utd 0-1
Gillingham v Peterborough Utd 3-3, 0-1
Grimsby T v Wolves 1-0
Guisborough T v Bury 0-1
Halifax T v York C 1-0
Hartlepool Utd v Wigan Ath 2-0
Huddersfield T v Rochdale 1-1, 4-3
Kettering T v Dartford 2-1
Mansfield T v Sheffield Utd 1-1, 1-2
Newport Co v Maidstone Utd 1-2
Preston NE v Tranmere R 1-1, 0-3
Reading v Hendon 4-2
Rotherham Utd v Barrow 3-1
Runcorn v Wrexham 2-2, 3-2
Scarborough v Stockport Co 2-1
Southport v Port Vale 0-2
Stafford Rgrs v Crew Alex 2-2, 2-3
Swansea C v Northampton T 3-1
Telford Utd v Carlisle Utd 1-1, 1-4
Torquay Utd v Fareham T 2-2, 3-2
Waterlooville v Aylesbury Utd 1-4
Welling Utd v Bromsgrove R 3-0
Woking v Cambridge Utd 1-4
Yeovil T v Merthyr Tydfil 3-2

Second Round
Aldershot v Bristol C 1-1, 0-0, 2-2, 0-1
Altrincham v Halifax T 0-3
Aylesbury Utd v Sutton Utd 0-1
Bath C v Welling Utd 0-0, 2-3
Blackpool v Bury 3-0
Bognor Regis T v Cambridge Utd 0-1
Bolton W v Port Vale 1-2
Colchester Utd v Swansea C 2-2, 3-1
Doncaster R v Sheffield Utd 1-3
Enfield v Cardiff C 1-4
Grimsby T v Rotherham Utd 3-2
Hartlepool Utd v Notts Co 1-0
Huddersfield T v Chester C 1-0
Kettering T v Bristol R 2-1
Northwich Vic v Tranmere R 1-2
Peterborough Utd v Brentford 0-0, 2-3
Reading v Maidstone Utd 1-1, 2-1
Runcorn v Crewe Alex 0-3
Scarborough v Carlisle Utd 0-1
Yeovil T v Torquay Utd 1-1, 0-1

Third Round
West Bromwich A v EVERTON 1-1, 0-1
Plymouth Arg v Cambridge Utd 2-0
Stoke C v Crystal Palace 1-0
Barnsley v Chelsea 4-0
Crewe Alex v Aston Villa 2-3
Birmingham C v Wimbledon 0-1
Middlesbrough v Grimsby T 1-2
Tranmere R v Reading 1-1, 1-2
Port Vale v Norwich C 1-3
Sutton Utd v Coventry C 2-1
Shrewsbury T v Colchester Utd 0-3
Huddersfield T v Sheffield Utd 0-1
Charlton Ath v Oldham Ath 2-1
Kettering T v Halifax T 1-1, 3-2
Portsmouth v Swindon T 1-1, 0-2
West Ham Utd v Arsenal 2-2, 1-0
Nottingham F v Ipswich T 3-0
Brighton & HA v Leeds Utd 1-2
Derby Co v Southampton 1-1, 2-1
Newcastle Utd v Watford 0-0, 2-2, 0-0, 0-1
Sunderland v Oxford Utd 1-1, 0-2
Manchester Utd v Queen's Park R 0-0, 2-2, 3-0
Harltepool Utd v Bristol C 1-0
Blackpool v AFC Bournemouth 0-1
Walsall v Brentford 1-1, 0-1
Manchester C v Leicester C 1-0
Sheffield Wed v Torquay Utd 5-1
Welling Utd v Blackburn R 0-1
Cardiff C v Hull 1-2
Bradford C v Tottenham H 1-0
Millwall v Luton T 3-2
Carlisle Utd v LIVERPOOL 0-3

The Princess of Wales meets the Liverpool players before the 1989 FA Cup Final, yet another all-Merseyside affair.

Fourth Round
Plymouth Arg v EVERTON 1-1, 0-4
Stoke C v Barnsley 3-3, 1-2
Aston Villa v Wimbledon 0-1
Grimsby T v Reading 1-1, 2-1
Norwich C v Sutton Utd 8-0
Sheffield Utd v Colchester Utd 3-3, 2-0
Charlton Ath v Kettering T 2-1
Swindon T v West Ham Utd 0-0, 0-1
Nottingham F v Leeds Utd 2-0
Watford v Derby Co 2-1
Manchester Utd v Oxford Utd 4-0
Hartlepool Utd v AFC Bournemouth 1-1, 2-5
Brentford v Manchester C 3-1
Blackburn R v Sheffield Wed 2-1
Bradford C v Hull C 1-2
Millwall v LIVERPOOL 0-2

Fifth Round
Barnsley v EVERTON 0-1
Wimbledon v Grimsby T 3-1
Norwich C v Sheffield Utd 3-2
Charlton Ath v West Ham Utd 0-1
Watford v Nottingham F 0-3
AFC Bournemouth v Manchester Utd 1-1, 0-1
Blackburn R v Brentford 0-2
Hull C v LIVERPOOL 2-3

Sixth Round
EVERTON v Wimbledon 1-0
West Ham Utd v Norwich C 0-0, 1-3
Manchester Utd v Nottingham F 0-1
LIVERPOOL v Brentford 4-0

Semi-final
EVERTON v Norwich C 1-0
Nottingham F v LIVERPOOL *0-0, 1-3

FINAL (Wembley Stadium)
LIVERPOOL 3
EVERTON 2
(after extra-time)

Liverpool: Grobbelaar; Ablett, Staunton(Venison), Nicol, Whelan, Hansen, Beardsley, Aldridge(Rush), Houghton, Barnes, McMahon.
Goalscorers: Aldridge, Rush 2
Everton: Southall; McDonald, Van den Hauwe, Ratcliffe, Watson, Bracewell(McCall), Nevin, Steven, Sharp, Cottee, Sheedy(Wilson).
Goalscorer: McCall 2
Referee: J.Worrall (Warrington)
Attendance: 82,800

*Abandoned after six minutes, crowd disaster.

1989-90

First Round
Aldershot v Cambridge Utd 0-1
Aylesbury v Southend Utd 1-0
Basingstoke v Bromsgrove 3-0
Bath C v Fulham 2-2, 1-2
Bishop Auckland v Tow Law 2-0
Blackpool v Bolton W 2-1
Brentford v Colchester Utd 0-1
Bristol C v Barnet 2-0
Bristol R v Reading 1-1, 1-1, 0-1
Burnley v Stockport Co 1-1, 2-1
Cardiff C v Halesowen T 1-0
Carlisle Utd v Wrexham 3-0
Crewe Alex v Congleton T 2-0
Darlington v Northwich Vic 6-2
Dartford v Exeter C 1-1, 1-4
Doncaster R v Notts Co 1-0
Farnborough T v Hereford Utd 0-1
Gillingham v Welling Utd 0-0, 0-1
Gloucester C v Dorchester 1-0
Hartlepool Utd v Huddersfield T 0-2
Kettering T v Northampton T 0-1
Kidderminster H v Swansea C 2-3
Leyton Orient v Birmingham C 0-1
Lincoln C v Billingham Synthonia 1-0
Macclesfield T v Chester C 1-1, 2-3
Maidstone Utd v Yeovil T 2-1
Marine v Rochdale 0-1
Peterborough Utd v Hayes 1-1, 1-0
Preston NE v Tranmere R 1-0
Redditch v Merthyr Tydfil 1-3
Rotherham Utd v Bury 0-0, 2-1
Scarborough v Whitley Bay 0-1
Scunthorpe Utd v Matlock T 4-1
Shrewsbury T v Chesterfield 2-3
Slough T v Woking 1-2
Stafford Rgrs v Halifax T 2-3
Sutton Utd v Torquay Utd 1-1, 0-4
Telford Utd v Walsall 0-3
Wigan Ath v Mansfield T 2-0
York C v Grimsby T 1-2

Second Round
Basingstoke v Torquay Utd 2-3
Blackpool v Chester C 3-0
Bristol C v Fulham 2-1
Cambridge Utd v Woking 3-1
Cardiff C v Gloucester C 2-2, 1-0
Chesterfield v Huddersfield T 0-2
Colchester Utd v Birmingham C 0-2
Crewe Alex v Bishop Auckland 1-1, 2-0
Darlington v Halifax T 3-0
Grimsby T v Doncaster R 1-0
Hereford Utd v Merthyr Tydfil 3-2
Maidstone Utd v Exeter C 1-1, 2-3
Northampton T v Aylesbury 0-0, 1-0
Reading v Welling Utd 0-0, 1-1, 0-0, 2-1
Rochdale v Lincoln C 3-0
Scunthorpe Utd v Burnley 2-2, 1-1, 0-5
Swansea C v Peterborough Utd 3-1
Walsall v Rotherham Utd 1-0
Whiltey Bay v Preston NE 2-0
Wigan Ath v Carlisle Utd 2-0

Third Round
Birmingham C v Oldham Ath 1-1, 0-1
Blackburn R v Aston Villa 2-2, 1-3
Blackpool v Burnley 1-0
Brighton & HA v Luton T 4-1
Bristol C v Swindon T 2-1
Cambridge Utd v Darlington 0-0, 3-1
Cardiff C v Queen's Park R 0-0, 0-2
Charlton Ath v Bradford C 1-1, 3-0
Chelsea v Crewe Alex 1-1, 2-0
CRYSTAL PALACE v Portsmouth 2-1
Exeter C v Norwich C 1-1, 0-2
Hereford Utd v Walsall 2-1
Huddersfield T v Grimsby T 3-1
Hull C v Newcastle Utd 0-1
Leeds Utd v Ipswich T 0-1
Leicester C v Barnsley 1-2
Manchester C v Millwall 0-0, 1-1, 1-3
Middlesbrough v Everton 0-0, 1-1, 0-1
Northampton T v Coventry C 1-0
Nottingham F v MANCHESTER UTD 0-1
Plymouth Arg v Oxford Utd 0-1
Port Vale v Derby Co 1-1, 3-2
Reading v Sunderland 2-1

Rochdale v Whitley Bay 1-0
Sheffield Utd v AFC Bournemouth 2-0
Stoke C v Arsenal 0-1
Swansea C v Liverpool 0-0, 0-8
Torquay Utd v West Ham Utd 1-0
Tottenham H v Southampton 1-3
Watford v Wigan Ath 2-0
West Bromwich A v Wimbledon 2-0
Wolves v Sheffield Wed 1-2

Fourth Round
Arsenal v Queen's Park R 0-0, 0-2
Aston Villa v Port Vale 6-0
Barnsley v Ipswich T 2-0
Blackpool v Torquay Utd 1-0
Bristol C v Chelsea 3-1
CRYSTAL PALACE v Huddersfield T 4-0
Hereford Utd v MANCHESTER UTD 0-1
Millwall v Cambridge Utd 1-1, 0-1
Norwich C v Liverpool 0-0, 1-3
Oldham Ath v Brighton & HA 2-1
Reading v Newcastle Utd 3-3, 1-4
Rochdale v Northampton T 3-0
Sheffield Utd v Watford 1-1, 2-1
Sheffield Wed v Everton 1-2
Southampton v Oxford Utd 1-0
West Bromwich A v Charlton Ath 1-0

Fifth Round
Blackpool v Queen's Park R 2-2, 0-0, 0-3
Bristol C v Cambridge Utd 0-0, 1-1, 1-5
CRYSTAL PALACE v Rochdale 1-0
Liverpool v Southampton 3-0
Newcastle Utd v MANCHESTER UTD 2-3
Oldham Ath v Everton 2-2, 1-1, 2-1
Sheffield Utd v Barnsley 2-2, 0-0, 1-0
West Bromwich A v Aston Villa 0-2

Sixth Round
Cambridge Utd v CRYSTAL PALACE 0-1
Oldham Ath v Aston Villa 3-0
Queen's Park R v Liverpool 2-2, 0-1
Sheffield Utd v MANCHESTER UTD 0-1

Semi-final
CRYSTAL PALACE v Liverpool 4-3
MANCHESTER UTD v Oldham Ath 3-3, 2-1

FINAL (Wembley Stadium)
MANCHESTER UNITED 1
CRYSTAL PALACE 0
(following a 3-3 draw after extra-time)

Manchester United: Sealey; Ince, Martin, Bruce, Phelan, Pallister, Robson, Webb, McClair, Hughes, Wallace. (Leighton played in place of Sealey in the first game with Blackmore substituting Martin and Robins for Pallister).
Goalscorer: Martin
Crystal Palace: Martyn; Pemberton, Shaw, Gray, O'Reilly, Thorn, Barber(Wright), Thomas, Bright, Salako(Madden), Pardew. (Madden substituted Gray in the first game).
Referee: A.Gunn (South Chailey) Attendance: 80,000

The first game was played at Wembley Stadium in front of 80,000 spectators. Robson and Hughes (2) scored for Manchester United with O'Reilly and Wright (2) for Crystal Palace.

Manchester United's young goalscorer Lee Martin celebrates a memorable 1990 Cup Final.

1990-91

First Round
Aldershot v Tiverton 6-2
Altrincham v Huddersfield T 1-2
Atherstone v Fleetwood 3-1
Aylesbury v Walsall 0-1
Barnet v Chelmsford C 2-2, 2-0
Birmingham C v Cheltenham T 1-0
Bishop Auckland v Barrow 0-1
Blackpool v Grimsby T 2-0
Boston Utd v Wycombe W 1-1, 0-4
AFC Bournemouth v Gillingham 2-1
Bradford C v Shrewsbury T 0-0, 1-2
Brentford v Yeovil T 5-0
Cardiff C v Hayes 0-0, 0-1
Chester C v Doncaster R 2-2, 2-1
Chesterfield v Spennymoor 3-2
Chorley v Bury 2-1
Colchester Utd v Reading 2-1
Darlington v York C 1-1, 0-1
Exeter C v Cambridge Utd 1-2
Fulham v Farnborough T 2-1
Halesowen T v Tranmere R 1-2
Halifax T v Wrexham 3-2
Hereford Utd v Peterborough Utd 1-1, 1-2
Leyton Orient v Southend Utd 3-2
Lincoln C v Crewe Alex 1-4
Littlehampton v Northampton T 0-4
Maidstone Utd v Torquay Utd 4-1
Merthyr Tydfil v Sutton Utd 1-1, 1-0
Preston NE v Mansfield T 0-1
Rochdale v Scunthorpe Utd 1-1, 1-2
Rotherham Utd v Stockport Co 1-0
Runcorn v Hartlepool Utd 0-3
Scarborough v Leek T 0-2
Stafford Rgrs v Burnley 1-3
Swansea C v Welling Utd 5-2
Tamworth v Whitley Bay 4-6
Telford Utd v Stoke C 0-0, 0-1
Wigan Ath v Carlisle Utd 5-0
Witton A v Bolton W 1-2
Woking v Kidderminster H 0-0, 1-1, 2-1

Second Round
Aldershot v Maidstone Utd 2-1
Barnet v Northampton T 0-0, 1-0
Birmingham C v Brentford 1-3
AFC Bournemouth v Hayes 1-0
Burnley v Stoke C 2-0
Chesterfield v Bolton W 3-4
Colchester Utd v Leyton Orient 0-0, 1-4
Crewe Alex v Atherstone 1-0
Fulham v Cambridge Utd 0-0, 1-2
Huddersfield T v Blackpool 0-2
Leek T v Chester C 1-1, 0-4
Mansfield T v York C 2-1
Rotherham Utd v Halifax T 1-1, 2-1
Scunthorpe Utd v Tranmere R 3-2
Shrewsbury T v Chorley 1-0
Swansea C v Walsall 2-1
Whitley Bay v Barrow 0-1
Wigan Ath v Hartlepool Utd 2-0
Woking v Merthyr Tydfil 5-1
Wycombe W v Peterborough Utd 1-1, 0-2

Third Round
Aldershot v West Ham Utd 0-0, 1-6
Arsenal v Sunderland 2-1
Aston Villa v Wimbledon 1-1, 0-1
Barnet v Portsmouth 0-5
Barnsley v Leeds Utd 1-1, 0-4
Blackburn R v Liverpool 1-1, 0-3
Blackpool v Tottenham H 0-1
Bolton W v Barrow 1-0
Brighton & HA v Scunthorpe Utd 3-2
Bristol R v Crewe Alex 0-2
Burnley v Manchester C 0-1
Charlton Ath v Everton 1-2
Chelsea v Oxford Utd 1-3
Chester C v AFC Bournemouth 2-3
Coventry C v Wigan Ath 1-1, 1-0
Crystal Palace v Nottingham F 0-0, 2-2, 0-3
Hull C v Notts Co 2-5
Leyton Orient v Swindon T 1-1, 0-1
Manchester Utd v Queen's Park R 2-1
Mansfield T v Sheffield Wed 0-2
Middlesbrough v Plymouth Arg 0-0, 2-1
Millwall v Leicester C 2-1
Newcastle Utd v Derby Co 2-0
Norwich C v Bristol C 2-1
Oldham Ath v Brentford 3-1
Port Vale v Peterborough Utd 2-1
Sheffield Utd v Luton T 1-3
Shrewsbury T v Watford 4-1
Southampton v Ipswich T 3-2
Swansea C v Rotherham Utd 0-0, 0-4
West Bromwich A v Woking 2-4
Wolves v Cambridge Utd 0-1

Fourth Round
Arsenal v Leeds Utd 0-0, 1-1, 0-0, 2-1
Cambridge Utd v Middlesbrough 2-0
Coventry C v Southampton 1-1, 0-2
Crewe Alex v Rotherham Utd 1-0
Liverpool v Brighton & HA 2-2, 3-2
Luton T v West Ham Utd 1-1, 0-5
Manchester Utd v Bolton W 1-0
Millwall v Sheffield Wed 4-4, 0-2
Newcastle Utd v Nottingham F 2-2, 0-3
Norwich C v Swindon T 3-1
Notts Co v Oldham Ath 2-0
Portsmouth v AFC Bournemouth 5-1
Port Vale v Manchester C 1-2
Shrewsbury T v Wimbledon 1-0
Tottenham H v Oxford Utd 4-2
Woking v Everton 0-1

Fifth Round
Cambridge Utd v Sheffield Wed 4-0
Liverpool v Everton 0-0, 4-4, 0-1
Norwich C v Manchester Utd 2-1
Notts Co v Manchester C 1-0
Portsmouth v Tottenham H 1-2
Shrewsbury T v Arsenal 0-1
Southampton v Nottingham F 1-1, 1-3
West Ham Utd v Crewe Alex 1-0

Sixth Round
Arsenal v Cambridge Utd 2-1
Norwich C v Nottingham F 0-1
Tottenham H v Notts Co 2-1
West Ham Utd v Everton 2-1

Semi-final
Arsenal v Tottenham H 1-3
Nottingham F v West Ham Utd 4-0

Gary Lineker with the FA Cup after Spurs' extra-time victory over Nottingham Forest.

FINAL (Wembley Stadium)
TOTTENHAM HOTSPUR 2
NOTTINGHAM FOREST 1
(after extra-time)

Tottenham Hotspur: Thorstvedt; Edinburgh, Van den Hauwe, Sedgeley, Howells, Mabbutt, Stewart, Gascoigne(Nayim), Samways(Walsh), Lineker, Allen.
Goalscorers: Stewart, Walker (og)
Nottingham Forest: Crossley; Charles, Pearce, Walker, Chettle, Keane, Crosby, Parker, Clough, Glover(Laws), Woan(Hodge).
Goalscorer: Pearce
Referee: R.G.Milford (Bristol) Attendance: 80,000

1991-92

First Round
Stockport Co v Lincoln C ... 3-1
Hartlepool Utd v Shrewsbury T ... 3-2
Witton A v Halifax T ... 1-1, 2-1
Chester C v Guiseley ... 1-0
Runcorn v Tranmere R ... 0-3
Scunthorpe Utd v Rotherham Utd* ... 1-1, 3-3
Emley v Bolton W ... 0-3
Mansfield T v Preston NE ... 0-1
Bury v Bradford C ... 0-1
Darlington v Chesterfield ... 2-1
Scarborough v Wigan Ath ... 0-2
Morecambe v Hull C ... 0-1
Huddersfield T v Lincoln Utd ... 6-0
Wrexham v Winsford Utd ... 5-2
Bridlington T v York C ... 1-2
Gretna v Rochdale ... 0-0, 1-3
Blackpool v Grimsby T ... 2-1
Stoke C v Telford Utd ... 0-0, 1-2
Burnley v Doncaster R ... 1-1, 3-1
Carlisle Utd v Crewe Alex ... 1-1, 3-5
Brentford v Gillingham ... 3-3, 3-1
Halesowen T v Farnborough T ... 2-2, 0-4
AFC Bournemouth v Bromsgrove R ... 3-1
Swansea C v Cardiff C ... 2-1
Kidderminster H v Aylesbury Utd ... 0-1
Leyton Orient v Welling Utd ... 2-1
West Bromwich A v Marlow ... 6-0
Crawley T v Northampton T ... 4-2
Peterborough Utd v Harlow T ... 7-0
Windsor & Eton v Woking ... 2-4
Maidstone Utd v Sutton Utd ... 1-0
Fulham v Hayes ... 0-2
Slough T v Reading ... 3-3, 1-2
Aldershot v Enfield ... 0-1
Yeovil T v Walsall ... 1-1, 1-0
Colchester Utd v Exeter C* ... 0-0, 0-0
Atherstone Utd v Hereford Utd ... 0-0, 0-3
Kettering T v Wycombe W ... 1-1, 2-0
Barnet v Tiverton T ... 5-0
Torquay Utd v Birmingham C ... 3-0

Second Round
Crewe Alex v Chester C ... 2-0
Rochdale v Huddersfield T ... 1-2
Wrexham v Telford Utd ... 1-0
Burnley v Rotherham Utd ... 2-0
York C v Tranmere R ... 1-1, 1-2
Darlington v Hartlepool Utd ... 1-2
Bolton W v Bradford C ... 3-1
Preston NE v Witton A ... 5-1
Blackpool v Hull C ... 0-1
Wigan Ath v Stockport Co ... 2-0
Aylesbury Utd v Hereford Utd ... 2-3
Leyton Orient v West Bromwich A ... 2-1
Peterborough Utd v Reading ... 0-0, 0-1
Enfield v Barnet ... 1-4
Woking v Yeovil T ... 3-0
Exeter C v Swansea C ... 0-0, 2-1
Hayes v Crawley T ... 0-2
Maidstone Utd v Kettering T ... 1-2
Torquay Utd v Farnborough T ... 1-1, 3-4
AFC Bournemouth v Brentford ... 2-1

Third Round
Huddersfield T v Millwall ... 0-4
Oxford Utd v Tranmere R ... 3-1
Leeds Utd v Manchester Utd ... 0-1
Notts Co v Wigan Ath ... 2-0
Sheffield Utd v Luton T ... 4-0
Aston Villa v Tottenham H ... 0-0
Tottenham H v Aston Villa ... 0-1
Norwich C v Barnsley ... 1-0
Burnley v Derby Co ... 2-2, 0-2
Nottingham F v Wolverhampton W ... 1-0
Woking v Hereford Utd ... 0-0, 1-2
Brighton & HA v Crawley T ... 5-0
Ipswich T v Hartlepool Utd ... 1-1, 2-0
Hull C v Chelsea ... 0-2
Bolton W v Reading ... 2-0
Bristol C v Wimbledon ... 1-1, 1-0
Preston NE v Sheffield Wed ... 0-2
Oldham Ath v Leyton Orient ... 1-1, 3-4
Swindon T v Watford ... 3-2
Wrexham v Arsenal ... 2-1
Bristol R v Plymouth Arg ... 5-0
Coventry C v Cambridge Utd ... 1-1, 0-1
Farnborough T v West Ham Utd ... 1-1, 0-1
Southampton v Queen's Park R ... 2-0
Leicester C v Crystal Palace ... 1-0
Exeter C v Portsmouth ... 1-2
Charlton Ath v Barnet ... 3-1
Middlesbrough v Manchester C ... 2-1
AFC Bournemouth v Newcastle Utd ... 0-0
Newcastle Utd v AFC Bournemouth ... 2-2
Everton v Southend Utd ... 1-0
Crewe Alex v LIVERPOOL ... 0-4
SUNDERLAND v Port Vale ... 3-0
Blackburn R v Kettering T ... 4-1

Top: Liverpool's Thomas volleys home the first goal in the 1992 FA Cup Final. Bottom: Ian Rush (partly hidden) sidefoots home the second goal and Sunderland are down and out.

Fourth Round
Bolton W v Brighton & HA ... 2-1
Portsmouth v Leyton Orient ... 2-0
Sheffield Wed v Middlesbrough ... 1-2
Oxford Utd v SUNDERLAND ... 2-3
Chelsea v Everton ... 1-0
Charlton Ath v Sheffield Utd ... 0-0, 1-3
Leicester C v Bristol C ... 1-2
Norwich C v Millwall ... 2-1
Southampton* v Manchester Utd ... 0-0, 2-2
West Ham Utd v Wrexham ... 2-2, 1-0
Notts Co v Blackburn R ... 2-1
Ipswich T v AFC Bournemouth ... 3-0
Nottingham F v Hereford Utd ... 2-0
Bristol R v LIVERPOOL ... 1-1, 1-2
Cambridge Utd v Swindon T ... 0-3
Derby Co v Aston Villa ... 3-4

Fifth Round
Chelsea v Sheffield Utd ... 1-0
Portsmouth v Middlesbrough ... 1-1, 4-2
Swindon T v Aston Villa ... 1-2
Norwich C v Notts Co ... 3-0
Bolton W v Southampton ... 2-2, 2-3
SUNDERLAND v West Ham Utd ... 1-1, 3-2
Nottingham F v Bristol C ... 4-1
Ipswich T v LIVERPOOL ... 0-0, 2-3

Sixth Round
Portsmouth v Nottingham F ... 1-0
Southampton v Norwich ... 0-0, 1-2
LIVERPOOL v Aston Villa ... 1-0
Chelsea v SUNDERLAND ... 1-1, 1-2

Semi-final
LIVERPOOL* v Portsmouth ... 1-1, 0-0
SUNDERLAND v Norwich ... 1-0

FINAL (Wembley Stadium)
LIVERPOOL ... 2
SUNDERLAND ... 0
Liverpool: Grobbelaar; Jones, Burrows, Nicol, Molby, Wright, Saunders, Houghton, I.Rush, McManaman, Thomas.
Goalscorers: Thomas, I.Rush
Sunderland: Norman; Owers, Ball, Bennett, Rogan, D.Rush(Handyman), Bracewell, Davenport, Armstrong(Hawke), Byrne, Atkinson.
Referee: P.Don (Middlesex) *Attendance: 79,544*
*Won on penalties.

The Football League Cup

1960-61

First Round
Bristol R v Fulham 2-1
West Ham Utd v Charlton Ath 3-1
Middlesbrough v Cardiff C 3-4
Colchester Utd v Newcastle Utd 4-1
Coventry C v Barrow 4-2
Hull C v Bolton W 0-0, 1-5
Millwall v Chelsea 1-7
Newport Co v Southampton 2-2, 2-2, 3-5
Rochdale v Scunthorpe Utd 1-1, 1-0
Stockport Co v Carlisle Utd 2-0
York C v Blackburn R 1-3
Ipswich T v Barnsley 0-2
Oldham Ath v Hartlepools Utd 2-1
Preston NE v Peterborough Utd 4-1
Watford v Derby Co 2-5
Chester v Leyton Orient 2-2, 0-1
Darlington v Crystal Palace 2-0
Everton v Accrington S 3-1
Leicester C v Mansfield T 4-0
Lincoln C v Bradford 2-2, 0-1
Plymouth Arg v Southport 2-0
Queen's Park R v Port Vale 2-2, 1-3
Exeter C v Manchester Utd 1-1, 1-4

Second Round
Leeds Utd v Blackpool 0-0, 3-1
Nottingham F v Halifax T 2-0
Aldershot v Bristol C 1-1, 0-3
Bury v Sheffield Utd 3-1
ASTON VILLA v Huddersfield T 4-1
Bournemouth & Bos Ath v Crewe Alex 1-1, 0-2
Reading v Bristol R 3-5
Swindon T v Shrewsbury T 1-1, 2-2, 0-2
Doncaster R v Stoke C 3-1
Manchester C v Stockport Co 3-0
Northampton T v Wrexham 1-1, 0-2
Swansea C v Blackburn R 1-2
Derby Co v Barnsley 3-0
Gillingham v Preston NE 1-1, 0-3
Liverpool v Luton T 1-1, 5-2
Notts Co v Brighton & HA 1-3
Cardiff C v Burnley 0-4
Chelsea v Workington 4-2
Darlington v West Ham Utd 3-2
Port Vale v Tranmere R 0-2
Brentford v Sunderland 4-3
Rochdale v Southend Utd 5-2
Bolton W v Grimsby T 6-2
Leicester C v ROTHERHAM UTD 1-2
Norwich C v Oldham Ath 6-2
Bradford v Birmingham C 0-1
Colchester Utd v Southampton 0-2
Everton v Walsall 3-1
Bradford C v Manchester Utd 2-1
Plymouth Arg v Torquay Utd 1-1, 2-1
Portsmouth v Coventry C 2-0
Leyton Orient v Chesterfield 0-1

Third Round
Birmingham C v Plymouth Arg 0-0, 1-3
Darlington v Bolton W 1-2
Derby Co v Norwich C 1-4

Aston Villa in 1961. Back row (left to right): O'Neill, Lynn, Dugdale, Sims, Dougan, Lee, McParland. Front row: Joe Mercer (manager), Wylie, Neal, Crowe, MacEwan, Thomson. On ground: Burrows, Deakin.

Nottingham F v Bristol C 2-1
Preston NE v ASTON VILLA 3-3, 1-3
Brighton & HA v Wrexham 0-2
Doncaster R v Chelsea 0-7
Liverpool v Southampton 1-2
Shrewsbury T v Bradford C 2-1
Tranmere R v Crewe Alex 2-0
Blackburn R v Rochdale 2-1
Portsmouth v Manchester C 2-0
Brentford v Burnley 1-1, 1-2
Chesterfield v Leeds Utd 0-4
Everton v Bury 3-1
ROTHERHAM UTD v Bristol R 2-0

Fourth Round
Blackburn R v Wrexham 1-1, 1-3
Southampton v Leeds Utd 5-4
ASTON VILLA v Plymouth Arg 3-3, 0-0, 5-3
Portsmouth v Chelsea 1-0
Shrewsbury T v Norwich C 1-0
Bolton W v ROTHERHAM UTD 0-2
Tranmere R v Everton 0-4
Burnley v Nottingham F 2-1

Fifth Round
Southampton v Burnley 2-4
ROTHERHAM UTD v Portsmouth 3-0
Shrewsbury T v Everton 2-1
ASTON VILLA v Wrexham 3-0

Semi-final (agg)
ROTHERHAM UTD v Shrewsbury T ... 3-2, 1-1 (4-3)
Burnley v ASTON VILLA 1-1, 2-2, 1-2 (4-5)

FINAL (First leg) (Millmoor)
ROTHERHAM UNITED 2
ASTON VILLA 0
Rotherham United: Ironside; Perry, Morgan, Lambert, Madden, Waterhouse, Webster, Weston, Houghton, Kirkman, Bambridge.
Goalscorers: Webster, Kirkman
Aston Villa: Sims; Lynn, Lee, Crowe, Dugdale, Deakin, MacEwan, Thomson, Brown, Wylie, McParland.
Referee. K.A.Collinge (Altrincham)
Attendance: 12,226

FINAL (Second leg) (Villa Park)
ASTON VILLA 3
ROTHERHAM UNITED 0
(after extra-time)
Aston Villa: Sidebottom; Neal, Lee, Crowe, Dugdale, Deakin, MacEwan, O'Neill, McParland, Thomson, Burrows.
Goalscorers: O'Neill, Burrows, McParland
Rotherham United: Unchanged from first leg.
Referee: C.W.Kingston (Newport) Attendance: 31.202

Aston Villa won 3-2 on aggregate.

1961-62

First Round
Bristol R v Hartlepools Utd 2-1
Darlington v Rotherham Utd 0-1
Hull C v Bradford 4-2
Ipswich T v Manchester C 4-2
Mansfield T v Exeter C 5-2
Newport Co v Shrewsbury T 0-0, 1-3
Nottingham F v Gillingham 4-1
Peterborough Utd v Blackburn R 1-3
Stockport Co v Leyton Orient 0-1
Watford v Halifax T 3-0
West Ham Utd v Plymouth Arg 3-2
Bury v Brighton & HA 5-1
Carlisle Utd v Huddersfield T 1-1, 0-3
Oldham Ath v Charlton Ath 1-4
Barnsley v Southport 3-2
Barrow v Portsmouth 0-2
Birmingham C v Swindon T 1-1, 0-2
Blackpool v Port Vale 2-1
Bolton W v Sunderland 1-1, 0-1
Bournemouth & Bos Ath v Torquay Utd 2-2, 1-0
Bradford C v Aston Villa 3-4
Cardiff C v Wrexham 2-0
Chesterfield v NORWICH C 2-3
Colchester Utd v Crewe Alex 1-2
Doncaster R v Grimsby T 3-2
Fulham v Sheffield Utd 1-1, 0-4
Leeds Utd v Brentford 4-1
Lincoln C v Accrington S 1-0
Luton T v Northampton T 2-1
Millwall v Walsall 1-2
Newcastle Utd v Scunthorpe Utd 2-0
Preston NE v Aldershot 3-1
Queen's Park R v Crystal Palace 5-2
Reading v Chester 4-2
Southampton v ROCHDALE 0-0, 1-2
Southend Utd v Stoke C 0-1
Tranmere R v Middlesbrough 3-6
Workington v Coventry C 3-0
York C v Bristol C 3-0
Notts Co v Derby Co 2-2, 2-3

Second Round
Bristol R v Blackburn R 1-1, 0-4
Sheffield Utd v Newcastle Utd 2-2, 2-0
Bury v Hull C 3-4
Swansea v Ipswich T 3-3, 2-3
Charlton Ath v Stoke C 4-1
Leeds Utd v Huddersfield T 3-2
Leyton Orient v Blackpool 1-1, 1-5
Luton T v Rotherham Utd 0-0, 0-2
Middlesbrough v Crewe Alex 3-1
NORWICH C v Lincoln C 3-2
Portsmouth v Derby Co 1-1, 4-2
ROCHDALE v Doncaster R 4-0
Sunderland v Walsall 5-2
Mansfield T v Cardiff C 1-1, 1-2
Preston NE v Swindon T 3-1
Barnsley v Workington 1-3
Shrewsbury T v Bournemouth & Bos Ath 1-3
West Ham Utd v Aston Villa 1-3
York C v Leicester C 2-1
Queen's Park R v Nottingham F 1-2
Watford v Reading 3-1

Third Round
Sheffield Utd v Portsmouth 1-0
Nottingham F v Blackburn R 1-2
Preston NE v Rotherham Utd 0-0, 0-3
ROCHDALE v Charlton Ath 1-0
Bournemouth & Bos Ath v Cardiff C 3-0
NORWICH C v Middlesbrough 3-2
Sunderland v Hull C 2-1
Workington v Blackpool 0-1
York C v Watford 1-1, 2-2, 3-2
Aston Villa v Ipswich T 2-3

Fourth Round
Blackburn R v Ipswich T 4-1
Rotherham Utd v Leeds Utd 1-1, 2-1
York C v Bournemouth & Bos Ath 1-0
Sunderland .... bye
Blackpool .... bye
NORWICH C .... bye
Sheffield Utd .... bye
ROCHDALE .... bye

Fifth Round
Blackpool v Sheffield Utd 0-0, 2-0
Rotherham Utd v Blackburn R 0-1
ROCHDALE v York C 2-1
Sunderland v NORWICH C 1-4

Semi-final **(agg)**
ROCHDALE v Blackburn R 3-1, 1-2 (4-3)
NORWICH C v Blackpool 4-1, 0-2 (4-3)

FINAL (First leg) **(Spotland)**
ROCHDALE 0
NORWICH CITY 3

Rochdale: Burgin; Milburn, Winton, Bodell, Aspden, Thompson, Wragg, Hepton, Bimpson, Cairns, Whitaker.
Norwich City: Kennon; McCrohan, Ashman, Burton, Butler, Mullett, Mannion, Lythgoe, Scott, Hill, Punton.
Goalscorers: Lythgoe 2, Punton
Referee: A.Holland (Barnsley) Attendance: 11,123

FINAL (Second leg) (Carrow Road)
NORWICH CITY 1
ROCHDALE 0
Norwich City: Unchanged from first leg.
Goalscorer: Hill
Rochdale: Burgin; Milburn, Winton, Bodell, Aspden, Thompson, Whyke, Richardson, Bimpson, Cairns, Whitaker.
Referee: R.H.Mann (Worcs) Attendance: 19,708
Norwich City won 4-0 on aggregate.

1962-63

First Round
Torquay Utd v Oxford Utd 2-0
Tranmere R v Carlisle Utd 2-3
Brentford v Wrexham 3-0
Aldershot v Exeter C 2-0
Barrow v Workington 3-2
Bradford C v Doncaster R 2-2, 0-2
Chester v Stockport Co 2-0
Crewe Alex v Oldham Ath 2-3
Darlington v Chesterfield 1-0
Newport Co v Gillingham 2-1
Shrewsbury T v Millwall 3-1
Southport v Rochdale 0-0, 2-1
York C v Lincoln C 2-2, 0-2
Hartlepools Utd v Barnsley 1-1, 1-2
Watford v Colchester Utd 1-2
Halifax T v Mansfield T 2-3

Second Round
ASTON VILLA v Peterborough Utd 6-1
Barrow v Shrewsbury T 3-1
Bury v Lincoln C 2-2, 3-2
Hull C v Middlesbrough 2-2, 1-1, 3-0
Manchester C v Blackpool 0-0, 3-3, 4-2
Queen's Park R v Preston NE 1-2
Southampton v Scunthorpe Utd 1-1, 2-2, 0-3
Southport v Luton T 1-3
Sunderland v Oldham Ath 7-1
Barnsley v Grimsby T 3-2
Brighton & HA v Portsmouth 1-5
Bristol C v Rotherham Utd 1-2
Walsall v Stoke C 1-2
Swindon T v Darlington 4-0
Aldershot v Newport Co 0-3
BIRMINGHAM C v Doncaster R 5-0
Bradford v Huddersfield T 3-1
Brentford v Sheffield Utd 1-4
Cardiff C v Reading 5-1
Chester v Mansfield T 2-2, 1-0
Coventry C v Swansea T 3-2
Derby Co v Blackburn R 1-1, 1-3
Fulham v Bournemouth & Bos Ath 4-0
Leeds Utd v Crystal Palace 2-1
Leicester C v Charlton Ath 4-4, 1-2
Newcastle Utd v Leyton Orient 1-1, 2-4
Northampton T v Colchester Utd 2-0
Norwich C v Bolton W 4-0
Southend Utd v Notts Co 2-3
Torquay Utd v Carlisle Utd 1-2
West Ham Utd v Plymouth Arg 6-0
Bristol R v Port Vale 2-0

Third Round
Barrow v BIRMINGHAM C 1-1, 1-5
Barnsley v Luton T 1-2
Bradford v Charlton Ath 2-2, 0-1
Carlisle Utd v Norwich C 1-1, 0-5
Northampton T v Preston NE 1-1, 1-2
Rotherham Utd v West Ham Utd 3-1
ASTON VILLA v Stoke C 3-1
Blackburn R v Leeds Utd 4-0
Hull C v Fulham 1-2
Leyton Orient v Chester 9-2
Notts Co v Swindon T 5-0
Portsmouth v Coventry C 5-1
Sunderland v Scunthorpe Utd 2-0
Bristol R v Cardiff C 2-0
Bury v Sheffield Utd 3-1
Newport Co v Manchester C 1-2

Fourth Round
ASTON VILLA v Preston NE 6-2
Leyton Orient v Charlton Ath 3-2
Bury v Bristol R 3-1
BIRMINGHAM C v Notts Co 3-2
Blackburn R v Rotherham Utd 4-1
Manchester C v Luton T 1-0
Norwich C v Fulham 1-0
Portsmouth v Sunderland 0-0, 1-2

Fifth Round
ASTON VILLA v Norwich C 4-1
Leyton Orient v Bury 0-2
Sunderland v Blackburn R 3-2
BIRMINGHAM C v Manchester C 6-0

Semi-final (agg)
Sunderland v ASTON VILLA 1-3, 0-0 (1-3)
BIRMINGHAM C v Bury 3-2, 1-1 (4-3)

FINAL (First leg) (St Andrew's)
BIRMINGHAM CITY 3
ASTON VILLA 1
Birmingham City: Schofield; Lynn, Green, Hennessey, Smith, Beard, Hellawell, Bloomfield, Harris, Leek, Auld.
Goalscorers: Leek 2, Bloomfield
Aston Villa: Sims; Fraser, Aitken, Crowe, Sleeuwenhoek, Lee, Baker, Graham, Thomson, Wylie, Burrows.
Goalscorer: Thomson
Referee: E.Crawford (Doncaster) Attendance: 31,580

FINAL (Second leg) (Villa Park)
ASTON VILLA 0
BIRMINGHAM CITY 0
Aston Villa: Sims; Fraser, Aitken, Crowe, Chatterley, Lee, Baker, Graham, Thomson, Wylie, Burrows.
Birmingham City: Unchanged from first leg
Referee: Attendance: 37,921
Birmingham City won 3-1 on aggregate.

1963-64

First Round
Aldershot v Queen's Park R 3-1
Bradford v Bradford C 7-3
Carlisle Utd v Crewe Alex 3-2
Chesterfield v Halifax T 0-1
Darlington v Barnsley 2-2, 2-6
Doncaster R v York C 0-0, 0-3
Gillingham v Bristol C 4-2
Lincoln C v Hartlepools Utd 3-2
Mansfield T v Watford 2-1
Newport Co v Millwall 3-4
Oldham Ath v Workington 3-5
Oxford Utd v Exeter C 0-1
Reading v Brentford 1-1, 0-2
Rochdale v Chester 1-1, 5-2
Shrewsbury T v Bristol R 1-1, 2-6
Southport v Barrow 2-1
Torquay Utd v Brighton & HA 1-2
Tranmere R v Stockport Co 2-0

Second Round
Aston Villa v Barnsley 3-1
Blackpool v Charlton Ath 7-1
Bradford v Middlesbrough 2-2, 3-2
Brentford v Bournemouth & Bos Ath 0-0, 0-2
Brighton & HA v Northampton T 1-1, 2-3
Bristol R v Crystal Palace 2-0
Cardiff C v Wrexham 2-2, 1-1, 0-3
Colchester Utd v Fulham 5-3
Gillingham v Bury 3-0
Grimsby T v Rotherham Utd 1-3
Halifax T v Rochdale 4-2
Hull C v Exeter C 1-0
Ipswich T v Walsall 0-0, 0-1
Leeds Utd v Mansfield T 5-1
LEICESTER C v Aldershot 2-0
Luton T v Coventry C 3-4
Manchester C v Carlisle Utd 2-0
Millwall v Peterborough Utd 3-2
Newcastle Utd v Preston NE 3-0
Norwich C v Birmingham C 2-0
Notts Co v Blackburn R 2-1
Plymouth Arg v Huddersfield T 2-2, 3-3, 1-2
Portsmouth v Derby Co 3-2
Scunthorpe Utd v STOKE C 2-2, 3-3, 0-1
Sheffield Utd v Bolton W 1-2
Southend Utd v Port Vale 2-1
Swansea T v Sunderland 3-1
Swindon T v Chelsea 3-0
Tranmere R v Southampton 2-0
West Ham Utd v Leyton Orient 2-1
Workington v Southport 3-0
York C v Lincoln C 1-1, 0-2

Third Round
Aston Villa v West Ham Utd 0-2
Halifax T v Walsall 2-0
Hull C v Manchester C 0-3
Swindon T v Southend Utd 3-0
Tranmere R v LEICESTER C 1-2
Leeds Utd v Swansea T 2-0
STOKE C v Bolton W 3-0
Norwich C v Blackpool 1-0
Bristol R v Gillingham 1-1, 1-3
Colchester Utd v Northampton T 4-1
Millwall v Lincoln C 1-1, 2-1
Rotherham Utd v Coventry C 4-2
Notts Co v Bradford 3-2
Workington v Huddersfield T 1-0
Wrexham v Portsmouth 3-5
Bournemouth & Bos Ath v Newcastle Utd 2-1

Fourth Round
Notts Co v Portsmouth 3-2
Swindon T v West Ham Utd 3-3, 1-4
Workington v Colchester Utd 2-1
Halifax T v Norwich C 1-7
LEICESTER C v Gillingham 3-1
Manchester C v Leeds Utd 3-1
Rotherham Utd v Millwall 5-2
STOKE C v Bournemouth & Bos Ath 2-1

Fifth Round
STOKE C v Rotherham Utd 3-2
West Ham Utd v Workington 6-0
Notts Co v Manchester C 0-1
Norwich C v LEICESTER C 1-1, 1-2

Semi-final (agg)
STOKE C v Manchester C 2-0, 0-1 (2-1)
LEICESTER C v West Ham Utd 4-3, 2-0 (6-3)

FINAL (First leg) (Victoria Ground)
STOKE CITY 1
LEICESTER CITY 1
Stoke City: Leslie; Asprey, Allen, Palmer, Kinnell, Skeels, Dobing, Viollet, Ritchie, McIlroy, Bebbington.
Goalscorer: Bebbington
Leicester City: Banks; Sjoberg, Appleton, Dougan, King, Cross, Riley, Heath, Keyworth, Gibson, Stringfellow.
Goalscorer: Gibson
Referee: W.Clements (West Bromwich) Attendance: 22,309

FINAL (Second leg) (Filbert Street)
LEICESTER CITY 3
STOKE CITY 2
Leicester City: Banks; Sjoberg, Norman, Cross, King, Appleton, Riley, Gibson, Keyworth, Sweenie, Stringfellow.
Goalscorers: Stringfellow, Gibson, Riley
Stoke City: Irvine; Asprey, Allen, Palmer, Kinnell, Skeels, Dobing, Viollet, Ritchie, McIlroy, Bebbington.
Goalscorers: Viollet, Kinnell
Referee: A.Jobing (Grimsby) Att: 25,372
Leicester City won 4-3 on aggregate.

1964-65

First Round
Barnsley v Lincoln C 2-1
Bradford C v York C 2-0
Brentford v Southend Utd 0-2
Brighton & HA v Millwall 2-2, 0-1
Chester v Wrexham 3-0
Chesterfield v Hartlepools Utd 3-0
Colchester Utd v Torquay Utd 1-1, 0-3
Doncaster R v Bradford 1-0
Exeter C v Gillingham 2-0
Halifax T v Darlington 1-3
Notts Co v Newport Co 3-2
Port Vale v Luton T 0-1
Queen's Park R v Aldershot 5-2
Southport v Carlisle Utd 0-0, 0-1
Stockport Co v Rochdale 1-3
Tranmere R v Crewe Alex 2-0
Walsall v Oxford Utd 1-1, 1-6
Workington v Barrow 9-1

Second Round
Birmingham C v CHELSEA 0-3
Blackpool v Newcastle Utd 3-0
Bolton W v Blackburn R 1-5
Bristol R v Chesterfield 0-2
Bournemouth & Bos Ath v Northampton T 0-2
Bury v Darlington 1-0
Carlisle Utd v Bristol C 4-1
Charlton Ath v Miiddlesbrough 2-1
Hull C v Southend Utd 0-0, 1-3
Watford v Portsmouth 2-2, 1-2
Chester v Derby Co 5-4
Coventry C v Ipswich T 4-1
Doncaster R v Preston NE 1-0
Exeter C v Bradford C 3-5
Fulham v Oxford Utd 2-0
Grimsby T v Oldham Ath 3-1
Leeds Utd v Huddersfield T 3-2
LEICESTER C v Peterborough Utd 0-0, 2-0
Leyton Orient v Barnsley 3-0
Luton T v Aston Villa 0-1

Manchester C v Mansfield T 3-5
Millwall v Norwich C 1-2
Plymouth Arg v Sheffield Utd 2-1
Reading v Queen's Park R 4-0
Rotherham Utd v Rochdale 2-0
Scunthorpe Utd v Workington 0-1
Southampton v Cardiff C 3-2
Stoke C v Shrewsbury T 1-1, 1-0
Swansea T v Swindon T 3-1
Torquay Utd v Notts Co 1-2
Tranmere R v Crystal Palace 0-2
Sunderland v West Ham Utd 4-1

Third Round
Bury v Plymouth Arg 0-1
CHELSEA v Notts Co 4-0
Charlton Ath v Leyton Orient 2-1
Chesterfield v Carlisle Utd 3-1
Coventry C v Mansfield T 3-2
Crystal Palace v Southampton 2-0
Doncaster R v Bradford C 2-3
Grimsby T v LEICESTER C 0-5
Leeds Utd v Aston Villa 2-3
Northampton T v Portsmouth 2-1
Norwich C v Chester 5-3
Reading v Fulham 1-1, 3-1
Rotherham Utd v Swansea T 2-2, 0-2
Stoke C v Southend Utd 3-1
Sunderland v Blackpool 4-1
Workington v Blackburn R 0-0, 5-1

Fourth Round
Aston Villa v Reading 3-1
Charlton Ath v Bradford C 0-1
LEICESTER C v Crystal Palace 0-0, 2-1
Northampton T v Chesterfield 4-1
Stoke C v Plymouth Arg 1-1, 1-3
Workington v Norwich C 3-0
Coventry C v Sunderland 4-2
CHELSEA v Swansea T 3-2

Fifth Round
Aston Villa v Bradford C 7-1
Plymouth Arg v Northampton T 1-0
Workington v CHELSEA 2-2, 0-2
Coventry C v LEICESTER C 1-8

Semi-final (agg)
Aston Villa v CHELSEA 2-3, 1-1 (3-4)
LEICESTER C v Plymouth Arg 3-2, 1-0 (4-2)

FINAL (First leg) (Stamford Bridge)
CHELSEA 3
LEICESTER CITY 2
Chelsea: Bonetti; Hinton, Row, Harris, Hollins, Young, Boyle, Murray, Graham, McCreadie, Venables, Tambling.
Goalscorers: Tambling, Venables (pen), McCreadie
Leicester City: Banks; Sjoberg, Norman, Chalmers, King, Appleton, Hodgson, Cross, Goodfellow, Gibson, Sweenie.
Goalscorers: Appleton, Goodfellow
Referee: J.Finney (Hereford) Attendance: 20,690

FINAL (Second leg) (Filbert Street)
LEICESTER CITY 0
CHELSEA 0
Leicester City: Banks; Walker, Norman, Roberts, Sjoberg, Appleton, Hodgson, Cross, Goodfellow, Gibson, Stringfellow.
Chelsea: Bonetti; Hinton, McCreadie, R.Harris, Mortimore, Upton, Murray, Boyle, Bridges, Venables, Tambling.
Referee: K.Howley (Middlesbrough)
Attendance: 26,958

Chelsea won 3-2 on aggregate.

Bobby Tambling's goal for Chelsea in the first leg of the 1965 League Cup Final.

1965-66

First Round
Barrow v Rochdale 1-1, 1-3
Bournemouth & Bos Ath v Aldershot 0-0, 1-2
Bradford v Halifax T 1-0
Colchester Utd v Exeter C 2-1
Crewe Alex v Southport 2-0
Doncaster R v Barnsley 2-2, 2-1
Hartlepools Utd v Bradford C 1-0
Lincoln C v York C 2-2, 2-4
Luton T v Brighton & HA 1-1, 0-2
Newport Co v Southend Utd 2-2, 1-3
Notts Co v Chesterfield 0-0, 1-2
Oldham Ath v Tranmere R 3-2
Oxford Utd v Millwall 0-1
Port Vale v Reading 2-2, 0-1
Queen's Park R v Walsall 1-1, 2-3
Scunthorpe Utd v Darlington 0-2
Shrewsbury T v Torquay Utd 3-0
Stockport Co v Workington 2-3
Wrexham v Chester 5-2

Second Round
Blackburn R v Northampton T 0-1
Brighton & HA v Ipswich T 1-2
Bristol R v WEST HAM UTD 3-3, 2-3
Bury v Huddersfield T 0-2
Charlton Ath v Carlisle Utd 4-1
Swansea T v Aston Villa 2-3
Blackpool v Gillingham 5-2
Bolton W v Aldershot 3-0
Chesterfield v Bradford 3-0
Colchester Utd v Middlesbrough 2-4
Crewe Alex v Cardiff C 1-1, 0-3
Crystal Palace v Grimsby T 0-1
Darlington v Swindon T 2-1
Doncaster R v Burnley 0-4
Hull C v Derby Co 2-2, 3-4
Leeds Utd v Hartlepools Utd 4-2
Leyton Orient v Coventry C 0-3
Manchester C v Leicester C 3-1
Mansfield T v Birmingham C 2-1
Millwall v York C 4-1
Newcastle Utd v Peterborough Utd 3-4
Oldham Ath v Portsmouth 1-2
Preston NE v Plymouth Arg 1-0
Reading v Southend Utd 5-1
Rotherham Utd v Watford 2-0
Shrewsbury T v Bristol C 1-0
Southampton v Rochdale 3-0
Stoke C v Norwich C 2-1
Sunderland v Sheffield Utd 2-1
WEST BROMWICH A v Walsall 3-1
Workington v Brentford 0-0, 2-1
Wrexham v Fulham 1-2

Third Round
Blackpool v Darlington 1-2
Burnley v Southampton 3-2
Cardiff C v Portsmouth 2-0
Chesterfield v Stoke C 2-2, 1-2
Derby Co v Reading 1-1, 0-2
Fulham v Northampton T 5-0
Grimsby T v Bolton W 4-2
Huddersfield T v Preston NE 0-1
Leeds Utd v WEST BROMWICH A 2-4
Manchester C v Coventry C 2-3
Middlesbrough v Millwall 0-0, 1-3
Peterborough Utd v Charlton Ath 4-3
Shrewsbury T v Rotherham Utd 2-5
Sunderland v Aston Villa 1-2
WEST HAM UTD v Mansfield T 4-0
Workington v Ipswich T 1-1, 1-3

Fourth Round
Cardiff C v Reading 5-1
Coventry C v WEST BROMWICH A 1-1, 1-6
Fulham v Aston Villa 1-1, 0-2
Grimsby T v Preston NE 4-0
Ipswich T v Darlington 2-0
Millwall v Peterborough Utd 1-4
Rotherham Utd v WEST HAM UTD 1-2
Stoke C v Burnley 0-0, 1-2

Fifth Round
Cardiff C v Ipswich T 2-1
Grimsby T v WEST HAM UTD 2-2, 0-1
Peterborough Utd v Burnley 4-0
WEST BROMWICH A v Aston Villa 3-1

Semi-final (agg)
WEST BROMWICH A v Peterborough Utd 2-1, 4-2 (6-3)
WEST HAM UTD v Cardiff C 5-2, 5-1 (10-3)

FINAL (First leg) (Upton Park)
WEST HAM UNITED 2
WEST BROMWICH ALBION 1
West Ham United: Standen; Burnett, Burkett, Peters, Brown, Moore, Brabrook, Boyce, Byrne, Hurst, Dear.
Goalscorers: Moore, Byrne
West Bromwich Albion: Potter; Cram, Fairfax, Fraser, Campbell, Williams, Brown, Astle, Kaye, Lovett, Clark.
Goalscorer: Astle
Referee: D.W.Smith (Stonehouse) Attendance: 28,341

FINAL (Second leg) (The Hawthorns)
WEST BROMWICH ALBION 4
WEST HAM UNITED 1
West Bromwich Albion: Potter; Cram, Fairfax, Fraser, Campbell, Williams, Brown, Astle, Kay, Hope, Clark.
Goalscorers: Kay, Brown, Clark, Williams
West Ham United: Standen; Burnett, Peters, Bovington, Brown, Brown, Brabrook, Boyce, Byrne, Hurst, Sissons.
Goalscorer: Peters
Referee: J.Mitchell (Whiston) Attendance: 31,925
West Bromwich Albion won 5-3 on aggregate.

1966-67

First Round
Bradford v Hartlepools Utd 2-2, 2-1
Bury v Rochdale 2-0
Halifax T v Darlington 0-0, 0-4
Port Vale v Walsall 1-3
Queen's Park R v Colchester Utd 5-0
Watford v Reading 1-1, 0-1
Aldershot v Luton T 2-2, 2-1
Barnsley v Grimsby T 1-2
Barrow v Oldham Ath 2-1
Bradford C v Doncaster R 1-1, 2-5
Brentford v Millwall 0-0, 1-0
Brighton & HA v Leyton Orient 1-0
Cardiff C v Bristol R 1-0
Chester v Tranmere R 2-5
Chesterfield v Scunthorpe Utd 2-1
Crewe Alex v Stockport Co 1-0
Exeter C v Torquay Utd 2-2, 2-1
Lincoln C v Hull C 1-0
Middlesbrough v York C 0-0, 1-2
Newport Co v Swansea T 1-2
Notts Co v Mansfield T 1-1, 0-3
Peterborough Utd v Oxford Utd 2-1
Southend Utd v Gillingham 0-0, 0-2
Southport v Workington 0-1
Shrewsbury T v Wrexham 6-1
Swindon T v Bournemouth & Bos Ath 2-1

Second Round
Arsenal v Gillingham 1-1, 1-1, 5-0
Brentford v Ipswich T 2-4
Bristol C v Swansea T 1-1, 1-2
Coventry C v Derby Co 2-1

West Brom's Astle, Clarke and Williams after the 1966 League Cup Final win over West Ham.

Fulham v Crystal Palace	2-0
Leeds Utd v Newcastle Utd	1-0
Nottingham F v Birmingham C	1-1, 1-2
Swindon T v Portsmouth	4-1
Walsall v Stoke C	2-1
Wolves v Mansfield T	2-1
York C v Chesterfield	3-2
Aldershot v QUEEN'S PARK R	1-1, 0-2
Blackburn R v Barrow	4-1
Blackpool v Manchester Utd	5-1
Bradford v Grimsby T	0-0, 1-3
Bury v Workington	2-3
Cardiff C v Exeter C	0-1
Carlisle Utd v Tranmere R	1-1, 2-0
Chelsea v Charlton Ath	5-2
Darlington v Doncaster R	1-1, 0-2
Leicester C v Reading	5-0
Lincoln C v Huddersfield T	2-1
Manchester C v Bolton W	3-1
Northampton T v Peterborough Utd	2-2, 2-0
Norwich C v Brighton & HA	0-1
Preston NE v Crewe Alex	2-0
Sheffield Wed v Rotherham Utd	0-1
Shrewsbury T v Burnley	1-1, 0-5
Southampton T v Plymouth Arg	4-3
Sunderland v Sheffield Utd	1-1, 0-1
WEST BROMWICH A v Aston Villa	6-1
West Ham Utd v Tottenham H	1-0

Third Round

Birmingham C v Ipswich T	2-1
Doncaster R v Swindon T	1-1, 2-4
Preston NE v Leeds Utd	1-1, 0-3
York C v Blackburn R	0-2
Arsenal v West Ham Utd	1-3
Blackpool v Chelsea	1-1, 3-1
Brighton & HA v Coventry C	1-1, 3-1
Exeter C v Walsall	1-2
Fulham v Wolves	5-0
Grimsby T v Workington	3-0
Leicester C v Lincoln C	5-0
Northampton T v Rotherham Utd	2-1
Sheffield Utd v Burnley	2-0
Southampton v Carlisle Utd	3-3, 1-2
WEST BROMWICH A v Manchester C	4-2
QUEEN'S PARK R v Swansea T	2-1

Fourth Round

Swindon T v WEST BROMWICH A	0-2
QUEEN'S PARK R v Leicester C	4-2
Blackpool v Fulham	4-2
Brighton & HA v Northampton T	1-1, 0-8
Carlisle Utd v Blackburn R	4-0
Grimsby T v Birmingham C	2-4
Sheffield Utd v Walsall	2-1
West Ham Utd v Leeds Utd	7-0

Fifth Round

Blackpool v West Ham Utd	1-3
Northampton T v WEST BROMWICH A	1-3
QUEEN'S PARK R v Carlisle Utd	2-1
Sheffield Utd v Birmingham C	2-3

Semi-final (agg)

Birmingham C v QUEEN'S PARK R	1-4, 1-3 (2-7)
WEST BROMWICH A v West Ham Utd	4-0, 2-2 (6-2)

Mark Lazarus (centre, white shirt) wheels around after scoring the winner for Third Division QPR in the 1967 Final.

FINAL (Wembley Stadium)

QUEEN'S PARK RANGERS	3
WEST BROMWICH ALBION	2

Queen's Park Rangers: Springett; Hazell, Langley, Sibley, Hunt, Keen, Lazarus, Sanderson, Allen, Marsh, R.Morgan.
Goalscorers: R.Morgan, Marsh, Lazarus
West Bromwich Albion: Sheppard; Cram, Williams, Collard, D.Clarke, Fraser, Brown, Astle, Kaye, Hope, C.Clark.
Goalscorer: C.Clarke 2
Referee: W.Crossley (Lancaster) *Attendance: 97,952*

1967-68

First Round

Bournemouth & Bos Ath v Watford	1-1, 0-0, 1-2
Middlesbrough v Barnsley	4-1
Orient v Gillingham	1-3
Port Vale v Chester	3-0
Swindon T v Newport Co	1-1, 0-2
Torquay Utd v Exeter C	0-0, 3-0
Walsall v Shrewsbury T	4-2
Aldershot v Cardiff C	2-3
Barrow v Southport	1-0
Brighton & HA v Colchester Utd	4-0
Crewe Alex v Stockport Co	1-1, 0-3
Darlington v York C	1-0
Doncaster R v Scunthorpe Utd	1-2
Grimsby T v Chesterfield	1-0
Halifax T v Bradford	5-0
Hartlepools Utd v Bradford C	2-0
Luton T v Charlton Ath	1-1, 2-1
Mansfield T v Lincoln C	2-3
Northampton T v Peterborough Utd	3-2
Notts Co v Rotherham Utd	0-1
Oxford Utd v Swansea T	3-1
Reading v Bristol R	3-0
Rochdale v Bury	0-1
Southend Utd v Brentford	1-0
Tranmere R v Wrexham	2-1
Workington v Oldham Ath	1-1, 1-1, 2-1

Second Round

Burnley v Cardiff C	2-1
Coventry C v ARSENAL	1-2
Grimsby T v Bury	2-2, 0-2
Huddersfield T v Wolves	1-0
Ipswich T v Southampton	5-2
Newport Co v Blackpool	0-1
Queen's Park R v Hull C	2-1
Barrow v Crystal Palace	1-0
Blackburn R v Brighton & HA	3-1
Bristol C v Everton	0-5
Carlisle Utd v Workington	0-2
Derby Co v Hartlepools Utd	4-0
Fulham v Tranmere R	1-0
Gillingham v Torquay Utd	2-2, 0-2
LEEDS UTD v Luton T	3-1
Lincoln C v Newcastle Utd	2-1
Liverpool v Bolton W	1-1, 2-3
Middlesbrough v Chelsea	2-1
Millwall v Sheffield Utd	3-2
Manchester C v Leicester C	4-0
Northampton T v Aston Villa	3-1
Norwich C v Rotherham Utd	1-1, 2-0
Oxford Utd v Preston NE	2-1
Plymouth Arg v Birmingham C	0-2
Portsmouth v Port Vale	3-1
Reading v West Bromwich A	3-1

Above: Terry Cooper scores the winner against Arsenal in the 1968 Final. Below: Billy Bremner with the League Cup after Leeds' win over the Gunners.

Scunthorpe Utd v Nottingham F 0-1
Southend Utd v Darlington 1-2
Stockport Co v Sheffield Wed 3-5
Stoke C v Watford 2-0
Sunderland v Halifax T 3-2
Walsall v West Ham Utd 1-5

Third Round
Burnley v Nottingham F 3-0
Queen's Park R v Oxford Utd 5-1
ARSENAL v Reading 1-0
Blackburn R v Middlesbrough 3-2
Darlington v Portsmouth 4-1
Derby Co v Birmingham C 3-1
Everton v Sunderland 2-3
LEEDS UTD v Bury 3-0
Lincoln C v Torquay Utd 4-2
Manchester C v Blackpool 1-1, 2-0
Northampton T v Millwall 0-0, 1-5
Norwich C v Huddersfield T 0-1
Sheffield Wed v Barrow 3-1
Stoke C v Ipswich T 2-1
West Ham Utd v Bolton W 4-1
Workington v Fulham 2-2, 2-6

Fourth Round
Darlington v Millwall 2-0
Queen's Park R v Burnley 1-2
ARSENAL v Blackburn R 2-1
Derby Co v Lincoln C 1-1, 3-0

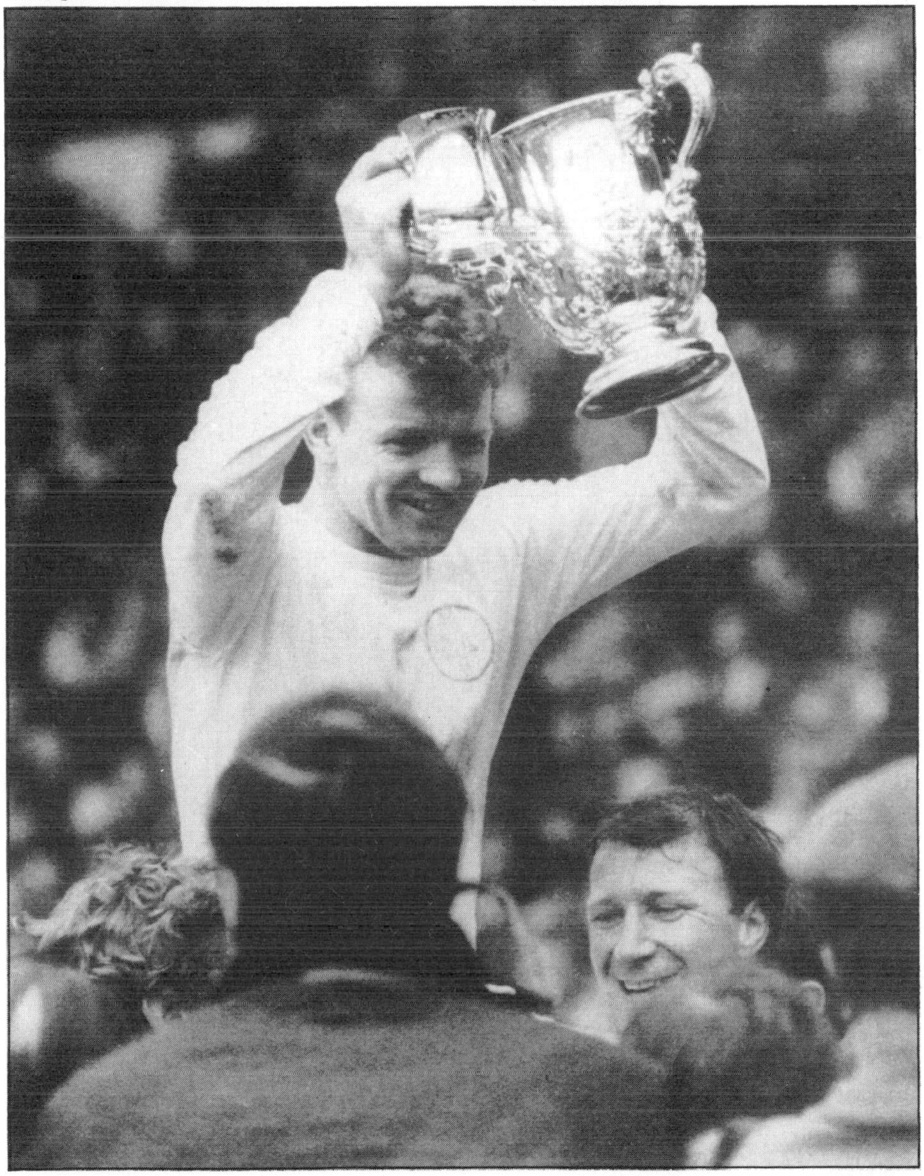

Fulham v Manchester C 3-2
Huddersfield T v West Ham Utd 2-0
Sheffield Wed v Stoke C 0-0, 1-2
Sunderland v LEEDS UTD 0-2

Fifth Round
Burnley v ARSENAL 3-3, 1-2
Derby Co v Darlington 5-4
Fulham v Huddersfield T 1-1, 1-2
LEEDS UTD v Stoke C 2-0

Semi-final (agg)
ARSENAL v Huddersfield T 3-2, 3-1 (6-3)
Derby Co v LEEDS UTD 0-1, 2-3 (2-4)

FINAL (Wembley Stadium)
LEEDS UNITED 1
ARSENAL 0
Leeds United: Sprake; Reaney, Cooper, Bremner, Charlton, Hunter, Greenhoff, Lorimer, Madeley, Giles, Gray(Belfitt).
Goalscorer: Cooper
Arsenal: Furnell; Storey, McNab, McLintock, Simpson, Ure, Radford, Jenkins(Neill), Graham, Sammels, Armstrong.
Referee: L.J.Hamer (Horwich) Attendance: 97,887

1968-69

First Round
Bournemouth & Bos Ath v Southend Utd 1-6
Bradford v Darlington 0-3
Bristol C v Newport Co 2-0
Bristol R v Swansea T 0-2
Bury v Stockport Co 1-1, 0-1
Chester v Tranmere R 0-0, 2-2, 1-1, 1-2
Colchester Utd v Reading 2-0
Derby Co v Chesterfield 3-0
Scunthorpe Utd v Rotherham Utd 2-1
SWINDON T v Torquay Utd 2-1
Walsall v Shrewsbury T 2-0
Aldershot v Brentford 2-4
Bradford C v Hartlepool 3-2
Brighton & HA v Oxford Utd 2-0
Doncaster R v Peterborough Utd 0-0, 0-1
Gillingham v Orient 2-2, 0-3
Grimsby T v Notts Co 0-0, 1-0
Halifax T v Hull C 0-3
Lincoln C v Mansfield T 2-1
Luton T v Watford 3-0
Northampton T v Crewe Alex 1-1, 0-1
Plymouth Arg v Exeter C 0-0, 0-0, 0-1
Preston NE v Oldham Ath 1-1, 1-0
Southport v Barrow 2-2, 3-1
Workington v Rochdale 2-1
Wrexham v Port Vale 2-0
York C v Barnsley 3-4

Second Round
Southport v Newcastle Utd 0-2
Barnsley v Millwall 1-1, 1-3
Birmingham C v Chelsea 0-1
Coventry C v Portsmouth 2-0
Everton v Tranmere R 4-0
Huddersfield T v Manchester C 0-0, 0-4
Ipswich T v Norwich C 2-4
Nottingham F v West Bromwich A 2-3
Orient v Fulham 1-0
Scunthorpe Utd v Lincoln C 2-1
Walsall v Swansea T 1-1, 2-3
Aston Villa v Tottenham H 1-4
ARSENAL v Sunderland 1-0
Blackburn R v Stoke C 1-1, 1-0
Bradford C v SWINDON T 1-1, 3-4
Brentford v Hull C 3-0
Brighton & HA v Luton T 1-1, 2-4
Bristol C v Middlesbrough 1-0
Carlisle Utd v Cardiff C 2-0
Colchester Utd v Workington 0-1
Crystal Palace v Preston NE 3-1
Darlington v Leicester C 1-2
Derby Co v Stockport Co 5-1
Exeter C v Sheffield Wed 3-1
Grimsby T v Burnley 1-1, 0-6
Leeds Utd v Charlton Ath 1-0
Liverpool v Sheffield Utd 4-0
Peterborough U v Queen's Park R 4-2
Southampton v Crewe Alex 3-1
West Ham Utd v Bolton W 7-2
Wolves v Southend Utd 1-0
Wrexham v Blackpool 1-1, 0-3

Third Round
Brentford v Norwich C 0-2
Carlisle Utd v Leicester C 0-3
Everton v Luton T 5-1
Orient v Crystal Palace 0-1
SWINDON T v Blackburn R 1-0
Blackpool v Manchester C 1-0
Chelsea v Derby Co 0-0, 1-3

Leeds Utd v Bristol C............2-1
Liverpool v Swansea T............2-0
Peterborough U v West Bromwich A............2-1
Scunthorpe Utd v ARSENAL............1-6
Southampton v Newcastle Utd............4-1
Tottenham H v Exeter C............6-3
West Ham Utd v Coventry C............0-0, 2-3
Wolves v Millwall............5-1
Workington v Burnley............0-1

Fourth Round
ARSENAL v Liverpool............2-1
Blackpool v Wolves............2-1
Burnley v Leicester C............4-0
Coventry C v SWINDON T............2-2, 0-3
Crystal Palace v Leeds Utd............2-1
Everton v Derby Co............0-0, 0-1
Norwich C v Southampton............0-4
Tottenham H v Peterborough Utd............1-0

Fifth Round
ARSENAL v Blackpool............5-1
Burnley v Crystal Palace............2-0
Derby Co v SWINDON T............0-0, 0-1
Tottenham H v Southampton............1-0

Semi-final (agg)
ARSENAL v Tottenham H............1-0, 1-1 (2-1)
Burnley v SWINDON T............1-2, 2-1, 2-3 (5-6)

FINAL (Wembley Stadium)
SWINDON TOWN............3
ARSENAL............1
Arsenal: Wilson; Storey, McNab, McLintock, Ure, Simpson(Graham), Radford, Sammels, Court, Gould, Armstrong.
Goalscorer: Gould
Swindon Town: Downsborough; Thomas, Trollope, Butler, Burrows, Harland, Heath, Smart, Smith, Noble(Penman), Rogers.
Goalscorers: Smart, Rogers 2
Referee: W.Handley (Cannock) *Attendance: 98,189*

1969-70

First Round
Bradford v Rotherham Utd............0-2
Newport Co v Swansea C............2-3
Scunthorpe Utd v Hartlepool............0-2
Southend Utd v Brentford............2-2, 0-0, 3-2
Aldershot v Gillingham............0-1
Barnsley v Halifax T............0-1
Bolton W v Rochdale............6-3
Bournemouth & Bos Ath v Bristol R............3-0
Bradford C v Chesterfield............1-1, 1-0
Brighton & HA v Portsmouth............1-0
Chester v Aston Villa............1-2
Colchester Utd v Reading............1-1, 3-0
Crewe Alex v Wrexham............0-0, 0-1
Darlington v York C............3-0
Exeter C v Bristol C............1-1, 2-3
Grimsby T v Doncaster R............0-2
Mansfield T v Notts Co............3-1
Orient v Fulham............0-0, 1-3
Oxford Utd v Northampton T............2-0
Peterborough Utd v Luton T............1-1, 2-5
Plymouth Arg v Torquay Utd............2-2, 0-1
Port Vale v Tranmere R............0-1
Preston NE v Bury............0-1
Shrewsbury T v Walsall............1-0
Southport v Oldham Ath............5-1
Stockport Co v Blackburn R............0-2
Watford v Lincoln C............2-1
Workington v Barrow............0-0, 1-3

Second Round
Bristol C v Leicester C............0-0, 0-0, 1-3
Carlisle Utd v Huddersfield T............2-0
Charlton Ath v Wrexham............0-2
Coventry C v Chelsea............0-1
Luton T v Millwall............2-2, 1-0
Sheffield Utd v Newcastle Utd............2-0
Shrewsbury T v Southend Utd............2-2, 0-2
Southampton v Arsenal............1-1, 0-2
Swansea C v Swindon T............1-3
Aston Villa v WEST BROMWICH A............1-2
Barrow v Nottingham F............1-2
Blackburn R v Doncaster R............4-2
Blackpool v Gillingham............3-1
Bolton W v Rotherham Utd............0-0, 3-3, 0-1
Brighton & HA v Birmingham C............2-0
Crystal Palace v Cardiff C............3-1
Darlington v Everton............0-1
Fulham v Leeds Utd............0-1
Hartlepool v Derby Co............1-3
Hull C v Norwich C............1-0
Ipswich T v Colchester Utd............4-0
Manchester Utd v Middlesbrough............1-0
Mansfield T v Queen's Park R............2-2, 0-4

Arsenal's Bob McNab (3) and Ian Ure watch as Third Division Swindon Town put Arsenal goalkeeper Bob Wilson under pressure in the 1969 Final.

Oxford Utd v Bury............4-1
Sheffield Wed v Bournemouth & Bos Ath............1-1, 0-1
Southport v MANCHESTER C............0-3
Stoke C v Burnley............0-2
Sunderland v Bradford C............1-2
Tranmere R v Torquay Utd............2-1
Watford v Liverpool............1-2
West Ham Utd v Halifax T............4-2
Wolves v Tottenham H............1-0

Third Round
Manchester Utd v Wrexham............2-0
Nottingham F v West Ham Utd............1-0
Queen's Park R v Tranmere R............6-0
Sheffield Utd v Luton T............3-0
Arsenal v Everton............0-0, 0-1
Bournemouth & Bos Ath v Leicester C............0-2
Bradford C v Southend Utd............2-1
Brighton & HA v Wolves............2-3
Crystal Palace v Blackpool............2-2, 1-0
Carlisle Utd v Blackburn R............2-1
Derby Co v Hull C............3-1
Ipswich T v WEST BROMWICH A............1-1, 0-2
Leeds Utd v Chelsea............1-1, 0-2
MANCHESTER C v Liverpool............3-2
Oxford Utd v Swindon T............1-0
Rotherham Utd v Burnley............1-1, 0-2

Fourth Round
Burnley v Manchester Utd............0-0, 0-1
Carlisle Utd v Chelsea............1-0
Crystal Palace v Derby Co............1-1, 0-3
Leicester C v Sheffield Utd............2-0
MANCHESTER C v Everton............2-0
Nottingham F v Oxford Utd............0-1
Queen's Park R v Wolves............3-1
WEST BROMWICH A v Bradford C............4-0

Fifth Round
Leicester C v WEST BROMWICH A............0-0, 1-2
MANCHESTER C v Queen's Park R............3-0
Oxford Utd v Carlisle Utd............0-0, 0-1
Derby Co v Manchester Utd............0-0, 0-1

Semi-final (agg)
Carlisle Utd v WEST BROMWICH A............1-0, 1-4 (2-4)
MANCHESTER C v Manchester Utd............2-1, 2-2 (4-3)

FINAL (Wembley Stadium)
MANCHESTER CITY............2
WEST BROMWICH ALBION............1
Manchester City: Corrigan; Book, Mann, Doyle, Booth, Oakes, Heslop, Bell, Summerbee(Bowyer), Lee, Pardoe.
Goalscorers: Doyle, Pardoe
West Bromwich Albion: Osborne; Fraser, Wilson, Brown, Talbut, Kaye, Cantello, Suggett, Astle, Hartford(Krzywicki), Hope.
Goalscorer: Astle
Referee: J.James (York) *Attendance: 97,963*

Veteran Tony Book carries the League Cup after Manchester City's win in 1970.

1970-71

First Round
Birmingham C v Wrexham 3-3, 3-2
Bristol R v Brighton & HA 1-0
Bury v Oldham Ath 1-3
Charlton Ath v Southend Utd 3-0
Crewe Alex v Tranmere R 2-2, 0-4
Exeter C v Swansea C 0-0, 2-4
Port Vale v Walsall 0-1
Aldershot v Brentford 1-0
Aston Villa v Notts Co 4-0
Torquay Utd v Bournemouth & Bos Ath 1-1, 2-1
Watford v Peterborough Utd 2-0
Workington v Barrow 2-0
Barnsley v Rotherham Utd 0-1
Chester v Shrewsbury T 2-1
Colchester Utd v Cambridge Utd 5-0
Doncaster R v Darlington 1-1, 1-3
Fulham v Orient 1-0
Halifax T v Bradford C 3-2
Hartlepool v York C 2-3
Gillingham v Luton T 0-1
Lincoln C v Grimsby T 2-1
Mansfield T v Chesterfield 6-2
Newport Co v Reading 2-1
Portsmouth v Plymouth Arg 2-0
Rochdale v Southport 1-0
Scunthorpe Utd v Northampton T 2-3
Stockport Co v Preston NE 0-1

Second Round
Bristol R v Newcastle Utd 2-1
Derby Co v Halifax T 3-1
Ipswich T v Arsenal 0-0, 0-4
Luton T v Workington 3-0
Mansfield T v Liverpool 0-0, 2-3
Oldham Ath v Middlesbrough 2-4
Queen's Park R v Cardiff C 4-0
Rotherham Utd v Bristol C 0-0, 0-4
Sheffield Utd v Leeds Utd 1-0
Swindon T v Watford 4-2
West Bromwich A v Charlton Ath 3-1
Aldershot v Manchester Utd 1-3
ASTON VILLA v Burnley 2-0
Blackpool v Newport Co 4-1
Bolton W v Blackburn R 1-0
Carlisle Utd v Manchester C 2-1
Colchester Utd v Birmingham C 1-1, 1-2
Crystal Palace v Rochdale 3-3, 3-1
Darlington v Fulham 0-4
Huddersfield T v Nottingham F 0-0, 0-2
Leicester C v Southampton 3-2
Lincoln C v Sunderland 2-1
Norwich C v Chester 0-0, 2-1
Oxford Utd v Wolves 1-0
Portsmouth v Walsall 1-0
Sheffield Wed v Chelsea 1-1, 1-2
Stoke C v Millwall 0-0, 1-2
Torquay Utd v Preston NE 1-3
TOTTENHAM H v Swansea C 3-0
Tranmere R v Coventry C 1-1, 1-2
West Ham Utd v Hull C 1-0
York C v Northampton T 0-0, 1-1, 1-2

Third Round
Birmingham C v Nottingham F 2-1
Carlisle Utd v Oxford Utd 3-1
Coventry C v West Ham Utd 3-1
Fulham v Queen's Park R 2-0
Luton T v Arsenal 0-1
Northampton T v ASTON VILLA 1-1, 0-3
Preston NE v West Bromwich A 0-1
Swindon T v Liverpool 2-0
Blackpool v Bristol C 0-1
Bolton W v Leicester C 1-1, 0-1
Chelsea v Middlesbrough 3-2
Crystal Palace v Lincoln C 4-0
Derby Co v Millwall 4-2
Norwich C v Bristol R 1-1, 1-3
TOTTENHAM H v Sheffield Utd 2-1
Manchester Utd v Portsmouth 1-0

Fourth Round
Bristol R v Birmingham C 3-0
Coventry C v Derby Co 1-0
Fulham v Swindon T 1-0
ASTON VILLA v Carlisle Utd 1-0
Crystal Palace v Arsenal 0-0, 2-0
Leicester C v Bristol C 2-2, 1-2
Manchester Utd v Chelsea 2-1
TOTTENHAM H v West Bromwich A 5-0

Fifth Round
Fulham v Bristol C 0-0, 0-1
Bristol R v ASTON VILLA 1-1, 0-1
Manchester Utd v Crystal Palace 4-2
TOTTENHAM H v Coventry C 4-1

Semi-final (agg)
Bristol C v TOTTENHAM H 1-1, 0-2 (1-3)
Manchester Utd v ASTON VILLA 1-1, 1-2 (2-3)

FINAL (Wembley Stadium)
TOTTENHAM HOTSPUR 2
ASTON VILLA 0
Tottenham Hotspur: Jennings; Kinnear, Knowles, Mullery, Collins, Beal, Gilzean, Perryman, Chivers, Peters, Neighbour. Sub: Pearce.
Goalscorer: Chivers 2
Aston Villa: Dunn; Bradley, Aitken, Godfrey, Turnbull, Tiler, McMahon, Rioch, Lochhead, Hamilton, Anderson.
Referee: J.Finney (Hereford) Attendance: 97,024

Alan Mullery after Spurs' win over Aston Villa in 1971.

1971-72

First Round
AFC Bournemouth v Portsmouth 2-1
Charlton Ath v Peterborough Utd 5-1
Fulham v Cambridge Utd 4-0
Grimsby T v Doncaster R 4-3
Newport Co v Torquay Utd 1-2
Oldham Ath v Bury 1-0
Orient v Notts Co 1-1, 1-3
Plymouth Arg v Bristol C 1-0
Rotherham Utd v Sheffield Wed 0-2
Swansea C v Brighton & HA 0-1
Aldershot v Southend Utd 1-1, 2-1
Aston Villa v Wrexham 2-2, 1-1, 4-3

Barnsley v Hartlepool	0-0, 1-0
Barrow v Preston NE	0-2
Blackburn R v Workington	2-0
Bradford C v Bolton W	1-1, 1-2
Chesterfield v Mansfield T	0-0, 5-0
Colchester Utd v Brentford	3-1
Crewe Alex v Southport	0-1
Darlington v York C	0-1
Exeter C v Bristol R	0-3
Gillingham v Reading	4-0
Halifax T v Rochdale	1-1, 2-2, 2-0
Port Vale v Shrewsbury T	0-2
Scunthorpe Utd v Lincoln C	0-1
Stockport Co v Walsall	1-0
Tranmere R v Chester	1-1, 3-1
Watford v Northampton T	2-0

Second Round

Bristol R v Sunderland	3-1
Carlisle Utd v Sheffield Wed	5-0
Charlton Ath v Leicester C	3-1
Coventry C v Burnley	0-1
Crystal Palace v Luton T	2-0
Grimsby T v Shrewsbury T	2-1
Huddersfield T v Bolton W	0-2
Ipswich T v Manchester Utd	1-3
Liverpool v Hull C	3-0
Nottingham F v Aldershot	5-1
Queen's Park R v Birmingham C	2-0
Sheffield Utd v Fulham	3-0
Southampton v Everton	2-1
Stockport Co v Watford	0-1
Arsenal v Barnsley	1-0
Blackburn R v Lincoln C	0-0, 1-4
AFC Bournemouth v Blackpool	0-2
CHELSEA v Plymouth Arg	2-0
Chesterfield v Aston Villa	2-3
Colchester Utd v Swindon T	4-1
Derby Co v Leeds Utd	0-0, 0-2
Manchester C v Wolves	4-3
Newcastle Utd v Halifax T	2-1
Norwich C v Brighton & HA	2-0
Notts Co v Gillingham	1-2
Oxford Utd v Millwall	1-0
Southport v STOKE C	1-2
Torquay Utd v Oldham Ath	2-1
Tranmere R v Preston NE	0-1
West Bromwich A v Tottenham H	0-1
West Ham Utd v Cardiff C	1-1, 2-1
York C v Middlesbrough	2-2, 2-1

Third Round

Blackpool v Colchester Utd	4-0
Bolton W v Manchester C	3-0
Bristol R v Charlton Ath	2-1
Crystal Palace v Aston Villa	2-2, 0-2
Liverpool v Southampton	1-0
Queen's Park R v Lincoln C	4-2
Sheffield Utd v York C	3-2
Arsenal v Newcastle Utd	4-0
Gillingham v Grimsby T	1-1, 0-1
Manchester Utd v Burnley	1-1, 1-0
Nottingham F v CHELSEA	1-1, 1-2
Norwich C v Carlisle Utd	4-1
Oxford Utd v STOKE C	1-1, 0-2
Torquay Utd v Tottenham H	1-4
Watford v Preston NE	1-1, 1-2
West Ham Utd v Leeds Utd	0-0, 1-0

Fourth Round

Arsenal v Sheffield Utd	0-0, 0-2
Blackpool v Aston Villa	4-1
Grimsby T v Norwich C	1-1, 1-3
Queen's Park R v Bristol R	1-1, 0-1
CHELSEA v Bolton W	1-1, 6-0
Manchester Utd v STOKE C	1-1, 0-0, 1-2
Tottenham H v Preston NE	1-1, 2-1
West Ham Utd v Liverpool	2-1

Fifth Round

Norwich C v CHELSEA	0-1
Tottenham H v Blackpool	2-0
West Ham Utd v Sheffield Utd	5-0
Bristol R v STOKE C	2-4

Semi-final (agg)

STOKE C v West Ham Utd	1-2, 1-0, 0-0, 3-2 (5-4)
CHELSEA v Tottenham H	3-2, 2-2 (5-4)

FINAL (Wembley Stadium)

STOKE CITY	2
CHELSEA	1

Stoke City: Banks; Marsh, Pejic, Bernard, Smith, Bloor, Conroy, Greenhoff(Mahoney), Ritchie, Dobing, Eastham.
Goalscorers: Conroy, Eastham
Chelsea: Bonetti; Mulligan(Balding), Harris, Hollins, Dempsey, Webb, Cooke, Garland, Osgood, Hudson, Houseman.
Goalscorer: Osgood
Referee: *Attendance: 99,998*

Peter Dobing assumes the classic winners' pose after Stoke City's victory over Chelsea in 1972.

1972-73

First Round

Halifax T v Bury	1-2
Northampton T v Charlton Ath	0-3
Plymouth Arg v AFC Bournemouth	0-2
Scunthorpe Utd v Chesterfield	0-0, 0-5
Swansea C v Newport Co	1-1, 0-3
Aston Villa v Hereford Utd	4-1
Barnsley v Grimsby T	0-0, 0-2
Blackburn R v Rochdale	0-1
Bolton W v Oldham Ath	3-0
Bradford C v Stockport Co	1-1, 1-1, 0-2
Brentford v Cambridge Utd	1-0
Brighton & HA v Exeter C	2-1
Cardiff C v Bristol R	2-2, 1-3
Chester v Shrewsbury T	4-3
Darlington v Rotherham Utd	0-1
Gillingham v Colchester Utd	1-0
Hartlepool v Doncaster R	1-0
Mansfield T v Lincoln C	3-1
Notts Co v York C	3-1
Orient v Watford	2-0
Oxford Utd v Peterborough Utd	4-0
Reading v Fulham	1-1, 1-1, 0-1
Southend Utd v Aldershot	2-1
Southport v Walsall	4-1
Torquay Utd v Portsmouth	1-2
Tranmere R v Port Vale	0-1
Workington v Preston NE	1-0
Wrexham v Crewe Alex	4-0

Second Round

TOTTENHAM H v Huddersfield T	2-1
Middlesbrough v Wrexham	2-0
Gillingham v Millwall	0-2
Portsmouth v Chesterfield	0-1
West Bromwich A v Queen's Park R	2-1
Carlisle Utd v Liverpool	1-1, 1-5
Nottingham F v Aston Villa	0-1
Leeds Utd v Burnley	4-0
Wolves v Orient	2-1
Sheffield Wed v Bolton W	2-0
Bristol R v Brighton & HA	4-0
Oxford Utd v Manchester Utd	2-2, 1-3
Port Vale v Newcastle Utd	1-3
AFC Bournemouth v Blackpool	0-0, 1-1, 1-2
Birmingham C v Luton T	1-1, 1-1, 1-0
Coventry C v Hartlepool	1-0
Bury v Grimsby T	1-0
Manchester C v Rochdale	4-0
Swindon T v Derby Co	0-1
Southend Utd v Chelsea	0-1
Southampton v Chester	0-0, 2-2, 2-0
Notts Co v Southport	3-2
Newport Co v Ipswich T	0-3
Stoke C v Sunderland	3-0
Workington v Sheffield Utd	0-1
Charlton Ath v Mansfield T	4-3
Arsenal v Everton	1-0
Rotherham Utd v Brentford	2-0
Crystal Palace v Stockport Co	0-1
West Ham Utd v Bristol C	2-1
Hull C v Fulham	1-0
NORWICH C v Leicester C	2-1

Third Round

Arsenal v Rotherham Utd	5-0
Birmingham C v Coventry C	2-1
Bristol R v Manchester Utd	1-1, 2-1
Bury v Manchester C	2-0
Hull C v NORWICH C	1-2
Ipswich T v Stoke C	1-2
Middlesbrough v TOTTENHAM H	1-1, 0-0, 1-2
Millwall v Chesterfield	2-0
Sheffield Utd v Charlton Ath	0-0, 2-2, 1-0
Southampton v Notts Co	1-3
West Bromwich A v Liverpool	1-1, 1-2
Aston Villa v Leeds Utd	1-1, 0-2
Derby Co v Chelsea	0-0, 2-3
Newcastle Utd v Blackpool	0-3
Stockport Co v West Ham Utd	2-1
Wolves v Sheffield Wed	3-1

Fourth Round

Blackpool v Birmingham C	2-0
Bury v Chelsea	0-1
Liverpool v Leeds Utd	2-2, 1-0
Notts Co v Stoke C	3-1
Sheffield Utd v Arsenal	1-2
Wolves v Bristol R	4-0
Stockport Co v NORWICH C	1-5
TOTTENHAM H v Millwall	2-0

Fifth Round

Arsenal v NORWICH C	0-3
Wolves v Blackpool	1-1, 1-0
Chelsea v Notts Co	3-1
Liverpool v TOTTENHAM H	1-1, 1-3

Semi-final (agg)

Chelsea v NORWICH C	0-2, 0-1 (0-3)
Wolves v TOTTENHAM H	1-2, 2-2 (3-4)

FINAL (Wembley Stadium)

TOTTENHAM HOTSPUR	1
NORWICH CITY	0

Tottenham Hotspur: Jennings; Kinnear, Knowles, Pratt(Coates), England, Beal, Gilzean, Perryman, Chivers, Peters, Pearce.
Goalscorer: Coates
Norwich City: Keelan; Payne, Butler, Stringer, Forbes, Briggs, Livermore, Blair(Howard), Cross, Paddon, Anderson.
Referee: *Attendance: 100,000*

1973-74

First Round

Bolton W v Preston NE	1-1, 2-0
Brentford v Orient	1-2
Bury v Oldham Ath	0-0, 3-2
Carlisle Utd v Workington	2-2, 1-0
Grimsby T v Northampton T	2-1
Halifax T v Barnsley	1-1, 1-0
Notts Co v Doncaster R	3-4

Tottenham's goalscorer Ralph Coates crowns himself after netting the winner in the 1973 League Cup Final against Norwich City.

Wolves skipper Mike Bailey and teammates after the Midlanders beat Manchester City in the 1974 Final.

Portsmouth v Southend Utd 2-1
Rotherham Utd v Lincoln C 2-1
Swansea C v Exeter C 1-1, 1-2
Swindon T v Newport Co 3-3, 2-1
Aldershot v Cambridge Utd 1-1, 0-3
AFC Bournemouth v Bristol R 1-0
Brighton & HA v Charlton Ath 1-2
Cardiff C v Hereford Utd 2-0
Chester v Wrexham 0-2
Chesterfield v Mansfield T 1-1, 1-0
Darlington v Bradford C 2-1
Gillingham v Colchester Utd 4-2
Peterborough Utd v Scunthorpe Utd 2-2, 1-2
Reading v Watford 2-2, 3-2
Rochdale v Hartlepool 5-3
Southport v Blackburn R 1-1, 1-3
Stockport Co v Port Vale 2-0
Torquay Utd v Plymouth Arg 0-2
Tranmere R v Crewe Alex 3-3, 1-0
Walsall v Shrewsbury T 6-1
York C v Huddersfield T 1-0

Second Round
Arsenal v Tranmere R 0-1
Walsall v MANCHESTER C 0-0, 0-0, 0-4
Coventry C v Darlington 5-1
Derby Co v Sunderland 2-2, 1-1, 0-3
Everton v Reading 1-0
Halifax T v WOLVES 0-3
Ipswich T v Leeds Utd 2-0
Leicester C v Hull C 3-3, 2-3
Manchester Utd v Middlesbrough 0-1
Newcastle Utd v Doncaster R 6-0
Queen's Park R v Tottenham H 1-0
Southampton v Charlton Ath 3-0
Stoke C v Chelsea 1-0
West Bromwich A v Sheffield Utd 2-1
West Ham Utd v Liverpool 2-2, 0-1
Blackpool v Birmingham C 1-1, 2-4
Bury v Cambridge Utd 2-0
Orient v Blackburn R 2-0
Plymouth Arg v Portsmouth 4-0
Scunthorpe Utd v Bristol C 0-0, 1-2
Stockport Co v Crystal Palace 1-0
York C v Aston Villa 1-0
AFC Bournemouth v Sheffield Wed 0-0, 2-2, 1-2
Cardiff C v Burnley 2-2, 2-3
Chesterfield v Swindon T 1-0
Gillingham v Carlisle Utd 1-2
Luton T v Grimsby T 1-1, 0-0, 2-0
Millwall v Nottingham F 0-0, 3-1
Norwich C v Wrexham 6-2
Oxford Utd v Fulham 1-1, 0-3
Rotherham Utd v Exeter C 1-4
Rochdale v Bolton W 0-4

Third Round
Birmingham C v Newcastle Utd 2-2, 1-0
Bristol C v Coventry C 2-2, 1-2
Burnley v Plymouth Arg 1-2
Everton v Norwich C 0-1
Southampton v Chesterfield 3-0
Fulham v Ipswich T 2-2, 1-2
Luton T v Bury 0-0, 3-2
Millwall v Bolton W 1-1, 2-1
Orient v York C 1-1, 1-2
Stoke C v Middlesbrough 1-1, 2-1
Tranmere R v WOLVES 1-1, 1-2
West Bromwich A v Exeter C 1-3
Carlisle Utd v MANCHESTER C 0-1
Hull C v Stockport Co 4-1
Queen's Park R v Sheffield Wed 8-2
Sunderland v Liverpool 0-2

Fourth Round
Coventry C v Stoke C 2-1
Queen's Park R v Plymouth Arg 0-3
WOLVES v Exeter C 5-1
Ipswich T v Birmingham C 1-3
Millwall v Luton T 3-1
Southampton v Norwich C 0-2
York C v MANCHESTER C 0-0, 1-4
Hull C v Liverpool 0-0, 1-3

Fifth Round
Birmingham C v Plymouth Arg 1-2
Coventry C v MANCHESTER C 2-2, 2-4
Millwall v Norwich C 1-1, 1-2
WOLVES v Liverpool 1-0

Semi-final (agg)
Norwich C v WOLVES 1-1, 0-1 (1-2)
Plymouth Arg v MANCHESTER C 1-1, 0-2 (1-3)

FINAL (Wembley Stadium)
WOLVERHAMPTON WANDERERS 2
MANCHESTER CITY 1
Wolverhampton Wanderers: Pierce; Palmer, Parkin, Bailey, Munro, McAlle, Sunderland, Hibbitt, Richards, Dougan, Wagstaffe(Powell).
Goalscorers: Hibbitt, Richards

Manchester City: MacRae; Pardoe, Donachie, Doyle, Booth, Towers, Summerbee, Bell, Lee, Law, Marsh.
Goalscorer: Bell
Referee: E.Wallace (Crewe) Attendance: 100,000

1974-75

First Round
Bristol C v Cardiff C 2-1
Barnsley v Halifax T 0-1
Bradford C v Darlington 2-1
Bristol R v Plymouth Arg 0-0, 1-0
Bury v Oldham Ath 2-0
Charlton Ath v Peterborough Utd 4-0
Colchester Utd v Oxford Utd 1-0
Doncaster R v Mansfield T 2-1
Newport Co v Torquay Utd 1-0
Northampton T v Port Vale 1-0
Preston NE v Rochdale 1-0
Rotherham Utd v Lincoln C 1-1, 1-1, 2-1
Scunthorpe Utd v Sheffield Wed 1-0
Swindon T v Portsmouth 0-1
Wrexham v Crewe Alex 1-2
Brentford v Aldershot 3-0
Chester v Walsall 2-1
Chesterfield v Grimsby T 3-0
Exeter C v Swansea C 3-1
Gillingham v AFC Bournemouth 1-1, 1-1, 1-2
Hereford Utd v Shrewsbury T 1-1, 1-0
Reading v Brighton & HA 0-0, 2-2, 0-0, 3-2
Southend Utd v Cambridge Utd 2-0
Southport v Tranmere R 0-2
Stockport Co v Blackburn R 0-2
Watford v Crystal Palace 1-1, 1-5
Workington v Hartlepool 1-2
York C v Huddersfield T 0-2

Second Round
Arsenal v Leicester C 1-1, 1-2
Bolton W v NORWICH C 0-0, 1-3
Bury v Doncaster R 2-0
Coventry C v Ipswich T 1-2
Crystal Palace v Bristol C 1-4
Huddersfield T v Leeds Utd 1-1, 1-1, 1-2
Liverpool v Brentford 2-1
Manchester C v Scunthorpe Utd 6-0
Northampton T v Blackburn R 2-2, 0-1
Nottingham F v Newcastle Utd 1-1, 0-3
Preston NE v Sunderland 2-0
Queen's Park R v Orient 1-1, 3-0
Sheffield Utd v Chesterfield 3-1
Southampton v Notts Co 1-0
West Bromwich A v Millwall 1-0
ASTON VILLA v Everton 1-1, 3-0
AFC Bournemouth v Hartlepool 1-1, 2-2, 1-1, 0-1
Bradford C v Carlisle Utd 0-1
Chelsea v Newport Co 4-2
Chester v Blackpool 3-1
Crewe Alex v Birmingham C 2-1
Exeter C v Hereford Utd 0-1
Hull C v Burnley 1-2
Luton T v Bristol R 1-0
Manchester Utd v Charlton Ath 5-1
Portsmouth v Derby Co 1-5
Reading v Rotherham Utd 4-2
Southend Utd v Colchester Utd 0-2
Tottenham H v Middlesbrough 0-4
Stoke C v Halifax T 3-0
Tranmere R v West Ham Utd 0-0, 0-6
Wolves v Fulham 1-3

Third Round
Bristol C v Liverpool 0-0, 0-4
Fulham v West Ham Utd 2-1
Ipswich T v Hereford Utd 4-1
Middlesbrough v Leicester C 1-0
Queen's Park R v Newcastle Utd 0-4
Sheffield Utd v Luton T 2-0
Southampton v Derby Co 5-0
Bury v Leeds Utd 1-2
Chelsea v Stoke C 2-2, 1-1, 2-6
Chester v Preston NE 1-0
Colchester Utd v Carlisle Utd 2-0
Crewe Alex v ASTON VILLA 2-2, 0-1
Hartlepool v Blackburn R 1-1, 2-1
Manchester Utd v Manchester C 1-0
Reading v Burnley 1-2
West Bromwich A v NORWICH C 1-1, 0-2

Fourth Round
Hartlepool v ASTON VILLA 1-1, 1-6
Ipswich T v Stoke C 2-1
Liverpool v Middlesbrough 0-1
Sheffield Utd v NORWICH C 2-2, 1-2
Chester v Leeds Utd 3-0
Colchester Utd v Southampton 0-0, 1-0
Manchester Utd v Burnley 3-2
Newcastle Utd v Fulham 3-0

Fifth Round
Colchester Utd v ASTON VILLA 1-2
Middlesbrough v Manchester Utd 0-0, 0-3
NORWICH C v Ipswich T 1-1, 2-1
Newcastle Utd v Chester 0-0, 0-1

Semi-final (agg)
Chester v ASTON VILLA 2-2, 2-3 (4-5)
Manchester Utd v NORWICH C 2-2, 0-1 (2-3)

FINAL (Wembley Stadium)
ASTON VILLA 1
NORWICH CITY 0
Aston Villa: Cumbes; Robson, Aitken, Ross, Nicholl, McDonald, Graydon, Little, Leonard, Hamilton, Carrodus.
Goalscorer: Graydon
Norwich City: Keelan; Machin, Sullivan, Morris, Forbes, Stringer, Miller, MacDougall, Boyer, Suggett, Powell.
Referee: G.Hill (Lancashire) Attendance: 95,946

1975-76

First Round (agg)
Port Vale v Hereford Utd 4-2, 0-2, 0-1 (4-5)
Brentford v Brighton & HA 2-1, 1-1 (3-2)
Bury v Rochdale 2-0, 2-0 (4-0)
Cambridge Utd v Charlton Ath 1-1, 0-3 (1-4)
Crystal Palace v Colchester Utd 3-0, 1-3 (4-3)
Darlington* v Sheffield Wed 0-2, 2-0, 0-0 (2-2)
Doncaster R v Grimsby T 3-1, 0-0 (3-1)
Halifax T v Hartlepool 4-1, 1-2 (5-3)
Huddersfield T v Barnsley 2-1, 1-1 (3-2)
Newport Co v Exeter C 1-1, 0-2 (1-3)
Oldham Ath v Workington 3-0, 3-1 (6-1)
Plymouth Arg v AFC Bournemouth 2-0, 2-1 (4-1)
Preston NE v Blackburn R 2-0, 0-0 (2-0)
Rotherham Utd v Nottingham F 1-2, 1-5 (2-7)
Swansea C v Torquay Utd 1-2, 3-5 (4-7)
Swindon T v Millwall 2-1, 1-0 (3-1)
Walsall v Shrewsbury T 0-0, 1-2 (1-2)
Watford v Northampton T 2-0, 1-1 (3-1)
Aldershot v Portsmouth 1-1, 1-2 (2-3)
Bradford C v York C 2-0, 0-3 (2-3)
Cardiff C v Bristol R 1-2, 1-1 (2-3)
Crewe Alex v Tranmere R 2-1, 1-2, 2-1 (5-4)
Lincoln C v Chesterfield 4-2, 2-3 (6-5)
Mansfield T v Scunthorpe Utd 4-0, 2-0 (6-0)
Reading v Gillingham 0-1, 1-1 (1-2)
Southend Utd v Peterborough Utd 2-0, 0-3 (2-3)
Southport v Stockport Co 3-1, 2-1 (5-2)
Wrexham v Chester 3-0, 0-0 (3-0)

Second Round
NEWCASTLE UTD v Southport 6-0
Birmingham C v Orient 4-0
Bury v Middlesbrough 1-2
Carlisle Utd v Gillingham 2-0
Charlton Ath v Oxford Utd 3-3, 1-1, 3-2
Doncaster R v Crystal Palace 2-1
Darlington v Luton T 2-1
Everton v Arsenal 2-2, 1-0
Hull C v Preston NE 4-2
Leeds Utd v Ipswich T 3-2
Notts Co v Sunderland 2-1
Portsmouth v Leicester C 1-1, 0-1
Shrewsbury T v Queen's Park R 1-4
Southampton v Bristol R 0-1
Swindon T v Wolves 2-2, 2-3
Watford v Tottenham H 0-1
York C v Liverpool 0-1
West Bromwich A v Fulham 1-1, 0-1
Peterborough Utd v Blackpool 2-0
Wrexham v Mansfield T 1-2
West Ham Utd v Bristol C 0-0, 3-1
Aston Villa v Oldham Ath 2-0
Manchester Utd v Brentford 2-1
Nottingham F v Plymouth Arg 1-0
Bolton W v Coventry C 1-3
Crewe Alex v Chelsea 1-0
Derby Co v Huddersfield T 2-1
Halifax T v Sheffield Utd 2-4
Torquay Utd v Exeter C 1-1, 2-1
Hereford Utd v Burnley 1-4
Lincoln C v Stoke C 2-1
Norwich C v MANCHESTER C 1-1, 2-2, 1-6

Third Round
Birmingham C v Wolves 0-2
Bristol R v NEWCASTLE UTD 1-1, 0-2
Hull C v Sheffield Utd 2-0
Liverpool v Burnley 1-1, 0-1
Middlesbrough v Derby Co 1-0
Queen's Park R v Charlton Ath 1-1, 3-0
Torquay Utd v Doncaster R 1-1, 0-3
Aston Villa v Manchester Utd 1-2
Crewe Alex v Tottenham H 0-2
Everton v Carlisle Utd 2-0
Fulham v Peterborough Utd 0-1
Leeds Utd v Notts Co 0-1
Leicester C v Lincoln C 2-1
MANCHESTER C v Nottingham F 2-1
Mansfield T v Coventry C 2-0
West Ham Utd v Darlington 3-0

Fourth Round 11 November
Burnley v Leicester C 2-0
Doncaster R v Hull C 2-1
Everton v Notts Co 2-2, 0-2
Middlesbrough v Peterborough Utd 3-0
Queen's Park R v NEWCASTLE UTD 1-3
MANCHESTER C v Manchester Utd 4-0
Mansfield T v Wolves 1-0
Tottenham H v West Ham Utd 0-0, 2-0

Fifth Round
Burnley v Middlesbrough 0-2
MANCHESTER C v Mansfield T 4-2
NEWCASTLE UTD v Notts Co 1-0
Tottenham H v Doncaster R 7-2

Semi-final (agg)
Middlesbrough v MANCHESTER C 1-0, 0-4 (1-4)
Tottenham H v NEWCASTLE UTD 1-0, 1-3 (2-3)

FINAL (Wembley Stadium)
MANCHESTER CITY 2
NEWCASTLE UNITED 1
Manchester City: Corrigan; Keegan, Donachie, Doyle, Watson, Oakes, Barnes, Booth, Royle, Hartford, Tueart.
Goalscorers: Barnes, Tueart
Newcastle United: Mahoney; Nattrass, Kennedy, Barrowclough, Keeley, Howard, Burns, Cassidy, Macdonald, Gowling, Craig.
Goalscorer: Gowling
Referee: J.K.Taylor (Wolverhampton)
Attendance: 100,000

*Won on penalties.

Manchester City's Dave Watson and Dennis Tueart (scorer of the winning goal) in 1976.

1976-77

First Round (agg)
Aldershot v Gillingham 1-1, 0-2 (1-3)
AFC Bournemouth v Torquay Utd 0-0, 0-1 (0-1)
Bradford C v Oldham Ath 1-1, 3-1 (4-2)
Bury v Preston NE 2-1, 1-1 (3-2)
Cardiff C v Bristol R 2-1, 4-4 (6-5)
Chester v Hereford Utd 2-0, 3-4 (5-4)
Chesterfield v Rotherham Utd 3-1, 0-3 (3-4)
Crewe Alex v Tranmere R 2-1, 1-3 (3-4)
Crystal Palace v Portsmouth 2-2, 1-0 (3-2)
Doncaster R* v Lincoln C 1-1, 1-1, 2-2 (4-4)
Grimsby T v Sheffield Wed 0-3, 0-0 (0-3)
Halifax T v Darlington 0-0, 1-1, 1-2 (2-3)
Huddersfield T v Hartlepool 2-0, 2-1 (4-1)
Mansfield T v Scunthorpe Utd 2-0, 0-2, 1-2 (3-4)
Millwall* v Colchester Utd 2-1, 1-2, 4-4 (7-7)
Oxford Utd v Cambridge Utd 1-0, 0-2 (1-2)
Plymouth Arg v Exeter C 0-1, 0-1 (0-2)
Port Vale v Wrexham 1-1, 0-1 (1-2)
Reading v Peterborough Utd 2-3, 1-0, 1-3 (4-6)
Rochdale v Blackburn R 0-1, 1-4 (1-5)
Shrewsbury T v Walsall 0-1, 0-1 (0-2)
Southend Utd v Brighton & HA 1-1, 1-2 (2-3)
Southport v Carlisle Utd 1-2, 1-0, 2-3 (4-5)
Swansea C v Newport Co 4-1, 0-1 (4-2)
Swindon T v Northampton T 3-2, 0-2 (3-4)
Watford v Brentford 1-1, 2-0 (3-1)
Workington v Stockport Co 0-0, 0-0, 0-2 (0-2)
York C v Barnsley 0-0, 0-0, 1-2 (1-2)

Second Round
EVERTON v Cambridge Utd 3-0
Arsenal v Carlisle Utd 3-2
Blackpool v Birmingham C 2-1
Bristol C v Coventry C 0-1

Chester v Swansea C 2-3
Crystal Palace v Watford 1-3
Doncaster R v Derby Co 1-2
Exeter C v Norwich C 1-3
Fulham v Peterborough Utd 1-1, 2-1
Ipswich T v Brighton & HA 0-0, 1-2
Liverpool v West Bromwich A 1-1, 0-1
Middlesbrough v Tottenham H 1-2
Northampton T v Huddersfield T 0-1
Orient v Hull C 1-0
Scunthorpe Utd v Notts Co 0-2
Southampton v Charlton Ath 1-1, 1-2
Sunderland v Luton T 3-1
Walsall v Nottingham F 2-4
Wolves v Sheffield Wed 1-2
ASTON VILLA v Manchester C 3-0
Blackburn R v Stockport Co 1-3
Bradford C v Bolton W 1-2
Bury v Darlington 2-1
Cardiff C v Queen's Park R 1-3
Chelsea v Sheffield Utd 3-1
Gillingham v Newcastle Utd 1-2
Manchester Utd v Tranmere R 5-0
Rotherham Utd v Millwall 1-2
Stoke C v Leeds Utd 2-1
Torquay Utd v Burnley 1-0
West Ham Utd v Barnsley 3-0
Wrexham v Leicester C 1-0

Third Round
Chelsea v Huddersfield T 2-0
Stockport Co v EVERTON 0-1
ASTON VILLA v Norwich C 2-1
Blackpool v Arsenal 1-1, 0-0, 0-2
Charlton Ath v West Ham Utd 0-1
Millwall v Orient 0-0, 0-0, 3-0
Nottingham F v Coventry C 0-3
Queen's Park R v Bury 2-1
Sheffield Wed v Watford 3-1
Derby Co v Notts Co 1-1, 2-1
Fulham v Bolton W 2-2, 2-2, 1-2
Manchester Utd v Sunderland 2-2, 2-2, 1-0
Newcastle Utd v Stoke C 3-0
Tottenham H v Wrexham 2-3
Torquay Utd v Swansea C 1-2
West Bromwich A v Brighton & HA 0-2

Fourth Round
Arsenal v Chelsea 2-1
Brighton & HA v Derby Co 1-1, 1-2
EVERTON v Coventry C 3-0
Swansea C v Bolton W 1-1, 1-5
ASTON VILLA v Wrexham 5-1
Manchester Utd v Newcastle Utd 7-2
Millwall v Sheffield Wed 3-0
West Ham Utd v Queen's Park R 0-2

Fifth Round
ASTON VILLA v Millwall 2-0
Derby Co v Bolton W 1-2
Manchester Utd v EVERTON 0-3
Queen's Park R v Arsenal 2-1

Semi-final (agg)
EVERTON v Bolton W 1-1, 1-0 (2-1)
Queen's Park R v ASTON VILLA 0-0, 2-2, 0-3 (2-5)

FINAL (Old Trafford, Manchester)
ASTON VILLA 3
EVERTON 2
(following a 0-0 and a 1-1 draw after extra-time)

Aston Villa: Burridge; Gidman(Smith), Robson, Phillips, Nicholl, Mortimer, Graydon, Little, Deehan, Cropley, Cowans.
Goalscorers: Little 2, Nicholl
Everton: Lawson; Robinson, Darracott, Lyons, McNaught, King, Hamilton, Dobson, Latchford, Pearson(Seargeant), Goodlass.
Goalscorers: Latchford, Lyons
Referee: C.G.Kew (Amersham) *Attendance: 54,749*

The first game was played at Wembley Stadium in front of 96,223 spectators and the second at Hillsborough, Sheffield with an attendance of 54,840. The referee remained the same for all three games. Deehan played in place of Graydon, Gray for Deehan and Carrodus for Cowans for Aston Villa in the first game. Cowans played in place of Cropley in the second game. Villa's goalscorer for the second game was Kenyon (own-goal). Jones played in place of Robinson and McKenzie for Pearson for Everton in the first game. Bernard played in place of Jones and Kenyon for Dobson in the second game with Pearson replacing Hamilton as substitute. Everton's goalscorer in the second game was Latchford.
*Won on penalties.

A happy trio: Aston Villa's Smith, Nicholl and Little after their 1977 replay victory over Everton. The Final went to three games following a three-game semi-final for Villa against QPR.

1977-78

First Round (agg)
Aldershot v Colchester Utd 1-1, 1-4 (2-5)
Brentford v Crystal Palace 2-1, 1-5 (3-6)
Bristol R v Walsall 1-2, 0-1 (1-3)
Burnley v Chester 2-0, 0-1 (2-1)
Bury v Crewe Alex 3-0, 1-1 (4-1)
Cambridge Utd v Brighton & HA 0-0, 0-0, 0-3 (0-3)
Chesterfield v Barnsley 4-1, 0-3, 2-0 (6-4)
Darlington v Scunthorpe Utd 0-0, 1-3 (1-3)
Exeter C v Plymouth Arg 2-2, 0-0, 1-0 (3-2)
Gillingham v Wimbledon 1-1, 1-3 (2-4)
Grimsby T v Hartlepool Utd 3-0, 2-1 (5-1)
Hereford Utd v AFC Bournemouth 2-0, 2-4, 1-2 (5-6)
Huddersfield T v Carlisle Utd 1-1, 2-2, 2-1 (5-4)
Mansfield T v Lincoln C 0-1, 0-0 (0-1)
Fulham v Orient 0-2, 2-1 (2-3)
Oxford Utd v Shrewsbury T 3-0, 2-2 (5-2)
Peterborough Utd v Bradford C 4-1, 1-1 (5-2)
Portsmouth v Newport Co 3-1, 2-3 (5-4)
Port Vale v Preston NE 2-1, 1-2, 1-2 (4-5)
Rochdale v Halifax T 1-1, 2-1 (3-2)
Rotherham Utd* v York C 3-0, 0-3, 1-1 (4-4)
Sheffield Wed v Doncaster R 5-2, 3-0 (8-2)
Southend Utd v Northampton T 2-3, 1-2 (3-5)
Swansea C v Swindon T 1-3, 1-2 (2-5)
Torquay Utd v Cardiff C 1-0, 2-3, 1-2 (4-5)
Tranmere R v Southport 0-1, 2-2 (2-3)
Watford v Reading 2-1, 0-1, 5-0 (7-2)
Wrexham v Stockport Co 1-0, 1-1 (2-1)

Second Round
Bristol C v Stoke C 1-0
Arsenal v Manchester Utd 3-2
Birmingham C v Notts Co 0-2
Blackpool v Sheffield Wed 2-2, 1-3
Bolton W v Lincoln C 1-0
Brighton & HA v Oldham Ath 0-0, 2-2, 1-2
Burnley v Norwich C 3-1
Charlton Ath v Wrexham 1-2
Crystal Palace v Southampton 0-0, 1-2
Grimsby T v Watford 1-2
Huddersfield T v Coventry C 0-2
Ipswich T v Northampton T 5-0
LIVERPOOL v Chelsea 2-0
NOTTINGHAM F v West Ham Utd 5-0
Peterborough Utd v Scunthorpe Utd 1-1, 1-0
Portsmouth v Leicester C 2-0
Sheffield Utd v Everton 0-3
Sunderland v Middlesbrough 2-2, 0-1
Swindon T v Cardiff C 5-1
Walsall v Preston NE 0-0, 1-0
Wolves v Luton T 1-3
Blackburn R v Colchester Utd 1-1, 0-4
Chesterfield v Manchester C 0-1
Derby Co v Orient 3-1
Exeter C v Aston Villa 1-3
Newcastle Utd v Millwall 0-2
Oxford Utd v Bury 1-1, 0-1
Queen's Park R v AFC Bournemouth 2-0
Rochdale v Leeds Utd 0-3
Southport v Hull C 2-2, 0-1
Tottenham H v Wimbledon 4-0
West Bromwich A v Rotherham Utd 4-0

Third Round
Arsenal v Southampton 2-0
Bolton W v Peterborough Utd 3-1
Burnley v Ipswich T 1-2
Everton v Middlesbrough 2-2, 2-1
Hull C v Oldham Ath 2-0
Luton T v Manchester C 1-1, 0-0, 2-3
Millwall v Bury 1-1, 0-2
NOTTINGHAM F v Notts Co 4-0
Portsmouth v Swindon T 1-1, 3-4
Sheffield Wed v Walsall 2-1
West Bromwich A v Watford 1-0
Aston Villa v Queen's Park R 1-0
Leeds Utd v Colchester Utd 4-0
LIVERPOOL v Derby Co 2-0
Tottenham H v Coventry C 2-3
Wrexham v Bristol C 1-0

Fourth Round
Arsenal v Hull C 5-1
Bury v West Bromwich A 1-0
Ipswich T v Manchester C 1-2
LIVERPOOL v Coventry C 2-2, 2-0
NOTTINGHAM F v Aston Villa 4-2
Sheffield Wed v Everton 1-3
Bolton W v Leeds Utd 1-3
Wrexham v Swindon T 2-0

Fifth Round
Bury v NOTTINGHAM F 0-3
Wrexham v LIVERPOOL 1-3
Leeds Utd v Everton 4-1
Manchester C v Arsenal 0-0, 0-1

Semi-final (agg)
LIVERPOOL v Arsenal 2-1, 0-0 (2-1)
Leeds Utd v NOTTINGHAM F 1-3, 2-4 (3-7)

FINAL (Old Trafford, Manchester)
NOTTINGHAM FOREST 1
LIVERPOOL 0
(following a 0-0 draw after extra-time)
Nottingham Forest: Woods; Anderson, Clark, O'Hare, Lloyd, Burns, O'Neill, Bowyer, Withe, Woodcock, Robertson.
Goalscorer: Robertson (pen)
Liverpool: Clemence; Neal, Smith, Thompson, Kennedy, Hughes, Dalglish, Case(Fairclough), Heighway, McDermott, Callaghan.
Referee: P.Partridge (Durham) *Attendance: 54,375*

The first game was played at Wembley Stadium in

front of 100,000 spectators. McGovern played in place of O'Hare in the first game for Nottingham Forest although O'Hare replaced McGovern in that game. Fairclough replaced Kennedy for Liverpool in the first game.
*Won on penalties.

1978-79

First Round

Aldershot v Millwall	0-1, 0-1 (0-2)
Barnsley v Chesterfield	1-2, 0-0 (1-2)
AFC Bournemouth v Exeter C	0-1, 1-1 (1-2)
Bradford C v Lincoln C	2-0, 1-1 (3-1)
Bristol R v Hereford Utd	2-1, 0-4 (2-5)
Cambridge Utd v Northampton T	2-2, 1-2 (3-4)
Cardiff C v Oxford Utd	1-2, 1-2 (2-4)
Carlisle Utd v Blackpool	2-2, 1-2 (3-4)
Colchester Utd v Charlton Ath	2-3, 0-0 (2-3)
Crewe Alex v Rochdale	1-0, 4-2 (5-2)
Doncaster R v Sheffield Wed	0-1, 1-0, 0-1 (1-2)
Grimsby T v York C	2-0, 3-0 (5-0)
Hull C v Peterborough Utd	0-1, 2-1, 0-1 (2-3)
Mansfield T v Darlington	0-1, 2-2 (2-3)
Newport Co v Swansea C	2-1, 0-5 (2-6)
Plymouth Arg v Torquay Utd	1-1, 2-1 (3-2)
Portsmouth v Swindon T	0-0, 2-4 (2-4)
Port Vale v Chester	0-3, 1-1 (1-4)
Preston NE v Huddersfield T	3-0, 2-2 (5-2)
Reading v Gillingham	3-1, 2-1 (5-2)
Rotherham Utd v Hartlepool Utd	5-0, 1-1 (6-1)
Scunthorpe Utd v Notts Co	0-1, 0-3 (0-4)
Shrewsbury T v Stockport Co	1-0, 1-3 (2-3)
Southend Utd v Wimbledon	1-0, 1-4 (2-4)
Tranmere R v Wigan Ath	1-1, 1-2 (2-3)
Walsall v Halifax T	2-1, 2-0 (4-1)
Watford v Brentford	4-0, 3-1 (7-1)
Wrexham v Bury	2-0, 2-1 (4-1)

Second Round

Aston Villa v Sheffield Wed	1-0
Birmingham C v SOUTHAMPTON	2-5
Blackpool v Ipswich T	2-0
Bolton W v Chelsea	2-1
Brighton & HA v Millwall	1-0
Bristol C v Crystal Palace	1-2
Burnley v Bradford C	1-1, 3-2
Chester v Coventry C	2-1
Crewe Alex v Notts Co	2-0
Everton v Wimbledon	8-0
Exeter C v Blackburn R	2-1
Fulham v Darlington	2-2, 0-1
Leicester C v Derby Co	0-1
Luton T v Wigan Ath	2-0
Manchester C v Grimsby T	2-0
Middlesbrough v Peterborough Utd	0-0, 0-1
Northampton T v Hereford Utd	0-0, 1-0
Oldham Ath v NOTTINGHAM F	0-0, 2-4
Oxford Utd v Plymouth Arg	1-1, 2-1
Orient v Chesterfield	1-2
Preston NE v Queen's Park R	1-3
Reading v Wolves	1-0
Rotherham Utd v Arsenal	3-1
Sheffield Utd v Liverpool	1-0
Stockport Co v Manchester Utd	2-3
Sunderland v Stoke C	0-2
Swansea C v Tottenham H	2-2, 3-1
Walsall v Charlton Ath	1-2
Watford v Newcastle Utd	2-1
West Bromwich A v Leeds Utd	0-0, 0-0, 0-1
West Ham Utd v Stoke C	1-2
Wrexham v Norwich C	1-3

Third Round

Burnley v Brighton & HA	1-3
Everton v Darlington	1-0
Luton T v Crewe Alex	2-1
Northampton T v Stoke C	1-3
Peterborough Utd v Swindon T	1-1, 2-0
Queen's Park R v Swansea T	2-0
Rotherham Utd v Reading	2-2, 0-1
SOUTHAMPTON v Derby Co	1-0
Blackpool v Manchester C	1-1, 0-3
Chester v Norwich C	0-2
Chesterfield v Charlton Ath	4-5
Exeter C v Bolton W	2-1
Manchester Utd v Watford	1-2
Oxford Utd v NOTTINGHAM F	0-5
Aston Villa v Crystal Palace	1-1, 0-0, 3-0
Sheffield Utd v Leeds Utd	1-4

Fourth Round

Brighton & HA v Peterborough Utd	1-0
Charlton Ath v Stoke C	2-3
Everton v NOTTINGHAM F	2-3
Queen's Park R v Leeds Utd	0-2
Aston Villa v Luton T	0-2
Exeter C v Watford	0-2
Norwich C v Manchester C	1-3
Reading v SOUTHAMPTON	0-0, 0-2

Fifth Round

Leeds Utd v Luton T	4-1
NOTTINGHAM F v Brighton & HA	3-1
Stoke C v Watford	0-0, 1-3
SOUTHAMPTON v Manchester C	2-1

Semi-final (agg)

NOTTINGHAM F v Watford	3-1, 0-0 (3-1)
Leeds Utd v SOUTHAMPTON	2-2, 0-1 (2-3)

FINAL (Wembley Stadium)

NOTTINGHAM FOREST	3
SOUTHAMPTON	2

Nottingham Forest: Shilton; Barrett, Clark, McGovern, Lloyd, Needham, O'Neill, Gemmill, Birtles, Woodcock, Robertson.
Goalscorers: Birtles 2, Woodcock
Southampton: Gennoe; Golac, Peach, Williams, Nicholl, Waldron, Ball, Boyer, Hayes(Sealey), Holmes, Curran.
Goalscorers: Peach, Holmes
Referee: P.Reeves (Leicester) *Attendance: 100,000*

1979-80

First Round (agg)

Blackpool v Rochdale	1-1, 1-0 (2-1)
Bradford C v Darlington	0-2, 3-0 (3-2)
Bury v Blackburn R	0-3, 2-3 (2-6)
Chester v Walsall	2-1, 0-0 (2-1)
Chesterfield v Hartlepool Utd	5-1, 1-2 (6-3)
Colchester Utd v Watford	2-0, 1-2 (3-2)
Gillingham v Luton T	3-0, 1-1 (4-1)
Grimsby T v Scunthorpe Utd	2-0, 0-0 (2-0)
Halifax T v Shrewsbury T	2-2, 0-1 (2-3)
Hereford Utd v Exeter C	1-3, 1-2 (2-5)
Huddersfield T v Crewe Alex	2-1, 3-1 (5-2)
Leicester C v Rotherham Utd	1-2, 0-3 (1-5)
Lincoln C v Barnsley*	2-1, 1-2 (3-3)
Mansfield T v York C†	1-0, 2-3 (3-3)
Newport Co v Plymouth Arg	1-0, 0-2 (1-2)
Northampton T v Millwall	2-1, 2-2 (4-3)
Oxford Utd v Reading	1-5, 1-2 (2-7)
Peterborough Utd v Charlton Ath	3-1, 1-1 (4-2)
Portsmouth v Swindon T	1-1, 0-2 (1-3)
Port Vale v Tranmere R	1-2, 0-1 (1-3)
Sheffield Utd v Doncaster R	1-1, 1-3 (2-4)
Sheffield Wed v Hull C	1-1, 2-1 (3-2)
Southend Utd v Brentford	2-1, 4-1 (6-2)
Stockport Co v Wigan Ath	2-1, 0-0 (2-1)
Swansea C v AFC Bournemouth	4-1, 0-0 (4-1)
Torquay Utd v Bristol R	1-2, 3-1 (4-3)
Wimbledon v Aldershot	4-1, 2-1 (6-2)
Wrexham v Carlisle Utd	1-1, 2-1 (3-2)

Second Round (agg)

Birmingham C v Preston NE	2-1, 1-0 (3-1)
Blackburn R v NOTTINGHAM F	1-1, 1-6 (2-7)
Bolton W v Southend Utd	1-2, 0-0 (1-2)
Brighton & HA v Cambridge Utd	2-0, 2-1 (4-1)
Bristol C v Rotherham Utd	1-0, 1-1 (2-1)
Burnley v WOLVES	1-1, 0-2 (1-3)
Chesterfield v Shrewsbury T	3-0, 0-0 (3-0)
Colchester Utd v Aston Villa*	0-2, 2-0 (2-2)
Derby Co v Middlesbrough	0-1, 1-1 (1-2)
Doncaster R v Exeter C	3-1, 1-5 (4-6)
Everton v Cardiff C	2-0, 0-1 (2-1)
Gillingham v Norwich C	1-1, 2-4 (3-5)
Grimsby T v Huddersfield T	1-0, 4-1 (5-1)
Ipswich T v Coventry C	0-1, 0-0 (0-1)
Leeds Utd v Arsenal	1-1, 0-7 (1-8)
Northampton T v Oldham Ath	3-0, 1-3 (4-3)
Notts Co v Torquay Utd	0-0, 1-0 (1-0)
Orient v Wimbledon*	2-2, 2-2 (4-4)
Peterborough Utd v Blackpool	0-0, 1-0 (1-0)
Plymouth Arg v Chelsea	2-2, 2-1 (4-3)
Queen's Park R v Bradford C	2-1, 2-0 (4-1)
Reading v Mansfield T	4-3, 2-4 (6-7)
Stockport Co v Crystal Palace	1-1, 0-7 (1-8)
Sheffield Wed v Manchester C	1-1, 1-2 (2-3)
Southampton v Wrexham	5-0, 3-0 (8-0)
Stoke C v Swansea C	1-1, 3-1 (4-2)
Sunderland* v Newcastle Utd	2-2, 2-2 (4-4)
Swindon T v Chester	1-0, 1-1 (2-1)
Tottenham H v Manchester Utd	2-1, 1-3 (3-4)
Tranmere R v Liverpool	0-0, 0-4 (0-4)
West Bromwich A v Fulham	1-1, 1-0 (2-1)
West Ham Utd v Barnsley	3-1, 2-0 (5-1)

Third Round

Arsenal v Southampton	2-1
Aston Villa v Everton	0-0, 1-4
Crystal Palace v WOLVES	1-2
Grimsby T v Notts Co	3-1
Liverpool v Chesterfield	3-1
Mansfield T v Queen's Park R	0-3
Middlesbrough v NOTTINGHAM F	1-3
Northampton T v Brighton & HA	0-1
Plymouth Arg v Wimbledon	0-0, 0-1
West Ham Utd v Southend Utd	1-1, 0-0, 5-1
Birmingham C v Exeter C	1-2
Manchester C v Sunderland	1-1, 0-1
Norwich C v Manchester Utd	4-1
Peterborough Utd v Bristol C	1-1, 0-4
Stoke C v Swindon T	2-2, 1-2
West Bromwich A v Coventry C	2-1

Fourth Round

Brighton & HA v Arsenal	0-0, 0-4
Bristol C v NOTTINGHAM F	1-1, 0-3
Grimsby T v Everton	2-1
Liverpool v Exeter C	2-0
Queen's Park R v WOLVES	1-1, 0-1
Wimbledon v Swindon T	1-2
Sunderland v West Ham Utd	1-1, 1-2
West Bromwich A v Norwich C	0-0, 0-3

Fifth Round

Arsenal v Swindon T	1-1, 3-4
Grimsby T v WOLVES	0-0, 1-1, 0-2
West Ham Utd v NOTTINGHAM F	0-0, 0-3
Norwich C v Liverpool	1-3

Semi-final (agg)

NOTTINGHAM F v Liverpool	1-0, 1-1 (2-1)
Swindon T v WOLVES	2-1, 1-3 (3-4)

FINAL (Wembley Stadium)

WOLVERHAMPTON WANDERERS	1
NOTTINGHAM FOREST	0

Former Anfield favourite Emlyn Hughes is used to all this. But this time he is in Wolves' colours after their 1980 win over Nottingham Forest.

Wolverhampton Wanderers: Bradshaw; Palmer, Parkin, Daniel, Berry, Hughes, Carr, Hibbitt, A.Gray, Richards, Eves.
Goalscorer: Gray
Nottingham Forest: Shilton; Anderson, F.Gray, McGovern, Needham, Burns, O'Neill, Bowyer, Birtles, Francis, Robertson.
Referee: D.Richardson (Great Harwood)
Attendance: 100,000

*Won on penalties. †Won on away-goals rule.

1980-81

First Round (agg)
Aldershot v Wimbledon 2-0, 1-4 (3-4)
Blackburn R† v Huddersfield T 0-0, 1-1 (1-1)
AFC Bournemouth v Swindon T 1-1, 0-2 (1-3)
Brentford v Charlton Ath 3-1, 0-5 (3-6)
Bury v Halifax T 2-2, 1-0 (3-2)
Carlisle Utd v Rochdale 2-0, 1-1 (3-1)
Chester v Stockport Co 1-1, 0-1 (1-2)
Chesterfield v Darlington 1-0, 2-1 (3-1)
Colchester Utd v Gillingham 0-2, 1-2 (1-4)
Doncaster R v Mansfield T 1-1, 1-2 (2-3)
Exeter C v Bristol R* 1-1, 1-1 (2-2)
Grimsby T v Notts Co 1-0, 0-3 (1-3)
Hereford Utd v Newport Co 1-0, 0-5 (1-5)
Lincoln C v Hull C 5-0, 2-0 (7-0)
Northampton T v Reading 0-2, 3-2 (3-4)
Peterborough Utd v Fulham 3-2, 1-1 (4-3)
Plymouth Arg v Portsmouth 0-1, 1-2 (1-3)
Port Vale v Tranmere R† 2-3, 1-0 (3-3)
Rotherham Utd v Bradford C 1-3, 0-0 (1-3)
Scunthorpe Utd v Barnsley 0-1, 1-2 (1-3)
Sheffield Wed v Sheffield Utd 2-0, 1-1 (3-1)
Southend Utd v Oxford Utd 1-0, 0-2 (1-2)
Torquay Utd v Cardiff C 0-0, 1-2 (1-2)
Walsall v Blackpool 2-3, 1-3 (3-6)
Watford v Millwall 2-1, 2-0 (4-1)
Wigan Ath v Crewe Alex 2-1, 2-2 (4-3)
Wrexham v Burnley 1-3, 1-2 (2-5)
York C v Hartlepool Utd 2-1, 0-0 (2-1)

Second Round (agg)
Birmingham C v Bristol C 2-1, 0-0 (2-1)
Bolton W v Crystal Palace 0-3, 1-2 (1-5)
Burnley v WEST HAM UTD 0-2, 0-4 (0-6)
Brighton & HA v Tranmere R 3-1, 4-2 (7-3)
Cambridge Utd v Wolves 3-1, 1-0 (4-1)
Carlisle Utd v Charlton Ath 1-2, 1-2 (2-4)
Chesterfield v Oxford Utd 3-1, 0-3 (3-4)
Everton v Blackpool 3-0, 2-2 (5-2)
Mansfield T v Barnsley 0-0, 2-4 (2-4)
Middlesbrough v Ipswich T 3-1, 0-3 (3-4)
Newport Co v Notts Co 1-1, 0-2 (1-3)
Oldham Ath v Portsmouth† 3-2, 0-1 (3-3)
Preston NE v Wigan Ath 1-0, 2-1 (3-1)
Queen's Park R* v Derby Co 0-0, 0-0 (0-0)
Shrewsbury T v Norwich C 1-1, 0-2 (1-3)
Southampton v Watford 4-0, 1-7 (5-7)
Swansea C v Arsenal 1-1, 1-3 (2-4)
West Bromwich A v Leicester C 1-0, 1-0 (2-0)
Wimbledon v Sheffield Wed 2-1, 1-3 (3-4)
Aston Villa v Leeds Utd 1-0, 3-1 (4-1)
Blackburn R v Gillingham 0-0, 2-1 (2-1)
Bradford C v LIVERPOOL 1-0, 0-4 (1-4)
Cardiff C v Chelsea 1-0, 1-1 (2-1)
Lincoln C v Swindon T 1-1, 0-2 (1-3)
Manchester Utd v Coventry C 0-1, 0-1 (0-2)
Newcastle Utd v Bury† 3-2, 0-1 (3-3)
Nottingham F v Peterborough Utd 3-0, 1-1 (4-1)
Orient v Tottenham H 0-1, 1-3 (1-4)
Reading v Luton T 0-2, 1-1 (1-3)
Stockport Co v Sunderland 1-1, 2-1 (3-2)
Stoke C v Manchester C 1-1, 0-3 (1-4)
York C v Bristol R† 2-1, 0-1 (2-2)

Third Round
Stockport Co v Arsenal 1-3
Barnsley v Cardiff C 3-2
Birmingham C v Blackburn R 1-0
Brighton & HA v Coventry C 1-2
Bristol R v Portsmouth 0-0, 0-2
Bury v Nottingham F 0-7
Cambridge Utd v Aston Villa 2-1
Charlton Ath v WEST HAM UTD 1-2
Ipswich T v Norwich C 1-1, 3-1
LIVERPOOL v Swindon T 5-0
Luton T v Manchester C 1-2
Notts Co v Queen's Park R 4-1
Preston NE v Oxford Utd 1-0
Sheffield Wed v Watford 1-2
Everton v West Bromwich A 1-2
Tottenham H v Crystal Palace 0-0, 3-1

Fourth Round
Birmingham C v Ipswich T 2-1
Coventry C v Cambridge Utd 1-1, 1-0
LIVERPOOL v Portsmouth 4-1
Watford v Nottingham F 4-1
WEST HAM UTD v Barnsley 2-1
Manchester C v Notts Co 5-1
West Bromwich A v Preston NE 0-0, 1-1, 2-1
Tottenham H v Arsenal 1-0

Fifth Round
LIVERPOOL v Birmingham C 3-1
Watford v Coventry C 2-2, 0-5
WEST HAM UTD v Tottenham H 1-0
Manchester C v West Bromwich A 2-1

Semi-final (agg)
Manchester C v LIVERPOOL 0-1, 1-1 (1-2)
Coventry C v WEST HAM UTD 3-2, 0-2 (3-4)

FINAL (Villa Park, Birmingham)
LIVERPOOL 2
WEST HAM UNITED 1
(following a 1-1 draw after extra-time)

Liverpool: Clemence; Neal, A.Kennedy, Thompson, R.Kennedy, Hansen, Dalglish, Lee, Rush, McDermott, Case.
Goalscorers: Dalglish, Hansen
West Ham United: Parkes; Stewart, Lampard, Bonds, Martin, Devonshire, Neighbour, Goddard, Cross, Brooking, Pike(Pearson).
Goalscorer: Goddard
Referee: C.Thomas (Treorchy) *Attendance: 36,693*

The first game was played at Wembley Stadium in front of 100,000 spectators. Irwin played in place of Thompson, Heighway(Case) for Rush and Souness for Case for Liverpool in the first game. Alan Kennedy scored for Liverpool. Pearson replaced Pike for West Ham United in the first game and Stewart (pen) scored the goal.
*Won on penalties. †Won on away-goals rule.

1981-82

First Round (agg)
Wigan Ath v Stockport Co 3-0, 2-1 (5-1)
Aldershot v Wimbledon 0-0, 3-1 (3-1)
AFC Bournemouth v Fulham 0-1, 0-2 (0-3)
Bolton W v Oldham Ath 2-1, 2-4 (4-5)
Bristol C v Walsall 2-0, 0-1 (2-1)
Bury v Carlisle Utd 3-3, 1-2 (4-5)
Colchester Utd v Gillingham 2-0, 1-1 (3-1)
Darlington v Rotherham Utd 1-3, 1-2 (2-5)
Doncaster R† v Chesterfield 0-0, 1-1 (1-1)
Halifax T v Preston NE 1-2, 0-0 (1-2)
Huddersfield T v Rochdale 3-1, 4-2 (7-3)
Northampton T v Hartlepool Utd 2-0, 1-2 (3-2)
Orient v Millwall 1-1, 2-3 (3-4)
Scunthorpe Utd v Mansfield T 0-0, 0-2 (0-2)
Sheffield Utd v York C 1-0, 1-1 (2-1)
Tranmere R v Burnley 4-2, 3-3 (7-5)
Wrexham v Swindon T 3-2, 2-0 (5-2)
Bradford C v Blackpool 3-1, 0-0 (3-1)
Cardiff C v Exeter C 2-1, 1-3 (3-4)
Chester v Plymouth Arg 1-1, 0-1 (1-2)
Crewe Alex v Bristol R 1-1, 0-1 (1-2)
Hereford Utd v Port Vale 1-1, 0-2 (1-3)
Lincoln C v Hull C 3-0, 1-1 (4-1)
Oxford Utd v Brentford 1-0, 2-0 (3-0)
Peterborough Utd v Barnsley 2-3, 0-6 (2-9)
Reading v Charlton Ath 2-2, 1-3 (3-5)
Southend Utd v Portsmouth 0-0, 1-4 (1-4)
Torquay Utd v Newport Co 2-3, 0-0 (2-3)

Second Round (agg)
Tranmere R v Port Vale 2-0, 2-1 (4-1)
Aldershot v Wigan Ath 2-2, 0-1 (2-3)
Barnsley v Swansea C 2-0, 2-3 (4-3)
Birmingham C v Nottingham F 2-3, 1-2 (3-5)
Bristol R v Northampton T 1-2, 1-3 (2-5)
Carlisle Utd v Bristol C 0-0, 1-2 (1-2)
Colchester Utd v Cambridge Utd 3-1, 2-3 (5-4)
Doncaster R v Crystal Palace 1-0, 0-2 (1-2)
Everton v Coventry C 1-1, 1-0 (2-1)
Grimsby T v Watford 1-0, 1-3 (2-3)
Huddersfield T v Brighton & HA 1-0, 0-2 (1-2)
Luton T v Wrexham 0-2, 1-0 (1-2)
Middlesbrough v Plymouth Arg 2-1, 0-0 (2-1)
Millwall v Oxford Utd 3-3, 0-1 (3-4)
Oldham v Newport Co 1-0, 0-0 (1-0)
Preston NE v Leicester C 1-0, 0-4 (1-4)
Queen's Park R v Portsmouth 5-0, 2-2 (7-2)
Sheffield Utd v Arsenal 1-0, 0-2 (1-2)
Shrewsbury T v West Bromwich A 3-3, 1-2 (4-5)
Southampton v Chelsea 1-1, 1-2 (2-3)
Aston Villa v Wolves 3-2, 2-1 (5-3)
Blackburn R v Sheffield Wed 1-1, 2-1 (3-2)
Bradford C v Mansfield T 3-4, 2-0 (5-4)
Derby Co v West Ham Utd 2-3, 0-2 (2-5)
Leeds Utd v Ipswich T 0-1, 0-3 (0-4)
Lincoln C v Notts Co 1-1, 3-2 (4-3)
LIVERPOOL v Exeter C 5-0, 6-0 (11-0)

Alan Kennedy's goal for Liverpool in the drawn 1981 League Cup Final against West Ham.

Manchester C* v Stoke C 2-0, 0-2 (2-2)
Newcastle Utd v Fulham 1-2, 0-2 (1-4)
Norwich C v Charlton Ath 1-0, 1-0 (2-0)
Sunderland v Rotherham Utd 2-0, 3-3 (5-3)
TOTTENHAM H v Manchester Utd 1-0, 1-0 (2-0)

Third Round
Arsenal v Norwich C 1-0
Barnsley v Brighton & HA 4-1
Ipswich T v Bradford C 1-1, 3-2
LIVERPOOL v Middlesbrough 4-1
Oldham Ath v Fulham 1-1, 0-3
Queen's Park R v Bristol C 3-0
Tranmere R v Colchester Utd 1-0
Watford v Lincoln C 2-2, 3-2
West Ham Utd v West Bromwich A 2-2, 1-1, 0-1
Blackburn R v Nottingham F 0-1
Everton v Oxford Utd 1-0

Liverpool's Graeme Souness after the Reds' 1982 win over Tottenham, in what was now the Milk Cup Final. All season the trophy had still been known as the League Cup but the sponsorship was announcd on the eve of the Wembley Final.

Leicester C v Aston Villa 0-0, 0-2
Manchester C v Northampton T 3-1
Sunderland v Crystal Palace 0-1
TOTTENHAM H v Wrexham 2-0
Wigan Ath v Chelsea 4-2

Fourth Round
Arsenal v LIVERPOOL 0-0, 0-3
Watford v Queen's Park R 4-1
Wigan Ath v Aston Villa 1-2
Barnsley v Manchester C 1-0
Nottingham F v Tranmere R 2-0
TOTTENHAM H v Fulham 1-0
Crystal Palace v West Bromwich A 1-3
Everton v Ipswich T 2-3

Fifth Round
LIVERPOOL v Barnsley 0-0, 3-1
Ipswich T v Watford 2-1
TOTTENHAM H v Nottingham F 1-0
Aston Villa v West Bromwich A 0-1

Semi-final (agg)
Ipswich T v LIVERPOOL 0-2, 2-2 (2-4)
West Bromwich A v TOTTENHAM H 0-0, 0-1 (0-1)

FINAL (Wembley Stadium)
LIVERPOOL 3
TOTTENHAM HOTSPUR 1
(after extra-time)
Liverpool: Grobbelaar; Neal, A.Kennedy, Thompson, Whelan, Lawrenson, Dalglish, Lee, Rush, McDermott(Johnson), Souness.
Goalscorers: Whelan 2, Rush
Tottenham Hotspur: Clemence; Hughton, Miller, Price, Hazard(Villa), Perryman, Ardíles, Archibald, Galvin, Hoddle, Crooks.
Goalscorer: Archibald
Referee: P.N.Willis (County Durham)
Attendance: 100,000
*Won on penalties. †Won on away-goals rule.

1982-83

First Round (agg)
Port Vale v Rochdale 1-0, 0-2 (1-2)
Stockport Co v Wigan Ath* 1-1, 1-1 (2-2)
Wimbledon v Brentford 1-1, 0-2 (1-3)
Bristol R v Torquay Utd 2-2, 4-0 (6-2)
Bury v Burnley 3-5, 1-3 (4-8)
Cardiff C v Hereford Utd 2-1, 2-1 (4-2)
Carlisle Utd v Bolton W 3-3, 0-4 (3-7)
Chesterfield v Hartlepool Utd 2-1, 0-2 (2-3)
Colchester Utd v Aldershot 2-0, 1-0 (3-0)
Crewe Alex v Tranmere R† 1-1, 0-0 (1-1)
Crystal Palace v Portsmouth 2-0, 1-1 (3-1)
Darlington v Peterborough Utd 0-2, 2-4 (2-6)
Gillingham v Orient 3-0, 0-2 (3-2)
Halifax T v Derby Co 2-1, 2-5 (4-6)
Huddersfield T v Doncaster R 1-1, 1-0 (2-1)
Millwall v Northampton T 0-2, 2-2 (2-4)
Plymouth Arg v AFC Bournemouth 2-0, 0-3 (2-3)
Scunthorpe Utd v Grimsby T 1-2, 0-0 (1-2)
Sheffield Utd v Hull C 3-1, 0-1 (3-2)
Swindon T v Bristol C 2-1, 0-2 (2-3)
Walsall v Preston NE 0-1, 1-1 (1-2)
Wrexham v Shrewsbury T 1-0, 0-2 (1-2)
York C v Lincoln C 2-1, 1-3 (3-4)
Bradford C v Mansfield T 1-0, 2-0 (3-0)
Exeter C v Newport Co 1-2, 0-6 (1-8)
Southend Utd v Fulham 1-0, 2-4 (3-4)
Reading v Oxford Utd 0-2, 0-2 (0-4)
Chester v Blackpool 1-2, 1-5 (2-7)

Second Round (agg)
Bristol C v Sheffield Wed 1-2, 1-1 (2-3)
Arsenal v Cardiff C 2-1, 3-1 (5-2)
Bolton W v Watford 1-2, 1-2 (2-4)
Brentford v Blackburn R 3-2, 0-0 (3-2)
Bristol R v Swansea C 1-0, 0-3 (1-3)
Burnley v Middlesbrough 3-2, 1-1 (4-3)
Fulham v Coventry C† 2-2, 0-0 (2-2)
Gillingham v Oldham Ath 2-0, 0-1 (2-1)
Huddersfield T v Oxford Utd 2-0, 0-1 (2-1)
Ipswich T v LIVERPOOL 1-2, 0-2 (1-4)
Luton T v Charlton Ath 3-0, 0-2 (3-2)
Newport Co v Everton 0-2, 2-2 (2-4)
Northampton T v Blackpool 1-1, 1-2 (2-3)
Rochdale v Bradford C 0-1, 0-4 (0-5)
Rotherham Utd v Queen's Park R 2-1, 0-0 (2-1)
Shrewsbury T v Birmingham C 1-1, 1-4 (2-5)
Wigan Ath v Manchester C 1-1, 0-2 (1-3)
Wolves v Sunderland 1-1, 0-5 (1-6)
Aston Villa v Notts Co 1-2, 0-1 (1-3)
Chelsea v Tranmere R 3-1, 2-1 (5-2)
Colchester Utd v Southampton 0-0, 2-4 (2-4)
Derby Co† v Hartlepool Utd 2-0, 2-4 (4-4)
Leeds Utd v Newcastle Utd 0-1, 4-1 (4-2)
Lincoln C v Leicester C 2-0, 1-0 (3-0)

MANCHESTER UTD v AFC Bournemouth 2-0, 2-2 (4-2)
Norwich C v Preston NE 2-1, 2-1 (4-2)
Nottingham F v West Bromwich A 6-1, 1-3 (7-4)
Peterborough Utd v Crystal Palace 0-2, 1-2 (1-4)
Stoke C v West Ham Utd 1-1, 1-2 (2-3)
Tottenham H v Brighton & HA 1-1, 1-0 (2-1)
Barnsley v Cambridge Utd 2-1, 3-1 (5-2)
Grimsby T v Sheffield Utd 3-3, 1-5 (4-8)

Third Round
Birmingham C v Derby Co 3-1
Brentford v Swansea C 1-1, 2-1
Coventry C v Burnley 1-2
Crystal Palace v Sheffield Wed 1-2
Everton v Arsenal 1-1, 0-3
Gilligham v Tottenham H 2-4
Luton T v Blackpool 4-2
Notts Co v Chelsea 2-0
Sheffield Utd v Barnsley 1-3
Bradford C v MANCHESTER UTD 0-0, 1-4
Leeds Utd v Huddersfield T 0-1
Lincoln C v West Ham Utd 1-1, 1-2
LIVERPOOL v Rotherham Utd 1-0
Manchester C v Southampton 1-1, 0-4
Nottingham F v Watford 7-3
Sunderland v Norwich C 0-0, 1-3

Fourth Round
Arsenal v Huddersfield T 1-0
Burnley v Birmingham C 3-2
LIVERPOOL v Norwich C 2-0
Sheffield Wed v Barnsley 1-0
MANCHESTER UTD v Southampton 2-0
Nottingham F v Brentford 2-0
Tottenham H v Luton T 1-0
Notts Co v West Ham Utd 3-3, 0-3

Fifth Round
Arsenal v Sheffield Wed 1-0
LIVERPOOL v West Ham Utd 2-1
MANCHESTER UTD v Nottingham F 4-0
Tottenham H v Burnley 1-4

Semi-final (agg)
LIVERPOOL v Burnley 3-0, 0-1 (3-1)
Arsenal v MANCHESTER UTD 2-4, 1-2 (3-6)

FINAL (Wembley Stadium)
LIVERPOOL 2
MANCHESTER UNITED 1
(after extra-time)

Liverpool: Grobbelaar; Neal, Kennedy, Lawrenson, Whelan, Hanson, Dalglish, Lee, Rush, Johnston(Fairclough), Souness.
Goalscorers: Kennedy, Whelan
Manchester United: Bailey; Duxbury, Albiston, Moses, Moran(Macari), McQueen, Wilkins, Muhren, Stapleton, Whiteside, Coppell.
Goalscorer: Whiteside
Referee: G.Courtney (Spennymoor)
Attendance: 100,000

From this season, after sponsorship from the Milk Marketing Board, the trophy was called the Milk Cup. *Won on penalties. †Won on away-goals rule.

Milk Cup winners again in 1983. Liverpool parade the trophy after beating Manchester United. The following year the Reds completed a hat-trick of successes in this competition.

1983-84

First Round (agg)
Bradford C v Sheffield Utd 0-1, 1-1 (1-2)
Millwall v Northampton T 3-0, 2-1 (5-1)
Southend Utd v Wimbledon 1-0, 4-6 (5-6)
Aldershot v Orient 3-1, 3-3 (6-4)
Blackpool v Walsall 2-1, 1-3 (3-4)
Bolton W v Chester C* 3-0, 0-3 (3-3)
AFC Bournemouth v Bristol R 1-2, 2-2 (3-4)
Brentford v Charlton Ath 3-0, 1-2 (4-2)
Colchester Utd† v Reading 3-2, 3-4 (6-6)
Crewe Alex v Burnley 1-0, 4-3 (5-3)
Crystal Palace v Peterborough Utd* 3-0, 0-3 (3-3)
Gillingham v Chelsea 1-2, 0-4 (1-6)
Halifax T v Darlington 0-1, 2-3 (2-4)
Hull C v Lincoln C 0-0, 1-3 (1-3)
Mansfield T v Huddersfield T 1-2, 1-5 (2-7)
Middlesbrough v Chesterfield* 0-1, 1-0 (1-1)
Newport Co v Torquay Utd 2-3, 0-1 (2-4)
Preston NE v Tranmere R 1-0, 0-0 (1-0)
Rochdale v Stockport Co 0-3, 2-2 (2-5)
Rotherham Utd v Hartlepool Utd 0-0, 1-0 (1-0)
Scunthorpe Utd v Doncaster R 1-1, 0-3 (1-4)
Swindon T v Plymouth Arg 1-0, 1-4 (2-4)
Wigan Ath v Bury 1-2, 0-2 (1-4)
York C v Grimsby T 2-1, 0-2 (2-3)
Exeter C v Cardiff C 2-3, 1-2 (3-5)
Hereford Utd v Portsmouth 3-2, 1-3 (4-5)
Oxford Utd v Bristol C 1-1, 1-0 (2-1)
Port Vale v Wrexham 3-1, 5-1 (8-2)

Second Round (agg)
Port Vale v Manchester Utd 0-1, 0-2 (0-3)
Stockport Co v Oldham Ath 0-2, 2-2 (2-4)
Aldershot v Notts Co 2-4, 1-4 (3-8)
Brighton & HA v Bristol R 4-2, 1-2 (5-4)
Bury v West Ham Utd 1-2, 0-10 (1-12)
Cambridge Utd v Sunderland 2-3, 3-4 (5-7)
Cardiff C v Norwich C 0-0, 0-3 (0-3)
Carlisle Utd v Southampton 2-0, 0-3 (2-3)
Chesterfield v EVERTON 0-1, 2-2 (2-3)
Grimsby T v Coventry C 0-0, 1-2 (1-2)
Huddersfield T v Watford 2-1, 2-2 (4-3)
Millwall v West Bromwich A 3-0, 1-5 (4-5)
Plymouth Arg v Arsenal 1-1, 0-1 (1-2)
Portsmouth v Aston Villa 2-2, 2-3 (4-5)
Queen's Park R v Crewe Alex 8-1, 0-3 (8-4)
Rotherham Utd v Luton T 2-3, 2-0 (4-3)
Sheffield Wed v Darlington 3-0, 4-2 (7-2)
Shrewsbury T v Sheffield Utd 2-1, 2-2 (4-3)
Swansea C v Colchester Utd 1-1, 0-1 (1-2)
Walsall v Barnsley 1-0, 2-0 (3-0)
Wimbledon v Nottingham F 2-0, 1-1 (3-1)
Wolves v Preston NE 2-3, 0-1 (2-4)
Brentford v LIVERPOOL 1-4, 0-4 (1-8)
Derby Co v Birmingham C 0-3, 0-4 (0-7)
Doncaster R v Fulham 1-3, 1-3 (2-6)
Ipswich T v Blackburn R 4-3, 2-1 (6-4)
Leeds Utd v Chester C 0-1, 4-1 (4-2)
Leicester C v Chelsea* 0-2, 2-0 (2-2)
Newcastle Utd v Oxford Utd 1-1, 1-2 (2-3)
Stoke C v Peterborough Utd 0-0, 2-1 (2-1)
Torquay Utd v Manchester C 0-0, 0-6 (0-6)
Tottenham H v Lincoln C 3-1, 1-2 (4-3)

Third Round
Birmingham C v Notts Co 2-2, 0-0, 0-0, 3-1
Colchester Utd v Manchester Utd 0-2
Fulham v LIVERPOOL 1-1, 1-1, 0-1
Preston NE v Sheffield Wed 0-2
Rotherham Utd v Southampton 2-1
Stoke C v Huddersfield T 0-0, 2-0
Walsall v Shrewsbury T 2-1
West Ham Utd v Brighton & HA 1-0
Wimbledon v Oldham Ath 3-1
Aston Villa v Manchester C 3-0
Chelsea v West Bromwich A 0-1
EVERTON v Coventry C 2-1
Ipswich T v Queen's Park R 3-2
Leeds Utd v Oxford Utd 1-1, 1-4
Norwich C v Sunderland 0-0, 2-1
Tottenham H v Arsenal 1-2

Fourth Round
Arsenal v Walsall 1-2
Rotherham Utd v Wimbledon 1-0
Ipswich T v Norwich C 0-1
Oxford Utd v Manchester Utd 1-1, 1-1, 2-1
Stoke C v Sheffield Wed 0-1
West Bromwich A v Aston Villa 1-2
West Ham Utd v EVERTON 2-2, 0-2
Birmingham C v LIVERPOOL 1-1, 0-3

Fifth Round
Norwich C v Aston Villa 0-2
Sheffield Wed v LIVERPOOL 2-2, 0-3
Oxford Utd v EVERTON 1-1, 1-4
Rotherham Utd v Walsall 2-4

Semi-final (agg)
LIVERPOOL v Walsall 2-2, 2-0 (4-2)
EVERTON v Aston Villa 2-0, 0-1 (2-1)

FINAL (Maine Road, Manchester)
LIVERPOOL 1
EVERTON 0
(following a 0-0 draw after extra-time)

Liverpool: Grobbelaar; Neal, Kennedy, Lawrenson, Whelan, Hansen, Dalglish, Lee, Rush, Johnston, Souness.
Goalscorer: Souness
Everton: Southall; Stevens, Bailey, Ratcliffe, Mountfield, Reid, Irvine(King), Heath, Sharp, Richardson, Harper.
Refereee: A.Robinson (Portsmouth)
Attendance: 52,089

The first game was played at Wembley Stadium in front of 100,000 spectators. Robinson came on as substitute for Johnston in the first game for Liverpool. Sheedy played in place of Harper (who replaced Sheedy during the game) in the first game for Everton.
*Won on penalties. †Won on away-goals rule.

1984-85

First Round (agg)
Crystal Palace v Northampton T 1-0, 0-0 (1-0)
Plymouth Arg v Torquay Utd 1-0, 1-0 (2-0)
Stockport Co v Rochdale 3-1, 2-1 (5-2)
Swindon T v Bristol R 1-5, 1-0 (2-5)
Aldershot v AFC Bournemouth 4-0, 1-0 (5-0)
Blackpool v Chester C 1-0, 3-0 (4-0)
Bolton W v Oldham Ath 2-1, 4-4 (6-5)
Brentford v Cambridge Utd 2-0, 0-1 (2-1)
Bristol C v Newport Co 2-1, 3-0 (5-1)
Burnley v Crewe Alex 1-2, 3-0 (4-2)
Darlington v Rotherham Utd 1-2, 0-4 (1-6)
Doncaster R v York C 2-3, 0-5 (2-8)
Gillingham v Colchester Utd 3-2, 2-0 (5-2)
Halifax T v Chesterfield 1-1, 2-1 (3-2)
Orient v Southend Utd 2-1, 0-0 (2-1)
Portsmouth v Wimbledon 3-0, 0-1 (3-1)
Port Vale† v Bury 1-0, 1-2 (2-2)
Scunthorpe Utd† v Mansfield T 0-1, 2-1 (2-2)
Swansea C v Walsall 0-2, 1-3 (1-5)
Sheffield Utd v Peterborough Utd 1-0, 2-2 (3-2)
Tranmere R v Preston NE 2-3, 2-2 (4-5)
Wrexham v Wigan Ath 0-3, 0-2 (0-5)
Bradford C v Middlesbrough 2-0, 2-2 (4-2)
Derby Co v Hartlepool Utd 5-1, 1-0 (6-1)
Exeter C v Cardiff C 1-0, 0-2 (1-2)
Hereford Utd v Oxford Utd 2-2, 3-5 (5-7)
Lincoln C v Hull C 0-2, 1-4 (1-6)
Reading v Millwall 1-1, 3-4 (4-5)

Second Round (agg)
Port Vale v Wolves 1-2, 0-0 (1-2)
Scunthorpe Utd v Aston Villa 2-3, 1-3 (3-6)
Stockport Co v Liverpool 0-0, 0-2 (0-2)
Arsenal v Bristol R 4-0, 1-1 (5-1)
Birmingham C v Plymouth Arg 4-1, 1-0 (5-1)
Blackburn R v Oxford Utd 1-1, 1-3 (2-4)
Brighton & HA v Aldershot 3-1, 0-3 (3-4)
Bristol C v West Ham Utd 2-2, 1-6 (3-8)
Charlton Ath v Notts Co 0-1, 0-2 (0-3)
Fulham v Carlisle Utd 2-0, 2-1 (4-1)
Gillingham v Leeds Utd 1-2, 2-3 (3-5)

Grimsby T v Barnsley 3-0, 1-1 (4-1)
Ipswich T v Derby Co 4-2, 1-1 (5-3)
Manchester C v Blackpool 4-2, 3-1 (7-3)
Orient v Luton T 1-4, 1-3 (2-7)
Portsmouth v Nottingham F 1-0, 0-3 (1-3)
Preston NE v NORWICH C 3-3, 1-6 (4-9)
Sheffield Wed v Huddersfield T 3-0, 1-2 (4-2)
Shrewsbury T v Bolton W 2-2, 1-2 (3-4)
Southampton v Hull C 3-2, 2-2 (5-4)
SUNDERLAND v Crystal Palace 2-1, 0-0 (2-1)
Walsall v Coventry C 1-2, 3-0 (4-2)
Watford v Cardiff C 3-1, 0-1 (3-2)
Wigan Ath v West Bromwich A 0-0, 1-3 (1-3)
York C v Queen's Park R 2-4, 1-4 (3-8)
Chelsea v Millwall 3-1, 1-1 (4-2)
Halifax T v Tottenham H 1-5, 0-4 (1-9)
Leicester C v Brentford 4-2, 2-0 (6-2)
Manchester Utd v Burnley 4-0, 3-0 (7-0)
Newcastle Utd v Bradford C 3-1, 1-0 (4-1)
Sheffield Utd v Everton 2-2, 0-4 (2-6)
Stoke C v Rotherham Utd 1-2, 1-1 (2-3)

Third Round
Birmingham C v West Bromwich A 0-0, 1-3
Ipswich T v Newcastle Utd 1-1, 2-1
Luton T v Leicester C 3-1
Manchester Utd v Everton 1-2
Notts Co v Bolton W 6-1
Queen's Park R v Aston Villa 1-0
Rotherham Utd v Grimsby T 0-0, 1-6
Sheffield Wed v Fulham 3-2
Southampton v Wolves 2-2, 2-0
Walsall v Chelsea 2-2, 0-3
Leeds Utd v Watford 0-4
Manchester C v West Ham Utd 0-0, 2-1
NORWICH C v Aldershot 0-0, 4-0
Nottingham F v SUNDERLAND 1-1, 0-1
Oxford Utd v Arsenal 3-2
Tottenham H v Liverpool 1-0

Fourth Round
Everton v Grimsby T 0-1
Ipswich T v Oxford Utd 2-1
Sheffield Wed v Luton T 4-2
Southampton v Queen's Park R 1-1, 0-0, 0-4
Watford v West Bromwich A 4-1
Chelsea v Manchester C 4-1
NORWICH C v Notts Co 3-0
SUNDERLAND v Tottenham H 0-0, 2-1

Fifth Round
Grimsby T v NORWICH C 0-1
Ipswich T v Queen's Park R 0-0, 2-1
Watford v SUNDERLAND 0-1
Chelsea v Sheffield Wed 1-1, 4-4, 2-1

Semi-final (agg)
SUNDERLAND v Chelsea 2-0, 3-2 (5-2)
Ipswich T v NORWICH C 1-0, 0-2 (1-2)

FINAL (Wembley Stadium)
NORWICH CITY 1
SUNDERLAND 0
Norwich City: Woods; Haylock, Van Wyk, Bruce, Mendham, Watson, Barham, Channon, Deehan, Hartford, Donowa.
Goalscorer: Chisholm (og)
Sunderland: Turner; Venison, Pickering, Bennett, Chisholm, Corner(Gayle), Daniel, Wallace, Hodgson, Berry, Walker.
Referee: N.Midgley (Salford) Attendance: 100,000
†Won on away-goals rule.

1985-86

First Round (agg)
Aldershot v Orient 1-3, 2-2 (3-5)
Bolton W v Stockport Co 4-1, 1-1 (5-2)
Bristol R v Newport Co 2-0, 0-1 (2-1)
Burnley v Bury 2-1, 3-5 (5-6)
Cambridge Utd v Brentford 1-1, 0-2 (1-3)
Cardiff C v Swansea C 2-1, 1-3 (3-4)
Charlton Ath v Crystal Palace 1-2, 1-1 (2-3)
Crewe Alex v Carlisle Utd 3-3, 4-3 (7-6)
Darlington v Scunthorpe Utd 3-2, 0-0 (3-2)
Halifax T v Hull C 1-1, 0-3 (1-4)
Notts Co† v Doncaster R 1-0, 1-2 (2-2)
Plymouth Arg v Exeter C 2-1, 0-2 (2-3)
Preston NE v Blackpool 2-1, 3-1 (5-2)
Rotherham Utd v Sheffield Utd 1-3, 1-5 (2-8)
Southend Utd v Gillingham 1-1, 0-2 (1-3)
Torquay Utd v Swindon T 1-2, 2-2 (3-4)
Walsall v Wolves 1-1, 1-0 (2-1)
Wigan Ath v Port Vale 2-1, 0-2 (2-3)
Wrexham v Rochdale 4-0, 1-2 (5-2)
York C v Lincoln C 2-1, 2-1 (4-2)
Bradford C v Chesterfield 2-2, 4-3 (6-5)
Colchester Utd v Millwall 2-3, 1-4 (3-7)
Derby Co v Hartlepool Utd 3-0, 0-2 (3-2)
Hereford Utd v Bristol C 5-1, 0-2 (5-3)
Mansfield T v Middlesbrough 2-0, 4-4 (6-4)
Peterborough Utd v Northampton T 0-0, 0-2 (0-2)
Reading v AFC Bournemouth 1-3, 0-2 (1-5)
Tranmere R v Chester C 1-3, 0-0 (1-3)

Second Round (agg)
Orient v Tottenham H 2-0, 0-4 (2-4)
Bristol R v Birmingham C 2-3, 1-2 (3-5)
Crewe Alex v Watford 1-3, 2-3 (3-6)
Crystal Palace v Manchester Utd 0-1, 0-1 (0-2)
Fulham v Notts Co 1-1, 4-2 (5-3)
Gillingham v Portsmouth 1-3, 1-2 (2-5)
Grimsby T v York C 1-1, 3-2 (4-3)
Ipswich T v Darlington 3-1, 4-1 (7-2)
Liverpool v Oldham Ath 3-0, 5-2 (8-2)
QUEEN'S PARK R v Hull C 3-0, 5-1 (8-1)
Sheffield Utd v Luton T 1-2, 1-3 (2-5)
Shrewsbury T v Huddersfield T 2-3, 2-0 (4-3)
Sunderland v Swindon T 3-2, 1-3 (4-5)
West Bromwich A v Port Vale 1-0, 2-2 (3-2)
West Ham Utd v Swansea C 3-0, 3-2 (6-2)
Wimbledon v Blackburn R 5-0, 1-2 (6-2)
Wrexham v Stoke C 0-1, 0-1 (0-2)
Brentford v Sheffield Wed 2-2, 0-2 (2-4)
Brighton & HA v Bradford C 5-2, 2-0 (7-2)
Bury v Manchester C 1-2, 1-2 (2-4)
Chester C v Coventry C 1-2, 2-7 (3-9)
Derby Co v Leicester C 2-0, 1-1 (3-1)
Everton v AFC Bournemouth 3-2, 2-0 (5-2)
Exeter C v Aston Villa 1-4, 1-8 (2-12)
Hereford Utd v Arsenal 0-0, 1-2 (1-2)
Leeds Utd v Walsall 0-0, 3-0 (3-0)
Mansfield T v Chelsea 2-2, 0-2 (2-4)
Millwall v Southampton* 0-0, 0-0 (0-0)
Newcastle Utd† v Barnsley 0-0, 1-1 (1-1)
Nottingham F v Bolton W 4-0, 3-0 (7-0)
OXFORD UTD v Northampton T 2-1, 2-0 (4-1)
Preston NE v Norwich C 1-1, 1-2 (2-3)

Third Round
Chelsea v Fulham 1-1, 1-0
Coventry C v West Bromwich A 0-0, 3-4
Grimsby T v Ipswich T 0-2
Liverpool v Brighton & HA 4-0
Luton T v Norwich C 0-2
Manchester Utd v West Ham Utd 1-0
Portsmouth v Stoke C 2-0
Shrewsbury T v Everton 1-4
Swindon T v Sheffield Wed 1-0
Watford v QUEEN'S PARK R 0-1
Birmingham C v Southampton 1-1, 0-3
Derby Co v Nottingham F 1-2
Leeds Utd v Aston Villa 0-3
Manchester C v Arsenal 1-2
OXFORD UTD v Newcastle Utd 3-1
Tottenham H v Wimbledon 2-0

Fourth Round
Arsenal v Southampton 0-0, 3-1
Aston Villa v West Bromwich A 2-2, 2-1
OXFORD UTD v Norwich C 3-1
Tottenham H v Portsmouth 0-0, 0-0, 0-1
QUEEN'S PARK R v Nottingham F 3-1
Chelsea v Everton 2-2, 2-1
Ipswich T v Swindon T 6-1
Liverpool v Manchester Utd 2-1

Ray Houghton carries the Milk Cup after Oxford United beat QPR in the 1986 Final.

Fifth Round
Liverpool v Ipswich T 3-0
Aston Villa v Arsenal 1-1, 2-1
OXFORD UTD v Portsmouth 3-1
QUEEN'S PARK R v Chelsea 1-1, 2-0

Semi-final (agg)
QUEEN'S PARK R v Liverpool 1-0, 2-2 (3-2)
Aston Villa v OXFORD UTD 2-2, 1-2 (3-4)

FINAL (Wembley Stadium)
OXFORD UNITED 3
QUEEN'S PARK RANGERS 0
Oxford United: Judge; Langan, Trewick, Phillips, Briggs, Shotton, Houghton, Aldridge, Charles, Hebberd, Brock.
Goalscorers: Hebberd, Houghton, Charles
Queen's Park Rangers: Barron; McDonald, Dawes, Neill, Wicks, Fenwick, Allen(Rosenior), James, Bannister, Byrne, Robinson.
Referee: K.Hackett (Sheffield) Attendance: 90,396
*Won on penalties. †Won on away-goals rule.

1986-87

First Round (agg)
Gillingham v Northampton T 1-0, 2-2 (3-2)
Aldershot v Fulham 1-3, 0-2 (1-5)
Blackpool v Preston NE 0-0, 1-2 (1-2)
AFC Bournemouth v Bristol C 0-1, 1-1 (1-2)
Bury v Bolton W 2-1, 0-0 (2-1)
Cardiff C v Plymouth Arg 5-4, 1-0 (6-4)
Chesterfield v Wrexham 0-2, 2-2 (2-4)
Colchester Utd v Peterborough Utd 0-0, 0-2 (0-2)
Doncaster R v Rotherham Utd 1-1, 1-4 (2-5)
Hartlepool Utd v Middlesbrough 1-1, 0-2 (1-3)
Huddersfield T v Halifax T 3-1, 2-2 (5-3)
Notts Co v Port Vale 1-3, 1-4 (2-7)
Orient v Cambridge Utd 2-2, 0-1 (2-3)
Rochdale v Burnley 1-1, 1-3 (2-4)
Scunthorpe Utd v Darlington 2-0, 2-1 (4-1)
Shrewsbury T v Crewe Alex 0-0, 4-0 (4-0)
Southend Utd v Brentford 1-0, 3-2 (4-2)
Stockport Co v Tranmere R 2-1, 3-3 (5-4)
Sunderland v York C† 2-4, 3-1 (5-5)
Swindon T v Torquay Utd 3-0, 3-2 (6-2)
Walsall v Mansfield T 1-0, 4-2 (5-2)
Wigan Ath v Blackburn R 1-3, 0-2 (1-5)
Wolves v Lincoln C† 1-2, 1-0 (2-2)
Bristol R v Reading 1-2, 0-4 (1-6)
Derby Co† v Chester C 0-1, 2-1 (2-2)
Exeter C v Newport Co 0-0, 0-1 (0-1)
Hereford Utd v Swansea C 3-3, 1-5 (4-8)
Carlisle Utd v Grimsby T 1-0, 0-2 (1-2)

Second Round ((agg)
ARSENAL v Huddersfield T 2-0, 1-1 (3-1)
Barnsley v Tottenham H 2-3, 3-5 (5-8)
Bradford C v Newcastle Utd 2-0, 0-1 (2-1)
Brighton & HA v Nottingham F 0-0, 0-3 (0-3)
Bristol C v Sheffield Utd 2-2, 0-3 (2-5)
Cambridge Utd† v Wimbledon 1-1, 2-2 (3-3)

Charlton Ath v Lincoln C....3-1, 1-0 (4-1)
Coventry C v Rotherham Utd....3-2, 1-0 (4-2)
Crystal Palace v Bury....0-0, 1-0 (1-0)
Derby Co v West Bromwich A....4-1, 1-0 (5-1)
Everton v Newport Co....4-0, 5-1 (9-1)
Hull C v Grimsby T....1-0, 1-1 (2-1)
LIVERPOOL v Fulham....10-0, 3-2 (13-2)
Luton T v Cardiff C‡....wo
Manchester Utd v Port Vale....2-0, 5-2 (7-2)
Middlesbrough v Birmingham C....2-2, 2-3 (4-5)
Oldham Ath v Leeds Utd....3-2, 1-0 (4-2)
Oxford Utd v Gillingham....6-0, 1-1 (7-1)
Peterborough Utd v Norwich C....0-0, 0-1 (0-1)
Preston NE v West Ham Utd....1-1, 1-4 (2-5)
Queen's Park R v Blackburn R....2-1, 2-2 (4-3)
Reading v Aston Villa....1-1, 1-4 (2-5)
Scunthorpe Utd v Ipswich T....1-2, 0-2 (1-4)
Sheffield Wed v Stockport Co....3-0, 7-0 (10-0)
Shrewsbury T v Stoke C....2-1, 0-0 (2-1)
Southampton v Swindon T....3-0, 0-0 (3-0)
Southend Utd v Manchester C....0-0, 1-2 (1-2)
Swansea C v Leicester C....0-2, 2-4 (2-6)
Walsall v Millwall....0-1, 2-3 (2-4)
Watford v Rochdale....1-1, 2-1 (3-2)
Wrexham v Portsmouth....1-2, 0-2 (1-4)
York C v Chelsea....1-0, 0-3 (1-3)

Third Round
ARSENAL v Manchester C....3-1
Cambridge Utd v Ipswich T....1-0
Cardiff C v Chelsea....2-1
Charlton Ath v Queen's Park R....1-0
Coventry C v Oldham Ath....2-1
Everton v Sheffield Wed....4-0
Shrewsbury T v Hull C....1-0
Bradford C v Portsmouth....3-1
Crystal Palace v Nottingham F....2-2, 0-1
Derby Co v Aston Villa....1-1, 1-2
LIVERPOOL v Leicester C....4-1
Manchester Utd v Southampton....0-0, 1-4
Norwich C v Millwall....4-1
Oxford Utd v Sheffield Utd....3-1
Tottenham H v Birmingham C....5-0
Watford v West Ham Utd....2-3

Fourth Round
ARSENAL v Charlton Ath....2-0
Shrewsbury T v Cardiff C....1-0
Southampton v Aston Villa....2-1
West Ham Utd v Oxford Utd....1-0
Bradford C v Nottingham F....0-5
Coventry C v LIVERPOOL....0-0, 1-3
Norwich C v Everton....1-4
Cambridge Utd v Tottenham H....1-3

Fifth Round
ARSENAL v Nottingham F....2-0
Everton v LIVERPOOL....0-1
Southampton v Shrewsbury T....1-0
West Ham Utd v Tottenham H....1-1, 0-5

Semi-final (agg)
ARSENAL v Tottenham H....0-1, 2-1, 2-1 (4-3)
Southampton v LIVERPOOL....0-0, 0-3 (0-3)

FINAL (Wembley Stadium)
ARSENAL....2
LIVERPOOL....1
Arsenal: Lukic; Anderson, Sansom, Williams, O'Leary, Adams, Rocastle, Davis, Quinn(Groves), Nicholas, Hayes(Thomas).
Goalscorer: Nicholas 2
Liverpool: Grobbelaar; Gillespie, Venison, Spackman, Whelan, Hansen, Walsh(Dalglish), Johnston, Rush, Molby, McMahon(Wark).
Goalscorer: Rush
Referee: L.Shapter (Torquay) *Attendance: 96,000*

From this season, after sponsorship from the Littlewoods Organisation, the trophy was called the Littlewoods Challenge Cup.
†Won on away-goals rule. ‡Cardiff City walked-over (wo) because Luton Town refused to allow visiting fans into their Kenilworth Road ground.

1987-88

First Round (agg)
Port Vale v Northampton T....0-1, 0-4 (0-5)
Blackpool v Chester C....2-0, 0-1 (2-1)
AFC Bournemouth v Exeter C....1-1, 3-1 (4-2)
Brentford v Southend Utd....2-1, 2-4 (4-5)
Bury v Preston NE....2-2, 3-2 (5-4)
Cambridge Utd v Aldershot....1-1, 4-1 (5-2)
Chesterfield v Peterborough Utd....2-1, 0-2 (2-3)
Fulham v Colchester Utd....3-1, 2-0 (5-1)
Gillingham* v Brighton & HA....1-0, 0-1 (1-1)
Grimsby T v Darlington†....3-2, 1-2 (4-4)
Halifax T v York C....1-1, 0-1 (1-2)
Leyton Orient v Millwall....1-1, 0-1 (1-2)

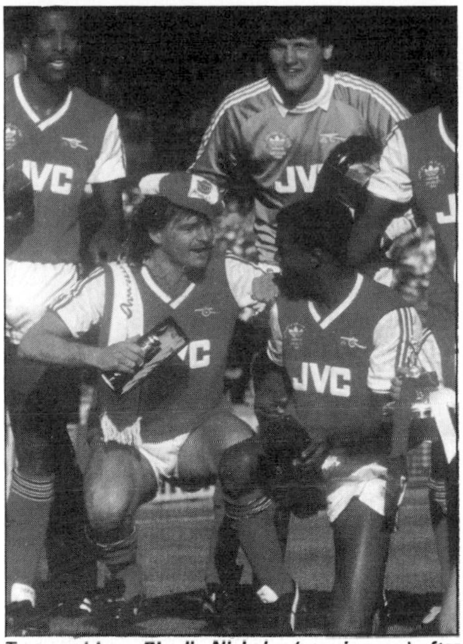

Two-goal hero Charlie Nicholas (wearing cap) after Arsenal's victory over Liverpool in 1987. The competition was now known as the Littlewoods Cup.

Mansfield T v Birmingham C....2-2, 1-0 (3-2)
Newport Co v Cardiff C....2-1, 2-2 (4-3)
Rochdale v Tranmere R....3-1, 0-1 (3-2)
Rotherham Utd v Huddersfield T....4-4, 3-1 (7-5)
Scunthorpe Utd v Hartlepool Utd....3-1, 1-0 (4-1)
Stockport Co v Carlisle Utd....0-1, 0-3 (0-4)
Sunderland v Middlesbrough....1-0, 0-2 (1-2)
Swindon T v Bristol C....3-0, 2-3 (5-3)
Torquay Utd v Swansea C....2-1, 1-1 (3-2)
Wigan Ath v Bolton W....2-3, 3-1 (5-4)
Wolves v Notts Co....3-0, 2-1 (5-1)
Wrexham v Burnley....1-0, 0-3 (1-3)
Bristol R v Hereford Utd....1-0, 0-2 (1-2)
Scarborough v Doncaster R....1-0, 1-3 (2-3)
West Bromwich A v Walsall....2-3, 0-0 (2-3)
Crewe Alex v Shrewsbury T....3-3, 1-4 (4-7)

Second Round
Everton v Rotherham Utd....3-2, 0-0 (3-2)
Blackburn R v Liverpool....1-1, 0-1 (1-2)
Leeds Utd v York C....1-1, 4-0 (5-1)
Carlisle Utd v Oldham Ath....4-3, 1-4 (5-7)
Darlington v Watford....0-3, 0-8 (0-11)
Swindon T v Portsmouth....3-1, 3-1 (6-2)
Nottingham F v Hereford Utd....5-0, 1-1 (6-1)
Manchester C v Wolves....1-2, 2-0 (3-2)
Shrewsbury T v Sheffield Wed....1-1, 1-2 (2-3)
Barnsley v West Ham Utd....0-0, 5-2 (5-2)
Torquay Utd Tottenham H....1-0, 0-3 (1-3)
Middlesbrough v Aston Villa....0-1, 0-1 (0-2)
Stoke C v Gillingham....2-0, 1-0 (3-0)
Burnley v Norwich C....1-1, 0-1 (1-2)
AFC Bournemouth v Southampton....1-0, 2-2 (3-2)
Doncaster R v ARSENAL....0-3, 0-1 (0-4)
Oxford Utd v Mansfield T....1-1, 2-0 (3-1)
Leicester C v Scunthorpe Utd....2-1, 2-1 (4-2)
Blackpool v Newcastle Utd....1-0, 1-4 (2-4)
Rochdale v Wimbledon....1-1, 1-2 (2-3)
Bury v Sheffield Utd....2-1, 1-1 (3-2)
Queen's Park R v Millwall....2-1, 0-0 (2-1)
Crystal Palace v Newport Co....4-0, 2-0 (6-0)
Manchester Utd v Hull C....5-0, 1-0 (6-0)
Fulham v Bradford C....1-5, 1-2 (2-7)
Charlton Ath v Walsall....3-0, 0-2 (3-2)
Peterborough Utd v Plymouth Arg....4-1, 1-1 (5-2)
Reading v Chelsea....3-1, 2-3 (5-4)
Ipswich T v Northampton T....1-1, 4-2 (5-3)
Southend Utd v Derby Co....1-0, 0-0 (1-0)
Cambridge Utd v Coventry C....0-1, 1-2 (1-3)
Wigan Ath v LUTON T....0-1, 2-4 (2-5)

Third Round
Liverpool v Everton....0-1
Leeds Utd v Oldham Ath....2-2, 2-4
Swindon T v Watford....1-1, 2-4
Manchester C v Nottingham F....3-0
Barnsley v Sheffield Wed....1-2
Aston Villa v Tottenham H....2-1
Stoke C v Norwich C....2-1
ARSENAL v AFC Bournemouth....3-0
Oxford Utd v Leicester C....0-0, 3-2
Wimbledon v Newcastle Utd....2-1
Bury v Queen's Park R....1-0
Manchester Utd v Crystal Palace....2-1
Charlton Ath v Bradford C....0-1
Peterborough Utd v Reading....0-0, 0-1
Ipswich T v Southend Utd....1-0
LUTON T v Coventry C....3-1

Fourth Round
Everton v Oldham Ath....2-1
Manchester C v Watford....3-1
Aston Villa v Sheffield Wed....1-2
ARSENAL v Stoke C....3-0
Oxford Utd v Wimbledon....2-1
Bury v Manchester Utd....1-2
Reading v Bradford C....0-0, 0-1
Ipswich T v LUTON T....0-1

Fifth Round
Everton v Manchester C....2-0
Sheffield Wed v ARSENAL....0-1
Oxford Utd v Manchester Utd....2-0
LUTON T v Bradford C....2-0

Semi-final (agg)
Everton v ARSENAL....0-1, 1-3 (1-4)
Oxford U v LUTON T....1-1, 0-2 (1-3)

FINAL (Wembley Stadium)
LUTON TOWN....3
ARSENAL....2
Luton Town: Dibble; Breacker, Johnson, Hill, Foster, Donaghy, Wilson, B.Stein, Harford(M.Stein), Preece(Grimes), Black.
Goalscorers: B.Stein 2, Wilson
Arsenal: Lukic; Winterburn, Sansom, Thomas, Caeser, Adams, Rocastle, Davis, Smith, Groves(Hayes), Richardson.
Goalscorers: Hayes, Smith
Referee: J.Worrall (Warrington) *Attendance: 95,732*

*Won on penalties. †Won on away-goals rule.

1988-89

First Round (agg)
Hereford Utd v Plymouth Arg....0-3, 2-3 (2-6)
Stockport Co v Tranmere R....0-1, 1-1 (1-2)
Wigan Ath v Preston NE....0-0, 0-1 (0-1)
Bolton W v Chester C....1-0, 1-3 (2-3)
AFC Bournemouth v Bristol R....1-0, 0-0 (1-0)
Bristol C v Exeter C....1-0, 1-0 (2-0)
Bury v Wrexham....2-1, 2-2 (4-3)
Cambridge Utd v Gillingham....1-2, 1-3 (2-5)
Cardiff C v Swansea C....0-1, 2-0 (2-1)
Carlisle Utd v Blackpool....1-1, 0-3 (1-4)
Colchester Utd v Northampton T....0-0, 0-5 (0-5)
Crewe Alex v Lincoln C....1-1, 1-2 (2-3)
Doncaster R v Darlington....1-1, 0-2 (1-3)
Fulham v Brentford....2-2, 0-1 (2-3)
Grimsby T v Rotherham Utd....0-1, 0-1 (0-2)
Hartlepool Utd v Sheffield Utd....2-2, 0-2 (2-4)
Leyton Orient v Aldershot....2-0, 0-0 (2-0)
Notts Co v Mansfield T....5-0, 0-1 (5-1)
Port Vale v Chesterfield....3-2, 1-1 (4-3)
Rochdale v Burnley....3-3, 1-2 (4-5)
Scunthorpe Utd v Huddersfield T....3-2, 2-2 (5-4)
Shrewsbury T v Walsall....2-2, 0-3 (2-5)
Southend Utd v Brighton & HA....2-0, 1-0 (3-0)
Torquay Utd v Reading....0-1, 1-3 (1-4)
Wolves v Birmingham C†....3-2, 0-1 (3-3)
York C v Sunderland....0-0, 0-4 (0-4)
Scarborough† v Halifax T....1-1, 2-2 (3-3)
West Bromwich A v Peterborough Utd 0-3, 2-0 (2-3)

Second Round (agg)
LUTON T v Burnley....1-1, 1-0 (2-1)
Peterborough Utd v Leeds Utd....1-2, 1-3 (2-5)
Manchester C v Plymouth Arg....1-0, 6-3 (7-3)
Sheffield Utd v Newcastle Utd....3-0, 0-2 (3-2)
Lincoln C v Southampton....1-1, 1-3 (2-4)
Portsmouth v Scarborough....2-2, 1-3 (3-5)
Notts Co v Tottenham H....1-1, 1-2 (2-3)
Blackburn R v Brentford....3-1, 3-4 (6-5)
Port Vale v Ipswich T....1-0, 0-3 (1-3)
Leyton Orient* v Stoke C....1-2, 2-1 (3-3)
Birmingham C v Aston Villa....0-2, 0-5 (0-7)
Millwall v Gillingham....3-0, 3-1 (6-1)
Liverpool v Walsall....1-0, 3-1 (4-1)
Hull C v Arsenal....1-2, 0-3 (1-5)
Derby Co v Southend Utd....1-0, 2-1 (3-1)
Sunderland v West Ham Utd....0-3, 1-2 (1-5)
NOTTINGHAM F v Chester....6-0, 4-0 (10-0)
AFC Bournemouth v Coventry C....0-4, 1-3 (1-7)
Leicester C v Watford....4-1, 2-2 (6-3)
Norwich C v Preston NE....2-0, 3-0 (5-0)
Queen's Park R v Cardiff C....3-0, 4-1 (7-1)
Northampton T v Charlton Ath....1-1, 1-2 (2-3)
Barnsley v Wimbledon....0-2, 1-0 (1-2)
Rotherham Utd v Manchester Utd....0-1, 0-5 (0-6)
Reading v Bradford C....1-1, 1-2 (2-3)
Scunthorpe Utd v Chelsea....4-1, 2-2 (6-3)
Everton v Bury....3-0, 2-2 (5-2)
Darlington v Oldham Ath....2-0, 2-4 (4-4)
Middlesbrough v Tranmere R....0-0, 0-1 (0-1)
Blackpool† v Sheffield Wed....2-0, 1-3 (3-3)
Swindon T v Crystal Palace....1-2, 0-2 (1-4)
Oxford Utd v Bristol C....2-4, 0-2 (2-6)

Third Round
Leeds Utd v LUTON T 0-2
Manchester C v Sheffield Utd 4-2
Scarborough v Southampton 2-2, 0-1
Tottenham H v Blackburn R 0-0, 2-1
Ipswich T v Leyton Orient 2-0
Aston Villa v Millwall 3-1
Liverpool v Arsenal 1-1, 0-0, 2-1
West Ham Utd v Derby Co 5-0
NOTTINGHAM F v Coventry C 3-2
Leicester C v Norwich C 2-0
Queen's Park R v Charlton Ath 2-1
Wimbledon v Manchester Utd 2-1
Bradford C v Scunthorpe Utd 1-1, 1-0
Everton v Oldham Ath 1-1, 2-0
Tranmere R v Blackpool 1-0
Bristol C v Crystal Palace 4-1

Fourth Round
LUTON T v Manchester C 3-1
Southampton v Tottenham H 2-1
Aston Villa v Ipswich T 6-2
West Ham Utd v Liverpool 4-1
Leicester C v NOTTINGHAM F 0-0, 1-2
Queen's Park R v Wimbledon 0-0, 1-0
Bradford C v Everton 3-1
Bristol C v Tranmere R 1-0

Fifth Round
LUTON T v Southampton 1-1, 2-1
West Ham Utd v Aston Villa 2-1
NOTTINGHAM F v Queen's Park R 5-2
Bradford C v Bristol C 0-1

Semi-final (agg)
West Ham Utd v LUTON T 0-3, 0-2 (0-5)
NOTTINGHAM F v Bristol C 1-1, 1-0 (2-1)

FINAL (Wembley Stadium)
NOTTINGHAM FOREST 3
LUTON TOWN 1
Nottingham Forest: Sutton; Laws, Pearce, Walker, Wilson, Hodge, Gaynor, Webb, Clough, Chapman, Parker.

Goalscorers: Clough 2 (1 pen), Webb
Luton Town: Sealey; Breacker, Grimes(McDonough), Preece, Foster, Beaumont, Wilson, Wegerle, Harford, Hill, Black.

Goalscorer: Harford
Referee: R.G.Milford (Bristol) Attendance: 76,130
*Won on penalties. †Won on away-goals rule.

1989-90

First Round (agg)
Birmingham C v Chesterfield 2-1, 1-1 (3-2)
Blackpool v Burnley 2-2, 1-0 (3-2)
Brighton & HA v Brentford 0-3, 1-1 (1-4)
Bristol C v Reading 2-3, 2-2 (4-5)
Bristol R v Portsmouth 1-0, 0-2 (1-2)
Cambridge Utd v Maidstone Utd 3-1, 1-0 (4-1)
Cardiff C v Plymouth Arg 0-3, 2-0 (2-3)
Colchester Utd v Southend Utd 3-4, 1-2 (4-6)
Crewe Alex v Chester C 4-0, 2-0 (6-0)
Exeter C v Swansea C 3-0, 1-1 (4-1)
Fulham v Oxford Utd 0-1, 5-3 (5-4)
Gillingham v Leyton Orient 1-4, 0-3 (1-7)
Halifax T v Carlisle Utd 3-1, 0-1 (3-2)
Hartlepool Utd v York C 3-3, 1-4 (4-7)
Huddersfield T v Doncaster R 1-1, 2-1 (3-2)
Hull C v Grimsby T 1-0, 0-2 (1-2)
Mansfield T v Northampton T 1-1, 2-0 (3-1)
Peterborough Utd v Aldershot 2-0, 2-6 (4-6)
Preston NE v Tranmere R 3-4, 1-3 (4-7)
Rochdale v Bolton W 2-1, 1-5 (3-6)
Scarborough v Scunthorpe Utd 2-0, 1-1 (3-1)
Sheffield Utd v Rotherham Utd 1-1, 0-1 (1-2)
Shrewsbury T v Notts Co 3-0, 1-3 (4-3)
Stockport Co v Bury 1-0, 1-1 (2-1)
Torquay Utd v Hereford Utd 0-1, 0-3 (0-4)
Walsall v Port Vale 1-2, 0-1 (1-3)
Wolves v Lincoln C 1-0, 2-0 (3-0)
Wrexham v Wigan Ath 0-0, 0-5 (0-5)

Second Round (agg)
Arsenal v Plymouth Arg 2-0, 6-1 (8-1)
Aston Villa v Wolves 2-1, 1-1 (3-2)
Barnsley v Blackpool* 1-1, 1-1 (2-2)
Birmingham C v West Ham Utd 1-2, 1-1 (2-3)
Bolton W v Watford 2-1, 1-1 (3-2)
Brentford v Manchester C 2-1, 1-4 (3-5)
Cambridge Utd v Derby Co 2-1, 0-5 (2-6)
Charlton Ath v Hereford Utd 3-1, 1-0 (4-1)
Chelsea v Scarborough 1-1, 2-3 (3-4)
Crewe Alex v AFC Bournemouth 0-0, 0-1 (0-1)
Crystal Palace† v Leicester C 1-2, 3-2 (4-4)
Exeter C v Blackburn R 3-0, 1-2 (4-2)
Grimsby T v Coventry C 3-1, 0-3 (3-4)
Ipswich T v Tranmere R 0-1, 0-1 (0-2)
Leyton Orient v Everton 0-2, 2-2 (2-4)
Liverpool v Wigan Ath 5-2, 3-0 (8-2)
Mansfield T v Luton T 3-4, 2-7 (5-11)
Middlesbrough v Halifax T 4-0, 1-0 (5-0)
Norwich C v Rotherham Utd 1-1, 2-0 (3-1)
NOTTINGHAM F† v Huddersfield T 1-1, 3-3 (4-4)
OLDHAM ATH v Leeds Utd 2-1, 2-1 (4-2)
Portsmouth v Manchester Utd 2-3, 0-0 (2-3)
Port Vale v Wimbledon 1-2, 0-3 (1-5)
Queen's Park R v Stockport Co 2-1, 0-0 (2-1)
Reading v Newcastle Utd 3-1, 0-4 (3-5)
Sheffield Wed v Aldershot 0-0, 8-0 (8-0)
Shrewsbury T v Swindon T 0-3, 1-3 (1-6)
Stoke C v Millwall 1-0, 0-2 (1-2)
Sunderland v Fulham 1-1, 3-0 (4-1)
Tottenham H† v Southend Utd 1-0, 2-3 (3-3)
West Bromwich A† v Bradford C 1-3, 5-3 (6-6)
York C v Southampton 0-1, 0-2 (0-3)

Third Round
Arsenal v Liverpool 1-0
Aston Villa v West Ham Utd 0-0, 0-1
Crystal P v NOTTINGHAM F 0-0, 0-5
Derby Co v Sheffield Wed 2-1
Everton v Luton T 3-0
Exeter C v Blackpool 3-0
Manchester C v Norwich C 3-1
Manchester Utd v Tottenham H 0-3
Middlesbrough v Wimbledon 1-1, 0-1
Newcastle Utd v West Bromwich A 0-1
OLDHAM ATH v Scarborough 7-0
Queen's Park R v Coventry C 1-2
Southampton v Charlton Ath 1-0
Sunderland v AFC Bournemouth 1-1, 1-0
Swindon T v Bolton W 3-3, 1-1, 1-1, 2-1
Tranmere R v Millwall 3-2

Fourth Round
Derby Co v West Bromwich A 2-0
Exeter C v Sunderland 2-2, 2-5
Manchester C v Coventry C 0-1
NOTTINGHAM F v Everton 1-0
OLDHAM ATH v Arsenal 3-1
Swindon T v Southampton 0-0, 2-4
Tranmere R v Tottenham H 2-2, 0-4
West Ham Utd v Wimbledon 1-0

Fifth Round
NOTTINGHAM F v Tottenham H 2-2, 3-2
Southampton v OLDHAM ATH 2-2, 0-2
Sunderland v Coventry C 0-0, 0-5
West Ham Utd v Derby Co 1-1, 0-0, 2-1

Semi-final (agg)
NOTTINGHAM F v Coventry C 2-1, 0-0 (2-1)
OLDHAM ATH v West Ham Utd 6-0, 0-3 (6-3)

FINAL (Wembley Stadium)
NOTTINGHAM FOREST 1
OLDHAM ATHLETIC 0
Nottingham Forest: Sutton; Laws, Pearce, Walker, Chettle, Hodge, Crosby, Parker, Clough, Jemson, Carr.

Goalscorer: Jemson
Oldham Athletic: Rhodes; Irwin, Barlow, Henry, Barrett, Warhurst, Adams, Ritchie, Bunn(Palmer), Milligan, R.Holden.
Referee: J.Martin (Alton) Attendance: 74,343
*Won on penalties. †Won on away-goals rule.

Nottingham Forest's Des Walker with the Littlewoods Cup in 1990. Forest had just beaten Oldham Athletic.

1990-91

First Round (agg)
Birmingham C v AFC Bournemouth 0-1, 1-1 (1-2)
Bradford C v Bury 2-0, 2-3 (4-3)
Brentford v Hereford Utd 2-0, 0-1 (2-1)
Brighton & HA v Northampton T 0-2, 1-1 (1-3)
Bristol R v Torquay Utd 1-2, 1-1 (2-3)
Carlisle Utd v Scunthorpe Utd 1-0, 1-1 (2-1)
Chesterfield v Hartlepool Utd 1-2, 2-2 (3-4)
Darlington† v Blackpool 0-0, 1-1 (1-1)
Doncaster R v Rotherham Utd 2-6, 1-2 (3-8)
Exeter C v Notts Co 1-1, 0-1 (1-2)
Fulham v Peterborough Utd 1-2, 0-1 (1-3)
Gillingham v Shrewsbury T 1-0, 0-2 (1-2)
Grimsby T v Crewe Alex† 2-1, 0-1 (2-2)
Halifax T v Lincoln C 2-0, 0-1 (2-1)
Huddersfield T v Bolton W 0-3, 1-2 (1-5)
Maidstone Utd v Leyton Orient 2-2, 1-4 (3-6)
Mansfield T v Cardiff C 1-1, 0-3 (1-4)
Middlesbrough v Tranmere R 1-1, 2-1 (3-2)
Preston NE v Chester C 2-0, 1-5 (3-5)
Reading v Oxford Utd 0-1, 1-2 (1-3)
Rochdale v Scarborough 4-0, 3-3 (7-3)
Southend Utd v Aldershot 2-1, 2-2 (4-3)
Stockport Co v Burnley 0-2, 1-0 (1-2)
Stoke C v Swansea C 0-0, 1-0 (1-0)
Walsall v Cambridge Utd 4-2, 1-2 (5-4)
West Bromwich A v Bristol C 2-2, 0-1 (2-3)
Wigan Ath v Barnsley* 0-1, 1-0 (1-1)
York C v Wrexham 0-1, 0-2 (0-3)

Second Round (agg)
Aston Villa v Barnsley 1-0, 1-0 (2-0)
AFC Bournemouth v Millwall 0-0, 1-2 (1-2)
Cardiff C v Portsmouth 1-1, 1-3 (2-4)
Carlisle Utd v Derby Co 1-1, 0-1 (1-2)
Charlton Ath v Leyton Orient 2-2, 0-1 (2-3)
Chester C v Arsenal 0-1, 0-5 (0-6)
Coventry C v Bolton W 4-2, 3-2 (7-4)
Crystal Palace v Southend Utd 8-0, 2-1 (10-1)
Darlington v Swindon T 3-0, 0-4 (3-4)
Halifax T v MANCHESTER UTD 1-3, 1-2 (2-5)
Hull C† v Wolves 0-0, 1-1 (1-1)
Leicester C v Leeds Utd 1-0, 0-3 (1-3)
Liverpool v Crewe Alex 5-1, 4-1 (9-2)
Luton T v Bradford C* 1-1, 1-1 (2-2)
Middlesbrough v Newcastle Utd 2-0, 0-1 (2-1)
Northampton T v Sheffield Utd 0-1, 1-2 (1-3)
Norwich C v Watford 2-0, 3-0 (5-0)
Nottingham F v Burnley 4-1, 1-0 (5-1)
Notts Co v Oldham Ath 1-0, 2-5 (3-5)
Plymouth Arg v Wimbledon 1-0, 2-0 (3-0)
Port Vale v Oxford Utd 0-2, 0-0 (0-2)
Queen's Park R v Peterborough Utd 3-1, 1-1 (4-2)
Rochdale v Southampton 0-5, 0-3 (0-8)
Rotherham Utd v Blackburn R 1-1, 0-1 (1-2)
SHEFFIELD WED v Brentford 1-1, 2-1 (3-2)
Shrewsbury T v Ipswich T 1-1, 0-3 (1-4)
Sunderland v Bristol C 0-1, 6-1 (6-2)
Torquay Utd v Manchester C 0-4, 0-0 (0-4)
Tottenham H v Hartlepool Utd 5-0, 2-1 (7-1)
Walsall v Chelsea 0-5, 1-4 (1-9)
West Ham Utd v Stoke C 3-0, 2-1 (5-1)
Wrexham v Everton 0-5, 0-6 (0-11)

Third Round
Aston Villa v Millwall 2-0
Chelsea v Portsmouth 0-0, 3-2
Coventry C v Hull C 3-0
Crystal Palace v Leyton Orient 0-0, 1-0
Derby Co v Sunderland 6-0
Ipswich T v Southampton 0-2
Leeds Utd v Oldham Ath 2-0
Manchester C v Arsenal 1-2
MANCHESTER UTD v Liverpool 3-1
Middlesbrough v Norwich C 2-0
Oxford Utd v West Ham Utd 2-1
Plymouth Arg v Nottingham F 1-2
Queen's Park R v Blackburn R 2-1
Sheffield Utd v Everton 2-1
SHEFFIELD WED v Swindon T 0-0, 1-0
Tottenham H v Bradford C 2-1

Fourth Round
Arsenal v MANCHESTER UTD 2-6
Aston Villa v Middlesbrough 3-2
Coventry C v Nottingham F 5-4
SHEFFIELD WED v Derby Co 1-1, 2-1
Oxford Utd v Chelsea 1-2
Queen's Park R v Leeds Utd 0-3
Sheffield Utd v Tottenham H 0-2
Southampton v Crystal Palace 2-0

Fifth Round
Leeds Utd v Aston Villa 4-1
Coventry C v SHEFFIELD WED 0-1
Chelsea v Tottenham H 0-0, 3-0
Southampton v MANCHESTER UTD 1-1, 2-3

Sheffield Wednesday's goalscoring hero John Sheridan proudly holds aloft the Rumbelows Cup after the Owls' single-goal victory over Manchester United.

Semi-final (agg)
MANCHESTER UTD v Leeds Utd 2-1, 1-0 (3-1)
Chelsea v SHEFFIELD WED 0-2, 1-3 (1-5)

FINAL (Wembley Stadium)
SHEFFIELD WEDNESDAY 1
MANCHESTER UNITED 0
Sheffield Wednesday: Turner; Nilsson, King, Harkes(Madden), Shirtliff, Pearson, Wilson, Sheridan, Hirst, Williams, Worthington.

Goalscorer: Sheridan
Manchester United: Sealey; Irwin, Blackmore, Bruce, Webb(Phelan), Pallister, Robson, Ince, McClair, Hughes, Sharpe.
Referee: R.Lewis (Great Bookham) Attendance: 80,000

From this season the trophy was called the Rumbelows Cup.

1991-92

First Round (agg)
Barnet v Brentford 5-5, 1-3 (6-8)
Blackburn R v Hull C 1-1, 0-1 (1-2)
Bolton W v York C 2-2, 2-1 (4-3)
Cambridge Utd v Reading 1-0, 3-0 (4-0)
Cardiff C v AFC Bournemouth 3-2, 1-4 (4-6)
Charlton Ath v Fulham 4-2, 1-1 (5-3)
Chester C† v Lincoln C 1-0, 3-4 (4-4)
Crewe Alex v Doncaster R 5-2, 4-2 (9-4)
Darlington v Huddersfield T 1-0, 0-4 (1-4)
Exeter C v Birmingham C 0-1, 0-4 (0-5)
Halifax T v Tranmere R 3-4, 3-4 (6-8)
Hartlepool Utd v Bury 1-0, 2-2 (3-2)
Leicester C v Maidstone Utd 3-0, 1-0 (4-0)
Leyton Orient v Northampton T 5-0, 0-2 (5-2)
Mansfield T v Blackpool 0-3, 2-4 (2-7)
Peterborough Utd v Aldershot 3-1, 2-1 (5-2)
Portsmouth v Gillingham 2-1, 4-3 (6-4)
Preston NE v Scarborough 5-4, 1-3 (6-7)
Rochdale v Carlisle Utd 5-1, 1-1 (6-2)
Rotherham Utd v Grimsby T 1-3, 0-1 (1-4)
Shrewsbury T† v Plymouth Arg 1-1, 2-2 (3-3)
Stockport Co v Bradford C 1-1, 1-3 (2-4)
Stoke C v Chesterfield 1-0, 2-1 (3-1)
Swansea C v Walsall 2-2, 1-0 (3-2)
Swindon T v West Bromwich A 2-0, 2-2 (4-2)
Torquay Utd v Hereford Utd 2-0, 1-2 (3-2)
Watford v Southend Utd 2-0, 1-1 (3-1)
Wigan Ath v Burnley 3-1, 3-2 (6-3)
Wrexham v Scunthorpe Utd 1-0, 0-3 (1-3)

Second Round (agg)
Blackpool v Barnsley 1-0, 0-2 (1-2)
Bradford C v Wrexham 1-1, 0-4 (1-5)
Brentford v Brighton & HA 4-1, 2-4 (6-5)
Bristol R† v Bristol C 1-3, 4-2 (5-5)

Top: Manchester United with the Rumbelows Cup after their Wembley victory over Nottingham Forest in 1992. Bottom: Brian McClair, scorer of the only goal in the Final, shares United's prize with a fan.

Fifth Round

Crystal Palace v NOTTINGHAM F 1-1, 2-4
Leeds Utd v MANCHESTER UTD 1-3
Peterborough Utd v Middlesbrough 0-0, 0-1
Tottenham H v Norwich C 2-1

Semi-final (agg)

NOTTINGHAM F v Tottenham H 1-1, 2-1 (3-2)
Middlesbrough v MANCHESTER UTD ... 0-0, 1-2 (1-2)

FINAL (Wembley Stadium)

MANCHESTER UNITED 1
NOTTINGHAM FOREST 0

Manchester United: Schmeichel; Parker, Irwin, Bruce, Phelan, Pallister, Kanchelskis(Sharpe), Ince, McClair, Hughes, Giggs.
Goalscorer: McClair
Nottingham Forest: Marriott; Charles(Laws), Williams, Walker, Wassall, Keane, Crosby, Gemmill, Clough, Sherringham, Black.
Referee: G.Courtney (Spennymoor) Attendance: 76,810

†Won on away-goals rule.

Charlton Ath v Norwich C 0-2, 0-3 (0-5)
Chelsea v Tranmere R 1-1, 1-3 (2-4)
Coventry C v Rochdale 4-0, 0-1 (4-1)
Crewe Alex v Newcastle Utd 3-4, 0-1 (3-5)
Derby Co v Ipswich T 0-0, 2-0 (2-0)
Everton v Watford 1-0, 2-1 (3-1)
Grimsby T v Aston Villa 0-0, 1-1 (1-1)
Hartlepool Utd v Crystal Palace 1-1, 1-6 (2-7)
Hull C v Queen's Park R 0-3, 1-5 (1-8)
Leicester C v Arsenal 1-1, 0-2 (1-3)
Leyton Orient v Sheffield Wed 0-0, 1-4 (1-4)
Liverpool v Stoke C 2-2, 3-2 (5-4)
Luton T v Birmingham C 2-2, 2-3 (4-5)
Manchester C v Chester C 3-1, 3-0 (6-1)
MANCHESTER UTD v Cambridge Utd ... 3-0, 1-1 (4-1)
Middlesbrough v AFC Bournemouth 1-1, 2-1 (3-2)
Millwall v Swindon T 2-2, 1-3 (3-5)
NOTTINGHAM F v Bolton W 4-0, 5-2 (9-2)
Oldham Ath v Torquay Utd 7-1, 2-0 (9-1)
Port Vale v Notts Co 2-1, 2-3 (4-4)
Portsmouth v Oxford Utd 0-0, 1-0 (1-0)
Scarborough v Southampton 1-3, 2-2 (3-5)
Scunthorpe Utd v Leeds Utd 0-0, 0-3 (0-3)
Sunderland v Huddersfield T 1-2, 0-4 (1-6)
Swansea C v Tottenham H 1-0, 1-5 (2-5)
Wigan Ath v Sheffield Utd 2-2, 0-1 (2-3)
Wimbledon v Peterborough Utd 1-2, 2-2 (3-4)
Wolves v Shrewsbury T 6-1, 1-3 (7-4)

Third Round

Birmingham C v Crystal Palace 1-1, 1-1, 1-2
Coventry C v Arsenal 1-0
Everton v Wolves 4-1
Grimsby T v Tottenham H 0-3
Huddersfield T v Swindon T 1-4
Leeds Utd v Tranmere R 3-1
Liverpool v Port Vale 2-2, 4-1
Manchester C v Queen's Park R 0-0, 3-1
MANCHESTER UTD v Portsmouth 3-1
Middlesbrough v Barnsley 1-0
Norwich C v Brentford 4-1
NOTTINGHAM F v Bristol R 2-0
Oldham Ath v Derby Co 2-1
Peterborough Utd v Newcastle Utd 1-0
Sheffield Utd v West Ham Utd 0-2
Sheffield Wed v Southampton 1-1, 0-1

Fourth Round

Coventry C v Tottenham H 1-2
Everton v Leeds Utd 1-4
MANCHESTER UTD v Oldham Ath 2-0
Middlesbrough v Manchester C 2-1
Norwich C v West Ham Utd 2-1
NOTTINGHAM F v Southampton 0-0, 1-0
Peterborough Utd v Liverpool 1-0
Swindon T v Crystal Palace 0-1